Patty -

Thank You so much for your friendship and support since I've known you. May it return to you three-fold during the course of your life.

Your friends,

Petar, Marija and Eva Nikolić

01/22/07

THE ORTHODOX STUDY BIBLE

NEW TESTAMENT AND PSALMS

PRESENTED TO

____

ON THIS __________ DAY OF ______________

____

BY ______________________________

____

THE ORTHODOX STUDY BIBLE

NEW TESTAMENT AND PSALMS
NEW KING JAMES VERSION

First Edition Participants

Project Director
Fr. Peter E. Gillquist

Managing Editor
Mr. Alan Wallerstedt

Initial Draft Prepared by the Academic Community
of St. Athanasius Orthodox Academy, Santa Barbara, California

General Editors

Joseph Allen, Th.D.
Jack Norman Sparks, Ph.D.
Michel Najim, Ph.D.
Theodore Stylianopoulos, Th.D.

Overview Committee

Archbishop IAKOVOS
Metropolitan THEODOSIUS
Metropolitan PHILIP
Metropolitan CHRISTOPHER
Bishop ANTHONY
Bishop DEMETRIOS
Bishop DMITRI
Bishop KALLISTOS
Bishop MAXIMOS
Bishop NICHOLAS
Bishop VSEVOLOD
Fr. Anthony Coniaris
Fr. Antony Gabriel
Fr. Stanley Harakas
Fr. Thomas Hopko
Fr. Alexander Veronis
Fr. Thaddeus Wojcik
Mr. Charles Ajalat
Dr. Apostolos Athanassakis
Dr. John Boojamra
Mr. Brian Gerich
Dr. Veselin Kesich
Dr. Petros Vasiliades
Mr. Ernest Villas

Thomas Nelson Publishers
Nashville, Tennessee

Contents

Section I

The Bible and the Orthodox Church

"[The Bible] is the mother of all books, just as it is the prayer above all prayers, and the guide to the Kingdom of heaven. It leads men on earth to the understanding of the Truth, and enables one to see God with the heart while still in the flesh, and in time to come allows one to enjoy face to face the sweet vision of the Holy Trinity." (Parthenios of Kiev, 19th century)

Introduction

What is the role of the Bible in the Orthodox Church? Outwardly, the Holy Scriptures occupy a position of great prominence in Orthodox worship. Encased in gold and covered with a protective veil, the Gospel Book rests conspicuously on the Holy Altar throughout the week. During Divine Liturgy it is carried in dignified procession by the clergy, preceded by incense, candles, and the processional cross. The solemn proclamation of the Gospel by priest or deacon becomes a focal point for the entire service, preparing worshippers for the final ascent to Holy Communion.

But is there substance beyond these external expressions? Does the Bible play as important a role in the internal life and spirituality of Orthodox Christianity as it does in the external elements of her worship? Is Orthodox theologian, Bishop Kallistos Ware, correct in stating, "The Christian Church is a scriptural Church; Orthodoxy believes this just as firmly, if not more firmly, than Protestantism. The Bible is the supreme expression of God's revelation to the human race, and Christians must always be 'People of the Book' "?

Listen first to the clear voice of the Church, speaking throughout the centuries concerning the place of the Scriptures in the life of the believer. Then we will see how the Church has historically understood those Scriptures, in both their composition and proper interpretation, and examine some of the issues surrounding certain Orthodox beliefs in light of their biblical foundation.

The Church Fathers Speak

On the Importance of Reading the Scriptures

"What then do I ask of you? That each of you take in hand that part of the Gospels which is to be read in your presence on the first day of the week or even on the Sabbath; and before that day comes, sit down at home and read it through; consider often and carefully its content, and examine all its parts well, noting what is clear, what is confusing, what seems to assist the position of the adversaries but really does not. And, in a word, when you have sounded every point, then go to hear it read. From such zeal as this there will be no small benefit both to you and to me." (St. John Chrysostom, 4th–5th century)

"For the soul who has chosen to meditate day and night on the law of God, nothing can be more beneficial than to search the Holy Scriptures. The design of the grace of the Spirit to be found therein overwhelms the senses of the mind with fulfillment, by removing it completely from earthly realities and visible things, taking it to the level of the angels and associating it with the life of the angels themselves." (St. Symeon the New Theologian, 10th–11th century)

"Holy Scripture is given by God not only to humanity in general, but to each individual, to me, to you, to every one. . . . Every time we either read it ourselves, or hear it read in church, we hear our God conversing with us." (St. Tikhon of Zadonsk, 18th century)

"If you, Christian, wish to learn to live a holy and truly Christian life, set before yourself the Holy Gospel and the irreproachable life of Christ, and learn from it." (St. Tikhon of Zadonsk, 18th century)

"It is necessary to satisfy the soul with the Word of God. . . . One must train oneself in such a way that the mind, as it were, swims in the Law of God, by the direction of which one must order one's life. For this exercise alone, apart from other good works, the Lord will not leave a man without His mercy, but will fulfill his gift of understanding." (St. Seraphim of Sarov, 19th century)

"I especially love to read the Holy Scriptures, both Testaments. I cannot live without this reading. They contain so much. So many laws for the life of man's soul are revealed there! A person striving for spiritual renewal can obtain so much guidance in being reborn from evil to good." (St. John of Kronstadt, 19th century)

"Read the Holy Gospel, be penetrated by its spirit, make it the rule of your life, your handbook; in every action and question of life act according to the study of the Gospel. This is the only light of our life." (Nikon of Optina, 20th century)

On the Divine Nature of the Scriptures:

"Brethren, be contentious and zealous for the things which lead to salvation! You have studied the Holy Scriptures, which are true and are of the Holy Spirit. You well know that nothing unjust or fraudulent is written in them." (St. Clement of Rome, 1st century)

"When you hear the words of the Prophets, spoken as it were personally, do not imagine that they are spoken by the inspired persons themselves. It is the Divine Word who moves them." (St. Justin Martyr, 2nd Century)

"Moreover, in regard to the righteousness which the law enjoined, the Prophets and the Gospels are found to be consistent with each other, because they all spoke as being inspired by the one Spirit of God." (St. Theophilus of Antioch, 2nd century)

"Divinely inspired Scripture, as the Divine Apostle calls it, is the Holy Spirit's writing. Its purpose is usefulness to men. 'All Scripture,' he says, 'is inspired of God and useful.'" (St. Gregory of Nyssa, 4th century)

"Some say that not all the Psalms are by David, but that some are by others. . . . About this I make no very strong affirmation. What difference does it make to me whether all of them or some of them [are David's], when it is clear in any case that all are written under the operation of the Divine Spirit?" (Theodoret of Cyr, 4th–5th century)

On the Proper Interpretation of Scripture:

"Every care should be taken to hold fast to what has been believed everywhere, always, and by all. This general rule will be truly applied if we follow the principles of universality, antiquity, and consent. We do so in regard to universality if we confess that faith alone to be true which the entire Church confesses all over the world. [We do so] in regard to antiquity if we in no way deviate from those interpretations which our ancestors and fathers have manifestly proclaimed as inviolable. [We do so] in regard to consent if, in this very antiquity, we adopt the definitions of all, or almost all, the bishops and pious theologians." (St. Vincent of Lerins, 5th century)

"Let us not knock casually [at the door of the Scriptures], but with eagerness and persistence, and let us not lose heart while knocking, for so it will be opened to us. Should we read once and then a second time and still not understand what we are reading, let us not be discouraged. Rather, let us persist, let us meditate and inquire, for it is written: 'Ask thy father, and he will declare to thee: thy elders and they will tell thee' (Deuteronomy 32:7)." (St. John of Damascus, 7th-8th century)

"I have learned to hold those books alone of the Scriptures that are now called canonical in such reverence and honor that I do most firmly believe that none of their authors has erred in anything that he has written therein. If I find anything in those writings which seems to be contrary to the truth, I presume that either the codex is inaccurate, or the translator has not followed what was said, or I have not properly understood it." (St. Augustine of Hippo, 4th–5th century)

"If, however, we are not able to find explanations for all those passages of Scripture which are investigated, we ought not on that account seek for another God besides Him who exists. This would indeed be the greatest impiety. Things of that kind we must leave to God, the One who made us, knowing full well that the Scriptures are certainly perfect, since they were spoken by the Word of God and by His Spirit." (St. Irenaeus, 2nd–3rd century)

"First, one must read [Scripture] with reverence, as the Word of God, and with prayer for understanding of it; second, one must read it with pure intention, for establishment in the faith and motivation to good works; third, one must understand it in accordance with the interpretation of the Orthodox Church and the Holy Fathers." (Metropolitan Philaret of Moscow, 19th century)

The Bible and Orthodox Tradition*

The Orthodox Church governs her life by Holy Tradition. Many, however, are confused as to what exactly Holy Tradition is.

The word "tradition" comes from the Latin *traditio,* which is a translation of a Greek word used frequently in the Scriptures, *paradosis*. Translated literally, this word means something that is handed on from one person to another, in the same way that a baton is handed over in a relay race. Something that is "traditioned" is passed on from one person or group of people to another. St. Paul clarifies in Galatians 1:11 that the Tradition of the Church is "not according to man." In other words, it is revealed by God. It is not a human product.

Tradition means an experience, an entire life—not simply a series of teachings, but the living out of those teachings that have come from the God who has revealed Himself to us. Tradition is the living out of the revelation of God by His people.

Where is this Tradition to be found? What are its sources?

Five Sources of Christian Tradition

1) The Holy Scriptures

The first place we give to the Holy Scriptures: the Bible, Old and New Testaments. The Bible is understood by Orthodox Christians to be the principal written record of the experience by God's people of God's revealing Himself to them. It is understood that the Church, therefore, wrote the Bible. The Bible is the word of God, but the word of God was not written directly and personally by God. The Holy Scriptures did not fall from heaven in a fully complete written form. By whom were the Scriptures written? They were written by human beings who were inspired by God. What they write is the truth about God. They write what they write as members of God's people.

For example, in the early years of the Christian Church, those most important books of Holy Scripture that we call the Gospels did not exist. Several decades passed after Pentecost before the first Gospel was written. It was the end of the first century by the time all four Gospels were written. Three hundred more years passed before a decision was made in the Church that there would be only four Gospels.

The books that are in the Holy Scriptures, both Old and New Testaments, are there because God's people, through those who were set aside as having the authority to make the decision, decided that these books would be part of the Bible, and other books would not. The Church, as God's people inspired by God, wrote the Bible. The Church produced the Bible. The Bible did not produce the Church.

The Holy Scriptures are the principal and most honored written record of

* This article is taken from the catechism series *What We Believe* by Fr. David Anderson (© 1997, Conciliar Press).

God's revelation to His people. But it is the understanding of the Orthodox that the Holy Scriptures cannot be completely, truthfully understood unless they are understood within the context of the Church that produced them, that declared them to be what they are. So the Bible is the Book of the Church, the first source of the Christian Tradition. We will speak of the Bible in greater detail later on.

2) *The Liturgy*

The second source is the liturgy of the Church. "Liturgy" is a word that means in Greek, "common work." The liturgy of the Church means the work of the Church when it comes together to be the people of God and to worship God. Liturgy includes the whole body of the Church's common worship: the services for the various hours of the day, the days of the week, the feast days and seasons of the Church, the sacraments of the Church (baptism, the Holy Eucharist, marriage, and others).

In all this public prayer of the Church we have a record of what the Church believes. In fact, there is a saying that has been popular among the Orthodox from the beginning: the rule of faith, the standard of what we believe, is established by the way we pray (in Latin, *lex orandi, lex est credendi*). The best Orthodox answer to the question, "What do you believe as Orthodox Christians? How can I find out what you believe?" would not be simply to say, "Come hear this talk or read this book." Teaching is essential in the life of the Church and always has been. But the first answer that an Orthodox Christian always gives to that question is, "Come and see."

That is always the Orthodox invitation. Come and see what we do when we assemble together to be the Church in the common worship of God. Anybody who exposes himself or herself intensely to the Church's common worship will have a better course in Orthodox Faith, doctrine, and practice than any book could give, and nothing can take the place of that. So the liturgy is the second source of the Tradition.

3) *The Councils*

The third source is the councils of the Church. A council is a meeting of those in the Church who have been given the authority to decide what is faithful to the Tradition of the Church and what is not. The first council that we hear described in the Holy Scripture (Acts 15) takes place in the Church of Jerusalem. This council was convened to decide the question of whether Gentiles could become Christians and whether they should be required to obey the Jewish Law. This was a situation that Jesus had not specifically prepared His Apostles to deal with. But He had given them the authority in the Church to distinguish between what was true and what was not, so they met to decide what to do with the Gentiles who wanted to become part of the Church.

The result of this council was a compromise: the Gentiles would be required to keep a few core principles of the Jewish law, but the rest of it was not binding on them. Moreover, the Apostles made it very clear that this was not merely a human decision. They were so bold as to say, "It seems good to the Holy Spirit and to us that this is how we answer this question."

Many councils have met through the centuries of the Church's life and they have decided many questions. The answers they give to the questions that have to be resolved come in two forms: creeds and canons.

Creeds are statements of faith. The most important of the Church's statements of faith is contained in the creed called the Nicene Creed. It is called "Nicene" because it was written at the First Ecumenical Council in Nicea in A.D. 325. ("Ecumenical" in this case means a council involving the whole Church throughout the known world.) The Nicene Creed appears on page 13 of this Bible. There are many other creeds used in the Church that come from other councils, and all of them together constitute one source of the Church's Tradition.

Councils also produce canons. The word "canon" comes from the Greek kanon , which means a ruler or a yardstick, something used to measure what is to be normative in the practice of the Church. Canons provide answers, for example, to questions of discipline or morality in the Church. What is to be done when people in the Church fall into sin? How are they to be reconciled to the Church? What is to be done when there are disputes between two churches, as there were disputes among the Apostles? There have always been disputes among the people of God. The people of God, though they receive the revelation of God, do not become perfect overnight, and most of them do not become perfect in this world. So the canons of the Church are a body of rules, or norms, to regulate the discipline of the Church, and their source is the Councils.

4) *The Saints*

The fourth source of the Church's Tradition, another double source, is the lives of the saints and the teaching of one particular group of saints who are called the Fathers (a group which includes some mothers).

In every generation in the life of the Church, there have been people who live the teachings of Christ faithfully, heroically, who attain while living in this world the destiny for which we as Christians believe God has created us: to share His own life.

The ultimate promise concerning the Christian revelation is that it is true. "You shall know the Truth, and the Truth shall make you free." Free from what? Free from error, free from sin, free from emptiness, and ultimately free from death in the negative sense. Those are the things that God frees us from. But He does this so that we can be free for something that is indescribably greater: to reach our destiny as partakers of the life of God Himself.

There are those in the Church who, by their faithful obedience and perfection in faith, hope, and love for God, are the greatest examples. We could call them the heroes of the Church. The icons in our churches show us the saints from every age. Those saints are present in the Church, are sources of the Church's experience to show the people who belong to the Church of God the way to life, the way to truth, to show each one of us that yes, it is possible. It is possible for the saints and it is possible for us to reach this destiny that God calls us to.

A certain group of those saints is called the Fathers. By a Father of the Church, we mean one who by his (or her) wisdom in teaching or defending Church doctrine, often at the cost of his life or in the face of great suffering, bore witness to the Tradition of the Church. When we read the Gospels, we say yes, what is written in the Gospel here is what the Church has always believed. In the same sense, when we read the writings of the great Fathers, we can find in them a faithful and true testimony to what the Church has always believed and experienced about God.

5) *Church Art*

The final source of the Christian Tradition we will call Church art. Now, it might come as a surprise to some that along with such exalted things as the Holy Scriptures and the liturgy of the Church and the saints and the Fathers, we would speak of Church art. In the minds of some people, art is simply a kind of decoration, a secondary thing. But the Orthodox understanding of the nature of the human being, of how God has made us, how God has revealed Himself to us, is that material creation is very much involved. One could say that the Orthodox Faith, the Orthodox experience is a holistic one. It involves the whole man. It involves the material creation. In fact, the Incarnation—the entry of God into the material world, God becoming man, God becoming matter—is uniquely at the heart of the Christian Faith.

Art is, by definition, the use of material things as the medium for the revelation of God. So for the Orthodox, art is not icing on the cake; it is something very central to what we know of how God has revealed Himself to us. One goes into an Orthodox Church building and is immediately surrounded by all sorts of things that appeal to the senses. We could divide them into three categories. Firstly, iconography: the way in which the images of Christ, His life, His Mother, and the saints are portrayed in the Church. Secondly, Church music: the way our Church services are sung, the chants that are used in the liturgical services. And finally, Church architecture: even the way an Orthodox church is traditionally built is a visible testimony to the Faith of the Church as it has been experienced throughout the ages. None of these is understood to be merely accidental or a frill. Rather, they are at the heart of our experience in the Church as the people of God.

So we have these five basic sources of the Orthodox Tradition, what has been passed on from one generation of the faithful to the next, from Christ and the Apostles even to the present time: the Scripture, the liturgy, the creeds and canons that have come from the Church councils, the lives of the saints and the teaching of the Fathers, and finally Orthodox Christian art.

The Unity of Tradition

It is the Church's understanding that all of these sources of Tradition hold together in unity. One is never used in isolation from the others. It will not work, for example, for a person to say, "Well, I can find all that I need to know by staying at home and reading the Bible by myself, and I don't have to go to church." Nor would it work for a person to say, "Well, all I have to do is go to Church and look at the icons and I don't have to know anything about the Holy Scriptures." In both cases, something is being taken outside the context, outside the boundaries in which it works. When you take something outside the boundaries in which it functions, it doesn't work the way it's supposed to work.

The Orthodox would claim that all the problems, all the false teaching, all the exaggerations, all the misunderstandings that have occurred in two thousand years of Christian history have taken place because people misguidedly have taken one or another source of Christian Tradition, isolated it from everything else, and treated it as an independent unit. The Orthodox Church is not Bible only. The Orthodox Church is not liturgy only. The Orthodox Church is not creed, council, and canon only. Rather, everything works together in unity, and when all of these sources of Tradition are accepted as the common fountain of the self-revelation of God, it is our faith that they will bring us to the life to which God has invited His creation, to the destiny that He has given us in sharing His own life, His own eternal communion—to know Him who has offered us the truth that will set us free.

The Bible

There is, however, something that holds the primacy, the place of honor in the sources of our Tradition—and that is the Bible. The word "bible" comes from the Greek *biblous*, which means "books," plural. The Bible is a collection of various books. The existence of the Bible as a single volume is a modern phenomenon made possible by the printing press. In the Bible, or the Scriptures (which simply means "writings"), we find books of various kinds with various contents. We find books of history, poetry and songs, books of wisdom and philosophy, collections of stories. We find Gospels, which are the Church's expression of who Jesus Christ is, what He taught, what He did. We find letters written by Apostles, also called epistles. (The word "epistle" simply means "letter.")

This collection of writings is inspired by the Holy Spirit. "Inspired" comes from "spirit," which means "breath." Something that has been inspired has had the breath of God breathed into it. It is an expression of God's truth. The Scriptures are those writings which the Church has produced which faithfully convey what God has revealed.

As has been said already, it is not the Bible that produced the Church. Rather, it is the Church that produced the Bible. It is the authority of the Church that decided which books would be considered as part of the Holy Scriptures, and which books would not be so considered. Many writings were being circulated, both among the Jews, over a period of a thousand years, and also among the early Christians. It is the authority of the Church that sorted through all these writings and gave the stamp of approval to those which faithfully expressed what had always been believed and experienced in the Church.

As we know, the Scriptures in the Orthodox Bible are divided up into the Old Testament and the New Testament. Although there is not a specifically Orthodox English translation of the Bible, there are some important differences between the various editions of the Scriptures, both Old and New Testaments.

The Orthodox Scriptures

The Old Testament, for the most part, was written in the Hebrew language, the language of Israel. At the time of Jesus and the Apostles, however, most of the Jews no longer lived in the territory that we call Israel. So Hebrew, the language in which the Old Testament was written, had ceased to be a commonly spoken language among the Jews. It was used in the temple, and to a certain extent in the synagogues, but the people, for the most part, did not speak it at home.

The language that was most common at that time was Greek. The New Testament is written in Greek because that was the language that was commonly spoken, the so-called lingua franca throughout the Roman Empire. So a couple of centuries before Christ, the Old Testament Scriptures were translated from Hebrew into Greek. According to the tradition of this translation, it was made by seventy translators in the city of Alexandria in Egypt, so this Greek translation is called the Septuagint (from the Greek word for "seventy").

At the time of Jesus and the Apostles, and during the period of the early Church, it was very rare for an individual person to have in his possession any kind of scroll of the Scriptures. They were too precious and valuable, and also treated with such reverence that it was considered inappropriate for an individual to have possession of them. A local church or synagogue would consider itself fortunate to have one complete text of the Scripture, one set of scrolls or books.

The language familiar to most of those hearing or reading the Scriptures in the early Church would have been Greek, so it is this Greek translation of the Old Testament called the Septuagint that is the official Old Testament of the Orthodox Church. Because nearly all currently available English Old Testaments are not translated from the Septuagint texts, but from the Hebrew texts, it's hard to get a Septuagint Old Testament. Why does the Orthodox Church insist that this remain the standard Old Testament text? It is because, particularly in the Psalms and the Prophets, the prophecies that are made regarding the coming of the Savior, the Messiah, are far more literal, far more precise, far more intense in the Septuagint text than they are in the Hebrew texts of the rabbis.

In the New King James Version, or any of the currently available English translations, the Old Testament is translated from the Hebrew text that was preserved by the rabbis and the Hebrew scribes. The Septuagint was actually based on an older set of manuscripts in Hebrew that are not available any more. This Septuagint translation was made before Christ, yet the prophecies of the coming of the Savior to Israel are far more intense in it than in the later texts. The early Christians saw in this the increased preparation of God revealing Himself to Israel. Of course, the ultimate revelation of the God of Israel is His own coming in the Person of Jesus Christ, His Son. The gradual intensification of the Messianic prophecies that one finds in the Septuagint text is understood by the Orthodox as being inspired by the Holy Spirit.

Secondly, whenever the New Testament quotes the Old Testament, the version that is quoted *almost without exception* is the Septuagint version. In the case of the Psalms and the Prophets, the differences between the Septuagint and the Hebrew text of the scribes are considerable. That's why, when we sing psalms or read from the Old Testament in Orthodox services, we take great care that what we are reading is faithful to the Septuagint text. Someday, by the grace of God, there will be a good translation of the complete Septuagint into modern English which will be readily available.

Thirdly, the other aspect of the Old Testament that is part of what the Orthodox accept as canonical Scripture is what is called the "longer canon." (Canonical means legitimate according to the canon, the rule of faith.) This consists of books that are found only in the Septuagint version and not in the Hebrew texts of the rabbis. Such books as Tobit, Judah, more chapters to the Book of Esther, more chapters to the Prophecy of Daniel, the Books of Maccabees, the Book of the Wisdom of Solomon, the Book of Sirach, the Prophecy of Baruch, the Prayer of Manasseh, because they are part of the longer canon that was accepted from the beginning by the early Church, are considered by the Orthodox to be fully part of the Old Testament.

Protestant translations which include these books refer to them as the "Apocrypha." The root of the word "apocrypha" means "that which is hidden." We don't use that word in the Orthodox Church to refer to the books that belong to the longer canon. Protestants use the term "Apocrypha" to imply that those books are not really part of the Old Testament, but are extra, less than fully Scriptural books. But in the Orthodox Church the books of the longer canon are understood to be fully part of the Old Testament.

The official Orthodox Greek text of the New Testament is frequently referred to as the "Received Text." Sometimes it's called the "Byzantine Text." It is the text of the Gospels and Epistles that has been read in the Greek Church from the beginning. The most easily available version of the New Testament which follows very strictly this traditional, received text, yet is written in understandable modern English, is the New King James Version.

Understanding the Scriptures within the Church

The Scriptures say of themselves that they are to be understood within the life and understanding of the people of God. It's important to realize that the Church of the New Testament existed for more than three hundred years before the books of the New Testament were put into their final form.

In 2 Thessalonians 2:15, we read this: "Therefore, brethren, stand fast and hold the traditions which you were taught, whether by word or our epistle." That is a very important expression, "the traditions which you were taught." Where do they come from? They are not all to be found in something you can pick up and read. There is an aspect of the Church's life which is conveyed orally, and has been from the beginning. There is another aspect of the Church's life which is conveyed through writing. But the essential thing to understand is that it is the Church itself that is the criterion of truth.

Another very important reference to that is found in 1 Timothy 3:14, 15, where St. Paul describes the Church as "the pillar and ground of the truth." The Scriptures themselves confess that the pillar and ground of truth is the Church. If we are to understand the Scriptures, we must understand them with the understanding of the Church.

St. Peter writes in his second epistle, 1:20, "No prophecy of Scripture is of any private interpretation, for prophecy never came by the will of man, but holy men of God spoke as they were moved by the Holy Spirit." The important context of those holy men of God is that they lived within the framework of the chosen people of God, whether Israel or the Church. So it is in the Church, through the Church, that the Scriptures are understood.

The Orthodox teaching is that if you divorce the Scriptures from their context, break them away from the Church which created themand declared them to be what they are, anything can happen. People through the centuries have, on the basis of private interpretation, concluded all sorts of things from reading Scripture that have not been believed or experienced by the people of God. We see, when we look at the world through Orthodox eyes, what happens when private interpretation becomes the criterion of truth.

Looking at the history of non-Orthodox Christians for the last thousand years, Orthodox observe a question, which is never satisfactorily answered. What is the criterion of truth? Where does one find the standard of truth? Is it found in one particular authority figure in the Church? Is it found in the Book, by itself, independently? Either one of those answers the Orthodox find unsatisfactory. As to the second answer, when you say, "All I need for salvation, I can find with me and my Bible alone," you are saying that the criterion of truth is me and what I think. The result of that, in Orthodox eyes, is the continual proliferation of various bodies that call themselves churches. New denominations are forming every week, all based primarily on private interpretation of the Scriptures.

Everywhere, Always, and by All

So the Orthodox Faith insists that the Scriptures are understood within the life of the Church. How do we understand that? There are three important criteria for determining whether something is traditional, of the life of the Church. First is the criterion of antiquity. Antiquity means it has been believed from the beginning. Secondly, the criterion of universality: you can find it taught and believed everywhere. And thirdly there is unanimity: it has been believed and taught by everyone who has ever been a member of the Church. Everything we believe and teach, the whole body of the Church's Tradition, is governed by these three factors.

As the Church lives through time and continually has to state the faith in words that are adequate to convey it, sometimes new expressions have to be formulated. But when a new expression is formulated it's not something new being added to the Faith. The most direct example is the use of the word Trinity. Nowhere in the Scriptures do you find the word Trinity. It doesn't exist. Great teachers in the Church in the fourth century made it up. Now, the Father, Son, and Holy Spirit are certainly in the Scriptures, from the beginning to the end. But there was a need in the fourth century to express what the Church meant by saying God is Father, Son, and Holy Spirit.

By the time the Church had been around for four hundred years and had finally been freed from persecution, there were people in the Church teaching all sorts of doctrine that was contrary to what had been believed from the beginning. The worst of those teachings denied that Christ was fully God. Later on there were those that denied that the Holy Spirit was fully God. They said if Christ is God and the Holy Spirit is God, then you don't have one God.

So the teachers of the Church were called upon. There was a need, not to invent a new doctrine, but to express with greater clarity what had been believed from the beginning. So it is in that way that such an expression as the Trinity began to be used by the Church. That is just one illustration of how the Church lives in time and addresses the need to continually express who she is, what she believes, what she has always believed. New things happen, but those new things are in concord with what has been believed and taught from the beginning, everywhere, by everyone.

So the Orthodox claim that what we profess is the Faith of the Apostles with nothing added to it, nothing subtracted from it. In the Church's efforts throughout time to be continually faithful to what she has received and passed on in her life, what we call her Tradition, all of these written sources, whether it be Scripture or any of the other things we mentioned, as they developed throughout the ages, all are faithful together to what has been revealed from the beginning, held together by this unity of faith and experience among the people of God that we call the Church.

That is why the Orthodox are not disturbed by what are sometimes described as discrepancies in Scripture. If you read the four Gospels, you will see that they are four very different books. They express both what Jesus said and what He did in different ways. For example, if you read the accounts of the Resurrection of the Lord, which is at the very heart of our faith, you find all kinds of different details in the different Gospels. But that has never troubled the Church.

Some people read these accounts and are troubled and say, "They should agree in every last little thing."But this reflects a mentality that tries to make the Gospel into something that it isn't. The Gospel never was intended to be some kind of newsreel playback. Maybe that's one of the reasons why the Gospel has lasted two thousand years, and we forget the news after one day. We modern people have a fascination with data. Data for us equal fact. But in the Gospel, the truth is often something far deeper than mere data are capable of expressing.

When something like the Resurrection of Christ takes place, something which brings the Kingdom of God finally into the human experience and makes it possible for us to have the life of God, it is actually impossible for human writers to find words to express it fully. That's why the Orthodox insist that no single source is isolated from the rest. We don't pick and choose. There's a verb in Greek that means to pick and choose, and from that verb comes the word "heresy." To be a heretic is to pick one part of what the historical Church has always believed and experienced and to ignore the rest. You end up unbalanced. That's why the Orthodox insist on the unity of all of the sources of Tradition. These are safeguards that we are given within the life of the Church, that not only our knowledge but our experience of God will be the complete revelation that He has made of Himself.

The Creed

The Nicene Creed was formulated at the first two Ecumenical Councils. At the first council, held in A.D. 325 at Nicaea, the first seven articles were adopted. The second council, which convened in A.D. 381 at Constantinople, added the last five articles of the Creed. The Creed expresses the belief of Orthodox worshippers, and is often referred to as "The Symbol of Faith." The Nicene Creed (together with the other formulations of the Seven Ecumenical Councils) distills the basic theology of the New Testament into a concise definition of what is to be believed, and serves as a guidepost for the interpretation of Scripture.

I believe in one God, the Father Almighty, Maker of heaven and earth, and of all things visible and invisible;

And in one Lord Jesus Christ, Son of God, the Only-begotten; begotten of the Father before all worlds;

Light of Light, Very God of Very God, begotten, not made; of one essence with the Father, by whom all things were made;

Who, for us men and for our salvation, came down from heaven, and was incarnate of the Holy Spirit and the Virgin Mary, and was made man;

And was crucified also for us under Pontius Pilate, and suffered and was buried;

And the third day He rose again, according to the Scriptures;

And ascended into heaven, and sits at the right hand of the Father;

And He shall come again with glory to judge the living and the dead;

Whose Kingdom shall have no end.

And I believe in the Holy Spirit, the Lord and Giver of life,

Who proceeds from the Father, who with the Father and the Son together is worshipped and glorified, who spoke by the prophets;

And I believe in One Holy Catholic and Apostolic Church.

I acknowledge one baptism for the remission of sins.

I look for the resurrection of the dead,

And the life of the world to come.

AMEN.

Some Orthodox Beliefs and Their Biblical Foundation

1. How does the Orthodox Church view the sacraments, specifically Communion?

Some teach that Communion or the Lord's Supper (which Orthodox call "the Eucharist") is only a sign or symbol. Most of Christendom, however, believes it is far more. The Orthodox Church has always believed that we, in a mystery, receive the Body and Blood of Christ in the Holy Eucharist. What do the Holy Scriptures teach concerning Communion?

a. Jesus said at the Last Supper: "This *is* My body" and "This cup *is* . . . My blood" (Luke 22:19, 20, italics added). The Lord states clearly that His gifts to us are more than just a sign or a mere memorial, and all of ancient Christendom took Him at His word.

The skeptic might say, "But Jesus also said, 'I am the door.' Certainly He did not mean He was a seven-foot wooden plank." No, and Christians have never interpreted His statement that way. But the Church does teach that He is our entrance into the Kingdom of God and that the bread and wine become, in a mystery, His Body and Blood.

b. In 1 Corinthians 11:29, 30, we read of people who became sick and even died through receiving Communion hypocritically. People are not affected in that manner by something that is merely "symbolic." In this sacrament we commune with God Himself.

c. In 1 Corinthians 10, Saint Paul is comparing the manna and water in the wilderness with the true bread and drink of the New Covenant. In 1 Corinthians 10:4 he writes, "And all drank the same spiritual drink. For they drank of that spiritual Rock that followed them, and that Rock was Christ." The question is, was the Rock Christ? Under laboratory observation, the rock would still most likely be granite. But the Word of God says, "The Rock was Christ." We do not subject the gifts to chemical analysis, but to the Word of God. It is *mystery*, but never magic. Christ was present in the Rock; He is present in the Holy Gifts.

d. In John 6:53 we read, "Then Jesus said to them, 'Most assuredly, I say to you, unless you eat the flesh of the Son of Man and drink His blood, you have no life in you.'" The Church receives this passage at face value—nothing added, nothing taken away. In Communion we become partakers of the Body and Blood of Christ. Just as the new birth (John 3) gives us life through water and the Holy Spirit, so the Body and Blood of Christ *sustain* His life in us.

e. There is also the fact (Heb. 9:11, 12) that Christ our High Priest enters the heavenly Sanctuary with His own Blood, and that it is in this heavenly Sanctuary that we worship (Heb. 10:19–25). There is only one Eucharist, the one in heaven, and we join in that one feast.

We must neither add to nor subtract from the Word of God. Therefore we confess with Holy Scripture that the consecrated bread and wine is the Body and Blood of Christ. It is a mystery: we do not pretend to know how or why. As always, we come to Christ in childlike faith, receive His gifts, and offer Him praise that He has called us to His heavenly banquet.

2. Why does the Orthodox Church continually honor and bless Mary?

Let us turn to the New Testament to learn what God says about Mary. A key passage is Luke 1:26–49.

a. The Archangel Gabriel calls the Virgin Mary "highly favored" with God and the most "blessed" of all women (Luke 1:28). The Church can never do less.

b. In Luke 1:42, 43, Elizabeth, the mother of John the Baptist, also calls Mary "blessed," and "the mother of my Lord." Can we not make the same confession? For centuries the Church with one voice has called Mary the mother of God. If God was not in her womb, we are dead in our sins. By calling her "mother of God" we do not mean, of course, that she is mother of the Holy Trinity. She is mother of the eternal Son of God in His humanity. Thus we call her the *Theotokos* or God-bearer.

c. Not only does Elizabeth call her blessed, but Mary herself, inspired by the Holy Spirit, predicts, "All generations will call me blessed" (Luke 1:48). This biblical prophecy explains the Orthodox hymn, "It is truly right to bless you, O Theotokos, the Mother of our God." One cannot believe the Bible and ignore Mary. Orthodox Christians bless her in obedience to God, fulfilling these holy words. We do not worship Mary. Worship is reserved only for God the Father, Son, and Holy Spirit. We honor or venerate her, as the Scriptures teach.

d. It is important to secure Mary's identity as the mother of God in order to protect the identity of her holy Son, "the Son of the Highest" (Luke 1:32), God in the flesh. Jesus assumed His human flesh from her! Mary's role is essential in understanding that Jesus is both fully God and fully man.

3. Does the Orthodox Church place tradition above or equal to Scripture?

The Church sees the Scriptures as inspired and authoritative Holy Tradition: the Word of God. It is crucial to understand how the word "tradition" is used in the New Testament, which condemns the tradition of men but calls us to follow Apostolic or Holy Tradition.

Tradition of Men

a. First of all, Jesus warned against holding to the "tradition of men" and "your tradition" in the strongest possible terms (see Mark 7:6–16). All Christians agree: The Bible says "no" to man-made religious teachings and traditions.

b. Secondly, Saint Paul warns in Colossians 2:8: "Beware lest anyone cheat you through philosophy and empty deceit, according to the tradition of men, according to the basic principles of the world, and not according to Christ." Here again, we notice the phrase "tradition of men," which the Orthodox Church condemns.

Holy Tradition

c. In distinction to the tradition of men, the Bible calls us to obey tradition which has God as its source. In 2 Thessalonians 2:15, Saint Paul writes, "Therefore, brethren, stand fast and hold the traditions which you were taught, whether by word or our epistle." In contrast to man-made tradition, Apostolic Tradition is our foundation in the Church.

d. Further, in 2 Thessalonians 3:6 we read, "But we command you, brethren, in the name of our Lord Jesus Christ, that you withdraw from every brother who walks disorderly and not according to the tradition which he received from us." Here again, we are dealing with Apostolic Tradition, the tradition which God planted in the Church. Thus, the Church is "the pillar and ground [or support] of the truth" (1 Tim. 3:15).

e. All true tradition comes from the same source: the Holy Spirit in the Church. The same One who inspired Holy Scripture prompted all the teaching of the Apostles, whether written or oral (2 Thess. 2:15). Further, it was on the basis of Church Tradition that the biblical canon was determined.

f. Tradition, as G.K. Chesterton wrote, is "giving our ancestors a vote." It is walking in the "paths of righteousness for His name's sake" (Psalm 23:3). Or, as Jeremiah writes, living by Holy Tradition is a call from God Himself. "Stand in the ways and see, and ask for the old paths, where the good way is, and walk in it; then you will find rest for your souls" (Jer. 6:16). Thus, there are two kinds of tradition: that of God and that of men. It is to the former only that the Orthodox Church is committed.

4. Do the icons of Orthodoxy border on idolatry?

In Orthodox Christianity, icons are never worshipped, but they are honored or venerated.

a. The Second Commandment says, "You shall not make for yourself any carved image, or any likeness of anything that is in heaven above, or that is in the earth beneath, or that is in the water under the earth" (Ex. 20:4, 5). The warning here is (1) that we are not to image things which are limited to heaven and therefore unseen, and (2) we never bow down to or worship created, earthly things such as the golden calf. Does this condemn all imagery in worship? The Bible speaks for itself, and the answer is no.

b. Just five chapters after the giving of the Ten Commandments, God, as recorded in Exodus 25, gives His divine blueprint, if you will, for the tabernacle. Specifically in verses 19 and 20, he commands images of cherubim to be placed above the mercy seat. Also, God promises to meet and speak with us through this imagery! (Ex. 25:22). It is not true imagery which is condemned in Scripture, but false imagery.

c. In Exodus 26:1, Israel was commanded in no uncertain terms to weave "artistic designs of cherubim" into the tabernacle curtains. Are these images? Absolutely! In fact, they could well be called Old Testament icons. And they are images which God *commanded* to be made.

From the beginning the Church has made images of heavenly things brought to earth: Christ Himself, the Cross (Gal. 6:14), and the saints of God (Heb. 11; 12). Worship is reserved for the Holy Trinity alone. But we honor the great men and women of the Faith by remembering them in the Orthodox Church via visual aids, called icons or "windows to heaven."

5. Why do Orthodox Christians honor the saints?

The Scriptures themselves call us to honor other Christians, both the living and departed.

a. In Acts 28:10, Saint Luke writes, "They also honored us [the apostolic band] in many ways." The biblical injunction concerning Mary, "All generations will call me blessed" (Luke 1:48), is an example of how we are to honor the saints for all time (see also Heb. 11:4–40).

b. We are to honor all believers and true authorities, not just departed ones. This is why Saint Paul exhorts us to honor one another (1 Tim. 5:17), and why Saint Peter tells husbands to honor their wives (1 Pet. 3:7). We are even called to obey and honor our civil authorities (Rom. 13:1–7).

c. In Orthodox worship, we see pictures or icons of the believers of history all around us. This is, in part, how we honor our forerunners in the Faith. In Hebrews 12:22–24 we read that in worship we join with the heavenly throng to praise and worship God. We come to join "an innumerable company of angels," "the general assembly and church of the firstborn who are registered in heaven," and "the spirits of just men made perfect." And as "in spirit and in truth" we join these angelic and redeemed heroes of the Faith, we do give them proper honor, as the Scripture teaches.

d. Modern Christianity tends to give notice primarily to living heroes—often newly believing athletes, beauty queens, and political figures. But throughout Church history, honor went to those who had finished the race (1 Cor. 9:24–27), not to those who have merely begun or who are still on the earthly track (Gal. 5:7). And these saints of old are not dead, but alive in Christ forever!

6. What do Orthodox Christians believe about liturgy?

Biblically and historically, true worship has consistently been liturgical. "Spontaneous" worship is an innovation of the last century or so.

a. Liturgical worship, written prayers (the Psalms), and feast days were the norm throughout the history of Israel (see Ex. 23:14–19; 24:1, 2).

b. The worship of heaven is liturgical (Is. 6:1–9; Heb. 8:1–3; Rev. 4).

c. The foundations of liturgical worship in the Church are apparent in the New Testament. The most oft-repeated prayer of the Church is there (Matt. 6:9–13). The words we say at baptism are there (Matt. 28:19). The words spoken at Holy Communion are there, with Saint Paul repeating Jesus' words (1 Cor. 11:23–26). Further, the believers in Acts 13:2, about A.D. 49, were seen in a liturgical service to the Lord: "As they ministered [Greek: *leitourgouaton*, the root word for "liturgy"] to the Lord and fasted, the Holy Spirit said. . . ." Note, too, in this passage that the Holy Spirit speaks to us during liturgical worship. Thus praise to God must never become dead form, but rather living worship, "in spirit and truth" (John 4:23, 24).

d. Some Protestant groups have reacted against Rome by dismissing liturgical worship (though everyone has patterned worship, "spontaneous" or not!). But the Bible and Church history are clear: liturgical worship is the norm for the people of God. Documents like the *Didache* (A.D. 70) and the writings of Saint Justin Martyr (A.D. 150) and Hipploytus (early 200s) all show that the worship of the early Church was, without exception, liturgical.

Section II

A Guide to the Spiritual Life

"One of the best known of the Desert Fathers of fourth-century Egypt, Saint Sarapion the Sindonite, traveled once on pilgrimage to Rome. Here he was told of a celebrated recluse, a woman who lived always in one small room, never going out. Skeptical about her way of life—for he was himself a great wanderer—Sarapion called on her and asked 'Why are you sitting here?' To this she replied: 'I am not sitting, I am on a journey.'

I am not sitting, I am on a journey. *Every Christian may apply these words to himself or herself. To be a Christian is to be a traveler. Our situation, say the Greek Fathers, is like that of the Israelite people in the desert of Sinai: we live in tents, not houses, for spiritually we are always on the move. We are on a journey through the inward space of the heart, a journey not measured by the hours of our watch or the days of the calendar, for it is a journey out of time into eternity." (Bishop Kallistos Ware,* The Orthodox Way, *SVS Press).*

Introduction

Having examined the role of the Bible in the Orthodox Church, let us now turn to a second, crucially important issue. What does it mean to be a true Christian—to walk as a committed disciple of Jesus Christ at the dawn of a new millennium of human existence? Once again, the Orthodox Church provides profound answers, based on two thousand years of Spirit-led experience.

In the teaching of the Orthodox Faith, salvation is never limited to a point in time. Salvation is not a one-dimensional event, a past-tense occurrence with merely philosophical or "positional" implications for the present. Rather, as illustrated above, salvation is perceived to be a lifetime experience—a journey "not measured by the hours of our watch or the days of the calendar, for it is a journey out of time into eternity." Like every journey, this journey must have a beginning. And like every journey, this journey continues until it reaches its final destination. By faith we come to Christ. Through His sacraments we walk with Him daily—hour by hour, moment by moment. And with hope and love we move ahead to that time when we will be eternally in His presence, worshipping with the angels. As Saint Paul says: "Now we see in a mirror, dimly, but then face to face. Now I know in part, but then I shall know just as I also am known" (1 Cor. 13:12).

We now turn to a brief examination of the Christian life—how we become Christians, and how we remain in communion with God throughout our entire lives.

Beginning the Journey to the Kingdom*

Most people, at one time or another, wonder if there is real meaning to life—an underlying pattern or purpose to it all. For me, that quest for meaning and purpose took place in college.

By the end of my junior year, I was ready to do a turn-around. I knew that Jesus Christ had a rightful claim on my life. And I had come to see that life apart from Him—even the enjoyable and constructive parts of life—held little meaning and satisfaction. I was into myself, out for myself, but at a point of wanting to start over.

That spring, I consciously committed my life to Christ. I acknowledged that I had shut Him out of my life, that I was honestly sorry for not following Him, and that I wanted Him to take full control of my life. Without much realization of what it would mean, I told Him, "From here on out, I'm Yours."

The inner results of my initial repentance and belief in Christ are difficult for me to describe. While some people have very dramatic turn-arounds, others experience few or no spiritual feelings. For me, there were no lightning bolts, no shock waves. But what I did sense was a distinct new awareness of the Lord's presence, and an accompanying peace in my heart and life. A love for God and a desire to please Him—experiences left behind in childhood—were rekindled. From that point on, I had an inner desire to know God, to live in abandonment to Him, and to attain to His heavenly Kingdom.

Of course, turning to Christ is nothing new, either to people in our age or to those in ages past. The fact is, Jesus Christ has changed the lives of countless men and women over the last two thousand years. People meet Him and are never the same again. Their lives are transformed. Christ has so deeply affected His followers that millions have willingly died for Him—and counted it an honor to have done so. But why?

Who is this Man who came into the world so unobtrusively, yet can change us so drastically, take away our loneliness, forgive our sins, restore and stabilize our minds and hearts, and even take us into the very Kingdom of God?

An Incomparable Life

Often when we think about the life of Christ, we start two thousand years ago at a manger in the Middle East, with the Baby, the Wise Men, the star. While these things concern His earthly birth, His story really begins in eternity past. Because before time began, before the world was ever made, before the beginning, Christ was there. For there never was a time when He did not exist!

The first words in the Bible are, "In the beginning God . . ." (Gen. 1:1). For God was there from the start, always existing in Three Persons: Father, Son, and Holy Spirit. From God the Father there was begotten or born from before all time God the Son. And eternally proceeding from the Father is God the Holy Spirit.

At the creation of the human race, we find God saying, "Let Us make man in

*This article is taken from the booklet *Entering God's Kingdom* by Fr. Peter E. Gillquist (© 1987, Conciliar Press).

Our image, according to Our likeness" (Gen. 1:26). Note the plurality of Persons in the Godhead. Thus, from before all ages, God the Son—also called in Scripture the Word of God—reigned with God the Father and God the Holy Spirit. This explains why the Gospels teach that God the Son, Jesus Christ, came to reveal the Father to us, and to send to us the Comforter, the Holy Spirit.

Throughout the history of ancient Israel, the Prophets foretold the coming of One who would be the Messiah of Israel, the Anointed One. They predicted He would be born in Bethlehem (Mic. 5:2), that a sign of His coming would be that a virgin would conceive Him (Is. 7:14), and that He would suffer and die for the sins of the people (Is. 53:5, 6). There are some three hundred references to His coming in the Old Testament Scriptures, all penned hundreds of years before He came.

Then, just as promised, in the fullness of time the angel appeared to a godly young Jewish virgin named Mary, and announced to her that she would bear a Son. "You shall call His name Jesus," the angel said, "for He will save His people from their sins" (Matt. 1:21). Thus, in the womb of the Virgin Mary, the humanity of Jesus Christ was formed. The Son of God became everything we are—except for sin—in order that we might become the recipients of everything He is. As Saint John writes, "The Word became flesh and dwelt among us" (John 1:14). God became man to reveal Himself to us.

Most of us ask ourselves at one time or another, "Does anyone else in all the world understand me?" The Incarnation—the "enfleshment"—of the Son of God answers that question once and for all—with a resounding Yes! Because Jesus Christ is fully God, He knows all things—even the number of the hairs on our heads (Luke 12:7). He created us. And because He is fully man, He is acquainted firsthand with our weaknesses, our disappointments, our sufferings. He knows about rejection, loneliness, hunger, and death because He went through them. Isaiah the Prophet wrote of Him, "Surely He has borne our griefs and carried our sorrows" (Is. 53:4).

Taking His flesh from His Holy Mother Mary, Jesus experienced birth and growth like all of us. In His early years He knew both servitude and apprenticeship to His earthly father, Joseph, in his trade of carpentry. And He knew the higher priority of obedience and submission to His heavenly Father, on one occasion staying behind in the temple to be about His Father's business instead of accompanying Mary and Joseph back home from a trip to Jerusalem.

He went through the adolescent years—he experienced what it was like to be thirteen, fifteen—and faced head-on the opportunities for loss of temper, moral compromise, dishonesty, and rebellion present in His day. He knows about human frailty because He was tempted in every way we are, yet He never succumbed to sin.

At the age of thirty, He was baptized by John the Baptist in the Jordan River. In doing so, He not only began His own public ministry, but also forever set apart water as the means of beginning our new life in Christ through the Holy Spirit. This is why the Church, His followers here on earth, has baptized her converts in "water and the Spirit" (John 3:5). Baptism is that God-given rite of passage into the Kingdom of God whose mystic power to change us surpasses all human reason.

Throughout His three-year public ministry, Jesus Christ worked countless miracles. He healed the sick, He brought sight to the blind, hearing to the deaf, and help to the helpless. He stilled a storm, cast out demons, and raised the dead. All these miracles established the presence of God's Kingdom and further affirmed that He was God. Those who knew Him but a short time said, "He has done all things well" (Mark 7:37). And when pressed on specifics, even His enemies could find no fault in Him (John 19:4, 6). The daily routines of entire towns and villages were cancelled or changed when He visited. Everything, it became apparent, was subject to Him.

After three years of His ministry the Jewish religious establishment could stand no more of Him. Because He was God and said so, calls for Jesus' death began to mount. Some of His followers saw the implications and fell away. Even the disciples whom He had hand-picked faltered, one of them denying Him three times. Finally, the religious and civil authorities teamed up against Him, put Him through a sham of a trial, and crucified Him as a common criminal between two thieves. In a few hours, He was dead. No one yet understood that He had died for the entire world, carrying our sins and transgressions with Him into the grave.

Then came the culmination, the most powerful and supernatural event of all history. Three days after dying, Jesus Christ was alive again. He rose from the grave, a champion over death. Death would never touch Him again, for He cancelled out its power. And to those who are joined to Him, His promise is, "Because I live, you will live also" (John 14:19). He had forever trampled down our greatest enemy, death, by His own death. And in His Resurrection He bestows life on the living as well as upon those long dead.

For forty days after His Resurrection, Jesus opened the Scriptures to the eyes of His disciples, teaching them about His everlasting Kingdom, and commissioning them to take the gospel to the whole world. He instructed them to build His Church, the expression of His Kingdom on the earth, and fulfilled for them His promise of the Holy Spirit to accomplish the task.

To be sure, the one thing Jesus Christ left behind in this world is His Church. The Scriptures describe that Church as an assembly of His people, a new nation, a royal priesthood, a dwelling place of God in the Spirit. Because those who make up His Church share in His Resurrection, they are called the Body of Christ, and He Himself is Head.

At the end of His forty days of teaching, while His disciples stood by as witnesses, Jesus Christ ascended in His glorified body into heaven. He reigns at the right hand of His Father. As our heavenly bishop, He is Lord of His Church. In Him, Saint Paul writes, all things "consist" or are held together (Col. 1:17).

One day Jesus Christ will return to earth, to confront the living and the dead. All humanity will appear before His awesome and dread judgment seat. The righteous will inherit eternal life; the wicked, everlasting darkness. The Kingdom of God will be established in its fullness, and Christ will reign, together with the Father and the Holy Spirit, forever.

Knowing God

Some years ago, I was speaking at Religious Emphasis Week at Washington State University. A student stepped forward with an important question. "What does it take for a person to truly become a Christian—what is the price tag for me?"

I told him that night there are two answers to his question. On the one hand, our salvation is a gift. It is freely given. There is nothing we can do to merit a relationship with God through Jesus Christ. That is what the Cross is all about. For when Jesus Christ died for us, He triumphed over the result of our sin, which is death. He died that we might live. Because of the mercy of God, we therefore read in the Scriptures that salvation is a free gift bestowed upon those who are joined to Christ.

That beloved passage, John 3:16, sums it up: "For God so loved the world that He gave His only begotten Son, that whoever believes in Him should not perish but have everlasting life." Saint Paul reminds us, "The gift of God is eternal life in Christ Jesus our Lord" (Rom. 6:23). Through Christ we are born from above through Holy Baptism into newness of life. We are given a fresh start in life—forgiven of all our sins, freed from the hold of evil in our lives, and filled with the Spirit of God to pursue a process of maturity in Christ. His grace to us is a gift.

But I also told my student friend there is a second answer to his question. "Let me say it as plainly as I can," I told him. "Coming to Christ will cost you everything you have. Your whole life must be changed—and keep changing—to become what He wants it to be. If you're into sexual immorality, it will cost you that. Cheating—you'll need to stop it. Drugs and drunkenness—you will need to turn from those. And if you are the sort of person who wants to withdraw from life and is not much interested in people, that will have to change as well."

You see, Jesus Christ preached one central message. It is called the gospel, the good news, and it is this: "Repent, for the kingdom of heaven is at hand!" (Matt. 3:2). To repent means to turn around, to commit one's life fully to Christ, to say "Yes" to the Lord and absolutely mean it. And why are we called to this life of repentance? Because to enter God's Kingdom there is one requirement. We must be righteous. We repent because we are unrighteous—we come far short of living lives that bring glory to God.

Isn't it true, when we look at our motives and actions, we see we must be an embarrassment to God? We have basically gone our own way; we have ignored His will and commands for us; we have acted in ways that have damaged other people—some even permanently. Sometimes we turn to God in a pinch, but when things smooth out we return to doing our own thing . . . and we know it.

When we first repent, we turn to the Lord Jesus Christ and tell Him we are sorry at heart for how we have lived. As undeserving sinners, we ask for His mercy and His forgiveness, and commit ourselves into His care for the rest of our lives.

Let's face it. If the Kingdom of God is worth anything, it's worth everything. We are called upon by Christ Himself to lay down everything that would keep us from entering it. That is why Jesus compared the Kingdom of God to a treasure hidden in a field. Once we realize the incredible value of that precious piece, we will sell everything we have to obtain it. This divesting of our private holdings is exactly what repentance means. We give up what we must not keep for the incomparable riches of Jesus Christ. This cost to us is the greatest bargain we can ever know.

When we turn to the Lord in this way, we begin the thrilling and adventuresome process of knowing God.

Consider one Saul of Tarsus who lived in the first century. We know him better, of course, as Saint Paul, the Apostle of Jesus Christ. Well educated under leading Jewish rabbis, the young Saul took it upon himself to persecute the early Christians at every turn. One day on the road leading to the city of Damascus, he was blinded by an overpowering light. Jesus Christ appeared to him from heaven asking, "Saul, Saul, why are you persecuting Me?"

Having been struck to the ground, Saul uttered his prayer of repentance. "Lord, what do You want me to do?" he asked, no doubt trembling. He was instructed by Christ to go into Damascus, where he would be told what to do. Ananias the prophet met him there and confirmed his faith and repentance. Saul was filled with the Holy Spirit, healed of his blindness, and baptized (Acts 9:1–19). He went on to bring the Word of God to countless men and women.

Or consider the venerable Polycarp, who was probably baptized into Christ as an infant or young child in about A.D. 70, still in the heart of the New Testament era. He was brought up to love and serve Christ, and became the bishop of Smyrna in Asia Minor just after the turn of the century. As persecutions of Christians intensified midway through the second century, Polycarp, now an old man, was given the choice of denying Christ or being burned alive. "I have served Him eighty-six years," replied Saint Polycarp, "and in no way has He dealt unjustly with me. So how can I blaspheme my King who has saved me?" (*Martyrdom of Polycarp,* chapter 9). Burned for his faith, Saint Polycarp is an example not of a dramatic adult conversion, but rather of a Christian privileged to live his whole life in peace and repentance.

I live in Santa Barbara, California, a city named for Saint Barbara, who lived in Nicomedia in the third century. Her father was an avowed pagan, a fanatical worshiper of idols, and he kept his daughter insulated from the outside world to keep her from contact with Christians. But in spite of it all Barbara heard the gospel of Christ, and turned to Him in Holy Baptism. When her father was told of her conversion, he marched her to the executioner's block and she was beheaded—possibly at her father's hand. Her pure and godly life, and her willingness to die for Jesus Christ, have brought great glory to Christ throughout history.

A century later in northern Africa, another Christian woman, Monica, gave birth to a son named Augustine. Though raised in a Christian home, Augustine, like many of us, determined to ignore God and live for himself. This gifted young man pursued a life of both academic achievement and immorality, and by his mid-twenties was miserable and empty. He tells in his classic autobiography, *Confessions,* of his surrender to Jesus Christ. "You have made us for yourself, O Lord," he writes, "and our hearts are restless until they find their rest in You." It was as though he came to Christ by the process of elimination. Nothing else worked. Under the guidance of his spiritual father, Ambrose, the young convert grew steadily in the grace of God. Saint Augustine went on to become a bishop in the Church and one of the most influential Christian writers and thinkers of all time.

Space does not permit us to tell of Saint Katherine of Alexandria, Saint John of Damascus, Saint Maximus the Confessor, Saints Cyril and Methodius, Saint Gregory Palamas, Saint Seraphim of Sarov, and the hosts of others who lived their lives under the lordship of Christ as fellow heirs of His Kingdom.

Besides their love for Christ, there is at least one other vital characteristic these people held in common. They all grew to know God and serve Him *in the Church*. This stands in stark contrast to much of what is taught today under the guise of Christianity. Tragically, some who still use His name have so willfully departed from the path which Christ set forth and those heroes and heroines of the Faith followed, that they have made knowing God nearly impossible. This, coupled with the churchless Christ of televangelism, has prompted people who sincerely desire to serve the Lord to try to make it on their own. But this option works no better.

Let me illustrate. Suppose you take a trip to Cairo, Egypt. You're sitting one afternoon at a table in a crowded sidewalk café having tea. A young man walks up and, with a heavy accent, asks to join you. A bit surprised, you invite him to sit down. You discover his name is Wong Lee, and he is an outspoken communist from China who is in Cairo for a brief summer tour.

Wong Lee asks you to tell him something about life in America, including what it's like to live in a democracy. You begin by talking about various opportunities in the business world, the possibility of owning property. Then you move on to the political arena, voting and the electoral process. You tell him about the checks and balances of the executive, legislative, and judicial branches of the federal government and something of how state and local governments work as well. You're honest about the shortcomings of the system, too, and start to wrap up your remarks about the essential freedoms under a democracy.

But before you can finish, Lee interrupts. "That's it!" he exclaims with the first real excitement of the afternoon in his voice. "This is what I want!"

"What do you mean?" you ask, bewildered.

"I mean, I want to embrace democracy! It's better than what we have as communists. Far better. Right now at this moment, I am telling you I am committing myself to democracy!"

You're stunned. You've never seen anything like this in your life. Half an hour ago, you barely knew this man. Now you have a new convert to democracy on your hands. You collect your thoughts for a minute, and then begin to offer some direction.

"Well, let's see, Lee. This is going to mean that we'll have to make arrangements to bring you into the country and make you an American citizen."

"What do you mean?" Lee asks. "Why should I move?"

"So you can live out your life under a democracy, so you can experience this freedom and opportunity," you explain.

"But my home is in Beijing," Lee retorts. "I have no intention of moving away from there. I'll study about democracy and learn on my own. I will memorize the Constitution and learn the Bill of Rights. And I can subscribe to the *Congressional Record*."

Your heart sinks. What he's saying will not work, and you know it won't work. How can anyone be committed to democracy and be perfectly satisfied to remain living under communism? It's impossible. But you can't get Lee to understand. He's into democracy merely on a mental level, and it will do him little or no good.

Such and worse is the plight of those who try to follow Christ—even zealously—but apart from the Church. They may be sincere, but they will never really get to know Him out there. For one must live within the Body of Christ, be fed by her sacraments, be instructed in her true Faith, and worship at her altar to attain the godliness and righteousness that lead to the Kingdom's open doors.

Coming to Christ and His Church

For two thousand years, the Orthodox Christian Church has held intact the fullness of Christ that we have discussed here. She has maintained this Faith in the face of almost indescribable persecution and suffering. Within the gates of Orthodox Christianity is the totality of the New Testament Faith, the Apostolic Church.

By the mercy of God, this Faith has never been reduced or diminished. Nor has it been added to or altered. The Orthodox Church is that one place, that zone of safety, if you will, where the God of the Scriptures—Father, Son, and Holy Spirit—can be fully known, loved, and worshipped.

One of the great Fathers of Orthodoxy is Saint John Chrysostom, a Bible teacher and preacher of the fourth century who has brought and still brings thousands of people to a saving knowledge of Jesus Christ through his writings. Whenever this man encountered a person who wanted to commit himself to Christ and learn to know Him, Saint John would agree to instruct him in the Orthodox Faith, after which would come Holy Baptism and the anointing with oil to receive the gift of the Holy Spirit.

But before the actual instruction was begun, the godly pastor would offer a prayer of enrollment by which the person was entrusted to Jesus Christ as his Lord and King. This prayer is still used today at the opening of the Orthodox service of baptism. Look carefully at how it begins:

"In Your Name, O Lord, God of truth,
And in the Name of Your Only-begotten Son,
And of your Holy Spirit,
I lay my hands upon your servant,
Who has been found worthy to flee to your Holy Name
And to take refuge under the shelter of Your wings."

Let me ask you a sincere question. Are you willing to flee to Jesus Christ for protection in His Holy Church, to learn to know Him, to be cleansed and changed? If so, a new life in Christ lies ahead for you. Your next step is to get to know an Orthodox priest in your area who can guide you through a time of preparation and instruction in the Faith, and then union with Christ in Holy Baptism.
Ask the person who gave you *The Orthodox Study Bible* to put you in touch with a priest. Or check the Yellow Pages of the phone book under "Orthodox" or "Eastern Orthodox," and call for an appointment to visit. Or you may write to Conciliar Press, P.O. Box 76, Ben Lomond, CA 95005, and we will try to refer you to an Orthodox church near your home.

Jesus said, "I am the way, the truth, and the life. No one comes to the Father except through Me" (John 14:6). Determine to follow Jesus Christ and learn to walk with Him on that path which leads to the knowledge of God. For Jesus Christ has promised, "The one who comes to Me I will by no means cast out" (John 6:37). The door has been opened to you, and He will receive you as His disciple.

How to Remain in Communion With God

There are many necessary elements for remaining in communion with God. Among the chief are:

- Regular attendance at Sunday Divine Liturgy, as well as consistent participation in the feasts and fasts of the Church year.
- Maintaining a daily prayer rule (for a basic outline, see *Morning Prayers* and *Evening Prayers* on pages 755 to 761).
- Daily reading and study of the Scripture (see either the Lectionary beginning on page 771, or the chart *How to Read the New Testament in a Year* on pages 781 to 783).
- Regularly partaking of the Eucharist.
- Regular repentance and confession of sins.

Spiritual Helps in the Examination of Your Conscience

The Seven Grievous Sins

1. PRIDE: the lack of humility befitting a creature of God.
2. GREED: too great a desire for money or worldly goods.
3. LUST: impure and unworthy desire for something evil.
4. ANGER: unworthy irritation and lack of self-control.
5. GLUTTONY: the habit of eating or drinking too much.
6. ENVY: jealousy of some other person's happiness.
7. SLOTH: laziness that keeps us from doing our duty to God and man.

The Seven Capital Virtues

The seven capital virtues are the opposite of the seven grievous sins.

1. Humility.
2. Liberality.
3. Chastity.
4. Mildness.
5. Temperance.
6. Contentment.
7. Diligence.

The Works of the Flesh

1. Adultery.
2. Fornication.
3. Uncleanness.
4. Licentiousness.
5. Idolatry.
6. Sorcery.
7. Hatred.
8. Contentions.
9. Jealousies.
10. Outbursts of wrath.
11. Selfish ambitions.
12. Dissensions.
13. Heresies.
14. Envy.
15. Murders.
16. Drunkenness.
17. Revelries.

(See Gal. 5:19–21)

Nine Ways of Participating in Another's Sin

1. By counsel.
2. By command.
3. By consent.
4. By provocation.
5. By praise or flattery.
6. By concealment.
7. By partaking.
8. By silence.
9. By defense of the sin committed.

The Fruit of the Holy Spirit

1. Love.
2. Joy.
3. Peace.
4. Longsuffering.
5. Kindness.
6. Goodness.
7. Faithfulness.
8. Gentleness.
9. Self-control.
10. Modesty.
11. Continence.
12. Chastity.

(See Gal. 5:22, 23)

The Three Theological Virtues

1. Faith.
2. Hope.
3. Love.

(See 1 Cor. 13:13)

The Chief Aids to Penitence

1. Prayer.
2. Fasting.
3. Performance of the spiritual and corporal works of mercy.

(See Matt. 6:1–18)

The Chief Corporal Works of Mercy

1. To feed the hungry.
2. To give drink to the thirsty.
3. To shelter the homeless.
4. To clothe the naked.
5. To visit those in prison.
6. To visit the sick.
7. To bury the dead.

(See Matt. 25:34–45)

The Ten Commandments

I am the LORD your God, who brought you out of the land of Egypt, out of the house of bondage.

1. You shall have no other gods before Me.
2. You shall not make for yourself any carved image, or any likeness of anything that is in heaven above, or that is in the earth beneath, or that is in the water under the earth; you shall not bow down to them nor serve them. For I, the LORD your God, am a jealous God, visiting the iniquity of the fathers on the children to the third and fourth generations of those who hate Me, but showing mercy to thousands, to those who love Me and keep My commandments.
3. You shall not take the name of the LORD your God in vain, for the LORD will not hold him guiltless who takes His name in vain.

4. Remember the Sabbath day, to keep it holy. Six days you shall labor and do all your work, but the seventh day is the Sabbath of the LORD your God. In it you shall do no work: you, nor your son, nor your daughter, nor your manservant, nor your maidservant, nor your cattle, nor your stranger who is within your gates. For in six days the LORD made the heavens and the earth, the sea, and all that is in them, and rested the seventh day. Therefore the LORD blessed the Sabbath day and hallowed it.
5. Honor your father and your mother, that your days may be long upon the land which the LORD your God is giving you.
6. You shall not murder.
7. You shall not commit adultery.
8. You shall not steal.
9. You shall not bear false witness against your neighbor.
10. You shall not covet your neighbor's house; you shall not covet your neighbor's wife, nor his manservant, nor his maidservant, nor his ox, nor his donkey, nor anything that is your neighbor's.

(Ex. 20:1–17)

Examination of Conscience Before Confession

Before going to confession, the penitent should make an appraisal of his or her personal shortcomings. For guidance, the following questions, based upon the Ten Commandments, are suitable for examination of one's conscience.

1. Have you experienced doubts in your faith? Have you failed to trust in God's mercies or spoken against the Lord in time of adversity? Have you doubted the Christian faith and the teachings of the Church?
2. Have you made an idol of any person or thing? Have you given to anyone or anything the worship that is due to God alone? Have you put your belief in fortune tellers or consulted those who presume to predict the future?
3. Have you taken the name of God in vain? Have you spoken lightly of religious matters or of sacred objects? Have you cursed yourself or others? Have you sworn a false oath or broken any solemn vow or promise?
4. Have you attended church regularly? Have you prayed regularly, remembering others in your prayers? Have you kept the Sabbath holy and refrained from doing any unnecessary work on Sundays? Have you spent the day in any unwholesome fashion or profaned it by improper conduct? Have you kept the fasts and Holy Days prescribed by the Church?
5. Have you honored your parents, superiors, teachers, and spiritual advisors? Have you done your duty towards your family? Have you been wanting in love or kindness towards your family in any way? Have you caused them pain by your words or actions, or neglected them, or failed to help them?
6. Have you oppressed anyone, held hatred for others, envied others, or desired revenge on anyone? Have you injured anyone by word or deed? Have you desired or hastened the death of anyone? Have you done anything to shorten your own life or that of someone else by injuring health or through intemperate living?
7. Have you willfully entertained impure thoughts or desires? Have you com-

mitted any unworthy actions alone or with others? Have you read immoral literature or been guilty of unchaste words or actions? Have you chosen bad companions or frequented unwholesome places? Have you led others to commit sinful acts?

8. Have you taken any property belonging to others or wished to do so? Have you kept anything that did not belong to you? Have you deceived anyone in business transactions? Have you paid your debts? Have you given to charitable causes in proportion to your means?
9. Have you witnessed falsely against anyone or passed unconfirmed judgment on anyone? Have you gossiped about anyone or harmed their reputation? Have you told lies, added to or subtracted from the truth, concealed the truth, or assisted in carrying out a lie?
10. Have you coveted the possessions of others? Have you been jealous of another's good fortune? Have you wished for things God has not given you, or been discontented with your lot?

Other useful preparations for confession include:

- Reflecting on the Lord's commandments (Matt. 22:37, 39).
- Reading and meditating upon the Beatitudes and the Sermon on the Mount (Matt. 5—7; Luke 6:17–49).
- Reading and meditating upon Psalm 50(51) and other penitential psalms.
- Reading the moral exhortations found in Romans 12 and 13; Galatians 5:14–25; Ephesians 4—6; and 1 Peter 2—4.

Where to Turn in the Psalms . . .

When you are tempted to compromise	Psalm 1:1–7
When you are unjustly criticized	Psalm 3:1–4
When you are lacking in joy	Psalm 5:11, 12
When you are being tested	Psalm 10:5–7
When you need encouragement	Psalm 17:6–8
If you doubt the Scriptures	Psalm 19:7–11
When you are lonely	Psalm 23:1–6
When you mourn	Psalm 30:10–12
When you need God's forgiveness	Psalm 32:1–5
When you are tempted to miss church	Psalm 34:1–10
When you are worried	Psalm 37:1–8
When you are sad	Psalm 43:3–5
Before you go to confession	Psalm 51:1–19
When you are depressed	Psalm 57:6–11
When you need God's protection	Psalm 61:1–8
When you need strength	Psalm 62:5–8
When enemies come against you	Psalm 70:1–5
When there is a shortage of money	Psalm 72:12–19
When you are deeply troubled	Psalm 77:1–15
When you feel insignificant	Psalm 84:5–12
When you wonder about life's meaning	Psalm 90:10–17
In times of anxiety	Psalm 94:16–19
If you are tempted to disobey God	Psalm 95:6–11
When you need God's mercy	Psalm 103:1–14
When you are discouraged	Psalm 109:21–31
When you have opportunity to serve God	Psalm 112:1–10
When a loved one dies	Psalm 116:1–19
When you need God's guidance	Psalm 119:9–16
Before leaving on a journey	Psalm 121:1–18
When you contemplate marriage	Psalm 127:1–5
To find a litany of prayer	Psalm 136:1–26
If God seems far away	Psalm 139:1–18
Before retiring for the night	Psalm 141:1–10
If you want to complain to God	Psalm 142:1–7
When you want to give praise to God	Psalm 150:1–6

Where to turn in the New Testament . . .

For the Sermon on the Mount	Matthew 5—7
When you are under pressure	Matthew 11:25–30
For Jesus' teaching on the Second Coming	Matthew 24:3–44
For the distribution of the Holy Eucharist	Matthew 26:26–30
For the Great Commission	Matthew 28:18–20
For Jesus' teaching on servanthood	Mark 10:42–45
For the Annunciation to Mary	Luke 1:26–56
For the earthly birth of Jesus Christ	Luke 2:1–20
For Jesus' teaching on eternal punishment	Luke 13:24–30
For the death, burial and resurrection of Christ	Luke 23:33—24:49
For how one is born again	John 3:1–8
For Jesus' teaching on the Eucharist	John 6:30–59
When you feel estranged from Christ	John 10:7–30
When you need comfort	John 14:1–6
To learn about union with Christ	John 15:1–17
For Jesus' teaching on the Holy Spirit	John 15:26—16:15
For the coming of the Holy Spirit	Acts 2:1–21
For the first Church Council	Acts 15:1–35
For the scriptural teaching on sexual immorality and homosexuality	Romans 1:18–32; 1 Corinthians 5:1–13; 6:15–20
For St. Paul's teaching on justification	Romans 5:1–21
For St. Paul's teaching on holy baptism	Romans 6:1–11
When the unexpected happens	Romans 8:28–39
When you are tempted to break the law	Romans 13:1–10
To learn of true Christian love	1 Corinthians 13:1–13
To learn of sin and righteousness	Galatians 5:19–26
To learn of faith and works	Ephesians 2:8–10
To learn of Christian marriage	Ephesians 5:22–33
To understand the unseen warfare	Ephesians 6:10–18
To learn of the communion of the saints	Hebrews 12:1–3, 22–24
To learn of Christian healing	James 5:13–16
For St. Peter's teaching on marriage	1 Peter 3:1–9
For St. Peter's teaching on false prophets	2 Peter 2:1–22
To learn about confession of sin	1 John 1:5—2:1
To learn about eternal life	1 John 5:11–13
To learn of the eternal kingdom	Revelation 21; 22

THE ORTHODOX STUDY BIBLE

NEW TESTAMENT AND PSALMS

NEW KING JAMES VERSION

First Edition Participants

Project Director
Fr. Peter E. Gillquist

Managing Editor
Mr. Alan Wallerstedt

Initial Draft Prepared by the Academic Community of St. Athanasius Orthodox Academy, Santa Barbara, California

General Editors

Joseph Allen, Th.D.
Michel Najim, Ph.D.
Jack Norman Sparks, Ph.D.
Theodore Stylianopoulos, Th.D.

Overview Committee

Archbishop IAKOVOS
Metropolitan THEODOSIUS
Metropolitan PHILIP
Metropolitan CHRISTOPHER
Bishop ANTHONY
Bishop DEMETRIOS
Bishop DMITRI
Bishop KALLISTOS
Bishop MAXIMOS
Bishop NICHOLAS
Bishop VSEVOLOD
Fr. Anthony Coniaris
Fr. Antony Gabriel
Fr. Stanley Harakas
Fr. Thomas Hopko
Fr. Alexander Veronis
Fr. Thaddeus Wojcik
Mr. Charles Ajalat
Dr. Apostolos Athanassakis
Dr. John Boojamra
Mr. Brian Gerich
Dr. Veselin Kesich
Dr. Petros Vasiliades
Mr. Ernest Villas

Thomas Nelson Publishers
Nashville, Tennessee

Printed in the United States of America

9 10 11 12 13 14 15---06

Contents

Articles

Introduction

You hold in your hands *The Orthodox Study Bible: New Testament and Psalms*. The first draft of the notes was compiled by the Academic Community of St. Athanasius Academy, Santa Barbara, California. The initial draft was then submitted to

The General Editors

Joseph Allen, Th.D., former professor of Pastoral Theology, St. Vladimir's Seminary, Crestwood, New York

Michel Najim, Ph.D., former dean of the Balamand Seminary, Lebanon

Jack Norman Sparks, Ph.D., dean of St. Athanasius Academy, Santa Barbara, California

Theodore Stylianopoulos, Th.D., professor of New Testament, Holy Cross Seminary, Boston, Massachusetts

This team of Orthodox Christian scholars reviewed, corrected, and expanded some 1150 manuscript pages of introductory material, notes, and commentaries on the twenty-seven New Testament books and the Psalms, plus the other instructional pieces which appear at the beginning and close of this volume and throughout the text. Serving as a special consultant and contributor at this phase of development was Fr. Thomas Hopko, Ph.D., dean of St. Vladimir's Seminary. The work of these editors was incorporated into a final manuscript which was submitted to the publisher as a final draft.

Overview Committee

Archbishop IAKOVOS
Metropolitan THEODOSIUS
Metropolitan PHILIP
Metropolitan CHRISTOPHER
Bishop ANTHONY
Bishop DEMETRIOS
Bishop DMITRI
Bishop KALLISTOS
Bishop MAXIMOS
Bishop NICHOLAS
Bishop VSEVOLOD
Fr. Anthony Coniaris
Fr. Antony Gabriel
Fr. Stanley Harakas
Fr. Thomas Hopko
Fr. Alexander Veronis
Fr. Thaddeus Wojcik
Mr. Charles Ajalat
Dr. Apostolos Athanassakis
Dr. John Boojamra
Mr. Brian Gerich
Dr. Veselin Kesich
Dr. Petros Vasiliades
Mr. Ernest Villas

The Overview Committee is composed of outstanding Orthodox clergy and lay leaders from around the world, representing numerous Orthodox patriarchates and jurisdictions. *The Orthodox Study Bible* has received enthusiastic support throughout the entire Orthodox Church. It is being made available throughout the English-speaking world and for translation and publication in Russia, Eastern and Western Europe and Greece.

Acknowledgments

The Academic Community at St. Athanasius Academy is chaired by Fr. Jack N. Sparks, dean, and includes Frs. Richard Ballew, Jon E. Braun, Michel Najim, Archdeacon John Finley, Jerry Cripe, Howard Lange, Dr. David Lewis, Carol McFarland, Christina Tassos, and Alan Wallerstedt. Fr. Peter E. Gillquist served as project director of *The Orthodox Study Bible,* and Mr. Alan Wallerstedt served as managing editor.

A number of clergy and lay scholars worked on the study material for one or more books of the New Testament and Psalms, and on the other supplemental sections. These contributors included Bishop KALLISTOS (Timothy) Ware and Frs. David Anderson, James Bernstein, David Barr, William Caldaroni, Marc Dunaway, John Elias, Antony Gabriel, George Gray, Peter Kreta, Michael Laffoon, John Morris, Constantine Nasr, Paul O'Callaghan, Gregory Rogers, and Gordon Walker. Lay scholars Dr. Apostolos Athanassakis, Dr. George Cronk, Paul DeMerritt and Jim Paffhausen provided valuable input. A special thanks goes to Dr. Petros Vasiliades for his work on the initial draft, and later editing by him and his colleagues at the University of Thessalonica. Additional help was supplied by the American Bible Society.

Undergirding this effort were more than three hundred individuals, churches, and organizations who served as benefactors for the project. Their gifts were contributed over a three-year span from 1989 through 1991 to underwrite the costs of biblical research and manuscript preparation. Thanks are due not only these donors but also to Mr. Sam Moore, president of Thomas Nelson Publishers, Inc., who established a generous matching gift program which motivated the great breadth of financial support for the project. It is in the memory of his mother, Marie Ziady, that this volume is published.

How to Use
The Orthodox Study Bible

The Orthodox Study Bible has been prepared as a lay- and clergy-oriented resource for personal Bible reading, group study, and the preparation of sermons and lessons. The Psalms have been included for Orthodox morning and evening prayers, which also appear in this volume. Other study and devotional helps include:

1. "Introducing the Orthodox Church" sets in historical context the development of the Church from her birth on the day of Pentecost, through the apostolic and post-apostolic eras, into the years of the Church Fathers and the seven Great Councils, down to the dawning of the twenty-first century.

2. "How to Read the Bible" by noted author Bishop KALLISTOS (Timothy) Ware provides help for all both in understanding the message of the New Testament and in gaining personal edification through its reading.

3. *Morning* and *Evening Prayers*. The text of these prayers can be traced back to the earliest centuries of the church.

4. "How to read the New Testament in a Year" is a systematic plan designed to guide readers into a more comprehensive reading of the New Testament Scriptures from beginning to end. Daily prayer and the reading of the Holy Scriptures are a part of the spiritual discipline of Orthodox Christians. In preparing *The Orthodox Study Bible*, all involved have maintained the hope and prayer that those who use this book will commit themselves to a life of prayer and Bible reading.

5. The Concordance, while not exhaustive, will be of significant help in locating passages for study reference.

6. The Glossary has been prepared by Orthodox scholars to assist those who love the Church and those who want to better understand her doctrines and practices. The words defined in the Glossary include both biblical and extrabiblical terms. In most entries, you will find one or more biblical references. In addition to these study aids, each book follows a consistent pattern of annotation.

The Annotations

An *Introduction*: Before reading a particular book, you have the opportunity to get a thorough overview of what you will read. Each introduction includes:

Author
Date
Major Theme(s)
Background Information
Outline of the Book

Footnotes: As you read, many passages will be footnoted to clarify meaning, historical context and other helpful insights. The footnotes will amplify the biblical text itself and its interpretation, Orthodox theology, liturgical use of a passage, people in the passage, and how the passage applies to our lives.

Headings and Sub-headings: Throughout the text, subject headings will help you follow the author's train of thought and provide continuity from subject to subject.

Cross-References in the center column enable you to look up passages that address similar subjects or contain parallel truths. Also, the center column will contain more literal translations and alternate renderings of certain words.

Articles: When the subject of a passage is dealt with at some length, the notes are included in a box under a subject heading. These are particularly helpful teaching aids.

The New King James Version

The text of *The Orthodox Study Bible* is the New King James Version. The translators and editors, while sensitive to English idiom, believe in the divine inspiration of Scripture and have adhered faithfully to the Hebrew, Aramaic, and Greek texts. The Koine Greek of the New Testament is influenced by the Hebrew background of the writers, for whom even the gospel narratives were not merely flat utterance but were often sung in various degrees of rhythm.

The **style** of the New King James Version is therefore designed to enhance the vividness and devotional quality of the Holy Scriptures: Words or phrases in *italics* indicate expressions in the original language which require clarification by additional English words; *textual notes* which will assist the reader to observe the variations between the different manuscript traditions of the New Testament; *oblique type* in the New Testament indicates a quotation from the Old Testament; *verse numbers in bold type* indicate the beginning of a paragraph; *prose divided into paragraphs* indicates the structure of thought; *poetry structured as contemporary verse* reflects the poetic form and beauty of the passage in the original language; and whenever the *covenant name of God* is quoted in the New Testament from a passage in the Old Testament, it has been translated from the Hebrew as LORD or GOD.

The **text** of the New Testament has more manuscript support than any other body of ancient literature. More than five thousand Greek, eight thousand Latin, and many more manuscripts in other languages attest the integrity of the New Testament. There is only one basic New Testament used by Protestants, Roman Catholics, and Orthodox, by conservatives and liberals. The traditional text of the Greek-speaking churches was first published in 1516, and later called the *Textus Receptus* or Received Text. Although based on the relatively few available manuscripts, these were representative of many more which existed at the time but only became known later. Those readings in the Textus Receptus which have weak support are indicated in the center reference column as being opposed by both Critical and Majority Texts.

Since the 1880s most contemporary translations of the New Testament have relied upon a relatively few manuscripts discovered chiefly in the late nineteenth and early twentieth centuries. Such translations depend primarily on two manuscripts, *Codex Vaticanus* and *Codex Sinaiticus*, because of their greater age. The Greek text obtained by using these sources and the related papyri (our most ancient manuscripts) is known as the *Alexandrian Text*. However, some scholars have grounds for doubting the faithfulness of Vaticanus and Sinaiticus, since they often disagree with one another, and Sinaiticus exhibits excessive omission.

Another viewpoint of New Testament scholarship holds that the best text is based on the consensus of the majority of existing Greek manuscripts. This text is called the *Majority Text*. Most of these manuscripts are in substantial agreement. Even though many are late, and none is earlier than the fifth century, usually their readings are verified by papyri, ancient versions, quotations from the early Church Fathers, or a combination of these. The Majority Text is similar to the Textus Receptus, but it corrects those readings which have little or no support in the Greek manuscript tradition.

Today, scholars agree that the science of New Testament textual criticism is in a state of flux. Very few scholars still favor the Textus Receptus as such, and then often for its historical prestige. For about a century most have followed a *Critical Text* which depends heavily upon the Alexandrian type of text, and more recently many have abandoned this Critical Text for one that is more eclectic. A small but growing number of scholars prefer the Majority Text, which is close to the traditional text except in the Revelation. Major Critical and Majority Text variant readings in the New King James Version are indicated in the center reference column, but it is most important to emphasize that fully eighty-five percent of the New Testament text is the same in the Textus Receptus, the Alexandrian Text, and the Majority Text.

Where significant variations occur in the New Testament Greek manuscripts, textual notes are classified as follows: (1) *NU-Text*: These variations from the traditional text generally represent the Alexandrian type of text. They are found in the Critical Text published in the twenty-sixth edition of the Nestle-Aland Greek New Testament (N) and in the United Bible Societies' third edition (U), hence the acronym, "NU-Text." (2) *M-Text*: This symbol indicates points of variation in the Majority Text from the traditional text. M stands for whatever reading is printed in the published *Greek New Testament According to the Majority Text*, whether supported by overwhelming, strong, or only a divided majority textual tradition.

A Challenge to Learn

Manuscript differences aside, we believe it is from an Orthodox Christian **perspective** that the Scriptures can best be understood. Here are some suggestions on how to do biblical study.

1. The New Testament is the place to begin. Try to read and understand one book at a time. One method is to read carefully and systematically, from Matthew to Revelation. Another strategy is to follow the Lectionary for daily Bible reading, which may be obtained at any Orthodox parish. You might choose to follow one method this year, another next year.

2. It is always helpful to study the epistle and Gospel reading for the coming Sunday as noted in your church calendar.

3. Many people benefit from taking notes in the margin of the Bible, and underlining verses which hold special meaning.

4. Set a goal to memorize a verse or more each week. It is not by accident that the Fathers of our faith have such a wonderful command of the Holy Scriptures: most spent long hours reading, memorizing, learning, absorbing.

5. Discuss what you are reading with your priest or spiritual director. Allow yourself to be spiritually formed by those who are mature in the faith, being careful to hold those opinions of the Scripture which are consistent with the historic creeds and councils of the church. For we follow not our private interpretations, but those which have been held by all, in all places at all times.

The Orthodox Christian faith is the faith revealed in the Bible. We listen to the Fathers because they listen to the Scriptures. We embrace the Creed for it distills the Gospel message. Therefore, it is imperative for us who want to be Orthodox to learn and live by the Gospel of our Lord Jesus Christ as it is revealed to us by His holy apostles in the New Testament.

Let us be a people who know and love the Word of God.

THE NEW TESTAMENT AND PSALMS

Words of Christ in Red

The Gospel According to

ST. MATTHEW

Author: *St. Matthew the Apostle*
Date: A.D. 50–75

Theme: *Immanuel, "God With Us"*

AUTHOR: Though the Gospel does not name Matthew as the author, all the early manuscripts attribute authorship to Matthew, one of the twelve disciples listed in the New Testament. His authorship is attested by the universal witness of the ancient Church.

DATE: Matthew could have been written as early as A.D. 50, but it is more likely that it was written after the fall of Jerusalem in A.D. 70. It was probably written over a period of years while Matthew resided in Antioch, where the church was a strong, mixed community of Jewish and Gentile Christians. St. Ignatius, Bishop of Antioch A.D. 67–107, is one of the earliest witnesses to the existence of this Gospel.

MAJOR THEME: Christ, the Incarnate God, Immanuel, has inaugurated the Kingdom of God and the New Covenant, which is realized in the true Israel, the Church.

Subthemes include:

(1) *The fulfillment of Old Testament prophecy*. Matthew shows conclusively that Christ, the incarnate Son of God, fulfills the prophecies of the Old Testament. He establishes the New Covenant through His death and Resurrection, and will continue to guide His Church, the true Israel of God, to the end of the age.

(2) *The revelation of the Kingdom of God*. Jesus proclaims that God's reign has come (4:17, 23), His power being manifested in His Son, but the fullness of the Kingdom will be consummated at Christ's Second Coming. The theme of the Kingdom of Heaven is present in:

(a) The *Person* of Jesus, at once God and Man, who radiates the immediacy of God's presence by His words and actions.

(b) The *preaching* of Jesus, whom Matthew depicts as the great Teacher, the interpreter of God's law through the Sermon on the Mount.

(c) The *miracles* of Jesus, which bear witness to His saving power, restoring health to creation and counteracting the deceit of Satan.

(d) The *authority* of Jesus to *forgive sins,* for God alone can forgive sins, and His forgiveness is fully realized only in His Kingdom.

(3) *A call to discipleship* (4:18–22; 8:18–22) through mission (ch. 10; 28:18–20), and the beginning of the gentile church (8:11, 12; 21:43; 28:19).

BACKGROUND INFORMATION: (1) *Matthew's personal background.* Matthew (meaning "gift of God") is identified as a tax collector (9:9; 10:3). In the other accounts of his meeting with Jesus (Mark 2:13, 14; Luke 5:27–29), he is called Levi. This use of two quite different names has led some scholars to argue for two different persons, due to the absence of Levi from the apostolic lists. Others, however, have argued that Matthew had a double name, because the Jews frequently carried two names—such as Simon/Peter and Saul/Paul. When he was called by Jesus (9:9), Matthew renounced the position of tax collector and became a disciple. According to Christian tradition, after Pentecost Matthew, filled with the Holy Spirit, preached the gospel in many places, especially to the Jews. He is commemorated in the Orthodox Church on November 16.

(2) *The Gospel to the Jews.* The Gospel of Matthew, though it has come down to us in Greek, has a Jewish/Hebraic flavor, which is evident in its Aramaic expressions and forms, and its use of numerous quotations and arguments from the Old Testament. Furthermore, Matthew gives details of Jewish religious observances, and often uses Jewish style and techniques of argument. God's final judgment, pictured in apocalyptic images common in Jewish writings, is also emphasized. Papias, a second-century Christian author, preserves the tradition that Matthew wrote the sayings of Christ in Aramaic, the common language of the Jews at the time of Christ, and that others later freely translated this work into Greek.

OUTLINE

I. The identity of Jesus Christ	1:1—2:23
A. Who Christ is	1:1–25
1. True Israel: Son of Abraham and David	1:1–17
2. True God: Immanuel, God with us	1:18–25
B. Events surrounding His birth	2:1–23
II. Jesus' public ministry: Revelation of the Kingdom	3:1—10:42
A. Beginning of the ministry: The Kingdom proclaimed	3:1—4:25
1. John the Baptist prepares the way	3:1–12
2. Jesus baptized and tested	3:13—4:11
3. Jesus' early ministry	4:12–25
B. Sermon on the Mount: Righteousness of the Kingdom	5:1—7:29
1. Blessings and responsibility of disciples	5:1–16
2. The righteousness of the Kingdom	5:17–48
3. The discipline of the Kingdom	6:1–18
4. The wisdom of the Kingdom	6:19—7:12
5. Admonitions and warnings	7:13–29

C. The mighty works of Christ: The power of the Kingdom 8:1—9:38
D. Discourse on mission 10:1–42

III. Responses to Christ: Belief and unbelief 11:1—25:46
A. Responses in Galilee 11:1—18:35
1. Belief and unbelief in the mystery of the Kingdom 11:1—13:52
a. Unbelief and hostility aroused 11:1—12:50
b. Parables of the Kingdom 13:1–52
2. Belief and unbelief intensify as Jesus manifests His deity 13:53—18:35
a. Examples of unbelief and hostility 13:53—14:12
b. The Pharisees' enmity increases 14:13—15:20
c. Jesus' mighty works for Gentiles 15:21–39
d. Jesus reveals His divinity to His disciples 16:1–20
e. Jesus reveals His coming death to His disciples 16:21—17:27
f. Discourse on life in the Kingdom 18:1–35
B. Responses in Judea and Jerusalem 19:1—25:46
1. On the way to Jerusalem: Jesus receives the lowly 19:1—20:34
2. Arrival in Jerusalem: Conflicts with Jewish leaders 21:1—23:39
3. Discourse on the end of the age 24:1—25:46
a. The events of the end 24:1–35
b. Active preparedness 24:36—25:30
c. The final judgment 25:31–46

IV. The Passion and Resurrection of Christ 26:1—28:20
A. Events prior to the arrest 26:1–46
B. Jesus' arrest 26:47—27:26
C. Crucifixion, death and burial 27:27–66
D. The Resurrection of Christ 28:1–15
E. The Great Commission 28:16–20

The Genealogy of Jesus
(Luke 3:23–38)

CHAPTER 1

1 The book of the [a]genealogy[1] of Jesus Christ, [b]the Son of David, [c]the Son of Abraham:†

2 [a]Abraham begot Isaac, [b]Isaac begot Jacob, and Jacob begot [c]Judah and his brothers.†

1 [a]Luke 3:23 [b]John 7:42 [c]Gen. 12:3; 22:18
[1]Lit. *generation*

2 [a]Gen. 21:2, 12 [b]Gen. 25:26; 28:14 [c]Gen. 29:35

1:1 Jesus means "O Lord, save," referring to Jesus' role as Savior (see v. 21). **Christ** means "the Anointed One," the Messiah, the One who is filled with the Spirit (see John 1:33). Though the Son alone became a man, God the Father and the Holy Spirit work in the Savior to save us.

Jesus became a man as a Jew, of the lineage of **Abraham,** the father of all Jews, with whom God established the covenant of circumcision (Gen. 17); and of **David,** Israel's greatest king, the prototype of the royal Messiah. Jesus fulfills the promise and the righteousness of the Jews, bringing those who are faithful and righteous to Himself, God incarnate. The **book of the genealogy** (vv. 1–17) reveals the history of God's choice of His servants and the preparation of humanity for His coming.

1:2 While Luke's genealogy runs from Jesus back to Adam, Matthew's list descends

(continued on next page)

Sunday of the Holy Fathers

Sunday before Christmas

1:1–25: God prepared the way for His Messiah through many generations.

3 [a]Judah begot Perez and Zerah
by Tamar, [b]Perez begot Hezron, and
Hezron begot Ram.†
4 Ram begot Amminadab, Amminadab begot Nahshon, and Nahshon begot Salmon.
5 Salmon begot [a]Boaz by Rahab,
Boaz begot Obed by Ruth, Obed begot Jesse,
6 and [a]Jesse begot David the king.
[b]David the king begot Solomon
by her [1]*who had been the wife* of
Uriah.†
7 [a]Solomon begot Rehoboam, Rehoboam begot [b]Abijah, and Abijah
begot [1]Asa.
8 Asa begot [a]Jehoshaphat, Jehoshaphat begot Joram, and Joram
begot [b]Uzziah.
9 Uzziah begot Jotham, Jotham
begot [a]Ahaz, and Ahaz begot
Hezekiah.
10 [a]Hezekiah begot Manasseh,
Manasseh begot [1]Amon, and Amon
begot [b]Josiah.
11 [a]Josiah begot [1]Jeconiah and his
brothers about the time they were
[b]carried away to Babylon.
12 And after they were brought
to Babylon, [a]Jeconiah begot Shealtiel, and Shealtiel begot [b]Zerubba-
bel.
13 Zerubbabel begot Abiud, Abiud
begot Eliakim, and Eliakim begot
Azor.
14 Azor begot Zadok, Zadok begot
Achim, and Achim begot Eliud.
15 Eliud begot Eleazar, Eleazar begot Matthan, and Matthan begot
Jacob.
16 And Jacob begot Joseph the husband of [a]Mary, of whom was born
Jesus who is called Christ.†
17 So all the generations from
Abraham to David *are* fourteen generations, from David until the captivity in Babylon *are* fourteen generations, and from the captivity in

3 [a]Gen. 38:27; 49:10 [b]Ruth 4:18–22 **5** [a]Ruth 2:1; 4:1–13 **6** [a]1 Sam. 16:1 [b]2 Sam. 7:12; 12:24 [1]Words in italic type have been added for clarity. They are not found in the original Greek. **7** [a]1 Chr. 3:10 [b]2 Chr. 11:20 [1]NU *Asaph* **8** [a]1 Chr. 3:10 [b]2 Kin. 15:13 **9** [a]2 Kin. 15:38 **10** [a]2 Kin. 20:21 [b]1 Kin. 13:2 [1]NU *Amos* **11** [a]1 Chr. 3:15, 16 [b]2 Kin. 24:14–16 [1]Or *Coniah* or *Jehoiachin* **12** [a]1 Chr. 3:17 [b]Ezra 3:2 **16** [a]Matt. 13:55

(continued from previous page)
from **Abraham,** the father of the believers of the Old Covenant, to Jesus (v. 16), the Messiah and the author of the New Covenant. Though all the families of the earth were to be blessed in Abraham through Israel (Gen. 12:3; 28:14; see Gal. 3:15–18), this promise was fulfilled through Abraham's greatest Son, Jesus, and the new people of God, the Church.

1:3 Jewish genealogical lists normally included only men. The mention of **Tamar** and other women (Rahab and Ruth, v. 5; Bathsheba [identified as "the wife of Uriah"], v. 6) is unusual. All those mentioned were Gentiles or sinners, which indicates God's graciousness. This passage underscores the role of women in the history of salvation and anticipates the crucial role of Mary.

1:6 King **David** mystically typifies the royalty of Christ (Ps. 110). Through his anointing by Samuel, David received the authority of kingship to lead Israel and preserve the covenant of God. As an adulterer and a murderer, however, he is a type of the repentant sinner. Although Jesus is David's descendant, He is a more exalted King, King of the Church, whose Kingdom cannot be destroyed.

1:16 The lists of both Matthew and Luke (Luke 3:23) name Joseph as Jesus' immediate predecessor, conferring legal paternity according to Jewish tradition. Some Church Fathers thought Mary, also, was of Davidic lineage. Old Testament marriage laws confer all hereditary rights on adopted as well as biological sons. Matthew, then, perhaps gives the succession of kings; Luke, a biological descent. **Of whom** is a feminine form in Greek, referring only to Mary, not to Joseph. Thus Matthew affirms that Jesus was born only of Mary. Joseph acted as Jesus' father, but he was not His begetter.

Babylon until the Christ *are* fourteen
generations.†

The Virgin Birth of Christ
(Luke 2:1–7)

18 Now the [a]birth of Jesus Christ
was as follows: After His mother
Mary was betrothed to Joseph, before they came together, she was
found with child [b]of the Holy Spirit.
19 Then Joseph her husband, being
[1]a just *man,* and not wanting [a]to
make her a public example, was
minded to put her away secretly.†
20 But while he thought about
these things, behold, an angel of the
Lord appeared to him in a dream,
saying, "Joseph, son of David, do
not be afraid to take to you Mary
your wife, [a]for that which is [1]con-
ceived in her is of the Holy Spirit.†
21 [a]"And she will bring forth a
Son, and you shall call His name
[1]JESUS, [b]for He will save His people
from their sins."

18 [a]Luke 1:27 [b]Luke 1:35
19 [a]Deut. 24:1 [1]*an upright*
20 [a]Luke 1:35 [1]Lit. *begotten*
21 [a]Luke 1:31; 2:21 [b]John 1:29 [1]Lit. *Savior*
23 [a]Is. 7:14 [1]Words in oblique type in the New Testament are quoted from the Old Testament.
25 [a]Luke 2:7, 21 [1]Kept her a virgin [2]NU *a Son*

CHAPTER 2

1 [a]Luke 2:4–7 [b]Gen. 25:6 [1]Gr. *magoi*
2 [a]Luke 2:11

22 So all this was done that it might
be fulfilled which was spoken by the
Lord through the prophet, saying:†
23 [a]*"Behold,*[1] *the virgin shall be
with child, and bear a Son, and they
shall call His name Immanuel,"*
which is translated, "God with us."†
24 Then Joseph, being aroused
from sleep, did as the angel of the
Lord commanded him and took to
him his wife,
25 and [1]did not know her till she
had brought forth [a]her[2] firstborn
Son. And he called His name JESUS.†

Gentiles Worship the Christ Child

2 Now after [a]Jesus was born in
Bethlehem of Judea in the days
of Herod the king, behold, [1]wise
men [b]from the East came to
Jerusalem,†
2 saying, [a]"Where is He who has
been born King of the Jews? For we

1:17 This selective list of Christ's ancestors (vv. 2–16) is arranged in three groups of **fourteen generations** each. *Fourteen* is the numerical value of the consonants in the name David, underlining Jesus' Davidic descent.

1:19 Joseph's righteousness—the righteousness of mercy, which transcends the Law—is seen in his unwillingness to expose Mary's supposed sin. Under Mosaic Law, betrothal involves almost the same commitment as marriage. Joseph cannot help but suspect a violation of divine law when he sees his betrothed pregnant. Although obliged by law to report the misconduct, he decides **to put her away secretly.**

1:20 An **angel** (or "messenger") **of the Lord** dispels the false reasoning of Joseph by announcing the utterly unreasonable: the pregnancy of the Virgin is by **the Holy Spirit.** Since being born of a virgin proves Jesus' divinity, only the revelation of God, in this case **a dream** (see also 2:12, 13, 19, 22; 27:19), could serve as adequate evidence of this miraculous conception.

The Bible calls engaged couples husband and wife before their marriage. Just as Rachel was called the wife of Jacob before marriage, because of her betrothal (Gen. 29:21; see also Deut. 20:7; 22:23, 24), so Joseph is called the "husband" of Mary (v. 19) and Mary is called the **wife** of Joseph. In the Orthodox Church, Joseph is remembered as the "Betrothed," pointing out Mary's ever-virginity.

1:22 Here is the first of Matthew's repeated uses of the formula **that it might be fulfilled which was spoken** (see also 2:15, 23; 4:14; 8:17; 12:17; 13:35; 21:4; 26:56; 27:35). The fulfillment of these prophecies not only underscores the intervention of God in history but also indicates His beginning the new creation.

1:23 The conception of Jesus fulfills Is. 7:14 in the Septuagint, where we are told that a **virgin** (Gr. *parthenos*) will conceive and **bear a Son.** He who is conceived in her is not a new Person coming into existence but the eternal Son of God, using her womb as His throne. The virginal conception through the Holy Spirit and the name of the incarnate Son, **Immanuel, God with us,** are clear declarations of Jesus' divinity.

1:25 This verse does not imply that Joseph did **know** Mary after Jesus' birth. **Firstborn** means having been born first and never implies the birth of others.

2:1 Matthew anticipates Jesus' mission to the Gentiles. The **wise men,** or Magi, who come **from the East,** that is, outside of Israel (perhaps from Persia), are the scholars of their time. In the OT, Balaam (Num. 23; 24) was one of their predecessors, a Gentile who also anticipated

(continued on next page)

The Birth of Our Lord Jesus Christ (Christmas)

December 25

2:1–12: Jesus is born in Bethlehem and honored by the wise men.

have seen [b]His star in the East and
have come to worship Him."†
3 When Herod the king heard
this, he was troubled, and all Jerusalem with him.
4 And when he had gathered all
[a]the chief priests and [b]scribes of the
people together, [c]he inquired of
them where the Christ was to be
born.†
5 So they said to him, "In Bethlehem of Judea, for thus it is written
by the prophet:

6 *'But[a] you, Bethlehem, in the*
land of Judah,
Are not the least among the
rulers of Judah;
For out of you shall come a
Ruler
[b]*Who will shepherd My people*
Israel.'"

7 Then Herod, when he had secretly called the [1]wise men, determined from them what time the
[a]star appeared.
8 And he sent them to Bethlehem
and said, "Go and search carefully
for the young Child, and when you
have found *Him,* bring back word to
me, that I may come and worship
Him also."
9 When they heard the king, they
departed; and behold, the star which
they had seen in the East went before
them, till it came and stood over
where the young Child was.
10 When they saw the star, they
rejoiced with exceedingly great joy.
11 And when they had come into
the house, they saw the young Child
with Mary His mother, and fell down
and worshiped Him. And when they
had opened their treasures, [a]they
presented gifts to Him: gold, frankincense, and myrrh.†
12 Then, being divinely warned
[a]in a dream that they should not return to Herod, they departed for
their own country another way.

2 [b][Num. 24:17]
4 [a]2 Chr. 36:14 [b]2 Chr. 34:13 [c]Mal. 2:7
6 [a]Mic. 5:2 [b][Rev. 2:27]
7 [a]Num. 24:17 [1]Gr. *magoi*
11 [a]Is. 60:6
12 [a]Matt. 1:20

(continued from previous page)
the Messiah. The worship of the Lord by the Magi is symbolic of the Church, the true Israel, in which membership is determined by faith, not by ethnic lineage.

One of the rare bits of chronological information in Matthew places this event in the reign of **Herod** the Great, **king** of Judea (37–4 B.C.). An underling of Rome, he was a great builder but a cruel ruler.

2:2 The **star** signifies the extraordinary importance of the birth of the Christ Child. In ancient times a star signified a god, a deified king (Num. 24:17). This *star* is a sign of the Messiah Himself, signifying the light He will shed upon the world.

2:4 Knowing little of the Jewish Messiah and fearful of losing his throne to a newborn king, Herod asks the **chief priests and scribes . . . where the Christ was to be born.** The *chief priests* of the temple in Jerusalem are the political and religious leaders of the Jews. They include the high priest, who alone can enter the Holiest of All (Heb. 9:7). They have no idea that the Messiah has been born. The *scribes,* high cabinet officers (2 Kin. 22; Jer. 36:10), know the Messiah is to be born, and where. But they have no revelation that He has come. God reveals His truth to those with "a noble and good heart" (Luke 8:15).

2:11 Matthew, writing for Jewish Christians, cites Gentiles as the first worshipers of Jesus. Luke, writing for Gentile Christians, cites as the first worshipers the Jewish poor—shepherds from surrounding fields (Luke 2:8–17). The Magi, firstfruits of the Gentiles, come to Christ bearing **gifts: gold,** for a King; **frankincense,** for God; and **myrrh,** for a Man who is to suffer and die. The wise men have received some knowledge about the newborn King through their observation of the star, but when they see Him, they recognize Him as the Sun of Righteousness (Mal. 4:2), the Orient (the rising sun) from on high (Is. 59:19), the Bright and Morning Star (Rev. 22:16).

Refuge in Egypt

13 Now when they had departed,
behold, an angel of the Lord appeared to Joseph in a dream, saying,
"Arise, take the young Child and His
mother, flee to Egypt, and stay there
until I bring you word; for Herod will
seek the young Child to destroy
Him."
14 When he arose, he took the
young Child and His mother by
night and departed for Egypt,†
15 and was there until the death
of Herod, that it might be fulfilled
which was spoken by the Lord
through the prophet, saying, [a]*"Out
of Egypt I called My Son."*†

The Holy Innocents

16 Then Herod, when he saw that
he was deceived by the wise men,
was exceedingly angry; and he sent
forth and put to death all the male
children who were in Bethlehem and
in all its districts, from two years old
and under, according to the time
which he had determined from the
wise men.†
17 Then was fulfilled what was
spoken by Jeremiah the prophet,
saying:†

18 *"A [a]voice was heard in Ramah,*
Lamentation, weeping, and
great mourning,
Rachel weeping for her children,
Refusing to be comforted,
Because they are no more."

Return from Exile
(Luke 2:39)

19 Now when Herod was dead, behold, an angel of the Lord appeared
in a dream to Joseph in Egypt,†
20 [a]saying, "Arise, take the young
Child and His mother, and go to the
land of Israel, for those who [b]sought
the young Child's life are dead."
21 Then he arose, took the young
Child and His mother, and came into
the land of Israel.
22 But when he heard that Archelaus was reigning over Judea instead
of his father Herod, he was afraid
to go there. And being warned by
God in a [a]dream, he turned aside
[b]into the region of Galilee.†
23 And he came and dwelt in a city
called [a]Nazareth, that it might be

15 [a]Hos. 11:1
18 [a]Jer. 31:15
20 [a]Luke 2:39 [b]Matt. 2:16
22 [a]Matt. 2:12, 13, 19 [b]Luke 2:39
23 [a]John 1:45, 46

2:14 Egypt is where Israel once took refuge and was made captive. As the Israelites fled from Egypt (Ex. 12:31–42), so Joseph flees into Egypt, **by night.** It is probable the gifts of the Magi paid for this journey. Some of the first steps of Jesus are taken in exile. This is one of a number of instances in Scripture where God's people must elude civil power in order to do His will.

2:15 Out of Egypt I called My Son refers to Israel in Hos. 11:1 (see Ex. 4:22; Num. 23:21, 22; 24:5–8). In the OT the *son* of God is Israel; here Jesus is the true Israel. He reenacts in His own life the history of Israel, without falling into sin.

2:16 The cruelty of Herod was prefigured at Moses' birth, when Pharaoh attempted to kill **all the male children** in order to destroy the first Israel (Ex. 1:16, 22).

2:17, 18 Jeremiah recorded the people of Jerusalem being led away to exile (Jer. 31:15). On their sad pilgrimage to an alien land, they passed **Ramah** (v. 18), where **Rachel,** wife of Jacob, lay buried (1 Sam. 10:2). In his prophecy Jeremiah pictures Rachel, who had long been dead, **weeping** even in her tomb for the fate that had befallen the people, **her children.** Now, the mothers of Bethlehem weep for the slaughter of their children, the Holy Innocents, who are regarded as saints and martyrs in the Orthodox Church. As Rachel was told her children would return from exile in Babylon (Jer. 31:16, 17), so Jesus will return from His exile in Egypt.

2:19 Herod the Great died in 4 B.C. The dating of Christ's birth on which the A.D. (*Anno Domini,* Latin for "in the year of the Lord") calendar was based was off by several years.

2:22 Archelaus was banished by Augustus Caesar to Gaul in A.D. 6, when the Jews, protesting the cruelty of Archelaus' rule, petitioned his removal. That very cruelty is foretold by the Lord as a warning to Joseph; hence the detour to Nazareth (v. 23), a town in **Galilee** governed by another son of Herod, called Herod Antipas (see Luke 3:1).

fulfilled [b]which was spoken by the
prophets, "He shall be called a
Nazarene."†

John the Baptist's Call to Repentance
(Mark 1:1–8; Luke 3:1–18; John 1:19–28)

3 In those days [a]John the Baptist
came preaching [b]in the wilderness of Judea,†
2 and saying, "Repent, for [a]the
kingdom of heaven is at hand!"
3 For this is he who was spoken
of by the prophet Isaiah, saying:

[a]"The voice of one crying in the
wilderness:
[b]'Prepare the way of the LORD;
Make His paths straight.' "

4 Now [a]John himself was clothed
in camel's hair, with a leather belt
around his waist; and his food was
[b]locusts and [c]wild honey.†
5 [a]Then Jerusalem, all Judea, and
all the region around the Jordan
went out to him
6 [a]and were baptized by him in
the Jordan, confessing their sins.†
7 But when he saw many of the
Pharisees and Sadducees coming to
his baptism, he said to them,
[a]"Brood of vipers! Who warned
you to flee from [b]the wrath to
come?†
8 "Therefore bear fruits worthy of
repentance,†

23 [b]Judg. 13:5

CHAPTER 3
1 [a]Mark 1:3–8 [b]Josh. 14:10
2 [a]Dan. 2:44
3 [a]Is. 40:3 [b]Luke 1:76
4 [a]Mark 1:6 [b]Lev. 11:22 [c]1 Sam. 14:25, 26
5 [a]Mark 1:5
6 [a]Acts 19:4, 18
7 [a]Matt. 12:34 [b][1 Thess. 1:10]

2:23 The prophecy here cannot be conclusively identified. It has been taken variously as a reference to the Branch (Heb. *neser*) of Isaiah (Is. 11:1) or to the Nazirite (Heb. *nazir*) of Judges (Judg. 13:7; see Num. 6:1–21). Or Matthew may be alluding to passages which speak of the Messiah as despised, since **Nazareth** did not have a good reputation among the Jews (John 1:46). **Nazarene** later became a designation for followers of Jesus, especially in the Semitic world, although "Christian" was the more common name.

3:1–3 The wilderness of Judea is the barren region descending from Jerusalem to the Dead Sea. Preparation for Jesus' ministry begins with the call of **John the Baptist** to **repent** (v. 2). The reason: the **kingdom . . . is at hand.** Repentance, which always accompanies belief, is a total about-face. It is a radical change of one's spirit, mind and heart, a complete reorientation of the whole of one's life and being. It is the necessary first step on **the way of the LORD** (v. 3) and is followed by the confession of sins, the decisive act of baptism, and an actual change in one's life, the "fruits worthy of repentance" (vv. 6, 8–12).

3:4 John's ascetic life-style is in conformity with that of the Jewish sects, such as the Essenes, who made their home in the wilderness and whose purpose was to prepare for the coming Kingdom of God. His clothing is typical of a prophet. Elijah, who also wore a **leather belt** (2 Kin. 1:8), was the prophet expected to prepare Israel for the Messiah (17:9–13; Mal. 4:5, 6). Monastics especially follow in Elijah's and the Baptist's mission of repentance and prophecy.

3:6 People are **baptized** by John, **confessing their sins,** so that they may be prepared to receive the Messiah. Such preparation is usual in coming to faith. Confession of sin is a sign of repentance and is essential to baptism even today. John's baptism, however, was for remission of sins only, purifying people for the coming of the Messiah and helping to deliver them from the wrath to come; it did not confer regeneration nor adoption as a child of God (v. 11), as does Christian baptism.

3:7 The Pharisees and Sadducees are skeptical of John's mission and oppose Jesus. *Sadducees,* members of the high-priestly and landowning class, controlled the temple and the internal political affairs of the Jews. Denying the resurrection of the dead, they had no messianic hope. The *Pharisees* were a lay religious movement centered on the study of the Law and on strict observance of all its regulations. They believed in resurrection and cherished a messianic hope, but taught that the resurrection to righteousness is attained solely on the power of one's good works according to Mosaic Law, and that the Messiah was only a glorious man. John's epithet for them, **brood of vipers** (12:34; 23:33), sharply denounces their malice as being influenced by "the snake," the Adversary, Satan (Job 1:6).

3:8 Repentance, confession, and baptism lead to **fruits worthy of repentance,** a way of life consonant with the expected messianic Kingdom (see Gal. 5:22–25). If no fruit appears, sacramental acts and spiritual discipline are useless. Thus in icons of John baptizing Jesus in the Jordan, often an ax is pictured on a fruitless tree (v. 10).

The Baptism of Our Lord Jesus Christ (Theophany) *January 6*

3:13–17: Jesus is publicly proclaimed the Son of God at His baptism.

9 "and do not think to say to
yourselves, [a]'We have Abraham as
our father.' For I say to you that God
is able to raise up children to Abraham from these stones.†
10 "And even now the ax is laid
to the root of the trees. [a]Therefore
every tree which does not bear good
fruit is cut down and thrown into
the fire.†
11 [a]"I indeed baptize you with water unto repentance, but He who is
coming after me is mightier than I,
whose sandals I am not worthy to
carry. [b]He will baptize you with the
Holy Spirit [1]and fire.†
12 [a]"His winnowing fan *is* in His
hand, and He will thoroughly clean
out His threshing floor, and gather
His wheat into the barn; but He will
[b]burn up the chaff with unquenchable fire."†

9 [a]John 8:33
10 [a]Matt. 7:19
11 [a]Luke 3:16 [b][Acts 2:3, 4] [1]M omits *and fire*
12 [a]Mal. 3:3 [b]Matt. 13:30

13 [a]Mark 1:9–11 [b]Matt. 2:22
16 [a]Mark 1:10 [b]John 1:32 [1]Or *he*
17 [a]John 12:28 [b]Ps. 2:7

The Baptism of Jesus
(Mark 1:9–11; Luke 3:21, 22; John 1:29–34)

13 [a]Then Jesus came [b]from Galilee
to John at the Jordan to be baptized
by him.
14 And John *tried to* prevent Him,
saying, "I need to be baptized by
You, and are You coming to me?"
15 But Jesus answered and said to
him, "Permit *it to be so* now, for thus
it is fitting for us to fulfill all righteousness." Then he allowed Him.†
16 [a]When He had been baptized,
Jesus came up immediately from the
water; and behold, the heavens were
opened to Him, and [1]He saw [b]the
Spirit of God descending like a dove
and alighting upon Him.†
17 [a]And suddenly a voice *came*
from heaven, saying, [b]"This is My

3:9 The warning that **from these stones** (Heb. *'ebanim*) God can **raise up children** (Heb. *banim*) is a Hebrew play on words. God does not admit fruitless children into His house; He creates new children from the Gentiles.

3:10 **Even now** shows that the Baptist anticipates divine judgment on God's people through the coming of the Messiah (v. 12). **Fire,** a symbol of destruction, often describes the final judgment (see Is. 33:11; 66:24; Ezek. 38:22; 39:6; Zeph. 1:18).

3:11 John's baptism of water only prepares for Christ's baptism of water and **the Holy Spirit.** Christ baptizes in **fire,** for as the grace of the Holy Spirit was poured out upon the Apostles in the form of tongues of *fire,* so is that grace poured out in baptism. In John's culture, a slave would **carry** the king's **sandals.** Thus John powerfully contrasts himself with God's Son, Jesus the Messiah.

3:12 The figure of **winnowing** the threshed grain from the **chaff** is a metaphor for divine judgment, which always separates good from evil.

3:15 Jesus did not need purification. But by making the purification of humanity His own, He would wash away the sin of humanity, grant regeneration, and reveal the mystery of the Holy Trinity. Thus, His baptism was necessary for the fulfillment of all God's righteousness. St. Gregory of Nyssa says, "Jesus enters the filthy [sinful] waters of the world and when He comes out, brings up [purifies] the entire world with Him."

3:16 The **Spirit of God** hovered over the water at the first creation (Gen. 1:2). Now, the Holy Spirit comes in the form of **a dove** to anoint the Messiah, the Son of God, at the beginning of the new creation. Jesus does not become the Son of God this day; rather, in His baptism the eternal Son of God is revealed to all humanity. The Holy Spirit always rests on Him. The feast day of Epiphany (a manifestation or revelation), or Theophany (a manifestation of God), commemorates this day and points to the age to come.

beloved Son, in whom I am well pleased."†

Jesus' Triumph over Satan

(Mark 1:12, 13; Luke 4:1–13)

4 Then [a]Jesus was led up by
[b]the Spirit into the wilderness to
be tempted by the devil.†
2 And when He had fasted forty
days and forty nights, afterward He
was hungry.†
3 Now when the tempter came to
Him, he said, "If You are the Son
of God, command that these stones
become bread."†
4 But He answered and said, "It
is written, [a]*'Man shall not live by
bread alone, but by every word that
proceeds from the mouth of God.'* "†
5 Then the devil took Him up
[a]into the holy city, set Him on the
pinnacle of the temple,†
6 and said to Him, "If You are the
Son of God, throw Yourself down.
For it is written:†

[a]*'He shall give His angels charge over you,'*

and,

[b]*'In their hands they shall bear you up,*

CHAPTER 4

1 [a]Matt. 4:1–11; Mark 1:12; Luke 4:1 [b]Ezek. 3:14; Acts 8:39

4 [a]Deut. 8:3

5 [a]Neh. 11:1, 18; Dan. 9:24; Matt. 27:53

6 [a]Ps. 91:11 [b]Ps. 91:12

3:17 This is a composite quotation from Ps. 2:7, "You are My Son, today I have begotten You," and Is. 42:1, "Behold! My Servant whom I uphold, My Elect One, in whom My soul delights!" The substitution of **Son** for "Servant" reveals the deity of Christ, the naturally and eternally begotten Son of God. Note how the baptism of Jesus reveals the great mystery of the Holy Trinity. The Father speaks; the Holy Spirit descends; the incarnate Son is baptized and anointed.

4:1 To be **tempted** is to be tested in fundamental areas of faith. As in Mark, the **Spirit** leads, or "throws," Jesus into **the wilderness** after His baptism to be tested by a struggle with **the devil.** We who are baptized into Him need not be defeated when temptations come along because, like Jesus, we are aided by the Spirit. *The wilderness* is a battleground, a picture of the world, at once the abode of demons and a source of divine tranquility and contemplation.

4:2–10 Jesus reverses Israel's dallying with temptation in the wilderness. The Israelites were tested 40 years in the wilderness, during which they were disloyal and disobedient. So God humbled them by letting them go hungry, then feeding them with manna, all to help them realize their dependence upon Him (Deut. 8:2, 3). Jesus is tested with hunger 40 days, but He does not sin. Jesus' answers to Satan are from Deuteronomy (see center-column references), and all of them call for loyalty to God: we are to live by that which God commands. Contrary to the opinions of His detractors, in His messiahship Jesus actually fulfills the Law. He is the loyal and obedient Son who triumphs over temptations.

Jesus **fasted** to overcome temptation, giving us an example of our own power and our limitations. The hunger of His flesh does not control Him; rather, He controls His flesh. Jesus' fasting **forty days** is the foundation of the Church's forty-day Lenten observance before Holy Week (and also of the fast before the Christmas and Epiphany feasts). It is a spiritual preparation for the Passion and Resurrection of Christ.

4:3 The devil challenges Jesus' relationship to the Father. **If You are the Son of God** calls into question the Father's declaration of Jesus' sonship at His baptism (3:17). The devil wants Jesus to abuse His divine powers, to act independently, detaching His will from the will of the Father. In His divine nature, the Son shares one will with the Father and the Spirit. He can do nothing of Himself (John 5:30); He has no operation that is distinct from His Father's. But in His humanity He possesses "free will" and at all times must choose to remain in communion with His Father, to be obedient to the divine will.

4:4 By rejecting the first temptation, Jesus rejects a kingdom based on materialism, earthly well-being, the "bread which perishes" (see John 6:1–40). He teaches us not to love ease and comfort, to accept willingly the struggle necessary to purify us from evil. While Adam and Eve disregarded the divine word given them, subordinating their souls to the passions of the body (Gen. 3), the New Adam conquers all temptations, that He might give our nature power to conquer the Adversary.

4:5 **The holy city** is Jerusalem.

4:6 Satan puts God's power of protection to the test. Will Jesus depend on spectacular signs and self-aggrandizement, or will He humbly submit to persecution, humiliation and death according to the Father's will?

Lest you dash your foot against
a stone.' "
7 Jesus said to him, "It is written
again, [a]*'You shall not* [1]*tempt the*
LORD your God.' "†
8 Again, the devil took Him up
on an exceedingly high mountain,
and [a]showed Him all the kingdoms
of the world and their glory.†
9 And he said to Him, "All these
things I will give You if You will fall
down and worship me."
10 Then Jesus said to him, [1]"Away
with you, Satan! For it is written,
[a]*'You shall worship the LORD your*
God, and Him only you shall
serve.' "†
11 Then the devil [a]left Him, and
behold, [b]angels came and ministered
to Him.

Repentance and the Kingdom

(Mark 1:14, 15; Luke 4:14, 15;
John 4:1–4)

12 [a]Now when Jesus heard that
John had been put in prison, He departed to Galilee.†
13 And leaving Nazareth, He came

7 [a]Deut. 6:16 [1]*test*
8 [a][Matt. 16:26; 1 John 2:15–17]
10 [a]Deut. 6:13; 10:20; Josh. 24:14 [1]M *Get behind Me*
11 [a][James 4:7] [b]Matt. 26:53; Luke 22:43; [Heb. 1:14]
12 [a]Matt. 14:3; Mark 1:14; Luke 3:20; John 4:43
15 [a]Is. 9:1, 2
16 [a]Is. 42:7; Luke 2:32
17 [a]Mark 1:14, 15 [b]Matt. 3:2; 10:7 [1]*has drawn near*
18 [a]Matt. 4:18–22; Mark 1:16–20; Luke 5:2–11; John 1:40–42 [b]Matt. 10:2; 16:18; John 1:40–42

and dwelt in Capernaum, which is
by the sea, in the regions of Zebulun
and Naphtali,
14 that it might be fulfilled which
was spoken by Isaiah the prophet,
saying:

15 *"The*[a] *land of Zebulun and the*
land of Naphtali,
By the way of the sea, beyond
the Jordan,
Galilee of the Gentiles:†
16 [a] *The people who sat in darkness*
have seen a great light,
And upon those who sat in the
region and shadow of death
Light has dawned."†

17 [a]From that time Jesus began to
preach and to say, [b]"Repent, for the
kingdom of heaven [1]is at hand."†

The First Disciples

(Mark 1:16–20; Luke 5:1–11)

18 [a]And Jesus, walking by the Sea
of Galilee, saw two brothers, Simon
[b]called Peter, and Andrew his
brother, casting a net into the sea;
for they were fishermen.†

4:7 God's Kingdom is not one of earthly spectacle and fame. Therefore we should never expose ourselves to danger just to test whether God is going to "protect" us. To do so is to **tempt the LORD.**

4:8 God's Kingdom is not one of earthly power and possessions. In the devil's offering of **the kingdoms of the world,** Jesus was being asked to choose worldly power over the Kingdom of God. The devil is "the ruler of this world" (John 12:31; 16:11), "the god of this age" (2 Cor. 4:4), because the whole world is in his power (1 John 5:19).

4:10 Jesus refuses to take a road that would lead Him away from the path of suffering and death for the redemption of the world. Jesus says simply, **away with you, Satan**—a command rather than a rebuke.

4:12 Jesus begins His ministry in Galilee, for the common people on the edge of Jewish territory are more receptive to His teaching than the Jewish leadership in Jerusalem.

4:15 The term **Galilee of the Gentiles** indicates that many non-Jews lived in this region, which became an Assyrian province in 734 B.C. By Jesus' time it had a mixed population and was not considered a genuinely Jewish land, even though many non-Jewish residents had converted to Judaism in the Maccabean period. Even the Jews who inhabited this area were influenced by Greek culture and were considered second-class by the Jews of Judea.

4:16 Darkness means ungodliness. To sit in *darkness* means to be overcome by spiritual ignorance and death. The **great light** shines on these people, anticipating the gospel being preached to all after the Resurrection.

4:17 Christ's first word, like that of John the Baptist, is **repent,** because repentance is necessary to enter and continue in His new way of life. Repentance is man's turning from himself to God (see note on 3:1–3). **The kingdom of heaven** is synonymous with "the kingdom of God"; it is present in Christ (12:28).

4:18–22 These first disciples of Christ had already heard the preaching of John the Baptist, which prepared them to accept the Messiah **immediately** (v. 22). Verse 19 may describe the

(continued on next page)

19 Then He said to them, "Follow
Me, and [a]I will make you fishers of
men."
20 [a]They immediately left *their* nets
and followed Him.
21 [a]Going on from there, He saw
two other brothers, James *the son* of
Zebedee, and John his brother, in the
boat with Zebedee their father,
mending their nets. He called them,
22 and immediately they left the
boat and their father, and followed
Him.

Summary of Jesus' Ministry

(Luke 6:17–19)

23 And Jesus went about all Galilee, [a]teaching in their synagogues,
preaching [b]the gospel of the kingdom, [c]and healing all kinds of sickness and all kinds of disease among
the people.†
24 Then [1]His fame went throughout all Syria; and they [a]brought to
Him all sick people who were afflicted with various diseases and torments, and those who were demon-

19 [a]Luke 5:10
20 [a]Mark 10:28
21 [a]Mark 1:19
23 [a]Matt. 9:35 [b][Matt. 24:14] [c]Mark 1:34
24 [a]Luke 4:40 [1]Lit. *the report of Him*

25 [a]Mark 3:7, 8 [1]Lit. *Ten Cities*

CHAPTER 5
1 [a]Mark 3:13
2 [a][Matt. 7:29]
3 [a]Luke 6:20–23
4 [a]Rev. 21:4
5 [a]Ps. 37:11 [b][Rom. 4:13] [1]Or *land*
6 [a]Luke 1:53

possessed, epileptics, and paralytics;
and He healed them.
25 [a]Great multitudes followed
Him—from Galilee, and *from*
[1]Decapolis, Jerusalem, Judea, and
beyond the Jordan.†

The Beatitudes: The Blessings of True Discipleship

(Luke 6:20–49)

5 And seeing the multitudes,
[a]He went up on a mountain, and
when He was seated His disciples
came to Him.†
2 Then He opened His mouth and
[a]taught them, saying:

3 "Blessed[a] *are* the poor in spirit,
For theirs is the kingdom of
heaven.†
4 [a]Blessed *are* those who mourn,
For they shall be comforted.†
5 [a]Blessed *are* the meek,
For [b]they shall inherit the
[1]earth.†
6 Blessed *are* those who
[a]hunger and thirst for
righteousness,

(continued from previous page)
second time Jesus has called three of these men (see center-column references). As His disciples, Jesus chooses men who have not been trained in any sacred school, most of whom are unlearned and illiterate, considered by the various religious groups within Judaism as "people of the land," or peasants. At Pentecost these men will be revealed to be the wisest of all, by the power of the Holy Spirit.

4:23 Here is a summary of Jesus' early activity: His miracles bear witness to the presence of the Kingdom (12:28) and serve as an introduction to the Sermon on the Mount.

4:25 Decapolis is a region located north and east of Galilee.

5:1 Seated is the traditional position of Jewish rabbis while teaching. Some early Christian preachers (St. John Chrysostom, for example) sat, while the people stood. To understand this sermon is to recognize this Rabbi is the one true Teacher of Israel.

5:3 Blessed in this context indicates heavenly, spiritual blessedness rather than earthly happiness or prosperity. In Hebrew, **"poor"** means both (1) the materially poor and (2) the faithful among God's people. **The poor in spirit,** the humble and lowly, have the heart of the poor and their total dependence upon God. These are truly the "spiritually rich."

5:4 By means of holy sorrow, we can keep watch over our hearts and learn self-control. **Those who mourn** over their sins and the suffering of mankind are genuinely repentant, to be **comforted** in the new age. Holy sorrow is part of conversion, the consummation of repentance, the firstfruit of infinite joy. It is distinguished from ungodly sorrow, a sadness which leads to despair (see 2 Cor. 7:10).

5:5 Mourning can extinguish the flame of anger and make a person **meek.** Meekness is an attitude of being content with both honor and dishonor. It is an imitation of Christ who said, "Learn from Me, for I am gentle [meek] and lowly in heart" (11:29). The meek are God-controlled, and through their prayers God gives them mastery over their passions—especially anger. Meekness is not passive gentleness, but strength under control. Jesus' promise of future blessings is not for the powerful, the rich and the violent, but for those who are meek and humble: they will **inherit the earth,** the new earth which is everlasting.

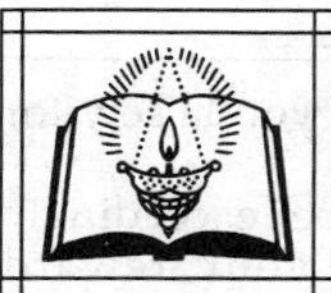

THE SERMON ON THE MOUNT

In the Sermon on the Mount (Matt. 5—7), Jesus introduces the kind of life those who seek the Kingdom of God must lead. His homily could properly be called, "The Righteousness of the Kingdom." It can be divided into several sections.

(1) *The Beatitudes* (Matt. 5:1–16): The sermon begins with the Beatitudes (the "blessings"), describing the joys of true discipleship, the blessed way of life. The people of God await the rewards of the promises Jesus makes.

(2) *The New Covenant* (Matt. 5:17–48): Then, as the Son of God whose authority is greater than Moses', Christ proclaims the new law, the righteousness leading toward perfection, to which the Mosaic Law and the Prophets pointed. Jesus reveals the deeper meaning of several Old Testament laws, broadening their implications.

(a) "You shall not murder" is expanded beyond the command against physically killing another (Matt. 5:21–26). Murder now includes anger, calling someone a fool, and failure to be reconciled with a friend or adversary.

(b) "You shall not commit adultery" no longer refers merely to the unlawful act of sex outside marriage. It now includes lust (Matt. 5:27).

(c) Divorce was allowable under the Old Testament law, but under the New Covenant, divorce is only permissible because of sexual immorality, and remarriage to a divorced person is not permitted (Matt. 5:31, 32).

(d) "Perform your oaths to the Lord" is the Old Testament law. Jesus instructs us to say "yes" or "no" without taking an oath, and to keep our word (Matt. 5:33–37).

(e) "An eye for an eye"—a graphic way of seeing justice from a human perspective—becomes "turn the other [cheek]" and "love your enemies." Not only must we forsake vengeance, even when it is just retribution; we must treat others as God treats us, with mercy and grace (Matt. 5:38–45).

(3) *Spiritual disciplines* (Matt. 6:1—7:12): Jesus assumes we will follow three disciplines which help us attain true righteousness (Matt. 6:1–18) and true wisdom (Matt. 6:19—7:12). These disciplines are a vital part of Christian tradition.

(a) Giving alms, or doing charitable deeds for the poor, should be done secretly, before God, not before men (Matt. 6:1–4).

(b) Prayer should follow the model of the Lord's Prayer, which Jesus here reveals to His Church (Matt. 6:5–15).

(c) Fasting should likewise be done for God, not for men (Matt. 6:16–18).

These disciplines help us find true wisdom, which consists of: (1) the love of God and pursuit of His righteousness by bringing our treasure (Matt. 6:19–26) as alms to God, our worries (Matt. 6:22—7:34) in prayer and fasting to Him; and (2) the love of human beings and pursuit of righteous reconciliation with them by submitting our judgments of them (Matt. 7:1–6) to God's severe mercy. For these difficult tasks we need divine discernment and guidance, which God provides to those who follow Jesus' spiritual rule (Matt. 7:7–12). Thus our natural impulses are redirected toward their proper goal: the righteousness of God in His Kingdom (Matt. 6:33).

(4) *Exhortations to righteousness* (Matt. 7:13–29): Jesus concludes with exhortations to true righteousness, warnings about hypocritical and deceitful professions of righteousness, and instructions to build on the rock of His teachings.

[b]For they shall be filled.†
7 Blessed *are* the merciful,
[a]For they shall obtain mercy.†
8 [a]Blessed *are* the pure in heart,
For [b]they shall see God.†
9 Blessed *are* the peacemakers,
For they shall be called sons
of God.†
10 [a]Blessed are those who are
persecuted for
righteousness' sake,
For theirs is the kingdom of
heaven.†
11 [a]"Blessed are you when they revile and persecute you, and say all
kinds of [b]evil against you falsely for
My sake.†
12 [a]"Rejoice and be exceedingly
glad, for great *is* your reward
in heaven, for [b]so they persecuted
the prophets who were before
you.

The Disciples in the World
(Mark 9:50; Luke 14:34, 35)

13 "You are the salt of the earth;
[a]but if the salt loses its flavor, how
shall it be seasoned? It is then good
for nothing but to be thrown out and
trampled underfoot by men.†

6 [b][Is. 55:1; 65:13] **7** [a]Ps. 41:1 **8** [a]Ps. 15:2; 24:4 [b]1 Cor. 13:12 **10** [a]1 Pet. 3:14 **11** [a]Luke 6:22 [b]1 Pet. 4:14 **12** [a]1 Pet. 4:13, 14 [b]Acts 7:52 **13** [a]Luke 14:34

5:6 Those who hunger and thirst for righteousness (Gr. *dikaiosune*, also translated "justification") see the presence of God and His Kingdom as the most important thing in their lives (see 6:33).

5:7 Mercy is love set in motion, love expressed in action. God's lovingkindness, His *mercy* in taking our sufferings upon Himself in order to grant us His Kingdom, sets us free from captivity to the evil one. In view of God's lovingkindness (Luke 6:36), we in turn are to be **merciful** to all others.

5:8 To be pure is to be unmixed with anything else. The **pure in heart** are devoted to the worship and service of God. With the aid of the Holy Spirit, they (1) practice all virtue, (2) are not conscious of any evil in themselves, and (3) live in temperance—a stage of spirituality attained by few in this life. When the soul is not dominated by sinful passions nor its energy dissipated by the things of this world, its only desire is God. Then the heart—holding fast to the new life in Christ and contemplating the glory of God (2 Cor. 3:18)—**shall see God** through communion with His Son.

5:9 Being Himself the source of peace, the Son of God found no price sufficient for peace but that of shedding His own blood. In doing so, Christ reveals Himself to us as the Reconciler, the Prince of Peace (Is. 9:6; Eph. 2:14, 16). The Holy Spirit gives peace, the sign of God's presence, to those who meditate on Christ and imitate Him. Peace brings communion with God and concord with all creation, the sign of our sanctity. Thus, **peacemakers** share God's peace with those around them, participating in the work of God's Son and becoming, by God's grace, **sons of God** themselves.

5:10 Children of God uphold God's truth and refuse to compromise with the ways of the world. They give themselves to no other (6:24, 33; see 1 Cor. 6:19, 20). It is not surprising then that they, like Jesus, should be **persecuted for righteousness' sake.** For Christ's **kingdom** is the crown awaiting the righteous.

5:11, 12 In willingness to suffer persecution, the Christian shows his loyalty and unity with Jesus Christ. He walks the road of the prophets, saints and martyrs. The Greek for **be exceedingly glad** (v. 12) means to "leap exceedingly with joy." Suffering for Christ is attended with inexpressible joy.

5:13–16 Salt (v. 13) and **light** (v. 14) illustrate the role of disciples in society. They are to manifest the *light* of patient goodness, bringing glory to their **Father in heaven.**

Because of its preservative powers, necessity for life and its ability to give flavor (Job 6:6; Sir. 39:26), *salt* had religious and sacrificial significance (Lev. 2:13; Ezra 6:9; Ezek. 43:24). It symbolized the making of a covenant (Lev. 2:13; see also Num. 18:19; 2 Chr. 13:5). To eat salt with someone meant to be bound together in loyalty. Thus as the *salt* of the earth, Christians are preservers of God's covenant and give proper flavor to society.

Light is a symbol of God who is the true, uncreated Light. In the OT light is symbolic of God (Is. 60:1–3), the divine Law (Ps. 119:105), or Israel in contrast to the Gentiles. In the NT the Son is called "light" (John 1:4, 5, 9; 1 John 1:5) and "the light of the world" (John 8:12). Light is necessary not only for clear vision but for life. Consequently, the life of faith relies on the divine light (Rom. 13:12; Eph. 1:18) and on the revelation which makes the believers "sons of light" (Luke 16:8; John 12:36; Eph. 5:8; 1 Thess. 5:5). With this knowledge of God in their hearts (2 Cor. 4:6), Christians shine as lights in a perverse world (Phil.

(continued on next page)

Commemoration of Holy Hierarchs

5:14–19: The Light of Christ shines brightly in the lives of these holy men who led His flock.

14 [a]"You are the light of the world.
A city that is set on a hill cannot be
hidden.
15 "Nor do they [a]light a lamp and
put it under a basket, but on a lampstand, and it gives light to all *who
are* in the house.
16 "Let your light so shine before
men, [a]that they may see your good
works and [b]glorify your Father in
heaven.✝

Righteousness: The Law Fulfilled

17 [a]"Do not think that I came to
destroy the Law or the Prophets. I
did not come to destroy but to
fulfill.✝
18 "For assuredly, I say to you,
[a]till heaven and earth pass away,
one [1]jot or one [2]tittle will by no
means pass from the law till all is
fulfilled.✝
19 [a]"Whoever therefore breaks one
of the least of these commandments,
and teaches men so, shall be called
least in the kingdom of heaven; but
whoever does and teaches *them,* he
shall be called great in the kingdom
of heaven.✝
20 "For I say to you, that unless
your righteousness exceeds [a]*the righteousness* of the scribes and Pharisees,
you will by no means enter the kingdom of heaven.✝

Righteousness Illustrated

21 "You have heard that it was said
to those [1]of old, [a]*'You shall not murder,* and whoever murders will be
in danger of the judgment.'✝

14 [a][John 8:12]
15 [a]Luke 8:16
16 [a]1 Pet. 2:12 [b][John 15:8]
17 [a]Rom. 10:4
18 [a]Luke 16:17 [1]Gr. *iota,* Heb. *yod,* the smallest letter [2]The smallest stroke in a Heb. letter
19 [a][James 2:10]
20 [a][Rom. 10:3]
21 [a]Ex. 20:13; Deut. 5:17 [1]*in ancient times*

(continued from previous page)
2:15), stimulating others to look to God and His righteousness. Thus in the Easter (Pascha) Liturgy a candle is brought forth with these words: "Come take the Light which is never overtaken by night."

5:16 Christian virtues have not only a personal but also a public function. By living according to the gospel, by *doing* the truth (John 3:21), we will bear **good works** and show the goodness of the **Father** to every person (see 1 Cor. 10:31; 1 Pet. 2:12).

5:17 Jesus fulfills **the Law** in His Person, words and actions by: (1) performing God's will in all its fullness (3:15); (2) transgressing none of the precepts of the Law (John 8:46; 14:30); (3) declaring the perfect fulfillment of the Law, which He was about to deliver to them; (4) granting righteousness—the goal of the Law—to us (Rom. 3:31; 8:3, 4; 10:4). He fulfills **the Prophets** by carrying out fully what they had foretold about Him.

5:18 Assuredly is *amen* in Greek, meaning "verily," "of a truth," "so be it." Christ uses it as a solemn affirmation, a form of oath, even using it to preface certain proclamations. He takes an oath by Himself to underline the authority of His words. A **jot** is the smallest letter in the Greek and Hebrew alphabets; a **tittle** is the small stroke in certain Hebrew letters. Thus, the whole of **the law** is the foundation of the new teaching. It is fulfilled by Christ and will not pass away **till heaven and earth pass away** (Mark 13:31; Luke 16:17).

5:19 Righteousness which is according to the Law is a unified whole: the observance of the **least of these** secures the observance of the greatest, while the violation of the very *least* is equivalent to the violation of the greatest.

To teach what one does not practice condemns the teacher (Rom. 2:21); to do right without guiding others lessens the reward of righteousness. Jesus Himself set the doing before the teaching. We ought to do right and teach ourselves, before we attempt to set others right.

5:20 Righteousness is more than proper behavior, such as **the scribes and Pharisees** were advocating, and holy thoughts. It centers upon our relationship with God (see notes on Rom. 1:17; 3:26).

5:21, 22 But I say to you indicates Jesus' authority (7:28, 29). Jesus, the Son of God, acting with the Father, created human nature and gave the Law of the OT. As the Old Law

(continued on next page)

22 "But I say to you that [a]whoever is angry with his brother [1]without a cause shall be in danger of the judgment. And whoever says to his brother, [b]'Raca!'[2] shall be in danger of the council. But whoever says, [3]'You fool!' shall be in danger of [4]hell fire.

23 "Therefore [a]if you bring your gift to the altar, and there remember that your brother has something against you,†

24 [a]"leave your gift there before the altar, and go your way. First be reconciled to your brother, and then come and offer your gift.

25 [a]"Agree with your adversary quickly, [b]while you are on the way with him, lest your adversary deliver you to the judge, the judge hand you over to the officer, and you be thrown into prison.†

26 "Assuredly, I say to you, you will by no means get out of there till you have paid the last penny.

27 "You have heard that it was said [1]to those of old, [a]*'You shall not commit adultery.'*†

28 "But I say to you that whoever [a]looks at a woman to lust for her has already committed adultery with her in his heart.

29 [a]"If your right eye causes you to [1]sin, [b]pluck it out and cast *it* from you; for it is more profitable for you that one of your members perish, than for your whole body to be cast into hell.†

30 "And if your right hand causes you to [1]sin, cut it off and cast *it* from you; for it is more profitable for you that one of your members perish, than for your whole body to be cast into hell.

31 "Furthermore it has been said, [a]'Whoever divorces his wife, let him give her a certificate of divorce. †

32 "But I say to you that [a]whoever divorces his wife for any reason except [1]sexual immorality causes her to commit adultery; and whoever marries a woman who is divorced commits adultery.

33 "Again you have heard that [a]it was said to those of [1]old, [b]'You shall not swear falsely, but [c]shall perform your oaths to the Lord.'

22 [a][1 John 3:15] [b][James 2:20; 3:6] [1]NU omits *without a cause* [2]Lit., in Aram., *Empty head* [3]Gr. *More* [4]Gr. *Gehenna*
23 [a]Matt. 8:4
24 [a][Job 42:8]
25 [a]Luke 12:58, 59 [b][Is. 55:6]
27 [a]Ex. 20:14; Deut. 5:18 [1]NU, M omit *to those of old*
28 [a]Prov. 6:25
29 [a]Mark 9:43 [b][Col. 3:5] [1]Lit. *stumble* or *offend*
30 [1]Lit. *stumble* or *offend*
31 [a]Deut. 24:1
32 [a][Luke 16:18] [1]Or *fornication*
33 [a]Matt. 23:16 [b]Lev. 19:12 [c]Deut. 23:23 [1]*ancient times*

(continued from previous page)
is fulfilled in the New Law, so human nature is healed by Christ. Jesus forbids sinful anger (see Ps. 4:4 and Eph. 4:26 for anger, or righteous indignation, that is not sinful), identifying such anger with **murder.** The **council** is the supreme legal body among the Jews. **Hell** (Gr. *Gehenna;* see 10:28 and note) is the final condition of sinners who resist God's grace.

5:23, 24 Peace with other believers takes primacy over duties of worship (Mark 11:25). In early Christian worship the liturgical "kiss of peace" at the beginning of the Communion prayers—not after—was a sign of reconciliation and forgiveness, preparing the Church to offer and receive the Eucharist (1 Cor. 16:20; 1 Pet. 5:14).

5:25, 26 Luke 12:57–59 places this teaching in a context dealing with the end of the age; here it is in the context of reconciliation. In both cases it is clear that quarrels must be settled **quickly,** not allowed to continue. Delaying reconciliation and good works gives room for the working of more evil (Eph. 4:26, 27).

5:27, 28 God sees the hidden desires which motivate our actions. The issue here is **lust,** not simply the God-given mutual attraction of men and women. Sin does not come out of nature, but out of internal self-indulgence. He who feasts on *lust* within himself brings sin into his heart through his thoughts. (Thoughts which enter the mind involuntarily are temptations, not sins. They become sins only when they are held onto and entertained.)

5:29 Jesus is speaking in vivid imagery, not literally, using the physical body as an illustration. To remove an eye would be to reproach the Creator (see 18:8, 9; Mark 9:43–48).

5:31, 32 In contrast to the easy access to divorce under the Mosaic Law, and because of the misuse of divorce in that day, Christ repeatedly condemns **divorce** (19:8, 9; Mark 10:2–9; Luke 16:18) and emphasizes the eternal character of marriage. However, the possibility of divorce on grounds of unchastity, for example, clearly shows that Christ considered that the marriage bond is not absolute: it can be destroyed by sin. The Orthodox Church thus allows divorce as a corrective measure of compassion when a marriage has unfortunately been broken. Human freedom implies the possibility of sin; sin can separate husband and **wife** from each other, and ultimately from the body of Christ and from God Himself. **Sexual immorality** is a grave sin against the divine Sacrament of Marriage.

34 "But I say to you, [a]do not swear at all: neither by heaven, for it is [b]God's throne;†

35 "nor by the earth, for it is His footstool; nor by Jerusalem, for it is the city of [a]the great King.

36 "Nor shall you swear by your head, because you cannot make one hair white or black.

37 [a]"But let [1]your 'Yes' be 'Yes,' and your 'No,' 'No.' For whatever is more than these is from the evil one.†

38 "You have heard that it was said, [a]*'An eye for an eye and a tooth for a tooth.'*

39 [a]"But I tell you not to resist an evil person. [b]But whoever slaps you on your right cheek, turn the other to him also.†

40 "If anyone wants to sue you and take away your tunic, let him have *your* cloak also.

41 "And whoever [a]compels you to go one mile, go with him two.

42 "Give to him who asks you, and [a]from him who wants to borrow from you do not turn away.

43 "You have heard that it was said, [a]*'You shall love your neighbor* [b]and hate your enemy.'

34 [a]James 5:12 [b]Is. 66:1
35 [a]Ps. 48:2
37 [a][Col. 4:6] [1]Lit. *your word be yes yes*
38 [a]Ex. 21:24; Lev. 24:20; Deut. 19:21
39 [a]Luke 6:29 [b]Is. 50:6
41 [a]Matt. 27:32
42 [a]Luke 6:30–34
43 [a]Lev. 19:18 [b]Deut. 23:3–6
44 [a]Luke 6:27 [b][Rom. 12:20] [c]Acts 7:60 [1]NU *But I say to you, love your enemies and pray for those who persecute you*
45 [a]Job 25:3
46 [a]Luke 6:32
47 [1]M *friends* [2]NU *Gentiles*
48 [a][Col. 1:28; 4:12] [b]Eph. 5:1

CHAPTER 6
2 [a]Rom. 12:8

44 [1]"But I say to you, [a]love your enemies, bless those who curse you, [b]do good to those who hate you, and pray [c]for those who spitefully use you and persecute you,†

45 "that you may be sons of your Father in heaven; for [a]He makes His sun rise on the evil and on the good, and sends rain on the just and on the unjust.

46 [a]"For if you love those who love you, what reward have you? Do not even the tax collectors do the same?

47 "And if you greet your [1]brethren only, what do you do more *than others?* Do not even the [2]tax collectors do so?

48 [a]"Therefore you shall be perfect, just [b]as your Father in heaven is perfect.†

How to Give Alms

6 "Take heed that you do not do your charitable deeds before men, to be seen by them. Otherwise you have no reward from your Father in heaven.†

2 "Therefore, [a]when you do a charitable deed, do not sound a

5:34–36 Jesus speaks against casual use of God's name and superficial oaths. The words of Jesus have not only a negative meaning, but a positive one also. They not only forbid us to **swear,** that is, to bind ourselves with an oath; they also command us to speak the truth and to keep our promises.

5:37 This is a well-known saying in the NT (James 5:12). Trust is secured not by an oath which exceeds **Yes** and **No,** but by inner integrity. Jesus teaches us to live in the simplicity of the present moment.

5:39 Jesus warned His disciples **not to resist** violence with more violence (contrary to Ex. 21:24; Lev. 24:20; Deut. 19:21). Evil, and the evil person, can be overcome only by good. This keeps us free from anger—from being poisoned by the evil directed against us and its destructive forces—and instructs others through Christian forbearance. It brings both us and our enemy under the yoke of God's love. This teaching does not, however, contradict a state's right to protect its citizens and to punish criminals.

5:44–47 Here is another radical command of Jesus: to **love** our **enemies** as a true expression of the life of the Kingdom. Having freed us from hate, sadness, and anger, He offers the greatest possession of all—perfect love. That is a gift which can only be possessed by the one who, by the grace of God and the power of the Spirit, manifests God's love for all. Such love calls us to **bless, do good,** and **pray**—even for enemies. Love of neighbor is the sign of having become a true child of God. Love is not merely an emotion. It is a divine grace—an uncreated divine energy—which inflames the soul and unites it to God and to other people (see 1 John 4:7–21).

5:48 This verse summarizes Jesus' teaching on God's standards. The Christian should grow into the perfection of the **Father** (Eph. 4:13; see also article, "Deification," at 2 Pet. 1). Christ is our guide, and He is able to bring us to participate in the very life of God, which is love.

6:1 In this chapter, Jesus calls us to practice three basic aspects of spiritual discipline, or

(continued on next page)

trumpet before you as the hypocrites
do in the synagogues and in the
streets, that they may have glory
from men. Assuredly, I say to you,
they have their reward.†
3 "But when you do a charitable
deed, do not let your left hand know
what your right hand is doing,†
4 that your charitable deed may
be in secret; and your Father who
sees in secret [a]will Himself reward
you [1]openly.

How to Pray
(Luke 11:1–4)

5 "And when you pray, you shall
not be like the [1]hypocrites. For they
love to pray standing in the synagogues and on the corners of the
streets, that they may be seen by
men. Assuredly, I say to you, they
have their reward.†
6 "But you, when you pray,
[a]go into your room, and when you
have shut your door, pray to your
Father who *is* in the secret *place;* and
your Father who sees in secret will
reward you [1]openly.
7 "And when you pray, [a]do not
use vain repetitions as the heathen
do. [b]For they think that they will be
heard for their many words.
8 "Therefore do not be like them.
For your Father [a]knows the things
you have need of before you ask
Him.
9 "In this [a]manner, therefore,
pray:

[b]Our Father in heaven,
Hallowed be Your [c]name.†
10 Your kingdom come.
[a]Your will be done
On earth [b]as *it is* in heaven.
11 Give us this day our [a]daily
bread.†

4 [a]Luke 14:12–14 [1]NU omits *openly*
5 [1]*pretenders*
6 [a]2 Kin. 4:33 [1]NU omits *openly*
7 [a]Eccl. 5:2 [b]1 Kin. 18:26
8 [a][Rom. 8:26, 27]
9 [a]Matt. 6:9–13; Luke 11:2–4; [John 16:24; Eph. 6:18; Jude 20] [b][Matt. 5:9, 16] [c]Mal. 1:11
10 [a]Matt. 26:42; Luke 22:42; Acts 21:14 [b]Ps. 103:20
11 [a][Job 23:12]; Prov. 30:8; Is. 33:16; Luke 11:3

(continued from previous page)
righteousness: (1) charitable giving (vv. 1–4), (2) prayer (vv. 5–15), and (3) fasting (vv. 16–18). These three disciplines relate directly to uprightness in the sight of God.

6:2 The original meaning of the word "hypocrite" was "actor." **Hypocrites** are play-actors practicing theatrical piety. They put on their show in synagogues and in the streets to please men, not God. Wearing masks of compassion, inwardly they are heartless. Their **reward** is the applause of men—nothing more.

6:3, 4 God is not impressed with what other people think of us, or even with our own opinion of ourselves. He sees who we really are, and He knows our motives as well as our deeds. Everything will be judged, and our good deeds will be rewarded **openly** (v. 4).

6:5–8 The hypocrites miss the spirit of prayer, which involves an intimate, personal relationship with God and leads to the vision of His glory (1 Cor. 2:9). Hypocrisy blocks out both the relationship and the vision. Mere **vain repetitions** (v. 7) do not establish such a relationship, for God does not need our "babble." To be made intimate with Him, be humbled, and be reminded of our sins, both silence and words are necessary. Therefore, we pray always (Luke 18:1), "without ceasing" (1 Thess. 5:17), and we do use **many words**—but they must come from the heart to seek God Himself. Here Jesus instructs us how to use words repetitiously (vv. 8–13). When we pray, we do not lecture God or make demands, but we are (1) humble (**go into your room,** v. 6), (2) personal and intimate with Him (**pray to your Father**), and (3) sincere (**do not use vain repetitions,** v. 7). It is not repetition *per se,* but *vain* repetition which Jesus condemns. Christian worship, with familiar psalms, hymns, prayers and readings from the Scriptures, brings God the praise "in spirit and truth" which He seeks (John 4:23). In no way do these liturgical acts violate Jesus' command against vain words and repetition.

6:9 The Father-Son relationship between God the Father and God the Son reveals the nature of our relationship with God. For Christ Himself, the Son of the Father by nature, grants us the privilege of calling the Creator **our Father** by the grace of adoption. As a "son" of God in Christ, the Christian is called to love, trust and serve God, as a son would his father. The emphasis in Scripture is not on a universal Fatherhood of God through creation, but on a saving and personal relationship with Him who is *our* Father by adoption through the Spirit (see Rom. 8:14–16).

6:11 Daily is a misleading translation of the Greek *epiousios,* which is literally "above the essence" or "supersubstantial." The expression **daily bread** indicates not merely bread for

(continued on next page)

Cheese Fare Sunday (Forgiveness Sunday) *Sunday before Lent*

6:14–21: Jesus exhorts His followers to forgive one another and to fast in truth.

12 And [a]forgive us our debts,
As we forgive our debtors.†
13 [a]And do not lead us into
temptation,
But [b]deliver us from the evil
one.
[1]For Yours is the kingdom and
the power and the glory
forever. Amen.†

14 [a]"For if you forgive men their
trespasses, your heavenly Father will
also forgive you.†
15 "But [a]if you do not forgive men
their trespasses, neither will your Father forgive your trespasses.

How to Fast

16 "Moreover, [a]when you fast, do
not be like the [1]hypocrites, with a sad countenance. For they disfigure their faces that they may appear to men to be fasting. Assuredly, I say to you, they have their reward.†
17 "But you, when you fast,
[a]anoint your head and wash your face,

12 [a][Matt. 18:21, 22]
13 [a][2 Pet. 2:9] [b]John 17:15 [1]NU omits the rest of v. 13.
14 [a]Mark 11:25
15 [a]Matt. 18:35
16 [a]Is. 58:3–7 [1]pretenders
17 [a]Ruth 3:3

(continued from previous page)
this day, taken for sustenance of life; it is bread for the eternal day of the Kingdom of God, for sustenance of our immortal life. It is living, "superessential" bread. This bread, prepared by God in the beginning for the immortality of our nature, is the Bread of Life which will triumph over the death brought about by sin.

Jesus commands us to seek first the Kingdom of God (v. 33). Here He tells us to ask not merely for material bread which keeps us in good physical health, but for the spiritual bread which gives us life—the Living Bread, Christ Himself, given in the Holy Eucharist to those who receive Him.

6:12 We request God to **forgive us . . . as we** are to **forgive** others. By using the plural, Jesus directs each of us to pray for the Father's forgiveness of all, and for all of us to forgive one another. Although God's forgiveness is primary, Jesus clearly teaches that there is a reciprocal relationship between divine and human forgiveness. We request God to be to us as we are to our neighbors. **Debts** refers to spiritual debts: when we sin, we "owe" restitution to our offended neighbor and to God.

6:13 We pray not only that our sins be forgiven (v. 12), but that we not yield to **temptation.** God tempts no one (James 1:13); temptations are from **the evil one,** the devil. They are aimed at the soul's willful yielding to the sinful passions of the flesh (Rom. 7:5). No one can live without at some time encountering *temptation*. But to yield to temptation and commit sin is blameworthy. Thus we pray that great temptations, tests beyond what we can bear (1 Cor. 10:13), should not come our way.

6:14, 15 Once again Jesus insists on mutual forgiveness between people as a precondition of God's forgiveness. Those who do not **forgive** are not forgiven. This teaching is repeated by Jesus in the parable of the unforgiving servant (18:23–35), which concludes with virtually the same words. The opinion that even unforgiving Christians are forgiven by God is contradicted by Christ Himself. The moral action of the faithful, when they *forgive* others **their trespasses,** is bound with the love of God: not to *forgive* others is willfully to alienate ourselves from the forgiveness of God.

6:16–18 Keeping **a sad countenance** while fasting, so that everyone can see how one is suffering, is mere external display. Jesus rejects such hypocrisy. For the one who fasts, the compassion of God outshines physical discomfort: joy overshadows sorrow. Thus, during seasons of fasting, the hymns of the Orthodox Church call the faithful to wash and anoint their faces. There is no "Ash Wednesday" in Orthodox practice. And fasting is not merely abstaining from eating. Physical fasting works together with spiritual fasting, or self-denial: it is a liberation of the spirit from its voluntary enslavement to sinful passions. Fasting is for the glory of God, not to impress people around us.

18 "so that you do not appear to men to be fasting, but to your Father who *is* in the secret *place;* and your Father who sees in secret will reward you [1]openly.

Trusting God Wholly
(Luke 16:13)

19 [a]"Do not lay up for yourselves treasures on earth, where moth and rust destroy and where thieves break in and steal;†

20 [a]"but lay up for yourselves treasures in heaven, where neither moth nor rust destroys and where thieves do not break in and steal.

21 "For where your treasure is, there your heart will be also.

22 [a]"The lamp of the body is the eye. If therefore your eye is [1]good, your whole body will be full of light.†

23 "But if your eye is [1]bad, your whole body will be full of darkness. If therefore the light that is in you is darkness, how great *is* that darkness!

24 [a]"No one can serve two masters; for either he will hate the one and love the other, or else he will be loyal to the one and despise the other. [b]You cannot serve God and [1]mammon.†

18 [1]NU, M omit *openly*
19 [a]Prov. 23:4; [1 Tim. 6:17; Heb. 13:5]; James 5:1
20 [a]Matt. 19:21; Luke 12:33; 18:22; 1 Tim. 6:19; 1 Pet. 1:4
22 [a]Luke 11:34, 35 [1]Clear, or healthy
23 [1]Evil, or unhealthy
24 [a]Luke 16:9, 11, 13 [b][Gal. 1:10; 1 Tim. 6:17; James 4:4; 1 John 2:15] [1]Lit., in Aram., *riches*
25 [a][Ps. 55:22]; Luke 12:22; [Phil. 4:6; 1 Pet. 5:7]
26 [a]Job 38:41; Ps. 147:9; Matt. 10:29; Luke 12:24
27 [1]About 18 inches [2]*height*
29 [1]*dressed*

Trusting God for Basic Needs
(Luke 12:22–31)

25 "Therefore I say to you, [a]do not worry about your life, what you will eat or what you will drink; nor about your body, what you will put on. Is not life more than food and the body more than clothing?†

26 [a]"Look at the birds of the air, for they neither sow nor reap nor gather into barns; yet your heavenly Father feeds them. Are you not of more value than they?

27 "Which of you by worrying can add one [1]cubit to his [2]stature?

28 "So why do you worry about clothing? Consider the lilies of the field, how they grow: they neither toil nor spin;

29 "and yet I say to you that even Solomon in all his glory was not [1]arrayed like one of these.

30 "Now if God so clothes the grass of the field, which today is, and tomorrow is thrown into the oven, *will He* not much more *clothe* you, O you of little faith?

31 "Therefore do not worry, saying, 'What shall we eat?' or 'What shall we drink?' or 'What shall we wear?'

32 "For after all these things the Gentiles seek. For your heavenly Father knows that you need all these things.†

6:19–21 By attaching themselves to **treasures on earth** people cut themselves off from heavenly treasures. They become slaves, not free in Christ. The heart of discipleship lies in (1) disentangling ourselves from the chains of earthly things, and (2) attaching ourselves to God, the true **treasure** (v. 21). We have need for certain material things (v. 25), but we use them according to God's will and purposes.

6:22, 23 Jesus refers to things within the reach of the senses so that we might more easily grasp His teaching. We all understand the value of light in our lives. As the **eye** is the **lamp of the body,** so the mind (Gr. *nous*) is the spiritual *eye* of the soul: it illuminates the whole inner man. Keeping our spiritual eyes **good,** that is, wholesome and pure, is fundamental to a Christian life.

6:24 As slaves serving **two masters,** people attempt to maintain an attachment both to earthly and to heavenly things. But this is impossible, for both demand full allegiance. Jesus calls **mammon** a master, not because it is by nature evil, but because of the absolute and wretched servility it exacts.

6:25–27 Severe anxiety, not thoughtful planning and care, is what is warned against here. Physical growth and length of life is dependent upon the providence of God more than upon **food, drink** and **clothing.** Persistent anxiety over the things of this world demonstrates internal insecurity and a weak or superficial faith.

6:32 The pagan worship of **the Gentiles** did not deliver them from their earthly cares, because it was focused upon nonexistent gods, that is, idols.

33 "But [a]seek first the kingdom of
God and His righteousness, and all
these things shall be added to you.†
34 "Therefore do not worry about
tomorrow, for tomorrow will worry
about its own things. Sufficient for
the day *is* its own trouble.

On Judging Others
(Luke 6:37, 38, 41, 42)

7 "Judge[1] [a]not, that you be not
judged.
2 "For with what [1]judgment you
judge, you will be judged; [a]and with
the measure you use, it will be measured back to you.†
3 [a]"And why do you look at the
speck in your brother's eye, but do
not consider the plank in your own
eye?†
4 "Or how can you say to your
brother, 'Let me remove the speck
from your eye'; and look, a plank *is*
in your own eye?
5 "Hypocrite! First remove the
plank from your own eye, and then
you will see clearly to remove the
speck from your brother's eye.
6 [a]"Do not give what is holy to
the dogs; nor cast your pearls before
swine, lest they trample them under
their feet, and turn and tear you in
pieces.†

Persevering in Prayer
(Luke 11:9–13)

7 [a]"Ask, and it will be given to
you; seek, and you will find; knock,
and it will be opened to you.†
8 "For [a]everyone who asks receives, and he who seeks finds, and
to him who knocks it will be opened.
9 [a]"Or what man is there among
you who, if his son asks for bread,
will give him a stone?
10 "Or if he asks for a fish, will
he give him a serpent?
11 "If you then, [a]being evil, know
how to give good gifts to your children, how much more will your Father who is in heaven give good
things to those who ask Him!†

33 [a]1 Kin. 3:13; Luke 12:31; [1 Tim. 4:8]

CHAPTER 7

1 [a]Matt. 7:1–5; Luke 6:37; Rom. 14:3; [1 Cor. 4:3, 4] [1]Condemn
2 [a]Mark 4:24; Luke 6:38 [1]Condemnation
3 [a]Luke 6:41
6 [a]Prov. 9:7, 8; Acts 13:45
7 [a][Matt. 21:22; Mark 11:24]; Luke 11:9–13; 18:1–8; [John 15:7; James 1:5, 6; 1 John 3:22]
8 [a]Prov. 8:17; Jer. 29:12
9 [a]Luke 11:11
11 [a]Gen. 6:5; 8:21; Ps. 84:11; Is. 63:7; [Rom. 8:32; James 1:17]; 1 John 3:1

6:33 The kingdom of God is the central theme of the teaching of Jesus, and **His righteousness** is the subject of the Sermon on the Mount. Calling us to be set free from anxiety about earthly things, Jesus directs us to look to heaven, to this greater "country" which will be received at the Day of the Lord, secure in the faith that God will provide needed earthly blessings.

7:2 We will be judged with our own **judgment** because we, the judges, are doing the very same things that we condemn in others (Rom. 2:1). We ourselves have failed to unceasingly remember our own sins and lay them aside (John 8:7; 2 Pet. 1:9). Condemnation of others and forgiveness do not mix (see Luke 6:27–38). It is the evil one, the slanderer of all, who urges us to pass judgment on others. To pass judgment on another is to usurp a prerogative of God, who knows all things and alone is able to judge (James 4:12).

The second part of this verse is found in Mark 4:24 and in Luke 6:38, each in a different context. Jesus no doubt used these words many times.

7:3–5 We ought to know our own sins better than those of others. The **hypocrite** sees the errors of others, ignoring his own, because he loves himself above all else.

7:6 Jesus warns His disciples to turn away from opponents and those incapable of receiving His message (1 Cor. 2:14), and to turn toward those who are receptive (10:13, 14). **Dogs** and **swine** refer to heathen peoples (Phil. 3:2; Rev. 22:15), but here Jesus' own Jewish contemporaries are obviously not excluded. According to the Church Fathers, *dogs* are those so deeply immersed in godlessness that they show no hope of change, while *swine* are those who habitually live an unchaste and immoral life-style. The **pearls** are Christ's teachings (13:46), or the "inner mysteries" of the Christian faith, particularly the Eucharist.

7:7–11 The threefold exhortation, **ask—be given, seek—find, knock—be opened,** promises the availability of God's help. The verbs are present progressives: be asking, be seeking, be knocking. Note the synergy: our effort is commanded, but never apart from the help of God. We *ask* in prayer; *seek* by learning God's truth; and *knock* by doing God's will.

7:11 Men are called **evil** not to condemn the whole race, but to contrast the goodness that is in men—which is from God but mixed with sin—with the goodness of God, which

(continued on next page)

Commemoration of Holy Monks

7:12–21: These holy men found the narrow way and bore good fruit.

12 "Therefore, [a]whatever you want men to do to you, do also to them, for [b]this is the Law and the Prophets.†

The Narrow Gate
(Luke 13:24)

13 [a]"Enter by the narrow gate; for wide *is* the gate and broad *is* the way that leads to destruction, and there are many who go in by it.†
14 [1]"Because narrow *is* the gate and [2]difficult *is* the way which leads to life, and there are few who find it.

Beware of False Prophets
(Luke 6:43, 44)

15 [a]"Beware of false prophets, [b]who come to you in sheep's clothing, but inwardly they are ravenous wolves.†

12 [a]Luke 6:31 [b]Gal. 5:14
13 [a]Luke 13:24
14 [1]NU, M *How narrow . . . !* [2]*confined*
15 [a]Jer. 23:16 [b]Mic. 3:5
16 [a]Matt. 7:20; 12:33 [b]Luke 6:43
17 [a]Matt. 12:33
19 [a][John 15:2, 6]
21 [a]Luke 6:46 [b]Rom. 2:13
22 [a]Num. 24:4
23 [a][2 Tim. 2:19] [b]Ps. 5:5; 6:8

16 [a]"You will know them by their
fruits. [b]Do men gather grapes from
thornbushes or figs from thistles?†
17 "Even so, [a]every good tree
bears good fruit, but a bad tree bears
bad fruit.
18 "A good tree cannot bear bad
fruit, nor *can* a bad tree bear good
fruit.
19 [a]"Every tree that does not bear
good fruit is cut down and thrown
into the fire.†
20 "Therefore by their fruits you
will know them.
21 "Not everyone who says to Me,
[a]'Lord, Lord,' shall enter the kingdom of heaven, but he who [b]does
the will of My Father in heaven.†
22 "Many will say to Me in that
day, 'Lord, Lord, have we [a]not
prophesied in Your name, cast out
demons in Your name, and done
many wonders in Your name?'
23 "And [a]then I will declare to
them, 'I never knew you; [b]depart

(continued from previous page)
is perfect (see 19:16, 17). If imperfect and even wicked people can do good, how much more can God, in whom there is no evil.

7:12 The Golden Rule fulfills the demands of the Law and the Prophets and is another version of the commandment to love one's neighbor as oneself (22:39, 40). The negative form of the Golden Rule ("Don't do to others what you don't want them to do to you") is well known in Judaism. Jesus' form, however, is positive: this is the action which brings us to the God who forgives.

7:13, 14 This description of the two ways is widespread in Judaism (Deut. 30:15–20; Ps. 1; Prov. 4:18, 19; 12:28; 15:24; Sir. 15:17), and in early Christian writings (Didache, Barnabas). Luke's version (Luke 13:24–30) is more eschatological, referring to the end of the age. Because we wrestle against human sins and weaknesses, as well as the spiritual forces of evil (Eph. 6:12), entering the Kingdom involves **difficult** (v. 14) labor and struggle (11:12).

7:15 Jesus charges us to **beware** because it is possible to be deceived by those who wear a mask of virtue but are **false prophets** (24:4, 24), or **wolves,** who live corrupt lives (10:16; Zeph. 3:3; John 10:12; Acts 20:29).

7:16–19 As long as a person is living in wickedness, he will not be able to **bear good fruit.** But Jesus does not say that there is no way for the wicked to change, or for the good to fall away. (See also 12:33–35.)

7:19 John the Baptist made the same statement (3:10).

7:21, 22 Here is a threefold testimony to the deity of Christ: (1) He calls Himself **Lord** (v. 21)—Yahweh of the OT; (2) He speaks of **the will of My Father** (v. 21), which He fully knows and shares; (3) v. 22 reveals Christ as judge and therefore God, for only God can execute judgment. **In that day** (v. 22) refers to the final judgment.

from Me, you who practice lawlessness!'

Hearing and Doing Jesus' Teachings
(Luke 6:47–49)

24 "Therefore [a]whoever hears
these sayings of Mine, and does
them, I will liken him to a wise man
who built his house on the rock:
25 "and the rain descended, the
floods came, and the winds blew and
beat on that house; and it did not
fall, for it was founded on the rock.
26 "But everyone who hears these
sayings of Mine, and does not do
them, will be like a foolish man who
built his house on the sand:
27 "and the rain descended, the
floods came, and the winds blew and
beat on that house; and it fell. And
great was its fall."
28 And so it was, when Jesus had
ended these sayings, that [a]the people were astonished at His teaching,
29 [a]for He taught them as one
having authority, and not as the
scribes.

A Leper Cleansed
(Mark 1:40–45; Luke 5:12–16)

8 When He had come down from
the mountain, great multitudes
followed Him.†
2 [a]And behold, a leper came and

24 [a]Matt. 7:24–27; Luke 6:47–49
28 [a]Matt. 13:54; Mark 1:22; 6:2; Luke 4:32; John 7:46
29 [a][John 7:46]

CHAPTER 8

2 [a]Matt. 8:2–4; Mark 1:40–45; Luke 5:12–14 [b]Matt. 2:11; 9:18; 15:25; John 9:38; Acts 10:25
3 [a]Matt. 11:5; Luke 4:27
4 [a]Matt. 9:30; Mark 5:43; Luke 4:41; 8:56; 9:21 [b]Lev. 14:3, 4, 10; Mark 1:44; Luke 5:14 [c]Lev. 14:4–32; Deut. 24:8
5 [a]Luke 7:1–3 [b]Matt. 27:54; Acts 10:1
8 [a]Luke 15:19, 21 [b]Ps. 107:20

[b]worshiped Him, saying, "Lord, if
You are willing, You can make me
clean."
3 Then Jesus put out *His* hand and
touched him, saying, "I am willing;
be cleansed." Immediately his leprosy [a]was cleansed.
4 And Jesus said to him, [a]"See
that you tell no one; but go your
way, show yourself to the priest, and
offer the gift that [b]Moses [c]com-
manded, as a testimony to them."

A Paralyzed Servant Healed
(Luke 7:1–10)

5 [a]Now when Jesus had entered
Capernaum, a [b]centurion came to
Him, pleading with Him,†
6 saying, "Lord, my servant is lying at home paralyzed, dreadfully
tormented."
7 And Jesus said to him, "I will
come and heal him."†
8 The centurion answered and
said, "Lord, [a]I am not worthy that
You should come under my roof. But
only [b]speak a word, and my servant
will be healed.†
9 "For I also am a man under authority, having soldiers under me.
And I say to this *one*, 'Go,' and he
goes; and to another, 'Come,' and
he comes; and to my servant, 'Do
this,' and he does *it*."
10 When Jesus heard *it*, He marveled, and said to those who followed, "Assuredly, I say to you, I

8:1–4 The biblical law concerning **leprosy** (v. 3) is found in Lev. 13; 14. Deuteronomy 24:8 describes the purification of lepers and leprous houses, which is a duty entrusted to the priests. *Leprosy* was considered a direct punishment for sins, and lepers were unclean, not permitted to live in the community or to worship God in synagogues or the temple. Touching the unclean was forbidden under Mosaic Law (Lev. 7:21). Jesus **touched** (v. 3) the leper, showing His compassion, and demonstrating He is not subject to the Law but over it. To the clean there is nothing unclean.

8:5 A **centurion** commanded 100 men in a Roman legion. The man is a Gentile (Luke 7:3–5). Jesus is the Savior of all; for Him ethnic and social distinctions are void.

8:7 I will come has been read as a question by many Greek language scholars: "Shall I come?" Regardless, Jesus is ready to deal graciously with a Gentile and even to enter his house, which would make Him unclean in the eyes of the Jews.

8:8, 9 The **centurion** recognizes Jesus' authority, calling Him **Lord.** Although the centurion has authority over men, he understands that only Jesus has authority over disease. The centurion's phrase, **Lord, I am not worthy that You should come under my roof,** is frequently quoted in the liturgical texts of the Orthodox Church. It is an ideal expression of our deep unworthiness before Christ.

have not found such great faith, not
even in Israel!†
11 "And I say to you that [a]many
will come from east and west, and
sit down with Abraham, Isaac, and
Jacob in the kingdom of heaven.†
12 "But [a]the sons of the kingdom
[b]will be cast out into outer darkness.
There will be weeping and gnashing
of teeth."
13 Then Jesus said to the centurion, "Go your way; and as you have
believed, *so* let it be done for you."
And his servant was healed that
same hour.

Power over All Infirmities
(Mark 1:29–34; Luke 4:38–41)

14 [a]Now when Jesus had come
into Peter's house, He saw [b]his
wife's mother lying sick with a
fever.†
15 So He touched her hand, and
the fever left her. And she arose and
served [1]them.
16 [a]When evening had come, they
brought to Him many who were
demon-possessed. And He cast out

11 [a][Gen. 12:3; Is. 2:2, 3; 11:10]; Mal. 1:11; Luke 13:29; [Acts 10:45; 11:18; 14:27; Rom. 15:9–13; Eph. 3:6]
12 [a][Matt. 21:43] [b]Matt. 13:42, 50; 22:13; 24:51; 25:30; Luke 13:28; 2 Pet. 2:17; Jude 13
14 [a]Matt. 8:14–16; Mark 1:29–31; Luke 4:38, 39 [b]1 Cor. 9:5
15 [1]NU, M *Him*
16 [a]Mark 1:32–34; Luke 4:40, 41
17 [a]Is. 53:4; 1 Pet. 2:24
19 [a]Matt. 8:19–22; Luke 9:57, 58
21 [a]Luke 9:59, 60 [b]1 Kin. 19:20

the spirits with a word, and healed
all who were sick,
17 that it might be fulfilled which
was spoken by Isaiah the prophet,
saying:

[a]*"He Himself took our infirmities*
And bore our sicknesses."

Unconditional Loyalty
(Luke 9:57–62)

18 And when Jesus saw great multitudes about Him, He gave a command to depart to the other side.
19 [a]Then a certain scribe came and
said to Him, "Teacher, I will follow
You wherever You go."
20 And Jesus said to him, "Foxes
have holes and birds of the air *have*
nests, but the Son of Man has nowhere to lay *His* head."†
21 [a]Then another of His disciples
said to Him, "Lord, [b]let me first go
and bury my father."
22 But Jesus said to him, "Follow
Me, and let the dead bury their own
dead."†

8:10 Twice in the Gospels it is said of Jesus that **He marveled:** (1) at the *unbelief* in His hometown, His rejection in Nazareth (Mark 6:6); and (2) at the *belief* of this centurion that Jesus could heal his servant by simply speaking the word.

8:11, 12 Jesus praises the centurion, a Gentile, and lifts him up as a model of faith. Jesus nullifies the ethnic supremacy of the Jews, saying that many from other nations will share the heavenly blessings with the Jewish patriarchs. The centurion's faith in Christ places him also in the kingdom of heaven. **The sons of the kingdom** are Jews, who had a sense of racial superiority as the chosen people of God. **Outer darkness** and **weeping and gnashing of teeth** are not OT references but descriptions of the state of the unrighteous dead in Sheol recorded in Jewish tradition (see Enoch 103:8; Parables of Enoch 60:12). These are common expressions in Matthew (13:42, 50; 22:13; 24:51; 25:30), also occurring once in Luke (Luke 13:28). This accentuates the critical situation of all—Jew and Gentile—who do not follow Christ.

8:14–17 This passage and 1 Cor. 9:5 (where Peter is called Cephas—see John 1:42) indicate Peter was married.

Jesus' healing miracles are diverse. In this case, He heals by touch; in v. 13 He healed by the power of His word. This healing is immediate and complete; others are gradual (see Mark 8:22–25) or require the cooperation of the person healed or of his or her loved ones (see Luke 8:54, 55). But as the quote in v. 17 indicates, all of Christ's miracles manifest His redemptive ministry on behalf of ailing humanity.

8:20 Since **Son of Man** refers to the Messiah (Dan. 7:13), it expresses *both* His humanity and divinity. Here it refers to Jesus' human condition; in 25:31–33 it describes His divine authority as Judge.

8:22 Jesus is not negating the command to honor parents. He means that nothing ought to be more urgent to us than the things of the Kingdom. Those who ignore heavenly priority are spiritually **dead.**

A Storm Calmed
(Mark 4:35–41; Luke 8:22–25)

23 Now when He got into a boat,
His disciples followed Him.†
24 [a]And suddenly a great tempest
arose on the sea, so that the boat was
covered with the waves. But He was
asleep.
25 Then His disciples came to *Him*
and awoke Him, saying, "Lord, save
us! We are perishing!"
26 But He said to them, "Why are
you fearful, O you of little faith?"
Then [a]He arose and rebuked the
winds and the sea, and there was a
great calm.
27 So the men marveled, saying,
[1]"Who can this be, that even the
winds and the sea obey Him?"

The Gergesene Demoniacs
(Mark 5:1–20; Luke 8:26–39)

28 [a]When He had come to the
other side, to the country of the
[1]Gergesenes, there met Him two
demon-possessed *men,* coming out
of the tombs, exceedingly fierce, so
that no one could pass that way.†
29 And suddenly they cried out,
saying, "What have we to do with
You, Jesus, You Son of God? Have
You come here to torment us before
the time?"
30 Now a good way off from them
there was a herd of many swine
feeding.
31 So the demons begged Him,
saying, "If You cast us out, [1]permit
us to go away into the herd of
swine."
32 And He said to them, "Go." So
when they had come out, they went
into the herd of swine. And suddenly the whole herd of swine ran
violently down the steep place into
the sea, and perished in the water.
33 Then those who kept *them* fled;
and they went away into the city and
told everything, including what *had
happened* to the demon-possessed
men.
34 And behold, the whole city
came out to meet Jesus. And when
they saw Him, [a]they begged *Him* to
depart from their region.

The Paralytic Restored
(Mark 2:1–12; Luke 5:17–26)

9 So He got into a boat, crossed
over, [a]and came to His own
city.†
2 [a]Then behold, they brought to
Him a paralytic lying on a bed.

24 [a]Mark 4:37; Luke 8:23–25
26 [a]Ps. 65:7; 89:9; 107:29
27 [1]Lit. *What sort of man is this*
28 [a]Mark 5:1–4; Luke 8:26–33
[1]NU *Gadarenes*
31 [1]NU *send us into*
34 [a]Deut. 5:25; 1 Kin. 17:18; Amos 7:12; Luke 5:8; Acts 16:39

CHAPTER 9

1 [a]Matt. 4:13; 11:23; Mark 5:21
2 [a]Mark 2:3–12; Luke 5:18–26

8:23–27 Jesus' mastery over creation is another powerful sign that He is the Messiah and is divine. Commands to the **sea** and **waves** (v. 24) cannot be issued by a mere human being, but only by God (Job 38:8–11; Ps. 65:5–8; 107:29). Jesus **was asleep** because He was truly fatigued and needed the rest. For in His Incarnation He assumed all the natural and blameless passions of humanity, of which sleep is one. His inactivity intensified the disciples' fear, giving this miracle a greater impact. The image of Christ and the disciples in a boat is traditionally used to depict the Lord and His Church. God permits storms, and delivers us from them, so that we can see His blessings and protection more clearly. Jesus, rebuking the storms, reminds us that He puts an end to the tempest of our souls.

8:28–34 The two Gergesene demoniacs are unsuitable for society and live at a great distance from the village. They are possessed by mental derangement, which makes them aggressive and self-destructive. The demons in them recognize Jesus as the **Son of God.** They know they have nothing in common with Him, for Jesus seeks man's salvation; but His presence torments them and expels them. They are surprised that their power is being terminated **before the time** of the last judgment. Thus, even before His Resurrection Jesus rescues people from the devil's control. Jesus does not yield to their request, but sends them out by His will: though the malice and deceitfulness of the demons is great, they can do nothing unless He permits them. Even the demoniacs had enjoyed God's providential care. The demons' entering into the **swine** (v. 32), which were unclean for the Jews, is a sign of the reality of the demoniacs' healing. Jesus' sovereign power is not only over physical infirmity, but over mental illness as well. It shows us the incomparable value of human beings, whose salvation is worth every sacrifice.

9:1 Jesus' **own city** is Capernaum (4:13; Mark 2:1), which served as His headquarters.

[b] When Jesus saw their faith, He said
to the paralytic, "Son, be of good
cheer; your sins are forgiven you. †
3 And at once some of the scribes
said within themselves, "This Man
blasphemes!"
4 But Jesus, [a]knowing their
thoughts, said, "Why do you think
evil in your hearts?
5 "For which is easier, to say,
'Your sins are forgiven you,' or to
say, 'Arise and walk'?
6 "But that you may know that
the Son of Man has power on earth
to forgive sins"—then He said to the
paralytic, "Arise, take up your bed,
and go to your house."
7 And he arose and departed to
his house.
8 Now when the multitudes saw
it, they [a]marveled[1] and glorified
God, who had given such power to
men.

Sinners Received
(Mark 2:13–17; Luke 5:27–32)

9 [a]As Jesus passed on from there,
He saw a man named Matthew sitting at the tax office. And He said
to him, "Follow Me." So he arose
and followed Him.†
10 [a]Now it happened, as Jesus sat
at the table in the house, *that* behold,
many tax collectors and sinners came
and sat down with Him and His
disciples.
11 And when the Pharisees saw *it*,
they said to His disciples, "Why does
your Teacher eat with [a]tax collectors
and [b]sinners?"
12 When Jesus heard *that*, He said
to them, "Those who are well have
no need of a physician, but those
who are sick.
13 "But go and learn what *this*
means: [a]*'I desire mercy and not sac-*
rifice.' For I did not come to call the
righteous, [b]but sinners, [1]to repentance."

The New Wine of the Kingdom
(Mark 2:18–22; Luke 5:33–39)

14 Then the disciples of John came
to Him, saying, [a]"Why do we and
the Pharisees fast [1]often, but Your
disciples do not fast?"†

2 [b]Matt. 8:10
4 [a]Ps. 139:2; Matt. 12:25; Mark 12:15; Luke 5:22; 6:8; 9:47; 11:17
8 [a]Matt. 8:27; John 7:15 [1]NU *were afraid*
9 [a]Mark 2:14; Luke 5:27
10 [a]Mark 2:15; Luke 5:29
11 [a]Matt. 11:19; Mark 2:16; Luke 5:30; 15:2 [b][Gal. 2:15]
13 [a]Hos. 6:6; [Mic. 6:6–8]; Matt. 12:7 [b]Mark 2:17; Luke 5:32; 1 Tim. 1:15 [1]NU omits *to repentance*
14 [a]Mark 2:18; Luke 5:33–35; 18:12 [1]NU brackets *often* as disputed.

9:2–8 As shown by the healing of the **paralytic,** faith is an indispensable condition for salvation (v. 2). And faith is collective as well as personal, for the faith of the paralytic's friends is required for his healing, and the saving faith of the paralytic impresses **the multitudes** (v. 8). Three signs of Jesus' divinity are shown: (1) He knows the secrets of hearts (v. 4; see 1 Sam. 16:7; 2 Chr. 6:30); (2) He grants the forgiveness of sins (v. 5), a power which belongs to God alone; and (3) this healing is performed merely by the power of His word (v. 6).

9:9–13 **Matthew** is also named Levi (Mark 2:14; Luke 5:27, 29). Roman overlords assigned specific areas to Jewish tax collectors, who were free to collect extra revenues for their own profit. Their collaboration with Gentiles, and their fraud and corruption, caused other Jews to hate the tax collectors and consider them unclean (11:19; Luke 15:1). Jesus, with power to forgive and undo all offenses, calls to this tax collector, **follow Me,** and then dines with him and other sinners. Thus His followers are not troubled later at seeing a tax collector entering into the company of the disciples. The Pharisees, however, are offended, and Jesus' defense is simple: He goes where the need for the **physician** is greatest. **I desire mercy and not sacrifice** does not mean that Jesus rejects the sacrifices of the temple, but that His priority is mercy—the forgiving love of God in action (see Ps. 51).

9:14–17 The Jews typically fasted twice a week (Luke 18:12), Monday and Thursday. In addition, public fasts were regularly observed or occasionally proclaimed (2 Chr. 20:3; Ezra 8:21; Neh. 1:4–11), especially on the Day of Atonement (Lev. 16:31–34) and in times of mourning (Zech. 7:5; 8:19). But the Jews saw the day of the Messiah as a wedding feast—a time of joy and gladness, not a time of mourning and sorrow. Jesus here proclaims that He is that Messiah/Bridegroom. Yet Jesus says the time will come when His disciples will fast. For His disciples, then, fasting is not gloomy but desirable, a bright sadness, for by fasting they gain self-control and prepare themselves for the Wedding Feast of the Lamb.

The **old garment** (v. 16) and **old wineskins** (v. 17) stand for the Old Covenant and Judaism,

(continued on next page)

15 And Jesus said to them, "Can [a]the [1]friends of the bridegroom mourn as long as the bridegroom is with them? But the days will come when the bridegroom will be taken away from them, and [b]then they will fast.
16 "No one puts a piece of unshrunk cloth on an old garment; for [1]the patch pulls away from the garment, and the tear is made worse.
17 "Nor do they put new wine into old wineskins, or else the wineskins [1]break, the wine is spilled, and the wineskins are ruined. But they put new wine into new wineskins, and both are preserved."

A Healing and a Resurrection
(Mark 5:21–43; Luke 8:40–56)

18 [a]While He spoke these things to them, behold, a ruler came and worshiped Him, saying, "My daughter has just died, but come and lay Your hand on her and she will live."†
19 So Jesus arose and followed him, and so *did* His [a]disciples.
20 [a]And suddenly, a woman who had a flow of blood for twelve years came from behind and [b]touched the hem of His garment.
21 For she said to herself, "If only I may touch His garment, I shall be made well."
22 But Jesus turned around, and when He saw her He said, "Be of good cheer, daughter; [a]your faith has made you well." And the woman was made well from that hour.
23 [a]When Jesus came into the ruler's house, and saw [b]the flute players and the noisy crowd wailing,
24 He said to them, [a]"Make room, for the girl is not dead, but sleeping." And they ridiculed Him.
25 But when the crowd was put outside, He went in and [a]took her by the hand, and the girl arose.
26 And the [a]report of this went out into all that land.

Two Blind Men Healed

27 When Jesus departed from there, [a]two blind men followed Him, crying out and saying, [b]"Son of David, have mercy on us!"†
28 And when He had come into the house, the blind men came to Him. And Jesus said to them, "Do you believe that I am able to do this?" They said to Him, "Yes, Lord."
29 Then He touched their eyes,

15 [a]John 3:29 [b]Acts 13:2, 3; 14:23 [1]Lit. *sons of the bride-chamber*
16 [1]Lit. *that which is put on*
17 [1]*burst*
18 [a]Luke 8:41–56
19 [a]Matt. 10:2–4
20 [a]Luke 8:43 [b]Matt. 14:36; 23:5
22 [a]Luke 7:50; 8:48; 17:19; 18:42
23 [a]Mark 5:38 [b]2 Chr. 35:25
24 [a]Acts 20:10
25 [a]Mark 1:31
26 [a]Matt. 4:24
27 [a]Matt. 20:29–34 [b]Luke 18:38, 39

(continued from previous page)
viewed as imperfect and temporary; the **new wineskins** are the New Covenant and the Church, those in Christ. Wine represents the spirit and energy devoted to a covenant; the **new wine** of the New Covenant is the Holy Spirit dwelling within renewed men, the inauguration of the long-awaited Kingdom.

9:18–26 Authority over life and death is in the hand of God alone (Deut. 32:39; 1 Sam. 2:6). Being of one essence with the Father, Jesus has this authority (John 5:21). The healing of the ailing woman is another demonstration of Christ's power to cleanse and make whole (see 8:1–4). In the OT, hemorrhage caused ceremonial defilement, imposing religious and social restrictions, for contact with blood was strictly prohibited (Lev. 15:25). This suffering woman, accounting herself unclean, approaches Jesus secretly, but with great faith. In v. 22, Jesus (1) brings her **good cheer** because of her simple faith; (2) corrects her thinking, for she could not hide her touch from Him; and (3) exhibits her **faith** to all, that they might imitate her. Note that Jesus was not so disturbed by the news of the death of the ruler's daughter that He could not also attend to the needs of the suffering woman.

9:27–34 According to the prophecy of Isaiah, the messianic age is signified when "the eyes of the blind shall be opened, and the ears of the deaf shall be unstopped" (Is. 35:5; see also Is. 29:18; 42:7). These healings are a sign that Christ is the Messiah. The use of the title **Son of David** expresses the faith of the **blind men** that Jesus is the Messiah. Jesus' statement, **let it be to you** (v. 29), somewhat echoes the command of God at creation (Gen. 1:3).

The Pharisees, full of malice and irritated by His healings, accuse Him of casting out demons **by the ruler of the demons** (v. 34)—which is impossible, for the aim of the devil is to consolidate the power of demons, not destroy it. Further, Jesus cleansed lepers, raised the dead, and remitted sins—works which demons could not perform.

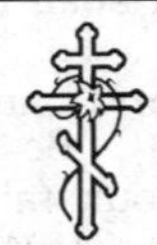

Commemoration of Holy Unmercenary Healers
10:1, 5–8: These saintly physicians obeyed Christ's call to heal the sick.

saying, "According to your faith let
it be to you."
30 And their eyes were opened.
And Jesus sternly warned them, saying, [a]"See *that* no one knows *it*."
31 [a]But when they had departed,
they [1]spread the news about Him in
all that [2]country.

A Demoniac Healed

32 [a]As they went out, behold, they
brought to Him a man, mute and
demon-possessed.
33 And when the demon was cast
out, the mute spoke. And the multitudes marveled, saying, "It was
never seen like this in Israel!"
34 But the Pharisees said, [a]"He
casts out demons by the ruler of the
demons."
35 Then Jesus went about all the
cities and villages, [a]teaching in their
synagogues, preaching the gospel of
the kingdom, and healing every sickness and every disease [1]among the
people.

A Plentiful Harvest

36 [a]But when He saw the multitudes, He was moved with compassion for them, because they were
[1]weary and scattered, [b]like sheep
having no shepherd.†
37 Then He said to His disciples,
[a]"The harvest truly *is* plentiful, but
the laborers *are* few.†
38 [a]"Therefore pray the Lord of the
harvest to send out laborers into His
harvest."

The Twelve Chosen
(Mark 3:13–19; Luke 6:12–16)

10 And [a]when He had called His
twelve disciples to *Him,* He
gave them power *over* unclean spirits, to cast them out, and to heal all
kinds of sickness and all kinds of
disease.†
2 Now the names of the twelve
apostles are these: first, Simon,
[a]who is called Peter, and Andrew his
brother; James the *son* of Zebedee,
and John his brother;
3 Philip and Bartholomew;
Thomas and Matthew the tax collector; James the *son* of Alphaeus, and
[1]Lebbaeus, whose surname was
Thaddaeus;
4 [a]Simon the [1]Cananite, and Judas [b]Iscariot, who also betrayed
Him.

30 [a]Matt. 8:4
31 [a]Mark 7:36 [1]Lit. *made Him known* [2]Lit. *land*
32 [a]Matt. 12:22, 24
34 [a]Luke 11:15
35 [a]Matt. 4:23 [1]NU omits *among the people*
36 [a]Mark 6:34 [b]Num. 27:17 [1]NU, M *harassed*
37 [a]Luke 10:2
38 [a]2 Thess. 3:1

CHAPTER 10

1 [a]Luke 6:13
2 [a]John 1:42
3 [1]NU omits *Lebbaeus, whose surname was*
4 [a]Acts 1:13 [b]John 13:2, 26 [1]NU *Cananaean*

9:36 Jesus does not see people as sinners to be condemned, but as lost sheep to be found and brought home. **Compassion** means "suffering with." **Like sheep having no shepherd,** drawn from the OT (Num. 27:17; 1 Kin. 22:17; Ezek. 34:5), is an accusation against Jewish leaders who, charged with the duty of shepherds, acted the part of wolves.

9:37, 38 The harvest suggests the abundance of those who are ready to accept the message of the Kingdom. Jesus, Himself the Sower, is also **Lord of the harvest** (v. 38). His disciples are sent not to sow but to reap what He had sown by the prophets. It is not the number of those who go which is most important, but the power given to those who are sent (10:1).

10:1–4 Disciples (v. 1) and **apostles** (v. 2) are interchangeable terms for the Twelve followers of Jesus. The Greek word for "disciple" means "learner." The word "apostle" means "one officially sent on a mission." **He gave them power** (v. 1) to perform miracles, while He performed miracles by His own power. Both Matthew and Luke 9:1 add to Mark 6:7 the power of healing diseases. The names of the Twelve, which are not exactly the same in all the NT lists, are arranged in pairs. This gives an interesting idea of who may have traveled with whom on this, the apostles' "first missionary journey," since Mark reports they were sent out two by two.

Commemoration of Holy Martyrs

10:16–22: Jesus' prophecy in this passage is fulfilled in the lives of His holy martyrs.

Mission and Instructions

(Mark 6:7–13; Luke 9:1–6)

5 **These twelve Jesus sent out and
commanded them, saying:** [a]"Do not
go into the way of the Gentiles, and
do not enter a city of [b]the
Samaritans.†
6 [a]"But go rather to the [b]lost
sheep of the house of Israel.
7 [a]"And as you go, preach, saying, [b]'The kingdom of heaven [1]is
at hand.'
8 "Heal the sick, [1]cleanse the lepers, [2]raise the dead, cast out demons.
[a]Freely you have received, freely
give.
9 [a]"Provide neither gold nor silver nor [b]copper in your money belts,
10 "nor bag for *your* journey, nor
two tunics, nor sandals, nor staffs;
[a]for a worker is worthy of his food.
11 [a]"Now whatever city or town
you enter, inquire who in it is worthy, and stay there till you go out.
12 "And when you go into a
household, greet it.†
13 [a]"If the household is worthy, let
your peace come upon it. [b]But if it
is not worthy, let your peace return
to you.
14 [a]"And whoever will not receive
you nor hear your words, when you
depart from that house or city,
[b]shake off the dust from your feet.†
15 "Assuredly, I say to you, [a]it
will be more tolerable for the land
of Sodom and Gomorrah in the day
of judgment than for that city!

Persecution and Martyrdom

16 [a]"Behold, I send you out as
sheep in the midst of wolves. [b]There-
fore be wise as serpents and [c]harm-
less[1] as doves.†
17 "But beware of men, for [a]they
will deliver you up to councils and
[b]scourge you in their synagogues.
18 [a]"You will be brought before
governors and kings for My sake, as
a testimony to them and to the
Gentiles.
19 [a]"But when they deliver you
up, do not worry about how or what

5 [a]Matt. 4:15 [b]John 4:9
6 [a]Matt. 15:24 [b]Jer. 50:6
7 [a]Luke 9:2 [b]Matt. 3:2 [1]*has drawn near*
8 [a][Acts 8:18] [1]NU *raise the dead, cleanse the lepers* [2]M omits *raise the dead*
9 [a]1 Sam. 9:7 [b]Mark 6:8
10 [a]1 Tim. 5:18
11 [a]Luke 10:8
13 [a]Luke 10:5 [b]Ps. 35:13
14 [a]Mark 6:11 [b]Acts 13:51
15 [a]Matt. 11:22, 24
16 [a]Luke 10:3 [b]Eph. 5:15 [c][Phil. 2:14–16] [1]*innocent*
17 [a]Mark 13:9 [b]Acts 5:40; 22:19; 26:11
18 [a]2 Tim. 4:16
19 [a]Luke 12:11, 12; 21:14, 15

10:5–10 The disciples' mission, like that of Jesus, is to **preach** (v. 7) and **heal** (v. 8). Jesus sends them only to the Jews (v. 6), the focus of His earthly ministry, that the Jews might not, after the Resurrection, blame the disciples for "going to uncircumcised men" (Acts 11:3), the Gentiles. Jesus carefully prepares His disciples to be single-minded: (1) He teaches them that His power is free—whatever they accomplish is a gift from God (v. 8). (2) He instructs them to carry no money (v. 9); they must depend on God for their sustenance. Also, this prevents any accusations of greed. (3) He frees them from worry about worldly provisions so that their only occupation is preaching the Word (vv. 7, 9, 10).

10:12, 13 Christ commissions His servants to give a greeting of **peace,** the same peace He offered when He said, "Peace I leave with you, My peace I give to you" (John 14:27). God's peace, proclaimed by the Prophets of the OT (see Is. 52:7), revealed as a fruit of the Holy Spirit (Gal. 5:22), is to this day given to the people through the Word of Christ, "Peace be to all," spoken by His priests in the Liturgy.

10:14, 15 People, and even cities, who don't respond and believe in Christ are left to the **judgment** of God. The example of God's judgment on those who do not believe is **Sodom and Gomorrah** (Gen. 18:16—19:29).

10:16 Persecution accompanies Christian mission because of humanity's sin and rebelliousness against God. Jesus instructed the disciples to **be wise as serpents** that they might not be unnecessarily wounded, and **harmless as doves** that they should not retaliate against those who do them wrong.

you should speak. For [b]it will be
given to you in that hour what you
should speak;
20 [a]"for it is not you who speak,
but the Spirit of your Father who
speaks in you.†
21 [a]"Now brother will deliver up
brother to death, and a father *his*
child; and children will rise up
against parents and cause them to
be put to death.
22 "And [a]you will be hated by all
for My name's sake. [b]But he who endures to the end will be saved.
23 [a]"When they persecute you in
this city, flee to another. For assuredly, I say to you, you will not
have [b]gone through the cities
of Israel [c]before the Son of Man
comes.†

Encouragement to Fearless Witness

24 [a]"A disciple is not above *his*
teacher, nor a servant above his
master.
25 "It is enough for a disciple that
he be like his teacher, and a servant
like his master. If [a]they have called
the master of the house [1]Beelzebub,
how much more *will they call* those
of his household!
26 "Therefore do not fear them.
[a]For there is nothing covered that
will not be revealed, and hidden that
will not be known.†
27 "Whatever I tell you in the dark,
[a]speak in the light; and what you
hear in the ear, preach on the
housetops.
28 [a]"And do not fear those who
kill the body but cannot kill the soul.
But rather [b]fear Him who is able to
destroy both soul and body in
[1]hell.†
29 "Are not two [a]sparrows sold for
a [1]copper coin? And not one of them
falls to the ground apart from your
Father's will.†
30 [a]"But the very hairs of your
head are all numbered.
31 "Do not fear therefore; you are
of more value than many sparrows.
32 [a]"Therefore whoever confesses
Me before men, [b]him I will also confess before My Father who is in
heaven.
33 [a]"But whoever denies Me before men, him I will also deny before
My Father who is in heaven.
34 [a]"Do not think that I came to

19 [b]Ex. 4:12
20 [a]2 Sam. 23:2
21 [a]Mic. 7:6
22 [a]Luke 21:17 [b]Mark 13:13
23 [a]Acts 8:1 [b][Mark 13:10] [c]Matt. 16:28
24 [a]John 15:20
25 [a]John 8:48, 52 [1]NU, M *Beelzebul;* a Philistine deity, 2 Kin. 1:2, 3
26 [a]Mark 4:22
27 [a]Acts 5:20
28 [a]Luke 12:4 [b]Luke 12:5 [1]Gr. *Gehenna*
29 [a]Luke 12:6, 7 [1]Gr. *assarion,* a coin worth about 1/16 of a denarius
30 [a]Luke 21:18
32 [a]Luke 12:8 [b][Rev. 3:5]
33 [a]2 Tim. 2:12
34 [a][Luke 12:49]

10:20 When the disciples bear witness to Jesus, the **Spirit** will speak through them and they will not be defeated (Mark 13:11; John 14:26), though they may be persecuted, even martyred. The work of the disciples in advancing the Kingdom of God is accompanied and empowered by the Spirit, who always accomplishes His purposes.

10:23 The disciples are never told to quit or even to flee far when they are persecuted—just to move on to the next **city** and thus to all **the cities of Israel. Before the Son of Man comes** is probably not a reference to the Second Coming, but to (1) the exaltation of the Messiah in His Passion and Resurrection, or (2) the destruction of Jerusalem in A.D. 70, which was a visitation of Christ in judgment.

10:26 Them refers to those unidentified people (v. 17) who persecute the disciples. **Do not fear** appears three times here (vv. 26, 28, 31) to embolden the community's witness in the face of adversity. Christ's disciples, then and now, must not be intimidated by persecutors nor fail to persevere in fearless preaching.

10:28 Kill the body refers to physical death, but the impossibility of killing **the soul** shows the immortality of the human soul, which is ours by God's grace. **Him** refers to God, not to the devil (see also Luke 1:50; 23:40; Acts 10:2; Col. 3:22; 1 Pet. 2:17; Rev. 15:4; 19:5). Christians are instructed to resist the devil (James 4:7), but not to fear him.

Hell is literally "Gehenna." In Jewish history Gehenna (the Valley of Hinnom) became a place of forbidden religious practices because a throne was established there for Molech, to whom children were offered as sacrifices (2 Chr. 28:3; Jer. 32:35). King Josiah put an end to these practices (2 Kin. 23:10). By Jesus' time the valley had become a garbage dump that smoldered ceaselessly. Because of these associations, Gehenna acquired the connotation of punishment in the afterlife.

10:29–31 If God takes care of **sparrows** (vv. 29, 31) and the **hairs of your head** (v. 30) are numbered, then He has the power of creating, sustaining, and providing for everything—even to the smallest details. Thus, **do not fear** (v. 31).

Sunday of All Saints *First Sunday after Pentecost*

10:32, 33, 37, 38; 19:27–30: These holy people left all to follow Christ and proclaim Him.

The Finding of the Head of John the Baptist *February 24, May 29*

11:2–15: Jesus explains John's ministry to the people.

bring peace on earth. I did not come
to bring peace but a sword.†
35 "For I have come to [a]*'set*[1] *a man against his father, a daughter against her mother, and a daughter-in-law against her mother-in-law';*†
36 "and [a]*'a man's enemies will be those of his own household.'*
37 [a]"He who loves father or mother more than Me is not worthy of Me. And he who loves son or daughter more than Me is not worthy of Me.
38 [a]"And he who does not take his cross and follow after Me is not worthy of Me.
39 [a]"He who finds his life will lose it, and he who loses his life for My sake will find it.
40 [a]"He who receives you receives Me, and he who receives Me receives Him who sent Me.†
41 [a]"He who receives a prophet in the name of a prophet shall receive a prophet's reward. And he who receives a righteous man in the name of a righteous man shall receive a righteous man's reward.
42 [a]"And whoever gives one of these little ones only a cup of cold *water* in the name of a disciple, assuredly, I say to you, he shall by no means lose his reward."

The Baptist's Question to Jesus
(Luke 7:18–23)

11 Now it came to pass, when Jesus finished commanding His twelve disciples, that He departed from there to [a]teach and to preach in their cities.
2 [a]And when John had heard [b]in prison about the works of Christ, he [1]sent two of his disciples
3 and said to Him, "Are You [a]the Coming One, or do we look for another?"†
4 Jesus answered and said to them, "Go and tell John the things which you hear and see:
5 [a]"*The* blind see and *the* lame walk; *the* lepers are cleansed and *the* deaf hear; *the* dead are raised up and

35 [a]Mic. 7:6 [1]*alienate a man from*
36 [a]John 13:18
37 [a]Luke 14:26
38 [a][Mark 8:34]
39 [a]John 12:25
40 [a]Luke 9:48
41 [a]1 Kin. 17:10
42 [a]Mark 9:41

CHAPTER 11

1 [a]Luke 23:5
2 [a]Luke 7:18–35 [b]Matt. 4:12; 14:3 [1]NU *sent by his*
3 [a]John 6:14
5 [a]Is. 29:18; 35:4–6

10:34, 35 Just before His Passion, the most violent of events, Christ promised peace to His disciples. But the message here is that the existence of evil necessitates war. The **earth** to which Christ came was under the authority of Satan (John 12:31; 2 Cor. 4:4), who deluded the whole world. It is therefore essential that Christ wage war against the leader of vice with His weapons of virtue.

10:35–39 The gospel can create sharp conflicts within families because of unbelief and evil in people. To carry **his cross** to the end, a true disciple must be ready, if absolutely necessary, to sacrifice even family relationships.

10:40–42 The disciples and missionaries are ambassadors who represent Jesus. All who extend help to them will receive God's **reward.**

11:3 According to the Church Fathers, John the Baptist asks this question in order to guide his own disciples to Jesus. It is also possible, according to modern interpretations, that John thought of the Messiah as judge only and was perplexed by the mercy of Jesus.

[b]*the* poor have the gospel preached
to them.†
6 "And blessed is he who is not
[a]offended because of Me."

John and Jesus Rejected
(Luke 7:24–35)

7 [a]**As they departed, Jesus began
to say to the multitudes concerning
John:** "What did you go out into the
wilderness to see? [b]A reed shaken
by the wind?
8 "But what did you go out to see?
A man clothed in soft garments? Indeed, those who wear soft *clothing*
are in kings' houses.
9 "But what did you go out to see?
A prophet? Yes, I say to you, [a]and
more than a prophet.
10 "For this is *he* of whom it is
written:

> [a]*'Behold, I send My messenger*
> *before Your face,*
> *Who will prepare Your way*
> *before You.'*

5 [b]Is. 61:1
6 [a][Rom. 9:32]
7 [a]Luke 7:24 [b][Eph. 4:14]
9 [a]Luke 1:76; 20:6
10 [a]Mal. 3:1
12 [a]Luke 16:16
13 [a]Mal. 4:4–6
14 [a]Luke 1:17
15 [a]Luke 8:8
16 [a]Luke 7:31
17 [1]Lit. *beat your breast*

11 "Assuredly, I say to you, among
those born of women there has not
risen one greater than John the
Baptist; but he who is least in the
kingdom of heaven is greater than
he.†
12 [a]"And from the days of John the
Baptist until now the kingdom of
heaven suffers violence, and the violent take it by force.†
13 [a]"For all the prophets and the
law prophesied until John.†
14 "And if you are willing to receive *it,* he is [a]Elijah who is to come.
15 [a]"He who has ears to hear, let
him hear!
16 [a]"But to what shall I liken this
generation? It is like children sitting
in the marketplaces and calling to
their companions,†
17 "and saying:

> 'We played the flute for you,
> And you did not dance;
> We mourned to you,
> And you did not [1]lament.'

18 "For John came neither eating
nor drinking, and they say, 'He has
a demon.'

11:5 Isaiah predicted that at the coming of the Messiah the **blind** would **see,** the **lame walk, lepers** would be **cleansed,** the **deaf** would **hear** (see Luke 7:22). Jesus fulfills the prophecies of Isaiah, bearing the fruit which only the Messiah can produce.

11:11 In terms of the OT Law, John is the greatest prophet. But the New Covenant inaugurated by Christ is of such incomparable value that everyone who shares in it is, as it were, greater than John. For by grace through faith under the New Covenant we become children of God and partakers of the Holy Spirit. John is honored because (1) he was righteous, (2) he prepared the way for the first coming of the Lord, and (3) he baptized Christ.

11:12 Suffers violence may mean that the Kingdom is under attack by opponents of John the Baptist and Jesus, or other **violent** men—messianic pretenders trying to bring in the Kingdom by using military **force** against the Romans. An ancient patristic interpretation is that the Kingdom itself breaks into this world "violently" (10:34). For instance, through powerful miracles, alert and daring people take hold of it aggressively. Whoever is a hearer and lover of the Word of God takes the Kingdom "by force," exerting all earnestness and desire to enter the reality of the Kingdom. For this martyrs shed their blood, making their confession of faith, being "made a spectacle to the world, both to angels and to men" (1 Cor. 4:9). The Kingdom of Heaven belongs not to the sleeping or lazy. Rather, **the violent take it by force.**

11:13, 14 The identification between John the Baptist and Elijah is quite explicit. It is not John who ascribes to himself the role of Elijah, but Jesus who assigns him this place in the history of salvation. John fulfilled the mission of Elijah (Luke 1:17, 76) and his destiny was similar to Elijah's. Yet John is honored over Elijah, for Jesus in comparing the prophets said, "There has not risen one greater than John" (v. 11).

11:16–19 A reference to an ancient game played among Jewish **children** in which the youthful **companions** divided into two groups: those pretending to play musical instruments or singing, and those responding appropriately by dancing or mourning. But in the case of John the Baptist and Jesus, their contemporaries—especially the Jewish leaders—refuse to respond to either one. They accuse John of being too ascetic and Jesus of being too liberal, **a friend of . . . sinners** (v. 19).

Commemoration of Holy Monks

11:27–30: These holy men found Jesus' yoke to be light.

19 "The Son of Man came eating
and drinking, and they say, 'Look,
a glutton and a [1]winebibber, [a]a
friend of tax collectors and sinners!'
[b]But wisdom is justified by her
[2]children."

Woe to the Cities of Galilee

20 [a]**Then He began to rebuke the
cities in which most of His mighty
works had been done, because they
did not repent:†**
21 "Woe to you, Chorazin! Woe to
you, Bethsaida! For if the mighty
works which were done in you had
been done in Tyre and Sidon, they
would have repented long ago [a]in
sackcloth and ashes.
22 "But I say to you, [a]it will be
more tolerable for Tyre and Sidon
in the day of judgment than for
you.
23 "And you, Capernaum, [a]who[1]
are exalted to heaven, will be
brought down to Hades; for if the
mighty works which were done in
you had been done in Sodom, it
would have remained until this day.
24 "But I say to you [a]that it shall
be more tolerable for the land of
Sodom in the day of judgment than
for you."

Rest in Christ

25 [a]**At that time Jesus answered
and said,** "I thank You, Father, Lord
of heaven and earth, that [b]You have
hidden these things from *the* wise
and prudent [c]and have revealed
them to babes.†
26 "Even so, Father, for so it
seemed good in Your sight.
27 [a]"All things have been delivered to Me by My Father, and no
one knows the Son except the Father. [b]Nor does anyone know the
Father except the Son, and *the one*
to whom the Son wills to reveal
Him.†
28 "Come to [a]Me, all *you* who labor
and are heavy laden, and I will give
you rest.†
29 "Take My yoke upon you [a]and
learn from Me, for I am [1]gentle and
[b]lowly in heart, [c]and you will find
rest for your souls.

19 [a]Matt. 9:10 [b]Luke 7:35 [1]*wine drinker* [2]NU *works*
20 [a]Luke 10:13–15, 18
21 [a]Jon. 3:6–8
22 [a]Matt. 10:15; 11:24
23 [a]Is. 14:13 [1]NU *will you be exalted to heaven? No, you will be*
24 [a]Matt. 10:15
25 [a]Luke 10:21, 22 [b]Ps. 8:2 [c]Matt. 16:17
27 [a]Matt. 28:18 [b]John 1:18; 6:46; 10:15
28 [a][John 6:35–37]
29 [a][Phil. 2:5] [b]Zech. 9:9 [c]Jer. 6:16 [1]*meek*

11:20–24 Severe judgment is pronounced on Galilean cities where Jesus preached and healed, but the people did not respond. This happened in **Chorazin** (v. 21), **Bethsaida** and most especially **Capernaum** (v. 23). **Sodom** (v. 23), the greatest offender, will receive some lenience **in the day of judgment** (v. 24), because that city never saw Jesus' **mighty works** (v. 23). "To whom much is given . . . much will be required" (Luke 12:48).

11:25 In Jesus' prayer of thanksgiving, the Father alone is the source of knowledge, and He alone opens the hearts of men to receive it. He communicates in a hidden way to responsive hearts. The paradox: the veiled reality of the Kingdom which Jesus reveals is seen by **babes,** simple fishermen, and sinners, not the **wise and prudent,** the Pharisees, Sadducees and scribes.

11:27 Another clear statement about the deity of Christ, **Son** of **the Father,** who knows the Father and reveals Him. The Son reveals only as much as we have the capacity to receive.

11:28–30 Jesus' **yoke** (vv. 29, 30) is submission to the Kingdom of God. A *yoke* may be the symbol of hardship, burdens and responsibilities (1 Kin. 12:1–11; Jer. 27:8—28:2; Sir. 40:1). Although it may feel heavy due to our sins (Ps. 38:4), Christ's *yoke* is easy. In Him the soul is refreshed and sees that the Lord is gracious (Ps. 34:9; Is. 55:2; Jer. 31:25). A sign of Jesus' lordship is His meekness—He is **gentle and lowly.** King David emphasized that the Lord would teach His ways to the meek (Ps. 25:9). Meekness is the mother of love, the foundation of discernment and the forerunner of all humility. Jesus finds rest in the hearts of the meek, while the turbulent spirit is home to the devil.

30 [a]"For My yoke *is* easy and My
burden is light."

The Pharisees' Hostility
(Mark 2:23—3:6; Luke 6:1–11)

12 At that time [a]Jesus went
through the grainfields on the
Sabbath. And His disciples were
hungry, and began to [b]pluck heads
of grain and to eat.†
2 And when the Pharisees saw *it,*
they said to Him, "Look, Your disciples are doing what is not lawful to
do on the Sabbath!"
3 But He said to them, "Have you
not read [a]what David did when he
was hungry, he and those who were
with him:†
4 "how he entered the house of
God and ate [a]the showbread which
was not lawful for him to eat, nor
for those who were with him,
[b]but only for the priests?
5 "Or have you not read in the
[a]law that on the Sabbath the priests
in the temple [1]profane the Sabbath,
and are blameless?
6 "Yet I say to you that in this
place there is [a]*One* greater than the
temple.†
7 "But if you had known what *this*
means, [a]*'I desire mercy and not sacrifice,'* you would not have condemned the guiltless.
8 "For the Son of Man is Lord
[1]even of the Sabbath."
9 [a]Now when He had departed
from there, He went into their
synagogue.
10 And behold, there was a man
who had a withered hand. And they
asked Him, saying, [a]"Is it lawful to
heal on the Sabbath?"—that they
might accuse Him.†
11 Then He said to them, "What
man is there among you who has one
sheep, and if it falls into a pit on the
Sabbath, will not lay hold of it and
lift *it* out?
12 "Of how much more value then
is a man than a sheep? Therefore
it is lawful to do good on the Sabbath."
13 Then He said to the man,
"Stretch out your hand." And he
stretched *it* out, and it was restored
as whole as the other.
14 Then [a]the Pharisees went out
and plotted against Him, how they
might destroy Him.

Isaiah's Servant of God
(Mark 3:7–12; Luke 6:17–19)

15 But when Jesus knew *it,* [a]He
withdrew from there. [b]And great
[1]multitudes followed Him, and He
healed them all.
16 Yet He [a]warned them not to
make Him known,†

30 [a][1 John 5:3]

CHAPTER 12

1 [a]Luke 6:1–5 [b]Deut. 23:25
3 [a]1 Sam. 21:6
4 [a]Lev. 24:5 [b]Ex. 29:32
5 [a]Num. 28:9 [1]*desecrate*
6 [a][Is. 66:1, 2]
7 [a][Hos. 6:6]
8 [1]NU, M omit *even*
9 [a]Mark 3:1–6
10 [a]John 9:16
14 [a]Mark 3:6
15 [a]Mark 3:7 [b]Matt. 19:2 [1]NU brackets *multitudes* as disputed.
16 [a]Matt. 8:4; 9:30; 17:9

12:1, 2 The Pharisees are rigid in their legalism. While the plucking of a few ears in a neighbor's field is permitted by the Law (Deut. 23:25), they consider it "reaping" and unlawful work **on the Sabbath** (v. 2).

12:3–5 Providing OT precedents of **blameless** (v. 5) violations of the **Sabbath** rule (Lev. 24:5–9; Num. 28:9, 10; 1 Sam. 21:1–6), Jesus demonstrates the **law** is not absolute over human need or service to God. The **showbread** (v. 4) suggests the Bread from heaven which is set upon holy tables of the **house of God,** the Church.

12:6–8 Jesus is **Lord even of the Sabbath,** thus Lord of all days including the Lord's Day, and the Author of the Law itself. He gives precedence to **mercy** rather than ritualistic observance.

12:10–13 Rabbis permitted healing on the Sabbath only if a person's life was in danger. Jesus goes further. The man with **a withered hand** (v. 10) is not in critical condition, but Jesus is merciful and heals him in the synagogue.

12:16–21 Jesus' refusal to fully disclose His identity as Messiah is foreseen by Isaiah. The reasons for secrecy include: (1) the growing hostility of the Jewish leaders, (2) the people's misunderstanding of messiahship as political and earthly, and (3) Jesus' desire to evoke the response of faith—He wants people to discover His identity for themselves. The **Servant** (v. 18) of God refers both to the Messiah and to all God's elect. Jesus also fulfills another prophecy of Isaiah, that of the Suffering Servant (see Is. 52:13—53:12). The mission to the **Gentiles** (v. 21) after Pentecost is also foreseen.

17 that it might be fulfilled which
was spoken by Isaiah the prophet,
saying:

18 *"Behold![a] My Servant whom I*
have chosen,
My Beloved [b]in whom My soul
is well pleased!
I will put My Spirit upon Him,
And He will declare justice to
the Gentiles.
19 *He will not quarrel nor cry out,*
Nor will anyone hear His voice
in the streets.
20 *A bruised reed He will not*
break,
And smoking flax He will not
quench,
Till He sends forth justice to
victory;
21 *And in His name Gentiles will*
trust."

Is Jesus from God?

(Mark 3:20–30; Luke 11:14–23)

22 [a]Then one was brought to Him
who was demon-possessed, blind
and mute; and He healed him, so
that the [1]blind and mute man both
spoke and saw.†
23 And all the multitudes were
amazed and said, "Could this be the
[a]Son of David?"
24 [a]Now when the Pharisees heard
it they said, "This *fellow* does not cast
out demons except by [1]Beelzebub,
the ruler of the demons."
25 But Jesus [a]knew their thoughts,
and said to them: "Every kingdom
divided against itself is brought to
desolation, and every city or house
divided against itself will not stand.
26 "If Satan casts out Satan, he is
divided against himself. How then
will his kingdom stand?
27 "And if I cast out demons by
Beelzebub, by whom do your sons
cast *them* out? Therefore they shall
be your judges.
28 "But if I cast out demons by the
Spirit of God, [a]surely the kingdom
of God has come upon you.
29 [a]"Or how can one enter a strong
man's house and plunder his goods,
unless he first binds the strong man?
And then he will plunder his house.
30 "He who is not with Me is
against Me, and he who does not
gather with Me scatters abroad.
31 "Therefore I say to you, [a]every
sin and blasphemy will be forgiven
men, [b]but the blasphemy *against* the
Spirit will not be forgiven men.
32 "Anyone who [a]speaks a word
against the Son of Man, [b]it will be
forgiven him; but whoever speaks
against the Holy Spirit, it will not be
forgiven him, either in this age or
in the *age* to come.†
33 "Either make the tree good and
[a]its fruit good, or else make the tree
bad and its fruit bad; for a tree is
known by *its* fruit.†

18 [a]Is. 42:1–4; 49:3 [b]Matt. 3:17; 17:5
22 [a]Matt. 9:32; [Mark 3:11]; Luke 11:14, 15 [1]NU omits *blind and*
23 [a]Matt. 9:27; 21:9
24 [a]Matt. 9:34; Mark 3:22; Luke 11:15 [1]NU, M *Beelzebul*, a Philistine deity
25 [a]Matt. 9:4; John 2:25; Rev. 2:23
28 [a][Dan. 2:44; 7:14; Luke 1:33]; 11:20; [17:20, 21; 1 John 3:8]
29 [a]Is. 49:24; [Luke 11:21–23]
31 [a]Mark 3:28–30; Luke 12:10; [Heb. 6:4–6; 10:26, 29; 1 John 5:16] [b]Acts 7:51
32 [a]Matt. 11:19; 13:55; John 7:12, 52 [b]1 Tim. 1:13
33 [a]Matt. 7:16–18; Luke 6:43, 44; [John 15:4–7]

12:22–30 Filled with pride and envy, the Pharisees found in this miracle a pretext to attack Jesus, accusing Him of having **Beelzebub** (v. 24) as the source of His power. Beelzebub/Baal was the prince perhaps of "the dung heap" or "the flies"—a god worshiped by the Philistines (2 Kin. 1:2–16); here he is called **ruler of the demons** (v. 24). Demons do not fight against themselves, but are cast out by God's power through the Holy **Spirit** (v. 28), whose action signals the present reality of the Kingdom.

12:32 Blasphemy **against the Holy Spirit** is blasphemy against the divine activity of the Spirit—the accusation that Jesus healed the demoniac by demonic power (v. 24) rather than by the power of the Holy Spirit (v. 28; see Mark 3:29, 30). Every sin **against the Son of Man** can be forgiven, because the Jews do not yet know much about Him. But blasphemy against the Spirit, whose divine activity they know from the OT, will not be forgiven. This blasphemy is willful hardness of heart. It attributes the saving action of the Spirit to Satan and refuses to accept God's forgiveness and mercy.

12:33–36 Jesus pronounces a severe judgment against the blasphemers of the Spirit. As the tree is revealed by its fruit, a human being is known by his works. He will *do* according to the kind of person he *is*. The blasphemers are a **brood of vipers** (v. 34; see 3:7; 23:33) because of their evil works and malice. Their heritage is of no value to them; they bear no fruit appropriate to a chosen people.

The **heart** (v. 35) in Scripture refers to the center of consciousness, the seat of the intellect

(continued on next page)

34 [a]"Brood[1] of vipers! How can you, being evil, speak good things? [b]For out of the abundance of the heart the mouth speaks.

35 "A good man out of the good treasure [1]of his heart brings forth good things, and an evil man out of the evil treasure brings forth evil things.

36 "But I say to you that for every idle word men may speak, they will give account of it in the day of judgment.

37 "For by your words you will be justified, and by your words you will be condemned."

Can Jesus Perform a Sign?
(Luke 11:24–26, 29–32)

38 **[a]Then some of the scribes and Pharisees answered, saying, "Teacher, we want to see a sign from You."†**

39 **But He answered and said to them,** "An evil and [a]adulterous generation seeks after a sign, and no sign will be given to it except the sign of the prophet Jonah.†

40 [a]"For as Jonah was three days and three nights in the belly of the great fish, so will the Son of Man be three days and three nights in the heart of the earth.

41 [a]"The men of Nineveh will rise up in the judgment with this generation and [b]condemn it, [c]because they repented at the preaching of Jonah; and indeed a greater than Jonah *is* here.

42 [a]"The queen of the South will rise up in the judgment with this generation and condemn it, for she came from the ends of the earth to hear the wisdom of Solomon; and indeed a greater than Solomon *is* here.

43 [a]"When an unclean spirit goes out of a man, [b]he goes through dry places, seeking rest, and finds none.†

44 "Then he says, 'I will return to my house from which I came.' And when he comes, he finds *it* empty, swept, and put in order.

45 "Then he goes and takes with him seven other spirits more wicked than himself, and they enter and dwell there; [a]and the last *state* of that man is worse than the first. So shall it also be with this wicked generation."

Jesus' Relatives Fail to Understand
(Mark 3:31–35; Luke 8:19–21)

46 **While He was still talking to the multitudes, [a]behold, His mother and [b]brothers stood outside, seeking to speak with Him.†**

47 **Then one said to Him,** "Look,

34 [a]Matt. 3:7; 23:33 [b]Luke 6:45 [1]*Offspring*
35 [1]NU, M omit *of his heart*
38 [a]Mark 8:11
39 [a]Matt. 16:4
40 [a]Jon. 1:17
41 [a]Luke 11:32 [b]Jer. 3:11 [c]Jon. 3:5
42 [a]1 Kin. 10:1–13
43 [a]Luke 11:24–26 [b][1 Pet. 5:8]
45 [a][2 Pet. 2:20–22]
46 [a]Luke 8:19–21 [b]John 2:12; 7:3, 5

(continued from previous page)
and the will, the source from which the whole of spiritual life proceeds. When grace permeates the *heart,* it masters the body and guides all actions and thoughts. When malice and evil capture the heart, a person becomes full of darkness and spiritual confusion.

12:38 In their request for **a sign,** some spectacular display, **the scribes and Pharisees** show their wickedness. After so many miracles, they now ask Jesus for such a sign? But Jesus will not cater to their hard-heartedness. His sign will be His Passion and Resurrection from the dead, beautifully displayed in icons in which Christ descends into Sheol and lifts Adam and Eve out of its open jaws.

12:39 Adulterous generation echoes the analogy of the prophets for the infidelity of Israel (Jer. 2:1–3, 20–25, 32, 33; 3:1–5; Hos. 2:2–13).

12:43–45 When, by the mercy of God, the Israelites were delivered out of Egypt, they did not repent of their impure ways, and unclean spirits again took up residence in them (Deut. 31:20; 32:15–18; Ps. 106:34–39). The same happens here. Unless there is full-hearted repentance and the Holy Spirit dwells in a person, the expelled demon will return with many others and reoccupy its abode.

12:46–50 Jesus' relatives have not yet understood His identity and mission. He points to a spiritual family based on obedience to **the will of My Father** (v. 50). In Jewish usage "brother" may also signify a stepbrother or other relative. Abram called his nephew Lot "brother" (Gen. 14:14); Boaz spoke of his relative Elimelech as his "brother" (Ruth 4:3); and

(continued on next page)

[a]Your mother and Your brothers are
standing outside, seeking to speak
with You."
48 But He answered and said to the
one who told Him, "Who is My
mother and who are My brothers?"
49 And He stretched out His hand
toward His disciples and said, "Here
are My mother and My [a]brothers!
50 "For [a]whoever does the will of
My Father in heaven is My brother
and sister and mother."

The Parable of the Sower
(Mark 4:1–9; Luke 8:4–8)

13 On the same day Jesus went
out of the house [a]and sat by
the sea.
2 [a]And great multitudes were
gathered together to Him, so that
[b]He got into a boat and sat; and the
whole multitude stood on the
shore.
3 Then He spoke many things to
them in parables, saying: [a]"Behold,
a sower went out to sow.†
4 "And as he sowed, some *seed*
fell by the wayside; and the birds
came and devoured them.
5 "Some fell on stony places,
where they did not have much earth;
and they immediately sprang up because they had no depth of earth.
6 "But when the sun was up they
were scorched, and because they had
no root they withered away.
7 "And some fell among thorns,
and the thorns sprang up and
choked them.
8 "But others fell on good ground
and yielded a crop: some [a]a hundredfold, some sixty, some thirty.
9 [a]"He who has ears to hear, let
him hear!"

The Mystery of Parables
(Mark 4:10–12; Luke 8:9, 10)

10 And the disciples came and said
to Him, "Why do You speak to them
in parables?"
11 He answered and said to them,
"Because [a]it has been given to you
to know the [1]mysteries of the kingdom of heaven, but to them it has
not been given.†
12 [a]"For whoever has, to him more
will be given, and he will have abundance; but whoever does not have,
even what he has will be taken away
from him.†
13 "Therefore I speak to them in
parables, because seeing they do not
see, and hearing they do not hear,
nor do they understand.
14 "And in them the prophecy of
Isaiah is fulfilled, which says:

[a]'Hearing you will hear and shall
not understand,
And seeing you will see and not
[b]perceive;
15 *For the hearts of this people*
have grown dull.
Their ears [a]are hard of hearing,

47 [a]Matt. 13:55, 56
49 [a]John 20:17
50 [a]John 15:14

CHAPTER 13
1 [a]Mark 4:1–12
2 [a]Luke 8:4 [b]Luke 5:3
3 [a]Luke 8:5
8 [a]Gen. 26:12
9 [a]Matt. 11:15
11 [a]Mark 4:10, 11 [1]*secret* or *hidden truths*
12 [a]Matt. 25:29
14 [a]Is. 6:9, 10 [b][John 3:36]
15 [a]Heb. 5:11

(continued from previous page)
Joab called Amasa, his first cousin (2 Sam. 17:25), "brother" just before he killed him (2 Sam. 20:9). Orthodox Christians believe that Jesus had relatives, not blood brothers. Indeed, at the Cross, Jesus commits His mother to the care of His disciple John, which would have been a crime against tradition had she had another child to care for her.

13:3–9 In the OT, metaphors of sowing and harvesting are common (Ps. 126:5, 6; Is. 55:10–13; Jer. 31:27–34; Hos. 2:21–23; and Joel 3:12–14), part of the daily lives of the people. In this parable Jesus is revealing Himself as the promised Messiah, the **sower** on earth (see the interpretation in vv. 18–23).

13:11 The mysteries of the kingdom are not mere esoteric concepts or a body of religious truth only for the elite. Nor is true understanding of the parables simply an intellectual apprehension. Even the disciples find His message hard to understand. Jesus preached and taught the same message to all; but it is the "babes," the simple and innocent, who are open to the gospel and have the faith to receive this mystery, which is the reality of the Kingdom.

13:12 When one has zeal, he **will be given** more from God. But if he does not use what he has, and fails to participate in the life of the Kingdom, God's gifts **will be taken away.** This is a hard saying, but true.

PARABLES

Parables are stories in word-pictures, revealing spiritual truth. The Hebrew and Aramaic words for *parable* also mean "allegory," "riddle," or "proverb." The Scriptures, especially the Gospels, are filled with parables—images drawn from daily life in the world to represent and communicate the deep things of God. Parables give us glimpses of Him whose thoughts are not our thoughts and whose ways are not our ways (Is. 55:8, 9).

The truth communicated by Jesus' parables, however, is not evident to all who hear them. One must have spiritual eyes to see and spiritual ears to hear, and even then there are degrees of understanding of the parables.

Thus, "to those who are outside, all things come in parables" (Mark 4:11) may be translated "to those who are outside, all things come in riddles." Jesus' quotation of Isaiah 6:9, 10 (Matt. 13:14, 15) does not mean He used parables to blind the people or to lead them to punishment. On the contrary, it demonstrates that the people are responsible for their own receptivity: having grown dull and insensitive, they are unwilling to accept the message of the parables. As the mission of Isaiah in the Old Testament was to open the eyes of Israel to see the acts of God, so the parables of Jesus are given to open the eyes of His hearers to the truth, and to lead them to produce the fruit of righteousness.

Parables challenge the hearer and call for faith to perceive the mysteries of the Kingdom. Insight into God's Kingdom does not come simply through an intellectual understanding of the parables. Spiritual enlightenment is communicated through faith in the Person, words, and deeds of the Lord Jesus Christ.

The use of parables was known in Jewish culture long before Jesus (2 Sam. 12:1–4; 1 Kin. 20:35–42; Is. 5:1–7). Jesus, however, brought the art of parables to perfection, relating aspects of the Kingdom and speaking of God Himself through vivid stories. His purpose was not only to reveal truth to those with hearts prepared. He also wished to draw responsive hearts past the entrance and into the very reality of God's Kingdom which He proclaimed and inaugurated.

Among the familiar parables read on Sundays throughout the Church year are: the Sower (Luke 8:5–15); the Good Samaritan (Luke 10:25–37); the Rich Man and His Crops (Luke 12:16–21); the Great Supper (Luke 14:16–24); the Talents (Matt. 25:14–30); the Pharisee and the Tax Collector (Luke 18:10–14); and the Prodigal Son (Luke 15:11–32).

In opening to us the door to the Kingdom of Heaven, the parables help us to love God and to know Him, to understand and believe His grace, mercy and forgiveness, and to order our lives according to His Holy Word.

And their eyes they have
[b]closed,
Lest they should see with their
eyes and hear with their ears,
Lest they should understand
with their hearts and turn,
So that I [1]should [c]heal them.'

16 "But [a]blessed *are* your eyes for
they see, and your ears for they hear;
17 "for assuredly, I say to you
[a]that many prophets and righteous
men desired to see what you see, and
did not see *it,* and to hear what you
hear, and did not hear *it.*

The Sower Explained

(Mark 4:13–20; Luke 8:11–15)

18 [a]"Therefore hear the parable of
the sower:
19 "When anyone hears the word
[a]of the kingdom, and does not understand *it,* then the wicked *one*
comes and snatches away what was
sown in his heart. This is he who
received seed by the wayside.
20 "But he who received the seed
on stony places, this is he who hears
the word and immediately [a]receives
it with joy;
21 "yet he has no root in himself,
but endures only for a while. For
when [a]tribulation or persecution
arises because of the word, immediately [b]he stumbles.
22 "Now [a]he who received seed
[b]among the thorns is he who hears
the word, and the cares of this world
and the deceitfulness of riches choke
the word, and he becomes unfruitful.
23 "But he who received seed on
the good ground is he who hears the
word and understands *it,* who indeed bears [a]fruit and produces:
some a hundredfold, some sixty,
some thirty."

15 [b]Luke 19:42 [c]Acts 28:26, 27 [1]NU, M *would*
16 [a]Luke 10:23, 24
17 [a]Heb. 11:13
18 [a]Mark 4:13–20
19 [a]Matt. 4:23
20 [a]Is. 58:2
21 [a][Acts 14:22] [b]Matt. 11:6
22 [a]1 Tim. 6:9 [b]Jer. 4:3
23 [a]Col. 1:6
30 [a]Matt. 3:12
31 [a]Luke 13:18, 19

The Wheat and the Tares

24 Another parable He put forth to
them, saying: "The kingdom of
heaven is like a man who sowed
good seed in his field;†
25 "but while men slept, his enemy
came and sowed tares among the
wheat and went his way.
26 "But when the grain had
sprouted and produced a crop, then
the tares also appeared.
27 "So the servants of the owner
came and said to him, 'Sir, did you
not sow good seed in your field?
How then does it have tares?'
28 "He said to them, 'An enemy
has done this.' The servants said to
him, 'Do you want us then to go and
gather them up?'
29 "But he said, 'No, lest while you
gather up the tares you also uproot
the wheat with them.
30 'Let both grow together until the
harvest, and at the time of harvest I
will say to the reapers, "First gather
together the tares and bind them in
bundles to burn them, but [a]gather
the wheat into my barn." ' "

The Mustard Seed and the Leaven

(Mark 4:30–32; Luke 13:18–21)

31 Another parable He put forth to
them, saying: [a]"The kingdom of
heaven is like a mustard seed, which
a man took and sowed in his field,†

13:24–30, 37–43 The parable of the wheat and tares builds on the previous parable of the sower. Here Christ the Sower gives attention to the work of the **enemy** (v. 25), the devil, who comes to sow his own seed after the fruits have multiplied. Falsehood comes in after truth: after the prophets came false prophets; after Christ will come the Antichrist. The devil fashions falsehood and heresy to resemble the true Faith: the weeds look somewhat like the wheat. The evil one also comes while everybody is asleep. While the devices of the evil one do not extend into heaven, in this age he intermingles the counterfeit with the Kingdom. This parable explains why the Church does not expel her nominal members. To weed out the **tares** is to disrupt the **wheat** (v. 29). Those who are watchful and remain faithful **will shine forth as the sun** (v. 43) forever.

13:31–33 These two short parables signify the startling success of God's Kingdom. A few weak fishermen will convert the whole world because of the divine power of the gospel.

32 "which indeed is the least of all
the seeds; but when it is grown it is
greater than the herbs and becomes
a [a]tree, so that the birds of the air
come and nest in its branches."
33 [a]Another parable He spoke to
them: "The kingdom of heaven is
like leaven, which a woman took and
hid in three [1]measures of meal till
[b]it was all leavened."

Parables Fulfill Prophecy
(Mark 4:33, 34)

34 [a]All these things Jesus spoke to
the multitude in parables; and without a parable He did not speak to
them,
35 that it might be fulfilled which
was spoken by the prophet, saying:

> [a]*"I will open My mouth in*
> *parables;*
> [b]*I will utter things kept secret*
> *from the foundation of the*
> *world."*

The Wheat and Tares Explained

36 Then Jesus sent the multitude
away and went into the house. And
His disciples came to Him, saying,
"Explain to us the parable of the
tares of the field."
37 He answered and said to them:
"He who sows the good seed is the
Son of Man.
38 [a]"The field is the world, the
good seeds are the sons of the kingdom, but the tares are [b]the sons of
the wicked *one.*
39 "The enemy who sowed them
is the devil, [a]the harvest is the end
of the age, and the reapers are the
angels.
40 "Therefore as the tares are gathered and burned in the fire, so it will
be at the end of this age.
41 "The Son of Man will send out
His angels, [a]and they will gather out
of His kingdom all things that offend, and those who practice
lawlessness,
42 [a]"and will cast them into the
furnace of fire. [b]There will be wailing
and gnashing of teeth.
43 [a]"Then the righteous will shine
forth as the sun in the kingdom of
their Father. [b]He who has ears to
hear, let him hear!

The Hidden Treasure and the Pearl of Great Price

44 "Again, the kingdom of heaven
is like treasure hidden in a field,
which a man found and hid; and for
joy over it he goes and [a]sells all that
he has and [b]buys that field.†
45 "Again, the kingdom of heaven
is like a merchant seeking beautiful
pearls,
46 "who, when he had found
[a]one pearl of great price, went and
sold all that he had and bought it.

The Dragnet

47 "Again, the kingdom of heaven
is like a dragnet that was cast into
the sea and [a]gathered some of every
kind,†
48 "which, when it was full, they
drew to shore; and they sat down
and gathered the good into vessels,
but threw the bad away.
49 "So it will be at the end of the
age. The angels will come forth,
[a]separate the wicked from among
the just,
50 "and cast them into the furnace
of fire. There will be wailing and
gnashing of teeth."

32 [a]Ps. 104:12; Ezek. 17:22–24; 31:3–9; Dan. 4:12
33 [a]Luke 13:20, 21 [b][1 Cor. 5:6; Gal. 5:9] [1]Gr. *sata,* same as a Heb. *seah;* approximately 2 pecks in all
34 [a]Mark 4:33, 34; John 10:6; 16:25
35 [a]Ps. 78:2 [b]Rom. 16:25, 26; 1 Cor. 2:7; Eph. 3:9; Col. 1:26
38 [a]Matt. 24:14; 28:19; Mark 16:15; Luke 24:47; Rom. 10:18; Col. 1:6 [b]Gen. 3:15; John 8:44; Acts 13:10
39 [a]Joel 3:13; Rev. 14:15
41 [a]Matt. 18:7; 2 Pet. 2:1, 2
42 [a]Matt. 3:12; Rev. 19:20; 20:10 [b]Matt. 8:12; 13:50
43 [a][Dan. 12:3; 1 Cor. 15:42, 43, 58] [b]Matt. 13:9
44 [a]Phil. 3:7, 8 [b][Is. 55:1; Rev. 3:18]
46 [a]Prov. 2:4; 3:14, 15; 8:10, 19
47 [a]Matt. 22:9, 10
49 [a]Matt. 25:32

13:44–46 The Kingdom of God is compared to an earthly **treasure** and a costly **pearl** (v. 46). The driving desire of men for wealth pictures the desire of the soul for heavenly riches. The jewel is described as **hidden** because it requires faith and perseverance to discover it.

13:47–50 The Kingdom is compared to a fishing net which gathers the good and the wicked, an image similar to that of the parable of the tares (vv. 36–43). The point is that the final judgment will finally disclose and separate the wicked from the righteous.

Old and New Wisdom

51 [1]Jesus said to them, "Have you
understood all these things?" They
said to Him, "Yes, [2]Lord."
52 Then He said to them, "Therefore every [1]scribe instructed [2]con-
cerning the kingdom of heaven is
like a householder who brings out
of his treasure [a]*things* new and
old."†
53 Now it came to pass, when Jesus had finished these parables, that
He departed from there.

Rejection at Nazareth
(Mark 6:1–6; Luke 4:16–30)

54 [a]When He had come to His own
country, He taught them in their
synagogue, so that they were astonished and said, "Where did this *Man*
get this wisdom and *these* mighty
works?
55 [a]"Is this not the carpenter's
son? Is not His mother called Mary?
And [b]His brothers [c]James, [1]Joses, Simon, and Judas?†
56 "And His sisters, are they not
all with us? Where then did this *Man*
get all these things?"
57 So they [a]were offended at Him.
But Jesus said to them, [b]"A prophet
is not without honor except in his
own country and in his own house."
58 Now [a]He did not do many
mighty works there because of their
unbelief.

Herod's Fears
(Mark 6:14–29; Luke 3:19, 20; 9:7–9)

14 At that time [a]Herod the tetrarch heard the report about
Jesus†
2 and said to his servants, "This
is John the Baptist; he is risen from
the dead, and therefore these powers
are at work in him."
3 [a]For Herod had laid hold of
John and bound him, and put *him*
in prison for the sake of Herodias,
his brother Philip's wife.
4 Because John had said to him,
[a]"It is not lawful for you to have
her."
5 And although he wanted to put
him to death, he feared the multitude, [a]because they counted him as
a prophet.
6 But when Herod's birthday was
celebrated, the daughter of Herodias
danced before them and pleased
Herod.
7 Therefore he promised with an
oath to give her whatever she might
ask.
8 So she, having been prompted
by her mother, said, "Give me John
the Baptist's head here on a platter."
9 And the king was sorry; nevertheless, because of the oaths and because of those who sat with him, he
commanded *it* to be given to *her*.
10 So he sent and had John beheaded in prison.
11 And his head was brought on
a platter and given to the girl, and
she brought *it* to her mother.
12 Then his disciples came and
took away the body and buried it,
and went and told Jesus.

Feeding the Five Thousand
(Mark 6:30–44; Luke 9:10–17; John 6:1–14)

13 [a]When Jesus heard *it*, He departed from there by boat to a

51 [1]NU omits *Jesus said to them* [2]NU omits *Lord*
52 [a]Song 7:13 [1]A scholar of the Old Testament [2]Or *for*
54 [a]Ps. 22:22; Matt. 2:23; Mark 6:1; Luke 4:16; John 7:15
55 [a]Is. 49:7; Mark 6:3; [Luke 3:23]; John 6:42 [b]Matt. 12:46 [c]Mark 15:40 [1]NU *Joseph*
57 [a]Matt. 11:6; Mark 6:3, 4 [b]Luke 4:24; John 4:44
58 [a]Mark 6:5, 6; John 5:44, 46, 47

CHAPTER 14

1 [a]Mark 6:14–29; Luke 9:7–9
3 [a]Matt. 4:12; Mark 6:17; Luke 3:19, 20
4 [a]Lev. 18:16; 20:21
5 [a]Matt. 21:26; Luke 20:6
13 [a]Matt. 10:23; 12:15; Mark 6:32–44; Luke 9:10–17; John 6:1, 2

13:52 Jesus does not reject the OT; rather, He commends it and calls it **treasure.** Fulfillment is found, however, in the NT, which leads to a complete understanding of the OT. This parable describes how Matthew, a Christian **scribe,** composed his Gospel.

13:55–58 Even in **his own country,** Nazareth, Jesus finds not acceptance but rejection (see John 1:11). In their envy, although they can find no fault in His words and miracles, the Nazarenes dismiss Him on the basis of the unimportance of His family.

14:1–12 The beheading of John the Baptist is permitted by God. In a world of shameful wickedness, the righteous are afflicted and suffer death, though they are great in the eyes of God. Through John's martyrdom the coming of the Savior is announced to souls in Hades, for John is considered to be a forerunner of Jesus there as well as on earth.

deserted place by Himself. But when
the multitudes heard it, they
followed Him on foot from the
cities.
14 And when Jesus went out He
saw a great multitude; and He
[a]was moved with compassion for
them, and healed their sick.†
15 [a]When it was evening, His disciples came to Him, saying, "This
is a deserted place, and the hour
is already late. Send the multitudes away, that they may go into
the villages and buy themselves
food."
16 But Jesus said to them, "They
do not need to go away. You give
them something to eat."
17 And they said to Him, "We
have here only five loaves and two
fish."
18 He said, "Bring them here to
Me."
19 Then He commanded the multitudes to sit down on the grass. And
He took the five loaves and the two
fish, and looking up to heaven,
[a]He blessed and broke and gave the
loaves to the disciples; and the disciples gave to the multitudes.†
20 So they all ate and were filled,
and they took up twelve baskets full
of the fragments that remained.
21 Now those who had eaten were
about five thousand men, besides
women and children.

14 [a]Matt. 9:36; Mark 6:34
15 [a]Mark 6:35; Luke 9:12
19 [a]1 Sam. 9:13; Matt. 15:36; 26:26; Mark 6:41; 8:7; 14:22; Luke 24:30; Acts 27:35; [Rom. 14:6]
22 [1]*invited, strongly urged*
23 [a]Mark 6:46; Luke 9:28; John 6:15
[b]John 6:16
24 [1]NU *many furlongs away from the land*
26 [a]Job 9:8
27 [a]Acts 23:11; 27:22, 25, 36
[1]*Take courage*
[2]Lit. *I am*
30 [1]NU brackets *that* and *boisterous* as disputed.

Walking on Water
(Mark 6:45–52; John 6:15–21)

22 Immediately Jesus [1]made His
disciples get into the boat and go before Him to the other side, while He
sent the multitudes away.†
23 [a]And when He had sent the
multitudes away, He went up on the
mountain by Himself to pray.
[b]Now when evening came, He was
alone there.
24 But the boat was now [1]in the
middle of the sea, tossed by the
waves, for the wind was contrary.
25 Now in the fourth watch of the
night Jesus went to them, walking
on the sea.
26 And when the disciples saw
Him [a]walking on the sea, they were
troubled, saying, "It is a ghost!" And
they cried out for fear.
27 But immediately Jesus spoke to
them, saying, [1]"Be of good [a]cheer!
[2]It is I; do not be afraid."†
28 And Peter answered Him and
said, "Lord, if it is You, command
me to come to You on the water."
29 So He said, "Come." And when
Peter had come down out of the
boat, he walked on the water to go
to Jesus.
30 But when he saw [1]that the wind
was boisterous, he was afraid; and
beginning to sink he cried out, saying, "Lord, save me!"†

14:14–21 The miracle of the feeding of the five thousand, reported by all four evangelists, shows Jesus feeding His people as God fed the Israelites in the desert. The Church Fathers see in this an image of the Eucharist, an idea also expressed in John 6, the discourse on the Bread of Life. In 15:32–39 and Mark 8:1–10 another miracle is mentioned, in which Jesus feeds four thousand people with seven loaves and a few small fish. This miracle is probably not a duplicate report of the first miracle, but another performed in a different place. **Moved with compassion** is used in very similar situations (see 20:34; Mark 1:41; 6:34; Luke 7:13) to show the Messiah's power and authority extending to those who suffer.

14:19 Jesus is teaching us not to eat until we first give thanks to God. The terminology reminds us of the Last Supper (see Luke 22:15–20) and leads to the Eucharistic interpretation of this miracle. The participation of the disciples in distributing the loaves and the fish is important. In the Church Jesus feeds His flock at the Eucharist through His servants, the priests.

14:22–33 This miracle implies the divinity of Jesus the Messiah (v. 33), because He holds dominion over nature.

14:27–29 In saying to the disciples, **be of good cheer! It is I; do not be afraid,** He is also assuring us He will be with His people in the midst of the storms of life (28:20). **Come** (v. 29) is the call of Christ in the midst of turmoil.

14:30 After Peter cries, **Lord, save me,** Jesus does just that. How clearly the Son of God answers prayer—including this, the shortest prayer in the Bible. The often-repeated liturgical

(continued on next page)

31 And immediately Jesus
stretched out *His* hand and caught
him, and said to him, "O you of
[a]little faith, why did you doubt?"†
32 And when they got into the
boat, the wind ceased.
33 Then those who were in the
boat [1]came and worshiped Him, saying, "Truly [a]You are the Son of
God."†

Healing Continues
(Mark 6:53–56)

34 [a]When they had crossed over,
they came [1]to the land of Gennesaret.
35 And when the men of that place
recognized Him, they sent out into
all that surrounding region, brought
to Him all who were sick,
36 and begged Him that they might
only [a]touch the hem of His garment.
And [b]as many as touched *it* were
made perfectly well.

Conflict over Cleanliness
(Mark 7:1–23)

15 Then [a]the scribes and Pharisees who were from Jerusalem came to Jesus, saying,†
2 [a]"Why do Your disciples transgress the tradition of the elders? For
they do not wash their hands when
they eat bread."
3 He answered and said to them,
"Why do you also transgress the

31 [a]Matt. 6:30; 8:26
33 [a]Ps. 2:7 [1]NU omits *came and*
34 [a]Mark 6:53 [1]NU *to land at*
36 [a][Mark 5:24–34] [b][Luke 6:19]

CHAPTER 15
1 [a]Mark 7:1
2 [a]Mark 7:5
4 [a][Deut. 5:16] [b]Ex. 21:17
5 [a]Mark 7:11, 12
6 [1]NU omits *or mother* [2]NU *word*
7 [a]Mark 7:6
8 [a]Is. 29:13 [1]NU omits *draw near to Me with their mouth, And*
9 [a][Col. 2:18–22]
10 [a]Mark 7:14
11 [a][Acts 10:15]
13 [a][John 15:2]
14 [a]Luke 6:39

commandment of God because of
your tradition?
4 "For God commanded, saying,
[a]*'Honor your father and your*
mother'; and, [b]*'He who curses father*
or mother, let him be put to death.'†
5 "But you say, 'Whoever says to
his father or mother, [a]"Whatever
profit you might have received from
me *is* a gift *to God*"—
6 'then he need not honor his father [1]or mother.' Thus you have
made the [2]commandment of God of
no effect by your tradition.
7 [a]"Hypocrites! Well did Isaiah
prophesy about you, saying:

8 *'These[a] people [1]draw near to Me*
with their mouth,
And honor Me with their lips,
But their heart is far from Me.
9 *And in vain they worship Me,*
[a]*Teaching as doctrines the*
commandments of men.' "

10 [a]When He had called the multitude to *Himself*, He said to them,
"Hear and understand:
11 [a]"Not what goes into the mouth
defiles a man; but what comes out
of the mouth, this defiles a man."
12 Then His disciples came and
said to Him, "Do You know that the
Pharisees were offended when they
heard this saying?"
13 But He answered and said,
[a]"Every plant which My heavenly
Father has not planted will be
uprooted.
14 "Let them alone. [a]They are

(continued from previous page)
refrain, "Lord, have mercy," is this same prayer; the Jesus Prayer, "Lord Jesus Christ, Son of God, have mercy on me a sinner," is an expansion of it.

14:31 The Greek term for **doubt** here means wavering, hesitation, or vacillation. Peter is not denying the faith, but he hesitates and weakens because he has taken his eyes off Christ and focused on the storm.

14:33 This is the first time the Apostles confess faith in Jesus as **the Son of God.** They know, as did the wise men before them (2:11), that only God should be **worshiped.**

15:1–20 The tradition of the elders (v. 2) refers to the interpretations of the Mosaic Law by Jewish teachers, here regarding ritual purity. Jesus sharply refutes their views that ritual purity depends on what a person does or doesn't do. Rather, He points to the **heart** (v. 8) as the source of evils which defile a person. We guard our hearts from evil to keep ourselves from error, to overcome unchastity, and to protect ourselves from any other sinful passion.

15:4–6 The commandment to honor one's father and mother is the first of the Ten Commandments which deals with human relations. A work of service or devotion to God is of no value if in carrying it out one ignores personal responsibility to others. Right human relationships are a necessary element of Christian devotion.

Commemoration of Female Martyrs

15:21–28: These holy women followed the Canaanite woman's example of persistence and faith.

blind leaders of the blind. And if the
blind leads the blind, both will fall
into a ditch."
15 [a]Then Peter answered and said
to Him, "Explain this parable to us."
16 So Jesus said, [a]"Are you also
still without understanding?
17 "Do you not yet understand
that [a]whatever enters the mouth
goes into the stomach and is
eliminated?
18 "But [a]those things which proceed out of the mouth come from the
heart, and they defile a man.
19 [a]"For out of the heart proceed
evil thoughts, murders, adulteries,
fornications, thefts, false witness,
blasphemies.
20 "These are *the things* which defile a man, but to eat with unwashed
hands does not defile a man."

A Gentile with Great Faith
(Mark 7:24–30)

21 [a]Then Jesus went out from there
and departed to the region of Tyre
and Sidon.†
22 And behold, a woman of Canaan came from that region and cried
out to Him, saying, "Have mercy on
me, O Lord, [a]Son of David! My

15 [a]Mark 7:17
16 [a]Matt. 16:9; Mark 7:18
17 [a][1 Cor. 6:13]
18 [a][Matt. 12:34]; Mark 7:20; [James 3:6]
19 [a]Gen. 6:5; 8:21; Prov. 6:14; Jer. 17:9; Mark 7:21; [Rom. 1:29–32; Gal. 5:19–21]
21 [a]Mark 7:24–30
22 [a]Matt. 1:1; 22:41, 42
24 [a]Matt. 10:5, 6; [Rom. 15:8]
26 [a]Matt. 7:6; Phil. 3:2
28 [a]Luke 7:9
29 [a]Matt. 15:29–31; Mark 7:31–37
[b]Matt. 4:18

daughter is severely demon-
possessed."
23 But He answered her not a
word. And His disciples came and
urged Him, saying, "Send her away,
for she cries out after us."
24 But He answered and said,
[a]"I was not sent except to the lost
sheep of the house of Israel."†
25 Then she came and worshiped
Him, saying, "Lord, help me!"
26 But He answered and said, "It
is not good to take the children's
bread and throw *it* to the little
[a]dogs."
27 And she said, "Yes, Lord, yet
even the little dogs eat the crumbs
which fall from their masters'
table."†
28 Then Jesus answered and said
to her, "O woman, [a]great *is* your
faith! Let it be to you as you desire."
And her daughter was healed from
that very hour.

Healing Among the Gentiles
(Mark 7:31–37)

29 [a]Jesus departed from there,
[b]skirted the Sea of Galilee, and went
up on the mountain and sat down
there.†

15:21–28 This story, of a humble Gentile woman who is tested and then praised by Jesus for her faith, is mentioned also in Mark 7:24–30 but with two major differences: (1) Matthew says **the lost sheep of the house of Israel** (v. 24), while Mark says only, "Let the children be filled first." (2) In Matthew the woman is recorded as shouting, **Have mercy on me, O Lord, Son of David** (v. 22). The Jewish orientation of Matthew's version accounts for his concern to show Jesus as the Son of David, endowed with divine majesty even in His humanity.

15:24 Jesus' answer should not be understood as an insult, but as a way to reveal the treasure of the woman's faith. In her can be envisioned the future Gentile Church, the true Israel, coming to Christ.

15:27 The faith and humility of this woman are shown in that (1) Jesus' hesitancy was not enough to discourage her; (2) in her answer, she implies that she is a dog, and she calls the Jews **masters.**

15:29–31 Jesus immediately bestows healing on other Gentiles as well, repeating what had been done among Jews (9:1–8, 27–33), that the **God of Israel** (v. 31) might be **glorified.**

(continued on next page)

30 [a]Then great multitudes came to
Him, having with them *the* lame,
blind, mute, [1]maimed, and many
others; and they laid them down at
Jesus' [b]feet, and He healed them.
31 So the multitude marveled
when they saw *the* mute speaking,
the [1]maimed made whole, *the* lame
walking, and *the* blind seeing; and
they [a]glorified the God of Israel.

Feeding the Four Thousand
(Mark 8:1–9)

32 [a]Now Jesus called His disciples
to *Himself* and said, "I have compassion on the multitude, because they
have now continued with Me three
days and have nothing to eat. And
I do not want to send them away
hungry, lest they faint on the way."†
33 [a]Then His disciples said to Him,
"Where could we get enough bread
in the wilderness to fill such a great
multitude?"
34 Jesus said to them, "How many
loaves do you have?" And they said,
"Seven, and a few little fish."
35 So He commanded the multitude to sit down on the ground.
36 And [a]He took the seven loaves
and the fish and [b]gave thanks, broke
them and gave *them* to His disciples;
and the disciples *gave* to the
multitude.
37 So they all ate and were filled,
and they took up seven large baskets
full of the fragments that were left.
38 Now those who ate were four
thousand men, besides women and
children.
39 [a]And He sent away the multitude, got into the boat, and came to
the region of [1]Magdala.

30 [a]Is. 35:5, 6; Matt. 11:5; Luke 7:22 [b]Mark 7:25; Luke 7:38; 8:41; 10:39 [1]*crippled*
31 [a]Luke 5:25, 26; 19:37, 38 [1]*crippled*
32 [a]Mark 8:1–10
33 [a]2 Kin. 4:43
36 [a]Matt. 14:19; 26:27; Luke 22:17, 19; John 6:11, 23; Acts 27:35; [Rom. 14:6] [b]1 Sam. 9:13; Luke 22:19
39 [a]Mark 8:10 [1]NU *Magadan*

CHAPTER 16

1 [a]Matt. 12:38; Mark 8:11; Luke 11:16; 12:54–56; 1 Cor. 1:22
3 [1]NU omits *Hypocrites*
4 [a]Prov. 30:12; Matt. 12:39; Luke 11:29; 24:46 [1]NU omits *the prophet*
5 [a]Mark 8:14

Jewish Leaders Test Jesus
(Mark 8:10–13)

16 Then the [a]Pharisees and Sadducees came, and testing Him
asked that He would show them a
sign from heaven.†
2 He answered and said to them,
"When it is evening you say, *'It will
be* fair weather, for the sky is red';
3 "and in the morning, *'It will be*
foul weather today, for the sky is red
and threatening.' [1]Hypocrites! You
know how to discern the face of the
sky, but you cannot *discern* the signs
of the times.
4 [a]"A wicked and adulterous generation seeks after a sign, and no
sign shall be given to it except the
sign of [1]the prophet Jonah." And He
left them and departed.†

The Pharisees' False Doctrine
(Mark 8:14–21)

5 Now [a]when His disciples had
come to the other side, they had forgotten to take bread.†

(continued from previous page)
Though Jesus focused on Jews, He taught and healed all who came to Him, thus transcending racial distinctions and prejudices.

15:32–39 This passage recounts a second feeding of a crowd, this one including many Gentiles (see 14:13–21). Again this may be connected to the Eucharist. This is another sign of Jesus' deity, for He created new matter which had not before existed—an attribute of God alone.

16:1–3 A sign from heaven implies some spectacular evidence proving Jesus' messiahship. All acknowledge that the time of the Messiah will be a time for signs. But they do not understand the signs already performed, for their hearts are hardened in disbelief. They can predict the rain and storms, but they cannot understand the Law, which points to Christ, even though they are supposed to be experts in it.

16:4 Jesus refuses to prove Himself to a **wicked and adulterous generation**—who refuse to see anyway—except by the **sign of the prophet Jonah,** a veiled prediction of His death and Resurrection. Just as Jonah was delivered safely from the belly of the great fish, Jesus will rise from the grave.

16:5–12 The leaven of the Pharisees (v. 6) is their **doctrine** (v. 12) and their hypocrisy (Luke 12:2). The disciples are painfully slow to understand, for they have **little faith** (v. 8). They do not fully understand Jesus' teaching until Pentecost, when the Spirit is given.

The Feast of Sts. Peter and Paul

June 29

16:13–19: Peter confesses Jesus as the Christ and is promised the keys of the kingdom.

6 Then Jesus said to them, [a]"Take
heed and beware of the [1]leaven
of the Pharisees and the Sadducees."
7 And they reasoned among
themselves, saying, "*It is* because we
have taken no bread."
8 But Jesus, being aware of *it*,
said to them, "O you of little faith,
why do you reason among yourselves because you [1]have brought
no bread?
9 [a]"Do you not yet understand,
or remember the five loaves of the
five thousand and how many baskets
you took up?
10 [a]"Nor the seven loaves of the
four thousand and how many large
baskets you took up?
11 "How is it you do not understand that I did not speak to you
concerning bread?—*but* to beware
of the [1]leaven of the Pharisees and
Sadducees."
12 Then they understood that He
did not tell *them* to beware of the
leaven of bread, but of the [1]doc-
trine of the Pharisees and Sadducees.

6 [a]Luke 12:1 [1]*yeast* **8** [1]NU *have no bread* **9** [a]Matt. 14:15–21 **10** [a]Matt. 15:32–38 **11** [1]*yeast* **12** [1]*teaching*

Jesus Is the Christ, the Son of God

(Mark 8:27–30; Luke 9:18–21)

13 When Jesus came into the region of Caesarea Philippi, He asked
His disciples, saying, [a]"Who do men
say that I, the Son of Man, am?"✝
14 So they said, [a]"Some *say* John
the Baptist, some Elijah, and others
Jeremiah or [b]one of the prophets."
15 He said to them, "But who do
[a]you say that I am?"
16 Simon Peter answered and said,
[a]"You are the Christ, the Son of the
living God."
17 Jesus answered and said to him,
"Blessed are you, Simon Bar-Jonah,
[a]for flesh and blood has not revealed
this to you, but [b]My Father who is
in heaven.
18 "And I also say to you that
[a]you are Peter, and [b]on this rock I
will build My church, and [c]the gates
of Hades shall not [1]prevail against
it.✝
19 [a]"And I will give you the keys
of the kingdom of heaven, and whatever you bind on earth [1]will be
bound in heaven, and whatever you

13 [a]Luke 9:18 **14** [a]Matt. 14:2 [b]Matt. 21:11 **15** [a]John 6:67 **16** [a]Acts 8:37; 9:20 **17** [a][Eph. 2:8] [b]Gal. 1:16 **18** [a]John 1:42 [b][Eph. 2:20] [c]Is. 38:10 [1]*be victorious* **19** [a]Matt. 18:18 [1]Or *will have been bound . . . will have been loosed*

16:13–20 Who do you say that I am? (v. 15) is the greatest question we can ever face. **You are the Christ, the Son of the living God** (v. 16) is Peter's ringing confession—an insight given to him by the **Father** (v. 17). Jesus' messianic identity and divinity, the mystery hidden from eternity, cannot be truly known by human reason, but only by God's revelation (1 Cor. 12:3). *Christ* means "the Anointed One." Christ is the Son of the living God, whom the Father has anointed with the Holy Spirit (Acts 10:38). David says, "Therefore God, Your God, has anointed You with the oil of gladness more than Your companions" (Ps. 45:7). Isaiah, speaking in the name of the Lord, says, "The Spirit of the Lord GOD is upon Me, because the LORD has anointed Me" (Is. 61:1).

16:18 Peter/rock is a play on the word for rock in Aramaic and Greek (*petros/petra*). *Rock* refers not to Peter himself but to the confession of his faith. The true Rock and foundation of the Church is, of course, Christ Himself. The Church rests upon this Rock by her unchanging faith, her confession. With this faith as the foundation, **the gates of Hades,** the powers of death, are powerless against her. In the OT *gates* suggest a fortified city (Gen. 22:17; 24:60; Is. 14:31). Hence, by shattering the gates, Christ is opening the stronghold of death to set free the souls of righteous men. In all the Gospels, **church** is mentioned twice by the Lord, here and in 18:17, describing the true Israel whose citizenship is heavenly. She is the body of Christ, the divine-human organism, and to her comes the call of Jesus for the whole of mankind to abide with Him and in Him (Eph. 1:23).

loose on earth will be loosed in
heaven."†
20 [a]Then He commanded His disciples that they should tell no one
that He was Jesus the Christ.

Jesus' Work: His Passion and Resurrection
(Mark 8:31—9:1; Luke 9:22–27)

21 From that time Jesus began
[a]to show to His disciples that He
must go to Jerusalem, and suffer
many things from the elders and
chief priests and scribes, and be
killed, and be raised the third
day.†
22 Then Peter took Him aside and
began to rebuke Him, saying,
[1]"Far be it from You, Lord; this shall
not happen to You!"
23 But He turned and said to Peter,
"Get behind Me, [a]Satan! [b]You are
[1]an offense to Me, for you are not
mindful of the things of God, but the
things of men."†
24 [a]Then Jesus said to His disciples, "If anyone desires to come after

20 [a]Luke 9:21
21 [a]Luke 9:22; 18:31; 24:46
22 [1]Lit. *Merciful to You* (May God be merciful)
23 [a]Matt. 4:10 [b][Rom. 8:7] [1]*a stumbling block*
24 [a][2 Tim. 3:12] [b][1 Pet. 2:21]
25 [a]John 12:25
26 [a]Luke 12:20, 21 [b]Ps. 49:7, 8
27 [a]Mark 8:38 [b][Dan. 7:10] [c]Rom. 2:6
28 [a]Luke 9:27
CHAPTER 17
1 [a]Mark 9:2–8

Me, let him deny himself, and take
up his cross, and [b]follow Me.†
25 "For [a]whoever desires to save
his life will lose it, but whoever loses
his life for My sake will find it.†
26 "For what [a]profit is it to a man
if he gains the whole world, and
loses his own soul? Or [b]what will a
man give in exchange for his soul?
27 "For [a]the Son of Man will come
in the glory of His Father [b]with His
angels, [c]and then He will reward
each according to his works.†
28 "Assuredly, I say to you,
[a]there are some standing here who
shall not taste death till they see the
Son of Man coming in His kingdom."†

The Transfiguration
(Mark 9:2–13; Luke 9:28–36)

17 Now [a]after six days Jesus
took Peter, James, and John
his brother, led them up on a high
mountain by themselves;†
2 and He was transfigured before
them. His face shone like the sun,

16:19 Keys of the kingdom clearly implies a special authority given to Peter himself, but never separated from his confession of faith. While Peter was a leader of the disciples and of the early Church, all the apostles were empowered with Christ's authority (18:18). Further, Peter was not a leader *over* the others but a leader *among* them, as seen at the Council of Jerusalem (Acts 15), where elders, or presbyters, met with the apostles together as equals. Papal claims in later centuries must not be confused with the NT witness regarding Peter, nor should the role of Peter in the NT be minimized in opposition to those claims.

Binding and loosing is a reference to the teaching, sacramental, and administrative powers of the Apostles which were transmitted to the bishops of the Church.

16:21–23 After Peter's confession, Jesus reveals the true nature of His messiahship, the mystery of the Passion. But **Peter took Him aside** (v. 22), expecting Him to enter Jerusalem and establish the Kingdom immediately (as Peter understood it, an earthly, political kingdom), not to go to the Cross and death. Peter thought the Messiah would reign forever, not die. But Jesus was to be a suffering Messiah, a scandalous idea to the Jews.

16:23 Christ did not call Peter **Satan** to insult him, but to rebuke him for unwittingly serving as a mouthpiece of the devil.

16:24 The **cross,** a dreaded instrument of Roman punishment, is also a symbol of suffering by Christians in imitation of Christ. Self-denial is for the sake of Christ and the gospel, for a better life; it is not a punitive end in itself.

16:25 Here Jesus states the central paradox of the Christian faith. In grasping the temporal, we lose the eternal; in sacrificing everything we can know, we gain unimaginable riches. In dying, we live.

16:27 When **the Son of Man** comes in **glory** to **reward each according to his works,** it will be shown that absolutely nothing exceeds the value of finding true life, the salvation of one's soul.

16:28 Seeing Jesus **coming in His kingdom** may refer to the Transfiguration, which occurs immediately after this.

17:1 A high mountain in Scripture is often a place of revelation (Ex. 19:3, 23; Is. 2:3; 2 Pet. 1:18).

THE TRANSFIGURATION

"And He was transfigured before them. His face shone like the sun, and His clothes became as white as the light" (Matt. 17:2).

The Transfiguration is a *theophany*—a manifestation of God, especially of the divinity of Christ, through a display of His uncreated, divine energy. Therefore, the Orthodox Church celebrates the Transfiguration of the Lord as a major feast day.

Several elements of the Transfiguration show that Christ is Messiah and God.

(1) Because God is light (1 John 1:5), the bright cloud, the shining of Jesus' face like the sun, and the whiteness of His garment (Matt. 17:2, 5) all demonstrate that Jesus is God. (In some icons this light is shown as *beyond* white, a blue-white, ineffable color, indicating its spiritual origin.)

(2) The Father bears witness from heaven concerning His Son. He does not say, "This has become My beloved Son," but "This is My beloved Son" (Matt. 17:5), indicating that this divine glory is Christ's by nature. From eternity past, infinitely before Jesus' Baptism and Transfiguration, He is God's Son, fully sharing in the essence of the Father: Jesus Christ is God of God.

(3) The Transfiguration not only proclaims Christ's divine sonship, but foreshadows His future glory when He as the Messiah will usher in the long-awaited Kingdom. The bright cloud recalls temple worship and the cloud that went before the Israelites in the wilderness, the visible sign of God being extraordinarily present. Peter sees this as a sign that the Kingdom has come. Knowing that the Feast of Tabernacles is the feast of the coming Kingdom, he asks to build booths (Matt. 17:4), as was done at that feast, to serve as symbols of God's dwelling among the just in the Kingdom.

(4) Moses represents the Law and all those who have died. Elijah represents the Prophets and—since he did not experience death—all those who are alive in Christ. Their presence shows that the Law and the Prophets, the living and the dead, all bear witness to Jesus as the Messiah, the fulfillment of the whole Old Testament.

The presence of Moses and Elijah also manifests the communion of the saints (Heb. 12:1). Both men are immediately recognizable, and talk with the Lord. The disciples are able to understand Jesus' words that "Elijah has come already" (Matt. 17:12) referring to John the Baptist. Their eyes have been opened to the fact that Malachi's prophecy (Matt. 4:5, 6) refers to one coming "in the spirit and power of Elijah" (Luke 1:17), rather than to Elijah himself.

(5) Finally, the Holy Trinity is manifest here, for Christ is transfigured (Matt. 17:2), the Father speaks from heaven testifying to Jesus' divine sonship (Matt. 17:5), and the Spirit is present in the form of a dazzling light surrounding Christ's Person, overshadowing the whole mountain (Matt. 17:5).

The Holy Transfiguration of Our Lord Jesus Christ

August 6

17:1–9: Peter, James, and John see Christ in the glory of His divinity.

and His clothes became as white as
the light.†
3 And behold, Moses and Elijah
appeared to them, talking with Him.
4 Then Peter answered and said
to Jesus, "Lord, it is good for us to
be here; if You wish, [1]let us make
here three tabernacles: one for You,
one for Moses, and one for Elijah."
5 [a]While he was still speaking, behold, a bright cloud overshadowed
them; and suddenly a voice came out
of the cloud, saying, [b]"This is My
beloved Son, [c]in whom I am well
pleased. [d]Hear Him!"
6 [a]And when the disciples heard
it, they fell on their faces and were
greatly afraid.
7 But Jesus came and [a]touched
them and said, "Arise, and do not
be afraid."
8 When they had lifted up their
eyes, they saw no one but Jesus only.
9 Now as they came down from
the mountain, Jesus commanded
them, saying, "Tell the vision to no
one until the Son of Man is risen
from the dead."
10 And His disciples asked Him,
saying, [a]"Why then do the scribes
say that Elijah must come first?"
11 Jesus answered and said to
them, "Indeed, Elijah is coming
[1]first and will [a]restore all things.
12 [a]"But I say to you that Elijah has
come already, and they [b]did not
know him but did to him whatever
they wished. Likewise [c]the Son of
Man is also about to suffer at their
hands."
13 [a]Then the disciples understood
that He spoke to them of John the
Baptist.

The Disciples Lack Faith

(Mark 9:14–29; Luke 9:37–42)

14 [a]And when they had come to
the multitude, a man came to Him,
kneeling down to Him and saying,†
15 "Lord, have mercy on my son,
for he is [1]an epileptic and suffers severely; for he often falls into the fire
and often into the water.
16 "So I brought him to Your disciples, but they could not cure him."
17 Then Jesus answered and said,
"O [1]faithless and [a]perverse generation, how long shall I be with you?
How long shall I bear with you?
Bring him here to Me."†
18 And Jesus [a]rebuked the demon,
and it came out of him; and the child
was cured from that very hour.
19 Then the disciples came to Jesus
privately and said, "Why could we
not cast it out?"
20 So Jesus said to them, "Because
of your [1]unbelief; for assuredly, I say
to you, [a]if you have faith as a mustard seed, you will say to this mountain, 'Move from here to there,' and
it will move; and nothing will be impossible for you.†

4 [1]NU *I will make*
5 [a]2 Pet. 1:17 [b]Mark 1:11 [c]Matt. 3:17; 12:18 [d][Deut. 18:15, 19]
6 [a]2 Pet. 1:18
7 [a]Dan. 8:18
10 [a]Mal. 4:5
11 [a][Mal. 4:6] [1]NU omits *first*
12 [a]Mark 9:12, 13 [b]Matt. 14:3, 10 [c]Matt. 16:21
13 [a]Matt. 11:14
14 [a]Mark 9:14–28
15 [1]Lit. *moonstruck*
17 [a]Phil. 2:15 [1]*unbelieving*
18 [a]Luke 4:41
20 [a]Luke 17:6 [1]NU *little faith*

17:2 See article, "The Transfiguration" at Matt. 17.

17:14–16 Kneeling and saying, **Lord, have mercy on my son,** (v. 15), the father of the **epileptic** expresses his desperate need and his unworthiness before Christ. Sickness, especially epilepsy, is often connected to demonic activity in Scripture. Yet the **disciples** (v. 16) could not banish Satan.

17:17 Jesus rebukes His disciples' powerlessness and their participation with the **faithless and perverse** (see Deut. 32:5). Nothing can withstand Jesus' power, for He is the Lord of all. To everyone in need He says, **Bring him here to Me!**

17:20, 21 Exorcisms require sincere **faith** (v. 20) combined with **prayer and fasting** (v. 21). *Faith* is a gift of God, either (1) an assent to the truth, which profits the soul (John

(continued on next page)

21 [1]"However, this kind does not
go out except by prayer and fasting."

Jesus' Suffering

(Mark 9:30–32; Luke 9:43–45)

22 [a]Now while they were [1]staying
in Galilee, Jesus said to them, "The
Son of Man is about to be betrayed
into the hands of men,†
23 "and they will kill Him, and the
third day He will be raised up." And
they were exceedingly [a]sorrowful.

Jesus Pays the Temple Tax

24 [a]When they had come to
[1]Capernaum, those who received the
[2]*temple* tax came to Peter and said,
"Does your Teacher not pay the *temple* tax?"†
25 He said, "Yes." And when he
had come into the house, Jesus anticipated him, saying, "What do you
think, Simon? From whom do the
kings of the earth take customs or
taxes, from their sons or from
[a]strangers?"
26 Peter said to Him, "From
strangers." Jesus said to him, "Then
the sons are free.
27 "Nevertheless, lest we offend
them, go to the sea, cast in a hook,
and take the fish that comes up first.
And when you have opened its
mouth, you will find a [1]piece of
money; take that and give it to them
for Me and you."

Who Is the Greatest?

(Mark 9:33–37; Luke 9:46–48)

18 At [a]that time the disciples
came to Jesus, saying, "Who
then is greatest in the kingdom of
heaven?"†
2 Then Jesus called a little [a]child
to Him, set him in the midst of them,
3 and said, "Assuredly, I say to
you, [a]unless you are converted and
become as little children, you will by
no means enter the kingdom of
heaven.
4 [a]"Therefore whoever humbles
himself as this little child is the greatest in the kingdom of heaven.
5 [a]"Whoever receives one little
child like this in My name receives
Me.

Scandals and Temptations

(Mark 9:42–48)

6 [a]"But whoever causes one of
these little ones who believe in Me
to sin, it would be better for him if
a millstone were hung around his
neck, and he were drowned in the
depth of the sea.†

21 [1]NU omits v. 21.
22 [a]Mark 8:31 [1]NU *gathering together*
23 [a]John 16:6; 19:30
24 [a]Mark 9:33 [1]NU *Capharnaum,* here and elsewhere [2]Lit. *double drachma*
25 [a][Is. 60:10–17]
27 [1]Gr. *stater,* the exact temple tax for two

CHAPTER 18
1 [a]Luke 9:46–48; 22:24–27
2 [a]Matt. 19:14
3 [a]Luke 18:16
4 [a][Matt. 20:27; 23:11]
5 [a][Matt. 10:42]
6 [a]Mark 9:42

(continued from previous page)
3:18; 5:24) or (2) a special gift bestowed by Christ which effects things beyond man's power (Mark 11:23; 1 Cor. 12:8, 9). But it is always *both* a belief and a trust.

17:22, 23 Jesus predicts His death and Resurrection a second time. **The Son of Man** (v. 22) is not led by compulsion, but He is going to the Passion willingly, so that "He, by the grace of God, might taste death for everyone" (Heb. 2:9).

17:24–27 The temple tax was an annual head tax on all male Jews 12 years of age and up, excepting priests and rabbis, for the maintenance of the temple. Jesus as Son of God is supremely free of this tax. Nevertheless, He does not refuse to pay it, nor does He tell His disciples to pay it for Him. But, having proved Himself not liable to it, He gives it. He pays it not as a debt, but in consideration of their weakness and to avoid unnecessary offense.

18:1–4 Who then is the greatest in the kingdom indicates selfish interests having to do with worldly power (see 20:20–24). But Jesus points to **a little child** (v. 2) as the model of the true disciple. For **little children** have the spiritual attitudes required to **enter the kingdom** (v. 3): humility, dependence, lowliness and simplicity. Humility, without which there is no virtue at all, is the acknowledgment of divine grace and mercy, and the constant denial of man's achievement.

In Orthodox iconography, St. Ignatius of Antioch is depicted as the child who was held in the arms of Jesus. In certain legends of saints, he is the boy who gave the loaves and fishes.

18:6 The **little ones** are the humble and simple, who may be ignored or offended by
(continued on next page)

SAINT JOHN THE FORERUNNER
IC XC
SEEST THOU
WHAT SUFFER
THOSE WHO
CENSURE, O
WORD OF GOD,
THE FAULTS
OF THE UNCLEAN,
NOT BEING
ABLE TO BEAR
CENSURE, LO
HEROD CUT
OFF MY HEAD
O SAV-
IOUR;

St. John the Forerunner, *by the hand of Father Gregory.* Courtesy of Dormition Skete, Buena Vista, Colorado.

By his own testimony, the ministry of John the Baptist is that of Forerunner: to prepare the way for Christ, pointing us to the One who was to come after him. Feast Day readings are Genesis 17:15–17, 19; 18:11–14; 21:1–8; Judges 13:2–8, 13, 14, 17, 18, 21; Isaiah 40:1–3, 9; 41:17, 18; 45:8; 48:20, 21; 54:1; Luke 1:1–15; 24, 25, 57–68, 76, 80; Romans 13:11—14:4.

See also Matthew 3:1–12; Mark 1:1–8; Luke 3:1–20; John 1:6–9, 19–28.

The Day of the Holy Spirit *Monday after Pentecost*
18:10–20: He is in the Church.

7 "Woe to the world because of
[1]offenses! For [a]offenses must come,
but [b]woe to that man by whom the
offense comes!
8 [a]"If your hand or foot causes
you to sin, cut it off and cast *it* from
you. It is better for you to enter into
life lame or maimed, rather than having two hands or two feet, to be cast
into the everlasting fire.†
9 "And if your eye causes you to
sin, pluck it out and cast *it* from you.
It is better for you to enter into life
with one eye, rather than having two
eyes, to be cast into [1]hell fire.

Finding the Lost Sheep

(Luke 15:3–7)

10 "Take heed that you do not despise one of these little ones, for I
say to you that in heaven [a]their angels always [b]see the face of My Father who is in heaven.†
11 [a]"For[1] the Son of Man has come
to save that which was lost.
12 [a]"What do you think? If a man
has a hundred sheep, and one of
them goes astray, does he not leave
the ninety-nine and go to the
mountains to seek the one that is
straying?†
13 "And if he should find it, assuredly, I say to you, he rejoices
more over that *sheep* than over the
ninety-nine that did not go astray.
14 "Even so it is not the [a]will
of your Father who is in heaven
that one of these little ones should
perish.

Discipline in the Church

15 "Moreover [a]if your brother sins
against you, go and tell him his fault
between you and him alone. If he
hears you, [b]you have gained your
brother.†
16 "But if he will not hear, take
with you one or two more, that
[a]*'by the mouth of two or three witnesses every word may be established.'*
17 "And if he refuses to hear them,
tell *it* to the church. But if he refuses
even to hear the church, let him be

7 [a][1 Cor. 11:19] [b]Matt. 26:24; 27:4, 5 [1]*enticements to sin* **8** [a]Matt. 5:29, 30 **9** [1]Gr. *Gehenna* **10** [a][Heb. 1:14] [b]Luke 1:19 **11** [a]Luke 9:56 [1]NU omits v. 11. **12** [a]Luke 15:4–7 **14** [a][1 Tim. 2:4] **15** [a]Lev. 19:17 [b][James 5:20] **16** [a]Deut. 17:6; 19:15

(continued from previous page)
more influential members of the Church, against whom Jesus issues severe warnings. Scandals may be inevitable, but those who cause them will be punished by God.

18:8 The reference to mutilating parts of the body suggests decisive action to avoid sin, not literal amputation (see 5:29). For instance, we cut off relations with friends and others, if they are seriously harmful to the soul.

18:10 No one should **despise** humble Christians, because their guardian **angels** occupy foremost positions before God. The *angels* **always see the face** of God, not in His divine essence, but in His divine glory, His energy, according to the measure of their capacity (John 6:46). Only the Son and the Holy Spirit can behold Him perfectly (11:27; 1 Cor. 2:10). It is not the nature of God, but the weakness of men, which requires the angels' service. They are sent for the sake of those who will inherit salvation (Heb. 1:14).

18:12 The search for the lost **sheep** is an act of God in mercy and love for each person who goes astray. No first-century Palestinian shepherd would dare leave **ninety-nine** to find **one,** lest the wolves come and devour the flock (Luke 15:4). But God's love is so great He would seek even the **one that is straying.**

18:15–20 These verses set forth a classic form of Church discipline based on mutual correction, in three expanding stages (in vv. 15, 16, and 17). Sin and repentance are private unless the offender refuses to repent; then the issue may have to be made public and corporate, coming before the whole Church. All discipline must be done with great care and humility, for it is easy to be hypocritical in the way we judge (see 7:1–5).

to you like a [a]heathen and a tax
collector.†
18 "Assuredly, I say to you,
[a]whatever you bind on earth will be
bound in heaven, and whatever you
loose on earth will be loosed in
heaven.†
19 [a]"Again[1] I say to you that if two
of you agree on earth concerning
anything that they ask, [b]it will be
done for them by My Father in
heaven.
20 "For where two or three are
gathered [a]together in My name, I am
there in the midst of them."

Forgiveness in the Church

21 **Then Peter came to Him and
said, "Lord, how often shall my
brother sin against me, and I forgive
him? [a]Up to seven times?"†**
22 **Jesus said to him,** "I do not say
to you, [a]up to seven times, but up
to seventy times seven.
23 "Therefore the kingdom of
heaven is like a certain king who
wanted to settle accounts with his
servants.
24 "And when he had begun to
settle accounts, one was brought to
him who owed him ten thousand
talents.
25 "But as he was not able to pay,
his master commanded [a]that he be
sold, with his wife and children and
all that he had, and that payment
be made.
26 "The servant therefore fell
down before him, saying, 'Master,
have patience with me, and I will pay
you all.'
27 "Then the master of that servant
was moved with compassion, released him, and forgave him the
debt.
28 "But that servant went out and
found one of his fellow servants who
owed him a hundred denarii; and he
laid hands on him and took *him* by
the throat, saying, 'Pay me what you
owe!'
29 "So his fellow servant fell down
[1]at his feet and begged him, saying,
'Have patience with me, and I will
pay you [2]all.'
30 "And he would not, but went
and threw him into prison till he
should pay the debt.
31 "So when his fellow servants
saw what had been done, they were
very grieved, and came and told
their master all that had been
done.
32 "Then his master, after he had
called him, said to him, 'You wicked
servant! I forgave you [a]all that debt
because you begged me.
33 'Should you not also have had
compassion on your fellow servant,
just as I had pity on you?'
34 "And his master was angry, and
delivered him to the torturers until

17 [a]Rom. 16:17; 1 Cor. 5:9; [2 Thess. 3:6, 14; 2 John 10]
18 [a]Matt. 16:19; [John 20:22, 23; 1 Cor. 5:4]
19 [a][1 Cor. 1:10] *b*[1 John 3:22; 5:14] [1]NU, M *Again, assuredly, I say*
20 [a]Acts 20:7; 1 Cor. 14:26
21 [a]Luke 17:4
22 [a][Matt. 6:14; Mark 11:25]; Col. 3:13
25 [a]Ex. 21:2; Lev. 25:39; 2 Kin. 4:1; Neh. 5:5, 8
29 [1]NU omits *at his feet* [2]NU, M omit *all*
32 [a]Luke 7:41–43

18:17 The term **church,** which occurs only in Matthew among the Gospels (here and 16:18), refers to the people of God, the community of faith. Jesus came to establish a congregation, gathered by Him and united with Him, in the power of the Holy Spirit.

18:18–20 Temporal rulers have the power of binding, but they bind only the body. God, however, binds with a bond which pertains to the soul itself, a power which God has not given even to angels. God is with us. He has a special presence in heaven and in every church as well, through His grace and the sacraments. Mutual correction, which sometimes necessitates expulsion from the community, makes the Church strong and invincible through the love of Christ.

18:21–35 Unlimited forgiveness toward a **brother** or sister is illustrated by this parable. Sin is portrayed as a debt to God (6:12), a debt originated by neglecting God's will. **Ten thousand talents** (v. 24)—an impossible sum, more than a laborer could earn in a lifetime—is contrasted to **a hundred denarii** (v. 28), equivalent to about a hundred days' wages. Just as the king shows mercy and severity toward the servant, so does God show love and strictness toward us depending on our willingness to forgive our brothers and sisters. The love of God is manifested in paying off the **debt,** a remission or letting go of sins. Because God forgives us, we in return are obliged to grant this gift of forgiveness to others. When each Christian forgives **from his heart** (v. 35), true reconciliation and healing come to the Church by God's grace.

he should pay all that was due to
him.
35 [a]"So My heavenly Father also
will do to you if each of you, from
his heart, does not forgive his
brother [1]his trespasses."

Divorce and Marriage
(Mark 10:1–12)

19 Now it came to pass, [a]when
Jesus had finished these sayings, *that* He departed from Galilee
and came to the region of Judea beyond the Jordan.†
2 [a]And great multitudes followed
Him, and He healed them there.
3 The Pharisees also came to Him,
testing Him, and saying to Him, "Is
it lawful for a man to divorce his wife
for *just* any reason?"
4 And He answered and said to
them, "Have you not read that He
who [1]made *them* at the beginning
[a]*'made them male and female,'*
5 "and said, [a]*'For this reason a*
man shall leave his father and
mother and be joined to his wife, and
[b]*the two shall become one flesh'*?†
6 "So then, they are no longer two
but one flesh. Therefore what God
has joined together, let not man
separate."
7 They said to Him, [a]"Why then
did Moses command to give a certificate of divorce, and to put her
away?"
8 He said to them, "Moses, because of the [a]hardness of your
hearts, permitted you to divorce
your [b]wives, but from the beginning
it was not so.
9 [a]"And I say to you, whoever divorces his wife, except for [1]sexual
immorality, and marries another,
commits adultery; and whoever marries her who is divorced commits
adultery."†
10 His disciples said to Him,
[a]"If such is the case of the man with
his wife, it is better not to marry."
11 But He said to them, [a]"All cannot accept this saying, but only *those*
to whom it has been given:
12 "For there are [1]eunuchs who
were born thus from *their* mother's
womb, and [a]there are eunuchs who
were made eunuchs by men, and
there are eunuchs who have made
themselves eunuchs for the kingdom
of heaven's sake. He who is able to
accept *it*, let him accept *it*."†

Receiving the Children
(Mark 10:13–16; Luke 18:15–17)

13 [a]Then little children were
brought to Him that He might put
His hands on them and pray, but the
disciples rebuked them.†

35 [a]James 2:13
[1]NU omits *his trespasses*

CHAPTER 19
1 [a]Mark 10:1–12
2 [a]Matt. 12:15
4 [a]Gen. 1:27; 5:2
[1]NU *created*
5 [a]Gen. 2:24
[b][1 Cor. 6:16; 7:2]
7 [a]Deut. 24:1–4
8 [a]Heb. 3:15
[b]Mal. 2:16
9 [a][Matt. 5:32]
[1]Or *fornication*
10 [a][Prov. 21:19]
11 [a][1 Cor. 7:2, 7, 9, 17]
12 [a][1 Cor. 7:32]
[1]Emasculated men
13 [a]Luke 18:15

19:1–12 The Pharisees come **testing Him** with the question of the legality of divorce, hoping to catch Him on the interpretation of Deut. 24:1–4, the basis of divorce among Jews. But Jesus looks further back to the original intent of God in creation (Gen. 1:27; 2:24) regarding monogamous marriage for life, and adds His own clear prohibition against divorce (v. 9).

19:5, 6 The yearning of a husband and wife for one another was planted in human nature by God before the Fall. The harmony of Adam and Eve with God and with each other was a great virtue. Adam considered Eve a part of himself (Gen. 2:23). When he cut himself off from the love of God, that harmony was broken. Jesus restores the marriage relationship to its original state, giving it a spiritual dimension.

19:9 Divorce is permitted only **for sexual immorality,** which destroys a marriage—a teaching held also by the stricter school of the Pharisees. The reasons for divorce were eventually increased in the ancient Church to include threat to one partner's life, desertion, and forced prostitution. The Orthodox Church may grant divorce, but regards it as a spiritual tragedy requiring great pastoral care.

19:12 Eunuchs are lifelong celibates. Jesus praises those **who have made themselves eunuchs,** that is, those who are celibate by free choice and according to God's will for them. Jesus does not endorse mutilation but the putting away of wicked thoughts. The first Ecumenical Council (A.D. 325) rejected willful mutilation.

19:13–15 Little children are given "equal opportunity" to live in **the kingdom of heaven**

(continued on next page)

14 But Jesus said, "Let the little children come to Me, and do not forbid them; for [a]of such is the kingdom of heaven."

15 And He laid *His* hands on them and departed from there.

Riches and the Kingdom

(Mark 10:17–31; Luke 18:18–30)

16 [a]Now behold, one came and said to Him, [b]"Good[1] Teacher, what good thing shall I do that I may have eternal life?"†

17 So He said to him, [1]"Why do you call Me good? [2]No one *is* [a]good but One, *that is*, God. But if you want to enter into life, [b]keep the commandments."

18 He said to Him, "Which ones?" Jesus said, [a]"*'You shall not murder,' 'You shall not commit adultery,' 'You shall not steal,' 'You shall not bear false witness,'*

19 [a]*'Honor your father and your mother,'* and, [b]*'You shall love your neighbor as yourself.'* "

20 The young man said to Him, "All these things I have [a]kept [1]from my youth. What do I still lack?"†

21 Jesus said to him, "If you want to be perfect, [a]go, sell what you have and give to the poor, and you will have treasure in heaven; and come, follow Me."†

22 But when the young man heard that saying, he went away sorrowful, for he had great possessions.

23 Then Jesus said to His disciples, "Assuredly, I say to you that [a]it is hard for a rich man to enter the kingdom of heaven.†

24 "And again I say to you, it is easier for a camel to go through the eye of a needle than for a rich man to enter the kingdom of God."

25 When His disciples heard *it*, they were greatly astonished, saying, "Who then can be saved?"

26 But Jesus looked at *them* and said to them, "With men this is impossible, but [a]with God all things are possible."

27 Then Peter answered and said to Him, "See, [a]we have left all and followed You. Therefore what shall we have?"

28 So Jesus said to them, "As-

14 [a]Matt. 18:3, 4
16 [a]Mark 10:17–30 [b]Luke 10:25 [1]NU omits *Good*
17 [a]Nah. 1:7 [b]Lev. 18:5 [1]NU *Why do you ask Me about what is good?* [2]NU *There is One who is good. But*
18 [a]Ex. 20:13–16
19 [a]Ex. 20:12–16; Deut. 5:16–20 [b]Lev. 19:18
20 [a][Phil. 3:6, 7] [1]NU omits *from my youth*
21 [a]Acts 2:45; 4:34, 35
23 [a][1 Tim. 6:9]
26 [a]Jer. 32:17
27 [a]Deut. 33:9

(continued from previous page)

(v. 14), for their humble openness accepts God's gifts. There is nothing about them, including their age or immaturity, to keep them from the Kingdom. Therefore children, like adults, participate in the Kingdom through baptism, chrismation, communion, confession, and anointing with oil for healing.

19:16–22 The young ruler sees Jesus as a man only, a **Good Teacher** of the written Law, not as God. Jesus answers him accordingly, **Why do you call Me good?** (v. 17). Jesus instructs him to **keep the commandments,** demonstrating the connection of virtue to salvation. In saying, **No one is good but One** (v. 17), our Lord rejects the worldly view that He is merely "a good man," at the same time teaching that goodness is in God alone. Then He exercises the duties of goodness by opening the treasures of heaven to the young man, offering Himself as the guide to them. In doing this the Lord reveals Himself as God.

19:20 Formal observance of the Law does not equal fulfillment of all the commandments of God. Indeed, saying that one has **kept** the letter of the Law can create a false satisfaction about virtue. Salvation does not depend upon external things, whether they be many or few, great or small, but on the virtues of the soul—faith, hope, and love—the reward of which is salvation. These virtues the young man still lacked.

19:21 God acts in cooperation with the human soul. To save the unwilling would be compulsion, but to save the willing is a show of grace. Perfection is voluntarily to sacrifice all and to follow Christ for the cause of the Kingdom. The Kingdom of God does not belong to sluggards, but to those who **want to be perfect.**

19:23–29 Various interpretations have been suggested for the impossible image of a **camel** going through **the eye of a needle:** e.g., that the word was not *camel*, but "rope"; or that *the eye of a needle* was a city gate through which the camel might barely squeeze. (The Talmud uses a similar expression, "for an elephant to go through the eye of the needle.") But whatever the phrase refers to, it displays the difficulty of salvation for those who are attached to riches. The disciples and others who give all will receive **a hundredfold** (v. 29) in the Kingdom.

suredly I say to you, that in the regeneration, when the Son of Man sits
on the throne of His glory, [a]you who
have followed Me will also sit on
twelve thrones, judging the twelve
tribes of Israel.
29 [a]"And everyone who has left
houses or brothers or sisters or father
or mother [1]or wife or children or
[2]lands, for My name's sake, shall receive a hundredfold, and inherit
eternal life.
30 [a]"But many *who are* first will be
last, and the last first.

The First and the Last

20 "For the kingdom of heaven
is like a landowner who went
out early in the morning to hire laborers for his vineyard.†
2 "Now when he had agreed with
the laborers for a denarius a day, he
sent them into his vineyard.
3 "And he went out about the
third hour and saw others standing
idle in the marketplace,
4 "and said to them, 'You also go
into the vineyard, and whatever is
right I will give you.' So they went.
5 "Again he went out about the
sixth and the ninth hour, and did
likewise.
6 "And about the eleventh hour
he went out and found others standing [1]idle, and said to them, 'Why
have you been standing here idle all
day?'
7 "They said to him, 'Because no
one hired us.' He said to them, 'You
also go into the vineyard, [1]and whatever is right you will receive.'

28 [a]Matt. 20:21; Luke 22:28–30; [1 Cor. 6:2; Rev. 2:26]
29 [a][Matt. 6:33]; Mark 10:29, 30; Luke 18:29, 30
[1]NU omits *or wife*
[2]Lit. *fields*
30 [a][Matt. 20:16; 21:31, 32]; Mark 10:31; Luke 13:30

CHAPTER 20
6 [1]NU omits *idle*
7 [1]NU omits the rest of v. 7.
11 [1]*grumbled*
15 [a][Rom. 9:20, 21]
[b]Deut. 15:9; Prov. 23:6; [Matt. 6:23]; Mark 7:22
16 [a]Matt. 19:30; Mark 10:31; Luke 13:30
[b]Matt. 22:14
[1]NU omits the rest of v. 16.
17 [a]Matt. 20:17–19; Mark 10:32–34; Luke 18:31–33; John 12:12
18 [a]Matt. 16:21; 26:47–57; Mark 14:42, 64; John 18:5; 19:7

8 "So when evening had come,
the owner of the vineyard said to his
steward, 'Call the laborers and give
them *their* wages, beginning with the
last to the first.'
9 "And when those came who
were hired about the eleventh hour,
they each received a denarius.
10 "But when the first came, they
supposed that they would receive
more; and they likewise received
each a denarius.
11 "And when they had received
it, they [1]complained against the
landowner,
12 "saying, 'These last *men* have
worked *only* one hour, and you made
them equal to us who have borne
the burden and the heat of the day.'
13 "But he answered one of them
and said, 'Friend, I am doing you
no wrong. Did you not agree with
me for a denarius?
14 'Take *what is* yours and go your
way. I wish to give to this last man
the same as to you.
15 [a]'Is it not lawful for me to do
what I wish with my own things?
Or [b]is your eye evil because I am
good?'
16 [a]"So the last will be first, and
the first last. [b]For[1] many are called,
but few chosen."

Jesus' Death and Resurrection
(Mark 10:32–34; Luke 18:31–34)

17 [a]**Now Jesus, going up to Jerusalem, took the twelve disciples aside
on the road and said to them,**
18 [a]"Behold, we are going up to
Jerusalem, and the Son of Man will

20:1–16 Jesus describes a startling reversal of positions (v. 16; 19:30). In this parable: (1) the **vineyard** is the life God gives us in the world; (2) the **day** is the time of laboring, the here and now; (3) the **laborers** are those He calls to fulfill His commandments; (4) **early in the morning** and the **third, sixth, ninth,** and **eleventh** hours refer to the different ages of those who draw near to God: those who from earliest youth, from mature age, or from very old age hold to virtue. God's generosity provides equal access to and enjoyment of rewards in the life of the Kingdom for both early and late comers. Jesus teaches the former they should neither be proud of their long service, nor question those called at the eleventh hour—lest they themselves lose all. To the latter, He teaches it is possible even in a short time to recover everything. In Jesus' ministry this parable applies to the Pharisees and sinners, while in the early Church it applies to Jews and Gentiles. St. John Chrysostom's famous Easter sermon is based on this parable; for him the reward is the Lord's rich banquet of the Easter Eucharist.

be betrayed to the chief priests and
to the scribes; and they will condemn
Him to death,
19 [a]"and deliver Him to the Gentiles to [b]mock and to [c]scourge and
to [d]crucify. And the third day He will
[e]rise again."

Leaders as Servants
(Mark 10:35–45)

20 [a]Then the mother of [b]Zebedee's
sons came to Him with her sons,
kneeling down and asking something from Him.†
21 And He said to her, "What do
you wish?" She said to Him, "Grant
that these two sons of mine [a]may
sit, one on Your right hand and the
other on the left, in Your kingdom."
22 But Jesus answered and said,
"You do not know what you ask. Are
you able to drink [a]the cup that I am
about to drink, [1]and be baptized with
[b]the baptism that I am baptized
with?" They said to Him, "We are
able."†
23 So He said to them, [a]"You will
indeed drink My cup, [1]and be baptized with the baptism that I am baptized with; but to sit on My right
hand and on My left is not Mine to
give, but *it is for those* for whom it
is prepared by My Father."
24 [a]And when the ten heard *it*,
they were greatly displeased with
the two brothers.
25 But Jesus called them to *Himself*
and said, "You know that the rulers
of the Gentiles lord it over them, and
those who are great exercise authority over them.
26 "Yet [a]it shall not be so among
you; but [b]whoever desires to become
great among you, let him be your
servant.†
27 [a]"And whoever desires to be
first among you, let him be your
slave—
28 [a]"just as the [b]Son of Man did
not come to be served, [c]but to serve,
and [d]to give His life a ransom
[e]for many."†

Two Blind Men Confess Jesus as Lord

29 [a]Now as they went out of Jericho, a great multitude followed Him.
30 And behold, [a]two blind men sitting by the road, when they heard
that Jesus was passing by, cried out,
saying, "Have mercy on us, O Lord,
[b]Son of David!"†
31 Then the multitude [a]warned
them that they should be quiet; but
they cried out all the more, saying,

19 [a]Matt. 27:2 [b]Matt. 26:67, 68; 27:29, 41 [c]Matt. 27:26 [d]Acts 3:13–15 [e]Matt. 28:5, 6
20 [a]Mark 10:35–45 [b]Matt. 4:21; 10:2
21 [a][Matt. 19:28]
22 [a]Luke 22:42 [b]Luke 12:50 [1]NU omits *and be baptized with the baptism that I am baptized with*
23 [a][Acts 12:2] [1]NU omits *and be baptized with the baptism that I am baptized with*
24 [a]Mark 10:41
26 [a][1 Pet. 5:3] [b]Matt. 23:11
27 [a][Matt. 18:4]
28 [a]John 13:4 [b][Phil. 2:6, 7] [c]Luke 22:27 [d][Is. 53:10, 11] [e][Rom. 5:15, 19]
29 [a]Mark 10:46–52 **30** [a]Matt. 9:27 [b][Ezek. 37:21–25] **31** [a]Matt. 19:13

20:20–28 Here is yet another discussion about greatness and rank among the disciples. Matthew reports that **the mother of Zebedee's sons** requested positions of honor for her sons, but John's and James's own involvement is revealed by the plural **you** in the Greek of v. 22 and by their answer, **We are able.**

20:22, 23 Christ calls His Crucifixion a **cup** and His death a **baptism.** The Cross is a *cup* because He drank it willingly (Heb. 12:2). His death is *baptism,* for He was completely immersed in it, and by it He cleansed the world. He does not say the seating arrangement **is not Mine to give** (v. 23) to diminish His own authority; He means that it is not His alone to give.

20:26 Here is a new definition of greatness. All offices and positions in the Church are for service of God's people based on love.

20:28 The Only Begotten Son possessed the power **to give His life** voluntarily, and to take it up again (John 10:17). Christ, the lover of man, did not shun death, for He wished to prevent the whole world from perishing in sin. **For many** in Aramaic means "for all."

20:30 This last miracle before Jesus' triumphal entrance into Jerusalem reveals the arrival of the messianic age. For this reason, the **two blind men** greet Him as **Lord,** the common name for God, and **Son of David,** a title deeply rooted in popular messianic expectation. Jesus knows beforehand what they want—and what we want. But He calls us to ask freely that He might answer us in mercy. Matthew reports two blind men; Mark mentions only one (Mark 10:46–52).

"Have mercy on us, O Lord, Son of David!"
32 So Jesus stood still and called
them, and said, "What do you want
Me to do for you?"
33 They said to Him, "Lord, that
our eyes may be opened."
34 So Jesus had [a]compassion and
touched their eyes. And immediately
their eyes received sight, and they
followed Him.

Palm Sunday: The Messianic King
(Mark 11:1–10; Luke 19:28–44; John 12:12–19)

21 Now [a]when they drew near
Jerusalem, and came to
[1]Bethphage, at [b]the Mount of Olives,
then Jesus sent two disciples,†
2 saying to them, "Go into the village opposite you, and immediately
you will find a donkey tied, and a
colt with her. Loose *them* and bring
them to Me.†
3 "And if anyone says anything
to you, you shall say, 'The Lord has
need of them,' and immediately he
will send them."
4 [1]All this was done that it might
be fulfilled which was spoken by the
prophet, saying:

5 *"Tell[a] the daughter of Zion,*
'Behold, your King is coming to you,
Lowly, and sitting on a donkey,
A colt, the foal of a donkey.'"

6 [a]So the disciples went and did
as Jesus commanded them.
7 They brought the donkey and
the colt, [a]laid their clothes on them,
[1]and set *Him* on them.
8 And a very great multitude
spread their clothes on the road;
[a]others cut down branches from
the trees and spread *them* on the
road.
9 Then the multitudes who went
before and those who followed cried
out, saying:†

"Hosanna to the Son of David!
[a]*'Blessed is He who comes in the name of the* Lord!*'*
Hosanna in the highest!"

10 [a]And when He had come into
Jerusalem, all the city was moved,
saying, "Who is this?"
11 So the multitudes said, "This is
Jesus, [a]the prophet from Nazareth
of Galilee."

Jesus Purifies the Temple
(Mark 11:11–18; Luke 19:45–48)

12 [a]Then Jesus went into the temple [1]of God and drove out all those
who bought and sold in the temple,
and overturned the tables of the

34 [a]Matt. 9:36; 14:14; 15:32; 18:27

CHAPTER 21

1 [a]Mark 11:1–10; Luke 19:29–38 [b][Zech. 14:4] [1]M *Bethsphage*
4 [1]NU omits *All*
5 [a]Is. 62:11; Zech. 9:9; John 12:15
6 [a]Mark 11:4
7 [a]2 Kin. 9:13 [1]NU *and He sat*
8 [a]Lev. 23:40; John 12:13
9 [a]Ps. 118:26; Matt. 23:39
10 [a]John 2:13, 15
11 [a][Deut. 18:15, 18]; Matt. 2:23; 16:14; Luke 4:16–29; John 6:14; 7:40; 9:17; [Acts 3:22, 23]
12 [a]Mal. 3:1; Mark 11:15–18; Luke 19:45–47; John 2:13–16 [1]NU omits *of God*

21:1–11 The Triumphal Entry is celebrated by the Church on Palm Sunday. By Jesus' time, Jewish nationalism had begun to rise, leading to the expectation of a political Messiah. Jewish leaders looked for a national king who would deliver them from the Roman yoke and reestablish David's kingdom. Many Jews wanted a king like Jehu (2 Kin. 9), who shed much blood and who would not hesitate to use the sword for the realization of nationalistic dreams. Others, responding to the messianic signs of Jesus—especially the raising of Lazarus (John 12:9–11)—expected more. In humility, Jesus shows He has not come to reestablish the earthly kingdom of David. He does not ride in a chariot but upon a donkey, an animal of peace. This is no mere earthly king, but the King of Glory who has come to reveal the Kingdom of God. Thus, the Church sees the Son of God entering not the earthly Jerusalem only, but more importantly the celestial Jerusalem, to establish His reign and His Kingdom (see Mark 11:10; Luke 19:38). He is taking the New Jerusalem to Himself as a pure bride, and the children celebrate His entrance as if it were a marriage (v. 15).

21:2 Matthew reports a second animal, **a colt,** possibly symbolizing the Gentiles who will advance from infidelity to faith.

21:9 As He enters Jerusalem, Jesus is hailed as Messiah with the words of Ps. 118:25, 26. The people knew this psalm well. Associated with messianic expectation, it was recited daily for six days during the Feast of Tabernacles, and seven times on the seventh day as branches were waved. **Hosanna** means "Save [we] pray."

[b]money changers and the seats of
those who sold doves.†
13 And He said to them, "It is written, [a]*'My house shall be called a
house of prayer,'* but you have made
it a [b]*'den of thieves.'"*
14 Then *the* blind and *the* lame
came to Him in the temple, and He
healed them.
15 But when the chief priests and
scribes saw the wonderful things
that He did, and the children crying
out in the temple and saying, "Hosanna to the [a]Son of David!" they
were [1]indignant
16 and said to Him, "Do You hear
what these are saying?" And Jesus
said to them, "Yes. Have you never
read,

> [a]*'Out of the mouth of babes and
> nursing infants
> You have perfected praise'?"*

17 Then He left them and [a]went
out of the city to Bethany, and He
lodged there.

Israel: The Withered Fig Tree
(Mark 11:19–26)

18 [a]Now in the morning, as He returned to the city, He was hungry.
19 [a]And seeing a fig tree by the
road, He came to it and found nothing on it but leaves, and said to it,
"Let no fruit grow on you ever
again." Immediately the fig tree
withered away.†
20 [a]And when the disciples saw *it*,
they marveled, saying, "How did the
fig tree wither away so soon?"
21 So Jesus answered and said to
them, "Assuredly, I say to you,
[a]if you have faith and [b]do not doubt,
you will not only do what was done
to the fig tree, [c]but also if you say
to this mountain, 'Be removed and
be cast into the sea,' it will be done.†
22 "And [a]whatever things you ask
in prayer, believing, you will
receive."†

Jewish Leaders Question Jesus
(Mark 11:27–33; Luke 20:1–8)

23 [a]Now when He came into the
temple, the chief priests and the elders of the people confronted Him
as He was teaching, and [b]said, "By
what authority are You doing these
things? And who gave You this
authority?"†
24 But Jesus answered and said to
them, "I also will ask you one thing,
which if you tell Me, I likewise will
tell you by what authority I do these
things:
25 "The [a]baptism of [b]John—where
was it from? From heaven or from
men?" And they reasoned among
themselves, saying, "If we say,

12 [b]Deut. 14:25
13 [a]Is. 56:7 [b]Jer. 7:11
15 [a]Matt. 1:1; John 7:42 [1]*angry*
16 [a]Ps. 8:2; Matt. 11:25
17 [a]Matt. 26:6; Mark 11:1, 11, 12; 14:3; Luke 19:29; 24:50; John 11:1, 18; 12:1
18 [a]Mark 11:12–14, 20–24
19 [a]Mark 11:13
20 [a]Mark 11:20
21 [a]Matt. 17:20 [b]James 1:6 [c]1 Cor. 13:2
22 [a]Matt. 7:7–11; Mark 11:24; Luke 11:9; [John 15:7; James 5:16; 1 John 3:22; 5:14]
23 [a]Mark 11:27–33; Luke 20:1–8 [b]Ex. 2:14; Acts 4:7; 7:27
25 [a][John 1:29–34] [b]John 1:15–28

21:12, 13 Those who bought and sold in the temple traded in animals used for sacrifices. The **money changers** were needed to provide currency acceptable to the temple, because Roman coins bearing the head of Caesar were considered defiling. When Jesus sees that worship has become commercialized, He acts against the abuses, boldly overturning **the tables** and casting the tradesmen out. The cleansing of the temple is seen as an image of the cleansing of our souls.

21:19 The **fig tree,** a symbol of prosperity and peace, withers because of its fruitlessness. This is a prophetic act, for after three years of preaching, teaching and healing, the Jews are destitute of spiritual fruit; therefore, He withers them with His reproach. He curses the tree to warn of the curse on those who will crucify Him. He submits Himself willingly to the Cross; He is the Suffering Servant who yields to their torture.

21:21 Jesus does not expect His disciples literally to move mountains, but this extravagant image accurately depicts the astonishing power of undoubting faith.

21:22 To receive **whatever things you ask in prayer,** one must have the faith and discernment to ask for what is in accordance with God's will. God cannot be manipulated by our prayers.

21:23 Since the **chief priests and the elders** cannot object to Jesus' miracles, they bring charges against Him for His chastisement of the tradesmen in the temple. Since He is not a Levitical priest and does not have the schooling normally required of a rabbi, Jesus is asked about His **authority** to cleanse the temple.

'From heaven,' He will say to us,
'Why then did you not believe
him?'†
26 "But if we say, 'From men,' we
[a]fear the multitude, [b]for all count
John as a prophet."
27 So they answered Jesus and
said, "We do not know." And He
said to them, "Neither will I tell you
by what authority I do these things.

Sinners Believe

28 "But what do you think? A man
had two sons, and he came to the
first and said, 'Son, go, work today
in my [a]vineyard.'
29 "He answered and said, 'I will
not,' but afterward he regretted it
and went.
30 "Then he came to the second
and said likewise. And he answered
and said, 'I *go,* sir,' but he did not
go.
31 "Which of the two did the will
of *his* father?" They said to Him,
"The first." Jesus said to them,
[a]"Assuredly, I say to you that tax
collectors and harlots enter the kingdom of God before you.†
32 "For [a]John came to you in the
way of righteousness, and you did
not believe him; [b]but tax collectors
and harlots believed him; and when
you saw *it,* you did not afterward
[1]relent and believe him.

Leaders Mistreat God's Messengers
(Mark 12:1–12; Luke 20:9–19)

33 "Hear another parable: There
was a certain landowner [a]who
planted a vineyard and set a hedge

26 [a]Matt. 14:5; 21:46; Luke 20:6 [b]Matt. 14:5; Mark 6:20
28 [a]Matt. 20:1; 21:33
31 [a]Luke 7:29, 37–50
32 [a]Luke 3:1–12; 7:29 [b]Luke 3:12, 13 [1]*regret it*
33 [a]Ps. 80:9; Mark 12:1–12; Luke 20:9–19 [b]Matt. 25:14
35 [a]2 Chr. 24:21; 36:16; [Matt. 23:34, 37; Acts 7:52; 1 Thess. 2:15]; Heb. 11:36, 37
37 [a][John 3:16]
38 [a][Ps. 2:8; Heb. 1:2] [b][Ps. 2:2]; John 11:53; Acts 4:27
39 [a][Matt. 26:50]; Mark 14:46; Luke 22:54; John 18:12; [Acts 2:23]
41 [a]Luke 20:16 [b][Luke 21:24] [c][Matt. 8:11; Acts 13:46; Rom. 9; 10] [1]*give*
42 [a]Ps. 118:22, 23; Is. 28:16; Mark 12:10; Luke 20:17; Acts 4:11; [Rom. 9:33]; Eph. 2:20; [1 Pet. 2:6, 7]
43 [a][Matt. 8:12]; Acts 13:46

around it, dug a winepress in it and
built a tower. And he leased it to
vinedressers and [b]went into a far
country.†
34 "Now when vintage-time drew
near, he sent his servants to the vinedressers, that they might receive its
fruit.
35 [a]"And the vinedressers took his
servants, beat one, killed one, and
stoned another.
36 "Again he sent other servants,
more than the first, and they did
likewise to them.
37 "Then last of all he sent his
[a]son to them, saying, 'They will respect my son.'
38 "But when the vinedressers saw
the son, they said among themselves, [a]'This is the heir. [b]Come, let
us kill him and seize his inheritance.'
39 [a]"So they took him and cast *him*
out of the vineyard and killed *him.*
40 "Therefore, when the owner of
the vineyard comes, what will he do
to those vinedressers?"
41 [a]They said to Him, [b]"He will
destroy those wicked men miserably,
[c]and lease *his* vineyard to other vinedressers who will [1]render to him the
fruits in their seasons."
42 Jesus said to them, "Have you
never read in the Scriptures:

[a]*'The stone which the builders rejected*
Has become the chief cornerstone.
This was the LORD*'s doing,*
And it is marvelous in our eyes'?

43 "Therefore I say to you, [a]the
kingdom of God will be taken from
you and given to a nation bearing
the fruits of it.

21:25 Because they are motivated by unbelief and hostility, Jesus does not answer, but confounds His adversaries with a question of His own.

21:31 He mentions the **tax collectors and harlots,** presumed to be great sinners, to jolt His hearers into obedience.

21:33–46 God the Father is the **landowner** who **planted a vineyard.** The tenant **vinedressers** are the religious leaders entrusted with the care of God's people. The landowner's **servants** (v. 34) are the prophets, sent by God to proclaim His word. For instead of tending the vineyard, the vinedressers had devoured it. Although they were obstinate toward His *servants,* God sent His Son (v. 37), our Lord Jesus Christ, whom they might honor. But in their greed and impiety they murdered the Son as well. The **nation bearing the fruits** (v. 43) of the Kingdom is the Church, the new people of God.

44 "And [a]whoever falls on this
stone will be broken; but on whomever it falls, [b]it will grind him to
powder."
45 **Now when the chief priests and
Pharisees heard His parables, they
[1]perceived that He was speaking of
them.**
46 **But when they sought to lay
hands on Him, they [a]feared the multitudes, because [b]they took Him for
a prophet.**

Who Enters into the Kingdom?
(Luke 14:15–24)

22 And Jesus answered [a]and
spoke to them again by parables and said:†
2 "The kingdom of heaven is like
a certain king who arranged a marriage for his son,
3 "and sent out his servants to call
those who were invited to the wedding; and they were not willing to
come.
4 "Again, he sent out other servants, saying, 'Tell those who are invited, "See, I have prepared my dinner; [a]my oxen and fatted cattle *are*
killed, and all things *are* ready. Come
to the wedding."'
5 "But they made light of it and
went their ways, one to his own
farm, another to his business.
6 "And the rest seized his servants, treated *them* [1]spitefully, and
killed *them.*

44 [a]Is. 8:14, 15; Zech. 12:3; Luke 20:18; [Rom. 9:33]; 1 Pet. 2:8 [b][Is. 60:12; Dan. 2:44]
45 [1]*knew*
46 [a]Matt. 21:26; Mark 11:18, 32 [b]Matt. 21:11; Luke 7:16; John 7:40

CHAPTER 22

1 [a]Luke 14:16; [Rev. 19:7–9]
4 [a]Prov. 9:2
6 [1]*insolently*
7 [a][Dan. 9:26]
8 [a]Matt. 10:11
10 [a]Matt. 13:38, 47, 48; [Acts 28:28]
11 [a][2 Cor. 5:3; Eph. 4:24; Col. 3:10, 12; Rev. 3:4; 16:15; 19:8]
12 [a][Rom. 3:19]
13 [a]Matt. 8:12; 25:30; Luke 13:28 [1]NU omits *take him away, and*
14 [a]Matt. 20:16
15 [a]Mark 12:13–17; Luke 20:20–26

7 "But when the king heard *about
it,* he was furious. And he sent out
[a]his armies, destroyed those murderers, and burned up their city.†
8 "Then he said to his servants,
'The wedding is ready, but those
who were invited were not [a]worthy.
9 'Therefore go into the highways, and as many as you find, invite to the wedding.'†
10 "So those servants went out into
the highways and [a]gathered together all whom they found, both
bad and good. And the wedding *hall*
was filled with guests.
11 "But when the king came in to
see the guests, he saw a man there
[a]who did not have on a wedding
garment.†
12 "So he said to him, 'Friend, how
did you come in here without a wedding garment?' And he was
[a]speechless.
13 "Then the king said to the servants, 'Bind him hand and foot,
[1]take him away, and cast *him* [a]into
outer darkness; there will be weeping and gnashing of teeth.'
14 [a]"For many are called, but few
are chosen."

A Trap for Jesus
(Mark 12:13–17; Luke 20:20–26)

15 **[a]Then the Pharisees went and
plotted how they might entangle
Him in *His* talk.†**

22:1–14 This is another parable proclaiming the transfer of the Kingdom from Jews to Gentiles, depicted as a joyful wedding banquet (see 25:1–13). John the Baptist calls Christ the "bridegroom" (John 3:29) and Paul also uses the marriage analogy (Eph. 5:22–33). Ancient tradition applies these two parables in Matthew to the process of initiation into the Church, because the sacraments of baptism and chrismation bring us into marriage or union with Christ, a union fully realized in the age to come.

22:7 Burned up their city refers to the destruction of Jerusalem in A.D. 70.

22:9 The highways are the Gentile world. Though the Apostles do not immediately understand it, this parable proclaims beforehand both the casting out of the unbelieving Jews, and the calling of the Gentiles into the **wedding** hall, the Kingdom of God. God calls all peoples to salvation in Christ—Jew and Gentile—carrying forth the plan of salvation to all humanity.

22:11 Jesus is speaking here of the judgment which is to come. The **wedding garment** is provided by the host. To be at the wedding improperly dressed indicates one who is uninvited or who, having been invited, rejects the host's hospitality. In the Church, the *wedding garment* is true repentance and righteousness—the way of salvation—gained only by the grace of God.

22:15 The Pharisees wish to **entangle Him** by showing Christ to be either a revolutionary against or a collaborator with the Romans.

16 And they sent to Him their disciples with the [a]Herodians, saying,
"Teacher, we know that You are
true, and teach the way of God in
truth; nor do You care about anyone,
for You do not [1]regard the person
of men.
17 "Tell us, therefore, what do You
think? Is it lawful to pay taxes to Caesar, or not?"
18 But Jesus [1]perceived their wickedness, and said, "Why do you test
Me, *you* hypocrites?†
19 "Show Me the tax money." So
they brought Him a denarius.
20 And He said to them, "Whose
image and inscription *is* this?"
21 They said to Him, "Caesar's."
And He said to them, [a]"Render[1]
therefore to Caesar the things that
are [b]Caesar's, and to God the things
that are [c]God's."†
22 When they had heard *these
words,* they marveled, and left Him
and went their way.

Resurrection of the Dead
(Mark 12:18–27; Luke 20:27–40)

23 [a]The same day the Sadducees,
[b]who say there is no resurrection,
came to Him and asked Him,†
24 saying: "Teacher, [a]Moses said
that if a man dies, having no children, his brother shall marry his wife
and raise up offspring for his
brother.
25 "Now there were with us seven
brothers. The first died after he had
married, and having no offspring,
left his wife to his brother.
26 "Likewise the second also, and
the third, even to the seventh.
27 "Last of all the woman died
also.
28 "Therefore, in the resurrection,
whose wife of the seven will she be?
For they all had her."
29 Jesus answered and said to
them, "You are [1]mistaken, [a]not
knowing the Scriptures nor the
power of God.†
30 "For in the resurrection they
neither marry nor are given in marriage, but [a]are like angels [1]of God
in heaven.
31 "But concerning the resurrection of the dead, have you not
read what was spoken to you by
God, saying,
32 [a]*'I am the God of Abraham, the
God of Isaac, and the God of Jacob'*?
God is not the God of the dead, but
of the living."
33 And when the multitudes heard
this, [a]they were astonished at His
teaching.

The Greatest Commandment
(Mark 12:28–34)

34 [a]But when the Pharisees heard
that He had silenced the Sadducees,
they gathered together.
35 Then one of them, [a]a lawyer,
asked *Him a question,* testing Him,
and saying,

16 [a]Mark 3:6; 8:15; 12:13 [1]Lit. *look at the face of*
18 [1]*knew*
21 [a]Matt. 17:25 [b][Rom. 13:1–7; 1 Pet. 2:13–15] [c][1 Cor. 3:23; 6:19, 20; 12:27] [1]*Pay*
23 [a]Mark 12:18–27; Luke 20:27–40 [b]Acts 23:8
24 [a]Deut. 25:5
29 [a]John 20:9 [1]*deceived*
30 [a][1 John 3:2] [1]NU omits *of God*
32 [a]Gen. 17:7; 26:24; 28:21; Ex. 3:6, 15; Mark 12:26; Luke 20:37; Acts 7:32; [Heb. 11:16]
33 [a]Matt. 7:28
34 [a]Mark 12:28–31; Luke 10:25–37
35 [a]Luke 7:30; 10:25; 11:45, 46, 52; 14:3; Titus 3:13

22:18 Jesus constantly demonstrates He is divine as well as human. Here again He does so by (1) revealing the secrets of their hearts, and (2) silencing them through His questions.

22:21 The distinction between **things that are Caesar's** and **things that are God's** does not imply a division of life into two domains, the secular and the sacred. Rather, God is Lord over all. We must fulfill legitimate governmental requirements which do not conflict with our responsibility toward God (Rom. 13:7). Paying taxes and similar duties are not detrimental to godliness. The fact that the Jewish establishment had a Roman coin in hand proved they accepted and used this coin, thereby accepting the earthly rule of the one who issued it.

22:23 Unlike the Pharisees, the **Sadducees** do not believe in the **resurrection** of the dead and try to ridicule this doctrine.

22:29 You are mistaken: There will be a resurrection, but not of the sort they think. (1) They are ignorant of **the Scriptures,** which say nothing about earthly laws of marriage being applicable to the future Kingdom. The resurrection is not merely life resuming where it left off, but a complete change of life. (2) They do not know **the power of God,** which transforms us from death to life. The "dead" even now are living before God (v. 32).

36 "Teacher, which *is* the great
commandment in the law?"†
37 Jesus said to him, [a]" '*You shall
love the* LORD *your God with all your
heart, with all your soul, and with
all your mind.*'†
38 "This is *the* first and great
commandment.
39 "And *the* second *is* like it:
[a]'*You shall love your neighbor as
yourself.*'
40 [a]"On these two commandments
hang all the Law and the Prophets."

David's Son Is His Lord
(Mark 12:35–37; Luke 20:41–44)

41 [a]While the Pharisees were gathered together, Jesus asked them,
42 saying, "What do you think
about the Christ? Whose Son is He?"
They said to Him, "*The* [a]*Son* of
David."†
43 He said to them, "How then
does David in the Spirit call Him
'*Lord,*' saying:†
44 '*The*[a] LORD *said to my Lord,
"Sit at My right hand,
Till I make Your enemies Your
footstool"* '?
45 "If David then calls Him '*Lord,*'
how is He his Son?"
46 [a]And no one was able to answer
Him a word, [b]nor from that day on
did anyone dare question Him anymore.

Abuses of Authority
(Mark 12:38, 39; Luke 20:45, 46)

23 Then Jesus spoke to the multitudes and to His disciples,†
2 saying: [a]"The scribes and the
Pharisees sit in Moses' seat.†
3 "Therefore whatever they tell
you [1]to observe, *that* observe and do,
but do not do according to their
works; for [a]they say, and do not do.†
4 [a]"For they bind heavy burdens,
hard to bear, and lay *them* on men's
shoulders; but they *themselves* will
not move them with one of their fingers.

37 [a]Deut. 6:5; 10:12; 30:6
39 [a]Lev. 19:18
40 [a][Matt. 7:12]
41 [a]Luke 20:41–44
42 [a]Matt. 1:1; 21:9
44 [a]Ps. 110:1
46 [a]Luke 14:6 [b]Mark 12:34

CHAPTER 23
2 [a]Neh. 8:4, 8
3 [a][Rom. 2:19]
[1]NU omits *to observe*
4 [a]Luke 11:46

22:36 The Pharisees, lay experts on the Scripture and the Law, had found 613 commandments in the Scriptures and argued interminably about which one was central. Thus they ask about the **great commandment.**

22:37–40 Jesus sets forth the **first . . . commandment** (v. 37) and the **second** (v. 39) as well, which together constitute the grand summary of the Law. He knows they are asking Him maliciously.

22:42 Jesus takes the offensive against the Pharisees, further exposing them as pseudo-scholars who do not understand the Bible. They suppose the Messiah to be a mere man, and therefore reply **Son of David** to Jesus' question.

22:43–45 David, as king of Israel, would not address anyone as "my Lord" except God Himself. Therefore, this psalm verse describes God talking to God—the Father to the Son—which contradicts the Pharisees' view of God as one Person, and introduces the doctrine of the Holy Trinity.

23:1–36 Jesus spoke His grand critique of the Pharisees in this chapter. (1) They have God-given authority and many God-given commandments, but they are personally ungodly, coldhearted and vainglorious. Their teaching is to be honored, but they are not to be imitated (vv. 2–7). (2) God is our true Father. A true teacher leads his people to God. The Pharisees do the opposite, placing themselves in God's stead (vv. 8–12). (3) In His eightfold indictment of the Pharisees (vv. 13–36), Jesus charges them with inverting God's values and with being mean-spirited, greedy, ambitious, absorbed in externals, hypocritical, and blindly self-righteous. How much worse will it be for Christians who lapse into patterns of religious life similar to the scribes' and Pharisees'!

23:2 Moses' seat was a special chair in the synagogue assigned to the most famous rabbi of the town.

23:3 The rabbinic teachers assumed an intrinsic value for their own office as the seat of authority. According to the prevailing system of the Pharisees, the student in rabbinic tradition submitted himself to his master's authority in a total and servile manner. The call of Jesus to His disciples differed radically from the rabbinic system in that (1) the disciples were not merely servants but beloved friends; (2) their calling did not imply they would themselves become independent masters; (3) the brotherhood of disciples would remain unified and loyal to Jesus.

5 "But all their works they do to [a]be seen by men. They make their phylacteries broad and enlarge the borders of their garments.†

6 [a]"They love the [1]best places at feasts, the best seats in the synagogues,

7 "greetings in the marketplaces, and to be called by men, 'Rabbi, Rabbi.'

8 [a]"But you, do not be called 'Rabbi'; for One is your [1]Teacher, [2]the Christ, and you are all brethren.

9 "Do not call anyone on earth your father; [a]for One is your Father, He who is in heaven.†

10 "And do not be called teachers; for One is your Teacher, the Christ.

11 "But [a]he who is greatest among you shall be your servant.

12 [a]"And whoever exalts himself will be [1]humbled, and he who humbles himself will be [2]exalted.

Pronouncement of Judgment

(Mark 12:40; Luke 20:47)

13 "But [a]woe to you, scribes and Pharisees, hypocrites! For you shut up the kingdom of heaven against men; for you neither go in *yourselves,* nor do you allow those who are entering to go in.†

14 [1]"Woe to you, scribes and Pharisees, hypocrites! [a]For you devour widows' houses, and for a pretense make long prayers. Therefore you will receive greater condemnation.

15 "Woe to you, scribes and Pharisees, hypocrites! For you travel land and sea to win one proselyte, and when he is won, you make him twice as much a son of [1]hell as yourselves.

16 "Woe to you, [a]blind guides, who say, [b]'Whoever swears by the temple, it is nothing; but whoever swears by the gold of the temple, he is obliged *to perform it.'*

17 "Fools and blind! For which is greater, the gold [a]or the temple that [1]sanctifies the gold?

18 "And, 'Whoever swears by the altar, it is nothing; but whoever swears by the gift that is on it, he is obliged *to perform it.'*

19 "Fools and blind! For which is greater, the gift [a]or the altar that sanctifies the gift?

20 "Therefore he who [1]swears by the altar, swears by it and by all things on it.

21 "He who swears by the temple, swears by it and by [a]Him who [1]dwells in it.

22 "And he who swears by heaven, swears by [a]the throne of God and by Him who sits on it.

23 "Woe to you, scribes and Pharisees, hypocrites! [a]For you pay tithe of mint and anise and cummin, and [b]have neglected the weightier *matters* of the law: justice and mercy and faith. These you ought to have done, without leaving the others undone.†

5 [a][Matt. 6:1–6, 16–18]
6 [a]Luke 11:43; 20:46 [1]Or *place of honor*
8 [a][James 3:1] [1]*Leader* [2]NU omits *the Christ*
9 [a][Mal. 1:6]
11 [a]Matt. 20:26, 27
12 [a]Luke 14:11; 18:14 [1]*put down* [2]*lifted up*
13 [a]Luke 11:52
14 [a]Mark 12:40 [1]NU omits v. 14.
15 [1]Gr. *Gehenna*
16 [a]Matt. 15:14; 23:24 [b][Matt. 5:33, 34]
17 [a]Ex. 30:29 [1]NU *sanctified*
19 [a]Ex. 29:37
20 [1]Swears an oath
21 [a]1 Kin. 8:13 [1]M *dwelt*
22 [a]Matt. 5:34
23 [a]Luke 11:42; 18:12 [b][Hos. 6:6]

23:5 Phylacteries and **borders of their garments** refer to articles worn by pious Jews to remind them of God's Law.

23:9, 10 Jesus warns against calling hypocrites **father** and **teacher.** Far from being a prohibition against using these terms under any circumstances, it is a warning not to use them undeservedly. Both terms are applied to men in the NT. "Father" is used in Luke 16:24; 1 Cor. 4:15; and Col. 3:21. In the earliest Christian communities, this term was applied to bishops and presbyters, because they represent the Father in the Church. "Teacher" is used in John 3:10; Acts 13:1; 1 Cor. 12:28; Eph. 4:11; and 2 Tim. 1:11.

23:13 The Pharisees perpetuate a systematic hypocrisy which creates a wall between people and God.

23:23–33 These warnings are especially important to Orthodox Christians. This historic Church has maintained the ancient liturgical obligations (vv. 23, 24), beautiful holy objects (vv. 25, 26), specific rituals which externally guard righteousness (vv. 27, 28), and imposing tradition, handed down through God-fearing fathers. These rites can be performed, invoked, defended and passed on without ever being taken by faith to heart; or they can be helps, safeguards and doorways into the true life of Christ in us, which transforms us from glory to glory.

23:23 Jesus is not against externals, but considers them of lesser significance. **The weightier matters** are of trust and obedience to God in **justice, mercy** and **faith.**

Commemoration of Holy Prophets

23:29–39: Jesus denounces the Jews for ignoring and persecuting the prophets of God.

24 "Blind guides, who strain out a
gnat and swallow a camel!†
25 "Woe to you, scribes and Pharisees, hypocrites! [a]For you cleanse
the outside of the cup and dish, but
inside they are full of extortion and
[1]self-indulgence.
26 "Blind Pharisee, first cleanse the
inside of the cup and dish, that the
outside of them may be clean also.
27 "Woe to you, scribes and Pharisees, hypocrites! [a]For you are like
whitewashed tombs which indeed
appear beautiful outwardly, but inside are full of dead *men's* bones and
all uncleanness.
28 "Even so you also outwardly
appear righteous to men, but inside
you are full of hypocrisy and
lawlessness.
29 [a]"Woe to you, scribes and Pharisees, hypocrites! Because you build
the tombs of the prophets and
[1]adorn the monuments of the
righteous,
30 "and say, 'If we had lived in the
days of our fathers, we would not
have been partakers with them in the
blood of the prophets.'
31 "Therefore you are witnesses
against yourselves that [a]you are
sons of those who murdered the
prophets.
32 [a]"Fill up, then, the measure of
your fathers' *guilt.*
33 "Serpents, [a]brood[1] of vipers!
How can you escape the condemnation of hell?
34 [a]"Therefore, indeed, I send you
prophets, wise men, and scribes:
[b]*some* of them you will kill and crucify, and [c]*some* of them you will
scourge in your synagogues and persecute from city to city,
35 [a]"that on you may come all the
righteous blood shed on the earth,
[b]from the blood of righteous Abel to
[c]the blood of Zechariah, son of Ber-
echiah, whom you murdered between the temple and the altar.
36 "Assuredly, I say to you, all
these things will come upon this
generation.

The Fate of Jerusalem
(Luke 13:34, 35)

37 [a]"O Jerusalem, Jerusalem, the
one who kills the prophets [b]and
stones those who are sent to her!
How often [c]I wanted to gather your
children together, as a hen gathers
her chicks [d]under *her* wings, but you
were not willing!
38 "See! Your house is left to you
desolate;
39 "for I say to you, you shall see
Me no more till you say, [a]*'Blessed
is He who comes in the name of the
LORD!'* "

Destruction of the Temple
(Mark 13:1–4; Luke 21:5–7)

24 **Then [a]Jesus went out and departed from the temple, and
His disciples came up to show Him
the buildings of the temple.†**

25 [a]Luke 11:39 [1]M *unrighteousness*
27 [a]Acts 23:3
29 [a]Luke 11:47, 48 [1]*decorate*
31 [a][Acts 7:51, 52]
32 [a][1 Thess. 2:16]
33 [a]Matt. 3:7; 12:34 [1]*offspring*
34 [a]Luke 11:49 [b]Acts 7:54–60; 22:19 [c]2 Cor. 11:24, 25
35 [a]Rev. 18:24 [b]Gen. 4:8 [c]2 Chr. 24:20, 21
37 [a]Luke 13:34, 35 [b]2 Chr. 24:20, 21; 36:15, 16 [c]Deut. 32:11, 12 [d]Ps. 17:8; 91:4
39 [a]Ps. 118:26
CHAPTER 24
1 [a]Mark 13:1

23:24 In the ancient world, strainers were attached to the mouths of decanters, because any liquid might contain foreign matter. Pharisaic observance used the strainer also to strain out any ritually unclean substance which one might accidentally consume. This **gnat** and **camel** analogy points out how carefully the scribes and the Pharisees observed the minutiae of the Law, while neglecting its most significant aspects.

24:1, 2 This is a prediction of the destruction of **the temple** in A.D. 70, which sets the

(continued on next page)

Holy Monday *Monday before Easter*

24:3–35: Shortly before His death, Jesus warns His disciples to prepare for Judgment.

2 And Jesus said to them, "Do
you not see all these things? Assuredly, I say to you, [a]not *one* stone
shall be left here upon another, that
shall not be thrown down."

The Beginning of Birth Pangs

(Mark 13:5–13; Luke 21:8–19)

3 **Now as He sat on the Mount
of Olives, [a]the disciples came to Him
privately, saying, [b]"Tell us, when
will these things be? And what *will*
be the sign of Your coming, and of
the end of the age?"†**
4 **And Jesus answered and said to
them:** [a]"Take heed that no one deceives you.
5 "For [a]many will come in My
name, saying, 'I am the Christ,'
[b]and will deceive many.
6 "And you will hear of [a]wars and
rumors of wars. See that you are not
troubled; for [1]all *these things* must
come to pass, but the end is not
yet.†
7 "For [a]nation will rise against nation, and kingdom against kingdom.
And there will be [b]famines, [1]pes-
tilences, and earthquakes in various
places.
8 "All these *are* the beginning of
sorrows.
9 [a]"Then they will deliver you up
to tribulation and kill you, and you
will be hated by all nations for My
name's sake.
10 "And then many will be offended, will betray one another, and
will hate one another.
11 "Then [a]many false prophets
will rise up and [b]deceive many.
12 "And because lawlessness will
abound, the love of many will grow
[a]cold.
13 [a]"But he who endures to the
end shall be saved.
14 "And this [a]gospel of the kingdom [b]will be preached in all the
world as a witness to all the nations,
and then the end will come.†

The Great Tribulation

(Mark 13:14–23; Luke 21:20–24)

15 [a]"Therefore when you see the
[b]*'abomination of desolation,'* spoken
of by Daniel the prophet, standing

2 [a]Luke 19:44
3 [a]Mark 13:3 [b][1 Thess. 5:1–3]
4 [a][Col. 2:8, 18]
5 [a]John 5:43 [b]Matt. 24:11
6 [a][Rev. 6:2–4] [1]NU omits *all*
7 [a]Hag. 2:22 [b]Rev. 6:5, 6 [1]NU omits *pestilences*
9 [a]Matt. 10:17
11 [a]2 Pet. 2:1 [b][1 Tim. 4:1]
12 [a][2 Thess. 2:3]
13 [a]Matt. 10:22
14 [a]Matt. 4:23 [b]Rom. 10:18
15 [a]Mark 13:14 [b]Dan. 9:27; 11:31; 12:11

(continued from previous page)
tone for Jesus' discourse on the end of the age (chs. 24; 25). The NT describes the end time in a variety of ways, so that no precise chronology can be determined (see Mark 13; Luke 21; 1 Cor. 15:51–55; 1 Thess. 4:13–17; 2 Thess. 2:1–10; and the Book of Revelation). Jesus' emphasis is on being prepared through watchfulness and stewardship rather than on constructing exacting chronologies. In this chapter the end is described as a process with three overlapping stages: (1) the beginning of sorrows (vv. 4–14), (2) the Great Tribulation (vv. 15–28) and (3) the coming of the Son of Man (vv. 29–31).

24:3–14 The question about the signs and the persecutions is connected in Matthew with the sign of His coming and the end of the age. The disciples dream of the hoped-for earthly kingdom, which they expect to appear almost immediately. Jesus knows their anticipation and sets out to prepare them for what is to come. He warns them to **take heed** (v. 4) not to (1) be seduced by any deception (v. 5); (2) be overpowered by the violence of afflictions which will come (vv. 6–9); or (3) stumble because of false brethren (vv. 10–12).

24:6 Jesus and the disciples are sitting on the Mount of Olives looking out over Jerusalem (v. 1). The immediate reference here is not to the **wars** of the world over the centuries, but to wars in Jerusalem.

24:14 All these calamities and tribulations will not prevent the progress of the **gospel;** the Good News **will be preached** everywhere (Rom. 10:18; Col. 1:6, 23).

in the holy place" [c](**whoever reads,
let him understand),†
16 "then let those who are in Judea
flee to the mountains.
17 "Let him who is on the housetop not go down to take anything
out of his house.
18 "And let him who is in the field
not go back to get his clothes.
19 "But [a]woe to those who are
pregnant and to those who are nursing babies in those days!
20 "And pray that your flight may
not be in winter or on the Sabbath.
21 "For [a]then there will be great
tribulation, such as has not been
since the beginning of the world
until this time, no, nor ever shall
be.
22 "And unless those days were
shortened, no flesh would be saved;
[a]but for the [1]elect's sake those days
will be shortened.
23 [a]"Then if anyone says to you,
'Look, here *is* the Christ!' or 'There!'
do not believe *it*.
24 "For [a]false christs and false
prophets will rise and show great
signs and wonders to deceive,
[b]if possible, even the elect.
25 "See, I have told you
beforehand.
26 "Therefore if they say to you,
'Look, He is in the desert!' do not
go out; *or* 'Look, *He is* in the inner
rooms!' do not believe *it*.
27 [a]"For as the lightning comes
from the east and flashes to the west,
so also will the coming of the Son
of Man be.†
28 [a]"For wherever the carcass is,
there the eagles will be gathered
together.

15 [c]Dan. 9:23
19 [a]Luke 23:29
21 [a]Dan. 9:26
22 [a]Is. 65:8, 9 [1]*chosen ones'*
23 [a]Luke 17:23
24 [a][2 Thess. 2:9] [b][2 Tim. 2:19]
27 [a]Luke 17:24
28 [a]Luke 17:37
29 [a][Dan. 7:11] [b]Ezek. 32:7
30 [a][Dan. 7:13, 14] [b]Zech. 12:12
31 [a][1 Cor. 15:52] [1]*chosen ones*
32 [a]Luke 21:29

The End

(Mark 13:24–27; Luke 21:25–28)

29 [a]"Immediately after the tribulation of those days [b]the sun will be
darkened, and the moon will not
give its light; the stars will fall from
heaven, and the powers of the heavens will be shaken.†
30 [a]"Then the sign of the Son of
Man will appear in heaven, [b]and
then all the tribes of the earth will
mourn, and they will see the Son of
Man coming on the clouds of heaven
with power and great glory.
31 [a]"And He will send His angels
with a great sound of a trumpet, and
they will gather together His [1]elect
from the four winds, from one end
of heaven to the other.

No One Knows the Hour

(Mark 13:28–32; Luke 21:29–36)

32 "Now learn [a]this parable from
the fig tree: When its branch has already become tender and puts forth
leaves, you know that summer *is*
near.

24:15 Daniel's prophecy of the **abomination of desolation** was fulfilled in A.D. 70, when the Roman general Titus, before ordering the temple burned, entered the Most Holy Place, thus defiling the temple. Jesus quotes this prophecy so that the disciples might know these things will happen while most of them are still alive. **Whoever reads, let him understand** are code words from the author to early Christians about the known meaning of what is written.

24:27 How will Christ come back? The event will be unmistakably visible to all. In the Orthodox Church we pray in the direction of the rising sun, because the East symbolizes Christ Himself who is the East of easts, Light of light. The great day of the Lord will be illuminated by the true Light, the "rising" (Is. 60:1, 3; Mal. 4:2; Luke 1:78; 2 Pet. 1:19). The very creation will be transfigured—not destroyed but superseded—by the light of His presence at the end of the age.

24:29–31 After He speaks about Jerusalem, He moves on to His own Second Coming, not for their sakes only, but for all of us who come after them. **The sign of the Son of Man** (v. 30) in His Second Coming is thought by many to be His glorious Cross, the memorial of His Passion. His **power and great glory** will be brighter than the sun, which will be darkened. The Lord Jesus will come from heaven in the same way the Apostles saw Him ascend to heaven (Acts 1:11).

Holy Tuesday *Tuesday before Easter*

24:36—26:2: Through parables, Jesus teaches His servants to be ready for His return.

33 "So you also, when you see all
these things, know [a]that [1]it is near—
at the doors!†
34 "Assuredly, I say to you,
[a]this generation will by no means
pass away till all these things take
place.
35 [a]"Heaven and earth will pass
away, but My words will by no
means pass away.
36 [a]"But of that day and hour no
one knows, not even the angels of
[1]heaven, [b]but My Father only.
37 "But as the days of Noah *were,*
so also will the coming of the Son
of Man be.
38 [a]"For as in the days before the
flood, they were eating and drinking, marrying and giving in marriage, until the day that Noah entered the ark,
39 "and did not know until the
flood came and took them all away,
so also will the coming of the Son
of Man be.
40 [a]"Then two *men* will be in the
field: one will be taken and the other
left.
41 "Two *women will be* grinding at
the mill: one will be taken and the
other left.
42 [a]"Watch therefore, for you do
not know what [1]hour your Lord is
coming.†
43 [a]"But know this, that if the master of the house had known what
[1]hour the thief would come, he
would have watched and not allowed his house to be broken
into.
44 [a]"Therefore you also be ready,
for the Son of Man is coming at an
hour you do not expect.

We Must Be Loyal
(Mark 13:33–37)

45 [a]"Who then is a faithful and
wise servant, whom his master made
ruler over his household, to give
them food [1]in due season?
46 [a]"Blessed *is* that servant whom
his master, when he comes, will find
so doing.
47 "Assuredly, I say to you that
[a]he will make him ruler over all his
goods.
48 "But if that evil servant says in
his heart, 'My master [a]is delaying
[1]his coming,'
49 "and begins to beat *his* fellow
servants, and to eat and drink with
the drunkards,
50 "the master of that servant will
come on a day when he is not looking for *him* and at an hour that he
is [a]not aware of,
51 "and will cut him in two and
appoint *him* his portion with the
hypocrites. [a]There shall be weeping
and gnashing of teeth.

33 [a][James 5:9] [1]Or *He*
34 [a][Matt. 10:23; 16:28; 23:36]
35 [a]Luke 21:33
36 [a]Acts 1:7 [b]Zech. 14:7 [1]NU adds *nor the Son*
38 [a][Gen. 6:3–5]
40 [a]Luke 17:34
42 [a]Matt. 25:13 [1]NU *day*
43 [a]Luke 12:39 [1]Lit. *watch of the night*
44 [a][1 Thess. 5:6]
45 [a]Luke 12:42–46 [1]*at the right time*
46 [a]Rev. 16:15
47 [a]Matt. 25:21, 23
48 [a][2 Pet. 3:4–9] [1]NU omits *his coming*
50 [a]Mark 13:32
51 [a]Matt. 8:12; 25:30

24:33–41 This generation (v. 34) probably refers to the new race of Christians. The end is always **near** (v. 33), just ahead of us. The unexpected suddenness of Christ's coming will catch people unaware and engaged in earthly pursuits, just as in **the days of Noah** (v. 37).

24:42–44 The Lord's purpose in this discourse is not to make the disciples "experts on prophecy." It is rather that they may **watch** (v. 42) and **be ready** (v. 44), continually engaged in virtuous action, obeying His commandments—remembering that we cannot know the time of His coming. These warnings are illustrated by the parable of the householder and **the thief** (v. 43), and three longer parables which follow (24:45—25:30). They urge us to (1) watchfulness (v. 43), (2) faithful responsibility (vv. 45–51), (3) preparedness (25:1–13), and (4) use of our spiritual gifts (25:14–30).

Commemoration of Holy Nuns

25:1–13: These holy women, like the wise virgins, were ready to meet their Bridegroom.

We Must Be Prepared

25 "Then the kingdom of heaven
shall be likened to ten virgins
who took their lamps and went out
to meet [a]the bridegroom.†
2 [a]"Now five of them were wise,
and five *were* foolish.
3 "Those who *were* foolish took
their lamps and took no oil with
them,
4 "but the wise took oil in their
vessels with their lamps.
5 "But while the bridegroom was
delayed, [a]they all slumbered and
slept.
6 "And at midnight [a]a cry was
heard: 'Behold, the bridegroom
[1]is coming; go out to meet him!'
7 "Then all those virgins arose
and [a]trimmed their lamps.
8 "And the foolish said to the
wise, 'Give us *some* of your oil, for
our lamps are going out.'
9 "But the wise answered, saying,
'*No,* lest there should not be enough
for us and you; but go rather to those
who sell, and buy for yourselves.'
10 "And while they went to buy,
the bridegroom came, and those who
were ready went in with him to the
wedding; and [a]the door was shut.
11 "Afterward the other virgins
came also, saying, [a]'Lord, Lord,
open to us!'
12 "But he answered and said, 'Assuredly,
I say to you, [a]I do not know
you.'
13 [a]"Watch therefore, for you
[b]know neither the day nor the hour
[1]in which the Son of Man is coming.

We Must Be Good Stewards

14 [a]"For *the kingdom of heaven is*
[b]like a man traveling to a far country,
who called his own servants and delivered
his goods to them.†
15 "And to one he gave five talents,
to another two, and to another
one, [a]to each according to his own
ability; and immediately he went on
a journey.
16 "Then he who had received the
five talents went and traded with

CHAPTER 25
1 [a][Eph. 5:29, 30]
2 [a]Matt. 13:47; 22:10
5 [a]1 Thess. 5:6
6 [a][1 Thess. 4:16] [1]NU omits *is coming*
7 [a]Luke 12:35
10 [a]Luke 13:25
11 [a][Matt. 7:21–23]
12 [a][Hab. 1:13]
13 [a]Mark 13:35 [b]Matt. 24:36, 42 [1]NU omits the rest of v. 13.
14 [a]Luke 19:12–27 [b]Matt. 21:33
15 [a][Rom. 12:6]

25:1–13 This parable illustrates preparedness, or lack of it, **while the bridegroom was delayed** (v. 5). The OT prophets portray the covenant between God and Israel as a marriage covenant. The marriage will finally be consummated when the Bridegroom returns at the end of the age and the righteous form a wedding party to go forth to meet Him. The Bridegroom represents Christ in His Passion, who dies out of love for His Church (Eph. 5:25–27).

That the wise virgins also **slumbered and slept** (v. 5) suggests that once prepared, a person rests as needed. Their refusal to give oil to the foolish ones is not lack of love. It portrays the fact that spiritual preparedness cannot be conveniently given or borrowed. This parable encourages the proper use of God's gifts: to bear fruit. Some interpreters say **lamps** indicate the gift of purity and holiness, and **oil,** works of mercy—the grace of the Holy Spirit. Traditionally, virginity has been considered a special "lamp," and almsgiving or help to the poor a special "oil."

25:14–30 This parable illustrates the use of gifts given by God. A talent was a great sum of money and came to designate a special gift or endowment. The Lord came **after a long time** (v. 19) but exacted full accountability. The **wicked and lazy servant** (v. 26) could not evade responsibility for ignoring his talent. We are stewards of every gift, using each for our own and our neighbor's salvation. Idleness is a renunciation of God's grace, as well as a lack of love for God and humanity. Since people are managers, or stewards, of God's gifts, each of us will give account of how we used the **abundance** (v. 29; see the note on 13:12) of gifts given to us.

Meat Fare Sunday (Sunday of the Last Judgment)

Second Sunday before Lent

25:31–46: Jesus teaches His disciples to be ready for the Judgment by practicing good works.

them, and made another five talents.
17 "And likewise he who *had received* two gained two more also.
18 "But he who had received one went and dug in the ground, and hid his lord's money.
19 "After a long time the lord of those servants came and settled accounts with them.
20 "So he who had received five talents came and brought five other talents, saying, 'Lord, you delivered to me five talents; look, I have gained five more talents besides them.'
21 "His lord said to him, 'Well *done,* good and faithful servant; you were [a]faithful over a few things, [b]I will make you ruler over many things. Enter into [c]the joy of your lord.'
22 "He also who had received two talents came and said, 'Lord, you delivered to me two talents; look, I have gained two more talents besides them.'
23 "His lord said to him, [a]'Well *done,* good and faithful servant; you have been faithful over a few things, I will make you ruler over many things. Enter into [b]the joy of your lord.'
24 "Then he who had received the one talent came and said, 'Lord, I knew you to be a hard man, reaping where you have not sown, and gathering where you have not scattered seed.
25 'And I was afraid, and went and hid your talent in the ground. Look, *there* you have *what is* yours.'
26 "But his lord answered and said to him, 'You [a]wicked and lazy servant, you knew that I reap where I have not sown, and gather where I have not scattered seed.
27 'So you ought to have deposited my money with the bankers, and at my coming I would have received back my own with interest.
28 'Therefore take the talent from him, and give *it* to him who has ten talents.
29 [a]'For to everyone who has, more will be given, and he will have abundance; but from him who does not have, even what he has will be taken away.
30 'And cast the unprofitable servant [a]into the outer darkness. [b]There will be weeping and [c]gnashing of teeth.'

The Judgment of Works

31 [a]"When the Son of Man comes in His glory, and all the [1]holy angels with Him, then He will sit on the throne of His glory.†

21 [a][1 Cor. 4:2] [b][Luke 12:44; 22:29, 30] [c][Heb. 12:2] **23** [a]Matt. 24:45, 47; 25:21 [b][Ps. 16:11]

26 [a]Matt. 18:32 **29** [a]Matt. 13:12 **30** [a]Matt. 8:12; 22:13 [b]Matt. 7:23; 8:12; 24:51 [c]Ps. 112:10 **31** [a][1 Thess. 4:16] [1]NU omits *holy*

25:31–46 Here is the majestic climax of the discourse, which is not simply a parable but an account of the universal judgment. Since the Cross is now near for Him, Jesus raises up the hearer to the sight of the glory of the Son of Man, His judgment seat, and the whole world before Him. He shows the heavens opened and **all the holy angels** (v. 31) present to witness His judgment. For if the first coming of the Son of Man was in humility, to serve and to die, the Second Coming will be in **glory,** as a King to judge **all the nations** (v. 32).

The standard of judgment is uncalculated mercy toward the needy. The works produced by faith are emphasized, for a saving faith produces righteous works. It is possible to fool ourselves about whether we truly believe, but what we do so reflects our true inner state that we will need no other evidence before God's court. The needy are the intimate **brethren** (v. 40) of Christ. **The least of these** (v. 45) may refer primarily to Christian missionaries or to needy Christians and, by extension, all who suffer. Jesus identifies Himself with the poor and the outcast and invites to brotherhood all who are kindled with love for others (1 John 4:20). These are crowned with grace.

Holy Wednesday and Holy Thursday

Wednesday and Thursday before Easter

26:1—27:2: Jesus eats the Last Supper with His disciples and is betrayed.

32 [a]"All the nations will be gathered before Him, and [b]He will separate them one from another, as a
shepherd divides *his* sheep from the
goats.
33 "And He will set the [a]sheep on
His right hand, but the goats on the
left.
34 "Then the King will say to those
on His right hand, 'Come, you
blessed of My Father, [a]inherit the
kingdom [b]prepared for you from the
foundation of the world:
35 [a]'for I was hungry and you gave
Me food; I was thirsty and you gave
Me drink; [b]I was a stranger and you
took Me in;
36 'I *was* [a]naked and you clothed
Me; I was sick and you visited Me;
[b]I was in prison and you came to
Me.'
37 "Then the righteous will answer
Him, saying, 'Lord, when did we see
You hungry and feed *You,* or thirsty
and give *You* drink?
38 'When did we see You a
stranger and take *You* in, or naked
and clothe *You?*
39 'Or when did we see You sick,
or in prison, and come to You?'
40 "And the King will answer and
say to them, 'Assuredly, I say to you,
[a]inasmuch as you did *it* to one of
the least of these My brethren, you
did *it* to Me.'
41 "Then He will also say to those
on the left hand, [a]'Depart from Me,
you cursed, [b]into the everlasting fire
prepared for [c]the devil and his
angels:
42 'for I was hungry and you gave
Me no food; I was thirsty and you
gave Me no drink;
43 'I was a stranger and you did
not take Me in, naked and you did
not clothe Me, sick and in prison and
you did not visit Me.'
44 "Then they also will answer
[1]Him, saying, 'Lord, when did we
see You hungry or thirsty or a
stranger or naked or sick or in
prison, and did not minister to You?'
45 "Then He will answer them,
saying, 'Assuredly, I say to you,
[a]inasmuch as you did not do *it* to
one of the least of these, you did not
do *it* to Me.'
46 "And [a]these will go away into
everlasting punishment, but the
righteous into eternal life."

32 a[2 Cor. 5:10] bEzek. 20:38
33 a[John 10:11, 27, 28]
34 a[Rom. 8:17] bMark 10:40
35 aIs. 58:7 b[Heb. 13:2]
36 a[James 2:15, 16] b2 Tim. 1:16
40 aMark 9:41
41 aMatt. 7:23 bMatt. 13:40, 42 c[2 Pet. 2:4]
44 1NU, M omit *Him*
45 aProv. 14:31
46 a[Dan. 12:2]

CHAPTER 26

2 aLuke 22:1, 2
3 aJohn 11:47 1NU omits *the scribes*
4 aActs 4:25–28 1*deception*
5 aMatt. 21:26

Wednesday: The Sanhedrin's Conspiracy
(Mark 14:1, 2; Luke 22:1, 2)

26 Now it came to pass, when
Jesus had finished all these
sayings, *that* He said to His disciples,
2 [a]"You know that after two days
is the Passover, and the Son of Man
will be delivered up to be crucified."†
3 [a]Then the chief priests, [1]the
scribes, and the elders of the people
assembled at the palace of the high
priest, who was called Caiaphas,
4 and [a]plotted to take Jesus by
[1]trickery and kill *Him.*
5 But they said, "Not during the
feast, lest there be an uproar among
the [a]people."

26:2 Jesus is **delivered up** to His Passion by His accusers, yet He goes willingly. Others, ignorant of their fate, die against their will. Or, if they know they are in danger, they seek to avoid it. Jesus foretells His Passion and approaches it with the joy of knowing its fruit: the Resurrection and our salvation (Heb. 12:2).

Anointing for Burial
(Mark 14:3–9; John 12:1–8)

6 And when Jesus was in [a]Beth-
any at the house of Simon the leper,†
7 a woman came to Him having
an alabaster flask of very costly fragrant oil, and she poured *it* on His
head as He sat *at the table.*
8 [a]But when His disciples saw *it,*
they were indignant, saying, "Why
this waste?
9 "For this fragrant oil might have
been sold for much and given to *the*
poor."
10 But when Jesus was aware of *it,*
He said to them, "Why do you trouble the woman? For she has done a
good work for Me.
11 [a]"For you have the poor with
you always, but [b]Me you do not
have always.
12 "For in pouring this fragrant oil
on My body, she did *it* for My
[a]burial.
13 "Assuredly, I say to you, wherever this gospel is preached in the
whole world, what this woman has
done will also be told as a memorial
to her."†

Judas Betrays Jesus
(Mark 14:10, 11; Luke 23:3–5)

14 [a]Then one of the twelve, called
[b]Judas Iscariot, went to the chief
priests†

6 [a]Matt. 8:2; Mark 14:3–9; Luke 7:37–39; John 11:1, 2; 12:1–8
8 [a]John 12:4
11 [a][Deut. 15:11; Mark 14:7]; John 12:8 [b][Matt. 18:20; 28:20; John 13:33; 14:19; 16:5, 28; 17:11]
12 [a]Matt. 27:60; Luke 23:53; John 19:38–42
14 [a]Mark 14:10, 11; Luke 22:3–6; John 13:2, 30 [b]Matt. 10:4
15 [a]Ex. 21:32; Zech. 11:12; Matt. 27:3
17 [a]Ex. 12:6, 18–20
18 [a]Luke 9:51; John 12:23; 13:1; 17:1
20 [a]Mark 14:17–21; Luke 22:14; John 13:21
21 [a]Matt. 26:46; Mark 14:42; Luke 22:21–23; John 6:70, 71; 13:21
23 [a]Ps. 41:9; Luke 22:21; John 13:18

15 and said, [a]"What are you willing to give me if I deliver Him to
you?" And they counted out to him
thirty pieces of silver.
16 So from that time he sought opportunity to betray Him.

Thursday: The Passover Meal
(Mark 14:12–21; Luke 22:7–16, 21–30; John 13:21–30)

17 [a]Now on the first *day of the Feast*
of Unleavened Bread the disciples
came to Jesus, saying to Him,
"Where do You want us to prepare
for You to eat the Passover?"†
18 And He said, "Go into the city
to a certain man, and say to him,
'The Teacher says, [a]"My time is at
hand; I will keep the Passover at
your house with My disciples." ' "
19 So the disciples did as Jesus had
directed them; and they prepared the
Passover.
20 [a]When evening had come, He
sat down with the twelve.
21 Now as they were eating, He
said, "Assuredly, I say to you, one
of you will [a]betray Me."
22 And they were exceedingly sorrowful, and each of them began to
say to Him, "Lord, is it I?"
23 He answered and said, [a]"He
who dipped *his* hand with Me in the
dish will betray Me.
24 "The Son of Man indeed goes

26:6–13 Should we give to charity or to the Church building fund? What specifically is to be done with our personal funds and the Church's money is not resolved here; but Christ establishes that a believer's gift of his very best to honor and glorify the Person of Christ is just as worthy as giving to **the poor** (v. 9). The material richness of Orthodox worship—the gold censers, elaborate vestments, grand iconostases—is our equivalent of anointing Christ with **very costly fragrant oil** (v. 7).

26:6 Simon the leper must have been healed by Jesus earlier, for lepers were forbidden to live in towns.

26:13 Because of her fervent faith, Jesus promises perpetual public memory of **this woman.** She is probably not the harlot of Luke 7 but Mary, the sister of Martha, as identified in John 12.

26:14–16 Judas on his own initiative seeks to betray Jesus, apparently out of greed. The Scriptures foretold the exact wages of betrayal, the price of our Lord's Crucifixion: **And they counted out to him thirty pieces of silver** (Zech. 11:12).

26:17–19 The **Passover** commemorates God's deliverance of Israel from slavery in Egypt to the Land of Promise. It prefigures the Passion of Christ, the new Passover, God's redemption of all humanity from sin and death to the promised Kingdom. **The first day of the Feast** is Thursday of Holy Week. Whether this was Passover or the day before Passover is debated. What is certain is that Jesus regarded the Thursday evening meal as the Passover meal for Himself and His disciples.

just [a]as it is written of Him, but
[b]woe to that man by whom the Son
of Man is betrayed! [c]It would have
been good for that man if he had not
been born."†
25 **Then Judas, who was betraying
Him, answered and said, "Rabbi, is
it I?" He said to him,** "You have said
it."

Institution of the Eucharist

(Mark 14:22–26; Luke 22:15–20)

26 **[a]And as they were eating,
[b]Jesus took bread, [1]blessed and
broke *it*, and gave *it* to the disciples
and said,** "Take, eat; [c]this is My
body."†
27 **Then He took the cup, and gave
thanks, and gave *it* to them, saying,**
[a]"Drink from it, all of you.
28 "For [a]this is My blood [b]of the
[1]new covenant, which is shed
[c]for many for the [2]remission of sins.
29 "But [a]I say to you, I will not
drink of this fruit of the vine from
now on [b]until that day when I drink
it new with you in My Father's
kingdom."†
30 **[a]And when they had sung a
hymn, they went out to the Mount
of Olives.**

Prediction of Peter's Denial

(Mark 14:27–31; Luke 22:31–38; John 13:36–38)

31 **Then Jesus said to them,** [a]"All
of you will [b]be [1]made to stumble be-

24 [a]1 Cor. 15:3 [b]Luke 17:1 [c]John 17:12
26 [a]Mark 14:22–25 [b]1 Cor. 11:23–25 [c][1 Pet. 2:24] [1]M *gave thanks for*
27 [a]Mark 14:23
28 [a][Ex. 24:8] [b]Jer. 31:31 [c]Matt. 20:28 [1]NU omits *new* [2]*forgiveness*
29 [a]Mark 14:25 [b]Acts 10:41
30 [a]Mark 14:26–31
31 [a]John 16:32 [b][Matt. 11:6] [c]Zech. 13:7 [1]*caused to take offense at Me*
32 [a]Matt. 28:7, 10, 16
33 [1]*caused to take offense at You*
34 [a]John 13:38
36 [a]Mark 14:32–35
37 [a]Matt. 4:21; 17:1
38 [a]John 12:27
39 [a][Heb. 5:7–9] [b]John 12:27 [c]Matt. 20:22

cause of Me this night, for it is
written:

[c]'I will strike the Shepherd,
And the sheep of the flock will
be scattered.'

32 "But after I have been raised,
[a]I will go before you to Galilee."
33 **Peter answered and said to
Him, "Even if all are [1]made to stumble because of You, I will never be
made to stumble."**
34 **Jesus said to him,** [a]"Assuredly,
I say to you that this night, before
the rooster crows, you will deny Me
three times."
35 **Peter said to Him, "Even if I
have to die with You, I will not deny
You!" And so said all the disciples.**

Gethsemane: Jesus' Prayers

(Mark 14:32–42; Luke 22:39–46; John 18:1)

36 **[a]Then Jesus came with them to
a place called Gethsemane, and said
to the disciples,** "Sit here while I go
and pray over there."
37 **And He took with Him Peter
and [a]the two sons of Zebedee, and
He began to be sorrowful and deeply
distressed.**
38 **Then He said to them,** [a]"My
soul is exceedingly sorrowful, even
to death. Stay here and watch with
Me."
39 **He went a little farther and fell
on His face, and [a]prayed, saying,**
[b]"O My Father, if it is possible,
[c]let this cup pass from Me; neverthe-

26:24, 25 It is written of Him does not cancel Judas's responsibility. God foresees, but does not cause, the evil actions of humans, who always have free will. Jesus does not expressly accuse Judas, but He does let Judas disclose his own guilt. Not even this, however, brings Judas to his senses.

26:26–28 Jesus institutes the Eucharist, the long-awaited messianic banquet, to which He admits even Judas, seeking by all means to save him. These words are repeated in the Divine Liturgy at the invitation of Christ to receive His **body** and **blood.** Thus it is clear we are invited to a feast, to the Last Supper, at which we become truly united to Christ. He **gave thanks** (v. 27) to teach us (1) how we should celebrate this sacrament, (2) that He comes willingly to His Passion, and (3) whatever we may suffer, to bear it as He did: thankfully.

The Old Covenant was sealed with the blood of bulls and goats. The New is sealed by the gift of Christ, who **shed** His own **blood** (v. 28) to reconcile us with God and reunite us to Himself. He calls it the **blood of the new covenant,** that is, God's promise, the new Law. By *new* He means we now have immortal and incorruptible Life. **For many** is a Semitic idiom meaning "for all."

26:29 Jesus Himself drinks of the cup, His own blood, in order to lead the disciples into

(continued on next page)

less, [d]not as I will, but as You *will*."†
40 Then He came to the disciples
and found them sleeping, and said
to Peter, "What? Could you not
watch with Me one hour?
41 [a]"Watch and pray, lest you enter into temptation. [b]The spirit indeed *is* willing, but the flesh *is*
weak."†
42 Again, a second time, He went
away and prayed, saying, "O My Father, [1]if this cup cannot pass away
from Me unless I drink it, Your will
be done."
43 And He came and found them
asleep again, for their eyes were
heavy.
44 So He left them, went away
again, and prayed the third time,
saying the same words.
45 Then He came to His disciples
and said to them, "Are *you* still
sleeping and resting? Behold, the
hour [1]is at hand, and the Son of Man
is being [a]betrayed into the hands of
sinners.
46 "Rise, let us be going. See, My
betrayer is at hand."

Betrayed, Arrested, Forsaken

(Mark 14:43–52; Luke 22:47–53;
John 18:2–12)

47 And [a]while He was still speaking, behold, Judas, one of the
twelve, with a great multitude with
swords and clubs, came from the
chief priests and elders of the people.
48 Now His betrayer had given
them a sign, saying, "Whomever I kiss, He is the One; seize
Him."
49 Immediately he went up to Jesus and said, "Greetings, Rabbi!"
[a]and kissed Him.
50 But Jesus said to him, [a]"Friend,
why have you come?" Then they
came and laid hands on Jesus and
took Him.
51 And suddenly, [a]one of those
who were with Jesus stretched out *his*
hand and drew his sword, struck the
servant of the high priest, and cut
off his ear.
52 But Jesus said to him, "Put your
sword in its place, [a]for all who take
the sword will [1]perish by the
sword.†
53 "Or do you think that I cannot
now pray to My Father, and He will
provide Me with [a]more than twelve
legions of angels?†
54 "How then could the Scriptures
be fulfilled, [a]that it must happen
thus?"†
55 In that hour Jesus said to the
multitudes, "Have you come out, as
against a robber, with swords and
clubs to take Me? I sat daily with

39 [d]John 5:30; 6:38
41 [a]Luke 22:40, 46 [b][Gal. 5:17]
42 [1]NU *if this may not pass away unless*
45 [a]Matt. 17:22, 23; 20:18, 19 [1]*has drawn near*
47 [a]Acts 1:16
49 [a]2 Sam. 20:9
50 [a]Ps. 41:9; 55:13
51 [a]John 18:10
52 [a]Rev. 13:10 [1]M *die*
53 [a]Dan. 7:10
54 [a]Is. 50:6; 53:2–11

(continued from previous page)
participation in the heavenly mysteries. **In My Father's kingdom** relates the Eucharist to the age to come, for the Last Supper inaugurates the future messianic banquet.

26:39 According to His divine nature, Jesus knows He must drink the cup. As man, He wishes the chalice to pass, for it is a mark of humanity to abhor death and struggle against it. He prays **if . . . possible** the suffering be taken from Him. Thus, He gives abundant proof that His flesh is true flesh, but without sin. Though Jesus' body is the temple of His divinity, we do not attribute to His divinity the properties of the humanity united to it: the Passion, the suffering and death.

26:41 **Watch and pray** is a key to Christian spirituality and our struggle against temptations. Hereby Jesus' soul is strengthened and He faces death courageously. For, while the divine will of the Father and the Son is one, the Lord becomes obedient to the Father in His humanity. In contrast to Jesus' vigilance, His disciples sleep. Since body and soul are united, the **spirit** is paralyzed by a lethargic body. A **willing** *spirit,* recognizing the weakness of the **flesh,** knows it needs God's presence and power. True faith is nourished by ardent, vigilant prayer.

26:52 Jesus rebukes Peter (identified in John 18:10) severely for using the **sword** and then heals the servant of the high priest, showing at once His patient forbearance and His great power.

26:53 A **legion** is 6,000 soldiers. Thus, the One who heals is the One who can also call for an army of 72,000 **angels!** But He does nothing of the kind. He goes to His Passion voluntarily.

26:54 By saying that **the Scriptures** must **be fulfilled** Jesus quenches the Apostles' anger, indicating what is happening is proper because it is in accordance with *the Scriptures*.

you, teaching in the temple, and you
did not seize Me.
56 "But all this was done that the
[a]Scriptures of the prophets might be
fulfilled." Then [b]all the disciples forsook Him and fled.

Before Caiaphas and the Sanhedrin
(Mark 14:53–65; Luke 22:54, 63–65;
John 18:13–24)

57 [a]And those who had laid hold
of Jesus led *Him* away to Caiaphas
the high priest, where the scribes
and the elders were assembled.
58 But [a]Peter followed Him at a
distance to the high priest's courtyard. And he went in and sat with
the servants to see the end.
59 Now the chief priests, [1]the elders, and all the council sought
[a]false testimony against Jesus to put
Him to death,
60 [1]but found none. Even though
[a]many false witnesses came forward,
they found none. But at last [b]two
[2]false witnesses came forward
61 and said, "This *fellow* said,
[a]'I am able to destroy the temple of
God and to build it in three days.' "†
62 [a]And the high priest arose and
said to Him, "Do You answer nothing? What *is it* these men testify
against You?"
63 But [a]Jesus kept silent. And the
high priest answered and said to
Him, [b]"I put You under oath by the
living God: Tell us if You are the
Christ, the Son of God!"
64 Jesus said to him, *"It is as* you
said. Nevertheless, I say to you,
[a]hereafter you will see the Son of
Man [b]sitting at the right hand of the
Power, and coming on the clouds of
heaven."†

56 [a]Lam. 4:20 [b]John 18:15
57 [a]John 18:12, 19–24
58 [a]John 18:15, 16
59 [a]Ps. 35:11 [1]NU omits *the elders*
60 [a]Mark 14:55 [b]Deut. 19:15 [1]NU *but found none, even though many false witnesses came forward.* [2]NU omits *false witnesses*
61 [a]John 2:19
62 [a]Mark 14:60
63 [a]Is. 53:7 [b]Lev. 5:1
64 [a]Dan. 7:13 [b][Acts 7:55]
65 [a]2 Kin. 18:37 [b]John 10:30–36
66 [a]Lev. 24:16
67 [a]Is. 50:6; 53:3 [b]Luke 22:63–65 [1]Or *rods,*
68 [a]Mark 14:65
69 [a]John 18:16–18, 25–27
73 [a]Luke 22:59
74 [a]Mark 14:71 [1]*call down curses* [2]Swear oaths
75 [a]Matt. 26:34

65 [a]Then the high priest tore his
clothes, saying, "He has spoken
blasphemy! What further need do we
have of witnesses? Look, now you
have heard His [b]blasphemy!
66 "What do you think?" They answered and said, [a]"He is deserving
of death."
67 [a]Then they spat in His face and
beat Him; and [b]others struck *Him*
with [1]the palms of their hands,
68 saying, [a]"Prophesy to us,
Christ! Who is the one who struck
You?"

Peter's Three Denials
(Mark 14:54, 66–72; Luke 22:54–62; John
18:15–18, 25–27)

69 [a]Now Peter sat outside in the
courtyard. And a servant girl came
to him, saying, "You also were with
Jesus of Galilee."
70 But he denied it before *them* all,
saying, "I do not know what you are
saying."
71 And when he had gone out to
the gateway, another *girl* saw him
and said to those *who were* there,
"This *fellow* also was with Jesus of
Nazareth."
72 But again he denied with an
oath, "I do not know the Man!"
73 And a little later those who
stood by came up and said to Peter,
"Surely you also are *one* of them, for
your [a]speech betrays you."
74 Then [a]he began to [1]curse and
[2]swear, *saying,* "I do not know the
Man!" Immediately a rooster
crowed.
75 And Peter remembered the
word of Jesus who had said to him,
[a]"Before the rooster crows, you will

26:61 The people misunderstand Jesus' words reported in John 2:19. Some Jews believed the temple would be destroyed and a new one rebuilt by the Messiah.

26:64–66 Quoting from Ps. 110 and the prophecy of Daniel (Dan. 7:13), Jesus confesses He is the Messiah, both fully man, indeed, the **Son of Man,** and fully God—for only God can sit **at the right hand of the Power,** sharing the authority of the Father. Jesus also proclaims He will yet establish the Kingdom of God in its fullness, coming in His glory on the **clouds of heaven.** His claim to be God is the real reason the high priest sentences Him to die (vv. 65, 66). Jesus' statement is befitting His divinity, but the high priest can neither comprehend nor endure such a thing.

Vespers of Great and Holy Friday *Friday before Easter*

27:1–61: Jesus is condemned, crucified, and buried.

deny Me three times." So he went
out and wept bitterly.†

Friday: The Sanhedrin Delivers Jesus to Pilate
(Mark 15:1; Luke 22:66—23:1)

27 When morning came, [a]all the
chief priests and elders of the
people plotted against Jesus to put
Him to death.
2 And when they had bound
Him, they led Him away and [a]deliv-
ered Him to [1]Pontius Pilate the
governor.†

The Death of Judas

3 [a]Then Judas, His betrayer, seeing that He had been condemned,
was remorseful and brought back the
thirty [b]pieces of silver to the chief
priests and elders,†
4 saying, "I have sinned by betraying innocent blood." And they
said, "What *is that* to us? You see *to
it!*"
5 Then he threw down the pieces
of silver in the temple and
[a]departed, and went and hanged
himself.
6 But the chief priests took the silver pieces and said, "It is not lawful
to put them into the treasury, because they are the price of blood."
7 And they consulted together
and bought with them the potter's
field, to bury strangers in.
8 Therefore that field has been
called [a]the Field of Blood to this day.
9 Then was fulfilled what was
spoken by Jeremiah the prophet,
saying, [a]*"And they took the thirty
pieces of silver, the value of Him
who was priced,* whom they of the
children of Israel priced,
10 *"and [a]gave them for the potter's
field, as the LORD directed me."*

"King of the Jews"
(Mark 15:1–5; Luke 23:1–7; John 18:28–38)

11 Now Jesus stood before the governor. [a]And the governor asked
Him, saying, "Are You the King of
the Jews?" Jesus said to him, [b]*"It is
as* you say."†
12 And while He was being accused by the chief priests and elders,
[a]He answered nothing.
13 Then Pilate said to Him, [a]"Do
You not hear how many things they
testify against You?"
14 But He answered him not one
word, so that the governor marveled
greatly.

Pilate Barters over Barabbas
(Mark 15:6–15; Luke 23:13–25; John 18:39, 40)

15 [a]Now at the feast the governor
was accustomed to releasing to the

CHAPTER 27
1 [a]Ps. 2:2; Mark 15:1; Luke 22:66; 23:1; John 18:28
2 [a]Matt. 20:19; Luke 18:32; Acts 3:13
[1]NU omits *Pontius*
3 [a]Matt. 26:14
[b]Matt. 26:15
5 [a]2 Sam. 17:23; Matt. 18:7; 26:24; John 17:12; Acts 1:18
8 [a]Acts 1:19
9 [a]Zech. 11:12
10 [a]Jer. 32:6–9; Zech. 11:12, 13
11 [a]Mark 15:2–5; Luke 23:2, 3; John 18:29–38
[b]John 18:37; 1 Tim. 6:13
12 [a]Ps. 38:13, 14; Matt. 26:63; John 19:9
13 [a]Matt. 26:62; John 19:10
15 [a]Mark 15:6–15; Luke 23:17–25; John 18:39—19:16

26:75 What is the proper response after sinning severely? Peter **wept bitterly,** beginning a process of repentance, confession, forgiveness, reconciliation and renewal (see notes on Luke 22:31, 32; John 21:15–19). "A broken and a contrite heart—these, O God, You will not despise" (Ps. 51:17).

27:2 Under Roman law, only **the governor** had authority to pronounce the death sentence.

27:3 Judas is **remorseful** but not repentant—a sharp contrast to Peter's sorrow after his denials. Two accounts of Judas's death are given, here and in Acts 1:16–19.

27:11–14 The Jews hide their real charge against Jesus, that Jesus claimed to be God (which did not concern the Romans), behind the political threat that He is **King of the Jews,** which would be a direct attack on Roman rule.

multitude one prisoner whom they
wished.
16 And at that time they had a notorious prisoner called [1]Barabbas.†
17 Therefore, when they had gathered together, Pilate said to them,
"Whom do you want me to release
to you? Barabbas, or Jesus who is
called Christ?"
18 For he knew that they had
handed Him over because of [a]envy.
19 While he was sitting on the
judgment seat, his wife sent to him,
saying, "Have nothing to do with
that just Man, for I have suffered
many things today in a dream because of Him."†
20 [a]But the chief priests and elders
persuaded the multitudes that they
should ask for Barabbas and destroy
Jesus.
21 The governor answered and
said to them, "Which of the two do
you want me to release to you?"
They said, [a]"Barabbas!"
22 Pilate said to them, "What then
shall I do with Jesus who is called
Christ?" *They* all said to him, "Let
Him be crucified!"
23 Then the governor said, [a]"Why,
what evil has He done?" But they
cried out all the more, saying, "Let
Him be crucified!"
24 When Pilate saw that he could
not prevail at all, but rather *that* a
[1]tumult was rising, he [a]took water
and washed *his* hands before the
multitude, saying, "I am innocent of
the blood of this [2]just Person. You
see *to it*."

16 [1]NU *Jesus Barabbas*
18 [a]Matt. 21:38
20 [a]Acts 3:14
21 [a]Acts 3:14
23 [a]Acts 3:13
24 [a]Deut. 21:6–8
[1]*an uproar*
[2]NU omits *just*
25 [a]Josh. 2:19
26 [a][Is. 50:6; 53:5]
[1]*flogged* with a Roman scourge
27 [a]Mark 15:16–20
[1]The governor's headquarters
[2]*cohort*
28 [a]John 19:2
[b]Luke 23:11
29 [a]Is. 53:3
[1]Lit. *woven*
30 [a]Matt. 26:67
31 [a]Is. 53:7
32 [a]Heb. 13:12
[b]Mark 15:21

25 And all the people answered
and said, [a]"His blood *be* on us and
on our children."†
26 Then he released Barabbas to
them; and when [a]he had [1]scourged
Jesus, he delivered *Him* to be
crucified.

Soldiers Mock Jesus as King
(Mark 15:16–20)

27 [a]Then the soldiers of the governor took Jesus into the [1]Praetorium
and gathered the whole [2]garrison
around Him.†
28 And they [a]stripped Him and
[b]put a scarlet robe on Him.†
29 [a]When they had [1]twisted a
crown of thorns, they put *it* on His
head, and a reed in His right hand.
And they bowed the knee before
Him and mocked Him, saying,
"Hail, King of the Jews!"
30 Then [a]they spat on Him, and
took the reed and struck Him on the
head.
31 And when they had mocked
Him, they took the robe off Him, put
His *own* clothes on Him, [a]and led
Him away to be crucified.

The Crucifixion
(Mark 15:20–32; Luke 23:26–43; John 19:16–27)

32 [a]Now as they came out, [b]they
found a man of Cyrene, Simon by

27:16 Barabbas, a popular rebel against the Romans, means "Son of Abbas." In Aramaic it sounds like "Son of the Father," who is Jesus.

27:19 Pilate is moved on Jesus' behalf. It is not that he knows who is being judged, but he fears his wife's **dream** which has been reported to him.

27:25 This verse is never to be used as a justification for persecuting Jews. The Jews were elected to represent all, and **His blood** is on us all. In the OT, the shedding of innocent blood is avenged by God. In the history of Israel, this curse was foreshadowed by the cursing of the fig tree (21:18, 19; Mark 11:12–14) and fulfilled by the destruction of Jerusalem in A.D. 70 (24:2).

27:27 The **Praetorium** was the governor's residence.

27:28–31 Every king is proclaimed by his soldiers. Thus it is fitting that Jesus should be crowned by the soldiers, although they are unaware of what they are doing. His **crown** (v. 29) of mockery shows Him "despised and rejected by men" (Is. 53:3) and thus the One who bears "the iniquity of us all" (Is. 53:6). Jesus is clothed in **scarlet** (Mark 15:17 and John 19:2 have "purple"), representing both His royalty and the sins of humanity which He has taken upon Himself (see Is. 1:18). That the Son of God would so humble Himself to release us from our sin and death should melt even a heart of stone.

name. Him they compelled to bear
His cross.†
33 [a]And when they had come to a
place called Golgotha, that is to say,
Place of a Skull,
34 [a]they gave Him [1]sour wine mingled with gall to drink. But when He
had tasted *it,* He would not drink.
35 [a]Then they crucified Him, and
divided His garments, casting lots,
[1]that it might be fulfilled which was
spoken by the prophet:

[b]"They divided My garments
among them,
And for My clothing they cast
lots."

36 [a]Sitting down, they kept watch
over Him there.
37 And they [a]put up over His head
the accusation written against Him:

THIS IS JESUS
THE KING OF THE JEWS.

38 [a]Then two robbers were crucified with Him, one on the right and
another on the left.
39 And [a]those who passed by blasphemed Him, wagging their heads
40 and saying, [a]"You who destroy
the temple and build *it* in three days,
save Yourself! [b]If You are the Son
of God, come down from the cross."
41 Likewise the chief priests also,
mocking with the [1]scribes and elders, said,

33 [a]John 19:17
34 [a]Ps. 69:21 [1]NU omits *sour*
35 [a]Luke 23:34 [b]Ps. 22:18 [1]NU, M omit the rest of v. 35.
36 [a]Matt. 27:54
37 [a]John 19:19
38 [a]Is. 53:9, 12
39 [a]Mark 15:29
40 [a]John 2:19 [b]Matt. 26:63
41 [1]M *scribes, the Pharisees, and the elders*
42 [a][John 3:14, 15] [1]NU omits *If* [2]NU, M *in Him*
43 [a]Ps. 22:8
44 [a]Luke 23:39–43
45 [a]Mark 15:33–41
46 [a][Heb. 5:7] [b]Ps. 22:1
48 [a]Ps. 69:21
50 [a]Luke 23:46 [b][John 10:18]

42 "He [a]saved others; Himself He
cannot save. [1]If He is the King of Israel, let Him now come down from
the cross, and we will believe [2]Him.
43 [a]"He trusted in God; let Him
deliver Him now if He will have
Him; for He said, 'I am the Son of
God.' "
44 [a]Even the robbers who were
crucified with Him reviled Him with
the same thing.

The Death of Jesus

(Mark 15:33–41; Luke 23:44–49; John 19:28–30)

45 [a]Now from the sixth hour until
the ninth hour there was darkness
over all the land.†
46 And about the ninth hour
[a]Jesus cried out with a loud voice,
saying, "Eli, Eli, lama sabachthani?"
that is, *[b]"My God, My God, why*
have You forsaken Me?"†
47 Some of those who stood there,
when they heard *that,* said, "This
Man is calling for Elijah!"
48 Immediately one of them ran
and took a sponge, [a]filled *it* with
sour wine and put *it* on a reed, and
offered it to Him to drink.
49 The rest said, "Let Him alone;
let us see if Elijah will come to save
Him."
50 And Jesus [a]cried out again with
a loud voice, and [b]yielded up His
spirit.†

27:32–44 Jesus endures the weakness of our body in His own body on the Cross to take upon Himself our sufferings. This He does by the reality of the union of His divine nature and human nature in the One Son of God. His humanity is indeed our very humanity. He endures pain, is struck, tortured and crucified: He is wounded on account of our sins (Is. 53:5). And though He has no sin, He Himself was made to be sin for us, that through His flesh He might condemn sin in the flesh (Rom. 8:3; 2 Cor. 5:21; Heb. 2:9).

27:45–56 The details of His Crucifixion were written in the OT, "It shall come to pass in that day that there will be no light; the lights will diminish. It shall be one day which is known to the LORD—neither day nor night. But at evening time it shall happen that it will be light" (Zech. 14:6, 7; see also Amos 8:9).

27:46 Jesus repeats a passage from Ps. 22, which corresponds exactly to the Crucifixion. Taken by itself, without any consideration of what follows, His cry of **My God, My God, why have You forsaken Me?** could be interpreted as an expression of despair. Since He appropriated our nature, Jesus experiences true separation from God in His humanity, knowing suffering and distress, and yet He does not despair. He speaks these words in the name of humanity, to put an end to the alienation of man from God. For as God He is never forsaken by the Father. With this cry humanity is accepted and saved.

27:50 **Yielded up His spirit** shows His death was a voluntary separation of the soul from the body, yet both remain in a binding relationship with His divine nature.

Matins of Holy Saturday

Saturday before Easter

27:62–66: Pilate agrees to set a guard at Jesus' tomb.

51 Then, behold, [a]the veil of the
temple was torn in two from top to
bottom; and the earth quaked, and
the rocks were split,†
52 and the graves were opened;
and many bodies of the saints who
had fallen asleep were raised;†
53 and coming out of the graves after His resurrection, they went into
the holy city and appeared to many.
54 [a]So when the centurion and
those with him, who were guarding
Jesus, saw the earthquake and the
things that had happened, they
feared greatly, saying, [b]"Truly this
was the Son of God!"†
55 And many women [a]who followed Jesus from Galilee, ministering to Him, were there looking on
from afar,
56 [a]among whom were Mary Magdalene, Mary the mother of James
and [1]Joses, and the mother of Zebedee's sons.†

The Burial of Jesus

(Mark 15:42–46; Luke 23:50–56; John 19:38–42)

57 Now [a]when evening had come,
there came a rich man from Arimathea, named Joseph, who himself
had also become a disciple of Jesus.†
58 This man went to Pilate and
asked for the body of Jesus. Then
Pilate commanded the body to be
given to him.
59 When Joseph had taken the
body, he wrapped it in a clean linen
cloth,
60 and [a]laid it in his new tomb
which he had hewn out of the rock;
and he rolled a large stone against
the door of the tomb, and departed.†
61 And Mary Magdalene was
there, and the other Mary, sitting
[1]opposite the tomb.

51 [a]Ex. 26:31; 2 Chr. 3:14; Zech. 11:10; Mark 15:38; Luke 23:45; Heb. 9:3
54 [a]Mark 15:39; Luke 23:47 [b]Matt. 14:33
55 [a]Mark 15:41; Luke 8:2, 3
56 [a]Matt. 28:1; Mark 15:40, 47; 16:9; Luke 8:2; John 19:25; 20:1, 18 [1]NU *Joseph*
57 [a]Mark 15:42–47; Luke 23:50–56; John 19:38–42
60 [a]Is. 53:9; Matt. 26:12
61 [1]*in front of*
63 [a]Matt. 16:21; 17:23; 20:19; 26:61; Mark 8:31; 10:34; Luke 9:22; 13:33; 24:6, 7; John 2:19
64 [1]NU omits *by night*

Saturday: Guards at the Tomb

62 On the next day, which followed the Day of Preparation, the
chief priests and Pharisees gathered
together to Pilate,
63 saying, "Sir, we remember,
while He was still alive, how that deceiver said, [a]'After three days I will
rise.'
64 "Therefore command that the
tomb be made secure until the third
day, lest His disciples come [1]by night
and steal Him *away*, and say to the

27:51 The **veil** or curtain that separated the Most Holy Place from the rest of the temple was a symbol of the separation between God and man. Christ's death opens the way into the presence of God for all people. Because His flesh, the true veil (Heb. 10:20), is dishonored, the figurative veil of the temple is **torn in two.** The **rocks were split,** because He is the "spiritual Rock" (1 Cor. 10:4).

27:52, 53 The completeness and scope of the salvation won by Christ are signified in the resurrection of **the saints,** the righteous of the OT. Considering this, no one ever need wonder whether the OT saints are also saved. The **holy city** (v. 53) where the saints appeared is an icon of the heavenly Jerusalem (Heb. 11:10; 12:22, 23; 13:14; Rev. 3:12; 21:2—22:5).

27:54 The **centurion,** a Gentile, realizes Jesus has dominion over nature, and therefore acknowledges He is **the Son of God**—something the Jews were unwilling to do. Tradition knows this soldier as St. Longinos.

27:56 Mary the mother of James and Joses is not to be confused with Mary the mother of Jesus; Jesus is never called "Joses" in the Bible.

27:57, 58 To ask for **the body of Jesus** for burial is a bold public act even for this influential and wealthy man.

27:60 He is buried in a **new tomb,** so that no suspicion might later arise that another had risen instead of Christ.

people, 'He has risen from the dead.'
So the last deception will be worse
than the first."
65 Pilate said to them, "You have
a guard; go your way, make *it* as secure as you know how."
66 So they went and made the
tomb secure, [a]sealing the stone and
setting the guard.

Sunday: Christ Is Risen
(Mark 16:1–8; Luke 24:1–12; John 20:1–10)

28 Now [a]after the Sabbath, as
the first *day* of the week began
to dawn, Mary Magdalene [b]and the
other Mary came to see the tomb.
2 And behold, there was a great
earthquake; for [a]an angel of the Lord
descended from heaven, and came
and rolled back the stone [1]from the
door, and sat on it.†
3 [a]His countenance was like lightning, and his clothing as white as
snow.
4 And the guards shook for fear
of him, and became like [a]dead *men*.
5 But the angel answered and said
to the women, "Do not be afraid, for
I know that you seek Jesus who was
crucified.†
6 "He is not here; for He is risen,
[a]as He said. Come, see the place
where the Lord lay.
7 "And go quickly and tell His
disciples that He is risen from the
dead, and indeed [a]He is going before
you into Galilee; there you will see
Him. Behold, I have told you."
8 So they went out quickly from
the tomb with fear and great joy, and
ran to bring His disciples word.

Jesus Appears to the Women

9 And [1]as they went to tell His
disciples, behold, [a]Jesus met them,
saying, "Rejoice!" So they came and
held Him by the feet and worshiped
Him.†
10 Then Jesus said to them, "Do
not be afraid. Go *and* tell [a]My brethren to go to Galilee, and there they
will see Me."

Deceit of Jewish Authorities

11 Now while they were going, behold, some of the guard came into
the city and reported to the chief
priests all the things that had
happened.
12 When they had assembled with
the elders and consulted together,
they gave a large sum of money to
the soldiers,
13 saying, "Tell them, 'His disciples came at night and stole Him
away while we slept.'
14 "And if this comes to the governor's ears, we will appease him and
make you secure."
15 So they took the money and did
as they were instructed; and this saying is commonly reported among the
Jews until this day.

The Great Commission
(Mark 16:14–18; Luke 24:44–49)

16 Then the eleven disciples went
away into Galilee, to the mountain
[a]which Jesus had appointed for
them.
17 When they saw Him, they worshiped Him; but some [a]doubted.
18 And Jesus came and spoke to
them, saying, [a]"All authority has
been given to Me in heaven and on
earth.†
19 [a]"Go [1]therefore and [b]make disciples of all the nations, baptizing

66 [a]Dan. 6:17

CHAPTER 28

1 [a]Luke 24:1–10 [b]Matt. 27:56, 61
2 [a]Mark 16:5 [1]NU omits *from the door*
3 [a]Dan. 7:9; 10:6
4 [a]Rev. 1:17
6 [a]Matt. 12:40; 16:21; 17:23; 20:19
7 [a]Mark 16:7
9 [a]John 20:14 [1]NU omits *as they went to tell His disciples*
10 [a]John 20:17
16 [a]Matt. 26:32; 28:7, 10
17 [a]John 20:24–29
18 [a][Dan. 7:13, 14]
19 [a]Mark 16:15 [b]Luke 24:47 [1]M omits *therefore*

28:2 The **earthquake** is a sign of Jesus' great victory over death, pointing to the general resurrection. Neither the earthquake nor the moving of **the stone** expedites Jesus' Resurrection; they are signs for the benefit of the women and the soldiers.

28:5 The two **women** are the first witnesses to the most amazing event in all history: the empty tomb, the first firm evidence of the Resurrection.

28:9 **Rejoice** is the first word of the risen Christ, a common greeting here filled with great blessing.

28:18 This is the terminology of exaltation and glorification. It manifests the power of His Resurrection, and the **authority** to bring human beings back to life.

them in the name of the Father and of the Son and of the Holy Spirit,†
20 [a]"teaching them to observe all things that I have commanded you; and lo, I am [b]with you always, *even* to the end of the age." [1]Amen.†

20 [a][Acts 2:42] [b][Acts 4:31; 18:10; 23:11]

[1]NU omits *Amen*

28:19 If we observe this context for the Lord's command to **make disciples of all the nations** and to baptize them **in the name of the Father and of the Son and of the Holy Spirit,** we see that making disciples cannot be done in the strength of man, but only in the power of God. The reality of the Resurrection refers not only to its historicity, apostolic witness, and necessity for faith, but also to its power in our Christian life and mission. The resurrected Son of God, living in us and energizing us, makes possible the salvation of all.

28:20 By saying He is **with you always,** Jesus means His Resurrection is neither of the past, nor of the future. It is always present in our lives through the Holy Spirit. We know Him directly, here and now, in the present, as our Savior and our Friend. **To the end of the age** does not by any means imply that we are to be separated from Him after that great consummation. He is with us now, and ever, and unto the ages of ages. **Amen.**

The Gospel According to

ST. MARK

Author: *St. Mark the Apostle*

Date: *A.D. 65–70*

Theme: *Jesus Christ as Servant and Sacrifice*

AUTHOR: Mark the Apostle, also known as John Mark, is widely attested by the ancient Church as the author of this Gospel. Some early writers suggest that the young man in the linen wrap (14:51, 52) is Mark himself. His mother's house was a meeting place for Christians in Jerusalem (Acts 12:12). Paul and Barnabas took John Mark with them to Antioch when they returned from the Jerusalem famine relief effort (Acts 12:25). He briefly assisted Paul and Barnabas on their first missionary journey (Acts 13:5), departed from them (Acts 13:13), then helped Barnabas (Acts 15:37–39; see Col. 4:10, 11), and eventually was reconciled to Paul (Philem. 24). Later he also aided Peter (1 Pet. 5:13) and, according to tradition, subsequently used Peter's teaching as his primary source for this Gospel, adding to it his personal experience and other Church traditions.

DATE: As with the other Gospels, the exact date of writing is uncertain. Because of its connection with Rome and its lack of any clear reference to the destruction of Jerusalem (13:2), the Gospel of Mark may be dated shortly before the fall of Jerusalem in A.D. 70. Many believe this was the first of the four Gospels to be written.

MAJOR THEME: Jesus Christ as Servant and Sacrifice. Subthemes in the book include:

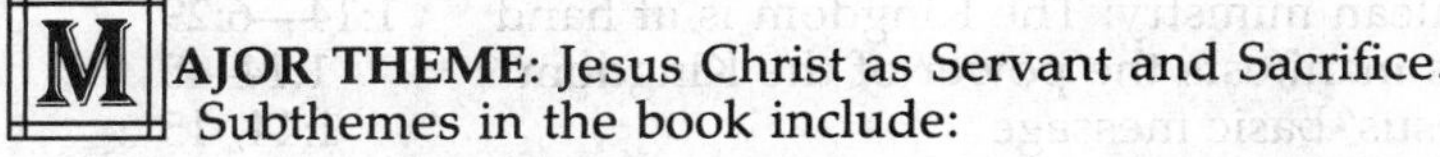

(1) *The suffering Messiah*. Christ, who acts with power and authority, is nevertheless a suffering Messiah (8:27–33), One who has come to serve and give His life for many (10:45). Jesus is clearly the Son of God (1:1, 11; 9:7; 14:61, 62), who has power over demons, heals the sick and forgives sins (1:23–25; 2:10, 11). But He also possesses a full humanity, expressed through the agony of Gethsemane and the suffering on the Cross.

(2) *The messianic secret*. Mark underscores the fact that Jesus veiled His messianic identity, in spite of His preaching and teaching, His miracles, His authority over evil spirits, and the forgiveness of sins He granted. He commanded demons, the people He healed, and even the disciples to keep silent about His messiahship (1:34, 44; 8:30) until He Himself revealed the mystery before the Sanhedrin (14:62). Jesus did not want to encourage popular political

ideas about the Messiah (see John 6:15). While the evangelist introduces the Gospel with Christ as the Son of God (1:1), the first confession of Him as God by a human being which Mark records is by an outsider, the centurion, as Jesus dies on the Cross (15:39). In this Gospel Peter confesses Jesus only as "the Christ" (8:29; contrast Matt. 16:16; John 6:69). Only after the Resurrection do His followers recognize Him as God (16:14).

(3) *Discipleship*. Though the word "disciple" never occurs in Mark, Jesus calls His followers to uncompromising and heroic commitment. True disciples take up their crosses and suffer with Jesus (8:34–38). He allows them to share in His ministry if they participate in His way of life.

BACKGROUND INFORMATION: (1) *Style*. The shortest of the Gospels, Mark has a style that features simplicity of language and a rapid pace of narration. By the end of the first chapter Christ has been baptized by John the Baptist and performed numerous miracles.

(2) *Audience*. According to some Church Fathers, Mark is writing for the Christian community of Rome, which either was experiencing the great persecution by Nero (beginning in A.D. 64), or was caught up in the apocalyptic fervor occasioned by the Jewish war (Jerusalem was destroyed in A.D. 70). Mark tells the story of Jesus so his readers may see their own suffering as a prelude to the glorious Second Coming of Jesus, and may discern the reward of those who endure to the end. The suffering and the glory are equally real: this was true for Jesus and will be true for all believers.

(3) *Ending*. The earliest manuscripts of Mark end abruptly at 16:8. Later manuscripts provide additional material (16:9–20), included in this and other versions, which the Church recognizes as inspired.

OUTLINE

Prologue: Preparation for the Ministry — 1:1–13
- A. The way prepared — 1:1–8
- B. The Messiah prepared: Baptism and temptation — 1:9–13

I. The Galilean ministry: The Kingdom is at hand — 1:14—6:29
- A. Jesus manifests the power of the Kingdom — 1:14–45
  1. Jesus' basic message — 1:14, 15
  2. Circle of disciples begun — 1:16–20
  3. Jesus' power over this world — 1:21–45
- B. Israel is divided over Jesus' authority — 2:1—5:43
  1. Opposition to Jesus: His authority over Israel — 2:1—3:6
     - a. Authority to forgive sins — 2:1–12
     - b. Authority to associate with sinners — 2:13–22
     - c. Authority over the Sabbath — 2:23—3:6
  2. Jesus and the people: Followers, foes, family — 3:7–35
  3. Jesus the teacher: The parables — 4:1–34
  4. Jesus the Messiah — 4:35—5:43
     - a. Lord over nature — 4:35–41
     - b. Lord over demons — 5:1–20
     - c. Lord over death — 5:21–43

John: Forerunner of Christ
(Matt. 3:1–12; Luke 3:1–18; John 1:19–23)

1 The [a]beginning of the gospel of Jesus Christ, [b]the Son of God.†
2 As it is written in [1]the Prophets:

[a]*"Behold, I send My messenger*
before Your face,
Who will prepare Your way
before You."†
3 *"The[a] voice of one crying in the*
wilderness:

CHAPTER 1
1 [a]Luke 3:22 [b]Matt. 14:33
2 [a]Mal. 3:1 [1]NU *Isaiah the prophet*
3 [a]Is. 40:3

1:1–8 See notes on Matt. 3:1–12; Luke 3:1–18; John 1:19–28.

1:1 Gospel refers not to Mark *per se,* but to the sacred story of the life, death and Resurrection of Christ, the Good News of salvation in the Kingdom of God (Matt. 4:17, 23).

(continued on page 85)

JOHN THE BAPTIST

"John came baptizing in the wilderness and preaching a baptism of repentance for the remission of sins" (Mark 1:4).

John the Baptist plays a crucial role in the history of salvation. Chosen before his birth to be the herald and forerunner of the Messiah (Luke 1:13–17), he knew his Lord from the beginning. Luke writes of the miraculous conception of John (Luke 1:24). He then records that when the Virgin Mary visited Elizabeth, who was then six months pregnant with John the Baptist, the baby in Elizabeth's womb leaped at the sound of Mary's voice (Luke 1:41).

Jesus taught that John fulfilled the prophecy of the return of Elijah (Matt. 11:14), who was to precede the Messiah as "the voice of one crying in the wilderness: 'Prepare the way of the LORD' " (Matt. 3:3; Mark 1:3; Luke 3:4; John 1:23).

Shortly before Jesus began His public ministry, John went out to the wilderness of Jordan to prepare the way for the Messiah. He carried out his prophetic role with a brotherhood of disciples characterized by: (1) repentance in expectation of the Kingdom, (2) baptism for forgiveness of sins, (3) bearing the fruit of righteousness, and (4) spiritual discipline. John himself lived by an ascetic rule of poverty and fasting; in fact, he may have been a lifelong Nazirite (see Luke 1:15; Num. 6). His eyes were set not on the body and its desires but upon Christ the Lord, and this influence was widespread (see Mark 11:32; Luke 7:29; Acts 18:25; 19:1–7).

John prophesied that the Messiah was coming, One immeasurably greater than himself, "whose sandal strap I am not worthy to stoop down and loose" (Mark 1:7). This One would baptize not only with water but with the Holy Spirit (Mark 1:8). When Jesus appeared before him to be baptized, John was humbled, realizing he himself was in need of being baptized by the Messiah, Jesus (Matt. 3:14). But Jesus knew what was fitting "to fulfill all righteousness" (Matt. 3:15), and John obeyed. Thus came the event so familiar in Orthodox icons: Christ in the Jordan, being baptized by John, the Holy Spirit descending on Him in the form of a dove. The Father's voice from heaven declares, "This is My beloved Son, in whom I am well pleased" (Matt. 3:17).

John's work was crucial to Jesus' ministry. Jesus considered John's testimony important—not because Jesus, the Son of God, needed to be validated by any human witness but because the people's acceptance of John as a godly man prepared them to accept Jesus as well (John 5:33–35). Jesus' first disciples came from John's brotherhood (John 1:35–39), and the vacancy in the apostolic college was filled by one who had been John's follower (Acts 1:21, 22).

John the Baptist died a martyr for Christ (Mark 6:24–29). The Orthodox Church commemorates him in special hymns every Tuesday, as well as on designated feast days throughout the year.

The Eve of the Baptism of Jesus Christ (Theophany) *January 5*

1:9–11: Jesus is revealed as the Son of God at His baptism.

'Prepare the way of the LORD;
Make His paths straight.' "

4 [a]John came baptizing in the wilderness and preaching a baptism of repentance [1]for the remission of sins.†
5 [a]Then all the land of Judea, and those from Jerusalem, went out to him and were all baptized by him in the Jordan River, confessing their sins.†
6 Now John was [a]clothed with camel's hair and with a leather belt around his waist, and he ate locusts and wild honey.†
7 And he preached, saying, [a]"There comes One after me who is mightier than I, whose sandal strap I am not worthy to stoop down and loose.
8 [a]"I indeed baptized you with water, but He will baptize you [b]with the Holy Spirit."†

Jesus Baptized and Tempted
(Matt. 3:13—4:11; Luke 3:21—4:13; John 1:29–34)

9 [a]It came to pass in those days *that* Jesus came from Nazareth of Galilee, and was baptized by John in the Jordan.†
10 [a]And immediately, coming up [1]from the water, He saw the heavens [2]parting and the Spirit [b]descending upon Him like a dove.†
11 Then a voice came from heaven,

4 [a]Matt. 3:1 [1]Or *because of forgiveness*
5 [a]Matt. 3:5
6 [a]Matt. 3:4
7 [a]John 1:27
8 [a]Acts 1:5; 11:16 [b]Is. 44:3
9 [a]Matt. 3:13–17
10 [a]Matt. 3:16 [b]Acts 10:38 [1]NU *out of* [2]*torn open*

(continued from page 83)
Beginning refers to the opening events of the ministry of Jesus, namely, the preparatory activity of John the Baptist and the baptism and temptation of **Jesus, the Christ, the Son of God.**

1:2, 3 Prepare Your way: John the Baptist, the last prophet of the OT period, fulfills prophecy and prepares the people of God for the Messiah's coming. Hearts are softened to receive the Light.

1:4 Baptism . . . for the remission of sins (lit. "to let go" of sins) is a major part of John's preparation of the people for Jesus' coming. Later, in Christian baptism, God not only forgives our sins, letting them go, but He also brings us into union with Christ. (See Rom. 6:5.)

1:5 All the land of Judea . . . went out to him indicates the sweeping impact of the ministry of John the Baptist. He is perhaps the leading religious figure outside of official and rabbinic Judaism.

1:6 John's clothing is similar to that of Elijah (2 Kin. 1:8), indicating that he fulfills the prophecy of Elijah's return (see article, "John the Baptist," at Mark 1).

1:8 Baptism **with the Holy Spirit** means that only Christ, the Son of God, fully possesses and gives the Spirit. So to receive the Spirit we must be **baptized** in Christ and adopted as children of God (see Gal. 3:27; Eph. 1:5). In adoption, Christians become anointed ones; it was of these God said, "Do not touch My anointed ones" (Ps. 105:15). For more on the ministry of John the Baptist see notes on Matt. 3:1–12.

1:9 Jesus and **John** were related through their mothers (Luke 1:36). Perhaps Jesus and John were acquainted.

1:10 By saying that He came **up from the water,** Mark suggests Jesus was immersed in water. Christ's rising from the water is symbolic of His Ascension, since the same Greek verb (*anabaino*) is also used to refer to that event (John 3:13; Acts 2:34; Eph. 4:8–10). The Church Fathers taught that in coming up, He lifts the whole world with Him. **The Spirit descending upon Him** foreshadows the Spirit's descent upon the first Christians at Pentecost (Acts 2:1–4). **Like a dove** does not mean the Holy Spirit is incarnated as a dove. Rather this is a special sign indicating the presence of the Spirit. A *dove* symbolizes purity, peace and wisdom.

[a]"You are My beloved Son, in whom
I am well pleased."†
12 [a]Immediately the Spirit [1]drove
Him into the wilderness.
13 And He was there in the wilderness forty days, tempted by Satan,
and was with the wild beasts;
[a]and the angels ministered to Him.†

Jesus Preaches: Repent and Believe

(Matt. 4:12–17; Luke 4:14, 15; John 4:1–3)

14 [a]Now after John was put in
prison, Jesus came to Galilee,
[b]preaching the gospel [1]of the kingdom of God,†
15 and saying, [a]"The time is fulfilled, and [b]the kingdom of God
[1]is at hand. Repent, and believe in
the gospel."†

The First Four Disciples

(Matt. 4:18–22; Luke 5:1–11)

16 [a]And as He walked by the Sea
of Galilee, He saw Simon and Andrew his brother casting a net into
the sea; for they were fishermen.†
17 Then Jesus said to them, "Follow Me, and I will make you become
[a]fishers of men."
18 [a]They immediately left their
nets and followed Him.†
19 When He had gone a little farther from there, He saw James the
son of Zebedee, and John his brother,
who also *were* in the boat mending
their nets.
20 And immediately He called
them, and they left their father Zebedee in the boat with the hired servants, and went after Him.†

Healings in Capernaum

(Matt. 8:14–17; Luke 4:31–41)

21 [a]Then they went into Capernaum, and immediately on the Sabbath He entered the [b]synagogue and
taught.
22 [a]And they were astonished at
His teaching, for He taught them as

11 [a]Matt. 3:17; 12:18
12 [a]Matt. 4:1–11
[1]*sent Him out*
13 [a]Matt. 4:10, 11
14 [a]Matt. 4:12
[b]Matt. 4:23
[1]NU omits *of the kingdom*
15 [a][Gal. 4:4]
[b]Matt. 3:2; 4:17
[1]*has drawn near*
16 [a]Luke 5:2–11
17 [a]Matt. 13:47, 48
18 [a][Luke 14:26]
21 [a]Luke 4:31–37
[b]Matt. 4:23
22 [a]Matt. 7:28, 29; 13:54

1:11 The **voice** of God the Father **from heaven** makes Jesus' baptism a manifestation or epiphany of the Holy Trinity. The Father is not adopting Jesus as His **Son,** but proclaiming that He is and always has been His Son. This divine proclamation, combining a messianic psalm (Ps. 2:7) with the first song of the Suffering Servant of the Lord (Is. 42:1), reveals who Jesus is. Thus Jesus' baptism anticipates His Transfiguration and Resurrection, the dawning of the new creation. (See notes on Matt. 3:13–17 and Luke 3:21, 22 for more on Jesus' baptism.)

1:13 As Jesus' baptism is the first revelation of His divinity, so His temptation inaugurates His role as the "Lamb of God" (John 1:29, 36), the suffering and obedient Son of God whose destiny is the Cross by God's will. **Forty days** echoes the forty years of Israel's temptations in the OT and becomes the basis for the forty-day period of Great Lent in later Christian tradition. Being with the **beasts** and served by the **angels** suggests a relationship between Christ and Adam, Christ being the New Adam. Even if we are subjected to evil, (the demons, the *beasts,*) God will never desert us as we struggle toward Him. The Church Fathers believed meditative seclusion is (1) conducive to freer communion with God and (2) effective preparation for great tasks ahead. (See notes on Matt. 4:1–11; Luke 4:1–13.)

1:14 Jesus preaches **the gospel of the kingdom of God:** the Good News of the royal reign of God revealed decisively through the Person, words and works of Jesus, the fullness of the faith of Christ.

1:15 To **repent** denotes an about-face in life, a necessary part of faith and the experience of the Kingdom as a present reality. The Kingdom is yet to come, but it is also **at hand,** already here. It is inaugurated but not yet **fulfilled.** (See notes on Matt. 4:12–17.)

1:16–20 Time has elapsed and many events have occurred between the temptation of Jesus and the call of the first disciples. Jesus chooses simple **fishermen** as messengers of the divine gospel.

1:18 This is not the first meeting of these men with Christ (John 1:40, 41). They obey Him and **immediately** leave their nets because He has already established a relationship with them, and they trust Him. (See also note on Matt. 4:18–22.)

1:20 **Called** suggests discipleship is an invitation issued by Jesus, the emphasis being on

(continued on next page)

one having authority, and not as the
scribes.†
23 Now there was a man in their
synagogue with an [a]unclean spirit.
And he cried out,†
24 saying, "Let *us* alone! [a]What
have we to do with You, Jesus of
Nazareth? Did You come to destroy
us? I [b]know who You are—the
[c]Holy One of God!"
25 But Jesus [a]rebuked him, saying,
[1]"Be quiet, and come out of him!"
26 And when the unclean spirit
[a]had convulsed him and cried out
with a loud voice, he came out of
him.
27 Then they were all amazed, so
that they questioned among themselves, saying, [1]"What is this? What
new [2]doctrine *is* this? For with authority He commands even the unclean spirits, and they obey Him."
28 And immediately His [a]fame
spread throughout all the region
around Galilee.
29 [a]Now as soon as they had come
out of the synagogue, they entered
the house of Simon and Andrew,
with James and John.†
30 But Simon's wife's mother lay
sick with a fever, and they told Him
about her at once.
31 So He came and took her by the
hand and lifted her up, and immediately the fever left her. And she
served them.
32 [a]At evening, when the sun had
set, they brought to Him all who
were sick and those who were
demon-possessed.
33 And the whole city was gathered together at the door.
34 Then He healed many who were
sick with various diseases, and
[a]cast out many demons; and He
[b]did not allow the demons to speak,
because they knew Him.

Tour of Galilee

(Matt. 4:23–25; Luke 4:42–44)

35 Now [a]in the morning, having
risen a long while before daylight,
He went out and departed to a
[1]solitary place; and there He
[b]prayed.†
36 And Simon and those *who were*
with Him searched for Him.
37 When they found Him, they
said to Him, [a]"Everyone [b]is looking
for You."
38 But He said to them, [a]"Let us
go into the next towns, that I may
preach there also, because [b]for this
purpose I have come forth."

23 [a][Matt. 12:43]
24 [a]Matt. 8:28, 29 [b]James 2:19 [c]Ps. 16:10
25 [a][Luke 4:39] [1]Lit. *Be muzzled*
26 [a]Mark 9:20
27 [1]NU *What is this? A new doctrine with authority. He* [2]*teaching*
28 [a]Matt. 4:24; 9:31
29 [a]Luke 4:38, 39
32 [a]Matt. 8:16, 17
34 [a]Luke 13:32 [b]Acts 16:17, 18
35 [a]Luke 4:42, 43 [b]Luke 5:16; 6:12; 9:28, 29 [1]*deserted*
37 [a]John 3:26; 12:19 [b][Heb. 11:6]
38 [a]Luke 4:43 [b][Is. 61:1, 2]

(continued from previous page)
His initiative—the opposite of rabbinic discipleship, where the student took the initiative to follow the leader (rabbi). Jesus does not hesitate to include groups of friends and relatives among His disciples. Here are two sets of brothers, and the two families are friends, perhaps even relatives.

1:22 The **scribes** speak by virtue of their official role and scholarly education. They quote others, usually earlier, well-known teachers; at times they must be boring. Jesus speaks and acts by an inner, divine **authority.** He needs no credentials nor the renown of others to back Him up.

1:23–26 Jesus demonstrates His authority not only by His teaching, but by dealing powerfully with this **unclean spirit** (v. 23). Not one demon ever successfully resists His command. Here a spirit tries to command Jesus: **Let us alone** (v. 24). It does not work. Jesus responds with two commands: (1) **be quiet,** and (2) **come out** (v. 25). The unclean spirit has no choice but to obey Jesus because God has authority over these spirits (Matt. 8:16). The demons recognize Jesus as God without having full understanding of what this means. But they do rightly fear that, with the coming of **the Holy One** (v. 24), the time of their confinement has come.

1:29–34 See notes on Matt. 8:14–17; Luke 4:38–41.

1:35–38 Mark is the only Gospel which gives us a full 24-hour day in Jesus' life, a day built around prayer and ministry. Jesus is the model for both, and He does not separate them. Jesus' priority is prayer to His Father: prayer before service. He goes to a **solitary place** (v. 35) to be free from distraction, despite the multitudes' need of Him. His ministry comes out of His relationship with His Father, not foremost out of people's need. Here He moves along to **the next towns** (v. 38). He knows His task, and performs it although the crowds clamor around Him.

Sunday of the Paralytic and Commemoration of St. Gregory Palamas *Second Sunday of Lent*

2:1–12: Jesus heals the paralytic in body and in soul, showing that the whole person is saved—not the spirit only.

39 [a]And He was preaching in their
synagogues throughout all Galilee,
and [b]casting out demons.

Uncleanness Cleansed: A Leper
(Matt. 8:1–4; Luke 5:12–16)

40 [a]Now a leper came to Him, imploring Him, kneeling down to Him and saying to Him, "If You are willing, You can make me clean."†
41 Then Jesus, moved with [a]compassion, stretched out *His* hand and touched him, and said to him, "I am willing; be cleansed."
42 As soon as He had spoken, [a]immediately the leprosy left him, and he was cleansed.
43 And He strictly warned him and sent him away at once,
44 and said to him, "See that you say nothing to anyone; but go your way, show yourself to the priest, and offer for your cleansing those things [a]which Moses commanded, as a testimony to them."
45 [a]However, he went out and began to proclaim *it* freely, and to spread the matter, so that Jesus could no longer openly enter the city, but was outside in deserted places; [b]and they came to Him from every direction.

39 [a]Ps. 22:22; Matt. 4:23; 9:35; Mark 1:21; 3:1; Luke 4:44 [b]Mark 5:8, 13; 7:29, 30
40 [a]Matt. 8:2–4; Luke 5:12–14
41 [a]Luke 7:13
42 [a]Matt. 15:28; Mark 5:29
44 [a]Lev. 14:1–32
45 [a]Matt. 28:15; Luke 5:15 [b]Mark 2:2, 13; 3:7; Luke 5:17; John 6:2

CHAPTER 2

1 [a]Matt. 9:1
2 [1]NU omits *Immediately*
3 [a]Matt. 4:24; 8:6; Acts 8:7; 9:33
7 [a]Job 14:4; Is. 43:25; Dan. 9:9

Sins Are Forgiven: A Paralytic
(Matt. 9:1–8; Luke 5:17–26)

2 And again [a]He entered Capernaum after *some* days, and it was heard that He was in the house.†
2 [1]Immediately many gathered together, so that there was no longer room to receive *them,* not even near the door. And He preached the word to them.†
3 Then they came to Him, bringing a [a]paralytic who was carried by four *men.*
4 And when they could not come near Him because of the crowd, they uncovered the roof where He was. So when they had broken through, they let down the bed on which the paralytic was lying.
5 When Jesus saw their faith, He said to the paralytic, "Son, your sins are forgiven you."
6 And some of the scribes were sitting there and reasoning in their hearts,†
7 "Why does this *Man* speak blasphemies like this? [a]Who can forgive sins but God alone?"†
8 But immediately, when Jesus perceived in His spirit that they reasoned thus within themselves, He said to them, "Why do you reason

1:40–45 As the dialogue between the leper and Jesus demonstrates, Jesus heals from **compassion**—not from duty or a need to prove Himself, or in order to gather a following. Jesus' authority is comprehensive: (1) in teaching, (2) over demons (vv. 21–28), and (3) over sickness—powerful testimony to His divinity. But He wishes this and His messiahship to be kept a secret (see notes on Matt. 8:1–4; Luke 5:12–16).

2:1–12 This passage, read on the second Sunday of Lent in the Orthodox Church, has a threefold symbolism relating to our preparation for Easter. (1) We must come to Christ in faith and let Him heal us of our spiritual paralysis. Sin is a paralysis of the soul. (2) We should let nothing deter us from getting to Christ, who alone can heal us, both in body and in soul. (3) We must help each other come to Christ.

2:2 Jesus **preached** (a vital part of His ministry) wherever there were people—in the synagogue, on the mountain, on the plain, and here in a house.

2:6 The **heart** in Scripture usually refers to the center of consciousness, including the will and reason.

2:7 The scribes are correct in saying that only God can **forgive sins.** They unwittingly confirm the divinity of Christ.

about these things in your hearts?
9 [a]"Which is easier, to say to the
paralytic, '*Your* sins are forgiven
you,' or to say, 'Arise, take up your
bed and walk'?†
10 "But that you may know that
the Son of Man has [1]power on earth
to forgive sins"—He said to the
paralytic,
11 "I say to you, arise, take up your
bed, and go to your house."
12 Immediately he arose, took up
the bed, and went out in the presence
of them all, so that all were
amazed and [a]glorified God, saying,
"We never saw *anything* like
this!"

9 [a]Matt. 9:5
10 [1]*authority*
12 [a]Matt. 15:31; [Phil. 2:11]

Sinners Are Welcome: Levi

(Matt. 9:9–13; Luke 5:27–32)

13 [a]Then He went out again by the
sea; and all the multitude came to
Him, and He taught them.
14 [a]As He passed by, He saw Levi
the *son* of Alphaeus sitting at the tax
office. And He said to him, [b]"Follow
Me." So he arose and [c]followed
Him.†
15 [a]Now it happened, as He was
dining in *Levi's* house, that many tax
collectors and sinners also sat together
with Jesus and His disciples;
for there were many, and they followed
Him.†
16 And when the scribes [1]and
Pharisees saw Him eating with the
tax collectors and sinners, they said
to His disciples, "How *is it* that He
eats and drinks with tax collectors
and sinners?"†
17 When Jesus heard *it*, He said to
them, [a]"Those who are well have no
need of a physician, but those who
are sick. I did not come to call *the*
righteous, but sinners, [1]to repentance."†

13 [a]Matt. 9:9
14 [a]Matt. 9:9–13; Luke 5:27–32 [b]Matt. 4:19; 8:22; 19:21; John 1:43; 12:26; 21:22 [c]Luke 18:28
15 [a]Matt. 9:10
16 [1]NU *of the*
17 [a]Matt. 9:12, 13; 18:11; Luke 5:31, 32; 19:10 [1]NU omits *to repentance*

Jesus Transcends the Fast

(Matt. 9:14–17; Luke 5:33–39)

18 [a]The disciples of John and of the
Pharisees were fasting. Then they
came and said to Him, "Why do the
disciples of John and of the Pharisees
fast, but Your disciples do not
fast?"
19 And Jesus said to them, "Can
the [1]friends of the bridegroom fast
while the bridegroom is with them?
As long as they have the bridegroom
with them they cannot fast.†
20 "But the days will come when
the bridegroom will be [a]taken away
from them, and then they will fast
in those days.†

18 [a]Matt. 9:14–17; Luke 5:33–38
19 [1]Lit. *sons of the bridechamber*
20 [a]Acts 1:9; 13:2, 3; 14:23

2:9 The point is not that either one **is easier,** but that One who can say, **Arise, take up your bed and walk** is also able to forgive sins.

2:14 Levi (Matthew) is the only one of the Twelve with a powerful position in society and presumably an education. He has probably already heard of Jesus. **Follow Me** is a divine call, a command, not merely a suggestion. Of course, Matthew, like anyone receiving a call, must respond by his own free will. (See notes on Matt. 9:9–13; Luke 5:27–32.)

2:15 In **dining** with sinners, Jesus shows the Kingdom's openness to the outcast, and its destruction of the barrier between sinful men and God. Jesus recognizes these people as a definable group. It is possible to follow Jesus and remain in one's social class; however, friends no longer come first.

2:16 The teachers of the Law sought to expel evil; Christ comes to transform it. Jesus does not become unclean by contact with the unclean. Rather, His touch makes the unclean clean.

2:17 Christ came to save and heal, not to judge (John 1:17; 3:17). There are **righteous** people who do dead works (actions which are good in themselves but are motivated by legalism rather than by love) and keep people from God. True righteousness comes through faith and is accompanied by wholesome works. Many Pharisees were masters of dead works; some tax collectors and many sinners would become masters of true righteousness.

2:19 An expression of the messianic joy which accompanies the presence of Christ. Some believe this episode suggests the Eucharist (see notes on Matt. 9:14–17; Luke 5:33–39).

2:20 Fasting is not to be neglected as unimportant, or as smacking of "works salvation." Jesus clearly states His disciples **will fast.** Refusal to fast is disobedience to Christ and causes one to miss a great spiritual blessing.

21 "No one sews a piece of unshrunk cloth on an old garment; or
else the new piece pulls away from
the old, and the tear is made worse.†
22 "And no one puts new wine
into old wineskins; or else the new
wine bursts the wineskins, the wine
is spilled, and the wineskins are
ruined. But new wine must be put
into new wineskins."

Jesus Transcends the Sabbath
(Matt. 12:1–14; Luke 6:1–11)

23 [a]Now it happened that He went
through the grainfields on the Sabbath; and as they went His disciples
began [b]to pluck the heads of grain.†
24 And the Pharisees said to Him,
"Look, why do they do what is
[a]not lawful on the Sabbath?"
25 But He said to them, "Have you
never read [a]what David did when
he was in need and hungry, he and
those with him:
26 "how he went into the house
of God *in the days* of Abiathar the
high priest, and ate the showbread,
[a]which is not lawful to eat except for
the priests, and also gave some to
those who were with him?"†
27 And He said to them, "The Sabbath was made for man, and not man
for the [a]Sabbath.†

23 [a]Matt. 12:1–8; Luke 6:1–5 [b]Deut. 23:25
24 [a]Ex. 20:10; 31:15
25 [a]1 Sam. 21:1–6
26 [a]Ex. 29:32, 33; Lev. 24:5–9
27 [a]Gen. 2:3; Ex. 23:12; Deut. 5:14; Neh. 9:14; Ezek. 20:12
28 [a]Matt. 12:8

CHAPTER 3

1 [a]Matt. 12:9–14; Luke 6:6–11
2 [a][Ps. 37:32]; Luke 14:1; 20:20 [b]Luke 13:14 [1]*bring charges against*
3 [1]Lit. *Arise into the midst*
5 [a]Zech. 7:12 [1]NU omits *as whole as the other*
6 [a]Ps. 2:2; Mark 12:13 [b]Matt. 22:16
7 [a]Matt. 4:25; Luke 6:17

28 "Therefore [a]the Son of Man is
also Lord of the Sabbath."

3 And [a]He entered the synagogue
again, and a man was there who
had a withered hand.†
2 So they [a]watched Him closely,
whether He would [b]heal him on the
Sabbath, so that they might [1]accuse
Him.†
3 And He said to the man who
had the withered hand, [1]"Step
forward."
4 Then He said to them, "Is it lawful on the Sabbath to do good or to
do evil, to save life or to kill?" But
they kept silent.
5 And when He had looked
around at them with anger, being
grieved by the [a]hardness of their
hearts, He said to the man, "Stretch
out your hand." And he stretched
it out, and his hand was restored
[1]as whole as the other.
6 [a]Then the Pharisees went out
and immediately plotted with [b]the
Herodians against Him, how they
might destroy Him.†

The People Follow Jesus
(Matt. 12:15–21; Luke 6:17–19)

7 But Jesus withdrew with His
disciples to the sea. And a great multitude from Galilee followed Him,
[a]and from Judea

2:21, 22 This is not a blanket condemnation of OT traditions, which Christ came to fulfill, not to destroy (Matt. 5:17). Rather, this verse stresses the newness of Christ's teaching. The old and the new cannot mix.

2:23, 24 This is **not lawful** because it was considered work, a violation of **the Sabbath**-rest. "Pharisaism" is a very real danger for all. Rules for religious practice are not bad in themselves, but when adherence to those rules triumphs over mercy and human need, the practice leads people away from God, not toward Him (see note on Matt. 12:1–8).

2:26 Abiathar was appointed **high priest** during David's reign (1 Sam. 23:6–11). His father, Ahimelech, provided David and his men, who were starving, with holy bread intended for **priests** only (1 Sam. 21:1–6).

2:27, 28 A similar saying is found in rabbinical literature: "The Sabbath has been given unto you; you have not been given unto the Sabbath." Jesus, however, puts what He teaches into practice, interpreting the Law with authority. Only God can say He is **Lord of the Sabbath** (v. 28).

3:1–6 See notes on Matt. 12:10–13; Luke 6:7.

3:2–4 Jesus is motivated by compassion. He does not deny Sabbath traditions, but teaches that it is more important to do good **on the Sabbath** than to maintain the strict observance of Sabbath rest. The religious leaders are motivated by zeal for the rigid performance of rabbinic tradition; for them outward performance is more important than doing good. The two perspectives are incompatible.

3:6 In their anger and self-deception, the **Pharisees** believe that in order to serve God, they must collaborate with their enemies, the **Herodians,** to murder the One who is the true Servant of God.

8 and Jerusalem and Idumea and
beyond the Jordan; and those from
Tyre and Sidon, a great multitude,
when they heard how [a]many things
He was doing, came to Him.
9 So He told His disciples that a
small boat should be kept ready for
Him because of the multitude, lest
they should crush Him.
10 For He healed [a]many, so that
as many as had afflictions pressed
about Him to [b]touch Him.
11 [a]And the unclean spirits, whenever they saw Him, fell down before
Him and cried out, saying, [b]"You are
the Son of God."†
12 But [a]He sternly warned them
that they should not make Him
known.

The Twelve
(Matt. 10:1–4; Luke 6:12–16)

13 [a]And He went up on the mountain and called to *Him* those He Himself wanted. And they came to Him.
14 Then He appointed twelve,
[1]that they might be with Him and
that He might send them out to
preach,†
15 and to have [1]power [2]to heal
sicknesses and to cast out demons:
16 [1]Simon, [a]to whom He gave the
name Peter;
17 James the *son* of Zebedee and
John the brother of James, to whom
He gave the name Boanerges, that
is, "Sons of Thunder";

8 [a]Mark 5:19
10 [a]Luke 7:21 [b]Matt. 9:21; 14:36
11 [a]Luke 4:41 [b]Matt. 8:29; 14:33
12 [a]Mark 1:25, 34
13 [a]Luke 9:1
14 [1]NU adds *whom He also named apostles*
15 [1]*authority* [2]NU omits *to heal sicknesses and*
16 [a]John 1:42 [1]NU *and He appointed the twelve: Simon . . .*

18 Andrew, Philip, Bartholomew,
Matthew, Thomas, James the *son* of
Alphaeus, Thaddaeus, Simon the
Cananite;†
19 and Judas Iscariot, who also betrayed Him. And they went into a
house.

A House Divided
(Matt. 12:22–37; Luke 11:14–23)

20 Then the multitude came together again, [a]so that they could not
so much as eat bread.†
21 But when His [a]own people
heard *about this,* they went out to lay
hold of Him, [b]for they said, "He is
out of His mind."†
22 And the scribes who came down
from Jerusalem said, [a]"He has Beelzebub," and, "By the [b]ruler of the
demons He casts out demons."
23 [a]So He called them to *Himself*
and said to them in parables: "How
can Satan cast out Satan?
24 "If a kingdom is divided against
itself, that kingdom cannot stand.
25 "And if a house is divided
against itself, that house cannot
stand.
26 "And if Satan has risen up
against himself, and is divided, he
cannot stand, but has an end.
27 [a]"No one can enter a strong
man's house and plunder his goods,
unless he first binds the strong man.
And then he will plunder his house.†

20 [a]Mark 6:31
21 [a]Mark 6:3 [b]John 7:5; 10:20
22 [a]Matt. 9:34; 10:25 [b][John 12:31; 14:30; 16:11]
23 [a]Matt. 12:25–29
27 [a][Is. 49:24, 25]

3:11, 12 The troublesome demons again recognize the divinity of Jesus (see 1:24), but Jesus commands them to be silent, that the messianic secret may be preserved.

3:14, 15 The appointing of the **twelve** sets forth: (1) Jesus' authority in calling people to ministry: many might have volunteered, but He **appointed** whom He would; (2) the requirement of discipleship before ministry: to **be with Him**—for intimate fellowship and training—and to follow Him in order to be sent by Him; and (3) the commission to share in Jesus' ministry of preaching, healing, and casting out demons. In Mark's view, demonic oppression is characteristic of human existence under the bondage of evil. The mission of Jesus' disciples is to liberate humanity from this bondage. Every age has its own manifestations of demonic power. Thus, we who are His disciples have a similar mission today—helping people to break loose from bondage and come to freedom in Christ.

3:18 Thaddaeus is probably the same man called Judas son of James in Luke 6:16 and Acts 1:13.

3:20–27 See notes on Matt. 12:22–30.

3:21 His own people are His relatives, who do not yet comprehend Jesus and His mission (see John 7:3–5).

3:27 Jesus clearly is plundering the **strong man,** the devil, whose **goods** were the people he oppressed. Jesus' work brings total triumph. Not one demon is able to resist Him.

28 [a]"Assuredly, I say to you, all
sins will be forgiven the sons of men,
and whatever blasphemies they may
utter;†
29 "but he who blasphemes
against the Holy Spirit never has forgiveness, but is subject to eternal
condemnation"—
30 because they [a]said, "He has an
unclean spirit."

Jesus' True Kinsmen
(Matt. 12:46–50; Luke 8:19–21)

31 [a]Then His brothers and His
mother came, and standing outside
they sent to Him, calling Him.†
32 And a multitude was sitting
around Him; and they said to Him,
"Look, Your mother and Your
brothers [1]are outside seeking You."
33 But He answered them, saying,
"Who is My mother, or My
brothers?"†
34 And He looked around in a circle at those who sat about Him, and
said, "Here are My mother and My
brothers!
35 "For whoever does the [a]will of
God is My brother and My sister and
mother."

The Parable of the Sower
(Matt. 13:1–9; Luke 8:4–8)

4 And [a]again He began to teach
by the sea. And a great multitude was gathered to Him, so that
He got into a boat and sat *in it* on
the sea; and the whole multitude was
on the land facing the sea.
2 Then He taught them many
things by parables, [a]and said to them
in His teaching:†
3 "Listen! Behold, a sower went
out to sow.
4 "And it happened, as he sowed,
that some *seed* fell by the wayside;
and the birds [1]of the air came and
devoured it.
5 "Some fell on stony ground,
where it did not have much earth;
and immediately it sprang up because it had no depth of earth.
6 "But when the sun was up it
was scorched, and because it had no
root it withered away.
7 "And some *seed* fell among
thorns; and the thorns grew up and
choked it, and it yielded no [1]crop.
8 "But other *seed* fell on good
ground and yielded a crop that
sprang up, increased and produced:
some thirtyfold, some sixty, and
some a hundred."
9 And He said [1]to them, "He who
has ears to hear, let him hear!"

Why Parables?
(Matt. 13:10–17; Luke 8:9, 10)

10 [a]But when He was alone, those
around Him with the twelve asked
Him about the parable.
11 And He said to them, "To you
it has been given to [a]know the
[1]mystery of the kingdom of God; but
to [b]those who are outside, all things
come in parables,†

28 [a]Matt. 12:31, 32; Luke 12:10; [1 John 5:16]
30 [a]Matt. 9:34; John 7:20; 8:48, 52; 10:20
31 [a]Matt. 12:46–50; Luke 8:19–21
32 [1]NU, M add *and Your sisters*
35 [a]Eph. 6:6; Heb. 10:36; 1 Pet. 4:2; [1 John 2:17]

CHAPTER 4
1 [a]Matt. 13:1–15; Luke 8:4–10
2 [a]Mark 12:38
4 [1]NU, M omit *of the air*
7 [1]Lit. *fruit*
9 [1]NU, M omit *to them*
10 [a]Matt. 13:10; Luke 8:9
11 [a][Matt. 11:25; 1 Cor. 2:10–16; 2 Cor. 4:6] [b][1 Cor. 5:12, 13; Col. 4:5; 1 Thess. 4:12; 1 Tim. 3:7] [1]*secret* or *hidden truths*

3:28–30 The "unforgivable sin" is the accusation that Jesus performs exorcisms by the power of a demonic **spirit** (v. 30) instead of **the Holy Spirit** (v. 29). This is blasphemy. (See notes on Matt. 12:32; Luke 12:10.)

3:31 In the Greek patristic tradition, these **brothers** are identified as stepbrothers of Jesus, sons of Joseph by a previous wife. In the Latin tradition, they are seen as relatives, such as cousins.

3:33–35 Jesus is not necessarily belittling His **mother** and relatives. Who was more obedient to the will of God than Mary who said, "Let it be to me according to your word" (Luke 1:38)? In effect Jesus is saying, "Be like My mother. Do the will of God as she does." In obeying God we become sons of God and brothers with other Christians—spiritual relationships which are more valuable than natural ones.

4:2 For comments on the meaning and mystery of **parables** (stories illustrating truth about the Kingdom as realized in Christ), see article, "Parables" at Matt. 13.

4:11 The **mystery** is the reality of the presence of the Kingdom itself, revealed in Jesus and perceived by faith.

12 "so that

[a]'Seeing they may see and not
perceive,
And hearing they may hear and
not understand;
Lest they should turn,
And their sins be forgiven
them.'"†

The Parable of the Sower Explained
(Matt. 13:18–23; Luke 8:11–15)

13 And He said to them, "Do you
not understand this parable? How
then will you understand all the
parables?†
14 [a]"The sower sows the word.†
15 "And these are the ones by the
wayside where the word is sown.
When they hear, Satan comes immediately and takes away the word that
was sown in their hearts.
16 "These likewise are the ones
sown on stony ground who, when
they hear the word, immediately receive it with gladness;
17 "and they have no root in themselves, and so endure only for a time.
Afterward, when tribulation or persecution arises for the word's sake,
immediately they stumble.
18 "Now these are the ones sown
among thorns; *they are* the ones who
hear the word,
19 "and the [a]cares of this world,
[b]the deceitfulness of riches, and the
desires for other things entering in
choke the word, and it becomes
unfruitful.
20 "But these are the ones sown
on good ground, those who hear the
word, [1]accept *it,* and bear [a]fruit:
some thirtyfold, some sixty, and
some a hundred."

The Lamp Under a Basket
(Matt. 5:14–16)

21 [a]Also He said to them, "Is a
lamp brought to be put under a basket or under a bed? Is it not to be
set on a lampstand?†
22 [a]"For there is nothing hidden
which will not be revealed, nor has
anything been kept secret but that
it should come to light.
23 [a]"If anyone has ears to hear, let
him hear."
24 Then He said to them, "Take
heed what you hear. [a]With the same
measure you use, it will be measured
to you; and to you who hear, more
will be given.†
25 [a]"For whoever has, to him more
will be given; but whoever does not

12 [a]Is. 6:9, 10; 43:8; Jer. 5:21; Ezek. 12:2; Matt. 13:14; Luke 8:10; John 12:40; Rom. 11:8
14 [a]Matt. 13:18–23; Luke 8:11–15
19 [a]Luke 21:34 [b]Prov. 23:5; Eccl. 5:13; Luke 18:24; 1 Tim. 6:9, 10, 17
20 [a][John 15:2, 5; Rom. 7:4] [1]*receive*
21 [a]Matt. 5:15; Luke 8:16; 11:33
22 [a]Eccl. 12:14; Matt. 10:26, 27; Luke 12:3; [1 Cor. 4:5]
23 [a]Matt. 11:15; 13:9, 43; Mark 4:9; Luke 8:8; 14:35; Rev. 3:6, 13, 22; 13:9
24 [a]Matt. 7:2; Luke 6:38; 2 Cor. 9:6
25 [a]Matt. 13:12; 25:29; Luke 8:18; 19:26

4:12 So that points to the fulfillment of Is. 6:9, 10, referring to hardness of heart as the cause of lack of understanding. Jesus is not disclosing truth to some while hiding it from others. He proclaims the Good News of the Kingdom openly to all, but only those who repent and believe can perceive the power of the Kingdom in Him and in their lives.

4:13 Discipleship requires both that we have a personal relationship with Christ and that we **understand** what He teaches.

4:14–20 The gospel of God's Kingdom is powerful, but our heart response determines its fruitfulness in our lives.

4:21, 22 Christ discloses truth, He does not hide it. His truth is like light, for it reveals all mysteries and exposes all secrets. That which is **hidden** (v. 22) is the Gospel, the presence of the Kingdom of God. The Gospel, at first a mystery explained only to the disciples, will be revealed to all (Luke 8:16–18). Everything done in secret will ultimately be revealed (Luke 12:1–3).

4:24 A call to attentive listening and discriminating response, both requisites for understanding and experiencing the truth of Christ. We must not only hear but hear properly. **More will be given** to those who respond to Jesus with open hearts; they will grow in understanding. "Do the good you know, and what you do not know will be revealed to you" (St. Mark the Ascetic, 6th century). See notes on Matt. 7:2; 13:12; Luke 6:37, 38; 8:18.

have, even what he has will be taken
away from him."†

The Parable of the Scattered Seed

26 And He said, [a]"The kingdom of
God is as if a man should [1]scatter
seed on the ground,†
27 "and should sleep by night and
rise by day, and the seed should
sprout and [a]grow, he himself does
not know how.
28 "For the earth [a]yields crops
by itself: first the blade, then the head,
after that the full grain in the head.
29 "But when the grain ripens, immediately [a]he puts in the sickle, because the harvest has come."

The Parable of the Mustard Seed
(Matt. 13:31, 32; Luke 13:18, 19)

30 Then He said, [a]"To what shall
we liken the kingdom of God? Or
with what parable shall we picture
it?†
31 "*It is* like a mustard seed which,
when it is sown on the ground, is
smaller than all the seeds on earth;
32 "but when it is sown, it grows
up and becomes greater than all
herbs, and shoots out large
branches, so that the birds of the air
may nest under its shade."

Jesus' Use of Parables
(Matt. 13:34, 35)

33 [a]And with many such parables
He spoke the word to them as they
were able to hear *it*.†
34 But without a parable He did
not speak to them. And when they
were alone, [a]He explained all things
to His disciples.†

A Storm Obeys Jesus
(Matt. 8:23–27; Luke 8:22–25)

35 [a]On the same day, when evening had come, He said to them, "Let
us cross over to the other side."†
36 Now when they had left the
multitude, they took Him along in
the boat as He was. And other little
boats were also with Him.
37 And a great windstorm arose,
and the waves beat into the boat, so
that it was already filling.
38 But He was in the stern, asleep
on a pillow. And they awoke Him
and said to Him, [a]"Teacher, [b]do You
not care that we are perishing?"
39 Then He arose and [a]rebuked the
wind, and said to the sea, [b]"Peace,[1]
be still!" And the wind ceased and
there was a great calm.
40 But He said to them, "Why are
you so fearful? [a]How[1] *is it* that you
have no faith?"
41 And they feared exceedingly,

26 [a][Matt. 13:24–30, 36–43]; Luke 8:1 [1]*sow*
27 [a][2 Cor. 3:18; 2 Pet. 3:18]
28 [a][John 12:24]
29 [a][Mark 13:30, 39]; Rev. 14:15
30 [a]Matt. 13:31, 32; Luke 13:18, 19; [Acts 2:41; 4:4; 5:14; 19:20]
33 [a]Matt. 13:34, 35; [John 16:12]
34 [a]Luke 24:27, 45
35 [a]Matt. 8:18, 23–27; Luke 8:22, 25
38 [a][Matt. 23:8–10] [b]Ps. 44:23
39 [a]Mark 9:25; Luke 4:39 [b]Ps. 65:7; 89:9; 93:4; 104:6, 7; Matt. 8:26; Luke 8:24 [1]Lit. *Be quiet*
40 [a]Matt. 14:31, 32; Luke 8:25 [1]NU *Have you still no faith?*

4:25 Satan, not God, takes away the Word that was sown in hearts too hard to receive it (v. 15). But to those who are able to receive His Word, God gives even **more.**

4:26–29 The kingdom of God is like the **seed** which by the power of God produces a harvest. This is an image of the mysterious working of the Kingdom—beyond human measures and expectations. This parable appears only in Mark.

4:30–32 The parable of the **mustard seed** contrasts humble beginnings with a bountiful crop. Jesus begins with poor fishermen, but in a few years the Christian faith will spread throughout the Roman Empire and beyond. The work of God may involve apparently insignificant people and circumstances, but the possibilities are limitless because of God's power. That being said, Jesus' followers must always be prepared for the "long haul." Jewish expectations in Jesus' day were for the Kingdom to appear suddenly and fully. But God's Kingdom takes time to grow and mature through adversity, and when it is fully formed it will be even greater than expected.

4:33 Jesus spoke in parables, **as they were able to hear.** Had the people turned to God in their hearts, their understanding would have cleared. People are accountable even for what they do not understand.

4:34 This is true here, but not at all times of His ministry. On other occasions, Jesus did teach the people **without a parable.**

4:35–41 The same Greek word (*phimoœ*) by which Jesus commands the storm to **be still** (v. 39) is used for His telling the demon to "be quiet" in 1:25. As Lord of all, He commands all. In obedience, the storm subsides instantly and fully.

and said to one another, "Who can this be, that even the wind and the sea obey Him!"

The Gadarene Demoniac

(Matt. 8:28–34; Luke 8:26–39)

5 Then [a]they came to the other side of the sea, to the country of the [1]Gadarenes.†

2 And when He had come out of the boat, immediately there met Him out of the tombs a man with an [a]unclean spirit,

3 who had *his* dwelling among the tombs; and no one could bind [1]him, not even with chains,†

4 because he had often been bound with shackles and chains. And the chains had been pulled apart by him, and the shackles broken in pieces; neither could anyone tame him.

5 And always, night and day, he was in the mountains and in the tombs, crying out and cutting himself with stones.

6 When he saw Jesus from afar, he ran and worshiped Him.†

7 And he cried out with a loud voice and said, "What have I to do with You, Jesus, Son of the Most High God? I [a]implore[1] You by God that You do not torment me."

8 For He said to him, [a]"Come out of the man, unclean spirit!"

9 Then He asked him, "What *is* your name?" And he answered, saying, "My name *is* Legion; for we are many."

10 Also he begged Him earnestly that He would not send them out of the country.†

11 Now a large herd of [a]swine was feeding there near the mountains.

12 So all the demons begged Him, saying, "Send us to the swine, that we may enter them."

13 And [1]at once Jesus gave them permission. Then the unclean spirits went out and entered the swine (there were about two thousand); and the herd ran violently down the steep place into the sea, and drowned in the sea.†

14 So those who fed the swine fled, and they told *it* in the city and in the country. And they went out to see what it was that had happened.

15 Then they came to Jesus, and saw the one *who had been* [a]demon-possessed and had the legion, [b]sitting and [c]clothed and in his right mind. And they were afraid.

16 And those who saw it told them how it happened to him *who had been* demon-possessed, and about the swine.

17 Then [a]they began to plead with Him to depart from their region.†

18 And when He got into the boat, [a]he who had been demon-possessed begged Him that he might be with Him.

19 However, Jesus did not permit him, but said to him, "Go home to your friends, and tell them what great things the Lord has done for you, and how He has had compassion on you."†

CHAPTER 5
1 [a]Matt. 8:28–34; Luke 8:26–37 [1]NU *Gerasenes*
2 [a]Mark 1:23; 7:25; [Rev. 16:13, 14]
3 [1]NU adds *anymore*
7 [a]Matt. 26:63; Mark 1:24; Acts 19:13 [1]*adjure*
8 [a]Mark 1:25; 9:25; [Acts 16:18]
11 [a]Lev. 11:7, 8; Deut. 14:8; Luke 15:15, 16
13 [1]NU *He gave*
15 [a]Matt. 4:24; 8:16; Mark 1:32 [b]Luke 10:39 [c][Is. 61:10]
17 [a]Matt. 8:34; Acts 16:39
18 [a]Luke 8:38, 39

5:1 The Gadarenes were Gentiles, so they could raise pigs (v. 11), which were considered unclean by Jews.

5:3 The tombs were caves cut out of soft rock.

5:6, 7 The deranged man **worshiped** Jesus (v. 6); the demons see Him and fear **torment** (v. 7). Not only are the demons unable to resist Jesus' command, they are unable to escape confrontation with Him. Though they have power over the man, they have no power over Jesus. Jesus' words accomplish in an instant (v. 13) what shackles and chains cannot.

5:10 Out of the country perhaps reflects both the wretched man's fear of being compelled to leave his homeland and the demons' fear of being cast out of the man.

5:13 The destruction of the unclean **swine** was appropriate according to Jewish law.

5:17 They ("those who fed the swine," v. 14) fear Jesus' power, which they do not understand, and possible further disturbance from Him. Their primary concern is with animals and property rights; Jesus is more concerned about the life of a demon-possessed man.

5:19 Jesus allows an exception to the messianic secret: this man may tell others. Perhaps in Gentile territory misunderstanding of Jesus' mission was not so much a problem, because the Gentiles had no preconceptions about the Messiah.

20 And he departed and began to
[a]proclaim in [1]Decapolis all that Jesus
had done for him; and all [b]marveled.

Jairus's Daughter
(Matt. 9:18, 19; Luke 8:40–42)

21 [a]Now when Jesus had crossed
over again by boat to the other side,
a great multitude gathered to Him;
and He was by the sea.
22 [a]And behold, one of the rulers
of the synagogue came, Jairus by
name. And when he saw Him, he
fell at His feet †
23 and begged Him earnestly, saying, "My little daughter lies at the
point of death. Come and [a]lay Your
hands on her, that she may be
healed, and she will live."
24 So *Jesus* went with him, and a
great multitude followed Him and
thronged Him.

The Woman with a Flow of Blood
(Matt. 9:20–22; Luke 8:43–48)

25 Now a certain woman [a]had a
flow of blood for twelve years,†
26 and had suffered many things
from many physicians. She had
spent all that she had and was no
better, but rather grew worse.
27 When she heard about Jesus,
she came behind *Him* in the crowd
and [a]touched His garment.
28 For she said, "If only I may
touch His clothes, I shall be made
well."
29 Immediately the fountain of her
blood was dried up, and she felt in
her body that she was healed of the
[1]affliction.
30 And Jesus, immediately knowing in Himself that [a]power had gone
out of Him, turned around in the
crowd and said, "Who touched My
clothes?"†
31 But His disciples said to Him,
"You see the multitude thronging
You, and You say, 'Who touched
Me?' "
32 And He looked around to see
her who had done this thing.
33 But the woman, [a]fearing and
trembling, knowing what had happened to her, came and fell down
before Him and told Him the whole
truth.
34 And He said to her, "Daughter,
[a]your faith has made you well.
[b]Go in peace, and be healed of your
affliction."†

Jairus's Daughter Raised
(Matt. 9:23–26; Luke 8:49–56)

35 [a]While He was still speaking,
some came from the ruler of the synagogue's *house* who said, "Your
daughter is dead. Why trouble the
Teacher any further?"
36 As soon as Jesus heard the word
that was spoken, He said to the ruler
of the synagogue, "Do not be afraid;
only [a]believe."†
37 And He permitted no one to follow Him except Peter, James, and
John the brother of James.†
38 Then He came to the house of

20 [a]Ex. 15:2; Ps. 66:16 [b]Matt. 9:8, 33; John 5:20; 7:21; Acts 3:12; 4:13 [1]Lit. *Ten Cities*
21 [a]Matt. 9:1; Luke 8:40
22 [a]Matt. 9:18–26; Luke 8:41–56; Acts 13:15
23 [a]Matt. 8:15; Mark 6:5; 7:32; 8:23, 25; 16:18; Luke 4:40; Acts 9:17; 28:8
25 [a]Lev. 15:19, 25; Matt. 9:20
27 [a]Matt. 14:35, 36; Mark 3:10; 6:56
29 [1]*suffering*
30 [a]Luke 6:19; 8:46
33 [a][Ps. 89:7]
34 [a]Matt. 9:22; Mark 10:52; Acts 14:9 [b]1 Sam. 1:17; 20:42; 2 Kin. 5:19; Luke 7:50; 8:48; Acts 16:36; [James 2:16]
35 [a]Luke 8:49
36 [a][Mark 9:23; John 11:40]

5:22 Not all Jewish leaders were opposed to Jesus.

5:25 Jesus never seems to be in a hurry, or ever interrupted from His mission. Here, He attends to both needs. The **woman** goes away healed (v. 29), Jairus is amazed and happy (v. 42), and Jesus is not detained! Only God in the flesh brings such things to pass.

5:30 Healing takes energy. Jesus is aware that divine energy **had gone out of Him** when He was **touched** (see 6:56). This **power** (Gr. *dynamis*) is a manifestation of the one, uncreated power of God, "the power of God to salvation" (Rom. 1:16).

5:34 God's power or energy is available to people as grace from Him. Jesus says, **Daughter, your faith has made you well,** showing that while divine power healed her, the woman's faith participated in the healing.

5:36 No situation is hopeless when Christ is present. As the woman needed faith to be healed, so these parents need to persist in faith, even now that their daughter's condition seems past hope.

5:37 **Peter, James and John:** the inner circle of the disciples, on whose faith and understanding Jesus could rely.

the ruler of the synagogue, and saw
[1]a tumult and those who [a]wept and
wailed loudly.
39 When He came in, He said to
them, "Why make this commotion
and weep? The child is not dead, but
[a]sleeping."
40 And they ridiculed Him. [a]But
when He had put them all outside,
He took the father and the mother
of the child, and those *who were* with
Him, and entered where the child
was lying.
41 Then He took the child by the
hand, and said to her, "Talitha,
cumi," which is translated, "Little
girl, I say to you, arise."†
42 Immediately the girl arose and
walked, for she was twelve years *of
age*. And they were [a]overcome with
great amazement.†
43 But [a]He commanded them
strictly that no one should know it,
and said that *something* should be
given her to eat.†

At Nazareth: No Honor
(Matt. 13:53–58; Luke 4:16–30)

6 Then [a]He went out from there
and came to His own country,
and His disciples followed Him.
2 And when the Sabbath had
come, He began to teach in the synagogue. And many hearing *Him* were
[a]astonished, saying, [b]"Where *did*
this Man *get* these things? And what
wisdom *is* this which is given to
Him, that such mighty works are
performed by His hands!
3 "Is this not the carpenter, the
Son of Mary, and [a]brother of James,
Joses, Judas, and Simon? And are
not His sisters here with us?" So they
[b]were offended at Him.†
4 But Jesus said to them, [a]"A
prophet is not without honor except
in his own country, among his own
relatives, and in his own house."
5 [a]Now He could do no mighty
work there, except that He laid His
hands on a few sick people and
healed *them*.†
6 And [a]He marveled because of
their unbelief. [b]Then He went about
the villages in a circuit, teaching.

The Mission of the Twelve
(Matt. 9:35—11:1; Luke 9:1–6)

7 [a]And He called the twelve to
Himself, and began to send them out
[b]two *by* two, and gave them power
over unclean spirits.†
8 He commanded them to take
nothing for the journey except a
staff—no bag, no bread, no copper
in *their* money belts—
9 but [a]to wear sandals, and not
to put on two tunics.
10 [a]Also He said to them, "In
whatever place you enter a house,
stay there till you depart from that
place.
11 [a]"And [1]whoever will not receive
you nor hear you, when you depart

38 [a]Acts 9:39 [1]*an uproar*
39 [a]John 11:4, 11
40 [a]Acts 9:40
42 [a]Mark 1:27; 7:37
43 [a][Matt. 8:4; 12:16–19; 17:9]

CHAPTER 6
1 [a]Matt. 13:54
2 [a]Matt. 7:28 [b]John 6:42
3 [a]Matt. 12:46 [b][Matt. 11:6]
4 [a]John 4:44
5 [a]Gen. 19:22; 32:25
6 [a]Is. 59:16 [b]Matt. 9:35
7 [a]Mark 3:13, 14 [b][Eccl. 4:9, 10]
9 [a][Eph. 6:15]
10 [a]Matt. 10:11
11 [a]Matt. 10:14 [1]NU *whatever place*

5:41 Jesus speaks Aramaic here, the spoken language of Jews in His time. Jesus commands demons and they obey, the stormy seas and they obey, and here, the dead and she "obeys."

5:42 The daughter of Jairus returns to life to the **great amazement** of those present. But like all of us, she will die again to await the resurrection of the dead at Christ's return.

5:43 Once again **He commanded** silence to avoid misunderstanding.

6:3 Jesus' teaching, wisdom, and miracles do not overcome the disbelief of those in His hometown. The people see Him as one of them, the carpenter they know. **They** are **offended** because they can do none of His works, and they are unwilling to accept a far greater role and dignity for Him. In Scripture the words **brothers** and **sisters** can refer to stepbrothers and stepsisters, as well as other relatives (see, for example, Abraham and Lot; compare Gen. 12:5 with 14:16). There is no NT evidence that Mary had other children besides Jesus. That Christ from the Cross committed His mother to the care of John suggests that (1) Joseph was by now deceased and (2) Jesus was Mary's only child.

6:5 Jealousy affects faith. Every person could have been restored. But in the absence of faith, Jesus does not release the divine power which is always His.

6:7 This is the first time **the twelve** are sent out, as it were, on a training mission, preparing them for taking the gospel to the ends of the earth. They go **two by two** for mutual support. (See notes on Matt. 10.)

The Beheading of John the Baptist

August 29

6:14–30: The Forerunner John is martyred for standing up for his convictions.

from there, [b]shake off the dust under
your feet as a testimony against
them. [2]Assuredly, I say to you, it will
be more tolerable for Sodom and Gomorrah in the day of judgment than
for that city!"†
12 So they went out and preached
that *people* should repent.
13 And they cast out many demons, [a]and anointed with oil many
who were sick, and healed *them*.†

The Baptist Beheaded
(Matt. 14:1–12; Luke 9:7–9)

14 [a]Now King Herod heard *of Him*,
for His name had become well
known. And he said, "John the Baptist is risen from the dead, and therefore [b]these powers are at work in
him."†
15 [a]Others said, "It is Elijah." And
others said, "It is [1]the Prophet,
[b]or like one of the prophets."
16 [a]But when Herod heard, he
said, "This is John, whom I beheaded; he has been raised from the
dead!"
17 For Herod himself had sent and
laid hold of John, and bound him
in prison for the sake of Herodias,
his brother Philip's wife; for he had
married her.†
18 Because John had said to Herod,
[a]"It is not lawful for you to have
your brother's wife."
19 Therefore Herodias [1]held it
against him and wanted to kill him,
but she could not;
20 for Herod [a]feared John, knowing that he *was* a just and holy man,
and he protected him. And when he
heard him, he [1]did many things, and
heard him gladly.†
21 [a]Then an opportune day came
when Herod [b]on his birthday gave
a feast for his nobles, the high officers, and the chief *men* of Galilee.
22 And when Herodias' daughter
herself came in and danced, and
pleased Herod and those who sat
with him, the king said to the girl,
"Ask me whatever you want, and I
will give *it* to you."
23 He also swore to her, [a]"Whatever you ask me, I will give you, up
to half my kingdom."
24 So she went out and said to her
mother, "What shall I ask?" And she
said, "The head of John the Baptist!"
25 Immediately she came in with
haste to the king and asked, saying,

11 [b]Acts 13:51; 18:6 [2]NU omits the rest of v. 11.
13 [a][James 5:14]
14 [a]Luke 9:7–9 [b]Luke 19:37
15 [a]Mark 8:28 [b]Matt. 21:11 [1]NU, M *a prophet, like one*
16 [a]Luke 3:19
18 [a]Lev. 18:16; 20:21
19 [1]*held a grudge*
20 [a]Matt. 14:5; 21:26 [1]NU *was very perplexed, yet*
21 [a]Matt. 14:6 [b]Gen. 40:20
23 [a]Esth. 5:3, 6; 7:2

6:11 Shake off the dust is a symbolic gesture of judgment.

6:13 Preaching is an earnest proclamation, and this present proclamation of the need for repentance is momentous. This is the first time the Twelve perform miracles. God gives His power, His energy, to human beings and through human beings—to and through those who repent. He shares with us by grace what is His by nature. The disciples **anointed with oil** as part of the act of healing, for by the Incarnation of Christ creation is renewed: oil and water become instruments of healing and renewal for the human race.

6:14 Herod is Herod Antipas, son of Herod the Great and governor of Galilee, called a **king** in popular language.

6:17–29 A flashback relating the circumstances of the death of John the Baptist, which give powerful testimony to his faith and zeal (see Matt. 11:11). Early Christians regarded John the Baptist with utmost esteem. Here, Mark shows John's fearlessness in telling the truth (v. 18). (See notes on Matt. 14:1–12; Luke 9:7–9.)

6:20 What a comment on the righteousness of John the Baptist: the king **feared John!** The royally clad Herod was frightened of a man clothed in camel's hair, a servant of God who lived out in the desert.

IC XC

Mother of God, *by the hand of Jan Isham.*

This icon of the Incarnation, the coming of the Son of God in the flesh, shows that Jesus took our humanity in the womb of His mother, the Virgin Mary. In so doing, God joins heaven and earth. Feast Day readings are Genesis 28:10–17; Exodus 3:1–8; Proverbs 8:22–30; 9:1–11; Ezekiel 43:27—44:4; Luke 1:39–49, 56; 10:38–42; 11:27, 28; Philippians 2:5–11. See also John 1:14; Colossians 2:9; 1 John 1:1.

"I want you to give me at once the
head of John the Baptist on a
platter."
26 [a]And the king was exceedingly
sorry; *yet*, because of the oaths and
because of those who sat with him,
he did not want to refuse her.
27 Immediately the king sent an
executioner and commanded his
head to be brought. And he went
and beheaded him in prison,
28 brought his head on a platter,
and gave it to the girl; and the girl
gave it to her mother.
29 When his disciples heard *of it*,
they came and [a]took away his corpse
and laid it in a tomb.

Feeding the Five Thousand

(Matt. 14:13–21; Luke 9:10–17;
John 6:1–14)

30 [a]Then the apostles gathered to
Jesus and told Him all things, both
what they had done and what they
had taught.†
31 [a]And He said to them, "Come
aside by yourselves to a deserted
place and rest a while." For [b]there
were many coming and going, and
they did not even have time to
eat.†
32 [a]So they departed to a deserted
place in the boat by themselves.
33 But [1]the multitudes saw them
departing, and many [a]knew Him
and ran there on foot from all the
cities. They arrived before them and
came together to Him.
34 [a]And Jesus, when He came out,
saw a great multitude and was
moved with compassion for them,
because they were like [b]sheep not
having a shepherd. So [c]He began to
teach them many things.
35 [a]When the day was now far
spent, His disciples came to Him and
said, "This is a deserted place, and
already the hour *is* late.
36 "Send them away, that they
may go into the surrounding country
and villages and buy themselves
[1]bread; for they have nothing to
eat."
37 But He answered and said to
them, "You give them something to
eat." And they said to Him, [a]"Shall
we go and buy two hundred denarii
worth of bread and give them *some-*
thing to eat?"†
38 But He said to them, "How
many loaves do you have? Go and
see." And when they found out they
said, [a]"Five, and two fish."
39 Then He [a]commanded them to
make them all sit down in groups
on the green grass.
40 So they sat down in ranks, in
hundreds and in fifties.
41 And when He had taken the five
loaves and the two fish, He [a]looked
up to heaven, [b]blessed and broke the
loaves, and gave *them* to His disciples
to set before them; and the two fish
He divided among *them* all.†
42 So they all ate and were filled.
43 And they took up twelve baskets full of fragments and of the fish.
44 Now those who had eaten the
loaves were [1]about five thousand
men.†

26 [a]Matt. 14:9
29 [a]1 Kin. 13:29, 30
30 [a]Luke 9:10
31 [a]Matt. 14:13 [b]Mark 3:20
32 [a]Matt. 14:13–21
33 [a][Col. 1:6] [1]NU, M *they*
34 [a]Matt. 9:36; 14:14 [b]Num. 27:17 [c]Luke 9:11
35 [a]Matt. 14:15
36 [1]NU *something to eat* and omits the rest of v. 36.
37 [a]2 Kin. 4:43
38 [a]John 6:9
39 [a]Matt. 15:35
41 [a]John 11:41, 42 [b]Matt. 15:36; 26:26
44 [1]NU, M omit *about*

6:30–44 See notes on Matt. 14:13–21; also Luke 9:10–17; John 6:1–14.

6:30 The word **apostle** (meaning "one who is sent," a messenger) is used frequently in the epistles but is rare in the gospels. It designates an official representative authorized to carry out a specific mission (see v. 7).

6:31 Jesus gives the disciples time to **rest a while.** They have just returned from a demanding assignment—preaching, healing and casting out demons—and it is time for solitude.

6:37–42 The feeding of the multitudes is both a messianic sign and an image of the Eucharist (see note on Matt. 14:14–21). Jesus' sustenance is never exhausted, just as His eucharistic body, multiplied and distributed, is "ever eaten and never consumed, sanctifying those who partake" (from the Divine Liturgy).

6:41–44 The disciples learn a great lesson here: whatever they have is enough to feed the people, whether physically or spiritually. God can multiply our resources so that everyone can be filled. But we must participate in His grace: Christ, along with the Father, blesses the **loaves** (v. 41), but the **disciples** distribute them.

6:44 There were also women and children present (Matt. 14:21), but according to cultural custom, only the approximate number of **men** is given.

Jesus Walks on Water
(Matt. 14:22–33; John 6:15–21)

45 [a]Immediately He [1]made His
disciples get into the boat and go
before Him to the other side, to Bethsaida, while He sent the multitude
away.
46 And when He had sent them
away, He [a]departed to the mountain
to pray.
47 Now when evening came, the
boat was in the middle of the sea;
and He *was* alone on the land.
48 Then He saw them straining at
rowing, for the wind was against
them. Now about the fourth watch
of the night He came to them, walking on the sea, and [a]would have
passed them by.
49 And when they saw Him walking on the sea, they supposed it was
a [a]ghost, and cried out;
50 for they all saw Him and were
troubled. But immediately He talked
with them and said to them, [a]"Be[1]
of good cheer! It is I; do not be
[b]afraid."†
51 Then He went up into the boat
to them, and the wind [a]ceased. And
they were greatly [b]amazed in themselves beyond measure, and
marveled.
52 For [a]they had not understood
about the loaves, because their
[b]heart was hardened.†

45 [a]John 6:15–21 [1]*invited, strongly urged*
46 [a]Luke 5:16
48 [a]Luke 24:28
49 [a]Matt. 14:26
50 [a]Matt. 9:2 [b]Is. 41:10 [1]*Take courage*
51 [a]Ps. 107:29 [b]Mark 1:27; 2:12; 5:42; 7:37
52 [a]Mark 8:17, 18 [b]Mark 3:5; 16:14
53 [a]Matt. 14:34–36
54 [1]Lit. *they*
56 [a]Matt. 9:20 [b]Num. 15:38, 39

CHAPTER 7
1 [a]Matt. 15:1–20
2 [a]Matt. 15:20 [1]NU omits *when* [2]NU omits *they found fault*
3 [a]Gal. 1:14 [1]Lit. *with the fist*

Many Made Whole
(Matt. 14:34–36)

53 [a]When they had crossed over,
they came to the land of Gennesaret
and anchored there.†
54 And when they came out of the
boat, immediately [1]the people recognized Him,
55 ran through that whole surrounding region, and began to carry
about on beds those who were sick
to wherever they heard He was.
56 Wherever He entered, into villages, cities, or the country, they laid
the sick in the marketplaces, and
begged Him that [a]they might just
touch the [b]hem of His garment. And
as many as touched Him were made
well.

The Traditions of the Pharisees
(Matt. 15:1–20)

7 Then [a]the Pharisees and some of
the scribes came together to
Him, having come from Jerusalem.†
2 Now [1]when they saw some of
His disciples eat bread with defiled,
that is, with [a]unwashed hands,
[2]they found fault.
3 For the Pharisees and all the
Jews do not eat unless they wash
their hands [1]in a special way, holding
the [a]tradition of the elders.

6:50 It is I, literally "I am" (Gr. *ego eimi*), especially used in the Gospel of John, is Jesus' own testimony to His deity. It reflects God's name as revealed to Moses at the burning bush (Ex. 3:14). Only God is self-existent, uncreated, the only being whose existence depends on no other but Himself; therefore He alone can truly say, "I am."

6:52 The knowledge of Christ is a matter of the **heart.** When our hearts are illumined by God, they become the seat of divine presence, grace and knowledge. In all the ascetic writings of the Orthodox Church, the heart is known as the "seat of knowledge."

6:53–56 Gennesaret is a region of Gentiles, where many respond to Jesus and are healed.

7:1–13 The issue here is not Jewish customs or traditions. Jesus does not prohibit them (Matt. 23:23). At issue is the raising of human tradition over the tradition or commandments of God (v. 8). The **tradition of the elders** (v. 3) is a body of interpretations of the Law handed down orally, which for **the Pharisees** and **the scribes** (v. 1) is as authoritative as the written Law of Moses. According to this tradition, purification—cleansing oneself from defiling contact with Gentiles or sinners (vv. 3, 4)—occurs by the outward act of ceremonial washing. Further, offerings to God may be made by promises. Thereby one could dedicate property or earnings to God (**Corban,** v. 11) to prevent their use by one's parents, but continue to use them oneself. These secondary traditions obscure the primary commandments of God and obedience to them. Traditions not from God must never supersede traditions from God, or Holy Tradition (2 Thess. 2:15; 3:6). Unlike Holy Tradition, human traditions can prevent people from coming to God (Rom. 2:24; Col. 2:8). See notes on Matt. 15:1–20.

4 *When they come* from the marketplace, they do not eat unless they
wash. And there are many other
things which they have received and
hold, *like* the washing of cups, pitchers, copper vessels, and couches.
5 [a]Then the Pharisees and scribes
asked Him, "Why do Your disciples
not walk according to the tradition
of the elders, but eat bread with unwashed hands?"
6 He answered and said to them,
"Well did Isaiah prophesy of you
[a]hypocrites, as it is written:

[b]'This people honors Me with
their lips,
But their heart is far from Me.
7 *And in vain they worship Me,*
Teaching as doctrines the
commandments of men.'

8 "For laying aside the commandment of God, you hold the tradition
of men—[1]the washing of pitchers
and cups, and many other such
things you do."
9 He said to them, "*All too* well
[a]you [1]reject the commandment of
God, that you may keep your
tradition.
10 "For Moses said, *[a]'Honor your*
father and your mother'; and,
[b]'He who curses father or mother,
let him be put to death.'
11 "But you say, 'If a man says to
his father or mother, [a]"Whatever
profit you might have received from
me *is* Corban"—' (that is, a gift *to*
God),
12 "then you no longer let him do
anything for his father or his mother,
13 "making the word of God of no
effect through your tradition which
you have handed down. And many
such things you do."
14 [a]When He had called all the
multitude to *Himself*, He said to

5 [a]Matt. 15:2
6 [a]Matt. 23:13–29
[b]Is. 29:13
8 [1]NU omits the rest of v. 8.
9 [a]Prov. 1:25
[1]*set aside*
10 [a]Ex. 20:12; Deut. 5:16
[b]Ex. 21:17
11 [a]Matt. 15:5; 23:18
14 [a]Matt. 15:10
[b]Matt. 16:9, 11, 12
15 [a]Is. 59:3
16 [a]Matt. 11:15
[1]NU omits v. 16.
17 [a]Matt. 15:15
18 [a][Heb. 5:11–14]
19 [1]NU sets off the final phrase as Mark's comment that Jesus has declared all foods clean.
20 [a]Ps. 39:1
21 [a]Gen. 6:5; 8:21
[b][Gal. 5:19–21]
[c]2 Pet. 2:14
[d]1 Thess. 4:3
22 [a]Luke 12:15
[b]Rom. 1:28, 29
[c]1 Pet. 4:3
[d]Rev. 2:9
[e]1 John 2:16
24 [a]Matt. 15:21
[b]Mark 2:1, 2
[1]NU omits *and Sidon*
25 [a]John 11:32
26 [1]*Gentile*
[2]A Syrian of Phoenicia

them, "Hear Me, everyone, and
[b]understand:
15 "There is nothing that enters a
man from outside which can defile
him; but the things which come out
of him, those are the things that
[a]defile a man.†
16 [a]"If[1] anyone has ears to hear,
let him hear!"
17 [a]When He had entered a house
away from the crowd, His disciples
asked Him concerning the parable.
18 So He said to them, [a]"Are you
thus without understanding also? Do
you not perceive that whatever enters a man from outside cannot defile
him,
19 "because it does not enter his
heart but his stomach, and is eliminated, [1]*thus* purifying all foods?"
20 And He said, [a]"What comes out
of a man, that defiles a man.
21 [a]"For from within, out of the
heart of men, [b]proceed evil
thoughts, [c]adulteries, [d]fornications,
murders,†
22 "thefts, [a]covetousness, wickedness, [b]deceit, [c]lewdness, an evil eye,
[d]blasphemy, [e]pride, foolishness.
23 "All these evil things come from
within and defile a man."

A Gentile Woman Believes

(Matt. 15:21–28)

24 [a]From there He arose and went
to the region of Tyre [1]and Sidon.
And He entered a house and wanted
no one to know *it*, but He could not
be [b]hidden.†
25 For a woman whose young
daughter had an unclean spirit heard
about Him, and she came and
[a]fell at His feet.
26 The woman was a [1]Greek, a
[2]Syro-Phoenician by birth, and she

7:15 Jesus teaches that nothing is of itself spiritually unclean. God makes all things good. Sins committed of our own free will, what comes from within us, **defile** and make the heart impure.

7:21–23 All these evil things (v. 23) are not what God created. We will them; we produce them; they are our sins coming from within us. They are a perversion of what God has made.

7:24 Tyre and Sidon: Gentile cities on the coast of Palestine.

kept [3]asking Him to cast the demon
out of her daughter.†
27 But Jesus said to her, "Let the
children be filled first, for it is not
good to take the children's bread and
throw *it* to the little dogs."
28 And she answered and said to
Him, "Yes, Lord, yet even the little
dogs under the table eat from the
children's crumbs."
29 Then He said to her, "For this
saying go your way; the demon has
gone out of your daughter."
30 And when she had come to her
house, she found the demon gone
out, and her daughter lying on the
bed.

The Healing of a Deaf Man
(Matt. 15:29–31)

31 [a]Again, departing from the region of Tyre and Sidon, He came
through the midst of the region of
Decapolis to the Sea of Galilee.
32 Then [a]they brought to Him one
who was deaf and had an impedi-
ment in his speech, and they begged
Him to put His hand on him.
33 And He took him aside from the
multitude, and put His fingers in his
ears, and [a]He spat and touched his
tongue.†
34 Then, [a]looking up to heaven,
[b]He sighed, and said to him, "Eph-
phatha," that is, "Be opened."†
35 [a]Immediately his ears were
opened, and the [1]impediment of his
tongue was loosed, and he spoke
plainly.
36 Then [a]He commanded them
that they should tell no one; but the
more He commanded them, the
more widely they proclaimed *it*.†
37 And they were [a]astonished beyond measure, saying, "He has done
all things well. He [b]makes both the
deaf to hear and the mute to speak."

Feeding the Four Thousand
(Matt. 15:32–39)

8 In those days, [a]the multitude being very great and having nothing to eat, Jesus called His disciples
to Him and said to them,†
2 "I have [a]compassion on the
multitude, because they have now
continued with Me three days and
have nothing to eat.
3 "And if I send them away hungry to their own houses, they will
faint on the way; for some of them
have come from afar."
4 Then His disciples answered
Him, "How can one satisfy these
people with bread here in the
wilderness?"
5 [a]He asked them, "How many
loaves do you have?" And they said,
"Seven."
6 So He commanded the multitude to sit down on the ground. And
He took the seven loaves and gave
thanks, broke *them* and gave *them* to
His disciples to set before *them;* and

26 [3]*begging*
31 [a]Matt. 15:29
32 [a]Luke 11:14
33 [a]Mark 8:23
34 [a]Mark 6:41 [b]John 11:33, 38
35 [a]Is. 35:5, 6 [1]Lit. *bond*
36 [a]Mark 5:43
37 [a]Mark 6:51; 10:26 [b]Matt. 12:22

CHAPTER 8
1 [a]Matt. 15:32–39
2 [a]Mark 1:41; 6:34
5 [a]Mark 6:38

7:26 That the mother **kept asking Him** for her daughter's deliverance teaches perseverance in prayer. Jesus resists her, not to make her persuade Him, but to test her faith. Such persistence the Lord seeks from all. (See notes on Matt. 15:21–28.)

7:33 Jesus heals in various ways. Sometimes He speaks a word (vv. 29, 30), sometimes He commands people to act (take up a bed, 2:10–12; wash in a pool, John 9:7), sometimes He touches people (1:40–42). Here He takes a man **aside** for a private and unusual act of healing. The ways of God at times do not make sense to us, not because He is illogical, but because His nature transcends our capacity to understand.

7:34 **Looking up to heaven** is a sign of intimacy with the Father in prayer. **He sighed** out of deep compassion for the man's pitiful condition.

7:36 Here Jesus' attempt to keep His messianic identity secret is foiled by the people's enthusiasm. The gospel is so powerful that it simply cannot be contained.

8:1–10 Mark here reports a second feeding of a **multitude,** which now includes many Gentiles in the region of the Decapolis (see 7:31), southeast of the Sea of Galilee. To feed the hungry in the wilderness is a messianic sign, fulfilling the prophecy, "Can God prepare a table in the wilderness? . . . Can He give bread also?" (Ps. 78:19, 20). This miracle has special significance: seldom does Jesus refer back to a miracle He has performed, but to the feeding of the four and five thousand He does (8:19–21).

they set *them* before the multitude.
7 They also had a few small fish;
and [a]having blessed them, He said
to set them also before *them*.
8 So they ate and were filled, and
they took up seven large baskets of
leftover fragments.
9 Now those who had eaten were
about four thousand. And He sent
them away,
10 [a]immediately got into the boat
with His disciples, and came to the
region of Dalmanutha.

Show Us a Sign
(Matt. 16:1–4)

11 [a]Then the Pharisees came out
and began to dispute with Him,
seeking from Him a sign from
heaven, testing Him.†
12 But He [a]sighed deeply in His
spirit, and said, "Why does this generation seek a sign? Assuredly, I say
to you, [b]no sign shall be given to
this generation."

The Leaven of the Pharisees
(Matt. 16:5–12)

13 And He left them, and getting
into the boat again, departed to the
other side.†
14 [a]Now [1]the disciples had forgotten to take bread, and they did not
have more than one loaf with them
in the boat.

7 [a]Matt. 14:19; Mark 6:41
10 [a]Matt. 15:39
11 [a]Matt. 12:38; 16:1; Luke 11:16; John 2:18; 6:30; 1 Cor. 1:22
12 [a]Mark 7:34 [b]Matt. 12:39
14 [a]Matt. 16:5 [1]NU, M *they*
15 [a]Matt. 16:6; Luke 12:1 [1]*yeast*
17 [a]Mark 6:52; 16:14 [1]NU omits *still*
19 [a]Matt. 14:20; Mark 6:43; Luke 9:17; John 6:13
20 [a]Matt. 15:37
21 [a][Mark 6:52]
22 [a]Matt. 9:27; John 9:1 [b]Luke 18:15
23 [a]Mark 7:33

15 [a]Then He charged them, saying, "Take heed, beware of the
[1]leaven of the Pharisees and the
leaven of Herod."
16 And they reasoned among
themselves, saying, "*It is* because we
have no bread."
17 But Jesus, being aware of *it*, said
to them, "Why do you reason because you have no bread? [a]Do you
not yet perceive nor understand? Is
your heart [1]still hardened?†
18 "Having eyes, do you not see?
And having ears, do you not hear?
And do you not remember?
19 [a]"When I broke the five loaves
for the five thousand, how many
baskets full of fragments did you
take up?" They said to Him,
"Twelve."
20 "Also, [a]when I broke the seven
for the four thousand, how many
large baskets full of fragments did
you take up?" And they said,
"Seven."
21 So He said to them, "How *is it*
[a]you do not understand?"

A Blind Man Healed

22 Then He came to Bethsaida;
and they brought a [a]blind man to
Him, and begged Him to [b]touch
him.
23 So He took the blind man by the
hand and led him out of the town.
And when [a]He had spit on his eyes

8:11, 12 A sign from heaven (v. 11) is an indisputable, spectacular act, the kind Jesus rejected in His temptations (see notes on Matt. 4:6, 7; Luke 4:9). Jesus has given countless signs by this time: causing the blind to see, the lame to walk, the deaf to hear, the dumb to speak, and the dead to rise. But these are not good enough for **the Pharisees.** Jesus **sighed deeply,** for they **seek a sign** (v. 12) out of hardness of heart, daring Jesus to force them to faith.

8:13 The other side is the northern shore of the Sea of Galilee, not far from Bethsaida (v. 22).

8:15 Leaven is frequently (but not always) a negative image in Scripture, symbolizing evil. Here it represents the erroneous understanding and evil intent of **the Pharisees** and **Herod** Antipas. Though they completely misunderstand the revelation of God in Christ, the Pharisees influence the people. Their teaching is like *leaven;* it permeates the whole. Their blatant legalism and hypocritical actions damage those who listen to them.

8:17–21 Jesus is concerned about His disciples. Men who do not yet understand the Lord's provision for them in the feeding of **the five thousand** (v. 19) and **the four thousand** (v. 20) are men whose hearts are **still hardened** (v. 17). Discipleship without an understanding of Christ is unthinkable.

and put His hands on him, He asked
him if he saw anything.†
24 And he looked up and said, "I
see men like trees, walking."
25 Then He put *His* hands on his
eyes again and made him look up.
And he was restored and saw everyone clearly.
26 Then He sent him away to his
house, saying, [1]"Neither go into
the town, [a]nor tell anyone in the
town."

Peter's Confession
(Matt. 16:13–20; Luke 9:18–21)

27 [a]Now Jesus and His disciples
went out to the towns of Caesarea
Philippi; and on the road He asked
His disciples, saying to them, "Who
do men say that I am?"†
28 So they answered, [a]"John the
Baptist; but some *say,* [b]Elijah; and
others, one of the prophets."
29 He said to them, "But who do
you say that I am?" Peter answered
and said to Him, [a]"You are the
Christ."†
30 [a]Then He strictly warned them
that they should tell no one about
Him.

Jesus' First Prophecy of His Passion
(Matt. 16:21–28; Luke 9:22–27)

31 And [a]He began to teach them
that the Son of Man must suffer
many things, and be [b]rejected by the
elders and chief priests and scribes,
and be [c]killed, and after three days
rise again.†
32 He spoke this word openly.
Then Peter took Him aside and began to rebuke Him.
33 But when He had turned
around and looked at His disciples,
He [a]rebuked Peter, saying, "Get behind Me, Satan! For you are not
[1]mindful of the things of God, but
the things of men."†
34 When He had called the people
to *Himself,* with His disciples also,
He said to them, [a]"Whoever desires
to come after Me, let him deny himself, and take up his cross, and follow Me.†
35 "For [a]whoever desires to save
his life will lose it, but whoever loses

26 [a]Mark 5:43; 7:36 [1]NU *Do not even go into the town.*
27 [a]Luke 9:18–20
28 [a]Matt. 14:2 [b]Luke 9:7, 8
29 [a]John 1:41; 4:42; 6:69; 11:27
30 [a]Matt. 8:4; 16:20
31 [a]Matt. 16:21; 20:19 [b]Mark 10:33 [c]Mark 9:31; 10:34
33 [a][Rev. 3:19] [1]*setting your mind on*
34 [a]Luke 14:27
35 [a]John 12:25

8:23–26 Jesus leads the man **out of the town** (v. 23), to a private place once again, for another special healing. This man is healed in stages, just as our ability to know God grows gradually. Again, He wishes His messianic secret not to be revealed (see vv. 27–30).

8:27 Caesarea Philippi, a major city rebuilt by Herod's son Philip, who named it after Tiberius Caesar and himself, was located some 20 miles north of the Sea of Galilee. Jesus chooses this Gentile area to challenge His disciples with the messianic question in private, apparently wishing to avoid popular repercussions among Jews.

8:29 Peter, on behalf of the disciples, confesses Jesus as **the Christ.** The Hebrew equivalent of *Christ* is "Messiah," meaning "the Anointed One." Because this title was fraught with popular nationalistic misunderstandings, Jesus uses it only rarely, but accepts it when questioned at His trial before the Sanhedrin (14:61, 62). The understanding of Christ's identity cannot be gained through human reason; nor do miracles divulge it. It comes only by revelation from the Father in heaven (Matt. 16:16, 17).

8:31, 32 Son of Man is a veiled OT messianic title (Dan. 7:13) which Jesus uses frequently, as it is more suitable than "the Christ" for this stage in Jesus' ministry. Jesus **must suffer:** This is the inscrutable divine will, and the very heart of His redemptive work. Suffering marks Jesus' redefinition of messiahship (see Is. 53). Peter is shocked by this unprecedented notion (v. 32). But Jesus is preparing His disciples—and Christians today—for adversity.

8:33 Peter unknowingly serves the intent of **Satan** other than the plan of God in attempting to lead Jesus away from the path of suffering.

8:34 After Peter's confession, Jesus injects a new, solemn tone into His ministry by speaking about suffering and by teaching the **people** and the **disciples** the cost of discipleship: self-denial, carrying one's cross (a symbol of suffering), and obedience to Christ. By saying **let him deny himself, and take up his cross,** Jesus means His followers should separate themselves from their sins and from the inclination of their hearts towards evil (Gen. 8:21), crucifying the flesh with its passions and desires (Gal. 5:24).

The Adoration of the Holy Cross *Third Sunday of Lent*

8:34—9:1: Jesus explains the meaning of the Cross in the life of the believer.

his life for My sake and the gospel's
will save it.†
36 "For what will it profit a man
if he gains the whole world, and
loses his own soul?†
37 "Or what will a man give in exchange for his soul?
38 [a]"For whoever [b]is ashamed of
Me and My words in this adulterous
and sinful generation, of him the Son
of Man also will be ashamed when
He comes in the glory of His Father
with the holy angels."

9 And He said to them, [a]"Assuredly, I say to you that there
are some standing here who will not
taste death till they see [b]the kingdom
of God [1]present with power."†

The Transfiguration
(Matt. 17:1–8; Luke 9:28–36)

2 [a]Now after six days Jesus took
Peter, James, and John, and led them
up on a high mountain apart by
themselves; and He was transfigured
before them.†
3 His clothes became shining, exceedingly [a]white, like snow, such as
no launderer on earth can whiten
them.
4 And Elijah appeared to them
with Moses, and they were talking
with Jesus.
5 Then Peter answered and said
to Jesus, "Rabbi, it is good for us to
be here; and let us make three tabernacles: one for You, one for Moses,
and one for Elijah"—†
6 because he did not know what
to say, for they were greatly
afraid.
7 And a [a]cloud came and overshadowed them; and a voice came
out of the cloud, saying, "This is
[b]My beloved Son. [c]Hear Him!"†
8 Suddenly, when they had
looked around, they saw no one

38 [a]Matt. 10:33 [b]2 Tim. 1:8, 9; 2:12

CHAPTER 9

1 [a]Luke 9:27 [b][Matt. 24:30] [1]*having come*
2 [a]Matt. 17:1–8
3 [a]Dan. 7:9
7 [a]Ex. 40:34 [b]Mark 1:11 [c]Acts 3:22

8:35 To **save** one's **life** means to base one's earthly life on self. This is the opposite of self-denial, and ultimately results in the loss of eternal life. To **lose** one's life is to accept suffering and sacrifice for the sake of Christ and His Kingdom, which ultimately brings salvation. Discipleship is costly: it requires giving up all claim to everything the world holds dear.

8:36, 37 Soul (Gr. *psyche*), also translated "life" (v. 35), can refer to our spiritual nature or the whole human being. Nothing is more valuable to us than our souls.

9:1 The kingdom of God present with power is connected to the previous words about the Son of Man coming in glory (8:38). A foretaste of this glory is granted at the Transfiguration, which anticipates future revelatory moments of God's great *power:* the Resurrection of Christ and Pentecost, as well as the consummation of *the Kingdom.*

9:2, 3 The **transfigured** radiance of Christ is His uncreated glory, a saving revelation at the heart of the Christian experience (2 Pet. 1:16–18). The Transfiguration assures the disciples that the Messiah, who is to suffer, is also the Lord of Glory (see 1 Cor. 2:8). Only His third-day Resurrection is a greater sign of His divinity than is His Transfiguration.

9:5 Although Christ is addressed as **Rabbi,** He has not passed through a rabbinical school, and His ministry has clearly gone beyond the established function of a rabbi, which was to teach. This title shows the Master-disciple relationship between Christ and the Twelve. Peter recognizes **Moses** and **Elijah,** representing the Law and the Prophets, who appear with Jesus. This is a glimpse of the glory that is to be revealed (Rom. 8:18), where introductions will not be needed.

9:7 A **cloud** is sometimes the sign of a theophany, the presence of God the Father. This revelation is for the benefit of the disciples, that their faith should be firm. For they are called to believe not only in Christ but in what is to come, the eternal Kingdom. The Greek verb for **hear** is in the present imperative form, meaning "listen always."

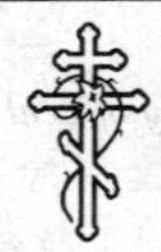

Commemoration of St. John of the Ladder *Fourth Sunday of Lent*

9:17–31: Fasting and prayer are necessary to spiritual life.

anymore, but only Jesus with themselves.

Is Elijah Coming?
(Matt. 17:9–13)

9 [a]Now as they came down from
the mountain, He commanded them
that they should tell no one the
things they had seen, till the Son of
Man had risen from the dead.†
10 So they kept this word to themselves, questioning [a]what the rising
from the dead meant.
11 And they asked Him, saying,
"Why do the scribes say [a]that Elijah
must come first?"†
12 Then He answered and told
them, "Indeed, Elijah is coming first
and restores all things. And [a]how is
it written concerning the Son of Man,
that He must suffer many things and
[b]be treated with contempt?
13 "But I say to you that [a]Elijah has
also come, and they did to him whatever they wished, as it is written of
him."

O Faithless Generation
(Matt. 17:14–21; Luke 9:37–42)

14 [a]And when He came to the disciples, He saw a great multitude
around them, and scribes disputing
with them.
15 Immediately, when they saw
Him, all the people were greatly
amazed, and running to *Him*,
greeted Him.
16 And He asked the scribes,
"What are you discussing with
them?"†
17 Then [a]one of the crowd answered and said, "Teacher, I brought
You my son, who has a mute spirit.
18 "And wherever it seizes him, it
throws him down; he foams at the
mouth, gnashes his teeth, and becomes rigid. So I spoke to Your disciples, that they should cast it out, but
they could not."
19 He answered him and said, "O
[a]faithless[1] generation, how long
shall I be with you? How long shall
I [2]bear with you? Bring him to Me."†
20 Then they brought him to Him.
And [a]when he saw Him, immediately the spirit convulsed him, and
he fell on the ground and wallowed,
foaming at the mouth.
21 So He asked his father, "How
long has this been happening to
him?" And he said, "From
childhood.
22 "And often he has thrown him
both into the fire and into the water
to destroy him. But if You can do
anything, have compassion on us
and help us."†
23 Jesus said to him, [a]"If[1] you can
believe, all things *are* possible to him
who believes."†

9 [a]Matt. 17:9–13; Mark 16:6; Luke 24:6, 7, 46
10 [a]John 2:19–22
11 [a]Mal. 4:5; Matt. 17:10
12 [a]Ps. 22:6; Is. 53:3; Dan. 9:26 [b]Luke 23:11; Phil. 2:7
13 [a]Mal. 4:5; Matt. 11:14; 17:12; Luke 1:17
14 [a]Matt. 17:14–19; Luke 9:37–42
17 [a]Matt. 17:14; Luke 9:38
19 [a]John 4:48 [1]*unbelieving* [2]*put up with*
20 [a]Mark 1:26; Luke 9:42
23 [a]Matt. 17:20; Mark 11:23; Luke 17:6; John 11:40 [1]NU *"If You can!' All things*

9:9 Christ's Resurrection is required for full disclosure of the messianic secret and for full understanding of messiahship.

9:11–13 The return of **Elijah,** expected as a preparation for the Messiah, has already been fulfilled through John the Baptist.

9:16 The Lord is loyal to His own. Jesus does not ask the disciples what they are **discussing** with **the scribes;** it is the scribes who must answer.

9:19 Faithless generation is said of all, including the father of the child and the disciples.

9:22 The man's comment, **but if you can do anything,** is prompted by the disciples' inability to cast out the demon. What Christ's disciples can or cannot do reflects on the Lord Himself.

9:23 All things are possible because of God's power released through faith. Jesus seeks to elicit faith from the child's father.

24 Immediately the father of the
child cried out and said with tears,
"Lord, I believe; [a]help my unbelief!"†
25 When Jesus saw that the people
came running together, He [a]rebuked
the unclean spirit, saying to it: "Deaf
and dumb spirit, I command you,
come out of him and enter him no
more!"
26 Then *the spirit* cried out, convulsed him greatly, and came out of
him. And he became as one dead,
so that many said, "He is dead."
27 But Jesus took him by the hand
and lifted him up, and he arose.
28 [a]And when He had come into
the house, His disciples asked Him
privately, "Why could we not cast
it out?"
29 So He said to them, "This kind
can come out by nothing but [a]prayer
[1]and fasting."†

Jesus' Second Prophecy of His Passion

(Matt. 17:22, 23; Luke 9:43–45)

30 Then they departed from there
and passed through Galilee, and He
did not want anyone to know *it*.†
31 [a]For He taught His disciples and
said to them, "The Son of Man is
being betrayed into the hands of
men, and they will [b]kill Him. And
after He is killed, He will [c]rise the
third day."
32 But they [a]did not understand
this saying, and were afraid to ask
Him.†

24 [a]Luke 17:5
25 [a]Mark 1:25
28 [a]Matt. 17:19
29 [a][James 5:16] [1]NU omits *and fasting*
31 [a]Luke 9:44 [b]Matt. 16:21; 27:50 [c]1 Cor. 15:4
32 [a]Luke 2:50; 18:34
33 [a]Matt. 18:1–5 [1]*discussed*
34 [a][Prov. 13:10] [b]Luke 22:24; 23:46; 24:46
35 [a]Luke 22:26, 27
36 [a]Mark 10:13–16
37 [a]Matt. 10:40
38 [a]Num. 11:27–29

The Way of Discipleship

(Matt. 18:1–35; Luke 9:46–50)

33 [a]Then He came to Capernaum.
And when He was in the house He
asked them, "What was it you
[1]disputed among yourselves on the
road?"
34 But they kept silent, for on the
road they had [a]disputed among
themselves who *would be the* [b]great-
est.†
35 And He sat down, called the
twelve, and said to them, [a]"If anyone desires to be first, he shall be
last of all and servant of all."†
36 Then [a]He took a little child and
set him in the midst of them. And
when He had taken him in His arms,
He said to them,
37 "Whoever receives one of these
little children in My name receives
Me; and [a]whoever receives Me, receives not Me but Him who sent
Me."
38 [a]Now John answered Him, saying, "Teacher, we saw someone who
does not follow us casting out demons in Your name, and we forbade
him because he does not follow us."†

9:24 The presence of doubt does not imply the absence of faith. Christ honors whatever faith we have and will increase faith when we sincerely desire Him.

9:29 Prayer and fasting are essential expressions of the life of faith. The inclusion of *and fasting* in the text is quite appropriate, though a number of ancient manuscripts lack it.

9:30 He did not want anyone to know it because He wished to spend time privately with His disciples.

9:32 The disciples **were afraid to ask Him,** perhaps because they were aware of their own dullness and had become sensitive to His rebukes; or perhaps because they did not want to face the fact of His coming death.

9:34 While Jesus is revealing His future suffering and death, the disciples are discussing personal ambitions, having possibly misunderstood Jesus' earlier words about His second and glorious coming (8:38) and the power of the Kingdom (v. 1). They miss the point of suffering and discipleship. For they have performed many miracles and have exercised great power, and now they are tempted by pride and desire for position. So serious is this issue that the remainder of this chapter is cast against its backdrop.

9:35 The passion for position must be displaced by a decision to **be last,** to serve all people. Beyond even humility, service is active care and love for others.

9:38–40 This discussion is the aftermath of the argument as to who would be the greatest. Sectarianism and triumphalism (the attitude that one creed is superior to all others) are forbidden, for God's working transcends our limited perceptions. One is either for or **against** (v. 40) Christ, but it is not always ours to know who is on which side.

39 But Jesus said, "Do not forbid
him, [a]for no one who works a miracle in My name can soon afterward
speak evil of Me.
40 "For [a]he who is not against
[1]us is on [2]our side.
41 [a]"For whoever gives you a cup
of water to drink in My name, because you belong to Christ, assuredly, I say to you, he will by no
means lose his reward.
42 [a]"But whoever causes one of
these little ones who believe in Me
[1]to stumble, it would be better for
him if a millstone were hung around
his neck, and he were thrown into
the sea.†
43 [a]"If your hand causes you to
sin, cut it off. It is better for you to
enter into life [1]maimed, rather than
having two hands, to go to [2]hell,
into the fire that shall never be
quenched—
44 [1]"where

> [a]*'Their worm does not die,*
> *And the fire is not quenched.'*

45 "And if your foot causes you to
sin, cut it off. It is better for you
to enter life lame, rather than having two feet, to be cast into [1]hell,
[2]into the fire that shall never be
quenched—
46 "where

> [a]*'Their worm does not die,*
> *And the fire is not quenched.'*

47 "And if your eye causes you to
sin, pluck it out. It is better for you
to enter the kingdom of God with
one eye, rather than having two
eyes, to be cast into [1]hell fire—
48 "where

> [a]*'Their worm does not die,*
> *And the [b]fire is not quenched.'*

49 "For everyone will be [a]seasoned
with fire, [b]and[1] every sacrifice will
be seasoned with salt.†
50 [a]"Salt *is* good, but if the salt
loses its flavor, how will you season
it? [b]Have salt in yourselves, and
[c]have peace with one another."

39 [a]1 Cor. 12:3
40 [a][Matt. 12:30] [1]M *you* [2]M *your*
41 [a]Matt. 10:42
42 [a]Luke 17:1, 2 [1]To fall into sin
43 [a]Matt. 5:29, 30; 18:8, 9 [1]*crippled* [2]Gr. *Gehenna*
44 [a]Is. 66:24 [1]NU omits v. 44.
45 [1]Gr. *Gehenna* [2]NU omits the rest of v. 45 and all of v. 46.
46 [a]Is. 66:24
47 [1]Gr. *Gehenna*
48 [a]Is. 66:24 [b]Jer. 7:20
49 [a][Matt. 3:11] [b]Lev. 2:13 [1]NU omits the rest of v. 49.
50 [a]Matt. 5:13 [b]Col. 4:6 [c]Rom. 12:18; 14:19

CHAPTER 10
1 [a]Matt. 19:1–9
2 [a]Matt. 19:3

What Is Marriage?
(Matt. 19:1–12)

10 Then [a]He arose from there
and came to the region of Judea by the other side of the Jordan.
And multitudes gathered to Him
again, and as He was accustomed,
He taught them again.†
2 [a]The Pharisees came and asked
Him, "Is it lawful for a man to divorce *his* wife?" testing Him.†

9:42–48 One of the sternest warnings Christ ever gave is here directed at the disciples. **Little ones,** like the "little children" (v. 37), are humble believers with no pretensions to greatness. Leaders are to be "last": faithful and serving. A major cause of stumbling for Christians is that their leaders seek to be great. To bring leaders to servanthood, Jesus requires not physical mutilation but uncompromising detachment, even from the most precious relationships or possessions, if they cause sin. As a negative motivation, He portrays eternal torment.

9:49, 50 This difficult passage, directed specifically to the disciples, mixes both negative and positive images of **salt.** This may be a combination of statements made by Jesus in different contexts: (1) The **fire** with which everyone **will be seasoned** (lit. "salted") seems to refer back to the fire of judgment (vv. 47, 48). (2) **Every sacrifice will be seasoned with salt** tells us suffering will happen to all who follow Christ, a positive experience when undertaken in humble faith. (3) **Salt is good** (v. 50) refers to the special quality of life expected of disciples, particularly those whom Christ has called to spread His gospel. **Have peace with one another** suggests that one way to lose flavor as salt is to be striving for greatness (v. 34).

10:1 Having completed His Galilean ministry, Jesus begins His Judean ministry, the focus of which is Jerusalem. Jesus **taught** regularly. Teaching is not all people need, but it is indispensable for effective Christian living.

10:2–4 The scribes and **Pharisees** often debated the legal basis of divorce in Judaism (Deut. 24:1–4). Here, the Pharisees seek to test Jesus. Divorce was very simple for a man during

(continued on next page)

3 And He answered and said to
them, "What did Moses command
you?"
4 They said, [a]"Moses permitted *a*
man to write a certificate of divorce,
and to dismiss *her*."
5 And Jesus answered and said to
them, "Because of the hardness of
your heart he wrote you this
[1]precept.†
6 "But from the beginning of the
creation, God [a]'*made them male and*
female.'†
7 [a]'*For this reason a man shall*
leave his father and mother and be
joined to his wife,
8 '*and the two shall become one*
flesh'; so then they are no longer
two, but one flesh.
9 "Therefore what God has joined
together, let not man separate."
10 In the house His disciples also
asked Him again about the same
matter.
11 So He said to them, [a]"Whoever
divorces his wife and marries another commits adultery against
her.†
12 "And if a woman divorces her
husband and marries another, she
commits adultery."

4 [a]Deut. 24:1–4; Matt. 5:31; 19:7
5 [1]*command*
6 [a]Gen. 1:27; 5:2
7 [a]Gen. 2:24; [1 Cor. 6:16]; Eph. 5:31
11 [a]Ex. 20:14; [Matt. 5:32; 19:9]; Luke 16:18; [Rom. 7:3]; 1 Cor. 7:10, 11
13 [a]Matt. 19:13–15; Luke 18:15–17
14 [a][1 Cor. 14:20; 1 Pet. 2:2]
15 [a]Matt. 18:3, 4; 19:14; Luke 18:17 [b]Luke 13:28
17 [a]Matt. 19:16–30; Luke 18:18–30 [b]John 6:28; Acts 2:37
18 [a]1 Sam. 2:2

Children Receive the Kingdom

(Matt. 19:13–15; Luke 18:15–17)

13 [a]Then they brought little children to Him, that He might touch
them; but the disciples rebuked
those who brought *them*.
14 But when Jesus saw *it*, He was
greatly displeased and said to them,
"Let the little children come to Me,
and do not forbid them; for [a]of such
is the kingdom of God.†
15 "Assuredly, I say to you,
[a]whoever does not receive the kingdom of God as a little child will
[b]by no means enter it."
16 And He took them up in His
arms, laid *His* hands on them, and
blessed them.†

The Danger of Riches

(Matt. 19:16–30; Luke 18:18–30)

17 [a]Now as He was going out on
the road, one came running, knelt
before Him, and asked Him, "Good
Teacher, what shall I [b]do that I may
inherit eternal life?"
18 So Jesus said to him, "Why do
you call Me good? No one *is* good
but One, *that is*, [a]God.†

(continued from previous page)
the time of Jesus: a mere **certificate** (v. 4) written by a dissatisfied husband was all that was needed.

10:5 Moses' legislation on divorce is a concession to a human weakness, **hardness** of **heart,** which is at the root of divorce on the part of one partner or both.

10:6–9 Jesus goes back to the original will of God for permanent, monogamous marriage, indicated by the creation of man and woman as well as by God's explicit command in Gen. 2:24. **Then they are no longer two, but one flesh** is the heart of the biblical teaching on marriage: Husband and wife are *one flesh,* joined together in oneness by God. This is not symbolic or merely moral but real—a man and woman are actually joined, creating a total unity which is unbreakable. Therefore, marriage is a sacrament by the grace of God. The issue in this passage is not whether divorce is permissible, but whether the union between husband and wife can be broken—even when a divorce occurs. (See notes on Matt. 19:1–12.) Consequently, v. 9 is a strong counsel against divorce.

10:11, 12 According to Jesus, remarriage after divorce is equivalent to **adultery. If a woman divorces her husband** is a case applicable only to Gentiles, for a Jewish woman could not legally divorce her husband. Mark does not report Matthew's exception for divorce, "except for sexual immorality" (Matt. 19:9). St. Paul also knew of Christ's command repudiating divorce (1 Cor. 7:10).

10:14, 15 Jesus rebukes the disciples not only because He has compassion for **children,** but because children are models of those who **receive the kingdom** (v. 15) in their openness and simple trust.

10:16 See note on Matt. 19:13–15.

10:18 The man approaches Jesus as a mere human and Jesus replies as such, not denying His own goodness but focusing the man's attention entirely on God: **No one is good but One, that is, God.**

19 "You know the command-
ments: [a]*'Do not commit adultery,'*
'Do not murder,' 'Do not steal,' 'Do
not bear false witness,' 'Do not defraud,' *'Honor your father and your*
mother.' "✝
20 **And he answered and said to**
Him, "Teacher, all these things I
have [a]kept from my youth."
21 **Then Jesus, looking at him,**
loved him, and said to him, "One
thing you lack: Go your way, [a]sell
whatever you have and give to the
poor, and you will have [b]treasure in
heaven; and come, [c]take up the
cross, and follow Me."✝
22 **But he was sad at this word, and**
went away sorrowful, for he had
great possessions.
23 [a]**Then Jesus looked around and**
said to His disciples, "How hard it
is for those who have riches to enter
the kingdom of God!"✝
24 **And the disciples were aston-**
ished at His words. But Jesus an-
swered again and said to them,
"Children, how hard it is [1]for those
[a]who trust in riches to enter the
kingdom of God!✝
25 "It is easier for a camel to go
through the eye of a needle than for
a [a]rich man to enter the kingdom of
God."✝
26 **And they were greatly aston-**
ished, saying among themselves,
"Who then can be saved?"
27 **But Jesus looked at them and**
said, "With men *it is* impossible, but
not [a]with God; for with God all
things are possible."
28 [a]**Then Peter began to say to**
Him, "See, we have left all and fol-
lowed You."✝
29 **So Jesus answered and said,**
"Assuredly, I say to you, there is no
one who has left house or brothers
or sisters or father or mother [1]or wife
or children or [2]lands, for My sake
and the gospel's,✝
30 [a]"who shall not receive a
hundredfold now in this time—
houses and brothers and sisters and
mothers and children and lands,
with [b]persecutions—and in the age
to come, eternal life.✝
31 [a]"But many *who are* first will be
last, and the last first."

Jesus' Third Prophecy of His Passion
(Matt. 20:17–19; Luke 18:31–34)

32 [a]**Now they were on the road,**
going up to Jerusalem, and Jesus was
going before them; and they were

19 [a]Ex. 20:12–16; Deut. 5:16–20
20 [a]Phil. 3:6
21 [a][Luke 12:33; 16:9] [b]Matt. 6:19, 20; 19:21 [c][Mark 8:34]
23 [a]Matt. 19:23
24 [a][1 Tim. 6:17] [1]NU omits *for those who trust in riches*
25 [a][Matt. 13:22; 19:24]
27 [a]Jer. 32:17
28 [a]Luke 18:28
29 [1]NU omits *or wife* [2]Lit. *fields*
30 [a]Luke 18:29, 30 [b][1 Pet. 4:12, 13]
31 [a]Luke 13:30
32 [a]Matt. 20:17–19

10:19 Jesus affirms obedience to the Ten **Commandments** as an essential aspect of the quest for righteousness and eternal life.

10:21 Jesus recognizes and approves the man's moral righteousness. But He tests him at his point of greatest vulnerability, where he needs to repent most. It is his money that is keeping him from salvation. Jesus challenges him with the ideal of total sacrifice for His sake. The command to **sell** all is for this man, or for any other whom Christ may call in this particular way, but should not be construed as a universal requirement. Christians are to use their possessions according to God's purposes, above all to help the poor and needy, but they are not to reject ownership of property. However, voluntary poverty is a legitimate part of a freely chosen way of life—for example, for monastics.

10:23, 24 Riches grip the heart like few other things. When people **trust in** (v. 24) money more than in God, refusing to return their wealth to Christ, they fail to gain eternal life.

10:25 Jesus uses an exaggerated image to indicate the extreme difficulty of entering **the kingdom** for those given to riches (see note on Matt. 19:23–29).

10:28 The disciples have done what Jesus asked the rich young man to do. Justification before God is never, in the OT or NT, said to be by faith *alone,* though it is by faith apart from the law (Gal. 2:16). God calls on people to believe *and* to act because they believe (see James 2:17).

10:29–31 Discipleship is radical self-denial, a total offering of oneself to God. This implies readiness to give up dear possessions or even relationships that stand in the way of following Christ.

10:30 That disciples will receive earthly rewards **a hundredfold now in this time** is not an absolute promise: countless saints and martyrs were not so rewarded. However, God

(continued on next page)

amazed. And as they followed they
were afraid. [b]Then He took the
twelve aside again and began to tell
them the things that would happen
to Him:†
33 "Behold, we are going up to Jerusalem, and the Son of Man will be
betrayed to the chief priests and to
the scribes; and they will condemn
Him to death and deliver Him to the
Gentiles;
34 "and they will mock Him, and
[1]scourge Him, and spit on Him, and
kill Him. And the third day He will
rise again."

True Greatness in Serving
(Matt. 20:20–28)

35 [a]Then James and John, the sons
of Zebedee, came to Him, saying,
"Teacher, we want You to do for us
whatever we ask."
36 And He said to them, "What do
you want Me to do for you?"
37 They said to Him, "Grant us
that we may sit, one on Your right
hand and the other on Your left, in
Your glory."
38 But Jesus said to them, "You do
not know what you ask. Are you able
to drink the [a]cup that I drink, and
be baptized with the [b]baptism that I
am baptized with?"†
39 They said to Him, "We are
able." So Jesus said to them, [a]"You
will indeed drink the cup that I
drink, and with the baptism I am
baptized with you will be baptized;
40 "but to sit on My right hand and
on My left is not Mine to give, but
it is for those [a]for whom it is
prepared."†
41 [a]And when the ten heard *it,*
they began to be greatly displeased
with James and John.
42 But Jesus called them to *Himself*
and said to them, [a]"You know that
those who are considered rulers over
the Gentiles lord it over them, and
their great ones exercise authority
over them.
43 [a]"Yet it shall not be so among
you; but whoever desires to become
great among you shall be your
servant.†
44 "And whoever of you desires to
be first shall be slave of all.
45 "For even [a]the Son of Man did
not come to be served, but to serve,
and [b]to give His life a ransom for
many."

The Blind Man Believes
(Luke 18:35–43)

46 [a]Now they came to Jericho. As
He went out of Jericho with His disciples and a great multitude, blind
Bartimaeus, the son of Timaeus, sat
by the road begging.
47 And when he heard that it was

32 [b]Mark 8:31; 9:31 **34** [1]*flog Him* with a Roman scourge **35** [a][James 4:3] **38** [a]John 18:11 [b]Luke 12:50 **39** [a]Acts 12:2

40 [a][Heb. 11:16] **41** [a]Matt. 20:24 **42** [a]Luke 22:25 **43** [a]Mark 9:35 **45** [a][Phil. 2:7, 8] [b][Titus 2:14] **46** [a]Luke 18:35–43

(continued from previous page)
has a way of returning and multiplying earthly blessings along **with persecutions** to faithful men and women according to His will.

10:32–34 Here Jesus gives a more detailed disclosure about the events of His Passion and Resurrection, including being handed over **to the Gentiles,** the Romans. His predictions are fulfilled in chs. 14—16.

10:38 Jesus says **you do not know what you ask** because He does not promise a visible kingdom on earth or an immediate, victorious and glorious consummation, but rather toils, struggles and conflicts. **Cup** and **baptism** are references to suffering and death. The disciples do not grasp this now. But they will meet both these realities in future persecutions and in the sacramental realities of the *cup* of the Eucharist (1 Cor. 11:26) and the death and resurrection of *baptism* (Col. 2:12).

10:40 A place of honor in the eternal Kingdom will be given by the Father to **those for whom it is prepared,** that is (according to the Church Fathers) not by God's arbitrary choice but according to a believer's sacrifice and suffering for Christ and the Kingdom.

10:43–45 Service is characteristic of true greatness. The model is Christ's incarnate life and death: the perfect man is the perfect **servant. Ransom** is the price paid for the release of someone held captive. In this case, humanity is released from the bondage of sin and death by Christ's redemptive sacrifice on the Cross (see notes on Matt. 20:20–28).

Jesus of Nazareth, he began to cry
out and say, "Jesus, [a]Son of David,
[b]have mercy on me!"†
48 Then many warned him to be
quiet; but he cried out all the more,
"Son of David, have mercy on me!"
49 So Jesus stood still and commanded him to be called. Then they
called the blind man, saying to him,
"Be of good cheer. Rise, He is calling
you."
50 And throwing aside his garment, he rose and came to Jesus.
51 So Jesus answered and said to
him, "What do you want Me to do
for you?" The blind man said to Him,
[1]"Rabboni, that I may receive my
sight."†
52 Then Jesus said to him, "Go
your way; [a]your faith has [1]made you
well." And immediately he received
his sight and followed Jesus on the
road.†

The Triumphal Entry
(Matt. 21:1–9; Luke 19:28–44;
John 12:12–19)

11 Now [a]when they drew near
Jerusalem, to [1]Bethphage and
Bethany, at the Mount of Olives, He
sent two of His disciples;†
2 and He said to them, "Go
into the village opposite you; and
as soon as you have entered it you
will find a colt tied, on which
no one has sat. Loose it and bring
it.†
3 "And if anyone says to you,
'Why are you doing this?' say, 'The
Lord has need of it,' and immediately he will send it here."†
4 So they went their way, and
found [1]the colt tied by the door outside on the street, and they loosed
it.
5 But some of those who stood
there said to them, "What are you
doing, loosing the colt?"
6 And they spoke to them just as
Jesus had commanded. So they let
them go.
7 Then they brought the colt to
Jesus and threw their clothes on it,
and He sat on it.
8 [a]And many spread their clothes
on the road, and others cut down
leafy branches from the trees and
spread *them* on the road.†
9 Then those who went before

47 [a]Jer. 23:5; Matt. 22:42; Rom. 1:3, 4; Rev. 22:16 [b]Matt. 15:22; Luke 17:13
51 [1]Lit. *My Great One*
52 [a]Matt. 9:22; Mark 5:34 [1]Lit. *saved you*

CHAPTER 11

1 [a]Matt. 21:1–9; Luke 19:29; John 2:13 [1]M *Bethsphage*
4 [1]NU, M *a*
8 [a]Matt. 21:8

10:47 Have mercy is a favorite phrase of prayer in the liturgical tradition of the Orthodox Church. *Mercy* is God's lovingkindness, His tender compassion toward repentant sinners.

10:51 Jesus knows all things, and knows this man is blind. Yet He asks, **What do you want Me to do for you?** The man could have asked, "Lord, give me grace to live with blindness," but he asks for his sight. Faith needs to be specific, and Jesus requests him to exercise his faith by asking for a specific need. **Rabboni** means "my teacher," showing the man's affection for Jesus.

10:52 Bartimaeus (v. 46) follows Jesus, becoming a disciple of His (**the road** is Gr. *hodos,* the same word used for "the Way" in Acts 9:2), and is not commanded to silence. Now that Jesus is heading toward an open confrontation with the Jewish leaders in the Holy City, the veiling of His identity (the messianic secret) is no longer necessary.

11:1 Jesus approaches Jerusalem from nearby villages directly to the east. **The Mount of Olives** rises higher than Jerusalem (about 2,700 feet above sea level) and has messianic significance, for the Messiah is to appear and enter Jerusalem triumphantly from there.

11:2 Jesus fully understands what He is about to do: He deliberately prepares His entry into Jerusalem as a messianic act, thus challenging the authorities. He also, therefore, makes a statement regarding humility in His Kingdom, for He has just commanded His disciples not to be as worldly rulers (10:40–45). He will practice what He preaches. The donkey is a symbol of peace. Jesus comes on a donkey's **colt** as a Messiah of peace, not on a chariot or a war-horse as a political or military deliverer. Using a donkey **on which no one has sat** is appropriate to the dignity of the messianic entry of Jesus.

11:3 There are many in Israel who love and follow Christ. It is not presumptuous of Jesus to request this colt, for the owner will be told, **The Lord** needs it—granting him the privilege of giving to God.

11:8–10 An excited crowd acclaims Jesus as messianic King, a dangerous act before the Jewish and Roman authorities. **Hosanna** (lit. "save now," quoted from Ps. 118:25) was sung at the Passover as a greeting or blessing with messianic significance. (See notes on Matt. 21:1–11.)

and those who followed cried out,
saying:

"Hosanna!
[a]'Blessed is He who comes in the
name of the LORD!'
10 Blessed *is* the kingdom of our
father David
That comes [1]in the name of the
Lord!
[a]Hosanna in the highest!"

11 [a]And Jesus went into Jerusalem and into the temple. So when
He had looked around at all things,
as the hour was already late, He
went out to Bethany with the
twelve.

The Barren Fig Tree
(Matt. 21:18, 19)

12 [a]Now the next day, when they
had come out from Bethany, He was
hungry.
13 [a]And seeing from afar a fig tree
having leaves, He went to see if perhaps He would find something on
it. When He came to it, He found
nothing but leaves, for it was not the
season for figs.†
14 In response Jesus said to it, "Let
no one eat fruit from you ever
again." And His disciples heard
it.

The Temple Cleansed
(Matt. 21:12–17; Luke 19:45–48)

15 [a]So they came to Jerusalem.
Then Jesus went into the temple and
began to drive out those who bought
and sold in the temple, and overturned the tables of the money changers and the seats of those who sold
[b]doves.†
16 And He would not allow anyone to carry wares through the
temple.
17 Then He taught, saying to them,
"Is it not written, [a]'*My house shall
be called a house of prayer for all
nations*'? But you have made it a
[b]'*den of thieves*.'"
18 And [a]the scribes and chief
priests heard it and sought how they
might destroy Him; for they feared
Him, because [b]all the people were
astonished at His teaching.
19 When evening had come, He
went out of the city.

The Fig Tree Withered
(Matt. 21:20–22)

20 [a]Now in the morning, as they
passed by, they saw the fig tree dried
up from the roots.†
21 And Peter, remembering, said
to Him, "Rabbi, look! The fig tree
which You cursed has withered
away."

9 [a]Ps. 118:25, 26; Matt. 21:9
10 [a]Ps. 148:1 [1]NU omits *in the name of the Lord*
11 [a]Matt. 21:12
12 [a]Matt. 21:18–22
13 [a]Matt. 21:19
15 [a]Mal. 3:1; Matt. 21:12–16; Luke 19:45–47; John 2:13–16 [b]Lev. 14:22
17 [a]Is. 56:7 [b]Jer. 7:11
18 [a]Ps. 2:2; Matt. 21:45, 46; Luke 19:47 [b]Matt. 7:28; Mark 1:22; 6:2; Luke 4:32
20 [a]Matt. 21:19–22

11:13, 14 It was not the season for figs means that this **fig tree** had sprouted an early full foliage, indicating a first crop, but without bearing any fruit. Jesus, finding not even one fig, condemns it. In Scripture a fig tree is often a symbol of Israel (Hos. 9:10). Her fruitfulness has ceased, so the Kingdom will be taken from her and given to another people, who will bear spiritual fruit (see Matt. 21:43; Gal. 5:22, 23; see note on Matt. 21:19).

11:15–17 John appears to report the cleansing of the temple as occurring early in Jesus' ministry (John 2:13–22), whereas the other Gospels place it in the week before His Passion. Perhaps there were two cleansings. More likely, John is not concerned with chronological order and places the event early for teaching purposes. (See notes on Matt. 21:12, 13; John 2:13–22.) Jesus acts as the King of Israel would, utterly in control. He disrupts business and makes a sweeping condemnation of the religious system, yet He is untouched. The religious rulers and the Roman soldiers are close by, but all are paralyzed. In the light of the imagery in the account of the fig tree (vv. 13, 14, 20, 21), **the temple** is all leaves and no fruit, a picture of the nation itself.

11:20, 21 The cursing and withering of **the fig tree** is a prophetic act, signifying the judgment of Israel. The disciples need to learn that Israel is being rejected. They will establish His Church, ultimately filled with Gentiles and Jews, and they need assurance that they are following His will. The fig tree will be an indelible image in their minds.

things that are God's." And they
marveled at Him.†

Jesus Explains the Resurrection
(Matt. 22:23–33; Luke 20:27–40)

18 [a]Then *some* Sadducees, [b]who
say there is no resurrection, came to
Him; and they asked Him, saying:†
19 "Teacher, [a]Moses wrote to us
that if a man's brother dies, and
leaves *his* wife behind, and leaves no
children, his brother should take his
wife and raise up offspring for his
brother.
20 "Now there were seven
brothers. The first took a wife; and
dying, he left no offspring.
21 "And the second took her, and
he died; nor did he leave any offspring. And the third likewise.
22 "So the seven had her and left
no offspring. Last of all the woman
died also.
23 "Therefore, in the resurrection,
when they rise, whose wife will she
be? For all seven had her as wife."
24 Jesus answered and said to
them, "Are you not therefore
[1]mistaken, because you do not know
the Scriptures nor the power of God?
25 "For when they rise from the

18 [a]Matt. 22:23–33; Luke 20:27–38 [b]Acts 23:8
19 [a]Deut. 25:5
24 [1]Or *deceived*
25 [a][1 Cor. 15:42, 49, 52]
26 [a][John 5:25, 28, 29]; Acts 26:8; Rom. 4:17; [Rev. 20:12, 13] [b]Ex. 3:6, 15
27 [1]Or *deceived*
28 [a]Matt. 22:34–40; Luke 10:25–28; 20:39 [1]NU *seeing* [2]*foremost*
29 [a]Deut. 6:4, 5; Is. 44:8; 45:22; 46:9; 1 Cor. 8:6 [1]*foremost*
30 [a][Deut. 10:12; 30:6]; Luke 10:27 [1]NU omits the rest of v. 30.

dead, they neither marry nor are
given in marriage, but [a]are like angels in heaven.†
26 "But concerning the dead, that
they [a]rise, have you not read in the
book of Moses, in the *burning* bush
passage, how God spoke to him, saying, [b]*'I am the God of Abraham, the*
God of Isaac, and the God of Jacob'?†
27 "He is not the God of the dead,
but the God of the living. You are
therefore greatly [1]mistaken."

The Greatest Commandment
(Matt. 22:34–40)

28 [a]Then one of the scribes came,
and having heard them reasoning together, [1]perceiving that He had answered them well, asked Him,
"Which is the [2]first commandment
of all?"†
29 Jesus answered him, "The
[1]first of all the commandments *is:*
[a]*'Hear, O Israel, the LORD our God,*
the LORD is one.†
30 *'And you shall [a]love the LORD*
your God with all your heart, with
all your soul, with all your mind, and
with all your strength.' [1]This *is* the
first commandment.
31 "And the second, like *it, is* this:

12:17 Civic and religious duties need not necessarily clash. While each has its own sphere, there is no separation between God and Caesar, because God is Lord over all. However, obedience to God takes precedence over obligations to the state, should conflict arise. (See note on Matt. 22:21.)

12:18 The **Saddducees** represent landowners and other wealthy families in Jerusalem. They held many high offices within Israel, controlling the temple and the Sanhedrin. They differed from the Pharisees in that they were politically prudent and they adapted to the presence of the Romans. They interpreted the Law even more rigidly than the Pharisees and, unlike them, the Sadducees rejected belief in angels and in the **resurrection** from the dead at the end of the age. The Sadducees completely disappeared after the destruction of Jerusalem. (See notes on Matt. 22:23, 29.)

12:25 At the Second Coming, the bodies of the faithful will be transformed into incorruptible bodies; there will no longer be marriage or begetting of children. That does not mean, however, that family relationships are broken or ignored. The Sadducees are taken off guard by Jesus' answer.

12:26, 27 This part of Jesus' answer is similar to what the Sadducees expect from the Pharisees, who are right about the resurrection. Old Testament passages such as Ex. 3:6, 15 were the foundation for the Pharisees' belief in the resurrection from the dead.

12:28 The **scribes** are a professional class of experts in the Mosaic Law. While most of them were hostile to Jesus, this scribe seems to be a sincere inquirer.

12:29–31 In response, Jesus quotes Deut. 6:4, 5, the greatest Jewish confession of faith, called the *shema'* (meaning "hear," the first word of the confession). In v. 31, He quotes Lev. 19:18, combining what is already in the OT to create a new understanding: love of neighbor is an expression of love of God.

and those who followed cried out,
saying:

"Hosanna!
[a]'*Blessed is He who comes in the*
name of the LORD!'
10 Blessed *is* the kingdom of our
father David
That comes [1]in the name of the
Lord!
[a]Hosanna in the highest!"

11 [a]And Jesus went into Jerusalem and into the temple. So when
He had looked around at all things,
as the hour was already late, He
went out to Bethany with the
twelve.

The Barren Fig Tree
(Matt. 21:18, 19)

12 [a]Now the next day, when they
had come out from Bethany, He was
hungry.
13 [a]And seeing from afar a fig tree
having leaves, He went to see if perhaps He would find something on
it. When He came to it, He found
nothing but leaves, for it was not the
season for figs.†
14 In response Jesus said to it, "Let
no one eat fruit from you ever
again." And His disciples heard
it.

9 [a]Ps. 118:25, 26; Matt. 21:9
10 [a]Ps. 148:1 [1]NU omits *in the name of the Lord*
11 [a]Matt. 21:12
12 [a]Matt. 21:18–22
13 [a]Matt. 21:19

The Temple Cleansed
(Matt. 21:12–17; Luke 19:45–48)

15 [a]So they came to Jerusalem.
Then Jesus went into the temple and
began to drive out those who bought
and sold in the temple, and overturned the tables of the money changers and the seats of those who sold
[b]doves.†
16 And He would not allow anyone to carry wares through the
temple.
17 Then He taught, saying to them,
"Is it not written, [a]'*My house shall*
be called a house of prayer for all
nations'? But you have made it a
[b]'*den of thieves.*'"
18 And [a]the scribes and chief
priests heard it and sought how they
might destroy Him; for they feared
Him, because [b]all the people were
astonished at His teaching.
19 When evening had come, He
went out of the city.

The Fig Tree Withered
(Matt. 21:20–22)

20 [a]Now in the morning, as they
passed by, they saw the fig tree dried
up from the roots.†
21 And Peter, remembering, said
to Him, "Rabbi, look! The fig tree
which You cursed has withered
away."

15 [a]Mal. 3:1; Matt. 21:12–16; Luke 19:45–47; John 2:13–16 [b]Lev. 14:22
17 [a]Is. 56:7 [b]Jer. 7:11
18 [a]Ps. 2:2; Matt. 21:45, 46; Luke 19:47 [b]Matt. 7:28; Mark 1:22; 6:2; Luke 4:32
20 [a]Matt. 21:19–22

11:13, 14 It was not the season for figs means that this **fig tree** had sprouted an early full foliage, indicating a first crop, but without bearing any fruit. Jesus, finding not even one fig, condemns it. In Scripture a fig tree is often a symbol of Israel (Hos. 9:10). Her fruitfulness has ceased, so the Kingdom will be taken from her and given to another people, who will bear spiritual fruit (see Matt. 21:43; Gal. 5:22, 23; see note on Matt. 21:19).

11:15–17 John appears to report the cleansing of the temple as occurring early in Jesus' ministry (John 2:13–22), whereas the other Gospels place it in the week before His Passion. Perhaps there were two cleansings. More likely, John is not concerned with chronological order and places the event early for teaching purposes. (See notes on Matt. 21:12, 13; John 2:13–22.) Jesus acts as the King of Israel would, utterly in control. He disrupts business and makes a sweeping condemnation of the religious system, yet He is untouched. The religious rulers and the Roman soldiers are close by, but all are paralyzed. In the light of the imagery in the account of the fig tree (vv. 13, 14, 20, 21), **the temple** is all leaves and no fruit, a picture of the nation itself.

11:20, 21 The cursing and withering of **the fig tree** is a prophetic act, signifying the judgment of Israel. The disciples need to learn that Israel is being rejected. They will establish His Church, ultimately filled with Gentiles and Jews, and they need assurance that they are following His will. The fig tree will be an indelible image in their minds.

22 So Jesus answered and said to
them, "Have faith in God.†
23 "For [a]assuredly, I say to you,
whoever says to this mountain, 'Be
removed and be cast into the sea,'
and does not doubt in his heart, but
believes that those things he says
will be done, he will have whatever
he says.
24 "Therefore I say to you, [a]what-
ever things you ask when you pray,
believe that you receive *them,* and
you will have *them.*
25 "And whenever you stand
praying, [a]if you have anything
against anyone, forgive him, that
your Father in heaven may also forgive you your trespasses.†
26 [1]"But [a]if you do not forgive, neither will your Father in heaven forgive your trespasses."

By Whose Authority?

(Matt. 21:23–27; Luke 20:1–8)

27 Then they came again to Jerusalem. [a]And as He was walking
in the temple, the chief priests, the
scribes, and the elders came to
Him.†
28 And they said to Him, "By what
[a]authority are You doing these
things? And who gave You this authority to do these things?"†
29 But Jesus answered and said to
them, "I also will ask you one question; then answer Me, and I will tell
you by what authority I do these
things:
30 "The [a]baptism of John—was it
from heaven or from men? Answer
Me."
31 And they reasoned among
themselves, saying, "If we say,
'From heaven,' He will say, 'Why
then did you not believe him?'
32 "But if we say, 'From men' "—
they feared the people, for [a]all
counted John to have been a prophet
indeed.
33 So they answered and said to
Jesus, "We do not know." And Jesus
answered and said to them, "Neither
will I tell you by what authority I
do these things."

The Wicked Vinedressers

(Matt. 21:33–46; Luke 20:9–19)

12 Then [a]He began to speak to
them in parables: "A man
planted a vineyard and set a hedge
around *it,* dug *a place for* the wine
vat and built a tower. And he leased

23 [a]Matt. 17:20; 21:21; Luke 17:6
24 [a]Matt. 7:7; Luke 11:9; [John 14:13; 15:7; 16:24; James 1:5, 6]
25 [a]Matt. 6:14; 18:23–35; Eph. 4:32; [Col. 3:13]
26 [a]Matt. 6:15; 18:35 [1]NU omits v. 26.
27 [a]Matt. 21:23–27; Luke 20:1–8
28 [a]John 5:27
30 [a][Mark 1:4, 5, 8]; Luke 7:29, 30
32 [a]Matt. 3:5; 14:5; Mark 6:20

CHAPTER 12

1 [a]Matt. 21:33–46; Luke 20:9–19

11:22–24 The cursing of the fig tree also demonstrates the power of **faith in God** and prayer. **This mountain** probably refers to the Mount of Olives, but Jesus speaks not of its physical relocation, but of great deeds done through undoubting faith. Neither Jesus nor the disciples moved any actual mountains, but they did turn society upside down with the message of the Kingdom. We all need such faith in our struggle for full repentance and life in Christ (hence the use of this event in the Orthodox Church in the first service of Holy Week). We can have assured faith in answered prayer, according to St. John Chrysostom, when we ask things worthy of the Lord and strive for holiness. Of course, human requests neither limit nor control God's omniscient freedom.

11:25, 26 A call to **forgive** follows the promise of nearly unlimited possibilities of faith in prayer (vv. 22–24). What can deter faith that is able to move mountains? Failure to forgive—the greatest hindrance to knowing God. Not only does unforgiveness cripple our prayers, but even the **Father in heaven** (v. 26) does not **forgive** the unforgiving. As the fig tree is rejected for bearing no fruit, so are unforgiving people rejected (see John 15:1–6).

11:27 In the opinion of the official leaders of Israel, Jesus has trespassed on their territory. If He is allowed to remain, they are totally discredited. The stage is set after the cleansing of the temple: they must destroy Him.

11:28–33 Answering the angry opposition's questions is often not wise. Their question **By what authority are You doing these things?** is logical, for Jesus' acts are messianic. And there is an answer: the authority is that of Himself and His Father. But, knowing they seek to entrap Him, He will not say so. He leaves them with their question unanswered, and in confusion over His question. Those who claim to have the answers are left admitting their ignorance.

it to [1]vinedressers and went into a
far country.†
2 "Now at vintage-time he sent a
servant to the vinedressers, that he
might receive some of the fruit of the
vineyard from the vinedressers.†
3 "And they took *him* and beat
him and sent *him* away empty-
handed.
4 "Again he sent them another
servant, [1]and at him they threw
stones, wounded *him* in the head,
and sent *him* away shamefully
treated.
5 "And again he sent another,
and him they killed; and many others, [a]beating some and killing
some.
6 "Therefore still having one son,
his beloved, he also sent him to them
last, saying, 'They will respect my
son.'
7 "But those [1]vinedressers said
among themselves, 'This is the heir.
Come, let us kill him, and the inheritance will be ours.'
8 "So they took him and [a]killed
him and cast *him* out of the vineyard.
9 "Therefore what will the owner
of the vineyard do? He will come and
destroy the vinedressers, and give
the vineyard to others.
10 "Have you not even read this
Scripture:

[a]*'The stone which the builders*
rejected
Has become the chief
cornerstone.
11 *This was the* LORD*'s doing,*
And it is marvelous in our
eyes'?"

12 [a]And they sought to lay hands
on Him, but feared the multitude,
for they knew He had spoken the
parable against them. So they left
Him and went away.†

Taxes to Caesar

(Matt. 22:15–22; Luke 20:20–26)

13 [a]Then they sent to Him some
of the Pharisees and the Herodians,
to catch Him in *His* words.†
14 When they had come, they said
to Him, "Teacher, we know that You
are true, and [1]care about no one; for
You do not [2]regard the person of
men, but teach the [a]way of God in
truth. Is it lawful to pay taxes to Caesar, or not?†
15 "Shall we pay, or shall we not
pay?" But He, knowing their [a]hy-
pocrisy, said to them, "Why do you
test Me? Bring Me a denarius that I
may see *it*."
16 So they brought *it*. And He said
to them, "Whose image and inscription *is* this?" They said to Him,
"Caesar's."
17 And Jesus answered and said to
them, [1]"Render to Caesar the things
that are Caesar's, and to [a]God the

1 [1]*tenant farmers*
4 [1]NU omits *and at him they threw stones*
5 [a]2 Chr. 36:16
7 [1]*tenant farmers*
8 [a][Acts 2:23]
10 [a]Ps. 118:22, 23
12 [a]Matt. 21:45, 46; Mark 11:18; John 7:25, 30, 44
13 [a]Matt. 22:15–22; Luke 20:20–26
14 [a]Acts 18:26
[1]Court no man's favor
[2]Lit. *look at the face of men*
15 [a]Matt. 23:28; Luke 12:1
17 [a][Eccl. 5:4, 5]
[1]*Pay*

12:1 In this parable, the **vineyard** is Israel, the **vinedressers** are the Jewish leaders. It is plainly told against the chief priests, the elders and the scribes—and in the presence of the multitude.

12:2 In the services of the Orthodox Church during Holy Week, the theme of fruit-bearing is prominent. Jesus has recently focused on fruit-bearing in the fig-tree incident (11:12–14, 20, 21). John reports more conversation of Jesus at this time on fruit-bearing (John 15:1–8)—the vine and the branches. The bearing of **fruit** is the mark of vital spiritual life.

12:12 With this parable, Jesus totally discredits the religious leaders of Israel and establishes Himself as Messiah. The religious leaders plainly understand Jesus' criticism and would have Him arrested, but they **feared the multitude** and a possible insurrection. The leaders in Jerusalem were often viewed by the people as collaborators with the Romans, seeking to maintain their positions. Therefore the people tended to favor popular charismatic figures such as Jesus.

12:13 The Herodians were Jewish political supporters of the ruling house of Herod the Great and thus willing servants of Rome.

12:14–17 The conflict intensifies. Jesus must be discredited, but their attempts fail. Even His enemies marvel at His answers. They are dealing with God in the flesh, their long-promised Messiah, but they are blind to that fact because of the hardness of their hearts.

things that are God's." And they
marveled at Him.†

Jesus Explains the Resurrection
(Matt. 22:23–33; Luke 20:27–40)

18 [a]Then *some* Sadducees, [b]who
say there is no resurrection, came to
Him; and they asked Him, saying:†
19 "Teacher, [a]Moses wrote to us
that if a man's brother dies, and
leaves *his* wife behind, and leaves no
children, his brother should take his
wife and raise up offspring for his
brother.
20 "Now there were seven
brothers. The first took a wife; and
dying, he left no offspring.
21 "And the second took her, and
he died; nor did he leave any offspring. And the third likewise.
22 "So the seven had her and left
no offspring. Last of all the woman
died also.
23 "Therefore, in the resurrection,
when they rise, whose wife will she
be? For all seven had her as wife."
24 Jesus answered and said to
them, "Are you not therefore
[1]mistaken, because you do not know
the Scriptures nor the power of God?
25 "For when they rise from the

18 [a]Matt. 22:23–33; Luke 20:27–38 [b]Acts 23:8
19 [a]Deut. 25:5
24 [1]Or *deceived*
25 [a][1 Cor. 15:42, 49, 52]
26 [a][John 5:25, 28, 29]; Acts 26:8; Rom. 4:17; [Rev. 20:12, 13] [b]Ex. 3:6, 15
27 [1]Or *deceived*
28 [a]Matt. 22:34–40; Luke 10:25–28; 20:39 [1]NU *seeing* [2]*foremost*
29 [a]Deut. 6:4, 5; Is. 44:8; 45:22; 46:9; 1 Cor. 8:6 [1]*foremost*
30 [a][Deut. 10:12; 30:6]; Luke 10:27 [1]NU omits the rest of v. 30.

dead, they neither marry nor are
given in marriage, but [a]are like angels in heaven.†
26 "But concerning the dead, that
they [a]rise, have you not read in the
book of Moses, in the *burning* bush
passage, how God spoke to him, saying, [b]*'I am the God of Abraham, the*
God of Isaac, and the God of Jacob'?†
27 "He is not the God of the dead,
but the God of the living. You are
therefore greatly [1]mistaken."

The Greatest Commandment
(Matt. 22:34–40)

28 [a]Then one of the scribes came,
and having heard them reasoning together, [1]perceiving that He had answered them well, asked Him,
"Which is the [2]first commandment
of all?"†
29 Jesus answered him, "The
[1]first of all the commandments *is:*
[a]*'Hear, O Israel, the* LORD *our God,*
the LORD *is one.*†
30 *'And you shall* [a]*love the* LORD
your God with all your heart, with
all your soul, with all your mind, and
with all your strength.' [1]This *is* the
first commandment.
31 "And the second, like *it, is* this:

12:17 Civic and religious duties need not necessarily clash. While each has its own sphere, there is no separation between God and Caesar, because God is Lord over all. However, obedience to God takes precedence over obligations to the state, should conflict arise. (See note on Matt. 22:21.)

12:18 The **Saddducees** represent landowners and other wealthy families in Jerusalem. They held many high offices within Israel, controlling the temple and the Sanhedrin. They differed from the Pharisees in that they were politically prudent and they adapted to the presence of the Romans. They interpreted the Law even more rigidly than the Pharisees and, unlike them, the Sadducees rejected belief in angels and in the **resurrection** from the dead at the end of the age. The Sadducees completely disappeared after the destruction of Jerusalem. (See notes on Matt. 22:23, 29.)

12:25 At the Second Coming, the bodies of the faithful will be transformed into incorruptible bodies; there will no longer be marriage or begetting of children. That does not mean, however, that family relationships are broken or ignored. The Sadducees are taken off guard by Jesus' answer.

12:26, 27 This part of Jesus' answer is similar to what the Sadducees expect from the Pharisees, who are right about the resurrection. Old Testament passages such as Ex. 3:6, 15 were the foundation for the Pharisees' belief in the resurrection from the dead.

12:28 The **scribes** are a professional class of experts in the Mosaic Law. While most of them were hostile to Jesus, this scribe seems to be a sincere inquirer.

12:29–31 In response, Jesus quotes Deut. 6:4, 5, the greatest Jewish confession of faith, called the *shema'* (meaning "hear," the first word of the confession). In v. 31, He quotes Lev. 19:18, combining what is already in the OT to create a new understanding: love of neighbor is an expression of love of God.

[a]*'You shall love your neighbor as*
yourself.' There is no other commandment greater than [b]these."
32 So the scribe said to Him, "Well
said, Teacher. You have spoken the
truth, for there is one God, [a]and
there is no other but He.†
33 "And to love Him with all the
heart, with all the understanding,
[1]with all the soul, and with all the
strength, and to love one's neighbor
as oneself, [a]is more than all the
whole burnt offerings and sacrifices."
34 Now when Jesus saw that he
answered wisely, He said to him,
"You are not far from the kingdom
of God." [a]But after that no one dared
question Him.†

David's Son and Lord
(Matt. 22:41–46; Luke 20:41–44)

35 [a]Then Jesus answered and said,
while He taught in the temple, "How
is it that the scribes say that the
Christ is the Son of David?†
36 "For David himself said [a]by the
Holy Spirit:

[b]*'The* L*ORD said to my Lord,*
"Sit at My right hand,
Till I make Your enemies Your
footstool."'

37 "Therefore David himself calls
Him *'Lord'*; how is He *then* his
[a]Son?" And the common people
heard Him gladly.

31 [a]Lev. 19:18 [b][Rom. 13:9]
32 [a]Deut. 4:39
33 [a][Hos. 6:6] [1]NU omits *with all the soul*
34 [a]Matt. 22:46
35 [a]Luke 20:41–44
36 [a]2 Sam. 23:2 [b]Ps. 110:1
37 [a][Acts 2:29–31]
38 [a]Mark 4:2 [b]Matt. 23:1–7 [c]Matt. 23:7
39 [a]Luke 14:7
40 [a]Matt. 23:14 [1]*for appearance' sake*
41 [a]Luke 21:1–4 [b]2 Kin. 12:9
42 [1]Gr. *lepta,* very small copper coins [2]A Roman coin
43 [a][2 Cor. 8:12]
44 [a]Deut. 24:6

CHAPTER 13

1 [a]Luke 21:5–36

Beware of the Scribes
(Matt. 23:1–13; Luke 20:45–47)

38 Then [a]He said to them in His
teaching, [b]"Beware of the scribes,
who desire to go around in long
robes, [c]*love* greetings in the
marketplaces,†
39 "the [a]best seats in the synagogues, and the best places at feasts,
40 [a]"who devour widows' houses,
and [1]for a pretense make long
prayers. These will receive greater
condemnation."

A Poor Widow Gives All
(Luke 21:1–4)

41 [a]Now Jesus sat opposite the
treasury and saw how the people put
money [b]into the treasury. And many
who were rich put in much.†
42 Then one poor widow came and
threw in two [1]mites, which make a
[2]quadrans.
43 So He called His disciples to
Himself and said to them, "Assuredly, I say to you that [a]this poor
widow has put in more than all those
who have given to the treasury;
44 "for they all put in out of their
abundance, but she out of her poverty put in all that she had, [a]her
whole livelihood."

The Destruction of the Temple
(Matt. 24:1, 2; Luke 21:5, 6)

13 Then [a]as He went out of the
temple, one of His disciples

12:32, 33 This scribe's insight has penetrated beyond the Pharisees' obsession with outward forms. He understands that the condition of the heart is central to righteousness.

12:34 This scribe's wisdom and honesty bring him **not far from the kingdom of God.** Only God can say who is, and who is not, far from His Kingdom.

12:35–37 The tables are turned: Jesus' interrogators are interrogated by Him. In the presence of the common people Jesus questions the scribes, and they are unable to answer (Matt. 22:46). The answer, of course, is that David **calls Him 'Lord'** in His divinity, yet Jesus is also David's Son in His humanity. (See notes on Matt. 22:42, 43–45.)

12:38 Jesus exposes His opponents publicly, warning, **Beware of the scribes.** By now they hate Him. Their plans have gone awry. Though expert in the Law, they have failed to answer Jesus' questions. Mark reports only briefly on Jesus' extended critique of the Jewish leaders.

12:41–44 As Jesus observes the temple **treasury,** a poor **widow** (v. 42) donates **two mites,** the least valuable coins. Jesus' deity is again manifest as He knows she **put in all that she had.** It is not the amount that counts with God, but the degree of sacrifice out of what a person possesses. Many who give the least give the most; some who give the most, give the least in proportion to their abundance. God takes note of our giving (Acts 10:4).

said to Him, "Teacher, see what
manner of stones and what buildings
are here!"†
2 And Jesus answered and said to
him, "Do you see these great buildings? [a]Not *one* stone shall be left
upon another, that shall not be
thrown down."†

The Beginning of Sorrows
(Matt. 24:3–14; Luke 21:7–19)

3 Now as He sat on the Mount
of Olives opposite the temple,
[a]Peter, [b]James, [c]John, and [d]Andrew
asked Him privately,†
4 [a]"Tell us, when will these
things be? And what *will be* the sign
when all these things will be
fulfilled?"†
5 And Jesus, answering them, began to say: [a]"Take heed that no one
deceives you.†
6 "For many will come in My
name, saying, 'I am *He*,' and will deceive many.
7 "But when you hear of wars and
rumors of wars, do not be troubled;
for *such things* must happen, but the
end *is* not yet.
8 "For nation will rise against nation, and [a]kingdom against kingdom. And there will be earthquakes
in various places, and there will be
famines [1]and troubles. [b]These *are* the
beginnings of [2]sorrows.†
9 "But [a]watch out for yourselves,
for they will deliver you up to councils, and you will be beaten in the
synagogues. You will [1]be brought
before rulers and kings for My sake,
for a testimony to them.†

2 [a]Luke 19:44
3 [a]Matt. 16:18; Mark 1:16 [b]Mark 1:19 [c]Mark 1:19 [d]John 1:40
4 [a]Matt. 24:3; Luke 21:7
5 [a]Jer. 29:8; Eph. 5:6; [Col. 2:8]; 1 Thess. 2:3; 2 Thess. 2:3
8 [a]Hag. 2:22 [b]Matt. 24:8 [1]NU omits *and troubles* [2]Lit. *birth pangs*
9 [a]Matt. 10:17, 18; 24:9; Acts 12:4; [Rev. 2:10] [1]NU, M *stand*

13:1–37 This passage has two points of focus: (1) the destruction of Jerusalem (vv. 2, 14–23) and (2) the end of the age (vv. 4–13, 24–37). These points converge in Jesus' teaching and guide our interpretation. **The temple** had been rebuilt by Herod the Great, including porticoes, courtyards and colonnades, covering about a sixth of the area of Jerusalem—an architectural marvel dominating the Holy City. Some of the **stones** were about 10×40×20 feet each.

13:2 The grandeur of the buildings made Jesus' comment about their destruction very dramatic. It would be hard for the listener at that time to imagine such great destruction. In A.D. 70 this prophecy of Christ came true when the Roman general Titus recaptured Jerusalem and leveled everything on the temple mount. It was rumored there was gold between the stones, so **not one stone** was left unturned. Only a retaining wall remained, later called the Wailing Wall, after Emperor Trajan (c. A.D. 135) permitted Jews to come to this site once a year to mourn the temple's fate. Jews still mourn at the Wailing Wall today.

13:3–37 Jesus' discourse on the end of the age highlights several crucial events and stages: (1) **the beginnings of sorrows** or trials (v. 8); (2) the great **tribulation** (v. 19); and (3) **the Son of Man coming** (v. 26), concluding with admonitions to watchfulness (vv. 28–37). Each evangelist presents a somewhat different arrangement of Jesus' predictions and admonitions. They cannot be exactly systematized and harmonized with other NT predictions of the end (see 1 Cor. 15:51, 52; 2 Thess. 2:1–10; and the Book of Revelation). The Church Fathers counsel Christians to be concerned with being watchful and prepared for the end, not with speculating about details and chronology.

13:4 Interest in the future and the end of the age is nothing new. The disciples want to know when all the things spoken about the end times will take place. Jesus obliges them.

13:5 Jesus' first word about the end of the age is a warning about deception. **Take heed** is a dominant note throughout the discourse. Do not fail because of deceit by impostors, speculation about dates, political upheavals, natural catastrophes, or persecutions. Today, popular preachers contradict one another with novel doctrines which are at odds with the historic interpretation of the Church. **Take heed that no one deceives you!**

13:8 **Sorrows** (lit. "birth pangs") is an image taken from childbearing and applied to the world-renewing events and crises at the consummation of the Kingdom.

13:9–11 Such experiences are recorded in the Book of Acts and Paul's Epistles. Until the return of Christ in glory (vv. 26, 27; 14:62), His followers will suffer and people will fall into apostasy (4:16, 17). Discipleship produces martyrs and confessors (those injured or maimed for confessing Christ before men). Jesus tells His disciples plainly what will happen to them. Tradition holds that of the Twelve, all but John died a martyr's death. The promise that the **Holy Spirit** will **speak** through us is not intended to discourage preparation for Christian teaching. It refers primarily to crises.

10 "And [a]the gospel must first be
preached to all the nations.
11 [a]"But when they arrest *you* and
deliver you up, do not worry beforehand, [1]or premeditate what you
will speak. But whatever is given
you in that hour, speak that; for it
is not you who speak, [b]but the Holy
Spirit.
12 "Now [a]brother will betray
brother to death, and a father *his*
child; and children will rise up
against parents and cause them to
be put to death.†
13 [a]"And you will be hated by
all for My name's sake. But [b]he
who [1]endures to the end shall be
saved.†

10 [a]Matt. 24:14
11 [a]Luke 12:11; 21:12–17
[b]Acts 2:4; 4:8, 31
[1]NU omits *or premeditate*
12 [a]Mic. 7:6
13 [a]Luke 21:17
[b]Matt. 10:22; 24:13
[1]*bears patiently*
14 [a]Matt. 24:15
[b]Dan. 9:27; 11:31; 12:11
[c]Luke 21:21
[1]NU omits *spoken of by Daniel the prophet*

Tribulation in Jerusalem
(Matt. 24:15–28; Luke 21:20–24)

14 [a]"So when you see the [b]*'abomination of desolation,'* [1]spoken of by
Daniel the prophet, standing where
it ought not" **(let the reader understand),** "then [c]let those who are in
Judea flee to the mountains.†
15 "Let him who is on the housetop not go down into the house, nor
enter to take anything out of his
house.
16 "And let him who is in the field
not go back to get his clothes.
17 [a]"But woe to those who are
pregnant and to those who are nursing babies in those days!
18 "And pray that your flight may
not be in winter.
19 [a]"For *in* those days there will
be tribulation, such as has not been
since the beginning of the creation
which God created until this time,
nor ever shall be.
20 "And unless the Lord had
shortened those days, no flesh
would be saved; but for the elect's
sake, whom He chose, He shortened
the days.
21 [a]"Then if anyone says to you,
'Look, here *is* the Christ!' or, 'Look,
He is there!' do not believe it.
22 "For false christs and false
prophets will rise and show signs
and [a]wonders to deceive, if possible,
even the [1]elect.
23 "But [a]take heed; see, I have told
you all things beforehand.

17 [a]Luke 21:23
19 [a]Dan. 9:26; 12:1
21 [a]Luke 17:23; 21:8
22 [a]Rev. 13:13, 14
[1]*chosen ones*
23 [a][2 Pet. 3:17]
24 [a]Zeph. 1:15

The Coming of the Son of Man
(Matt. 24:29–31; Luke 21:25–28)

24 [a]"But in those days, after that
tribulation, the sun will be darkened,

13:12 One sign of the end times is the breakdown of family loyalties. This very situation seems to constitute a worldwide crisis today.

13:13 There is security of salvation for him **who endures to the end,** but it is not ours to say when the race is over. The modern innovative doctrine of "eternal security"—once saved, always saved—is not the teaching of Jesus; rather, He teaches the endurance of the faithful through God's strength and grace.

13:14–23 The destruction of Jerusalem in A.D. 70, culminating in the burning of the temple, appears to be the major focal point in these verses. The Roman general Titus defiled the temple by first entering into it and **standing where** [he] **ought not** (i.e. in the Most Holy Place). Heeding prophecies, the Church in Jerusalem fled before this great **tribulation** (v. 19) occurred (vv. 15–18). This was a time of great suffering and consternation (vv. 19–22), vividly recounted by the Jewish historian Josephus, an eyewitness.

Christians have suffered many great tribulations throughout the centuries—in the twentieth century alone, many millions have been martyred—and there will likely be great trials in the future. However, the speculation popular in some Christian circles about a single tribulation period, conceived in various conflicting forms, is unwarranted on the basis of biblical and patristic teaching. Further, Orthodox Christians reject any teaching that (1) conveniently "delivers" them from tribulation (Jesus teaches to prepare for tribulation) or (2) speaks of a secret Second Coming of Christ. Christian consensus is, "He shall come again with glory to judge the living and the dead" (Nicene Creed). There is nothing secret here. The Scriptures teach that many events spoken of in the OT regarding the end will not be understood until they happen (v. 29). "Many shall run to and fro, and knowledge shall increase" (Dan. 12:4). Dazzling words claiming to set forth God's prophetic scenario for the end times are at best speculative, and at worst, heretical.

and the moon will not give its light;†
25 "the stars of heaven will fall,
and the powers in the heavens will
be [a]shaken.
26 [a]"Then they will see the Son of
Man coming in the clouds with great
power and glory.
27 "And then He will send His angels, and gather together His [1]elect
from the four winds, from the farthest part of earth to the farthest part
of heaven.

When Will He Return?
(Matt. 24:32–44; Luke 21:29–36)

28 [a]"Now learn this parable from
the fig tree: When its branch has already become tender, and puts forth
leaves, you know that summer is
near.†
29 "So you also, when you see
these things happening, know that
[1]it is near—at the doors!
30 "Assuredly, I say to you, this
generation will by no means pass
away till all these things take place.
31 "Heaven and earth will pass
away, but [a]My words will by no
means pass away.
32 "But of that day and hour
[a]no one knows, not even the angels
in heaven, nor the Son, but only the
[b]Father.†
33 [a]"Take heed, watch and pray;
for you do not know when the time
is.†
34 [a]"*It is* like a man going to a far
country, who left his house and gave
[b]authority to his servants, and to
each his work, and commanded the
doorkeeper to watch.
35 [a]"Watch therefore, for you do
not know when the master of the
house is coming—in the evening, at
midnight, at the crowing of the
rooster, or in the morning—
36 "lest, coming suddenly, he find
you sleeping.
37 "And what I say to you, I say
to all: Watch!"

The Conspiracy to Kill Jesus
(Matt. 26:1–5; Luke 22:1, 2)

14 After [a]two days it was the
Passover and [b]*the Feast* of Unleavened Bread. And the chief
priests and the scribes sought how
they might take Him by [1]trickery and
put *Him* to death.†
2 But they said, "Not during the
feast, lest there be an uproar of the
people."

25 [a]Is. 13:10; 34:4
26 [a][Dan. 7:13, 14]
27 [1]*chosen ones*
28 [a]Luke 21:29
29 [1]Or *He*
31 [a]Is. 40:8
32 [a]Matt. 25:13 [b]Acts 1:7
33 [a]1 Thess. 5:6
34 [a]Matt. 24:45; 25:14 [b][Matt. 16:19]
35 [a]Matt. 24:42, 44

CHAPTER 14

1 [a]Luke 22:1, 2 [b]Ex. 12:1–27 [1]*deception*

13:24–26 In those days refers to the end of time, when Christ will return bodily. The Second Coming is neither secretive nor figurative.

13:28–31 The **parable from the fig tree** warns us to be watchful and ready for the events of the final days (see note on Matt. 24:33–41). Each generation since Pentecost has looked for the Second Coming of Christ, and that is proper. Jesus' teaching is that we will know the end is **near** when we see **these things** (v. 29) taking place.

13:32 Since **of that day and hour no one knows,** believers should always be ready in watchfulness and prayer (see note on Matt. 24:42–44). Many Church Fathers consider that **nor the Son** speaks of Christ's having limited knowledge in His humanity. This shows the depth of Christ's condescension, because in His divine nature He is as omniscient as the Father. Other Church Fathers do not accept any limitation of knowledge in Christ, and interpret this as His deliberate accommodation to the disciples' weakness. Exact knowledge of the Second Coming could lead otherwise serious believers to moral carelessness, inactive faith, and lack of daily perseverance.

13:33 To propose schemes of how and when He will come will not prepare anyone for the coming of Christ. But to **take heed, watch and pray** does prepare us.

14:1 The Feast of Unleavened Bread begins with the **Passover** meal on the evening of 15 Nisan and lasts seven days (Ex. 12:12–20). Both feasts commemorate Israel's liberation from Egypt. The word "Passover" does not refer to the crossing of the Red Sea, but to the angel of death "passing over" Hebrew homes when killing the firstborn of the Egyptians (Ex. 12:13). Unleavened bread is a reminder of the haste with which the Hebrews left Egypt. It also symbolized holiness unmixed with evil. Passover prefigures the new deliverance of humanity by Christ from the power of sin and death.

The Anointing at Bethany
(Matt. 26:6–13; John 12:1–8)

3 [a]And being in Bethany at the
house of Simon the leper, as He sat
at the table, a woman came having
an alabaster flask of very costly
[1]oil of spikenard. Then she broke the
flask and poured *it* on His head.†
4 But there were some who were
indignant among themselves, and
said, "Why was this fragrant oil
wasted?
5 "For it might have been sold for
more than three hundred [a]denarii
and given to the poor." And they
[b]criticized[1] her sharply.
6 But Jesus said, "Let her alone.
Why do you trouble her? She has
done a good work for Me.
7 [a]"For you have the poor with
you always, and whenever you wish
you may do them good; [b]but Me you
do not have always.
8 "She has done what she could.
She has come beforehand to anoint
My body for burial.†
9 "Assuredly, I say to you, wherever this gospel is [a]preached in the
whole world, what this woman has
done will also be told as a memorial
to her."

Judas Betrays Jesus
(Matt. 26:14–16; Luke 22:3–6)

10 [a]Then Judas Iscariot, one of the
twelve, went to the chief priests to
betray Him to them.
11 And when they heard *it,* they
were glad, and promised to give him
money. So he sought how he might
conveniently betray Him.

Preparations for the Passover
(Matt. 26:17–19; Luke 22:7–13)

12 [a]Now on the first day of Unleavened Bread, when they [1]killed the
Passover *lamb,* His disciples said to
Him, "Where do You want us to go
and prepare, that You may eat the
Passover?"†
13 And He sent out two of His disciples and said to them, "Go into the
city, and a man will meet you carrying a pitcher of water; follow him.†
14 "Wherever he goes in, say to the
master of the house, 'The Teacher
says, "Where is the guest room in
which I may eat the Passover with
My disciples?"'†
15 "Then he will show you a large
upper room, furnished *and* prepared;
there make ready for us."
16 So His disciples went out, and
came into the city, and found it just
as He had said to them; and they
prepared the Passover.

The Last Supper: The Eucharist Instituted
(Matt. 26:20–35; Luke 22:14–38; John 13:1–38)

17 [a]In the evening He came with
the twelve.

3 [a]Matt. 26:6; Luke 7:37; John 12:1, 3 [1]Perfume of pure nard
5 [a]Matt. 18:28; Mark 12:15 [b]Matt. 20:11; John 6:61 [1]*scolded*
7 [a]Deut. 15:11; Matt. 26:11; John 12:8 [b][John 7:33; 8:21; 14:2, 12; 16:10, 17, 28]
9 [a]Matt. 28:19, 20; Mark 16:15; Luke 24:47
10 [a]Ps. 41:9; 55:12–14; Matt. 10:2–4
12 [a]Ex. 12:8; Matt. 26:17–19; Luke 22:7–13 [1]*sacrificed*
17 [a]Matt. 26:20–24; Luke 22:14, 21–23

14:3–6 Knowledge of religious things is good, but devotion to Christ is more important. Here a woman who knows less about religion than her critics expresses her deep love and devotion to Christ, devotion He accepts with gratitude. Those **who were indignant** are the disciples themselves, according to Matt. 26:8, while John 12:4, 5 specifies Judas Iscariot. (See notes on Matt. 26:2–16.)

14:8 Often we do not fully understand the implications of what we do for Christ. This woman was expressing her love for Jesus; she may or may not have known that she was anointing the body of Jesus for burial (see Matt. 26:12).

14:12 The first day of Unleavened Bread is 14 Nisan, when **the Passover** lambs were ritually slaughtered at noontime. Passover and the Feast of Unleavened Bread actually begin after sunset of that same day, which is then 15 Nisan, because the Jewish calendar counts days from sunset to sunset.

14:13 The deity of Christ again shows through. Jesus knows they will meet a man carrying a pitcher of water, and He knows how that man will respond. (See notes on Matt. 26:17–25.)

14:14 As with the colt (see note on 11:3), so with the upper room. Jesus is not presumptuous in the use of the room. It was a gift to the man to have the Son of God use it and thus forever set it apart as holy. Whatever gifts God asks of us today are similarly sanctified.

18 Now as they sat and ate, Jesus said, "Assuredly, I say to you, [a]one of you who eats with Me will betray Me."

19 And they began to be sorrowful, and to say to Him one by one, "*Is* it I?" [1]And another *said, "Is* it I?"

20 He answered and said to them, "*It is* one of the twelve, who dips with Me in the dish.

21 [a]"The Son of Man indeed goes just as it is written of Him, but woe to that man by whom the Son of Man is betrayed! It would have been good for that man if he had never been born."†

22 [a]And as they were eating, Jesus took bread, blessed and broke *it*, and gave *it* to them and said, "Take, [1]eat; this is My [b]body."†

23 Then He took the cup, and when He had given thanks He gave *it* to them, and they all drank from it.

24 And He said to them, "This is My blood of the [1]new covenant, which is shed for many.†

25 "Assuredly, I say to you, I will no longer drink of the fruit of the vine until that day when I drink it new in the kingdom of God."

26 [a]And when they had sung [1]a hymn, they went out to the Mount of Olives.†

27 [a]Then Jesus said to them, "All of you will be made to stumble [1]because of Me this night, for it is written:

[b]'I will strike the Shepherd,
And the sheep will be scattered.'

28 "But [a]after I have been raised, I will go before you to Galilee."

29 [a]Peter said to Him, "Even if all are made to [1]stumble, yet I *will* not *be*."†

30 Jesus said to him, "Assuredly, I say to you that today, *even* this night, before the rooster crows twice, you will deny Me three times."

31 But he spoke more vehemently, "If I have to die with You, I will not deny You!" And they all said likewise.

Gethsemane

(Matt. 26:36–46; Luke 22:39–46; John 18:1)

32 [a]Then they came to a place which was named Gethsemane; and He said to His disciples, "Sit here while I pray."†

18 [a]John 6:70, 71; 13:18
19 [1]NU omits the rest of v. 19.
21 [a]Luke 22:22
22 [a]1 Cor. 11:23–25 [b][1 Pet. 2:24] [1]NU omits *eat*
24 [1]NU omits *new*
26 [a]Matt. 26:30 [1]Or *hymns*
27 [a]Matt. 26:31–35 [b]Zech. 13:7 [1]NU omits *because of Me this night*
28 [a]Mark 16:7
29 [a]John 13:37, 38 [1]*fall away*
32 [a]Luke 22:40–46

14:21 Jesus says this not in deprecation of this man, His own creation, but in deprecation of that man's choice and rashness. For it was the rashness of Judas's own will that made the Creator's gift of goodness useless to him (see note on Matt. 26:24, 25). Divine foreknowledge of the betrayal takes away neither Judas's moral freedom nor his accountability. For God all things are a present reality; He foresees all human actions, but does not cause them.

14:22–26 This Passover meal is the first Eucharist, the heart of Christian worship, which celebrates the New Covenant and sacramental union with Christ (see notes on Matt. 26:26–29). By uttering the solemn words **this is My body** and **this is My blood,** Jesus clearly refers to the bread and wine He offers to His disciples as His own body and blood. Orthodox teaching has always affirmed the truth of Jesus' words, no more and no less, but without scrutinizing or theorizing about this great mystery of faith. *The body* denotes the totality of man. On behalf of all mankind, Christ offers Himself in the totality of His Person.

14:24 For many is the Semitic way of saying for all, for an innumerable people (see Matt. 26:28).

14:26 A **hymn** means a psalm from a group of psalms (Ps. 115—118) traditionally sung after the Passover meal. A detailed prophecy of the Crucifixion is found in Ps. 22:1–21. Psalm 22:22, as quoted from the Septuagint in Heb. 2:12, reads, "I will declare Your name to My brethren; in the midst of the assembly I will sing praise to You." On the night of His arrest, Jesus sang praise to God "in the midst of the assembly."

14:29 Peter still does not understand the need for divine help to remain faithful. Peter's desire is right, but his source of strength—himself—is wrong.

14:32 Gethsemane, meaning "oil press," is an orchard of olive trees at the foot of the Mount of Olives where oil was extracted from olives.

33 And He [a]took Peter, James, and John with Him, and He began to be troubled and deeply distressed.

34 Then He said to them, [a]"My soul is exceedingly sorrowful, *even* to death. Stay here and watch."

35 He went a little farther, and fell on the ground, and prayed that if it were possible, the hour might pass from Him.†

36 And He said, [a]"Abba, Father, [b]all things *are* possible for You. Take this cup away from Me; [c]nevertheless, not what I will, but what You *will*."

37 Then He came and found them sleeping, and said to Peter, "Simon, are you sleeping? Could you not watch one hour?

38 [a]"Watch and pray, lest you enter into temptation. [b]The spirit indeed *is* willing, but the flesh *is* weak."†

39 Again He went away and prayed, and spoke the same words.

40 And when He returned, He found them asleep again, for their eyes were heavy; and they did not know what to answer Him.

41 Then He came the third time and said to them, "Are you still sleeping and resting? It is enough! [a]The hour has come; behold, the Son of Man is being betrayed into the hands of sinners.

42 [a]"Rise, let us be going. See, My betrayer is at hand."

33 [a]Mark 5:37; 9:2; 13:3
34 [a]Is. 53:3, 4; Matt. 26:38; John 12:27
36 [a]Rom. 8:15; Gal. 4:6 [b][Heb. 5:7] [c]Is. 50:5; John 5:30; 6:38
38 [a]Luke 21:36 [b][Rom. 7:18, 21–24; Gal. 5:17]
41 [a]John 13:1; 17:1
42 [a]Matt. 26:46; Mark 14:18; Luke 9:44; John 13:21; 18:1, 2
43 [a]Ps. 3:1; Matt. 26:47–56; Luke 22:47–53; John 18:3–11
44 [a][Prov. 27:6]
48 [a]Matt. 26:55; Luke 22:52
49 [a]Matt. 21:23 [b]Ps. 22:6; Is. 53:7; Luke 22:37; 24:44
50 [a]Ps. 88:8; Zech. 13:7; Matt. 26:31; Mark 14:27

Jesus Is Arrested
(Matt. 26:47–56; Luke 22:47–53; John 18:2–12)

43 [a]And immediately, while He was still speaking, Judas, one of the twelve, with a great multitude with swords and clubs, came from the chief priests and the scribes and the elders.†

44 Now His betrayer had given them a signal, saying, "Whomever I [a]kiss, He is the One; seize Him and lead *Him* away safely."

45 As soon as he had come, immediately he went up to Him and said to Him, "Rabbi, Rabbi!" and kissed Him.

46 Then they laid their hands on Him and took Him.

47 And one of those who stood by drew his sword and struck the servant of the high priest, and cut off his ear.†

48 [a]Then Jesus answered and said to them, "Have you come out, as against a robber, with swords and clubs to take Me?

49 "I was daily with you in the temple [a]teaching, and you did not seize Me. But [b]the Scriptures must be fulfilled."

50 [a]Then they all forsook Him and fled.

51 Now a certain young man followed Him, having a linen cloth thrown around *his* naked *body*. And the young men laid hold of him,†

14:35, 36 Abba in Aramaic is the familiar form for **Father,** equivalent to "Daddy" or "Papa," indicating Christ's intimacy with God the Father. Jesus prays to be spared **this cup,** His death by crucifixion, but obediently entrusts Himself to the will of God (see note on Matt. 26:39). It is not as God that He asks **the hour might pass,** but as man. His divinity cannot suffer; His humanity can and does.

14:38 To **watch and pray** is the way to avoid entering into **temptation**—at any time, anywhere. The **spirit** of the disciples, their inner selves, is ready to die with Jesus (v. 31), but their **flesh,** their physical bodies, is weak and given to sleep.

14:43, 44 The fact that a signal, the **kiss** (v. 44), is needed here is a commentary on the kind of people who make up the mob that has come to take Jesus. Had the chief priests, the scribes and the elders come, they would have recognized Him. Even most of the common people would recognize Him. But these are armed Jewish servants, usually confined in the temple area to maintain order under the authority of the **chief priests** (v. 43). According to John 18:3, a band of Roman soldiers collaborated with them. Orthodox Christians pray during every Eucharist not to give Jesus a kiss as did Judas.

14:47 See note on Matt. 26:52.

14:51 There is some conjecture that this young man who fled naked is the Apostle John.

(continued on next page)

52 and he left the linen cloth and
fled from them naked.

Jesus Before the Sanhedrin
(Matt. 26:57–68; Luke 22:54, 63–71; John 18:13–24)

53 [a]And they led Jesus away to the
high priest; and with him were
[b]assembled all the [c]chief priests, the
elders, and the scribes.
54 But [a]Peter followed Him at a
distance, right into the courtyard of
the high priest. And he sat with the
servants and warmed himself at the
fire.
55 [a]Now the chief priests and all
the council sought testimony against
Jesus to put Him to death, but found
none.
56 For many bore [a]false witness
against Him, but their testimonies
[1]did not agree.†
57 Then some rose up and bore
false witness against Him, saying,
58 "We heard Him say, [a]'I will destroy this temple made with hands,
and within three days I will build another made without hands.' "
59 But not even then did their testimony agree.
60 [a]And the high priest stood up
in the midst and asked Jesus, saying,
"Do You answer nothing? What *is*
it these men testify against You?"
61 But [a]He kept silent and answered nothing. [b]Again the high
priest asked Him, saying to Him,
"Are You the Christ, the Son of the
Blessed?"
62 Jesus said, "I am. [a]And you will
see the Son of Man sitting at the right
hand of the Power, and coming with
the clouds of heaven."†
63 Then the high priest tore his
clothes and said, "What further need
do we have of witnesses?†
64 "You have heard the [a]blas-
phemy! What do you think?" And
they all condemned Him to be deserving of [b]death.
65 Then some began to [a]spit on
Him, and to blindfold Him, and
to beat Him, and to say to Him,
"Prophesy!" And the officers [1]struck
Him with the palms of their hands.

Peter's Denials
(Matt. 26:58, 69–75; Luke 22:54–62; John 18:15–18, 25–27)

66 [a]Now as Peter was below in the
courtyard, one of the servant girls
of the high priest came.†
67 And when she saw Peter warm-
ing himself, she looked at him and
said, "You also were with [a]Jesus of
Nazareth."
68 But he denied it, saying, "I neither know nor understand what you
are saying." And he went out on the
porch, and a rooster crowed.
69 [a]And the servant girl saw him
again, and began to say to those who
stood by, "This is one of them."
70 But he denied it again. [a]And a

53 [a]Matt. 26:57–68 [b]Mark 15:1 [c]John 7:32; 18:3; 19:6 **54** [a]John 18:15 **55** [a]Matt. 26:59 **56** [a]Ex. 20:16 [1]*were not consistent* **58** [a]John 2:19 **60** [a]Matt. 26:62 **61** [a]Is. 53:7 [b]Luke 22:67–71 **62** [a]Luke 22:69 **64** [a]John 10:33, 36 [b]John 19:7 **65** [a]Is. 50:6; 52:14 [1]NU *received Him with slaps* **66** [a]John 18:16–18, 25–27 **67** [a]John 1:45 **69** [a]Matt. 26:71 **70** [a]Luke 22:59

(continued from previous page)
Another tradition holds the young man is Mark himself. The latter view would explain why the incident is mentioned by him, but with no name given—a traditional way of talking about oneself.

14:56 Those who oppose Jesus and testify **against Him** cannot agree on their testimony. They stand in perpetual self-contradiction.

14:62 Jesus' answer is a revelation of the mystery of His Person. **I am** is a direct answer given only in Mark. **Power** is a substitute for the name of God, which pious Jews would not pronounce. Jesus' bold declaration that He, the Son of Man coming in glory, will share the authority of God brings the charge of blasphemy and condemnation to death (v. 64).

14:63, 64 By the symbolic act of tearing his mantle, the **high priest** shows his belief that Jesus is guilty of **blasphemy** (v. 64). Thus, according to Jewish law (which, under Roman domination, the priests could not enforce), Jesus is sentenced to **death** (Lev. 24:16), though the charge of blasphemy will not be mentioned before Pilate.

14:66–72 Of the remaining faithful disciples, Peter and John (see John 18:15, 16) alone have the courage to follow Jesus. Peter denies the Lord, but at least he is there to do so. His intentions are commendable (v. 29), but his strength fails.

little later those who stood by said
to Peter again, "Surely you are *one*
of them; [b]for you are a Galilean,
[1]and your [2]speech shows *it*."
71 Then he began to curse and
swear, "I do not know this Man of
whom you speak!"
72 [a]A second time *the* rooster
crowed. Then Peter called to mind
the word that Jesus had said to him,
"Before the rooster crows twice, you
will deny Me three times." And
when he thought about it, he wept.†

Jesus Before Pilate

(Matt. 27:1, 2, 11–26; Luke 23:1–25; John 18:28—19:16)

15 Immediately, [a]in the morning, the chief priests held a
consultation with the elders and
scribes and the whole council; and
they bound Jesus, led *Him* away, and
[b]delivered *Him* to Pilate.†
2 [a]Then Pilate asked Him, "Are
You the King of the Jews?" He answered and said to him, "*It is as* you
say."†
3 And the chief priests accused
Him of many things, but He [a]an-
swered nothing.†

70 [b]Acts 2:7 [1]NU omits the rest of v. 70. [2]accent
72 [a]Matt. 26:75

CHAPTER 15
1 [a]Ps. 2:2 [b]Acts 3:13
2 [a]Matt. 27:11–14
3 [a]John 19:9
4 [a]Matt. 27:13 [1]NU *of which they accuse You*
5 [a]Is. 53:7
6 [a]Matt. 27:15–26
8 [1]NU *going up*
11 [a]Acts 3:14
12 [a]Mic. 5:2

4 [a]Then Pilate asked Him again,
saying, "Do You answer nothing?
See how many things [1]they testify
against You!"
5 [a]But Jesus still answered nothing, so that Pilate marveled.
6 Now [a]at the feast he was accustomed to releasing one prisoner to
them, whomever they requested.
7 And there was one named Barabbas, *who was* chained with his fellow rebels; they had committed murder in the rebellion.†
8 Then the multitude, [1]crying
aloud, began to ask *him to do* just as
he had always done for them.†
9 But Pilate answered them, saying, "Do you want me to release to
you the King of the Jews?"
10 For he knew that the chief
priests had handed Him over because of envy.
11 But [a]the chief priests stirred up
the crowd, so that he should rather
release Barabbas to them.
12 Pilate answered and said to
them again, "What then do you want
me to do *with Him* whom you call
the [a]King of the Jews?"
13 So they cried out again, "Crucify Him!"
14 Then Pilate said to them, "Why,

14:72 When he thought about it, he wept. All of us fail; Peter bursts into tears of repentance over his denial (for his restoration by Christ, see 16:7 and John 21:15–17).

15:1 The Sanhedrin waits to reach the official decision **in the morning,** probably because by law sessions at night were not allowed. **Pilate:** the Roman procurator of Judea, A.D. 26–36. The **council** is greatly deluded. They think they are going to take away the life of the Son of God! Jesus said, "Therefore My Father loves Me, because I lay down My life that I may take it again" (John 10:17).

15:2 Are You the King of the Jews? is a political question, to which a positive answer would be tantamount to treason against Rome. Jesus answers indirectly, **It is as you say.**

15:3–5 It is not that Jesus **answered nothing** to any of the charges. He does indirectly acknowledge being "the King of the Jews" (v. 2) and He affirms that He is "the Christ, the Son of the Blessed" (14:61). But against false charges He makes no defense. (See notes on Matt. 27:2, 11–14.)

15:7 Barabbas and **his fellow rebels** are Jewish nationalists who have already participated in some local insurrection against the Romans. Barabbas means "son of Abba" or, literally, "son of the father." A variant reading in Matt. 27:16 (see center-column note there) and a patristic tradition also attribute the name Jesus to him, thus underscoring the bitter irony that the false "savior" and "son of the father" is released, whereas the true Savior and Son of the Father is condemned to death.

15:8 This **multitude,** stirred up by the Jewish leaders, is quite likely a crowd of their own supporters hastily gathered in the early morning. It is probably not the same crowd which welcomed Jesus at His Triumphal Entry (11:9), nor the general populace feared by the Jewish leaders (14:2). However, just days before on Palm Sunday, no doubt some of these same people had praised Him. The multitudes were always interested in Christ. Now they turn against Him. Why? The multitude is fickle. The crowd follows the crowd. It loves good teaching and prophetic insight, but avoids discipleship, suffering and perseverance.

[a]what evil has He done?" But they
cried out all the more, "Crucify
Him!"
15 [a]So Pilate, wanting to gratify the
crowd, released Barabbas to them;
and he delivered Jesus, after he
had scourged *Him,* to be [b]cruci-
fied.†

Mocked by Soldiers
(Matt. 27:27–31)

16 [a]Then the soldiers led Him
away into the hall called [1]Praeto-
rium, and they called together the
whole garrison.†
17 And they clothed Him with purple; and they twisted a crown of
thorns, put it on His *head,*
18 and began to salute Him, "Hail,
King of the Jews!"†
19 Then they [a]struck Him on the
head with a reed and spat on Him;
and bowing the knee, they worshiped Him.†
20 And when they had [a]mocked
Him, they took the purple off Him,

14 [a]1 Pet. 2:21–23
15 [a]Matt. 27:26 [b][Is. 53:8]
16 [a]Matt. 27:27–31 [1]The governor's headquarters
19 [a][Is. 50:6; 52:14; 53:5]
20 [a]Luke 22:63; 23:11
21 [a]Matt. 27:32
22 [a]John 19:17–24
23 [a]Matt. 27:34
24 [a]Ps. 22:18
25 [a]John 19:14
26 [a]Matt. 27:37 [1]*crime*

put His own clothes on Him, and
led Him out to crucify Him.

The Crucifixion
(Matt. 27:31–44; Luke 23:26–43; John
19:17–27)

21 [a]Then they compelled a certain
man, Simon a Cyrenian, the father
of Alexander and Rufus, as he was
coming out of the country and passing by, to bear His cross.†
22 [a]And they brought Him to the
place Golgotha, which is translated,
Place of a Skull.
23 [a]Then they gave Him wine mingled with myrrh to drink, but He did
not take *it.*
24 And when they crucified Him,
[a]they divided His garments, casting
lots for them to determine what
every man should take.†
25 Now [a]it was the third hour, and
they crucified Him.†
26 And [a]the inscription of His
[1]accusation was written above:

THE KING OF THE JEWS.†

15:15 The envy of the Jews brought Jesus to Pilate. The cowardice of Pilate allows envy to have its way. How pathetic is Pilate: known in history by billions of people for his complicity, perhaps the greatest coward of all time. **Scourged** means flogged with a Roman whip consisting of several leather strips with small pieces of bone and lead at the tips.

15:16 The **Praetorium** is the residence of the Roman governor. Pilate may have resided either in Herod's palace or in the Fortress Antonia near the temple.

15:18 The mockery by the Roman soldiers includes the salute **Hail, King of the Jews,** a parody of the salute to Caesar. It is astonishing that the King of kings humbly condescends to be shamefully treated as a criminal. One cannot help but grieve for those who abuse Jesus, for most of them also will reject the reality of His Resurrection and His victory over sin and death.

15:19 Even in their mockery they prefigure things to come. They will bow **the knee** to Him once more, for "at the name of Jesus every knee should bow" (Phil. 2:10).

15:21–32 See notes on Matt. 27:32–44.

15:21, 22 Compelled signifies the right of soldiers to press civilians into service. **Cyrenian:** that is, from Cyrene, a city on the coast of Libya, North Africa, where many Jews lived. **Simon** has the unique privilege of helping the Son of God, weakened by flogging, to carry His Cross to **Golgotha** (v. 22).

15:24 That **they divided His garments** was a right of the squad of executioners. It also fulfills the prophesy of Psalm 22:18.

15:25 Crucifixion was a horrifying means of Roman execution reserved for rebellious slaves, violent criminals, and those charged with high treason. Roman citizens were spared crucifixion. **The third hour** is 9:00 A.M. or thereabouts. The Evangelist John reports a time closer to noon (John 19:14).

15:26 The inscription on the Cross was in accordance with a Roman custom of indicating the official charge against the prisoner. Whereas the Jewish authorities condemn Jesus for blasphemy, in Roman eyes Jesus dies as a potential political agitator. St. Paul writes, "None of the rulers of this age knew; for had they known, they would not have crucified the Lord of glory" (1 Cor. 2:8).

27 [a]With Him they also crucified two robbers, one on His right and the other on His left.†

28 [1]So the Scripture was fulfilled which says, [a]*"And He was numbered with the transgressors."*

29 And [a]those who passed by blasphemed Him, [b]wagging their heads and saying, "Aha! [c]*You* who destroy the temple and build *it* in three days,

30 "save Yourself, and come down from the cross!"

31 Likewise the chief priests also, [a]mocking among themselves with the scribes, said, "He saved [b]others; Himself He cannot save.†

32 "Let the Christ, the King of Israel, descend now from the cross, that we may see and [1]believe." Even [a]those who were crucified with Him reviled Him.

Jesus Dies

(Matt. 27:45–56; Luke 23:44–49; John 19:28–37)

33 Now [a]when the sixth hour had come, there was darkness over the whole land until the ninth hour.†

34 And at the ninth hour Jesus cried out with a loud voice, saying, "Eloi, Eloi, lama sabachthani?" which is translated, [a]*"My God, My God, why have You forsaken Me?"*†

35 Some of those who stood by, when they heard *that*, said, "Look, He is calling for Elijah!"

36 Then [a]someone ran and filled a sponge full of sour wine, put *it* on a reed, and [b]offered *it* to Him to drink, saying, "Let Him alone; let us see if Elijah will come to take Him down."†

37 [a]And Jesus cried out with a loud voice, and breathed His last.†

38 Then [a]the veil of the temple was torn in two from top to bottom.†

39 So [a]when the centurion, who stood opposite Him, saw that [1]He cried out like this and breathed His last, he said, "Truly this Man was the Son of God!"

40 [a]There were also women looking on [b]from afar, among whom were Mary Magdalene, Mary the mother of James the Less and of Joses, and Salome,

41 who also [a]followed Him and ministered to Him when He was in Galilee, and many other women who came up with Him to Jerusalem.

The Burial

(Matt. 27:57–61; Luke 23:50–56; John 19:38–42)

42 [a]Now when evening had come, because it was the Preparation Day, that is, the day before the Sabbath,

43 Joseph of Arimathea, a prominent council member, who [a]was himself waiting for the kingdom of God, coming and taking courage, went in to Pilate and asked for the body of Jesus.†

44 Pilate marveled that He was

27 [a]Luke 22:37
28 [a]Is. 53:12
[1]NU omits v. 28.
29 [a]Ps. 22:6, 7; 69:7
[b]Ps. 109:25
[c]John 2:19–21
31 [a]Luke 18:32
[b]John 11:43, 44
32 [a]Matt. 27:44
[1]M *believe Him*
33 [a]Luke 23:44–49
34 [a]Ps. 22:1
36 [a]John 19:29
[b]Ps. 69:21
37 [a]Matt. 27:50
38 [a]Ex. 26:31–33
39 [a]Luke 23:47
[1]NU *He thus breathed His last*
40 [a]Matt. 27:55
[b]Ps. 38:11
41 [a]Luke 8:2, 3
42 [a]John 19:38–42
43 [a]Luke 2:25, 38; 23:51

15:27 The ancient Jewish historian Josephus defines **robbers** (Gr. *lestes*) as insurrectionists, that is, militant nationalist Jews who fought against Romans and Jewish collaborators.

15:31 This is the hour of greatest scandal, a seeming triumph for the chief priests and the scribes, but one short-lived.

15:33 When the Creator suffers, the creation suffers with Him. The lights of heaven hide themselves and are darkened **until the ninth hour** as God hangs suspended upon a Cross. (See notes on Matt. 27:45–56.)

15:34 In His humanity, Christ is really **forsaken:** in, and with, and for us, who are *forsaken* and abandoned. **Eloi** is an Aramaic form which means "my God."

15:36 Many believed Elijah would come to rescue the pious.

15:37 The Greek verb for **breathed His last** or "expired" connotes a voluntary death. Jesus' death is that of the suffering Messiah, whose cry is not a defeat but a sign of the separation between the soul and the body, a turning point towards the triumph over death, the trampling down of death by death.

15:38 The dividing wall of hostility separating man from God is symbolically represented by **the veil of the temple,** which **was torn in two** by the death of Jesus.

15:43 Not all members of the Sanhedrin are opposed to Jesus. **Joseph of Arimathea** is an

(continued on next page)

Sunday of the Myrrhbearing Women, Joseph of Arimathea and Nicodemus

Second Sunday after Easter (Third Sunday of Pascha)

15:43—16:8: Joseph of Arimathea buries Jesus; the faithful women come to anoint Him and discover He is risen.

already dead; and summoning the
centurion, he asked him if He had
been dead for some time.†
45 So when he found out from the
centurion, he granted the body to
Joseph.
46 [a]Then he bought fine linen,
took Him down, and wrapped Him
in the linen. And he laid Him in a
tomb which had been hewn out of
the rock, and rolled a stone against
the door of the tomb.†
47 And Mary Magdalene and Mary
the mother of Joses observed where
He was laid.

The Empty Tomb

(Matt. 28:1–8; Luke 24:1–12; John 20:1–10)

16 Now [a]when the Sabbath was
past, Mary Magdalene, Mary
the mother of James, and Salome
[b]bought spices, that they might
come and anoint Him.†
2 [a]Very early in the morning, on
the first *day* of the week, they came
to the tomb when the sun had risen.
3 And they said among themselves,
"Who will roll away the stone
from the door of the tomb for us?"
4 But when they looked up, they
saw that the stone had been rolled
away—for it was very large.†
5 [a]And entering the tomb, they
saw a young man clothed in a long
white robe sitting on the right side;
and they were alarmed.†
6 [a]But he said to them, "Do not
be alarmed. You seek Jesus of Nazareth,
who was crucified. He is risen!
He is not here. See the place where
they laid Him.
7 "But go, tell His disciples—and
Peter—that He is going [1]before you

46 [a]Matt. 27:59, 60

CHAPTER 16

1 [a]John 20:1–8 [b]Luke 23:56

2 [a]Luke 24:1

5 [a]John 20:11, 12

6 [a]Matt. 28:6

7 [1]*ahead of*

(continued from previous page)
exception, as is Nicodemus (John 3:1–4; 7:50; 19:39). Joseph was **waiting for the kingdom of God,** sympathetic to the message of Jesus. According to tradition, Joseph went on to evangelize the British Isles.

15:44 Pilate marveled because crucified men usually lived for many hours, or even days, after being hung on the cross.

15:46 According to custom, tombs were carved out of soft rock in a cavelike fashion, sometimes with several chambers. Then a flat, circular **stone** was rolled into a prepared groove to shut the opening. This verse is spoken by the priest in the Liturgy of St. John Chrysostom as the Gifts (the bread and the wine) are placed on the altar after the Great Entrance. They are followed by an awesome proclamation of who this Jesus is who is crucified: "In the grave with Your body, but in hell with Your soul as God, in Paradise with the thief, and on the throne with Your Father and the Spirit, O Christ You are uncontained."

16:1 At least some of the mothers of Jesus' disciples were involved in His life and ministry (see 15:40). **Mary the mother of James** is probably the mother of James, son of Alphaeus (also called James the Less), one of the Twelve. Salome is probably the mother of James and John, sons of Zebedee, two of the Twelve (compare to Matt. 27:56). They **bought spices,** aromatic oils, **when the Sabbath was past,** out of respect for the Sabbath-rest. Anointing the body, but not embalming it, was a Jewish custom. The women seek to fulfill this custom, in their courage exhibiting their great love and devotion for Jesus, in contrast to the scattered disciples. They are rewarded by the honor of being the first witnesses to the Resurrection.

16:4 The stone had been rolled away not to accommodate Jesus' Resurrection, but to show that the tomb is empty.

16:5 Entering the tomb, that is, the first chamber, they see **a young man** who is actually an angel. The details vary among the Gospels: Matthew reports the angel as sitting outside on the stone (Matt. 28:2), while Luke recounts two angels in the vicinity (Luke 24:4).

into Galilee; there you will see Him,
[a]as He said to you."†
8 So they went out [1]quickly and
fled from the tomb, for they trembled
and were amazed. [a]And they said
nothing to anyone, for they were
afraid.

The Risen Christ Appears

(Matt. 28:9, 10; Luke 24:13–43; John 20:11—21:25)

9 [1]Now when *He* rose early on the
first *day* of the week, He appeared
first to Mary Magdalene, [a]out of
whom He had cast seven demons.†
10 [a]She went and told those who
had been with Him, as they
mourned and wept.
11 [a]And when they heard that He
was alive and had been seen by her,
they did not believe.
12 After that, He appeared in another form [a]to two of them as they
walked and went into the country.†
13 And they went and told *it* to the
rest, *but* they did not believe them
either.

The Great Commission

(Matt. 28:16–20; Luke 24:44–49)

14 [a]Later He appeared to the
eleven as they sat at the table; and
He rebuked their unbelief and hardness of heart, because they did not
believe those who had seen Him after He had risen.†
15 [a]And He said to them, "Go into
all the world [b]and preach the gospel
to every creature.†
16 [a]"He who believes and is baptized will be saved; [b]but he who does
not believe will be condemned.†
17 "And these [a]signs will follow
those who [1]believe: [b]In My name
they will cast out demons; [c]they will
speak with new tongues;†
18 [a]"they[1] will take up serpents;

7 [a]Matt. 26:32; 28:16, 17
8 [a]Matt. 28:8 [1]NU, M omit *quickly*
9 [a]Luke 8:2 [1]Vv. 9–20 are bracketed in NU as not in the original text. They are lacking in Codex Sinaiticus and Codex Vaticanus, although nearly all other mss. of Mark contain them.
10 [a]Luke 24:10
11 [a]Luke 24:11, 41
12 [a]Luke 24:13–35
14 [a]1 Cor. 15:5
15 [a]Matt. 28:19 [b][Col. 1:23]
16 [a][John 3:18, 36] [b][John 12:48]
17 [a]Acts 5:12 [b]Luke 10:17 [c][Acts 2:4] [1]*have believed*
18 [a]Acts 28:3–6 [1]NU *and in their hands they will*

16:7 And Peter indicates Christ's loving concern and encouraging word for the disciple who had denied Him. **Galilee,** an area to the north of Israel and removed from the center of Jewish life, is already inhabited by Gentiles and represents Christ's mission to the Gentiles. The plan of God progresses toward the goal of offering salvation and glory to all mankind. So, in Mark, He instructs His disciples to return to Galilee after the Resurrection (14:28; as in Matt. 26:32; 28:7, 10, 16; but in contrast to Luke 24:49).

16:9–20 Some manuscripts do not include this longer ending. Later traditions testify to several endings. The Church, however, has always regarded this ending as canonical and inspired.

16:9 Mary Magdalene is the first to break the news of the Resurrection. She who at one time had **seven demons** now becomes the first to see the risen Lord.

16:12 Another form: Christ's resurrected body transcends not only time and space, but physical appearance as well. He was sometimes recognizable to His disciples and sometimes not.

16:14 Failure to believe the report of the Resurrection is worthy of blame. Jesus **rebuked** the disciples for **unbelief** and **hardness of heart** even as they experience the joy of intimacy with the risen Lord in meals alluding to the Eucharist. The Holy Spirit comes to lead them to a full understanding of the mystery of Christ and His mission.

16:15–18 The Resurrection launches the Church toward her **world** mission. This passage is read at Orthodox baptisms, the sacramental initiation of a Christian's discipleship. All nations are to be His disciples and to bear witness to His Resurrection. Further, **every creature,** the entire cosmos, is affected by it.

16:16 Jesus commends the task of baptism not to the public but to His Apostles. Salvation includes faith and baptism.

16:17 To invoke the **name** of the incarnate Son of God is also to call upon the Father and the Holy Spirit: three Persons, one in divine nature and divine power. The power to **cast out demons** had already been given to the disciples (6:7). Now future believers are also promised the gift of exorcism. Speaking with **new tongues** was a gift highly valued by the Corinthian Christians (1 Cor. 13:1; 14:2–28). For the Church Fathers this was the miraculous ability to speak foreign tongues in order to spread the gospel, as at Pentecost (Acts 2:6–11).

and if they drink anything deadly,
it will by no means hurt them;
[b]they will lay hands on the sick, and
they will recover."†

The Ascension
(Luke 24:50–53)

19 So then, [a]after the Lord had
spoken to them, He was [b]received
up into heaven, and [c]sat down at
the right hand of God.†
20 And they went out and
preached everywhere, the Lord
working with *them* [a]and confirming
the word through the accompanying
signs. Amen.

18 [b]James 5:14
19 [a]Acts 1:2, 3
[b]Luke 9:51; 24:51
[c][Ps. 110:1]
20 [a][Heb. 2:4]

16:18 Paul took up a **serpent** and was not harmed by its bite (Acts 28:3–6). According to a tradition preserved by the Church historian Eusebius, Barsabas Justus (Acts 1:23) in his later life, while tested by unbelievers, drank poison and survived. The Church Fathers strictly prohibited deliberate, harmful acts against oneself as demonstrations of Christian faith.

16:19, 20 Note the sequence: Ascension, sitting down **at the right hand of God,** mission. This sitting down refers to (1) Christ's enthronement in glory and (2) the immovable stability of His royal state, His eternal sharing in the divine power and lordship of the Father. He will cooperate with the apostles, **working with them and confirming** the gospel they will preach, in part through **accompanying signs.** The book of Acts provides ample evidence of this ongoing synergy between man and God.

The Gospel According to
ST. LUKE

Author: *St. Luke, the "beloved physician"*

Date: A.D. *70–80*

Theme: *The Universality of the Gospel Message*

AUTHOR: All the early sources emphasize that the third Gospel was written by Luke, who is mentioned in Colossians 4:14; 2 Timothy 4:11, and Philemon 24. Luke was a Gentile from Antioch by birth, and a physician by profession. He was a fellow worker of Paul's: the plural "we" (Acts 20:6ff.) indicates Luke was with Paul as he traveled the coast of Asia Minor on his way to Jerusalem. Luke has left us two New Testament books: this Gospel and the Acts of the Apostles.

DATE: In his preface to the Gospel (1:1), Luke indicates knowledge of other written sources. Most scholars believe he used Mark as a source. He probably wrote his Gospel either from Greece or from Asia Minor in A.D. 70–80.

MAJOR THEME: *The Universality of the Gospel Message*. Luke has been called a "historian" because he dates biblical events by reference to secular history (2:1, 2; 3:1). Since this is a Gospel written for Christians of Gentile background, it emphasizes more than the other Gospels the challenge of mission and evangelization. Salvation is described as "a light to bring revelation to the Gentiles" (2:32). At the end of the Gospel, the risen Lord instructs His disciples to preach repentance and the forgiveness of sins "to all nations" (24:47).

BACKGROUND INFORMATION: Three aspects of the Christian life are emphasized throughout Luke, perhaps revealing the author's own spiritual gifts and strengths.

(1) *Prayer*. The early chapters lift up the example of righteous men and women offering gifts, hymns and prayers to God (1:10, 13, 46–55, 64; 2:20, 28–32). Jesus is portrayed frequently at prayer, especially before every important step in His ministry (3:21; 5:16; 6:12; 9:18, 28; 11:1; 22:32, 41; 23:46). The Gospel ends with the disciples "continually in the temple praising and blessing God" (24:53).

(2) *The activity of the Holy Spirit*. The inspirational work of the Holy Spirit is everywhere evident in the Gospel. Mary is "overshadowed" by the Spirit

(1:35). The Spirit leads Zacharias to prophesy (1:67) and prompts Simeon's actions (2:25–27). Jesus conducts His ministry in the fullness of the Spirit (3:22; 4:1, 18; 10:21). The disciples were to embark upon their world mission after receiving "power from on high" (24:49), the gift of the Spirit.

(3) *A deep concern for sinners.* Luke reports Jesus' concern and love for sinners, with a confident hope of their repentance and forgiveness (5:1–11; 7:36–50; 9:51–56; 10:29–37; 19:1–10; 23:39–43).

OUTLINE

Introduction	1:1–4
I. Jesus' birth and early life	1:5—2:52
A. The two annunciations	1:5–38
1. To Zacharias concerning John the Baptist	1:5–25
2. To Mary concerning the Son of God	1:26–38
B. Mary and Elizabeth wait together	1:39–56
1. Elizabeth and her unborn child magnify Mary	1:39–45
2. Mary's hymn of praise: The *Magnificat*	1:46–56
C. John's birth and early life	1:57–80
1. John is named	1:57–66
2. Zacharias' song: The *Benedictus*	1:67–79
3. John's childhood and early manhood	1:80
D. Jesus' birth and early life	2:1–52
1. His birth	2:1–38
2. His childhood and early manhood	2:39–52
II. The Messiah manifested	3:1—4:13
A. The Forerunner's message: Repentance and expectation	3:1–20
B. Jesus' anointing as Messiah	3:21—4:13
1. His baptism and chrismation	3:21, 22
2. His identity: Son of David, Son of God	3:23–38
3. His temptation	4:1–13
III. The great Galilean ministry	4:14—9:50
A. The contrast of law and grace	4:14—6:11
1. Lord over fallen humanity	4:14–44
2. Lord over the Law of Moses	5:1–39
3. Lord over worship: The Sabbath	6:1–11
B. The separation of law from grace	6:12—7:50
1. The new government	6:12–19
2. The new law: The Sermon	6:20–49
3. The new citizens	7:1–50
a. The dead become citizens	7:1–35
b. Sinners become citizens	7:36–50
C. The new Kingdom is hidden from the old	8:1–56
1. A veiled form of teaching: The parables	8:1–18
2. A new, spiritual family	8:19–21
3. Renewed but secret miracles	8:22–56
D. A new Israel: New manna, new glory revealed	9:1–50
1. New apostolate: The Twelve sent out	9:1–10
2. New sacrament: Jesus' manna from heaven	9:11–17

3. New creed: Jesus is Messiah 9:18–27
4. Renewed humanity: The Transfiguration 9:28–36
5. In contrast to the old 9:37–50

IV. Later Judean and Perean ministries 9:51—18:30

A. The new rule for new Israel 9:51—11:13
1. New rule of discipleship 9:51–62
2. New goal of service 10:1–24
3. New rule of spirituality 10:25—11:13

B. The new critiques the old (Judean Ministry) 11:14—13:21
1. Lack of spiritual perception 11:14–36
2. The arrogant pride of externalism 11:37–54
3. Hypocrisy 12:1–12
4. Greed and anxiety 12:13–34
5. Laziness, forgetfulness 12:35–48
6. Blindness, lack of discernment 12:49–59
7. Conclusion: Repent or perish! 13:1–9
8. Test of a Pharisee: A Sabbath healing 13:10–21

C. Striving for the Kingdom (Perean Ministry) 13:22—17:10
1. Desire for God: Strive to enter! 13:22–35
2. Lowliness: Be kind to the poor 14:1–24
3. Desire for God: Costly discipleship 14:25–35
4. Lowliness: Associate with sinners 15:1–32
5. Stewardship 16:1—17:10
a. Its wisdom 16:1–18
b. Its compassion 16:19–31
c. Its humility 17:1–10

D. Waiting for the coming Kingdom (on to Jerusalem) 17:11—18:30
1. Gratitude and remembrance 17:11–19
2. Renunciation and wakefulness 17:20–37
3. Prayer: Persistent and contrite 18:1–14
4. Total, willful commitment 18:15–30

V. Holy Week: The New Covenant made 18:31—24:53

A. Public fulfillment and rejection 18:31—21:38
1. Christ as Suffering Servant 18:31—19:27
a. Glory through humility 18:31—19:10
b. Patient responsibility 19:11–27
2. Christ as King: Great entrance of Palm Sunday 19:28–44
3. Christ as High Priest: Cleansing of the temple 19:45, 46
4. Christ as Teacher 19:47—21:4
a. Interrogation by Jewish leaders 19:47—20:40
b. Cross-examination 20:41–44
c. Christ's summation 20:45—21:4
5. Christ as Prophet 21:5–38
a. What are the signs? 21:5–28
b. When is the time? 21:29–33
c. What shall we do? 21:34–38

B. Private preparation and faithfulness 22:1—24:53
1. Passover nears 22:1–13
2. Sacrament: The old meal and the new 22:14–23

3. Headship: True greatness, true reward 22:24–30
4. Christ's Kingdom in this world 22:31–38
C. Christ's Passion: Passover fulfilled 22:39—23:56
1. The Mount of Olives 22:39–53
2. Trials 22:54—23:25
3. Crucifixion 23:26–49
4. Burial 23:50–56
D. Resurrection 24:1–49
1. The empty tomb 24:1–12
2. Resurrection appearances 24:13–49
a. To two, on the road to Emmaus 24:13–35
b. To the ten apostles 24:36–49
E. Ascension 24:50–53

Preface

1 Inasmuch as many have taken in
hand to set in order a narrative
of those [a]things which [1]have been
fulfilled among us,
2 just as those who [a]from the beginning were [b]eyewitnesses and
ministers of the word [c]delivered
them to us,†
3 it seemed good to me also, having [1]had perfect understanding of all
things from the very first, to write
to you an orderly account, [a]most excellent Theophilus,†
4 [a]that you may know the certainty of those things in which you
were instructed.

John's Birth Announced to Zacharias

5 There was [a]in the days of
Herod, the king of Judea, a certain
priest named Zacharias, [b]of the division of [c]Abijah. His [d]wife *was* of the
daughters of Aaron, and her name
was Elizabeth.†
6 And they were both righteous
before God, walking in all the commandments and ordinances of the
Lord blameless.†
7 But they had no child, because
Elizabeth was barren, and they were
both well advanced in years.
8 So it was, that while he was
serving as priest before God in the
order of his division,†
9 according to the custom of the
priesthood, [1]his lot fell [a]to burn incense when he went into the temple
of the Lord.
10 [a]And the whole multitude of
the people was praying outside at
the hour of incense.
11 Then an angel of the Lord appeared to him, standing on the right
side of [a]the altar of incense.

CHAPTER 1
1 [a]John 20:31 [1]Or *are most surely believed*
2 [a]Acts 1:21, 22 [b]Acts 1:2 [c]Heb. 2:3
3 [a]Acts 1:1 [1]Lit. *accurately followed*
4 [a][John 20:31]
5 [a]Matt. 2:1 [b]1 Chr. 24:1, 10 [c]Neh. 12:4 [d]Lev. 21:13, 14
9 [a]Ex. 30:7, 8 [1]*he was chosen by lot*
10 [a]Lev. 16:17
11 [a]Ex. 30:1

1:2 As **eyewitnesses** of Jesus Christ, the disciples listened to His Good News and saw His miracles firsthand. As Luke himself was not one of the original disciples of Jesus, his Gospel is anchored on the testimony of these witnesses.

1:3, 4 Luke addresses himself to **Theophilus** (see Acts 1:1), a prominent Gentile who has received Christian instruction, but is otherwise unknown to us. The Gospel is written as **an orderly account** to provide greater **certainty** about the details of Jesus' ministry.

1:5–80 Luke is the only Evangelist who provides information about the birth and infancy of John the Baptist.

1:6, 7 Zacharias and Elizabeth are a **righteous** (v. 6) couple of a priestly lineage, living always to fulfill God's will. But Elizabeth, like other well-known women of the Bible—Sarah (Gen. 16:1), Rebekah (Gen. 25:21), Hannah (1 Sam. 1:2) and others—is **barren** (v. 7), which was a public reproach (v. 25).

1:8, 9 Each priest was assigned to a **division** (v. 8; see 1 Chr. 23:3–6; 28:13). There were 24 divisions in all, each serving a week at a time by rotation. The responsibilities of the priests in the division were decided by **lot** (v. 9).

MARY

"For behold, all generations will call me blessed." (Luke 1:48)

For two thousand years the Church has preserved the memory of the Virgin Mary as the prototype of all Christians—the model of what we are to become in Christ. Mary was truly pure and unconditionally obedient to God. The tradition of the Church holds that Mary remained a virgin all her life (see note on Matt. 12:46–50). While lifelong celibacy is not a model for all Christians to follow, Mary's spiritual purity, her wholehearted devotion to God, is certainly to be emulated.

Mary is also our model in that she was the first person to receive Jesus Christ. As Mary bore Christ in her womb physically, all Christians now have the privilege of bearing God within them spiritually. By God's grace and mercy we are purified and empowered to become like Him.

The honor we give to Mary also signifies our view of who Jesus is. From early times the Church has called her Mother of God (Gr. *Theotokos,* lit. God-Bearer), a title which implies that her Son is both fully man and fully God. As His mother, Mary was the source of Jesus' human nature; yet, the One she bore in her womb was also the eternal God.

Therefore, because of her character and especially because of her role in God's plan of salvation, Christians appropriately honor Mary as the first among the saints. The archangel Gabriel initiated this honor in his address to her: "Rejoice, highly favored one, the Lord is with you; blessed are you among women!" (Luke 1:28). This salutation clearly indicates that God Himself had chosen to honor Mary. Her favored status was confirmed when she went to visit her cousin Elizabeth, who was then six months pregnant with John the Baptist. Elizabeth greeted Mary with these words: "Blessed are you among women, and blessed is the fruit of your womb! But why is this granted to me, that the mother of my Lord should come to me?" (Luke 1:42, 43). And Mary herself, by the inspiration of the Holy Spirit, predicted the honor that would be paid her throughout history: "For behold, henceforth all generations will call me blessed" (Luke 1:48).

In obedience to God's clear intention, therefore, the Orthodox Church honors Mary in icons, hymns, and special feast days. We entreat her, as the human being who was most intimate with Christ on earth, to intercede with her Son on our behalf. We ask her, as the first believer and the mother of the Church, for guidance and protection. We venerate her—but we do not worship her, for worship belongs to God alone.

In Matins, Vespers, and all the services of the hours of prayer, we sing this hymn, which expresses Mary's unique place in creation.

> It is truly right to bless you, O Theotokos, ever-blessed and most pure, and the mother of our God. More honorable than the Cherubim, and more glorious beyond compare than the Seraphim, without defilement you gave birth to God the Word: True Theotokos, we magnify you.

The Birth of John the Baptist *June 24*

1:1–15, 57–68, 76, 80: John's birth is announced, accomplished, and celebrated.

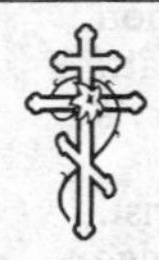

The Conception of John the Baptist *September 23*

1:5–25: John's coming birth is announced to his father, Zacharias.

12 And when Zacharias saw *him,*
[a]he was troubled, and fear fell upon
him.
13 But the angel said to him, "Do
not be afraid, Zacharias, for your
prayer is heard; and your wife Elizabeth will bear you a son, and [a]you
shall call his name John.†
14 "And you will have joy and
gladness, and [a]many will rejoice at
his birth.
15 "For he will be [a]great in the
sight of the Lord, and [b]shall drink
neither wine nor strong drink. He
will also be filled with the Holy
Spirit, [c]even from his mother's
womb.†
16 "And he will turn many of the
children of Israel to the Lord their
God.
17 [a]"He will also go before Him in
the spirit and power of Elijah, *'to
turn the hearts of the fathers to the
children,'* and the disobedient to the
wisdom of the just, to make ready
a people prepared for the Lord."
18 And Zacharias said to the angel,
[a]"How shall I know this? For I am
an old man, and my wife is well advanced in years."†
19 And the angel answered and
said to him, "I am [a]Gabriel, who
stands in the presence of God, and
was sent to speak to you and bring
you [1]these glad [b]tidings.
20 "But behold, [a]you will be mute
and not able to speak until the day
these things take place, because you
did not believe my words which will
be fulfilled in their own time."†
21 And the people waited for
Zacharias, and marveled that he lingered so long in the temple.
22 But when he came out, he could
not speak to them; and they perceived that he had seen a vision in
the temple, for he beckoned to them
and remained speechless.
23 So it was, as soon as [a]the days
of his service were completed, that
he departed to his own house.
24 Now after those days his wife
Elizabeth conceived; and she hid
herself five months, saying,
25 "Thus the Lord has dealt with
me, in the days when He looked on

12 [a]Judg. 6:22; Dan. 10:8; Luke 2:9; Acts 10:4; Rev. 1:17
13 [a]Luke 1:57, 60, 63
14 [a]Luke 1:58
15 [a][Luke 7:24–28] [b]Num. 6:3; Judg. 13:4; Matt. 11:18 [c]Jer. 1:5; Gal. 1:15
17 [a]Mal. 4:5, 6; Matt. 3:2; 11:14; Mark 1:4; 9:12
18 [a]Gen. 17:17
19 [a]Dan. 8:16; [Matt. 18:10]; Heb. 1:4 [b]Luke 2:10 [1]*this good news*
20 [a]Ezek. 3:26; 24:27
23 [a]2 Kin. 11:5; 1 Chr. 9:25

1:13 Zacharias has prayed often for **a son** and now his prayer is answered. **The angel** (Gabriel, v. 19) promises a son who will be named **John,** meaning "the grace of God."

1:15–17 Note the description of the character and role of John the Baptist as an ascetic prophet who is to prepare the Jewish people for the coming of the Messiah. Elijah (v. 17), one of the greatest prophets of Israel, was expected to reappear from heaven in order to anoint the Messiah.

1:18 Zacharias's question indicates a lack of complete faith in God's promise. Compare this with Abram's response when he was promised a son: "he believed in the LORD" (Gen. 15:3–6).

1:20 Losing his speech serves both as discipline for Zacharias's unbelief and as a sign of the truth of Gabriel's announcement.

The Announcement to the Virgin Mary *March 25*

1:24–38: The coming birth of the Lord Jesus Christ is announced to His mother, Mary.

me, to [a]take away my reproach
among people."

Christ's Birth Announced to Mary

26 Now in the sixth month the angel Gabriel was sent by God to a city
of Galilee named Nazareth,
27 to a virgin [a]betrothed to a man
whose name was Joseph, of the
house of David. The virgin's name
was Mary.†
28 And having come in, the angel
said to her, [a]"Rejoice, highly favored
one, [b]the Lord *is* with you; [1]blessed
are you among women!"†
29 But [1]when she saw *him,* [a]she
was troubled at his saying, and considered what manner of greeting this
was.
30 Then the angel said to her, "Do
not be afraid, Mary, for you have
found [a]favor with God.
31 [a]"And behold, you will conceive in your womb and bring forth
a Son, and [b]shall call His name
JESUS.†
32 "He will be great, [a]and will be
called the Son of the Highest; and
[b]the Lord God will give Him the
[c]throne of His [d]father David.
33 [a]"And He will reign over the

25 [a]Gen. 30:23
27 [a]Matt. 1:18
28 [a]Dan. 9:23 [b]Judg. 6:12 [1]NU omits *blessed are you among women*
29 [a]Luke 1:12 [1]NU omits *when she saw him*
30 [a]Luke 2:52
31 [a]Is. 7:14 [b]Luke 2:21
32 [a]Mark 5:7 [b]2 Sam. 7:12, 13, 16 [c]2 Sam. 7:14–17 [d]Matt. 1:1
33 [a][Dan. 2:44]
34 [1]Am a virgin
35 [a]Matt. 1:20 [b][Heb. 1:2, 8]
37 [a]Jer. 32:17
39 [a]Josh. 21:9

house of Jacob forever, and of His
kingdom there will be no end."
34 Then Mary said to the angel,
"How can this be, since I [1]do not
know a man?"
35 And the angel answered and
said to her, [a]"*The* Holy Spirit will
come upon you, and the power of
the Highest will overshadow you;
therefore, also, that Holy One who
is to be born will be called [b]the Son
of God.†
36 "Now indeed, Elizabeth your
relative has also conceived a son in
her old age; and this is now the sixth
month for her who was called
barren.
37 "For [a]with God nothing will be
impossible."
38 Then Mary said, "Behold the
maidservant of the Lord! Let it
be to me according to your word."
And the angel departed from
her.†

Elizabeth Praises Mary, Mother of God

39 Now Mary arose in those days
and went into the hill country with
haste, [a]to a city of Judah,

1:27 Mary (lit., "exalted one") is **betrothed** to **Joseph,** a man of royal lineage, of **the house** (family) **of David.** Luke says twice for emphasis that Mary is a **virgin.**

1:28 Highly favored (Gr. *charitoo*) can also be translated "full of grace." Mary is greeted with an exalted salutation because, in her destiny to be the mother of Christ, she is the most **blessed** woman of all time. In accord with Luke's picture of her, Mary is praised in the Orthodox Church as being surrounded with divine grace and shining with holiness.

1:31–33 What a description of the expected Messiah!

1:35 Holy Spirit and **power of the Highest** are synonymous; this is a case of repetition for emphasis. **Holy One** is a messianic title. That He is **to be born** of Mary demonstrates Christ's human nature. But that the Virgin will conceive and bear **the Son of God** reveals the divine nature of Christ. We note especially the reference to the Holy Trinity: God the Father (**the Highest**), the Son, and the Holy Spirit.

1:38 Mary's faithful response makes her the highest model of obedience to God. The Incarnation of the Son of God is not only the work of the Trinity, but also the work of the will and the faith of the Virgin. Therefore, the Virgin Mary is honored not only because God chose her, or because she bore the Son of God in the flesh, but also because she herself chose to believe and obey God firmly.

40 and entered the house of Zacharias and greeted Elizabeth.
41 And it happened, when Elizabeth heard the greeting of Mary, that
the babe leaped in her womb; and
Elizabeth was [a]filled with the Holy
Spirit.†
42 Then she spoke out with a loud
voice and said, [a]"Blessed *are* you
among women, and blessed *is* the
fruit of your womb!†
43 "But why *is* this *granted* to me,
that the mother of my Lord should
come to me?†
44 "For indeed, as soon as the
voice of your greeting sounded in my
ears, the babe leaped in my womb
for joy.
45 [a]"Blessed *is* she who [1]believed,
for there will be a fulfillment of those
things which were told her from the
Lord."

Mary Exults in God: The Magnificat

46 And Mary said:

[a]"My soul [1]magnifies the Lord,†
47 And my spirit has [a]rejoiced in
[b]God my Savior.
48 For [a]He has regarded the lowly
state of His maidservant;
For behold, henceforth [b]all
generations will call me
blessed.
49 For He who is mighty [a]has done
great things for me,
And [b]holy *is* His name.
50 And [a]His mercy *is* on those who
fear Him
From generation to generation.
51 [a]He has shown strength with His
arm;
[b]He has scattered *the* proud in
the imagination of their
hearts.
52 [a]He has put down the mighty
from *their* thrones,
And exalted *the* lowly.
53 He has [a]filled *the* hungry with
good things,
And *the* rich He has sent away
empty.
54 He has helped His [a]servant
Israel,
[b]In remembrance of *His* mercy,
55 [a]As He spoke to our [b]fathers,
To Abraham and to his
[c]seed forever."

56 And Mary remained with her
about three months, and returned to
her house.

John Born and Named

57 Now Elizabeth's full time came
for her to be delivered, and she
brought forth a son.
58 When her neighbors and relatives heard how the Lord had shown

41 [a]Acts 6:3 **42** [a]Judg. 5:24 **45** [a]John 20:29 [1]Or *believed that there* **46** [a]1 Sam. 2:1–10 [1]Declares the greatness of **47** [a]Hab. 3:18 [b]1 Tim. 1:1; 2:3 **48** [a]Ps. 138:6 [b]Luke 11:27 **49** [a]Ps. 71:19; 126:2, 3 [b]Ps. 111:9 **50** [a]Ps. 103:17 **51** [a]Ps. 98:1; 118:15 [b][1 Pet. 5:5] **52** [a]1 Sam. 2:7, 8 **53** [a][Matt. 5:6] **54** [a]Is. 41:8 [b][Jer. 31:3] **55** [a]Gen. 17:19 [b][Rom. 11:28] [c]Gen. 17:7

1:41 The babe, John the Baptist in his sixth month of gestation, **leaped in her womb** (see v. 15) as a joyous response to the presence of God, the Lord Jesus Christ, in Mary's womb.

1:42 Mary receives veneration from both angels and humans. For as did Gabriel (v. 28), Elizabeth also calls Mary **blessed.** Mary is the model of womanhood. None other has ever received the glory given to her, either in Scripture or in Church history.

1:43 Mary is confessed as **the mother of my Lord** by Elizabeth. This was no mere man Mary carried. The title "Theotokos" (the mother of God), given to the Virgin Mary by the Church, was derived from the truth of this confession. For unless that One in her womb was God, the world is still enslaved to sin.

1:46–56 This passage (called the *Magnificat,* the first word of this song in Latin) is a remarkable hymn of praise to God. It comes from the heart of Mary, who was probably only 16 or 17 years old at this time, but also from Hannah, advanced in years, who first uttered this inspired prayer (1 Sam. 2:1–10), which had been prayed by expectant Jewish mothers for centuries. From this NT passage we learn: (1) Christian believers for all time will honor or venerate the Virgin, for **all generations will call me blessed** (v. 48). It is not possible to believe and obey the Bible and not bless the Mother of God. (2) Identity between Mary and **Israel** is implicit here as the Israel of God, the Church, receives **His mercy** (v. 54). (3) The reign of God is over (a) our **hearts** (v. 51), (b) kings and rulers (v. 52), (c) the poor (v. 52) and the **rich** (v. 53), and (d) the faithful of God (v. 54).

great mercy to her, they [a]rejoiced
with her.
59 So it was, [a]on the eighth day,
that they came to circumcise the
child; and they would have called
him by the name of his father,
Zacharias.†
60 His mother answered and said,
[a]"No; he shall be called John."
61 But they said to her, "There is
no one among your relatives who is
called by this name."
62 So they made signs to his father—what he would have him
called.
63 And he asked for a writing tablet, and wrote, saying, "His name
is John." So they all marveled.
64 Immediately his mouth was
opened and his tongue *loosed*, and
he spoke, praising God.
65 Then fear came on all who dwelt
around them; and all these sayings
were discussed throughout all the
hill country of Judea.
66 And all those who heard *them*
[a]kept *them* in their hearts, saying,
"What kind of child will this be?"
And [b]the hand of the Lord was with
him.

Zacharias' Song: The Benedictus

67 Now his father Zacharias
[a]was filled with the Holy Spirit, and
prophesied, saying:†

68 "Blessed[a] *is* the Lord God of
Israel,
For [b]He has visited and
redeemed His people,
69 [a]And has raised up a horn of
salvation for us
In the house of His servant
David,
70 [a]As He spoke by the mouth of
His holy prophets,
Who *have been* [b]since the world
began,
71 That we should be saved from
our enemies
And from the hand of all who
hate us,
72 [a]To perform the mercy *promised*
to our fathers
And to remember His holy
covenant,
73 [a]The oath which He swore to our
father Abraham:
74 To grant us that we,
Being delivered from the hand
of our enemies,
Might [a]serve Him without
fear,
75 [a]In holiness and righteousness
before Him all the days of our
life.

76 "And you, child, will be called
the [a]prophet of the Highest;
For [b]you will go before the face
of the Lord to prepare His
ways,
77 To give [a]knowledge of salvation
to His people
By the remission of their sins,
78 Through the tender mercy of
our God,
With which the [1]Dayspring
from on high [2]has visited
us;†
79 [a]To give light to those who sit
in darkness and the shadow
of death,
To [b]guide our feet into the way
of peace."

John's Growth

80 So [a]the child grew and became
strong in spirit, and [b]was in the

58 [a][Rom. 12:15]
59 [a]Gen. 17:12; Lev. 12:3; Luke 2:21; Phil. 3:5
60 [a]Luke 1:13, 63
66 [a]Luke 2:19 [b]Gen. 39:2; Acts 11:21
67 [a]Joel 2:28
68 [a]1 Kin. 1:48; Ps. 106:48 [b]Ex. 3:16
69 [a]2 Sam. 22:3; Ps. 132:17; Ezek. 29:21
70 [a]Jer. 23:5; Rom. 1:2 [b]Acts 3:21
72 [a]Lev. 26:42
73 [a]Gen. 12:3; 22:16–18; [Heb. 6:13]
74 [a][Rom. 6:18; Heb. 9:14]
75 [a]Jer. 32:39; [Eph. 4:24; 2 Thess. 2:13]
76 [a]Matt. 3:3; 11:9; Mark 3:2, 3; Luke 3:4; John 1:23 [b]Is. 40:3; Mal. 3:1; Matt. 11:10
77 [a][Jer. 31:34; Mark 1:4]; Luke 3:3
78 [1]Lit. *Dawn;* the Messiah [2]NU *shall visit*
79 [a]Is. 9:2; Matt. 4:16; [Acts 26:18; 2 Cor. 4:6; Eph. 5:14] [b][John 10:4; 14:27; 16:33]
80 [a]Luke 2:40 [b]Matt. 3:1

1:59 Circumcision was a most important ritual by which a male child was initiated into the covenant people of God. After Christ, circumcision was fulfilled in Christian baptism. (See article, "Holy Baptism," at Rom. 6.)

1:67–79 The song of the priest Zacharias (often called the *Benedictus,* the first word of the song in Latin) is a prophetic hymn of praise to God. God is blessed for His gracious and redeeming acts among His people in fulfillment of the messianic promises now at hand. Verses 76 and 77 speak of John and his role as **the prophet** of God preparing the people to receive Christ.

1:78, 79 Dayspring from on high is a reference to the Messiah who is coming like the rising sun to bring **light to those . . . in darkness** (v. 79).

The Eve of the Birth of Jesus Christ (Christmas Eve) *December 24*

2:1–20: Jesus' birth in Bethlehem is heralded by angels and shepherds.

deserts till the day of his manifestation to Israel.†

Christ Born in the City of David
(Matt. 1:18–25)

2 And it came to pass in those days *that* a decree went out from Caesar Augustus that all the world should be registered.†
2 [a]This census first took place while Quirinius was governing Syria.†
3 So all went to be registered, everyone to his own city.
4 Joseph also went up from Galilee, out of the city of Nazareth, into Judea, to [a]the city of David, which is called Bethlehem, [b]because he was of the house and lineage of David,
5 to be registered with Mary, [a]his betrothed [1]wife, who was with child.†
6 So it was, that while they were there, the days were completed for her to be delivered.
7 And [a]she brought forth her firstborn Son, and wrapped Him in swaddling cloths, and laid Him in a [1]manger, because there was no room for them in the inn.†

The Witness of the Shepherds

8 Now there were in the same country shepherds living out in the fields, keeping watch over their flock by night.†
9 And [1]behold, an angel of the Lord stood before them, and the glory of the Lord shone around them, [a]and they were greatly afraid.†
10 Then the angel said to them, [a]"Do not be afraid, for behold, I bring you good tidings of great joy [b]which will be to all people.
11 [a]"For there is born to you this

CHAPTER 2
2 [a]Acts 5:37
4 [a]1 Sam. 16:1 [b]Matt. 1:16
5 [a][Matt. 1:18] [1]NU omits *wife*
7 [a]Matt. 1:25 [1]*feed trough*
9 [a]Luke 1:12 [1]NU omits *behold*
10 [a]Luke 1:13, 30 [b]Gen. 12:3
11 [a]Is. 9:6

1:80 Two things in particular are important for **the child** John: (1) he needs to grow strong physically, and (2) he needs to grow **strong in spirit.** Like some OT prophets, especially Elijah, John practiced solitude with God until he was called to begin his ministry.

2:1 Octavian, who as emperor was called **Caesar Augustus,** ruled the Roman Empire at the zenith of its expansion and power (31 B.C.–A.D. 14). The registration is for the purpose of taxation.

2:2 This **census** probably began about 6–5 B.C.

2:5 Though **Mary** is **with child,** the Gospel does not call her Joseph's wife but rather **his betrothed wife,** for she is still a virgin. Some manuscripts read simply "his betrothed." Although betrothal was binding in the Jewish tradition, the couple did not engage in sexual relations during this period.

2:7 The **firstborn Son** is "holy to the LORD" (v. 23) and has special significance as primary heir and carrier of patriarchal blessings. *Firstborn* does not necessarily mean others will be born after Him, but only that no child was born before Him. **Manger:** a feeding trough for livestock. The hills around Bethlehem held many caves where domestic animals were kept by night. It was in such a humble cave that Jesus was born.

2:8 Not to kings, priests or biblical scholars, but to **Shepherds living out in the fields** do the angels announce the birth of Him who would be Lamb of God and Shepherd of the sheep.

2:9 The appearance of the **angel** and the radiance of the **glory of the Lord** underscore the divine event that is taking place, the birth of the eternal Son of God in His human nature.

The Presentation of the Lord in the Temple *February 2*

2:22–40: As the firstborn of His mother, Jesus is taken to the temple to be dedicated to the Lord.

day in the city of David [b]a Savior,
[c]who is Christ the Lord.†
12 "And this *will be* the sign to you:
You will find a Babe wrapped in
swaddling cloths, lying in a
[1]manger."
13 [a]And suddenly there was with
the angel a multitude of the heavenly
host praising God and saying:

14 "Glory[a] to God in the highest,
And on earth [b]peace, [c]goodwill[1]
toward men!"†

15 So it was, when the angels had
gone away from them into heaven,
that the shepherds said to one another, "Let us now go to Bethlehem
and see this thing that has come to
pass, which the Lord has made
known to us."
16 And they came with haste and
found Mary and Joseph, and the
Babe lying in a manger.
17 Now when they had seen *Him,*
they made [1]widely known the saying
which was told them concerning this
Child.†
18 And all those who heard *it* marveled at those things which were told
them by the shepherds.
19 [a]But Mary kept all these things
and pondered *them* in her heart.
20 Then the shepherds returned,
glorifying and [a]praising God for all
the things that they had heard and
seen, as it was told them.

The Naming of Jesus

21 [a]And when eight days were
completed [1]for the circumcision of
the Child, His name was called
[b]JESUS, the name given by the angel
[c]before He was conceived in the
womb.†

Jesus Dedicated in the Temple

22 Now when [a]the days of her purification according to the law of Moses were completed, they brought
Him to Jerusalem to present *Him* to
the Lord†
23 [a](as it is written in the law of
the Lord, [b]*"Every male who opens
the womb shall be called holy to the
LORD"*),
24 and to offer a sacrifice according
to what is said in the law of the Lord,
[a]*"A pair of turtledoves or two young
pigeons."*

Simeon's Song: The Nunc Dimittis

25 And behold, there was a man
in Jerusalem whose name was

11 [b]Matt. 1:21 [c]Acts 2:36
12 [1]*feed trough*
13 [a]Dan. 7:10
14 [a]Luke 19:38 [b]Is. 57:19 [c][Eph. 2:4, 7] [1]NU *toward men of goodwill*
17 [1]NU omits *widely*
19 [a]Gen. 37:11
20 [a]Luke 19:37
21 [a]Lev. 12:3 [b][Matt. 1:21] [c]Luke 1:31 [1]NU *for His circumcision*
22 [a]Lev. 12:2–8
23 [a]Deut. 18:4 [b]Ex. 13:2, 12, 15
24 [a]Lev. 12:2, 8

2:11 Christ means "the Anointed One," the Messiah. The title **Lord** shows He is God; **Savior** shows that He will save His people from the power of sin and death.

2:14 Christ comes to bring **peace** and **goodwill** toward men, for He is the incarnate love of God, reconciling humanity to God and people to each other.

2:17 The lowly shepherds become the first to share the message of salvation with others.

2:21 Because He fulfills the Law, **Jesus** receives **circumcision** according to the precepts of the Mosaic Law—which He follows during His life and ministry. After the Resurrection, baptism replaced circumcision as the universal sacrament of salvation and initiation into the Church. In the Orthodox Church it is an ancient tradition to **name** a child on the eighth day.

2:22 Days of . . . purification: Forty days after birth (see Lev. 12:2–4), Jesus is **brought** to the temple to be blessed according to Jewish tradition. In the Orthodox Church women and their infants, male or female, also come for a blessing on the fortieth day.

Simeon, and this man was just and devout, [a]waiting for the Consolation of Israel, and the Holy Spirit was upon him.†

26 And it had been revealed to him by the Holy Spirit that he would not [a]see death before he had seen the Lord's Christ.†

27 So he came [a]by the Spirit into the temple. And when the parents brought in the Child Jesus, to do for Him according to the custom of the law,

28 he took Him up in his arms and blessed God and said:

29 "Lord, [a]now You are letting Your
servant depart in peace,
According to Your word;†
30 For my eyes [a]have seen Your
salvation
31 Which You have prepared
before the face of all peoples,
32 [a]A light to *bring* revelation to the
Gentiles,
And the glory of Your people
Israel."

33 [1]And Joseph and His mother marveled at those things which were spoken of Him.

34 Then Simeon blessed them, and said to Mary His mother, "Behold, this *Child* is destined for the [a]fall and rising of many in Israel, and for [b]a sign which will be spoken against

35 "(yes, [a]a sword will pierce through your own soul also), that the thoughts of many hearts may be revealed."†

Anna's Prophecy

36 Now there was one, Anna, a prophetess, the daughter of Phanuel, of the tribe of [a]Asher. She was of a great age, and had lived with a husband seven years from her virginity;

37 and this woman *was* a widow [1]of about eighty-four years, who did not depart from the temple, but served *God* with fastings and prayers [a]night and day.†

38 And coming in that instant she gave thanks to [1]the Lord, and spoke of Him to all those who [a]looked for redemption in Jerusalem.

Jesus' Childhood in Nazareth

(Matt. 2:19–23)

39 So when they had performed all things according to the law of the Lord, they returned to Galilee, to their *own* city, Nazareth.

40 [a]And the Child grew and became strong [1]in spirit, filled with wisdom; and the grace of God was upon Him.†

25 [a]Mark 15:43
26 [a][Heb. 11:5]
27 [a]Matt. 4:1
29 [a]Gen. 46:30
30 [a][Is. 52:10]
32 [a]Acts 10:45; 13:47; 28:28
33 [1]NU *And His father and mother*
34 [a][1 Pet. 2:7, 8] [b]Acts 4:2; 17:32; 28:22
35 [a]Ps. 42:10
36 [a]Josh. 19:24
37 [a]1 Tim. 5:5 [1]NU *until she was eighty-four*
38 [a]Mark 15:43 [1]NU *God*
40 [a]Luke 1:80; 2:52 [1]NU omits *in spirit*

2:25 The Consolation of Israel: the joy of the deliverance that the Messiah is expected to bring to Israel.

2:26 Lord's: God the Father's.

2:29–32 This "Canticle of Simeon," called the *Nunc Dimittis* (the first words of the prayer in Latin), is still sung daily at evening prayers in the Orthodox Church, as the contemporary confession and experience of all worshiping Christians. Christ is still the **salvation** God **prepared** for **all peoples,** the **light** of the **Gentiles** and the **glory of Israel.**

2:35 At the time of the Passion of Christ, Mary will suffer the **sword** of pain which (according to tradition) she escaped in childbirth. Seeing her Son on the Cross, her **soul** will be pierced in grief.

2:37 God reveals Himself to those who do **not depart** from Him. This woman has served God for many years, and she is prepared to meet her Messiah. For the elderly and lonely who wonder what they can do to serve God, Anna's **fastings and prayers** are a wonderful example.

2:40 The Incarnation means that Jesus experiences normal human physical, emotional and intellectual growth, but under the special overshadowing grace of God which fills Him with **wisdom** and strength.

Jesus in His Father's House

41 His parents went to [a]Jerusalem
[b]every year at the Feast of the
Passover.†
42 And when He was twelve years
old, they went up to Jerusalem
according to the [a]custom of the
feast.
43 When they had finished the
[a]days, as they returned, the Boy
Jesus lingered behind in Jerusalem.
And [1]Joseph and His mother did not
know *it;*
44 but supposing Him to have been
in the company, they went a day's
journey, and sought Him among
their relatives and acquaintances.
45 So when they did not find Him,
they returned to Jerusalem, seeking
Him.
46 Now so it was *that* after three
days they found Him in the temple,
sitting in the midst of the teachers,
both listening to them and asking
them questions.
47 And [a]all who heard Him were
astonished at His understanding and
answers.
48 So when they saw Him, they
were amazed; and His mother said
to Him, "Son, why have You done
this to us? Look, Your father and I
have sought You anxiously."
49 And He said to them, "Why did
you seek Me? Did you not know that
I must be [a]about [b]My Father's
business?"†
50 But [a]they did not understand
the statement which He spoke to
them.

Jesus' Growth

51 Then He went down with them
and came to Nazareth, and was
[1]subject to them, but His mother
[a]kept all these things in her heart.†
52 And Jesus [a]increased in wisdom
and stature, [b]and in favor with God
and men.†

The Baptist's Call for Repentance
(Matt. 3:1–12; Mark 1:1–8; John 1:19–28)

3 Now in the fifteenth year of the
reign of Tiberius Caesar, [a]Pon-
tius Pilate being governor of Judea, Herod being tetrarch of Galilee, his brother Philip tetrarch of
Iturea and the region of Trachonitis, and Lysanias tetrarch of Abilene,†
2 [1]while [a]Annas and Caiaphas
were high priests, the word of God
came to [b]John the son of Zacharias
in the wilderness.†
3 [a]And he went into all the region
around the Jordan, preaching a baptism of repentance [b]for the remission
of sins,†

41 [a]John 4:20 [b]Deut. 16:1, 16
42 [a]Ex. 23:14, 15
43 [a]Ex. 12:15 [1]NU *His parents*
47 [a]Matt. 7:28; 13:54; 22:33
49 [a]John 9:4 [b][Luke 4:22, 32]
50 [a]John 7:15, 46
51 [a]Dan. 7:28 [1]*obedient*
52 [a][Col. 2:2, 3] [b]1 Sam. 2:26

CHAPTER 3

1 [a]Matt. 27:2
2 [a]Acts 4:6 [b]Luke 1:13 [1]NU, M *in the high priesthood of Annas and Caiaphas*
3 [a]Mark 1:4
3 [b]Luke 1:77

2:41 Pilgrimages to **Jerusalem** on three great feasts, **Passover,** Pentecost, and Tabernacles, were customary for all except those who lived at great distances. Entire clans and villages would travel together.

2:49 **My Father's business** means God's will in preparation for Jesus' ministry. This is the first statement about God as Jesus' Father. What He does is righteous, but His parents do not understand it at the time.

2:51 Jesus is **subject** to His parents, showing humble obedience to His earthly mother and father.

2:52 Jesus increases in **wisdom, stature** and **favor with God and men,** bringing into plain view the wisdom and grace inherent in Him. In His Incarnation Jesus makes humanity completely His own, including progress in wisdom and grace. He experiences and sanctifies every stage of human life. Since He is at once both God and man, He increases humanly in the grace and wisdom which are already fully His in His divine nature. Indeed, that growth of His humanity prefigures our own growth into union with Him.

3:1 **Tiberius** ruled as sole Roman emperor in A.D. 14–37, but had authority over the provinces from A.D. 11 on. Thus the ministries of John the Baptist and Jesus began sometime between A.D. 26 and 28. **Pilate** was **governor of Judea** from A.D. 26–36.

3:2 **Caiaphas** was the sole official high priest (A.D. 18–36), but people recognized behind him the power of his father-in-law, **Annas,** a previous high priest deposed by the Romans.

3:3 The call to **repentance** was typical of the OT prophets, but John's **baptism for the**

(continued on next page)

4 as it is written in the book of
the words of Isaiah the prophet,
saying:

[a]*"The voice of one crying in the*
wilderness:
'Prepare the way of the LORD;
Make His paths straight.†
5 *Every valley shall be filled*
And every mountain and hill
brought low;
The crooked places shall be
made straight
And the rough ways smooth;
6 *And [a]all flesh shall see the*
salvation of God.' "

7 Then he said to the multitudes
that came out to be baptized by him,
[a]"Brood[1] of vipers! Who warned
you to flee from the wrath to
come?
8 "Therefore bear fruits [a]worthy
of repentance, and do not begin to
say to yourselves, 'We have Abraham as *our* father.' For I say to
you that God is able to raise up
children to Abraham from these
stones.†
9 "And even now the ax is laid
to the root of the trees. Therefore
[a]every tree which does not bear good
fruit is cut down and thrown into
the fire."
10 So the people asked him, saying, [a]"What shall we do then?"
11 He answered and said to them,
[a]"He who has two tunics, let him
give to him who has none; and he
who has food, [b]let him do likewise."
12 Then [a]tax collectors also came
to be baptized, and said to him,
"Teacher, what shall we do?"
13 And he said to them, [a]"Collect
no more than what is appointed for
you."
14 Likewise the soldiers asked him,
saying, "And what shall we do?" So
he said to them, "Do not [1]intimidate
anyone [a]or accuse falsely, and be
content with your wages."
15 Now as the people were in expectation, and all reasoned in their
hearts about John, whether he was
the Christ *or* not,
16 John answered, saying to all,
[a]"I indeed baptize you with water;
but One mightier than I is coming,
whose sandal strap I am not worthy
to loose. He will [b]baptize you with
the Holy Spirit and fire.†
17 "His winnowing fan *is* in His
hand, and He will thoroughly clean
out His threshing floor, and [a]gather
the wheat into His barn; but the chaff
He will burn with unquenchable
fire."
18 And with many other exhortations he preached to the people.
19 [a]But Herod the tetrarch, being
rebuked by him concerning Herodias, his [1]brother Philip's wife, and
for all the evils which Herod had
done,†

4 [a]Is. 40:3–5
6 [a]Is. 52:10
7 [a]Matt. 3:7; 12:34; 23:33 [1]*Offspring*
8 [a][2 Cor. 7:9–11]
9 [a]Matt. 7:19
10 [a][Acts 2:37, 38; 16:30, 31]
11 [a]2 Cor. 8:14 [b]Is. 58:7
12 [a]Luke 7:29
13 [a]Luke 19:8
14 [a]Ex. 20:16; 23:1 [1]Lit. *shake down* for money
16 [a]Matt. 3:11, 12 [b]John 7:39; 20:22
17 [a]Matt. 13:24–30
19 [a]Mark 6:17 [1]NU *brother's wife*

(continued from previous page)
remission of sins sounds a deeper note: a symbolic washing away of sins, prefiguring that which will come. As Paul writes in Rom. 6:1–6, those who come to Christ will be buried with Him in baptism, rising to new life.

3:4 Isaiah the prophet foresaw the momentous significance of the period of the Messiah and the preparation necessary for it (vv. 4–6).

3:8 Ethnic or "spiritual" ancestry does not guarantee security in the face of God's judgment. Only faithful **repentance** and good works **worthy** of it bring salvation. **Stones** symbolize Gentile Christians who became children of God.

3:16 With a clear understanding of his own mission, John points to Christ as **coming** Messiah who **will baptize . . . with the Holy Spirit and fire.** Although baptism is practiced by Jesus' circle of disciples (John 4:1, 2), the prophecy here describes the baptismal gift of the Spirit at Pentecost (Acts 2:1–4). *Fire* in this context seems to imply judgment, the same as the images of the winnowing fan and of burning the chaff (v. 17). John understands that the coming of the Messiah brings judgment, as the Apostle John writes, "This is the condemnation, that the light has come into the world, and men loved darkness rather than light, because their deeds were evil" (John 3:19).

3:19 John **rebuked Herod** Antipas because he had divorced his wife and married Herodias, his brother Philip's wife, while Philip was still living.

20 also added this, above all, that
he shut John up in prison.

Jesus Is Baptized
(Matt. 3:13–17; Mark 1:9–11; John 1:29–34)

21 When all the people were baptized, [a]it came to pass that Jesus also
was baptized; and while He prayed,
the heaven was opened.†
22 And the Holy Spirit descended
in bodily form like a dove upon Him,
and a voice came from heaven which
said, "You are My beloved Son; in
You I am [a]well pleased."†

Jesus: Son of David, the Son of God
(Matt. 1:1–17)

23 Now Jesus Himself began *His
ministry at* [a]about thirty years of age,
being (as was supposed) [b]*the* son of
Joseph, *the son* of Heli,†
24 *the son* of Matthat, *the son* of
Levi, *the son* of Melchi, *the son* of
Janna, *the son* of Joseph,
25 *the son* of Mattathiah, *the son* of
Amos, *the son* of Nahum, *the son* of
Esli, *the son* of Naggai,

21 [a]Matt. 3:13–17; John 1:32
22 [a]Ps. 2:7; [Is. 42:1]; Matt. 3:17; 17:5; Mark 1:11; Luke 1:35; 9:35; 2 Pet. 1:17
23 [a][Num. 4:3, 35, 39, 43, 47] [b]Matt. 13:55; John 6:42
27 [a]Ezra 2:2; 3:8
31 [a]Zech. 12:12 [b]2 Sam. 5:14; 7:12; 1 Chr. 3:5; 17:11; Is. 9:7; Jer. 23:5
32 [a]Ruth 4:18–22; 1 Chr. 2:10–12; Is. 11:1, 10
34 [a]Gen. 11:24, 26–30; 12:3; Num. 24:17; 1 Chr. 1:24–27

26 *the son* of Maath, *the son* of Mattathiah, *the son* of Semei, *the son* of
Joseph, *the son* of Judah,
27 *the son* of Joannas, *the son* of
Rhesa, *the son* of [a]Zerubbabel, *the son*
of Shealtiel, *the son* of Neri,
28 *the son* of Melchi, *the son* of Addi,
the son of Cosam, *the son* of Elmodam,
the son of Er,
29 *the son* of Jose, *the son* of Eliezer,
the son of Jorim, *the son* of Matthat,
the son of Levi,
30 *the son* of Simeon, *the son* of Judah, *the son* of Joseph, *the son* of
Jonan, *the son* of Eliakim,
31 *the son* of Melea, *the son* of
Menan, *the son* of Mattathah, *the son*
of [a]Nathan, [b]*the son* of David,
32 [a]*the son* of Jesse, *the son* of Obed,
the son of Boaz, *the son* of Salmon,
the son of Nahshon,
33 *the son* of Amminadab, *the son*
of Ram, *the son* of Hezron, *the son*
of Perez, *the son* of Judah,
34 *the son* of Jacob, *the son* of Isaac,
the son of Abraham, [a]*the son* of Terah,
the son of Nahor,
35 *the son* of Serug, *the son* of Reu,
the son of Peleg, *the son* of Eber, *the
son* of Shelah,

3:21 Jesus comes to be **baptized,** recognizing John's ministry. Jesus does not need baptism for forgiveness of sins, for He is sinless. Rather He is baptized to be revealed to Israel (John 1:31). In this baptism, He identifies Himself with His church that is to be, prefiguring our going down to death in baptism (see Rom. 6:1–6). By thus entering the waters of Jordan, He sanctifies forever the waters of baptism (and indeed, all of creation), by mystery restoring it to its original condition through union with Him.

3:22 The dove in **bodily form** is not an incarnation of the Spirit, but a temporary sign showing the invisible descent of the fullness of the Spirit on Jesus. The **voice** of the Father testifies to the divine nature of Christ, completing the revealing (epiphany) of the Holy Trinity at the baptism of Jesus. The church sets aside January 6th as a day to celebrate this Epiphany or Theophany (lit. "appearance of God") of our Lord.

3:23 Joseph is the legal father of Jesus. The genealogy of Luke (vv. 23–38) moves in the opposite direction from that of Matthew, going all the way back beyond Abraham to Adam, who was originally the son of God (v. 38). Luke's purpose is to emphasize the Lord's unity with the entire human race, and to underline the office of divine sonship (John 1:12), made available to all in Christ. Both Luke and Matthew underscore Christ's Davidic descent through Joseph, and His virginal conception and birth. Both show Him to be the preexistent Son of God.

Luke's genealogy differs somewhat from Matthew's. The probable explanation is that Matthew derives the Davidic ancestry through King Solomon, a son of David, while Luke traces Christ's ancestry through another son of David, Nathan.

Luke describes Joseph as the son of Heli (3:23). Matthew says Jacob begot Joseph (Matt. 1:16). There was a law (Deut. 25:5, 6) that the brother of a man who died without a child should marry the wife of the deceased and raise up an heir for his brother. The most likely explanation is that Jacob and Heli were born of the same mother, but of different fathers. When Heli died after a childless marriage, his brother Jacob married the widow, who became the mother of Joseph.

36 [a]*the son* of Cainan, *the son* of
[b]Arphaxad, [c]*the son* of Shem, *the son*
of Noah, *the son* of Lamech,
37 *the son* of Methuselah, *the son* of
Enoch, *the son* of Jared, *the son* of Ma-
halalel, *the son* of Cainan,
38 *the son* of Enosh, *the son* of Seth,
the son of Adam, [a]*the son* of God.

The Temptation
(Matt. 4:1–11; Mark 1:12, 13)

4 Then [a]Jesus, being filled with
the Holy Spirit, returned from
the Jordan and [b]was led by the Spirit
[1]into the wilderness,†
2 being [1]tempted for forty days by
the devil. And [a]in those days He ate
nothing, and afterward, when they
had ended, He was hungry.
3 And the devil said to Him, "If
You are [a]the Son of God, command
this stone to become bread."†
4 But Jesus answered him, saying,
"It is written, [a]*'Man shall not live*
by bread alone, [1]*but by every word*
of God.' "†
5 [1]Then the devil, taking Him up
on a high mountain, showed Him
all the kingdoms of the world in a
moment of time.
6 And the devil said to Him, "All
this authority I will give You, and
their glory; for [a]*this* has been delivered to me, and I give it to whomever
I wish.†
7 "Therefore, if You will worship
before me, all will be Yours."
8 And Jesus answered and said to
him, [1]"Get behind Me, Satan! [2]For
it is written, [a]*'You shall worship the*
LORD your God, and Him only you
shall serve.' "
9 [a]Then he brought Him to Jerusalem, set Him on the pinnacle of
the temple, and said to Him, "If You
are the Son of God, throw Yourself
down from here.†
10 "For it is written:

[a]*'He shall give His angels charge*
over you,
To keep you,'

11 "and,

[a]*'In their hands they shall bear*
you up,
Lest you dash your foot against
a stone.' "

12 And Jesus answered and said to
him, "It has been said, [a]*'You shall*
not [1]*tempt the LORD your God.'* "
13 Now when the devil had ended
every [1]temptation, he departed from
Him [a]until an opportune time.†

Jesus' Galilean Ministry Begins
(Matt. 4:12; Mark 1:14, 15; John 4:1–4, 43–45)

14 [a]Then Jesus returned [b]in the
power of the Spirit to [c]Galilee, and
[d]news of Him went out through all
the surrounding region.
15 And He [a]taught in their synagogues, [b]being glorified by all.

36 [a]Gen. 11:12 [b]Gen. 10:22, 24; 11:10–13 [c]Gen. 5:6–32; 9:27; 11:10
38 [a]Gen. 5:1, 2

CHAPTER 4

1 [a]Matt. 4:1–11 [b]Luke 2:27 [1]NU *in*
2 [a]Ex. 34:28 [1]*tested*
3 [a]John 20:31
4 [a]Deut. 8:3 [1]NU omits *but by every word of God*
5 [1]NU *And taking Him up, he showed Him*
6 [a][Rev. 13:2, 7]
8 [a]Deut. 6:13; 10:20 [1]NU omits *Get behind Me, Satan* [2]NU, M omit *For*
9 [a]Matt. 4:5–7
10 [a]Ps. 91:11
11 [a]Ps. 91:12
12 [a]Deut. 6:16 [1]*test*
13 [a][Heb. 4:15] [1]*testing*
14 [a]Matt. 4:12 [b]John 4:43 [c]Acts 10:37 [d]Matt. 4:24
15 [a]Matt. 4:23 [b]Is. 52:13

4:1 This exodus of Jesus **into the wilderness** following His baptism has a dual symbolism: (1) the OT type of Israel in the wilderness Exodus following the "baptism" in the Red Sea; and (2) our new exodus of salvation from darkness to light, though yet in this world.

4:3 Satan's attempt here was to exploit the extreme hunger which the Lord experienced in His humanity. The phrase, **if You are the Son of God,** shows Satan was seeking to generate self-doubt in Christ concerning His divinity, and to control His actions.

4:4 The fullness of life sought by mankind is not found in material satisfaction, but in the revealed **word of God.**

4:6 The devil claims to be the possessor of all worldly power and wealth, and attempts to turn Jesus from His true sonship and ministry. Christ does not dispute the claim, but declares that man is to worship God alone (v. 8).

4:9 The third temptation (second in Matthew's order) concerns self-aggrandizement and vanity. Is Jesus to base His ministry on new, spectacular acts designed to get people's attention? He declares one is not to tempt God (v. 12), that is, to test His providential love and care by thoughtless and vain acts.

4:13 In Luke's account of the temptations, the devil will bide his **time** for another opportunity to test Jesus.

Unbelief at Nazareth

16 So He came to [a]Nazareth,
where He had been brought up. And
as His custom was, [b]He went into
the synagogue on the Sabbath day,
and stood up to read.
17 And He was handed the book
of the prophet Isaiah. And when He
had opened the book, He found the
place where it was written:

18 *"The[a] Spirit of the LORD is upon*
Me,
Because He has anointed Me
To preach the gospel to the poor;
He has sent Me [1]to heal the
brokenhearted,
To proclaim liberty to the
captives
And recovery of sight to the
blind,
To [b]set at liberty those who are
[2]oppressed;†
19 *To proclaim the acceptable year*
of the LORD."

20 Then He closed the book, and
gave *it* back to the attendant and sat
down. And the eyes of all who were
in the synagogue were fixed on Him.
21 And He began to say to them,
"Today this Scripture is [a]fulfilled in
your hearing."
22 So all bore witness to Him, and
[a]marveled at the gracious words
which proceeded out of His mouth.
And they said, [b]"Is this not Joseph's
son?"†
23 He said to them, "You will
surely say this proverb to Me, 'Physician, heal yourself! Whatever we
have heard done in [a]Capernaum,[1]
do also here in [b]Your country.'"

16 [a]Mark 6:1 [b]Acts 13:14–16; 17:2
18 [a]Is. 49:8, 9; 61:1, 2 [b][Dan. 9:24] [1]NU omits *to heal the broken-hearted* [2]*downtrodden*
21 [a]Acts 13:29
22 [a][Ps. 45:2] [b]John 6:42
23 [a]Matt. 4:13; 11:23 [b]Matt. 13:54 [1]NU *Capharnaum,* here and elsewhere
24 [a]John 4:44
25 [a]1 Kin. 17:9
26 [1]Gr. *Sarepta*
27 [a]2 Kin. 5:1–14
28 [a]Luke 6:11 [1]*rage*
29 [a]John 8:37; 10:31
30 [a]John 8:59; 10:39
31 [a]Matt. 4:13
32 [a]Matt. 7:28, 29 [b][John 6:63; 7:46; 8:26, 28, 38, 47; 12:49, 50]
33 [a]Mark 1:23

24 Then He said, "Assuredly, I say
to you, no [a]prophet is accepted in
his own country.†
25 "But I tell you truly, [a]many widows were in Israel in the days of Elijah, when the heaven was shut up
three years and six months, and
there was a great famine throughout
all the land;
26 "but to none of them was Elijah
sent except to [1]Zarephath, *in the re-*
gion of Sidon, to a woman *who was*
a widow.
27 [a]"And many lepers were in Israel in the time of Elisha the prophet,
and none of them was cleansed except Naaman the Syrian."
28 So all those in the synagogue,
when they heard these things, were
[a]filled with [1]wrath,
29 [a]and rose up and thrust Him
out of the city; and they led Him to
the brow of the hill on which their
city was built, that they might throw
Him down over the cliff.
30 Then [a]passing through the
midst of them, He went His way.†

Power over a Demon
(Mark 1:21–28)

31 Then [a]He went down to Capernaum, a city of Galilee, and was
teaching them on the Sabbaths.†
32 And they were [a]astonished at
His teaching, [b]for His word was with
authority.†
33 [a]Now in the synagogue there
was a man who had a spirit of an
unclean demon. And he cried out
with a loud voice,
34 saying, "Let *us* alone! What
have we to do with You, Jesus of

4:18 Isaiah speaks of the anointing of Christ by the Holy Spirit. The **Spirit of the LORD** descended upon Jesus at His baptism (3:22). Jesus will bring blessings long awaited by the Jewish people, thus fulfilling the prophecy of Isaiah.

4:22 They **marveled** at His **words,** but could not believe that Jesus, a fellow villager, could be the Messiah.

4:24–27 Jesus exposes their unbelief. Through examples of God's mercy to Gentiles, He warns them that their heritage alone will not save them.

4:30 They seek to destroy Him but He miraculously passes **through the midst of them** unharmed.

4:31 **Capernaum** was a major city on the northern shore of the Lake of **Galilee.**

4:32 Jesus derives His **authority** from His messianic identity—unlike the scribes and Pharisees, who claim authority because of their academic credentials as teachers of the Law.

Nazareth? Did You come to destroy
us? [a]I know who You are—[b]the Holy
One of God!"†
35 But Jesus rebuked him, saying,
[1]"Be quiet, and come out of him!"
And when the demon had thrown
him in *their* midst, it came out of him
and did not hurt him.
36 Then they were all amazed and
spoke among themselves, saying,
"What a word this *is!* For with authority and power He commands the
unclean spirits, and they come out."
37 And the report about Him went
out into every place in the surrounding region.

Power over Diseases

(Matt. 8:14–17; Mark 1:29–34)

38 [a]Now He arose from the synagogue and entered Simon's house.
But Simon's wife's mother was
[1]sick with a high fever, and they
[b]made request of Him concerning
her.†
39 So He stood over her and
[a]rebuked the fever, and it left her.
And immediately she arose and
served them.
40 [a]When the sun was setting, all
those who had any that were sick
with various diseases brought them
to Him; and He laid His hands on
every one of them and healed them.†
41 [a]And demons also came out of
many, crying out and saying, [b]"You
are [1]the Christ, the Son of God!"
And He, [c]rebuking *them,* did not al-

34 [a]Luke 4:41 [b]Ps. 16:10; Is. 49:7; Dan. 9:24; Luke 1:35
35 [1]Lit. *Be muzzled*
38 [a]Matt. 8:14, 15; Mark 1:29–31 [b]Mark 5:23 [1]*afflicted with*
39 [a]Luke 8:24
40 [a]Matt. 8:16, 17; Mark 1:32–34
41 [a]Mark 1:34; 3:11; Acts 8:7 [b]Mark 8:29 [c]Mark 1:25, 34; 3:11; Luke 4:34, 35 [1]NU omits *the Christ* [2]Or *say that they knew*
42 [a]Mark 1:35–38; Luke 9:10
43 [a]Mark 1:14; [John 9:4]
44 [a]Matt. 4:23; 9:35; Mark 1:39 [1]NU *Judea*

CHAPTER 5

1 [a]Matt. 4:18–22; Mark 1:16–20; John 1:40–42 [b]Acts 13:44
3 [a]John 8:2
4 [a]John 21:6

low them to [2]speak, for they knew
that He was the Christ.†

Preaching Throughout Galilee

(Matt. 4:23; Mark 1:35–39)

42 [a]Now when it was day, He departed and went into a deserted
place. And the crowd sought Him
and came to Him, and tried to keep
Him from leaving them;
43 but He said to them, "I must
[a]preach the kingdom of God to the
other cities also, because for this purpose I have been sent."†
44 [a]And He was preaching in the
synagogues of [1]Galilee.

Four Fishermen Called

(Matt. 4:18–22; Mark 1:16–20)

5 So [a]it was, as the multitude
pressed about Him to [b]hear the
word of God, that He stood by the
Lake of Gennesaret,†
2 and saw two boats standing by
the lake; but the fishermen had gone
from them and were washing *their*
nets.
3 Then He got into one of the
boats, which was Simon's, and asked
him to put out a little from the land.
And He [a]sat down and taught the
multitudes from the boat.
4 When He had stopped speaking, He said to Simon, [a]"Launch out
into the deep and let down your nets
for a catch."†

4:34 The demon and the possessed man speak in the plural **we,** expressing their fear before the divine presence of Jesus. The demon recognizes Jesus as the **Holy One of God,** but is rebuked (v. 35) for his hostile boldness.

4:38, 39 See note on Matt. 8:14–17.

4:40 Jesus performed many miracles, healing countless people and releasing many from demonic spirits. No sickness could resist His power; no demon could refuse His word.

4:41 Jesus prohibits the demons from identifying Him for two reasons: (1) theirs is not a confession of faith, and (2) He reveals Himself to the people in His own way and time.

4:43 Jesus' ministry was not based on the wants and needs of people in any given locality (vv. 42–44). Nor was the primary purpose of His ministry to heal. Rather His purpose was to **preach the kingdom of God.** Thus He moved to **other cities,** the miracles testifying to the power of the gospel message which He preached.

5:1 The Lake of Gennesaret, also known as the Sea of Galilee, is about 13 miles long and 7 miles wide.

5:4 Simon Peter does not know that Jesus' request to **launch out into the deep** will mean a radical change of life for him (see v. 10).

5 But Simon answered and said
to Him, "Master, we have toiled all
night and caught [a]nothing; nevertheless [b]at Your word I will let down
the net."†
6 And when they had done this,
they caught a great number of fish,
and their net was breaking.
7 So they signaled to *their* partners
in the other boat to come and help
them. And they came and filled both
the boats, so that they began to
sink.
8 When Simon Peter saw *it*, he fell
down at Jesus' knees, saying, [a]"Depart from me, for I am a sinful man,
O Lord!"†
9 For he and all who were with
him were [a]astonished at the catch of
fish which they had taken;
10 and so also *were* James and John,
the sons of Zebedee, who were partners with Simon. And Jesus said to
Simon, "Do not be afraid. [a]From
now on you will catch men."†
11 So when they had brought their
boats to land, [a]they [1]forsook all and
followed Him.

Jesus Cleanses a Leper
(Matt. 8:1–4; Mark 1:40–45)

12 [a]And it happened when He was
in a certain city, that behold, a man
who was full of [b]leprosy saw Jesus;
and he fell on *his* face and [1]implored
Him, saying, "Lord, if You are willing, You can make me clean."†
13 Then He put out *His* hand and
touched him, saying, "I am willing;
be cleansed." [a]Immediately the leprosy left him.†
14 [a]And He charged him to tell no
one, "But go and show yourself to
the priest, and make an offering for
your cleansing, as a testimony to
them, [b]just as Moses commanded."†
15 However, [a]the report went
around concerning Him all the more;
and [b]great multitudes came together
to hear, and to be healed by Him of
their infirmities.
16 [a]So He Himself *often* withdrew
into the wilderness and [b]prayed.†

Jesus Forgives Sins
(Matt. 9:1–8; Mark 2:1–12)

17 Now it happened on a certain
day, as He was teaching, that there
were Pharisees and teachers of the
law sitting by, who had come out
of every town of Galilee, Judea, and
Jerusalem. And the power of the
Lord was *present* [1]to heal them.
18 [a]Then behold, men brought on
a bed a man who was paralyzed,
whom they sought to bring in and
lay before Him.
19 And when they could not find
how they might bring him in, because of the crowd, they went up
on the housetop and let him down
with *his* bed through the tiling into
the midst [a]before Jesus.
20 When He saw their faith, He
said to him, "Man, your sins are forgiven you."
21 [a]And the scribes and the Pharisees began to reason, saying, "Who

5 [a]John 21:3 [b]Ps. 33:9
8 [a]1 Kin. 17:18
9 [a]Mark 5:42; 10:24, 26
10 [a]Matt. 4:19
11 [a]Matt. 4:20; 19:27 [1]*left behind*
12 [a]Mark 1:40–44 [b]Lev. 13:14 [1]*begged*
13 [a]John 5:9
14 [a]Matt. 8:4 [b]Lev. 13:1–3; 14:2–32
15 [a]Mark 1:45 [b]John 6:2
16 [a]Luke 9:10 [b]Matt. 14:23
17 [1]NU *with Him to heal*
18 [a]Mark 2:3–12
19 [a]Matt. 15:30
21 [a]Mark 2:6, 7

5:5 Peter both called Jesus **Master** and did whatever his Master asked him to do. Allegiance and obedience go together.

5:8 **Peter** kneels and confesses Jesus as **Lord,** showing a profound awareness both of the divinity of Christ and of his own human sinfulness.

5:10, 11 The first disciples, partners in fishing, were to become partners also in the work of mission and evangelism in the early Church.

5:12 **Leprosy** was one of the most dreaded diseases of this time. It brought great physical suffering, and total banishment from society.

5:13 Jesus touched this man, both sick and an outcast. In the healing of this leper, the Lord also demonstrates there is no one in society who is to be left untouched by His gospel.

5:14 Jesus instructs the man to **tell no one** because He wants to avoid public misunderstanding of His messiahship. But He makes one exception, instructing the former leper to obey the Law and give **testimony** before the Jewish leaders. By tradition, the man needs an official certificate that he is cured before he can rejoin society.

5:16 There are always more people to teach, to heal, to be freed from demons. But Jesus still takes time for prayer.

is this who speaks blasphemies?
[b]Who can forgive sins but God
alone?"
22 But when Jesus [a]perceived their
thoughts, He answered and said to
them, "Why are you reasoning in
your hearts?
23 "Which is easier, to say, 'Your
sins are forgiven you,' or to say, 'Rise
up and walk'?†
24 "But that you may know that
the Son of Man has power on earth
to forgive sins"—He said to the man
who was paralyzed, [a]"I say to you,
arise, take up your bed, and go to
your house."
25 Immediately he rose up before
them, took up what he had been lying on, and departed to his own
house, [a]glorifying God.
26 And they were all amazed, and
they [a]glorified God and were filled
with fear, saying, "We have seen
strange things today!"

Jesus Invites Matthew, a Sinner

(Matt. 9:9–13; Mark 2:13–17)

27 [a]After these things He went out
and saw a tax collector named Levi,
sitting at the tax office. And He said
to him, [b]"Follow Me."†
28 So he left all, rose up, and
[a]followed Him.
29 [a]Then Levi gave Him a great
feast in his own house. And [b]there
were a great number of tax collectors
and others who sat down with
them.†
30 [1]And their scribes and the Pharisees [2]complained against His disciples, saying, [a]"Why do You eat and
drink with tax collectors and
sinners?"
31 Jesus answered and said to
them, "Those who are well have no
need of a physician, but those who
are sick.
32 [a]"I have not come to call *the*
righteous, but sinners, to repentance."†

When Does Jesus Fast?

(Matt. 9:14–17; Mark 2:18–22)

33 Then they said to Him, [a]"Why[1]
do the disciples of John fast often
and make prayers, and likewise
those of the Pharisees, but Yours eat
and drink?"†
34 And He said to them, "Can you
make the friends of the bridegroom
fast while the [a]bridegroom is with
them?
35 "But the days will come when
the bridegroom will be taken away
from them; then they will fast in
those days."
36 [a]Then He spoke a parable to
them: "No one [1]puts a piece from a
new garment on an old one; otherwise the new makes a tear, and also
the piece that was *taken* out of the
new does not match the old.
37 "And no one puts new wine
into old wineskins; or else the new
wine will burst the wineskins and be
spilled, and the wineskins will be
ruined.
38 "But new wine must be put into
new wineskins, [1]and both are preserved.

21 [b]Is. 43:25
22 [a]John 2:25
24 [a]Luke 7:14
25 [a]Acts 3:8
26 [a]Luke 1:65; 7:16
27 [a]Matt. 9:9–17
[b]John 12:26; 21:19, 22
28 [a]Mark 10:28
29 [a]Matt. 9:9, 10
[b]Luke 15:1
30 [a]Luke 15:2
[1]NU *But the Pharisees and their scribes*
[2]*grumbled*
32 [a]1 Tim. 1:15
33 [a]Matt. 9:14
[1]NU omits *Why do,* making the verse a statement
34 [a]John 3:29
36 [a]Mark 2:21, 22
[1]NU *tears a piece from a new garment and puts it on an old one*
38 [1]NU omits *and both are preserved*

5:23 The powers to forgive **sins** and to heal belong to God alone. Jesus' exercise of these powers shows that He is the incarnate Son of God. (See the notes on Matt. 9:2–8; Mark 2:1–12.)

5:27 **Levi** (Matthew) answers Christ's call, **follow me,** and leaves his occupation to become a disciple. From the beginning of His ministry Christ has been a friend of tax collectors and sinners, which is one of the Pharisees' complaints against Him (v. 30). Levi may also have been one of those tax collectors prepared for Christ by John the Baptist (3:12).

5:29 This **feast** expresses Matthew's joy and gratitude. The guest register is a stirring demonstration of the fruit of Jesus' love and forgiveness.

5:32 Christ has **come to call** only those who know they need Him. **Sinners** know it, but the scribes and Pharisees do not.

5:33–39 Jesus' earthly life is a time of joyous blessings. But there will come a time when His followers will practice fasting (see notes on Matt. 9:14–17; Mark 2:20).

39 "And no one, having drunk old
wine, [1]immediately desires new; for
he says, 'The old is [2]better.' "†

The Lord of the Sabbath
(Matt. 12:1–8; Mark 2:23–28)

6 Now [a]it happened [1]on the second Sabbath after the first that
He went through the grainfields.
And His disciples plucked the heads
of grain and ate *them*, rubbing *them*
in *their* hands.
2 And some of the Pharisees said
to them, "Why are you doing [a]what
is not lawful to do on the Sabbath?"†
3 But Jesus answering them said,
"Have you not even read this,
[a]what David did when he was hungry, he and those who were with
him:
4 "how he went into the house
of God, took and ate the showbread,
and also gave some to those with
him, [a]which is not lawful for any but
the priests to eat?"
5 And He said to them, "The Son
of Man is also Lord of the Sabbath."†

Healing on the Sabbath
(Matt. 12:9–14; Mark 3:1–6)

6 [a]Now it happened on another
Sabbath, also, that He entered the
synagogue and taught. And a man
was there whose right hand was
withered.
7 So the scribes and Pharisees
watched Him closely, whether He
would [a]heal on the Sabbath, that
they might find an [b]accusation
against Him.†
8 But He [a]knew their thoughts,

39 [1]NU omits *immediately* [2]NU *good*

CHAPTER 6

1 [a]Matt. 12:1–8; Mark 2:23–28 [1]NU *on a Sabbath that He went*
2 [a]Ex. 20:10
3 [a]1 Sam. 21:6
4 [a]Lev. 24:9
6 [a]Matt. 12:9–14; Mark 3:1–6; Luke 13:14; 14:3; John 9:16
7 [a]Luke 13:14; 14:1–6 [b]Luke 20:20
8 [a]Matt. 9:4; John 2:24, 25
9 [a]John 7:23 [1]M *to kill*
10 [1]NU, M *him* [2]NU omits *as whole as the other*
12 [a]Matt. 14:23; Mark 1:35; Luke 5:16; 9:18; 11:1
13 [a]John 6:70 [b]Matt. 10:1
14 [a]John 1:42
16 [a]Jude 1 [b]Luke 22:3–6

and said to the man who had the
withered hand, "Arise and stand
here." And he arose and stood.
9 Then Jesus said to them, "I will
ask you one thing: [a]Is it lawful on
the Sabbath to do good or to do evil,
to save life or [1]to destroy?"
10 And when He had looked
around at them all, He said to
[1]the man, "Stretch out your hand."
And he did so, and his hand was
restored [2]as whole as the other.
11 But they were filled with rage,
and discussed with one another
what they might do to Jesus.

The Twelve Chosen
(Matt. 10:1–4; Mark 3:13–19)

12 Now it came to pass in those
days that He went out to the mountain to pray, and continued all night
in [a]prayer to God.†
13 And when it was day, He called
His disciples to *Himself*; [a]and from
them He chose [b]twelve whom He
also named apostles:
14 Simon, [a]whom He also named
Peter, and Andrew his brother;
James and John; Philip and
Bartholomew;
15 Matthew and Thomas; James
the *son* of Alphaeus, and Simon
called the Zealot;
16 Judas [a]*the son* of James, and
[b]Judas Iscariot who also became a
traitor.

Crowds Follow Jesus
(Matt. 4:24, 25; 12:15, 16; Mark 3:7–12)

17 And He came down with them
and stood on a level place with a

5:39 This is a difficult verse, appearing only in Luke. Either it means that Jewish traditionalists are not ready to receive the new **wine** of Jesus' teaching, or this is a warning not to reject the Jewish heritage altogether.

6:2 The correct observance of the **Sabbath**-rest is a major point of controversy between the Pharisees and Jesus (see notes on Matt. 12:1–8 and Mark 2:23, 24).

6:5 This is a reminder that Jesus is God in the flesh—that He is both God and Man.

6:7 According to the **scribes and Pharisees,** healing was considered work and was not permissible on the Sabbath. They believed they served God by being zealous for traditions they had built up around the Law, and they saw Jesus as a lawbreaker. Their dedication to rigid legalism made them insensitive to God's priorities.

6:12 Jesus prays **all night** before He selects the Twelve whom He will train to continue His mission in the world.

Commemoration of Hierarchs, Hieromartyrs, and Monks

6:17–23; 10:22–24; 14:25–35: Having left all to follow Christ, these holy ones have obtained the rewards of the blessed.

crowd of His disciples [a]and a great multitude of people from all Judea and Jerusalem, and from the seacoast of Tyre and Sidon, who came to hear Him and be healed of their diseases,
18 as well as those who were tormented with unclean spirits. And they were healed.
19 And the whole multitude [a]sought to [b]touch Him, for [c]power went out from Him and healed *them* all.

The Beatitudes, the Woes
(Matt. 5:1–12)

20 Then He lifted up His eyes toward His disciples, and said:

[a]"Blessed *are you* poor,
For yours is the kingdom of God.†
21 [a]Blessed *are you* who hunger now,
For you shall be [b]filled.[1]
[c]Blessed *are you* who weep now,
For you shall [d]laugh.
22 [a]Blessed are you when men hate you,
And when they [b]exclude you,
And revile *you*, and cast out your name as evil,
For the Son of Man's sake.
23 [a]Rejoice in that day and leap for joy!
For indeed your reward *is* great in heaven,
For [b]in like manner their fathers did to the prophets.

24 "But[a] woe to you [b]who are rich,
For [c]you have received your consolation.†
25 [a]Woe to you who are full,
For you shall hunger.
[b]Woe to you who laugh now,
For you shall mourn and [c]weep.
26 [a]Woe [1]to you when [2]all men speak well of you,
For so did their fathers to the false prophets.

Love of Enemies
(Matt. 5:38–48)

27 [a]"But I say to you who hear: Love your enemies, do good to those who hate you,
28 [a]"bless those who curse you, and [b]pray for those who spitefully use you.
29 [a]"To him who strikes you on the *one* cheek, offer the other also. [b]And from him who takes away your cloak, do not withhold *your* tunic either.
30 [a]"Give to everyone who asks of you. And from him who takes away your goods do not ask *them* back.
31 [a]"And just as you want men to do to you, you also do to them likewise.
32 [a]"But if you love those who love you, what credit is that to you? For even sinners love those who love them.
33 "And if you do good to those who do good to you, what credit is

17 [a]Matt. 4:25; Mark 3:7, 8
19 [a]Matt. 9:21; 14:36 [b]Mark 5:27, 28 [c]Luke 8:46
20 [a]Matt. 5:3–12; [11:5]
21 [a]Is. 55:1; 65:13 [b][Rev. 7:16] [c][Is. 61:3] [d]Ps. 126:5 [1]*satisfied*
22 [a]1 Pet. 2:19; 3:14; 4:14 [b][John 16:2]
23 [a]James 1:2 [b]Acts 7:51
24 [a]James 5:1–6 [b]Luke 12:21 [c]Luke 16:25
25 [a][Is. 65:13] [b][Prov. 14:13] [c]James 4:9
26 [a][John 15:19] [1]NU, M omit *to you* [2]M omits *all*
27 [a]Rom. 12:20
28 [a]Rom. 12:14 [b]Acts 7:60
29 [a]Matt. 5:39–42 [b][1 Cor. 6:7]
30 [a]Deut. 15:7, 8
31 [a]Matt. 7:12
32 [a]Matt. 5:46

6:20–49 This teaching is similar in content to the Sermon on the Mount (Matt. 5—7) but not as extensive. This has been called the Sermon on the Plain because Jesus "stood on a level place" (v. 17) when He delivered it. Jesus taught many of the same things over a period of three years in a setting of hills, plains, the lakeshore and the cities, and we have His teachings in various versions. (See notes on Matt. 5—7.)

6:24 Luke also reports four "woes" (vv. 24–26) in addition to his four Beatitudes.

that to you? For even sinners do the
same.
34 [a]"And if you lend *to those* from
whom you hope to receive back,
what credit is that to you? For even
sinners lend to sinners to receive as
much back.
35 "But [a]love your enemies,
[b]do good, and [c]lend, [1]hoping for
nothing in return; and your reward
will be great, and [d]you will be sons
of the Most High. For He is kind to
the unthankful and evil.
36 [a]"Therefore be merciful, just as
your Father also is merciful.

Be Merciful
(Matt. 7:1–5)

37 [a]"Judge not, and you shall not
be judged. Condemn not, and you
shall not be condemned. [b]Forgive,
and you will be forgiven.†
38 [a]"Give, and it will be given to
you: good measure, pressed down,
shaken together, and running over
will be put into your [b]bosom. For
[c]with the same measure that you
use, it will be measured back to
you."
39 **And He spoke a parable to**
them: [a]"Can the blind lead the
blind? Will they not both fall into the
ditch?†
40 [a]"A disciple is not above his
teacher, but everyone who is perfectly trained will be like his teacher.
41 [a]"And why do you look at the
speck in your brother's eye, but do
not perceive the plank in your own
eye?
42 "Or how can you say to your
brother, 'Brother, let me remove the

34 [a]Matt. 5:42
35 [a][Rom. 13:10] [b]Heb. 13:16 [c]Lev. 25:35–37; Ps. 37:26 [d]Matt. 5:46 [1]*expecting*
36 [a]Matt. 5:48; Eph. 4:32
37 [a]Matt. 7:1–5; Rom. 14:4; [1 Cor. 4:5] [b]Matt. 18:21–35
38 [a][Prov. 19:17; 28:27] [b]Ps. 79:12; Is. 65:6, 7; Jer. 32:18 [c]Matt. 7:2; Mark 4:24; James 2:13
39 [a]Matt. 15:14; 23:16; Rom. 2:19
40 [a]Matt. 10:24; [John 13:16; 15:20]
41 [a]Matt. 7:3
43 [a]Matt. 7:16–18, 20
44 [a]Matt. 12:33
45 [a]Matt. 12:35 [b]Prov. 15:2, 28; 16:23; 18:21; Matt. 12:34 [1]NU omits *treasure of his heart*
46 [a]Mal. 1:6; Matt. 7:21; 25:11; Luke 13:25
47 [a]Matt. 7:24–27; [John 14:21]; James 1:22–25
48 [1]NU *well built*
49 [1]NU *collapsed*

speck that *is* in your eye,' when you
yourself do not see the plank that *is*
in your own eye? Hypocrite! First remove the plank from your own eye,
and then you will see clearly to
remove the speck that is in your
brother's eye.

Beware of Hypocrisy
(Matt. 7:15–27)

43 [a]"For a good tree does not bear
bad fruit, nor does a bad tree bear
good fruit.
44 "For [a]every tree is known by its
own fruit. For *men* do not gather figs
from thorns, nor do they gather
grapes from a bramble bush.
45 [a]"A good man out of the good
treasure of his heart brings forth
good; and an evil man out of the evil
[1]treasure of his heart brings forth
evil. For out [b]of the abundance of
the heart his mouth speaks.
46 [a]"But why do you call Me 'Lord,
Lord,' and not do the things which
I say?
47 [a]"Whoever comes to Me, and
hears My sayings and does them, I
will show you whom he is like:†
48 "He is like a man building a
house, who dug deep and laid the
foundation on the rock. And when
the flood arose, the stream beat vehemently against that house, and
could not shake it, for it was
[1]founded on the rock.
49 "But he who heard and did
nothing is like a man who built a
house on the earth without a foundation, against which the stream beat
vehemently; and immediately it
[1]fell. And the ruin of that house was
great."

6:37, 38 The Kingdom of God calls us to a way of life in which mercy abounds. We must:
(1) Refrain from judging. By definition, human judgment precludes mercy.
(2) Do not condemn. Condemnation causes us to depart from mercy.
(3) Forgive. Forgiveness can only come out of a heart of mercy.
(4) Give. When we give abundantly we receive from God in the same measure.

6:39, 40 Spoken to the disciples, these words are an exhortation to discernment and imitation of Christ in their training for the apostolic ministry.

6:47–49 Hearing the gospel is not enough, according to Jesus. We must do what He says. Jesus did not preach that faith alone is all God requires for salvation. Spiritual foundations are made secure with both faithful hearing and faithful doing of the words of Christ.

A Gentile Soldier's Faith
(Matt. 8:5–13)

7 Now when He concluded all His
sayings in the hearing of the
people, He [a]entered Capernaum.
2 And a certain centurion's servant, who was dear to him, was sick
and ready to die.†
3 So when he heard about Jesus,
he sent elders of the Jews to Him,
pleading with Him to come and heal
his servant.
4 And when they came to Jesus,
they begged Him earnestly, saying
that the one for whom He should
do this was deserving,
5 "for he loves our nation, and
has built us a synagogue."
6 Then Jesus went with them.
And when He was already not far
from the house, the centurion sent
friends to Him, saying to Him,
"Lord, do not trouble Yourself, for
I am not worthy that You should enter under my roof.
7 "Therefore I did not even think
myself worthy to come to You. But
[a]say the word, and my servant will
be healed.
8 "For I also am a man placed under [a]authority, having soldiers under me. And I say to one, 'Go,' and
he goes; and to another, 'Come,' and
he comes; and to my servant, 'Do
this,' and he does *it*."
9 When Jesus heard these things,
He marveled at him, and turned
around and said to the crowd that
followed Him, "I say to you, I have
not found such great faith, not even
in Israel!"
10 And those who were sent, returning to the house, found the servant well [1]who had been sick.

A Widow's Son Is Raised

11 Now it happened, the day after,
that He went into a city called Nain;
and many of His disciples went with
Him, and a large crowd.†
12 And when He came near the
gate of the city, behold, a dead man
was being carried out, the only son
of his mother; and she was a widow.
And a large crowd from the city was
with her.
13 When the Lord saw her, He had
[a]compassion on her and said to her,
[b]"Do not weep."
14 Then He came and touched the
open coffin, and those who carried
him stood still. And He said, "Young
man, I say to you, [a]arise."
15 So he who was dead [a]sat up and
began to speak. And He [b]presented
him to his mother.
16 [a]Then fear [1]came upon all, and
they [b]glorified God, saying, [c]"A
great prophet has risen up among
us"; and, [d]"God has visited His people."†

CHAPTER 7
1 [a]Matt. 8:5–13
7 [a]Ps. 33:9; 107:20
8 [a][Mark 13:34]
10 [1]NU omits *who had been sick*
13 [a]Lam. 3:32; John 11:35; [Heb. 4:15] [b]Luke 8:52
14 [a]Mark 5:41; Luke 8:54; John 11:43; Acts 9:40; [Rom. 4:17]
15 [a]Matt. 11:5; Luke 8:55; John 11:44 [b]1 Kin. 17:23; 2 Kin. 4:36
16 [a]Luke 1:65 [b]Luke 5:26 [c]Luke 24:19; John 4:19; 6:14; 9:17 [d]Luke 1:68 [1]*seized them all*

7:2–10 This **centurion** is an unusual Roman officer. He is attracted to the Jewish people and their religious tradition, and greatly commended by Jesus. The characteristics which he possesses are notable:

(1) He has *compassion* for his servant (v. 2).

(2) He is a man of *humility* (v. 3). He does not consider himself worthy to go to Christ (v. 7), so he asks that the elders go. He clearly does not consider himself worthy to have Christ enter his home (v. 6).

(3) He has *love* for the Jewish people (v. 5).

(4) He is *considerate* (v. 6).

(5) He possesses great *faith* (vv. 7–9), more than Jesus had found thus far in His ministry.

7:11–17 This account is reported only by Luke, and shows Jesus' deep compassion toward the mourning **widow** of **Nain** who has lost her only son and provider. The raising of the son is performed by **the Lord** (v. 13) who has power over life and death. Jesus also raises Jairus's daughter (8:41–56) and Lazarus (John 11:1–44). But note: these were all acts of resuscitation, which is different from resurrection. They were brought back to life, but would eventually die again physically. Nevertheless their new life manifests Christ's divinity, and gives assurance of His Resurrection and ours, a transformation to glory.

7:16 Through the three miraculous resurrections performed by Jesus—the son of the widow of Nain, Jairus's daughter, and Lazarus—**God** is **glorified.** In the glorification of the Father

(continued on next page)

17 And this report about Him went
throughout all Judea and all the surrounding region.

John's Messengers Inquire of Jesus
(Matt. 11:2–19)

18 [a]Then the disciples of John reported to him concerning all these
things.
19 And John, calling two of his disciples to *him,* sent *them* to [1]Jesus, saying, "Are You [a]the Coming One, or
[2]do we look for another?"†
20 When the men had come to
Him, they said, "John the Baptist has
sent us to You, saying, 'Are You the
Coming One, or do we look for
another?' "
21 And that very hour He cured
many of [1]infirmities, afflictions, and
evil spirits; and to many blind He
gave sight.
22 [a]Jesus answered and said to
them, "Go and tell John the things
you have seen and heard: [b]that *the*
blind [c]see, *the* lame [d]walk, *the* lepers
are [e]cleansed, *the* deaf [f]hear, *the* dead
are raised, [g]*the* poor have the gospel
preached to them.
23 "And blessed is *he* who is not
[1]offended because of Me."
24 [a]When the messengers of John
had departed, He began to speak to
the multitudes concerning John:
"What did you go out into the wilderness to see? A reed shaken by the
wind?

18 [a]Matt. 11:2–19
19 [a][Mic. 5:2; Zech. 9:9; Mal. 3:1–3] [1]NU *the Lord* [2]*should we expect*
21 [1]*illnesses*
22 [a]Matt. 11:4 [b]Is. 35:5 [c]John 9:7 [d]Matt. 15:31 [e]Luke 17:12–14 [f]Mark 7:37 [g][Is. 61:1–3; Luke 4:18]
23 [1]*caused to stumble*
24 [a]Matt. 11:7
27 [a]Is. 40:3; Mal. 3:1; Matt. 11:10; Mark 1:2
28 [a][Luke 1:15] [1]NU *none greater than John;*
29 [a]Matt. 3:5; Luke 3:12 [1]*declared the righteousness of*
30 [a]Acts 20:27 [1]*the experts in the law*
31 [a]Matt. 11:16 [1]NU, M omit *And the Lord said,*

25 "But what did you go out to see?
A man clothed in soft garments? Indeed those who are gorgeously ap-
pareled and live in luxury are in
kings' courts.
26 "But what did you go out to see?
A prophet? Yes, I say to you, and
more than a prophet.
27 "This is *he* of whom it is written:

[a]*'Behold, I send My messenger*
before Your face,
Who will prepare Your way
before You.'

28 "For I say to you, among those
born of women there is [1]not a
[a]greater prophet than John the Baptist; but he who is least in the kingdom of God is greater than he."†
29 And when all the people heard
Him, even the tax collectors [1]justified
God, [a]having been baptized with the
baptism of John.
30 But the Pharisees and [1]lawyers
rejected [a]the will of God for themselves, not having been baptized by
him.†
31 [1]And the Lord said, [a]"To what
then shall I liken the men of this generation, and what are they like?
32 "They are like children sitting
in the marketplace and calling to one
another, saying:

'We played the flute for you,
And you did not dance;
We mourned to you,
And you did not weep.'†

(continued from previous page)
through these incidents, the Son of God is Himself glorified. In raising these who were dead, though they would return to death one day, Christ shows forth His divinity and gives assurance to all who believe of His Resurrection and ours.

7:19 John had been imprisoned shortly after he baptized Jesus. He probably has not heard Jesus teach, nor seen His many miracles. John also anticipates that Jesus will judge at His first coming, whereas Jesus comes to save and heal. John's question indicates either a desire to obtain secure knowledge or an intent to guide his own disciples to Jesus. Christ answers the question indirectly by pointing to His miraculous messianic deeds.

7:28 Christ recognizes John as the greatest **prophet.** John belongs to the period of the Old Covenant; the Kingdom of God is inaugurated through Christ. The New Covenant so far surpasses the old that the **least in the kingdom** is **greater** than John.

7:30 Luke makes a blunt observation: anyone who **rejected** the baptism of John is out of step with the **will of God.** Such a spurning by the Pharisees and the lawyers indicates a hardness of heart and no receptivity to the grace of the Kingdom of God. It is a sobering thought that some today reject the baptism of Christ.

7:32 This verse describes an ancient game which children played in two groups; here

(continued on next page)

Commemoration of Holy Nuns

7:36–50: These holy women had a great love for Jesus, like the woman who anointed His feet.

33 "For [a]John the Baptist came
[b]neither eating bread nor drinking
wine, and you say, 'He has a
demon.'
34 "The Son of Man has come
[a]eating and drinking, and you say,
'Look, a glutton and a [1]winebibber,
a friend of tax collectors and sinners!'
35 [a]"But wisdom is justified by all
her children."

Forgiveness of a Sinful Woman

36 [a]Then one of the Pharisees
asked Him to eat with him. And He
went to the Pharisee's house, and sat
down to eat.
37 And behold, a woman in the
city who was a sinner, when she
knew that *Jesus* sat at the table in the
Pharisee's house, brought an alabaster flask of fragrant oil,
38 and stood at His feet behind
Him weeping; and she began to wash
His feet with her tears, and wiped
them with the hair of her head; and
she kissed His feet and anointed *them*
with the fragrant oil.
39 Now when the Pharisee who
had invited Him saw *this,* he spoke
to himself, saying, [a]"This Man, if He
were a prophet, would know who
and what manner of woman *this is*
who is touching Him, for she is a
sinner."†
40 And Jesus answered and said to
him, "Simon, I have something to
say to you." **So he said, "Teacher,
say it."**
41 "There was a certain creditor
who had two debtors. One owed five
hundred [a]denarii, and the other
fifty.
42 "And when they had nothing
with which to repay, he freely forgave them both. Tell Me, therefore,
which of them will love him more?"
43 **Simon answered and said, "I
suppose the *one* whom he forgave
more."** And He said to him, "You
have rightly judged."
44 **Then He turned to the woman
and said to Simon,** "Do you see this
woman? I entered your house; you
gave Me no [a]water for My feet, but
she has washed My feet with her
tears and wiped *them* with the hair
of her head.
45 "You gave Me no [a]kiss, but this
woman has not ceased to kiss My
feet since the time I came in.
46 [a]"You did not anoint My head
with oil, but this woman has
anointed My feet with fragrant oil.
47 [a]"Therefore I say to you, her
sins, *which are* many, are forgiven,
for she loved much. But to whom
little is forgiven, *the same* loves
little."†
48 **Then He said to her,** [a]"Your
sins are forgiven."
49 **And those who sat at the table
with Him began to say to them-**

33 [a]Matt. 3:1 [b][Matt. 3:4]; Luke 1:15
34 [a]Luke 15:2 [1]An excessive drinker
35 [a]Matt. 11:19
36 [a]Matt. 26:6; Mark 14:3; John 11:2
39 [a]Luke 15:2
41 [a]Matt. 18:28; Mark 6:37
44 [a]Gen. 18:4; 19:2; 43:24; Judg. 19:21; 1 Tim. 5:10
45 [a]Rom. 16:16
46 [a]2 Sam. 12:20; Ps. 23:5; Eccl. 9:8; Dan. 10:3
47 [a][1 Tim. 1:14]
48 [a]Matt. 9:2; Mark 2:5

(continued from previous page)
one group would not cooperate, neither dancing nor weeping (see note on Matt. 11:16–19). Similarly, as was true of the Pharisees and scribes, unregenerate religious people will neither **dance** nor **weep!** John the Baptist is to them a stern ascetic; Jesus, "a glutton and a winebibber" (v. 34).

7:39 Some Pharisees were open to Jesus' mission, as indicated by their gesture of hospitality towards Him (v. 36). Yet they could not entirely free themselves from their suspicions and prejudices.

7:47 This is a great encouragement to all who feel so much of their lives has been given over to sin. In the mercy of God, a sinful past is not a hopeless liability. Forgiveness comes to those who truly love Christ.

selves, [a]"Who is this who even forgives sins?"
50 Then He said to the woman,
[a]"Your faith has saved you. Go in
peace."†

Women Who Served Jesus

8 Now it came to pass, afterward,
that He went through every city
and village, preaching and [1]bringing
the glad tidings of the kingdom of
God. And the twelve *were* with
Him,†
2 and [a]certain women who had
been healed of evil spirits and
[1]infirmities—Mary called Magdalene, [b]out of whom had come seven
demons,
3 and Joanna the wife of Chuza,
Herod's steward, and Susanna, and
many others who provided for
[1]Him from their [2]substance.

Parable of the Sower
(Matt. 13:1–23; Mark 4:1–20)

4 [a]And when a great multitude
had gathered, and they had come to
Him from every city, He spoke by a
parable:
5 "A sower went out to sow his
seed. And as he sowed, some fell
by the wayside; and it was trampled
down, and the birds of the air devoured it.
6 "Some fell on rock; and as soon
as it sprang up, it withered away because it lacked moisture.
7 "And some fell among thorns,
and the thorns sprang up with it and
choked it.
8 "But others fell on good ground,
sprang up, and yielded [1]a crop a
hundredfold." When He had said
these things He cried, [a]"He who has
ears to hear, let him hear!"
9 [a]Then His disciples asked Him,
saying, "What does this parable
mean?"†
10 And He said, "To you it has
been given to know the [1]mysteries
of the kingdom of God, but to the
rest *it is given* in parables, that

> [a]*'Seeing they may not see,*
> *And hearing they may not*
> *understand.'*

11 [a]"Now the parable is this: The
seed is the [b]word of God.†
12 "Those by the wayside are the
ones who hear; then the devil comes
and takes away the word out of their
hearts, lest they should believe and
be saved.
13 "But the ones on the rock *are*
those who, when they hear, receive
the word with joy; and these have
no root, who believe for a while and
in time of [1]temptation fall away.
14 "Now the ones *that* fell among
thorns are those who, when they
have heard, go out and are choked
with cares, [a]riches, and pleasures of
life, and bring no fruit to maturity.
15 "But the ones *that* fell on the
good ground are those who, having
heard the word with a noble and
good heart, keep *it* and bear fruit
with [a]patience.[1]

Take Care How You Hear
(Mark 4:21–25)

16 [a]"No one, when he has lit a
lamp, covers it with a vessel or puts

49 [a]Luke 5:21
50 [a]Matt. 9:22

CHAPTER 8

1 [1]*proclaiming the good news*
2 [a]Matt. 27:55
[b]Mark 16:9
[1]*sicknesses*
3 [1]NU, M *them*
[2]*possessions*
4 [a]Mark 4:1–9
8 [a]Luke 14:35
[1]Lit. *fruit*
9 [a]Matt. 13:10–23
10 [a]Is. 6:9
[1]*secret* or *hidden truths*
11 [a][1 Pet. 1:23]
[b]Luke 5:1; 11:28
13 [1]*testing*
14 [a]1 Tim. 6:9, 10
15 [a][Heb. 10:36–39]
[1]*endurance*
16 [a]Luke 11:33

7:50 The Scriptures speak of many things that contribute to our salvation: a believing spouse (1 Cor. 7:14–16), prayer (James 5:15) and baptism (1 Pet. 3:21). Here Jesus names a basic one: personal **faith.**

8:1–3 The group that accompanied Jesus as He went about teaching and healing was not limited to **the twelve.** A number of **women** (v. 2) were part of that band as well, and they **provided for** (v. 3) Jesus from their possessions (Matt. 27:55).

8:9, 10 The **mysteries of the kingdom** are revealed to the faithful, but hidden from those with unresponsive hearts (see notes on Matt. 13:11 and Mark 4:10–12).

8:11 The explanation of the parable is easily grasped. But only with the eyes of faith does one see and know that Jesus Himself is truly the Savior (see notes on Matt. 13:18–23; Mark 4:13–20).

it under a bed, but sets *it* on a lampstand, that those who enter may see the [b]light.
17 [a]"For nothing is secret that will not be [b]revealed, nor *anything* hidden that will not be known and come to light.
18 "Therefore take heed how you hear. [a]For whoever has, to him *more* will be given; and whoever does not have, even what he [1]seems to [b]have will be taken from him."†

Jesus' True Kinsmen
(Matt. 12:46–50; Mark 3:31–35)

19 [a]Then His mother and brothers came to Him, and could not approach Him because of the crowd.†
20 And it was told Him *by some,* who said, "Your mother and Your brothers are standing outside, desiring to see You."
21 But He answered and said to them, "My mother and My brothers are these who hear the word of God and do it."†

Jesus Calms a Storm
(Matt. 8:23–27; Mark 4:35–41)

22 [a]Now it happened, on a certain day, that He got into a boat with His disciples. And He said to them, "Let us cross over to the other side of the lake." And they launched out.
23 But as they sailed He fell asleep. And a windstorm came down on the lake, and they were filling *with water,* and were in [1]jeopardy.

16 [b]Matt. 5:14
17 [a]Luke 12:2 [b][2 Cor. 5:10]
18 [a]Matt. 25:29 [b]Matt. 13:12 [1]*thinks that he has*
19 [a]Mark 3:31–35
22 [a]Matt. 8:23–27
23 [1]*danger*

24 And they came to Him and awoke Him, saying, "Master, Master, we are perishing!" Then He arose and rebuked the wind and the raging of the water. And they ceased, and there was a calm.
25 But He said to them, [a]"Where is your faith?" And they were afraid, and marveled, saying to one another, [b]"Who can this be? For He commands even the winds and water, and they obey Him!"†

The Gadarene Demoniac
(Matt. 8:28–34; Mark 5:1–20)

26 [a]Then they sailed to the country of the [1]Gadarenes, which is opposite Galilee.†
27 And when He stepped out on the land, there met Him a certain man from the city who had demons [1]for a long time. And he wore no clothes, nor did he live in a house but in the tombs.
28 When he saw Jesus, he [a]cried out, fell down before Him, and with a loud voice said, [b]"What have I to do with [c]You, Jesus, Son of the Most High God? I beg You, do not torment me!"†
29 For He had commanded the unclean spirit to come out of the man. For it had often seized him, and he was kept under guard, bound with chains and shackles; and he broke the bonds and was driven by the demon into the wilderness.
30 Jesus asked him, saying, "What is your name?" And he said, "Le-

25 [a]Luke 9:41 [b]Luke 4:36; 5:26
26 [a]Mark 5:1–17 [1]NU *Gerasenes*
27 [1]NU *and for a long time wore no clothes*
28 [a]Mark 1:26; 9:26 [b]Mark 1:23, 24 [c]Luke 4:41

8:18 Taking **heed** to **hear** Jesus, the Word of God, brings light (vv. 16, 17) within the soul. It must not be covered but allowed to shine forth. The more one permits God's light to shine, the more light is given.

8:19 Luke does not report why Jesus' family wanted to see Him. His **brothers** are either stepbrothers, sons of Joseph by a previous wife (the opinion of some Church Fathers), or other relatives (see notes on Matt. 12:46–50; Mark 3:31–35).

8:21 Jesus declares His true family is a spiritual one—those who hear and do God's word.

8:25 In the most difficult moments of life, **faith** unites us with Christ and gives us His strength and comfort.

8:26 The **country of the Gadarenes** was Gentile territory where people could raise swine (v. 32), which were considered unclean by the Jews (see notes on Matt. 8:28–34; Mark 5:1–20).

8:28 Christ draws forth the reluctant confession of the demons. Their displeasure at being forced to obey Christ (v. 31) testifies to the strength of Jesus' divine nature. His power overcomes them, and they are forced to abandon immediately the man they possessed.

gion," because many demons had
entered him.
31 And they begged Him that He
would not command them to go out
[a]into the abyss.
32 Now a herd of many [a]swine was
feeding there on the mountain. So
they begged Him that He would permit them to enter them. And He permitted them.
33 Then the demons went out of
the man and entered the swine, and
the herd ran violently down the
steep place into the lake and
drowned.
34 When those who fed *them* saw
what had happened, they fled and
told *it* in the city and in the country.
35 Then they went out to see what
had happened, and came to Jesus,
and found the man from whom the
demons had departed, [a]sitting at the
[b]feet of Jesus, clothed and in his
[c]right mind. And they were afraid.
36 They also who had seen *it* told
them by what means he who had
been demon-possessed was [1]healed.
37 [a]Then the whole multitude of
the surrounding region of the
[1]Gadarenes [b]asked Him to [c]depart
from them, for they were seized with
great [d]fear. And He got into the boat
and returned.
38 Now [a]the man from whom the
demons had departed begged Him
that he might be with Him. But Jesus
sent him away, saying,
39 "Return to your own house, and
tell what great things God has done
for you." And he went his way and
proclaimed throughout the whole
city what great things Jesus had done
for him.†

31 [a]Rom. 10:7; [Rev. 20:1, 3]
32 [a]Lev. 11:7; Deut. 14:8
35 [a][Matt. 11:28] [b]Matt. 28:9; Mark 7:25; Luke 10:39; 17:16; John 11:32 [c][2 Tim. 1:7]
36 [1]*delivered*
37 [a]Matt. 8:34 [b]Mark 1:24; Luke 4:34 [c]Job 21:14; Acts 16:39 [d]Luke 5:26 [1]NU *Gerasenes*
38 [a]Mark 5:18–20
41 [a]Matt. 9:18–26; Mark 5:22–43
42 [a]Luke 7:2
43 [a]Matt. 9:20 [b]Luke 15:19–22
44 [a]Mark 6:56; Luke 5:13
45 [1]NU omits *and those with him* [2]NU omits the rest of v. 45.
46 [a]Mark 5:30; Luke 6:19
48 [a]Mark 5:34; Luke 7:50 [b]John 8:11 [1]NU omits *be of good cheer*

Jairus's Daughter Raised, a Woman Healed
(Matt. 9:18–26; Mark 5:21–43)

40 So it was, when Jesus returned,
that the multitude welcomed Him,
for they were all waiting for Him.
41 [a]And behold, there came a man
named Jairus, and he was a ruler of
the synagogue. And he fell down at
Jesus' feet and begged Him to come
to his house,†
42 for he had an only daughter
about twelve years of age, and she
[a]was dying. But as He went, the
multitudes thronged Him.
43 [a]Now a woman, having a
[b]flow of blood for twelve years, who
had spent all her livelihood on physicians and could not be healed by
any,
44 came from behind and [a]touched
the border of His garment. And immediately her flow of blood stopped.
45 And Jesus said, "Who touched
Me?" When all denied it, Peter
[1]and those with him said, "Master,
the multitudes throng and press
You, [2]and You say, 'Who touched
Me?' "
46 But Jesus said, "Somebody
touched Me, for I perceived [a]power
going out from Me."†
47 Now when the woman saw that
she was not hidden, she came trembling; and falling down before Him,
she declared to Him in the presence
of all the people the reason she had
touched Him and how she was
healed immediately.
48 And He said to her, "Daughter,
[1]be of good cheer; [a]your faith has
made you well. [b]Go in peace."

8:39 Jesus does not call all whom He saves to join His band of disciples. This man, wonderfully healed, is sent back home to witness to the power of Christ there.

8:41–56 This double miracle is also reported by Matthew and Mark (see notes on Matt. 9:18–26 and Mark 5:22–43).

8:46 Healing **power** flows from Christ. That which Jesus touches or which touches Him, is sanctified. The power to heal comes through the garment (v. 44) of Jesus but originates within Him. Similarly, we use physical things in the Orthodox Church because in the context of faith and prayer, the power of Christ works through them. There is power in the paint or wood of an icon, or in the metal of a cross, or in oil or water, only if it is sanctified by Christ. Jesus taught that one thing sanctifies another: "Fools and blind! For which is greater, the gold or the temple that sanctifies the gold?" (Matt. 23:17). Therefore, to trustingly touch the border of His garment was to touch Him. Others may have touched Christ, but this woman's faith draws His power as well.

49 [a]While He was still speaking,
someone came from the ruler of the
synagogue's *house,* saying to him,
"Your daughter is dead. Do not trouble the [1]Teacher."
50 But when Jesus heard *it,* He answered him, saying, "Do not be
afraid; [a]only believe, and she will be
made well."†
51 When He came into the house,
He permitted no one to go [1]in except
[2]Peter, James, and John, and the father and mother of the girl.
52 Now all wept and mourned for
her; but He said, [a]"Do not weep; she
is not dead, [b]but sleeping."
53 And they ridiculed Him, knowing that she was dead.
54 But He [1]put them all outside,
took her by the hand and called, saying, "Little girl, [a]arise."†
55 Then her spirit returned, and
she arose immediately. And He commanded that she be given *something*
to eat.
56 And her parents were astonished, but [a]He charged them to tell
no one what had happened.

The Twelve Sent Out
(Matt. 9:35—11:1; Mark 6:7–13)

9 Then [a]He called His twelve disciples together and [b]gave them
power and authority over all demons, and to cure diseases.†
2 [a]He sent them to preach the
kingdom of God and to heal the
sick.
3 [a]And He said to them, "Take
nothing for the journey, neither
staffs nor bag nor bread nor money;
and do not have two tunics apiece.
4 [a]"Whatever house you enter,
stay there, and from there depart.
5 [a]"And whoever will not receive
you, when you go out of that
city, [b]shake off the very dust from
your feet as a testimony against
them."
6 [a]So they departed and went
through the towns, preaching the
gospel and healing everywhere.
7 [a]Now Herod the tetrarch heard
of all that was done by Him; and he
was perplexed, because it was said
by some that John had risen from
the dead,†
8 and by some that Elijah had appeared, and by others that one of the
old prophets had risen again.
9 Herod said, "John I have beheaded, but who is this of whom I
hear such things?" [a]So he sought to
see Him.
10 [a]And the apostles, when they
had returned, told Him all that they
had done. [b]Then He took them and
went aside privately into a deserted
place belonging to the city called
Bethsaida.†

Feeding the Five Thousand
(Matt. 14:13–21; Mark 6:30–44; John 6:1–14)

11 But when the multitudes knew
it, they followed Him; and He received them and spoke to them
about the kingdom of God, and
healed those who had need of
healing.
12 [a]When the day began to wear
away, the twelve came and said to

49 [a]Mark 5:35 [1]NU adds *anymore*
50 [a][Mark 11:22–24]
51 [1]NU adds *with Him* [2]NU, M *Peter, John, and James*
52 [a]Luke 7:13 [b][John 11:11, 13]
54 [a]Luke 7:14; John 11:43 [1]NU omits *put them all outside*
56 [a]Matt. 8:4; 9:30; Mark 5:43

CHAPTER 9

1 [a]Matt. 10:1, 2; Mark 3:13; 6:7 [b]Mark 16:17, 18; [John 14:12]
2 [a]Matt. 10:7, 8; Mark 6:12; Luke 10:1, 9
3 [a]Matt. 10:9–15; Mark 6:8–11; Luke 10:4–12; 22:35
4 [a]Matt. 10:11; Mark 6:10
5 [a]Matt. 10:14 [b]Luke 10:11; Acts 13:51
6 [a]Mark 6:12; Luke 8:1
7 [a]Matt. 14:1, 2; Mark 6:14
9 [a]Luke 23:8
10 [a]Mark 6:30 [b]Matt. 14:13
12 [a]Matt. 14:15; Mark 6:35; John 6:1, 5

8:50 Jesus exhorts the parents, **only believe.** We are to believe God, even when it appears there is no hope. These parents do keep believing, and their daughter is made well.

8:54 Christ's divinity works together with His humanity to accomplish His miracles. Here, taking the child by the hand and calling her to **arise** is an action of His humanity. Her being restored to life is an action of His divinity. These two operations, however, are inseparable because He is One undivided Person.

9:1, 2 After being with His disciples for a considerable period, Jesus sends them out on their first mission, giving them **power and authority** to perform exorcisms and healings as well as to preach the dawn of the kingdom (v. 2; see notes on Matt. 10).

9:7 This is **Herod** Antipas (a son of Herod the Great), ruler of Galilee under Rome. This is the Herod who had John the Baptist beheaded (v. 9), and the one in Jerusalem at Jesus' trial, to whom Pilate sent Jesus.

9:10 The disciples are called **apostles** (meaning "those officially sent on a mission"), their proper title after Jesus' Resurrection.

Him, "Send the multitude away, that
they may go into the surrounding
towns and country, and lodge and
get provisions; for we are in a deserted place here."†
13 But He said to them, "You give
them something to eat." And they
said, "We have no more than five
loaves and two fish, unless we go
and buy food for all these people."
14 For there were about five thousand men. Then He said to His disciples, "Make them sit down in groups
of fifty."
15 And they did so, and made
them all sit down.
16 Then He took the five loaves
and the two fish, and looking up to
heaven, He [a]blessed and broke *them,*
and gave *them* to the disciples to set
before the multitude.
17 So they all ate and were [1]filled,
and twelve baskets of the leftover
fragments were taken up by them.

Peter's Confession: Jesus Is the Christ

(Matt. 16:13–20; Mark 8:27–30)

18 [a]And it happened, as He was
alone praying, *that* His disciples
joined Him, and He asked them,
saying, "Who do the crowds say that
I am?"†
19 So they answered and said,
[a]"John the Baptist, but some *say* Elijah; and others *say* that one of the
old prophets has risen again."
20 He said to them, "But who do
you say that I am?" [a]Peter answered
and said, "The Christ of God."†

16 [a]Luke 22:19; 24:30
17 [1]*satisfied*
18 [a]Matt. 16:13–16; Mark 8:27–29
19 [a]Matt. 14:2
20 [a]Matt. 16:16; John 6:68, 69
21 [a]Matt. 8:4; 16:20; Mark 8:30
22 [a]Matt. 16:21; 17:22; Luke 18:31–33; 23:46; 24:46
23 [a]Matt. 10:38; 16:24; Mark 8:34; Luke 14:27 [1]M omits *daily*
24 [a]Matt. 10:39; Luke 17:33; [John 12:25]
25 [a]Matt. 16:26; Mark 8:36; [Luke 16:19–31]; Acts 1:18, 25
26 [a][Rom. 1:16] [b]Matt. 10:33; Mark 8:38; Luke 12:9; 2 Tim. 2:12
27 [a]Matt. 16:28; Mark 9:1; Acts 7:55, 56; Rev. 20:4
28 [a]Matt. 17:1–8; Mark 9:2–8

First Prediction of the Passion

(Matt. 16:21–28; Mark 8:31—9:1)

21 [a]And He strictly warned and
commanded them to tell this to no
one,†
22 saying, [a]"The Son of Man must
suffer many things, and be rejected
by the elders and chief priests and
scribes, and be killed, and be raised
the third day."†
23 [a]Then He said to *them* all, "If
anyone desires to come after Me, let
him deny himself, and take up his
cross [1]daily, and follow Me.
24 [a]"For whoever desires to save
his life will lose it, but whoever loses
his life for My sake will save it.
25 [a]"For what profit is it to a man
if he gains the whole world, and is
himself destroyed or lost?
26 [a]"For whoever is ashamed of
Me and My words, of him the Son
of Man will be [b]ashamed when He
comes in His *own* glory, and *in His*
Father's, and of the holy angels.
27 [a]"But I tell you truly, there are
some standing here who shall not
taste death till they see the kingdom
of God."

The Transfiguration

(Matt. 17:1–9; Mark 9:2–10)

28 [a]Now it came to pass, about
eight days after these sayings, that
He took Peter, John, and James and
went up on the mountain to pray.
29 As He prayed, the appearance
of His face was altered, and His robe
became white *and* glistening.†

9:12–17 All are satisfied when Jesus feeds them. No one need go away hungry. This feeding of the 5,000 is a messianic sign (see comments on Matt. 14:14–21).

9:18 What **the crowds** have to say about Jesus is of little importance (v. 19). The disciples learn that lesson here. In the NT, the opinion of the crowd is seldom, if ever, clear, and often completely wrong.

9:20 A great moment in the ministry of Jesus comes when **Peter,** on behalf of the disciples, acknowledges Jesus as **the Christ of God** (see notes on Matt. 16:13–20; Mark 8:29).

9:21 Jesus desires to keep His messiahship hidden to avoid (1) popular political misunderstanding and (2) quick intervention by the Romans.

9:22 Luke omits Peter's objection to Jesus' announcement of His Passion (see notes on Matt. 16:21–23 and Mark 8:31—9:1).

9:29 The Transfiguration demonstrates Jesus is the Lord of glory, despite the fact that He will later suffer and die on the Cross (see "The Transfiguration" at Matt. 17). Jesus' humanity

(continued on next page)

30 And behold, two men talked with Him, who were [a]Moses and [b]Elijah,†

31 who appeared in glory and spoke of His [1]decease which He was about to accomplish at Jerusalem.†

32 But Peter and those with him [a]were heavy with sleep; and when they were fully awake, they saw His glory and the two men who stood with Him.

33 Then it happened, as they were parting from Him, *that* Peter said to Jesus, "Master, it is good for us to be here; and let us make three [1]tabernacles: one for You, one for Moses, and one for Elijah"—not knowing what he said.

34 While he was saying this, a cloud came and overshadowed them; and they were fearful as they entered the [a]cloud.

35 And a voice came out of the cloud, saying, [a]"This is [1]My beloved Son. [b]Hear Him!"

36 When the voice had ceased, Jesus was found alone. [a]But they kept quiet, and told no one in those days any of the things they had seen.†

The Unbelieving World
(Matt. 17:14–21; Mark 9:14–29)

37 [a]Now it happened on the next day, when they had come down from the mountain, that a great multitude met Him.

38 Suddenly a man from the multitude cried out, saying, "Teacher, I implore You, look on my son, for he is my only child.

39 "And behold, a spirit seizes him, and he suddenly cries out; it convulses him so that he foams *at the mouth;* and it departs from him with great difficulty, bruising him.

40 "So I implored Your disciples to cast it out, but they could not."

41 Then Jesus answered and said, "O [1]faithless and perverse generation, how long shall I be with you and [2]bear with you? Bring your son here."

42 And as he was still coming, the demon threw him down and convulsed *him.* Then Jesus rebuked the unclean spirit, healed the child, and gave him back to his father.

Second Prediction of the Passion
(Matt. 17:22, 23; Mark 9:30–32)

43 And they were all amazed at the majesty of God. But while everyone marveled at all the things which Jesus did, He said to His disciples,†

44 [a]"Let these words sink down into your ears, for the Son of Man is about to be betrayed into the hands of men."†

45 [a]But they did not understand

30 [a]Heb. 11:23–29 [b]2 Kin. 2:1–11
31 [1]Death, lit. *departure*
32 [a]Dan. 8:18; 10:9; Matt. 26:40, 43; Mark 14:40
33 [1]*tents*
34 [a]Ex. 13:21; Acts 1:9
35 [a]Ps. 2:7; [Is. 42:1; Matt. 3:17; 12:18]; Mark 1:11; Luke 3:22 [b]Acts 3:22 [1]NU *My Son, the Chosen One*
36 [a]Matt. 17:9; Mark 9:9
37 [a]Matt. 17:14–18; Mark 9:14–27
41 [1]*unbelieving* [2]*put up with*
44 [a]Matt. 17:22; Mark 10:33; 14:53; Luke 22:54; John 18:12
45 [a]Mark 9:32; Luke 2:50; 18:34

(continued from previous page)
was filled with splendor, was made Godlike, deified. His Transfiguration is the most evident expression of our hope for glorification in God's eternal Kingdom. St. Paul writes, "Behold, I tell you a mystery: We shall not all sleep, but we shall all be changed" (1 Cor. 15:51). And St. John writes, "We know that when He is revealed, we shall be like Him, for we shall see Him as He is" (1 John 3:2). For eternity, we shall be like Jesus as He appeared on the Mount of Transfiguration.

9:30 Christ's Transfiguration is witnessed to by **Moses and Elijah,** appearing in the glory (v. 31) which reveals the transfiguration of our humanity. Moses and Elijah, as representatives of the Law and the Prophets, appear to the apostles showing that Jesus is the fulfillment of the OT.

9:31 Decease in Greek is *exodos.* This term makes it clear that through His death Jesus will perform an exodus from Jerusalem, in which He will deliver mankind from the slavery of the evil one. It is revealed to the disciples at His Transfiguration that He will suffer, so when they see Him crucified, they will remember this day of glory and that His suffering is completely volitional.

9:36 Peter, James and John **kept quiet** because the Lord commanded them not to speak of this experience **in those days,** meaning until after the Resurrection.

9:43 The majesty of God is His greatness and power shown through Jesus' miracles.

9:44 See notes on Matt. 17:22, 23 and Mark 9:30–32.

this saying, and it was hidden from
them so that they did not perceive
it; and they were afraid to ask Him
about this saying.

Who Is the Greatest?

(Matt. 18:1–5; Mark 9:33–37)

46 [a]Then a dispute arose among
them as to which of them would be
greatest.†
47 And Jesus, [a]perceiving the
thought of their heart, took a [b]little
child and set him by Him,
48 and said to them, [a]"Whoever
receives this little child in My name
receives Me; and [b]whoever receives
Me [c]receives Him who sent Me.
[d]For he who is least among you all
will be great."

The Rights of Jesus' Disciples

(Mark 9:38–41)

49 [a]Now John answered and said,
"Master, we saw someone casting
out demons in Your name, and we
forbade him because he does not follow with us."†
50 But Jesus said to him, "Do not
forbid *him*, for [a]he who is not against
[1]us is on [2]our side."

46 [a]Matt. 18:1–5
47 [a]Matt. 9:4 [b]Luke 18:17
48 [a]Matt. 18:5 [b]John 12:44 [c]John 13:20 [d]Eph. 3:8
49 [a]Mark 9:38–40
50 [a]Luke 11:23 [1]NU *you* [2]NU *your*
51 [a]Mark 16:19
53 [a]John 4:4, 9
54 [a]Mark 3:17 [b]2 Kin. 1:10, 12 [1]NU omits *just as Elijah did*
55 [a][2 Tim. 1:7] [1]NU omits the rest of v. 55.
56 [a]John 3:17; 12:47 [1]NU omits *For the Son of Man did not come to destroy men's lives but to save them.*
57 [a]Matt. 8:19–22

Kindness Toward the Inhospitable

51 Now it came to pass, when the
time had come for [a]Him to be received up, that He steadfastly set His
face to go to Jerusalem,†
52 and sent messengers before His
face. And as they went, they entered
a village of the Samaritans, to prepare for Him.†
53 But [a]they did not receive Him,
because His face was *set* for the journey to Jerusalem.
54 And when His disciples [a]James
and John saw *this,* they said, "Lord,
do You want us to command fire to
come down from heaven and consume them, [1]just as [b]Elijah did?"
55 But He turned and rebuked
them, [1]and said, "You do not know
what manner of [a]spirit you are of.
56 [1]"For [a]the Son of Man did not
come to destroy men's lives but to
save *them.*" And they went to another village.

Undivided Commitment

(Matt. 8:18–22)

57 [a]Now it happened as they journeyed on the road, *that* someone said
to Him, "Lord, I will follow You
wherever You go."†

9:46–48 The disciples themselves are not above the desire for worldly glory and power. One of the last lessons they will learn before Christ's Ascension is that of humility and service. Jesus teaches them by a simple illustration: a **little child** (v. 48)—an icon of dependency. (See notes on Matt. 18:1–4 and Mark 9:30–32.)

9:49, 50 This is an example of Jesus' tolerance and breadth of vision. It is a temptation for us to want everyone to have a spiritual practice exactly like ours, to do things the way we do, and to be in our group. How many schisms have occurred in Church history because people missed Jesus' lesson here!

9:51 He steadfastly set His face to go to Jerusalem marks a turning point in Jesus' life and ministry. From this point in the Gospel, Jerusalem and the Passion is the next step of Jesus' journey. The Greek verb **received up** describes the Ascension, the ultimate goal of His Passion and Resurrection.

9:52, 53 Jesus does not exclude the **Samaritans** (v. 52) from salvation, even though this **village** refuses to **receive Him** (v. 53). Other Samaritans welcome Him (John 4).

9:57–62 I will follow You: There is a cost to discipleship. Jesus talks of three such costs:

(1) Provision for personal security does not mix with true discipleship. The disciple will be no more secure than the Teacher. If the Teacher has nowhere to lay His head (v. 58), neither will the disciple.

(2) Discipleship demands singular commitment to the Kingdom of God. A disciple must be willing to let the spiritually dead bury the physically dead (v. 60).

(3) Discipleship does not look back to reconsider, or operate by delayed response. It means taking hold of the commission given by Christ and moving forward.

58 And Jesus said to him, "Foxes
have holes and birds of the air *have*
nests, but the Son of Man [a]has nowhere to lay *His* head."
59 [a]Then He said to another, "Follow Me." But he said, "Lord, let me
first go and bury my father."
60 Jesus said to him, "Let the dead
bury their own dead, but you go and
preach the kingdom of God."
61 And another also said, "Lord,
[a]I will follow You, but let me first
go *and* bid them farewell who are at
my house."
62 But Jesus said to him, "No one,
having put his hand to the plow, and
looking back, is [a]fit for the kingdom
of God."

The Seventy Sent Out

10 After these things the Lord
appointed [1]seventy others
also, and [a]sent them two by two
before His face into every city and
place where He Himself was about
to go.†
2 Then He said to them, [a]"The
harvest truly *is* great, but the laborers
are few; therefore [b]pray the Lord of
the harvest to send out laborers into
His harvest.†
3 "Go your way; [a]behold, I send
you out as lambs among wolves.†
4 [a]"Carry neither money bag,
knapsack, nor sandals; and [b]greet no
one along the road.†
5 [a]"But whatever house you enter, first say, 'Peace to this house.'
6 "And if a son of peace is there,
your peace will rest on it; if not, it
will return to you.
7 [a]"And remain in the same
house, [b]eating and drinking such
things as they give, for [c]the laborer
is worthy of his wages. Do not go
from house to house.†
8 "Whatever city you enter, and
they receive you, eat such things as
are set before you.
9 [a]"And heal the sick there, and
say to them, [b]'The kingdom of God
has come near to you.'†
10 "But whatever city you enter,
and they do not receive you, go out
into its streets and say,
11 [a]'The very dust of your city
which clings to [1]us we wipe off
against you. Nevertheless know this,
that the kingdom of God has come
near you.'
12 [1]"But I say to you that [a]it will
be more tolerable in that Day for
Sodom than for that city.
13 [a]"Woe to you, Chorazin! Woe
to you, Bethsaida! [b]For if the mighty
works which were done in you
had been done in Tyre and Sidon,
they would have repented long
ago, sitting in sackcloth and
ashes.†
14 "But it will be more tolerable for
Tyre and Sidon at the judgment than
for you.
15 [a]"And you, Capernaum, [1]who
are [b]exalted to heaven, [c]will be
brought down to Hades.

58 [a]Luke 2:7; 8:23
59 [a]Matt. 8:21, 22
61 [a]1 Kin. 19:20
62 [a]2 Tim. 4:10

CHAPTER 10

1 [a]Mark 6:7 [1]NU *seventy-two others*
2 [a]John 4:35 [b]2 Thess. 3:1
3 [a]Matt. 10:16
4 [a]Luke 9:3–5 [b]2 Kin. 4:29
5 [a]Matt. 10:12
7 [a]Matt. 10:11 [b]1 Cor. 10:27 [c]1 Tim. 5:18
9 [a]Mark 3:15 [b]Matt. 3:2; 10:7
11 [a]Acts 13:51 [1]NU *our feet*
12 [a]Matt. 10:15; 11:24 [1]NU, M omit *But*
13 [a]Matt. 11:21–23 [b]Ezek. 3:6
15 [a]Matt. 11:23 [b]Is. 14:13–15 [c]Ezek. 26:20 [1]NU *will you be exalted to heaven? You will be thrust down to Hades!*

10:1 Only Luke reports a sending of **seventy others** besides the Twelve, but the instructions to the two groups are similar (see Matt. 10:1–15). The Seventy **appointed** by Christ may fulfill the type of the seventy elders appointed by Moses (Ex. 18:21, 22; 24:1). The Orthodox Church commemorates the Seventy as saints.

10:2 Missionary endeavors are accomplished by God's initiative and power. We **pray to the Lord,** and it is He who calls and sends out the workers. We have the assurance, however, that **the harvest truly is great.**

10:3 Lambs speaks of the sacrificial life of the missionaries, their innocence, while the world into which they are sent is hostile and cruel.

10:4 The missionary of Christ travels light, moving easily from place to place, and avoids superficial conversation.

10:7 Going **from house to house** implies looking for better accommodations.

10:9 The gospel of Christ is not simply that there is a divine Kingdom somewhere, but that **the kingdom of God has come near** to us. It breaks into our lives through the work of Christ and His sent ones.

10:13–16 Judgment is more severe against those who witness Jesus' **mighty works,** or hear His word but reject it, as in the case of these Galilean cities (see note on Matt. 11:20–24).

THE SEVENTY

In Luke 10:1ff the Lord appointed seventy men to go out as missionaries—as apostles. Though not so prominent as the Twelve, the Seventy carried out their missions with fervor and enthusiasm. The Tradition of the Church confirms that the Seventy remained true to the Lord and their calling, fulfilling a vital role in the spread of the gospel. These were not random choices or accidental volunteers but true disciples, true apostles, whose labors carried the message of their Lord throughout the Roman Empire and beyond.

Though lists of the Seventy vary somewhat, all are remembered in the calendar of the Church (see chart, "The Seventy," on page 818). One day, January 4, is set aside to remember them all, and the record of their work is preserved in accounts handed down through the centuries from place to place, especially in those locations where they labored.

To tell the stories passed down in the Church concerning all of the Seventy would fill a book of considerable size, but the compromise of telling the stories of a few, both prominent and relatively obscure members, will relate the conviction and faith of this illustrious body.

Barnabas, a Jew of the tribe of Levi, was born in Cyprus of wealthy parents. He is said to have studied under Gamaliel with Saul of Tarsus, who was to become Paul the Apostle. Originally named Joseph, he was called Barnabas (Son of Consolation) by the apostles (Acts 4:36) because he had a rare gift of comforting the hearts of people. He sought out Paul when everyone else was afraid of him, bringing him to the apostles. And it was Barnabas who was first sent by the apostles to Antioch to find out what was going on there (Acts 11:22). Barnabas sought out Paul to work with him, and their long association was broken only when Barnabas was determined to take his cousin Mark, whom Paul did not trust just then, on a missionary journey. The mutual relationships among the three were later healed (Col. 4:10). Many ancient accounts say Barnabas was the first to preach in Rome and the first in Milan, but he was martyred in Cyprus, then buried by Mark at the western gate of the city of Salamis.

Among the more prominent of the Seventy was the Apostle Titus, whom Paul called his brother (2 Cor. 12:18) and his son (Titus 1:4). Born in Crete, Titus was educated in Greek philosophy, but after reading the Prophet Isaiah he began to doubt the value of all he had been taught. Hearing the news of the coming of Jesus Christ, he joined some others from Crete who went to Jerusalem to see for themselves. After hearing Jesus speak and seeing His works, the young Titus joined those who followed. Baptized by the Apostle Paul, he worked with and served the great apostle to the Gentiles, traveling with him until Paul sent him to Crete, making him bishop of that city. It is said that he was in Rome at the time of the beheading of St. Paul and that he buried the body of his spiritual father before returning home. Back in Crete, he converted and baptized many people, governing the Church on that island until he entered into rest at the age of ninety-four.

There are many less prominent among the Seventy who also labored for Christ unto death. Aristarchus, whom Paul mentions several times (cf. Acts 19:29; Col. 4:10; Philem. 24), calling him a "fellow laborer," became bishop of Apamea in Syria. Sosthenes (Acts 18:17; 1 Cor. 1:1) became bishop of Caesarea, and Tychicus (Acts 20:4; Eph. 6:21; Col. 4:7; 2 Tim. 4:12; Titus 3:12) succeeded him in that city. Simeon (Matt. 13:55; Mark 6:3), son of Cleopas (who was the brother of Joseph the betrothed of the Virgin Mary), succeeded James as bishop of Jerusalem. Aristobulus (Rom. 16:10), the brother of the Apostle Barnabas, preached the gospel in Britain and died peacefully there.

The lives of these few are quite representative of the Seventy who were instrumental in helping to plant the Church throughout the world. Many became bishops, but the names of all are numbered in heaven in the Book of Life, as faithful servants of the Lord, apostles and foundations of the Church.

Commemoration of the Holy Archangels

November 8

10:16–21: The Archangels war against Satan in the name of Christ.

16 [a]"He who hears you hears Me,
[b]he who rejects you rejects Me, and
[c]he who rejects Me rejects Him who
sent Me."
17 Then [a]the [1]seventy returned
with joy, saying, "Lord, even the demons
are subject to us in Your
name."
18 And He said to them, [a]"I saw
Satan fall like lightning from
heaven.†
19 "Behold, [a]I give you the authority
to trample on serpents and scorpions,
and over all the power of the
enemy, and nothing shall by any
means hurt you.
20 "Nevertheless do not rejoice in
this, that the spirits are subject to
you, but [1]rather rejoice because
[a]your names are written in heaven."
21 [a]In that hour Jesus rejoiced in
the Spirit and said, "I thank You,
Father, Lord of heaven and earth,
that You have hidden these things
from *the* wise and prudent and
revealed them to babes. Even so,
Father, for so it seemed good in
Your sight.†
22 [a]"All[1] things have been delivered
to Me by My Father, and
[b]no one knows who the Son is except
the Father, and who the Father is except
the Son, and *the one* to whom
the Son wills to reveal *Him.*"†
23 Then He turned to *His* disciples
and said privately, [a]"Blessed *are*
the eyes which see the things you
see;
24 "for I tell you [a]that many prophets
and kings have desired to see
what you see, and have not seen *it*,
and to hear what you hear, and have
not heard *it*."†

The Good Samaritan

25 And behold, a certain [1]lawyer
stood up and tested Him, saying,
[a]"Teacher, what shall I do to inherit
eternal life?"†
26 He said to him, "What is written
in the law? What is your reading *of*
it?"
27 So he answered and said,
[a]"*'You shall love the* LORD *your God*
with all your heart, with all your
soul, with all your strength, and with
all your mind,' and [b]*'your neighbor*
as yourself.'"
28 And He said to him, "You have
answered rightly; do this and [a]you
will live."
29 But he, wanting to [a]justify himself,
said to Jesus, "And who is my
neighbor?"
30 Then Jesus answered and said:
"A certain *man* went down from Je-

16 [a]John 13:20 [b]1 Thess. 4:8 [c]John 5:23
17 [a]Luke 10:1 [1]NU *seventy-two*
18 [a]John 12:31
19 [a]Mark 16:18
20 [a]Is. 4:3 [1]NU, M omit *rather*
21 [a]Matt. 11:25–27
22 [a]John 3:35; 5:27; 17:2 [b][John 1:18; 6:44, 46] [1]M *And turning to the disciples He said, "All*
23 [a]Matt. 13:16, 17
24 [a]1 Pet. 1:10, 11
25 [a]Matt. 19:16–19; 22:35 [1]*expert in the law*
27 [a]Deut. 6:5 [b]Lev. 19:18
28 [a]Ezek. 20:11, 13, 21
29 [a]Luke 16:15

10:18–20 I saw Satan fall . . . from heaven is probably a reference by Jesus to Is. 14:12–15. Note the five "I wills" in that passage. Because he pursued his own will, Satan is both fallen from heaven, and he is defeated and dethroned from his demonic lordship over the world by the ministry of Christ and His disciples (v. 19). The joy of discipleship is not in authority over demonic power, but in the citizenship of God's Kingdom.

10:21 These things are the mysteries of the Kingdom manifested through the words and works of Jesus. They are received by **babes,** people of simple and open hearts, rather than by the scribes and Pharisees, the **wise and prudent.**

10:22 Jesus is **the Son** of God in the absolute. He shares fully **all** authority and knowledge of the Father, and is the sole and eternal revealer of God to humanity.

10:24 Many prophets and kings of the OT anticipated the coming of Jesus, but they did not experience the blessing of His Incarnation and the presence of His Kingdom.

10:25–27 What shall I do to inherit eternal life? This is a momentous question for every person. The answer of Jesus is to love God above all else, and to love one's neighbor (v. 27).

The Feasts of the Virgin Mary: Her Birth *September 8*
Protection *October 1*
Entry into the Temple *November 21*
Lifegiving Spring *Friday after Easter*
Falling Asleep *August 15*
10:38–42; 11:27, 28: Mary, the mother of God, was the most devoted and obedient of all His disciples.

rusalem to Jericho, and fell among
[1]thieves, who stripped him of his
clothing, wounded *him,* and departed, leaving *him* half dead.†
31 "Now by chance a certain priest
came down that road. And when he
saw him, [a]he passed by on the other
side.
32 "Likewise a Levite, when he arrived at the place, came and looked,
and passed by on the other side.†
33 "But a certain [a]Samaritan, as he
journeyed, came where he was. And
when he saw him, he had [b]com-
passion.†
34 "So he went to *him* and bandaged his wounds, pouring on oil
and wine; and he set him on his own
animal, brought him to an inn, and
took care of him.
35 "On the next day, [1]when he departed, he took out two [a]denarii,
gave *them* to the innkeeper, and said
to him, 'Take care of him; and whatever more you spend, when I come
again, I will repay you.'
36 "So which of these three do you
think was neighbor to him who fell
among the thieves?"
37 And he said, "He who showed
mercy on him." Then Jesus said to
him, [a]"Go and do likewise."

30 [1]*robbers*
31 [a]Ps. 38:11
33 [a]John 4:9
[b]Luke 15:20
35 [a]Matt. 20:2
[1]NU omits *when he departed*
37 [a]Prov. 14:21; [Matt. 9:13; 12:7]

Mary and Martha

38 Now it happened as they went
that He entered a certain village; and
a certain woman named [a]Martha
welcomed Him into her house.†
39 And she had a sister called
Mary, [a]who also [b]sat at [1]Jesus' feet
and heard His word.
40 But Martha was distracted with
much serving, and she approached
Him and said, "Lord, do You not
care that my sister has left me to
serve alone? Therefore tell her to
help me."†
41 And [1]Jesus answered and said
to her, "Martha, Martha, you are
worried and troubled about many
things.
42 "But [a]one thing is needed, and
Mary has chosen that good part,
which will not be taken away from
her."

38 [a]John 11:1; 12:2, 3
39 [a][1 Cor. 7:32–40]
[b]Luke 8:35; Acts 22:3
[1]NU *the Lord's*
41 [1]NU *the Lord*
42 [a][Ps. 27:4; John 6:27]

How to Pray
(Matt. 6:9–13)

11 Now it came to pass, as He
was praying in a certain place,
when He ceased, *that* one of His disciples said to Him, "Lord, teach us

10:30–37 The Parable of the Good Samaritan occurs only in Luke, and illustrates Jesus' teaching of who our **neighbor** is: anyone in immediate need, even a supposed enemy. Symbolically, the Good Samaritan is Christ Himself, the wounded man is humanity set upon by demons, and the inn is the Church. Love for neighbor proves our love for God.

10:32 Levite: an official helper in the temple.

10:33 The **Samaritan,** a presumed enemy of Jews, is highlighted as the good neighbor because of his loving actions toward the wounded Jew ignored by fellow Jews.

10:38, 39 Martha (v. 38) and **Mary** (v. 39) are the sisters of Lazarus, whom Jesus raised from the dead (John 11:1).

10:40–42 Martha was distracted (v. 40) and **troubled about many things** (v. 41) in providing hospitality for Jesus. But the **one thing** (v. 42) needed was for her to listen to Christ, to hear His words—a priority which certainly does not exclude serving Him.

to pray, as John also taught his disciples."†
2 So He said to them, "When you
pray, say:

[a]Our[1] Father [2]in heaven,
Hallowed be Your name.
Your kingdom come.
[3]Your will be done
On earth as *it is* in heaven.†
3 Give us day by day our daily
bread.†
4 And [a]forgive us our sins,
For we also forgive everyone
who is indebted to us.
And do not lead us into
temptation,
[1]But deliver us from the evil
one."†

5 And He said to them, "Which
of you shall have a friend, and go
to him at midnight and say to him,
'Friend, lend me three loaves;
6 'for a friend of mine has come
to me on his journey, and I have
nothing to set before him';
7 "and he will answer from within
and say, 'Do not trouble me; the door
is now shut, and my children are
with me in bed; I cannot rise and
give to you'?
8 "I say to you, [a]though he will
not rise and give to him because he
is his friend, yet because of his persistence he will rise and give him as
many as he needs.†
9 [a]"So I say to you, ask, and it
will be given to you; [b]seek, and you
will find; knock, and it will be
opened to you.†
10 "For everyone who asks receives, and he who seeks finds, and
to him who knocks it will be opened.
11 [a]"If a son asks for [1]bread from
any father among you, will he give
him a stone? Or if *he asks* for a fish,
will he give him a serpent instead
of a fish?
12 "Or if he asks for an egg, will
he offer him a scorpion?
13 "If you then, being evil, know
how to give [a]good gifts to your children, how much more will *your*
heavenly Father give the Holy Spirit
to those who ask Him!"†

Jesus and the Devil

(Matt. 12:22–24; Mark 3:22)

14 [a]And He was casting out a demon, and it was mute. So it was,

CHAPTER 11
2 [a]Matt. 6:9–13
[1]NU omits *Our*
[2]NU omits *in heaven*
[3]NU omits the rest of v. 2.
4 [a][Eph. 4:32]
[1]NU omits *But deliver us from the evil one*
8 [a][Luke 18:1–5]
9 [a]Ps. 50:14, 15; Jer. 33:3; [Matt. 7:7; 21:22; Mark 11:24; John 15:7; James 1:5, 6; 1 John 3:22; 5:14, 15]
[b]Is. 55:6
11 [a]Matt. 7:9
[1]NU omits *bread from any father among you, will he give him a stone? Or if he asks for*
13 [a]James 1:17
14 [a]Matt. 9:32–34; 12:22, 24

11:1 Lord, teach us to pray expresses a universal spiritual need, and leads Jesus to teach the Lord's Prayer to the disciples.

11:2 Matthew's record of the Lord's Prayer (Matt. 6:9–13) has a slightly stronger liturgical flavor, and is the one prayed in the Orthodox liturgy.

Our Father signifies (1) the unique privilege of being children of God by the grace of adoption, and (2) the unity of Christians who commonly call God "Our" Father. God's **name** is **hallowed** when we praise and glorify Him by righteous words and deeds. God's **kingdom** and **will** are closely related: we pray they may be actualized **on earth** as they are **in heaven,** where God's reign is gloriously manifest.

11:3 Daily (Gr. *epiousios*) can also mean the "essential" bread which many Church Fathers understood as (1) the truth of God's Word for daily sustenance, or (2) the sacramental bread of the Eucharist, Christ Himself.

11:4 Willingness to **forgive everyone** is a prerequisite to being forgiven by God. To be **indebted** means to have committed a sin against another. Although God tests us, He does **not lead us into temptation.** Deliverance **from the evil one** (rather than from evil in the abstract) is the classic patristic understanding of this petition. (See comments on Matt. 6:9–13.)

11:8 Jesus praises **persistence** even if it seems inopportune and bothersome. Persistence in prayer helps us to focus our attention on God.

11:9 We **ask** in prayer, **seek** through study, and **knock** through righteous living.

11:13 Evil is used here in the general sense of all human beings being weak and sinful. If Jesus promises to **give the Holy Spirit to those who ask Him,** how is it that we ask? The Church, since the early days, has provided this prayer: "O Heavenly King, O Comforter, the Spirit of truth, who are in all places and fill all things, the Treasure of good things, and Giver of life, come and abide in us, cleanse us from every stain and save our souls, O Good One."

when the demon had gone out, that
the mute spoke; and the multitudes
marveled.
15 But some of them said, [a]"He
casts out demons by [1]Beelzebub, the
ruler of the demons."†
16 Others, testing *Him*, [a]sought
from Him a sign from heaven.†

Spiritual Power, Spiritual War

(Matt. 12:24–32, 43–45; Mark 3:23–30)

17 [a]But [b]He, knowing their
thoughts, said to them: "Every kingdom divided against itself is brought
to desolation, and a house *divided*
against a house falls.
18 "If Satan also is divided against
himself, how will his kingdom
stand? Because you say I cast out demons by Beelzebub.
19 "And if I cast out demons by
Beelzebub, by whom do your sons
cast *them* out? Therefore they will be
your judges.†
20 "But if I cast out demons
[a]with the finger of God, surely the
kingdom of God has come upon
you.†
21 [a]"When a strong man, fully
armed, guards his own palace, his
goods are in peace.
22 "But [a]when a stronger than he
comes upon him and overcomes
him, he takes from him all his armor
in which he trusted, and divides his
[1]spoils.

15 [a]Matt. 9:34; 12:24 [1]NU, M *Beelzebul*
16 [a]Matt. 12:38; 16:1; Mark 8:11
17 [a]Matt. 12:25–29; Mark 3:23–27 [b]Matt. 9:4; John 2:25
20 [a]Ex. 8:19
21 [a]Matt. 12:29; Mark 3:27
22 [a][Is. 53:12; Col. 2:15] [1]*plunder*
23 [a]Matt. 12:30; Mark 9:40
24 [a]Matt. 12:43–45; Mark 1:27; 3:11; 5:13; Acts 5:16; 8:7
26 [a]John 5:14; [Heb. 6:4–6; 10:26; 2 Pet. 2:20]
27 [a]Luke 1:28, 48
28 [a]Ps. 1:1, 2; 112:1; 119:1, 2; Is. 48:17, 18; [Matt. 7:21; Luke 8:21]; James 1:25
29 [a]Matt. 12:38–42 [b]1 Cor. 1:22 [1]NU omits *the prophet*
30 [a]Jon. 1:17; 2:10; 3:3–10; Luke 24:46; Acts 10:40; 1 Cor. 15:4

23 [a]"He who is not with Me is
against Me, and he who does not
gather with Me scatters.†
24 [a]"When an unclean spirit goes
out of a man, he goes through dry
places, seeking rest; and finding
none, he says, 'I will return to my
house from which I came.'†
25 "And when he comes, he finds
it swept and put in order.
26 "Then he goes and takes with
him seven other spirits more wicked
than himself, and they enter and
dwell there; and [a]the last *state* of that
man is worse than the first."
27 And it happened, as He spoke
these things, that a certain woman
from the crowd raised her voice and
said to Him, [a]"Blessed *is* the womb
that bore You, and *the* breasts which
nursed You!"†
28 But He said, [a]"More than that,
blessed *are* those who hear the word
of God and keep it!"

Spiritual Perception: A Sign

(Matt. 12:38–42)

29 [a]And while the crowds were
thickly gathered together, He began
to say, "This is an evil generation.
It seeks a [b]sign, and no sign will be
given to it except the sign of Jonah
[1]the prophet.†
30 "For as [a]Jonah became a sign to
the Ninevites, so also the Son of Man
will be to this generation.

11:15 Beelzebub: a pagan god, derided by Jews as "The Lord of the Flies." Here it is a direct reference to Satan (v. 18).

11:16 A sign from heaven would be a spectacular miracle validating Jesus' authority. Jesus refused to do such a sign in His temptations in the wilderness by the devil, and He declines here as well (vv. 29, 30).

11:19 Exorcisms were part of the tradition of the Jews (see Acts 19:13).

11:20 The **finger of God** is the Holy Spirit (Matt. 12:28).

11:23 This verse is seemingly the opposite of 9:50: "He who is not against us is on our side." Here however, the unique action of gathering or scattering is the issue: each person does one or the other.

11:24–26 Those who have been cleansed are here warned not to be careless. **Dry places,** deserts, were thought to be the abode of demons.

11:27, 28 God's blessing falls not upon those who have prominent family connections, but upon those **who hear the word of God and keep it.** Jesus is stating a principle, not denigrating His mother: she both heard God's word and kept it, and thus became the most blessed of women (1:28–38, 42).

11:29–32 The sign of Jonah is **the preaching of Jonah** (v. 32) under which the Ninevites repented. By contrast, this **evil generation** (v. 29) did not repent under Jesus' preaching,

(continued on next page)

31 [a]"The queen of the South will
rise up in the judgment with the men
of this generation and condemn
them, for she came from the ends
of the earth to hear the wisdom of
Solomon; and indeed a [b]greater than
Solomon *is* here.
32 "The men of Nineveh will rise
up in the judgment with this generation and condemn it, for [a]they repented at the preaching of Jonah;
and indeed a greater than Jonah *is*
here.

Spiritual Perception: A Light to See By

33 [a]"No one, when he has lit a
lamp, puts *it* in a secret place or under a [b]basket, but on a lampstand,
that those who come in may see the
light.†
34 [a]"The lamp of the body is the
eye. Therefore, when your eye is
[1]good, your whole body also is full
of light. But when *your eye* is [2]bad,
your body also *is* full of darkness.
35 "Therefore take heed that the
light which is in you is not darkness.
36 "If then your whole body *is* full
of light, having no part dark, *the*
whole *body* will be full of light, as
when the bright shining of a lamp
gives you light."

The Pride of the Pharisees

37 And as He spoke, a certain
Pharisee asked Him to dine with
him. So He went in and sat down
to eat.
38 [a]When the Pharisee saw *it,* he
marveled that He had not first
washed before dinner.†
39 [a]Then the Lord said to him,
"Now you Pharisees make the outside of the cup and dish clean, but
[b]your inward part is full of [1]greed
and wickedness.
40 "Foolish ones! Did not [a]He who
made the outside make the inside
also?
41 [a]"But rather give alms of [1]such
things as you have; then indeed all
things are clean to you.†
42 [a]"But woe to you Pharisees! For
you tithe the mint and rue and all manner of herbs, and [b]pass by justice
and the [c]love of God. These you
ought to have done, without leaving
the others undone.†
43 [a]"Woe to you Pharisees! For
you love the [1]best seats in the synagogues and greetings in the
marketplaces.
44 [a]"Woe to you, [1]scribes and
Pharisees, hypocrites! [b]For you are
like graves which are not seen, and
the men who walk over *them* are not
aware *of them.*"
45 Then one of the lawyers answered and said to Him, "Teacher,
by saying these things You reproach
us also."
46 And He said, "Woe to you also,
lawyers! [a]For you load men with
burdens hard to bear, and you yourselves do not touch the burdens with
one of your fingers.
47 [a]"Woe to you! For you build the
tombs of the prophets, and your fathers killed them.
48 "In fact, you bear witness that
you approve the deeds of your fa-

31 [a]1 Kin. 10:1–9; 2 Chr. 9:1–8 [b][Is. 9:6; Rom. 9:5]
32 [a]Jon. 3:5
33 [a]Matt. 5:15; Mark 4:21; Luke 8:16 [b]Matt. 5:15
34 [a]Matt. 6:22, 23 [1]Clear, or healthy [2]Evil, or unhealthy
38 [a]Matt. 15:2; Mark 7:2, 3
39 [a]Matt. 23:25 [b]Gen. 6:5; Titus 1:15 [1]Lit. *eager grasping* or *robbery*
40 [a]Gen. 1:26, 27
41 [a]Is. 58:7; Dan. 4:27; [Luke 12:33; 16:9] [1]Or *what is inside*
42 [a]Matt. 23:23 [b][Mic. 6:7, 8] [c]John 5:42
43 [a]Matt. 23:6; Mark 12:38, 39; Luke 14:7; 20:46 [1]Or *places of honor*
44 [a]Matt. 23:27 [b]Ps. 5:9 [1]NU omits *scribes and Pharisees, hypocrites*
46 [a]Matt. 23:4
47 [a]Matt. 23:29; Acts 7:52

(continued from previous page)
which is far **greater than Jonah** (v. 32). In Matthew, the sign of Jonah is also Jonah's three-day sojourn in the belly of the great fish, a picture of Christ's death and Resurrection (Matt. 12:40).

11:33–36 Spiritual sight is compared to physical sight: if the eyes of both body and soul are healthy, a person is full of light (see notes on Matt. 5:13–16; 6:22, 23).

11:38 Washing the hands before eating was an important religious ritual for the Pharisees. They are concerned about outward cleanliness; Jesus says internal purity is more important.

11:41 Deeds of love toward people, such as giving **alms,** purify the inward man. External things like food and clothing cannot defile one who is inwardly pure.

11:42–52 After their testy attacks against Him, Jesus pronounces a series of denunciations against the Pharisees and scribes. (In v. 45, **lawyers** are experts in the Mosaic Law; for comments on the woes see Matt. 23.)

Commemoration of Holy Prophets

11:47–54: Jesus reproaches the Jews for their treatment of the prophets.

Commemoration of a Holy Martyr

12:1–12: The holy martyrs proclaimed the Word of God fearlessly and in faith.

thers; for they indeed killed them, and you build their tombs.

49 "Therefore the wisdom of God also said, [a]'I will send them prophets and apostles, and *some* of them they will kill and persecute,'

50 "that the blood of all the prophets which was shed from the foundation of the world may be required of this generation,

51 [a]"from the blood of Abel to [b]the blood of Zechariah who perished between the altar and the temple. Yes, I say to you, it shall be required of this generation.

52 [a]"Woe to you lawyers! For you have taken away the key of knowledge. You did not enter in yourselves, and those who were entering in you hindered."

53 [1]And as He said these things to them, the scribes and the Pharisees began to assail *Him* vehemently, and to cross-examine Him about many things,

54 lying in wait for Him, [1]and [a]seeking to catch Him in something He might say, [2]that they might accuse Him.

Against Hypocrisy

12 In [a]the meantime, when an innumerable multitude of people had gathered together, so that they trampled one another, He began to say to His disciples first *of all*, [b]"Beware of the [1]leaven of the Pharisees, which is hypocrisy.†

2 [a]"For there is nothing covered that will not be revealed, nor hidden that will not be known.

3 "Therefore whatever you have spoken in the dark will be heard in the light, and what you have spoken in the ear in inner rooms will be proclaimed on the housetops.

4 [a]"And I say to you, [b]My friends, do not be afraid of those who kill the body, and after that have no more that they can do.†

5 "But I will show you whom you should fear: Fear Him who, after He has killed, has power to cast into hell; yes, I say to you, [a]fear Him!

6 "Are not five sparrows sold for two [1]copper coins? And [a]not one of them is forgotten before God.

7 "But the very hairs of your head are all numbered. Do not fear therefore; you are of more value than many sparrows.

8 [a]"Also I say to you, whoever confesses Me [b]before men, him the Son of Man also will confess before the angels of God.†

9 "But he who [a]denies Me before men will be denied before the angels of God.

49 [a]Matt. 23:34
51 [a]Gen. 4:8 [b]2 Chr. 24:20, 21
52 [a]Matt. 23:13
53 [1]NU *And when He left there*
54 [a]Mark 12:13 [1]NU omits *and seeking* [2]NU omits *that they might accuse Him*

CHAPTER 12

1 [a]Mark 8:15 [b]Matt. 16:12 [1]*yeast*
2 [a]Matt. 10:26; [1 Cor. 4:5]
4 [a]Is. 51:7, 8, 12, 13 [b][John 15:13–15]
5 [a]Ps. 119:120
6 [a]Matt. 6:26 [1]Gr. *assarion*, a coin worth about 1/16 of a denarius
8 [a]Matt. 10:32 [b]Ps. 119:46
9 [a]Matt. 10:33

12:1–3 Jesus warns against **hypocrisy** (v. 1). All pretense and hidden evils will be exposed by God's light.

12:4–7 In the face of persecution and dangers the disciples are to fear only God, in whose power and providential care lies each person's ultimate destiny.

12:8, 9 True discipleship means public confession of Jesus as **the Son of Man** (Dan. 7:13), who is the Messiah and the eternal Son of God.

10 "And [a]anyone who speaks a
word against the Son of Man, it will
be forgiven him; but to him who
blasphemes against the Holy Spirit,
it will not be forgiven.†
11 [a]"Now when they bring you to
the synagogues and magistrates and
authorities, do not worry about how
or what you should answer, or what
you should say.
12 "For the Holy Spirit will [a]teach
you in that very hour what you
ought to say."

Against Greed and Anxiety

13 **Then one from the crowd said
to Him, "Teacher, tell my brother to
divide the inheritance with me."†**
14 **But He said to him,** [a]"Man, who
made Me a judge or an arbitrator
over you?"
15 **And He said to them,** [a]"Take
heed and beware of [1]covetousness,
for one's life does not consist in the
abundance of the things he
possesses."
16 **Then He spoke a parable to
them, saying:** "The ground of a certain rich man yielded plentifully.†
17 "And he thought within himself, saying, 'What shall I do, since
I have no room to store my
crops?'
18 "So he said, 'I will do this: I will
pull down my barns and build
greater, and there I will store all my
crops and my goods.
19 'And I will say to my soul,
[a]"Soul, you have many goods laid
up for many years; take your ease;
[b]eat, drink, *and* be merry." '
20 "But God said to him, 'Fool!
This night [a]your soul will be required of you; [b]then whose will
those things be which you have
provided?'
21 "So *is* he who lays up treasure
for himself, [a]and is not rich toward
God."
22 **Then He said to His disciples,**
"Therefore I say to you, [a]do not
worry about your life, what you will
eat; nor about the body, what you
will put on.†
23 "Life is more than food, and the
body *is more* than clothing.
24 "Consider the ravens, for they
neither sow nor reap, which have
neither storehouse nor barn; and
[a]God feeds them. Of how much
more value are you than the
birds?
25 "And which of you by worrying
can add one cubit to his stature?
26 "If you then are not able to do
the least, why [1]are you anxious for
the rest?
27 "Consider the lilies, how they
grow: they neither toil nor spin; and
yet I say to you, even [a]Solomon in
all his glory was not [1]arrayed like one
of these.
28 "If then God so clothes the
grass, which today is in the field and
tomorrow is thrown into the oven,
how much more *will He clothe* you,
O *you* of [a]little faith?
29 "And do not seek what you
should eat or what you should drink,
nor have an anxious mind.
30 "For all these things the nations
of the world seek after, and your Father [a]knows that you need these
things.
31 [a]"But seek [1]the kingdom of
God, and all these things shall be
added to you.
32 "Do not fear, little flock, for

10 [a][Matt. 12:31, 32; Mark 3:28; 1 John 5:16]
11 [a]Matt. 6:25; 10:19; Mark 13:11
12 [a][John 14:26]
14 [a][John 18:36]
15 [a][1 Tim. 6:6–10] [1]NU *all covetousness*
19 [a]Eccl. 11:9; 1 Cor. 15:32; James 5:5 [b][Eccl. 2:24; 3:13; 5:18; 8:15]
20 [a]Job 27:8; Ps. 52:7; [James 4:14] [b]Ps. 39:6; Jer. 17:11
21 [a][Matt. 6:20; Luke 12:33; 1 Tim. 6:18, 19; James 2:5; 5:1–5]
22 [a]Matt. 6:25–33
24 [a]Job 38:41; Ps. 147:9
26 [1]*do you worry*
27 [a]1 Kin. 10:4–7; 2 Chr. 9:3–6 [1]*clothed*
28 [a]Matt. 6:30; 8:26; 14:31; 16:8
30 [a]Matt. 6:31, 32
31 [a]Matt. 6:33 [1]NU *His kingdom, and these things*

12:10 To say **a word against the Son of Man** is to reject His messianic claims. To many people, before their conversion, Jesus seems a mere man. Later, they are enlightened, repent and are **forgiven.** On the blasphemy **against the Holy Spirit,** see note on Matt. 12:32.

12:13–15 It was a tradition for respected rabbis to arbitrate personal disputes over property or money. But Jesus refuses to play the role of **judge** (v. 14) regarding material things, and instead issues a stern warning about greed (v. 15).

12:16–21 The rich man is a fool, despite his material success, because he vainly puts all his trust in his possessions rather than in God. To be **rich toward God** (v. 21) is to have a life of close communion with Him through faith and works.

12:22–31 This is an exhortation against **worry** (v. 22) and anxiety (v. 26), not against God-ordained planning and earnest work (see notes on Matt. 6:25–33).

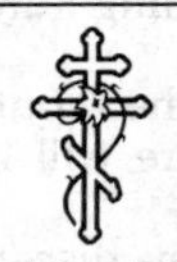

Commemoration of a Priest Martyr

12:32–40: The priest martyrs served God's flock faithfully at the expense of their lives.

[a]it is your Father's good pleasure to give you the kingdom.†
33 [a]"Sell what you have and give [b]alms; [c]provide yourselves money bags which do not grow old, a treasure in the heavens that does not fail, where no thief approaches nor moth destroys.†
34 "For where your treasure is, there your heart will be also.†

Against Laziness and Forgetfulness

35 [a]"Let your waist be girded and [b]*your* lamps burning;†
36 "and you yourselves be like men who wait for their master, when he will return from the wedding, that when he comes and knocks they may open to him immediately.†
37 [a]"Blessed *are* those servants whom the master, when he comes, will find watching. Assuredly, I say to you that he will gird himself and have them sit down *to eat,* and will come and serve them.†
38 "And if he should come in the second watch, or come in the third watch, and find *them* so, blessed are those servants.
39 [a]"But know this, that if the master of the house had known what hour the thief would come, he would [1]have watched and not allowed his house to be broken into.
40 [a]"Therefore you also be ready, for the Son of Man is coming at an hour you do not expect."†
41 **Then Peter said to Him, "Lord, do You speak this parable *only* to us, or to all *people?*"†**
42 **And the Lord said,** [a]"Who then is that faithful and wise steward, whom *his* master will make ruler over his household, to give *them their* portion of food [1]in due season?
43 "Blessed *is* that servant whom his master will find so doing when he comes.†
44 [a]"Truly, I say to you that he will make him ruler over all that he has.
45 [a]"But if that servant says in his heart, 'My master is delaying his coming,' and begins to beat the male and female servants, and to eat and drink and be drunk,
46 "the master of that servant will come on a [a]day when he is not looking for *him,* and at an hour when he is not aware, and will cut him in two and appoint *him* his portion with the unbelievers.
47 "And [a]that servant who [b]knew his master's will, and did not prepare

32 [a][Matt. 11:25, 26]
33 [a]Matt. 19:21 [b]Luke 11:41 [c]Matt. 6:20
35 [a][1 Pet. 1:13] [b][Matt. 25:1–13]
37 [a]Matt. 24:46
39 [a]Rev. 3:3; 16:15 [1]NU *not have allowed*
40 [a]Mark 13:33
42 [a]Matt. 24:45, 46; 25:21 [1]*at the right time*
44 [a]Matt. 24:47; 25:21
45 [a]2 Pet. 3:3, 4
46 [a]1 Thess. 5:3
47 [a]Deut. 25:2 [b][James 4:17]

12:32 Little flock: the band of disciples who have left everything behind in total commitment to Christ and the Kingdom.

12:33 Material riches suffer corruption; spiritual riches abide eternally.

12:34 This verse expresses a basic principle of human behavior: a strong warning to guard the heart, the door of inner spirituality.

12:35 A **girded** waist (as in a suit of military armor; see Eph. 6:14) renders one ready for action. **Lamps burning** suggests alertness in doing God's will.

12:36 This verse echoes the parable of the wise and foolish virgins (Matt. 25:1–13).

12:37–48 This is a longer version of a parable more simply recounted by Matthew (see Matt. 24:45–51).

12:40 The point of Christ's admonitions is that we should constantly be prepared for His Second Coming, the date being unannounced.

12:41 The nature of these admonitions suggests Jesus is speaking about matters of concern **to all people.**

12:43–48 The master requires not merely vigilant waiting, but also actively **doing** God's appointed tasks.

himself or do according to his will,
shall be beaten with many *stripes*.
48 [a]"But he who did not know, yet
committed things deserving of
stripes, shall be beaten with few. For
everyone to whom much is given,
from him much will be required; and
to whom much has been committed,
of him they will ask the more.

Against Lack of Discernment

49 [a]"I came to send fire on the
earth, and how I wish it were already
kindled!†
50 "But [a]I have a baptism to be
baptized with, and how distressed I
am till it is [b]accomplished!†
51 [a]"Do *you* suppose that I came
to give peace on earth? I tell you,
not at all, [b]but rather division.†
52 [a]"For from now on five in one
house will be divided: three against
two, and two against three.
53 [a]"Father will be divided against
son and son against father, mother
against daughter and daughter
against mother, mother-in-law
against her daughter-in-law and
daughter-in-law against her mother-
in-law."
54 Then He also said to the multitudes, [a]"Whenever you see a cloud
rising out of the west, immediately

48 [a][Lev. 5:17]; Num. 15:29; [1 Tim. 1:13]
49 [a]Luke 12:51
50 [a]Matt. 20:18, 22, 23; Mark 10:38 [b]John 12:27; 19:30
51 [a]Matt. 10:34–36 [b]Mic. 7:6; John 7:43; 9:16; 10:19; Acts 14:4
52 [a]Matt. 10:35; Mark 13:12
53 [a]Matt. 10:21, 36
54 [a]Matt. 16:2, 3
55 [a]Job 37:17
56 [a]Luke 19:41–44
58 [a]Prov. 25:8; Matt. 5:25, 26 [b][Ps. 32:6; Is. 55:6]

CHAPTER 13
1 [1]*mixed*

you say, 'A shower is coming'; and
so it is.†
55 "And when you see the [a]south
wind blow, you say, 'There will be
hot weather'; and there is.
56 "Hypocrites! You can discern
the face of the sky and of the earth,
but how *is it* you do not discern
[a]this time?
57 "Yes, and why, even of yourselves, do you not judge what is
right?†
58 [a]"When you go with your adversary to the magistrate, make
every effort [b]along the way to settle
with him, lest he drag you to the
judge, the judge deliver you to the
officer, and the officer throw you into
prison.
59 "I tell you, you shall not depart
from there till you have paid the very
last mite."

What Happens to the Unrepentant

13 There were present at that
season some who told Him
about the Galileans whose blood Pilate had [1]mingled with their sacrifices.†
2 And Jesus answered and said to
them, "Do you suppose that these
Galileans were worse sinners than all
other Galileans, because they suffered such things?

12:49 Fire on the earth is either (1) the fire of judgment and the anticipated divisions resulting from uncompromising loyalty to Christ, or (2) the gift of the Holy Spirit poured out as tongues of fire upon the disciples on Pentecost.

12:50 Baptism here is a reference to Christ's Passion.

12:51–53 Jesus' words are tinged with irony. Indeed He came to bring peace to the world, but uncompromising witness to truth inevitably causes controversies and divisions even within households.

12:54–56 These **hypocrites** are those who pretend to have insight into all things (here, the weather) but cannot see that in Jesus' words and works the long-awaited Kingdom of God is dawning.

12:57–59 Jesus gives another warning concerning discerning **what is right.** Just as one should know when to negotiate a reconciliation with an opponent before suffering greater loss, so also one should know to come to terms with the claims of Christ before having to face His dread judgment.

13:1–5 These two historical incidents (vv. 1 and 4) are reported in no other source except Luke. The slain **Galileans** were probably Zealots, Jewish nationalists who triggered some disturbance against the Romans in the temple area. The collapse of the **tower in Siloam** may have been simply an accident, rather than an act of sabotage, which people thought of as divine justice on sinners. Jesus passes judgment on neither group. He only registers these tragic events to warn that, unless His listeners respond to His message and repent, they would **all likewise perish** (v. 5). Perish may have the double meaning of both physical and spiritual death.

3 "I tell you, no; but unless you
repent you will all likewise perish.
4 "Or those eighteen on whom
the tower in Siloam fell and killed
them, do you think that they were
worse sinners than all *other* men who
dwelt in Jerusalem?
5 "I tell you, no; but unless you
repent you will all likewise perish."

The Critical Time of Repentance

6 He also spoke this parable:
[a]"A certain *man* had a fig tree
planted in his vineyard, and he came
seeking fruit on it and found none.†
7 "Then he said to the keeper of
his vineyard, 'Look, for three years
I have come seeking fruit on this fig
tree and find none. Cut it down; why
does it [1]use up the ground?'
8 "But he answered and said to
him, 'Sir, let it alone this year also,
until I dig around it and fertilize *it*.
9 [1]'And if it bears fruit, *well*. But
if not, after that you can [a]cut it
down.' "

A Woman Healed on the Sabbath

10 Now He was teaching in one of
the synagogues on the Sabbath.
11 And behold, there was a woman
who had a spirit of infirmity eighteen
years, and was bent over and could
in no way [1]raise *herself* up.
12 But when Jesus saw her, He
called *her* to *Him* and said to her,
"Woman, you are loosed from your
[a]infirmity."
13 [a]And He laid *His* hands on her,
and immediately she was made
straight, and glorified God.
14 But the ruler of the synagogue
answered with indignation, because
Jesus had [a]healed on the Sabbath;
and he said to the crowd, [b]"There
are six days on which men ought to
work; therefore come and be healed
on them, and [c]not on the Sabbath
day."†
15 The Lord then answered him
and said, [1]"Hypocrite! [a]Does not
each one of you on the Sabbath loose
his ox or donkey from the stall, and
lead *it* away to water it?
16 "So ought not this woman,
[a]being a daughter of Abraham,
whom Satan has bound—think of
it—for eighteen years, be loosed
from this bond on the Sabbath?"
17 And when He said these things,
all His adversaries were put to
shame; and all the multitude rejoiced
for all the glorious things that were
[a]done by Him.

Parables of the Kingdom

(Matt. 13:31, 32; Mark 4:30–32)

18 [a]Then He said, "What is the
kingdom of God like? And to what
shall I compare it?
19 "It is like a mustard seed, which
a man took and put in his garden;
and it grew and became a [1]large tree,
and the birds of the air nested in its
branches."†
20 And again He said, "To what
shall I liken the kingdom of God?
21 "It is like [1]leaven, which a
woman took and hid in three
[a]measures[2] of meal till it was all leavened."†

6 [a]Is. 5:2; Matt. 21:19
7 [1]*waste*
9 [a][John 15:2] [1]NU *And if it bears fruit after that, well. But if not, you can*
11 [1]*straighten up*
12 [a]Luke 7:21; 8:2
13 [a]Mark 16:18; Acts 9:17
14 [a][Luke 6:6–11; 14:1–6]; John 5:16 [b]Ex. 20:9; 23:12 [c]Matt. 12:10; Mark 3:2; Luke 6:7; 14:3
15 [a][Matt. 7:5; 23:13]; Luke 14:5 [1]NU, M *Hypocrites*
16 [a]Luke 19:9
17 [a]Mark 5:19, 20
18 [a]Matt. 13:31, 32; Mark 4:30–32
19 [1]NU omits *large*
21 [a]Matt. 13:33 [1]*yeast* [2]Gr. *sata*, same as Heb. *seah*; approximately 2 pecks in all

---

13:6–9 Here Luke gives his account of the fruitless **fig tree.** It is spared from the curse, at least for a time. (See notes on Matt. 21:19 and Mark 11:13, 14, 20–24.) In the OT the fig tree symbolizes Israel, which receives God's loving care in the expectation of a fruitful harvest. **Three years** (v. 7) probably represents the three-year ministry of Christ. Because of the pleading of an unknown vineyard **keeper,** the Master allows additional time for true repentance and fruitfulness before judgment occurs.

13:14–16 Acts of help toward others **on the Sabbath** were considered work and were forbidden, except in life-threatening situations. Jesus notes that if animals needing water were cared for on the Sabbath, certainly a woman of Israel could be delivered from Satan's bondage on the Sabbath.

13:19 The **mustard seed** is tiny, but the plant grows to a height of about 10 feet in Palestine.

13:21 A small amount of **leaven** inevitably penetrates the entire dough. Such is the power of the Kingdom. (See note on Matt. 13:31–33.)

Strive to Be Saved

22 [a]And He went through the cities and villages, teaching, and journeying toward Jerusalem.
23 Then one said to Him, "Lord, are there [a]few who are saved?" And He said to them,
24 [a]"Strive to enter through the narrow gate, for [b]many, I say to you, will seek to enter and will not be able.†
25 [a]"When once the Master of the house has risen up and [b]shut the door, and you begin to stand outside and knock at the door, saying, [c]'Lord, Lord, open for us,' and He will answer and say to you, [d]'I do not know you, where you are from,'
26 "then you will begin to say, 'We ate and drank in Your presence, and You taught in our streets.'
27 [a]"But He will say, 'I tell you I do not know you, where you are from. [b]Depart from Me, all you workers of iniquity.'†
28 [a]"There will be weeping and gnashing of teeth, [b]when you see Abraham and Isaac and Jacob and all the prophets in the kingdom of God, and yourselves thrust out.
29 "They will come from the east and the west, from the north and the south, and sit down in the kingdom of God.†
30 [a]"And indeed there are last who will be first, and there are first who will be last."

Jesus Presses on Toward Jerusalem

31 [1]On that very day some Pharisees came, saying to Him, "Get out and depart from here, for Herod wants to kill You."†
32 And He said to them, "Go, tell that fox, 'Behold, I cast out demons and perform cures today and tomorrow, and the third *day* [a]I shall be [1]perfected.'†
33 "Nevertheless I must journey today, tomorrow, and the *day* following; for it cannot be that a prophet should perish outside of Jerusalem.†
34 [a]"O Jerusalem, Jerusalem, the one who kills the prophets and stones those who are sent to her! How often I wanted to gather your children together, as a hen *gathers* her brood under *her* wings, but you were not willing!†
35 "See! [a]Your house is left to you desolate; and [1]assuredly, I say to you, you shall not see Me until *the time* comes when you say, [b]*'Blessed is He who comes in the name of the* LORD!' "†

22 [a]Mark 6:6
23 [a][Matt. 7:14; 20:16]
24 [a][Matt. 7:13] [b][John 7:34; 8:21; 13:33]
25 [a]Is. 55:6 [b]Matt. 25:10 [c]Luke 6:46 [d]Matt. 7:23; 25:12
27 [a][Matt. 7:23; 25:41] [b]Ps. 6:8
28 [a]Matt. 8:12; 13:42; 24:51 [b]Matt. 8:11
30 [a][Matt. 19:30; 20:16]
31 [1]NU *In that very hour*
32 [a][Heb. 2:10; 5:9; 7:28] [1]Resurrected
34 [a]Matt. 23:37–39
35 [a]Lev. 26:31, 32 [b]Ps. 118:26; Matt. 21:9 [1]NU, M omit *assuredly*

13:24 The narrow gate is a path to salvation marked by Jesus' teaching on discipleship and its cost.

13:27 Jesus says **I do not know you** because they are **workers of iniquity.** If a person is not abiding in Christ, neither verbal confessions (**"Lord, Lord,"** v. 25) nor previous experiences with Christ (v. 26) will be of any avail at the Judgment.

13:29, 30 People of humble faith from all parts of the earth will join together in God's consummated Kingdom. Those who vainly think themselves secure because of honored status **will be last.**

13:31 This warning of **some Pharisees** may well be sincere, or it could be a cunning way to get Jesus to Judea so they could enforce their authority against Him. **Herod** Antipas imprisoned and beheaded John the Baptist.

13:32 Jesus does not mince words in calling Herod **fox** for his sly craftiness. **Perfected** refers to the completion of Jesus' mission through His Passion and Resurrection in Jerusalem. He has nothing to fear from Herod.

13:33 Jerusalem, the center of religious authority, often was the site of the judgment and persecution of God's prophets (v. 34). Jesus speaks with prophetic irony here.

13:34 Jesus' tender lament and judgment over unrepentant Jerusalem show He loves His adversaries as we are to love ours.

13:35 The time referred to is Palm Sunday, when Jesus will be acclaimed at His Triumphal Entry into Jerusalem.

A Man Healed on the Sabbath

14 Now it happened, as He went into the house of one of the rulers of the Pharisees to eat bread on the Sabbath, that they watched Him closely.†

2 And behold, there was a certain man before Him who had dropsy.†

3 And Jesus, answering, spoke to the lawyers and Pharisees, saying, [a]"Is it lawful to heal on the [1]Sabbath?"

4 But they kept silent. And He took *him* and healed him, and let him go.

5 Then He answered them, saying, [a]"Which of you, having a [1]donkey or an ox that has fallen into a pit, will not immediately pull him out on the Sabbath day?"

6 And they could not answer Him regarding these things.

Be Lowly

7 So He told a parable to those who were invited, when He noted how they chose the best places, saying to them:

8 "When you are invited by anyone to a wedding feast, do not sit down in the best place, lest one more honorable than you be invited by him;†

9 "and he who invited you and him come and say to you, 'Give place to this man,' and then you begin with shame to take the lowest place.

10 [a]"But when you are invited, go and sit down in the lowest place, so that when he who invited you comes he may say to you, 'Friend, go up higher.' Then you will have glory in the presence of those who sit at the table with you.

11 [a]"For whoever exalts himself will be [1]humbled, and he who humbles himself will be exalted."

Be Hospitable to the Lowly

12 Then He also said to him who invited Him, "When you give a dinner or a supper, do not ask your friends, your brothers, your relatives, nor rich neighbors, lest they also invite you back, and you be repaid.†

13 "But when you give a feast, invite [a]*the* poor, *the* [1]maimed, *the* lame, *the* blind.

14 "And you will be [a]blessed, because they cannot repay you; for you shall be repaid at the resurrection of the just."

Worldly Entanglements, Poor Excuses

(Matt. 22:1–14)

15 Now when one of those who sat at the table with Him heard these things, he said to Him, [a]"Blessed *is* he who shall eat [1]bread in the kingdom of God!"†

16 [a]Then He said to him, "A certain man gave a great supper and invited many,†

17 "and [a]sent his servant at supper time to say to those who were invited, 'Come, for all things are now ready.'

CHAPTER 14
3 [a]Matt. 12:10 [1]NU adds *or not*
5 [a][Ex. 23:5; Deut. 22:4]; Luke 13:15 [1]NU, M *son*
10 [a]Prov. 25:6, 7
11 [a]Job 22:29; Ps. 18:27; Prov. 29:23; Matt. 23:12; Luke 18:14; James 4:6; [1 Pet. 5:5] [1]*put down*
13 [a]Neh. 8:10, 12 [1]*crippled*
14 [a][Matt. 25:34–40]
15 [a]Rev. 19:9 [1]M *dinner*
16 [a]Matt. 22:2–14
17 [a]Prov. 9:2, 5

14:1 The **Pharisees** again exemplify a paradoxical, cunning combination of interest and suspicion. They receive Jesus for a meal and yet watch to catch Him as a lawbreaker.

14:2–5 Jesus' illustration builds on His words in 13:15.

14:8–11 This parable of good manners, found only in Luke, contrasts the virtue of humility with the vice of self-exaltation. Compare James 4:6: "God resists the proud, but gives grace to the humble."

14:12–14 This story of God's compassion toward the poor appears only in Luke. To share hospitality with the needy is to imitate God's love which welcomes the lowly into the banquet of His Kingdom.

14:15 This is an inspirational, although little-known, beatitude. The purpose of life is to join in the sharing of **bread in the kingdom of God,** a partaking of the eternal love of God.

14:16–24 This parable exemplifies God's Kingdom, imaged in the ministry of Christ and later in the Church. The Kingdom is filled with outcasts and Gentiles, while the unresponsive privileged guests shut themselves out with their **excuses** (v. 18). (See notes on Matt. 22:1–14.)

Sunday of the Holy Ancestors of Christ *Two Sundays before Christmas*
14:16–24: These faithful ones will taste of the Great Supper in the Kingdom.

18 "But they all with one *accord* began to make excuses. The first said
to him, 'I have bought a piece of
ground, and I must go and see it. I
ask you to have me excused.'
19 "And another said, 'I have
bought five yoke of oxen, and I am
going to test them. I ask you to have
me excused.'
20 "Still another said, 'I have married a wife, and therefore I cannot
come.'
21 "So that servant came and reported these things to his master.
Then the master of the house, being
angry, said to his servant, 'Go out
quickly into the streets and lanes of
the city, and bring in here *the* poor
and *the* [1]maimed and *the* lame and
the blind.'
22 "And the servant said, 'Master,
it is done as you commanded, and
still there is room.'
23 "Then the master said to the
servant, 'Go out into the highways
and hedges, and compel *them* to
come in, that my house may be
filled.†
24 'For I say to you [a]that none of
those men who were invited shall
taste my supper.' "

The Cost of Discipleship

25 Now great multitudes went
with Him. And He turned and said
to them,
26 [a]"If anyone comes to Me [b]and
does not hate his father and mother,
wife and children, brothers and sisters, [c]yes, and his own life also, he
cannot be My disciple.†
27 "And [a]whoever does not bear
his cross and come after Me cannot
be My disciple.†
28 "For [a]which of you, intending
to build a tower, does not sit down
first and count the cost, whether he
has *enough* to finish *it*—
29 "lest, after he has laid the
foundation, and is not able to
finish, all who see *it* begin to mock
him,
30 "saying, 'This man began to
build and was not able to finish.'
31 "Or what king, going to make
war against another king, does not
sit down first and consider whether
he is able with ten thousand to meet
him who comes against him with
twenty thousand?
32 "Or else, while the other is still
a great way off, he sends a delegation and asks conditions of
peace.
33 "So likewise, whoever of you
[a]does not forsake all that he has cannot be My disciple.
34 [a]"Salt *is* good; but if the salt has
lost its flavor, how shall it be
seasoned?†
35 "It is neither fit for the land nor
for the [1]dunghill, *but* men throw it
out. He who has ears to hear, let him
hear!"

21 [1]*crippled*
24 [a][Matt. 21:43; 22:8; Acts 13:46]
26 [a]Deut. 13:6; 33:9; Matt. 10:37 [b]Rom. 9:13 [c]Rev. 12:11
27 [a]Matt. 16:24; Mark 8:34; Luke 9:23; [2 Tim. 3:12]
28 [a]Prov. 24:27
33 [a]Matt. 19:27
34 [a]Matt. 5:13; [Mark 9:50]
35 [1]*rubbish heap*

14:23 Compel them indicates that God's plan is to fill His messianic banquet, and that even with refusals, His desire to fill His **house** will not be frustrated.

14:26 God has commanded man to love and honor, not to **hate his father and mother.** The word "hate" here represents a Semitic expression used in reference to ultimate commitments (see 16:13; Matt. 6:24). A follower of Christ works for loving relationships toward all, but his commitment to God carries absolute priority even over family ties.

14:27–33 Jesus gives several examples of what it means to carry one's cross, the cost of discipleship. To be a disciple means to count the cost, and pay it.

14:34, 35 To recover lost **flavor,** the true quality of discipleship, is not easy. Without it, a disciple becomes as useless as salt without seasoning power.

Sunday of the Prodigal Son *Third Sunday before Lent*

15:11–32: This great parable reminds us of our distance from God and our need for forgiveness.

The Lost Sheep
(Matt. 18:10–14)

15 Then [a]all the tax collectors
and the sinners drew near to
Him to hear Him.
2 And the Pharisees and scribes
complained, saying, "This Man
[1]receives sinners [a]and eats with
them."†
3 So He spoke this parable to
them, saying:
4 [a]"What man of you, having a
hundred sheep, if he loses one of
them, does not leave the ninety-nine
in the wilderness, and go after the
one which is lost until he finds it?
5 "And when he has found *it,* he
lays *it* on his shoulders, rejoicing.
6 "And when he comes home, he
calls together *his* friends and neighbors, saying to them, [a]'Rejoice with
me, for I have found my sheep
[b]which was lost!'
7 "I say to you that likewise there
will be more joy in heaven over one
sinner who repents [a]than over
ninety-nine [1]just persons who
[b]need no repentance.†

The Lost Coin

8 "Or what woman, having ten
silver [1]coins, if she loses one coin,
does not light a lamp, sweep the
house, and search carefully until she
finds *it?*
9 "And when she has found *it,*
she calls *her* friends and neighbors
together, saying, 'Rejoice with me,
for I have found the piece which I
lost!'
10 "Likewise, I say to you, there
is joy in the presence of the angels
of God over one sinner who
repents."

The Prodigal Son

11 **Then He said:** "A certain man
had two sons.†
12 "And the younger of them said
to *his* father, 'Father, give me the
portion of goods that falls *to me.*' So
he divided to them [a]*his* livelihood.†
13 "And not many days after, the
younger son gathered all together,
journeyed to a far country, and there
wasted his possessions with [1]prod-
igal living.
14 "But when he had spent all,
there arose a severe famine in that
land, and he began to be in want.
15 "Then he went and joined himself to a citizen of that country, and
he sent him into his fields to feed
swine.†
16 "And he would gladly have
filled his stomach with the [1]pods that
the swine ate, and no one gave him
anything.
17 "But when he came to himself,
he said, 'How many of my father's
hired servants have bread enough

CHAPTER 15
1 [a][Matt. 9:10–13]
2 [a]Acts 11:3; Gal. 2:12
[1]*welcomes*
4 [a]Matt. 18:12–14; 1 Pet. 2:25
6 [a][Rom. 12:15]
[b][Luke 19:10; 1 Pet. 2:10, 25]
7 [a][Luke 5:32]
[b][Mark 2:17]
[1]*upright*
8 [1]Gr. *drachma,* a valuable coin often worn in a ten-piece garland by married women
12 [a]Mark 12:44
13 [1]*wasteful*
16 [1]*carob pods*

15:2 Mealtime fellowship with tax collectors and sinners was considered to be defiling for pious Jews.

15:7 Joy in heaven for the repentance of each sinner is the main theme of this chapter. Jesus connects repentance with joy, not sadness.

15:11–32 This parable, perhaps the most magnificent of all parables, occurs only in Luke and illustrates God's unconditional love and forgiveness for the repentant sinner.

15:12 The **father** fulfills the request of the son out of profound respect for his freedom, and he lets him go for the same reason. God neither holds nor pulls anyone by force.

15:15 Consenting **to feed swine,** unclean and despised animals to Jews, is an act of utter desperation.

and to spare, and I perish with
hunger!†
18 'I will arise and go to my father,
and will say to him, "Father, [a]I have
sinned against heaven and before
you,
19 "and I am no longer worthy to
be called your son. Make me like one
of your hired servants."'
20 "And he arose and came to his
father. But [a]when he was still a great
way off, his father saw him and had
compassion, and ran and fell on his
neck and kissed him.†
21 "And the son said to him, 'Father, I have sinned against heaven
[a]and in your sight, and am no longer
worthy to be called your son.'
22 "But the father said to his servants, [1]'Bring out the best robe and
put *it* on him, and put a ring on his
hand and sandals on *his* feet.†
23 'And bring the fatted calf here
and kill *it*, and let us eat and be
merry;
24 [a]'for this my son was dead and
is alive again; he was lost and is
found.' And they began to be merry.
25 "Now his older son was in the
field. And as he came and drew near
to the house, he heard music and
dancing.†
26 "So he called one of the servants
and asked what these things meant.
27 "And he said to him, 'Your
brother has come, and because he
has received him safe and sound,
your father has killed the fatted
calf.'
28 "But he was angry and would
not go in. Therefore his father came
out and pleaded with him.
29 "So he answered and said to *his*
father, 'Lo, these many years I have
been serving you; I never transgressed your commandment at any
time; and yet you never gave me a
young goat, that I might make merry
with my friends.
30 'But as soon as this son of yours
came, who has devoured your livelihood with harlots, you killed the fatted calf for him.'
31 "And he said to him, 'Son, you
are always with me, and all that I
have is yours.
32 'It was right that we should
make merry and be glad, [a]for your
brother was dead and is alive again,
and was lost and is found.'"

The Unjust Steward

16 He also said to His disciples:
"There was a certain rich man
who had a steward, and an accusation was brought to him that this
man was [1]wasting his goods.†
2 "So he called him and said to
him, 'What is this I hear about you?
Give an [a]account of your stewardship, for you can no longer be
steward.'
3 "Then the steward said within
himself, 'What shall I do? For my
master is taking the stewardship
away from me. I cannot dig; I am
ashamed to beg.

18 [a]Ex. 9:27; 10:16; Num. 22:34; Josh. 7:20; 1 Sam. 15:24, 30; 26:21; 2 Sam. 12:13; 24:10, 17; Ps. 51:4; Matt. 27:4
20 [a][Jer. 3:12]; Matt. 9:36; [Acts 2:39; Eph. 2:13, 17]
21 [a]Ps. 51:4
22 [1]NU *Quickly bring*
24 [a]Matt. 8:22; Luke 9:60; 15:32; Rom. 11:15; [Eph. 2:1, 5; 5:14; Col. 2:13; 1 Tim. 5:6]
32 [a]Luke 15:24

CHAPTER 16

1 [1]*squandering*
2 [a][Rom. 14:12; 2 Cor. 5:10; 1 Pet. 4:5, 6]

15:17 Extreme need brings the prodigal son to his senses, but what draws him homeward is probably his father's love.

15:20 The father's tender actions show he never ceased looking for the return of his son, just as God always longs for the return of every sinner to His forgiving embrace. In Jewish culture, it was considered undignified for an older man to run, but that did not stop this **father.**

15:22–24 The father does not censure the contrite son, but celebrates his homecoming as of one who came alive from the dead. The symbolic significance of the **robe** is righteousness (Is. 61:10), the **ring** (a signet ring) is family identity (Hag. 2:23), and **sandals** refer to walking according to the gospel (Eph. 6:15).

15:25–32 The father also has to deal with the resentful **older son** (v. 25) and does so with the same gentle kindness shown to the younger. By contrast, this son shows a pharisaic attitude of self-righteousness and contempt for his brother, much like a Church member who does not wish to be bothered with visitors or new converts.

16:1, 2 Steward: a manager of a wealthy man's household and property. He is called to **give an account** (v. 2) because he is being dismissed, as his master no longer trusts him.

4 'I have resolved what to do, that when I am put out of the stewardship, they may receive me into their houses.'

5 "So he called every one of his master's debtors to *him*, and said to the first, 'How much do you owe my master?'

6 "And he said, 'A hundred [1]measures of oil.' So he said to him, 'Take your bill, and sit down quickly and write fifty.'

7 "Then he said to another, 'And how much do you owe?' So he said, 'A hundred [1]measures of wheat.' And he said to him, 'Take your bill, and write eighty.'

8 "So the master commended the unjust steward because he had dealt shrewdly. For the sons of this world are more shrewd in their generation than [a]the sons of light.†

9 "And I say to you, [a]make friends for yourselves by unrighteous [1]mammon, that when [2]you fail, they may receive you into an everlasting home.†

10 [a]"He who *is* faithful in *what is* least is faithful also in much; and he who is unjust in *what is* least is unjust also in much.†

11 "Therefore if you have not been faithful in the unrighteous mammon, who will commit to your trust the true *riches?*†

12 "And if you have not been faithful in what is another man's, who will give you what is your [a]own?†

13 [a]"No servant can serve two masters; for either he will hate the one and love the other, or else he will be loyal to the one and despise the other. You cannot serve God and mammon."†

Press for the Kingdom

14 Now the Pharisees, [a]who were lovers of money, also heard all these things, and they [1]derided Him.

15 And He said to them, "You are those who [a]justify yourselves [b]before men, but [c]God knows your hearts. For [d]what is highly esteemed among men is an abomination in the sight of God.†

16 [a]"The law and the prophets *were* until John. Since that time the kingdom of God has been preached, and everyone is pressing into it.†

17 [a]"And it is easier for heaven and earth to pass away than for one [1]tittle of the law to fail.†

18 [a]"Whoever divorces his wife and marries another commits adultery; and whoever marries her who is divorced from *her* husband commits adultery.†

6 [1]Gr. *batos,* same as Heb. *bath;* 8 or 9 gallons each
7 [1]Gr. *koros,* same as Heb. *kor;* 10 or 12 bushels each
8 [a][Eph. 5:8]
9 [a]Dan. 4:27 [1]Lit., in Aram., *wealth* [2]NU *it fails*
10 [a]Matt. 25:21
12 [a][1 Pet. 1:3, 4]
13 [a]Matt. 6:24
14 [a]Matt. 23:14 [1]Lit. *turned up their nose at*
15 [a]Luke 10:29 [b][Matt. 6:2, 5, 16] [c]Ps. 7:9 [d]1 Sam. 16:7
16 [a]Matt. 3:1–12; 4:17; 11:12, 13
17 [a]Is. 40:8; 51:6 [1]The smallest stroke in a Heb. letter
18 [a]1 Cor. 7:10, 11

16:8 The steward is **unjust** in his actions, which are not condoned, but his shrewdness is praised. This is meant as a lesson for **the sons of light,** the Christian believers, who ought to be as shrewd about their pursuit of godliness as unbelievers are about their businesses.

16:9 The reference to **unrighteous mammon** is a warning about the dangers of money, which can corrupt. The right use of wealth is to **make friends** among the poor and needy by sharing it with them. At death, these poor friends will be the first to welcome their benefactor into the eternal Kingdom.

16:10 Faithful means trustworthy. It is essential for a Christian disciple to be trustworthy in small as well as in great things.

16:11 True riches signify spiritual treasures.

16:12 What is your own implies one's own property. If one is not trustworthy in managing someone else's property, one can hardly expect to be given property of one's own.

16:13 Ultimate loyalty cannot be divided. Life is devoted either to God first or riches first, not both.

16:15 What is highly esteemed presumably refers to money.

16:16 The law and the prophets represent the OT period, ending with John the Baptist. **Pressing** into the Kingdom means earnestly seeking to enter into it.

16:17 Tittle: a tiny punctuation mark in written Hebrew. The smallest part of God's purposes behind His law will not fail to be accomplished.

16:18 Jesus, teaching the permanence of marriage, lays down a new rule, a standard of life in the Kingdom.

The Rich Man and Lazarus

19 "There was a certain rich man
who was clothed in purple and fine
linen and [1]fared sumptuously every
day.
20 "But there was a certain beggar
named Lazarus, full of sores, who
was laid at his gate,
21 "desiring to be fed with [1]the
crumbs which fell from the rich
man's table. Moreover the dogs came
and licked his sores.
22 "So it was that the beggar died,
and was carried by the angels to
[a]Abraham's bosom. The rich man
also died and was buried.†
23 "And being in torments in
Hades, he lifted up his eyes and saw
Abraham afar off, and Lazarus in his
bosom.
24 "Then he cried and said, 'Father
Abraham, have mercy on me, and
send Lazarus that he may dip the
tip of his finger in water and [a]cool
my tongue; for I [b]am tormented in
this flame.'
25 "But Abraham said, 'Son, [a]re-
member that in your lifetime you received your good things, and likewise Lazarus evil things; but now he
is comforted and you are tormented.†
26 'And besides all this, between
us and you there is a great gulf fixed,
so that those who want to pass from
here to you cannot, nor can those
from there pass to us.'†
27 "Then he said, 'I beg you therefore, father, that you would send
him to my father's house,
28 'for I have five brothers, that he
may testify to them, lest they also
come to this place of torment.'
29 "Abraham said to him, [a]'They
have Moses and the prophets; let
them hear them.'†
30 "And he said, 'No, father Abraham; but if one goes to them from
the dead, they will repent.'
31 "But he said to him, [a]'If they
do not hear Moses and the prophets,
[b]neither will they be persuaded
though one rise from the dead.' "

Leadership Is a Stewardship

(Matt. 18:6, 7, 15; Mark 9:42)

17 **Then He said to the disciples,**
[a]"It is impossible that no
[1]offenses should come, but [b]woe *to*
him through whom they do come!
2 "It would be better for him if a
millstone were hung around his
neck, and he were thrown into the
sea, than that he should [1]offend one
of these little ones.†
3 "Take heed to yourselves.
[a]If your brother sins [1]against you,
[b]rebuke him; and if he repents, forgive him.
4 "And if he sins against you
seven times in a day, and seven
times in a day returns [1]to you, saying, 'I repent,' you shall forgive
him."†
5 **And the apostles said to the**
Lord, "Increase our faith."†
6 [a]**So the Lord said,** "If you have
faith as a mustard seed, you can say
to this mulberry tree, 'Be pulled up
by the roots and be planted in the
sea,' and it would obey you.†

19 [1]*lived in luxury*
21 [1]NU *what fell*
22 [a]Matt. 8:11
24 [a]Zech. 14:12 [b][Is. 66:24; Mark 9:42–48]
25 [a]Job 21:13; Luke 6:24; James 5:5
29 [a]Is. 8:20; 34:16; [John 5:39, 45]; Acts 15:21; 17:11; [2 Tim. 3:15]
31 [a][John 5:46] [b]John 12:10, 11

CHAPTER 17

1 [a][1 Cor. 11:19] [b]Matt. 18:6, 7; 26:24; Mark 9:42; [2 Thess. 1:6]; Jude 11 [1]*stumbling blocks*
2 [1]*cause one of these little ones to stumble*
3 [a][Matt. 18:15, 21] [b]Lev. 19:17; [Prov. 17:10; Gal. 6:1; James 5:19, 20] [1]NU omits *against you*
4 [1]M omits *to you*
6 [a]Matt. 17:20; 21:21; [Mark 9:23; 11:23]; Luke 13:19

16:22 Abraham's bosom means heaven.

16:25 This conversation is not between God and the rich man, but between Abraham and the rich man.

16:26 A great gulf between Lazarus and the rich man signifies there is no possibility of transfer between heaven and hell after death. It should also be noted that neither poverty nor riches, in themselves, gain Lazarus and the rich man their irreversible places. The rich man goes to hell because of his hardness of heart; Lazarus to heaven because of his humble faith.

16:29 Moses and the prophets, that is, the OT Scriptures which testify to God.

17:2 Little ones: small children or those of humble status who are unable to defend themselves, but are under God's care.

17:4 Christians are to practice unlimited forgiveness (see note on Matt. 18:21–35).

17:5 Although **faith** is a gift from God, it can **increase** in strength and wisdom by God's grace and human willingness.

17:6 Jesus uses a deliberate exaggeration to emphasize the strength of genuine faith.

7 "And which of you, having a
servant plowing or tending sheep,
will say to him when he has come
in from the field, 'Come at once and
sit down to eat'?†
8 "But will he not rather say to
him, 'Prepare something for my supper, and gird yourself [a]and serve me
till I have eaten and drunk, and afterward you will eat and drink'?
9 "Does he thank that servant because he did the things that were
commanded [1]him? I think not.
10 "So likewise you, when you
have done all those things which you
are commanded, say, 'We are [a]un-
profitable servants. We have done
what was our duty to do.' "

The Ten Cleansed Lepers

11 Now it happened [a]as He went
to Jerusalem that He passed through
the midst of Samaria and Galilee.
12 Then as He entered a certain village, there met Him ten men who
were lepers, [a]who stood afar off.†
13 And they lifted up *their* voices
and said, "Jesus, Master, have mercy
on us!"
14 So when He saw *them*, He said
to them, [a]"Go, show yourselves to
the priests." And so it was that as
they went, they were cleansed.
15 And one of them, when he saw
that he was healed, returned, and
with a loud voice [a]glorified God,
16 and fell down on *his* face at His
feet, giving Him thanks. And he was
a [a]Samaritan.†

8 [a][Luke 12:37]
9 [1]NU omits the rest of v. 9; M omits *him*
10 [a]Rom. 3:12; 11:35
11 [a]Luke 9:51, 52
12 [a]Lev. 13:46
14 [a]Matt. 8:4
15 [a]Luke 5:25; 18:43
16 [a]2 Kin. 17:24
19 [a]Matt. 9:22
21 [a]Luke 17:23 [b][Rom. 14:17] [1]NU reverses *here* and *there* [2]*in your midst*
22 [a]Matt. 9:15
23 [a]Matt. 24:23 [1]NU reverses *here* and *there*
24 [a]Matt. 24:27
25 [a]Mark 8:31; 9:31; 10:33 [b]Luke 9:22
26 [a]Matt. 24:37–39 [b][Gen. 6:5–7] [c][Gen. 6:8–13] [d]1 Pet. 3:20

17 So Jesus answered and said,
"Were there not ten cleansed? But
where *are* the nine?
18 "Were there not any found who
returned to give glory to God except
this foreigner?"
19 [a]And He said to him, "Arise,
go your way. Your faith has made
you well."

The Coming of the Kingdom

20 Now when He was asked by the
Pharisees when the kingdom of God
would come, He answered them and
said, "The kingdom of God does not
come with observation;†
21 [a]"nor will they say, [1]'See here!'
or 'See there!' For indeed, [b]the kingdom of God is [2]within you."†
22 Then He said to the disciples,
[a]"The days will come when you will
desire to see one of the days of the
Son of Man, and you will not see
it.†
23 [a]"And they will say to you,
[1]'Look here!' or 'Look there!' Do not
go after *them* or follow *them*.
24 [a]"For as the lightning that
flashes out of one *part* under heaven
shines to the other *part* under
heaven, so also the Son of Man will
be in His day.
25 [a]"But first He must suffer many
things and be [b]rejected by this
generation.
26 [a]"And as it [b]was in the [c]days
of [d]Noah, so it will be also in the
days of the Son of Man:†
27 "They ate, they drank, they

17:7–10 The purest faith is that which recognizes that we are servants who owe everything we are and have to God our Master. Thus, after fulfilling His commandments, we should humbly recognize that we are still **unprofitable** (v. 10), never worthy of all His gifts.

17:12 The lepers **stood afar off** because they were not permitted to approach people or enter into the villages.

17:16 Only **a Samaritan,** despised by Jews, sets the example of gratitude for his healing. God's blessings are all too easily taken for granted or forgotten.

17:20 With observation implies by external or tangible means measurable by man.

17:21 The **kingdom of God** is an invisible, spiritual reality present **within** the Christian believer. The Greek for "within you" can also be translated "among you" or "in your midst." To eyes that see, the mystery of the Kingdom is a radiant spiritual glory throughout creation.

17:22–24 Prior to Christ's Second Coming, Christians should not be misled by deceptive calls or signs. The glorious return of Christ will be as evident as **lightning.**

17:26–30 These verses are a warning to be prepared. The coming of Christ will be like a fire of judgment on many who are preoccupied with daily pursuits, but are oblivious of the things of God.

married wives, they were given in
marriage, until the [a]day that Noah
entered the ark, and the flood came
and [b]destroyed them all.
28 [a]"Likewise as it was also in the
days of Lot: They ate, they drank,
they bought, they sold, they planted,
they built;
29 "but on [a]the day that Lot went
out of Sodom it rained fire and brimstone from heaven and destroyed
them all.
30 "Even so will it be in the day
when the Son of Man [a]is revealed.
31 "In that day, he [a]who is on the
housetop, and his [1]goods *are* in the
house, let him not come down to
take them away. And likewise the
one who is in the field, let him not
turn back.†
32 [a]"Remember Lot's wife.
33 [a]"Whoever seeks to save his life
will lose it, and whoever loses his
life will preserve it.
34 [a]"I tell you, in that night there
will be two [1]*men* in one bed: the one
will be taken and the other will be
left.†
35 [a]"Two *women* will be grinding
together: the one will be taken and
the other left.
36 [1]"Two *men* will be in the field:
the one will be taken and the other
left."
37 And they answered and said to
Him, [a]"Where, Lord?" So He said
to them, "Wherever the body is,
there the eagles will be gathered together."†

The Tenacious Widow

18 Then He spoke a parable to
them, that men [a]always
ought to pray and not lose heart,†
2 saying: "There was in a certain
city a judge who did not fear God
nor [1]regard man.†
3 "Now there was a widow in that
city; and she came to him, saying,
[1]'Get justice for me from my adversary.'
4 "And he would not for a while;
but afterward he said within himself,
'Though I do not fear God nor regard
man,
5 [a]'yet because this widow troubles me I will [1]avenge her, lest by
her continual coming she weary
me.'"
6 Then the Lord said, "Hear what
the unjust judge said.
7 "And [a]shall God not avenge His
own elect who cry out day and night
to Him, though He bears long with
them?
8 "I tell you [a]that He will avenge
them speedily. Nevertheless, when
the Son of Man comes, will He really
find faith on the earth?"

The Pharisee and the Publican

9 Also He spoke this parable to
some [a]who trusted in themselves
that they were righteous, and despised others:
10 "Two men went up to the tem-

27 [a]Gen. 7:1–16 [b]Gen. 7:19–23
28 [a]Gen. 19
29 [a]Gen. 19:16, 24, 29
30 [a][2 Thess. 1:7]
31 [a]Mark 13:15 [1]*possessions*
32 [a]Gen. 19:26
33 [a]Matt. 10:39; 16:25
34 [a][1 Thess. 4:17] [1]Or *people*
35 [a]Matt. 24:40, 41
36 [1]NU, M omit v. 36.
37 [a]Matt. 24:28

CHAPTER 18
1 [a]Luke 11:5–10
2 [1]*respect*
3 [1]*Avenge me on*
5 [a]Luke 11:8 [1]*vindicate*
7 [a]Rev. 6:10
8 [a]Heb. 10:37
9 [a]Luke 10:29; 16:15

17:31–33 The absolute value of God's Kingdom requires urgent preparedness and decisive action to **preserve** one's life eternally.

17:34–36 The coming of Christ will entail a sudden, unexpected separation of destinies for friends and coworkers alike, depending on their preparedness for the Kingdom. **One will be taken and the other left** (v. 36): One *will be taken* to a place of judgment and death.

17:37 This proverb used by Jesus signifies that His glorious return will come as inevitably and clearly as birds of prey can be seen from afar gathering around a carcass (see Matt. 24:28). The disciples' question, **Where, Lord?** seems to refer to Jesus' earlier words (vv. 34–36).

18:1 To pray and not lose heart is a vital step in preparation for the coming of the Lord.

18:2–8 This parable, found only in Luke, illustrates the results of persistent prayer. If a helpless widow wins her case by persistent pleading before even a callous judge, how much more will God's **elect** find quick justice before a loving and righteous Father? Will Christ, upon His return, **find faith on the earth** (v. 8)? Each of us must take care to be part of His faithful remnant.

Sunday of the Publican and Pharisee *Fourth Sunday before Lent*

18:10–14: This parable reminds us to imitate the humility of the tax collector, not the pride of the Pharisee.

ple to pray, one a Pharisee and the
other a tax collector.†
11 "The Pharisee [a]stood and
prayed thus with himself, [b]'God, I
thank You that I am not like other
men—extortioners, unjust, adulterers, or even as this tax collector.†
12 'I fast twice a week; I give tithes
of all that I possess.'
13 "And the tax collector, standing
afar off, would not so much as raise
his eyes to heaven, but beat his
breast, saying, 'God, be merciful to
me a sinner!'†
14 "I tell you, this man went down
to his house justified *rather* than
the other; [a]for everyone who exalts
himself will be [1]humbled, and
he who humbles himself will be
exalted."†

Receive the Kingdom as a Child
(Matt. 19:13–15; Mark 10:13–16)

15 **[a]Then they also brought infants
to Him that He might touch them;
but when the disciples saw *it*, they
rebuked them.†**
16 **But Jesus called them to *Him*
and said,** "Let the little children
come to Me, and do not forbid them;
for [a]of such is the kingdom of God.

11 [a]Ps. 135:2 [b]Is. 1:15; 58:2; Rev. 3:17
14 [a]Job 22:29; Matt. 23:12; Luke 14:11; [James 4:6; 1 Pet. 5:5] [1]*put down*
15 [a]Matt. 19:13–15; Mark 10:13–16
16 [a]Matt. 18:3; 1 Cor. 14:20; 1 Pet. 2:2
17 [a]Matt. 18:3; 19:14; Mark 10:15
18 [a]Matt. 19:16–29; Mark 10:17–30
19 [a]Ps. 86:5; 119:68
20 [a]Ex. 20:12–16; Deut. 5:16–20; Mark 10:19; Rom. 13:9 [b]Eph. 6:2; Col. 3:20
21 [a]Phil. 3:6
22 [a]Matt. 6:19, 20; 19:21; [1 Tim. 6:19]

17 [a]"Assuredly, I say to you, whoever does not receive the kingdom
of God as a little child will by no
means enter it."

The Rich Young Man
(Matt. 19:16–26; Mark 10:17–23)

18 **[a]Now a certain ruler asked Him,
saying, "Good Teacher, what shall I
do to inherit eternal life?"†**
19 **So Jesus said to him,** "Why do
you call Me good? No one *is* good
but [a]One, *that is,* God.
20 "You know the command-
ments: [a]*'Do not commit adultery,'
'Do not murder,' 'Do not steal,' 'Do
not bear false witness,'* [b]*'Honor your
father and your mother.'* "
21 **And he said, "All [a]these things
I have kept from my youth."**
22 **So when Jesus heard these
things, He said to him,** "You still lack
one thing. [a]Sell all that you have and
distribute to the poor, and you will
have treasure in heaven; and come,
follow Me."
23 **But when he heard this, he became very sorrowful, for he was very
rich.**
24 **And when Jesus saw that he
became very sorrowful, He said,**

18:10 The sharp contrast between the two men is deliberately drawn by Jesus. The **Pharisee** is highly respected as a zealous observer of God's Law, whereas the **tax collector** is despised as a public sinner, collaborating with the Romans, cheating the people.

18:11 The Pharisee **prayed thus with himself** and not to God!

18:13 The tax collector's posture and words express his deep humility and contrition, the opposite of the Pharisee's attitude.

18:14 Justified: forgiven and made right with God. Jesus reverses the expected conclusion. In the eyes of God, it is the tax collector who is *justified* because of his humility. The Pharisee is condemned because of his self-righteousness and self-exaltation.

18:15–17 The blessing of children by respected rabbis was customary. Jesus uses the image of the child to convey the ideal of childlike simplicity and humility required to enter the Kingdom. (See note on Matt. 19:13–15.)

18:18–23 A rich ruler is challenged by Jesus not only to observe the Ten Commandments but also to sacrifice all things and follow Him. (See note on Matt. 19:16–22.) St. John Chrysostom teaches that because Jesus loved the man (Mark 10:21), He named these conditions for his particular need.

[a]"How hard it is for those who have
riches to enter the kingdom of God!†
25 "For it is easier for a camel to
go through the eye of a needle than
for a rich man to enter the kingdom
of God."
26 And those who heard it said,
"Who then can be saved?"
27 But He said, [a]"The things which
are impossible with men are possible
with God."

The Reward of Renunciation
(Matt. 19:27–30; Mark 10:28–31)

28 [a]Then Peter said, "See, we have
left [1]all and followed You."
29 So He said to them, "Assuredly,
I say to you, [a]there is no one who
has left house or parents or brothers
or wife or children, for the sake of
the kingdom of God,
30 [a]"who shall not receive many
times more in this present time, and
in the age to come eternal life."†

The Third Prophecy of the Passion
(Matt. 20:17–19; Mark 10:32–34)

31 [a]Then He took the twelve aside
and said to them, "Behold, we are
going up to Jerusalem, and all things
[b]that are written by the prophets
concerning the Son of Man will be
[1]accomplished.
32 "For [a]He will be delivered to the
Gentiles and will be mocked and insulted and spit upon.
33 "They will scourge *Him* and kill
Him. And the third day He will rise
again."
34 [a]But they understood none of
these things; this saying was hidden

24 [a]Prov. 11:28; Matt. 19:23; Mark 10:23
27 [a]Job 42:2; Jer. 32:17; Zech. 8:6; Matt. 19:26; Luke 1:37
28 [a]Matt. 19:27
[1]NU *our own*
29 [a]Deut. 33:9
30 [a]Job 42:10
31 [a]Matt. 16:21; 17:22; 20:17; Mark 10:32; Luke 9:51
[b]Ps. 22; [Is. 53]
[1]*fulfilled*
32 [a]Matt. 26:67; 27:2, 29, 41; Mark 14:65; 15:1, 19, 20, 31; Luke 23:1; John 18:28; Acts 3:13
34 [a]Mark 9:32; Luke 2:50; 9:45; [John 10:6; 12:16]
35 [a]Matt. 20:29–34; Mark 10:46–52
38 [a]Matt. 9:27
42 [a]Luke 17:19
43 [a]Luke 5:26; Acts 4:21; 11:18

CHAPTER 19

1 [a]Josh. 6:26; 1 Kin. 16:34
3 [a]John 12:21

from them, and they did not know
the things which were spoken.†

The Blind Man of Jericho Healed
(Mark 10:46–52)

35 [a]Then it happened, as He was
coming near Jericho, that a certain
blind man sat by the road begging.†
36 And hearing a multitude passing by, he asked what it meant.
37 So they told him that Jesus of
Nazareth was passing by.
38 And he cried out, saying,
"Jesus, [a]Son of David, have mercy
on me!"
39 Then those who went before
warned him that he should be quiet;
but he cried out all the more, "Son
of David, have mercy on me!"
40 So Jesus stood still and commanded him to be brought to Him.
And when he had come near, He
asked him,
41 saying, "What do you want Me
to do for you?" He said, "Lord, that
I may receive my sight."
42 Then Jesus said to him, "Receive your sight; [a]your faith has
made you well."
43 And immediately he received
his sight, and followed Him, [a]glorify-
ing God. And all the people, when
they saw *it*, gave praise to God.

Zacchaeus Is Restored

19 Then *Jesus* entered and
passed through [a]Jericho.
2 Now behold, *there was* a man
named Zacchaeus who was a chief
tax collector, and he was rich.†
3 And he sought to [a]see who

18:24–30 God's power can save even a rich man. And those who have turned their backs on riches and forsaken earthly goods altogether for the cause of the Kingdom will reap abundant rewards from God. (See note on Matt. 19:23–29.)

18:30 **More in this present time** does not necessarily signify more material things.

18:34 The **saying was hidden** not deliberately, but because the disciples could not comprehend the reality and meaning of the Passion events predicted by Jesus.

18:35 Luke and Mark report one blind man, whereas Matthew mentions two. But the lesson remains the same (see notes on Matt. 20:30 and Mark 10:47–52).

19:2–10 This delightful account occurs only in Luke. **Zacchaeus** means "the pure and innocent one." Being a tax collector, he does not live up to his name, by his own admission.

(continued on next page)

Zacchaeus Sunday *Fifth Sunday before Lent*

19:1–10: The story of this man, little in stature but big in heart, exhorts us to repent wholeheartedly.

Jesus was, but could not because of
the crowd, for he was of short
stature.
4 So he ran ahead and climbed up
into a sycamore tree to see Him, for
He was going to pass that *way*.
5 And when Jesus came to the
place, He looked up [1]and saw him,
and said to him, "Zacchaeus, [2]make
haste and come down, for today I
must stay at your house."
6 So he [1]made haste and came
down, and received Him joyfully.
7 But when they saw *it*, they all
[1]complained, saying, [a]"He has gone
to be a guest with a man who is a
sinner."
8 Then Zacchaeus stood and said
to the Lord, "Look, Lord, I give half
of my goods to the [a]poor; and if I
have taken anything from anyone by
[b]false accusation, [c]I restore fourfold."
9 And Jesus said to him, "Today
salvation has come to this house, because [a]he also is [b]a son of Abraham;
10 [a]"for the Son of Man has come
to seek and to save that which was
lost."

The Parable of the Minas
(Matt. 25:14–30)

11 Now as they heard these things,
He spoke another parable, because
He was near Jerusalem and because
[a]they thought the kingdom of God
would appear immediately.
12 [a]Therefore He said: "A certain
nobleman went into a far country to
receive for himself a kingdom and
to return.†
13 "So he called ten of his servants,
delivered to them ten [1]minas, and
said to them, 'Do business till I
come.'
14 [a]"But his citizens hated him,
and sent a delegation after him, saying, 'We will not have this *man* to
reign over us.'
15 "And so it was that when he
returned, having received the kingdom, he then commanded these servants, to whom he had given the
money, to be called to him, that he
might know how much every man
had gained by trading.
16 "Then came the first, saying,
'Master, your mina has earned ten
minas.'
17 "And he said to him, [a]'Well
done, good servant; because you
were [b]faithful in a very little, have
authority over ten cities.'
18 "And the second came, saying,
'Master, your mina has earned five
minas.'
19 "Likewise he said to him, 'You
also be over five cities.'
20 "Then another came, saying,
'Master, here is your mina, which
I have kept put away in a hand-
kerchief.
21 [a]'For I feared you, because you
are [1]an austere man. You collect
what you did not deposit, and reap
what you did not sow.'
22 "And he said to him, [a]'Out of
your own mouth I will judge you,

5 [1]NU omits *and saw him* [2]*hurry*
6 [1]*hurried*
7 [a]Matt. 9:11; Luke 5:30; 15:2 [1]*grumbled*
8 [a][Ps. 41:1] [b]Luke 3:14 [c]Ex. 22:1; Lev. 6:5; Num. 5:7; 1 Sam. 12:3; 2 Sam. 12:6
9 [a]Luke 3:8; 13:16; [Rom. 4:16; Gal. 3:7] [b][Luke 13:16]
10 [a]Matt. 18:11; [Luke 5:32; Rom. 5:8]
11 [a]Acts 1:6
12 [a]Matt. 25:14–30; Mark 13:34
13 [1]Gr. *mna*, same as Heb. *minah*, each worth about three months' salary
14 [a][John 1:11]
17 [a]Matt. 25:21, 23 [b]Luke 16:10
21 [a]Matt. 25:24 [1]*a severe*
22 [a]2 Sam. 1:16; Job 15:6; [Matt. 12:37]

(continued from previous page)
Nevertheless, he comes to have a heart for Christ and becomes a changed man (v. 8). Because he has been richly blessed, he gladly offers to do something voluntarily, which the rich ruler would not (18:22, 23). Exactly what happened in the house of Zacchaeus is unknown (v. 9), but the joy rings out in Christ's words: **Today salvation has come to this house.**

19:12–27 A noble ruler gives the same sum of money to ten servants; only three give an accounting to him. (See note on Matt. 25:14–30.) A **mina:** a measure of money equivalent to about three months' wages. Rather than waiting for the Kingdom in lazy occupation, we are to anticipate and plan for the Kingdom to come through wise use of the King's resources.

you wicked servant. [b]You knew that
I was an austere man, collecting
what I did not deposit and reaping
what I did not sow.
23 'Why then did you not put my
money in the bank, that at my coming I might have collected it with
interest?'
24 "And he said to those who
stood by, 'Take the mina from him,
and give *it* to him who has ten
minas.'
25 ("But they said to him, 'Master,
he has ten minas.')
26 'For I say to you, [a]that to everyone who has will be given; and from
him who does not have, even what
he has will be taken away from
him.
27 'But bring here those enemies
of mine, who did not want me to
reign over them, and slay *them* before
me.' "

The Colt Borrowed
(Matt. 21:1–7; Mark 11:1–7)

28 When He had said this, [a]He
went on ahead, going up to
Jerusalem.†
29 [a]And it came to pass, when He
drew near to [1]Bethphage and [b]Beth-
any, at the mountain called [c]Olivet,
that He sent two of His disciples,
30 saying, "Go into the village opposite *you,* where as you enter you
will find a colt tied, on which no one
has ever sat. Loose it and bring *it*
here.
31 "And if anyone asks you, 'Why
are you loosing *it?*' thus you shall
say to him, 'Because the Lord has
need of it.' "
32 So those who were sent went
their way and found *it* just [a]as He
had said to them.
33 But as they were loosing the
colt, the owners of it said to them,
"Why are you loosing the colt?"
34 And they said, "The Lord has
need of him."

The Triumphal Entry
(Matt. 21:8, 9; Mark 11:8–10;
John 12:12–19)

35 Then they brought him to Jesus.
[a]And they threw their own clothes
on the colt, and they set Jesus on
him.
36 And as He went, *many* spread
their clothes on the road.
37 Then, as He was now drawing
near the descent of the Mount of Olives, the whole multitude of the disciples began to [a]rejoice and praise
God with a loud voice for all the
mighty works they had seen,
38 saying:

[a]" *'Blessed is the King who comes*
in the name of the L*ORD*!'
[b]Peace in heaven and glory in the
highest!"

39 And some of the Pharisees
called to Him from the crowd,
"Teacher, rebuke Your disciples."
40 But He answered and said to
them, "I tell you that if these should
keep silent, [a]the stones would immediately cry out."

Lament over Jerusalem

41 Now as He drew near, He saw
the city and [a]wept over it,†
42 saying, "If you had known,
even you, especially in this [a]your
day, the things *that* [b]*make* for your
[c]peace! But now they are hidden
from your eyes.†

22 [b]Matt. 25:26
26 [a]Matt. 13:12; 25:29; Mark 4:25; Luke 8:18
28 [a]Mark 10:32
29 [a]Matt. 21:1; Mark 11:1
[b]Matt. 26:6; John 12:1
[c]John 8:1; Acts 1:12
[1]M *Bethsphage*
32 [a]Luke 22:13
35 [a]2 Kin. 9:13; Matt. 21:7; Mark 11:7
37 [a]Luke 13:17; 18:43
38 [a]Ps. 118:26; Luke 13:35
[b]Luke 2:14; [Eph. 2:14]
40 [a]Hab. 2:11
41 [a]Is. 53:3; John 11:35
42 [a]Ps. 95:7, 8; Heb. 3:13
[b][Luke 1:77–79; Acts 10:36]
[c][Rom. 5:1]

19:28–40 The Triumphal Entry marks a public, messianic acclamation of Jesus, which He accepts as His mission draws toward its climax. The people hail Him as **King** (v. 38), but His kingship is not as they think (see notes on Matt. 21:1–11).

19:41 Jesus **wept over** the Holy City because, in spite of its beauty and spiritual significance, it lay in unbelief and impending judgment.

19:42–44 Luke recounts two occasions of Jesus lamenting over Jerusalem (see 13:34, 35). The second half of the name Jerusalem means "peace," but **the things that make for** . . .

(continued on next page)

43 "For days will come upon you
when your enemies will [a]build an
embankment around you, surround
you and close you in on every side,
44 [a]"and level you, and your children within you, to the ground; and
[b]they will not leave in you one stone
upon another, [c]because you did not
know the time of your visitation."

Cleansing the Temple

(Matt. 21:10–17; Mark 11:11, 15–17)

45 [a]Then He went into the temple
and began to drive out those who
[1]bought and sold in it,†
46 saying to them, "It is written,
[a]*'My house [1]is a house of prayer,'*
but you have made it a *[b]'den of
thieves.'* "

Jesus' Popularity

(Mark 11:18, 19)

47 And He [a]was teaching daily in
the temple. But [b]the chief priests, the
scribes, and the leaders of the people
sought to destroy Him,
48 and were unable to do anything;
for all the people were very attentive
to [a]hear Him.

What Is Jesus' Authority?

(Matt. 21:23–27; Mark 11:27–33)

20 Now [a]it happened on one of
those days, as He taught the
people in the temple and preached
the gospel, *that* the chief priests and
the scribes, together with the elders,
confronted *Him*
2 and spoke to Him, saying, "Tell
us, [a]by what authority are You doing
these things? Or who is he who gave
You this authority?"†
3 But He answered and said to
them, "I also will ask you one thing,
and answer Me:†
4 "The [a]baptism of John—was it
from heaven or from men?"
5 And they reasoned among
themselves, saying, "If we say,
'From heaven,' He will say, 'Why
[1]then did you not believe him?'
6 "But if we say, 'From men,' all
the people will stone us, [a]for they
are persuaded that John was a
prophet."
7 So they answered that they did
not know where *it was* from.
8 And Jesus said to them, "Neither will I tell you by what authority
I do these things."

The Wicked Vineyard Tenants

(Matt. 21:33–46; Mark 12:1–12)

9 Then He began to tell the people
this parable: [a]"A certain man
planted a vineyard, leased it to
[1]vinedressers, and went into a far
country for a long time.†
10 "Now at [1]vintage-time he
[a]sent a servant to the vinedressers,
that they might give him some of the
fruit of the vineyard. But the vinedressers beat him and sent *him* away
empty-handed.
11 "Again he sent another servant;
and they beat him also, treated *him*

43 [a]Jer. 6:3, 6
44 [a]1 Kin. 9:7, 8 [b]Matt. 24:2 [c][1 Pet. 2:12]
45 [a]Mark 11:11, 15–17 [1]NU *were selling, saying*
46 [a]Is. 56:7 [b]Jer. 7:11 [1]NU *shall be*
47 [a]Luke 21:37; 22:53 [b]John 7:19; 8:37
48 [a]Luke 21:38

CHAPTER 20

1 [a]Matt. 21:23–27
2 [a]Acts 4:7; 7:27
4 [a]John 1:26, 31
5 [1]NU, M omit *then*
6 [a]Luke 7:24–30
9 [a]Mark 12:1–12 [1]*tenant farmers*
10 [a][1 Thess. 2:15] [1]Lit. *the season*

(continued from previous page)
peace are **hidden** from its eyes because of unbelief. The predicted destruction occurred in A.D. 70 at the hands of the Romans, who recaptured Jerusalem by storm and burned the temple. **The time of your visitation** is Christ's ministry as a visitation from God, either for salvation or judgment.

19:45, 46 Into the temple refers to the temple area, where a precinct was used for the selling and buying of animals offered in sacrifices. This was regulated by the Law, but to Jesus the atmosphere reeks of commercialism (see notes on Matt. 21:12, 13).

20:2 Jesus is questioned about His **authority. These things** include the cleansing of the temple (19:45) and His preaching of the gospel (v. 1) with messianic claims.

20:3–8 Perceiving their intent to trap Him, Jesus answers with a question of His own—and reduces His opponents to silence (v. 7).

20:9–16 This parable recounts the history of Israel. God the Father is the owner. The **vineyard** is Israel. The **vinedressers** are the religious leaders. The **servants** are the prophets. The **beloved son** is Jesus the Messiah. The **others** are the Gentiles.

shamefully, and sent *him* away
empty-handed.
12 "And again he sent a third; and
they wounded him also and cast *him*
out.
13 "Then the owner of the vineyard said, 'What shall I do? I will
send my beloved son. Probably they
will respect *him* when they see
him.'
14 "But when the vinedressers saw
him, they reasoned among themselves, saying, 'This is the [a]heir.
Come, [b]let us kill him, that the inheritance may be [c]ours.'
15 "So they cast him out of the
vineyard and [a]killed *him*. Therefore
what will the owner of the vineyard
do to them?
16 "He will come and destroy
those vinedressers and give the vineyard to [a]others." And when they
heard *it* they said, "Certainly not!"
17 Then He looked at them and
said, "What then is this that is
written:

> [a]*'The stone which the builders rejected*
> *Has become the chief cornerstone'* ?†

18 "Whoever falls on that stone
will be [a]broken; but [b]on whomever
it falls, it will grind him to powder."†
19 And the chief priests and the
scribes that very hour sought to lay
hands on Him, but they [1]feared the
people—for they knew He had spoken this parable against them.

14 [a][Heb. 1:1–3] [b]Matt. 27:21–23 [c]John 11:47, 48
15 [a]Luke 23:33; Acts 2:22, 23; 3:15
16 [a][John 1:11–13]; Rom. 11:1, 11; 1 Cor. 6:15; Gal. 2:17; 3:21; 6:14
17 [a]Ps. 118:22; Matt. 21:42; 1 Pet. 2:7, 8
18 [a]Is. 8:14, 15 [b][Dan. 2:34, 35, 44, 45]; Matt. 21:44
19 [1]M *were afraid—for*
20 [a]Matt. 22:15
21 [a]Matt. 22:16; Mark 12:14
23 [1]NU omits *Why do you test Me?*
25 [a]Matt. 17:24–27; Rom. 13:7; [1 Pet. 2:13–17] [1]*Pay*
27 [a]Matt. 22:23–33; Mark 12:18–27 [b]Acts 23:6, 8

Do We Pay Taxes to Caesar?
(Matt. 22:15–22; Mark 12:13–17)

20 [a]So they watched *Him*, and sent
spies who pretended to be righteous,
that they might seize on His words,
in order to deliver Him to the power
and the authority of the governor.†
21 Then they asked Him, saying,
[a]"Teacher, we know that You say
and teach rightly, and You do not
show personal favoritism, but teach
the way of God in truth:
22 "Is it lawful for us to pay taxes
to Caesar or not?"
23 But He perceived their craftiness, and said to them, [1]"Why do
you test Me?
24 "Show Me a denarius. Whose
image and inscription does it have?"
They answered and said, "Caesar's."
25 And He said to them, [a]"Render[1]
therefore to Caesar the things that
are Caesar's, and to God the things
that are God's."
26 But they could not catch Him
in His words in the presence of the
people. And they marveled at His
answer and kept silent.

The Mystery of Resurrection
(Matt. 22:23–33; Mark 12:18–27)

27 [a]Then some of the Sadducees,
[b]who deny that there is a resurrection, came to *Him* and asked
Him,†

20:17 This quotation from Ps. 118:22 refers to Christ, the foundation **stone** rejected by the religious leaders, who becomes **chief cornerstone** of the Church.

20:18 To attack or resist Christ means to suffer judgment and utter destruction.

20:20–26 The question on Roman taxation is designed to trap Jesus between the Roman government and the Jewish people. A "yes" would turn the people against Him. A "no" would bring a charge of treason by the Roman governor. His answer defeats their cunning, and shows that no conflict need exist between civic and religious duties. Christians can render the state its due while serving God. As the coin bears the image of the emperor and is properly paid to him, so each person bears the image of God and belongs to Him. Conflict arises when the state demands of Christians what belongs only to God.

20:27–38 The **Sadducees:** the high priestly and landowning class which controlled the temple and the Jewish Council. In a striking difference with the Pharisees, the Sadducees rejected the resurrection of the dead and they came to Christ to dispute it. Jesus' answer is concise and irrefutable. Since God **is not the God of the dead but of the living,** both those who are physically alive and those who are deceased, such as Abraham, Isaac, and Jacob, **all live to Him** (vv. 37, 38).

28 saying: "Teacher, Moses wrote
to us *that* if a man's brother dies,
having a wife, and he dies without
children, his brother should take his
wife and raise up offspring for his
brother.
29 "Now there were seven brothers. And the first took a wife, and
died without children.
30 "And the second [1]took her as
wife, and he died childless.
31 "Then the third took her, and
in like manner the seven [1]also;
and they left no children, and
died.
32 "Last of all the woman died
also.
33 "Therefore, in the resurrection,
whose wife does she become? For all
seven had her as wife."
34 Jesus answered and said to
them, "The sons of this age marry
and are given in marriage.
35 "But those who are [a]counted
worthy to attain that age, and
the resurrection from the dead,
neither marry nor are given in marriage;
36 "nor can they die anymore, for
[a]they are equal to the angels and are
sons of God, [b]being sons of the
resurrection.
37 "But even Moses showed in the
burning bush *passage* that the dead
are raised, when he called the Lord
[a]*'the God of Abraham, the God of
Isaac, and the God of Jacob.'*
38 "For He is not the God of the
dead but of the living, for [a]all live
to Him."
39 Then some of the scribes answered and said, "Teacher, You
have spoken well."
40 But after that they dared not
question Him anymore.

30 [1]NU omits the rest of v. 30.
31 [1]NU, M *also left no children*
35 [a]Phil. 3:11
36 [a][1 Cor. 15:42, 49, 52; 1 John 3:2] [b]Rom. 8:23
37 [a]Ex. 3:1–6, 15; Acts 7:30–32
38 [a][Rom. 6:10, 11; 14:8, 9; Heb. 11:16]
41 [a]Matt. 22:41–46; Mark 12:35–37
42 [a]Ps. 110:1; Acts 2:34, 35
44 [a]Acts 13:22, 23; Rom. 1:3; 9:4, 5
45 [a]Matt. 23:1–7; Mark 12:38–40
46 [a]Matt. 23:5 [b]Luke 11:43; 14:7
47 [a]Matt. 23:14 [b][Matt. 6:5, 6]

CHAPTER 21

1 [a]Mark 12:41–44
2 [a][2 Cor. 6:10] [b]Mark 12:42 [1]Gr. *lepta,* very small copper coins

Son of David, Son of God
(Matt. 22:41–46; Mark 12:35–37)

41 And He said to them, [a]"How
can they say that the Christ is the
Son of David?
42 "Now David himself said in the
Book of Psalms:

[a]*'The* LORD *said to my Lord,*
"Sit at My right hand,†
43 *Till I make Your enemies Your*
footstool."'

44 "Therefore David calls Him
'Lord'; [a]how is He then his Son?"†

Beware of the Scribes
(Matt. 23:1–36; Mark 12:38–40)

45 [a]Then, in the hearing of all
the people, He said to His disciples,†
46 [a]"Beware of the scribes, who
desire to go around in long robes,
[b]love greetings in the marketplaces,
the best seats in the synagogues, and
the best places at feasts,
47 [a]"who devour widows' houses,
and for a [b]pretense make long
prayers. These will receive greater
condemnation."

Imitate the Poor Widow
(Mark 12:41–44)

21 And He looked up [a]and saw
the rich putting their gifts into
the treasury,
2 and He saw also a certain
[a]poor widow putting in two
[b]mites.[1]†

20:42 The first reference to LORD applies to God the Father, the second to Christ—whom David, the writer of this Psalm, calls **my Lord.**

20:44 The riddle has its solution in that the Messiah is David's Son in His humanity, yet David calls Him **Lord** in His eternal deity.

20:45–47 These verses criticize the **scribes,** a professional class of teachers and experts in Mosaic Law, for glorying in their influential roles while practicing injustice.

21:2 A **mite:** a Jewish copper coin of the lowest value, like a penny. Yet this sacrificial offering by the **poor widow** is praised by Christ. The value of a gift derives from the spirit in which it is given. A gift that seeks recognition loses spiritual value; a gift made from the heart gains immense value.

Commemoration of Holy Martyrs

21:12–19: Jesus predicts the fate of those who confess His name.

3 So He said, "Truly I say to you
[a]that this poor widow has put in
more than all;
4 "for all these out of their abundance have put in offerings [1]for
God, but she out of her poverty
put in [a]all the livelihood that she
had."

Signs of the End

(Matt. 24:1–14; Mark 13:1–13)

5 [a]Then, as some spoke of the
temple, how it was [1]adorned with
beautiful stones and donations, He
said,†
6 "These things which you see—
the days will come in which [a]not *one*
stone shall be left upon another that
shall not be thrown down."
7 So they asked Him, saying,
"Teacher, but when will these things
be? And what sign *will there be*
when these things are about to take
place?"
8 And He said: [a]"Take heed that
you not be deceived. For many will
come in My name, saying, 'I am
He,' and, 'The time has drawn
near.' [1]Therefore do not [2]go after
them †
9 "But when you hear of [a]wars
and commotions, do not be terrified;
for these things must come to pass
first, but the end *will not come*
immediately."
10 [a]Then He said to them, "Nation
will rise against nation, and kingdom
against kingdom.
11 "And there will be great
[a]earthquakes in various places, and
famines and pestilences; and there
will be fearful sights and great signs
from heaven.
12 [a]"But before all these things,
they will lay their hands on you
and persecute *you*, delivering *you*
up to the synagogues and [b]pris-
ons. [c]You will be brought before
kings and rulers [d]for My name's
sake †
13 "But [a]it will turn out for you as
an occasion for testimony.
14 [a]"Therefore settle *it* in your
hearts not to meditate beforehand on
what you will [1]answer;
15 "for I will give you a mouth and
wisdom [a]which all your adversaries
will not be able to contradict or
[1]resist.
16 [a]"You will be betrayed even by
parents and brothers, relatives and
friends; and they will put [b]*some* of
you to death.
17 "And [a]you will be hated by all
for My name's sake.
18 [a]"But not a hair of your head
shall be lost †
19 "By your patience possess your
souls †

3 [a][2 Cor. 8:12]
4 [a][2 Cor. 8:12] [1]NU omits *for God*
5 [a]Mark 13:1 [1]*decorated*
6 [a]Luke 19:41–44
8 [a]Eph. 5:6 [1]NU omits *Therefore* [2]*follow*
9 [a]Rev. 6:4
10 [a]Matt. 24:7
11 [a]Rev. 6:12
12 [a][Rev. 2:10] [b]Acts 4:3; 5:18; 12:4; 16:24 [c]Acts 25:23 [d]1 Pet. 2:13
13 [a][Phil. 1:12–14, 28]
14 [a]Luke 12:11 [1]*say in defense*
15 [a]Acts 6:10 [1]*withstand*
16 [a]Mic. 7:6 [b]Acts 7:59; 12:2
17 [a]Matt. 10:22
18 [a]Matt. 10:30

21:5, 6 In Luke, the discourse of Christ on the destruction of Jerusalem and the end of the age (vv. 5–38) occurs in the temple area and is addressed to the public. (See notes on Matt. 24 and Mark 13.) The Lord's warnings about the future are intended to alert people to live righteously in the present.

21:8 Not to **be deceived** is the first caution Christians ought to **heed** when people talk about the signs of the end.

21:12, 13 Persecutions against Christians will provide them with opportunities to give **testimony** to their faith.

21:18 This is an ancient expression meaning that not even death (v. 16) can harm a soul that is in God's hands.

21:19 Endurance assures a place for us in the kingdom of God (see 1 Cor. 9:24; Heb. 12:1).

The Destruction of Jerusalem
(Matt. 24:15–28; Mark 13:14–20)

20 [a]"But when you see Jerusalem
surrounded by armies, then know
that its desolation is near †
21 "Then let those who are in Judea flee to the mountains, let those
who are in the midst of her depart,
and let not those who are in the
country enter her.
22 "For these are the days of vengeance, that [a]all things which are
written may be fulfilled.
23 [a]"But woe to those who are
pregnant and to those who are nursing babies in those days! For there
will be great distress in the land and
wrath upon this people.
24 "And they will fall by the edge
of the sword, and be led away captive into all nations. And Jerusalem
will be trampled by Gentiles [a]until
the times of the Gentiles are fulfilled.

Cosmic Signs
(Matt. 24:29–31; Mark 13:24–27)

25 [a]"And there will be signs in the
sun, in the moon, and in the stars,
and on the earth distress of nations,
with perplexity, the sea and the
waves roaring †
26 "men's hearts failing them from
fear and the expectation of those
things which are coming on the
earth, [a]for the powers of the heavens
will be shaken.
27 "Then they will see the Son of
Man [a]coming in a cloud with power
and great glory.
28 "Now when these things begin
to happen, look up and lift up your
heads, because [a]your redemption
draws near."

The Time of His Coming
(Matt. 24:32–36; Mark 13:28–32)

29 [a]Then He spoke to them a parable: "Look at the fig tree, and all the
trees.
30 "When they are already bud-
ding, you see and know for yourselves that summer is now near.
31 "So you also, when you see
these things happening, know that
the kingdom of God is near.
32 "Assuredly, I say to you, this
generation will by no means pass
away till all things take place †
33 [a]"Heaven and earth will pass
away, but My [b]words will by no
means pass away.

Be Watchful and Pray

34 "But [a]take heed to yourselves,
lest your hearts be weighed down
with [1]carousing, drunkenness, and
[b]cares of this life, and that Day come
on you unexpectedly †
35 "For [a]it will come as a snare on
all those who dwell on the face of
the whole earth.
36 [a]"Watch therefore, and [b]pray
always that you may [1]be counted
[c]worthy to escape all these things
that will come to pass, and [d]to stand
before the Son of Man."
37 [a]And in the daytime He was
teaching in the temple, but [b]at night
He went out and stayed on the
mountain called Olivet.†
38 Then early in the morning all
the people came to Him in the temple to hear Him.

20 [a]Mark 13:14
22 [a][Dan. 9:24–27]
23 [a]Matt. 24:19
24 [a][Dan. 9:27; 12:7]
25 [a][2 Pet. 3:10–12]
26 [a]Matt. 24:29
27 [a]Rev. 1:7; 14:14
28 [a][Rom. 8:19, 23]
29 [a]Mark 13:28
33 [a]Matt. 24:35
[b]Is. 40:8
34 [a]1 Thess. 5:6
[b]Luke 8:14
[1]*dissipation*
35 [a]Rev. 3:3; 16:15
36 [a]Matt. 24:42; 25:13
[b]Luke 18:1
[c]Luke 20:35
[d][Eph. 6:13]
[1]NU *have strength to*
37 [a]John 8:1, 2
[b]Luke 22:39

21:20–24 A prediction of the siege and capture of Jerusalem by Titus, son of the Emperor Vespasian, in A.D. 70. Damage included the total destruction of the temple.

21:25–28 Cosmic as well as historical upheavals will precede **the Son of Man coming in a cloud with power and great glory.** The expectation of Christ's return sums up the Christian hope and constitutes an important doctrine of the Church.

21:32 This difficult verse may be interpreted in two ways: (1) **this generation** refers to Jesus' contemporaries and **all things** pertain to the capture of Jerusalem; or (2) *this generation* is the new Christian generation and *all things* include the return of Christ. The latter is the preferred interpretation of the Church Fathers.

21:34–36 Jesus concludes His discourse with a final admonition to vigilance in the face of the unpredictable time of His return.

21:37 Olivet is the Mount of Olives, a hill on the east side of Jerusalem where pilgrims stayed when the city was overcrowded during festivals such as the Passover.

The Chief Priests and Judas

(Matt. 26:1–5, 14–16; Mark 14:1, 2, 10, 11)

22 Now [a]the Feast of Unleavened Bread drew near, which is called Passover.†

2 And [a]the chief priests and the scribes sought how they might kill Him, for they feared the people.†

3 [a]Then Satan entered Judas, surnamed Iscariot, who was numbered among the [b]twelve.

4 So he went his way and conferred with the chief priests and captains, how he might betray Him to them.

5 And they were glad, and [a]agreed to give him money.

6 So he promised and sought opportunity to [a]betray Him to them in the absence of the multitude.

Preparation for the Passover

(Matt. 26:17–19; Mark 14:12–26)

7 [a]Then came the Day of Unleavened Bread, when the Passover must be [1]killed.†

8 And He sent Peter and John, saying, "Go and prepare the Passover for us, that we may eat."

9 So they said to Him, "Where do You want us to prepare?"

10 And He said to them, "Behold, when you have entered the city, a man will meet you carrying a pitcher of water; follow him into the house which he enters.

11 "Then you shall say to the master of the house, 'The Teacher says to you, "Where is the guest room where I may eat the Passover with My disciples?" '

12 "Then he will show you a large, furnished upper room; there make ready."

13 So they went and [a]found it just as He had said to them, and they prepared the Passover.

The Eucharist Instituted

(Matt. 26:20, 26–29; Mark 14:22–25; John 13:1–38)

14 [a]When the hour had come, He sat down, and the [1]twelve apostles with Him.

15 Then He said to them, "With *fervent* desire I have desired to eat this Passover with you before I suffer;†

16 "for I say to you, I will no longer eat of it [a]until it is fulfilled in the kingdom of God."

17 Then He took the cup, and gave thanks, and said, "Take this and divide *it* among yourselves;†

18 "for [a]I say to you, [1]I will not drink of the fruit of the vine until the kingdom of God comes."

19 [a]And He took bread, gave thanks and broke *it*, and gave *it* to them, saying, "This is My [b]body which is given for you; [c]do this in remembrance of Me."†

20 Likewise He also *took* the cup

CHAPTER 22

1 [a]Matt. 26:2–5; Mark 14:1, 2
2 [a]Ps. 2:2; John 11:47; Acts 4:27
3 [a]Matt. 26:14–16; Mark 14:10, 11; John 13:2, 27 [b]Matt. 10:2–4
5 [a]Zech. 11:12
6 [a]Ps. 41:9
7 [a]Matt. 26:17–19; Mark 14:12–16 [1]Sacrificed
13 [a]Luke 19:32
14 [a]Matt. 26:20; Mark 14:17 [1]NU omits *twelve*
16 [a]Luke 14:15; [Acts 10:41; Rev. 19:9]
18 [a]Matt. 26:29; Mark 14:25 [1]NU adds *from now on*
19 [a]Matt. 26:26; Mark 14:22 [b][1 Pet. 2:24] [c]1 Cor. 11:23–26

22:1 These two feasts were distinct but largely overlapping; thus they could be identified as one (see note on Matt. 26:17–19).

22:2 That the religious leaders **feared the people** means the populace at large favored charismatic figures such as Jesus. Therefore, there is need for treachery, night arrest, and quick trial.

22:7 The **Passover** lambs were ritually slaughtered about noon on the first **Day of Unleavened Bread,** roasted in the afternoon, and eaten that evening—marking the beginning of the Passover Festival. Unleavened bread was eaten in remembrance of the urgent Exodus from Egypt, in which there was not time for the bread to rise.

22:15, 16 The Passover signifies deliverance of the Hebrew people from Egypt. Now Jesus, with **fervent desire,** anticipates the great deliverance of humanity from the power of sin, which will be accomplished through His saving death, establishing the New Covenant (v. 20). This Passover meal is the Last Supper, continued in the Eucharist of the Church, which is to be **fulfilled in the kingdom of God.**

22:17 Luke reports the partaking of two cups (vv. 17, 20). Several cups were offered during the Passover meal.

22:19 Christ is the Lamb of God who gives Himself as a sacrifice on the Cross for the

(continued on next page)

THE BAPTISM
OF OUR LORD

The Baptism of Christ, *by the hand of Fr. Luke Dingman.*

In humility, God the Creator submits to baptism by the hand of John. With glory the Trinity is revealed: God the Son is manifest in the flesh; the voice of God the Father proclaims, "This is My Beloved Son;" and God the Holy Spirit descends upon Christ in the form of a dove. Feast Day readings are Matthew 3:1–11; 1 Timothy 3:14—4:5.

See also Matthew 3:13–17; Mark 1:9–11; Luke 3:21, 22.

after supper, saying, [a]"This cup *is*
the new covenant in My blood,
which is shed for you.

Deception and Betrayal

(Matt. 26:21–25; Mark 14:18–21; John 13:21–30)

21 [a]"But behold, the hand of My
betrayer *is* with Me on the table.
22 [a]"And truly the Son of Man
goes [b]as it has been determined, but
woe to that man by whom He is
betrayed!"†
23 [a]Then they began to question
among themselves, which of them
it was who would do this thing.

Greatness Is Service

(Matt. 20:24–28; Mark 10:35–45)

24 [a]Now there was also a dispute
among them, as to which of them
should be considered the greatest.†
25 [a]And He said to them, "The
kings of the Gentiles exercise lordship over them, and those who exercise authority over them are called
'benefactors.'†
26 [a]"But not so *among* you; on the
contrary, [b]he who is greatest among
you, let him be as the younger, and
he who governs as he who serves.†
27 [a]"For who *is* greater, he who
sits at the table, or he who serves?
Is it not he who sits at the table? Yet
[b]I am among you as the One who
serves.

Christ Rewards His Servants

28 "But you are those who have
continued with Me in [a]My trials.†
29 "And [a]I bestow upon you a
kingdom, just as My Father bestowed *one* upon Me,
30 "that [a]you may eat and drink
at My table in My kingdom, [b]and sit
on thrones judging the twelve tribes
of Israel."

Peter's Denials Predicted

(Matt. 26:30–35; Mark 14:26–31; John 13:36–38)

31 [1]And the Lord said, "Simon, Simon! Indeed, [a]Satan has asked for
you, that he may [b]sift *you* as wheat.†
32 "But [a]I have prayed for you,
that your faith should not fail; and
when you have returned to *Me*,
[b]strengthen your brethren."
33 But he said to Him, "Lord, I am
ready to go with You, both to prison
and to death."
34 [a]Then He said, "I tell you, Peter, the rooster shall not crow this
day before you will deny three times
that you know Me."

A Time of Crisis

35 [a]And He said to them, "When
I sent you without money bag, knapsack, and sandals, did you lack anything?" So they said, "Nothing."
36 Then He said to them, "But

20 [a]1 Cor. 10:16
21 [a]John 13:21, 26, 27
22 [a]Matt. 26:24 [b]Acts 2:23
23 [a]John 13:22, 25
24 [a]Mark 9:34
25 [a]Mark 10:42–45
26 [a][1 Pet. 5:3] [b]Luke 9:48
27 [a][Luke 12:37] [b]Phil. 2:7
28 [a][Heb. 2:18; 4:15]
29 [a]Matt. 24:47
30 [a][Matt. 8:11] [b][Rev. 3:21]
31 [a]1 Pet. 5:8 [b]Amos 9:9 [1]NU omits *And the Lord said*
32 [a][John 17:9, 11, 15] [b]John 21:15–17
34 [a]John 13:37, 38
35 [a]Matt. 10:9

(continued from previous page)
salvation of the world. **Remembrance** in its biblical significance is a reliving of the original event. We do this through the sacred act of the Eucharist (see notes on Matt. 26:26–28, 29).

22:22 With these words Jesus looks ahead to His arrest (see v. 51 and note) and suffering (see 23:34 and note).

22:24 In view of Jesus' willingness to die for the world, the concern of the disciples over who among them is **the greatest** is reprehensibly small-minded.

22:25 Some kings called themselves **benefactors,** a title which is not without irony considering their tyrannical rule.

22:26, 27 Jesus Himself is the supreme example of His teaching that greatness consists in humble service to others.

22:28–30 Jesus is not speaking of two different kingdoms but of one **kingdom** (v. 29) which will be fully revealed at His glorious return. Then, the disciples will **sit on thrones** (v. 30) occupying honorary positions as reward for sharing Christ's **trials** (v. 28).

22:31, 32 Jesus sees **Simon** Peter's denial as a violent attack by Satan, which Peter endures through Jesus' intercessory prayer. After his tearful repentance and the experience of the Resurrection, Peter indeed **returned** to Christ and was able to **strengthen** the early Church as one of its leaders.

Holy Thursday *Thursday before Easter*

22:43–45: Jesus prays in agony while His disciples sleep.

now, he who has a money bag, let
him take *it,* and likewise a knapsack;
and he who has no sword, let him
sell his garment and buy one. †
37 "For I say to you that this which
is written must still be [1]accomplished
in Me: [a]*'And He was numbered with
the transgressors.'* For the things
concerning Me have an end." †
38 So they said, "Lord, look, here
are two swords." And He said to
them, "It is enough." †

Jesus Watches in the Garden
(Matt. 26:30, 36–46; Mark 14:26, 32–42; John 18:1)

39 [a]Coming out, [b]He went to the
Mount of Olives, as He was accustomed, and His disciples also followed Him.
40 [a]When He came to the place, He
said to them, "Pray that you may not
enter into temptation." †
41 [a]And He was withdrawn from
them about a stone's throw, and He
knelt down and prayed,
42 saying, "Father, if it is Your will,
take this cup away from Me; nevertheless [a]not My will, but Yours, be
done." †
43 [1]Then [a]an angel appeared to
Him from heaven, strengthening
Him. †
44 [a]And being in agony, He
prayed more earnestly. Then His
sweat became like great drops of
blood falling down to the ground.
45 When He rose up from prayer,
and had come to His disciples, He
found them sleeping from sorrow.
46 Then He said to them, "Why
[a]do you sleep? Rise and [b]pray, lest
you enter into temptation."

Arrest
(Matt. 26:47–56; Mark 14:43–52; John 18:2–12)

47 And while He was still speaking, [a]behold, a multitude; and he
who was called [b]Judas, one of the
twelve, went before them and drew
near to Jesus to kiss Him.
48 But Jesus said to him, "Judas,
are you betraying the Son of Man
with a [a]kiss?" †
49 When those around Him saw
what was going to happen, they said
to Him, "Lord, shall we strike with
the sword?"
50 And [a]one of them struck the
servant of the high priest and cut off
his right ear.

37 [a]Is. 53:12 [1]*fulfilled*
39 [a]John 18:1 [b]Luke 21:37
40 [a]Mark 14:32–42
41 [a]Matt. 26:39
42 [a]John 4:34; 5:30; 6:38; 8:29
43 [a]Matt. 4:11 [1]NU brackets vv. 43 and 44 as not in the original text.
44 [a][Heb. 5:7]
46 [a]Luke 9:32 [b]Luke 22:40
47 [a]John 18:3–11 [b]Acts 1:16, 17
48 [a][Prov. 27:6]
50 [a]Matt. 26:51

22:36 In view of the coming death of Christ and the persecutions against the disciples, Jesus instructs them to be ready for anything. The sword suggests resistance against the evil one (Eph. 6:17).

22:37 The transgressors were the two criminals crucified with Jesus. **Have an end** means come to fulfillment.

22:38 It is enough does not signify approval (vv. 49–51). The expression, according to most interpreters, is either ironical—two swords would hardly suffice as a means of defense—or an abrupt censure by Jesus, meaning, "Enough of this!" (see Deut. 3:26).

22:40 One of the fundamental purposes of prayer is to strengthen us against **temptation** in terms of inner sin and outward trials.

22:42 Jesus exemplifies what He taught in the Lord's Prayer—"Your will be done" (11:2).

22:43, 44 These details, reported only by Luke, indicate the human agony of Jesus and the divine help given to Him as He contemplates His Crucifixion.

22:48 Son of Man is an expression that Jesus used for Himself which could mean (1) simply "man"—that is, "me"—or (2) the heavenly figure of Dan. 7:13, a title which both revealed and veiled Jesus' messianic identity.

51 But Jesus answered and said,
"Permit even this." And He touched
his ear and healed him.†
52 [a]Then Jesus said to the chief
priests, captains of the temple,
and the elders who had come to
Him, "Have you come out, as
against a [b]robber, with swords and
clubs?†
53 "When I was with you daily in
the [a]temple, you did not try to seize
Me. But this is your [b]hour, and the
power of darkness."

Peter's Denials
(Matt. 26:57, 58, 69–75; Mark 14:53, 54, 66–72; John 18:13–18, 25–27)

54 [a]Having arrested Him, they led
Him and brought Him into the high
priest's house. [b]But Peter followed
at a distance.
55 [a]Now when they had kindled
a fire in the midst of the courtyard
and sat down together, Peter sat
among them.
56 And a certain servant girl, seeing him as he sat by the fire, looked
intently at him and said, "This man
was also with Him."
57 But he denied [1]Him, saying,
"Woman, I do not know Him."
58 [a]And after a little while another
saw him and said, "You also are of
them." But Peter said, "Man, I am
not!"
59 [a]Then after about an hour had
passed, another confidently affirmed, saying, "Surely this *fellow*
also was with Him, for he is a
[b]Galilean."
60 But Peter said, "Man, I do not
know what you are saying!" Immediately, while he was still speaking,
[1]the rooster crowed.

52 [a]Matt. 26:55 [b]Luke 23:32
53 [a]Luke 19:47, 48 [b][John 12:27]
54 [a]Matt. 26:57 [b]John 18:15
55 [a]Mark 14:66–72
57 [1]NU *it*
58 [a]John 18:25
59 [a]Mark 14:70 [b]Acts 1:11; 2:7
60 [1]NU, M *a rooster*
61 [a]Matt. 26:75 [b]John 13:38 [1]NU adds *today*
63 [a]Ps. 69:1, 4, 7–9 [b]Is. 50:6
64 [a]Zech. 13:7 [1]NU *And having blindfolded Him, they asked Him*
66 [a]Matt. 27:1 [b]Acts 4:26
67 [a]Matt. 26:63–66 [b]Luke 20:5–7
68 [1]NU omits *also* [2]NU omits the rest of v. 68.
69 [a]Heb. 1:3; 8:1
70 [a]Matt. 26:64; 27:11
71 [a]Mark 14:63

61 And the Lord turned and looked
at Peter. Then [a]Peter remembered
the word of the Lord, how He had
said to him, [b]"Before the rooster
[1]crows, you will deny Me three
times."†
62 So Peter went out and wept
bitterly.
63 [a]Now the men who held Jesus
mocked Him and [b]beat Him.
64 [1]And having blindfolded Him,
they [a]struck Him on the face and
asked Him, saying, "Prophesy! Who
is the one who struck You?"
65 And many other things they
blasphemously spoke against Him.

Before the Sanhedrin
(Matt. 26:57–68; Mark 14:55–65; John 18:19–24)

66 [a]As soon as it was day, [b]the
elders of the people, both chief
priests and scribes, came together
and led Him into their council,
saying,†
67 [a]"If You are the Christ, tell
us." But He said to them, "If I
tell you, you will [b]by no means believe.
68 "And if I [1]also ask *you*, you will
by no means answer [2]Me or let *Me*
go.
69 [a]"Hereafter the Son of Man will
sit on the right hand of the power
of God."†
70 Then they all said, "Are You
then the Son of God?" So He said
to them, [a]"You *rightly* say that I
am."
71 [a]And they said, "What further
testimony do we need? For we have
heard it ourselves from His own
mouth."

22:51 Permit even this: permit the arrest and let events take their course in fulfillment of God's will.

22:52 Luke reports only the Jewish participants of the arresting party, whereas John reveals a contingent of Roman soldiers was involved as well (John 18:3, 12).

22:61 That **the Lord turned and looked at Peter** is an intimate detail reported only by Luke. One can imagine the profound meaning of their mutual glance.

22:66 The official sessions of the council could take place only by daylight.

22:69 To **sit on the right hand of the power of God** signifies Christ's equality with God the Father.

Before Pilate
(Matt. 27:1, 2, 11–14; Mark 15:1–5;
John 18:28–38)

23 Then [a]the whole multitude of
them arose and led Him to
[b]Pilate.
2 And they began to [a]accuse Him,
saying, "We found this *fellow* [b]per-
verting [1]the nation, and [c]forbidding
to pay taxes to Caesar, saying [d]that
He Himself is Christ, a King."†
3 [a]Then Pilate asked Him, saying,
"Are You the King of the Jews?" He
answered him and said, "*It is as* you
say."†
4 So Pilate said to the chief priests
and the crowd, [a]"I find no fault in
this Man."
5 But they were the more fierce,
saying, "He stirs up the people,
teaching throughout all Judea, beginning from [a]Galilee to this place."

Before Herod

6 When Pilate heard [1]of Galilee,
he asked if the Man were a Galilean.
7 And as soon as he knew that
He belonged to [a]Herod's jurisdiction, he sent Him to Herod, who was
also in Jerusalem at that time.†
8 Now when Herod saw Jesus,
[a]he was exceedingly glad; for he had
desired for a long *time* to see Him,
because [b]he had heard many things
about Him, and he hoped to see
some miracle done by Him.
9 Then he questioned Him with
many words, but He answered him
[a]nothing.
10 And the chief priests and scribes
stood and vehemently accused Him.
11 [a]Then Herod, with his [1]men of

CHAPTER 23
1 [a]John 18:28 [b]Luke 3:1; 13:1
2 [a]Acts 24:2 [b]Acts 17:7 [c]Matt. 17:27 [d]John 19:12 [1]NU *our*
3 [a]1 Tim. 6:13
4 [a][1 Pet. 2:22]
5 [a]John 7:41
6 [1]NU omits *of Galilee*
7 [a]Luke 3:1; 9:7; 13:31
8 [a]Luke 9:9 [b]Matt. 14:1
9 [a]John 19:9
11 [a]Is. 53:3 [1]*troops*

12 [a]Acts 4:26, 27
13 [a]Mark 15:14
14 [a]Luke 23:1, 2 [b]Luke 23:4
15 [1]NU *he sent Him back to us*
16 [a]John 19:1
17 [a]John 18:39 [1]NU omits v. 17.
18 [a]Acts 3:13–15

war, treated Him with contempt and
mocked *Him,* arrayed Him in a gor-
geous robe, and sent Him back to
Pilate.
12 That very day [a]Pilate and Herod
became friends with each other, for
previously they had been at enmity
with each other.†

Jesus or Barabbas?
(Matt. 27:15–26; Mark 15:6–15;
John 18:39—19:16)

13 [a]Then Pilate, when he had
called together the chief priests, the
rulers, and the people,
14 said to them, [a]"You have
brought this Man to me, as one who
misleads the people. And indeed,
[b]having examined *Him* in your presence, I have found no fault in this
Man concerning those things of
which you accuse Him;
15 "no, neither did Herod, for
[1]I sent you back to him; and indeed
nothing deserving of death has been
done by Him.
16 [a]"I will therefore chastise Him
and release *Him*"†
17 [a](for[1] it was necessary for him
to release one to them at the feast).
18 And [a]they all cried out at once,
saying, "Away with this *Man,* and
release to us Barabbas"—
19 who had been thrown into
prison for a certain rebellion made
in the city, and for murder.
20 Pilate, therefore, wishing to release Jesus, again called out to them.
21 But they shouted, saying, "Crucify *Him,* crucify Him!"
22 Then he said to them the third
time, "Why, what evil has He done?
I have found no reason for death in

23:2 These false accusations seek to label Jesus as a political Messiah and a threat to Roman rule.

23:3, 4 The Greek behind **it is as you say** can also be translated "you say so," as an ambiguous answer. Jesus is **the King of the Jews,** but not in a political sense. Pilate's response (v. 4) shows he does not take the political charge seriously.

23:7 Pilate sends Jesus to **Herod** Antipas, ruler of Galilee, as a way of either gaining favor or getting rid of an unwanted case.

23:12 The two cruel and cunning enemies reconcile by sharing in the mistreatment of the innocent Jesus, a tragic footnote on human sinfulness.

23:16 To **chastise** means to scourge, a Roman punishment using a whip made from several leather strips with small bones or metal bits tied at the tips.

Him. I will therefore chastise Him
and let *Him* go."
23 But they were insistent, demanding with loud voices that He
be crucified. And the voices of these
men [1]and of the chief priests
prevailed.†
24 So [a]Pilate gave sentence that it
should be as they requested.
25 [a]And he released [1]to them the
one they requested, who for rebellion and murder had been thrown
into prison; but he delivered Jesus
to their will.†

The Procession to Golgotha
(Matt. 27:31–33; Mark 15:20–22;
John 19:17)

26 [a]Now as they led Him away,
they laid hold of a certain man, Simon a Cyrenian, who was coming
from the country, and on him they
laid the cross that he might bear *it*
after Jesus.†
27 And a great multitude of the
people followed Him, and women
who also mourned and lamented
Him.†
28 But Jesus, turning to them, said,
"Daughters of Jerusalem, do not
weep for Me, but weep for yourselves and for your children.
29 [a]"For indeed the days are coming in which they will say, 'Blessed
are the barren, wombs that never
bore, and breasts which never
nursed!'
30 "Then they will begin [a]*'to say
to the mountains, "Fall on us!" and
to the hills, "Cover us!"'*
31 [a]"For if they do these things in
the green wood, what will be done
in the dry?"†
32 [a]There were also two others,
criminals, led with Him to be put to
death.

The Compassionate Christ
(Matt. 27:33–43; Mark 15:22–32;
John 19:17–29)

33 And [a]when they had come to
the place called Calvary, there they
crucified Him, and the criminals, one
on the right hand and the other on
the left.†
34 [1]Then Jesus said, "Father, [a]for-
give them, for [b]they do not know
what they do." And [c]they divided
His garments and cast lots.†
35 And [a]the people stood looking
on. But even the [b]rulers with them
sneered, saying, "He saved others;
let Him save Himself if He is the
Christ, the chosen of God."†
36 The soldiers also mocked Him,
coming and offering Him [a]sour
wine,

23 [1]NU omits *and of the chief priests*
24 [a]Mark 15:15
25 [a]Is. 53:8 [1]NU, M omit *to them*
26 [a]Matt. 27:32
29 [a]Matt. 24:19
30 [a]Hos. 10:8; Rev. 6:16, 17; 9:6
31 [a][Jer. 25:29]
32 [a]Is. 53:9, 12
33 [a]John 19:17–24
34 [a]1 Cor. 4:12 [b]Acts 3:17 [c]Matt. 27:35 [1]NU brackets the first sentence as a later addition.
35 [a]Ps. 22:17 [b]Matt. 27:39
36 [a]Ps. 69:21

23:23 These men were the sympathizers of the Jewish leaders, not the general public whom the leaders feared (see 22:2, 6).

23:25 Here is a tragic irony. The murderer is released and the innocent Jesus is given up to be murdered, a failure of both the Roman and Jewish systems of justice.

23:26 What a great privilege to carry **the cross** of Christ. **Simon** the **Cyrenian** is a model of humble service for every Christian.

23:27–30 Daughters of Jerusalem: women of Jerusalem lamenting Jesus, mentioned only by Luke. In His words to them, Jesus envisions the calamity to befall Jerusalem.

23:31 This is a proverb comparing the fate of Jesus and the fate of Jerusalem. If the innocent Jesus (**the green wood**) suffered so, the sufferings of guilty Jerusalem (the **dry** wood) will be incomparably greater.

23:33 The Greek word for **Calvary** means "skull," and the English "Calvary" comes from the Latin word for skull. The place of crucifixion was so called either because the hill resembled a skull or because it was a place of death.

23:34 Father, forgive them is a remarkable prayer, showing the boundless mercy of the crucified Jesus. **They do not know what they do** means *they*—both leaders and executioners—have no insight into the profound mystery that they are crucifying the Lord of glory (1 Cor. 2:6–8).

23:35 The people are merely onlookers. The sinister **rulers** and their sympathizers, who pushed for Jesus' Crucifixion, jeer Him. It is unlikely the general public would actually insult one of their own as He was being crucified by the Romans.

Vespers of Great and Holy Friday

Friday before Easter

23:39–43: Jesus speaks with the two thieves from the Cross.

37 and saying, "If You are the King
of the Jews, save Yourself."
38 [a]And an inscription also was
[1]written over Him in letters of Greek,
Latin, and Hebrew:

THIS IS THE KING OF THE JEWS.

Two Thieves, Two Ways

(Matt. 27:44; Mark 15:32)

39 [a]Then one of the criminals who
were hanged blasphemed Him, saying, [1]"If You are the Christ, save
Yourself and us."
40 But the other, answering, rebuked him, saying, "Do you not
even fear God, seeing you are under
the same condemnation?
41 "And we indeed justly, for we
receive the due reward of our deeds;
but this Man has done [a]nothing
wrong."
42 Then he said [1]to Jesus, "Lord,
remember me when You come into
Your kingdom."†
43 And Jesus said to him, "Assuredly, I say to you, today you will
be with Me in [a]Paradise."

Darkness and Death

(Matt. 27:45–56; Mark 15:33–41;
John 19:28–30)

44 [a]Now it [1]was about the sixth
hour, and there was darkness over
all the earth until the ninth hour.†
45 Then the sun was [1]darkened,
and [a]the veil of the temple was torn
in [2]two.
46 And when Jesus had cried out
with a loud voice, He said, "Father,
[a]*'into Your hands I commit My
spirit.'*" [b]Having said this, He
breathed His last.†
47 [a]So when the centurion saw
what had happened, he glorified
God, saying, "Certainly this was a
righteous Man!"
48 And the whole crowd who came
together to that sight, seeing what
had been done, beat their breasts
and returned.
49 [a]But all His acquaintances, and
the women who followed Him from
Galilee, stood at a distance, watching
these things.

Burial

(Matt. 27:57–61; Mark 15:42–47;
John 19:38–42)

50 [a]Now behold, *there was* a man
named Joseph, a council member, a
good and just man.†
51 He had not consented to their
decision and deed. *He was* from Arimathea, a city of the Jews, [a]who[1]
himself was also waiting for the
kingdom of God.
52 This man went to Pilate and
asked for the body of Jesus.

38 [a]John 19:19 [1]NU omits *written* and *in letters of Greek, Latin, and Hebrew*
39 [a]Mark 15:32 [1]NU *Are You not the Christ? Save*
41 [a][Heb. 7:26]
42 [1]NU *"Jesus, remember me*
43 [a][Rev. 2:7]
44 [a]Matt. 27:45–56 [1]NU adds *already*
45 [a]Matt. 27:51 [1]NU *obscured* [2]*the middle*
46 [a]Ps. 31:5 [b]John 19:30
47 [a]Mark 15:39
49 [a]Ps. 38:11
50 [a]Matt. 27:57–61
51 [a]Luke 2:25, 38 [1]NU *who was waiting*

23:42, 43 The repentant criminal is the first person to enter **Paradise** (see Glossary) with Christ! This dramatic detail, reported only in Luke, demonstrates the unmerited grace of God toward penitent sinners, a magnificent expression of the heart of the gospel. The prayer, **Lord, remember me when You come into Your kingdom,** is highlighted in the hymns and worship of the Orthodox Church.

23:44 Jesus the Lamb of God died on the Cross at **the sixth hour,** noon, about the same time the paschal lambs were ritually killed.

23:46 Luke omits the cry of Christ (Matt. 27:46; Mark 15:34) and underscores His total trust in God to His last human breath.

23:50–53 This is a crucial reference indicating that not all Jewish leaders were opposed to Christ. Matthew calls this man (Joseph of Arimathea) "a disciple of Jesus" (see notes on Matt. 27:57–60).

53 [a]Then he took it down,
wrapped it in linen, and laid it in a
tomb *that was* hewn out of the rock,
where no one had ever lain before.
54 That day was [a]the Preparation,
and the Sabbath drew near.
55 And the women [a]who had come
with Him from Galilee followed after, and [b]they observed the tomb
and how His body was laid.
56 Then they returned and [a]pre-
pared spices and fragrant oils. And
they rested on the Sabbath [b]accord-
ing to the commandment.

The Women Find the Tomb Empty
(Matt. 28:1–8; Mark 16:1–8; John 20:1–18)

24 Now [a]on the first *day* of the
week, very early in the morn-
ing, they, [1]and certain *other women*
with them, came to the tomb [b]bring-
ing the spices which they had
prepared.†
2 [a]But they found the stone rolled
away from the tomb.
3 [a]Then they went in and did not
find the body of the Lord Jesus.
4 And it happened, as they were
[1]greatly perplexed about this, that
[a]behold, two men stood by them in
shining garments.†
5 Then, as they were afraid and
bowed *their* faces to the earth, they
said to them, "Why do you seek the
living among the dead?
6 "He is not here, but is risen!
[a]Remember how He spoke to you
when He was still in Galilee,†
7 "saying, 'The Son of Man must
be [a]delivered into the hands of sinful

53 [a]Mark 15:46
54 [a]Matt. 27:62
55 [a]Luke 8:2 [b]Mark 15:47
56 [a]Mark 16:1 [b]Ex. 20:10

CHAPTER 24

1 [a]John 20:1–8 [b]Luke 23:56 [1]NU omits *and certain other women with them*
2 [a]Mark 16:4
3 [a]Mark 16:5
4 [a]John 20:12 [1]NU omits *greatly*
6 [a]Luke 9:22
7 [a]Luke 9:44; 11:29, 30; 18:31–33
8 [a]John 2:19–22
9 [a]Mark 16:10
10 [a]Luke 8:3
11 [a]Luke 24:25 [1]*nonsense*
12 [a]John 20:3–6 [1]NU omits *lying*
13 [a]Mark 16:12 [1]Lit. *60 stadia*
15 [a][Matt. 18:20]
16 [a]John 20:14; 21:4
17 [1]NU *walk? And they stood still, looking sad.*
18 [a]John 19:25

men, and be crucified, and the third
day rise again.' "
8 And [a]they remembered His
words.
9 [a]Then they returned from the
tomb and told all these things to the
eleven and to all the rest.†
10 It was Mary Magdalene, [a]Jo-
anna, Mary *the mother* of James, and
the other *women* with them, who told
these things to the apostles.
11 [a]And their words seemed to
them like [1]idle tales, and they did
not believe them.
12 [a]But Peter arose and ran to the
tomb; and stooping down, he saw
the linen cloths [1]lying by themselves;
and he departed, marveling to himself at what had happened.

Jesus Appears: The Road to Emmaus
(Mark 16:12, 13)

13 [a]Now behold, two of them were
traveling that same day to a village
called Emmaus, which was [1]seven
miles from Jerusalem.†
14 And they talked together of all
these things which had happened.
15 So it was, while they conversed
and reasoned, that [a]Jesus Himself
drew near and went with them.†
16 But [a]their eyes were restrained,
so that they did not know Him.
17 And He said to them, "What
kind of conversation *is* this that you
have with one another as you
[1]walk and are sad?"
18 Then the one [a]whose name was
Cleopas answered and said to Him,
"Are You the only stranger in Jerusalem, and have You not known the

24:1 The first day of the week was the first day after the Sabbath, which is Sunday, called the Lord's Day in Christian tradition.

24:4 The **men . . . in shining garments** were angels (v. 23).

24:6 He **is risen!** The news of great joy, heralding the new dispensation, resounds throughout the whole world, transforming the creation and the lives of millions of men and women.

24:9 The women going to inform **the eleven and . . . all the rest** implies that the group of faithful followers of Jesus was larger than the eleven disciples (see Acts 1:14, 15).

24:13–35 This is a delightful account of a resurrection appearance of Christ to two perplexed followers: (1) **Cleopas** (v. 18), whom tradition identifies as the brother of Joseph, Mary's husband, and thus Jesus' uncle; and (2) the unnamed follower who, according to tradition, is the evangelist Luke himself.

24:15–17 The risen Christ appears to them in a veiled way. He shows tender concern for the feelings of the two men.

things which happened there in
these days?"†
19 And He said to them, "What
things?" So they said to Him, "The
things concerning Jesus of Nazareth,
[a]who was a Prophet [b]mighty in deed
and word before God and all the
people,†
20 [a]"and how the chief priests and
our rulers delivered Him to be condemned to death, and crucified
Him.†
21 "But we were hoping [a]that it
was He who was going to redeem
Israel. Indeed, besides all this, today
is the third day since these things
happened.
22 "Yes, and [a]certain women of
our company, who arrived at the
tomb early, astonished us.
23 "When they did not find His
body, they came saying that they
had also seen a vision of angels who
said He was alive.
24 "And [a]certain of those *who were*
with us went to the tomb and found
it just as the women had said; but
Him they did not see."
25 Then He said to them, "O foolish ones, and slow of heart to believe
in all that the prophets have
spoken!†
26 [a]"Ought not the Christ to have
suffered these things and to enter
into His [b]glory?"
27 And beginning at [a]Moses and
[b]all the Prophets, He [1]expounded to
them in all the Scriptures the things
concerning Himself.
28 Then they drew near to the village where they were going, and
[a]He [1]indicated that He would have
gone farther.
29 But [a]they constrained Him, saying, [b]"Abide with us, for it is toward
evening, and the day is far spent."
And He went in to stay with them.
30 Now it came to pass, as [a]He sat
at the table with them, that He took
bread, blessed and broke *it*, and gave
it to them†.
31 Then their eyes were opened
and they knew Him; and He van-
ished from their sight.
32 And they said to one another,
"Did not our heart burn within us
while He talked with us on the road,
and while He opened the Scriptures
to us?"
33 So they rose up that very hour
and returned to Jerusalem, and
found the eleven and those *who were*
with them gathered together,
34 saying, "The Lord is risen indeed, and [a]has appeared to
Simon!"†
35 And they told about the things
that had happened on the road, and
how He was [1]known to them in the
breaking of bread.

Jesus Appears to the Apostles
(Mark 16:14; John 20:19–23)

36 [a]Now as they said these things,
Jesus Himself stood in the midst of
them, and said to them, "Peace to
you."†
37 But they were terrified and

19 [a]Matt. 21:11 [b]Acts 7:22
20 [a]Acts 13:27, 28
21 [a]Luke 1:68; 2:38
22 [a]Mark 16:10
24 [a]Luke 24:12
26 [a]Acts 17:2, 3 [b][1 Pet. 1:10–12]
27 [a][Deut. 18:15] [b][Is. 7:14; 9:6] [1]*explained*
28 [a]Mark 6:48 [1]*acted as if*
29 [a]Gen. 19:2, 3 [b][John 14:23]
30 [a]Matt. 14:19
34 [a]1 Cor. 15:5
35 [1]*recognized*
36 [a]Mark 16:14

24:18 These disciples are incredulous that anyone could have been in Jerusalem for the Passover and not be aware of the tragic events of the Passion.

24:19 These two followers think of Jesus as a great **Prophet** who is to redeem Israel (v. 21), probably in the nationalistic sense.

24:20 They recognize that the responsibility for the death of Christ lies on the leaders, **the chief priests** and **rulers.**

24:25–27 The risen Lord censures them for their weak faith, explaining the prophecies of the OT which were fulfilled through His Passion and Resurrection. **To enter into His glory** means to enter into the glorified order of existence, the Resurrection.

24:30–32 The Lord broke bread with them in the same manner as during the Last Supper. Christ's actions and the experience of the meal by the two men image the Eucharist. At each Eucharist, as we continue to share the Lord's Supper, the risen Christ comes to open our eyes to His mystical presence and to leave our hearts burning with His love.

24:34 A resurrection appearance to **Simon,** the Apostle Peter, without any detailed description, is also reported by St. Paul (1 Cor. 15:3–5).

24:36 The resurrectional greeting of **Peace to you** frequently resounds in Orthodox worship.

The Ascension of Our Lord Jesus Christ *Sixth Thursday after Easter*

24:36–53: Jesus appears to His disciples after His Resurrection, then ascends into heaven.

frightened, and supposed they had
seen [a]a spirit.
38 And He said to them, "Why are
you troubled? And why do doubts
arise in your hearts?†
39 "Behold My hands and My feet,
that it is I Myself. [a]Handle Me and
see, for a [b]spirit does not have flesh
and bones as you see I have."
40 [1]When He had said this, He
showed them His hands and His
feet.
41 But while they still did not believe [a]for joy, and marveled, He said
to them, [b]"Have you any food
here?"
42 So they gave Him a piece of
a broiled fish [1]and some honeycomb.
43 [a]And He took *it* and ate in their
presence.

Jesus Enlightens the Apostles

(Matt. 28:16–20; Mark 16:15–18)

44 Then He said to them, [a]"These
are the words which I spoke to you
while I was still with you, that all
things must be fulfilled which were
written in the Law of Moses and *the*
Prophets and *the* Psalms concerning
Me."†
45 And [a]He opened their understanding, that they might comprehend the Scriptures.†
46 Then He said to them, [a]"Thus
it is written, [1]and thus it was necessary for the Christ to suffer
and to rise from the dead the third
day,
47 "and that repentance and [a]re-
mission of sins should be preached
in His name [b]to all nations, beginning at Jerusalem.†
48 "And [a]you are witnesses of
these things.
49 [a]"Behold, I send the Promise of
My Father upon you; but tarry in
the city [1]of Jerusalem until you
are endued with power from on
high."†

The Ascension

(Mark 16:19, 20)

50 And He led them out [a]as far as
Bethany, and He lifted up His hands
and blessed them.†

37 [a]Mark 6:49
39 [a]John 20:20, 27 [b][1 Cor. 15:50]
40 [1]Some printed New Testaments omit v. 40. It is found in nearly all Gr. mss.
41 [a]Gen. 45:26 [b]John 21:5
42 [1]NU omits *and some honeycomb*
43 [a]Acts 10:39–41
44 [a]Matt. 16:21; 17:22; 20:18
45 [a]Acts 16:14
46 [a]Acts 17:3 [1]NU *that the Christ should suffer and rise*
47 [a]Acts 5:31; 10:43; 13:38; 26:18 [b][Jer. 31:34]
48 [a][Acts 1:8]
49 [a]Joel 2:28 [1]NU omits *of Jerusalem*
50 [a]Acts 1:12

24:38–43 To counter the fears and doubts of the disciples, the Lord demonstrates the reality of His Resurrection by inviting them to touch Him and by eating with them. This is a special instance, since the glorified body of Christ needs no food for sustenance.

24:44 The Law, the Prophets, and the Psalms were the three sections of the Hebrew Scriptures—also called the Pentateuch, the Prophets, and the Writings.

24:45 Understanding is not merely intellectual, but a full experiential, spiritual understanding. To comprehend and receive the spiritual value of the Scriptures is a gift of the risen Lord through the power of the Holy Spirit.

24:47 Repentance and remission of sins are part of the gospel, which is to be proclaimed **in His name to all nations.**

24:49 Endued with power from on high means filled with the Holy Spirit, which occurs on Pentecost (Acts 1:8; 2:2–4). The apostles are to wait in Jerusalem, because their divine mission can be accomplished only with the enabling of divine power. Luke concludes his gospel with this reference to **the Promise of My Father** and begins the Book of Acts with the fulfillment of it.

24:50–53 Luke alone records the event of the Ascension (see also Acts 1:9). The Ascension signifies Jesus' full glorification and lordship over all. He is *Pantokrator,* the All-ruling Christ, sharing equal glory, authority, and honor with the Father. The Ascension is as great a mystery as the Resurrection, and should not be understood simply in terms of time and space. The

(continued on next page)

51 [a]Now it came to pass, while He
blessed them, that He was parted
from them and carried up into
heaven.
52 [a]And they worshiped Him, and
returned to Jerusalem with great joy,
53 and were continually [a]in the
temple [1]praising and blessing God.
[2]Amen.

51 [a]Mark 16:19
52 [a]Matt. 28:9
53 [a]Acts 2:46 [1]NU omits *praising and*
[2]NU omits *Amen.*

(continued from previous page)
risen Lord Jesus Christ is now enthroned, sharing fully the ruling power of the Father together with the all-Holy Spirit. The disciples **worshiped Him** (v. 52) because His Resurrection and Ascension fully reveal His divine nature. They also continue to meet together, **praising and blessing God** (v. 53) for all the gifts of salvation in the Son. **Joy** (v. 52) dominates their lives through the renewing experience of His Resurrection.

The Gospel According to

ST. JOHN

Author: *St. John the Apostle*

Date: *about* A.D. *96*

Theme: *The Eternal Son of God Has Come in the Flesh*

AUTHOR: According to tradition, St. John the Apostle was assisted by St. Prochoros in writing this Gospel. John, "Son of Thunder" (Mark 3:17), was one of the Twelve Apostles of Jesus. John and his brother, the Apostle James, were fishermen by trade, like their father Zebedee. John is believed to be the youngest Apostle and also "the beloved disciple" of Christ (13:23; 21:7, 20). On the Cross, Jesus entrusted His mother, the Virgin Mary, to John's care (19:26, 27). John was a "pillar" of the church in Jerusalem, and later moved to Ephesus. He served as the leading authority ("Elder," lit. "presbyter," in 2 John 1) of Ephesus for the remainder of his ministry. During the reign of the tyrannical Roman Emperor Domitian (A.D. 81–96), John was exiled to the nearby island of Patmos, where he wrote Revelation. Upon the emperor's death he returned to Ephesus to resume his episcopacy and to write his Gospel.

John is the first of only three saints in history to be named by the Church "the Theologian," because of the profundity of his Gospel, which has been called "the spiritual Gospel." The New Testament contains four other books attributed to John: three letters (1, 2, and 3 John), written about A.D. 90, and the Book of Revelation, written about A.D. 95.

St. John the Apostle was almost one hundred years old when he died, about A.D. 96–100.

DATE: This Gospel, written about A.D. 96, is usually considered the last of the four Gospels to be written, supplementing the other three.

MAJOR THEME: The eternal Son of God has come in the flesh. The Gospel was written "that you may believe that Jesus is the Christ, the Son of God, and that believing you may have life in His name" (20:31).

The Gospel of John has many theological themes. They include the following:

(1) *The Trinity*. In his Gospel, John is quite explicit about the Persons of the Trinity and their relationships. The Son has one and the same nature as the Father (1:1; 10:30). When Jesus declares, "I AM" (Gr. *ego eimi*, 8:58; see 4:26; 6:20; 8:24, 28; 13:19; 18:6), He is calling Himself by the name of the LORD of the Old Testament and therefore declaring Himself to be God. The difference

between the Father and the Son is that of person: the Son is the Only Begotten (1:18; 3:16, 18); by implication, the Father is the Unbegotten. While He is the source of the Son, the Father has given all things to the Son (3:35; 13:3; 17:2), and their relationship is reciprocal (10:15; 14:10, 11, 20; 17:21–23). This relationship is the model for life in the Church (10:14; 14:20; 17:23). Similarly, the Holy Spirit is distinguished from the Father in person, *proceeding* from Him (15:26). By nature, the Holy Spirit has everything the Son has (16:13–15) and everything the Father has. In their activity in the world, neither the Son nor the Holy Spirit acts on His own, but both are "sent" (3:17, 34; 14:26; 15:26; 17:3, 18, 21, 25).

(2) *Glory*. Glorification is a prominent theme in John's theology. The glory of God is the radiance and power of His saving acts in history. It is preeminently manifested or revealed in Christ's earthly ministry—His Person, words, and works—but His glory is also experienced by the Church in the power of the Holy Spirit, the Helper or Paraclete (14:16, 26; 15:26; 16:7). In John, the gift of the Holy Spirit is not something peripheral or additional to salvation. Rather, it is the final, decisive act of salvation, the energizing power of the new creation. Glorification begins not in the next life, but now, commencing with the Incarnation of Christ and continuing with those who receive a new birth (1:12; 3:3, 5; 7:38) and are in union with Christ (14:20–23; 15:1–7; 17:22, 24). We "are being transformed . . . from glory to glory" (2 Cor. 3:18). In John:

(a) We behold Christ's glory through the Incarnation (1:14).

(b) Jesus manifests His glory to us so we might believe (2:11; 11:40).

(c) Jesus seeks glory for the Father (7:18), but not for Himself (8:50).

(d) The Father's glory is given to us by the Son (17:22).

(e) We will behold God's glory when we are with Him in eternity (17:24).

(3) *The spiritual dimension*. John's Gospel is not strictly historical. The Evangelist presents the grandeur of the divine nature of Christ as he more fully understood it after Jesus' Resurrection, aided by the Holy Spirit (see 2:22; 16:13). This is a "spiritual Gospel" because the mystical, theological perspective dominates, and it is reflected to this day in the theology and liturgical practices of the Orthodox Church. Everything in life is conditioned by the realm and activity of God the Trinity, whose eternal glory, life and light is shared with those who believe. The Christian receives heavenly birth and beholds heavenly things (1:12, 14, 51; 3:3, 5, 12; 14:12). This revelation of divine life and light is resisted by this age, however, resulting in great spiritual warfare: the Kingdom of God versus "the world" as a fallen entity in rebellion against God. John describes this conflict with terms such as light and darkness (1:5; 3:19; 8:12; 12:35), truth and falsehood (3:20, 21; 8:32, 44; 18:37), life and death (3:16, 36; 5:24, 29; 10:28; 11:25), and spirit and flesh (3:6; 6:63).

(4) *The sacramental dimension*. A sacrament is an event in which God's grace works together with our faith to bring us into closer communion with Him. The sacraments are called "mysteries" (Gr. *mysterion*) for by them God, through the action of grace, bestows divine life on all who live in faith and obedience, a foretaste of the fulfillment of salvation in the age to come.

The early Church was a community of prayer and worship centered on the mysteries of baptism and the Lord's Supper (Acts 2:38, 42; 8:36–38; Rom. 6:3–11; 1 Cor. 10:16, 17; 11:23–29). John stresses the mysterious and sacramental presence and activity of God in the world, linking the saving work of Christ to baptism (3:5) and the Eucharist (6:52–59). In the context of true faith, these mysteries contribute to our salvation. The sacraments are not magical, nor are they laws or ordinances to be obeyed; they are mystical expressions of the life of faith. There is no dichotomy between the sacred and the profane, word and sacrament, faith and works. Jesus came to redeem and sanctify all of life and all of creation.

In the Gospel of John, there are direct references, as well as many allusions, to the sacraments:

(a) *Baptism:* As water is a necessity for life, so the water of baptism, together with the Holy Spirit, is necessary for eternal life—fulfilling Isaiah's prophecy that God's people will joyfully draw water from the wells of salvation (Is. 12:3; 58:11). From the wedding at Cana (2:9), to the conversation with Nicodemus (3:5), to the encounter with the woman at the well (4:14), the significance and transforming power of water and the Spirit are made manifest.

(b) *Anointing by the Spirit (chrismation):* In the Gospel of John it is difficult to distinguish a baptismal reference from a chrismational one. Jesus speaks to Nicodemus about "water and the Spirit" (3:5). To the Samaritan woman He promises the gift of "living water" (4:10, 14), which the evangelist himself interprets as the new life by the gift of the Spirit (7:38, 39).

(c) *The Eucharist:* The Church Fathers found allusions to the Eucharist in the wine at Cana and the bread for feeding the five thousand, an event which provided the setting for Jesus' discourse on the bread of life. Certainly 6:52–59 is a powerful biblical expression of the sacramental and eucharistic basis of Christian life. In this passage Christ speaks not merely of eating the bread of life through faith alone, but of the eating of His *flesh* and the drinking of His *blood*—which can only refer to the Eucharist as a mystical-sacramental act uniting us with Him.

(5) *The Church.* The Gospel of John testifies to a strong sense of community among the disciples, expressed through the plural "we" (1:14, 16). True disciples are those who believe in Jesus as the incarnate Son of the Father, who are united with Him, and who here and now express the life of divine love given by Christ. The foot-washing in chapter 13 shows the Church is to be characterized by humble service and mutual love, which is the New Commandment (13:34). The symbolism of the vine and branches (15:1–8) shows the Church in intimate and abiding unity with the incarnate Son. The "High Priestly Prayer" of chapter 17 shows the Church to be one, holy, catholic, and apostolic—manifesting universal truth and moving toward the glory of God.

(6) *The Paschal theme.* Time in John is often marked by the feasts of the Jews, especially the Passover (Heb. *pascha*). Three Passovers are specifically mentioned, hence the tradition that the public ministry of Jesus encompassed a three-year period: (a) at 2:13, when Jesus cleanses the temple as a symbol of the Resurrection of His body; (b) at 6:4, when Jesus delivers His discourse on the bread of life, His own body being offered for the life of the world; and (c) at 11:55, when Jesus, during the Passover, leads His followers to a new Passover through His death and Resurrection.

Christ is called the Lamb of God (1:29, 36). He is crucified at about noon, before the Passover meal, the time at which the paschal lambs were ritually slaughtered (see 1 Cor. 5:7). In Orthodox tradition, the Paschal theme of John is heightened by the liturgical practice of reading his Gospel during the Easter period, up until Pentecost. This continues the tradition, going back perhaps as far as the second century, in which catechumens were baptized on Resurrection Sunday (Pascha or Easter) and then admitted to the full liturgy of the Church. Here, they heard John's Gospel read for fifty days until Pentecost. Thus the new converts learned of the change that had taken place in them and the glories of their union with Christ.

(7) *The Redemption of the World.* In John's perspective, the Divine Word, the Son of God, came into the world to save the world and, through the life of the Church, to offer the whole world up to God. Christ and His Church begin this transformation now.

OUTLINE

- I. The witness, John the Baptist — 1:1–51
  - A. Prologue — 1:1–18
    - 1. The Word is God — 1:1–5
    - 2. John's witness: The Word became man — 1:6–13
    - 3. The Word made flesh reveals the Father — 1:14–18
  - B. The mission of John the Baptist — 1:19–51
    - 1. His mission: Preparation for the Messiah — 1:19–28
    - 2. The Lamb, the Son of God — 1:29–34
    - 3. The Baptist's disciples follow Jesus — 1:35–51
- II. The Word incarnate transfigures creation — 2:1–10:42
  - A. The new creation prefigured — 2:1–25
    - 1. Water changed to wine — 2:1–12
    - 2. Jesus cleanses the temple — 2:13–25
  - B. Baptism manifested — 3:1—5:47
    - 1. In Jerusalem with Nicodemus: Water and the Spirit — 3:1–21
    - 2. In Judea with John the Baptist: Jesus is God! — 3:22–36
    - 3. In Samaria: The Samaritan woman at the well — 4:1–42
    - 4. In Galilee: Healing of a Gentile — 4:43–54
    - 5. In Jerusalem: Healing at a pool — 5:1–47
  - C. The Eucharist manifested: Feeding of 5,000 — 6:1–71
    - 1. Feeding of the five thousand — 6:1–21
    - 2. Jesus is the Bread of Life — 6:22–71
  - D. The old creation transformed — 7:1—10:42
    - 1. The Feast of Tabernacles fulfilled — 7:1—10:21
      - a. By the Son and the Holy Spirit — 7:1—8:11
      - b. By the Light of the World — 8:12—9:38
      - c. By true love: The caring Shepherd — 9:39—10:21
    - 2. The Feast of Dedication (Hanukkah) fulfilled — 10:22–42
- III. The Word incarnate transfigures all humanity — 11:1—17:26
  - A. Through death and resurrection: Lazarus — 11:1—12:11
  - B. Through ascension into the Kingdom: Palm Sunday — 12:12–50
  - C. Through the messianic Banquet of the Kingdom — 13:1—17:26

1. The New Commandment: Love 13:1–38
2. The New Covenant 14:1—16:15
   a. Approaching the Father 14:1–6
   b. The presence of the Trinity 14:7–31
   c. Union and communion with God incarnate 15:1–17
   d. Opposition in this world 15:18—16:4
   e. The work of the Holy Spirit 16:5–15
3. Preparation for the Passion 16:16–33
4. Prayer for the Church 17:1–26

IV. The Paschal offering: Death and Resurrection 18:1—21:25
A. Death: The Passion of Christ 18:1—19:42
1. Betrayal and arrest 18:1–11
2. Trials: Before Annas, Caiaphas, Pilate 18:12—19:16
3. Crucifixion 19:17–37
4. Burial 19:38–42

B. Resurrection of Christ 20:1—21:25
1. The tomb is empty 20:1–10
2. Jesus appears to Mary Magdalene 20:11–18
3. Jesus appears to His disciples 20:19–29
4. First epilogue: Purpose of this Gospel 20:30, 31
5. Further appearances of Christ 21:1–14
6. Peter is restored and commissioned 21:15–23
7. Second epilogue: John's personal witness 21:24, 25

The Word Is God

1 In the beginning [a]was the Word,
and the [b]Word was [c]with God,
and the Word was [d]God.†
2 [a]He was in the beginning with
God.
3 [a]All things were made through
Him, and without Him nothing was
made that was made.†
4 [a]In Him was life, and [b]the life
was the light of men.†

CHAPTER 1
1 [a]1 John 1:1 [b]Rev. 19:13 [c][John 17:5] [d][1 John 5:20]
2 [a]Gen. 1:1
3 [a][Col. 1:16, 17]
4 [a][1 John 5:11] [b]John 8:12; 9:5; 12:46

1:1–18 John's well-known "Prologue" proclaims Christ is God. It is read during the Easter (Pascha) liturgy.

1:1 In the beginning recalls the creation but speaks of the Creator Himself. As Gen. 1:1 introduces the original creation, by itself an incomplete existence, this verse reveals the new creation, a fulfilled and complete existence.

Was the Word (Gr. *logos*): *Was* indicates existence without reference to a starting point. Therefore, *In the beginning was the Word* emphasizes (1) the Word's eternal existence in the Father without beginning, and (2) His oneness with Him in essence. *Logos* signifies wisdom and reason as well as word: the Creator. ("Creation" is Gr. *logikos*, participating in the Divine *Word*.) With the Incarnation, the *Logos* fully participates in human nature.

The Word was with God: *With* in the Greek shows that the Word, the Son, is (1) a distinct Person from the Father, and (2) in communion with the Father.

The Word was God: The OT prophets saw the Word of God as the presence of the Lord. This phrase reveals He is not only from the Father, He is coequal and coeternal with the Father: one in divinity with Him. "I and My Father are one" (10:30).

Some mistranslate this phrase "the Word was *a god*" to propagate their heresy that the Son is a created being, not fully divine. Such a translation is unwarranted and false.

1:3 The Word is co-Creator of all things with the Father (Gen. 1 and Ps. 33:6, 9), not merely an "instrument" or a "servant" of creation. Will, operation, and power are seen to be one in the Father, Son and Holy Spirit. **Through Him** shows the Word is not included in **all things** created by the Father. His eternal birth is by generation from the Father, whereas

(continued on page 211)

CHRISTOLOGY

The center of Christianity is the Lord Jesus Christ Himself. In fact, He is the centerpiece of all history. But the world struggles with His identity. Who is He? Is He God? Is He man? Both? The Scriptures clearly answer these crucial questions.

In his Gospel, John gives a specific and definitive explanation of who Christ is. "In the beginning was the Word, and the Word was with God, and the Word was God" (1:1). John the Baptist, the forerunner of Christ, revealed God the Word as "the Light" (1:6, 7). "The Word became flesh and dwelt among us" (1:14). Who then is Jesus Christ?

(1) He is God, for He was with God from before all time. Clearly, the One born Jesus of Nazareth did not have His beginning in His earthly birth. Rather, He is the eternal Son of God, without beginning. There never was a time when the Son of God did not exist.

(2) He is also man, for He "became flesh." He has become one of us, being like us in all things but without sin.

(3) He acts both as God and as man, doing what is appropriate for each nature in the unity provided by His one divine Person. Never does divine nature and activity become changed into human nature and activity. The two are in union without confusion. Christ does, however, "energize" human nature with divine energy so that human nature is redeemed from sin and death and brought into union with God. He thus "deifies" humanity.

The miracle of these incomparable truths is known as the knowledge of Christ, or "Christology." Many documents have expounded on Christology, but the definitive text is the Nicene Creed, the outcome of the first and second Ecumenical Councils in the fourth century. The Creed of Chalcedon (issued by the fourth Ecumenical Council, A.D. 451) embodies other truths concerning the Incarnation of the Word. These creeds set the doctrinal fences outside of which we do not wander in our knowledge of Christ.

The Apostle John bears witness to Christ: "That which was from the beginning, which we have heard, which we have seen with our eyes, which we have looked upon, and our hands have handled, concerning the Word of life—the life was manifested, and we have seen, and bear witness, and declare to you that eternal life which was with the Father and was manifested to us—that which we have seen and heard we declare to you, that you also may have fellowship with us; and truly our fellowship is with the Father and with His Son Jesus Christ" (1 John 1:1–3).

We, too, bear witness to Jesus Christ. For since God became man, and we are united with Him in baptism, we experience His Incarnation in our lives. The miracle of Christology for us is that, as the Son of God became man, we in turn may partake of God.

Easter (Pascha)—The Resurrection of Christ

1:1–17: Jesus Christ is God become Man that men might become children of God.

5 And [a]the light shines in the
darkness, and the darkness did not
[1]comprehend it.†

The Baptist's Witness to the Word

6 There was a [a]man sent from
God, whose name *was* John.
7 This man came for a [a]witness,
to bear witness of the Light, that all
through him might [b]believe.
8 He was not that Light, but *was*
sent to bear witness of that [a]Light.
9 [a]That[1] was the true Light which
gives light to every man coming into
the world.†
10 He was in the world, and the
world was made through Him, and
[a]the world did not know Him.
11 [a]He came to His [1]own, and His
[2]own did not receive Him.†
12 But [a]as many as received Him,
to them He gave the [1]right to become
children of God, to those who believe in His name:†
13 [a]who were born, not of blood,
nor of the will of the flesh, nor of
the will of man, but of God.†

The Word Becomes Flesh to Reveal the Father

14 [a]And the Word [b]became [c]flesh
and dwelt among us, and [d]we be-

5 [a][John 3:19] [1]Or *overcome* **6** [a]Matt. 3:1–17 **7** [a]John 3:25–36; 5:33–35 [b][John 3:16] **8** [a]Is. 9:2; 49:6 **9** [a]Is. 49:6 [1]Or *That was the true Light which, coming into the world, gives light to every man.* **10** [a]Heb. 1:2 **11** [a][Luke 19:14] [1]His own things or domain [2]His own people **12** [a]Gal. 3:26 [1]*authority* **13** [a][1 Pet. 1:23] **14** [a]Rev. 19:13 [b]Gal. 4:4 [c]Heb. 2:11 [d]Is. 40:5

(continued from page 209)
the works of creation are made. Thus, the heavens and the earth are the works of the One who made them, while the Son alone is born from the Father. Even when He comes in human flesh, the Word forever remains God, the Creator.

1:4 As the Divine Word incarnate, Christ is also the source of **life** and enlightenment. Because the Word is God, He is life: only God has life in Himself.

And the life was the light: By seeing and participating in Christ's *life* believers become *light* and children of light (12:36). Moses saw this light in the burning bush (Ex. 3:2), Isaiah saw it in his heavenly vision (Is. 6:1–5), and Peter, James and John saw it on the Mount of Transfiguration (Matt. 17:2). In the Divine Liturgy at Easter, light breaks forth from the night at the proclamation of the Resurrection: "Come, take light from the light that is never overtaken by night. Come, glorify Christ, risen from the dead."

1:5 Darkness: the satanic wickedness which actively opposes the light. Though the world has embraced darkness (3:19), the Word freely offers light to all. **Comprehend:** see center-column note. Darkness will oppose the light, yet cannot defeat the light.

1:9, 10 The **true Light**, Jesus Christ, enlightens every person, but **the world** refuses to receive and live in this light, and does not **know Him** (v. 10). The Orthodox Church sings, in the hymn after Communion, "We have seen the true light . . . worshiping the undivided Trinity."

1:11 Most of **His own** people, the Jews, failed to **receive Him.**

1:12 Right: see center-column note. This is a gift, not an inalienable right. Those who receive Christ are given His power, His grace, to **become children of God**—no longer servants, but friends of Christ (15:15). The Jews were children of God by descent from Abraham, the father of the people of God. But now divine sonship is a gift of grace through faith in Jesus. Whether we are of a privileged race or not, we are born into the family of God and saved not by "the faith of our fathers," but by our own faith in Christ. **His name:** His identity, the Word, the Son of God, the Messiah and Savior, who in His humanity is called Jesus. To **believe** means to trust oneself completely to Him: who He is, what He does, what He teaches.

1:13 Who were born: This spiritual birth from God is a mystery of the Holy Spirit (3:8) which is closely integrated with Holy Baptism (3:5; see Titus 3:5).

held His glory, the glory as of the
only begotten of the Father, [e]full of
grace and truth.†
15 [a]John bore witness of Him and
cried out, saying, "This was He of
whom I said, [b]'He who comes after
me [1]is preferred before me, [c]for He
was before me.' "
16 [1]And of His [a]fullness we have
all received, and grace for grace.†
17 For [a]the law was given through
Moses, *but* [b]grace and [c]truth came
through Jesus Christ.
18 [a]No one has seen God at any
time. [b]The only begotten [1]Son, who
is in the bosom of the Father, He has
declared *Him.*†

14 [e][John 8:32; 14:6; 18:37] **15** [a]John 3:32 [b][Matt. 3:11] [c][Col. 1:17] [1]*ranks higher than I* **16** [a][Col. 1:19; 2:9] [1]NU *For* **17** [a][Ex. 20:1] [b][Rom. 5:21; 6:14] [c][John 8:32; 14:6; 18:37] **18** [a]Ex. 33:20 [b]1 John 4:9 [1]NU *God*

Who Is John the Baptist?

(Matt. 3:1–6; Mark 1:1–6; Luke 3:1–6)

19 Now this is [a]the testimony of
John, when the Jews sent priests and
Levites from Jerusalem to ask him,
"Who are you?"†

19 [a]John 5:33

1:14 The Word became flesh: Here we turn to the humanity of Jesus. The Word became man without ceasing to be fully God: the mystery of God incarnate! He assumed complete human nature, both a physical body and a rational soul—everything we are, except for sin. As God and man in one Person, Christ accomplishes a redemption that fully heals and saves fallen humanity. He **dwelt among us:** "We" are the disciples, the people of God, pilgrims in this transient world. In the OT, God's glory, His radiant power, *dwelt* ("tabernacled") in the temple. Here, the eternal Word in His divine glory comes to dwell in the midst of humanity through the Incarnation.

We beheld His glory: The *glory* of the Word which the Apostles *beheld* was the manifestation of the very presence of God, shown in His words and deeds (2:11), and more fully *beheld* in His Transfiguration and His Resurrection.

Only begotten of the Father: The Son was eternally born from the Father; the Son has no beginning but He has His source in the Father. He is called *Only* Begotten because there is no other born from the Father. Thus, the Son Himself is God. (The Holy Spirit exists eternally from the Father through another mystery called "procession"—15:26.)

Full of grace and truth: This phrase qualifies not only "the Word" but also "the glory." *Grace* is Jesus' uncreated energy manifested to us through His lovingkindness and redeeming love. *Truth* includes His faithfulness to His promises and covenants, and the abiding reality of His gifts. By His grace and truth we enjoy a life in union and communion with God through Christ.

1:16 And of His fullness we have all received: Because Christ is God by nature, God's uncreated grace filled His human nature, thus deifying it (see article, "Deification," at 2 Pet. 1). In union with Christ's deified humanity, we participate in the fullness of grace. Through Christ, God's children become gods *by grace* (10:34, 35), without ceasing to be human by nature. As metal thrust into fire takes on the heat of the fire without ceasing to be itself, so human nature immersed in God's uncreated grace and truth becomes godlike without ceasing to be human. **Grace for grace:** A Semitic expression signifying an abundance of grace.

1:18 No one has seen God at any time: No one has had a direct vision of the nature of God. To see God is to die (Ex. 33:20). Moses saw only the "back" of God. Isaiah beheld God's glory (see 12:41; Is. 6:1). Since to see God in His essence is to be God, the Son who is **in the bosom of the Father** can **declare** God. He is one with the Father, and He (together with the Holy Spirit) sees the Father in His essence. As "Light of Light," Jesus reveals the Father: when we see Jesus Christ we see the Father (14:9).

1:19–51 Here the theological Prologue ends and the focus shifts to the witness of John the Baptist (vv. 19–34; see also 3:22–36) and to Jesus calling the first Apostles (vv. 35–51). The account covers four successive days:

(1) The first day (vv. 19–28)—John the Baptist is a witness to Jesus in the presence of the Jews.

(2) The second day (vv. 29–34)—the Baptist speaks to his own disciples.

(3) The third day (vv. 35–42)—John the Baptist guides two of his disciples to Jesus, and they acknowledge Him as the Messiah.

(4) The fourth day (vv. 43–51)—Jesus calls Philip and Nathanael.

John the Baptist denies he is himself the Messiah (vv. 19, 20), but claims to be the prophetic forerunner of Christ spoken of by Isaiah (vv. 21–23; see Is. 40:3). He will announce that the Messiah is present in the world (vv. 24–28), and that Jesus is He (vv. 29–34).

20 [a]He confessed, and did not
deny, but confessed, "I am not the
Christ."
21 And they asked him, "What
then? Are you Elijah?" He said, "I
am not." "Are you [a]the Prophet?"
And he answered, "No."†
22 Then they said to him, "Who
are you, that we may give an answer
to those who sent us? What do you
say about yourself?"
23 He said: [a]"I *am*

[b]*'The voice of one crying in the wilderness:*
"Make straight the way of the LORD,"'

as the prophet Isaiah said."

Why Does John Baptize?
(Luke 3:15–18)

24 Now those who were sent were
from the Pharisees.†
25 And they asked him, saying,
"Why then do you baptize if you are
not the Christ, nor Elijah, nor the
Prophet?"
26 John answered them, saying,
[a]"I baptize with water, [b]but there
stands One among you whom you
do not know.†
27 [a]"It is He who, coming after me,
[1]is preferred before me, whose
sandal strap I am not worthy to
loose."
28 These things were done [a]in
[1]Bethabara beyond the Jordan,
where John was baptizing.

20 [a]Luke 3:15 **21** [a]Deut. 18:15, 18 **23** [a]Matt. 3:3 [b]Is. 40:3 **26** [a]Matt. 3:11 [b]Mal. 3:1 **27** [a]Acts 19:4 [1]*ranks higher than I* **28** [a]Judg. 7:24 [1]NU, M *Bethany*

The Baptist's Testimony to Christ
(Matt. 3:13–17; Mark 1:9–11; Luke 3:21, 22)

29 The next day John saw Jesus
coming toward him, and said, "Behold! [a]The Lamb of God [b]who takes
away the sin of the world!†
30 "This is He of whom I said, 'After me comes a Man who [1]is preferred before me, for He was before
me.'
31 "I did not know Him; but that
He should be revealed to Israel,
[a]therefore I came baptizing with
water."
32 [a]And John bore witness, saying,
"I saw the Spirit descending from
heaven like a dove, and He remained
upon Him.†
33 "I did not know Him, but He
who sent me to baptize with water
said to me, 'Upon whom you see the
Spirit descending, and remaining on
Him, [a]this is He who baptizes with
the Holy Spirit.'
34 "And I have seen and testified
that this is the [a]Son of God."

The Baptist's Disciples Follow Jesus
(Matt. 4:18–22; Mark 1:16–20; Luke 5:1–11)

35 Again, the next day, John stood
with two of his disciples.†
36 And looking at Jesus as He
walked, he said, [a]"Behold the Lamb
of God!"
37 The two disciples heard him

29 [a]Rev. 5:6–14 [b][1 Pet. 2:24] **30** [1]*ranks higher than I* **31** [a]Matt. 3:6 **32** [a]Mark 1:10 **33** [a]Matt. 3:11 **34** [a]John 11:27 **36** [a]John 1:29

1:21 The Baptist is a prophet, but not **the Prophet,** the messianic Moses-like figure expected by the Jews (Deut. 18:15, 18).

1:24 The Pharisees refuse to repent. They see neither Jesus as the light (v. 26) nor the Father whom He revealed (8:19). Practicing external religion, they lack inward enlightenment.

1:26 John baptizes with **water** as a sign of repentance, but baptism with the Spirit can come only through Christ.

1:29 John's naming Jesus publicly as the **Lamb of God** recalls Isaiah's "Servant of God" who dies for the transgressions of His people (Is. 53:4–12). Christ, the true Paschal *Lamb,* offers Himself for our deliverance from darkness and death (1 Pet. 1:18, 19).

1:32 The Spirit **remained upon Him** because Christ possesses the Holy Spirit in His fullness.

1:35–45 Jesus' first disciples had been followers of John the Baptist. They were (1) **Andrew** (v. 40); (2) an unnamed disciple (v. 40), probably the author of this Gospel; (3) Andrew's **brother, Simon** (v. 41), given the name **Cephas,** which is equivalent to the Greek "Peter," meaning "rock" (v. 42); (4) **Philip** (v. 43); and (5) **Nathanael** (v. 45), also known as Bartholomew.

Sunday of Orthodoxy

First Sunday of Lent

1:43–51: We shall see Heaven.

speak, and they [a]followed Jesus.
38 Then Jesus turned, and seeing
them following, said to them, "What
do you seek?" They said to Him,
"Rabbi" (which is to say, when
translated, Teacher), "where are You
staying?"
39 He said to them, "Come and
see." They came and saw where He
was staying, and remained with Him
that day (now it was about the tenth
hour).
40 One of the two who heard John
speak, and followed Him, was [a]An-
drew, Simon Peter's brother.
41 He first found his own brother
Simon, and said to him, "We have
found the [1]Messiah" (which is translated, the Christ).
42 And he brought him to Jesus.
Now when Jesus looked at him, He
said, "You are Simon the son of
[1]Jonah. [a]You shall be called Cephas"
(which is translated, [2]A Stone).
43 The following day Jesus wanted
to go to Galilee, and He found
[a]Philip and said to him, "Follow
Me."†
44 Now [a]Philip was from Bethsaida, the city of Andrew and
Peter.
45 Philip found [a]Nathanael and
said to him, "We have found Him
of whom [b]Moses in the law, and also
the [c]prophets, wrote—Jesus [d]of
Nazareth, the [e]son of Joseph."
46 And Nathanael said to him,
[a]"Can anything good come out of
Nazareth?" Philip said to him,
"Come and see."
47 Jesus saw Nathanael coming toward Him, and said of him, "Behold,
[a]an Israelite indeed, in whom is no
deceit!"†
48 Nathanael said to Him, "How
do You know me?" Jesus answered
and said to him, "Before Philip called
you, when you were under the fig
tree, I saw you."†
49 Nathanael answered and said to
Him, "Rabbi, [a]You are the Son of
God! You are [b]the King of Israel!"
50 Jesus answered and said to him,
"Because I said to you, 'I saw you
under the fig tree,' do you believe?
You will see greater things than
these."
51 And He said to him, "Most assuredly, I say to you, [a]hereafter[1] you
shall see heaven open, and the angels of God ascending and descending upon the Son of Man."†

The First Sign at Cana

2 On the third day there was a
[a]wedding in [b]Cana of Galilee,

37 [a]Matt. 4:20, 22
40 [a]Matt. 4:18
41 [1]Lit. *Anointed One*
42 [a]Matt. 16:18
[1]NU *John*
[2]Gr. *Petros,* usually translated *Peter*
43 [a]John 6:5; 12:21, 22; 14:8, 9
44 [a]John 12:21
45 [a]John 21:2
[b]Luke 24:27
[c][Zech. 6:12]
[d][Matt. 2:23]
[e]Luke 3:23
46 [a]John 7:41, 42, 52
47 [a]Ps. 32:2; 73:1
49 [a]Matt. 14:33
[b]Matt. 21:5
51 [a]Gen. 28:12
[1]NU omits *hereafter*

CHAPTER 2

1 [a][Heb. 13:4]
[b]John 4:46

1:43 Follow Me: Philip immediately obeys, perhaps because he already knows about Jesus, or beholds the divine presence in Him.

1:47 No deceit implies a pure heart which is capable of recognizing Christ.

1:48, 49 Jesus' foreknowledge stirs Nathanael to a joyous confession of faith.

1:51 In ancient Jewish thought, the **Son of Man** is a mysterious being of heavenly origin who is to usher in the Kingdom of God (see Dan. 7:13, 14). Jesus is this One (see Matt. 24:30, 31). In OT prophecy, Jacob dreamed of a ladder connecting earth and heaven, upon which the angels of God were ascending and descending (see Gen. 28:12–15). Jesus—the Son of Man—is "Jacob's Ladder," man's access to God, the final and fullest revelation of God. In His Incarnation, God and man are united. In the teachings and miracles of His public ministry, the Kingdom of God on earth is inaugurated. His Cross, set up on earth like Jacob's ladder, reaches into heaven. Through His Resurrection, Ascension, and exaltation to the right hand of God, human nature is raised into heaven. And through His Second Coming, all things will be reconciled to God. In Christ, heaven and earth are joined.

and the [c]mother of Jesus was there.†
2 Now both Jesus and His disciples were invited to the wedding.
3 And when they ran out of wine,
the mother of Jesus said to Him,
"They have no wine."†
4 Jesus said to her, [a]"Woman,
[b]what does your concern have to do
with Me? [c]My hour has not yet
come."†
5 His mother said to the servants,
"Whatever He says to you, do *it*."†
6 Now there were set there six
waterpots of stone, [a]according to the
manner of purification of the Jews,
containing twenty or thirty gallons
apiece.†
7 Jesus said to them, "Fill the
waterpots with water." And they
filled them up to the brim.†
8 And He said to them, "Draw
some out now, and take *it* to the master of the feast." And they took *it*.
9 When the master of the feast
had tasted [a]the water that was made
wine, and did not know where it
came from (but the servants who had
drawn the water knew), the master
of the feast called the bridegroom.†
10 And he said to him, "Every man
at the beginning sets out the good
wine, and when the *guests* have well
drunk, then the inferior. You have
kept the good wine until now!"
11 This [a]beginning of signs Jesus
did in Cana of Galilee, [b]and [1]mani-
fested His glory; and His disciples believed in Him.†
12 After this He went down to
[a]Capernaum, He, His mother,

1 [c]John 19:25
4 [a]John 19:26 [b]2 Sam. 16:10 [c]John 7:6, 8, 30; 8:20
6 [a][Mark 7:3]
9 [a]John 4:46
11 [a]John 4:54 [b][John 1:14] [1]*revealed*
12 [a]Matt. 4:13

2:1–11 The **wedding in Cana** is the setting for the first of the seven signs performed by Jesus in the Gospel of John. These signs are: (1) changing water into wine; (2) curing the nobleman's son (4:46–54); (3) healing the paralytic (5:1–15); (4) feeding the 5,000 (6:1–14); (5) walking on water (6:15–21); (6) giving sight to the blind man (9:1–41); and (7) raising Lazarus from the dead (11:38–44).

The setting is significant. In the OT, marriage feasts symbolize the union of God with His bride, Israel. Jesus begins His ministry at a wedding in **Galilee,** which was largely Gentile territory (see note on Matt. 4:15): thus this sign becomes a symbol of the joy of the Kingdom being spread beyond Judea to all the world. It is **the third day** from the call of the first disciples (1:35). **The mother of Jesus was there,** perhaps as a relative of the bride or groom. (Tradition names Simon the Zealot as the groom.) By His presence at this wedding, Jesus declares marriage to be holy and honorable (Heb. 13:4); therefore this passage is read at Orthodox weddings.

2:3 Here is an example of Mary's gift of intercession. The Orthodox Church believes Mary continually speaks to her Son on our behalf. **Wine** was diluted with water in the ancient world; the Jews diluted it in a proportion of one part wine to three parts water, to discourage drunkenness.

2:4 Woman is a title of respect and distinction. Jesus addresses His mother from the Cross in the same way (19:26) as He does the woman at the well (4:21), the adulteress (8:10), and Mary Magdalene (20:13, 15), thus giving great dignity to womanhood. **What does your concern have to do with Me?** is literally, "What to Me and to you?" A better translation is, "What concern is that to Me and to you?" or, "Why do you intervene?" In His answer to His mother, Jesus is neither refusing Mary's request nor embarrassing her, but reminding her that the time for His full and public self-disclosure has not yet arrived. **My hour** refers primarily to the time of His "glorification"—His Passion, death, Resurrection, and Ascension.

2:5 Despite Jesus' reply, **His mother** expects her Son will act.

2:6 Waterpots were made **of stone** because, according to rabbinical teaching, stone would not contract ritual impurity. That there are six (one less than the perfect seven) may indicate that Levitical law (Lev. 11:29–38), typified by this water, was partial, incomplete, imperfect. The water, symbolizing the old dispensation, is changed into wine, symbolizing the new dispensation revealed by Christ. The abundant **gallons** of wine are probably symbolic of the abundance of grace and truth in Christ.

2:7, 8 There is no overt action on the part of the Lord. His word alone is sufficient to work the miracle (see 4:49–53; Matt. 8:8; also Gen. 1:3, 6, 9; Is. 55:11).

2:9 The Church Fathers saw in the transformation of **the water** into **wine** an anticipation of the transformation of the bread and wine into Christ's Body and Blood at the Eucharist.

2:11 The seven **signs** of this Gospel (see note on 2:1–11) point to something beyond them-

(continued on next page)

[b]His brothers, and His disciples; and
they did not stay there many days.

Cleansing the Temple

(Matt. 21:12, 13; Mark 11:15–17; Luke
19:45, 46)

13 [a]Now the Passover of the Jews
was at hand, and Jesus went up to
Jerusalem.†
14 [a]And He found in the temple
those who sold oxen and sheep and
doves, and the money changers
[1]doing business.
15 When He had made a whip of
cords, He drove them all out of the
temple, with the sheep and the oxen,
and poured out the changers' money
and overturned the tables.
16 And He said to those who sold
doves, "Take these things away! Do
not make [a]My Father's house a
house of merchandise!"†
17 Then His disciples remembered
that it was written, [a]*"Zeal for Your
house [1]has eaten Me up."*
18 So the Jews answered and said
to Him, [a]"What sign do You show
to us, since You do these things?"†
19 Jesus answered and said to
them, [a]"Destroy this temple, and in
three days I will raise it up."
20 Then the Jews said, "It has
taken forty-six years to build this
temple, and will You raise it up in
three days?"†
21 But He was speaking [a]of the
temple of His body.
22 Therefore, when He had risen
from the dead, [a]His disciples remembered that He had said this
[1]to them; and they believed the
Scripture and the word which Jesus
had said.
23 Now when He was in Jerusalem
at the Passover, during the feast,
many believed in His name when
they saw the [a]signs which He did.†
24 But Jesus did not commit Himself to them, because He [a]knew all
men,†
25 and had no need that anyone
should testify of man, for [a]He knew
what was in man.

New Birth: Entering the Kingdom

3 There was a man of the Pharisees
named Nicodemus, a ruler of the
Jews.†

12 [b]Matt. 12:46; 13:55
13 [a]Deut. 16:1–6
14 [a]Mark 11:15, 17
[1]Lit. *sitting*
16 [a]Luke 2:49
17 [a]Ps. 69:9
[1]NU, M *will eat*
18 [a]Matt. 12:38
19 [a]Matt. 26:61; 27:40
21 [a][1 Cor. 3:16; 6:19]
22 [a]Luke 24:8
[1]NU, M omit *to them*
23 [a][Acts 2:22]
24 [a]Rev. 2:23
25 [a]Matt. 9:4

(continued from previous page)
selves: the mystery of the Incarnate God at work in His mighty and saving acts; the Kingdom of God being inaugurated by Jesus. The disciples see His **glory**—His divine power which reveals that He comes from the Father—and are strengthened in their faith in Him.

2:13–17 By transferring this incident from Holy Week (where it is related in the synoptic Gospels) to the beginning of Jesus' ministry, John emphasizes that Jesus' ministry is not, like that of the prophets, merely to renew faith under the Old Covenant. Rather, He is instituting a new kind of worship altogether. Interestingly, St. John Chrysostom believes Jesus cleansed the temple twice, at the beginning and again at the end of His public ministry. **The Passover:** Jesus performs His miracles during the major Jewish feasts (5:1; 6:4; 11:55), demonstrating that the Old Law is fulfilled in Jesus Himself.

2:16 By this cleansing, Jesus vigorously protects the purity of worship against commercialism. Likewise, He zealously desires His Church to be a holy, pure house of prayer.

2:18, 19 What sign do You show to us? The question concerns Jesus' authority in cleansing the temple. He answers in a hidden way: the ultimate *sign* will be His death and Resurrection.

2:20 The Jews misunderstand Jesus' words as referring to the temple which Herod the Great began to rebuild in 20 B.C.

2:23 Unlike the other Gospels, John reports three **Passover** feasts during Jesus' ministry (see 6:4; 11:55), which scholars believe is historically accurate.

2:24 In His divine foreknowledge Jesus **knew** many were misreading His signs.

3:1, 2 Nicodemus believed Jesus was **from God** (v. 2). Afraid of being seen with Him by his peers, he **came to Jesus by night** (v. 2). Following this conversation with Jesus, Nicodemus disappears from John's Gospel until he seeks to defend Jesus' legal rights before the Sanhedrin (7:50, 51). At the end, with Joseph of Arimathea, he prepares and entombs the body of Jesus (19:39–42)—a bold public expression of faith. His memory is celebrated with that of the myrrh-bearing women and Joseph of Arimathea on the second Sunday after Easter. According to some early sources, Nicodemus was baptized by Peter, and consequently was removed from the Sanhedrin and forced to leave Jerusalem.

THE NEW BIRTH

Early in His ministry Jesus revealed the way to enter God's eternal Kingdom. We must be "born again" (John 3:3), a birth from above brought about by water and the Spirit.

In His conversation with Nicodemus, Christ states: "Unless one is born of water and the Spirit, he cannot enter the kingdom of God" (John 3:5). From the beginning the Church has recognized "water" to be the waters of baptism, "the Spirit" to be the Holy Spirit. Therefore, the new birth is being joined to Christ in the water of baptism, and receiving the Holy Spirit through anointing or "chrismation."

Salvation, then, is more than forgiveness of sins, more than a mental acceptance of Christ and His teachings. For in salvation we are given union with God through Christ, a right and full relationship with the Holy Trinity, and the restoration of our full humanity. All these things are accomplished through the Incarnation, the union of God and man in the Person of Jesus Christ. Salvation, then, is founded upon a substantial union of the believer with Christ in His full humanity, a flesh-to-flesh relationship. Paul likens it to the joining of husband and wife (Eph. 5:23–32).

Throughout their letters the apostles remind us that the new birth is necessary for salvation. We die to sin; then, buried with Christ and risen with Him, we are united to Christ and to His body, the Church. We are cleansed, justified and sanctified—all in baptism, "the washing of regeneration and renewing of the Holy Spirit" (Titus 3:5). Without our repentance and faith, however, immersion in water would be of no effect.

Some Christians bypass baptism and stress only faith. Why is the mystery of the water necessary? Because just as Christ actually died on a cross, was buried, and rose again—all through His faith and God's grace—so we must be actually immersed in the sacramental waters of baptism, made effectual through our faith and God's grace.

The basic form of baptism is simple. The person to be born again, joined to Christ, is immersed in the water three times in the name of the Father, and of the Son, and of the Holy Spirit (Matt. 28:19). One first-century document teaches, "If you do not have running water, use whatever is available. And if you cannot do it in cold water, use warm. But if you have neither, pour water on the head three times—in the name of Father, Son and Holy Spirit" (*The Teaching of the Twelve Apostles* [*The Didache*], 7:1–3).

In the new birth, a true mystery takes place. For in the sacrament of baptism, we die, going down into the water to be mystically united to Christ in His death, and we live again, rising up out of the water in His resurrected humanity. In short, we are born again.

2 [a]This man came to Jesus by
night and said to Him, "Rabbi, we
know that You are a teacher come
from God; for [b]no one can do these
signs that You do unless [c]God is
with him."
3 Jesus answered and said to him,
"Most assuredly, I say to you,
[a]unless one is born [1]again, he cannot
see the kingdom of God."†
4 Nicodemus said to Him, "How
can a man be born when he is old?
Can he enter a second time into his
mother's womb and be born?"†
5 Jesus answered, "Most assuredly, I say to you, [a]unless one is
born of water and the Spirit, he cannot enter the kingdom of God.†
6 "That which is born of the flesh
is [a]flesh, and that which is born of
the Spirit is spirit.
7 "Do not marvel that I said to
you, 'You must be born again.'
8 [a]"The wind blows where it
wishes, and you hear the sound of
it, but cannot tell where it comes
from and where it goes. So is everyone who is born of the Spirit."†
9 Nicodemus answered and said
to Him, [a]"How can these things be?"

CHAPTER 3
2 [a]John 7:50; 19:39 [b]John 9:16, 33 [c][Acts 10:38]
3 [a][1 Pet. 1:23] [1]Or *from above*
5 [a][Acts 2:38]
6 [a]1 Cor. 15:50
8 [a]Eccl. 11:5
9 [a]John 6:52, 60
11 [a][Matt. 11:27] [b]John 3:32; 8:14
13 [a]Eph. 4:9 [1]NU omits *who is in heaven*
14 [a]Num. 21:9 [b]John 8:28; 12:34; 19:18
15 [a]John 6:47 [b]John 3:36 [1]NU omits *not perish but*
16 [a]Rom. 5:8 [b][Is. 9:6]
17 [a]Luke 9:56

10 Jesus answered and said to him,
"Are you the teacher of Israel, and
do not know these things?
11 [a]"Most assuredly, I say to you,
We speak what We know and testify
what We have seen, and [b]you do not
receive Our witness.
12 "If I have told you earthly things
and you do not believe, how will you
believe if I tell you heavenly things?†
13 [a]"No one has ascended to
heaven but He who came down from
heaven, *that is,* the Son of Man
[1]who is in heaven.
14 [a]"And as Moses lifted up the
serpent in the wilderness, even so
[b]must the Son of Man be lifted up,†
15 "that whoever [a]believes in Him
should [1]not perish but [b]have eternal
life.

Life in the Kingdom

16 [a]"For God so loved the world
that He gave His only begotten
[b]Son, that whoever believes in Him
should not perish but have everlasting life.†
17 [a]"For God did not send His Son

3:3 Again: more accurately, "from above," speaking of the heavenly birth from God through faith in Christ (1:12, 13). Whereas God the Word is born from the Father before all ages, Christians are **born** from the Son in His human nature within time by Holy Baptism. Being *born again,* however, is but the beginning of spiritual life. The goal is to **see the kingdom of God,** a phrase frequently used in the synoptic Gospels but found only here in John (vv. 3, 5). Its equivalent in John is "life" or "eternal life."

3:4 Nicodemus misunderstands, thinking of a second physical birth. A typical feature in John's Gospel (see 4:10, 11, 32, 33) is the elevation of an idea from its superficial meaning in this age to its spiritual meaning in the Kingdom.

3:5 Birth from above is **of water and the Spirit,** a clear reference to Christian baptism. While the workings of the Holy Spirit are mysterious (v. 8), nevertheless spiritual birth is integrated with baptism here and throughout the NT.

3:8 A play on words: the Greek word *pneuma* can mean either **wind** or **Spirit.** The working of the Holy Spirit in the new birth is as mysterious as the source or destination of the blowing wind.

3:12, 13 This is a difficult passage. St. John Chrysostom interprets **earthly things** as being the mystery of new birth through baptism (v. 5) and **heavenly things** as being the eternal generation of the Son from the Father (v. 13). The new birth is an incomparable spiritual gift, but compared to Christ's eternal birth from the Father, it is *earthly.*

3:14 Moses lifted up a bronze **serpent** to cure the Israelites from the deadly bites of poisonous snakes. Christ will be **lifted up** on the Cross. As the believer beholds the crucified Christ through faith as Savior, the poisonous bite of that old *serpent,* the devil, and the bite of sin and death, is counteracted and cured. The moment of Christ's greatest humiliation becomes the moment of exaltation for completing His redeeming work (19:30). This is the first of many instances in John's Gospel where Jesus teaches that He is the fulfillment of an OT type.

3:16 The essence of the gospel: God's gift of His **Son** as the ultimate expression of His love for **the world.**

into the world to condemn the
world, but that the world through
Him might be saved.†
18 [a]"He who believes in Him is not
condemned; but he who does not believe is condemned already, because
he has not believed in the name of
the only begotten Son of God.
19 "And this is the condemnation,
[a]that the light has come into the
world, and men loved darkness
rather than light, because their deeds
were evil.†
20 "For [a]everyone practicing evil
hates the light and does not come
to the light, lest his deeds should be
exposed.
21 "But he who does the truth
comes to the light, that his deeds
may be clearly seen, that they have
been [a]done in God."

The Preaching of John the Baptist

22 After these things Jesus and His
disciples came into the land of Judea,
and there He remained with them
[a]and baptized.†
23 Now John also was baptizing in
Aenon near [a]Salim, because there
was much water there. [b]And they
came and were baptized.
24 For [a]John had not yet been
thrown into prison.
25 Then there arose a dispute between *some* of John's disciples and
the Jews about purification.
26 And they came to John and said
to him, "Rabbi, He who was with
you beyond the Jordan, [a]to whom
you have testified—behold, He is
baptizing, and all [b]are coming to
Him!"
27 John answered and said, [a]"A
man can receive nothing unless it has
been given to him from heaven.
28 "You yourselves bear me witness, that I said, [a]'I am not the
Christ,' but, [b]'I have been sent before Him.'
29 [a]"He who has the bride is the
bridegroom; but [b]the friend of the
bridegroom, who stands and hears
him, rejoices greatly because of the
bridegroom's voice. Therefore this
joy of mine is fulfilled.†
30 [a]"He must increase, but I *must*
decrease.†
31 [a]"He who comes from above
[b]is above all; [c]he who is of the earth
is earthly and speaks of the earth.
[d]He who comes from heaven is
above all.†
32 "And [a]what He has seen and
heard, that He testifies; and no one
receives His testimony.
33 "He who has received His testimony [a]has certified that God is
true.
34 [a]"For He whom God has sent
speaks the words of God, for God
does not give the Spirit [b]by measure.
35 [a]"The Father loves the Son, and
has given all things into His hand.
36 [a]"He who believes in the Son
has everlasting life; and he who does
not believe the Son shall not see life,
but the [b]wrath of God abides on
him."

18 [a]John 5:24; 6:40, 47; 20:31
19 [a][John 1:4, 9–11]
20 [a]Eph. 5:11, 13
21 [a]1 Cor. 15:10
22 [a]John 4:1, 2
23 [a]1 Sam. 9:4 [b]Matt. 3:5, 6
24 [a]Matt. 4:12; 14:3
26 [a]John 1:7, 15, 27, 34 [b]Mark 2:2; 3:10; 5:24
27 [a]1 Cor. 3:5, 6; 4:7
28 [a]John 1:19–27 [b]Mal. 3:1
29 [a][2 Cor. 11:2] [b]Song 5:1
30 [a][Is. 9:7]
31 [a]John 3:13; 8:23 [b]Matt. 28:18 [c]1 Cor. 15:47 [d]John 6:33
32 [a]John 3:11; 15:15
33 [a]1 John 5:10
34 [a]John 7:16 [b]John 1:16
35 [a][Heb. 2:8]
36 [a]John 3:16, 17; 6:47 [b]Rom. 1:18

3:17, 18 The purpose of Christ's coming is to save; but the result is also condemnation for those who will not believe.

3:19–21 A profound insight: Goodness and a pure heart welcome the **light,** whereas evil deeds and malice resist the light and seek to hide in the **darkness.**

3:22–36 John the Baptist gives his final witness to Jesus as the One who is greater. Jesus has the Spirit in fullness, He possesses all the authority of the Father, and He grants eternal life to those who believe.

3:29 John the Baptist is called the **friend** (the equivalent of a modern "best man"), but it is Christ who is the **bridegroom; the bride** is God's people. As God was the Lord of His people in the OT, so Christ is the *Bridegroom* of the Church in the NT.

3:30 The Forerunner expresses profound humility and acceptance of his role in the service of God. He renounces all earthly glory and reputation and glories only in Christ. John's aspirations of hope and joy as a minister and servant of God have now been fulfilled.

3:31–36 John gives a summary of the teaching of the Gospel about the origin, dignity, and saving work of Christ.

The Samaritan Woman

(Matt. 4:12; Mark 1:14; Luke 4:14)

4 Therefore, when the Lord knew
that the Pharisees had heard that
Jesus made and [a]baptized more disciples than John†
2 (though Jesus Himself did not
baptize, but His disciples),
3 He left Judea and departed
again to Galilee.
4 But He needed to go through
Samaria.†
5 So He came to a city of Samaria
which is called Sychar, near the plot
of ground that [a]Jacob [b]gave to his
son Joseph.†
6 Now Jacob's well was there.
Jesus therefore, being wearied from
His journey, sat thus by the well. It
was about the sixth hour.†
7 A woman of Samaria came to
draw water. Jesus said to her, "Give
Me a drink."
8 For His disciples had gone away
into the city to buy food.
9 Then the woman of Samaria
said to Him, "How is it that You,
being a Jew, ask a drink from me, a
Samaritan woman?" For [a]Jews have
no dealings with [b]Samaritans.†
10 Jesus answered and said to her,
"If you knew the [a]gift of God, and
who it is who says to you, 'Give Me
a drink,' you would have asked Him,
and He would have given you
[b]living water."†
11 The woman said to Him, "Sir,
You have nothing to draw with, and
the well is deep. Where then do You
get that living water?
12 "Are You greater than our father Jacob, who gave us the well, and
drank from it himself, as well as his
sons and his livestock?"†
13 Jesus answered and said to her,
"Whoever drinks of this water will
thirst again,
14 "but [a]whoever drinks of the water that I shall give him will never
thirst. But the water that I shall give
him [b]will become in him a fountain
of water springing up into everlasting life."†
15 [a]The woman said to Him, "Sir,
give me this water, that I may not

CHAPTER 4
1 [a]John 3:22, 26; 1 Cor. 1:17
5 [a]Gen. 33:19; Josh. 24:32 [b]Gen. 48:22; Josh. 4:12
9 [a]Acts 10:28 [b]2 Kin. 17:24; Matt. 10:5, 6; Luke 9:52; 10:33; 17:16; John 8:48
10 [a][Rom. 5:15] [b]Is. 12:3; 44:3; Jer. 2:13; Zech. 13:1; 14:8; John 7:38
14 [a][John 6:35, 58] [b]John 7:37, 38
15 [a]John 6:34, 35; 17:2, 3; [Rom. 6:23; 1 John 5:20]

4:1–3 Because of the growing opposition of **the Pharisees** to His work done in Judea (3:22–36), Jesus leaves for Galilee. The Pharisees earlier took note of the activity of John the Baptist (1:19, 24) and now show interest in Jesus' ministry, since it has gained momentum.

4:4 Samaria was the region to the north, between Judea and Galilee.

4:5 Sychar: a town identified by scholars with Shechem or a village nearby.

4:6, 7 The OT does not mention **Jacob's well,** but Jacob did own property in the area (Gen. 33:19). Wells and springs are significant in Scripture because of their rarity in desert life. In the OT they often symbolize the life given by God, especially a life of blessedness (Ps. 36:8, 9; 46:4; Is. 55:1). This particular well, located at the foot of Mt. Gerizim, is maintained as a shrine and pilgrims can drink from it to this day. Jesus is **wearied** and thirsty from the labors of His journey, showing His complete humanity which He voluntarily assumed. The **sixth hour** is noontime.

4:9 The **Samaritans** were a mixed race and traditional enemies of the **Jews.** Although they worshiped the God of Israel and were awaiting a redeemer, they accepted only the first five books of the OT (the Pentateuch) as their Scriptures. They had built their own temple on Mt. Gerizim, which the Jews destroyed in 128 B.C.

4:10 Living water in the ordinary sense means fresh, flowing water, from a spring rather than a pond or cistern. In the spiritual sense it symbolizes true life from God, who is the fountain of life (Jer. 2:13; Ezek. 47:1–12; Zech. 14:8; Rev. 21:6; 22:1).

4:12 The woman initially misunderstands Jesus' words, a typical case in this Gospel, and asks, **Are You greater than our father Jacob . . . ?** According to the Church Fathers, the patriarch Jacob, who received the revelation of the divine ladder (Gen. 28:12), is a prefiguration of Christ. Jesus is thus greater than Jacob; He is the final revelation of God (see note on 1:51) and giver of life and refreshment to all.

4:14 The living water given by Jesus is the gift of the Holy Spirit which believers receive (7:37–39). And the Holy Spirit becomes **a fountain of water** which flows with eternal life. That this extraordinary water is **springing** (or leaping) **up** denotes the vigor of true life from God.

thirst, nor come here to draw."†
16 Jesus said to her, "Go, call your
husband, and come here."
17 The woman answered and said,
"I have no husband." Jesus said to
her, "You have well said, 'I have no
husband,'
18 "for you have had five husbands, and the one whom you now
have is not your husband; in that you
spoke truly."
19 The woman said to Him, "Sir,
[a]I perceive that You are a prophet.
20 "Our fathers worshiped on
[a]this mountain, and you *Jews* say
that in [b]Jerusalem is the place where
one ought to worship."†
21 Jesus said to her, "Woman, believe Me, the hour is coming [a]when
you will neither on this mountain,

19 [a]Luke 7:16, 39; 24:19
20 [a]Judg. 9:7 [b]Deut. 12:5, 11
21 [a]1 Tim. 2:8
22 [a][2 Kin. 17:28–41] [b][Rom. 3:1; 9:4, 5]
23 [a][Heb. 13:10–14] [b]Phil. 3:3 [c][John 1:17]
24 [a]2 Cor. 3:17
25 [a]Deut. 18:15 [b]John 4:29, 39
26 [a]Matt. 26:63, 64

nor in Jerusalem, worship the
Father.†
22 "You worship [a]what you do
not know; we know what we
worship, for [b]salvation is of the
Jews.†
23 "But the hour is coming, and
now is, when the true worshipers
will [a]worship the Father in [b]spirit
[c]and truth; for the Father is seeking
such to worship Him.†
24 [a]"God *is* Spirit, and those who
worship Him must worship in spirit
and truth."
25 The woman said to Him, "I
know that Messiah [a]is coming" (who
is called Christ). "When He comes,
[b]He will tell us all things."
26 Jesus said to her, [a]"I who speak
to you am *He*."†

4:15–19 The woman does not yet understand the significance of what is being offered, so Jesus initiates a new direction in the dialogue (v. 16). When the Lord reveals to her that He knows that her present partner, following a chain of spouses, is not her husband at all, she is prompted to think Jesus **a prophet** (v. 19). Though the Samaritans did not accept any prophet after Moses, they did look forward to the promise of the Moses-like Prophet (Deut. 18:15–18), the Restorer, the true Teacher, the Messiah. The supernatural knowledge possessed by Jesus is manifested in many instances in John: regarding Nathanael (1:47–50); Lazarus's death (11:14); Peter's denial (13:38); what would befall Him after His arrest (18:4). By reporting these insights John underscores the divinity of the Messiah.

4:20 The Samaritan version of the Ten Commandments decreed they worship on Mt. Gerizim, whereas the Jews worshiped on Mt. Zion in Jerusalem. The woman, thinking Jesus was a prophet, posed to Him this burning dispute between Jew and Samaritan.

4:21 The **hour** that is coming is the death of the Savior on the Cross, when the sacrifice made once and for all will supplant the necessity for any temple anywhere. The idea that worship must be performed only at a specific place of revelation—Mt. Zion or Mt. Gerizim—will give way to His revolutionary teaching about worship in spirit and in truth (v. 23).

4:22 Salvation is of the Jews: Jesus Christ affirms that valid revelation comes from Judaism (see Ps. 76:1). "The commonwealth of Israel was the school of the knowledge of God for all the nations" (St. Athanasius). Note that Jesus' disputes with the Jews involve chiefly the Jewish leaders, not the people themselves, and certainly not the spiritual heritage of Judaism. The Messiah was prophesied within Judaism; the Incarnation took place among the Jewish people. God's universal gift of salvation arises within the context of His promises to the Jews and their religious tradition.

4:23, 24 While the Jews and Samaritans historically argued about *where* true **worship** takes place, Jesus teaches that worship is not tied to any certain geographical place. Instead He turns to the heart of the matter: the object of worship, God Himself, and how worship takes place. **The Father** (v. 23) is worshiped **in spirit**—that is, in the Holy Spirit who is given upon the completion of Christ's mission (15:26; 16:13; 20:22)—**and truth** (v. 24), which is Jesus Christ Himself (14:6) and His revelation. **God is Spirit** (v. 24), that is, He possesses a spiritual nature which cannot be confined to a particular geographic location. Those who believe in the revelation of Christ and have the power of the Holy Spirit can truly worship God anywhere.

4:26 I who speak to you am He: Literally, "I AM (Gr. *ego eimi*), who speak to you." "I AM" is the name of God; its use indicates a theophany, or revelation of God (Gen. 17:1; Ex. 3:14). This is the first instance in John of Jesus' use of this formula of self-revelation (see 6:35; 8:12, 58; 11:25). Jesus reveals Himself to be more than the Mosaic Prophet and more than the Jewish Messiah; indeed, He is the Incarnate God Himself.

The Harvest Is Ready
(Matt. 4:13–17; Mark 1:14, 15;
Luke 4:14, 15)

27 And at this *point* His disciples
came, and they marveled that He
talked with a woman; yet no one
said, "What do You seek?" or, "Why
are You talking with her?"†
28 The woman then left her water-
pot, went her way into the city, and
said to the men,†
29 "Come, see a Man [a]who told me
all things that I ever did. Could this
be the Christ?"
30 Then they went out of the city
and came to Him.
31 In the meantime His disciples urged Him, saying, "Rabbi,
eat."†
32 But He said to them, "I have
food to eat of which you do not
know."
33 Therefore the disciples said to
one another, "Has anyone brought
Him *anything* to eat?"
34 Jesus said to them, [a]"My food
is to do the will of Him who sent
Me, and to [b]finish His work.
35 "Do you not say, 'There are still
four months and *then* comes [a]the
harvest'? Behold, I say to you, lift
up your eyes and look at the fields,
[b]for they are already white for
harvest!†
36 [a]"And he who reaps receives
wages, and gathers fruit for eternal
life, that [b]both he who sows and he
who reaps may rejoice together.†
37 "For in this the saying is true:
[a]'One sows and another reaps.'
38 "I sent you to reap that for
which you have not labored; [a]others
have labored, and you have entered
into their labors."†
39 And many of the Samaritans of
that city believed in Him [a]because
of the word of the woman who testified, "He told me all that I *ever*
did."
40 So when the Samaritans had
come to Him, they urged Him to stay
with them; and He stayed there two
days.
41 And many more believed because of His own [a]word.
42 Then they said to the woman,
"Now we believe, not because of
what you said, for [a]we ourselves
have heard *Him* and we know that
this is indeed [1]the Christ, the Savior
of the world."†
43 Now after the two days He departed from there and went to
Galilee.
44 For [a]Jesus Himself testified that

29 [a]John 4:25
34 [a]Ps. 40:7, 8; Heb. 10:9 [b]Job 23:12; [John 6:38; 17:4; 19:30]
35 [a]Gen. 8:22 [b]Matt. 9:37; Luke 10:2
36 [a]Dan. 12:3; Rom. 6:22 [b]1 Thess. 2:19
37 [a]1 Cor. 3:5–9
38 [a]Jer. 44:4; [1 Pet. 1:12]
39 [a]John 4:29
41 [a]Luke 4:32; [John 6:63]
42 [a]John 17:8; 1 John 4:14 [1]NU omits *the Christ*
44 [a]Matt. 13:57; Mark 6:4; Luke 4:24

4:27 They marveled because Jews were not allowed to converse publicly **with a woman,** and a Samaritan at that. Jesus' words and actions transcend ethnic and gender-related customs of the time. (For further instances of the Lord's dealings with women, see 7:53—8:11; 11:20–33; Luke 7:36–50; 8:2, 3; 10:38–42.)

4:28–30 The Samaritan woman becomes the first evangelist, testifying to the advent of Christ and bringing others to Him (v. 39). According to an early tradition, after the Resurrection of Christ she was baptized and given the Christian name Photini, "the enlightened one." Along with her two sons and five daughters she went to Carthage to spread the gospel. There they were arrested, taken to Rome under Nero, imprisoned, and later martyred. According to tradition, St. Photini, who first met Christ beside a well, was martyred for Christ by being thrown into a well. The Church remembers her on March 20.

4:31–34 The disciples, too, misunderstand Jesus' words. Once again we see revealed in John's Gospel Jesus' typical means of moving from the surface meaning of a statement on to a deeper truth. His **food** is to bring people to believe in Him and be saved.

4:35 The townspeople (traditionally thought to have been dressed in **white**) approach the well with the Samaritan woman. Our Lord urges the disciples to look up and see the ripe **fields** (that is, these Samaritans) ready for **harvest.**

4:36 The Father is the sower; Jesus is the reaper. Jesus will send the disciples to reap (17:18; 20:21); their apostolic mission has been implicit from their initial calling.

4:38 The **others** are all those who have prepared the way for the coming of the Messiah: the OT patriarchs, prophets, St. John the Baptist and more.

4:42 The Samaritans are the first to recognize Jesus as **Savior of the world.** The gospel is for all people.

a prophet has no honor in his own
country.†
45 So when He came to Galilee, the
Galileans received Him, [a]having
seen all the things He did in Jerusalem at the feast; [b]for they also had
gone to the feast.

A Nobleman's Son Is Healed

46 So Jesus came again to Cana of
Galilee [a]where He had made the water wine. And there was a certain
[1]nobleman whose son was sick at
Capernaum.†
47 When he heard that Jesus had
come out of Judea into Galilee, he
went to Him and implored Him to
come down and heal his son, for he
was at the point of death.
48 Then Jesus said to him, [a]"Unless you *people* see signs and wonders, you will by no means
believe."†
49 The nobleman said to Him, "Sir,
come down before my child dies!"†
50 Jesus said to him, "Go your

45 [a]John 2:13, 23; 3:2 [b]Deut. 16:16
46 [a]John 2:1, 11 [1]*royal official*
48 [a]John 6:30; Rom. 15:19; 1 Cor. 1:22; 2 Cor. 12:12; [2 Thess. 2:9]; Heb. 2:4

CHAPTER 5

1 [a]Lev. 23:2; Deut. 16:16 [b]John 2:13
2 [a]Neh. 3:1, 32; 12:39

way; your son lives." So the man believed the word that Jesus spoke to
him, and he went his way.
51 And as he was now going
down, his servants met him and told
him, saying, "Your son lives!"
52 Then he inquired of them
the hour when he got better. And
they said to him, "Yesterday at
the seventh hour the fever left
him."
53 So the father knew that *it was*
at the same hour in which Jesus said
to him, "Your son lives." And he
himself believed, and his whole
household.†
54 This again *is* the second sign
Jesus did when He had come out of
Judea into Galilee.

A Paralytic Is Healed

5 After [a]this there was a feast of
the Jews, and Jesus [b]went up to
Jerusalem.†
2 Now there is in Jerusalem [a]by
the Sheep *Gate* a pool, which is called

4:44, 45 Jesus' statement concerning the **prophet** without **honor** is reported in all four Gospels (see center column). **His own country** refers to Galilee (as John stresses: 1:46; 2:1; 7:42, 52; 19:19). Galileans were present in Jerusalem during the Passover, when He won many devotees because of the signs He performed (2:13–25). Because they gave Him only this minimal honor based upon their wonder at His signs, and not true glory based upon belief in His messianic vocation, He knew not to trust Himself to them.

4:46–54 This is the second of Christ's signs reported in John (see note on 2:1–11). In **Cana of Galilee,** Nathanael's hometown (21:2), Jesus had demonstrated, by identifying Nathanael from afar, that He could see at a distance (1:47, 48). He now shows He can heal at a distance—He can heal the unseen. The royal (Herodian) official may be the centurion of Matt. 8:5–13 and Luke 7:1–10, although there are many differences between the synoptic story and the Johannine account.

4:48 Once again, recognizing humanity's need for **signs and wonders,** Jesus manifests His power to reveal Himself as God. The Lord admonishes the Galileans (in the person of this official), a people whose faith depends on "signs and wonders" (Ex. 7:3 [LXX]; Deut. 4:34; Is. 8:18; Jer. 32:20). Faith based upon the miraculous alone is inadequate, but not unacceptable (see 14:11; 20:29–31). The Galileans, however, according to this account, lack authentic faith.

4:49–52 The official approaches Jesus out of urgent need for his little **son.** Jesus gives the official no sign, but simply the command to **go** (v. 50) and the word that his child **lives.** But that is enough for the official to have faith. Thus, the official manifests true belief (unlike the people of v. 48). The **seventh hour** (v. 52) is about 1:00 P.M.

4:53 This is the third time the phrase **your son lives** is reported. The very word of the One who is the resurrection and the life (11:25) gives life as well.

5:1–15 This healing (the third sign recorded by John; see note on 2:1–11) exemplifies Jesus' divine power to give life.

St. John Chrysostom and other Fathers state that this **feast** is the Jewish Feast of Pentecost (or the Feast of Weeks), due to the references to the Law of Moses later in the chapter. The Feast of Pentecost centers around the theme of the giving of the Law on Mt. Sinai.

in Hebrew, [1]Bethesda, having five
porches.†
3 In these lay a great multitude
of sick people, blind, lame, [1]para-
lyzed, [2]waiting for the moving of the
water.†
4 For an angel went down at a certain time into the pool and stirred
up the water; then whoever stepped
in first, after the stirring of the water,
was made well of whatever disease
he had.
5 Now a certain man was there
who had an infirmity thirty-eight
years.
6 When Jesus saw him lying
there, and knew that he already had
been *in that condition* a long time, He
said to him, "Do you want to be
made well?"†
7 The sick man answered Him,
"Sir, I have no man to put me into
the pool when the water is stirred
up; but while I am coming, another
steps down before me."
8 Jesus said to him, [a]"Rise, take
up your bed and walk."

2 [1]NU *Bethzatha*
3 [1]*withered* [2]NU omits the rest of v. 3 and all of v. 4.
8 [a]Matt. 9:6; Mark 2:11; Luke 5:24
9 [a]John 9:14
10 [a]Ex. 20:10; Neh. 13:19; Jer. 17:21, 22; Matt. 12:2; Mark 2:24; Luke 6:2
13 [a]Luke 13:14; 22:51
14 [a]Matt. 12:45; [Mark 2:5]; John 8:11

9 And immediately the man was
made well, took up his bed, and
walked. And [a]that day was the
Sabbath.
10 The Jews therefore said to him
who was cured, "It is the Sabbath;
[a]it is not lawful for you to carry your
bed."†
11 He answered them, "He who
made me well said to me, 'Take up
your bed and walk.' "
12 Then they asked him, "Who is
the Man who said to you, 'Take up
your bed and walk'?"
13 But the one who was [a]healed
did not know who it was, for Jesus
had withdrawn, a multitude being
in *that* place.
14 Afterward Jesus found him in
the temple, and said to him, "See,
you have been made well. [a]Sin no
more, lest a worse thing come upon
you."†
15 The man departed and told the
Jews that it was Jesus who had made
him well.

5:2 This double-basin pool, believed to have curative powers, has been discovered by archaeologists about 100 yards north of the temple area, near **the Sheep Gate**. The water for this high-ground pool came from underground springs, and it was used to wash down the sacrificial lambs before they were slain. The pool has led some Christians to see in this imagery a prefiguration of baptism.

The Type: the Pool of Bethesda	*The Fulfillment: Jesus Christ*
A place of miracles	A Person of miracles
For one person at one time	For everyone at any time
Through angelic mediation	Without angelic mediation
For physical and temporal well-being	For spiritual and eternal well-being which begins with baptism.

5:3, 4 This passage, explaining the presence of the sick around the pool, is often omitted from modern English translations because it appears in none of the oldest extant Greek manuscripts. Tertullian (c. A.D. 200) is the first Latin writer, and St. John Chrysostom (c. A.D. 400) the first Greek writer, to refer to it. The disturbance of the water may actually have been caused by bubbling up of the intermittent underground springs, which was understood as an angelic action. On the other hand, it is possible that angelic activity was indeed the cause for the stirring of the water. The role of spiritual powers in the world must never be discounted.

5:6 Jesus asks an obvious question to stimulate the man's faith.

5:10 Although the law of the **Sabbath** (Ex. 20:8–11; Deut. 5:12–15) does not specifically prohibit the carrying of burdens, this activity is mentioned in Jer. 17:21 and Neh. 13:19 and was explicitly forbidden by rabbinical regulations. **The Jews** again refers not to the Jewish people (for the paralytic was a Jew), but to the authorities, who thought of themselves as guardians of the Law.

5:14 It was a common belief that illness and misfortune were divine retribution for **sin.** The Savior, however, does not ratify this as an absolute principle (see 9:1–3). The paralytic's cure is to lead to conversion and a righteous life.

Commemoration of the Dead

5:17–30; 6:35–44, 48–54: Jesus gives the promise of resurrection and eternal life to those who love Him and partake of His body and blood.

Father and Son Work Together

16 For this reason the Jews [a]perse-
cuted Jesus, [1]and sought to kill Him,
because He had done these things
on the Sabbath.†
17 But Jesus answered them,
[a]"My Father has been working until
now, and I have been working."
18 Therefore the Jews [a]sought all
the more to kill Him, because He not
only broke the Sabbath, but also said
that God was His Father, [b]making
Himself equal with God.
19 Then Jesus answered and said
to them, "Most assuredly, I say to
you, [a]the Son can do nothing of
Himself, but what He sees the Father
do; for whatever He does, the Son
also does in like manner.†
20 "For [a]the Father loves the Son,
and [b]shows Him all things that He
Himself does; and He will show Him
greater works than these, that you
may marvel.
21 "For as the Father raises the
dead and gives life to *them,* [a]even
so the Son gives life to whom He
will.
22 "For the Father judges no one,
but [a]has committed all judgment to
the Son,†

16 [a]John 8:37; 10:39 [1]NU omits *and sought to kill Him*
17 [a][John 9:4; 17:4]
18 [a]John 7:1, 19 [b]John 10:30
19 [a]John 5:30; 6:38; 8:28; 12:49; 14:10
20 [a]Matt. 3:17 [b][Matt. 11:27]
21 [a][John 11:25]
22 [a][Acts 17:31]
23 [a]1 John 2:23
24 [a]John 3:16, 18; 6:47 [b][1 John 3:14]
25 [a][Col. 2:13]
26 [a]Ps. 36:9 [b]1 Cor. 15:45
27 [a][Acts 10:42; 17:31] [b]Dan. 7:13
28 [a][1 Thess. 4:15–17]
29 [a]Is. 26:19 [b]Dan. 12:2
30 [a]John 5:19

23 "that all should honor the Son
just as they honor the Father.
[a]He who does not honor the Son
does not honor the Father who sent
Him.
24 "Most assuredly, I say to you,
[a]he who hears My word and believes
in Him who sent Me has everlasting
life, and shall not come into judgment, [b]but has passed from death
into life.†
25 "Most assuredly, I say to you,
the hour is coming, and now is,
when [a]the dead will hear the voice
of the Son of God; and those who
hear will live.
26 "For [a]as the Father has life in
Himself, so He has granted the Son
to have [b]life in Himself,
27 "and [a]has given Him authority
to execute judgment also, [b]because
He is the Son of Man.
28 "Do not marvel at this; for the
hour is coming in which all who are
in the graves will [a]hear His voice
29 [a]"and come forth—[b]those who
have done good, to the resurrection
of life, and those who have done
evil, to the resurrection of condemnation.
30 [a]"I can of Myself do nothing.
As I hear, I judge; and My judgment

5:16–18 Confronted by His Jewish critics, Jesus argues that God's sustaining and redeeming work in the world does not cease on the Sabbath. Hearing these words, **the Jews** are doubly offended: Jesus not only violates scribal law, but also presents Himself as **equal with God** (v. 18).

5:19–30 The discourse here shows the Father and the Son are so united in nature, will, and action that the Son fully shares the divine attributes of giving life and executing judgment. This judgment is based on both faith (v. 24) and works (v. 29). The two can be distinguished, but they cannot be separated. Those who respond to the Son of God in faith (v. 24) and who do good (v. 29) will receive the gift of eternal life.

5:22 Has committed all judgment to the Son: Christ in His glory will be the Judge of the world at the Second Coming.

5:24–30 This passage is read at the Orthodox funeral service. These verses refer to the general resurrection of the dead at the end of days. However, that "hour" is already present and "now is" (v. 25) in that an encounter with Christ results in life or judgment as a present reality, depending upon one's response. Those who believe in Christ have already **passed from death into life** (v. 24).

is righteous, because [b]I do not seek
My own will but the will of the Father who sent Me.†
31 [a]"If I bear witness of Myself, My
witness is not [1]true.†
32 [a]"There is another who bears
witness of Me, and I know that the
witness which He witnesses of Me
is true.
33 "You have sent to John, [a]and
he has borne witness to the truth.
34 "Yet I do not receive testimony
from man, but I say these things that
you may be saved.†
35 "He was the burning and
[a]shining lamp, and [b]you were willing for a time to rejoice in his light.
36 "But [a]I have a greater witness
than John's; for [b]the works which
the Father has given Me to finish—
the very [c]works that I do—bear witness of Me, that the Father has sent
Me.
37 "And the Father Himself, who
sent Me, [a]has testified of Me. You
have neither heard His voice at any
time, [b]nor seen His form.
38 "But you do not have His word
abiding in you, because whom He
sent, Him you do not believe.
39 [a]"You search the Scriptures, for
in them you think you have eternal
life; and [b]these are they which testify
of Me.
40 [a]"But you are not willing to
come to Me that you may have life.

30 [b]Matt. 26:39
31 [a]John 8:14 [1]*valid* as testimony
32 [a][Matt. 3:17]
33 [a][John 1:15, 19, 27, 32]
35 [a]2 Pet. 1:19 [b]Mark 6:20
36 [a]1 John 5:9 [b]John 3:2; 10:25; 17:4 [c]John 9:16; 10:38
37 [a]Matt. 3:17 [b]1 John 4:12
39 [a]Is. 8:20; 34:16 [b]Luke 24:27
40 [a][John 1:11; 3:19]
41 [a]1 Thess. 2:6
44 [a]John 12:43 [b][Rom. 2:29]
45 [a]Rom. 2:12
46 [a]Deut. 18:15, 18
47 [a]Luke 16:29, 31

CHAPTER 6
1 [a]Mark 6:32 [b]John 6:23; 21:1
2 [a]Matt. 4:23; 8:16; 9:35; 14:36; 15:30; 19:2 [1]*sick*

41 [a]"I do not receive honor from
men.
42 "But I know you, that you do
not have the love of God in you.†
43 "I have come in My Father's
name, and you do not receive Me;
if another comes in his own name,
him you will receive.
44 [a]"How can you believe, who receive honor from one another, and
do not seek [b]the honor that *comes*
from the only God?
45 "Do not think that I shall accuse
you to the Father; [a]there is *one* who
accuses you—Moses, in whom you
trust.
46 "For if you believed Moses, you
would believe Me; [a]for he wrote
about Me.
47 "But if you [a]do not believe his
writings, how will you believe My
words?"

Feeding of the Five Thousand
(Matt. 14:13–21; Mark 6:30–44;
Luke 9:10–17)

6 After [a]these things Jesus went
over the Sea of Galilee, which is
the Sea of [b]Tiberias.†
2 Then a great multitude followed
Him, because they saw His signs
which He performed on those who
were [a]diseased.[1]†

5:30 The divine will is common to the Persons of the Trinity, for all share the same divine energy. In their manifestation in the world, however, all energy originates in the Father, being communicated through the Son in the Holy Spirit. Here there is a sense that the Son obeys the Father. This is because, in His human nature, the Son has human energy—including human will—which He offers to God the Father as the source of all. This is His **own will** which must do **the will of the Father.**

5:31–47 In Jewish tradition, a valid testimony requires two witnesses (Deut. 17:6). Jesus offers four witnesses to His messiahship and divine Sonship: (1) God the Father (vv. 32, 37, 38); (2) John the Baptist (vv. 33–35); (3) His own works (v. 36); and (4) the OT Scriptures, through which Moses gives his testimony (vv. 39–47).

5:34 The **testimony from man** is that of John the Baptist.

5:42 Jesus is aware they do not possess the **love of God:** it does not remain in them because they do not receive Him who comes in the name of His Father.

6:1 The theme of Christ as the Giver of Life is continued throughout this chapter. Jesus, who gives Himself "for the life of the world" (v. 51), is depicted as the Bread of Life which is received through faith and sacrament. The **Sea of Galilee** is actually a lake about 7 miles wide and 13 miles long. Its crossing by the Savior (vv. 16–21) is reminiscent of the crossing of the Red Sea by Moses and the Israelites.

6:2–14 The feeding of the multitude is the fourth of Jesus' miraculous signs reported by John (see note on 2:1–11); it is recorded in all four Gospels. Placed against the background

(continued on next page)

3 And Jesus went up on the
mountain, and there He sat with His
disciples.
4 [a]Now the Passover, a feast of
the Jews, was near.†
5 [a]Then Jesus lifted up *His* eyes,
and seeing a great multitude coming
toward Him, He said to [b]Philip,
"Where shall we buy bread, that
these may eat?"†
6 But this He said to test him, for
He Himself knew what He would
do.
7 Philip answered Him, [a]"Two
hundred denarii worth of bread is
not sufficient for them, that every
one of them may have a little."†
8 One of His disciples, [a]Andrew,
Simon Peter's brother, said to
Him,
9 "There is a lad here who has five
barley loaves and two small fish,
[a]but what are they among so
many?"†
10 Then Jesus said, "Make the people sit down." Now there was much
grass in the place. So the men sat
down, in number about five
thousand.
11 And Jesus took the loaves, and
when He had given thanks He distributed *them* [1]to the disciples, and
the disciples to those sitting down;
and likewise of the fish, as much as
they wanted.†
12 So when they were filled, He
said to His disciples, "Gather up the
fragments that remain, so that nothing is lost."†
13 Therefore they gathered *them*
up, and filled twelve baskets with
the fragments of the five barley
loaves which were left over by those
who had eaten.
14 Then those men, when they had
seen the sign that Jesus did, said,
"This is truly [a]the Prophet who is
to come into the world."†

4 [a]Lev. 23:5, 7; Deut. 16:1; John 2:13
5 [a]Matt. 14:14; Mark 6:35; Luke 9:12
[b]John 1:43
7 [a]Num. 11:21, 22
8 [a]John 1:40
9 [a]2 Kin. 4:43
11 [1]NU omits *to the disciples, and the disciples*
14 [a]Gen. 49:10; Deut. 18:15, 18; John 1:21; 7:40; Acts 3:22; 7:37
15 [a][John 18:36]
16 [a]Matt. 14:23; Mark 6:47

Walking on Rough Seas
(Matt. 14:22–33; Mark 6:45–52)

15 Therefore when Jesus perceived
that they were about to come and
take Him by force to make Him
[a]king, He departed again to the
mountain by Himself alone.
16 [a]Now when evening came, His
disciples went down to the sea,†

(continued from previous page)
of the **Passover** (v. 4), this sign is a fulfillment of OT messianic prophecies and types, especially the miraculous gift of manna which fed the Israelites in the wilderness after the Exodus (vv. 31, 32; Ex. 16:15). Jesus **took the loaves,** gave **thanks,** and **distributed them** (v. 11), a description which has eucharistic overtones.

6:4 The Passover coincided with the Feast of Unleavened Bread which commemorated not only the Exodus from Egypt, but the first food from grain eaten in the Promised Land after the crossing of the Jordan.

6:5, 6 Philip is tested (v. 6) because he needs to understand who Christ is (14:8–10). Andrew (vv. 8, 9) sees the loaves and fish, yet he sees no potential in them.

6:7 Two hundred denarii corresponds to about 200 days' wages for a laborer.

6:9 Barley was generally used by the poorer people—it cost less than wheat and was ready for harvest in the springtime at Passover.

6:11 Given thanks is from the Greek verb *eucharisto* (v. 23; see also Matt. 15:36; 26:27; Mark 8:6; 14:23; Luke 22:17–19; 1 Cor. 11:24; Eph. 5:20). The multiplication of the loaves provides the context for the following day's discourse on the Bread of Life. Note the process: (1) giving of thanks; (2) distribution of the gifts, first to the disciples and then by the disciples to the people; and (3) partaking. What a remarkable preview of the Eucharist!

6:12, 13 As with the manna in the wilderness (Ex. 16:16–21), **nothing** of the gift of God should be **lost** (v. 12). In contrast to the manna, here we have an abundance of **twelve baskets** (v. 13) of leftovers, one for each disciple.

6:14, 15 The Galilean Jews, with their misguided messianic enthusiasm, equate Jesus with **the Prophet** of Deut. 18:15–19, whom they expect to be an earthly, political leader who will lead them against the occupying Romans, as Moses led his people out of bondage (see note on 7:40). Because He is not to fulfill these expectations, Jesus withdraws from the crowd.

6:16–21 This, the fifth of Christ's miracles reported by John (see note on 2:1–11), reenacts

(continued on next page)

17 got into the boat, and went over
the sea toward Capernaum. And it
was already dark, and Jesus had not
come to them.
18 Then the sea arose because a
great wind was blowing.
19 So when they had rowed about
[1]three or four miles, they saw Jesus
walking on the sea and drawing near
the boat; and they were [a]afraid.
20 But He said to them, [a]"It is I;
do not be afraid."
21 Then they willingly received
Him into the boat, and immediately
the boat was at the land where they
were going.

Work for Heavenly Bread

22 On the following day, when the
people who were standing on the
other side of the sea saw that there
was no other boat there, except
[1]that one [2]which His disciples had
entered, and that Jesus had not
entered the boat with His disciples,
but His disciples had gone away
alone—
23 however, other boats came from
Tiberias, near the place where they
ate bread after the Lord had given
thanks—
24 when the people therefore saw
that Jesus was not there, nor His disciples, they also got into boats and
came to Capernaum, [a]seeking Jesus.
25 And when they found Him on
the other side of the sea, they said
to Him, "Rabbi, when did You come
here?"
26 Jesus answered them and said,
"Most assuredly, I say to you, you
seek Me, not because you saw the
signs, but because you ate of the
loaves and were filled.
27 [a]"Do not labor for the food
which perishes, but [b]for the food
which endures to everlasting life,
which the Son of Man will give you,
[c]because God the Father has set His
seal on Him."†
28 Then they said to Him, "What
shall we do, that we may work the
works of God?"
29 Jesus answered and said to
them, [a]"This is the work of God, that
you believe in Him whom He sent."†

Jesus, the Bread of Life

30 Therefore they said to Him,
[a]"What sign will You perform then,
that we may see it and believe You?
What work will You do?
31 [a]"Our fathers ate the manna in
the desert; as it is written, [b]*'He gave
them bread from heaven to eat.'*"
32 Then Jesus said to them, "Most
assuredly, I say to you, Moses did
not give you the bread from heaven,
but [a]My Father gives you the true
bread from heaven.
33 "For the bread of God is He who
comes down from heaven and gives
life to the world."
34 [a]Then they said to Him, "Lord,
give us this bread always."
35 And Jesus said to them, [a]"I am
the bread of life. [b]He who comes to
Me shall never hunger, and he who
believes in Me shall never [c]thirst.
36 [a]"But I said to you that you
have seen Me and yet [b]do not
believe.
37 [a]"All that the Father gives Me
will come to Me, and [b]the one who

19 [a]Matt. 17:6 [1]Lit. *25 or 30 stadia*
20 [a]Is. 43:1, 2
22 [1]NU omits *that* [2]NU omits *which His disciples had entered*
24 [a]Luke 4:42
27 [a]Matt. 6:19 [b]John 4:14 [c]Acts 2:22
29 [a][1 John 3:23]
30 [a]Matt. 12:38; 16:1
31 [a]Ex. 16:15 [b]Ex. 16:4, 15; Neh. 9:15; Ps. 78:24
32 [a]John 3:13, 16
34 [a]John 4:15
35 [a]John 6:48, 58 [b]John 4:14; 7:37 [c]Is. 55:1, 2
36 [a]John 6:26, 64; 15:24 [b]John 10:26
37 [a]John 6:45 [b]2 Tim. 2:19

(continued from previous page)
ancient Israel's passage through the Red Sea. Moses led the old Israel through the sea to liberty. Christ walks on top of the water and leads His disciples over the sea to **the land where they were going** (v. 21). Christ's **walking on the sea** (v. 19) is a sign of His lordship over creation.

6:27 The multitude had continued to pursue Jesus in the hope that He might miraculously solve all of their earthly problems as He had miraculously provided them with food. He tries to turn their minds to spiritual concerns, telling them not to labor for perishable food but for the food of eternal life, which is available in **the Son of Man.** He does not chide them for seeking and working, but for pursuing temporary satisfaction rather than eternal fulfillment.

6:29 The most fundamental **work of God** is true faith in Christ!

comes to Me I will [1]by no means cast
out.†
38 "For I have come down from
heaven, [a]not to do My own will,
[b]but the will of Him who sent Me.†
39 "This is the will of the Father
who sent Me, [a]that of all He has
given Me I should lose nothing, but
should raise it up at the last day.
40 "And this is the will of Him who
sent Me, [a]that everyone who sees
the Son and believes in Him may
have everlasting life; and I will raise
him up at the last day."
41 The Jews then [1]complained
about Him, because He said, "I am
the bread which came down from
heaven."
42 And they said, [a]"Is not this
Jesus, the son of Joseph, whose father and mother we know? How is
it then that He says, 'I have come
down from heaven'?"
43 Jesus therefore answered and
said to them, [1]"Do not murmur
among yourselves.
44 [a]"No one can come to Me unless the Father who sent Me [b]draws
him; and I will raise him up at the
last day.
45 "It is written in the prophets,
[a]*'And they shall all be taught by
God.'* [b]Therefore everyone who
[1]has heard and learned from the Father comes to Me.

37 [1]*certainly not*
38 [a]Matt. 26:39
[b]John 4:34
39 [a]John 10:28; 17:12; 18:9
40 [a]John 3:15, 16; 4:14; 6:27, 47, 54
41 [1]*grumbled*
42 [a]Matt. 13:55
43 [1]*Stop grumbling*
44 [a]Song 1:4
[b][Phil. 1:29; 2:12, 13]
45 [a]Is. 54:13
[b]John 6:37
[1]M *hears and has learned*
46 [a]John 1:18
[b]Matt. 11:27
47 [a][John 3:16, 18]
[1]NU omits *in Me*
48 [a]John 6:33, 35
49 [a]John 6:31, 58
50 [a]John 6:51, 58
51 [a]John 3:13
[b]Heb. 10:5
52 [a]John 7:43; 9:16; 10:19
53 [a]Matt. 26:26
54 [a]John 4:14; 6:27, 40

46 [a]"Not that anyone has seen the
Father, [b]except He who is from God;
He has seen the Father.
47 "Most assuredly, I say to you,
[a]he who believes [1]in Me has everlasting life.
48 [a]"I am the bread of life.
49 [a]"Your fathers ate the manna in
the wilderness, and are dead.
50 [a]"This is the bread which comes
down from heaven, that one may eat
of it and not die.

Eat His Flesh, Drink His Blood

51 "I am the living bread [a]which
came down from heaven. If anyone
eats of this bread, he will live forever;
and [b]the bread that I shall give is
My flesh, which I shall give for the
life of the world."†
52 The Jews therefore [a]quarreled
among themselves, saying, "How
can this Man give us *His* flesh to
eat?"
53 Then Jesus said to them, "Most
assuredly, I say to you, unless
[a]you eat the flesh of the Son of Man
and drink His blood, you have no
life in you.†
54 [a]"Whoever eats My flesh and
drinks My blood has eternal life,
and I will raise him up at the last
day.†

6:37–40 Since the Son and the Father are united in essence and will, those who are chosen by the Father will also believe in Jesus and receive eternal life.

6:38 Since the Son is of one essence with the Father, He shares the one will of God the Father. In His Incarnation, of course, the Son of God gains a human nature and a human will as well. Thus, the Council of Chalcedon (A.D. 451) teaches that, in the Person of Christ, there are united a complete divine nature and a complete human nature. Similarly, the Third Council of Constantinople (A.D. 680–681) proclaims there are two natural wills in Christ, not contrary to one another, although "His human will follows, not as resisting or reluctant but rather as subject to His Divinity and omnipotent will." (See the note on 5:30.)

6:51–59 The eucharistic significance of this passage is indisputable. Jesus' declaration that He is Himself **the living bread** which brings us life is intended to reveal the eucharistic feast. His offering is not for His people only but **for the life of the world.**

6:53 Christ's body was crucified and His blood shed on the Cross. We receive the benefits of Christ's sacrifice by coming to Him in faith (v. 35), and by communion with Him: we **eat** His **flesh** and **drink His blood.** These words refer directly to the Eucharist, the mystery of Christ our life. His words are clear: To receive everlasting life, we must partake of His eucharistic *flesh* and *blood*. St. John Chrysostom (*Homily 47:2*) teaches we must not understand the sacrament carnally, that is, according to the laws of physical nature, but spiritually (v. 63), perceiving a true but mystical presence of Christ in the Eucharist.

6:54, 55 St. Hilary of Poitiers writes, "What we say concerning the reality of Christ's

(continued on next page)

55 "For My flesh is [1]food indeed,
and My blood is [2]drink indeed.
56 "He who eats My flesh and
drinks My blood [a]abides in Me, and
I in him.
57 "As the living Father sent Me,
and I live because of the Father, so
he who feeds on Me will live because
of Me.
58 [a]"This is the bread which came
down from heaven—not [b]as your fathers ate the manna, and are dead.
He who eats this bread will live
forever."
59 **These things He said in the
synagogue as He taught in Capernaum.**

The Words of Eternal Life

60 [a]Therefore many of His disciples, when they heard *this,* said,
"This is a [1]hard saying; who can
understand it?"†
61 When Jesus knew in Himself
that His disciples [1]complained about
this, He said to them, "Does this
[2]offend you?
62 [a]"*What* then if you should see
the Son of Man ascend where He
was before?
63 [a]"It is the Spirit who gives life;
the [b]flesh profits nothing. The
[c]words that I speak to you are spirit,
and *they* are life.
64 "But [a]there are some of you
who do not believe." For [b]Jesus
knew from the beginning who they
were who did not believe, and who
would betray Him.
65 And He said, "Therefore [a]I have
said to you that no one can come to
Me unless it has been granted to him
by My Father."
66 [a]From that *time* many of His disciples went [1]back and walked with
Him no more.†
67 Then Jesus said to the twelve,
"Do you also want to go away?"
68 But Simon Peter answered Him,
"Lord, to whom shall we go?
You have [a]the words of eternal
life.†
69 [a]"Also we have come to believe
and know that You are the [1]Christ,
the Son of the living God."
70 Jesus answered them, [a]"Did I
not choose you, the twelve, [b]and one
of you is a devil?"
71 He spoke of [a]Judas Iscariot, *the
son* of Simon, for it was he who
would [b]betray Him, being one of the
twelve.

Jesus at the Feast of Tabernacles

7 After these things Jesus walked
in Galilee; for He did not want
to walk in Judea, [a]because the
[1]Jews sought to kill Him.†

55 [1]NU *true food* [2]NU *true drink*
56 [a][1 John 3:24; 4:15, 16]
58 [a]John 6:49–51 [b]Ex. 16:14–35
60 [a]John 6:66 [1]*difficult*
61 [1]*grumbled* [2]*make you stumble*
62 [a]Acts 1:9; 2:32, 33
63 [a]2 Cor. 3:6 [b]John 3:6 [c][John 6:68; 14:24]
64 [a]John 6:36 [b]John 2:24, 25; 13:11
65 [a]John 6:37, 44, 45
66 [a]Luke 9:62 [1]Or *away;* lit. *to the back*
68 [a]Acts 5:20
69 [a]Luke 9:20 [1]NU *Holy One of God.*
70 [a]Luke 6:13 [b][John 13:27]
71 [a]John 12:4; 13:2, 26 [b]Matt. 26:14–16

CHAPTER 7

1 [a]John 5:18; 7:19, 25; 8:37, 40 [1]The ruling authorities

(continued from previous page)
nature within us would be foolish and impious were we not taught by His very words. . . . There is no room left for doubt about the reality of His flesh and blood, because we have both the witness of His words and our own faith. Thus, when we eat and drink these elements we are in Christ and Christ is in us" (*On the Trinity,* Book VIII, 14).

This reality, however, is a profound mystery of faith and grace. Orthodox theology teaches that in the Eucharist we partake not simply of the physical/material, but of the deified and glorified Body and Blood of Christ which give resurrection life.

6:60, 61 Even His disciples took Christ's teaching on His Body and Blood as **a hard saying** (v. 60), and many of them departed from Him (v. 66). The Lord Jesus is aware of the thoughts of men.

6:66 To reject Jesus' teaching on the sacramental eating of His Body and drinking of His Blood is to walk **with Him no more.**

6:68, 69 This confession of faith is a pivotal moment in the life of Peter and the disciples on behalf of whom he spoke.

7:1 This section (chs. 7—9) tells of Jesus' visit to Jerusalem for the Feast of Tabernacles (v. 2). At this festival, during the last year of His earthly life, Jesus taught in the temple and attracted a great deal of public attention. Some thought Him mad, others believed Him to be the Messiah, and still others (Sadducees and Pharisees who were members of the Sanhedrin) considered Him a threat to the religious and political status quo (ch. 7). The **Jews,** that is, the Jewish leaders, **sought to kill Him** (see 5:16).

2 [a]Now the Jews' Feast of Tabernacles was at hand.†
3 [a]His brothers therefore said to
Him, "Depart from here and go into
Judea, that Your disciples also may
see the works that You are doing.†
4 "For no one does anything
in secret while he himself seeks to
be known openly. If You do
these things, show Yourself to the
world."
5 For [a]even His [b]brothers did not
believe in Him.
6 Then Jesus said to them, [a]"My
time has not yet come, but your time
is always ready.
7 [a]"The world cannot hate you,
but it hates Me [b]because I testify of
it that its works are evil.
8 "You go up to this feast. I am
not [1]yet going up to this feast,
[a]for My time has not yet fully come."
9 When He had said these things
to them, He remained in Galilee.
10 But when His brothers had gone
up, then He also went up to the
feast, not openly, but as it were in
secret.†
11 Then [a]the Jews sought Him at
the feast, and said, "Where is
He?"
12 And [a]there was much complaining among the people concerning
Him. [b]Some said, "He is good";
others said, "No, on the contrary,
He deceives the people."
13 However, no one spoke openly
of Him [a]for fear of the Jews.

Jesus Teaches at the Feast

14 Now about the middle of the
feast Jesus went up into the temple
and [a]taught.
15 [a]And the Jews marveled, saying, "How does this Man know letters, having never studied?"
16 [1]Jesus answered them and said,
[a]"My doctrine is not Mine, but His
who sent Me.
17 [a]"If anyone wills to do His will,
he shall know concerning the doctrine, whether it is from God or
whether I speak on My own *authority*.†
18 [a]"He who speaks from himself
seeks his own glory; but He who
[b]seeks the glory of the One who sent
Him is true, and [c]no unrighteousness is in Him.
19 [a]"Did not Moses give you the
law, yet none of you keeps the law?
[b]Why do you seek to kill Me?"
20 The people answered and said,
[a]"You have a demon. Who is seeking to kill You?"
21 Jesus answered and said to
them, "I did one work, and you all
marvel.
22 [a]"Moses therefore gave you
circumcision (not that it is from
Moses, [b]but from the fathers),
and you circumcise a man on the
Sabbath.
23 "If a man receives circumcision
on the Sabbath, so that the law of
Moses should not be broken, are you
angry with Me because [a]I made a

2 [a]Lev. 23:34
3 [a]Matt. 12:46
5 [a]Ps. 69:8 [b]Mark 3:21
6 [a]John 2:4; 8:20
7 [a][John 15:19] [b]John 3:19
8 [a]John 8:20 [1]NU omits *yet*
11 [a]John 11:56
12 [a]John 9:16; 10:19 [b]Luke 7:16
13 [a][John 9:22; 12:42; 19:38]
14 [a]Mark 6:34
15 [a]Matt. 13:54
16 [a]John 3:11 [1]NU, M *So Jesus*
17 [a]John 3:21; 8:43
18 [a]John 5:41 [b]John 8:50 [c][2 Cor. 5:21]
19 [a]Deut. 33:4 [b]Matt. 12:14
20 [a]John 8:48, 52
22 [a]Lev. 12:3 [b]Gen. 17:9–14
23 [a]John 5:8, 9, 16

7:2 The **Feast of Tabernacles** (Heb. *succoth*) is an eight-day autumn harvest festival commemorating the wanderings of ancient Israel in the wilderness of Sinai, a time when the chosen people lived in tents (or "tabernacles"). Along with Passover and Pentecost, Tabernacles was one of the three most important festivals of the ancient Jews.

7:3 His **brothers** are members of His wider family clan who themselves do not believe in Him (v. 5). The Eastern Fathers understood "brothers" as stepbrothers, sons of Joseph by a previous wife; while the Western Fathers understood them to be first or second cousins Never are they called sons of Mary.

7:10 **Not openly** means not publicly, as in the case of the Triumphal Entry (12:12–16).

7:17 Jesus identifies the source of spiritual blindness: unwillingness to do the will of God. St. John Chrysostom paraphrases the words of Christ: "Rid yourselves of wickedness: the anger, and the envy, and the hatred which have arisen in your hearts—entirely without provocation—against Me, and you will have no difficulty in realizing that My words are actually those of God. For, as it is, these passions darken your understanding and distort the sound judgment that shines there, while, if you remove these passions, you will no longer be thus afflicted" (*Homily 49*).

man completely well on the Sabbath?†
24 [a]"Do not judge according to appearance, but judge with righteous
judgment."
25 Now some of them from Jerusalem said, "Is this not He whom they
seek to [a]kill?
26 "But look! He speaks boldly,
and they say nothing to Him.
[a]Do the rulers know indeed that this
is [1]truly the Christ?
27 [a]"However, we know where
this Man is from; but when the
Christ comes, no one knows where
He is from."†
28 Then Jesus cried out, as He
taught in the temple, saying, [a]"You
both know Me, and you know where
I am from; and [b]I have not come of
Myself, but He who sent Me [c]is true,
[d]whom you do not know.
29 [1]"But [a]I know Him, for I am
from Him, and He sent Me."
30 Therefore [a]they sought to take
Him; but [b]no one laid a hand on
Him, because His hour had not yet
come.†
31 And [a]many of the people believed in Him, and said, "When the
Christ comes, will He do more signs
than these which this *Man* has
done?"
32 The Pharisees heard the crowd
murmuring these things concerning Him, and the Pharisees and the
chief priests sent officers to take
Him.
33 Then Jesus said [1]to them,
[a]"I shall be with you a little while
longer, and *then* I [b]go to Him who
sent Me.†
34 "You [a]will seek Me and not find
Me, and where I am you [b]cannot
come."
35 Then the Jews said among
themselves, "Where does He intend
to go that we shall not find Him?
Does He intend to go to [a]the Dispersion among the Greeks and teach the
Greeks?†
36 "What is this thing that He
said, 'You will seek Me and not
find Me, and where I am you cannot come'?"

The Promise of Pentecost

37 [a]On the last day, that great *day*
of the feast, Jesus stood and cried
out, saying, [b]"If anyone thirsts, let
him come to Me and drink.†
38 [a]"He who believes in Me, as the
Scripture has said, [b]out of his heart
will flow rivers of living water."
39 [a]But this He spoke concerning
the Spirit, whom those [1]believing in
Him would receive; for the [2]Holy

24 [a]Prov. 24:23
25 [a]Matt. 21:38; 26:4
26 [a]John 7:48
[1]NU omits *truly*
27 [a]Luke 4:22
28 [a]John 8:14
[b]John 5:43
[c]Rom. 3:4
[d]John 1:18; 8:55
29 [a]Matt. 11:27
[1]NU, M omit *But*
30 [a]Mark 11:18
[b]John 7:32, 44; 8:20; 10:39
31 [a]Matt. 12:23
33 [a]John 13:33
[b][1 Pet. 3:22]
[1]NU, M omit *to them*
34 [a]Hos. 5:6
[b][Matt. 5:20]
35 [a]James 1:1
37 [a]Lev. 23:36
[b][Is. 55:1]
38 [a]Deut. 18:15
[b]Is. 12:3; 43:20; 44:3; 55:1
39 [a]Is. 44:3
[1]NU *who believed*
[2]NU omits *Holy*

7:23 Jesus implies that healing the paralytic **on the Sabbath** is a greater obedience to the will of God than circumcising on the Sabbath.

7:27 This is an ignorant claim filled with irony: they know Jesus' human origin, but not His divine origin.

7:30 His hour is the time of His suffering and death. Jesus Christ shows Himself to be Lord of time, a prerogative possessed by God alone. He comes to the Cross of His own free will and in His time, not as a result of the political machinations of the Sadducees, Pharisees, and Romans.

7:33–35 Jesus speaks of His death, Resurrection, and Ascension. His hearers, as is so often the case, do not understand Him.

7:35 Among the Greeks means among the Gentiles. In those days, there were communities of Jews scattered throughout the Mediterranean world, especially in Syria, Asia Minor, Greece and Egypt. Their question bears a tinge of irony. By the time this Gospel was written, the Christian faith had spread throughout much of the Gentile world.

7:37–39 The **last day, that great day of the feast** is probably the seventh or eighth day of the Feast of Tabernacles. Ceremonies include a procession from the pool of Siloam, carrying water and pouring it as a libation at the temple. This commemorates the water flowing from the rock which Moses struck in the wilderness (Ex. 17:1–7), and provides the context for the Lord's words, **if anyone thirsts. Living water** (v. 38) is the gift of the **Spirit** (v. 39) and the new life which springs forth by the power of the Spirit. Christ gives the Holy Spirit, and the believer's heart consequently flows with new life. Christ does not force us, but is always available if we desire Him.

Pentecost (Trinity Sunday)—The Descent of the Holy Spirit on the Disciples *Seventh Sunday after Easter*

7:37–52; 8:12: Jesus gives the promise of the Holy Spirit to His disciples.

Spirit was not yet *given,* because Jesus was not yet [b]glorified.

Reaction to Jesus' Teaching

40 Therefore [1]many from the crowd, when they heard this saying, said, "Truly this is [a]the Prophet."†
41 Others said, "This is [a]the Christ." But some said, "Will the Christ come out of Galilee?†
42 [a]"Has not the Scripture said that the Christ comes from the seed of David and from the town of Bethlehem, [b]where David was?"
43 So [a]there was a division among the people because of Him.
44 Now [a]some of them wanted to take Him, but no one laid hands on Him.

39 [b]John 12:16; 13:31; 17:5
40 [a]Deut. 18:15, 18
[1]NU *some*
41 [a]John 4:42; 6:69
42 [a]Mic. 5:2
[b]1 Sam. 16:1, 4
43 [a]John 7:12
44 [a]John 7:30
46 [a]Luke 4:22
50 [a]John 3:1, 2; 19:39
[1]Lit. *Him*
[2]NU *before*
51 [a]Deut. 1:16, 17; 19:15
52 [a][Is. 9:1, 2]
[1]NU *is to rise*

45 Then the officers came to the chief priests and Pharisees, who said to them, "Why have you not brought Him?"†
46 The officers answered, [a]"No man ever spoke like this Man!"
47 Then the Pharisees answered them, "Are you also deceived?
48 "Have any of the rulers or the Pharisees believed in Him?
49 "But this crowd that does not know the law is accursed."
50 Nicodemus [a](he who came to [1]Jesus [2]by night, being one of them) said to them,†
51 [a]"Does our law judge a man before it hears him and knows what he is doing?"
52 They answered and said to him, "Are you also from Galilee? Search and look, for [a]no prophet [1]has arisen out of Galilee."

7:40 The Prophet: Many Jews of those days were looking not only for the Messiah (or Christ) but also for a prophet who would be a new Moses, one who would lead Israel out of bondage (Deut. 18:15–19). Reference is often made during the Holy (Passion) Week services to the "Great Moses," especially on Holy Saturday.

7:41–44 We know that Jesus did come from the line of **David** and was born in **Bethlehem,** as had been prophesied (see center column). But the people think He is from Nazareth in Galilee. Far more significantly, throughout his Gospel John uses occasions like this to bring out the truth concerning Jesus' eternal origin from the Father (see 7:28; 8:14, 23). No arrest could be made before Jesus' "hour" had come (v. 44).

7:45, 46 The enemies of Jesus increasingly scheme to destroy Him. The officers of the temple were sent out to Him in the middle of the Feast (v. 32), and it is now the last day. They came back saying, **No man ever spoke like this Man!** (v. 46). St. John Chrysostom writes: "The Pharisees and the Scribes . . . who even witnessed miracles and read Scriptures, derived no benefit from all this. . . . The attendants [the officers], on the other hand, though they could lay claim to none of this, were captivated by a single sermon. . . . For when the mind is open to conviction there is no need of long speeches. Truth is like that" (*Homily 52*).

7:50–52 Nicodemus (v. 50) has spoken with Jesus (3:1–21), and may well be on his way to becoming a follower (19:39). Others also believed in Christ, but were afraid of repercussions (12:42). Nicodemus's defense of Jesus (v. 51) is based upon legal grounds: they should first listen to Jesus' words before He is arrested. (See Ex. 23:1, forbidding false reporting; Deut. 1:16, requiring that both sides of the case be heard; see also Josephus *Antiquities* 14:167.) The Pharisees fail to uphold the law, making a sarcastic response to Nicodemus (v. 52). But their statement condemns them and shows their blindness to the Scriptures: the **prophet** Jonah came from Gath Hepher, a town in Galilee only 3 miles from Nazareth (2 Kin. 14:25).

53 [1]And everyone went to his *own*
house.†

8 But Jesus went to the Mount of
Olives.
2 Now [1]early in the morning He
came again into the temple, and all
the people came to Him; and He sat
down and [a]taught them.

Jesus Restores the Adulterous Woman

3 Then the scribes and Pharisees
brought to Him a woman caught in
adultery. And when they had set her
in the midst,
4 they said to Him, "Teacher,
[1]this woman was caught in [a]adul-
tery, in the very act.
5 [a]"Now [1]Moses, in the law, commanded us [2]that such should be
stoned. But what do You [3]say?"†
6 This they said, testing Him, that
they [a]might have *something* of which
to accuse Him. But Jesus stooped
down and wrote on the ground with
His finger, [1]as though He did not
hear.†
7 So when they continued asking
Him, He [1]raised Himself up and said
to them, [a]"He who is without sin
among you, let him throw a stone
at her first."
8 And again He stooped down
and wrote on the ground.
9 Then those who heard *it*,
[a]being[1] convicted by *their* conscience, went out one by one, beginning with the oldest *even* to
the last. And Jesus was left alone,
and the woman standing in the
midst.
10 When Jesus had raised Himself
up [1]and saw no one but the woman,
He said to her, "Woman, where are
those accusers [2]of yours? Has no one
condemned you?"
11 She said, "No one, Lord." And
Jesus said to her, [a]"Neither do
I condemn you; go [1]and [b]sin no
more."†

Jesus, Light of the World

12 Then Jesus spoke to them again,
saying, [a]"I am the light of the world.
He who [b]follows Me shall not walk
in darkness, but have the light of
life."†
13 The Pharisees therefore said to
Him, [a]"You bear witness of Yourself;
Your witness is not [1]true."†

53 [1]NU brackets 7:53 through 8:11 as not in the original text. They are present in over 900 mss. of John.

CHAPTER 8

2 [a]John 8:20; 18:20 [1]M *very early*
4 [a]Ex. 20:14 [1]M *we found this woman*
5 [a]Lev. 20:10 [1]M *in our law Moses commanded* [2]NU, M *to stone such* [3]M adds *about her*
6 [a]Matt. 22:15 [1]NU, M omit *as though He did not hear*
7 [a]Deut. 17:7 [1]M *He looked up*
9 [a]Rom. 2:22 [1]NU, M omit *being convicted by their conscience*
10 [1]NU omits *and saw no one but the woman;* M *He saw her and said,*
[2]NU, M omit *of yours*
11 [a][John 3:17] [b][John 5:14] [1]NU, M add *from now on*
12 [a]John 1:4; 9:5; 12:35 [b]1 Thess. 5:5
13 [a]John 5:31 [1]*valid* as testimony

7:53—8:11 This passage, the story of the adulterous woman, forcefully demonstrates the grace and power of Christ to redeem and reclaim all sinners, in contrast to the judgmental attitude of the scribes and Pharisees. Interestingly, this passage is read on one of the two days on which St. Mary of Egypt, a reformed prostitute, is commemorated.

8:5 The passage in **the law** is: "The man who commits adultery with another man's wife, he who commits adultery with his neighbor's wife, the adulterer and the adulteress, shall surely be put to death" (Lev. 20:10). This law was not observed to the letter in the days of Jesus; they are forcing application to test Him.

8:6 Testing Him: If Jesus refuses to condemn the woman, He will be accused as a lawbreaker; if He approves her condemnation, He will be inconsistent in His mercy to sinners. This (and v. 8) is the only NT reference that Christ **wrote** anything. Speculation abounds as to what He wrote, one theory being that He wrote the names of those accusers who were themselves guilty of adultery.

8:11 Go and sin no more: God forgives and does not condemn the repentant sinner. But true repentance includes striving to *sin no more.*

8:12 I am the light of the world: During the Feast of Tabernacles, torches were lit in the temple court, and singing and dancing continued each night. In this context Jesus is the One who gives **the light of life.** In the NT God is light (1 John 1:5); the followers of Jesus are the light (Matt. 5:14); and believers shine as lights in the world (Phil. 2:15). In these and other references in John, God is the source of this uncreated, life-giving light (see 1:4–10; 3:19; 12:35, 36).

8:13–29 In the face of resistance and disbelief Jesus continues to proclaim His relationship with the Father. **The Pharisees** either were unable to understand Jesus' words or were simply astonished that Jesus was claiming God as His own Father.

14 **Jesus answered and said to**
them, "Even if I bear witness of Myself, My witness is true, for I know
where I came from and where I am
going; but [a]you do not know where
I come from and where I am going.
15 [a]"You judge according to the
flesh; [b]I judge no one.
16 "And yet if I do judge, My judgment is true; for [a]I am not alone, but
I *am* with the Father who sent Me.
17 [a]"It is also written in your law
that the testimony of two men is
true.
18 "I am One who bears witness
of Myself, and [a]the Father who sent
Me bears witness of Me."
19 **Then they said to Him, "Where**
is Your Father?" Jesus answered,
[a]"You know neither Me nor My Father. [b]If you had known Me, you
would have known My Father
also."†
20 These words Jesus spoke in
[a]the treasury, as He taught in the
temple; and [b]no one laid hands on
Him, for [c]His hour had not yet
come.
21 Then Jesus said to them again,
"I am going away, and [a]you will
seek Me, and [b]will die in your sin.
Where I go you cannot come."†
22 **So the Jews said, "Will He kill**
Himself, because He says, 'Where I
go you cannot come'?"
23 And He said to them, [a]"You are
from beneath; I am from above.
[b]You are of this world; I am not of
this world.
24 [a]"Therefore I said to you that
you will die in your sins; [b]for if you
do not believe that I am *He,* you will
die in your sins."
25 **Then they said to Him, "Who**
are You?" And Jesus said to them,
"Just what I [a]have been saying to
you from the beginning.†
26 "I have many things to say and
to judge concerning you, but [a]He
who sent Me is true; and [b]I speak
to the world those things which I
heard from Him."
27 **They did not understand that**
He spoke to them of the Father.
28 **Then Jesus said to them,** "When
you [a]lift[1] up the Son of Man, [b]then
you will know that I am *He,* and
[c]*that* I do nothing of Myself; but
[d]as My Father taught Me, I speak
these things.†
29 "And [a]He who sent Me is with
Me. [b]The Father has not left Me
alone, [c]for I always do those things
that please Him."
30 **As He spoke these words,**
[a]**many believed in Him.**

The Truth Shall Make You Free

31 **Then Jesus said to those Jews**
who believed Him, "If you [a]abide in
My word, you are My disciples
indeed.†
32 "And you shall know the
[a]truth, and [b]the truth shall make you
free."†
33 **They answered Him,** [a]**"We are**
Abraham's descendants, and have
never been in bondage to anyone.
How *can* You say, 'You will be made
free'?"
34 Jesus answered them, "Most assuredly, I say to you, [a]whoever commits sin is a slave of sin.
35 "And [a]a slave does not abide in
the house forever, *but* a son abides
forever.

14 [a]John 7:28; 9:29
15 [a]John 7:24 [b][John 3:17; 12:47; 18:36]
16 [a]John 16:32
17 [a]Deut. 17:6; 19:15
18 [a]John 5:37
19 [a]John 16:3 [b]John 14:7
20 [a]Mark 12:41, 43 [b]John 2:4; 7:30 [c]John 7:8
21 [a]John 7:34; 13:33 [b]John 8:24
23 [a]John 3:31 [b]1 John 4:5
24 [a]John 8:21 [b][Mark 16:16]
25 [a]John 4:26
26 [a]John 7:28 [b]John 3:32; 15:15
28 [a]John 3:14; 12:32; 19:18 [b][Rom. 1:4] [c]John 5:19, 30 [d]John 3:11 [1]Crucify
29 [a]John 14:10 [b]John 8:16; 16:32 [c]John 4:34; 5:30; 6:38
30 [a]John 7:31; 10:42; 11:45
31 [a][John 14:15, 23]
32 [a][John 1:14, 17; 14:6] [b][Rom. 6:14, 18, 22]
33 [a][Matt. 3:9]
34 [a]2 Pet. 2:19
35 [a]Gal. 4:30

8:19 Because the Son and the Father share the same nature, one cannot be known apart from the other. St. John Chrysostom writes: "Indeed, if He were not of the same nature as the Father, He would not have spoken as He did."

8:21 Going away refers to His death and Resurrection.

8:25 St. John Chrysostom writes: "Oh, what stupidity! After so long a time and miracles, and teaching, they asked 'Who art thou?'"

8:28 Lift up has the double meaning of being nailed to the Cross and of being exalted by the Father upon the completion of His work.

8:31 Jesus expects all who follow Him to be **disciples** (learners). Abiding in His **word** is not something reserved for an elite class of zealots.

8:32 Being **free** refers specifically to freedom from bondage to sin (v. 34), granted by the Redeemer through His death and Resurrection.

36 [a]"Therefore if the Son makes
you free, you shall be free indeed.

Sons of the Devil Reject the Son of God

37 "I know that you are Abraham's
descendants, but [a]you seek to kill
Me, because My word has no place
in you.†
38 [a]"I speak what I have seen with
My Father, and you do what you
have [1]seen with your father."
39 **They answered and said to Him,**
[a]**"Abraham is our father." Jesus said**
to them, [b]"If you were Abraham's
children, you would do the works
of Abraham.
40 [a]"But now you seek to kill Me,
a Man who has told you the truth
[b]which I heard from God. Abraham
did not do this.
41 "You do the deeds of your father." **Then they said to Him, "We**
were not born of fornication; [a]**we**
have one Father—God."†
42 **Jesus said to them,** [a]"If God
were your Father, you would love
Me, for [b]I proceeded forth and came
from God; [c]nor have I come of Myself, but He sent Me.†
43 [a]"Why do you not understand
My speech? Because you are not able
to listen to My word.†
44 [a]"You are of *your* father the
devil, and the [b]desires of your father
you want to [c]do. He was a murderer
from the beginning, and [d]does not
stand in the truth, because there is
no truth in him. When he speaks a
lie, he speaks from his own *resources,*
for he is a liar and the father of it.
45 "But because I tell the truth, you
do not believe Me.
46 "Which of you convicts Me of
sin? And if I tell the truth, why do
you not believe Me?
47 [a]"He who is of God hears God's
words; therefore you do not hear,
because you are not of God."
48 **Then the Jews answered and**
said to Him, "Do we not say rightly
that You are a Samaritan and [a]**have**
a demon?"†
49 **Jesus answered,** "I do not have
a demon; but I honor My Father, and
[a]you dishonor Me.
50 "And [a]I do not seek My *own*
glory; there is One who seeks and
judges.
51 "Most assuredly, I say to you,
[a]if anyone keeps My word he shall
never see death."

The Father Honors the Son

52 **Then the Jews said to Him,**
"Now we know that You [a]**have a de-**
mon! [b]**Abraham is dead, and the**
prophets; and You say, 'If anyone
keeps My word he shall never taste
death.'
53 **"Are You greater than our fa-**
ther Abraham, who is dead? And the
prophets are dead. [a]**Who do You**
make Yourself out to be?"
54 **Jesus answered,** [a]"If I honor
Myself, My honor is nothing. [b]It is
My Father who honors Me, of whom
you say that He is [1]your God.
55 "Yet [a]you have not known Him,
but I know Him. And if I say, 'I do

36 [a]Gal. 5:1
37 [a]John 7:19
38 [a][John 3:32; 5:19, 30; 14:10, 24] [1]NU *heard from*
39 [a]Matt. 3:9 [b][Rom. 2:28]
40 [a]John 8:37 [b]John 8:26
41 [a]Is. 63:16
42 [a]1 John 5:1 [b]John 16:27; 17:8, 25 [c]Gal. 4:4
43 [a][John 7:17]
44 [a]Matt. 13:38 [b]1 John 2:16, 17 [c][1 John 3:8–10, 15] [d][Jude 6]
47 [a]1 John 4:6
48 [a]John 7:20; 10:20
49 [a]John 5:41
50 [a]John 5:41; 7:18
51 [a]John 5:24; 11:26
52 [a]John 7:20; 10:20 [b]Zech. 1:5
53 [a]John 10:33; 19:7
54 [a]John 5:31, 32 [b]Acts 3:13 [1]NU, M *our*
55 [a]John 7:28, 29

8:37–44 Who are the true children of Abraham? Jesus makes it clear that one lives either by God's way or the devil's way (vv. 37–59). There is no middle ground (vv. 42–44).

8:41 St. John Chrysostom writes: "[Jesus] wished to detach them from this racial pride and to deflate their excessive conceit, and to persuade them no longer to place their hope of salvation in Abraham, or in nobility of race according to nature, but in that according to free will. For, this was the thing that prevented them from coming to Christ; namely, they thought their descent from Abraham sufficed for their salvation."

8:42 Proceeded here, referring to Christ, translates the Greek *exerchomai,* whereas "proceeds" in 15:26, referring to the Holy Spirit, translates the Greek *ekporeuomai.* Christ's eternal relationship to the Father is one of Sonship rather than procession.

8:43 They are **not able to listen** to His word because they are not willing to learn from Him. Spiritual truth can be genuinely heard only if there is willingness to know God and to do His will.

8:48 Samaritans were viewed as demon-possessed heretics.

not know Him,' I shall be a liar like you; but I do know Him and [b]keep His word.

56 "Your father Abraham [a]rejoiced to see My day, [b]and he saw *it* and was glad."

57 Then the Jews said to Him, "You are not yet fifty years old, and have You seen Abraham?"

58 Jesus said to them, "Most assuredly, I say to you, [a]before Abraham was, [b]I AM."†

59 Then [a]they took up stones to throw at Him; but Jesus hid Himself and went out of the temple, [b]going[1] through the midst of them, and so passed by.†

The Man Born Blind Sees

9 Now as *Jesus* passed by, He saw a man who was blind from birth.†

2 And His disciples asked Him, saying, "Rabbi, [a]who sinned, this man or his parents, that he was born blind?"

3 Jesus answered, "Neither this man nor his parents sinned, [a]but that the works of God should be revealed in him.†

4 [a]"I[1] must work the works of Him who sent Me while it is [b]day; *the* night is coming when no one can work.†

5 "As long as I am in the world, [a]I am the light of the world."

6 When He had said these things, [a]He spat on the ground and made clay with the saliva; and He anointed the eyes of the blind man with the clay.†

7 And He said to him, "Go, wash [a]in the pool of Siloam" (which is translated, Sent). So [b]he went and washed, and came back seeing.†

8 Therefore the neighbors and

55 [b][John 15:10]
56 [a]Luke 10:24
[b]Heb. 11:13
58 [a]Mic. 5:2
[b]Rev. 1:8
59 [a]John 10:31; 11:8
[b]Luke 4:30
[1]NU omits the rest of v. 59.

CHAPTER 9

2 [a]John 9:34
3 [a]John 11:4
4 [a][John 4:34; 5:19, 36; 17:4]
[b]John 11:9, 10; 12:35
[1]NU *We*
5 [a][John 1:5, 9; 3:19; 8:12; 12:35, 46]
6 [a]Mark 7:33; 8:23
7 [a]Neh. 3:15
[b]2 Kin. 5:14

8:58 I AM (Gr. *ego eimi*) is a name of God in the OT, first revealed to Moses at the burning bush (Ex. 3:13–15; Is. 43:10; see also John 4:26; 6:20; 8:24, 28; 13:19; 18:5–8). To the Jews this pronouncement was a direct, explicit, and unmistakable claim to perfect equality with God. John places special emphasis on the use of the expression for the purpose of revealing Christ as God. In context, this statement illuminates what He began saying in v. 51, that those who keep His word will neither see nor taste death. Only God has power over death, and Jesus is claiming such power.

8:59 The Jews regarded Jesus' claim to be one with God (v. 58) as the most abominable form of blasphemy. They **took up stones** because death by stoning was the penalty for blasphemy required by the Mosaic Law. But Jesus departs from their midst by divine power, without being harmed.

9:1–38 Of all the miracle stories in the Bible, this is the only one in which the person was **blind from birth.** This man is symbolic of all humanity: all need illumination by Christ, the Light of the world. This passage is also a picture of baptism, which is also called "holy illumination." This healing is the sixth sign of Jesus in John's Gospel (see note on 2:1–11). In the ancient Church this passage, along with chs. 3 and 5, was read on the Saturday night of Easter, when Christian catechumens were baptized. It reiterates the paschal themes of washing, illumination, healing, faith, conversion, and salvation.

9:3 The Savior rejects the assumption (common in the ancient world) that trouble and malady are necessarily a consequence of personal sin (see Ex. 20:5; Ezek. 18:20). Rather, this man's blindness provides the occasion for God's mighty works to be revealed. However, it is true that suffering and death entered the world as a result of sin (Rom. 5:12), and some sinful acts bring about sickness and death (1 Cor. 11:30). There would be no sickness in the world if there were no sin, but by no means is all sickness the result of a specific person's sin.

9:4 Jesus speaks of the urgency of bringing light into the darkened world, for the duration of His time upon the earth is limited.

9:6 Made clay with the saliva: St. Irenaeus sees in this mixture of dust and spittle a type of the creation of humanity from the earth (Gen. 2:7). Jesus reveals His deity by restoring part of creation in the same way He had created humanity in the beginning.

9:7 The **pool of Siloam** (Gr. for *Shiloah*) was on the outskirts of Jerusalem, a considerable distance from the temple. What a spectacle was this man, blind and eyes covered with mud, making his way across the city, from the temple to the pool, in faithful expectation of

(continued on next page)

those who previously had seen that
he was [1]blind said, "Is not this he
who sat and begged?"
9 Some said, "This is he." Others
said, [1]"He is like him." He said, "I
am *he.*"
10 Therefore they said to him,
"How were your eyes opened?"†
11 He answered and said, [a]"A
Man called Jesus made clay and
anointed my eyes and said to me,
'Go to [1]the pool of Siloam and wash.'
So I went and washed, and I received
sight."
12 Then they said to him, "Where
is He?" He said, "I do not know."

Those Who See, Those Who Do Not

13 They brought him who formerly
was blind to the Pharisees.
14 Now it was a Sabbath when
Jesus made the clay and opened his
eyes.
15 Then the Pharisees also asked
him again how he had received his
sight. He said to them, "He put clay
on my eyes, and I washed, and I
see."
16 Therefore some of the Pharisees
said, "This Man is not from God, because He does not [1]keep the Sabbath." Others said, [a]"How can a
man who is a sinner do such signs?"
And [b]there was a division among
them.†
17 They said to the blind man
again, "What do you say about Him
because He opened your eyes?" He
said, [a]"He is a prophet."
18 But the Jews did not believe
concerning him, that he had been
blind and received his sight, until
they called the parents of him who
had received his sight.†
19 And they asked them, saying,
"Is this your son, who you say was
born blind? How then does he now
see?"
20 His parents answered them and
said, "We know that this is our son,
and that he was born blind;
21 "but by what means he now
sees we do not know, or who opened
his eyes we do not know. He is of
age; ask him. He will speak for
himself."
22 His parents said these *things* because [a]they feared the Jews, for the
Jews had agreed already that if anyone confessed *that* He *was* Christ, he
[b]would be put out of the synagogue.
23 Therefore his parents said, "He
is of age; ask him."
24 So they again called the man
who was blind, and said to him,
[a]"Give God the glory! [b]We know
that this Man is a sinner."†
25 He answered and said,
"Whether He is a sinner *or not* I do
not know. One thing I know: that
though I was blind, now I see."
26 Then they said to him again,
"What did He do to you? How did
He open your eyes?"
27 He answered them, "I told you
already, and you did not listen. Why

8 [1]NU *a begger*
9 [1]NU *"No, but he is like him."*
11 [a]John 9:6, 7 [1]NU omits *the pool of*
16 [a]John 3:2; 9:33 [b]John 7:12, 43; 10:19 [1]*observe*
17 [a][John 4:19; 6:14]
22 [a]John 7:13; 12:42; 19:38; Acts 5:13 [b]John 16:2
24 [a]Josh. 7:19; 1 Sam. 6:5; Ezra 10:11; Rev. 11:13 [b]John 9:16

(continued from previous page)
Christ's promised healing! It was from this pool that water was taken for the rites connected with the Feast of Tabernacles (see note for 7:37–39). Siloam, **translated, Sent,** symbolizes Christ, the One sent by the Father.

9:10 That the Lord **opened** the **eyes** of the blind man recalls Is. 35:5, with its messianic significance. As the story progresses (vv. 14–41), the once-blind man gradually comes to an awareness of who Jesus is, while the Pharisees lapse into deeper darkness.

9:16 The Jewish authorities try to discredit the miracle by discrediting Jesus. They claim that because He works on the Sabbath, contrary to their law, He cannot be from God.

9:18 The Jewish authorities again try to discredit the miracle by denying that this man was **blind** from birth. His **parents** are called in, even though the age of legal responsibility was 13.

9:24 With Jesus not present, the Pharisees harshly call Him a **sinner**—but earlier when Jesus asked them face-to-face, "Which of you convicts Me of sin?" (8:46), they answered by evading the question. **Give God the glory** is an oath formula, used before giving testimony or before confessing guilt. Ironically, the formerly blind man will indeed give glory to God (v. 38). The more he is pressed, the more tenacious he becomes in his belief.

do you want to hear *it* again? Do you also want to become His disciples?"

28 Then they reviled him and said, "You are His disciple, but we are Moses' disciples.

29 "We know that God [a]spoke to [b]Moses; *as for* this *fellow,* [c]we do not know where He is from."

30 The man answered and said to them, [a]"Why, this is a marvelous thing, that you do not know where He is from; yet He has opened my eyes!

31 "Now we know that [a]God does not hear sinners; but if anyone is a worshiper of God and does His will, He hears him.

32 "Since the world began it has been unheard of that anyone opened the eyes of one who was born blind.

33 [a]"If this Man were not from God, He could do nothing."

34 They answered and said to him, [a]"You were completely born in sins, and are you teaching us?" And they [1]cast him out.

35 Jesus heard that they had cast him out; and when He had [a]found him, He said to him, "Do you [b]believe in [c]the Son of [1]God?"†

36 He answered and said, "Who is He, Lord, that I may believe in Him?"

37 And Jesus said to him, "You have both seen Him and [a]it is He who is talking with you."

38 Then he said, "Lord, I believe!" And he [a]worshiped Him.

39 And Jesus said, [a]"For judgment I have come into this world, [b]that those who do not see may see, and that those who see may be made blind."

40 Then *some* of the Pharisees who were with Him heard these words, [a]and said to Him, "Are we blind also?"

41 Jesus said to them, [a]"If you were blind, you would have no sin; but now you say, 'We see.' Therefore your sin remains.

Jesus, the Good Shepherd

10 "Most assuredly, I say to you, he who does not enter the sheepfold by the door, but climbs up some other way, the same is a thief and a robber.†

2 "But he who enters by the door is the shepherd of the sheep.

3 "To him the doorkeeper opens, and the sheep hear his voice; and he calls his own sheep by [a]name and leads them out.

4 "And when he brings out his own sheep, he goes before them; and the sheep follow him, for they know his voice.

5 "Yet they will by no means follow a [a]stranger, but will flee from him, for they do not know the voice of strangers."

6 Jesus used this illustration, but they did not understand the things which He spoke to them.

7 Then Jesus said to them again, "Most assuredly, I say to you, I am the door of the sheep.†

8 "All who *ever* came [1]before Me are thieves and robbers, but the sheep did not hear them.

29 [a]Ex. 19:19, 20; 33:11; 34:29; Num. 12:6–8 [b][John 5:45–47] [c]John 7:27, 28; 8:14
30 [a]John 3:10
31 [a]Job 27:9; 35:12; Ps. 18:41; Prov. 1:28; 15:29; 28:9; Is. 1:15; Jer. 11:11; 14:12; Ezek. 8:18; Mic. 3:4; Zech. 7:13; [James 5:16]
33 [a]John 3:2; 9:16
34 [a]Ps. 51:5; John 9:2 [1]Excommunicated him
35 [a]John 5:14 [b]John 1:7; 16:31 [c]Matt. 14:33; 16:16; Mark 1:1; John 10:36; 1 John 5:13 [1]NU *Man*
37 [a]John 4:26
38 [a]Matt. 8:2
39 [a][John 3:17; 5:22, 27; 12:47] [b]Matt. 13:13; 15:14
40 [a][Rom. 2:19]
41 [a]John 15:22, 24

CHAPTER 10

3 [a]John 20:16
5 [a][2 Cor. 11:13–15]
8 [1]M omits *before Me*

9:35–41 Having opened the blind man's eyes, Jesus also opens the eyes of his heart, offering spiritual illumination. The man, "seeing" the divinity of the Son of Man, **worshiped Him** (v. 38). Jesus' coming brought **judgment** (v. 39) by increasing the accountability of those who saw and heard Him, but did not believe. The brilliance of Christ's light becomes an illumination to some, but a blinding glare to others (v. 41).

10:1–18 Jesus' conversation with the Pharisees continues (there is no break between 9:41 and 10:1). Christ tells the Pharisees that they, not the blind man, are alienated from God. They are blind, and false shepherds of God's people.

10:1–16 This parable of salvation uses the symbolism of the shepherd and his flock. This is the Gospel reading on the days the Church honors her true bishops and theologians.

10:7 In calling Himself **the door,** Jesus signifies He will bring His flock into an enclosed sheepfold with a central gate. Normally a hired guard would tend the gate while the shepherds rested through the night. But Jesus is the tireless Shepherd, always guarding the entrance. No one can enter except by way of Him.

Commemoration of a Holy Hierarch

10:9–16: These holy men were good shepherds to the Lord's flock.

9 [a]"I am the door. If anyone enters by Me, he will be saved, and
will go in and out and find pasture.

Jesus Gives His Life for the Sheep

10 "The thief does not come except
to steal, and to kill, and to destroy.
I have come that they may have life,
and that they may have *it* more
abundantly.†
11 [a]"I am the good shepherd. The
good shepherd gives His life for the
sheep.†
12 "But a [1]hireling, *he who is* not
the shepherd, one who does not own
the sheep, sees the wolf coming and
[a]leaves the sheep and flees; and the
wolf catches the sheep and scatters
them.†
13 "The hireling flees because he
is a hireling and does not care about
the sheep.
14 "I am the good shepherd; and
[a]I know My *sheep,* and [b]am known
by My own.
15 [a]"As the Father knows Me,
even so I know the Father; [b]and I
lay down My life for the sheep.
16 "And [a]other sheep I have which

9 [a][Eph. 2:18]
11 [a]Is. 40:11
12 [a]Zech. 11:16, 17
[1]*hired man*
14 [a]2 Tim. 2:19
[b]2 Tim. 1:12
15 [a]Matt. 11:27
[b][John 15:13; 19:30]
16 [a]Is. 42:6; 56:8
[b]Eph. 2:13–18
17 [a]John 5:20
[b][Heb. 2:9]
18 [a][John 2:19; 5:26]
[b][John 6:38; 14:31; 17:4; Acts 2:24, 32]
19 [a]John 7:43; 9:16
20 [a]John 7:20
[1]*insane*
21 [a][Ex. 4:11]
[b]John 9:6, 7, 32, 33

are not of this fold; them also I must
bring, and they will hear My voice;
[b]and there will be one flock *and* one
shepherd.†
17 "Therefore My Father [a]loves
Me, [b]because I lay down My life that
I may take it again.†
18 "No one takes it from Me, but
I lay it down of Myself. I [a]have
power to lay it down, and I have
power to take it again. [b]This command I have received from My
Father."
19 Therefore [a]there was a division
again among the Jews because of
these sayings.
20 And many of them said, [a]"He
has a demon and is [1]mad. Why do
you listen to Him?"
21 Others said, "These are not the
words of one who has a demon.
[a]Can a demon [b]open the eyes of the
blind?"

Jesus Gives Eternal Life to the Sheep

22 Now it was the Feast of Dedication in Jerusalem, and it was
winter.†

10:10 The **thief**—the devil—steals, kills and destroys the virtues of Christian life and lays waste those who follow his heresies. Life **more abundantly** is the life of God's Kingdom, offered us by Christ Himself (see Ps. 23:5).

10:11 This is a prophecy of Jesus' impending death, through which His people are to be reconciled to God the Father. The **good shepherd,** Christ, and His under-shepherds look after the sheep even to the point of giving their lives for them.

10:12 The **hireling** (vv. 12–15), the noncommitted religious leader, is contrasted with the **shepherd,** one who considers the **sheep** his own. The hired hand looks primarily after himself.

10:16 Other sheep are the Gentiles, who will be brought into the **one flock** under the **one shepherd.** Hence, the Church cannot be divided along denominational, ethnic, cultural or family lines.

10:17, 18 The Lord makes it clear this atoning death will be voluntary. Though He is God, He does nothing apart from the authority of His Father. If we seek to experience God's love and His power, we do so as Christ Himself does: by obeying willingly the Father's commands. As He laid down His life for us, we lay down our lives for Him, willingly and out of love.

10:22 This encounter with the Jewish authorities in Jerusalem takes place approximately *(continued on next page)*

23 And Jesus walked in the temple,
[a]in Solomon's porch.
24 Then the Jews surrounded Him
and said to Him, "How long do You
keep us in [1]doubt? If You are the
Christ, tell us plainly."
25 Jesus answered them, "I told
you, and you do not believe. [a]The
works that I do in My Father's name,
they [b]bear witness of Me.
26 "But [a]you do not believe, because you are not of My sheep,
[1]as I said to you.
27 [a]"My sheep hear My voice, and
I know them, and they follow Me.
28 • "And I give them eternal life,
and they shall never perish; neither
shall anyone snatch them out of My
hand.

I and My Father Are One

29 [a]"My Father, [b]who has given
them to Me, is greater than all; and
no one is able to snatch *them* out of
My Father's hand.
30 [a]"I and *My* Father are one."†
31 Then [a]the Jews took up stones
again to stone Him.
32 Jesus answered them, "Many
good works I have shown you from
My Father. For which of those works
do you stone Me?"
33 The Jews answered Him, saying, "For a good work we do not
stone You, but for [a]blasphemy, and
because You, being a Man, [b]make
Yourself God."

23 [a]Acts 3:11; 5:12
24 [1]Suspense
25 [a]John 5:36; 10:38 [b]Matt. 11:4
26 [a][John 8:47] [1]NU omits *as I said to you*
27 [a]John 10:4, 14
29 [a]John 14:28 [b][John 17:2, 6, 12, 24]
30 [a]John 17:11, 21–24
31 [a]John 8:59
33 [a]Matt. 9:3 [b]John 5:18
34 [a]Ps. 82:6
35 [a]Matt. 5:17, 18 [b]1 Pet. 1:25
36 [a]John 6:27 [b]John 3:17 [c]John 5:17, 18 [d]Luke 1:35
37 [a]John 10:25; 15:24
38 [a]John 5:36 [b]John 14:10, 11 [1]NU *understand*
39 [a]John 7:30, 44
40 [a]John 1:28
41 [a][John 1:29, 36; 3:28–36; 5:33]

CHAPTER 11

1 [a]Luke 10:38, 39
2 [a]Matt. 26:7

34 Jesus answered them, "Is it not
written in your law, [a]*'I said, "You
are gods"'*?†
35 "If He called them gods, [a]to
whom the word of God came (and
the Scripture [b]cannot be broken),
36 "do you say of Him [a]whom the
Father sanctified and [b]sent into the
world, 'You are blaspheming,'
[c]because I said, 'I am [d]the Son of
God'?
37 [a]"If I do not do the works of
My Father, do not believe Me;
38 "but if I do, though you do not
believe Me, [a]believe the works, that
you may know and [1]believe [b]that the
Father *is* in Me, and I in Him."
39 [a]Therefore they sought again to
seize Him, but He escaped out of
their hand.
40 And He went away again beyond the Jordan to the place [a]where
John was baptizing at first, and there
He stayed.
41 Then many came to Him and
said, "John performed no sign,
[a]but all the things that John spoke
about this Man were true."
42 And many believed in Him
there.

Lazarus Dies

11 Now a certain *man* was sick,
Lazarus of Bethany, the town
of [a]Mary and her sister Martha.†
2 [a]It was *that* Mary who anointed
the Lord with fragrant oil and wiped

(continued from previous page)
three months after the Feast of Tabernacles (chs. 7—9). The occasion of Christ's presence in Jerusalem is again a religious festival, the **Feast of Dedication** (Hanukkah), the festival of lights. This Feast commemorates the rededication of the temple to the God of Israel after the Seleucid king, Antiochus Epiphanes, desecrated the temple in 167 B.C. (see 1 Macc. 1—4). The leaders of Israel's past are commemorated, many of whom were literal shepherds.

10:30–33 Responding to their question (v. 24), Jesus reveals Himself as fully God: **one** means one in nature. He was God before the Incarnation, and He remains fully God after that union of God and man in His one Person. The verb **are** indicates the Father and the Son are two Persons. They are always distinct, but united in essence, will and action. Jesus' bold claim causes a violent reaction: they attempt to stone Him, accusing Him of blasphemy.

10:34–36 Jesus' question comes in response to the Pharisees' charge of blasphemy (v. 33). What the Lord is saying, according to St. John Chrysostom, is this: "If those who have received this honor by grace are not found with fault for calling themselves gods, how can He who has this by nature deserve to be rebuked?"

11:1–45 The account of the raising of Lazarus exemplifies the truth that Christ is **the**

(continued on next page)

Lazarus Saturday

Saturday before Palm Sunday

11:1–45: The resurrection of Lazarus prefigures Christ's Resurrection and our own.

His feet with her hair, whose brother
Lazarus was sick.†
3 Therefore the sisters sent to
Him, saying, "Lord, behold, he
whom You love is sick."
4 When Jesus heard *that*, He said,
"This sickness is not unto death, but
for the glory of God, that the Son
of God may be glorified through it."†
5 Now Jesus loved Martha and
her sister and Lazarus.
6 So, when He heard that he was
sick, [a]He stayed two more days in
the place where He was.†
7 Then after this He said to *the*
disciples, "Let us go to Judea again."
8 *The* disciples said to Him,
"Rabbi, lately the Jews sought to
[a]stone You, and are You going there
again?"†
9 Jesus answered, "Are there not
twelve hours in the day? [a]If anyone
walks in the day, he does not stumble, because he sees the [b]light of this
world.
10 "But [a]if one walks in the night,
he stumbles, because the light is not
in him."
11 These things He said, and after
that He said to them, "Our friend
Lazarus [a]sleeps, but I go that I may
wake him up."†
12 Then His disciples said, "Lord,
if he sleeps he will get well."
13 However, Jesus spoke of his
death, but they thought that He was
speaking about taking rest in sleep.
14 Then Jesus said to them plainly,
"Lazarus is dead.
15 "And I am glad for your sakes
that I was not there, that you may
believe. Nevertheless let us go to
him."
16 Then [a]Thomas, who is called
the Twin, said to his fellow disciples,
"Let us also go, that we may die with
Him."†

I Am the Resurrection and the Life

17 So when Jesus came, He found
that he had already been in the tomb
four days.†
18 Now Bethany was near Jerusalem, about [1]two miles away.
19 And many of the Jews had
joined the women around Martha
and Mary, to comfort them concerning their brother.†
20 Then Martha, as soon as she

6 [a]John 10:40
8 [a]John 8:59; 10:31
9 [a]Luke 13:33; John 9:4; 12:35 [b]Is. 9:2
10 [a]John 12:35
11 [a]Deut. 31:16; [Dan. 12:2]; Matt. 9:24; Acts 7:60; [1 Cor. 15:18, 51]
16 [a]Matt. 10:3; Mark 3:18; Luke 6:15; John 14:5; 20:26–28; Acts 1:13
18 [1]Lit. *15 stadia*

(continued from previous page)
resurrection and the life (v. 25). This miracle is the last of our Lord's seven signs in the Gospel of John (see note on 2:1–11): the sign which sealed the decision of the Jewish authorities to put Jesus to death. **Bethany** is on the eastern slope of the Mount of Olives, about 2 miles from Jerusalem (v. 18). Lazarus is the same name as Eleazar (lit. "God helps").

11:2 The Evangelist assumes his readers already know of the anointing of Jesus by Mary, an account he places later in his Gospel (12:1–8).

11:4 Lazarus' **sickness** would not result in permanent **death** because he would be brought back to life by Christ, an act which would bring **glory** to the Father and the Son.

11:6 So, when He heard is a conclusion drawn from v. 3. Jesus delays to allow for the assured death of Lazarus (v. 17), which will underscore the magnitude of the miracle.

11:8 In Jerusalem at the Feast of Dedication, the Jewish authorities sought to kill Jesus (10:22–39). **Going there again** would incur the risk of death.

11:11 Sleep is often used to signify death (Acts 7:60; 1 Cor. 15:6).

11:16 Thomas, if not with full understanding, speaks the truth: dying with Christ, in baptism and sometimes in martyrdom, will become the seal of Christian discipleship.

11:17 There existed a rabbinic opinion that the soul lingered about the body for three days, but from the fourth day on there was no hope of resuscitation.

11:19 Official mourning began on the same day as death and burial (immediate burial

(continued on next page)

+ Ἡ ΜΕΤΑ ΜΟΡΦΩCΙC
ΗΛΙΑC
ΙC ΧC
ΜΩΫCΗC

The Transfiguration of Christ, *by the hand of Photios Kontoglu.* Courtesy of Dormition Skete, Buena Vista, Colorado.

Christ came in fulfillment of the Law and the Prophets, represented by Moses and Elijah appearing with Him on Mount Tabor. The apostles stand in amazement, seeing the glory of God as Christ is transfigured before them. Feast Day readings are Exodus 24:12–18; 33:11–23; 34:4–6, 8; 1 Kings 19:3–9, 11–13, 15, 16; Matthew 17:1–9; Luke 9:28–36; 2 Peter 1:10–19.

heard that Jesus was coming, went
and met Him, but Mary was sitting
in the house.†
21 Now Martha said to Jesus,
"Lord, if You had been here, my
brother would not have died.
22 "But even now I know that
[a]whatever You ask of God, God will
give You."
23 Jesus said to her, "Your brother
will rise again."†
24 Martha said to Him, [a]"I know
that he will rise again in the resurrection at the last day."
25 Jesus said to her, "I am [a]the resurrection and the life. [b]He who believes in Me, though he may [c]die,
he shall live.
26 "And whoever lives and believes in Me shall never die. Do you
believe this?"
27 She said to Him, "Yes, Lord,
[a]I believe that You are the Christ,
the Son of God, who is to come into
the world."
28 And when she had said these
things, she went her way and secretly called Mary her sister, saying,
"The Teacher has come and is calling
for you."
29 As soon as she heard *that*, she
arose quickly and came to Him.
30 Now Jesus had not yet come
into the town, but [1]was in the place
where Martha met Him.
31 [a]Then the Jews who were with
her in the house, and comforting
her, when they saw that Mary rose
up quickly and went out, followed
her, [1]saying, "She is going to the
tomb to weep there."
32 Then, when Mary came where
Jesus was, and saw Him, she [a]fell
down at His feet, saying to Him,
[b]"Lord, if You had been here, my
brother would not have died."
33 Therefore, when Jesus saw her
weeping, and the Jews who came
with her weeping, He groaned in the
spirit and was troubled.
34 And He said, "Where have you
laid him?" They said to Him, "Lord,
come and see."
35 [a]Jesus wept.†
36 Then the Jews said, "See how
He loved him!"
37 And some of them said, "Could
not this Man, [a]who opened the eyes
of the blind, also have kept this man
from dying?"

Lazarus Is Raised

38 Then Jesus, again groaning in
Himself, came to the tomb. It was a
cave, and a [a]stone lay against it.†
39 Jesus said, "Take away the
stone." Martha, the sister of him
who was dead, said to Him, "Lord,
by this time there is a stench, for he
has been *dead* four days."
40 Jesus said to her, "Did I not say
to you that if you would believe you
would [a]see the glory of God?"†

22 [a][John 9:31; 11:41]
24 [a][Luke 14:14; John 5:29]
25 [a]John 5:21; 6:39, 40, 44; [Rev. 1:18] [b]John 3:16, 36; 1 John 5:10 [c]1 Cor. 15:22; [Heb. 9:27]
27 [a]Matt. 16:16; Luke 2:11; John 4:42; 6:14, 69
30 [1]NU *was still*
31 [a]John 11:19, 33 [1]NU *supposing that she was going*
32 [a]Mark 5:22; 7:25; Rev. 1:17 [b]John 11:21
35 [a]Luke 19:41
37 [a]John 9:6, 7
38 [a]Matt. 27:60, 66; Mark 15:46; Luke 24:2; John 20:1
40 [a][John 11:4, 23]

(continued from previous page)
was necessary in warm climates). Weeping and wailing lasted three days; lamentation lasted the rest of the week; general mourning lasted 30 days following death. During this time mourners constantly came and went from the home of the deceased.

11:20 Not unlike the incident of Luke 10:38–42, the two sisters react differently to what occurs. As the one busily responsible for the duties of hospitality, **Martha** heads out to meet Jesus, while **Mary** remains at home. **Sitting** is the correct posture when mourning and greeting mourners (see Job 2:8, 13; Ezek. 8:14).

11:23–26 Your brother will rise again (v. 23) is misunderstood by Martha as indicating the final resurrection. Thus Jesus declares, **I am the resurrection and the life** (v. 25). Whoever believes in Christ already has eternal life and therefore **shall never die** (v. 26) spiritually.

11:35 As true man Jesus shows by example that weeping is the natural human response to death. As true God He shows compassion upon His creation when the soul is torn from the body.

11:38, 39 Jesus comes to the place of burial. A corpse that has by the fourth day begun to deteriorate is enough reason for Martha's warning. Embalming was prohibited in Judaism. The body was simply anointed with spices and other aromatic substances which would keep the stench of decomposition at bay for a time.

11:40 The Savior responds to Martha's cautionary note (v. 39) by reminding her of His earlier words (vv. 25, 26).

41 Then they took away the stone
[1]*from the place* where the dead man
was lying. And Jesus lifted up *His*
eyes and said, "Father, I thank You
that You have heard Me.†
42 "And I know that You always
hear Me, but [a]because of the people
who are standing by I said *this*, that
they may believe that You sent Me."
43 Now when He had said these
things, He cried with a loud voice,
"Lazarus, come forth!"†
44 And he who had died came out
bound hand and foot with [a]grave-
clothes, and [b]his face was wrapped
with a cloth. Jesus said to them,
"Loose him, and let him go."†
45 Then many of the Jews who had
come to Mary, [a]and had seen the
things Jesus did, believed in Him.
46 But some of them went away to
the Pharisees and [a]told them the
things Jesus did.

The Sanhedrin Plots to Kill Jesus

47 [a]Then the chief priests and the
Pharisees gathered a council and
said, [b]"What shall we do? For this
Man works many signs.†
48 "If we let Him alone like this,
everyone will believe in Him, and
the Romans will come and take away
both our place and nation."
49 And one of them, [a]Caiaphas,
being high priest that year, said
to them, "You know nothing at
all,†
50 [a]"nor do you consider that it is
expedient for [1]us that one man
should die for the people, and not
that the whole nation should
perish."
51 Now this he did not say on his
own *authority;* but being high priest
that year he prophesied that Jesus
would die for the nation,
52 and [a]not for that nation only,
but [b]also that He would gather together in one the children of God
who were scattered abroad.
53 Then, from that day on, they
plotted to [a]put Him to death.
54 [a]Therefore Jesus no longer
walked openly among the Jews, but
went from there into the country
near the wilderness, to a city called
[b]Ephraim, and there remained with
His disciples.
55 [a]And the Passover of the Jews
was near, and many went from the
country up to Jerusalem before the
Passover, to [b]purify themselves.†
56 [a]Then they sought Jesus, and
spoke among themselves as they
stood in the temple, "What do you
think—that He will not come to the
feast?"
57 Now both the chief priests and
the Pharisees had given a command,
that if anyone knew where He was,

41 [1]NU omits *from the place where the dead man was lying*
42 [a]John 12:30; 17:21
44 [a]John 19:40 [b]John 20:7
45 [a]John 2:23; 10:42; 12:11, 18
46 [a]John 5:15
47 [a]Ps. 2:2 [b]Acts 4:16
49 [a]Luke 3:2
50 [a]John 18:14 [1]NU *you*
52 [a]Is. 49:6 [b][Eph. 2:14–17]
53 [a]Matt. 26:4
54 [a]John 4:1, 3; 7:1 [b]2 Chr. 13:19
55 [a]John 2:13; 5:1; 6:4 [b]Num. 9:10, 13; 31:19, 20
56 [a]John 7:11

11:41, 42 Again we see the Evangelist's insistence on relating Jesus' dependence upon the Father for all His works. Jesus prays for the bystanders, that they may have the insight to see the glory of God in the miracle.

11:43 Jesus' **loud** cry for all to hear is reminiscent of His earlier words, "The hour is coming in which all who are in the graves will hear His voice and come forth" (5:28, 29).

11:44 That Lazarus **came out** bound in his linen **graveclothes** is interpreted by patristic writers as an indication he will need them once again: he will eventually die. The Savior's grave linens, by contrast, were left in the tomb. He will have no more use for them, for He will never die again.

11:47, 48 The Jewish leaders acknowledge Jesus' **signs** and are concerned that the **Romans** will intervene militarily if a popular movement around Jesus gains momentum and threatens the established order.

11:49–52 Caiaphas, being high priest of Israel, is given through his office the authority to speak prophetically. Caiaphas means only that the death of Jesus would spare the nation from Roman intervention. But the greater prophetic meaning of his words is that the death of Jesus will be for the salvation of the Jewish people and many others throughout the world.

11:55 Because Jesus is the Lamb of God (1:29), the connection between the **Passover** and the death of Jesus is important, and John emphasizes it over and again (see 2:13, 23; 6:4; 12:1; 13:1; 18:28, 39; 19:14, 42).

Palm Sunday—The Entrance of the Lord into Jerusalem *Sunday before Easter*

12:1–18: Jesus is prepared for burial before being hailed as King by the people.

he should report *it*, that they might
[a]seize Him.

Jesus Anointed for His Burial

12 Then, six days before the
Passover, Jesus came to Bethany, [a]where Lazarus was [1]who had
been dead, whom He had raised
from the dead.†
2 [a]There they made Him a supper; and Martha served, but Lazarus
was one of those who sat at the table
with Him.
3 Then [a]Mary took a pound of
very costly oil of [b]spikenard,
anointed the feet of Jesus, and wiped
His feet with her hair. And the house
was filled with the fragrance of the
oil.†
4 But one of His disciples, [a]Judas
Iscariot, Simon's *son*, who would betray Him, said,
5 "Why was this fragrant oil not
sold for [1]three hundred denarii and
given to the poor?"
6 This he said, not that he cared
for the poor, but because he was
a thief, and [a]had the money box;
and he used to take what was put
in it.
7 But Jesus said, "Let her alone;
[1]she has kept this for the day of My
burial.

57 [a]Matt. 26:14–16

CHAPTER 12

1 [a]Matt. 21:17; John 11:1, 43
[1]NU omits *who had been dead*
2 [a]Matt. 26:6; Mark 14:3; Luke 10:38–41
3 [a]Luke 10:38, 39; John 11:2
[b]Song 1:12
4 [a]John 13:26
5 [1]About one year's wages for a worker
6 [a]John 13:29
7 [1]NU *that she may keep*
8 [a]Deut. 15:11; Matt. 26:11; Mark 14:7; John 17:11
9 [a]John 11:43, 44
10 [a]Luke 16:31
11 [a]John 11:45; 12:18
12 [a]Matt. 21:4–9; Mark 11:7–10; Luke 19:35–38
13 [a]Ps. 118:25, 26
14 [a]Matt. 21:7

8 "For [a]the poor you have with
you always, but Me you do not have
always."
9 Now a great many of the Jews
knew that He was there; and they
came, not for Jesus' sake only, but
that they might also see Lazarus,
[a]whom He had raised from the
dead.
10 [a]But the chief priests plotted to
put Lazarus to death also,
11 [a]because on account of him
many of the Jews went away and believed in Jesus.

The Triumph of Palm Sunday
(Matt. 21:1–9; Mark 11:1–11; Luke 19:28–40)

12 [a]The next day a great multitude
that had come to the feast, when
they heard that Jesus was coming to
Jerusalem,†
13 took branches of palm trees and
went out to meet Him, and cried out:

"Hosanna!
[a]*'Blessed is He who comes in the name of the* LORD*!'*
The King of Israel!"†

14 [a]Then Jesus, when He had
found a young donkey, sat on it; as
it is written:†

12:1 Six days before the Passover, the third Passover mentioned in John, begins the last week of Christ's earthly ministry, which is narrated in careful detail. The time for signs and miracles has passed. It remains for the Son of Man to be glorified through the completion of His mission (12:23; 13:31; 17:1, 5). As Passover draws near, the Lord returns to **Bethany** to spend the Saturday before Palm Sunday at the home of His close friends, **Lazarus,** Mary, and Martha (see 11:5).

12:3 The account of the anointing contrasts Mary's act of devotion—the "extravagance of love"—with Judas's bitter cynicism. Anticipating His death, Jesus considers the anointing to be a symbol of preparation of His body for burial (vv. 7, 8).

12:12 Earlier Jesus had come to Jerusalem in a hidden, private way (7:10). But now He enters the Holy City publicly.

12:13 Hosanna is a liturgical shout which means "save now" (Ps. 118:25).

12:14 Jesus' deliberate action of riding in on a **donkey** signifies He is the prophesied

(continued on next page)

15 *"Fear*[a] *not, daughter of Zion;*
Behold, your King is coming,
Sitting on a donkey's colt."

16 [a]His disciples did not understand these things at first; [b]but when
Jesus was glorified, [c]then they remembered that these things were
written about Him and *that* they had
done these things to Him.
17 Therefore the people, who were
with Him when He called Lazarus
out of his tomb and raised him from
the dead, bore witness.
18 [a]For this reason the people also
met Him, because they heard that
He had done this sign.

Dying to This World

19 The Pharisees therefore said
among themselves, [a]"You see that
you are accomplishing nothing.
Look, the world has gone after
Him!"
20 Now there [a]were certain Greeks
among those [b]who came up to worship at the feast.†
21 Then they came to Philip,
[a]who was from Bethsaida of Galilee,
and asked him, saying, "Sir, we wish
to see Jesus."
22 Philip came and told Andrew,
and in turn Andrew and Philip told
Jesus.
23 But Jesus answered them, saying, [a]"The hour has come that the
Son of Man should be glorified.†
24 "Most assuredly, I say to you,
[a]unless a grain of wheat falls into the
ground and dies, it remains alone;
but if it dies, it produces much
[1]grain.†
25 [a]"He who loves his life will lose
it, and he who hates his life in this
world will keep it for eternal life.
26 "If anyone serves Me, let him
[a]follow Me; and [b]where I am, there
My servant will be also. If anyone
serves Me, him *My* Father will
honor.
27 [a]"Now My soul is troubled, and
what shall I say? 'Father, save Me
from this hour'? [b]But for this purpose I came to this hour.†
28 "Father, glorify Your name."
[a]Then a voice came from heaven,
saying, "I have both glorified *it* and
will glorify *it* again."†

Judgment of This World: The Cross

29 Therefore the people who stood
by and heard *it* said that it had thundered. Others said, "An angel has
spoken to Him."
30 Jesus answered and said,
[a]"This voice did not come because
of Me, but for your sake.
31 "Now is the judgment of this
world; now [a]the ruler of this world
will be cast out.†

15 [a]Zech. 9:9
16 [a]Luke 18:34 [b]John 7:39; 12:23 [c][John 14:26]
18 [a]John 12:11
19 [a]John 11:47, 48
20 [a]Acts 17:4 [b]1 Kin. 8:41, 42
21 [a]John 1:43, 44; 14:8–11
23 [a]John 13:32
24 [a]1 Cor. 15:36 [1]Lit. *fruit*
25 [a]Mark 8:35
26 [a][Matt. 16:24] [b]John 14:3; 17:24
27 [a][Matt. 26:38, 39] [b]Luke 22:53
28 [a]Matt. 3:17; 17:5
30 [a]John 11:42
31 [a][2 Cor. 4:4]

(continued from previous page)
Messiah of peace (Zech. 9:9), for kings and military leaders rode on horses or in chariots. The Triumphal Entry marks a high point in Jesus' ministry as He brings His message to the Holy City and encounters the central authorities. This event is celebrated on Palm Sunday, an acclamation of the lordship of Christ as King of kings.

12:20, 21 These **Greeks** are Gentiles attracted to Judaism, either God-fearing or full proselytes, who came to participate in the Passover festivities.

12:23 The hour has come: the great hour of salvation through the death and Resurrection of Jesus, leading to the salvation of the human race.

12:24, 25 The image of the **grain of wheat** dying in order to bear fruit signifies that Christ will die in order to give life, a principle of self-sacrifice which applies to all those who follow the way of Christ.

12:27 This verse gives a glimpse of the Gethsemane experience of Jesus (Matt. 26:36–46).

12:28 The Father's **name** is an extension of His Person. The Son worked for the glory of the Father, and His death is now to be offered up to complete that purpose (v. 27) and to show the Father's love for all people. The divine **voice** gives assurance that the death of Jesus is not humiliation but glorification through the fulfillment of God's plan for the redemption of the world.

12:31, 32 Lifted up (v. 32; see also 3:14, 15; 8:28): a reference to the lifting up of Christ

(continued on next page)

32 "And I, [a]if I am [1]lifted up from
the earth, will draw [b]all *peoples* to
Myself."
33 [a]This He said, signifying by
what death He would die.
34 The people answered Him,
[a]"We have heard from the law that
the Christ remains forever; and how
can You say, 'The Son of Man must
be lifted up'? Who is this Son of
Man?"

Become Sons of Light

35 Then Jesus said to them, "A little while longer [a]the light is with
you. [b]Walk while you have the light,
lest darkness overtake you; [c]he who
walks in darkness does not know
where he is going.†
36 "While you have the light, believe in the light, that you may become [a]sons of light." These things
Jesus spoke, and departed, and
[b]was hidden from them.

Who Has Believed Jesus' Words?

37 But although He had done so
many [a]signs before them, they did
not believe in Him,†
38 that the word of Isaiah the
prophet might be fulfilled, which he
spoke:

[a]*"Lord, who has believed our*
report?
And to whom has the arm of
the LORD *been revealed?"*

39 Therefore they could not believe, because Isaiah said again:

40 *"He[a] has blinded their eyes and*
hardened their hearts,
[b]*Lest they should see with their*
eyes,
Lest they should understand
with their hearts and turn,
So that I should heal them."

41 [a]These things Isaiah said [1]when
he saw His glory and spoke of
Him.†
42 Nevertheless even among the
rulers many believed in Him, but
[a]because of the Pharisees they did
not confess *Him,* lest they should be
put out of the synagogue;†
43 [a]for they loved the praise of
men more than the praise of God.

Jesus' Words: From the Father

44 Then Jesus cried out and said,
[a]"He who believes in Me, [b]believes

32 [a]John 3:14; 8:28 [b][Rom. 5:18] [1]Crucified
33 [a]John 18:32; 21:19
34 [a]Mic. 4:7
35 [a][John 1:9; 7:33; 8:12] [b]Eph. 5:8 [c][1 John 2:9–11]
36 [a]Luke 16:8 [b]John 8:59
37 [a]John 11:47
38 [a]Is. 53:1
40 [a]Is. 6:9, 10 [b]Matt. 13:14
41 [a]Is. 6:1 [1]NU *because*
42 [a]John 7:13; 9:22
43 [a]John 5:41, 44
44 [a]Mark 9:37 [b][John 3:16, 18, 36; 11:25, 26]

(continued from previous page)
on the Cross, which is His glorification and will lead to the salvation of the human race. At the same time this event is a **judgment** (v. 31) on the unbelieving world of darkness and the abolition of the power of **the ruler of this world,** Satan.

We live in a state of tension between the victory won (see 1 John 2:13) and that yet to be won (see 1 John 5:4, 5). In a vespers hymn for the Feast of the Exaltation of the Cross we sing: "Lifted high upon the Cross, O Master, with Yourself You have raised up Adam and the whole of fallen nature. Therefore, exalting Your undefiled Cross, O You who love mankind, we ask You for Your strength from above, crying: O God Most High, in Your mercy save those who honor the sacred light-giving and divine Exaltation of Your Cross."

12:35, 36 The theme of Jesus as the **light** receives renewed emphasis. The crowd wants to know the identity of the Son of Man. But Jesus challenges them to come to the light while there is still time to become children of light. Christ is "light from Light" (Nicene Creed). In union with Him, we partake of His light, becoming children of light (v. 36).

12:37–40 Failure to believe in Jesus as the Incarnate Word, despite His many miracles, is due to willful spiritual blindness and hardness of heart, as foretold by **Isaiah the prophet** (v. 38). According to St. John Chrysostom, Isaiah's prophecy is descriptive, but does not cause the willful blindness of people. They did not become blind because Isaiah spoke, but rather Isaiah spoke because he foresaw their blindness.

12:41 In about 700 B.C., Isaiah reports that in a vision, "I saw the Lord" (Is. 6:1). He saw the **glory** of the Son of God and **spoke of Him** (see v. 38).

12:42, 43 Nicodemus (3:1) was one of these **rulers,** a "hidden" disciple during Christ's ministry.

Holy Thursday *Thursday before Easter*

13:3–17: Jesus gives His disciples an example of service by washing their feet.

not in Me [c]but in Him who sent Me.†
45 "And [a]he who sees Me sees
Him who sent Me.
46 [a]"I have come *as* a light into the
world, that whoever believes in Me
should not abide in darkness.
47 "And if anyone hears My words
and does not [1]believe, [a]I do not
judge him; for [b]I did not come to
judge the world but to save the
world.
48 [a]"He who rejects Me, and does
not receive My words, has that
which judges him—[b]the word that I
have spoken will judge him in the
last day.
49 "For [a]I have not spoken on My
own *authority;* but the Father who
sent Me gave Me a command,
[b]what I should say and what I
should speak.
50 "And I know that His command
is everlasting life. Therefore, whatever I speak, just as the Father has
told Me, so I [a]speak."

44 [c][John 5:24]
45 [a][John 14:9]
46 [a]John 1:4, 5; 8:12; 12:35, 36
47 [a]John 5:45 [b]John 3:17 [1]NU *keep them*
48 [a][Luke 10:16] [b]Deut. 18:18, 19
49 [a]John 8:38 [b]Deut. 18:18
50 [a]John 5:19; 8:28

CHAPTER 13

1 [a]Matt. 26:2 [b]John 12:23; 17:1 [c]John 15:9
2 [a]Luke 22:3 [1]NU *during supper*
3 [a]Acts 2:36 [b]John 8:42; 16:28 [c]John 17:11; 20:17
4 [a][Luke 22:27]

Jesus Washes the Disciples' Feet

13 Now [a]before the Feast of the
Passover, when Jesus knew
that [b]His hour had come that He
should depart from this world to the
Father, having loved His own who
were in the world, He [c]loved them
to the end.†
2 And [1]supper being ended,
[a]the devil having already put it into
the heart of Judas Iscariot, Simon's
son, to betray Him,†
3 Jesus, knowing [a]that the Father
had given all things into His hands,
and that He [b]had come from God
and [c]was going to God,
4 [a]rose from supper and laid aside
His garments, took a towel and
girded Himself.
5 After that, He poured water into
a basin and began to wash the disciples' feet, and to wipe *them* with the

12:44–50 Jesus' last public appeal sums up His message about His unique relationship to the Father, His mission in the world, and the destiny of the people—damnation or eternal life, depending on their response.

13:1 John's magnificent account of Jesus' discourses during the Last Supper (v. 2) is contained in chs. 13—17. The Jewish **Passover** commemorated the Lord passing over the Israelites when He killed the firstborn of the Egyptians (Ex. 12) and is also linked with "crossing over" the Red Sea (Ex. 14). In Christ, we escape death and pass over from this world, enslaved in sin, to the true land of promise, the Kingdom of God. When Jesus has eaten the old Passover with His disciples, He makes a New Covenant, in which eternal life is granted. **His hour had come** signals the departure of Jesus from **this world to the Father** through the events of the Cross, Resurrection and Ascension. At this crucial time of salvation, Jesus' heart is filled with love for **His own who were in the world,** His disciples and all those who believed in Him.

13:2 Supper: This account does not directly mention the Eucharist (which is clearly reflected in 6:51–59), for by the time John was writing (about A.D. 90) the traditions concerning the Last Supper recorded in the synoptic Gospels were well known. Jesus' "farewell" discourses (chs. 13—17) in the intimate setting of the meal reveal to the disciples the mystery of Christ in His divine grandeur, His mission in the world, His departure from the world, and His relationship to the disciples, as well as their life and mission in the world.

There are two ways **the devil** influences the human **heart:** (1) through ideas or thoughts; and (2) through conceptual images, as clearly taught in 2 Cor. 10:5. With **Judas,** Satan has done his work in both areas. Christians must learn to exercise their wills to reject the thoughts and images suggested by the devil—the moment they occur. Judas cooperated with the devil's will and carried it out. Far from being a victim, Judas was the devil's willing co-conspirator.

towel with which He was girded.†
6 Then He came to Simon Peter.
And *Peter* said to Him, [a]"Lord, are
You washing my feet?"
7 Jesus answered and said to him,
"What I am doing you [a]do not
understand now, [b]but you will know
after this."
8 Peter said to Him, "You shall
never wash my feet!" Jesus answered him, [a]"If I do not wash you,
you have no part with Me."†
9 Simon Peter said to Him, "Lord,
not my feet only, but also *my* hands
and *my* head!"†
10 Jesus said to him, "He who is
bathed needs only to wash *his* feet,
but is completely clean; and [a]you are
clean, but not all of you."†
11 For [a]He knew who would betray Him; therefore He said, "You
are not all clean."
12 So when He had washed their
feet, taken His garments, and sat
down again, He said to them, "Do
you [1]know what I have done to
you?†
13 [a]"You call Me Teacher and
Lord, and you say well, for *so* I am.
14 [a]"If I then, *your* Lord and
Teacher, have washed your feet,
[b]you also ought to wash one another's feet.
15 "For [a]I have given you an example, that you should do as I have
done to you.†
16 [a]"Most assuredly, I say to you,
a servant is not greater than his master; nor is he who is sent greater than
he who sent him.
17 [a]"If you know these things,
blessed are you if you do them.

The Betrayer in Their Midst
(Matt. 26:21–25; Mark 14:18–21; Luke 22:21–23)

18 "I do not speak concerning all
of you. I know whom I have chosen;
but that the [a]Scripture may be fulfilled, [b]*'He who eats [1]bread with Me
has lifted up his heel against Me.'*†
19 [a]"Now I tell you before it

6 [a]Matt. 3:14
7 [a]John 12:16; 16:12 [b]John 13:19
8 [a][1 Cor. 6:11]
10 [a][John 15:3]
11 [a]John 6:64; 18:4
12 [1]*understand*
13 [a]Matt. 23:8, 10
14 [a]Luke 22:27 [b][Rom. 12:10]
15 [a][1 Pet. 2:21–24]
16 [a]Matt. 10:24
17 [a][James 1:25]
18 [a]John 15:25; 17:12 [b]Ps. 41:9 [1]NU *My bread has*
19 [a]John 14:29; 16:4

13:5 The foot-washing (vv. 3–17) is an act of love and humble service. That Jesus is God in the flesh renders His humility all the more profound. A hymn of Matins on the Sunday of the Publican and the Pharisee emphasizes this incident: "The Savior and Master, ever leading us to divine exaltation, in His actions revealed to us the humility that raises us on high. For with His own hands, He washed the feet of the disciples."

13:8 The washing of feet was a common expression of hospitality in the ancient Middle East, but it was normally done by slaves or house servants. **You shall never wash my feet!** shows the Apostles are understandably shocked when their Lord stoops like a slave at their feet. **If I do not wash you, you have no part with Me** alludes to the cleansing power of Jesus' death and Resurrection. For the early Church, these words and the foot-washing took on sacramental significance, for in washing His disciples' feet, Jesus set forth a symbol of baptism.

13:9 Peter's response is a remarkable reversal of v. 8. For as he hears the Lord's words, he says **not my feet only, but also my hands and my head.** In other words, "If this is the way for me to be a part of You, then wash all of me." Significantly, the icon of the washing of the feet shows Peter pointing to his head.

13:10 In baptism we enter into the death and Resurrection of Christ; in the Eucharist we have communion in the Body and Blood of our risen Lord—and we are made **completely clean** by the power of Christ's death and Resurrection. In ancient times, people bathed at a bath house, walked home and then bathed their feet again before stepping into their houses. As Christians, we are bathed and cleansed by Christ in Holy Baptism, and have periodic "foot-washings" by Him in the sacrament of repentance or confession.

13:12–20 After the foot-washing, Jesus explains its significance: As He Himself is a Servant of God and mankind, so we are to serve God and our fellowman. As Christ has made salvation available to the world, so the Apostles ("sent ones") are to carry that salvation to all nations. To be a leader in the Church, one must be as a humble servant—a reversal of the values of the world.

13:15 To this day, some Orthodox churches have preserved the ancient practice of foot-washing on Thursday of Holy Week, following the Lord's instruction here literally.

13:18–30 The betrayal by Judas is a moral low point in the Gospel of John. It is a fearful

(continued on next page)

comes, that when it does come to
pass, you may believe that I am *He.*
20 [a]"Most assuredly, I say to you,
he who receives whomever I send
receives Me; and he who receives Me
receives Him who sent Me."
21 [a]When Jesus had said these
things, [b]He was troubled in spirit,
and testified and said, "Most assuredly, I say to you, [c]one of you
will betray Me."
22 Then the disciples looked at one
another, perplexed about whom He
spoke.
23 Now [a]there was [1]leaning on
Jesus' bosom one of His disciples,
whom Jesus loved.
24 Simon Peter therefore motioned
to him to ask who it was of whom
He spoke.
25 Then, leaning [1]back on Jesus'
breast, he said to Him, "Lord, who
is it?"
26 Jesus answered, "It is he to
whom I shall give a piece of bread
when I have dipped *it.*" And having
dipped the bread, He gave *it* to
[a]Judas Iscariot, *the son* of Simon.†
27 [a]Now after the piece of bread,
Satan entered him. Then Jesus said
to him, "What you do, do quickly."
28 But no one at the table knew for
what reason He said this to him.
29 For some thought, because
[a]Judas had the money box, that Jesus
had said to him, "Buy *those things*

20 [a]Matt. 10:40
21 [a]Luke 22:21
[b]John 12:27
[c]1 John 2:19
23 [a]John 19:26; 20:2; 21:7, 20
[1]*reclining*
25 [1]NU, M add *thus*
26 [a]John 6:70, 71; 12:4
27 [a]Luke 22:3
29 [a]John 12:6
31 [a]John 12:23
[b][1 Pet. 4:11]
32 [a]John 12:23
33 [a]John 12:35; 14:19; 16:16–19
[b][John 7:34; 8:21]
34 [a]1 Thess. 4:9
35 [a]1 John 2:5
36 [a]John 13:33; 14:2; 16:5
[b]2 Pet. 1:14

we need for the feast," or that he
should give something to the poor.
30 Having received the piece of
bread, he then went out immediately. And it was night.†

The New Commandment

31 So, when he had gone out, Jesus
said, [a]"Now the Son of Man is glorified, and [b]God is glorified in Him.†
32 "If God is glorified in Him, God
will also glorify Him in Himself, and
[a]glorify Him immediately.
33 "Little children, I shall be with
you a [a]little while longer. You will
seek Me; [b]and as I said to the Jews,
'Where I am going, you cannot
come,' so now I say to you.
34 [a]"A new commandment I give
to you, that you love one another;
as I have loved you, that you also
love one another.†
35 [a]"By this all will know that you
are My disciples, if you have love
for one another."

Peter's Denials Foretold

(Matt. 26:31–35; Mark 14:27–31;
Luke 22:31–38)

36 Simon Peter said to Him, "Lord,
where are You going?" Jesus answered him, "Where I [a]am going
you cannot follow Me now, but
[b]you shall follow Me afterward."†

(continued from previous page)
thing to willfully turn one's back on the Son of God. Far from being soft on Judas, Jesus will call him "the son of perdition" (17:12).

13:26 These words appear to be spoken privately to the beloved disciple (see vv. 23–25), for the others do not perceive why Judas left their company (vv. 28, 29).

13:30 Judas' exit from the Last Supper was at night, symbolizing spiritual darkness. Holy Friday is the one day of Holy Week when the Eucharist cannot be celebrated. Great and Holy Friday has also been called "the day of this world," the day the entire human race rejected Jesus Christ.

13:31 After Judas leaves, Jesus presents the final teachings of His earthly ministry (13:31—16:33), often called "the Farewell Discourse," His last major teaching in John. In calling His death "glorification" (vv. 31–33), He shows He does not fear death. The Father and the Son are **glorified.** For through the death of Jesus, God is victorious over the powers of darkness. And through Christ's Resurrection, the love of God for mankind will be manifest to all creation.

13:34 What is **new** about Christ's **commandment?** In the Law of Moses, the command was to love your neighbor "as yourself." In Christ's command, we love one another **as I have loved you.** This means Christ's love for us is the true measure for how we are to love our neighbor.

13:36 Jesus is saying, "You cannot die with Me now, but you shall later." This is a prediction of Peter's martyrdom (see 21:18, 19).

37 Peter said to Him, "Lord, why
can I not follow You now? I
will [a]lay down my life for Your
sake."
38 Jesus answered him, "Will you
lay down your life for My sake? Most
assuredly, I say to you, the rooster
shall not [a]crow till you have denied
Me three times.

The Way to the Father

14 "Let [a]not your heart be troubled; you believe in God, believe also in Me.
2 "In My Father's house are many
[1]mansions; if *it were* not *so*, [2]I would
have told you. [a]I go to prepare a
place for you.†
3 "And if I go and prepare a place
for you, [a]I will come again and receive you to Myself; that [b]where I
am, *there* you may be also.
4 "And where I go you know, and
the way you know."
5 [a]Thomas said to Him, "Lord,
we do not know where You are going, and how can we know the
way?"
6 Jesus said to him, "I am [a]the
way, [b]the truth, and [c]the life.
[d]No one comes to the Father [e]except
through Me.†
7 [a]"If you had known Me, you
would have known My Father also;
and from now on you know Him and
have seen Him."
8 Philip said to Him, "Lord, show
us the Father, and it is sufficient for
us."
9 Jesus said to him, "Have I been
with you so long, and yet you have
not known Me, Philip? [a]He who has
seen Me has seen the Father; so
how can you say, 'Show us the
Father'?†
10 "Do you not believe that [a]I am
in the Father, and the Father in Me?
The words that I speak to you
[b]I do not speak on My own *authority;*
but the Father who dwells in Me
does the works.†
11 "Believe Me that I *am* in the Father and the Father in Me, [a]or else
believe Me for the sake of the works
themselves.
12 [a]"Most assuredly, I say to you,
he who believes in Me, the works
that I do he will do also; and greater
works than these he will do, because
I go to My Father.†
13 [a]"And whatever you ask in My

37 [a]Mark 14:29–31
38 [a]John 18:25–27

CHAPTER 14

1 [a][John 14:27; 16:22, 24]
2 [a]John 13:33, 36
[1]Lit. *dwellings*
[2]NU *would I have told you that I go* or *I would have told you; for I go*
3 [a][Acts 1:11] [b][John 12:26]
5 [a]Matt. 10:3
6 [a][Heb. 9:8; 10:19, 20] [b][John 1:14, 17; 8:32; 18:37] [c][John 11:25] [d]1 Tim. 2:5 [e][John 10:7–9]
7 [a]John 8:19
9 [a]Col. 1:15
10 [a]John 10:38; 14:11, 20 [b]John 5:19; 14:24
11 [a]John 5:36; 10:38
12 [a]Luke 10:17
13 [a]Matt. 7:7

14:2, 3 Many mansions is literally "many dwelling places," a word-picture of numerous living units surrounding a central courtyard—an abundance of living accommodations. *Mansions* also speak of the multiplicity of blessings which await those who enter the Kingdom of God.

14:6 The way, the truth, and the life is a Person, our Lord Jesus Christ. He is so because of His perfect union with His Father (vv. 9, 11). *The way* we reach the Father is forever established through the Son. Jesus is *the truth* because He is the unique revelation of the Father, who is the goal of our journey through life. Christ is *the life,* the uncreated eternal life manifest in the flesh, so that we might have life. Because of this, **No one comes to the Father except through** the Son. While aspects of goodness and truth are found among all people by virtue of their being created in the image and likeness of God, salvation comes through Christ alone.

14:9 He who has seen Me has seen the Father: Our relationship with Christ determines our relationship with the Father. If we reject Christ, then we will not find the Father; but if we believe in Christ and follow Him, then we ourselves become "sons of God," living eternally in the love of the Father (see 16:16, 20–28).

14:10 While human beings are made in God's image, the Incarnate Son is the exact image of the Father (Col. 1:15). He did not say, "I am the Father," for He is not. Instead, He declared, **I am in the Father, and the Father in Me.** This means He and the Father are one in essence and undivided.

14:12 As shown in the Book of Acts, the disciples will later do even **greater works** in spreading the gospel throughout the world because Jesus will have completed the work of salvation and they will be endowed with the Spirit. In Christ, and through the Holy Spirit, the Church makes God's salvation available to all in every age.

name, that I will do, that the Father
may be [b]glorified in the Son.†
14 "If you [1]ask anything in My
name, I will do *it.*

The Coming of the Holy Spirit

15 [a]"If you love Me, [1]keep My
commandments.
16 "And I will pray the Father, and
[a]He will give you another [1]Helper,
that He may abide with you forever—†
17 [a]"the Spirit of truth, [b]whom the
world cannot receive, because it neither sees Him nor knows Him; but
you know Him, for He dwells with
you [c]and will be in you.†

The Son's Presence

18 [a]"I will not leave you orphans;
[b]I will come to you.
19 "A little while longer and the
world will see Me no more, but
[a]you will see Me. [b]Because I live,
you will live also.†
20 "At that day you will know that
[a]I *am* in My Father, and you in Me,
and I in you.†
21 [a]"He who has My commandments and keeps them, it is he who
loves Me. And he who loves Me will
be loved by My Father, and I will
love him and [1]manifest Myself to
him."†
22 **[a]Judas (not Iscariot) said to
Him, "Lord, how is it that You will
manifest Yourself to us, and not to
the world?"**
23 **Jesus answered and said to him,**
"If anyone loves Me, he will keep
My word; and My Father will love
him, [a]and We will come to him and
make Our home with him.†
24 "He who does not love Me does
not keep My words; and [a]the word
which you hear is not Mine but the
Father's who sent Me.
25 "These things I have spoken
to you while being present with
you.
26 "But [a]the [1]Helper, the Holy
Spirit, whom the Father will [b]send
in My name, [c]He will teach you all
things, and bring to your [d]re-
membrance all things that I said
to you.†

13 [b]John 13:31
14 [1]NU *ask Me*
15 [a]1 John 5:3 [1]NU *you will keep*
16 [a]Rom. 8:15 [1]*Comforter*, Gr. *Parakletos*
17 [a][1 John 4:6; 5:7] [b][1 Cor. 2:14] [c][1 John 2:27]
18 [a][Matt. 28:20] [b][John 14:3, 28]
19 [a]John 16:16, 22 [b][1 Cor. 15:20]
20 [a]John 10:38; 14:11
21 [a]1 John 2:5 [1]*reveal*
22 [a]Luke 6:16
23 [a]Rev. 3:20; 21:3
24 [a]John 5:19
26 [a]Luke 24:49 [b]John 15:26 [c]1 Cor. 2:13 [d]John 2:22; 12:16 [1]*Comforter*, Gr. *Parakletos*

14:13 We pray in Jesus' **name** because when we are in union with Him, our will corresponds with His will. Thus what we ask for is exactly what Christ wants to give (see also 15:16 and 16:23). Prayer is for the glory of God the Father, not for our own glory, so we also pray, "Our Father."

14:16–18 This is the first of three passages in the Farewell Discourse (chs. 14—16) which deals with the ministry of the Holy Spirit (15:26, 27; 16:5–15). The Apostles did not fully understand the teachings and works of Christ prior to their reception of the Holy Spirit on Pentecost (see Acts 2).

14:17 Jesus calls us to know **the Spirit of truth** who is in us and helps us pray. Thus prayer in Jesus' name (see note on v. 13) relates to all three Persons of the Holy Trinity. Jesus gives assurance that such prayer (v. 14) is answered for those who are united with Him.

14:19 The brief separation of Jesus from the disciples, due to His arrest and Crucifixion, will lead to a deeper mystical union after the Resurrection and the gift of the Holy Spirit at Pentecost.

14:20 At that day refers to the Resurrection of Jesus followed by the Ascension and the giving of the Holy Spirit at Pentecost, all of which, working together, make the fullness of divine life available to all believers.

14:21 Love for Christ is shown through obedience to Him. Jesus tells us if we have His **commandments** and keep them, He will **manifest** Himself (reveal, make Himself real) to us.

14:23 To experience the benefits of Christ's completed work, Christians must be steadfast in their love for Him and obedience of Him. It is on this basis that the Father and the Son—together with the Holy Spirit (v. 17)—come to dwell in the believer and **make** their **home with him.**

14:26 We have confidence in the Apostles' doctrine (Acts 2:42) because the Holy Spirit is their Teacher and brings Christ's words to their remembrance. We have confidence in the

(continued on next page)

The Son's Departure

27 [a]"Peace I leave with you, My
peace I give to you; not as the world
gives do I give to you. Let not your
heart be troubled, neither let it be
afraid.†
28 "You have heard Me [a]say to
you, 'I am going away and coming
back to you.' If you loved Me, you
would rejoice because [1]I said, [b]'I am
going to the Father,' for [c]My Father
is greater than I.†
29 "And [a]now I have told you before it comes, that when it does come
to pass, you may believe.†
30 "I will no longer talk much with
you, [a]for the ruler of this world is
coming, and he has [b]nothing in
Me.†
31 "But that the world may know
that I love the Father, and [a]as
the Father gave Me commandment, so I do. Arise, let us go from
here.

27 [a][Phil. 4:7]
28 [a]John 14:3, 18
[b]John 16:16
[c][Phil. 2:6]
[1]NU omits *I said*
29 [a]John 13:19
30 [a][John 12:31]
[b][Heb. 4:15]
31 [a]John 10:18

CHAPTER 15

2 [a]Matt. 15:13
[b][Matt. 13:12]
[1]Or *lifts up*
3 [a][John 13:10; 17:17]
4 [a][Col. 1:23]
5 [a]Hos. 14:8
[b]2 Cor. 3:5
6 [a]Matt. 3:10

Union and Communion with Christ

15 "I am the true vine, and My
Father is the vinedresser.†
2 [a]"Every branch in Me that does
not bear fruit He [1]takes away; and
every *branch* that bears fruit He
prunes, that it may bear [b]more fruit.
3 [a]"You are already clean because
of the word which I have spoken to
you.
4 [a]"Abide in Me, and I in you.
As the branch cannot bear fruit of
itself, unless it abides in the vine,
neither can you, unless you abide in
Me.†
5 "I am the vine, you *are* the
branches. He who abides in Me, and
I in him, bears much [a]fruit; for without Me you can do [b]nothing.†
6 "If anyone does not abide in
Me, [a]he is cast out as a branch and
is withered; and they gather them
and throw *them* into the fire, and
they are burned.

(continued from previous page)
Church, the guardian of the Faith, because the Holy Spirit is our Teacher as well. He leads us into all truth (16:13). St. Irenaeus wrote, "Where the Church is, there is the Holy Spirit and the fullness of grace."

14:27 Peace was the customary Jewish word of both greeting and farewell. Perfect peace is brought by the Messiah, who carries out the work of salvation and reconciles humanity with God. Together with "grace," peace is part of the traditional greeting of Christians to each other (see Rom. 1:7; 1 Cor. 1:3). Today it remains as "Peace be to all" in the Divine Liturgy of the Orthodox Church.

14:28 My Father is greater than I does not mean the Father is greater than the Son in nature or essence, for the Father is in the Son and the Son is in the Father (v. 11). Rather, it means the Father as the Fountainhead of the Trinity is the eternal cause of the Son, for He begot the Son before all time and ages. The Son is "begotten" of the Father before all worlds, and not made. Indeed, the Incarnate Son receives His whole existence from the Father and carries out His mission in full obedience to the Father.

14:29 I have told you before it comes refers to the whole sequence of death, Resurrection, Ascension and the sending of the Spirit. His disciples will recognize the fulfillment when it comes.

14:30 The ruler of this world, the devil, dominates the realm of those who do not love Christ or keep His commandments. Jesus said the devil **has nothing in Me** because there can be no compromise between Christ—or us—and the devil. Jesus became man, but was never stained with the sin of men, nor was He under the authority of the devil.

15:1 The vine is a symbol of Israel (see Is. 5:1–7; Jer. 2:21). In contrast to disobedient and unfruitful Israel, Jesus calls Himself the **true vine** which, together with its branches, constitutes a new and fruitful people of God, the Church.

15:4 Abiding in Christ is living out our union with Him in faith, baptism, love, obedience, and Eucharist. The figure of the vine and branches shows: (1) our union with Christ is intimate and real—we are a new people in Christ; (2) life flows from the vine to the branches—abiding in Christ is not static nor "positional," but dynamic and vitalizing; and (3) the fruit we bear is both good works and mission (v. 16, "go and bear fruit"; see 17:18). Those who do not abide in Christ bear no fruit, and are cut off from Him (v. 6).

15:5 Without Christ we **can do nothing**—nothing which is properly motivated and gives glory to God.

Commemoration of a Holy Martyr

15:17—16:2: The martyrs' love for God brought them persecution from men.

7 "If you abide in Me, and My
words [a]abide in you, [b]you[1] will ask
what you desire, and it shall be done
for you.
8 [a]"By this My Father is glorified,
that you bear much fruit; [b]so you will
be My disciples.
9 "As the Father [a]loved Me, I also
have loved you; abide in My love.
10 [a]"If you keep My commandments, you will abide in My love,
just as I have kept My Father's commandments and abide in His love.†
11 "These things I have spoken to
you, that My joy may remain in you,
and [a]*that* your joy may be full.
12 [a]"This is My [b]commandment,
that you love one another as I have
loved you.†
13 [a]"Greater love has no one than
this, than to lay down one's life for
his friends.
14 [a]"You are My friends if you do
whatever I command you.†
15 "No longer do I call you servants, for a servant does not know
what his master is doing; but I have
called you friends, [a]for all things that
I heard from My Father I have made
known to you.
16 [a]"You did not choose Me, but
I chose you and [b]appointed you that
you should go and bear fruit, and
that your fruit should remain, that
whatever you ask the Father [c]in My
name He may give you.
17 "These things I command you,
that you love one another.

7 [a]1 John 2:14 [b]John 14:13; 16:23 [1]NU omits *you will*
8 [a][Matt. 5:16] [b]John 8:31
9 [a]John 5:20; 17:26
10 [a]John 14:15
11 [a]1 John 1:4
12 [a]1 John 3:11 [b]Rom. 12:9
13 [a]1 John 3:16
14 [a][Matt. 12:50; 28:20]
15 [a]Gen. 18:17
16 [a]John 6:70; 13:18; 15:19 [b][Col. 1:6] [c]John 14:13; 16:23, 24
18 [a]1 John 3:13
19 [a]1 John 4:5 [b]John 17:14
20 [a]John 13:16 [b]Ezek. 3:7
21 [a]Matt. 10:22; 24:9
22 [a]John 9:41; 15:24

The World's Hatred

18 [a]"If the world hates you, you
know that it hated Me before *it hated*
you.†
19 [a]"If you were of the world, the
world would love its own. Yet
[b]because you are not of the world,
but I chose you out of the world,
therefore the world hates you.
20 "Remember the word that I said
to you, [a]'A servant is not greater
than his master.' If they persecuted
Me, they will also persecute you.
[b]If they kept My word, they will
keep yours also.
21 "But [a]all these things they will
do to you for My name's sake, because they do not know Him who
sent Me.
22 [a]"If I had not come and spoken
to them, they would have no sin,

15:10 The fact is, God does love us unconditionally, no matter what our response. But His unconditional love does us no good unless we keep His commandments and abide in His love. We show our love for God by obeying Him.

15:12 Just as God loves us unconditionally, so we are to love each other unconditionally in Christ's name—whether there is a response or not!

15:14, 15 Friendship is higher than servanthood. A servant obeys his master out of fear; a friend is a servant who obeys out of love. Abraham was called a "friend of God" (James 2:23) because he believed and obeyed God. The disciples and the saints are honored as friends of Christ and heirs of God: "and if children, then heirs—heirs of God and joint heirs with Christ" (Rom. 8:17; see also Gal. 4:7). Here Jesus tells his **friends** those things He has heard from His Father, the truths and blessings which He reveals in this Gospel.

15:18–25 Regarding **the world** we learn that: (1) while union with Christ brings love, joy and peace, it also brings the world's hatred and persecution (v. 19; see also 16:1–4); (2) the citizens of the world who hate Christians do so because they do not know the Father (v. 21); (3) a person cannot say he loves God but not God's Son, for those who hate Christ also hate God the Father (vv. 23, 24); and (4) hatred for Jesus Christ is without legitimate cause (v. 25), for He brings God's love and truth to the world.

[b]but now they have no excuse for
their sin.
23 [a]"He who hates Me hates My
Father also.
24 "If I had not done among them
[a]the works which no one else did,
they would have no sin; but now
they have [b]seen and also hated both
Me and My Father.
25 "But *this happened* that the word
might be fulfilled which is written
in their law, [a]*'They hated Me without a cause.'*
26 [a]"But when the [1]Helper comes,
whom I shall send to you from the
Father, the Spirit of truth who proceeds from the Father, [b]He will testify of Me.†
27 "And [a]you also will bear witness, because [b]you have been with
Me from the beginning.
16 "These things I have spoken
to you, that you [a]should not
be made to stumble.
2 [a]"They will put you out of the
synagogues; yes, the time is coming
[b]that whoever kills you will think
that he offers God service.
3 "And [a]these things they will do
[1]to you because they have not
known the Father nor Me.
4 "But these things I have told
you, that when [1]the time comes, you
may remember that I told you of
them. And these things I did not say
to you at the beginning, because I
was with you.

The Work of the Holy Spirit

5 "But now I [a]go away to Him
who sent Me, and none of you asks
Me, 'Where are You going?'
6 "But because I have said these
things to you, [a]sorrow has filled
your heart.†
7 "Nevertheless I tell you the
truth. It is to your advantage that I
go away; for if I do not go away,
the Helper will not come to you; but
[a]if I depart, I will send Him to you.†
8 "And when He has [a]come, He
will convict the world of sin, and of
righteousness, and of judgment:†
9 [a]"of sin, because they do not believe in Me;
10 [a]"of righteousness, [b]because I
go to My Father and you see Me no
more;
11 [a]"of judgment, because [b]the
ruler of this world is judged.
12 "I still have many things to say
to you, [a]but you cannot bear *them*
now.
13 "However, when He, [a]the Spirit
of truth, has come, [b]He will guide
you into all truth; for He will not
speak on His own *authority,* but
whatever He hears He will speak;
and He will tell you things to come.†

22 [b][James 4:17]
23 [a]1 John 2:23
24 [a]John 3:2 [b]John 14:9
25 [a]Ps. 35:19; 69:4; 109:3–5
26 [a]Luke 24:49 [b]1 John 5:6 [1]*Comforter,* Gr. *Parakletos*
27 [a]Luke 24:48 [b]Luke 1:2

CHAPTER 16

1 [a]Matt. 11:6
2 [a]John 9:22 [b]Acts 8:1
3 [a]John 8:19; 15:21 [1]NU, M omit *to you*
4 [1]NU *their*
5 [a]John 7:33; 13:33; 14:28; 17:11
6 [a][John 16:20, 22]
7 [a]Acts 2:33
8 [a]Acts 1:8; 2:1–4, 37
9 [a]Acts 2:22
10 [a]Acts 2:32 [b]John 5:32
11 [a]Acts 26:18 [b][Luke 10:18]
12 [a]Mark 4:33
13 [a][John 14:17] [b]John 14:26

15:26 While, with respect to God's work in the world, the Son will give or **send . . . the Spirit . . . from the Father,** with respect to His divinity, the Spirit originates or **proceeds from the Father** alone: The Spirit receives His eternal existence only from the Father. In conformity with Christ's words, the Nicene Creed confesses belief "in the Holy Spirit, the Lord and giver of life, who proceeds from the Father." By contrast, the Son is eternally begotten of the Father (3:16). The source, the fountainhead, of both is the Father.

16:6 The word **sorrow** means "extreme grief, leading to a state of severe depression," which is a sinful passion. Thus, St. John Chrysostom writes, "Great is the tyranny of despondency." This sin is also constantly referred to in the writings of the Desert Fathers. Even when the world hates true Christians, they must not become despondent, but take comfort from the Holy Spirit (vv. 5–15). The disciples are troubled not only because Jesus is leaving them, but also because of the ongoing struggle between light and darkness, between Jesus and the prince of this world.

16:7 The **advantage** is that the Holy Spirit, **the Helper,** will come.

16:8–11 Through the illumination of the Holy Spirit, the world will be convicted, that is, proved wrong and judged about: (1) **sin**—the ultimate sin is not to believe in Jesus as God and man, crucified and resurrected; (2) **righteousness** (v. 10)—a right relationship with God, possible only through Christ, risen, ascended, and righteous before God; (3) **judgment** (v. 11)—all who reject Christ, and are under the sway of the devil, will be given the same penalty their **ruler** has already received.

16:13 Because the Church is given this promise of being guided **into all truth,** she trusts the work of **the Spirit** on behalf of those who have gone before: Holy Tradition.

14 [a]"He will glorify Me, for He will
take of what is Mine and declare *it*
to you.
15 [a]"All things that the Father has
are Mine. Therefore I said that He
[1]will take of Mine and declare *it* to
you. †

Death, Resurrection, Ascension Foretold

16 "A [a]little while, and you will
not see Me; and again a little while,
and you will see Me, [b]because I go
to the Father." †
17 Then *some* of His disciples said
among themselves, "What is this
that He says to us, 'A little while,
and you will not see Me; and again
a little while, and you will see Me';
and, 'because I go to the Father'?"
18 They said therefore, "What is
this that He says, 'A little while'? We
do not [1]know what He is saying."
19 Now Jesus knew that they desired to ask Him, and He said to
them, "Are you inquiring among
yourselves about what I said, 'A little
while, and you will not see Me; and
again a little while, and you will see
Me'?
20 "Most assuredly, I say to you
that you will weep and [a]lament, but
the world will rejoice; and you will
be sorrowful, but your sorrow will
be turned into [b]joy.
21 [a]"A woman, when she is in labor, has sorrow because her hour has
come; but as soon as she has given
birth to the child, she no longer remembers the anguish, for joy that a
human being has been born into the
world. †
22 "Therefore you now have sorrow; but I will see you again and
[a]your heart will rejoice, and your joy
no one will take from you. †
23 "And in that day you will ask
Me nothing. [a]Most assuredly, I say
to you, whatever you ask the Father
in My name He will give you.
24 "Until now you have asked
nothing in My name. Ask, and you
will receive, [a]that your joy may be
[b]full. †
25 "These things I have spoken to
you in figurative language; but the
time is coming when I will no longer
speak to you in figurative language,
but I will tell you [a]plainly about the
Father. †
26 "In that day you will ask in
My name, and I do not say to you
that I shall pray the Father for
you; †
27 [a]"for the Father Himself loves
you, because you have loved Me,

14 [a]John 15:26 **15** [a]Matt. 11:27 [1]NU, M *takes of Mine and will declare* **16** [a]John 7:33; 12:35; 13:33; 14:19; 19:40–42; 20:19 [b]John 13:3 **18** [1]*understand* **20** [a]Mark 16:10 [b]Luke 24:32, 41 **21** [a]Is. 13:8; 26:17; 42:14 **22** [a]1 Pet. 1:8 **23** [a]Matt. 7:7 **24** [a]John 17:13 [b]John 15:11 **25** [a]John 7:13 **27** [a][John 14:21, 23]

16:15 All things that the Father has are Mine: Jesus Christ, the incarnate Son of God, possesses all things the Father has and is fully equal to the Father.

16:16 The first **little while** is the period of the arrest, death and burial of Jesus; the second *little while* is the time He is in the tomb.

16:21 Jesus uses the powerful image of **a woman** giving **birth** to express both the pain and **joy** of the birth of His new creation.

16:22 Joy will come with the revelation of Christ risen from the dead, after the **sorrow** of the Cross. Jesus does not promise *sorrow* will be removed. His promise is that no one can remove our *joy*. In Phil. 3:10 we see this same combination of sorrow and joy—the sufferings of Christ combined with His Resurrection, giving us entrance into the Kingdom of God.

16:24 They **asked nothing in** His **name** because Jesus was not yet glorified (see 14:13, 14).

16:25 The time is coming when Jesus will speak plainly, not in parables. That time, according to St. John Chrysostom, refers to the post-Resurrection 40 days, as confirmed by Acts 1:3.

16:26–28 We know that prayer may be made in the name of God the Father, for Jesus Himself prayed "Our Father" (Matt. 6:9) and "Father, the hour has come" (17:1). Through Christ, we have direct access to the Father. Here, however, our Lord teaches us we may also pray in the name of God the Son. After Pentecost, we learn "the [Holy] Spirit Himself makes intercession for us" (Rom. 8:26) and we are instructed to be "praying always . . . in the Spirit" (Eph. 6:18). Therefore, as Orthodox Christians we pray continually and with confidence to all three Persons of the Trinity, "in the name of the Father and the Son and the Holy Spirit."

and [b]have believed that I came forth
from God.
28 [a]"I came forth from the Father
and have come into the world.
Again, I leave the world and go to
the Father."
29 His disciples said to Him, "See,
now You are speaking plainly, and
using no figure of speech!
30 "Now we are sure that [a]You
know all things, and have no need
that anyone should question You. By
this [b]we believe that You came forth
from God."
31 Jesus answered them, "Do you
now believe?
32 [a]"Indeed the hour is coming,
yes, has now come, that you will be
scattered, [b]each to his [1]own, and will
leave Me alone. And [c]yet I am not
alone, because the Father is with Me.
33 "These things I have spoken to
you, that [a]in Me you may have
peace. [b]In the world you [1]will have
tribulation; but be of good cheer,
[c]I have overcome the world."†

Christ's Prayer for Himself

17 Jesus spoke these words,
lifted up His eyes to heaven,
and said: "Father, [a]the hour has
come. Glorify Your Son, that Your
Son also may glorify You,†
2 [a]"as You have given Him authority over all flesh, that He [1]should
give eternal life to as many [b]as You
have given Him.
3 "And [a]this is eternal life, that
they may know You, [b]the only true
God, and Jesus Christ [c]whom You
have sent.†
4 [a]"I have glorified You on the
earth. [b]I have finished the work
[c]which You have given Me to do.†
5 "And now, O Father, glorify Me
together [1]with Yourself, with the
glory [a]which I had with You before
the world was.

Christ's Prayer for the Apostles

6 [a]"I have [1]manifested Your name
to the men [b]whom You have given
Me out of the world. [c]They were
Yours, You gave them to Me, and
they have kept Your word.†
7 "Now they have known that all
things which You have given Me are
from You.
8 "For I have given to them the

27 [b]John 3:13
28 [a]John 13:1, 3; 16:5, 10, 17
30 [a]John 21:17 [b]John 17:8
32 [a]Matt. 26:31, 56 [b]John 20:10 [c]John 8:29 [1]*own things* or *place*
33 [a][Eph. 2:14] [b]2 Tim. 3:12 [c]Rom. 8:37 [1]NU, M omit *will*

CHAPTER 17

1 [a]John 12:23
2 [a]John 3:35 [b]John 6:37, 39; 17:6, 9, 24 [1]M *shall*
3 [a]Jer. 9:23, 24 [b]1 Cor. 8:4 [c]John 3:34
4 [a]John 13:31 [b]John 4:34; 19:30 [c]John 14:31
5 [a]Phil. 2:6 [1]Lit. *alongside*
6 [a]Ps. 22:22 [b]John 6:37 [c]Ezek. 18:4 [1]*revealed*

16:33 Despite persecution and suffering, Christians can maintain the peace and joy of Jesus Christ who has **overcome the world** of darkness through His saving work.

17:1–13 This passage is read at the Divine Liturgy on the seventh Sunday of Easter, which falls between Ascension Thursday and Pentecost. On this day the Church commemorates the Fathers who met at the First Ecumenical Council (Nicea I) in A.D. 325. It was at this Council that the heresy of Arianism (which held that the Son was created by God; there was a time when the Son of God did not exist) was condemned, and the basis of the Nicene Creed was ratified. We find our Lord's words bearing witness to His divinity and His filial relationship with the Father (see v. 5)—testimony sufficient in itself to dismiss Arianism.

The hour has come signifies Christ is in charge of time. He cannot be crucified until He is ready (10:18); He "voluntarily willed to ascend the Cross in His flesh" (hymn of Orthodoxy Sunday). **Glorify** refers to the exaltation as well as the eternal glory of the preexistent Christ (v. 5). The "hour" is that of His death: the sacrifice of the Lamb of God made once and for all (13:1; 19:30). This is Jesus' exaltation upon the Cross—the completion of the work of salvation for which He was sent by the Father. In this, both the Father and the Son are victoriously glorified. This is why the Cross, a sign of death, is glorified in the Orthodox Church as "life-giving." God is glorified when salvation and eternal life come to His people.

17:3 The knowledge of God, which is **eternal life,** goes far beyond rational or academic pursuit; it is participation in divine life and communion with God. Thus, *eternal life*—life proper to the age to come—is an ongoing, loving knowledge of God in Christ.

17:4 For Christians, there are two important and interrelated aspects of Christ: (1) who He is: the eternal Son of God incarnate; and (2) His **work:** accomplished through His Incarnation. His work is not limited to the Cross. It incorporates everything from His conception in the womb of Mary to His Ascension and enthronement in the eternal Kingdom.

17:6 **The men whom You have given Me** are the Apostles. It is the Apostles who receive

(continued on next page)

words [a]which You have given Me;
and they have received *them,* [b]and
have known surely that I came forth
from You; and they have believed
that [c]You sent Me.
9 "I pray for them. [a]I do not pray
for the world but for those whom
You have given Me, for they are
Yours.†
10 "And all Mine are Yours, and
[a]Yours are Mine, and I am glorified
in them.
11 [a]"Now I am no longer in the
world, but these are in the world,
and I come to You. Holy Father,
[b]keep[1] through Your name those
whom You have given Me, that they
may be one [c]as We *are.*†
12 "While I was with them [1]in
the world, [a]I kept them in [2]Your
name. Those whom You gave Me
I have kept; and [b]none of them
is [3]lost [c]except the son of [4]perdi-
tion, [d]that the Scripture might be
fulfilled.
13 "But now I come to You, and
these things I speak in the world,
that they may have My joy fulfilled
in themselves.
14 "I have given them Your word;
[a]and the world has hated them because they are not of the world,
[b]just as I am not of the world.†
15 "I do not pray that You should
take them out of the world, but
[a]that You should keep them from the
evil one.
16 "They are not of the world, just
as I am not of the world.
17 [a]"Sanctify[1] them by Your truth.
[b]Your word is truth.†
18 [a]"As You sent Me into the
world, I also have sent them into the
world.
19 "And [a]for their sakes I sanctify

8 [a]John 8:28 [b]John 8:42; 16:27, 30 [c]Deut. 18:15, 18
9 [a][1 John 5:19]
10 [a]John 16:15
11 [a]John 13:1 [b][1 Pet. 1:5] [c]John 10:30 [1]NU, M *keep them through Your name which You have given Me*
12 [a]Heb. 2:13 [b]1 John 2:19 [c]John 6:70 [d]Ps. 41:9; 109:8 [1]NU omits *in the world* [2]NU *Your name which You gave Me. And I guarded them* (or *it;*) [3]*destroyed* [4]*destruction*

14 [a]John 15:19 [b]John 8:23 **15** [a]1 John 5:18 **17** [a][Eph. 5:26] [b]Ps. 119:9, 142, 151 [1]*Set them apart* **18** [a]John 4:38; 20:21 **19** [a][Heb. 10:10]

(continued from previous page)
the Word of the Father from the Son and pass it on to those "who will believe in Me through their word" (v. 20). The Apostles as a body—not primarily Peter, nor any individual preacher or teacher—are the ones through whom God's Word comes to us. This is what is meant by apostolic tradition. Isaiah 52:6 prophesies that in the messianic days the knowledge of the Name, which is an extension of the being and power of God, will be revealed (see Rev. 3:12; 22:4). **Your name:** In OT times the term "the Name" was reverently used as a substitute for God's actual name, "Yahweh." Although all humans belong to God, the fuller revelation of the Name was given only to those who were given to the Savior from out of the world. The **word** they have **kept** is Jesus' revelation, and especially the new commandment to love one another, which is a definitive mark of discipleship (13:34).

17:9 Although God loves the whole world (3:16), and the Son came with a specific mission to **the world,** Jesus prays here for the disciples, the Twelve. He will later extend His prayer to all believers to come (vv. 20–26). But He does not pray for *the world* as such in terms of society, governments, nations. Here *the world* is that portion of humanity which exists in direct opposition to Him; preferring darkness to His light; refusing to come to the light; rejecting Him (15:18–25; 16:1–4, 8–11) and thus standing under judgment.

17:11, 12 Holy Father is echoed in the eucharistic prayer of *Didache* 10:2: "We give You thanks, Holy Father, for Your Holy Name which You have made to dwell in our hearts, and for the knowledge and faith and immortality which You have made known to us through Your Son Jesus." **The son of perdition** ("destruction") is Judas Iscariot (6:70, 71). Old Testament prophecy (Ps. 41:9; 109:2–13) alludes to Judas. Judas's actions also herald the "falling away" that will occur in the last days (see 2 Thess. 2:3, where "son of perdition" refers to the Antichrist).

17:14, 15 Inasmuch as Jesus comes from the realm of divine existence, He confers a heavenly identity and life on those who are joined to Him. In fellowship with Him, the disciples attract the world's hatred. The second-century *Letter to Diognetus* (6:3) states: "Christians dwell in the world but do not belong to the world." Reborn in Christ, Christians have their citizenship in the Kingdom of God (3:1–5). Yet their vocation is in the world, where they are protected by God against the evil one. "Remember, O Lord, Your Church to deliver it from all evil . . ." (*Didache* 10:5).

17:17 Sanctify: to consecrate, make holy, separate, set apart from the world, and bring into the sphere of the sacred for God's use. St. John Chrysostom interprets this verse: "Make them holy through the gift of the Spirit and by correct doctrine."

Myself, that they also may be sanctified by the truth.

Christ's Prayer for the Church

20 "I do not pray for these alone,
but also for those who [1]will believe
in Me through their word;†
21 [a]"that they all may be one, as
[b]You, Father, *are* in Me, and I in You;
that they also may be one in Us, that
the world may believe that You sent
Me.
22 "And the [a]glory which You
gave Me I have given them, [b]that
they may be one just as We are one:
23 "I in them, and You in Me;
[a]that they may be made perfect in
one, and that the world may know
that You have sent Me, and have
loved them as You have loved Me.

Christ's Prayer for All

24 [a]"Father, I desire that they also
whom You gave Me may be with Me
where I am, that they may behold
My glory which You have given Me;
[b]for You loved Me before the foundation of the world.
25 "O righteous Father! [a]The
world has not known You, but
[b]I have known You; and [c]these have
known that You sent Me.
26 [a]"And I have declared to them
Your name, and will declare *it,* that
the love [b]with which You loved Me
may be in them, and I in them."†

20 [1]NU, M omit *will*
21 [a][Gal. 3:28] [b]John 10:38; 17:11, 23
22 [a]1 John 1:3 [b][2 Cor. 3:18]
23 [a][Col. 3:14]
24 [a][1 Thess. 4:17] [b]John 17:5
25 [a]John 15:21 [b]John 7:29; 8:55; 10:15 [c]John 3:17; 17:3, 8, 18, 21, 23
26 [a]John 17:6 [b]John 15:9

CHAPTER 18

1 [a]Mark 14:26, 32 [b]2 Sam. 15:23
2 [a]Luke 21:37; 22:39
3 [a]Luke 22:47–53
4 [a]John 6:64; 13:1, 3; 19:28
5 [a]Matt. 21:11 [b]Ps. 41:9 [1]Lit. *the Nazarene*
9 [a][John 6:39; 17:12]
10 [a]Matt. 26:51

Jesus' Betrayal and Arrest

(Matt. 26:47–56; Mark 14:43–52;
Luke 22:47–53)

18 When Jesus had spoken these
words, [a]He went out with His
disciples over [b]the Brook Kidron,
where there was a garden, which He
and His disciples entered.†
2 And Judas, who betrayed Him,
also knew the place; [a]for Jesus often
met there with His disciples.†
3 [a]Then Judas, having received a
detachment *of troops,* and officers
from the chief priests and Pharisees,
came there with lanterns, torches,
and weapons.
4 Jesus therefore, [a]knowing all
things that would come upon Him,
went forward and said to them,
"Whom are you seeking?"
5 They answered Him, [a]"Jesus
[1]of Nazareth." Jesus said to them,
"I am *He.*" And Judas, who [b]be-
trayed Him, also stood with them.
6 Now when He said to them, "I
am *He,*" they drew back and fell to
the ground.†
7 Then He asked them again,
"Whom are you seeking?" And they
said, "Jesus of Nazareth."
8 Jesus answered, "I have told
you that I am *He.* Therefore, if you
seek Me, let these go their way,"
9 that the saying might be fulfilled
which He spoke, [a]"Of those whom
You gave Me I have lost none."
10 [a]Then Simon Peter, having a
sword, drew it and struck the high
priest's servant, and cut off his right

17:20, 21 Who will believe: Jesus prays for the future Church, which participates in the life and glory of the Father and the Son by the power of the Holy Spirit. Christians enjoy two kinds of unity: vertical, with the Trinity, and horizontal, with one another, the latter rooted in the former.

17:26 We cannot have **love** for God the Father, or receive His love, apart from the knowledge of (communion with) the Father. The purpose of the knowledge of God is to impart the love of God.

18:1 The **garden** here is at the foot of the Mount of Olives (Mark 14:26).

18:2–14 Jesus' capture and Crucifixion was accomplished by the cooperation of: (1) Judas (vv. 2–5); (2) the Roman authorities (**detachment of troops,** vv. 3, 12); and (3) the Jews—the chief priests and Pharisees, the religious establishment (vv. 3, 10, 12).

18:6–11 Since Christ is Lord of all in a kingdom not of this world (v. 36), He is Lord even of His Passion. He is not overcome, but goes to the Cross "for us and for our salvation" willingly, voluntarily, as shown by these details: (1) the troops **drew back and fell to the ground** in awe; (2) He tells His captors to let His disciples go (v. 8); (3) His betrayal fulfills OT prophetic Scripture (Ps. 41:9; 109:2–13); and (4) by His will He drinks the cup His Father gives to Him (v. 11). Thus, Jesus teaches, "I lay down My life" (10:17, 18).

ear. The servant's name was Mal-
chus.
11 So Jesus said to Peter, "Put your
sword into the sheath. Shall I not
drink [a]the cup which My Father has
given Me?"

Before the High Priests; Peter's Denials

(Matt. 26:57–75; Mark 14:53–72; Luke 22:54–71)

12 Then the detachment *of troops*
and the captain and the officers of
the Jews arrested Jesus and bound
Him.
13 And [a]they led Him away to
[b]Annas first, for he was the father-
in-law of [c]Caiaphas who was high
priest that year.†
14 [a]Now it was Caiaphas who advised the Jews that it was [1]expedient
that one man should die for the
people.
15 [a]And Simon Peter followed
Jesus, and so *did* [b]another[1] disciple. Now that disciple was known
to the high priest, and went with
Jesus into the courtyard of the high
priest.
16 [a]But Peter stood at the door outside. Then the other disciple, who
was known to the high priest, went
out and spoke to her who kept the
door, and brought Peter in.
17 Then the servant girl who kept
the door said to Peter, "You are not
also *one* of this Man's disciples, are
you?" He said, "I am [a]not."†
18 Now the servants and officers
who had made a fire of coals stood
there, for it was cold, and they
warmed themselves. And Peter
stood with them and warmed himself.

11 [a]Matt. 20:22; 26:39
13 [a]Matt. 26:57 [b]Luke 3:2 [c]Matt. 26:3
14 [a]John 11:50 [1]*advantageous*
15 [a]Mark 14:54 [b]John 20:2–5 [1]M *the other*
16 [a]Matt. 26:69
17 [a]Matt. 26:34
20 [a]Luke 4:15 [b]John 6:59 [c]Mark 14:49 [1]NU *all the Jews meet*
21 [a]Mark 12:37
22 [a]Jer. 20:2 [1]Lit. *gave Jesus a slap,*
24 [a]Matt. 26:57 [b]John 11:49
25 [a]Luke 22:58–62
27 [a]John 13:38
28 [a]Mark 15:1 [b]Acts 10:28; 11:3 [1]The governor's headquarters

19 The high priest then asked Jesus
about His disciples and His doctrine.†
20 Jesus answered him, [a]"I spoke
openly to the world. I always taught
[b]in synagogues and [c]in the temple, where [1]the Jews always
meet, and in secret I have said nothing.
21 "Why do you ask Me? Ask
[a]those who have heard Me what I
said to them. Indeed they know
what I said."
22 And when He had said these
things, one of the officers who stood
by [a]struck[1] Jesus with the palm of
his hand, saying, "Do You answer
the high priest like that?"
23 Jesus answered him, "If I have
spoken evil, bear witness of the
evil; but if well, why do you strike
Me?"
24 [a]Then Annas sent Him bound
to [b]Caiaphas the high priest.
25 Now Simon Peter stood and
warmed himself. [a]Therefore they
said to him, "You are not also *one*
of His disciples, are you?" He denied
it and said, "I am not!"
26 One of the servants of the high
priest, a relative *of him* whose ear Peter cut off, said, "Did I not see you
in the garden with Him?"
27 Peter then denied again; and
[a]immediately a rooster crowed.

Jesus Before Pilate

(Matt. 27:1, 2, 11–27; Mark 15:1–15; Luke 23:1–22)

28 [a]Then they led Jesus from Caiaphas to the Praetorium, and it was
early morning. [b]But they themselves
did not go into the [1]Praetorium, lest

18:13 Annas was the previous high priest, the power behind the religious establishment. **Caiaphas** was **high priest that year,** the year of the Crucifixion of Christ. He held that office from A.D. 18–36.

18:17 I am not: Peter's denial of Christ, reported here, is threefold (vv. 25–27; Matt. 26:69–75). After the Resurrection of Christ, the Lord extends to Peter a threefold restoration and commission (21:15–17).

18:19 The **high priest** is seeking to find evidence of subversive activity with which to accuse Jesus before Pilate. Note the two points of question put to Jesus: He is asked about His **disciples** and His **doctrine,** two essential aspects of the Church.

they should be defiled, but that they
might eat the Passover.†
29 [a]Pilate then went out to them
and said, "What accusation do you
bring against this Man?"†
30 They answered and said to him,
"If He were not [1]an evildoer, we
would not have delivered Him up
to you."
31 Then Pilate said to them, "You
take Him and judge Him according
to your law." Therefore the Jews said
to him, "It is not lawful for us to
put anyone to death,"
32 [a]that the saying of Jesus might
be fulfilled which He spoke, [b]sig-
nifying by what death He would
die.
33 [a]Then Pilate entered the [1]Prae-
torium again, called Jesus, and
said to Him, "Are You the King of
the Jews?"
34 Jesus answered him, "Are you
speaking for yourself about this, or
did others tell you this concerning
Me?"†
35 Pilate answered, "Am I a Jew?
Your own nation and the chief
priests have delivered You to me.
What have You done?"
36 [a]Jesus answered, [b]"My kingdom is not of this world. If My kingdom were of this world, My servants
would fight, so that I should not be
delivered to the Jews; but now My
kingdom is not from here."
37 Pilate therefore said to Him,
"Are You a king then?" Jesus answered, "You say *rightly* that I am a
king. For this cause I was born, and
for this cause I have come into the
world, [a]that I should bear [b]witness
to the truth. Everyone who [c]is of the
truth [d]hears My voice."
38 Pilate said to Him, "What is
truth?" And when he had said this,
he went out again to the Jews, and
said to them, [a]"I find no fault in Him
at all.
39 [a]"But you have a custom that I
should release someone to you at the
Passover. Do you therefore want me
to release to you the King of the
Jews?"
40 [a]Then they all cried again, saying, "Not this Man, but Barabbas!"
[b]Now Barabbas was a robber.

19 So then [a]Pilate took Jesus and
scourged *Him*.†
2 And the soldiers twisted a
crown of thorns and put *it* on His
head, and they put on Him a purple
robe.
3 [1]Then they said, "Hail, King of
the Jews!" And they [a]struck Him
with their hands.
4 Pilate then went out again, and
said to them, "Behold, I am bringing
Him out to you, [a]that you may know
that I find no fault in Him."

Pilate's Judgment

(Matt. 27:28–31; Mark 15:16–20;
Luke 23:23–25)

5 Then Jesus came out, wearing
the crown of thorns and the purple
robe. And *Pilate* said to them, "Behold the Man!"

29 [a]Matt. 27:11–14
30 [1]*a criminal*
32 [a]Matt. 20:17–19; 26:2 [b]John 3:14; 8:28; 12:32, 33
33 [a]Matt. 27:11 [1]The governor's headquarters
36 [a]1 Tim. 6:13 [b][Dan. 2:44; 7:14]
37 [a][Matt. 5:17; 20:28] [b]Is. 55:4 [c][John 14:6] [d]John 8:47; 10:27
38 [a]John 19:4, 6
39 [a]Luke 23:17–25
40 [a]Acts 3:14 [b]Luke 23:19

CHAPTER 19
1 [a]Matt. 20:19; 27:26
3 [a]Is. 50:6 [1]NU *And they came up to Him and said*
4 [a]John 18:33, 38

18:28 Jesus is taken to the **Praetorium,** the military quarters of Pilate, where the Jewish leaders do not enter. They fear being **defiled** (ritual pollution by contact with Gentiles)—a supreme irony in view of their evil intentions against Jesus. According to this Gospel the main trial of Jesus occurs before Pilate (18:28—19:16). In this dramatic account, Pilate goes back and forth between Jesus and the Jewish leaders.

18:29–33 While the Jews' true charge against Jesus is blasphemy, which according to Jewish law was a crime deserving death, under Roman law the Jewish leaders could not put anyone to death. Pilate, as Roman governor, has the power to enforce the death penalty, but the charge of blasphemy means nothing to him; he must have a serious political charge in order to condemn Jesus. Therefore, the Jews tell Pilate that Jesus claims to be a political King-Messiah—a threat to Roman rule in Palestine.

18:34–38 Jesus testifies His messiahship is of a spiritual character, that He bears **witness** to God's **truth** (v. 37). This declaration receives only an apparently cynical response from Pilate (v. 38).

19:1–4 Scourging was a Roman punishment performed with a whip made of several leather strips with bits of metal or bone at the tips. Pilate hopes in vain to satisfy Jesus' accusers by having Him whipped and released (v. 4).

The Exaltation of the Holy Cross *September 14*

19:6–11, 13–20, 25–28, 30–35: We read of the Crucifixion as we remember St. Helen's finding of the True Cross of Christ.

6 [a]Therefore, when the chief
priests and officers saw Him, they
cried out, saying, "Crucify *Him*, crucify *Him!*" Pilate said to them, "You
take Him and crucify *Him*, for I find
no fault in Him."
7 The Jews answered him, [a]"We
have a law, and according to [1]our
law He ought to die, because [b]He
made Himself the Son of God."†
8 Therefore, when Pilate heard
that saying, he was the more afraid,
9 and went again into the Praetorium, and said to Jesus, "Where are
You from?" [a]But Jesus gave him no
answer.
10 Then Pilate said to Him, "Are
You not speaking to me? Do You not
know that I have [1]power to crucify
You, and [1]power to release You?"
11 Jesus answered, [a]"You could
have no power at all against Me unless it had been given you from
above. Therefore [b]the one who delivered Me to you has the greater sin."†
12 From then on Pilate sought to
release Him, but the Jews cried out,
saying, "If you let this Man go, you
are not Caesar's friend. [a]Whoever
makes himself a king speaks against
Caesar."†
13 [a]When Pilate therefore heard
that saying, he brought Jesus out and
sat down in the judgment seat in a
place that is called *The* Pavement, but
in Hebrew, Gabbatha.
14 Now [a]it was the Preparation
Day of the Passover, and about the
sixth hour. And he said to the Jews,
"Behold your King!"†
15 But they cried out, "Away with
Him, away with *Him!* Crucify Him!"
Pilate said to them, "Shall I crucify
your King?" The chief priests answered, [a]"We have no king but
Caesar!"†
16 [a]Then he delivered Him to them
to be crucified. So they took Jesus
[1]and led *Him* away.†

Crucifixion
(Matt. 27:32–44; Mark 15:21–32;
Luke 23:26–43)

17 [a]And He, bearing His cross,
[b]went out to a place called *the Place*
of a Skull, which is called in Hebrew,
Golgotha,
18 where they crucified Him, and
[a]two others with Him, one on either
side, and Jesus in the center.
19 [a]Now Pilate wrote a title and

6 [a]Acts 3:13
7 [a]Lev. 24:16 [b]Matt. 26:63–66 [1]NU *the law*
9 [a]Is. 53:7
10 [1]*authority*
11 [a][Luke 22:53] [b]Rom. 13:1
12 [a]Luke 23:2
13 [a]1 Sam. 15:24
14 [a]Matt. 27:62
15 [a][Gen. 49:10]
16 [a]Luke 23:24 [1]NU omits *and led Him away*
17 [a]Mark 15:21, 22 [b]Num. 15:36
18 [a]Is. 53:12
19 [a]Matt. 27:37

19:7 The Jewish leaders convicted Jesus on a charge of blasphemy: **He made Himself the Son of God.** What they miss, of course, is the gospel: Jesus not only claims to be, but indeed *is* the Son of God!

19:11 God controls all **power.** With all Rome's force, and with all the relentless persistence of the Jewish authorities, their power was permitted by God. **The one who delivered** Jesus to Pilate is, according to many interpreters, the high priest Caiaphas (18:28); however, the phrase may refer to Judas.

19:12 The Jewish leaders apply hard political pressure on Pilate to gain their ends. Confronted with the choice between Christ and **Caesar,** Pilate chooses his emperor, Tiberius Caesar (reigned A.D. 14–37).

19:14 **Preparation Day** is the day before **Passover.** The synoptic Gospels date the Crucifixion of Jesus on Friday, the first day of the *Passover*.

19:15 The Jewish leadership ironically rejects the King of the Jews and accepts Caesar, a foreign king who ruled Palestine as a result of conquest. In their blind hatred for Jesus, they deny the essential element of their nation's hopes.

19:16 Crucifixion was the method of execution employed by the Romans in capital cases involving rebellious slaves and the worst criminals.

put *it* on the cross. And the writing
was:

JESUS OF NAZARETH,
THE KING OF THE JEWS.

20 Then many of the Jews read this
title, for the place where Jesus was
crucified was near the city; and it was
written in Hebrew, Greek, *and* Latin.
21 Therefore the chief priests of the
Jews said to Pilate, "Do not write,
'The King of the Jews,' but, 'He said,
"I am the King of the Jews." ' "
22 Pilate answered, "What I have
written, I have written."†
23 [a]Then the soldiers, when they
had crucified Jesus, took His garments and made four parts, to each
soldier a part, and also the tunic.
Now the tunic was without seam,
woven from the top in one piece.†
24 They said therefore among
themselves, "Let us not tear it, but
cast lots for it, whose it shall be,"
that the Scripture might be fulfilled
which says:

[a]"*They divided My garments*
among them,
And for My clothing they cast
lots."

Therefore the soldiers did these
things.

Care for Mary

25 [a]Now there stood by the cross
of Jesus His mother, and His
mother's sister, Mary the *wife* of
[b]Clopas, and Mary Magdalene.†
26 When Jesus therefore saw His
mother, and [a]the disciple whom He
loved standing by, He said to His
mother, [b]"Woman, behold your
son!"
27 Then He said to the disciple,
"Behold your mother!" And from
that hour that disciple took her
[a]to his own *home*.

Jesus' Death
(Matt. 27:45–50; Mark 15:33–37;
Luke 23:44–49)

28 After this, Jesus, [1]knowing that
all things were now accomplished,
[a]that the Scripture might be fulfilled,
said, "I thirst!"†
29 Now a vessel full of sour wine
was sitting there; and [a]they filled a
sponge with sour wine, put *it* on
hyssop, and put *it* to His mouth.
30 So when Jesus had received the
sour wine, He said, [a]"It is finished!"
And bowing His head, He gave up
His spirit.†

His Side Is Pierced

31 [a]Therefore, because it was the
Preparation *Day*, [b]that the bodies
should not remain on the cross on
the Sabbath (for that Sabbath was a
[c]high day), the Jews asked Pilate that
their legs might be broken, and *that*
they might be taken away.

23 [a]Matt. 27:35; Mark 15:24; Luke 23:34
24 [a]Ps. 22:18
25 [a]Matt. 27:55; Mark 15:40; Luke 2:35; 23:49 [b]Luke 24:18
26 [a]John 13:23; 20:2; 21:7, 20, 24 [b]John 2:4
27 [a]Luke 18:28; John 1:11; 16:32; Acts 21:6
28 [a]Ps. 22:15 [1]M *seeing*
29 [a]Ps. 69:21; Matt. 27:48, 50; Mark 15:36; Luke 23:36
30 [a]Dan. 9:26; Zech. 11:10, 11; John 17:4
31 [a]Matt. 27:62; Mark 15:42; Luke 23:54 [b]Deut. 21:23; Josh. 8:29; 10:26 [c]Ex. 12:16; Lev. 23:6, 7

19:22 Pilate, a Gentile, insists on the kingship of Jesus, possibly seeking to humiliate the Jewish leaders in retaliation for their earlier pressure against him.

19:23 Many of the Fathers teach Jesus' seamless robe is symbolic of the unity of the Church.

19:25–27 We note three important truths concerning **His mother:** (1) In calling Mary **woman** (v. 26), Jesus is using a term of dignity and affection. (2) In saying to **the disciple whom** Jesus **loved** (v. 26), that is, to John, **Behold your mother** (v. 27), Jesus symbolically establishes Mary's role as mother of all faithful disciples—of the entire Church. (3) If Mary had other offspring, Jesus would not have placed her under the care of John. The Church's teaching concerning Mary's eternal virginity is ratified by Christ's action.

19:28 I thirst: God the Son, through the Incarnation, has fully assumed our weakness in order that we may be delivered from thirst (4:13, 14; 7:37, 38) by partaking of His salvation.

19:30 It is finished: The work of salvation for the redemption of sinful humanity is completed with the death of Christ on the Cross. His Resurrection, Ascension, and gift of the Spirit will inaugurate the age of new creation until the consummation in the Kingdom. **Bowing His head, He gave up His spirit:** "Christ did not, after He expired, bow His head, as happens with us," says St. John Chrysostom. "But when He had bent His head, then He expired, showing He was Lord of all."

Vespers of Great and Holy Friday

Friday before Easter

19:31–37: On the Cross, Jesus' side is pierced, fulfilling prophecy.

32 Then the soldiers came and broke the legs of the first and of the other who was crucified with Him.
33 But when they came to Jesus and saw that He was already dead, they did not break His legs.
34 But one of the soldiers pierced His side with a spear, and immediately [a]blood and water came out.†
35 And he who has seen has testified, and his testimony is [a]true; and he knows that he is telling the truth, so that you may [b]believe.
36 For these things were done that the Scripture should be fulfilled, [a]*"Not one of His bones shall be broken."*
37 And again another Scripture says, [a]*"They shall look on Him whom they pierced."*

The Burial of Jesus

(Matt. 27:57–60; Mark 15:42–47; Luke 23:50–56)

38 [a]After this, Joseph of Arimathea, being a disciple of Jesus, but secretly, [b]for fear of the Jews, asked Pilate that he might take away the body of Jesus; and Pilate gave *him* permission. So he came and took the body of Jesus.†
39 And [a]Nicodemus, who at first came to Jesus by night, also came, bringing a mixture of [b]myrrh and aloes, about a hundred pounds.
40 Then they took the body of Jesus, and [a]bound it in strips of linen with the spices, as the custom of the Jews is to bury.
41 Now in the place where He was crucified there was a garden, and in the garden a new tomb in which no one had yet been laid.
42 So [a]there they laid Jesus, [b]because of the Jews' Preparation *Day*, for the tomb was nearby.

The Tomb Is Empty

(Matt. 28:1–8; Mark 16:1–8; Luke 24:1–12)

20 Now on the [a]first *day* of the week Mary Magdalene went to the tomb early, while it was still dark, and saw *that* the [b]stone had been taken away from the tomb.†
2 Then she ran and came to Simon Peter, and to the [a]other disciple, [b]whom Jesus loved, and said to them, "They have taken away the

34 a[1 John 5:6, 8]
35 aJohn 21:24
b[John 20:31]
36 a[Ex. 12:46; Num. 9:12]; Ps. 34:20
37 aZech. 12:10; 13:6
38 aLuke 23:50–56
b[John 7:13; 9:22; 12:42]
39 aJohn 3:1, 2; 7:50
bMatt. 2:11
40 aJohn 20:5, 7
42 aIs. 53:9
bJohn 19:14, 31

CHAPTER 20
1 aMatt. 28:1–8
bMatt. 27:60, 66; 28:2
2 aJohn 21:23, 24
bJohn 13:23; 19:26; 21:7, 20, 24

19:34 Blood and water may well symbolize the sacraments. For the water speaks of our baptism, and in partaking of the eucharistic cup we are "drinking from His very side" (St. John Chrysostom). It is literally the forgiveness of sins that gushed out from Jesus' side; the water gushed unto regeneration and the washing away of sin, and the blood as drink productive of life everlasting (see also 1 John 5:6–8). Some of the early Church literature records "from His side came water and blood"—in that order.

19:38, 39 Two prominent Jews take responsibility for the burial of Jesus. **Joseph of Arimathea** (v. 38) was a "hidden" disciple, one who believed in Jesus but made no public acknowledgment of his belief. **Nicodemus** (v. 39) had come to talk with Jesus by night (3:2) and later tried to speak in His defense (7:50–52). Now, by burying Him, both Joseph and Nicodemus show their devotion to Jesus publicly, in stark contrast to the fearful disciples who had scattered. **About a hundred pounds** (v. 39) of aromatic substances is a symbolic number exalting the dignity of Christ as King.

20:1 First day of the week: The theme of Sunday is the Resurrection, "the living monument" of Christianity (St. Athanasius). In no way is Sunday the "Old Testament Saturday" or Sabbath. The Resurrection transforms time, marking Sunday as both the eighth day (symbolic of eternity) and the first day of the week (symbolic of the first day of creation).

Lord out of the tomb, and we do not
know where they have laid Him."†
3 [a]Peter therefore went out, and
the other disciple, and were going
to the tomb.
4 So they both ran together, and
the other disciple outran Peter and
came to the tomb first.†
5 And he, stooping down and
looking in, saw [a]the linen cloths lying *there;* yet he did not go in.
6 Then Simon Peter came, following him, and went into the tomb;
and he saw the linen cloths lying
there,†
7 and [a]the [1]handkerchief that had
been around His head, not lying
with the linen cloths, but folded together in a place by itself.
8 Then the [a]other disciple, who
came to the tomb first, went in also;
and he saw and believed.†
9 For as yet they did not [1]know
the [a]Scripture, that He must rise
again from the dead.
10 Then the disciples went away
again to their own homes.

Jesus Appears to Mary Magdalene

11 [a]But Mary stood outside by the
tomb weeping, and as she wept she
stooped down *and looked* into the
tomb.
12 And she saw two angels in
white sitting, one at the head and
the other at the feet, where the body
of Jesus had lain.

3 [a]Luke 24:12
5 [a]John 19:40
7 [a]John 11:44 [1]*face cloth*
8 [a]John 21:23, 24
9 [a]Ps. 16:10; Acts 2:25, 31; 13:34, 35 [1]*understand*
11 [a]Mark 16:5
14 [a]Matt. 28:9; Mark 16:9 [b][Luke 24:16, 31]; John 21:4
16 [a]John 10:3 [1]NU adds *in Hebrew*
17 [a]Mark 16:19; Luke 24:5; Acts 1:9; 2:34–36; Eph. 4:8–10; Heb. 4:14 [b]Ps. 22:22; Matt. 18:10; Rom. 8:29; Heb. 2:11 [c]John 16:28; 17:11 [d]Eph. 1:17
18 [a]Matt. 28:10; Luke 24:10, 23 [1]NU *disciples, "I have seen the Lord,"*
19 [a]Mark 16:14; Luke 24:36; John 14:27; 1 Cor. 15:5 [b]John 9:22; 19:38 [1]NU omits *assembled*

13 Then they said to her, "Woman,
why are you weeping?" She said to
them, "Because they have taken
away my Lord, and I do not know
where they have laid Him."
14 [a]Now when she had said this,
she turned around and saw Jesus
standing *there,* and [b]did not know
that it was Jesus.†
15 Jesus said to her, "Woman, why
are you weeping? Whom are you
seeking?" She, supposing Him to be
the gardener, said to Him, "Sir, if
You have carried Him away, tell me
where You have laid Him, and I will
take Him away."
16 Jesus said to her, [a]"Mary!" She
turned and said to [1]Him, "Rabboni!"
(which is to say, Teacher).†
17 Jesus said to her, "Do not cling
to Me, for I have not yet [a]ascended
to My Father; but go to [b]My brethren and say to them, [c]'I am ascending to My Father and your
Father, and *to* [d]My God and your
God.' "
18 [a]Mary Magdalene came and
told the [1]disciples that she had seen
the Lord, and *that* He had spoken
these things to her.†

Jesus Appears to Ten Disciples

19 [a]Then, the same day at evening,
being the first *day* of the week, when
the doors were shut where the disciples were [1]assembled, for [b]fear of the
Jews, Jesus came and stood in the

20:2 John does not mention the other myrrh-bearing women, but Mary Magdalene's use of "we" indicates they were present. The empty tomb is the first major testimony to the Resurrection of Jesus.

20:4, 5 The beloved disciple, John the Evangelist, who is younger, outruns Peter to the tomb. He does not enter, perhaps out of awe and fear.

20:6, 7 True to his character, Peter boldly **went into the tomb** (v. 6). He finds Jesus' burial clothes still in the tomb and the face cloth neatly **folded** (v. 7), indicating His body was resurrected, not stolen as Mary Magdalene first thought (v. 2).

20:8 Faith in Jesus' Resurrection begins to take hold in the disciples' hearts when they see the empty tomb and burial clothes.

20:14–18 This is the first of four post-Resurrection appearances (epiphanies) of Christ reported in John. He also appears to ten of the Apostles that evening (20:19–23); eight days after the Resurrection to the eleven Apostles, including Thomas (20:24–29); and to seven of the Apostles as they are fishing in Galilee (21:1–19).

20:16 Mary's eyes are mysteriously held from recognizing Jesus until He calls her name. **Rabboni:** an affectionate term meaning "my dear Teacher."

20:18 Mary Magdalene is the first to see the risen Christ and becomes "the apostle to the Apostles."

Thomas Sunday

Sunday after Easter (Second Sunday of Pascha)

20:19–31: St. Thomas requires proof of Christ's resurrection.

midst, and said to them, [c]"Peace *be*
with you."
20 When He had said this, He
[a]showed them *His* hands and His
side. [b]Then the disciples were glad
when they saw the Lord.
21 So Jesus said to them again,
"Peace to you! [a]As the Father has
sent Me, I also send you."†
22 And when He had said this, He
breathed on *them,* and said to them,
"Receive the Holy Spirit.
23 [a]"If you forgive the sins of any,
they are forgiven them; if you retain the *sins* of any, they are retained."
24 Now Thomas, [a]called the Twin,
one of the twelve, was not with them
when Jesus came.
25 The other disciples therefore
said to him, "We have seen the
Lord." So he said to them, "Unless
I see in His hands the print of
the nails, and put my finger into
the print of the nails, and put my
hand into His side, I will not believe."†
26 And after eight days His disciples were again inside, and Thomas
with them. Jesus came, the doors being shut, and stood in the midst, and
said, "Peace to you!"
27 Then He said to Thomas,
"Reach your finger here, and look
at My hands; and [a]reach your hand
here, and put *it* into My side. Do
not be [b]unbelieving, but believing."†
28 And Thomas answered and said
to Him, "My Lord and my God!"
29 Jesus said to him, [1]"Thomas, because you have seen Me, you have
believed. [a]Blessed *are* those who
have not seen and *yet* have believed."†

The Purpose of John's Gospel

30 And [a]truly Jesus did many other
signs in the presence of His disciples, which are not written in this
book;†
31 [a]but these are written that
[b]you may believe that Jesus [c]is the
Christ, the Son of God, [d]and that believing you may have life in His
name.†

19 [c]John 14:27; 16:33; Eph. 2:17
20 [a]Acts 1:3 [b]John 16:20, 22
21 [a][Matt. 28:18–20]; John 17:18, 19; [2 Tim. 2:2]; Heb. 3:1
23 [a]Matt. 16:19; 18:18
24 [a]John 11:16
27 [a]Ps. 22:16; Zech. 12:10; 13:6; 1 John 1:1 [b]Mark 16:14
29 [a]2 Cor. 5:7; 1 Pet. 1:8 [1]NU, M omit *Thomas*
30 [a]John 21:25
31 [a]Luke 1:4 [b]John 19:35; 1 John 5:13 [c]Luke 2:11; 1 John 5:1 [d]John 3:15, 16; 5:24; [1 Pet. 1:8, 9]

20:21–23 Christ commissions the disciples to continue His mission on earth, granting them **the Holy Spirit** (v. 22) and the power to **forgive . . . sins** (v. 23). These words of Christ are among the scriptural foundations of the sacraments of holy orders (see article, "Ordination," at Acts 14) and repentance (see article, "Confession," at 1 John 1). Through the consecration and empowerment of the Apostles by the Lord, and through their ordination of others to continue their apostolic mission, Christ's own Holy Priesthood is communicated to the bishops and priests of the Church.

20:25 The disbelief of Thomas, in view of the evidence and the disciples' testimony, is difficult to explain. It shows either perplexity about the miracle or a certain stubbornness of character.

20:27, 28 Thomas, upon Jesus' invitation, does not actually touch Jesus for proof. His magnificent confession, **My Lord and my God,** testifies both to the lordship and deity of Christ.

20:29 Doubting **Thomas** required direct proof of the Resurrection. A **blessed** faith is one which trusts in the risen Christ without proof.

20:30 Signs are the selected miracles (also called "works") of Jesus reported in this Gospel (see note on 2:1–11).

20:31 Here is John's main purpose in writing his Gospel: to lead people to faith in Jesus as **the Christ, the Son of God,** that they may receive eternal **life in His name.**

Jesus Eats with the Eleven

21 After these things Jesus showed Himself again to the disciples at the [a]Sea of Tiberias, and in this way He showed *Himself*:†

2 Simon Peter, [a]Thomas called the Twin, [b]Nathanael of [c]Cana in Galilee, [d]the *sons* of Zebedee, and two others of His disciples were together.

3 Simon Peter said to them, "I am going fishing." They said to him, "We are going with you also." They went out and [1]immediately got into the boat, and that night they caught nothing.

4 But when the morning had now come, Jesus stood on the shore; yet the disciples [a]did not know that it was Jesus.†

5 Then [a]Jesus said to them, "Children, have you any food?" They answered Him, "No."

6 And He said to them, [a]"Cast the net on the right side of the boat, and you will find *some*." So they cast, and now they were not able to draw it in because of the multitude of fish.†

7 Therefore [a]that disciple whom Jesus loved said to Peter, "It is the Lord!" Now when Simon Peter heard that it was the Lord, he put on *his* outer garment (for he had removed it), and plunged into the sea.†

8 But the other disciples came in the little boat (for they were not far from land, but about two hundred cubits), dragging the net with fish.

9 Then, as soon as they had come to land, they saw a fire of coals there, and fish laid on it, and bread.

10 Jesus said to them, "Bring some of the fish which you have just caught."

11 Simon Peter went up and dragged the net to land, full of large fish, one hundred and fifty-three; and although there were so many, the net was not broken.†

12 Jesus said to them, [a]"Come *and* eat breakfast." Yet none of the disciples dared ask Him, "Who are You?"—knowing that it was the Lord.†

13 Jesus then came and took the bread and gave it to them, and likewise the fish.†

14 This *is* now [a]the third time Jesus showed Himself to His disciples after He was raised from the dead.

Jesus Restores and Commissions Peter

15 So when they had eaten breakfast, Jesus said to Simon Peter, "Simon, *son* of [1]Jonah, do you love Me more than these?" He said to Him,

CHAPTER 21
1 [a]John 6:1
2 [a]John 20:24 [b]John 1:45–51 [c]John 2:1 [d]Matt. 4:21
3 [1]NU omits *immediately*
4 [a]John 20:14
5 [a]Luke 24:41
6 [a]Luke 5:4, 6, 7
7 [a]John 13:23; 20:2
12 [a]Acts 10:41
14 [a]John 20:19, 26
15 [a]Acts 20:28 [1]NU *John*

21:1 The Lake of Galilee is also called the **Sea of Tiberias,** especially by Hellenized Gentiles, because the city of Tiberias (built c. 20 B.C. in honor of Tiberius Caesar) is on its shores.

21:4–7 Like Mary Magdalene (20:14–16), the disciples do not initially recognize Jesus.

21:6 The disciples' miraculous catch of fish during this fourth appearance of the risen Christ symbolizes their commissioning as apostles to preach the gospel and to be "fishers of men" (Matt. 4:19).

21:7 The beloved disciple (John) is the first to perceive that the stranger on shore is **the Lord,** suggesting that love brings spiritual insight. Peter **had removed** his **outer garment** to work.

21:11 Peter takes initiative in dragging **the net to land,** an act symbolic of his leadership role in the early Church. Various connotations have been given to the number of fish, 153. The ancient Christians took it as a symbol of the universal character of the Christian Church, taken to every race of humanity. A modern scholar has pointed out the letters in the phrase we translate "children of God" have the numerical value of 153.

21:12 The meal has certain overtones of the Eucharist.

21:13 The **fish** becomes a symbol of identity for Christians, a picture of the Last Supper according to Orthodox tradition. The initials of the phrase "Jesus Christ, God's Son, Savior" in Greek form the acronym *ICHTHYS,* which is Greek for "fish."

"Yes, Lord; You know that I [2]love
You." He said to him, [a]"Feed My
lambs."†
16 He said to him again a second
time, "Simon, *son* of [1]Jonah, do
you love Me?" He said to Him,
"Yes, Lord; You know that I [2]love
You." [a]He said to him, "Tend My
[b]sheep."
17 He said to him the third time,
"Simon, *son* of [1]Jonah, do you
[2]love Me?" Peter was grieved because He said to him the third
time, "Do you [2]love Me?" And he
said to Him, "Lord, [a]You know
all things; You know that I [2]love
You." Jesus said to him, "Feed My
sheep.†
18 [a]"Most assuredly, I say to you,
when you were younger, you girded
yourself and walked where you
wished; but when you are old, you
will stretch out your hands, and another will gird you and carry *you*
where you do not wish."†
19 This He spoke, signifying [a]by
what death he would glorify God.
And when He had spoken this, He
said to him, [b]"Follow Me."

The Beloved Disciple and His Book

20 Then Peter, turning around,
saw the disciple [a]whom Jesus loved
following, [b]who also had leaned on
His breast at the supper, and said,
"Lord, who is the one who betrays
You?"†
21 Peter, seeing him, said to Jesus,
"But Lord, what *about* this man?"
22 Jesus said to him, "If I [1]will that
he remain [a]till I come, what *is that*
to you? You follow Me."†
23 Then this saying went out
among the brethren that this disciple
would not die. Yet Jesus did not say
to him that he would not die, but,
"If I will that he remain till I come,
what *is that* to you?"†
24 This is the disciple who [a]tes-
tifies of these things, and wrote these
things; and we know that his testimony is true.†
25 [a]And there are also many other
things that Jesus did, which if they
were written one by one, [b]I suppose
that even the world itself could not
contain the books that would be
written. Amen.†

15 [2]*have affection for*
16 [a]Heb. 13:20 [b]Ps. 79:13 [1]NU *John* [2]*have affection for*
17 [a]John 2:24, 25; 16:30 [1]NU *John* [2]*have affection for*
18 [a]Acts 12:3, 4
19 [a]2 Pet. 1:13, 14 [b][Matt. 4:19; 16:24]
20 [a]John 13:23; 20:2 [b]John 13:25
22 [a][Rev. 2:25; 3:11; 22:7, 20] [1]*desire*
24 [a]John 19:35
25 [a]John 20:30 [b]Amos 7:10

21:15 More than these is a reference to the other disciples. Before the Passion of Christ, Peter had expressed absolute loyalty to Him, even if the others were to be scattered (Matt. 26:33). Now the risen Lord asks Peter whether he really means what he says, and if so, to concentrate his efforts on serving the flock.

21:17 Since Peter denied Christ three times (Matt. 26:69–75), Jesus asks Peter three times to confess his love for Him. Peter is thus restored to leadership in the early Church to continue his ministry of shepherding Christ's flock.

21:18, 19 This is a veiled prophecy of the martyrdom of Peter. These words imply that Peter would thenceforth be a steadfast follower of Christ, even though faithful discipleship would bring the Apostle to his death. Peter, according to Christian tradition, was martyred in A.D. 64–68 under Nero Caesar, by being crucified upside down.

21:20 The disciple whom Jesus loved: the Apostle John, according to the common witness of ancient Tradition.

21:22 What is that to you? You follow Me. We are not to concern ourselves with what the Lord has in store for others. Our job is to follow Christ and to pursue the mission He has given to us.

21:23 The Apostle John lived a long life, dying at about the age of 100 (c. A.D. 95–100). Early Christians marvelled at his longevity and remembered the words of Christ recorded here. It is possible some Christians thought John would not die before the return of Christ, and that this view is corrected with the words, **Yet Jesus did not say to him that he would not die.**

21:24 This is the testimony of the Evangelist's assistants, as the plural **we know** indicates. Tradition holds that a certain scribe named Prochoros actually committed the Evangelist's words and teachings to writing.

21:25 This is a conscious exaggeration to make a point: the Gospel of John contains only a small part of the works of Jesus. Many more are reported in the Gospels of Matthew, Mark, and Luke, but even these records are not exhaustive.

THE ACTS

of the Apostles

Author: *St. Luke*

Date: *A.D. 75–85*

Theme: *The Apostles Spread the Gospel*

AUTHOR: Traditionally, Acts is ascribed to Luke—"the beloved physician," as Paul calls him (Col. 4:14); the "disciple of Paul," as St. John Chrysostom describes him. It is a continuation by Luke of the account given in his Gospel (see note on 1:1).

DATE: Acts was written about A.D. 75–85, sometime after the composition of the Gospel of Luke.

MAJOR THEME: The spread of the gospel by the Apostles, from Jerusalem to the whole world (1:8).

The Book of Acts recounts the triumphant march of the Christian mission from Jerusalem to Samaria, Syria, Cyprus, Asia Minor, Greece, and finally Rome, the capital of the Empire. This achievement points to the work of the Holy Spirit, who descended on the early Church, empowering the Apostles and other missionaries to bring the Good News of salvation to the known world. At the same time Acts narrates the expansion of the Church by means of small congregations throughout the Greco-Roman world. The story concludes in an open-ended way when St. Paul, the great missionary hero of Acts, comes to Rome as a prisoner but continues to preach the gospel of the Kingdom unimpeded (28:30, 31).

The primary subtheme of Acts is the same as the major theme of the Gospel of Luke: Immanuel, "God with us." In Luke's Gospel, God is with us in His incarnate Son, and Luke reports "all that Jesus began both to do and teach, until the day in which He was taken up" (1:1, 2). In Acts, the Incarnate Son of God, ascended into heaven and is seated at the right hand of the Father, is yet present in the Church by the power of the Holy Spirit.

BACKGROUND INFORMATION: (1) *The scope of Acts.* Acts moves from the Ascension of the Lord (1:9), through that first meeting of the Twelve and the One-Hundred-Twenty for prayer (1:12–15), the labors and lessons of Peter (1:15—6:7), the conversion and missionary journeys of Paul (7:58—28:31), to the rapid spread of the Church throughout the Mediterranean world (9:31—21:14).

(2) *A record of Church growth.* Our objective in studying this book is not simply to acquire objective knowledge about the Church, but to gain an intuitive sense of how the Church, seen through the actions of the early Christians and filled with God's presence, developed. For the Acts of the Apostles is a spiritual and theological record as well as a historical one, and we are the spiritual children of the Lord's Apostles.

Yet this book is not to be read as a blueprint for reproducing the specific details and aspects of the Church which we read there. They cannot be reproduced. Such an effort would, at best, create only a poor copy of the New Testament Church. Our task is not to be forever starting the Church over, but to enter more fully into her contemporary expression in our time and world.

This book is of great importance for understanding the organization and structure of the Church: its method of resolving controversies; the role of apostles, bishops, priests (elders) and deacons; and the spiritual life of the Church.

(3) *The organization of Acts.* Chapters 1—12 focus largely on the ministry of Peter, while chapters 13—28 concentrate almost exclusively on Paul. With Peter we see the Church being established. With Paul we see the expansion of the Church throughout the Roman world.

OUTLINE

Introduction	1:1–3
I. The birth of the Church	1:4—12:24
A. Preparation for the Church	1:4–26
B. Beginning of the Church	2:1—4:37
1. Pentecost: The gift of the Holy Spirit	2:1–47
2. A pattern of confirming signs begins	3:1–26
3. Immediate opposition develops	4:1–37
C. Life in the Church	5:1—7:60
1. Purging of sin	5:1–11
2. Signs and wonders continue	5:12–16
3. Persecution continues	5:17–42
4. The expansion of the ministry	6:1–7
5. Stephen, the first Christian martyr	6:8—7:60
D. Persecution and expansion of the Church	8:1—12:24
1. Saul persecutes the Church	8:1–3
2. The Church goes to Samaria	8:4–25
3. Roots for the Church in Africa	8:26–40
4. The conversion of Saul	9:1–30
5. The Church outside Jerusalem	9:31–43
6. The Church of the Gentiles	10:1—11:18
7. The Church in Antioch	11:19–30
8. Death for James, prison for Peter	12:1–24
II. The growth of the Church from Antioch: The labor of Paul	12:25—28:31
A. Barnabas and Saul commissioned	12:25—13:3
B. The first missionary journey	13:4—14:28
C. The Jerusalem Council	15:1–35
D. The second missionary journey	15:36—18:22

Easter (Pascha)—The Resurrection of Christ

1:1–8: Jesus promises the Holy Spirit to His disciples and commands them to be His witnesses.

From Passover to Pentecost

1 The former account I made, O
[a]Theophilus, of all that Jesus began both to do and teach,†
2 [a]until the day in which [1]He was
taken up, after He through the Holy
Spirit [b]had given commandments to
the apostles whom He had chosen,†

Days 1–39: Jesus' Promise of the Holy Spirit

3 [a]to whom He also presented
Himself alive after His suffering by
many [1]infallible proofs, being seen
by them during forty days and
speaking of the things pertaining to
the kingdom of God.†
4 [a]And being assembled together
with *them,* He commanded them not
to depart from Jerusalem, but to wait
for the Promise of the Father,
"which," *He said,* "you have [b]heard
from Me;†
5 [a]"for John truly baptized with
water, [b]but you shall be baptized
with the Holy Spirit not many days
from now."
6 Therefore, when they had come
together, they asked Him, saying,

CHAPTER 1
1 [a]Luke 1:3
2 [a]Mark 16:19 [b]Matt. 28:19 [1]He ascended into heaven.
3 [a]Mark 16:12, 14 [1]*unmistakable*
4 [a]Luke 24:49 [b][John 14:16, 17, 26; 15:26]
5 [a]Matt. 3:11 [b][Joel 2:28]

1:1 The former account is the Gospel of Luke (Luke 1:3). The Gospel covers over 30 years of Jesus' earthly life; Acts covers over 30 years of early Church life. Luke addresses **Theophilus** in both books. Ancient writers would sometimes dedicate a work to one person, intending it to be read by many. This may be the case here.

1:2 Jesus Christ is the model for all things done in the Church. Even as He in His earthly life worked **through the Holy Spirit,** so will the Apostles. During the Last Supper, Jesus promised to teach His disciples by the Holy Spirit (John 16:13). Now, after His Resurrection, His promise will be fulfilled.

1:3 In these **forty days** His Apostles are forever changed by the reality of Jesus' Resurrection. The same men who denied Him and fled at His arrest are being transformed—powerful evidence of the truth of the Resurrection of Christ.

1:4, 5 The **Promise of the Father:** the gift of the Holy Spirit to be poured out on God's faithful, according to Jewish expectations.

The Ascension of Our Lord Jesus Christ

Sixth Thursday after Easter

1:1–12: Jesus appears to His disciples one last time before His Ascension.

"Lord, will You at this time restore
the kingdom to Israel?"†
7 And He said to them, [a]"It is not
for you to [b]know times or seasons
which the Father has put in His own
authority.†
8 [a]"But you shall receive power
[b]when the Holy Spirit has come
upon you; and [c]you shall be
[1]witnesses to Me in Jerusalem, and
in all Judea and [d]Samaria, and to the
[e]end of the earth."

Day 40: The Ascension

9 [a]Now when He had spoken
these things, while they watched,
[b]He was taken up, and a cloud received Him out of their sight.†
10 And while they looked steadfastly toward heaven as He went up,
behold, two men stood by them
[a]in white apparel,
11 who also said, "Men of Galilee,
why do you stand gazing up
into heaven? This *same* Jesus,
who was taken up from you
into heaven, [a]will so come in like
manner as you saw Him go into
heaven."

Days 40–49: Preparation for Pentecost

12 [a]Then they returned to Jerusalem from the mount called Olivet,
which is near Jerusalem, a Sabbath
day's journey.†
13 And when they had entered,
they went up [a]into the upper room
where they were staying: [b]Peter,
James, John, and Andrew; Philip and
Thomas; Bartholomew and Matthew;
James *the son* of Alphaeus and
[c]Simon the Zealot; and [d]Judas *the son*
of James.†
14 [a]These all continued with one
[1]accord in prayer [2]and supplication,

7 [a]1 Thess. 5:1 [b]Matt. 24:36 **8** [a][Acts 2:1, 4] [b]Luke 24:49 [c]Luke 24:48 [d]Acts 8:1, 5, 14 [e]Col. 1:23 [1]NU *My witnesses* **9** [a]Luke 24:50, 51 [b]Acts 1:2 **10** [a]John 20:12 **11** [a]Dan. 7:13 **12** [a]Luke 24:52 **13** [a]Acts 9:37, 39; 20:8 [b]Matt. 10:2–4 [c]Luke 6:15 [d]Jude 1 **14** [a]Acts 2:1, 46 [1]*purpose* or *mind* [2]NU omits *and supplication*

1:6 The concern of the disciples is still fixed on the idea of an earthly kingdom which would liberate the Jews from the humiliation of subjection to Rome. Only after Pentecost do the disciples have a clear understanding of Jesus' messianic mission and the establishment of the Kingdom of God.

1:7, 8 Jesus' concern is with another Kingdom, one ruled in the power of the Holy Spirit. Note how all three Persons of the Holy Trinity are clearly related in the work of salvation. The power of the Holy Spirit will energize the disciples to go to the entire world with the gospel.

1:9–11 Peter and the others are witnesses to the Ascension. Christ's Ascension is His enthronement in the fullness of divine authority and glory. In the Orthodox Church we sing, "When the Disciples beheld You, O Christ, ascending unto the Father and sitting down beside Him, the angels rejoiced, shouting, 'Lift up you gates, lift up; for the King has ascended unto the glory of His Nature's light' " (Vespers for the Feast of the Ascension).

Certain Orthodox icons of the Ascension represent Christ in such a way that one cannot tell whether He is going into heaven or coming again. This captures the profound truth that we are already living under His reign while awaiting His return to establish the Kingdom in its fullness. We are not to stand idly **gazing up into heaven** (v. 11), but to prepare ourselves soberly as His servants, filled with the Spirit, expecting His return, living lives of righteousness.

1:12 A Sabbath day's journey is the distance the Jews could travel without breaking the Sabbath—something under a mile.

1:13, 14 Obedient to Christ's command (v. 4), the Apostles, with the other disciples including the Virgin Mary and members of Jesus' extended family, all wait in **the upper room** for the coming of the Holy Spirit, devoting themselves to **prayer.**

with [b]the women and Mary the
mother of Jesus, and with [c]His
brothers.
15 And in those days Peter stood
up in the midst of the [1]disciples (altogether the number [a]of names was
about a hundred and twenty), and
said,
16 "Men *and* brethren, this Scripture had to be fulfilled, [a]which the
Holy Spirit spoke before by the
mouth of David concerning Judas,
[b]who became a guide to those who
arrested Jesus;†
17 "for [a]he was numbered with us
and obtained a part in [b]this
ministry."
18 [a](Now this man purchased a
field with [b]the [1]wages of iniquity;
and falling headlong, he burst open
in the middle and all his [2]entrails
gushed out.†
19 And it became known to all
those dwelling in Jerusalem; so that
field is called in their own language,
Akel Dama, that is, Field of Blood.)
20 "For it is written in the Book of
Psalms:

[a]*'Let his dwelling place be*
[1]desolate,
And let no one live in it';†

and,

[b]*'Let another take his [2]office.'*

14 [b]Luke 23:49, 55 [c]Matt. 13:55
15 [a]Rev. 3:4 [1]NU *brethren*
16 [a]Ps. 41:9 [b]Luke 22:47
17 [a]Matt. 10:4 [b]Acts 1:25
18 [a]Matt. 27:3–10 [b]Mark 14:21 [1]*reward of unrighteousness* [2]*intestines*
20 [a]Ps. 69:25 [b]Ps. 109:8 [1]*deserted* [2]Gr. *episkopen,* position of overseer
22 [a]Acts 1:9 [b]Acts 1:8; 2:32
23 [a]Acts 15:22
24 [a]1 Sam. 16:7
25 [a]Acts 1:17

CHAPTER 2

1 [a]Lev. 23:15 [b]Acts 1:14 [1]NU *together*
2 [a]Acts 4:31
3 [1]Or *tongues as of fire, distributed and resting on each*

21 "Therefore, of these men who
have accompanied us all the time
that the Lord Jesus went in and out
among us,
22 "beginning from the baptism of
John to that day when [a]He was taken
up from us, one of these must
[b]become a witness with us of His
resurrection."
23 And they proposed two: Joseph
called [a]Barsabas, who was surnamed
Justus, and Matthias.
24 And they prayed and said,
"You, O Lord, [a]who know the hearts
of all, show which of these two You
have chosen
25 [a]"to take part in this ministry
and apostleship from which Judas by
transgression fell, that he might go
to his own place."
26 And they cast their lots, and the
lot fell on Matthias. And he was
numbered with the eleven apostles.†

Day 50: Pentecost

2 When [a]the Day of Pentecost had
fully come, [b]they were all
[1]with one accord in one place.†
2 And suddenly there came a
sound from heaven, as of a rushing
mighty wind, and [a]it filled the whole
house where they were sitting.
3 Then there appeared to them
[1]divided tongues, as of fire, and *one*
sat upon each of them.†

1:16 That **Scripture had to be fulfilled** does not imply strict predestination. Scripture prophetically reveals what people will do, but does not cause them to do it. Because the Apostles had been enlightened by Christ to understand the OT more fully (Luke 24:27), Peter is able to apply two prophetic psalms (Ps. 69:25; 109:8) to the case of Judas.

1:18, 19 Luke does not give details of Judas' death in his Gospel. This account is perhaps an expansion of Matthew's report (Matt. 27:3–10).

1:20 The Greek word *episkope* (lit. "supervisorship"), here rendered **office,** refers to the apostolic office. The authority of overseeing the life of the Church continued in the bishops of the Church who stand in apostolic succession. The Greek word for "bishop" is *episkopos,* literally "overseer."

1:26 They cast their lots in the conviction that God would control the lots and thereby make the final choice. **Matthias** is the twelfth apostle.

2:1 The **Day of Pentecost** (also called the Feast of Weeks) in the OT (Lev. 23:16) comes 50 days after Passover and is a celebration of the firstfruits of harvest. Since Jesus was crucified at Passover, the events of ch. 2 occur 50 days after His death. On the first Christian Pentecost the believers are gathered together **with one accord in one place,** that is, they are united in an assembly. Their unity creates an environment in which the Holy Spirit will come.

2:3 This phenomenon of **tongues, as of fire** fulfills the prophecy of John the Baptist that Christ would "baptize you with the Holy Spirit and fire" (Luke 3:16; see Matt. 3:11). This *fire* is a manifestation of the uncreated energy of God. (Because God is outside the bounds

(continued on page 275)

CHRISMATION

From earliest times the church has practiced chrismation immediately following baptism. In the sacrament of chrismation (Gr. *chrismatis,* "anointing") the newly baptized person receives the Holy Spirit through anointing with oil by the bishop or priest. The roots of this sacrament are clear in both the Old and New Testaments, and are especially brought to light on the Day of Pentecost.

Promises of the Holy Spirit from the Old Testament. In his sermon on Pentecost, St. Peter quotes the well-known prophecy of Joel, "I will pour out my Spirit on all flesh" (Acts 2:17; see Joel 2:28). This promise was significant because under the Old Covenant, the gift of the Spirit had been given only to a few—the patriarchs, the prophets, and some of the judges. Certain leaders of Israel were indwelt with the Holy Spirit to accomplish their tasks. Joel, however, prophesied that the Holy Spirit would be given to all God's people, "all flesh." This was fulfilled at Pentecost, for Peter exclaims, "this [outpouring of the Spirit] is what was spoken by the prophet Joel" (Acts 2:16).

Other Old Testament prophets who speak of this same promise of the Spirit include Jeremiah (Jer. 31:31–34) and Ezekiel (Ezek. 36:25–27). In fact, the Ezekiel passage ties together the water and the Spirit in a prophetic vision of baptism and chrismation.

Jesus promises the Holy Spirit. Our Lord Jesus Christ repeatedly promised the gift of the Holy Spirit to His disciples. Early in His public ministry He said, " 'If anyone thirsts, let him come to Me and drink. He who believes in Me, as the Scripture has said, out of his heart will flow rivers of living water.' But this He spoke concerning the Spirit . . . " (John 7:37–39). Jesus also said, "I will pray the Father, and He will give you another Helper, that He may abide with you forever" (John 14:16).

Christ promised the Holy Spirit would reveal truth to the Church. "When He, the Spirit of truth, has come, He will guide you into all truth; for He will not speak on His own authority, but whatever He hears He will speak; and He will tell you things to come. He will glorify Me, for He will take of what is Mine and declare it to you" (John 16:13, 14). Jesus says the Holy Spirit will bring glory to Christ. This gives us an excellent means of testing whether or not acts attributed to the Holy Spirit are indeed valid.

The last words of Christ before His Ascension include a promise: "John truly baptized with water, but you shall be baptized with the Holy Spirit not many days from now" (Acts 1:5). This word was fulfilled ten days later on the Day of Pentecost.

How is the Holy Spirit given to us? The people who heard Peter speak at Pentecost asked him how they might receive salvation. He answered, "Repent, and let every one of you be baptized in the name of Jesus Christ for the remission of sins; and you shall receive the gift of the Holy Spirit" (Acts 2:38). We repent (turn from our sins and toward Christ); we are baptized; we are given "the gift of the Holy Spirit," chrismation. That practice has never changed.

In Acts 8, Philip, the deacon and evangelist, preached in Samaria (Acts 8:5–8). Many believed and were baptized (Acts 8:12). The apostles came and later confirmed these new believers with the gift of the Holy Spirit through the laying on of hands (Acts 8:14–17). Here is the sacrament of chrismation following Holy Baptism. Later, the Apostle Paul met some disciples of John the Baptist who had not been present when Peter spoke at Pentecost (Acts 19:1–7). They believed in Christ, "were baptized" (Acts 19:5) and "the Holy Spirit came upon them" (Acts 19:6), again through the hands of an apostle.

The promise of God includes both our union with Christ in Holy Baptism and the gift of the Holy Spirit at chrismation.

Pentecost (Trinity Sunday)—The Descent of the Holy Spirit on the Disciples

Seventh Sunday after Easter

2:1–11: The disciples receive the Holy Spirit and speak in many languages.

4 And [a]they were all filled with
the Holy Spirit and began [b]to speak
with other tongues, as the Spirit gave
them utterance.†

Witness to the World

5 And there were dwelling in Jerusalem Jews, [a]devout men, from
every nation under heaven.
6 And when this sound occurred,
the [a]multitude came together, and
were confused, because everyone
heard them speak in his own
language.
7 Then they were all amazed and
marveled, saying to one another,
"Look, are not all these who speak
[a]Galileans?
8 "And how *is it that* we hear,
each in our own [1]language in which
we were born?
9 "Parthians and Medes and
Elamites, those dwelling in Mesopotamia, Judea and [a]Cappadocia, Pontus and Asia,†
10 "Phrygia and Pamphylia, Egypt
and the parts of Libya adjoining Cyrene, visitors from Rome, both Jews
and proselytes,
11 "Cretans and [1]Arabs—we hear
them speaking in our own tongues
the wonderful works of God."
12 So they were all amazed and
perplexed, saying to one another,
"Whatever could this mean?"
13 Others mocking said, "They are
full of new wine."

Witness to the Jews: Peter's Sermon

14 But Peter, standing up with the
eleven, raised his voice and said to
them, "Men of Judea and all who
dwell in Jerusalem, let this be known
to you, and heed my words.†
15 "For these are not drunk, as you
suppose, [a]since it is *only* [1]the third
hour of the day.

The Holy Spirit Has Come

16 "But this is what was spoken by
the prophet Joel:†

17 *'And[a] it shall come to pass in the*
last days, says God,
[b]That I will pour out of My Spirit
on all flesh;

4 [a]Acts 1:5 [b]Mark 16:17
5 [a]Acts 8:2
6 [a]Acts 4:32
7 [a]Acts 1:11
8 [1]*dialect*
9 [a]1 Pet. 1:1
11 [1]*Arabians*
15 [a]1 Thess. 5:7
[1]9 A.M.
17 [a]Joel 2:28–32 [b]Acts 10:45

(continued from page 273)
of all that is created, He and all that comes from His uncreated nature, including His power or energy, are called uncreated.) Pentecost so transcends man's understanding that human language cannot describe this experience, but only point to it.

2:4–8 This is a fulfillment of the prophecy of Joel (Joel 2:28, 29) concerning the Holy Spirit. The words spoken by the Apostles are in the actual languages of people from all over the empire who have come to Jerusalem for the feast. They hear the Good News and praises of God in their respective languages from people who do not know those languages.

2:9–11 The people and places mentioned here are important, for many of these locations will soon become the sites of new churches recorded later in Acts.

2:14–40 Peter's sermon focuses on two prophetic themes: (1) the promised coming of the Holy Spirit, and (2) the Resurrection of Christ from the dead. This pattern of showing OT prophecy fulfilled in Christ is a major theme of apostolic preaching, leading to repentance, baptism for the remission of sins, and the receiving of the Holy Spirit (vv. 38, 39).

2:16–21 Joel was one of the early prophets (ninth century B.C.) who proclaimed God's sovereign lordship and judgment in the last days. On Pentecost the first part of this prophecy is fulfilled in the outpouring of God's Spirit. The second part will be fulfilled with the Second Coming of Christ.

Your sons and [c]your daughters
shall prophesy,
Your young men shall see
visions,
Your old men shall dream
dreams.
18 *And on My menservants and on*
My maidservants
I will pour out My Spirit in those
days;
[a]*And they shall prophesy.*
19 [a]*I will show wonders in heaven*
above
And signs in the earth beneath:
Blood and fire and vapor of
smoke.
20 [a]*The sun shall be turned into*
darkness,
And the moon into blood,
Before the coming of the great
and awesome day of the
LORD.
21 *And it shall come to pass*
That [a]*whoever calls on the name*
of the LORD
Shall be saved.'

Jesus Is the Messiah

22 "Men of Israel, hear these
words: Jesus of Nazareth, a Man attested by God to you [a]by miracles,
wonders, and signs which God did
through Him in your midst, as you
yourselves also know—
23 "Him, [a]being delivered by the
determined purpose and foreknowledge of God, [b]you [1]have taken by
lawless hands, have crucified, and
put to death;
24 [a]"whom God raised up, having
[1]loosed the [2]pains of death, because
it was not possible that He should
be held by it.
25 "For David says concerning
Him:

[a]*'I foresaw the LORD always*
before my face,
For He is at my right hand, that
I may not be shaken.†
26 *Therefore my heart rejoiced,*
and my tongue was glad;
Moreover my flesh also will rest
in hope.
27 *For You will not leave my soul*
in Hades,
Nor will You allow Your Holy
One to see [a]*corruption.*
28 *You have made known to me*
the ways of life;
You will make me full of joy in
Your presence.'

29 "Men *and* brethren, let *me* speak
freely to you [a]of the patriarch David,
that he is both dead and buried, and
his tomb is with us to this day.
30 "Therefore, being a prophet,
[a]and knowing that God had sworn
with an oath to him that of the fruit
of his body, [1]according to the flesh,
He would raise up the Christ to sit
on his throne,
31 "he, foreseeing this, spoke concerning the resurrection of the
Christ, [a]that His soul was not left
in Hades, nor did His flesh see
corruption.
32 [a]"This Jesus God has raised up,
[b]of which we are all witnesses.
33 "Therefore [a]being exalted
[1]to [b]the right hand of God, and
[c]having received from the Father the
promise of the Holy Spirit, He
[d]poured out this which you now see
and hear.†
34 "For David did not ascend into
the heavens, but he says himself:

[a]*'The LORD said to my Lord,*
"Sit at My right hand,
35 *Till I make Your enemies Your*
footstool."'

36 "Therefore let all the house of
Israel know assuredly that God has
made this Jesus, whom you crucified, both Lord and Christ."†

17 [c]Acts 21:9 **18** [a]1 Cor. 12:10 **19** [a]Joel 2:30 **20** [a]Matt. 24:29 **21** [a]Rom. 10:13 **22** [a]John 3:2; 5:6 **23** [a]Luke 22:22 [b]Acts 5:30 [1]NU omits *have taken* **24** [a][Rom. 8:11] [1]*destroyed* or *abolished* [2]Lit. *birth pangs* **25** [a]Ps. 16:8–11

27 [a]Acts 13:30–37 **29** [a]Acts 13:36 **30** [a]Ps. 132:11 [1]NU *He would seat one on his throne,* **31** [a]Ps. 16:10 **32** [a]Acts 2:24 [b]Acts 1:8; 3:15 **33** [a][Acts 5:31] [b][Heb. 10:12] [c][John 14:26] [d]Acts 2:1–11, 17; 10:45 [1]Possibly *by* **34** [a]Ps. 68:18; 110:1

2:25–32 A prophetic psalm of David is here applied to the incorruptible death and Resurrection of Christ.

2:33 The age of the Kingdom of the trinitarian God begins with the Ascension of Christ into the heavens, His enthronement at the **right hand of God** the Father, and the outpouring of the Holy Spirit.

2:36 The verb **made** refers to Christ's Incarnation and glorification, not to His eternal existence as Lord and God. As God's Only Begotten Son, Jesus is uncreated.

What Shall We Do?

37 Now when they heard *this*,
[a]they were cut to the heart, and said
to Peter and the rest of the apostles,
"Men *and* brethren, what shall we
do?"†
38 Then Peter said to them, [a]"Repent, and let every one of you be baptized in the name of Jesus Christ for
the [1]remission of sins; and you shall
receive the gift of the Holy Spirit.†
39 "For the promise is to you and
[a]to your children, and [b]to all who
are afar off, as many as the Lord our
God will call."

The First Converts Baptized

40 And with many other words he
testified and exhorted them, saying,
"Be saved from this [1]perverse
generation."
41 Then those who [1]gladly received his word were baptized; and
that day about three thousand souls
were added *to them.*

The Life of the First Church

42 [a]And they continued steadfastly
in the apostles' [1]doctrine and fellowship, in the breaking of bread, and
in prayers.†
43 Then fear came upon every
soul, and [a]many wonders and signs
were done through the apostles.
44 Now all who believed were together, and [a]had all things in
common,†
45 and [1]sold their possessions and
goods, and [a]divided[2] them among
all, as anyone had need.
46 [a]So continuing daily with one
accord [b]in the temple, and [c]breaking
bread from house to house, they ate
their food with gladness and simplicity of heart,
47 praising God and having favor
with all the people. And [a]the Lord
added [1]to the church daily those who
were being saved.

Evangelism: A Lame Man Is Healed

3 Now Peter and John went up together [a]to the temple at the hour
of prayer, [b]the ninth *hour*.†
2 And [a]a certain man lame from
his mother's womb was carried,
whom they laid daily at the gate of
the temple which is called Beautiful,
[b]to [1]ask alms from those who entered the temple;

37 [a]Luke 3:10, 12, 14
38 [a]Luke 24:47 [1]*forgiveness*
39 [a]Joel 2:28, 32 [b]Eph. 2:13
40 [1]*crooked*
41 [1]NU omits *gladly*
42 [a]Acts 1:14 [1]*teaching*
43 [a]Acts 2:22
44 [a]Acts 4:32, 34, 37; 5:2
45 [a]Is. 58:7 [1]*would sell* [2]*distributed*
46 [a]Acts 1:14 [b]Luke 24:53 [c]Acts 2:42; 20:7
47 [a]Acts 5:14 [1]NU omits *to the church*

CHAPTER 3

1 [a]Acts 2:46 [b]Ps. 55:17
2 [a]Acts 14:8 [b]John 9:8 [1]Beg

2:37 Peter's listeners are **cut to the heart** because they understand what he is saying. Almost half of Peter's message is the quotation of OT Scriptures promising the Messiah. The evidence that Jesus Christ is Lord is overwhelming to them.

2:38, 39 Peter's call to respond to the gospel requires specific actions which define Christian life within the Church. We must: (1) **repent,** (2) **be baptized,** and (3) **receive the gift of the Holy Spirit.** To this day, people come to Christ in precisely this same manner in the baptismal service of the Orthodox Church. They (1) repent, renouncing the devil; (2) are baptized by immersion in water for the remission of sins; and (3) are chrismated (anointed) for the receiving of the Holy Spirit. This sacramental action inaugurates our new life in Christ (Rom. 8:9; 1 Cor. 6:17; 12:13; Gal. 4:6, 7; Phil. 1:6; 1 John 3:2).

2:42 Central elements of Orthodox worship—apostolic teaching, liturgical prayer and the Eucharist—are present from the very beginning of the Church. **Prayers** is literally "the prayers" in Greek, referring to specific liturgical prayers. The Jews had practiced liturgical prayer for centuries; many of their prayers are contained in the Book of Psalms. The early Christians adapted these prayers for use in the Church. The **breaking of bread** is, of course, the Eucharist, Holy Communion.

2:44–47 The earliest days of the church of Jerusalem were filled with love, unity, and joy in which Christians shared **all things in common.** Communal life was practiced because it was necessary to care for all of the new converts who were away from their homes. It is still appropriate in times of need, though surely not necessary at all times. We should, however, always regard all of our possessions as belonging to God.

3:1 At the hour of prayer, the ninth hour, indicates the Apostles were observing regular hours of prayer, such as the Jews had observed for centuries (see Ps. 55:17; Dan. 6:10). The

(continued on next page)

3 who, seeing Peter and John
about to go into the temple, asked
for alms.
4 And fixing his eyes on him, with
John, Peter said, "Look at us."
5 So he gave them his attention,
expecting to receive something from
them.
6 Then Peter said, "Silver and
gold I do not have, but what I do
have I give you: [a]In the name of
Jesus Christ of Nazareth, rise up and
walk."
7 And he took him by the right
hand and lifted *him* up, and immediately his feet and ankle bones received strength.
8 So he, [a]leaping up, stood and
walked and entered the temple with
them—walking, leaping, and praising God.
9 [a]And all the people saw him
walking and praising God.
10 Then they knew that it was he
who [a]sat begging alms at the Beautiful Gate of the temple; and they
were filled with wonder and
amazement at what had happened
to him.

Peter's Sermon at Solomon's Porch

11 Now as the lame man who was
healed held on to Peter and John,
all the people ran together to them
in the porch [a]which is called Solomon's, greatly amazed.†
12 So when Peter saw *it*, he responded to the people: "Men of Israel, why do you marvel at this? Or
why look so intently at us, as though
by our own power or godliness we
had made this man walk?†
13 [a]"The God of Abraham, Isaac,
and Jacob, the God of our fathers,
[b]glorified His Servant Jesus, whom
you [c]delivered up and [d]denied in the
presence of Pilate, when he was determined to let *Him* go.
14 "But you denied [a]the Holy One
[b]and the Just, and [c]asked for a murderer to be granted to you,
15 "and killed the [1]Prince of life,
[a]whom God raised from the dead,
[b]of which we are witnesses.
16 [a]"And His name, through faith
in His name, has made this man
strong, whom you see and know.
Yes, the faith which *comes* through
Him has given him this perfect
soundness in the presence of you
all.
17 "Yet now, brethren, I know that
[a]you did *it* in ignorance, as *did* also
your rulers.
18 "But [a]those things which God
foretold [b]by the mouth of all His
prophets, that the Christ would suffer, He has thus fulfilled.
19 [a]"Repent therefore and be converted, that your sins may be blotted

6 [a]Acts 4:10
8 [a]Is. 35:6
9 [a]Acts 4:16, 21
10 [a]John 9:8
11 [a]John 10:23
13 [a]John 5:30 [b]John 7:39; 12:23; 13:31 [c]Matt. 27:2 [d]Matt. 27:20
14 [a]Mark 1:24 [b]Acts 7:52 [c]John 18:40
15 [a]Acts 2:24 [b]Acts 2:32 [1]Or *Originator*
16 [a]Matt. 9:22
17 [a]Luke 23:34
18 [a]Acts 26:22 [b]1 Pet. 1:10
19 [a][Acts 2:38; 26:20]

(continued from previous page)
practice of praying at the first (6:00 A.M.), third (9:00 A.M.), sixth (12:00 noon) and ninth (3:00 P.M.) hours of the day was carried over into the Church from the start. It continues today in Orthodox monasteries and in many Orthodox parishes, especially during Advent and Lent (see also 10:3, 9, 30).

3:1–10 The Apostles are empowered not only to preach and teach, but also to continue Christ's healing ministry—a sacrament of the church—as an authentication of the gospel.

3:11 Solomon's porch is in the temple area.

3:12–26 Peter's homily is both brief and full. He explains:

(1) The identity of Jesus, by whose **power** the lame man was healed: He is God's Suffering **Servant** (v. 13), the **Holy One** (v. 14) of God, **the Prince of life** (v. 15), the Christ foretold by the prophets (v. 18).

(2) Jesus' rejection by the Jews: The religious leaders had Him **killed** (v. 15), but God brought Him back to life, and the Apostles are **witnesses** to that Resurrection (v. 15).

(3) What that rejection means: It shows profound ignorance of God's saving activity as prophesied by Scripture (vv. 18–20).

(4) What people need to do: **repent** (v. 19) and convert (experience a thorough change of heart and mind), which is essential for participation in the Kingdom (v. 19).

(5) The results of conversion: forgiveness of sins, renewal, and confident expectation of the Second Coming of Christ (vv. 19–26).

out, so that times of refreshing may
come from the presence of the Lord,†
20 "and that He may send [1]Jesus
Christ, who was [2]preached to you
before,
21 [a]"whom heaven must receive
until the times of [b]restoration of all
things, [c]which God has spoken by
the mouth of all His holy prophets
since [1]the world began.
22 "For Moses truly said to the fathers, [a]*'The* LORD *your God will raise
up for you a Prophet like me from
your brethren. Him you shall hear
in all things, whatever He says to
you.*
23 *'And it shall be that every soul
who will not hear that Prophet shall
be utterly destroyed from among the
people.'*
24 "Yes, and [a]all the prophets,
from Samuel and those who follow,
as many as have spoken, have also
[1]foretold these days.
25 [a]"You are sons of the prophets,
and of the covenant which God
made with our fathers, saying to
Abraham, [b]*'And in your seed all
the families of the earth shall be
blessed.'*
26 "To you [a]first, God, having
raised up His Servant Jesus, sent
Him to bless you, [b]in turning away
every one *of you* from your iniquities."†

Peter and John Arrested

4 Now as they spoke to the people, the priests, the captain of
the temple, and the [a]Saddducees
came upon them,†
2 being greatly disturbed that
they taught the people and preached

20 [1]NU, M *Christ Jesus* [2]NU, M *ordained for you before*
21 [a]Acts 1:11 [b]Matt. 17:11; [Rom. 8:21] [c]Luke 1:70 [1]Or *time*
22 [a]Deut. 18:15, 18, 19; Acts 7:37
24 [a]2 Sam. 7:12; Luke 24:25 [1]NU, M *proclaimed*
25 [a]Acts 2:39; [Rom. 9:4, 8; Gal. 3:26] [b]Gen. 12:3; 18:18; 22:18; 26:4; 28:14
26 [a]Matt. 15:24; John 4:22; Acts 13:46; [Rom. 1:16; 2:9] [b]Is. 42:1; Matt. 1:21

CHAPTER 4

1 [a]Matt. 22:23
6 [a]Luke 3:2; John 11:49; 18:13
7 [a]Ex. 2:14; Matt. 21:23; Acts 7:27
8 [a]Luke 12:11, 12
10 [a]Acts 2:22; 3:6, 16 [b]Acts 2:24
11 [a]Ps. 118:22; Is. 28:16; Matt. 21:42
12 [a]Is. 42:1, 6, 7; 53:11; Dan. 9:24; [Matt. 1:21; John 14:6; Acts 10:43; 1 Tim. 2:5, 6]

in Jesus the resurrection from the
dead.
3 And they laid hands on them,
and put *them* in custody until the
next day, for it was already evening.
4 However, many of those who
heard the word believed; and the
number of the men came to be about
five thousand.

Before the Sanhedrin

5 And it came to pass, on the next
day, that their rulers, elders, and
scribes,
6 as well as [a]Annas the high
priest, Caiaphas, John, and Alexander, and as many as were of the family of the high priest, were gathered
together at Jerusalem.
7 And when they had set them
in the midst, they asked, [a]"By what
power or by what name have you
done this?"
8 [a]Then Peter, filled with the
Holy Spirit, said to them, "Rulers of
the people and elders of Israel:
9 "If we this day are judged for
a good deed *done* to a helpless man,
by what means he has been made
well,
10 "let it be known to you all, and
to all the people of Israel, [a]that by
the name of Jesus Christ of Nazareth, whom you crucified, [b]whom
God raised from the dead, by
Him this man stands here before
you whole.
11 "This is the [a]*'stone which was
rejected by you builders, which has
become the chief cornerstone.'*
12 [a]"Nor is there salvation in any
other, for there is no other name

3:19 On the Day of Pentecost, Peter preached that the outcome of repentance is receiving the Holy Spirit (2:38). Here, he says the outcome is that **times of refreshing may come from the presence of the Lord.** This second outcome illuminates the first. Receiving the Holy Spirit brings refreshing renewal from the Lord—the presence of the Lord in the eucharistic assembly.

3:26 Repentance always brings blessing from the Lord. Some fear **turning away** from sin makes life hard to bear. On the contrary, through repentance mere existence is transformed into an abundant life of faith, love, and joy.

4:1, 2 The **Sadducees** were the Jewish leaders who controlled the temple and its worship. They taught that there is no **resurrection.** False religious convictions prevent them from believing the Good News, that **Jesus** (v. 2) was raised **from the dead.**

under heaven given among men by
which we must be saved."†
13 Now when they saw the boldness of Peter and John, [a]and perceived that they were uneducated
and untrained men, they marveled.
And they realized that they had been
with Jesus.†
14 And seeing the man who had
been healed [a]standing with them,
they could say nothing against it.
15 But when they had commanded
them to go aside out of the council,
they conferred among themselves,
16 saying, [a]"What shall we do to
these men? For, indeed, that a
[1]notable miracle has been done
through them *is* [b]evident[2] to all who
dwell in Jerusalem, and we cannot
deny *it*.†
17 "But so that it spreads no further among the people, let us severely threaten them, that from now
on they speak to no man in this
name."
18 [a]So they called them and commanded them not to speak at all nor
teach in the name of Jesus.
19 But Peter and John answered
and said to them, [a]"Whether it is
right in the sight of God to listen to
you more than to God, you judge.†
20 [a]"For we cannot but speak the
things which [b]we have seen and
heard."
21 So when they had further
threatened them, they let them go,
finding no way of punishing them,
[a]because of the people, since they
all [b]glorified God for [c]what had been
done.
22 For the man was over forty
years old on whom this miracle of
healing had been performed.

Prayer and Power

23 And being let go, [a]they went to
their own *companions* and reported
all that the chief priests and elders
had said to them.
24 So when they heard that, they
raised their voice to God with one
accord and said: "Lord, [a]You *are*
God, who made heaven and earth
and the sea, and all that is in them,†
25 "who [1]by the mouth of Your
servant David have said:

[a]'*Why did the nations rage,*
And the people plot vain
things?
26 *The kings of the earth took their*
stand,
And the rulers were gathered
together
Against the LORD *and against*
His Christ.'

27 "For [a]truly against [b]Your holy
Servant Jesus, [c]whom You anointed,
both Herod and Pontius Pilate, with
the Gentiles and the people of Israel,
were gathered together†
28 [a]"to do whatever Your hand
and Your purpose determined before
to be done.

13 [a]Matt. 11:25; [1 Cor. 1:27]
14 [a]Acts 3:11
16 [a]John 11:47 [b]Acts 3:7–10 [1]*remarkable sign* [2]*well known*
18 [a]Acts 5:28, 40
19 [a]Acts 5:29
20 [a]Acts 1:8; 2:32 [b]Acts 22:15; [1 John 1:1, 3]
21 [a]Matt. 21:26; Luke 20:6, 19; 22:2; Acts 5:26 [b]Matt. 15:31 [c]Acts 3:7, 8
23 [a]Acts 2:44–46; 12:12
24 [a]Ex. 20:11; 2 Kin. 19:15; Neh. 9:6; Ps. 146:6
25 [a]Ps. 2:1, 2 [1]NU *through the Holy Spirit, by the mouth of our father, Your servant David,*
27 [a]Matt. 26:3; Luke 22:2; 23:1, 8 [b][Luke 1:35] [c]Luke 4:18; John 10:36
28 [a]Acts 2:23; 3:18

4:12 The response of the Apostles to the questions of the Jewish Council (vv. 7–11) is unequivocal: Salvation is in the **name** of Christ alone.

4:13 The Apostles' lack of education and training stands in contrast to the theological expertise of the Sanhedrin. The work of the Holy Spirit is not limited by lack of education.

4:16 It is apparent to the Council that a **notable miracle** has been performed, but it makes little impression on them. As in their response to the miracles of Jesus, their hardness of heart prevents them from believing the obvious.

4:19, 20 The Apostles were totally committed to obeying God rather than the Jewish Council. Peter and John make it clear: Obedience to God is of higher value than obedience to public authorities. They were thoroughly willing to pay the price for this choice, even to accept martyrdom.

4:24–30 This prayer is not spontaneous, but likely an established liturgical prayer. This explains how the people are able to pray the same words simultaneously, **with one accord.** Notice they did not pray for deliverance from danger, but for **boldness** (v. 29) in the face of it.

4:27, 28 The Lord God is master over all, even over evil. What all these diverse people did to Jesus was foreseen by God and used for His redemptive purposes.

29 "Now, Lord, look on their
threats, and grant to Your servants
[a]that with all boldness they may
speak Your word,
30 "by stretching out Your hand to
heal, [a]and that signs and wonders
may be done [b]through the name of
[c]Your holy Servant Jesus."
31 And when they had prayed,
[a]the place where they were assembled together was shaken; and they
were all filled with the Holy Spirit,
[b]and they spoke the word of God
with boldness.†

Giving for the Common Good

32 Now the multitude of those who
believed [a]were of one heart and one
soul; [b]neither did anyone say that
any of the things he possessed was
his own, but they had all things in
common.†
33 And with [a]great power the
apostles gave [b]witness to the resurrection of the Lord Jesus. And
[c]great grace was upon them all.
34 Nor was there anyone among
them who lacked; [a]for all who were
possessors of lands or houses sold
them, and brought the proceeds of
the things that were sold,
35 [a]and laid *them* at the apostles'
feet; [b]and they distributed to each
as anyone had need.
36 And [1]Joses, who was also
named Barnabas by the apostles
(which is translated Son of [2]En-
couragement), a Levite of the country of Cyprus,
37 [a]having land, sold *it*, and
brought the money and laid *it* at the
apostles' feet.

Ananias and Sapphira

5 But a certain man named Ananias, with Sapphira his wife,
sold a possession.†
2 And he kept back *part* of the
proceeds, his wife also being aware
of it, and brought a certain part and
laid *it* at the apostles' feet.
3 [a]But Peter said, "Ananias, why
has [b]Satan filled your heart to lie to
the Holy Spirit and keep back *part*
of the price of the land for yourself?
4 "While it remained, was it not
your own? And after it was sold, was
it not in your own control? Why have
you conceived this thing in your
heart? You have not lied to men but
to God."
5 Then Ananias, hearing these
words, [a]fell down and breathed his
last. So great fear came upon all
those who heard these things.
6 And the young men arose and
[a]wrapped him up, carried *him* out,
and buried *him*.
7 Now it was about three hours
later when his wife came in, not
knowing what had happened.
8 And Peter answered her, "Tell
me whether you sold the land for
so much?" She said, "Yes, for so
much."
9 Then Peter said to her, "How
is it that you have agreed together
[a]to test the Spirit of the Lord? Look,
the feet of those who have buried

29 [a]Acts 4:13, 31; 9:27; 13:46; 14:3; 19:8; 26:26; Eph. 6:19
30 [a]Acts 2:43; 5:12 [b]Acts 3:6, 16 [c]Acts 4:27
31 [a]Matt. 5:6; Acts 2:2, 4; 16:26 [b]Acts 4:29
32 [a]Acts 5:12; Rom. 15:5, 6; 2 Cor. 13:11; Phil. 1:27; 2:2; 1 Pet. 3:8 [b]Acts 2:44
33 [a][Acts 1:8] [b]Acts 1:22 [c]Rom. 6:15
34 [a][Matt. 19:21]; Acts 2:45
35 [a]Acts 4:37; 5:2 [b]Acts 2:45; 6:1
36 [1]NU *Joseph* [2]Or *Consolation*
37 [a]Acts 4:34, 35; 5:1, 2

CHAPTER 5

3 [a]Num. 30:2; Deut. 23:21; Eccl. 5:4 [b]Matt. 4:10; Luke 22:3; John 13:2, 27
5 [a]Ezek. 11:13; Acts 5:10, 11
6 [a]John 19:40
9 [a]Matt. 4:7; Acts 5:3, 4

4:31 Although the Holy Spirit abides in the Church as a permanent gift, His presence is experienced again and again in the liturgical assemblies of the Church as recurring pentecostal outpourings. He gives both **boldness** and confidence to the Church.

4:32–37 The spiritual life of the early days of the church of Jerusalem continues (see note on 2:44–47). The precedent set here for the Church is not that of communal living *per se*, but of the willingness to do what is necessary for the good of the community. **Barnabas** is highlighted as an example of Christian sharing, and is destined to play a leading role in the church of Antioch.

5:1–4 **Ananias** and **Sapphira** are accountable for allowing Satan to fill their hearts and to break the trust and integrity of the early Church. They were not helpless in the face of temptation, nor are we. And though they **lied to men,** namely Peter and the other Apostles, this is a lie to the Holy Spirit, who reigns in the love and voluntary sharing of the Church. They have not been forced to sell their possessions, nor to give everything to the Church. Their sin is in lying to God, and causing mistrust in the communal life of holiness and purity in the Spirit.

Thomas Sunday *Sunday after Easter (Second Sunday of Pascha)*

5:12–20: Miraculous signs accompany the early work of the disciples.

your husband *are* at the door, and
they will carry you out."
10 [a]Then immediately she fell
down at his feet and breathed her
last. And the young men came
in and found her dead, and carrying *her* out, buried *her* by her husband.
11 [a]So great fear came upon all the
church and upon all who heard these
things.

Evangelism in the Spirit

12 And [a]through the hands of the
apostles many signs and wonders
were done among the people.
[b]And they were all with one accord
in Solomon's Porch.†
13 Yet [a]none of the rest dared join
them, [b]but the people esteemed
them highly.
14 And believers were increasingly
added to the Lord, multitudes of
both men and women,
15 so that they brought the sick out
into the streets and laid *them* on beds
and couches, [a]that at least the
shadow of Peter passing by might
fall on some of them.
16 Also a multitude gathered from
the surrounding cities to Jerusalem,
bringing [a]sick people and those who
were tormented by unclean spirits,
and they were all healed.

The Apostles Arrested

17 [a]Then the high priest rose up,
and all those who *were* with him
(which is the sect of the Sadducees),
and they were filled with [1]indig-
nation,
18 [a]and laid their hands on the
apostles and put them in the common prison.
19 But at night [a]an angel of the
Lord opened the prison doors and
brought them out, and said,
20 "Go, stand in the temple and
speak to the people [a]all the words
of this life."
21 And when they heard *that*, they
entered the temple early in the
morning and taught. [a]But the high
priest and those with him came and
called the [1]council together, with all
the [2]elders of the children of Israel,
and sent to the prison to have them
brought.
22 But when the officers came and
did not find them in the prison, they
returned and reported,
23 saying, "Indeed we found the
prison shut securely, and the guards
standing [1]outside before the doors;
but when we opened them, we
found no one inside!"
24 Now when [1]the high priest,
[a]the captain of the temple, and the
chief priests heard these things, they
wondered what the outcome would
be.
25 So one came and told them,
[1]saying, "Look, the men whom you
put in prison are standing in the temple and teaching the people!"
26 Then the captain went with the
officers and brought them without
violence, [a]for they feared the people,
lest they should be stoned.†
27 And when they had brought
them, they set *them* before the council. And the high priest asked them,

10 [a]Ezek. 11:13; Acts 5:5
11 [a]Acts 2:43; 5:5; 19:17
12 [a]Acts 2:43; 4:30; 6:8; 14:3; 15:12; [Rom. 15:19]; 2 Cor. 12:12; Heb. 2:4 [b]Acts 3:11; 4:32
13 [a]John 9:22 [b]Acts 2:47; 4:21
15 [a]Matt. 9:21; 14:36; Acts 19:12
16 [a]Mark 16:17, 18; [John 14:12]
17 [a]Matt. 3:7; Acts 4:1, 2, 6 [1]*jealousy*
18 [a]Luke 21:12; Acts 4:3; 16:37
19 [a]Matt. 1:20, 24; 2:13, 19; 28:2; Luke 1:11; 2:9; Acts 12:7; 16:26
20 [a][John 6:63, 68; 17:3; 1 John 5:11]
21 [a]Acts 4:5, 6 [1]Sanhedrin [2]*council of elders* or *senate*
23 [1]NU, M omit *outside*
24 [a]Luke 22:4; Acts 4:1; 5:26 [1]NU omits *the high priest*
25 [1]NU, M omit *saying*
26 [a]Matt. 21:26

5:12–21 This passage reminds us that life in the infant Church was characterized by (1) unity, (2) the power of God, and (3) persecution.

5:26 In the early days of the Church, as in the ministry of Jesus, the primary opponents of the Christian movement are the Jewish leaders.

28 saying, [a]"Did we not strictly
command you not to teach in this
name? And look, you have filled Jerusalem with your doctrine, [b]and intend to bring this Man's [c]blood on
us!"†
29 But Peter and the *other* apostles
answered and said: [a]"We ought to
obey God rather than men.
30 [a]"The God of our fathers raised
up Jesus whom you murdered by
[b]hanging on a tree.
31 [a]"Him God has exalted to His
right hand *to be* [b]Prince and [c]Savior,
[d]to give repentance to Israel and forgiveness of sins.
32 "And [a]we are His witnesses to
these things, and *so* also *is* the Holy
Spirit [b]whom God has given to those
who obey Him."†
33 When they heard *this,* they were
[a]furious[1] and plotted to kill them.
34 Then one in the council stood
up, a Pharisee named [a]Gamaliel, a
teacher of the law held in respect by
all the people, and commanded them
to put the apostles outside for a little
while.†
35 And he said to them: "Men of
Israel, [1]take heed to yourselves what
you intend to do regarding these
men.
36 "For some time ago Theudas
rose up, claiming to be somebody.
A number of men, about four hundred, [1]joined him. He was slain, and
all who obeyed him were scattered
and came to nothing.†
37 "After this man, Judas of Galilee
rose up in the days of the census,
and drew away many people after

28 [a]Acts 4:17, 18 [b]Acts 2:23, 36 [c]Matt. 23:35
29 [a]Acts 4:19
30 [a]Acts 3:13, 15 [b][1 Pet. 2:24]
31 [a][Acts 2:33, 36] [b]Acts 3:15 [c]Matt. 1:21 [d]Luke 24:47
32 [a]John 15:26, 27 [b]Acts 2:4; 10:44
33 [a]Acts 2:37; 7:54 [1]*cut to the quick*
34 [a]Acts 22:3
35 [1]*be careful*
36 [1]*followed*
39 [a]1 Cor. 1:25 [b]Acts 7:51; 9:5
40 [a]Acts 4:18 [b]Matt. 10:17
41 [a][1 Pet. 4:13–16] [1]NU *the name;* M *the name of Jesus*
42 [a]Acts 2:46 [b]Acts 4:20, 29

CHAPTER 6

1 [a]Acts 2:41; 4:4 [b]Acts 9:29; 11:20 [c]Acts 4:35; 11:29 [1]Greek-speaking Jews

him. He also perished, and all who
obeyed him were dispersed.
38 "And now I say to you, keep
away from these men and let them
alone; for if this plan or this work
is of men, it will come to nothing;
39 [a]"but if it is of God, you cannot
overthrow it—lest you even be found
[b]to fight against God."
40 And they agreed with him, and
when they had [a]called for the apostles [b]and beaten *them,* they commanded that they should not speak
in the name of Jesus, and let them
go.

Apostolic Evangelism

41 So they departed from the presence of the council, [a]rejoicing that
they were counted worthy to suffer
shame for [1]His name.†
42 And daily [a]in the temple, and
in every house, [b]they did not cease
teaching and preaching Jesus *as* the
Christ.

Deacons Ordained

6 Now in those days, [a]when *the
number of* the disciples was multiplying, there arose a complaint
against the Hebrews by the [b]Hellen-
ists,[1] because their widows were
neglected [c]in the daily distribution.†
2 Then the twelve summoned the
multitude of the disciples and said,

5:28 Miracles did not necessarily soften hard hearts in Jesus' ministry; this is true also in the case of the Apostles.

5:32 How do Christ's disciples find the strength to serve Him? **The Holy Spirit** is given by God **to those who obey Him.**

5:34–39 Gamaliel was a famous rabbi under whom Paul studied (22:3).

5:36, 37 Theudas and **Judas of Galilee** were two of many who made false messianic claims. They raised the sword of rebellion against Rome and were crushed, as reported by the contemporary Jewish historian Josephus.

5:41 The Apostles do not regard suffering as something to be avoided at all costs, or as evidence of a lack of faith.

6:1 The Hebrews: Jewish Christians of the Jerusalem area who spoke Aramaic, the contemporary language of the Jews. **Hellenists:** Greek-speaking Jewish Christians from other places of the Hellenized world who had moved to the Holy City. They complain that **their widows were neglected** in the program of **daily distribution** of food by the Apostles as practiced by the early Jerusalem church.

Sunday of the Myrrhbearing Women, Joseph of Arimathea and Nicodemus *Second Sunday after Easter (Third Sunday of Pascha)*

6:1–7: Seven deacons are chosen, continuing the tradition of faithful service begun by the myrrhbearing women.

[a]"It is not desirable that we should
leave the word of God and serve
tables.†
3 "Therefore, brethren, [a]seek out
from among you seven men of *good*
reputation, full of the Holy Spirit and
wisdom, whom we may appoint
over this [b]business;†
4 "but we [a]will give ourselves
continually to prayer and to the ministry of the word."
5 And the saying pleased the
whole multitude. And they chose
Stephen, [a]a man full of faith and the
Holy Spirit, and [b]Philip, Prochorus,
Nicanor, Timon, Parmenas, and
[c]Nicolas, a proselyte from Antioch,†
6 whom they set before the apostles; and [a]when they had prayed,
[b]they laid hands on them.†
7 Then [a]the word of God spread,
and the number of the disciples multiplied greatly in Jerusalem, and a
great many [b]of the priests were obedient to the faith.†

2 [a]Ex. 18:17
3 [a]1 Tim. 3:7 [b]1 Tim. 3:8–13
4 [a]Acts 2:42
5 [a]Acts 6:3; 11:24 [b]Acts 8:5, 26; 21:8 [c]Rev. 2:6, 15
6 [a]Acts 1:24 [b][2 Tim. 1:6]
7 [a]Acts 12:24 [b]John 12:42
8 [a]Acts 2:43; 5:12; 8:15; 14:3 [1]NU *grace*
10 [a]Luke 21:15
11 [a]1 Kin. 21:10, 13
13 [1]NU omits *blasphemous*

Evangelism by the Deacons

8 And Stephen, full of [1]faith and
power, did great [a]wonders and signs
among the people.†
9 Then there arose some from
what is called the Synagogue of the
Freedmen (Cyrenians, Alexandrians,
and those from Cilicia and Asia), disputing with Stephen.†
10 And [a]they were not able to resist the wisdom and the Spirit by
which he spoke.
11 [a]Then they secretly induced
men to say, "We have heard him
speak blasphemous words against
Moses and God."†
12 And they stirred up the people,
the elders, and the scribes; and they
came upon *him*, seized him, and
brought *him* to the council.
13 They also set up false witnesses
who said, "This man does not cease
to speak [1]blasphemous words
against this holy place and the law;

6:2 The Apostles recognize the need for assistants to serve the growing Church, a first indication of various offices and ministries which would be developed in the history of the Church. **Disciples** in the Book of Acts generally refers to all Christians, whereas **the twelve** are usually termed "Apostles."

6:3 The qualifications for deacons are: (1) having a good reputation, (2) being full of the Holy Spirit, and (3) being full of wisdom.

6:5 All those chosen have Greek names, a popular practice especially of Jews who lived outside Palestine. One of them, **Nicolas,** was a **proselyte,** that is, a Gentile convert to Judaism who had become a Christian. Eusebius, the fourth-century historian, claims he later apostatized and formed the heretical group known as the Nicolaitans (Rev. 2:6).

6:6 The first ordination of deacons (lit. "servants") is performed by the Apostles themselves.

6:7 The priests: Jewish priests who became Christians but did not continue to function in a priestly capacity within the Church. Priesthood in Judaism was inherited.

6:8 Stephen was the leader of the deacons because of his special gifts and attributes.

6:9 These **Freedmen** were Jews who had formerly been held captive under the Romans, usually as a result of rebelliousness. A number of them and their descendants had gained their freedom and in their zeal returned to Jerusalem where they had their own synagogue.

6:11 Unable to refute Stephen's inspired wisdom, the Freedmen, misunderstanding Stephen's words, resort to charging him with blasphemy **against Moses and God.** Stephen is among the first Christians to proclaim that the Christian faith and worship is for all people, not only the Jews. Although Christianity includes changes in the Mosaic Law and in temple worship (7:48–50; 11:1–3, 17, 18; 15:1–11), these changes are according to God's will—not blasphemous, as these opponents believe.

14 [a]"for we have heard him say
that this Jesus of Nazareth will destroy this place and change the customs which Moses delivered to us."†
15 And all who sat in the council,
looking steadfastly at him, saw his
face as the face of an angel.†

Stephen's Defense

7 Then the high priest said, "Are
these things so?"†
2 And he said, [a]"Brethren and fathers, listen: The [b]God of glory appeared to our father Abraham when
he was in Mesopotamia, before he
dwelt in [c]Haran,
3 "and said to him, [a]*'Get out of*
your country and from your rela-
tives, and come to a land that I will
show you.'
4 "Then [a]he came out of the land
of the Chaldeans and dwelt in
Haran. And from there, when his
father was [b]dead, He moved
him to this land in which you now
dwell.
5 "And *God* gave him no inheritance in it, not even *enough* to set
his foot on. But even when *Abraham*
had no child, [a]He promised to give
it to him for a possession, and to his
descendants after him.
6 "But God spoke in this way:
[a]that his descendants would dwell
in a foreign land, and that they
would bring them into [b]bondage and
oppress *them* four hundred years.†
7 [a]*'And the nation to whom they*
will be in bondage I will [b]*judge,'* said
God, [c]*'and after that they shall come*
out and serve Me in this place.'

14 [a]Acts 10:38; 25:8
CHAPTER 7
2 [a]Acts 22:1 [b]Ps. 29:3 [c]Gen. 11:31, 32
3 [a]Gen. 12:1
4 [a]Gen. 11:31; 15:7 [b]Gen. 11:32
5 [a]Gen. 12:7; 13:15; 15:3, 18; 17:8; 26:3
6 [a]Gen. 15:13, 14, 16; 47:11, 12 [b]Ex. 1:8–14; 12:40, 41
7 [a]Gen. 15:14 [b]Ex. 14:13–31 [c]Ex. 3:12
8 [a]Gen. 17:9–14 [b]Gen. 21:1–5 [c]Gen. 25:21–26 [d]Gen. 29:31—30:24; 35:18, 22–26
9 [a]Gen. 37:4, 11, 28 [b]Gen. 37:28 [c]Gen. 39:2, 21, 23
10 [a]Gen. 41:38–44
11 [a]Gen. 41:54; 42:5 [1]*affliction*
12 [a]Gen. 42:1, 2
13 [a]Gen. 45:4, 16
14 [a]Gen. 45:9, 27 [b]Deut. 10:22 [1]Or *seventy,* Ex. 1:5
15 [a]Gen. 46:1–7 [b]Gen. 49:33

8 [a]"Then He gave him the covenant of circumcision; [b]and so *Abra-*
ham begot Isaac and circumcised him
on the eighth day; [c]and Isaac *begot*
Jacob, and [d]Jacob *begot* the twelve
patriarchs.†
9 [a]"And the patriarchs, becoming
envious, [b]sold Joseph into Egypt.
[c]But God was with him
10 "and delivered him out of all his
troubles, [a]and gave him favor and
wisdom in the presence of Pharaoh, king of Egypt; and he made
him governor over Egypt and all
his house.
11 [a]"Now a famine and great
[1]trouble came over all the land of
Egypt and Canaan, and our fathers
found no sustenance.
12 [a]"But when Jacob heard that
there was grain in Egypt, he sent out
our fathers first.
13 "And the [a]second *time* Joseph
was made known to his brothers,
and Joseph's family became known
to the Pharaoh.
14 [a]"Then Joseph sent and called
his father Jacob and [b]all his relatives
to *him,* [1]seventy-five people.
15 [a]"So Jacob went down to Egypt;
[b]and he died, he and our fathers.
16 "And [a]they were carried back
to Shechem and laid in [b]the tomb
that Abraham bought for a sum of
money from the sons of Hamor, *the*
father of Shechem.
17 "But when [a]the time of the
promise drew near which God had
sworn to Abraham, [b]the people grew
and multiplied in Egypt

16 [a]Josh. 24:32 [b]Gen. 23:16 17 [a]Gen. 15:13 [b]Ex. 1:7–9

6:14 The charge that Jesus would destroy the temple was leveled against Him by false witnesses at His trial before the Council (Matt. 26:61). This was a misinterpretation of two of Jesus' sayings: (1) "Destroy this temple, and in three days I will raise it up" (John 2:19)—referring to His own body; and (2) His prophecy of the destruction of the temple (Matt. 24:1, 2). This prophecy was fulfilled in A.D. 70, when the Romans destroyed the temple in reprisal against a Jewish rebellion.

6:15 A divine radiance, the very uncreated energy of God, was reflected in Stephen's **face,** a foretaste of glory of the age to come for all of the people of God (see 2 Cor. 3:18).

7:1 Stephen does not answer the question of the **high priest** yes or no. To provide a proper context in which to answer his accusers, he embarks on a review of salvation history to show how the Jews consistently missed the purpose of God's dealings with them because of their hardness of heart (v. 51). Stephen has a remarkable knowledge of the OT Scriptures.

7:6 This is a reference to Israel's time of **bondage** in Egypt.

7:8 God's **covenant of circumcision** is a mark of identity for the posterity of **Abraham.**

18 "till another king [a]arose who
did not know Joseph.
19 "This man dealt treacherously
with our people, and oppressed our
forefathers, [a]making them expose
their babies, so that they might not
live.
20 [a]"At this time Moses was born,
and [b]was well pleasing to God; and
he was brought up in his father's
house for three months.
21 "But [a]when he was set out,
[b]Pharaoh's daughter took him away
and brought him up as her own
son.
22 "And Moses was learned in
all the wisdom of the Egyptians,
and was [a]mighty in words and
deeds.
23 [a]"Now when he was forty years
old, it came into his heart to visit his
brethren, the children of Israel.
24 "And seeing one of *them* suffer
wrong, he defended and avenged
him who was oppressed, and struck
down the Egyptian.
25 "For he supposed that his brethren would have understood that God
would deliver them by his hand, but
they did not understand.
26 "And the next day he appeared
to two of them as they were fighting,
and *tried to* reconcile them, saying,
'Men, you are brethren; why do you
wrong one another?'
27 "But he who did his neighbor
wrong pushed him away, saying,
[a]*'Who made you a ruler and a judge
over us?*
28 *'Do you want to kill me as you
did the Egyptian yesterday?'*
29 [a]"Then, at this saying, Moses
fled and became a dweller in the
land of Midian, where he [b]had two
sons.
30 [a]"And when forty years had
passed, an Angel [1]of the Lord appeared to him in a flame of fire in a
bush, in the wilderness of Mount
Sinai.†
31 "When Moses saw *it*, he marveled at the sight; and as he drew
near to observe, the voice of the Lord
came to him,
32 *"saying,* [a]*'I am the God of your
fathers—the God of Abraham, the
God of Isaac, and the God of Jacob.'*
And Moses trembled and dared not
look.
33 [a]*'Then the* Lord *said to him,
"Take your sandals off your feet, for
the place where you stand is holy
ground.*†
34 *"I have surely* [a]*seen the oppression of My people who are in Egypt;
I have heard their groaning and have
come down to deliver them. And
now come, I will* [b]*send you to
Egypt."'*
35 "This Moses whom they rejected, saying, [a]*'Who made you a
ruler and a judge?'* is the one God
sent *to be* a ruler and a deliverer
[b]by the hand of the Angel who appeared to him in the bush.
36 [a]"He brought them out, after he
had [b]shown wonders and signs in
the land of Egypt, [c]and in the Red
Sea, [d]and in the wilderness forty
years.
37 "This is that Moses who said to
the children of Israel, [a]*'The* Lord
*your God will raise up for you a
Prophet like me from your brethren.*
[b]*Him*[1] *you shall hear.'*
38 [a]"This is he who was in the
[1]congregation in the wilderness with
[b]the Angel who spoke to him on
Mount Sinai, and *with* our fathers,
[c]the one who received the living
[d]oracles[2] to give to us,†
39 "whom our fathers [a]would not
obey, but rejected. And in their
hearts they turned back to Egypt,

18 [a]Ex. 1:8
19 [a]Ex. 1:22
20 [a]Ex. 2:1, 2 [b]Heb. 11:23
21 [a]Ex. 2:3, 4 [b]Ex. 2:5–10
22 [a]Luke 24:19
23 [a]Ex. 2:11, 12
27 [a]Ex. 2:14
29 [a]Heb. 11:27 [b]Ex. 2:15, 21, 22; 4:20; 18:3
30 [a]Ex. 3:1–10 [1]NU omits *of the Lord*
32 [a]Ex. 3:6, 15
33 [a]Ex. 3:5, 7, 8, 10
34 [a]Ex. 2:24, 25 [b]Ps. 105:26
35 [a]Ex. 2:14 [b]Ex. 14:21
36 [a]Ex. 12:41; 33:1 [b]Ps. 105:27 [c]Ex. 14:21 [d]Ex. 16:1, 35
37 [a]Deut. 18:15, 18, 19 [b]Matt. 17:5 [1]NU, M omit *Him you shall hear*
38 [a]Ex. 19:3 [b]Gal. 3:19 [c]Deut. 5:27 [d]Heb. 5:12 [1]Gr. *ekklesia, assembly* or *church* [2]*sayings*
39 [a]Ps. 95:8–11

7:30 The **Angel** (or Messenger) **of the Lord** who **appeared** to Moses and spoke with "the voice of the Lord" (v. 31) is the eternal Christ, according to the interpretation of the Church Fathers. Christ is the agent of creation and revelation (John 1:1–4), and thus was already active in the OT in a hidden way.

7:33 The place of revelation is **holy ground.** It is the presence of God that makes things holy, and we experience God in time and space through holy places and things—for example, icons—as Moses did at the burning bush.

7:38 The **congregation** of Israel under the Old Covenant was a type or picture of the Church in the New Covenant (see note in center column).

40 [a]"saying to Aaron, *'Make us
gods to go before us; as for this Moses
who brought us out of the land of
Egypt, we do not know what has become of him.'*
41 [a]"And they made a calf in those
days, offered sacrifices to the idol,
and [b]rejoiced in the works of their
own hands.
42 "Then [a]God turned and gave
them up to worship [b]the host of
heaven, as it is written in the book
of the Prophets:

[c]*'Did you offer Me slaughtered*
animals and sacrifices during
forty years in the wilderness,
O house of Israel?
43 *You also took up the tabernacle*
of Moloch,
And the star of your god
Remphan,
Images which you made to
worship;
And [a]I will carry you away
beyond Babylon.'

44 "Our fathers had the tabernacle
of witness in the wilderness, as He
appointed, instructing Moses [a]to
make it according to the pattern that
he had seen,
45 [a]"which our fathers, having received it in turn, also brought with
Joshua into the land possessed by
the Gentiles, [b]whom God drove out
before the face of our fathers until
the [c]days of David,
46 [a]"who found favor before God
and [b]asked to find a dwelling for the
God of Jacob.
47 [a]"But Solomon built Him a
house.†
48 "However, [a]the Most High does
not dwell in temples made with
hands, as the prophet says:

49 *'Heaven[a] is My throne,*
And earth is My footstool.
What house will you build for
Me? says the LORD,
Or what is the place of My rest?
50 *Has My hand not [a]made all*
these things?'

51 *"You* [a]stiff-necked[1] and [b]uncir-
cumcised in heart and ears! You always resist the Holy Spirit; as your
fathers *did*, so *do* you.†
52 [a]"Which of the prophets did
your fathers not persecute? And they
killed those who foretold the coming
of [b]the Just One, of whom you now
have become the betrayers and
murderers,
53 [a]"who have received the law by
the direction of angels and have not
kept *it*."

Stephen's Martyrdom

54 [a]When they heard these things
they were [1]cut to the heart, and they
gnashed at him with *their* teeth.
55 But he, [a]being full of the Holy
Spirit, gazed into heaven and saw
the [b]glory of God, and Jesus standing at the right hand of God,†
56 and said, "Look! [a]I see the heavens opened and the [b]Son of Man
standing at the right hand of God!"
57 Then they cried out with a loud
voice, stopped their ears, and ran at
him with one accord;
58 and they cast *him* out of the city
and stoned *him*. And [a]the witnesses
laid down their clothes at the feet
of a young man named Saul.

40 [a]Ex. 32:1, 23
41 [a]Deut. 9:16 [b]Ex. 32:6, 18, 19
42 [a][2 Thess. 2:11] [b]2 Kin. 21:3 [c]Amos 5:25–27
43 [a]Jer. 25:9–12
44 [a][Heb. 8:5]
45 [a]Josh. 3:14; 18:1; 23:9 [b]Ps. 44:2 [c]2 Sam. 6:2–15
46 [a]2 Sam. 7:1–13 [b]1 Chr. 22:7
47 [a]1 Kin. 6:1–38; 8:20, 21
48 [a]1 Kin. 8:27
49 [a]Is. 66:1, 2
50 [a]Ps. 102:25
51 [a]Ex. 32:9 [b]Lev. 26:41 [1]*stubborn*
52 [a]2 Chr. 36:16 [b]Acts 3:14; 22:14
53 [a]Ex. 20:1
54 [a]Acts 5:33 [1]*furious*
55 [a]Acts 6:5 [b][Ex. 24:17]
56 [a]Matt. 3:16 [b]Dan. 7:13
58 [a]Acts 22:20

7:47–50 Stephen recounts the history of the temple as God's earthly sanctuary. But God is limitless and **does not dwell in temples made with hands.** As seen in Jesus' teaching (John 4:21–24), the temple was not the absolute and exclusive dwelling place of God.

7:51 Israel resisted **the Holy Spirit** in that they did not heed God's guidance through the prophets, but rebelled against it. By implication, Stephen is saying that the contemporary Jewish leaders and their followers are still resisting the Holy Spirit in rejecting the mission of Jesus and the Church.

7:55–58 Stephen's vision of the enthroned Christ (vv. 55, 56) appears as the ultimate blasphemy to his opponents. The OT penalty for blasphemy is stoning (Lev. 24:16). **Saul,** an indirect participant in the martyrdom of Stephen, is the great persecutor of the early Christians. Later he will be called by Christ to be His apostle and will become the great Christian missionary, Paul of Tarsus (see Acts 9:1–22).

59 And they stoned Stephen as he
was calling on *God* and saying, "Lord
Jesus, [a]receive my spirit."
60 Then he knelt down and cried
out with a loud voice, [a]"Lord, do not
charge them with this sin." And
when he had said this, he fell
asleep.†

The First General Persecution

8 Now Saul was consenting to his
death. At that time a great persecution arose against the church
which was at Jerusalem; and [a]they
were all scattered throughout the regions of Judea and Samaria, except
the apostles.†
2 And devout men carried Stephen *to his burial,* and [a]made great
lamentation over him.
3 As for Saul, [a]he made havoc of
the church, entering every house,
and dragging off men and women,
committing *them* to prison.

The Church in Samaria

4 Therefore [a]those who were scattered went everywhere preaching
the word.
5 Then [a]Philip went down to
[1]the city of Samaria and preached
Christ to them.†
6 And the multitudes with one accord heeded the things spoken by
Philip, hearing and seeing the miracles which he did.
7 For [a]unclean spirits, crying with
a loud voice, came out of many who
were possessed; and many who were
paralyzed and lame were healed.
8 And there was great joy in that
city.
9 But there was a certain man
called Simon, who previously [a]prac-
ticed [1]sorcery in the city and [b]aston-
ished the [2]people of Samaria, claiming that he was someone great,†
10 to whom they all gave heed,
from the least to the greatest, saying,
"This man is the great power of
God."
11 And they heeded him because
he had astonished them with his
[1]sorceries for a long time.
12 But when they believed Philip
as he preached the things [a]concern-
ing the kingdom of God and the
name of Jesus Christ, both men and
women were baptized.
13 Then Simon himself also believed; and when he was baptized
he continued with Philip, and was
amazed, seeing the miracles and
signs which were done.

The Samaritan Pentecost

14 Now when the [a]apostles who
were at Jerusalem heard that Samaria
had received the word of God, they
sent Peter and John to them,†
15 who, when they had come
down, prayed for them [a]that they
might receive the Holy Spirit.
16 For [a]as yet He had fallen upon
none of them. [b]They had only been
baptized in [c]the name of the Lord
Jesus.†

59 [a]Ps. 31:5
60 [a]Matt. 5:44; Luke 23:34
CHAPTER 8
1 [a]John 16:2; Acts 8:4; 11:19
2 [a]Gen. 23:2
3 [a]Acts 7:58; 1 Cor. 15:9; Gal. 1:13; Phil. 3:6; 1 Tim. 1:13
4 [a]Matt. 10:23
5 [a]Acts 6:5; 8:26, 30 [1]Or *a*
7 [a]Mark 16:17
9 [a]Acts 8:11; 13:6 [b]Acts 5:36 [1]*magic* [2]Or *nation*
11 [1]*magic arts*
12 [a]Acts 1:3; 8:4
14 [a]Acts 5:12, 29, 40
15 [a]Acts 2:38; 19:2
16 [a]Acts 19:2 [b]Matt. 28:19; Acts 2:38 [c]Acts 10:48; 19:5

7:60 Stephen's words are reminiscent of Christ's words from the Cross (Luke 23:34).

8:1 The martyrdom of St. Stephen, called the Protomartyr, was the beginning of the first widespread **persecution** of the early Christians. In response to it they **scattered throughout the regions** of Palestine, using the opportunity to spread the gospel (v. 4).

8:5 Philip the deacon (not the Apostle) is the first evangelist to **Samaria,** the capital city of the district of Samaria. Philip carries on both an evangelistic and a healing (v. 7) ministry.

8:9 Simon is a magician who converts to Christianity and is fascinated by miracles. His conversion, however, is not based on pure motives, for he seeks to trade with the power of the Spirit (which is now called "simony") and is rebuked by the Apostles (vv. 18–24). According to later tradition, Simon returned to the practice of magic and became a fierce antagonist of the Church.

8:14 The church of **Jerusalem** exercises apostolic supervision over the new communities of Christians, showing the unity of the Church.

8:16, 17 The acts of baptism and chrismation (receiving **the Holy Spirit,** v. 17), were

(continued on next page)

17 Then [a]they laid hands on them,
and they received the Holy Spirit.
18 And when Simon saw that
through the laying on of the apostles'
hands the Holy Spirit was given, he
offered them money,
19 saying, "Give me this power
also, that anyone on whom I lay
hands may receive the Holy Spirit."
20 But Peter said to him, "Your
money perish with you, because
[a]you thought that [b]the gift of God
could be purchased with money!
21 "You have neither part nor portion in this matter, for your [a]heart
is not right in the sight of God.
22 "Repent therefore of this your
wickedness, and pray God [a]if perhaps the thought of your heart may
be forgiven you.†
23 "For I see that you are [a]poi-
soned by bitterness and bound by
iniquity."
24 Then Simon answered and said,
[a]"Pray to the Lord for me, that none
of the things which you have spoken
may come upon me."
25 So when they had testified and
preached the word of the Lord, they
returned to Jerusalem, preaching the
gospel in many villages of the
Samaritans.

The Ethiopian Eunuch

26 Now an angel of the Lord spoke
to [a]Philip, saying, "Arise and go toward the south along the road which
goes down from Jerusalem to Gaza."
This is [1]desert.†
27 So he arose and went. And behold, [a]a man of Ethiopia, a eunuch
of great authority under Candace the
queen of the Ethiopians, who had
charge of all her treasury, and
[b]had come to Jerusalem to worship,†
28 was returning. And sitting in his
chariot, he was reading Isaiah the
prophet.
29 Then the Spirit said to Philip,
"Go near and overtake this chariot."†
30 So Philip ran to him, and heard
him reading the prophet Isaiah, and
said, "Do you understand what you
are reading?"†
31 And he said, "How can I, unless
someone guides me?" And he asked
Philip to come up and sit with him.
32 The place in the Scripture which
he read was this:

[a]"He was led as a sheep to the
slaughter;
And as a lamb before its shearer
is silent,
[b]So He opened not His mouth.†
33 *In His humiliation His [a]justice*
was taken away,
And who will declare His
generation?
For His life is [b]taken from the
earth."

34 So the eunuch answered Philip
and said, "I ask you, of whom does

17 [a]Acts 6:6; 19:6; Heb. 6:2 **20** [a]2 Kin. 5:16; Is. 55:1; Dan. 5:17; [Matt. 10:8] [b][Acts 2:38; 10:45; 11:17] **21** [a]Jer. 17:9 **22** [a]Dan. 4:27; 2 Tim. 2:25 **23** [a]Heb. 12:15 **24** [a]Gen. 20:7, 17; Ex. 8:8; Num. 21:7; 1 Kin. 13:6; Job 42:8; James 5:16 **26** [a]Acts 6:5 [1]Or *a deserted place*

27 [a]Ps. 68:31; 87:4; Is. 56:3; Zeph. 3:10 [b]1 Kin. 8:41, 42; John 12:20 **32** [a]Is. 53:7, 8 [b]Matt. 26:62, 63; 27:12, 14; John 19:9 **33** [a]Luke 23:1–25 [b]Luke 23:33–46

(continued from previous page)
distinguished from earliest times. Baptism was sometimes performed in Christ's name alone, but baptism in the name of the Holy Trinity (Matt. 28:19) became standard throughout the Church.

8:22–24 Faith is necessary to our salvation. Saving faith is accompanied by true repentance, without which one is not justified before God. Simon believed (v. 13), but he was not justified because he was **poisoned by bitterness and bound by iniquity.** He wanted Christianity on his terms, to prosper from it. The modern "prosperity gospel," faith without works, and the self-help message are deadly deviations from apostolic preaching.

8:26 Gaza is a city near the coast of Palestine, southeast of **Jerusalem** and on the way to Egypt.

8:27 A **eunuch** was an unmarried man totally devoted to the service of his master. The Ethiopian eunuch is a follower of Judaism, perhaps a Jewish proselyte who had fully converted to Judaism and had come to **worship** in **Jerusalem.**

8:29 Effective mission is prompted and led by the Holy Spirit.

8:30, 31 The eunuch is aware he needs guidance. Here **Philip** answers that need with basic catechism, something all seekers and new believers need.

8:32, 33 This quote is a prophecy of the death of Christ. These words are repeated by the priest as the bread is being prepared for the Eucharist.

the prophet say this, of himself or
of some other man?"
35 Then Philip opened his mouth,
[a]and beginning at this Scripture,
preached Jesus to him.
36 Now as they went down the
road, they came to some water. And
the eunuch said, "See, *here is* water.
[a]What hinders me from being
baptized?"†
37 [1]Then Philip said, [a]"If you believe with all your heart, you may."
And he answered and said, [b]"I believe that Jesus Christ is the Son of
God."
38 So he commanded the chariot
to stand still. And both Philip and
the eunuch went down into the water, and he baptized him.
39 Now when they came up out of
the water, [a]the Spirit of the Lord
caught Philip away, so that the eunuch saw him no more; and he went
on his way rejoicing.
40 But Philip was found at
[1]Azotus. And passing through, he
preached in all the cities till he came
to [a]Caesarea.†

Saul Converted

9 Then [a]Saul, still breathing
threats and murder against the
disciples of the Lord, went to the
high priest†
2 and asked [a]letters from him to
the synagogues of Damascus, so that
if he found any who were of the
Way, whether men or women, he
might bring them bound to Jerusalem.
3 [a]As he journeyed he came near
Damascus, and suddenly a light
shone around him from heaven.
4 Then he fell to the ground, and
heard a voice saying to him, "Saul,
Saul, [a]why are you persecuting
Me?"†
5 And he said, "Who are You,
Lord?" Then the Lord said, "I am
Jesus, whom you are persecuting.
[1]It *is* hard for you to kick against the
goads."†
6 So he, trembling and astonished, said, "Lord, what do You
want me to do?" Then the Lord *said*
to him, "Arise and go into the city,
and you will be told what you must
do."
7 And [a]the men who journeyed
with him stood speechless, hearing
a voice but seeing no one.
8 Then Saul arose from the
ground, and when his eyes were
opened he saw no one. But they led
him by the hand and brought *him*
into Damascus.†
9 And he was three days without
sight, and neither ate nor drank.
10 Now there was a certain disciple
at Damascus [a]named Ananias; and
to him the Lord said in a vision,
"Ananias." And he said, "Here I am,
Lord."†
11 So the Lord *said* to him, "Arise

35 [a]Luke 24:27
36 [a]Acts 10:47; 16:33
37 [a][Mark 16:16] [b]Matt. 16:16 [1]NU, M omit v. 37. It is found in Western texts, including the Latin tradition.
39 [a]Ezek. 3:12, 14
40 [a]Acts 21:8 [1]Same as Heb. *Ashdod*

CHAPTER 9
1 [a]Acts 7:57; 8:1, 3; 26:10, 11
2 [a]Acts 22:5
3 [a]1 Cor. 15:8
4 [a][Matt. 25:40]
5 [1]NU, M omit the rest of v.5 and begin v. 6 with *But arise and go*
7 [a][Acts 22:9; 26:13]
10 [a]Acts 22:12

8:36–39 One does not make oneself a Christian. Baptism is a crucial act of entry into salvation—into the Church. The apostolic pattern of conversion is: (1) hearing Christ preached, (2) acceptance of Christ by faith, and (3) baptism.

8:40 Philip conducts a wide evangelistic ministry. This Philip is one of the seven deacons (6:3), not to be confused with the Apostle Philip, one of the Twelve (John 1:43–48).

9:1, 2 Saul, or Paul, as persecutor acts officially within the legal structure of Judaism. His purpose is to arrest and prosecute Jewish Christians; he has no authority over Gentile Christians, who are few at this time. Note that Christianity is called **the Way** (v. 2): Jesus said, "I am the way" (John 14:6), and following Him is a *way* of life.

9:4 To persecute the Church is to persecute Christ Himself (see Matt. 25:40; Eph. 5:23, 30).

9:5 Goads are spikes. This expression is part of a proverb implying the futility of action against an invincible force.

9:8 Saul is temporarily blinded by the light of the risen Christ. This is a way of leading him into the Church. It is when Saul loses his eyesight that he sees Christ by the grace of the Spirit.

9:10 Ananias is probably one of the Christian leaders in Damascus whom Saul is coming to arrest.

and go to the street called Straight,
and inquire at the house of Judas for
one called Saul [a]of Tarsus, for behold, he is praying.
12 "And in a vision he has seen a
man named Ananias coming in and
putting *his* hand on him, so that he
might receive his sight."
13 Then Ananias answered, "Lord,
I have heard from many about this
man, [a]how much [1]harm he has done
to Your saints in Jerusalem.
14 "And here he has authority
from the chief priests to bind all
[a]who call on Your name."
15 But the Lord said to him, "Go,
for [a]he is a chosen vessel of Mine
to bear My name before [b]Gentiles,
[c]kings, and the [d]children[1] of Israel.†
16 "For [a]I will show him how
many things he must suffer for My
[b]name's sake."
17 [a]And Ananias went his way and
entered the house; and [b]laying his
hands on him he said, "Brother Saul,
the Lord [1]Jesus, who appeared to
you on the road as you came, has
sent me that you may receive your
sight and [c]be filled with the Holy
Spirit."†
18 Immediately there fell from his
eyes *something* like scales, and he received his sight at once; and he arose
and was baptized.

Saul's First Preaching

19 So when he had received food,
he was strengthened. [a]Then Saul
spent some days with the disciples
at Damascus.†
20 Immediately he preached [1]the
Christ in the synagogues, that He is
the Son of God.
21 Then all who heard were
amazed, and said, [a]"Is this not he
who destroyed those who called on
this name in Jerusalem, and has
come here for that purpose, so that
he might bring them bound to the
chief priests?"
22 But Saul increased all the more
in strength, [a]and confounded the
Jews who dwelt in Damascus, proving that this *Jesus* is the Christ.
23 Now after many days were past,
[a]the Jews plotted to kill him.
24 [a]But their plot became known
to Saul. And they watched the gates
day and night, to kill him.
25 Then the disciples took him by
night and [a]let *him* down through the
wall in a large basket.†

Saul in Jerusalem

26 And [a]when Saul had come to
Jerusalem, he tried to join the disciples; but they were all afraid of him,
and did not believe that he was a
disciple.
27 [a]But Barnabas took him and
brought *him* to the apostles. And he
declared to them how he had seen
the Lord on the road, and that He
had spoken to him, [b]and how he had
preached boldly at Damascus in the
name of Jesus.
28 So [a]he was with them at Jerusalem, coming in and going out.
29 And he spoke boldly in the
name of the Lord Jesus and disputed
against the [a]Hellenists,[1] [b]but they attempted to kill him.†

11 [a]Acts 21:39; 22:3
13 [a]Acts 9:1 [1]*bad things*
14 [a]Acts 7:59; 9:2, 21
15 [a]Eph. 3:7, 8 [b]Rom. 1:5; 11:13 [c]Acts 25:22, 23; 26:1 [d]Rom. 1:16; 9:1–5 [1]Lit. *sons*
16 [a]Acts 20:23 [b]2 Cor. 4:11
17 [a]Acts 22:12, 13 [b]Acts 8:17 [c]Acts 2:4; 4:31; 8:17; 13:52 [1]M omits *Jesus*
19 [a]Acts 26:20
20 [1]NU *Jesus*
21 [a]Gal. 1:13, 23
22 [a]Acts 18:28
23 [a]2 Cor. 11:26
24 [a]2 Cor. 11:32
25 [a]Josh. 2:15
26 [a]Acts 22:17–20; 26:20
27 [a]Acts 4:36; 13:2 [b]Acts 9:20, 22
28 [a]Gal. 1:18
29 [a]Acts 6:1; 11:20 [b]2 Cor. 11:26 [1]Greek-speaking Jews

9:15 Saul is **a chosen vessel** of God's work and becomes known as Paul, the Apostle to the Gentiles.

9:17, 18 Remarkably, **Ananias** calls this former persecutor of Christians **brother,** a sign that Saul had already believed in Christ. To enter into the fullness of Christ, he is **baptized** (v. 18) and **filled with the Holy Spirit** (v. 17).

9:19 The existence of a group of **disciples at Damascus** demonstrates significant growth during the first three to five years of the Church's life. Today, this same strong church is still in Damascus and the Patriarchate of Antioch is based there, on the street called Straight (v. 11).

9:25 The former persecutor is now himself persecuted and has to escape over the walls of the city in a **basket** (see 2 Cor. 11:33).

9:29 **Hellenists** here are Greek-speaking Jews in Jerusalem who are *not* Christian believers, in contrast to those mentioned in 6:1.

30 When the brethren found out,
they brought him down to Caesarea
and sent him out to Tarsus.
31 [a]Then the [1]churches throughout
all Judea, Galilee, and Samaria had
peace and were [b]edified.[2] And walking in the [c]fear of the Lord and in
the [d]comfort of the Holy Spirit, they
were [e]multiplied.†

Peter in Gentile Judea

32 Now it came to pass, as Peter
went [a]through all *parts of the country,*
that he also came down to the saints
who dwelt in Lydda.†
33 There he found a certain man
named Aeneas, who had been bedridden eight years and was
paralyzed.
34 And Peter said to him, "Aeneas,
[a]Jesus the Christ heals you. Arise
and make your bed." Then he arose
immediately.†
35 So all who dwelt at Lydda and
[a]Sharon saw him and [b]turned to the
Lord.†
36 At Joppa there was a certain disciple named [1]Tabitha, which is translated [2]Dorcas. This woman was full
[a]of good works and charitable deeds
which she did.†
37 But it happened in those days
that she became sick and died. When
they had washed her, they laid *her*
in [a]an upper room.
38 And since Lydda was near
Joppa, and the disciples had heard
that Peter was there, they sent two
men to him, imploring *him* not to delay in coming to them.†
39 Then Peter arose and went with
them. When he had come, they
brought *him* to the upper room. And
all the widows stood by him weeping, showing the tunics and garments which Dorcas had made while
she was with them.
40 But Peter [a]put them all out, and
[b]knelt down and prayed. And turning to the body he [c]said, "Tabitha,
arise." And she opened her eyes,
and when she saw Peter she sat up.†
41 Then he gave her *his* hand and
lifted her up; and when he had called
the saints and widows, he presented
her alive.
42 And it became known throughout all Joppa, [a]and many believed
on the Lord.
43 So it was that he stayed many
days in Joppa with [a]Simon, a tanner.

Cornelius's Vision

10 There was a certain man in
[a]Caesarea called Cornelius, a
centurion of what was called the Ital-
ian [1]Regiment,†

31 [a]Acts 5:11; 8:1; 16:5 [b][Eph. 4:16, 29] [c]Ps. 34:9 [d]John 14:16 [e]Acts 16:5 [1]NU *church . . . was* [2]*built up*
32 [a]Acts 8:14
34 [a][Acts 3:6, 16; 4:10]
35 [a]1 Chr. 5:16; 27:29; Is. 33:9; 35:2; 65:10 [b]Acts 11:21; 15:19
36 [a]1 Tim. 2:10; Titus 3:8 [1]Lit., in Aram., *Gazelle* [2]Lit., in Gr., *Gazelle*
37 [a]Acts 1:13; 9:39
40 [a]Matt. 9:25 [b]Luke 22:41; Acts 7:60 [c]Mark 5:41, 42; John 11:43
42 [a]John 11:45
43 [a]Acts 10:6

CHAPTER 10
1 [a]Acts 8:40; 23:23 [1]*Cohort*

9:31 This is the first mention in the Book of Acts of **churches** in the plural scattered throughout **Judea, Galilee, and Samaria.** The Church is not "invisible" but seeable and locatable.

9:32 Lydda is about 25 miles northwest of Jerusalem. **Saints** in the terminology of the early Church refers to all Christians, who are sanctified by the Holy Spirit and participate in the holiness of God.

9:34 Peter brings Christ's healing to a paralytic in Lydda. In the Gospel of John, Jesus healed the paralytic at the Pool of Bethesda (John 5:1–15). As there was power with Christ to heal during His earthly ministry, so there is power in His Church to continue His healing ministry.

9:35 Sharon was a region north of Lydda, extending about 10 miles in width and 50 miles in length along the Mediterranean seacoast. The impact of the healing of the paralytic Aeneas in Lydda is felt for miles around. Many in that region **turned to the Lord.** As the Apostles go out, signs and miracles accompany them as a witness to the truth, intended to produce repentance.

9:36 Tabitha, or **Dorcas,** was a model Christian woman in the church at Joppa.

9:38 Joppa, a seaport city at the southwest end of the plain of Sharon, was 35 miles northwest of Jerusalem. Peter's lengthy stay (v. 43) is in part occasioned by the interest generated from the raising of Dorcas from the dead (vv. 36–41).

9:40 Peter's raising of **Tabitha** from the dead parallels Jesus' raising of the synagogue ruler's daughter (Matt. 9:22–25).

10:1 Caesarea was a seaport about 25 miles north of Joppa on the coast. Here begins a

(continued on next page)

2 [a]a devout *man* and one who
[b]feared God with all his household,
who gave [1]alms generously to the
people, and prayed to God always.†
3 About [1]the ninth hour of the
day [a]he saw clearly in a vision an
angel of God coming in and saying
to him, "Cornelius!"†
4 And when he observed him, he
was afraid, and said, "What is it,
lord?" So he said to him, "Your
prayers and your alms have come up
for a memorial before God.
5 "Now [a]send men to Joppa, and
send for Simon whose surname is
Peter.
6 "He is lodging with [a]Simon, a
tanner, whose house is by the sea.
[b]He[1] will tell you what you must
do."
7 And when the angel who spoke
to him had departed, Cornelius
called two of his household servants
and a devout soldier from among
those who waited on him continually.†
8 So when he had explained all
these things to them, he sent them
to Joppa.

Peter's Vision

9 The next day, as they went on
their journey and drew near the city,
[a]Peter went up on the housetop to
pray, about [1]the sixth hour.†

2 [a]Acts 8:2; 9:22; 22:12 [b][Acts 10:22, 35; 13:16, 26] [1]*charitable gifts*
3 [a]Acts 10:30; 11:13 [1]3 P.M.
5 [a]Acts 11:13, 14
6 [a]Acts 9:43 [b]Acts 11:14 [1]NU, M omit the rest of v. 6.
9 [a]Acts 10:9–32; 11:5–14 [1]Noon
11 [a]Ezek. 1:1; Matt. 3:16; Acts 7:56; Rev. 4:1; 19:11
14 [a]Lev. 11:4; 20:25; Deut. 14:3, 7; Ezek. 4:14
15 [a][Matt. 15:11; Mark 7:19]; Acts 10:28; [Rom. 14:14]; 1 Cor. 10:25; [1 Tim. 4:4; Titus 1:15] [1]Declared clean
17 [1]*was perplexed*
19 [a]Acts 11:12
20 [a]Acts 15:7–9

10 Then he became very hungry
and wanted to eat; but while they
made ready, he fell into a trance
11 and [a]saw heaven opened and
an object like a great sheet bound
at the four corners, descending to
him and let down to the earth.
12 In it were all kinds of four-
footed animals of the earth, wild
beasts, creeping things, and birds of
the air.
13 And a voice came to him, "Rise,
Peter; kill and eat."
14 But Peter said, "Not so, Lord!
[a]For I have never eaten anything
common or unclean."†
15 And a voice *spoke* to him again
the second time, [a]"What God has
[1]cleansed you must not call
common."
16 This was done three times. And
the object was taken up into heaven
again.
17 Now while Peter [1]wondered
within himself what this vision
which he had seen meant, behold,
the men who had been sent from
Cornelius had made inquiry for Simon's house, and stood before the
gate.
18 And they called and asked
whether Simon, whose surname was
Peter, was lodging there.
19 While Peter thought about the
vision, [a]the Spirit said to him, "Behold, three men are seeking you.
20 [a]"Arise therefore, go down and

(continued from previous page)
whole new chapter in Church history. Membership in the Church was initially limited to Jews and later expanded to include Samaritans (see 8:5–25). With the conversion of **Cornelius,** the gates are for all time opened to the Gentiles.

10:2 "Fearer of God" was a formal designation for a Gentile who followed precepts of the Jewish religion but had not yet become a "proselyte" or full convert. Two things characterize the devotion of Cornelius: he **gave alms generously** (charitable giving) and he **prayed.** His devotion did not make him a Christian, but his prayers and alms came "up for a memorial before God" (v. 4). God rewarded his devotion by bringing Peter to him to explain more fully the way of Christ.

10:3, 9 The sixth hour is noon (v. 9) and **the ninth hour** is 3:00 P.M. (v. 3)—two specific times set aside for prayer for the Jews, and now for Christians (see also 3:1 and note). Cornelius and Peter were accustomed to observing these regular hours where liturgical, not privately composed, prayers were used.

10:7 The state of Cornelius' heart is apparent in that he immediately obeyed the instructions given to him by **the angel.**

10:9 Palestinian homes had flat roofs which were used for various activities.

10:14, 15 Peter needs convincing because he is asked to deviate from the Jewish custom of not eating the meat of animals considered unclean. He is taught symbolically that nothing which God has made is of itself unclean.

go with them, doubting nothing; for
I have sent them."
21 Then Peter went down to the
men [1]who had been sent to him from
Cornelius, and said, "Yes, I am he
whom you seek. For what reason
have you come?"
22 And they said, "Cornelius *the*
centurion, a just man, one who fears
God and [a]has a good reputation
among all the nation of the Jews, was
divinely instructed by a holy angel
to summon you to his house, and
to hear words from you."
23 Then he invited them in and
lodged *them.* On the next day Peter
went away with them, [a]and some
brethren from Joppa accompanied
him.

Peter Preaches to Gentiles

24 And the following day they entered Caesarea. Now Cornelius was
waiting for them, and had called together his relatives and close friends.
25 As Peter was coming in, Cornelius met him and fell down at his feet
and worshiped *him.*†
26 But Peter lifted him up, saying,
[a]"Stand up; I myself am also a man."
27 And as he talked with him, he
went in and found many who had
come together.
28 Then he said to them, "You
know how [a]unlawful it is for a Jewish man to keep company with or
go to one of another nation. But
[b]God has shown me that I should
not call any man common or unclean.†
29 "Therefore I came without objection as soon as I was sent for. I
ask, then, for what reason have you
sent for me?"
30 So Cornelius said, [1]"Four days
ago I was fasting until this hour;
and at the ninth hour I prayed
in my house, and behold, [a]a man
stood before me [b]in bright clothing,†
31 "and said, 'Cornelius, [a]your
prayer has been heard, and [b]your
[1]alms are remembered in the sight
of God.
32 'Send therefore to Joppa and call
Simon here, whose surname is Peter.
He is lodging in the house of Simon,
a tanner, by the sea. [1]When he
comes, he will speak to you.'
33 "So I sent to you immediately,
and you have done well to come.
Now therefore, we are all present before God, to hear all the things commanded you by God."†
34 Then Peter opened *his* mouth
and said: [a]"In truth I perceive that
God shows no partiality.†
35 "But [a]in every nation whoever
fears Him and works righteousness
is [b]accepted by Him.†
36 "The word which *God* sent to
the [1]children of Israel, [a]preaching
peace through Jesus Christ—[b]He is
Lord of all—
37 "that word you know, which
was proclaimed throughout all Judea, and [a]began from Galilee after
the baptism which John preached:
38 "how [a]God anointed Jesus of
Nazareth with the Holy Spirit and
with power, who [b]went about doing
good and healing all who were op-

21 [1]NU, M omit *who had been sent to him from Cornelius*
22 [a]Acts 22:12
23 [a]Acts 10:45; 11:12
26 [a]Acts 14:14, 15
28 [a]John 4:9; 18:28 [b][Acts 10:14, 35; 15:8, 9]
30 [a]Acts 1:10 [b]Matt. 28:3 [1]NU *Four days ago to this hour, at the ninth hour*
31 [a]Dan. 10:12 [b]Heb. 6:10 [1]*charitable gifts*
32 [1]NU omits the rest of v. 32.
34 [a]Deut. 10:17
35 [a][Eph. 2:13] [b]Ps. 15:1, 2
36 [a]Is. 57:19 [b]Rom. 10:12 [1]Lit. *sons*
37 [a]Luke 4:14
38 [a]Luke 4:18 [b]Matt. 4:23

10:25, 26 A powerful Roman commander falls **down at his feet,** worshiping **Peter** in awe of the spiritual power he represents. But Peter humbly corrects this gesture of devotion as belonging properly to God, not to created human beings.

10:28 Peter understands and acknowledges the meaning of his earlier vision (vv. 10–16). The unclean animals represent Gentiles, who were thought to be unclean by Jews.

10:30 A man . . . in bright clothing signifies an angel.

10:33 Cornelius and those with him are **present before God, to hear.** "So then faith comes by hearing, and hearing by the word of God" (Rom. 10:17). Devoted people still need to hear the gospel.

10:34–43 Peter gives the people a summary of the gospel, focusing on the ministry and the saving work of Christ.

10:35 Justification is not merely a once-for-all event, but a dynamic, ongoing process. Two conditions are given here: God accepts whoever (1) **fears Him** and (2) **works righteousness.** This in no way denies justification by faith; but it is not by faith *alone.* And God supplies the grace necessary for us to fear Him and work righteousness.

pressed by the devil, [c]for God was
with Him.†
39 "And we are [a]witnesses of all
things which He did both in the land
of the Jews and in Jerusalem, whom
[1]they [b]killed by hanging on a tree.
40 "Him [a]God raised up on the
third day, and showed Him openly,
41 [a]"not to all the people, but to
witnesses chosen before by God,
even to us [b]who ate and drank with
Him after He arose from the dead.
42 "And [a]He commanded us to
preach to the people, and to testify
[b]that it is He who was ordained by
God *to be* Judge [c]of the living and
the dead.
43 [a]"To Him all the prophets witness that, through His name,
[b]whoever believes in Him will receive [c]remission[1] of sins."

The Gentile Pentecost

44 While Peter was still speaking
these words, [a]the Holy Spirit fell
upon all those who heard the word.†
45 [a]And [1]those of the circumcision
who believed were astonished, as
many as came with Peter, [b]because
the gift of the Holy Spirit had been
poured out on the Gentiles also.
46 For they heard them speak with
tongues and magnify God. Then Peter answered,
47 "Can anyone forbid water, that
these should not be baptized who
have received the Holy Spirit [a]just
as we *have?"*
48 [a]And he commanded them to
be baptized [b]in the name of the Lord.
Then they asked him to stay a few
days.†

38 [c]John 3:2; 8:29
39 [a]Acts 1:8 [b]Acts 2:23 [1]NU, M *they also*
40 [a]Acts 2:24
41 [a][John 14:17, 19, 22; 15:27] [b]Luke 24:30, 41–43
42 [a]Matt. 28:19 [b]John 5:22, 27 [c]1 Pet. 4:5
43 [a]Zech. 13:1 [b]Gal. 3:22 [c]Acts 13:38, 39 [1]*forgiveness*
44 [a]Acts 4:31
45 [a]Acts 10:23 [b]Acts 11:18 [1]The Jews
47 [a]Acts 2:4; 10:44; 11:17; 15:8
48 [a]1 Cor. 1:14–17 [b]Acts 2:38; 8:16; 19:5

CHAPTER 11

2 [a]Acts 10:45
3 [a]Acts 10:28 [b]Gal. 2:12
4 [a]Luke 1:3
5 [a]Acts 10:9
12 [a][John 16:13] [b]Acts 10:23
13 [a]Acts 10:30

The Apostles in Jerusalem

11 Now the apostles and brethren who were in Judea heard
that the Gentiles had also received
the word of God.
2 And when Peter came up to Jerusalem, [a]those of the circumcision
contended with him,†
3 saying, [a]"You went in to uncircumcised men [b]and ate with them!"
4 But Peter explained *it* to them
[a]in order from the beginning, saying:
5 [a]"I was in the city of Joppa praying; and in a trance I saw a vision,
an object descending like a great
sheet, let down from heaven by four
corners; and it came to me.
6 "When I observed it intently
and considered, I saw four-footed
animals of the earth, wild beasts,
creeping things, and birds of the air.
7 "And I heard a voice saying to
me, 'Rise, Peter; kill and eat.'
8 "But I said, 'Not so, Lord! For
nothing common or unclean has at
any time entered my mouth.'
9 "But the voice answered me
again from heaven, 'What God has
cleansed you must not call common.'
10 "Now this was done three
times, and all were drawn up again
into heaven.
11 "At that very moment, three
men stood before the house where
I was, having been sent to me from
Caesarea.
12 "Then [a]the Spirit told me to go
with them, doubting nothing. Moreover [b]these six brethren accompanied me, and we entered the man's
house.
13 [a]"And he told us how he had
seen an angel standing in his house,

10:38 It was in His humanity that Jesus was anointed by the Holy Spirit. Note all three Persons of the Holy Trinity are mentioned here.

10:44 The giving of **the Holy Spirit** prior to baptism is something the Church had not seen before (v. 45). This unusual occurrence is a sign that God has accepted the Gentiles and therefore baptism should not be denied them.

10:48 To be baptized is of monumental importance. Even after the household of Cornelius has received the Holy Spirit, baptism is essential. The Book of Acts amply demonstrates the crucial importance of the sacraments—baptism (2:41), chrismation through the laying on of hands (8:17), and the Eucharist (20:7).

11:2 Those of the circumcision are conservative Jewish Christians who insist that circumcision and other ritual laws of the OT are necessary for salvation (see 15:1; Gal. 2:12). These Christians also advocate separation from Gentiles.

who said to him, 'Send men to
Joppa, and call for Simon whose surname is Peter,
14 'who will tell you words by
which you and all your household
will be saved.'†
15 "And as I began to speak, the
Holy Spirit fell upon them, [a]as upon
us at the beginning.
16 "Then I remembered the word
of the Lord, how He said, [a]'John indeed baptized with water, but
[b]you shall be baptized with the Holy
Spirit.'
17 [a]"If therefore God gave them
the same gift as *He gave* us when we
believed on the Lord Jesus Christ,
[b]who was I that I could withstand
God?"†
18 When they heard these things
they became silent; and they glorified God, saying, [a]"Then God has
also granted to the Gentiles repentance to life."

The Gentile Church: Antioch

19 [a]Now those who were scattered
after the persecution that arose over
Stephen traveled as far as Phoenicia,
Cyprus, and Antioch, preaching the
word to no one but the Jews only.†
20 But some of them were men
from Cyprus and Cyrene, who,
when they had come to Antioch,
spoke to [a]the Hellenists, preaching
the Lord Jesus.†
21 And [a]the hand of the Lord was
with them, and a great number believed and [b]turned to the Lord.
22 Then news of these things came
to the ears of the church in Jerusalem, and they sent out [a]Barnabas to
go as far as Antioch.†
23 When he came and had seen the
grace of God, he was glad, and
[a]encouraged them all that with purpose of heart they should continue
with the Lord.
24 For he was a good man, [a]full
of the Holy Spirit and of faith.
[b]And a great many people were
added to the Lord.
25 Then Barnabas departed for
[a]Tarsus to seek Saul.†
26 And when he had found him,
he brought him to Antioch. So it was
that for a whole year they assembled
with the church and taught a great
many people. And the disciples were
first called Christians in Antioch.†

Aid to Jewish Christians

27 And in these days [a]prophets
came from Jerusalem to Antioch.†
28 Then one of them, named
[a]Agabus, stood up and showed by

15 [a]Acts 2:1–4; 15:7–9
16 [a]Matt. 3:11; Mark 1:8; John 1:26, 33; Acts 1:5; 19:4 [b]Is. 44:3
17 [a][Acts 15:8, 9] [b]Acts 10:47
18 [a]Is. 42:1, 6; 49:6; Luke 2:32; John 11:52; Rom. 10:12, 13; 15:9, 16
19 [a]Acts 8:1, 4
20 [a]Acts 6:1; 9:29
21 [a]Luke 1:66; Acts 2:47 [b]Acts 9:35; 14:1
22 [a]Acts 4:36; 9:27
23 [a]Acts 13:43; 14:22
24 [a]Acts 6:5 [b]Acts 5:14; 11:21
25 [a]Acts 9:11, 30
27 [a]Acts 2:17; 13:1; 15:32; 21:9; 1 Cor. 12:28; Eph. 4:11
28 [a]John 16:13; Acts 21:10

11:14 Words by which we **will be saved** are the words of the message of salvation through Christ. A marvelous challenge to those who preach the Gospel: There are *words* that must be heard for salvation.

11:17, 18 The apostolic church of Jerusalem recognizes God's special initiative and concludes that Gentiles, too, are to be saved and received into the life of the Church. Although the risen Christ charged the Apostles to preach a universal gospel (Matt. 28:19), the early Church recognizes this truth gradually. Much debate will come over the requirements of the OT Law for Gentiles who have become Christians (see ch. 15).

11:19 Phoenicia was the coastland in the area of Tyre and Sidon, the southern part of modern Lebanon. **Antioch** was a major city near the Mediterranean coast of Syria.

11:20 As Jesus proclaimed the gospel in Sychar (John 4:5–42), a city of Samaria, to those who were not Jews, so here the gospel is proclaimed to Gentile Greeks. **Hellenists** here refers to Greeks, not to Hellenistic Jews (as in 6:1). The church of Antioch marked a new page in history by admitting numerous Gentiles into its life.

11:22 Here is a clear example of apostolic authority. Barnabas does not go to Antioch on his own. He is **sent.**

11:25 Barnabas is a clear-sighted Christian who knows when he needs help! **Tarsus,** a Greek city near the eastern coast of southern Asia Minor, was the hometown of Saul.

11:26 Note three key actions here: (1) they **assembled** a great number of people; (2) they **taught** apostolic doctrine; (3) they made **disciples** (see also 6:1; 9:1, 26, 38).

11:27 Prophets refers to Christian prophets within the Church (see 1 Cor. 12:29; 14:3, 29).

Commemoration of a Holy Martyr

12:1–11: Peter is delivered from prison by an angel, showing that the martyrdom of God's servants is always in His hands.

the Spirit that there was going to be
a great famine throughout all the
world, which also happened in the
days of [b]Claudius Caesar.†
29 Then the disciples, each according to his ability, determined to send
[a]relief to the brethren dwelling in
Judea.†
30 [a]This they also did, and sent it
to the elders by the hands of Barnabas and Saul.†

Jerusalem Shaken

12 Now about that time Herod
the king stretched out *his*
hand to harass some from the
church.†
2 Then he killed James [a]the
brother of John with the sword.
3 And because he saw that it
pleased the Jews, he proceeded further to seize Peter also. Now it was
during [a]the Days of Unleavened
Bread.†
4 So [a]when he had arrested him,
he put *him* in prison, and delivered
him to four [1]squads of soldiers to
keep him, intending to bring him before the people after Passover.
5 Peter was therefore kept in
prison, but [1]constant prayer was offered to God for him by the church.

28 [b]Acts 18:2
29 [a]Rom. 15:26; 1 Cor. 16:1; 2 Cor. 9:1
30 [a]Acts 12:25

CHAPTER 12

2 [a]Matt. 4:21; 20:23
3 [a]Ex. 12:15; 23:15; Acts 20:6
4 [a]John 21:18 [1]Gr. *tetrads,* squads of four
5 [1]NU *constantly* or *earnestly*
6 [1]*guarding*
7 [a]Acts 5:19
9 [a]Ps. 126:1 [b]Acts 10:3, 17; 11:5
10 [a]Acts 5:19; 16:26
11 [a][Ps. 34:7]; Dan. 3:28; 6:22; [Heb. 1:14] [b]Job 5:19; [Ps. 33:18, 19; 34:22; 41:2]; 2 Cor. 1:10; [2 Pet. 2:9]

6 And when Herod was about to
bring him out, that night Peter was
sleeping, bound with two chains between two soldiers; and the guards
before the door were [1]keeping the
prison.
7 Now behold, [a]an angel of the
Lord stood by *him,* and a light shone
in the prison; and he struck Peter on
the side and raised him up, saying,
"Arise quickly!" And his chains fell
off *his* hands.
8 Then the angel said to him,
"Gird yourself and tie on your sandals"; and so he did. And he said
to him, "Put on your garment and
follow me."
9 So he went out and followed
him, and [a]did not know that what
was done by the angel was real, but
thought [b]he was seeing a vision.
10 When they were past the first
and the second guard posts, they
came to the iron gate that leads to
the city, [a]which opened to them of
its own accord; and they went out
and went down one street, and immediately the angel departed from
him.
11 And when Peter had come to
himself, he said, "Now I know for
certain that [a]the Lord has sent His
angel, and [b]has delivered me from
the hand of Herod and *from* all the

11:28 This **famine** came to pass in A.D. 44–51, beginning in Judea and spreading to Greece and Italy.

11:29 These Christians **determined to send relief** to their brothers and sisters in Christ. This is not general "welfare" but a "family" effort, for the household of God (Eph. 2:19).

11:30 This is the first mention in Acts of **elders** (or presbyters) in the Church.

12:1–19 Herod is Herod Agrippa, the grandson of Herod the Great who had sought to kill Jesus as a child. Herod Agrippa ruled as king in Judea and Palestine under Rome in A.D. 41–44. The dates of his reign determine the period in which James, the brother of John, was killed (v. 2) and Peter imprisoned (v. 3). James is the first of the Twelve Apostles to be martyred. Herod had in mind to "oppress" or "hurt," as the word for **harass** is translated elsewhere (7:6, 19; 18:10). This incident reveals that by A.D. 44 there was growing popular displeasure against Christians, and limited persecution by Jews.

12:3 The Days of Unleavened Bread mark the Passover period, since these two feasts were largely overlapping.

expectation of the Jewish people."
12 So, when he had considered
this, [a]he came to the house of Mary,
the mother of [b]John whose surname
was Mark, where many were gathered together [c]praying.†
13 And as Peter knocked at the
door of the gate, a girl named Rhoda
came to answer.
14 When she recognized Peter's
voice, because of *her* gladness she
did not open the gate, but ran in and
announced that Peter stood before
the gate.
15 But they said to her, "You are
beside yourself!" Yet she kept insist-
ing that it was so. So they said,
[a]"It is his angel."†
16 Now Peter continued knocking;
and when they opened *the door* and
saw him, they were astonished.
17 But [a]motioning to them with his
hand to keep silent, he declared to
them how the Lord had brought him
out of the prison. And he said, "Go,
tell these things to James and to the
brethren." And he departed and
went to another place.†
18 Then, as soon as it was day,
there was no small [1]stir among the
soldiers about what had become of
Peter.
19 But when Herod had searched
for him and not found him, he examined the guards and commanded
that *they* should be put to death. And
he went down from Judea to Caesarea, and stayed *there*.

12 [a]Acts 4:23 [b]Acts 13:5, 13; 15:37; 2 Tim. 4:11; Philem. 24; 1 Pet. 5:13 [c]Acts 12:5
15 [a]Gen. 48:16; [Matt. 18:10]
17 [a]Acts 13:16; 19:33; 21:40
18 [1]*disturbance*
20 [a]Matt. 11:21 [b]1 Kin. 5:11; Ezra 3:7; Ezek. 27:17 [1]*who was in charge of the king's bedchamber* [2]Lit. *nourished*
23 [a]1 Sam. 25:38; 2 Sam. 24:16, 17; 2 Kin. 19:35; Acts 5:19 [b]Ps. 115:1 [1]*breathed his last*
24 [a]Is. 55:11; Acts 6:7; 19:20
25 [a]Acts 11:30 [b]Acts 11:30 [c]Acts 13:5, 13 [d]Acts 12:12; 15:37 [1]NU, M *to*

CHAPTER 13
1 [a]Acts 14:26 [b]Acts 11:22 [c]Rom. 16:21

Herod Dies

20 Now Herod had been very angry with the people of [a]Tyre and Sidon; but they came to him with one
accord, and having made Blastus
[1]the king's personal aide their friend,
they asked for peace, because
[b]their country was [2]supplied with
food by the king's *country*.
21 So on a set day Herod, arrayed
in royal apparel, sat on his throne
and gave an oration to them.
22 And the people kept shouting,
"The voice of a god and not of a
man!"†
23 Then immediately an angel of
the Lord [a]struck him, because
[b]he did not give glory to God. And
he was eaten by worms and [1]died.
24 But [a]the word of God grew and
multiplied.†
25 And [a]Barnabas and Saul returned [1]from Jerusalem when they
had [b]fulfilled *their* ministry, and they
also [c]took with them [d]John whose
surname was Mark.

Antioch Sends Barnabas and Saul

13 Now [a]in the church that was
at Antioch there were certain
prophets and teachers: [b]Barnabas,
Simeon who was called Niger,
[c]Lucius of Cyrene, Manaen who had
been brought up with Herod the tetrarch, and Saul.†

12:12 John . . . Mark later became a coworker of Saul and Barnabas (v. 25; Col. 4:10) and still later of Peter (1 Pet. 5:13).

12:15 It is his angel indicates these Christians believed: (1) in angels, (2) in angels assigned to people, and (3) that some point of recognition existed between a person and his angel, since the girl had recognized Peter's voice (v. 14). The Orthodox Church emphatically believes Christians have guardian angels, and prays in its liturgy "for an angel of peace, a faithful guide and guardian of our souls and bodies."

12:17 This James is not one of the Twelve (that James had already been martyred; see v. 2). **James** here is the "brother" of the Lord (see note on Matt. 12:46–50), and by this time he is the bishop, the leader of the local church, in Jerusalem (see 15:13; 21:18; Gal. 1:19; James 1:1). **The brethren** are all Christians of the Jerusalem church. Peter **departed** from Jerusalem to escape Herod Agrippa's persecution.

12:22 Herod Agrippa committed a form of idolatry in receiving the people's worship, and in consequence was stricken by a fatal disease.

12:24 The enemies of God cannot stop the growth of **the word of God.**

13:1 Among the **prophets and teachers** of the church of Antioch are listed **Barnabas** and **Saul** (Paul), coworkers in mission. **Manaen** was brought up in his youth with **Herod** Antipas, the tetrarch of Galilee (39–4 B.C.), and was one of the early Christians with noble family connections.

2 As they ministered to the Lord
and fasted, the Holy Spirit said,
[a]"Now separate to Me Barnabas and
Saul for the work [b]to which I have
called them."†
3 Then, [a]having fasted and
prayed, and laid hands on them,
they sent *them* away.†

Churches Established on Cyprus

4 So, being sent out by the Holy
Spirit, they went down to Seleucia,
and from there they sailed to
[a]Cyprus.
5 And when they arrived in Salamis, [a]they preached the word of
God in the synagogues of the Jews.
They also had [b]John as *their*
assistant.†
6 Now when they had gone
through [1]the island to Paphos, they
found [a]a certain sorcerer, a false
prophet, a Jew whose name *was* Bar-
Jesus,
7 who was with the proconsul,
Sergius Paulus, an intelligent man.
This man called for Barnabas and
Saul and sought to hear the word
of God.
8 But [a]Elymas the sorcerer (for so
his name is translated) [1]withstood

2 [a]Num. 8:14; Acts 9:15; 22:21; Rom. 1:1; Gal. 1:15; 2:9 [b]Matt. 9:38; Acts 14:26; Rom. 10:15; Eph. 3:7, 8; 1 Tim. 2:7; 2 Tim. 1:11; Heb. 5:4
3 [a]Matt. 9:15; Mark 2:20; Luke 5:35; Acts 6:6
4 [a]Acts 4:36
5 [a][Acts 13:46] [b]Acts 12:25; 15:37
6 [a]Acts 8:9 [1]NU *the whole island*
8 [a]Ex. 7:11; 2 Tim. 3:8 [1]*opposed*
9 [a]Acts 2:4; 4:8
10 [a]Matt. 13:38; John 8:44; [1 John 3:8]
11 [a]Ex. 9:3; 1 Sam. 5:6; Job 19:21; Ps. 32:4; Heb. 10:31
13 [a]Acts 15:38
14 [a]Acts 16:13

them, seeking to turn the proconsul
away from the faith.
9 Then Saul, who also *is called*
Paul, [a]filled with the Holy Spirit,
looked intently at him†
10 and said, "O full of all deceit
and all fraud, [a]*you* son of the devil,
you enemy of all righteousness, will
you not cease perverting the straight
ways of the Lord?
11 "And now, indeed, [a]the hand
of the Lord *is* upon you, and you
shall be blind, not seeing the sun for
a time." And immediately a dark
mist fell on him, and he went around
seeking someone to lead him by the
hand.
12 Then the proconsul believed,
when he saw what had been done,
being astonished at the teaching of
the Lord.†

The Church in Pisidia

13 Now when Paul and his party
set sail from Paphos, they came to
Perga in Pamphylia; and [a]John, departing from them, returned to
Jerusalem.†
14 But when they departed from
Perga, they came to Antioch in Pisidia, and [a]went into the synagogue
on the Sabbath day and sat down.†

13:2 Ministered (Gr. *leitourgeo*) means "to perform ritual acts." It is the same root word from which "liturgy" is derived. Literally translated, this passage would read, "As they liturgized to the Lord and fasted." Liturgical worship did not originate in Antioch. The Christians in Antioch were taught how to worship by Saul and Barnabas (11:22, 25, 26). It is in the midst of this liturgy that the **Holy Spirit** speaks. Worship and fasting go together; they are part of Orthodox life. **Separate** means "set apart" from the rest of the Christians for a special service.

13:3 Laid hands on them is a reference to the Sacrament of Ordination. Here is a case of multiple ordinations. The work of the Church is the work of the Holy Spirit—it is the Church that sends them out, and it is the Holy Spirit who sends them out (v. 4). Saul and Barnabas are sent, not self-ordained or self-appointed, on this first missionary journey (chronicled in 13:4—14:28).

13:5 The synagogues are the initial places of Christian preaching because Christianity first arose within Judaism. Just as Jesus preached in the synagogues regularly, so also Saul and Barnabas proclaim Jesus in the synagogues. **John** is John Mark, the author of the Gospel According to St. Mark.

13:9 This is the first use in Acts of the name **Paul** for **Saul** of Tarsus. No particular significance is noted. Paul comes from the Roman name "Paulus" (lit. "little") and Saul from the Hebrew name "Saoul" (lit. "asked"). Many Jews of this time had two names, one Jewish and another Greek or Roman, often chosen for the similarity of sound.

13:12 This is the first instance of a conversion of a high Roman official.

13:13 Pamphylia: a region on the southern coast of modern Turkey.

13:14 Antioch in Pisidia was in Phrygia, in the Roman province of Galatia (in what is

(continued on next page)

The Beheading of John the Baptist

August 29

13:25–32: Paul preaches about the ministry of John and about Christ's death in fulfillment of prophecy.

15 And [a]after the reading of the
Law and the Prophets, the rulers of
the synagogue sent to them, saying,
"Men *and* brethren, if you have
[b]any word of [1]exhortation for the
people, say on."
16 Then Paul stood up, and mo-
tioning with *his* hand said, "Men of
Israel, and [a]you who fear God,
listen:†
17 "The God of this people [1]Israel
[a]chose our fathers, and exalted the
people [b]when they dwelt as strangers in the land of Egypt, and with
[2]an uplifted arm He [c]brought them
out of it.
18 "Now [a]for a time of about forty
years He put up with their ways in
the wilderness.
19 "And when He had destroyed
[a]seven nations in the land of Canaan, [b]He distributed their land to
them by allotment.
20 "After that [a]He gave *them*
judges for about four hundred and
fifty years, [b]until Samuel the
prophet.
21 [a]"And afterward they asked for
a king; so God gave them [b]Saul the
son of Kish, a man of the tribe of
Benjamin, for forty years.†
22 "And [a]when He had removed
him, [b]He raised up for them David
as king, to whom also He gave testimony and said, [c]'*I have found
David* the *son* of Jesse, [d]*a man after
My own heart,* who will do all My
will.'
23 [a]"From this man's seed, according [b]to *the* promise, God raised up
for Israel [c]a[1] Savior—Jesus—†
24 [a]"after John had first preached,
before His coming, the baptism of
repentance to all the people of Israel.
25 "And as John was finishing his
course, he said, [a]'Who do you think
I am? I am not *He.* But behold,
[b]there comes One after me, the sandals of whose feet I am not worthy
to loose.'
26 "Men *and* brethren, sons of the
[1]family of Abraham, and [a]those
among you who fear God, [b]to you
the [2]word of this salvation has been
sent.†
27 "For those who dwell in Jerusalem, and their rulers, [a]because they

15 [a]Luke 4:16 [b]Heb. 13:22 [1]*encouragement*
16 [a]Acts 10:35
17 [a]Deut. 7:6–8 [b]Acts 7:17 [c]Ex. 14:8 [1]M omits *Israel* [2]Mighty power
18 [a]Num. 14:34
19 [a]Deut. 7:1 [b]Josh. 14:1, 2; 19:51
20 [a]Judg. 2:16 [b]1 Sam. 3:20
21 [a]1 Sam. 8:5 [b]1 Sam. 10:20–24
22 [a]1 Sam. 15:23, 26, 28 [b]1 Sam. 16:1, 12, 13 [c]Ps. 89:20 [d]1 Sam. 13:14
23 [a]Is. 11:1 [b]Ps. 132:11 [c][Matt. 1:21] [1]M *salvation, after*
24 [a][Luke 3:3]
25 [a]Mark 1:7 [b]John 1:20, 27 **26** [a]Ps. 66:16 [b]Matt. 10:6 [1]*stock* [2]*message*
27 [a]Luke 23:34

(continued from previous page)
now Turkey). It is not to be confused with Antioch of Syria, from which Paul and Barnabas were sent out. The population included numerous Roman army veterans, a large Jewish settlement, and many native Phrygians. This may have been the first predominantly Gentile church. This Antioch was 3,300 feet higher in altitude than **Perga** and 160 miles away. The route was extremely dangerous. John Mark apparently left the others before this arduous journey (15:37–41).

13:16 You who fear God: Gentile followers of Judaism who are not full converts through circumcision; they are also called "God-fearers" (see note on 10:2). This begins Paul's speech (vv. 16–41) in which he demonstrates from Jewish history God's working with Israel—a message similar to Stephen's speech before the Council (ch. 7).

13:21, 22 The Lord **removed** King Saul by rejecting him as **king** of Israel (1 Sam. 15:28), and removing him from the lineage of salvation in favor of **David** (Is. 9:7).

13:23, 24 Paul is teaching that: (1) his gospel is the very heart, **the promise** (v. 23), of the Jewish faith; (2) Jesus is of the **seed** (v. 23) or house of David; and (3) Jesus is the One **John** the Baptist **preached** (v. 24).

13:26 Paul is careful to include the Gentiles, those **who fear God** (see v. 16; 10:2 and notes), in the salvation he is proclaiming.

did not know Him, nor even the voices of the Prophets which are read every Sabbath, have fulfilled *them* in condemning *Him*.†

28 [a]"And though they found no cause for death *in Him*, they asked Pilate that He should be put to death.

29 [a]"Now when they had fulfilled all that was written concerning Him, [b]they took *Him* down from the tree and laid *Him* in a tomb.

30 [a]"But God raised Him from the dead.

31 [a]"He was seen for many days by those who came up with Him from Galilee to Jerusalem, who are His witnesses to the people.

32 "And we declare to you glad tidings—[a]that promise which was made to the fathers.

33 "God has fulfilled this for us their children, in that He has raised up Jesus. As it is also written in the second Psalm:†

> [a]*'You are My Son,*
> *Today I have begotten You.'*

34 "And that He raised Him from the dead, no more to return to [1]corruption, He has spoken thus:

> [a]*'I will give you the sure*
> *[2]mercies of David.'*

35 "Therefore He also says in another *Psalm:*

> [a]*'You will not allow Your Holy*
> *One to see corruption.'*

36 "For David, after he had served [1]his own generation by the will of God, [a]fell asleep, was buried with his fathers, and [2]saw corruption;

37 "but He whom God raised up [1]saw no corruption.

38 "Therefore let it be known to you, brethren, that [a]through this Man is preached to you the forgiveness of sins;†

39 "and [a]by Him everyone who believes is justified from all things from which you could not be justified by the law of Moses.

40 "Beware therefore, lest what has been spoken in the prophets come upon you:

> 41 *'Behold,[a] you despisers,*
> *Marvel and perish!*
> *For I work a work in your days,*
> *A work which you will by no*
> *means believe,*
> *Though one were to declare it*
> *to you.'"*

42 [1]So when the Jews went out of the synagogue, the Gentiles begged that these words might be preached to them the next Sabbath.

43 Now when the congregation had broken up, many of the Jews and devout proselytes followed Paul and Barnabas, who, speaking to them, [a]persuaded them to continue in [b]the grace of God.

Apostles to the Gentiles

44 On the next Sabbath almost the whole city came together to hear the word of God.

45 But when the Jews saw the multitudes, they were filled with envy; and contradicting and blaspheming, they [a]opposed the things spoken by Paul.†

46 Then Paul and Barnabas grew

28 [a]Matt. 27:22, 23
29 [a]Luke 18:31 [b]Matt. 27:57–61
30 [a]Matt. 12:39, 40; 28:6
31 [a]Acts 1:3, 11
32 [a][Gen. 3:15]
33 [a]Ps. 2:7
34 [a]Is. 55:3 [1]*the state of decay* [2]*blessings*
35 [a]Ps. 16:10
36 [a]Acts 2:29 [1]*in his* [2]*underwent decay*
37 [1]*underwent no decay*
38 [a]Jer. 31:34
39 [a][Is. 53:11]
41 [a]Hab. 1:5
42 [1]Or *And when they went out of the synagogue of the Jews;* NU *And when they went out of the synagogue, they begged*
43 [a]Acts 11:23 [b]Titus 2:11
45 [a]1 Pet. 4:4

13:27 Jesus alone **fulfilled** the message of all the OT **Prophets** who wrote concerning the Messiah. Paul consistently presses this home to the Jews: If the OT is properly understood, it is clear that Jesus is the Messiah. Even the Jewish leaders' rejection of Jesus as the One of whom the prophets wrote is a fulfillment of prophecy (Matt. 21:42–45; see John 11:49–52).

13:33 Psalm 2:7 is a prophecy of the Messiah and is quoted to prove the one **raised up** is the Son of God.

13:38, 39 Besides the Resurrection of Christ (vv. 30–37), two continually recurring themes in apostolic preaching are: (1) **forgiveness of sins** (v. 38) and (2) that no one is justified by **the law of Moses** (v. 39).

13:45 The majority of **the Jews** disputed and rejected the gospel of salvation for all people

(continued on next page)

bold and said, [a]"It was necessary
that the word of God should be spoken to you first; but [b]since you reject
it, and judge yourselves unworthy
of everlasting life, behold, [c]we turn
to the Gentiles.
47 "For so the Lord has commanded us:

> [a]'I have set you as a light to the Gentiles,
> That you should be for salvation to the ends of the earth.'"

48 Now when the Gentiles heard
this, they were glad and glorified the
word of the Lord. [a]And as many as
had been appointed to eternal life
believed.
49 And the word of the Lord was
being spread throughout all the
region.
50 But the Jews stirred up the devout and prominent women and the
chief men of the city, [a]raised up persecution against Paul and Barnabas,
and expelled them from their region.
51 [a]But they shook off the dust
from their feet against them, and
came to Iconium.
52 And the disciples [a]were filled
with joy and [b]with the Holy Spirit.

The Church in Iconium, Galatia

14 Now it happened in Iconium
that they went together to the
synagogue of the Jews, and so spoke
that a great multitude both of the
Jews and of the [a]Greeks believed.†
2 But the unbelieving Jews stirred
up the Gentiles and [1]poisoned their
[2]minds against the brethren.†
3 Therefore they stayed there a
long time, speaking boldly in the
Lord, [a]who was bearing witness to
the word of His grace, granting signs
and [b]wonders to be done by their
hands.
4 But the multitude of the city was
[a]divided: part sided with the Jews,
and part with the [b]apostles.
5 And when a violent attempt was
made by both the Gentiles and Jews,
with their rulers, [a]to abuse and stone
them,
6 they became aware of it and
[a]fled to Lystra and Derbe, cities of
Lycaonia, and to the surrounding
region.
7 And they were preaching the
gospel there.

In Lystra and Derbe, Galatia

8 [a]And in Lystra a certain man
without strength in his feet was sitting, a cripple from his mother's
womb, who had never walked.†
9 *This* man heard Paul speaking.
[1]Paul, observing him intently and
seeing that he had faith to be healed,
10 said with a loud voice, [a]"Stand
up straight on your feet!" And he
leaped and walked.
11 Now when the people saw what
Paul had done, they raised their
voices, saying in the Lycaonian *language,* [a]"The gods have come down
to us in the likeness of men!"
12 And Barnabas they called

46 [a]Matt. 10:6; Acts 3:26; Rom. 1:16 [b]Ex. 32:10; Deut. 32:21; Is. 55:5; Matt. 21:43; Rom. 10:19 [c]Acts 18:6
47 [a]Is. 42:6; 49:6; Luke 2:32
48 [a][Acts 2:47]
50 [a]Acts 7:52; 2 Tim. 3:11
51 [a]Matt. 10:14; Mark 6:11; [Luke 9:5]
52 [a]Matt. 5:12; John 16:22 [b]Acts 2:4; 4:8, 31; 13:9

CHAPTER 14

1 [a]John 7:35; Acts 18:4; Rom. 1:14, 16; 1 Cor. 1:22
2 [1]*embittered* [2]Lit. *souls*
3 [a]Mark 16:20; Acts 4:29; 20:32; Heb. 2:4 [b]Acts 5:12
4 [a]Luke 12:51 [b]Acts 13:2, 3
5 [a]2 Tim. 3:11
6 [a]Matt. 10:23
8 [a]Acts 3:2
9 [1]Lit. *Who*
10 [a][Is. 35:6]
11 [a]Acts 8:10; 28:6

(continued from previous page)
through Christ (see also v. 50), so Paul and Barnabas turn directly to the Gentiles. This becomes an established pattern throughout Acts: the gospel is preached first to the Jews because they were the chosen people, then to the Gentiles (see Rom. 1:16).

14:1 Iconium, located off the Roman military highway between Antioch and Lystra, was the capitol of Lycaonia in Asia Minor and had a large Jewish population. An interesting second-century account tells of a man from Iconium who went to meet Paul at the junction on the highway. He was looking for "a small man in size with meeting eyebrows, with a rather large nose, bald, bow-legged, strongly built, full of grace, who at times seemed to have the face of an angel" (from *The Acts of Thekla*).

14:2 Unbelieving could also be translated "disobedient." It is from the common Greek verb *apeitheo,* meaning "to disobey." Unbelief is a form of disobedience to the gospel of Christ.

14:8 Lystra was a small mountain town which had served as a Roman garrison.

ORDINATION

Sacraments (or mysteries) are holy actions of the Church by which spiritual life is imparted to those receiving them. Ordination, which means "to set in place" or "to select by the outstretched hand," is one of several Orthodox sacraments. It is extended specifically to bishops, presbyters (priests) and deacons, and generally to all through Holy Baptism.

(1) *Bishops*. In His ministry Christ ordained or "set in place" the Twelve, assuring them, "You did not choose Me, but I chose you and appointed you that you should go and bear fruit, and that your fruit should remain" (John 15:16).

Both the New Testament and the Church Fathers recognize the Twelve as the first bishops or overseers in the Church. When Judas had fallen away and the disciples were considering his successor, Peter said, "Let another take his office" (Gr. *episkopen*, lit. "bishopric"; Acts 1:20). This bishopric was given to Matthias (Acts 1:26).

The apostles—these first bishops—in turn ordained presbyters and deacons.

(2) *Deacons*. The account of the first ordination of deacons (Acts 6:1–6) is quite detailed. "Seek out from among you seven men of good reputation, full of the Holy Spirit and wisdom," the apostles said, "whom we may appoint [Gr. *kathistemi*, "to set down" or "ordain"] over this business" (Acts 6:3). The manner of this appointment is clear: "They laid hands on them" (Acts 6:6). The ordination of deacons in the Orthodox Church takes place in this same manner today, through the laying on of hands by the bishop.

(3) *Presbyters*. The first account of the ordination of elders or presbyters is in Acts 14:23. The apostles Paul and Barnabas "appointed [literally, "elected by stretching forth the hand"] elders in every church, and prayed with fasting," then "commended them to the Lord in whom they had believed." Similarly, Paul reminds his apostolic apprentice, Titus, "For this reason I left you in Crete, that you should set in order the things that are lacking, and appoint [set in place, ordain] elders in every city as I commanded you" (Titus 1:5).

The Titus passage brings to mind the first prayer the bishop prays over the one being ordained to the Orthodox priesthood: "The grace divine, which always heals that which is weak, and completes that which is lacking, elevates through the laying on of my hands this most devout deacon to be priest."

The bishop continues to ask God to "fill with the gift of the Holy Spirit this man . . . that he may be worthy to stand in innocence before Your holy altar, to proclaim the gospel of Your Kingdom, to minister the word of Your truth, to offer You spiritual gifts and sacrifices, to renew Your people through the laver of regeneration."

A dramatic moment in the service of ordination comes when the candidate is led around the altar three times, kissing or venerating the four corners of the altar. This symbolizes his marriage to Christ, his death with Christ, and his willingness to serve the Church sacrificially after the example of his Master.

Ordination is seen as an eternal appointment, "for the gifts and the calling of God are irrevocable" (Rom. 11:29). It is in this spirit that during each Divine Liturgy the priest prays for his bishop that "the Lord God remember him in His Kingdom always, now and ever, and unto ages of ages."

Through the sacrament of ordination in His Church, Christ entrusts to the shepherd the very salvation of His people's souls.

[1]Zeus, and Paul, [2]Hermes, because he was the chief speaker.†

13 Then the priest of Zeus, whose temple was in front of their city, brought oxen and garlands to the gates, [a]intending to sacrifice with the multitudes.

14 But when the apostles Barnabas and Paul heard this, [a]they tore their clothes and ran in among the multitude, crying out

15 and saying, "Men, [a]why are you doing these things? [b]We also are men with the same nature as you, and preach to you that you should turn from [c]these useless things [d]to the living God, [e]who made the heaven, the earth, the sea, and all things that are in them,†

16 [a]"who in bygone generations allowed all nations to walk in their own ways.

17 [a]"Nevertheless He did not leave Himself without witness, in that He did good, [b]gave us rain from heaven and fruitful seasons, filling our hearts with [c]food and gladness."

18 And with these sayings they could scarcely restrain the multitudes from sacrificing to them.

19 [a]Then Jews from Antioch and Iconium came there; and having persuaded the multitudes, [b]they stoned Paul *and* dragged *him* out of the city, supposing him to be [c]dead.†

12 [1]*Jupiter* [2]*Mercury* **13** [a]Dan. 2:46 **14** [a]Matt. 26:65 **15** [a]Acts 10:26 [b]James 5:17 [c]1 Cor. 8:4 [d]1 Thess. 1:9 [e]Rev. 14:7 **16** [a]Ps. 81:12 **17** [a]Rom. 1:19, 20 [b]Deut. 11:14 [c]Ps. 145:16 **19** [a]Acts 13:45, 50; 14:2–5 [b]2 Cor. 11:25 [c][2 Cor. 12:1–4]

21 [a]Matt. 28:19 **22** [a]Acts 11:23 [b][2 Tim. 2:12; 3:12] **23** [a]Titus 1:5

20 However, when the disciples gathered around him, he rose up and went into the city. And the next day he departed with Barnabas to Derbe.

Return Visit

21 And when they had preached the gospel to that city [a]and made many disciples, they returned to Lystra, Iconium, and Antioch,

22 strengthening the souls of the disciples, [a]exhorting *them* to continue in the faith, and *saying,* [b]"We must through many tribulations enter the kingdom of God."†

23 So when they had [a]appointed elders in every church, and prayed with fasting, they commended them to the Lord in whom they had believed.†

24 And after they had passed through Pisidia, they came to Pamphylia.

25 Now when they had preached the word in Perga, they went down to Attalia.

Report Back to Antioch

26 From there they sailed to Antioch, where they had been commended to the grace of God for the work which they had completed.

14:12 Barnabas apparently had an impressive stature and is thus viewed as **Zeus,** the chief of the Greek gods, whereas **Paul** took the initiative in speaking and is thus viewed as **Hermes,** the gods' messenger.

14:15 The apostles react strongly to the idolatrous sacrifice being prepared on their behalf (vv. 13–18) and provide correct teaching about **the living God.** Note the difference between apostolic preaching to Jews and to Gentiles. To a Gentile audience, Paul speaks not of prophecy and its fulfillment, but of God as Creator (see note on 17:32).

14:19–21 Jesus had instructed the disciples, "When they persecute you in this city, flee to another" (Matt. 10:23). Leaving town in the face of persecution displays wisdom, not lack of faith. Had Paul and Barnabas remained they might have brought persecution on the new disciples. The short reference to **Derbe** (v. 20) does not imply a short stay by Paul and Barnabas. They were there long enough to make **many disciples** (v. 21). Derbe is 45 miles southwest of Iconium, 20 miles from Lystra. They returned to Antioch by way of the same cities, including Lystra, to strengthen the Christians there (v. 22).

14:22 Christians have a great need to have strong **souls**—the inner man, the heart—especially in times of adversity. The ultimate goal of NT preaching is that people might **enter the kingdom of God,** the very purpose of the New Birth (John 3:5). The Kingdom is the goal; being spiritually reborn is the means.

14:23 Though **elders** are mentioned earlier (11:30), this is the first reference to appointing or ordaining *elders* or presbyters as leaders in the churches Paul and Barnabas had established. The word translated **appointed** (Gr. *cheirotoneo*) means "to ordain by the laying on of hands."

27 Now when they had come and
gathered the church together,
[a]they reported all that God had done
with them, and that He had [b]opened
the door of faith to the Gentiles.
28 So they stayed there a long time
with the disciples.

Circumcision in Antioch

15 And [a]certain *men* came down
from Judea and taught the
brethren, [b]"Unless you are circumcised according to the custom of Moses, you cannot be saved."†
2 Therefore, when Paul and Barnabas had no small dissension and
dispute with them, they determined
that [a]Paul and Barnabas and certain
others of them should go up to Jerusalem, to the apostles and elders,
about this question.†
3 So, [a]being sent on their way by
the church, they passed through
Phoenicia and Samaria, [b]describing
the conversion of the Gentiles; and
they caused great joy to all the
brethren.
4 And when they had come to Jerusalem, they were received by the
church and the apostles and the elders; and they reported all things that
God had done with them.†

27 [a]Acts 15:4, 12 [b]2 Cor. 2:12

CHAPTER 15

1 [a]Gal. 2:12 [b]Phil. 3:2
2 [a]Gal. 2:1
3 [a]Rom. 15:24 [b]Acts 14:27; 15:4, 12

7 [a]Acts 10:20
8 [a]Acts 1:24 [b]Acts 2:4; 10:44, 47 [1]*bore witness to*
9 [a]Rom. 10:12 [b]Acts 10:15, 28
10 [a]Matt. 23:4
11 [a]Rom. 3:4; 5:15 [1]NU, M omit *Christ*

5 But some of the sect of the Pharisees who believed rose up, saying,
"It is necessary to circumcise them,
and to command *them* to keep the
law of Moses."

The Council in Jerusalem

6 Now the apostles and elders
came together to consider this
matter.†
7 And when there had been much
dispute, Peter rose up and said to
them: [a]"Men and brethren, you
know that a good while ago God
chose among us, that by my mouth
the Gentiles should hear the word
of the gospel and believe.
8 "So God, [a]who knows the
heart, [1]acknowledged them by
[b]giving them the Holy Spirit, just as
He did to us,†
9 [a]"and made no distinction between us and them, [b]purifying their
hearts by faith.
10 "Now therefore, why do you
test God [a]by putting a yoke on the
neck of the disciples which neither
our fathers nor we were able to bear?
11 "But [a]we believe that through
the grace of the Lord Jesus [1]Christ
we shall be saved in the same manner as they."†

15:1 The **certain men** who advocate circumcision as a requirement for salvation are conservative Jewish Christians (11:2; Gal. 2:12), some of whom had belonged to the sect of the Pharisees (v. 5).

15:2 The first major **dispute** in the Church: Must Gentile converts keep the Law of Moses, particularly the rite of circumcision? This controversy would be settled not in Antioch (14:26), but by the Apostles and elders in Jerusalem. Some Jewish Christians never accepted the decision, but opposed Paul and Barnabas for the rest of their days.

Some view the early Church as ideal, perfect; yet in this controversy there is **no small dissension.** However, the Christian community has a way to resolve doctrinal disputes: in council. This has always been and still is the practice of the Orthodox Church.

15:4 Paul and Barnabas are not on trial, but their work among the Gentiles has to be judged by the consensus or common agreement of the Church. For the sake of the unity of the Church, Paul and Barnabas are humbly willing to submit to God's judgment in council.

15:6 This is the Apostolic Council (c. A.D. 49), a precedent of tremendous importance for the government of the Church. The Orthodox Church is known as the Church of the Councils, for it continues the practice of solving disputes in council.

15:8–11 Peter emphasizes that: (1) God **acknowledged** (v. 8) the sincere faith of the Gentile hearts at Cornelius' house by giving them the Holy Spirit; and (2) God purified their hearts from all defilement (10:47, 48). God makes **no distinction** (v. 9) between races in offering the gift of salvation in Christ, free from the **yoke** (v. 10) of the Mosaic Law.

15:11 Apostolic preaching understands salvation in three tenses: (1) past: we have been saved, in baptism; (2) present: we are being saved, working out our salvation in cooperation with God (Phil. 2:12, 13); and (3) future: **we shall be saved** at the Judgment.

12 Then all the multitude kept silent and listened to Barnabas and
Paul declaring how many miracles
and wonders God had [a]worked
through them among the Gentiles.
13 And after they had [1]become silent, [a]James answered, saying,
"Men *and* brethren, listen to me:†
14 [a]"Simon has declared how God
at the first visited the Gentiles to take
out of them a people for His name.
15 "And with this the words of the
prophets agree, just as it is written:†

16 *'After[a] this I will return*
And will rebuild the tabernacle
of David, which has fallen
down;
I will rebuild its ruins,
And I will set it up;
17 *So that the rest of mankind may*
seek the LORD,
Even all the Gentiles who are
called by My name,
Says the [1]LORD *who does all*
these things.'

18 [1]"Known to God from eternity
are all His works.
19 "Therefore [a]I judge that we
should not trouble those from among
the Gentiles who [b]are turning to
God,†
20 "but that we [a]write to them to
abstain [b]from things polluted by
idols, [c]*from* [1]sexual immorality,
[d]*from* things strangled, and *from*
blood.†
21 "For Moses has had throughout
many generations those who preach
him in every city, [a]being read in the
synagogues every Sabbath."

12 [a]Acts 14:27; 15:3, 4
13 [a]Acts 12:17 [1]*stopped speaking*
14 [a]Acts 15:7
16 [a]Amos 9:11, 12
17 [1]NU LORD, *who makes these things*
18 [1]NU (continuing v. 17) *known from eternity (of old).'*
19 [a]Acts 15:28; 21:25 [b]1 Thess. 1:9
20 [a]Acts 21:25 [b][1 Cor. 8:1; 10:20, 28] [c][1 Cor. 6:9] [d]Lev. 3:17 [1]Or *fornication*
21 [a]Acts 13:15, 27
22 [a]Acts 1:23 [1]NU, M *Barsabbas*
24 [a]Titus 1:10, 11 [b]Gal. 1:7; 5:10 [1]NU omits *saying, "You must be circumcised and keep the law"*
25 [1]*purpose* or *mind*
26 [a]Acts 13:50; 14:19
29 [a]Acts 15:20; 21:25 [b]Lev. 17:14

The Decree: Early Canon Law

22 Then it pleased the apostles and
elders, with the whole church, to
send chosen men of their own company to Antioch with Paul and Barnabas, *namely,* Judas who was also
named [a]Barsabas,[1] and Silas, leading
men among the brethren.
23 They wrote this *letter* by them:

The apostles, the elders, and the
brethren,

To the brethren who are of the
Gentiles in Antioch, Syria, and
Cilicia:

Greetings.†

24 Since we have heard that
[a]some who went out from us
have troubled you with words,
[b]unsettling your souls, [1]saying,
"You must be circumcised and
keep the law"—to whom we
gave no *such* commandment—
25 it seemed good to us, being
assembled with one [1]accord, to
send chosen men to you with
our beloved Barnabas and Paul,
26 [a]men who have risked their
lives for the name of our Lord
Jesus Christ.
27 We have therefore sent Judas
and Silas, who will also report
the same things by word of
mouth.
28 For it seemed good to the Holy
Spirit, and to us, to lay upon
you no greater burden than
these necessary things:†
29 [a]that you abstain from things
offered to idols, [b]from blood,

15:13 James, the "brother" of the Lord (see note on Matt. 12:46–50), speaks as the bishop of the Jerusalem church, which ancient records reveal him to be.

15:15 Agree here translates *sumphoneo,* the Greek word from which we get "symphony." In essence James is saying, "This is in symphony with what God said through the prophets. Therefore, it is the work of God."

15:19 Therefore I judge does not mean "I think," or "in my opinion." James is making the final decision here. However, this is not his private opinion; he is summarizing the consensus of the council. His speaking last suggests he is the bishop.

15:20 The four prohibited acts seem to reflect Lev. 17; 18 and are viewed as minimal requirements on Christian Gentiles.

15:23–29 This is the earliest known apostolic letter, sent from the church of Jerusalem to the church of Antioch, and is a kind of canon law.

15:28 It seemed good to the Holy Spirit, and to us demonstrates the unity between the

(continued on next page)

from things strangled, and from [c]sexual[1] immorality. If you keep yourselves from these, you will do well.

Farewell.

The Decree Received in Antioch

30 So when they were sent off, they came to Antioch; and when they had gathered the multitude together, they delivered the letter.
31 When they had read it, they rejoiced over its encouragement.
32 Now Judas and Silas, themselves being [a]prophets also, [b]exhorted and strengthened the brethren with many words.
33 And after they had stayed *there* for a time, they were [a]sent back with greetings from the brethren to [1]the apostles.
34 [1]However, it seemed good to Silas to remain there.
35 [a]Paul and Barnabas also remained in Antioch, teaching and preaching the word of the Lord, with many others also.†

Paul and Barnabas Separate

36 Then after some days Paul said to Barnabas, "Let us now go back and visit our brethren in every city where we have preached the word of the Lord, *and see* how they are doing."†
37 Now Barnabas [1]was determined to take with them [a]John called Mark.
38 But Paul insisted that they should not take with them [a]the one who had departed from them in Pamphylia, and had not gone with them to the work.
39 Then the contention became so sharp that they parted from one another. And so Barnabas took Mark and sailed to [a]Cyprus;
40 but Paul chose Silas and departed, [a]being [1]commended by the brethren to the grace of God.
41 And he went through Syria and Cilicia, [a]strengthening the churches.

The Call to Europe

16 Then he came to [a]Derbe and Lystra. And behold, a certain disciple was there, [b]named Timothy, [c]*the* son of a certain Jewish woman who believed, but his father *was* Greek.†
2 He was well spoken of by the brethren who were at Lystra and Iconium.
3 Paul wanted to have him go on with him. And he [a]took *him* and circumcised him because of the Jews who were in that region, for they all knew that his father was Greek.†
4 And as they went through the cities, they delivered to them the [a]decrees to keep, [b]which were determined by the apostles and elders at Jerusalem.†

29 [c]Col. 3:5 [1]Or *fornication*
32 [a]Eph. 4:11 [b]Acts 14:22; 18:23
33 [a]Heb. 11:31 [1]NU *those who had sent them*
34 [1]NU, M omit v. 34.
35 [a]Acts 13:1
37 [a]Acts 12:12, 25 [1]*resolved*
38 [a]Acts 13:13
39 [a]Acts 4:36; 13:4
40 [a]Acts 11:23; 14:26 [1]*committed*
41 [a]Acts 16:5

CHAPTER 16

1 [a]Acts 14:6 [b]Rom. 16:21 [c]2 Tim. 1:5; 3:15
3 [a][Gal. 2:3; 5:2]
4 [a]Acts 15:19–21 [b]Acts 15:28, 29

(continued from previous page)
work of the Holy Spirit and the Church. The Holy Spirit is speaking through the human agency of the Council, the Church cooperating with God.

15:35 Paul and Barnabas have already spent a year in the church of Antioch (11:25, 26), and now continue **teaching and preaching** there. Worship is indispensable, but so also is instruction.

15:36–40 This disagreement was eventually resolved and Mark later rejoined Paul, who wrote, "he is useful to me for ministry" (2 Tim. 4:11).

16:1 Timothy is destined to become one of the chief coworkers of Paul and the recipient of two of Paul's epistles.

16:3 Since Timothy is partly of Jewish heritage, Paul has him **circumcised** to accommodate Jewish sensibilities. But in the case of Titus, a Gentile, Paul refuses to do this, in order to maintain the principle that Christian Gentiles are not required to be circumcised in order to be saved (Gal. 2:3).

16:4 Decrees translates the Greek word *dogma*. The Church preserves her dogmas or doctrines, and they are not up for periodic renegotiation. In an age when popular opinion holds that what one believes is optional, there is one true faith which was once for all delivered to the saints. This faith is kept securely intact in the Orthodox Church.

5 [a]So the churches were strengthened in the faith, and increased in
number daily.
6 Now when they had gone
through Phrygia and the region of
[a]Galatia, they were forbidden by the
Holy Spirit to preach the word in
[1]Asia.†
7 After they had come to Mysia,
they tried to go into Bithynia, but
the [1]Spirit did not permit them.
8 So passing by Mysia, they
[a]came down to Troas.†
9 And a vision appeared to Paul
in the night. A [a]man of Macedonia
stood and pleaded with him, saying,
"Come over to Macedonia and help
us."
10 Now after he had seen the vision, immediately we sought to go
[a]to Macedonia, concluding that the
Lord had called us to preach the gospel to them.†

The First European Convert

11 Therefore, sailing from Troas,
we ran a straight course to Samo-
thrace, and the next *day* came to Neapolis,†
12 and from there to [a]Philippi,
which is the [1]foremost city of that
part of Macedonia, a colony. And we
were staying in that city for some
days.†
13 And on the Sabbath day we
went out of the city to the riverside,
where prayer was customarily made;
and we sat down and spoke to the
women who met *there*.†
14 Now a certain woman named
Lydia heard *us*. She was a seller of
purple from the city of [a]Thyatira,
who worshiped God. [b]The Lord
opened her heart to heed the things
spoken by Paul.†
15 And when she and her household were baptized, she begged *us*,
saying, "If you have judged me to
be faithful to the Lord, come to my
house and stay." So [a]she persuaded
us.

Exorcism of a Spirit

16 Now it happened, as we went
to prayer, that a certain slave girl
[a]possessed with a spirit of divina-
tion met us, who brought her
masters [b]much profit by fortune-
telling.†
17 This girl followed Paul and us,
and cried out, saying, "These men
are the servants of the Most High
God, who proclaim to us the way
of salvation."
18 And this she did for many days.
But Paul, [a]greatly [1]annoyed, turned
and said to the spirit, "I command
you in the name of Jesus Christ to
come out of her." [b]And he came out
that very hour.

5 [a]Acts 2:47; 15:41
6 [a]Acts 18:23; Gal. 1:1, 2 [1]The Roman province of Asia
7 [1]NU adds *of Jesus*
8 [a]Acts 16:11; 20:5; 2 Cor. 2:12; 2 Tim. 4:13
9 [a]Acts 10:30
10 [a]2 Cor. 2:13
12 [a]Acts 20:6; Phil. 1:1; 1 Thess. 2:2 [1]Lit. *first*
14 [a]Rev. 1:11; 2:18, 24 [b]Luke 24:45
15 [a]Gen. 19:3; 33:11; Judg. 19:21; Luke 24:29; [Heb. 13:2]
16 [a]Lev. 19:31; 20:6, 27; Deut. 18:11; 1 Sam. 28:3, 7; 2 Kin. 21:6; 1 Chr. 10:13; Is. 8:19 [b]Acts 19:24
18 [a]Mark 1:25, 34 [b]Mark 16:17 [1]*distressed*

16:6, 7 While no clue is given as to how or why Paul, Silas and Timothy **were forbidden by the Holy Spirit** (v. 6) from preaching in Asia and **Bithynia** (v. 7; regions in northwestern Asia Minor), they do not question the immediate direction of the Holy Spirit. God does not always give reasons for His instruction.

16:8 Troas was a coastal city at the northwestern tip of Asia Minor.

16:10 The first-person plural **we** indicates Luke, the author of Acts, has joined Paul, Silas, and Timothy in Troas. This is the first of several "we" passages in Acts indicating Luke's presence as an eyewitness and participant.

16:11 Neapolis is contemporary Karalla on the coast of northern Greece. Here St. Paul first set foot on European soil.

16:12 Philippi was a Roman **colony,** a city of Roman administration, where many retired soldiers and their families lived.

16:13 A place of **prayer** was usually a synagogue, but in Philippi, where few Jews lived, it may have been a private outdoor gathering place for lack of an actual synagogue.

16:14, 15 Paul is the "church planter" *par excellence*, and his work remains the model for building churches. He starts with people attuned to God. **Lydia,** a woman **who worshiped God** (that is, a believer in the true God of Judaism) is Paul's first Gentile convert to Christ in Europe. Lydia is a well-to-do businesswoman with a large home sufficient to host the Christian missionaries. Again, faith leads immediately to baptism. The household of Lydia probably included children.

16:16–18 Apostolic ministry includes exorcisms in the name of Christ. St. Paul is **greatly annoyed** (v. 18) at the evil spirit which torments the slave girl.

Paul and Silas Imprisoned

19 But [a]when her masters saw that
their hope of profit was gone, they
seized Paul and Silas and [b]dragged
them into the marketplace to the
authorities.†
20 And they brought them to the
magistrates, and said, "These men,
being Jews, [a]exceedingly trouble our
city;†
21 "and they teach customs which
are not lawful for us, being Romans,
to receive or observe."
22 Then the multitude rose up together against them; and the magistrates tore off their clothes [a]and commanded *them* to be beaten with
rods.†
23 And when they had laid many
stripes on them, they threw *them* into
prison, commanding the jailer to
keep them securely.
24 Having received such a charge,
he put them into the inner prison
and fastened their feet in the stocks.

The Philippian Jailer

25 But at midnight Paul and Silas
were praying and singing hymns to
God, and the prisoners were listening to them.†
26 [a]Suddenly there was a great
earthquake, so that the foundations
of the prison were shaken; and immediately [b]all the doors were
opened and everyone's chains were
loosed.
27 And the keeper of the prison,
awaking from sleep and seeing the
prison doors open, supposing the
prisoners had fled, drew his sword
and was about to kill himself.†
28 But Paul called with a loud
voice, saying, "Do yourself no harm,
for we are all here."
29 Then he called for a light, ran
in, and fell down trembling before
Paul and Silas.
30 And he brought them out and
said, [a]"Sirs, what must I do to be
saved?"†
31 So they said, [a]"Believe on the
Lord Jesus Christ, and you will be
saved, you and your household."
32 Then they spoke the word of the
Lord to him and to all who were in
his house.
33 And he took them the same
hour of the night and washed *their*
stripes. And immediately he and all
his family were baptized.†
34 Now when he had brought
them into his house, [a]he set food before them; and he rejoiced, having
believed in God with all his
household.

The Apostles Released

35 And when it was day, the magistrates sent the [1]officers, saying,
"Let those men go."†

19 [a]Acts 16:16; 19:25, 26 [b]Matt. 10:18
20 [a]1 Kin. 18:17; Acts 17:8
22 [a]2 Cor. 6:5; 11:23, 25; 1 Thess. 2:2
26 [a]Acts 4:31 [b]Acts 5:19; 12:7, 10
30 [a]Luke 3:10; Acts 2:37; 9:6; 22:10
31 [a][John 3:16, 36; 6:47; Acts 13:38, 39; Rom. 10:9–11; 1 John 5:10]
34 [a]Matt. 5:4; Luke 5:29; 19:6
35 [1]*lictors*, lit. *rod bearers*

16:19 The **marketplace** (Gr. *agora*) was the public square where the city offices and jail were located.

16:20 The acts of hostility against Paul and Silas are committed by Gentiles exploiting prejudices against **Jews.** Timothy was not with them on this day; thus he was not arrested.

16:22 **Beaten with rods:** a form of flogging, a Roman punishment.

16:25 Although beaten and imprisoned, the Christian missionaries were **praying and singing.** Literally, this reads, "But at midnight Paul and Silas, while praying, were singing hymns to God." Bearing persecution with joy is a powerful testimony to Christian faith.

16:27 The jailer would answer with his life if the prisoners escaped.

16:30 The jailer's question, **What must I do to be saved?,** implies he has already heard his prisoners proclaiming "the way of salvation" (v. 17). The witness of the prisoners and the dramatic event of the earthquake (v. 26) causes him to fall before them in repentance. Then he takes them to his own home (v. 32) to care for them, no longer fearing they will escape.

16:33 Again confession of faith and immediate baptism mark the entrance to salvation. Presumably **all his family** includes his wife and children.

16:35–40 Having already punished them for public disturbance, the magistrates order the

(continued on next page)

36 So the keeper of the prison reported these words to Paul, saying,
"The magistrates have sent to let you
go. Now therefore depart, and go in
peace."
37 But Paul said to them, "They
have beaten us openly, uncondemned [a]Romans, *and* have thrown
us into prison. And now do they
put us out secretly? No indeed! Let
them come themselves and get
us out."
38 And the officers told these
words to the magistrates, and they
were afraid when they heard that
they were Romans.
39 Then they came and pleaded
with them and brought *them* out, and
[a]asked *them* to depart from the city.
40 So they went out of the prison
[a]and entered *the house of* Lydia; and
when they had seen the brethren,
they encouraged them and departed.

The Church in Thessalonica

17 Now when they had passed
through Amphipolis and
Apollonia, they came to [a]Thessalo-
nica, where there was a synagogue
of the Jews.†

37 [a]Acts 22:25–29
39 [a]Matt. 8:34
40 [a]Acts 16:14

CHAPTER 17
1 [a]Acts 17:11, 13; 20:4; 27:2; Phil. 4:16; 1 Thess. 1:1; 2 Thess. 1:1; 2 Tim. 4:10
2 [a]Luke 4:16; Acts 9:20; 13:5, 14; 14:1; 16:13; 19:8 [b]1 Thess. 2:1–16
3 [a]Luke 24:26, 46; Acts 18:5, 28; Gal. 3:1
4 [a]Acts 28:24 [b]Acts 15:22, 27, 32, 40
5 [a]Acts 13:45 [b]Acts 17:6, 7, 9; Rom. 16:21 [1]NU omits *who were not persuaded* [2]M omits *becoming envious*
6 [a][Acts 16:20]
7 [a]Luke 23:2; John 19:12; 1 Pet. 2:13 [1]*welcomed*

2 Then Paul, as his custom was,
[a]went in to them, and for three Sabbaths [b]reasoned with them from the
Scriptures,†
3 explaining and demonstrating
[a]that the Christ had to suffer and rise
again from the dead, and *saying*,
"This Jesus whom I preach to you
is the Christ."
4 [a]And some of them were persuaded; and a great multitude of the
devout Greeks, and not a few of the
leading women, joined Paul and
[b]Silas.†
5 But the Jews [1]who were not persuaded, [2]becoming [a]envious, took
some of the evil men from the
marketplace, and gathering a
mob, set all the city in an uproar
and attacked the house of [b]Jason,
and sought to bring them out to the
people.
6 But when they did not find
them, they dragged Jason and some
brethren to the rulers of the city, crying out, [a]"These who have turned
the world upside down have come
here too.
7 "Jason has [1]harbored them, and
these are all acting contrary to the
decrees of Caesar, [a]saying there is
another king—Jesus."†

(continued from previous page)
secret release of Paul and Silas. They, however, refuse to leave secretly as if they are guilty of a crime. They appeal to their Roman citizenship and gain public release by the magistrates in order to give testimony to their innocence. They leave the city voluntarily to continue their missionary work. Lydia's house has become the center of a Christian congregation to which St. Paul will later write the Epistle to the Philippians.

17:1 These cities were located along the Egnatian Way, a heavily traveled Roman road. **Thessalonica** is a large coastal city in northern Greece and was the capital of the Roman province of Macedonia. The largest and most important city in Macedonia, Thessalonica was very cosmopolitan, possessing an excellent harbor and superior commerce. With the flow of goods, communication, and people to and from the city, it is not surprising that word spread of what was happening in Thessalonica. Thus the church there became influential: "The word of the Lord has sounded forth" from them "not only in Macedonia and Achaia, but also in every place" (1 Thess. 1:8).

17:2, 3 The preaching of the gospel does not depend on reasoned argument as such. **Reasoned** (v. 2; Gr. *dialegomai*) here means "conducted a discussion." Elsewhere in Acts the same word is translated "speaking" (20:9). St. Paul was simply presenting the gospel in the light of OT Scriptures, **explaining and demonstrating** (v. 3) the truth of Christ's death and Resurrection.

17:4 Devout means "God-fearing," the formal expression for uncircumcised Gentiles who accepted the Jewish faith and participated in synagogue worship. Many of the earliest converts to Christ were from this class of Gentiles.

17:7 The trumped-up charge that Christians claimed **another king—Jesus** is reminiscent of the charges brought against Jesus of being a political king. Paul was proclaiming the Kingdom of God, with Jesus as King (see 14:22; 19:8; 20:25).

8 And they troubled the crowd
and the rulers of the city when they
heard these things.
9 So when they had taken security
from Jason and the rest, they let
them go.†

The Church in Berea

10 Then [a]the brethren immediately
sent Paul and Silas away by night
to Berea. When they arrived, they
went into the synagogue of the
Jews.†
11 These were more [1]fair-minded
than those in Thessalonica, in that
they received the word with all readiness, and [a]searched the Scriptures
daily *to find out* whether these things
were so.†
12 Therefore many of them believed, and also not a few of the
Greeks, prominent women as well
as men.
13 But when the Jews from Thessalonica learned that the word of
God was preached by Paul at Berea,
they came there also and stirred up
the crowds.†
14 [a]Then immediately the brethren
sent Paul away, to go to the sea; but
both Silas and Timothy remained
there.†
15 So those who conducted Paul
brought him to Athens; and [a]receiv-
ing a command for Silas and Timothy to come to him with all speed,
they departed.

The Church in Athens

16 Now while Paul waited for them
at Athens, [a]his spirit was provoked
within him when he saw that the city
was [1]given over to idols.†
17 Therefore he reasoned in the
synagogue with the Jews and with
the *Gentile* worshipers, and in the
marketplace daily with those who
happened to be there.†
18 [1]Then certain Epicurean and
Stoic philosophers encountered him.
And some said, "What does this
[2]babbler want to say?" Others said,
"He seems to be a proclaimer of foreign gods," because he preached to
them [a]Jesus and the resurrection.†
19 And they took him and brought
him to the [1]Areopagus, saying,
"May we know what this new doctrine *is* of which you speak?
20 "For you are bringing some
strange things to our ears. Therefore
we want to know what these things
mean."
21 For all the Athenians and the
foreigners who were there spent
their time in nothing else but either
to tell or to hear some new thing.
22 Then Paul stood in the midst of
the [1]Areopagus and said, "Men of
Athens, I perceive that in all things
you are very religious;†

10 [a]Acts 9:25; 17:14
11 [a]Is. 34:16; Luke 16:29; John 5:39 [1]Lit. *noble*
14 [a]Matt. 10:23
15 [a]Acts 18:5
16 [a]2 Pet. 2:8 [1]*full of idols*
18 [a]1 Cor. 15:12 [1]NU, M add *also* [2]Lit. *seed picker,* an idler who makes a living picking up scraps
19 [1]Lit. *Hill of Ares,* or *Mars' Hill*
22 [1]Lit. *Hill of Ares,* or *Mars' Hill*

17:9 Security: a sum of money as bond to guarantee public peace in the future.

17:10 Berea is 60 miles southwest of Thessalonica, off the Egnatian Way. These events, described succinctly in Acts, probably took weeks rather than days to develop. Christian churches were established in both Thessalonica and Berea.

17:11 With all readiness could be translated, "with all goodwill."

17:13 Those unwilling to search the Scriptures (v. 11) to verify Paul's teaching *are* willing to travel 60 miles to Berea in order to stir up trouble there for the apostles.

17:14 The brethren: the new Christians.

17:16 Athens, the chief city of Greece, was also the intellectual capital of the empire.

17:17 In freethinking Athens, Paul moves beyond the synagogue and makes open contact with Gentiles in the marketplace. The Epicurean and Stoic philosophers bring him to the Areopagus, or Mars' Hill, a place of open-air public debate (vv. 18–21).

17:18 Both the Epicureans and the Stoics believed that fulfillment could be achieved in this life through emotional calm and impassivity; however, they approached this goal differently. The Epicureans pursued pleasure, while the Stoics renounced it.

17:22–31 Paul's speech at the Areopagus is highlighted by Luke and gives evidence of how the Christian faith was proclaimed to Gentiles in language and categories of thought familiar to them. With the Jews, Paul referred to the Law and the Prophets, explaining messianic prophecies. With the Gentile Athenians he spoke more philosophically of: (1) God

(continued on next page)

23 "for as I was passing through
and considering the objects of your
worship, I even found an altar with
this inscription:

TO THE UNKNOWN GOD.

Therefore, the One whom you worship without knowing, Him I proclaim to you:
24 [a]"God, who made the world
and everything in it, since He is
[b]Lord of heaven and earth, [c]does
not dwell in temples made with
hands.
25 "Nor is He worshiped with
men's hands, as though He needed
anything, since He [a]gives to all life,
breath, and all things.
26 "And He has made from one
[1]blood every nation of men to dwell
on all the face of the earth, and has
determined their preappointed times
and [a]the boundaries of their
dwellings,
27 [a]"so that they should seek the
Lord, in the hope that they might
grope for Him and find Him,
[b]though He is not far from each one
of us;
28 "for [a]in Him we live and move
and have our being, [b]as also some
of your own poets have said, 'For
we are also His offspring.'
29 "Therefore, since we are the offspring of God, [a]we ought not to
think that the Divine Nature is like
gold or silver or stone, something
shaped by art and man's devising.
30 "Truly, [a]these times of ignorance God overlooked, but [b]now
commands all men everywhere to
repent,
31 "because He has appointed
a day on which [a]He will judge
the world in righteousness by
the Man whom He has ordained.
He has given assurance of this
to all by [b]raising Him from the
dead."
32 And when they heard of the resurrection of the dead, some mocked,
while others said, "We will hear you
again on this *matter*."†
33 So Paul departed from among
them.
34 However, some men joined him
and believed, among them Di-
onysius the Areopagite, a woman
named Damaris, and others with
them.†

The Church in Corinth

18 After these things Paul departed from Athens and went
to Corinth.†
2 And he found a certain Jew
named [a]Aquila, born in Pontus, who
had recently come from Italy with
his wife Priscilla (because Claudius
had commanded all the Jews to
depart from Rome); and he came to
them.†
3 So, because he was of the same
trade, he stayed with them [a]and

24 [a]Acts 14:15 [b]Matt. 11:25 [c]Acts 7:48–50
25 [a]Is. 42:5
26 [a]Deut. 32:8 [1]NU omits *blood*
27 [a][Rom. 1:20] [b]Jer. 23:23, 24
28 [a][Heb. 1:3] [b]Titus 1:12
29 [a]Is. 40:18, 19
30 [a][Rom. 3:25] [b][Titus 2:11, 12]
31 [a]Acts 10:42 [b]Acts 2:24

CHAPTER 18
2 [a]1 Cor. 16:19
3 [a]Acts 20:34

(continued from previous page)
as the Creator of all; (2) God as the giver of life; (3) God's concern that all people seek Him; (4) repentance toward God; (5) God as the Judge of all; and (6) the Resurrection of Christ from the dead.

17:32 The resurrection of the dead is inevitably the point at which the Gentile philosophers react negatively, while God as Creator, life-giver, and Lord of the affairs of heaven and humans, repentance and even judgment were not challenged. Many philosophers, especially in the Platonic tradition, taught the existence of an eternal soul and viewed the body as a temporary prison-house for the soul, unworthy of salvation.

17:34 To join Paul and to believe meant to enter the Church as the corporate expression of Christian existence.

18:1 Corinth was a major commercial and cultural city, the capital of the Roman province of Achaia. Paul spent several years in Corinth, where he established a prominent church.

18:2, 3 Since Paul does not preach to or convert **Aquila** and **Priscilla,** they must have already been Christians. This couple became Christian leaders and coworkers of Paul in Corinth and later in Ephesus (vv. 18, 19; 1 Cor. 16:19).

worked; for by occupation they were
tentmakers.
4 [a]And he reasoned in the synagogue every Sabbath, and persuaded
both Jews and Greeks.†
5 [a]When Silas and Timothy had
come from Macedonia, Paul was
[b]compelled [1]by the Spirit, and testified to the Jews *that* Jesus *is* the
Christ.

Teaching in Corinth

6 But [a]when they opposed him
and blasphemed, [b]he shook *his* garments and said to them, [c]"Your
blood *be* upon your *own* heads;
[d]I *am* clean. [e]From now on I will go
to the Gentiles."†
7 And he departed from there and
entered the house of a certain *man*
named [1]Justus, *one* who worshiped
God, whose house was next door to
the synagogue.†
8 [a]Then Crispus, the ruler of the
synagogue, believed on the Lord
with all his household. And many
of the Corinthians, hearing, believed
and were baptized.
9 Now [a]the Lord spoke to Paul in
the night by a vision, "Do not be
afraid, but speak, and do not keep
silent;
10 [a]"for I am with you, and no one
will attack you to hurt you; for I have
many people in this city."
11 And he continued *there* a year
and six months, teaching the word
of God among them.

4 [a]Acts 17:2
5 [a]Acts 17:14, 15
[b]Acts 18:28
[1]Or *in his spirit* or *in the Spirit*
6 [a]Acts 13:45
[b]Neh. 5:13; Matt. 10:14; Acts 13:51
[c]Lev. 20:9, 11, 12; 2 Sam. 1:16; 1 Kin. 2:33; Ezek. 18:13; 33:4, 6, 8; Matt. 27:25; Acts 20:26
[d][Ezek. 3:18, 19]
[e]Acts 13:46–48; 28:28
7 [1]NU *Titius Justus*
8 [a]1 Cor. 1:14
9 [a]Acts 23:11
10 [a]Jer. 1:18, 19
12 [1]Gr. *bema*
15 [a]Acts 23:29; 25:19
17 [a]1 Cor. 1:1
[1]NU *they all*
18 [a]Num. 6:2, 5, 9, 18; Acts 21:24
[b]Rom. 16:1
[1]Lit. *many days*

The Proconsul's Refusal

12 When Gallio was proconsul of
Achaia, the Jews with one accord
rose up against Paul and brought
him to the [1]judgment seat,†
13 saying, "This *fellow* persuades
men to worship God contrary to the
law."
14 And when Paul was about to
open *his* mouth, Gallio said to the
Jews, "If it were a matter of wrongdoing or wicked crimes, O Jews,
there would be reason why I should
bear with you.
15 "But if it is a [a]question of words
and names and your own law, look
to it yourselves; for I do not want to
be a judge of such *matters*."
16 And he drove them from the
judgment seat.
17 Then [1]all the Greeks took
[a]Sosthenes, the ruler of the synagogue, and beat *him* before the judgment seat. But Gallio took no notice
of these things.†

Report to Jerusalem and Antioch

18 So Paul still remained [1]a good
while. Then he took leave of the
brethren and sailed for Syria, and
Priscilla and Aquila *were* with him.
[a]He had *his* hair cut off at [b]Cenchrea,
for he had taken a vow.†
19 And he came to Ephesus, and
left them there; but he himself entered the synagogue and reasoned
with the Jews.

18:4 The **Greeks** were Gentile converts to Judaism, or "God-fearers."
18:6 Shaking out **his garments** is a gesture of judgment. Paul also uses words from the OT to declare the fulfillment of his responsibility, and the Jews' full accountability for rejecting the gospel (Ezek. 18:13; 2 Sam. 1:16).
18:7 Justus is another Gentile interested in Judaism who became a Christian.
18:12 Gallio was governor of Corinth and Achaia in A.D. 51–52, a firm historical reference for dating Paul's first visit to Corinth.
18:17 All the Greeks are likely the Gentiles present at the tribunal attempting to "teach the Jews a lesson" by beating their leader for bringing things to court. However, other ancient manuscripts (see note in center column) suggest that it was the Jews who beat Sosthenes, another official of the synagogue who had become a Christian (1 Cor. 1:1).
18:18 Cenchrea, 9 miles from Corinth, was a seaport on the Aegean Sea. The **vow** Paul makes is probably a modified form of the Nazirite vow (Num. 6:1–21) taken in thanksgiving for his deliverance from danger in Corinth, and with prayer for his intended trip to Jerusalem for Passover. Paul was a Jew to the Jews as he was a Gentile to Gentiles (1 Cor. 9:19, 20). Nevertheless, he does not regard obedience to the Law as a requirement for salvation (Gal. 2:16).

20 When they asked *him* to stay a
longer time with them, he did not
consent,
21 but took leave of them, saying,
[a]"I[1] must by all means keep this
coming feast in Jerusalem; but I will
return again to you, [b]God willing."
And he sailed from Ephesus.†
22 And when he had landed at
[a]Caesarea, and [1]gone up and greeted
the church, he went down to
Antioch.†

In Ephesus: Apollos Instructed

23 After he had spent some time
there, he departed and went over the
region of [a]Galatia and Phrygia
[1]in order, [b]strengthening all the
disciples.
24 [a]Now a certain Jew named
Apollos, born at Alexandria, an eloquent man *and* mighty in the Scriptures, came to Ephesus.†
25 This man had been instructed
in the way of the Lord; and being
[a]fervent in spirit, he spoke and
taught accurately the things of the
Lord, [b]though he knew only the baptism of John.
26 So he began to speak boldly in
the synagogue. When Aquila and
Priscilla heard him, they took him
aside and explained to him the way
of God more accurately.
27 And when he desired to cross
to Achaia, the brethren wrote, exhorting the disciples to receive him;
and when he arrived, [a]he greatly
helped those who had believed
through grace;
28 for he vigorously refuted the
Jews publicly, [a]showing from the
Scriptures that Jesus is the Christ.

Disciples of John the Baptist

19 And it happened, while
[a]Apollos was at Corinth, that
Paul, having passed through [b]the
upper regions, came to Ephesus.
And finding some disciples†
2 he said to them, "Did you receive the Holy Spirit when you believed?" So they said to him, [a]"We
have not so much as heard whether
there is a Holy Spirit."
3 And he said to them, "Into what
then were you baptized?" So they
said, [a]"Into John's baptism."
4 Then Paul said, [a]"John indeed
baptized with a baptism of repentance, saying to the people that they
should believe on Him who would
come after him, that is, on Christ
Jesus."

21 [a]Acts 19:21; 20:16 [b]1 Cor. 4:19 [1]NU omits *I must by all means keep this coming feast in Jerusalem*
22 [a]Acts 8:40 [1]To Jerusalem
23 [a]Gal. 1:2 [b]Acts 14:22; 15:32, 41 [1]*successively*
24 [a]Titus 3:13
25 [a]Rom. 12:11 [b]Acts 19:3
27 [a]1 Cor. 3:6
28 [a]Acts 9:22; 17:3; 18:5

CHAPTER 19

1 [a]1 Cor. 1:12; 3:5, 6 [b]Acts 18:23
2 [a]1 Sam. 3:7
3 [a]Acts 18:25
4 [a]Matt. 3:11

18:21 God willing underscores Paul's constant reliance upon God. Paul's interest in going to Jerusalem is not frivolous. He wants to **keep this . . . feast** (v. 21), which will soon give way to Christian Easter (Pascha). Considering dates from secular history concerning Gallio in Corinth (see v. 12) during the reign of the emperor Claudius, this was likely A.D. 53, when Passover fell on March 22.

18:22, 23 Luke gives a very condensed account of this period of time. Paul's second missionary journey ends in **Antioch** (v. 22), and his third journey begins as he departs for **Galatia** and **Phrygia** (v. 23).

18:24–28 Two outstanding qualities characterize **Apollos:** (1) He is **fervent in spirit** (v. 25). A *fervent* person (see also Rom. 12:11) can be useful to God, even if he is not yet well taught. Apollos apparently was not yet in the Church, but he was speaking **boldly in the synagogue** (v. 26). (2) He is humble. This eloquent man, powerful in his command of the Scriptures, is willing to receive instruction from two humble tentmakers—one a woman, which would be offensive to most men in his culture. **Aquila and Priscilla** displayed great decency and propriety: they did not correct Apollos publicly, but **took him aside** privately to complete his instruction in **the way of God** (v. 26).

19:1 Ephesus was a large, magnificent city, the capital of the Roman province of Asia Minor. Located on the main route from Rome to the East, it was a major center of trade and commerce, not only in goods but also in ideas. Paul remained there for at least two years and three months. Because of its strategic location, this city became a center of outreach for the growing Church. Churches were formed in almost every city and town in the province within three years, including the churches to which the Seven Letters in the Book of Revelation are addressed (Rev. 2; 3).

5 When they heard *this*, they were
baptized [a]in the name of the Lord
Jesus.†
6 And when Paul had [a]laid hands
on them, the Holy Spirit came upon
them, and [b]they spoke with tongues
and prophesied.
7 Now the men were about twelve
in all.

Two Years in Ephesus

8 [a]And he went into the synagogue and spoke boldly for three
months, reasoning and persuading
[b]concerning the things of the kingdom of God.†
9 But [a]when some were hardened
and did not believe, but spoke evil
[b]of the Way before the multitude, he
departed from them and withdrew
the disciples, reasoning daily in the
school of Tyrannus.†
10 And [a]this continued for two
years, so that all who dwelt in Asia
heard the word of the Lord Jesus,
both Jews and Greeks.

Occultists Converted

11 Now [a]God worked unusual miracles by the hands of Paul,†
12 [a]so that even handkerchiefs or
aprons were brought from his body
to the sick, and the diseases left them
and the evil spirits went out of
them.
13 [a]Then some of the itinerant Jewish exorcists [b]took it upon themselves to call the name of the Lord
Jesus over those who had evil spirits,
saying, [1]"We [2]exorcise you by the
Jesus whom Paul [c]preaches."
14 Also there were seven sons of
Sceva, a Jewish chief priest, who did
so.
15 And the evil spirit answered
and said, "Jesus I know, and Paul I
know; but who are you?"
16 Then the man in whom the evil
spirit was leaped on them,
[1]overpowered them, and prevailed
against [2]them, so that they fled out
of that house naked and wounded.
17 This became known both to all
Jews and Greeks dwelling in Ephesus; and [a]fear fell on them all, and
the name of the Lord Jesus was
magnified.
18 And many who had believed
came [a]confessing and telling their
deeds.
19 Also, many of those who had
practiced magic brought their books
together and burned *them* in the sight
of all. And they counted up the value
of them, and *it* totaled fifty thousand
pieces of silver.
20 [a]So the word of the Lord grew
mightily and prevailed.†
21 [a]When these things were accomplished, Paul [b]purposed in the
Spirit, when he had passed through
[c]Macedonia and Achaia, to go to Jerusalem, saying, "After I have been
there, [d]I must also see Rome."
22 So he sent into Macedonia two
of those who ministered to him,

5 [a]Acts 8:12, 16; 10:48
6 [a]Acts 6:6; 8:17 [b]Acts 2:4; 10:46
8 [a]Acts 17:2; 18:4 [b]Acts 1:3; 28:23
9 [a]2 Tim. 1:15 [b]Acts 9:2; 19:23; 22:4; 24:14
10 [a]Acts 19:8; 20:31
11 [a]Mark 16:20
12 [a]Acts 5:15
13 [a]Matt. 12:27 [b]Mark 9:38 [c]1 Cor. 1:23; 2:2 [1]NU *I* [2]*adjure,* solemnly command
16 [1]M *and they overpowered them* [2]NU *both of them*
17 [a]Luke 1:65; 7:16
18 [a]Matt. 3:6
20 [a]Acts 6:7; 12:24
21 [a]Rom. 15:25 [b]Acts 20:22 [c]Acts 20:1 [d]Rom. 1:13; 15:22–29

19:5, 6 In the Church, the laying on of hands for the receiving of the Holy Spirit immediately follows baptism. The two events are distinct but not separated. The Orthodox Church continues this apostolic sacramental practice.

19:8 Faithful preaching of the gospel demands preaching the Kingdom of God. A personal relationship with Christ without the reality of His Kingdom—as it is experienced in the Church and in the age to come—falls far short of true Christianity (see 1:3; 8:12; 14:22; 20:25; 28:31).

19:9 Once again Paul, after sufficient testimony to the Jews, turns to proclaim the gospel to the Gentiles. **The school of Tyrannus** was probably a lecture hall bearing the name of its owner or of an otherwise unknown philosopher.

19:11–19 The miracles and events described here parallel and continue those of Jesus' earthly ministry: diseases are cured and the powers of evil are overcome. Such is the authority of the Kingdom of God. That physical objects (**handkerchiefs** and **aprons**) are instruments of healing demonstrates the truth of the gospel that God became Man in order to redeem all creation and make all creation a vehicle of grace.

19:20 The **word** of God is living and dynamic and cannot be confined. Here in Ephesus (1) it **grew mightily** as more people believed, and (2) it **prevailed** regardless of the opposition.

[a]Timothy and [b]Erastus, but he himself stayed in Asia for a time.

A Greek Goddess Defended

23 And [a]about that time there
arose a great commotion about
[b]the Way.
24 For a certain man named Demetrius, a silversmith, who made silver
shrines of [1]Diana, brought [a]no small
profit to the craftsmen.
25 He called them together with
the workers of similar occupation,
and said: "Men, you know that we
have our prosperity by this trade.
26 "Moreover you see and hear
that not only at Ephesus, but
throughout almost all Asia, this Paul
has persuaded and turned away
many people, saying that [a]they are
not gods which are made with
hands.†
27 "So not only is this trade of ours
in danger of falling into disrepute,
but also the temple of the great
goddess Diana may be despised
and [1]her magnificence destroyed,
whom all Asia and the world worship."†
28 Now when they heard *this*, they
were full of wrath and cried out, saying, "Great *is* Diana of the
Ephesians!"
29 So the whole city was filled with
confusion, and rushed into the theater with one accord, having seized
[a]Gaius and [b]Aristarchus, Macedonians, Paul's travel companions.†
30 And when Paul wanted to go
in to the people, the disciples would
not allow him.†
31 Then some of the [1]officials of
Asia, who were his friends, sent to
him pleading that he would not ven-
ture into the theater.
32 Some therefore cried one thing
and some another, for the assembly
was confused, and most of them did
not know why they had come
together.
33 And they drew Alexander out
of the multitude, the Jews putting
him forward. And [a]Alexander
[b]motioned with his hand, and
wanted to make his defense to the
people.†
34 But when they found out that
he was a Jew, all with one voice cried
out for about two hours, "Great *is*
Diana of the Ephesians!"
35 And when the city clerk had
quieted the crowd, he said: "Men of
Ephesus, what man is there who
does not know that the city of the
Ephesians is temple guardian of the
great goddess [1]Diana, and of the *im-*
age which fell down from [2]Zeus?†
36 "Therefore, since these things
cannot be denied, you ought to be
quiet and do nothing rashly.
37 "For you have brought these
men here who are neither robbers
of temples nor blasphemers of
[1]your goddess.

22 [a]1 Tim. 1:2 [b]Rom. 16:23; 2 Tim. 4:20
23 [a]2 Cor. 1:8 [b]Acts 9:2
24 [a]Acts 16:16, 19 [1]Gr. *Artemis*
26 [a]Deut. 4:28; Ps. 115:4; Is. 44:10–20; Jer. 10:3; Acts 17:29; 1 Cor. 8:4; 10:19; Rev. 9:20
27 [1]NU *she be deposed from her magnificence*
29 [a]Acts 20:4; Rom. 16:23; 1 Cor. 1:14; 3 John 1 [b]Acts 20:4; 27:2; Col. 4:10; Philem. 24
31 [1]*Asiarchs, rulers of Asia,* the province
33 [a]1 Tim. 1:20; 2 Tim. 4:14 [b]Acts 12:17
35 [1]Gr. *Artemis* [2]*heaven*
37 [1]NU *our*

19:26 The Church, when it is vital, will have an impact on the culture in which it exists. Conflict is to be expected.

19:27 The **temple** of **Diana** (Gr. *Artemis*), a fertility goddess, was one of the seven wonders of the ancient world. It was approximately 360 feet long and 180 feet wide and was supported by 100 solid marble columns. The artistic decorations inside were remarkable. In the center of the temple was the statue of Diana, which had supposedly fallen from heaven from Zeus (v. 35). The cult of Diana was widely popular in the pagan world of that time.

19:29 Gaius, from Asia Minor (20:4), is perhaps the same person mentioned in Rom. 16:23 and 1 Cor. 1:14. **Aristarchus** is a Thessalonian (20:4; 27:2; Col. 4:10).

19:30 Paul is eager to preach to the crowds but the Ephesian Christians do **not allow him,** fearing for his life.

19:33 Alexander was put forward by **the Jews** presumably to plead their own innocence and to accuse the Christians.

19:35–37 The behavior of Christians, especially leaders, needs to be above reproach. **The city clerk** (v. 35), a just and wise man judging by his words, testifies that **these** Christian **men** (v. 37, Aristarchus and Gaius), far from being criminals, had not blasphemed the **goddess** of the Ephesians. A lesson for us: we need not slander the gods of others to get our point across.

38 "Therefore, if Demetrius and his
fellow craftsmen have a [1]case against
anyone, the courts are open and
there are proconsuls. Let them bring
charges against one another.
39 "But if you have any other inquiry to make, it shall be determined
in the lawful assembly.
40 "For we are in danger of being
[1]called in question for today's uproar, there being no reason which we
may give to account for this disorderly gathering."
41 And when he had said these
things, he dismissed the assembly.

Return Visit to Greece

20 After the uproar had ceased,
Paul called the disciples to
himself, embraced *them,* and [a]de-
parted to go to Macedonia.
2 Now when he had gone over
that region and encouraged them
with many words, he came to
[a]Greece
3 and stayed three months. And
[a]when the Jews plotted against him
as he was about to sail to Syria, he
decided to return through Macedonia.
4 And Sopater of Berea accompanied him to Asia—also [a]Aristarchus
and Secundus of the Thessalonians,
and [b]Gaius of Derbe, and [c]Timothy,
and [d]Tychicus and [e]Trophimus of
Asia.†
5 These men, going ahead, waited
for us at [a]Troas.†
6 But we sailed away from Philippi after [a]the Days of Unleavened
Bread, and in five days joined them
[b]at Troas, where we stayed seven
days.

38 [1]Lit. *matter*
40 [1]Or *charged with rebellion concerning today*

CHAPTER 20
1 [a]1 Cor. 16:5; 1 Tim. 1:3
2 [a]Acts 17:15; 18:1
3 [a]Acts 9:23; 23:12; 25:3; 2 Cor. 11:26
4 [a]Acts 19:29; Col. 4:10 [b]Acts 19:29 [c]Acts 16:1 [d]Eph. 6:21; Col. 4:7; 2 Tim. 4:12; Titus 3:12 [e]Acts 21:29; 2 Tim. 4:20
5 [a]2 Cor. 2:12; 2 Tim. 4:13
6 [a]Ex. 12:14, 15 [b]Acts 16:8; 2 Cor. 2:12; 2 Tim. 4:13
7 [a]1 Cor. 16:2; Rev. 1:10 [b]Acts 2:42, 46; 20:11; 1 Cor. 10:16
8 [a]Acts 1:13 [1]NU, M *we*
10 [a]1 Kin. 17:21; 2 Kin. 4:34 [b]Matt. 9:23, 24; Mark 5:39
13 [1]*arranged it*

Back in Asia: Eutychus Raised

7 Now on [a]the first *day* of the
week, when the disciples came together [b]to break bread, Paul, ready
to depart the next day, spoke to them
and continued his message until
midnight.†
8 There were many lamps [a]in the
upper room where [1]they were gathered together.
9 And in a window sat a certain
young man named Eutychus, who
was sinking into a deep sleep. He
was overcome by sleep; and as Paul
continued speaking, he fell down
from the third story and was taken
up dead.†
10 But Paul went down, [a]fell on
him, and embracing *him* said, [b]"Do
not trouble yourselves, for his life is
in him."†
11 Now when he had come up,
had broken bread and eaten, and
talked a long while, even till day-
break, he departed.
12 And they brought the young
man in alive, and they were not a
little comforted.

Paul's Farewell Address

13 Then we went ahead to the ship
and sailed to Assos, there intending
to take Paul on board; for so he had
[1]given orders, intending himself to
go on foot.
14 And when he met us at Assos,
we took him on board and came to
Mitylene.
15 We sailed from there, and the
next *day* came opposite Chios. The
following *day* we arrived at Samos
and stayed at Trogyllium. The next
day we came to Miletus.

20:4 Paul is not a lone evangelist. He always seeks to build up a missionary team, to raise up local leaders.

20:5 The first-person plural **us** indicates the presence of Luke in the following passage.

20:7 The first day of the week was Sunday, the Church's customary day **to break bread**—to celebrate the Eucharist. Occasional communion has no NT precedence.

20:9 Young man refers to a male in early adulthood, perhaps late teens through early 30's. It is the same word used for Paul (Saul) himself when he was holding the garments of those stoning Stephen (7:58).

20:10 Paul's actions in bringing the young man back to life reflect those of Elisha the Prophet (2 Kin. 4:34).

16 For Paul had decided to sail past
Ephesus, so that he would not have
to spend time in Asia; for [a]he was
hurrying [b]to be at Jerusalem, if
possible, on [c]the Day of Pentecost.†
17 From Miletus he sent to Ephesus and called for the elders of the
church.†
18 And when they had come to
him, he said to them: "You know,
[a]from the first day that I came to
Asia, in what manner I always lived
among you,
19 "serving the Lord with all humility, with many tears and trials
which happened to me [a]by the plotting of the Jews;†
20 "how [a]I kept back nothing that
was helpful, but proclaimed it to
you, and taught you publicly and
from house to house,
21 [a]"testifying to Jews, and also to
Greeks, [b]repentance toward God
and faith toward our Lord Jesus
Christ.†
22 "And see, now [a]I go bound in
the spirit to Jerusalem, not knowing
the things that will happen to me
there,
23 "except that [a]the Holy Spirit testifies in every city, saying that chains
and tribulations await me.
24 [1]"But [a]none of these things
move me; nor do I count my life dear
to myself, [b]so that I may finish my
[2]race with joy, [c]and the ministry
[d]which I received from the Lord
Jesus, to testify to the gospel of the
grace of God.
25 "And indeed, now I know that
you all, among whom I have gone
preaching the kingdom of God, will
see my face no more.
26 "Therefore I testify to you this
day that I *am* [a]innocent[1] of the blood
of all *men*.†
27 "For I have not [1]shunned to declare to you [a]the whole counsel of
God.
28 [a]"Therefore take heed to yourselves and to all the flock, among
which the Holy Spirit [b]has made you
overseers, to shepherd the church
[1]of God [c]which He purchased
[d]with His own blood.†
29 "For I know this, that after my
departure [a]savage wolves will come
in among you, not sparing the
flock.†

16 [a]Acts 18:21; 19:21; 21:4 [b]Acts 24:17 [c]Acts 2:1
18 [a]Acts 18:19; 19:1, 10; 20:4, 16
19 [a]Acts 20:3
20 [a]Acts 20:27
21 [a]Acts 18:5; 19:10 [b]Mark 1:15
22 [a]Acts 19:21
23 [a]Acts 21:4, 11
24 [a]Acts 21:13 [b]2 Tim. 4:7 [c]Acts 1:17 [d]Gal. 1:1 [1]NU *But I do not count my life of any value or dear to myself* [2]*course*
26 [a]Acts 18:6 [1]Lit. *clean*
27 [a]Luke 7:30 [1]*avoided declaring*
28 [a]1 Pet. 5:2 [b]1 Cor. 12:28 [c]Eph. 1:7, 14 [d]Heb. 9:14 [1]M *of the Lord and God*
29 [a]Matt. 7:15

20:16 Paul and his companions travel quickly down the coast of Asia Minor in order to arrive in **Jerusalem** by **Pentecost.** The ancient Church kept track of the calendar by reference to sacred days. In that tradition, the Orthodox Church's calendar today still revolves around the feasts and special days of the year.

20:17–38 Paul meets with the **elders** of **Ephesus** and gives his stirring farewell discourse to them. He defends his ministry and offers pastoral instruction. We learn from this meeting that: (1) the Church is living and growing; (2) it has already developed a pattern of permanent leadership in terms of *elders* (presbyters, v. 17) and **overseers** (bishops, v. 28); and (3) false teachers and heresies will arise from inside the Church, and she must be protected through godly clergy and laity.

20:19 Christians are not exempt from **tears and trials.** Paul writes the Corinthians, "I have fought with beasts at Ephesus" (1 Cor. 15:32). And he admits despair to them, "For we do not want you to be ignorant, brethren, of our trouble which came to us in Asia [where Ephesus is]: that we were burdened beyond measure, above strength, so that we despaired even of life" (2 Cor. 1:8). "Tribulations render men more illustrious both in the presence of God and of man, if they know how to bear them with fortitude" (St. John Chrysostom).

20:21–25 Paul summarizes three basic elements in his preaching: **repentance toward God, faith toward our Lord Jesus Christ** (see 1 Cor. 2:2) and **the kingdom of God** (v. 25).

20:26 Innocent of the blood means not accountable for their lives, insofar as he has fulfilled his responsibility of preaching the gospel to them (see 18:6 and note).

20:28 Blood in biblical language signifies life. Christ gave His own life on the Cross to redeem His people and establish His Church.

20:29, 30 These are references to external and internal trials and persecutions in the future. Ephesus would be the scene of the Third Ecumenical Council in A.D. 431, which preserved the doctrine of the two natures of Christ in one divine Person against the heresy of Nestorius.

30 "Also [a]from among yourselves
men will rise up, speaking [1]perverse
things, to draw away the disciples
after themselves.
31 "Therefore watch, and remember that [a]for three years I did not
cease to warn everyone night and
day with tears.
32 "So now, brethren, I commend
you to God and [a]to the word of His
grace, which is able [b]to build you up
and give you [c]an inheritance among
all those who are sanctified.
33 "I have coveted no one's silver
or gold or apparel.†
34 [1]"Yes, you yourselves know
[a]that these hands have provided for
my necessities, and for those who
were with me.
35 "I have shown you in every
way, [a]by laboring like this, that you
must support the weak. And remember the words of the Lord Jesus, that
He said, 'It is more blessed to give
than to receive.' "
36 And when he had said these
things, he knelt down and prayed
with them all.
37 Then they all [a]wept [1]freely, and
[b]fell on Paul's neck and kissed
him,†
38 sorrowing most of all for the
words which he spoke, that they
would see his face no more. And
they accompanied him to the ship.

Palestine and Jerusalem: Don't Go!

21 Now it came to pass, that
when we had departed from
them and set sail, running a straight
course we came to Cos, the following
day to Rhodes, and from there to
Patara.†
2 And finding a ship sailing over
to Phoenicia, we went aboard and
set sail.
3 When we had sighted Cyprus,
we passed it on the left, sailed
to Syria, and landed at Tyre; for
there the ship was to unload her
cargo.
4 And finding [1]disciples, we
stayed there seven days. [a]They told
Paul through the Spirit not to go up
to Jerusalem.
5 When we had come to the end
of those days, we departed and went
on our way; and they all accompanied us, with wives and children, till *we were* out of the city. And
[a]we knelt down on the shore and
prayed.
6 When we had taken our leave
of one another, we boarded the ship,
and they returned [a]home.
7 And when we had finished *our*
voyage from Tyre, we came to Ptolemais, greeted the brethren, and
stayed with them one day.
8 On the next *day* we [1]who were
Paul's companions departed and
came to [a]Caesarea, and entered the
house of Philip [b]the evangelist,
[c]who was *one* of the seven, and
stayed with him.†
9 Now this man had four virgin
daughters [a]who prophesied.†
10 And as we stayed many days,
a certain prophet named [a]Agabus
came down from Judea.†

30 [a]1 Tim. 1:20 [1]*misleading*
31 [a]Acts 19:8, 10; 24:17
32 [a]Heb. 13:9 [b]Acts 9:31 [c][Heb. 9:15]
34 [a]Acts 18:3 [1]NU, M omit *Yes*
35 [a]Rom. 15:1
37 [a]Acts 21:13 [b]Gen. 45:14 [1]Lit. *much*

CHAPTER 21
4 [a][Acts 20:23; 21:12] [1]NU *the disciples*
5 [a]Acts 9:40; 20:36
6 [a]John 1:11
8 [a]Acts 8:40; 21:16 [b]Eph. 4:11 [c]Acts 6:5 [1]NU omits *who were Paul's companions*
9 [a]Joel 2:28
10 [a]Acts 11:28

20:33–35 Itinerant philosophers and teachers were often motivated by greed. Paul, on the contrary, worked with his own hands to support himself, but also accepted material help for his basic needs (see Phil. 4:15–19). In v. 35 Paul quotes a saying of Jesus not recorded in the Gospels.

20:37, 38 The parting acts of prayer and farewell are moving testimony to the love and devotion of the early Christians.

21:1 The journey is resumed along the eastern shores of Asia Minor.

21:8 This is the **Philip, one of the seven** deacons (6:5), who preached the gospel first in Samaria (8:5–25) and then to the Ethiopian eunuch (8:26–40), and who had settled in **Caesarea** (8:40).

21:9 The gift of prophecy is given to both men and women. Many holy women were prophets, including Miriam, sister of Moses (Ex. 15:20, 21), Deborah (Judg. 4:4), Huldah (2 Kin. 22:14), Isaiah's wife (Is. 8:3), the Virgin Mary (Luke 1:46–55), and Anna (Luke 2:36–38).

21:10, 11 The same **Agabus** is mentioned in 11:28. Here, he gives the prophecy of Paul's

(continued on next page)

11 When he had come to us, he
took Paul's belt, bound his *own*
hands and feet, and said, "Thus says
the Holy Spirit, [a]'So shall the Jews
at Jerusalem bind the man who owns
this belt, and deliver *him* into the
hands of the Gentiles.' "
12 Now when we heard these
things, both we and those from that
place pleaded with him not to go up
to Jerusalem.
13 Then Paul answered, [a]"What
do you mean by weeping and breaking my heart? For I am ready not
only to be bound, but also to die at
Jerusalem for the name of the Lord
Jesus."
14 So when he would not be persuaded, we ceased, saying, [a]"The
will of the Lord be done."
15 And after those days we
[1]packed and went up to Jerusalem.
16 Also some of the disciples from
Caesarea went with us and brought
with them a certain Mnason of Cyprus, an early disciple, with whom
we were to lodge.

In Jerusalem

17 [a]And when we had come to Jerusalem, the brethren received us
gladly.†
18 On the following *day* Paul went
in with us to [a]James, and all the elders were present.
19 When he had greeted them,
[a]he told in detail those things which
God had done among the Gentiles
[b]through his ministry.
20 And when they heard *it*, they
glorified the Lord. And they said to
him, "You see, brother, how many
myriads of Jews there are who have
believed, and they are all [a]zealous
for the law;
21 "but they have been informed
about you that you teach all the Jews
who are among the Gentiles to forsake Moses, saying that they ought
not to circumcise *their* children nor
to walk according to the customs.
22 [1]"What then? The assembly
must certainly meet, for they will
hear that you have come.
23 "Therefore do what we tell you:
We have four men who have taken
a vow.
24 "Take them and be purified
with them, and pay their expenses
so that they may [a]shave *their* heads,
and that all may know that those
things of which they were informed
concerning you are nothing, but *that*
you yourself also walk orderly and
keep the law.
25 "But concerning the Gentiles
who believe, [a]we have written *and*
decided [1]that they should observe no
such thing, except that they should
keep themselves from *things* offered
to idols, from blood, from things
strangled, and from [2]sexual immorality."

Temple Riot, Paul Arrested

26 Then Paul took the men, and
the next day, having been purified
with them, [a]entered the temple
[b]to announce the [1]expiration of the
days of purification, at which time
an offering should be made for each
one of them.

11 [a]Acts 20:23; 21:33; 22:25
13 [a]Acts 20:24, 37
14 [a]Matt. 6:10; 26:42; Luke 11:2; 22:42
15 [1]*made preparations*
17 [a]Acts 15:4
18 [a]Acts 15:13; Gal. 1:19; 2:9
19 [a]Acts 15:4, 12; Rom. 15:18, 19 [b]Acts 1:17; 20:24; 1 Tim. 2:7
20 [a]Acts 15:1; 22:3; [Rom. 10:2]; Gal. 1:14
22 [1]NU *What then is to be done? They will certainly hear*
24 [a]Num. 6:2, 13, 18; Acts 18:18
25 [a]Acts 15:19, 20, 29 [1]NU omits *that they should observe no such thing, except* [2]*fornication*
26 [a]John 11:55; Acts 21:24; 24:18 [b]Num. 6:13; Acts 24:18 [1]*completion*

(continued from previous page)
arrest in the style of the OT prophets, using an ordinary object to illustrate his point (see Is. 20:2; Jer. 13:1).

21:17–25 Paul meets with **James** (v. 18), the overseer of the Jerusalem church. James reports that numerous Jewish Christians, **zealous for the law** (v. 20), are ill-disposed toward Paul on account of rumors that he advocates noncompliance with the Law even for Jews living outside Palestine. James agrees that Gentiles are not required to practice the Mosaic Law, as the Apostolic Council had decided (ch. 15). Jewish Christians are not being asked to behave like Gentile Christians, but neither are the Gentile Christians asked to be like Jewish Christians. Differences in tradition are recognized and treated with charity.

The **vow** (v. 23) of Paul is no compromise with Judaism. It is an expression of Christian charity from Paul, a Jewish Christian, toward the Jewish Christians in Jerusalem in order to dispel false rumors and to build their trust.

27 Now when the seven days were
almost ended, [a]the Jews from Asia,
seeing him in the temple, stirred up
the whole crowd and [b]laid hands on
him,
28 crying out, "Men of Israel, help!
This is the man [a]who teaches all *men*
everywhere against the people, the
law, and this place; and furthermore
he also brought Greeks into the temple and has defiled this holy place."†
29 (For they had [1]previously seen
[a]Trophimus the Ephesian with him
in the city, whom they supposed that
Paul had brought into the temple.)
30 And [a]all the city was disturbed;
and the people ran together, seized
Paul, and dragged him out of the
temple; and immediately the doors
were shut.
31 Now as they were [a]seeking to
kill him, news came to the commander of the [1]garrison that all Jerusalem was in an uproar.†
32 [a]He immediately took soldiers
and centurions, and ran down to
them. And when they saw the commander and the soldiers, they
stopped beating Paul.
33 Then the [a]commander came
near and took him, and [b]com-
manded *him* to be bound with two
chains; and he asked who he was
and what he had done.
34 And some among the multitude
cried one thing and some another.
So when he could not ascertain the
truth because of the tumult, he commanded him to be taken into the barracks.

27 [a]Acts 20:19; 24:18 [b]Acts 26:21
28 [a]Acts 6:13; 24:6
29 [a]Acts 20:4 [1]M omits *previously*
30 [a]Acts 16:19; 26:21
31 [a]2 Cor. 11:23 [1]*cohort*
32 [a]Acts 23:27; 24:7
33 [a]Acts 24:7 [b]Acts 20:23; 21:11
36 [a]John 19:15
38 [a]Acts 5:36
39 [a]Acts 9:11; 22:3 [1]*insignificant*
40 [a]Acts 12:17 [b]Acts 22:2

CHAPTER 22
1 [a]Acts 7:2
2 [a]Acts 21:40
3 [a]2 Cor. 11:22 [b]Deut. 33:3 [c]Acts 5:34 [d]Acts 23:6; 26:5 [e]Gal. 1:14

35 When he reached the stairs, he
had to be carried by the soldiers because of the violence of the mob.
36 For the multitude of the people
followed after, crying out, [a]"Away
with him!"†
37 Then as Paul was about to be
led into the barracks, he said to the
commander, "May I speak to you?"
He replied, "Can you speak Greek?
38 [a]"Are you not the Egyptian who
some time ago stirred up a rebellion
and led the four thousand assassins
out into the wilderness?"†
39 But Paul said, [a]"I am a Jew from
Tarsus, in Cilicia, a citizen of no
[1]mean city; and I implore you, permit me to speak to the people."
40 So when he had given him permission, Paul stood on the stairs and
[a]motioned with his hand to the people. And when there was a great silence, he spoke to *them* in the
[b]Hebrew language, saying,†

Paul's Defense at the Temple

22 "Brethren[a] and fathers, hear
my defense before you
now."†
2 And when they heard that he
spoke to them in the [a]Hebrew language, they kept all the more silent.
Then he said:
3 [a]"I am indeed a Jew, born in
Tarsus of Cilicia, but brought up in
this city [b]at the feet of [c]Gamaliel,
taught [d]according to the strictness of
our fathers' law, and [e]was zealous

21:28 Jewish opponents of Paul from Asia Minor, who had also come to Jerusalem for the Feast of Pentecost, raise false charges and work up the crowd against Paul. For a Gentile to enter prohibited precincts of the **temple** area is a serious offense punishable by death.

21:31 Since **Jerusalem** is under Roman rule, any disturbance would be investigated by the soldiers stationed there. The commander (v. 33), Claudius Lysias, is simply doing his duty.

21:36 Away with him echoes the mob's outcry against Jesus during His trial (Luke 23:18).

21:38 The Egyptian, according to Josephus the historian, claimed to be a prophet and led a group of 30,000 (probably an exaggerated number) to the Mount of Olives, telling them the walls of the city would fall at his word. Felix, the Roman governor, attacked the rebels and killed thousands of them, but this false prophet and some of his followers fled into the wilderness.

21:40 The Hebrew language may refer to Aramaic, which was the spoken language of Jews in the time of Jesus.

22:1 Brethren and fathers is a polite Jewish form of address, used earlier by St. Stephen in speaking to the Council (7:2). Paul is respectful and gracious to a crowd seeking to kill him.

toward God [f]as you all are today.†
4 [a]"I persecuted this Way to the
death, binding and delivering into
prisons both men and women,
5 "as also the high priest bears me
witness, and [a]all the council of the
elders, [b]from whom I also received
letters to the brethren, and went to
Damascus [c]to bring in chains even
those who were there to Jerusalem
to be punished.
6 "Now [a]it happened, as I journeyed and came near Damascus at
about noon, suddenly a great light
from heaven shone around me.†
7 "And I fell to the ground and
heard a voice saying to me, 'Saul,
Saul, why are you persecuting Me?'
8 "So I answered, 'Who are You,
Lord?' And He said to me, 'I am
Jesus of Nazareth, whom you are
persecuting.'
9 "And [a]those who were with me
indeed saw the light [1]and were
afraid, but they did not hear the
voice of Him who spoke to me.
10 "So I said, 'What shall I do,
Lord?' And the Lord said to me,
'Arise and go into Damascus, and
there you will be told all things
which are appointed for you to
do.'
11 "And since I could not see for
the glory of that light, being led by
the hand of those who were with me,
I came into Damascus.
12 "Then [a]a certain Ananias, a devout man according to the law,
[b]having a good testimony with all
the [c]Jews who dwelt *there*,†

3 [f][Rom. 10:2]
4 [a]1 Tim. 1:13
5 [a]Acts 23:14; 24:1; 25:15 [b]Luke 22:66 [c]Acts 9:2
6 [a]Acts 9:3; 26:12, 13
9 [a]Acts 9:7 [1]NU omits *and were afraid*
12 [a]Acts 9:17 [b]Acts 10:22 [c]1 Tim. 3:7
14 [a]Acts 3:13; 5:30 [b]Acts 9:15; 26:16 [c]Acts 3:14; 7:52 [d]1 Cor. 9:1; 15:8 [e]Gal. 1:12
15 [a]Acts 23:11 [b]Acts 4:20; 26:16
16 [a]Heb. 10:22 [b]Rom. 10:13
17 [a]Acts 9:26; 26:20
18 [a]Acts 22:14 [b]Matt. 10:14
19 [a]Acts 8:3; 22:4 [b]Matt. 10:17
20 [a]Acts 7:54—8:1 [b]Luke 11:48 [1]NU omits *to his death*
21 [a]Acts 9:15

13 "came to me; and he stood and
said to me, 'Brother Saul, receive
your sight.' And at that same hour
I looked up at him.
14 "Then he said, [a]'The God of our
fathers [b]has chosen you that you
should [c]know His will, and [d]see the
Just One, [e]and hear the voice of His
mouth.†
15 [a]'For you will be His witness to
all men of [b]what you have seen and
heard.
16 'And now why are you waiting?
Arise and be baptized, [a]and wash
away your sins, [b]calling on the name
of the Lord.'†
17 "Now [a]it happened, when I returned to Jerusalem and was praying
in the temple, that I was in a trance†
18 "and [a]saw Him saying to me,
[b]'Make haste and get out of Jerusalem quickly, for they will not receive
your testimony concerning Me.'
19 "So I said, 'Lord, [a]they know
that in every synagogue I imprisoned
and [b]beat those who believe on
You.
20 [a]'And when the blood of Your
martyr Stephen was shed, I also was
standing by [b]consenting [1]to his
death, and guarding the clothes of
those who were killing him.'
21 "Then He said to me, 'Depart,
[a]for I will send you far from here to
the Gentiles.'"

An Appeal to Roman Citizenship

22 And they listened to him until
this word, and *then* they raised their

22:3 Paul seeks to win the trust of the crowd by reference to his former zeal for the Law and the Jewish traditions. **Tarsus** was a prominent city and cultural center in southeastern Asia Minor. **Gamaliel** (5:34) was a famous and highly respected rabbi, renowned for his knowledge of religious law and tradition.

22:6–10 This is a second account of the **Damascus** vision with some new details and slight variations (see 9:3–8).

22:12 The faithfulness of **Ananias** to the Jewish tradition is stressed for the benefit of the crowd.

22:14, 15 Ananias validates Paul's Damascus experience as coming from God. Its purpose is fourfold: (1) Paul is to **know** God's **will.** (2) He is to **see the Just One** (the Lord Jesus Christ). (3) He is to **hear the voice of His** (Christ's) **mouth.** (4) He is to **be His witness to all men** (v. 15).

22:16 Paul links cleansing from **sins** with baptism.

22:17, 18 Upon his return to Jerusalem after the Damascus experience (see Gal. 1:18, 19), Paul prays in the temple and has another vision of the risen Christ who directs him to the Gentile mission (see 2 Cor. 12:1–4). **Trance** means religious ecstasy, as in the case of Stephen's vision (7:55, 56).

voices and said, [a]"Away with such
a *fellow* from the earth, for [b]he is not
fit to live!"
23 Then, as they cried out and
[1]tore off *their* clothes and threw dust
into the air,
24 the commander ordered him to
be brought into the barracks, and
said that he should be examined under scourging, so that he might
know why they shouted so against
him.†
25 And as they bound him with
thongs, Paul said to the centurion
who stood by, [a]"Is it lawful for you
to scourge a man who is a Roman,
and uncondemned?"
26 When the centurion heard *that*,
he went and told the commander,
saying, "Take care what you do, for
this man is a Roman."
27 Then the commander came and
said to him, "Tell me, are you a Roman?" He said, "Yes."
28 The commander answered,
"With a large sum I obtained this citizenship." And Paul said, "But I was
born *a citizen*."
29 Then immediately those who
were about to examine him withdrew from him; and the commander
was also afraid after he found out
that he was a Roman, and because
he had bound him.

Before the Sanhedrin

30 The next day, because he
wanted to know for certain why he
was accused by the Jews, he released
him from *his* bonds, and commanded
the chief priests and all their council
to appear, and brought Paul down
and set him before them.

23 Then Paul, looking earnestly
at the council, said, "Men *and*
brethren, [a]I have lived in all good
conscience before God until this
day."†
2 And the high priest Ananias
commanded those who stood by him
[a]to strike him on the mouth.†
3 Then Paul said to him, "God
will strike you, *you* whitewashed
wall! For you sit to judge me according to the law, and [a]do you command me to be struck contrary to the
law?"†
4 And those who stood by said,
"Do you revile God's high priest?"
5 Then Paul said, [a]"I did not
know, brethren, that he was the high
priest; for it is written, [b]*'You shall
not speak evil of a ruler of your
people.'*"
6 But when Paul perceived that
one part were Sadducees and the
other Pharisees, he cried out in the
council, "Men *and* brethren, [a]I am a
Pharisee, the son of a Pharisee;
[b]concerning the hope and resurrection of the dead I am being
judged!"†
7 And when he had said this, a
dissension arose between the Pharisees and the Sadducees; and the assembly was divided.
8 [a]For Sadducees say that there is
no resurrection—and no angel or
spirit; but the Pharisees confess both.
9 Then there arose a loud outcry.

22 [a]Acts 21:36; 1 Thess. 2:16 [b]Acts 25:24
23 [1]Lit. *threw*
25 [a]Acts 16:37

CHAPTER 23
1 [a]Acts 24:16; 1 Cor. 4:4; 2 Cor. 1:12; 4:2; 2 Tim. 1:3; Heb. 13:18
2 [a]1 Kin. 22:24; Jer. 20:2; John 18:22
3 [a]Lev. 19:35; Deut. 25:1, 2; John 7:51
5 [a]Lev. 5:17, 18 [b]Ex. 22:28; Eccl. 10:20; 2 Pet. 2:10
6 [a]Acts 26:5; Phil. 3:5 [b]Acts 24:15, 21; 26:6; 28:20
8 [a]Matt. 22:23; Mark 12:18; Luke 20:27

22:24–29 To extract a confession, the Romans bound their prisoners in a stooping position, their hands tied behind their backs for **scourging,** whipping them with leather lashes. Paul appeals to his **Roman** (v. 25) citizenship because it was not **lawful** to punish a citizen until he was proven guilty of a crime.

23:1 The Jewish **council,** or Sanhedrin, is the highest Jewish governing body.

23:2 **Ananias** was **high priest** during A.D. 47–59, according to Josephus. He was a hard and violent man who was later assassinated by his own people at the start of the Jewish war against the Romans (A.D. 70). It is not clear why he commands Paul to be struck, an illegal action at a court hearing.

23:3–5 Paul initially reacts boldly, accusing Ananias of the ultimate hypocrisy: violating the Law while posing as a judge according to the Law. But then, once he realizes that Ananias is the **high priest** (v. 4), Paul quickly becomes conciliatory.

23:6 Knowing that his interrogators will not hear him impartially, Paul brings up the issue of the **resurrection** to divide the Council. The **Pharisees** believe in a resurrection; the **Sadducees** do not.

And the scribes of the Pharisees'
party arose and protested, saying,
[a]"We find no evil in this man;
[1]but [b]if a spirit or an angel has spoken to him, [c]let us not fight against
God."
10 Now when there arose a great
dissension, the commander, fearing
lest Paul might be pulled to pieces
by them, commanded the soldiers to
go down and take him by force from
among them, and bring *him* into the
barracks.
11 But [a]the following night the
Lord stood by him and said, [1]"Be of
good cheer, Paul; for as you have testified for Me in [b]Jerusalem, so you
must also bear witness at [c]Rome."†

The Murder Plot Against Paul

12 And when it was day, [a]some of
the Jews banded together and bound
themselves under an oath, saying
that they would neither eat nor drink
till they had [b]killed Paul.†
13 Now there were more than forty
who had formed this conspiracy.
14 They came to the chief priests
and [a]elders, and said, "We have
bound ourselves under a great oath
that we will eat nothing until we
have killed Paul.
15 "Now you, therefore, together
with the council, suggest to the commander that he be brought down to
you [1]tomorrow, as though you were
going to make further inquiries concerning him; but we are ready to kill
him before he comes near."
16 So when Paul's sister's son
heard of their ambush, he went and
entered the barracks and told Paul.†
17 Then Paul called one of the centurions to *him* and said, "Take this
young man to the commander, for
he has something to tell him."
18 So he took him and brought *him*
to the commander and said, "Paul
the prisoner called me to *him* and
asked *me* to bring this young man
to you. He has something to say to
you."
19 Then the commander took him
by the hand, went aside, and asked
privately, "What is it that you have
to tell me?"
20 And he said, [a]"The Jews have
agreed to ask that you bring Paul
down to the council tomorrow, as
though they were going to inquire
more fully about him.
21 "But do not yield to them, for
more than forty of them lie in wait
for him, men who have bound themselves by an oath that they will neither eat nor drink till they have killed
him; and now they are ready, waiting for the promise from you."
22 So the commander let the young
man depart, and commanded *him*,
"Tell no one that you have revealed
these things to me."

Paul Imprisoned in Caesarea

23 And he called for two centurions, saying, "Prepare two hundred
soldiers, seventy horsemen, and two
hundred spearmen to go to [a]Caes-
area at the third hour of the night;†
24 "and provide mounts to set Paul
on, and bring *him* safely to Felix the
governor."†

9 [a]Acts 25:25; 26:31 [b]John 12:29; Acts 22:6, 7, 17, 18 [c]Acts 5:39 [1]NU *what if a spirit or an angel has spoken to him?* omitting the last clause
11 [a]Acts 18:9; 27:23, 24 [b]Acts 21:18, 19; 22:1–21 [c]Acts 28:16, 17, 23 [1]*Take courage*
12 [a]Acts 23:21, 30; 25:3 [b]Acts 9:23, 24; 25:3; 26:21; 27:42; 1 Thess. 2:15
14 [a]Acts 4:5, 23; 6:12; 22:5; 24:1; 25:15
15 [1]NU omits *tomorrow*
20 [a]Acts 23:12
23 [a]Acts 8:40; 23:33

23:11 The Lord comforts His servant **Paul** with another personal revelation, hinting at his destiny of martyrdom in Rome.

23:12–15 A number of **Jews** conspire to assassinate Paul. The enemies of the gospel, even the most religious of people, do not hesitate to employ treachery, deceit and hypocrisy in their war against the Christian faith. Even those who condemn violence can quickly stoop to it.

23:16 This is an interesting historical note which partly explains Paul's coming to live in Jerusalem as a young man. His nephew providentially exposes the plot.

23:23 The commander was determined to prevent the assassination. The Church did not have an army to protect Paul, but God selected hundreds of Roman soldiers to do the job. **Caesarea,** a city on the coast of Palestine, was the seat of the Roman governor for the area. The **third hour** of the night was 9:00 P.M.

23:24 Felix: the Roman governor (A.D. 52–59).

25 He wrote a letter in the following manner:†

26 Claudius Lysias,

To the most excellent governor
Felix:

Greetings.

27 [a]This man was seized by the
Jews and was about to be killed
by them. Coming with the
troops I rescued him, having
learned that he was a Roman.
28 [a]And when I wanted to know
the reason they accused him, I
brought him before their
council.
29 I found out that he was accused
[a]concerning questions of their
law, [b]but had nothing charged
against him deserving of death
or chains.
30 And [a]when it was told me that
[1]the Jews lay in wait for the
man, I sent him immediately to
you, and [b]also commanded his
accusers to state before you the
charges against him.

Farewell.

31 Then the soldiers, as they were
commanded, took Paul and brought
him by night to Antipatris.†
32 The next day they left the horsemen to go on with him, and returned
to the barracks.
33 When they came to [a]Caesarea
and had delivered the [b]letter to the
governor, they also presented Paul
to him.

27 [a]Acts 21:30, 33; 24:7
28 [a]Acts 22:30
29 [a]Acts 18:15; 25:19 [b]Acts 25:25; 26:31
30 [a]Acts 23:20 [b]Acts 24:8; 25:6 [1]NU *there would be a plot against the man*
33 [a]Acts 8:40 [b]Acts 23:26–30
34 [a]Acts 6:9; 21:39
35 [a]Acts 24:1, 10; 25:16 [b]Matt. 27:27 [1]Headquarters

CHAPTER 24

1 [a]Acts 21:27 [b]Acts 23:2, 30, 35; 25:2
2 [1]Or *reforms are*
4 [1]*graciousness*
5 [a]Luke 23:2; Acts 6:13; 16:20; 17:6; 21:28; 1 Pet. 2:12, 15
6 [a]Acts 21:28 [b]John 18:31 [1]NU ends the sentence here and omits the rest of v. 6, all of v. 7, and the first clause of v. 8.
7 [a]Acts 21:33; 23:10

34 And when the governor had
read *it*, he asked what province he
was from. And when he understood
that *he was* from [a]Cilicia,
35 he said, [a]"I will hear you when
your accusers also have come." And
he commanded him to be kept in
[b]Herod's [1]Praetorium.†

The Trial Before Felix

24 Now after [a]five days [b]Ana-
nias the high priest came
down with the elders and a certain
orator *named* Tertullus. These gave
evidence to the governor against
Paul.†
2 And when he was called upon,
Tertullus began his accusation, saying: "Seeing that through you we enjoy great peace, and [1]prosperity is
being brought to this nation by your
foresight,
3 "we accept *it* always and in all
places, most noble Felix, with all
thankfulness.
4 "Nevertheless, not to be tedious
to you any further, I beg you to hear,
by your [1]courtesy, a few words from
us.
5 [a]"For we have found this man
a plague, a creator of dissension
among all the Jews throughout the
world, and a ringleader of the sect
of the Nazarenes.†
6 [a]"He even tried to profane the
temple, and we seized him, [1]and
wanted [b]to judge him according to
our law.
7 [a]"But the commander Lysias
came by and with great violence took
him out of our hands,

23:25 The commander's **letter** (vv. 26–30) conveys a Roman view of the matter and seeks to refer this difficult problem to higher authority.

23:31 Antipatris, a town about halfway between Jerusalem and Caesarea, served as a military outpost. Since Paul had been moved beyond the reach of the would-be assassins, the whole Roman escort was no longer required.

23:35 Herod's Praetorium: a palace which also served as a fortress. It was built by Herod the Great and later was taken over by the Roman governors as their official residence.

24:1 The presence of **the high priest** himself indicates the seriousness with which the Jewish Council sought the demise of Paul. **Tertullus** is engaged as a lawyer to present the case against Paul, and seeks to win the favor of Felix through flattery (vv. 2, 3).

24:5, 6 There is no real transgression against Roman law. The Jews' tactic is to present Paul as a constant agitator, potentially dangerous, who might stir up trouble at any time. Roman authorities were extremely wary of troublemakers in this politically restive part of the Empire.

8 [a]"commanding his accusers to
come to you. By examining him
yourself you may ascertain all these
things of which we accuse him."
9 And the Jews also [1]assented,
maintaining that these things were
so.

Paul's Defense

10 Then Paul, after the governor
had nodded to him to speak, answered: "Inasmuch as I know that
you have been for many years a
judge of this nation, I do the more
cheerfully answer for myself,
11 "because you may ascertain that
it is no more than twelve days since
I went up to Jerusalem [a]to worship.†
12 [a]"And they neither found me in
the temple disputing with anyone
nor inciting the crowd, either in the
synagogues or in the city.
13 "Nor can they prove the things
of which they now accuse me.
14 "But this I confess to you, that
according to [a]the Way which they
call a sect, so I worship the [b]God of
my fathers, believing all things
which are written in [c]the Law and
in the Prophets.†
15 [a]"I have hope in God, which
they themselves also accept, [b]that
there will be a resurrection [1]of *the*
dead, both of *the* just and *the* unjust.
16 [a]"This *being* so, I myself always
strive to have a conscience without
offense toward God and men.
17 "Now after many years [a]I came
to bring alms and offerings to my
nation,†
18 [a]"in the midst of which some

8 [a]Acts 23:30
9 [1]NU, M *joined the attack*
11 [a]Acts 21:15, 18, 26, 27; 24:17
12 [a]Acts 25:8; 28:17
14 [a]Acts 9:2; 24:22 [b]2 Tim. 1:3 [c]Acts 26:22; 28:23
15 [a]Acts 23:6; 26:6, 7; 28:20 [b][Dan. 12:2] [1]NU omits *of the dead*
16 [a]Acts 23:1
17 [a]Rom. 15:25–28
18 [a]Acts 21:27; 26:21 [b]Acts 21:26
19 [a][Acts 23:30; 25:16]
20 [1]NU, M *what wrongdoing they found*
21 [a][Acts 23:6; 24:15; 28:20]
22 [a]Acts 9:2; 18:26; 19:9, 23; 22:4 [b]Acts 23:26; 24:7
23 [a]Acts 23:16; 27:3; 28:16
24 [a][Rom. 10:9]
26 [a]Ex. 23:8 [1]NU omits *that he might release him*

Jews from Asia found me [b]purified
in the temple, neither with a mob
nor with tumult.
19 [a]"They ought to have been here
before you to object if they had anything against me.
20 "Or else let those who are *here*
themselves say [1]if they found any
wrongdoing in me while I stood before the council,
21 "unless *it is* for this one statement which I cried out, standing
among them, [a]'Concerning the resurrection of the dead I am being
judged by you this day.'"

The Decision

22 But when Felix heard these
things, having more accurate knowledge of *the* [a]Way, he adjourned the
proceedings and said, "When
[b]Lysias the commander comes
down, I will make a decision on your
case."
23 So he commanded the centurion
to keep Paul and to let *him* have liberty, and [a]told him not to forbid any
of his friends to provide for or visit
him.
24 And after some days, when Felix came with his wife Drusilla, who
was Jewish, he sent for Paul and
heard him concerning the [a]faith in
Christ.
25 Now as he reasoned about righteousness, self-control, and the judgment to come, Felix was afraid and
answered, "Go away for now; when
I have a convenient time I will call
for you."†
26 Meanwhile he also hoped that
[a]money would be given him by Paul,
[1]that he might release him. Therefore

24:11, 12 Paul denies the charges against him in part by pointing out that he had not been in **Jerusalem** long enough to start a riot.

24:14 Paul affirms the harmony between the **Way** of the Christian Church and God's promises in the OT.

24:17 This is the only place Acts mentions a main reason Paul came to Jerusalem together with so many companions: to bring funds collected for the poor of Jerusalem which he had promised at the Apostolic Council (see Rom. 15:25–28; 1 Cor. 16:1–4; Gal. 2:10).

24:25 Paul's conversation with **Felix** and Drusilla gives insight into Christian ethical issues he considered crucial: (1) **righteousness,** (2) **self-control,** and (3) **the judgment to come.** Felix reacts with **"Go away,"** for, according to Josephus, he had an adulterous marriage and was dishonest, as his desire for a bribe from Paul shows (v. 26).

he sent for him more often and conversed with him.
27 But after two years Porcius Festus succeeded Felix; and Felix,
[a]wanting to do the Jews a favor, left
Paul bound.†

The Trial Before Festus

25 Now when Festus had come
to the province, after three
days he went up from [a]Caesarea to
Jerusalem.†
2 [a]Then the [1]high priest and the
chief men of the Jews informed him
against Paul; and they petitioned
him,
3 asking a favor against him, that
he would summon him to Jerusalem—[a]while *they* lay in ambush
along the road to kill him.†
4 But Festus answered that Paul
should be kept at Caesarea, and that
he himself was going *there* shortly.
5 "Therefore," he said, "let those
who have authority among you go
down with *me* and accuse this man,
to see [a]if there is any fault in him."
6 And when he had remained
among them more than ten days, he
went down to Caesarea. And the
next day, sitting on the judgment
seat, he commanded Paul to be
brought.†
7 When he had come, the Jews
who had come down from Jerusalem
stood about [a]and laid many serious
complaints against Paul, which they
could not prove,†
8 while he answered for himself,
[a]"Neither against the law of the
Jews, nor against the temple, nor
against Caesar have I offended in
anything at all."
9 But Festus, [a]wanting to do the
Jews a favor, answered Paul and
said, [b]"Are you willing to go up to
Jerusalem and there be judged before
me concerning these things?"
10 So Paul said, "I stand at Caesar's judgment seat, where I ought
to be judged. To the Jews I have
done no wrong, as you very well
know.
11 [a]"For if I am an offender, or
have committed anything deserving
of death, I do not object to dying;
but if there is nothing in these things
of which these men accuse me, no
one can deliver me to them. [b]I appeal
to Caesar."†
12 Then Festus, when he had conferred with the council, answered,
"You have appealed to Caesar? To
Caesar you shall go!"

Festus's Plan

13 And after some days King
Agrippa and Bernice came to Caesarea to greet Festus.†
14 When they had been there
many days, Festus laid Paul's case
before the king, saying: [a]"There is

27 [a]Ex. 23:2; Acts 12:3; 23:35; 25:9, 14

CHAPTER 25
1 [a]Acts 8:40; 25:4, 6, 13
2 [a]Acts 24:1; 25:15
[1]NU *chief priests*
3 [a]Acts 23:12, 15
5 [a]Acts 18:14; 25:18
7 [a]Mark 15:3; Luke 23:2, 10; Acts 24:5, 13
8 [a]Acts 6:13; 24:12; 28:17
9 [a]Acts 12:2; 24:27
[b]Acts 25:20
11 [a]Acts 18:14; 23:29; 25:25; 26:31
[b]Acts 26:32; 28:19
14 [a]Acts 24:27

24:27 Festus succeeded **Felix** about A.D. 60, after the latter had been recalled to Rome to answer charges of misrule.

25:1 Festus is eager to get to **Jerusalem** to establish his presence there as the new procurator.

25:3, 4 Two years after his arrest (24:27), Paul's Jewish opponents are still determined **to kill** him. The new governor, **Festus** (v. 4), denies their request for a trial in **Jerusalem** (v. 3). This is not so much to protect Paul (v. 9) as to underscore Festus's authority in the early days of his rule by having the trial at his headquarters in **Caesarea** (v. 4).

25:6 Judgment seat: the official bench from which sentence is pronounced.

25:7 Paul's innocence is evident. There is no proof of any religious or political crime committed by him.

25:11 Perceiving that Festus might yield to the wishes of the Jewish authorities, Paul appeals to **Caesar.** It was a right of Roman citizens to be tried before the imperial tribunal in Rome.

25:13 King Agrippa is Herod Agrippa II, ruler of Galilee. He is the son of Herod Agrippa I (12:1–23), who beheaded James and imprisoned Peter; and the grandson of Herod the Great (Matt. 2:1). **Bernice** is Agrippa's sister. There was scandal associated with her constant companionship with Agrippa. Paul's words must have pricked the conscience of this decadent ruler (see 26:28).

a certain man left a prisoner by
Felix,†
15 [a]"about whom the chief priests
and the elders of the Jews informed
me, when I was in Jerusalem, asking
for a judgment against him.†
16 [a]"To them I answered, 'It is not
the custom of the Romans to deliver
any man [1]to destruction before the
accused meets the accusers face to
face, and has opportunity to answer
for himself concerning the charge
against him.'
17 "Therefore when they had come
together, [a]without any delay, the
next day I sat on the judgment seat
and commanded the man to be
brought in.
18 "When the accusers stood up,
they brought no accusation against
him of such things as I [1]supposed,
19 [a]"but had some questions
against him about their own religion
and about a certain Jesus, who had
died, whom Paul affirmed to be
alive.†
20 "And because I was uncertain
of such questions, I asked whether
he was willing to go to Jerusalem and
there be judged concerning these
matters.
21 "But when Paul [a]appealed to be
reserved for the decision of Augustus, I commanded him to be kept till
I could send him to Caesar."
22 Then [a]Agrippa said to Festus,
"I also would like to hear the man
myself." "Tomorrow," he said, "you
shall hear him."

15 [a]Acts 24:1; 25:2, 3
16 [a]Acts 25:4, 5
[1]NU omits *to destruction,* although it is implied
17 [a]Acts 25:6, 10
18 [1]*suspected*
19 [a]Acts 18:14, 15; 23:29
21 [a]Acts 25:11, 12
22 [a]Acts 9:15
23 [a]Acts 9:15
[1]*pageantry*
24 [a]Acts 25:2, 3, 7
[b]Acts 21:36; 22:22
25 [a]Acts 23:9, 29; 26:31
[b]Acts 25:11, 12

CHAPTER 26

2 [a][1 Pet. 3:14; 4:14]
[b][1 Pet. 3:15, 16]

23 So the next day, when Agrippa
and Bernice had come with great
[1]pomp, and had entered the auditorium with the commanders and the
prominent men of the city, at Festus'
command [a]Paul was brought in.†
24 And Festus said: "King Agrippa
and all the men who are here present
with us, you see this man about
whom [a]the whole assembly of the
Jews petitioned me, both at Jerusalem and here, crying out that he was
[b]not fit to live any longer.
25 "But when I found that [a]he had
committed nothing deserving of
death, [b]and that he himself had appealed to Augustus, I decided to
send him.†
26 "I have nothing certain to write
to my lord concerning him. Therefore I have brought him out before
you, and especially before you, King
Agrippa, so that after the examination has taken place I may have
something to write.†
27 "For it seems to me unreasonable to send a prisoner and not to
specify the charges against him."

Paul's Defense

26 Then Agrippa said to Paul,
"You are permitted to speak
for yourself." So Paul stretched out
his hand and answered for himself:†
2 "I think myself [a]happy, King
Agrippa, because today I shall answer [b]for myself before you concern-

---

25:14 Festus wants to present Paul to King Agrippa, hoping to get more information for his report to the imperial tribunal (v. 26).

25:15, 16 The Jewish authorities had from the first (vv. 2, 3, 24) asked for the death sentence against Paul. But Roman law prohibited the sentence of judgment without fair trial and the opportunity of the accused to offer a defense.

25:19 The dispute is not only over **Jesus** but also over the Jewish traditions as requirements for salvation. To the Jewish authorities Paul seems an apostate, questioning the saving validity of circumcision and other Jewish rituals.

25:23 Agrippa's interest in Paul's message brought a whole **auditorium** full of people—including the **prominent** people of the city—under the sound of the gospel.

25:25 Augustus: a title of the Roman Emperors, who were also called "lord" (v. 26) or Caesar. Nero was the Emperor at this time.

25:26, 27 A report of the charges against a prisoner was required in the Roman judicial process. A new governor, after all, would not want to look bad before the emperor. There is a twist of humor here. The charges against Paul are groundless. He is about to be sent to Caesar for judgment, and there is nothing to say against him!

26:1 Being of higher rank, **Agrippa** opens the proceedings. Paul **stretched out his hand,** a common gesture for an ancient public speaker.

ing all the things of which I am
[c]accused by the Jews,†
3 "especially because you are expert in all customs and questions
which have to do with the Jews.
Therefore I beg you to hear me
patiently.†
4 "My manner of life from my
youth, which was spent from the beginning among my own nation at Jerusalem, all the Jews know.
5 "They knew me from the first,
if they were willing to testify, that
according to [a]the strictest sect of our
religion I lived a Pharisee.
6 [a]"And now I stand and am
judged for the hope of [b]the promise
made by God to our fathers.
7 "To this *promise* [a]our twelve
tribes, earnestly serving *God* [b]night
and day, [c]hope to attain. For this
hope's sake, King Agrippa, I am accused by the Jews.
8 "Why should it be thought incredible by you that God raises the
dead?
9 [a]"Indeed, I myself thought I
must do many things [1]contrary to the
name of [b]Jesus of Nazareth.
10 [a]"This I also did in Jerusalem,
and many of the saints I shut up in
prison, having received authority
[b]from the chief priests; and when
they were put to death, I cast my
vote against *them*.
11 [a]"And I punished them often in
every synagogue and compelled *them*
to blaspheme; and being exceedingly
enraged against them, I persecuted
them even to foreign cities.†
12 [a]"While thus occupied, as I

2 [c]Acts 21:28; 24:5, 6
5 [a]Phil. 3:5
6 [a]Acts 23:6 [b]Acts 13:32
7 [a]James 1:1 [b]1 Thess. 3:10 [c]Phil. 3:11
9 [a]1 Tim. 1:12, 13 [b]Acts 2:22; 10:38 [1]*against*
10 [a]Acts 8:1–3; 9:13 [b]Acts 9:14
11 [a]Acts 22:19
12 [a]Acts 9:3–8; 22:6–11; 26:12–18
16 [a]Acts 22:15
17 [a]Acts 22:21 [1]*rescue* [2]NU, M omit *now*
18 [a]Is. 35:5; 42:7, 16 [b]1 Pet. 2:9 [c]Luke 1:77 [d]Col. 1:12 [e]Acts 20:32 [1]*set apart*
20 [a]Acts 9:19, 20, 22; 11:26

journeyed to Damascus with authority and commission from the chief
priests,†
13 "at midday, O king, along the
road I saw a light from heaven,
brighter than the sun, shining
around me and those who journeyed
with me.†
14 "And when we all had fallen to
the ground, I heard a voice speaking
to me and saying in the Hebrew language, 'Saul, Saul, why are you persecuting Me? *It is* hard for you to
kick against the goads.'
15 "So I said, 'Who are You, Lord?'
And He said, 'I am Jesus, whom you
are persecuting.
16 'But rise and stand on your feet;
for I have appeared to you for this
purpose, [a]to make you a minister
and a witness both of the things
which you have seen and of the
things which I will yet reveal to
you.†
17 'I will [1]deliver you from the *Jewish* people, as well as *from* the Gentiles, [a]to whom I [2]now send you,
18 [a]'to open their eyes, *in order*
[b]to turn *them* from darkness to light,
and *from* the power of Satan to God,
[c]that they may receive forgiveness
of sins and [d]an inheritance among
those who are [e]sanctified[1] by faith
in Me.'
19 "Therefore, King Agrippa, I was
not disobedient to the heavenly
vision,†
20 "but [a]declared first to those in
Damascus and in Jerusalem, and
throughout all the region of Judea,
and *then* to the Gentiles, that they

26:2 No accusers are present. Paul is free to proceed as he pleases, though he uses the Jews' charges as his point of reference.

26:3 We know also from secular history that Agrippa was knowledgeable in **customs and questions** which had to do with **the Jews.**

26:11 As part of Paul's earlier persecution against Jewish Christians, he forced them to **blaspheme** or curse the name of Christ (see 1 Cor. 12:3).

26:12–18 This is the third account of Paul's **Damascus** vision (see notes on 9:3–8).

26:13 Paul describes the **light** he saw on the road to Damascus as **brighter than the sun** (see 9:3; 22:6). The context (v. 14) suggests it is the glorified Christ Himself (see v. 16; 9:17; 22:14; 1 Cor. 9:1; 15:8).

26:16 The risen Christ commissions Paul as His **witness,** just as He charged the Apostles (1:8).

26:19, 20 A direct call from God constitutes the highest authority. Paul obeys this **heavenly vision,** declaring to both Jews and **Gentiles** (v. 20) that they should: (1) **repent,** (2) **turn to God,** and (3) **do works befitting repentance.**

should repent, turn to God, and do
[b]works befitting repentance.
21 "For these reasons the Jews
seized me in the temple and tried
to kill *me*.
22 "Therefore, having obtained
help from God, to this day I stand,
witnessing both to small and great,
saying no other things than those
[a]which the prophets and [b]Moses
said would come—
23 [a]"that the Christ would suffer,
[b]that He would be the first to rise
from the dead, and [c]would proclaim
light to the *Jewish* people and to the
Gentiles."

The Tribunal's Reaction

24 Now as he thus made his defense, Festus said with a loud voice,
"Paul, [a]you are beside yourself!
Much learning is driving you
mad!"
25 But he said, "I am not [1]mad,
most noble Festus, but speak the
words of truth and reason.†
26 "For the king, before whom I
also speak freely, [a]knows these
things; for I am convinced that none
of these things escapes his attention,
since this thing was not done in a
corner.†
27 "King Agrippa, do you believe
the prophets? I know that you do
believe."†
28 Then Agrippa said to Paul,
"You almost persuade me to become
a Christian."
29 And Paul said, [a]"I would to

20 [b]Matt. 3:8
22 [a]Rom. 3:21
[b]John 5:46
23 [a]Luke 24:26
[b]1 Cor. 15:20, 23
[c]Luke 2:32
24 [a][1 Cor. 1:23; 2:13, 14; 4:10]
25 [1]*out of my mind*
26 [a]Acts 26:3
29 [a]1 Cor. 7:7
31 [a]Acts 23:9, 29; 25:25
32 [a]Acts 28:18
[b]Acts 25:11

CHAPTER 27
1 [a]Acts 25:12, 25
2 [a]Acts 19:29
3 [a]Acts 24:23; 28:16

God that not only you, but also all
who hear me today, might become
both almost and altogether such as
I am, except for these chains."
30 When he had said these things,
the king stood up, as well as the governor and Bernice and those who sat
with them;†
31 and when they had gone aside,
they talked among themselves, saying, [a]"This man is doing nothing deserving of death or chains."
32 Then Agrippa said to Festus,
"This man might have been set
[a]free [b]if he had not appealed to
Caesar."

The Voyage to Rome Begins

27 And when [a]it was decided
that we should sail to Italy,
they delivered Paul and some other
prisoners to *one* named Julius, a
centurion of the Augustan Regiment.
2 So, entering a ship of Adramyt-
tium, we put to sea, meaning to sail
along the coasts of Asia. [a]Aristar-
chus, a Macedonian of Thessalonica,
was with us.†
3 And the next *day* we landed at
Sidon. And Julius [a]treated Paul
kindly and gave *him* liberty to go to
his friends and receive care.†
4 When we had put to sea from
there, we sailed under *the shelter of*
Cyprus, because the winds were
contrary.
5 And when we had sailed over
the sea which is off Cilicia and Pam-

26:25 The Greek word for **reason** (*sophrosune*) could more aptly be translated "good judgment."

26:26 This thing was not done in a corner is a proverb, here applied to the death and Resurrection of Christ; they are public events, fulfilling the OT and now widely known.

26:27 Agrippa was of Jewish blood. If he believed in the authority of the OT prophets, as one might expect, he would have had to take Paul's proclamation seriously, as Agrippa himself suggests (v. 28).

26:30–32 Agrippa recognizes Paul's innocence. But the appeal to **Caesar** (v. 32) is not an error. Paul still needs protection from the Jews who were seeking to kill him, and he wants to go to Rome.

27:2 We indicates Luke is with Paul, and Paul's Thessalonian companion **Aristarchus** is present as well (19:29; 20:4; Philem. 24).

27:3–5 From Caesarea the company sails to **Sidon,** then on past the north side of **Cyprus** (v. 4), hugging the coast of southern Asia Minor for protection from the extremely dangerous elements. Paul's **friends** (v. 3) are local Christians.

phylia, we came to Myra, *a city* of Lycia.

6 There the centurion found [a]an Alexandrian ship sailing to Italy, and he put us on board.

7 When we had sailed slowly many days, and arrived with difficulty off Cnidus, the wind not permitting us to proceed, we sailed under *the shelter of* [a]Crete off Salmone.

8 Passing it with difficulty, we came to a place called Fair Havens, near the city *of* Lasea.

9 Now when much time had been spent, and sailing was now dangerous [a]because [1]the Fast was already over, Paul advised them,†

10 saying, "Men, I perceive that this voyage will end with disaster and much loss, not only of the cargo and ship, but also our lives."

11 Nevertheless the centurion was more persuaded by the helmsman and the owner of the ship than by the things spoken by Paul.

12 And because the harbor was not suitable to winter in, the majority advised to set sail from there also, if by any means they could reach Phoenix, a harbor of Crete opening toward the southwest and northwest, *and* winter *there*.

Storm and Shipwreck

13 When the south wind blew softly, supposing that they had obtained *their* desire, putting out to sea, they sailed close by Crete.

14 But not long after, a tempestuous head wind arose, called [1]Euroclydon.†

15 So when the ship was caught, and could not head into the wind, we let *her* [1]drive.

16 And running under *the shelter of* an island called [1]Clauda, we secured the skiff with difficulty.†

17 When they had taken it on board, they used cables to undergird the ship; and fearing lest they should run aground on the [1]Syrtis *Sands*, they struck sail and so were driven.†

18 And because we were exceedingly tempest-tossed, the next *day* they lightened the ship.†

19 On the third *day* [a]we threw the ship's tackle overboard with our own hands.

20 Now when neither sun nor stars appeared for many days, and no small tempest beat on *us*, all hope that we would be saved was finally given up.†

21 But after long abstinence from food, then Paul stood in the midst of them and said, "Men, you should have listened to me, and not have sailed from Crete and incurred this disaster and loss.†

22 "And now I urge you to take [1]heart, for there will be no loss of life among you, but only of the ship.

23 [a]"For there stood by me this night an angel of the God to whom I belong and [b]whom I serve,

24 "saying, 'Do not be afraid, Paul; you must be brought before Caesar; and indeed God has granted you all those who sail with you.'

25 "Therefore take heart, men, [a]for I believe God that it will be just as it was told me.

26 "However, [a]we must run aground on a certain island."

27 Now when the fourteenth night had come, as we were driven up and

6 [a]Acts 28:11
7 [a]Acts 2:11; 27:12, 21; Titus 1:5, 12
9 [a]Lev. 16:29–31; 23:27–29; Num. 29:7 [1]The Day of Atonement, late September or early October
14 [1]A southeast wind that stirs up broad waves; NU *Euraquilon*, a northeaster
15 [1]*be driven*
16 [1]NU *Cauda*
17 [1]M *Syrtes*
19 [a]Jon. 1:5
22 [1]*courage*
23 [a]Acts 18:9; 23:11; 2 Tim. 4:17 [b]Dan. 6:16; Rom. 1:9; 2 Tim. 1:3
25 [a]Luke 1:45; Rom. 4:20, 21; 2 Tim. 1:12
26 [a]Acts 28:1

27:9–12 This was a time of the year when sailing was not advisable because of winter storms (see note in center column).

27:14 The Greek word translated **tempestuous** is *tuphonikos,* from which we derive the word "typhoon."

27:16 **The skiff:** a small boat or dinghy pulled by the ship.

27:17 **The Syrtis Sands:** a sandbank on the coast of North Africa.

27:18 **They lightened the ship** by dumping some of the cargo (see v. 19).

27:20 Unable to see the **sun** or the **stars,** they lost all sense of direction in the stormy sea.

27:21–26 Having been proven correct once, Paul again speaks to the passengers to reassure them of their own safety, but not that of the ship itself. Paul's intimate communion with God and his prophetic gifts are evident.

down in the Adriatic *Sea*, about midnight the sailors sensed that they
were drawing near some land.
28 And they took soundings and
found *it* to be twenty fathoms; and
when they had gone a little farther,
they took soundings again and
found *it* to be fifteen fathoms.
29 Then, fearing lest we should run
aground on the rocks, they dropped
four anchors from the stern, and
[1]prayed for day to come.
30 And as the sailors were seeking
to escape from the ship, when they
had let down the skiff into the sea,
under pretense of putting out anchors from the prow,
31 Paul said to the centurion and
the soldiers, "Unless these men stay
in the ship, you cannot be saved."
32 Then the soldiers cut away
the ropes of the skiff and let it fall
off.
33 And as day was about to dawn,
Paul implored *them* all to take food,
saying, "Today is the fourteenth day
you have waited and continued
without food, and eaten nothing.
34 "Therefore I urge you to take
nourishment, for this is for your sur-
vival, [a]since not a hair will fall from
the head of any of you."
35 And when he had said these
things, he took bread and [a]gave
thanks to God in the presence of
them all; and when he had broken
it he began to eat.†
36 Then they were all encouraged,
and also took food themselves.
37 And in all we were two hundred
and seventy-six [a]persons on the
ship.
38 So when they had eaten
enough, they lightened the ship and
threw out the wheat into the sea.
39 When it was day, they did not
recognize the land; but they observed a bay with a beach, onto
which they planned to run the ship
if possible.
40 And they [1]let go the anchors
and left *them* in the sea, meanwhile
loosing the rudder ropes; and they
hoisted the mainsail to the wind and
made for shore.
41 But striking [1]a place where two
seas met, [a]they ran the ship
aground; and the prow stuck fast
and remained immovable, but the
stern was being broken up by the
violence of the waves.
42 And the soldiers' plan was to
kill the prisoners, lest any of them
should swim away and escape.
43 But the centurion, wanting to
save Paul, kept them from *their* purpose, and commanded that those
who could swim should jump *overboard* first and get to land,
44 and the rest, some on boards
and some on *parts* of the ship. And
so it was [a]that they all escaped safely
to land.

Winter at Malta

28 Now when they had escaped,
they then found out that
[a]the island was called Malta.†
2 And the [a]natives[1] showed us
unusual kindness; for they kindled
a fire and made us all welcome, because of the rain that was falling and
because of the cold.†
3 But when Paul had gathered a
bundle of sticks and laid *them* on
the fire, a viper came out because
of the heat, and fastened on his
hand.†
4 So when the natives saw the
creature hanging from his hand, they
said to one another, "No doubt this
man is a murderer, whom, though
he has escaped the sea, yet justice
does not allow to live."
5 But he shook off the creature
into the fire and [a]suffered no harm.
6 However, they were expecting
that he would swell up or suddenly

29 [1]Or *wished*
34 [a]1 Kin. 1:52; [Matt. 10:30; Luke 12:7; 21:18]
35 [a]1 Sam. 9:13; Matt. 15:36; Mark 8:6; John 6:11; [1 Tim. 4:3, 4]
37 [a]Acts 2:41; 7:14; Rom. 13:1; 1 Pet. 3:20
40 [1]*cast off*
41 [a]2 Cor. 11:25 [1]A reef
44 [a]Acts 27:22, 31

CHAPTER 28

1 [a]Acts 27:26
2 [a]Acts 28:4; Rom. 1:14; 1 Cor. 14:11; Col. 3:11 [1]Lit. *barbarians*
5 [a]Mark 16:18; Luke 10:19

27:35 Paul's actions express the Jewish tradition of giving **thanks to God** before a meal, but they also have eucharistic overtones.
28:1 **Malta:** a small **island** south of Sicily.
28:2 **Natives** (lit. "barbarians") refers to those who are not cultured and do not speak Greek.
28:3 The **viper,** common to that area, is a highly poisonous snake.

fall down dead. But after they had
looked for a long time and saw no
harm come to him, they changed
their minds and [a]said that he was a
god.†
7 In that region there was an estate of the [1]leading citizen of the island, whose name was Publius, who
received us and entertained us cour-
teously for three days.
8 And it happened that the father
of Publius lay sick of a fever and dys-
entery. Paul went in to him and
[a]prayed, and [b]he laid his hands on
him and healed him.†
9 So when this was done, the rest
of those on the island who had diseases also came and were healed.
10 They also honored us in many
[a]ways; and when we departed, they
provided such things as were
[b]necessary.

From Malta to Rome

11 After three months we sailed in
[a]an Alexandrian ship whose figurehead was the [1]Twin Brothers, which
had wintered at the island.†
12 And landing at Syracuse, we
stayed three days.†
13 From there we circled round
and reached Rhegium. And after one
day the south wind blew; and the
next day we came to Puteoli,†
14 where we found [a]brethren, and
were invited to stay with them seven
days. And so we went toward Rome.

6 [a]Acts 12:22; 14:11
7 [1]Magistrate
8 [a]Acts 9:40; [James 5:14, 15] [b]Matt. 9:18; Mark 5:23; 6:5; 7:32; 16:18; Luke 4:40; Acts 19:11, 12; [1 Cor. 12:9, 28]
10 [a]Matt. 15:6; 1 Tim. 5:17 [b][Phil. 4:19]
11 [a]Acts 27:6 [1]Gr. *Dioskouroi,* Zeus's sons Castor and Pollux
14 [a]Rom. 1:8
16 [a]Acts 23:11; 24:25; 27:3
17 [a]Acts 23:29; 24:12, 13; 26:31 [b]Acts 21:33
18 [a]Acts 22:24; 24:10; 25:8; 26:32
19 [a]Acts 25:11, 21, 25 [1]The ruling authorities
20 [a]Acts 26:6, 7 [b]Acts 26:29; Eph. 3:1; 4:1; 6:20; 2 Tim. 1:8, 16; Philem. 10, 13

15 And from there, when the
brethren heard about us, they came
to meet us as far as Appii Forum and
Three Inns. When Paul saw them,
he thanked God and took courage.

Paul's Ministry in Rome

16 Now when we came to Rome,
the centurion delivered the prisoners
to the captain of the guard; but
[a]Paul was permitted to dwell by himself with the soldier who guarded
him.
17 And it came to pass after three
days that Paul called the leaders of
the Jews together. So when they had
come together, he said to them:
"Men *and* brethren, [a]though I have
done nothing against our people or
the customs of our fathers, yet
[b]I was delivered as a prisoner from
Jerusalem into the hands of the
Romans,
18 "who, [a]when they had examined me, wanted to let *me* go, because there was no cause for putting
me to death.
19 "But when the [1]Jews spoke
against *it,* [a]I was compelled to appeal
to Caesar, not that I had anything
of which to accuse my nation.†
20 "For this reason therefore I have
called for you, to see *you* and speak
with *you,* because [a]for the hope
of Israel I am bound with [b]this
chain."†

28:6 For the second time Paul is taken for **a god.** At Lystra, he and Barnabas were taken for Hermes and Zeus (14:12).

28:8–10 The people of Malta showed great kindness to them after Publius' **father** and the rest of the sick people on the island were **healed** (v. 9) through Paul. It would appear (v. 7) this occurred very early in their stay.

28:11 The **Twin Brothers,** according to Greek mythology, were sons of Zeus and protectors of sailors.

28:12 **Syracuse:** a major seaport in Sicily.

28:13, 14 **Rhegium** and **Puteoli:** towns on the western coast of Italy. By A.D. 60 there were numerous churches scattered throughout the empire, including one in Puteoli. From here Paul's company travelled to Rome on foot.

28:19 **The Jews** had a strong and well-organized community in Rome. Paul speaks first to the Jewish leaders, recapitulating the false charges against him and defending his innocence. He tells them the truth up front, not later when they might think he had deceived them.

28:20 The **hope of Israel** is another reference to the Resurrection, which Paul has made central in his apologetic speeches. **This chain** may be figurative of his imprisonment under house arrest.

21 Then they said to him, "We neither received letters from Judea concerning you, nor have any of the brethren who came reported or spoken any evil of you.

22 "But we desire to hear from you what you think; for concerning this sect, we know that [a]it is spoken against everywhere."

23 So when they had appointed him a day, many came to him at *his* lodging, [a]to whom he explained and solemnly testified of the kingdom of God, persuading them concerning Jesus [b]from both the Law of Moses and the Prophets, from morning till evening.†

24 And [a]some were persuaded by the things which were spoken, and some disbelieved.

25 So when they did not agree among themselves, they departed after Paul had said one word: "The Holy Spirit spoke rightly through Isaiah the prophet to [1]our fathers,

26 "saying,

> [a]*'Go to this people and say:*
> *"Hearing you will hear, and shall not understand;*
> *And seeing you will see, and not perceive;*

27 *For the hearts of this people have grown dull.*
> *Their ears are hard of hearing,*
> *And their eyes they have closed,*
> *Lest they should see with their eyes and hear with their ears,*
> *Lest they should understand with their hearts and turn,*
> *So that I should heal them."'*

28 "Therefore let it be known to you that the salvation of God has been sent [a]to the Gentiles, and they will hear it!"

29 [1]And when he had said these words, the Jews departed and had a great dispute among themselves.

30 Then Paul dwelt two whole years in his own rented house, and received all who came to him,

31 [a]preaching the kingdom of God and teaching the things which concern the Lord Jesus Christ with all confidence, no one forbidding him.†

22 [a]Luke 2:34; Acts 24:5, 14; [1 Pet. 2:12; 3:16; 4:14, 16]
23 [a]Luke 24:27; [Acts 17:3; 19:8] [b]Acts 26:6, 22
24 [a]Acts 14:4; 19:9
25 [1]NU *your*
26 [a]Is. 6:9, 10; Jer. 5:21; Ezek. 12:2; Matt. 13:14, 15; Mark 4:12; Luke 8:10; John 12:40, 41; Rom. 11:8
28 [a]Is. 42:1, 6; 49:6; Matt. 21:41; Luke 2:32; Rom. 11:11
29 [1]NU omits v. 29.
31 [a]Acts 4:31; Eph. 6:19

28:23 Although these Jewish leaders know that Christianity is **spoken against everywhere** (v. 22), Paul is granted the opportunity to present the gospel of **the kingdom of God** and Christ as prophesied by the OT.

28:31 Paul's preaching finishes where it began: (1) proclaiming **the kingdom of God** and (2) **things** concerning **the Lord Jesus Christ.** These two related items are still the content of the preaching and teaching of the true Christian faith. **With all confidence, no one forbidding him**—the last words of Acts—can be translated simply "boldly and without hindrance." The story of the Acts of the Apostles and their successors continues to this day.

The Epistle of Paul the Apostle to the

ROMANS

Author: *St. Paul the Apostle*

Date: A.D. 55–57

Theme: *God's Righteousness Revealed in Christ for Our Salvation*

AUTHOR: While Pauline authorship of some epistles has been questioned, the Church has universally accepted Paul as the author of Romans.

DATE: Romans was probably written in A.D. 55–57 during the latter part of Paul's third missionary journey (Acts 20:3—21:16), most likely while he was in Corinth.

MAJOR THEME: God's righteousness revealed in Christ for our salvation (1:16, 17). Righteousness is the basis of a faithful relationship between God and humanity. God Himself freely offers this living and growing relationship to all through Christ. Subthemes in Romans include:

(1) The natural mortality and actual sinfulness of all (1:18—3:20).

(2) Salvation through Christ apart from the Mosaic Law (3:21—4:25): we live by faith in response to grace, rather than by the dead works of the law.

(3) New life in Christ: freedom from sin, death and the law through our sacramental identity with Christ, established in Holy Baptism (chs. 5—7).

(4) New life in the Holy Spirit: the power to be Godlike, established in chrismation (ch. 8).

(5) God's plan for Jews and Gentiles, and their reconciliation in Christ (chs. 9—11).

(6) Christian life in the Church and in the world (chs. 12—16).

BACKGROUND INFORMATION: (1) *Dichotomies and Synergies*. Paul's logic in Romans proceeds largely from the use of dichotomies, in which two concepts are placed in opposition to each other; and synergies, in which two concepts work together. However, many modern commentators have seen opposition between pairs of concepts where Paul intends cooperation. These pairs of concepts include:

Law and Grace
Faith and Works
Old Testament and New Testament
Nature and Grace
Spirit and Body
Reality and Symbol
God's Faithfulness and Humanity's Faithfulness
Secular and Sacred
Church and State

The areas in which Paul truly sees opposition are fewer and more fundamental:

Living Faith vs. Dead Faith
Living Works vs. Dead Works
Good vs. Evil
Righteousness vs. Unrighteousness
Natural vs. Unnatural
Faithfulness vs. Unfaithfulness

(2) *Jew and Gentile.* In Romans and Galatians, Paul deals extensively with the relation of the Old Covenant to belief in Christ, and how Gentiles can be full members of the New Covenant by grace through faith.

(3) *The uniqueness of Romans.* Romans has several qualities which set it apart from the rest of Paul's epistles.

(a) *Romans is Paul's most significant letter.* It summarizes the entire gospel. St. John Chrysostom calls Romans "a spiritual trumpet."

(b) *Romans is Paul's most logical letter.* He argues his case like a lawyer.

(c) *Romans is the only letter Paul wrote to a church he had not yet visited* (1:11; 15:22). Paul was hoping to obtain Rome's support for his planned mission to Spain (15:24, 28, 29). Some have suggested Romans contains what Paul preached and taught when he visited churches in person.

(d) *Romans is Paul's most doctrinally oriented letter.* While most of Paul's epistles correct doctrinal or moral problems, Romans proclaims the faith more completely and systematically, addressing few specific problems. St. John Chrysostom says: "[Paul] abounded more than all the rest in the word of doctrine."

OUTLINE

Introduction: The righteousness of God available for all — 1:1–17

- I. God's faithfulness to all: His judgment and salvation — 1:18—4:25
  - A. Judgment on all who disbelieve: The unfaithfulness of Jew and Gentile — 1:18—3:20
  - B. Salvation for all who believe: Through faith apart from the law — 3:21—4:25
- II. Faithful union between God and His Church — 5:1—8:39
  - A. Righteous living through the reign of Christ — 5:1–21
  - B. Resurrection life through union with Christ — 6:1—7:6

Greeting

1 Paul, a bondservant of Jesus
Christ, [a]called *to be* an apostle, [b]separated to the gospel of
God†
2 [a]which He promised before
[b]through His prophets in the Holy
Scriptures,
3 concerning His Son Jesus Christ
our Lord, who [1]was [a]born of the
seed of David according to the
flesh,†
4 *and* [a]declared *to be* the Son of
God with power according [b]to the
Spirit of holiness, by the resurrection
from the dead.†
5 Through Him [a]we have received grace and apostleship for
[b]obedience to the faith among all nations [c]for His name,†
6 among whom you also are the
called of Jesus Christ;†

7 To all who are in Rome, beloved
of God, [a]called *to be* saints:

CHAPTER 1
1 [a]1 Tim. 1:11 [b]Acts 9:15; 13:2
2 [a]Acts 26:6 [b]Gal. 3:8
3 [a]Gal. 4:4 [1]*came*
4 [a]Acts 9:20; 13:33 [b][Heb. 9:14]
5 [a]Eph. 3:8 [b]Acts 6:7 [c]Acts 9:15
7 [a]1 Cor. 1:2, 24

1:1–4 Paul is **a bondservant** (literally, a slave; see note on Titus 1:1) as **an apostle** (a sent one) totally devoted to Christ. The **gospel of God:** the Good News of salvation in Christ. The restoration of union between God and humanity leads to human participation in divine life (deification) and the fulfillment of all creation. The gospel: (1) fulfills God's promise in the OT (v. 2); (2) reveals the saving work of the Holy Trinity: it is from the Father (**God,** v. 1), **concerning His Son** (v. 3), and **according to the Spirit** (v. 4); (3) is realized in the Incarnation: as One of the Holy Trinity, the Son becomes Man without ceasing to be God (v. 3) and restores human nature through His Resurrection and Ascension into heaven (v. 4).

1:3 Jesus is the Son of God, one in essence with the Father and the Holy Spirit. Even the OT calls the Messiah **"Lord"** (Ps. 110:1), "Son" of God (Ps. 2:7) and "God" (Ps. 45:6, 7). **According to the flesh** means in Christ's human nature. (Incarnation is literally "enfleshment.") Thus Christ is one divine Person with two natures.

1:4 Christ's **resurrection declared** Him to be the **Son of God,** but did not make Him so. What had been partially hidden was now openly and undeniably demonstrated: This Man is God from before all time. The heart of the gospel is not simply the death of Christ, but His death *and* Resurrection (see 6:8–10; 15:3, 4). By His life-giving death and glorious Resurrection, Christ has conquered sin and death. Now that He is ascended and reigning with the Father, His uncreated deity will be forever declared to all. **The Spirit of holiness,** the Holy Spirit, was also at work in the Resurrection of Jesus, even as the Son later sends the Spirit to testify of Himself.

1:5 Obedience to the faith means acceptance of the Christian faith by the Gentiles. Some translate the phrase "obedience of faith," meaning obedience which belongs to faith. The faith which saves is the faith which obeys. While the NT separates faith from the works of the law, it never isolates faith from obedience. How may we acquire this faith and obedience? With the assistance of the **apostleship,** the episcopal ministry, as it is energized by God's **grace.**

1:6 Christians are **the called of Jesus Christ** with a purpose: to join the Church of the Apostles. It is not up to us to create the Church; God brings us into the community which is already there.

[b]Grace to you and peace from God our Father and the Lord Jesus Christ.†

Desire to Visit Rome

8 First, [a]I thank my God through Jesus Christ for you all, that [b]your faith is spoken of throughout the whole world.†
9 For [a]God is my witness, [b]whom I serve [1]with my spirit in the gospel of His Son, that [c]without ceasing I make mention of you always in my prayers,
10 making request if, by some means, now at last I may find a way in the will of God to come to you.
11 For I long to see you, that [a]I may impart to you some spiritual gift, so that you may be established—†
12 that is, that I may be encouraged together with you by [a]the mutual faith both of you and me.†
13 Now I do not want you to be unaware, brethren, that I often planned to come to you (but [a]was hindered until now), that I might have some [b]fruit among you also, just as among the other Gentiles.†
14 I am a debtor both to Greeks and to barbarians, both to wise and to unwise.†
15 So, as much as is in me, *I am* ready to preach the gospel to you who are in Rome also.

The Theme: The Righteousness of God Through Faith in Christ

16 For [a]I am not ashamed of the gospel [1]of Christ, for [b]it is the power of God to salvation for everyone who believes, [c]for the Jew first and also for the Greek.†
17 For [a]in it the righteousness of God is revealed from faith to faith; as it is written, [b]*"The just shall live by faith."*†

7 [b]1 Cor. 1:3
8 [a]1 Cor. 1:4 [b]Rom. 16:19
9 [a]Rom. 9:1 [b]Acts 27:23 [c]1 Thess. 3:10 [1]Or *in*
11 [a]Rom. 15:29
12 [a]Titus 1:4
13 [a][1 Thess. 2:18] [b]Phil. 4:17
16 [a]Ps. 40:9, 10 [b]1 Cor. 1:18, 24 [c]Acts 3:26 [1]NU omits *of Christ*
17 [a]Rom. 3:21; 9:30 [b]Hab. 2:4

1:7 Called to be saints refers to a present reality. In the NT all who are true Christians are called *saints* (1 Cor. 1:2; Eph. 3:8; 2 Thess. 1:10; Jude 3). But from among all Christians, the Orthodox Church has specially recognized those who have been holy, faithful, and victorious in finishing the course: St. Paul, St. Ignatius, St. Irenaeus, and St. Athanasius are examples.

1:8–12 Paul shows a pastoral concern for the Roman Christians even though he is not technically their pastor. He (1) thanks God for them, (2) prays for them daily, and (3) longs to see them for mutual benefit.

1:11 Paul had not yet visited Rome when he wrote this letter. He wrote to the Romans what he preached to other churches: the core of true apostolic doctrine, necessary for the full foundation of a church. For this reason the Orthodox Church reads Romans immediately following Pentecost, the birthday of the Church, and the season when the ancient Church completed the instruction of those who had been baptized at Easter (Pascha).

1:12 The mutual faith in Christ unites and strengthens Christians (see vv. 5, 17; 3:26). By our faith we participate in the faith of Christ Himself, who alone has perfect faith and helps us grow in ours.

1:13 Paul wanted to visit Rome, but until this time had not been able. One of the "hindrances" was his desire to complete his missionary work in the Eastern part of the Roman Empire (15:22–24). Like all true servants, he does not question the Master's will, but simply obeys Him. **Fruit** includes both spiritual benefits and new converts.

1:14 Barbarians: those not culturally Greek and unable to speak Greek. Obviously the Romans are "Greeks" in the cultural sense, for Paul is writing to them in Greek. Paul did not discriminate between cultured and uncultured, educated and uneducated. God loves all equally and unites differing national groups—from "every nation, tribe, tongue, and people" (Rev. 14:6)—into one body, the Church. Culture is subservient to the gospel. A shepherd filled with the love of God opens God's Kingdom to all.

1:16 What gives the gospel **power** for **salvation?** The Holy Spirit uniting us to the living Christ. Paul is **not ashamed** (see Luke 9:26), continually bearing witness fearlessly to Christ.

1:17 The **righteousness of God:** a right relationship with God, which originates with Him. God's plan for our reception of His righteousness is the Incarnation of the Son. Christ's righteousness is given to us, and by our own cooperation with God we continue to grow in

(continued on next page)

THE RESURRECTION

The Resurrection of Christ, *by the hand of Robin Armstrong.*

By His glorious death and Resurrection, Jesus Christ defeats the power of the devil and delivers fallen mankind from the depths of hell. Feast Day readings are John 1:1–17; Acts 1:1–8.

See also Matthew 28:1–15; Mark 16:1–19; Luke 24:1–12; John 20:1–18; 1 Corinthians 15:12–28.

Judgment of Sinning Humanity

18 [a]For the wrath of God is revealed from heaven against all ungodliness and [b]unrighteousness of
men, who [1]suppress the truth in
unrighteousness,†
19 because [a]what may be known
of God is [1]manifest [2]in them, for
[b]God has shown *it* to them.
20 For since the creation of the
world [a]His invisible *attributes* are
clearly seen, being understood by
the things that are made, *even* His
eternal power and [1]Godhead, so that
they are without excuse,†
21 because, although they knew
God, they did not glorify *Him* as
God, nor were thankful, but [a]be-
came futile in their thoughts, and
their foolish hearts were darkened.†
22 [a]Professing to be wise, they became fools,
23 and changed the glory of the
[a]incorruptible [b]God into an image
made like [1]corruptible man—and
birds and four-footed animals and
creeping things.
24 [a]Therefore God also gave them
up to uncleanness, in the lusts of
their hearts, [b]to dishonor their bodies [c]among themselves,
25 who exchanged [a]the truth of
God [b]for the lie, and worshiped and
served the creature rather than the
Creator, who is blessed forever.
Amen.
26 For this reason God gave them
up to [a]vile passions. For even their
[1]women exchanged the natural use
for what is against nature.†
27 Likewise also the [1]men, leaving
the natural use of the [2]woman,
burned in their lust for one another,
[1]men with [1]men committing what is
shameful, and receiving in themselves the penalty of their error
which was due.
28 And even as they did not like
to retain God in *their* knowledge,
God gave them over to a debased
mind, to do those things [a]which are
not fitting;
29 being filled with all unrighteousness, [1]sexual immorality, wickedness, [2]covetousness, [3]mali-
ciousness; full of envy, murder,
strife, deceit, evil-mindedness; *they*
are whisperers,†

18 [a][Acts 17:30] [b]2 Thess. 2:10 [1]*hold down*
19 [a][Acts 14:17; 17:24] [b][John 1:9] [1]*evident* [2]*among*
20 [a]Ps. 19:1–6 [1]*divine nature, deity*
21 [a]Jer. 2:5
22 [a]Jer. 10:14
23 [a]1 Tim. 1:17; 6:15, 16 [b]Deut. 4:16–18 [1]*perishable*
24 [a]Eph. 4:18, 19 [b]1 Cor. 6:18 [c]Lev. 18:22
25 [a]1 Thess. 1:9 [b]Is. 44:20
26 [a]Lev. 18:22 [1]Lit. *females*
27 [1]Lit. *males* [2]Lit. *female*
28 [a]Eph. 5:4
29 [1]NU omits *sexual immorality* [2]*greed* [3]*malice*

(continued from previous page)
it. This is **revealed from faith to faith:** we receive the incarnate Son through faith, and then live by faith. Humanity has always, in the OT and the NT, participated in God's righteousness on the basis of faith.

The just shall live by faith is the most often internally quoted passage in the entire Bible. It shows the harmony of teaching of the two Testaments, and embodies the theme of Romans: Faith is a way of life. The faithful (*just* means "righteous" or "faithful") actively participate in God's righteousness through their response of belief and obedience. Living by faith in Christ, we exhibit the fruit of the Holy Spirit (14:17; 15:13).

1:18, 19 The wrath of God is His righteous and holy judgment. It involves no loss of temper or self-control; it is calm and impartial, free from emotion and bias, and is based on the truth. God's *wrath* falls on those who knowingly and willfully **suppress the truth in unrighteousness.** Although sin has wounded the ability of humanity to relate to God, even the most terrible sin cannot destroy the image of God in us.

1:20 All humanity knows "natural revelation," that is, God's energy (**power**) and His transcendence (**Godhead**), revealed through the order of the universe and in humanity. But all freely thwart the truth. In their hardness of heart, the ungodly despise the goodness of God revealed in creation. They refuse to repent.

1:21–25 Humanity by nature worships, if not the one uncreated God, then something created. Sin is the result of our failure to know God because we refuse to **glorify** Him and to be **thankful.** Refusing to worship God, men first turned inward to their own spiritual center without regard for God, cutting themselves off from light (v. 21) and true wisdom (v. 22). They then lifted up created things as objects of worship (v. 25).

1:26, 27 Error means delusion. Paul, and the rest of Scripture, is clear. To claim that homosexuality is natural or an "alternative life-style" is delusion. Rather, it is unnatural, shameful and unacceptable to God.

1:29 Sex, of course, is not evil, for it is a gift of God. But sex outside of marriage is
(continued on next page)

30 backbiters, haters of God, violent, proud, boasters, inventors of
evil things, disobedient to parents,†
31 [1]undiscerning, untrustworthy,
unloving, [2]unforgiving, unmerciful;†
32 who, [a]knowing the righteous
judgment of God, that those who
practice such things [b]are deserving
of death, not only do the same but
also [c]approve of those who practice
them.†

Judgment of Each Conscience

2 Therefore you are [a]inexcusable,
O man, whoever you are who
judge, [b]for in whatever you judge
another you condemn yourself; for
you who judge practice the same
things.†
2 But we know that the judgment
of God is according to truth against
those who practice such things.†
3 And do you think this, O man,
you who judge those practicing such
things, and doing the same, that you
will escape the judgment of God?
4 Or do you despise [a]the riches
of His goodness, [b]forbearance, and
[c]longsuffering, [d]not knowing that
the goodness of God leads you to
repentance?
5 But in accordance with your
hardness and your [1]impenitent heart
[a]you are [2]treasuring up for yourself
wrath in the day of wrath and revelation of the righteous judgment of
God,
6 who [a]*"will render to each one
according to his deeds"*:
7 eternal life to those who by
patient continuance in doing good
seek for glory, honor, and immortality;
8 but to those who are self-
seeking and [a]do not obey the truth,
but obey unrighteousness—indignation and wrath,
9 tribulation and anguish, on every soul of man who does evil, of
the Jew [a]first and also of the [1]Greek;
10 [a]but glory, honor, and peace to
everyone who works what is good,
to the Jew first and also to the Greek.
11 For [a]there is no partiality with
God.
12 For as many as have sinned
without law will also perish without
law, and as many as have sinned in
the law will be judged by the law
13 (for [a]not the hearers of the law
are just in the sight of God, but the
doers of the law will be justified;
14 for when Gentiles, who do not
have the law, by nature do the things

31 [1]*without understanding* [2]NU omits *unforgiving*
32 [a][Rom. 2:2] [b][Rom. 6:21] [c]Hos. 7:3

CHAPTER 2

1 [a][Rom. 1:20] [b][Matt. 7:1–5]
4 [a][Eph. 1:7, 18; 2:7] [b][Rom. 3:25] [c]Ex. 34:6 [d]Is. 30:18
5 [a][Deut. 32:34] [1]*unrepentant* [2]*storing*
6 [a]Ps. 62:12; Prov. 24:12
8 [a][2 Thess. 1:8]
9 [a]1 Pet. 4:17 [1]Gentile
10 [a][1 Pet. 1:7]
11 [a]Deut. 10:17
13 [a][James 1:22, 25]

(continued from previous page)
immoral, for it violates God's law. **Covetousness,** wanting something that belongs to someone else, is a sinful passion which corrupts our desires. It leads the soul to grasp for more, regardless of the will of God. The object pursued may, in itself, be good, such as needed possessions or a job. But the motivation is personal pleasure, and the eventual outcome is always more sin. **Murder** may seem far from us, but it is a child of anger, and anger is common to all. For sinful desire arouses anger, anger eventually leads to hate, and hate in turn may lead to *murder*.

1:30 Inventors of evil things are those who cooperate with Satan to create new forms of evil. The devil, the author of all the vices, energizes ungodly people. Those **disobedient to parents** who raised them in godliness bring dishonor not only to their parents, but to God.

1:31 Unloving refers to people without natural tenderness, such as fathers or mothers who neglect, abuse or abandon their children, or children who neglect aged parents. **Unmerciful** are those filled with a critical, judgmental and condemning spirit: judgment overrules mercy in their hearts.

1:32 God will also judge those who **approve** of unrighteousness. All humanity (even the ungodly) knows God's righteousness through creation (v. 20) and conscience (2:14, 15). While those who excuse themselves may form an unrighteous brotherhood with the vices, all will know they are **deserving of death** at the final judgment.

2:1 Not only will the unrighteous experience God's righteous judgment (1:18–32); so will the self-righteous. Characterized by a condemning spirit, the self-righteous judge the immoral person for his or her vices. If, however, one knows what is righteous, one is responsible for being righteous—and extending mercy. But the self-righteous **practice the same things** they condemn.

2:2–16 See article, "The Basis of God's Judgment," p. 341.

THE BASIS OF GOD'S JUDGMENT

Even as believing Christians, we must not take the outcome of God's final judgment for granted. In every Divine Liturgy Orthodox Christians pray, "For a good defense before the dread Judgment Seat of Christ, let us pray to the Lord: Lord have mercy." Romans 2:2–16 describes God's righteous judgment, showing how we can prepare ourselves for it. God's judgment will be:

(1) *According to truth* (*Rom. 2:2, 3*): Nothing is hidden from God. He sees everything and knows the truth about each of us. One of mankind's great self-deceptions is to say, "Who sees us?" (Is. 29:15) and think there is no judgment.

(2) *According to impenitent hearts* (*Rom. 2:4, 5*): An unrepentant or hard heart despises God's goodness, treasuring up the wrath of God at the judgment. A repentant heart, on the other hand, is grateful for God's patience and abides in Christ, practicing a lifetime of repentance, which produces confidence before Him at the judgment (1 John 2:28).

(3) *According to our deeds* (*Rom. 2:6–15*): The "doing good" referred to in v. 7 is not trying to gain merit with God. Rather, it is the unity of intentions with actions, faith with works. Even unbelievers are rewarded for good works, apart from spiritual understanding (Rom. 2:14, 15). But note the following:

(a) "Doing good" means seeking God's glory, not one's own glory; God's honor, not one's own honor; the eternal reward of immortality, not reward here and now. "Doing good" is seeking first the Kingdom of God (Matt. 6:33).

(b) Good intentions alone, or faith without works, will not save (Rom. 2:13). Simply to hear and not do is religion without reality. Those with true faith, "the doers" of the truth, practice virtue from pure and repentant hearts (James 1:21–27).

(c) "By nature" (Rom. 2:14) people are inspired by and cooperate with God's grace. Therefore, good deeds are natural to us, whereas evil deeds are contrary to nature. Because we all fail, we need God's mercy (Rom. 3:9–19). The presence of God's law in our conscience (Rom. 2:15) condemns anything we do which is contrary to true human nature. Therefore, even Gentiles—people not under the Law of Moses, those who do not know of Christ—have an internal law from God, the natural law written in their hearts, according to which God will judge them. Melchizedek, Job, and the Ninevites are Old Testament examples of non-Jews who were judged to be righteous. Jews, then, have two laws from God—the Law of Moses and conscience—and are accountable to Him for both (v. 12).

(d) Those who are condemned *choose* to reject God. There is no automatic, fated condemnation: God's just judgment of us is based on our exercise of free will. Although sin impairs our powers, it does not destroy God's image in us or our free will.

(4) *By Jesus Christ* (*Rom. 2:16*): In the day of judgment we are not judged directly by God the Father, whom we cannot see, but by the incarnate Son whom we do see, Christ Jesus (Acts 17:31; see John 3:16–21, 35, 36). Christ will judge on the basis of the light He Himself has given to each of us (John 1:9) and our response to His light (John 3:16–21). "The secrets of men" are "the thoughts and intents of the heart" (Heb. 4:12).

in the law, these, although not having the law, are a law to themselves,
15 who show the [a]work of the law
written in their hearts, their [b]con-
science also bearing witness, and between themselves *their* thoughts accusing or else excusing *them*)
16 [a]in the day when God will judge
the secrets of men [b]by Jesus Christ,
[c]according to my gospel.

Judgment of the Jews

17 [1]Indeed [a]you are called a Jew,
and [b]rest[2] on the law, [c]and make
your boast in God,†
18 and [a]know *His* will, and [b]ap-
prove the things that are excellent,
being instructed out of the law,
19 and [a]are confident that you
yourself are a guide to the blind, a
light to those who are in darkness,
20 an instructor of the foolish, a
teacher of babes, [a]having the form
of knowledge and truth in the
law.
21 [a]You, therefore, who teach another, do you not teach yourself?
You who preach that a man should
not steal, do you steal?
22 You who say, "Do not commit
adultery," do you commit adultery?
You who abhor idols, [a]do you rob
temples?
23 You who [a]make your boast in
the law, do you dishonor God
through breaking the law?
24 For [a]*"the name of God is*
[b]*blasphemed among the Gentiles be-*
cause of you," as it is written.
25 [a]For circumcision is indeed
profitable if you keep the law; but if

15 [a]1 Cor. 5:1 [b]Acts 24:25
16 [a][Matt. 25:31] [b]Acts 10:42; 17:31 [c]1 Tim. 1:11
17 [a]John 8:33 [b]Mic. 3:11 [c]Is. 48:1, 2 [1]NU *But if* [2]*rely*
18 [a]Deut. 4:8 [b]Phil. 1:10
19 [a]Matt. 15:14
20 [a][2 Tim. 3:5]
21 [a]Matt. 23:3
22 [a]Mal. 3:8
23 [a]Rom. 2:17; 9:4
24 [a]Ezek. 16:27 [b]Is. 52:5; Ezek. 36:22
25 [a][Gal. 5:3]
26 [a][Acts 10:34]
27 [a]Matt. 12:41 [1]Lit. *letter*
28 [a][Gal. 6:15]
29 [a][1 Pet. 3:4] [b]Phil. 3:3 [c]Deut. 30:6 [d][1 Cor. 4:5] [1]A play on words—*Jew* is literally *praise.*

CHAPTER 3

2 [a]Deut. 4:5–8 [1]*sayings,* Scriptures
3 [a]Heb. 4:2 [b][2 Tim. 2:13]
4 [a]Job 40:8 [b][John 3:33]

you are a breaker of the law, your
circumcision has become uncircumcision.†
26 Therefore, [a]if an uncircumcised
man keeps the righteous requirements of the law, will not his uncircumcision be counted as
circumcision?
27 And will not the physically uncircumcised, if he fulfills the law,
[a]judge you who, *even* with *your*
[1]written *code* and circumcision, *are* a
transgressor of the law?†
28 For [a]he is not a Jew who *is one*
outwardly, nor *is* circumcision that
which *is* outward in the flesh;
29 but *he is* a Jew [a]who *is one* inwardly; and [b]circumcision *is that* of
the heart, [c]in the Spirit, not in the
letter; [d]whose [1]praise *is* not from
men but from God.†

The Jews' Unfaithfulness

3 What advantage then has the
Jew, or what *is* the profit of
circumcision?
2 Much in every way! Chiefly because [a]to them were committed the
[1]oracles of God.
3 For what if [a]some did not believe? [b]Will their unbelief make
the faithfulness of God without effect?
4 [a]Certainly not! Indeed, let
[b]God be [1]true but [c]every man a liar.
As it is written:

[d]*"That You may be justified in*
Your words,

[c]Ps. 62:9 [d]Ps. 51:4 [1]Found true

2:17–24 Many Jews relied on the letter of **the law** for righteousness, praising their possession of it and their knowledge of it (vv. 18–20). Yet they did not keep it (vv. 21–23). Such hypocrisy dishonors God (vv. 23, 24); nobody else wants to join them (v. 24). Lesson: the letter of the law must be united with the spirit of the law.

2:25 **Circumcision** is not condemned; it is valued. But religious externals must be accompanied by internal conversion (vv. 28, 29) and virtuous action for the glory of God.

2:27 Paul despises a juridical, or "by-the-letter" view of the law, calling it **your written code.**

2:29 The name **Jew** is from "Judah," which means "the Lord be praised." A true *Jew* seeks only **praise . . . from God.** (A Gentile who keeps the natural law of the conscience is righteous and counted as a Jew. The legalist's goal is vainglory, praise **from men;** the spiritual man, Jew or Gentile, has the goal of pleasing God. True circumcision, and true baptism, is **of the heart, in the Spirit,** leading from repentance to obedience.

THE LAW

One key to understanding Romans is to properly distinguish between the several ways Paul uses the word "law" in this epistle.

(1) *The Mosaic Law* (Rom. 2:12, 13) was written by God on tablets of stone (2 Cor. 3:3, 7) and given to the Jews through Moses. This Law reveals God's righteousness to prepare men for the Messiah and for God's grace. When Paul speaks of "the law" he is most often referring to the Mosaic Law.

The Law is good, but cannot be kept. It is revelation from God, but it is not an end in itself. The purpose of the Mosaic Law is to: (a) reveal the difference between good and evil; (b) make the world accountable to God (Rom. 3:19); (c) manifest sin (Rom. 3:20); and (d) be a schoolmaster to lead us to Christ (Gal. 3:24). Though it is not opposed to the grace of God, the Law cannot save us or make us righteous.

(2) *The natural law* (Rom. 2:14, 15) has been "written" by God in the heart of every human who has ever lived. This is the voice of conscience. It is a reliable guide to God's righteousness for those who are pure in heart; but it can be dulled or obscured completely by habitual sin.

(3) *The law of works* (Rom. 3:27) is our attempt to establish righteousness before God on the basis of keeping the natural law and/or the Mosaic Law. This law reveals human weakness and sin.

(4) *The law of faith* (Rom. 3:27) is the synergy, the cooperation, of our faithfulness with God's. It alone is the means by which we attain the righteousness of God. God has been revealing His righteousness by this law little by little since the Creation, but now has revealed it fully in Christ. As both the natural law and the Mosaic Law bear witness to the law of faith, so those who become righteous by grace through faith fulfill in Christ both the natural and the Mosaic Law.

(5) *The law of sin* (Rom. 7:25; 8:2) is the power of the sinful passions in our mortal humanity. Passions—desires for such things as food, sex, praise, possessions—are natural; their sinful over-indulgence is not. Carnal (physical) passions are especially strong. They aid the unnatural domination of the body over the soul. Sometimes carnal passions overpower the will. The law of sin coupled with the Mosaic Law breeds intense warfare between sin and righteousness. Only God's grace can bring victory for righteousness.

(6) *The law of the Spirit* (Rom. 8:2) is also called "the law of Christ" (Gal. 6:2) and "the law of liberty" (James 1:25; 2:12). It is the power and life of the Holy Spirit active in those who by faith in Christ live out their baptism and chrismation to the fullest possible degree. This makes the righteousness of God gained by faith real in one's life. Coupled with the law of faith, the law of the Spirit defeats the law of sin and fulfills the natural and Mosaic Law. It orients one's innermost being toward God and restores the power of the spirit over the flesh, the soul over the body.

And may overcome when You
are judged."†

5 But if our unrighteousness demonstrates the righteousness of God,
what shall we say? *Is* God unjust
who inflicts wrath? [a](I speak as a
man.)
6 Certainly not! For then [a]how
will God judge the world?
7 For if the truth of God has increased through my lie to His glory,
why am I also still judged as a
sinner?
8 And *why* not *say*, [a]"Let us do
evil that good may come"?—as we
are slanderously reported and as
some affirm that we say. Their
[1]condemnation is just.

Conclusion: All Are Unfaithful

9 What then? Are we better *than*
they? Not at all. For we have previously charged both Jews and Greeks
that [a]they are all under sin.†
10 As it is written:

[a]*"There is none righteous, no, not one;*†
11 *There is none who understands;*
There is none who seeks after God.
12 *They have all turned aside;*
They have together become unprofitable;
There is none who does good, no, not one."
13 *"Their*[a] *throat is an open* [1]*tomb;*
With their tongues they have practiced deceit";
[b]*"The poison of asps is under their lips";*
14 *"Whose*[a] *mouth is full of cursing and bitterness."*
15 *"Their*[a] *feet are swift to shed blood;*
16 *Destruction and misery are in their ways;*
17 *And the way of peace they have not known."*
18 *"There*[a] *is no fear of God before their eyes."*

19 Now we know that whatever
[a]the law says, it says to those who
are under the law, that [b]every mouth
may be stopped, and all the world
may become [1]guilty before God.†
20 Therefore [a]by the deeds of the
law no flesh will be justified in His
sight, for by the law *is* the knowledge
of sin.†

Righteousness in Christ Fulfills the Law

21 But now [a]the righteousness of
God apart from the law is revealed,
[b]being witnessed by the Law [c]and
the Prophets,†
22 even the righteousness of God,
through faith in Jesus Christ, to all
[1]and on all who believe. For [a]there
is no difference;

5 [a]Rom. 6:19; 1 Cor. 9:8; 15:32; Gal. 3:15
6 [a][Gen. 18:25]
8 [a]Rom. 5:20 [1]Lit. *judgment*
9 [a]Rom. 3:19, 23; 11:32; Gal. 3:22
10 [a]Ps. 14:1–3; 53:1–3; Eccl. 7:20
13 [a]Ps. 5:9 [b]Ps. 140:3 [1]*grave*
14 [a]Ps. 10:7
15 [a]Prov. 1:16; Is. 59:7, 8
18 [a]Ps. 36:1
19 [a]John 10:34 [b]Job 5:16; Ps. 107:42 [1]*accountable*
20 [a]Ps. 143:2; [Acts 13:39; Gal. 2:16]
21 [a]Acts 15:11 [b]John 5:46 [c]1 Pet. 1:10
22 [a]Rom. 10:12; [Gal. 3:28; Col. 3:11] [1]NU omits *and on all*

3:4 While man changes and may be unfaithful, God does not change and He remains faithful.

3:9 Are Gentiles, with only the law of nature, **better** off than Jews who also must follow the Law of Moses? No. All humanity is **under sin.** All "fall short of the glory of God" (v. 23).

3:10–18 This OT quote speaks to the questions Paul asks in vv. 1–9.

3:19 As Gentiles fail to keep the natural law, so Jews fail to keep **the law** of Moses. All are sinners before God.

3:20 Salvation by obedience to law would require perfect obedience. If we offend in a single point, we become guilty of the whole (Lev. 18:5; James 2:10). Therefore, by law-keeping alone one cannot be **justified.** How the Law of Moses arouses knowledge of sin is explained in 7:7–11.

3:21, 22 The law may be kept by (1) obedience (Lev. 18:5) and (2) faith (Deut. 30:14). Becoming righteous by obedience without faith—keeping God's law, natural or Mosaic, as a legalistic instrument—fails. Becoming righteous is possible through faith that works, **apart from the law** (v. 21). Faith has always been accessible. But only now, in Christ, is it **revealed** (v. 21) fully, **through faith in Jesus Christ** (v. 22), which we receive as a gift (Eph. 2:8).

23 for [a]all have sinned and fall
short of the glory of God,†
24 being justified [1]freely [a]by His
grace [b]through the redemption that
is in Christ Jesus,†
25 whom God set forth [a]*as* a
[1]propitiation [b]by His blood, through
faith, to demonstrate His righteousness, because in His forbearance God
had passed over [c]the sins that were
previously committed,†
26 to demonstrate at the present
time His righteousness, that He
might be just and the justifier of the
one who has faith in Jesus.†
27 [a]Where *is* boasting then? It is excluded. By what law? Of works? No,
but by the law of faith.†
28 Therefore we conclude [a]that a
man is [1]justified by faith apart from
the deeds of the law.
29 Or *is He* the God of the Jews
only? *Is He* not also the God of the
Gentiles? Yes, of the Gentiles also,
30 since [a]*there is* one God who will
justify the circumcised by faith and
the uncircumcised through faith.
31 Do we then make void the law
through faith? Certainly not! On the
contrary, we establish the law.

23 [a]Gal. 3:22 **24** [a][Eph. 2:8] [b][Heb. 9:12, 15] [1]*without any cost* **25** [a]Lev. 16:15 [b]Col. 1:20 [c]Acts 14:16; 17:30 [1]*mercy seat* **27** [a][1 Cor. 1:29] **28** [a]Gal. 2:16 [1]*declared righteous* **30** [a][Gal. 3:8, 20]

Abraham, Model of Faith

4 What then shall we say that
[a]Abraham our [b]father[1] has
found according to the flesh?†

CHAPTER 4

1 [a]Is. 51:2 [b]James 2:21

[1]Or *(fore)father according to the flesh has found?*

3:23 The ultimate purpose of man's existence is to attain **the glory of God.** Even if we should keep the law, we would still **fall short** of God's *glory,* for we would still die and need salvation. The way to God is both perfect righteousness and eternal life. But how can we attain that? Jesus Christ alone lived in complete righteousness, He alone was resurrected to eternal life. Therefore, He alone is our way to God (John 14:6); He is the *glory* of God.

3:24 Being justified requires **redemption:** a sacrifice capable of (1) setting us free from sin and death and (2) uniting us with righteousness and life. In the OT, this sacrifice was imperfectly pictured by blood sacrifices, the killing of physically perfect animals (Heb. 9). In the NT, Christ, the once-for-all Sacrifice, fulfills both requirements. Though we are not worthy of God's **grace** of justification, He **freely** gives it to us in Christ.

3:25 Propitiation refers to the mercy seat in the tabernacle where God was thought to have His throne (Ex. 25:17–22). Once a year, on the Day of Atonement, the blood of the sacrifice was sprinkled on the mercy seat, a picture of forgiveness of sins and hope for eternal life in God's presence. Heaven holds the true mercy seat (Heb. 9:23–26; 10:19–22) and Christ's atoning blood is sprinkled on it. But **His blood** is effective because Christ is righteous and immortal, conquering death. **Passed over** means freely forgiven.

3:26 Christ is faithful in His "propitiation" (v. 25), through which God's **righteousness** may become ours. How can we benefit from this? By **faith in Jesus.** Justification by faith is not merely the equivalent of a one-time "not guilty" verdict delivered by a court of law. Further, righteousness is not credited, as money to a bank account. Why? God's righteousness is Christ Himself (1 Cor. 1:30). To have His righteousness is to have Christ living within us, to be in union with Him, a relationship that is dynamic and substantial. It is personal: a relationship between Shepherd and sheep, Master and friend, Father and child—not judge and defendant.

3:27–31 What, then, does the **law** teach us? (1) Attaining righteousness through **works,** human effort alone, is impossible (v. 27). (2) Righteousness is attained only on the basis of **faith,** which is given to man as a gift (vv. 27, 28). (3) God is impartial; Jews and Gentiles are justified on the same basis, faith in Christ (vv. 29, 30). **By faith** and **through faith** (v. 30) are synonymous. (4) Justification by faith in Christ fulfills the law, for Christ's faithfulness in doing His works satisfies the law. Those who have true faith in Christ are made truly righteous (v. 31).

4:1–5 Even **Abraham** became righteous in the sight of God not through works—human actions designed to attain righteousness—but through faith. If this holds true of the Jews' founding father, it is true for all Jews. When the Son of God came to Abraham in a vision (Gen. 15:1) and Abraham called Him "Lord GOD" (Gen. 15:2), the Son proclaimed to Abraham His coming in the flesh: "So shall your descendants be" (Gen. 15:5; "descendants" is lit. "seed," which is singular, not plural, referring to Christ; see Gal. 3:16). Because Abraham responded in **faith** (v. 5) he was **accounted** righteous (v. 3; Gen. 15:6), or justified (v. 5). Such a relationship transforms a person from being **ungodly** to being made righteous and godly, as was Abraham (v. 5).

2 For if Abraham was [a]justified by
works, he has *something* to boast
about, but not before God.
3 For what does the Scripture say?
[a]*"Abraham believed God, and it was*
[1]*accounted to him for righ-*
teousness."
4 Now [a]to him who works, the
wages are not counted [1]as grace but
[1]as debt.
5 But to him who [a]does not work
but believes on Him who justifies
[b]the ungodly, his faith is accounted
for righteousness,
6 just as David also [a]describes the
blessedness of the man to whom
God imputes righteousness apart
from works:†

7 *"Blessed[a] are those whose lawless*
deeds are forgiven,
And whose sins are covered;
8 *Blessed is the man to whom the*
LORD shall not impute sin."

9 *Does* this blessedness then *come*
upon the circumcised *only,* or upon
the uncircumcised also? For we say
that faith was accounted to Abraham
for righteousness.

2 [a]Rom. 3:20, 27
3 [a]Gen. 15:6; Rom. 4:9, 22; Gal. 3:6; James 2:23 [1]*imputed, credited, reckoned, counted*
4 [a]Rom. 11:6 [1]*according to*
5 [a][Gal. 2:16; Eph. 2:8, 9] [b]Josh. 24:2
6 [a]Ps. 32:1, 2
7 [a]Ps. 32:1, 2

11 [a]Gen. 17:10 [b]Luke 19:9; Rom. 4:16
12 [a]Rom. 4:18–22
13 [a]Gen. 17:4–6; 22:17
14 [a]Gal. 3:18

10 How then was it accounted?
While he was circumcised, or uncircumcised? Not while circumcised,
but while uncircumcised.
11 And [a]he received the sign of circumcision, a seal of the righteousness of the faith which *he had while*
still uncircumcised, that [b]he might be
the father of all those who believe,
though they are uncircumcised, that
righteousness might be imputed to
them also,†
12 and the father of circumcision
to those who not only *are* of the circumcision, but who also walk in the
steps of the faith which our father
[a]Abraham *had while still* uncircumcised.

Abraham's Children: Faithful Believers

13 For the promise that he would
be the [a]heir of the world *was* not to
Abraham or to his seed through the
law, but through the righteousness
of faith.†
14 For [a]if those who are of the law

4:6–8 Faith not only predated the Mosaic Law (vv. 1–5), it was active during the time of the law. For **David** (v. 6) made the same discovery that Abraham had, that being **forgiven** (v. 7) of sins comes from God by repentance and faith (Ps. 32:5, 10), and the resulting **righteousness** (v. 6) is as real as is the forgiveness of sins (Ps. 32:2, 11).

4:11, 12 Abraham was living by faith when he was 75 but was not circumcised until he was 99 (Gen. 12:4; 17:24). He was the father of Gentiles who live by faith before he became the father of faithful Jews. Circumcision was **sign** and **seal** (v. 11) for Israel, a lesser reality—emphasizing the external and physical—pointing to a greater reality, the righteousness of faith. The Jews mistook the lesser reality for the greater. But outward circumcision points to inward circumcision, which consists in putting off the sins of the flesh (Col. 2:11–13) and being kept by the Spirit in the heart (2:29).

Imputed (v. 11) means "reckoned" or "rendered." This is not merely juridical or external, for true **righteousness** transcends the law, as shown with both Abraham and David. Rather, by **faith** we actively participate in God's grace given to us, His *righteousness.* By continuing in it we are gradually transformed internally *and* externally into His likeness. Those who relegate God's righteousness to something external and "spiritual" by saying righteousness is not really ours, but only "imputed" to us, miss the truth. They externalize God's righteousness as much as did many Jews. Faith and righteousness lead to the greater reality of internal circumcision, the life of faith, of the Spirit in us, the **walk in the steps of the faith** (v. 12).

4:13–18 Righteousness is not through physical descent. For if one has to become a Jew to inherit **the world** (God's Kingdom, v. 13), Abraham's salvation, based on his **faith** and God's **promise,** is **made void** (v. 14). **The law** which requires physical descent **brings about wrath** (v. 15); only grace has the power to satisfy the law so there is no **transgression.** The righteous, then, are those of faith, not those **of the law** (v. 14), that is, merely physical descendants of Abraham. Abraham's true offspring are spiritual—he is the father of all who believe, Jew and Gentile (vv. 16, 17). And the righteous "seed" or descendant (not **descendants,** v. 18; see Gal. 3:16) of Abraham is Jesus Christ the Messiah.

are heirs, faith is made void and the promise made of no effect,

15 because [a]the law brings about wrath; for where there is no law *there is* no transgression.

16 Therefore *it is* of faith that *it might be* [a]according to grace, [b]so that the promise might be [1]sure to all the seed, not only to those who are of the law, but also to those who are of the faith of Abraham, [c]who is the father of us all

17 (as it is written, [a]*"I have made you a father of many nations"*) in the presence of Him whom he believed—God, [b]who gives life to the dead and calls those [c]things which do not exist as though they did;

18 who, contrary to hope, in hope believed, so that he became the father of many nations, according to what was spoken, [a]*"So shall your descendants be."*

19 And not being weak in faith, [a]he did not consider his own body, already dead (since he was about a hundred years old), [b]and the deadness of Sarah's womb.

20 He did not waver at the promise of God through unbelief, but was strengthened in faith, giving glory to God,†

21 and being fully convinced that what He had promised [a]He was also able to perform.

22 And therefore [a]*"it was accounted to him for righteousness."*

23 Now [a]it was not written for his sake alone that it was imputed to him,

24 but also for us. It shall be imputed to us who believe [a]in Him who raised up Jesus our Lord from the dead,

25 [a]who was delivered up because of our offenses, and [b]was raised because of our justification.†

15 [a]Rom. 3:20
16 [a][Rom. 3:24] [b][Gal. 3:22] [c]Is. 51:2 [1]*certain*
17 [a]Gen. 17:5 [b][Rom. 8:11] [c]Rom. 9:26
18 [a]Gen. 15:5
19 [a]Gen. 17:17 [b]Heb. 11:11
21 [a][Heb. 11:19]
22 [a]Gen. 15:6
23 [a]Rom. 15:4
24 [a]Acts 2:24
25 [a]Is. 53:4, 5 [b][1 Cor. 15:17]

CHAPTER 5

1 [a]Is. 32:17 [b][Eph. 2:14] [1]Some ancient mss. *let us have*
2 [a][Eph. 2:18; 3:12] [b]1 Cor. 15:1 [c]Heb. 3:6
3 [a]Matt. 5:11, 12 [b]James 1:3 [1]*endurance*
4 [a][James 1:12] [1]*approved character*
5 [a]Phil. 1:20 [b]2 Cor. 1:22
6 [a][Rom. 4:25; 5:8; 8:32] [1]*at the right time*
8 [a][John 3:16; 15:13]

Righteousness as a Living Reality

5 Therefore, [a]having been justified by faith, [1]we have [b]peace with God through our Lord Jesus Christ,†

2 [a]through whom also we have access by faith into this grace [b]in which we stand, and [c]rejoice in hope of the glory of God.

3 And not only *that*, but [a]we also glory in tribulations, [b]knowing that tribulation produces [1]perseverance;

4 [a]and perseverance, [1]character; and character, hope.

5 [a]Now hope does not disappoint, [b]because the love of God has been poured out in our hearts by the Holy Spirit who was given to us.

6 For when we were still without strength, [1]in due time [a]Christ died for the ungodly.†

7 For scarcely for a righteous man will one die; yet perhaps for a good man someone would even dare to die.

8 But [a]God demonstrates His own love toward us, in that while we were still sinners, Christ died for us.

4:20 Our model for being an heir of the Kingdom of God is Abraham. He was strong **in faith.** He believed in creation and resurrection (v. 17), and that God could cause Sarah to conceive (v. 19) and give him a son of promise and of faith (vv. 20, 21). Further, he gave **glory to God** (v. 20).

4:25 Jesus died for the forgiveness of **our offenses.** If He had been a sinner, the law would have condemned Him as it did everyone else. But He is perfect love, and love is self-sacrifice on behalf of the beloved. The purpose of His death and Resurrection was **our justification,** to bring us into a living relationship with God.

5:1 **Faith** in Christ makes us **justified**—in a right and faithful relationship with God—and therefore at **peace with God.** The Greek word *pistis* can be translated both "faith" and "faithfulness." Faith is the conviction that something is true; faithfulness is loyalty and obedience to God. Faith, therefore, is far more than possessing mental belief. Since neither faith nor righteousness originates in us but in our all-merciful God, true faith transforms our lives, making us Godlike, bearing the fruit of the Spirit.

5:6 **Christ died for the ungodly,** those who lack the capacity to become righteous due to alienation from their Creator. Those who recognize their failure, their ungodliness, can appropriate God's love.

JUSTIFICATION BY FAITH

For most of Church history, salvation was seen as comprehending all of life: Christians believed in Christ, were baptized, and were nurtured in their salvation in the Church. Key doctrines of the faith centered around the Holy Trinity, the Incarnation of the Son of God, and the atonement.

In Western Europe during the sixteenth century, however, and even before, justifiable concern arose among the Reformers over a prevailing understanding that salvation depended on human works of merit, and not upon the grace and mercy of God. Many involved with the Reformation experienced a rediscovery of Romans 5. Their slogan of salvation became *sola fides* (Lat.): justification was by *faith alone*.

This Reformation debate in the West was late-breaking news for the Orthodox East: why this new polarization of faith and works? It had been settled since the apostolic era that salvation was granted by the mercy of God to righteous men and women. Those baptized into Christ were called to believe in Him and do good works. A discussion of faith *versus* works was unprecedented in Orthodox thought.

The Orthodox understanding of justification differs from the Protestant in several ways.

(1) *Justification and the New Covenant*. When Orthodox Christians approach the doctrine of salvation, the discussion centers around the New Covenant. Justification (being or becoming righteous) by faith in God is part of being brought into a covenant relationship with Him. Whereas Israel was under the Old Covenant, wherein salvation came through faith as revealed in the law, the Church is under the New Covenant. Salvation comes through faith in Christ who fulfills the law, and we receive the gift of the Holy Spirit who dwells in us, leading us to the knowledge of God the Father. Whereas some Christians focus on justification as a legal acquittal before God, Orthodox believers see justification by faith as a covenant relationship with Him, centered in union with Christ (Rom. 6:1–6).

(2) *Justification and God's mercy*. Orthodoxy emphasizes it is first God's mercy—not our faith—which saves us. "Therefore, having been justified by faith, we have peace with God through our Lord Jesus Christ, through whom also we have access by faith into this grace in which we stand, and rejoice in hope of the glory of God" (Rom. 5:1, 2). It is God who initiates or makes the New Covenant with us.

(3) *Justification by faith is dynamic, not static*. For Orthodox Christians, faith is living, dynamic, continuous—never static or merely point-in-time. Faith is not something a Christian exercises only at one critical moment, expecting it to cover all the rest of his life. True faith is not just a decision, it's a way of life.

This is why the modern evangelical Protestant question, "Are you saved?" gives pause to an Orthodox believer. As the subject of salvation is addressed in Scripture, the Orthodox Christian would see it in at least three aspects: (a) I have been saved, being joined to Christ in baptism; (b) I am being saved, growing in Christ through the sacramental life of the Church; and (c) I will be saved, by the mercy of God at the Last Judgment.

A final difficulty for Orthodox Christians is the word *alone*. Justification by faith, though not the major New Testament doctrine for Orthodox as it is for Protestants, poses no problem. But justification by faith *alone* brings up an objection. It contradicts Scripture, which says: "You see then that a man is justified by works, and not by faith only" (James 2:24). We are "justified by faith apart from the deeds of the law" (Rom. 3:28), but nowhere does the Bible say we are justified by faith "alone." On the contrary, "faith by itself, if it does not have works, is dead" (James 2:17).

As Christians we are no longer under the demands of the Old Testament law (Rom. 3:20), for Christ has fulfilled the law (Gal. 2:21; 3:5, 24). By God's mercy, we are brought into a New Covenant relationship with Him. We who believe are granted entrance into His Kingdom by His grace. Through His mercy we are justified by faith and empowered by God for good works or deeds of righteousness which bring glory to Him.

9 Much more then, having now
been justified [a]by His blood, we shall
be saved [b]from wrath through
Him.†
10 For [a]if when we were enemies
[b]we were reconciled to God through
the death of His Son, much more,
having been reconciled, we shall be
saved [c]by His life.†
11 And not only *that,* but we also
[a]rejoice in God through our Lord
Jesus Christ, through whom we have
now received the reconciliation.

Reign of Sin, Reign of Grace

12 Therefore, just as [a]through one
man sin entered the world, and
[b]death through sin, and thus death
spread to all men, because all
sinned—†
13 (For until the law sin was in the
world, but [a]sin is not imputed when
there is no law.†
14 Nevertheless death reigned
from Adam to Moses, even over
those who had not sinned according
to the likeness of the transgression
of Adam, [a]who is a type of Him who
was to come.†
15 But the free gift *is* not like the
[1]offense. For if by the one man's offense many died, much more the
grace of God and the gift by the grace
of the one Man, Jesus Christ,
abounded [a]to many.†
16 And the gift *is* not like *that which
came* through the one who sinned.
For the judgment *which came* from
one *offense resulted* in condemnation,
but the free gift *which came* from
many [1]offenses *resulted* in justification.
17 For if by the one man's [1]offense
death reigned through the one,
much more those who receive abundance of grace and of the gift of righteousness will reign in life through
the One, Jesus Christ.)
18 Therefore, as through [1]one
man's offense *judgment* came to
all men, resulting in condemnation, even so through [a]one[2] Man's

9 [a]Eph. 2:13 [b]1 Thess. 1:10 **10** [a][Rom. 8:32] [b]2 Cor. 5:18 [c]John 14:19 **11** [a][Gal. 4:9] **12** [a][1 Cor. 15:21] [b]Gen. 2:17 **13** [a]1 John 3:4

14 [a][1 Cor. 15:21, 22] **15** [a][Is. 53:11] [1]*trespass* or *false step* **16** [1]*trespasses* **17** [1]*trespass* **18** [a][1 Cor. 15:21, 45] [1]Or *one trespass* [2]Or *one righteous act*

5:9 It is not the Son alone who saves us from **wrath** that belongs to the Father alone. Rather, both wrath and salvation belong to all three Persons: Father, Son and Holy Spirit.

5:10 Those who appropriate Christ's love are **reconciled** to God. "To reconcile" means to change or reestablish, as in a broken friendship—to return to peace and communion. God has not ceased to be our Friend, for He is unchangeable. Thus, His wrath is His unchangeable love for us spurned. We are the ones who have changed, and need changing. Christ's death and Resurrection, then, bring about a change in repentant sinners, who are changed from being **enemies** of God to being His friends.

5:12 Which comes first, **death** or **sin?** For Adam, sin came first (the original sin) and then death. For us, it is the opposite: death, mortality, we inherit from Adam, and sin follows after.

5:13 **Until the law** of Moses came, the law of **sin** was working **in the world:** from Adam to Moses, people suffered from mortality and committed transgressions, and were accountable to God for their sins under natural law (2:14, 15). But without the written Law the seriousness of their sin often remained clouded. God gave the Mosaic Law to expose the law of sin and death in the world.

5:14 After **Adam,** our sin could not be said to be in the **likeness** of his sin, because only Adam's sin brought mortality to our race. Yet the law of sin and death **reigned** because of people's refusal to keep the law. However, among both Gentiles and Jews, some kept the law (of nature or of Moses) on the basis of the law of faith. Adam is a **type,** a prefigurement, of Christ as the Head of humanity. Adam causes death and the law of sin; Christ brings life and the law of the Spirit, righteousness.

5:15–17 As immortality is not the opposite and equal of mortality but far outstrips it, so the **grace** of Christ far excels our inheritance from Adam. For by grace not only is Adam's offense covered and our bondage to death overthrown, but the sins of the whole world (the **many offenses** of v. 16) are covered as well. **Justification** (v. 16) through Christ far exceeds **condemnation** through Adam. As we all inherit Adam's mortality (**many died,** v. 15, all of us), we all shall be raised to immortality. But the saving **gift** of **Jesus Christ,** though it is **free** (v. 15), must be received through the life of faith. Thus, some shall be raised to life, others to condemnation.

righteous act *the free gift came* [b]to all
men, resulting in justification of
life.†
19 For as by one man's disobedience many were made sinners, so
also by [a]one Man's obedience many
will be made righteous.†
20 Moreover [a]the law entered that
the offense might abound. But where
sin abounded, grace [b]abounded
much more,†
21 so that as sin reigned in death,
even so grace might reign through
righteousness to eternal life through
Jesus Christ our Lord.†

Baptism: Dead to Sin, Alive in Christ

6 What shall we say then? [a]Shall
we continue in sin that grace
may abound?†
2 Certainly not! How shall we
who [a]died to sin live any longer in
it?†
3 Or do you not know that
[a]as many of us as were baptized into
Christ Jesus [b]were baptized into His
death?†
4 Therefore we were [a]buried with
Him through baptism into death,
that [b]just as Christ was raised from
the dead by [c]the glory of the Father,
[d]even so we also should walk in
newness of life.†
5 [a]For if we have been united together in the likeness of His death,
certainly we also shall be *in the likeness* of *His* resurrection,†
6 knowing this, that [a]our old man
was crucified with *Him*, that [b]the
body of sin might be [1]done away
with, that we should no longer be
slaves of sin.†

18 [b][John 12:32]
19 [a][Phil. 2:8]
20 [a]John 15:22
[b]1 Tim. 1:14

CHAPTER 6

1 [a]Rom. 3:8; 6:15
2 [a][Gal. 2:19]
3 [a][Gal. 3:27]
[b][1 Cor. 15:29]
4 [a]Col. 2:12
[b]1 Cor. 6:14
[c]John 2:11
[d][Gal. 6:15]
5 [a]Phil. 3:10
6 [a]Gal. 2:20; 5:24; 6:14
[b]Col. 2:11
[1]*rendered inoperative*

5:18 One Man's righteous act refers primarily to Christ's Passion, His voluntary death and Resurrection. But it also relates to His entire incarnate life, which reunites human nature with God. Christ's obedience in all things (see Matt. 3:15) brings us the gift of eternal life. **Justification,** or righteousness, and **life** are wedded together.

5:19 Paul contrasts Adam's **disobedience** with Christ's **obedience. Many were made sinners** refers to mortality and subjection to the law of sin (see vv. 12, 16, 18), not to an inherited guilt or an inevitability of sin. However, the first thing damaged in Adam's nature was his will, and in the death and corruption we inherit our will is also weakened.

In Christ are two wills, human and divine; His human will is obedient to His divine will. Through His obedience, His salvation brings healing to our will. Therefore, **many**—that is, those who believe in Christ—are **made righteous** and able by grace to participate willfully by faith in God's righteousness.

5:20 The law of Moses **entered** as a temporary measure on God's part to reveal sin and to lead us to faith in Christ (Gal. 3:23–25). But instead of decreasing, **sin abounded** even more—it got worse—not because of God's good Law but because of human weakness (8:3). Such increase in sin's power amplifies our need of God's grace in Jesus Christ.

5:21 Again, **sin** and **death,** and **righteousness** and **life,** are paired. Christ not only delivers us from the tyranny of human weakness, but also crowns us with **eternal life.**

6:1–14 Opponents of Paul twisted his summary of God's past dealings with humanity and applied it to individuals, accusing him of saying, "Sin increases grace, so let us increase sin!" (3:8, paraphrased). But this argument does not take into account the fact that a person must be allied with one side or the other, either with sin and death or with righteousness and life. If one is living in sin, he cannot be in union with God's grace. Even if grace is increasing, he is hurting himself, and for that he is responsible. However, in union with Christ we become dead to the law of sin and alive to God. And this is the "increase" in grace which honors God.

6:2 The argument implied in v. 1 is an absurdity. We **died to sin,** how can we possibly live **in it**? To be dead to sin does not mean our human nature dies; Christ did not die on the Cross in order to kill human nature. Nor do we die in the flesh on the Cross as Christ did. Rather, being dead to sin means that we do not obey it any more. We are to be unmovable towards it, as something dead would be.

6:3 Paul grounds freedom from sin in the Sacrament of Baptism: **Do you not know?** Ignorance of what happens when we are **baptized** is a great enemy. For because of ignorance many are miserably defeated in their battle against sin. What Christ accomplished on the Cross—an actual and real death to sin—baptism is to us: an actual and real death to sin, a liberation from it. Thus, in our union with Christ through baptism, in His death and Resur-

(continued on next page)

7 For [a]he who has died has been
[1]freed from sin.†
8 Now [a]if we died with Christ, we
believe that we shall also live with
Him,†
9 knowing that [a]Christ, having
been raised from the dead, dies no
more. Death no longer has dominion
over Him.†
10 For *the death* that He died,
[a]He died to sin once for all; but *the*
life that He lives, [b]He lives to God.†

7 [a]1 Pet. 4:1
[1]*cleared*
8 [a]2 Tim. 2:11
9 [a]Rev. 1:18
10 [a]Heb. 9:27
[b]Luke 20:38
11 [a][Rom. 6:2; 7:4, 6]
[b][Gal. 2:19]
[1]*consider*
12 [a]Ps. 19:13
13 [a]Col. 3:5
[b]1 Pet. 2:24; 4:2

11 Likewise you also, [1]reckon
yourselves to be [a]dead indeed to sin,
but [b]alive to God in Christ Jesus our
Lord.†
12 [a]Therefore do not let sin reign
in your mortal body, that you should
obey it in its lusts.†
13 And do not present your [a]mem-
bers *as* [1]instruments of unrighteousness to sin, but [b]present yourselves

[1]Or *weapons*

(continued from previous page)
rection, lies the power for victory over the law, the power, of sin. In this sense baptism is an exact likeness to Christ's death on the Cross. Baptism is reality! It is not something that somehow "stands for" reality. The Cross is the power of God for overcoming sin (1 Cor. 1:18), and baptism is our Cross! There we tap into the power of God to say no to sin's commands and temptations.

6:4 If Christ was buried for us, how are we **buried with Him? Through baptism.** For what Christ accomplished in the grave—an actual and real burial of sin—baptism is to us: an actual and real burial of sin. Our old, mortal nature is replaced by a renewed nature capable of living righteously.

6:5 **United together** refers to being planted and growing together, clearly implying the expectation of fruit. **In the likeness of His death** means baptism has a real unity with Christ's death. For the Holy Spirit unites the reality of being immersed in the water to the reality of Christ going to the Cross and the grave. Yet we are not "united together in His death," but in the *likeness* of His death. We did not die in our flesh with Christ on the Cross, nor does our human nature die. **We also shall be in the likeness of His resurrection** is literally translated "we shall be of the resurrection." The *likeness of His resurrection* is the new life received in baptism. But Paul is referring here to the future resurrection of the body. If we truly participate in baptism's *likeness* to Christ's *death*, then we are prepared for the *resurrection* of the body.

6:6 **Knowing this** is understanding baptism and its reality in the Christian life. **Old man** does not refer to human nature as such but to the power of sin in human nature; **the body** (the complete whole) **of sin** refers to the whole self, body and soul, under the law of sin and of death. And so it is *sin* that is **crucified with Him,** not some kind of "sinful nature." We and human nature are not destroyed, sin is. Not only are we dead to sin, but sin is dead to us. The law of sin is completely defeated, and we are no longer to be its servants.

6:7 Just as a physical body, once dead, has no more response to its environment, so we who die with Christ in baptism ought not to respond to the law of sin. In our union with Christ through Holy Baptism, we are dead to sin and alive to God! The tyranny of sinful passions no longer reigns in us. We must be careful to remain free **from sin** by remaining dead to it.

6:8 In our union with Christ through baptism we are also raised with Him to share His Resurrection life: both a life of faith ("walk in newness of life," v. 4) and bodily resurrection with Him in the eternal Kingdom. Faith (**we believe**) maintains union with Christ as a living and dynamic reality.

6:9 Christ **dies no more,** for by His death, death died (as did death's companion, sin; 1 Cor. 15:56) and He lives eternally.

6:10 Christ was subject neither to **death** nor to **sin,** yet He voluntarily died **to sin** for our sake. In Christ, through the power of God, we, too, can voluntarily "die" to sin in baptism. But Christ's death is **once,** and now **He lives to God.** As He will never die again, so there is never second baptism. We lay hold of our one baptism and continue in communion with God.

6:11 A shift in emphasis comes here, from what Christ has done for us (vv. 1–10) to what we do in response (vv. 11–14). **Reckon** is an action word, relating to faith: we lay hold of our union with Christ and thereby lay hold of every virtue.

6:12 **Do not let sin reign** implies that sin's power over us is not inevitable; it is something
(continued on page 353)

HOLY BAPTISM

What Is Baptism? Simply put, baptism is our death, burial, and resurrection in union with Jesus Christ. It is a rite of passage, given by Christ to the Church, as an entrance into the Kingdom of God and eternal life.

The Apostle Paul describes the promise of God in this "mystery," as most Orthodox call it, most succinctly when he writes, "Therefore we were buried with Him through baptism into death, that just as Christ was raised from the dead by the glory of the Father, even so we also should walk in newness of life" (Rom. 6:4). To baptize (Gr. *baptizo*) literally means to immerse, to put into. Historically, the Orthodox Church has baptized by triple immersion, "in the name of the Father, and of the Son, and of the Holy Spirit" (Matt. 28:19).

In the Old Testament, baptism was pictured by the passage of God's people with Moses through the Red Sea (1 Cor. 10:1, 2). John the Baptist, the last prophet of the Old Covenant, baptized in water unto repentance (Mark 1:4; Acts 19:4). John's baptism was received by Jesus, who thereby transformed the water and baptism itself. In the New Covenant, baptism is the means by which we enter the Kingdom of God (John 3:5), are joined to Christ (Rom. 6:3), and are granted the remission of our sins and the gift of the Holy Spirit (Acts 2:38).

What Results from Baptism? From the start, the Church has understood baptism as:

(1) *A first and second dying*. Our first dying with Christ in baptism was our death with Him on the Cross. In the fourth century, Cyril of Jerusalem instructed his new converts: "You were led by the hand to the holy pool of divine baptism . . . and each of you was asked if he believed in the Name of the Father, and of the Son, and of the Holy Ghost. And you made that saving confession, you descended into the water and came up again three times. In the very same moment you died and were born."

The second death of baptism is continual—dying to sin daily as we walk in newness of life. St. Paul writes to the Colossians concerning baptism (Col. 2:12) and concludes by saying, "Therefore put to death your members which are upon the earth: fornication, uncleanness, passion, evil desire, and covetousness, which is idolatry" (Col. 3:5).

(2) *The resurrection of righteousness*. This is our life in Christ, our new birth and entrance into God's Kingdom (John 3:3), our "newness of life" (Rom. 6:4). It is our being joined to Christ in His glorified humanity and indwelt by God Himself (John 14:23). Our relationship with God is not something static, a legal fiction given to us by a Divine Judge. Rather, this is a dynamic and real life in Christ, holding the promise of everlasting life. Our resurrection to new life now forms a prelude to the resurrection of our body at Christ's Second Coming.

(3) *An intimate and continual communion with God*. We are raised to new life for a purpose: union and communion with God. In this sense baptism is the beginning of eternal life. For this reason, Peter writes that baptism now saves us (1 Pet. 3:21)—it is not the mere removal of dirt from our bodies, but it provides us with "a good conscience toward God."

Because of these promises, the priest prays for the newly baptized, thanking God "who has given us, unworthy though we be, blessed purification through holy water, and divine sanctification through life-giving chrismation, and who now also has been pleased to bring new life to Your servant newly illuminated by water and the Spirit, and granted remission of sins—voluntary and involuntary."

to God as being alive from the dead,
and your members *as* [1]instruments
of righteousness to God.†
14 For [a]sin shall not have dominion over you, for you are not under
law but under grace.

Baptism: Freedom from Sin, Under Grace

15 What then? Shall we sin [a]be-
cause we are not under law but under grace? Certainly not!†
16 Do you not know that [a]to whom
you present yourselves slaves to
obey, you are that one's slaves
whom you obey, whether of sin *leading* to death, or of obedience *leading*
to righteousness?†
17 But God be thanked that *though*
you were slaves of sin, yet you
obeyed from the heart [a]that form of
doctrine to which you were
[1]delivered.†
18 And [a]having been set free from
sin, you became slaves of righteousness.†
19 I speak in human *terms* because
of the weakness of your flesh. For
just as you presented your members
as slaves of uncleanness, and of lawlessness *leading* to *more* lawlessness,
so now present your members *as*
slaves *of* righteousness [1]for holiness.†
20 For when you were [a]slaves of
sin, you were free in regard to
righteousness.†
21 [a]What fruit did you have then
in the things of which you are now

13 [1]Or *weapons*
14 [a][Gal. 5:18]
15 [a]1 Cor. 9:21
16 [a]2 Pet. 2:19
17 [a]2 Tim. 1:13 [1]*entrusted*
18 [a]John 8:32
19 [1]*unto sanctification*
20 [a]John 8:34
21 [a]Rom. 7:5

(continued from page 351)
we allow by our free will. Man's will was the first aspect of human nature damaged in the Fall and, therefore, is the first thing Christ heals. His healing enables us to make right choices, especially against sin. For the Christian, sin is no longer a power which reigns and puts one in bondage. Though our **mortal body** demands pleasures, we can direct it rather than allowing it to direct us. **Lusts,** the sinful passions, we can resist, for sin has no power but what we give it. Only our own listlessness, dejection, indifference or laziness can defeat us. In Christ, we have no excuses. We can "help it," we can avoid sin. For in Christ, we are restored to what God intended human nature to be.

6:13 Instruments (lit. "weapons of war") are in this case various aspects of human nature, especially the body. Though God created our members good, we may use them to serve either of two rulers, **sin** or **God.** For those who actively live in their baptism, proper loyalty is clear, for we are **alive from the dead.** Though difficult warfare faces us, our weapons bear the **righteousness** of **God.**

6:15 Having completed his references to baptism, Paul initiates another discussion: Christians are no longer to sin as those who sinned during the period of the law. Those **under law** dealt with a swarm of passions, yet did not have the power of baptism, the power of the Cross, the fullness of the Spirit. The law exhorted mankind to battle, promising crowns after warfare: **grace** crowns us first, then leads us to the arena.

6:16 Though we choose freely, we are never without a master, either Satan or God, law or grace. If one should defect from grace and return to his former master, the law of **sin,** he will find himself led to **death,** the "second death" (Rev. 20:14). But those "under grace" (vv. 14, 15), who lovingly and willingly take on God as master, practice **obedience** and grow in God's free gift of **righteousness.** They cannot keep on sinning (John 14:15).

6:17 Baptism frees us from being **slaves of sin** and makes us servants of God *if* we continue with a willing spirit and submissiveness to God. For (1) the **form of doctrine,** the basic teaching of the Church, calls us to love God and to obey **from the heart.** But (2) without the assistance of God, to whom we **were delivered,** we could neither understand doctrine nor do virtuous deeds.

6:18 Set free from sin is described in vv. 1–14; **slaves of righteousness,** in 6:15—7:6. But this "slavery" is our true home and our true dignity, voluntarily accepted and lived. Christians are voluntary slaves, better off by far than "free men" in the world.

6:19 Human terms are the images of slavery by which Paul expresses the fallen human condition. We must serve someone, and if we served sin and the devil so well, certainly we can serve God and **righteousness** even better.

6:20 Freedom is a great dignity, but by itself it is neutral. For if we are **free** to **sin,** we become sin's **slaves** and alienated from **righteousness,** which is no freedom at all. True freedom is joined to virtue.

ashamed? For [b]the end of those
things *is* death.†
22 But now [a]having been set free
from sin, and having become slaves
of God, you have your fruit [1]to holiness, and the end, everlasting life.†
23 For [a]the wages of sin *is* death,
but [b]the [1]gift of God *is* eternal life
in Christ Jesus our Lord.†

Baptism: Freedom from Law, Union with Christ

7 Or do you not know, brethren
(for I speak to those who know
the law), that the law [1]has dominion
over a man as long as he lives?†
2 For [a]the woman who has a husband is bound by the law to *her* husband as long as he lives. But if the
husband dies, she is released from
the law of *her* husband.
3 So then [a]if, while *her* husband
lives, she marries another man, she
will be called an adulteress; but if her
husband dies, she is free from that
law, so that she is no adulteress,
though she has married another
man.
4 Therefore, my brethren, you
also have become [a]dead to the law
through the body of Christ, that you
may be married to another—to Him
who was raised from the dead, that
we should [b]bear fruit to God.
5 For when we were in the flesh,
the sinful passions which were
aroused by the law [a]were at work
in our members [b]to bear fruit to
death.†
6 But now we have been delivered
from the law, having died to what
we were held by, so that we should
serve [a]in the newness of the Spirit
and not *in* the oldness of the letter.

Sin Uses What Is Holy to Produce Death

7 What shall we say then? *Is* the
law sin? Certainly not! On the contrary, [a]I would not have known sin
except through the law. For I would
not have known covetousness unless
the law had said, [b]*"You shall not
covet."*†
8 But [a]sin, taking opportunity by

21 [b]Rom. 1:32
22 [a]Rom. 6:18; 8:2
[1]*unto sanctification*
23 [a]Gen. 2:17
[b]1 Pet. 1:4
[1]*free gift*

CHAPTER 7

1 [1]*rules*
2 [a]1 Cor. 7:39
3 [a][Matt. 5:32]
4 [a]Gal. 2:19; 5:18
[b]Gal. 5:22
5 [a]Rom. 6:13
[b]James 1:15
6 [a]Rom. 2:29
7 [a]Rom. 3:20
[b]Ex. 20:17; Deut. 5:21; Acts 20:33
8 [a]Rom. 4:15

6:21 While one is freely enslaved to sin, he is not even aware of it; he does not know enough to be **ashamed.** But **now**—having received the gospel—one knows all actions have serious consequences: sin bears the fruit of shame and ends in the second **death** (see v. 23).

6:22 Slavery to God, initiated in baptism, is true freedom. The **fruit** of baptism is **holiness,** or sanctification, and it ends in **everlasting life.** Thus salvation is a process of transformation from sinner to saint. We are saved through baptism, and we are being saved, that is, being transformed by the uncreated grace of God to be like Him, in anticipation of eternal life.

6:23 Sin's reward is **death,** but God's **gift** in Christ is **eternal life.** Eternal *death* we earn by our own actions: it is the horrible **wages** of sin. We cannot earn *eternal life*. We do, however, participate in it, and must not become listless in our Christian life.

7:1–4 Paul has affirmed that justification, a right relationship to God, comes by faith in Christ and not by adherence to works of the Mosaic Law (3:21, 22, 28; 4:10–16). This passage paradoxically illustrates freedom from the law by examples taken from the law. Under the Law of Moses, only death releases from marriage and allows the living spouse to remarry (v. 2). Divorce cannot give that freedom (v. 3).

7:5, 6 Paul restates freedom from the law in theological terms, contrasting two situations. (1) **Flesh** here refers to the whole unredeemed man under the power of sin and death. In this condition **sinful passions** are constantly energized when man faces the demands of the law (see vv. 7–10). **Aroused by** (v. 5) is properly translated "aroused through." The law merely brings to light our willful bondage to sin, with accusations and powerless words. (2) But Christians live in a new mode of existence by the power of the Holy Spirit. We have been liberated by Christ from the mode of the *flesh,* freed from the law, and, in our marriage to Christ, we are expected to bear godly fruit (v. 4). For the Holy Spirit energizes us with the power of God (see Matt. 5:20; Luke 12:48). **Letter** (v. 6) refers to the Mosaic Law.

7:7–12 The law of Moses is not our problem. For it is from God (v. 12, see v. 14) and its ultimate aim is to bring us to grace. But we, imperfect and without power, cannot keep it. Therefore, it can only reveal our problems (vv. 7, 13) and intensify our failure and rebellion (vv. 8, 9). Unredeemed human nature always wants to do what is forbidden.

the commandment, produced in me
all *manner of evil* desire. For [b]apart
from the law sin *was* dead.
9 I was alive once without the
law, but when the commandment
came, sin revived and I died.
10 And the commandment, [a]which
was to *bring* life, I found to *bring*
death.
11 For sin, taking occasion by the
commandment, deceived me, and by
it killed *me*.
12 Therefore [a]the law *is* holy, and
the commandment holy and just and
good.

The Flesh Uses What Is Good to Produce Sin

13 Has then what is good become
death to me? Certainly not! But sin,
that it might appear sin, was produc-
ing death in me through what is
good, so that sin through the commandment might become exceedingly sinful.†
14 For we know that the law is
spiritual, but I am carnal, [a]sold under sin.
15 For what I am doing, I do not
understand. [a]For what I will to do,
that I do not practice; but what I
hate, that I do.
16 If, then, I do what I will not to
do, I agree with the law that *it is*
good.
17 But now, *it is* no longer I who
do it, but sin that dwells in me.
18 For I know that [a]in me (that is,
in my flesh) nothing good dwells; for
to will is present with me, but *how*
to perform what is good I do not
find.†
19 For the good that I will *to do*, I
do not do; but the evil I will not *to*
do, that I practice.
20 Now if I do what I will not *to*
do, it is no longer I who do it, but
sin that dwells in me.
21 I find then a law, that evil is
present with me, the one who wills
to do good.
22 For I [a]delight in the law of God
according to [b]the inward man.
23 But [a]I see another law in [b]my
members, warring against the law of
my mind, and bringing me into captivity to the law of sin which is in
my members.
24 O wretched man that I am! Who
will deliver me [a]from this body of
death?†
25 [a]I thank God—through Jesus
Christ our Lord! So then, with the
mind I myself serve the law of
God, but with the flesh the law of
sin.†

The Spirit Defeats Sin and the Flesh

8 *There is* therefore now no condemnation to those who are in
Christ Jesus, [a]who[1] do not walk according to the flesh, but according
to the Spirit.†
2 For [a]the law of [b]the Spirit of
life in Christ Jesus has made me
free from [c]the law of sin and
death.†
3 For [a]what the law could not do
in that it was weak through the flesh,

8 [b]1 Cor. 15:56
10 [a]Lev. 18:5
12 [a]Ps. 19:8
14 [a]2 Kin. 17:17
15 [a][Gal. 5:17]
18 [a][Gen. 6:5; 8:21]
22 [a]Ps. 1:2 [b][2 Cor. 4:16]
23 [a][Gal. 5:17] [b]Rom. 6:13, 19
24 [a][1 Cor. 15:51, 52]
25 [a]1 Cor. 15:57

CHAPTER 8

1 [a]Gal. 5:16 [1]NU omits the rest of v. 1.
2 [a]Rom. 6:18, 22 [b][1 Cor. 15:45] [c]Rom. 7:24, 25
3 [a]Acts 13:39

7:13–17 The problem then, is not the law but **sin,** as manifested in our carnality (v. 14), our bondage to sinful passions. These passions are only strengthened when we attempt to obey the letter of the law. Without Christ's healing and power, they only get worse, resulting in the second death (v. 13; see v. 11).

7:18–23 Paul gives another dramatic description of the tragedy of fallen man, this time in the first person.

7:24 This question is answered in 8:1–4.

7:25 This conclusion of vv. 7–25 describes neither Paul's own spiritual journey, nor fallen man, as hopeless. Rather, it vindicates the law and lays the blame on sin.

8:1 No condemnation is based on (1) being **in Christ Jesus** by faith and baptism, and (2) walking in the power of **the Spirit.**

8:2 Two laws are contrasted: **the law of sin and death** (humanity united with mortal Adam and under the power of sin and death) and **the law of the Spirit** (the new humanity united with Christ and energized by the Spirit).

[b]God *did* by sending His own Son
in the likeness of sinful flesh, on account of sin: He condemned sin in
the flesh,†
4 that the righteous requirement of the law might be fulfilled
in us who [a]do not walk according
to the flesh but according to the
Spirit.
5 For [a]those who live according
to the flesh set their minds on the
things of the flesh, but those *who live*
according to the Spirit, [b]the things
of the Spirit.†
6 For [a]to be [1]carnally minded *is*
death, but to be spiritually minded
is life and peace.
7 Because [a]the [1]carnal mind *is* enmity against God; for it is not subject
to the law of God, [b]nor indeed can
be.
8 So then, those who are in the
flesh cannot please God.

3 [b][2 Cor. 5:21]
4 [a]Gal. 5:16, 25
5 [a]John 3:6 [b][Gal. 5:22–25]
6 [a]Gal. 6:8 [1]*fleshly*
7 [a]James 4:4 [b]1 Cor. 2:14 [1]*fleshly*

11 [a]Acts 2:24 [b]1 Cor. 6:14 [1]Or *because of*
12 [a][Rom. 6:7, 14]
13 [a]Gal. 6:8 [b]Eph. 4:22

9 But you are not in the flesh but
in the Spirit, if indeed the Spirit of
God dwells in you. Now if anyone
does not have the Spirit of Christ,
he is not His.†
10 And if Christ *is* in you, the
body *is* dead because of sin, but the
Spirit *is* life because of righteousness.†
11 But if the Spirit of [a]Him who
raised Jesus from the dead dwells in
you, [b]He who raised Christ from the
dead will also give life to your mortal
bodies [1]through His Spirit who
dwells in you.
12 [a]Therefore, brethren, we are
debtors—not to the flesh, to live according to the flesh.
13 For [a]if you live according to the
flesh you will die; but if by
the Spirit you [b]put to death
the deeds of the body, you will
live.†

8:3, 4 The **law** of Moses failed because of **the flesh,** the weakness of human nature, which is not inherently **sinful** but is taken captive by sin (7:14–25). The law and human nature are **fulfilled** by the Incarnation. For the Son took on flesh, human nature as beset with troubles. Aided by the power of the **Spirit** Christ did not sin, for He was only in the **likeness** of our sinfulness. Moreover, it was by the flesh and in the Spirit that Christ **condemned sin,** destroying its power for believers. In Him the flesh, human nature, by the divine power of the Spirit, is the victor, crowned with honor.

8:5–8 Two ways of human existence are expounded. The "mind" here is far more than intellectual capacity. It is the highest knowing faculty of the soul (Gr. *nous*), the spirit behind all we think and do. To repent means to have "a change of mind"—not a change of intelligence, but a change of heart. **To be carnally minded** (v. 6; lit. "to have the mind of the flesh") means to choose to have one's whole existence, soul and body, captivated by sin. This is a turning against God and His righteousness, an **enmity** (v. 7) with God rather than peace with Him. The *carnally minded* cannot be **subject** to (v. 7) or **please** (v. 8) God. "A bad tree [cannot] bear good fruit" (Matt. 7:18), but it can choose to become a good tree through repentance. **To be spiritually minded** (lit. "to have the mind of the Spirit") means to choose to be liberated by the Holy Spirit, so that one's whole nature becomes spiritual, body and soul. Christians are free to **set their minds** on the Holy Spirit, allowing Him to have His way (His **things**) and actively pursuing virtue and goodness.

When fire penetrates iron, the iron becomes fiery hot without ceasing to be iron. So our human nature, body and soul, in its union with Christ becomes like God without ceasing to be human; it is interpenetrated by the energy and grace of the Holy Spirit. We become spiritual. Self-indulgence and sinful pleasure are scorned, and all the pains and sufferings of the Christian life may be endured with joy.

8:9 The Spirit of Christ refers to the intimacy of the Holy Spirit's working with Christ. The Son sends the Holy Spirit into the world (John 16:7), but eternally the Spirit proceeds only from the Father (John 15:26).

8:10 Participation in Christ and the Spirit leads to fullness of **life.** Though **the body is dead**—that is mortal—**because of** sin's entry into the world, the Holy **Spirit** gives new *life,* the pledge of resurrection (v. 11).

8:13 The gift of new life is not magical, but requires the cooperation of the believer in obedience to God. For we are His children (v. 14), as He leads us by the power of **the Spirit.** Therefore, **the body** becomes the follower, not the leader. We personally choose the way of the Spirit and deliberately **put to death** sinful **deeds.**

The Spirit Conveys Divine Sonship

14 For [a]as many as are led by the
Spirit of God, these are sons of
God.†
15 For [a]you did not receive the
spirit of bondage again [b]to fear, but
you received the [c]Spirit of adoption
by whom we cry out, [d]"Abba,[1]
Father."†
16 [a]The Spirit Himself bears witness with our spirit that we are children of God,†
17 and if children, then [a]heirs—
heirs of God and joint heirs with
Christ, [b]if indeed we suffer with
Him, that we may also be glorified
together.†

The Spirit Assists Us Through Suffering

18 For I consider that [a]the sufferings of this present time are not worthy *to be compared* with the glory
which shall be revealed in us.†
19 For [a]the earnest expectation of
the creation eagerly waits for the revealing of the sons of God.
20 For [a]the creation was subjected
to futility, not willingly, but because
of Him who subjected *it* in hope;
21 because the creation itself also
will be delivered from the bondage
of [1]corruption into the glorious
[a]liberty of the children of God.†
22 For we know that the whole creation [a]groans and labors with birth
pangs together until now.†
23 Not only *that,* but we also who
have [a]the firstfruits of the Spirit,
[b]even we ourselves groan [c]within
ourselves, eagerly waiting for the
adoption, the [d]redemption of our
body.
24 For we were saved in this hope,
but [a]hope that is seen is not hope;
for why does one still hope for what
he sees?†
25 But if we hope for what we do
not see, we eagerly wait for *it* with
perseverance.
26 Likewise the Spirit also helps in
our weaknesses. For [a]we do not
know what we should pray for as
we ought, but [b]the Spirit Himself
makes intercession [1]for us with
groanings which cannot be uttered.†

14 [a][Gal. 5:18]
15 [a]Heb. 2:15 [b]2 Tim. 1:7 [c][Is. 56:5] [d]Mark 14:36 [1]Lit., in Aram., *Father*
16 [a]Eph. 1:13
17 [a]Acts 26:18 [b]Phil. 1:29
18 [a]2 Cor. 4:17
19 [a][2 Pet. 3:13]
20 [a]Gen. 3:17–19
21 [a][2 Cor. 3:17] [1]*decay*
22 [a]Jer. 12:4, 11
23 [a]2 Cor. 5:5 [b]2 Cor. 5:2, 4 [c][Luke 20:36] [d]Eph. 1:14; 4:30
24 [a]Heb. 11:1
26 [a]Matt. 20:22 [b]Eph. 6:18 [1]NU omits *for us*

8:14–17 Christians are **sons of God, children** (vv. 16, 17) and **heirs** (v. 17) by **adoption** (v. 15). Thus we become like God—not by nature but according to God's grace or uncreated energy. *Adoption* moves from fact to experience as the Holy Spirit, stirring in our hearts, prompts us to pray to the Father with the intimate **Abba,** "Daddy" (v. 15; see Gal. 4:5–7). This process of growth as children of God the Orthodox Church calls deification.

8:15 The spirit of bondage is **fear** of the letter of the Law of Moses (2:28, 29) and its demands. Israel feared God as a slave would a stern master.

8:16 The human **spirit** is the deepest part of the soul, by which we have communion with God.

8:17 Joint heirs with Christ are all **children** of **God,** all believers, who are destined to receive God's glory as their inheritance. But the present Christian life is grace mingled with hardship: **we suffer with Him.**

8:18 Note the contrast: **sufferings** and **glory.** As Christians, we have God's *glory* **in us** and we experience "the firstfruits" (v. 23), though His glory is not yet fully **revealed** (see Col. 3:3, 4). In the Orthodox Church, the icon of the Incarnation of the Son of God (Blessed Mary and her Child) is placed on the left side of the altar. The icon of Christ as Ruler on the throne in glory is on the right. We are thereby taught that we live in a tension between our present and future experience of the Kingdom. We live between Christ's first and His second coming.

8:21 Glorious liberty is the freedom of future resurrection life. Then our wills, free from **corruption,** will be in complete harmony with God's.

8:22 The groaning is a desire for greater things, the transformation of all creation to be eternally in harmony with God's sovereign rule.

8:24 Hope is more than optimism; it is settled confidence about things to come—so secure that we can patiently wait through much suffering for Christ's coming.

8:26 The Holy **Spirit** not only brings us strength, He empowers us in **our weaknesses,** especially helping us to pray. Prayer in the spirit, also called prayer without words, is the

(continued on next page)

Commemoration of Martyrs and Monk Martyrs

8:28–39: This passage is our great assurance that, in life or in death, we are in God's hands.

27 Now [a]He who searches the
hearts knows what the mind of the
Spirit *is,* because He makes intercession for the saints [b]according to *the*
will of God.

The Father Ensures Our Destiny

28 And we know that all things
work together for good to those
who love God, to those [a]who are
the called according to *His* purpose.†
29 For whom [a]He foreknew,
[b]He also predestined [c]*to be* conformed to the image of His Son,
[d]that He might be the firstborn
among many brethren.
30 Moreover whom He predestined, these He also [a]called; whom
He called, these He also [b]justified;
and whom He justified, these He
also [c]glorified.†

27 [a]1 Chr. 28:9 [b]1 John 5:14
28 [a]2 Tim. 1:9
29 [a]2 Tim. 2:19 [b]Eph. 1:5, 11 [c][2 Cor. 3:18] [d]Heb. 1:6
30 [a][1 Pet. 2:9; 3:9] [b][Gal. 2:16] [c]John 17:22
31 [a]Num. 14:9
32 [a]Rom. 5:6, 10 [b][Rom. 4:25]
33 [a]Is. 50:8, 9
34 [a]John 3:18 [b]Mark 16:19 [c]Heb. 7:25; 9:24

The Father's Love Triumphs in Christ

31 What then shall we say to these
things? [a]If God *is* for us, who *can be*
against us?†
32 [a]He who did not spare His own
Son, but [b]delivered Him up for us
all, how shall He not with Him also
freely give us all things?
33 Who shall bring a charge against
God's elect? [a]*It is* God who justifies.
34 [a]Who *is* he who condemns? *It*
is Christ who died, and furthermore
is also risen, [b]who is even at the right
hand of God, [c]who also makes intercession for us.
35 Who shall separate us from the
love of Christ? *Shall* tribulation,
or distress, or persecution, or
famine, or nakedness, or peril, or
sword?
36 As it is written:

(continued from previous page)
highest form of prayer. The Fathers identify three stages: (1) saying the words of the prayers; (2) saying the words with meaning and full concentration; (3) praying without words, when one is so filled with the Holy Spirit and so in union with God that words are inadequate.

8:28, 29 For those who love God, the Scriptures and experience bear witness: **all things work together for good.** Setbacks and difficulties there will be, but God turns them into "light affliction" (2 Cor. 4:17, 18; 12:9, 10). This passage (vv. 28–39) is read on the Feasts of Martyrs, for being **conformed to the image of His Son** (v. 29) includes conformity to Christ's death out of His love for the Father. God foreknows all things, but He does not predetermine all. For God is free and man is free. God freely offers salvation to all, and man freely responds to it. All are **called,** but all do not respond. Those who refuse to love God are not forced to change; God compels no one. "God does not will evil to be done, nor does He force virtue" (St. John of Damascus). Based on His foreknowledge, God assures or predestines that those who choose to love and obey Him will be fulfilled, being *conformed to the image of His Son.* The model for the creation of man is the Son incarnate, and the eternal goal of man is conformity to the incarnate Son. Thus, everything the Only Begotten Son is by nature we become by the grace of the Incarnation. In relation to the Father, the Son is the Only Begotten, but in relation to us He is **the firstborn** of **many brethren.**

8:30 Paul writes of the overall breadth of salvation. **Glorified** is in the past tense, but it also refers to the future glorification of believers through the resurrection.

8:31–39 This passage begins a summary of chs. 1—8. Because of (1) God's love for us in our union with Christ, (2) His victory over sin and death, and (3) our life in His Kingdom, we can withstand all the assaults of the world and the devil and come out of the attacks **more than conquerors** (v. 37).

[a]"For Your sake we are killed all
day long;
We are accounted as sheep for
the slaughter."†

37 [a]Yet in all these things we are
more than conquerors through Him
who loved us.†
38 For I am persuaded that neither
death nor life, nor angels nor [a]prin-
cipalities nor powers, nor things
present nor things to come,†
39 nor height nor depth, nor any
other created thing, shall be able
to separate us from the love of
God which is in Christ Jesus our
Lord.

Unbelief of the Jews, Despite God's Blessings

9 I [a]tell the truth in Christ, I am
not lying, my conscience also
bearing me witness in the Holy
Spirit,†
2 [a]that I have great sorrow and
continual grief in my heart.
3 For [a]I could wish that I myself
were accursed from Christ for my
brethren, my [1]countrymen according
to the flesh,

36 [a]Ps. 44:22
37 [a]1 Cor. 15:57
38 [a][Eph. 1:21]

CHAPTER 9
1 [a]2 Cor. 1:23
2 [a]Rom. 10:1
3 [a]Ex. 32:32
[1]Or *relatives*
4 [a]Ex. 4:22
[b]1 Sam. 4:21
[c]Acts 3:25
[d]Ps. 147:19
[e]Heb. 9:1, 6
[f][Acts 2:39; 13:32]
5 [a]Deut. 10:15
[b][Luke 1:34, 35; 3:23]
[c]Jer. 23:6
6 [a]Num. 23:19
[b][Gal. 6:16]
7 [a][Gal. 4:23]
[b]Gen. 21:12
8 [a]Gal. 4:28
9 [a]Gen. 18:10, 14
10 [a]Gen. 25:21

4 who are Israelites, [a]to whom
pertain the adoption, [b]the glory,
[c]the covenants, [d]the giving of the
law, [e]the service *of God,* and [f]the
promises;
5 [a]of whom *are* the fathers and
from [b]whom, according to the flesh,
Christ *came,* [c]who is over all, *the* eternally blessed God. Amen.

God Is Sovereign, Faithful to Israel

6 [a]But it is not that the word of
God has taken no effect. For [b]they
are not all Israel who *are* of Israel,†
7 [a]nor *are they* all children because
they are the seed of Abraham;
but, [b]*"In Isaac your seed shall be*
called."
8 That is, those who *are* the children of the flesh, these *are* not the
children of God; but [a]the children of
the promise are counted as the seed.
9 For this *is* the word of promise:
[a]*"At this time I will come and Sarah*
shall have a son."
10 And not only *this,* but when
[a]Rebecca also had conceived by one
man, *even* by our father Isaac†
11 (for *the children* not yet being
born, nor having done any good or

8:36 It is not ultimately for men nor for anything in this life that we endure suffering (v. 35), but for the **sake** of the King of Glory.

8:37 The conquering power is God's, not ours.

8:38, 39 Paul knew all this by personal experience (see 2 Cor. 1:8, 9; 4:7–15; 11:23–28). **Angels, principalities** and **powers** are spirit beings.

9:1–5 Paul has a strong word for any who accuse him of failing to love his fellow Jews.

9:6–13 The paradox of Jewish unbelief is understood in part by Paul's description of a twofold Israel: one spiritual, the other physical. God is faithful to all Israel, but the issue is, who is a true child **of Abraham** (v. 7)?

(1) Not a natural or biological offspring of Abraham, for if this were the case the children of Hagar (Gen. 16:4, 15) and of Keturah (Gen. 25:1–4) would be Israelites. Further, not all those in Isaac's line are Israelites (otherwise Esau and the Edomites would be) but only those who are **"in Isaac"** (v. 7)—in other words, faithful believers. Being a child **of God** (v. 8) has never been based on race, or family.

(2) **Children of the promise**—that is, those *in Isaac,* or faithful believers—are the true children of Abraham (see Gal. 4:28). For Isaac was conceived by **the word of promise** (v. 9), not just by the natural procreative powers of his elderly parents (Gen. 18:10–15; 21:1–7).

9:10–13 It was being argued that since Ishmael was the son of a slave woman, whereas Sarah was free, Isaac was the seed and Ishmael was not. However, the fact that **Rebecca** was free and the mother of both **Jacob** and **Esau** (v. 13) proves the argument wrong. For if being God's children is based on the flesh, then Esau must also be counted in the inheritance. Jacob is the seed, not because of his human parentage, but because he is the child of promise.

Both Jacob and Esau were called to salvation, for God loves all equally. But God foreknew

(continued on page 361)

IS GOD FAITHFUL TO ISRAEL?

In the early chapters of Romans (Rom. 1—8), Paul expounds the gospel of God's righteousness for the salvation of all who believe in Christ, both Jews and Gentiles. In the middle chapters of the epistle (Rom. 9—11) he grapples with the perplexing theme of Jewish unbelief in their own promised Messiah. This is a matter which not only causes him great anguish, but also raises questions about God's faithfulness to the Jewish people.

An accusation was circulating in the first century that God had not kept His promises to Israel—that Israel had been unjustly abandoned by God in favor of idol-worshiping Gentiles. Although many Jews believed in Christ, the majority of the Jewish people adhered to their former leaders and traditions. Meanwhile, increasing numbers of Gentiles were becoming Christians.

How was one to view these developments? What was God's plan for Jews and Gentiles in this decisive period of the history of salvation? Why were most Jews unresponsive or opposed to the gospel while Gentiles were becoming the majority in the young Church?

Paul's letter to the Romans indicates how important such questions were to Christians in the sixth decade of the first century. Has God been fair to Israel? Paul's conclusion is yes: He has been faithful to Israel, and, through them, to the Gentiles. God's unchanging faithfulness is seen in several ways.

(1) *Through Paul* (Rom. 9:1–3). God miraculously saved the Jewish zealot Saul (Acts 9:1–22), who later, as Paul the Apostle, confesses, "I am indeed a Jew" (Acts 22:3). The faithfulness of God to Israel and to the Gentiles is witnessed "in the Holy Spirit" (Rom. 9:1) through Paul, who is even willing to be "accursed from Christ" (Rom. 9:3) if by that Israel could be saved.

(2) *Through Providence* (Rom. 9:4, 5). God the Father shows His sovereign care for Israel, and to the Gentiles, through bestowing on them His adoption, glory, covenants, law, service (Gr. *latreia*—a reference to proper worship) and promises. The gospel itself came to "the Jew first" (Rom. 1:16), then to the Gentile.

(3) *Through the Patriarchs* (Rom. 9:6–13). God has been faithful to Israel and thus to the Gentiles through His servants Abraham (v. 7), Isaac (v. 10) and Jacob (v. 13). As Isaac's birth came by the promise of God (vv. 6–9), so does the new birth come for us. For just as it was possible to be in the nation of Israel, but not truly a child of God, so being born into a Christian home, church and culture does not *de facto* guarantee our faithfulness. We must, like Isaac, be born of God's promise. For the Christian this new birth comes from the watery womb of baptism, with the injunction that we grow to serve the Lord with all our heart, mind, and strength.

(4) *Through the Prophets* (Rom. 9:14–29). Beginning with Moses (v. 15), and including Hosea (vv. 25, 26) and Isaiah (vv. 27–29), the Prophets reveal God's faithfulness in His sovereign mercy and election of His faithful—Jew and Gentile alike. The "potter" has "power over the clay" (v. 21), "that He might make known the riches of His glory on the vessels of mercy" (v. 23).

We therefore conclude that God is faithful to Israel as He is to the Gentiles. But we also see that to benefit from His faithfulness to us, we must be faithful to Him.

evil, that the purpose of God according to election might stand, not of
works but of [a]Him who calls),
12 it was said to her, [a]*"The older*
shall serve the younger."
13 As it is written, [a]*"Jacob I have*
loved, but Esau I have hated."

God Is Just in His Choice

14 What shall we say then? [a]*Is there*
unrighteousness with God? Certainly not!†
15 For He says to Moses, [a]*"I will*
have mercy on whomever I will have
mercy, and I will have compassion
on whomever I will have com-
passion."
16 So then *it is* not of him who
wills, nor of him who runs, but of
God who shows mercy.
17 For [a]the Scripture says to the
Pharaoh, [b]*"For this very purpose*
I have raised you up, that I may
show My power in you, and that My
name may be declared in all the
earth."†
18 Therefore He has mercy on
whom He wills, and whom He wills
He [a]hardens.
19 You will say to me then, "Why
does He still find fault? For [a]who has
resisted His will?"†
20 But indeed, O man, who are
you to reply against God? [a]Will the
thing formed say to him who formed
it, "Why have you made me like
this?"
21 Does not the [a]potter have
power over the clay, from the same
lump to make [b]one vessel for honor
and another for dishonor?
22 *What* if God, wanting to show
His wrath and to make His power
known, endured with much longsuffering [a]the vessels of wrath [b]pre-
pared for destruction,†
23 and that He might make known
[a]the riches of His glory on the vessels of mercy, which He had [b]pre-
pared beforehand for glory,
24 *even* us whom He [a]called,
[b]not of the Jews only, but also of the
Gentiles?
25 As He says also in Hosea:

[a]*"I will call them My people, who*
were not My people,

11 [a][Rom. 4:17; 8:28] **12** [a]Gen. 25:23 **13** [a]Mal. 1:2, 3 **14** [a]Deut. 32:4 **15** [a]Ex. 33:19 **17** [a]Gal. 3:8 [b]Ex. 9:16 **18** [a]Ex. 4:21 **19** [a]2 Chr. 20:6 **20** [a]Is. 29:16 **21** [a]Prov. 16:4 [b]2 Tim. 2:20 **22** [a][1 Thess. 5:9] [b][1 Pet. 2:8] **23** [a][Col. 1:27] [b][Rom. 8:28–30] **24** [a][Rom. 8:28] [b]Rom. 3:29 **25** [a]Hos. 2:23

(continued from page 359)
how these two would freely respond to His call: Esau was **hated** (v. 13), or rejected, only because God knew he would choose wrongly and be wicked. Jacob was **loved** and chosen because God knew he would participate in the faith of Abraham and serve God's purposes. Similarly, though at one time Paul persecuted Christians, God foreknew he would repent and had elected him before he was born (Gal. 1:15). God knows the end even before the beginning.

9:14–16 Paul does not yield ground but rather emphasizes the point even more. At Mt. Sinai some idolatrous Jews perished while others survived (Ex. 32; 33) by God's inscrutable mercy explained to no one. God is not a capricious tyrant, but His will is unquestionable. For the basis of salvation is God's **mercy** and **compassion** (v. 15), not human free will or faith or works. Though man must freely accept God's grace and righteousness, God knows who will do this.

9:17, 18 Paul brings forward **Pharaoh** as another example of God's sovereign will. Even though this ruler of Egypt arrogantly deified himself, he was under God's controlling hand. His defeat manifested God's **name,** His glory (Ex. 9:15, 16), a great **show** of divine **power.** Thus, God shows **mercy** (v. 18) or judgment on whomever **He wills.**

9:19–21 An objector to God's sovereignty has no complaint, any more than **clay** (v. 21) can question **the potter** about how he fashions it. When one truly understands who God is, the objections vanish (see Job 42:5, 6). It is ours to obey, not to call God to account. We yield our wills to God's will, as *clay* yields itself to *the potter* (v. 21)—an image not of necessity but of responsibility.

9:22–24 Paul applies his teaching on God's free will to his contemporary situation. **The vessels of wrath** are the unbelieving Jews to whom God is showing **longsuffering** by not destroying them. The **vessels of mercy** (v. 23) are believing Jews and Gentiles to whom God is revealing **the riches of His glory** in Christ. The implied conclusion: the paradox of the unbelief of the majority of Jews, and the belief of other Jews and many Gentiles, is all according to God's sovereign will.

And her beloved, who was not
beloved."†
26 *"And[a] it shall come to pass in the*
place where it was said to
them,
'You are not My people,'
There they shall be called sons
of the living God."

27 Isaiah also cries out concerning
Israel:

[a]*"Though the number of the*
children of Israel be as the
sand of the sea,
[b]*The remnant will be saved.*
28 *For [1]He will finish the work and*
cut it short in righteousness,
[a]*Because the* LORD *will make*
a short work upon the
earth."

29 And as Isaiah said before:

[a]*"Unless the* LORD *of [1]Sabaoth had*
left us a seed,
[b]*We would have become like*
Sodom,
And we would have been made
like Gomorrah."

Israel Pursues Self-Righteousness

30 What shall we say then? [a]That
Gentiles, who did not pursue righteousness, have attained to righteousness, [b]even the righteousness
of faith;†
31 but Israel, [a]pursuing the law of
righteousness, [b]has not attained to
the law [1]of righteousness.
32 Why? Because *they did* not *seek*
it by faith, but as it were, [1]by the
works of the law. For [a]they stumbled
at that stumbling stone.
33 As it is written:

[a]*"Behold, I lay in Zion a*
stumbling stone and rock of
offense,
And [b]whoever believes on
Him will not be put to
shame."

10 Brethren, my heart's desire
and prayer to God for [1]Israel
is that they may be saved.†
2 For I bear them witness [a]that
they have a zeal for God, but not
according to knowledge.
3 For they being ignorant of
[a]God's righteousness, and seeking to
establish their own [b]righteousness,
have not submitted to the righteousness of God.
4 For [a]Christ *is* the end of the law
for righteousness to everyone who
believes.†

26 [a]Hos. 1:10
27 [a]Is. 10:22, 23
[b]Rom. 11:5
28 [a]Is. 10:23; 28:22
[1]NU *the* LORD *will finish the work and cut it short upon the earth*
29 [a]Is. 1:9
[b]Is. 13:19
[1]Lit., in Heb., *Hosts*
30 [a]Rom. 4:11
[b]Rom. 1:17; 3:21; 10:6
31 [a][Rom. 10:2–4]
[b][Gal. 5:4]
[1]NU omits *of righteousness*
32 [a][1 Cor. 1:23]
[1]NU *by works,* omitting *of the law*
33 [a]Is. 8:14; 28:16
[b]Rom. 5:5; 10:11

CHAPTER 10

1 [1]NU *them*
2 [a]Acts 21:20
3 [a][Rom. 1:17]
[b][Phil. 3:9]
4 [a][Gal. 3:24; 4:5]

9:25–29 The OT prophets had foreseen God's sovereignty and man's salvation in several ways: (1) He makes the outcasts, the Gentiles, His **people** and **sons** (vv. 25, 26); (2) He saves only a small portion, a **remnant,** of the Jews (vv. 27, 28); and (3) He does not utterly destroy the unbelieving Jews because of the faithful remnant (v. 29). Receiving God's mercy or rejecting it is not complicated, but simple or **short** (v. 28): either we have faith in Christ or we do not.

9:30–33 The first answer to the paradox of Jewish unbelief is from God's standpoint: His sovereign will (vv. 6–29). The second answer to the paradox is from humanity's standpoint (9:30—10:21): faith. For "the righteousness of God is revealed from faith to faith" (1:17), equally for Jews and Gentiles. The Gentiles, who had been unconcerned about **righteousness,** now attain it by their **faith** in Christ. God mercifully overlooks their former unrighteousness practiced in ignorance (Acts 17:30). By contrast the Jews fail to attain even the righteousness of **the law,** for they do not pursue the law **by faith** (v. 32) but by **works.** Seeing only the letter of **the law,** not its spirit, they miss Christ in the law and try to keep the commandments apart from Him. They substitute what was "shadow" (Col. 2:16, 17; Heb. 10:1) for substance. Jesus Christ becomes their **stumbling** block (v. 32).

10:1–3 Paul wishes nothing but good for the people of **Israel.** He prays for their salvation, and knows of their **zeal for God** (v. 2). But their zeal is without insight into **God's righteousness** (v. 3) in Christ. By rejecting the gospel and adhering to the law, they seek to establish **their own righteousness.** Their ignorance of God's righteousness, a rejection of Christ Himself, is willful and self-imposed.

10:4 Christ has always been the way of salvation in both Testaments. Christ puts an **end**

(continued on next page)

God's Righteousness Is by Faith

5 For Moses writes about the righteousness which is of the law,
[a]*"The man who does those things
shall live by them."*†
6 But the righteousness of faith
speaks in this way, [a]*"Do not say in
your heart, 'Who will ascend into
heaven?' "* (that is, to bring Christ
down *from above*)
7 or, [a]*" 'Who will descend into
the abyss?' "* (that is, to bring Christ
up from the dead).
8 But what does it say? [a]*"The
word is near you, in your mouth and
in your heart"* (that is, the word of
faith which we preach):
9 that [a]if you confess with your
mouth the Lord Jesus and believe in
your heart that God has raised Him
from the dead, you will be saved.†
10 For with the heart one believes
unto righteousness, and with the
mouth confession is made unto
salvation.
11 For the Scripture says, [a]*"Whoever believes on Him will not be put
to shame."*†
12 For [a]there is no distinction between Jew and Greek, for [b]the same
Lord over all [c]is rich to all who call
upon Him.
13 For [a]*"whoever calls* [b]*on the
name of the* LORD *shall be saved."*

Israel Rejects, Gentiles Receive the Gospel

14 How then shall they call on Him
in whom they have not believed?
And how shall they believe in Him
of whom they have not heard? And
how shall they hear [a]without a
preacher?†
15 And how shall they preach unless they are sent? As it is written:

[a]*"How beautiful are the feet of
those who* [1]*preach the gospel
of peace,
Who bring glad tidings of good
things!"*

5 [a]Lev. 18:5
6 [a]Deut. 30:12–14
7 [a]Deut. 30:13
8 [a]Deut. 30:14
9 [a]Luke 12:8
11 [a]Is. 28:16
12 [a]Rom. 3:22, 29 [b]Acts 10:36 [c]Eph. 1:7
13 [a]Joel 2:32 [b]Acts 9:14
14 [a]Titus 1:3
15 [a]Is. 52:7; Nah. 1:15 [1]NU omits *preach the gospel of peace, Who*

(continued from previous page)
to **the law** as a way for people to try to gain **righteousness** without Him (see v. 5). Thus, He terminates the Old Covenant without nullifying its law as useless. For He fulfills the law; His righteousness is superior to that of the law. **Everyone who believes** in Christ participates in His incomparable righteousness.

10:5–13 The way of **the law** and the way of **faith** (v. 6) are contrasted. Whereas mere obedience to the law has always failed, faith in Christ as **LORD** (v. 13) always succeeds (vv. 11–13). For: (1) Faith does not doubt, though righteousness is beyond human possibility without **Christ** (v. 6). (2) Faith is not a distant accomplishment but **is near** (v. 8), having a vision of Christ as present and easily accessible (vv. 6–8). (3) Faith transforms the whole person; the soul (**heart,** vv. 8, 9) working with the body (**mouth**) makes it real (vv. 8–10). (4) True faith is accessible to all equally, as even the OT prophets teach (vv. 11–13).

10:9, 10 What does the **mouth . . . confess** and the **heart . . . believe?** The *mouth* confesses **the Lord Jesus,** that the Savior (Jesus) is God (Lord). The *heart* believes that the Father **raised** the Son from the dead. That is, it believes in the Trinity, the Resurrection and in the works of the incarnate Son.

10:11–13 Believing and confessing are OT themes—Isaiah emphasizing the faith of the heart (v. 11), and Joel, the confession of the mouth (v. 13). Both prophets teach that grace and faith are universal: God makes **no distinction** (v. 12) between persons. All may come freely if they will.

10:14–21 From 9:1—10:13 Paul has left the Jews with no excuse for rejecting the Gospel. Paul insists God fulfilled His part completely. The Jews had extraordinary opportunities to come to faith. For God sent His message through preachers (v. 15) and throughout all creation (v. 18). Israel did indeed hear (vv. 16, 18), but did not believe (vv. 16, 21). Therefore, God turned to the Gentiles, who heard and believed (vv. 19, 20). The Jews of Jesus' time demanded a sign, yet they always had a higher sign than miracles; they had God's own words, and creation itself. When they failed to heed the prophets, God gave them a sign of fulfilled prophecy, the conversion of the Gentiles. **Jealousy** (v. 19) is a powerful motivator. To see those deemed far inferior to you, whom you detest, adopted and inheriting your promises and dreams should arouse great indignation.

16 But they have not all obeyed the
gospel. For Isaiah says, [a]*"LORD, who
has believed our report?"*
17 So then faith *comes* by hearing,
and hearing by the word of God.
18 But I say, have they not heard?
Yes indeed:

> [a]*"Their sound has gone out to all*
> *the earth,*
> [b]*And their words to the ends of*
> *the world."*

19 But I say, did Israel not know?
First Moses says:

> [a]*"I will provoke you to jealousy*
> *by those who are not a nation,*
> *I will move you to anger by a*
> [b]*foolish nation."*

20 But Isaiah is very bold and says:

> [a]*"I was found by those who did*
> *not seek Me;*
> *I was made manifest to those*
> *who did not ask for Me."*

21 But to Israel he says:

> [a]*"All day long I have stretched out*
> *My hands*
> *To a disobedient and contrary*
> *people."*

God Elects a Remnant of Israel

11 I say then, [a]has God cast
away His people? [b]Certainly
not! For [c]I also am an Israelite, of
the seed of Abraham, *of* the tribe of
Benjamin.†
2 God has not cast away His people whom [a]He foreknew. Or do you
not know what the Scripture says of
Elijah, how he pleads with God
against Israel, saying,
3 [a]*"LORD, they have killed Your
prophets and torn down Your altars,
and I alone am left, and they seek
my life"*?
4 But what does the divine response say to him? [a]*"I have reserved
for Myself seven thousand men
who have not bowed the knee to
Baal."*
5 [a]Even so then, at this present
time there is a remnant according to
the election of grace.
6 And [a]if by grace, then *it is* no
longer of works; otherwise grace is
no longer grace. [1]But if *it is* of works,
it is no longer grace; otherwise work
is no longer work.
7 What then? [a]Israel has not obtained what it seeks; but the elect
have obtained it, and the rest were
[b]blinded.
8 Just as it is written:

> [a]*"God has given them a spirit of*
> *stupor,*
> [b]*Eyes that they should not see*
> *And ears that they should not*
> *hear,*
> *To this very day."*

9 And David says:

> [a]*"Let their table become a snare*
> *and a trap,*
> *A stumbling block and a*
> *recompense to them.*

10 *Let their eyes be darkened, so*
> *that they do not see,*
> *And bow down their back*
> *always."*

16 [a]Is. 53:1; John 12:38
18 [a]Ps. 19:4; Matt. 24:14; Mark 16:15; Rom. 1:8; Col. 1:6, 23; 1 Thess. 1:8 [b]1 Kin. 18:10; Matt. 4:8
19 [a]Deut. 32:21; Rom. 11:11 [b]Titus 3:3
20 [a]Is. 65:1; Rom. 9:30
21 [a]Is. 65:2

CHAPTER 11

1 [a]Ps. 94:14; Jer. 46:28 [b]1 Sam. 12:22; Jer. 31:37 [c]2 Cor. 11:22; Phil. 3:5
2 [a][Rom. 8:29]
3 [a]1 Kin. 19:10, 14
4 [a]1 Kin. 19:18
5 [a]2 Kin. 19:4; Rom. 9:27
6 [a]Rom. 4:4 [1]NU omits the rest of v. 6.
7 [a]Rom. 9:31 [b]Mark 6:52; Rom. 9:18; 11:25; 2 Cor. 3:14
8 [a]Is. 29:10, 13 [b]Deut. 29:3, 4; Is. 6:9; Matt. 13:13, 14; John 12:40; Acts 28:26, 27
9 [a]Ps. 69:22, 23

11:1–10 Jewish unbelief in Christ raises the question whether **God cast away His people**? And the answer is "no." For had He done so, He would have saved none of them. Paul himself, an Israelite, was not cast away (v. 1); and there is **a remnant** (v. 5), a minority, of Jews who choose to believe. Elijah testifies to this, for he thought he was the only one **left** (vv. 2–4)! As only a few heeded Elijah in his day, so only a few heed Jesus, the Apostles and Paul (9:27, 29; 1 Thess. 2:14–16) in theirs.

God's grace saves the willing, not the unwilling: those who will receive grace by faith and obey God (vv. 5, 6). Israel is not willing, for she **seeks** (v. 7) righteousness on her own terms: through the works of the law, not through the grace of Christ. She stubbornly and freely hardens herself in unrepentance (2:4). God does not cast the people away; they remove themselves. **God has given them a spirit of stupor** (v. 8).

Gentiles Are Being Saved

11 I say then, have they stumbled
that they should fall? Certainly not!
But [a]through their [1]fall, to provoke
them to [b]jealousy, salvation *has come*
to the Gentiles.†
12 Now if their [1]fall *is* riches for the
world, and their failure riches for the
Gentiles, how much more their
fullness!
13 For I speak to you Gentiles; inasmuch as [a]I am an apostle to the
Gentiles, I magnify my ministry,
14 if by any means I may provoke
to jealousy *those who are* my flesh and
[a]save some of them.
15 For if their being cast away *is*
the reconciling of the world, what
will their acceptance *be* [a]but life from
the dead?

God Will Yet Restore Israel

16 For if [a]the firstfruit *is* holy, the
lump *is* also *holy;* and if the root *is*
holy, so *are* the branches.†
17 And if [a]some of the branches
were broken off, [b]and you, being a
wild olive tree, were grafted in
among them, and with them became
a partaker of the root and [1]fatness
of the olive tree,
18 [a]do not boast against the
branches. But if you do boast, *remem-*
ber that you do not support the root,
but the root supports you.
19 You will say then, "Branches
were broken off that I might be
grafted in."
20 Well *said.* Because of [a]unbelief
they were broken off, and you stand
by faith. Do not be haughty, but fear.
21 For if God did not spare the natural branches, He may not spare you
either.
22 Therefore consider the goodness and severity of God: on those
who fell, severity; but toward you,
[1]goodness, [a]if you continue in *His*
goodness. Otherwise [b]you also will
be cut off.
23 And they also, [a]if they do not
continue in unbelief, will be grafted
in, for God is able to graft them in
again.
24 For if you were cut out of the
olive tree which is wild by nature,
and were grafted contrary to nature
into a cultivated olive tree, how
much more will these, who *are* natural *branches,* be grafted into their own
olive tree?†
25 For I do not desire, brethren,
that you should be ignorant of this
mystery, lest you should be [a]wise in
your own [1]opinion, that [b]blindness
in part has happened to Israel
[c]until the fullness of the Gentiles has
come in.†
26 And so all Israel will be [1]saved,
as it is written:

11 [a]Is. 42:6, 7; Acts 28:28 [b]Deut. 32:21; Acts 13:46; Rom. 10:19 [1]*trespass*
12 [1]*trespass*
13 [a]Acts 9:15; 22:21; Gal. 1:16; 2:7–9; Eph. 3:8
14 [a]1 Cor. 9:22; 1 Tim. 4:16; James 5:20
15 [a][Is. 26:16–19]
16 [a]Lev. 23:10; [James 1:18]
17 [a]Jer. 11:16; [John 15:2] [b]Acts 2:39; [Eph. 2:12] [1]*richness*
18 [a][1 Cor. 10:12]
20 [a]Heb. 3:19
22 [a]1 Cor. 15:2; Heb. 3:6, 14 [b][John 15:2] [1]NU adds *of God*
23 [a][2 Cor. 3:16]
25 [a]Rom. 12:16 [b]2 Cor. 3:14 [c]Luke 21:24; John 10:16; Rom. 11:12 [1]*estimation*
26 [1]Or *delivered*

11:11–15 Has Israel **stumbled that** it **should fall** permanently? Since the people have fallen away because of Christ, are they beyond salvation? No, for through Israel's failure to believe, **salvation has come to the Gentiles** (v. 11). Further, through the Gentiles' faith, Israel's opportunity for salvation is renewed. God's presence among the Gentiles provokes the Jews to **jealousy** and anger (vv. 11, 14; 10:19) that they might believe and experience the **fullness** (v. 12) of grace. As **their being cast away** (v. 15) is caused by their own unbelief (vv. 20, 23), their return through faith would be so glorious, it would be as **life from the dead** (v. 15), the final resurrection itself.

11:16–22 Paul admonishes Christian Gentiles not to be boastful and contemptuous toward unbelieving Jews. For (1) Israel's heritage is holy and ought to make Christians humble. Jewish tradition and righteous Jews are **the root** (v. 16). Gentile believers are a wild branch **grafted in** (v. 17). Thus, the Church is one with Israel, as its consummation, its ultimate fruition, the true fulfillment of Israel. (2) Israel's unbelief is a warning to the Church to remain faithful. We **also will be cut off** (v. 22) unless we continue in faith. God has both **goodness and severity** (v. 22)—He respects man's free choices.

11:24 Continuing in faith produces fruit. Before faith we were barren, **wild by nature,** choosing unbelief and unruly behavior. Belief yields to being **cultivated** by God. It produces self-control and the fruit of the Spirit (Gal. 5:22, 23).

11:25–27 Here is Paul's final answer to the paradox of Jewish unbelief, which is the

(continued on next page)

[a]"*The Deliverer will come out of*
Zion,
And He will turn away
ungodliness from Jacob;
27 *For* [a]*this is My covenant with*
them,
When I take away their sins."

28 Concerning the gospel *they are*
enemies for your sake, but concerning the election *they are* [a]beloved for
the sake of the fathers.†
29 For the gifts and the calling of
God *are* [a]irrevocable.
30 For as you [a]were once disobedient to God, yet have now
obtained mercy through their disobedience,
31 even so these also have now
been disobedient, that through the
mercy shown you they also may obtain mercy.
32 For God has [1]committed them
[a]all to disobedience, that He might
have mercy on all.

Doxology to God's Ways

33 Oh, the depth of the riches both
of the wisdom and knowledge of
God! How unsearchable *are* His
judgments and His ways past finding out!

34 *"For who has known the*
[a]*mind of the* LORD?
Or [b]*who has become His*
counselor?"
35 *"Or*[a] *who has first given to Him*
And it shall be repaid to him?"

36 For [a]of Him and through Him
and to Him *are* all things, [b]to whom
be glory forever. Amen.†

Christian Renewal

12 I [a]beseech[1] you therefore,
brethren, by the mercies of
God, that you present your bodies
[b]a living sacrifice, holy, acceptable to
God, *which is* your [2]reasonable
service.†
2 And [a]do not be conformed to
this world, but [b]be transformed by
the renewing of your mind, that
you may [c]prove what *is* that good
and acceptable and perfect will of
God.†

26 [a]Is. 59:20, 21
27 [a]Is. 27:9
28 [a]Deut. 7:8; 10:15
29 [a]Num. 23:19
30 [a][Eph. 2:2]
32 [a][Gal. 3:22]
[1]*shut them all up in*
34 [a]Is. 40:13; Jer. 23:18
[b]Job 36:22
35 [a]Job 41:11
36 [a]Heb. 2:10
[b]Heb. 13:21

CHAPTER 12
1 [a]2 Cor. 10:1–4
[b]Heb. 10:18, 20
[1]*urge*
[2]*rational*
2 [a]1 John 2:15
[b]Eph. 4:23
[c][1 Thess. 4:3]

(continued from previous page)
revelation of a **mystery** (v. 25) from God and which censures conceit by Christian Gentiles. For while the Gentiles are being gathered in between Christ's two comings, so are the elect among the Jews. Then **all Israel will be saved** (v. 26)—that is, true Israel (see 9:6), those who truly believe, not all physical descendants of Jacob.

11:28, 29 True Israel is those who freely believe, the elect of God.

11:36 Paul ends this discourse by celebrating God's wisdom in dealing with both Jews and Gentiles. **Forever:** literally "unto ages of ages."

12:1 Service (Gr. *latreia,* lit. "bow down") is better translated "worship" (see 1:9, 25; Heb. 9:14). This is the worship of God through the whole life of the Church, beginning with a renewed mind and integrity of heart (see John 4:23, 24). In union with Christ, we are brought from worshiping the creature to worshiping the Creator in all we do. This worship is:

(1) Physical: **Bodies** suggests both the physical aspect of human nature and human nature generally—ourselves.

(2) **Living:** A contrast to the Old Covenant under which sacrifices were put to death. Under the New Covenant, to die is also to be resurrected. Sacrifice is not a final act but the firstfruit, the foundation, for all other spiritual fruit.

(3) Virtuous (**holy, acceptable**): OT sacrifice was unacceptable and temporary. Animals are not substitutes for humanity or true holiness (Ps. 50:13, 14, 23; 69:30, 31).

(4) **Reasonable,** or "spiritual" (Gr. *logike*): Though worship of God has its logical side, it is more than this—even as Christ, the *Logos,* possesses reason but is far more than reason. To be *reasonable* is to live according to Christ, with renewed hearts and minds.

12:2 Faithful relationship to God changes our relationship to the world. (1) We renounce the pretenses of "this present evil age" (Gal. 1:4). **Conformed to this world** is to be identified with and shaped by the world's values and pleasures. (2) We are **transformed,** starting with the inward man, the **mind,** by virtue, the keeping of God's commandments. *Mind* here is more than the rational faculty; it is the highest faculty of human nature: "the eyes of your heart" (Eph. 1:18, literal translation), by which one sees and comprehends God.

A Life of Unity in the Church

3 For I say, [a]through the grace
given to me, to everyone who is
among you, [b]not to think *of himself*
more highly than he ought to think,
but to think soberly, as God has dealt
[c]to each one a measure of faith.†
4 For [a]as we have many members
in one body, but all the members do
not have the same function,
5 so [a]we, *being* many, are one
body in Christ, and individually
members of one another.
6 Having then gifts differing according to the grace that is [a]given
to us, *let us use them:* if prophecy,
let us [b]*prophesy* in proportion to our
faith;
7 or ministry, *let us use it* in *our*
ministering; [a]he who teaches, in
teaching;
8 [a]he who exhorts, in exhortation;
[b]he who gives, with liberality;
[c]he who leads, with diligence; he
who shows mercy, [d]with cheerfulness.

A Life of Mercy for All Men

9 [a]*Let* love *be* without hypocrisy.
[b]Abhor what is evil. Cling to what
is good.†
10 [a]*Be* kindly affectionate to one
another with brotherly love, [b]in
honor giving preference to one
another;
11 not lagging in diligence, fervent
in spirit, serving the Lord;
12 [a]rejoicing in hope, [b]patient[1] in
tribulation, [c]continuing steadfastly
in prayer;

3 [a]Gal. 2:9 [b]Prov. 25:27 [c][Eph. 4:7]
4 [a]1 Cor. 12:12–14
5 [a][1 Cor. 10:17]
6 [a][John 3:27] [b]Acts 11:27
7 [a]Eph. 4:11
8 [a]Acts 15:32 [b][Matt. 6:1–3] [c][Acts 20:28] [d]2 Cor. 9:7
9 [a]1 Tim. 1:5 [b]Ps. 34:14
10 [a]Heb. 13:1 [b]Phil. 2:3
12 [a]Luke 10:20 [b]Luke 21:19 [c]Luke 18:1 [1]*persevering*
13 [a]1 Cor. 16:1 [b]1 Tim. 3:2 [1]Lit. *pursuing*
14 [a][Matt. 5:44]
15 [a][1 Cor. 12:26]
16 [a][Phil. 2:2; 4:2] [b]Jer. 45:5
17 [a][Matt. 5:39] [b]2 Cor. 8:21 [1]Or *Provide good*
18 [a]Heb. 12:14
19 [a]Lev. 19:18 [b]Deut. 32:35
20 [a]Prov. 25:21, 22
21 [a][Rom. 12:1, 2]

CHAPTER 13
1 [a]1 Pet. 2:13
2 [a][Titus 3:1]

13 [a]distributing to the needs of the
saints, [b]given[1] to hospitality.
14 [a]Bless those who persecute you;
bless and do not curse.
15 [a]Rejoice with those who rejoice,
and weep with those who weep.
16 [a]Be of the same mind toward
one another. [b]Do not set your mind
on high things, but associate with
the humble. Do not be wise in your
own opinion.
17 [a]Repay no one evil for evil.
[b]Have[1] regard for good things in the
sight of all men.†
18 If it is possible, as much as depends on you, [a]live peaceably with
all men.
19 Beloved, [a]do not avenge yourselves, but *rather* give place to wrath;
for it is written, [b]*"Vengeance is*
Mine, I will repay," says the Lord.
20 Therefore

[a]*"If your enemy is hungry, feed*
him;
If he is thirsty, give him a drink;
For in so doing you will heap
coals of fire on his head."

21 Do not be overcome by evil, but
[a]overcome evil with good.

Duties to the State

13 Let every soul be [a]subject to
the governing authorities. For
there is no authority except from
God, and the authorities that exist
are appointed by God.†
2 Therefore whoever resists
[a]the authority resists the ordinance

12:3–8 We live out this faithful relationship to God in the Church, the body of Christ, with (1) humility—contentedness with one's role (v. 3); (2) self-control (**to think soberly,** v. 3), especially control over the sinful passions; (3) proper use of spiritual gifts and ministries (vv. 4–8). Ministry requires functioning together, fitting into the corporate whole of the Church. Each person has a **measure of faith** (v. 3) and divine gifting. Paul gives seven examples of gifts (vv. 6–8), but there are many more.

12:9–16 These timeless exhortations to practice specific virtues are reminders to the Romans and to us that true Christian faith is a faith that works.

12:17–21 Paul explains principles of relating to the world. **Vengeance** (v. 19), here meaning just judgment, belongs to God alone. **Evil** is **overcome** (v. 21) only by **good,** for doing good is participating in the power of God.

13:1 The source of civil government, of all **authorities,** is God, for He alone is sovereign.

Cheese Fare Sunday (Forgiveness Sunday) *Sunday before Lent June 24*
The Birth of John the Baptist

13:11—14:4: Paul exhorts us to awaken and put on the armor of light—this was the ministry of John the Baptist, and is appropriate preparation for Lent.

of God, and those who resist will
[1]bring judgment on themselves.
3 For rulers are not a terror to
good works, but to evil. Do you want
to be unafraid of the authority?
[a]Do what is good, and you will have
praise from the same.†
4 For he is God's minister to you
for good. But if you do evil, be afraid;
for he does not bear the sword in
vain; for he is God's minister, an
avenger to *execute* wrath on him who
practices evil.
5 Therefore [a]*you* must be subject,
not only because of wrath [b]but also
for conscience' sake.†
6 For because of this you also pay
taxes, for they are God's ministers
attending continually to this very
thing.
7 [a]Render therefore to all their
due: taxes to whom taxes *are due,*
customs to whom customs, fear to
whom fear, honor to whom honor.

Love of Neighbor

8 Owe no one anything except to
love one another, for [a]he who loves
another has fulfilled the law.†
9 For the commandments, [a]*"You
shall not commit adultery," "You
shall not murder," "You shall not
steal,"* [1]*"You shall not bear false witness," "You shall not covet,"* and if
there is any other commandment, are
all summed up in this saying,
namely, [b]*"You shall love your neighbor as yourself."*
10 Love does no harm to a neigh-
bor; therefore [a]love *is* the fulfillment
of the law.

"The Day" Is at Hand

11 And *do* this, knowing the time,
that now *it is* high time [a]to awake
out of sleep; for now our salvation
is nearer than when we *first*
believed.†
12 The night is far spent, the day
is at hand. [a]Therefore let us cast off
the works of darkness, and [b]let us
put on the armor of light.†
13 [a]Let us walk [1]properly, as in the
day, [b]not in revelry and drunkenness, [c]not in lewdness and lust,
[d]not in strife and envy.
14 But [a]put on the Lord Jesus
Christ, and [b]make no provision for
the flesh, to *fulfill its* lusts.

Christian Liberty in Serving God

14 Receive[a] one who is weak in
the faith, *but* not to disputes
over doubtful things.†

2 [1]Lit. *receive*
3 [a]1 Pet. 2:14
5 [a]Eccl. 8:2 [b][1 Pet. 2:13, 19]
7 [a]Matt. 22:21
8 [a][Gal. 5:13, 14]
9 [a]Ex. 20:13–17; Deut. 5:17–21 [b]Lev. 19:18 [1]NU omits *"You shall not bear false witness,"*
10 [a][Matt. 7:12; 22:39, 40]
11 [a][1 Cor. 15:34]
12 [a]Eph. 5:11 [b][Eph. 6:11, 13]
13 [a]Phil. 4:8 [b]Prov. 23:20 [c][1 Cor. 6:9] [d]James 3:14 [1]*decently*
14 [a]Gal. 3:27 [b][Gal. 5:16]
CHAPTER 14
1 [a][1 Cor. 8:9; 9:22]

13:3 The purpose of civil government is to produce a social order that is grounded in goodness, not **evil.** The government is, in fact, responsible to punish evildoers.

13:5–7 Paul calls Christians to submit to good government, to obey both God and man. The Kingdom of Heaven and earthly kingdoms are called to work together. The Church and state for Paul are certainly distinct, but they are not separated or isolated from one another. On the other hand, a government that upholds evil, forcing it on her people, is an abusive authority and in such cases, "we ought to obey God rather than men" (Acts 5:29).

13:8–10 Love fulfills **the law** (vv. 8, 10). A person who loves his neighbor will have no problem obeying a just government. Breaking God's commandments fragments society.

13:11 Expectation of future **salvation** through the glorious coming of Christ motivates us to vigilance and proper conduct.

13:12 The night is this life under the influence of evil powers. **The day** is the glorious coming of the Lord.

14:1 In Orthodox Christianity, there are things that cannot be compromised; there are

(continued on next page)

2 For one believes he [a]may eat all
things, but he who is weak eats *only*
vegetables.
3 Let not him who eats despise
him who does not eat, and [a]let not
him who does not eat judge him who
eats; for God has received him.
4 [a]Who are you to judge another's
servant? To his own master he
stands or falls. Indeed, he will be
made to stand, for God is able to
make him stand.
5 [a]One person esteems *one* day
above another; another esteems
every day *alike*. Let each be fully convinced in his own mind.
6 He who [a]observes the day, observes *it* to the Lord; [1]and he who
does not observe the day, to the Lord
he does not observe *it*. He who eats,
eats to the Lord, for [b]he gives God
thanks; and he who does not eat, to
the Lord he does not eat, and gives
God thanks.†
7 For [a]none of us lives to himself,
and no one dies to himself.
8 For if we [a]live, we live to the
Lord; and if we die, we die to the
Lord. Therefore, whether we live or
die, we are the Lord's.
9 For [a]to this end Christ died
[1]and rose and lived again, that He
might be [b]Lord of both the dead and
the living.
10 But why do you judge your
brother? Or why do you show contempt for your brother? For [a]we shall
all stand before the judgment seat
of [1]Christ.
11 For it is written:

[a]*"As I live, says the* LORD,
Every knee shall bow to Me,
And every tongue shall confess
to God."

12 So then [a]each of us shall give
account of himself to God.

Loving Fellow Christians

13 Therefore let us not judge one
another [1]anymore, but rather resolve
this, [a]not to put a stumbling block
or a cause to fall in *our* brother's
way.
14 I know and am convinced by the
Lord Jesus [a]that *there is* nothing unclean of itself; but to him who considers anything to be unclean, to him
it is unclean.†
15 Yet if your brother is grieved because of *your* food, you are no longer
walking in love. [a]Do not destroy
with your food the one for whom
Christ died.
16 [a]Therefore do not let your good
be spoken of as evil;†
17 [a]for the kingdom of God is not
eating and drinking, but righteousness and [b]peace and joy in the Holy
Spirit.
18 For he who serves Christ in
[1]these things [a]*is* acceptable to God
and approved by men.
19 [a]Therefore let us pursue the
things *which make* for peace and the
things by which [b]one may [1]edify
another.
20 [a]Do not destroy the work
of God for the sake of food. [b]All
things indeed *are* pure, [c]but *it is*
evil for the man who eats with [1]of-
fense.

2 [a][Titus 1:15]
3 [a][Col. 2:16]
4 [a]James 4:11, 12
5 [a]Gal. 4:10
6 [a]Gal. 4:10 [b][1 Tim. 4:3] [1]NU omits the rest of this sentence.
7 [a][Gal. 2:20]
8 [a]2 Cor. 5:14, 15
9 [a]2 Cor. 5:15 [b]Acts 10:36 [1]NU omits *and rose*
10 [a]2 Cor. 5:10 [1]NU *God*
11 [a]Is. 45:23
12 [a]1 Pet. 4:5
13 [a]1 Cor. 8:9 [1]*any longer*
14 [a]1 Cor. 10:25
15 [a]1 Cor. 8:11
16 [a][Rom. 12:17]
17 [a]1 Cor. 8:8 [b][Rom. 8:6]
18 [a]2 Cor. 8:21 [1]NU *this thing*
19 [a]Rom. 12:18 [b]1 Cor. 14:12 [1]*build up*
20 [a]Rom. 14:15 [b]Acts 10:15 [c]1 Cor. 8:9–12 [1]A feeling of giving offense

---

(continued from previous page)
also grey areas. God is gracious and allows diversity in **doubtful things** (v. 1), matters not involving Christian dogma. Those **weak in the faith** are Christians of immature conscience and wisdom who may attach primary importance to secondary matters, such as foods and religious festivals (see vv. 2–6).

14:6–9 Christ is **the Lord** of the community, its religious practices and observances. It is when we make ourselves, our prejudices, and our cultural heritage the focal point that we lose sight of our oneness in Christ.

14:14 A mature conscience in Christ knows no food is **unclean of itself**. But an immature conscience must be free to follow stricter rules if it sees fit.

14:16–21 Although Paul theologically stands with the mature in conscience, practically he supports the weak. The superior principle is to sacrifice one's rights and refrain from causing spiritual harm to another, **for the kingdom** is **righteousness and peace and joy** (v. 17).

21 *It is* good neither to eat [a]meat
nor drink wine nor *do anything* by
which your brother stumbles [1]or is
offended or is made weak.
22 [1]Do you have faith? Have *it* to
yourself before God. [a]Happy *is* he
who does not condemn himself in
what he approves.†
23 But he who doubts is condemned if he eats, because *he does*
not *eat* from faith; for [a]whatever *is*
not from faith is [1]sin.

Christian Unity for God's Glory

15 We [a]then who are strong
ought to bear with the
[1]scruples of the weak, and not to
please ourselves.†
2 [a]Let each of us please *his* neighbor for *his* good, leading to [1]edi-
fication.
3 [a]For even Christ did not please
Himself; but as it is written, [b]*"The
reproaches of those who reproached
You fell on Me."*†
4 For [a]whatever things were written before were written for our learning, that we through the [1]patience
and comfort of the Scriptures might
have hope.
5 [a]Now may the God of patience
and comfort grant you to be like-
minded toward one another, according to Christ Jesus,
6 that you may [a]with one mind
and one mouth glorify the God and
Father of our Lord Jesus Christ.
7 Therefore [a]receive one another,
just [b]as Christ also received [1]us, to
the glory of God.†

Christ's Priestly Work for Gentiles

8 Now I say that [a]Jesus Christ has
become a [1]servant to the circumcision for the truth of God, [b]to confirm
the promises *made* to the fathers,
9 and [a]that the Gentiles might
glorify God for *His* mercy, as it is
written:

[b]*"For this reason I will confess to*
You among the Gentiles,
And sing to Your name."†

10 And again he says:

[a]*"Rejoice, O Gentiles, with His*
people!"

11 And again:

[a]*"Praise the LORD, all you*
Gentiles!
Laud Him, all you peoples!"

12 And again, Isaiah says:

[a]*"There shall be a root of Jesse;*
And He who shall rise to reign
over the Gentiles,
In Him the Gentiles shall hope."

13 Now may the God of hope fill
you with all [a]joy and peace in believing, that you may abound
in hope by the power of the Holy
Spirit.

Paul's Missionary Work to the Gentiles

14 Now [a]I myself am confident
concerning you, my brethren, that
you also are full of goodness, [b]filled
with all knowledge, able also to admonish [1]one another.†

21 [a]1 Cor. 8:13
[1]NU omits the rest of v. 21.
22 [a][1 John 3:21]
[1]NU *The faith which you have—have*
23 [a]Titus 1:15
[1]M puts Rom. 16:25–27 here.

CHAPTER 15

1 [a][Gal. 6:1, 2]
[1]*weaknesses*
2 [a]1 Cor. 9:22; 10:24, 33
[1]*building up*
3 [a]Matt. 26:39
[b]Ps. 69:9
4 [a]1 Cor. 10:11
[1]*perseverance*
5 [a]1 Cor. 1:10
6 [a]Acts 4:24
7 [a]Rom. 14:1, 3
[b]Rom. 5:2
[1]NU, M *you*
8 [a]Matt. 15:24
[b]2 Cor. 1:20
[1]*minister*
9 [a]John 10:16
[b]2 Sam. 22:50; Ps. 18:49
10 [a]Deut. 32:43
11 [a]Ps. 117:1
12 [a]Is. 11:1, 10
13 [a]Rom. 12:12; 14:17
14 [a]2 Pet. 1:12
[b]1 Cor. 1:5; 8:1, 7, 10
[1]M *others*

14:22, 23 A conscience informed by faith is the best guide in matters that do not concern other people. If one violates his conscience informed by faith, he sins.

15:1 The mature in faith, with whom Paul theologically identifies, are here called **strong** and are exhorted to be patient regarding **the scruples of the weak.**

15:3 Christ is the supreme example of sacrificing personal rights and not pleasing **Himself.**

15:7 Paul addresses Jewish and Gentile Christians on their cultural differences regarding foods and festivals. Both are exhorted to mutual acceptance, just as both are accepted by Christ for **the glory of God.**

15:9–12 The OT had foreseen the unity of faith and joy of believing Jews and Gentiles joined in Christ (vv. 7–9).

15:14–16 Paul recognizes that his lengthy letter to Rome—a church he did not found—is bold in teaching and counsel. He seeks to soften possible offense by expressing confidence

(continued on next page)

15 Nevertheless, brethren, I have
written more boldly to you on *some*
points, as reminding you, [a]because
of the grace given to me by God,
16 that [a]I might be a minister of
Jesus Christ to the Gentiles, ministering the gospel of God, that the
[b]offering [1]of the Gentiles might be
acceptable, sanctified by the Holy
Spirit.†
17 Therefore I have reason to glory
in Christ Jesus [a]in the things *which*
pertain to God.
18 For I will not dare to speak of
any of those things [a]which Christ
has not accomplished through me,
in word and deed, [b]to make the Gentiles obedient—†
19 [a]in mighty signs and wonders,
by the power of the Spirit of God,
so that from Jerusalem and round
about to Illyricum I have fully
preached the gospel of Christ.
20 And so I have made it my aim
to preach the gospel, not where
Christ was named, [a]lest I should
build on another man's foundation,†
21 but as it is written:

[a]*"To whom He was not*
announced, they shall see;
And those who have not heard
shall understand."

Paul's Plan to Visit Rome

22 For this reason [a]I also have been
much hindered from coming to
you.
23 But now no longer having a
place in these parts, and [a]having a
great desire these many years to
come to you,
24 whenever I journey to Spain,
[1]I shall come to you. For I hope to
see you on my journey, [a]and to be
helped on my way there by you, if
first I may [b]enjoy your *company* for
a while.
25 But now [a]I am going to Jerusalem to [1]minister to the saints.
26 For [a]it pleased those from
Macedonia and Achaia to make
a certain contribution for the poor
among the saints who are in Jerusalem.
27 It pleased them indeed, and
they are their debtors. For [a]if the
Gentiles have been partakers of their
spiritual things, [b]their duty is also
to minister to them in material
things.†
28 Therefore, when I have performed this and have sealed to them
[a]this fruit, I shall go by way of you
to Spain.
29 [a]But I know that when I come
to you, I shall come in the fullness
of the blessing [1]of the gospel of
Christ.
30 Now I beg you, brethren,
through the Lord Jesus Christ, and
[a]through the love of the Spirit,
[b]that you strive together with me in
prayers to God for me,
31 [a]that I may be delivered from
those in Judea who [1]do not believe, and that [b]my service for Jerusalem may be acceptable to the
saints,
32 [a]that I may come to you with
joy [b]by the will of God, and may
[c]be refreshed together with you.

15 [a]Rom. 1:5; 12:3
16 [a]Rom. 11:13 [b][Is. 66:20] [1]Consisting of
17 [a]Heb. 2:17; 5:1
18 [a]Acts 15:12; 21:19 [b]Rom. 1:5
19 [a]Acts 19:11
20 [a][2 Cor. 10:13, 15, 16]
21 [a]Is. 52:15
22 [a]Rom. 1:13
23 [a]Acts 19:21; 23:11
24 [a]Acts 15:3 [b]Rom. 1:12 [1]NU omits *I shall come to you* and joins *Spain* with the next sentence.
25 [a]Acts 19:21 [1]*serve*
26 [a]1 Cor. 16:1
27 [a]Rom. 11:17 [b]1 Cor. 9:11
28 [a]Phil. 4:17
29 [a][Rom. 1:11] [1]NU omits *of the gospel*
30 [a]Phil. 2:1 [b]2 Cor. 1:11
31 [a]2 Tim. 3:11; 4:17 [b]2 Cor. 8:4 [1]*are disobedient*
32 [a]Rom. 1:10 [b]Acts 18:21 [c]1 Cor. 16:18

(continued from previous page)
in their own gifts and by referring to his special commission from God to be the Apostle to the Gentiles, including those in Rome (see 1:13–15).

15:16 Minister is literally "liturgist" (Gr. *leitourgos*); **ministering** is doing the work of a priest. **Offering** is the word that came to be used for the bread of the Eucharist (Gr. *prosphora*). **Sanctified by the Holy Spirit** is the action called for in the *epiclesis,* the invocation for the sending down of the Holy Spirit upon the eucharistic gifts of bread and wine.

15:18 The goal of preaching of the full gospel (v. 19), is to bring hearers to be **obedient** to God—the fulfillment of faith with righteous works.

15:20–24 Paul's missionary strategy was to preach the gospel in virgin territories, where the name of Christ had not been heard. He knew a church in Rome had long existed. **Spain** (v. 24), however, apparently was mostly unevangelized.

15:27 The Jewish Christians have passed on to the Gentiles the great gift of the gospel. The least the Gentiles can do in return is to share their **material things** with them.

Commemoration of the Departed

16:6–9: Paul's greetings remind us of the communion of all saints, living and departed.

33 Now [a]the God of peace *be* with
you all. Amen.

Paul's Personal Greetings

16 I commend to you Phoebe our
sister, who is a servant of the
church in [a]Cenchrea,†
2 [a]that you may receive her in the
Lord [b]in a manner worthy of the
saints, and assist her in whatever
business she has need of you; for indeed she has been a helper of many
and of myself also.
3 Greet [a]Priscilla and Aquila, my
fellow workers in Christ Jesus,†
4 who risked their own necks for
my life, to whom not only I give
thanks, but also all the churches of
the Gentiles.
5 Likewise *greet* [a]the church that
is in their house. Greet my beloved
Epaenetus, who is [b]the firstfruits of
[1]Achaia to Christ.
6 Greet Mary, who labored much
for us.
7 Greet Andronicus and Junia, my
countrymen and my fellow prisoners, who are of note among the
[a]apostles, who also [b]were in Christ
before me.†
8 Greet Amplias, my beloved in
the Lord.
9 Greet Urbanus, our fellow
worker in Christ, and Stachys, my
beloved.
10 Greet Apelles, approved in
Christ. Greet those who are of the
household of Aristobulus.
11 Greet Herodion, my [1]coun-
tryman. Greet those who are of the
household of Narcissus who are in the
Lord.
12 Greet Tryphena and Tryphosa,
who have labored in the Lord. Greet
the beloved Persis, who labored
much in the Lord.
13 Greet Rufus, [a]chosen in the
Lord, and his mother and mine.
14 Greet Asyncritus, Phlegon, Her-
mas, Patrobas, Hermes, and the
brethren who are with them.
15 Greet Philologus and Julia, Ne-
reus and his sister, and Olympas,
and all the saints who are with
them.
16 [a]Greet one another with a holy
kiss. [1]The churches of Christ greet
you.

Warning About Divisive Teachers

17 Now I urge you, brethren, note
those [a]who cause divisions and offenses, contrary to the doctrine

33 [a]1 Cor. 14:33
CHAPTER 16
1 [a]Acts 18:18
2 [a]Phil. 2:29 [b]Phil. 1:27
3 [a]Acts 18:2, 18, 26
5 [a]1 Cor. 16:19 [b]1 Cor. 16:15 [1]NU *Asia*
7 [a]Acts 1:13, 26 [b]Gal. 1:22
11 [1]Or *relative*
13 [a]2 John 1
16 [a]1 Cor. 16:20 [1]NU *All the churches*
17 [a][Acts 15:1]

16:1–16 How did Paul know so many people in Rome? Some conjecture that a copy of this letter was sent elsewhere and that our present letter contains the greetings to the people in that place. Many of the people mentioned are in the traditional list of the Seventy Apostles (see article, "The Seventy," at Luke 10), first sent out by the Lord (Luke 10:1, 17).

16:1, 2 Phoebe was a leading Christian woman of **the church in Cenchrea,** the point of Corinth on the Aegean Sea, who apparently was involved in missionary work.

16:3–5 Priscilla and Aquila were married Jewish business people and coworkers of Paul who had come to Corinth from Italy. Later they moved on with Paul to Ephesus, where they hosted the church in their house (see Acts 18:2, 18; 1 Cor. 16:19). They may have **risked their own necks** for Paul's life during the mob disturbance in Ephesus (Acts 19:26–41).

16:7 We know of no imprisonment of Paul in Corinth, where Romans was probably written. It is likely he was imprisoned in Ephesus for a time; perhaps **Andronicus and Junia** were his **fellow prisoners** there.

which you learned, and [b]avoid
them.†
18 For those who are such do not
serve our Lord [1]Jesus Christ, but
[a]their own belly, and [b]by smooth
words and flattering speech deceive
the hearts of the simple.
19 For [a]your obedience has become
known to all. Therefore I am glad
on your behalf; but I want you to
be [b]wise in what is good, and
[1]simple concerning evil.†
20 And [a]the God of peace [b]will
crush Satan under your feet shortly.
[c]The grace of our Lord Jesus Christ
be with you. Amen.

Greetings from Paul's Friends

21 [a]Timothy, my fellow worker,
and [b]Lucius, [c]Jason, and [d]Sosipater,
my countrymen, greet you.
22 I, Tertius, who wrote *this* epistle, greet you in the Lord.†
23 [a]Gaius, my host and *the host* of
the whole church, greets you.
[b]Erastus, the treasurer of the city,
greets you, and Quartus, a brother.
24 [a]The[1] grace of our Lord Jesus
Christ *be* with you all. Amen.

Benediction

25 [1]Now [a]to Him who is able to establish you [b]according to my gospel
and the preaching of Jesus Christ,
[c]according to the revelation of the
mystery [d]kept secret since the world
began†
26 but [a]now made manifest, and
by the prophetic Scriptures made
known to all nations, according to
the commandment of the everlasting God, for [b]obedience to the
faith—†
27 to [a]God, alone wise, *be* glory
through Jesus Christ forever.
Amen.†

17 [b][1 Cor. 5:9]
18 [a]Phil. 3:19 [b]Col. 2:4 [1]NU, M omit *Jesus*
19 [a]Rom. 1:8 [b]Matt. 10:16 [1]*innocent*
20 [a]Rom. 15:33 [b]Gen. 3:15 [c]1 Cor. 16:23
21 [a]Acts 16:1 [b]Acts 13:1 [c]Acts 17:5 [d]Acts 20:4
23 [a]1 Cor. 1:14 [b]Acts 19:22
24 [a]1 Thess. 5:28 [1]NU omits v. 24.
25 [a][Eph. 3:20] [b]Rom. 2:16 [c]Eph. 1:9 [d]Col. 1:26; 2:2; 4:3 [1]M puts Rom. 16:25–27 after Rom. 14:23.
26 [a]Eph. 1:9 [b]Rom. 1:5 **27** [a]Jude 25

16:17, 18 Divisions caused by those who serve **their own belly** (v. 18) is perhaps the same problem as in 14:1–23, only in this case involving Jewish Christians who insisted on the necessity of eating kosher foods and observing Jewish festivals. **Simple** here (Gr. *akakos*) does not mean stupid, but innocent of evil, guileless, trusting.

16:19 Simple here (Gr. *akeraios*) means "innocent" or "pure."

16:22 Paul apparently used a scribe, or secretary, in the composition of many of his letters (see also 1 Cor. 16:21; Gal. 6:11; Col. 4:18; 2 Thess. 2:17; Philem. 19).

16:25–27 This letter seems to have multiple conclusions (15:33; 16:20, 24, 27). Dismissals in Orthodox services are patterned after scriptural benedictions such as this one by Paul.

16:25 Paul uses **mystery,** a word also found both in Jewish apocalyptic literature and in other religions, to designate God's plan of salvation revealed in Jesus Christ.

16:26 Obedience to the faith includes both surrender of the will to God and acceptance of apostolic doctrine. It is therefore significant that before the Eucharist in the Orthodox Church, the Nicene Creed is recited by all, showing that all have the same faith in God the Father, His Son our Lord Jesus Christ, the Holy Spirit, and the Church.

16:27 Forever is literally "unto ages of ages"—a frequent refrain in Orthodox liturgy.

The First Epistle of Paul the Apostle to the

CORINTHIANS

Author: *St. Paul the Apostle*

Date: *c.* A.D. *55*

Theme: *Communion with God vs. Communion with Darkness*

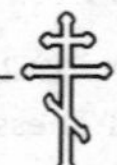
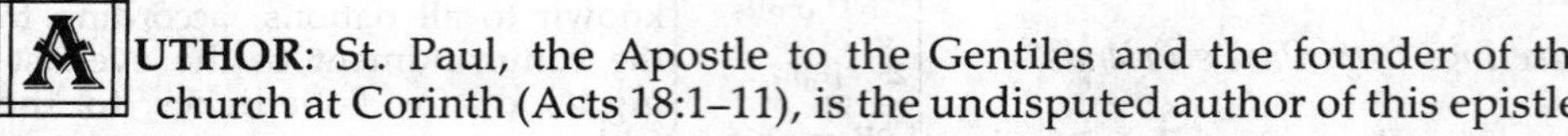

AUTHOR: St. Paul, the Apostle to the Gentiles and the founder of the church at Corinth (Acts 18:1–11), is the undisputed author of this epistle.

DATE: First Corinthians was probably written from Ephesus around A.D. 55, during Paul's third missionary journey (Acts 19:1—20:1).

MAJOR THEME: *Communion with God vs. communion with darkness.* We are created for communion (Gr. *koinonia*) with God and with each other. *Koinonia* is concretely experienced in the life of the Church, which is the body of Christ and the temple of the Holy Spirit. But communion is not automatic; we pursue it. And while we may cooperate with evil, we are created to cooperate with God and with each other.

The subthemes of this epistle are found in the sections Paul writes to answer specific problems or concerns in the church: (1) factionalism (1:10—3:23); (2) civil lawsuits (4:1–21; 6:1–8); (3) sexual immorality (5:1–13; 6:9—7:40); (4) meat sacrificed to idols (8:1—9:27); (5) eucharistic theology and practice (10:1—11:34); (6) spiritual gifts (12:1—14:40); and (7) resurrection life (15:1—16:24).

BACKGROUND INFORMATION: (1) *The problems at Corinth.* There were a number of problems in the Corinthian church to which Paul responds in this letter. These problems include:

(a) *Church disunity.* Many Corinthian Christians had broken into several factions based on improper loyalty to particular Christian leaders (1:12). These factions included: (1) followers of Paul, the founder of the church at Corinth (3:10; 4:15; Acts 18:1–19); (2) followers of Apollos, a master rhetorician and expositor of Scripture, who had preached at Corinth (Acts 18:24–28); (3) followers of Peter (Cephas), the chief of the Apostles; and (4) those who simply claimed to be "of Christ."

(b) *Doctrinal speculations.* Erroneous teaching thrived in Corinth. Some have thought there was an organized theological clique in the church, the "Christ Party" (from 1:12), which taught the "true Jesus," the "true gospel" (2 Cor. 11:4), in a gnostic manner. Components of this error were: (1) The true gospel is known only by certain Christians through "spiritual" means, of which the apostles are ignorant; therefore the apostles are not to be heeded (chs. 1—4). The "spiritual" people are in charge. (2) Gaining this "spiritual knowledge" is the way to spiritual growth (3:18–23; 8:1–3, 10, 11; 13:2). (3) True freedom is release from all moral and corporate restraints. "All things are lawful for me" (6:12; 10:23) is probably a slogan of the "Christ Party." (4) The primary sign of one's spirituality is the possession of spiritual gifts (chs. 12—14). (5) The body cannot enter into the age to come, as in the Jewish and Christian notion of bodily resurrection. Thus the body is insignificant now (6:12–20; 9:24–27) and forever.

(c) *Moral failure.* The Corinthian church, free from persecution, became spiritually weak and succumbed to the moral failure for which the city was famous. A verb had even been coined, to "Corinthize," meaning to be immoral (with drunken carousing). Greed, sexual lust, drunkenness, polytheism, Hellenistic free thought, and divisiveness were accepted even by some "Christians."

(d) *Dealing with pagan religions.* Christians in Corinth could not agree about how to respond to idolatry. Some were offended by the seemingly shallow treatment of idolatry by others. These in turn belittled what seemed to them as superstition on the part of the former. Christians did not just have different opinions; they were insulting one another.

(e) *Self-centeredness and spiritual gifts.* Corinth was brilliantly endowed with spiritual gifts, perhaps as the Holy Spirit's counter to the hedonism there. But the self-centeredness of the gifted ones brought dishonor to God.

(2) *Paul's answer to the problems at Corinth.* Seeing that Corinth's problems derived from incomplete and distorted understandings of the Church and the Kingdom, Paul shows that *everything*—both life within the Church and life in general—is sacramental, an offering to God. Even now, in this life, everything must begin to conform to the standards of the Kingdom of God. The Christian community, therefore, must be a Church that is (1) one (chs. 1—4), (2) holy (chs. 5; 6), (3) catholic (chs. 7—14), and (4) apostolic (ch. 15, as well as chs. 3; 4).

Paul touches on many other important theological issues while solving the problems in Corinth, such as the sanctification of the body, the supremacy of love, and the resurrection of the body.

(3) *Paul's steps toward a solution at Corinth.* Paul took a number of steps toward reestablishing the Corinthian church on a firm foundation:

(a) At Ephesus on his third missionary journey (Acts 19:1—20:1), Paul heard of the immorality of the Corinthian church and wrote a letter, now lost, espousing Christian morality and Church discipline (5:9–11).

(b) Paul received two more negative reports from Corinth, sent Timothy there (4:17; 16:10, 11) and wrote another letter, 1 Corinthians. Chapters 1—6 reply to the first report (1:11); chapters 7—16 reply to the second report (7:1).

(c) Paul learned of further immorality in Corinth and the defiance of his apostolic authority. He traveled there, perhaps unexpectedly (the "sorrowful" visit, 2 Cor. 2:1; 12:21—13:2), and exhorted them.

(d) Returning to Ephesus, Paul wrote a third letter (the "sorrowful" letter, 2 Cor. 2:4–11; 7:8), also lost, which was hand-delivered by Titus (2 Cor. 7:6, 7, 13–15).

(e) Titus and Paul later met while Paul was on his way back to Corinth (2 Cor. 2:12, 13; 7:5, 6). Titus reported the church had obeyed Paul (2 Cor. 2:9; 7:15), but a minority still attacked his authority, claiming other leaders.

(f) Paul wrote a fourth letter, our 2 Corinthians (c. A.D. 57), to defend his apostleship, and to request alms for the Jerusalem church.

OUTLINE

Introduction	1:1–9
A. Greeting	1:1–3
B. Thanksgiving for spiritual gifts	1:4–9
I. Response to reports received	1:10—6:20
A. The Church is one	1:10—4:21
1. The report	1:10–12
2. Unity and baptism	1:13–16
3. Unity and doctrine	1:17—3:4
a. Crucified in Christ: Baptism	1:17—2:5
b. Taught by the Spirit: Chrismation	2:6—3:4
4. Unity and the Church	3:5—4:16
5. Paul answers his Corinthian critics	4:17–21
B. The Church is holy	5:1—6:20
1. The Church is pure	5:1–13
2. The Church has discernment	6:1–11
3. The Church is the temple of the Holy Spirit	6:12–20
II. Response to questions asked	7:1—15:58
A. The Church is catholic	7:1—14:40
1. Questions about marriage and virginity	7:1–40
2. Questions about food offered to idols	8:1—11:1
a. The balance between knowledge and love	8:1–13
b. A superb example: Paul's graciousness	9:1–27
c. A bad example: Israel's apostasy	10:1–13
d. All worship is sacramental	10:14–22
e. Offend no man, glorify God	10:23—11:1
3. Questions about corporate worship	11:2—14:40
a. Conduct of women	11:2–16
b. Unity of the Eucharist	11:17–34
c. Spiritual gifts in worship	12:1—14:40
B. The Church is apostolic: The Resurrection	15:1–58
1. The importance of the Resurrection	15:1–34
2. The manner of the Resurrection	15:35–58
Conclusion	16:1–24
A. Collection for the Jerusalem church	16:1–4
B. Paul's plans	16:5–12
C. Exhortations, greetings and benediction	16:13–24

Greeting

1 Paul, [a]called *to be* an apostle of
Jesus Christ [b]through the will of
God, and [c]Sosthenes *our* brother,†

2 To the church of God which is
at Corinth, to those who [a]are
[1]sanctified in Christ Jesus, [b]called *to*
be saints, with all who in every place
call on the name of Jesus Christ
[c]our Lord, [d]both theirs and ours:†

Thanksgiving for God's Grace at Corinth

3 [a]Grace to you and peace from
God our Father and the Lord Jesus
Christ.†

4 [a]I thank my God always concerning you for the grace of God
which was given to you by Christ
Jesus,†
5 that you were enriched in every
thing by Him [a]in all [1]utterance and
all knowledge,
6 even as [a]the testimony of Christ
was confirmed [1]in you,
7 so that you come short in no
gift, eagerly [a]waiting for the revelation of our Lord Jesus Christ,†
8 [a]who will also confirm you to
the end, [b]*that you may be* blameless in the day of our Lord Jesus
Christ.
9 [a]God *is* faithful, by whom you
were called into [b]the fellowship of
His Son, Jesus Christ our Lord.

Reported Contentiousness in the Church

10 Now I plead with you, brethren,
by the name of our Lord Jesus Christ,
[a]that you all [1]speak the same thing,
and *that* there be no [2]divisions
among you, but *that* you be perfectly
joined together in the same mind
and in the same judgment.†
11 For it has been declared to me
concerning you, my brethren, by
those of Chloe's *household*, that there
are [1]contentions among you.†
12 Now I say this, that [a]each of you
says, "I am of Paul," or "I am of
[b]Apollos," or "I am of [c]Cephas," or
"I am of Christ."†

CHAPTER 1
1 [a]Rom. 1:1 [b]2 Cor. 1:1 [c]Acts 18:17
2 [a][Acts 15:9] [b]Rom. 1:7 [c][1 Cor. 8:6] [d][Rom. 3:22] [1]*set apart*
3 [a]Rom. 1:7
4 [a]Rom. 1:8
5 [a][1 Cor. 12:8] [1]*speech*
6 [a]2 Tim. 1:8 [1]Or *among*
7 [a]Phil. 3:20
8 [a]1 Thess. 3:13; 5:23 [b]Col. 1:22; 2:7
9 [a]Is. 49:7 [b][John 15:4]
10 [a]2 Cor. 13:11 [1]Have a uniform testimony [2]*schisms* or *dissensions*
11 [1]*quarrels*
12 [a]1 Cor. 3:4 [b]Acts 18:24 [c]John 1:42

1:1 Since Paul is **called to be an apostle** by **the will of God,** men cannot remove him as some were trying to do. A **Sosthenes** is also mentioned in Acts 18:17 as the ruler of the synagogue at Corinth. Probably this is he: there are stories of his spectacular conversion in early records, which also report that Sosthenes became bishop of Caesarea.

1:2 Despite disorder, disunity and error among the Corinthians, the Apostle still calls them **the church of God, sanctified in Christ,** and **saints,** those set apart to God. Baptized into Christ, united with Him, this church by His mercy is one with the faithful everywhere.

1:3 **Grace** is God's unlimited, unconditional, uncreated love, freely given to those who do not deserve it. **Peace** is our reconciliation with God and with each other. "Peace to you," found repeatedly in the OT, is the common everyday greeting then and now throughout the Middle East. "Peace be to you" in the Orthodox Divine Liturgy is connected to the reading of the gospel, the kiss of peace, and the Lord's Prayer. Jesus gave to the disciples the gift of *peace,* which is the presence of the Holy Spirit (John 14:27; 20:19).

1:4–9 Though he will later rebuke this church severely, Paul's assurance concerning their gifts and calling is sincere. For God's grace is given to the Church in every place, even in Corinth.

1:4 Nothing is so acceptable to God as our thankfulness for His grace, both to us and to others.

1:7 **Revelation** implies that although He is not seen, yet the **Lord Jesus Christ** is present even now, and then shall appear in glory. The Second Coming of Christ is a main point in Paul's teaching, for then our salvation will be clearly revealed and fully known.

1:10 Here for the first time Paul rebukes the Corinthians, pleading with them in the name of the Lord to put away **divisions** and maintain unity in the church.

1:11 Chloe was a prominent woman who hosted the Corinthian church in her home and who faithfully reported these **contentions** to Paul.

1:12 **Apollos** was a learned Jew from Alexandria, Egypt, "mighty in the Scriptures" (Acts

(continued on next page)

The Exaltation of the Holy Cross *September 14*

1:18–24: The message of the Cross is foolishness to the world, but to Christians it is the power of God.

The Sacrament of Unity: Baptism

13 [a]Is Christ divided? Was Paul crucified for you? Or were you baptized in the name of Paul?†
14 I thank God that I baptized [a]none of you except [b]Crispus and [c]Gaius,†
15 lest anyone should say that I had baptized in my own name.†
16 Yes, I also baptized the household of [a]Stephanas. Besides, I do not know whether I baptized any other.

The Message of Unity: Exaltation of the Cross

17 For Christ did not send me to baptize, but to preach the gospel, [a]not with wisdom of words, lest the cross of Christ should be made of no effect.†
18 For the [1]message of the cross is [a]foolishness to [b]those who are perishing, but to us [c]who are being saved it is the [d]power of God.†
19 For it is written:

[a]*"I will destroy the wisdom of the wise,*
And bring to nothing the understanding of the prudent."

20 [a]Where *is* the wise? Where *is* the scribe? Where *is* the [1]disputer of this age? [b]Has not God made foolish the wisdom of this world?
21 For since, in the [a]wisdom of God, the world through wisdom did

13 [a]2 Cor. 11:4
14 [a]John 4:2 [b]Acts 18:8 [c]Rom. 16:23
16 [a]1 Cor. 16:15, 17
17 [a][1 Cor. 2:1, 4, 13]
18 [a]1 Cor. 2:14 [b]2 Cor. 2:15 [c][1 Cor. 15:2] [d]Rom. 1:16 [1]Lit. *word*
19 [a]Is. 29:14
20 [a]Is. 19:12; 33:18 [b]Job 12:17 [1]*debater*
21 [a]Dan. 2:20

(continued from previous page)
18:24). Originally a follower of "the baptism of John" (Acts 18:25), he was taught more fully about Christ by Priscilla and Aquila at Ephesus, and he later preached at Corinth where some saw him as a rival to Paul. Tradition tells us Apollos became the first bishop of Crete (see Titus 3:13). Paul makes it plain that he and Apollos are partners in apostolic work and that Apollos would not approve of the factionalism in Corinth (3:4–6; 4:6; 16:12).

1:13 Is Christ divided? Or is the Church? The answer to all questions in this passage is *no*. One can leave the Church, but not divide it! Factionalism, however, brings great harm to the Church, for it seeks to give to the apostle a place which only Christ should occupy (vv. 13–17). Many looked upon the apostles as teachers of philosophy rather than preachers of the Cross (1:18—2:5). The factious do not accept true wisdom, which is bestowed by the Spirit (2:6—3:4), and they misrepresent the apostles as rivals to each other rather than as fellow workers with Christ (3:5–23).

1:14 Crispus had been the ruler of the synagogue at Corinth (Acts 18:8). Converted through the preaching of Paul, then baptized, he was apparently succeeded as ruler by Sosthenes (Acts 18:17). **Gaius** was a resident of Corinth, with whom Paul was staying when he wrote the Epistle to the Romans (Rom. 16:23). The third epistle of John (see 3 John 1) seems to have been directed to this same Gaius.

1:15–17 Paul's denial does not degrade baptism; he is simply emphasizing the baptizing is not his primary role. As an apostle, Paul's primary job is to **preach the gospel** (v. 17), teaching those seeking God to be baptized. The one who performs a baptism is God's instrument; the convert's loyalty must be to God alone.

1:17–25 Wisdom of words (v. 17) refers especially to philosophical thought and rhetorical devices. Such human wisdom by itself does not promote salvation or an understanding of how God works in the world and what He wishes us to do.

1:18 Why is the **message of the cross** . . . **foolishness** to unbelievers? St. John Chrysostom answers that "it is a mark of them that perish not to recognize the things which lead to salvation." We who bear witness to Christ must not be discouraged when those outside of Him mock, for so did once even Paul himself. **Being saved,** present tense, refers to the process by which the Cross transforms us with the **power of God.**

not know God, it pleased God
through the foolishness of the message preached to save those who
believe.
22 For [a]Jews request a sign, and
Greeks seek after wisdom;†
23 but we preach Christ crucified,
[a]to the Jews a [1]stumbling block and
to the [2]Greeks [b]foolishness,
24 but to those who are called, both
Jews and Greeks, Christ [a]the power
of God and [b]the wisdom of
God.†
25 Because the foolishness of God
is wiser than men, and the weakness
of God is stronger than men.
26 For [1]you see your calling, brethren, [a]that not many wise according
to the flesh, not many mighty, not
many [2]noble, *are called*.
27 But [a]God has chosen the foolish
things of the world to put to shame
the wise, and God has chosen the
weak things of the world to put
to shame the things which are
mighty;
28 and the [1]base things of the
world and the things which are despised God has chosen, and the
things which are not, to bring to
nothing the things that are,†
29 that no flesh should glory in His
presence.
30 But of Him you are in Christ
Jesus, who became for us wisdom
from God—and [a]righteousness and
sanctification and redemption—

22 [a]Matt. 12:38
23 [a]Luke 2:34 [b][1 Cor. 2:14] [1]Gr. *skandalon, offense* [2]NU *Gentiles*
24 [a][Rom. 1:4] [b]Col. 2:3
26 [a]John 7:48 [1]*consider* [2]*well-born*
27 [a]Matt. 11:25
28 [1]*insignificant* or *lowly*
30 [a][2 Cor. 5:21]
31 [a]Jer. 9:23, 24

CHAPTER 2

1 [1]NU *mystery*
2 [a]Gal. 6:14
3 [a]Acts 18:1 [b][2 Cor. 4:7]
4 [a]2 Pet. 1:16 [b]Rom. 15:19 [1]NU omits *human*
5 [a]1 Thess. 1:5
7 [1]*predetermined*
8 [a]Luke 23:34 [b]Matt. 27:33–50

31 that, as it is written, [a]*"He who
glories, let him glory in the* L*ORD*."
2 And I, brethren, when I came to
you, did not come with excellence of speech or of wisdom declaring to you the [1]testimony of
God.
2 For I determined not to know
anything among you [a]except Jesus
Christ and Him crucified.
3 [a]I was with you [b]in weakness,
in fear, and in much trembling.
4 And my speech and my preaching [a]*were* not with persuasive words
of [1]human wisdom, [b]but in demonstration of the Spirit and of power,†
5 that your faith should not be in
the wisdom of men but in the
[a]power of God.

Understanding Unity: Wisdom of the Spirit

6 However, we speak wisdom
among those who are mature, yet
not the wisdom of this age, nor of
the rulers of this age, who are coming to nothing.†
7 But we speak the wisdom of
God in a mystery, the hidden *wisdom*
which God [1]ordained before the ages
for our glory,
8 which none of the rulers of this
age knew; for [a]had they known, they
would not have [b]crucified the Lord
of glory.†

1:22 To those who **request a sign,** the Church offers one: the Cross! The Cross is to be adored, for wherever the sign may be, there Jesus will be.

1:24 Since **Christ** is the **power** and **wisdom** of **God** the Father—the brightness of the Father's glory (Heb. 1:3), the substantial and perfect image of the invisible God—where He is, there is the uncreated and saving grace of God. His Cross restores man to immortality and stirs up desire for the things of heaven.

1:28 The base things of the world are "those persons who are considered to be nothing because of their great insignificance" (St. John Chrysostom). There is no such thing as a "no-account" Christian (v. 27; 2 Cor. 12:9).

2:4, 5 Great preaching is not with "swelling words" (2 Pet. 2:18) but with (1) the anointing of the Holy **Spirit** and (2) the dynamic of God's **power.**

2:6, 7 The **mature** (Gr. *teleioi*) are the "spiritual" (Gr. *pneumatikoi*) of v. 15. **Mystery** here is the gospel of the Kingdom (see Rom. 16:25; Eph. 3:3, 4, 9; 6:19; Col. 4:3; 1 Tim. 3:9, 16), which neither angels nor any other creature knew before it was revealed by Christ, even though the Incarnation of the Son was God's plan from eternity for transforming creation. Moreover, that gospel is hidden from those who perish (2 Cor. 4:3). Those who will not believe do not grasp what is clear to the faithful.

2:8 The **Lord of glory** demonstrates that the dignity and honor of Jesus is that of God the Father Himself (Ex. 24:16–18). The incarnate Son of God, who clothes Himself "with

(continued on next page)

9 But as it is written:

[a]*"Eye has not seen, nor ear heard,*
Nor have entered into the heart
of man
The things which God has
prepared for those who love
Him."†

10 But [a]God has revealed *them* to
us through His Spirit. For the Spirit
searches all things, yes, the deep
things of God.†
11 For what man knows the things
of a man except the [a]spirit of the man
which is in him? [b]Even so no one
knows the things of God except the
Spirit of God.
12 Now we have received, not the
spirit of the world, but [a]the Spirit
who is from God, that we might
know the things that have been
freely given to us by God.†
13 These things we also speak, not
in words which man's wisdom
teaches but which the [1]Holy Spirit
teaches, comparing spiritual things
with spiritual.
14 [a]But the natural man does not
receive the things of the Spirit of
God, for they are foolishness to him;
nor can he know *them,* because they
are spiritually discerned.
15 But he who is spiritual judges
all things, yet he himself is *rightly*
judged by no one.
16 For [a]*"who has known the mind*
of the L*ORD* *that he may instruct*
Him?" [b]But we have the mind of
Christ.†

3 And I, brethren, could not speak
to you as to spiritual *people* but
as to carnal, as to [a]babes in Christ.†
2 I fed you with [a]milk and not
with solid food; [b]for until now you
were not able *to receive it,* and even
now you are still not able;
3 for you are still carnal. For
where *there are* envy, strife, and divisions among you, are you not carnal
and [1]behaving like *mere* men?
4 For when one says, "I am of

9 [a][Is. 64:4; 65:17]
10 [a]Matt. 11:25; 13:11; 16:17; [Gal. 1:12; Eph. 3:3, 5]
11 [a]Job 32:8; Eccl. 12:7; [1 Cor. 6:20; James 2:26] [b]Rom. 11:33
12 [a][Rom. 8:15]
13 [1]NU omits *Holy*
14 [a]Matt. 16:23
16 [a]Job 15:8; Is. 40:13; Rom. 11:34 [b][John 15:15]

CHAPTER 3

1 [a]1 Cor. 2:6; Eph. 4:14; Heb. 5:13
2 [a]Heb. 5:12; 1 Pet. 2:2 [b]John 16:12
3 [1]Lit. *walking according to man*

(continued from previous page)
light as with a garment" (Ps. 104:2), stood naked before human judges, receiving blows from hands which He had formed. The Lord of Glory, the Son of the Father, was crucified in His humanity (Acts 2:36). They crucified God!

2:9 Paul seems to have collected phrases from several passages (Is. 52:15; 64:4; 65:17; Jer. 3:16; Sir. 1:10), though this may have come from an early hymn.

2:10—3:4 We come to know God's wisdom through the Holy Spirit, for the Holy Spirit **knows the things of God** (v. 11), just as **the spirit of the man** knows what is in man. Note Paul's threefold classification of humanity:

(1) The **natural man** (v. 14; lit. "soulish") is one not yet joined to Christ, unenlightened and unregenerate. For such people, divine **things** appear to be **foolishness** because they inquire into divine things by human and natural reasoning, rather than receiving these by faith.

(2) The **spiritual** man (v. 15) is filled with the Holy Spirit given at chrismation, and is maturing in his knowledge of Christ.

(3) The **carnal** man (fleshly; 3:1) is the person who, while in the Church, has his mind set on earthly things, still trying to satisfy personal wants and selfish desires.

We reveal our spiritual condition by our relationships with other Christians. The lesson is plain: Growth in our fellowship with God demands living in the overcoming strength of the Holy Spirit, who brings unity to the Church and great victory over petty, egocentric squabblings.

2:12–15 Enlightenment from God in itself is beyond all words, and even beyond evaluation by other men (v. 15). Nevertheless, the Holy Spirit speaks through spiritual people words that truly reflect the unspeakable knowledge of faith. This language of faith in turn leads spiritually minded people to know God better, although it baffles the **natural man** (v. 14).

2:16 The **mind of Christ** is enlightenment by the Holy Spirit (v. 10). He brings those chrismated into communion with Christ and others of like mind in His body, the Church. The *mind of Christ,* then, is not private but is given to all: it is the mind of the Church.

3:1–4 Note the gospel was first communicated through the spoken word of the apostles. Since God inspires both oral (apostolic preaching) and written (scriptural) communication of His Word, oral and written Tradition form a seamless whole.

Paul," and another, "I *am* of Apollos," are you not carnal?

Wisdom in the Apostolic Ministry

5 Who then is Paul, and who *is*
Apollos, but [a]ministers through
whom you believed, as the Lord
gave to each one?
6 [a]I planted, [b]Apollos watered,
[c]but God gave the increase.†
7 So then [a]neither he who plants
is anything, nor he who waters, but
God who gives the increase.
8 Now he who plants and he who
waters are one, [a]and each one will
receive his own reward according to
his own labor.
9 For [a]we are God's fellow workers; you are God's field, *you are*
[b]God's building.†
10 [a]According to the grace of God
which was given to me, as a wise
master builder I have laid [b]the foundation, and another builds on it. But
let each one take heed how he builds
on it.
11 For no other foundation can
anyone lay than [a]that which is laid,
[b]which is Jesus Christ.
12 Now if anyone builds on this
foundation *with* gold, silver, precious
stones, wood, hay, straw,
13 each one's work will become
clear; for the Day [a]will declare it, because [b]it will be revealed by fire; and

5 [a]2 Cor. 3:3, 6; 4:1; 5:18; 6:4
6 [a]Acts 18:4 [b]Acts 18:24–27 [c][2 Cor. 3:5]
7 [a][Gal. 6:3]
8 [a]Ps. 62:12
9 [a]2 Cor. 6:1 [b][Eph. 2:20–22]
10 [a]Rom. 1:5 [b]1 Cor. 4:15
11 [a]Is. 28:16 [b]Eph. 2:20
13 [a]1 Pet. 1:7 [b]Luke 2:35
16 [a]2 Cor. 6:16
17 [1]*destroys*
18 [a]Prov. 3:7
19 [a]Job 5:13
20 [a]Ps. 94:11
21 [a][2 Cor. 4:5]
23 [a]2 Cor. 10:7

the fire will test each one's work, of
what sort it is.
14 If anyone's work which he has
built on *it* endures, he will receive a
reward.
15 If anyone's work is burned, he
will suffer loss; but he himself will
be saved, yet so as through fire.
16 [a]Do you not know that you are
the temple of God and *that* the Spirit
of God dwells in you?
17 If anyone [1]defiles the temple of
God, God will destroy him. For the
temple of God is holy, which *temple*
you are.

Wisdom in Christ's Church

18 [a]Let no one deceive himself.
If anyone among you seems to
be wise in this age, let him become a fool that he may become
wise.†
19 For the wisdom of this world is
foolishness with God. For it is written, [a]*"He catches the wise in their*
own craftiness";
20 and again, [a]*"The LORD knows*
the thoughts of the wise, that they
are futile."
21 Therefore let no one boast in
men. For [a]all things are yours:†
22 whether Paul or Apollos or Cephas, or the world or life or death,
or things present or things to come—
all are yours.
23 And [a]you *are* Christ's, and
Christ *is* God's.

3:6–17 The Church is an organic whole: (1) it is **planted** (vv. 6–9), (2) a **building** (vv. 9–11), (3) a **temple** (vv. 16, 17). In vv. 16, 17 **you** is plural and refers to the whole Church. One who would break this unity would desecrate a sacred place.

3:9 Fellow workers (Gr. *synergoi*) is the biblical concept of synergism, shown here by how the Apostles work together with God in carrying out the ministry. So too, we as God's fellow workers cooperate with Him to do His will. By this cooperation or synergy with God, we do not mean a working together of equals, or a so-called fifty-fifty arrangement. Rather we mean that He is the Lord, and we His servants are called to participate obediently in His work.

3:18–20 The **wisdom of this world** (v. 19) is attractive and reasonable, and on the surface appears to be true. But such earthly wisdom denies God and leads us away from Him—not to fulfillment, but to death. True wisdom and life are found only in Christ, in our total abandonment to the love of God and neighbor.

3:21–23 Yours and **you** here are plural. They refer not to the individual but to the corporate Church. The Church possesses the whole, **all things,** because the Church is the body of Christ—His perfect and glorified humanity—and Christ is God. Individual opinion in doctrine and private interpretation of Scripture which stand apart from that of the Church, or outside of apostolic tradition, are marks of worldly wisdom.

Wisdom in Spiritual Fatherhood

4 Let a man so consider us, as
[a]servants of Christ [b]and stewards of the mysteries of God.
2 Moreover it is required in stewards that one be found faithful.
3 But with me it is a very small
thing that I should be judged by you
or by a human [1]court. In fact, I do
not even judge myself.†
4 For I know of nothing against
myself, yet I am not justified by
this; but He who judges me is the
Lord.
5 [a]Therefore judge nothing before
the time, until the Lord comes, who
will both bring to [b]light the hidden
things of darkness and [c]reveal the
[1]counsels of the hearts. [d]Then each
one's praise will come from God.
6 Now these things, brethren, I
have figuratively transferred to myself and Apollos for your sakes, that
you may learn in us not to think beyond what is written, that none of
you may be [1]puffed up on behalf of
one against the other.†
7 For who [1]makes you differ *from
another?* And [a]what do you have that
you did not receive? Now if you did
indeed receive *it,* why do you boast
as if you had not received *it?*†
8 You are already full! [a]You are
already rich! You have reigned as
kings without us—and indeed I
could wish you did reign, that we
also might reign with you!
9 For I think that God has displayed us, the apostles, last, as men
condemned to death; for we have
been made a [a]spectacle[1] to the
world, both to angels and to men.
10 We *are* [a]fools for Christ's sake,
but you *are* wise in Christ! [b]We
are weak, but you *are* strong! You
are distinguished, but we *are* dishonored!†
11 To the present hour we both
hunger and thirst, and we are poorly
clothed, and beaten, and homeless.
12 [a]And we labor, working with
our own hands. [b]Being reviled, we
bless; being persecuted, we endure;†
13 being defamed, we [1]entreat.
[a]We have been made as the filth of
the world, the offscouring of all
things until now.

Appeal and Warning

14 I do not write these things to
shame you, but [a]as my beloved children I warn *you.*†
15 For though you might have ten
thousand instructors in Christ, yet
you do not *have* many fathers; for

CHAPTER 4
1 [a]Col. 1:25 [b]Titus 1:7
3 [1]Lit. *day*
5 [a]Matt. 7:1 [b]Matt. 10:26 [c]1 Cor. 3:13 [d]Rom. 2:29 [1]*motives*
6 [1]*arrogant*
7 [a]John 3:27 [1]*distinguishes you*
8 [a]Rev. 3:17
9 [a]Heb. 10:33 [1]Lit. *theater*
10 [a]Acts 17:18; 26:24 [b]2 Cor. 13:9
12 [a]Acts 18:3; 20:34 [b]Matt. 5:44
13 [a]Lam. 3:45 [1]*exhort, encourage*
14 [a]1 Thess. 2:11

4:3 Here, as in 2:15, **judge** (Gr. *anakrinein*) is difficult to render in English. *Anakrinein* is comparable to the investigation that takes place before and during a trial, and preceding judgment; *krinein* (v. 5; Matt. 7:1), to rendering of a verdict. Many Corinthians prejudged Paul as an unfaithful steward; some denied his apostolic authority (see Introduction to 2 Corinthians). For Paul it is improper for them, or even for himself, to prejudge his life, for Christ is the Judge.

4:6 In the expression, **beyond what is written,** most likely Paul refers to the whole OT, reminding the Corinthians that all Scripture urges us not to be proud or contentious. **Puffed up** in Greek suggests the swollen inflammation around an infected wound, and may be rendered "arrogant" (vv. 18, 19; 5:2).

4:7 Paul directs a series of sharp questions to the Corinthians to deflate their pride. Nothing justifies thinking ourselves better or above anyone else.

4:10 Irony and sarcasm are bitter medicine, and Paul uses them here (vv. 8–13) with full force. The three parallel statements **we are fools, we are weak, we are dishonored** are heaped upon each other in a stinging series. The relative comfort of the Corinthian Christians is contrasted with the persecuted, poverty-stricken and uncertain life of the apostles (vv. 11–13; see Mark 6:4; 9:35; 10:31).

4:12, 13 The apostles have endured all kinds of humiliation, being treated as **filth,** and instead of fighting back have responded with love toward their persecutors—all for the joy of serving Christ and reconciling the world to God.

4:14–16 Paul soothes the soreness of his rebuke by reminding them of his fatherhood (see the note on Matt. 23:9, 10). As in a family, so in the Church, maturing children need parental guidance. The Apostle to the Gentiles—thus to most Christians—writes **imitate me** because he imitates Christ (11:1).

Matins of Holy Saturday *Saturday before Easter*
5:6–8: Christ, our Passover, has been sacrificed for us.

[a]in Christ Jesus I have begotten you
through the gospel.
16 Therefore I urge you, [a]imitate
me.
17 For this reason I have sent
[a]Timothy to you, [b]who is my beloved and faithful son in the Lord,
who will [c]remind you of my ways
in Christ, as I [d]teach everywhere
[e]in every church.
18 [a]Now some are [1]puffed up, as
though I were not coming to you.†
19 [a]But I will come to you shortly,
[b]if the Lord wills, and I will know,
not the word of those who are puffed
up, but the power.
20 For [a]the kingdom of God *is* not
in word but in [b]power.
21 What do you want? [a]Shall I
come to you with a rod, or in love
and a spirit of gentleness?

Incest: The Church Must Be Pure

5 It is actually reported *that there*
is sexual immorality among you,
and such sexual immorality as is
not even [1]named among the Gentiles—that a man has his father's
[a]wife!†
2 [a]And you are [1]puffed up, and
have not rather [b]mourned, that he
who has done this deed might be
taken away from among you.†
3 [a]For I indeed, as absent in body
but present in spirit, have already
judged (as though I were present)
him who has so done this deed.
4 In the [a]name of our Lord Jesus
Christ, when you are gathered
together, along with my spirit,
[b]with the power of our Lord Jesus
Christ,†
5 [a]deliver such a one to [b]Satan for
the destruction of the flesh, that his
spirit may be saved in the day of the
Lord [1]Jesus.†
6 [a]Your glorying *is* not good. Do
you not know that [b]a little leaven
leavens the whole lump?†

15 [a]Gal. 4:19 **16** [a][1 Cor. 11:1] **17** [a]Acts 19:22 [b]1 Tim. 1:2, 18 [c]1 Cor. 11:2 [d]1 Cor. 7:17 [e]1 Cor. 14:33 **18** [a]1 Cor. 5:2 [1]*arrogant* **19** [a]Acts 19:21; 20:2 [b]Acts 18:21 **20** [a]1 Thess. 1:5 [b]1 Cor. 2:4 **21** [a]2 Cor. 10:2

CHAPTER 5

1 [a]Lev. 18:6–8 [1]NU omits *named* **2** [a]1 Cor. 4:18 [b]2 Cor. 7:7–10 [1]*arrogant* **3** [a]Col. 2:5 **4** [a][Matt. 18:20] [b][John 20:23]

5 [a]1 Tim. 1:20 [b][Acts 26:18] [1]NU omits *Jesus* **6** [a]1 Cor. 3:21 [b]Gal. 5:9

4:18–20 Paul will soon visit Corinth and face those who prejudge him, to see if any **power** (Gr. *dunamis*) lies behind their **word.** Citizenship in **the kingdom of God,** discovered in the Church, does not consist in mere talk but is manifested in a growing life of grace.

5:1 Sexual immorality (Gr. *porneia,* from which we get "pornography") originally meant prostitution, later immorality in general. In this case of incest, **his father's wife** is not the man's own mother, but a stepmother. Even so, this sin is grievous among Jews and Gentiles alike.

5:2 The Greek word for **mourned** (*pentheo*) is also used in the Septuagint to refer to (1) grieving for the dead, and (2) sorrow over unrepentant sinners (see Neh. 8:9; Is. 24:4; Dan. 10:2; Amos 8:8). **Taken away from among you** refers to excommunication.

5:4 My spirit (Gr. *pneuma*) is Paul's human spirit, which is being sanctified by the Holy Spirit.

5:5 In the Church there is protection from the destructive power of **Satan** (Matt. 16:18). This protection is here removed through excommunication, in the hope that, having experienced the difference between God's rule and Satan's, this offender may repent and in the end **be saved. The flesh** (Gr. *sarx*) is not synonymous with "body" (Gr. *soma;* see v. 3). Paul is calling for the **destruction** not of the body but rather of the lusts of *the flesh.*

5:6–8 The Israelites were to remove the **leaven** (v. 7) from their houses in preparation for Passover (Ex. 12:1–30), the remembrance of their freedom from Pharaoh's bondage. Christ, crucified and risen, is our Paschal Lamb, **our Passover.** United to Him in baptism, our life becomes an unending deliverance from evil. Since our life in Christ includes keeping **the feast** (v. 8), Passover fulfilled in Eucharist, the old leaven of **malice and wickedness** must be continually removed from us personally and corporately.

7 Therefore [1]purge out the old
leaven, that you may be a new lump,
since you truly are unleavened. For
indeed [a]Christ, our [b]Passover, was
sacrificed [2]for us.
8 Therefore [a]let us keep the feast,
[b]not with old leaven, nor [c]with the
leaven of malice and wickedness, but
with the unleavened *bread* of sincerity and truth.
9 I wrote to you in my epistle
[a]not to [1]keep company with sexually
immoral people.†
10 Yet *I* certainly *did* not *mean* with
the sexually immoral people of this
world, or with the covetous, or extortioners, or idolaters, since then
you would need to go [a]out of the
world.
11 But now I have written to you
not to keep company [a]with anyone
named a brother, who is sexually immoral, or covetous, or an idolater,
or a reviler, or a drunkard, or an ex-
tortioner—[b]not even to eat with such
a person.
12 For what *have* I *to do* with judging those also who are outside? Do
you not judge those who are inside?†
13 But those who are outside God
judges. Therefore [a]*"put away from
yourselves the evil person."*

Lawsuits: The Church Has Discernment

6 Dare any of you, having a matter
against another, go to law before
the unrighteous, and not before the
[a]saints?†
2 Do you not know that [a]the
saints will judge the world? And if
the world will be judged by you, are
you unworthy to judge the smallest
matters?†
3 Do you not know that we shall
[a]judge angels? How much more,
things that pertain to this life?
4 If then you have [1]judgments
concerning things pertaining to this
life, do you appoint those who are
least esteemed by the church to
judge?
5 I say this to your shame. Is it
so, that there is not a wise man
among you, not even one, who will
be able to judge between his
brethren?
6 But brother goes to law against
brother, and that before unbelievers!
7 Now therefore, it is already an
utter failure for you that you go to
law against one another. [a]Why do
you not rather accept wrong? Why
do you not rather *let yourselves* be
cheated?†
8 No, you yourselves do wrong
and cheat, and *you do* these things
to your brethren!
9 Do you not know that the unrighteous will not inherit the kingdom of God? Do not be deceived.
[a]Neither fornicators, nor idolaters,
nor adulterers, nor [1]homosexuals,
nor [2]sodomites,†
10 nor thieves, nor covetous, nor
drunkards, nor revilers, nor extor-

7 [a]Is. 53:7 [b]John 19:14 [1]*clean out* [2]NU omits *for us*
8 [a]Ex. 12:15 [b]Deut. 16:3 [c]Matt. 16:6
9 [a]2 Cor. 6:14 [1]*associate*
10 [a]John 17:15
11 [a]Matt. 18:17 [b]Gal. 2:12
13 [a]Deut. 13:5; 17:7, 12; 19:19; 21:21; 22:21, 24; 24:7

CHAPTER 6

1 [a]Dan. 7:22
2 [a]Ps. 49:14
3 [a]2 Pet. 2:4
4 [1]*courts*
7 [a][Prov. 20:22]
9 [a]Gal. 5:21 [1]*catamites, those submitting to homosexuals* [2]*male homosexuals*

5:9 My epistle to which Paul refers is apparently lost. There is evidence Paul wrote letters which were lost and not incorporated in the NT canon (see Col. 4:16).

5:12, 13 Those who are outside is an ancient Semitic expression for those outside the community of God (see Ecclesiasticus, The Prologue; Mark 4:11; Col. 4:5; 1 Thess. 4:12; 1 Tim. 3:7).

6:1 Before the unrighteous refers to judges of secular courts at Corinth. Paul asks, why seek justice before the unjust and not before **the saints,** their fellow Christians? This is the biblical basis for Church courts.

6:2, 3 Saints will judge the world (v. 2) and **angels** (v. 3) because in Christ, Christians share in His authority to judge (see Matt. 19:28; John 5:22, 27; 2 Pet. 2:4; Jude 6; Rev. 20:4). This being so, **how much more** are we able to judge the everyday concerns of **this life** (v. 3).

6:7 Love of litigation is a love of greed, hatred, and retaliation. Christians ought to be possessed of generosity, mercy and forgiveness. To **let yourselves be cheated** is to turn the other cheek (see Matt. 5:39).

6:9, 10 As to those who will **not inherit the kingdom of God,** see 15:50; Gal. 5:19–21; Eph. 5:5; Rev. 21:7, 8; 22:15.

Sunday of the Prodigal Son *Third Sunday before Lent*

6:12–20: We must keep our bodies pure because they are members of Christ and the temple of the Holy Spirit.

tioners will inherit the kingdom of
God.
11 And such were [a]some of you.
[b]But you were washed, but you were
[1]sanctified, but you were justified in
the name of the Lord Jesus and by
the Spirit of our God.†

Immorality: The Church Is a Temple

12 [a]All things are lawful for me,
but all things are not [1]helpful. All
things are lawful for me, but I will
not be brought under the power of
[2]any.†
13 [a]Foods for the stomach and the
stomach for foods, but God will destroy both it and them. Now the
body *is* not for [b]sexual immorality
but [c]for the Lord, [d]and the Lord for
the body.†
14 And [a]God both raised up the
Lord and will also raise us up
[b]by His power.
15 Do you not know that [a]your
bodies are members of Christ? Shall
I then take the members of Christ
and make *them* members of a harlot?
Certainly not!†
16 Or do you not know that he
who is joined to a harlot is one body
with her? For [a]*"the two,"* He says,
"shall become one flesh."
17 [a]But he who is joined to the
Lord is one spirit *with Him.*
18 [a]Flee sexual immorality. Every
sin that a man does is outside the
body, but he who commits sexual
immorality sins [b]against his own
body.
19 Or [a]do you not know that your
body is the temple of the Holy
Spirit *who is* in you, whom you
have from God, [b]and you are not
your own?†
20 For [a]you were bought at a price;
therefore glorify God in your body
[1]and in your spirit, which are
God's.

Concerning Marriage

7 Now concerning the things of
which you wrote to me: [a]*It is*
good for a man not to touch a
woman.†
2 Nevertheless, because of sexual
immorality, let each man have his

11 [a][1 Cor. 12:2] [b]Heb. 10:22 [1]*set apart*
12 [a]1 Cor. 10:23 [1]*profitable* [2]Or *anything*
13 [a]Matt. 15:17 [b]Gal. 5:19 [c]1 Thess. 4:3 [d][Eph. 5:23]
14 [a]2 Cor. 4:14 [b]Eph. 1:19
15 [a]Rom. 12:5
16 [a]Gen. 2:24
17 [a][John 17:21–23]
18 [a]Heb. 13:4 [b]Rom. 1:24
19 [a]2 Cor. 6:16 [b]Rom. 14:7
20 [a]2 Pet. 2:1 [1]NU omits the rest of v. 20.

CHAPTER 7

1 [a]1 Cor. 7:8, 26

6:11 Salvation includes being **washed** in Holy Baptism, **sanctified** through the giving of the Holy Spirit in the oil of chrismation, and **justified** through our faith. **Such were some of you** shows that in Christ we can be set free from the very worst of sins (see vv. 8–10).

6:12 All things are lawful for me may be a statement Paul made in Corinth sometime earlier (perhaps regarding the Mosaic cleanliness code) which the libertines took out of context as their slogan. The Apostle sets the record straight: without discipline and discernment through obedience to Christ, freedom from law is slavery to sin.

6:13 The libertines in Corinth—as some do today—argued that illicit sex (adultery and fornication) is as necessary for the body as eating, and both are irrelevant to the spiritual life. Paul contends **the body** belongs to God, and everything is relevant to the spiritual life. Therefore, dealing with sin means controlling our bodies. This is why in the Orthodox Church abstinence from **foods** is the first discipline of the Fast, which also includes prayer and charitable giving.

6:15 When Paul calls our bodies **members of Christ** (see 12:12; Rom. 6:13; 12:4, 5), he is reminding us of our union with Christ in baptism (see Rom. 6:3–10). Fornication is therefore a sin to be fled in horror, for it joins Christ to harlots. St. John Chrysostom writes, "We have many improper wishes, but we must repress them, for we can."

6:19 Temple here refers to the individual Christian as a dwelling place of the Spirit.

7:1 Paul's personal preference is for celibacy, but he knows this is a "gift from God" (v. 7) which is not given to all.

own wife, and let each woman have
her own husband.
3 [a]Let the husband render to his
wife the affection due her, and likewise also the wife to her husband.
4 The wife does not have authority over her own body, but the husband *does*. And likewise the husband
does not have authority over his own
body, but the wife *does*.†
5 [a]Do not deprive one another except with consent for a time, that you
may give yourselves to fasting and
prayer; and come together again so
that [b]Satan does not tempt you because of your lack of self-control.†
6 But I say this as a concession,
[a]not as a commandment.
7 For [a]I wish that all men were
even as I myself. But each one has
his own gift from God, one in this
manner and another in that.
8 But I say to the unmarried and
to the widows: [a]It is good for them
if they remain even as I am;†
9 but [a]if they cannot exercise self-
control, let them marry. For it is
better to marry than to burn *with
passion*.
10 Now to the married I command,
yet not I but the [a]Lord: [b]A wife is
not to depart from *her* husband.
11 But even if she does depart, let
her remain unmarried or be reconciled to *her* husband. And a husband
is not to divorce *his* wife.†
12 But to the rest I, not the Lord,
say: If any brother has a wife who
does not believe, and she is willing
to live with him, let him not divorce
her.
13 And a woman who has a husband who does not believe, if he is
willing to live with her, let her not
divorce him.
14 For the unbelieving husband is
sanctified by the wife, and the unbelieving wife is sanctified by the
husband; otherwise [a]your children
would be unclean, but now they are
holy.†
15 But if the unbeliever departs, let
him depart; a brother or a sister is
not under bondage in such *cases*. But
God has called us [a]to peace.
16 For how do you know, O wife,
whether you will [a]save *your* husband? Or how do you know, O husband, whether you will save *your*
wife?
17 But as God has distributed to
each one, as the Lord has called each
one, so let him walk. And [a]so I
[1]ordain in all the churches.†
18 Was anyone called while circumcised? Let him not become uncircumcised. Was anyone called
while uncircumcised? [a]Let him not
be circumcised.
19 [a]Circumcision is nothing and
uncircumcision is nothing, but
[b]keeping the commandments of God
is what matters.
20 Let each one remain in the same
calling in which he was called.
21 Were you called *while* a slave?

3 [a]Ex. 21:10
5 [a]Joel 2:16 [b]1 Thess. 3:5
6 [a]2 Cor. 8:8
7 [a]Acts 26:29
8 [a]1 Cor. 7:1, 26
9 [a]1 Tim. 5:14
10 [a]Mark 10:6–10 [b]Mal. 2:14; [Matt. 5:32]
14 [a]Ezra 9:2; Mal. 2:15
15 [a]Rom. 12:18
16 [a]Rom. 11:14; 1 Pet. 3:1
17 [a]1 Cor. 4:17 [1]*direct*
18 [a]Acts 15:1
19 [a][Rom. 2:27, 29; Gal. 3:28; 5:6; 6:15; Col. 3:11] [b][John 15:14]

7:4 The mutuality of marriage, the equality of commitment, which Paul enjoins here is unprecedented in his era. Speaking of husband and wife, St. John Chrysostom teaches neither "is master of himself . . . they are servants to each other."

7:5 While periodic ascetic practices, including temporary abstinence from sexual relations for the sake of prayer, are good, sexual abstinence by married people for other reasons and at other times is usually unwise.

7:8, 9 It is wise to consider marriage rather than to insist upon the virtue of chastity and fight a losing battle against sexual passion.

7:11 If a Christian couple cannot stay together, the two alternatives are to **remain unmarried,** that is, separated, or **be reconciled. Divorce** is hated by God (Mal. 2:16), a last measure, a great calamity. Paul forbids remarriage while the first spouse is still living (v. 39).

7:14 In Judaism the family was joined to the covenant through the father. But in the Church, the family is **holy** if either spouse is a believer (see also 2 Tim. 1:5). This does not mean that all are saved, but all are affected by the faith of a Christian spouse. The family is a spiritual unit: if one member is a Christian, the whole family is set apart by God's grace.

7:17–28 When the **Lord has called** (v. 17) us into His salvation, we do not change our ethnic identity (vv. 18, 19) or our occupations (vv. 20–23), and we certainly do not rush out and get married or divorced (vv. 25–28)—though Paul's counsel is a preferred option, not a command. **Keeping the commandments of God is what matters** (v. 19).

Η ΑΓΙΑ
ΠΕΝΤΗΚΟΣΗ

Pentecost: The Coming of the Holy Spirit, *by the hand of Constantine Youssis.* Courtesy of the Department of Religious Education, Greek Orthodox Archdiocese of America.

As the disciples gather in the upper room in obedience to Christ, the Holy Spirit comes upon them and rests on them with tongues of fire. Feast Day readings are Numbers 11:16, 17, 24–29; Ezekiel 36:24–28; Joel 2:23–32; John 7:37–52; 8:12; 20:19–23; Acts 2:1–11.

Do not be concerned about it; but if
you can be made free, rather use *it*.
22 For he who is called in the Lord
while a slave is [a]the Lord's freedman.
Likewise he who is called *while* free
is [b]Christ's slave.
23 [a]You were bought at a price; do
not become slaves of men.
24 Brethren, let each one remain
with [a]God in that *state* in which he
was called.

Concerning Virginity

25 Now concerning virgins: [a]I have
no commandment from the Lord; yet
I give judgment as one [b]whom the
Lord in His mercy *has made*
[c]trustworthy.
26 I suppose therefore that this is
good because of the present distress—[a]that *it is* good for a man to
remain as he is:†
27 Are you bound to a wife? Do
not seek to be loosed. Are you loosed
from a wife? Do not seek a wife.
28 But even if you do marry, you
have not sinned; and if a virgin marries, she has not sinned. Nevertheless such will have trouble in the
flesh, but I would spare you.
29 But [a]this I say, brethren, the
time *is* short, so that from now on
even those who have wives should
be as though they had none,†
30 those who weep as though they
did not weep, those who rejoice as
though they did not rejoice, those
who buy as though they did not
possess,
31 and those who use this world
as not [a]misusing *it*. For [b]the form
of this world is passing away.
32 But I want you to be without
[1]care. [a]He who is unmarried [2]cares
for the things of the Lord—how he
may please the Lord.
33 But he who is married cares
about the things of the world—how
he may please *his* wife.
34 There is a difference between a
wife and a virgin. The unmarried
woman [a]cares about the things of the
Lord, that she may be holy both in
body and in spirit. But she who is
married cares about the things of the
world—how she may please *her*
husband.
35 And this I say for your own
profit, not that I may put a leash on
you, but for what is proper, and that
you may serve the Lord without
distraction.
36 But if any man thinks he is be-
having improperly toward his
[1]virgin, if she is past the flower of
youth, and thus it must be, let him
do what he wishes. He does not sin;
let them marry.†
37 Nevertheless he who stands
steadfast in his heart, having no necessity, but has power over his own
will, and has so determined in his
heart that he will keep his [1]virgin,
does well.
38 [a]So then he who gives [1]*her* in
marriage does well, but he who does
not give *her* in marriage does better.

Concerning Widowhood

39 [a]A wife is bound by law as long
as her husband lives; but if her husband dies, she is at liberty to be married to whom she wishes, [b]only in
the Lord.†
40 But she is happier if she remains
as she is, [a]according to my judgment—and [b]I think I also have the
Spirit of God.

22 [a][John 8:36]; Rom. 6:18; Philem. 16 [b][1 Cor. 9:21; Gal. 5:13]; Eph. 6:6; Col. 3:24; 1 Pet. 2:16
23 [a]Lev. 25:42; 1 Cor. 6:20; 1 Pet. 1:18, 19; Rev. 5:9
24 [a][Eph. 6:5–8; Col. 3:22–24]
25 [a]2 Cor. 8:8 [b]2 Cor. 4:1; 1 Tim. 1:13, 16 [c]1 Tim. 1:12
26 [a]1 Cor. 7:1, 8
29 [a][Rom. 13:11]; 1 Cor. 7:31; 1 Pet. 4:7; [2 Pet. 3:8, 9]
31 [a]1 Cor. 9:18 [b]Ps. 39:6; 1 Cor. 7:29; James 1:10; 4:14; 1 Pet. 1:24; 4:7; [1 John 2:17]
32 [a]1 Tim. 5:5 [1]*concern* [2]*is concerned about*
34 [a]Luke 10:40
36 [1]Or *virgin daughter*
37 [1]Or *virgin daughter*
38 [a]Heb. 13:4 [1]NU *his own virgin*
39 [a]Rom. 7:2 [b]2 Cor. 6:14
40 [a]1 Cor. 7:6, 25 [b]1 Thess. 4:8

7:26 The present distress probably refers to the trials and tribulation of life just before the glorious coming of Christ, which Paul perceived as imminent (vv. 29–33).

7:29–35 Paul expects an imminent end of this age. **The time is short;** it is better to minimize obligations in this age—without being irresponsible—in order to be prepared for the age to come.

7:36–38 It is not clear whether **any man** is the father or the fiancé of the **virgin,** but in any case the option of her marriage is left open.

7:39, 40 Though Paul once again recommends the unmarried state, he affirms the holiness of marriage and gives the widow a choice: **to be married . . . in the Lord** (v. 39), that is to another Christian, or remain **as she is** (v. 40).

Meat Fare Sunday *Second Sunday before Lent*

8:8—9:2: We should abstain from meat, or anything else, if it causes our brother to stumble.

Love Reigns over Knowledge

8 Now [a]concerning things offered
to idols: We know that we all
have [b]knowledge. [c]Knowledge
[1]puffs up, but love [2]edifies.
2 And [a]if anyone thinks that he
knows anything, he knows nothing
yet as he ought to know.
3 But if anyone loves God, this
one is known by Him.
4 Therefore concerning the eating
of things offered to idols, we know
that [a]an idol *is* nothing in the world,
[b]and that *there is* no other God but
one.†
5 For even if there are [a]so-called
gods, whether in heaven or on earth
(as there are many gods and many
lords),
6 yet [a]for us *there is* one God, the
Father, [b]of whom *are* all things, and
we for Him; and [c]one Lord Jesus
Christ, [d]through whom *are* all
things, and [e]through whom we
live.†
7 However, *there is* not in everyone that knowledge; for some,
[a]with consciousness of the idol, until
now eat *it* as a thing offered to an
idol; and their conscience, being
weak, is [b]defiled.
8 But [a]food does not commend us
to God; for neither if we eat are we
the better, nor if we do not eat are
we the worse.
9 But [a]beware lest somehow this
liberty of yours become [b]a [1]stum-
bling block to those who are weak.
10 For if anyone sees you who have
knowledge eating in an idol's temple, will not [a]the conscience of him
who is weak be emboldened to eat
those things offered to idols?
11 And [a]because of your knowledge shall the weak brother perish,
for whom Christ died?
12 But [a]when you thus sin against
the brethren, and wound their weak
conscience, you sin against Christ.
13 Therefore, [a]if food makes my
brother stumble, I will never again
eat meat, lest I make my brother
stumble.

A Good Example: Paul's Rights

9 Am [a]I not an apostle? Am I not
free? [b]Have I not seen Jesus
Christ our Lord? [c]Are you not my
work in the Lord?†
2 If I am not an apostle to others,
yet doubtless I am to you. For you
are [a]the [1]seal of my apostleship in
the Lord.†
3 My defense to those who examine me is this:
4 [a]Do we have no [1]right to eat and
drink?
5 Do we have no right to take
along [1]a believing wife, as *do* also the

CHAPTER 8
1 [a]Acts 15:20 [b]Rom. 14:14 [c]Rom. 14:3 [1]*makes arrogant* [2]*builds up*
2 [a][1 Cor. 13:8–12]
4 [a]Is. 41:24 [b]Deut. 4:35, 39; 6:4
5 [a][John 10:34]
6 [a]Mal. 2:10 [b]Acts 17:28 [c]John 13:13 [d]John 1:3 [e]Rom. 5:11
7 [a][1 Cor. 10:28] [b]Rom. 14:14, 22
8 [a][Rom. 14:17]
9 [a]Gal. 5:13 [b]Rom. 14:13, 21 [1]*cause of offense*
10 [a]1 Cor. 10:28
11 [a]Rom. 14:15, 20
12 [a]Matt. 25:40
13 [a]Rom. 14:21

CHAPTER 9
1 [a]Acts 9:15 [b]1 Cor. 15:8 [c]1 Cor. 3:6; 4:15
2 [a]2 Cor. 12:12 [1]*certification*

4 [a][1 Thess. 2:6, 9] [1]*authority* 5 [1]Lit. *a sister, a wife*

8:4–13 Throughout the Roman Empire, animals were sacrificed to pagan "gods" at feasts and public occasions. Part of each offering was used in a ceremonial meal or went to the donor; the remainder was often sold in public meat markets. Christians had a dilemma. Should they eat meat which had been offered before idols? The Jews had prohibitions, but the Christians believed an **idol is nothing.** Paul answers they are correct in principle (v. 8), but they must think about other people's consciences (vv. 9, 10). Love of God and of fellow Christians compels Paul not to eat such meat (v. 13).

8:6 **Of whom** and **through whom** do not speak of the divine nature, but of the relationship of the Father and the Son to us.

9:1 Paul's apostleship is under attack; in this chapter he defends it.

9:2 The effectiveness of the clergy is certified by the spiritual condition of the sheep.

other apostles, [a]the brothers of the
Lord, and [b]Cephas?
6 Or *is it* only Barnabas and I
[a]*who* have no right to refrain from
working?
7 Who ever [a]goes to war at his
own expense? Who [b]plants a vineyard and does not eat of its fruit?
Or who [c]tends a flock and does not
drink of the milk of the flock?
8 Do I say these things as a *mere*
man? Or does not the law say the
same also?
9 For it is written in the law of
Moses, [a]*"You shall not muzzle an*
ox while it treads out the grain." Is
it oxen God is concerned about?
10 Or does He say *it* altogether for
our sakes? For our sakes, no doubt,
this is written, that [a]he who plows
should plow in hope, and he who
threshes in hope should be partaker
of his hope.
11 [a]If we have sown spiritual
things for you, *is it* a great thing if
we reap your material things?†
12 If others are partakers of *this*
right over you, *are* we not even
more? [a]Nevertheless we have not
used this right, but endure all things
[b]lest we hinder the gospel of Christ.
13 [a]Do you not know that those
who minister the holy things eat *of*
the things of the [b]temple, and those
who serve at the altar partake of *the*
offerings of the altar?
14 Even so [a]the Lord has commanded [b]that those who preach the
gospel should live from the gospel.

Paul's Obligations

15 But [a]I have used none of these
things, nor have I written these
things that it should be done so to
me; for [b]it *would be* better for me to
die than that anyone should make
my boasting void.
16 For if I preach the gospel, I have
nothing to boast of, for [a]necessity is
laid upon me; yes, woe is me if I
do not preach the gospel!
17 For if I do this willingly, [a]I
have a reward; but if against my
will, [b]I have been entrusted with a
stewardship.
18 What is my reward then? That
[a]when I preach the gospel, I may
present the gospel [1]of Christ without
charge, that I [b]may not abuse my authority in the gospel.
19 For though I am [a]free from all
men, [b]I have made myself a servant to all, [c]that I might win the
more;
20 and [a]to the Jews I became as a
Jew, that I might win Jews; to those
who are under the law, as under the
[1]law, that I might win those *who are*
under the law;
21 [a]to [b]those *who are* without law,
as without law [c](not being without
[1]law toward God, but under [2]law toward Christ), that I might win those
who are without law;
22 [a]to the weak I became [1]as weak,
that I might win the weak. [b]I have
become all things to all *men,* [c]that I
might by all means save some.
23 Now this I do for the gospel's
sake, that I may be partaker of it with
you.

Paul's Spiritual Discipline

24 Do you not know that those
who run in a race all run, but one
receives the prize? [a]Run in such a
way that you may [1]obtain *it.*†
25 And everyone who competes *for*
the prize [1]is temperate in all things.
Now they *do it* to obtain a perishable
crown, but we *for* [a]an imperishable
crown.
26 Therefore I run thus: [a]not with

5 [a]Matt. 13:55 [b]Matt. 8:14
6 [a]Acts 4:36
7 [a]2 Cor. 10:4 [b]Deut. 20:6 [c]John 21:15
9 [a]Deut. 25:4
10 [a]2 Tim. 2:6
11 [a]Rom. 15:27
12 [a][Acts 18:3; 20:33] [b]2 Cor. 11:12
13 [a]Lev. 6:16, 26; 7:6, 31 [b]Num. 18:8–31
14 [a]Matt. 10:10 [b]Rom. 10:15
15 [a]Acts 18:3; 20:33 [b]2 Cor. 11:10
16 [a][Rom. 1:14]
17 [a]1 Cor. 3:8, 14; 9:18 [b]Gal. 2:7
18 [a]1 Cor. 10:33 [b]1 Cor. 7:31; 9:12 [1]NU omits *of Christ*
19 [a]1 Cor. 9:1 [b]Gal. 5:13 [c]Matt. 18:15
20 [a]Acts 16:3; 21:23–26 [1]NU adds *though not being myself under the law*
21 [a][Gal. 2:3; 3:2] [b][Rom. 2:12, 14] [c][1 Cor. 7:22] [1]NU *God's law* [2]NU *Christ's law*
22 [a]Rom. 14:1; 15:1 [b]1 Cor. 10:33 [c]Rom. 11:14 [1]NU omits *as*
24 [a]Gal. 2:2 [1]*win*
25 [a]James 1:12 [1]*exercises self-control*
26 [a]2 Tim. 2:5

9:11 Clergy must be given **material** support to be free to sow **spiritual things.** God saw to this under the Old Covenant (vv. 8, 9) and Paul implies that most Christian pastors are similarly supported (vv. 5, 6).

9:24–27 Using contemporary terms from the sports of running (vv. 24, 25) and boxing (vv. 26, 27), Paul shows the proper use of ascetic practices in the life of faith. They are valuable not in themselves, but for the sake of the goal of salvation. As training prepares an athlete, so spiritual **discipline** prepares a Christian to exercise faith and enter the Kingdom.

The Eve of the Baptism of Jesus Christ (Theophany) *January 5*

10:1–4: The crossing of the Red Sea prefigures our baptism.

uncertainty. Thus I fight: not as *one*
who beats the air.
27 [a]But I discipline my body and
[b]bring *it* into subjection, lest, when
I have preached to others, I myself
should become [c]disqualified.

A Bad Example: Israel's Apostasy

10 Moreover, brethren, I do not
want you to be unaware that
all our fathers were under [a]the
cloud, all passed through [b]the sea,†
2 all were baptized into Moses in
the cloud and in the sea,†
3 all ate the same [a]spiritual food,
4 and all drank the same [a]spiritual
drink. For they drank of that spiritual
Rock that followed them, and that
Rock was Christ.
5 But with most of them God was
not well pleased, for *their bodies*
[a]were scattered in the wilderness.†
6 Now these things became our
examples, to the intent that we
should not lust after evil things as
[a]they also lusted.†
7 [a]And do not become idolaters
as *were* some of them. As it is written, [b]*"The people sat down to eat*
and drink, and rose up to play."
8 [a]Nor let us commit sexual immorality, as [b]some of them did, and
[c]in one day twenty-three thousand
fell;
9 nor let us [1]tempt Christ, as
[a]some of them also tempted, and
[b]were destroyed by serpents;
10 nor complain, as [a]some of them
also complained, and [b]were destroyed by [c]the destroyer.
11 Now [1]all these things happened
to them as examples, and [a]they were
written for our [2]admonition, [b]upon
whom the ends of the ages have
come.
12 Therefore [a]let him who thinks
he stands take heed lest he fall.
13 No temptation has overtaken
you except such as is common to
man; but [a]God *is* faithful, [b]who will
not allow you to be tempted beyond
what you are able, but with the
temptation will also make the way
of escape, that you may be able to
[1]bear *it*.

Worship Is Sacramental

14 Therefore, my beloved, [a]flee
from idolatry.
15 I speak as to [a]wise men; judge
for yourselves what I say.
16 [a]The cup of blessing which we
bless, is it not the [1]communion of
the blood of Christ? [b]The bread
which we break, is it not the communion of the body of Christ?†

27 [a][Rom. 8:13] [b][Rom. 6:18] [c]Jer. 6:30

CHAPTER 10

1 [a]Ex. 13:21, 22 [b]Ex. 14:21, 22, 29
3 [a]Ex. 16:4, 15, 35
4 [a]Ex. 17:5–7
5 [a]Num. 14:29, 37; 26:65
6 [a]Num. 11:4, 34
7 [a]1 Cor. 5:11; 10:14 [b]Ex. 32:6
8 [a]Rev. 2:14 [b]Num. 25:1–9 [c]Ps. 106:29
9 [a]Ex. 17:2, 7 [b]Num. 21:6–9 [1]*test*
10 [a]Ex. 16:2 [b]Num. 14:37 [c]Ex. 12:23
11 [a]Rom. 15:4 [b]Phil. 4:5 [1]NU omits *all* [2]*instruction*
12 [a]Rom. 11:20
13 [a]1 Cor. 1:9 [b]Ps. 125:3 [1]*endure*
14 [a]2 Cor. 6:17
15 [a]1 Cor. 8:1
16 [a]Matt. 26:26–28 [b]Acts 2:42 [1]*fellowship* or *sharing*

10:1 Paul often uses **I do not want you to be unaware** or a similar formula (Rom. 11:25; 12:1; 2 Cor. 1:8; Col. 2:1; 1 Thess. 4:13) to introduce a matter vital to the Christian faith.

10:2–4 Israel's liberation from Egypt by Moses prefigures our liberation from sin by Christ (see Deut. 32:4, 15, 18, 30–32; 2 Sam. 22:2, 32, 47; Ps. 18:2, 3). **The cloud** is a symbol of the Holy Spirit; **the sea,** of water and baptism; the **Rock** (v. 4), of the body of Christ, His humanity; and the **spiritual drink,** of Christ's blood. Jesus Himself linked these events of the Passover with the Eucharist when He established it (Matt. 26:17–29).

10:5–8 In spite of her baptism in the Red Sea (v. 2) and her spiritual eating and drinking (vv. 3, 4), Israel still fell into idolatry and sexual immorality.

10:6 The lessons of the OT, here those surrounding the Passover (vv. 1–5), are **examples** for us, that we might not repeat the same mistakes.

10:16, 17 The English word **communion** (Gr. *koinonia*) is the correct translation; the alternative, "fellowship," is too weak. For at Communion, at the Eucharist, there is a real participa-

(continued on next page)

17 For [a]we, *though* many, are one
bread *and* one body; for we all partake of that one bread.
18 Observe [a]Israel [b]after the flesh:
[c]Are not those who eat of the sacrifices [1]partakers of the altar?†
19 What am I saying then? [a]That
an idol is anything, or what is offered
to idols is anything?†
20 Rather, that the things which
the Gentiles [a]sacrifice [b]they sacrifice
to demons and not to God, and I do
not want you to have fellowship with
demons.
21 [a]You cannot drink the cup of
the Lord and [b]the cup of demons;
you cannot partake of the [c]Lord's table and of the table of demons.
22 Or do we [a]provoke the Lord to
jealousy? [b]Are we stronger than
He?

Offend No Man, Glorify God

23 All things are lawful [1]for me,
but not all things are [a]helpful; all
things are lawful [1]for me, but not all
things [2]edify.†
24 Let no one seek his own, but
each one [a]the other's *well-being.*
25 [a]Eat whatever is sold in the
meat market, asking no questions for
conscience' sake;†
26 for [a]"*the earth is the* LORD'*s,*
and all its fullness."

17 [a]1 Cor. 12:12, 27
18 [a]Rom. 4:12 [b]Rom. 4:1 [c]Lev. 3:3; 7:6, 14 [1]*fellowshippers* or *sharers*
19 [a]1 Cor. 8:4
20 [a]Lev. 17:7 [b]Deut. 32:17
21 [a]2 Cor. 6:15, 16 [b]Deut. 32:38 [c][1 Cor. 11:23–29]
22 [a]Deut. 32:21 [b]Ezek. 22:14
23 [a]1 Cor. 6:12 [1]NU omits *for me* [2]*build up*
24 [a]Phil. 2:4
25 [a][1 Tim. 4:4]
26 [a]Ps. 24:1
27 [a]Luke 10:7, 8
28 [a][1 Cor. 8:7, 10, 12] [b]Ps. 24:1 [1]NU omits the rest of v. 28.
29 [a]Rom. 14:16
30 [a]Rom. 14:6
31 [a]Col. 3:17
32 [a]Rom. 14:13
33 [a]Rom. 15:2

CHAPTER 11
1 [a]Eph. 5:1

27 If any of those who do not believe invites you *to dinner,* and you
desire to go, [a]eat whatever is set before you, asking no question for conscience' sake.
28 But if anyone says to you, "This
was offered to idols," do not eat it
[a]for the sake of the one who told
you, and for conscience' sake;
[1]for [b]"*the earth is the* LORD'*s, and*
all its fullness."
29 "Conscience," I say, not your
own, but that of the other. For
[a]why is my liberty judged by another
man's conscience?
30 But if I partake with thanks,
why am I evil spoken of for *the food*
[a]over which I give thanks?
31 [a]Therefore, whether you eat or
drink, or whatever you do, do all to
the glory of God.
32 [a]Give no offense, either to the
Jews or to the Greeks or to the
church of God,
33 just [a]as I also please all *men* in
all *things,* not seeking my own profit,
but the *profit* of many, that they may
be saved.
11 Imitate[a] me, just as I also *imi-*
tate Christ.

The Conduct of Women

2 Now I praise you, brethren, that
you remember me in all things and

(continued from previous page)
tion in the Body and Blood of Christ. Just as Christ's human body is united to Him, so we are united to Him. As many grains become one loaf, those who take this *communion* become one in Christ.

10:18 Israel after the flesh is the Israel of Judaism as contrasted to the true Israel, which is the Church, the Israel of God (see Gal. 6:16).

10:19–22 All worship is sacramental, even false worship. To genuinely offer a sacrifice is to unite spiritually with the object of that offering. An **idol** (v. 19) by itself is nothing, but behind them lurk **demons** (v. 20) waiting for someone to partake of them. The Christian offering is the once-for-all sacrifice of Jesus Christ. We are not to engage in any worship contrary to, or in competition with, the Eucharist of Christ.

10:23, 24 Christians are obligated to obey only one law: the law of Christ, the law of love. This obligates us to what is **helpful** (v. 23), and edifies, to **the other's well-being** (v. 24). We therefore continually seek the good of others in every way.

10:25–33 Since God created everything, everything is clean (v. 26), even what was once used in idolatrous worship (vv. 25, 27). However, offending a fellow Christian in nonessential matters breaks the law of love, the bond of unity (vv. 28–30). If we say that it affects no one but ourselves, yet we must **do** what is **to the glory of God** (v. 31), or else we offend God. The salvation of all is greater than the rights of the individual (v. 33). A right is never inalienable if it alienates us from others. Note that Paul assumes Christians say a prayer at meals (v. 30).

THE EUCHARIST

"For I received from the Lord that which I also delivered to you: that the Lord Jesus on the same night in which He was betrayed took bread; and when He had given thanks [Gr. *eucharistesas*], He broke it and said, 'Take, eat; this is My body which is broken for you; do this in remembrance of Me.' In the same manner He also took the cup after supper, saying, 'This cup is the new covenant in My blood. This do, as often as you drink it, in remembrance of Me' " (1 Cor. 11:23–25).

With these words—quoting the same words of Christ in Luke 22:19, 20—St. Paul instructs the Corinthians concerning the Eucharist, the giving of thanks. Some two thousand years after Jesus gave Himself "for the life of the world" (John 6:51), there are in Christendom at least three different interpretations of His words.

How Do We View the Eucharist? For the first thousand years of Christian history, when the Church was visibly one and undivided, the holy gifts of the Body and Blood of Christ were received as just that: His Body and Blood. The Church confessed this was a mystery: The bread is truly His Body, and that which is in the cup is truly His Blood, but one cannot say *how* they become so.

The eleventh and twelfth centuries brought on the scholastic era, the Age of Reason in the West. The Roman Church, which had become separated from the Orthodox Church in A.D. 1054, was pressed by the rationalists to define *how* the transformation takes place. They answered with the word *transubstantiation*, meaning a change of substance. The elements are no longer bread and wine; they are physically changed into flesh and blood. The sacrament, which only faith can comprehend, was subjected to a philosophical definition. This second view of the Eucharist was unknown in the ancient Church.

Not surprisingly, one of the points of disagreement between Rome and the sixteenth-century reformers was this issue of transubstantiation. Unable to accept this explanation of the sacrament, the radical reformers, who were rationalists themselves, took up the opposite point of view: the gifts are nothing but bread and wine, period. They only represent Christ's Body and Blood; they have no spiritual reality. This third, symbol-only view helps explain the infrequency with which some Protestants partake of the Eucharist.

The Scriptures and the Eucharist. What do the Scriptures teach concerning the Eucharist?

(1) Jesus said, "This *is* My body . . . this *is* My blood." (Luke 22:19, 20). There is never a statement that these gifts merely symbolize His Body and Blood. Critics have charged that Jesus also said of Himself, "I am the door" (John. 10:7), and He certainly is not a seven-foot wooden plank. The flaw in that argument is obvious: at no time has the Church ever believed He was a literal door. But she has always believed the consecrated gifts of bread and wine are truly His Body and Blood.

(2) In the New Testament, those who receive Christ's Body and Blood unworthily are said to bring condemnation upon themselves. "For this reason many are weak and sick among you, and many sleep" (literally, "are dead"; 1 Cor. 11:30). A mere symbol, a quarterly reminder, could hardly have the power to cause sickness and death!

(3) Historically, from the New Testament days on, the central act of worship, the very apex of spiritual sacrifice, took place "on the first day of the week, when the disciples came together to break bread" (Acts 20:7). The Eucharist has always been that supreme act of thanksgiving and praise to God in His Church.

keep the traditions just as I delivered *them* to you.†

3 But I want you to know that [a]the head of every man is Christ, [b]the head of woman *is* man, and [c]the head of Christ *is* God.

4 Every man praying or [a]prophesying, having *his* head covered, dishonors his head.

5 But every woman who prays or prophesies with *her* head uncovered dishonors her head, for that is one and the same as if her head were [a]shaved.

6 For if a woman is not covered, let her also be shorn. But if it is [a]shameful for a woman to be shorn or shaved, let her be covered.

7 For a man indeed ought not to cover *his* head, since [a]he is the image and glory of God; but woman is the glory of man.

8 For man is not from woman, but woman [a]from man.

9 Nor was man created for the woman, but woman [a]for the man.

10 For this reason the woman ought to have *a symbol of* authority on *her* head, because of the angels.

11 Nevertheless, [a]neither *is* man independent of woman, nor woman independent of man, in the Lord.

12 For as woman *came* from man, even so man also *comes* through woman; but all things are from God.

13 Judge among yourselves. Is it proper for a woman to pray to God with her head uncovered?

14 Does not even nature itself teach you that if a man has long hair, it is a dishonor to him?

15 But if a woman has long hair, it is a glory to her; for *her* hair is given [1]to her for a covering.

16 But [a]if anyone seems to be contentious, we have no such custom, [b]nor *do* the churches of God.

Unity at the Eucharist

17 Now in giving these instructions I do not praise *you,* since you come together not for the better but for the worse.†

18 For first of all, when you come together as a church, [a]I hear that there are divisions among you, and in part I believe it.

19 For [a]there must also be factions among you, [b]that those who are approved may be [1]recognized among you.

20 Therefore when you come together in one place, it is not to eat the Lord's Supper.†

21 For in eating, each one takes his own supper ahead of *others;* and one is hungry and [a]another is drunk.

22 What! Do you not have houses to eat and drink in? Or do you despise [a]the church of God and [b]shame [1]those who have nothing? What shall I say to you? Shall I praise you in this? I do not praise *you.*

23 For [a]I received from the Lord that which I also delivered to you: [b]that the Lord Jesus on the *same* night in which He was betrayed took bread;†

3 [a]Eph. 1:22; 4:15; 5:23 [b]Gen. 3:16 [c]John 14:28
4 [a]1 Cor. 12:10
5 [a]Deut. 21:12
6 [a]Num. 5:18
7 [a]Gen. 1:26, 27; 5:1; 9:6
8 [a]Gen. 2:21–23
9 [a]Gen. 2:18
11 [a][Gal. 3:28]

15 [1]M omits *to her*
16 [a]1 Tim. 6:4 [b]1 Cor. 7:17
18 [a]1 Cor. 1:10–12; 3:3
19 [a]1 Tim. 4:1 [b][Deut. 13:3] [1]Lit. *manifest, evident*
21 [a]Jude 12
22 [a]1 Cor. 10:32 [b]James 2:6 [1]The poor
23 [a]1 Cor. 15:3 [b]Matt. 26:26–28

11:2 Remember is primarily a word of liturgical prayer: The Corinthians constantly pray for their apostle in their corporate prayers. **Delivered** (Gr. *paredoka*) refers to the passing on of authentic apostolic tradition. **Keep the traditions** refers to obedience to what has been *delivered*—God-given oral tradition, from which Paul taught. He makes no distinction between the authority of his written and his oral instruction.

11:17–19 When the Corinthians come **together** (v. 17) as the Church, they reveal the world, not heaven. For **divisions** (v. 18, Gr. *schismata*) and **factions** (v. 19, Gr. *haireseis*), are contrary to the Church, which is one and indivisible. Paul finds only one good thing in this ungodly disorder: God's **approved** (v. 19) faithful are shown to be trustworthy.

11:20–22 The Agape meal held before or after **the Lord's Supper** (see vv. 33, 34; also 2 Pet. 2:13; Jude 12), was intended to build and unify the community in Christ. It gave the rich opportunity to serve the poor, for everyone brought food and shared it—an ancient potluck supper. When the Corinthians **come together,** however, they experience drunkenness and gluttony, not Christ and His body, manifesting not God's love (Gr. *agape*) but self love.

11:23–26 Received (Gr. *parelabon*) and **delivered** (v. 23) refer to the transmission of Holy

(continued on next page)

Holy Thursday

Thursday before Easter

11:23–32: Paul recounts the institution of the Eucharist on Holy Thursday.

24 and when He had given thanks,
He broke *it* and said, [1]"Take, eat;
this is My body which is [2]broken
for you; do this in remembrance
of Me."
25 In the same manner *He* also *took*
the cup after supper, saying, "This
cup is the new covenant in My
blood. This do, as often as you drink
it, in remembrance of Me."
26 For as often as you eat this bread
and drink this cup, you proclaim the
Lord's death [a]till He comes.
27 Therefore whoever eats [a]this
bread or drinks *this* cup of the Lord
in an unworthy manner will be
guilty of the body and [1]blood of the
Lord.†
28 But [a]let a man examine himself,
and so let him eat of the bread and
drink of the cup.†
29 For he who eats and drinks
[1]in an unworthy manner eats and
drinks judgment to himself, not discerning the [2]Lord's body.†
30 For this reason many *are* weak
and sick among you, and many
[1]sleep.
31 For [a]if we would judge ourselves, we would not be judged.†
32 But when we are judged, [a]we
are chastened by the Lord, that we
may not be condemned with the
world.
33 Therefore, my brethren, when
you [a]come together to eat, wait for
one another.†
34 But if anyone is hungry, let him
eat at home, lest you come together
for judgment. And the rest I will set
in order when I come.

24 [1]NU omits *Take, eat* [2]NU omits *broken*
26 [a]John 14:3
27 [a][John 6:51] [1]NU, M *the blood*
28 [a]2 Cor. 13:5
29 [1]NU omits *in an unworthy manner* [2]NU omits *Lord's*
30 [1]Are dead
31 [a][1 John 1:9]
32 [a]Ps. 94:12
33 [a]1 Cor. 14:26

(continued from previous page)

Tradition. These words were part of the Eucharistic celebration in the first century just as they are today. **Remembrance** (vv. 24, 25; Gr. *anamnesis*) is far more than thinking back about something; it is participation in it. In the Eucharist we participate in Christ's human nature, His **body** and His **blood.** The Jews were permitted to eat meat but not blood, for the life is in the blood (Lev. 17:11), and life belongs to God. Now, the Israel of God, the Church, breaks this fast and feasts, as it were, by eating Christ's body and drinking His blood in the Divine Liturgy. We **proclaim the Lord's death till He comes** (v. 26) for we presently celebrate the Eucharist in Christ's invisible presence, though one day we will feast with Him face-to-face in His Kingdom.

11:27 To receive Christ's Body and Blood **in an unworthy manner** means coming to Him with hidden immorality (6:18–20), disunity (v. 18), doctrinal heresy (v. 19), or disorder (vv. 21, 22), failing to see the gifts of God as holy things for holy people.

11:28 We prepare for the Eucharist by examining ourselves. This includes confessing our sins and being reconciled to one another in the sacrament of repentance (Matt. 5:23–26). In the Orthodox Church this confession before God is done in the presence of a priest, who visibly represents Christ (Matt. 16:19; 18:18–20; John 20:23), and in general prayers of confession. Being "worthy" does not mean being sinless, but being cleansed. It is not legalism but commitment to walk in righteousness before God.

11:29, 30 There is such power in the Body and Blood of Christ communicated to us in the eating and drinking of His gifts (John 6:54–56) that to do so in willful disregard of the Lord could result in sickness and even death.

11:31, 32 God's promise is if we **judge ourselves** we will not be **condemned with the world** (v. 32).

11:33, 34 The Agape meal, connected to the Eucharist, was conducted with the same dignity as the Eucharist. While the Corinthian church ate before communion, and present-day Orthodox Christians fast, the spirit of their eating was the same as our fasting: preparation.

Spiritual Gifts

12 Now [a]concerning spiritual
gifts, brethren, I do not want
you to be ignorant:†
2 You know [a]that[1] you were Gentiles, carried away to these [b]dumb[2]
idols, however you were led.†
3 Therefore I make known to you
that no one speaking by the Spirit
of God calls Jesus [1]accursed, and
[a]no one can say that Jesus is Lord
except by the Holy Spirit.†
4 [a]There are [1]diversities of gifts,
but [b]the same Spirit.†
5 [a]There are differences of ministries, but the same Lord.
6 And there are diversities of activities, but it is the same God
[a]who works [1]all in all.
7 But the manifestation of the
Spirit is given to each one for the
profit *of all:*†
8 for to one is given [a]the word of
wisdom through the Spirit, to another [b]the word of knowledge
through the same Spirit,†
9 [a]to another faith by the same
Spirit, to another [b]gifts of healings
by [1]the same Spirit,
10 [a]to another the working of miracles, to another [b]prophecy, to another [c]discerning of spirits, to another [d]*different* kinds of tongues, to
another the interpretation of
tongues.
11 But one and the same Spirit
works all these things, [a]distributing
to each one individually [b]as He wills.
12 For [a]as the body is one and has
many members, but all the members
of that one body, being many, are
one body, [b]so also *is* Christ.†
13 For [a]by one Spirit we were all
baptized into one body—[b]whether
Jews or Greeks, whether slaves or
free—and [c]have all been made to
drink [1]into one Spirit.
14 For in fact the body is not one
member but many.†
15 If the foot should say, "Because
I am not a hand, I am not of the
body," is it therefore not of the
body?
16 And if the ear should say, "Because I am not an eye, I am not of
the body," is it therefore not of the
body?
17 If the whole body *were* an eye,
where *would be* the hearing? If the
whole *were* hearing, where *would be*
the smelling?
18 But now [a]God has set the members, each one of them, in the body
[b]just as He pleased.

CHAPTER 12
1 [a]1 Cor. 12:4; 14:1, 37
2 [a]Eph. 2:11 [b]Ps. 115:5 [1]NU, M *that when* [2]*mute, silent*
3 [a]Matt. 16:17 [1]Gr. *anathema*
4 [a]Rom. 12:3–8 [b]Eph. 4:4 [1]*allotments* or *various kinds*
5 [a]Rom. 12:6
6 [a]1 Cor. 15:28 [1]*all things in*
8 [a]1 Cor. 2:6, 7 [b]Rom. 15:14
9 [a]2 Cor. 4:13 [b]Mark 3:15; 16:18 [1]NU *one*
10 [a]Mark 16:17 [b]Rom. 12:6 [c]1 John 4:1 [d]Acts 2:4–11
11 [a]Rom. 12:6 [b][John 3:8]
12 [a]Rom. 12:4, 5 [b][Gal. 3:16]
13 [a][Rom. 6:5] [b]Col. 3:11 [c][John 7:37–39] [1]NU omits *into*
18 [a]1 Cor. 12:28 [b]Rom. 12:3

12:1 The Corinthians were not **ignorant** of the spiritual gifts but of how they were to be used in service to God.

12:2 It is possible to get **carried away,** and **led** into error. For not all gifts are from the Holy Spirit. Demons lurk behind **dumb idols** (v. 2), speaking evil prophecies through the religious ecstasies of their priests (see Acts 16:16). Religious ecstasy or enthusiasm is no proof of spirituality.

12:3 The sign of the **Holy Spirit** speaking is when Christians say from the heart, **Jesus is Lord.** Every time we say the Nicene Creed sincerely at the Divine Liturgy, for example, we are gifted by the Holy Spirit to do so.

12:4–6 Every true gift and ministry in the Church manifests the Holy Trinity: the **Spirit** (v. 4), the Son, the **Lord** (v. 5) Jesus Christ, and the Father, **God** (v. 6). While the working out of our chrismation is primarily the grace of the Holy Spirit, it is the work of the whole of the Trinity as well. Note there are **diversities** or **differences** of **gifts** and **activities;** no two Christians are alike.

12:7 The purpose of spiritual gifts is the growth of the whole Church. "A charism is a gift of the Holy Spirit given for the benefit of others. But no person possesses all the gifts" (St. Basil the Great).

12:8–10 This list of nine gifts is not exhaustive (see 14:1–5; Rom. 12:6–8; Eph. 4:7–12).

12:12, 13 Paul here moves from the gifts in the Church to **the members** of the **one body** of Christ. Note how the **many members** are to work as **one.**

12:14–18 A remarkable passage which leaves no room for a spiritual inferiority complex (see also vv. 22–24). Every member of Christ's body is important to the overall life and work of the Church.

Commemoration of Holy Unmercenary Healers

12:27—13:8: Healing is a great gift, but not as great as love, which these saints showed abundantly.

19 And if they *were* all one member, where *would* the body *be?*
20 But now indeed *there are* many members, yet one body.
21 And the eye cannot say to the hand, "I have no need of you"; nor again the head to the feet, "I have no need of you."
22 No, much rather, those members of the body which seem to be weaker are necessary.
23 And those *members* of the body which we think to be less honorable, on these we bestow greater honor; and our unpresentable *parts* have greater modesty,
24 but our presentable *parts* have no need. But God composed the body, having given greater honor to that *part* which lacks it,
25 that there should be no [1]schism in the body, but *that* the members should have the same care for one another.
26 And if one member suffers, all the members suffer with *it;* or if one member is honored, all the members rejoice with *it.*†
27 Now [a]you are the body of Christ, and [b]members individually.
28 And [a]God has appointed these in the church: first [b]apostles, second [c]prophets, third teachers, after that [d]miracles, then [e]gifts of healings, [f]helps, [g]administrations, varieties of tongues.†
29 *Are* all apostles? *Are* all prophets? *Are* all teachers? *Are* all workers of miracles?
30 Do all have gifts of healings? Do all speak with tongues? Do all interpret?

Love, Superior to Gifts

31 But [a]earnestly desire the [1]best gifts. And yet I show you a more excellent way.

13 Though I speak with the tongues of men and of angels, but have not love, I have become sounding brass or a clanging cymbal.†
2 And though I have *the gift of* [a]prophecy, and understand all mysteries and all knowledge, and though I have all faith, [b]so that I could remove mountains, but have not love, I am nothing.†
3 And [a]though I bestow all my goods to feed *the poor,* and though I give my body [1]to be burned, but have not love, it profits me nothing.†

25 [1]*division*
27 [a]Rom. 12:5 [b]Eph. 5:30
28 [a]Eph. 4:11 [b][Eph. 2:20; 3:5] [c]Acts 13:1 [d]1 Cor. 12:10, 29 [e]1 Cor. 12:9, 30 [f]Num. 11:17 [g]Rom. 12:8
31 [a]1 Cor. 14:1, 39 [1]NU *greater*

CHAPTER 13
2 [a]1 Cor. 12:8–10, 28; 14:1 [b]Matt. 17:20; 21:21
3 [a]Matt. 6:1, 2 [1]NU *so I may boast*

12:26 There is no such thing as an "individual" Christian. Being "knit together in love" (Col. 2:2), we are called in Christ to **suffer** together, be **honored** together and **rejoice** together.

12:28–31 There is a hierarchy of honor in the Church of the NT as there is in the Church today. The apostolic work, that of the bishop, sets the pace for all the rest. When the oversight is in order, the rest of the Church is free to function at the optimal level. But seen with all the gifts in place and operative there is something even **more excellent** (v. 31). It is the love of God, the true sign of the presence of the Holy Spirit.

13:1 St. Basil the Great teaches there are three reasons, all biblical and all God-given, why people follow the Lord: (1) fear (Prov. 1:7); (2) obedience, a recognition that because He is God we must follow Him (Acts 5:29); and (3) **love** (1 John 4:19). And while Basil teaches we must aim to do all things out of love, we also must not cease fearing God and obeying Him. To a church preoccupied with **tongues,** Paul teaches the ultimate gift: love.

13:2 Love outshines **prophecy** and **all faith.** It is of far greater value than the miraculous ability to **remove mountains.**

13:3 Jesus urges us to "give to the poor" (Matt. 19:21) and to lay down our lives for others (John 15:13). But even such a selfless act done without **love, profits** us **nothing.**

4 [a]Love suffers long *and* is [b]kind;
love [c]does not envy; love does not
parade itself, is not [1]puffed up;†
5 does not behave rudely, [a]does
not seek its own, is not provoked,
[1]thinks no evil;
6 [a]does not rejoice in iniquity, but
[b]rejoices in the truth;
7 [a]bears all things, believes all
things, hopes all things, endures all
things.
8 Love never fails. But whether
there are prophecies, they will fail;
whether *there are* tongues, they will
cease; whether *there is* knowledge, it
will vanish away.†
9 [a]For we know in part and we
prophesy in part.
10 But when that which is [1]perfect
has come, then that which is in part
will be done away.
11 When I was a child, I spoke as
a child, I understood as a child, I
thought as a child; but when I became a man, I put away childish
things.†
12 For [a]now we see in a mirror,
dimly, but then [b]face to face. Now I
know in part, but then I shall know
just as I also am known.
13 And now abide faith, hope,
love, these three; but the greatest of
these *is* love.

4 [a]Prov. 10:12; 17:9 [b]Eph. 4:32 [c]Gal. 5:26 [1]*arrogant*
5 [a]1 Cor. 10:24 [1]*keeps no accounts of evil*
6 [a]Rom. 1:32 [b]2 John 4
7 [a]Gal. 6:2
9 [a]1 Cor. 8:2; 13:12
10 [1]*complete*
12 [a]Phil. 3:12 [b][1 John 3:2]

Prophecy, Superior to Tongues

14 Pursue love, and [a]desire spiritual *gifts,* [b]but especially that
you may prophesy.†
2 For he who [a]speaks in a tongue
does not speak to men but to God,
for no one understands *him;* however, in the spirit he speaks
mysteries.†
3 But he who prophesies speaks
[a]edification and [b]exhortation and
comfort to men.
4 He who speaks in a tongue edifies himself, but he who prophesies
edifies the church.
5 I wish you all spoke with
tongues, but even more that you
prophesied; [1]for he who prophesies
is greater than he who speaks with
tongues, unless indeed he interprets,

CHAPTER 14
1 [a]1 Cor. 12:31; 14:39 [b]Num. 11:25, 29
2 [a]Acts 2:4; 10:46
3 [a]Rom. 14:19; 15:2 [b]1 Tim. 4:13
5 [1]NU *and*

13:4–8 How do we know we are acting with **love** (v. 4)? This passage gives specific characteristics of love: (1) it **suffers long,** is patient (1 Thess. 5:14); (2) it is **kind,** gentle, especially with those who hurt (Eph. 4:32); (3) it **does not envy,** is not jealous of what others have (Prov. 23:17); (4) it **does not parade itself,** put itself on display (John 3:30); (5) it **is not puffed up,** arrogant, proud (Gal. 6:3); (6) it **does not** act **rudely,** brashly, mean-spiritedly, insulting others (Eccl. 5:2); (7) it **does not seek its own** way, act pushy (10:24); (8) it **is not provoked** or angered (Prov. 19:11); (9) it **thinks no evil,** does not keep score on others (Heb. 10:17); (10) it rejoices not **in iniquity,** takes no pleasure when others fall into sin (Mark 3:5); (11) it **rejoices in the truth,** is joyful when righteousness prevails (2 John 4); (12) it **bears all things,** handles the burdensome (Gal. 6:2); (13) it **believes all things,** trusts in God no matter what (Prov. 3:5); (14) it **hopes all things,** keeps looking up, does not despair (Phil. 3:13); (15) it **endures all things,** "puts up with everything" (St. John Chrysostom), does not wear out (Gal. 6:9); (16) it **never fails.** The only thing love cannot do is fail (16:14).

13:8–13 The gifts of the Spirit, wonderful as they are, are temporary and incomplete. They are for this age, while we are "children" (v. 11). But **love** continues into the age to come: it is eternal, complete and fulfilling.

13:11 The Scriptures differentiate between being dependent upon God, or childlike (Matt. 18:3), and being **childish** or immature.

14:1 We are to **desire** or want the gifts of the Spirit, but **pursue** the **love** of God. St. John Chrysostom notes the difference. "Chase" love, he writes. "Make every effort" to retain her. To find this love one "strains himself, and leaves not off until he lay hold of it."

14:2 In the Orthodox Church, what about one **who speaks in a tongue?** Historically, God judged the builders of the Tower of Babel (Gen. 11:1–9), dividing their unity by confusing their language. At Pentecost Vespers we hear, "Of old there was confusion of tongues because of the boldness of the tower builders." Then, "God condemned the infidels." But at Pentecost, "the Spirit of Christ illuminated the fishermen." At Babel, there was "confusion of tongues." At Pentecost, "the vision of tongues has been renewed. . . ." In the Church, as in the NT, the gift of tongues is last on the list of the gifts (12:10, 28), temporary (13:8), primarily for the edification of the one who speaks (v. 4), and difficult to understand (vv. 11, 14). St. John Chrysostom concludes that tongues are "neither altogether useless, nor very profitable."

Commemoration of Holy Prophets

14:20–25: Paul commends the gift of prophecy.

that the church may receive
edification.
6 But now, brethren, if I come to
you speaking with tongues, what
shall I profit you unless I speak to
you either by [a]revelation, by knowledge, by prophesying, or by
teaching?
7 Even things without life,
whether flute or harp, when they
make a sound, unless they make a
distinction in the sounds, how will
it be known what is piped or played?
8 For if the trumpet makes an uncertain sound, who will prepare for
battle?
9 So likewise you, unless you utter by the tongue words easy to
understand, how will it be known
what is spoken? For you will be
speaking into the air.
10 There are, it may be, so many
kinds of languages in the world, and
none of them *is* without [1]signifi-
cance.
11 Therefore, if I do not know the
meaning of the language, I shall be
a [1]foreigner to him who speaks, and
he who speaks *will be* a foreigner to
me.
12 Even so you, since you are
[1]zealous for spiritual *gifts, let it be* for
the [2]edification of the church *that* you
seek to excel.
13 Therefore let him who speaks in
a tongue pray that he may [a]interpret.
14 For if I pray in a tongue, my
spirit prays, but my understanding
is unfruitful.
15 What is *the conclusion* then? I will
pray with the spirit, and I will also
pray with the understanding. [a]I will
sing with the spirit, and I will also
sing [b]with the understanding.

6 [a]1 Cor. 14:26
10 [1]*meaning*
11 [1]Lit. *barbarian*
12 [1]*eager* [2]*building up*
13 [a]1 Cor. 12:10
15 [a]Col. 3:16 [b]Ps. 47:7

16 Otherwise, if you bless with the
spirit, how will he who occupies the
place of the uninformed say "Amen"
[a]at your giving of thanks, since he
does not understand what you say?
17 For you indeed give thanks
well, but the other is not edified.
18 I thank my God I speak with
tongues more than you all;
19 yet in the church I would rather
speak five words with my understanding, that I may teach others
also, than ten thousand words in a
tongue.
20 Brethren, [a]do not be children in
understanding; however, in malice
[b]be babes, but in understanding be
mature.
21 [a]In the law it is written:

[b]*"With men of other tongues and*
other lips
I will speak to this people;
And yet, for all that, they will
not hear Me,"

says the Lord.
22 Therefore tongues are for a
[a]sign, not to those who believe but
to unbelievers; but prophesying is
not for unbelievers but for those who
believe.†
23 Therefore if the whole church
comes together in one place, and all
speak with tongues, and there come
in *those who are* uninformed or unbelievers, [a]will they not say that you
are [1]out of your mind?
24 But if all prophesy, and an unbeliever or an uninformed person
comes in, he is convinced by all, he
is convicted by all.
25 [1]And thus the secrets of his
heart are revealed; and so, falling

16 [a]1 Cor. 11:24
20 [a]Ps. 131:2 [b][1 Pet. 2:2]
21 [a]John 10:34 [b]Is. 28:11, 12
22 [a]Mark 16:17
23 [a]Acts 2:13 [1]*insane*
25 [1]NU omits *And thus*

14:22, 23 Spiritual gifts are for all men, Christians and non-Christians. But tongues do not edify most Christians and fail to convert **unbelievers** (v. 22), instead repelling them and suggesting that Christians are **out of** their **mind** (v. 23).

down on *his* face, he will worship God and report [a]that God is truly among you.

Order in Worship

26 How is it then, brethren? Whenever you come together, each of you has a psalm, [a]has a teaching, has a tongue, has a revelation, has an interpretation. [b]Let all things be done for [1]edification.†
27 If anyone speaks in a tongue, *let there be* two or at the most three, *each* in turn, and let one interpret.
28 But if there is no interpreter, let him keep silent in church, and let him speak to himself and to God.
29 Let two or three prophets speak, and [a]let the others judge.
30 But if *anything* is revealed to another who sits by, [a]let the first keep silent.
31 For you can all prophesy one by one, that all may learn and all may be encouraged.
32 And [a]the spirits of the prophets are subject to the prophets.
33 For God is not *the author* of [1]confusion but of peace, [a]as in all the churches of the saints.
34 [a]Let [1]your women keep silent in the churches, for they are not permitted to speak; but *they are* to be submissive, as the [b]law also says.†
35 And if they want to learn something, let them ask their own husbands at home; for it is shameful for women to speak in church.
36 Or did the word of God come *originally* from you? Or *was it* you only that it reached?
37 [a]If anyone thinks himself to be a prophet or spiritual, let him acknowledge that the things which I write to you are the commandments of the Lord.†
38 But [1]if anyone is ignorant, let him be ignorant.
39 Therefore, brethren, [a]desire earnestly to prophesy, and do not forbid to speak with tongues.
40 [a]Let all things be done decently and in order.

Witnesses to the Resurrection

15 Moreover, brethren, I declare to you the gospel [a]which I preached to you, which also you received and [b]in which you stand,
2 [a]by which also you are saved, if you hold fast that word which I preached to you—unless [b]you believed in vain.
3 For [a]I delivered to you first of all that [b]which I also received: that Christ died for our sins [c]according to the Scriptures,†

25 [a]Is. 45:14
26 [a]1 Cor. 12:8–10; 14:6 [b][2 Cor. 12:19] [1]*building up*
29 [a]1 Cor. 12:10
30 [a][1 Thess. 5:19, 20]
32 [a]1 John 4:1
33 [a]1 Cor. 11:16 [1]*disorder*
34 [a]1 Tim. 2:11 [b]Gen. 3:16 [1]NU omits *your*
37 [a]2 Cor. 10:7
38 [1]NU *if anyone does not recognize this, he is not recognized.*
39 [a]1 Cor. 12:31
40 [a]1 Cor. 14:33

CHAPTER 15

1 [a][Gal. 1:11] [b][Rom. 5:2; 11:20]
2 [a]Rom. 1:16 [b]Gal. 3:4
3 [a]1 Cor. 11:2, 23 [b][Gal. 1:12] [c]Ps. 22:15

14:26–33 This is a compassionate exhortation to the one who claims to possess the gift of tongues. This passage explains why the practice of tongues is not a part of the Divine Liturgy, which is to be entered into as God's living word. In worship we know **God is truly among** us (v. 25) because we have His prophetic word in our ears and upon our lips. Paul is here guiding a church that is severely out of balance. **God is not the author of confusion** (v. 33), and the truly spiritual can control themselves (v. 32). True spirituality is manifested in preparedness, propriety and order, courtesy, and control. If the Spirit is truly moving, there is **peace.** This is already a tradition of the Church (v. 33).

14:34–36 An early tradition in the Church is that women shall **keep silent** and not talk during the Liturgy. While they are permitted to prophesy (11:5) they are not allowed to simply converse (see also 1 Tim. 2:12). With the spiritual gifts (12:12–27), all are equal in Christ, while the order of the original creation remains in the new creation.

14:37 One can picture Paul as he writes, thinking back over his hard sayings in chs. 12—14. He is clear: this is God's word, not man's.

15:3, 4 This concise statement of the gospel is probably part of an early creed or catechism. (See Ps. 79:9; Gal. 1:4; 1 John 2:2; 4:10.)

15:3 Paul **delivered** an apostolic tradition of Christ's Resurrection which is unchanging and sufficient for salvation (v. 2). How had Paul **received** his gospel? By direct experience with the risen Lord (v. 8), confirmed by his interactions with the original Apostles (Gal. 2:2–10) and the whole Church. It is impossible to decipher what he learned where; in Paul's mind, his gospel forms a seamless whole. "To receive" designates the passing on of tradition (see 11:2, 23; Gal. 1:9; Phil. 4:9; 1 Thess. 2:13; 4:1).

Commemoration of the Dead

15:20–28, 39–57: Paul gives assurance of the bodily resurrection of the faithful.

4 and that He was buried, and
that He rose again the third day
[a]according to the Scriptures,
5 [a]and that He was seen by
[1]Cephas, then [b]by the twelve.†
6 After that He was seen by over
five hundred brethren at once, of
whom the greater part remain to the
present, but some have [1]fallen
asleep.
7 After that He was seen by
James, then [a]by all the apostles.
8 [a]Then last of all He was seen
by me also, as by one born out of
due time.
9 For I am [a]the least of the apostles, who am not worthy to be called
an apostle, because [b]I persecuted the
church of God.
10 But [a]by the grace of God I am
what I am, and His grace toward me
was not in vain; but I labored more
abundantly than they all, [b]yet not I,
but the grace of God *which was* with
me.
11 Therefore, whether *it was* I or
they, so we preach and so you
believed.

The Centrality of the Resurrection

12 Now if Christ is preached that
He has been raised from the dead,
how do some among you say that
there is no resurrection of the dead?†
13 But if there is no resurrection
of the dead, [a]then Christ is not
risen.
14 And if Christ is not risen, then
our preaching *is* empty and your
faith *is* also empty.
15 Yes, and we are found false witnesses of God, because [a]we have testified of God that He raised up
Christ, whom He did not raise up—
if in fact the dead do not rise.
16 For if *the* dead do not rise, then
Christ is not risen.
17 And if Christ is not risen, your
faith *is* futile; [a]you are still in your
sins!
18 Then also those who have
[1]fallen [a]asleep in Christ have
perished.
19 [a]If in this life only we have hope
in Christ, we are of all men the most
pitiable.

The Resurrection and the Kingdom

20 But now [a]Christ is risen from
the dead, *and* has become [b]the firstfruits of those who have [1]fallen
asleep.†
21 For [a]since by man *came* death,
[b]by Man also *came* the resurrection
of the dead.
22 For as in Adam all die, even
so in Christ all shall [a]be made
alive.†

4 [a]Ps. 16:9–11; 68:18; 110:1
5 [a]Luke 24:34 [b]Matt. 28:17 [1]Peter
6 [1]Died
7 [a]Acts 1:3, 4
8 [a][Acts 9:3–8; 22:6–11; 26:12–18]
9 [a]Eph. 3:8 [b]Acts 8:3
10 [a]Eph. 3:7, 8 [b]Phil. 2:13
13 [a][1 Thess. 4:14]
15 [a]Acts 2:24
17 [a][Rom. 4:25]
18 [a]Job 14:12 [1]Died
19 [a]2 Tim. 3:12
20 [a]1 Pet. 1:3 [b]Acts 26:23 [1]Died
21 [a]Rom. 5:12; 6:23 [b]John 11:25
22 [a][John 5:28, 29]

15:5–8 Paul lists those who would testify to the truth of the Resurrection, from the first witnesses to Paul himself.

15:12–19 What is Christianity without the resurrection—both Christ's and ours? His death does us no good without it. What use is forgiveness if we remain dead? His disciples were transformed by His Resurrection; and this they preached above all. On Easter morning Orthodox Christians sing, "Christ is risen from the dead, trampling down death by death, and upon those in the tombs bestowing life."

15:20 As **the firstfruits** in the OT were consecrated to God representative of the promise of later fruits (Ex. 23:16), so the Resurrection of Jesus from the dead is the first offering of the resurrection of all who are His (v. 23).

15:22 All people share the same human nature, but Christians have two fathers: first **Adam,** who became the father of mortality and earthly life, and now **Christ,** the father of immortality and spiritual life.

23 But [a]each one in his own order:
Christ the firstfruits, afterward those
who are Christ's at His coming.
24 Then *comes* the end, when He
delivers [a]the kingdom to God the Father, when He puts an end to all rule
and all authority and power.†
25 For He must reign [a]till He has
put all enemies under His feet.
26 [a]The last enemy *that* will be destroyed *is* death.
27 For [a]*"He has put all things under His feet."* But when He says "all
things are put under *Him," it is* evident that He who put all things under Him is excepted.
28 [a]Now when all things are made
subject to Him, then [b]the Son Himself will also be subject to Him who
put all things under Him, that God
may be all in all.
29 Otherwise, what will they do
who are baptized for the dead, if the
dead do not rise at all? Why then
are they baptized for the dead?†
30 And [a]why do we stand in
[1]jeopardy every hour?
31 I affirm, by [a]the boasting in you
which I have in Christ Jesus our
Lord, [b]I die daily.
32 If, in the manner of men,
[a]I have fought with beasts at Ephesus, what advantage *is it* to me? If
the dead do not rise, [b]*"Let us eat and
drink, for tomorrow we die!"*†

23 [a][1 Thess. 4:15–17]
24 [a][Dan. 2:44; 7:14, 27]
25 [a]Ps. 110:1
26 [a][2 Tim. 1:10]
27 [a]Ps. 8:6
28 [a][Phil. 3:21] [b]1 Cor. 3:23; 11:3; 12:6
30 [a]2 Cor. 11:26 [1]*danger*
31 [a]1 Thess. 2:19 [b]Rom. 8:36
32 [a]2 Cor. 1:8 [b]Is. 22:13; 56:12
33 [a][1 Cor. 5:6]
34 [a]Rom. 13:11 [b][1 Thess. 4:5] [c]1 Cor. 6:5
35 [a]Ezek. 37:3
36 [a]John 12:24
39 [1]NU, M omit *of flesh*
40 [1]*heavenly* [2]*earthly*
42 [a][Dan. 12:3]

33 Do not be deceived: [a]"Evil company corrupts good habits."
34 [a]Awake to righteousness, and
do not sin; [b]for some do not have
the knowledge of God. [c]I speak *this*
to your shame.

The Manner of the Resurrection

35 But someone will say, [a]"How
are the dead raised up? And with
what body do they come?"†
36 Foolish one, [a]what you sow is
not made alive unless it dies.
37 And what you sow, you do not
sow that body that shall be, but mere
grain—perhaps wheat or some other
grain.
38 But God gives it a body as He
pleases, and to each seed its own
body.
39 All flesh *is* not the same flesh,
but *there is* one *kind* [1]*of* flesh of men,
another flesh of animals, another of
fish, *and* another of birds.
40 *There are* also [1]celestial bodies
and [2]terrestrial bodies; but the glory
of the celestial *is* one, and the *glory*
of the terrestrial *is* another.
41 *There is* one glory of the sun, another glory of the moon, and another
glory of the stars; for *one* star differs
from *another* star in glory.
42 [a]So also *is* the resurrection of

15:24–28 The end is the consummation of the Kingdom when Christ's lordship over all will be fulfilled and He will offer creation up to God the Father (see Rom. 8:19–23, 32–39). Although **the Son** (v. 28) shares the same divine nature and dignity as the Father, He is **subject to** the Father because only the Father is the source of divinity. God being **all in all** refers to the common lordship of the Trinity over all things, not to pantheism.

15:29 The meaning of **baptized for the dead** is much disputed. Many understand this as vicarious baptism of baptized Christians for deceased catechumens. St. John Chrysostom considered it a derisive comment about the practices of the Marcionite heretics. Epiphanius says it refers to a practice of the followers of Cerinthus, another Gnostic teacher.

15:32 Fighting **with beasts at Ephesus** may refer to persecutions there (16:8, 9; Acts 19:21–31).

15:35–54 How will **the dead** rise? What is the resurrection **body** like? Paul's most basic contrast is that between the **natural** (literally "soulish"; Gr. *psychikon*) and the **spiritual** (Gr. *pneumatikon,* v. 44), that is, between the present body and the deified body. Other contrasts are **corruption** vs. **incorruption** (v. 42), **dishonor** vs. **glory** (v. 43), **weakness** vs. **power** (v. 43), **living** "soul" (literal translation) vs. **life-giving spirit** (v. 45), **of the earth** vs. **from heaven** (v. 47), **of dust** vs. **heavenly** (v. 48), the **mortal** vs. the immortal (v. 54).

This present body is only a **seed** (v. 38) of the body to come. The "spiritual" body is not a pale shadow of the material world we now know; the opposite is true. The resurrection body is the fulfillment of what God intends for our present body. It is the material fulfilled, not dematerialized.

the dead. *The body* is sown in corruption, it is raised in incorruption.

43 [a]It is sown in dishonor, it is raised in glory. It is sown in weakness, it is raised in power.

44 It is sown a natural body, it is raised a spiritual body. There is a natural body, and there is a spiritual body.

The One Who Resurrects Us

45 And so it is written, [a]*"The first man Adam became a living being."* [b]The last Adam *became* [c]a life-giving spirit.†

46 However, the spiritual is not first, but the natural, and afterward the spiritual.

47 [a]The first man *was* of the earth, [b]*made*[1] of dust; the second Man *is* [2]the Lord [c]from heaven.

48 As *was* the [1]*man* of dust, so also *are* those *who are* [1]*made* of dust; [a]and as *is* the heavenly *Man*, so also *are* those *who are* heavenly.

49 And [a]as we have borne the image of the *man* of dust, [b]we[1] shall also bear the image of the heavenly *Man*.

The Time of the Resurrection

50 Now this I say, brethren, that [a]flesh and blood cannot inherit the kingdom of God; nor does corruption inherit incorruption.†

51 Behold, I tell you a [1]mystery: [a]We shall not all sleep, [b]but we shall all be changed—

52 in a moment, in the twinkling of an eye, at the last trumpet. [a]For the trumpet will sound, and the dead will be raised incorruptible, and we shall be changed.

53 For this corruptible must put on incorruption, and [a]this mortal *must* put on immortality.

Hymn: Triumph over Death

54 So when this corruptible has put on incorruption, and this mortal has put on immortality, then shall be brought to pass the saying that is written: [a]*"Death is swallowed up in victory."*

55 *"O[a][1] Death, where is your sting?*
O Hades, where is your
victory?"

56 The sting of death *is* sin, and [a]the strength of sin *is* the law.†

57 [a]But thanks *be* to God, who gives us [b]the victory through our Lord Jesus Christ.

58 [a]Therefore, my beloved brethren, be steadfast, immovable, always abounding in the work of the Lord, knowing [b]that your labor is not in vain in the Lord.†

Collection for Jerusalem

16 Now concerning [a]the collection for the saints, as I have given orders to the churches of Galatia, so you must do also:†

2 [a]On the first *day* of the week let each one of you lay something aside, storing up as he may prosper, that

43 [a][Phil. 3:21]
45 [a]Gen. 2:7 [b][Rom. 5:14] [c]John 5:21; 6:57
47 [a]John 3:31 [b]Gen. 2:7; 3:19 [c]John 3:13 [1]*earthy* [2]NU omits *the Lord*
48 [a]Phil. 3:20 [1]*earthy*
49 [a]Gen. 5:3 [b]Rom. 8:29 [1]M *let us also bear*
50 [a][John 3:3, 5]
51 [a][1 Thess. 4:15] [b][Phil. 3:21] [1]*hidden truth*
52 [a]Matt. 24:31
53 [a]2 Cor. 5:4
54 [a]Is. 25:8
55 [a]Hos. 13:14 [1]NU *O Death, where is your victory? O Death, where is your sting?*
56 [a][Rom. 3:20; 4:15; 7:8]
57 [a][Rom. 7:25] [b][1 John 5:4]
58 [a]2 Pet. 3:14 [b][1 Cor. 3:8]

CHAPTER 16

1 [a]Gal. 2:10
2 [a]Acts 20:7

15:45–49 Whose body is this? As our present body is Adam's, so the resurrection body is the last Adam's, Christ's.

15:50 Flesh and blood (v. 50) refers to human nature in its present weak and imperfect condition.

15:56 Our basic mortal condition is manifested in sin. We are born mortal; we then become sinful. Thus does **death** "sting" us before we die. Being a Christian is more than having one's sins forgiven or being good; it is being alive.

The law is not sinful, but it exposes sin. And, since it does not provide the power to obey it, it increases sinfulness in unchanged humans (Rom. 3:20; 4:15; 5:13, 20; 7:7; Gal. 3:19–22).

15:58 The doctrine of the resurrection has a practical consequence: It is to move us to do the works that God would have us do, **the work of the Lord.**

16:1–4 See 2 Cor. 8; 9.

there be no collections when I come.
3 And when I come, [a]whomever
you approve by *your* letters I will
send to bear your gift to Jerusalem.
4 [a]But if it is fitting that I go also,
they will go with me.

Paul's Plans

5 Now I will come to you [a]when
I pass through Macedonia (for I am
passing through Macedonia).
6 And it may be that I will remain,
or even spend the winter with you,
that you may [a]send me on my journey, wherever I go.
7 For I do not wish to see you now
on the way; but I hope to stay a while
with you, [a]if the Lord permits.
8 But I will tarry in Ephesus until
[a]Pentecost.
9 For [a]a great and effective door
has opened to me, and [b]*there are*
many adversaries.
10 And [a]if Timothy comes, see that
he may be with you without fear; for
[b]he does the work of the Lord, as I
also *do*.
11 [a]Therefore let no one despise
him. But send him on his journey
[b]in peace, that he may come to me;
for I am waiting for him with the
brethren.
12 Now concerning *our* brother
[a]Apollos, I strongly urged him to
come to you with the brethren, but
he was quite unwilling to come at
this time; however, he will come
when he has a convenient time.

3 [a]2 Cor. 3:1; 8:18
4 [a]2 Cor. 8:4, 19
5 [a]2 Cor. 1:15, 16
6 [a]Acts 15:3
7 [a]James 4:15
8 [a]Lev. 23:15–22
9 [a]Acts 14:27 [b]Acts 19:9
10 [a]Acts 19:22 [b]Phil. 2:20
11 [a]1 Tim. 4:12 [b]Acts 15:33
12 [a]1 Cor. 1:12; 3:5

Final Exhortations and Greetings

13 [a]Watch, [b]stand fast in the faith,
be brave, [c]be strong.
14 [a]Let all *that* you *do* be done with
love.
15 I urge you, brethren—you know
[a]the household of Stephanas, that it
is [b]the firstfruits of Achaia, and *that*
they have devoted themselves to
[c]the ministry of the saints—
16 [a]that you also submit to such,
and to everyone who works and
[b]labors with *us*.
17 I am glad about the coming of
Stephanas, Fortunatus, and Achai-
cus, [a]for what was lacking on your
part they supplied.†
18 [a]For they refreshed my spirit
and yours. Therefore [b]acknowledge
such men.
19 The churches of Asia greet you.
Aquila and Priscilla greet you heartily in the Lord, [a]with the church that
is in their house.†
20 All the brethren greet you.
[a]Greet one another with a holy kiss.
21 [a]The salutation with my own
hand—Paul's.†
22 If anyone [a]does not love the
Lord Jesus Christ, [b]let him be
[1]accursed. [c]O[2] Lord, come!
23 [a]The grace of our Lord Jesus
Christ *be* with you.
24 My love *be* with you all in Christ
Jesus. Amen.

13 [a]Matt. 24:42 [b]Phil. 1:27; 4:1 [c][Eph. 3:16; 6:10]
14 [a][1 Pet. 4:8]
15 [a]1 Cor. 1:16 [b]Rom. 16:5 [c]2 Cor. 8:4
16 [a]Heb. 13:17 [b][Heb. 6:10]
17 [a]2 Cor. 11:9
18 [a]Col. 4:8 [b]Phil. 2:29
19 [a]Rom. 16:5
20 [a]Rom. 16:16
21 [a]Col. 4:18
22 [a]Eph. 6:24 [b]Gal. 1:8, 9 [c]Jude 14, 15 [1]Gr. *anathema*

[2]Aram. *Marana tha* or *Maranatha;* possibly *Maran atha, Our Lord has come* **23** [a]Rom. 16:20

16:17, 18 These men apparently were the carriers of the letter which Paul answers in chs. 7—15 (7:1). Paul's displeasure with Corinth does not affect his joy for certain Corinthians.

16:19 Aquila and Priscilla were Jews who had been among those expelled from Rome by Claudius in A.D. 49–50, had resided in Corinth for a while (Acts 18:2) and then moved to Ephesus (Acts 18:26).

16:21 Paul often dictated his letters to a secretary. The proof that he composed this letter is his closing signature.

The Second Epistle of Paul the Apostle to the

CORINTHIANS

Author: *St. Paul the Apostle*

Date: *c. A.D. 55*

Theme: *Reconciliation and Communion*

AUTHOR: St. Paul the Apostle is identified as the author in 1:1 and there is no reason to doubt his authorship.

DATE: Second Corinthians was written the same year as 1 Corinthians (c. A.D. 55) from Macedonia, where Titus rejoined Paul with a report about the Corinthian church (see Introduction to 1 Corinthians).

MAJOR THEME: Reconciliation and communion. This theme is clearly seen in Paul's attempt to be reconciled to the Corinthian church. Other aspects of this theme include:

(1) *The communion of saints.* Second Corinthians presupposes an understanding on the part of the reader that the Church is the body of Christ: a corporate unity of all members in all things.

(2) *Apostleship and the Church.* Paul battles for a principle: the faith of properly ordained and recognized apostles is essential to the life of the Church. If there is no apostolic faith, there is no Church. For Paul, the apostolic ministry is part of "the ministry of the Spirit" (3:8) and is necessary for the manifestation of the Trinity in the body of Christ. The apostles have real authority, a loving, serving authority, based on and empowered by the mercy of God. The relationship between the apostles and the laity is a communion of love, as is the relationship between father and child, between the Father and the Son.

The primary duty of apostles is to preach the gospel, both to the Church and to the world: the Good News that Jesus is the Christ, the Son of God, and He is risen. His Resurrection is the basis for all else: doctrine, sacrament, and the Christian life. Through the Resurrection, Christ takes His human nature into heaven and opens the possibility of all of creation being reconciled to God.

(3) *The unity of the Church.* The collection for Jerusalem (chs. 8; 9) demonstrates the love and unity between the Gentile and the Judaic elements in the Church—manifested in sacrificial giving.

(4) *The Church and the world.* Christianity does not renounce and forsake the world, but renews it. Things are not divided into categories of secular or

sacred, profane or holy, for God made all and continues to be in all; but things are divided into old and new (5:17). The old is deeply affected by corruption, doomed to unfulfillment, and temporary. The new alone participates in incorruption, perfection, and eternity. The task of the Church is to reconcile all men and all of creation to God (5:18–20). Then God makes all things new, transforms all things into what He originally intended them to be.

BACKGROUND INFORMATION: For the historical setting of 2 Corinthians, see the Introduction to 1 Corinthians.

A major purpose of this second epistle is Paul's defense of his apostleship and his polemic against false apostles in Corinth.

(1) *The charges against Paul.* Outsiders have shown up in Corinth calling themselves "the most eminent apostles" (11:5; 12:11), or "super-apostles." They claim to be better than Paul, alleging that he does not measure up (13:5–7). They seek to prove Paul an impostor, charging that he is indecisive (1:17), cowardly (1:23; 13:2), cruel (2:2), weak (11:21; 13:9, 10), and unattractive—no more than walking death (2:16; 4:7–18)! He has no letters of recommendation (3:1), no teaching credentials (3:5), no special revelatory experiences (3:7–18; 12:1–10), no miraculous powers (12:12), and little knowledge (11:6). Yet he boastfully asserts his authority (3:1; 4:5; 12:1, 17). He is a terrible administrator, lacking the wisdom necessary to be a leader; perhaps he is mad (5:13; 11:1, 16). He is not even a good preacher (2:17; 4:2; 10:10; 11:6). Further, say these false apostles, Paul and his cronies tricked Corinth into thinking he received no support from them (7:2; 11:7–9; 12:14, 17, 18), while he may even have been an embezzler (8:20, 21).

(2) *The claims of the false apostles.* They point to (1) their own letters of recommendation (3:1); (2) their Jewish, Greek, and Christian credentials (3:5, 6; 11:15, 22, 23); (3) their resumés of success, backed up by the public acclaim of non-Christians (1:12; 4:8–11; 6:4–10; 10:7; 11:18); and (4) their own claims to personal greatness (4:7; 5:12; 10:12, 17, 18). Apparently they compare their experiences of God to those of Moses (3:7–18).

In their preaching they elevate themselves (4:5) and present a different gospel from Paul's (11:4). They depend upon speaking skills to influence their audience with unorthodox ideas (2:17; 4:2). They teach that Christians must have exalted spiritual experiences and lead successful, painless lives, and should not be concerned about moral purity and holiness (6:14—7:1).

(3) *Paul's response.* Paul perceives all of this false teaching as a vain, earthly show, having nothing to do with God, the gospel, or the Kingdom (5:11–19). He reveals the false apostles as agents of Satan (4:3, 4; 6:15; 11:3, 13–15).

OUTLINE

Greeting	1:1, 2
I. Paul's reconciliation to the Corinthian church	1:3—7:16
A. Thanksgiving for comfort in affliction	1:3–11
B. Is Paul sincere?	1:12—2:17
1. Paul's pure conscience toward Corinth	1:12–14
2. Paul's intended visit to Corinth	1:15—2:17

Greeting

1 Paul, [a]an apostle of Jesus Christ by the will of God, and [b]Timothy *our* brother,

To the church of God which is at Corinth, [c]with all the saints who are in all Achaia:

2 [a]Grace to you and peace from God our Father and the Lord Jesus Christ.

Sharing Suffering, Sharing Comfort

3 [a]Blessed *be* the God and Father of our Lord Jesus Christ, the Father of mercies and God of all comfort,†
4 who [a]comforts us in all our tribulation, that we may be able to comfort those who are in any [1]trouble, with the comfort with which we ourselves are comforted by God.
5 For as [a]the sufferings of Christ abound in us, so our [1]consolation also abounds through Christ.
6 Now if we are afflicted, [a]*it is* for your consolation and salvation, which is effective for enduring the same sufferings which we also suffer. Or if we are comforted, *it is* for your consolation and salvation.†
7 And our hope for you *is* steadfast, because we know that [a]as you are partakers of the sufferings, so also *you will partake* of the consolation.

Sharing in Adversity by Prayer

8 For we do not want you to be ignorant, brethren, of [a]our [1]trouble

CHAPTER 1
1 [a]2 Tim. 1:1 [b]1 Cor. 16:10 [c]Col. 1:2
2 [a]Rom. 1:7
3 [a]1 Pet. 1:3
4 [a]Is. 51:12; 66:13 [1]*tribulation*
5 [a]2 Cor. 4:10 [1]*comfort*
6 [a]2 Cor. 4:15; 12:15
7 [a][Rom. 8:17]
8 [a]Acts 19:23 [1]*tribulation*

1:3–11 The *source* of afflictions is the sin of humanity. The *purpose* of afflictions, if we use them properly, may be our comfort and salvation, as the Father Himself preserves us through them (v. 3). The *means* of facing our afflictions is a hope in God which allows us to enter into the afflictions of others in actual, experiential knowledge. In this case, this means people empathizing with their apostle's trials. The communion of saints, spiritual solidarity, is to begin now in the pains of this life.

1:6 The godly suffer, in part, so that having experienced God's comfort they in turn can comfort others. Thus, Paul shows the fallacy in his opponents' idea that Christians should never suffer and should be concerned only with their own salvation.

which came to us in Asia: that we
were burdened beyond measure,
above strength, so that we despaired
even of life.†
9 Yes, we had the sentence of
death in ourselves, that we should
[a]not trust in ourselves but in God
who raises the dead,
10 [a]who delivered us from so great
a death, and [1]does deliver us; in
whom we trust that He will still deliver *us,*
11 you also [a]helping together in
prayer for us, that thanks may be
given by many persons on [1]our behalf [b]for the gift *granted* to us
through many.

Paul's Pure Conscience Toward Corinth

12 For our boasting is this: the testimony of our conscience that we
conducted ourselves in the world in
[1]simplicity and [a]godly sincerity,
[b]not with fleshly wisdom but by the
grace of God, and more abundantly
toward you.
13 For we are not writing any other
things to you than what you read
or understand. Now I trust you will
understand, even to the end†
14 (as also you have understood us
in part), [a]that we are your boast as
[b]you also *are* ours, in the day of the
Lord Jesus.

9 [a]Jer. 17:5, 7
10 [a][2 Pet. 2:9] [1]NU *shall*
11 [a]Rom. 15:30 [b]2 Cor. 4:15; 9:11 [1]M *your behalf*
12 [a]2 Cor. 2:17 [b][1 Cor. 2:4] [1]The opposite of duplicity
14 [a]2 Cor. 5:12 [b]Phil. 2:16
15 [a]1 Cor. 4:19 [b]Rom. 1:11; 15:29
16 [a]1 Cor. 16:3–6
17 [a]2 Cor. 10:2; 11:18
18 [a]1 John 5:20 [1]*message*
19 [a]Mark 1:1 [b]1 Pet. 5:12 [c]2 Cor. 1:1 [d][Heb. 13:8]
20 [a][Rom. 15:8, 9]
21 [a][1 John 2:20, 27]
22 [a][Eph. 4:30] [b][Eph. 1:14]

Paul Does Not Vacillate

15 And in this confidence [a]I intended to come to you before, that
you might have [b]a second benefit—†
16 to pass by way of you to Macedonia, [a]to come again from Macedonia to you, and be helped by you
on my way to Judea.
17 Therefore, when I was planning
this, did I do it lightly? Or the things
I plan, do I plan [a]according to the
flesh, that with me there should be
Yes, Yes, and No, No?
18 But *as* God *is* [a]faithful, our
[1]word to you was not Yes and
No.
19 For [a]the Son of God, Jesus
Christ, who was preached among
you by us—by me, [b]Silvanus, and
[c]Timothy—was not Yes and No,
[d]but in Him was Yes.†
20 [a]For all the promises of God in
Him *are* Yes, and in Him Amen, to
the glory of God through us.†
21 Now He who establishes us
with you in Christ and [a]has anointed
us *is* God,†
22 who [a]also has sealed us and
[b]given us the Spirit in our hearts as
a guarantee.

1:8 What this **trouble** is for Paul is not clear—perhaps a physical malady, or persecution. But whatever its nature, it makes him more aware of death and of his dependence upon God (v. 9)—and more appreciative of the fellowship of other Christians, and of the power of the Church's corporate prayer (v. 11).

1:13 Paul was accused by the dissidents/schismatics in Corinth of speaking murkily, indirectly, by allusion and not by clear, direct statement.

1:15 Paul has changed his travel plans. (1) In his earlier letter, he planned to travel to Corinth, passing through Macedonia in northern Greece (1 Cor. 16:5–7). (2) When he felt compelled to go to Corinth immediately, the "sorrowful visit," he planned to visit Corinth twice (vv. 15, 16); but he actually came only once. (3) In the "sorrowful" letter (now lost), written after that visit, his plan was to travel directly from Ephesus to Corinth. Instead, he travelled up through Macedonia (2:12, 13). This was perceived as vacillation by some in Corinth. (See Introduction to 1 Corinthians for a summary of Paul's dealings with Corinth.)

1:19 Silvanus is Silas, Paul's longtime coworker (Acts 15:40).

1:20 Christ is **Yes.** He affirms and fulfills God-given **promises,** though His ways may at times seem strange to men. Therefore, the Church may always affirm **Amen to Him**—which explains the repeated use of that response in liturgical practice.

1:21, 22 Note again the NT roots of Orthodox sacramental life. We are established **in Christ** (v. 21) through baptism and are **anointed** and **sealed** (v. 22) in **the Spirit** through chrismation.

Paul Is Merciful

23 Moreover [a]I call God as witness
against my soul, [b]that to spare you
I came no more to Corinth.†
24 Not [a]that we [1]have dominion
over your faith, but are fellow workers for your joy; for [b]by faith you
stand.

2 But I determined this within myself, [a]that I would not come
again to you in sorrow.
2 For if I make you [a]sorrowful,
then who is he who makes me glad
but the one who is made sorrowful
by me?
3 And I wrote this very thing to
you, lest, when I came, [a]I should
have sorrow over those from whom
I ought to have joy, [b]having confidence in you all that my joy is *the
joy* of you all.
4 For out of much [1]affliction and
anguish of heart I wrote to you, with
many tears, [a]not that you should be
grieved, but that you might know
the love which I have so abundantly
for you.†

Restore the Penitent Offender

5 But [a]if anyone has caused grief,
he has not [b]grieved me, but all of
you to some extent—not to be too
severe.†
6 This punishment which *was inflicted* [a]by the majority *is* sufficient
for such a man,

23 [a]Gal. 1:20 [b]1 Cor. 4:21
24 [a][1 Pet. 5:3] [b]Rom. 11:20 [1]*rule*

CHAPTER 2

1 [a]2 Cor. 1:23
2 [a]2 Cor. 7:8
3 [a]2 Cor. 12:21 [b]Gal. 5:10
4 [a][2 Cor. 2:9; 7:8, 12] [1]*tribulation*
5 [a][1 Cor. 5:1] [b]Gal. 4:12
6 [a]1 Cor. 5:4, 5
7 [a]Gal. 6:1
9 [a]2 Cor. 7:15; 10:6
10 [1]NU *indeed, what I have forgiven, if I have forgiven anything, I did it for your sakes*
12 [a]Acts 16:8 [b]1 Cor. 16:9 [1]Opportunity
13 [a]2 Cor. 7:6, 13; 8:6
14 [1]*manifests*
15 [a][1 Cor. 1:18] [b][2 Cor. 4:3]

7 [a]so that, on the contrary, you
ought rather to forgive and comfort
him, lest perhaps such a one be swallowed up with too much sorrow.
8 Therefore I urge you to reaffirm
your love to him.
9 For to this end I also wrote, that
I might put you to the test, whether
you are [a]obedient in all things.
10 Now whom you forgive any-
thing, I also *forgive.* For [1]if indeed I
have forgiven anything, I have forgiven that one for your sakes in the
presence of Christ,
11 lest Satan should take advantage of us; for we are not ignorant
of his devices.

God Triumphs in His Apostles

12 Furthermore, [a]when I came to
Troas to *preach* Christ's gospel, and
[b]a [1]door was opened to me by the
Lord,
13 [a]I had no rest in my spirit, because I did not find Titus my brother;
but taking my leave of them, I departed for Macedonia.
14 Now thanks *be* to God who always leads us in triumph in Christ,
and through us [1]diffuses the fragrance of His knowledge in every
place.†
15 For we are to God the fragrance
of Christ [a]among those who are being saved and [b]among those who are
perishing.

1:23, 24 The real reason for Paul's change in itinerary is graciousness: to **spare** them a confrontation. The purpose of Church discipline is never for the leader to exercise **dominion** or harsh authority; rather it is to call for (1) repentance, (2) reconciliation with the Church and (3) renewal in the **joy** (v. 24) of the Spirit.

2:4 True pastoral correction brings both agony for the overseer—**affliction, anguish of heart, many tears**—and abundant **love** for the one being disciplined (see Heb. 12:5, 6, 11).

2:5–11 Church discipline must not **be too severe;** that is, it must not go farther than the sin. And not to **forgive and comfort** (v. 7) the one who repents is itself a sin. Undue separation from the Church through excessive and prolonged discipline increases tension (**too much sorrow,** v. 7) and even division. This pleases **Satan** (v. 11), the author of strife and discord; it does not please God.

2:14–17 Our **triumph in Christ** (v. 14), taken in an ancient Roman context, suggests a magnificent picture of unwilling captive soldiers paraded before the victorious commander's chariot, while fragrant flowers are strewn along the way in celebration. The victor is Christ; the captives are the powers of darkness; His **fragrance** is the apostolic ministry, especially its preaching (v. 17). Christians are the winning forces who triumph through the hearing of the **word of God** (v. 17) and joining the great procession of thanksgiving **leading to life** (v. 16).

16 [a]To the one *we are* the aroma of
death *leading* to death, and to the
other the aroma of life *leading* to life.
And [b]who *is* sufficient for these
things?
17 For we are not, as [1]so many,
[a]peddling[2] the word of God; but
as [b]of sincerity, but as from God,
we speak in the sight of God in
Christ.

Paul's Letter of Recommendation

3 Do [a]we begin again to commend
ourselves? Or do we need, as
some *others*, [b]epistles of commendation to you or *letters* of commendation from you?†
2 [a]You are our epistle written in
our hearts, known and read by all
men;†
3 clearly *you are* an epistle of
Christ, [a]ministered by us, written
not with ink but by the Spirit of the
living God, not [b]on tablets of stone
but [c]on tablets of flesh, *that is,* of the
heart.

Paul's Sufficiency: The Life-Giving Spirit

4 And we have such trust through
Christ toward God.†

16 [a]Luke 2:34 [b][1 Cor. 15:10]
17 [a]2 Pet. 2:3 [b]2 Cor. 1:12 [1]M *the rest* [2]*adulterating for gain*

CHAPTER 3

1 [a]2 Cor. 5:12; 10:12, 18; 12:11 [b]Acts 18:27
2 [a]1 Cor. 9:2
3 [a]1 Cor. 3:5 [b]Ex. 24:12; 31:18; 32:15 [c]Ps. 40:8
5 [a][John 15:5] [b]1 Cor. 15:10
6 [a]1 Cor. 3:5 [b]Jer. 31:31 [c]Rom. 2:27 [d]Gal. 3:10 [e]John 6:63 [1]Or *spirit*
7 [a]Rom. 7:10 [b]Ex. 34:1 [c]Ex. 34:29
8 [a][Gal. 3:5]
9 [a][Rom. 1:17; 3:21]

5 [a]Not that we are sufficient of
ourselves to think of anything as *being* from ourselves, but [b]our sufficiency *is* from God,
6 who also made us sufficient as
[a]ministers of [b]the new covenant, not
[c]of the letter but of the [1]Spirit; for
[d]the letter kills, [e]but the Spirit gives
life.

Paul's Ministry: The Glory of God

7 But if [a]the ministry of death,
[b]written *and* engraved on stones,
was glorious, [c]so that the children
of Israel could not look steadily at
the face of Moses because of the
glory of his countenance, which *glory*
was passing away,†
8 how will [a]the ministry of the
Spirit not be more glorious?
9 For if the ministry of condemnation *had* glory, the ministry [a]of righteousness exceeds much more in
glory.
10 For even what was made glorious had no glory in this respect, because of the glory that excels.
11 For if what is passing away *was*
glorious, what remains *is* much more
glorious.

3:1 The outsiders who came to Corinth as prominent apostles demanded evidence of Paul's sincerity. They themselves carried forged **letters of commendation**—letters which Paul could not match. They maintained Paul was not a genuine apostle.

3:2, 3 Paul does not need a commendation in **ink** (v. 3), for the Corinthians have all experienced the fruit of his ministry; this fruit is of more value than any written **epistle.** Paul compares the difference between sterile epistles and living spiritual fruit to the difference between the Old Covenant, written **on tablets of stone,** and the New, written **on tablets . . . of the heart.** The impostors in Corinth are lifeless legalists. Paul is ministering **Christ** through the **Spirit** of **God.**

3:4–6 This passage holds great hope for the Christian ministry. "Who is sufficient for these things?" (2:16)—the one who places **trust through Christ** in **God** (v. 4). The minister gives his all in study and service, but ultimately human power is not sufficient for ministry or for salvation: we must depend utterly upon God.

3:7–9 The Old Covenant was external, temporary, and powerless. Under it God was present, and it **was glorious** with the presence of God. But it was imperfect, and imparted a **ministry of death** because men were unable to keep the Law. There was an access to God, but **Israel** generally failed to apprehend it. The inner veil of the temple and the veil over **the face of Moses** spoke of the veil over the hearts of fallen human nature: men could neither adequately approach nor adequately see God. Many even fail to see the Godhead veiled in Jesus' flesh. By contrast, the New Covenant is internal, eternal, and powerful. Under it God is fully present as an unlimited, life-giving **glory** (v. 9), through **the ministry of the Spirit** (v. 8) and **of righteousness** (v. 9). Christians have bold access to God, for there is no veil to separate us (v. 16). The New Covenant is therefore **more glorious** (v. 8).

Paul's Relationship with God

12 Therefore, since we have such
hope, [a]we use great boldness of
speech—
13 unlike Moses, [a]*who* put a veil
over his face so that the children of
Israel could not look steadily at
[b]the end of what was passing away.
14 But [a]their minds were blinded.
For until this day the same veil remains unlifted in the reading of the
Old Testament, because the *veil* is
taken away in Christ.
15 But even to this day, when
Moses is read, a veil lies on their
heart.
16 Nevertheless [a]when one turns
to the Lord, [b]the veil is taken away.†
17 Now [a]the Lord is the Spirit; and
where the Spirit of the Lord *is,* there
is [b]liberty.†
18 But we all, with unveiled face,
beholding [a]as in a mirror [b]the glory
of the Lord, [c]are being transformed
into the same image from glory to
glory, just as [1]by the Spirit of the
Lord.

12 [a]Eph. 6:19
13 [a]Ex. 34:33–35
[b][Gal. 3:23]
14 [a]Acts 28:26
16 [a]Rom. 11:23
[b]Is. 25:7
17 [a][1 Cor. 15:45]
[b]Gal. 5:1, 13
18 [a]1 Cor. 13:12
[b][2 Cor. 4:4, 6]
[c][Rom. 8:29, 30]
[1]Or *from the Lord, the Spirit*

CHAPTER 4

1 [a]1 Cor. 7:25
[b]2 Cor. 4:16
2 [a]2 Cor. 5:11
[1]*adulterating the word of God*
3 [a][1 Cor. 1:18]
4 [a]John 12:31
[b]John 12:40
[c][2 Cor. 3:8, 9]
[d][John 1:18]

Paul's Faithfulness to the Gospel

4 Therefore, since we have this
ministry, [a]as we have received
mercy, we [b]do not lose heart.†
2 But we have renounced the hidden things of shame, not walking in
craftiness nor [1]handling the word of
God deceitfully, but by manifestation
of the truth [a]commending ourselves
to every man's conscience in the
sight of God.
3 But even if our gospel is veiled,
[a]it is veiled to those who are
perishing,
4 whose minds [a]the god of this
age [b]has blinded, who do not believe, lest [c]the light of the gospel of
the glory of Christ, [d]who is the image of God, should shine on them.
5 [a]For we do not preach ourselves, but Christ Jesus the Lord, and
[b]ourselves your bondservants for
Jesus' sake.†
6 For it is the God [a]who com-

5 [a]1 Cor. 1:13 [b]1 Cor. 9:19 6 [a]Gen. 1:3

3:16–18 The Lord here is a title. In the NT *Lord* usually refers to the Son. The Father is sometimes called Lord (Matt. 11:25; 22:44; Luke 1:32; 4:12, 18; 10:21; Acts 3:22; 4:26; Rev. 11:15; 21:22), and **the Spirit** is referred to as Lord here (v. 17) and in the Nicene Creed: "I believe in the Holy Spirit, the Lord and giver of life."

There is difference of opinion as to which of the Divine Persons *the Lord* refers to in each usage here. But Orthodox interpreters all agree that: (1) The Father, the Son and the Holy Spirit are in no way confused here—Paul has in mind one Person or another. The Son, for example, cannot be the Holy Spirit. (2) *The Spirit* is a Divine Person, not an impersonal force—though elsewhere in the NT "spirit" occasionally refers to a realm or way of existence. (3) This title here describes how God reigns in the world. It does not describe the eternal relationship of the Persons of the Trinity: the Spirit, for instance, does not proceed from the Son.

Paul is transforming the understanding of one God, the Lord, in the Old Covenant into Jesus' revelation of one God in three Persons, each of whom is Lord, in the New Covenant. So **when one turns to the Lord** (v. 16) he turns not just to the Father but also to the Incarnate Son (v. 16), in the power of the Holy Spirit (v. 17).

3:17, 18 The work of the Holy Spirit brings **liberty** (v. 17), freeing us to behold God and have open access to Him. Created as the image of God, we see His uncreated **image,** the Son, the **glory of the Lord** (v. 18; see 4:4–6), in two ways: (1) through the Son's deified humanity (see 1 Cor. 13:12; James 1:23–25) and (2) in the power of the Spirit. As we behold Him, we become what we were created to be. God is infinite; therefore, growing in His *image* and *glory* has no limits. We shall ever see God more clearly and ever be **transformed** into His likeness.

4:1 In the face of numerous onslaughts, challenges to his apostleship, and his responsibility "for all the churches" (11:28), Paul still writes, **we do not lose heart** (see v. 16). For he is preoccupied with the glories of the **ministry** of Christ and the **mercy** by which it is given to him.

4:3, 4 The veil is not over the gospel or the apostle, but over the hearts and minds of those who will not believe.

4:5 The goal in preaching is not to glorify **ourselves,** but **Christ.**

The Finding of the Head of John the Baptist *February 24, May 29*

4:6–12: Like Paul, John the Baptist faced death that he might show forth the light of Christ.

manded light to shine out of darkness, who has [b]shone in our hearts to *givee* the light of the knowledge of the glory of God in the face of Jesus Christ.

The Power of an Apostle

7 But we have this treasure in earthen vessels, [a]that the excellence of the power may be of God and not of us.†

8 *We are* [a]hard pressed on every side, yet not crushed; *we are* perplexed, but not in despair;†

9 persecuted, but not [a]forsaken; [b]struck down, but not destroyed—

10 [a]always carrying about in the body the dying of the Lord Jesus, [b]that the life of Jesus also may be manifested in our body.

11 For we who live [a]are always delivered to death for Jesus' sake, that the life of Jesus also may be manifested in our mortal flesh.

12 So then death is working in us, but life in you.

13 And since we have [a]the same spirit of faith, according to what is written, [b]"*I believed and therefore I spoke,*" we also believe and therefore speak,

14 knowing that [a]He who raised up the Lord Jesus will also raise us up with Jesus, and will present *us* with you.

15 For [a]all things *are* for your sakes, that [b]grace, having spread through the many, may cause thanksgiving to abound to the glory of God.

Seeing the Unseen

16 Therefore we [a]do not lose heart. Even though our outward man is perishing, yet the inward *man* is [b]being renewed day by day.†

17 For [a]our light affliction, which is but for a moment, is working for us a far more exceeding *and* eternal weight of glory,†

18 [a]while we do not look at the things which are seen, but at the things which are not seen. For the things which are seen *are* temporary, but the things which are not seen *are* eternal.†

6 [b]2 Pet. 1:19
7 [a]1 Cor. 2:5
8 [a]2 Cor. 1:8; 7:5
9 [a][Heb. 13:5] [b]Ps. 37:24
10 [a]Phil. 3:10 [b]Rom. 8:17
11 [a]Rom. 8:36
13 [a]2 Pet. 1:1 [b]Ps. 116:10
14 [a][Rom. 8:11]
15 [a]Col. 1:24 [b]2 Cor. 1:11
16 [a]2 Cor. 4:1 [b][Is. 40:29, 31]
17 [a]Rom. 8:18
18 [a][Heb. 11:1, 13]

4:7 The **treasure** is the light of God's glory in Christ (v. 6); **earthen vessels** refers to our humanity. As this light shines in and through us, people will see that **the power** is **of God** and not of man.

4:8–12 This is victorious, but not trouble-free, Christianity. These trials "show both the power of God and, more, disclose His Grace" (St. John Chrysostom).

4:16 The Orthodox Faith teaches that salvation in Christ includes: (1) *a passage* from death to life, from darkness to light (John 3:1–6; Col. 1:13, 14), through repentance, faith, and baptism ("I have been saved"); (2) *a process* of spiritual growth and maturation (2 Pet. 1:2–8) through ongoing repentance, faith, and communion, often called deification ("I am being saved"); and (3) *a promise* of eternal life (5:9–11; John 14:1–6), calling us to perseverance and righteousness ("I shall be saved"). It is this second element, the process of our salvation, which Paul describes here, saying that our inner life **is being renewed day by day.**

4:17 Despite Paul's hardships (vv. 8–12), he sees God's everlasting **glory** and calls his trials **light affliction.**

4:18 As part of our inner renewal in Christ (v. 16) we gain the gift of seeing the unseen, **the things which are . . . eternal.**

Commemoration of the Departed

5:1–10: Paul looks forward to the resurrection of the body.

The Hope of the Resurrection

5 For we know that if [a]our earthly
[1]house, *this* tent, is destroyed,
we have a building from God, a
house [b]not made with hands, eternal
in the heavens.†
2 For in this [a]we groan, earnestly
desiring to be clothed with our
[1]habitation which is from heaven,
3 if indeed, [a]having been clothed,
we shall not be found naked.
4 For we who are in *this* tent
groan, being burdened, not because
we want to be unclothed, [a]but further clothed, that mortality may be
swallowed up by life.
5 Now He who has prepared us
for this very thing *is* God, who also
[a]has given us the Spirit as [1]a
guarantee.†
6 So *we are* always confident,
knowing that while we are at home
in the body we are absent from the
Lord.
7 For [a]we walk by faith, not by
sight.
8 We are confident, yes, [a]well
pleased rather to be absent from the
body and to be present with the
Lord.
9 Therefore we make it our aim,
whether present or absent, to be well
pleasing to Him.
10 [a]For we must all appear before
the judgment seat of Christ, [b]that
each one may receive the things
done in the body, according to
what he has done, whether good or
bad.†

Apostolic Motivation: Fearing and Loving God

11 Knowing, therefore, [a]the terror
of the Lord, we persuade men; but
we are well known to God, and I
also trust are well known in your
consciences.†
12 For [a]we do not commend ourselves again to you, but give you opportunity [b]to boast on our behalf,
that you may have *an answer* for
those who boast in appearance and
not in heart.
13 For [a]if we are beside ourselves,
it is for God; or if we are of sound
mind, *it is* for you.
14 For the love of Christ compels
us, because we judge thus: that
[a]if One died for all, then all died;

CHAPTER 5
1 [a]Job 4:19 [b]Mark 14:58 [1]Physical body
2 [a]Rom. 8:23 [1]*dwelling*
3 [a]Rev. 3:18
4 [a]1 Cor. 15:53
5 [a]Rom. 8:23 [1]*down payment, earnest*
7 [a]Heb. 11:1
8 [a]Phil. 1:23
10 [a]Rom. 2:16; 14:10, 12 [b]Eph. 6:8
11 [a][Heb. 10:31; 12:29]
12 [a]2 Cor. 3:1 [b]2 Cor. 1:14
13 [a]2 Cor. 11:1, 16; 12:11
14 [a][Rom. 5:15; 6:6]

5:1–4 Fear of death is overcome by: (1) hope in the resurrection, (2) faith in the Holy Trinity (vv. 5, 7), and (3) the love of Christ and our union with Christ (v. 14). **Our earthly house** (v. 1) is our present mortal body. The **building from God,** the one **which is from heaven** (v. 2), is the immortal, deified body we shall have in heaven (see 1 Cor. 15). The soul is **naked** (v. 3), or **unclothed** (v. 4), when it departs the body, that is, when one dies. Paul longs not for death but for resurrection; he knows God created us not to die, but to be transformed from **mortality** to **life** (v. 4; see v. 5). So he speaks not of the bliss of the soul without a body, but of the union of the soul with the glorified body.

5:5–8 Being **always confident** (v. 6) in the resurrection means we are being **prepared** by **God** the Father and **the Spirit** (v. 5) to join **the Lord** (v. 8), Jesus Christ.

5:10 Following his discourse on suffering, death and resurrection (4:16—5:8), Paul now turns to the **judgment. We must all appear,** not only the unbelievers, to be judged according to **what** we have **done.** For Christians, right belief gives power and motivation for right behavior. Here again, the NT unifies faith and works.

5:11–15 In his gospel, Paul seeks to **persuade men** (v. 11) on two fronts: (1) by **the terror of the Lord** (v. 11), the possibility of judgment to eternal death; and (2) by **the love of Christ** (v. 14), the divine invitation to **live** for Christ (v. 15), to eternal life. The heart of Paul's gospel is baptism, where life and death meet: Christ died and rose for us that we may die and rise in Him.

Commemoration of Female Martyrs

6:1–10: These holy women endured sufferings and persecution similar to Paul's.

15 and He died for all, [a]that those
who live should live no longer for
themselves, but for Him who died
for them and rose again.

Apostolic Vision: The New Creation

16 [a]Therefore, from now on, we regard no one according to the flesh.
Even though we have known Christ
according to the flesh, [b]yet now we
know *Him thus* no longer.†
17 Therefore, if anyone [a]*is* in
Christ, *he is* [b]a new creation; [c]old
things have passed away; behold, all
things have become [d]new.

Apostolic Ministry: Reconciliation

18 Now all things *are* of God,
[a]who has reconciled us to Himself through Jesus Christ, and has
given us the ministry of reconciliation,†
19 that is, that [a]God was in Christ
reconciling the world to Himself, not
[1]imputing their trespasses to them,
and has committed to us the word
of reconciliation.
20 Now then, we are [a]ambassadors
for Christ, as though God were
pleading through us: we implore *you*
on Christ's behalf, be reconciled to
God.
21 For [a]He made Him who knew
no sin *to be* sin for us, that we might
become [b]the righteousness of God in
Him.

15 [a][Rom. 6:11]
16 [a]2 Cor. 10:3 [b][Matt. 12:50]
17 [a][John 6:63] [b][Rom. 8:9] [c]Is. 43:18; 65:17 [d][Rom. 6:3–10]
18 [a]Rom. 5:10
19 [a][Rom. 3:24] [1]*reckoning*
20 [a]Eph. 6:20
21 [a]Is. 53:6, 9 [b][Rom. 1:17; 3:21]

The Marks of Apostleship

6 We then, *as* [a]workers together
with Him also [b]plead with *you*
not to receive the grace of God in
vain.†
2 For He says:

[a]*"In an acceptable time I have*
heard you,
And in the day of salvation I
have helped you."

Behold, now *is* the accepted time;
behold, now *is* the day of salvation.
3 [a]We give no offense in anything, that our ministry may not be
blamed.
4 But in all *things* we commend
ourselves [a]as ministers of God: in
much [1]patience, in tribulations, in
needs, in distresses,

CHAPTER 6
1 [a]1 Cor. 3:9 [b]2 Cor. 5:20
2 [a]Is. 49:8
3 [a]Rom. 14:13
4 [a]1 Cor. 4:1 [1]*endurance*

5:16, 17 Paul did not know "the historical Jesus," as He voluntarily took on our mortality, lived on earth and was known **according to the flesh** (v. 16). Nobody knows Jesus that way after His Ascension, for his mortal *flesh* has been transformed into an immortal body. Even so, our **old** bodies are transformed into **a new creation** (v. 17) in Christ. Because God created **all things** through Christ, He will transform and reunite *all things*—material as well as spiritual—to Himself through Christ.

5:18–21 How was Christ made **to be sin for us?** He, the incarnate Son of God, voluntarily assumed the consequences of our sin—corruption and death—without sinning Himself. And He submitted to unjust suffering because of the sinful passions of men and of angels. This means salvation is far more than forgiveness of sins. It is new life: our reconciliation to God (vv. 18–20) and our becoming new creatures (v. 17), participants in the very **righteousness of God** (v. 21). This means our salvation is not just juridical (the static, legal pronouncement of a judge) but it is personal and relational (the dynamic, sacrificial love of a father for his child).

6:1–10 Here is an authentic apostle! His life demonstrates the paradox of God's strength working in human weakness, of renouncing the world in order to master it. **The day of salvation** is **now** (v. 2), always the present moment in the period before Christ's return.

5 [a]in stripes, in imprisonments, in
tumults, in labors, in sleeplessness,
in fastings;
6 by purity, by knowledge, by
longsuffering, by kindness, by the
Holy Spirit, by [1]sincere love,
7 [a]by the word of truth, by
[b]the power of God, by [c]the armor
of righteousness on the right hand
and on the left,
8 by honor and dishonor, by evil
report and good report; as deceivers,
and *yet* true;
9 as unknown, and [a]*yet* well
known; [b]as dying, and behold we
live; [c]as chastened, and *yet* not
killed;
10 as sorrowful, yet always rejoicing; as poor, yet making many
[a]rich; as having nothing, and *yet* possessing all things.

A Plea for Holiness

11 O Corinthians! [1]We have spoken openly to you, [a]our heart is wide
open.†
12 You are not restricted by us, but
[a]you are restricted by your *own*
affections.
13 Now in return for the same
[a](I speak as to children), you also be
open.
14 [a]Do not be unequally yoked together with unbelievers. For [b]what
[1]fellowship has righteousness with
lawlessness? And what [2]communion
has light with darkness?†

5 [a]2 Cor. 11:23
6 [1]Lit. *unhypocritical*
7 [a]2 Cor. 7:14 [b]1 Cor. 2:4 [c]2 Cor. 10:4
9 [a]2 Cor. 4:2; 5:11 [b]1 Cor. 4:9, 11 [c]Ps. 118:18
10 [a][2 Cor. 8:9]
11 [a]2 Cor. 7:3 [1]Lit. *Our mouth is open*
12 [a]2 Cor. 12:15
13 [a]1 Cor. 4:14
14 [a]1 Cor. 5:9 [b]Eph. 5:6, 7, 11 [1]*in common* [2]*fellowship*
16 [a][1 Cor. 3:16, 17; 6:19] [b]Ezek. 37:26, 27 [1]NU *we*
17 [a]Is. 52:11
18 [a]2 Sam. 7:14 [b][Rom. 8:14]

CHAPTER 7

1 [a][1 John 3:3]
2 [a]Acts 20:33
3 [a]2 Cor. 6:11, 12
4 [a]2 Cor. 3:12 [b]1 Cor. 1:4 [c]Phil. 2:17

15 And what accord has Christ
with Belial? Or what part has a believer with an unbeliever?
16 And what agreement has the
temple of God with idols? For
[a]you[1] are the temple of the living
God. As God has said:

[b]*"I will dwell in them*
And walk among them.
I will be their God,
And they shall be My people."

17 Therefore

[a]*"Come out from among them*
And be separate, says the Lord.
Do not touch what is unclean,
And I will receive you."
18 *"I* [a]*will be a Father to you,*
And you shall be My [b]*sons and daughters,*
Says the LORD *Almighty."*

7 Therefore,[a] having these promises, beloved, let us cleanse ourselves from all filthiness of the flesh
and spirit, perfecting holiness in the
fear of God.†
2 Open *your hearts* to us. We have
wronged no one, we have corrupted
no one, [a]we have cheated no one.
3 I do not say *this* to condemn;
for [a]I have said before that you are
in our hearts, to die together and to
live together.
4 [a]Great *is* my boldness of speech
toward you, [b]great *is* my boasting on
your behalf. [c]I am filled with com-

6:11—7:1 This passage is the spiritual perspective of the New Covenant holiness code: Love of God and His Church requires a spurning of immorality and false religions, and a devotion to **perfecting holiness in the fear of God** (7:1).

6:14 One important application of this passage is that the Church calls us to marriage between those of like faith.

6:17 This verse extends an invitation from God to **come out** of the world and false religion.

7:1 An escape from **filthiness** requires more than thinking repentant thoughts. For we are enmeshed in a spiritual war zone, entrenched in patterns of sin which become habitual. Often, darkness becomes imprinted in our souls and bodies, so that even our wills are bypassed and we sin automatically. To **cleanse ourselves** means that by the **promises** of God, we embark on a sustained struggle for **holiness.** This cleansing includes genuine sorrow for our sins, confession, and repentance. It means a willful avoidance of sin-arousing situations, reconciliation with those we have wronged, the resolute practice of Christian virtue, and cleaving to God through faith and prayer. It calls us to participation in the holy sacraments. Is this too difficult for us humans? Yes. Thus it is the Holy Spirit, who cleanses us from every stain and heals our infirmities, who empowers us to live this life of peace with God and repentance before Him.

fort. I am exceedingly joyful in all
our tribulation.

Desire and Diligence

5 For indeed, [a]when we came to
Macedonia, our bodies had no rest,
but [b]we were troubled on every side.
[c]Outside *were* conflicts, inside *were*
fears.†
6 Nevertheless [a]God, who comforts the downcast, comforted us by
[b]the coming of Titus,
7 and not only by his coming, but
also by the [1]consolation with which
he was comforted in you, when he
told us of your earnest desire, your
mourning, your zeal for me, so that
I rejoiced even more.
8 For even if I made you [a]sorry
with my letter, I do not regret it;
[b]though I did regret it. For I perceive
that the same epistle made you
sorry, though only for a while.
9 Now I rejoice, not that you were
made sorry, but that your sorrow led
to repentance. For you were made
sorry in a godly manner, that you
might suffer loss from us in
nothing.†
10 For [a]godly sorrow produces repentance *leading* to salvation, not to
be regretted; [b]but the sorrow of the
world produces death.
11 For observe this very thing, that
you sorrowed in a godly manner:
What diligence it produced in you,
what [a]clearing *of yourselves, what* indignation, *what* fear, *what* vehement
desire, *what* zeal, *what* vindication!
In all *things* you proved yourselves
to be [b]clear in this matter.
12 Therefore, although I wrote to
you, *I did* not *do it* for the sake of
him who had done the wrong, nor
for the sake of him who suffered
wrong, [a]but that our care for you in
the sight of God might appear to
you.
13 Therefore we have been comforted in your comfort. And we rejoiced exceedingly more for the joy
of Titus, because his spirit [a]has been
refreshed by you all.
14 For if in anything I have boasted
to him about you, I am not ashamed.
But as we spoke all things to you in
truth, even so our boasting to Titus
was found true.
15 And his affections are greater
for you as he remembers [a]the obedience of you all, how with fear and
trembling you received him.
16 Therefore I rejoice that [a]I have
confidence in you in everything.

Models to Imitate

8 Moreover, brethren, we make
known to you the grace of God
bestowed on the churches of Macedonia:†

5 [a]Rom. 15:26; 2 Cor. 2:13 [b]2 Cor. 4:8 [c]Deut. 32:25
6 [a]Is. 49:13; 2 Cor. 1:3, 4 [b]2 Cor. 2:13; 7:13
7 [1]*comfort*
8 [a]2 Cor. 2:2 [b]2 Cor. 2:4
10 [a]2 Sam. 12:13; Ps. 32:10; Matt. 26:75 [b]Prov. 17:22
11 [a]Eph. 5:11 [b]2 Cor. 2:5–11
12 [a]2 Cor. 2:4
13 [a]Rom. 15:32
15 [a]2 Cor. 2:9; Phil. 2:12
16 [a]2 Cor. 2:3; 8:22; 2 Thess. 3:4; Philem. 8, 21

7:5–15 For the background of this passage, see the Introduction to 1 Corinthians.

7:9–11 Feeling sorry is not enough. Heartfelt, **godly sorrow** produces **repentance** and **diligence** (v. 11). True *repentance* cleanses us from sin and alienation, and *diligence* zealously pursues holiness and reconciliation. We hereby continue on the path of **salvation** to eternal life. The **sorrow of the world** (v. 10) is feeling sorry we were caught. It centers upon ourselves, upon our embarrassment over the predicament we find ourselves in. It stops short of repentance and reconciliation to God.

8:1—9:15 The subject of this passage is a collection from the churches in Asia Minor for the church in Jerusalem. Beyond the material help that Jerusalem needs, for Paul this appears to be an important theological matter as well. It (1) relates to the unity of Jew and Gentile in the Church, (2) underscores the messianic age as having indeed come in Christ, and (3) demonstrates that the charismatic effects of Pentecost are continuing and maturing in the Church.

Paul had given the Corinthians the same instruction he gave to Galatia, to contribute systematically to the fund (1 Cor. 16:1–4). Titus is to make sure they actually have begun to do so (8:6). Paul has told the Macedonians that Corinth was exemplary in giving (9:2), but he has his doubts. So he sends Titus to Corinth to be sure the Corinthians will comply (9:3–5). Some in Corinth feel pressure, saying that Paul is "crafty"; he gets his way "by cunning" (12:16). Paul encourages the Corinthians by holding up the generosity of the poorer

(continued on next page)

2 that in a great trial of affliction
the abundance of their joy and
[a]their deep poverty abounded in the
riches of their liberality.
3 For I bear witness that according
to *their* ability, yes, and beyond *their*
ability, *they were* freely willing,
4 imploring us with much urgency [1]that we would receive the gift
and [a]the fellowship of the ministering to the saints.
5 And not *only* as we had hoped,
but they first [a]gave themselves to the
Lord, and *then* to us by the [b]will of
God.†
6 So [a]we urged Titus, that as he
had begun, so he would also complete this grace in you as well.
7 But as [a]you abound in everything—in faith, in speech, in knowledge, in all diligence, and in your
love for us—*see* [b]that you abound in
this grace also.
8 [a]I speak not by commandment, but I am testing the sincerity
of your love by the diligence of
others.
9 For you know the grace of our
Lord Jesus Christ, [a]that though He
was rich, yet for your sakes He became poor, that you through His
poverty might become [b]rich.†

The Ideal of Mutual Giving

10 And in this [a]I give advice:
[b]It is to your advantage not only to
be doing what you began and
[c]were desiring to do a year ago;
11 but now you also must complete
the doing *of it;* that as *there was* a
readiness to desire *it,* so *there* also
may be a completion out of what *you*
have.
12 For [a]if there is first a willing
mind, *it is* accepted according to
what one has, *and* not according to
what he does not have.
13 For *I do* not *mean* that others
should be eased and you burdened;
14 but by an equality, *that* now at
this time your abundance *may supply*
their lack, that their abundance also
may supply your lack—that there
may be equality.
15 As it is written, [a]*"He who gath-*
ered much had nothing left over,
and he who gathered little had no
lack."

Accountability for this Collection

16 But thanks *be* to God who
[1]puts the same earnest care for you
into the heart of Titus.
17 For he not only accepted the exhortation, but being more diligent,
he went to you of his own accord.
18 And we have sent with him
[a]the brother whose praise *is* in the
gospel throughout all the churches,
19 and not only *that,* but who was
also [a]chosen by the churches to
travel with us with this gift, which
is administered by us [b]to the glory
of the Lord Himself and *to show* your
ready mind,
20 avoiding this: that anyone
should blame us in this lavish gift
which is administered by us—
21 [a]providing honorable things,
not only in the sight of the Lord, but
also in the sight of men.
22 And we have sent with them
our brother whom we have often
proved diligent in many things, but
now much more diligent, because of
the great confidence which *we have*
in you.
23 If *anyone inquires* about [a]Titus,
he is my partner and fellow worker
concerning you. Or if our brethren

CHAPTER 8
2 [a]Mark 12:44
4 [a]Rom. 15:25, 26
[1]NU, M omit *that we would receive,* thus changing text to *urgency for the favor and fellowship*
5 [a][Rom. 12:1, 2]
[b][Eph. 6:6]
6 [a]2 Cor. 8:17; 12:18
7 [a][1 Cor. 1:5; 12:13]
[b]2 Cor. 9:8
8 [a]1 Cor. 7:6
9 [a]Phil. 2:6, 7
[b]Rom. 9:23
10 [a]1 Cor. 7:25, 40
[b][Heb. 13:16]
[c]2 Cor. 9:2
12 [a]Mark 12:43, 44
15 [a]Ex. 16:18
16 [1]NU *has put*
18 [a]2 Cor. 12:18
19 [a]1 Cor. 16:3, 4
[b]2 Cor. 4:15
21 [a]Rom. 12:17
23 [a]2 Cor. 7:13, 14

(continued from previous page)
Macedonians (8:1–5). The Corinthians actually do contribute to the fund, and Paul is pleased with them (Rom. 15:25–28).

8:5 Note the progression: **They first gave themselves to the Lord** ("They offered up themselves"—St. John Chrysostom) **and then to us,** to the Church, to the apostles. If our lives are an offering to God, they will be an offering to His people as well.

8:9 What was Christ's **poverty?** He emptied Himself (Phil. 2:5–8) of His heavenly glory to join our humanity to His divinity, and to suffer and die on our behalf. He did not owe this to us, but did so by His **grace,** that we **might become rich** in His salvation.

are *inquired about, they are* [b]messen-
gers[1] of the churches, the glory of
Christ.
24 Therefore show to them, [1]and
before the churches the proof of your
love and of our [a]boasting on your
behalf.†

9 Now concerning [a]the ministering to the saints, it is superfluous
for me to write to you;
2 for I know your willingness,
about which I boast of you to the
Macedonians, that Achaia was ready
a [a]year ago; and your zeal has stirred
up the majority.
3 [a]Yet I have sent the brethren,
lest our boasting of you should be
in vain in this respect, that, as I said,
you may be ready;†
4 lest if *some* Macedonians come
with me and find you unprepared,
we (not to mention you!) should be
ashamed of this [1]confident boasting.
5 Therefore I thought it necessary
to [1]exhort the brethren to go to you
ahead of time, and prepare your generous gift beforehand, which *you had*
previously promised, that it may be
ready as *a matter of* generosity and
not as a [2]grudging obligation.

Cheerful Giving

6 [a]But this *I say:* He who sows
sparingly will also reap sparingly,
and he who sows [1]bountifully will
also reap [1]bountifully.†
7 *So let* each one *give* as he purposes in his heart, [a]not grudgingly
or of [1]necessity; for [b]God loves a
cheerful giver.
8 [a]And God *is* able to make all
grace abound toward you, that you,
always having all sufficiency in all
things, may have an abundance for
every good work.
9 As it is written:

[a]*"He has dispersed abroad,*
He has given to the poor;
His righteousness endures
forever."

10 Now [1]may He who [a]supplies
seed to the sower, and bread for
food, [2]supply and multiply the seed
you have *sown* and increase the fruits
of your [b]righteousness,
11 while *you are* enriched in everything for all liberality, [a]which causes
thanksgiving through us to God.
12 For the administration of this
service not only [a]supplies the needs
of the saints, but also is abounding
through many thanksgivings to God,
13 while, through the proof of this
ministry, they [a]glorify God for the
obedience of your confession to the
gospel of Christ, and for *your* liberal
[b]sharing with them and all *men,*
14 and by their prayer for you, who
long for you because of the exceeding [a]grace of God in you.
15 Thanks *be* to God [a]for His indescribable gift!

Spiritual Warfare

10 Now [a]I, Paul, myself am
pleading with you by the
meekness and gentleness of Christ—
[b]who in presence *am* lowly among
you, but being absent am bold toward you.†

23 [b]Phil. 2:25 [1]Lit. *apostles, "sent ones"*
24 [a]2 Cor. 7:4, 14; 9:2 [1]NU, M omit *and*

CHAPTER 9

1 [a]Gal. 2:10
2 [a]2 Cor. 8:10
3 [a]2 Cor. 8:6, 17
4 [1]NU *confidence.*
5 [1]*encourage* [2]Lit. *covetousness*
6 [a]Prov. 11:24; 22:9 [1]*with blessings*
7 [a]Deut. 15:7 [b]Rom. 12:8 [1]*compulsion*
8 [a][Prov. 11:24]
9 [a]Ps. 112:9
10 [a]Is. 55:10 [b]Hos. 10:12 [1]NU omits *may* [2]NU *will supply*
11 [a]2 Cor. 1:11
12 [a]2 Cor. 8:14
13 [a][Matt. 5:16] [b][Heb. 13:16]
14 [a]2 Cor. 8:1
15 [a][James 1:17]

CHAPTER 10

1 [a]Rom. 12:1 [b]1 Thess. 2:7

8:24 The proof of God's love for us is that He gave us His Son through His Incarnation and death (Rom. 5:8). The **proof** of our **love** for God is in the giving of our gifts to Him and **the churches.**

9:3 Paul has stuck his neck out. The Corinthians' "zeal" had caused many in Macedonia to give to Jerusalem (v. 2). Yet, to make sure Corinth will stay zealous, Paul has **sent the brethren.**

9:6–15 Here is Paul's landmark teaching on Christian stewardship. The metaphor is not the giving of money but the sowing of seed for a harvest. And where does the seed come from? God Himself (v. 10).

10:1 Paul replies to the charges of his opponents: far from being weak, he is extraordinarily strong. But strength in spiritual warfare sometimes appears as weakness to the world. **the meekness and gentleness of Christ** is sometimes communicated in a **lowly** or humble fashion, and sometimes boldly (see vv. 10, 11).

2 But I beg *you* [a]that when I am
present I may not be bold with that
confidence by which I intend to be
bold against some, who think of us
as if we walked according to the
flesh.
3 For though we walk in the flesh,
we do not war according to the
flesh.†
4 [a]For the weapons [b]of our warfare *are* not [1]carnal but [c]mighty in
God [d]for pulling down strongholds,†
5 [a]casting down arguments and
every high thing that exalts itself
against the knowledge of God,
bringing every thought into captivity
to the obedience of Christ,
6 [a]and being ready to punish all
disobedience when [b]your obedience
is fulfilled.

Paul's Authority in Christ

7 [a]Do you look at things according to the outward appearance?
[b]If anyone is convinced in himself
that he is Christ's, let him again
consider this in himself, that just
as he *is* Christ's, even [1]so [c]we *are*
Christ's.†
8 For even if I should boast somewhat more [a]about our authority,
which the Lord gave [1]us for
[2]edification and not for your destruction, [b]I shall not be ashamed—
9 lest I seem to terrify you by
letters.
10 "For *his* letters," they say, "*are*
weighty and powerful, but [a]*his* bodily presence *is* weak, and *his* [b]speech
contemptible."
11 Let such a person consider this,
that what we are in word by letters when we are absent, such *we
will* also *be* in deed when we are
present.

The Sphere of Labor

12 [a]For we dare not class ourselves
or compare ourselves with those
who commend themselves. But they,
measuring themselves by themselves, and comparing themselves
among themselves, are not wise.†
13 [a]We, however, will not boast
beyond measure, but within the limits of the sphere which God appointed us—a sphere which especially includes you.
14 For we are not overextending
ourselves (as though *our authority* did
not extend to you), [a]for it was to you
that we came with the gospel of
Christ;
15 not boasting of things beyond
measure, *that is,* [a]in other men's labors, but having hope, *that* as your
faith is increased, we shall be greatly
enlarged by you in our sphere,
16 to preach the gospel in the *regions* beyond you, *and* not to boast
in another man's sphere of
accomplishment.
17 But [a]"*he who glories, let him
glory in the* LORD."
18 For [a]not he who commends
himself is approved, but [b]whom the
Lord commends.

2 [a]1 Cor. 4:21; 2 Cor. 13:2, 10
4 [a]Eph. 6:13 [b]1 Cor. 9:7; [2 Cor. 6:7]; 1 Tim. 1:18 [c]Acts 7:22 [d]Jer. 1:10; [2 Cor. 10:8; 13:10] [1]*of the flesh*
5 [a]1 Cor. 1:19
6 [a]2 Cor. 13:2, 10 [b]2 Cor. 7:15
7 [a][John 7:24]; 2 Cor. 5:12 [b]1 Cor. 1:12; 14:37 [c][Rom. 14:8]; 1 Cor. 3:23 [1]NU *as we are.*
8 [a]2 Cor. 13:10 [b]2 Cor. 7:14 [1]NU omits *us* [2]*building up*
10 [a]1 Cor. 2:3, 4; 2 Cor. 12:7; Gal. 4:13 [b][1 Cor. 1:17]; 2 Cor. 11:6
12 [a]2 Cor. 5:12
13 [a]2 Cor. 10:15
14 [a]1 Cor. 3:5, 6
15 [a]Rom. 15:20
17 [a]Is. 65:16; Jer. 9:24; 1 Cor. 1:31
18 [a]Prov. 27:2 [b]Rom. 2:29; [1 Cor. 4:5]

10:3 In the flesh refers to fallen human nature.

10:4–6 The battlefield of spiritual **warfare** includes (1) entrenched spiritual fortresses (**strongholds**), (2) human reason (**arguments,** v. 5), (3) human and angelic powers (**every high thing that exalts itself**), (4) ideas (**thought**) and (5) the will (**obedience**). Our **weapons** include the Cross, prayer, and the Word of God. Both our thoughts (v. 5) and our actions (v. 6) together are to be submissive to Christ. The Church is God's fortress, marching against the **strongholds** of **disobedience** (vv. 4, 6).

10:7, 8 Some teachers in Corinth had claimed a special knowledge of or an esoteric relationship to Christ. Paul here counters their claim by boasting **somewhat more** of his **authority**—not because he wants to boast (11:1, 16–19; 12:1, 11), but because the boastfulness of his enemies must be shown to be not only empty, but ruinous for those who believe them.

10:12–18 Paul's opponents had stepped into Paul's **sphere** (v. 13) after he had evangelized and established the church in Corinth—and then claimed they were responsible for raising up this church, and commended themselves (v. 18) for doing so.

Paul Preaches the True Gospel

11 Oh, that you would bear with
me in a little [a]folly—and indeed you do bear with me.†
2 For I am [a]jealous for you with
godly jealousy. For [b]I have betrothed
you to one husband, [c]that I may
present *you* [d]*as* a chaste virgin to
Christ.
3 But I fear, lest somehow, as
[a]the serpent deceived Eve by his
craftiness, so your minds [b]may be
corrupted from the [1]simplicity that
is in Christ.
4 For if he who comes preaches
another Jesus whom we have not
preached, or *if* you receive a different
spirit which you have not received,
or a [a]different gospel which you
have not accepted—you may well
put up with it!†
5 For I consider that [a]I am not at
all inferior to the most eminent
apostles.
6 Even though [a]*I am* untrained in
speech, yet *I am* not [b]in knowledge.
But [c]we have [1]been thoroughly manifested among you in all things.

Serving out of Love

7 Did I commit sin in [1]humbling
myself that you might be exalted, because I preached the gospel of God
to you [a]free of charge?†
8 I robbed other churches, taking
wages *from them* to minister to you.
9 And when I was present with
you, and in need, [a]I was a burden
to no one, for what I lacked [b]the
brethren who came from Macedonia
supplied. And in everything I kept
myself from being burdensome to
you, and so I will keep *myself.*
10 [a]As the truth of Christ is in me,
[b]no one shall stop me from this
boasting in the regions of Achaia.
11 Why? [a]Because I do not love
you? God knows!
12 But what I do, I will also continue to do, [a]that I may cut off the
opportunity from those who desire
an opportunity to be regarded just
as we are in the things of which they
boast.
13 For such [a]*are* false apostles,
[b]deceitful workers, transforming
themselves into apostles of Christ.†
14 And no wonder! For Satan himself transforms himself into [a]an angel of light.
15 Therefore *it is* no great thing if
his ministers also transform themselves into ministers of righteousness, [a]whose end will be according to their works.

Paul's Reluctant Boasting

16 I say again, let no one think me
a fool. If otherwise, at least receive
me as a fool, that I also may boast a
little.†
17 What I speak, [a]I speak not according to the Lord, but as it were,

CHAPTER 11
1 [a]2 Cor. 11:4, 16, 19
2 [a]Gal. 4:17 [b]Hos. 2:19 [c]Col. 1:28 [d]Lev. 21:13
3 [a]Gen. 3:4, 13 [b]Eph. 6:24 [1]NU adds *and purity*
4 [a]Gal. 1:6–8
5 [a]2 Cor. 12:11
6 [a][1 Cor. 1:17] [b][Eph. 3:4] [c][2 Cor. 12:12] [1]NU omits *been*
7 [a]1 Cor. 9:18 [1]*putting myself down*
9 [a]Acts 20:33 [b]Phil. 4:10
10 [a]Rom. 1:9; 9:1 [b]1 Cor. 9:15
11 [a]2 Cor. 6:11; 12:15
12 [a]1 Cor. 9:12
13 [a]Phil. 1:15 [b]Phil. 3:2
14 [a]Gal. 1:8
15 [a][Phil. 3:19]
17 [a]1 Cor. 7:6

11:1–3 Paul compares the reality of the New Covenant to the Garden of Eden, where Christ is Adam and the Church is Eve, and where Satan is up to his same **craftiness** (v. 3). Paul's desire is to present a pure Church, **a chaste virgin** (v. 2), **to Christ** at the Second Coming.

11:4–6 The first element of a "chaste virgin" (v. 2) is the purity of Orthodox doctrine. Not human persuasiveness (v. 6) but apostolic content is important. Paul is a part of the apostolic college (v. 5) which continues in line with the original Twelve Apostles.

11:7–12 Pure doctrine is taught out of pure motives. A mark of apostolic authenticity is the refusal of excessive money. The clergy draw their living from the Church, but not to the point of getting rich (see 1 Cor. 9:4–18; 1 Tim. 6:3–10; Titus 1:11). Paul's opponents dared not make this claim.

11:13–15 Although **Satan** (v. 14) imitates the Kingdom of God, telltale signs reveal his sham, such as nonapostolic doctrine (vv. 4–6) and a lucrative ministry (vv. 7–12).

11:16–21 The Corinthians thought they were **wise** (v. 19) enough to evaluate Church leaders. They had become enamored with false apostles who championed themselves, using the methods and values of the world, full of outward show and crafty talk. They disparaged Paul, seeing him as a weakling without credentials. As a result they were in **bondage**

(continued on next page)

The Feast of Sts. Peter and Paul *June 29*

11:21—12:9: Paul defends his apostleship, recounting his sufferings, visions, and weaknesses.

foolishly, in this confidence of
boasting.
18 Seeing that many boast according to the flesh, I also will boast.
19 For you put up with fools
gladly, [a]since you *yourselves* are wise!
20 For you put up with it [a]if one
brings you into bondage, if one devours *you*, if one takes *from you*, if
one exalts himself, if one strikes you
on the face.
21 To *our* shame [a]I say that we
were too weak for that! But [b]in whatever anyone is bold—I speak foolishly—I am bold also.

Jewish and Christian Credentials

22 Are they [a]Hebrews? So *am* I.
Are they Israelites? So *am* I. Are they
the seed of Abraham? So *am* I.†
23 Are they ministers of Christ?—
I speak as a fool—I *am* more: [a]in labors more abundant, [b]in stripes
above measure, in prisons more frequently, [c]in deaths often.
24 From the Jews five times I received [a]forty [b]*stripes* minus one.
25 Three times I was [a]beaten with
rods; [b]once I was stoned; three times
I [c]was shipwrecked; a night and a
day I have been in the deep;
26 *in* journeys often, *in* perils of
waters, *in* perils of robbers, [a]*in* perils
of *my own* countrymen, [b]in perils of
the Gentiles, *in* perils in the city, *in*
perils in the wilderness, *in* perils in
the sea, *in* perils among false
brethren;
27 in weariness and toil, [a]in sleeplessness often, [b]in hunger and thirst,
in [c]fastings often, in cold and nakedness—
28 besides the other things, what
comes upon me daily: [a]my deep concern for all the churches.
29 [a]Who is weak, and I am not
weak? Who is made to stumble, and
I do not burn *with indignation*?
30 If I must boast, [a]I will boast in
the things which concern my
[1]infirmity.
31 [a]The God and Father of our
Lord Jesus Christ, [b]who is blessed
forever, knows that I am not lying.
32 [a]In Damascus the governor, under Aretas the king, was guarding
the city of the Damascenes with a
garrison, desiring to arrest me;
33 but I was let down in a basket
through a window in the wall, and
escaped from his hands.

Paul's Visions

12 It is [1]doubtless not profitable
for me to boast. I will come
to [a]visions and [b]revelations of the
Lord:†

19 [a]1 Cor. 4:10
20 [a][Gal. 2:4; 4:3, 9; 5:1]
21 [a]2 Cor. 10:10 [b]Phil. 3:4
22 [a]Phil. 3:4–6
23 [a]1 Cor. 15:10 [b]Acts 9:16 [c]1 Cor. 15:30
24 [a]Deut. 25:3 [b]2 Cor. 6:5
25 [a]Acts 16:22, 23; 21:32 [b]Acts 14:5, 19 [c]Acts 27:1–44
26 [a]Acts 9:23, 24; 13:45, 50; 17:5, 13 [b]Acts 14:5, 19; 19:23; 27:42
27 [a]Acts 20:31 [b]1 Cor. 4:11 [c]Acts 9:9; 13:2, 3; 14:23
28 [a]Acts 20:18
29 [a][1 Cor. 8:9, 13; 9:22]
30 [a][2 Cor. 12:5, 9, 10] [1]*weakness*
31 [a]1 Thess. 2:5 [b]Rom. 9:5
32 [a]Acts 9:19–25

CHAPTER 12

1 [a]Acts 16:9; 18:9; 22:17, 18; 23:11; 26:13–15; 27:23 [b][Gal. 1:12; 2:2] [1]NU *necessary, though not profitable, to boast*

(continued from previous page)
(v. 20), defrauded and even brutalized. Paul, playing the devil's advocate, takes up the methods of these false apostles to show them as **fools** (v. 19). He satirizes them in the hope the Corinthians will thereby see through their charade.

11:22–33 Using his opponents' level of argument, Paul lists his Jewish and Christian credentials. If genealogy means anything, which it does to the Jews, Paul has it (v. 22). If "Christian experience" means anything, no one can compare with him: his sufferings (vv. 23–27); his compassionate, involved concern for his people (vv. 28, 29); even his bizarre adventures (vv. 30–33).

12:1–6 Paul's opponents probably boasted of **visions and revelations** (v. 1), for Paul men-
(continued on next page)

2 I know a man [a]in Christ who
fourteen years ago—whether in the
body I do not know, or whether out
of the body I do not know, God
knows—such a one [b]was caught up
to the third heaven.
3 And I know such a man—
whether in the body or out of the
body I do not know, God knows—
4 how he was caught up into
[a]Paradise and heard inexpressible
words, which it is not lawful for a
man to utter.
5 Of such a one I will boast; yet
of myself I will not [a]boast, except in
my infirmities.
6 For though I might desire to
boast, I will not be a fool; for I will
speak the truth. But I refrain, lest
anyone should think of me above
what he sees me *to be* or hears from
me.

A Thorn in the Flesh

7 And lest I should be exalted
above measure by the abundance of
the revelations, a [a]thorn in the flesh
was given to me, [b]a messenger of
Satan to [1]buffet me, lest I be exalted
above measure.†
8 [a]Concerning this thing I
pleaded with the Lord three times
that it might depart from me.
9 And He said to me, "My grace
is sufficient for you, for My strength
is made perfect in weakness. Therefore most gladly [a]I will rather boast
in my infirmities, [b]that the power of
Christ may rest upon me.
10 Therefore [a]I take pleasure in infirmities, in reproaches, in needs, in
persecutions, in distresses, for
Christ's sake. [b]For when I am weak,
then I am strong.

Paul's Miracles

11 I have become [a]a fool [1]in boasting; you have compelled me. For I
ought to have been commended by
you; for [b]in nothing was I behind the
most eminent apostles, though
[c]I am nothing.†
12 [a]Truly the signs of an apostle
were accomplished among you with
all perseverance, in signs and [b]won-
ders and mighty [c]deeds.
13 For what is it in which you were
inferior to other churches, except
that I myself was not burdensome
to you? Forgive me this wrong!

A Love Rejected

14 [a]Now *for* the third time I am
ready to come to you. And I will not
be burdensome to you; for [b]I do not
seek yours, but you. [c]For the children ought not to lay up for the parents, but the parents for the children.
15 And I will very gladly spend
and be spent [a]for your souls; though
[b]the more abundantly I love you, the
less I am loved.†
16 But be that *as it may,* [a]I did not
burden you. Nevertheless, being
crafty, I caught you by cunning!
17 Did I take advantage of you by
any of those whom I sent to you?
18 I urged Titus, and sent our

2 [a]Rom. 16:7 [b]Acts 22:17
4 [a]Luke 23:43
5 [a]2 Cor. 11:30
7 [a]Ezek. 28:24 [b]Job 2:7 [1]*beat*
8 [a]Matt. 26:44
9 [a]2 Cor. 11:30 [b][1 Pet. 4:14]
10 [a][Rom. 5:3; 8:35] [b]2 Cor. 13:4
11 [a]2 Cor. 5:13; 11:1, 16; 12:6 [b]2 Cor. 11:5 [c]1 Cor. 3:7; 13:2; 15:9 [1]NU omits *in boasting*
12 [a]Rom. 15:18 [b]Acts 15:12 [c]Acts 14:8–10; 16:16–18; 19:11, 12; 20:6–12; 28:1–10
14 [a]2 Cor. 1:15; 13:1, 2 [b][1 Cor. 10:24–33] [c]1 Cor. 4:14
15 [a][2 Tim. 2:10] [b]2 Cor. 6:12, 13
16 [a]2 Cor. 11:9

(continued from previous page)
tions one of his. **Fourteen years ago** would date the event before his missionary journeys. Paul employs two terms used by Jews to describe heavenly realms: **the third heaven** (v. 2) is the highest heaven; **Paradise** (v. 4), where God is surrounded by the assembly of the just, is the city of God.

12:7–10 Unlike his opponents, who publicly proclaimed their own greatness in their mystical experiences, Paul sees his **thorn in the flesh** (v. 7) as **given to** him precisely so he might not **be exalted.** What was this *thorn?* Perhaps a chronic physical problem, or deluded Christian leaders, or hard-hearted Israelites. Nevertheless, for Paul, his **weakness** (v. 9; see v. 5), not his mystical experiences (vv. 2–4), is the means of **the power of Christ** remaining in him.

12:11–13 By **signs of an apostle** (v. 12; see Rom. 15:19; 1 Cor. 2:4; 4:20; 12:28, 29; Heb. 2:4) Paul seems to be referring to miracles which lead men to God and the Church, for with these **signs and wonders** (v. 12) the Corinthians are greatly impressed.

12:15 This is the experience through history of the godly shepherd.

[a]brother with *him*. Did Titus take advantage of you? Did we not walk in
the same spirit? Did *we* not *walk* in
the same steps?
19 [a]Again,[1] do you think that we
excuse ourselves to you? [b]We speak
before God in Christ. [c]But *we do* all
things, beloved, for your edification.
20 For I fear lest, when I come, I
shall not find you such as I wish,
and *that* [a]I shall be found by you
such as you do not wish; lest *there*
be contentions, jealousies, outbursts
of wrath, selfish ambitions, backbitings, whisperings, conceits,
tumults;†
21 lest, when I come again, my
God [a]will humble me among you,
and I shall mourn for many [b]who
have sinned before and have not repented of the uncleanness, [c]fornica-
tion, and lewdness which they have
practiced.

Resolution: A Coming Visit

13 This *will be* [a]the third *time* I
am coming to you. [b]*"By the*
mouth of two or three witnesses
every word shall be established."
2 [a]I have told you before, and
foretell as if I were present the second time, and now being absent
[1]I write to those [b]who have sinned
before, and to all the rest, that if I
come again [c]I will not spare—
3 since you seek a proof of Christ
[a]speaking in me, who is not weak
toward you, but mighty [b]in you.
4 [a]For though He was crucified in
weakness, yet [b]He lives by the
power of God. For [c]we also are weak
in Him, but we shall live with Him
by the power of God toward you.
5 Examine yourselves *as to*
whether you are in the faith. Test
yourselves. Do you not know yourselves, [a]that Jesus Christ is in
you?—unless indeed you [1]are [b]dis-
qualified.†
6 But I trust that you will know
that we are not disqualified.
7 Now [1]I pray to God that you do
no evil, not that we should appear
approved, but that you should do
what is honorable, though [a]we may
seem disqualified.
8 For we can do nothing against
the truth, but for the truth.
9 For we are glad [a]when we are
weak and you are strong. And this
also we pray, [b]that you may be made
complete.
10 [a]Therefore I write these things
being absent, lest being present I
should use sharpness, according to
the [b]authority which the Lord has
given me for edification and not for
destruction.

Greetings and Benediction

11 Finally, brethren, farewell. Become complete. [a]Be of good comfort,
be of one mind, live in peace; and
the God of love [b]and peace will be
with you.
12 [a]Greet one another with a holy
kiss.†
13 All the saints greet you.
14 [a]The grace of the Lord Jesus
Christ, and the love of God, and
[b]the [1]communion of the Holy Spirit
be with you all. Amen.†

18 [a]2 Cor. 8:18
19 [a]2 Cor. 5:12 [b][Rom. 9:1, 2] [c]1 Cor. 10:33 [1]NU *You have been thinking for a long time that we*
20 [a]1 Cor. 4:21
21 [a]2 Cor. 2:1, 4 [b]2 Cor. 13:2 [c]1 Cor. 5:1

CHAPTER 13

1 [a]2 Cor. 12:14 [b]Deut. 17:6; 19:15
2 [a]2 Cor. 10:2 [b]2 Cor. 12:21 [c]2 Cor. 1:23; 10:11 [1]NU omits *I write*
3 [a]Matt. 10:20 [b][1 Cor. 9:2]
4 [a][1 Pet. 3:18] [b][Rom. 1:4; 6:4] [c][2 Cor. 10:3, 4]
5 [a][Gal. 4:19] [b]1 Cor. 9:27 [1]*do not stand the test*
7 [a]2 Cor. 6:9 [1]NU *we*
9 [a]1 Cor. 4:10 [b][1 Thess. 3:10]
10 [a]1 Cor. 4:21 [b]2 Cor. 10:8
11 [a]Rom. 12:16, 18 [b]Rom. 15:33
12 [a]Rom. 16:16
14 [a]Rom. 16:24 [b]Phil. 2:1 [1]*fellowship*

12:20—13:4 Paul is more impressed with the miracle of unity and harmony than with physical miracles. He fears he may have to exercise the supreme apostolic power, that of excluding people who **have not repented** (v. 21) from the Church.

13:5 In this context, the test of being in Christ is a humble, virtuous life lived in communion with the Church.

13:12 The **holy kiss,** the kiss of peace, is an established liturgical tradition. Perhaps the final test of whether one is a Christian is whether one can give this kiss with an uncondemning conscience.

13:14 This trinitarian blessing is also an ancient and contemporary liturgical practice.

The Epistle of Paul the Apostle to the

GALATIANS

Author: *St. Paul the Apostle*

Date: *A.D. 49 or 53–56*

Theme: *The True Gospel vs. the False Gospel*

AUTHOR: St. Paul had established churches in a number of cities in the Roman province of Galatia in Asia Minor. This is the only New Testament letter which Paul addressed to a group of churches (1:2).

DATE: The references to time and place in Galatians are unclear; therefore its exact historical setting and date are uncertain.

MAJOR THEME: *The true gospel vs. the false gospel.* After initially believing in the gospel of Jesus Christ as a gift of God, many in Galatia had turned to the teaching of the Jewish legalizers, who claimed that Christians must also follow the laws of the Old Covenant. Paul writes to call them back to "the grace of Christ" (1:6).

While Galatians calls people away from slavery to OT law, calling it also "bondage," a "curse," a "tutor" or schoolmaster, we must be careful to see that the Apostle is not pitting faith against good works. False teaching often separates or isolates two things which God only distinguishes between. In Paul's view, under the Old Covenant, God's promise takes theological precedence over the law, and faith takes precedence over circumcision. In the New Covenant, faith takes precedence over baptism, and love over obedience. But Paul sees these as distinctions between things in union—one cannot exist without the other. Being bound to something is not the same as being in bondage to it. We used to be in bondage to the law and the flesh; now we are bound by our own free will to righteousness and the Spirit.

Spiritual discipline, then, is not bondage. It is a rejection of bondage, a pursuit of holiness while gaining freedom from legalism and sinful passions. The freedom of grace is known through the discipline of being bound to God the Father, to Christ and to the Holy Spirit. Christ fulfilled the law with its demands that we might be free in Him, justified by faith, to live fruitful and righteous lives, obeying the truth. Thus Paul exhorts the Galatians, "Do not grow weary while doing good" (6:9) and, "Do good to all" (6:10).

Subthemes include: (1) a defense of Paul's apostolic authority (1:1—2:21); (2) the gift of the Holy Spirit to the Church (5:1—6:18); (3) the Cross of Christ (6:11–15); and (4) the life of faith (2:15—4:7).

OUTLINE

Introduction	1:1–10
A. Greeting	1:1, 2
B. Theme: The true gospel vs. the false gospel	1:3–10
I. The apostolic authority of the true gospel	1:11—2:15
A. The call to apostleship	1:11–24
B. Apostles are guided by councils	2:1–10
C. Apostles are guided by conscience	2:11–14
II. The content of the true gospel	2:15—4:31
A. Jesus Christ and faith	2:15–21
B. Jesus Christ and the Holy Spirit	3:1–14
C. Jesus Christ and sonship	3:15—4:31
III. Living in the true gospel	5:1—6:10
A. The liberty of the Spirit	5:1–12
B. Living in the love of the Spirit	5:13—6:10
1. By warring against the flesh	5:13–26
2. By doing good to all	6:1–10
Concluding remarks	6:11–18
A. The rule of faith	6:11–17
B. Benediction	6:18

Greeting

1 Paul, an apostle (not from men
nor through man, but [a]through
Jesus Christ and God the Father
[b]who raised Him from the dead),†
2 and all the brethren who are
with me,

To the churches of Galatia:

Warning: True Gospel vs. False Gospel

3 Grace to you and peace from
God the Father and our Lord Jesus
Christ,†
4 [a]who gave Himself for our sins,
that He might deliver us [b]from this
present evil age, according to the will
of our God and Father,
5 to whom *be* glory forever and
ever. Amen.
6 I marvel that you are turning
away so soon [a]from Him who called
you in the grace of Christ, to a different gospel,†
7 [a]which is not another; but there
are some [b]who trouble you and
want to [c]pervert[1] the gospel of
Christ.
8 But even if [a]we, or an angel
from heaven, preach any other gos-

CHAPTER 1
1 [a]Acts 9:6 [b]Acts 2:24
4 [a][Matt. 20:28] [b]Heb. 2:5
6 [a]Gal. 1:15; 5:8
7 [a]2 Cor. 11:4 [b]Gal. 5:10, 12 [c]2 Cor. 2:17 [1]*distort*
8 [a]1 Cor. 16:22

1:1, 2 The Judaizers invading Galatia argued that Paul was not a true apostle. Paul introduces himself with a threefold defense: (1) The source of his apostleship is God (v. 1). (2) He has witnessed the resurrected Christ (Acts 9:27), just as the Twelve have. (3) His apostleship is confirmed by **all the brethren** (v. 2) with him. An additional proof of Paul's apostleship is that he founded **the churches of Galatia** (v. 2).

1:3–5 Paul's greeting encapsulates the true gospel which he is defending in this epistle. Several points may be drawn from this greeting: (1) The true gospel comes from God Himself (v. 3). (2) Christ **gave Himself for our sins** not only in His death, but in every phase of His Incarnation, from conception to Ascension (see 2:20). (3) Christ delivers us **from this present evil age** (v. 4) to enter the age to come. (4) This deliverance is accomplished **according to the will of our God** (v. 4), the Son in His human nature cooperating with the divine will (John 5:30; 6:38). The Father's will is done by Jesus, and then by us, "on earth as it is in heaven" (Matt. 6:10).

1:6–10 Different (Gr. *heteros,* v. 6) means different in kind, whereas **another** (Gr. *allos,* v. 7) means another of the same kind. Paul is saying that the teaching the Galatians are

(continued on next page)

pel to you than what we have
preached to you, let him be [1]ac-
cursed.
9 As we have said before, so now
I say again, if anyone preaches any
other gospel to you [a]than what you
have received, let him be accursed.
10 For [a]do I now [b]persuade men,
or God? Or [c]do I seek to please men?
For if I still pleased men, I would
not be a bondservant of Christ.

God's Call: Paul the Apostle

11 [a]But I make known to you,
brethren, that the gospel which was
preached by me is not according to
man.†
12 For [a]I neither received it from
man, nor was I taught *it,* but *it came*
[b]through the revelation of Jesus
Christ.
13 For you have heard of my former conduct in Judaism, how [a]I persecuted the church of God beyond measure and [b]*tried to* destroy
it.†
14 And I advanced in Judaism beyond many of my contemporaries in
my own nation, [a]being more exceedingly zealous [b]for the traditions of
my fathers.
15 But when it pleased God,
[a]who separated me from my
mother's womb and called *me*
through His grace,
16 [a]to reveal His Son in me, that
[b]I might preach Him among the Gentiles, I did not immediately confer
with [c]flesh and blood,
17 nor did I go up to Jerusalem to
those *who were* apostles before me;
but I went to Arabia, and returned
again to Damascus.

Paul's Gospel: That of the Twelve

18 Then after three years [a]I went
up to Jerusalem to see [1]Peter, and
remained with him fifteen days.†

8 [1]Gr. *anathema*
9 [a]Deut. 4:2
10 [a]1 Thess. 2:4 [b]1 Sam. 24:7 [c]1 Thess. 2:4
11 [a]1 Cor. 15:1
12 [a]1 Cor. 15:1 [b][Eph. 3:3–5]
13 [a]Acts 9:1 [b]Acts 8:3; 22:4, 5
14 [a]Acts 26:9 [b]Jer. 9:14
15 [a]Is. 49:1, 5
16 [a][2 Cor. 4:5–7] [b]Acts 9:15 [c]Matt. 16:17
18 [a]Acts 9:26 [1]NU *Cephas*

(continued from previous page)
listening to is not a harmless variation of the truth, but a completely different, false **gospel.** This "gospel": (1) is a **turning away** from **the grace of Christ** (v. 6); (2) brings **trouble** to the faithful; (3) will **pervert the gospel of Christ** (v. 7)—it is a distortion of the truth, a mixture of truth and falsehood; (4) is **accursed** or anathematized by the Church (v. 8); (5) is intended to **please men** (v. 10), not God.

Paul's warning about **we, or an angel from heaven** is not hypothetical. Angels can and have delivered the gospel to us: they announced Christ's conception (Luke 1:26–38), birth (Luke 2:9–15), Resurrection (Matt. 28:5–7), and Ascension (Acts 1:9–11). But angelic messages are not necessarily true; they may come from fallen angels, who are **accursed.**

1:11—2:14 The true gospel is taught by true apostles, but many declare themselves to be apostles. How can we know true apostles from false?

(1) True apostles are called by God. They learn the gospel by revelation, either directly from the risen Son, as did the original Apostles (1:11, 12), or by the revelation of apostolic tradition (2 Tim. 2:2). They are called by grace, not according to works or a "proper" background (1:13–17). A true apostle brings glory to God, not to himself (1:18–23).

(2) True apostles form one Church government, holding the same doctrine and working by agreement reached in council (2:6–10).

(3) True apostles stand firm in matters of conscience and are correctable when mistaken (2:11–14). Thus Paul rebukes Peter sharply in public for his hypocritical ethnic elitism.

1:11, 12 Apostolic tradition is grounded in divine **revelation** from **Jesus Christ.** Just as the Twelve were called by Christ, so was Paul (v. 1). Just as the Twelve received the gospel directly from Christ, so did Paul (Acts 9:3–6; 26:13–18). Just as the Twelve stood together as one, so Paul entered their unity in consensus and mutual submission.

1:13–17 People are called by God not according to **former conduct** (v. 13)—good or bad—but by God's **grace** (v. 15). Paul, whom God called in mercy, received grace from Ananias' hands and the waters of baptism (Acts 9:10–19). **Separated me from my mother's womb** (v. 15) refers not to Paul's physical birth but to God's call to apostolic ministry before he was born (see Ps. 139:15, 16; Is. 49:1; Jer. 1:5; Luke 1:35, 43, 44, 48). As with Paul, God's intentions for a person may lie hidden for years.

1:18–20 As a true apostle, Paul submits himself to the Church and her apostles rather

(continued on next page)

19 But [a]I saw none of the other
apostles except [b]James, the Lord's
brother.†
20 (Now *concerning* the things
which I write to you, indeed, before
God, I do not lie.)
21 [a]Afterward I went into the regions of Syria and Cilicia.
22 And I was unknown by face to
the churches of Judea which [a]*were*
in Christ.
23 But they were [a]hearing only,
"He who formerly [b]persecuted us
now preaches the faith which he
once *tried to* destroy."
24 And they [a]glorified God in me.†

The Apostles in Jerusalem: One Doctrine

2 Then after fourteen years [a]I went
up again to Jerusalem with Barnabas, and also took Titus with *me.*
2 And I went up [1]by revelation,
and communicated to them that gospel which I preach among the Gentiles, but [a]privately to those who
were of reputation, lest by any
means [b]I might run, or had run, in
vain.†
3 Yet not even Titus who *was* with
me, being a Greek, was compelled
to be circumcised.
4 And *this occurred* because of
[a]false brethren secretly brought in
(who came in by stealth to spy out
our [b]liberty which we have in Christ
Jesus, [c]that they might bring us into
bondage),†
5 to whom we did not yield submission even for an hour, that
[a]the truth of the gospel might continue with you.
6 But from those [a]who seemed to
be something—whatever they were,
it makes no difference to me; [b]God
[1]shows personal favoritism to no
man—for those who seemed *to be
something* [c]added nothing to me.†
7 But on the contrary, [a]when they
saw that the gospel for the uncircumcised [b]had been committed to me,
as *the gospel* for the circumcised *was*
to Peter†
8 (for He who worked effectively
in Peter for the apostleship to the
[a]circumcised [b]also [c]worked effectively in me toward the Gentiles),†
9 and when James, [1]Cephas, and
John, who seemed to be [a]pillars, perceived [b]the grace that had been
given to me, they gave me and Barnabas the right hand of fellowship,

19 [a]1 Cor. 9:5 [b]Matt. 13:55
21 [a]Acts 9:30
22 [a]Rom. 16:7
23 [a]Acts 9:20, 21 [b]Acts 8:3
24 [a]Acts 11:18

CHAPTER 2
1 [a]Acts 15:2
2 [a]Acts 15:1–4 [b]Phil. 2:16 [1]*because of*
4 [a]Acts 15:1, 24 [b]Gal. 3:25; 5:1, 13 [c]Gal. 4:3, 9
5 [a][Gal. 1:6; 2:14; 3:1]
6 [a]Gal. 2:9; 6:3 [b]Acts 10:34 [c]2 Cor. 11:5; 12:11 [1]Lit. *does not receive the face of a man*
7 [a]Acts 9:15; 13:46; 22:21 [b]1 Thess. 2:4
8 [a]1 Pet. 1:1 [b]Acts 9:15 [c][Gal. 3:5]
9 [a]Matt. 16:18 [b]Rom. 1:5 [1]Peter

(continued from previous page)
than elevating himself. Paul knows his encounter with Christ, instruction in the gospel, and call to apostleship are highly unusual—in a private revelation the only other witness is God (v. 20). But he also knows he must teach the same gospel as the other apostles.

1:19 James is James the Just, the first bishop of Jerusalem and author of the Epistle of James. **Brother** also means cousin or close relation (see the Introduction to the Epistle of James).

1:24 Glory goes to God, not to the apostle.

2:2 Communicated (Gr. *anatithemai*) means "laid before" or "submitted." Paul submitted to the Apostles James, Peter and John (v. 9) what he had been teaching **among the Gentiles** so that he might not **run . . . in vain,** that is, teach error. He did so **privately** because the Judaizers were slandering him, giving apostolic honor only **to those** they considered **of reputation,** the original Apostles.

2:4, 5 The **false brethren** are not those "of reputation" (v. 2) in the Church, but the Judaizers, whom no one had recognized as apostolic.

2:6 Seemed to be something is more correctly translated "were of reputation," as in v. 2. To the Judaizers, only the original Apostles had valid authority. But the Judaizers were wrong. Paul is not putting down the Twelve; rather he is saying that **it makes no difference** that all his fellow apostles were formerly "blue collar" workers, not scholars like Paul himself. **God** does not show **personal favoritism.** As for correcting Paul's gospel, they **added nothing to** his teaching.

2:7 Peter and Paul were each responsible to reach one segment of the population in the central part of the Roman Empire: **Peter** the **circumcised** (Jews), Paul the **uncircumcised** (Gentiles). The others of the Twelve also did evangelistic work, as did the Seventy (see article, "The Seventy," at Luke 10).

2:8 One God gave one gospel through two apostles, to two different ethnic groups.

[c]that we *should go* to the Gentiles and
they to the circumcised.†
10 *They desired* only that we should
remember the poor, [a]the very thing
which I also was eager to do.†

True Apostles Are Correctable

11 [a]Now when [1]Peter had come to
Antioch, I [2]withstood him to his face,
because he was to be blamed;†
12 for before certain men came
from James, [a]he would eat with the
Gentiles; but when they came, he
withdrew and separated himself,
fearing [1]those who were of the
circumcision.†
13 And the rest of the Jews also
played the hypocrite with him, so
that even Barnabas was carried away
with their hypocrisy.
14 But when I saw that they
were not straightforward about [a]the
truth of the gospel, I said to Peter
[b]before *them* all, [c]"If you, being a
Jew, live in the manner of Gentiles and not as the Jews, [1]why do
you compel Gentiles to live as
[2]Jews?†
15 [a]"We *who are* Jews by nature, and not [b]sinners of the Gentiles,†

The Source of Faith Is Christ

16 [a]"knowing that a man is not
[1]justified by the works of the law but
[b]by faith in Jesus Christ, even we
have believed in Christ Jesus, that
we might be justified by faith in
Christ and not [c]by the works of the
law; for by the works of the law no
flesh shall be justified.†
17 "But if, while we seek to be

9 [c]Acts 13:3
10 [a]Acts 11:30
11 [a]Acts 15:35
[1]NU *Cephas*
[2]*opposed*
12 [a][Acts 10:28; 11:2, 3]
[1]Jewish Christians
14 [a]Gal. 1:6; 2:5
[b]1 Tim. 5:20
[c][Acts 10:28]
[1]NU *how can you*
[2]Some interpreters stop the quotation here.
15 [a][Acts 15:10]
[b]Matt. 9:11
16 [a]Acts 13:38, 39
[b]Rom. 1:17
[c]Ps. 143:2
[1]*declared righteous*

2:9 The right hand of fellowship indicates consensus, not merely friendship. The apostles are united in preaching the same gospel.

2:10 Apostles are also united in caring for **the poor,** which in this case probably refers to the Jerusalem church (see Acts 11:27–30).

2:11 No individual apostle (or bishop or patriarch) is infallible. Even when he speaks officially (*ex officio*) he is correctable. Unchecked, Peter could have caused a schism.

2:12, 13 The **men** who **came from James** were probably trying to force the culture of the Jerusalem church on the Gentiles—and they were not necessarily representing James. Jerusalem was Jewish, but to impose that culture on Gentiles was **hypocrisy** (v. 13). And to mistake culture—any culture—for the gospel is even worse! God had already shown that Jewish dietary laws were obsolete (Acts 10:11–16), for the law is fulfilled in Christ.

2:14–21 Paul recounts the speech he gave in Antioch when he confronted Peter.

2:15 Gentiles were considered **sinners** by the Jews.

2:16—4:31 In this section, Paul gives the content of the true gospel by contrasting it with the false gospel, that of the Judaizers.

(1) The source of justification is faith, not the works of the law (2:16–21). (a) Works of the law deal with man in his fallen state, in his corruption; faith "crucifies" man's corrupt condition and deals with the new man in Christ. (b) Works of the law begin with the action of man; faith begins with the action of God. Every work of faith is the action of both God and man, a cooperation (synergy) between the divine and human wills. This faith and these actions find their source and fulfillment in God-made-Man, Christ. We experience them through our union with Christ brought about in baptism.

(2) The Holy Spirit gives us power for the ongoing life of righteousness in Christ, the life of blessing (3:1–14). (a) Father Abraham is the father of faith and of the blessing of the Spirit. (b) But Judaizers, who have based their righteousness on the works of the law, have received a curse, not the blessing of the Spirit.

(3) The status conferred by righteousness is sonship. We become children of God through union with God incarnate (3:15—4:31). (a) The source of sonship is God, not humanity; divine promise, not human deeds; faith, not works. (b) God introduced the works of the law to protect mankind until the time of divine sonship, the time when our union with the Son of God became possible. (c) The purpose of sonship is for us to become like God and to enter heaven.

2:16 What does it mean to be **justified?** See article, "Justification by Faith," at Romans 5. **Faith in Jesus Christ** is grammatically parallel to **the works of the law,** and should be translated "the faith of Jesus Christ." The faith of Christ is the gospel. As the source of

(continued on next page)

justified by Christ, we ourselves also
are found [a]sinners, *is* Christ therefore a minister of sin? Certainly
not!†
18 "For if I build again those things
which I destroyed, I make myself a
transgressor.†
19 "For I [a]through the law [b]died
to the law that I might [c]live to
God.†
20 "I have been [a]crucified with
Christ; it is no longer I who live, but
Christ lives in me; and the *life* which
I now live in the flesh [b]I live by faith
in the Son of God, [c]who loved me
and gave Himself for me.†
21 "I do not set aside the grace of
God; for [a]if righteousness *comes*
through the law, then Christ died
[1]in vain."†

17 [a][1 John 3:8]
19 [a]Rom. 8:2 [b][Rom. 6:2, 14; 7:4] [c][Rom. 6:11]
20 [a][Rom. 6:6] [b]2 Cor. 5:15 [c]Eph. 5:2
21 [a]Heb. 7:11 [1]*for nothing*

CHAPTER 3

1 [1]NU omits *that you should not obey the truth* [2]NU omits *among you*
2 [a]Rom. 10:16, 17
3 [a][Gal. 4:9] [b]Heb. 7:16

The Life of Faith Is in the Spirit

3 O foolish Galatians! Who has
bewitched you [1]that you should
not obey the truth, before whose
eyes Jesus Christ was clearly portrayed [2]among you as crucified?†
2 This only I want to learn from
you: Did you receive the Spirit by
the works of the law, [a]or by the hearing of faith?
3 Are you so foolish? [a]Having begun in the Spirit, are you now being
made perfect by [b]the flesh?
4 [a]Have you suffered so [1]many
things in vain—if indeed *it was* in
vain?

4 [a]Heb. 10:35 [1]Or *great*

(continued from previous page)
works is *the* law, so the source of *faith* is *Christ*. It is the faith of Christ—His belief, His trust, His obedience—that justifies us, not our faith as such. Christ's faith is seen in His entire life on earth, not just in His more spectacular works.

2:17 By Christ should be "in Christ." Justification is not merely legal but actual—effected by our real, personal union with Christ in His glorified human nature. That we could be **found sinners** shows this union never takes away our free will, and explains how some defected to Judaism.

2:18 Those things which I destroyed are "the works of the law" (v. 16). Paul *destroyed* them in the sense of proving their ineffectiveness for salvation. The real **transgressor** here is one who tries to reinstitute the Jewish Law.

2:19 We die **through the law,** not bypassing or dishonoring it, but by recognizing that: (1) it is holy; (2) we deserve its consequence, death; and (3) we voluntarily die **to the law** through our death with Christ. Being crucified with Christ, through baptism, we come alive to the law of the Spirit, which perfects the intention of the OT *law*. There is no contradiction between law and gospel. The law is "holy and just and good" (Rom. 7:12). However, the law is "weak" (Rom. 8:3) and "obsolete" (Heb. 8:13), for it is fulfilled in the gospel, in Christ Himself.

2:20 I have been crucified with Christ means our sinful "passions and desires" (5:24) have been crucified. This is not the crucifixion of human nature, but of **the flesh,** the corruption into which humanity has fallen. This crucifixion must be willingly and freely accepted, just as Christ freely accepted His death. Living **in the flesh** (Gr. *en sarki*) is contrasted with living "in the faith" (Gr. *en pistei*), translated here **by faith.** Just as living *in the flesh* involves the whole person, body and soul, so living "in the faith" involves the whole person. Justification therefore constitutes substantial union with Christ, not just an abstract position of the believer with respect to God.

While **it is no longer I who live** under the dominion of sinful passions and desires, I do **live** a crucified life in Christ. As we are not saved by works alone, nowhere does the NT say we are saved by faith alone. We are saved by faith, but not faith *alone*.

2:21 Set aside the grace of God is what Peter and Barnabas had done (vv. 12, 13). The faith of Christ is not opposed to the works of the law, but it is opposed to using works to justify oneself before God. As Moses himself looked ahead to Christ (Heb. 11:26), so the law is a shadow, an icon, pointing toward Christ Himself who brings us life.

3:1–5 The **Galatians** had believed in **Jesus Christ** (v. 1) and received **the Spirit** through **the hearing of faith** (v. 2). But they are **foolish** because they have rejected ongoing life in Christ and the Spirit, teaching instead that we are **made perfect by the flesh** (v. 3)—circumcision. Paul argues they do not understand righteousness, nor how men have always participated in it.

Matins of Holy Saturday *Saturday before Easter*

3:13, 14: Christ's death redeems us from the curse of the law.

5 Therefore He who supplies the Spirit to you and works miracles among you, *does He do it* by the works of the law, or by the hearing of faith?—
6 just as Abraham [a]*"believed God, and it was accounted to him for righteousness."*†

Faith Brings Sonship

7 Therefore know that *only* [a]those who are of faith are sons of Abraham.
8 And [a]the Scripture, foreseeing that God would justify the Gentiles by faith, preached the gospel to Abraham beforehand, *saying,* [b]*"In you all the nations shall be blessed."*
9 So then those who *are* of faith are blessed with believing Abraham.

6 [a]Gen. 15:6
7 [a]John 8:39
8 [a]Rom. 9:17 [b]Gen. 12:3; 18:18; 22:18; 26:4; 28:14
10 [a]Deut. 27:26
11 [a]Hab. 2:4 [1]*declared righteous*
12 [a]Rom. 4:4, 5 [b]Lev. 18:5
13 [a][Rom. 8:3] [b]Deut. 21:23
14 [a][Rom. 4:1–5, 9, 16] [b]Rom. 3:29, 30 [c]Is. 32:15

Free from the Curse

10 For as many as are of the works of the law are under the curse; for it is written, [a]*"Cursed is everyone who does not continue in all things which are written in the book of the law, to do them."*†
11 But that no one is [1]justified by the law in the sight of God *is* evident, for [a]*"the just shall live by faith."*
12 Yet [a]the law is not of faith, but [b]*"the man who does them shall live by them."*†
13 [a]Christ has redeemed us from the curse of the law, having become a curse for us (for it is written, [b]*"Cursed is everyone who hangs on a tree"*),†
14 [a]that the blessing of Abraham might come upon the [b]Gentiles in Christ Jesus, that we might receive [c]the promise of the Spirit through faith.†

3:6–9 Who are the **sons of Abraham? Those who are of faith** (v. 7)—true Christians. Jews saw Abraham as their father. Paul shows that Abraham's **righteousness** (v. 6) does not consist in keeping the law, but in **believing** God (v. 9). *Righteousness* is a heart-centered belief in and obedience to God, with the blessing of the Holy Spirit.

Accounted (v. 6) in our day suggests bookkeeping, debits and credits. To "account" here (Gr. *logizomai*) refers rather to faithful participation. When God "accounted" Abraham righteous, Abraham was participating with God in the fruit of the Holy Spirit and faith (v. 5).

With believing Abraham (v. 9) is literally "in the faith of Abraham," that which he believed and did. This shows that Jesus' words, "If you were Abraham's children, you would do the works of Abraham" (John 8:39), underscore the fact that separating faith from works is impossible. To **justify** (v. 8) means to make righteous and so to be righteous. Therefore, to be **blessed** (v. 9) in Abraham is to participate with him, body and soul, in communion with God and His goodness.

3:10 While the works of the law are good, those who **are of the works of the law** are **cursed** because they cannot become righteous by keeping the law. Even on their own premise they fail, for no one has kept *all* the law.

3:12 The law is not of faith because the law came before the true faith (v. 23). This is not to say that no one believed before Christ, or that the law cannot be obeyed out of faith. Abraham is the father of faith! But his faith was a type of the faith of Christ, for his faith is perfected in the faith of Christ.

3:13 Christ perfectly obeyed **the law** and accepted its **curse.** In Christ, we are redeemed from the curse and participate in His perfect faith and obedience.

3:14 How is God's promised **blessing** obtained? The Judaizers believed they were progressing toward perfection by obeying the law. Paul argues by contrast that the blessing comes through **the promise of the Spirit through faith,** a participation in the very life of God.

Commemoration of Female Martyrs and Holy Nuns

3:23–29: Women are equal partakers with men in all the blessings of Christ.

Sonship: Promise, Not Law

15 Brethren, I speak in the manner
of men: [a]Though *it is* only a man's
covenant, yet *if it is* confirmed, no
one annuls or adds to it.†
16 Now to Abraham and his Seed
were the promises made. He does
not say, "And to seeds," as of many,
but as of [a]one, [b]*"And to your Seed,"*
who is [c]Christ.
17 And this I say, *that* the law,
[a]which was four hundred and thirty
years later, cannot annul the covenant that was confirmed before by
God [1]in Christ, [b]that it should make
the promise of no effect.
18 For if [a]the inheritance *is* of the
law, [b]*it is* no longer of promise; but
God gave *it* to Abraham by promise.

The Law Our Tutor

19 What purpose then *does* the law
serve? [a]It was added because of
transgressions, till the [b]Seed should
come to whom the promise was
made; *and it was* [c]appointed through
angels by the hand [d]of a mediator.†
20 Now a mediator does not *medi-
ate* for one *only,* [a]but God is one.†
21 *Is* the law then against the
promises of God? Certainly not! For
if there had been a law given which
could have given life, truly righteousness would have been by the
law.
22 But the Scripture has confined
[a]all under sin, [b]that the promise by
faith in Jesus Christ might be given
to those who believe.†
23 But before faith came, we were
kept under guard by the law, [1]kept
for the faith which would afterward
be revealed.
24 Therefore [a]the law was our
[1]tutor *to bring us* to Christ, [b]that we
might be justified by faith.
25 But after faith has come, we are
no longer under a tutor.

Sonship by Faith and Baptism

26 For you [a]are all sons of God
through faith in Christ Jesus.†

15 [a]Heb. 9:17 **16** [a]Gen. 22:18 [b]Gen. 12:3, 7; 13:15; 24:7 [c][1 Cor. 12:12] **17** [a]Ex. 12:40 [b][Rom. 4:13] [1]NU omits *in Christ* **18** [a][Rom. 8:17] [b]Rom. 4:14 **19** [a]John 15:22 [b]Gal. 4:4 [c]Acts 7:53 [d]Ex. 20:19 **20** [a][Rom. 3:29] **22** [a]Rom. 11:32 [b]Rom. 4:11 **23** [1]Lit. *confined* **24** [a]Rom. 10:4 [b]Acts 13:39 [1]In a household, the guardian responsible for the care and discipline of the children **26** [a]John 1:12

3:15–18 The Jews were blinded by the multitude of details of the law. They failed to see that their sonship was founded on God's **promises** (the covenant) **made to Abraham** (v. 16). Since a **covenant that was confirmed** (v. 17) cannot be added to, changed, or annulled, the law, which comes later (v. 17), cannot alter the covenant's promise (v. 15). The Jews thought they were sons of Abraham (**seeds**) through physical genealogy. They overlooked the fact that **Seed** (v. 16) is singular, referring to Christ.

3:19 Why was **the law** given then? Because Israel was transgressing what they knew of God's law through conscience and nature. So God put it in writing! The law was never a savior, but a tutor (v. 24) to convict Israel of **transgressions** and to lead her to Christ.

3:20 For Christ to be the **mediator** between **God** and man (see also 1 Tim. 2:5), He had to be both God and man. **God is one** is a reference to the one divine nature, and does not deny the existence of three divine Persons. (Priests, by the way, are not seen as mediators between God and man: their role is to lead people to the Mediator.)

3:22–25 Faith in (v. 22) is "faith of." Two faiths are cooperating: first and foremost, Christ's faith; secondarily, the faith of **those who believe.** While OT people had faith, they could not participate in Christ's faith, for Christ had not yet come.

3:26, 27 Paul directly relates saving **faith** (v. 26) and being **baptized,** connecting them as the most intimate of friends.

Verse 27 is the ancient hymn perhaps already being sung at Christian baptisms during the procession of the newly regenerated into the assembly—and sung at every Orthodox baptismal service to this day.

The Birth of Our Lord Jesus Christ (Christmas) *December 25*

4:4–7: Christ was born of a woman that we might become sons of God.

27 For [a]as many of you as were
baptized into Christ [b]have put on
Christ.
28 [a]There is neither Jew nor Greek,
[b]there is neither slave nor free, there
is neither male nor female; for you
are all [c]one in Christ Jesus.†
29 And [a]if you *are* Christ's, then
you are Abraham's [b]seed, and
[c]heirs according to the promise.

Sons of God Through Christ and the Spirit

4 Now I say *that* the heir, as long
as he is a child, does not differ
at all from a slave, though he is master of all,†
2 but is under guardians and
stewards until the time appointed by
the father.
3 Even so we, when we were children, [a]were in bondage under the
elements of the world.†
4 But [a]when the fullness of the
time had come, God sent forth His
Son, [b]born[1] [c]of a woman, [d]born under the law,†
5 [a]to redeem those who were under the law, [b]that we might receive
the adoption as sons.
6 And because you are sons, God
has sent forth [a]the Spirit of His Son
into your hearts, crying out, [1]"Abba,
Father!"†
7 Therefore you are no longer a
slave but a son, [a]and if a son, then
an heir [1]of God [2]through Christ.

27 [a][Rom. 6:3] [b]Rom. 10:12; 13:14 **28** [a]Col. 3:11 [b][1 Cor. 12:13] [c][Eph. 2:15, 16] **29** [a]Gen. 21:10 [b]Rom. 4:11 [c]Rom. 8:17

CHAPTER 4

3 [a]Col. 2:8, 20 **4** [a][Gen. 49:10] [b][John 1:14] [c]Gen. 3:15 [d]Luke 2:21, 27 [1]Or *made* **5** [a][Matt. 20:28] [b][John 1:12]

6 [a][Rom. 5:5; 8:9, 15, 16] [1]Lit., in Aram., *Father* **7** [a][Rom. 8:16, 17] [1]NU *through God* [2]NU omits *through Christ*

3:28, 29 We share one human nature in Christ. Therefore, valuing people based on (1) opinions and ethnicity (**neither Jew nor Greek**), (2) pride and social status (**neither slave nor free**), and (3) gender (**neither male nor female**) has no place in the Church. **All** are **one** in nature and so all are equal in dignity.

4:1, 2 Child refers not to age but to understanding. **guardians and stewards** provide the special discipline and protection required for growth. **Slave** refers to one under the rule of a taskmaster, in this case, the law.

4:3 The elements of the world are the philosophies and traditions developed by humanity without regard to God (Col. 2:8).

4:4, 5 Son refers to Christ as God by nature. God, then, is **born of a woman,** and so Mary is rightly called the mother of God (Theotokos). Since Jesus is **born under the law** He can redeem those under the law. Jesus fulfilled the law as an infant by being circumcised on the eighth day, and being presented in the temple forty days after His birth. Both of these events are remembered in the liturgical cycle of the Orthodox Church.

Why does God **redeem those who were under the law?** To fulfill His promise to Abraham. He pays ransom, as it were, to Himself, according to His own vow. God owes no one anything—He certainly does not owe us salvation.

Whereas the Son is God by nature, we become sons of God by **adoption.** We cannot become members of the Godhead by nature because we are human by nature. But we do become members of His family by grace. In adoption we become everything God is, except in nature. Because we are given new life, *adoption* is also called a new birth, being born again.

4:6, 7 The ongoing growth into adoption, being **an heir of God** (v. 7), is called deification (see article, "Deification," at 2 Pet.). This means we are becoming by grace what God is by nature. Each Person of the Trinity, **Spirit, Son,** and **Father** (v. 6), is involved in this process of transformation. Therefore, to become sons of God by grace, one must believe in and know the Father, the Son and the Holy Spirit.

The Danger of the Law

8 But then, indeed, [a]when you
did not know God, [b]you served
those which by nature are not
gods.
9 But now [a]after you have known
God, or rather are known by God,
[b]how *is it that* you turn again to
[c]the weak and beggarly elements, to
which you desire again to be in
bondage?
10 [a]You observe days and months
and seasons and years.†
11 I am afraid for you, [a]lest I have
labored for you in vain.
12 Brethren, I urge you to become
like me, for I *became* like you. [a]You
have not injured me at all.
13 You know that [a]because of
physical infirmity I preached the gospel to you at the first.†
14 And my trial which was in my
flesh you did not despise or reject,
but you received me [a]as an [1]angel
of God, [b]*even* as Christ Jesus.†
15 [1]What then was the blessing
you *enjoyed?* For I bear you witness
that, if possible, you would have
plucked out your own eyes and
given them to me.
16 Have I therefore become your
enemy because I tell you the truth?
17 They [a]zealously court you, *but*
for no good; yes, they want to exclude you, that you may be zealous
for them.
18 But it is good to be zealous in
a good thing always, and not only
when I am present with you.
19 [a]My little children, for whom I
labor in birth again until Christ is
formed in you,
20 I would like to be present with
you now and to change my tone; for
I have doubts about you.

An Allegory: Slavery and Sonship

21 Tell me, you who desire to be
under the law, do you not hear the
law?†
22 For it is written that Abraham had two sons: [a]the one by a
bondwoman, [b]the other by a freewoman.
23 But he *who was* of the bond-

8 [a]1 Cor. 1:21; Eph. 2:12; 1 Thess. 4:5; 2 Thess. 1:8 [b]Rom. 1:25
9 [a][1 Cor. 8:3] [b]Gal. 3:1–3; Col. 2:20 [c]Heb. 7:18
10 [a]Rom. 14:5; Col. 2:16
11 [a]1 Thess. 3:5
12 [a]2 Cor. 2:5
13 [a]1 Cor. 2:3
14 [a]Mal. 2:7 [b][Luke 10:16] [1]Or *messenger*
15 [1]NU *Where*
17 [a]Rom. 10:2
19 [a]1 Cor. 4:15
22 [a]Gen. 16:15 [b]Gen. 21:2

4:10 The Judaizers were making their "holy-day calendar" an end in itself. Although God gave Israel her holy days, they point beyond themselves to Christ and His Kingdom. The OT holy days are fulfilled in the great feasts of the Church. Passover becomes Easter, while Pentecost, the celebration of the giving of the Law on Mt. Sinai, becomes the descent of the Holy Spirit—a renewed calendar for a renewed creation.

4:13 The nature of Paul's **physical infirmity** is not known. Perhaps it was simply the sufferings of his work for the gospel.

4:14–19 The **angel of God** in the OT was a preincarnate appearance (theophany) of the Son, whom we know as **Christ Jesus.**

A priest in the Church is called to be a manifestation of Christ and is to be **received** as Christ, but he is neither identical with Christ nor a mediator between a Christian and Christ. He must both win the love of his people (v. 15), and adamantly confront bad behavior and wrong belief (vv. 16–18). A true priest seeks spiritual growth, deification, for his people (v. 19), even if his people do not want the truth (v. 16).

4:21–31 By saying that Abraham's **two sons** and related events are **symbolic** (v. 24, Gr. *allegoreo*) Paul is not implying that they are not historical. Rather he asserts that OT history is announcing something far greater than itself. **Hagar** and **Mount Sinai** symbolize earthly **Jerusalem** and the Jews under the law (v. 25). Sarah, the **freewoman** (vv. 22, 23), symbolizes the heavenly Jerusalem, that is, the Church (v. 26). **The desolate** are those in the Church, especially the Gentiles; **she who has a husband** is Israel (v. 27). Furthermore, Sarah is a type of Mary, the Mother of God, for Sarah's son was born **through promise** (v. 23), the promise of God.

In commenting on v. 23, St. John Chrysostom teaches that Isaac "was the issue of bodies that were dead, and of a womb that was dead. His conception was not by the flesh, nor his birth by the seed, for the womb was dead both through age and barrenness. But the Word of God fashioned him . . . He that was not according to the flesh was more honorable than he that was born after the flesh. Therefore let it not disturb you that you were not born after the flesh. For from the very reason that you are not so born, are you most of all Abraham's kindred."

The Conception of John the Baptist *September 23*

4:22–31: Like Isaac, John was a child of promise, born to barren parents in their old age.

woman [a]was born according to the
flesh, [b]and he of the freewoman
through promise,
24 which things are symbolic. For
these are [1]the two covenants: the one
from Mount [a]Sinai which gives birth
to bondage, which is Hagar—
25 for this Hagar is Mount Sinai in
Arabia, and corresponds to Jerusalem which now is, and is in bondage
with her children—
26 but the [a]Jerusalem above is free,
which is the mother of us all.
27 For it is written:

[a]*"Rejoice, O barren,*
You who do not bear!
Break forth and shout,
You who are not in labor!
For the desolate has many more
children
Than she who has a husband."

28 Now [a]we, brethren, as Isaac
was, are [b]children of promise.
29 But, as [a]he who was born according to the flesh then persecuted
him *who was born* according to the
Spirit, [b]even so *it is* now.
30 Nevertheless what does [a]the
Scripture say? [b]*"Cast out the bond-*
woman and her son, for [c]*the son of*
the bondwoman shall not be heir
with the son of the freewoman."
31 So then, brethren, we are not
children of the bondwoman but of
the free.

23 [a]Rom. 9:7, 8 [b]Heb. 11:11
24 [a]Deut. 33:2 [1]NU, M omit *the*
26 [a][Is. 2:2]
27 [a]Is. 54:1
28 [a]Gal. 3:29 [b]Acts 3:25
29 [a]Gen. 21:9 [b]Gal. 5:11
30 [a][Gal. 3:8, 22] [b]Gen. 21:10, 12 [c][John 8:35]

CHAPTER 5
1 [a]Phil. 4:1 [b]Acts 15:10 [1]NU *For freedom Christ has made us free; stand fast therefore, and*
2 [a]Acts 15:1
3 [a][Rom. 2:25] [1]*obligated*
4 [a][Rom. 9:31] [b]Heb. 12:15
5 [a]Rom. 8:24
6 [a][Gal. 6:15] [b]1 Thess. 1:3

Liberty of the Spirit

5 [a]Stand[1] fast therefore in the liberty by which Christ has made
us free, and do not be entangled
again with a [b]yoke of bondage.†
2 Indeed I, Paul, say to you that
[a]if you become circumcised, Christ
will profit you nothing.
3 And I testify again to every man
who becomes circumcised [a]that he
is [1]a debtor to keep the whole law.
4 [a]You have become estranged
from Christ, you who *attempt to* be
justified by law; [b]you have fallen
from grace.
5 For we through the Spirit
eagerly [a]wait for the hope of righteousness by faith.†
6 For [a]in Christ Jesus neither circumcision nor uncircumcision avails
anything, but [b]faith working
through love.†

5:1–5 The **yoke of bondage** is the law. It mistakes the lesser reality, its rules and regulations, its externals, for the greater reality, God, who produced the law and to whom the externals point. The law in this sense includes: (1) circumcision as a prerequisite (v. 2); (2) an obligation to perfectly obey **the whole law** (v. 3); (3) being **justified by law**—trying to establish one's own righteousness under the law (v. 4); (4) continuing **bondage** to sin (v. 1); (5) dependence upon the "flesh,"—the drive of sinful passions; (6) alienation **from Christ** and **from grace** (v. 4), which Christ calls "labor" and being "heavy laden" (Matt. 11:28).

By contrast, Christ's yoke is life in the Spirit and it includes: (1) the regeneration of baptism (3:27), the renewal of the complete person in Christ, the circumcision of the heart; (2) obedience to Christ and growth in perfection (Matt. 5:48); (3) being justified by grace, God's righteousness which becomes ours; (4) freedom or **liberty** (v. 1) from the power of sin; (5) dependence upon **the Spirit** (v. 5) and access to the perfect and glorified humanity of Christ; (6) union with Christ and the grace of God. Christ calls this yoke "rest," for it is "easy" and "light" (Matt. 11:30).

5:5 The hope of righteousness is the Kingdom of God.

5:6–12 To believe in Christ involves **faith working through love** (v. 6). Those who stop

(continued on next page)

Commemoration of Holy Monks

5:22—6:2: The holy monks crucified their flesh that they might bear the burdens of others.

Liberty of the Apostles

7 You [a]ran well. Who hindered
you from obeying the truth?
8 This persuasion does not *come*
from Him who calls you.
9 [a]A little leaven leavens the
whole lump.
10 I have confidence in you, in the
Lord, that you will have no other
mind; but he who troubles you shall
bear his judgment, whoever he is.
11 And I, brethren, if I still preach
circumcision, [a]why do I still suffer
persecution? Then [b]the offense of
the cross has ceased.
12 [a]I could wish that those [b]who
trouble you would even [1]cut themselves off!

War Against the Flesh

13 For you, brethren, have been
called to liberty; only [a]do not *use* liberty as an [b]opportunity for the flesh,
but [c]through love serve one
another.†
14 For [a]all the law is fulfilled in one
word, *even* in this: [b]*"You shall love
your neighbor as yourself."*
15 But if you bite and devour one
another, beware lest you be consumed by one another!

7 [a]1 Cor. 9:24
9 [a]1 Cor. 5:6
11 [a]1 Cor. 15:30
[b][1 Cor. 1:23]
12 [a]Josh. 7:25
[b]Acts 15:1, 2
[1]*mutilate themselves*
13 [a]1 Cor. 8:9
[b]1 Pet. 2:16
[c]1 Cor. 9:19
14 [a]Matt. 7:12; 22:40
[b]Lev. 19:18
16 [a]Rom. 6:12
17 [a]Rom. 7:18, 22, 23; 8:5
[b]Rom. 7:15
18 [a][Rom. 6:14; 7:4; 8:14]
19 [a]Eph. 5:3, 11
[1]NU omits *adultery*
[2]*sexual immorality*
21 [a]1 Cor. 6:9, 10
[1]NU omits *murders*
22 [a][John 15:2]
[b][Col. 3:12–15]
[c]Rom. 15:14
[d]1 Cor. 13:7
23 [a]1 Tim. 1:9
[1]*meekness*
24 [a]Rom. 6:6
25 [a][Rom. 8:4, 5]

16 I say then: [a]Walk in the Spirit,
and you shall not fulfill the lust of
the flesh.†
17 For [a]the flesh lusts against the
Spirit, and the Spirit against the
flesh; and these are contrary to one
another, [b]so that you do not do the
things that you wish.
18 But [a]if you are led by the Spirit,
you are not under the law.
19 Now [a]the works of the flesh are
evident, which are: [1]adultery,
[2]fornication, uncleanness, lewdness,
20 idolatry, sorcery, hatred, contentions, jealousies, outbursts of
wrath, selfish ambitions, dissensions, heresies,
21 envy, [1]murders, drunkenness,
revelries, and the like; of which I tell
you beforehand, just as I also told
you in time past, that [a]those who
practice such things will not inherit
the kingdom of God.
22 But [a]the fruit of the Spirit is
[b]love, joy, peace, longsuffering,
kindness, [c]goodness, [d]faithfulness,
23 [1]gentleness, self-control.
[a]Against such there is no law.
24 And those *who are* Christ's
[a]have crucified the flesh with its passions and desires.
25 [a]If we live in the Spirit, let us
also walk in the Spirit.†

(continued from previous page)
short of love, **hindered** by legalism (v. 7), miss the message of the Cross (v. 11). For by His death Christ abolished the law, and by His Resurrection He granted us sonship with God. For **those who trouble you** (v. 12) with circumcision, Paul wishes they would **cut themselves off**—referring to complete castration. Why does he speak so strongly? Christ broke the bonds of the law, not that our standard may be lowered, but that it may be exalted. We who are free from the law must not return to its bondage.

5:13–15 The way of life in the Spirit, the way of faith and love, is expressed through service to God and **one another** (v. 13). We must avoid at all costs competitive comparisons of each other's deeds.

5:16 By **the flesh,** Paul does not mean the body. *The flesh* here is a general term for evil actions, the depraved will, the earthly mind, the slothful and careless soul—things that are under one's control, not part of human nature. This *flesh* is crucified with Christ (v. 24). It is not human nature that is mortified, but its evil deeds.

5:25 A **walk in the Spirit** comes from life **in the spirit.**

26 [a]Let us not become conceited,
provoking one another, envying one
another.

Do Good to All

6 Brethren, if a man is [1]overtaken
in any trespass, you who *are*
spiritual restore such a one in a spirit
of [a]gentleness, considering yourself
lest you also be tempted.†
2 [a]Bear one another's burdens,
and so fulfill [b]the law of Christ.†
3 For [a]if anyone thinks himself to
be something, when [b]he is nothing,
he deceives himself.
4 But [a]let each one examine his
own work, and then he will have rejoicing in himself alone, and [b]not in
another.
5 For [a]each one shall bear his own
load.
6 [a]Let him who is taught the word
share in all good things with him
who teaches.†
7 Do not be deceived, God is not
mocked; for [a]whatever a man sows,
that he will also reap.
8 For he who sows to his flesh will
of the flesh reap corruption, but he
who sows to the Spirit will of the
Spirit reap [a]everlasting life.
9 And [a]let us not grow weary
while doing good, for in due season
we shall reap [b]if we do not lose
heart.
10 [a]Therefore, as we have opportu-

26 [a]Phil. 2:3

CHAPTER 6
1 [a]Eph. 4:2 [1]*caught*
2 [a]Rom. 15:1 [b][James 2:8]
3 [a]Rom. 12:3 [b][2 Cor. 3:5]
4 [a]1 Cor. 11:28 [b]Luke 18:11
5 [a][Rom. 2:6]
6 [a]1 Cor. 9:11, 14
7 [a][Rom. 2:6]
8 [a][Rom. 6:8]
9 [a]1 Cor. 15:58 [b][James 5:7, 8]
10 [a]Prov. 3:27 [b]Titus 3:8 [c]Rom. 12:13
12 [a]Gal. 5:11
14 [a][1 Cor. 1:18] [b]Col. 2:20 [1]Or *which,* the cross
15 [a]1 Cor. 7:19

nity, [b]let us do good to all, [c]espe-
cially to those who are of the household of faith.

The Rule of Faith

11 See with what large letters I
have written to you with my own
hand!
12 As many as desire to make a
good showing in the flesh, these
would compel you to be circumcised,
[a]only that they may not suffer persecution for the cross of Christ.†
13 For not even those who are circumcised keep the law, but they desire to have you circumcised that
they may boast in your flesh.
14 But God forbid that I should
boast except in the [a]cross of our Lord
Jesus Christ, by [1]whom the world
has been crucified to me, and [b]I to
the world.†
15 For [a]in Christ Jesus neither circumcision nor uncircumcision avails
anything, but a new creation.†
16 And as many as walk according
to this rule, peace and mercy *be* upon
them, and upon the Israel of God.†
17 From now on let no one trouble
me, for I bear in my body the marks
of the Lord Jesus.†

Benediction

18 Brethren, the grace of our Lord
Jesus Christ *be* with your spirit.
Amen.

6:1 To be able to administer correction with **gentleness** is a spiritual gift.

6:2 Paul admonishes us to **bear one another's burdens.** But moments later, he notes that "each one shall bear his own load" (v. 5). Both are true. We are called to initiate caregiving in the Church, *and* not to be needless burdens to others.

6:6 See Num. 31:47; 35:1–8; 1 Cor. 9:14. The teacher and the **taught** form a bond, and the sharing here is in material blessings.

6:12 The legalizers choose to offend God that they may please human beings.

6:14 How does one **boast . . . in the cross?** Throughout the history of the Church, Christians have preached the Cross, displayed the Cross in their homes and altars, venerated the Cross in the liturgy and signed themselves with the Cross in worship of the Holy Trinity and during times of fear or temptation.

6:15 The **new creation** is our way of life **in Christ Jesus.**

6:16 Paul calls the Church **Israel.**

6:17 Paul is no hypocrite or coward. He has persevered through much for what he is teaching, and he bears in his **body** the **marks** to prove it.

The Epistle of Paul the Apostle to the

EPHESIANS

Author: *St. Paul the Apostle*

Date: A.D. *61–63*

Theme: *The Riches of Christ in the Church*

AUTHOR: Some have cited differences in style, vocabulary and doctrinal emphasis between Ephesians and other Pauline epistles to dispute Paul's authorship of Ephesians. However, the epistle itself claims to be written by Paul (1:1), and the Church has recognized Paul as the author, writing under the inspiration of the Holy Spirit. Because Paul dictated some of his letters, differences in content and style would be expected.

DATE: Paul probably wrote Ephesians from Rome during his imprisonment in A.D. 61–63, as recorded in Acts 28:16–31.

MAJOR THEME: *The riches of Christ in the Church*. The mystery of salvation in the Church, the body of Christ, is not only for all mankind but for all creation, affecting this age and the age to come. The body of Christ is the center and life of all.

Subthemes include:

(1) The work of the Holy Trinity in our salvation (1:3–14, 17; 2:18, 22; 3:4, 5, 14–17, 20, 21; 4:3–6; 5:18–21).

(2) The blessings of Christ to the Church (1:1—3:21).

(3) Our response to God's grace (4:1—6:24).

(4) God's strength for spiritual warfare (1:19—2:10; 4:17–31; 6:10–18).

BACKGROUND INFORMATION: (1) *To whom was the letter written?* Some of the early manuscripts do not have "in Ephesus" in verse 1. Further, the content of Ephesians is general, which gives it the character of a book rather than a letter. It includes no personal greetings, although it is addressed to a city where Paul had spent two and a half years in the mid 50's (Acts 19:8, 10; 20:17, 31). It is probable, then, that this letter was intended not just for the Ephesians, but for circulation among the churches of western Asia Minor which Paul had founded from Ephesus during his third missionary journey. It is possible Ephesians is the "letter to the Laodiceans" mentioned in Colossians 4:16.

The messenger who delivered Ephesians, Tychicus (6:21, 22), was also carrying Colossians (which is similar to Ephesians). Tychicus had Onesimus with him (Col. 4:7–9) and so probably had letters for Philemon (Philem. 10–12) and the Laodiceans (Col. 4:16), and perhaps an extra copy of the letter to the Ephesians as well.

(2) *The purpose of Ephesians.* (a) Paul continued his oversight of churches in the area surrounding Ephesus while he was in prison. Letters and personal envoys were his means. He combats Gnosticism and the magic, mystery and fertility religions with a message of the unspeakable fullness of the apostolic faith. He uses the language of these other spiritual, religious and philosophical systems to impress upon his hearers the total and universal nature of Christian salvation.

(b) Paul uses letters to encourage the Church in evangelism. The Christians have grown dispirited at the news of his imprisonment (3:13). They see his weakness, but Paul sees God's strength. In chains to be sure, he is still an ambassador for Christ. He needs their bold intercessions (6:18–20). They are not helpless spectators but active participants.

(3) *Sacramental theology.* Paul writes not only of the Trinity (see Major Theme) but of the sacraments of the Church. He alludes to baptism (1:5, 6; 2:1–6; 4:5, 22–24; 5:8–14, 26–32), chrismation (1:13, 14; 4:3, 4, 7; 5:18), and the Eucharist (1:7; 5:2, 19, 20). Matrimony is treated in an eloquent discourse (5:22–33) which is the epistle reading for the Orthodox Christian wedding service.

The general priesthood and the different gifts within the body of Christ, conveyed by these sacraments, are given great prominence (2:20–22; 3:5, 6, 9–13; 4:11–16). Participation in the sacraments and the exercise of the spiritual gifts are key elements in the life of the Church.

OUTLINE

Greeting	1:1, 2
I. Praise of God's plan for the world	1:3–23
A. The creative sovereignty of the Father	1:3–6
B. The redemptive administration of the Son	1:7–12
C. The perfecting faithfulness of the Spirit	1:13, 14
D. A prayer for revelation	1:15–23
II. Theology of Christ and His Church	2:1—3:21
A. Salvation as a gift for all	2:1–10
B. The Church as one household for all	2:11–22
C. The apostles as faithful messengers	3:1–13
D. A prayer for the deification of the Church	3:14–21
III. Conduct of the body of Christ	4:1—6:20
A. As the body of Christ	4:1–16
1. Oneness in Christ	4:1–6
2. Diversity in Christ	4:7–16
B. As children of God	4:17—5:5
1. The source of sonship	4:17–24
2. The characteristics of sonship	4:25—5:5
C. As partakers of light	5:6–21
1. Separate from darkness	5:6, 7
2. Walk in Christ the light	5:8–10

3. Expose darkness 5:11–14
4. Live in God's will 5:15–17
5. Be filled with the Spirit 5:18–21
D. As families in the Church 5:22—6:9
1. Wives and husbands 5:22–33
2. Children and parents 6:1–4
3. Slaves and masters 6:5–9
E. As soldiers of Christ 6:10–20
1. Spiritual warfare 6:10–12
2. Spiritual weaponry 6:13–17
3. Spiritual readiness 6:18–20
Conclusion 6:21–24

Greeting

1 Paul, an apostle of Jesus Christ
by the will of God,

To the saints who are in Ephesus,
and faithful in Christ Jesus:†

2 Grace to you and peace from
God our Father and the Lord Jesus
Christ.

The Sovereignty of the Father

3 [a]Blessed *be* the God and Father
of our Lord Jesus Christ, who has
blessed us with every spiritual blessing in the heavenly *places* in Christ,†
4 just as [a]He chose us in Him
[b]before the foundation of the world,
that we should [c]be holy and without
blame before Him in love,†
5 [a]having predestined us to
[b]adoption as sons by Jesus Christ to
Himself, [c]according to the good
pleasure of His will,
6 to the praise of the glory of His
grace, [a]by which He [1]made us accepted in [b]the Beloved.

The Administration of the Son

7 [a]In Him we have redemption
through His blood, the forgiveness

CHAPTER 1
3 [a]2 Cor. 1:3
4 [a]Rom. 8:28
[b]1 Pet. 1:2
[c]Luke 1:75
5 [a][Rom. 8:29]
[b]John 1:12
[c][1 Cor. 1:21]
6 [a][Rom. 3:24]
[b]Matt. 3:17
[1]Lit. *bestowed grace (favor) upon us*
7 [a][Heb. 9:12]

1:1, 2 Saints and **faithful** are biblical and historic references to Christian believers. Here, **God** (v. 2) refers to the Father, **Lord** (Gr. *kyrios*) refers to the Son. Early Christian usage of these words indicates an identity of nature but distinction of Persons between the Father and the Son.

1:3–14 In the original Greek, this is all one sentence. Paul's opening theme is the preeminence of God's initiative. We say, simply, "Blessed is the Father, and the Son, and the Holy Spirit." Paul's doxology is more detailed: The Father has all power (vv. 3–6); the Son, all rule (vv. 7–12); the Spirit, all caretaking (vv. 13, 14).

1:3 God blesses and so is **blessed.** The Christian life is a response to God's initiative, especially that of the **Father** but also that of the Son, **our Lord Jesus Christ. Spiritual blessing** is primarily the work of the Spirit. **The heavenly places,** where the risen and ascended Christ reigns, are experienced **in Christ,** that is, by the life that is begun when one is joined with Christ in baptism (see Rom. 6:3–5).

1:4–6 Everything comes from God, and everything should be drawn back to Him. God's original intent for the Incarnation was not redemption from the fall but **adoption as sons** of God (v. 5), that is, deification. For when God contemplated creating the world, He planned on bringing it into union with Himself through the Incarnation of His Son, that is, through the Son's union with human nature. That is why St. Athanasius can say, "God became man that man might become god."

The Father **chose us in Him** (v. 4), the Son. Christ, who is God by nature, became man by choice. If we choose Him, we, who are human by nature, become "gods" by grace. If we are in Christ, the Son of God, we are sons of God. Paul is not addressing individuals as such but **us,** the community, the Church. And he is not addressing the issue of human will in salvation but the will of God: the will of God is that all are chosen (see Rom. 11:32;

(continued on next page)

of sins, according to [b]the riches of
His grace†
8 which He made to abound
toward us in all wisdom and
[1]prudence,
9 [a]having made known to us the
mystery of His will, according to His
good pleasure [b]which He purposed
in Himself,†
10 that in the dispensation of
[a]the fullness of the times [b]He might
gather together in one [c]all things in
Christ, [1]both which are in heaven
and which are on earth—in Him.
11 [a]In Him also we have obtained
an inheritance, being predestined according to [b]the purpose of Him who
works all things according to the
counsel of His will,†
12 [a]that we [b]who first trusted in
Christ should be to the praise of His
glory.

7 [b][Rom. 3:24, 25]
8 [1]*understanding*
9 [a][Rom. 16:25] [b][2 Tim. 1:9]
10 [a]Gal. 4:4 [b]1 Cor. 3:22 [c][Col. 1:16, 20] [1]NU, M omit *both*
11 [a]Rom. 8:17 [b]Is. 46:10
12 [a]2 Thess. 2:13 [b]James 1:18
13 [a]John 1:17 [b][2 Cor. 1:22]
14 [a]2 Cor. 5:5 [b]Rom. 8:23 [c][Acts 20:28] [d]1 Pet. 2:9 [1]NU *which* [2]*down payment, earnest*
15 [a]Col. 1:4
16 [a]Rom. 1:9

The Faithfulness of the Spirit

13 In Him you also *trusted*, after
you heard [a]the word of truth, the
gospel of your salvation; in whom
also, having believed, [b]you were
sealed with the Holy Spirit of
promise,†
14 [a]who[1] is the [2]guarantee of our
inheritance [b]until the redemption of
[c]the purchased possession, [d]to the
praise of His glory.

Prayer for Revelation

15 Therefore I also, [a]after I heard
of your faith in the Lord Jesus and
your love for all the saints,†
16 [a]do not cease to give thanks for
you, making mention of you in my
prayers:

(continued from previous page)
1 Tim. 2:4; 2 Pet. 3:9). But being **predestined** (v. 5) by God does not nullify human will: in everything, God is the originator, the initiator; we merely respond, but our response is necessary. Becoming a Christian is not so much inviting Christ into one's life as getting oneself into Christ's life. What is true of Christ must become true of one who is in Him.

1:7, 8 The sacraments of baptism (**redemption**) and the Eucharist (**His blood**) are alluded to as the necessary foundation for drawing near to God. *Redemption* has a technical meaning relative to the freeing of slaves. Here, the bondage is to **sins;** the act of releasing is **forgiveness;** the price of *redemption* is *blood*—the human life of Christ given over to death for the sake of new life. This beginning of life in Christ is not merely legal, nor instantaneous, but living and dynamic.

1:9, 10 The **mystery** is the plan of salvation, the gospel, the Kingdom of God, the Church. This mystery centers on Christ Himself (Col. 2:2), from the Incarnation (1 Tim. 3:16), to the Cross (1 Cor. 2:8), to the restoration and culmination of all things (v. 10). It is **the fullness** (v. 10) of all, not only for humanity but for the whole creation. Although it was announced by the prophets (Rom. 16:25, 26), God revealed it through Christ, and it is made known to us through the apostles (3:1–5; 1 Cor. 2:6, 7, 10–16; 4:1). The *mystery* is made manifest in history by the fact that Gentiles and Jews compose one body (3:6; Col. 1:26–28). The *mystery* is experienced in the sacraments of the Church, which are called the "mysteries."

1:11–14 The gospel unites all humanity: the Jews (vv. 11, 12) and the Gentiles (vv. 13, 14). The Jews, especially those who **trusted in Christ** (v. 12)—one of whom was Paul, hence the use of **we** (v. 11)—were the first witnesses to the coming of the Messiah. In **the fullness of the times** (v. 10) they were joined by the Gentiles.

1:13, 14 The outpouring of the Holy Spirit was an evidence that the last times, the day of the Lord, had come. Hence, Pentecost was a proof to the Jews that Jesus indeed was the Messiah. And the outpouring of the Holy Spirit upon the Gentiles (Acts 10:44–48) was a proof they were equal to the Jews in this final age. After baptism one is **sealed with the Holy Spirit,** called "chrismation." (The word "seal" is repeated by Orthodox Christians as the priest or bishop anoints the newly baptized with oil of chrism.)

The guarantee (v. 14) is a first installment in kind, a down payment or earnest of what is later to be completed: we both are redeemed and shall be redeemed.

1:15–23 This is an intercessory prayer which Paul prayed often and repetitiously (v. 16). He asks that his hearers might understand the redemption he outlined in vv. 3–14. Like vv. 3–14, this section is also one long sentence in Greek.

1:15 This is a way of restating the two great commandments: love God and love man.

17 that [a]the God of our Lord Jesus
Christ, the Father of glory, [b]may give
to you the spirit of wisdom and revelation in the knowledge of Him,
18 [a]the eyes of your [1]under-
standing being enlightened; that you
may know what is [b]the hope of His
calling, what are the riches of the
glory of His inheritance in the
saints,†
19 and what *is* the exceeding greatness of His power toward us who
believe, [a]according to the working of
His mighty power
20 which He worked in Christ
when [a]He raised Him from the dead
and [b]seated *Him* at His right hand
in the heavenly *places,*
21 [a]far above all [b]principality[1] and
[2]power and [3]might and dominion,
and every name that is named, not
only in this age but also in that which
is to come.†
22 And [a]He put all *things* under
His feet, and gave Him [b]*to be* head
over all *things* to the church,
23 [a]which is His body, [b]the fullness of Him [c]who fills all in all.

Transfiguration by Grace

2 And [a]you *He made alive,* [b]who
were dead in trespasses and
sins,†
2 [a]in which you once walked according to the [1]course of this world,
according to [b]the prince of the power
of the air, the spirit who now works
in [c]the sons of disobedience,
3 [a]among whom also we all once
conducted ourselves in [b]the lusts of
our flesh, fulfilling the desires of the
flesh and of the mind, and [c]were by
nature children of wrath, just as the
others.
4 But God, [a]who is rich in mercy,
because of His [b]great love with
which He loved us,
5 [a]even when we were dead in
trespasses, [b]made us alive together
with Christ (by grace you have been
saved),
6 and raised *us* up together, and
made *us* sit together [a]in the heavenly
places in Christ Jesus,
7 that in the ages to come He
might show the exceeding riches of
His grace in [a]*His* kindness toward
us in Christ Jesus.
8 [a]For by grace you have been
saved [b]through faith, and that not
of yourselves; [c]*it is* the gift of God,†
9 not of [a]works, lest anyone
should [b]boast.
10 For we are [a]His workmanship,

17 [a]John 20:17 [b]Col. 1:9
18 [a]Acts 26:18 [b]Eph. 2:12 [1]NU, M *hearts*
19 [a]Col. 2:12
20 [a]Acts 2:24 [b]Ps. 110:1
21 [a]Phil. 2:9, 10 [b][Rom. 8:38, 39] [1]*rule* [2]*authority* [3]*power*
22 [a]Ps. 8:6; 110:1 [b]Heb. 2:7
23 [a]Rom. 12:5 [b]Col. 2:9 [c][1 Cor. 12:6]

CHAPTER 2

1 [a]Col. 2:13 [b]Eph. 4:18
2 [a]Col. 1:21 [b]Eph. 6:12 [c]Col. 3:6 [1]Gr. *aion,* aeon
3 [a]1 Pet. 4:3 [b]Gal. 5:16 [c][Ps. 51:5]
4 [a]Rom. 10:12 [b]John 3:16
5 [a]Rom. 5:6, 8 [b][Rom. 6:4, 5]
6 [a]Eph. 1:20
7 [a]Titus 3:4
8 [a][2 Tim. 1:9] [b]Rom. 4:16 [c][John 1:12, 13]
9 [a]Rom. 4:4, 5; 11:6 [b]Rom. 3:27
10 [a]Is. 19:25

1:18 Understanding should be translated "heart." The prayer that Orthodox Christians pray before the reading of the gospel begins, "Illumine our hearts, O Master who love mankind, with the pure light of your divine knowledge."

1:21–23 Principality, power, might and **dominion** (v. 21) are orders of angelic beings. Because Christ transcends all (v. 21), everything submits to Him (v. 22). Because He is intimately united with **the church** (v. 22) as a **head** to its **body** (v. 23), the Church has the greatest glory of all creation. The Church is God's masterpiece (v. 23). Since Christ as God is infinite, the Church never ceases becoming "full."

2:1–7 Two unequal kingdoms are at war. Each is spiritual in nature, each stamps its image on its subjects and requires strict obedience. Yet they are opposites.

The king of the lesser realm is a created being, Satan. His domain is **of the air** (v. 2), neither fully of earth nor of heaven. He is the author of **disobedience** (v. 2), rebellion. The beginning of his rule is spiritual death (v. 1). The **desires** of his subjects are lustful, **of the flesh and of the mind** (v. 3). Their deeds are **trespasses and sins** (v. 1). The result of his rule is **wrath** (v. 3), and hence eternal death.

The King of the other Kingdom is uncreated, **God** the Father (v. 4). His realm is **the heavenly places** (v. 6). He rules by **mercy** and **love** (v. 4). The beginning of His rule is redemption to eternal life (v. 5). The desires of His subjects are thankfulness and glorifying God. Their deeds are righteous, as is proper to those who reign with Christ. The result of His rule is **exceeding riches** and **kindness** (v. 7), and hence eternal life.

2:8–10 How can one get from the one kingdom to the other (vv. 1–7)? By the unity of

(continued on page 442)

"WORKS" IN PAUL'S WRITING

St. Paul uses the term "works" extensively in his letters, and we encounter his use of the word especially in Romans, Galatians, and Ephesians. By this term, he means human activities which he generally classifies in two categories:

(1) *Dead works*: These are (a) works which are evil, such as murder, adultery, idol worship, and robbery. These the Scriptures also call "works of the flesh" (Gal. 5:19) and obviously condemn. But, in addition, dead works are (b) works—even good works—done for the wrong reasons. These are works which are good in themselves, such as fasting, giving money, and feeding the poor, but are done to call attention to oneself or to gain standing in the community. Selfish motivation turns good works to dead works. (The solution to this problem is not to cease fasting, giving or helping but to turn from the sin of self-glorification.)

(2) *Living works*: These are deeds which are both good in themselves and done for a good purpose: to glorify God. Good works the Scriptures commend. Paul teaches they are an outgrowth of our salvation when he writes, "For we are His workmanship, created in Christ Jesus for good works, which God has prepared beforehand that we should walk in them" (Eph. 2:10). They contribute to our faith, as James teaches, "You see then that a man is justified by works, and not by faith only [or alone]" (James 2:24). When we do living works, we seek to bring glory to God, not to ourselves, through what we do, and we rely upon the strength and the grace of God.

Some have erroneously understood Paul, particularly in Romans 4, to be condemning all works. A careful reading of Romans, however, reveals that Paul is not putting down works in general, but *dead works*. St. Maximos the Confessor, writing in the seventh century, states clearly the view of the Church concerning dead works:

> Many human activities, good in themselves, are not good because of the motive for which they are done. For example, fasting, vigils, prayer, psalmody [the singing of hymns], acts of charity and hospitality are by nature good. But when performed for the sake of self-esteem [vainglory, self-glorification] they are not good. In everything we do, God searches out our purpose to see whether we do it for Him or for some other motive . . . quite clearly He bestows blessings only when something is done for the right purpose. For God's judgment looks not at the actions, but at the purpose behind them.

Thus, the Christian actively cultivates a habit of doing good works for the glory of God, and as a way of life. The writings of Paul are clear. If we are joined to Christ and cleansed from the dishonor of the past, we become "a vessel for honor, sanctified and useful for the Master, prepared for every good work" (2 Tim. 2:21). God sets us apart to Himself so we will be productive and useful to Him.

"Therefore, my beloved brethren," Paul tells the Corinthians, "be steadfast, immovable, always abounding in the work of the Lord, knowing that your labor is not in vain in the Lord" (1 Cor. 15:58).

created in Christ Jesus for good works, which God prepared beforehand that we should walk in them.

The Former Alienation of the Gentiles

11 Therefore remember that you, once Gentiles in the flesh—who are called Uncircumcision by what is called [a]the Circumcision made in the flesh by hands—†

12 that at that time you were without Christ, being aliens from the commonwealth of Israel and strangers from the covenants of promise, having no hope and without God in the world.

The Means of Union

13 But now in Christ Jesus you who once were far off have been brought near by the blood of Christ.†

14 For He Himself is our peace, who has made both one, and has broken down the middle wall of separation,

15 having abolished in His flesh the enmity, *that is,* the law of commandments *contained* in ordinances, so as to create in Himself one [a]new man *from* the two, *thus* making peace,

16 and that He might [a]reconcile them both to God in one body through the cross, thereby [b]putting to death the enmity.

17 And He came and preached peace to you who were afar off and to those who were near.

18 For [a]through Him we both have access [b]by one Spirit to the Father.

The Unity of Jew and Gentile in Christ

19 Now, therefore, you are no longer strangers and foreigners, but fellow citizens with the saints and members of the household of God,†

20 having been [a]built [b]on the foundation of the [c]apostles and prophets, Jesus Christ Himself being [d]the chief corner*stone,*

21 in whom the whole building, being fitted together, grows into [a]a holy temple in the Lord,

11 [a][Rom. 2:28; Col. 2:11]
15 [a]Gal. 6:15
16 [a]2 Cor. 5:18; [Col. 1:20–22] [b][Rom. 6:6]
18 [a]John 10:9 [b]1 Cor. 12:13; Eph. 4:4
20 [a]1 Pet. 2:4 [b]Matt. 16:18; 1 Cor. 3:10, 11; Rev. 21:14 [c]1 Cor. 12:28; Eph. 3:5 [d]Ps. 118:22; Luke 20:17
21 [a]1 Cor. 3:16, 17

(continued from page 440)
grace, faith, and **works** (vv. 7–9). Not that these are equal, for grace is uncreated and infinite, our faith is limited and can grow, and good works flow out of authentic faith. Works cannot earn us this great treasure—it is a pure gift—but those who receive this gift do good. We are not saved *by* good works, but **for good works** (v. 10).

2:11, 12 Since salvation involves the renewal of all mankind in Christ, the old distinction between Jew and Gentile no longer exists. This ethnic distinction was based on **the flesh** (v. 11), the Gentiles being uncircumcised and the Jews being circumcised. While Israel was especially blessed by God (v. 12), both Jews and Gentiles had to become *true* Israel (see vv. 13–18).

2:13–18 Man's brokenness was twofold: man was separated from man, that is, Gentile from Jew (vv. 13–15); and man was separated from God (vv. 16–18). The healing is likewise twofold: the creation of a unified humanity, the Church, and the raising of this unified humanity to God. The Incarnation of the Son of God did the former; His death and Resurrection did the latter. The whole Trinity, Father, Son, and Holy Spirit, act together (v. 18; see v. 22).

The middle wall of separation (v. 14) probably refers to the barrier in the temple separating the Court of the Gentiles from the Court of the Jews. This barrier manifested the limitations of the Old Covenant. It did not heal humanity's self-alienation, and it actually increased human hostility. Now that this wall is **broken down,** both Gentiles and Jews are reconciled and one in Christ.

2:19–22 The Church, humanity unified and renewed through union with the incarnate Son of God (vv. 11–18), is built upon a foundation of **Jesus Christ** and **the apostles** and **prophets** (v. 20). From this foundation come the Scriptures and all doctrine. In 4:11 these gifts are implied to be a continuing reality in the Church. And the spiritual building is one: the Church is designed to be united.

22 [a]in whom you also are being
built together for a [b]dwelling place
of God in the Spirit.

Paul's Revelation

3 For this reason I, Paul, the prisoner of Christ Jesus for you Gentiles—†
2 if indeed you have heard of
the [1]dispensation of the grace of
God [a]which was given to me for
you,
3 [a]how that by revelation [b]He
made known to me the mystery (as
I have briefly written already,†
4 by which, when you read, you
may understand my knowledge in
the mystery of Christ),
5 which in other ages was not
made known to the sons of men, as
it has now been revealed by the
Spirit to His holy apostles and
prophets:†
6 that the Gentiles [a]should be fellow heirs, of the same body, and partakers of His promise in Christ
through the gospel,†

22 [a]1 Pet. 2:5 [b]John 17:23
CHAPTER 3
2 [a]Acts 9:15 [1]*stewardship*
3 [a]Acts 22:17, 21; 26:16 [b][Rom. 11:25; 16:25]
6 [a]Gal. 3:28, 29
7 [a]Rom. 15:16 [b]Rom. 1:5 [c]Rom. 15:18
8 [a][1 Cor. 15:9] [b][Col. 1:27; 2:2, 3]
9 [a]Heb. 1:2 [1]NU, M *stewardship* (dispensation) [2]NU omits *through Jesus Christ*
10 [a]1 Pet. 1:12 [b][1 Tim. 3:16] [c]Col. 1:16; 2:10, 15 [1]*variegated* or *many-sided* [2]*rulers*
11 [a][Eph. 1:4, 11]

Paul's Apostolic Commission

7 [a]of which I became a minister
[b]according to the gift of the grace of
God given to me by [c]the effective
working of His power.
8 To me, [a]who am less than the
least of all the saints, this grace was
given, that I should preach among
the Gentiles [b]the unsearchable riches
of Christ,†
9 and to make all see what *is* the
[1]fellowship of the mystery, which
from the beginning of the ages has
been hidden in God who [a]created all
things [2]through Jesus Christ;
10 [a]to the intent that now [b]the
[1]manifold wisdom of God might be
made known by the church [c]to the
[2]principalities and powers in the
heavenly *places*,†
11 [a]according to the eternal purpose which He accomplished in
Christ Jesus our Lord,
12 in whom we have boldness and
access [a]with confidence through
faith in Him.†

12 [a]Heb. 4:16; 10:19, 35

3:1–13 How does Paul fit into God's plan for creation described in 1:3–14 and 2:1–22? God has revealed this plan to him (vv. 1–6) so that he can reveal it to all, especially to the Gentiles (vv. 7–13).

3:1, 2 Prisoner (Paul is in prison in Rome as he writes this letter) is a title of honor and a mark of apostleship (Luke 21:12; 2 Cor. 6:4, 5). Paul is not only an apostle (see v. 5), but one with a special role, a special **dispensation** (v. 2, Gr. *oikonomia*). All NT leaders, "apostles and prophets" (v. 5; 2:20), know the doctrine of the unity in the Church of Christ; Paul has received the special commission to extend this Church to the Gentiles (v. 8).

3:3 God's **revelation** to Paul began on the road to Damascus (Acts 22:3–21). God was gracious to Paul not for his own sake but for others (see Acts 9:15, 16).

3:5 The apostolate is the special bearer of divine revelation necessary for the life of the Church in this age.

3:6 This is the content of the revelation mentioned in v. 3: that **through the gospel** the **Gentiles** should be united with the Jews, so that a united and renewed humanity is brought to God.

3:8 Why did God choose a Jew to preach to the Gentiles? Because if God can redeem Saul, the persecutor of the Church and hater of Gentiles, then God can certainly redeem the Gentiles through Saul.

3:10 Not only did men not know of God's mystery (v. 5), neither did the angels. They hear of it from men. How can this be? Because **the church** affects all elements of creation, from the material to the immaterial. The united, renewed humanity made possible by Christ is the basis of the reconciliation of the heavens and the earth. Therefore, the Church ascends above the angels, **the principalities and powers.** The basis of such an astounding work by men is Christ's Resurrection and exaltation (v. 11).

3:12 The wonder of the mystery of God, surprising even to angels, is that mere humans, earthly creatures, can have **boldness** and confident **access** to God the Father.

13 [a]Therefore I ask that you do not
lose heart at my tribulations for you,
[b]which is your glory.†

Prayer for Deification

14 For this reason I bow my knees
to the [a]Father [1]of our Lord Jesus
Christ,†
15 from whom the whole family in
heaven and earth is named,†
16 that He would grant you,
[a]according to the riches of His glory,
[b]to be strengthened with might
through His Spirit in [c]the inner man,
17 [a]that Christ may dwell in your
hearts through faith; that you,
[b]being rooted and grounded in love,
18 [a]may be able to comprehend
with all the saints [b]what *is* the
width and length and depth and
height—†
19 to know the love of Christ which
passes knowledge; that you may be
filled [a]with all the fullness of God.

Doxology to the Father

20 Now [a]to Him who is able to do
exceedingly abundantly [b]above all
that we ask or think, [c]according to
the power that works in us,†
21 [a]to Him *be* glory in the church
by Christ Jesus to all generations,
forever and ever. Amen.

Live in Unity

4 I, therefore, the prisoner [1]of the
Lord, [2]beseech you to [a]walk
worthy of the calling with which you
were called,†
2 with all lowliness and gentleness, with longsuffering, bearing
with one another in love,†

13 [a]Phil. 1:14 [b]2 Cor. 1:6 **14** [a]Eph. 1:3 [1]NU omits *of our Lord Jesus Christ* **16** [a][Phil. 4:19] [b]Col. 1:11 [c]Rom. 7:22 **17** [a]John 14:23 [b]Col. 1:23 **18** [a]Eph. 1:18 [b]Rom. 8:39 **19** [a]Eph. 1:23 **20** [a]Rom. 16:25 [b]1 Cor. 2:9 [c]Col. 1:29 **21** [a]Rom. 11:36

CHAPTER 4

1 [a]1 Thess. 2:12 [1]Lit. *in* [2]*exhort, encourage*

3:13 Paul sees that even his sufferings are a part of his apostolic work. His **tribulations** are **for you,** that is, for the Church, for us. So our sufferings can be for others.

3:14–19 Paul picks up where he left off in v. 1, beginning a prayer for his hearers. **I bow my knees** shows his special earnestness, since standing would have been a more common posture for prayer. The whole Trinity is involved in our deification: Father (vv. 14, 15, 19–21), Son (vv. 14, 17, 19, 21), and Holy Spirit (v. 16).

3:15 Family or clan (Gr. *patria*) is a group descended from one ancestor. God the Father (Gr. *pater,* v. 14), is the ultimate source of every living being. As there is only one uncreated Father, so the whole of creation is called to form one family under the fatherhood of God.

3:18, 19 How do we **comprehend** (v. 18) and **know** (v. 19)? It is something other than a scientific fact or intellectual awareness. It is (1) a revelation, a divine gift which illumines and transforms our intellect; and (2) a reciprocal encounter, a personal bond with the personal God, who reveals Himself to us through communion with Him. This revelation and personal communion, this faith, is best known (1) **with all the saints** (v. 18), that is, in personal communion with the corporate Church; and (2) through an experience of the great gift of grace, **the love of Christ** (v. 19). Theological knowledge is first personal and experiential, and then thought out and verbalized. A theologian witnesses to what he knows through experience.

3:20, 21 A benediction that falls in the middle of the epistle acknowledges that God's work goes far beyond what we envision, **above all that we ask or think.** The goal of deification, "that you may be filled with all the fullness of God" (v. 19), is accomplished by the working together, the synergism, of our faith and love with God's **power** and Spirit **in us** (v. 20).

4:1 Paul implores his hearers to realize what has been given to them, and to be in practice what they are in Christ. So he turns the focus of his letter from what God does for us to what we are to do in response. How you believe must affect how you live; creed must influence conduct.

4:2, 3 The basic characteristics of Christians are the virtues which contribute to **unity:** though we are many persons, we share one new nature. Though we are members of the most exalted body, the greatness is of God, not of ourselves. Even the cohesiveness of this body is God's work in the **Spirit** (v. 3). So, there is no place for quarreling. To live in the heavenlies we are to walk in solidarity and humility on earth. Note that the one virtue listed not common to Greco-Roman philosophy is **lowliness,** taught in word and in deed by Jesus Himself.

THE CHURCH

One of the tragic aberrations of so-called modern religion is the presence of "Churchless Christianity." The assertion is that it is Christ who saves us, not the Church, so "all you need is Jesus."

Few who claim to be Christians would argue against the statement that it is Christ who saves. For He is the eternal Son of God who has assumed human flesh, and has done so "for us and for our salvation." Thus Paul writes, "For there is one God and one Mediator between God and men, the Man Christ Jesus" (1 Tim. 2:5).

But because this Mediator established the Church which is His body, we who are joined to Him are joined to His Church as well. To say we love Christ, who is Head of the Church, and at the same time reject His body is to deny New Testament teaching.

The Gospel and Acts: The first use of the word "church" (Gr. *ecclesia)* in the New Testament comes in the Gospel of Matthew, when our Lord gives His approval of Peter's confession of faith and promises, "I will build My church" (Matt. 16:18). Jesus Christ builds and we cooperate with Him.

The Book of Acts discloses more of what Jesus meant in Matthew 16. When Peter's sermon on the Day of Pentecost concludes, those present ask for guidance toward salvation: "What shall we do?" (Acts 2:37). Following Peter's word, they are baptized and join with the other believers, three thousand of them (Acts 2:38, 41).

Having been joined to Christ and His Church, these baptized believers begin living as the body of Christ. We find them looking after each other, using their personal resources for the care of each other, continuing together in prayer and in the Eucharist (Acts 2:42–47). From this point on "the Lord added to the church daily those who were being saved" (Acts 2:47), and throughout Acts, the Church is being built as the gospel of Christ spreads.

The Epistles: Paul's instructions in his letters to the churches throughout the eastern Mediterranean clearly show what it means to be members of Christ: to be the Church and to be in the Church. Nowhere in the New Testament is Paul's teaching on the Church more fully disclosed than in Ephesians 4. He instructs us that:

(1) The Church is *one,* "endeavoring to keep the unity of the Spirit in the bond of peace" (Eph. 4:3). There is one Church, one God, one doctrine, one baptism.

(2) The Church is *people,* men and women who are energized by the Holy Spirit. For "to each one of us grace was given according to the measure of Christ's gift" (Eph. 4:7). We are not all given the same gifts, but together we are equipped to do God's will.

(3) The Head of the Church is *Christ,* "from whom the whole body [is] joined and knit together" (Eph. 4:14, 16).

(4) The Church is "the *new man*" (Eph. 4:24), the new creation, made to be righteous and holy. We are no longer alienated from God (Eph. 4:18) but we are being renewed together (Eph. 4:23), "members of one another" (Eph. 4:25).

The Church, then, is that place established by Christ where we each may become what we are created to be, maturing and being perfected, while the Church receives what it needs from each of us, so that it, too, is being perfected. The Church as the body of Christ carries us beyond our petty and worldly personal concerns, stretching our vision to the eternal and the heavenly as we ascend together to worship the Father, the Son and the Holy Spirit.

3 endeavoring to keep the unity
of the Spirit [a]in the bond of peace.
4 [a]*There is* one body and one
Spirit, just as you were called in one
hope of your calling;†
5 [a]one Lord, [b]one faith, [c]one
baptism;
6 [a]one God and Father of all, who
is above all, and [b]through all, and
in [1]you all.

Use the Spiritual Gifts

7 But [a]to each one of us grace was
given according to the measure of
Christ's gift.†
8 Therefore He says:

[a]*"When He ascended on high,*
He led captivity captive,
And gave gifts to men."†

9 [a](Now this, *"He ascended"*—
what does it mean but that He also
[1]first descended into the lower parts
of the earth?
10 He who descended is also the
One [a]who ascended far above all the
heavens, [b]that He might fill all
things.)
11 And He Himself gave some *to
be* apostles, some prophets, some
evangelists, and some pastors and
teachers,†
12 for the equipping of the saints
for the work of ministry, [a]for the
[1]edifying of [b]the body of Christ,
13 till we all come to the unity of
the faith [a]and of the knowledge of
the Son of God, to [b]a perfect man,
to the measure of the stature of the
fullness of Christ;
14 that we should no longer be
[a]children, tossed to and fro and carried
about with every wind of doctrine,
by the trickery of men, in the
cunning craftiness of [b]deceitful
plotting,
15 but, speaking the truth in love,
may grow up in all things into Him
who is the [a]head—Christ—
16 [a]from whom the whole body,
joined and knit together by what
every joint supplies, according to the
effective working by which every

3 [a]Col. 3:14
4 [a]Rom. 12:5
5 [a]1 Cor. 1:13 [b]Jude 3 [c][Heb. 6:6]
6 [a]Mal. 2:10 [b]Rom. 11:36 [1]NU omits *you;* M *us*
7 [a][1 Cor. 12:7, 11]
8 [a]Ps. 68:18
9 [a]John 3:13; 20:17 [1]NU omits *first*
10 [a]Acts 1:9 [b][Eph. 1:23]
12 [a]1 Cor. 14:26 [b]Col. 1:24 [1]*building up*
13 [a]Col. 2:2 [b]1 Cor. 14:20
14 [a]1 Cor. 14:20 [b]Rom. 16:18
15 [a]Eph. 1:22
16 [a]Col. 2:19

4:4–6 Here is the manifold unity of the Church. Christian morality is not based upon ideas but upon a living reality: the life of the Holy Trinity in the Church. Paul combines the three Persons of the Trinity (**one Spirit . . . one Lord . . . one God**) with the Church, the sacrament of **baptism** (v. 5), and the theological virtues of **hope** (v. 4) and **faith** (v. 5) into one grand reality, the concrete basis for holy living. Each Person of the Trinity sanctifies, but the sanctification is one, because the baptism is one, and the grace of the sacrament is one.

4:7–16 While the Church is one in essence, it is diverse in gifts and function. Unity does not mean uniformity. Each member is unique before God, with gifts and roles granted by Him. Diversity in operation is (1) based on the ascent of the Son and the descent of the Spirit (vv. 8–10), (2) guided by specially gifted people (v. 11), (3) for the sake of the maturity and stability of the body (vv. 12–16).

4:8–10 Paul's rabbinic way of intertwining the Ascension of Christ (**He ascended**) with the descent of the Spirit (**gave gifts**) reveals the relationship between the body of Christ and the gifts of the Spirit. **The lower parts of the earth** is either (1) the earth itself, referring to the Incarnation, or (2) burial or Hades, the place of the dead, referring to Christ's death and descent into hell (1 Pet. 3:19). Only Christ, as God and man, can **fill all things** (v. 10), that is, reign over the unification and fulfillment of creation.

4:11–16 The gifts listed in v. 11 are given to those who lead the Church. The Holy Spirit extends gifts to each person at chrismation, but the "ministry gifts" listed here form one leadership group responsible for **equipping** the laity for **the work of ministry** (v. 12).

Why is there a diversity of persons and giftings in the Church? (1) For unity of service (vv. 12, 13), (2) for the preservation of truth (v. 14), and (3) for the operation of **love** (vv. 15, 16), the primary quality of Christian growth. The Church, in which Christian life develops, is not primarily an organization, but an organism whose parts or members receive their edifying power from Christ to grow up into Christ. Paul does not look at the Christian as an isolated individual walking towards perfection, but as a member of the body, striving to reach the perfect faith and full knowledge of the Son of God. Thus unity of faith cannot be separated from knowledge of the Son of God.

part does its share, causes growth
of the body for the edifying of itself
in love.

Put Off the Old, Put On the New

17 This I say, therefore, and testify
in the Lord, that you should [a]no
longer walk as [1]the rest of the Gentiles walk, in the futility of their
mind,†
18 having their understanding
darkened, being alienated from the
life of God, because of the ignorance
that is in them, because of the
[a]blindness of their heart;
19 [a]who, being past feeling,
[b]have given themselves over to
lewdness, to work all uncleanness
with greediness.
20 But you have not so learned
Christ,
21 if indeed you have heard Him
and have been taught by Him, as the
truth is in Jesus:
22 that you [a]put off, concerning
your former conduct, the old man
which grows corrupt according to
the deceitful lusts,
23 and [a]be renewed in the spirit of
your mind,
24 and that you [a]put on the new
man which was created according to
God, in true righteousness and
holiness.

Be Children of God

25 Therefore, putting away lying,
[a]*"Let each one of you speak truth
with his neighbor,"* for [b]we are
members of one another.†
26 [a]*"Be angry, and do not sin"*: do
not let the sun go down on your
wrath,†
27 [a]nor give [1]place to the devil.
28 Let him who stole steal no
longer, but rather [a]let him labor,
working with *his* hands what is
good, that he may have something
[b]to give him who has need.†
29 [a]Let no corrupt word proceed
out of your mouth, but [b]what is good
for necessary [1]edification, [c]that it
may impart grace to the hearers.
30 And [a]do not grieve the Holy
Spirit of God, by whom you were
sealed for the day of redemption.

17 [a]Eph. 2:2; 4:22 [1]NU omits *the rest of*
18 [a]Rom. 1:21
19 [a]1 Tim. 4:2 [b]1 Pet. 4:3
22 [a]Col. 3:8
23 [a][Rom. 12:2]
24 [a][Rom. 6:4; 7:6; 12:2]
25 [a]Zech. 8:16 [b]Rom. 12:5
26 [a]Ps. 4:4; 37:8
27 [a][Rom. 12:19] [1]*an opportunity*
28 [a]Acts 20:35 [b]Luke 3:11
29 [a]Col. 3:8 [b]1 Thess. 5:11 [c]Col. 3:16 [1]*building up*
30 [a]Is. 7:13

4:17–24 The process of Christian growth requires our free-will commitment to walk in **righteousness and holiness** (v. 24). A child of the light can no longer act as a child of darkness. A change of life-style is possible because of Christ, the original **new man** (v. 24). So Christ must be **learned** (v. 20), and relationship with Him must **be renewed** (v. 23), a process implying intimate relationship. Further, Christ must be **put on** (v. 24), a clothing metaphor, an allusion to baptism and the baptismal robe. While spiritual grace makes man heavenly, righteousness is both a gift and a goal, a present reality and a promise to be striven for.

4:25—5:5 The way we live affects our relationship not only with God but also with each other—for in Christ we are **members of one another** (4:25). The moral standard for the new humanity is the life appropriate to a child of God (5:1)—of the Father (4:32—5:1), the Son (5:2), and the **Holy Spirit** (4:30). Such a child fulfills the two great commandments: (1) love of man, demonstrated in self-sacrificing service (5:2; **given Himself for us**); and (2) love of God, manifested in worship (**an offering and a sacrifice to God**).

Paul especially emphasizes that Christians must avoid sexual immorality, not just the act but thinking and talking about it also (5:4); and greed, which treats things as if they were gods (5:5). Ungodly thoughts as well as behavior can keep believers out of the Kingdom.

4:25 Lying hurts the entire body of the Church. It is as if the eye were to see a trap and not tell the foot, or the tongue to taste poison and not spit it out.

4:26, 27 "If you fail to master your anger on the first day, then on the next day and even sometimes for a whole year you will still be dragging it out . . . Anger will cause us to suspect that words spoken in one sense were meant in another. And we will even do the same with gestures and every little thing . . . Be angry with the devil and not your own member. This is why God has armed us with anger. Not that we should thrust the sword against our own bodies, but that we should baptize the whole blade in the devil's breast." (St. John Chrysostom)

4:28 We are to work, not for personal gain and luxury, but in order to serve.

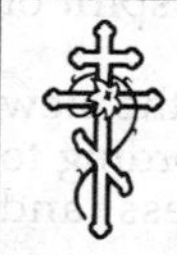

The Day of the Holy Spirit *Monday after Pentecost*

5:9–19: Paul exhorts us to be filled with the Spirit rather than partaking of darkness.

31 [a]Let all bitterness, wrath, anger,
[1]clamor, and [b]evil speaking be put
away from you, [c]with all malice.†
32 And [a]be kind to one another,
tenderhearted, [b]forgiving one another, even as God in Christ forgave
you.†

5 Therefore[a] be imitators of God
as dear [b]children.
2 And [a]walk in love, [b]as Christ
also has loved us and given Himself for us, an offering and a sacrifice to God [c]for a sweet-smelling
aroma.†
3 But fornication and all [a]uncleanness or [b]covetousness, let it not
even be named among you, as is fitting for saints;
4 [a]neither filthiness, nor [b]foolish
talking, nor coarse jesting, [c]which
are not fitting, but rather [d]giving of
thanks.†
5 For [1]this you know, that no fornicator, unclean person, nor covetous man, who is an idolater, has any
[a]inheritance in the kingdom of
Christ and God.

Separate from Darkness

6 Let no one deceive you with
empty words, for because of these
things the wrath of God comes upon
the sons of disobedience.†
7 Therefore do not be [a]partakers
with them.

Walk in Christ the Light

8 For you were once darkness, but
now *you are* [a]light in the Lord. Walk
as children of light†
9 (for [a]the fruit of the [1]Spirit *is* in
all goodness, righteousness, and
truth),
10 [a]finding out what is acceptable
to the Lord.

Expose Darkness

11 And have [a]no fellowship with
the unfruitful works of darkness, but
rather [1]expose *them*.†
12 [a]For it is shameful even to speak
of those things which are done by
them in secret.
13 But [a]all things that are exposed
are made manifest by the light, for
whatever makes manifest is light.
14 Therefore He says:

31 [a]Col. 3:8, 19 [b]James 4:11 [c]Titus 3:3 [1]*loud quarreling*
32 [a]2 Cor. 6:10 [b][Mark 11:25]

CHAPTER 5

1 [a]Luke 6:36 [b]1 Pet. 1:14–16
2 [a]1 Thess. 4:9 [b]Gal. 1:4 [c]2 Cor. 2:14, 15
3 [a]Col. 3:5–7 [b][Luke 12:15]
4 [a]Matt. 12:34, 35 [b]Titus 3:9 [c]Rom. 1:28 [d]Phil. 4:6
5 [a]1 Cor. 6:9, 10 [1]NU *know this*
7 [a]1 Tim. 5:22
8 [a]1 Thess. 5:5
9 [a]Gal. 5:22 [1]NU *light*
10 [a][Rom. 12:1, 2]
11 [a]2 Cor. 6:14 [1]*reprove*
12 [a]Rom. 1:24 [1]*reproved*
13 [a][John 3:20, 21]

4:31, 32 "Cut off clamor and you will clip the wings of anger . . . There is but one thing in which it is useful to cry aloud—in preaching and in teaching." (St. John Chrysostom)

4:32 We cannot be content only to root out the weeds mentioned in v. 31; we must plant good fruit as well.

5:2–15 "Walk worthy of the calling," Paul says in 4:1 (see 2:10). Here he defines this **walk:** Walk in love (v. 2); walk in light (v. 8); walk in wisdom (v. 15). *Walk* implies a slow, steady pace; a daily effort; a marathon, not a sprint.

5:4 "Just as clamor was the fuel of wrath, so foul talk is the fuel of lust." (St. John Chrysostom)

5:6, 7 The sharp contrast between the two ways, the way of darkness and the way of light, is begun. The animosity between the two ways is in thoughts, words (vv. 6–10) and actions (vv. 8–12).

5:8–10 We must judge what the world says is reasonable on the basis of what God says is true.

5:11–14 Besides separating from darkness, Christians are also to **expose** (v. 11) it. But we

(continued on page 450)

MARRIAGE

The Bible and human history begin and end with weddings. Adam and Eve come together in marital union in Paradise, before the Fall, revealing marriage as a part of God's eternal purpose for humanity in the midst of creation (Gen. 2:22–25). History closes with the marriage of the Bride to the Lamb (Rev. 19:7–9), earthly marriage being fulfilled in the heavenly, showing the eternal nature of the sacrament.

Between these bookend events of history are the accounts of numerous other unions of man and wife. In the centuries-old Christian wedding ceremony used to this day in the Orthodox Church, several of these historic marriages are remembered: Abraham and Sarah (Gen. 11:29—23:20); Isaac and Rebecca (Gen. 24); Joachim and Anna, the parents of the Virgin Mary; and Zacharias and Elizabeth (Luke 1:5–58).

The marriage most prominently featured in the wedding ceremony, however, is the one at Cana of Galilee, described in the Gospel passage read at every Orthodox wedding (John 2:1–11). In attending this wedding and performing His first miracle there, Jesus Christ, the Son of God, forever sanctifies marriage. As with all the Christian sacraments, marriage is sacramental because it is blessed by God.

Parenthetically, it is at this wedding at Cana that Mary first intercedes with Christ on behalf of others: "They have no wine" (John 2:3). Then she calls all humanity to obey Him: "Whatever He says to you, do it" (John 2:5).

In modern society, as well as in Christendom, a recurring debate is going on. It deals with the tension between equality of the partners in marriage and office or order in marriage. Often, this tension has turned into a polarity between men and women, and sometimes even breeds hostility. There are two elements in the Orthodox service of marriage which serve to heal such tension, while making clear the teaching of the Church on the twin themes of equality and order concerning husband and wife.

As to equality, during the ceremony crowns are placed on the heads of the bride and groom. This act is symbolic of their citizenship in the Kingdom of God, where "there is neither male nor female" (Gal. 3:28) and of their dying to each other (the crown is often a symbol of martyrdom; see Rev. 2:10). The words of St. Paul are clear on marital equality: "The wife does not have authority over her own body, but the husband does. And likewise also the husband does not have authority over his own body, but the wife does" (1 Cor. 7:4). Husband and wife belong to each other as martyrs, they belong to God as royalty, and they are called to treat each other accordingly.

But within marital equality there is also order. The epistle passage read at the Sacrament of Marriage is Ephesians 5:20–33, the exhortation to husbands and wives which begins with a call to submit to each other (Eph. 5:21). The husband is to serve God as head of his wife, as Christ is head of the Church (Eph. 5:23). The wife is to be subject to her husband as the Church is subject to Christ (Eph. 5:24). There is nothing here to suggest that the wife is oppressed in marriage, anymore than one would call the Church oppressed in relationship to Christ. He who calls us "brethren" (Heb. 2:11) and "friends" (John. 15:15) exhorts the husband to love his wife, to nourish and cherish her as He Himself does the Church (Eph. 5:28, 29).

Thus, marriage is a sacrament—holy, blessed, and everlasting in the sight of God and His Church. Within the bonds of marriage, husband and wife experience a union with one another in love, and hopefully the fruit of children and one day the joy of grandchildren. And within the bonds of marriage there is both a fullness of equality between husband and wife, and a clarity of order with the husband as the icon of Christ, the wife as the icon of the Church.

[a]"Awake, you who sleep,
Arise from the dead,
And Christ will give you light."

Walk in God's Will

15 [a]See then that you walk [1]cir-
cumspectly, not as fools but as wise,†
16 [a]redeeming the time, [b]because
the days are evil.
17 [a]Therefore do not be unwise,
but [b]understand [c]what the will of
the Lord *is*.

Be Filled with the Spirit

18 And [a]do not be drunk with
wine, in which is dissipation; but be
filled with the Spirit,†
19 speaking to one another [a]in
psalms and hymns and spiritual
songs, singing and making [b]melody
in your heart to the Lord,†
20 [a]giving thanks always for all
things to God the Father [b]in the
name of our Lord Jesus Christ,
21 [a]submitting to one another in
the fear of [1]God.†

The Mystery of Marriage

22 Wives, [a]submit to your own
husbands, as to the Lord.†
23 For [a]the husband is head of the
wife, as also [b]Christ is head of the
church; and He is the Savior of
the body.
24 Therefore, just as the church is
subject to Christ, so *let* the wives *be*
to their own husbands [a]in everything.
25 [a]Husbands, love your wives,
just as Christ also loved the church
and [b]gave Himself for her,
26 that He might [1]sanctify and
cleanse her [a]with the washing of water [b]by the word,

14 [a][Is. 26:19; 60:1]
15 [a]Col. 4:5 [1]*carefully*
16 [a]Col. 4:5 [b]Eccl. 11:2
17 [a]Col. 4:5 [b][Rom. 12:2] [c]1 Thess. 4:3
18 [a]Prov. 20:1; 23:31
19 [a]Acts 16:25 [b]James 5:13
20 [a]Ps. 34:1 [b][1 Pet. 2:5]
21 [a][Phil. 2:3] [1]NU *Christ*
22 [a]Col. 3:18—4:1
23 [a][1 Cor. 11:3] [b]Col. 1:18
24 [a]Titus 2:4, 5
25 [a]Col. 3:19 [b]Acts 20:28
26 [a]John 3:5 [b][John 15:3; 17:17] [1]*set it apart*

(continued from page 448)
must first come out of hiding in order to be exposed ourselves. That is, we must confess our sins and repent of them (see John 3:19–21). Orthodox Christians do this before baptism, before the Eucharist, and also in a separate sacrament of repentance. The hymn in v. 14 is an early baptismal hymn: baptism is illumination (see Acts 26:18; 2 Cor. 4:6; Heb. 6:4; 10:32). To walk in the light is to walk in one's baptism.

5:15–17 The goal is not to abandon the world, but to keep oneself in Christ and salvage as much as possible from the evil world. Christians renounce the fallenness of the world, not creation itself.

5:18–20 Following repentance, a surge of life and joy wells forth. A distinctive spirit, a kind of elation, energizes both darkness and light. For darkness this spirit is like drunkenness, artificial and temporary. For Christians, it is the Holy **Spirit** (v. 18), and the joy is New Covenant worship of the Holy Trinity, the Eucharist (**giving thanks,** v. 20): to the Father, through the Son incarnate (**Lord** in v. 19; **Lord Jesus Christ** in v. 20), in the Spirit (v. 18). He who is made drunk with wine totters and sways, but he who is inebriated with the Holy Spirit is rooted in Christ, and gloriously sober.

5:19–21 Quoting Scripture and singing hymns are not spiritual if there is not also true humility, submission and the **fear of God** (v. 21).

5:21—6:9 Verse 21 is a transition to the theme of the next section, where Paul applies the idea of mutual submission to the most basic human relationships—those in the household.

5:22–33 The model is **Christ and the church** (v. 32), which is then applied to marriage. Yet Christian marriage helps us to understand the mystery of the Church.

(1) For wives, concerning headship (vv. 22–24): In both the Church and marriage, there is one who acts as head, who leads. As Man, Christ is first among equals, not superior to us in nature; yet He alone is the **head of the church** (v. 23). Likewise, wives are called to submit to their husbands as equals.

(2) For husbands, concerning sacrificial love (vv. 25–31): Paul writes three sentences to wives, but writes at greater length to impress on husbands that they should love their wives. Just as the wife's submission is to accept the headship of the husband, the husband's submission to his wife is to sacrifice himself for her. In ancient Israel, the bride would bathe and dress and be escorted to the bridegroom by his friends. In the Church, baptism is that bathing and dressing in which we put on Christ (v. 26), and the groom Himself, Christ, escorts us (v. 27). In the Church, the baptized are one humanity, one flesh with Christ; in marriage, husband and wife are one flesh with each other.

27 [a]that He might present her to
Himself a glorious church, [b]not having spot or wrinkle or any such
thing, but that she should be holy
and without blemish.
28 So husbands ought to love their
own wives as their own bodies; he
who loves his wife loves himself.
29 For no one ever hated his own
flesh, but nourishes and cherishes it,
just as the Lord *does* the church.
30 For [a]we are members of His
body, [1]of His flesh and of His bones.
31 [a]*"For this reason a man shall*
leave his father and mother and be
joined to his wife, and the [b]*two shall*
become one flesh."
32 This is a great mystery, but I
speak concerning Christ and the
church.
33 Nevertheless [a]let each one of
you in particular so love his own wife
as himself, and let the wife *see* that
she [b]respects *her* husband.

Children and Parents

6 Children, [a]obey your parents in
the Lord, for this is right.†
2 [a]*"Honor your father and*
mother," which is the first commandment with promise:
3 *"that it may be well with you*
and you may live long on the earth."
4 And [a]you, fathers, do not provoke your children to wrath, but
[b]bring them up in the training and
admonition of the Lord.

27 [a]Col. 1:22
[b]Song 4:7
30 [a]Gen. 2:23
[1]NU omits the rest of v. 30.
31 [a]Gen. 2:24
[b][1 Cor. 6:16]
33 [a]Col. 3:19
[b]1 Pet. 3:1, 6

CHAPTER 6
1 [a]Col. 3:20
2 [a]Deut. 5:16
4 [a]Col. 3:21
[b]Gen. 18:19

5 [a][1 Tim. 6:1]
[b]2 Cor. 7:15
[c]1 Chr. 29:17
6 [a]Col. 3:22
8 [a]Rom. 2:6
9 [a]Col. 4:1
[b]Rom. 2:11
[1]NU *He who is both their Master and yours is*
11 [a][2 Cor. 6:7]
[1]*schemings*
12 [a]Rom. 8:38
[b]Luke 22:53
[1]NU *this darkness,*

Slaves and Masters

5 [a]Bondservants, be obedient to
those who are your masters according to the flesh, [b]with fear and trembling, [c]in sincerity of heart, as to
Christ;†
6 [a]not with eyeservice, as men-
pleasers, but as bondservants of
Christ, doing the will of God from
the heart,
7 with goodwill doing service, as
to the Lord, and not to men,
8 [a]knowing that whatever good
anyone does, he will receive the
same from the Lord, whether *he is* a
slave or free.
9 And you, masters, do the same
things to them, giving up threatening, knowing that [1]your own [a]Mas-
ter also is in heaven, and [b]there is
no partiality with Him.†

Spiritual Warfare

10 Finally, my brethren, be strong
in the Lord and in the power of His
might.†
11 [a]Put on the whole armor of
God, that you may be able to stand
against the [1]wiles of the devil.
12 For we do not wrestle against
flesh and blood, but against [a]princi-
palities, against powers, against
[b]the rulers of [1]the darkness of this
age, against spiritual *hosts* of wickedness in the heavenly *places.*

6:1–4 Children are expected to **obey** and respect their parents. The meaning of the Greek word for *obey (hupakouo)* begins with the idea of listening attentively. The caution regarding the fathers puts a restraint and a requirement of godly instruction on the parent.

6:5–8 As with marriage, Paul does not seek to alter the existing social structure. But he does insist that both marriage and the master-slave relationship (nowadays, employer-employee) are different when Christians are involved. The expectations for the slave are similar to those for a wife and for children: sincere obedience. Paul, however, unlike the culture around him, insists that, in God's eyes, the good done by a slave is the same as that done by a free man. Before Christ they are equal.

6:9 Masters are curtly warned against intimidation. They must remember their own **Master,** who is not biased in their favor just because they are earthly masters.

6:10–17 All who stand for good must wage a constant battle with the forces of evil. For the demons still have power in the world (v. 12) until Christ comes again in glory. This is clearly acknowledged in the prayers at the conclusion of Orthodox baptism. Christians fight back with God's arms, that is, His uncreated divine energy, given to us (1:19–23; 3:16–21) and actively used by us. The Christian has "put on" (4:24) at baptism all of the qualities listed as armor in vv. 14–17. These qualities must be exercised in the conflict of growth: no struggle, no deification.

Commemoration of Holy Confessors

6:10–17: The Holy Confessors withstood evil by putting on the armor of God.

Spiritual Weaponry

13 aTherefore take up the whole armor of God, that you may be able to withstand bin the evil day, and having done all, to stand.
14 Stand therefore, ahaving girded your waist with truth, bhaving put on the breastplate of righteousness,
15 aand having shod your feet with the preparation of the gospel of peace;
16 above all, taking athe shield of faith with which you will be able to quench all the fiery darts of the wicked one.
17 And atake the helmet of salvation, and bthe sword of the Spirit, which is the word of God;

Spiritual Readiness

18 apraying always with all prayer and supplication in the Spirit, bbeing watchful to this end with all perseverance and csupplication for all the saints—†
19 and for me, that utterance may be given to me, athat I may open my mouth boldly to make known the mystery of the gospel,
20 for which aI am an ambassador in chains; that in it I may speak boldly, as I ought to speak.

Commendation and Benediction

21 But that you also may know my affairs *and* how I am doing, aTychicus, a beloved brother and bfaithful minister in the Lord, will make all things known to you;†
22 awhom I have sent to you for this very purpose, that you may know our affairs, and *that* he may bcomfort your hearts.
23 Peace to the brethren, and love with faith, from God the Father and the Lord Jesus Christ.†
24 Grace *be* with all those who love our Lord Jesus Christ in sincerity. Amen.

13 a[2 Cor. 10:4] bEph. 5:16
14 aIs. 11:5; Luke 12:35; 1 Pet. 1:13 bIs. 59:17; Rom. 13:12; Eph. 6:13; 1 Thess. 5:8
15 aIs. 52:7; Rom. 10:15
16 a1 John 5:4
17 a1 Thess. 5:8 bIs. 49:2; Hos. 6:5; [Heb. 4:12]
18 aLuke 18:1; Col. 1:3; 4:2; 1 Thess. 5:17 b[Matt. 26:41] cPhil. 1:4
19 aActs 4:29; Col. 4:3
20 a2 Cor. 5:20; Philem. 9
21 aActs 20:4; 2 Tim. 4:12; Titus 3:12 b1 Cor. 4:1, 2
22 aCol. 4:8 b2 Cor. 1:6

6:18–20 Just as important as spiritual armor is a Christian's readiness and alertness: diligent prayer and watchfulness in submission to the Holy Spirit (see 1:16; 3:14–21; 5:20). Those on the "front lines," apostles and evangelists in this case, require the back up power of a praying Church.

6:21, 22 Tychicus presumably was the bearer of the letter (see the Introduction).

6:23, 24 This final benediction parallels the greeting (1:3–14).

The Epistle of Paul the Apostle to the

PHILIPPIANS

Author: *St. Paul the Apostle*

Date: A.D. *61–63*

Theme: *The Dynamic of Our Life in Christ*

AUTHOR: The early Church unanimously agreed that Paul wrote Philippians. Paul founded the church in Philippi, which was the first church in Europe, on his second missionary journey, A.D. 50–51 (Acts 16:11–40). On his third misionary journey he made two brief visits to Philippi, about A.D. 57–58 (Acts 20:1, 6).

DATE: Paul probably wrote Philippians while he was under house arrest in Rome in about A.D. 61–63 (Acts 28:16–31). At that time he was free to receive visitors and to correspond by letter.

MAJOR THEME: *The dynamic of our life in Christ*. Salvation is a dynamic, ongoing experience which is not merely personal, but shared among believers. St. Paul urges the believers in Philippi toward continued unity, humility, selfless generosity and joy in Christ. Subthemes include the alerting of the Philippian church to (1) interference from self-serving evangelists (1:12–18), (2) persecution from the world (1:27–30; 2:14–18), and (3) antagonism from heretics, particularly the legalistic Judaizers (3:1–11).

BACKGROUND INFORMATION: (1) *The church*. The church in Philippi was noted for its generosity in support of the apostolic ministry (1:5, 4:15, 16; Acts 16:15, 40). Recently, it had sent Epaphroditus to visit Paul in prison with a financial gift for the Apostle and with instructions that Epaphroditus remain there with Paul. But Epaphroditus apparently was so devoted to his work that he forgot his own physical health (2:30). The Philippian church heard this, and was concerned for him.

(2) *The ministry*. In the meantime, Paul's trial had started (1:7) and he hoped for an early release (1:25; 2:24). Thus, the Apostle wrote this letter of thanks to Philippi, with the comforting word that he would send Epaphroditus home (2:25–30), and that he would shortly dispatch Timothy to Philippi (2:19).

OUTLINE

Greeting	1:1, 2
I. Life in Christ amidst persecution	1:3—2:30
A. Exemplary lives of the Philippians and Paul	1:3–30
1. The Philippians	1:3–11
2. Paul	1:12–26
3. Encouragement to the Philippians	1:27–30
B. Exhortation to persevere amidst persecution	2:1–30
1. The Church is one	2:1, 2
2. The Church is catholic (universal)	2:3–5
3. A hymn of Christ's humility	2:6–11
4. The Church is apostolic in her obedience	2:12, 13
5. The Church is holy	2:14–16
6. The Church is apostolic in her ambassadors	2:17–30
II. Life in Christ in the face of heresy	3:1—4:9
A. Exhortation to righteousness; warning against legalism	3:1–21
1. What is true circumcision?	3:1–3
2. How is true righteousness attained?	3:4–21
B. Exhortation to unity; warning against schism	4:1–9
1. Live in harmony	4:1–3
2. Live in patience and prayer	4:4–7
3. Live in accordance with apostolic teaching	4:8, 9
Conclusion	4:10–23
A. Gratitude for financial help	4:10–20
B. Greeting and benediction	4:21–23

Greeting

1 Paul and Timothy, bondservants
of Jesus Christ,

To all the saints in Christ Jesus
who are in Philippi, with the
[1]bishops and [a]deacons:†

2 Grace to you and peace from
God our Father and the Lord Jesus
Christ.

CHAPTER 1
1 [a][1 Tim. 3:8–13]
[1]Lit. *overseers*
3 [a]1 Cor. 1:4
4 [a]Eph. 1:16; 1 Thess. 1:2
5 [a][Rom. 12:13]

Thanksgiving

3 [a]I thank my God upon every remembrance of you,
4 always in [a]every prayer of mine
making request for you all with
joy,
5 [a]for your fellowship in the
gospel from the first day until
now,†
6 being confident of this very

1:1 This is the only epistle in which St. Paul includes the clergy, the **bishops and deacons,** in his address. St. John Chrysostom says it is because it was the clergy in Philippi who collected the funds Paul so badly needed, and sent them to him by Epaphroditus. *Bishops* are the leading presbyters. By the time this letter was written, around A.D. 63, not only were bishops present in Philippi, but James was presiding over the church in Jerusalem (Acts 15:13) and tradition reveals that Peter was bishop in Antioch—and later in Rome. (Tradition sometimes refers to the men Peter designated his successors in those places as the "first" bishops, affirming the difference between the apostles and the overseers they appointed.) Paul's Pastoral Epistles outline the qualifications for the office of bishop (1 Tim. 3:1–7; Titus 1:7–9).

1:5 **Fellowship,** the Greek word *koinonia,* is central to this epistle and to Orthodox Chris-

(continued on next page)

thing, that He who has begun [a]a good work in you will complete *it* until the day of Jesus Christ;

7 just as it is right for me to think this of you all, because I have you in my heart, inasmuch as both in my chains and in the defense and confirmation of the gospel, you all are partakers with me of grace.

8 For God is my witness, how greatly I long for you all with the affection of Jesus Christ.

9 And this I pray, that your love may abound still more and more in knowledge and all discernment,†

10 that you may approve the things that are excellent, that you may be sincere and without offense till the day of Christ,

11 being filled with the fruits of righteousness [a]which *are* by Jesus Christ, [b]to the glory and praise of God.

Paul's Suffering in Prison

12 But I want you to know, brethren, that the things *which happened* to me have actually turned out for the furtherance of the gospel,

13 so that it has become evident [a]to the whole [1]palace guard, and to all the rest, that my chains are in Christ;

14 and most of the brethren in the Lord, having become confident by my chains, are much more bold to speak the word without fear.

15 Some indeed preach Christ even from envy and strife, and some also from goodwill:

16 [1]The former preach Christ from selfish ambition, not sincerely, supposing to add affliction to my chains;

6 [a][John 6:29]
11 [a][Eph. 2:10]; Col. 1:6 [b]John 15:8
13 [a]Phil. 4:22 [1]Or *Praetorium*
16 [1]NU reverses vv. 16 and 17.

17 but the latter out of love, knowing that I am appointed for the defense of the gospel.

18 What then? Only *that* in every way, whether in pretense or in truth, Christ is preached; and in this I rejoice, yes, and will rejoice.

19 For I know that [a]this will turn out for my deliverance through your prayer and the supply of the Spirit of Jesus Christ,†

20 according to my earnest expectation and hope that in nothing I shall be ashamed, but [a]with all boldness, as always, so now also Christ will be magnified in my body, whether by life [b]or by death.

21 For to me, to live *is* Christ, and to die *is* gain.

22 But if *I* live on in the flesh, this *will mean* fruit from *my* labor; yet what I shall choose I [1]cannot tell.

23 [1]For I am hard-pressed between the two, having a [a]desire to depart and be with Christ, *which is* [b]far better.

24 Nevertheless to remain in the flesh *is* more needful for you.

25 And being confident of this, I know that I shall remain and continue with you all for your progress and joy of faith,

26 that [a]your rejoicing for me may be more abundant in Jesus Christ by my coming to you again.

Be Steadfast in Suffering

27 Only [a]let your conduct be worthy of the gospel of Christ, so that whether I come and see you or am absent, I may hear of your affairs, that you stand fast in one spirit,

19 [a]Job 13:16, LXX
20 [a]Eph. 6:19, 20 [b][Rom. 14:8]
22 [1]*do not know*
23 [a][2 Cor. 5:2, 8]; 2 Tim. 4:6 [b][Ps. 16:11] [1]NU, M *But*
26 [a]2 Cor. 1:14
27 [a]Eph. 4:1

(continued from previous page)
tianity in general. It implies true communion, a more fundamental community of life and worship than is usually conveyed by the word "fellowship."

1:9–11 And this I pray: This prayer of Paul shows his love and pastoral care for the Philippians. Their behavior makes him confident that God will continue to perfect them—and those who follow in their footsteps.

1:19–21 Our witness for Christ goes beyond the words of our mouths, to the way we live and the way we die: the totality of what we are and do. St. Paul expects **deliverance** (v. 19), though not necessarily for his **body** (v. 20). His **expectation and hope** (v. 20) is of eternal life.

[b]with one mind [c]striving together for
the faith of the gospel,
28 and not in any way terrified by
your adversaries, which is to them
a proof of perdition, but [1]to you of
salvation, and that from God.
29 For to you [a]it has been granted
on behalf of Christ, [b]not only to believe in Him, but also to [c]suffer for
His sake,†
30 [a]having the same conflict
[b]which you saw in me and now hear
is in me.

Preserve Unity in Humility

2 Therefore if *there is* any [1]con-
solation in Christ, if any comfort of love, if any fellowship of
the Spirit, if any [a]affection and
mercy,
2 [a]fulfill my joy [b]by being like-
minded, having the same love, *being*
of [c]one accord, of one mind.
3 [a]*Let* nothing *be done* through
selfish ambition or conceit, but
[b]in lowliness of mind let each esteem
others better than himself.†
4 [a]Let each of you look out not
only for his own interests, but also
for the interests of [b]others.
5 [a]Let this mind be in you which
was also in Christ Jesus,†
6 who, [a]being in the form of God,
did not consider it [1]robbery to be
equal with God,†
7 [a]but [1]made Himself of no reputation, taking the form [b]of a bondservant, *and* [c]coming in the likeness
of men.†
8 And being found in appearance
as a man, He humbled Himself
and [a]became [b]obedient to *the point
of* death, even the death of the
cross.
9 [a]Therefore God also [b]has highly
exalted Him and [c]given Him the
name which is above every name,

27 [b]Eph. 4:3 [c]Jude 3
28 [1]NU *of your salvation*
29 [a][Matt. 5:11, 12] [b]Eph. 2:8 [c][2 Tim. 3:12]
30 [a]Col. 1:29; 2:1 [b]Acts 16:19–40

CHAPTER 2
1 [a]Col. 3:12 [1]Or *encouragement*
2 [a]John 3:29 [b]Rom. 12:16 [c]Phil. 4:2
3 [a]Gal. 5:26 [b]Rom. 12:10
4 [a]1 Cor. 13:5 [b]Rom. 15:1, 2
5 [a][Matt. 11:29]
6 [a]2 Cor. 4:4 [1]Or *something to be held onto to be equal*
7 [a]Ps. 22:6 [b]Is. 42:1 [c][John 1:14] [1]*emptied Himself* of His privileges
8 [a]Matt. 26:39 [b]Heb. 5:8
9 [a]Heb. 2:9 [b]Acts 2:33 [c]Eph. 1:21

1:29 To suffer for His sake is a repeated theme in this epistle. Suffering not only bears witness to others, as Paul's chains have done (see vv. 7, 13), but also can serve to increase our faith. Suffering is a gift from Christ, as is faith: it is a participation in His grace.

2:3 Conceit, or vainglory, is a common and fatal vice. It hinders spiritual growth, for *conceit* causes us to despise those who have a different way of life, thinking we are better than they. St. John Climacus says, "The spirit of despair exults at the sight of mounting vice, the spirit of vainglory at the sight of the growing treasures of virtue." To be conceited is a form of idolatry, and it captures those who say they want to please God, but secretly wish to please other people more.

2:5–11 This passage is a hymn already in use in the Church, quoted here by St. Paul because it calls us to ponder the humility of Christ, a truth necessary for suffering Christians to understand and live out. The passage has been incorporated into many hymns of the Orthodox Church. Christ is He who, being in **the form of God,** is also in the **form of a bondservant** (v. 7), in our likeness (see Gen. 1:26), and is voluntarily subject to death. He who has died, God has exalted and given the name **Lord** (v. 11), a name which God the Son shares with God the Father from all eternity.

2:6 The form (Gr. *morphe*) **of God,** a concept parallel with "the image (Gr. *eikon*) of God" (Col. 1:15), refers to the Son's sharing in full the divine nature. **Robbery** (Gr. *harpagmon,* a prize or booty) refers to an object stolen and tightly clutched. Christ has equality with God not by seizure but by nature, and with absolute security. There is, therefore, no threat, loss, or any change in the divine nature of the Son of God when He takes our humanity to Himself and offers us salvation.

2:7, 8 Made Himself of no reputation (v. 7; lit. "emptied Himself") deals with the Son's will, not His nature. He emptied Himself not by laying down His divine nature or setting it aside, but by voluntarily taking on our human nature. To human beings He looks just like another human being, for being truly incarnate, He is fully man by nature. He took **the form of a bondservant,** voluntarily sharing our human condition except for one thing: sin. In His humanity, He showed the fullness of humility by His obedience to the death which has enslaved humanity. To die on a **cross,** the death of a criminal, was repulsive to the Romans and considered a curse by the Jews. But His death brings life to all who are joined to Him.

The Feasts of the Virgin Mary: Her Birth *September 8*
Protection *October 1*
Entry into the Temple *November 21*
Lifegiving Spring *Friday after Easter*
Falling Asleep *August 15*

2:5–11: Through the humble obedience of His mother, Mary, Christ came in the likeness of men.

10 [a]that at the name of Jesus every
knee should bow, of those in
heaven, and of those on earth, and
of those under the earth,
11 and [a]*that* every tongue should
confess that Jesus Christ *is* Lord, to
the glory of God the Father.

Strive for Obedience

12 Therefore, my beloved, [a]as you
have always obeyed, not as in my
presence only, but now much more
in my absence, [b]work out your own
salvation with [c]fear and trembling;†
13 for [a]it is God who works in you
both to will and to do [b]for *His* good
pleasure.
14 Do all things [a]without [1]com-
plaining and [b]disputing,[2]
15 that you may become blameless
and [1]harmless, children of God without fault in the midst of a crooked
and perverse generation, among
whom you shine as [a]lights in the
world,
16 holding fast the word of life, so
that [a]I may rejoice in the day of
Christ that [b]I have not run in vain
or labored in [c]vain.

Apostolic Support for Philippi

17 Yes, and if [a]I am being poured
out *as a drink offering* on the sacrifice
[b]and service of your faith, [c]I am glad
and rejoice with you all.†
18 For the same reason you also be
glad and rejoice with me.
19 But I trust in the Lord Jesus to
send [a]Timothy to you shortly, that
I also may be encouraged when I
know your [1]state.†
20 For I have no one [a]like-minded,
who will sincerely care for your state.
21 For all seek their own, not the
things which are of Christ Jesus.
22 But you know his proven character, [a]that as a son with *his* father
he served with me in the gospel.
23 Therefore I hope to send him at
once, as soon as I see how it goes
with me.
24 But I trust in the Lord that I myself shall also come shortly.
25 Yet I considered it necessary to
send to you [a]Epaphroditus, my
brother, fellow worker, and [b]fellow
soldier, [c]but your messenger and
[d]the one who ministered to my need;
26 [a]since he was longing for you
all, and was distressed because you
had heard that he was sick.

10 [a]Is. 45:23 **11** [a]John 13:13 **12** [a]Phil. 1:5, 6; 4:15 [b]John 6:27, 29 [c]Eph. 6:5 **13** [a]Heb. 13:20, 21 [b]Eph. 1:5 **14** [a]1 Pet. 4:9 [b]Rom. 14:1 [1]*grumbling* [2]*arguing* **15** [a]Matt. 5:15, 16 [1]*innocent* **16** [a]2 Cor. 1:14 [b]Gal. 2:2 [c]1 Thess. 3:5 **17** [a]2 Tim. 4:6 [b]Rom. 15:16 [c]2 Cor. 7:4 **19** [a]Rom. 16:21 [1]*condition* **20** [a]2 Tim. 3:10 **22** [a]1 Cor. 4:17 **25** [a]Phil. 4:18 [b]Philem. 2 [c]2 Cor. 8:23 [d]2 Cor. 11:9 **26** [a]Phil. 1:8

2:12, 13 Therefore, because of Christ's sacrifice, we are to take hold of what God offers, accepting His grace, and working toward becoming mature in Christ. Note the cooperation: we **work out** our **own salvation** (v. 12) while **it is God who works in** us to do His **will** (v. 13).

2:17 Service is literally "liturgy." St. Paul sees himself being **poured out** as an **offering,** a participation in Christ's **sacrifice,** for he also participates in Christ's sufferings. In all this, we see that attitude which prevailed throughout the entire early Church: there is no separation between worship and life. They are one. To worship Christ is to live for Him and in Him.

2:19–30 These verses portray the leadership and the laity in the primitive Church working together. Paul is confident of his authority **to send Timothy** (v. 19) to Philippi, which demonstrates Paul's apostolic or episcopal role. Timothy is an apostle as well, sent to care for this church. **Epaphroditus** is a **fellow worker** and **fellow soldier** (v. 25) who earns high praise. Early tradition tells us Epaphroditus later became bishop of Philippi, and died a martyr.

27 For indeed he was sick almost
unto death; but God had mercy on
him, and not only on him but on me
also, lest I should have sorrow upon
sorrow.
28 Therefore I sent him the more
eagerly, that when you see him again
you may rejoice, and I may be less
sorrowful.
29 Receive him therefore in the
Lord with all gladness, and hold
such men in esteem;
30 because for the work of Christ
he came close to death, [1]not regarding his life, [a]to supply what was
lacking in your service toward me.

Beware of Judaizers

3 Finally, my brethren, [a]rejoice in
the Lord. For me to write the
same things to you *is* not tedious,
but for you *it is* safe.
2 [a]Beware of dogs, beware of
[b]evil workers, [c]beware of the
mutilation!†
3 For we are [a]the circumcision,
[b]who worship [1]God in the Spirit, rejoice in Christ Jesus, and have no
confidence in the flesh,
4 though [a]I also might have confidence in the flesh. If anyone else
thinks he may have confidence in the
flesh, I [b]more so:
5 circumcised the eighth day, of
the stock of Israel, [a]*of* the tribe of
Benjamin, [b]a Hebrew of the Hebrews; concerning the law, [c]a
Pharisee;
6 concerning zeal, [a]persecuting
the church; concerning the righteousness which is in the law,
blameless.
7 But [a]what things were gain to
me, these I have counted loss for
Christ.†
8 Yet indeed I also count all things
loss [a]for the excellence of the knowledge of Christ Jesus my Lord, for
whom I have suffered the loss of all
things, and count them as rubbish,
that I may gain Christ
9 and be found in Him, not having [a]my own righteousness, which
is from the law, but [b]that which *is*
through faith in Christ, the righteousness which is from God by
faith;†
10 that I may know Him and the
[a]power of His resurrection, and
[b]the fellowship of His sufferings, being conformed to His death,
11 if, by any means, I may [a]at-
tain[1] to the resurrection from the
dead.

Press Toward True Righteousness

12 Not that I have already [a]at-
tained,[1] or am already [b]perfected;
but I press on, that I may lay hold
of that for which Christ Jesus has
also laid hold of me.†

30 [a]1 Cor. 16:17 [1]*risking*

CHAPTER 3

1 [a]1 Thess. 5:16
2 [a]Gal. 5:15 [b]Ps. 119:115 [c]Rom. 2:28
3 [a]Deut. 30:6 [b]Rom. 7:6 [1]NU, M *in the Spirit of God*
4 [a]2 Cor. 5:16; 11:18 [b]2 Cor. 11:22, 23
5 [a]Rom. 11:1 [b]2 Cor. 11:22 [c]Acts 23:6
6 [a]Acts 8:3; 22:4, 5; 26:9–11
7 [a]Matt. 13:44
8 [a]Jer. 9:23
9 [a]Rom. 10:3 [b]Rom. 1:17
10 [a]Eph. 1:19, 20 [b][Rom. 6:3–5]
11 [a]Acts 26:6–8 [1]Lit. *arrive at*
12 [a][1 Tim. 6:12, 19] [b]Heb. 12:23 [1]*obtained it*

3:2, 3 The Judaizers were teaching that Christians needed to submit themselves to the Law of Moses, especially emphasizing the rite of **circumcision** (v. 3). Paul boldly tags them with the name they gave to Gentiles—**dogs** (v. 2)—and compares their circumcision to the self-inflicted **mutilation** (v. 2) of some pagan cults. True Israel, the Church, does not rely on outward observance of the law. She is the mystical body of **Christ Jesus,** composed of those **who worship God in the Spirit** (v. 3).

3:4–6 Though Paul could boast concerning his ancestry, his circumcision, his keeping of the **law** (v. 5)—he is a more zealous Jew than they are—he knows this is not true righteousness.

3:7–9 True righteousness is **the knowledge of Christ Jesus** (v. 8). He is the "pearl of great price," and eternal life (John 17:3). A faith which obeys Christ is the very content and meaning of life, and it is for this that we suffer **the loss of all things** (v. 8) and deny ourselves. Everything about us must be subordinated to Christ and His Kingdom (see Matt. 6:19–34; 24:36—25:46).

3:9–11 Faith is the name of the relationship which gives us full participation in the life of Christ, and in **His resurrection** (v. 10). Faith includes our assent to articles of belief, but it is also our openness to God's action in our lives. The meaning of our suffering comes in sharing in Christ's suffering and death, becoming like Him. Why? So that we may be with Him in glory.

Commemoration of Holy Hieromartyrs

3:20—4:3: These holy men stood fast in the Lord and attained to heavenly citizenship.

13 Brethren, I do not count myself
to have [1]apprehended; but one thing
I do, [a]forgetting those things which
are behind and [b]reaching forward to
those things which are ahead,
14 [a]I press toward the goal for the
prize of [b]the upward call of God in
Christ Jesus.
15 Therefore let us, as many as are
[a]mature, [b]have this mind; and if in
anything you think otherwise,
[c]God will reveal even this to you.
16 Nevertheless, to *the degree* that
we have already [1]attained, [a]let us
walk [b]by the same [2]rule, let us be
of the same mind.
17 Brethren, [a]join in following my
example, and note those who so
walk, as [b]you have us for a pattern.†
18 For many walk, of whom I
have told you often, and now
tell you even weeping, *that they
are* [a]the enemies of the cross of
Christ:†
19 [a]whose end *is* destruction,
[b]whose god *is their* belly, and [c]*whose*
glory *is* in their shame—[d]who set
their mind on earthly things.
20 For [a]our citizenship is in
heaven, [b]from which we also [c]ea-
gerly wait for the Savior, the Lord
Jesus Christ,
21 [a]who will transform our lowly
body that it may be [b]conformed to
His glorious body, [c]according to the
working by which He is able even
to [d]subdue all things to Himself.

4 Therefore, my beloved and
[a]longed-for brethren, [b]my joy
and crown, so [c]stand fast in the
Lord, beloved.

Exhortation for Daily Living

2 I implore Euodia and I implore
Syntyche [a]to be of the same mind
in the Lord.†
3 [1]And I urge you also, true companion, help these women who
[a]labored with me in the gospel, with
Clement also, and the rest of my fellow workers, whose names *are* in
[b]the Book of Life.†
4 [a]Rejoice in the Lord always.
Again I will say, rejoice!†

13 [a]Luke 9:62 [b]Heb. 6:1 [1]*laid hold of it* **14** [a]2 Tim. 4:7 [b]Heb. 3:1 **15** [a]1 Cor. 2:6 [b]Gal. 5:10 [c]Hos. 6:3 **16** [a]Gal. 6:16 [b]Rom. 12:16; 15:5 [1]*arrived* [2]NU omits *rule* and the rest of v. 16. **17** [a][1 Cor. 4:16; 11:1] [b]Titus 2:7, 8 **18** [a]Gal. 1:7 **19** [a]2 Cor. 11:15 [b]1 Tim. 6:5 [c]Hos. 4:7 [d]Rom. 8:5 **20** [a]Eph. 2:6, 19 [b]Acts 1:11 [c]1 Cor. 1:7 **21** [a][1 Cor. 15:43–53] [b]1 John 3:2 [c]Eph. 1:19 [d][1 Cor. 15:28]

CHAPTER 4

1 [a]Phil. 1:8 [b]2 Cor. 1:14 [c]Phil. 1:27 **2** [a]Phil. 2:2; 3:16 **3** [a]Rom. 16:3 [b]Luke 10:20 [1]NU, M *Yes* **4** [a]Rom. 12:12

3:12–16 What is the goal (v. 14) of the maturing Christian? For Paul it is that we be engaged in the struggle of faith, confident that Christ has made us His own, but knowing we are not yet **perfected.** Thus we are zealous to **press on** (v. 12) toward the completion of our salvation, **the prize of the upward call of God** (v. 14)—the resurrection to eternal life.

3:17 Because St. Paul and other saints set an **example** for us, **a pattern** for us to follow, we do follow in their steps (tradition) and honor them in the process (veneration).

3:18–21 The enemies of the cross of Christ (v. 18) is a reference to those made captive to dietary laws, circumcision, and discipline. Christian spirituality, by contrast, is based in the age to come, knowing we have no glory in this age. The passage from humiliation to exaltation which Christ experienced (2:5–11) is promised to those Christians who in perseverance follow Him. **Transform our lowly body** (v. 21) implies a change not in substance but to **His glorious body,** a change from corruption to incorruption.

4:2 Euodia and **Syntyche** are two women who assisted Paul in his ministry in Philippi.

4:3 It is most likely this **Clement,** a disciple of Paul, who later became the bishop of Rome. A long letter, still in existence, to the Corinthian church is attributed to him.

4:4, 6 Paul often uses the word **always** in relation to prayer. Rejoicing *always* is a fruit of perseverance in daily prayers (see 1 Thess. 5:16–18).

Palm Sunday—The Entrance of the Lord into Jerusalem *Sunday before Easter*

4:4–9: Let us rejoice, for the Lord is at hand!

5 Let your [1]gentleness be known
to all men. [a]The Lord *is* at hand.†
6 [a]Be anxious for nothing, but in
everything by prayer and supplication, with [b]thanksgiving, let your requests be made known to God;
7 and [a]the peace of God, which
surpasses all understanding, will
guard your hearts and minds
through Christ Jesus.
8 Finally, brethren, whatever
things are [a]true, whatever things *are*
[b]noble, whatever things *are* [c]just,
[d]whatever things *are* pure, whatever
things *are* [e]lovely, whatever things
are of good report, if *there is* any virtue and if *there is* anything praise-
worthy—meditate on these things.
9 The things which you learned
and received and heard and saw in
me, these do, and [a]the God of peace
will be with you.

Gratitude for Assistance

10 But I rejoiced in the Lord greatly
that now at last [a]your[1] care for me
has flourished again; though you
surely did care, but you lacked
opportunity.
11 Not that I speak in regard to
need, for I have learned in whatever
state I am, [a]to be content:†
12 [a]I know how to [1]be abased, and
I know how to [2]abound. Everywhere
and in all things I have learned both
to be full and to be hungry, both to
abound and to suffer need.
13 I can do all things [a]through
[1]Christ who strengthens me.
14 Nevertheless you have done
well that [a]you shared in my distress.
15 Now you Philippians know also
that in the beginning of the gospel,
when I departed from Macedonia,
[a]no church shared with me concerning giving and receiving but you
only.
16 For even in Thessalonica you
sent *aid* once and again for my
necessities.
17 Not that I seek the gift, but I
seek [a]the fruit that abounds to your
account.
18 Indeed I [1]have all and abound.
I am full, having received from
[a]Epaphroditus the things *sent* from
you, [b]a sweet-smelling aroma,
[c]an acceptable sacrifice, well pleasing to God.
19 And my God [a]shall supply all
your need according to His riches in
glory by Christ Jesus.
20 [a]Now to our God and Father *be*
glory forever and ever. Amen.

Greetings and Benediction

21 Greet every saint in Christ
Jesus. The brethren [a]who are with
me greet you.
22 All the saints greet you, but especially those who are of Caesar's
household.
23 The grace of our Lord Jesus
Christ be with [1]you all. Amen.

5 [a][James 5:7–9] [1]*graciousness or forbearance*
6 [a]Matt. 6:25 [b][1 Thess. 5:17, 18]
7 [a][John 14:27]
8 [a]Eph. 4:25 [b]2 Cor. 8:21 [c]Deut. 16:20 [d]1 Thess. 5:22 [e]1 Cor. 13:4–7
9 [a]Rom. 15:33
10 [a]2 Cor. 11:9 [1]*you have revived your care*
11 [a]1 Tim. 6:6, 8
12 [a]1 Cor. 4:11 [1]*live humbly* [2]*live in prosperity*
13 [a]John 15:5 [1]NU *Him who*
14 [a]Phil. 1:7
15 [a]2 Cor. 11:8, 9
17 [a]Titus 3:14
18 [a]Phil. 2:25 [b]Heb. 13:16 [c]2 Cor. 9:12 [1]Or *have received all*
19 [a]Ps. 23:1
20 [a]Rom. 16:27
21 [a]Gal. 1:2
23 [1]NU *your spirit*

4:5–9 How do we handle the daily pressures of life? By (1) faith that **the Lord is at hand,** present with us (v. 5); (2) refusing to worry, being **anxious for nothing** (v. 6); (3) **prayer** (v. 6); (4) **thanksgiving . . . to God** (v. 6); (5) meditation on that which is virtuous (v. 8); and (6) imitating the godly (v. 9).

4:11–13 Here is the secret of contentment.

The Epistle of Paul the Apostle to the COLOSSIANS

Author: *St. Paul the Apostle*

Date: *A.D. 61–63*

Theme: *Living by the Will of God*

AUTHOR: All early Church testimony credits Paul with the authorship of Colossians. Some of the vocabulary is unusual for Paul because he is combatting first-century Gnosticism using its own terminology—thereby deepening his own understanding of Christ.

DATE: Colossians was written at the same time as Ephesians and Philemon. These epistles, along with Philippians, were most likely composed during Paul's Roman captivity, about A.D. 61–63 (see 4:3, 10, 18; Eph. 3:1; 4:1; 6:20; Philem. 9, 10, 13).

MAJOR THEME: *Living by the will of God vs. dying by false human schemes.* The primary purpose of this epistle was to combat a form of gnosticism which was taking hold in the Colossian church. Paul preaches the true gospel to the Colossians once more, emphasizing those aspects which the prevalent heresy disputed (see below).

BACKGROUND INFORMATION: (1) *The Colossian church.* The city of Colosse was in the region of Ephesus. The church there was probably founded while Paul was in Ephesus for more than two years during his third missionary journey. Perhaps it was Epaphras, a native of Colosse, who started the church (1:7; 4:12), along with Philemon, who was its largest financial supporter and who opened his home for meetings. Epaphras visited Paul, probably in Rome, to seek Paul's apostolic guidance concerning the inroads of speculation into the community.

(2) *The Colossian heresy.* Error in Colosse was a local blend of Jewish (perhaps Essene) and Oriental ideas. The heretics thought they were "supplementing" apostolic Christianity, which they saw as primitive, with greater knowledge and better access to spiritual things. They imagined that (1) the hierarchy of celestial powers (the "angels" in some Jewish thought) was supreme, rather than Christ; (2) Christ was not unique in His divine nature nor in His actions, for He was not God but one of several mediators; (3) sin resulted from a lack of knowledge (Gr. *gnosis*), a particular sort of knowledge in which the heretics were specialists; and (4) salvation consisted in having this *gnosis*

imparted by a series of rituals and ascetic practices (among which Jewish rites were prized, but Christian baptism was considered a mere low-level initiation).

(3) *Apostolic tradition.* Paul's strategy is to contrast the full truth with the partial truth of the heresy. He uses the terminology of the heretics to show how they distort the truth. Apostolic tradition within the Church (2:6, 7) teaches Christ alone is the Lord and He alone is sufficient. Paul confronts false knowledge and worldly, legalistic asceticism with true knowledge and holy, gracious asceticism.

(4) *True spiritual life.* For Paul, true spirituality is life in Christ in the apostolic Church. Through Christ's Incarnation, Passion and Resurrection, which we join in by means of baptism and grow into through transformation of life, we have direct access to God's fullness and are capable of becoming Godlike (2:8–15; 3:1–17). Spiritual discipline centers on Christ Himself, the incarnate God, not on other "realities" (2:16–23). Further, Jesus Christ is known primarily in His body, the Church, a community of redeemed people. The Church is the new creation and through the Church all creation will be renewed (1:18–20).

OUTLINE

Introduction	1:1–14
A. Greeting	1:1, 2
B. Thanksgiving for the Colossians' growth	1:3–8
C. Prayer for continued growth and victory	1:9–14
I. Apostolic Christology: The basis for living in God's will	1:15—2:23
A. Christ is supreme over all	1:15—2:3
B. Christ is sufficient for all	2:4–23
1. Continue in Christ	2:4–8
2. Christ is over angels and creation	2:9–15
3. Christ is reality	2:16–23
II. Apostolic spirituality	3:1—4:6
A. Baptismal spirituality	3:1–17
1. Union with Christ in glory	3:1–4
2. The death of Christ and old sinful passions	3:5–11
3. The resurrection of Christ and new righteous virtues	3:12–14
4. The peace of Christ in one body	3:15–17
B. In relationships between Christians	3:18—4:1
C. For the world	4:2–6
Conclusion	4:7–18
A. Commendations	4:7–9
B. Greetings	4:10–14
C. Instructions	4:15–18

Greeting

1 Paul, [a]an apostle of Jesus Christ
by the will of God, and Timothy
our brother,

2 To the saints [a]and faithful brethren in Christ *who are* in Colosse:

[b]Grace to you and peace from God
our Father [1]and the Lord Jesus
Christ.

Thanksgiving for Abundant Growth

3 [a]We give thanks to the God and
Father of our Lord Jesus Christ,
praying always for you,†
4 [a]since we heard of your faith in
Christ Jesus and of [b]your love for all
the saints;
5 because of the hope [a]which is
laid up for you in heaven, of which
you heard before in the word of the
truth of the gospel,
6 which has come to you, [a]as *it*
has also in all the world, and [b]is
bringing forth [1]fruit, as *it is* also
among you since the day you heard
and knew [c]the grace of God in
truth;
7 as you also learned from [a]Epa-
phras, our dear fellow servant, who
is [b]a faithful minister of Christ on
your behalf,
8 who also declared to us your
[a]love in the Spirit.

CHAPTER 1
1 [a]Eph. 1:1
2 [a]1 Cor. 4:17 [b]Gal. 1:3 [1]NU omits *and the Lord Jesus Christ*
3 [a]Phil. 1:3
4 [a]Eph. 1:15 [b][Heb. 6:10]
5 [a][1 Pet. 1:4]
6 [a]Matt. 24:14 [b]John 15:16 [c]Eph. 3:2 [1]NU, M add *and growing*
7 [a]Philem. 23 [b]2 Cor. 11:23
8 [a]Rom. 15:30
9 [a]Eph. 1:15–17 [b]1 Cor. 1:5 [c][Rom. 12:2] [d]Eph. 1:8
10 [a]Eph. 4:1 [b]1 Thess. 4:1 [c]Heb. 13:21 [d]2 Pet. 3:18
11 [a][Eph. 3:16; 6:10] [b]Eph. 4:2 [c][Acts 5:41]
12 [a][Eph. 5:20] [b]Eph. 1:11
13 [a]Eph. 6:12 [b]2 Pet. 1:11 [1]*transferred*
14 [a]Eph. 1:7 [1]NU, M omit *through His blood*
15 [a]2 Cor. 4:4 [b]Rev. 3:14
16 [a]Heb. 1:2, 3

Petition for Continued Growth

9 [a]For this reason we also, since
the day we heard it, do not cease to
pray for you, and to ask [b]that you
may be filled with [c]the knowledge
of His will [d]in all wisdom and spiritual understanding;†
10 [a]that you may walk worthy of
the Lord, [b]fully pleasing *Him,*
[c]being fruitful in every good work
and increasing in the [d]knowledge of
God;
11 [a]strengthened with all might,
according to His glorious power,
[b]for all patience and longsuffering
[c]with joy;
12 [a]giving thanks to the Father
who has qualified us to be partakers
of [b]the inheritance of the saints in
the light.†
13 He has delivered us from [a]the
power of darkness [b]and [1]conveyed
us into the kingdom of the Son of
His love,
14 [a]in whom we have redemption
[1]through His blood, the forgiveness
of sins.

Apostolic Christology: A Hymn

15 He is [a]the image of the invisible
God, [b]the firstborn over all creation.†
16 For [a]by Him all things were created that are in heaven and that are

---

1:3–8 Giving **thanks** for the church in Colosse, Paul commends them with his **faith, hope, love** trilogy (vv. 4, 5). Note the gospel is the same in Colosse as **in all the world** (v. 6), indicating the catholic (universal) nature of the faith in the first century. Elements of this gospel include: (1) **faith in Christ Jesus** alone, no other (v. 4); (2) **love for all the saints** (v. 4); (3) **hope** in the Kingdom of **heaven** (v. 5); (4) true preaching (v. 6); and (5) godly ministry, as established by **Epaphras** (vv. 7, 8).

1:9–14 A summary of progress in a truly spiritual life: from discernment of God's **will** (v. 9) to doing God's will (v. 10), with divine energy and virtue (v. 11), within the Church, the baptized and eucharistic assembly. In the apostolic tradition, this life is open to all the saints, not to just a few.

1:12, 13 Being a Christian goes beyond changing masters from Satan to God, to a change of kingdoms as well—from that of **darkness** to the **kingdom of the Son.**

1:15–20 This passage is an ancient christological hymn, perhaps expanded upon by Paul, in two stanzas: (1) Christ the Head of creation (vv. 15–17) and (2) Christ the Head of the new creation (vv. 18–20). This hymn may have been part of the early baptismal liturgy; if so, Paul could be using it to bring the Colossians back to their original profession.

1:15 No clear distinction is made between Christ as God and Christ as Man, but the point of the verse is obvious. As God, Christ is eternally and consubstantially (of one essence)

(continued on next page)

on earth, visible and invisible,
whether thrones or [b]dominions or
[1]principalities or [2]powers. All things
were created [c]through Him and for
Him.†
17 [a]And He is before all things,
and in Him [b]all things consist.
18 And [a]He is the head of the
body, the church, who is the beginning, [b]the firstborn from the dead,
that in all things He may have the
preeminence.†
19 For it pleased *the Father that*
[a]in Him all the fullness should
dwell,†
20 and [a]by Him to reconcile [b]all
things to Himself, by Him, whether
things on earth or things in heaven,
[c]having made peace through the
blood of His cross.

Salvation with Perseverance

21 And you, [a]who once were alienated and enemies in your mind
[b]by wicked works, yet now He has
[c]reconciled
22 [a]in the body of His flesh
through death, [b]to present you holy,
and blameless, and above reproach
in His sight—†
23 if indeed you continue [a]in the
faith, grounded and steadfast, and
are [b]not moved away from the hope
of the gospel which you heard,
[c]which was preached to every creature under heaven, [d]of which I, Paul,
became a minister.

Paul's Sacrificial Service

24 [a]I now rejoice in my sufferings
[b]for you, and fill up in my flesh
[c]what is lacking in the afflictions of
Christ, for [d]the sake of His body,
which is the church,†
25 of which I became a minister according to [a]the [1]stewardship from
God which was given to me for you,
to fulfill the word of God,†

16 [b][Eph. 1:20, 21] [c]Heb. 2:10 [1]*rulers* [2]*authorities*
17 [a][John 17:5] [b]Heb. 1:3
18 [a]Eph. 1:22 [b]Rev. 1:5
19 [a]John 1:16
20 [a]Eph. 2:14 [b]2 Cor. 5:18 [c]Eph. 1:10
21 [a][Eph. 2:1] [b]Titus 1:15 [c]2 Cor. 5:18, 19
22 [a]2 Cor. 5:18 [b][Eph. 5:27]
23 [a]Eph. 3:17 [b][John 15:6] [c]Col. 1:6 [d]Col. 1:25
24 [a]2 Cor. 7:4 [b]Eph. 3:1, 13 [c][2 Cor. 1:5; 12:15] [d]Eph. 1:23
25 [a]Gal. 2:7 [1]*dispensation* or *administration*

(continued from previous page)
the **image** (Gr. *eikon,* "icon") of the Father. As Man, Christ is the *image* in which man was made and toward which man is moving. In both natures, He fully represents and manifests the Father. As God, Christ is **the firstborn over all creation** in that the Father created everything through Him, as the Only Begotten Son of God. As Man, Christ is *the firstborn over all creation* in that He has authority over creation. In either case, creation is fully subject to Him. Contrary to the Colossian heresy, in which He was considered one of the created mediators, Christ is the only Mediator and Lord of all.

1:16 Thrones, dominions, principalities, and **powers** are ranks of angels. Christ is not only the source (**through Him**) of creation—of all things, on earth and in heaven—but also its goal (**for Him;** see Eph. 1:10).

1:18 The head and **the body** have one and the same nature. In this case *the body* comes from, submits to and continues to exist in *the head,* so the one nature is the glorified humanity of Christ. As Christ has supreme and life-giving authority (**the firstborn**) over the original creation, where life is temporary, so He has supreme and life-giving authority over the new creation, where life is eternal. But now He is Head through the body, **the church.** The Church, then, is the source of the restoration and fulfillment of creation in Christ.

1:19, 20 The fullness was a term used by the gnostic heretics to describe all the spiritual beings and forces they saw as intervening between man and God. Of these, Jesus was seen as but one mediator in one level of existence with one force. Paul differs, saying Christ is Himself *the fullness.* Jesus is everything, God in all fullness; and in His human nature, resurrected and ascended, He is the created and glorified Head of all creation. Jesus Christ ends the alienation between God and creation, bringing creation as a sacrament into a living union with God.

1:22 The body of His flesh is the mortal (capable of dying) humanity of Christ before His resurrection. The heretics' angels cannot save us because they have not become one of us. We cannot be saved unless we become one with Christ, by becoming united with Him in His death. Through His death, we die with Him.

1:24 Christ and the Church are so intimately united that, as we suffer and die with Him (beginning at baptism), so Christ suffers with us in our work of reconciliation. (See Matt. 25:40; Luke 10:16; John 15:18–21; Acts 9:1, 4, 5; Rom. 8:17; 2 Cor. 1:5; 4:10; Phil. 1:20; 3:10.)

1:25 The Colossian church is bound not only to its confession of faith (vv. 15–20) but also to its divinely appointed apostle.

26 [a]the [1]mystery which has been
hidden from ages and from generations, [b]but now has been revealed
to His saints.†
27 [a]To them God willed to make
known what are [b]the riches of the
glory of this mystery among the
Gentiles: [1]which is [c]Christ in you,
[d]the hope of glory.
28 Him we preach, [a]warning every
man and teaching every man in all
wisdom, [b]that we may present every
man perfect in Christ Jesus.
29 To this *end* I also labor, striving
according to His working which
works in me [a]mightily.

Paul's Concern for Their Salvation

2 For I want you to know what a
great [a]conflict[1] I have for you
and those in Laodicea, and *for* as
many as have not seen my face in
the flesh,
2 that their hearts may be encouraged, being knit together in love,
and *attaining* to all riches of the
full assurance of understanding,
to the knowledge of the mystery
of God, [1]both of the Father and of
Christ,
3 [a]in whom are hidden all the
treasures of wisdom and knowledge.†
4 Now this I say [a]lest anyone
should deceive you with persuasive
words.
5 For [a]though I am absent in the
flesh, yet I am with you in spirit, re-

26 [a][1 Cor. 2:7] [b][2 Tim. 1:10] [1]*secret* or *hidden truth*
27 [a]2 Cor. 2:14 [b]Rom. 9:23 [c][Rom. 8:10, 11] [d]1 Tim. 1:1 [1]M *who*
28 [a]Acts 20:20 [b]Eph. 5:27
29 [a]Eph. 3:7

CHAPTER 2

1 [a]Phil. 1:30 [1]*struggle*
2 [1]NU omits *both of the Father and*
3 [a]1 Cor. 1:24, 30
4 [a]Rom. 16:18
5 [a]1 Thess. 2:17 [b]1 Cor. 14:40 [c]1 Pet. 5:9 [1]Lit. *and seeing*
6 [a]1 Thess. 4:1
7 [a]Eph. 2:21 [1]NU omits *in it*
8 [a]Gal. 1:14 [b]Gal. 4:3, 9, 10 [1]Lit. *plunder you* or *take you captive*
9 [a][John 1:14] [1]*in bodily form*

joicing [1]to see [b]your *good* order and
the [c]steadfastness of your faith in
Christ.

Against False Theology

6 [a]As you therefore have received
Christ Jesus the Lord, so walk in
Him,
7 [a]rooted and built up in Him and
established in the faith, as you have
been taught, abounding [1]in it with
thanksgiving.
8 Beware lest anyone [1]cheat you
through philosophy and empty deceit, according to [a]the tradition of
men, according to the [b]basic principles of the world, and not according
to Christ.†
9 For [a]in Him dwells all the fullness of the Godhead [1]bodily;†
10 and you are complete in Him,
who is the [a]head of all [1]principality
and power.
11 In Him you were also [a]circum-
cised with the circumcision made
without hands, by [b]putting off the
body [1]of the sins of the flesh, by the
circumcision of Christ,†
12 [a]buried with Him in baptism, in
which you also were raised with *Him*
through [b]faith in the working of
God, [c]who raised Him from the
dead.

10 [a][Eph. 1:20, 21] [1]*rule and authority* **11** [a]Deut. 10:16 [b]Rom. 6:6; 7:24 [1]NU omits *of the sins* **12** [a]Rom. 6:4 [b]Eph. 1:19, 20 [c]Acts 2:24

1:26 Mystery: See Eph. 1:9, 10 and note; see also *Glossary*.

2:3 For those who seek the secrets of the universe, a desire the Colossian heretics fed upon, Paul assures us Christ knows everything. Most of this is **hidden** to us, so we must seek Christ alone, who is God's Wisdom. In the Incarnation He became for us a Servant, taking on our weak and mortal existence, but He always remains Lord of all.

2:8 The basic principles of the world include (1) the basic elements of *matter;* (2) the *laws* that regulate the universe, including those conditioning fallen human life, such as death, sin, the flesh and the Mosaic Law; (3) the *spirits* who use these conditions to oppose Christ and are at the core of the pagan cults and systems of knowledge; and (4) *human traditions* opposed to God's tradition.

2:9, 10 See John 1:14. Do we need to rise through manifold levels of being to get to God? No! The incarnate Christ is fully God and fully Man—He fulfills human nature and all levels of being submit to Him. Do we need to rise slowly through a humanly conceived spiritual bureaucracy to God? No! We go directly through Christ, for He is the sovereign power, **the head** over angelic beings.

2:11–14 Do we need to perform man-made rituals and works in order to gain a hearing

(continued on next page)

13 And you, being dead in your trespasses and the uncircumcision of your flesh, He has made alive together with Him, having forgiven you all trespasses,

14 [a]having wiped out the [1]handwriting of requirements that was against us, which was contrary to us. And He has taken it out of the way, having nailed it to the cross.

15 [a]Having disarmed [b]principalities and powers, He made a public spectacle of them, triumphing over them in it.†

Against False Spirituality

16 So let no one [a]judge you in food or in drink, or regarding a [1]festival or a new moon or sabbaths,†

17 [a]which are a shadow of things to come, but the [1]substance is of Christ.

18 Let no one cheat you of your reward, taking delight in *false* humility and worship of angels, intruding into those things which he has [1]not seen, vainly puffed up by his fleshly mind,

19 and not holding fast to [a]the Head, from whom all the body, nourished and knit together by joints and ligaments, [b]grows with the increase *that is* from God.

20 [1]Therefore, if you [a]died with Christ from the basic principles of the world, [b]why, as *though* living in the world, do you subject yourselves to regulations—

21 [a]"Do not touch, do not taste, do not handle,"

22 which all concern things which perish with the using—[a]according to the commandments and doctrines of men?

23 [a]These things indeed have an appearance of wisdom in self-imposed religion, *false* humility, and [1]neglect of the body, *but are* of no value against the indulgence of the flesh.

Spirituality in the Church

3 If then you were [a]raised with Christ, seek those things which are above, [b]where Christ is, sitting at the right hand of God.†

14 [a][Eph. 2:15, 16] [1]*certificate of debt with its*
15 [a][Is. 53:12] [b]Eph. 6:12
16 [a]Rom. 14:3 [1]*feast day*
17 [a]Heb. 8:5; 10:1 [1]Lit. *body*
18 [1]NU omits *not*
19 [a]Eph. 4:15 [b]Eph. 1:23; 4:16
20 [a]Rom. 6:2–5 [b]Gal. 4:3, 9 [1]NU, M omit *Therefore*
21 [a]1 Tim. 4:3
22 [a]Titus 1:14
23 [a]1 Tim. 4:8 [1]*severe treatment, asceticism*

CHAPTER 3

1 [a]Col. 2:12 [b]Eph. 1:20

(continued from previous page)
before the Redeemer? No! We come through God's work, Holy **baptism,** to be joined to Christ. For Jesus Christ triumphs over the conditions of fallen existence—sin, death, the flesh, the law, and evil spirits—by His death and resurrection. In the OT rite of **circumcision** only a small piece of flesh is removed; in **the circumcision of Christ,** our baptism, we die to the flesh and live to God.

2:15 Don't the dark powers still have ability to take power over us? No! All of these created **principalities and powers,** the angels who are the hidden powers behind fallen human existence, are defeated by the Resurrection. Even the law has been fulfilled and thus transcended (v. 14). Christ triumphs, and He rides in triumphal procession, leading out the prisoners of war in chains before Him, while He follows behind in His glorious shining victor's chariot, the Cross.

2:16–23 Here Paul speaks against false worship (vv. 16, 17), false mysticism (vv. 18, 19) and false asceticism (vv. 20–23). He says **let no one judge you** (v. 16) and do not submit to **the basic principles of the world** (v. 20, see v. 8). For man does not live by **shadow,** the law, but by **the substance** (lit. "body") which produces the *shadow* (v. 17), which is the body of Christ, the Church. Man-centered superstitious ritualism is deadly. The fulfilling liturgy is that of the body of Christ, culminating in the Eucharist. (For Paul on liturgical worship, see 1 Cor. 11—14.) Mystical experiences are not wrong in themselves, but we must beware of deception, pride, schism, and a mind controlled by passions and the body. (For Paul on mystical experiences, see 2 Cor. 12; Eph. 1; 3.) Ascetic practices—prayer, fasting, almsgiving—are taught by God (Matt. 6), but there are enemies who lie along that path as well. Submitting to created realities, heeding human traditions, the deception of feeding the flesh when you think that you are denying it, is a false asceticism and is condemned as pride. (For Paul on asceticism, see 1 Cor. 9; 1 Tim. 6:12; 2 Tim. 2:3–6).

3:1–17 Using baptism as his backdrop, Paul counters the practices of the heretics in Colosse
(continued on next page)

Sunday of the Holy Ancestors of Christ *Two Sundays before Christmas*
3:4–11: Although they lived before Christ, His ancestors partake of His newness of life.

2 Set your mind on things above,
not on things on the [a]earth.
3 [a]For you died, [b]and your life is
hidden with Christ in God.
4 [a]When Christ *who is* [b]our life appears, then you also will appear with
Him in [c]glory.
5 [a]Therefore put to death [b]your
members which are on the earth:
[c]fornication, uncleanness, passion,
evil desire, and covetousness,
[d]which is idolatry.†
6 [a]Because of these things the
wrath of God is coming upon [b]the
sons of disobedience,
7 [a]in which you yourselves once
walked when you lived in them.
8 [a]But now you yourselves are to
put off all these: anger, wrath, malice, blasphemy, filthy language out
of your mouth.
9 Do not lie to one another, since
you have put off the old man with
his deeds,
10 and have put on the new *man*
who [a]is renewed in knowledge
[b]according to the image of Him who
[c]created him,†
11 where there is neither [a]Greek
nor Jew, circumcised nor uncircumcised, barbarian, Scythian, slave *nor*
free, [b]but Christ *is* all and in all.
12 Therefore, [a]as *the* elect of God,
holy and beloved, [b]put on tender
mercies, kindness, humility, meekness, longsuffering;
13 [a]bearing with one another, and
forgiving one another, if anyone has
a complaint against another; even as
Christ forgave you, so you also *must*
do.
14 [a]But above all these things
[b]put on love, which is the [c]bond of
perfection.
15 And let [a]the peace of God rule
in your hearts, [b]to which also you
were called [c]in one body; and
[d]be thankful.†
16 Let the word of Christ dwell in
you richly in all wisdom, teaching
and admonishing one another
[a]in psalms and hymns and spiritual
songs, singing with grace in your
hearts to the Lord.
17 And [a]*whatever* you do in word
or deed, *do* all in the name of the
Lord Jesus, giving thanks to God the
Father through Him.

2 [a][Matt. 6:19–21]
3 [a][Rom. 6:2] [b][2 Cor. 5:7]
4 [a][1 John 3:2] [b]John 14:6 [c]1 Cor. 15:43
5 [a][Rom. 8:13] [b][Rom. 6:13] [c]Eph. 5:3 [d]Eph. 4:19; 5:3, 5
6 [a]Rom. 1:18 [b][Eph. 2:2]
7 [a]1 Cor. 6:11
8 [a]Eph. 4:22
10 [a]Rom. 12:2 [b][Rom. 8:29] [c][Eph. 2:10]
11 [a]Gal. 3:27, 28 [b]Eph. 1:23
12 [a][1 Pet. 1:2] [b]1 John 3:17
13 [a][Mark 11:25]
14 [a]1 Pet. 4:8 [b][1 Cor. 13] [c]Eph. 4:3
15 [a][John 14:27] [b]1 Cor. 7:15 [c]Eph. 4:4 [d][1 Thess. 5:18]
16 [a]Eph. 5:19
17 [a]1 Cor. 10:31

(continued from previous page)
(2:16–23) with the practices of the apostolic Church: true mysticism (vv. 1–4), true asceticism (vv. 5–14), and true liturgical experience (vv. 15–17).

3:1–4 True mysticism: Christians both have received Christ's exalted resurrection life in baptism, and need to keep on seeking the ultimate and spiritual glories of the age to come. Remember your baptism! Live according to His resurrection! Seek your true life in Christ, awaiting the heavenly and glorious final revelation!

3:5–14 True asceticism: As baptized Christians, we are becoming in practice what we are already in spirit. As we died with Christ, so we must will to experience death daily by "killing" old sinful and disintegrating passions (vv. 5–9). As we were raised with Christ, so we must will to experience life daily by the virtuous and unifying desires of the **new man** which we all are in the body of Christ (vv. 10–14).

3:10 The **new man** grows from one stage of perfection to another, becoming **the image** of Jesus Christ and throughout eternity remaining *the image* of **Him who created him.**

3:15–17 True liturgical experience: Note how the liturgy of worship can be experienced as divine through the unity and holiness of the Church—the one New Man in Christ. Worship is experienced in: (1) **the word of Christ** including the Scriptures and their exposition; (2) the **hymns and spiritual songs;** (3) the Eucharist (**giving thanks to God**).

Spirituality in the Home

18 [a]Wives, submit to your own husbands, [b]as is fitting in the Lord.†

19 [a]Husbands, love your wives and do not be [b]bitter toward them.

20 [a]Children, obey your parents [b]in all things, for this is well pleasing to the Lord.

21 [a]Fathers, do not provoke your children, lest they become discouraged.

22 [a]Bondservants, obey in all things your masters according to the flesh, not with eyeservice, as men-pleasers, but in sincerity of heart, fearing God.

23 [a]And whatever you do, do it heartily, as to the Lord and not to men,

24 [a]knowing that from the Lord you will receive the reward of the inheritance; [b]for[1] you serve the Lord Christ.

25 But he who does wrong will be repaid for what he has done, and [a]there is no partiality.

4 Masters,[a] give your bondservants what is just and fair, knowing that you also have a Master in heaven.

Spirituality for the World

2 [a]Continue earnestly in prayer, being vigilant in it [b]with thanksgiving;†

3 [a]meanwhile praying also for us, that God would [b]open to us a door for the word, to speak [c]the [1]mystery of Christ, [d]for which I am also in chains,

4 that I may make it manifest, as I ought to speak.

5 [a]Walk in [b]wisdom toward those who are outside, [c]redeeming the time.

6 *Let* your speech always *be* [a]with grace, [b]seasoned with salt, [c]that you may know how you ought to answer each one.

Greetings and Instructions

7 [a]Tychicus, a beloved brother, faithful minister, and fellow servant in the Lord, will tell you all the news about me.†

8 [a]I am sending him to you for this very purpose, that [1]he may know your circumstances and comfort your hearts,

9 with [a]Onesimus, a faithful and beloved brother, who is *one* of you. They will make known to you all things which *are happening* here.

10 [a]Aristarchus my fellow prisoner greets you, with [b]Mark the cousin of Barnabas (about whom you received instructions: if he comes to you, welcome him),

11 and Jesus who is called Justus. These *are my* only fellow workers for the kingdom of God who are of the circumcision; they have proved to be a comfort to me.

12 [a]Epaphras, who is *one* of you, a bondservant of Christ, greets you, always [b]laboring fervently for you in prayers, that you may stand [c]perfect and [1]complete in all the will of God.

13 For I bear him witness that he has a great [1]zeal for you, and those who are in Laodicea, and those in Hierapolis.

14 [a]Luke the beloved physician and [b]Demas greet you.

15 Greet the brethren who are in Laodicea, and [1]Nymphas and [a]the church that *is* in [2]his house.

18 [a]1 Pet. 3:1 [b][Eph. 5:22—6:9]
19 [a][Eph. 5:25] [b]Eph. 4:31
20 [a]Eph. 6:1 [b]Eph. 5:24
21 [a]Eph. 6:4
22 [a]Eph. 6:5
23 [a][Eccl. 9:10]
24 [a]Eph. 6:8 [b]1 Cor. 7:22 [1]NU omits *for*
25 [a]Rom. 2:11

CHAPTER 4

1 [a]Eph. 6:9
2 [a]Luke 18:1 [b]Col. 2:7
3 [a]Eph. 6:19 [b]1 Cor. 16:9 [c]Eph. 3:3, 4; 6:19 [d]Eph. 6:20 [1]*hidden truth*
5 [a]Eph. 5:15 [b][Matt. 10:16] [c]Eph. 5:16
6 [a]Eccl. 10:12 [b]Mark 9:50 [c]1 Pet. 3:15
7 [a]2 Tim. 4:12
8 [a]Eph. 6:22 [1]NU *you may know our circumstances and he may comfort*
9 [a]Philem. 10
10 [a]Acts 19:29; 20:4; 27:2 [b]2 Tim. 4:11
12 [a]Philem. 23 [b]Rom. 15:30 [c]Matt. 5:48 [1]NU *fully assured*
13 [1]NU *concern*
14 [a]2 Tim. 4:11 [b]2 Tim. 4:10
15 [a]Rom. 16:5 [1]NU *Nympha* [2]NU *her*

3:18—4:1 Life in the home is **in the Lord;** the family is a little church and is to live in the baptismal and eucharistic life of the Church. Duties are reciprocal, everyone having the same standing before the same Master. All authority is for the sake of loving service (all authority is humbling) and all submission is to God (all submission is glorious).

4:2–6 Paul expects the church to be at corporate **prayer** often. Not only are the apostles to **speak the mystery of Christ,** but every member of the church is to have **speech . . . with grace** so as **to answer** those seeking the true faith.

4:7–9 Tychicus is the courier for this letter as well as for those to the Ephesians (Eph. 6:21) and to Philemon.

16 Now when [a]this epistle is read
among you, see that it is read also
in the church of the Laodiceans, and
that you likewise read the epistle
from Laodicea.†
17 And say to [a]Archippus, "Take
heed to [b]the ministry which you
have received in the Lord, that you
may fulfill it."
18 [a]This salutation by my own
hand—Paul. [b]Remember my chains.
Grace *be* with you. Amen.

16 [a]1 Thess. 5:27
17 [a]Philem. 2
[b]2 Tim. 4:5
18 [a]1 Cor. 16:21
[b]Heb. 13:3

4:16 Paul expected his letters to be read aloud to the churches and at least sometimes to be sent on to neighboring churches. (Colosse and Laodicea are less than 15 miles apart). Paul's letter coming from Laodicea probably is the one we know as Ephesians.

The First Epistle of Paul the Apostle to the THESSALONIANS

Author: *St. Paul the Apostle*

Date: *A.D. 50–51*

Theme: *A Holy Life Leads to Eternal Life*

AUTHOR: The greeting identifies Paul as the author, and also mentions Silvanus (Silas) and Timothy. They were coworkers with Paul in establishing the church in Thessalonica on his second missionary journey (Acts 17:1–9).

DATE: First Thessalonians was written in Corinth in A.D. 50–51, about six months after the church in Thessalonica was founded. It is probably the first of Paul's New Testament epistles, and perhaps the first of all the twenty-seven New Testament books to be written.

MAJOR THEME: *A holy life leads to eternal life.* An encouragement to be holy (3:13; 4:3; 5:23), with particular calls to (1) continue as examples to others (1:7), (2) walk worthy of God's calling (2:12), (3) stand fast in the faith (3:8), and (4) maintain moral purity (4:3). The letter closes with instruction and comfort concerning the Second Coming of Christ (4:13—5:11), along with other exhortations concerning the spiritual life.

BACKGROUND INFORMATION: (1) *The church in Thessalonica* was founded in the summer of A.D. 50 during Paul's second missionary journey (Acts 15:36—18:22). Built on the Aegean Sea, Thessalonica was the most prominent city in the Roman province of Macedonia, and served as a naval and commercial center. While many of the early churches were composed primarily of Jews who believed in Christ, the Thessalonian believers were mostly Gentiles, former idol-worshipers (1:9).

(2) *The historical setting.* When Paul left Thessalonica, the new church was exemplary (1:3, 7–10; 4:9, 10), but young and unstable. A few months later, while Paul was in Athens (3:1), he grew concerned about how the Thessalonian church was handling persecution by fellow citizens, stirred up by the Jews (1:6; 2:14; Acts 17:5–9). He was prevented from visiting Thessalonica (2:17, 18), so he sent Timothy to encourage the faithful and return with a report. Timothy met Paul in Corinth with the report, which could be summarized as follows:

(1) Regarding evangelism and endurance through persecution, the Thessalonians are remarkably strong (1:8).

(2) Some, however, have difficulty maintaining chastity in a place where the culture sees sexual purity as a laughable novelty (4:3–8).

(3) The people are doing well in Christian love and charity, but some have given in to that "getting even" syndrome which had been part of their pre-Christian lives (5:15).

(4) Their hope of Christ's imminent return has degenerated into irresponsibility. Some neglect the duties of daily life and work. Others are grieving over those who have died before Christ's coming. Many are too curious, engaging in calculations and date-setting for the Second Coming (4:13—5:11).

(5) There is some tension and insubordination regarding Church leaders (2:10–12; 5:12, 13).

(6) People are sceptical about spiritual gifts (5:19–21).

(7) Paul is charged with (a) cowardice (2:2, 17, 18), (b) seeking popularity (2:4, 5), (c) greed (2:5, 9), (d) self-aggrandizement (2:6), (e) hard-hearted pride (2:6–8), and (f) self-indulgent laziness (2:9–12).

3. *Paul's purpose in 1 Thessalonians* is to respond to Timothy's report, correct the Thessalonians and encourage them to greater spiritual excellence (3:10; 4:1).

OUTLINE

Introduction: Greeting and Thanksgiving	1:1–10
I. The power of the gospel in Paul's behavior	2:1—3:13
A. Paul's past work prepared them to endure persecution	2:1–16
B. Paul's present relationship with them is unchanged	2:17—3:13
II. The power of the gospel in the Church's behavior	4:1—5:22
A. Power for holiness	4:1–12
B. Power for right belief, catholic and apostolic	4:13—5:11
1. Christians who die before the Second Coming	4:13–18
2. Preparing for the Second Coming	5:1–11
C. Power for unity	5:12–22
Concluding prayer and instructions	5:23–28

Greeting and Thanksgiving

1 Paul, [a]Silvanus, and Timothy,
To the church of the [b]Thessaloni-
ans in God the Father and the Lord
Jesus Christ:

Grace to you and peace [1]from God
our Father and the Lord Jesus
Christ.†

2 [a]We give thanks to God always
for you all, making mention of you
in our prayers,†
3 remembering without ceasing
[a]your work of faith, [b]labor of love,
and patience of hope in our Lord
Jesus Christ in the sight of our God
and Father,†
4 knowing, beloved brethren,
[a]your election by God.
5 For [a]our gospel did not come to
you in word only, but also in power,
[b]and in the Holy Spirit [c]and in much
assurance, as you know what kind
of men we were among you for your
sake.
6 And [a]you became followers of
us and of the Lord, having received
the word in much affliction, [b]with
joy of the Holy Spirit,†
7 so that you became examples to
all in Macedonia and Achaia who
believe.†
8 For from you the word of the
Lord [a]has sounded forth, not only
in Macedonia and Achaia, but also
[b]in every place. Your faith toward
God has gone out, so that we do not
need to say anything.
9 For they themselves declare
concerning us [a]what manner of entry we had to you, [b]and how you
turned to God from idols to serve
the living and true God,
10 and [a]to wait for His Son from
heaven, whom He raised from the
dead, *even* Jesus who delivers us
[b]from the wrath to come.†

Defense of Paul's Past Work

2 For you yourselves know, brethren, that our coming to you was
not in vain.†
2 But [1]even after we had suffered
before and were spitefully treated at
[a]Philippi, as you know, we were

CHAPTER 1
1 [a]1 Pet. 5:12 [b]Acts 17:1–9 [1]NU omits *from God our Father and the Lord Jesus Christ*
2 [a]Rom. 1:8
3 [a]John 6:29 [b]Rom. 16:6
4 [a]Col. 3:12
5 [a]Mark 16:20 [b]2 Cor. 6:6 [c]Heb. 2:3
6 [a]1 Cor. 4:16; 11:1 [b]Acts 5:41; 13:52
8 [a]Rom. 10:18 [b]Rom. 1:8; 16:19
9 [a]1 Thess. 2:1 [b]1 Cor. 12:2
10 [a][Rom. 2:7] [b]Rom. 5:9

CHAPTER 2
2 [a]Acts 14:5; 16:19–24 [1]NU, M omit *even*

1:1 In the first-century Greek world, there was a general pattern by which all letters were begun: name of sender(s), the addressee(s), the greeting itself. As with most of Paul's epistles, this pattern is followed here but Christianized.

1:2 Give thanks in NT Greek is *eucharisto,* from which we get our English word "Eucharist." A spirit of thanksgiving constantly pervades the prayers of Paul, as here when he specifically remembers the Christians in Thessalonica.

1:3 Remembering and **without ceasing** describe effective prayer (see 2:13; 5:16–18). **Faith, hope** and **love** are three Christian virtues which Paul links together in other letters (1 Cor. 13:13; Col. 1:4, 5). These virtues are connected to actions: Faith works, love labors, hope produces **patience,** showing that salvation goes beyond attitudes to action.

1:6 Followers (lit. "imitators") of Christ also imitate spiritual leaders—pastors, bishops, in this case the apostles—even in their suffering. St. Ignatius of Antioch in the early second century writes, "Let [others] be instructed by you, at least by your deeds. With their wrath you be mild, with their boastful speech you be humble-minded, with their abuse you offer prayers, with their deceit you be firm in faith, with their cruelty you be gentle, not eager to imitate them" (*To the Ephesians*). The **joy of the Holy Spirit** is not an easy emotional high but comes with the struggle proper to spiritual life, including persevering through affliction. The one who suffers is the one who is comforted.

1:7–10 What a tribute to the Thessalonian believers. People everywhere were speaking of them!

1:10 The early Christians expected Christ to return in their lifetime. This hope helped purge their lives of sin.

2:1–16 Paul defends his apostolic work, claiming he has served with courage (vv. 1, 2), humility (vv. 3–6), love (vv. 7, 8), financial integrity (v. 9) and godly authority (vv. 10–12). Following his example, the Thessalonians can manifest similar holiness amidst hostility (vv. 13–16).

[b]bold in our God to speak to you
the gospel of God in much conflict.†
3 [a]For our exhortation *did* not
come from error or uncleanness, nor
was it in deceit.
4 But as [a]we have been approved
by God [b]to be entrusted with the
gospel, even so we speak, [c]not as
pleasing men, but God [d]who tests
our hearts.†
5 For [a]neither at any time did we
use flattering words, as you know,
nor a [1]cloak for covetousness—[b]God
is witness.
6 [a]Nor did we seek glory from
men, either from you or from others,
when [b]we might have [c]made demands [d]as apostles of Christ.
7 But [a]we were gentle among
you, just as a nursing *mother* cherishes her own children.†
8 So, affectionately longing for
you, we were well pleased [a]to impart
to you not only the gospel of God,
but also [b]our own lives, because you
had become dear to us.
9 For you remember, brethren,
our [a]labor and toil; for laboring night
and day, [b]that we might not be a
burden to any of you, we preached
to you the gospel of God.
10 [a]You *are* witnesses, and God
also, [b]how devoutly and justly and
blamelessly we behaved ourselves
among you who believe;
11 as you know how we exhorted,
and comforted, and [1]charged every
one of you, as a father *does* his own
children,†

2 [b]Acts 17:1–9
3 [a]2 Cor. 7:2
4 [a]1 Cor. 7:25 [b]Titus 1:3 [c]Gal. 1:10 [d]Prov. 17:3
5 [a]2 Cor. 2:17 [b]Rom. 1:9 [1]*pretext for greed*
6 [a]1 Tim. 5:17 [b]1 Cor. 9:4 [c]2 Cor. 11:9 [d]1 Cor. 9:1
7 [a]1 Cor. 2:3
8 [a]Rom. 1:11 [b]2 Cor. 12:15
9 [a]Acts 18:3; 20:34, 35 [b]2 Cor. 12:13
10 [a]1 Thess. 1:5 [b]2 Cor. 7:2
11 [1]NU, M *implored*
12 [a]Eph. 4:1 [b]1 Cor. 1:9
13 [a]1 Thess. 1:2, 3 [b]Mark 4:20 [c][Gal. 4:14] [d][1 Pet. 1:23]
14 [a]Gal. 1:22 [b]Acts 17:5
15 [a]Acts 2:23 [b]Matt. 5:12; 23:34, 35 [c]Esth. 3:8 [1]*hostile*
16 [a]Luke 11:52 [b]Gen. 15:16 [c]Matt. 24:6

12 [a]that you would walk worthy of
God [b]who calls you into His own
kingdom and glory.

Fruit of Paul's Work: They Endured Persecution

13 For this reason we also thank
God [a]without ceasing, because when
you [b]received the word of God
which you heard from us, you welcomed *it* [c]not *as* the word of men,
but as it is in truth, the word of God,
which also effectively [d]works in you
who believe.
14 For you, brethren, became imitators [a]of the churches of God which
are in Judea in Christ Jesus. For
[b]you also suffered the same things
from your own countrymen, just as
they *did* from the Judeans,†
15 [a]who killed both the Lord Jesus
and [b]their own prophets, and have
persecuted us; and they do not
please God [c]and are [1]contrary to all
men,
16 [a]forbidding us to speak to the
Gentiles that they may be saved, so
as always [b]to fill up *the measure of*
their sins; [c]but wrath has come upon
them to the uttermost.

Paul's Present Relationship with Thessalonica

17 But we, brethren, having been
taken away from you for a short time

2:2 Christians are repeatedly challenged in the NT to be **bold** in confessing Christ before others (see Acts 4:29–31; Rom. 1:16).

2:4–6 Paul has been accused of seeking his own glory, but he knows God does not share His glory with any other (Is. 48:11). As His servants, we must step outside the circle of world-pleasers and into the arena of pleasing God, whatever the cost.

2:7, 8 Spreading the gospel means putting our lives on the line for those we seek to reach, as a mother sacrifices herself for her children. Thus, the holy martyrs gave their lives with great joy for Christ and His Church.

2:11 Note the three verbs Paul uses to describe his apostolic preaching to the Thessalonians: (1) **exhorted,** which can also mean encouraged; (2) **comforted;** and (3) **charged** or implored. These elements are just as important for preaching today!

2:14, 15 While the persecution in Thessalonica comes primarily from Greeks, Paul, a Jew, is frank concerning his countrymen of that day who reject their Messiah, noting that they: (1) **killed . . . the Lord Jesus** (v. 15), (2) killed **their own prophets,** (3) **persecuted** the apostles, (4) **do not please God** and (5) act with hostility to **all men.** This is a strong indictment. But Paul's love for the Jews never wavers. He wishes himself to be cursed if that could cause his fellow Jews to turn to Christ for salvation (Rom. 9:3; 10:1).

[a]in presence, not in heart, endeav-
ored more eagerly to see your face
with great desire.
18 Therefore we wanted to come
to you—even I, Paul, time and
again—but [a]Satan hindered us.†
19 For [a]what *is* our hope, or joy,
or [b]crown of rejoicing? *Is it* not even
you in the [c]presence of our Lord
Jesus Christ [d]at His coming?†
20 For you are our glory and joy.

Timothy's Visit in Paul's Stead

3 Therefore, when we could no
longer endure it, we thought it
good to be left in Athens alone,†
2 and sent [a]Timothy, our brother
and minister of God, and our fellow
laborer in the gospel of Christ, to establish you and encourage you concerning your faith,†
3 [a]that no one should be shaken
by these afflictions; for you yourselves know that [b]we are appointed
to this.
4 [a]For, in fact, we told you before
when we were with you that we
would suffer tribulation, just as it
happened, and you know.
5 For this reason, when I could
no longer endure it, I sent to know
your faith, [a]lest by some means the
tempter had tempted you, and
[b]our labor might be in vain.

Timothy's Report, Paul's Joy

6 [a]But now that Timothy has
come to us from you, and brought
us good news of your faith and love,
and that you always have good
remembrance of us, greatly desiring to see us, [b]as we also *to see*
you—†
7 therefore, brethren, in all our affliction and distress [a]we were comforted concerning you by your faith.
8 For now we live, if you [a]stand
fast in the Lord.
9 For what thanks can we render
to God for you, for all the joy with
which we rejoice for your sake before
our God,
10 night and day praying exceedingly that we may see your face
[a]and perfect what is lacking in your
faith?
11 Now may our God and Father
Himself, and our Lord Jesus Christ,
[a]direct our way to you.
12 And may the Lord make you increase and [a]abound in love to one
another and to all, just as we *do* to
you,
13 so that He may establish [a]your
hearts blameless in holiness before
our God and Father at the coming
of our Lord Jesus Christ with all His
saints.†

Reminders Concerning Holiness

4 Finally then, brethren, we urge
and exhort in the Lord Jesus
[a]that you should abound more and
more, [b]just as you received from us
how you ought to walk and to please
God;†
2 for you know what command-

17 [a]1 Cor. 5:3
18 [a]Rom. 1:13; 15:22
19 [a]2 Cor. 1:14 [b]Prov. 16:31 [c]Jude 24 [d]1 Cor. 15:23

CHAPTER 3

2 [a]Rom. 16:21
3 [a]Eph. 3:13 [b]John 16:2; Acts 9:16; 14:22; 1 Cor. 4:9; 2 Tim. 3:12; 1 Pet. 2:21
4 [a]Acts 20:24
5 [a]1 Cor. 7:5 [b]Gal. 2:2
6 [a]Acts 18:5 [b]Phil. 1:8
7 [a]2 Cor. 1:4
8 [a][Eph. 6:13, 14]; Phil. 4:1
10 [a]2 Cor. 13:9; Col. 4:12
11 [a]Mark 1:3
12 [a]Phil. 1:9; 1 Thess. 4:1, 10; 2 Thess. 1:3
13 [a]2 Thess. 2:17

CHAPTER 4

1 [a]1 Cor. 15:58 [b]Phil. 1:27; Col. 1:10

2:18 Though unable to prevail against the Church (Matt. 16:18) or overcome the faithful (Eph. 6:11–13; Rev. 12:11), the enemy at times is permitted to hinder faithful Christians. Remember that God's promise applies: "Resist the devil and he will flee from you" (James 4:7).

2:19, 20 This passage shows all the trials and disappointments of the Christian life and ministry are worthwhile!

3:1–5 As healthy as the Thessalonian church is, Paul takes nothing for granted. Even well-grounded, deeply committed Christians need encouragement, instruction, and prayer.

3:2 Minister is from the Greek *diakonon,* from which we get "deacon." **Fellow Laborer** is Greek *synergon,* from which we get "synergy." As ministers, we not only represent God, we work together with Him and our fellow Christians.

3:6 Always and **remembrance** probably speak of prayer life.

3:13 Paul's goal here is for all Christians.

4:1–12 Holiness includes sexual purity (vv. 3–8), mutual love (vv. 9, 10) and honest labor

(continued on next page)

Commemoration of the Departed

4:13–17: Paul offers assurance of the resurrection of the body.

ments we gave you through the Lord
Jesus.
3 For this is [a]the will of God,
[b]your sanctification: [c]that you
should abstain from sexual immorality;
4 [a]that each of you should know
how to possess his own vessel in
sanctification and honor,†
5 [a]not in passion of lust, [b]like the
Gentiles [c]who do not know God;
6 that no one should take advantage of and defraud his brother in
this matter, because the Lord [a]*is* the
avenger of all such, as we also fore-
warned you and testified.
7 For God did not call us to uncleanness, [a]but in holiness.
8 [a]Therefore he who rejects *this*
does not reject man, but God,
[b]who[1] has also given us His Holy
Spirit.
9 But concerning brotherly love
you have no need that I should write
to you, for [a]you yourselves are
taught by God [b]to love one another;
10 and indeed you do so toward
all the brethren who are in all Macedonia. But we urge you, brethren,
[a]that you increase more and more;
11 that you also aspire to lead a
quiet life, [a]to mind your own business, and [b]to work with your own
hands, as we commanded you,†

3 [a][Rom. 12:2] [b]Eph. 5:27 [c][1 Cor. 6:15–20]
4 [a]Rom. 6:19
5 [a]Col. 3:5 [b]Eph. 4:17, 18 [c]1 Cor. 15:34
6 [a]2 Thess. 1:8
7 [a]Lev. 11:44
8 [a]Luke 10:16 [b]1 Cor. 2:10 [1]NU *who also gives*
9 [a][Jer. 31:33, 34] [b]Matt. 22:39
10 [a]1 Thess. 3:12
11 [a]2 Thess. 3:11 [b]Acts 20:35
12 [a]Rom. 13:13
13 [a]Lev. 19:28 [b][Eph. 2:12] [1]Died
14 [a]1 Cor. 15:13 [b]1 Cor. 15:20, 23 [1]Or *through Jesus sleep*
15 [a]1 Kin. 13:17; 20:35 [b]1 Cor. 15:51, 52 [1]Dead

12 [a]that you may walk properly toward those who are outside, and *that*
you may lack nothing.

Who Will Participate in Christ's Return

13 But I do not want you to be ignorant, brethren, concerning those
who have fallen [1]asleep, lest you
sorrow [a]as others [b]who have no
hope.†
14 For [a]if we believe that Jesus died
and rose again, even so God will
bring with Him [b]those who [1]sleep
in Jesus.
15 For this we say to you [a]by the
word of the Lord, that [b]we who are
alive *and* remain until the coming of
the Lord will by no means precede
those who are [1]asleep.
16 For [a]the Lord Himself will descend from heaven with a shout,
with the voice of an archangel, and
with [b]the trumpet of God. [c]And the
dead in Christ will rise first.
17 [a]Then we who are alive *and* remain shall be caught up together
with them [b]in the clouds to meet the

16 [a][Matt. 24:30, 31] [b][1 Cor. 15:52] [c][1 Cor. 15:23] 17 [a][1 Cor. 15:51–53] [b]Acts 1:9

(continued from previous page)
(vv. 11, 12). As for knowing God's will, this passage comes through in brilliant simplicity. God's will is our **sanctification** (v. 3), our being set apart to the Lord as His special possession. We are being sanctified as we walk with Him in faith and obedience.

4:4 His own vessel speaks of the entire human being (Jer. 18:6; Rom. 9:20–23; 2 Cor. 4:7; 2 Tim. 2:20, 21), probably one's own self, perhaps one's wife (or husband). In either case one's *vessel* must be possessed with purity, self-control and chastity.

4:11 The bedrock practicality of the Scriptures: In Paul's time and ours, we are to (1) live quietly, (2) mind our own business, and (3) work hard.

4:13–18 This is one of the clearest NT passages on the Second Coming of Christ. The first-century document, *The Didache*, lists three signs that will mark the return of the Lord: (1) "the sign spread out in the heavens"—Christ and His hosts; (2) "the sign of the trumpet"; and (3) "the resurrection of the dead." For the righteous, the return of Christ is a comfort (v. 18), not a threat.

Lord in the air. And thus [c]we shall
always be with the Lord.
18 [a]Therefore comfort one another
with these words.

How to Await His Coming

5 But concerning [a]the times and
the seasons, brethren, you have
no need that I should write to
you.†
2 For you yourselves know perfectly that [a]the day of the Lord so
comes as a thief in the night.
3 For when they say, "Peace and
safety!" then [a]sudden destruction
comes upon them, [b]as labor pains
upon a pregnant woman. And they
shall not escape.
4 [a]But you, brethren, are not in
darkness, so that this Day should
overtake you as a thief.
5 You are all [a]sons of light and
sons of the day. We are not of the
night nor of darkness.
6 [a]Therefore let us not sleep, as
others *do*, but [b]let us watch and be
[1]sober.
7 For [a]those who sleep, sleep at
night, and those who get drunk
[b]are drunk at night.
8 But let us who are of the day
be sober, [a]putting on the breastplate

17 [c]John 14:3; 17:24
18 [a]1 Thess. 5:11

CHAPTER 5

1 [a]Matt. 24:3
2 [a][2 Pet. 3:10]
3 [a]Is. 13:6–9 [b]Hos. 13:13
4 [a]1 John 2:8
5 [a]Eph. 5:8
6 [a]Matt. 25:5 [b][1 Pet. 5:8] [1]*self-controlled*
7 [a][Luke 21:34] [b]Acts 2:15
8 [a]Eph. 6:14
9 [a]Rom. 9:22 [b][2 Thess. 2:13]
10 [a]2 Cor. 5:15
11 [1]Or *encourage* [2]*build one another up*
12 [a]1 Cor. 16:18 [1]*instruct* or *warn*
13 [a]Mark 9:50
14 [a]2 Thess. 3:6, 7, 11 [b]Heb. 12:12 [c]Rom. 14:1; 15:1 [d]Gal. 5:22 [1]*encourage* [2]*insubordinate* or *idle*

of faith and love, and *as* a helmet
the hope of salvation.
9 For [a]God did not appoint us to
wrath, [b]but to obtain salvation
through our Lord Jesus Christ,
10 [a]who died for us, that whether
we wake or sleep, we should live together with Him.
11 Therefore [1]comfort each other
and [2]edify one another, just as you
also are doing.

Reminders Concerning Unity

12 And we urge you, brethren,
[a]to recognize those who labor among
you, and are over you in the Lord
and [1]admonish you,†
13 and to esteem them very highly
in love for their work's sake. [a]Be at
peace among yourselves.
14 Now we [1]exhort you, brethren,
[a] warn those who are [2]unruly, [b]com-
fort the fainthearted, [c]uphold the
weak, [d]be patient with all.
15 [a]See that no one renders evil for
evil to anyone, but always [b]pursue
what is good both for yourselves and
for all.†
16 [a]Rejoice always,†

15 [a]Lev. 19:18 [b]Gal. 6:10 **16** [a][2 Cor. 6:10]

5:1–11 The Thessalonian Christians had been speculating about the return of the Lord and making their own predictions. Paul tells them, **you have no need** (v. 1) for that kind of information (indeed, it is not available!). Does **a thief in the night** (v. 2) announce his coming? The disciples had gotten the same kind of answers to their questions on the Second Coming from Christ Himself (Matt. 24:36; Acts 1:6, 7). And suppose we know the end; what is this to us? Christians are called not to set dates but to make themselves ready to meet the Lord by being watchful and **sober** (v. 6). Our place is to be ceaselessly aware of the primacy of God's Kingdom and to have full control over our spiritual faculties.

5:12–22 The requirements of harmonious life in community include the honoring of sacramental leadership (vv. 12–14), pursuit of good works (v. 15), continual prayer and thanksgiving in worship (vv. 16–18), and proper regard for the prophetic gift and spiritual discernment (vv. 19–22).

5:12 The Greek term for **over you** has a liturgical connotation. It refers to the leader of the congregation in the Eucharistic assembly. **To recognize** is a weaker translation of "to know" (see 4:5). In a healthy church the people recognize their pastor as their leader in Christ, and willingly follow his admonitions.

5:15 When is it proper to return **evil for evil?** From the Sermon on the Mount (Matt. 5:44) to the end of the NT, the answer is, "Never."

5:16–18 In Paul's writings, words such as **rejoice, always** (v. 16), **without ceasing** or "constantly" (v. 17), and **give thanks** (v. 18) refer primarily to prayer. The spiritual Fathers of the Church teach that unceasing prayer is a proper goal, for spiritual growth comes through such discipline. For centuries, Christian people have used the "Jesus Prayer" as a way to pray unceasingly from the heart: "O Lord Jesus Christ, Son of God, have mercy on me, a sinner."

17 [a]pray without ceasing,
18 in everything give thanks; for
this is the will of God in Christ Jesus
for you.
19 [a]Do not quench the Spirit.†
20 [a]Do not despise prophecies.
21 [a]Test all things; [b]hold fast what
is good.
22 Abstain from every form of evil.

Prayer and Instructions

23 Now may [a]the God of peace
Himself [b]sanctify[1] you completely;
and may your whole spirit, soul,
and body [c]be preserved blameless
at the coming of our Lord Jesus
Christ.†
24 He who calls you *is* [a]faithful,
who also will [b]do *it*.
25 Brethren, pray for us.
26 Greet all the brethren with a
holy kiss.
27 I charge you by the Lord that
this [1]epistle be read to all the [2]holy
brethren.†
28 The grace of our Lord Jesus
Christ *be* with you. Amen.

17 [a]Eph. 6:18
19 [a]Eph. 4:30
20 [a]1 Cor. 14:1, 31
21 [a]1 John 4:1 [b]Phil. 4:8
23 [a]Phil. 4:9 [b]1 Thess. 3:13 [c]1 Cor. 1:8, 9 [1]*set you apart*
24 [a][1 Cor. 10:13] [b]Phil. 1:6
27 [1]*letter* [2]NU omits *holy*

5:19–22 The Holy Spirit is to be actively present in the life of the Church. But there is constant need of discernment and testing so as to avoid being misled (see 1 Cor. 12—14).

5:23–27 Note the liturgical overtones with regard to the corporate meetings. There is (1) the benediction (v. 23), (2) intercessory prayer (v. 25), (3) the kiss of peace (v. 26), and (4) the public reading of the Scriptures (v. 27). The practice of **a holy kiss** very early became a part of the worship liturgy (see Rom. 16:16; 1 Cor. 16:20; 2 Cor. 13:12; 1 Pet. 5:14). Just prior to Communion, the faithful would exchange the kiss of peace, on one cheek and then the other, to show their reconciliation in Christ. Thus, Christ is in our midst and ever shall be!

5:27 The Bible is to be **read** aloud during corporate worship.

The Second Epistle of Paul the Apostle to the
THESSALONIANS

Author: *St. Paul the Apostle*

Date: *A.D. 51*

Theme: *Stand Fast Through Apostolic Teaching*

AUTHOR: Silvanus (Silas) and Timothy are named with the author, Paul (as they are at the opening of 1 Thessalonians), because they were his colaborers in establishing the Thessalonian church (see Acts 17:1–9).

DATE: This epistle was written in A.D. 51, probably from Corinth.

MAJOR THEME: *Stand fast through apostolic teaching*. Some of the Thessalonians had been shaken in their faith by speculations on Christ's return; some even said the day of the Lord had already come (2:2). As a result, these people had lost holiness of life. Paul counters such traditions of men with apostolic tradition (2:15; 3:6). Subthemes include Paul's gratitude for the people's faithfulness (1:3; 2:13) and for God's faithfulness to His people (3:3).

BACKGROUND INFORMATION: (1) *Historical setting*. Paul had not paid a return visit to Thessalonica since the establishment of the church a year earlier. St. John Chrysostom observes he was "filling up by his writings what was lacking of his presence." But a few months after writing 1 Thessalonians, Paul received another report. The Thessalonians' faith amidst persecution was still firm, but speculations concerning the Second Coming were increasing, claiming to be based on Paul's teaching (2:2). Some became so excited about the end times that they abandoned their jobs and lived off the charity of the church (3:6–13). Others grew despondent and wavered in hope (2:13–17).

(2) *Purpose*. Paul wrote this letter (a) to encourage further endurance in persecution, (b) to correct mistaken ideas concerning the Second Coming of Christ and improper life-styles arising from these ideas, and (c) to offer assurance that his teaching is apostolic (2:15).

(3) *Theological significance*. Second Thessalonians was written approximately twenty years after the Ascension, and already people were speculating on the Lord's return. Such dazzling speculations surrounding the Second Coming will probably always be with us.

(4) *Does 2 Thessalonians contradict 1 Thessalonians?* Some say 1 Thessalonians teaches the *suddenness* of the Second Coming, whereas 2 Thessalonians

teaches that it is preceded by *signs.* But 1 Thessalonians does acknowledge the existence of signs (1 Thess. 5:3) while emphasizing (a) our incapacity to predict the time and (b) the importance of having our spiritual lives in order. And 2 Thessalonians acknowledges suddenness, for it never suggests a specific timetable: instead the signs serve to heighten the suddenness of His coming. In His end-time discourses (Matt. 24; Mark 13) Jesus Himself teaches both signs and suddenness, but He emphasizes a call to live lives of faithful stewardship (Matt. 24:45–51) and constant vigilance (Mark 13:34–37).

OUTLINE

Greeting

1 Paul, Silvanus, and Timothy,

To the church of the Thessalonians in God our Father and the Lord Jesus Christ:

2 [a]Grace to you and peace from God our Father and the Lord Jesus Christ.

The Present Persecution

3 We are bound to thank God always for you, brethren, as it is fitting, because your faith grows exceedingly, and the love of every one
of you all abounds toward each
other,†

4 so that [a]we ourselves boast of
you among the churches of God
[b]for your patience and faith [c]in all
your persecutions and [1]tribulations
that you endure,

5 *which is* [a]manifest[1] evidence of
the righteous judgment of God, that
you may be counted worthy of the
kingdom of God, [b]for which you also
suffer;

6 [a]since *it is* a righteous thing
with God to repay with [1]tribulation
those who trouble you,

7 and to *give* you who are troubled
[a]rest with us when [b]the Lord Jesus
is revealed from heaven with His
mighty angels,

8 in flaming fire taking vengeance
on those who do not know God, and
on those who do not obey the gospel
of our Lord Jesus Christ.

CHAPTER 1
2 [a]1 Cor. 1:3
4 [a]2 Cor. 7:4; [1 Thess. 2:19] [b]1 Thess. 1:3 [c]1 Thess. 2:14 [1]*afflictions*
5 [a]Phil. 1:28 [b]1 Thess. 2:14 [1]*plain*
6 [a]Rev. 6:10 [1]*affliction*
7 [a]Rev. 14:13 [b][1 Thess. 4:16]; Jude 14

1:3–10 This passage on God's judgment teaches (1) suffering is redemptive for the Christian (v. 5); (2) God promises to return tribulation to our enemies (vv. 6, 8); (3) punishment of the wicked is everlasting (v. 9); and (4) God's glory will be displayed in His saints (v. 10), for as Christ was transfigured, so will be His faithful (see Matt. 13:43; Col. 3:4).

Why does God reveal His dread judgment and His glory to us? To help us toward righteousness. Chrysostom comments on this passage: "If the fear of an earthly king withdraws us from so many evils, how much more the fear of the King Eternal!" How we bear up under unjust persecution now is **manifest evidence** (v. 5) of how we will stand at the final judgment.

9 [a]These shall be punished with
everlasting destruction from the
presence of the Lord and [b]from the
glory of His power,
10 when He comes, in that Day,
[a]to be [b]glorified in His saints and to
be admired among all those who
[1]believe, because our testimony
among you was believed.
11 Therefore we also pray always
for you that our God would [a]count
you worthy of *this* calling, and fulfill
all the good pleasure of *His* goodness
and [b]the work of faith with power,†
12 [a]that the name of our Lord Jesus
Christ may be glorified in you, and
you in Him, according to the grace
of our God and the Lord Jesus
Christ.

False Teaching on the Second Coming

2 Now, brethren, [a]concerning the
coming of our Lord Jesus Christ
[b]and our gathering together to Him,
we ask you,
2 [a]not to be soon shaken in mind
or troubled, either by spirit or by
word or by letter, as if from us, as
though the day of [1]Christ had come.

True Tradition on the Second Coming

3 Let no one deceive you by any
means; for *that Day will not come*
[a]unless the falling away comes first,
and [b]the man of [1]sin is revealed,
[c]the son of perdition,†
4 who opposes and [a]exalts himself [b]above all that is called God or
that is worshiped, so that he sits
[1]as God in the temple of God, showing himself that he is God.
5 Do you not remember that
when I was still with you I told you
these things?
6 And now you know what is restraining, that he may be revealed
in his own time.
7 For [a]the [1]mystery of lawlessness
is already at work; only [2]He who
now restrains *will do so* until [2]He is
taken out of the way.
8 And then the lawless one will
be revealed, [a]whom the Lord will
consume [b]with the breath of His
mouth and destroy [c]with the brightness of His coming.
9 The coming of the *lawless one* is
[a]according to the working of Satan,
with all power, [b]signs, and lying
wonders,
10 and with all unrighteous deception among [a]those who perish, because they did not receive [b]the love
of the truth, that they might be
saved.
11 And [a]for this reason God will
send them strong delusion, [b]that
they should believe the lie,
12 that they all may be condemned
who did not believe the truth but
[a]had pleasure in unrighteousness.

Stand Fast in the Faith

13 But we are [1]bound to give
thanks to God always for you, brethren beloved by the Lord, because
God [a]from the beginning [b]chose you
for salvation [c]through [2]sanctifica-

9 [a]Phil. 3:19 [b]Deut. 33:2
10 [a]Matt. 25:31 [b]John 17:10 [1]NU, M *have believed*
11 [a]Col. 1:12 [b]1 Thess. 1:3
12 [a][Col. 3:17]

CHAPTER 2

1 [a][1 Thess. 4:15–17] [b]Matt. 24:31
2 [a]Matt. 24:4 [1]NU *the Lord*
3 [a]1 Tim. 4:1 [b]Dan. 7:25; 8:25; 11:36 [c]John 17:12 [1]NU *lawlessness*
4 [a]Is. 14:13, 14 [b]1 Cor. 8:5 [1]NU omits *as God*
7 [a]1 John 2:18 [1]*hidden truth* [2]Or *he*
8 [a]Dan. 7:10 [b]Is. 11:4 [c]Heb. 10:27
9 [a]John 8:41 [b]Deut. 13:1
10 [a]2 Cor. 2:15 [b]1 Cor. 16:22
11 [a]Rom. 1:28 [b]1 Tim. 4:1
12 [a]Rom. 1:32
13 [a]Eph. 1:4 [b]1 Thess. 1:4 [c][1 Pet. 1:2] [1]*under obligation* [2]*being set apart by*

1:11, 12 Some say Paul and James contradict each other, but here is the essence of James 2. Paul teaches that God's **calling** and the **work of faith** are a unity through our cooperation with God's power.

2:3–12 While we are warned against predicting the Day of the Lord (Matt. 24:36; Acts 1:7; 1 Thess. 5:1), there will be signs preceding His Coming. Paul instructs the Thessalonians concerning two such signs: (1) a general **falling away** (v. 3; apostasy) from Christ and the Church and (2) the revealing of **the man of sin, the son of perdition** (v. 3), who is the Antichrist of 1 and 2 John, similar to the Dragon and the Beast of Rev. 13. This lawless one is described in the OT (Dan. 7:25; 8:25; 11:36), mentioned by Christ (Matt. 24:15), and discussed by Paul on his first visit to Thessalonica (v. 5). The devil incites divisions among people so they will readily receive the Antichrist when he comes. The man of sin is a counterfeit messiah with a counterfeit kingdom. He (1) exalts himself above God (v. 4), (2) performs *(continued on next page)*

tion by the Spirit and belief in the
truth,
14 to which He called you by our
gospel, for [a]the obtaining of the
glory of our Lord Jesus Christ.
15 Therefore, brethren, [a]stand fast
and hold [b]the traditions which you
were taught, whether by word or our
[1]epistle.†
16 Now may our Lord Jesus Christ
Himself, and our God and Father,
[a]who has loved us and given *us* everlasting consolation and [b]good hope
by grace,
17 comfort your hearts [a]and [1]estab-
lish you in every good word and
work.

Pray for Us

3 Finally, brethren, [a]pray for us,
that the word of the Lord may
run *swiftly* and be glorified, just as
it is with you,
2 and [a]that we may be delivered
from unreasonable and wicked men;
[b]for not all have faith.
3 But [a]the Lord is faithful, who
will establish you and [b]guard *you*
from the evil one.
4 And [a]we have confidence in the
Lord concerning you, both that you
do and will do the things we command you.
5 Now may [a]the Lord direct your
hearts into the love of God and into
the patience of Christ.

Be Industrious

6 But we command you, brethren,
in the name of our Lord Jesus Christ,
[a]that you withdraw [b]from every
brother who walks [c]disorderly and
not according to the tradition which
[1]he received from us.†
7 For you yourselves know how
you ought to follow us, for we were
not disorderly among you;
8 nor did we eat anyone's bread
[1]free of charge, but worked with
[a]labor and toil night and day, that
we might not be a burden to any of
you,
9 not because we do not have
[a]authority, but to make ourselves an
example of how you should follow
us.
10 For even when we were with
you, we commanded you this: If
anyone will not work, neither shall
he eat.
11 For we hear that there are some
who walk among you in a disorderly
manner, not working at all, but are
[a]busybodies.
12 Now those who are such we
command and [1]exhort through our
Lord Jesus Christ [a]that they work in
quietness and eat their own bread.
13 But *as for* you, brethren, [a]do not
grow weary *in* doing good.†

Preserve Unity

14 And if anyone does not obey
our word in this [1]epistle, note that

14 [a]1 Pet. 5:10
15 [a]1 Cor. 16:13 [b]1 Cor. 11:2 [1]*letter*
16 [a][Rev. 1:5] [b]1 Pet. 1:3
17 [a]1 Cor. 1:8 [1]*strengthen*

CHAPTER 3
1 [a]Eph. 6:19
2 [a]Rom. 15:31 [b]Acts 28:24
3 [a]1 Cor. 1:9 [b]John 17:15
4 [a]2 Cor. 7:16
5 [a]1 Chr. 29:18
6 [a]Rom. 16:17 [b]1 Cor. 5:1 [c]1 Thess. 4:11 [1]NU, M *they*
8 [a]1 Thess. 2:9 [1]Lit. *for nothing*
9 [a]1 Cor. 9:4, 6–14
11 [a]1 Pet. 4:15
12 [a]Eph. 4:28 [1]*encourage*
13 [a]Gal. 6:9
14 [1]*letter*

(continued from previous page)
deceptive miracles and wonders through satanic power (v. 9), (3) will fool the unrighteous into following him (vv. 10–12) and (4) will be removed from power by Christ Himself at His Second Coming (v. 8).

Paul instructs that when the world gets worse Christians must not be distressed or be deceived (vv. 11, 12) but rather persevere as good stewards (vv. 13–17).

2:15; 3:6 In the NT we read of two types off **traditions:** (1) *The tradition of men* (Matt. 15:1–9; Col. 2:8) is soundly condemned. Jesus (quoting Is. 29:13) describes this as "teaching as doctrines the commandments of men" (Matt. 15:9). (2) *The tradition of the apostles* or "Holy Tradition," by contrast, is to be preserved by the Church, for God is its source. Holy Tradition is that which Jesus taught to the apostles, and which they, in turn, taught the Church under the inspiration of the Holy Spirit in (a) their instructions as they visited the churches and (b) their writings. Under the guidance of the Holy Spirit we adhere to Holy Tradition as it is present in the apostles' writings and as it is resident in the Church to which the truth is promised (John 16:13).

3:6 See 2:15.

3:13 Here is a warning filled with great wisdom. While sin is burdensome, we can also grow tired and fatigued by **doing good.** Paul, as our spiritual director, cautions us not to cease or tire of good works.

person and [a]do not keep company
with him, that he may be ashamed.
15 [a]Yet do not count *him* as an enemy, [b]but [1]admonish *him* as a
brother.

Benediction

16 Now may [a]the Lord of peace
Himself give you peace always in
every way. The Lord *be* with you
all.
17 [a]The salutation of Paul with my
own hand, which is a sign in every
[1]epistle; so I write.†
18 [a]The grace of our Lord Jesus
Christ *be* with you all. Amen.

14 [a]Matt. 18:17
15 [a]Lev. 19:17 [b]Titus 3:10 [1]*warn*
16 [a]Rom. 15:33
17 [a]1 Cor. 16:21 [1]*letter*
18 [a]Rom. 16:20, 24

3:17 Paul's authorship is emphasized here because of the fraudulent letters mentioned in 2:2.

The First Epistle of Paul the Apostle to

TIMOTHY

Author: *St. Paul the Apostle*

Date: *Probably* A.D. *64–65*

Theme: *Pastoral Care of the Faithful*

AUTHOR: St. Ignatius, St. Polycarp, Tertullian and St. Clement of Alexandria are among the early Church writers who speak of St. Paul's authorship of this epistle.

DATE: The Pastoral Epistles, 1 and 2 Timothy and Titus, appear to have been written after the events of Acts 28. If so, 1 Timothy was written in A.D. 64–65, before Paul's second imprisonment in Rome, perhaps from Macedonia (1:3).

MAJOR THEME: *Pastoral care of the faithful*. The Church is to manifest the Kingdom of God on earth. Therefore, the government of the Church is integrally connected with both apostolic doctrine (1:1–20; 3:14—4:5) and worship (2:1–15).

Subthemes include: (1) the role of the clergy, (2) combatting heresy, (3) care for women, widows, and slaves, and (4) money and the ministry.

BACKGROUND INFORMATION: (1) *A Pastoral epistle*. First Timothy is both personal and pastoral. Whereas most of Paul's letters are addressed to the church in a particular location, the Pastoral Epistles are written to instruct specific leaders—in this case Timothy, Bishop of Ephesus. Paul speaks as an experienced mentor instructing his student, his "son," in his role as apostle and bishop.

(2) *Historical setting*. After his release from house arrest in Rome, Paul apparently fulfilled his dream of going to Spain and preaching there (Rom. 15:28). St. Clement of Rome, the *Muratorian Canon*, St. John Chrysostom, and Church historian Eusebius all write of such a trip. Upon his return to Rome he traveled to Crete (Titus 1:5), Asia (Ephesus, Titus 1:3), Macedonia (Nicopolis, Titus 3:12), and then back to Rome again as a prisoner, passing through Corinth (in Achaia) and Miletus (in Asia, 2 Tim. 4:20).

In Ephesus, where Paul had left Timothy as bishop or overseer, some church members were promoting a variety of theological opinions—from the irrelevant to the dangerously heretical (1:3–7; 4:1, 2, 7; 6:3–5). Paul found it necessary to excommunicate a couple of the speculators (1:19, 20). The church was also dealing with external pressures: from the Hellenistic mystery religions, which made much misuse of the terms "salvation" and "savior"; and from the cult of emperor worship, according to which Caesar is "lord."

(3) *Purpose of the letter.* Paul writes to guide Timothy as he encounters pastoral challenges and questions.

(a) Paul opposes false doctrine with the apostolic doctrine, showing that (1) the true spirit of Jewish law is love, not legalism (1:5–11); (2) ascetic practices are for the sanctification of the physical world, not its denial (4:4, 5); (3) the world is not inherently evil (it is sin that is evil) but good, for God created the world (6:13); (4) salvation is not by knowledge, attainable only by a few self-purified intellectuals, but by faith, which calls people out of their sinful condition (1:15; 2:3–6); (5) Jesus Christ is at once fully God and fully man (2:5, 6), sharing fully our humanity (3:16; 6:13).

(b) Paul opposes false leaders by upholding godly apostolic leaders (1:12–20; 3:1–16), especially Timothy, who had long been one of Paul's chosen missionaries. (Timothy is mentioned as accompanying Paul on his second missionary journey, in 1 Thess. 3:1, 2; late in his third journey, in 1 Cor. 4:17; 16:10; and late in his first Roman captivity, in Phil. 2:19–22.)

(c) Paul sets up administrative guidelines for the Church, but makes it clear there must be no enmity between the Church as structure (the institutional element) and the Church energized by the Spirit (the charismatic element).

(d) Paul encourages Timothy to overcome his apprehensions concerning his pastoral abilities (1:18–20; 4:6–11; 6:11–16, 20, 21; see 1 Cor. 16:10, 11), his youth (4:12), and his stomach ailments (5:23).

(4) *Spiritual direction.* The Pastoral Epistles hold incomparable insight into the historical workings of the early Church as guided by the Holy Spirit, and are a foundational source for pastoral theology, for clergy and their relationship to the Church.

(5) *Church government in the Pastorals.* Paul uses *episkopos* (Gr.; translated "bishop") synonymously with *presbyteros* (Gr.; translated "presbyter," "elder" or "priest"). Timothy and Titus have extraordinary assignments. They are responsible for several communities (Titus 1:5); they take part with the presbytery in ordinations (5:22) and bring unity to the presbyters (5:17–22). The original apostles soon will face death and are passing on their apostolic authority to a new generation of Church leaders. Not only are different types of ministry, or clerical orders, firmly established in 1 Timothy, but written creeds and specific liturgical practices are apparent as well.

OUTLINE

Greeting — 1:1, 2

I. Faithful ministry in doctrine and worship — 1:3—2:15
   - A. Faithful doctrine — 1:3–20
     1. Opposes false doctrine — 1:3, 4
     2. Opposes false conduct — 1:5–17
        - a. Use of the law without grace — 1:5–11
        - b. Paul's example: Triumph of grace over law — 1:12–17

3. Strengthens Timothy's apostolic commission 1:18–20
B. Faithful worship 2:1–15
1. Includes liturgical prayer 2:1–7
2. Requires godly living 2:8–15
II. Faithful ministry in conduct and care 3:1—6:19
A. Faithful clergy 3:1–16
1. Moral and spiritual requirements 3:1–13
2. Doctrinal requirement: An early creed 3:14–16
B. Faithful care 4:1—6:19
1. Over spiritual life 4:1–16
a. Replacing false asceticism with true spirituality 4:1–11
b. The overseer and his ministry 4:12–16
2. Directives for specific groups 5:1–25
3. The problem of money 6:1–19
a. Insubordinate Christian slaves 6:1, 2
b. Prideful teachers advocating greed 6:3–10
c. The solution to greed: Pursue godliness 6:11–16
d. A warning: Beware of riches 6:17–19
Conclusion: Keep the tradition! 6:20, 21

Greeting

1 Paul, an apostle of Jesus Christ,
by the commandment of God
our Savior and the Lord Jesus Christ,
our hope,†
2 To Timothy, a [a]true son in the
faith:

[b]Grace, mercy, *and* peace from
God our Father and Jesus Christ our
Lord.

Opposing Speculations with Faith

3 As I urged you [a]when I went
into Macedonia—remain in Ephesus
that you may [1]charge some [b]that
they teach no other doctrine,
4 [a]nor give heed to fables and
endless genealogies, which cause
disputes rather than godly edification which is in faith.†
5 Now [a]the purpose of the commandment is love [b]from a pure
heart, *from* a good conscience, and
from [1]sincere faith,

Opposing Legalism with Grace

6 from which some, having
strayed, have turned aside to [a]idle
talk,
7 desiring to be teachers of the
law, understanding neither what

CHAPTER 1
2 [a]Acts 16:1, 2; Rom. 1:7; 2 Tim. 1:2; Titus 1:4 [b]Gal. 1:3
3 [a]Acts 20:1, 3 [b]Rom. 16:17; 2 Cor. 11:4; Gal. 1:6, 7; 1 Tim. 6:3 [1]*command*
4 [a]1 Tim. 6:3, 4, 20; Titus 1:14
5 [a]Rom. 13:8–10; Gal. 5:14 [b]Eph. 6:24 [1]Lit. *unhypocritical*
6 [a]1 Tim. 6:4, 20

1:1, 2 Like all of Paul's epistles, 1 Timothy begins with the traditional Greco-Roman format of greeting (see note on 1 Thess. 1:1)—but in this case it is addressed not to a church, but to a **true son in the faith,** Timothy. (The disciple of a rabbi was called his "son.") This relationship supports Paul's title of "father" (1 Cor. 4:15) and, by application, the use of "Father" for priests.

God the Father is called **Savior** (see 2:3; 4:10; Titus 1:3; 2:10; 3:4), for every work of the Trinity is the work of all three Persons, in which each Person participates.

1:4 Paul's faithful flock is plagued by Jewish **fables and endless genealogies,** energetic disputation over myth and human tradition for argument's sake. St. John Chrysostom states, "The Jews wasted their whole course on these unprofitable points [for] historical knowledge and research."

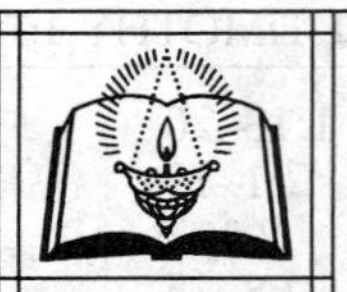

THE FOUR "ORDERS" IN CHURCH GOVERNMENT

An ancient visitor to modern Christendom would be shocked to find that factions have pulled away from Apostolic Christianity not just over doctrinal matters but even over the issue of how the Church is governed. Thus, in quite a recent development, some religious bodies call themselves *congregational* (ruled by the people), others are *presbyterian* (ruled by the elders), still others are *episcopal* (ruled by the bishops).

The New Testament teaches that all four "orders" which form the government of the Church—laity, deacons, presbyters, and bishops—are necessary to the proper functioning of the body of Christ. All four are clearly visible in Paul's first letter to Timothy.

(1) *The laity* are also called "saints" (Rom. 1:7; 2 Cor. 1:1; 1 Tim. 5:10), the "faithful" (Eph. 1:1), and "brethren" (Col. 1:2). The laity (Gr. *laos*) are all the people of God, the "priesthood" (1 Pet. 2:4–10). Technically "laity" includes clergy, though in our day the word usually refers to those in the Church who are not ordained. It is from among the laity that the other three orders emerge.

(2) *The deacons,* literally "servants," are ordained to serve the Church and must meet high qualifications (1 Tim. 3:8–13). The Apostles were the first to take on the service tasks of deacons, and when the workload became too great they called for "seven men of good reputation, full of the Holy Spirit and wisdom, whom we may appoint over this business" (Acts 6:3). Besides serving the material needs of the people, deacons occupy a crucial role in the liturgical life of the Church.

(3) *The presbyters,* or elders, are visible throughout the New Testament. Their ministry from the start was to "rule," "labor in the word" and teach true "doctrine" (1 Tim. 5:17) in the local congregation. Paul "appointed elders in every church" (Acts 14:23) and later instructed his apostolic apprentice, Titus, to do the same in Crete (Titus 1:5). From the word "presbyter" came the shorter form "prest," which was used in the early Church and finally became "priest." In no way is the ordained Christian priesthood seen as a throwback to or a reenacting of the Old Testament priesthood. Rather, joined to Christ who is our High Priest "according to the order of Melchizedek" (Heb. 5:6, 10), the Orthodox priest is likewise a minister of a New Covenant which supersedes the old.

(4) *The bishop* is the "overseer" of the congregation and clergy in a given area. Often the terms "bishop" and "elder" are interchangeable in the New Testament (Acts 20:17, 28), with the bishop being the leader of the elders. The qualifications for bishop listed in 1 Timothy 3:1–7 and Titus 1:7–9 underscore this role. Nonetheless, "bishop" is a specific office both in the New Testament and in the early Church. The Twelve were the first to hold this office (in Acts 1:20 "office" is literally translated "bishopric") and they in turn consecrated other bishops to follow them. For example, Timothy and Titus are clearly of a separate order from that of elder (see 1 Tim. 5:17–22; Titus 1:5). Early records show James was bishop of Jerusalem by A.D. 49 and functioned accordingly at the first council there (Acts 15:13–22). Peter is on record as the first bishop of Antioch prior to A.D. 53, and later first bishop of Rome, where he was martyred about A.D. 65.

Perhaps the strongest early reference outside the New Testament to the presence of the four orders in Church government occurs in the writings of Ignatius, bishop of Antioch from A.D. 67–107, the very heart of the New Testament era. To the church at Philadelphia (see Rev. 3:7–13) he writes of "Christians [*laity*] at one with the *bishop* and the *presbyters* and the *deacons* . . ." (Ign. Phil., salutation; italics added).

In the Orthodox Church, authority is resident in all four orders, with the bishop providing the center of unity. His authority is not over the Church but within the Church. He is an icon of Jesus Christ, "the Shepherd and Overseer [literally, "Bishop"] of your souls" (1 Pet. 2:25). Church leadership is not one or more of the orders functioning without the others. Rather the Church, with Christ as Head, is conducted like a symphony orchestra, a family, the body of Christ, where all the members in their given offices work together as the dwelling place of the Holy Trinity.

Commemoration of a Monk Martyr

1:8–18: Christ can redeem even the worst of sinners to become His faithful servants.

they say nor the things which they
affirm.†
8 But we know that the law *is*
[a]good if one uses it lawfully,†
9 knowing this: that the law is not
made for a righteous person, but for
the lawless and insubordinate, for *the*
ungodly and for sinners, for *the* unholy and profane, for murderers of
fathers and murderers of mothers,
for manslayers,
10 for fornicators, for sodomites,
for kidnappers, for liars, for perjur-
ers, and if there is any other thing
that is [1]contrary to sound doctrine,
11 according to the glorious gospel
of the [a]blessed God which was
[b]committed to my trust.

Paul's Example: Salvation by Grace

12 And I thank Christ Jesus our
Lord who has [a]enabled me, [b]because
He counted me faithful, [c]putting *me*
into the ministry,†
13 although [a]I was formerly a blasphemer, a persecutor, and an [1]in-
solent man; but I obtained mercy
because [b]I did *it* ignorantly in unbelief.
14 [a]And the grace of our Lord was
exceedingly abundant, [b]with faith
and love which are in Christ Jesus.
15 [a]This *is* a faithful saying and
worthy of all acceptance, that [b]Christ
Jesus came into the world to save
sinners, of whom I am chief.†
16 However, for this reason I obtained mercy, that in me first Jesus
Christ might show all longsuffering,
as a pattern to those who are going
to believe on Him for everlasting life.
17 Now to [a]the King eternal, [b]im-
mortal, [c]invisible, to [1]God [d]who
alone is wise, [e]*be* honor and glory
forever and ever. Amen.

Timothy Called to Faithfulness

18 This [1]charge I commit to you,
son Timothy, according to the
prophecies previously made concerning you, that by them you may
wage the good warfare,
19 having faith and a good conscience, which some having rejected,
concerning the faith have suffered
shipwreck,
20 of whom are [a]Hymenaeus and
[b]Alexander, whom I delivered to
Satan that they may learn not to
[c]blaspheme.†

Faithfulness in Prayer

2 Therefore I [1]exhort first of all that
supplications, prayers, interces-

8 [a]Rom. 7:12, 16
10 [1]*opposed*
11 [a]1 Tim. 6:15 [b]1 Cor. 9:17
12 [a]1 Cor. 15:10 [b]1 Cor. 7:25 [c]Col. 1:25
13 [a]Acts 8:3 [b]John 4:21 [1]*violently arrogant*
14 [a]Rom. 5:20 [b]2 Tim. 1:13; 2:22
15 [a]2 Tim. 2:11 [b]Matt. 1:21; 9:13
17 [a]Ps. 10:16 [b]Rom. 1:23 [c]Heb. 11:27 [d]Rom. 16:27 [e]1 Chr. 29:11 [1]NU *the only God,*
18 [1]*command*
20 [a]2 Tim. 2:17, 18 [b]2 Tim. 4:14 [c]Acts 13:45
CHAPTER 2
1 [1]*encourage*

1:7 The law is the Old Covenant Mosaic Law, not the commandments of Christ in the Gospels or the canons of the Church.

1:8 The law is good because God gave it (Rom. 7:16). It was (1) a schoolmaster for God's chosen people, to confront and control their sin until the Incarnation of His Son fulfilled the law; and (2) a guide to lead all people to Christ.

1:12–17 Paul, as a former rebel toward God and persecutor of the Church (Acts 9:1–3, "Saul"), gives glory to God for his calling as an apostle. Throughout the OT, NT and Church history, the greatest sinners have often become most notable saints: for instance, Moses, Rahab, David, Photini (the Samaritan woman at the well), Matthew, Paul, and St. Mary of Egypt (a notorious harlot before her conversion).

1:15 This verse is used in Orthodox liturgical prayer and is said by all approaching the chalice for Holy Communion.

1:20 Paul is an example of those who receive God's grace. Here are two men who rejected this grace and stand as a warning to all.

sions, *and* giving of thanks be made
for all men,†
2 [a]for kings and [b]all who are in
[1]authority, that we may lead a quiet
and peaceable life in all godliness
and [2]reverence.
3 For this *is* [a]good and acceptable
in the sight [b]of God our Savior,†
4 [a]who desires all men to be
saved [b]and to come to the knowledge of the truth.
5 [a]For *there is* one God and
[b]one Mediator between God and
men, *the* Man Christ Jesus,†
6 [a]who gave Himself a ransom for
all, to be testified in due time,†
7 [a]for which I was appointed a
preacher and an apostle—I am
speaking the truth [1]in Christ *and* not
lying—[b]a teacher of the Gentiles in
faith and truth.

Faithful Lives Fitting for Prayer

8 I desire therefore that the men
pray [a]everywhere, [b]lifting up holy
hands, without wrath and doubting;†
9 in like manner also, that the
[a]women adorn themselves in modest apparel, with propriety and
[1]moderation, not with braided hair
or gold or pearls or costly clothing,
10 [a]but, which is proper for
women professing godliness, with
good works.
11 Let a woman learn in silence
with all submission.
12 And [a]I do not permit a
woman to teach or to have authority over a man, but to be in
silence.†
13 For Adam was formed first,
then Eve.
14 And Adam was not deceived,
but the woman being deceived, fell
into transgression.
15 Nevertheless she will be saved
in childbearing if they continue in
faith, love, and holiness, with self-
control.†

2 [a]Ezra 6:10 [b][Rom. 13:1] [1]*a prominent place* [2]*dignity*
3 [a]Rom. 12:2 [b]2 Tim. 1:9
4 [a]Ezek. 18:23, 32 [b][John 17:3]
5 [a]Gal. 3:20 [b][Heb. 9:15]
6 [a]Mark 10:45
7 [a]Eph. 3:7, 8 [b][Gal. 1:15, 16] [1]NU omits *in Christ*
8 [a]Luke 23:34 [b]Ps. 134:2
9 [a]1 Pet. 3:3 [1]*discretion*
10 [a]1 Pet. 3:4
12 [a]1 Cor. 14:34

2:1, 2 Intercessory prayers are to be offered for all without partiality, but special attention is given to prayer for those **in authority.** Thus, Orthodox Christians repeatedly pray for "all civil authorities."

2:3–5 The religions of the Greek world were pluralistic and elite. In contrast, Paul teaches that there is one **Savior** (v. 3), **one God and one Mediator** (v. 5). This God offers salvation equally to all, for He created us to share in His goodness; for this end He became a **Man** like us.

2:5 Some who are opposed to the established Church have used this verse to claim that all you need is Jesus—not the church, her clergy, or her sacraments. But the Son became the **one Mediator** by becoming **Man** through the Holy Spirit and a virgin—that is, through **God and men.** He "built" His humanity not from Himself alone but from another, the Virgin Mary. Likewise, as the *Mediator* He says, "I will build My church" (Matt. 16:18); He establishes her leaders and her worship. As Mary gives us Christ in His humanity, the Church introduces us to Him, who alone is our *Mediator*.

2:6 In the context of ancient slavery, a **ransom** was paid not so much to purchase a slave as it was to free him from his bondage to experience liberty.

2:8 Prayer must be united with quiet and godly behavior. Does this contradict Christ's command to pray secretly, not to be seen by men (Matt. 6:5, 6)? No. That warning is against spiritual showmanship, not against congregational prayer. The secret "room" (Matt. 6:6) is a person's innermost being; so praying secretly is perfectly consistent with praying **everywhere.** In contrast to the Jewish emphasis upon one primary earthly place for prayer (the temple in Jerusalem), Christians can experience the fullness of prayer wherever they may be.

2:12 The Church's greatest Saint is a woman, the Virgin Mary, Mother of God. Some women, including Mary Magdalene, are called "equal to the Apostles," while others serve as deacons (Rom. 16:1). While sharing full equality in Christ, women are not ordained to the offices of bishop and presbyter in the Orthodox Church.

2:15 This verse does not imply that a woman must have children in order to be saved. If salvation is comprehensive, involving all of one's life, then women who do have children are **saved,** in part, by motherhood, *if* they persevere in godliness. Our God-given role in life is the place of our salvation.

Qualifications for Bishops

3 This *is* a faithful saying: If a man desires the position of a [1]bishop, he desires a good work.†

2 A bishop then must be blameless, the husband of one wife, temperate, sober-minded, of good behavior, hospitable, able to teach;†

3 not [1]given to wine, not violent, [2]not greedy for money, but gentle, not quarrelsome, not [3]covetous;

4 one who rules his own house well, having *his* children in submission with all reverence

5 (for if a man does not know how to rule his own house, how will he take care of the church of God?);

6 not a [1]novice, lest being puffed up with pride he fall into the *same* condemnation as the devil.

7 Moreover he must have a good testimony among those who are outside, lest he fall into reproach and the [a]snare of the devil.

Qualifications for Deacons

8 Likewise deacons *must be* reverent, not double-tongued, [a]not given to much wine, not greedy for money,†

9 holding the [1]mystery of the faith with a pure conscience.

10 But let these also first be tested; then let them serve as deacons, being *found* blameless.

11 Likewise, *their* wives *must be* reverent, not [1]slanderers, temperate, faithful in all things.†

12 Let deacons be the husbands of one wife, ruling *their* children and their own houses well.

13 For those who have served well as deacons [a]obtain for themselves a good standing and great boldness in the faith which is in Christ Jesus.

The Guide for Faithfulness: An Early Creed

14 These things I write to you, though I hope to come to you shortly;

15 but if I am delayed, *I write* so that you may know how you ought to conduct yourself in the house of God, which is the church of the living God, the pillar and [1]ground of the truth.†

16 And without controversy great is the [1]mystery of godliness:

[a]God[2] was manifested in the flesh,
[b]Justified in the Spirit,
[c]Seen by angels,
[d]Preached among the Gentiles,
[e]Believed on in the world,
[f]Received up in glory.†

False Teachers, False Rules

4 Now the Spirit [1]expressly says that in latter times some will depart from the faith, giving heed [a]to deceiving spirits and doctrines of demons,

2 [a]speaking lies in hypocrisy,

CHAPTER 3
1 [1]Lit. *overseer*
3 [1]*addicted* [2]NU omits *not greedy for money* [3]*loving money*
6 [1]*new convert*
7 [a]1 Tim. 6:9; 2 Tim. 2:26
8 [a]Ezek. 44:21
9 [1]*hidden truth*
11 [1]*malicious gossips*
13 [a]Matt. 25:21
15 [1]*foundation, mainstay*
16 [a][John 1:14; 1 Pet. 1:20; 1 John 1:2; 3:5, 8] [b][Matt. 3:16; Rom. 1:4] [c]Matt. 28:2 [d]Acts 10:34; Rom. 10:18 [e]Rom. 16:26; 2 Cor. 1:19; Col. 1:6, 23 [f]Luke 24:51 [1]*hidden truth* [2]NU *Who*

CHAPTER 4
1 [a]2 Tim. 3:13; Rev. 16:14 [1]*explicitly*
2 [a]Matt. 7:15

3:1 Bishop (Gr. *episkopos*) means "overseer," an elder (4:14; 5:17). Later in the first century *bishop* came to designate a presiding elder.

3:2 St. John Chrysostom on **blameless:** "Every virtue is implied in this word. [The bishop's] life should be unspotted so that all should look up to him, and make his life the model of their own." In the early Church, a bishop could be married. Today married men may be ordained to the Orthodox priesthood. The Sixth Ecumenical Council (A.D.681) sanctioned celibacy for bishops, but only as a special dispensation.

3:8 For qualifications for the first **deacons,** see Acts 6:1–6.

3:11 Wives could be translated "women," referring to deaconesses.

3:15 While the Scriptures are the inspired truth of God in human words (2 Tim. 3:15–17), the Church is **the pillar and ground** of that truth.

3:16 Paul quotes an ancient Christian creed or hymn which is especially clear about the divinity of Jesus Christ. Another such creed is found in 2 Tim. 2:11–13. (See also 6:15, 16; Eph. 1:3–14; 5:14; Phil. 2:6–11; Col. 1:15–20.) Thus, when the early councils met and issued creeds, they were well within the bounds of biblical precedent.

Zacchaeus Sunday *Fifth Sunday before Lent*

4:9–15: Zacchaeus repented and acted upon that repentance—as should we.

having their own conscience [b]seared
with a hot iron,†
3 forbidding to marry, *and commanding*
to abstain from foods which
God created to be received with
thanksgiving by those who believe
and know the truth.†

Orthodox Doctrine, Orthodox Spirituality

4 For every creature of God *is*
good, and nothing is to be refused
if it is received with thanksgiving;
5 for it is [1]sanctified by the word
of God and prayer.†
6 If you instruct the brethren in
these things, you will be a good minister
of Jesus Christ, [a]nourished in
the words of faith and of the good
doctrine which you have carefully
followed.
7 But [a]reject profane and old
wives' fables, and [b]exercise yourself
toward godliness.†
8 For [a]bodily exercise profits a little,
but godliness is profitable for all
things, [b]having promise of the life
that now is and of that which is to
come.
9 This *is* a faithful saying and worthy
of all acceptance.
10 For to this *end* [1]we both labor
and suffer reproach, because we
trust in the living God, [a]who is *the*
Savior of all men, especially of those
who believe.
11 These things command and
teach.

Self-Discipline in Ministry

12 Let no one [1]despise your youth,
but be an [a]example to the believers
in word, in conduct, in love, [2]in
spirit, in faith, in purity.
13 Till I come, give attention to
reading, to exhortation, to [1]doctrine.†
14 [a]Do not neglect the gift that is
in you, which was given to you by

2 [b]Eph. 4:19
5 [1]*set apart*
6 [a]2 Tim. 3:14
7 [a]2 Tim. 2:16; Titus 1:14 [b]Heb. 5:14
8 [a]1 Cor. 8:8 [b]Ps. 37:9
10 [a]Ps. 36:6 [1]NU *we labor and strive,*
12 [a]Phil. 3:17; Titus 2:7; 1 Pet. 5:3 [1]*look down on your youthfulness* [2]NU omits *in spirit*
13 [1]*teaching*
14 [a]2 Tim. 1:6

4:2 A **conscience seared with a hot iron** describes the reality that repeated willful sin blunts our sensitivity to good and evil. This is a grim warning to all Christians to reject evil in all forms and thereby maintain a softness of heart toward God.

4:3–5 Whereas sexual abstinence and fasting can be important aids to spiritual discipline, neither marriage nor any particular food is forbidden to Christians. We control our passions not because the material world is evil, but because we are corrupt and tend to sin. Sex and food are not unclean, but willful disobedience, an unthankful disposition, and uncontrolled desires are. The Church is here to bring the whole world back to God.

4:5, 6 The **word** (Gr. *logos*) **of God** is the Son (John 1:1; Heb. 4:12; 1 Pet. 1:23; 1 John 1:1; Rev. 19:13). A "word of God" in the NT can refer to a blessing using God's name, God's creative will (2 Pet. 3:5, 7), the OT (Mark 7:9–13), the gospel itself (Acts 4:31; 6:7; 13:5, 26; 15:7, 36; 1 Thess. 2:13), or a special message from God. Sometimes it is difficult to tell whether "word" means Christ Himself or words about Him (Col. 1:25). To spread the word of God is to bring Christ Himself to others. **Words of faith** (v. 6) means speech consonant with the gospel. **Doctrine,** or teaching, is the content of the gospel. Thus, the rich and manifold speech concerning salvation deepens our communion with Christ, the Word of God. He is the reason these words are vital and powerful. Using words without the Word is vain.

4:7, 8 Paul is no stranger to physical **exercise** and its benefits (see 1 Cor. 9:24–27), but he prefers spiritual exercise, for it leads to life eternal.

4:13 Reading, whether personal reading or the public reading of Scripture during worship, is tied to **exhortation** (preaching) and **doctrine** (teaching). The early Christians had a liturgical worship structure—including the reading of Scripture and a homily—the roots of which were in the synagogue.

prophecy [b]with the laying on of the hands of the eldership.†
15 Meditate on these things; give yourself entirely to them, that your progress may be evident to all.
16 Take heed to yourself and to the doctrine. Continue in them, for in doing this you will save both yourself and those who hear you.

General Pastoral Care

5 Do not rebuke an older man, but exhort *him* as a father, younger men as brothers,
2 older women as mothers, younger women as sisters, with all purity.

Care for Widows

3 Honor widows who are really widows.†
4 But if any widow has children or grandchildren, let them first learn to show piety at home and [a]to repay their parents; for this is [1]good and acceptable before God.
5 Now she who is really a widow, and left alone, trusts in God and continues in supplications and prayers [a]night and day.
6 But she who lives in [1]pleasure is dead while she lives.
7 And these things command, that they may be blameless.
8 But if anyone does not provide for his own, [a]and especially for those of his household, [b]he has denied the faith [c]and is worse than an unbeliever.
9 Do not let a widow under sixty years old be taken into the number, *and not unless* she has been the wife of one man,
10 well reported for good works: if she has brought up children, if she has lodged strangers, if she has washed the saints' feet, if she has relieved the afflicted, if she has diligently followed every good work.
11 But [1]refuse *the* younger widows; for when they have begun to grow wanton against Christ, they desire to marry,
12 having condemnation because they have cast off their first [1]faith.
13 And besides they learn *to be* idle, wandering about from house to house, and not only idle but also gossips and busybodies, saying things which they ought not.
14 Therefore I desire that *the* younger *widows* marry, bear children, manage the house, give no opportunity to the adversary to speak reproachfully.
15 For some have already turned aside after Satan.
16 If any believing [1]man or woman has widows, let them [2]relieve them, and do not let the church be burdened, that it may relieve those who are really widows.

Care for Elders

17 Let the elders who rule well be counted worthy of double honor, especially those who labor in the word and doctrine.
18 For the Scripture says, [a]*"You shall not muzzle an ox while it treads out the grain,"* and, [b]"The laborer *is* worthy of his wages."†

14 [b]Acts 6:6; 1 Tim. 5:22

CHAPTER 5

4 [a]Gen. 45:10 [1]NU, M omit *good and*
5 [a]Acts 26:7
6 [1]*indulgence*
8 [a]Is. 58:7; 2 Cor. 12:14 [b]2 Tim. 3:5 [c]Matt. 18:17
11 [1]Refuse to enroll
12 [1]Or *solemn promise*
16 [1]NU omits *man or* [2]*give aid to*
18 [a]Deut. 25:4; 1 Cor. 9:7–9 [b]Lev. 19:13; Deut. 24:15; Matt. 10:10; Luke 10:7; 1 Cor. 9:14

4:14 This verse refers to Timothy's ordination as presbyter (priest), which was conferred by the apostles, as it is by the bishop today (2 Tim. 1:6; see Acts 6:6). In continuity with the NT, Orthodox ordination to the diaconate and priesthood comes through the **laying on of . . . hands** by the bishop. In 5:22 Paul warns Timothy not to ordain anyone hastily.

5:3–16 This section contains specific advice on caring for **widows.** If there are no family members to care for a widow, the parish must do so, for a widow has God as her guardian (Deut. 10:17, 18; Ps. 68:5; 146:9). A "real" widow (vv. 3, 5, 16), however, in turn cares for the parish through prayer (v. 5) and works of compassion (v. 10), while maintaining a pure and holy life (vv. 6, 7, 11–16). Special qualifications are given for those who are on the register of widows (vv. 9, 10); perhaps this was an "order" for charitable service. Widows have from the start constituted a definable group within the Church (Acts 6:1; 9:39, 41).

5:18 This quotation of a saying of Jesus (Matt. 10:10; Luke 10:7) may be the first quotation of the Gospels as Scripture.

19 Do not receive an accusation against an elder except [a]from two or three witnesses.
20 Those who are sinning rebuke in the presence of all, that the rest also may fear.
21 I charge *you* before God and the Lord Jesus Christ and the [1]elect angels that you observe these things without [a]prejudice, doing nothing with partiality.
22 Do not lay hands on anyone hastily, nor [a]share in other people's sins; keep yourself pure.
23 No longer drink only water, but use a little wine for your stomach's sake and your frequent [1]infirmities.†
24 Some men's sins are [a]clearly evident, preceding *them* to judgment, but those of some *men* follow later.
25 Likewise, the good works *of some* are clearly evident, and those that are otherwise cannot be hidden.

Insubordinate Christian Slaves

6 Let as many [a]bondservants as are under the yoke count their own masters worthy of all honor, so that the name of God and *His* doctrine may not be blasphemed.
2 And those who have believing masters, let them not despise *them* because they are brethren, but rather serve *them* because those who are benefited are believers and beloved. Teach and exhort these things.

Ministers of Greed

3 If anyone teaches otherwise and does not consent to [a]wholesome words, *even* the words of our Lord Jesus Christ, [b]and to the [1]doctrine which accords with godliness,
4 he is proud, knowing nothing, but is obsessed with disputes and arguments over words, from which come envy, strife, reviling, evil suspicions,
5 [1]useless wranglings of men of corrupt minds and destitute of the truth, who suppose that godliness is a *means of* gain. [2]From [a]such withdraw yourself.
6 Now godliness with [a]contentment is great gain.
7 For we brought nothing into *this* world, [1]*and it is* [a]certain we can carry nothing out.
8 And having food and clothing, with these we shall be [a]content.
9 But those who desire to be rich fall into temptation and a snare, and *into* many foolish and harmful lusts which drown men in destruction and perdition.
10 For the love of money is a root of all *kinds of* evil, for which some have strayed from the faith in their greediness, and pierced themselves through with many sorrows.

Pursue Spirituality Instead

11 But you, O man of God, flee these things and pursue righteousness, godliness, faith, love, patience, gentleness.†
12 Fight the good fight of faith, lay hold on eternal life, to which you were also called and have confessed the good confession in the presence of many witnesses.†
13 I urge you in the sight of God who gives life to all things, and *before* Christ Jesus [a]who witnessed the good confession before Pontius Pilate,
14 that you keep *this* commandment without spot, blameless until our Lord Jesus Christ's appearing,
15 which He will manifest in His

19 [a]Deut. 17:6; 19:15; Matt. 18:16
21 [a]Deut. 1:17
[1]*chosen*
22 [a]Eph. 5:6, 7; 2 John 11
23 [1]*illnesses*
24 [a]Gal. 5:19–21

CHAPTER 6
1 [a]Eph. 6:5; Titus 2:9; 1 Pet. 2:18
3 [a]2 Tim. 1:13 [b]Titus 1:1
[1]*teaching*
5 [a]2 Tim. 3:5
[1]NU, M *constant friction*
[2]NU omits the rest of v. 5.
6 [a]Phil. 4:11; Heb. 13:5
7 [a]Job 1:21; Ps. 49:17; Eccl. 5:15
[1]NU omits *and it is certain*
8 [a]Prov. 30:8, 9
13 [a]Matt. 27:2; John 18:36, 37

5:23 Timothy's physical problems—perhaps arising from strict water-fasts—are not miraculously overcome. Paul does not suggest breaking the fasts, only decreasing their rigor.

6:11–16 This is a remarkable challenge for all who serve God, especially the ordained clergy.

6:11 The beginning of repentance is to flee from sin and to abstain from passions.

6:12 Confessed the good confession is a reference to Timothy's words at his baptism or ordination.

own time, *He who is* the blessed and
only [1]Potentate, the King of kings
and Lord of lords,
16 who alone has immortality,
dwelling in [a]unapproachable light,
[b]whom no man has seen or can see,
to whom *be* honor and everlasting
power. Amen.

Warning to Wealthy Christians

17 Command those who are rich in
this present age not to be haughty,
nor to trust in uncertain [a]riches but
in the living God, who gives us richly
all things [b]to enjoy.
18 *Let them* do good, that they be
rich in good works, ready to give,
willing to share,
19 [a]storing up for themselves a
good foundation for the time to
come, that they may lay hold on eternal life.

Keep the Tradition

20 O Timothy! [a]Guard what was
committed to your trust, [b]avoiding
the profane *and* [1]idle babblings and
contradictions of what is falsely
called knowledge—†
21 by professing it some have
strayed concerning the faith. Grace
be with you. Amen.

15 [1]*Sovereign*
16 [a]Dan. 2:22 [b]John 6:46
17 [a]Jer. 9:23; 48:7 [b]Eccl. 5:18, 19
19 [a][Matt. 6:20, 21; 19:21]
20 [a][2 Tim. 1:12, 14] [b]Titus 1:14 [1]*empty chatter*

6:20 The faith and worship of the Church is a sacred **trust,** to be preserved intact, without changes based on personal preference, and without regard for personal gain.

The Second Epistle of Paul the Apostle to

TIMOTHY

Author: *St. Paul the Apostle*

Date: *A.D. 65–67*

Theme: *Overcoming Hardship in the Ministry*

AUTHOR: By the second half of the second century the whole Church accepted 2 Timothy as Pauline and canonical.

DATE: This letter was written from Rome (1:17) in A.D. 65–67, when Paul was chained, suffering, and near his execution (unlike the freedom of his first confinement, described in Ephesians, Philippians, Colossians and Philemon).

MAJOR THEME: *Overcoming hardship in the ministry.* Ordained ministers utilize their spiritual gifts in the Church to keep and pass on her living tradition (1:13, 14; 2:2, 8, 11–13, 15; 3:14–17; 4:3). Through living tradition—the Bible and the ongoing life of the Holy Spirit in the body of Christ—the Church remains essentially as she was at her inception.

BACKGROUND INFORMATION: (1) *Historical setting.* Paul has been a prisoner in Rome for some time. Onesiphorus, a Christian from Ephesus, sought him out and visited him (1:16, 17). Although no one stood with Paul at his first hearing, he successfully defended himself and "was delivered out of the mouth of the lion" (4:16, 17). Nonetheless, Paul has no hope for acquittal. He knows his end is at hand (4:6–8). Worse, friends have turned against him (1:15; 4:16–18); only Luke is assisting him. Paul longs to see Timothy once more.

This is probably Paul's last letter. He knows his martyrdom is near and he looks forward to being with the Lord (4:8). Paul was martyred under Emperor Nero about A.D. 67.

(2) *Purpose.* Paul bids Timothy to come to him before winter seas make travel impossible (1:4; 4:9, 21). He urges Timothy to continue in perseverance and purity; he knows Timothy will face apostasy and harassment within the Church (1:8–15; 2:14–26; 4:3–5) and contamination from outside (3:1–9).

This letter is laced with warmth and affection, for the veteran apostle and missionary will soon depart. His "beloved son" (1:2) will now fight "the good fight" (4:7) without Paul's earthly guidance.

OUTLINE

Greeting	1:1, 2
I. Ministry: Exhortation to strength	1:3—2:13
A. To the Bishop, Timothy: Be bold!	1:3–18
1. In faith	1:3–5
2. In using the gift of ordination	1:6, 7
3. In loyalty to the gospel	1:8—2:1
B. To other faithful men	2:2–13
1. The task: Transmit the tradition	2:2
2. The means: Loyalty, discipline, hard work	2:3–6
3. The goal: Salvation and glory	2:7–13
II. Orthodoxy: Exhortation to faith and practice	2:14—4:22
A. Against false teachers	2:14–26
1. The teaching ministry of the bishop	2:14–19
2. The bishop's way of life	2:20–26
B. In the face of persecution	3:1—4:8
1. A description of the last days	3:1–9
2. Our defense: Steadfastness	3:10—4:8
a. The pastor's defense: Steadfastness in the tradition	3:10–17
b. The people's defense: Hearing Orthodox preaching	4:1–5
c. Our example: Paul	4:6–8
III. Conclusion	4:9–22
A. Fellow workers and evil workers	4:9–15
B. Paul's first defense	4:16–18
C. Greetings and benediction	4:19–22

Greeting

1 Paul, an apostle of [1]Jesus Christ
by the will of God, according to
the [a]promise of life which is in Christ
Jesus,

2 To Timothy, a [a]beloved son:

Grace, mercy, *and* peace from God
the Father and Christ Jesus our Lord.

Thanksgiving for Timothy

3 I thank God, whom I serve with
a pure conscience, as *my* [a]forefathers
did, as without ceasing I remember
you in my prayers night and day,
4 greatly desiring to see you, being mindful of your tears, that I may
be filled with joy,
5 when I call to remembrance
[a]the [1]genuine faith that is in you,
which dwelt first in your grand-
mother Lois and [b]your mother Eunice, and I am persuaded is in you
also.

Timothy's Gift, the Power of God

6 Therefore I remind you [a]to stir
up the gift of God which is in you
through the laying on of my hands.†
7 For [a]God has not given us a

CHAPTER 1
1 [a]Titus 1:2 [1]NU, M *Christ Jesus*
2 [a]1 Tim. 1:2; 2 Tim. 2:1; Titus 1:4
3 [a]Acts 24:14
5 [a]1 Tim. 1:5; 4:6 [b]Acts 16:1 [1]Lit. *unhypocritical*
6 [a]1 Tim. 4:14
7 [a]John 14:27; Rom. 8:15; 1 John 4:18

1:6 The gift of God is the grace of the Holy Spirit, or charism, given to Timothy at his ordination. This grace fills up that which is lacking and gives authenticity to the priesthood. But it is not automatic. We must **stir up** and rekindle it.

Commemoration of a Holy Martyr

2:1–10: The holy martyrs followed Paul's instructions to endure all things for Christ's sake.

spirit of fear, [b]but of power and of
love and of a sound mind.†
8 [a]Therefore do not be ashamed
of [b]the testimony of our Lord, nor
of me [c]His prisoner, but share with
me in the sufferings for the gospel
according to the power of God,
9 who has saved us and called *us*
with a holy calling, [a]not according
to our works, but [b]according to His
own purpose and grace which was
given to us in Christ Jesus [c]before
time began,†
10 but [a]has now been revealed by
the appearing of our Savior Jesus
Christ, *who* has abolished death and
brought life and immortality to light
through the gospel,†
11 [a]to which I was appointed a
preacher, an apostle, and a teacher
[1]of the Gentiles.
12 For this reason I also suffer
these things; nevertheless I am not
ashamed, [a]for I know whom I have
believed and am persuaded that He
is able to keep what I have committed to Him until that Day.

Fidelity in Spite of Desertions

13 [a]Hold fast [b]the pattern of
[c]sound words which you have heard
from me, in faith and love which are
in Christ Jesus.†
14 That good thing which was
committed to you, keep by the Holy
Spirit who dwells in us.
15 This you know, that all those in
Asia have turned away from me,
among whom are Phygellus and
Hermogenes.
16 The Lord grant mercy to the
[a]household of Onesiphorus, for he
often refreshed me, and was not
ashamed of my chain;
17 but when he arrived in Rome,
he sought me out very zealously and
found *me*.
18 The Lord [a]grant to him that he
may find mercy from the Lord
[b]in that Day—and you know very
well how many ways he [c]ministered
[1]*to me* at Ephesus.†

Transmitting the Faith

2 You therefore, [a]my son, [b]be
strong in the grace that is in
Christ Jesus.
2 And the things that you have
heard from me among many witnesses, commit these to faithful men

7 [b][Acts 1:8]
8 [a][Mark 8:38; Luke 9:26; Rom. 1:16]; 2 Tim. 1:12, 16
[b]1 Tim. 2:6
[c]Eph. 3:1; 2 Tim. 1:16
9 [a][Rom. 3:20]; Eph. 2:8, 9
[b]Rom. 8:28
[c]Rom. 16:25; Eph. 1:4; Titus 1:2
10 [a]Eph. 1:9
11 [a]Acts 9:15
[1]NU omits *of the Gentiles*
12 [a]1 Pet. 4:19
13 [a]2 Tim. 3:14; Titus 1:9
[b]Rom. 2:20; 6:17
[c]1 Tim. 6:3
16 [a]2 Tim. 4:19
18 [a]Matt. 6:4; Mark 9:41
[b]2 Thess. 1:10
[c]Heb. 6:10
[1]*to me* from Vg., a few Gr. mss.

CHAPTER 2
1 [a]1 Tim. 1:2
[b]Eph. 6:10

1:7 While any Christian may be persecuted (John 15:20; see Matt. 5:11, 12 and note), we reject feelings of fear or timidity. We do not "quench the Spirit" (1 Thess. 5:19), but act with power and courage (2:12; see Matt. 10:33; Luke 9:26).

1:9 Our salvation and **calling** are based on His **grace** and love, not on anything we have done to merit God's favor (Eph. 2:8–10; Titus 3:5, 6).

1:10 The second-century *Letter of Barnabas* notes that: "He submitted [to suffering] so that he might break the power of Death and demonstrate the resurrection from the dead—thus it was necessary for him to be manifested in flesh. Also [he submitted] so that he might fulfill the promise to the fathers and, while he was preparing the new people for himself and while he was still on earth, to prove that after he has brought about the resurrection he will judge" (Barn. 5:6, 7).

1:13, 14 The pattern of sound words (v. 13) is oral apostolic tradition **which you have heard.** It holds the same weight as written apostolic tradition (see 2:2; 2 Thess. 2:5). Oral or written, this Holy Tradition is rooted in **Christ Jesus** (v. 13) and kept by **the Holy Spirit who dwells in us** (v. 14).

1:18 Perhaps Onesiphorus is dead. The Church has never hesitated to pray for her de-

(continued on next page)

who will be able to teach others
also.†

Strengthening Others: Discipline and Suffering

3 You therefore must [a]endure[1]
hardship [b]as a good soldier of Jesus
Christ.†
4 [a]No one engaged in warfare entangles himself with the affairs of *this*
life, that he may please him who enlisted him as a soldier.
5 And also [a]if anyone competes
in athletics, he is not crowned unless
he competes according to the rules.
6 The hardworking farmer must
be first to partake of the crops.
7 Consider what I say, and
[1]may the Lord [a]give you understanding in all things.
8 Remember that Jesus Christ,
[a]of the seed of David, [b]was raised
from the dead [c]according to my
gospel,†
9 [a]for which I suffer trouble as an
evildoer, [b]*even* to the point of chains;
[c]but the word of God is not chained.
10 Therefore [a]I endure all things
for the sake of the [1]elect, [b]that they
also may obtain the salvation which
is in Christ Jesus with eternal glory.
11 *This is* a faithful saying:

For [a]if we died with *Him,*
We shall also live with *Him.*
12 [a]If we endure,
We shall also reign with
Him.
[b]If we deny *Him,*
He also will deny us.
13 If we are faithless,
He remains faithful;
He [a]cannot deny Himself.

Apostolic Teaching vs. Error

14 Remind *them* of these things,
[a]charging *them* before the Lord not
to [1]strive about words to no profit,
to the ruin of the hearers.
15 [a]Be diligent to present yourself
approved to God, a worker who does
not need to be ashamed, rightly dividing the word of truth.†
16 But shun profane *and* [1]idle babblings, for they will [2]increase to more
ungodliness.†
17 And their message will spread
like cancer. [a]Hymenaeus and Philetus are of this sort,†
18 who have strayed concerning
the truth, [a]saying that the resurrection is already past; and they
overthrow the faith of some.
19 Nevertheless [a]the solid foundation of God stands, having this seal:
"The Lord [b]knows those who are
His," and, "Let everyone who
names the name of [1]Christ depart
from iniquity."

3 [a]2 Tim. 4:5 [b]1 Tim. 1:18 [1]NU *You must share*
4 [a][2 Pet. 2:20]
5 [a][1 Cor. 9:25]
7 [a]Prov. 2:6 [1]NU *the Lord will give you*
8 [a]Rom. 1:3, 4 [b]1 Cor. 15:4 [c]Rom. 2:16
9 [a]Acts 9:16 [b]Eph. 3:1 [c]Acts 28:31
10 [a]Eph. 3:13 [b]2 Cor. 1:6 [1]*chosen ones*
11 [a]Rom. 6:5, 8
12 [a][Rom. 5:17; 8:17] [b]Matt. 10:33
13 [a]Num. 23:19
14 [a]Titus 3:9 [1]*battle*
15 [a]2 Pet. 1:10
16 [1]*empty chatter* [2]*lead*
17 [a]1 Tim. 1:20
18 [a]1 Cor. 15:12
19 [a][1 Cor. 3:11] [b][Nah. 1:7] [1]NU, M *the Lord*

(continued from previous page)
parted, that they **may find mercy** from God on the **Day** of **the Lord.** (The first *Lord* in the verse refers to the Son, the second to the Father.)

2:2 Paul establishes a clear chain of witnesses to oral tradition. Christian tradition is for all believers; it is "catholic," belonging to the whole Church, and must be passed down to others unhindered. This stands in clear contrast to the elitism of the major religions of the first-century Roman world, including Gnosticism and the various mystery religions.

2:3–6 Faithful ministry requires discipline: obedience, self-denial and struggle. Our examples here are the **soldier** (vv. 3, 4), the athlete (v. 5), and the **farmer** (v. 6).

2:8–13 Verses 11–13 may be an early baptismal hymn. Ministry is based on union with Christ and immovable loyalty to Him. The end, for the minister and his hearers, is life with Christ in the eternal Kingdom.

2:15 The last phrase of this verse is quoted in an Orthodox liturgical prayer for the bishops.

2:16 Profane and idle babblings (like nonsense syllables) is an apt description of heresy.

2:17, 18 What is the heresy of **Hymenaeus and Philetus?** Perhaps a super-spiritual interpretation of **the resurrection** (v. 18) as affecting only the soul and not the whole person (Greek philosophy thought bodily resurrection absurd); thus resurrection is thought to be **already past,** having occurred at baptism. They use the language of baptism but in a non-Orthodox way. Let us not be naive: unchecked, this sort of novel doctrine can spread through the community **like cancer** (v. 17).

Apostolic Conduct vs. Error

20 But in a great house there are
not only [a]vessels of gold and silver,
but also of wood and clay, some for
honor and some for dishonor.†
21 Therefore if anyone cleanses
himself from the latter, he will be a
vessel for honor, [1]sanctified and useful for the Master, [a]prepared for
every good work.
22 [a]Flee also youthful lusts; but
pursue righteousness, faith, love,
peace with those who call on the
Lord out of a pure heart.
23 But avoid foolish and ignorant
disputes, knowing that they generate strife.
24 And [a]a servant of the Lord must
not quarrel but be gentle to all,
[b]able to teach, [c]patient,†
25 [a]in humility correcting those
who are in opposition, [b]if God perhaps will grant them repentance,
[c]so that they may know the truth,
26 and *that* they may come to their
senses *and* [a]*escape* the snare of the
devil, having been taken captive by
him to *do* his will.

Moral Decline in the Last Days

3 But know this, that [a]in the last
days [1]perilous times will come:†

20 [a]Rom. 9:21
21 [a]2 Tim. 3:17
[1]*set apart*
22 [a]1 Tim. 6:11
24 [a]Titus 3:2
[b]Titus 1:9
[c]1 Tim. 3:3
25 [a]Gal. 6:1
[b]Acts 8:22
[c]1 Tim. 2:4
26 [a]1 Tim. 3:7

CHAPTER 3
1 [a]1 Tim. 4:1
[1]*times of stress*

3 [1]*irreconcilable*
4 [a]2 Pet. 2:10
5 [a]Titus 1:16
[b]1 Tim. 5:8
[c]2 Thess. 3:6
6 [a]Matt. 23:14
7 [a]1 Tim. 2:4
8 [a]Ex. 7:11, 12, 22; 8:7; 9:11
[b]1 Tim. 6:5
[c]Rom. 1:28
9 [a]Ex. 7:11, 12; 8:18; 9:11
10 [a]1 Tim. 4:6

2 For men will be lovers of themselves, lovers of money, boasters,
proud, blasphemers, disobedient to
parents, unthankful, unholy,
3 unloving, [1]unforgiving, slanderers, without self-control, brutal, de-
spisers of good,
4 [a]traitors, headstrong, haughty,
lovers of pleasure rather than lovers
of God,
5 [a]having a form of godliness but
[b]denying its power. And [c]from such
people turn away!†
6 For [a]of this sort are those who
creep into households and make captives of gullible women loaded down
with sins, led away by various lusts,
7 always learning and never able
[a]to come to the knowledge of the
truth.
8 [a]Now as Jannes and Jambres resisted Moses, so do these also resist
the truth: [b]men of corrupt minds,
[c]disapproved concerning the faith;†
9 but they will progress no further, for their folly will be manifest
to all, [a]as theirs also was.

The Pastor's Defense Against Apostasy: Loyalty to Tradition

10 [a]But you have carefully followed my doctrine, manner of life,

2:20–23 Heresy corrupts: bad theology leads to bad behavior. The Church on earth is a mixture of wheat and tares sown together (vv. 19–21). Membership in the Church guarantees nothing—even the baptismal confession (quoted in v. 19) acknowledges the necessity of struggle.

2:24–26 Good theology helps us along the path to good behavior. Although the truth stands firm and unalterable and cannot tolerate the false (see 1 Cor. 5:1–13; 2 Cor. 6:14–18), it instills a reasonable patience and gentleness toward all people. This attitude extends even to false teachers, although one must not forget that they are enemies and to be avoided (3:5).

3:1–9 While technically we have been **in the last days** since Christ walked the earth, the Church has seen this and other warnings as a reference to the days just before His coming again. A great decay in morals (see Matt. 24; Mark 13; 2 Thess. 2; 2 Pet. 2; compare Rom. 1:28–32) will even infiltrate the Church (v. 5; see Matt. 7:15–27; 1 Cor. 5:1–5; 1 Tim. 4:1–11). Like the prominent men of Cain's city (Gen. 4:16–24), these offenders willfully reject law and morals out of love of self and love of pleasure.

3:5 The **form** and **power** of **godliness** are intended to be inseparable. We normally do not have the *power* of *godliness* without the *form*. Charismatic power, however, can be twisted for evil and greed (Acts 8:9–20). Outward forms, even of liturgical worship, can be carried on without *power* or conviction (see Matt. 7:15; 24:4, 5, 24). As faith without works is a *form* without substance (James 2:26), so is religion without *power*. This is a stern warning to those of us committed to proper form.

3:8 In Jewish tradition, **Jannes** and **Jambres** are the Egyptian magicians who opposed Moses in Ex. 7.

Sunday of the Publican and Pharisee *Fourth Sunday before Lent*

3:10–15: As we strive to live godly lives, we must expect persecution.

purpose, faith, longsuffering, love,
perseverance,†
11 persecutions, afflictions, which
happened to me [a]at Antioch, [b]at Iconium, [c]at Lystra—what persecutions
I endured. And [d]out of *them* all the
Lord delivered me.
12 Yes, and [a]all who desire to live
godly in Christ Jesus will suffer
persecution.
13 [a]But evil men and impostors
will grow worse and worse, deceiving and being deceived.
14 But you must [a]continue in the
things which you have learned and
been assured of, knowing from
whom you have learned *them*,†
15 and that from childhood you
have known [a]the Holy Scriptures,
which are able to make you wise for
salvation through faith which is in
Christ Jesus.
16 [a]All Scripture *is* given by inspiration of God, [b]and *is* profitable for
doctrine, for reproof, for correction,
for [1]instruction in righteousness,
17 [a]that the man of God may be
complete, [b]thoroughly equipped for
every good work.

The People's Defense Against Apostasy: Orthodox Preaching

4 I [a]charge *you* [1]therefore before
God and the Lord Jesus Christ,
[b]who will judge the living and the
dead [2]at His appearing and His kingdom:

11 [a]Acts 13:44–52 [b]Acts 14:1–6, 19 [c]Acts 14:8–20 [d]Ps. 34:19
12 [a][Ps. 34:19]
13 [a]2 Thess. 2:11
14 [a]2 Tim. 1:13
15 [a]John 5:39
16 [a][2 Pet. 1:20] [b]Rom. 4:23; 15:4 [1]*training, discipline*
17 [a]1 Tim. 6:11 [b]2 Tim. 2:21

CHAPTER 4
1 [a]1 Tim. 5:21 [b]Acts 10:42 [1]NU omits *therefore* [2]NU *and by*
2 [a]Titus 2:15 [b]1 Tim. 5:20 [c]1 Tim. 4:13
3 [a]2 Tim. 3:1 [b]1 Tim. 1:10 [c]2 Tim. 3:6
4 [a]1 Tim. 1:4
5 [a]2 Tim. 1:8 [b]Acts 21:8
6 [a]Phil. 2:17 [b][Phil. 1:23]
7 [a]1 Cor. 9:24–27
8 [a]James 1:12 [b]John 5:22 [c]2 Tim. 1:12

2 Preach the word! Be ready in
season *and* out of season. [a]Convince,
[b]rebuke, [c]exhort, with all longsuffering and teaching.
3 [a]For the time will come when
they will not endure [b]sound doctrine, [c]but according to their own desires, *because* they have itching ears,
they will heap up for themselves
teachers;
4 and they will turn *their* ears
away from the truth, and [a]be turned
aside to fables.
5 But you be watchful in all
things, [a]endure afflictions, do the
work of [b]an evangelist, fulfill your
ministry.

Paul's Example

6 For [a]I am already being poured
out as a drink offering, and the time
of [b]my departure is at hand.†
7 [a]I have fought the good fight, I
have finished the race, I have kept
the faith.†
8 Finally, there is laid up for me
[a]the crown of righteousness, which
the Lord, the righteous [b]Judge, will
give to me [c]on that Day, and not to
me only but also to all who have
loved His appearing.

Request to See Timothy

9 Be diligent to come to me
quickly;

3:10–13 Paul's life exhibits what the Lord taught: In this world, godliness elicits persecution (see John 15:20).

3:14–17 Having exhorted Timothy with the example of his own steadfastness (vv. 10–13), Paul now issues a reminder of the depth of Timothy's training, which combined both oral and written instruction (see Matt. 28:16–20; 1 Cor. 11:2; 2 Thess. 2:15; 3:6). A part of this tradition is Scripture. Paul, of course, speaks of the OT since the NT did not yet exist.

4:6 A **drink offering** is a wine, water, or oil offering poured over animal or grain sacrifices at the conclusion of both Jewish and pagan rites.

4:7 The race is the life and work that God gave Paul. The comparison of the spiritual life to an athletic contest (see 1 Cor. 9:24–27) is common in the writings of the ascetic Fathers.

10 for [a]Demas has forsaken me,
[b]having loved this present world,
and has departed for Thessalonica—
Crescens for Galatia, Titus for Dalmatia.†
11 Only Luke is with me. Get
[a]Mark and bring him with you, for
he is useful to me for ministry.†
12 And [a]Tychicus I have sent to
Ephesus.
13 Bring the cloak that I left with
Carpus at Troas when you come—
and the books, especially the parchments.
14 [a]Alexander the coppersmith did
me much harm. May the Lord repay
him according to his works.
15 You also must beware of him,
for he has greatly resisted our
words.

Paul's First Defense

16 At my first defense no one stood
with me, but all forsook me. [a]May
it not be charged against them.
17 [a]But the Lord stood with me
and strengthened me, [b]so that the
message might be preached fully
through me, and *that* all the Gentiles
might hear. Also I was delivered
[c]out of the mouth of the lion.
18 [a]And the Lord will deliver me
from every evil work and preserve
me for His heavenly kingdom.
[b]To Him *be* glory forever and ever.
Amen!

Farewell

19 Greet [a]Prisca and Aquila, and
the household of [b]Onesiphorus.
20 [a]Erastus stayed in Corinth, but
[b]Trophimus I have left in Miletus
sick.
21 Do your utmost to come before
winter. Eubulus greets you, as well
as Pudens, Linus, Claudia, and all
the brethren.†
22 The Lord [1]Jesus Christ be with
your spirit. Grace be with you.
Amen.

10 [a]Col. 4:14 [b]1 John 2:15
11 [a]Acts 12:12, 25; 15:37–39
12 [a]Acts 20:4
14 [a]1 Tim. 1:20
16 [a]Acts 7:60
17 [a]Acts 23:11 [b]Acts 9:15 [c]1 Sam. 17:37
18 [a]Ps. 121:7 [b]Rom. 11:36
19 [a]Acts 18:2 [b]2 Tim. 1:16
20 [a]Rom. 16:23 [b]Acts 20:4; 21:29
22 [1]NU omits *Jesus Christ*

4:10 Demas provides a sobering footnote to Paul's ministry. He was Paul's companion in Rome, his colaborer in apostleship, and a close friend of Luke (Col. 4:14; Philem. 24). Yet Demas—after these great and glorious years of service with the Apostle—forsakes Paul, **having loved this present world.** It is in the face of tragedies such as this that the Scriptures, the Fathers, the prayers and hymns of the Church together call us repeatedly to a life of humility and repentance—that we should not think of ourselves more highly than we ought.

4:11 Paul is now reconciled with (John) **Mark** (see Acts 15:37–40). The sharp contention between Barnabas and Paul is forgotten and the true love of Christ reigns.

4:21 Of **Linus,** St. Irenaeus writes in the late second century: "The blessed Apostles Peter and Paul, having founded and established the Church of Rome, handed over the office of bishop to Linus—of whom Paul makes mention in his second letter to Timothy" (*Against Heresies*, 3,3,3). Eusebius, writing in the fourth century (*History of the Church*, 3,2), says the same.

The Epistle of Paul the Apostle to

TITUS

Author: *St. Paul the Apostle*

Date: *A.D. 63–65*

Theme: *Overseeing the Church According to the True Faith*

AUTHOR: The greeting (1:1) and Church tradition both affirm that Paul is the author.

DATE: The circumstances, content and organization of Titus are similar to 1 Timothy. The two books were probably written about the same time, in A.D. 63–65. Paul's work with Titus on Crete does not fit into the time covered by the Book of Acts, so it probably occurred after Paul's release from his first imprisonment in Rome.

MAJOR THEME: *Overseeing the Church according to the true faith*. As the Church grew, it naturally developed theology and structure, and encountered heresy and sub-Christian behavior among its members, as had been prophesied. Paul here advises Titus as he faces these issues.

BACKGROUND INFORMATION: (1) *The recipient, Titus*. Titus was a Gentile converted to Christ by St. Paul (1:4). He became an associate of Barnabas and Paul at Antioch and went to Jerusalem with them, receiving the approval of the Twelve to remain uncircumcised (Gal. 2:1–5).

Toward the end of Paul's third missionary journey, about A.D. 57, Titus was sent from Ephesus to Corinth with the "Sorrowful Letter" (Paul's third letter to Corinth). He restored the Corinthian Church to proper order and reported back to Paul, who was by then in Macedonia (2 Cor 2:13; 7:6, 7, 13–15). Shortly afterward, Paul sent Titus with two other trustworthy Christians back to Corinth to complete the collection for the Jerusalem relief fund, and to deliver the letter we call 2 Corinthians (2 Cor. 8:16, 17; 12:18).

After Paul was released from prison in Rome, about A.D. 63, he and Titus visited Crete (1:5). When Paul moved on, he appointed Titus as apostolic overseer of Crete. Thereafter, Paul wrote this letter asking Titus to meet him in Nicopolis (probably the Nicopolis on the western coast of Greece) as soon as possible (3:12). When Paul was again imprisoned in Rome he sent Titus to Dalmatia in Illyricum, present-day Yugoslavia (2 Tim. 4:10). According to tradition, Titus became Bishop of Crete and died there in old age.

(2) *Historical setting*. After Paul left Titus in charge of consolidating and organizing the church on the island of Crete, he found theological problems

there similar to those being confronted by Timothy in Asia Minor (specifically in Ephesus): elements of Judaism being forced on Christians, and early gnosticism. But Titus faced an even greater challenge, for the native culture of Crete was more antagonistic toward the Church than those cultures found in Asia Minor. Further, whereas Timothy was restoring order in established churches, Titus was establishing order in young churches.

OUTLINE

Greeting	1:1–4
I. Godly government	1:5–16
A. Organization: Ordination of sound presbyters	1:5–9
B. Danger and urgency concerning false teachers	1:10–16
II. Godly people	2:1—3:11
A. Right behavior in the Church and in the home	2:1–10
B. The purity of the eternal Kingdom	2:11–15
C. Right behavior toward the government and society	3:1, 2
D. Salvation by grace in baptism and chrismation	3:3–8
E. Discipline of heretical and schismatic members	3:9–11
Conclusion: Requests, greetings and benediction	3:12–15

Greeting

1 Paul, a bondservant of God and
an apostle of Jesus Christ, according to the faith of God's elect
and [a]the acknowledgment of the
truth [b]which accords with godliness,†
2 in hope of eternal life which
God, who [a]cannot lie, promised before time began,
3 but has in due time manifested
His word through preaching, which
was committed to me according to
the commandment of God our Savior;
4 To [a]Titus, a true son in *our* common faith:
Grace, mercy, *and* peace from God
the Father and [1]the Lord Jesus Christ
our Savior.

Ordination of Sound Elders

5 For this reason I left you in
Crete, that you should [a]set in order
the things that are lacking, and appoint elders in every city as I commanded you—†
6 if a man is blameless, the husband of one wife, [a]having faithful
children not accused of [1]dissipation
or insubordination.†
7 For a [1]bishop must be blameless, as a steward of God, not self-

CHAPTER 1
1 [a]2 Tim. 2:25 [b][1 Tim. 3:16]
2 [a]Num. 23:19
4 [a]2 Cor. 2:13; 8:23; Gal. 2:3; 2 Tim. 4:10 [1]NU *Christ Jesus*
5 [a]1 Cor. 11:34
6 [a]1 Tim. 3:2–4; Titus 1:6–8 [1]*debauchery,* lit. *incorrigibility*
7 [1]Lit. *overseer*

1:1 In the Roman world, a **bondservant** (Gr. *doulos*) was in a pitiful position: he had no name, rights, will or even time of his own. But in the world of the OT, a bondservant was often the king's right-hand man—one of the most honored positions. Moses and other OT prophets were the bondservants of the Lord. Paul, of course, knew of both usages. An **apostle,** "one sent out," was a New Covenant equivalent to an OT bondservant.

Acknowledgment (Gr. *epignosis*) is deeper than mental knowledge; it is experiential, not theoretical. Knowledge (**the truth**) and action (**godliness**) are a unity; knowledge that does not change one's life does not save.

1:5 When Paul evangelized an area, he did not leave it unattended (1 Cor. 3:6–10; Col. 1:7).

1:6–9 All Christians are priests in Christ. Candidates for eldership, that is, for the special

(continued on next page)

willed, not quick-tempered, [a]not given to wine, not violent, not greedy for money,

8 but hospitable, a lover of what is good, sober-minded, just, holy, self-controlled,

9 holding fast the faithful word as he has been taught, that he may be able, by sound doctrine, both to exhort and convict those who contradict.

Opposition to False Teachers

10 For there are many insubordinate, both idle [a]talkers and deceivers, especially those of the circumcision,†

11 whose mouths must be stopped, who subvert whole households, teaching things which they ought not, [a]for the sake of dishonest gain.

12 [a]One of them, a prophet of their own, said, "Cretans *are* always liars, evil beasts, lazy gluttons."

13 This testimony is true. [a]Therefore rebuke them sharply, that they may be sound in the faith,

14 not giving heed to Jewish fables and [a]commandments of men who turn from the truth.

15 [a]To the pure all things are pure, but to those who are defiled and unbelieving nothing is pure; but even their mind and conscience are defiled.

16 They profess to [a]know God, but [b]in works they deny Him, being [1]abominable, disobedient, [c]and disqualified for every good work.

7 [a]Lev. 10:9
10 [a]James 1:26
11 [a]1 Tim. 6:5
12 [a]Acts 17:28
13 [a]2 Cor. 13:10; 2 Tim. 4:2
14 [a]Is. 29:13
15 [a]Luke 11:41; Rom. 14:14, 20; 1 Cor. 6:12
16 [a]Matt. 7:20–23; 25:12; 1 John 2:4
[b][2 Tim. 3:5, 7]
[c]Rom. 1:28
[1]*detestable*

Sound Doctrine Produces Proper Behavior

2 But as for you, speak the things which are proper for sound doctrine:†

2 that the older men be sober, reverent, temperate, sound in faith, in love, in patience;

3 the older women likewise, that they be reverent in behavior, not slanderers, not given to much wine, teachers of good things—†

4 that they admonish the young women to love their husbands, to love their children,

5 to be discreet, chaste, [a]homemakers, good, [b]obedient to their own husbands, [c]that the word of God may not be blasphemed.

6 Likewise, exhort the young men to be sober-minded,

7 in all things showing yourself *to be* [a]a pattern of good works; in doctrine *showing* integrity, reverence, [b]incorruptibility,[1]

8 sound speech that cannot be condemned, that one who is an opponent may be ashamed, having nothing evil to say of [1]you.

9 *Exhort* [a]bondservants to be obedient to their own masters, to be well pleasing in all *things,* not answering back,

10 not [1]pilfering, but showing all good [2]fidelity, that they may adorn the doctrine of God our Savior in all things.

CHAPTER 2
5 [a]1 Tim. 5:14
[b]1 Cor. 14:34; 1 Tim. 2:11
[c]Rom. 2:24
7 [a]Phil. 3:17; 1 Tim. 4:12
[b]Eph. 6:24
[1]NU omits *incorruptibility*
8 [1]NU, M *us*
9 [a]Eph. 6:5; 1 Tim. 6:1
10 [1]*thieving*
[2]*honesty*

(continued from previous page)
priesthood within the general priesthood of all, should exhibit (1) a wholesome and united family life (v. 6), (2) control over passions and emotions (v. 7), (3) loving and righteous relations with others (v. 8), and (4) careful adherence to tradition (v. 9; see also 1 Tim. 3:1–16; 5:21; 2 Tim. 2:2).

1:10–16 False leaders also exhibit certain characteristics. They (1) upset rather than reconcile (v. 11), (2) have an eye for personal profit (v. 11), (3) lack discipline and integrity (vv. 12, 13), (4) misjudge reality—here setting up external laws when the uncleanness is internal (vv. 14, 15), and (5) are immoral. Bad theology leads to bad behavior (v. 16).

2:1–10 Good theology helps lead us to good behavior. Various classes, distinguished here primarily by age and sex, have characteristic problems and responsibilities.

2:3–5 Note the opportunity for older women to be role models and teachers in the Church for young wives and mothers.

The Baptism of Our Lord Jesus Christ (Theophany) *January 6*

2:11–14; 3:4–7: The grace of God, saves us through baptism in Jesus Christ, the Holy Spirit.

Proper Behavior Supports Sound Doctrine

11 For [a]the grace of God that
brings salvation has appeared to all
men,†
12 teaching us that, denying ungodliness and worldly lusts, we
should live soberly, righteously, and
godly in the present age,
13 [a]looking for the blessed [b]hope
and glorious appearing of our great
God and Savior Jesus Christ,†
14 [a]who gave Himself for us, that
He might redeem us from every lawless deed [b]and purify for Himself
[c]*His* own special people, zealous for
good works.
15 Speak these things, [a]exhort,
and rebuke with all authority. Let no
one despise you.

Kindness Toward All Men

3 Remind them [a]to be subject to
rulers and authorities, to obey,
[b]to be ready for every good work,
2 to speak evil of no one, to be
peaceable, gentle, showing all humility to all men.

God's Kindness to Us

3 For [a]we ourselves were also
once foolish, disobedient, deceived,
serving various lusts and pleasures,
living in malice and envy, hateful
and hating one another.
4 But when [a]the kindness and the
love of [b]God our Savior toward man
appeared,
5 [a]not by works of righteousness
which we have done, but according
to His mercy He saved us, through
[b]the washing of regeneration and renewing of the Holy Spirit,†
6 [a]whom He poured out on us
abundantly through Jesus Christ our
Savior,
7 that having been justified by His
grace [a]we should become heirs according to the hope of eternal life.†

11 [a][Rom. 5:15]
13 [a]1 Cor. 1:7 [b][Col. 3:4]
14 [a]Is. 53:12; Gal. 1:4 [b]Ezek. 37:23; [Heb. 1:3; 9:14; 1 John 1:7] [c]Ex. 15:16
15 [a]1 Tim. 4:13; 5:20; 2 Tim. 4:2

CHAPTER 3

1 [a][Rom. 13:1]; 1 Pet. 2:13 [b]Col. 1:10
3 [a]1 Cor. 6:11; 1 Pet. 4:3
4 [a]Titus 2:11 [b]1 Tim. 2:3
5 [a][Rom. 3:20]; Eph. 2:4–9 [b]John 3:3
6 [a]Ezek. 36:26
7 [a][Matt. 25:34]; Mark 10:17; [Rom. 8:17, 23, 24; Titus 1:2]

2:11–15 While Christian ethical teaching often appears similar to other systems—Paul uses both Roman and Jewish ethical terms—the basis of Christian ethics is unique. Christians are good not merely because of obedience to law or harmony with nature, or in order to gain immortal bliss for the soul. Rather, they are righteous in anticipation of the age to come, the *eschaton* (Gr.), the age of the fullness of creation in the incarnate Son of God. **Grace** (v. 11) is the uncreated energy of God, the gift of the Holy Spirit, through which He gives His gifts to man in tender mercy and good will. It is a formative power, the rule of life of the age to come, requiring our determined participation. To belong to God is to become like God. To be ransomed, or "owned," by God (v. 14) is not simply a legal and static condition, but a life in communion with Him: a blessed, victorious struggle.

2:13 The Church Fathers regard the phrase, **our great God and Savior Jesus Christ** as a landmark statement on the divinity of Christ (see Rom. 9:5; 2 Pet. 1:1). In Paul's thought, "God" refers usually to the Person of the Father, not to the divine nature.

As Paul grew older, it seems his sense of the difference between this age and the age to come deepened. In his earlier letters, he emphasized the present realization of God's power; now he speaks more of our future transfiguration.

3:5 The washing of regeneration, baptism, and **renewing of the Holy Spirit,** chrismation, form a unity in our salvation, which is clear throughout the NT. Jesus taught we are born from above through "water and the Spirit" (John 3:5); Peter preached salvation in Christ through being "baptized" and receiving "the gift of the Holy Spirit" (Acts 2:38). Now Paul calls us to the *washing* of the water and the *renewing of the Holy Spirit*.

3:7, 8 While Paul is painfully aware that we are awaiting the consummation of the age to

(continued on page 506)

THE SECOND COMING OF CHRIST

The Orthodox understanding of the Second Coming of Christ is clear: the Lord Jesus Christ truly will return. His second advent is not a myth, nor an empty promise, nor is it a metaphor. In fact, each time the Divine Liturgy is celebrated, the priest makes a proclamation to the Father which reveals how the Church responds not only to the Second Coming of Christ, but to all of His work.

> Remembering this saving commandment [Jesus' command to eat His flesh and drink His blood] and all that has been done for us— the Cross, the Tomb, the Resurrection on the third day, the Ascension into Heaven, the sitting at the right hand and the Second and glorious Coming—we offer You Your own, from what is Your own, on behalf of all and for all.

Orthodox Christians also believe the New Testament revelation of the Second Coming of Christ is meant to stimulate our preparation for it, not our speculation about it. This explains the relative simplicity with which the Nicene Creed, the most universal confession of faith in all of Christendom, addresses Christ's return: "He . . . will come again, with glory, to judge the living and the dead, whose Kingdom shall have no end." The emphasis of historic Orthodoxy is *that* Jesus will come again, not *when* He will come again.

Thus, St. Paul writes, "denying ungodliness and worldly lusts, we should live soberly, righteously, and godly in the present age, looking for the blessed hope and glorious appearing of our great God and Savior Jesus Christ, who gave Himself for us, that He might redeem us from every lawless deed and purify for Himself His own special people, zealous for good works" (Titus 2:12–14).

There are signs of Christ's coming, to be sure. Jesus prophesied many events that would take place in the world prior to His return (Matt. 24; Luke 21:7–36). But even here the teachings of Jesus in these gospels close with His exhortation to virtue, righteousness, and preparation for the Judgment. Christ and His apostles issue severe warnings, implicit and explicit, against second-guessing the time of His coming (Matt. 24:3–8, 36, 43, 44, 50; Luke 21:7–9, 34; Acts 1:7; 1 Thess. 5:1–3; 2 Pet. 3:8–10).

Much of modern Christendom has succumbed to divisive speculation regarding Christ's return. We are divided into pre-millennial, post-millennial, and a-millennial camps. Breaking it down even further, there are pre-tribulation, mid-tribulation, and post-tribulation adherents. Christians part ways and new denominations spring up around interpretations of events which have not yet even come to pass!

Throughout history the Orthodox Church has steadfastly insisted on the reality of the Second Coming of Christ as a settled belief, but granted liberty on the question of when it will occur. In the last chapter of Revelation, Jesus speaks the words, "I am coming quickly" three different times (Rev. 2:21:7, 12, 20). His coming will occur on a day, at an hour when it is not expected. The Apostle John, the author of Revelation, concludes his book with a warning:

> "For I testify to everyone who hears the words of the prophecy of this book: If anyone adds to these things, God will add to him the plagues that are written in this book; and if anyone takes away from the words of the book of this prophecy, God shall take away his part from the Book of Life, from the holy city, and from the things which are written in this book" (Rev. 22:18, 19).

To confess the return of Christ is to stand squarely within the apostolic tradition. To add "when" to the promise of His coming is warned against in the Scriptures. As members of the Bride of Christ, let us attend instead to being ready.

8 [a]This is a faithful saying, and
these things I want you to affirm
constantly, that those who have
believed in God should be careful
to maintain good works. These
things are good and profitable to
men.

Heretical and Schismatic Members

9 But [a]avoid foolish disputes,
genealogies, contentions, and strivings about the law; for they are unprofitable and useless.
10 [a]Reject a divisive man after the
first and second [1]admonition,†
11 knowing that such a person is
warped and sinning, being self-
condemned.

Conclusion

12 When I send Artemas to you,
or [a]Tychicus, be diligent to come to
me at Nicopolis, for I have decided
to spend the winter there.
13 Send Zenas the lawyer and
[a]Apollos on their journey with haste,
that they may lack nothing.
14 And let our *people* also learn to
maintain good works, to *meet* urgent
needs, that they may not be
unfruitful.
15 All who *are* with me greet you.
Greet those who love us in the faith.
Grace *be* with you all. Amen.

8 [a]1 Tim. 1:15
9 [a]1 Tim. 1:4; 2 Tim. 2:23
10 [a]Matt. 18:17 [1]*warning*
12 [a]Acts 20:4; Eph. 6:21; Col. 4:7; 2 Tim. 4:12
13 [a]Acts 18:24; 1 Cor. 16:12

(continued from page 504)
come (2:13), he knows we already participate in the life of the Kingdom. Baptism and chrisma-tion are the beginning, the rite of passage toward a progressive life of renewal in Christ (see 2 Cor. 3:16–18).

3:10, 11 A **divisive** person is one who "picks" or "chooses from" the whole truth. A sect is a group that follows its own choices, independent of Holy Tradition. Incomplete or erroneous beliefs result in immoral behavior.

The Epistle of Paul the Apostle to

PHILEMON

Author: *St. Paul the Apostle*

Date: *A.D.61–63*

Theme: *Our Brotherhood in Christ*

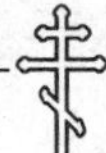

AUTHOR: Paul often used an assistant to whom he dictated his letters (Rom. 16:22; 1 Cor. 16:21; Gal. 6:11; Col. 4:18; 2 Thess. 3:17), but he wrote Philemon with his own hand (v. 19).

DATE: Philemon was written at the same time as Colossians (A.D. 61–63), most likely from Rome.

MAJOR THEME: We are no longer slaves, but brothers and sisters in Christ.

BACKGROUND INFORMATION: (1) *Philemon and Colossians.* Philemon is a sister letter to Colossians and therefore also closely related to Ephesians. In both Philemon and Colossians, Onesimus' mission is mentioned (v. 12; Col. 4:4, 9), Paul's companions are the same (vv. 23, 24; Col. 4:10–14), and Archippus is addressed (v. 2; Col. 4:17). Philemon and Colossians were written from prison, most likely during Paul's first Roman captivity (c. A.D. 61–63), but possibly during an unrecorded imprisonment in Ephesus.

(2) *The early Church and slavery.* The New Testament Church did not directly promote the abolition of slavery, but it did undermine the philosophy which allowed slavery to exist for all people are made in God's image. Further, citizenship in the Kingdom of God makes one's earthly status irrelevant. God is no respecter of persons. The basis for slavery was undone as master and slave became brethren in Christ: "there is neither slave nor free" (Gal. 3:28). Here, Paul transforms a slave into a beloved brother (see 1 Cor. 7:20–24; Eph. 6:5–9; Col. 3:22—4:1; 1 Tim. 6:1, 2; Titus 2:9).

(3) *Who is Philemon?* Philemon (lit. "Affectionate") had been converted by Paul (v. 19) and was a member of the Church in Colosse (Col. 4:9). Onesimus (lit. "Useful") had been a useless slave of Philemon, for he had run away, providing for his needs from the stolen treasury of his master—an offense punishable by death. Somehow Onesimus reached Paul, most likely in Rome. Paul then brought Onesimus to Christ and Onesimus became "useful" to Paul.
According to Roman law, Onesimus still belonged to Philemon. So Paul

sent Onesimus back to Colosse with this letter, under the care of Tychicus, who was also carrying the letters to the Colossians and the Ephesians. Paul urges Philemon to receive Onesimus with forgiveness as a brother in the Lord. And he hints that he would not be displeased if Philemon released Onesimus from bondage in order to free him for service to Paul.

According to ancient tradition, Philemon was consecrated bishop of Colosse and later martyred. Onesimus is perhaps the same Onesimus whom St. Ignatius mentions as bishop of Ephesus, forty years after this incident (*Ad. Eph.* 1:1).

OUTLINE

Greeting	vv. 1–3
I. Commendation of Philemon	vv. 4–7
II. Plea for Onesimus	vv. 8–21
Conclusion: Request, greetings and benediction	vv. 22–25

Greeting

Paul, a [a]prisoner of Christ Jesus,
and Timothy *our* brother,

To Philemon our beloved *friend*
and fellow laborer,†
2 to [1]the beloved Apphia, [a]Ar-
chippus our fellow soldier, and to the
church in your house:

3 Grace to you and peace from
God our Father and the Lord Jesus
Christ.

Commendation of Philemon

4 [a]I thank my God, making mention of you always in my prayers,†
5 [a]hearing of your love and
faith which you have toward the
Lord Jesus and toward all the
saints,†
6 that the sharing of your faith
may become effective [a]by the
acknowledgment of [b]every good
thing which is in [1]you in Christ
Jesus.†
7 For we [1]have great [2]joy and
[3]consolation in your love, because
the [4]hearts of the saints have been
refreshed by you, brother.

Plea for Onesimus

8 Therefore, though I might be
very bold in Christ to command you
what is fitting,†
9 *yet* for love's sake I rather appeal
to you—being such a one as Paul, the
aged, and now also a prisoner of
Jesus Christ—

1 [a]Eph. 3:1
2 [a]Col. 4:17
[1]NU *our sister Apphia*
4 [a]Eph. 1:16; 1 Thess. 1:2; 2 Thess. 1:3
5 [a]Eph. 1:15; Col. 1:4; 1 Thess. 3:6
6 [a]Phil. 1:9; [Col. 1:9; 3:10; James 2:14–17] [b][1 Thess. 5:18] [1]NU, M *us*
7 [1]NU *had* [2]M *thanksgiving* [3]*comfort* [4]Lit. *inward parts,* heart, liver, and lungs

1 It is not known whether **Philemon** was yet ordained as a presbyter/bishop; he is recognized for his kindness, hospitality and gracious spirit.

4–7 Paul's apostolic spirit is manifest in his affection, benevolence and regular intercessions for his fellow laborers.

5 Love and **faith** go together. As true faith includes works, so true faith includes love. We cannot believe in God without loving others.

6 Faith unites a person not only to Christ but to all who are in Him—including those who have greatly wronged us, as Onesimus had wronged Philemon.

8, 9 Paul does not appeal to Philemon on the basis of his own apostolic authority (v. 8; see Introduction to 2 Corinthians). Instead he appeals on the basis of (1) his age, (2) his being **a prisoner of Jesus Christ** (v. 9)—for whom we should be quick to do all that we can, and (3) Philemon's Christian conscience (see v. 14).

10 I appeal to you for my son
[a]Onesimus, whom I have begotten
while in my chains,†
11 who once was unprofitable to
you, but now is profitable to you and
to me.†
12 I am sending him [1]back. You
therefore receive him, that is, my
own [2]heart,
13 whom I wished to keep with
me, that on your behalf he might
minister to me in my chains for the
gospel.
14 But without your consent I
wanted to do nothing, [a]that your
good deed might not be by compulsion, as it were, but voluntary.†
15 For perhaps he departed for a
while for this *purpose*, that you might
receive him forever,
16 no longer as a slave but more
than a slave—a beloved brother, especially to me but how much more
to you, both in the [a]flesh and in the
Lord.
17 If then you count me as a partner, receive him as *you would* me.
18 But if he has wronged you or
owes anything, put that on my
account.†
19 I, Paul, am writing with my own
[a]hand. I will repay—not to mention
to you that you owe me even your
own self besides.†
20 Yes, brother, let me have joy
from you in the Lord; refresh my
heart in the Lord.
21 [a]Having confidence in your obedience, I write to you, knowing that
you will do even more than I say.†

Personal Request, Greetings, and Benediction

22 But, meanwhile, also prepare a
guest room for me, for [a]I trust that
[b]through your prayers I shall be
granted to you.
23 [a]Epaphras, my fellow prisoner
in Christ Jesus, greets you,
24 *as do* [a]Mark, [b]Aristarchus,
[c]Demas, [d]Luke, my fellow laborers.
25 [a]The grace of our Lord Jesus
Christ *be* with your spirit. Amen.

10 [a]Col. 4:9
12 [1]NU *back to you in person, that is, my own heart,*
[2]See v. 7.
14 [a]2 Cor. 9:7; 1 Pet. 5:2
16 [a]Eph. 6:5; Col. 3:22
19 [a]1 Cor. 16:21; Gal. 6:11; 2 Thess. 3:17
21 [a]2 Cor. 7:16
22 [a]Phil. 1:25; 2:24
[b]2 Cor. 1:11
23 [a]Col. 1:7; 4:12
24 [a]Acts 12:12, 25; 15:37–39; Col. 4:10
[b]Acts 19:29; 27:2; Col. 4:10
[c]Col. 4:14; 2 Tim. 4:10
[d]2 Tim. 4:11
25 [a]2 Tim. 4:22

10 Paul became Onesimus' spiritual father by leading him to Christ (see 1 Cor. 4:15; Gal. 4:19).

11–13 Paul sees to it that Onesimus fulfills his legal responsibilities by returning to his master. A slave is morally obligated to remain with his master despite the inherent injustice of his condition (Eph. 6:5).

14–17 While the master-slave relationship continues, it is transcended by brotherhood in Christ.

18 Apparently Onesimus stole from or otherwise wronged Philemon when he ran away. **Put that on my account** is reminiscent of how Christ has taken away our sins that we might go free (2 Cor. 5:21; 8:9).

19 Paul had also brought Philemon to Christ.

21 Perhaps Paul hopes Philemon will not only receive Onesimus with forgiveness, but will also free him and return him to Paul.

The Epistle to the HEBREWS

Author: *Unknown, but usually ascribed to St. Paul.*

Date: *About* A.D. *70*

Theme: *Persevering Faith in the Incarnate Son*

AUTHOR: In the early centuries of the Church, several differing opinions circulated as to the authorship of Hebrews. Tertullian (c. A.D. 160–225) cited Barnabas. St. Clement of Alexandria (c. A.D. 150–215) suggested Paul wrote Hebrews in Aramaic, the language of the Hebrew people, and Luke translated it into Greek. St. Irenaeus (c. A.D. 130–200) and St. Hippolytus (c. A.D. 170–236) questioned Paul's authorship. Origen (c. A.D. 185–254) saw the content of Hebrews as Pauline, but not the style and expression. Several early scholars believed Hebrews was written by a Hellenistic Jew, such as Apollos (Acts 18:24).

By the fourth century most witnesses ascribed Hebrews to St. Paul, including St. John Chrysostom (d. A.D. 407) and St. Athanasius (d. A.D. 373). Church historian Eusebius (d. c. A.D. 340) included Hebrews in his list of Paul's epistles, but noted that Rome rejected the letter because it was not Pauline. A Council at Carthage (A.D. 397) canonized Hebrews as one of fourteen epistles of Paul. All Orthodox lectionaries introduce Hebrews as "The Reading from the Epistle of the Holy Apostle Paul to the Hebrews." Nevertheless, most biblical scholars today agree that the authorship of the letter is uncertain.

DATE: The content of the epistle and the witness of the early Church argue for a date of composition near A.D. 70. One possible date is prior to the destruction of the temple in Jerusalem in A.D. 70. There is no reference to the fall of the city, and temple worship is described as if ongoing (although the author could be describing the Old Testament tabernacle). The other possible date is just after A.D. 70, during a persecution. Timothy is still alive (13:23) and eyewitnesses of the Lord, probably the Twelve, are still personally remembered (2:3). But the initial leaders of the churches addressed appear to be no longer alive (13:7). St. Clement of Rome referred to Hebrews in his letter to Corinth late in the first century.

MAJOR THEME: *Persevering faith in the incarnate Son.* Jesus Christ is superior to the prophets, angels, Moses and Aaron. He offers a better priesthood, sanctuary, and sacrifice, for in worshiping Him we enter heaven. Therefore, we must faithfully hold fast to Him.

BACKGROUND INFORMATION: (1) *The intended reader*. Hebrews seems to be written to Greek-speaking Jewish Christians, perhaps in Palestine, who were being drawn back to Judaism. Indeed, some had returned entirely to their Jewish roots, partly because of a low view of Jesus. Thus the subthemes of the book: (a) the superiority of Christ and His sacrifice over Judaism, and (b) encouragement to continue in the Christian faith. The Fathers generally considered the letter to be addressed to Palestinian Jewish Christians, not to the Diaspora living in Gentile lands, though numerous Jewish Christians were living in Rome (13:24). In the decade of A.D. 60 there was intense pressure for Jewish Christians to return to Judaism.

(2) *Historical setting*. The people addressed had previously demonstrated a deep faith (6:10), firmly enduring persecution themselves and aiding others under persecution (10:32–34). But now they were in a war of attrition. Internally, there was the perpetual battle with sin (12:1), and they had become dispirited and lax (12:2–4, 12, 13). Externally, there was the pressure of public contempt from their fellow Jews (13:13). The results of these pressures were: (a) they had ceased to grow in their faith (5:11–14); (b) they neglected corporate worship (10:25); (c) some possibly had already apostatized (6:4–8); (d) all were in danger of falling away (3:12) and of reverting to Judaism (13:9–14), enticed by its splendid worship and by its status as a legal religion, with economic and political connections.

(3) *Purpose*. Hebrews is not primarily a theological treatise but a rescue operation, a "word of exhortation" (13:22) to hold fast to the faith and persevere (3:6, 14; 10:23, 35–39; 12:1, 2).

(4) *Christological significance*. Nevertheless, Hebrews serves as one of the earliest treatises on the doctrine of Christ. It reveals that Jesus Christ is the Son of God, and what He has done, is doing, and will do forever in His earthly and heavenly ministry.

(5) *Liturgical significance*. Hebrews also serves as a treatise on Christian liturgical theology. It shows how the New Covenant fulfills and perfects Old Covenant liturgy, how New Covenant worship "enters into" heaven itself. For in the Eucharist, we participate in Christ's once-for-all sacrifice (9:26–28). It is He who offers and is offered—the perfect priest and perfect sacrifice in the heavenly liturgy and sanctuary. As Christ enters into heaven bodily, in His full human nature, so do we. The physical is in no way profane, but is truly sanctified.

(6) *Personal application*. As we come to know Christ and His work for us, we must stand firm and never reject God's grace. We serve and please Him through participation in His once-for-all sacrifice, tasting of the heavenly gift, sharing in the Holy Spirit. The Christian life is one of faith, love, and good works.

OUTLINE

I. The superiority of Christ 1:1—10:18
  A. Introduction: The supreme revelation 1:1–4
  B. Christ's authority is superior to the angels' 1:5—2:18

The Eve of the Birth of Jesus Christ (Christmas Eve) *December 24*

1:1–12: Jesus Christ, the Son of God Incarnate, is God's supreme revelation to man.

The Supreme Revelation of the Son of God

1 God, who [1]at various times and
[a]in various ways spoke in time
past to the fathers by the prophets,†
2 has in these last days spoken
to us by *His* Son, whom He has
appointed heir of all things,
through whom also He made the
[1]worlds;†
3 [a]who being the brightness of
His glory and the express [b]image
of His person, and [c]upholding
all things by the word of His
power, [d]when He had [1]by Himself
[2]purged [3]our sins, [e]sat down at
the right hand of the Majesty on
high,
4 having become so much better
than the angels, as [a]He has by inheritance obtained a more excellent
name than they.†

CHAPTER 1
1 [a]Num. 12:6, 8 [1]Or *in many portions*
2 [1]Or *ages,* Gr. *aiones,* aeons
3 [a]John 1:14 [b]2 Cor. 4:4 [c]Col. 1:17 [d][Heb. 7:27] [e]Ps. 110:1 [1]NU omits *by Himself* [2]*cleansed* [3]NU omits *our*
4 [a][Phil. 2:9, 10]

1:1–4 These verses provide an introductory summary to 1:1—10:18. The New Covenant is superior to the Old, for the Old is incomplete and preparatory whereas the New is complete and final. In the New Covenant man enters into the heavenly realm through Christ and is glorified (see Phil. 2:5–11 for a close parallel).

1:1, 2 In time past and **to the fathers** (v. 1) are contrasted with **in these last days** and **to us** (v. 2). In OT times God spoke constantly through the Holy Spirit in the Law and **the prophets,** leading His people into greater truth. Now He speaks to us directly, through His own incarnate Son. *The fathers* are the leaders of Israel, and representative of all the spiritual ancestors of the New Israel, the Church.

1:2, 3 Through whom also He made the worlds (v. 2; see John 1:3) and **upholding all things by the word of His power** (v. 3; see Col. 1:16, 17): These two phrases reveal the Son as God acting in the world. The Lord Jesus Christ is (1) the One who created the universe, together with the Father and the Holy Spirit, and is therefore (2) the One who sustains the creation and has absolute authority over it. It is natural, then, that the Son, as both God and man, is **heir of all things** (v. 2). If the sons of Abraham hoped to be heirs of the Promised Land, the sons of God in Christ can hope to be heirs of the whole universe.

The first half of v. 3 is quoted verbatim in the Liturgy of St. Basil the Great. The **brightness of His glory** expresses the Son's nature, His origin from and identity of nature with the Father. He is the Father's *brightness* because He is begotten from the Father beyond time and without change. Thus the Nicene Creed speaks of "Light of Light." As the sun does not exist without radiating light, so the Father does not exist without His Son.

Thus, the Son reflects His Father's glory in this world. The unapproachable light of divinity, the divine energy (1 Tim. 6:16; 1 Pet. 2:9; 1 John 1:7), is approachable only in the incarnate Christ (John 12:36). God's *brightness,* though it had been experienced at the burning bush (Ex. 3:2–4), known by Israel (Ex. 10:23; 13:21; 14:20), and spoken of by the prophets (Ps. 36:9; 104:2; Is. 9:1; 10:17; Hab. 3:4), is more fully revealed in Christ's birth (Luke 1:79; 2:32; John 1:4–9), the Transfiguration (Matt. 17:2) and the Resurrection.

The express image of His person (Gr. *hypostasis*) speaks of the Son's Person as being distinct from the Father. The Son is the perfect and eternal "icon" of the Father. Thus, the personal distinction of God as Trinity is known only through the Lord Jesus Christ (see John 14:9). No one knows the Father but through the Son.

Having conquered sin and death, the Son **sat down at the right hand of the Majesty on high,** a reference to the Father, showing Christ's exaltation as Man.

1:4 It is Christ's human nature, not His divine nature, which has **become so much better than the angels** (with regard to their role in the Old Covenant). His divine nature, of course, is eternally superior to the angels. The **name** inherited is an open declaration that this Man is the Son of God. In Hebrews this *name* is "Son;" in Phil. 2:11 it is "Lord."

Sunday of the Paralytic and Commemoration of St. Gregory Palamas *Second Sunday of Lent*

1:10—2:3: We dare not neglect the salvation granted in God the Son.

Christ's Dominion over Creation

5 For to which of the angels did
He ever say:

[a]*"You are My Son,*
Today I have begotten You"?†

And again:

[b]*"I will be to Him a Father,*
And He shall be to Me a Son"?

6 But when He again brings
[a]the firstborn into the world, He
says:

[b]*"Let all the angels of God*
worship Him."†

7 And of the angels He says:

[a]*"Who makes His angels spirits*
And His ministers a flame of
fire."

8 But to the Son *He says:*

[a]*"Your throne, O God, is forever*
and ever;
A [1]*scepter of righteousness is*
the scepter of Your kingdom.†
9 *You have loved righteousness*
and hated lawlessness;
Therefore God, Your God,
[a]*has anointed You*
With the oil of gladness more
than Your companions."†

Christ Without Beginning, Creator of All

10 And:

[a]*"You, LORD, in the beginning laid*
the foundation of the earth,
And the heavens are the work
of Your hands.
11 [a]*They will perish, but You*
remain;
And [b]*they will all grow old like*
a garment;
12 *Like a cloak You will fold them*
up,

5 [a]Ps. 2:7; Acts 13:33; Heb. 5:5 [b]2 Sam. 7:14
6 [a]Ps. 89:27; [Rom. 8:29] [b]Deut. 32:43, LXX, DSS; Ps. 97:7; 1 Pet. 3:22; Rev. 5:11–13
7 [a]Ps. 104:4
8 [a]Ps. 45:6, 7 [1]A ruler's staff
9 [a]Is. 61:1, 3
10 [a]Ps. 102:25–27
11 [a][Is. 34:4] [b]Is. 50:9; 51:6; Heb. 8:13

1:5–14 Much of first-century Judaism believed angels were present at creation and had mediated the Old Covenant. By using the rabbinic method of demonstration, Hebrews proves to lovers of Judaism that even the OT argues for the superiority of the Son.

1:5 Christ is superior to the angels. They are, in some Judaic thought, only "sons of God," whereas Christ is *the* **Son** of God. (The LXX at Deut. 32:43, which Hebrews paraphrases in v. 6, literally reads "sons of God," not "angels of God.") While Christ was recognized as God's eternal Son at His Baptism and the Transfiguration, it is His enthronement in heaven which settles the matter (vv. 3, 4; see Rom. 1:4). **Begotten** is a reference to the Son in His divine, eternal nature. The Nicene Creed states He is "begotten, not made, begotten from the Father from before all time." **Today** is eternity. There never was a time when God the Son did not exist.

1:6 Christ is **the firstborn** (1) of *God,* in that He is the Father's one and only eternal Son; (2) of all *creation,* in that He is the image (icon) by which creation was made and toward which creation is to move; and (3) of *man,* in that Christ Incarnate is the model for man's creation and the goal of man's existence. **The angels . . . worship Him** because He is God.

1:8 Psalm 45 (quoted in vv. 8, 9) celebrates a royal enthronement and wedding. The groom is a king who has conquered for righteousness and is called "god" (Heb. *Elohim*), though the king is distinct from God. This celebration is fulfilled with the messianic enthronement and wedding in the Kingdom of God. The OT gives the title "god" to Moses, Samuel, descendants of David, and angels, but it is primarily the Messiah who embodies this title. Here, God the Father calls **the Son, "God."**

1:9–12 In the Septuagint, this is in the third person. God the Father (v. 9) is addressing Another as "LORD," that is, as God.

Commemoration of the Holy Archangels *November 8*

2:2–10: This passage explains the place of angels in relationship to Christ.

And they will be changed.
But You are the [a]same,
And Your years will not fail."

13 But to which of the angels has
He ever said:

[a]*"Sit at My right hand,*
Till I make Your enemies Your
footstool"?

14 [a]Are they not all ministering
spirits sent forth to minister for those
who will [b]inherit salvation?†

Beware of Willful Negligence

2 Therefore we must give [1]the
more earnest heed to the things
we have heard, lest we drift away.†
2 For if the word [a]spoken through
angels proved steadfast, and [b]every
transgression and disobedience received a just [1]reward,
3 [a]how shall we escape if we neglect so great a salvation, [b]which at
the first began to be spoken by the

12 [a]Heb. 13:8
13 [a]Ps. 110:1
14 [a]Ps. 103:20 [b]Rom. 8:17

CHAPTER 2

1 [1]*all the more careful attention*
2 [a]Acts 7:53 [b]Num. 15:30 [1]*retribution or penalty*
3 [a]Heb. 10:28 [b]Matt. 4:17 [c]Luke 1:2
4 [a]Mark 16:20 [b]Acts 2:22, 43 [c]1 Cor. 12:4, 7, 11 [d]Eph. 1:5, 9 [1]*distributions*
5 [a][2 Pet. 3:13]
6 [a]Ps. 8:4–6
7 [1]Or *for a little while* [2]NU, M omit the rest of v. 7.
8 [a]Matt. 28:18

Lord, and was [c]confirmed to us by
those who heard *Him,*
4 [a]God also bearing witness
[b]both with signs and wonders, with
various miracles, and [c]gifts[1] of the
Holy Spirit, [d]according to His own
will?
5 For He has not put [a]the world
to come, of which we speak, in subjection to angels.†
6 But one testified in a certain
place, saying:

[a]*"What is man that You are*
mindful of him,
Or the son of man that You take
care of him?†
7 *You have made him [1]a little*
lower than the angels;
You have crowned him with
glory and honor,
[2]*And set him over the works of*
Your hands.
8 [a]*You have put all things in*
subjection under his feet."

For in that He put all in subjection
under him, He left nothing *that is* not

1:14 The role of angels is **to minister for those who will inherit salvation.** During the NT era, many Jews believed angels mediated the Old Covenant. Certainly they served the Angel of the Lord, the Son of God. In the New Covenant, they serve Him in His humanity. Instead of ruling over man, angels are partners in service with us.

2:1–4 These verses are an admonition against willful negligence and carelessness by a slow process of attrition, a **drift** (v. 1). **If** (v. 2) and **how** (v. 3) suggest a conditional statement or question. *If* Israel was to obey the words of created angels or suffer punishment, *how* much more must we heed what God Incarnate has said through His apostles—especially when the word has been **confirmed** (v. 3) by many **miracles** (v. 4) of the Spirit, proof that the Kingdom has come upon us. When we ask in the Liturgy for "pardon and remission of our sins and transgressions" and a "good defense before the dread judgment seat of Christ," we affirm there is **a just reward** (v. 2), or retribution, a very real judgment.

2:5–18 The Jews expected the Messiah to be an earthly, conquering king—a political success story, not a failure. They would naturally ask, if Jesus is superior to the angels—indeed, a divine being, as portrayed in ch. 1—why did He die, especially in such a degrading way? Hebrews answers, Christ's humiliation (1) is only temporary (v. 9), (2) is the only means of redeeming mortal man (vv. 14–16), and (3) reestablishes man's God-intended dominion over all creation, including the **angels** (vv. 5–8).

2:6–8 Hebrews applies the discussion in Ps. 8 about man to Jesus Christ, the perfect Man. Psalm 8:4 in Hebrew reads, "For You have made him little less than God (Heb. *Elohim*)"; Hebrews is quoting from the LXX, which reads **angels** instead of God.

The Annunciation: God's Message to the Virgin Mary *March 25*

2:11—18: Christ had to become man so that He could be our High Priest.

put under him. But now [b]we do not
yet see all things put under him.
9 But we see Jesus, [a]who was
made [1]a little lower than the angels,
for the suffering of death [b]crowned
with glory and honor, that He, by
the grace of God, might taste death
[c]for everyone.†
10 For it was fitting for Him,
[a]for whom *are* all things and by
whom *are* all things, in bringing
many sons to glory, to make the captain of their salvation [b]perfect
through sufferings.†

Why God Became Man

11 For [a]both He who [1]sanctifies
and those who are being sanctified
[b]*are* all of one, for which reason
[c]He is not ashamed to call them
brethren,
12 saying:

[a]*"I will declare Your name to My*
brethren;
In the midst of the assembly I
will sing praise to You."

8 [b]1 Cor. 15:25, 27
9 [a]Phil. 2:7–9 [b]Acts 2:33; 3:13 [c][John 3:16] [1]Or *for a little while*
10 [a]Col. 1:16 [b]Heb. 5:8, 9; 7:28
11 [a]Heb. 10:10 [b]Acts 17:26 [c]Matt. 28:10 [1]*sets apart*
12 [a]Ps. 22:22
13 [a]2 Sam. 22:3; Is. 8:17 [b]Is. 8:18
14 [a]John 1:14 [b]Col. 2:15 [c]2 Tim. 1:10
15 [a][Luke 1:74]
16 [1]Or *take on* the nature of [2]Or *take on*
17 [a]Phil. 2:7 [b][Heb. 4:15; 5:1–10]
18 [a][Heb. 4:15, 16]

13 And again:

[a]*"I will put My trust in Him."*

And again:

[b]*"Here am I and the children*
whom God has given Me."

14 Inasmuch then as the children
have partaken of flesh and blood, He
[a]Himself likewise shared in the
same, [b]that through death He might
destroy him who had the power of
[c]death, that is, the devil,†
15 and release those who [a]through
fear of death were all their lifetime
subject to bondage.†
16 For indeed He does not [1]give aid
to angels, but He does [2]give aid to
the seed of Abraham.
17 Therefore, in all things He had
[a]to be made like *His* brethren, that
He might be [b]a merciful and faithful
High Priest in things *pertaining* to
God, to make propitiation for the
sins of the people.†
18 [a]For in that He Himself has suf-

2:9 See Phil. 2:5–11. **Made a little lower than the angels** refers to the Incarnation, the Son becoming Man. Christ's **suffering** and **death** has highly exalted Him. The Cross, which should have brought shame and reproach, has brought Christ **glory and honor.** All of this is not something God has owed to man; it is **by the grace of God,** it is His gift. **Taste death** means to experience it fully, to know it intimately. Christ's death was a real death. He died for **everyone,** for the whole world, not for the faithful only.

2:10, 11 To make . . . perfect through sufferings does not suggest there was imperfection in Christ before the Cross. Rather, He voluntarily took on human nature (**all of one** nature, v. 11), which can be saved and perfected only by the suffering of death. Christ is the pioneering **captain** of the narrow path to God in His suffering for sin, death, descent into hell, Resurrection and Ascension. In salvation we take on Christ's way of suffering. Our perfection requires a growth that is manifested in suffering.

2:14 In the Incarnation, God did not come in appearance only; He truly assumed **flesh and blood** from the Virgin Mary, Mother of God, and became **the same** as we are, so that He could truly enter **death** and bring us salvation. Christ destroyed the devil's power by using the devil's strongest weapon—death itself.

2:15 There is a relationship between sin and death: each one leads to the other. Sin causes death, and the **fear of death** leads one to sin and thus to **bondage** (Rom. 5:12). Christ sets us free from this *bondage* of sin and death.

2:17, 18 In all things He had to be made like His brethren—Christ was even **tempted**—

(continued on next page)

fered, being [1]tempted, He is able to
aid those who are tempted.

Christ Is Faithful in a Superior Office

3 Therefore, holy brethren, partakers of the heavenly calling,
consider the Apostle and High Priest
of our confession, Christ Jesus,†
2 who was faithful to Him who
appointed Him, as [a]Moses also *was*
faithful in all His house.
3 For this One has been counted
worthy of more glory than Moses,
inasmuch as [a]He who built the
house has more honor than the
house.†
4 For every house is built by
someone, but [a]He who built all
things *is* God.
5 [a]And Moses indeed *was* faithful
in all His house as [b]a servant,
[c]for a testimony of those things
which would be spoken *afterward*,
6 but Christ as [a]a Son over His
own house, [b]whose house we are
[c]if we hold fast the confidence and
the rejoicing of the hope [1]firm to the
end.
7 Therefore, as [a]the Holy Spirit
says:

18 [1]*tested*

CHAPTER 3

2 [a]Num. 12:7
3 [a]Zech. 6:12, 13
4 [a][Eph. 2:10]
5 [a]Heb. 3:2 [b]Ex. 14:31 [c]Deut. 18:15, 18, 19
6 [a]Heb. 1:2 [b][1 Cor. 3:16] [c][Matt. 10:22] [1]NU omits *firm to the end*
7 [a]Acts 1:16 [b]Ps. 95:7–11

13 [1]*encourage*

[b]*"Today, if you will hear His*
voice,†
8 *Do not harden your hearts as*
in the rebellion,
In the day of trial in the
wilderness,
9 *Where your fathers tested Me,*
tried Me,
And saw My works forty years.
10 *Therefore I was angry with that*
generation,
And said, 'They always go
astray in their heart,
And they have not known My
ways.'
11 *So I swore in My wrath,*
'They shall not enter My rest.' "

Beware of Faithlessness

12 Beware, brethren, lest there be
in any of you an evil heart of unbelief
in departing from the living God;†
13 but [1]exhort one another daily,
while it is called *"Today,"* lest any
of you be hardened through the deceitfulness of sin.
14 For we have become partakers
of Christ if we hold the beginning

(continued from previous page)
for what is not assumed is not healed, and what is united to God is saved. The Son is like us in His human nature; we do not become like Him in His divine nature. Hebrews moves without transition from Christ as sacrifice to Christ as **High Priest,** for He is both the Offering and Offerer. He is **merciful** in behalf of those He serves and **faithful** in His ministry to God.

3:1 Christians are **holy brethren;** to be in Christ is a **heavenly calling,** one that separates those in Christ from those who have not heeded His call. As **Apostle** and **High Priest,** Christ is both God's representative to man and man's Mediator before God. In Him the offices of prophet and priest—of Moses and Aaron—are combined.

3:3–6 The glory of the building goes to the architect rather than to the structure itself. Thus **Moses** (v. 5) glorifies Christ, and the Church is consecrated to the glory of God, **whose house we are** (v. 6).

3:7–11 This reference is to the rebellion of those who left Egypt during the Exodus. Due to their unbelief, the whole **generation** (v. 10) was forbidden to enter into Canaan, the Promised Land, and thus could not enter God's **rest** (v. 11). Rest (Gr. *sabbatismos*) literally means a Sabbath rest or Sabbath observance.

There are three types of God's rest known to the Jews: (1) *the Sabbath rest,* the day on which God rested from His works (Gen. 2:2, 3); (2) *the rest from Egyptian bondage,* which the Israelites coming out of Egypt experienced in Canaan; (3) *the rest in the Kingdom,* the ultimate Sabbath rest found in heaven established by Messiah. Hebrews uses this OT quote (Ps. 95:7–11) concerning Canaan to refer to that rest which exists in the Kingdom of Heaven. Significantly, we experience this rest now, as we ascend to God in worship (4:4–11).

3:12 Those in Christ are not immune from turning away from God. There is a temporary attractiveness in sin, which leads to a hardened **heart** and ultimately to apostasy. Constant care must be taken not to be deceived and thus fall away (see Mark 4:5, 6, 16, 17).

of our confidence steadfast to the
end,†
15 while it is said:

[a]*"Today, if you will hear His*
voice,
Do not harden your hearts as
in the rebellion."

16 [a]For who, having heard, rebelled? Indeed, *was it* not all who
came out of Egypt, *led* by Moses?†
17 Now with whom was He angry
forty years? *Was it* not with those
who sinned, [a]whose corpses fell in
the wilderness?
18 And [a]to whom did He swear
that they would not enter His rest,
but to those who did not obey?
19 So we see that they could not
enter in because of [a]unbelief.

Entering God's Rest

4 Therefore, since a promise remains of entering His rest,
[a]let us fear lest any of you seem to
have come short of it.†
2 For indeed the gospel was
preached to us as well as to them;
but the word which they heard did
not profit them, [1]not being mixed
with faith in those who heard *it.*
3 For we who have believed do
enter that rest, as He has said:

[a]*"So I swore in My wrath,*
'They shall not enter My rest,' "

although the works were finished
from the foundation of the world.

15 [a]Ps. 95:7, 8
16 [a]Num. 14:2, 11, 30
17 [a]Num. 14:22, 23
18 [a]Num. 14:30
19 [a]1 Cor. 10:11, 12

CHAPTER 4

1 [a]Heb. 12:15
2 [1]NU, M *since they were not united by faith with those who heeded it*
3 [a]Ps. 95:11

4 [a]Gen. 2:2
5 [a]Ps. 95:11
7 [a]Ps. 95:7, 8
8 [a]Josh. 22:4 [1]Gr. *Jesus,* same as Heb. *Joshua*
11 [a]2 Pet. 1:10
12 [a]Ps. 147:15 [b]Is. 49:2

4 For He has spoken in a certain
place of the seventh *day* in this way:
[a]*"And God rested on the seventh*
day from all His works";
5 and again in this *place:* [a]*"They*
shall not enter My rest."

Christ's Rest Is Superior

6 Since therefore it remains that
some *must* enter it, and those to
whom it was first preached did not
enter because of disobedience,†
7 again He designates a certain
day, saying in David, *"Today,"* after
such a long time, as it has been said:

[a]*"Today, if you will hear His*
voice,
Do not harden your hearts."

8 For if [1]Joshua had [a]given them
rest, then He would not afterward
have spoken of another day.†
9 There remains therefore a rest
for the people of God.†
10 For he who has entered His rest
has himself also ceased from his
works as God *did* from His.

Work to Enter His Rest

11 [a]Let us therefore be diligent to
enter that rest, lest anyone fall according to the same example of
disobedience.†
12 For the word of God *is* [a]living
and powerful, and [b]sharper than any

3:14 Union with Christ belongs to those who persevere in their faith to **the end,** not to those who stop with a one-time profession of faith.

3:16–19 The five questions in this text demonstrate the consequences of Israel's disobedience and her failure to believe God in the wilderness. Once again, faith (v. 19) and works (v. 18) are distinguished but not separated. As the fundamental component of entering God's **rest** (v. 18) is faith, so the primary cause of failing to **enter** (v. 19) is **unbelief.**

4:1 Fear: Keep constant watch.

4:6 Faith (3:19) and obedience are inseparable. Lack of one is lack of the other. Lack of either bars entrance into rest.

4:8 Joshua and Caleb were the only two men who left Egypt and entered into Canaan (Num. 14:28–32; Deut. 1:34–40). They had not participated in the disobedience of Israel. The possession of Canaan under Joshua, though, was not the promised **rest.** Otherwise David would not have spoken centuries later of a rest still remaining for us (v. 3).

4:9 Rest here is a reference to the third type of rest (see note on 3:11), the perfect, final rest of the Kingdom of Heaven.

4:11 Man must labor to enter the rest of God, for rest implies prior work.

The Adoration of the Holy Cross *Third Sunday of Lent*

4:14—5:6: Christ is our High Priest, offering Himself on the Cross as a sacrifice for our sins.

[c]two-edged sword, piercing even to
the division of soul and spirit, and
of joints and marrow, and is [d]a discerner of the thoughts and intents
of the heart.†
13 [a]And there is no creature hidden from His sight, but all things *are*
[b]naked and open to the eyes of Him
to whom we *must give* account.

Our Merciful High Priest

14 Seeing then that we have a great
[a]High Priest who has passed
through the heavens, Jesus the Son
of God, [b]let us hold fast *our* confession.†
15 For [a]we do not have a High
Priest who cannot sympathize with
our weaknesses, but [b]was in all
points tempted as *we are*, [c]*yet* without
sin.†
16 [a]Let us therefore come boldly to
the throne of grace, that we may obtain mercy and find grace to help in
time of need.†

12 [c]Eph. 6:17 [d]1 Cor. 14:24, 25
13 [a]Ps. 33:13–15; 90:8 [b]Job 26:6
14 [a]Heb. 2:17; 7:26 [b]Heb. 10:23
15 [a]Is. 53:3–5 [b]Luke 22:28 [c]2 Cor. 5:21
16 [a][Eph. 2:18]

CHAPTER 5
1 [a]Heb. 2:17; 8:3
2 [a]Heb. 7:28 [1]*deal gently with*
3 [a]Lev. 9:7; 16:6
4 [a]Ex. 28:1
5 [a]John 8:54 [b]Ps. 2:7

Qualifications for Priesthood: Aaron and Melchizedek

5 For every high priest taken from
among men [a]is appointed for
men in things *pertaining* to God, that
he may offer both gifts and sacrifices
for sins.†
2 He can [1]have compassion on
those who are ignorant and going
astray, since he himself is also subject to [a]weakness.
3 Because of this he is required as
for the people, so also for [a]himself,
to offer *sacrifices* for sins.
4 And no man takes this honor
to himself, but he who is called by
God, just as [a]Aaron *was.*
5 [a]So also Christ did not glorify
Himself to become High Priest, *but*
it was He who said to Him:

[b]*"You are My Son,*
Today I have begotten You."†

6 As *He* also *says* in another *place:*

4:12, 13 The word of God and the **sword** here are **living and powerful.** The phrase **His sight** (v. 13) tells us this reference is not to the written word, Holy Scripture, but to the Word of God Himself, our Lord Jesus Christ (see John 1:1–18). Nothing is able to escape the discernment of Christ, the Word of God.

4:14 Passed through the heavens refers to the Ascension of Christ. It is seen in the context of the Son sitting "at the right hand of the Majesty on high" (1:3). Christ has accomplished His work on earth and has entered into His Sabbath rest.

4:15 Christ's empathy with sinners rests on His being **tempted** in every way **we are.**

4:16 Christ, enthroned at the right hand of the Father, sits on a **throne of grace** rather than of judgment, granting **mercy** and **grace to help in time of need.** The normal position for a priest is standing, not sitting. There is significant power in our enthroned Priest, for He has accomplished and fulfilled the sacrificial offering.

5:1–4 To qualify as priest in the OT one must (1) be **taken from among men** (v. 1), i.e., be fully human; (2) be **appointed for men** (v. 1), specifically for liturgical service; (3) offer **sacrifices** (v. 1); (4) **have compassion** (v. 2); and (5) be **called by God** (v. 4). In the Aaronic priesthood a priest identified himself with humanity and had sympathy for his fellowmen because he sinned as other men sinned. The sacrifices were vicarious offerings of animals.

5:5–11 Christ assumes and fulfills the OT priesthood (see 5:1–4): like **Melchizedek** (v. 6; see 7:1–21; Gen. 14:18–20), Jesus is both Priest and King. He does not sin, His sacrifice is the human sacrifice of Himself and His perfect priesthood continues in the Church to this day.

Commemoration of Holy Hieromartyrs

5:4–10: Following the example of Christ, the hieromartyrs offered their lives for their flock.

[a]*"You are a priest forever*
According to the order of
Melchizedek";

7 who, in the days of His flesh,
when He had [a]offered up prayers
and supplications, [b]with vehement
cries and tears to Him [c]who was able
to save Him from death, and was
heard [d]because of His godly fear,†
8 though He was a Son, *yet* He
learned [a]obedience by the things
which He suffered.†
9 And [a]having been perfected, He
became the author of eternal salvation to all who obey Him,
10 called by God as High Priest
[a]*"according to the order of Mel-*
chizedek,"

Beware of Immaturity

11 of whom [a]we have much to say,
and hard to explain, since you have
become [b]dull of hearing.†
12 For though by this time you
ought to be teachers, you need *some-*
one to teach you again the first principles of the [1]oracles of God; and you
have come to need [a]milk and not
solid food.
13 For everyone who partakes
only of milk *is* unskilled in the
word of righteousness, for he is [a]a
babe.
14 But solid food belongs to those
who are [1]of full age, *that is,* those
who by reason of [2]use have their
senses exercised [a]to discern both
good and evil.

6 Therefore, [a]leaving the discussion of the elementary *principles*
of Christ, let us go on to [1]perfection,
not laying again the foundation of
repentance from [b]dead works and of
faith toward God,†
2 [a]of the doctrine of baptisms,
[b]of laying on of hands, [c]of resurrection of the dead, [d]and of eternal
judgment.†

6 [a]Ps. 110:4
7 [a]Matt. 26:39, 42, 44 [b]Ps. 22:1 [c]Matt. 26:53 [d]Matt. 26:36
8 [a]Phil. 2:8
9 [a]Heb. 2:10
10 [a]Ps. 110:4
11 [a][John 16:12] [b][Matt. 13:15]
12 [a]1 Cor. 3:1–3 [1]*sayings,* Scriptures
13 [a]Eph. 4:14
14 [a]Is. 7:15 [1]*mature* [2]*practice*

CHAPTER 6
1 [a]Heb. 5:12 [b][Heb. 9:14] [1]*maturity*
2 [a]Acts 19:3–5 [b][Acts 8:17] [c]Acts 17:31 [d]Acts 24:25

5:7 Cries and tears is probably a reference to our Lord's agonizing prayer in the Garden of Gethsemane (Matt. 26:36–46; Mark 14:32–42; Luke 22:39–46).

5:8, 9 Christ **learned obedience** in his human will, which continually and freely submitted to the divine will. In the agony of injustice and in physical pain He submits to the will of the Father. This perfecting of human activity in communion with God shows Christ alone to be the Savior (v. 9).

5:11—6:20 How can one understand and enter into the message of the book of Hebrews? By (1) repenting of laziness (5:11; 6:12); (2) exercising one's spiritual senses, especially in doctrinal matters (5:12—6:8); (3) diligently doing good in all things, especially in loving service to others (6:9–12); and (4) firmly believing in Christ and the access He provides to God (6:13–20).

5:11–14 When Christians are not growing spiritually, doctrine is difficult to explain to them. Let us repent of being **dull of hearing** (v. 11)—a constant criticism Christ and the prophets had of God's people—and habitually and vigorously exercise ourselves in spiritual matters. According to St. John Chrysostom, the primary spiritual exercise is the study and knowledge of the Scriptures.

6:1–3 This passage gives a glimpse of some features of oral apostolic tradition.

6:1 Perfection is Christian maturity, the result of spiritual growth. **Dead works** are done without God's grace and without faith. Works of the Law are *dead* to those who know the New Covenant. Good works are done in **faith towards God.**

6:2 Baptisms are all the rites of washing, including those of the OT and of John the Baptist, fulfilled by Christ in the sacrament of Holy Baptism. **Laying on of hands** has several uses in the NT, such as for healing, prophetic commission, ordination, and reception of the Holy Spirit (chrismation).

3 And this [1]we will do if God
permits.
4 For *it is* impossible for those
who were once enlightened, and
have tasted [a]the heavenly gift, and
[b]have become partakers of the Holy
Spirit,†
5 and have tasted the good word
of God and the powers of the age
to come,†
6 [1]if they fall away, to renew them
again to repentance, [a]since they crucify again for themselves the Son of
God, and put *Him* to an open
shame.†
7 For the earth which drinks in
the rain that often comes upon it,
and bears herbs useful for those by
whom it is cultivated, [a]receives
blessing from God;†
8 [a]but if it bears thorns and
briers, *it is* rejected and near to
being cursed, whose end *is* to be
burned.

3 [1]M *let us do*
4 [a][John 4:10]; Eph. 2:8
[b][Gal. 3:2, 5]; Heb. 2:4
6 [a]Heb. 10:29
[1]Or *and have fallen away*
7 [a]Ps. 65:10
8 [a]Is. 5:6
10 [a]Rom. 3:4
[b]1 Thess. 1:3
[c]Rom. 15:25; Heb. 10:32–34
[1]NU omits *labor of*
11 [a]Col. 2:2
12 [a]Heb. 10:36
[1]*lazy*

Pursue the Promise with Persistence

9 But, beloved, we are confident
of better things concerning you, yes,
things that accompany salvation,
though we speak in this manner.
10 For [a]God *is* not unjust to forget
[b]your work and [1]labor of love which
you have shown toward His name,
in that you have [c]ministered to the
saints, and do minister.†
11 And we desire that each one of
you show the same diligence [a]to the
full assurance of hope until the end,
12 that you do not become
[1]sluggish, but imitate those who
through faith and patience [a]inherit
the promises.†

God Confirms the Promise by an Oath

13 For when God made a promise
to Abraham, because He could swear

6:4–6 This refers to those who have apostatized—that is those who, after being baptized, have rejected Christ and His saving power. Historically, these verses have been used extensively in discussions of repentance. For example, Tertullian, the Montanists and other ancient schismatics used these verses to argue there is no repentance from apostasy. The Church holds that those who apostatize may repent and be brought back into the Church after a period of repentance (see Canons VIII, X and XIV of I Nicea; Canon II of St. Gregory of Nyssa; and the Canons of the Council of Ancyra, A.D. 314). Nevertheless, such "second conversions" are difficult and rare—thus this sober warning.

6:4 The basic sacraments are crucial to salvation: One is **once enlightened** in baptism, which is unrepeatable and called the sacrament of illumination (see Eph. 5:14). **Tasted the heavenly gift** (see 1 Pet. 2:3) may refer to the grace of baptism—St. John Chrysostom says this *gift* is especially the forgiveness of sin experienced in baptism—and it most certainly refers to the Eucharist. **Become partakers of the Holy Spirit** refers to the fruit of chrismation, the experience of knowing the Holy Spirit.

6:5 Besides the sacraments (v. 4), belief and life experience are also essential: **tasted the good word of God** refers to the message of the gospel and the true doctrine of the Church, especially the confession of faith. **The powers of the age to come** are manifold: incorruption and eternal life, the presence of the future Kingdom here and now, and also miracles and spiritual gifts (Matt. 7:22, 23; 12:28).

6:6 Those who revert to Judaism **crucify** Christ **again**—they become like those who hung Christ on the Cross, who denied His deity and His saving power. They put themselves in a position of needing to be baptized again, which is impossible, for baptism is death and the dead cannot be put to death. To deny one's baptism is to mock Christ's death. Such may not be renewed **again to repentance.**

6:7, 8 This metaphor is reminiscent of John the Baptist's and Jesus' images and parables of trees and their fruit (Matt. 3:8–10; 7:16–20; 12:33; 21:19).

6:10 To **minister** is to serve someone else's will. The word has a liturgical dimension. In part, ministry flows out of liturgical worship (see 2 Cor. 9:12, where "the administration of this service" is more literally translated "the service of this worship"). Prayer leads to action: the supreme NT example is the collection for the church in Jerusalem (Rom. 15:25, 31; 2 Cor. 8:4).

6:12 For examples, see vv. 13–15 and ch. 11.

Commemoration of Holy Prophets *Fourth Sunday of Lent*
Commemoration of St. John of the Ladder
6:13–20: God has promised a steadfast Hope.

by no one greater, [a]He swore by Himself,†

14 saying, [a]*"Surely blessing I will bless you, and multiplying I will multiply you."*

15 And so, after he had patiently endured, he obtained the [a]promise.

16 For men indeed swear by the greater, and [a]an oath for confirmation *is* for them an end of all dispute.

17 Thus God, determining to show more abundantly to [a]the heirs of promise [b]the [1]immutability of His counsel, [2]confirmed *it* by an oath,†

18 that by two [1]immutable things, in which it *is* impossible for God to [a]lie, we [2]might have strong consolation, who have fled for refuge to lay hold of the hope [b]set before *us*.

19 This *hope* we have as an anchor of the soul, both sure and steadfast, [a]and which enters the Presence *behind* the veil,†

20 [a]where the forerunner has entered for us, *even* Jesus, [b]having become High Priest forever according to the order of Melchizedek.†

13 [a]Gen. 22:16, 17
14 [a]Gen. 22:16, 17
15 [a]Gen. 12:4; 21:5
16 [a]Ex. 22:11
17 [a]Heb. 11:9 [b]Rom. 11:29 [1]*unchangeableness of His purpose* [2]*guaranteed*
18 [a]Num. 23:19 [b][Col. 1:5] [1]*unchangeable* [2]M omits *might*
19 [a]Lev. 16:2, 15
20 [a][Heb. 4:14] [b]Heb. 3:1; 5:10, 11

Priestly Orders: Levi and Melchizedek

CHAPTER 7

7 For this [a]Melchizedek, king of Salem, priest of the Most High God, who met Abraham returning from the slaughter of the kings and blessed him,†

2 to whom also Abraham gave a tenth part of all, first being translated "king of righteousness," and then also king of Salem, meaning "king of peace,"

3 without father, without mother, without genealogy, having neither beginning of days nor end of life, but made like the Son of God, remains a priest continually.

4 Now consider how great this man *was,* to whom even the patriarch Abraham gave a tenth of the [1]spoils.

5 And indeed [a]those who are of the sons of Levi, who receive the priesthood, have a commandment to receive tithes from the people according to the law, that is, from their brethren, though they have come from the loins of Abraham;

6 but he whose genealogy is not derived from them received tithes from Abraham [a]and blessed [b]him who had the promises.

The Rules of the Priestly Orders

7 Now beyond all contradiction the lesser is blessed by the better.

8 Here mortal men receive tithes, but there he *receives them,* [a]of whom it is witnessed that he lives.

1 [a]Gen. 14:18–20
4 [1]*plunder*
5 [a]Num. 18:21–26
6 [a]Gen. 14:19, 20 [b][Rom. 4:13]
8 [a]Heb. 5:6; 6:20

6:13–15 The promise made to Abraham was that of a son, an heir through whom God would greatly **multiply** (v. 14) him.

6:17, 18 The **two immutable things** are God's promise and God's oath.

6:19 Behind the veil (see the note on 9:1–5) is heaven.

6:20 Melchizedek: The author picks up the argument from 5:10.

7:1–10 Persecuted Christians are encouraged not to apostatize to Judaism because the founding father of Christ's priesthood, Melchizedek, is superior to the OT priesthood of Levi.

Note the importance of the tithe: the desire to enter into the ministrations of a priesthood is fulfilled when such a liturgical offering is made. Throughout the OT, Israelites showed their continuing desire for God's priesthood by giving a **tenth** of all they received. Biblically, the tithe is a crucial element of worship.

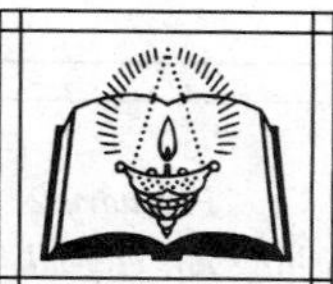

THE PRIESTHOOD—EARTHLY AND ETERNAL

A major theme of the Book of Hebrews is the contrast between the earthly, or Levitical, priesthood, and the eternal priesthood of Melchizedek, which is fulfilled in Christ.

The Levitical priesthood, established by Aaron of the tribe of Levi, is limited simply because those who fill it are ordinary human beings. The Levitical priests carry out God's instructions and assist the people in their worship, but they cannot ultimately reconcile people to God.

The mysterious figure of Melchizedek, on the other hand, represents an entirely different kind of priesthood. Melchizedek appears in Genesis (Gen. 14:18-20), long before the establishment of the Levitical priesthood. He is given no genealogy, and nothing is said of his death. He receives tithes from Abraham, implying he is superior to Abraham in rank—and by extension, superior to Abraham's descendants, the Levites. Melchizedek is not only a priest but a king as well. In this dual office he is able to reconcile the justice of God (the business of a king) with His mercy (the business of a priest). His name means "King of Righteousness," and his title "King of Salem" (Gen. 14:18) means "King of Peace." He may be a theophany—a preincarnate appearance of Christ; at the very least he is a type of Christ, as the author of Hebrews explains in detail.

There are several specific points of contrast between the Levitical priesthood and the priesthood of Melchizedek, which is fulfilled in Christ.

The Priesthood of Levi	The Priesthood of Melchizedek
(1) *Genealogical requirement*: The Levitical priesthood is limited to one tribe. It cannot transform mortal and corrupt humanity, because it consists of mere men.	As Melchizedek was without earthly genealogy, so is Christ by virtue of His virgin birth. He is God incarnate, immortal and sinless, and therefore His priesthood is able to transform humanity.
(2) *Ordination*: The power given at ordination is incomplete. The Levitical priesthood is weak, its sacrifices have to be repeated, and it cannot perfect the worshipers. It cannot reconcile people to God, nor give them the inner power to obey. The ordination is without direct confirmation from God.	The power given at ordination is strong and effective. The power of Christ's priesthood is perfect and draws us near to God. His sacrifice is offered once for all. The Father Himself ordains the Son.
(3) *Term of office*: The Levitical priesthood is temporary. Since it is composed of mortal men, it requires many members.	Since Christ is immortal, the priesthood of Melchizedek needs only one, eternal priest.
(4) *Moral and spiritual requirements*: These must be less than perfection, for the Levitical priests are all created beings subject to sin.	The requirement of perfect holiness is met in Christ, the only sinless One. He is more than mere man—He is the Son of God.

The Presentation of the Lord in the Temple *February 2*

7:7–17: In obeying the law, Christ fulfilled and transcended the law, establishing His eternal priesthood.

9 Even Levi, who receives tithes,
paid tithes through Abraham, so to
speak,
10 for he was still in the loins of
his father when Melchizedek met
him.
11 [a]Therefore, if perfection were
through the Levitical priesthood (for
under it the people received the law),
what further need *was there* that another priest should rise according to
the order of Melchizedek, and not
be called according to the order of
Aaron?†
12 For the priesthood being
changed, of necessity there is also a
change of the law.
13 For He of whom these things are
spoken belongs to another tribe,
from which no man has [1]officiated
at the altar.
14 For *it is* evident that [a]our Lord
arose from [b]Judah, of which tribe
Moses spoke nothing concerning
[1]priesthood.
15 And it is yet far more evident
if, in the likeness of Melchizedek,
there arises another priest
16 who has come, not according to
the law of a fleshly commandment,
but according to the power of an
endless life.
17 For [1]He testifies:

[a]*"You are a priest forever*
According to the order of
Melchizedek."

18 For on the one hand there is an
annulling of the former commandment because of [a]its weakness and
unprofitableness,
19 for [a]the law made nothing
[1]perfect; on the other hand, *there is*
the bringing in of [b]a better hope,
through which [c]we draw near to
God.
20 And inasmuch as *He was* not
made priest without an oath
21 (for they have become priests
without an oath, but He with an oath
by Him who said to Him:

[a]*"The LORD has sworn*
And will not relent,
'You are a priest [1]*forever*
According to the order of
Melchizedek'"),

22 by so much more Jesus has become a [1]surety of a [a]better covenant.
23 Also there were many priests,
because they were prevented by
death from continuing.
24 But He, because He continues
forever, has an unchangeable priesthood.
25 Therefore He is also [a]able to
save [1]to the uttermost those who
come to God through Him, since He
always lives [b]to make intercession
for them.
26 For such a High Priest was fitting for us, [a]*who is* holy, [1]harmless,
undefiled, separate from sinners,
[b]and has become higher than the
heavens;
27 who does not need daily, as
those high priests, to offer up sacrifices, first for His [a]own sins and then
for the people's, for this He did once
for all when He offered up Himself.
28 For the law appoints as high
priests men who have weakness, but
the word of the oath, which came

11 [a][Rom. 7:7–14]; Gal. 2:21; Heb. 7:18; 8:7
13 [1]*served*
14 [a]Gen. 49:8–10; Num. 24:17; Is. 1:1; Mic. 5:2; Matt. 1:3; 2:6; Rev. 5:5 [b]Matt. 1:2 [1]NU *priests*
17 [a]Ps. 110:4; Heb. 5:6; 6:20; 7:21 [1]NU *it is testified*
18 [a][Rom. 8:3]; Gal. 3:21; Heb. 7:11
19 [a][Acts 13:39]; Rom. 3:20; 7:7; Gal. 2:16; 3:21; Heb. 9:9; 10:1 [b]Heb. 6:18, 19 [c]Lam. 3:57; Rom. 5:2; [Eph. 2:18]; Heb. 4:16; James 4:8 [1]*complete*
21 [a]Ps. 110:4; Heb. 5:6; 7:17 [1]NU ends the quotation after *forever.*
22 [a]Heb. 8:6 [1]*guarantee*
25 [a]Jude 24 [b]Rom. 8:34; 1 Tim. 2:5; Heb. 9:24; 1 John 2:1 [1]*completely* or *forever*
26 [a][2 Cor. 5:21]; Heb. 4:15 [b]Eph. 1:20 [1]*innocent*
27 [a]Lev. 9:7; 16:6; Heb. 5:3

7:11–28 Not only is the founder of the New Covenant priesthood superior to that of the Old Covenant, the rules of the New Covenant's priestly order are also superior. Priesthood is so intertwined with a covenant that if the priesthood is changed, so is the covenant (vv. 11–15).

Commemoration of a Holy Hierarch

7:26—8:2: Priests of the New Covenant serve as representatives of the Great High Priest, Jesus Christ.

after the law, *appoints* the Son who has been perfected forever.

The Old Worship, an Earthly Shadow

8 Now *this is* the main point of the
things we are saying: We have
such a High Priest, [a]who is seated
at the right hand of the throne of
the Majesty in the heavens,†
2 a Minister of [a]the [1]sanctuary
and of [b]the true tabernacle which the
Lord erected, and not man.
3 For [a]every high priest is appointed to offer both gifts and sacrifices. Therefore [b]*it is* necessary that this One also have something to offer.
4 For if He were on earth, He
would not be a priest, since there are
priests who offer the gifts according
to the law;
5 who serve [a]the copy and [b]shadow of the heavenly things, as Moses
was divinely instructed when he was
about to make the tabernacle. For He
said, [c]*"See that you make all things according to the pattern shown you on the mountain."*
6 But now [a]He has obtained a
more excellent ministry, inasmuch as
He is also Mediator of a [b]better covenant, which was established on better promises.†

CHAPTER 8
1 [a]Col. 3:1
2 [a]Heb. 9:8, 12
[b]Heb. 9:11, 24
[1]Lit. *holies*
3 [a]Heb. 5:1; 8:4
[b][Eph. 5:2]
5 [a]Heb. 9:23, 24
[b]Col. 2:17
[c]Ex. 25:40
6 [a][2 Cor. 3:6–8]
[b]Heb. 7:22
7 [a]Ex. 3:8; 19:5
8 [a]Jer. 31:31–34
10 [a]Jer. 31:33
[b]Zech. 8:8
11 [a]Is. 54:13
[b]Jer. 31:34
12 [a]Rom. 11:27
[1]NU omits *and their lawless deeds*
13 [a][2 Cor. 5:17]

The Old Covenant Pleads for a New One

7 For if that [a]first *covenant* had
been faultless, then no place would
have been sought for a second.
8 Because finding fault with them,
He says: [a]*"Behold, the days are coming, says the LORD, when I will make a new covenant with the house of Israel and with the house of Judah—*
9 *"not according to the covenant that I made with their fathers in the day when I took them by the hand to lead them out of the land of Egypt; because they did not continue in My covenant, and I disregarded them, says the LORD.*
10 *"For this is the covenant that I will make with the house of Israel after those days, says the* [a]*LORD: I will put My laws in their mind and write them on their hearts; and* [b]*I will be their God, and they shall be My people.*
11 [a]*"None of them shall teach his neighbor, and none his brother, saying, 'Know the* [b]*LORD,' for all shall know Me, from the least of them to the greatest of them.*
12 *"For I will be merciful to their unrighteousness,* [a]*and their sins* [1]*and their lawless deeds I will remember no more."*
13 [a]In that He says, *"A new cov-*

8:1 Majesty is a biblical name for God the Father. A high priest sitting on the right hand of *majesty* would have to be both human and divine. **Seated:** No one but an equal sits in the presence of a king—much less in the presence of God.

8:6–13 Christ's covenant solves the problems that Moses' could not. Both covenants come from God's grace and require man's willed response. However, Moses' covenant (1) is external to man and cannot solve the root of man's problem, sin and death; (2) cannot reunite and reintegrate man's soul; (3) is learned by teaching; (4) is heeded with fearful compliance; and (5) gives imperfect forgiveness.

Christ's covenant (1) is internal—it heals our nature; (2) unifies the inner man—heart and mind are joined in union with God; (3) is therefore grasped intuitively; (4) is heeded with willing cooperation (synergy); and (5) gives perfect forgiveness, even of those sins the Old Covenant was powerless to deal with.

The Protection of the Virgin Mary *October 1*
The Entry of the Virgin Mary into the Temple *November 21*
9:1–7: The Virgin became the holy tabenacle of the Lord whom she bore in her womb.

enant," He has made the first obsolete. Now what is becoming obsolete
and growing old is ready to vanish
away.

The Earthly Sanctuary and Liturgy

9 Then indeed, even the first *cov-*
enant had ordinances of divine
service and [a]the earthly sanctuary.†
2 For a tabernacle was prepared:
the first *part,* in which *was* the lampstand, the table, and the showbread,
which is called the [1]sanctuary;
3 [a]and behind the second veil, the
part of the tabernacle which is called
the Holiest of All,†
4 which had the [a]golden censer
and [b]the ark of the covenant overlaid
on all sides with gold, in which *were*
[c]the golden pot that had the manna,
[d]Aaron's rod that budded, and
[e]the tablets of the covenant;†
5 and [a]above it were the cherubim
of glory overshadowing the mercy
seat. Of these things we cannot now
speak in detail.†
6 Now when these things had
been thus prepared, [a]the priests always went into the first part of the
tabernacle, performing *the services.*†
7 But into the second part the
high priest *went* alone [a]once a year,
not without blood, which he offered
for [b]himself and *for* the people's sins
committed in ignorance;
8 the Holy Spirit indicating this,
that [a]the way into the Holiest of All
was not yet made manifest while
the first tabernacle was still standing.

CHAPTER 9
1 [a]Ex. 25:8
2 [1]*holy place,* lit. *holies*
3 [a]Ex. 26:31–35; 40:3
4 [a]Lev. 16:12 [b]Ex. 25:10 [c]Ex. 16:33 [d]Num. 17:1–10 [e]Ex. 25:16; 34:29
5 [a]Lev. 16:2
6 [a]Num. 18:2–6; 28:3
7 [a]Ex. 30:10 [b]Heb. 5:3
8 [a][John 14:6]

9:1–5 These verses give a description of the Mosaic tabernacle, which is a copy of the heavenly altar. This passage is read during feasts of the Virgin Mary and Advent to describe the mystery of the Incarnation of the Son of God. Mary's womb was prepared to be Christ's tabernacle, the very dwelling place of God.

9:3 A most important detail in Hebrews is the inner veil, **the second veil.** It separates the holy place (v. 2, **the sanctuary**) from the Most Holy Place (v. 3, **the Holiest of All**) which contains the ark of the covenant and into which only the high priest can enter, and only once a year. The inner veil forms the locus of the liturgical practice of the Old Covenant (vv. 6–10) and reveals its imperfection. The people could not draw near to God (see especially v. 8). At His death, Christ resolved this alienation (Matt. 27:51).

9:4 The **ark of the covenant** contained the relics, as it were, of Israel: the **pot** of **manna, Aaron's rod,** and **the tablets** of the Law.

9:5 God is enthroned upon the **cherubim;** hence, God's throne in Israel's midst, **the mercy seat,** has a cherub on each side (the Orthodox Christian altar is also flanked by cherubim). These representations, along with the pictures of cherubim on the inner veil (Ex. 26:31) and the beauty and detailed workmanship of everything made for the tabernacle, serve as the icons of the OT. This, and numerous other passages, help put to rest the fear that the Second Commandment (Ex. 20:4–6) prohibits all imagery. God cannot be represented because divine nature is unknowable and hence cannot be depicted. However, when the Son becomes Man the human nature of God the Son can be, and is, imaged.

9:6–10 While priests entered the holy place daily, only the high priest could enter the Most Holy Place and only once a year, on the Day of Atonement (Heb. *yom kippur*). He entered with the animal blood of the atonement sacrifice, which was first for his own sins and then for the sins of the people. This annual sacrifice reveals the imperfect, temporary status of the Old Covenant, for: (1) only one man can enter God's presence; (2) that man cannot enter continually; (3) he must enter occasionally to repeat the sacrifice for sins, a sacrifice good only for a limited time; (4) this sacrifice deals entirely with materials from this age, which are imperfect and impermanent—it cannot begin a participation in the age to come (v. 10, **the time of reformation**); (5) it deals mainly with the outer man—it is superficial and cannot purify man's heart and mind, let alone restore fallen human nature.

9 It *was* symbolic for the present
time in which both gifts and sacrifices are offered [a]which cannot make
him who performed the service perfect in regard to the conscience—
10 *concerned* only with [a]foods and
drinks, [b]various [1]washings, [c]and
fleshly ordinances imposed until the
time of reformation.

The Heavenly Sanctuary and Liturgy

11 But Christ came *as* High Priest
of [a]the good things [1]to come, with
the greater and more perfect tabernacle not made with hands, that is, not
of this creation.†
12 Not [a]with the blood of goats
and calves, but [b]with His own blood
He entered the Most Holy Place
[c]once for all, [d]having obtained eternal redemption.
13 For if [a]the blood of bulls and
goats and [b]the ashes of a heifer,
sprinkling the unclean, [1]sanctifies for
the [2]purifying of the flesh,
14 how much more shall the blood
of Christ, who through the eternal
Spirit offered Himself without
[1]spot to God, [a]cleanse your conscience from [b]dead works [c]to serve
the living God?†

The New Covenant: The Blood of Christ

15 And for this reason [a]He is the
Mediator of the new covenant, by
means of death, for the redemption
of the transgressions under the first
covenant, that [b]those who are called
may receive the promise of the eternal inheritance.†
16 For where there *is* a testament,
there must also of necessity be the
death of the testator.
17 For [a]a testament *is* in force after
men are dead, since it has no power
at all while the testator lives.
18 [a]Therefore not even the first
covenant was dedicated without
blood.
19 For when Moses had spoken
every [1]precept to all the people according to the law, [a]he took the
blood of calves and goats, [b]with water, scarlet wool, and hyssop, and
sprinkled both the book itself and all
the people,
20 saying, [a]*"This is the* [b]*blood of
the covenant which God has commanded you."*
21 Then likewise [a]he sprinkled
with blood both the tabernacle and
all the vessels of the ministry.†
22 And according to the law almost
all things are [1]purified with blood,

9 [a][Gal. 3:21]; Heb. 7:19
10 [a]Lev. 11:2; Col. 2:16 [b]Num. 19:7 [c]Eph. 2:15 [1]Lit. *baptisms*
11 [a][Eph. 1:3–11]; Heb. 10:1 [1]NU *that have come*
12 [a]Heb. 10:4 [b]Is. 53:12; Eph. 1:7 [c]Zech. 3:9 [d][Dan. 9:24]
13 [a]Lev. 16:14, 15; Heb. 9:19; 10:4 [b]Num. 19:2 [1]*sets apart* [2]*cleansing*
14 [a]1 John 1:7 [b]Heb. 6:1 [c]Luke 1:74 [1]*blemish*
15 [a]Rom. 3:25 [b]Heb. 3:1
17 [a]Gal. 3:15
18 [a]Ex. 24:6
19 [a]Ex. 24:5, 6 [b]Lev. 14:4, 7; Num. 19:6, 18 [1]*command*
20 [a][Matt. 26:28] [b]Ex. 24:3–8
21 [a]Ex. 29:12, 36
22 [1]*cleansed*

9:11–14 Christ, in contrast to the OT high priest (see note on vv. 6–10), is High Priest of the New Covenant. He enters the heavenly sanctuary (1) **once for all** (v. 12)—Christ's one sacrifice covers all sins by all people for all time—and (2) with **the blood of Christ** (v. 14), His own human blood, which (a) heals our corrupt humanity (v. 13, **the flesh**); (b) restores us to our proper relationship to God, pure (v. 14, **cleanse our conscience**) and holy; and (c) draws us near to God in liturgical worship (v. 14, **serve the living God**). **Dead works** (see 6:1) are human activity in and of this age, participating in mortality and corruption (and normally even in sin). Liturgically *dead works* are the actions of Old Covenant worship.

9:14 This reference to the **eternal Spirit** is proof that the Holy Spirit is fully God.

9:15–23 Hebrews contrasts the Day of Atonement (once every year for forgiveness) with the Covenant Ceremony (once at the beginning to establish the covenant). In Christ's one sacrificial offering, He effects what all the sacrifices of the Old Covenant did not. He even covers those saints departed under the Old Covenant, that they might enter God's presence as they had been promised.

The Greek word *diatheke* means both **covenant** (vv. 15, 18, 20) and last will and **testament** (vv. 16, 17). (1) As with a *testament*, a **death** (vv. 16, 17) is required to initiate the covenant's conditions. This death is a death to sinning; the new condition initiated by the testament is that of the resurrection, the reformation of our nature. (2) As with a *covenant*, sprinkling **with blood** (v. 21) is necessary to consecrate all dedicated things into the covenantal reality. The locus of life is blood (Lev. 17:11). So blood, our mortal life, is offered to God, who is life, and establishes us in a new relationship with Him (vv. 19–21).

9:21–23 Why was the earthly sanctuary sprinkled with consecrated blood? Because it had

(continued on next page)

and [a]without shedding of blood there is no [2]remission.
23 Therefore *it was* necessary that [a]the copies of the things in the heavens should be [1]purified with these, but the heavenly things themselves with better sacrifices than these.†

The New Worship Is Heavenly Reality

24 For [a]Christ has not entered the holy places made with hands, *which are* [1]copies of [b]the true, but into heaven itself, now [c]to appear in the presence of God for us;
25 not that He should offer Himself often, as [a]the high priest enters the Most Holy Place every year with blood of another—
26 He then would have had to suffer often since the foundation of the world; but now, once at the end of the ages, He has appeared to put away sin by the sacrifice of Himself.
27 [a]And as it is appointed for men to die once, [b]but after this the judgment,
28 so [a]Christ was [b]offered once to bear the sins [c]of many. To those who [d]eagerly wait for Him He will appear a second time, apart from sin, for salvation.

The New Worship Accomplishes God's Will

10 For the law, having a [a]shadow of the good things to come, *and* not the very image of the things, [b]can never with these same sacrifices, which they offer continually year by year, make those who approach perfect.†
2 For then would they not have ceased to be offered? For the worshipers, once [1]purified, would have had no more consciousness of sins.†
3 But in those *sacrifices there is* a reminder of sins every year.
4 For [a]*it is* not possible that the blood of bulls and goats could take away sins.
5 Therefore, when He came into the world, He said:

[a]*"Sacrifice and offering You did not desire,*
But a body You have prepared for Me.
6 *In burnt offerings and sacrifices for sin*
You had no pleasure.
7 *Then I said, 'Behold, I have come—*
In the volume of the book it is written of Me—
To do Your will, O God.'"

8 Previously saying, *"Sacrifice and offering, burnt offerings, and offerings for sin You did not desire, nor had pleasure in them"* (which are offered according to the law),†
9 then He said, *"Behold, I have come to do Your will, [1]O God."* He takes away the first that He may establish the second.

22 [a]Lev. 17:11 [2]*forgiveness*
23 [a]Heb. 8:5 [1]*cleansed*
24 [a]Heb. 6:20 [b]Heb. 8:2 [c]Rom. 8:34 [1]*representations*
25 [a]Heb. 9:7
27 [a]Gen. 3:19; Eccl. 3:20 [b][2 Cor. 5:10]; 1 John 4:17
28 [a]Rom. 6:10 [b]Is. 53:12; 1 Pet. 2:24 [c]Matt. 26:28 [d]1 Cor. 1:7; Titus 2:13

CHAPTER 10

1 [a]Heb. 8:5 [b]Heb. 7:19; 9:9
2 [1]*cleansed*
4 [a]Mic. 6:6, 7
5 [a]Ps. 40:6–8
9 [1]NU, M omit *O God*

(continued from previous page)
to be cleansed, being of this mortal and corrupt realm, and it also needed to be consecrated to God. The heavenly sanctuary, of course, never was unclean, but there was a need for worship to be inaugurated there.

9:23–28 Hebrews moves back to the sacrificial act of the Day of Atonement (from vv. 11–14). The blood sprinkled here brings the life of the covenantal people into God's presence: it reconciles God and man. The final reconciliation, the eternal one, is the presentation of Christ's sacrificial blood (12:24) to God in heaven.

10:1 Worship in **shadow** has no power because it has no substance of its own and does not participate directly in the spiritual reality. True Christian worship, however, is **the very image** (Gr. *eikon,* from which "icon" is derived) **of the things.** It is united with eternal realities and participates in the Kingdom to come by participating in the voluntary Passion and exaltation of the incarnate Son (v. 10), the only release from our mortal and corrupt existence.

10:2–7 Although OT sacrifices prefigured Christ's sacrifice, they were powerless in themselves. An effective sacrifice requires **a body . . . prepared** (v. 5), a righteous human being who voluntarily obeys the Father (v. 7).

10:8–10 This is a common prophetic theme throughout the OT (see 1 Sam. 15:22;
(continued on next page)

10 [a]By that will we have been
[1]sanctified [b]through the offering of
the body of Jesus Christ once *for all.*

The New Worship Gives Boldness

11 And every priest stands [a]minis-
tering daily and offering repeatedly
the same sacrifices, which can never
take away sins.†
12 [a]But this Man, after He had offered one sacrifice for sins forever,
sat down [b]at the right hand of God,
13 from that time waiting [a]till His
enemies are made His footstool.
14 For by one offering He has perfected forever those who are being
[1]sanctified.†
15 But the Holy Spirit also witnesses to us; for after He had said
before,
16 [a]*"This is the covenant that I will
make with them after those days,
says the* LORD: *I will put My laws
into their hearts, and in their minds
I will write them,"*
17 *then He adds,* [a]*"Their sins and
their lawless deeds I will remember
no more."*
18 Now where there is [1]remission
of these, *there is* no longer an offering
for sin.

10 [a]John 17:19; [Eph. 5:26; Heb. 2:11; 10:14, 29; 13:12] [b][Heb. 9:12] [1]*set apart*
11 [a]Num. 28:3
12 [a]Col. 3:1; Heb. 1:3 [b]Ps. 110:1
13 [a]Ps. 110:1; Heb. 1:13
14 [1]*set apart*
16 [a]Jer. 31:33, 34; Heb. 8:10
17 [a]Jer. 31:34
18 [1]*forgiveness*
19 [a][Eph. 2:18]; Heb. 4:16 [b]Heb. 9:8, 12 [1]*confidence*
20 [a]John 14:6; [Heb. 7:24, 25]
22 [a]Heb. 7:19; 10:1 [b]Eph. 3:12
23 [a]1 Cor. 1:9; 10:13; 1 Thess. 5:24; Heb. 11:11
25 [a]Acts 2:42 [b]Rom. 13:11 [c]Phil. 4:5
26 [a]Num. 15:30 [b]2 Pet. 2:20 [c]Heb. 6:6

Continue to Enter and Draw Near

19 Therefore, brethren, having
[a]boldness[1] to enter [b]the Holiest by
the blood of Jesus,
20 by a new and [a]living way which
He consecrated for us, through the
veil, that is, His flesh,
21 and *having* a High Priest over
the house of God,
22 let us [a]draw near with a true
heart [b]in full assurance of faith, having our hearts sprinkled from an evil
conscience and our bodies washed
with pure water.†
23 Let us hold fast the confession
of *our* hope without wavering, for
[a]He who promised *is* faithful.
24 And let us consider one another
in order to stir up love and good
works,†
25 [a]not forsaking the assembling of
ourselves together, as *is* the manner
of some, but exhorting *one another,*
and [b]so much the more as you see
[c]the Day approaching.†

The Danger of Apostasy

26 For [a]if we sin willfully [b]after we
have received the knowledge of the
truth, there [c]no longer remains a sacrifice for sins,†

(continued from previous page)
Ps. 50:8–15; Is. 1:10–17; Jer. 7:21–26; Hos. 6:6). This is not in opposition to liturgical, sacramental worship, but a statement of priority: obedience comes before praise. Sacrifice pleasing to God requires voluntary human sacrifice, not the slaughter of dumb animals. The primary instance of this is Christ, who did God's will in a liturgical, sacramental act (v. 10).

10:11, 12 A priest **stands,** a king sits. Christ is both. Old Testament priests stood **daily** and vainly repeated ineffectual **sacrifices.** Christ offers His **one** perfect **sacrifice** (v. 12) and sits. His work is completed. The Church **repeatedly** does certain things, but she does not repeat Christ's sacrifices; she participates in Christ's once-for-all *sacrifice.*

10:14–18 The completeness of Christ's sacrifice establishes the prophesied New Covenant: Sacrifice for sin is complete, sanctification is perfect.

10:22 Full assurance of faith: With no doubts or second thoughts. **Sprinkled . . . washed** are past participles referring to a single action in the past, i.e., to baptism.

10:24 Love and good works go hand-in-hand, as attitude and action. They are almost synonymous.

10:25 Assembling: The assembly in the OT (Heb. *koheleth*) is translated *ekklesia* in Greek, which we translate as "church." God instructs the faithful not to forsake *assembling* as the church. Corporate worship on a daily basis, such as morning prayers or matins, increases our expectation of **the Day,** the coming of the Kingdom.

10:26, 27 While many sins are willful, to **sin willfully** here means defiant sin or a deliberate repudiation of God (see 5:2; 6:4–6). Christ is the offering for all sin—voluntary and involuntary—which demonstrates God's incomparable grace toward us. But if we deliberately and with full knowledge reject the sacrifice of Christ—which is all-encompassing and final—then where can we possibly turn to obtain forgiveness?

27 but a certain fearful expectation
of judgment, and [a]fiery indignation
which will devour the adversaries.
28 Anyone who has rejected Moses' law dies without mercy on the
testimony of two or three [a]wit-
nesses.
29 [a]Of how much worse punishment, do you suppose, will he be
thought worthy who has trampled
the Son of God underfoot, [b]counted
the blood of the covenant by which
he was sanctified a common thing,
[c]and insulted the Spirit of grace?
30 For we know Him who said,
[a]*"Vengeance is Mine, I will repay,"*
[1]says the Lord. And again, [b]*"The*
LORD will judge His people."
31 [a]It is a fearful thing to fall into
the hands of the living God.

Continue to Persevere

32 But [a]recall the former days in
which, after you were [1]illuminated,
you endured a great struggle with
sufferings:†
33 partly while you were made
[a]a spectacle both by reproaches and
tribulations, and partly while [b]you
became companions of those who
were so treated;
34 for you had compassion on
[1]me [a]in my chains, and [b]joyfully accepted the plundering of your
[2]goods, knowing that [c]you have a
better and an enduring possession
for yourselves [3]in heaven.
35 Therefore do not cast away your
confidence, [a]which has great reward.
36 [a]For you have need of endurance, so that after you have done the
will of God, [b]you may receive the
promise:

27 [a]Zeph. 1:18
28 [a]Deut. 17:2–6; 19:15
29 [a][Heb. 2:3] [b]1 Cor. 11:29 [c][Matt. 12:31]
30 [a]Deut. 32:35 [b]Deut. 32:36 [1]NU omits *says the Lord*
31 [a][Luke 12:5]
32 [a]Gal. 3:4 [1]*enlightened*
33 [a]1 Cor. 4:9 [b]Phil. 1:7
34 [a]2 Tim. 1:16 [b]Matt. 5:12 [c]Matt. 6:20 [1]NU *the prisoners* instead of *me in my chains* [2]*possessions* [3]NU omits *in heaven*
35 [a]Matt. 5:12
36 [a]Luke 21:19 [b][Col. 3:24]
37 [a]Luke 18:8 [b]Hab. 2:3, 4 [1]Or *that which* [2]*delay*
38 [a]Rom. 1:17 [1]NU *My just one*
39 [a]2 Pet. 2:20 [b]Acts 16:31 [1]*destruction*

CHAPTER 11

1 [a]Rom. 8:24 [1]*realization* [2]Or *confidence*
3 [a]Ps. 33:6 [1]Or *ages*, Gr. *aiones*, aeons
4 [a]Gen. 4:3–5 [b]Heb. 12:24
5 [a]Gen. 5:21–24

37 *"For [a]yet a little while,*
And [b]He[1] who is coming will
come and will not [2]tarry.
38 *Now [a]the[1] just shall live by*
faith;
But if anyone draws back,
My soul has no pleasure in
him."

39 But we are not of those [a]who
draw back to [1]perdition, but of those
who [b]believe to the saving of the
soul.

Faith's Hope

11 Now faith is the [1]substance of
things hoped for, the [2]evi-
dence [a]of things not seen.†
2 For by it the elders obtained a
good testimony.
3 By faith we understand that
[a]the [1]worlds were framed by the
word of God, so that the things
which are seen were not made of
things which are visible.

Faith from Creation to the Flood

4 By faith [a]Abel offered to God a
more excellent sacrifice than Cain,
through which he obtained witness
that he was righteous, God testifying
of his gifts; and through it he being
dead still [b]speaks.
5 By faith Enoch was taken away
so that he did not see death, [a]*"and*
was not found, because God had
taken him"; for before he was taken
he had this testimony, that he
pleased God.
6 But without faith *it is* impossible
to please *Him*, for he who comes to
God must believe that He is, and *that*

10:32 Illuminated: Illumination, or enlightenment, refers to baptism (see 6:4; Rom. 6:4; Eph. 5:14).

11:1 This is not so much a definition of fa th as it is a description of how faith works, especially during hard times. It encourages Jewish Christians discouraged by persecution. **Things hoped for** and **not seen,** a vision of the future, have encouraged the people of God throughout history: the invisible is often more real than the visible. In the past, mighty works of faith were done by those whose faith was unfulfilled (they did not see redemption in their lifetime). How much more should those persevere who have inherited the promise, knowing God under the New Covenant (vv. 39, 40).

Sunday of the Holy Fathers *Sunday before Christmas*

11:9, 10, 17–23, 32–40: The Holy Fathers continue the great tradition of faith of these Old Testament saints.

He is a rewarder of those who diligently seek Him.

7 By faith [a]Noah, being divinely warned of things not yet seen, moved with godly fear, [b]prepared an ark for the saving of his household, by which he condemned the world and became heir of [c]the righteousness which is according to faith.

Faith from Abraham to Joseph

8 By faith [a]Abraham obeyed when he was called to go out to the place which he would receive as an inheritance. And he went out, not knowing where he was going.†

9 By faith he dwelt in the land of promise as *in* a foreign country, [a]dwelling in tents with Isaac and Jacob, [b]the heirs with him of the same promise;

10 for he waited for [a]the city which has foundations, [b]whose builder and maker *is* God.

11 By faith [a]Sarah herself also received strength to conceive seed, and [b]she[1] bore a child when she was past the age, because she judged Him [c]faithful who had promised.

12 Therefore from one man, and him as good as [a]dead, were born *as many* as the [b]stars of the sky in multitude—innumerable as the sand which is by the seashore.

13 These all died in faith, [a]not having received the [b]promises, but [c]having seen them afar off [1]were assured of them, embraced *them* and [d]confessed that they were strangers and pilgrims on the earth.

14 For those who say such things [a]declare plainly that they seek a homeland.

15 And truly if they had called to mind [a]that *country* from which they had come out, they would have had opportunity to return.

16 But now they desire a better, that is, a heavenly *country*. Therefore God is not ashamed [a]to be called their God, for He has [b]prepared a city for them.

17 By faith Abraham, [a]when he was tested, offered up Isaac, and he who had received the promises offered up his only begotten *son,*

18 [1]of whom it was said, [a]*"In Isaac your seed shall be called,"*

19 concluding that God [a]*was* able to raise *him* up, even from the dead, from which he also received him in a figurative sense.

20 By faith [a]Isaac blessed Jacob and Esau concerning things to come.

21 By faith Jacob, when he was dying, [a]blessed each of the sons of Joseph, and worshiped, *leaning* on the top of his staff.†

22 By faith [a]Joseph, when he was dying, made mention of the departure of the children of Israel, and gave instructions concerning his bones.

Faith from Moses to Joshua

23 By faith [a]Moses, when he was born, was hidden three months by

7 [a]Gen. 6:13–22 [b]1 Pet. 3:20 [c]Rom. 3:22
8 [a]Gen. 12:1–4
9 [a]Gen. 12:8; 13:3, 18; 18:1, 9 [b]Heb. 6:17
10 [a][Heb. 12:22; 13:14] [b][Rev. 21:10]
11 [a]Gen. 17:19; 18:11–14; 21:1, 2 [b]Luke 1:36 [c]Heb. 10:23 [1]NU omits *she bore a child*
12 [a]Rom. 4:19 [b]Gen. 15:5; 22:17; 32:12
13 [a]Heb. 11:39 [b]Gen. 12:7 [c]John 8:56 [d]Ps. 39:12 [1]NU, M omit *were assured of them*
14 [a]Heb. 13:14
15 [a]Gen. 11:31
16 [a]Ex. 3:6, 15; 4:5 [b][Rev. 21:2]
17 [a]James 2:21
18 [a]Gen. 21:12 [1]*to*
19 [a]Rom. 4:17
20 [a]Gen. 27:26–40
21 [a]Gen. 48:1, 5, 16, 20
22 [a]Gen. 50:24, 25
23 [a]Ex. 2:1–3

11:8–12 Faith is simple, but it becomes many-splendored in our lives. For Abraham and Sarah it became (1) a venturesome action (v. 8), (2) obedience (v. 8), (3) patience (vv. 9, 10), (4) trust (v. 11), and (5) confidence (v. 11). Faith moves from the impermanence and discomfort of living **in tents** made by man (v. 9) to the permanence and solace of **the city** built by **God** (v. 10).

11:21 Jacob . . . blessed Joseph's **sons** with his hands crossed (Gen. 48:14), an action which prefigures the Cross.

Sunday of Orthodoxy *First Sunday of Lent*
Sunday of All Saints *First Sunday after Pentecost*
11:24–26; 11:32—12:2: The foundation of the Church is the sufferings of her saints.

his parents, because they saw *he was*
a beautiful child; and they were not
afraid of the king's [b]command.
24 By faith [a]Moses, when he became of age, refused to be called the
son of Pharaoh's daughter,
25 choosing rather to suffer affliction with the people of God than to
enjoy the [1]passing pleasures of sin,
26 esteeming [a]the [1]reproach of
Christ greater riches than the treasures [2]in Egypt; for he looked to the
[b]reward.
27 By faith [a]he forsook Egypt, not
fearing the wrath of the king; for he
endured as seeing Him who is
invisible.
28 By faith [a]he kept the Passover
and the sprinkling of blood, lest he
who destroyed the firstborn should
touch them.
29 By faith [a]they passed through
the Red Sea as by dry *land, whereas*
the Egyptians, attempting *to do* so,
were drowned.
30 By faith [a]the walls of Jericho fell
down after they were encircled for
seven days.
31 By faith [a]the harlot Rahab did
not perish with those who [1]did not
believe, when [b]she had received the
spies with peace.

Faith of Other Israelites

32 And what more shall I say? For
the time would fail me to tell of
[a]Gideon and [b]Barak and [c]Samson
and [d]Jephthah, also *of* [e]David and
[f]Samuel and the prophets:
33 who through faith subdued
kingdoms, worked righteousness,
obtained promises, [a]stopped the
mouths of lions,
34 [a]quenched the violence of fire,
escaped the edge of the sword, out
of weakness were made strong, became valiant in battle, turned to
flight the armies of the aliens.
35 [a]Women received their dead
raised to life again. Others were
[b]tortured, not accepting deliverance,
that they might obtain a better
resurrection.
36 Still others had trial of mockings
and scourgings, yes, and [a]of chains
and imprisonment.
37 [a]They were stoned, they were
sawn in two, [1]were tempted, were
slain with the sword. [b]They wandered about [c]in sheepskins and
goatskins, being destitute, afflicted,
tormented—†
38 of whom the world was not
worthy. They wandered in deserts
and mountains, [a]*in* dens and caves
of the earth.†

Faith's Perfection

39 And all these, [a]having obtained
a good testimony through faith, did
not receive the promise,
40 God having provided something better for us, that they should
not be [a]made perfect apart from us.†

Look to Jesus

12 Therefore we also, since we
are surrounded by so great a

23 [b]Ex. 1:16, 22
24 [a]Ex. 2:11–15
25 [1]*temporary*
26 [a]Heb. 13:13
[b]Rom. 8:18
[1]*reviling because of*
[2]NU, M *of*
27 [a]Ex. 10:28
28 [a]Ex. 12:21
29 [a]Ex. 14:22–29
30 [a]Josh. 6:20
31 [a]Josh. 2:9; 6:23
[b]Josh. 2:1
[1]*were disobedient*
32 [a]Judg. 6:11; 7:1–25
[b]Judg. 4:6–24
[c]Judg. 13:24—16:31
[d]Judg. 11:1–29; 12:1–7
[e]1 Sam. 16; 17
[f]1 Sam. 7:9–14
33 [a]Dan. 6:22
34 [a]Dan. 3:23–28
35 [a]1 Kin. 17:22
[b]Acts 22:25
36 [a]Gen. 39:20
37 [a]1 Kin. 21:13
[b]2 Kin. 1:8
[c]Zech. 13:4
[1]NU omits *were tempted*
38 [a]1 Kin. 18:4, 13; 19:9
39 [a]Heb. 11:2, 13
40 [a]Heb. 5:9

11:37 Sawn in two: Some traditions say that Isaiah was killed in this manner by Manasseh (see the pseudepigraphal *Martyrdom of Isaiah*). See also Jer. 26:23; 2 Macc. 5:26, 27; 6:12—7:42; Matt. 23:29–36.

11:38 Caves: See 2 Macc. 6:11; 10:6.

11:40 See 9:15. Christ's Incarnation, and all that He accomplished for us in the flesh, redeems the OT saints who by faith participate in His Resurrection and His Kingdom.

cloud of witnesses, [a]let us lay aside
every weight, and the sin which so
easily ensnares *us,* and [b]let us run
[c]with endurance the race that is set
before us,†
2 looking unto Jesus, the [1]author
and [2]finisher of *our* faith, [a]who for
the joy that was set before Him
[b]endured the cross, despising the
shame, and [c]has sat down at the
right hand of the throne of God.†
3 [a]For consider Him who endured
such hostility from sinners against
Himself, [b]lest you become weary
and discouraged in your souls.

Do Not Despise God's Chastening

4 [a]You have not yet resisted to
bloodshed, striving against sin.†
5 And you have forgotten the exhortation which speaks to you as to
sons:

> [a]"*My son, do not despise the*
> *[1]chastening of the* LORD,
> *Nor be discouraged when you*
> *are rebuked by Him;*
>
> 6 *For [a]whom the* LORD *loves He*
> *chastens,*
> *And scourges every son whom*
> *He receives."*

7 [a]If[1] you endure chastening, God
deals with you as with sons; for what
[b]son is there whom a father does not
chasten?
8 But if you are without chastening, [a]of which all have become partakers, then you are illegitimate and
not sons.
9 Furthermore, we have had
human fathers who corrected *us,*
and we paid *them* respect. Shall we
not much more readily be in subjection to [a]the Father of spirits and
live?
10 For they indeed for a few days
chastened *us* as seemed *best* to them,
but He for *our* profit, [a]that *we* may
be partakers of His holiness.
11 Now no [1]chastening seems to be
joyful for the present, but painful;
nevertheless, afterward it yields
[a]the peaceable fruit of righteousness
to those who have been trained by
it.
12 Therefore [a]strengthen the
hands which hang down, and the
feeble knees,
13 and make straight paths for
your feet, so that what is lame may

CHAPTER 12
1 [a]Col. 3:8 [b]1 Cor. 9:24 [c]Rom. 12:12
2 [a]Luke 24:26 [b]Phil. 2:8 [c]Ps. 110:1 [1]*originator* [2]*perfecter*
3 [a]Matt. 10:24 [b]Gal. 6:9
4 [a][1 Cor. 10:13]
5 [a]Prov. 3:11, 12 [1]*discipline*
6 [a]Rev. 3:19
7 [a]Deut. 8:5 [b]Prov. 13:24; 19:18; 23:13 [1]NU, M *It is for discipline that you endure; God*
8 [a]1 Pet. 5:9
9 [a][Job 12:10]
10 [a]Lev. 11:44
11 [a]James 3:17, 18 [1]*discipline*
12 [a]Is. 35:3

12:1–29 This entire passage (beginning with 10:19) is a progressive discourse imploring us to seek God's Kingdom first. Under the New Covenant, we can ascend to this heavenly place in worship and in prayer. Christians experience this heavenly dimension fundamentally in the Divine Liturgy. We ascend to that place where we are surrounded by a **great . . . cloud of witnesses** (v. 1). This is not a physical place (v. 18) but a spiritual place (v. 22), inhabited by God, the angels, and **the spirits of just men made perfect** (v. 23). Here, the communion of the saints is established in the NT.

In 9:11, 12 we saw Christ come to the greater and more perfect tabernacle, obtaining eternal redemption for us. In 12:22 this tabernacle is that same spiritual place, showing that we enter the holy place with Christ by virtue of our union with Him (10:19, 20). This is done fundamentally (1) in corporate worship (10:25), (2) by faith (11:1–3), and (3) in order to show gratitude to God (12:28, 29). The content of this worship includes remembering the departed righteous (11:4–40; see also Ps. 112:1–6; Prov. 10:7).

12:1 The **cloud of witnesses** includes not only the OT saints mentioned in ch. 11, but also the saints and martyrs of the Lord in all ages. If they made it, so can we. We persevere by (1) getting rid of **sin,** the **weight** which keeps us from heeding the truth; (2) setting as our destination the heavenly city, running **the race** of faith; and (3) keeping our attention focused on Jesus Christ our Lord and King (v. 2). This race is not a sprint but a marathon of **endurance:** it does not end until we fully enter the age to come (see 1 Cor. 9:24–27).

12:2, 3 Christ is both the **author** (initiator) and **finisher** (perfecter) of **faith.** His **joy** was to do God's will. He **endured the cross** in that He voluntarily accepted humiliation and death. We are to follow His determination and perseverance.

12:4–11 Unpleasant circumstances, which tempt us to complain, may be the **chastening of the LORD** (v. 5). If the loving discipline of our **human** fathers brought us to respect them, how much more deserving of respect is the discipline of **the Father of spirits** (v. 9), our Creator whose breath gives us life (Gen. 1:26; 2:7).

not be *dislocated,* but rather be
healed.†
14 [a]Pursue peace with all *people,*
and holiness, [b]without which no one
will see the Lord:†
15 looking carefully lest anyone
[a]fall short of the grace of God; lest
any [b]root of bitterness springing up
cause trouble, and by this many become defiled;
16 lest there *be* any [a]fornicator or
[1]profane person like Esau, [b]who for
one morsel of food sold his birthright.
17 For you know that afterward,
when he wanted to inherit the blessing, he was [a]rejected, for he found
no place for repentance, though he
sought it diligently with tears.

The Heavenly Jerusalem

18 For you have not come [1]to
[a]the mountain that may be touched
and that burned with fire, and to
blackness and [2]darkness and tempest,†
19 and the sound of a trumpet and
the voice of words, so that those who
heard *it* [a]begged that the word
should not be spoken to them
anymore.
20 (For they could not endure what
was commanded: [a]*"And if so much*
as a beast touches the mountain, it
shall be stoned [1]*or shot with an*
arrow."
21 And so terrifying was the sight
that Moses said, [a]*"I am exceedingly*
afraid and trembling.")
22 But you have come to Mount
Zion and to the city of the living
God, the heavenly Jerusalem, to an
innumerable company of angels,†
23 to the [1]general assembly and
church of [a]the firstborn [b]*who are* registered in heaven, to God [c]the Judge
of all, to the spirits of just men
[d]made perfect,

14 [a]Ps. 34:14 [b]Matt. 5:8
15 [a]Heb. 4:1 [b]Deut. 29:18
16 [a][1 Cor. 6:13–18] [b]Gen. 25:33 [1]*godless*
17 [a]Gen. 27:30–40
18 [a]Deut. 4:11; 5:22 [1]NU *to that which* [2]NU *gloom*
19 [a]Ex. 20:18–26
20 [a]Ex. 19:12, 13 [1]NU, M omit the rest of v. 20.
21 [a]Deut. 9:19
23 [a][James 1:18] [b]Luke 10:20 [c]Ps. 50:6; 94:2 [d][Phil. 3:12] [1]*festal gathering*

12:13 Straight paths as a metaphor for following God's will is a theme found throughout both the OT and the NT. See especially Deut. 6:6 and Matt. 7:13, 14.

12:14–17 An especially heavy "weight" (v. 1) is **bitterness,** a spirit of habitual complaining. Bitterness refuses God's chastening and defiles us before God. **Esau** became bitter about Jacob's easy, favored life in contrast to his own life of difficulty. Bitterness blinded him to what is truly valuable, so that he traded his family honor, **his birthright,** for one small meal (Gen. 25:27–34). For this Esau is called a **fornicator** (v. 16), being unfaithful to God and uniting his spirit to this temporary age. Later, when he changed his mind, his father Isaac would not relent. Esau missed his blessing (Gen. 27:30–40). Thus, our two clear choices for life are bitterness or blessing.

12:18–21 The mountain (v. 18) of the New Covenant, Mt. Zion, is the fulfillment of the mountain of the Old Covenant, Mt. Sinai. Sinai is remembered as the place where God first called Israel to meet Him (Ex. 19:9–23; 20:18–21; Deut. 4:11, 12; 5:22–26). It was a place of fear, a place not to be approached or touched, out in the desert where Israel could not live permanently. Israel met God, and God spoke, but Israel could not fully enter into God's holiness.

12:22–24 We are encouraged to approach and touch the **heavenly** mountain, for we already participate in the Kingdom and dwell there. It is more like **Mount Zion** and **Jerusalem** (v. 22) than Sinai (popular Jewish images at that time), for Jerusalem was a habitable place and Zion a place of God's holy presence. This Kingdom is not earthly but *heavenly,* inhabited by **angels** (v. 22) as well as men. There is an unending **assembly** (v. 23), the divinely instituted gathering of God's people of all ages where they know themselves as **church.** There all are collectively **firstborn** (v. 23) and have inherited all. There **blood** (v. 24) cries not for vengeance and further death—as did Abel's (see 11:4; Gen. 4:10)—but for mercy, forgiveness, atonement and unending life. This is the blood of Christ given to us in the Eucharist.

Heaven is not a place of the separation of the soul from the body. There, soul and body together are transformed into a **better** (v. 24) humanity. For **the spirits of just men made perfect** (v. 23; see 11:40) are in unity with their bodies *made perfect:* glorified, divinely energized, without the limitations we now experience. This passage is quoted in hymns for both the Trisagion and Funeral services of the Orthodox Church. **The blood of sprinkling** (v. 24) is that of Christ which effects the New Covenant—real blood, effective for people with a physical nature.

Lazarus Saturday *Saturday before Palm Sunday*
12:28—13:8: As Lazarus was raised, so is our hope in Christ's Resurrection.

24 to Jesus [a]the Mediator of the
new covenant, and to [b]the blood of
sprinkling that speaks better things
[c]than *that of* Abel.
25 See that you do not refuse Him
who speaks. For [a]if they did not escape who refused Him who spoke
on earth, much more *shall we not es-*
cape if we turn away from Him who
speaks from heaven,†
26 whose voice then shook the
earth; but now He has promised,
saying, [a]*"Yet once more I* [1]*shake not*
only the earth, but also heaven."†
27 Now this, *"Yet once more,"* indicates the [a]removal of those things
that are being shaken, as of things
that are made, that the things which
cannot be shaken may remain.

The Purity of Christian Community

28 Therefore, since we are receiving a kingdom which cannot be
shaken, let us have grace, by which
we [1]may [a]serve God acceptably with
reverence and godly fear.
29 For [a]our God *is* a consuming
fire.

13 Let [a]brotherly love continue.†
2 [a]Do not forget to enter-
tain strangers, for by so *doing* [b]some
have unwittingly entertained angels.
3 [a]Remember the prisoners as if
chained with them—those who are
mistreated—since you yourselves are
in the body also.
4 [a]Marriage *is* honorable among
all, and the bed undefiled; [b]but fornicators and adulterers God will judge.
5 *Let your* conduct *be* without covetousness; *be* content with such
things as you have. For He Himself
has said, [a]*"I will never leave you nor*
forsake you."
6 So we may boldly say:

[a]*"The LORD is my helper;*
I will not fear.
What can man do to me?"

Remember Those Who Rule over You

7 Remember those who [1]rule over
you, who have spoken the word of
God to you, whose faith follow, considering the outcome of *their* conduct.†
8 Jesus Christ *is* [a]the same yesterday, today, and forever.†

24 [a]Heb. 8:6; 9:15 [b]Ex. 24:8 [c]Gen. 4:10
25 [a]Heb. 2:2, 3
26 [a]Hag. 2:6 [1]NU *will shake*
27 [a][Is. 34:4; 54:10; 65:17]
28 [a]Heb. 13:15, 21 [1]M omits *may*
29 [a]Ex. 24:17

CHAPTER 13

1 [a]Rom. 12:10
2 [a]Matt. 25:35 [b]Gen. 18:1–22; 19:1
3 [a]Matt. 25:36
4 [a]Prov. 5:18, 19 [b]1 Cor. 6:9
5 [a]Deut. 31:6, 8; Josh. 1:5
6 [a]Ps. 27:1; 118:6
7 [1]*lead*
8 [a]Heb. 1:12

12:25 He **who speaks from heaven** is Christ at the right hand of the Father.

12:26–28 What can be **shaken** (v. 27) is that which is created: temporal, impermanent, imperfect—except for the final consummation of the **kingdom** (v. 28), which is unshakable. There, life is a eucharistic liturgy. The **grace** we can possess (v. 28) is gratitude that leads to serving God and worshiping Him in an acceptable way, with proper **reverence and godly fear.**

13:1–3 Practical **brotherly love** is to be shown toward all Christians, but especially for the lowly, the powerless and the victims of injustice. **Strangers** (v. 2) are travelers in need of hospitality. Abraham's hospitality is recalled (Gen. 18:1–8; also 19:1–3). **Prisoners** (v. 3) are to be prayed for, and aided if possible, for all those **in the body** of Christ, the Church, are members of one another (1 Cor. 12:12–27).

13:7 Those who rule are especially the leaders of the sacraments (bishops and priests). These Christian leaders are not only to be prayed for (see v. 3) but followed as models of Christian life as well. The **faith** of Christian leaders is that faith they both teach and live by.

13:8 Such a faith does not disappoint. Since Christ is God and does not change, His gospel does not change. If Christians in the past attained the eternal Kingdom through faith, so can we. Thus the Church strives to keep her doctrine pure and without change.

Commemoration of a Hieromartyr

13:7–16: The hieromartyrs made the greatest sacrifice saints of God can offer—their own lives.

Loyalty to Orthodox Doctrine and Worship

9 Do not be carried [1]about with various and strange doctrines. For *it is* good that the heart be established by grace, not with foods which have not profited those who have been occupied with them.†
10 We have an altar from which those who serve the tabernacle have no right to eat.†
11 For the bodies of those animals, whose blood is brought into the sanctuary by the high priest for sin, are burned outside the camp.†
12 Therefore Jesus also, that He might [1]sanctify the people with His own blood, suffered outside the gate.
13 Therefore let us go forth to Him, outside the camp, bearing [a]His reproach.†
14 For here we have no continuing city, but we seek the one to come.
15 [a]Therefore by Him let us continually offer [b]the sacrifice of praise to God, that is, [c]the fruit of *our* lips, [1]giving thanks to His name.†
16 [a]But do not forget to do good and to share, for [b]with such sacrifices God is well pleased.

9 [1]NU, M *away*
12 [1]*set apart*
13 [a]1 Pet. 4:14
15 [a]Eph. 5:20 [b]Lev. 7:12 [c]Hos. 14:2 [1]Lit. *confessing*
16 [a]Rom. 12:13 [b]Phil. 4:18

13:9 Strange doctrines are "foreign" ones, those not coming from the One, Holy, Catholic and Apostolic Church. In this case, the outside teaching is Jewish and legalistic. Kosher laws dealing with food do no spiritual good if **grace** is not at the heart of one's actions. Such has always been the teaching of the Church with regard to fasting (See 9:9, 10).

13:10 In the OT, priests were given part of most sacrifices for food, but lay people had **no right to eat** this food. Under the New Covenant, all Christians may eat the food of the **altar.**

13:11, 12 On the only day of the year when the Most Holy Place could be entered, the Day of Atonement, only the High Priest could be brought in and then only with the blood of sin offerings. The bodies of these animals were not eaten but **burned outside the camp.** Christ identified with this supreme sacrifice of the OT in that He **suffered** and died **outside the gate** (v. 12). His blood was not carried into the temple in Jerusalem by another human, however. Rather, He carried His own blood into the heavenly Most Holy Place in the eternal "today." This great entrance of Christ shows the Divine Liturgy is eternal and for all under the New Covenant. We, being members of our High Priest, Jesus Christ, may always enter in.

13:13, 14 The camp here is the Old Covenant, Israel and all its institutions and worship. The **city** (v. 14) is the earthly Jerusalem, the temple city of the Jews (see 11:10, 13–16; 12:22). One cannot follow both the New Covenant and the Old Covenant. The early church in Jerusalem (A.D. 30–70) retained its Jewish customs, even the religious traditions, but it was under only the New Covenant and so bore the ire of Jews still under the Old Covenant. Likewise, every Christian must be prepared to bear men's scorn and see himself as in exile in this life. The heavenly city we **seek** is the one to which we have already come (12:22): such a tension is no problem for the author of Hebrews.

13:15–19 These verses constitute a summarizing exhortation: (1) We experience the heavenly city and the heavenly Most Holy Place when we **sacrifice** our whole being, body and soul, in the Divine Liturgy—a mystery in which our part is that of praise consistent with true doctrine (v. 15; see vv. 9–14). (2) **Good** works and life in community (**to share,** Gr. *koinonias*) must be united with worship (v. 16; see vv. 1–6). (3) Priests and spiritual leaders must be respected and obeyed (v. 17; see vv. 7, 8), a reference to "spiritual fatherhood" in the Church. They will give account of their ministry at the judgment. The author sees himself among the leaders, and asks for prayer for his living an exemplary life (see v. 7).

Commemoration of Holy Hierarchs

13:17–21: The faithful are exhorted to be submissive to their earthly shepherds as representatives of the Great Shepherd, Christ.

The Holy Life Summarized

17 [a]Obey those who [1]rule over
you, and be submissive, for [b]they
watch out for your souls, as those
who must give account. Let them do
so with joy and not with grief, for
that would be unprofitable for you.
18 [a]Pray for us; for we are confident that we have [b]a good conscience, in all things desiring to live
honorably.
19 But I especially urge *you* to do
this, that I may be restored to you
the sooner.

Conclusion

20 Now may [a]the God of peace
[b]who brought up our Lord Jesus
from the dead, [c]that great Shepherd
of the sheep, [d]through the blood of
the everlasting covenant,†
21 make you [1]complete in every
good work to do His will, [a]working
in [2]you what is well pleasing in
His sight, through Jesus Christ, to
whom *be* glory forever and ever.
Amen.
22 And I appeal to you, brethren,
bear with the word of exhortation,
for I have written to you in few
words.
23 Know that *our* brother Timothy
has been set free, with whom I shall
see you if he comes shortly.
24 Greet all those who [1]rule over
you, and all the saints. Those from
Italy greet you.
25 Grace *be* with you all. Amen.

17 [a]Phil. 2:29 [b]Is. 62:6; Ezek. 3:17; Acts 20:28 [1]*lead*
18 [a]Eph. 6:19 [b]Acts 23:1
20 [a]Rom. 5:1, 2, 10; 15:33 [b]Ps. 16:10, 11; Hos. 6:2; Rom. 4:24 [c]Ps. 23:1; Is. 40:11; 63:11; John 10:11; 1 Pet. 2:25; 5:4 [d]Zech. 9:11; Heb. 10:29
21 [a]Phil. 2:13 [1]*perfect* [2]NU, M *us*
24 [1]*lead*

13:20, 21 The benediction notes: (1) The sufficiency of the **blood** of Christ is realized in His Resurrection as Christ offers His blood in the eternal sanctuary and thereby inaugurates a new, **everlasting covenant.** (2) The *everlasting covenant* makes us **complete** as we cooperate with God (synergy) in all things and progress toward sainthood.

The General Epistle of

JAMES

Author: *St. James the Just*

Date: A.D. *55–60*

Theme: *The Harmony of Faith and Works*

AUTHOR: The author identifies himself as "James, a bondservant of God and of the Lord Jesus Christ" (1:1). Early Church tradition ascribes this letter to James, the "brother," or kinsman, of our Lord, known as James the Just.

DATE: James the Just was martyred about A.D. 62. Although 1 and 2 Thessalonians likely pre-date it, some consider James' letter the earliest New Testament book, after the martyrdom of Stephen and the dispersion of Christians from Jerusalem (Acts 8:1).

MAJOR THEME: *The harmony of faith and works.* The letter has many direct parallels with the Sermon on the Mount. James does not teach that we are saved by works, but he does teach that a dead faith, one without works, does not save. This is an early polemic against invisible religion, or mental faith, wherein salvation by faith does not require visible works; and against antinomianism, the teaching that moral behavior is irrelevant to salvation. James is clear: the human will is not bypassed in salvation; grace does not nullify personal responsibility.

BACKGROUND INFORMATION: (1) *The life of James.* St. James was probably converted by a postresurrection appearance of Christ (1 Cor. 15:7). The apostles made him the first bishop of Jerusalem (see Acts 12:17; 21:17, 18; Gal. 1:18, 19; 2:9), where he presided over the Jerusalem Council (Acts 15:13).

James was the ideal bishop for Jerusalem. He lived a strict and holy life, praying in the temple so frequently he was called "camel-kneed." The Jews considered him incorruptible, for he obeyed the Law of Moses better than they. And they found no fault with him, except that he confessed Jesus to be the Messiah. It was the Jews who called this bishop of the Church "Just"!

According to tradition, James was executed at the prompting of the Sanhedrin, being thrown from the temple walls and then clubbed to death. October 23 is the remembrance of his martyrdom.

(2) *On Paul vs. James; faith vs. works.* Some have considered James's writings on works and faith to contradict Paul's. The contradiction is only apparent,

not real. The difference between Paul and James is one of emphasis and vocabulary.

Paul, concerned with Judaizing preachers and the self-righteousness of Jewish legal piety, argues that "works" (meaning Jewish deeds of formal, legalistic obedience) do not earn salvation. The root problem, mortality and bondage to unrighteousness, is solved by God's grace received by faith.

James, concerned with dead, legalistic Christianity, argues that a "faith" which is a mere intellectual assent to Christian doctrine does not save. He upholds "works," meaning willed actions flowing from belief, as the life of faith—the true evangelical ethic. Both Paul and James distinguish between faith and works, but they never separate them! For faith that works forms a living unity, a singular reality, which is true Christianity.

(3) *Recipients of the Epistle.* Unlike most New Testament letters, James does not address a particular church, or a geographical region, but "the twelve tribes which are scattered abroad" (1:1). Though James was a Jewish Christian and he assumes the recipients are familiar with the Old Testament, the letter is written in elegant Greek. There is no indication that it addresses only Jewish Christians. Furthermore, the New Testament identifies the whole Church as the New Israel (Gal. 6:15; Phil. 3:3; 1 Pet. 1:1; Rev. 7:4–8).

(4) *Historical setting.* The people James addresses are experiencing various trials: persecution, deception, economic injustice and poverty, apostasy, and divisions in the Church. In response to these trials, the people are tempted by: (a) *depression* over being snubbed and persecuted by the Jews; (b) *anger* at having their good will taken advantage of; (c) *bitterness* over being so poor when godless Jews were so rich; and (d) *impatience* over the delay in the return of Jesus. But they are plagued most by the classic sin of *hypocrisy*—the cleavage between profession and practice, between faith and works, which is manifested in distrust, dissension and quarrels.

(5) *Approach.* James uses his authority as bishop for spiritual discipline. He concentrates on rekindling true living faith and on the practice of repentance, trust, humility, patience, and self-control.

(6) *Liturgical use of James.* The most familiar reading from this letter (5:10–17) occurs in the sacrament of healing (oil, or Holy Unction). In addition, the epistle reading for the feast days of the various Old Testament prophets is 5:10–20.

(7) *Style.* James could be called "New Testament wisdom literature." It is more a sermon than a letter, rephrasing sayings both from the Jewish wisdom tradition and from Jesus. It is a series of admonitions, a Christian handbook on ethics. The letter is most often quoted in the spiritual and theological writings of the Church in affirming the completion of faith by works.

OUTLINE

Greeting	1:1
I. Trials and endurance: Love God!	1:2–27
A. The role of trials	1:2–12
B. God's place in trials	1:13–27

Greeting

CHAPTER 1

1 James, [a]a bondservant of God and of the Lord Jesus Christ,

To the twelve tribes which are scattered abroad:

Greetings.†

The Purpose of Trials

2 My brethren, [a]count it all joy
[b]when you fall into various trials,†
3 [a]knowing that the testing of
your faith produces [1]patience.
4 But let patience have *its* perfect
work, that you may be [1]perfect and
complete, lacking nothing.

Wisdom for Trials

5 [a]If any of you lacks wisdom,
[b]let him ask of God, who gives to
all liberally and without reproach,
and [c]it will be given to him.†
6 [a]But let him ask in faith, with
no doubting, for he who doubts is
like a wave of the sea driven and
tossed by the wind.†
7 For let not that man suppose

1 [a]Acts 12:17
2 [a]Acts 5:41 [b]1 Pet. 1:6
3 [a]Rom. 5:3–5 [1]*endurance* or *perseverance*
4 [1]*mature*
5 [a]1 Kin. 3:9; James 3:17 [b]Prov. 2:3–6; Matt. 7:7 [c]Jer. 29:12
6 [a][Mark 11:23, 24]; Acts 10:20

1:1 James establishes his authority, not as a relative of Christ or bishop of Jerusalem, but as **a bondservant** (self-indentured slave) **of God.** For the Jews, God is the only ruler and true honor comes from Him. *God* refers to the Father, and **Lord Jesus Christ** to the Son of God Incarnate. **Scattered abroad** (Gr. *diaspora*) refers to Jews in exile, but James applies it to the Church—Jewish and Gentile Christians alike—on pilgrimage.

1:2 Trials, the world's oppression, take place by God's permission. The issue is not trials *per se,* but our response to them. Properly received, trials reveal where our hearts are. They help to increase faith, which cannot remain static, but must grow or die. The godly reaction to trials is joy and perseverance (Matt. 5:11, 12; Acts 5:41; Rom. 5:2, 3; 8:18; Heb. 12:11; 1 Pet. 2:19). Though difficult circumstances are from the evil one, to be angry at circumstances is to be angry at God, who permits them.

1:5 Wisdom, the practical and spiritual knowledge required for godly living, comes to those who **ask of God,** in prayer. While James loves God's law, for him faith is found not in rules, as the Pharisees believe, but in a relationship with God.

1:6–8 Prayer as petition is effective when it is done **in faith, with no doubting** (v. 6). We

(continued on next page)

that he will receive anything from
the Lord;
8 *he is* [a]a double-minded man,
unstable in all his ways.
9 Let the lowly brother glory in
his exaltation,†
10 but the rich in his humiliation,
because [a]as a flower of the field he
will pass away.
11 For no sooner has the sun risen
with a burning heat than it withers
the grass; its flower falls, and its
beautiful appearance perishes. So
the rich man also will fade away in
his pursuits.

Temptations

12 [a]Blessed *is* the man who endures temptation; for when he has
been approved, he will receive
[b]the crown of life [c]which the Lord
has promised to those who love
Him.†
13 Let no one say when he is
tempted, "I am tempted by God";
for God cannot be tempted by evil,
nor does He Himself tempt anyone.†
14 But each one is tempted when
he is drawn away by his own desires
and enticed.†
15 Then, [a]when desire has conceived, it gives birth to sin; and sin,
when it is full-grown, [b]brings forth
death.
16 Do not be deceived, my beloved
brethren.
17 [a]Every good gift and every perfect gift is from above, and comes
down from the Father of lights,
[b]with whom there is no variation or
shadow of turning.†
18 [a]Of His own will He brought us
forth by the [b]word of truth, [c]that we
might be a kind of firstfruits of His
creatures.†

The Corrective: Hear and Do

19 [1]So then, my beloved brethren,
let every man be swift to hear,

8 [a]James 4:8
10 [a]Job 14:2
12 [a]James 5:11 [b][1 Cor. 9:25] [c]Matt. 10:22
15 [a]Job 15:35 [b][Rom. 5:12; 6:23]
17 [a]John 3:27 [b]Num. 23:19
18 [a]John 1:13 [b][1 Pet. 1:3, 23] [c][Eph. 1:12, 13]
19 [1]NU *Know this* or *This you know*

(continued from previous page)
need (1) an unquestioning loyalty to God and (2) the confidence that comes from a life that is stable in all its ways (v. 8). While James teaches the necessity of works, for him works represent a living *faith.* By contrast, *doubting* (v. 6) means questioning God. One who is **double-minded** (v. 8) is one who has two loyalties, love of the world competing with love for God (see Matt. 6:24). Such **unstable** life deadens our conscience and turns us aside from the truth.

1:9–11 Note the reverse of the order of the world. **The lowly** (v. 9), those who have the least here, will have the most in the Kingdom of Heaven (see 2:5; Matt. 5:3; Luke 1:52), but they are tempted to be bitter and envious. **The rich** (v. 10) may perceive their goods as passing, but they are tempted to be greedy and arrogant and may thereby lose true wealth (see 5:1–12).

1:12 We are to rejoice even in temptations. Our attitude toward them reveals whether or not we are prepared for heaven (see 1 Cor. 9:25).

1:13 James has discussed outward trials (vv. 1–11). He now turns to inward temptations, which deceive us and lead us into sin. God tries us, but He never tempts us.

1:14, 15 Temptation originates in our own sinful passions, which the devil energizes. Temptation begins with **desires** or lustful thoughts. When we entertain these thoughts and delight in them (**when desire has conceived**), we soon end up acting on them (**it gives birth to sin**). We fall to temptation because we allow ourselves to do so. Neither God nor circumstance forces us to yield.

1:17 As **Father of lights,** God reigns over both the visible and invisible creation. He is Creator of all and the giver of spiritual gifts. The first part of this verse is used in the Divine Liturgy, in the prayer before Christ's icon.

1:18 God provides our salvation **of His own will,** not of necessity. **Brought us forth:** He "begot" us, a reference to baptism, by which we become children of God by grace. **The word of truth** is the gospel, the precious, unchanging doctrines of the faith. We are the **firstfruits of His creatures:** in salvation we benefit not by taking on the essence or nature of God, but by putting on a new humanity consecrated to God (as *firstfruits* in the OT were consecrated). Humanity is preeminent over all creation, and through our salvation all creation is likewise being changed. The first half of this verse appears in the Divine Liturgy in the prayer of thanksgiving after the faithful receive communion.

[a]slow to speak, [b]slow to wrath;†
20 for the wrath of man does not
produce the righteousness of God.
21 Therefore [a]lay aside all filthiness and [1]overflow of wickedness,
and receive with meekness the implanted word, [b]which is able to save
your souls.†
22 But [a]be doers of the word, and
not hearers only, deceiving yourselves.
23 For [a]if anyone is a hearer of the
word and not a doer, he is like a man
observing his natural face in a mirror;
24 for he observes himself, goes
away, and immediately forgets what
kind of man he was.
25 But [a]he who looks into the perfect law of liberty and continues *in*
it, and is not a forgetful hearer but
a doer of the work, [b]this one will
be blessed in what he does.†
26 If anyone [1]among you thinks he
is religious, and [a]does not bridle his
tongue but deceives his own heart,
this one's religion *is* useless.†
27 [a]Pure and undefiled religion before God and the Father is this:
[b]to visit orphans and widows in their
trouble, [c]*and* to keep oneself unspotted from the world.

The Law of Love

2 My brethren, do not hold the
faith of our Lord Jesus Christ,
[a]*the Lord* of glory, with [b]partiality.†
2 For if there should come into
your assembly a man with gold
rings, in [1]fine apparel, and there
should also come in a poor man in
[2]filthy clothes,
3 and you [1]pay attention to the
one wearing the fine clothes and say
to him, "You sit here in a good
place," and say to the poor man,
"You stand there," or, "Sit here at
my footstool,"
4 have you not [1]shown partiality
among yourselves, and become
judges with evil thoughts?
5 Listen, my beloved brethren:
[a]Has God not chosen the poor of this
world *to be* [b]rich in faith and heirs
of the kingdom [c]which He promised
to those who love Him?†
6 But [a]you have dishonored the

19 [a]Prov. 10:19; 17:27 [b]Prov. 14:17; 16:32
21 [a]Col. 3:8 [b]Acts 13:26 [1]*abundance*
22 [a]Matt. 7:21–28
23 [a]Luke 6:47
25 [a]James 2:12 [b]John 13:17
26 [a]Ps. 34:13 [1]NU omits *among you*
27 [a]Matt. 25:34–36 [b]Is. 1:17 [c][Rom. 12:2]

CHAPTER 2
1 [a]1 Cor. 2:8 [b]Lev. 19:15
2 [1]*bright* [2]*vile*
3 [1]Lit. *look upon*
4 [1]*differentiated*
5 [a]1 Cor. 1:27 [b]Luke 12:21 [c]Ex. 20:6
6 [a]1 Cor. 11:22

1:19, 20 The wrath of man is unjust, ungracious and severe. It proceeds from uncontrolled anger and it is not God's judgment. For us to discern **the righteousness of God** requires patience, graciousness, and controlled passions.

1:21 While the **word** was **implanted** in baptism, Christians continue to **receive** Him throughout their lives.

1:25 James takes the Jewish notion of freedom—obedience to the Law—and applies it to Christ's Law, His commandment to love others as He loved us. James uses the OT form of the commandment in 2:8.

1:26, 27 Here are three examples of the relationship between faith and works. (1) *Mastery over speech:* What proceeds out of the mouth flows from the heart, for sooner or later our tongue will reveal the quality of our faith in God. (2) *Ministry to the needy:* Faithful Christians must be the guardians of the poor, especially of those **orphans and widows** who have lost their natural guardians. St. Ignatius of Antioch, writing to Polycarp, bishop of Smyrna, at the beginning of the second century, observes: "Do not let the widows be neglected; after the Lord, you must be their guardian" (*Ign. Polyc.* 4:1). (3) *Moral purity in thought and deed:* A faith that works produces moral purity. One of the hymns sung at Vespers during the week before Lent tells it well: "Let us make haste to wash away through fasting the filth of our transgressions, and through acts of mercy and compassion to the needy let us enter into the bridal chamber of the Bridegroom Christ, who grants to us great mercy."

2:1–4 Unjustly judging others is an example of fainthearted faith being manifested in unjust works. Favoring the rich over the poor is contrary to true faith. A person's dignity and worth come from God, not from fellow humans. So we must not judge others by the earthly standards of rank, wealth, attainments and appearance.

2:5–7 God does not show partiality to anyone. The **poor** are more likely to repent and renounce this world for the sake of the kingdom, for they more easily see the emptiness of earthly things. The **rich** (v. 6), on the other hand, tend to prize earthly things, desire material things, and even hurt others to gain them (see Luke 6:21–25; 1 Cor. 1:26–28). They may mock Christians for the **name by which** (v. 7) they **are called,** the *name* invoked at baptism.

poor man. Do not the rich oppress
you [b]and drag you into the courts?
7 Do they not blaspheme that noble name by which you are [a]called?
8 If you really fulfill *the* royal law
according to the Scripture, [a]*"You*
shall love your neighbor as your-
self," you do well;†
9 but if you [1]show partiality, you
commit sin, and are convicted by the
law as [a]transgressors.
10 For whoever shall keep the
whole law, and yet [a]stumble in one
point, [b]he is guilty of all.
11 For He who said, [a]*"Do not com-*
mit adultery," also said, [b]*"Do not*
murder." Now if you do not commit
adultery, but you do murder, you
have become a transgressor of the
law.
12 So speak and so do as those who
will be judged by [a]the law of liberty.
13 For [a]judgment is without mercy
to the one who has shown [b]no
[c]mercy. [d]Mercy triumphs over judgment.

6 [b]Acts 13:50
7 [a]1 Pet. 4:16
8 [a]Lev. 19:18
9 [a]Deut. 1:17 [1]Lit. *receive the face*
10 [a]Gal. 3:10 [b]Deut. 27:26
11 [a]Ex. 20:14; Deut. 5:18 [b]Ex. 20:13; Deut. 5:17
12 [a]James 1:25
13 [a]Job 22:6 [b]Prov. 21:13 [c]Mic. 7:18 [d]Rom. 12:8
14 [a]Matt. 7:21–23, 26; 21:28–32
15 [a]Luke 3:11
16 [a][1 John 3:17, 18]
18 [a]Heb. 6:10 [b]James 3:13 [1]NU omits *your* [2]NU omits *my*
20 [1]NU *useless*

Faith that Works

14 [a]What *does it* profit, my brethren, if someone says he has faith but
does not have works? Can faith save
him?†
15 [a]If a brother or sister is naked
and destitute of daily food,
16 and [a]one of you says to them,
"Depart in peace, be warmed and
filled," but you do not give them the
things which are needed for the
body, what *does it* profit?
17 Thus also faith by itself, if it
does not have works, is dead.
18 But someone will say, "You
have faith, and I have works."
[a]Show me your faith without [1]your
works, [b]and I will show you my faith
by [2]my works.
19 You believe that there is one
God. You do well. Even the demons
believe—and tremble!
20 But do you want to know, O
foolish man, that faith without works
is [1]dead?†

2:8–13 The true standard of judgment is perfect faith manifested in perfect works. The **royal law** (v. 8), **the law of liberty** (v. 12; 1:25), is the second great commandment of Christ: love your neighbor (John 13:34). The standard by which we judge is that by which we will be judged; the mercy we give will be the mercy we receive.

At Matins on Friday of the week before Lent, Orthodox Christians sing: "God has shown mercy to us. Let us in our turn show mercy: let us feed the poor, and with the divine water of fasting let us wash the defilement from our souls." Then we add, "O heavenly angels, entreat the Giver of good to accept in His infinite mercy our poor and mean repentance," for we know the weakness of our hearts.

2:14–19 The faith that saves is a complete faith: not just the mind believing and the tongue confessing, but the whole man trusting in the living God. This means our faith and our relationship with God—our justification—are dynamic and living. Our faith grows and affects our actions, or it dies. "Faith alone" (**by itself,** v. 17), static faith, does not save. We must nurture our faith in God and love for Him through our works. This point is well made by St. Maximus the Confessor (c. A.D. 580–662), "Do not say you are the temple of the Lord, writes Jeremiah [see Jer. 7:4]; nor should you say that faith alone in our Lord Jesus Christ can save you, for this is impossible unless you acquire love for Him through your works. As for faith by itself, 'the devils also believe, and tremble.'" (*The Philokalia,* Vol. II, p. 56).

2:20–24 The faith of **Abraham** is living and active. (1) In Gen. 12:1–3, when Abraham was 75 years old, he received a call to forsake all and follow God. (2) In Gen. 15:6, when Abraham was almost 85, after he had proven his faith through years of renouncing his land, family, property and privileges, God promised him that he would ultimately regain everything he had given up. Abraham's faith in God's promise was "reckoned to him as righteousness." God fulfilled Abraham's faith by making a covenant with him, an OT liturgical and sacramental act. (3) In Gen. 22:1–19, Abraham was at least 110 years old. He had been tested for years concerning God's promise of a son. Now, after the covenant sacrament of initiation (circumcision) had been given in Gen. 17, came Abraham's supreme test: the sacrifice of Isaac, his son of promise (Gen. 15:6).

James reveals that Gen. 15:6 is fulfilled in Gen. 22. This is a crucial lesson for us in our understanding of justification by faith. Neither Abraham's faith nor his justification is merely momentary, static or once-and-for-all. It is dynamic, a growth process which finds its natural

(continued on next page)

21 Was not Abraham our father
justified by works [a]when he offered
Isaac his son on the altar?
22 Do you see [a]that faith was
working together with his works,
and by [b]works faith was made
[1]perfect?
23 And the Scripture was fulfilled
which says, [a]*"Abraham believed*
God, and it was [1]*accounted to him*
for righteousness." And he was
called [b]the friend of God.
24 You see then that a man is justified by works, and not by faith only.
25 Likewise, [a]was not Rahab the
harlot also justified by works when
she received the messengers and
sent *them* out another way?
26 For as the body without the
spirit is dead, so faith without works
is dead also.†

The Work of Faith: Controlling What We Say

3 My brethren, [a]let not many of
you become teachers, [b]knowing
that we shall receive a stricter
judgment.†
2 For [a]we all stumble in many
things. [b]If anyone does not stumble
in word, [c]he *is* a [1]perfect man, able
also to bridle the whole body.
3 [1]Indeed, [a]we put bits in horses'
mouths that they may obey us, and
we turn their whole body.
4 Look also at ships: although
they are so large and are driven by
fierce winds, they are turned by a
very small rudder wherever the pilot
desires.
5 Even so [a]the tongue is a little
member and [b]boasts great things.
See how great a forest a little fire
kindles!
6 And [a]the tongue *is* a fire, a
world of [1]iniquity. The tongue is so
set among our members that it
[b]defiles the whole body, and sets on
fire the course of [2]nature; and it is
set on fire by [3]hell.
7 For every kind of beast and bird,
of reptile and creature of the sea, is
tamed and has been tamed by
mankind.
8 But no man can tame the
tongue. *It is* an unruly evil, [a]full of
deadly poison.
9 With it we bless our God and
Father, and with it we curse men,
who have been made [a]in the
[1]similitude of God.
10 Out of the same mouth proceed
blessing and cursing. My brethren,
these things ought not to be so.
11 Does a spring send forth fresh
water and bitter from the same
opening?
12 Can a [a]fig tree, my brethren,
bear olives, or a grapevine bear figs?
[1]Thus no spring yields both salt
water and fresh.

Godly Counsel

13 [a]Who *is* wise and understanding among you? Let him show by
good conduct *that* his works *are done*
in the meekness of wisdom.†

21 [a]Gen. 22:9, 10, 12, 16–18
22 [a]Heb. 11:17 [b]John 8:39 [1]*complete*
23 [a]Gen. 15:6 [b]2 Chr. 20:7 [1]*credited*
25 [a]Heb. 11:31

CHAPTER 3

1 [a][Matt. 23:8] [b]Luke 6:37
2 [a]1 Kin. 8:46 [b]Ps. 34:13 [c][Matt. 12:34–37] [1]*mature*
3 [a]Ps. 32:9 [1]NU *Now if*
5 [a]Prov. 12:18; 15:2 [b]Ps. 12:3; 73:8
6 [a]Prov. 16:27 [b][Matt. 12:36; 15:11, 18] [1]*unrighteousness* [2]*existence* [3]Gr. *Gehenna*
8 [a]Ps. 140:3
9 [a]Gen. 1:26; 5:1; 9:6 [1]*likeness*
12 [a]Matt. 7:16–20 [1]NU *Neither can a salty spring produce fresh water.*
13 [a]Gal. 6:4

(continued from previous page)
and normal realization in good works. Far from being just point-in-time, Abraham's justification is realized at least 25 years after God first declared Abraham just. It is living and active faith which saves!

2:26 This summary of the organic relationship of faith and works (see Matt. 7:21; 25:31–46; John 14:15; Gal. 5:6) shows that only God can save.

3:1–12 What we say reveals what we are. If we can control what we say, we can control what we do (vv. 2–8)! For James, this is a manifestation of the relationship of faith and works, and a major battleground of spiritual warfare. James even warns against becoming a Christian teacher (v. 1), and expresses astonishment at how hypocritical and contradictory our speech can be (vv. 9–12).

3:13–18 James also cautions us about counseling others, for what is offered as wisdom can be based on pride and other sinful passions. Self-centered faith will manifest itself in self-centered works, in this case "helping" others in an unhelpful manner. True wisdom comes from God and proves itself by action (v. 13). **Sensual** (v. 15; Gr. *psychike*) here means unspiritual, not possessing the Spirit of God.

14 But if you have [a]bitter envy and
[1]self-seeking in your hearts, [b]do not
boast and lie against the truth.
15 [a]This wisdom does not descend
from above, but *is* earthly, sensual,
demonic.
16 For [a]where envy and self-
seeking *exist,* confusion and every
evil thing *are* there.
17 But [a]the wisdom that is from
above is first pure, then peaceable,
gentle, willing to yield, full of mercy
and good fruits, [b]without partiality
[c]and without hypocrisy.
18 [a]Now the fruit of righteousness
is sown in peace by those who make
peace.

Lack of Faith and Works: Quarrels in the Church

4 Where do [1]wars and fights *come*
from among you? Do *they* not
come from your *desires for* pleasure
[a]that war in your members?†
2 You lust and do not have. You
murder and covet and cannot obtain.
You fight and [1]war. [2]Yet you do not
have because you do not ask.
3 [a]You ask and do not receive,
[b]because you ask amiss, that you
may spend *it* on your pleasures.
4 [1]Adulterers and adulteresses!
Do you not know that [a]friendship

14 [a]Rom. 13:13 [b]Rom. 2:17 [1]*selfish ambition*
15 [a]Phil. 3:19
16 [a]1 Cor. 3:3
17 [a]1 Cor. 2:6, 7 [b]James 2:1 [c]Rom. 12:9
18 [a]Prov. 11:18

CHAPTER 4

1 [a]Rom. 7:23 [1]*battles*
2 [1]*battle* [2]NU, M omit *Yet*
3 [a]Job 27:8, 9 [b][Ps. 66:18]
4 [a]1 John 2:15 [b]Gal. 1:4 [1]NU omits *Adulterers and*
5 [a]Gen. 6:5
6 [a]Prov. 3:34
7 [a][Eph. 4:27; 6:11]
8 [a]2 Chr. 15:2 [b]Is. 1:16 [c]1 Pet. 1:22
9 [a]Matt. 5:4
10 [a]Job 22:29
11 [a]1 Pet. 2:1–3 [b][Matt. 7:1–5]

with the world is enmity with God?
[b]Whoever therefore wants to be a
friend of the world makes himself an
enemy of God.
5 Or do you think that the Scripture says in vain, [a]"The Spirit who
dwells in us yearns jealously"?
6 But He gives more grace. Therefore He says:

[a]*"God resists the proud,*
But gives grace to the humble."

7 Therefore submit to God. [a]Re-
sist the devil and he will flee from
you.
8 [a]Draw near to God and He will
draw near to you. [b]Cleanse *your*
hands, *you* sinners; and [c]purify *your*
hearts, *you* double-minded.
9 [a]Lament and mourn and weep!
Let your laughter be turned to
mourning and *your* joy to gloom.
10 [a]Humble yourselves in the sight
of the Lord, and He will lift you up.

Criticizing Others

11 [a]Do not speak evil of one another, brethren. He who speaks evil
of a brother [b]and judges his brother,
speaks evil of the law and judges the
law. But if you judge the law, you
are not a doer of the law but a
judge.†

4:1–10 Wars and fights in the Church are another example of the result of faith without works. Such disputes come from **desires** or passions which bring disruption in the body of Christ. These passions are divisive (v. 1), self-centered (v. 3), of this world (v. 4), energized by Satan (v. 7), and therefore at **enmity with God** (v. 4). God does not answer prayers for our selfish desires (v. 3). **Adulterers and adulteresses:** The image of unfaithfulness in marriage for the faithlessness of God's people is common throughout the OT .

How do we conquer arrogant pleasure-seeking? (1) Stop praying for self-centered pleasures (vv. 2, 3). (2) Renounce the world and build a friendship with God (v. 4). (3) Yield to the Holy **Spirit who dwells in us** through chrismation (v. 5). In seeking the Holy Spirit we gain the Holy Trinity! (4) Be **humble,** recognizing that **God resists the proud** (v. 6). (5) **Resist** (be insubordinate to) Satan and **submit to God** (v. 7). (6) Approach God in worship (**draw near**). Take special care to **cleanse your hands** and **purify your hearts** through repentance in preparation for worship (vv. 8, 9). Never laugh off God's call to mourn for sin.

St. Maximus the Confessor summarizes: "The rewards for the toils of virtue are dispassion and spiritual knowledge. For these are the mediators of the kingdom of heaven, just as passions and ignorance are the mediators of eternal punishment. It is because of this that he who seeks these rewards for the sake of human glory and not for their intrinsic goodness is rebuked by the words of Scripture: 'You ask, and do not receive, because you ask wrongly.' " (*The Philokalia,* Vol. II, p. 71).

4:11, 12 Belittling criticism of others is another way pride is revealed in our speech. It is a lack of faith united with evil works, an offense both to the person criticized and to God.

(continued on next page)

12 There is one [1]Lawgiver, [a]who is
able to save and to destroy. [b]Who[2]
are you to judge [3]another?

Being Overly Confident

13 Come now, you who say, "Today or tomorrow [1]we will go to such
and such a city, spend a year there,
buy and sell, and make a profit";†
14 whereas you do not know what
will happen tomorrow. For what *is*
your life? [a]It is even a vapor that appears for a little time and then van-
ishes away.
15 Instead you *ought* to say, [a]"If
the Lord wills, we shall live and do
this or that."
16 But now you boast in your arrogance. [a]All such boasting is evil.
17 Therefore, [a]to him who knows
to do good and does not do *it*, to
him it is sin.

Warning to Rich Oppressors

5 Come now, *you* [a]rich, weep and
howl for your miseries that are
coming upon *you!*†
2 Your [a]riches [1]are corrupted, and
[b]your garments are moth-eaten.
3 Your gold and silver are cor-
roded, and their corrosion will be a
witness against you and will eat your
flesh like fire. [a]You have heaped up
treasure in the last days.
4 Indeed [a]the wages of the laborers who mowed your fields, which
you kept back by fraud, cry out; and
[b]the cries of the reapers have
reached the ears of the Lord of
[1]Sabaoth.
5 You have lived on the earth in
pleasure and [1]luxury; you have
[2]fattened your hearts [3]as in a day of
slaughter.
6 You have condemned, you have
murdered the just; he does not resist
you.

Encouragement to the Oppressed

7 Therefore be patient, brethren,
until the coming of the Lord. See *how*
the farmer waits for the precious fruit
of the earth, waiting patiently for it
until it receives the early and latter
rain.†
8 You also be patient. Establish
your hearts, for the coming of the
Lord [1]is at hand.
9 Do not [1]grumble against one another, brethren, lest you be [2]con-
demned. Behold, the Judge is standing at the door!
10 [a]My brethren, take the prophets, who spoke in the name of the
Lord, as an example of suffering and
[b]patience.†
11 Indeed [a]we count them blessed
who [b]endure. You have heard of
[c]the perseverance of Job and seen
[d]the end *intended by* the Lord—that
[e]the Lord is very compassionate and
merciful.
12 But above all, my brethren,
[a]do not swear, either by heaven or
by earth or with any other oath. But
let your "Yes" be "Yes," and *your*
"No," "No," lest you fall into
[1]judgment.†

12 [a][Matt. 10:28] [b]Rom. 14:4 [1]NU adds *and Judge* [2]NU, M *But who* [3]NU *a neighbor*
13 [1]M *let us*
14 [a]Job 7:7
15 [a]Acts 18:21
16 [a]1 Cor. 5:6
17 [a][Luke 12:47]

CHAPTER 5

1 [a][Luke 6:24]
2 [a]Matt. 6:19 [b]Job 13:28 [1]*have rotted*
3 [a]Rom. 2:5
4 [a]Lev. 19:13 [b]Deut. 24:15 [1]Lit., in Heb., *Hosts*
5 [1]*indulgence* [2]Lit. *nourished* [3]NU omits *as*
8 [1]*has drawn near*
9 [1]Lit. *groan* [2]NU, M *judged*
10 [a]Matt. 5:12 [b]Heb. 10:36
11 [a][Ps. 94:12] [b][James 1:12] [c]Job 1:21, 22; 2:10 [d]Job 42:10 [e]Num. 14:18
12 [a]Matt. 5:34–37 [1]M *hypocrisy*

(continued from previous page)
God's will is that we love others (2:8) with humility and mercy, even if they are in the wrong (see 3:13–18).

4:13–16 True faith (a) depends completely on God and (b) seeks ways to do good works. But to plan as if we know exactly what will happen is arrogance.

5:1–6 The terrible fate of the unjust **rich** is that their wealth will condemn them.

5:7–12 The **early and latter rain** (v. 7) refer to the pattern of rainfall—at planting time and just before harvest—in Palestine. We are to put away grumbling at each other, and we must not demand that life be "fair." Patience, forbearance and a right vision of the ultimate Judge are true works of living faith.

5:10, 11 The faithful prophets, true saints of God, are models or examples for us in how to practice **suffering and patience.** Consequently Christians, from the NT era even till today, have honored or venerated the prophets—indeed, all the saints—counting them **blessed.**

5:12 This is a polemic against a bad custom stemming from bad faith: the common practice

(continued on page 548)

HEALING

"Is anyone among you sick? Let him call for the elders of the church, and let them pray over him, anointing him with oil in the name of the Lord. And the prayer of faith will save the sick, and the Lord will raise him up. And if he has committed sins, he will be forgiven" (James 5:14, 15).

One of the great prophetic themes of the Old Testament concerning the promised Messiah is that the Father would send His Son "to heal the brokenhearted, and to proclaim liberty to the captives and recovery of sight to the blind." (Luke 4:18; see Is. 61:1). The ministry of Christ was one of numerous occurrences of healings of "all kinds of sickness and all kinds of disease" (Matt. 4:23). In addition, Jesus healed darkened hearts and minds as He released people from demonic oppression.

Like their Master before them, the early apostles participated in God's work of healing as well, attributing their miracles to the risen and ascended Christ. "Jesus the Christ heals you," Peter told a newly restored man, who had been bedridden for eight years (Acts 9:34). St. Paul identified healing as a gift of the Holy Spirit (1 Cor. 12:9). Thus the New Testament foundation was established for the healing ministry to be a part of the sacramental life of the Church (James 5:14, 15).

Healings throughout history. The Orthodox Church has never believed or behaved as though the gifts of the Spirit or the healing miracles of Christ have somehow passed away. Did not Jesus promise, "He who believes in Me, the works that I do he will do also; and greater works than these he will do, because I go to My Father" (John 14:12)?

St. Ireneaus, writing at the close of the second century, speaks of miracles in his day: "Some drive out devils . . . some have foreknowledge of the future . . . others heal the sick through the laying on of hands . . . and even the dead have been raised up before now and have remained with us for many years." The writings of other Church Fathers speak often of miracles within the Church.

Quite widely known are the supernatural healings which Christ performed through St. Seraphim of Sarov, a nineteenth century Russian monk. He was blessed with the gift of healing during his lifetime, and even after his death people would be restored to wholeness at his graveside.

The practice of the Church today. To this day, the Orthodox practice of prayer for the sick follows the New Testament instruction of St. James. The Orthodox Church has a special service of healing, which may be performed at any time. The presbyter prays for the ill person, anointing him with oil and saying:

"O Lord Almighty, Healer of our souls and bodies, who puts down and raises up, who chastises and heals also, visit now in Your mercy our brother or sister, N______, who is ill. Stretch forth Your arm that is full of healing and health, and raise (him, her) up from this bed and cure this illness. Put away the spirit of disease and every malady and pain and fever. And if (he, she) has committed sins and transgressions, grant remission and forgiveness, because You love mankind.

As Orthodox Christians we pray, neither commanding God to heal, nor doubting His ability to heal, but pleading for His promised mercy upon all who are ill.

Commemoration of Holy Prophets

5:10–20: The prophets are our example of suffering and patience, and our inspiration to fervent prayer.

The Work of Faith: Healing

13 Is anyone among you suffering?
Let him [a]pray. Is anyone cheerful?
[b]Let him sing psalms.†
14 Is anyone among you sick? Let
him call for the elders of the church,
and let them pray over him, [a]anoint-
ing him with oil in the name of the
Lord.
15 And the prayer of faith will save
the sick, and the Lord will raise him
up. [a]And if he has committed sins,
he will be forgiven.
16 [1]Confess *your* trespasses to one
another, and pray for one another,
that you may be healed. [a]The effective, [2]fervent prayer of a righteous
man avails much.†
17 Elijah was a man [a]with a nature
like ours, and [b]he prayed earnestly
that it would not rain; and it did not
rain on the land for three years and
six months.
18 And he prayed [a]again, and the
heaven gave rain, and the earth produced its fruit.

Restoration

19 Brethren, if anyone among you
wanders from the truth, and someone [a]turns him back,†
20 let him know that he who turns
a sinner from the error of his way
[a]will save [1]a soul from death and
[b]cover a multitude of sins.

13 [a]Ps. 50:14, 15 [b]Eph. 5:19
14 [a]Mark 6:13; 16:18
15 [a]Is. 33:24
16 [a]Num. 11:2 [1]NU *Therefore confess your sins* [2]*supplication*
17 [a]Acts 14:15 [b]1 Kin. 17:1; 18:1
18 [a]1 Kin. 18:1, 42
19 [a]Gal. 6:1
20 [a]Rom. 11:14 [b][1 Pet. 4:8] [1]NU *his soul*

(continued from page 546)
of swearing by God or something that signifies God (as if swearing is a proof of truthfulness). We may swear when required to, but the solution to lack of trust is good faith—our integrity, truthfulness between a person and God. (See Matt. 5:33–37.)

5:13–15 The sick person is to **call for the elders** (presbyters) for prayer. Salvation deals with the whole person, for each human being is a unity, body and soul. Hence, this sacrament has a double purpose: not only for healing but for forgiveness also. The presbyter (shortened form: priest) is given certain gifts of the ministry at ordination by the laying on of hands (see 1 Tim. 4:14). Prayer is combined with olive **oil**—not only the primary medicine of ancient times, but also a symbol of the Holy Spirit in the Church—in a single sacrament which effects a healing for the whole person. Thus, the elements of the sacrament of healing include (1) the presbyter or priest (v. 14); (2) **the prayer of** (the) **faith** which **will save** (v. 15); (3) the work of Christ Himself, for **the Lord will raise** us **up;** (4) the work of the Holy Spirit, manifested in the oil; and (5) confession of sins just prior to the anointing with oil, which explains why James writes that the sick person **will be forgiven** (v. 15). In the Orthodox Church, this sacrament is granted anyone who is sick, whether in danger of dying or not.

5:16–18 Some allege that confessing sins to God before a priest is not biblical. The ancient Christian custom was to **confess your trespasses to one another** (v. 16). When a Christian was guilty of sin, the matter was confessed before the whole church as an act of repentance. As the Church grew, and those not part of the community came to observe, the pressure in such public confession became so great that the priest alone would hear the confession, representing the people. What is not taught in Scripture is a private confession only to God, which is a refusal to acknowledge sin to the community (1 John 1:8, 10). Thus, the Church has effected healing through such works of faith as confession of sins and the power of intercessory prayer.

5:19, 20 These verses describe the work of faith in restoring the apostate.

The First General Epistle of

PETER

Author: *St. Peter the Apostle*

Date: *A.D. 50–67*

Theme: *Rejoice in Sharing the Sufferings of Christ*

AUTHOR: After Peter had helped to establish the church in Antioch, he preached the gospel to Jews and Gentile converts to Judaism throughout northern Asia Minor (1:1). Later, in Rome, hearing the churches of Asia Minor were being persecuted, he wrote them this letter of encouragement.

DATE: First Peter was composed at Rome (5:13) in the period from A.D. 50–67. The exact date that Peter arrived in Rome is unclear; tradition says he was martyred there later in Nero's reign, c. A.D. 67.

MAJOR THEME: *Rejoice in sharing the sufferings of Christ*. The first letter of Peter is an exhortation for Christians suffering persecution to remember and live in their baptism. Peter teaches that as baptism is a death and a resurrection, so Christians must enter into unjust suffering with a spirit of death and resurrection. Indeed, every trouble of life can be entered into as a baptismal experience, an ongoing acceptance of death in this life in order to grow in the qualities of the life to come. We undergo hardship in a spirit of joy, of transformed life, of awareness that the end of this age is imminent. Our goal is the fulfillment of baptism—heaven—for through the resurrection reality of baptism, our true and eternal homeland is the Kingdom of God. Attaining this goal requires unwavering commitment in this life to: (1) holiness (1:3—2:10), (2) submission in the roles we have in life (2:11—3:12), (3) patient suffering in this age as we prepare for the age to come (3:13—4:19), and (4) disciplined unity in the Church (5:1–11).

BACKGROUND INFORMATION: The Dispersion of which Peter speaks (1:1) is unknown. After the martyrdom of Stephen, many Christians fled (c. A.D. 33) from persecution in Jerusalem. Perhaps some also fled after the martyrdom of James the Just, Bishop of Jerusalem, in A.D. 62. Or it could be that Peter is speaking more generally of Christians at large, who were often ill-treated and forced into exile because of their faith. We are told these Christians live in five provinces of Asia Minor (1:1), located in the central and northern segments of the peninsula.

OUTLINE

Greeting

1 Peter, an apostle of Jesus Christ,
To the [1]pilgrims [a]of the Dispersion
in Pontus, Galatia, Cappadocia,
Asia, and Bithynia,†
2 [a]elect [b]according to the foreknowledge of God the Father, [c]in sanctification of the Spirit, for [d]obedience and [e]sprinkling of the blood of Jesus Christ:†

CHAPTER 1

1 [a]James 1:1 [1]*sojourners,* temporary residents
2 [a]Eph. 1:4 [b][Rom. 8:29] [c]2 Thess. 2:13 [d]Rom. 1:5 [e]Heb. 10:22; 12:24

1:1 Pilgrims, or "sojourners," are aliens, those who stay for a while in a strange place with no intention of permanently residing there. This is said of God's people in this world (see 2:11; Lev. 25:23; Ps. 39:12; Heb. 11:13), for they are citizens of the heavenly world to come (Phil. 3:20).

1:2 Note the Apostle's clear reference to all three divine Persons of the Holy Trinity.

God's **foreknowledge** does not preclude or bind human will. Rather, it has to do with His Providence, His sovereign control of history. The **sprinkling of the blood** connects OT sacramental rites with Christ and the NT. Through the blood sprinkled on the doorposts of their homes, the people of Israel escaped death in Egypt and the power of Satan (Ex. 12:13). When the covenant between God and the Israelites was made at Sinai, Moses sprinkled the blood of the covenant upon the people, thereby empowering Israel to participate in the life of God (Ex. 24:8). On the Day of Atonement, the blood of a goat was sprinkled on the

(continued on next page)

[f]Grace to you and peace be multiplied.

Born to a Heavenly Hope

3 [a]Blessed *be* the God and Father
of our Lord Jesus Christ, who
[b]according to His abundant mercy
[c]has begotten us again to a living
hope [d]through the resurrection of
Jesus Christ from the dead,†
4 to an inheritance [1]incorruptible
and undefiled and that does not fade
away, [a]reserved in heaven for you,†
5 [a]who are kept by the power of
God through faith for salvation ready
to be revealed in the last time.†

Tested for Genuine Faith

6 [a]In this you greatly rejoice,
though now [b]for a little while, if
need be, [c]you have been [1]grieved by
various trials,†

2 [f]Rom. 1:7
3 [a]Eph. 1:3
[b]Gal. 6:16
[c][John 3:3, 5]
[d]1 Cor. 15:20
4 [a]Col. 1:5
[1]*imperishable*
5 [a]John 10:28
6 [a]Matt. 5:12
[b]2 Cor. 4:17
[c]James 1:2
[1]*distressed*
7 [a]James 1:3
[b]Job 23:10
[c][Rom. 2:7]
8 [a]1 John 4:20
[b]John 20:29
[1]M *known*
11 [a]2 Pet. 1:21
12 [1]NU, M *you*

7 that [a]the genuineness of your
faith, *being* much more precious than
gold that perishes, though [b]it is
tested by fire, [c]may be found to
praise, honor, and glory at the revelation of Jesus Christ,
8 [a]whom having not [1]seen you
love. [b]Though now you do not see
Him, yet believing, you rejoice with
joy inexpressible and full of glory,†
9 receiving the end of your faith—
the salvation of *your* souls.
10 Of this salvation the prophets
have inquired and searched carefully, who prophesied of the grace
that would come to you,†
11 searching what, or what manner
of time, [a]the Spirit of Christ who was
in them was indicating when He testified beforehand the sufferings of
Christ and the glories that would
follow.
12 To them it was revealed that,
not to themselves, but to [1]us they
were ministering the things which
now have been reported to you

(continued from previous page)
mercy seat of the tabernacle (Lev. 16:15). As people of the New Covenant, we enter into God's life more intimately: "Unless you . . . drink [His] blood, you have no life in you" (John 6:53). Through Christ's blood communicated to us in the Holy Eucharist (1 Cor. 11:25) we are united with Him in His incorrupt human nature.

We are to be in **obedience** to Jesus Christ because of the *obedience* **of Jesus Christ.** In contrast to the disobedience of the first Adam, the second Adam, Christ, fulfilled the Law completely and performed all righteousness. Through His obedience, corrupt human nature will be transformed into incorrupt human nature.

1:3 We are **begotten again to a living hope** in baptism. As Jesus told Nicodemus, we enter the Kingdom of God by being "born of water and the Spirit" (John 3:5). This new birth in baptism unites us with Christ and His **resurrection** (Rom. 6:3). The words and actions of Peter also confirm this sacramental reality. (See Acts 2:37, 38, 41; 10:43, 47, 48. See also the "washing of regeneration" in Titus 3:5, where baptism and God's mercy are coupled.) Here the sacrament of baptism (vv. 3–6) is the power by which we suffer faithfully (vv. 7–9). Being regenerated, given new life in Christ, we have a hope by which to live. This grace of God sustains us in the trials of life. (Verses 3–12 in the original constitute one long sentence.)

1:4 Note that the home for which we yearn, our inheritance, is also described in the context of baptism (1:3).

1:5 The incorruptible inheritance is reserved for those who have true faith, the faith that by God's grace perseveres to the end.

1:6, 7 To reach the joy and blessing of eternal life in Christ, we first experience the sadness of the passing world, along with the afflictions we must face here (see also James 1:1–12). To the watching world the perseverance of the faithful during affliction appears foolish and even contemptible. But Peter shows that faith under trial is precious indeed, bearing more glory and honor as it continues to stand under trial (see Matt. 25:31–46; 1 Cor. 3:10–15).

1:8 Peter knew by experience the failure to perceive the truth until he saw it with his eyes (see Luke 24:8–12; Acts 10:39–43). Here he addresses those who believe in Him whom they have **not seen.** This is the faith of baptism and the faith of eternal life.

1:10, 11 The prophets had supernatural knowledge of the events to come—even so far as **the glories that would follow** the sufferings of Christ, His Resurrection, Ascension, and Second Coming.

through those who have preached
the gospel to you by the Holy Spirit
sent from heaven—things which
[a]angels desire to look into.†

Be Holy!

13 Therefore gird up the loins of
your mind, be sober, and rest *your*
hope fully upon the grace that is to
be brought to you at the revelation
of Jesus Christ;†
14 as obedient children, not [a]con-
forming yourselves to the former
lusts, *as* in your ignorance;
15 [a]but as He who called you *is*
holy, you also be holy in all *your*
conduct,
16 because it is written, [a]*"Be holy,
for I am holy."*†
17 And if you call on the Father,
who [a]without partiality judges according to each one's work, conduct
yourselves throughout the time of
your [1]stay *here* in fear;†
18 knowing that you were not redeemed with [1]corruptible things, *like*
silver or gold, from your aimless conduct *received* by tradition from your
fathers,†
19 but [a]with the precious blood of
Christ, [b]as of a lamb without blemish
and without spot.
20 [a]He indeed was foreordained
before the foundation of the world,
but was [1]manifest [b]in these last times
for you
21 who through Him believe in
God, [a]who raised Him from the dead
and [b]gave Him glory, so that your
faith and hope are in God.

Love Each Other

22 Since you [a]have purified your
souls in obeying the truth [1]through
the Spirit in [2]sincere [b]love of the
brethren, love one another fervently
with a pure heart,
23 [a]having been born again, not of
[1]corruptible seed but [2]incorruptible,
[b]through the word of God which
lives and abides [3]forever,†
24 because

[a]*"All flesh is as grass,*
And all [1]the glory of man as the
flower of the grass.
The grass withers,
And its flower falls away,†
25 [a]*But the [1]word of the* LORD
endures forever."

12 [a]Eph. 3:10
14 [a][Rom. 12:2]
15 [a][2 Cor. 7:1]
16 [a]Lev. 11:44, 45; 19:2; 20:7
17 [a]Acts 10:34 [1]*sojourning, dwelling* as resident aliens
18 [1]*perishable*
19 [a]Acts 20:28 [b]Ex. 12:5
20 [a]Rom. 3:25 [b]Gal. 4:4 [1]*revealed*
21 [a]Acts 2:24 [b]Acts 2:33
22 [a]Acts 15:9 [b]Heb. 13:1 [1]NU omits *through the Spirit* [2]Lit. *unhypocritical*
23 [a]John 1:13 [b]James 1:18 [1]*perishable* [2]*imperishable* [3]NU omits *forever*
24 [a]Is. 40:6–8 [1]NU *its glory as*
25 [a]Is. 40:8 [1]*spoken word*

1:12 Even the **angels** desire to deepen their vision both of the uncreated glory and of what God has in store for creation. The angels beheld and worshiped Christ in His divine nature; what is new and amazing to them is His human nature.

1:13 The Israelites ate the original Passover with **loins** girded, that is, with their long outer garments tucked into their belts so as to free their legs for movement. Similarly, Christians are to live always in the spirit of Passover, prepared for the journey of obedience and virtue.

1:16 See Matt. 5:48. The cleanliness code (Lev. 11—15) instructed Israel how to prepare for worship (Lev. 1—10). Holiness belongs to God, and we, who cannot attain holiness on our own but receive it from Him, are called to live a **holy** life before Him. Indeed, Christians are called to holiness in every area of their lives. In the Lord's prayer we say, "Hallowed be Your Name." It is not that we want God's name to be made holy by our prayers, but that His name may be made holy in us.

1:17 Why should we pray **in fear?** Because the **Father** we serve will judge us **according to each one's work.** While being certain of God's mercy, we **conduct** ourselves with care.

1:18, 19 Our salvation has been purchased by the infinitely **precious blood of Christ** (v. 19). We are not our own and are to conduct ourselves in a manner worthy of the price paid for our redemption (see 1 Cor. 6:19, 20).

1:23 See John 1:12, 13. The Lord's suffering and death is **incorruptible** and **abides forever,** and is the foundation of our baptism through which we are **born again** (see John 3:1–6 and Rom. 6:3–5).

1:24, 25 This passage from Is. 40:6–8 sets in sharp contrast the difference between human and divine seed. Our present human condition will have an end, of course, as witnessed by the ever-presence of corruption, and will meet that end in death. But in the glorified,

(continued on next page)

[b]Now this is the word which by the
gospel was preached to you.

Desire Christ

2 Therefore, [a]laying aside all malice, all deceit, hypocrisy, envy,
and all evil speaking,†
2 [a]as newborn babes, desire the
pure [b]milk of the word, that you may
grow [1]thereby,†
3 if indeed you have [a]tasted that
the Lord *is* gracious.

The New Priesthood

4 Coming to Him *as to* a living
stone, [a]rejected indeed by men, but
chosen by God *and* precious,†
5 you also, as living stones, are
being built up a spiritual house, a
holy priesthood, to offer up spiritual
sacrifices acceptable to God through
Jesus Christ.†
6 Therefore it is also contained in
the Scripture,

[a]*"Behold, I lay in Zion*
A chief cornerstone, elect,
precious,
And he who believes on Him
will by no means be put to
shame."

7 Therefore, to you who believe,
He is precious; but to those who
[1]are disobedient,

[a]*"The stone which the builders*
rejected
Has become the chief
cornerstone,"

8 and

[a]*"A stone of stumbling*
And a rock of offense."

[b]They stumble, being disobedient to
the word, [c]to which they also were
appointed.
9 But you *are* a chosen generation,
a royal priesthood, a holy nation, His
own special people, that you may
proclaim the praises of Him who
called you out of [a]darkness into His
marvelous light;†
10 [a]who once *were* not a people but
are now the people of God, who had
not obtained mercy but now have
obtained mercy.

25 [b][John 1:1]
CHAPTER 2
1 [a]Heb. 12:1
2 [a][Matt. 18:3; 19:14] [b]1 Cor. 3:2 [1]NU adds *up to salvation*
3 [a]Heb. 6:5
4 [a]Ps. 118:22
6 [a]Is. 28:16
7 [a]Ps. 118:22 [1]NU *disbelieve*
8 [a]Is. 8:14 [b]1 Cor. 1:23 [c]Rom. 9:22
9 [a][Acts 26:18]
10 [a]Hos. 1:9, 10; 2:23

(continued from previous page)
incarnate Son, **the word of the LORD** (v. 25), we gain incorrupt and immortal humanity, both in body and in soul.

2:1 The duty—the necessity—for Christians to be holy in their conduct is the issue pursued in this passage. The Apostle Paul has written that new Christians (indeed, all Christians) are to put off the old manner of life, corrupted by evil and deception (Eph. 4:22). Similarly, those addressed here are to turn away from evil.

2:2, 3 The pure milk of the word is apostolic doctrine (Acts 2:42), the basic teaching of the Church—both written (1:10–12) and spoken (1:25). This leads us to the meat of the word (1 Cor. 3:2), the sacraments of the Church, and continual growth in the Christian life. Having **tasted that the Lord is gracious,** we should long for this spiritual nourishment.

2:4–10 Peter likens the growth of the Church to the OT temple, with its attending priesthood and its sacrifice and worship, Christ Himself being the fulfillment of this imagery. Thus, in Christ we become **living stones, a spiritual house, a royal priesthood** (v. 5; see Ex. 19:5, 6), **the people of God** who have **obtained mercy** (v. 10; see 1 Cor. 3:16, 17; 2 Cor. 6:16; Eph. 2:19–22). This is salvation in all its fullness.

2:5 In the true temple, one sacrifice is offered, the unrepeatable sacrifice of Christ. But in Him, in baptism, we also are sacrificed, "a living sacrifice" (Rom. 12:1) **acceptable to God.** Our whole life is to be lived in this baptism as an offering to Christ our life. This is the **spiritual** offering of the Church in the Eucharist, the offering by which she lives.

2:9 In the true temple there is one offerer, one Priest, who, again, is Christ. In baptism we all are anointed with grace as priests in the Kingdom of God; for the spiritual Kingdom is also the spiritual priesthood. Moreover, as the body of Christ, we have a priestly ministry to the world, fulfilling the very priesthood and intercession of the Lord Himself, so that to the whole universe we **may proclaim the praises of Him** who called us **out of darkness into His marvelous light.**

All Men and Women: Bondservants of God

11 Beloved, I beg *you* as sojourners
and pilgrims, abstain from fleshly
lusts [a]which war against the soul,†
12 [a]having your conduct honorable
among the Gentiles, that when they
speak against you as evildoers,
[b]they may, by *your* good works
which they observe, glorify God in
the day of visitation.
13 [a]Therefore submit yourselves to
every [1]ordinance of man for the
Lord's sake, whether to the king as
supreme,†
14 or to governors, as to those who
are sent by him for the punishment
of evildoers and *for the* praise of those
who do good.
15 For this is the will of God, that
by doing good you may put to silence the ignorance of foolish men—
16 [a]as free, yet not [b]using liberty
as a cloak for [1]vice, but as bondservants of God.
17 Honor all *people.* Love the brotherhood. Fear [a]God. Honor the king.

Servants: Submissive to Masters

18 [a]Servants, *be* submissive to *your*
masters with all fear, not only to the
good and gentle, but also to the
harsh.†
19 For this *is* [a]commendable, if because of conscience toward God one
endures grief, suffering wrongfully.
20 For [a]what credit *is it* if, when
you are beaten for your faults, you
take it patiently? But when you do
good and suffer, if you take it patiently, this *is* commendable before
God.
21 For [a]to this you were called, because Christ also suffered for [1]us,
[b]leaving [2]us an example, that you
should follow His steps:

22 *"Who[a] committed no sin,*
Nor was deceit found in His
mouth";†

23 [a]who, when He was reviled, did
not revile in return; when He suffered, He did not threaten, but
[b]committed *Himself* to Him who
judges righteously;
24 [a]who Himself bore our sins in
His own body on the tree, [b]that we,
having died to sins, might live for
righteousness—[c]by whose [1]stripes
you were healed.
25 For [a]you were like sheep going
astray, but have now returned
[b]to the Shepherd and [1]Overseer of
your souls.†

11 [a]James 4:1
12 [a]Phil. 2:15 [b]Matt. 5:16; 9:8
13 [a]Matt. 22:21 [1]*institution*
16 [a]Rom. 6:14, 20, 22 [b]Gal. 5:13 [1]*wickedness*
17 [a]Prov. 24:21
18 [a]Eph. 6:5–8
19 [a]Matt. 5:10
20 [a]Luke 6:32–34
21 [a]Matt. 16:24 [b][1 John 2:6] [1]NU *you* [2]NU, M *you*
22 [a]Is. 53:9
23 [a]Is. 53:7 [b]Luke 23:46
24 [a][Heb. 9:28] [b]Rom. 7:6 [c]Is. 53:5 [1]*wounds*
25 [a]Is. 53:5, 6 [b][Ezek. 34:23] [1]Gr. *Episkopos*

2:11 To this point Peter has been addressing the whole of the Church, describing the benefits and challenges of salvation. Now he speaks to various groups of Christians—citizens, servants, wives, husbands, pastors—exhorting all to forsake sinful passions and to live as true **sojourners and pilgrims** in the world.

2:13–17 (See also Matt. 22:21; Rom. 13:1–7; Titus 3:1.) Peter urges his readers to be obedient to civil government. While Christians serve a higher authority, God Himself, God also calls us to **submit** to earthly leaders **for the Lord's sake** (v. 13). This is not a call to "separate" Church from state, but rather a call to cooperate with and enhance the state—realizing that at times Church and state have been at great odds. When ultimate loyalty and obedience to Christ and His gospel are at stake, Peter's actions show that we are to obey God rather than man, even to the point of imprisonment or death (Acts 4:19, 20).

2:18–24 This advice to **servants** is applicable to anyone who is employed by another. Christ is our **example** for service and for our response to mistreatment. He is shown to be the suffering Servant, offering Himself on our behalf, **by whose stripes you were healed** (v. 24; see Is. 53).

2:22 No washing away of sins was necessary for Christ, who did **no sin.** It was done for us, who do sin. We should live, then, for Him who did not spare His own Son, that in His body He might crucify our passions. For Christ died for us, that we might live in His renewed body, the Church.

2:25 Peter (according to tradition the first bishop of Antioch, mother church of the Eastern Mediterranean, and later bishop of Rome, mother church of the Western Mediterranean), the one charged by Christ to tend His sheep (John 21:16), sees all of us as **sheep,** under the care of Christ, our universal **shepherd** and **overseer** (lit. "bishop"). Peter calls himself "a fellow elder" in 5:1, for bishops and priests are both shepherds in God's flock.

Wives: Submissive to Husbands

3 Wives, likewise, *be* [a]submissive
to your own husbands, that even
if some do not obey the word,
[b]they, without a word, may [c]be won
by the conduct of their wives,†
2 [a]when they observe your chaste
conduct *accompanied* by fear.
3 [a]Do not let your adornment be
merely outward—arranging the hair,
wearing gold, or putting on *fine* apparel—
4 rather *let it be* [a]the hidden person of the heart, with the
[1]incorruptible *beauty* of a gentle and
quiet spirit, which is very precious
in the sight of God.
5 For in this manner, in former
times, the holy women who trusted
in God also adorned themselves, being submissive to their own husbands,
6 as Sarah obeyed Abraham,
[a]calling him lord, whose daughters
you are if you do good and are not
afraid with any terror.

Husbands: Honor Your Wives

7 [a]Husbands, likewise, dwell
with *them* with understanding, giving honor to the wife, [b]as to the
weaker vessel, and as *being* heirs together of the grace of life, [c]that your
prayers may not be hindered.

Christians: Bless Others

8 Finally, all *of you be* of one mind,
having compassion for one another;
love as brothers, *be* tenderhearted,
be [1]courteous;†
9 [a]not returning evil for evil or reviling for reviling, but on the contrary [b]blessing, knowing that you
were called to this, [c]that you may
inherit a blessing.
10 For

[a]"He who would love life
And see good days,
[b]Let him [1]refrain his tongue from
evil,
And his lips from speaking
deceit.
11 *Let him [a]turn away from evil*
and do good;
[b]Let him seek peace and pursue
it.
12 *For the eyes of the* LORD *are on*
the righteous,
[a]And His ears are open to their
prayers;
But the face of the LORD *is*
against those who do evil."

Suffering for Righteousness

13 [a]And who *is* he who will harm
you if you become followers of what
is good?†
14 [a]But even if you should suffer
for righteousness' sake, *you are*
blessed. [b]*"And do not be afraid of*
their threats, nor be troubled."
15 But [1]sanctify [2]the Lord God in
your hearts, and always [a]*be* ready to
give a defense to everyone who asks
you a reason for the [b]hope that is
in you, with meekness and fear;†

CHAPTER 3
1 [a]Gen. 3:16; 1 Cor. 14:34; Eph. 5:22; Col. 3:18
[b]1 Cor. 7:16
[c]Matt. 18:15
2 [a]1 Pet. 2:12; 3:6
3 [a]Is. 3:18; 1 Tim. 2:9
4 [a]Rom. 2:29
[1]*imperishable*
6 [a]Gen. 18:12
7 [a]1 Cor. 7:3; [Eph. 5:25]; Col. 3:19
[b]1 Cor. 12:23
[c]Job 42:8
8 [1]NU *humble*
9 [a][Prov. 17:13]
[b]Matt. 5:44
[c]Matt. 25:34
10 [a]Ps. 34:12–16
[b]James 1:26
[1]*restrain*
11 [a]Ps. 37:27
[b]Rom. 12:18
12 [a]John 9:31
13 [a]Prov. 16:7
14 [a]James 1:12
[b]Is. 8:12
15 [a]Ps. 119:46
[b][Titus 3:7]
[1]*set apart*
[2]NU *Christ as Lord*

3:1–7 A stunning call to contentment in Christian marriage, whether we live in the first century or the twenty-first. The dignity and modesty of a woman—and her good conduct—have the power to call her husband to faith and devotion. Nor are husbands to take advantage of this superior conduct on the part of their wives, but are to reciprocate, indeed to give honor. Peter's image of marriage is one of sacramental union, not merely of legal contract. Contrary to the inheritance customs of the time, husband and wife are **heirs together of the grace of life** (v. 7). Failure to live **with understanding** with one's spouse even affects one's relationship with God (see Eph. 5:22–33).

3:8–12 Our behavior today has consequences for the future. The Church as a corporate priesthood is to express God's graciousness to the entire world. As we have been blessed so must we bless (see Matt. 7:12).

3:13–17 As the royal priesthood follows Christ in His obedience and His mercifulness, so it follows Him in His suffering.

3:15 A challenge to all—clergy and laity alike—to answer when asked about our **hope** in Christ **with meekness and fear.**

16 [a]having a good conscience, that
when they defame you as evildoers,
those who revile your good conduct
in Christ may be ashamed.
17 For *it is* better, if it is the will
of God, to suffer for doing good than
for doing evil.†

Involved in Christ's Suffering

18 For Christ also suffered once for
sins, the just for the unjust, that He
might bring [1]us to God, being put
to death in the flesh but made alive
by the Spirit,†
19 by whom also He went and
preached to the spirits in prison,
20 who formerly were disobedient,
[1]when once the Divine longsuffering
waited in the days of Noah, while
the ark was being prepared, in which
a few, that is, eight souls, were saved
through water.
21 [a]There is also an antitype which
now saves us—baptism [b](not the removal of the filth of the flesh,
[c]but the answer of a good conscience
toward God), through the resurrection of Jesus Christ,†
22 who has gone into heaven and
[a]is at the right hand of God, [b]angels
and authorities and powers having
been made subject to Him.

Crucifying Passions

4 Therefore, since Christ suffered
[1]for us in the flesh, arm yourselves also with the same mind, for
he who has suffered in the flesh has
ceased from sin,†
2 that he no longer should live the
rest of *his* time in the flesh for the
lusts of men, [a]but for the will of God.
3 For we *have spent* enough of our
past [1]lifetime in doing the will of the
Gentiles—when we walked in lewdness, lusts, drunkenness, revelries,
drinking parties, and abominable
idolatries.
4 In regard to these, they think it
strange that you do not run with
them in the same flood of dissipation,
speaking evil of *you*.
5 They will give an account to
Him who is ready [a]to judge the living and the dead.
6 For this reason [a]the gospel was
preached also to those who are dead,
that they might be judged according
to men in the flesh, but [b]live according to God in the spirit.†

Prepare for Heaven by Serving

7 But [a]the end of all things is at
hand; therefore be serious and
watchful in your prayers.†
8 And above all things have fervent love for one another, for [a]*"love
will cover a multitude of sins."*
9 [a]*Be* hospitable to one another
[b]without grumbling.
10 [a]As each one has received a gift,
minister it to one another, [b]as good

16 [a]Heb. 13:18
18 [1]NU, M *you*
20 [1]NU, M *when the longsuffering of God waited patiently*
21 [a]Eph. 5:26 [b][Titus 3:5] [c][Rom. 10:10]
22 [a]Ps. 110:1 [b]Rom. 8:38

CHAPTER 4

1 [1]NU omits *for us*
2 [a]John 1:13
3 [1]NU *time*
5 [a]Acts 10:42
6 [a]1 Pet. 1:12; 3:19 [b][Rom. 8:9, 13]
7 [a]Rom. 13:11
8 [a][Prov. 10:12]
9 [a]Heb. 13:2 [b]2 Cor. 9:7
10 [a]Rom. 12:6–8 [b]1 Cor. 4:1, 2

3:17 Not all of our suffering is because we have been righteous.

3:18–20 As Noah preached righteousness, suffered unjustly, and rescued those who were with him, so also does Christ. Christ descended to those in darkness and death that light might shine on them and that He might deliver them from death. As Christ fearlessly faced His tormentors, death, and hell, so we, through Him, can confidently face mockers and tormentors—and bring His light to them.

3:21, 22 The Flood is an OT mystery of the salvation of the human race. Noah was saved from a godless society—not so much saved *from* the water, as *through* the water, from evil. For through the water of **baptism** the resurrected Christ, having taken His place in **heaven** itself, gives us a clean **conscience.**

4:1–5 Though Peter refers here to specific activities and vices prevalent in that day in Asia Minor—where excessive drinking, along with unspeakable practices took place in connection with the worship of various deities—there can be no doubt of the direct application of this passage to our own day and the condition from which many of us have come into the Kingdom.

4:6 The **dead** are most likely those preached to "in prison," in Hades (3:19).

4:7–11 Whatever gifts God has given to His people are to be used for the glory of God and in a spirit of love (see Rom. 12:4–10; 1 Cor. 12—14).

stewards of [c]the manifold grace of
God.
11 [a]If anyone speaks, *let him speak*
as the [1]oracles of God. If anyone
ministers, *let him do it* as with the
ability which God supplies, that
[b]in all things God may be glorified
through Jesus Christ, to whom belong the glory and the [2]dominion forever and ever. Amen.

Prepare for the End by Suffering

12 Beloved, do not think it strange
concerning the fiery trial which is to
try you, as though some strange
thing happened to you;†
13 but rejoice [a]to the extent that
you partake of Christ's sufferings,
that [b]when His glory is revealed, you
may also be glad with exceeding joy.
14 If you are [1]reproached for the
name of Christ, [a]blessed *are you,* for
the Spirit of glory and of God rests
upon you. [2]On their part He is blasphemed, [b]but on your part He is
glorified.
15 But let none of you suffer as a
murderer, a thief, an evildoer, or as
a [1]busybody in other people's matters.
16 Yet if *anyone suffers* as a Christian, let him not be ashamed, but let
him glorify God in this [1]matter.
17 For the time *has come* [a]for judgment to begin at the house of God;
and if *it begins* with us first, [b]what

10 [c][1 Cor. 12:4]
11 [a]Eph. 4:29 [b][1 Cor. 10:31] [1]*utterances* [2]*sovereignty*
13 [a]James 1:2 [b]2 Tim. 2:12
14 [a]Matt. 5:11 [b]Matt. 5:16 [1]*insulted* or *reviled* [2]NU omits the rest of v. 14.
15 [1]*meddler*
16 [1]NU *name*
17 [a]Is. 10:12 [b]Luke 10:12
18 [a]Prov. 11:31
19 [a]2 Tim. 1:12

CHAPTER 5

1 [a]Matt. 26:37 [b]Rom. 8:17, 18
2 [a]Acts 20:28 [b]1 Cor. 9:17 [c]1 Tim. 3:3 [1]NU adds *according to God*
3 [a]Ezek. 34:4 [b]Ps. 33:12 [c]Phil. 3:17 [1]*masters*
4 [a]Heb. 13:20 [b]2 Tim. 4:8
5 [a]Eph. 5:21

will *be* the end of those who do not
obey the gospel of God?†
18 Now

[a]*"If the righteous one is scarcely*
saved,
Where will the ungodly and the
sinner appear?"

19 Therefore let those who suffer
according to the will of God [a]commit
their souls *to Him* in doing good, as
to a faithful Creator.

Suffering as the Church

5 The elders who are among you
I exhort, I who am a fellow elder
and a [a]witness of the sufferings of
Christ, and also a partaker of the
[b]glory that will be revealed:†
2 [a]Shepherd the flock of God
which is among you, serving as overseers, [b]not by compulsion but
[1]willingly, [c]not for dishonest gain
but eagerly;
3 nor as [a]being [1]lords over [b]those
entrusted to you, but [c]being examples to the flock;†
4 and when [a]the Chief Shepherd
appears, you will receive [b]the crown
of glory that does not fade away.
5 Likewise you younger people,
submit yourselves to *your* elders.
Yes, [a]all of *you* be submissive to one
another, and be clothed with humility, for

4:12, 13 The **fiery trial** is the suffering of tribulations which tempt us to unfaithfulness, to the ruin of our faith. God's people have always suffered unjustly, but in baptism the **sufferings** in which we partake are those of Christ Himself, and will ultimately bring great **joy** (v. 13).

4:17–19 Slander and persecution purify the Church for **judgment** (v. 13), but persecutors and **the ungodly** (v. 18) are heaping condemnation upon themselves. The severity of the present judgment of **the righteous** is evidence that the ungodly face a fearsome fate. Christians who suffer can always be confident that God is **faithful** (v. 19) and good.

5:1–4 (See John 21:15–17.) From Christ Himself and throughout the history of the Church these words have been delivered in exhortation to the shepherds or leaders of **the flock** (v. 2). Pastoral work is to be undertaken **willingly** and cheerfully, with neither financial **gain** nor power in mind. For faithful service is done on behalf of Christ, **the Chief Shepherd** (v. 4), and awaits an eternal **crown of glory.**

5:3 (See Mark 10:42–45; 2 Cor. 4:5.) **Those entrusted to you** (Gr. *kleron*) means those who have "the inheritance," and is the source of our word "clergy." In the OT the Levites were the *kleros;* their inheritance was the Lord. In the NT all are *kleros,* a royal priesthood, equally inheriting the Lord. While there are "orders" of clergy in the Church—bishops, presbyters, deacons—a separation or isolation between priests and laity is unknown in the NT.

[b]*"God resists the proud,*
But [c]gives grace to the
humble."†

6 Therefore humble yourselves
under the mighty hand of God, that
He may exalt you in due time,
7 casting all your care upon Him,
for He cares for you.
8 Be [1]sober, be [2]vigilant; [3]because
your adversary the devil walks about
like a roaring lion, seeking whom he
may devour.†
9 Resist him, steadfast in the
faith, knowing that the same sufferings are experienced by your brotherhood in the world.
10 But [1]may the God of all grace,
[a]who called [2]us to His eternal glory
by Christ Jesus, after you have suffered a while, [3]perfect, establish,
strengthen, and settle *you.*
11 [a]To Him *be* the glory and the
dominion forever and ever. Amen.

Farewell and Greeting

12 By [a]Silvanus, our faithful
brother as I consider him, I have
written to you briefly, exhorting and
testifying [b]that this is the true grace
of God in which you stand.
13 She who is in Babylon, elect together with *you,* greets you; and *so
does* [a]Mark my son.†
14 Greet one another with a kiss
of love. Peace to you all who are in
Christ Jesus. Amen.†

5 [b]Prov. 3:34 [c]Is. 57:15
8 [1]*self-controlled* [2]*watchful* [3]NU, M omit *because*
10 [a]1 Cor. 1:9 [1]NU *the God of all grace,* [2]NU, M *you* [3]NU *will perfect*
11 [a]Rev. 1:6
12 [a]2 Cor. 1:19 [b]Acts 20:24
13 [a]Acts 12:12, 25; 15:37, 39

5:5–7 Humility is the foundation of virtue, and it is learned through submission and obedience to godly **elders.** In submitting to one another, we **humble** ourselves **under the mighty hand of God** (see 1 Thess. 5:12, 13; Heb. 13:7, 17).

5:8, 9 The **devil** and his angels explore us individually, looking for our weaknesses. The enemy offers appealing visions to our eyes, music to our ears, to each of our senses setting forth whatever might tempt us to sin. He arouses our tongues to speak evil about others, and urges our hands to injure them. He sets forth profits to be earned by shady and immoral means, and holds out earthly honors and false values to be preferred to heavenly ones. When he is unable to tempt us, he brings forth a threat of persecution so that fear may cause us to betray the faith. Thus we must always be alert for his many-faceted attacks, ready to **resist** him at every turn.

5:13 Babylon here is almost certainly a reference to ancient Rome, which, like the more ancient Babylon (itself of no significance in the days of the early Church), was a source of confusion and tribulation for the people of God. Peter himself was martyred in Rome.

5:14 The **kiss of love,** or of peace, is already a liturgical practice. In St. John Chrysostom's liturgy the kiss of peace occurs between the Great Entrance and the Creed; historically, and in some congregations today, the entire Church took part in it. This embrace signifies forgiveness, reconciliation, and banishment of every remembrance of injury. It recalls the command of Christ, "If you bring your gift to the altar, and there remember that your brother has something against you, leave your gift there before the altar, and go your way. First be reconciled to your brother, and then come and offer your gift" (Matt. 5:23, 24).

The Second General Epistle of

PETER

Author: *St. Peter the Apostle*

Date: *A.D. 63–67*

Theme: *True Knowledge vs. False Knowledge*

AUTHOR: While the Orthodox Church is clear on the canonicity of 2 Peter, some modern scholars consider the letter to be pseudonymous, that is, written by someone else based on what Peter taught.

Arguments favoring Peter's authorship include: (1) his signature (1:1); (2) the prediction of his death (1:14); (3) the reference to his eyewitness account of the Transfiguration (1:16–18); (4) the common themes of 1 and 2 Peter—Noah and the flood, angels, warning against error, the Second Coming of Christ, life in Christ as a process of growth; (5) the clear reference to his first letter (3:1).

DATE: Given Peter's authorship, the date of the letter is most likely A.D. 63–67, during Peter's imprisonment in Rome.

MAJOR THEME: *True knowledge vs. false knowledge.* Though the world disbelieves, deceives and mocks, Christians must maintain apostolic doctrine and the Christian way of life. We are to grow continually in holiness and virtue and pursue an entrance into "the everlasting kingdom" (1:11) which is to come.

BACKGROUND INFORMATION: (1) *Canonicity.* Of the 27 New Testament books, the canonicity of 2 Peter has been questioned most. However, there is unmistakable evidence that it was known and used in the early Church, and its canonicity was settled in the fourth century.

(2) *Historical setting.* Peter apparently wrote his second epistle from Roman imprisonment. The people addressed know the author (1:16) and seem to be Gentiles, former pagans, in territories evangelized by Paul (3:15, 16).

(3) *The presence of false teachers.* The Church has been infiltrated by gnostic-sounding, antinomian teachers. (Antinomianism—lit. "against the law"—is the teaching that faith alone, isolated from repentance, works, or virtue, saves.) They deny that (1) the Second Coming is a physical, historical event and that (2) morality is relevant to salvation. The whole Church is threatened, especially the new converts; some have already fallen away.

(4) *The heretics' lack of integrity.* They appear to be orthodox but are not. They desire to create a schismatic group. Since for them moral behavior is irrelevant to salvation, they promote immoral pleasure-seeking, advocating sexual gratification at will, and they infiltrate Christian love feasts with their carousing. Even non-Christians find them disgusting, but mistakenly associate them with the Church. The motivation of these false teachers is self-centered: greed and sensual pleasure—religion is merely a way to make a living.

(5) *The goal.* The Second Coming is at hand (as it always is), and morality is connected to salvation. What happened to the disobedient angels, to Noah's contemporaries, and to Sodom and Gomorrah will happen again. But this time, judgment will extend to the whole world, and will be so complete that it will never have to happen again. However, rescue and reward await the righteous.

OUTLINE

Greeting

1 Simon Peter, a bondservant and
[a]apostle of Jesus Christ,

To those who have [1]obtained
[b]like[2] precious faith with us by the
righteousness of our God and Savior
Jesus Christ:†

2 [a]Grace and peace be multiplied
to you in the knowledge of God and
of Jesus our Lord,†

CHAPTER 1
1 [a]Gal. 2:8 [b]Eph. 4:5 [1]*received* [2]*faith of the same value*
2 [a]Dan. 4:1

1:1 Whereas 1 Peter introduces the author simply as "Peter, an apostle of Jesus Christ," 2 Peter adds **Simon,** the pre-Christian name of Peter, and **a bondservant. God** refers to Jesus Christ (as in Titus 2:13). What Peter teaches in this letter is apostolic consensus: **Like precious faith with us.** He reminds and exhorts his hearers to full Christian belief and virtue.

1:2 Gnostics, who were infiltrating the Church, claimed that they had access to a special knowledge, unknown by ordinary people. Peter teaches the true **knowledge of God,** and it is in the Church this knowledge is found.

DEIFICATION

Deification is the ancient theological word used to describe the process by which a Christian becomes more like God. St. Peter speaks of this process when he writes, "As His divine power has given to us all things that pertain to life and godliness . . . you may be partakers of the divine nature" (2 Pet. 1:3, 4).

What does it mean to partake of the divine nature, and how do we experience it? To give an answer, we must first address what deification is not, then describe what it is.

What deification is not. When the Church calls us to pursue godliness, to be more like God, this does not mean that human beings then become divine. We do not become like God in His nature. That would not only be heresy, it would be impossible. For we are human, always have been human, and always will be human. We cannot take on the nature of God.

St. John of Damascus, writing in the eighth century, makes a remarkable observation. The word "God" in the Scriptures refers not to the divine nature or essence, for that is unknowable. "God" refers rather to the divine energies—the power and grace of God which we can perceive in this world. The Greek word for God, *theos*, comes from a verb meaning "run," "see," or "burn." These are energy words, so to speak, not essence words.

In John 10:34, Jesus, quoting Psalm 82:6, repeats the passage, "You are gods." The fact that He was speaking to a group of hypocritical religious leaders who were accusing Him of blasphemy makes the meaning doubly clear: Jesus is not using "god" to refer to divine nature. We are gods in that we bear His image, not His nature.

What deification is. Deification means we are to become more like God through His grace or divine energies. In creation, humans were made in the image and likeness of God (Gen. 1:26) according to human nature. In other words, humanity by nature is an icon or image of deity: The divine image is in all humanity. Through sin, however, this image and likeness of God was marred, and we fell.

When the Son of God assumed our humanity in the womb of the blessed Virgin Mary, the process of our being renewed in God's image and likeness was begun. Thus, those who are joined to Christ through faith in Holy Baptism begin a re-creation process, being renewed in God's image and likeness. We become, as St. Peter writes, "partakers of the divine nature" (2 Pet. 1:4).

Because of the Incarnation of the Son of God, because the fullness of God has inhabited human flesh, being joined to Christ means that it is again possible to experience *deification*, the fulfillment of our human destiny. That is, through union with Christ, we become by grace what God is by nature—we "become children of God" (John 1:12). His deity interpenetrates our humanity.

Historically, deification has often been illustrated by the "sword and fire" example. A steel sword is thrust into a hot fire until the sword takes on a red glow. The energy of the fire interpenetrates the sword. The sword never becomes fire, but it picks up the properties of fire.

By application, the divine energies interpenetrate the human nature of Christ. Being joined to Christ, our humanity is interpenetrated with the energies of God through Christ's glorified flesh. Nourished by the Body and Blood of Christ, we partake of the grace of God—His strength, His righteousness, His love—and are enabled to serve Him and glorify Him. Thus we, being human, are being deified.

The Holy Transfiguration of Our Lord Jesus Christ *August 6*

1:10–19: St. Peter describes his experience of the glory of Christ, reminding us to be prepared for His return.

Partakers of the Divine Nature

3 as His [a]divine power has given
to us all things that *pertain* to life and
godliness, through the knowledge of
Him [b]who called us by glory and
virtue,†
4 [a]by which have been given to
us exceedingly great and precious
promises, that through these you
may be [b]partakers of the divine nature, having escaped the [1]corrup-
tion *that is* in the world through
lust.†
5 But also for this very reason,
[a]giving all diligence, add to your
faith virtue, to virtue [b]knowledge,†
6 to knowledge self-control, to
self-control [1]perseverance, to perseverance godliness,
7 to godliness brotherly kindness,
and [a]to brotherly kindness love.
8 For if these things are yours and
abound, *you will be* neither [1]barren
[a]nor unfruitful in the knowledge of
our Lord Jesus Christ.†
9 For he who lacks these things
is [a]shortsighted, even to blindness,
and has forgotten that he was
cleansed from his old sins.†
10 Therefore, brethren, be even
more diligent [a]to make your call and
election sure, for if you do these
things you will never stumble;
11 for so an entrance will be supplied to you abundantly into the

3 [a]1 Pet. 1:5 [b]1 Thess. 2:12; 2 Thess. 2:14; 1 Pet. 5:10
4 [a]2 Cor. 1:20; 7:1 [b][2 Cor. 3:18] [1]*depravity*
5 [a]2 Pet. 3:18 [b]2 Pet. 1:2
6 [1]*patience*
7 [a]Gal. 6:10
8 [a][John 15:2] [1]*useless*
9 [a]1 John 2:9–11
10 [a]2 Cor. 13:5; 1 John 3:19

1:3 Peter assures us we have no need for anything other than what we have received. For God has given us His energy (**life**) and His personal presence (**godliness,** or piety, devotion), in which we may grow.

Virtue (Gr. *arete*) may also be translated as "excellence" or "power." It is spiritual and moral excellence attained by vigorous and courageous faith.

1:4 Being renewed by God's power, we become **partakers of the divine nature.** This does *not* mean we become divine by nature. If we participated in God's *essence* or nature, the distinction between God and man would be abolished. What this *does* mean is that we participate in God's divine *energy,* described by a number of terms in Scripture, such as glory, life, love, virtue, and power. We are to become like God by His grace, and truly His adopted children, but we never become God by nature. According to some Church Fathers, this transformation especially occurs through the Eucharist, for when Christ's body and blood become one with ours, we become Christ-bearers and *partakers of the divine nature.* (See article "Deification," at 2 Peter 1.)

St. Cyril of Alexandria (5th century), commenting on John 1:13, writes: "We that are made worthy to participate in Him [the Holy Spirit] through faith in Christ are brought to perfection as participants of the divine nature (1:4), and are said to be born of God, and on that account are given the title gods, not flying up to the glory above us by grace alone, but as already having God indwelling and taking lodging in us, according to what is set forth in the Prophet, 'I shall dwell among them and walk about in their midst' (Lev. 26:12; 2 Cor. 6:16)."

1:5–7 How do we who know Christ grow in our participation in the divine nature through grace? By the cultivation of a progression of spiritual qualities. As in v. 3, **virtue** refers to the vigor and courage behind attaining moral excellence. **Love** (v. 7) is adjoined to **brotherly kindness** (affection among Christians), for love of God cannot be perfected except through love of one's neighbor (see 1 John 4:20).

1:8 This **knowledge** (Gr. *epignosis,* as also in v. 2) is not primarily mental but spiritual and personal. It is experienced as we have faith and bear good fruit in the **Lord Jesus Christ.**

1:9 Gnostics claimed to know God without becoming godlike. Peter makes it plain this is not Christian, for we reach participation with God through the increase of spiritual virtues, not the absence of them. Here, as with all eschatological warnings in the NT, admittance to God's Kingdom is conditional upon a faith which exhibits perseverance and holiness.

everlasting kingdom of our Lord and Savior Jesus Christ.†

Pursue God

12 For this reason [a]I will not be negligent to remind you always of these things, [b]though you know and are established in the present truth.
13 Yes, I think it is right, [a]as long as I am in this [1]tent, [b]to stir you up by reminding *you*,†
14 [a]knowing that shortly I *must* [1]put off my tent, just as [b]our Lord Jesus Christ showed me.
15 Moreover I will be careful to ensure that you always have a reminder of these things after my [1]decease.

The Apostles' Report Is True

16 For we did not follow [a]cunningly devised fables when we made known to you the [b]power and [c]coming of our Lord Jesus Christ, but were [d]eyewitnesses of His majesty.†
17 For He received from God the Father honor and glory when such a voice came to Him from the Excellent Glory: [a]"This is My beloved Son, in whom I am well pleased."
18 And we heard this voice which came from heaven when we were with Him on [a]the holy mountain.

Interpreting Prophecy

19 [1]And so we have the prophetic word confirmed, which you do well to heed as a [a]light that shines in a dark place, [b]until [c]the day dawns and the morning star rises in your [d]hearts;†
20 knowing this first, that [a]no prophecy of Scripture is of any private [1]interpretation,
21 for [a]prophecy never came by the will of man, [b]but [1]holy men of God spoke *as they were* moved by the Holy Spirit.

The Deceptions of False Teachers

2 But there were also false prophets among the people, even as there will be [a]false teachers among

12 [a]Phil. 3:1 [b]1 Pet. 5:12
13 [a][2 Cor. 5:1, 4] [b]2 Pet. 3:1 [1]Body
14 [a][2 Tim. 4:6] [b]John 13:36; 21:18, 19 [1]Die and leave this body
15 [1]Lit. *exodus, departure*
16 [a]1 Cor. 1:17 [b][Eph. 1:19–22] [c][1 Pet. 5:4] [d]Matt. 17:1–5
17 [a]Matt. 17:5
18 [a]Matt. 17:1
19 [a][John 1:4, 5, 9] [b]Prov. 4:18 [c]Rev. 2:28; 22:16 [d][2 Cor. 4:5–7] [1]Or *We also have the more sure prophetic word*
20 [a][Rom. 12:6] [1]Or *origin*
21 [a][2 Tim. 3:16] [b]2 Sam. 23:2 [1]NU *men spoke from God*

CHAPTER 2
1 [a]1 Tim. 4:1, 2

1:11 The primary truth with which Peter is dealing (which he has only indirectly touched upon to this point) is the Second Coming of Christ and His **everlasting kingdom.**

1:13 One lives in a **tent** when one is on a journey or during war. As long as we are in this body we live in "tents," which bear witness to the long journey of life and to the ongoing battle against enemy forces of darkness.

1:16–18 Peter has been an eyewitness to the **majesty** of Christ in many ways—and here reminds us especially that he was one of those present with the Lord on the Mount of Transfiguration (Matt. 17:1–8). What Peter is going to repeat about the Second Coming is the common apostolic tradition, which is buttressed by the eyewitness testimony of the Apostles. It is not an elaborate scheme of **fables,** such as the gnostics propounded. In all the Gospel accounts, the Transfiguration is a proof and foretaste of the coming of Christ in glory.

1:19–21 The testimony of the apostles both (1) confirms **prophetic word** (v. 19) concerning the Second Coming and (2) shows us how to interpret prophecy. Just as **Scripture** (v. 20) was not written by the mere volition of men but by the inspiration of the **Holy Spirit** (v. 21), so Scripture is to be interpreted by holy men guided by the Holy Spirit. Heretics (ch. 2) and unstable Christians (3:16) interpret incorrectly. The apostles (the **we** of v. 19) are guided by the *Holy Spirit* (v. 21), trusting in the promise of true interpretation (John 16:13). The Church, founded by the apostles, likewise receives the Holy Spirit. "For the apostles, like a rich man in a bank, deposited with her [the Church] most copiously everything which pertains to the truth. And everyone who wishes, draws from her the drink of life. For she is the entrance to life, while all the rest are thieves and robbers. That is why it is surely necessary to avoid them, while cherishing with the utmost diligence the things pertaining to the church, and to lay hold of the tradition of truth" (St. Irenaeus of Lyons, 2nd century).

you, who will secretly bring in destructive heresies, even denying the Lord who bought them, *and* bring on themselves swift destruction.†
2 And many will follow their destructive ways, because of whom the way of truth will be blasphemed.
3 By covetousness they will exploit you with deceptive words; for a long time their judgment has not been idle, and their destruction [1]does not slumber.

The Doom of False Teachers

4 For if God did not spare the angels who sinned, but cast *them* down to [1]hell and delivered *them* into chains of darkness, to be reserved for judgment;†
5 and did not spare the ancient world, but saved Noah, *one of* eight *people,* a preacher of righteousness, bringing in the flood on the world of the ungodly;
6 and turning the cities of [a]Sodom and Gomorrah into ashes, condemned *them* to destruction, making *them* an example to those who afterward would live ungodly;
7 and [a]delivered righteous Lot, *who was* oppressed by the filthy conduct of the wicked
8 (for that righteous man, dwelling among them, [a]tormented *his* righteous soul from day to day by seeing and hearing *their* lawless deeds)—
9 *then* [a]the Lord knows how to deliver the godly out of temptations and to reserve the unjust under punishment for the day of judgment,

The Depravity of False Teachers

10 and especially [a]those who walk according to the flesh in the lust of uncleanness and despise authority. [b]*They are* presumptuous, self-willed. They are not afraid to speak evil of [1]dignitaries,
11 whereas [a]angels, who are greater in power and might, do not bring a reviling accusation against them before the Lord.
12 But these, [a]like natural brute beasts made to be caught and destroyed, speak evil of the things they do not understand, and will utterly perish in their own corruption,†
13 [a]*and* will receive the wages of unrighteousness, *as* those who count it pleasure [b]to [1]carouse in the daytime. [c]*They are* spots and blemishes, [2]carousing in their own deceptions while [d]they feast with you,
14 having eyes full of [1]adultery and that cannot cease from sin, enticing unstable souls. [a]*They have* a heart trained in covetous practices, *and are* accursed children.
15 They have forsaken the right way and gone astray, following the way of [a]Balaam the *son* of Beor, who loved the wages of unrighteousness;
16 but he was rebuked for his iniquity: a dumb donkey speaking with

3 [1]M *will not*
4 [1]Lit. *Tartarus*
6 [a]Gen. 19:1–26; Jude 7
7 [a]Gen. 19:16, 29
8 [a]Ps. 119:139
9 [a]Ps. 34:15–19; 1 Cor. 10:13; Rev. 3:10
10 [a]Jude 4, 7, 8 [b]Ex. 22:28; Jude 8 [1]*glorious ones,* lit. *glories*
11 [a]Jude 9
12 [a]Jude 10
13 [a]Phil. 3:19 [b]Rom. 13:13 [c]Jude 12 [d]1 Cor. 11:20, 21 [1]*revel* [2]*reveling*
14 [a]Jude 11 [1]Lit. *an adulteress*
15 [a]Num. 22:5, 7; Deut. 23:4; Neh. 13:2; Jude 11; Rev. 2:14

2:1–3 Peter now reaches his main concern: **False teachers** who are unholy and communicate heresy. They are arrogant, sensual, and greedy, and they deny accountability in their lives. Isolating themselves from apostolic doctrine concerning Christ, they hold their own "private interpretations," misconstruing doctrines about the Second Coming and the ultimate authority of Christ over us. Being deceivers, they teach as though they possess true apostolicity.

2:4–10 God's past judgments indicate what awaits the heretics: He will divide the holy from the unholy in the life to come. We already have the example of the **angels who sinned** (v. 4), imprisoned in the lowest part of **hell** (Gr. *tartarus*) while awaiting the final **judgment.** Verse 10 repeats two major sins of heretics: (1) immorality, and (2) disdain for **authority,** especially that of Christ.

Noah is called **a preacher of righteousness** (v. 5) in part because his life was an example of righteousness (see Heb. 11:7).

2:12–17 False teachers are condemned for both their words and their actions. Those who are **natural** cannot **understand** spiritual **things** (1 Cor. 2:14) and will be destroyed, as false prophets have been in the past. For the story of **Balaam** (v. 15) see Num. 22:1—25:9; 31:8, 16; Deut. 23:4, 5; Josh. 13:22; Jude 11.

a man's voice restrained the madness
of the prophet.
17 [a]These are wells without water,
[1]clouds carried by a tempest, for
whom is reserved the blackness of
darkness [2]forever.
18 For when they speak great
swelling *words* of emptiness, they al-
lure through the lusts of the flesh,
through lewdness, the ones who
[1]have actually escaped from those
who live in error.
19 While they promise them liberty, they themselves are slaves of
[1]corruption; [a]for by whom a person
is overcome, by him also he is
brought into [2]bondage.†

The Tragedy of Apostasy

20 For if, after they [a]have escaped
the pollutions of the world through
the knowledge of the Lord and
Savior Jesus Christ, they are [b]again
entangled in them and overcome,
the latter end is worse for them than
the beginning.
21 For [a]it would have been better
for them not to have known the way
of righteousness, than having
known *it,* to turn from the holy commandment delivered to them.
22 But it has happened to them according to the true proverb: [a]*"A dog
returns to his own vomit,"* and, "a
sow, having washed, to her wallow-
ing in the mire."

Where Is His Coming?

3 Beloved, I now write to you this
second epistle (in *both of* which
[a]I stir up your pure minds by way
of reminder),
2 that you may be mindful of the
words [a]which were spoken before by
the holy prophets, [b]and of the commandment of [1]us, the apostles of the
Lord and Savior,
3 knowing this first: that scoffers
will come in the last days, [a]walking
according to their own lusts,
4 and saying, "Where is the
promise of His coming? For since the
fathers fell asleep, all things continue
as *they were* from the beginning of
[a]creation."†
5 For this they willfully forget:
that [a]by the word of God the heavens were of old, and the earth
[b]standing out of water and in the
water,
6 [a]by which the world *that* then
existed perished, being flooded with
water.
7 But [a]the heavens and the earth
which are now preserved by the same
word, are reserved for [b]fire until the
day of judgment and [1]perdition of
ungodly men.
8 But, beloved, do not forget this
one thing, that with the Lord one
day *is* as a thousand years, and
[a]a thousand years as one day.
9 [a]The Lord is not slack concerning *His* promise, as some count
slackness, but [b]is longsuffering toward [1]us, [c]not willing that any
should perish but [d]that all should
come to repentance.†
10 But [a]the day of the Lord will
come as a thief in the night, in which
[b]the heavens will pass away with a
great noise, and the elements will
melt with fervent heat; both the earth

17 [a]Jude 12, 13 [1]NU *and mists* [2]NU omits *forever*
18 [1]NU *are barely escaping*
19 [a]John 8:34 [1]*depravity* [2]*slavery*
20 [a]Matt. 12:45 [b][Heb. 6:4–6]
21 [a]Luke 12:47
22 [a]Prov. 26:11

CHAPTER 3
1 [a]2 Pet. 1:13
2 [a]2 Pet. 1:21 [b]Jude 17 [1]NU, M *the apostles of your Lord and Savior* or *your apostles of the Lord and Savior*
3 [a]2 Pet. 2:10
4 [a]Gen. 6:1–7
5 [a]Gen. 1:6, 9 [b]Ps. 24:2; 136:6
6 [a]Gen. 7:11, 12, 21–23
7 [a]2 Pet. 3:10, 12 [b][2 Thess. 1:8] [1]*destruction*
8 [a]Ps. 90:4
9 [a]Hab. 2:3 [b]Is. 30:18 [c]Ezek. 33:11 [d][Rom. 2:4] [1]NU *you*
10 [a]Rev. 3:3; 16:15 [b]Ps. 102:25, 26

2:19 A common misunderstanding of **liberty** or freedom is to see it as standing apart from all moral restraints, to say there is no such thing as sin. But this results in slavery of the worst kind, **bondage** to egotistic and sensual passions. True Christian freedom begins with freedom from sin, freedom from immoral activity. A Christian is called to live in purity in an impure world.

3:4 "It is clear to all who love His coming that the mind must be controlled rather moderately in this conjecture. We must surmise neither that the aforesaid day of the Lord is near and will come quite quickly, nor again that it is coming too slowly. But we should be diligent in seeing to this alone: that whether it comes sooner or later, it may find us ready when it does come" (The Venerable Bede).

3:9 These words are not just for the false teachers, but for us all. We are granted more time primarily that we might achieve fuller **repentance.** (See v. 15 and 2 Cor. 7:9, 10.)

and the works that are in it will be [1]burned up.†

Purified by Waiting

11 Therefore, since all these things will be dissolved, what manner *of persons* ought you to be [a]in holy conduct and godliness,
12 [a]looking for and hastening the coming of the day of God, because of which the heavens will [b]be dissolved, being on fire, and the elements will [c]melt with fervent heat?
13 Nevertheless we, according to His promise, look for [a]new heavens and a [b]new earth in which righteousness dwells.†
14 Therefore, beloved, looking forward to these things, be diligent [a]to be found by Him in peace, without spot and blameless;

The Truth of Apostolic Teaching

15 and consider *that* [a]the longsuffering of our Lord *is* salvation—as also our beloved brother Paul, according to the wisdom given to him, has written to you,†
16 as also in all his [a]epistles, speaking in them of these things, in which are some things hard to understand, which untaught and unstable *people* twist to their own destruction, as *they do* also the [b]rest of the Scriptures.†
17 You therefore, beloved, [a]since you know *this* beforehand, [b]beware lest you also fall from your own steadfastness, being led away with the error of the wicked;†
18 [a]but grow in the grace and knowledge of our Lord and Savior Jesus Christ. [b]To Him *be* the glory both now and forever. Amen.

10 [1]NU *laid bare*, lit. *found*
11 [a]1 Pet. 1:15
12 [a]1 Cor. 1:7, 8 [b]Ps. 50:3 [c]Mic. 1:4
13 [a]Is. 65:17; 66:22 [b]Rev. 21:1
14 [a]1 Cor. 1:8; 15:58
15 [a]Rom. 2:4
16 [a]1 Cor. 15:24 [b]2 Tim. 3:16
17 [a]Mark 13:23 [b]Eph. 4:14
18 [a]Eph. 4:15 [b]2 Tim. 4:18

3:10–12 Because this world will pass away, we ought to be **holy** (v. 11) and godly, living as citizens of the new heaven and earth. Christians can actually hasten **the coming of** that **day** (v. 12). How? Through evangelism (Matt. 24:14; Mark 13:10), prayer (especially the Lord's Prayer, "Thy Kingdom come"), holy living (1 Pet. 2:12), and repentance and obedience (Acts 3:19–21).

3:13 We look for not other **heavens** and **earth,** but the same ones transfigured for the better. For a beautiful prophetic description of the new heaven and earth, see Rev. 21, 22 and Is. 65:17–25.

3:15 **Longsuffering** can be **salvation** only if our salvation in Christ includes a lifelong process of maturing.

3:16 The author knows of a collection of Paul's letters and regards it as equal in authority to Scripture, that is, to the OT. This is the first indication of the collection of a NT canon.

3:17, 18 The danger of deception is high for everyone. The defense against deception is to stay connected (1) to the true apostles and (2) to their doctrines, which encourage our growth in the **knowledge of our Lord . . . Jesus Christ** (v. 18).

The First Epistle of JOHN

Author: *St. John the Apostle*

Date: *A.D. 90–95*

Theme: *Tests of True Christian Life*

AUTHOR: First John is so similar to the Gospel of John in language, style, and theology, that few have ever disputed that the two books were written by the same man: St. John the Apostle.

DATE: The letter cannot be dated with certainty. Its similarity to John's Gospel, the presence among the recipients of a Christianized form of gnosticism, and the apparent age of its author suggest a time late in John's life, about the same time as he wrote his Gospel (A.D. 90–95).

MAJOR THEME: *Tests of true Christian life.* Jesus Christ, the Incarnate God, reveals the light (1:5–7), love (4:7–11) and life (5:11–13) of the Father, as contrasted with the darkness (1:6), hatred (2:9–11) and death (5:12) of the present world. Thus, 1 John can be read as a commentary on the reality of baptism, chrismation and the Eucharist in our lives.

Subthemes include:

(1) Our participation or communion with God and with each other. "Fellowship" (1:7; Gr. *koinonia*) speaks of our personal participation in something possessed in common, and describes communion—the inner reality of true worship. The bread and cup of the Eucharist, the body and blood of Christ, God's divine life in the life of the Church, involve a deep communion of persons, a participation together in the life of Christ.

(2) The close relationship of faith, love, obedience, and *life*—the all-inclusive term for salvation. Without confession of sin and love of other Christians, knowing God is impossible.

(3) The close relationship between the first great commandment, love of God, and the second, love of others—especially of fellow Christians. Words, thoughts, and feelings are not primarily in view here. *Acts* of love and mercy are the hard evidence of faith in God.

(4) The crucial importance of holding true faith. True love of God is inseparable from true doctrine, especially the doctrines of (1) the Holy Trinity and (2) the Lord Jesus Christ. Regarding Christ, (a) the Son is God along with

the Father (2:23, 24; 5:5, 9–12, 20) and (b) Jesus Christ is one divine Person in two complete natures, divine and human (2:22; 4:2, 3; 5:1, 6, 8). (It is obvious to John that the Holy Spirit is also God—see 2:20; 3:24; 4:2; 5:6, 7.)

(5) A stark, eschatological contrast between the children of God and the children of the world.

BACKGROUND INFORMATION: (1) *Denunciation of false teaching.* The polemic is mostly pastoral and positive, written to protect God's people. Living the truth is the best argument against what is false. For John, a theologian is one who lives in God, knows God, and therefore does what is true. First John is a polemic against two identifiable groups.

(a) False teachers with a gnostic bent. Gnosticism was based on a dualism between spirit and matter in which spirit is good and matter is evil (see *Glossary:* gnosticism). Gnostics used Christian words with redefined meanings—they could sound orthodox without being so. One early gnostic, for example, taught that the "heavenly Christ" was an emanation from the Father and not true God, and that his spirit fled from the man Jesus before His Passion so that only the "human Jesus" suffered and died. Therefore, according to this opinion, "Christ" came "by water" but not "by blood" (5:6–8); and sacrament, morality, and suffering have no place in true spiritual life.

(b) Former members of the Church who had left (2:19) and were a threat to the faith of Christians (2:26; 3:7). They decried the Church, her sacraments, and her theology—especially belittling apostolic teaching on the Incarnation and the Trinity. They had become pseudo-spiritual, and saw themselves as a new elite, superior to Christ's apostles (1:1–4; 2:24). They claimed special, unimpeded access to God (2:4, 6, 9; 4:20) and prophetic revelation from the Holy Spirit (4:1). John sees them as being not of the Holy Spirit, but of the spirit of error (4:6); not of Christ, but of the Antichrist (2:18, 22; 4:3); and not of God, but of the world (4:5).

(2) *Danger of worldliness.* Some Christians are so romanced by the world (2:15–17) that they stand in danger of falling away from God (5:21). John exhorts us to detach ourselves from the world in order to serve the living God.

(3) *The structure of the letter.* First John centers on three themes: baptism, chrismation, and the Eucharist. Making an outline of the book is difficult, even inadequate,—though an attempt, which follows, is made—it is best read prayerfully, with little effort to find John's structure. The style is rhythmic, using repetition and contrasts.

(4) *Audience.* While the addressee is not mentioned, perhaps this is an encyclical (a letter meant to be circulated among a group of churches) to John's archdiocese of Asia.

OUTLINE

Introduction: The apostolic witness to the Incarnation 1:1–4
- I. Live in the light 1:5—2:27
  - A. Walk in the light of confessed sin 1:5—2:2
  - B. Keep Christ's commandments of love 2:3–17
  - C. Remain in the true teaching about Christ 2:18–27

II. Live as God's children 2:28—4:6
A. Be righteous 2:28—3:9
B. Love one another 3:10–24
C. Confess that Jesus is God in the flesh 4:1–6
III. Live in love and faith 4:7—5:13
A. God's love becomes our love 4:7—5:2
1. God's love for us: The Incarnation 4:7–11
2. The Holy Trinity lives in us 4:12–16
3. Confidence at the judgment 4:17–19
4. Love of God requires love of others 4:20—5:2
B. Faith brings strength and life 5:3–13
1. Faith overcomes the world 5:3–5
2. The divine witnesses to faith 5:6–10
3. Eternal life is in the Son 5:11–13
Summary: Live in God 5:14–21
A. Pray according to God's will 5:14–17
B. Separate from sin and evil 5:18, 19
C. Live in Jesus Christ 5:20, 21

Introduction: The Incarnation

1 That [a]which was from the
beginning, which we have
heard, which we have [b]seen with
our eyes, [c]which we have looked
upon, and [d]our hands have handled, concerning the [e]Word of
life—†
2 [a]the life [b]was manifested, and
we have seen, [c]and bear witness,
and declare to you that eternal life
which was [d]with the Father and was
manifested to us—†
3 that which we have seen and
heard we declare to you, that you
also may have fellowship with us;
and truly our fellowship *is* [a]with the
Father and with His Son Jesus
Christ.†

1 a[John 1:1] bJohn 1:14 c2 Pet. 1:16 dLuke 24:39 e[John 1:1, 4, 14]
2 aJohn 1:4 bRom. 16:26 cJohn 21:24 d[John 1:1, 18; 16:28]
3 a1 Cor. 1:9

1:1–4 Contrary to the heretics who claim communion (Gr. *koinonia*) directly with God through "spiritual" (nonmaterial) means, John teaches communion with God through the incarnate Son. Especially in view here is the Eucharist, which the heretics find repulsive because it manifests the physical nature of Christ.

1:1 We means the apostles. Their testimony is true; that of the false apostles is not. While John makes a distinction between divine revelation (**which was from the beginning, the Word of life**) and human sensory perception (**heard, have seen, looked upon, handled**), he has no problem connecting them. Note John's clarity of teaching on Christ's two natures: divine (*from the beginning, the word of life*) and human (*heard, seen, handled*). (See Luke 24:39; John 1:14; 20:27, 28.)

St. Clement of Alexandria writes: "When [John] says: 'which was from the beginning,' he touches upon the generation without beginning of the Son, who is coexistent with the Father. 'Was,' therefore, indicates eternity without beginning, just as the Word Himself, the Son, being one with the Father in regard to equality of substance, is eternal and uncreated. That the Word always existed is signified by the words: 'In the beginning was the Word (John 1:1).' " (*Fragment of Commentary on the First Epistle of John*).

1:2 The divinity of Jesus **was manifested** in His **life,** especially His teaching and His miracles (see John 2:11).

1:3 *Koinonia* (Gr.) is far more than "fellowship." It is our personal participation with other believers in the life of Christ. **Fellowship with us** means communion—especially Eucharistic communion—within the apostolic Church. It is inconceivable to John that the Church not be one and united (see John 17:11, 20, 21) or that *fellowship* not be founded on doctrine (the theological implication of **with the Father and with His Son Jesus Christ**) and sacrament (the liturgical implication of *koinonia*).

4 And these things we write to
you [a]that [1]your joy may be full.†
5 [a]This is the message which we
have heard from Him and declare to
you, that [b]God is light and in Him
is no darkness at all.†

Walk in the Light: Confession

6 [a]If we say that we have fellowship with Him, and walk in darkness, we lie and do not practice the
truth.†
7 But if we [a]walk in the light as
He is in the light, we have fellowship
with one another, and [b]the blood of
Jesus Christ His Son cleanses us from
all sin.
8 If we say that we have no sin,
we deceive ourselves, and the truth
is not in us.
9 If we [a]confess our sins, He is
[b]faithful and just to forgive us *our*
sins and to [c]cleanse us from all unrighteousness.

4 [a]John 15:11; 16:24 [1]NU, M *our*
5 [a]1 John 3:11 [b][1 Tim. 6:16]
6 [a][1 John 2:9–11]
7 [a]Is. 2:5 [b][1 Cor. 6:11]
9 [a]Prov. 28:13 [b][Rom. 3:24–26] [c]Ps. 51:2
10 [a]1 John 5:10

CHAPTER 2

1 [a]Heb. 7:25; 9:24
2 [a][Rom. 3:25] [b]John 1:29
4 [a]Rom. 3:4
5 [a]John 14:21, 23 [b][1 John 4:12] [1]*has been completed*
6 [a]John 15:4

10 If we say that we have not
sinned, we [a]make Him a liar, and
His word is not in us.

2 My little children, these things I
write to you, so that you may
not sin. And if anyone sins, [a]we
have an Advocate with the Father,
Jesus Christ the righteous.

Keep God's Commandments of Love

2 And [a]He Himself is the propitiation for our sins, and not for ours
only but [b]also for the whole world.
3 Now by this we know that we
know Him, if we keep His commandments.†
4 He who says, "I know Him,"
and does not keep His commandments, is a [a]liar, and the truth is not
in him.
5 But [a]whoever keeps His word,
truly the love of God [1]is perfected
[b]in him. By this we know that we
are in Him.
6 [a]He who says he abides in Him

1:4 See John 15:11; 16:24; 17:13; Phil. 2:2.

1:5 For John, **light** is divine energy manifested as (1) truth (true doctrine), (2) virtue and holiness (true behavior), and (3) communion with God in the Church (true spirituality). The strongest of all weapons against **darkness** is our love for God, a strong, vibrant relationship with Him.

We recall the Evening Hymn of Vespers: "O joyful light of the holy glory of the immortal Father, heavenly, holy, blessed Jesus Christ: now that we are coming to the setting of the sun and behold the evening light, we sing in praise to God the Father, Son, and Holy Spirit. It is meet at all times to praise You in hymns with happy voice, O Son of God who grants life: therefore the world gives You glory."

1:6—2:2 John addresses three false gnostic teachings on "sin." Their intertwined errors are that: (1) union with God is indifferent to sin (vv. 6, 7); (2) sin does not exist (vv. 8, 9); (3) one in union with God cannot sin (1:10—2:2).

John answers by saying: (1) Faith must be seen in works, that is, it must produce moral purity (**practice the truth,** v. 6). To have a right relationship with God includes living a holy and righteous life. And faith must seek forgiveness and cleansing for sin (v. 7). (2) Sin does exist, and the practice of confession is the established basis for growth toward righteousness (v. 9). (3) Though we do sin, we should strive not to sin. Salvation in Christ is a process of growth into sinlessness (v. 7).

2:3–11 The ancient gnostics held two false teachings on God's "light": that knowledge of God requires neither (1) obedience (vv. 3–8) nor (2) love of others (vv. 9–11). John answers:

(1) To know God is to obey Him. **His commandments** (vv. 3, 4) are not a legal code; they form the essence of life in Christ, the way of love (vv. 5, 6). Those outside of Christ will not become partakers of His life unless they, by God's grace, practice what He says. ("In vain do we applaud Him whose commandments we do not keep"—The Venerable Bede; see also Luke 9:23; James 2:18, 19). The **new commandment** (v. 7) is Christ's, that we love as Christ loved us (John 13:34; 15:12, 17).

(2) To love God (to be **in the light,** vv. 9, 10) is also to love each other. ("Anyone who comes hating his brother to the font of life where he is to be reborn, to the cup of that precious blood whereby he is to be redeemed, even though he may think he is enlightened by the Lord, is still in darkness. He cannot in any way have put off the darkness of his sins when he did not take care to put on the fundamentals of love"—The Venerable Bede.)

CONFESSION

Perhaps the most misunderstood sacrament of the Christian Church is confession. How did it originate? What role does a priest play? Is there a special procedure for confession? The Scriptures hold answers to these questions.

Concerning our sins, God's Word gives a marvelous promise. "If we confess our sins, He is faithful and just to forgive us our sins and to cleanse us from all unrighteousness" (1 John 1:9). The faithful are to bring their sins to God in repentance and receive cleansing and forgiveness.

The early Christian community had a specific practice in this regard. People would stand and confess their sins to God in the presence of the whole congregation! Had not Jesus encouraged His followers to walk in the light together, to confront problems corporately, to "tell it to the church" (Matt. 18:17)? Thus James writes, "Confess your trespasses to one another" (James 5:16). But as time went on and the Church grew in numbers, strangers came to visit and public confession became more difficult. Out of mercy, priests began to witness confessions of sin privately on behalf of the Church.

Jesus gave His disciples the authority to forgive sin. "If you forgive the sins of any, they are forgiven them; if you retain the sins of any, they are retained" (John 20:23; see also Matt. 16:19). From the beginning, Christians understood that the grace of ordination endowed the shepherd of the flock with the discernment and compassion to speak the words of remission, on behalf of Christ, regarding the sins of those who confess and turn from sin. For God has promised the removing of sin from us "as far as the east is from the west" (Ps. 103:12).

"You did not choose Me," Jesus told the Twelve, "but I chose you and appointed [ordained] you." (John 15:16). To these same disciples Jesus promised, "It is not you who speak but the Holy Spirit" (Mark 13:11). Whom God calls, He equips. Paul writes to Timothy, "Stir up the gift of God which is in you through the laying on of my hands" (2 Tim. 1:6). It is the grace of the Holy Spirit which enables the priest to serve God and the people.

Thus the Church has encouraged her faithful: If you know you have committed a specific sin, do not hide it but confess it before coming to the Holy Eucharist. St. Paul wrote, "Let a man examine himself, and so let him eat of the bread and drink of the cup" (1 Cor. 11:28), and "If we would judge ourselves, we would not be judged" (1 Cor. 11:31).

King David learned a lesson regarding his sin which is recorded for our benefit. For about a year, he had hidden his sins of adultery with Bathsheba and the murder of her husband (2 Sam. 11:1—12:13). Then, confronted by Nathan the prophet, David repented from his heart and confessed his sin in a psalm which is used for general confession to this day (Ps. 51). The joy of salvation was restored to him.

People ask, "Can't I confess to God privately?" Certainly, though there is no clear biblical basis for it. Even general confession occurs in the Church. In His mercy, God provides the sacrament of confession (more properly called the sacrament of repentance) to give us deliverance from sin and from what psychologists call denial. It is easy to pray in isolation, yet never come clean. It is far more effective to confess aloud to God before a priest, and benefit from his guidance and help.

Thus we come before the holy icon of Christ, to whom we confess, and are guided by the priest, our spiritual father, in a cleansing inventory of our lives. When we tell God all, naming our sins and failures, we hear those glorious words of freedom which announce Christ's promise of forgiveness of all our sins. We resolve to "go and sin no more" (John 8:11).

[b]ought himself also to walk just as
He walked.
7 [1]Brethren, I write no new commandment to you, but an old commandment which you have had
[a]from the beginning. The old commandment is the word which you
heard [2]from the beginning.
8 Again, [a]a new commandment I
write to you, which thing is true in
Him and in you, [b]because the darkness is passing away, and [c]the true
light is already shining.
9 [a]He who says he is in the light,
and hates his brother, is in darkness
until now.
10 [a]He who loves his brother
abides in the light, and [b]there is no
cause for stumbling in him.
11 But he who [a]hates his brother
is in darkness and [b]walks in darkness, and does not know where he
is going, because the darkness has
blinded his eyes.

12 I write to you, little children,
Because [a]your sins are for-
given you for His name's
sake.†
13 I write to you, fathers,
Because you have known
Him *who is* [a]from the begin-
ning.
I write to you, young men,
Because you have overcome
the wicked one.
I write to you, little children,
Because you have [b]known the
Father.
14 I have written to you, fathers,
Because you have known
Him *who is* from the begin-
ning.
I have written to you, young
men,
Because [a]you are strong, and
the word of God abides in
you,
And you have overcome the
wicked one.

15 [a]Do not love the world or the
things in the world. [b]If anyone loves
the world, the love of the Father is
not in him.†
16 For all that *is* in the world—the
lust of the flesh, [a]the lust of the eyes,
and the pride of life—is not of the
Father but is of the world.†
17 And [a]the world is passing
away, and the lust of it; but he who
does the will of God abides forever.

The Truth: Jesus Is God

18 [a]Little children, [b]it is the last
hour; and as you have heard that
[c]the[1] Antichrist is coming, [d]even
now many antichrists have come, by
which we know [e]that it is the last
hour.†

6 [b]1 Pet. 2:21 **7** [a]1 John 3:11, 23; 4:21 [1]NU *Beloved* [2]NU omits *from the beginning* **8** [a]John 13:34; 15:12 [b]Rom. 13:12 [c][John 1:9; 8:12; 12:35] **9** [a][1 Cor. 13:2] **10** [a][1 John 3:14] [b]2 Pet. 1:10 **11** [a][1 John 2:9; 3:15; 4:20] [b]John 12:35 **12** [a][1 Cor. 6:11] **13** [a]John 1:1 [b][Rom. 8:15–17] **14** [a]Eph. 6:10 **15** [a][Rom. 12:2] [b]James 4:4 **16** [a][Eccl. 5:10, 11] **17** [a]1 Cor. 7:31 **18** [a]John 21:5 [b]1 Pet. 4:7 [c]2 Thess. 2:3 [d]2 John 7 [e]1 Tim. 4:1 [1]NU omits *the*

2:12–14 These verses are a poem of comfort and encouragement. John addresses three stages of Christian growth. (1) **Little children** are the newly converted (see Luke 10:21), who see clearly that their **sins are forgiven** (v. 12) and who know **the Father** (v. 13). (2) **Fathers,** are the mature in understanding who know Christ (vv. 13, 14). (3) **Young men** are those who war against the devil (vv. 13, 14), who are **strong** (v. 14) and who have **the word of God** (v. 14) living in them.

2:15 The world here is the creation after the Fall and under the dominion of Satan. It is creation no longer oriented toward God, but dominated by inordinate passions, and subject to death (see Matt. 6:24; Luke 16:13; 1 Cor. 7:29–31).

2:16 The world distorts every realm of God's good creation (see James 1:13, 14). There are (1) sensual pleasures **of the flesh** (physical passions), (2) intellectual attainments and capacities **of the eyes** (the soul's passions), and (3) inordinate possessions, power and honors **of life** (the pride of the human spirit). Biblical ascetic practices—prayer, fasting, almsgiving (see Matt. 6:1–18)—help us overcome these distortions and live lives of virtue.

2:18 The last hour is the era of the New Covenant, the "eleventh hour" (Matt. 20:6). The deceptions at hand are in view, rather than a specific prediction of the end of the world. **Many antichrists** are the heretics, through whom the Antichrist of the end time (see 2 Thess. 2) is doing his spadework.

Very early in the second century, on his way to martyrdom in Rome, St. Ignatius of Antioch wrote, in a letter to the church most closely associated with John's old age: "These

(continued on next page)

19 [a]They went out from us, but
they were not of us; for [b]if they had
been of us, they would have continued with us; but *they went out*
[c]that they might be made manifest,
that none of them were of us.†
20 But [a]you have an anointing
[b]from the Holy One, and [c]you[1]
know all things.†
21 I have not written to you because you do not know the truth,
but because you know it, and that
no lie is of the truth.
22 [a]Who is a liar but he who denies
that [b]Jesus is the Christ? He is antichrist who denies the Father and the
Son.†
23 [a]Whoever denies the Son does
not have the [b]Father either; [c]he who
acknowledges the Son has the Father
also.
24 Therefore let that abide in you
[a]which you heard from the beginning. If what you heard from the beginning abides in you, [b]you also will
abide in the Son and in the Father.†
25 [a]And this is the promise that He
has promised us—eternal life.
26 These things I have written to
you concerning those who *try to*
[1]deceive you.

19 [a]Deut. 13:13 [b]Matt. 24:24 [c]1 Cor. 11:19
20 [a]2 Cor. 1:21 [b]Acts 3:14 [c][John 16:13] [1]NU *you all know.*
22 [a]2 John 7 [b]1 John 4:3
23 [a]John 15:23 [b]John 5:23 [c]1 John 4:15; 5:1
24 [a]2 John 5, 6 [b]John 14:23
25 [a]John 3:14–16; 6:40; 17:2, 3
26 [1]*lead you astray*
27 [a][John 14:16; 16:13] [b][Jer. 31:33] [c][John 14:16] [1]NU omits *will*
28 [a]1 John 3:21; 4:17; 5:14 [1]NU *if*
29 [a]Acts 22:14 [b]1 John 3:7, 10

27 But the [a]anointing which you
have received from Him abides in
you, and [b]you do not need that anyone teach you; but as the same
anointing [c]teaches you concerning
all things, and is true, and is not a
lie, and just as it has taught you, you
[1]will abide in Him.

Practice Righteousness: Do Not Sin

28 And now, little children, abide
in Him, that [1]when He appears, we
may have [a]confidence and not be
ashamed before Him at His coming.
29 [a]If you know that He is righteous, you know that [b]everyone who
practices righteousness is born of
Him.

3 Behold [a]what manner of love the
Father has bestowed on us, that
[b]we should be called children of
[1]God! Therefore the world does not
know [2]us, [c]because it did not know
Him.†
2 Beloved, [a]now we are children

CHAPTER 3

1 [a][1 John 4:10] [b][John 1:12] [c]John 15:18, 21; 16:3 [1]NU adds *And we are.* [2]M *you*
2 [a][Rom. 8:15, 16]

(continued from previous page)
are the last times [see 1 Cor. 7:29]. Let us then be ashamed and fear God's patience so that it may not become condemnation for us. We should either fear the wrath to come or love the grace which is present, one of the two, just so that we may be found in Christ Jesus for true life [see Acts 17:30; 1 Thess. 1:10]. Nothing should seem fitting to you apart from him in whom I bear my bonds as spiritual pearls. May I rise again in them by your prayer, in which I may always participate so that I may be found in the lot apportioned to the Ephesian Christians, who have always agreed with the apostles by the power of Jesus Christ" (*Letter to the Ephesians*, 11:1, 2).

2:19 Being "on the roll" of the Church, even receiving the sacraments, is not enough. We must continue in our belief and manifest the fruit of faith.

2:20, 21 Anointing (Gr. *criso*, the root of "chrismation") recalls the coronation of kings and the ordinations of priests and prophets in the OT, which activated the spiritual gifts and energies needed for their offices. The NT anointing is the Holy Spirit, given to every member of the Church to preserve her in the truth (John 14:26; 16:13–15). **You** is plural. Anointing is not for independent action but for the good of the One Holy Church.

2:22, 23 Theologically, the issues are, (1) Does God the Father have a consubstantial Son? and (2) Is the man Jesus the same Person as God the Son? These, of course, are the two basic issues of Christology: Jesus Christ is one divine Person in two natures.

2:24–27 To **abide** in Christ is not merely to give mental assent to the doctrine of the Incarnation. It is a sacramental union with Him, effected in baptism and nourished in the Eucharist (John 6:53–59; 15:1–8). For John, apostolic teaching and writing (vv. 24–26) is identical with being taught by God (v. 27). Without both the work of the Spirit and apostolic doctrine, we would remain in darkness.

3:1 The Venerable Bede says that at the judgment, the people of the world "will say to

(continued on next page)

of God; and [b]it has not yet been revealed what we shall be, but we
know that when He is revealed,
[c]we shall be like Him, for [d]we shall
see Him as He is.†
3 [a]And everyone who has this
hope in Him purifies himself, just as
He is pure.
4 Whoever commits sin also commits lawlessness, and [a]sin is lawlessness.†
5 And you know [a]that He was
manifested [b]to take away our sins,
and [c]in Him there is no sin.
6 Whoever abides in Him does
not sin. Whoever sins has neither
seen Him nor known Him.
7 Little children, let no one deceive you. He who practices righteousness is righteous, just as He is
righteous.
8 [a]He who sins is of the devil, for
the devil has sinned from the beginning. For this purpose the Son of
God was manifested, [b]that He might
destroy the works of the devil.
9 Whoever has been [a]born of God
does not sin, for [b]His seed remains
in him; and he cannot sin, because
he has been born of God.

Love One Another

10 In this the children of God
and the children of the devil are
manifest: Whoever does not practice righteousness is not of God,
nor *is* he who does not love his
brother.
11 For this is the message that you
heard from the beginning, [a]that we
should love one another,
12 not as [a]Cain *who* was of the
wicked one and murdered his
brother. And why did he murder
him? Because his works were evil
and his brother's righteous.†
13 Do not marvel, my brethren, if
[a]the world hates you.
14 We know that we have passed
from death to life, because we love
the brethren. He who does not love
[1]*his* brother abides in death.
15 [a]Whoever hates his brother is a
murderer, and you know that
[b]no murderer has eternal life abiding
in him.†
16 [a]By this we know love, [b]because
He laid down His life for us. And
we also ought to lay down *our* lives
for the brethren.

2 [b][Rom. 8:18, 19, 23] [c]Rom. 8:29 [d][Ps. 16:11]
3 [a]1 John 4:17
4 [a]Rom. 4:15
5 [a]1 John 1:2; 3:8 [b]John 1:29 [c][2 Cor. 5:21]
8 [a]Matt. 13:38 [b]Luke 10:18
9 [a]John 1:3; 3:3 [b]1 Pet. 1:23
11 [a][John 13:34; 15:12]
12 [a]Gen. 4:4, 8
13 [a][John 15:18; 17:14]
14 [1]NU omits *his brother*
15 [a]Matt. 5:21 [b][Gal. 5:20, 21]
16 [a][John 3:16] [b]John 10:11; 15:13

(continued from previous page)
one another, groaning and repenting, 'These are they whom we once held in derision and, as it were, a byword for taunts; witless we judged their life madness and their end without honor. How have they been numbered among the children of God, and is their lot among the saints?' " Christians, of course, are **children of God** by grace while remaining human by nature.

3:2 Made in God's image and likeness, we are fulfilled by becoming **like Him,** a process called sanctification or deification. Being "partakers of the divine nature" (2 Pet. 1:4), we are "transformed into the same image, from glory to glory" (2 Cor. 3:18). When we **see Him as He is,** in the fullness of His glory at the last day, this process will be supremely magnified. John had seen the foretaste of this glory on the Mount of Transfiguration (Matt. 17:1–9; Mark 9:2–9; Luke 9:28–36).

How shall we see Him? Through our likeness to Him; our human nature will be glorified with the glorified humanity of the Son (see Col. 3:3, 4) and through a knowledge of all three Persons of the Trinity. (Note Paul's expressions, "face to face" and "with unveiled face" in 1 Cor. 13:12 and 2 Cor. 3:18.)

3:4–9 John is talking in general terms, contrasting this world with the world to come. The Christian, though sinful, **does not sin** (v. 9; lit., "does not keep on sinning") as the world does. The Church lives under God's influence; the world under Satan's **lawlessness** (v. 4) is living without law, in a hardened enmity to God. **The devil** (v. 8; "slanderer" or "opposer"), is a creature, a fallen archangel. **From the beginning** (v. 8) refers to Satan's ceaseless sinning since his fall.

3:12 We are to give our attention to deeds, not just to words. Abel showed himself **righteous,** a child of faith and love; **Cain** showed himself **evil,** self-centered and envious (see Gen. 4:4, 8; Heb. 11:4; 12:24).

3:15 John Cassian writes (*On the Three Vices*): "If then we wish to receive the Lord's blessings we should restrain not only the outward expression of anger, but also angry thoughts.

(continued on next page)

17 But [a]whoever has this world's goods, and sees his brother in need, and shuts up his heart from him, how does the love of God abide in him?

18 My little children, [a]let us not love in word or in tongue, but in deed and in truth.

19 And by this we [1]know [a]that we are of the truth, and shall [2]assure our hearts before Him.

20 [a]For if our heart condemns us, God is greater than our heart, and knows all things.

21 Beloved, if our heart does not condemn us, [a]we have confidence toward God.

22 And [a]whatever we ask we receive from Him, because we keep His commandments [b]and do those things that are pleasing in His sight.

23 And this is His commandment: that we should believe on the name of His Son Jesus Christ [a]and love one another, as He gave [1]us commandment.

24 Now [a]he who keeps His commandments [b]abides in Him, and He in him. And [c]by this we know that He abides in us, by the Spirit whom He has given us.

The Spirit's Witness: The Incarnation

4 Beloved, do not believe every spirit, but [a]test the spirits, whether they are of God; because [b]many false prophets have gone out into the world.

2 By this you know the Spirit of God: [a]Every spirit that confesses that Jesus Christ has come in the flesh is of God,

3 and every spirit that does not confess [1]that Jesus [2]Christ has come in the flesh is not of God. And this is the *spirit* of the Antichrist, which you have heard was coming, and is now already in the world.†

4 You are of God, little children, and have overcome them, because He who is in you is greater than [a]he who is in the world.

5 [a]They are of the world. Therefore they speak *as* of the world, and [b]the world hears them.

6 We are of God. He who knows God hears us; he who is not of God does not hear us. [a]By this we know the spirit of truth and the spirit of error.†

God Redeems Us in Love

7 [a]Beloved, let us love one another, for love is of God; and everyone who [b]loves is born of God and knows God.†

8 He who does not love does not know God, for God is love.

9 [a]In this the love of God was manifested toward us, that God has sent His only begotten [b]Son into the world, that we might live through Him.

17 [a]Deut. 15:7
18 [a]Ezek. 33:31
19 [a]John 18:37
[1]NU *shall know*
[2]*persuade, set at rest*
20 [a][1 Cor. 4:4, 5]
21 [a][1 John 2:28; 5:14]
22 [a]Ps. 34:15
[b]John 8:29
23 [a]Matt. 22:39
[1]M omits *us*
24 [a]John 14:23
[b]John 14:21; 17:21
[c]Rom. 8:9, 14, 16

CHAPTER 4

1 [a]1 Cor. 14:29
[b]Matt. 24:5
2 [a]1 Cor. 12:3
3 [1]NU omits *that*
[2]NU omits *Christ has come in the flesh*
4 [a]John 14:30; 16:11
5 [a]John 3:31
[b]John 15:19; 17:14
6 [a][1 Cor. 2:12–16]
7 [a]1 John 3:10, 11, 23
[b]1 Thess. 4:9
9 [a]Rom. 5:8
[b]John 3:16

(continued from previous page)
More beneficial than controlling our tongue in a moment of anger and refraining from angry words is purifying our heart from rancor and not harboring malicious thoughts against our brethren. The Gospel teaches us to cut off the roots of our sins and not merely their fruits. When we have dug the root of anger out of our heart, we will no longer act with hatred or envy. 'Whoever hates his brother is a murderer' (3:15), for he kills him with the hatred in his mind. The blood of a man who has been slain by the sword can be seen by men, but blood shed by the hatred in the mind is seen by God, who rewards each man with punishment or a crown not only for his acts but for his thoughts and intentions as well. (*Philokalia*, Vol. I, p. 86).

4:3 Antichrist is anyone who **does not confess** that the Son of God became Man while remaining God.

4:6 We refers to the apostles and their followers.

4:7–11 God is love (v. 8) is not a definition of who God is, but rather a description of His relationship to us as our Father. As the **only begotten Son** (v. 9) sacrificially gave Himself **that we might live through Him** (v. 9), so we are to give ourselves to Him and to **one another** (v. 11).

10 In this is love, [a]not that we
loved God, but that He loved us and
sent His Son [b]*to be* the propitiation
for our sins.†
11 Beloved, [a]if God so loved us, we
also ought to love one another.

God Abides in Us

12 [a]No one has seen God at any
time. If we love one another, God
abides in us, and His love has been
perfected in us.†
13 [a]By this we know that we abide
in Him, and He in us, because He
has given us of His Spirit.
14 And [a]we have seen and testify
that [b]the Father has sent the Son *as*
Savior of the world.
15 [a]Whoever confesses that Jesus
is the Son of God, God abides in him,
and he in God.
16 And we have known and believed the love that God has for us.
God is love, and [a]he who abides
in love abides in God, and God
[b]in him.

Love Overcomes Fear

17 Love has been perfected among
us in this: that [a]we may have boldness in the day of judgment; because
as He is, so are we in this world.
18 There is no fear in love; but perfect love casts out fear, because fear
involves torment. But he who fears
has not been made perfect in love.
19 [a]We love [1]Him because He first
loved us.

10 [a]Titus 3:5 [b]1 John 2:2
11 [a]Matt. 18:33
12 [a]John 1:18
13 [a]John 14:20
14 [a]John 1:14 [b]John 3:17; 4:42
15 [a][Rom. 10:9]
16 [a][1 John 3:24] [b][John 14:23]
17 [a]1 John 2:28
19 [a]1 John 4:10 [1]NU omits *Him*
20 [a][1 John 2:4] [b]1 John 4:12 [1]NU *he cannot*
21 [a][Matt. 5:43, 44; 22:39]

CHAPTER 5

1 [a]1 John 2:22; 4:2, 15 [b]John 1:13
2 [a]John 15:10
3 [a]John 14:15 [b]Matt. 11:30; 23:4
4 [a]John 16:33 [b]1 John 2:13; 4:4 [1]M *your*
5 [a]1 Cor. 15:57
6 [a]John 1:31–34 [b][John 14:17]

Love of God Means Love of Others

20 [a]If someone says, "I love God,"
and hates his brother, he is a liar;
for he who does not love his brother
whom he has seen, [1]how can he love
God [b]whom he has not seen?
21 And [a]this commandment we
have from Him: that he who loves
God *must* love his brother also.

5 Whoever believes that [a]Jesus is
the Christ is [b]born of God, and
everyone who loves Him who begot
also loves him who is begotten of
Him.†
2 By this we know that we love
the children of God, when we love
God and [a]keep His commandments.

Faith Overcomes the World

3 [a]For this is the love of God, that
we keep His commandments. And
[b]His commandments are not burdensome.†
4 For [a]whatever is born of God
overcomes the world. And this is the
victory that [b]has overcome the
world—[1]our faith.
5 Who is he who overcomes the
world, but [a]he who believes that
Jesus is the Son of God?

God Validates Our Faith

6 This is He who came [a]by water
and blood—Jesus Christ; not only by
water, but by water and blood.
[b]And it is the Spirit who bears witness, because the Spirit is truth.†

4:10 What a statement of God's mercy and grace! (See also v. 19.)

4:12–16 How can we know God lives in us? John gives a fourfold answer: (1) **if we love one another** (v. 12); (2) if we have been given **His Spirit** (v. 13); (3) if we can confess **Jesus is the Son of God** (v. 15); and (4) if we abide in the **love** of **God** (v. 16).

5:1, 2 Who is it that truly **believes that Jesus is the Christ**? Those who live in the way Christ commanded, who love others.

5:3 How is it that God's **commandments are not burdensome**? We live these *commandments* by faith and in God's love, which makes them light on our fallen nature. They are hard and rough only to those who are living a sinful life. That the Kingdom of Heaven belongs to those who suffer makes even suffering sweet.

5:6–12 By water and blood (v. 6) is a reference (1) to the constancy of the incarnate Son throughout His life; (2) to the mingled water and blood which poured from Jesus' side (John 19:34), which is a type of baptism. Similarly, **the Spirit, the water, and the blood** (v. 8) refers to the unity of the basic sacraments: chrismation, baptism and the Eucharist.

7 For there are three that bear witness [1]in heaven: the Father, [a]the
Word, and the Holy Spirit; [b]and
these three are one.
8 And there are three that bear
witness on earth: [a]the Spirit, the water, and the blood; and these three
agree as one.
9 If we receive [a]the witness of
men, the witness of God is greater;
[b]for this is the witness of [1]God which
He has testified of His Son.
10 He who believes in the Son of
God [a]has the witness in himself; he
who does not believe God [b]has made
Him a liar, because he has not believed the testimony that God has
given of His Son.

Faith Brings Eternal Life

11 And this is the testimony: that
God has given us eternal life, and
this life is in His Son.
12 [a]He who has the Son has
[1]life; he who does not have the Son
of God does not have [1]life.
13 These things I have written to
you who believe in the name of the
Son of God, that you may know that
you have eternal life, [1]and that you
may *continue to* believe in the name
of the Son of God.†

Pray According to God's Will

14 Now this is the confidence that
we have in Him, that [a]if we ask anything according to His will, He hears
us.
15 And if we know that He hears
us, whatever we ask, we know that
we have the petitions that we have
asked of Him.
16 If anyone sees his brother sinning a sin *which does* not *lead* to death,
he will ask, and [a]He will give him
life for those who commit sin not
leading to death. [b]There is sin *leading*
to death. [c]I do not say that he should
pray about that.†
17 [a]All unrighteousness is sin, and
there is sin not *leading* to death.

Separate from Sin

18 We know that [a]whoever is born
of God does not sin; but he who has
been born of God [b]keeps[1] [2]himself,
and the wicked one does not touch
him.
19 We know that we are of God,
and [a]the whole world lies *under the
sway of* the wicked one.

Live in Christ

20 And we know that the [a]Son of
God has come and [b]has given us an
understanding, [c]that we may know
Him who is true; and we are in Him
who is true, in His Son Jesus Christ.
[d]This is the true God [e]and eternal
life.
21 Little children, keep yourselves
from idols. Amen.†

7 [a][John 1:1] [b]John 10:30 [1]NU, M omit the words from *in heaven* (v. 7) through *on earth* (v. 8). Only 4 or 5 very late mss. contain these words in Greek.
8 [a]John 15:26
9 [a]John 5:34, 37; 8:17, 18 [b][Matt. 3:16, 17] [1]NU *God, that*
10 [a][Rom. 8:16] [b]John 3:18, 33
12 [a][John 3:15, 36; 6:47; 17:2, 3] [1]Or *the life*
13 [1]NU omits the rest of v. 13.
14 [a][1 John 2:28; 3:21, 22]
16 [a]Job 42:8 [b][Matt. 12:31] [c]Jer. 7:16; 14:11
17 [a]1 John 3:4
18 [a][1 Pet. 1:23] [b]James 1:27 [1]*guards* [2]NU *him*
19 [a]Gal. 1:4
20 [a]1 John 4:2 [b]Luke 24:45 [c]John 17:3 [d]Is. 9:6 [e]1 John 5:11, 12

5:13 When we **know** we have been given the gift of **eternal life,** we are to **continue to believe** and follow **the Son of God.**

5:16 What about those Christians who are not living righteously? John says God will forgive them if fellow Christians pray for them. **Sin leading to death**—that which is beyond our prayer—is willful, continual disbelief in the grace of the Holy Spirit toward us. (See Matt. 12:28, 31, 32; Heb. 6:4–6; 10:26–31.)

5:21 **Idols** are (1) false gods or (2) things that turn us away from God (Col. 3:5).

The Second Epistle of

JOHN

Author: *St. John the Apostle*

Date: *A.D. 90–95*

Theme: *Tests of True Christian Care*

AUTHOR: Although some in the third and fourth centuries doubted John's authorship, the early witnesses favor John and express no alternative.

DATE: There is no firm evidence for fixing a date. The epistle's similarities to the Gospel of John, 1 John and 3 John suggest a date of composition close to that of these other books (A.D. 90–95).

MAJOR THEME: *Tests of true Christian care.* The love of our Incarnate God brings promised victory over the Antichrist.

BACKGROUND INFORMATION: (1) *Recipients.* "The elect lady" (v. 1; Gr. *kyria*) is most likely a parish under John's oversight. The Church elsewhere is called the "bride" of Christ the Lord (Gr. *kyrios*). Thus it would be natural to refer to her as *kyria* ("lady"), the feminine of *kyrios*.

(2) *A warning against deceivers.* The "deceivers" (v. 7) are heretics, as evidenced by their denial of the Incarnation of the Son of God. These false apostles visited various churches, posing as true disciples and taking advantage of Christian hospitality.

OUTLINE

I. Greeting and benediction	vv. 1–3
II. Follow the law of love	vv. 4–6
III. Beware of deceiving heretics	vv. 7–11
IV. John's plans and farewell	vv. 12, 13

Ο ΑΓ. ΙΩ.
Ο ΘΕΟΛΟΓΟΣ
Ο ΑΓ. ΠΡΟΧΟΡΟΣ
ΕΝ ΑΡΧΗ ΗΝ Ο ΛΟΓΟΣ.
ΚΑΙ Ο ΛΟΓΟΣ
ΑΦΙΕΡΩΜΑ ΔΗΜ. ΣΕΝΤΟΥΚΑ
ΤΗ ΙΕΡΑ ΘΕΟΛΟΓΙΚΗ ΣΧΟΛΗ
ΕΠΙ ΔΙΕΥΘΥΝΣΕΩΣ ΘΕΟΦΙΛΕΣΤΑΤΟΥ
Κ.Κ. ΑΘΗΝΑΓΟΡΑ ΕΠΙΣΚΟΠΟΥ ΕΛΑΙΑΣ
ΧΕΙΡ ΔΗΜ. ΣΕΝΤΟΥΚΑ (DUKAS)

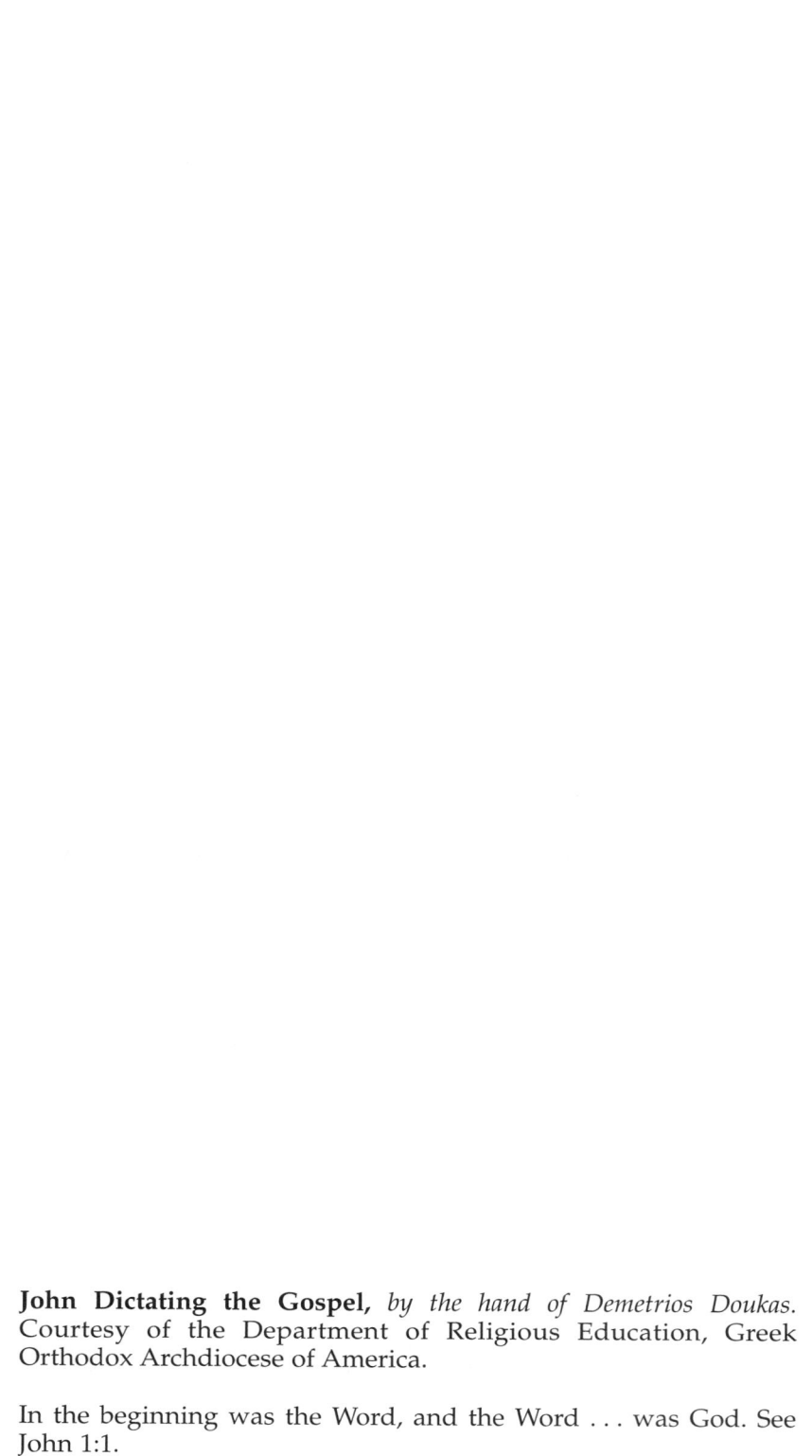

John Dictating the Gospel, *by the hand of Demetrios Doukas.* Courtesy of the Department of Religious Education, Greek Orthodox Archdiocese of America.

In the beginning was the Word, and the Word . . . was God. See John 1:1.

Greeting and Benediction

The Elder,

To the [1]elect lady and her children,
whom I love in truth, and not only
I, but also all those who have known
[a]the truth,†
2 because of the truth which
abides in us and will be with us forever:

3 [a]Grace, mercy, *and* peace will be
with [1]you from God the Father and
from the Lord Jesus Christ, the Son
of the Father, in truth and love.†

Follow the Law of Love

4 I [a]rejoiced greatly that I have
found *some* of your children walking
in truth, as we received commandment from the Father.†
5 And now I plead with you, lady,
not as though I wrote a new commandment to you, but that which we
have had from the beginning:
[a]that we love one another.
6 [a]This is love, that we walk according to His commandments. This
is the commandment, that [b]as you
have heard from the beginning, you
should walk in it.

Beware of Deceiving Heretics

7 For [a]many deceivers have gone
out into the world [b]who do not confess Jesus Christ *as* coming in the
flesh. [c]This is a deceiver and an
antichrist.†
8 [a]Look to yourselves, [b]that [1]we
do not lose those things we worked
for, but *that* [1]we may receive a full
reward.
9 [a]Whoever [1]transgresses and
does not abide in the doctrine of
Christ does not have God. He who
abides in the doctrine of Christ has
both the Father and the Son.†
10 If anyone comes to you and
[a]does not bring this doctrine, do not
receive him into your house nor
greet him;†
11 for he who greets him shares in
his evil deeds.

John's Plans and Farewell

12 [a]Having many things to write
to you, I did not wish *to do so* with
paper and ink; but I hope to come
to you and speak face to face,
[b]that our joy may be full.
13 [a]The children of your elect sister
greet you. Amen.†

1 [a]Col. 1:5 [1]*chosen*
3 [a]Rom. 1:7; 1 Tim. 1:2 [1]NU, M *us*
4 [a]1 Thess. 2:19, 20; 3 John 3, 4
5 [a][John 13:34, 35; 15:12, 17]; 1 John 3:11; 4:7, 11
6 [a]John 14:15; 1 John 2:5; 5:3 [b]1 John 2:24
7 [a]1 John 2:19; 4:1 [b]1 John 4:2 [c]1 John 2:22
8 [a]Mark 13:9 [b]Gal. 3:4 [1]NU *you*
9 [a]John 7:16; 8:31; 1 John 2:19, 23, 24 [1]NU *goes ahead*
10 [a]1 Kin. 13:16; Rom. 16:17; 2 Thess. 3:6, 14; Titus 3:10
12 [a]3 John 13, 14 [b]John 17:13
13 [a]1 Pet. 5:13

---

1 John calls himself **the Elder,** or presbyter. He is confident that those who stand against the apostolic Church are in the minority. He assumes the Church is one, a true, concrete unity, and that it follows one rule of faith, whereas the heteroorthodox agree mainly in their rejection of this common faith.

3 The Son of the Father strongly refutes the deceivers and gnostics. Jesus is the Son, and the Son is by nature what His Father is, and He does what His Father does (see John 5:19).

4–6 False teachers were introducing new, nontraditional practices and breaking the covenant of unity based on God's love—the heart of New Covenant life.

7 The heretics here deny either Jesus' full humanity or His full divinity (or the full divinity of the Holy Spirit). The Jews were denying that **Jesus** is "the Christ," the Messiah. All these deny that Jesus is our "Archpriest" in His human nature, and that He will come in His glorified human body to judge the dead and the living.

9 The Orthodox doctrine of the Incarnation (**the doctrine of Christ**) is, according to John, necessary for knowledge and communion with God. **God** is synonymous with **the Father,** but, according to *the doctrine of Christ,* **the Son,** Christ, is also God.

10, 11 It is reported that one day John went into a public bathhouse and found there the well-known gnostic heretic, Cerinthus. The apostle ran out crying, "Let us get out of here, for fear the place falls in, now that Cerinthus, the enemy of the truth, is inside." (See Titus 3:10, 11.)

13 The children of your elect sister probably refers to the church from which John is writing, namely Ephesus.

The Third Epistle of JOHN

Author: *St. John the Apostle*

Date: A.D. *90–95*

Theme: *Genuine Leadership vs. False Leadership*

AUTHOR: Third John has the same author as 2 John. The language and style are the same. Both are closely related to 1 John, and both are written by "the Elder," a name by which John was known in Asia Minor in his old age—probably not a title in the Church but a term of endearment. All the Apostles, however, could legitimately call themselves "elders" in terms of Church government, as Peter does in 1 Peter 5:1.

DATE: As with 2 John, there is no firm evidence for fixing a date. It is probable that all of John's letters were written about the same time (A.D. 90–95).

MAJOR THEME: *Genuine leadership vs. false leadership*. Third John exhorts the Church to persevere in the true faith which she has received. True Christian leaders will adhere to that faith and respect those who passed it on to them. John especially notes the traditions concerning the Incarnation and Christian love.

BACKGROUND INFORMATION: (1) *Historical background*. One of the parishes under John's oversight is having a jurisdictional dispute. Evangelists sent out by John have reported back to their home church, probably Ephesus, testifying that Gaius—full of love and loyalty—had liberally supported their mission. On the other hand, Diotrephes, apparently the local bishop, or one aspiring to be so, had vigorously opposed them and lorded over the church instead of leading it. He was resistant to apostolic oversight (v. 9) and the traditional ways of the Church and, as a power play, forbade the welcoming of missionaries from John. It may be that Demetrius (v. 12) is another missionary whom John intends to send that way and who also will be in need of hospitality. Thus John writes to Diotrephes' parish, but he does not trust Diotrephes with his letter (v. 9).

(2) *Purpose of the letter*. Third John, then, has three practical purposes: (1) to praise Gaius, (2) to confirm the condemnation of Diotrephes and (3) to commend Demetrius and ensure hospitality for him from Gaius.

OUTLINE

I. Greeting to Gaius vv. 1–4
II. Commendation of Gaius vv. 5–8
III. Condemnation of Diotrephes vv. 9–11
IV. Recommendation of Demetrius v. 12
V. Farewell vv. 13, 14

Greeting to Gaius

The Elder,

To the beloved Gaius, [a]whom I
love in truth:†

2 Beloved, I pray that you may
prosper in all things and be in health,
just as your soul prospers.
3 For I [a]rejoiced greatly when
brethren came and testified of the
truth *that is* in you, just as you walk
in the truth.†
4 I have no greater [a]joy than to
hear that [b]my children walk in
[1]truth.

Commendation of Gaius

5 Beloved, you do faithfully whatever
you do for the brethren [1]and
for strangers,†
6 who have borne witness of your
love before the church. *If* you send
them forward on their journey in a
manner worthy of God, you will do
well,
7 because they went forth for His
name's sake, [a]taking nothing from
the Gentiles.†
8 We therefore ought to [a]receive[1]
such, that we may become fellow
workers for the truth.†

Condemnation of Diotrephes

9 I wrote to the church, but Diotrephes,
who loves to have the
preeminence among them, does not
receive us.†
10 Therefore, if I come, I will call
to mind his deeds which he does,
[a]prating[1] against us with malicious
words. And not content with that,
he himself does not receive the
brethren, and forbids those who
wish to, putting *them* out of the
church.
11 Beloved, [a]do not imitate what
is evil, but what is good. [b]He who

1 [a]2 John 1
3 [a]2 John 4
4 [a]1 Thess. 2:19, 20; 2 John 4 [b][1 Cor. 4:15] [1]NU *the truth*
5 [1]NU *and especially for*
7 [a]1 Cor. 9:12, 15
8 [a]Matt. 10:40; Rom. 12:13; Heb. 13:2; 1 Pet. 4:9 [1]NU *support*
10 [a]Prov. 10:8, 10 [1]*talking nonsense*
11 [a]Ps. 34:14; 37:27; Rom. 14:19; 1 Thess. 5:15; 1 Tim. 6:11; 2 Tim. 2:22 [b][1 John 2:29; 3:10]

---

1 This is probably not the same **Gaius** as the one mentioned in Rom. 16:23 and 1 Cor. 1:14.

3, 4 Truth here does not refer to doctrine or thought, but to the Christian's manner of life. Like all fathers, John finds his greatest pleasure in seeing his children walking in truth.

5 Strangers are probably the missionaries sent by John.

7 The missionaries went forth for the specific purpose of preaching the gospel of the Lord Jesus Christ.

8 One way we may participate in ministry is in giving material help to those with spiritual gifts. The donor becomes a **fellow worker** in spiritual things (see Matt. 10:41).

9, 10 Diotrephes means "nursed or nourished by Zeus." Early Christians kept their original names after their baptism. Diotrephes loves being preeminent—not the first among equals but peerless, with a passion for personal aggrandizement. This sin results in insubordination: Diotrephes slanders John, the last of the Twelve Apostles, by refusing to accept John as either an apostle or a presbyter. By rejecting John's missionaries he rejects John himself. And he disdains the apostolic, catholic ways of the Church, setting himself up as a petty tyrant.

does good is of God, [1]but he who
does evil has not seen [c]God.

Recommendation of Demetrius

12 Demetrius [a]has a *good* testimony
from all, and from the truth itself.
And we also [1]bear witness, [b]and
you know that our testimony is
true.†

11 c[1 John 3:10] 1NU, M omit *but*
12 aActs 6:3; 1 Tim. 3:7 bJohn 19:35; 21:24 1*testify*
13 a2 John 12

Farewell

13 [a]I had many things to write, but
I do not wish to write to you with
pen and ink;
14 but I hope to see you shortly,
and we shall speak face to face. Peace
to you. Our friends greet you. Greet
the friends by name.

---

12 Demetrius is either a member of Diotrephes' party, or one of the emissaries already sent by John, or yet another emissary from John—perhaps the carrier of this letter.

The General Epistle of

JUDE

Author: *St. Jude, the relative of Christ*

Date: *A.D. 60–80*

Theme: *Contending Earnestly for the Faith*

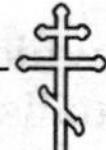

AUTHOR: Jude, a relative of Jesus (called the "brother" of the Lord in Matt. 13:55 and Mark 6:3) and the brother of James the Just (bishop of Jerusalem and author of James), is the author of this epistle. This is not the Jude who was one of the Twelve and was also called Thaddaeus or Lebbaeus (v. 17; see Matt. 10:3; Mark 3:18; Luke 6:16; Acts 1:13).

Jude, or Judas (Gr. *Ioudas*), was a popular name among the first-century Jews because Judas Maccabaeus ("the Hammer," died c. 160 B.C.) became a national hero as the leader of the Jewish resistance to Syria's attempt to destroy Judaism.

DATE: The date of the letter is uncertain, but sometime in the period A.D.60–80 seems reasonable. Time indicators in the letter suggest a maturing first-century faith and include the following:

(1) The basic doctrines of the faith are seen as fixed and already handed down (v. 3, further evidence of the role of oral tradition in the early Church).

(2) The founding utterances of the apostles are described as being in the past (vv. 17, 18).

(3) The Faith is seen as something to be maintained, not discovered (v. 20).

MAJOR THEME: *Contending earnestly for the faith.* Jude is a polemic directed against false teachers within the Church who are jeopardizing the salvation of many. Jude supports his attack with examples from the OT, and the tradition of God's dealing harshly with those who assault His people.

BACKGROUND INFORMATION: (1) *The canonicity of Jude.* The Epistle of Jude was not accepted as Scripture by some because it refers to pseudepigraphal books, the *Book of Enoch* (1:9; 10:4–13; 18:13–16) in vv. 6, 14, 15 (vv. 14, 15 are almost a direct quote); and the *Assumption of Moses* in v. 9. But to quote a book is not to believe that it is inspired.

Paul alludes to nonbiblical sources (1 Cor. 10:4; 2 Tim. 3:8), and John does so in Revelation. Jude uses these books as contemporary authorities and takes from them what is pertinent. Jude was eventually accepted as canonical because of its antiquity and because of the respect shown by its use in the Church.

(2) *The relation of Jude to 2 Peter.* These books share a similar purpose and similar language (compare vv. 3–18 with 2 Pet. 1:5; 2:1–18). Many scholars believe that 2 Peter refers to Jude.

(3) *Audience.* To whom Jude writes is difficult to discern. James the Just and Jude are associated with Palestine, and Jude makes use of Jewish tradition as if his readers would understand it. But the immorality which Jude attacks is associated more with Gentiles. Some scholars have suggested, then, that the addressees are Christians from a Hellenistic Jewish background.

(4) *The antagonists.* The heresy which Jude opposes seems to be an early form of gnosticism. In this system, dualism, which valued the immaterial and despised the material, resulted in licentiousness. Another error was the belief in a multilevel spiritual realm, in which angels were thought to be low-ranking beings, and Jesus was often ranked even lower than angels.

These heretics are still present in the Church (vv. 4, 12, 22, 23), carrying on an aggressive campaign of propaganda and subversion: (a) they question authority—they are disobedient to the laws which control the world and to the custodians of world order (v. 8), while loudly asserting their own authority (v. 16); (b) they attend the agape (love) feast in subterfuge (v. 12); (c) they do not hide their licentiousness (v. 13), yet set themselves up as dispensers of true grace; (d) they ridicule true Christianity (v. 18); (e) they are schismatic, worldly and devoid of the Spirit (v. 19).

Jude's mode of attack is more *ad hominem,* that is, a censure of persons, than theological: We will know them by their fruits, he says. These heretics are obviously bad trees; they are not to be honored with a theological rebuttal. Warnings against heretics became a part of traditional Christian instruction for baptism (catechesis).

(5) *Purpose of the letter.* Jude's purposes, then, are (a) to rouse the Church to declare war on heterodoxy (v. 3); (b) to exhort the Church to orthodox faith and practice (vv. 20, 21); (c) to rescue the weak and fallen where possible (vv. 22, 23); and (d) to instill confidence that God is indeed the Lord of *all* (vv. 1, 24, 25).

OUTLINE

I. Greeting	vv. 1, 2
II. Presence of false teachers	vv. 3, 4
III. Judgment of false teachers	vv. 5–7
IV. Character of false teachers	vv. 8–16
V. Resistance to false teachers	vv. 17–23
VI. Doxology	vv. 24, 25

Greeting

Jude, a bondservant of Jesus
Christ, and [a]brother of James,

To those who are [b]called,
[1]sanctified by God the Father, and
[c]preserved in Jesus Christ:†

2 Mercy, [a]peace, and love be multiplied to you.

The Presence of False Teachers

3 Beloved, while I was very diligent to write to you [a]concerning our
common salvation, I found it necessary to write to you exhorting
[b]you to contend earnestly for the
faith which was once for all delivered
to the saints.†
4 For certain men have crept in
unnoticed, who long ago were
marked out for this condemnation,
ungodly men, who turn the grace of
our God into lewdness and deny the
only Lord [1]God and our Lord Jesus
Christ.†

The Judgment of Such False Teachers

5 But I want to remind you,
though you once knew this, that
[a]the Lord, having saved the people
out of the land of Egypt, afterward
destroyed those who did not believe.†
6 And the angels who did not
keep their [1]proper domain, but left
their own abode, He has reserved in
everlasting chains under darkness
for the judgment of the great day;
7 as [a]Sodom and Gomorrah, and
the cities around them in a similar
manner to these, having given themselves over to sexual immorality and
gone after strange flesh, are set forth
as an example, suffering the
[1]vengeance of eternal fire.

The Character of False Teachers

8 [a]Likewise also these dreamers
defile the flesh, reject authority, and
[b]speak evil of [1]dignitaries.†
9 Yet Michael the archangel, in
[1]contending with the devil, when he

1 [a]Acts 1:13 [b]Rom. 1:7 [c]John 17:11, 12 [1]NU *beloved*
2 [a]1 Pet. 1:2
3 [a]Titus 1:4 [b]Phil. 1:27
4 [1]NU omits *God*
5 [a]1 Cor. 10:5–10
6 [1]*own*
7 [a]Gen. 19:24 [1]*punishment*
8 [a]2 Pet. 2:10 [b]Ex. 22:28 [1]*glorious ones,* lit. *glories*
9 [1]*arguing*

---

1 To be **preserved in Jesus Christ** is a promise of God to all the faithful. But not all are so faithful, as Jude will relate in this letter (see John 10:27–30; 2 Tim. 1:12; Heb. 12:25).
3 Jude had intended to write a more general letter on salvation, but the danger of false teachers caused him to write a polemic instead. There is one salvation which is the same for all the elect, **our common salvation.** This salvation is set in apostolic tradition **once for all delivered to the saints,** and it cannot be changed.
4 This condemnation involves body and soul (see John 5:29). **Only Lord God** is better translated "only Sovereign" (Gr. *despotes*).
5–7 The recipients of this letter **once knew this** (v. 5), the mysteries of the faith, because the totality of that faith had already been delivered to them (v. 3). Jude gives three arresting examples of the danger of departing from truth and righteousness:
(1) In the Exodus from **Egypt** (v. 5), all were saved through the baptism of the Red Sea, but not all responded to their deliverance with ongoing deeds of repentance and godliness (Num. 14:26–37; see 1 Cor. 10:1–13). The lesson for us as Christians is to keep walking in our union with Christ.
(2) The **proper domain** (v. 6) of the angels is in their likeness and proximity to God. Their **own abode** is heaven, though they may serve elsewhere. Those who left their proper place are confined far from God, having become bound to spiritual darkness. They await **the judgment** (2 Pet. 2:4), when their bonds with God will be demolished forever. The lesson for Christians is that their *proper domain* is in being children of God by grace, and their *own abode* is in the One Holy Church.
(3) The men in the plains around **Sodom and Gomorrah** (v. 7) lusted after angels because of their sin of immorality and homosexuality (Gen. 19:1–29). The lesson for Christians is to live under God's call to a chaste and pure life.
8 Authority (lit. "lordships"; also translated "dominion"; see Eph. 1:21; Col. 1:16) and **dignitaries** (lit. "glories") refer to angels, perhaps in this case to fallen angels (see the parallel in 2 Pet. 2:10). Although they are hostile to God, they are nonetheless to be treated dispassionately.

disputed about the body of Moses,
dared not bring against him a reviling accusation, but said, [a]"The Lord
rebuke you!"†
10 [a]But these speak evil of whatever they do not know; and whatever they know naturally, like brute
beasts, in these things they corrupt
themselves.†
11 Woe to them! For they have
gone in the way [a]of Cain, [b]have run
greedily in the error of Balaam for
profit, and perished [c]in the rebellion
of Korah.†
12 These are [1]spots in your love
feasts, while they feast with you
without fear, serving *only* themselves. *They are* clouds without water, carried [2]about by the winds; late
autumn trees without fruit, twice
dead, pulled up by the roots;†

9 [a]Zech. 3:2
10 [a]2 Pet. 2:12
11 [a]Gen. 4:3–8 [b]2 Pet. 2:15 [c]Num. 16:1–3, 31–35
12 [1]*stains,* or *hidden reefs* [2]NU, M *along*
13 [a]Is. 57:20 [b][Phil. 3:19] [c]2 Pet. 2:17
15 [a]1 Sam. 2:3
16 [a]2 Pet. 2:18 [b]Prov. 28:21

13 [a]raging waves of the sea,
[b]foaming up their own shame; wandering stars [c]for whom is reserved
the blackness of darkness forever.†
14 Now Enoch, the seventh from
Adam, prophesied about these men
also, saying, "Behold, the Lord
comes with ten thousands of His
saints,†
15 "to execute judgment on all, to
convict all who are ungodly among
them of all their ungodly deeds
which they have committed in an
ungodly way, and of all the [a]harsh
things which ungodly sinners have
spoken against Him."
16 These are grumblers, complainers, walking according to their own
lusts; and they [a]mouth great swelling *words,* [b]flattering people to gain
advantage.†

9 This incident is apparently taken from the pseudepigraphal book *The Assumption of Moses* (see Deut. 34:5, 6 for the possibility of the assumption of Moses; also Zech. 3:1, 2). The people of God are defended by holy angels. This is also a gracious warning to believers concerning vehement accusations against God's enemies: let God judge. Michael showed this restraint even though he was dealing with the devil himself.

10 Know naturally: that is, by their own natural instincts, apart from any specific revelation of the Holy Spirit. God has given all persons a measure of "common sense."

11 This is a threefold **woe** or warning of great sorrow, using a triad of the Bible's most famous offenders: (1) **Cain** (Gen. 4:3–24) sinned by faithlessness and envy, especially envy of an honor given to another. His sin led to murder (Gen. 4:8, 16–24). (2) **Balaam** (Num. 22—24) sinned by greed, which led to lying and an all-out assault upon the truth (which he knew) as well. (3) **Korah** (Num. 16:1–40) sinned by ambition, pride and arrogance, grasping for leadership against God's will. His sin led to blatant rebellion against God.

12 Jude has a gift for using graphic word pictures. **Spots** should be rendered "hidden reefs," those underwater razor-sharp growths which can damage and sink great ships. The **love feast,** or "agape," was a liturgical banquet tied to the Eucharist. Designed to be a peaceful, joyful meal, it was sabotaged by the false teachers, the hidden reefs in this peaceful ocean of loving friendship. **Clouds without water** are spiritually dry teachers who don't possess what they claim to have (Prov. 25:14). Being **carried about by the winds** is the effect of obeying their own passions and listening to the suggestions of invisible spirits. **Twice dead** means they were *dead* before they believed and *dead* a second time after they turned their backs on Christ.

If barrenness is worthy of being cast into the fire (Matt. 3:10), how much worse is bearing rotten fruit (Matt. 7:17–19)? In contrast to the saints who are firmly rooted in Christ (Eph. 3:17; Col. 2:7), the false teachers are **pulled up by the roots** and so cannot remain with Christ or in His Church (Matt. 13:24–30; John 15:6).

13 Raging waves are perverse teachers—restless, dark, bitter, destructive, and persistent (Is. 57:20, 21)—who are **foaming up** as they hit the breakwater of the Church. The higher they raise themselves, the more disorderly and dissipated they become: they crash and perish. In astronomy a **wandering star** is either (1) a planet that never rises or sets in the same place, or (2) a "shooting star," a comet, which shines brilliantly, but only briefly, and then burns out in **darkness.** These are probably fallen angels, for in the *Book of Enoch* and other late Jewish apocalyptic literature, "star" often means "angel."

14, 15 Thus has God always judged the wicked who dwell among the righteous.

16 Those who are consistently **grumblers** and **complainers** are often telegraphing a deeper

(continued on next page)

Resistance to False Teachers

17 [a]But you, beloved, remember
the words which were spoken before
by the apostles of our Lord Jesus
Christ:
18 how they told you that [a]there
would be mockers in the last time
who would walk according to their
own ungodly lusts.
19 These are [1]sensual persons,
who cause divisions, not having the
Spirit.†
20 But you, beloved, [a]building
yourselves up on your most holy
faith, [b]praying in the Holy Spirit,†
21 keep yourselves in the love
of God, [a]looking for the mercy of
our Lord Jesus Christ unto eternal
life.
22 And on some have compassion,
[1]making a distinction;
23 but [a]others save [1]with fear,
[b]pulling *them* out of the [2]fire, hating
even [c]the garment defiled by the
flesh.

Doxology

24 [a]Now to Him who is able to keep
[1]you from stumbling,
And [b]to present *you* faultless
Before the presence of His glory
with exceeding joy,†
25 To [1]God our Savior,
[2]Who alone is wise,
Be glory and majesty,
Dominion and [3]power,
Both now and forever.
Amen.

17 [a]2 Pet. 3:2 **18** [a][1 Tim. 4:1] **19** [1]*soulish* or *worldly* **20** [a]Col. 2:7 [b][Rom. 8:26] **21** [a]Titus 2:13 **22** [1]NU *who are doubting* (or *making distinctions*) **23** [a]Rom. 11:14 [b]Amos 4:11 [c][Zech. 3:4, 5] [1]NU omits *with fear* [2]NU adds *and on some have mercy with fear* **24** [a][Eph. 3:20] [b]Col. 1:22 [1]M *them*

25 [1]NU *the only God our Savior,* [2]NU *Through Jesus Christ our Lord, Be glory* [3]NU adds *Before all time,*

(continued from previous page)
problem, that is **walking according to** one's **own lusts.** The more a person truly desires the fullness of life in Christ, the easier it becomes to renounce those things which are contrary to godliness.

19 Sensual (Gr. *psychikoi*) means operating by the powers of the human soul alone without the indwelling power of the Spirit, that which makes one "spiritual" (see 1 Cor. 2:13–15; 15:44–46). **Cause divisions:** Having separated themselves from the way of the righteous and the life of the Spirit, the divisive "do not have the glue of charity" (The Venerable Bede).

20, 21 Our chief safeguards against heresy are: (1) growing in the **faith** of the Church—vital dependence upon God the Father, the Son and the Holy Spirit—and (2) maintaining *faith* by **praying.**

24, 25 Jude is quoting an ancient Christian benediction or doxology, probably taken from an early liturgical tradition.

THE REVELATION

of Jesus Christ

Author: *St. John the Apostle*

Date: *c.* A.D. *95*

Theme: *Faithfulness in Tribulation*

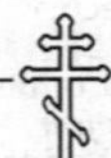

AUTHOR: Traditionally, Revelation (also called the Apocalypse) has been considered to have been written by the Apostle John during a forced exile on the Isle of Patmos (see 1:10) during the reign of the Emperor Domitian.

DATE: The vast majority of scholars hold that the Revelation was composed during the fierce persecution that occurred in the latter part of the reign of the Roman Emperor Domitian (A.D. 81–96).

MAJOR THEME: *Faithfulness in tribulation*. "Revelation" (Gr. *apokalypsis*) means the uncovering of something which has previously been hidden, in this case the final triumph of the Kingdom of God. Since the final triumph of the Kingdom of God is assured, our faithfulness and loyalty now—before its full revelation—will lead to our ultimate victory. Subthemes include (1) divine judgment of human wickedness, and (2) the symbolic presentation of most major New Testament teaching concerning eschatology, the last things.

BACKGROUND INFORMATION: (1) *The interpretation of Revelation*. This difficult book has been interpreted in many ways throughout the history of the Church. However, three basic approaches to its interpretation stand out:

(a) The *contemporaneous* approach assumes that Revelation was written for a specific group of churches (1:11) with specific needs at a specific time. The work is therefore interpreted in terms of what it was meant to say to those to whom it was immediately addressed.

(b) The *futurist* approach assumes that Revelation is a book of prophecy addressing a time far distant from its era of composition, predicting actual future events.

(c) The *idealist* approach assumes that Revelation is an exposition of the ongoing relationships and conflicts between God and His Kingdom, humanity, and Satan. It reveals things in the past, present, and future.

These three approaches are not contradictory, but must be used in conjunction. Revelation is for those to whom it is addressed and, equally, for us all.

(2) *The liturgical use of Revelation in the Church.* While seen as canonical and inspired by God, Revelation is the only New Testament book not publicly read in the services of the Orthodox Church. This is partly because the book was only gradually accepted as canonical in many parts of Christendom. In addition, in the second and third centuries Revelation was widely twisted and sensationally misinterpreted, and the resulting erroneous teachings brought troublesome confusion to Christians. These issues, coupled with the presence of admittedly obscure and difficult passages, caused the Church to adopt a cautious approach to the interpretation of Revelation.

(3) *The literary features of Revelation.* This book is unique within New Testament literature because it combines three important literary types: apocalyptic, prophetic, and epistolary writing.

(a) The *apocalyptic* form was especially popular in Judaic and Christian literature from about 200 B.C. to A.D. 200. It abounds with features such as divine visions, vivid and even grotesque imagery, and symbolic numerology. Apocalyptic works offered hope and encouraged steadfastness to groups undergoing persecution or severe crisis. Revelation was written for churches suffering persecution.

(b) Revelation is distinctly *prophetic,* speaking God's word directly to the seven Asian churches in their tribulation. It prophetically envisions the final victory of God over evil, including the last judgment and the establishment of His eternal Kingdom.

(c) The *epistolary* character of Revelation is also pronounced. Fundamentally, it is an epistle, a letter, from an early Church leader to specific churches, full of exhortation directed toward their particular situations.

(4) *The historic backdrop of Revelation.* The early Church was convinced that the Second Coming was near (1 Cor. 7:29; 1 John 2:18). This expectation was no doubt heightened during the time of Emperor Domitian, as Christians were persecuted because of their refusal to worship this Emperor, who had declared himself a "god." John's vision was a reminder from God to the churches not to give in to their adversaries, but to hold fast to their faith. They were called to overcome, be it against pressure from the state, slander and harassment from the synagogues, false teachers within the Church, or the corruption resulting from prosperity.

OUTLINE

I. Prologue	1:1—3:22
A. Introduction	1:1–3
B. Greeting	1:4–8
C. John's vision of the Son of Man	1:9–20
D. The seven letters	2:1—3:22
II. Warnings of the coming judgment	4:1—16:21
A. The seven seals	4:1—8:1
1. Preparation for the seals	4:1—5:14
a. The heavenly temple and its liturgy	4:1–11
b. The enthronement of the Lamb	5:1–14

2. The seven seals opened	6:1—8:1
a. Seals 1–6	6:1–17
b. Interlude: God's servants sealed and gathered	7:1–17
c. The seventh seal	8:1
B. The seven trumpets	8:2—14:20
1. The trumpets sound	8:2—11:19
a. Introduction: The heavenly altar of incense	8:2–5
b. Trumpets 1–4; the angel's warning	8:6–13
c. Trumpets 5 and 6, woes 1 and 2	9:1–21
d. The little book	10:1–11
e. The two witnesses	11:1–13
f. Trumpet 7, woe 3: The heavenly liturgy	11:14–19
2. The warfare of the trumpets	12:1—14:20
a. The woman and the dragon	12:1–4
b. The Child	12:5, 6
c. The dragon: Defeated in heaven	12:7–17
d. The dragon's beasts	13:1—14:5
e. The final harvest: Blessing and wrath	14:6–20
C. The seven bowls: The day of wrath	15:1—16:21
1. The liturgy of preparation	15:1–8
2. The first four bowls	16:1–9
3. The last three bowls	16:10–21
III. The judgment: Of Babylon, the beast and Satan	17:1—20:15
A. Babylon destroyed by a great angel	17:1—19:10
1. Babylon's wickedness: The great harlot	17:1–18
2. Babylon's fall	18:1–24
3. Litany of triumph in heaven	19:1–10
B. Powers of evil destroyed: Beast and dragon	19:11—20:10
1. The appearance of Christ	19:11–16
2. The beast and false prophets defeated on Earth	19:17–21
3. The dragon captured, released, defeated in heaven	20:1–10
C. The last judgment	20:11–15
IV. The new order	21:1—22:5
A. A new creation: Heaven, earth, city	21:1–8
B. The New Jerusalem: Bride of the Lamb	21:9—22:5
V. Conclusion	22:6–21
A. Testimonies	22:6–16
B. Petition of the Spirit and the bride	22:17
C. Warning against tampering with the text	22:18, 19
D. Petition of John	22:20
E. Benediction	22:21

Introduction and Blessing

1 The Revelation of Jesus Christ,
[a]which God gave Him to show
His servants—things which must
[1]shortly take place. And [b]He sent
and signified *it* by His angel to His
servant John,†
2 [a]who bore witness to the word
of God, and to the testimony of
Jesus Christ, to all things [b]that he
saw.†
3 [a]Blessed *is* he who reads and
those who hear the words of this
prophecy, and keep those things
which are written in it; for [b]the time
is near.†

CHAPTER 1
1 [a]John 3:32
[b]Rev. 22:6
[1]*quickly* or *swiftly*
2 [a]1 Cor. 1:6
[b]1 John 1:1
3 [a]Luke 11:28
[b]James 5:8
4 [a]Ex. 3:14
[b]John 1:1
[c][Is. 11:2]
5 [a]John 8:14
[b]Is. 55:4
[c][Col. 1:18]
[d]Rev. 17:14
[e]John 13:34
[f]Heb. 9:14

Greeting to the Seven Churches

4 John, to the seven churches
which are in Asia:

Grace to you and peace from Him
[a]who is and [b]who was and who is
to come, [c]and from the seven Spirits
who are before His throne,†
5 and from Jesus Christ, [a]the
faithful [b]witness, the [c]firstborn from
the dead, and [d]the ruler over the
kings of the earth. To Him [e]who
[1]loved us [f]and washed us from our
sins in His own blood,†

[1]NU *loves us and freed,* M *loves us and washed*

1:1 Revelation or "Apocalypse" (Gr. *apokalypsis*) means literally to unconceal, unveil or reveal. It was used anciently referring to a coded message which must get through without falling into the wrong hands. God Himself is the ultimate source of all revelation (see Dan. 2:28, 29, 45), but it is the Son, Jesus Christ—who revealed Himself to the prophets of the OT before He became flesh, and now is made flesh—who mediates this unveiling (see John 1:18; 8:26, 40; 15:15; 17:8). This revelation is not only of the age to come, but of certain things from the past and from this present age as well. **Things which must** tells us this is not a haphazard presentation. **Shortly take place** describes God's time, which is always imminent. It may take a great deal of earth's time.

1:2 The word of God refers to the Son of God. **Testimony of Jesus** means John's testimony concerning Jesus (John 21:24), not Jesus testifying of Himself. **Bore witness** (from Gr. *martyreo,* a verb) and *testimony* (from Gr. *martyria,* a noun) are forms of the word from which we obtain the word "martyr." Persecution is the consequence of witnessing. The martyrs (see Heb. 12:1) are those who testify or bear witness, sealing their testimony with their blood in death.

1:3 A blessing is promised to those who read and hear this prophecy (see Luke 11:28). This is the first of the seven beatitudes of the Revelation; the others are found in 14:13; 16:15; 19:9; 20:6; 22:7,14. **Blessed** here are both the reader and the hearers (the assembled faithful), provided that they heed what is read—for faith and works are inseparable. **Time** (Gr. *kairos*) here means an eschatological "decisive moment," a time of judgment, the time when all is fulfilled.

1:4–6 Church tradition maintains St. John the Theologian dwelt in Ephesus and was bishop there (in the early Church, the bishop was the leader of one church). **The seven churches** were located near Ephesus along a major roadway. The number *seven* signifies fullness, suggesting the entire Church is also in view.

The doxology (glorification of God) in these three verses is trinitarian, involving the Father (vv. 4, 6), the Spirit (v. 4), and the Son (vv. 5, 6). This initial greeting (lit. "the Existing, the Was, and the Coming") may express the Father, the one **who is** (Ex. 3:14); the Son, **who was** (John 1:1); and the Holy Spirit, **who is to come** (Acts 2) at Pentecost and shall always be present. Or it may simply denote the character of God, who is eternally present and exercises lordship throughout history (see Heb. 13:8). God reveals the meaning of the present in light of the past and of the age to come. This title may be a paraphrase of the OT name for God, "I AM" (Ex. 3:14).

The **seven Spirits** of God most likely refers to the Holy Spirit and His several gifts, as this phrase is included in the blessing with the Father and the Son (see note on 3:1). Alternately the term could refer to the seven archangels who, according to Jewish tradition, stand before the throne of God (Ezek. 9:2; Tob. 12:15).

1:5 Jesus Christ is presented as the Risen Savior, Lord of all (see Zech. 12:10), giving hope to the early Christians that the Church will not always be dominated by a cruel state. Instead of **washed** (v. 5) many Greek texts read "freed." The term **witness** (Gr. *martys*),

(continued on next page)

6 and has [a]made us [1]kings and
priests to His God and Father,
[b]to Him *be* glory and dominion forever and ever. Amen.†
7 Behold, He is coming with
[a]clouds, and every eye will see Him,
even [b]they who pierced Him. And
all the tribes of the earth will mourn
because of Him. Even so, Amen.
8 [a]"I am the Alpha and the
Omega, [1]*the* Beginning and *the*
End," says the [2]Lord, [b]"who is and
who was and who is to come, the
[c]Almighty."†

Vision and Commission of Christ

9 I, John, [1]both your brother and
[a]companion in the tribulation and
[b]kingdom and patience of Jesus
Christ, was on the island that is
called Patmos for the word of God
and for the testimony of Jesus
Christ.†
10 [a]I was in the Spirit on [b]the
Lord's Day, and I heard behind me
[c]a loud voice, as of a trumpet,†
11 saying, [1]"I am the Alpha and
the Omega, the First and the Last,"
and, "What you see, write in a book
and send *it* to the seven churches
[2]which are in Asia: to Ephesus, to
Smyrna, to Pergamos, to Thyatira,
to Sardis, to Philadelphia, and to
Laodicea."†

6 [a]1 Pet. 2:5, 9 [b]1 Tim. 6:16 [1]NU, M *a kingdom* 7 [a]Matt. 24:30 [b]Zech. 12:10–14 8 [a]Is. 41:4 [b]Rev. 4:8; 11:17 [c]Is. 9:6 [1]NU, M omit *the Beginning and the End* [2]NU, M *Lord God* 9 [a]Phil. 1:7 [b][2 Tim. 2:12] [1]NU, M omit *both* 10 [a]Acts 10:10 [b]Acts 20:7 [c]Rev. 4:1 **11** [1]NU, M omit *"I am the Alpha and the Omega, the First and the Last," and,* [2]NU, M omit *which are in Asia*

(continued from previous page)
used only twice in the entire NT (see 3:14), refers to Christ, the authentic *witness* of all divine revelation; all that God has revealed is summed up in His life, witness, Passion, Resurrection, and exaltation. He has inaugurated the new age, for He is **firstborn from the dead** in His humanity, and has achieved a universal sovereignty by His death, Resurrection and revelation of His Kingdom for the world's salvation.

1:6 Those joined to the body of Christ in baptism comprise the messianic royal priesthood promised of old (see Ex. 19:5, 6; Is. 61:6; 1 Pet. 2:9; and the Anaphora of the Liturgy of St. Basil). This priestly ministry is to offer the world back to God in a sacrifice of praise and thanksgiving—eucharistically—as in the Orthodox Church's Divine Liturgy. The universe itself thus becomes hallowed, transfigured, and sacramental. **Amen** is a Semitic word. It signifies ratification: an acknowledgment of something trustworthy.

1:8 Alpha and **Omega,** the first and last letters of the Greek alphabet, along with **Beginning** and **End,** signify the eternality of God, who is the origin and destiny of all things. Its attribution to the Son proves His divinity. History—in fact, all of creation—begins and is completed in the Creator (Is. 44:6). **Almighty** (Gr. *Pantokrator*) is used throughout the OT (LXX), and is found ten times in the NT—nine of which are in Revelation. The inscription which adorns the central dome of a properly appointed Orthodox temple bears the words of this verse; the fresco depicts the Lord Jesus, since He is the One who shows us the Father, and since He has used the title "Alpha and Omega" for Himself (22:13).

1:9 Patmos was a small rocky island 40 miles off the west coast of modern Turkey, 50 miles south of Ephesus, to which the Romans exiled criminals. John's preaching must have been considered a seditious threat to the public interest for him to have been imprisoned there.

1:10 In the Spirit may mean John received the revelation in a visionary ecstasy (see Ezek. 3:12), but more probably it means that he was in the worship ("in Spirit and in truth") of the Lord. **The Lord's Day** here is the earliest reference to the Christian name for Sunday. The *Didache* (14:1) and St. Ignatius of Antioch (Ign. Magn. 9:1) show this name was used very early for the day when Christians gathered to celebrate the Resurrection in the holy Eucharist. As a fulfillment of the first day of the week of the old creation, Sunday becomes the "eighth day," the "first day of the new creation." The term "eighth day" is seen in 2 Enoch 33:1; it inaugurates the first day of the timeless age to come. The **loud voice, as of a trumpet** is a traditional, eschatological, apocalyptic introduction describing an appearance of the Lord (see Ex. 19:16, 19; Matt. 24:31; 1 Thess. 4:16).

1:11, 12 The glorified Christ introduces himself as **the Alpha and the Omega, the First and Last,** thus identifying Himself with God the Father (v. 8; 22:13). His position amidst the seven lampstands signifies His presence in the Church. The **seven golden lampstands**—a fusion of the great Menorah of the temple, with its seven lamps (see Ex. 25:31–37;
(continued on next page)

12 Then I turned to see the voice
that spoke with me. And having
turned [a]I saw seven golden lampstands,
13 [a]and in the midst of the seven
lampstands [b]*One* like the Son of
Man, [c]clothed with a garment down
to the feet and [d]girded about the
chest with a golden band.†
14 His head and [a]hair *were* white
like wool, as white as snow, and
[b]His eyes like a flame of fire;
15 [a]His feet *were* like fine brass, as
if refined in a furnace, and [b]His voice
as the sound of many waters;†
16 [a]He had in His right hand seven
stars, [b]out of His mouth went a
sharp two-edged sword, [c]and His
countenance *was* like the sun shining
in its strength.†

12 [a]Ex. 25:37 **13** [a]Rev. 2:1 [b]Ezek. 1:26 [c]Dan. 10:5 [d]Rev. 15:6 **14** [a]Dan. 7:9 [b]Dan. 10:6 **15** [a]Ezek. 1:7 [b]Ezek. 1:24; 43:2 **16** [a]Rev. 1:20; 2:1; 3:1 [b]Is. 49:2 [c]Matt. 17:2

17 [a]Ezek. 1:28 [b]Dan. 8:18; 10:10, 12 [c]Is. 41:4; 44:6; 48:12 [1]NU, M omit *to me* **18** [a]Rom. 6:9 [b]Rev. 4:9 [c]Ps. 68:20

17 And [a]when I saw Him, I fell at
His feet as dead. But [b]He laid His
right hand on me, saying [1]to me,
"Do not be afraid; [c]I am the First and
the Last.†
18 [a]"I *am* He who lives, and was
dead, and behold, [b]I am alive forevermore. Amen. And [c]I have the keys
of [1]Hades and of Death.
19 [1]"Write the things which you
have [a]seen, [b]and the things which
are, [c]and the things which will take
place after this.†
20 "The [1]mystery of the seven stars
which you saw in My right hand,

[1]Lit. *Unseen;* the unseen realm **19** [a]Rev. 1:9–18 [b]Rev. 2:1 [c]Rev. 4:1 [1]NU, M *Therefore, write* **20** [1]*hidden truth*

(continued from previous page)
Zech. 4:2; Heb. 9:2), and the golden candlesticks of Solomon's temple (1 Kin. 7:49)—represent the fullness of God's presence. Also symbolized are the seven Asian churches which receive the letters of chs. 2 and 3. This reference prompts some scholars to suggest John was in the Church in a liturgical setting when he received the Revelation.

1:13–16 One like the Son of Man (v. 13) recalls Daniel's messianic figure (Dan. 7:13, repeated by Stephen at his martyrdom, Acts 7:56). Christ called Himself *Son of Man* (see Matt. 24:30–44) for He is the fulfillment of Daniel's prophecy. Additional parallels to this description may be seen in both the Old and New Testaments (Ezek. 43:2; Dan. 10:6; Matt. 17:2; Heb. 4:12). We also see Christ vested in high-priestly garments (see Ex. 28:4; 29:5; Lev. 16:4). The gold with which He is girded is both royal (1 Macc. 10:89) and priestly.

Further, Christ is here described as God, His **hair** (v. 14) being like that of Daniel's vision of God as the "Ancient of Days" (Dan. 7:9; see 1 Enoch 46:1). His **eyes** signify knowledge; His **feet** (v. 15), permanence and stability; His **voice,** authority or teaching; His **right hand** (v. 16), power; His **two-edged sword,** complete discernment. This imagery continues throughout Revelation to affirm the preexistence and eternal divinity of the Son of Man (see also John 1:1–18). Thus, in Christ man (v. 14) and God (vv. 15, 16) are united.

1:15 Daniel 2:31–45 indicates this mysterious metal foundation not only provides stability but has the ability to forcibly crush all opposition as well. These images are contrasted with the feet of clay found in Dan. 2:33, 44: The kingdoms of this world are not permanent, nor ultimately triumphant.

1:16 The Lord holds the **stars** which represent the angels of the seven churches (1:20), and hence, the whole Church. For Christ is Lord of the Church. In His just judgment, the **sword** He wields is the Word of God, which cuts effortlessly to the very marrow and heart of humanity (see 2:16; Is. 11:4; Eph. 6:17; Heb. 4:12). The brilliance of His face recalls the Uncreated Light seen by John radiating from the Savior at the Transfiguration on Mt. Tabor.

1:17, 18 Mortal humanity cannot bear the revelation of divine glory: this is a frequent biblical theme (see Ex. 19:21, 33:20; Is. 6:5). Just as John fell prostrate at Mt. Tabor (Matt. 17:6), so he does here, in the presence of the glorified Savior (see also Ezek. 1:28; Dan. 10:8–10; 1 Enoch 14:24). **Do not be afraid** is a revelatory formula from the OT. It was carried over into the NT as preparation for a theophany (see the Annunciation, Luke 1:30; Jesus walking upon the water, Matt. 14:27; the Transfiguration, Matt. 17:7). In the OT God was called "the First and . . . the Last" (Is. 44:6; 48:12), and so, too, was the Messiah. Some early heresies (e.g. docetism) held that Jesus only seemed to die. But the Lord Himself testified **I . . . was dead** affirming the authenticity of His death; and **am alive evermore,** affirming His resurrection—the power of which effects His lordship over **Death** and its realm. The Orthodox icon of the resurrected Christ depicts Him with these **keys** (v. 18) in hand, standing triumphantly upon the open gates of **Hades.**

1:19 John's visions have to do with both the present (**things which are**) and the future.

and the seven golden lampstands:
The seven stars are [a]the [2]angels of
the seven churches, and [b]the seven
lampstands [3]which you saw are the
seven churches.†

Ephesus: Loveless

2 "To the [1]angel of the church of
Ephesus write,
'These things says [a]He who holds
the seven stars in His right hand,
[b]who walks in the midst of the seven
golden lampstands:†
2 [a]"I know your works, your
labor, your [1]patience, and that
you cannot [2]bear those who are
evil. And [b]you have tested those
[c]who say they are apostles and
are not, and have found them
liars;†
3 "and you have persevered and
have patience, and have labored for
My name's sake and have [a]not become weary.
4 "Nevertheless I have *this* against
you, that you have left your first
love.
5 "Remember therefore from
where you have fallen; repent and
do the first works, [a]or else I will
come to you quickly and remove
your lampstand from its place—unless you repent.
6 "But this you have, that you
hate the deeds of the Nicolaitans,
which I also hate.†
7 [a]"He who has an ear, let him
hear what the Spirit says to the
churches. To him who overcomes I
will give [b]to eat from [c]the tree of life,
which is in the midst of the Paradise
of God." '†

20 [a]Rev. 2:1 [b]Zech. 4:2 [2]Or *messengers* [3]NU, M omit *which you saw*

CHAPTER 2

1 [a]Rev. 1:16 [b]Rev. 1:13 [1]Or *messenger*
2 [a]Ps. 1:6 [b]1 John 4:1 [c]2 Cor. 11:13 [1]*perseverance* [2]*endure*
3 [a]Gal. 6:9
5 [a]Matt. 21:41
7 [a]Matt. 11:15 [b][Rev. 22:2, 14] [c][Gen. 2:9; 3:22]

1:20 The angels of the seven churches have been variously interpreted as being: (1) the guardian angels of the church communities; (2) the pastoral leadership of these local churches; (3) a personification of the prevailing spirit of the given congregations; or (4) simply the messengers responsible for delivering the letters. The term "angel" (heavenly or earthly messenger) is used over 60 times in Revelation.

2:1 The letters to the seven churches all follow a standard format: (1) John is commanded to write to **the angel of the church.** (2) A short introduction of Christ with a descriptive title follows. (3) The state of the church is summarized, beginning with Jesus' saying "I know," with praise or rebuke. (4) Exhortations are given. (5) The message concludes with "He who has ears to hear, let him hear," and a special promise to him who "overcomes."

Ephesus, the provincial Roman capital (Gr. *Metropolis*) for Asia Minor, was a populous, prosperous city located on important trade routes. Besides the official cults of Artemis (Diana) and the emperor, various occult practices flourished there (see Acts 19). The church had been founded by Paul about A.D. 53–56, and according to tradition, both the Apostle John and the Virgin Mary (whom Christ had committed to John's care) lived in Ephesus.

2:2–5 The Ephesian church had persevered in orthodox faith and moral uprightness, but had left her **first love** (v. 4), presumably meaning love for God and each other. False apostles were a serious problem in the early Church (see 2 Cor. 11:13–23), and Paul warned they would ravage the church of Ephesus (Acts 20:29). However, in the early second century St. Ignatius of Antioch praised the Ephesians for their continuing resistance to heresy (Ign. Eph. 6:2; 9:1). The **lampstand** (v. 5) is probably the Ephesian church's honor as the metropolitan church of Asia.

2:6 Most scholars believe **the Nicolaitans** to be an early gnostic sect that tolerated idolatry and encouraged fornication. Some of the Church Fathers held the founder of this sect to be an apostate Nicolas, one of the original seven deacons (Acts 6:5).

2:7 The message of the Spirit to the churches is explicitly a message to all Christians. In Hebrew, "conquering" and "saving" are synonymous: salvation is victory. He **who overcomes** does so by participating in Christ's victory, which is salvation. In contrast to members of the false Nicolaitan sect, "overcomers" remain faithful to Christ until the end, in spite of all obstacles. Further, they fulfill the original destiny of man by partaking of **the tree of life** (Gen. 2:9). To eat of this *tree* is to receive eternal life. (See vv. 11, 17, 26; 3:5, 12, 21; 21:7; 2 Cor. 4:7–18.) The fruit of the tree is the spiritual food of 1 Cor. 10:3, the "medicine of immortality." *Tree of life* is also an allusion to the Cross, upon which all Christians must be cocrucified with Christ (Gal. 2:20), partaking in the death of Christ in order to participate in His Resurrection. **The Paradise of God** is heaven (Luke 23:43; 2 Cor. 12:2–4), the city of God, the New Jerusalem (see 21:1—22:5), contrasted to the original earthly paradise.

Smyrna: Persecuted

8 "And to the [1]angel of the church
in Smyrna write,
'These things says [a]the First and
the Last, who was dead, and came
to life:†
9 "I know your works, tribulation, and poverty (but you are
[a]rich); and *I know* the blasphemy of
[b]those who say they are Jews and
are not, [c]but *are* a [1]synagogue of
Satan.†
10 [a]"Do not fear any of those
things which you are about to suffer.
Indeed, the devil is about to throw
some of you into prison, that you may
be tested, and you will have tribulation ten days. [b]Be faithful until
death, and I will give you [c]the crown
of life.†
11 [a]"He who has an ear, let him
hear what the Spirit says to the
churches. He who overcomes shall
not be hurt by [b]the second death."'

Pergamos: Compromising

12 "And to the [1]angel of the church
in Pergamos write,
'These things says [a]He who has
the sharp two-edged sword:†
13 "I know your works, and where
you dwell, where Satan's throne *is*.
And you hold fast to My name, and
did not deny My faith even in the
days in which Antipas *was* My faithful martyr, who was killed among
you, where Satan dwells.†
14 "But I have a few things against
you, because you have there those
who hold the doctrine of [a]Balaam,
who taught Balak to put a stumbling
block before the children of Israel,
[b]to eat things sacrificed to idols,
[c]and to commit sexual immorality.†

8 [a]Rev. 1:8, 17, 18 [1]Or *messenger*
9 [a]Luke 12:21 [b]Rom. 2:17 [c]Rev. 3:9 [1]*congregation*
10 [a]Matt. 10:22 [b]Matt. 24:13 [c]James 1:12
11 [a]Rev. 13:9 [b][Rev. 20:6, 14; 21:8]
12 [a]Is. 49:2; Rev. 1:16; 2:16 [1]Or *messenger*
14 [a]Num. 31:16 [b]Num. 25; Acts 15:29; [1 Cor. 10:20]; Rev. 2:20 [c]1 Cor. 6:13

2:8 Smyrna (Izmir in modern Turkey) was, like Ephesus, a beautiful and prosperous city, maintaining a strong allegiance to Rome. A large and influential Jewish population actively opposed Christianity there. St. Polycarp, bishop of Smyrna, was one of the first of the early hierarchs to be martyred. He was burned to death on a pyre, confessing he had served Christ faithfully "for 86 years." Polycarp was probably a youth in Smyrna when John addressed the letter to the church there. St. Ignatius of Antioch also wrote to the Smyrnans—and to Polycarp, as well.

2:9 The Smyrnan Church was poor, perhaps because of the persecution, but spiritually rich—the opposite of Laodicea. The Jews of the **synagogue of Satan** may be (1) Jews in name only (see Rom. 2:28, 29) who were insincere in their profession of Judaism, and compromising in their beliefs (John 8:31–47); or (2) Jews who refused to embrace the Messiah and His Church (Rom. 2:28; Gal. 6:15).

2:10, 11 The persecution would be completed in **ten days** (a limited time, probably not to be taken literally) and some could undergo martyrdom. Christ encourages faithfulness to the end. The **crown of life,** an allusion to the wreath awarded to a victor in an arena (Phil. 3:14; 2 Tim. 2:5; 1 Pet. 5:4), is the reward of eternal life granted to those who conquer in Christ. The **second death** (v. 11) indicates eternal damnation, the "lake of fire," wherein sinners will receive their reward of final and lasting estrangement from God (20:6, 14, 15; 21:8).

2:12 Pergamos (modern Bergama), northeast of Smyrna, was a distinguished city built on top of a 1,000 foot hill 10 miles inland from the Aegean Sea. It boasted of an outstanding library (the word "parchment" is derived from its name). Four important pagan cults were centered there, and emperor worship was popular. The **sharp two-edged sword** is the Lord's two-edged message of terror to some and of joy to others—the just judgment of God.

2:13 Satan's throne refers to the city as a seat for idol worship. Pergamos was the first city in Asia to build a temple dedicated to the worship of a living emperor. Hence, *Satan's throne,* where he holds court, can also indicate the altar where Caesar was worshiped as Lord, and/or where the Roman governor sat in his judgment seat, dealing out capital punishment by the "law of the sword." According to tradition, the early martyr **Antipas** was bishop of Pergamos and was martyred in A.D.92 by being burned to death inside a heated bronze bull, having witnessed before the Roman governor that Jesus is Lord.

2:14 A group in this church holds **the doctrine of Balaam.** Balaam is the biblical prototype of all corrupt teachers and religious compromisers. He encouraged immorality, idolatrous feasting and infidelity against the Lord (Num. 22—24; 25:1–3; 31:16; 2 Pet. 2:15; Jude 11).

15 "Thus you also have those who
hold the doctrine of the Nicolaitans,
[1]which thing I hate.
16 "Repent, or else I will come to
you quickly and [a]will fight against
them with the sword of My mouth.†
17 "He who has an ear, let him
hear what the Spirit says to the
churches. To him who overcomes I
will give some of the hidden [a]manna
to eat. And I will give him a white
stone, and on the stone [b]a new name
written which no one knows except
him who receives *it*." '†

Thyatira: Corrupt

18 "And to the [1]angel of the church
in Thyatira write,
'These things says the Son of
God, [a]who has eyes like a flame
of fire, and His feet like fine
brass:†
19 [a]"I know your works, love,
[1]service, faith, and your [2]patience;
and *as* for your works, the last *are*
more than the first.
20 "Nevertheless I have [1]a few
things against you, because you allow [2]that woman [a]Jezebel, who calls
herself a prophetess, [3]to teach and
seduce My servants [b]to commit sexual immorality and eat things sacrificed to idols.†
21 "And I gave her time [a]to [1]repent
of her sexual immorality, and she did
not repent.
22 "Indeed I will cast her into a
sickbed, and those who commit
adultery with her into great tribulation, unless they repent of [1]their
deeds.†
23 "I will kill her children with
death, and all the churches shall
know that I am He who [a]searches[1]
the minds and hearts. And I will give
to each one of you according to your
works.
24 "Now to you I say, [1]and to the
rest in Thyatira, as many as do not
have this doctrine, who have not
known the [a]depths of Satan, as they
say, [b]I [2]will put on you no other
burden.†
25 "But hold fast [a]what you have
till I come.
26 "And he who overcomes, and
keeps [a]My works until the end,
[b]to him I will give power over the
nations—

27 *'He[a] shall rule them with a rod*
of iron;
They shall be dashed to pieces
like the potter's vessels'—

as I also have received from My Father;

15 [1]NU, M *likewise.* 16 [a]2 Thess. 2:8 17 [a]Ex. 16:33, 34 [b]Rev. 3:12 18 [a]Rev. 1:14, 15 [1]Or *messenger* 19 [a]Rev. 2:2 [1]NU, M *faith, service* [2]*perseverance* 20 [a]1 Kin. 16:31; 21:25 [b]Ex. 34:15 [1]NU, M *against you that you tolerate* [2]M *your wife Jezebel* [3]NU, M *and teaches and seduces* 21 [a]Rev. 9:20; 16:9, 11 [1]NU, M *repent, and she does not want to repent of her sexual immorality.* 22 [1]NU, M *her* 23 [a]Jer. 11:20; 17:10 [1]*examines* 24 [a]2 Tim. 3:1–9 [b]Acts 15:28 [1]NU, M omit *and* [2]NU, M omit *will* 25 [a]Rev. 3:11 26 [a][John 6:29] [b][Matt. 19:28] 27 [a]Ps. 2:8, 9

2:16 The sword of My mouth is simply the Word of the Lord, the very articulation of which is just and righteous judgment.

2:17 Hidden manna is an allusion to the bread of heaven (or the bread of angels), the bread of the Almighty (Ex. 16:4; Ps. 78:24, 25; John 6:31–35, 48–51). To eat it is to partake of the messianic banquet in the Kingdom (Luke 22:28–30), the Eucharist of the age to come. In sharp contrast to communion with the pagan cult, it restores our original communion with God. The **white stone** upon which a **new name** is inscribed indicates a new identity with Christ. Unlike pagan amulets inscribed with mysterious formulae, the *new name* of Christ is received by His faithful at their baptismal rebirth.

2:18 Thyatira lay southeast of Pergamos and was a commercial city known for its trade guilds (Acts 16:14). Guild meetings frequently included cultic meals in their patronal temples. This was a problem for Christian tradesmen, for the meetings involved idol worship and sexual debauchery. Christ's **eyes** and **feet** allude to the vision of the Son of Man in Dan. 10.

2:20 The false prophetess is called **Jezebel** after Ahab's queen, who vigorously promoted idolatry in Israel (1 Kin. 16:29–34; 2 Kin. 9). The church in Thyatira has allowed a new *Jezebel* (a member of the Nicolaitan sect) to exert an influential "prophetic" leadership in the community, leading many of the faithful astray.

2:22, 23 Those who commit adultery (v. 22) are those who accept the teaching of the false prophetess; **her children** (v. 23) are her followers.

2:24 The depths of Satan: The infidels claimed to know deep spiritual things, but Christ labels their claims as Satanic delusion.

28 "and I will give him [a]the morning star.†
29 "He who has an ear, let him
hear what the Spirit says to the
churches." '

Sardis: Dead

3 "And to the [1]angel of the church
in Sardis write,
'These things says He who [a]has
the seven Spirits of God and the
seven stars: "I know your works,
that you have a name that you are
alive, but you are dead.†
2 "Be watchful, and strengthen
the things which remain, that are
ready to die, for I have not found
your works perfect before [1]God.†
3 [a]"Remember therefore how you
have received and heard; hold fast
and [b]repent. [c]Therefore if you will
not watch, I will come upon you
[d]as a thief, and you will not know
what hour I will come upon you.
4 [1]"You have [a]a few names
[2]even in Sardis who have not
[b]defiled their garments; and they
shall walk with Me [c]in white, for
they are worthy.†
5 "He who overcomes [a]shall be
clothed in white garments, and I will
not [b]blot out his name from the
[c]Book of Life; but [d]I will confess his
name before My Father and before
His angels.†
6 [a]"He who has an ear, let him
hear what the Spirit says to the
churches." '

Philadelphia: Faithful

7 "And to the [1]angel of the church
in Philadelphia write,
'These things says [a]He who is
holy, [b]He who is true, [c]*"He who has
the key of David,* [d]*He who opens
and no one shuts, and* [e]*shuts and
no one opens"*:†

28 [a]2 Pet. 1:19

CHAPTER 3

1 [a]Rev. 1:4, 16
[1]Or *messenger*
2 [1]NU, M *My God*
3 [a]1 Tim. 6:20
[b]Rev. 3:19
[c]Matt. 24:42, 43
[d][Rev. 16:15]
4 [a]Acts 1:15
[b][Jude 23]
[c]Rev. 4:4; 6:11
[1]NU, M *Nevertheless you*
[2]NU, M omit *even*
5 [a][Rev. 19:8]
[b]Ex. 32:32
[c]Phil. 4:3
[d]Luke 12:8
6 [a]Rev. 2:7
7 [a]Acts 3:14
[b]1 John 5:20
[c]Is. 9:7; 22:22
[d][Matt. 16:19]
[e]Job 12:14

[1]Or *messenger*

2:28 The morning star is Christ Himself (22:16). He is the Dayspring from on high (Luke 1:78; see 2 Pet. 1:19), the true Light which enlightens all who come into the world (John 1:9). The phrase may also refer to eternal life and a share in the reign of Christ.

3:1 Sardis, 30 miles southeast of Thyatira, was known for its wealth and unassailable fortifications. It was an ancient city, once very powerful, but by the first century it had fallen into decline. The church there was also in decline, not falling into heresy or immorality, but into death. For the church in Sardis had so completely compromised with the surrounding pagan world that although it appeared to be **alive,** it was spiritually **dead** (Matt. 21:19). There is irony in Christ's accusation: Sardis boasted of a venerable temple to the Asiatic mother-goddess Cybele, who was purportedly able to restore the dead to life. The earliest recorded interpreter of Revelation, St. Melito, was bishop of Sardis around A.D. 190.

In the letter to Ephesus (2:1–7), the **seven stars** represented the angels who guided the churches. The **seven Spirits of God** is an expression indicating the fullness of God's powerful presence in the Church, or an allusion to the sevenfold operation of the Spirit of God spoken of by Isaiah (11:2), a connection proposed by St. Justin (Dial. 87).

3:2 Christ's exhortation to vigilance would be especially relevant to the citizens of Sardis. Though its fortress was considered impregnable, the city was overconfident and had twice fallen because of the failure of its guards to **be watchful.**

3:4, 5 White garments: basic vestments for priests, a symbol of the resurrected body. They also symbolize spiritual purity, victory and love; immersion or baptism into New Life in Christ; immortality; and a place at the messianic wedding banquet (Matt. 22:11–14).

3:5 The Book of Life (13:8; 17:8; 20:12, 15; Ex. 32:32; Luke 10:20) is God's register naming all who will inherit eternal life. By the fourth century, the Church had the custom of enrolling the names of the catechumens in a church record book termed "The Heavenly Book," or "The Book of the Church," at the beginning of Lent (see Theodore of Mopsuestia, Sts. John Chrysostom and Gregory of Nyssa). The Son speaks of His **Father** and **His angels,** but He also calls them His own angels (Matt. 13:41; 24:31), showing His equality with the Father.

3:7 Philadelphia (modern Alashehier) was a smaller and newer city than the other six, situated 30 miles southeast of Sardis. **The key of David** (Is. 22:22) is a messianic reference to the One who may judge in God's Name and admit or exclude from the City of David, the New Jerusalem, which is the Church (see Eph. 1:22). St. Ignatius calls Christ "the Door to the Father" (Ign. Phil. 9:1).

8 [a]"I know your works. See, I
have set before you [b]an open door,
[1]and no one can shut it; for you have
a little strength, have kept My word,
and have not denied My name.†
9 "Indeed I will make [a]*those* of the
synagogue of Satan, who say they
are Jews and are not, but lie—indeed
[b]I will make them come and worship
before your feet, and to know that I
have loved you.†
10 "Because you have kept [1]My
command to persevere, [a]I also will
keep you from the hour of trial which
shall come upon [b]the whole world,
to test those who dwell [c]on the
earth.†
11 [1]"Behold, [a]I am coming quickly!
[b]Hold fast what you have, that no
one may take [c]your crown.
12 "He who overcomes, I will
make him [a]a pillar in the temple of
My God, and he shall [b]go out no
more. [c]I will write on him the name
of My God and the name of the city
of My God, the [d]New Jerusalem,
which [e]comes down out of heaven
from My God. [f]And *I will write on*
him My new name.†
13 [a]"He who has an ear, let him
hear what the Spirit says to the
churches." '

Laodicea: Lukewarm

14 "And to the [1]angel of the church
[2]of the Laodiceans write,
[a]'These things says the Amen,
[b]the Faithful and True Witness,
[c]the Beginning of the creation of
God:†
15 [a]"I know your works, that you
are neither cold nor hot. I could wish
you were cold or hot.†
16 "So then, because you are luke-

8 [a]Rev. 3:1 [b]1 Cor. 16:9 [1]NU, M *which no one can shut* **9** [a]Rev. 2:9 [b]Is. 45:14; 49:23; 60:14 **10** [a]2 Pet. 2:9 [b]Luke 2:1 [c]Is. 24:17 [1]Lit. *the word of My patience* **11** [a]Phil. 4:5 [b]Rev. 2:25 [c][Rev. 2:10] [1]NU, M omit *Behold* **12** [a]1 Kin. 7:21 [b]Ps. 23:6 [c][Rev. 14:1; 22:4] [d][Heb. 12:22] [e]Rev. 21:2 [f][Rev. 2:17; 22:4] **13** [a]Rev. 2:7 **14** [a]2 Cor. 1:20 [b]Rev. 1:5; 3:7; 19:11 [c][Col. 1:15] [1]Or *messenger* [2]NU, M *in Laodicea* **15** [a]Rev. 3:1

3:8 The Philadelphians had probably been excommunicated from the local synagogue, hence Christ's assurance of an **open door** to His Kingdom.

3:9 **Worship** here is better translated "bow down." Jesus will force the unbelieving Jews to humble themselves before the Philadelphian Christians, but not literally to worship them.

3:10 To those faithful to Him, the Lord Jesus will in turn be faithful during the **hour of trial** which will come to **the whole world** by preserving them through that trial (see John 17:15) and protecting them from demonic assaults. Although the faithful will not be rescued from sufferings, persecution and martyrdom, they will be sustained and supported so as to persevere in their faithfulness. The *hour of trial* is an apocalyptic image (Dan. 12:2; John 17:6, 15; 2 Thess. 2:1–12), referring to the testing and tribulation (chs. 8; 9; 16) preceding the manifestation of the eternal Kingdom of God. **Those who dwell on the earth** is a commonly used term for the ungodly.

3:12 The coming down of the **New Jerusalem** represents the union of heaven and earth and the liberation of all creation from bondage. A **pillar** indicates permanence; **My new name** is Christ's full revelation at His Second and glorious Coming.

3:14 Laodicea (modern Eski-hisar) was 40 miles southeast of Philadelphia on the same road. It was the most prosperous city of the area, boasting a special type of wool, a large banking industry, and a famous medical school. Many Jews lived there. Paul wrote a letter to Laodicea (which no longer exists, unless it was identical to what we know as Ephesians) to be exchanged with the Colossians (see Col. 4:16).

Amen is a divine title applied here to Christ, who is the final ratification and accomplishment of the promise of God (2 Cor. 1:19, 20). This title affirms His sureness and steadfastness, amplified by the title **Faithful and True Witness.** The word **Beginning** (Gr. *arche*) has been seized upon by ancient Arians and modern Jehovah's Witnesses who attempt to prove Christ is created, thus denying His eternal existence. However, the term is more accurately translated as "source" or "origin," signifying He is the Master of all. Christ *the Beginning* is the principle, the source of God's creation (see John 1:1–3; 1 Cor. 8:6; Col. 1:16, 17), the creative Word and Wisdom of God.

3:15, 16 Six miles from Laodicea, hot springs at Hierapolis gave forth water that became **lukewarm** (v. 16) by the time it reached Laodicea. It was contaminated with many minerals, impossible to drink and nauseating. The Laodiceans are lukewarm in spiritual fervor and good works; their lack of commitment is revolting to the Lord, who would have them go one way or the other.

warm, and neither [1]cold nor hot, I
will vomit you out of My mouth.
17 "Because you say, [a]'I am rich,
have become wealthy, and have
need of nothing'—and do not know
that you are wretched, miserable,
poor, blind, and naked—†
18 "I counsel you [a]to buy from Me
gold refined in the fire, that you may
be rich; and [b]white garments, that
you may be clothed, *that* the shame
of your nakedness may not be revealed; and anoint your eyes with
eye salve, that you may see.
19 [a]"As many as I love, I rebuke
and [b]chasten.[1] Therefore be [2]zealous
and repent.
20 "Behold, [a]I stand at the door
and knock. [b]If anyone hears My
voice and opens the door, [c]I will
come in to him and dine with him,
and he with Me.†
21 "To him who overcomes [a]I will
grant to sit with Me on My throne,
as I also overcame and sat down with
My Father on His throne.†
22 [a]"He who has an ear, let him
hear what the Spirit says to the
churches." ' "

16 [1]NU, M *hot nor cold*
17 [a]Hos. 12:8
18 [a]Is. 55:1 [b]2 Cor. 5:3
19 [a]Job 5:17 [b]Heb. 12:6 [1]*discipline* [2]*eager*
20 [a]Song 5:2 [b]Luke 12:36, 37 [c][John 14:23]
21 [a]Matt. 19:28
22 [a]Rev. 2:7

CHAPTER 4

1 [a]Ezek. 1:1 [b]Rev. 1:10
2 [a]Rev. 1:10 [b]Is. 6:1
3 [1]M omits *And He who sat there was,* making the following a description of the throne.

Heavenly Temple, Heavenly Worship

4 After these things I looked, and
behold, a door *standing* [a]open in
heaven. And the first voice which I
heard *was* like a [b]trumpet speaking
with me, saying, "Come up here,
and I will show you things which
must take place after this."†
2 Immediately [a]I was in the Spirit;
and behold, [b]a throne set in heaven,
and *One* sat on the throne.†
3 [1]And He who sat there was

3:17, 18 Preoccupation with material wealth and comfort has deadened the fervor of the Laodiceans. They have fallen into a complacent self-satisfaction which is denounced by the Physician of our souls and bodies. Christ counsels them to seek spiritual wealth, forgiveness, resurrection life, and enlightenment. He offers a loving chastisement which can bring about true healing, true and lasting riches. **Gold, white garments** and **eye salve** (v. 18) correspond to the three leading Laodicean industries.

3:20 I will . . . dine with him if there is cooperation, the synergy of an open **door.** For God does not force anyone to cooperate with Him. He keeps knocking, awaiting a response. This promise looks toward both the messianic banquet, the Wedding Supper of the Lamb of God (19:9), and the Holy Eucharist, which is a foretaste of the heavenly feast. Faithful disciples are promised they will eat and drink at table with Him (Luke 22:28–30) in the ultimate fulfillment of the Kingdom of Heaven. Note the parallels with the parable of the bridegroom (Matt. 25:1–13) and with the teaching about those who will shut themselves out of the feast of the Kingdom (Luke 13:25–30).

3:21 The one who cooperates with God **overcomes,** or conquers. Those who heed God's rebuke and chastening (v. 19) and conquer lukewarmness become "hot" in their spiritual lives (vv. 15, 16). Those who share Christ's trials will share His table and His **throne** in His kingdom (4:4; 20:4–6; 22:3–5; Luke 22:30; 2 Tim. 2:12).

4:1 After this does not refer to a chronological order within the text of chs. 1—4, but instead connects this next sequence with the initial vision, a vision which beholds past, present and future as one whole. St. John writes, as it were, from inside the eye of an apocalyptic tornado, recording glimpses of the eschatological events which whirl by. The single open **door** through the vaulted firmament (Gen. 1:7, 8) allows vision into the depths of all mysteries, the celestial throne. Since earthly events have their origin in **heaven,** true insight into history can be attained only from that vantage point (see Gen. 28:17; Ezek. 1:1; Mark 1:10; Acts 7:56). **Come up,** reminiscent of Moses' invitation from God to ascend Mt. Sinai (Ex. 19:24), is a command with liturgical overtones: to enter God's sanctuary, His "high place."

4:2, 3 God is seen in biblical visions as sitting on a **throne,** a symbol of His sovereign Lordship (Ps. 47:8; Is. 6:1; Ezek. 1:26–28; Matt. 23:22). The image of this throne occurs over 40 times in Revelation and is further described as "a great white throne" (20:11), a throne of judgment. But here His throne is surrounded by **a rainbow** (v. 3), the sign of God's everlasting covenant according to which He will not judge man again as He did at the Flood (Gen. 9:12–17). Mercy triumphs over judgment (Matt. 9:13). Thus, in the Orthodox Church, the altar table is sometimes called "the throne."

LITURGY IN THE NEW TESTAMENT CHURCH

Virtually all students of the Bible realize there was liturgical worship in Israel. Immediately after the giving of the Ten Commandments (Ex. 20:1–17), instructions for building the altar were set forth (Ex. 20:24–26). Then comes instruction concerning keeping the Sabbath (Ex. 23:10–13), the annual feasts (Ex. 23:14–19) and the various offerings and furnishings in the sanctuary (Ex. 25:1–40). Following this, chapters 26—30 deal with such matters as the design of the tabernacle, the altar, and the outer court, the priests' vestments and their consecration, and instructions for daily offerings.

Most Bible scholars also find liturgical worship in heaven, which is to be expected, since God instructed Moses to make the earthly place of worship as a "copy and shadow of the heavenly things" (Heb. 8:5; see Ex. 25:40). Heavenly worship is revealed in such passages as Isaiah 6:1–8, where we see the prophet caught up to heaven for the liturgy, and Revelation 4, which records the Apostle John's vision of heaven's liturgy.

But these same scholars often fail to see that there is also liturgy in the New Testament Church.

The key to comprehending liturgy in the New Testament is to understand the work of the High Priest, our Lord Jesus Christ, who inaugurates the New Covenant. Christ is "a priest forever" (Heb. 7:17, 21). It is unthinkable that Christ would be a priest but not serve liturgically: "forever" suggests He serves continually, without ceasing, in the heavenly tabernacle. Further, He is called not only a priest but a liturgist: "a Minister (Gr. *leitourgos,* "liturgist") of the sanctuary and of the true tabernacle which the Lord erected" (Heb. 8:2). Christian worship on earth, to be fully Christian, must mirror the worship of Christ in heaven.

Moreover, Christ is "Mediator of a better covenant" (Heb. 8:6). What is that covenant? In the words of the Lord, "This cup is the new covenant in My blood" (1 Cor. 11:25). Just as the blood of bulls and goats in the Old Covenant prefigured Christ's sacrifice to come, so the Eucharistic Feast brings to us the fullness of His New Covenant offering, completed at the Cross and fulfilled in His Resurrection. This once-for-all offering of Himself (Heb. 7:27) which He as High Priest presents at the heavenly altar, is an offering in which we participate through the Divine Liturgy in the Church. This is the worship of the New Testament Church!

Given this biblical background, a number of New Testament passages take on new meaning.

(1) *Acts 13:2:* "As they ministered to the Lord [literally, "as they were in the liturgy of the Lord"] and fasted, the Holy Spirit said, 'Now separate to Me Barnabas and Saul . . .' " We learn that (a) these two apostles were called by God during worship, and (b) the Holy Spirit speaks in a liturgical setting.

(2) *Acts 20:7:* "Now on the first day of the week, when the disciples came together to break bread, Paul, ready to depart the next day, spoke to them." Communion was held each Sunday.

(3) *Rom. 16:16:* "Greet one another with a holy kiss." A kiss of greeting was common in this ancient culture. The "holy kiss," however, was an element of the Christian liturgy which signified that the people of God were reconciled to one another, so that they might receive the Body and Blood of Christ in peace.

(4) *Eph. 5:14:* "Awake, you who sleep, arise from the dead, and Christ will give you light." Biblical scholars tell us this is an ancient baptismal hymn, already in use by the time Ephesians was written. (Note other preexisting New Testament creeds and hymns such as 1 Tim. 3:16 and 2 Tim. 2:11–13.)

(5) *Heb. 13:10:* "We have an altar" reveals the continuation of the altar in New Testament worship.

(6) *Rev. 1:10:* "I was in the Spirit on the Lord's Day." Many scholars believe John saw his vision of Christ during the Sunday liturgy, as the Lord appeared to him "in the midst of the seven lampstands" (Rev. 1:13). Lampstands would be found in the Christian sanctuary just as they were in the Hebrew temple.

[a]like a jasper and a sardius stone in
appearance; [b]and *there was* a rainbow
around the throne, in appearance
like an emerald.
4 [a]Around the throne *were*
twenty-four thrones, and on the
thrones I saw twenty-four elders sitting, [b]clothed in white [1]robes; and
they had crowns of gold on their
heads.†
5 And from the throne proceeded
[a]lightnings, [1]thunderings, and
voices. [b]Seven lamps of fire *were*
burning before the throne, which are
[c]the[2] seven Spirits of God.
6 Before the throne *there* [1]*was*
[a]a sea of glass, like crystal. [b]And in
the midst of the throne, and around
the throne, *were* four living creatures
full of eyes in front and in back.†
7 [a]The first living creature *was* like
a lion, the second living creature like
a calf, the third living creature had
a face like a man, and the fourth living creature *was* like a flying eagle.
8 *The* four living creatures, each
having [a]six wings, were full of eyes
around and within. And they do not
rest day or night, saying:†

[b]"Holy,[1] holy, holy,
[c]Lord God Almighty,
[d]Who was and is and is to come!"

9 Whenever the living creatures
give glory and honor and thanks to
Him who sits on the throne, [a]who
lives forever and ever,
10 [a]the twenty-four elders fall
down before Him who sits on the
throne and worship Him who lives
forever and ever, and cast their
crowns before the throne, saying:†

3 [a]Rev. 21:11 [b]Ezek. 1:28
4 [a]Rev. 11:16 [b]Rev. 3:4, 5 [1]NU, M *robes, with crowns*
5 [a]Rev. 8:5; 11:19; 16:18 [b]Ex. 37:23 [c][Rev. 1:4] [1]NU, M *voices, and thunderings.* [2]M omits *the*
6 [a]Rev. 15:2 [b]Ezek. 1:5 [1]NU, M add *something like*
7 [a]Ezek. 1:10; 10:14
8 [a]Is. 6:2 [b]Is. 6:3 [c]Rev. 1:8 [d]Rev. 1:4 [1]M has *holy* nine times.
9 [a]Rev. 1:18
10 [a]Rev. 5:8, 14; 7:11; 11:16; 19:4

4:4 The **twenty-four elders** are usually interpreted to be elders of the Old and New Covenants: the twelve sons of Jacob and the Twelve Apostles, the fullness of both covenants. They are the foundation of the people of God (7:4; Matt. 19:28). These elders continually fall down before God in worship, adoration and praise (4:11; 5:9, 10, 14; 11:16–18; 19:4).

4:6, 7 The **sea of glass, like crystal** (see Ezek. 1:22–26) surrounding God's throne has a double significance: (1) God is approached by fallen men only through waters of death which produce life. As Israel journeyed through the Red Sea as if on hard ground, so Christians pass through the waters of baptism, entering into Christ's death and Resurrection. If the *sea* is not of *glass* (that is, hard as solid ground), there is death, not new life. (2) God is vast and overpowering, as a sea of light would be. The hosts of angels surround Him (Dan. 7:10) as a sea of purity.

The **four living creatures** are angelic beings similar to those of Ezekiel (Ezek. 1:5, 21) and Isaiah (Is. 6:2). Their number is representative of the whole world, the cosmos; thus the living creatures portray creation—beasts, men and angels—as the Kingdom of God. Traditional iconography depicts them as symbols for the four evangelists (Matthew—man, Mark—lion, Luke—calf, John—eagle). Their worship of God is unceasing, an ideal which inspires the around-the-clock services of Orthodox monastic communities.

4:8 The **six wings** (Is. 6:2) may symbolize the swiftness with which God's will is enacted in His world. **Full of eyes around and within** (see the wheels of Ezek. 1:18) indicates the absolute vigilance of these creatures. **They do not rest day or night** suggests the essence of their ceaseless activity: to praise God (the very liturgy which the whole cosmos is called to make) and pray without ceasing (Ps. 103:20–22; 148; 150; 1 Thess. 5:17).

Their hymn, **Holy, holy, holy,** like that of Isaiah's seraphim (Is. 6:3), praises God who is Lord of history and fills heaven and earth with His glory. Isaiah's doxology was part of synagogue worship and was incorporated into the worship of the Church (1 Clem. 34:6, 7). Another form of this hymn, the Trisagion ("Holy God, Holy Mighty, Holy Immortal, have mercy on us!") reverberates throughout the services of the Orthodox Church. Ambrose wrote a similar hymn, the "Te Deum." The Eucharistic Prayer of the Divine Liturgies of Sts. John Chrysostom, Basil, and James refers to the perpetual thrice-holy hymn of the "cherubim and the seraphim," thus blending the visions of Ezekiel, Isaiah, and St. John, and underscoring that the Divine Liturgy on earth is one with the heavenly liturgy of the angels and glorified saints.

4:10 The elders participate in the heavenly worship through the physical acts of prostration (falling down; see 1 Kin. 11:16) and casting down **their crowns.** Prostration, a significant feature of historic Christian worship, is based in Scripture and signifies humility before God. The casting of *crowns* shows that the honor and glory of the saints derives from, and belongs to, God.

11 "You[a] are worthy, [1]O Lord,
To receive glory and honor and
power;
[b]For You created all things,
And by [c]Your will they
[2]exist and were created."†

The Lamb Opens the Scroll

5 And I saw in the right *hand* of
Him who sat on the throne
[a]a scroll written inside and on the
back, [b]sealed with seven seals.†
2 Then I saw a strong angel proclaiming with a loud voice, [a]"Who
is worthy to open the scroll and to
loose its seals?"†
3 And no one in heaven or on the
earth or under the earth was able to
open the scroll, or to look at it.
4 So I wept much, because no one
was found worthy to open [1]and read
the scroll, or to look at it.
5 But one of the elders said to me,
"Do not weep. Behold, [a]the Lion of
the tribe of [b]Judah, [c]the Root of David, has [d]prevailed to open the scroll
[e]and [1]to loose its seven seals."
6 And I looked, [1]and behold, in
the midst of the throne and of the
four living creatures, and in the
midst of the elders, stood [a]a Lamb
as though it had been slain, having
seven horns and [b]seven eyes, which
are [c]the seven Spirits of God sent
out into all the earth.†
7 Then He came and took the
scroll out of the right hand [a]of Him
who sat on the throne.
8 Now when He had taken the
scroll, [a]the four living creatures and
the twenty-four elders fell down
before the Lamb, each having a
harp, and golden bowls full of incense, which are the [b]prayers of the
saints.†

11 [a]Rev. 1:6; 5:12 [b]Gen. 1:1 [c]Col. 1:16 [1]NU, M *our Lord and God* [2]NU, M *existed*

CHAPTER 5

1 [a]Ezek. 2:9, 10 [b]Is. 29:11
2 [a]Rev. 4:11; 5:9
4 [1]NU, M omit *and read*
5 [a]Gen. 49:9 [b]Heb. 7:14 [c]Is. 11:1, 10 [d]Rev. 3:21 [e]Rev. 6:1 [1]NU, M omit *to loose*
6 [a][John 1:29] [b]Zech. 3:9; 4:10 [c]Rev. 1:4; 3:1; 4:5

[1]NU, M *I saw in the midst . . . a Lamb standing* 7 [a]Rev. 4:2 8 [a]Rev. 4:8–10; 19:4 [b]Rev. 8:3

4:11 This doxology (glorification of God) is typical of many in the Apocalypse. It is offered to the Father and to Christ. Doxologies are a prominent aspect of Orthodox Liturgy, ascribing **glory, honor,** and **power** to God.

5:1 The **scroll** contains the secret decrees of God concerning the judgment and salvation of humanity (see Ps. 139:16; Ezek. 2:10). Included in it is the greatest of all mysteries—God's will concerning the events of the end times (see Dan. 10:21), sealed up securely **with seven seals** until the time comes for it to be fulfilled. In the 23 references to scrolls or books in Revelation there are five types: (1) the unsealed letters to the churches of Asia (chs. 2; 3); (2) the unsealed Book of Life (13:8); (3) the unsealed books of judgment (20:12); (4) the little book which is eaten (10:8–10); and (5) the present sealed scroll.

5:2–5 Who can know the mysteries of **the scroll** and the **seals**? Who but Christ, the Son of God Himself, can understand the greatest of all mysteries and how God deals with man in history? **The Lion of . . . Judah** and **Root of David** are messianic titles with parallels in the OT and apocryphal books (see Gen. 49:9, 10; Is. 11:1–10). The One who has conquered Satan decisively, once and for all, in His self-sacrifice on the Cross and in His Resurrection, is alone **worthy** to open the scroll of destiny, reveal its message, and carry out its words.

5:6, 7 Jesus is called the **Lamb** of God in John 1:29. Isaiah compares the Messiah's voluntary self-sacrifice to a lamb being led to slaughter (Is. 53). The central theme of Revelation is victory through sacrifice. This *lamb* stands between **the throne, the four living creatures,** and **the elders.** St. Ignatius (Ign. Magn. 3:1; 6:1) refers to the bishop standing at the center of his flock, as an image of both the Father and the Son. In the development of episcopal vesture, the bishop's outer garment was for a time woven of wool to image the Lamb. **Seven horns** and **seven eyes** represent the fullness of Christ's power and knowledge; through Him also the Holy Spirit (**the seven Spirits of God**) is sent upon His mission to the world. Intertestamental Jewish apocalyptic literature portrayed the Messiah as a horned lamb who would fight for His people and conquer the forces of evil. The Jews, however, never expected this warrior-lamb to suffer and die, and did not consider Him to be God. The warrior-lamb is both with God (**in the midst of the throne**) and with man (**in the midst of the elders**), for He is the union of God and man without the merging of the two natures.

5:8 The four angelic beings, (**living creatures**), and the glorified saints of all ages represented by **the twenty-four elders,** worship Jesus, thus recognizing His deity. And they present

(continued on next page)

9 And [a]they sang a new song, saying:

[b]"You are worthy to take the scroll,
And to open its seals;
For You were slain,
And [c]have redeemed us to God
[d]by Your blood
Out of every tribe and tongue
and people and nation,†
10 And have made [1]us [a]kings[2] and
[b]priests to our God;
And [3]we shall reign on the
earth."

11 Then I looked, and I heard the
voice of many angels around the
throne, the living creatures, and
the elders; and the number of them
was ten thousand times ten thousand, and thousands of thousands,
12 saying with a loud voice:

"Worthy is the Lamb who was
slain
To receive power and riches and
wisdom,
And strength and honor and
glory and blessing!"

13 And [a]every creature which is in
heaven and on the earth and under
the earth and such as are in the sea,
and all that are in them, I heard
saying:

[b]"Blessing and honor and glory
and power
Be to Him [c]who sits on the
throne,
And to the Lamb, forever and
[1]ever!"

14 Then the four living creatures
said, "Amen!" And the [1]twenty-four
elders fell down and worshiped
[2]Him who lives forever and ever.

Seal One: The Conqueror

6 Now [a]I saw when the Lamb
opened one of the [1]seals; and I
heard [b]one of the four living creatures saying with a voice like thunder, "Come and see."†
2 And I looked, and behold,
[a]a white horse. [b]He who sat on it
had a bow; [c]and a crown was given
to him, and he went out [d]conquering
and to conquer.†

9 [a]Rev. 14:3 [b]Rev. 4:11 [c]John 1:29 [d][Heb. 9:12]
10 [a]Ex. 19:6 [b]Is. 61:6 [1]NU, M *them* [2]NU *a kingdom* [3]NU, M *they*
13 [a]Phil. 2:10 [b]1 Chr. 29:11 [c]Rev. 4:2, 3; 6:16; 20:11 [1]M adds *Amen*
14 [1]NU, M omit *twenty-four* [2]NU, M omit *Him who lives forever and ever*

CHAPTER 6
1 [a][Rev. 5:5–7, 12; 13:8] [b]Rev. 4:7 [1]NU, M *seven seals*
2 [a]Zech. 1:8; 6:3 [b]Ps. 45:4, 5, LXX [c]Zech. 6:11 [d]Matt. 24:5

(continued from previous page)
the prayers of the saints still on earth, manifested in the **incense,** to God (8:3, 4; see Ps. 141:2). In the ancient world, incense was used in both secular and liturgical life. Altars, people, and objects were censed as a sign of honor and dedication. In the services of the Church, incense is also a symbol of prayer.

5:9–14 Three doxologies are sung by successively greater choruses. (1) The elders with the most eminent angels sing **a new song,** more perfect than any hymn before, to the Lamb (Christ), for He has inaugurated the new age (21:1, 5; Is. 42:9). (2) The Church joined by all the holy angels—much as the priests are followed by the choir and then by the entire Church—sends up to the Lamb a fullness of divine ascriptions in a sevenfold doxology (v. 12). (3) All creation, the whole cosmos, joins in a hymn of glory addressed to the Father and to the Son. When we sing to God in the Divine Liturgy, we "represent the cherubim," who are singing to Him in heaven. The Church has always been first and foremost a worshiping community, with the Divine Liturgy empowering and inspiring evangelism, social service, instruction and all other activities.

6:1–17 With the Lamb's opening of the seals, John begins a description of the "signs of the end" (Matt. 24:3), much of it already set forth by Jesus in the Gospels (Matt. 24; Mark 13; Luke 21). The seals are consequences of man's condition, an overview of conditions manifest since the birth of the Church and which will continue until Christ's Second Coming. The four horsemen (see Zech. 1:8–17; 6:1–8 for the model of this imagery) personify the scourges which, through the prophets, God has threatened as judgment upon the faithless: war, famine, plague, and natural disasters.

6:2 The first rider (on the **white horse,** carrying a **bow**) represents the spirit of conquest, reminiscent of fierce divine judgment in the OT, usually wrought through the military power of adversaries (Ps. 46:9; Jer. 51:56; Ezek. 5:16; Hab. 3:8, 9). Jesus taught "nation will rise against nation" (Matt. 24:7). The presence of the figure here probably represents liberators of the oppressed people of God.

Seal Two: Conflict on Earth

3 When He opened the second seal, [a]I heard the second living creature saying, "Come [1]and see."†

4 [a]Another horse, fiery red, went out. And it was granted to the one who sat on it to [b]take peace from the earth, and that *people* should kill one another; and there was given to him a great sword.

Seal Three: Scarcity on Earth

5 When He opened the third seal, [a]I heard the third living creature say, "Come and see." So I looked, and behold, [b]a black horse, and he who sat on it had a pair of [c]scales[1] in his hand.†

6 And I heard a voice in the midst of the four living creatures saying, "A [1]quart of wheat for a [2]denarius, and three quarts of barley for a denarius; and [a]do not harm the oil and the wine."

Seal Four: Widespread Death

7 When He opened the fourth seal, [a]I heard the voice of the fourth living creature saying, "Come and see."†

8 [a]So I looked, and behold, a pale horse. And the name of him who sat on it was Death, and Hades followed with him. And [1]power was given to them over a fourth of the earth, [b]to kill with sword, with hunger, with death, [c]and by the beasts of the earth.

Seal Five: Cry of the Martyrs

9 When He opened the fifth seal, I saw under [a]the altar [b]the souls of those who had been slain [c]for the word of God and for [d]the testimony which they held.†

10 And they cried with a loud voice, saying, [a]"How long, O Lord, [b]holy and true, [c]until You judge and avenge our blood on those who dwell on the earth?"

11 Then a [a]white robe was given to each of them; and it was said to them [b]that they should rest a little while longer, until both *the number of* their fellow servants and their brethren, who would be killed as they *were,* was completed.

Seal Six: Cosmic Disturbances

12 I looked when He opened the sixth seal, [a]and [1]behold, there was a great earthquake; and [b]the sun be-

3 [a]Rev. 4:7 [1]NU, M omit *and see*
4 [a]Zech. 1:8; 6:2 [b]Matt. 24:6, 7
5 [a]Rev. 4:7 [b]Zech. 6:2, 6 [c]Matt. 24:7 [1]*balances*
6 [a]Rev. 7:3; 9:4 [1]Gr. *choinix,* about 1 quart [2]About 1 day's wage for a worker
7 [a]Rev. 4:7
8 [a]Zech. 6:3 [b]Ezek. 5:12, 17; 14:21; 29:5 [c]Lev. 26:22 [1]*authority*
9 [a]Rev. 8:3 [b][Rev. 20:4] [c]Rev. 1:2, 9 [d]2 Tim. 1:8
10 [a]Zech. 1:12 [b]Rev. 3:7 [c]Rev. 11:18
11 [a]Rev. 3:4, 5; 7:9 [b]Heb. 11:40
12 [a]Matt. 24:7 [b]Joel 2:10, 31; 3:15 [1]NU, M omit *behold*

6:3, 4 The second rider represents war, violent bloodshed and death—removal of **peace from the earth,** the result of the conquests of the first rider. Jesus predicted there will be "wars and rumors of war" (Matt. 24:6, 7).

6:5, 6 The third rider represents famine and inflation, a frequent accompaniment of war.

6:7, 8 The fourth horseman represents widespread human **death, pale** green being the color of rotting flesh. Pestilence and starvation follow the famine of warfare.

6:9–11 The cry of the martyrs for vengeance is not vindictive; they are pleading with God to hasten the end of persecution and the consummation of His plans for the world. In the interim, the martyrs are consoled by the **white robe** (v. 11)—a Jewish symbol of resurrection from the dead. Elsewhere it is a symbol of blessedness, good deeds, innocence, victory, purity, new and eternal life, transfiguration, a resurrected and glorified body, being clothed with Christ, and the wedding garment of salvation (3:5; 7:9, 13–17; 19:8, 9; Ex. 28:4; Is. 61:10; Dan. 10:5; Matt. 22:1–4; Gal. 3:27). The martyrs are called to have patience until the fullness of their number is complete. The vision of **the souls** of the martyrs **under the altar** (v. 9) is derived from the OT practice of pouring the blood (the physical manifestation of the life of the soul) of sin offerings at the base of the altar of burnt offering. It is a basis for the historic Christian practices of building church buildings over tombs of martyrs, placing relics of saints in the altar when a church is consecrated, and burying baptized people under the altar. Thus, in the Divine Liturgy Orthodox Christians remember "those who lie asleep here, and in all the world."

came black as sackcloth of hair, and
the [2]moon became like blood.†
13 [a]And the stars of heaven fell to
the earth, as a fig tree drops its late
figs when it is shaken by a mighty
wind.
14 [a]Then the sky [1]receded as a
scroll when it is rolled up, and
[b]every mountain and island was
moved out of its place.
15 And the [a]kings of the earth, the
great men, [1]the rich men, the commanders,
the mighty men, every
slave and every free man, [b]hid themselves
in the caves and in the rocks
of the mountains,
16 [a]and said to the mountains and
rocks, "Fall on us and hide us from
the face of Him who [b]sits on the
throne and from the wrath of the
Lamb!
17 "For the great day of His wrath
has come, [a]and who is able to
stand?"

Angels Visit Earth

7 After these things I saw four angels
standing at the four corners
of the earth, [a]holding the four winds
of the earth, [b]that the wind should
not blow on the earth, on the sea,
or on any tree.†
2 Then I saw another angel ascending
from the east, having the
seal of the living God. And he cried
with a loud voice to the four angels
to whom it was granted to harm the
earth and the sea,
3 saying, [a]"Do not harm the
earth, the sea, or the trees till we
have sealed the servants of our God
[b]on their foreheads."
4 [a]And I heard the number of
those who were sealed. [b]One hundred
and forty-four thousand [c]of all
the tribes of the children of Israel
were sealed:†

Sealing God's Servants

5 of the tribe of Judah
twelve thousand *were* sealed;
of the tribe of Reuben
twelve thousand *were* [1]sealed;
of the tribe of Gad
twelve thousand *were* sealed;
6 of the tribe of Asher
twelve thousand *were* sealed;
of the tribe of Naphtali
twelve thousand *were* sealed;
of the tribe of Manasseh
twelve thousand *were* sealed;
7 of the tribe of Simeon
twelve thousand *were* sealed;
of the tribe of Levi
twelve thousand *were* sealed;
of the tribe of Issachar
twelve thousand *were* sealed;
8 of the tribe of Zebulun
twelve thousand *were* sealed;
of the tribe of Joseph
twelve thousand *were* sealed;
of the tribe of Benjamin
twelve thousand *were* sealed.

12 [2]NU, M *whole moon*
13 [a]Matt. 24:29; Mark 13:25; Rev. 8:10; 9:1
14 [a]Ps. 102:26; Is. 34:4; [2 Pet. 3:10]; Rev. 20:11; 21:1 [b]Jer. 3:23; Rev. 16:20 [1]Or *split apart*
15 [a]Ps. 2:2–4 [b]Is. 2:10, 19, 21; 24:21; Rev. 19:18 [1]NU, M *the commanders, the rich men,*
16 [a]Hos. 10:8; Luke 23:29, 30; Rev. 9:6 [b]Rev. 20:11
17 [a]Is. 63:4; Jer. 30:7; Joel 1:15; 2:1, 11, 31; Zeph. 1:14; Rev. 16:14

CHAPTER 7

1 [a]Jer. 49:36; Dan. 7:2; Zech. 6:5; Matt. 24:31 [b]Rev. 7:3; 8:7; 9:4
3 [a]Rev. 6:6 [b]Ezek. 9:4, 6; Rev. 22:4
4 [a]Rev. 9:16 [b]Rev. 14:1, 3 [c]Gen. 49:1–27
5 [1]NU, M omit *sealed* in vv. 5b–8b.

6:12–17 The sixth seal presents the cosmic disturbances that often accompany descriptions of "the day of the Lord," the return of Christ (Joel 2:30, 31; Matt. 24:29, 30). People in rebellion against God (v. 15) are terror-stricken before God's judgmental wrath.

7:1–17 The seventh (and final) seal will yet be opened (8:1). The visions here of the faithful Church form an interlude, wherein the Lord's faithful are "sealed" against His wrath. "Who is able to stand" (6:17)? The faithful, who will be sealed and will then assemble for worship.

7:1–3 The four winds are symbolic "winds of judgment," as in Jewish apocalyptic literature (Is. 11:12; Dan. 8:8; Zech. 2:6; Mark 13:27). They are restrained until God's **servants** (Is. 44:5; 2 Cor. 1:22; 2 Tim. 2:19) are **sealed** (v. 3), that is, given a special protection from the ensuing judgments (Ezek. 9:1–11).

7:4–8 The servants of God are **sealed** (v. 4) by the Holy Spirit. Extensive debates have taken place regarding the meaning of the 144,000. Some regard the number as symbolizing the entire faithful Church as the new Israel (12 tribes × the churches of the 12 apostles × 1,000—a number which means "a great amount"). Thus, the contention is that the number simply stands for completeness and perfection: 12 × 12 equals the perfect square. In a slightly different view, some see the 144,000 as the Church militant (the Church on earth), and the white-robed multitude (vv. 9, 10) as the Church triumphant (those who have fallen asleep).

Final Ingathering and Worship

9 After these things I looked, and behold, [a]a great multitude which no one could number, [b]of all nations, tribes, peoples, and tongues, standing before the throne and before the Lamb, [c]clothed with white robes, with palm branches in their hands,†

10 and crying out with a loud voice, saying, [a]"Salvation *belongs* to our God [b]who sits on the throne, and to the Lamb!"

11 [a]All the angels stood around the throne and the elders and the four living creatures, and fell on their faces before the throne and [b]worshiped God,

12 [a]saying:

"Amen! Blessing and glory and
wisdom,
Thanksgiving and honor and
power and might,
Be to our God forever and ever.
Amen."

13 Then one of the elders answered, saying to me, "Who are these arrayed in [a]white robes, and where did they come from?"

14 And I said to him, [1]"Sir, you know." So he said to me, [a]"These are the ones who come out of the great tribulation, and [b]washed their robes and made them white in the blood of the Lamb.

15 "Therefore they are before the throne of God, and serve Him day and night in His temple. And He who sits on the throne will [a]dwell among them.†

16 [a]"They shall neither hunger anymore nor thirst anymore; [b]the sun shall not strike them, nor any heat;

17 "for the Lamb who is in the midst of the throne [a]will shepherd them and lead them to [1]living fountains of waters. [b]And God will wipe away every tear from their eyes."

Seal Seven: Prelude to the Trumpets

8 When[a] He opened the seventh seal, there was silence in heaven for about half an hour.†

2 [a]And I saw the seven angels who stand before God, [b]and to them were given seven trumpets.†

3 Then another angel, having a golden censer, came and stood at the altar. He was given much incense, that he should offer *it* with [a]the prayers of all the saints upon [b]the golden altar which was before the throne.†

9 [a]Rom. 11:25 [b]Rev. 5:9 [c]Rev. 3:5, 18; 4:4; 6:11
10 [a]Ps. 3:8 [b]Rev. 5:13
11 [a]Rev. 4:6 [b]Rev. 4:11; 5:9, 12, 14; 11:16
12 [a]Rev. 5:13, 14
13 [a]Rev. 7:9
14 [a]Rev. 6:9 [b][Heb. 9:14] [1]NU, M *My lord*
15 [a]Is. 4:5, 6
16 [a]Is. 49:10 [b]Ps. 121:6
17 [a]Ps. 23:1 [b]Rev. 21:4 [1]NU, M *fountains of the waters of life*

CHAPTER 8
1 [a]Rev. 6:1
2 [a][Matt. 18:10] [b]2 Chr. 29:25–28
3 [a]Rev. 5:8 [b]Ex. 30:1

7:9–14 The scene shifts to heaven, where an innumerable **multitude** from **all nations** worships before the throne of God. Their **white robes** and **palm branches** (v. 9) symbolize purity and victory. The vast *multitude* represents either the entire faithful Church that lives in the spirit of its baptism (**washed . . . in the blood of the Lamb,** v. 14), or the righteous from all nations who were not members of the "12 × 12 × 1,000," Old Covenant Israel and the Church. These pass victoriously through the great tribulation to inherit the Kingdom. See also note on 22:14.

7:15–17 The heavenly life is pictured as one of unending worship, **day and night** (v. 15), from which all suffering has been banished. Here we have the ultimate sanctification of time, the consecration of all life to the service and worship of God, carried out along with the heavenly hosts. Isaiah 49:10 inspires the statement of v. 16. John's descriptions of the victorious Church and the blessings of heaven were written to encourage and console Christians of the first century who faced severe persecution for their faith—and His faithful of all generations may find consolation in them as well.

8:1–4 The **silence** (v. 1), **trumpets** (v. 2) and offering of **incense** (vv. 3, 4) were features of the Jewish temple liturgy. The half-hour silence (v. 1) dramatically indicates profound awe at the opening of the seventh seal (see Hab. 2:20; Zeph. 1:7, 8; Zech. 2:13).

8:2 The **seven angels** receive the **seven trumpets.** These bodiless powers represent the OT priests, who also sounded their trumpets during the temple liturgy (see Josh. 6:13; 1 Chr. 16:6; Ps. 96:6).

8:3 Much incense is present in heaven (see 5:8). It symbolizes **the prayers of all the saints.** Incense is: (a) commanded by God to Moses for use in Israel's worship (Ex. 25:6; Is. 4:5; 6:4; Luke 1:9–11); (b) used throughout Israel's history under the Old Covenant (1 Chr. 23:13); (c) prophesied by the Lord Himself, to be used in the Church: incense will be offered "among

(continued on next page)

4 And [a]the smoke of the incense,
with the prayers of the saints, ascended before God from the angel's
hand.
5 Then the angel took the censer,
filled it with fire from the altar, and
threw *it* to the earth. And [a]there
were noises, thunderings, [b]light-
nings, [c]and an earthquake.†
6 So the seven angels who had the
seven trumpets prepared themselves
to sound.†

Trumpet One: Vegetation Struck

7 The first angel sounded: [a]And
hail and fire followed, mingled with
blood, and they were thrown [b]to the
[1]earth. And a third [c]of the trees were
burned up, and all green grass was
burned up.†

Trumpet Two: The Seas Struck

8 Then the second angel sounded:
[a]And *something* like a great mountain
burning with fire was thrown into
the sea, [b]and a third of the sea
[c]became blood.†
9 [a]And a third of the living creatures in the sea died, and a third of
the ships were destroyed.

Trumpet Three: Fresh Waters Struck

10 Then the third angel sounded:
[a]And a great star fell from heaven,
burning like a torch, [b]and it fell on
a third of the rivers and on the
springs of water.†
11 [a]The name of the star is Wormwood. [b]A third of the waters became
wormwood, and many men died
from the water, because it was made
bitter.

Trumpet Four: The Heavens Struck

12 [a]Then the fourth angel
sounded: And a third of the sun was
struck, a third of the moon, and a
third of the stars, so that a third of
them were darkened. A third of the

4 [a]Ps. 141:2
5 [a]Rev. 11:19; 16:18
[b]Rev. 4:5
[c]2 Sam. 22:8
7 [a]Ezek. 38:22
[b]Rev. 16:2
[c]Rev. 9:4, 15–18
[1]NU, M add *and a third of the earth was burned up*
8 [a]Jer. 51:25
[b]Ex. 7:17
[c]Ezek. 14:19
9 [a]Rev. 16:3
10 [a]Is. 14:12
[b]Rev. 14:7; 16:4
11 [a]Ruth 1:20
[b]Ex. 15:23

(continued from previous page)
the Gentiles in every place" (Mal. 1:11); (d) brought by the Magi as a gift to Jesus (Matt. 2:11); (e) used in Christian worship from the beginning even till today, in both East and West.

8:5 The casting of **the censer** to **the earth** (v. 5) shows that the prayers of the saints for vengeance (6:9–11) have been heard. The **thunderings** and **earthquake** signify that the judgment of God is imminent.

8:6 The **seven angels** with the **seven trumpets** form a double image of (1) the temple liturgy of the Old Covenant (2 Chr. 5:11–13) and (2) the fall of Jericho (Josh. 6).

The relationship of the "seal judgments" (5:1—8:1), "trumpet judgments" (8:2—11:19) and "bowl judgments" (15:1—16:21) in Revelation is complex. There is some repetition and summarizing. The trumpets and bowls also give increasing specificity to God's judgments. They may not describe a chronological unfolding of events or even actual events. The trumpets speak of God's final warning to the world, especially seen in the "one-third" formula, calling the world to repentance before utter destruction comes. This stage of judgment can be seen as the prelude—manifested in the natural world—to the great tribulation (Matt. 24:15–22), playing a role much like that of the ten plagues of Exodus; the end itself is "not yet." The Church is not mentioned until ch. 11, where the calamities of the earth are overcome by the Kingdom of God (11:15–19).

8:7 Only vegetation is affected by this trumpet. The seventh plague in Egypt is recalled (Ex. 9:13–33; see also Ezek. 5:12; Zech. 13:8, 9). The reference to **blood** echoes the prophecy of Joel (Joel 2:31; see Acts 2:19). **Hail, fire** and *blood* are typical features of apocalyptic pictures of judgment.

8:8, 9 This plague is like the first plague of Egypt (Ex. 7:14–25). The **sea,** marine life and maritime commerce, is affected.

8:10, 11 Reminiscent of the first Egyptian plague, this judgment affects fresh waters. **Wormwood** (in Slavonic, "chernobyl"), an extremely bitter plant that would make water undrinkable, symbolizes the bitter fruits of idolatry and sorrow to those who pursue adulterous liaisons with the heathen Gentiles (see Jer. 9:12–16; 23:15; Lam. 3:19).

day [1]did not shine, and likewise the
night.†
13 And I looked, [a]and I heard an
[1]angel flying through the midst of
heaven, saying with a loud voice,
[b]"Woe, woe, woe to the inhabitants
of the earth, because of the remaining blasts of the trumpet of the
three angels who are about to
sound!"

Trumpet Five, Woe One: The Locusts

9 Then the fifth angel sounded:
[a]And I saw a star fallen from
heaven to the earth. To him was
given the key to [b]the [1]bottomless
pit.†
2 And he opened the bottomless
pit, and smoke arose out of the pit
like the smoke of a great furnace.
So the [a]sun and the air were darkened because of the smoke of the
pit.
3 Then out of the smoke locusts
came upon the earth. And to them
was given power, [a]as the scorpions
of the earth have power.†
4 They were commanded [a]not to
harm [b]the grass of the earth, or any
green thing, or any tree, but only
those men who do not have [c]the seal
of God on their foreheads.
5 And [1]they were not given *au-*
thority to kill them, [a]but to torment
them *for* five months. Their torment
was like the torment of a scorpion
when it strikes a man.†
6 In those days [a]men will seek
death and will not find it; they will
desire to die, and death will flee from
them.
7 [a]The shape of the locusts was
like horses prepared for battle.
[b]On their heads were crowns of
something like gold, [c]and their faces
were like the faces of men.†
8 They had hair like women's
hair, and [a]their teeth were like lions'
teeth.
9 And they had breastplates like
breastplates of iron, and the sound
of their wings *was* [a]like the sound
of chariots with many horses running into battle.
10 They had tails like scorpions,
and there were stings in their tails.
Their power *was* to hurt men five
months.
11 And they had as king over them
[a]the angel of the bottomless pit,
whose name in Hebrew *is* [1]Abaddon,
but in Greek he has the name
[2]Apollyon.†

12 [a]Is. 13:10 [1]*had no light*
13 [a]Rev. 14:6; 19:17 [b]Rev. 9:12; 11:14; 12:12 [1]NU, M *eagle*

CHAPTER 9

1 [a]Rev. 8:10 [b]Luke 8:31 [1]Lit. *shaft of the abyss*
2 [a]Joel 2:2, 10
3 [a]Judg. 7:12
4 [a]Rev. 6:6 [b]Rev. 8:7 [c]Rev. 7:2, 3
5 [a][Rev. 9:10; 11:7] [1]The locusts
6 [a]Jer. 8:3
7 [a]Joel 2:4 [b]Nah. 3:17 [c]Dan. 7:8
8 [a]Joel 1:6
9 [a]Joel 2:5–7
11 [a]Eph. 2:2 [1]Lit. *Destruction* [2]Lit. *Destroyer*

8:12 A three-day period of darkness was the ninth Egyptian plague (Ex. 10:21–29). An unnatural darkness is one of the signs of the end of days (Mark 13:24). Darkening of the **sun, moon,** and **stars** portends cosmic catastrophe. The darkness is partial to indicate it is a warning.

9:1, 2 While the **star** may refer to an angel, the same angel as the one of 20:1 (such symbolism was known in Judaism: see Job 38:7; 1 Enoch 21:6), it may also be the fallen world powers, a fallen angel, or Satan himself (v. 11; Is. 14:12). His "fall" may mean "descent": an angel is sent from heaven by God to unlock **the bottomless pit,** the abyss below the earth, the place of confinement for evil spirits (11:7; 17:8; 20:1–3; also Luke 8:31). The **smoke** from the *pit* causes a darkness on the earth; this may symbolize the spiritual darkness covering the earth during the last times. Compare with 1:18, in which the key to Death and Hades is given to the Risen One.

9:3, 4 These new plagues are again reminiscent of the plagues on Egypt (see the sixth, eighth, and ninth in Ex. 9; 10). From the smoke come **locusts,** representing demonic entities who rise from the pit to torture those who do not belong to God's Kingdom. **The seal of** (the name of) **God on their foreheads** is given to the 144,000 servants (5:4; 7:2–4; 14:1; 22:3, 4 in contrast with 13:16–18) for their spiritual identity. At chrismation, Orthodox Christians receive "the seal of the gift of the Holy Spirit" by holy oil placed on their foreheads.

9:5, 6 The period of torture is limited; it is likened to the sting of the scorpion, one of the most painful known to man. Because of its intensity, the afflicted will seek death, but it is not permitted to them.

9:7–10 This is a terrifying picture of the demonic oppression of sinners in the last times.

9:11 Apollyon means "destroyer," but there may be an allusion here to the Greek god Apollo, with whom the Emperors Caligula, Nero, and Domitian claimed a relationship.

12 [a]One woe is past. Behold, still
two more woes are coming after
these things.

Trumpet Six, Woe Two: The Plagues

13 Then the sixth angel sounded:
And I heard a voice from the four
horns of the [a]golden altar which is
before God,†
14 saying to the sixth angel who
had the trumpet, "Release the four
angels who are bound [a]at the great
river Euphrates."
15 So the four angels, who had
been prepared for the hour and day
and month and year, were released
to kill a [a]third of mankind.
16 Now [a]the number of the army
[b]of the horsemen *was* two hundred
million; [c]I heard the number of
them.
17 And thus I saw the horses in
the vision: those who sat on them
had breastplates of fiery red, hyacinth blue, and sulfur yellow; [a]and
the heads of the horses *were* like the
heads of lions; and out of their
mouths came fire, smoke, and
brimstone.†
18 By these three *plagues* a third of
mankind was killed—by the fire and
the smoke and the brimstone which
came out of their mouths.
19 For [1]their power is in their
mouth and in their tails; [a]for their
tails *are* like serpents, having heads;
and with them they do harm.
20 But the rest of mankind, who
were not killed by these plagues,
[a]did not repent of the works of their
hands, that they should not worship
[b]demons, [c]and idols of gold, silver,
brass, stone, and wood, which can
neither see nor hear nor walk.†
21 And they did not repent of their
murders [a]or their [1]sorceries or their
sexual immorality or their thefts.

Mighty Angel, Little Book

10 I saw still another mighty angel coming down from
heaven, clothed with a cloud.
[a]And a rainbow *was* on [b]his head,
his face *was* like the sun, and [c]his
feet like pillars of fire.†
2 He had a little book open in his
hand. [a]And he set his right foot on
the sea and *his* left *foot* on the land,
3 and cried with a loud voice, as
when a lion roars. When he cried out,
[a]seven thunders uttered their
voices.†

12 [a]Rev. 8:13; 11:14
13 [a]Rev. 8:3
14 [a]Rev. 16:12
15 [a]Rev. 8:7–9; 9:18
16 [a]Dan. 7:10 [b]Ezek. 38:4 [c]Rev. 7:4
17 [a]Is. 5:28, 29
19 [a]Is. 9:15 [1]NU, M *the power of the horses*
20 [a]Deut. 31:29 [b]1 Cor. 10:20 [c]Dan. 5:23
21 [a]Rev. 21:8; 22:15 [1]NU, M *drugs*

CHAPTER 10

1 [a]Rev. 4:3 [b]Rev. 1:16 [c]Rev. 1:15
2 [a]Matt. 28:18
3 [a]Ps. 29:3–9

9:13–16 The four-horned **altar** is based on the OT prototype (Ex. 27:2). The **voice** is a command from God allowing **the four angels** (v. 14) to create the spiritual conditions for the destruction of **a third of mankind** (v. 15). The **Euphrates** (v. 14) was the border of the empire beyond which fierce and menacing peoples (such as the Parthians) were often feared to dwell. The number **two hundred million** (v. 16) makes it unlikely any earthly army is in view; as with the locusts, another infernal, demonic host is probably envisioned.

9:17–19 The description given is for horse and rider combined. Some may imagine modern armaments, but this would have been completely foreign to the communities for whom the book was written. The various features are intended to present an awesome spectacle of the horrific plagues visited upon those who resist God.

9:20, 21 Unfortunately, humanity is so addicted to sin that even these terrifying plagues do not cause the survivors to repent (see Ps. 115:4–8; Jer. 10:3–5; 1 Cor. 8:4). Paul (1 Cor. 10:20, 21) and early Fathers such as St. Justin Martyr and St. Irenaeus also connected idol worship with the **worship** of **demons.**

10:1—11:13 This is a parenthesis between the sixth and seventh trumpets. The passage consists of two visions: (1) the angel with the book, and (2) the two witnesses. Daniel 12 provides many of the images.

10:1, 2 John once again beholds from earth the angel's descent. God's message comes to him in a **little book** (v. 2), or scroll. The descriptive features of the angel are common symbols for divine glory (Ezek. 1:26–28; Matt. 17:2). His feet **on the sea** and **land** (v. 2) show his immensity and his authority to speak to the whole earth.

10:3, 4 The angel's **voice, as when a lion roars,** reminds us of God readying Himself for judgment (Jer. 25:30; Joel 3:16; Amos 1:2). The **seven thunders** probably refer to the divine

(continued on next page)

4 Now when the seven thunders
[1]uttered their voices, I was about to
write; but I heard a voice from
heaven saying [2]to me, [a]"Seal up the
things which the seven thunders uttered, and do not write them."
5 The angel whom I saw standing
on the sea and on the land [a]raised
up his [1]hand to heaven†
6 and swore by Him who lives
forever and ever, [a]who created
heaven and the things that are in it,
the earth and the things that are in
it, and the sea and the things that
are in it, [b]that there should be delay
no longer,
7 but [a]in the days of the sounding
of the seventh angel, when he is
about to sound, the mystery of God
would be finished, as He declared
to His servants the prophets.

John Eats the Book

8 Then the voice which I heard
from heaven spoke to me again and
said, "Go, take the little book which
is open in the hand of the angel who
stands on the sea and on the earth."†
9 So I went to the angel and said
to him, "Give me the little book."
And he said to me, [a]"Take and eat
it; and it will make your stomach bitter, but it will be as sweet as honey
in your mouth."
10 Then I took the little book out
of the angel's hand and ate it,
[a]and it was as sweet as honey in my
mouth. But when I had eaten it,
[b]my stomach became bitter.
11 And [1]he said to me, "You must
prophesy again about many peoples,
nations, tongues, and kings."

The Two Witnesses

11 Then I was given [a]a reed like
a measuring rod. [1]And the
angel stood, saying, [b]"Rise and measure the temple of God, the altar,
and those who worship there.†

4 [a]Dan. 8:26; 12:4, 9 [1]NU, M *sounded,* [2]NU, M omit *to me*
5 [a]Dan. 12:7 [1]NU, M *right hand*
6 [a]Rev. 4:11 [b]Rev. 16:17
7 [a]Rev. 11:15
9 [a]Jer. 15:16
10 [a]Ezek. 3:3 [b]Ezek. 2:10
11 [1]NU, M *they*

CHAPTER 11
1 [a]Ezek. 40:3—42:20 [b]Num. 23:18 [1]NU, M omit *And the angel stood*

(continued from previous page)
voice (Ps. 29:3–9; John 12:28, 29), a fullness of terror, power and magnificence. In Dan. 12, God tells the prophet to **seal up** (v. 4) what has been written in his book. So, too, St. John is told, regarding what the *seven thunders* have revealed. This command not to write down the utterance shows John's revelation does not exhaust divine decrees for humanity: undisclosed mysteries remain (2 Cor. 12:4).

10:5–7 The angel, lifting **his hand** in the form for taking an oath (see Gen. 14:22; Dan. 12:7), swears that the fullness of time has arrived and God's plan for history (**the mystery of God,** v. 7) is to be completed. This recalls Ps. 119:126, proclaimed by the deacon at the beginning of the Divine Liturgy: "It is time for the Lord to act!" as an answer to the question of the martyrs dwelling under the altar (6:10, 11). **Forever and ever** (v. 6) is literally "unto ages of ages," the closing phrase of most Orthodox Christian prayers.

10:8–11 The voice of God directs John to take the **book.** The symbolism of eating refers to receiving a revelation from God: John's account has many parallels to the commissioning of Ezekiel (Ezek. 2:8—3:3; also Ps. 119:103; Jer. 15:16). The contrast between sweetness in the mouth and bitterness in the stomach shows the sweetness of receiving God's revelation (announcing God's victory for His people) as opposed to the bitterness of its message of woe (announcing God's terrible judgments, as well as sufferings for His faithful ones).

11:1, 2 The measurement of the **temple** recalls Ezekiel's vision (Ezek. 40—42). Here the measurement indicates the preservation of the temple, not restoration. Commentators variously interpret the temple as (1) a literal temple to be rebuilt in Jerusalem in the future, (2) a symbol of the Church (see Eph. 2:19–22; 1 Pet. 2:5), or (3) the Jewish-Christian Church of the first century. The reference to **the holy city** (v. 2) shows the setting of the temple to be Jerusalem. The synoptic Gospels also teach that Jerusalem would fall (Matt. 24; Mark 13; Luke 21); Luke mentions specifically that the Gentiles would trample Jerusalem for a certain period (21:24). In patristic tradition the temple is usually seen as a symbol of the Church.

The **forty-two months** (v. 2) is three and a half years, one-half of seven, symbolizing what is not full or final but temporary, incomplete. It recalls Daniel's "a time, two times, and half a time" (Dan. 12:7), the three-and-a-half-year period when the temple was to be profaned (Dan. 9:27). John affirms that the true temple, the Church, will be preserved during this Gentile onslaught. "Temple" is a frequent NT symbol for the Church (1 Cor. 3:16, 17; 2 Cor. 6:16; Eph. 2:19–22).

2 "But leave out [a]the court which
is outside the temple, and do not
measure it, [b]for it has been given to
the Gentiles. And they will [c]tread
the holy city underfoot *for* [d]forty-two
months.
3 "And I will give *power* to my two
[a]witnesses, [b]and they will prophesy
[c]one thousand two hundred and
sixty days, clothed in sackcloth."†
4 These are the [a]two olive trees
and the two lampstands standing before the [1]God of the earth.†
5 And if anyone wants to harm
them, [a]fire proceeds from their
mouth and devours their enemies.
[b]And if anyone wants to harm them,
he must be killed in this manner.†
6 These [a]have power to shut
heaven, so that no rain falls in the
days of their prophecy; and they
have power over waters to turn them
to blood, and to strike the earth with
all plagues, as often as they desire.
7 When they [a]finish their testimony, [b]the beast that ascends
[c]out of the bottomless pit [d]will make
war against them, overcome them,
and kill them.†
8 And their dead bodies *will lie* in
the street of [a]the great city which
spiritually is called Sodom and
Egypt, [b]where also [1]our Lord was
crucified.†
9 [a]Then *those* from the peoples,
tribes, tongues, and nations [1]will see
their dead bodies three-and-a-half
days, [b]and not allow their dead bodies to be put into graves.†
10 [a]And those who dwell on the
earth will rejoice over them, make
merry, [b]and send gifts to one another, [c]because these two prophets
tormented those who dwell on the
earth.
11 [a]Now after the three-and-a-half
days [b]the breath of life from God entered them, and they stood on their
feet, and great fear fell on those who
saw them.†
12 And [1]they heard a loud voice
from heaven saying to them, "Come
up here." [a]And they ascended to
heaven [b]in a cloud, [c]and their enemies saw them.
13 In the same hour [a]there was a
great earthquake, [b]and a tenth of the

2 [a]Ezek. 40:17, 20 [b]Ps. 79:1 [c]Dan. 8:10 [d]Rev. 12:6; 13:5
3 [a]Rev. 20:4 [b]Rev. 19:10 [c]Rev. 12:6
4 [a]Zech. 4:2, 3, 11, 14 [1]NU, M *Lord*
5 [a]2 Kin. 1:10–12 [b]Num. 16:29
6 [a]1 Kin. 17:1
7 [a]Luke 13:32 [b]Rev. 13:1, 11; 17:8 [c]Rev. 9:1, 2 [d]Dan. 7:21
8 [a]Rev. 14:8 [b]Heb. 13:12 [1]NU, M *their*
9 [a]Rev. 17:15 [b]Ps. 79:2, 3 [1]NU, M *see . . . and will not allow*
10 [a]Rev. 12:12 [b]Esth. 9:19, 22 [c]Rev. 16:10
11 [a]Rev. 11:9 [b]Ezek. 37:5, 9, 10
12 [a]Is. 14:13 [b]Acts 1:9 [c]2 Kin. 2:11, 12 [1]M *I*
13 [a]Rev. 6:12; 8:5; 11:19; 16:18 [b]Rev. 16:19

11:3 The identity of the **two witnesses** is much disputed. The most common opinion of the Church Fathers is that they represent Elijah and Enoch, who were said in Scripture to have ascended to heaven (Gen. 5:24; 2 Kin. 2:11). In Jewish tradition, Moses is frequently substituted for Enoch, on the basis of the tradition that he, too, ascended to heaven. It was Moses who appeared with Elijah at the Transfiguration of Jesus. John most likely drew on the Jewish tradition that Elijah would return to preach in the last days (Mal. 4:5; Matt. 17:10–12). Although Jesus identified the Elijah figure with John the Baptist, many continued to believe in an actual appearance of Elijah before the end. **Sackcloth** was the ancient garb of penitence (see Jer. 4:8; Matt. 11:21). Their prophecy will continue for 1,260 days (42 months or 3½ years; see Dan. 7:25; 12:7). This period may be interpreted as "fullness" (i.e., seven) arrested halfway, imperfect, impermanent: it is not necessarily to be taken in a numerically literal manner.

11:4 These **two olive trees . . . two lampstands** who stand **before . . . God** are the eschatological agents of God at work on earth. This symbolic description of the witnesses is derived from Zechariah's vision (Zech. 4) concerning Zerubbabel the governor and Joshua the high priest, who are described as standing "beside the Lord of the whole earth" (Zech. 4:14).

11:5, 6 These features are reminiscent of Elijah's and Elisha's ministries (1 Kin. 17; 2 Kin. 8—14) and of the plagues God visited upon the Egyptians through Moses (Ex. 7—11).

11:7 The beast is either the Antichrist or the Roman Empire (see 13:1–10; Dan. 7).

11:8 The great city . . . where also our Lord was crucified, is clearly Jerusalem (who kills the prophets, Luke 13:34). Like **Sodom** and **Egypt,** Jerusalem becomes self-sufficient and rebels against God.

11:9, 10 The peoples, tribes, tongues, and nations represent the whole world in rebellion against God. They rejoice at the sight of the **dead** prophets because their preaching had tormented the rebels' consciences.

11:11 The breath of life is a biblical term for the animating life force manifest in the breath. The resurrection of the witnesses is conceivable because of the traditions regarding the ascensions of Enoch, Elijah, and Moses (see, as well, the dry bones of Ezek. 37).

city fell. In the earthquake seven
thousand people were killed, and the
rest were afraid [c]and gave glory to
the God of heaven.
14 [a]The second woe is past. Behold, the third woe is coming quickly.

Trumpet Seven: The Kingdom Proclaimed

15 Then [a]the seventh angel
sounded: [b]And there were loud
voices in heaven, saying, [c]"The
[1]kingdoms of this world have become *the kingdoms* of our Lord and
of His Christ, [d]and He shall reign
forever and ever!"†
16 And [a]the twenty-four elders
who sat before God on their thrones
fell on their faces and [b]worshiped
God,†
17 saying:

"We give You thanks, O Lord
God Almighty,
The One [a]who is and who was
[1]and who is to come,
Because You have taken Your
great power [b]and reigned.
18 The nations were [a]angry, and
Your [1]wrath has come,
And the time of the [b]dead, that
they should be judged,
And that You should reward
Your servants the prophets
and the saints,
And those who fear Your name,
small and great,
And should destroy those who
destroy the earth."

19 Then [a]the temple of God was
opened in heaven, and the ark of
[1]His covenant was seen in His temple. And [b]there were lightnings,
noises, thunderings, an earthquake,
[c]and great hail.

The Woman, Her Child and the Dragon

12 Now a great sign appeared in
heaven: a woman clothed
with the sun, with the moon under
her feet, and on her head a garland
of twelve stars.†
2 Then being with child, she cried
out [a]in labor and in pain to give
birth.
3 And another sign appeared in
heaven: behold, [a]a great, fiery red
dragon having seven heads and ten

13 [c]Rev. 14:7; 16:9; 19:7
14 [a]Rev. 8:13; 9:12
15 [a]Rev. 8:2; 10:7 [b]Is. 27:13 [c]Rev. 12:10 [d]Ex. 15:18 [1]NU, M *kingdom . . . has become the kingdom*
16 [a]Rev. 4:4 [b]Rev. 4:11; 5:9, 12, 14; 7:11
17 [a]Rev. 16:5 [b]Rev. 19:6 [1]NU, M omit *and who is to come*
18 [a]Ps. 2:1 [b]Dan. 7:10 [1]*anger*
19 [a]Rev. 4:1; 15:5, 8 [b]Rev. 8:5 [c]Rev. 16:21 [1]M *the covenant of the Lord*

CHAPTER 12

2 [a]Is. 26:17; 66:6–9
3 [a]Rev. 13:1; 17:3, 7, 9

11:15 These heavenly **voices,** which introduce an interlude with the scene shifting back to heaven, provide for us the pivotal verse of the whole of Revelation. Once again (as in 10:5–7) the proclamation is made that the fullness of time has arrived: **the kingdoms of this world** are subject to the Kingdom of God. This is the mystery of mysteries alluded to in 10:7, which our Lord Himself mentioned, as recorded in John 12:31: The judgment of the world and the casting out of Satan are effected by the Crucifixion. The voices state this has already occurred once and for all, at Calvary. Up to this point, Revelation has recorded only the prelude to God's judgment. From now on, the book records the judgment of God in all its power!

11:16–18 The twenty-four elders concelebrate the consummation of God's Kingdom in the heavenly liturgy. This carries a message of consolation to the Church. **Those who destroy the earth** (v. 18) are the morally wicked, not merely the ecologically irresponsible (although ecological irresponsibility is a form of moral wickedness). Perhaps the pagan Roman Empire is in view.

12:1 This verse begins an extensive parenthesis in the center of Revelation dealing with the conflict between the Church and the powers of evil (12:1—14:20). The **great sign in heaven,** the **woman,** is either the Virgin Mary (Theotokos) or true Israel, the Church (Is. 7:14). Orthodoxy sees the Theotokos (lit. "God-bearer") as the perfect symbol of Israel and the Church. She is the antithesis of the harlot of ch. 17, for she is a radiant bride (Song 6:4, 10; Jer. 2:2), adorned with splendor (Gen. 37:9). The **twelve stars** indicate the twelve tribes (and possibly the Twelve Apostles) and **the moon under her feet** symbolizes her preeminence among all that is created. Her birth-giving (**a male Child,** v. 5) is that of the Messiah, and she bears other offspring as well (v. 17), a likely reference to the Church.

horns, and seven diadems on his
heads.†
4 [a]His tail drew a third [b]of the
stars of heaven [c]and threw them to
the earth. And the dragon stood
[d]before the woman who was ready
to give birth, [e]to devour her Child
as soon as it was born.

The Child

5 She bore a male Child [a]who was
to rule all nations with a rod of iron.
And her Child was [b]caught up to
God and His throne.†
6 Then [a]the woman fled into the
wilderness, where she has a place
prepared by God, that they should
feed her there [b]one thousand two
hundred and sixty days.†

War in Heaven

7 And war broke out in heaven:
[a]Michael and his angels fought
[b]with the dragon; and the dragon
and his angels fought,†
8 but they [1]did not prevail, nor
was a place found for [2]them in
heaven any longer.
9 So [a]the great dragon was cast
out, [b]that serpent of old, called
the Devil and Satan, [c]who deceives
the whole world; [d]he was cast to the
earth, and his angels were cast out
with him.
10 Then I heard a loud voice saying
in heaven, [a]"Now salvation, and
strength, and the kingdom of our
God, and the power of His Christ
have come, for the accuser of our
brethren, [b]who accused them before
our God day and night, has been cast
down.
11 "And [a]they overcame him by
the blood of the Lamb and by the
word of their testimony, [b]and they
did not love their lives to the death.
12 "Therefore [a]rejoice, O heavens,
and you who dwell in them! [b]Woe
to the inhabitants of the earth and
the sea! For the devil has come down
to you, having great wrath, [c]because
he knows that he has a short time."

War on Earth

13 Now when the dragon saw that
he had been cast to the earth, he persecuted [a]the woman who gave birth
to the male *Child*.†

4 [a]Rev. 9:10, 19 [b]Rev. 8:7, 12 [c]Dan. 8:10 [d]Rev. 12:2 [e]Matt. 2:16
5 [a]Ps. 2:9 [b]Acts 1:9–11
6 [a]Rev. 12:4, 14 [b]Rev. 11:3; 13:5
7 [a]Dan. 10:13, 21; 12:1 [b]Rev. 20:2
8 [1]*were not strong enough* [2]M *him*
9 [a]John 12:31 [b]Gen. 3:1, 4 [c]Rev. 20:3 [d]Rev. 9:1
10 [a]Rev. 11:15 [b]Zech. 3:1
11 [a]Rom. 16:20 [b]Luke 14:26
12 [a]Ps. 96:11 [b]Rev. 8:13 [c]Rev. 10:6
13 [a]Rev. 12:5

12:3, 4 The **dragon** is clearly identified as Satan (12:9). **A third of the stars of heaven** (v. 4) is usually interpreted to mean that Satan drew a third of the angels with him when he fell. His intention is to destroy the Messiah.

12:5 True Israel brings forth Christ, who after completion of His saving work, ascends to heaven (Ps. 2:7–9).

12:6 The flight of **the woman** may refer to the flight of the Jerusalem church (embodying true Israel) to Pella before the outbreak of the Roman war. It illustrates there is no permanent safe **place** for the Church in this age. The 1,260 days, or three and a half years, is the classic period of apocalyptic woe (see 11:1, 2 and note): as bad as it is, it is temporary, not the end of things.

12:7–12 This passage begins an interlude describing Satan's role in stimulating persecution of the Church. The **war** with **Michael** and the good **angels** is usually interpreted to picture an event before the creation of the world. However, the context places it just before the end of the world. Satan has been accusing the **brethren** (v. 10), the Christians, and his downfall (see Luke 10:18) presages the consummation of the Kingdom. Satan is overcome by Christ's self-sacrifice and that of the martyrs (v. 11)—those who **did not love their lives to the death.** The **short time** (v. 12) Satan has is the period of tribulation just prior to the end.

12:13–16 Satan hates Christ and His mother. The Virgin Mary was saved by the inspiration of the angel who told Joseph to run into Egypt. Likewise, Satan hates Christ and the Church (John 15:21) and attacks the one through the other, since they are identified with each other. One of his first activities is to persecute true Israel. The **wings of a great eagle** (v. 14) refers to the original Exodus (Ex. 19:4; see Deut. 32:11; Is. 40:31), as the **flood** (vv. 15, 16) may also be the threat of drowning in the Red Sea. However, Satan is unable to prevail. The

(continued on next page)

14 [a]But the woman was given two
wings of a great eagle, [b]that she
might fly [c]into the wilderness to her
place, where she is nourished
[d]for a time and times and half a time,
from the presence of the serpent.
15 So the serpent [a]spewed water
out of his mouth like a flood after
the woman, that he might cause her
to be carried away by the flood.
16 But the earth helped the
woman, and the earth opened its
mouth and swallowed up the flood
which the dragon had spewed out
of his mouth.
17 And the dragon was enraged
with the woman, and he went to
make war with the rest of her offspring, who keep the commandments of God and have the testimony of Jesus [1]Christ.†

The Beast Against the Saints

13 Then [1]I stood on the sand of
the sea. And I saw [a]a beast
rising up out of the sea, [b]having
[2]seven heads and ten horns, and on
his horns ten crowns, and on his
heads a [c]blasphemous name.†
2 Now the beast which I saw was
like a leopard, his feet were like *the*
feet of a bear, and his mouth like the
mouth of a lion. The [a]dragon gave
him his power, his throne, and great
authority.
3 And *I saw* one of his heads
[a]as if it had been mortally wounded,
and his deadly wound was healed.
And [b]all the world marveled and followed the beast.
4 So they worshiped the dragon
who gave authority to the beast; and
they worshiped the beast, saying,
[a]"Who *is* like the beast? Who is able
to make war with him?"†
5 And he was given [a]a mouth
speaking great things and blasphemies, and he was given authority to
[1]continue for [b]forty-two months.†
6 Then he opened his mouth in
blasphemy against God, to blas-

14 [a]Ex. 19:4 [b]Rev. 12:6 [c]Rev. 17:3 [d]Dan. 7:25; 12:7
15 [a]Is. 59:19
17 [1]NU, M omit *Christ*

CHAPTER 13

1 [a]Dan. 7:2, 7 [b]Rev. 12:3 [c]Rev. 17:3 [1]NU *he* [2]NU, M *ten horns and seven heads*
2 [a]Rev. 12:3, 9; 13:4, 12
3 [a]Rev. 13:12, 14 [b]Rev. 17:8
4 [a]Rev. 18:18
5 [a]Dan. 7:8, 11, 20, 25; 11:36 [b]Rev. 11:2 [1]M *make war*

(continued from previous page)
Jewish Church safely completes its exodus and is preserved during its apocalyptic period. And the Church in general will be preserved: the gates of hell cannot prevail against her (Matt. 16:18). For Jesus' warnings about this flight, see Matt. 24:15–21.

12:17 Satan then turns his attention to the rest of true Israel's **offspring,** obviously the Gentile Church, which has inherited from her both **the commandments of God** and faith in **Christ.**

13:1–3 The **beast** (monster) **rising up out of the sea,** a composite of the four beasts of Dan. 7, is the epitome of a worldly kingdom opposed to God and His Kingdom. For John, this was the Roman Empire: a monstrous creature with **ten horns** (very powerful), **seven heads** (the emperors), **ten crowns,** and **a blasphemous name** on its heads (emperors who assumed titles of divinity such as "Lord and God," "Savior," "Son of God," etc.). In a parody of 5:12–14, where the sacrificed Lamb is enthroned, the beast is given **power,** not to bless the Church but to persecute it. One of the heads of this monster appeared "as though it had been slaughtered to death" (literal translation)—another parody of the Lamb, which was standing even though it had been slain (5:6).

The **deadly wound** might refer to the mad emperor Nero's death (inflicted by a slit throat in the manner of temple sacrifice). For despite his death in A.D. 68, the empire lived on, revived under Vespasian. Many believed Nero himself would rise from the dead. Domitian (A.D. 81–96, the emperor at the time of the writing of Revelation) was considered to be "Nero reincarnate" because his cruelty surpassed Nero's. Christian tradition has also seen the beast as an image of the Antichrist, the false Messiah who presents himself in the last times as God Incarnate and is accepted by the world (see John 5:43; 2 Thess. 2:3, 4; 1 John 2:18). Since there are "many antichrists" (1 John 2:18), there may be more than one application of the beast figure.

13:4 People **worshiped the dragon** (Satan), for it had given **authority to the beast:** a reference to emperor worship, which Domitian ruthlessly enforced. **"Who is like the beast?"** is an allusion to Michael the Archangel, whose name means "Who is like God?" It is also a parody of God, the incomparable (Ex. 15:11; Ps. 89:6). Citizens are awed by the power and authority of the empire.

13:5 Forty-two months is the final period of apocalyptic conflict. It is one-half of seven

(continued on next page)

pheme His name, [a]His tabernacle,
and those who dwell in heaven.†
7 It was granted to him [a]to make
war with the saints and to overcome
them. And [b]authority was given him
over every [1]tribe, tongue, and
nation.
8 All who dwell on the earth will
worship him, [a]whose names have
not been written in the Book of Life
of the Lamb slain [b]from the foundation of the world.
9 [a]If anyone has an ear, let him
hear.
10 [a]He who leads into captivity
shall go into captivity; [b]he who kills
with the sword must be killed with
the sword. [c]Here is the [1]patience and
the faith of the saints.†

The Deception

11 Then I saw another beast
[a]coming up out of the earth, and he
had two horns like a lamb and spoke
like a dragon.†

6 [a][Col. 2:9]
7 [a]Dan. 7:21
[b]Rev. 11:18
[1]NU, M add *and people*
8 [a]Ex. 32:32
[b]Rev. 17:8
9 [a]Rev. 2:7
10 [a]Is. 33:1
[b]Gen. 9:6
[c]Rev. 14:12
[1]*perseverance*
11 [a]Rev. 11:7
12 [a]Rev. 13:3, 4
13 [a]Matt. 24:24
[b]1 Kin. 18:38
14 [a]Rev. 12:9
[b]2 Thess. 2:9
[c]2 Kin. 20:7
[1]M *my own people*
15 [a]Rev. 16:2
16 [a]Rev. 7:3; 14:9; 20:4

12 And he exercises all the authority of the first beast in his presence,
and causes the earth and those who
dwell in it to worship the first beast,
[a]whose deadly wound was healed.
13 [a]He performs great signs,
[b]so that he even makes fire come
down from heaven on the earth in
the sight of men.†
14 [a]And he deceives [1]those who
dwell on the earth [b]by those signs
which he was granted to do in the
sight of the beast, telling those who
dwell on the earth to make an image
to the beast who was wounded by
the sword [c]and lived.
15 He was granted *power* to give
breath to the image of the beast, that
the image of the beast should both
speak [a]and cause as many as would
not worship the image of the beast
to be killed.
16 He causes all, both small and
great, rich and poor, free and slave,
[a]to receive a mark on their right
hand or on their foreheads,†

(continued from previous page)
years, not the final end of things. Thus, the nations trample over the holy city for 3½ years (11:2); the two witnesses prophesy for 3½ years (11:3); they were left unburied for 3½ days (11:9, 11); the woman is protected in the wilderness for 3½ years (12:6, 14). Nero's persecution lasted approximately 42 months.

13:6 The beast, the Roman Empire, utters **blasphemy against God,** for the emperor came to see himself as God. Domitian demanded to be called divine, and on Roman coins divine titles were associated with the likenesses of deceased emperors. The **tabernacle** is God's Church; **those who dwell in heaven** are the angels and glorified saints. Christians saw emperor worship as worship of Satan (v. 2; 2:13), and the ultimate offense against God that His creatures would worship earthly authority, itself under demonic rule. Nevertheless, by God's permission, the Antichrist rules over the whole earth and appears to vanquish the Church.

13:10 The first sentence would be better rendered "he who is *destined* for captivity . . . , he who is *destined* for the sword . . . ," referring to Christians facing persecution (see Jer. 15:2).

13:11, 12 Another beast appears, which has **two horns** (power) **like a lamb** (Christ, gentle and giving), and speaks **like a dragon** (Satan, whose speech is seductive): this is worldly religion. Its minister of propaganda, so to speak, mimics John the Baptist and the Holy Spirit: it is a false prophet (see 16:13; 19:20; 20:10; Dan. 7:3, LXX) calling all to worship the first beast (false divinity). This monster completes the unholy triumvirate—dragon (Satan, false god), beast from the sea (worldly authority and power, false incarnation), and beast from the earth (worldly religion, false prophet)—a blasphemous parody of the Holy Trinity.

13:13–15 In a parody of Pentecost, this monstrous cult leader is able to make **fire come down** by means of deception and sorcery (see Deut. 13:1–3; Matt. 24:24; Acts 13:6–12; Didache 16:3, 4)—luring people into making an **image** of **the beast** (v. 14; the goddess of Rome or the emperor). Statues were often "brought to life" by sorcery. St. Irenaeus, Clement, Justin, and Eusebius note that the sorcerer Simon Magus (Acts 8:9–24) used illusion and occult practices to make idols seem alive. This beast is able to enforce the sentence of death upon those who will not worship him (see Nebuchadnezzar's statue in Dan. 3).

13:16, 17 This is a parody of God's seal of 7:3. It also alludes to the Hebrew phylactery
(continued on next page)

17 and that no one may buy or sell
except one who has [1]the mark or
[a]the name of the beast, [b]or the number of his name.
18 [a]Here is wisdom. Let him who
has [b]understanding calculate [c]the
number of the beast, [d]for it is the
number of a man: His number *is*
666.†

The Lamb and the 144,000

14 Then I looked, and behold,
[1]a [a]Lamb standing on Mount
Zion, and with Him [b]one hundred
and forty-four thousand, [2]having His
Father's name [c]written on their
foreheads.†
2 And I heard a voice from
heaven, [a]like the voice of many waters, and like the voice of loud thunder. And I heard the sound of
[b]harpists playing their harps.†
3 They sang as it were a new song
before the throne, before the four living creatures, and the elders; and no
one could learn that song [a]except the
hundred *and* forty-four thousand
who were redeemed from the earth.
4 These are the ones who were
not defiled with women, [a]for they
are virgins. These are the ones
[b]who follow the Lamb wherever He
goes. These [c]were [1]redeemed from
among men, [d]*being* firstfruits to God
and to the Lamb.†

17 [a]Rev. 14:9–11 [b]Rev. 15:2 [1]NU, M *the mark, the name*
18 [a]Rev. 17:9 [b][1 Cor. 2:14] [c]Rev. 15:2 [d]Rev. 21:17

CHAPTER 14

1 [a]Rev. 5:6 [b]Rev. 7:4; 14:3 [c]Rev. 7:3; 22:4 [1]NU, M *the* [2]NU, M add *His name and*
2 [a]Rev. 1:15; 19:6 [b]Rev. 5:8
3 [a]Rev. 5:9
4 [a][2 Cor. 11:2] [b]Rev. 3:4; 7:17 [c]Rev. 5:9 [d]James 1:18 [1]M adds *by Jesus*

(continued from previous page)
of Deut. 6:8, where God's Law is kept on the forehead and the left hand, and to chrismation. The **mark** is gained by worshiping **the beast** (v. 17); it signifies that the beast is the owner of those who wear it—their protector, and the one to whom they owe their livelihoods. This mark is not necessarily a visible and physical mark on the person, but it is required to do business. There is then an economic bias against those who do not bear the beast's mark (the faithful who will not render demonic worship to the state).

13:18 The letters of the alphabet were used as numbers in ancient times (as in "Roman numerals"). Thus the numerical value of names could easily be calculated. "The name of the beast" (v. 17) is the numerical equivalent to the letters of the name of **a man** (some texts read "616" instead of the well-known **666**). John may be purposefully enigmatic, using a secret code to protect against a charge of sedition.

This is a predictably misunderstood passage, for the text itself says it requires **wisdom** and **understanding.** In the Bible, the number six stands for falling short, incompleteness, imperfection; seven, for perfection, fullness, completion; eight, for eschatological perfection, a superabundance of fullness (see 2 Enoch 33:1). The sixth day, Friday, is the day of preparation; the seventh, the Sabbath, Saturday, a picture of the rest to come; the eighth day, Sunday, the day of the Resurrection, the final establishment of God's Kingdom. The numerical equivalent of "Jesus" in Greek is 888. The numerical equivalent of "Nero Caesar" transliterated from Greek into Hebrew is 666, meaning the epitome of created inadequacy. The numerical equivalent of "Nero Caesar" transliterated from Latin into Hebrew is 616. If John were referring to Domitian, whom some considered to be Nero reincarnated, it would be safer to refer not to the present persecutor but to the one long gone. Some believe that "666" is a symbol rather than a cryptogram, falling short of perfection in each of its digits: failure upon failure upon failure, an evil trinity which always falls short of the Holy Trinity ("777"). Many have attempted to identify "666", but writing only one hundred years after John, St. Irenaeus had no idea to whom John was referring!

14:1 Mount Zion, the location of the temple in Jerusalem, is the Church (Heb. 12:22, 23). It is where the **Lamb** of God and His **hundred and forty-four thousand** faithful (see 7:4) assemble. Instead of the mark of the beast (13:16–18) they have the "mark" of the Father (see 7:3).

14:2, 3 The **voice from heaven** that made the sound of many **waters . . . ; loud thunder . . . harps** recalls the sounds of the temple liturgy. This *voice* sings **a new song** (v. 3; see 5:8–10; Ps. 98:1; Is. 42:10) which only the **redeemed** faithful **from the earth** are able to learn.

14:4, 5 Virgins: In the OT, prostitution and adultery symbolize idolatry, and virginity signifies faithfulness to God. Thus, the 144,000 have kept themselves pure from the idolatrous worship of the beast. Instead, they are faithful and **follow** the Lord **wherever He goes** (see
(continued on next page)

5 And [a]in their mouth was found
no [1]deceit, for [b]they are without fault
[2]before the throne of God.

Proclamation of Angels

6 Then I saw another angel
[a]flying in the midst of heaven,
[b]having the everlasting gospel to
preach to those who dwell on the
earth—[c]to every nation, tribe,
tongue, and people—†
7 saying with a loud voice,
[a]"Fear God and give glory to Him,
for the hour of His judgment has
come; [b]and worship Him who made
heaven and earth, the sea and
springs of water."
8 And another angel followed,
saying, [a]"Babylon[1] is fallen, is fallen, that great city, because [b]she
has made all nations drink of the
wine of the wrath of her fornication."†
9 Then a third angel followed
them, saying with a loud voice,
[a]"If anyone worships the beast and
his image, and receives *his* [b]mark on
his forehead or on his hand,†
10 "he himself [a]shall also drink of
the wine of the wrath of God, which
is [b]poured out full strength into
[c]the cup of His indignation. [d]He
shall be tormented with [e]fire and
brimstone in the presence of the holy
angels and in the presence of the
Lamb.
11 "And [a]the smoke of their torment ascends forever and ever; and
they have no rest day or night, who
worship the beast and his image, and
whoever receives the mark of his
name."

Harvest of Blessing: The Martyrs

12 [a]Here is the [1]patience of the
saints; [b]here[2] *are* those who keep the
commandments of God and the faith
of Jesus.†
13 Then I heard a voice from
heaven saying [1]to me, "Write:
[a]'Blessed *are* the dead [b]who die in
the Lord from now on.'" "Yes,"
says the Spirit, [c]"that they may rest
from their labors, and their works
follow [d]them."

5 [a]Ps. 32:2 [b]Eph. 5:27 [1]NU, M *falsehood* [2]NU, M omit the rest of v. 5.
6 [a]Rev. 8:13 [b]Eph. 3:9 [c]Rev. 13:7
7 [a]Rev. 11:18 [b]Neh. 9:6
8 [a]Is. 21:9 [b]Jer. 51:7 [1]NU *Babylon the great is fallen, is fallen, which has made;* M *Babylon the great is fallen. She has made*
9 [a]Rev. 13:14, 15; 14:11 [b]Rev. 13:16
10 [a]Ps. 75:8 [b]Rev. 18:6 [c]Rev. 16:19 [d]Rev. 20:10 [e]2 Thess. 1:7
11 [a]Is. 34:8–10
12 [a]Rev. 13:10 [b]Rev. 12:17 [1]*steadfastness, perseverance* [2]NU, M omit *here are those*
13 [a]Eccl. 4:1, 2 [b]1 Cor. 15:18 [c]Heb. 4:9, 10 [d][1 Cor. 3:11–15; 15:58] [1]NU, M omit *to me*

(continued from previous page)
Ruth 1:16–18) as sheep follow a shepherd (and here, the Shepherd is **the Lamb**), unlike adulterous Israel (Hos. 3:1). These martyred faithful who love not their lives even unto death are the **firstfruits** offered to God from among humanity: the faithful remnant. They are truthful (having nothing to do with the Father of Lies) and unblemished (a technical term in OT temple sacrifice; see Ex. 12:5; Eph. 5:25–27; 1 Pet. 1:19). We shall later encounter them as the bride of the Lamb (19:8; 21:2).

14:6, 7 Here is a universal summons to worship the one true God in the face of His approaching judgment.

14:8 Babylon (Rome) has **fallen** (Jer. 51:8), an anticipation of the dirge over Babylon in 18:1—19:4 (see Is. 21:9). Rome has made the **nations,** peoples of the empire, subservient by making them drink the **wine** of her **fornication,** the sensual, unholy eucharist of her idolatry and self-divinization. This wine is intoxicating, and results in the **wrath** of man: corruption, anger and murder, including the shedding of the blood of the saints (6:10).

14:9–11 The wrath of God (v. 10) shall be poured out like **wine, full strength** (unmixed, with no water to dilute it), to be drunk by those who compromise with the evil one. Like a smoldering caldron, this **cup** is agonizing, the same bath of **fire and brimstone** (the fate of Sodom and Gomorrah, Gen. 19:24) reserved for Satan, the beast, and the false prophet (19:20; 20:10; 21:8). Even the presence of God, **the Lamb,** and His good servants, **the holy angels,** is a torment (see the townspeople in Luke 8:37). And, as the refuse piles in the Valley of Hinnom (Gehenna) smoldered unceasingly outside Jerusalem, this agony continues **forever and ever,** an eternal contrast to the never-ending joy of worship of God (7:14–17).

14:12, 13 Christians, when persecuted, must exercise **patience** and **faith,** with **labors** and good **works** (v. 13)—the unity of *faith* and *works.* The alternative, eternal damnation, is too horrible (vv. 9–11).

Harvest of Wrath: The Grapes

14 Then I looked, and behold, a
white cloud, and on the cloud sat
One like the Son of Man, having on
His head a golden crown, and in His
hand a sharp sickle.†
15 And another angel [a]came out of
the temple, crying with a loud voice
to Him who sat on the cloud,
[b]"Thrust in Your sickle and reap, for
the time has come [1]for You to reap,
for the harvest [c]of the earth is ripe."
16 So He who sat on the cloud
thrust in His sickle on the earth, and
the earth was reaped.
17 Then another angel came out of
the temple which is in heaven, he
also having a sharp sickle.
18 And another angel came out
from the altar, [a]who had power over
fire, and he cried with a loud cry to
him who had the sharp sickle, saying, [b]"Thrust in your sharp sickle
and gather the clusters of the vine
of the earth, for her grapes are fully
ripe."†
19 So the angel thrust his sickle
into the earth and gathered the vine
of the earth, and threw *it* into
[a]the great winepress of the wrath of
God.
20 And [a]the winepress was trampled [b]outside the city, and blood
came out of the winepress, [c]up to
the horses' bridles, for one thousand
six hundred [1]furlongs.†

The Liturgy of Preparation

15 Then [a]I saw another sign in
heaven, great and marvelous:
[b]seven angels having the seven last
plagues, [c]for in them the wrath of
God is complete.†
2 And I saw *something* like [a]a sea
of glass [b]mingled with fire, and
those who have the victory over the
beast, [c]over his image and [1]over his
mark *and* over the [d]number of his
name, standing on the sea of glass,
[e]having harps of God.†
3 They sing [a]the song of Moses,
the servant of God, and the song of
the [b]Lamb, saying:

[c]"Great and marvelous *are* Your
works,
Lord God Almighty!
[d]Just and true *are* Your ways,
O King of the [1]saints!

15 [a]Rev. 16:17 [b]Joel 3:13 [c]Jer. 51:33 [1]NU, M omit *for You*
18 [a]Rev. 16:8 [b]Joel 3:13
19 [a]Rev. 19:15
20 [a]Is. 63:3 [b]Heb. 13:12 [c]Is. 34:3 [1]Lit. *stadia,* about 184 miles in all

CHAPTER 15
1 [a]Rev. 12:1, 3 [b]Rev. 21:9 [c]Rev. 14:10
2 [a]Rev. 4:6 [b][Matt. 3:11] [c]Rev. 13:14, 15 [d]Rev. 13:17 [e]Rev. 5:8 [1]NU, M omit *over his mark*
3 [a]Ex. 15:1–21 [b]Rev. 15:3 [c]Deut. 32:3, 4 [d]Ps. 145:17 [1]NU, M *nations*

14:14–20 This passage presents two images of judgment, a grain harvest (vv. 14–16) and a grape harvest, complete with the treading of a wine press (vv. 17–20).

14:14, 15 The **Son of Man,** royal conqueror (**golden crown**) and judge (**sharp sickle**), appears, seated on a **white cloud** (see Mark 13:26), and reaps **the harvest of the earth** (v. 15), the beginning of the final judgment of the earth (see Matt. 13:24–30, 36–43; Mark 4:26–29).

14:18 The **angel . . . from the altar** with **power over fire** (see 1 Enoch 60:11–21) recalls 6:9; 8:3–5; and 11:1, 18. The prayers of the martyrs under the altar and the saints on earth for a hasty destruction of the destroyers are answered.

14:20 The trampling of the wicked who were gathered **outside the city** recalls the bloodshed (the Crucifixion, Heb. 13:12; the martyrdom of Stephen, Acts 7:58–60) that took place outside the walls of Jerusalem. The whole world is judged as the Jews would judge the Gentiles (Joel 3:2, 12; Zech. 14:2–12). The absurdly large amount of blood (**one thousand six hundred furlongs** is about 184 miles) suggests the severity and completeness (1600 = 4 × 4 × 100) of God's judgment.

15:1 This verse introduces the bowl plagues, the culmination of God's judgment of the earth.

15:2–4 This is the victory celebration for those who refuse to submit to Antichrist, including a hymn that may have been used in the liturgy of the early Church. In contrast to the idolatry of the beast, this hymn emphasizes the worthiness of the true God. The **song of Moses and the Lamb** (v. 3) is prefigured in the hymns of Ex. 15:1–8 and Deut. 32:1–43, where victory over the oppression of Pharaoh and the Egyptians is celebrated. The Jews incorporated these into the Sabbath liturgy, and the Church also sings them at various times of the year (for example, in Matins, and the Vespers of Holy Saturday in the Orthodox Church). The Church sings this *song of the Lamb* in baptism and at the Great Blessing of Water on Epiphany.

4 [a]Who shall not fear You, O Lord,
and glorify Your name?
For *You* alone *are* [b]holy.
For [c]all nations shall come and
worship before You,
For Your judgments have been
manifested."

5 After these things I looked, and
[1]behold, [a]the [2]temple of the tabernacle of the testimony in heaven was
opened.†
6 And out of the [1]temple came the
seven angels having the seven
plagues, [a]clothed in pure bright
linen, and having their chests girded
with golden bands.
7 [a]Then one of the four living
creatures gave to the seven angels
seven golden bowls full of the wrath
of God [b]who lives forever and ever.
8 [a]The temple was filled with
smoke [b]from the glory of God and
from His power, and no one was able
to enter the temple till the seven
plagues of the seven angels were
completed.†

16

Then I heard a loud voice
from the temple saying
[a]to the seven angels, "Go and pour
out the [1]bowls [b]of the wrath of God
on the earth."†

Bowl One: Loathsome Sores

2 So the first went and poured out
his bowl [a]upon the earth, and a
[1]foul and [b]loathsome sore came
upon the men [c]who had the mark
of the beast and those [d]who worshiped his image.†

Bowl Two: The Sea Turns to Blood

3 Then the second angel poured
out his bowl [a]on the sea, and [b]it became blood as of a dead *man;* [c]and
every living creature in the sea died.

Bowl Three: Fresh Waters Turn to Blood

4 Then the third angel poured out
his bowl [a]on the rivers and springs
of water, [b]and they became blood.

4 [a]Ex. 15:14 [b]Lev. 11:44 [c]Is. 66:23
5 [a]Num. 1:50 [1]NU, M omit *behold* [2]*sanctuary,* the inner shrine
6 [a]Ex. 28:6 [1]*sanctuary,* the inner shrine
7 [a]Rev. 4:6 [b]1 Thess. 1:9
8 [a]Ex. 19:18; 40:34 [b]2 Thess. 1:9

CHAPTER 16

1 [a]Rev. 15:1 [b]Rev. 14:10 [1]NU, M *seven bowls*
2 [a]Rev. 8:7 [b]Ex. 9:9–11 [c]Rev. 13:15–17; 14:9 [d]Rev. 13:14 [1]*severe and malignant,* lit. *bad and evil*
3 [a]Rev. 8:8; 11:6 [b]Ex. 7:17–21 [c]Rev. 8:9
4 [a]Rev. 8:10 [b]Ex. 7:17–20

15:5–7 The **temple of the tabernacle of the testimony** is the prototype of the "tabernacle of witness" (Num. 17:7), containing the witness of God's covenant, the tablets of the Law brought down from Mt. Sinai by Moses (Ex. 32:15). The tabernacle was itself the archetype of the temple of Jerusalem (see Ex. 25:9, 40; Heb. 8:5; 9:11; 13:10). **Seven angels** (v. 6) appear out of the temple, in priestly vesture (Ezek. 9:2; Dan. 10:5). They are given **golden bowls** (see the vessels used by the priests in the Jerusalem temple: 5:8; Ex. 27:3; Num. 7) by one of the **living creatures** (v. 7; see 4:6). God's judgment is meted out within this liturgical framework.

15:8 The temple was filled with smoke (see Is. 6:4; Ezek. 10:3, 4), so that none could **enter** (see Ex. 40:35, where Moses was unable to enter the tent; and 1 Kin. 8:10, 11 where the priests were unable to enter the temple for the same reason). No one may enter to intercede for the earth or to divert the coming catastrophe of God's sworn judgment.

16:1 Although the trumpet and bowl plagues are quite similar, the trumpet plagues are partial, a warning and call to repentance, whereas the bowl judgments are final and total. The difference is that dreadful step from the "beginning of sorrows" to final judgment. This chapter, as well as ch. 15, contains many elements foreshadowed in Joel 3:9–17, which is read in the Church on the Wednesday before Great Lent.

The **loud voice from the** celestial **temple** is presumably God's voice. **Pour out** is a liturgical term (Lev. 4:7, 18, 25, LXX) referring to the blood and the wine poured out with the offering of the daily sacrifice and the Feast of Dedication. On the Day of Atonement, blood was sprinkled seven times toward the inner veil, more was then smeared upon the horns of the altar, and the remainder was poured out at the altar's base. Here, the seven angelic priests pour out the bowls of God's wrath as a ritual answer to the cry of the martyrs from under the altar for vengeance (6:9, 10; see Ps. 69:24; Jer. 10:25; Zeph. 3:8).

16:2–4 The **first . . . bowl** is poured out and **the mark of the beast** breaks out upon those who received it in **foul** and **loathsome** sores (see Wisd. 11:16), like the sixth plague of Ex. 9:8–11. The **second** (v. 3) and **third** (v. 4) bowls are like the first plague (Ex. 7:20, 21; see Rev. 8:8–11).

5 And I heard the angel of the waters saying:

[a]"You are righteous, [1]O Lord,
The One [b]who is and who
[2]was and who is to be,
Because You have judged these
things.†
6 For [a]they have shed the blood
[b]of saints and prophets,
[c]And You have given them blood
to drink.
[1]For it is their just due."

7 And I heard [1]another from the
altar saying, "Even so, [a]Lord God
Almighty, [b]true and righteous *are*
Your judgments."

Bowl Four: Men Are Scorched

8 Then the fourth angel poured
out his bowl [a]on the sun, [b]and
power was given to him to scorch
men with fire.†
9 And men were scorched with
great heat, and they [a]blasphemed
the name of God who has power
over these plagues; [b]and they did
not repent [c]and give Him glory.

5 [a]Rev. 15:3, 4
[b]Rev. 1:4, 8
[1]NU, M omit *O Lord*
[2]NU, M *was, the Holy One*
6 [a]Matt. 23:34
[b]Rev. 11:18
[c]Is. 49:26
[1]NU, M omit *For*
7 [a]Rev. 15:3
[b]Rev. 13:10; 19:2
[1]NU, M omit *another from*
8 [a]Rev. 8:12
[b]Rev. 9:17, 18
9 [a]Rev. 16:11
[b]Dan. 5:22
[c]Rev. 11:13
10 [a]Rev. 13:2
[b]Rev. 8:12; 9:2
[c]Rev. 11:10
12 [a]Rev. 9:14
[b]Jer. 50:38
[c]Is. 41:2, 25; 46:11
13 [a]1 John 4:1
[b]Rev. 12:3, 9
[c]Rev. 13:11, 14; 19:20; 20:10
14 [a]2 Thess. 2:9
[b]Luke 2:1

Bowl Five: Darkness and Pain

10 Then the fifth angel poured out
his bowl [a]on the throne of the beast,
[b]and his kingdom became full of
darkness; [c]and they gnawed their
tongues because of the pain.†
11 They blasphemed the God of
heaven because of their pains and
their sores, and did not repent of
their deeds.

Bowl Six: Euphrates Dries Up

12 Then the sixth angel poured out
his bowl [a]on the great river Euphrates, [b]and its water was dried up,
[c]so that the way of the kings from
the east might be prepared.†
13 And I saw three unclean [a]spirits
like frogs *coming* out of the mouth
of [b]the dragon, out of the mouth of
the beast, and out of the mouth of
[c]the false prophet.†
14 For they are spirits of demons,
[a]performing signs, *which* go out to
the kings [1]of the earth and of [b]the

[1]NU, M omit *of the earth and*

16:5–7 This judgment becomes the occasion for a doxology to God from **the angel of the waters,** the element just affected by God's wrath (vv. 3, 4). In biblical thought, spiritual or angelic powers have charge of the physical realm; all elements of the material world have angelic guardians. In response, a voice from the altar (possibly the voice of the martyrs—see 6:9; 8:3–5; 9:13) proclaims God's **judgments** are **true and righteous** (v. 7).

There is a parallel here with "the song of Moses" (15:3, 4). Indeed, there is a parallel here with the hymnodic interlude in the Jerusalem temple liturgy between the preparation and the offering of the sacrificed lamb. **It is their just due** (v. 6) is literally "they are worthy" (Gr. *axios*), the antithesis of the worthiness of the Lamb sung about in 5:9, 12. At the ordination of a deacon, priest, or bishop, the assembly sings *"Axios"* as an assent to the candidate's worthiness.

16:8, 9 The spiritually hardened followers of the beast cannot repent, but only blaspheme at the judgments of God. In contrast to Dan. 3:22, 27, where the holy youths who refuse to worship Nebuchadnezzar's image are not even singed by the furnace's heat, here those who worship the beast and its image are **scorched with great heat** (v. 9).

16:10 The plague of darkness is similar to the ninth Egyptian plague (Ex. 10:21–29). Here the **throne** is Rome (in contrast to 2:13, where "Satan's throne" is Pergamos), and the **kingdom** is the empire. Satan has shared his dominion with "the beast from the land," the false prophet (13:11).

16:12 As in 9:13–21, the Roman Empire is threatened by peoples from beyond the Euphrates. This river formed a natural defensive line for Rome against **the kings from the east,** the Parthians (see also 6:2; 17:12, 13). The OT miracles of crossing over a river on dry land (Ex. 14:21; Josh. 3:17) are repeated (see also Is. 11:15; Jer. 51:36; Zech. 10:11).

16:13 This is an allusion to the second Egyptian plague (Ex. 8:1–11). The **unclean spirits** (see 1 Tim. 4:1) are **like frogs** (included in the unclean animals of Lev. 11:10).

whole world, to gather them to
[c]the battle of that great day of God
Almighty.†
15 [a]"Behold, I am coming as a
thief. Blessed *is* he who watches, and
keeps his garments, [b]lest he walk
naked and they see his shame."†
16 [a]And they gathered them together to the place called in Hebrew,
[1]Armageddon.†

Bowl Seven: Earth Utterly Shaken

17 Then the seventh angel poured
out his bowl into the air, and a loud
voice came out of the temple of
heaven, from the throne, saying,
[a]"It is done!"†
18 And [a]there were noises and
thunderings and lightnings; [b]and
there was a great earthquake, such
a mighty and great earthquake
[c]as had not occurred since men were
on the earth.
19 Now [a]the great city was divided
into three parts, and the cities of the
nations fell. And [b]great Babylon
[c]was remembered before God,
[d]to give her the cup of the wine of
the fierceness of His wrath.
20 Then [a]every island fled away,
and the mountains were not found.
21 And great hail from heaven fell
upon men, *each hailstone* about the
weight of a talent. Men blasphemed
God because of the plague of the
hail, since that plague was exceedingly great.

The Great Harlot and Her Beast

17 Then [a]one of the seven angels
who had the seven bowls
came and talked with me, saying
[1]to me, "Come, [b]I will show you the
judgment of [c]the great harlot [d]who
sits on many waters,†
2 [a]"with whom the kings of the
earth committed fornication, and
[b]the inhabitants of the earth were

14 [c]Rev. 17:14; 19:19; 20:8
15 [a]Matt. 24:43 [b]2 Cor. 5:3
16 [a]Rev. 19:19 [1]Lit. *Mount Megiddo;* M *Megiddo*
17 [a]Rev. 10:6; 21:6
18 [a]Rev. 4:5 [b]Rev. 11:13 [c]Dan. 12:1
19 [a]Rev. 14:8 [b]Rev. 17:5, 18 [c]Rev. 14:8; 18:5 [d]Is. 51:17
20 [a]Rev. 6:14; 20:11

CHAPTER 17

1 [a]Rev. 1:1; 21:9 [b]Rev. 16:19 [c]Nah. 3:4 [d]Jer. 51:13 [1]NU, M omit *to me*
2 [a]Rev. 2:22; 18:3, 9 [b]Jer. 51:7

16:14 Spirits of demons, performing signs are predicted by our Lord (Mark 13:22; see also Acts 13:6; 2 Thess. 2:9). **The great day of God Almighty** (6:17; foreshadowed in Joel 2:11 and Zeph. 1:14; graphically described in 2 Pet. 3:12) is the eschatological Day of the Lord.

16:15 In a parenthetical comment, we are told that this Day of the Lord will see Him **coming** unexpectedly like **a thief** (see 3:3; Matt. 24:42–44; 1 Thess. 5:2). Like the wise virgins who stand in readiness for the Bridegroom who comes at midnight (Matt. 25:1–13), the **blessed** faithful are here exhorted to remain vigilant as well. It is said that the officer on duty at the Jerusalem temple was to see that his night guards kept awake during their watch. If they were caught asleep, they were beaten. If caught a second time, they were stripped of their **garments,** their vesture, then and there. A Christian's garment is his white baptismal robe, "the garment of righteousness," the putting on of Christ.

16:16 Decisive battles in Israel's history were fought in the strategic pass near Megiddo (see 2 Kin. 9:27). **Armageddon**—the word is found only here in Scripture—means "the hill of Megiddo"; the nearest hill to Megiddo is Mt. Carmel, where Elijah confronted the prophets of Baal (1 Kin. 18:19–40). In the final conflict at *Armageddon,* evil spirits (vv. 13, 14) lead apostate mankind against God. This battle is more fully recorded in 20:7–10, and foreshadowed in Ezek. 39 and Joel 3.

16:17–21 The last **bowl** is a conclusive act of judgment; **a loud voice** from God's **throne** declares, **"It is done!"** (repeated at 21:6; see John 19:30). Cosmic signs of God's presence are manifest which evoke His appearance on Mt. Sinai and other theophanies (see 4:5; 8:5; 11:10), and are quite similar to those of the last trumpet (11:19)—especially **a great earthquake,** causing worldwide destruction (v. 20). Yet even 75-pound (75 lbs. = one **talent**) hailstones fail to induce repentance. The **great city** (v. 19) is probably Jerusalem (see 11:8), since Rome is mentioned separately as **great Babylon.**

17:1 The **great harlot** is Rome, the empire with its claims of divinity, sovereignty, and eternity (see vv. 9, 18) opposed to God and the Church: symbolic of all evil rule. In the Bible, harlotry frequently symbolizes apostasy and idolatry (see Jer. 2:20–31; Ezek. 16; Hos. 4:12). The **many waters** on which the harlot is seated portray both the waters of Babylon—the canals and tributaries of the Euphrates (Ps. 137:1; Jer. 51:13)—and the waters of Rome, the seas surrounding Italy. They symbolize the nations who submit to the harlot's rule (v. 15).

made drunk with the wine of her fornication."†
3 So he carried me away in the
Spirit [a]into the wilderness. And I
saw a woman sitting [b]on a scarlet
beast *which was* full of [c]names of blasphemy, having seven heads and ten horns.†
4 The woman [a]was arrayed in
purple and scarlet, [b]and adorned with gold and precious stones and pearls, [c]having in her hand a golden cup [d]full of abominations and the filthiness of [1]her fornication.†
5 And on her forehead a name *was*
written:

[a]MYSTERY, BABYLON THE GREAT, THE MOTHER OF HARLOTS AND OF THE ABOMINATIONS OF THE EARTH.†

6 I saw [a]the woman, drunk
[b]with the blood of the saints and with the blood of [c]the martyrs of Jesus. And when I saw her, I marveled with great amazement.

3 [a]Rev. 12:6, 14; 21:10 [b]Rev. 12:3 [c]Rev. 13:1
4 [a]Rev. 18:12, 16 [b]Dan. 11:38 [c]Jer. 51:7 [d]Rev. 14:8 [1]M *the fornication of the earth*
5 [a]2 Thess. 2:7
6 [a]Rev. 18:24 [b]Rev. 13:15 [c]Rev. 6:9, 10

The Meaning of the Harlot and Her Beast

7 But the angel said to me, "Why
did you marvel? I will tell you the [1]mystery of the woman and of the beast that carries her, which has the seven heads and the ten horns.
8 "The beast that you saw was,
and is not, and [a]will ascend out of the bottomless pit and [b]go to [1]perdition. And those who [c]dwell on the earth [d]will marvel, [e]whose names are not written in the Book of Life from the foundation of the world, when they see the beast that was, and is not, and [2]yet is.†
9 [a]"Here *is* the mind which has
wisdom: [b]The seven heads are seven mountains on which the woman sits.
10 "There are also seven kings.
Five have fallen, one is, *and* the other

7 [1]*hidden truth*
8 [a]Rev. 11:7 [b]Rev. 13:10; 17:11 [c]Rev. 3:10 [d]Rev. 13:3 [e]Rev. 13:8 [1]*destruction* [2]NU, M *shall be present*
9 [a]Rev. 13:18 [b]Rev. 13:1

17:2 Fornication, committed by the **kings of the earth** with this harlot, is a metaphor for infidelity to the Lord (Jer. 3; Ezek. 16; 23; Hos. 2). The vassal kingdoms within the Roman Empire have accepted the cults of Rome and her emperors, have solidified their obeisance with political and economic obligations—and have fallen into moral decadence. The **wine** of this fornication has made **the inhabitants of the earth** to become **drunk,** seduced and stupefied by a hideous eucharist of death, focused on the persecution and martyrdom of Christians (v. 6; see Jer. 51:7).

17:3 The woman's position on the **beast** shows the Roman system supported by the Antichrist-Emperor. The **names of blasphemy** may be the divine titles assumed by the emperors.

17:4 The harlot is **arrayed** in abominable luxury: **purple** (an extremely expensive and rare dye obtained from the murex shellfish of Phoenicia, reserved for royalty), **scarlet, gold, jewels,** and **pearls.** Contrast this with the pure linen in which the Bride is arrayed in 19:8. The harlot's **cup** contains the spiritual pollutions by which she contaminates humanity. In Jer. 51:7, Babylon is pictured as a golden cup in the hand of the Lord which makes all the earth madly intoxicated.

17:5 Roman law stated harlots must wear headbands exhibiting their name. This great harlot bears the mysterious name of **BABYLON . . . MOTHER OF HARLOTS.** For the late-first-century Christians, *Babylon* was incarnate in Rome (see 1 Pet. 5:13), but it is primarily a spiritual reality, a "mystery," transcending concrete manifestations. For *Babylon* has always stood for rebellion against God (see Gen. 11:1–9; Babel = Babylon): self-exaltation and idolatry. She is the *mother* **OF THE ABOMINATIONS OF THE EARTH** (lit. "detestable things"), the prostitution of God's creation. And she finds her life in a perverse eucharist, the death of those united with Life Incarnate.

17:8–11 The **beast that was, and is not, and yet is** (v. 8) is the Roman Empire or the hellish Antichrist, who seems to have been destroyed only to rise again, in imitation of the true Christ. The **seven mountains** (v. 9) was a well-known description of Rome herself. Numerous interpretations have been made of these verses. A likely historical explanation is that *the beast* is Nero, who was expected to return to life after he died; the **five** who **have fallen** (v. 10) are Augustus through Nero; Vespasian is the **one** who **is;** and **the beast** who is **himself also the eighth** (v. 11) is Domitian, seen as Nero revived. But again, the reality seems to be transcendent, as well. Certainly, at least, *the eighth*—the number eight signifying complete abundance—is a type of the final Antichrist.

has not yet come. And when he
comes, he must [a]continue a short
time.
11 "The [a]beast that was, and is
not, is himself also the eighth, and
is of the seven, and is going to
[1]perdition.
12 [a]"The ten horns which you saw
are ten kings who have received no
kingdom as yet, but they receive authority for one hour as kings with
the beast.†
13 "These are of one mind, and
they will give their power and authority to the beast.
14 [a]"These will make war with the
Lamb, and the Lamb will [b]overcome
them, [c]for He is Lord of lords and
King of kings; [d]and those *who are*
with Him *are* called, chosen, and
faithful."
15 Then he said to me, [a]"The waters which you saw, where the harlot
sits, [b]are peoples, multitudes, nations, and tongues.†
16 "And the ten horns which you
[1]saw on the beast, [a]these will hate
the harlot, make her [b]desolate
[c]and naked, eat her flesh and
[d]burn her with fire.
17 [a]"For God has put it into their
hearts to fulfill His purpose, to be
of one mind, and to give their king-

10 [a]Rev. 13:5
11 [a]Rev. 13:3, 12, 14; 17:8 [1]*destruction*
12 [a]Dan. 7:20
14 [a]Rev. 16:14; 19:19 [b]Rev. 19:20 [c]1 Tim. 6:15 [d]Jer. 50:44
15 [a]Is. 8:7 [b]Rev. 13:7
16 [a]Jer. 50:41 [b]Rev. 18:17, 19 [c]Ezek. 16:37, 39 [d]Rev. 18:8 [1]NU, M *saw, and the beast*
17 [a]2 Thess. 2:11 [b]Rev. 10:7
18 [a]Rev. 11:8; 16:19 [b]Rev. 12:4

CHAPTER 18

1 [a]Rev. 17:1, 7 [b]Ezek. 43:2
2 [a]Is. 13:19; 21:9 [b]Is. 13:21; 34:11, 13–15 [c]Is. 14:23 [1]NU, M omit *mightily*
3 [a]Rev. 14:8 [b]Is. 47:15 [1]Lit. *strengths*
4 [a]Is. 48:20

dom to the beast, [b]until the words
of God are fulfilled.
18 "And the woman whom you
saw [a]is that great city [b]which reigns
over the kings of the earth."

The Judgment of Babylon

18 After[a] these things I saw another angel coming down
from heaven, having great authority,
[b]and the earth was illuminated with
his glory.†
2 And he cried [1]mightily with a
loud voice, saying, [a]"Babylon the
great is fallen, is fallen, and [b]has become a dwelling place of demons, a
prison for every foul spirit, and
[c]a cage for every unclean and hated
bird!†
3 "For all the nations [a]have drunk
of the wine of the wrath of her fornication, the kings of the earth have
committed fornication with her,
[b]and the merchants of the earth have
become rich through the [1]abundance
of her luxury."
4 And I heard another voice from
heaven saying, [a]"Come out of her,
my people, lest you share in her
sins, and lest you receive of her
plagues.†

17:12 The **ten kings** may be symbolic of all the nations allied with Antichrist in his war against the Church. They completely give themselves over to the beast, but the **authority** they **receive** is of very short duration (symbolically, **one hour**). Though they join the beast in his persecution fury, ultimately Christ and his faithful triumph (19:11–21).

17:15–18 The **peoples, multitudes, nations and tongues** represent the diverse population of the Roman Empire (see v. 18). Reaping what she sows, Rome will be conquered as she has conquered. That the **ten horns** (vassal kings) and the **beast** (false prophet) will rise up against **the harlot** (v. 16) indicates the self-destructiveness of evil (see Ezek. 23:11–35). The Antichrist proves himself (in contrast to the true Christ, v. 14) the traitor of traitors. Rome will be stripped, devoured and burned (see Lev. 21:9, where death by fire is required for a harlot who is the daughter of a priest).

18:1 As God is Light (4:3; Ps. 104:1, 2; 1 Tim. 6:16), so the **angel coming down from heaven** exudes a lingering radiance (see Moses in Ex. 34:29–35).

18:2 This dirge over **fallen Babylon** recalls Is. 13:19–22 and 34:11–15, where the prophet speaks of the total destruction of the enemies of God's people (see also Jer. 3:2; Hos. 4:10). The city is a haunt of demonic, foul, and hateful spirits.

18:4–8 God's people are called to **come out of her** so as not to partake of her punishment, destruction and devastation (see Num. 33:51–56; Is. 52:11; Jer. 50:8; 51:6, 45). Separation from this world is spiritual—not necessarily a physical move, but a refusal to participate in the works of darkness (2 Cor. 6:14–18). This was one cause for the development of monasticism when the world (culture, society, empire) recognized Christianity. The monastics felt the Church joined the world.

As Babylon (Rome) has proclaimed her own sovereign greatness, sitting **as queen** (v. 7),

(continued on next page)

5 [a]"For her sins have [1]reached to
heaven, and [b]God has remembered
her iniquities.
6 [a]"Render to her just as she rendered [1]to you, and repay her double
according to her works; [b]in the cup
which she has mixed, [c]mix double
for her.
7 [a]"In the measure that she glorified herself and lived [1]luxuriously,
in the same measure give her torment and sorrow; for she says in her
heart, 'I sit *as* [b]queen, and am
no widow, and will not see sorrow.'
8 "Therefore her plagues will
come [a]in one day—death and
mourning and famine. And [b]she will
be utterly burned with fire, [c]for
strong *is* the Lord God who [1]judges
her.

The World Mourns for Babylon

9 [a]"The kings of the earth who
committed fornication and lived lux-
uriously with her [b]will weep and lament for her, [c]when they see the
smoke of her burning,†
10 "standing at a distance for fear
of her torment, saying, [a]'Alas, alas,
that great city Babylon, that mighty
city! [b]For in one hour your judgment
has come.'
11 "And [a]the merchants of the
earth will weep and mourn over her,
for no one buys their merchandise
anymore:†

5 [a]Gen. 18:20 [b]Rev. 16:19 [1]NU, M *have been heaped up*
6 [a]Ps. 137:8 [b]Rev. 14:10 [c]Rev. 16:19 [1]NU, M omit *to you*
7 [a]Ezek. 28:2–8 [b]Is. 47:7, 8 [1]*sensually*
8 [a]Rev. 18:10 [b]Rev. 17:16 [c]Jer. 50:34 [1]NU, M *has judged*
9 [a]Ezek. 26:16; 27:35 [b]Jer. 50:46 [c]Rev. 19:3
10 [a]Is. 21:9 [b]Rev. 18:17, 19
11 [a]Ezek. 27:27–34
12 [a]Rev. 17:4
13 [a]Ezek. 27:13
14 [1]NU, M *been lost to you*
16 [a]Rev. 17:18 [b]Rev. 17:4
17 [a]Rev. 18:10 [b]Is. 23:14 [1]*have been laid waste*
18 [a]Ezek. 27:30 [b]Rev. 13:4
19 [a]Josh. 7:6

12 [a]"merchandise of gold and silver, precious stones and pearls, fine
linen and purple, silk and scarlet,
every kind of citron wood, every
kind of object of ivory, every kind
of object of most precious wood,
bronze, iron, and marble;
13 "and cinnamon and incense,
fragrant oil and frankincense, wine
and oil, fine flour and wheat, cattle
and sheep, horses and chariots, and
bodies and [a]souls of men.
14 "The fruit that your soul longed
for has gone from you, and all the
things which are rich and splendid
have [1]gone from you, and you shall
find them no more at all.
15 "The merchants of these things,
who became rich by her, will stand
at a distance for fear of her torment,
weeping and wailing,
16 "and saying, 'Alas, alas, [a]that
great city [b]that was clothed in fine
linen, purple, and scarlet, and
adorned with gold and precious
stones and pearls!
17 [a]'For in one hour such great
riches [1]came to nothing.' [b]Every
shipmaster, all who travel by ship,
sailors, and as many as trade on the
sea, stood at a distance
18 [a]"and cried out when they saw
the smoke of her burning, saying,
[b]'What *is* like this great city?'
19 [a]"They threw dust on their
heads and cried out, weeping and
wailing, and saying, 'Alas, alas, that
great city, in which all who had ships

(continued from previous page)
so her **sins have reached to heaven** (v. 5), recalling the Tower of Babel (Gen. 11:4), a symbol of excessive arrogance. God's judgment will be swift, **in one day** (v. 8). In Hebrew *day* is not so much a chronological unit as an indication of a completed act.

18:9, 10 The kings of the earth will mourn (but from a distance), stunned by the judgment of Rome and the specter of their own economic loss, when they see her devastation (see Ps. 76:12; Nah. 3:4–7). What happened to Sodom (Gen. 19:28) and Edom (Is. 34:10) is befalling Rome.

18:11–19 Like the political leaders (vv. 9, 10), the economic leaders, **the merchants,** stand astonished at Rome's sudden destruction and their own loss of revenues. Verses 11–13 list luxury items in Rome's flow of trade (see Ezek. 27:12–24). It was said by the rabbis, "Ten measures of wealth came down into the world; Rome received nine and all the world received one." These goods together with their profit made Rome queen (v. 7) of the world. While worldly possessions are not in themselves good or bad, their misuse leads to sin, complacency, and a fatal lack of poverty of spirit (see 3:17–20). Therefore, excessive wealth can easily conflict with authentic Christian discipleship (see Matt. 6:24). The last item in this list, **bodies and souls** (v. 13), refers to slaves, sold at auction as human livestock for domestic service, prostitution, and gladiatorial amusements.

on the sea became rich by her wealth!
[b]For in one hour she [1]is made
desolate.'
20 [a]"Rejoice over her, O heaven,
and *you* [1]holy apostles and prophets,
for [b]God has avenged you on her!"†

The Finality of Babylon's Fall

21 Then a mighty angel took up a
stone like a great millstone and
threw *it* into the sea, saying, [a]"Thus
with violence the great city Babylon
shall be thrown down, and [b]shall not
be found anymore.†
22 [a]"The sound of harpists, musicians, flutists, and trumpeters shall
not be heard in you anymore. No
craftsman of any craft shall be found
in you anymore, and the sound of
a millstone shall not be heard in you
anymore.
23 [a]"The light of a lamp shall not
shine in you anymore, [b]and the
voice of bridegroom and bride shall
not be heard in you anymore. For
[c]your merchants were the great men
of the earth, [d]for by your sorcery all
the nations were deceived.
24 "And [a]in her was found the
blood of prophets and saints, and of
all who [b]were slain on the earth."

19 [b]Rev. 18:8 [1]*have been laid waste*
20 [a]Jer. 51:48 [b]Luke 11:49 [1]NU, M *saints and apostles*
21 [a]Jer. 51:63, 64 [b]Rev. 12:8; 16:20
22 [a]Jer. 7:34; 16:9; 25:10
23 [a]Jer. 25:10 [b]Jer. 7:34; 16:9 [c]Is. 23:8 [d]2 Kin. 9:22
24 [a]Rev. 16:6; 17:6 [b]Jer. 51:49

CHAPTER 19

1 [a]Rev. 11:15; 19:6 [b]Rev. 4:11 [1]NU, M add *something like* [2]NU, M omit *the Lord*
2 [a]Rev. 15:3; 16:7 [b]Deut. 32:43
3 [a]Is. 34:10
4 [a]Rev. 4:4, 6, 10 [b]1 Chr. 16:36
5 [a]Ps. 134:1 [b]Rev. 11:18 [1]NU, M omit *both*

Litany of Triumph in Heaven

19 After these things [a]I [1]heard a
loud voice of a great multitude in heaven, saying, "Alleluia!
[b]Salvation and glory and honor and
power *belong* to [2]the Lord our God!†
2 "For [a]true and righteous *are* His
judgments, because He has judged
the great harlot who corrupted the
earth with her fornication; and He
[b]has avenged on her the blood of His
servants *shed* by her."†
3 Again they said, "Alleluia!
[a]Her smoke rises up forever and
ever!"†
4 And [a]the twenty-four elders
and the four living creatures fell
down and worshiped God who sat
on the throne, saying, [b]"Amen!
Alleluia!"
5 Then a voice came from the
throne, saying, [a]"Praise our God, all
you His servants and those who fear
Him, [b]both[1] small and great!"
6 [a]And I heard, as it were, the
voice of a great multitude, as the
sound of many waters and as the
sound of mighty thunderings, saying, "Alleluia! For [b]the[1] Lord God
Omnipotent reigns!†

6 [a]Ezek. 1:24 [b]Rev. 11:15 [1]NU, M *our*

18:20 The opposite reaction to that of the kings in vv. 9–19 is seen in heaven: Justice has prevailed!

18:21–24 The **great millstone** thrown **into the sea** recalls Babylon's disasters and annihilation (Jer. 51:59–64; Nah. 3:4). Her spell of idolatry, vice, and murder bound the whole civilized world with a bewitching belief that she was immortal and secure. But as her influence was total, so her destruction is total. No signs of life are seen or heard; an eerie silence pervades. **In her was found the blood of prophets and saints** (v. 24; see Jer. 51:49) here alludes directly to the massacres of Christians under such emperors as Nero and Domitian. However, **Babylon** as the center of opposition to God and self-deification of creation continues beyond the immediate incarnation to be seen in the Roman Empire.

19:1 In contrast to the song of doom for Babylon (ch. 18), the scene returns to the heavenly liturgy with an outburst of celestial triumph. **Alleluia,** appearing in the NT only here (vv. 1, 3, 4, 6), is from the Hebrew for "Praise the Lord." It was used in the Great Hallel (Praise) of the Jerusalem temple liturgy (Ps. 104—106; 111—118; 134; 135; 145—150) and in the synagogue as a response by the people (see Tob. 13:8; 3 Macc. 7:13). Within Christendom, the *Alleluia* has been a part of liturgical and private prayers since earliest times.

19:2 The **judgments** of God are **righteous,** in contrast to the slander of the "accuser of our brethren" (12:10; see 2:9) which resulted in the persecutions of Christians.

19:3–5 Her (the harlot, Rome) **smoke rises up forever and ever,** in contrast to the ascent of incense (5:8; 8:4) in eternal heavenly worship. The Church on earth is united with this liturgy in heaven; a deacon calls from the altar, as it were, for all to **praise our God** (v. 5).

19:6–9 At the Passover, deliverance from Egypt (the "Babylon" of Moses' day) was united

(continued on next page)

7 "Let us be glad and rejoice and
give Him glory, for [a]the marriage of
the Lamb has come, and His wife
has made herself ready."
8 And [a]to her it was granted to
be arrayed in fine linen, clean and
bright, [b]for the fine linen is the righteous acts of the saints.
9 Then he said to me, "Write:
[a]'Blessed *are* those who are called to
the marriage supper of the Lamb!'"
And he said to me, [b]"These are the
true sayings of God."
10 And [a]I fell at his feet to worship
him. But he said to me, [b]"See *that
you do* not *do that!* I am your [c]fellow
servant, and of your brethren [d]who
have the testimony of Jesus. Worship
God! For the [e]testimony of Jesus is
the spirit of prophecy."†

7 [a][Matt. 22:2; 25:10]
8 [a]Ezek. 16:10 [b]Ps. 132:9
9 [a]Luke 14:15 [b]Rev. 22:6
10 [a]Rev. 22:8 [b]Acts 10:26 [c][Heb. 1:14] [d]1 John 5:10 [e]Luke 24:27
11 [a]Rev. 15:5 [b]Rev. 6:2; 19:19, 21 [c]Rev. 3:7, 14 [d]Is. 11:4
12 [a]Rev. 1:14 [b]Rev. 2:17; 19:16 [1]M adds *names written, and*
13 [a]Is. 63:2, 3 [b][John 1:1, 14]

The Word and His Army

11 [a]Now I saw heaven opened,
and behold, [b]a white horse. And He
who sat on him *was* called [c]Faithful
and True, and [d]in righteousness He
judges and makes war.†
12 [a]His eyes *were* like a flame of
fire, and on His head *were* many
crowns. [b]He [1]had a name written
that no one knew except Himself.
13 [a]He *was* clothed with a robe
dipped in blood, and His name is
called [b]The Word of God.†
14 [a]And the armies in heaven,
[b]clothed in [1]fine linen, white and
clean, followed Him on white
horses.†

14 [a]Rev. 14:20 [b]Matt. 28:3 [1]NU, M *pure white linen*

(continued from previous page)
with the theme of Israel's betrothal to the Lord (for further nuptial imagery, see Song of Solomon; Rom. 7:1–6). For marriage is a symbol of the union of God with His people (see Is. 54:1–8; Ezek. 16:7–14; Hos. 2:1–23), of Christ with His Church (Matt. 22:1–14; 2 Cor. 11:2; Eph. 5:22–32). This union is fulfilled in the rest of Revelation: Jesus, the Passover Lamb (1 Cor. 5:7) whose death has ransomed the New Israel, is also the divine Bridegroom (Matt. 25:1–13).

A wedding in the Middle East consisted of two parts: the betrothal and the wedding proper. The wedding itself began with the procession of the groom to the bride's home and concluded with the procession of the entire party back to the bridegroom's home for the wedding supper. The Church is now betrothed to Christ by faith. She awaits the coming of the Bridegroom for the **marriage supper of the Lamb** (v. 9), the final eschatological union of Christ and His Church.

The recompense to the faithful for having remained steadfast and pure under persecution (see Matt. 5:12; 1 Pet. 4:13) is to be **arrayed in fine linen, clean and bright** (v. 8; see 3:4, 5; 7:14)—the clothing of grace, holiness and incorruption—and to participate in this mystical *supper* both as guest (v. 9) and as bride (in apocalyptic literature it is not uncommon to find mixed images). This supper has already begun in the Eucharist, a foretaste of the Kingdom (see Matt. 26:29; Luke 22:30). The Orthodox sing on Pascha (Easter): "Shine, shine, O New Jerusalem; the glory of the Lord has shone on you. . . . Grant that we may evermore perfectly partake of You in the neverending Day of Your Kingdom."

19:6 The term here translated **Omnipotent** (Gr. *Pantokrator*) is elsewhere translated "Almighty" (see 1:8; 4:8; 11:17; 15:3; 16:7, 14; 19:15; 21:22). *Pantokrator* also occurs in the LXX version of Hos. 12:5 and Amos 4:13. It is used in the NT only in Revelation, and once in 2 Cor. 6:18, where it is quoted from the OT. The word means all-mighty, all-powerful.

19:10 Orthodoxy makes a strict distinction between the veneration proper to saints and angels (Gr. *doulia*), and the **worship** (Gr. *latria*) due to God alone (see 22:8, 9).

19:11, 12 Heaven being **opened** is a standard formula of revelation (4:1; Ezek. 1:1; Matt. 3:16; John 1:51). Christ is presented as the Warrior-Messiah, a triumphant King. In Semitic thought a name expressed one's essential nature. Some of the names of the rider are understandable: **Faithful and True** (see 3:13), "Word of God" (v. 13; see John 1:1, 14), "KING OF KINGS AND LORD OF LORDS" (v. 16; see 17:14; Deut. 10:17; 1 Tim. 6:15). But He has a secret name which only He can understand (v. 12; see 2:17), for He is God, and only God can fully comprehend God (John 1:18).

19:13 His **robe dipped in blood** (see Gen. 49:10, 11; Is. 63:1–6) unites Christ's sacrifice on the Cross, granting forgiveness of sin and fulfilling all righteousness, with His making war "in righteousness" (v. 11), judging sin.

19:14 The **armies in heaven, clothed in fine linen** are probably the 144,000 faithful (14:3–5)

(continued on next page)

Ο
Ω
Ν
IC
XC
THE SAVIOUR
OF THE WORLD
A NEW COMMANDMENT I GIVE UNTO YOU, THAT YE LOVE ONE ANOTHER; AS I HAVE LOVED
YOU, THAT YE ALSO LOVE ONE ANOTHER. BY THIS SHALL ALL MEN KNOW YE ARE MY DISCIPLES.

Jesus Christ, the Savior of the World, *by the hand of Father Gregory.* Courtesy of St. George Cathedral, Wichita, Kansas, and Dormition Skete, Buena Vista, Colorado.

Now at the right hand of the Father, Jesus Christ is coming again, with glory, to judge the living and the dead. See Psalm 68:18; 110:1; Ephesians 1:20, 21; 4:8–10; Colossians 1:13–18; 3:1; Hebrews 12:22–24; 1 Peter 4:5.

15 Now [a]out of His mouth goes a
[1]sharp sword, that with it He should
strike the nations. And [b]He Himself
will rule them with a rod of iron.
[c]He Himself treads the winepress of
the fierceness and wrath of Almighty
God.†
16 And [a]He has on *His* robe and
on His thigh a name written:

[b]KING OF KINGS
AND LORD OF LORDS.

Defeat of the Beast and False Prophet

17 Then I saw an angel standing
in the sun; and he cried with a loud
voice, saying to all the birds that fly
in the midst of heaven, [a]"Come and
gather together for the [1]supper of the
great God,†
18 [a]"that you may eat the flesh of
kings, the flesh of captains, the flesh
of mighty men, the flesh of horses
and of those who sit on them, and
the flesh of all *people,* [1]free and slave,
both small and great."
19 [a]And I saw the beast, the kings
of the earth, and their armies, gathered together to make war against
Him who sat on the horse and
against His army.
20 [a]Then the beast was captured,
and with him the false prophet who
worked signs in his presence, by
which he deceived those who received the mark of the beast and
[b]those who worshiped his image.
[c]These two were cast alive into the
lake of fire [d]burning with brimstone.†
21 And the rest [a]were killed with
the sword which proceeded from the
mouth of Him who sat on the horse.
[b]And all the birds [c]were filled with
their flesh.

The Millennial Age

20 Then I saw an angel coming
down from heaven, [a]having
the key to the bottomless pit and a
great chain in his hand.†
2 He laid hold of [a]the dragon, that
serpent of old, who is *the* Devil and
Satan, and bound him for a thousand
years;†
3 and he cast him into the bottom-

15 [a]Is. 11:4 [b]Ps. 2:8, 9 [c]Is. 63:3–6 [1]M *sharp two-edged*
16 [a]Rev. 2:17; 19:12 [b]Dan. 2:47
17 [a]Ezek. 39:17 [1]NU, M *great supper of God*
18 [a]Ezek. 39:18–20 [1]NU, M *both free*
19 [a]Rev. 16:13–16
20 [a]Rev. 16:13 [b]Rev. 13:8, 12, 13 [c]Dan. 7:11 [d]Rev. 14:10
21 [a]Rev. 19:15 [b]Rev. 19:17, 18 [c]Rev. 17:16

CHAPTER 20

1 [a]Rev. 1:18; 9:1
2 [a]2 Pet. 2:4

(continued from previous page)
who, having survived the great tribulation in purity, have washed their robes in the blood of the Lamb (7:14).

19:15 The **sharp sword** from the **mouth** is judgment, the prophetic word fulfilled (1:16; 2:12; Is. 11:4); the **rod of iron** (2:27; 12:5; Ps. 2:9) is rule. He **treads the winepress,** executing God's wrath on earth (14:19, 20; Is. 63:3; Jer. 25:30; Lam. 1:15).

19:17, 18 This is a graphic portrayal of the triumph of Christ over Antichrist, forming a macabre contrast with the wedding supper of the Lamb of God (v. 9; 2:17; 3:20). The destruction is total (see Is. 34:1–7; Ezek. 39:17–20; Matt. 24:28).

19:20, 21 Worldly authority and worldly religion are overthrown. The first **beast** (false deity) and the second beast (**false prophet**) of 13:11–15 are captured and **cast alive into the lake of fire,** hell. Hell is symbolized by Gehenna, the noxious, smoldering garbage dump just outside Jerusalem in the Valley of Hinnom. In the past, pagan rituals, including child sacrifice, had occurred in this valley. It came to be associated with the abode of the wicked dead, either awaiting final judgment or actually experiencing eternal torment (see Gen. 19:24; Matt. 18:9). **Brimstone,** a yellow sulphurous substance that burns easily, exuding a foul odor, is found in the Dead Sea region. While the beast and the false prophet were judged immediately, **the rest were killed** (v. 21) in order to arise later for final judgment.

20:1 The **bottomless pit** (abyss) is the great nether region (Ps. 88:6) where the disobedient are confined awaiting final judgment. The demons fear it (see Luke 8:31; Jude 6). It is reached through a chasm, the **key** to which is in the hand of the **angel.** The **great chain** binds Satan.

20:2 Though most did not, a few early Fathers and writers believed in a literal **thousand years** binding of Satan and reign of Christ and the saints on earth (vv. 2–7). The Church, however, authoritatively rejected this teaching (called *chiliasm*) at the Second Ecumenical Council. In apocalyptic literature, numbers have symbolic significance. "Thousand" is often used in the Scriptures to denote a long period of time, a great quantity, completion, perfection,

(continued on next page)

less pit, and shut him up, and
[a]set a seal on him, [b]so that he should
deceive the nations no more till the
thousand years were finished. But
after these things he must be released for a little while.†
4 And I saw [a]thrones, and they
sat on them, and [b]judgment was
committed to them. Then *I saw*
[c]the souls of those who had been beheaded for their witness to Jesus and
for the word of God, [d]who had not
worshiped the beast [e]or his image,
and had not received *his* mark on
their foreheads or on their hands.
And they [f]lived and [g]reigned with
Christ for [1]a thousand years.†
5 But the rest of the dead did not
live again until the thousand years
were finished. This *is* the first
resurrection.
6 Blessed and holy *is* he who has
part in the first resurrection. Over
such [a]the second death has no
power, but they shall be [b]priests of
God and of Christ, [c]and shall reign
with Him a thousand years.

After the Millennium

7 Now when the thousand years
have expired, Satan will be released
from his prison†
8 and will go out [a]to deceive the
nations which are in the four corners
of the earth, [b]Gog and Magog,
[c]to gather them together to battle,
whose number *is* as the sand of the
sea.
9 [a]They went up on the breadth
of the earth and surrounded the
camp of the saints and the beloved
city. And fire came down from God
out of heaven and devoured them.
10 The devil, who deceived them,
was cast into the lake of fire and
brimstone [a]where[1] the beast and the

3 [a]Dan. 6:17 [b]Rev. 12:9; 20:8, 10
4 [a]Dan. 7:9 [b][1 Cor. 6:2, 3] [c]Rev. 6:9 [d]Rev. 13:12 [e]Rev. 13:15 [f]John 14:19 [g]Rom. 8:17 [1]M *the*
6 [a][Rev. 2:11; 20:14] [b]Is. 61:6 [c]Rev. 20:4
8 [a]Rev. 12:9; 20:3, 10 [b]Ezek. 38:2; 39:1, 6 [c]Rev. 16:14
9 [a]Ezek. 38:9, 16
10 [a]Rev. 19:20; 20:14, 15 [1]NU, M *where also*

(continued from previous page)
thoroughness (Ps. 50:10; 2 Pet. 3:8). Here, a *thousand years* (vv. 2–7) is interpreted as the Church age, when Jesus reigns on earth in those who believe. It is that era between the First and Second Comings of Christ, also called the "last times," when Satan's effectiveness at deceit is restricted through the Cross and Resurrection of Christ, and the saints share in Christ's earthly reign through the Church. For these persecuted Christians threatened by martyrdom, this is a consoling hope.

20:3 The devil is thrown, **shut** and sealed into the pit for one **thousand years** (i.e., a long period of time) to allow the Church to be planted, to grow and to overcome, even in time of persecution and trial. The word "millennium" is synonymous with *thousand years*, and carries with it no connotations of peace and prosperity. The Bible teaches that Satan was bound at the completion of Christ's saving work (Matt. 12:28, 29; Luke 10:17, 18; John 12:31, 32; Col. 2:15). He is not totally inactive (Acts 5:3; 1 Cor. 5:5; Eph. 6:11), but he cannot **deceive the nations** by keeping the gospel from them. At the close of the millennium or Church age, Satan will be **released for a while** (vv. 7, 8).

20:4–6 Those who have died **for their witness to Jesus** are in heaven living and reigning with Him (Matt. 19:28; 2 Tim. 2:12) as royal **priests** (1:6; 5:9, 10; Is. 61:6; 1 Pet. 2:9, 10) while the Church serves Him here on earth. **The first resurrection** (v. 6) is the heavenly life of souls who have died in Christ before His Second Coming. Those not in Christ who die are in Hades awaiting the resurrection of the body at His coming. For the righteous saints with Christ, the **second death has no power** (v. 6). These righteous spirits (Heb. 12:23) await only the reuniting of soul and body after the final judgment, when all things are made new (21:1). Hell or Hades (Sheol), where sinners' souls are separated from their bodies, will give up its dead to Gehenna (vv. 13, 14), the lake of fire which burns with sulphur (21:8), eternal damnation (Matt. 25:41), and these will be excluded from the blessedness of the age to come. Hell cannot harm the victorious in Christ (2:11).

20:7–10 The lengthy, millennial period of Satan's binding and the saints' heavenly reign (vv. 1–6) is concluded by the release of Satan and the final battle of history (probably the same as that of 19:14–21; 16:12–16). **Gog and Magog** (v. 8; see Ezek. 38, 39) are nations hostile to God's people, gathered for one final assault directed against **the beloved city** (v. 9), Jerusalem as the Church. As Elijah called down **fire . . . out of heaven** upon his persecutors (2 Kin. 1:10–12), so here God sends a consuming fire (see Gen. 19:24; 1 Kin. 18:38; Ezek. 38:22; 39:6). The **devil** joins **the beast and the false prophet** in the **lake of fire,** the second death of eternal damnation, and is no longer a threat to the world.

false prophet *are.* And they [b]will be
tormented day and night forever and
ever.

The Great White Throne Judgment

11 Then I saw a great white throne
and Him who sat on it, from whose
face [a]the earth and the heaven fled
away. [b]And there was found no
place for them.†
12 And I saw the dead, [a]small and
great, standing before [1]God, [b]and
books were opened. And another
[c]book was opened, which is *the Book*
of Life. And the dead were judged
[d]according to their works, by the
things which were written in the
books.†
13 The sea gave up the dead who
were in it, [a]and Death and Hades
delivered up the dead who were in
them. [b]And they were judged, each
one according to his works.†
14 Then [a]Death and Hades were
cast into the lake of fire. [b]This is the
second [1]death.
15 And anyone not found written
in the Book of Life [a]was cast into the
lake of fire.

A New Creation

21 Now [a]I saw a new heaven
and a new earth, [b]for the first
heaven and the first earth had
passed away. Also there was no
more sea.†
2 Then I, [1]John, saw [a]the holy
city, New Jerusalem, coming down
out of heaven from God, prepared
[b]as a bride adorned for her
husband.†
3 And I heard a loud voice from
heaven saying, "Behold, [a]the tabernacle of God *is* with men, and He
will dwell with them, and they shall
be His people. God Himself will be
with them *and be* their God.†
4 [a]"And God will wipe away

10 [b]Rev. 14:10
11 [a]2 Pet. 3:7 [b]Dan. 2:35
12 [a]Rev. 19:5 [b]Dan. 7:10 [c]Ps. 69:28 [d]Matt. 16:27 [1]NU, M *the throne*
13 [a]Rev. 1:18; 6:8; 21:4 [b]Rev. 2:23; 20:12
14 [a]1 Cor. 15:26 [b]Rev. 21:8 [1]NU, M *death, the lake of fire.*
15 [a]Rev. 19:20

CHAPTER 21

1 [a][2 Pet. 3:13] [b]Rev. 20:11
2 [a]Is. 52:1 [b]2 Cor. 11:2 [1]NU, M omit *John*
3 [a]Lev. 26:11
4 [a]Is. 25:8

20:11 God executes judgment from the **great white throne** (see Dan. 7:9; 1 Enoch 18:8). The One who sits on the *throne* in Revelation is God the Father (4:2–9; 5:1, 7, 13; 6:16; 7:10). However, in the rest of the NT Christ is the judge upon the throne (Matt. 25:31–46; Acts 10:42; 2 Cor. 5:10). John is about to show their unity: "the throne of God and the Lamb" (22:1). **Earth and heaven** flee **away** (Matt. 24:35; 2 Pet. 3:10–13) in terror—a cosmic sign of the great Day of the Lord and the coming of the New Heaven and Earth (21:1).

20:12 Standing before God at His throne at the final judgment, **the dead** are confronted with **their works. The books** of judgment (Dan. 7:10) contain a record of men's own deeds; their own works will judge them (Ps. 62:12; Jer. 17:10). This judging of believers' works is a common NT theme (Matt. 16:27; Rom. 2:6; 2 Cor. 5:10; 1 Pet. 1:17; see also the anaphora of the Liturgy of St. Basil, and the hymns for the Sunday of the Last Judgment). In contrast, **the Book of Life** contains the names of all who are saved by grace (see Ex. 32:32; Is. 4:3; Dan. 12:1, 2): God's mercy is far greater than human works, good or bad. The Orthodox liturgy thus petitions God for a "good account before the dread judgment seat of Christ."

20:13–15 The **sea, Death and Hades**—the powers that held men captive—all give up their dead, showing that all the dead of the world are judged. That Christ has the keys to *Death* and *Hades* (1:18) expresses not His power to put men to death, but His trampling of death by death. He is victorious over death. The *sea* as a symbol of turbulence, chaos and the unknown will be no more (21:1). *Death,* the "last enemy to be destroyed" (1 Cor. 15:26), and *Hades,* the intermediate state between death and resurrection, will end. They are cast into hell, **the lake of fire** (vv. 14, 15), along with all who reject the grace of God.

21:1 The NT teaching that the present world will pass away (see Matt. 5:18; 2 Pet. 3:10–13; 1 John 2:17) does not mean the present creation will be utterly destroyed. It will be totally renewed (21:5; Is. 65:17–25; Rom. 8:19–22; 2 Pet. 3:13): freed from corruption, purified, transfigured, glorified. The first cosmos will pass away; the **sea** will be **no more** (symbolic of chaos, turbulence, and unrest that will one day cease).

21:2 The holy city, New Jerusalem is the city built by God (Heb. 11:10). It is the perfected Church, the **bride** ready for **her husband,** Christ, the abode of the righteous eternally. The OT prophesied a restored and exalted Jerusalem (Is. 60:1–22; 65:17–25; Ezek. 40—48).

21:3, 4 The OT also prophesied that God would dwell with His people. The Immanuel prophecy (Ps. 46:4–7; Is. 7:14) is fulfilled in the Incarnation (John 1:14; 17:22), but comes to

(continued on page 631)

THE ETERNAL KINGDOM

Few saints have been blessed with a vision of heaven while still in this life. Isaiah was one who saw heaven (Is. 6:1–8), as did Ezekiel (Ezek. 1:1–28), and the Apostle John saw a new heaven—God's eternal Kingdom revealed as a city (Rev. 21:1—22:5).

When we read these passages, we note an abundance of mystical, apocalyptic imagery, but the strong similarities between these passages suggest an inspired consistency of reporting on the visions. The living creatures, the light, the cherubic beings, the throne, and the glory of the Lord all work together to unveil a Kingdom of celestial majesty and splendor.

While confessing with the Prophet Isaiah and the Apostle Paul that "eye has not seen, nor ear heard, nor have entered into the heart of man the things which God has prepared for those who love Him" (1 Cor. 2:9), we can find, taking the Scriptures as a whole, certain things which can be said about the eternal Kingdom.

(1) *The saints who inhabit God's Kingdom live in active fulfillment of His eternal plan.* In the Kingdom, humanity becomes all it is meant to be. There is nothing at all in Scripture to suggest that eternal life means people strumming on harps or passively afloat on huge white clouds unto the ages of ages.

Originally created to inhabit Paradise, our first parents chose to sin against God and were expelled from the Garden. The Kingdom of God was closed to mankind (Gen. 3:24). But God in His love called His creation back to Himself, speaking to us through the Law and the prophets and ultimately through His incarnate Son. Through new life in Jesus Christ, we are brought back by God's mercy into the new creation, His everlasting Kingdom. As kings and priests we will reign with Him forever (Rev. 1:6).

(2) *We experience a foretaste of the Kingdom in the Church.* The very first words of the Divine Liturgy spoken by the priest are: "Blessed is the Kingdom of the Father and of the Son and of the Holy Spirit now and ever and unto ages of ages." The Church at worship enters or ascends to the heavenly Kingdom. For it is in the Church that we are seated "together in the heavenly places in Christ Jesus" (Eph. 2:6) and are raised to "where Christ is, sitting at the right hand of God" (Col. 3:1).

In worship we join the heavenly hosts—the saints and the angels—in giving praise to our God. As the body of Christ we participate with that "great cloud of witnesses" (Heb. 12:1) surrounding us as we come to "the throne of God" (Heb. 12:2). We come liturgically "to the city of the living God, the heavenly Jerusalem, to an innumerable company of angels, to the general assembly and church of the firstborn who are registered in heaven, to God the Judge of all" (Heb. 12:22, 23). With this heavenly vision, the Orthodox Church each Sunday remembers not only those in the parish but "all those who in faith have gone on before us to their rest."

(3) *Knowledge of the Kingdom motivates us to live in complete devotion to Christ.* In this life, we have a foretaste of the Kingdom which inspires us to seek its fullness. In Paul's words, "For now we see in a mirror dimly, but then face to face" (1 Cor. 13:12). Worship is not a solitary act. Rather it is the Bride of Christ, the one Church—those on earth joining with those in heaven—giving thanks to our God and King, who has made us citizens of His magnificent domain.

The Apostle John writes, "Beloved, now we are children of God and it has not yet been revealed what we shall be, but we know that when He is revealed, we shall be like Him, for we shall see Him as He is. And everyone who has this hope in Him purifies himself, just as He is pure" (1 John 3:2, 3).

every tear from their eyes; [b]there
shall be no more death, [c]nor sorrow,
nor crying. There shall be no more
pain, for the former things have
passed away."
5 Then [a]He who sat on the throne
said, [b]"Behold, I make all things
new." And He said [1]to me, "Write,
for [c]these words are true and
faithful."
6 And He said to me, [a]"It[1] is
done! [b]I am the Alpha and the
Omega, the Beginning and the End.
[c]I will give of the fountain of the water of life freely to him who thirsts.†
7 "He who overcomes [1]shall inherit all things, and [a]I will be his God
and he shall be My son.
8 [a]"But the cowardly, [1]unbe-
lieving, abominable, murderers, sexually immoral, sorcerers, idolaters,
and all liars shall have their part in
[b]the lake which burns with fire and
brimstone, which is the second
death."

The New Jerusalem

9 Then one of [a]the seven angels
who had the seven bowls filled with
the seven last plagues came [1]to me
and talked with me, saying, "Come,
I will show you [b]the [2]bride, the
Lamb's wife."†
10 And he carried me away [a]in the
Spirit to a great and high mountain,
and showed me [b]the [1]great city, the
[2]holy Jerusalem, descending out of
heaven from God,†
11 [a]having the glory of God. Her
light *was* like a most precious stone,
like a jasper stone, clear as crystal.
12 Also she had a great and high
wall with [a]twelve gates, and twelve
angels at the gates, and names written on them, which are *the names* of
the twelve tribes of the children of
Israel:†
13 [a]three gates on the east, three
gates on the north, three gates on
the south, and three gates on the
west.
14 Now the wall of the city had
twelve foundations, and [a]on them
were the [1]names of the twelve apostles of the Lamb.
15 And he who talked with me

4 [b]1 Cor. 15:26 [c]Is. 35:10; 51:11; 65:19
5 [a]Rev. 4:2, 9; 20:11 [b]Is. 43:19 [c]Rev. 19:9; 22:6 [1]NU, M omit *to me*
6 [a]Rev. 10:6; 16:17 [b]Rev. 1:8; 22:13 [c]John 4:10 [1]M omits *It is done*
7 [a]Zech. 8:8 [1]M *I shall give him these things*
8 [a]1 Cor. 6:9 [b]Rev. 20:14 [1]M adds *and sinners,*
9 [a]Rev. 15:1 [b]Rev. 19:7; 21:2 [1]NU, M omit *to me* [2]M *woman, the Lamb's bride*
10 [a]Rev. 1:10 [b]Ezek. 48 [1]NU, M omit *great* [2]NU, M *holy city, Jerusalem*
11 [a]Rev. 15:8; 21:23; 22:5
12 [a]Ezek. 48:31–34 **13** [a]Ezek. 48:31–34
14 [a]Eph. 2:20 [1]NU, M *twelve names*

(continued from page 629)
completion in the messianic age when God will fully dwell (lit. "in-tent") with His people, restoring the paradise of old (Gen. 2; Ezek. 37:26, 27; 2 Cor. 6:16). Therefore joy displaces the sorrows and sufferings, a great consolation for persecuted believers.

21:6–8 The **water of life** ("living water," 7:17; John 4:10–14; 7:37–39; see Is. 55:1) is the grace of the Holy Spirit, bestowed along with baptism in chrismation. Only the one **who thirsts** will be given the *water* forever (v. 6). And, repeating the concluding exhortation of each of the seven letters (chs. 2; 3), only **he who overcomes** (v. 7), who persists in his allegiance to God, will **inherit,** becoming a permanent son of God. Those who fall away through cowardice or unbelief face instead **the lake** of fire (v. 8). They lose God's inheritance, receiving instead the damning recompense of sin and death (see 20:15; 22:15), in company with the beast, the false prophet, Death, and Hades.

21:9–11 In stark contrast to the harlot arrayed in gaudy finery (17:3), the Messiah's **bride** comes from God and so reflects God's splendor.

21:10 Like Ezekiel, John has the vantage point of a **high mountain** (Ezek. 40:2); the perfected Church he sees resembles Ezekiel's new temple (Ezek. 40—48). The New **Jerusalem** descends **out of heaven from God,** for God Himself completes the reunion of heaven and earth. The New Jerusalem completes and fulfills the old Jerusalem (see 1 Kin. 5:17; Is. 54:11, 12) just as the New Covenant fulfills the Old.

21:12–14 The splendor described is fitting for the place where God will dwell with His people (vv. 3, 7). As the breastplate of the High Priest was adorned with twelve jewels corresponding to the twelve tribes (Ex. 28:16–21), so the Church is founded on the twelve precious foundation stones of the **apostles** (v. 14; see vv. 19, 20). All who are espoused to Christ, who feast at the Wedding Supper, and who dwell in the Holy City, are members of the royal priesthood (1:6; 5:10; 20:6; 1 Pet. 2:9).

[a]had a gold reed to measure the city,
its gates, and its wall.†
16 The city is laid out as a square;
its length is as great as its breadth.
And he measured the city with the
reed: twelve thousand [1]furlongs. Its
length, breadth, and height are
equal.
17 Then he measured its wall: one
hundred *and* forty-four cubits, *accord-*
ing to the measure of a man, that
is, of an angel.
18 The construction of its wall was
of jasper; and the city *was* pure gold,
like clear glass.
19 [a]The foundations of the wall of
the city *were* adorned with all kinds
of precious stones: the first foundation *was* jasper, the second sapphire,
the third chalcedony, the fourth
emerald,
20 the fifth sardonyx, the sixth sardius, the seventh chrysolite, the
eighth beryl, the ninth topaz, the
tenth chrysoprase, the eleventh ja-
cinth, and the twelfth amethyst.
21 The twelve gates *were* twelve
[a]pearls: each individual gate was
of one pearl. [b]And the street of the
city *was* pure gold, like transparent
glass.

Healing of the Nations

22 [a]But I saw no temple in it, for
the Lord God Almighty and the
Lamb are its temple.†
23 [a]The city had no need of the sun
or of the moon to shine [1]in it, for
the [2]glory of God illuminated it. The
Lamb *is* its light.†
24 [a]And the nations [1]of those who
are saved shall walk in its light, and
the kings of the earth bring their
glory and honor [2]into it.
25 [a]Its gates shall not be shut at
all by day [b](there shall be no night
there).
26 [a]And they shall bring the glory
and the honor of the nations into
[1]it.
27 But [a]there shall by no means enter it anything [1]that defiles, or causes
an abomination or a lie, but only
those who are written in the Lamb's
[b]Book of Life.

Paradise Regained

22 And he showed me [a]a [1]pure
river of water of life, clear as
crystal, proceeding from the throne
of God and of the Lamb.†

15 [a]Ezek. 40:3
16 [1]Lit. *stadia,* about 1,380 miles in all
19 [a]Is. 54:11
21 [a]Matt. 13:45, 46 [b]Rev. 22:2
22 [a]John 4:21, 23
23 [a]Is. 24:23; 60:19, 20 [1]NU, M omit *in it* [2]M *very glory*
24 [a]Is. 60:3, 5; 66:12 [1]NU, M omit *of those who are saved* [2]M *of the nations to Him*
25 [a]Is. 60:11 [b]Is. 60:20
26 [a]Rev. 21:24 [1]M adds *that they may enter in.*
27 [a]Joel 3:17 [b]Phil. 4:3 [1]NU, M *profane, nor one who causes*

CHAPTER 22

1 [a]Ezek. 47:1 [1]NU, M omit *pure*

21:15–21 As in Ezekiel's vision, the angel measures **the city** (Ezek. 40—42). It is a colossal cube (see center-column note, v. 16), recalling the shape of the Most Holy Place (1 Kin. 6:19, 20; Ezek. 41:4). The dimensions of the city are symbolic of its perfection: the multiples of 12 symbolize the people of God; 1,000 shows its greatness. The **precious stones** (v. 19) portray its glory. As the priests in the Jerusalem temple walked on pavements of gold (1 Kin. 6:30), so the new, royal priesthood will walk on a **street** of **pure gold** (v.21).

21:22 There is **no** material **temple** in the New Jerusalem (John 4:21). **Its temple** is the presence of God in all its inhabitants (1 Cor. 15:28; 1 Pet. 2:4–10). The Church itself is the temple.

21:23–27 The OT prophecies concerning the glorification of Jerusalem are fulfilled in the eternal Kingdom (see Is. 60). Created light is unnecessary, for the everlasting Uncreated Light (Is. 60:19, 20) will illumine all (Ps. 36:9) with true and clear vision to see things as they really are. The true Light, the Light of the World (John 8:12), was incarnate (John 1:9), and even while on earth He shone with Uncreated Light (Mark 9:2–8; 2 Pet. 1:16–18). As prophesied, all the earth will stream to the Holy City to honor it (Is. 55:5; Jer. 16:19–21; Tobit 13:11)—it has no enemies—but only the pure will live within it (Matt. 5:8).

22:1 The **river of** the **water of life** manifests the Giver of Life, the Holy Spirit (see 21:6; also Ezek. 47:1–12; Zech. 14:8). The OT Feast of Tabernacles, the festival of the messianic Kingdom, emphasized light and water. As in his Gospel, so here John shows these themes are fulfilled by Christ and His Church. Christ is the Light of the World (21:23–26 and 22:5 with John 8:12); the Holy Spirit is the Water of Life (vv. 1, 2 and 21:6 with John 7:37–39). The Church is the messianic Kingdom.

God the Father and **the Lamb,** the Son incarnate, share one **throne,** for they are consubstantial and one worship is offered them. With the Spirit **proceeding from** the *throne,* the entire Trinity is here.

2 [a]In the middle of its street, and
on either side of the river, *was*
[b]the tree of life, which bore twelve
fruits, each *tree* yielding its fruit
every month. The leaves of the tree
were [c]for the healing of the nations.†
3 And [a]there shall be no more
curse, [b]but the throne of God and
of the Lamb shall be in it, and His
[c]servants shall serve Him.
4 [a]They shall see His face, and
[b]His name *shall be* on their foreheads.†
5 [a]There shall be no night there:
They need no lamp nor [b]light of the
sun, for [c]the Lord God gives them
light. [d]And they shall reign forever
and ever.†

The Angel's Testimony

6 Then he said to me, [a]"These
words *are* faithful and true." And the
Lord God of the [1]holy prophets
[b]sent His angel to show His servants
the things which must [c]shortly take
place.
7 [a]"Behold, I am coming quickly!

2 [a]Ezek. 47:12
[b]Gen. 2:9
[c]Rev. 21:24
3 [a]Zech. 14:11
[b]Ezek. 48:35
[c]Rev. 7:15
4 [a][Matt. 5:8]
[b]Rev. 14:1
5 [a]Rev. 21:23
[b]Rev. 7:15
[c]Ps. 36:9
[d]Dan. 7:18, 27
6 [a]Rev. 19:9
[b]Rev. 1:1
[c]Heb. 10:37
[1]NU, M *spirits of the prophets*
7 [a][Rev. 3:11]
[b]Rev. 1:3
8 [a]Rev. 19:10
[1]NU, M *am the one who heard and saw*
9 [a]Rev. 19:10
[1]NU, M omit *For*
10 [a]Dan. 8:26
[b]Rev. 1:3
11 [1]NU, M *do right*
12 [a]Is. 40:10; 62:11
[b]Rev. 20:12

[b]Blessed *is* he who keeps the words
of the prophecy of this book."†
8 Now I, John, [1]saw and heard
these things. And when I heard and
saw, [a]I fell down to worship before
the feet of the angel who showed me
these things.†
9 Then he said to me, [a]"See *that*
you do not *do that*. [1]For I am your
fellow servant, and of your brethren
the prophets, and of those who keep
the words of this book. Worship
God."

Christ's Testimony

10 [a]And he said to me, "Do not
seal the words of the prophecy of
this book, [b]for the time is at hand.†
11 "He who is unjust, let him be
unjust still; he who is filthy, let him
be filthy still; he who is righteous,
let him [1]be righteous still; he who is
holy, let him be holy still."
12 "And behold, I am coming
quickly, and [a]My reward *is* with Me,
[b]to give to every one according to
his work.†

22:2, 3 The tree of life, a symbol of Christ Himself, gives immortality. It fulfills the Tree of Life in Paradise (Gen. 3:22) and the other Tree of Life, the Cross of the Savior—a tree of curse (Gal. 3:13). But there is **no more curse** (v. 3) in the Holy City: the curse of Gen. 3:14–19 is reversed. The **fruits** and **leaves** of the *tree* are completely and universally therapeutic, reversing the effects of the fruit of the tree of disobedience (Gen. 3:2–11).

22:4 The **face** of God is that of the glorified Christ (see John 14:9; 1 John 3:2). The *face* which cannot be seen is the hidden essence of God (John 1:18; 1 Tim. 6:16). Normally, to **see** even an indirect manifestation of God is not possible in this life (Ex. 33:20, 23; Matt. 5:8; 1 Cor. 13:12; Heb. 12:14). But in the age to come the faithful, who bear Jesus' Name **on their foreheads,** may *see* Him ceaselessly. In the OT only the high priest bore the unspeakable *name of* ***God on his*** **forehead,** and that he did externally, on a golden plate attached to his turban (Ex. 28:36–39). In the NT, all who believe are granted His *name*. (See 3:12; 7:3; Ezek. 9:4–6.)

22:5 The Lord God gives them light perfects the priestly blessing of Num. 6:23–27, a concluding benediction of the daily morning and evening sacrifices of the OT Temple. When you have God's Uncreated Light, there can be **no night** (see 21:23; Is. 60:19, 20).

22:7 Keeping **the words . . . of this book** refers to repentance, faithfulness and steadfastness, no matter the circumstances of life. The "overcomers" are **blessed.**

22:8, 9 John repeats his error of attempting to worship **the angel** (see 19:10). The fact is, even mature Christians and leaders sometimes err. But we press on to change and to continue with Christ. The command to John is, **Worship God** (v. 9). The angel affirms that John is a brother of **the prophets** (v. 9).

22:10, 11 The command not to **seal the words of the prophecy** is a reversal of 10:4 and Dan. 8:26; 12:4, 9. Those prophecies were for a future time, but the message of Revelation is for the contemporary communities John is addressing. Some—those who still persist in their wickedness—are unable to repent (see Is. 6:9, 10; Ezek. 3:27; Dan. 12:10; Mark 4:12). The **righteous** are encouraged to be steadfast.

22:12 Divine **reward** (Is. 40:10; Jer. 17:10) will be visited upon the earth soon.

13 [a]"I am the Alpha and the
Omega, *the* [1]Beginning and *the* End,
the First and the Last."†
14 [a]Blessed *are* those who [1]do His
commandments, that they may have
the right [b]to the tree of life, [c]and may
enter through the gates into the
city.†
15 [1]But [a]outside *are* [b]dogs and sorcerers and sexually immoral and murderers and idolaters, and whoever loves and practices a lie.
16 [a]"I, Jesus, have sent My angel
to testify to you these things in the
churches. [b]I am the Root and the
Offspring of David, [c]the Bright and
Morning Star."†

The Church's Testimony

17 And the Spirit and [a]the bride
say, "Come!" And let him who hears
say, "Come!" [b]And let him who
thirsts come. Whoever desires, let
him take the water of life freely.†
18 [1]For I testify to everyone who
hears the words of the prophecy of
this book: [a]If anyone adds to these
things, [2]God will add to him the
plagues that are written in this
book;†
19 and if anyone takes away from
the words of the book of this prophecy, [a]God[1] shall take away his part
from the [2]Book of Life, from the holy
city, and *from* the things which are
written in this book.
20 He who testifies to these things
says, "Surely I am coming quickly."
Amen. Even so, come, Lord Jesus!†

Benediction

21 The grace of our Lord Jesus
Christ *be* [1]with you all. Amen.†

13 [a]Is. 41:4 [1]NU, M *First and the Last, the Beginning and the End.*
14 [a]Dan. 12:12 [b][Prov. 11:30] [c]Rev. 21:27 [1]NU *wash their robes,*
15 [a]1 Cor. 6:9 [b]Phil. 3:2 [1]NU, M omit *But*
16 [a]Rev. 1:1 [b]Rev. 5:5 [c]Num. 24:17
17 [a][Rev. 21:2, 9] [b]Is. 55:1
18 [a]Deut. 4:2; 12:32 [1]NU, M omit *For* [2]M *may God add*
19 [a]Ex. 32:33 [1]M *may God take away* [2]NU, M *tree of life with all the saints*
21 [1]NU *with all;* M

22:13 For the meaning of these divine titles, see note on 1:8 (see also 1:17; 21:6; Is. 44:6; 48:12).

22:14, 15 A clear distinction is drawn between the eternal state of the blessed and that of the damned (see 21:8). Many texts read "wash their robes" (see 3:4; 7:14; 16:15) rather than **do His commandments.** The point is the same: it is the pure in Christ who enter the Kingdom. **Dogs** (v. 15) refers to the impure (Deut. 23:18; Phil. 3:2; 2 Pet. 2:22).

22:16 Jesus confirms this is His message. It fulfills the intent of OT prophecy, for He Himself is the prophesied Messiah.

22:17 This is a liturgical dialogue, a reflection of eucharistic theology. The Church as bound to God, **the bride** in union with the Holy **Spirit,** invites Christ to **"Come!"** We plead for His return (see His answer in v. 20). Those who desire God (21:6; Ps. 63:1; Is. 26:9; John 6:35) but who are not yet overcoming the world, are in turn invited to **come** to Christ.

22:18, 19 This severe warning refers to the Book of Revelation, not to the Bible as a whole, and admonishes those in the communities addressed not to distort its message. To do so is to threaten one's very salvation (see Deut. 4:2; 12:32; Gal. 1:8, 9).

22:20 This is a liturgical benediction to the book. The bride, recognizing the voice of her Beloved as He testifies to His Advent, runs out to meet Him (see Matt. 25:6) and in her joy proclaims: **Amen . . . come, Lord Jesus!** This echoes "Maranatha" (1 Cor. 16:22), which was part of the eucharistic dialogue of the early Church (Didache 10, 6).

22:21 This is an appropriate final benediction, considering the book was to be read aloud in **all** seven churches.

The Book of PSALMS

Authors: *David and others*

Date: *About 1000–400* B.C.

Theme: *The Songs of God's People*

AUTHOR: Among the authors of the Psalms are David, the temple musicians (such as Asaph and Jeduthun), Ethan the Ezrahite and the "sons of Korah."

DATE: The Psalms were written at various times, most likely beginning in the time of David (c. 1000 B.C.) and for several centuries thereafter.

MAJOR THEME: *The songs of God's people.* The Psalms are the hymnbook of Israel, and now of the Church. Each psalm has its own theme, as noted in the titles.

BACKGROUND INFORMATION: (1) *Types of psalms:* The Psalms are of many types, including: (a) prophecies of the coming Messiah, (b) prayers for the king, (c) personal lamentations (d) songs of praise, and (e) hymns for special feasts.

(2) *The prayer book of the Church:* The Psalms have become for the Church, as for ancient Israel, a book of prayer and praise. All reach their fulfillment in Christ, the Son of God. Not only do the Psalms predict specific events of Christ's life, but in them He Himself intercedes for and with His people before the Father. The Psalms could also be seen as a dialogue between the Church, the body of Christ, and Christ her Head. Therefore, they make the most sense to us when they are prayed, not simply read.

(3) *Uses in the Church:* The Book of Psalms, or Psalter, is used in the Orthodox Church in three primary ways:

(a) In the *daily* cycle of prayers. The liturgical tradition appoints certain psalms as "fixed" portions of the daily services. These will be pointed out in the notes throughout the text as psalms for morning prayers, evening prayers, and prayers of the hours.

(b) In the *weekly* order of the morning and evening services (Matins and Vespers). When these are done in their entirety, as in the monasteries, all 150 psalms are chanted in the course of the week, starting at Saturday Vespers and concluding at Matins the following Saturday.

(c) In the observance of the Church *year*, the liturgical tradition selects particular psalms or verses for special feasts or seasons as prophetic statements illustrating the work of Christ for us. For example, the Passion Song of Psalm 22 ("they pierced My hands and My feet") is used in the Church on Good Friday. This use of the Psalms is crucial to our understanding of the fullness of Christ's ministry to His people. By far the majority of our notes pertain to this third category.

(4) *Purpose:* The Psalms serve many functions. They (a) foretell coming events, (b) recall history, (c) frame laws for life, (d) suggest what must be done to obey God's word, (e) are a treasury of good doctrine, (f) help overcome the passions which exercise dominion over our souls, through the power of poetic expression to take over and gradually transform our thoughts.

(5) *The two texts of the Psalms:* In the ancient Church, and yet today in the Orthodox Church, the preferred text of the Old Testament is the Septuagint (LXX), a Greek translation completed by the second century B.C. Septuagint means "seventy" (hence the Roman numeral shorthand "LXX"), deriving from the tradition that Ptolemy Philadelphius (285–246 B.C.) directed 70 or 72 scholars to translate the Hebrew Old Testament into Greek for use in his library at Alexandria. By the time of Christ, most Jews scattered throughout the Greek-speaking world did not know Hebrew and therefore used the Septuagint text. Even in Israel the Jews used the Septuagint or an Aramaic (the language of the people) text, rather than the Hebrew. Consequently, Christ and the New Testament writers generally quoted the Old Testament from the Septuagint. As the early Church spread throughout the Empire where Greek was the common language, she used the Septuagint version of the Scriptures. Thus it was only natural for the Church to use the Septuagint in her liturgical texts.

Some thirty years after the fall of Jerusalem in A.D. 70, the remaining Jewish leadership in the area called a council of Jewish teachers at Jamnia, near Joppa, which, according to tradition, decided a distinctively Jewish Old Testament text was required, written in Hebrew. Scholars (the "masoretes") edited and copied that Hebrew version from the sixth to tenth centuries A.D.; thus it is known as the Masoretic Text (MT).

The Church continued to prefer the Septuagint, however, because the Greek language was known by most Christians, and because of its messianic and prophetic sense. But later in the West, Latin became the dominant language and a Latin Old Testament (the Vulgate) came to overshadow other texts. Thus, until the Reformation, Christian worship and doctrine developed from Greek and Latin Old Testament versions.

Steered by the Renaissance concept of appeal to antiquity, and by their own antagonism to anything Roman Catholic, the Reformers bypassed Rome's Vulgate and the Septuagint used by the Eastern Church to claim the "original" text and its abbreviated canon, the Masoretic Text. The NKJV Book of Psalms is, therefore, translated from the Masoretic Text.

While no suitable English translation of the Septuagint is currently available, some compensation is provided by giving the Septuagint text (author's translation) in the notes for certain psalms. Differences in psalm numbering between the Septuagint and the Masoretic Text are also indicated.

BOOK ONE: Psalms 1–41

PSALM 1†

The Way of the Righteous and the Way of the Ungodly

BLESSED [a]*is* the man
Who walks not in the counsel of the [1]ungodly,
Nor stands in the path of sinners,
[b]Nor sits in the seat of the scornful;
2 But [a]his delight *is* in the law of the LORD,
[b]And in His law he [1]meditates day and night.
3 He shall be like a tree
[a]Planted by the [1]rivers of water,
That brings forth its fruit in its season,
Whose leaf also shall not wither;
And whatever he does shall [b]prosper.

4 The ungodly *are* not so,
But *are* [a]like the chaff which the wind drives away.
5 Therefore the ungodly shall not stand in the judgment,
Nor sinners in the congregation of the righteous.

6 For [a]the LORD knows the way of the righteous,
But the way of the ungodly shall perish.

PSALM 1
1 [a]Prov. 4:14 [b]Jer. 15:17 [1]*wicked*
2 [a]Ps. 119:14, 16, 35 [b][Josh. 1:8] [1]*ponders* by talking to himself
3 [a]Jer. 17:8 [b]Gen. 39:2, 3, 23 [1]*channels*
4 [a]Job 21:18
6 [a]Ps. 37:18

PSALM 2†

The Begotten One

WHY [a]do the [1]nations [2]rage,
And the people plot a [3]vain thing?
2 The kings of the earth set themselves,
And the [a]rulers take counsel together,
Against the LORD and against His [b]Anointed,[1] *saying,*
3 "Let [a]us break Their bonds in pieces
And cast away Their cords from us."

4 He who sits in the heavens [a]shall laugh;
The LORD shall hold them in derision.
5 Then He shall speak to them in His wrath,
And distress them in His deep displeasure:
6 "Yet I have [1]set My King
[2]On My holy hill of Zion."

7 "I will declare the [1]decree:
The LORD has said to Me,
[a]'You *are* My Son,
Today I have begotten You.
8 Ask of Me, and I will give *You*

PSALM 2
1 [a]Acts 4:25, 26 [1]*Gentiles* [2]*throng tumultuously* [3]*worthless* or *empty*
2 [a][Mark 3:6; 11:18] [b][John 1:41] [1]Christ, Commissioned One, Heb. *Messiah*
3 [a]Luke 19:14
4 [a]Ps. 37:13
6 [1]Lit. *installed* [2]Lit. *Upon Zion, the hill of My holiness*
7 [a][Heb. 1:5; 5:5] [1]Or *decree of the LORD: He said to Me*

---

1 This psalm serves as an introduction to the entire Psalter with its depiction of the "two ways": the way of the **righteous** and the way of the **ungodly** (v. 6).

The psalmist dedicates the beginning of His prophecy to Christ **the LORD** (vv. 2, 6). For this reason, he pronounces those who have trusted in Him happy and **blessed** (v. 1). He sets forth three acts which must be guarded against: (1) walking in the **counsel of the ungodly,** or taking the advice of unbelievers; (2) standing in the **path of sinners,** or associating with those who refuse to do God's will; (3) sitting on the **seat of the scornful,** or adopting the attitude of those who blaspheme God.

2 This is a messianic psalm, containing a collection of prophecies about Jesus Christ, centered around the fact that the Son is the Lord (Heb. *Yahweh*). Consequently, it is no surprise that we find it used in the Christmas Eve and Good Friday services. On Christmas Eve this is the psalm used in the refrain (called the prokeimenon or gradual) before the Epistle is read in the Vesperal (evening) Liturgy. On Good Friday, the entire psalm is sung in the First Hour prayers. The theme of the psalm is the Anointed One entering into history. We read of the eternal generation of the Son from the Father before all time (v. 7; quoted in the NT, Heb. 1:5; 5:5). Interestingly, St. Paul quotes v. 7 as referring also to the Resurrection (Acts 13:32, 33).

The nations *for* Your inheritance,
And the ends of the earth *for* Your possession.
9 [a]You shall [1]break them with a rod of iron;
You shall dash them to pieces like a potter's vessel.' "

10 Now therefore, be wise, O kings;
Be instructed, you judges of the earth.
11 Serve the LORD with fear,
And rejoice with trembling.
12 [1]Kiss the Son, lest [2]He be angry,
And you perish *in* the way,
When [a]His wrath is kindled but a little.
[b]Blessed *are* all those who put their trust in Him.

PSALM 3†

Help for the Afflicted

A Psalm of David [a]when he fled from Absalom his son.

LORD, how they have increased who trouble me!
Many *are* they who rise up against me.
2 Many *are* they who say of me,
"*There is* no help for him in God." Selah

3 But You, O LORD, *are* [a]a shield [1]for me,
My glory and [b]the One who lifts up my head.

9 [a]Ps. 89:23; 110:5, 6; [Rev. 2:26, 27; 12:5; 19:15] [1]So with MT, Tg.; LXX, Syr., Vg. *rule* (cf. Rev. 2:27)
12 [a][Rev. 6:16, 17] [b][Ps. 5:11; 34:22] [1]LXX, Vg. *Embrace discipline;* Tg. *Receive instruction* [2]LXX *the* LORD

PSALM 3
title [a]2 Sam. 15:13–17
3 [a]Ps. 5:12; 28:7 [b]Ps. 9:13; 27:6 [1]Lit. *around*
4 [a]Ps. 4:3; 34:4 [b]Ps. 2:6; 15:1; 43:3
5 [a]Lev. 26:6; Ps. 4:8; Prov. 3:24
6 [a]Ps. 23:4; 27:3
7 [a]Job 16:10
8 [a]Ps. 28:8; 35:3; [Is. 43:11]

PSALM 4
title [1]*Choir Director*
1 [1]*Be gracious to me*

4 I cried to the LORD with my voice,
And [a]He heard me from His [b]holy hill. Selah

5 [a]I lay down and slept;
I awoke, for the LORD sustained me.
6 [a]I will not be afraid of ten thousands of people
Who have set *themselves* against me all around.

7 Arise, O LORD;
Save me, O my God!
[a]For You have struck all my enemies on the cheekbone;
You have broken the teeth of the ungodly.
8 [a]Salvation *belongs* to the LORD.
Your blessing *is* upon Your people. Selah

PSALM 4†

The Security of God's People

To the [1]Chief Musician. With stringed instruments. A Psalm of David.

HEAR me when I call, O God of my righteousness!
You have relieved me in *my* distress;
[1]Have mercy on me, and hear my prayer.

2 How long, O you sons of men,
Will you turn my glory to shame?
How long will you love worthlessness

3 Psalm 3 is used throughout Christendom as a morning prayer (see v. 5), and so serves as the first of the six psalms of the Matins service (Ps. 3; 38; 63; 88; 103; 143). This psalm originally referred to David himself, for the expression **many are they who rise up against me** (v. 1) speaks of those who had previously belonged to the faithful, but were now rebelling against him. The psalm refers also to humanity in general, which has sinned and was delivered to spiritual enemies, yet is ultimately saved by God. **I awoke** (v. 5) refers to our resurrection; **arise, O LORD** (v. 7) refers to Christ's Resurrection.

4 An evening prayer (v. 8), Ps. 4 is used as a prokeimenon (gradual) at daily Vespers on Monday. It is one of the psalms for Great Compline (the last service of the day) during Lent.

Accused of wrongdoing (v. 2), the psalmist replies by declaring his innocence. He is sure of God's help, and relief when he is in distress: **You have put gladness in my heart** (v. 7). **The light of** God's **countenance** (v. 6) is Christ, who teaches us all good things and through whom we obtain true *gladness* of mind and heart.

And seek falsehood? Selah
3 But know that [a]the LORD has
[1]set apart for Himself him
who is godly;
The LORD will hear when I call
to Him.

4 [a]Be[1] angry, and do not sin.
[b]Meditate within your heart on
your bed, and be still. Selah
5 Offer [a]the sacrifices of
righteousness,
And [b]put your trust in the
LORD.

6 *There are* many who say,
"Who will show us *any* good?"
[a]LORD, lift up the light of Your
countenance upon us.
7 You have put [a]gladness in my
heart,
More than in the season that
their grain and wine
increased.
8 [a]I will both lie down in peace,
and sleep;
[b]For You alone, O LORD, make
me dwell in safety.

PSALM 5†

A Prayer for Guidance

To the Chief Musician. With [1]flutes. A Psalm of David.

GIVE [a]ear to my words, O LORD,
Consider my [1]meditation.
2 Give heed to the voice of my
cry,
My King and my God,
For to You I will pray.
3 My voice You shall hear in the
morning, O LORD;
[a]In the morning I will direct *it*
to You,
And I will look up.

4 For You *are* not a God who takes
pleasure in wickedness,
Nor shall evil [1]dwell with You.
5 The [a]boastful shall not [b]stand in
Your sight;
You hate all workers of iniquity.
6 You shall destroy those who
speak falsehood;
The LORD abhors the
[a]bloodthirsty and deceitful
man.

7 But as for me, I will come into
Your house in the multitude
of Your mercy;
In fear of You I will worship
toward [1]Your holy temple.
8 [a]Lead me, O LORD, in Your
righteousness because of my
enemies;
Make Your way straight before
my face.

9 For *there is* no [1]faithfulness in
their mouth;
Their inward part *is* destruction;
[a]Their throat *is* an open tomb;
They flatter with their tongue.
10 Pronounce them guilty, O God!
Let them fall by their own
counsels;
Cast them out in the multitude
of their transgressions,
For they have rebelled against
You.

11 But let all those rejoice who put
their trust in You;
Let them ever shout for joy,
because You [1]defend them;
Let those also who love Your
name
Be joyful in You.
12 For You, O LORD, will bless the
righteous;
With favor You will surround
him as *with* a shield.

3 [a][2 Tim. 2:19] [1]Many Heb. mss., LXX, Tg., Vg. *made wonderful*
4 [a][Ps. 119:11; Eph. 4:26] [b]Ps. 77:6 [1]Lit. *Tremble* or *Be agitated*
5 [a]Deut. 33:19; Ps. 51:19 [b]Ps. 37:3, 5; 62:8
6 [a]Num. 6:26; Ps. 80:3, 7, 19
7 [a]Ps. 97:11, 12; Is. 9:3; Acts 14:17
8 [a]Job 11:19; Ps. 3:5 [b][Lev. 25:18]; Deut. 12:10

PSALM 5
title [1]Heb. *nehiloth*
1 [a]Ps. 4:1 [1]Lit. *groaning*
3 [a]Ps. 55:17; 88:13
4 [1]Lit. *sojourn*
5 [a][Hab. 1:13] [b]Ps. 1:5
6 [a]Ps. 55:23
7 [1]Lit. *the temple of Your holiness*
8 [a]Ps. 25:4, 5; 27:11; 31:3
9 [a]Rom. 3:13 [1]*uprightness*
11 [1]*protect*, lit. *cover*

5 A **morning** prayer (v. 3), Ps. 5 is used as one of the fixed psalms of the First Hour. In ancient Israel, this was the prayer of the priest preparing to offer the sacrifice. For that reason, in Orthodox Christian use, v. 7 is often prayed by the priest when he enters the Church prior to his vesting for the Divine Liturgy. In his prayer, the psalmist asks for three things: (1) For himself, that the LORD will **lead** him (v. 8); (2) for God's enemies, that they will **fall** (v. 10); and (3) for the **righteous** faithful, that God will **bless** them (v. 12).

PSALM 6†

A Psalm of Repentance

To the Chief Musician. With stringed instruments. [a]On [1]an eight-stringed harp. A Psalm of David.

O LORD, [a]do not rebuke me in
Your anger,
Nor chasten me in Your hot
displeasure.
2 Have mercy on me, O LORD, for
I *am* weak;
O LORD, [a]heal me, for my bones
are troubled.
3 My soul also is greatly
[a]troubled;
But You, O LORD—how long?

4 Return, O LORD, deliver me!
Oh, save me for Your mercies'
sake!
5 [a]For in death *there is* no
remembrance of You;
In the grave who will give You
thanks?

6 I am weary with my groaning;
[1]All night I make my bed swim;
I drench my couch with my
tears.
7 [a]My eye wastes away because of
grief;
It grows old because of all my
enemies.

8 [a]Depart from me, all you
workers of iniquity;
For the LORD has [b]heard the
voice of my weeping.
9 The LORD has heard my
supplication;
The LORD will receive my
prayer.
10 Let all my enemies be ashamed
and greatly troubled;
Let them turn back *and* be
ashamed suddenly.

PSALM 6
title [a]Ps. 12:title [1]Heb. *sheminith*
1 [a]Ps. 38:1; 118:18; [Jer. 10:24]
2 [a]Ps. 41:4; 147:3; [Hos. 6:1]
3 [a]Ps. 88:3; John 12:27
5 [a]Ps. 30:9; 88:10–12; 115:17; [Eccl. 9:10]; Is. 38:18
6 [1]Or *Every night*
7 [a]Job 17:7; Ps. 31:9
8 [a][Matt. 25:41] [b]Ps. 3:4; 28:6

PSALM 7
title [a]Hab. 3:1 [b]2 Sam. 16 [1]Heb. *Shiggaion*
1 [a]Ps. 31:15
2 [a]Ps. 57:4; Is. 38:13 [b]Ps. 50:22
3 [a]2 Sam. 16:7 [b]1 Sam. 24:11
4 [a]1 Sam. 24:7; 26:9
6 [a]Ps. 94:2 [b]Ps. 35:23; 44:23 [1]So with MT, Tg., Vg.; LXX *O LORD my God*

PSALM 7†

Prayer and Praise for Deliverance from Enemies

A [a]Meditation[1] of David, which he sang to the LORD [b]concerning the words of Cush, a Benjamite.

O LORD my God, in You I put
my trust;
[a]Save me from all those who
persecute me;
And deliver me,
2 [a]Lest they tear me like a lion,
[b]Rending *me* in pieces, while
there is none to deliver.

3 O LORD my God, [a]if I have done
this:
If there is [b]iniquity in my hands,
4 If I have repaid evil to him who
was at peace with me,
Or [a]have plundered my enemy
without cause,
5 Let the enemy pursue me and
overtake *me;*
Yes, let him trample my life to
the earth,
And lay my honor in the dust.
Selah

6 Arise, O LORD, in Your anger;
[a]Lift Yourself up because of the
rage of my enemies;
[b]Rise up [1]for me *to* the judgment
You have commanded!
7 So the congregation of the
peoples shall surround You;
For their sakes, therefore,
return on high.

---

6 A psalm of repentance, this is used both as a prayer of confession and as an evening prayer in the Church (Great Compline during Lent). Verse 1 is a frequently repeated refrain in liturgical hymnography throughout the Church year. Psalm 6 includes (1) a calling out to God (vv. 1–5); (2) the matter of complaint (vv. 6, 7); (3) a petition for deliverance (v. 8); and (4) an expression of confidence (vv. 9, 10).

7 This is a psalm of David, who prays to be saved from his persecutors (v. 1). His words show the fierce enmities bred by religious and political strife within the community (vv. 2, 6–16), and his defense against the accusations of the enemy (vv. 3–5).

8 The LORD shall judge the
peoples;
[a]Judge me, O LORD, [b]according
to my righteousness,
And according to my integrity
within me.

9 Oh, let the wickedness of
the wicked come to an
end,
But establish the just;
[a]For the righteous God tests the
hearts and [1]minds.
10 [1]My defense *is* of God,
Who saves the [a]upright in
heart.

11 God *is* a just judge,
And God is angry *with the wicked*
every day.
12 If he does not turn back,
He will [a]sharpen His sword;
He bends His bow and makes
it ready.
13 He also prepares for Himself
instruments of death;
He makes His arrows into fiery
shafts.

14 [a]Behold, *the wicked* brings forth
iniquity;
Yes, he conceives trouble and
brings forth falsehood.
15 He made a pit and dug it out,
[a]And has fallen into the ditch
which he made.
16 [a]His trouble shall return upon
his own head,
And his violent dealing shall
come down on [1]his own
crown.

17 I will praise the LORD according
to His righteousness,
And will sing praise to the name
of the LORD Most High.

8 [a]Ps. 26:1; 35:24; 43:1 [b]Ps. 18:20; 35:24 **9** [a][1 Sam. 16:7] [1]Lit. *kidneys,* the most secret part of man **10** [a]Ps. 97:10, 11; 125:4 [1]Lit. *My shield is upon God* **12** [a]Deut. 32:41 **14** [a]Job 15:35; Is. 59:4; [James 1:15] **15** [a][Job 4:8]; Ps. 57:6 **16** [a]Esth. 9:25; Ps. 140:9 [1]The crown of his own head

PSALM 8

title [1]Heb. *Al Gittith* **1** [a]Ps. 148:13 [b]Ps. 113:4 **2** [a]Matt. 21:16; [1 Cor. 1:27] [b]Ps. 44:16 [1]*established* **3** [a]Ps. 111:2 **4** [a]Job 7:17, 18; [Heb. 2:6–8] [b][Job 10:12] [1]*give attention to* or *care for* **5** [1]Heb. *Elohim, God;* LXX, Syr., Tg., Jewish tradition *angels* **6** [a][Gen. 1:26, 28] [b][1 Cor. 15:27; Eph. 1:22; Heb. 2:8] **9** [a]Ps. 8:1

PSALM 8†

The Glory of the Lord in Creation

To the Chief Musician. [1]On the instrument of Gath. A Psalm of David.

O LORD, our Lord,
How [a]excellent *is* Your name in
all the earth,
Who have [b]set Your glory above
the heavens!

2 [a]Out of the mouth of babes and
nursing infants
You have [1]ordained strength,
Because of Your enemies,
That You may silence [b]the
enemy and the avenger.

3 When I [a]consider Your heavens,
the work of Your fingers,
The moon and the stars, which
You have ordained,
4 [a]What is man that You are
mindful of him,
And the son of man that You
[b]visit[1] him?
5 For You have made him a little
lower than [1]the angels,
And You have crowned him
with glory and honor.

6 [a]You have made him to have
dominion over the works of
Your hands;
[b]You have put all *things* under
his feet,
7 All sheep and oxen—
Even the beasts of the field,
8 The birds of the air,
And the fish of the sea
That pass through the paths of
the seas.

9 [a]O LORD, our Lord,
How excellent *is* Your name in
all the earth!

---

8 This psalm is the communion hymn on Lazarus Saturday (the day before Palm Sunday) and is also sung at Palm Sunday Matins. Jesus teaches that this prophecy (v. 2) is fulfilled by the children praising Him on Palm Sunday as He enters Jerusalem (Matt. 21:15, 16).
The best commentary on this passage (vv. 4, 5) is found in the Book of Hebrews (Heb. 2:5–9), where we see that Jesus is made "a little lower than the angels" so that He can taste death for all and thus exalt humanity above the angels.

PSALM 9†

God's Righteous Judgment upon Enemies

To the Chief Musician. To *the tune of* [1]"Death of the Son." A Psalm of David.

I WILL praise *You,* O LORD, with
my whole heart;
I will tell of all Your marvelous
works.
2 I will be glad and [a]rejoice in
You;
I will sing praise to Your name,
[b]O Most High.

3 When my enemies turn back,
They shall fall and perish at
Your presence.
4 For You have maintained my
right and my cause;
You sat on the throne judging
in righteousness.
5 You have rebuked the [1]nations,
You have destroyed the wicked;
You have [a]blotted out their
name forever and ever.

6 O enemy, destructions are
finished forever!
And you have destroyed cities;
Even their memory has
[a]perished.
7 [a]But the LORD shall endure
forever;
He has prepared His throne for
judgment.
8 [a]He shall judge the world in
righteousness,
And He shall administer
judgment for the peoples in
uprightness.

9 The LORD also will be a
[a]refuge[1] for the oppressed,
A refuge in times of trouble.
10 And those who [a]know Your
name will put their trust in
You;
For You, LORD, have not
forsaken those who seek You.

11 Sing praises to the LORD, who
dwells in Zion!
[a]Declare His deeds among the
people.
12 [a]When He avenges blood, He
remembers them;
He does not forget the cry of the
[1]humble.

13 Have mercy on me, O LORD!
Consider my trouble from those
who hate me,
You who lift me up from the
gates of death,
14 That I may tell of all Your praise
In the gates of [1]the daughter of
Zion.
I will [a]rejoice in Your salvation.

15 [a]The [1]nations have sunk down
in the pit *which* they made;
In the net which they hid, their
own foot is caught.
16 The LORD is [a]known *by* the
judgment He executes;
The wicked is snared in the
work of his own hands.
[b]Meditation.[1] Selah

17 The wicked shall be turned into
hell,
And all the [1]nations [a]that forget
God.
18 [a]For the needy shall not always
be forgotten;
[b]The expectation of the poor
shall *not* perish forever.

19 Arise, O LORD,
Do not let man prevail;
Let the [1]nations be judged in
Your sight.
20 Put them in fear, O LORD,
That the [1]nations may know
themselves *to be but* men.
Selah

PSALM 9
title [1]Heb. *Muth Labben*
2 [a]Ps. 5:11; 104:34 [b][Ps. 83:18; 92:1]
5 [a]Prov. 10:7 [1]*Gentiles*
6 [a][Ps. 34:16]
7 [a]Ps. 102:12, 26; Heb. 1:11
8 [a][Ps. 96:13; 98:9; Acts 17:31]
9 [a]Ps. 32:7; 46:1; 91:2 [1]Lit. *secure height*
10 [a]Ps. 91:14
11 [a]Ps. 66:16; 107:22
12 [a][Gen. 9:5; Ps. 72:14] [1]*afflicted*
14 [a]Ps. 13:5; 20:5; 35:9 [1]Jerusalem
15 [a]Ps. 7:15, 16 [1]*Gentiles*
16 [a]Ex. 7:5 [b]Ps. 92:3 [1]Heb. *Higgaion*
17 [a]Job 8:13; Ps. 50:22 [1]*Gentiles*
18 [a]Ps. 9:12; 12:5 [b][Ps. 62:5; 71:5]; Prov. 23:18
19 [1]*Gentiles*
20 [1]*Gentiles*

9 At Psalm 9 the numerical divergence begins between the Septuagint (LXX) and the Masoretic Text (see Introduction). In the LXX Ps. 9 and 10 are combined. Both 9 and 10 are militant psalms, dealing with the destruction of the enemies of the Lord; they are seen as being fulfilled in the Resurrection of Christ. Both psalms declare the many works of Christ in triumphing over His enemies.

PSALM 10

A Song of Confidence in God's Triumph over Evil

WHY do You stand afar off, O LORD?
Why do You hide in times of trouble?
2 The wicked in *his* pride [1]persecutes the poor;
[a]Let them be caught in the plots which they have devised.

3 For the wicked [a]boasts of his heart's desire;
[1]He [b]blesses the greedy *and* renounces the LORD.
4 The wicked in his proud countenance does not seek *God;*
[1]God *is* in none of his [a]thoughts.

5 His ways [1]are always prospering;
Your judgments *are* far above, out of his sight;
As for all his enemies, he sneers at them.
6 [a]He has said in his heart,
"I shall not be moved;
[b]I shall never be in adversity."
7 [a]His mouth is full of cursing and [b]deceit and oppression;
Under his tongue *is* trouble and iniquity.

8 He sits in the lurking places of the villages;
In the secret places he murders the innocent;
His eyes are secretly fixed on the helpless.
9 He lies in wait secretly, as a lion in his den;
He lies in wait to catch the poor;
He catches the poor when he draws him into his net.
10 So [1]he crouches, he lies low,
That the helpless may fall by his [2]strength.
11 He has said in his heart,
"God has forgotten;
He hides His face;
He will never see."

PSALM 10
2 [a]Ps. 7:16; 9:16 [1]*hotly pursues*
3 [a]Ps. 49:6; 94:3, 4 [b]Prov. 28:4 [1]Or *The greedy man curses and spurns the* LORD
4 [a]Ps. 14:1; 36:1 [1]Or *All his thoughts are, "There is no God"*
5 [1]Lit. *are strong*
6 [a]Ps. 49:11; [Eccl. 8:11] [b]Rev. 18:7
7 [a][Rom. 3:14] [b]Ps. 55:10, 11
10 [1]Or *he is crushed, is bowed* [2]Or *mighty ones*
12 [a]Ps. 17:7; 94:2; Mic. 5:9 [b]Ps. 9:12
14 [a][Ps. 11:4] [b][2 Tim. 1:12] [c]Ps. 68:5; Hos. 14:3 [1]Lit. *leaves, entrusts*
16 [a]Ps. 29:10
18 [1]*vindicate* [2]*terrify*

PSALM 11
1 [a]Ps. 56:11
2 [a]Ps. 64:3, 4 [1]Lit. *in darkness*
3 [a]Ps. 82:5; 87:1; 119:152
4 [a]Ps. 2:4; [Is. 66:1]; Matt. 5:34; 23:22; [Acts 7:49]; Rev. 4:2 [b][Ps. 33:18; 34:15, 16]

12 Arise, O LORD!
O God, [a]lift up Your hand!
Do not forget the [b]humble.
13 Why do the wicked renounce God?
He has said in his heart,
"You will not require *an account.*"

14 But You have [a]seen, for You observe trouble and grief,
To repay *it* by Your hand.
The helpless [b]commits[1] himself to You;
[c]You are the helper of the fatherless.
15 Break the arm of the wicked and the evil *man;*
Seek out his wickedness *until* You find none.

16 [a]The LORD *is* King forever and ever;
The nations have perished out of His land.
17 LORD, You have heard the desire of the humble;
You will prepare their heart;
You will cause Your ear to hear,
18 To [1]do justice to the fatherless and the oppressed,
That the man of the earth may [2]oppress no more.

PSALM 11

Faith in the Lord's Righteousness

To the Chief Musician. A Psalm of David.

IN [a]the LORD I put my trust;
How can you say to my soul,
"Flee *as* a bird to your mountain"?
2 For look! [a]The wicked bend *their* bow,
They make ready their arrow on the string,
That they may shoot [1]secretly at the upright in heart.
3 [a]If the foundations are destroyed,
What can the righteous do?

4 The LORD *is* in His holy temple,
The LORD's [a]throne *is* in heaven;
[b]His eyes behold,
His eyelids test the sons of men.

5 The LORD [a]tests the righteous,
But the wicked and the one who loves violence His soul hates.
6 Upon the wicked He will rain coals;
Fire and brimstone and a burning wind
[a]*Shall be* [1]the portion of their cup.

7 For the LORD *is* righteous,
He [a]loves righteousness;
[1]His countenance beholds the upright.

PSALM 12†

Man's Treachery and God's Constancy

To the Chief Musician. [a]On [1]an eight-stringed harp. A Psalm of David.

HELP,[1] LORD, for the godly man [a]ceases!
For the faithful disappear from among the sons of men.
2 [a]They speak idly everyone with his neighbor;
With flattering lips *and* [1]a double heart they speak.

3 May the LORD [1]cut off all flattering lips,
And the tongue that speaks [2]proud things,
4 Who have said,
"With our tongue we will prevail;
Our lips *are* our own;
Who *is* lord over us?"

5 "For the oppression of the poor, for the sighing of the needy,
Now I will arise," says the LORD;
"I will set *him* in the safety for which he yearns."

6 The words of the LORD *are* [a]pure words,
Like silver tried in a furnace of earth,
Purified seven times.
7 You shall keep them, O LORD,
You shall preserve them from this generation forever.

8 The wicked prowl on every side,
When vileness is exalted among the sons of men.

PSALM 13†

Trust in the Salvation of the Lord

To the Chief Musician. A Psalm of David.

HOW long, O LORD? Will You forget me forever?
[a]How long will You hide Your face from me?
2 How long shall I take counsel in my soul,
Having sorrow in my heart daily?
How long will my enemy be exalted over me?

3 Consider *and* hear me, O LORD my God;
[a]Enlighten my eyes,
[b]Lest I sleep the *sleep of* death;
4 Lest my enemy say,
"I have prevailed against him";
Lest those who trouble me rejoice when I am moved.

5 But I have trusted in Your mercy;
My heart shall rejoice in Your salvation.
6 I will sing to the LORD,
Because He has dealt bountifully with me.

5 [a]Gen. 22:1; [James 1:12]
6 [a]1 Sam. 1:4; Ps. 75:8; Ezek. 38:22 [1]Their allotted portion or serving
7 [a]Ps. 33:5; 45:7 [1]Or *The upright beholds His countenance*

PSALM 12
title [a]Ps. 6:title [1]Heb. *sheminith*
1 [a][Is. 57:1]; Mic. 7:2 [1]*Save*
2 [a]Ps. 10:7; 41:6 [1]An inconsistent mind
3 [1]*destroy* [2]*great*
6 [a]2 Sam. 22:31; Ps. 18:30; 119:140; Prov. 30:5

PSALM 13
1 [a]Job 13:24; Ps. 89:46
3 [a]1 Sam. 14:29; Ezra 9:8; Job 33:30; Ps. 18:28 [b]Jer. 51:39

12 (11, LXX) This psalm presents a contrast between the constancy of the Lord and the perversity of the sons of men. Verse 7 is a regular prokeimenon, or gradual, at the Sunday Liturgy, and is also chanted before the Gospel in the marriage ceremony as a prayer for the preservation of the union of husband and wife. This psalm was sung by David during the period of his repentance. Within its context, salvation is declared to us and we have an example of how we should approach God if we have fallen into sins.

13 (12, LXX) This psalm is an evening prayer (v. 3), used in Great Compline and in the Lenten services.

PSALM 14†

Folly of the Godless, and God's Final Triumph

To the Chief Musician. A Psalm of David.

THE [a]fool has said in his heart,
"*There is* no God."
They are corrupt,
They have done abominable works,
There is none who does good.

2 [a]The LORD looks down from heaven upon the children of men,
To see if there are any who understand, who seek God.
3 [a]They have all turned aside,
They have together become corrupt;
There is none who does good,
No, not one.

4 Have all the workers of iniquity no knowledge,
Who eat up my people *as* they eat bread,
And [a]do not call on the LORD?
5 There they are in great fear,
For God *is* with the generation of the righteous.
6 You shame the counsel of the poor,
But the LORD *is* his [a]refuge.

7 [a]Oh,[1] that the salvation of Israel *would come* out of Zion!
[b]When the LORD brings back [2]the captivity of His people,
Let Jacob rejoice *and* Israel be glad.

PSALM 14
1 [a]Ps. 10:4; 53:1
2 [a]Ps. 33:13, 14; 102:19; Rom. 3:11
3 [a]Rom. 3:12
4 [a]Ps. 79:6; Is. 64:7; Jer. 10:25; Amos 8:4; Mic. 3:3
6 [a]Ps. 9:9; 40:17; 46:1; 142:5
7 [a]Ps. 53:6; [Rom. 11:25–27] [b]Deut. 30:3; Job 42:10 [1]Lit. *Who will give out of Zion the salvation of Israel?* [2]Or *His captive people*

PSALM 15
1 [a]Ps. 24:3–5 [1]*sojourn*
2 [a]Zech. 8:16; [Eph. 4:25]
3 [a][Lev. 19:16–18] [b]Ex. 23:1 [1]*receive*
4 [a]Esth. 3:2 [b]Lev. 5:4
5 [a]2 Pet. 1:10

PSALM 16
title [a]Ps. 56—60
1 [1]*Watch over*

PSALM 15†

A Song of the Righteous

A Psalm of David.

LORD, [a]who may [1]abide in Your tabernacle?
Who may dwell in Your holy hill?

2 He who walks uprightly,
And works righteousness,
And speaks the [a]truth in his heart;
3 He *who* [a]does not backbite with his tongue,
Nor does evil to his neighbor,
[b]Nor does he [1]take up a reproach against his friend;
4 [a]In whose eyes a vile person is despised,
But he honors those who fear the LORD;
He *who* [b]swears to his own hurt and does not change;
5 He *who* does not put out his money at usury,
Nor does he take a bribe against the innocent.

He who does these *things* [a]shall never be moved.

PSALM 16†

Our Hope in the Messiah

A [a]Michtam of David.

PRESERVE[1] me, O God, for in You I put my trust.

---

14 (13, LXX) In the Ninth Hour prayers on Good Friday, at the hour of Christ's death, the Church intones, **The fool has said in his heart, "There is no God"** (v. 1). Even the pagan centurion who saw Christ our God crucified on the Cross believed in Him. Only the **corrupt** (v. 3) could see Him die and deny that He exists!

15 (14, LXX) This is a psalm of a righteous man. Verse 1 is used in the prayers of the service of Christ's Transfiguration. Herein we are taught how to prepare our hearts and lives in order to attain the blessed inheritance—to **abide** in the **tabernacle** of the Lord (v. 1).

16 (15, LXX) Verses 8–11 of this great messianic psalm are quoted twice in the Acts of the Apostles (in Acts 2:25–31 by St. Peter and in Acts 13:35–37 by St. Paul). In both cases, the Apostles in their preaching assure us the reference is not to David, who died and saw

(continued on next page)

2 *O my soul,* you have said to the LORD,
"You *are* my Lord,
[a]My goodness is nothing apart from You."
3 As for the saints who *are* on the earth,
"They are the excellent ones, in [a]whom is all my delight."

4 Their sorrows shall be multiplied who hasten *after* another *god;*
Their drink offerings of [a]blood I will not offer,
[b]Nor take up their names on my lips.

5 O LORD, *You are* the portion of my inheritance and my cup;
You [1]maintain my lot.
6 The lines have fallen to me in pleasant *places;*
Yes, I have a good inheritance.

7 I will bless the LORD who has given me counsel;
My [1]heart also instructs me in the night seasons.
8 [a]I have set the LORD always before me;
Because *He is* at my right hand I shall not be moved.

9 Therefore my heart is glad, and my glory rejoices;
My flesh also will [1]rest in hope.
10 [a]For You will not leave my soul in [1]Sheol,
Nor will You allow Your Holy One to [2]see corruption.
11 You will show me the [a]path of life;
In Your presence *is* fullness of joy;
At Your right hand *are* pleasures forevermore.

2 [a]Job 35:7
3 [a]Ps. 119:63
4 [a]Ps. 106:37, 38 [b][Ex. 23:13]; Josh. 23:7
5 [1]Lit. *uphold*
7 [1]Mind, lit. *kidneys*
8 [a][Acts 2:25–28]
9 [1]Or *dwell securely*
10 [a]Ps. 49:15; 86:13; Acts 2:31, 32; Heb. 13:20 [1]The abode of the dead [2]*undergo*
11 [a]Ps. 139:24; [Matt. 7:14]

PSALM 17†

The Righteous Prevail

A Prayer of David.

HEAR a just cause, O LORD,
Attend to my cry;
Give ear to my prayer *which is* not from deceitful lips.
2 Let my vindication come from Your presence;
Let Your eyes look on the things that are upright.

3 You have tested my heart;
You have visited *me* in the night;
[a]You have [1]tried me and have found [2]nothing;
I have purposed that my mouth shall not [b]transgress.
4 Concerning the works of men,
By the word of Your lips,
I have kept away from the paths of the destroyer.
5 [a]Uphold my steps in Your paths,
That my footsteps may not slip.

6 [a]I have called upon You, for You will hear me, O God;
Incline Your ear to me, *and* hear my speech.
7 Show Your marvelous lovingkindness by Your right hand,
O You who [1]save those who trust *in You*
From those who rise up *against them.*
8 Keep me as the [1]apple of Your eye;
Hide me under the shadow of Your wings,
9 From the wicked who oppress me,
From my deadly enemies who surround me.

PSALM 17
3 [a]Job 23:10; Ps. 66:10; Zech. 13:9; [1 Pet. 1:7] [b]Ps. 39:1 [1]*examined* [2]Nothing evil
5 [a]Job 23:11; Ps. 44:18; 119:133
6 [a]Ps. 86:7; 116:2
7 [1]*deliver*
8 [1]*pupil*

(continued from previous page)
corruption, but to the Lord Jesus Christ Himself. Significantly, both apostles quote Ps. 16 from the LXX, not the MT.

Verse 3 is often used in Orthodox services honoring the saints, the **excellent ones** who are a **delight** to the Lord. This present prophecy deals with the calling of the Gentiles, and with the disobedience of Israel. It also refers to the Resurrection of Jesus Christ, the Savior of mankind (see Acts 2:25).

17 (16, LXX) This psalm is sung during the Third Hour prayers of the Church. It is a contrast between the wicked and the righteous who awake in God's glory (v. 15).

10 They have closed up their
[a]fat *hearts;*
With their mouths they
[b]speak proudly.
11 They have now surrounded us
in our steps;
They have set their eyes,
crouching down to the earth,
12 As a lion is eager to tear his
prey,
And like a young lion lurking
in secret places.

13 Arise, O LORD,
Confront him, cast him down;
Deliver my life from the wicked
with Your sword,
14 With Your hand from men,
O LORD,
From men of the world *who have*
their portion in *this* life,
And whose belly You fill with
Your hidden treasure.
They are satisfied with children,
And leave the rest of their
possession for their babes.

15 As for me, [a]I will see Your face
in righteousness;
[b]I shall be satisfied when I
[c]awake in Your likeness.

PSALM 18†

The Victory of David Fulfilled in the Messiah

To the Chief Musician. A Psalm of David [a]the servant of the LORD, who spoke to the LORD the words of [b]this song on the day that the LORD delivered him from the hand of all his enemies and from the hand of Saul. And he said:

1 I [a]WILL love You, O LORD, my
strength.
2 The LORD is my rock and my
fortress and my deliverer;
My God, my [1]strength,
[a]in whom I will trust;
My shield and the [2]horn of my
salvation, my stronghold.
3 I will call upon the LORD,
[a]*who is worthy* to be praised;
So shall I be saved from my
enemies.

4 [a]The pangs of death surrounded
me,
And the floods of [1]ungodliness
made me afraid.
5 The sorrows of Sheol
surrounded me;
The snares of death confronted
me.
6 In my distress I called upon the
LORD,
And cried out to my God;
He heard my voice from His
temple,
And my cry came before Him,
even to His ears.

7 [a]Then the earth shook and
trembled;
The foundations of the hills also
quaked and were shaken,
Because He was angry.
8 Smoke went up from His
nostrils,
And devouring fire from His
mouth;
Coals were kindled by it.
9 [a]He bowed the heavens also, and
came down
With darkness under His feet.
10 [a]And He rode upon a cherub,
and flew;
[b]He flew upon the wings of the
wind.
11 He made darkness His secret
place;
[a]His canopy around Him *was*
dark waters
And thick clouds of the skies.
12 [a]From the brightness before
Him,

10 [a]Ezek. 16:49 [b][1 Sam. 2:3]
15 [a][1 John 3:2] [b]Ps. 4:6, 7; 16:11 [c][Is. 26:19]

PSALM 18

title [a]Ps. 36:title [b]2 Sam. 22
1 [a]Ps. 144:1
2 [a]Heb. 2:13 [1]Lit. *rock* [2]Strength
3 [a]Ps. 76:4; Rev. 5:12
4 [a]Ps. 116:3 [1]Lit. *Belial*
7 [a]Acts 4:31
9 [a]Ps. 144:5
10 [a]Ps. 80:1; 99:1 [b][Ps. 104:3]
11 [a]Ps. 97:2
12 [a]Ps. 97:3; 140:10; Hab. 3:11

18 (17, LXX) This psalm of the victory of David is fulfilled in the victory of Christ over death and hell. Verses 46–50 are sung on appointed Sundays immediately before the reading of the Holy Gospel, announcing the Word of Christ our Victor and our life. We see herein: (1) strife caused by enemies, and resultant calling upon God for help (vv. 1–15); (2) the coming down and Ascension of the Only Begotten Son (vv. 16–42); and (3) the calling of the Gentiles (vv. 43–50).

His thick clouds passed with
hailstones and coals of fire.
13 The LORD thundered from
heaven,
And the Most High uttered
[a]His voice,
[1]Hailstones and coals of fire.
14 [a]He sent out His arrows and
scattered [1]the foe,
Lightnings in abundance, and
He vanquished them.
15 Then the channels of the sea
were seen,
The foundations of the world
were uncovered
At Your rebuke, O LORD,
At the blast of the breath of
Your nostrils.

16 [a]He sent from above, He took
me;
He drew me out of many
waters.
17 He delivered me from my
strong enemy,
From those who hated me,
For they were too strong for me.
18 They confronted me in the day
of my calamity,
But the LORD was my support.
19 [a]He also brought me out into a
broad place;
He delivered me because He
delighted in me.

20 [a]The LORD rewarded me
according to my
righteousness;
According to the cleanness of
my hands
He has recompensed me.
21 For I have kept the ways of the
LORD,
And have not wickedly
departed from my God.
22 For all His judgments *were*
before me,
And I did not put away His
statutes from me.
23 I was also blameless [1]before
Him,
And I kept myself from my
iniquity.
24 [a]Therefore the LORD has
recompensed me according to
my righteousness,
According to the cleanness of
my hands in His sight.

25 [a]With the merciful You will show
Yourself merciful;
With a blameless man You will
show Yourself blameless;
26 With the pure You will show
Yourself pure;
And [a]with the devious You will
show Yourself shrewd.
27 For You will save the humble
people,
But will bring down [a]haughty
looks.

28 [a]For You will light my lamp;
The LORD my God will enlighten
my darkness.
29 For by You I can [1]run against a
troop,
By my God I can leap over a
wall.
30 *As for* God, [a]His way *is* perfect;
[b]The word of the LORD is
[1]proven;
He *is* a shield [c]to all who trust
in Him.

31 [a]For who *is* God, except the
LORD?
And who *is* a rock, except our
God?
32 *It is* God who [a]arms me with
strength,
And makes my way perfect.
33 [a]He makes my feet like the *feet*
of deer,
And [b]sets me on my high
places.
34 [a]He teaches my hands to make
war,
So that my arms can bend a bow
of bronze.

35 You have also given me the
shield of Your salvation;
Your right hand has held me
up,
Your gentleness has made me
great.
36 You enlarged my path under
me,
[a]So my feet did not slip.

37 I have pursued my enemies and
overtaken them;

13 [a][Ps. 29:3–9; 104:7] [1]So with MT, Tg., Vg.; a few Heb. mss., LXX omit *Hailstones and coals of fire*
14 [a]Josh. 10:10; Ps. 144:6; Is. 30:30; Hab. 3:11 [1]Lit. *them*
16 [a]Ps. 144:7
19 [a]Ps. 4:1; 31:8; 118:5
20 [a]1 Sam. 24:19; [Job 33:26]; Ps. 7:8
23 [1]*with*
24 [a]1 Sam. 26:23; Ps. 18:20
25 [a][1 Kin. 8:32; Ps. 62:12]; Matt. 5:7
26 [a][Lev. 26:23–28]; Prov. 3:34
27 [a][Ps. 101:5]; Prov. 6:17
28 [a]1 Kin. 15:4; Job 18:6; [Ps. 119:105]
29 [1]Or *run through*
30 [a][Deut. 32:4]; Rev. 15:3 [b]Ps. 12:6; 119:140; [Prov. 30:5] [c][Ps. 17:7] [1]Lit. *refined*
31 [a][Deut. 32:31, 39; 1 Sam. 2:2; Ps. 86:8–10; Is. 45:5]
32 [a][Ps. 91:2]
33 [a]2 Sam. 2:18; Hab. 3:19 [b]Deut. 32:13; 33:29
34 [a]Ps. 144:1
36 [a]Ps. 66:9; Prov. 4:12

Neither did I turn back again till
they were destroyed.
38 I have wounded them,
So that they could not rise;
They have fallen under my feet.
39 For You have armed me with
strength for the battle;
You have [1]subdued under me
those who rose up against
me.
40 You have also given me the
necks of my enemies,
So that I destroyed those who
hated me.
41 They cried out, but *there was*
none to save;
[a]*Even* to the LORD, but He did not
answer them.
42 Then I beat them as fine as the
dust before the wind;
I [a]cast them out like dirt in the
streets.

43 You have delivered me from the
strivings of the people;
[a]You have made me the head of
the [1]nations;
[b]A people I have not known shall
serve me.
44 As soon as they hear of me they
obey me;
The foreigners [1]submit to me.
45 [a]The foreigners fade away,
And come frightened from their
hideouts.

46 The LORD lives!
Blessed *be* my Rock!
Let the God of my salvation be
exalted.
47 *It is* God who avenges me,
[a]And subdues the peoples under
me;
48 He delivers me from my
enemies.
[a]You also lift me up above those
who rise against me;
You have delivered me from the
violent man.
49 [a]Therefore I will give thanks to
You, O LORD, among the
[1]Gentiles,
And sing praises to Your name.

50 [a]Great deliverance He gives to
His king,
And shows mercy to His
anointed,
To David and his [1]descendants
forevermore.

39 [1]Lit. *caused to bow*
41 [a]Job 27:9; Prov. 1:28; Is. 1:15; Ezek. 8:18; Zech. 7:13
42 [a]Zech. 10:5
43 [a]2 Sam. 8; Ps. 89:27 [b]Is. 52:15 [1]*Gentiles*
44 [1]*feign submission*
45 [a]Mic. 7:17
47 [a]Ps. 47:3
48 [a]Ps. 27:6; 59:1
49 [a]2 Sam. 22:50; Rom. 15:9 [1]*nations*
50 [a]2 Sam. 7:12; Ps. 21:1; 144:10 [1]Lit. *seed*

PSALM 19†

The Revelation of God in Creation and in the Law

To the Chief Musician. A Psalm of David.

THE [a]heavens declare the glory of
God;
And the [b]firmament[1] shows
[2]His handiwork.
2 Day unto day utters speech,
And night unto night reveals
knowledge.
3 *There is* no speech nor language
Where their voice is not heard.
4 [a]Their [1]line has gone out through
all the earth,
And their words to the end of
the world.

In them He has set a [2]tabernacle
for the sun,
5 Which *is* like a bridegroom
coming out of his chamber,
[a]*And* rejoices like a strong man
to run its race.
6 Its rising *is* from one end of
heaven,
And its circuit to the other end;
And there is nothing hidden
from its heat.

PSALM 19
1 [a]Is. 40:22; [Rom. 1:19, 20] [b]Gen. 1:6, 7 [1]*expanse of heaven* [2]*the work of His hands*
4 [a]Rom. 10:18 [1]LXX, Syr., Vg. *sound;* Tg. *business* [2]*tent*
5 [a]Eccl. 1:5

19 (18, LXX) **Their line** (v. 4) is better translated in the LXX as "their proclamation." It is, in context, the proclamation of the glory of God in creation, but it is often used liturgically and even in the NT (Rom. 10:18) as a reference to the preaching of the apostles.

Verse 5 describes the sun emerging from the chambers of heaven, but it is sung on Christmas Day during the "Alleluia" to show forth the newborn Christ, the Son of God, as our Sun who has come to bring us light and life.

An undercurrent of the psalm is praise of the Creator by the sun, the heavens and all the elements (which the Gentiles worshiped) for the initiation of instruction to the Gentiles concerning God and His ways.

7 [a]The law of the LORD *is* perfect,
[1]converting the soul;
The testimony of the LORD *is*
sure, making [b]wise the
simple;
8 The statutes of the LORD *are*
right, rejoicing the heart;
The commandment of the LORD
is pure, enlightening the eyes;
9 The fear of the LORD *is* clean,
enduring forever;
The judgments of the LORD *are*
true *and* righteous altogether.
10 More to be desired *are they* than
[a]gold,
Yea, than much fine gold;
Sweeter also than honey and
the [1]honeycomb.
11 Moreover by them Your servant
is warned,
And in keeping them *there is*
great reward.

12 Who can understand *his* errors?
[a]Cleanse me from secret *faults.*
13 Keep back Your servant also
from [a]presumptuous *sins;*
Let them not have [b]dominion
over me.
Then I shall be blameless,
And I shall be innocent of
[1]great transgression.

14 [a]Let the words of my mouth and
the meditation of my heart
Be acceptable in Your sight,
O LORD, my [1]strength and my
[b]Redeemer.

7 [a]Ps. 111:7; [Rom. 7:12] [b]Ps. 119:130 [1]*restoring*
10 [a]Ps. 119:72, 127; Prov. 8:10, 11, 19 [1]*honey in the combs*
12 [a][Ps. 51:1, 2]
13 [a]Num. 15:30 [b]Ps. 119:133; [Rom. 6:12–14] [1]Or *much*
14 [a]Ps. 51:15 [b]Ps. 31:5; Is. 47:4 [1]Lit. *rock*

PSALM 20†

A Prayer for the King

To the Chief Musician. A Psalm of David.

MAY the LORD answer you in the
day of trouble;
May the name of the God of
Jacob [1]defend you;
2 May He send you help from the
sanctuary,
And strengthen you out of Zion;
3 May He remember all your
offerings,
And accept your burnt sacrifice.
Selah

4 May He grant you according to
your heart's *desire,*
And [a]fulfill all your [1]purpose.
5 We will rejoice in your
salvation,
And in the name of our God we
will set up *our* banners!
May the LORD fulfill all your
petitions.

6 Now I know that the LORD saves
His [1]anointed;
He will answer him from His
holy heaven
With the saving strength of His
right hand.

7 Some *trust* in chariots, and some
in [a]horses;
But we will remember the name
of the LORD our God.
8 They have bowed down and
fallen;
But we have risen and stand
upright.

9 Save, LORD!
May the King answer us when
we call.

PSALM 20
1 [1]Lit. *set you on high*
4 [a]Ps. 21:2 [1]*counsel*
6 [1]Commissioned one, Heb. *messiah*
7 [a]Deut. 20:1; Ps. 33:16, 17; Prov. 21:31; Is. 31:1

PSALM 21†

A Royal Psalm of Salvation

To the Chief Musician. A Psalm of David.

THE king shall have joy in Your
strength, O LORD;

20 (19, LXX) This prayer for **the King** of Israel (v. 9) was prayed by Christians in the Old World as a petition for their Emperor, and was known as the Royal Psalm.
21 (20, LXX) This is also a Royal Psalm as is Ps. 20, but it is much more directly messianic (especially vv. 3–7). It is understood by the Church as the triumph of Christ in His Ascension. The exalted Lord sends us the Holy Spirit: vv. 1–6, 13 are used in the Divine Liturgy on Pentecost Sunday. In the psalm, the friends of the king are singing, while he himself is rejoicing, for from his descent the Savior of the world will be born.

And in Your salvation how
greatly shall he rejoice!
2 You have given him his heart's
desire,
And have not withheld the
[a]request of his lips. Selah
3 For You meet him with the
blessings of goodness;
You set a crown of pure gold
upon his head.
4 [a]He asked life from You, *and* You
gave *it* to him—
Length of days forever and
ever.
5 His glory *is* great in Your
salvation;
Honor and majesty You have
placed upon him.
6 For You have made him most
blessed forever;
[a]You have made him
[1]exceedingly glad with Your
presence.
7 For the king trusts in the LORD,
And through the mercy of the
Most High he shall not be
[1]moved.

8 Your hand will find all Your
enemies;
Your right hand will find those
who hate You.
9 You shall make them as a fiery
oven in the time of Your
anger;
The LORD shall swallow them up
in His wrath,
And the fire shall devour them.
10 Their offspring You shall
destroy from the earth,
And their [1]descendants from
among the sons of men.
11 For they intended evil against
You;
They devised a plot *which* they
are not able *to* [a]*perform.*
12 Therefore You will make them
turn their back;
You will make ready *Your arrows*
on Your string toward their
faces.

13 Be exalted, O LORD, in Your
own strength!
We will sing and praise Your
power.

PSALM 21

2 [a]2 Sam. 7:26–29
4 [a]Ps. 61:5, 6; 133:3
6 [a]Ps. 16:11; 45:7
[1]Lit. *joyful with gladness*
7 [1]*shaken*
10 [1]Lit. *seed*
11 [a]Ps. 2:1–4

PSALM 22

title [1]Heb. *Aijeleth Hashahar*
1 [a][Matt. 27:46; Mark 15:34]

PSALM 22†

A Prophetic Psalm of the Messiah

To the Chief Musician. Set to [1]"The Deer of the Dawn." A Psalm of David.

MY [a]God, My God, why have
You forsaken Me?
Why are You so far from helping
Me,
And from the words of My
groaning?

---

22 (21, LXX) This is the most specifically prophetic psalm of Christ's Passion in the entire Psalter. It makes no sense apart from its fulfillment in Christ's suffering and death. Verses 1, 2 express the sufferings of Christ; vv. 22–31 describe His victory. The LXX heads this psalm "for help in the morning," for the Only Begotten Son has delivered humanity from the darkness of evil.

Liturgically, Ps. 22 is used throughout the Matins, First Hour and Vespers of Good Friday, and also on the Feast of the Exaltation of the Cross.

Verse 1 is prayed by Christ on the Cross (Matt. 27:46), suggesting He is praying the whole psalm to the Father. These words do not describe the Father turning His back, as it were, on the Son, for there can be no sundering of the Holy Deity. However, the Son does experience, in His humanity, some sense of forsakenness while on the Cross. Further, the question of v. 1 is resolved with **You** (the Father) **have answered Me** (the Son—v. 21, and the verses which follow).

Verse 8: These are the words by which Christ was mocked as He hung on the Cross (Matt. 27:43).

Verse 16 describes the piercing of Christ's **hands and feet.**

Verse 18, quoted in the Gospels (Matt. 27:35; John 19:24), is the prophecy of the casting of lots for Christ's garments. The clarity of this verse continues to this day to baffle both the Jews who have rejected Him as the Messiah, and modern unbelieving biblical scholars.

Verse 22 reveals Christ will be preached to the Jews.

Verse 27 shows Christ will be worshiped by people of all nations.

2 O My God, I cry in the daytime,
but You do not hear;
And in the night season, and
am not silent.

3 But You *are* holy,
Enthroned in the [a]praises of
Israel.
4 Our fathers trusted in You;
They trusted, and You delivered
them.
5 They cried to You, and were
delivered;
[a]They trusted in You, and were
not ashamed.

6 But I *am* [a]a worm, and no man;
[b]A reproach of men, and
despised by the people.
7 [a]All those who see Me ridicule
Me;
They [1]shoot out the lip, they
shake the head, *saying*,
8 "He[a] [1]trusted in the LORD, let
Him rescue Him;
[b]Let Him deliver Him, since He
delights in Him!"

9 [a]But You *are* He who took Me
out of the womb;
You made Me trust *while* on My
mother's breasts.
10 I was cast upon You from birth.
From My mother's womb
[a]You *have been* My God.
11 Be not far from Me,
For trouble *is* near;
For *there is* none to help.

12 [a]Many bulls have surrounded
Me;
Strong *bulls* of [b]Bashan have
encircled Me.
13 [a]They [1]gape at Me *with* their
mouths,
Like a raging and roaring lion.

14 I am poured out like water,
[a]And all My bones are out of
joint;
My heart is like wax;
It has melted [1]within Me.
15 [a]My strength is dried up like a
potsherd,
And [b]My tongue clings to My
jaws;
You have brought Me to the
dust of death.

16 For dogs have surrounded Me;
The congregation of the wicked
has enclosed Me.
[a]They[1] pierced My hands and
My feet;
17 I can count all My bones.
[a]They look *and* stare at Me.
18 [a]They divide My garments
among them,
And for My clothing they cast
lots.

19 But You, O LORD, do not be far
from Me;
O My Strength, hasten to help
Me!
20 Deliver Me from the sword,
[a]My[1] precious *life* from the power
of the dog.
21 [a]Save Me from the lion's mouth
And from the horns of the wild
oxen!

[b]You have answered Me.

22 [a]I will declare Your name to
[b]My brethren;
In the midst of the assembly I
will praise You.
23 [a]You who fear the LORD, praise
Him!
All you [1]descendants of Jacob,
glorify Him,
And fear Him, all you offspring
of Israel!
24 For He has not despised nor
abhorred the affliction of the
afflicted;
Nor has He hidden His face
from Him;
But [a]when He cried to Him, He
heard.

25 [a]My praise *shall be* of You in the
great assembly;
[b]I will pay My vows before those
who fear Him.
26 The poor shall eat and be
satisfied;
Those who seek Him will praise
the LORD.
Let your heart live forever!

27 All the ends of the world
Shall remember and turn to the
LORD,

PSALM 22
3 [a]Deut. 10:21
5 [a]Is. 49:23
6 [a]Is. 41:14 [b][Is. 53:3]
7 [a]Matt. 27:39 [1]Show contempt with their mouth
8 [a]Matt. 27:43 [b]Ps. 91:14 [1]LXX, Syr., Vg. *hoped;* Tg. *praised*
9 [a][Ps. 71:5, 6]
10 [a][Is. 46:3; 49:1]
12 [a]Ps. 22:21; 68:30 [b]Deut. 32:14
13 [a]Job 16:10 [1]Lit. *have opened their mouths at Me*
14 [a]Dan. 5:6 [1]Lit. *in the midst of My bowels*
15 [a]Prov. 17:22 [b]John 19:28
16 [a]Matt. 27:35 [1]So with some Heb. mss., LXX, Syr., Vg.; MT *Like a lion* instead of *They pierced*
17 [a]Luke 23:27, 35
18 [a]Matt. 27:35
20 [a]Ps. 35:17 [1]Lit. *My only one*
21 [a]2 Tim. 4:17 [b]Is. 34:7
22 [a]Heb. 2:12 [b][Rom. 8:29]
23 [a]Ps. 135:19, 20 [1]Lit. *seed*
24 [a]Heb. 5:7
25 [a]Ps. 35:18; 40:9, 10 [b]Eccl. 5:4

And all the families of the
[1]nations
Shall worship before [2]You.
28 [a]For the kingdom *is* the LORD's,
And He rules over the nations.

29 [a]All the prosperous of the earth
Shall eat and worship;
[b]All those who go down to
[1]the dust
Shall bow before Him,
Even he who cannot keep
himself alive.

30 A posterity shall serve Him.
It will be recounted of the Lord
to the *next* generation,
31 They will come and declare His
righteousness to a people
who will be born,
That He has done *this*.

PSALM 23†

The Lord the Shepherd of His People

A Psalm of David.

THE LORD *is* [a]my shepherd;
[b]I shall not [1]want.
2 [a]He makes me to lie down in
[1]green pastures;
[b]He leads me beside the
[2]still waters.
3 He restores my soul;
[a]He leads me in the paths of
righteousness
For His name's sake.

4 Yea, though I walk through the
valley of [a]the shadow of
death,
[b]I will fear no evil;
[c]For You *are* with me;
Your rod and Your staff, they
comfort me.

5 You [a]prepare a table before me
in the presence of my
enemies;
You [b]anoint my head with oil;
My cup runs over.
6 Surely goodness and mercy
shall follow me
All the days of my life;
And I will [1]dwell in the house
of the LORD
[2]Forever.

PSALM 24†

The Entrance of the King

A Psalm of David.

THE [a]earth *is* the LORD's, and all
its fullness,
The world and those who dwell
therein.

27 [1]*Gentiles* [2]So with MT, LXX, Tg.; Arab., Syr., Vg. *Him*
28 [a]Matt. 6:13
29 [a]Ps. 17:10; 45:12 [b][Is. 26:19] [1]Death

PSALM 23

1 [a][Is. 40:11] [b][Phil. 4:19] [1]*lack*
2 [a]Ezek. 34:14 [b][Rev. 7:17] [1]Lit. *pastures of tender grass* [2]Lit. *waters of rest*
3 [a]Ps. 5:8; 31:3
4 [a]Job 3:5; 10:21, 22; 24:17 [b][Ps. 3:6; 27:1] [c][Is. 43:2]
5 [a]Ps. 104:15 [b]Ps. 92:10
6 [1]So with LXX, Syr., Tg., Vg.; MT *return* [2]Or *To the end of my days*, lit. *For length of days*

PSALM 24

1 [a]1 Cor. 10:26, 28

23 (22, LXX) Psalm 23 is chanted in the name of the Gentiles, who rejoice because the Lord is their shepherd. They recount the mystical supper the Shepherd has put among them. Paradoxically, the most beloved of all the psalms—frequently sung by the congregation during Holy Communion on Sundays—is used quite sparingly in the services, and is not mentioned in the NT. The psalm makes mention of water (v. 2), oil (v. 5) and the spreading of the table (v. 5) and is understood therefore as a sacramental psalm. Psalm 23 appears in the order for the prayers prior to Holy Communion and is the prokeimenon (gradual) in Tuesday Vespers.

24 (23, LXX) This psalm declares the Ascension of Christ and His teaching that the Gentiles will become worthy to dwell in the heavenly dwelling places. This is the psalm of the Entrance of the **King** (v. 7), said over the grave of the newly departed faithful as earth is scattered in the form of a cross over the resting place. **The earth is the LORD's** (v. 1) gives Christians who remain the assurance that the departed loved one, body and soul, is entrusted to God's care.

Verses 7–10 are proclaimed as the priest knocks on the door of the church on Easter morning, signalling our triumphant entrance into the Kingdom of Heaven through Christ's glorious Resurrection. This same action takes place at the consecration of a church building throughout the Orthodox Christian world.

The LXX renders v. 7, "Lift up your gates, O Priests" (the leaders of angelic hosts), a far more comprehensible rendering, which explains its use on Ascension Thursday woven into liturgical poetry.

2 For He has [a]founded it upon the seas,
And established it upon the [1]waters.

3 [a]Who may ascend into the hill of the LORD?
Or who may stand in His holy place?
4 He who has [a]clean hands and [b]a pure heart,
Who has not lifted up his soul to an idol,
Nor [c]sworn deceitfully.
5 He shall receive blessing from the LORD,
And righteousness from the God of his salvation.
6 This *is* Jacob, the generation of those who [a]seek Him,
Who seek Your face. Selah

7 [a]Lift up your heads, O you gates!
And be lifted up, you everlasting doors!
[b]And the King of glory shall come in.
8 Who *is* this King of glory?
The LORD strong and mighty,
The LORD mighty in [a]battle.
9 Lift up your heads, O you gates!
Lift up, you everlasting doors!
And the King of glory shall come in.
10 Who is this King of glory?
The LORD of hosts,
He *is* the King of glory. Selah

2 [a]Ps. 89:11 [1]Lit. *rivers* 3 [a]Ps. 15:1–5 4 [a][Job 17:9]; Ps. 26:6 [b]Ps. 51:10; 73:1; [Matt. 5:8] [c]Ps. 15:4 6 [a]Ps. 27:4, 8 7 [a]Ps. 118:20; Is. 26:2 [b]Ps. 29:2, 9; 97:6; Hag. 2:7; Acts 7:2; [1 Cor. 2:8] 8 [a]Rev. 19:13–16

PSALM 25
1 [a]Ps. 86:4; 143:8 2 [a]Ps. 34:8 [b]Ps. 13:4; 41:11
3 [1]Waits for You in faith 4 [a]Ex. 33:13; Ps. 5:8; 27:11; 86:11; 119:27; 143:8 6 [a]Ps. 103:17; 106:1 7 [a]Job 13:26; [Jer. 3:25] [b]Ps. 51:1 11 [a]Ps. 31:3; 79:9; 109:21; 143:11 12 [a][Ps. 25:8; 37:23] [1]Or *he* 13 [a][Prov. 19:23] [b]Ps. 37:11; 69:36; Matt. 5:5 [1]Lit. *goodness* 14 [a][Prov. 3:32; John 7:17]

PSALM 25†

A Prayer for All of Life

A Psalm of David.

TO [a]You, O LORD, I lift up my soul.
2 O my God, I [a]trust in You;
Let me not be ashamed;
[b]Let not my enemies triumph over me.
3 Indeed, let no one who [1]waits on You be ashamed;
Let those be ashamed who deal treacherously without cause.

4 [a]Show me Your ways, O LORD;
Teach me Your paths.
5 Lead me in Your truth and teach me,
For You *are* the God of my salvation;
On You I wait all the day.

6 Remember, O LORD, [a]Your tender mercies and Your lovingkindnesses,
For they *are* from of old.
7 Do not remember [a]the sins of my youth, nor my transgressions;
[b]According to Your mercy remember me,
For Your goodness' sake, O LORD.

8 Good and upright *is* the LORD;
Therefore He teaches sinners in the way.
9 The humble He guides in justice,
And the humble He teaches His way.
10 All the paths of the LORD *are* mercy and truth,
To such as keep His covenant and His testimonies.
11 [a]For Your name's sake, O LORD,
Pardon my iniquity, for it *is* great.

12 Who *is* the man that fears the LORD?
[a]Him shall [1]He teach in the way [1]He chooses.
13 [a]He himself shall dwell in [1]prosperity,
And [b]his descendants shall inherit the earth.
14 [a]The secret of the LORD *is* with those who fear Him,
And He will show them His covenant.

25 (24, LXX) This psalm is a personal prayer of **trust** (v. 2), for guidance (v. 4), for forgiveness (v. 7), for deliverance (v. 15), and for **mercy** (v. 16). Overall, this psalm speaks about those who have been gathered to follow the spiritual life. It is a prayer which covers all of life for us. These words may be recited prayerfully during times of persecution. This psalm is read in Great Compline, and in the Third Hour prayers.

15 [a]My eyes *are* ever toward the LORD,
For He shall [1]pluck my feet out of the net.

16 [a]Turn Yourself to me, and have mercy on me,
For I *am* [1]desolate and afflicted.
17 The troubles of my heart have enlarged;
Bring me out of my distresses!
18 [a]Look on my affliction and my pain,
And forgive all my sins.
19 Consider my enemies, for they are many;
And they hate me with [1]cruel hatred.
20 Keep my soul, and deliver me;
Let me not be ashamed, for I put my trust in You.
21 Let integrity and uprightness preserve me,
For I wait for You.

22 [a]Redeem Israel, O God,
Out of all their troubles!

PSALM 26†

The Prayer of the Priest

A Psalm of David.

VINDICATE [a]me, O LORD,
For I have [b]walked in my integrity.
[c]I have also trusted in the LORD;
I shall not slip.
2 [a]Examine me, O LORD, and [1]prove me;
Try my mind and my heart.
3 For Your lovingkindness *is* before my eyes,
And [a]I have walked in Your truth.
4 I have not [a]sat with idolatrous mortals,
Nor will I go in with hypocrites.
5 I have [a]hated the assembly of evildoers,
And will not sit with the wicked.

6 I will wash my hands in innocence;
So I will go about Your altar, O LORD,
7 That I may proclaim with the voice of thanksgiving,
And tell of all Your wondrous works.
8 LORD, [a]I have loved the habitation of Your house,
And the place [1]where Your glory dwells.

9 [a]Do[1] not gather my soul with sinners,
Nor my life with bloodthirsty men,
10 In whose hands *is* a sinister scheme,
And whose right hand is full of [a]bribes.

11 But as for me, I will walk in my integrity;
Redeem me and be merciful to me.
12 [a]My foot stands in an even place;
In the congregations I will bless the LORD.

15 [a][Ps. 123:2; 141:8] [1]Lit. *bring out* 16 [a]Ps. 69:16 [1]*lonely* 18 [a]2 Sam. 16:12; Ps. 31:7 19 [1]*violent hatred* 22 [a][Ps. 130:8]

PSALM 26
1 [a]Ps. 7:8 [b]2 Kin. 20:3; [Prov. 20:7] [c][Ps. 13:5; 28:7] 2 [a]Ps. 17:3; 139:23 [1]*test me* 3 [a]2 Kin. 20:3; Ps. 86:11 4 [a]Ps. 1:1; Jer. 15:17 5 [a]Ps. 31:6; 139:21 8 [a]Ps. 27:4; 84:1–4, 10 [1]Lit. *of the tabernacle of Your glory* 9 [a]Ps. 28:3 [1]*Do not take away* 10 [a]1 Sam. 8:3 12 [a]Ps. 40:2

PSALM 27
1 [a]Ps. 18:28; 84:11; [Is. 60:19, 20; Mic. 7:8]

PSALM 27†

Song of the Newly Enlightened

A Psalm of David.

THE LORD *is* my [a]light and my salvation;

26 (25, LXX) Verse 6 is prayed by the priest in the Orthodox Church just after he has put on his vestments, as he washes his hands prior to the Divine Liturgy. This psalm pictures those who believe in Christ rejecting association with hypocrites who have gathered together against the Lord and His Christ.

27 (26, LXX) This is the song of the Newly Baptized in the Orthodox Church, sung before the reading of the Epistle, Rom. 6:3–11, at the sacrament of baptism. It is also sung on the eve of Epiphany, the feast of the Baptism of the Lord Jesus Christ. The psalm itself is a confirmation of faith in the midst of adversity. Just as Christ's temptations followed His baptism, so we who are joined to Christ in Holy Baptism are readied for the battle of unseen warfare that lies ahead.

Whom shall I fear?
The [b]LORD *is* the strength of my life;
Of whom shall I be afraid?
2 When the wicked came against me
To [a]eat[1] up my flesh,
My enemies and foes,
They stumbled and fell.
3 [a]Though an army may encamp against me,
My heart shall not fear;
Though war may rise against me,
In this I *will be* confident.

4 [a]One *thing* I have desired of the LORD,
That will I seek:
That I may [b]dwell in the house of the LORD
All the days of my life,
To behold the [1]beauty of the LORD,
And to inquire in His temple.
5 For [a]in the time of trouble
He shall hide me in His pavilion;
In the secret place of His tabernacle
He shall hide me;
He shall [b]set me high upon a rock.

6 And now [a]my head shall be [1]lifted up above my enemies all around me;
Therefore I will offer sacrifices of [2]joy in His tabernacle;
I will sing, yes, I will sing praises to the LORD.

7 Hear, O LORD, *when* I cry with my voice!
Have mercy also upon me, and answer me.
8 *When You said,* "Seek My face,"
My heart said to You, "Your face, LORD, I will seek."
9 [a]Do not hide Your face from me;
Do not turn Your servant away in anger;
You have been my help;
Do not leave me nor forsake me,
O God of my salvation.
10 [a]When my father and my mother forsake me,
Then the LORD will take care of me.

11 [a]Teach me Your way, O LORD,
And lead me in a smooth path, because of my enemies.
12 Do not deliver me to the will of my adversaries;
For [a]false witnesses have risen against me,
And such as breathe out violence.
13 *I would have lost heart,* unless I had believed
That I would see the goodness of the LORD
[a]In the land of the living.

14 [a]Wait[1] on the LORD;
Be of good courage,
And He shall strengthen your heart;
Wait, I say, on the LORD!

PSALM 28†

A Prayer for God's Help

A Psalm of David.

TO You I will cry, O LORD my Rock:
[a]Do not be silent to me,
[b]Lest, if You *are* silent to me,
I become like those who go down to the pit.

1 [b]Ex. 15:2; Ps. 62:7; 118:14; Is. 12:2; 33:2
2 [a]Ps. 14:4 [1]*devour*
3 [a]Ps. 3:6
4 [a]Ps. 26:8; 65:4 [b]Luke 2:37 [1]*delightfulness*
5 [a]Ps. 31:20; 91:1 [b]Ps. 40:2
6 [a]Ps. 3:3 [1]Lifted up in honor [2]*joyous shouts*
9 [a]Ps. 69:17; 143:7
10 [a]Is. 49:15
11 [a]Ps. 25:4; 86:11; 119:33
12 [a]Deut. 19:18; Ps. 35:11; Matt. 26:60; Mark 14:56; John 19:33
13 [a]Job 28:13; Ps. 52:5; 116:9; 142:5; Is. 38:11; Jer. 11:19; Ezek. 26:20
14 [a]Ps. 25:3; 37:34; 40:1; 62:5; 130:5; Prov. 20:22; Is. 25:9; [Hab. 2:3] [1]Wait in faith

PSALM 28
1 [a]Ps. 35:22; 39:12; 83:1 [b]Ps. 88:4; 143:7; Prov. 1:12

28 (27, LXX) Psalm 28 is supplication for God's help. Verse 9 is sung repeatedly in the Orthodox Church, by itself and also woven into numerous hymns, showing the Church as God's inheritance. David was **anointed** (v. 8) three times: (1) by Samuel in Bethlehem (1 Sam. 16:1–13); (2) in Hebron (2 Sam. 2:4); (3) by all the tribes of Israel, after the death of Saul (2 Sam. 5:3).

This psalm was written before David's second anointing. It is chanted on behalf of those who believe in Christ. The psalmist implores God to help us in our distress.

2 Hear the voice of my
supplications
When I cry to You,
[a]When I lift up my hands
[b]toward Your holy
sanctuary.

3 Do not [1]take me away with the
wicked
And with the workers of
iniquity,
[a]Who speak peace to their
neighbors,
But evil *is* in their hearts.
4 [a]Give them according to their
deeds,
And according to the
wickedness of their
endeavors;
Give them according to the
work of their hands;
Render to them what they
deserve.
5 Because [a]they do not regard the
works of the LORD,
Nor the operation of His
hands,
He shall destroy them
And not build them up.

6 Blessed *be* the LORD,
Because He has heard the voice
of my supplications!
7 The LORD *is* [a]my strength and
my shield;
My heart [b]trusted in Him, and
I am helped;
Therefore my heart greatly
rejoices,
And with my song I will praise
Him.

8 The LORD *is* [1]their strength,
And He *is* the [a]saving refuge of
His [2]anointed.
9 Save Your people,
And bless [a]Your inheritance;
Shepherd them also,
[b]And bear them up forever.

2 [a]Ps. 5:7 [b]Ps. 138:2
3 [a]Ps. 12:2; 55:21; 62:4; Jer. 9:8 [1]*drag*
4 [a][Ps. 62:12]; 2 Tim. 4:14; [Rev. 18:6; 22:12]
5 [a]Is. 5:12
7 [a]Ps. 18:2; 59:17 [b]Ps. 13:5; 112:7
8 [a]Ps. 20:6 [1]So with MT, Tg.; LXX, Syr., Vg. *the strength of His people* [2]Commissioned one, Heb. *messiah*
9 [a][Deut. 9:29; 32:9; 1 Kin. 8:51; Ps. 33:12]; 106:40 [b]Deut. 1:31; Is. 63:9

PSALM 29†

The Voice of the Lord

A Psalm of David.

GIVE[1] [a]unto the LORD, O you
mighty ones,
Give unto the LORD glory and
strength.
2 [1]Give unto the LORD the glory
[2]due to His name;
Worship the LORD in [a]the
[3]beauty of holiness.

3 The voice of the LORD *is* over the
waters;
[a]The God of glory thunders;
The LORD *is* over many waters.
4 The voice of the LORD *is*
powerful;
The voice of the LORD *is* full of
majesty.

5 The voice of the LORD breaks
[a]the cedars,
Yes, the LORD splinters the
cedars of Lebanon.
6 [a]He makes them also skip like a
calf,
Lebanon and [b]Sirion like a
young wild ox.
7 The voice of the LORD [1]divides
the flames of fire.

8 The voice of the LORD shakes the
wilderness;
The LORD shakes the Wilderness
of [a]Kadesh.
9 The voice of the LORD makes the
[a]deer give birth,
And strips the forests bare;
And in His temple everyone
says, "Glory!"

10 The [a]LORD sat *enthroned* at the
Flood,
And [b]the LORD sits as King
forever.
11 [a]The LORD will give strength to
His people;

PSALM 29
1 [a]1 Chr. 16:28, 29 [1]*Ascribe*
2 [a]2 Chr. 20:21; Ps. 110:3 [1]*Ascribe* [2]Lit. *of His name* [3]*majesty*
3 [a][Job 37:4, 5]; Ps. 18:13; Acts 7:2
5 [a]Judg. 9:15; 1 Kin. 5:6; Ps. 104:16; Is. 2:13; 14:8
6 [a]Ps. 114:4 [b]Deut. 3:9
7 [1]*stirs up*, lit. *hews out*
8 [a]Num. 13:26
9 [a]Job 39:1
10 [a]Gen. 6:17; Job 38:8, 25 [b]Ps. 10:16
11 [a]Ps. 28:8; 68:35; [Is. 40:29]

29 (28, LXX) This psalm is used repeatedly throughout the season of Epiphany, specifically vv. 3, 4, which are seen as fulfilled in the Baptism of Christ when God the Father spoke from heaven, "This is My beloved Son in whom I am well pleased" (Matt. 3:17; Mark 1:11; Luke 3:22).

The LORD will bless His people
with peace.

PSALM 30†

A Hymn of Resurrection

A Psalm. A Song [a]at the dedication of the house of David.

I WILL extol You, O LORD, for You
have [a]lifted me up,
And have not let my foes
[b]rejoice over me.
2 O LORD my God, I cried out to
You,
And You [a]healed me.
3 O LORD, [a]You brought my soul
up from the grave;
You have kept me alive,
[1]that I should not go down to
the pit.

4 [a]Sing praise to the LORD, you
saints of His,
And give thanks at the
remembrance of [1]His holy
name.
5 For [a]His anger *is but for* a
moment,
[b]His favor *is for* life;
Weeping may endure for a
night,
But [1]joy *comes* in the morning.

6 Now in my prosperity I said,
"I shall never be [1]moved."
7 LORD, by Your favor You have
made my mountain stand
strong;
[a]You hid Your face, *and* I was
troubled.

8 I cried out to You, O LORD;
And to the LORD I made
supplication:
9 "What profit *is there* in my blood,
When I go down to the pit?
[a]Will the dust praise You?
Will it declare Your truth?
10 Hear, O LORD, and have mercy
on me;
LORD, be my helper!"

11 [a]You have turned for me my
mourning into dancing;
You have put off [1]my sackcloth
and clothed me with
gladness,
12 To the end that *my* [1]glory may
sing praise to You and not be
silent.
O LORD my God, I will give
thanks to You forever.

PSALM 31†

The Lord a Fortress in Adversity

To the Chief Musician. A Psalm of David.

IN [a]You, O LORD, I [1]put my trust;
Let me never be ashamed;
Deliver me in Your
righteousness.
2 [a]Bow down Your ear to me,
Deliver me speedily;
Be my rock of [1]refuge,
A [2]fortress of defense to save
me.
3 [a]For You *are* my rock and my
fortress;
Therefore, [b]for Your name's
sake,
Lead me and guide me.
4 Pull me out of the net which
they have secretly laid for me,
For You *are* my strength.
5 [a]Into Your hand I commit my
spirit;
You have redeemed me, O LORD
God of [b]truth.

PSALM 30

title [a]Deut. 20:5
1 [a]Ps. 28:9 [b]Ps. 25:2
2 [a]Ps. 6:2; 103:3; [Is. 53:5]
3 [a]Ps. 86:13 [1]So with Qr., Tg.; Kt., LXX, Syr., Vg. *from those who descend to the pit*
4 [a]Ps. 97:12 [1]Or *His holiness*
5 [a]Ps. 103:9; Is. 26:20; 54:7, 8 [b]Ps. 63:3 [1]*a shout of joy*
6 [1]*shaken*
7 [a][Deut. 31:17; Ps. 104:29; 143:7]
9 [a][Ps. 6:5]
11 [a]Eccl. 3:4; Is. 61:3; Jer. 31:4 [1]The sackcloth of my mourning
12 [1]*soul*

PSALM 31

1 [a]Ps. 22:5 [1]*have taken refuge*
2 [a]Ps. 17:6; 71:2; 86:1; 102:2 [1]*strength* [2]Lit. *house of fortresses*
3 [a][Ps. 18:2] [b]Ps. 23:3; 25:11
5 [a]Luke 23:46 [b][Deut. 32:4]; Ps. 71:22

---

30 (29, LXX) In numerous biblical commentaries of the early Church Fathers, Ps. 30—especially vv. 3, 5—is seen as being wonderfully fulfilled in Christ's Resurrection.

31 (30, LXX) According to St. Luke (Luke 23:46), v. 5 represents the last words of Christ on the Cross. This is a psalm of confidence in God, used as a song in Great Compline during the season of Lent. Psalm 31 has often been compared to Ps. 22, the Passion Psalm, because it expresses the cry of all who seek help and deliverance from the Lord in the midst of terrible suffering and pain. David sang this psalm when he repented from his sin, imploring God to deliver him from it. He gives thanks to God, because He accepted his repentance.

6 I have hated those [a]who regard useless idols;
But I trust in the LORD.
7 I will be glad and rejoice in Your mercy,
For You have considered my trouble;
You have [a]known my soul in [1]adversities,
8 And have not [a]shut[1] me up into the hand of the enemy;
[b]You have set my feet in a wide place.

9 Have mercy on me, O LORD, for I am in trouble;
[a]My eye wastes away with grief,
Yes, my soul and my [1]body!
10 For my life is spent with grief,
And my years with sighing;
My strength fails because of my iniquity,
And my bones waste away.
11 [a]I am a [1]reproach among all my enemies,
But [b]especially among my neighbors,
And *am* repulsive to my acquaintances;
[c]Those who see me outside flee from me.
12 [a]I am forgotten like a dead man, out of mind;
I am like a [1]broken vessel.
13 [a]For I hear the slander of many;
[b]Fear *is* on every side;
While they [c]take counsel together against me,
They scheme to take away my life.

14 But as for me, I trust in You, O LORD;
I say, "You *are* my God."
15 My times *are* in Your [a]hand;
Deliver me from the hand of my enemies,
And from those who persecute me.
16 [a]Make Your face shine upon Your servant;
Save me for Your mercies' sake.
17 [a]Do not let me be ashamed,
O LORD, for I have called upon You;
Let the wicked be ashamed;
[b]Let them be silent in the grave.
18 [a]Let the lying lips be put to silence,
Which [b]speak insolent things proudly and contemptuously against the righteous.

19 [a]Oh, how great *is* Your goodness,
Which You have laid up for those who fear You,
Which You have prepared for those who trust in You
In the presence of the sons of men!
20 [a]You shall hide them in the secret place of Your presence
From the plots of man;
[b]You shall keep them secretly in a [1]pavilion
From the strife of tongues.

21 Blessed *be* the LORD,
For [a]He has shown me His marvelous kindness in a [1]strong city!
22 For I said in my haste,
"I am cut off from before Your eyes";
Nevertheless You heard the voice of my supplications
When I cried out to You.

23 Oh, love the LORD, all you His saints!
For the LORD preserves the faithful,
And fully repays the proud person.
24 [a]Be of good courage,
And He shall strengthen your heart,
All you who hope in the LORD.

6 [a]Jon. 2:8 **7** [a][John 10:27] [1]*troubles* **8** [a][Deut. 32:30]; Ps. 37:33 [b][Ps. 4:1; 18:19] [1]*given me over* **9** [a]Ps. 6:7 [1]Lit. *belly* **11** [a][Is. 53:4] [b]Job 19:13; Ps. 38:11; 88:8, 18 [c]Ps. 64:8 [1]*despised thing* **12** [a]Ps. 88:4, 5 [1]Lit. *perishing* **13** [a]Ps. 50:20; Jer. 20:10 [b]Lam. 2:22 [c]Ps. 62:4; Matt. 27:1 **15** [a][Job 14:5; 24:1] **16** [a]Ps. 4:6; 80:3 **17** [a]Ps. 25:2, 20 [b][1 Sam. 2:9]; Ps. 94:17; 115:17 **18** [a]Ps. 109:2; 120:2 [b][1 Sam. 2:3]; Ps. 94:4; [Jude 15] **19** [a]Ps. 145:7; [Rom. 2:4; 11:22] **20** [a][Ps. 27:5; 32:7] [b]Job 5:21 [1]*shelter* **21** [a][Ps. 17:7] [1]*fortified* **24** [a][Ps. 27:14]

PSALM 32†

The Joy of Forgiveness

A Psalm of David. A [1]Contemplation.

BLESSED *is he whose* [a]transgression *is* forgiven,
Whose sin *is* covered.

PSALM 32 **title** [1]Heb. *Maschil* **1** [a][Ps. 85:2; 103:3]; Rom. 4:7, 8

32 (31, LXX) This psalm of forgiveness is sung in the Orthodox Church when the newly baptized are brought up out of the water and given their white garments. Note both the *(continued on next page)*

2 Blessed *is* the man to whom the
LORD [a]does not [1]impute
iniquity,
And [b]in whose spirit *there is* no
deceit.

3 When I kept silent, my bones
grew old
Through my groaning all the
day long.
4 For day and night Your
[a]hand was heavy upon me;
My vitality was turned into the
drought of summer. Selah
5 I acknowledged my sin to You,
And my iniquity I have not
hidden.
[a]I said, "I will confess my
transgressions to the LORD,"
And You forgave the iniquity of
my sin. Selah

6 [a]For this cause everyone who is
godly shall [b]pray to You
In a time when You may be
found;
Surely in a flood of great waters
They shall not come near him.
7 [a]You *are* my hiding place;
You shall preserve me from
trouble;
You shall surround me with
[b]songs of deliverance. Selah

8 I will instruct you and teach you
in the way you should go;
I will guide you with My eye.
9 Do not be like the [a]horse *or* like
the mule,
Which have no understanding,
Which must be harnessed with
bit and bridle,
Else they will not come near
you.

10 [a]Many sorrows *shall be* to the
wicked;
But [b]he who trusts in the LORD,
mercy shall surround him.
11 [a]Be glad in the LORD and rejoice,
you righteous;
And shout for joy, all *you*
upright in heart!

PSALM 33†

The Glory of God the Creator

REJOICE [a]in the LORD, O you
righteous!
For praise from the upright is
beautiful.
2 Praise the LORD with the harp;
[1]Make melody to Him with an
instrument of ten strings.
3 Sing to Him a new song;
Play skillfully with a shout of
joy.

4 For the word of the LORD *is*
right,
And all His work *is done* in
truth.
5 He loves righteousness and
justice;
The earth is full of the goodness
of the LORD.

6 [a]By the word of the LORD the
heavens were made,
And all the [b]host of them
[c]by the breath of His mouth.
7 [a]He gathers the waters of the sea
together [1]as a heap;
He lays up the deep in
storehouses.

2 [a][2 Cor. 5:19] [b]John 1:47 [1]*charge his account with*
4 [a]1 Sam. 5:6; Ps. 38:2; 39:10
5 [a]2 Sam. 12:13; Ps. 38:18; [Prov. 28:13; 1 John 1:9]
6 [a][1 Tim. 1:16] [b]Ps. 69:13; Is. 55:6
7 [a]Ps. 9:9 [b]Ex. 15:1; Judg. 5:1; [Ps. 40:3]
9 [a]Prov. 26:3
10 [a]Ps. 16:4; [Prov. 13:21; Rom. 2:9] [b][Ps. 5:11, 12]; Prov. 16:20
11 [a]Ps. 64:10; 68:3; 97:12

PSALM 33

1 [a]Ps. 32:11; 97:12; Phil. 3:1; 4:4
2 [1]Lit. *Sing to Him*
6 [a]Gen. 1:6, 7; Ps. 148:5; [Heb. 11:3; 2 Pet. 3:5] [b]Gen. 2:1 [c][Job 26:13]
7 [a]Gen. 1:9; Job 26:10; 38:8 [1]LXX, Tg., Vg. *in a vessel*

(continued from previous page)
clear promise that our sins are fully and utterly forgiven in Christ (vv. 1–7) and our assurance that we will be taught by God and given understanding as we live in Him in His Church (vv. 8, 9). The psalmist shows the sufferings he endures during the time of his repentance, and pronounces joyfully those who have obtained the remission of sins by regeneration.

33 (32, LXX) God is glorified as Creator. Verse 1 is a communion refrain, sung on days of commemorating great saints of the Church. Of special note is v. 6, which in the LXX reads, "By the Word [the Son] of the Lord [the Father] the heavens were made, and all the host of them [the angels] by the Spirit of His mouth," a majestic revelation of the Trinity. Appropriately, this verse is sung at Pentecost. Verse 22 is a favorite Orthodox prayer asking God for His continued mercy. The psalmist teaches believers in Christ to praise their Lord, for He will save all those who have hope in Him.

8 Let all the earth fear the LORD;
Let all the inhabitants of the world stand in awe of Him.
9 For [a]He spoke, and it was *done;*
He commanded, and it stood fast.

10 [a]The LORD brings the counsel of the nations to nothing;
He makes the plans of the peoples of no effect.
11 [a]The counsel of the LORD stands forever,
The plans of His heart to all generations.
12 Blessed *is* the nation whose God *is* the LORD,
The people He has [a]chosen as His own inheritance.

13 [a]The LORD looks from heaven;
He sees all the sons of men.
14 From the place of His dwelling He looks
On all the inhabitants of the earth;
15 He fashions their hearts individually;
[a]He [1]considers all their works.

16 [a]No king *is* saved by the multitude of an army;
A mighty man is not delivered by great strength.
17 [a]A horse *is* a [1]vain hope for safety;
Neither shall it deliver *any* by its great strength.

18 [a]Behold, the eye of the LORD *is* on those who fear Him,
On those who hope in His mercy,
19 To deliver their soul from death,
And [a]to keep them alive in famine.

20 Our soul waits for the LORD;
He *is* our help and our shield.

9 [a]Gen. 1:3; Ps. 148:5
10 [a][Ps. 2:1–3]; Is. 8:10; 19:3
11 [a][Job 23:13; Prov. 19:21]
12 [a][Ex. 19:5; Deut. 7:6]; Ps. 28:9
13 [a]Job 28:24; [Ps. 14:2]
15 [a][2 Chr. 16:9]; Job 34:21; [Jer. 32:19] [1]*understands*
16 [a]Ps. 44:6; 60:11; [Jer. 9:23, 24]
17 [a][Ps. 20:7; 147:10; Prov. 21:31] [1]*false*
18 [a][Job 36:7]; Ps. 32:8; 34:15; [1 Pet. 3:12]
19 [a]Job 5:20; Ps. 37:19

PSALM 34
title [a]1 Sam. 21:10–15
1 [a][Eph. 5:20; 1 Thess. 5:18]
4 [a][2 Chr. 15:2; Ps. 9:10; Matt. 7:7; Luke 11:9]
7 [a][Ps. 91:11]; Dan. 6:22 [b]2 Kin. 6:17 [1]Or *Angel*
8 [a]Ps. 119:103; [Heb. 6:5]; 1 Pet. 2:3 [b]Ps. 2:12

21 For our heart shall rejoice in Him,
Because we have trusted in His holy name.
22 Let Your mercy, O LORD, be upon us,
Just as we hope in You.

PSALM 34†

Communing with God

A Psalm of David [a]when he pretended madness before Abimelech, who drove him away, and he departed.

I WILL [a]bless the LORD at all times;
His praise *shall* continually *be* in my mouth.
2 My soul shall make its boast in the LORD;
The humble shall hear *of it* and be glad.
3 Oh, magnify the LORD with me,
And let us exalt His name together.

4 I [a]sought the LORD, and He heard me,
And delivered me from all my fears.
5 They looked to Him and were radiant,
And their faces were not ashamed.
6 This poor man cried out, and the LORD heard *him,*
And saved him out of all his troubles.
7 [a]The [1]angel of the LORD [b]encamps all around those who fear Him,
And delivers them.

8 Oh, [a]taste and see that the LORD *is* good;
[b]Blessed *is* the man *who* trusts in Him!

34 (33, LXX) Historically and liturgically, this is the favorite psalm of the Church to accompany the receiving of Holy Communion. Verse 8 is seen throughout the Orthodox Church as describing the act of receiving the Body and Blood of Christ. In present Orthodox practice, Ps. 39 (38, LXX) is sung, with 34:8 as the refrain, during communion at the Liturgy of the Presanctified Gifts during Lent. Verse 8 was the communion hymn on all Sundays of the year for many centuries. In the Russian tradition, it is sung before the dismissal of the faithful at the Divine Liturgy.

9 Oh, fear the LORD, you His saints!
There is no [1]want to those who fear Him.
10 The young lions lack and suffer hunger;
[a]But those who seek the LORD shall not lack any good *thing*.

11 Come, you children, listen to me;
[a]I will teach you the fear of the LORD.
12 [a]Who *is* the man *who* desires life,
And loves *many* days, that he may see good?
13 Keep your tongue from evil,
And your lips from speaking [a]deceit.
14 [a]Depart from evil and do good;
[b]Seek peace and pursue it.

15 [a]The eyes of the LORD *are* on the righteous,
And His ears *are open* to their cry.
16 [a]The face of the LORD *is* against those who do evil,
[b]To [1]cut off the remembrance of them from the earth.

17 *The righteous* cry out, and [a]the LORD hears,
And delivers them out of all their troubles.
18 [a]The LORD *is* near [b]to those who have a broken heart,
And saves such as [1]have a contrite spirit.

19 [a]Many *are* the afflictions of the righteous,
[b]But the LORD delivers him out of them all.
20 He guards all his bones;
[a]Not one of them is broken.
21 [a]Evil shall slay the wicked,
And those who hate the righteous shall be [1]condemned.
22 The LORD [a]redeems the soul of His servants,
And none of those who trust in Him shall be condemned.

9 [1]*lack*
10 [a][Ps. 84:11]
11 [a]Ps. 32:8
12 [a][1 Pet. 3:10–12]
13 [a][Eph. 4:25]
14 [a]Ps. 37:27 [b][Rom. 14:19]
15 [a]Job 36:7
16 [a]Lev. 17:10 [b][Prov. 10:7] [1]*destroy*
17 [a]Ps. 34:6; 145:19
18 [a][Ps. 145:18] [b][Is. 57:15] [1]*are crushed in spirit*
19 [a]Prov. 24:16 [b]Ps. 34:4, 6, 17
20 [a]John 19:33, 36
21 [a]Ps. 94:23; 140:11 [1]*held guilty*
22 [a]1 Kin. 1:29

PSALM 35†

The Lord the Avenger of His People

A Psalm of David.

PLEAD[1] *my cause*, O LORD, with those who strive with me;
Fight against those who fight against me.
2 Take hold of shield and [1]buckler,
And stand up for my help.
3 Also draw out the spear,
And stop those who pursue me.
Say to my soul,
"I *am* your salvation."

4 [a]Let those be put to shame and brought to dishonor
Who seek after my life;
Let those be [b]turned back and brought to confusion
Who plot my hurt.
5 [a]Let them be like chaff before the wind,
And let the [1]angel of the LORD chase *them*.
6 Let their way be [a]dark and slippery,
And let the angel of the LORD pursue them.
7 For without cause they have [a]hidden their net for me *in* a pit,
Which they have dug without cause for my life.
8 [1]Let [a]destruction come upon him unexpectedly,
And let his net that he has hidden catch himself;
Into that very destruction let him fall.

9 And my soul shall be joyful in the LORD;
It shall rejoice in His salvation.

PSALM 35
1 [1]*Contend for me*
2 [1]A small shield
4 [a]Ps. 40:14, 15; 70:2, 3 [b]Ps. 129:5
5 [a]Job 21:18 [1]Or *Angel*
6 [a]Ps. 73:18
7 [a]Ps. 9:15
8 [a][1 Thess. 5:3] [1]Lit. *Let destruction he does not know come upon him,*

35 (34, LXX) Asking God to vindicate us before our enemies, this is a Good Friday psalm, portraying the deliverance of Christ in His sufferings on the Cross. Verse 11 refers to the false witnesses at the trial of Christ, as do vv. 15, 16, 21, 22. The psalmist introduces the person of Jesus as well as Jesus' Passion, so that those who are attacked for the sake of God will have patience. Thus, Ps. 35 is known as a Passion psalm, and is prayed at the Third Hour on Good Friday.

10 [a]All my bones shall say,
"LORD, [b]who *is* like You,
Delivering the poor from him
who is too strong for him,
Yes, the poor and the needy
from him who plunders
him?"

11 Fierce witnesses rise up;
They ask me *things* that I do not
know.
12 [a]They reward me evil for good,
To the sorrow of my soul.
13 But as for me, [a]when they were
sick,
My clothing *was* sackcloth;
I humbled myself with fasting;
And my prayer would return to
my own [1]heart.
14 I paced about as though *he were*
my friend *or* brother;
I bowed down [1]heavily, as one
who mourns *for his* mother.

15 But in my [1]adversity they
rejoiced
And gathered together;
Attackers gathered against me,
And I did not know *it;*
They tore *at me* and did not
cease;
16 With ungodly mockers at feasts
They gnashed at me with their
teeth.

17 Lord, how long will You
[a]look on?
Rescue me from their
destructions,
My precious *life* from the lions.
18 I will give You thanks in the
great assembly;
I will praise You among
[1]many people.
19 [a]Let them not rejoice over me
who are wrongfully my
enemies;
Nor let them wink with the eye
who hate me without a cause.
20 For they do not speak peace,
But they devise deceitful
matters

10 [a]Ps. 51:8 [b][Ex. 15:11]; Ps. 71:19; 86:8; [Mic. 7:18]
12 [a]Ps. 38:20; 109:5; Jer. 18:20; John 10:32
13 [a]Job 30:25 [1]Lit. *bosom*
14 [1]*in mourning*
15 [1]*limping, stumbling*
17 [a]Ps. 13:1; [Hab. 1:13]
18 [1]*a mighty*
19 [a]Ps. 69:4; 109:3; Lam. 3:52; [John 15:25]

26 [a]Ps. 109:29
27 [a]Rom. 12:15

Against *the* quiet ones in the
land.
21 They also opened their mouth
wide against me,
And said, "Aha, aha!
Our eyes have seen *it*."

22 *This* You have seen, O LORD;
Do not keep silence.
O Lord, do not be far from me.
23 Stir up Yourself, and awake to
my vindication,
To my cause, my God and my
Lord.
24 Vindicate me, O LORD my God,
according to Your
righteousness;
And let them not rejoice over
me.
25 Let them not say in their hearts,
"Ah, so we would have it!"
Let them not say, "We have
swallowed him up."

26 Let them be ashamed and
brought to mutual confusion
Who rejoice at my hurt;
Let them be [a]clothed with
shame and dishonor
Who exalt themselves against
me.

27 [a]Let them shout for joy and be
glad,
Who favor my righteous cause;
And let them say continually,
"Let the LORD be magnified,
Who has pleasure in the
prosperity of His servant."
28 And my tongue shall speak of
Your righteousness
And of Your praise all the day
long.

PSALM 36†

The Wickedness of Sinners and the Goodness of God

To the Chief Musician. A Psalm of David the servant of the LORD.

AN oracle within my heart
concerning the transgression
of the wicked:

36 (35, LXX) This psalm has two distinct parts: vv. 1–4 show the wickedness of sinners; vv. 5–12 reveal the goodness of God. The psalmist reproves the haughtiness of the people,
(continued on next page)

[a]*There is* no fear of God before his eyes.
2 For he flatters himself in his own eyes,
When he finds out his iniquity *and* when he hates.
3 The words of his mouth *are* wickedness and deceit;
[a]He has ceased to be wise *and* to do good.
4 [a]He devises wickedness on his bed;
He sets himself [b]in a way *that is* not good;
He does not [1]abhor [c]evil.

5 Your mercy, O LORD, *is* in the heavens;
Your faithfulness *reaches* to the clouds.
6 Your righteousness *is* like the [1]great mountains;
[a]Your judgments *are* a great deep;
O LORD, You preserve man and beast.

7 How precious *is* Your lovingkindness, O God!
Therefore the children of men [a]put their trust under the shadow of Your wings.
8 [a]They are abundantly satisfied with the fullness of Your house,
And You give them drink from [b]the river of Your pleasures.
9 [a]For with You *is* the fountain of life;
[b]In Your light we see light.

10 Oh, continue Your lovingkindness to those who know You,
And Your righteousness to the upright in heart.
11 Let not the foot of pride come against me,
And let not the hand of the wicked drive me away.
12 There the workers of iniquity have fallen;
They have been cast down and are not able to rise.

PSALM 36
1 [a]Rom. 3:18
3 [a]Ps. 94:8; Jer. 4:22
4 [a]Prov. 4:16; [Mic. 2:1] [b]Is. 65:2 [c][Ps. 52:3; Rom. 12:9] [1]*reject, loathe*
6 [a]Job 11:8; Ps. 77:19; [Rom. 11:33] [1]Lit. *mountains of God*
7 [a]Ruth 2:12; Ps. 17:8; 57:1; 91:4
8 [a]Ps. 63:5; 65:4; Is. 25:6; Jer. 31:12–14 [b]Ps. 46:4; Rev. 22:1
9 [a][Jer. 2:13; John 4:10, 14] [b][1 Pet. 2:9]

PSALM 37†

God Vindicates His Righteous Ones

A Psalm of David.

Do[a] not fret because of evildoers,
Nor be envious of the workers of iniquity.
2 For they shall soon be cut down [a]like the grass,
And wither as the green herb.

3 Trust in the LORD, and do good;
Dwell in the land, and feed on His faithfulness.
4 [a]Delight yourself also in the LORD,
And He shall give you the desires of your [b]heart.

5 [a]Commit[1] your way to the LORD,
Trust also in Him,
And He shall bring *it* to pass.
6 [a]He shall bring forth your righteousness as the light,
And your justice as the noonday.

7 Rest in the LORD, [a]and wait patiently for Him;
Do not fret because of him who [b]prospers in his way,
Because of the man who brings wicked schemes to pass.

PSALM 37
1 [a]Ps. 73:3; [Prov. 23:17; 24:19]
2 [a]Job 14:2; Ps. 90:5, 6; 92:7; James 1:11
4 [a]Job 22:26; Ps. 94:19; Is. 58:14 [b]Ps. 21:2; 145:19; [Matt. 7:7, 8]
5 [a][Ps. 55:22; Prov. 16:3; 1 Pet. 5:7] [1]Lit. *Roll off onto*
6 [a]Job 11:17; [Is. 58:8, 10]
7 [a]Ps. 40:1; 62:5; [Lam. 3:26] [b][Ps. 73:3–12]

(continued from previous page)
and rebukes their evil doings. He praises the goodwill through which God created the world. Two verses, vv. 9, 10, are very familiar to Orthodox Christians, for they have found their way into the Great Doxology sung at the close of Sunday Matins.

37 (36, LXX) Patristic commentators refer often to this psalm, which describes how God vindicates the righteous even though it appears the situation continues to go badly for them. Our lesson: God always rescues the faithful believer *in the end*—that is, at the judgment—whether or not we see relief from our adversaries in this life. Verses 30, 31 are used in the Orthodox Church to commemorate St. John the Baptist and other followers of Christ who have endured martyrdom.

8 [a]Cease from anger, and forsake wrath;
[b]Do not fret—*it* only *causes* harm.
9 For evildoers shall be [1]cut off;
But those who wait on the LORD,
They shall [a]inherit the earth.
10 For [a]yet a little while and the wicked *shall be* no *more;*
Indeed, [b]you will look carefully for his place,
But it *shall be* no *more.*
11 [a]But the meek shall inherit the earth,
And shall delight themselves in the abundance of peace.

12 The wicked plots against the just,
[a]And gnashes at him with his teeth.
13 [a]The Lord laughs at him,
For He sees that [b]his day is coming.
14 The wicked have drawn the sword
And have bent their bow,
To cast down the poor and needy,
To slay those who are of upright conduct.
15 Their sword shall enter their own heart,
And their bows shall be broken.

16 [a]A little that a righteous man has
Is better than the riches of many wicked.
17 For the arms of the wicked shall be broken,
But the LORD upholds the righteous.

18 The LORD knows the days of the upright,
And their inheritance shall be forever.
19 They shall not be ashamed in the evil time,
And in the days of famine they shall be satisfied.
20 But the wicked shall perish;
And the enemies of the LORD,
Like the splendor of the meadows, shall vanish.
Into smoke they shall vanish away.
21 The wicked borrows and does not repay,
But [a]the righteous shows mercy and gives.
22 [a]For *those* blessed by Him shall inherit the earth,
But *those* cursed by Him shall be [1]cut off.

23 [a]The steps of a *good* man are [1]ordered by the LORD,
And He delights in his way.
24 [a]Though he fall, he shall not be utterly cast down;
For the LORD upholds *him with* His hand.

25 I have been young, and *now* am old;
Yet I have not seen the righteous forsaken,
Nor his descendants begging bread.
26 [a]*He is* [1]ever merciful, and lends;
And his descendants *are* blessed.

27 Depart from evil, and do good;
And dwell forevermore.
28 For the LORD loves justice,
And does not forsake His saints;
They are preserved forever,
But the descendants of the wicked shall be cut off.
29 [a]The righteous shall inherit the land,
And dwell in it forever.

30 [a]The mouth of the righteous speaks wisdom,
And his tongue talks of justice.
31 The law of his God *is* in his heart;
None of his steps shall [1]slide.

32 The wicked [a]watches the righteous,
And seeks to slay him.
33 The LORD [a]will not leave him in his hand,
Nor condemn him when he is judged.

34 [a]Wait on the LORD,
And keep His way,
And He shall exalt you to inherit the land;

8 [a][Eph. 4:26] [b]Ps. 73:3
9 [a]Ps. 25:13; Prov. 2:21; [Is. 57:13; 60:21; Matt. 5:5] [1]*destroyed*
10 [a][Heb. 10:37] [b]Job 7:10; Ps. 37:35, 36
11 [a][Matt. 5:5]
12 [a]Ps. 35:16
13 [a]Ps. 2:4; 59:8 [b]1 Sam. 26:10; Job 18:20
16 [a]Prov. 15:16; 16:8; [1 Tim. 6:6]
21 [a]Ps. 112:5, 9
22 [a][Prov. 3:33] [1]*destroyed*
23 [a][1 Sam. 2:9]; Ps. 40:2; 66:9; 119:5 [1]*established*
24 [a]Prov. 24:16
26 [a][Deut. 15:8]; Ps. 37:21 [1]Lit. *all the day*
29 [a]Ps. 37:9; Prov. 2:21
30 [a][Matt. 12:35]
31 [1]*slip*
32 [a]Ps. 10:8; 17:11
33 [a]Ps. 31:8; [2 Pet. 2:9]
34 [a]Ps. 27:14; 37:9

When the wicked are cut off, you shall see *it*.
35 I have seen the wicked in great power,
And spreading himself like a native green tree.
36 Yet [1]he passed away, and behold, he *was* no *more;*
Indeed I sought him, but he could not be found.

37 Mark the blameless *man,* and observe the upright;
For the future of *that* man *is* peace.
38 [a]But the transgressors shall be destroyed together;
The future of the wicked shall be cut off.

39 But the salvation of the righteous *is* from the LORD;
He is their strength [a]in the time of trouble.
40 And [a]the LORD shall help them and deliver them;
He shall deliver them from the wicked,
And save them,
[b]Because they trust in Him.

PSALM 38†

A Psalm of Repentance

A Psalm of David. [a]To bring to remembrance.

O LORD, do not [a]rebuke me in Your wrath,
Nor chasten me in Your hot displeasure!
2 For Your arrows pierce me deeply,
And Your hand presses me down.

3 *There is* no soundness in my flesh
Because of Your anger,
Nor *any* health in my bones
Because of my sin.
4 For my iniquities have gone over my head;
Like a heavy burden they are too heavy for me.
5 My wounds are foul *and* festering
Because of my foolishness.

6 I am [1]troubled, I am bowed down greatly;
I go mourning all the day long.
7 For my loins are full of inflammation,
And *there is* no soundness in my flesh.
8 I am feeble and severely broken;
I groan because of the turmoil of my heart.

9 Lord, all my desire *is* before You;
And my sighing is not hidden from You.
10 My heart pants, my strength fails me;
As for the light of my eyes, it also has gone from me.

11 My loved ones and my friends [a]stand aloof from my plague,
And my relatives stand afar off.
12 Those also who seek my life lay snares *for me;*
Those who seek my hurt speak of destruction,
And plan deception all the day long.

13 But I, like a deaf *man,* do not hear;
And *I am* like a mute *who* does not open his mouth.
14 Thus I am like a man who does not hear,
And in whose mouth *is* no response.

36 [1]So with MT, LXX, Tg.; Syr., Vg. *I passed by*
38 [a][Ps. 1:4–6; 37:20, 28]
39 [a]Ps. 9:9; 37:19
40 [a]Ps. 22:4; Is. 31:5; Dan. 3:17; 6:23 [b]1 Chr. 5:20; Ps. 34:22

PSALM 38
title [a]Ps. 70:title
1 [a]Ps. 6:1

6 [1]Lit. *bent down*
11 [a]Ps. 31:11; 88:18

38 (37, LXX) A psalm of repentance, this is the second of the six psalms used in the Matins service (see note on Ps. 3). The psalmist remembers the sufferings which he endured because of his sins. He asks God to deliver him from all calamities and misfortunes. But it is also seen as a psalm of the Lord in His Passion, bearing the sins of the whole world. Verse 17 is used in the Third Hour prayers on Good Friday, before the scriptural readings. The LXX renders v. 17 as, "I am ready for wounds, and My pain is with Me always."

15 For [1]in You, O LORD, [a]I hope;
You will [2]hear, O Lord my God.
16 For I said, "*Hear me,* lest they
rejoice over me,
Lest, when my foot slips, they
exalt *themselves* against me."

17 [a]For I *am* ready to fall,
And my sorrow *is* continually
before me.
18 For I will [a]declare my iniquity;
I will be [b]in [1]anguish over my
sin.
19 But my enemies *are* vigorous,
and they are strong;
And those who hate me
wrongfully have multiplied.
20 Those also [a]who render evil for
good,
They are my adversaries,
because I follow *what is* good.

21 Do not forsake me, O LORD;
O my God, [a]be not far from me!
22 Make haste to help me,
O Lord, my salvation!

PSALM 39

Prayer for Wisdom and Forgiveness

To the Chief Musician. To Jeduthun. A Psalm of David.

I SAID, "I will guard my ways,
Lest I sin with my [a]tongue;
I will restrain my mouth with a
muzzle,
While the wicked are before
me."
2 [a]I was mute with silence,
I held my peace *even* from good;
And my sorrow was stirred up.
3 My heart was hot within me;
While I was [1]musing, the fire
burned.
Then I spoke with my tongue:

4 "LORD, [a]make me to know my
end,
And what *is* the measure of my
days,
That I may know how frail I *am.*
5 Indeed, You have made my
days *as* handbreadths,
And my age *is* as nothing before
You;
Certainly every man at his best
state *is* but [a]vapor. Selah
6 Surely every man walks about
like a shadow;
Surely they [1]busy themselves in
vain;
He heaps up *riches,*
And does not know who will
gather them.

7 "And now, Lord, what do I wait
for?
My [a]hope *is* in You.
8 Deliver me from all my
transgressions;
Do not make me [a]the reproach
of the foolish.
9 [a]I was mute, I did not open my
mouth,
Because it was [b]You who did *it.*
10 [a]Remove Your plague from me;
I am consumed by the blow of
Your hand.
11 When with rebukes You correct
man for iniquity,
You make his beauty [a]melt
away like a moth;
Surely every man *is* vapor.
Selah

12 "Hear my prayer, O LORD,
And give ear to my cry;
Do not be silent at my tears;
For I *am* a stranger with You,
A sojourner, [a]as all my fathers
were.
13 [a]Remove Your gaze from me,
that I may regain strength,
Before I go away and [b]am no
more."

PSALM 40†

A Messianic Psalm of Strength

To the Chief Musician. A Psalm of David.

I [a]WAITED patiently for the LORD;
And He inclined to me,
And heard my cry.

15 [a][Ps. 39:7] [1]*I wait for You, O LORD* [2]*answer*
17 [a]Ps. 51:3
18 [a]Ps. 32:5 [b][2 Cor. 7:9, 10] [1]*anxiety*
20 [a]Ps. 35:12
21 [a]Ps. 22:19; 35:22

PSALM 39

1 [a]Job 2:10; Ps. 34:13; [James 3:5–12]
2 [a]Ps. 38:13
3 [1]*meditating*
4 [a]Ps. 90:12; 119:84
5 [a]Ps. 62:9; [Eccl. 6:12]
6 [1]*make an uproar for nothing*
7 [a]Ps. 38:15
8 [a]Ps. 44:13; 79:4; 119:22
9 [a]Ps. 39:2 [b]2 Sam. 16:10; Job 2:10
10 [a]Job 9:34; 13:21
11 [a]Job 13:28; [Ps. 90:7]; Is. 50:9
12 [a]Gen. 47:9; Lev. 25:23; 1 Chr. 29:15; Ps. 119:19; Heb. 11:13; 1 Pet. 2:11
13 [a]Job 7:19; 10:20, 21; 14:6; Ps. 102:24 [b][Job 14:10]

PSALM 40

1 [a]Ps. 25:5; 27:14; 37:7

40 (39, LXX) This is a messianic psalm, notable because vv. 6–8 are quoted in Heb. 10:5–9. But note the added clarity in Hebrews, which is quoted from the LXX, not the MT. In

(continued on next page)

2 He also brought me up out of
a horrible pit,
Out of [a]the miry clay,
And [b]set my feet upon a rock,
And established my steps.
3 [a]He has put a new song in my
mouth—
Praise to our God;
Many will see *it* and fear,
And will trust in the LORD.

4 [a]Blessed *is* that man who makes
the LORD his trust,
And does not respect the proud,
nor such as turn aside to lies.
5 [a]Many, O LORD my God, *are*
Your wonderful works
Which You have done;
[b]And Your thoughts toward us
Cannot be recounted to You in
order;
If I would declare and speak *of*
them,
They are more than can be
numbered.

6 [a]Sacrifice and offering You did
not desire;
My ears You have opened.
Burnt offering and sin offering
You did not require.
7 Then I said, "Behold, I come;
In the scroll of the book *it is*
written of me.
8 [a]I delight to do Your will, O my
God,
And Your law *is* [b]within my
heart."

9 [a]I have proclaimed the good
news of righteousness
In the great assembly;
Indeed, [b]I do not restrain my
lips,
O LORD, You Yourself know.
10 [a]I have not hidden Your
righteousness within my
heart;
I have declared Your
faithfulness and Your
salvation;
I have not concealed Your
lovingkindness and Your
truth
From the great assembly.

11 Do not withhold Your tender
mercies from me, O LORD;
[a]Let Your lovingkindness and
Your truth continually
preserve me.
12 For innumerable evils have
surrounded me;
[a]My iniquities have overtaken
me, so that I am not able to
look up;
They are more than the hairs of
my head;
Therefore my heart fails me.
13 [a]Be pleased, O LORD, to deliver
me;
O LORD, make haste to help me!
14 [a]Let them be ashamed and
brought to mutual confusion
Who seek to destroy my
[1]life;
Let them be driven backward
and brought to dishonor
Who wish me evil.
15 Let them be [a]confounded
because of their shame,
Who say to me, "Aha, aha!"

16 [a]Let all those who seek You
rejoice and be glad in You;
Let such as love Your salvation
[b]say continually,
"The LORD be magnified!"
17 [a]But I *am* poor and needy;
Yet the LORD thinks upon me.
You *are* my help and my
deliverer;
[b]Do not delay, O my God.

PSALM 41†

Blessedness and Suffering of the Righteous One

To the Chief Musician. A Psalm of David.

BLESSED *is* he who considers the
[1]poor;

2 [a]Ps. 69:2, 14; Jer. 38:6 [b]Ps. 27:5 **3** [a]Ps. 32:7; 33:3 **4** [a]Ps. 34:8; 84:12 **5** [a]Job 9:10 [b]Ps. 139:17; [Is. 55:8] **6** [a][1 Sam. 15:22]; Ps. 51:16; Is. 1:11; [Jer. 6:20; 7:22, 23]; Amos 5:22; [Mic. 6:6–8; Heb. 10:5–9] **8** [a][Matt. 26:39; John 4:34; 6:38]; Heb. 10:7 [b][Ps. 37:31; Jer. 31:33; 2 Cor. 3:3] **9** [a]Ps. 22:22, 25 [b]Ps. 119:13 **10** [a]Acts 20:20, 27

11 [a]Ps. 61:7; Prov. 20:28 **12** [a]Ps. 38:4; 65:3 **13** [a]Ps. 70:1 **14** [a]Ps. 35:4, 26; 70:2; 71:13 [1]Lit. *soul* **15** [a]Ps. 73:19 **16** [a]Ps. 70:4 [b]Ps 35:27 **17** [a]Ps. 70:5; 86:1; 109:22 [b]Ps. 40:5; 1 Pet. 5:7

PSALM 41

1 [1]*helpless* or *powerless*

(continued from previous page)
v. 6 we see a major difference between the Hebrew and the Septuagint. Where the Hebrew reads, **My ears You have opened,** the Greek reads, "You have prepared a body for me."
41 (40, LXX) This is a Passion psalm predicting Christ's betrayal. Verse 9 is quoted by the Lord (John 13:18), an obvious reference to Judas himself. Psalm 41 is used liturgically on Holy Thursday and Good Friday.

The LORD will deliver him in
time of trouble.
2 The LORD will preserve him and
keep him alive,
And he will be blessed on the
earth;
[a]You will not deliver him to the
will of his enemies.
3 The LORD will strengthen him
on his bed of illness;
You will [1]sustain him on his
sickbed.

4 I said, "LORD, be merciful to me;
[a]Heal my soul, for I have sinned
against You."
5 My enemies speak evil of me:
"When will he die, and his name
perish?"
6 And if he comes to see *me,* he
speaks [1]lies;
His heart gathers iniquity to
itself;
When he goes out, he tells *it.*

7 All who hate me whisper
together against me;
Against me they [1]devise my
hurt.
8 "An[1] evil disease," *they say,*
"clings to him.
And *now* that he lies down, he
will rise up no more."
9 [a]Even my own familiar friend in
whom I trusted,
[b]Who ate my bread,
Has [1]lifted up *his* heel against
me.

10 But You, O LORD, be merciful
to me, and raise me up,
That I may repay them.
11 By this I know that You are well
pleased with me,
Because my enemy does not
triumph over me.
12 As for me, You uphold me in
my integrity,
And [a]set me before Your face
forever.

13 [a]Blessed *be* the LORD God of
Israel
From everlasting to everlasting!
Amen and Amen.

BOOK TWO: Psalms 42–72

PSALM 42†

Yearning for God in the Midst of Distresses

To the Chief Musician. A [1]Contemplation of the sons of Korah.

AS the deer [1]pants for the water
brooks,
So pants my soul for You,
O God.
2 [a]My soul thirsts for God, for the
[b]living God.
When shall I come and
[1]appear before God?
3 [a]My tears have been my food day
and night,
While they continually say to
me,
[b]"Where *is* your God?"

4 When I remember these *things,*
[a]I pour out my soul within me.
For I used to go with the
multitude;
[b]I went with them to the house
of God,
With the voice of joy and praise,
With a multitude that kept a
pilgrim feast.

5 [a]Why are you [1]cast down, O my
soul?
And *why* are you disquieted
within me?
[b]Hope in God, for I shall yet
praise Him
[2]*For* the help of His countenance.

6 [1]O my God, my soul is cast down
within me;

---

2 [a]Ps. 27:12
3 [1]*restore*
4 [a]Ps. 6:2; 103:3; 147:3
6 [1]*empty words*
7 [1]*plot*
8 [1]Lit. *A thing of Belial*
9 [a]2 Sam. 15:12 [b]John 13:18, 21–30 [1]Acted as a traitor
12 [a][Job 36:7]
13 [a]Ps. 72:18, 19; 89:52; 106:48; 150:6

PSALM 42

title [1]Heb. *Maschil*
1 [1]Lit. *longs for*
2 [a]Ps. 63:1; 84:2; 143:6 [b]1 Thess. 1:9 [1]So with MT, Vg.; some Heb. mss., LXX, Syr., Tg. *I see the face of God*
3 [a]Ps. 80:5; 102:9 [b]Ps. 79:10; 115:2
4 [a]Job 30:16 [b]Is. 30:29
5 [a]Ps. 42:11; 43:5 [b]Lam. 3:24 [1]Lit. *bowed down* [2]So with MT, Tg.; a few Heb. mss., LXX, Syr., Vg. *The help of my countenance, my God*
6 [1]So with MT, Tg.; a few Heb. mss., LXX, Syr., Vg. put *my God* at the end of v. 5

---

42 (41, LXX) This has been called a psalm of personal longing for God. Great teachers of the Church have been taken with vv. 1, 2 as a beautiful expression of the soul's desire for union with God. Because of the frequent water references (vv. 1, 6, 7), this psalm is used on all the days before the Feast of Epiphany, and is prayed at the Third Hour of Epiphany Eve.

Therefore I will remember You
from the land of the Jordan,
And from the heights of
Hermon,
From [2]the Hill Mizar.
7 Deep calls unto deep at the
noise of Your waterfalls;
[a]All Your waves and billows
have gone over me.
8 The LORD will [a]command His
lovingkindness in the
daytime,
And [b]in the night His song *shall*
be with me—
A prayer to the God of my life.

9 I will say to God my Rock,
[a]"Why have You forgotten me?
Why do I go mourning because
of the oppression of the
enemy?"
10 *As* with a [1]breaking of my
bones,
My enemies [2]reproach me,
[a]While they say to me all day
long,
"Where *is* your God?"

11 [a]Why are you cast down, O my
soul?
And why are you disquieted
within me?
Hope in God;
For I shall yet praise Him,
The [1]help of my countenance
and my God.

PSALM 43†

A Prayer Before the Altar

VINDICATE [a]me, O God,
And [b]plead my cause against an
ungodly nation;
Oh, deliver me from the
deceitful and unjust man!
2 For You *are* the God of my
strength;
Why do You cast me off?
[a]Why do I go mourning because
of the oppression of the
enemy?

3 [a]Oh, send out Your light and
Your truth!
Let them lead me;
Let them bring me to [b]Your holy
hill
And to Your [1]tabernacle.
4 Then I will go to the altar of
God,
To God my exceeding joy;
And on the harp I will praise
You,
O God, my God.

5 [a]Why are you cast down, O my
soul?
And why are you disquieted
within me?
Hope in God;
For I shall yet praise Him,
The [1]help of my countenance
and my God.

PSALM 44†

The Works of God for Israel

To the Chief Musician. A [a]Contemplation[1] of the sons of Korah.

WE have heard with our ears,
O God,
[a]Our fathers have told us,
The deeds You did in their days,
In days of old:
2 [a]You drove out the [1]nations with
Your hand,
But them You planted;
You afflicted the peoples, and
cast them out.
3 For [a]they did not gain
possession of the land by their
own sword,
Nor did their own arm save
them;
But it was Your right hand,
Your arm, and the light of

---

6 [2]Or *Mount*
7 [a]Ps. 69:1, 2; 88:7
8 [a]Deut. 28:8 [b]Job 35:10
9 [a]Ps. 38:6
10 [a]Joel 2:17 [1]Lit. *shattering* [2]*revile*
11 [a]Ps. 43:5 [1]Lit. *salvation*

PSALM 43
1 [a][Ps. 26:1; 35:24] [b]Ps. 35:1
2 [a]Ps. 42:9
3 [a][Ps. 40:11] [b]Ps. 3:4 [1]*dwelling places*
5 [a]Ps. 42:5, 11 [1]Lit. *salvation*

PSALM 44
title [a]Ps. 42:title [1]Heb. *Maschil*
1 [a][Ex. 12:26, 27]
2 [a]Ex. 15:17 [1]*Gentiles, heathen*
3 [a][Deut. 8:17, 18]

---

43 (42, LXX) The Israelites will come during the last days and ask for salvation through Jesus Christ. In the OT, this was a prayer of the priest before he served at the altar.

44 (43, LXX) Here is an historical summary of the mighty deeds of God in ages past with the question, where is He now (vv. 23–26)? This psalm is a cry of God's people in a lowly state. It is prayed at the Matins of Holy Saturday, and v. 26 is sung before the reading of Ezekiel's prophecy of the dry bones coming to life.

Your countenance,
[b]Because You favored them.

4 [a]You are my King, [1]O God;
[2]Command victories for Jacob.
5 Through You [a]we will push
down our enemies;
Through Your name we will
trample those who rise up
against us.
6 For [a]I will not trust in my bow,
Nor shall my sword save me.
7 But You have saved us from our
enemies,
And have put to shame those
who hated us.
8 [a]In God we boast all day long,
And praise Your name forever.
Selah

9 But [a]You have cast *us* off and
put us to shame,
And You do not go out with our
armies.
10 You make us [a]turn back from
the enemy,
And those who hate us have
taken [1]spoil for themselves.
11 [a]You have given us up like sheep
intended for food,
And have [b]scattered us among
the nations.
12 [a]You sell Your people for *next to*
nothing,
And are not enriched by selling
them.

13 [a]You make us a reproach to our
neighbors,
A scorn and a derision to those
all around us.
14 [a]You make us a byword among
the nations,
[b]A shaking of the head among
the peoples.
15 My dishonor *is* continually
before me,
And the shame of my face has
covered me,
16 Because of the voice of him who
reproaches and reviles,
[a]Because of the enemy and the
avenger.

3 [b][Deut. 4:37; 7:7, 8]
4 [a][Ps. 74:12] [1]So with MT, Tg.; LXX, Vg. *and my God* [2]So with MT, Tg.; LXX, Syr., Vg. *who commands*
5 [a][Dan. 8:4]
6 [a]Ps. 33:16
8 [a]Ps. 34:2
9 [a]Ps. 60:1
10 [a]Lev. 26:17 [1]*plunder*
11 [a]Rom. 8:36 [b]Deut. 4:27; 28:64
12 [a]Is. 52:3, 4
13 [a]Jer. 24:9
14 [a]Deut. 28:37 [b]Job 16:4
16 [a]Ps. 8:2

17 [a]Dan. 9:13
18 [a]Job 23:11
19 [a]Is. 34:13 [b][Ps. 23:4]
20 [a][Deut. 6:14] [1]Worshiped
21 [a][Ps. 139:1, 2]
22 [a]Rom. 8:36
23 [a]Ps. 7:6
24 [a]Job 13:24
25 [a]Ps. 119:25 [1]Ground, in humiliation

PSALM 45
title [a]Ps. 69:title [1]Heb. *Shoshannim* [2]Heb. *Maschil*
1 [1]*skillful*

17 [a]All this has come upon us;
But we have not forgotten You,
Nor have we dealt falsely with
Your covenant.
18 Our heart has not turned back,
[a]Nor have our steps departed
from Your way;
19 But You have severely broken
us in [a]the place of jackals,
And covered us [b]with the
shadow of death.

20 If we had forgotten the name of
our God,
Or [a]stretched[1] out our hands to
a foreign god,
21 [a]Would not God search this out?
For He knows the secrets of the
heart.
22 [a]Yet for Your sake we are killed
all day long;
We are accounted as sheep for
the slaughter.

23 [a]Awake! Why do You sleep,
O Lord?
Arise! Do not cast *us* off forever.
24 [a]Why do You hide Your face,
And forget our affliction and our
oppression?
25 For [a]our soul is bowed down to
the [1]dust;
Our body clings to the ground.
26 Arise for our help,
And redeem us for Your
mercies' sake.

PSALM 45†

A Wedding Hymn: The Messiah and the Bride

To the Chief Musician. [a]Set to [1]"The Lilies." A [2]Contemplation of the sons of Korah. A Song of Love.

MY heart is overflowing with a
good theme;
I recite my composition
concerning the King;
My tongue *is* the pen of a
[1]ready writer.

45 (44, LXX) These words refer to Christ, who came and changed idolatry into real worship of God. The wedding hymn is sung in the third person to the Messiah and His bride. Verses

(continued on next page)

2 You are fairer than the sons of men;
[a]Grace is poured upon Your lips;
Therefore God has blessed You forever.
3 [1]Gird Your [a]sword upon *Your* thigh, [b]O Mighty One,
With Your [c]glory and Your majesty.
4 [a]And in Your majesty ride prosperously because of truth, humility, *and* righteousness;
And Your right hand shall teach You awesome things.
5 Your arrows *are* sharp in the heart of the King's enemies;
The peoples fall under You.

6 [a]Your throne, O God, *is* forever and ever;
A [b]scepter of righteousness *is* the scepter of Your kingdom.
7 You love righteousness and hate wickedness;
Therefore God, Your God, has [a]anointed You
With the oil of [b]gladness more than Your companions.
8 All Your garments are [a]scented with myrrh and aloes *and* cassia,
Out of the ivory palaces, by which they have made You glad.
9 [a]Kings' daughters *are* among Your honorable women;
[b]At Your right hand stands the queen in gold from Ophir.

10 Listen, O daughter,
Consider and incline your ear;
[a]Forget your own people also, and your father's house;
11 So the King will greatly desire your beauty;
[a]Because He *is* your Lord, worship Him.
12 And the daughter of Tyre *will come* with a gift;
[a]The rich among the people will seek your favor.

13 The royal daughter *is* all glorious within *the palace;*
Her clothing *is* woven with gold.
14 [a]She shall be brought to the King in robes of many colors;
The virgins, her companions who follow her, shall be brought to You.
15 With gladness and rejoicing they shall be brought;
They shall enter the King's palace.

16 Instead of Your fathers shall be Your sons,
[a]Whom You shall make princes in all the earth.
17 [a]I will make Your name to be remembered in all generations;
Therefore the people shall praise You forever and ever.

2 [a]Luke 4:22
3 [a][Is. 49:2; Heb. 4:12]; Rev. 1:16 [b][Is. 9:6] [c]Jude 25 [1]*Belt on*
4 [a]Rev. 6:2
6 [a][Ps. 93:2]; Heb. 1:8, 9 [b][Num. 24:17]
7 [a]Ps. 2:2 [b]Ps. 21:6; Heb. 1:8, 9
8 [a]Song 1:12, 13
9 [a]Song 6:8 [b]1 Kin. 2:19
10 [a]Deut. 21:13; Ruth 1:16, 17
11 [a]Ps. 95:6; [Is. 54:5]
12 [a]Is. 49:23
14 [a]Song 1:4
16 [a][1 Pet. 2:9; Rev. 1:6; 20:6]
17 [a]Mal. 1:11

PSALM 46
title [a]1 Chr. 15:20
1 [a]Ps. 62:7, 8

PSALM 46†

God Dwells Within His People

To the Chief Musician. A Psalm of the sons of Korah. A Song [a]for Alamoth.

GOD *is* our [a]refuge and strength,

(continued from previous page)
1–9 refer explicitly to Christ as Bridegroom and Savior. Verses 6, 7 establish the Messiah as God, not simply a human deliverer (see as quoted in Heb. 1:8, 9). Verse 16 shows how the sons replace the fathers, the interpretation being that the sons of the New Covenant are in a higher place than the fathers of the Old Covenant.

Verses 9–17 are seen throughout the Church as a reference to the Virgin Mary, **the queen** (v. 9), as a personification of the Church (**virgins,** v. 14), the bride of the Messiah. This passage is sung on all the feast days of Mary, and v. 9b is said by the priest as he commemorates Mary in the preparation service. Although the NKJV capitalizes **Your** in v. 17 as referring to God, the Church historically has seen this verse as a reference to Mary, as echoed in the Magnificat: "All generations will call me blessed" (Luke 1:48).

Psalm 45 is also sung at the First Hour on Christmas Eve Day, and the messianic verses (vv. 3, 4, 7) are sung on the Sunday of the Samaritan Woman (John 4:25, 26), the first woman to whom Christ revealed Himself as Messiah.

46 (45, LXX) This psalm refers to the call of the Gentiles, and to the banishment of evil

(continued on next page)

[b]A[1] very present help in trouble.
2 Therefore we will not fear,
Even though the earth be removed,
And though the mountains be carried into the [1]midst of the sea;
3 [a]*Though* its waters roar *and* be troubled,
Though the mountains shake with its swelling. Selah

4 *There is* a [a]river whose streams shall make glad the [b]city of God,
The holy *place* of the [1]tabernacle of the Most High.
5 God *is* [a]in the midst of her, she shall not be [1]moved;
God shall help her, just [2]at the break of dawn.
6 [a]The nations raged, the kingdoms were moved;
He uttered His voice, the earth melted.

7 The [a]LORD of hosts *is* with us;
The God of Jacob *is* our refuge. Selah

8 Come, behold the works of the LORD,
Who has made desolations in the earth.
9 [a]He makes wars cease to the end of the earth;
[b]He breaks the bow and cuts the spear in two;
[c]He burns the chariot in the fire.
10 Be still, and know that I *am* God;
[a]I will be exalted among the nations,
I will be exalted in the earth!
11 The LORD of hosts *is* with us;
The God of Jacob *is* our refuge. Selah

1 [b][Deut. 4:7; Ps. 145:18] [1]*An abundantly available help*
2 [1]Lit. *heart*
3 [a][Ps. 93:3, 4]
4 [a][Ezek. 47:1–12] [b]Ps. 48:1, 8; Is. 60:14 [1]*dwelling places*
5 [a][Deut. 23:14; Is. 12:6]; Ezek. 43:7; Hos. 11:9; [Joel 2:27; Zeph. 3:15; Zech. 2:5, 10, 11; 8:3] [1]*shaken* [2]Lit. *at the turning of the morning*
6 [a]Ps. 2:1, 2
7 [a]Num. 14:9; 2 Chr. 13:12
9 [a]Is. 2:4 [b]Ps. 76:3 [c]Ezek. 39:9
10 [a][Is. 2:11, 17]

PSALM 47
2 [a]Deut. 7:21; Neh. 1:5; Ps. 76:12
3 [a]Ps. 18:47
4 [a][1 Pet. 1:4]
5 [a]Ps. 68:24, 25
7 [a]Zech. 14:9 [b]1 Cor. 14:15
8 [a]1 Chr. 16:31 [b]Ps. 97:2 [c]Ps. 48:1
9 [a][Rom. 4:11, 12] [b][Ps. 89:18]

PSALM 47†

Song of Ascent

To the Chief Musician. A Psalm of the sons of Korah.

OH, clap your hands, all you peoples!
Shout to God with the voice of triumph!
2 For the LORD Most High *is* awesome;
He is a great [a]King over all the earth.
3 [a]He will subdue the peoples under us,
And the nations under our feet.
4 He will choose our [a]inheritance for us,
The excellence of Jacob whom He loves. Selah

5 [a]God has gone up with a shout,
The LORD with the sound of a trumpet.
6 Sing praises to God, sing praises!
Sing praises to our King, sing praises!
7 [a]For God *is* the King of all the earth;
[b]Sing praises with understanding.

8 [a]God reigns over the nations;
God [b]sits on His [c]holy throne.
9 The princes of the people have gathered together,
[a]The people of the God of Abraham.
[b]For the shields of the earth *belong* to God;
He is greatly exalted.

(continued from previous page) spirits. It describes the indwelling of God within His people. Verses 4, 5 refer to the OT temple, or the city of God, Jerusalem, which is fulfilled in the Church and in the Mother of God, the first in whom He dwelt. Verse 10 is quoted repeatedly by the great teachers of prayer.

47 (46, LXX) This is an Ascension psalm, used in the services of the Feast of the Ascension in the Church.

PSALM 48†

The Glory of God in Zion

A Song. A Psalm of the sons of Korah.

GREAT *is* the LORD, and greatly
to be praised
In the [a]city of our God,
In His holy mountain.
2 [a]Beautiful in [1]elevation,
The joy of the whole earth,
Is Mount Zion *on* the sides of
the north,
The city of the great King.
3 God *is* in her palaces;
He is known as her refuge.

4 For behold, [a]the kings
assembled,
They passed by together.
5 They saw *it, and* so they
marveled;
They were troubled, they
hastened away.
6 Fear [a]took hold of them there,
And pain, as of a woman in birth
pangs,
7 *As when* You break the [a]ships
of Tarshish
With an east wind.

8 As we have heard,
So we have seen
In the city of the LORD of hosts,
In the city of our God:
God will [a]establish it forever.
Selah

9 We have thought, O God, on
[a]Your lovingkindness,
In the midst of Your temple.
10 According to [a]Your name,
O God,
So *is* Your praise to the ends of
the earth;
Your right hand is full of
righteousness.
11 Let Mount Zion rejoice,
Let the daughters of Judah be
glad,
Because of Your judgments.

12 Walk about Zion,
And go all around her.
Count her towers;
13 Mark well her bulwarks;
Consider her palaces;
That you may [a]tell *it* to the
generation following.
14 For this *is* God,
Our God forever and ever;
[a]He will be our guide
[1]*Even* to death.

PSALM 49†

Wisdom and Foolishness

To the Chief Musician. A Psalm of the sons of Korah.

HEAR this, all peoples;
Give ear, all inhabitants of the
world,
2 Both low and high,
Rich and poor together.
3 My mouth shall speak wisdom,
And the meditation of my heart
shall give understanding.
4 I will incline my ear to a
proverb;
I will disclose my [1]dark saying
on the harp.

5 Why should I fear in the days
of evil,
When the iniquity at my heels
surrounds me?
6 Those who [a]trust in their wealth
And boast in the multitude of
their riches,
7 None *of them* can by any means
redeem *his* brother,
Nor [a]give to God a ransom for
him—
8 For [a]the redemption of their
souls *is* costly,
And it shall cease forever—

PSALM 48
1 [a]Ps. 46:4; 87:3; Matt. 5:35
2 [a]Ps. 50:2 [1]*height*
4 [a]2 Sam. 10:6, 14
6 [a]Ex. 15:15
7 [a]1 Kin. 10:22; Ezek. 27:25
8 [a][Ps. 87:5; Is. 2:2]; Mic. 4:1
9 [a]Ps. 26:3
10 [a][Deut. 28:58]; Josh. 7:9; Mal. 1:11
13 [a][Ps. 78:5–7]
14 [a]Is. 58:11 [1]So with MT, Syr.; LXX, Vg. *Forever*

PSALM 49
4 [1]*riddle*
6 [a]Job 31:24; Ps. 52:7; [Prov. 11:28; Mark 10:23,24]
7 [a]Job 36:18, 19
8 [a][Matt. 16:26]

48 (47, LXX) This is a city of God or temple of God psalm. Note that Zion is referred to in the feminine, fulfilled both by the Virgin and by the bride, who is the Church. Specifically, vv. 12–14 are seen as a reference to the Church, the Zion of God.

49 (48, LXX) This is a psalm of wisdom and foolishness, used on the feast days of the Great Fathers of the Church. The psalm is one of the few times in the OT that redemption is spoken of with the hope that there is communion with God after death (v. 15). Usually in the Old Covenant **the grave** is seen as a place of shadows.

9 That he should continue to live
eternally,
And [a]not [1]see the Pit.

10 For he sees wise men die;
Likewise the fool and the
senseless person perish,
And leave their wealth to
others.
11 [1]Their inner thought *is that* their
houses *will last* forever,
Their dwelling places to all
generations;
They [a]call *their* lands after their
own names.
12 Nevertheless man, *though* in
honor, does not [1]remain;
He is like the beasts *that* perish.

13 This is the way of those who *are*
[a]foolish,
And of their posterity who
approve their sayings. Selah
14 Like sheep they are laid in the
grave;
Death shall feed on them;
[a]The upright shall have
dominion over them in the
morning;
[b]And their beauty shall be
consumed in [1]the grave, far
from their dwelling.
15 But God [a]will redeem my soul
from the power of [1]the
grave,
For He shall [b]receive me.
Selah

16 Do not be afraid when one
becomes rich,
When the glory of his house is
increased;
17 For when he dies he shall carry
nothing away;
His glory shall not descend after
him.
18 Though while he lives [a]he
blesses himself
(For *men* will praise you when
you do well for yourself),
19 He shall go to the generation of
his fathers;
They shall never see [a]light.[1]

9 [a]Ps. 89:48 [1]*experience corruption*
11 [a]Gen. 4:17; Deut. 3:14 [1]LXX, Syr., Tg., Vg. *Their graves shall be their houses forever*
12 [1]So with MT, Tg.; LXX, Syr., Vg. *understand* (cf. v. 20)
13 [a][Luke 12:20]
14 [a]Ps. 47:3; [Dan. 7:18; 1 Cor. 6:2; Rev. 2:26] [b]Job 4:21 [1]Or *Sheol*
15 [a][Hos. 13:4]; Mark 16:6, 7; Acts 2:31, 32 [b]Ps. 73:24 [1]Or *Sheol*
18 [a]Deut. 29:19; Luke 12:19
19 [a]Job 33:30 [1]The light of life
20 [a]Eccl. 3:19

PSALM 50

1 [a]Is. 9:6
2 [a]Deut. 33:2; Ps. 80:1
3 [a]Lev. 10:2; Num. 16:35; [Ps. 97:3]
4 [a]Deut. 4:26; 31:28; 32:1; Is. 1:2
5 [a]Deut. 33:3 [b]Ex. 24:7 [1]Lit. *cut*
6 [a][Ps. 97:6] [b]Ps. 75:7
7 [a]Ex. 20:2
8 [a]Jer. 7:22 [b]Is. 1:11; [Hos. 6:6] [1]*reprove*
9 [a]Ps. 69:31

20 A man *who is* in honor, yet does
not understand,
[a]Is like the beasts *that* perish.

PSALM 50†

God the Righteous Judge

A Psalm of Asaph.

THE [a]Mighty One, God the LORD,
Has spoken and called the earth
From the rising of the sun to its
going down.
2 Out of Zion, the perfection of
beauty,
[a]God will shine forth.
3 Our God shall come, and shall
not keep silent;
[a]A fire shall devour before Him,
And it shall be very
tempestuous all around Him.

4 [a]He shall call to the heavens from
above,
And to the earth, that He may
judge His people:
5 "Gather [a]My saints together to
Me,
[b]Those who have [1]made a
covenant with Me by
sacrifice."
6 Let the [a]heavens declare His
righteousness,
For [b]God Himself *is* Judge.
Selah

7 "Hear, O My people, and I will
speak,
O Israel, and I will testify
against you;
[a]I *am* God, your God!
8 [a]I will not [1]rebuke you [b]for your
sacrifices
Or your burnt offerings,
Which are continually before Me.
9 [a]I will not take a bull from your
house,
Nor goats out of your folds.
10 For every beast of the forest *is*
Mine,

50 (49, LXX) God is coming to judge His people, and does not need their sacrifices. What He wants (vv. 14–23) is the sacrifice of thanksgiving and praise fulfilled in the Holy Eucharist!

And the cattle on a thousand hills.
11 I know all the birds of the mountains,
And the wild beasts of the field *are* Mine.

12 "If I were hungry, I would not tell you;
[a]For the world *is* Mine, and all its fullness.
13 [a]Will I eat the flesh of bulls,
Or drink the blood of goats?
14 [a]Offer to God thanksgiving,
And [b]pay your vows to the Most High.
15 [a]Call upon Me in the day of trouble;
I will deliver you, and you shall glorify Me."

16 But to the wicked God says:
"What *right* have you to declare My statutes,
Or take My covenant in your mouth,
17 [a]Seeing you hate instruction
And cast My words behind you?
18 When you saw a thief, you [a]consented[1] with him,
And have been a [b]partaker with adulterers.
19 You give your mouth to evil,
And [a]your tongue frames deceit.
20 You sit *and* speak against your brother;
You slander your own mother's son.
21 These *things* you have done, and I kept silent;
[a]You thought that I was altogether like you;
But I will rebuke you,
And [b]set *them* in order before your eyes.

22 "Now consider this, you who [a]forget God,
Lest I tear *you* in pieces,
And *there be* none to deliver:
23 Whoever offers praise glorifies Me;
And [a]to him who orders *his* conduct *aright*
I will show the salvation of God."

12 [a]Ex. 19:5; [Deut. 10:14; Job 41:11]; 1 Cor. 10:26
13 [a][Ps. 51:15–17]
14 [a]Hos. 14:2; Heb. 13:15 [b]Num. 30:2; Deut. 23:21
15 [a]Job 22:27; [Zech. 13:9]
17 [a]Neh. 9:26; Rom. 2:21
18 [a][Rom. 1:32] [b]1 Tim. 5:22 [1]LXX, Syr., Tg., Vg. *ran*
19 [a]Ps. 52:2
21 [a][Rom. 2:4] [b][Ps. 90:8]
22 [a][Job 8:13]
23 [a]Gal. 6:16

PSALM 51†

A Prayer of Repentance

To the Chief Musician. A Psalm of David [a]when Nathan the prophet went to him, after he had gone in to Bathsheba.

HAVE mercy upon me, O God,
According to Your lovingkindness;
According to the multitude of Your tender mercies,
[a]Blot out my transgressions.
2 [a]Wash me thoroughly from my iniquity,
And cleanse me from my sin.

3 For I acknowledge my transgressions,
And my sin *is* always before me.
4 [a]Against You, You only, have I sinned,
And done *this* evil [b]in Your sight—
[c]That You may be found just [1]when You speak,
And blameless when You judge.

PSALM 51
title [a]2 Sam. 12:1
1 [a][Is. 43:25; 44:22; Acts 3:19; Col. 2:14]
2 [a]Jer. 33:8; Ezek. 36:33; [Heb. 9:14; 1 John 1:7, 9]
4 [a]2 Sam. 12:13 [b][Luke 5:21] [c]Rom. 3:4 [1]LXX, Tg., Vg. *in Your words*

51 (50, LXX) This is a psalm of repentance and God's mercy, and a prophecy about salvation through baptism (vv. 2, 7). It is also a teaching about worship in spirit (vv. 17–19). Of all 150 psalms, this is the one most used in the Orthodox Church. It is a psalm of repentance said three times daily—Matins, Third Hour, and Compline—as well as in every Divine Liturgy, where it is recited by the priest as a sign of repentance while he censes before the Great Entrance. Historically, this psalm is David's prayer of confession after his sin with Bathsheba (2 Sam. 12:1–15).

Verse 5 is clarified in the LXX: "Behold I was brought forth in iniquities and in sins [plural] did my mother conceive me." Far from seeing conception and childbirth as sinful in themselves, or as a means of passing on Adam's guilt, this passage tells us every action in this fallen world is accomplished by sinful people in sinful circumstances.

This psalm is a liturgical deposit of gold in the Church, prayed by clergy and laity, expressing the most basic things that need to be said by the faithful before their God. It is best learned and understood through its use in prayer.

5 [a]Behold, I was brought forth in
iniquity,
And in sin my mother
conceived me.
6 Behold, You desire truth in the
inward parts,
And in the hidden *part* You will
make me to know wisdom.

7 [a]Purge me with hyssop, and I
shall be clean;
Wash me, and I shall be
[b]whiter than snow.
8 Make me hear joy and gladness,
That the bones You have broken
[a]may rejoice.
9 Hide Your face from my sins,
And blot out all my iniquities.

10 [a]Create in me a clean heart,
O God,
And renew a steadfast spirit
within me.
11 Do not cast me away from Your
presence,
And do not take Your [a]Holy
Spirit from me.

12 Restore to me the joy of Your
salvation,
And uphold me *by Your*
[a]generous Spirit.
13 *Then* I will teach transgressors
Your ways,
And sinners shall be converted
to You.

14 Deliver me from the guilt of
bloodshed, O God,
The God of my salvation,
And my tongue shall sing aloud
of Your righteousness.
15 O Lord, open my lips,
And my mouth shall show forth
Your praise.
16 For [a]You do not desire sacrifice,
or else I would give *it;*
You do not delight in burnt
offering.
17 [a]The sacrifices of God *are* a
broken spirit,
A broken and a contrite heart—
These, O God, You will not
despise.

18 Do good in Your good pleasure
to Zion;
Build the walls of Jerusalem.
19 Then You shall be pleased with
[a]the sacrifices of
righteousness,
With burnt offering and whole
burnt offering;
Then they shall offer bulls on
Your altar.

PSALM 52†

The End of the Wicked and the Peace of the Godly

To the Chief Musician. A [1]Contemplation of David [a]when Doeg the Edomite went and [b]told Saul, and said to him, "David has gone to the house of Ahimelech."

WHY do you boast in evil,
O mighty man?
The goodness of God *endures*
continually.
2 Your tongue devises
destruction,
Like a sharp razor, working
deceitfully.
3 You love evil more than good,
Lying rather than speaking
righteousness. Selah
4 You love all devouring words,
You deceitful tongue.

5 God shall likewise destroy you
forever;
He shall take you away, and
pluck you out of *your* dwelling
place,
And uproot you from the land
of the living. Selah
6 The righteous also shall see and
fear,
And shall laugh at him,
saying,
7 "Here is the man *who* did not
make God his strength,
But trusted in the abundance of
his riches,
And strengthened himself in his
[1]wickedness."

5 [a][Job 14:4; Ps. 58:3; John 3:6; Rom. 5:12]
7 [a]Ex. 12:22; Lev. 14:4; Num. 19:18; Heb. 9:19 [b][Is. 1:18]
8 [a][Matt. 5:4]
10 [a][Ezek. 18:31; Eph. 2:10]
11 [a][Luke 11:13]
12 [a][2 Cor. 3:17]
16 [a][1 Sam. 15:22]; Ps. 50:8–14; [Mic. 6:6–8]
17 [a]Ps. 34:18; [Is. 57:15]; 66:2
19 [a]Ps. 4:5

PSALM 52
title [a]1 Sam. 22:9 [b]Ezek. 22:9 [1]Heb. *Maschil*
7 [1]Lit. *desire,* in evil sense

52 (51, LXX) Although it refers to the Jewish people, this psalm has a promise of the good things to come and of the dwelling of the saints in the house of God (v. 9).

8 But I *am* [a]like a green olive tree
in the house of God;
I trust in the mercy of God
forever and ever.
9 I will praise You forever,
Because You have done *it;*
And in the presence of Your
saints
I will wait on Your name, for *it*
[1]*is* good.

8 [a]Jer. 11:16
9 [1]Or *has a good reputation*

PSALM 53†

Folly of the Godless, and God's Final Triumph

To the Chief Musician. Set to "Mahalath." A [1]Contemplation of David.

THE [a]fool has said in his heart,
"*There is* no God."
They are corrupt, and have
done abominable iniquity;
[b]*There is* none who does
good.

2 God looks down from heaven
upon the children of men,
To see if there are *any* who
understand, who [a]seek
God.
3 Every one of them has turned
aside;
They have together become
corrupt;
There is none who does good,
No, not one.

4 Have the workers of iniquity
[a]no knowledge,
Who eat up my people *as* they
eat bread,
And do not call upon God?
5 [a]There they are in great fear
Where no fear was,
For God has scattered the bones
of him who encamps against
you;
You have put *them* to shame,
Because God has despised
them.

6 [a]Oh, that the salvation of Israel
would come out of Zion!
When God brings back
[1]the captivity of His people,
Let Jacob rejoice *and* Israel be
glad.

PSALM 53
title [1]Heb. *Maschil*
1 [a]Ps. 10:4 [b]Rom. 3:10–12
2 [a][2 Chr. 15:2]
4 [a]Jer. 4:22
5 [a]Lev. 26:17, 36; Prov. 28:1
6 [a]Ps. 14:7 [1]Or *His captive people*

PSALM 54†

A Prayer for Rescue from Adversity

To the Chief Musician. With [1]stringed instruments. A [2]Contemplation of David [a]when the Ziphites went and said to Saul, "Is David not hiding with us?"

SAVE me, O God, by Your name,
And vindicate me by Your
strength.
2 Hear my prayer, O God;
Give ear to the words of my
mouth.
3 For strangers have risen up
against me,
And oppressors have sought
after my life;
They have not set God before
them. Selah

4 Behold, God *is* my helper;
The Lord *is* with those who
[1]uphold my life.
5 He will repay my enemies for
their evil.
[1]Cut them off in Your [2]truth.

6 I will freely sacrifice to You;
I will praise Your name,
O LORD, for *it is* good.
7 For He has delivered me out of
all trouble;
[a]And my eye has seen *its desire*
upon my enemies.

PSALM 54
title [a]1 Sam. 23:19 [1]Heb. *neginoth* [2]Heb. *Maschil*
4 [1]*sustain my soul*
5 [1]*Destroy them* [2]Or *faithfulness*
7 [a]Ps. 59:10

53 (52, LXX) Without any explanation, this psalm is almost identical to Ps. 14. It refers to the incidents which would come to pass before the coming of the Lord, so that He could show the benefits of His coming.

54 (53, LXX) The prokeimenon (gradual) of Wednesday Vespers, this psalm is also used in the daily prayers at the Sixth Hour—noontime. It is a prayer said in adversity, with the underlying assumption that noonday is the hour of greatest adversity (see 91:6 and note).

PSALM 55†

The Agony of Betrayal

To the Chief Musician. With [1]stringed instruments. A [2]Contemplation of David.

GIVE ear to my prayer, O God,
And do not hide Yourself from
my supplication.
2 Attend to me, and hear me;
I [a]am[1] restless in my complaint,
and moan noisily,
3 Because of the voice of the
enemy,
Because of the oppression of the
wicked;
[a]For they bring down trouble
upon me,
And in wrath they hate me.

4 [a]My heart is severely pained
within me,
And the terrors of death have
fallen upon me.
5 Fearfulness and trembling have
come upon me,
And horror has overwhelmed
me.
6 So I said, "Oh, that I had wings
like a dove!
I would fly away and be at rest.
7 Indeed, I would wander far
off,
And remain in the wilderness.
Selah
8 I would hasten my escape
From the windy storm *and*
tempest."

9 Destroy, O Lord, *and* divide
their [1]tongues,
For I have seen [a]violence and
strife in the city.
10 Day and night they go around
it on its walls;
[a]Iniquity and trouble *are* also in
the midst of it.
11 Destruction *is* in its midst;
[a]Oppression and deceit do not
depart from its streets.

12 [a]For *it is* not an enemy *who*
reproaches me;
Then I could bear *it*.
Nor *is it* one *who* hates me who
has [b]exalted *himself* against
me;
Then I could hide from him.
13 But *it was* you, a man my equal,
[a]My companion and my
acquaintance.
14 We took sweet counsel
together,
And [a]walked to the house of
God in the throng.

15 Let death seize them;
Let them [a]go down alive into
[1]hell,
For wickedness *is* in their
dwellings *and* among them.

16 As for me, I will call upon God,
And the LORD shall save me.
17 [a]Evening and morning and at
noon
I will pray, and cry aloud,
And He shall hear my voice.
18 He has redeemed my soul in
peace from the battle *that was*
against me,
For [a]there were many against
me.
19 God will hear, and afflict them,
[a]Even He who abides from of
old. Selah
Because they do not change,
Therefore they do not fear God.

20 He has [a]put forth his hands
against those who [b]were at
peace with him;
He has broken his [1]covenant.
21 [a]*The words* of his mouth were
smoother than butter,

PSALM 55
title [1]Heb. *neginoth* [2]Heb. *Maschil*
2 [a]Is. 38:14; 59:11; Ezek. 7:16 [1]*wander*
3 [a]2 Sam. 16:7, 8
4 [a]Ps. 116:3
9 [a]Jer. 6:7 [1]*speech,* their counsel
10 [a]Ps. 10:7
11 [a]Ps. 10:7
12 [a]Ps. 41:9 [b]Ps. 35:26; 38:16
13 [a]2 Sam. 15:12
14 [a]Ps. 42:4
15 [a]Num. 16:30, 33 [1]Or *Sheol*
17 [a]Dan. 6:10; Luke 18:1; Acts 3:1; 10:3, 30
18 [a]2 Chr. 32:7, 8
19 [a][Deut. 33:27]
20 [a]Acts 12:1 [b]Ps. 7:4 [1]*treaty*
21 [a]Ps. 28:3; 57:4; [Prov. 5:3, 4; 12:18]

55 (54, LXX) This psalm is very similar to Ps. 41 because of its many references to betrayal. It is a prayer for deliverance from personal enemies—particularly the psalmist's chief enemy, a former friend. On a deeper level, it expresses the mental agony, the interior sufferings of the Messiah (vv. 1–5; 12–14). The verses of Ps. 55 go back and forth between the pain of betrayal and our confidence in God in the midst of all evil. For the Christian, for the Church, when the betrayal of a longtime friend or communicant occurs, there is no greater description of the pain than vv. 12–14 and 20–22. Psalm 55 is prayed daily at the Sixth Hour and, in part, on Holy Thursday and Good Friday.

But war *was* in his heart;
His words were softer than oil,
Yet they *were* drawn swords.

22 [a]Cast your burden on the LORD,
And [b]He shall sustain you;
He shall never permit the
righteous to be [1]moved.

23 But You, O God, shall bring
them down to the pit of
destruction;
[a]Bloodthirsty and deceitful men
[b]shall not live out half their
days;
But I will trust in You.

PSALM 56†

Prayer for Relief from Tormentors

To the Chief Musician. Set to [1]"The Silent Dove in Distant Lands." A Michtam of David when the [a]Philistines captured him in Gath.

BE [a]merciful to me, O God, for
man would swallow me up;
Fighting all day he oppresses
me.
2 My enemies would [a]hound *me*
all day,
For *there are* many who fight
against me, O Most High.

3 Whenever I am afraid,
I will trust in You.
4 In God (I will praise His word),
In God I have put my trust;
[a]I will not fear.
What can flesh do to me?

5 All day they twist my words;
All their thoughts *are* against me
for evil.
6 They gather together,
They hide, they mark my steps,
When they lie in wait for my
life.
7 Shall they escape by iniquity?
In anger cast down the peoples,
O God!

8 You number my wanderings;
Put my tears into Your bottle;
[a]*Are they* not in Your book?

22 [a][Ps. 37:5; Matt. 6:25–34; Luke 12:22–31; 1 Pet. 5:7] [b]Ps. 37:24 [1]*shaken*
23 [a]Ps. 5:6 [b]Prov. 10:27

PSALM 56
title [a]1 Sam. 21:11 [1]Heb. *Jonath Elem Rechokim*
1 [a]Ps. 57:1
2 [a]Ps. 57:3
4 [a]Ps. 118:6; Is. 31:3; [Heb. 13:6]
8 [a][Mal. 3:16]
9 [a][Ps. 118:6; Rom. 8:31]
13 [a]Ps. 116:8, 9 [b]Job 33:30

PSALM 57
title [a]1 Sam. 22:1 [1]Heb. *Al Tashcheth*
1 [a]Ruth 2:12; Ps. 17:8; 63:7 [b]Is. 26:20
2 [a][Ps. 138:8]
3 [a]Ps. 144:5, 7 [b]Ps. 43:3 [1]*snaps at* or *hounds me*, or *crushes me*

9 When I cry out *to You*,
Then my enemies will turn
back;
This I know, because [a]God *is* for
me.
10 In God (I will praise *His* word),
In the LORD (I will praise *His*
word),
11 In God I have put my trust;
I will not be afraid.
What can man do to me?

12 Vows *made* to You *are binding*
upon me, O God;
I will render praises to You,
13 [a]For You have delivered my soul
from death.
Have You not *kept* my feet from
falling,
That I may walk before God
In the [b]light of the living?

PSALM 57†

Prayer for Safety from Enemies

To the Chief Musician. Set to [1]"Do Not Destroy." A Michtam of David [a]when he fled from Saul into the cave.

BE merciful to me, O God,
be merciful to me!
For my soul trusts in You;
[a]And in the shadow of Your
wings I will make my refuge,
[b]Until *these* calamities have
passed by.

2 I will cry out to God Most High,
To God [a]who performs *all things*
for me.
3 [a]He shall send from heaven and
save me;
He reproaches the one who
[1]would swallow me up.
Selah
God [b]shall send forth His mercy
and His truth.

4 My soul *is* among lions;
I lie *among* the sons of men
Who are set on fire,

56—59 (55—58, LXX) Much the same as Ps. 55, these are prayers for comfort and deliverance from evildoers.

[a]Whose teeth *are* spears and arrows,
And their tongue a sharp sword.
5 [a]Be exalted, O God, above the heavens;
Let Your glory *be* above all the earth.

6 [a]They have prepared a net for my steps;
My soul is bowed down;
They have dug a pit before me;
Into the midst of it they *themselves* have fallen. Selah

7 [a]My heart is steadfast, O God, my heart is steadfast;
I will sing and give praise.
8 Awake, [a]my glory!
Awake, lute and harp!
I will awaken the dawn.

9 [a]I will praise You, O Lord, among the peoples;
I will sing to You among the [1]nations.
10 [a]For Your mercy reaches unto the heavens,
And Your truth unto the clouds.

11 [a]Be exalted, O God, above the heavens;
Let Your glory *be* above all the earth.

PSALM 58†

The Just Judgment of the Wicked

To the Chief Musician. Set to [1]"Do Not Destroy." A Michtam of David.

DO you indeed speak righteousness, you silent ones?
Do you judge uprightly, you sons of men?
2 No, in heart you work wickedness;
You weigh out the violence of your hands in the earth.

3 [a]The wicked are estranged from the womb;
They go astray as soon as they are born, speaking lies.
4 [a]Their poison *is* like the poison of a serpent;
They are like the deaf cobra *that* stops its ear,
5 Which will not [a]heed the voice of charmers,
Charming ever so skillfully.

6 [a]Break[1] their teeth in their mouth, O God!
Break out the fangs of the young lions, O LORD!
7 [a]Let them flow away as waters *which* run continually;
When he bends *his bow*,
Let his arrows be as if cut in pieces.
8 *Let them be* like a snail which melts away as it goes,
[a]*Like* a stillborn child of a woman, that they may not see the sun.

9 Before your [a]pots can feel *the burning* thorns,
He shall take them away [b]as with a whirlwind,
As in His living and burning wrath.
10 The righteous shall rejoice when he sees the [a]vengeance;
[b]He shall wash his feet in the blood of the wicked,
11 [a]So that men will say,
"Surely *there is* a reward for the righteous;
Surely He is God who [b]judges in the earth."

PSALM 59†

The Assured Judgment of the Wicked

To the Chief Musician. Set to [1]"Do Not Destroy." A Michtam of David [a]when Saul sent men, and they watched the house in order to kill him.

DELIVER me from my enemies, O my God;
[1]Defend me from those who rise up against me.
2 Deliver me from the workers of iniquity,
And save me from bloodthirsty men.

---

4 [a]Prov. 30:14 **5** [a]Ps. 108:5 **6** [a]Ps. 9:15 **7** [a]Ps. 108:1–5 **8** [a]Ps. 16:9 **9** [a]Ps. 108:3 [1]*Gentiles* **10** [a]Ps. 103:11 **11** [a]Ps. 57:5

PSALM 58
title [1]Heb. *Al Tashcheth* **3** [a][Ps. 53:3; Is. 48:8] **4** [a]Eccl. 10:11 **5** [a]Jer. 8:17 **6** [a]Job 4:10 [1]*Break away* **7** [a]Josh. 2:11; 7:5; Ps. 112:10; Is. 13:7; Ezek. 21:7 **8** [a]Job 3:16 **9** [a]Ps. 118:12; Eccl. 7:6 [b]Job 27:21; Prov. 10:25 **10** [a][Deut. 32:43]; Jer. 11:20 [b]Ps. 68:23 **11** [a]Ps. 92:15; Prov. 11:18; [2 Cor. 5:10] [b]Ps. 50:6; 75:7

PSALM 59
title [a]1 Sam. 19:11 [1]Heb. *Al Tashcheth* **1** [1]Lit. *Set me on high*

3 For look, they lie in wait for my life;
[a]The mighty gather against me,
Not *for* my transgression nor *for* my sin, O LORD.
4 They run and prepare themselves through no fault *of mine*.

[a]Awake to help me, and behold!
5 You therefore, O LORD God of hosts, the God of Israel,
Awake to punish all the [1]nations;
Do not be merciful to any wicked transgressors. Selah

6 [a]At evening they return,
They growl like a dog,
And go all around the city.
7 Indeed, they belch with their mouth;
[a]Swords *are* in their lips;
For *they say*, [b]"Who hears?"

8 But [a]You, O LORD, shall laugh at them;
You shall have all the [1]nations in derision.
9 I will wait for You, O You [1]his Strength;
[a]For God *is* my [2]defense.
10 [1]My God of mercy shall [a]come to meet me;
God shall let [b]me see *my desire* on my enemies.

11 Do not slay them, lest my people forget;
Scatter them by Your power,
And bring them down,
O Lord our shield.
12 [a]*For* the sin of their mouth *and* the words of their lips,
Let them even be taken in their pride,
And for the cursing and lying *which* they speak.
13 [a]Consume *them* in wrath, consume *them*,
That they *may* not *be*;
And [b]let them know that God rules in Jacob
To the ends of the earth. Selah

14 And [a]at evening they return,
They growl like a dog,
And go all around the city.
15 They [a]wander up and down for food,
And [1]howl if they are not satisfied.

16 But I will sing of Your power;
Yes, I will sing aloud of Your mercy in the morning;
For You have been my defense
And refuge in the day of my trouble.
17 To You, [a]O my Strength, I will sing praises;
For God *is* my defense,
My God of mercy.

PSALM 60†

A Prayer for Restoration and Healing

To the Chief Musician. [a]Set to [1]"Lily of the Testimony." A Michtam of David. For teaching. [b]When he fought against Mesopotamia and Syria of Zobah, and Joab returned and killed twelve thousand Edomites in the Valley of Salt.

O GOD, [a]You have cast us off;
You have broken us down;
You have been displeased;
Oh, restore us again!
2 You have made the earth tremble;
You have broken it;
[a]Heal its breaches, for it is shaking.
3 [a]You have shown Your people hard things;
[b]You have made us drink the wine of [1]confusion.

4 [a]You have given a banner to those who fear You,
That it may be displayed because of the truth. Selah
5 [a]That Your beloved may be delivered,
Save *with* Your right hand, and hear me.

3 [a]Ps. 56:6
4 [a]Ps. 35:23
5 [1]*Gentiles*
6 [a]Ps. 59:14
7 [a]Ps. 57:4; Prov. 12:18 [b]Job 22:13; Ps. 10:11
8 [a]Prov. 1:26 [1]*Gentiles*
9 [a][Ps. 62:2] [1]So with MT, Syr.; some Heb. mss., LXX, Tg., Vg. *my Strength* [2]Lit. *fortress*
10 [a]Ps. 21:3 [b]Ps. 54:7 [1]So with Qr.; some Heb. mss., LXX, Vg. *My God, His mercy;* Kt., some Heb. mss., Tg. *O God, my mercy;* Syr. *O God, Your mercy*
12 [a]Prov. 12:13
13 [a]Ps. 104:35 [b]Ps. 83:18
14 [a]Ps. 59:6
15 [a]Job 15:23 [1]So with LXX, Vg.; MT, Syr., Tg. *spend the night*
17 [a]Ps. 18:1

PSALM 60

title [a]Ps. 80 [b]2 Sam. 8:3, 13; 1 Chr. 18:3 [1]Heb. *Shushan Eduth*
1 [a]Ps. 44:9
2 [a][2 Chr. 7:14]; Is. 30:26
3 [a]Ps. 71:20 [b]Is. 51:17, 22; Jer. 25:15 [1]*staggering*
4 [a]Ps. 20:5; Is. 5:26; 11:12; 13:2
5 [a]Ps. 108:6–13

60 (59, LXX) This psalm is a communal prayer for restoration and healing. The **banner** (v. 4) is the inspiration for many Orthodox hymns concerning the Cross of Christ.

6 God has [a]spoken in His holiness:
"I will rejoice;
I will [b]divide [c]Shechem
And measure out [d]the Valley of Succoth.
7 Gilead *is* Mine, and Manasseh *is* Mine;
[a]Ephraim also *is* the [1]helmet for My head;
[b]Judah *is* My lawgiver.
8 [a]Moab *is* My washpot;
[b]Over Edom I will cast My shoe;
[c]Philistia, shout in triumph because of Me."

9 Who will bring me *to* the strong city?
Who will lead me to Edom?
10 *Is it* not You, O God, [a]*who* cast us off?
And You, O God, *who* did [b]not go out with our armies?
11 Give us help from trouble,
[a]For the help of man *is* useless.
12 Through God [a]we will do valiantly,
For *it is* He *who* shall tread down our enemies.

PSALM 61†

A Prayer for Protection

To the Chief Musician. On [1]a stringed instrument. A Psalm of David.

HEAR my cry, O God;
Attend to my prayer.
2 From the end of the earth I will cry to You,
When my heart is overwhelmed;
Lead me to the rock that is higher than I.

3 For You have been a shelter for me,
[a]A strong tower from the enemy.
4 I will abide in Your [1]tabernacle forever;
[a]I will trust in the shelter of Your wings. Selah
5 For You, O God, have heard my vows;
You have given *me* the heritage of those who fear Your name.
6 You will prolong the king's life,
His years as many generations.
7 He shall abide before God forever.
Oh, prepare mercy [a]and truth, *which* may [1]preserve him!

8 So I will sing praise to Your name forever,
That I may daily perform my vows.

6 [a]Ps. 89:35 [b]Josh. 1:6 [c]Gen. 12:6 [d]Josh. 13:27 7 [a]Deut. 33:17 [b][Gen. 49:10] [1]Lit. *protection* 8 [a]2 Sam. 8:2 [b]2 Sam. 8:14; Ps. 108:9 [c]2 Sam. 8:1 10 [a]Ps. 108:11 [b]Josh. 7:12 11 [a]Ps. 118:8; 146:3 12 [a]Num. 24:18

PSALM 61
title [1]Heb. *neginah* 3 [a]Prov. 18:10 4 [a]Ps. 91:4 [1]*tent* 7 [a]Ps. 40:11 [1]Lit. *guard* or *keep*

PSALM 62

Waiting for God's Salvation

To the Chief Musician. To [a]Jeduthun. A Psalm of David.

TRULY [a]my soul silently *waits* for God;
From Him *comes* my salvation.
2 He only *is* my rock and my salvation;
He is my [1]defense;
I shall not be greatly [a]moved.[2]

3 How long will you attack a man?
You shall be slain, all of you,
[a]Like a leaning wall and a tottering fence.
4 They only consult to cast *him* down from his high position;
They [a]delight in lies;
They bless with their mouth,
But they curse inwardly. Selah

5 My soul, wait silently for God alone,
For my [1]expectation *is* from Him.
6 He only *is* my rock and my salvation;

PSALM 62
title [a]1 Chr. 25:1 1 [a]Ps. 33:20 2 [a]Ps. 55:22 [1]*strong tower* [2]*shaken* 3 [a]Is. 30:13 4 [a]Ps. 28:3 5 [1]*hope*

61 (60, LXX) The psalmist gives thanks to the Lord, for himself and for the people, who have been saved by faith. He promises God he will sing praise to His name until the end. This psalm is used as a prayer for protection. **The heritage of those who fear Your name** (v. 5) is the salvation of God Himself. This is prayed as the evening prokeimenon (gradual) of Sunday Vespers during Lent.

He is my defense;
I shall not be [1]moved.
7 [a]In God *is* my salvation and my glory;
The rock of my strength,
And my refuge, *is* in God.

8 Trust in Him at all times, you people;
[a]Pour out your heart before Him;
God *is* a refuge for us. Selah

9 [a]Surely men of low degree *are* [1]a vapor,
Men of high degree *are* a lie;
If they are weighed on the scales,
They *are* altogether *lighter* than vapor.
10 Do not trust in oppression,
Nor vainly hope in robbery;
[a]If riches increase,
Do not set *your* heart *on them.*

11 God has spoken once,
Twice I have heard this:
That power *belongs* to God.
12 Also to You, O Lord, *belongs* mercy;
For [a]You [1]render to each one according to his work.

PSALM 63†

Friendship with God

A Psalm of David [a]when he was in the wilderness of Judah.

O GOD, You *are* my God;
Early will I seek You;
[a]My soul thirsts for You;
My flesh longs for You
In a dry and thirsty land
Where there is no water.
2 So I have looked for You in the sanctuary,

6 [1]*shaken*
7 [a][Jer. 3:23]
8 [a]1 Sam. 1:15; Ps. 42:4; Lam. 2:19
9 [a]Job 7:16; Ps. 39:5; Is. 40:17
[1]*vanity*
10 [a]Job 31:25; [Mark 10:24; Luke 12:15; 1 Tim. 6:10]
12 [a][Matt. 16:27]; Rom. 2:6; 1 Cor. 3:8
[1]*reward*

PSALM 63
title [a]1 Sam. 22:5
1 [a]Ps. 42:2; [Matt. 5:6]

2 [a]Ps. 27:4
3 [a]Ps. 138:2
4 [a]Ps. 28:2; 143:6
5 [1]Lit. *fat*
[2]Abundance
6 [a]Ps. 42:8
10 [1]Lit. *pour him out by the hand of the sword*
[2]Prey
11 [a]Deut. 6:13; [Is. 45:23; 65:16]

PSALM 64
1 [1]*complaint*

To see [a]Your power and Your glory.

3 [a]Because Your lovingkindness *is* better than life,
My lips shall praise You.
4 Thus I will bless You while I live;
I will [a]lift up my hands in Your name.
5 My soul shall be satisfied as with [1]marrow and [2]fatness,
And my mouth shall praise You with joyful lips.

6 When [a]I remember You on my bed,
I meditate on You in the *night* watches.
7 Because You have been my help,
Therefore in the shadow of Your wings I will rejoice.
8 My soul follows close behind You;
Your right hand upholds me.

9 But those *who* seek my life, to destroy *it,*
Shall go into the lower parts of the earth.
10 They shall [1]fall by the sword;
They shall be [2]a portion for jackals.

11 But the king shall rejoice in God;
[a]Everyone who swears by Him shall glory;
But the mouth of those who speak lies shall be stopped.

PSALM 64†

Preservation from Oppression

To the Chief Musician. A Psalm of David.

HEAR my voice, O God, in my [1]meditation;

63 (62, LXX) This is a psalm of the soul, which used to be empty of any good thing, but is now restored through the grace of Christ. It is the most common and most beloved of the morning psalms of the Church. St. Basil the Great said if there were a perfect prayer to be prayed in the morning, it is Ps. 63. It is the third of the six Matins psalms (see note on Ps. 3) and also a psalm of vigil during the night (vv. 6–8).
64 (63, LXX) The psalmist speaks on behalf of believers, who implore God to save them

(continued on next page)

Preserve my life from fear of the enemy.
2 Hide me from the secret plots of the wicked,
From the rebellion of the workers of iniquity,
3 Who sharpen their tongue like a sword,
[a]And bend *their bows to shoot* their arrows—bitter words,
4 That they may shoot in secret at the blameless;
Suddenly they shoot at him and do not fear.

5 They encourage themselves *in* an evil matter;
They talk of laying snares secretly;
[a]They say, "Who will see them?"
6 They devise iniquities:
"We have perfected a shrewd scheme."
Both the inward thought and the heart of man are deep.

7 But God shall shoot at them *with* an arrow;
Suddenly they shall be wounded.
8 So He will make them stumble over their own tongue;
[a]All who see them shall flee away.
9 All men shall fear,
And shall [a]declare the work of God;
For they shall wisely consider His doing.

10 [a]The righteous shall be glad in the LORD, and trust in Him.
And all the upright in heart shall glory.

3 [a]Ps. 58:7
5 [a]Ps. 10:11; 59:7
8 [a]Ps. 31:11
9 [a]Jer. 50:28; 51:10
10 [a]Job 22:19; Ps. 32:11

PSALM 65†

In Praise of Salvation and Creation

To the Chief Musician. A Psalm of David. A Song.

PRAISE is awaiting You, O God, in Zion;
And to You the [1]vow shall be performed.
2 O You who hear prayer,
[a]To You all flesh will come.
3 Iniquities prevail against me;
As for our transgressions,
You will [a]provide atonement for them.

4 [a]Blessed *is the man* You [b]choose,
And cause to approach *You,*
That he may dwell in Your courts.
[c]We shall be satisfied with the goodness of Your house,
Of Your holy temple.

5 *By* awesome deeds in righteousness You will answer us,
O God of our salvation,
You who are the confidence of all the ends of the earth,
And of the far-off seas;
6 Who established the mountains by His strength,
[a]*Being* clothed with power;
7 [a]You who still the noise of the seas,
The noise of their waves,
[b]And the tumult of the peoples.
8 They also who dwell in the farthest parts are afraid of Your signs;
You make the outgoings of the morning and evening [1]rejoice.

PSALM 65
1 [1]A promised deed
2 [a][Is. 66:23]
3 [a]Ps. 51:2; 79:9; Is. 6:7; [Heb. 9:14; 1 John 1:7, 9]
4 [a]Ps. 33:12 [b]Ps. 4:3 [c]Ps. 36:8
6 [a]Ps. 93:1
7 [a]Matt. 8:26 [b]Is. 17:12, 13
8 [1]*shout for joy*

(continued from previous page)
from the deceitful plots and scheming of evildoers. But they will be delivered through their rejoicing in the Lord. Verse 10 is used in our commemorations of St. John the Baptist and all martyrs.

65 (64, LXX) The psalmist prays for those who have been fruitless, and have become full of good harvest through their faith in God. In itself, the psalm is unusual in that it starts with a theme of salvation and worship (vv. 1–4) and ends with a section on God and creation (vv. 5–13)—two almost separate themes. In the Orthodox Church, v. 4 is used often in prayers for the departed, and for their rest in a place of peace.

9 You [1]visit the earth and
[a]water it,
You greatly enrich it;
[b]The river of God is full of water;
You provide their grain,
For so You have prepared it.
10 You water its ridges
abundantly,
You settle its furrows;
You make it soft with showers,
You bless its growth.

11 You crown the year with Your
goodness,
And Your paths drip *with*
abundance.
12 They drop *on* the pastures of the
wilderness,
And the little hills rejoice on
every side.
13 The pastures are clothed with
flocks;
[a]The valleys also are covered
with grain;
They shout for joy, they also
sing.

PSALM 66†

Praise to God for His Awesome Works

To the Chief Musician. A Song. A Psalm.

MAKE [a]a joyful shout to God, all
the earth!
2 Sing out the honor of His name;
Make His praise glorious.
3 Say to God,
"How [a]awesome are Your works!
[b]Through the greatness of Your
power
Your enemies shall submit
themselves to You.
4 [a]All the earth shall worship You
And sing praises to You;
They shall sing praises *to* Your
name." Selah

5 Come and see the works of God;
He is awesome *in His* doing
toward the sons of men.
6 [a]He turned the sea into dry *land;*
[b]They went through the river on
foot.
There we will rejoice in Him.
7 He rules by His power forever;
His eyes observe the nations;
Do not let the rebellious exalt
themselves. Selah

8 Oh, bless our God, you peoples!
And make the voice of His
praise to be heard,
9 Who keeps our soul among the
living,
And does not allow our feet to
[1]be moved.
10 For [a]You, O God, have tested
us;
[b]You have refined us as silver is
refined.
11 [a]You brought us into the net;
You laid affliction on our backs.
12 [a]You have caused men to ride
over our heads;
[b]We went through fire and
through water;
But You brought us out to
[1]rich *fulfillment*.

9 [a][Deut. 11:12]; Jer. 5:24 [b]Ps. 46:4; 104:13; 147:8 [1]*give attention to* 13 [a]Is. 44:23; 55:12

PSALM 66

1 [a]Ps. 100:1 3 [a]Ps. 65:5 [b]Ps. 18:44

4 [a]Ps. 117:1; Zech. 14:16 6 [a]Ex. 14:21 [b]Josh. 3:14–16 9 [1]*slip* 10 [a]Job 23:10; Ps. 17:3 [b][Is. 48:10; Zech. 13:9; Mal. 3:3; 1 Pet. 1:7] 11 [a]Lam. 1:13; Ezek. 12:13 12 [a]Is. 51:23 [b]Is. 43:2 [1]*abundance*

66—68 (65—67, LXX) These psalms are a unit in their usage in the Orthodox Church, all three psalms being used as paschal psalms throughout the Easter services and Bright Week.

Psalm 66 is a psalm of *praise,* commemorating the Exodus in Israel's history, which is seen in the Church as being perfected in Christ in His exodus from the grave to heaven.

Psalm 67 speaks of the *salvation* of all the nations—the Gentile people—not only of Israel. The promises of Ps. 67 are fulfilled in Christ in His offer of salvation to every nation, tongue and tribe.

Psalm 68 speaks of God arising—*the Resurrection.* Verses 1–3 are sung all through the paschal season with the refrain, "Christ is risen from the dead, trampling down death by death." In the OT context, this psalm describes God's procession in Israel, and His triumph over death. Ephesians 4:8–10 quotes v. 18 as a specific reference to the Ascension of Christ and His sending of the Holy Spirit at Pentecost. The psalmist teaches that God is He who delivers the sons of Israel from Egypt, and he promises them they will receive the Holy Spirit if they accept God's Word. He also consoles believers, promising they will ultimately be delivered from every affliction and from every spiritual captivity.

13 [a]I will go into Your house with burnt offerings;
[b]I will pay You my [1]vows,
14 Which my lips have uttered
And my mouth has spoken when I was in trouble.
15 I will offer You burnt sacrifices of fat animals,
With the sweet aroma of rams;
I will offer bulls with goats. Selah

16 Come *and* hear, all you who fear God,
And I will declare what He has done for my soul.
17 I cried to Him with my mouth,
And He was [1]extolled with my tongue.
18 [a]If I regard iniquity in my heart,
The Lord will not hear.
19 *But* certainly God [a]has heard *me;*
He has attended to the voice of my prayer.

20 Blessed *be* God,
Who has not turned away my prayer,
Nor His mercy from me!

PSALM 67†

Salvation for the Gentiles

To the Chief Musician. On [1]stringed instruments. A Psalm. A Song.

GOD be merciful to us and bless us,
And [a]cause His face to shine upon us, Selah
2 That [a]Your way may be known on earth,
[b]Your salvation among all nations.

3 Let the peoples praise You, O God;
Let all the peoples praise You.
4 Oh, let the nations be glad and sing for joy!
For [a]You shall judge the people righteously,
And govern the nations on earth. Selah

13 [a]Ps. 100:4; 116:14, 17–19 [b][Eccl. 5:4] [1]Promised deeds
17 [1]*praised*
18 [a]Job 27:9; [Prov. 15:29; 28:9]; Is. 1:15; [John 9:31; James 4:3]
19 [a]Ps. 116:1, 2

PSALM 67
title [1]Heb. *neginoth*
1 [a]Num. 6:25
2 [a]Acts 18:25 [b]Is. 52:10; Titus 2:11
4 [a][Ps. 96:10, 13; 98:9]

6 [a]Lev. 26:4; Ps. 85:12; [Ezek. 34:27]; Zech. 8:12 [1]*give her produce*

PSALM 68
1 [a]Num. 10:35
2 [a][Is. 9:18]; Hos. 13:3 [b]Ps. 97:5; Mic. 1:4
3 [a]Ps. 32:11
4 [a]Deut. 33:26 [b][Ex. 6:3] [1]*Praise* [2]MT *deserts;* Tg. *heavens* (cf. v. 34 and Is. 19:1) [3]Lit. LORD, a shortened Heb. form
5 [a][Ps. 10:14, 18; 146:9]
6 [a]Ps. 107:4–7 [b]Acts 12:6–11 [c]Ps. 107:34
7 [a]Ex. 13:21; [Hab. 3:13]

5 Let the peoples praise You, O God;
Let all the peoples praise You.
6 [a]*Then* the earth shall [1]yield her increase;
God, our own God, shall bless us.
7 God shall bless us,
And all the ends of the earth shall fear Him.

PSALM 68†

Let God Arise

To the Chief Musician. A Psalm of David. A Song.

LET [a]God arise,
Let His enemies be scattered;
Let those also who hate Him flee before Him.
2 [a]As smoke is driven away,
So drive *them* away;
[b]As wax melts before the fire,
So let the wicked perish at the presence of God.
3 But [a]let the righteous be glad;
Let them rejoice before God;
Yes, let them rejoice exceedingly.

4 Sing to God, sing praises to His name;
[a]Extol[1] Him who rides on the [2]clouds,
[b]By His name [3]YAH,
And rejoice before Him.

5 [a]A father of the fatherless, a defender of widows,
Is God in His holy habitation.
6 [a]God sets the solitary in families;
[b]He brings out those who are bound into prosperity;
But [c]the rebellious dwell in a dry *land.*

7 O God, [a]when You went out before Your people,
When You marched through the wilderness, Selah
8 The earth shook;
The heavens also dropped *rain* at the presence of God;
Sinai itself *was moved* at the

presence of God, the God of
Israel.
9 [a]You, O God, sent a plentiful
rain,
Whereby You confirmed Your
inheritance,
When it was weary.
10 Your congregation dwelt in it;
[a]You, O God, provided from
Your goodness for the poor.

11 The Lord gave the word;
Great *was* the [1]company of those
who proclaimed *it:*
12 "Kings[a] of armies flee, they
flee,
And she who remains at home
divides the [1]spoil.
13 [a]Though you lie down among
the [1]sheepfolds,
[b]*You will be* like the wings of a
dove covered with silver,
And her feathers with yellow
gold."
14 [a]When the Almighty scattered
kings in it,
It was *white* as snow in Zalmon.

15 A mountain of God *is* the
mountain of Bashan;
A mountain *of many* peaks *is* the
mountain of Bashan.
16 Why do you [1]fume with envy,
you mountains of *many*
peaks?
[a]*This is* the mountain *which* God
desires to dwell in;
Yes, the LORD will dwell *in it*
forever.

17 [a]The chariots of God *are* twenty
thousand,
Even thousands of thousands;
The Lord is among them *as in*
Sinai, in the Holy *Place.*
18 [a]You have ascended on high,
[b]You have led captivity captive;
[c]You have received gifts among
men,
Even *from* [d]the rebellious,
[e]That the LORD God might dwell
there.

19 Blessed *be* the Lord,
Who daily loads us *with benefits,*
The God of our salvation!
Selah

9 [a]Deut. 11:11
10 [a]Deut. 26:5
11 [1]*host*
12 [a]Josh. 10:16
[1]*plunder*
13 [a]Ps. 81:6
[b]Ps. 105:37
[1]Or *saddlebags*
14 [a]Josh. 10:10
16 [a][Deut. 12:5]
[1]Lit. *stare*
17 [a]Deut. 33:2
18 [a]Eph. 4:8
[b]Judg. 5:12
[c]Acts 2:4, 33; 10:44–46
[d][1 Tim. 1:13]
[e]Ps. 78:60
20 [a][Deut. 32:39]
21 [a]Hab. 3:13
[b]Ps. 55:23
22 [a]Num. 21:33
[b]Ex. 14:22
23 [a]Ps. 58:10
[b]1 Kin. 21:19
[1]LXX, Syr., Tg., Vg. *you may dip your foot*
24 [1]Lit. *goings*
25 [a]1 Chr. 13:8
26 [a]Deut. 33:28
27 [a]1 Sam. 9:21
[1]*throng*
28 [a]Is. 26:12
[1]LXX, Syr., Tg., Vg. *Command, O God*
29 [a]Ps. 45:12; 72:10
30 [a]Ps. 22:12
[b]2 Sam. 8:2
31 [a]Is. 19:19–23
[b]Is. 45:14
[c]Ps. 44:20

20 Our God *is* the God of salvation;
And [a]to GOD the Lord *belong*
escapes from death.

21 But [a]God will wound the head
of His enemies,
[b]The hairy scalp of the one who
still goes on in his trespasses.
22 The Lord said, "I will bring
[a]back from Bashan,
I will bring *them* back [b]from the
depths of the sea,
23 [a]That [1]your foot may crush *them*
in blood,
[b]And the tongues of your dogs
may have their portion from
your enemies."

24 They have seen Your
[1]procession, O God,
The procession of my God, my
King, into the sanctuary.
25 [a]The singers went before, the
players on instruments
followed after;
Among *them were* the maidens
playing timbrels.
26 Bless God in the congregations,
The Lord, from [a]the fountain of
Israel.
27 [a]There *is* little Benjamin, their
leader,
The princes of Judah *and* their
[1]company,
The princes of Zebulun *and* the
princes of Naphtali.

28 [1]Your God has [a]commanded
your strength;
Strengthen, O God, what You
have done for us.
29 Because of Your temple at
Jerusalem,
[a]Kings will bring presents to
You.
30 Rebuke the beasts of the reeds,
[a]The herd of bulls with the calves
of the peoples,
Till everyone [b]submits himself
with pieces of silver.
Scatter the peoples *who* delight
in war.
31 [a]Envoys will come out of Egypt;
[b]Ethiopia will quickly [c]stretch
out her hands to God.

32 Sing to God, you [a]kingdoms of the earth;
Oh, sing praises to the Lord, Selah
33 To Him [a]who rides on the heaven of heavens, *which were* of old!
Indeed, He sends out His voice, a [b]mighty voice.
34 [a]Ascribe strength to God;
His excellence *is* over Israel,
And His strength *is* in the clouds.
35 O God, [a]*You are* more awesome than Your holy places.
The God of Israel *is* He who gives strength and power to *His* people.

Blessed *be* God!

PSALM 69†

A Song of Suffering

To the Chief Musician. Set to [1]"The Lilies." A Psalm of David.

SAVE me, O God!
For [a]the waters have come up to *my* [1]neck.
2 [a]I sink in deep mire,
Where *there is* no standing;
I have come into deep waters,
Where the floods overflow me.
3 [a]I am weary with my crying;
My throat is dry;
[b]My eyes fail while I wait for my God.

4 Those who [a]hate me without a cause
Are more than the hairs of my head;
They are mighty who would destroy me,
Being my enemies wrongfully;

32 [a][Ps. 67:3, 4]
33 [a]Deut. 33:26; Ps. 18:10
[b]Ps. 46:6; Is. 30:30
34 [a]Ps. 29:1
35 [a]Ps. 76:12

PSALM 69
title [1]Heb. *Shoshannim*
1 [a]Job 22:11; Jon. 2:5
[1]Lit. *soul*
2 [a]Ps. 40:2
3 [a]Ps. 6:6
[b]Deut. 28:32; Ps. 119:82, 123; Is. 38:14
4 [a]Ps. 35:19; John 15:25

6 [1]Wait in faith
[2]*dishonored*
8 [a]Is. 53:3; Mark 3:21; Luke 8:19; John 7:3–5
9 [a]John 2:17
[b]Rom. 15:3
11 [1]Symbolic of sorrow
12 [a]Job 30:9
[1]Sit as judges

Though I have stolen nothing,
I *still* must restore *it*.

5 O God, You know my foolishness;
And my sins are not hidden from You.
6 Let not those who [1]wait for You, O Lord GOD of hosts, be ashamed because of me;
Let not those who seek You be [2]confounded because of me, O God of Israel.
7 Because for Your sake I have borne reproach;
Shame has covered my face.
8 [a]I have become a stranger to my brothers,
And an alien to my mother's children;
9 [a]Because zeal for Your house has eaten me up,
[b]And the reproaches of those who reproach You have fallen on me.
10 When I wept *and chastened* my soul with fasting,
That became my reproach.
11 I also [1]made sackcloth my garment;
I became a byword to them.
12 Those who [1]sit in the gate speak against me,
And I *am* the song of the [a]drunkards.

13 But as for me, my prayer *is* to You,
O LORD, *in* the acceptable time;
O God, in the multitude of Your mercy,
Hear me in the truth of Your salvation.
14 Deliver me out of the mire,
And let me not sink;
Let me be delivered from those who hate me,
And out of the deep waters.

69 (68, LXX) This is an explicit Passion psalm. The first half of v. 9 is quoted by the disciples (John 2:17) as Christ cleanses the temple in their presence. Verse 9b is quoted in Rom. 15:3 by St. Paul in the context of bearing the pains of the weak, just as Christ bore the reproach of others. Verses 17, 18 are used in the Forgiveness Sunday service to usher in the season of Lent. Verse 21 is quoted in all four Gospels as being fulfilled with the giving of the vinegar to Christ on the Cross (see center-column references). Thus, the whole psalm is related to Christ's Passion.

15 Let not the floodwater overflow me,
Nor let the deep swallow me up;
And let not the pit shut its mouth on me.

16 Hear me, O LORD, for Your lovingkindness *is* good;
Turn to me according to the multitude of Your tender mercies.
17 And do not hide Your face from Your servant,
For I am in trouble;
Hear me speedily.
18 Draw near to my soul, *and* redeem it;
Deliver me because of my enemies.

19 You know [a]my reproach, my shame, and my dishonor;
My adversaries *are* all before You.
20 Reproach has broken my heart,
And I am full of [1]heaviness;
[a]I looked *for someone* to take pity, but *there was* none;
And for [b]comforters, but I found none.
21 They also gave me gall for my food,
[a]And for my thirst they gave me vinegar to drink.

22 [a]Let their table become a snare before them,
And their well-being a trap.
23 [a]Let their eyes be darkened, so that they do not see;
And make their loins shake continually.
24 [a]Pour out Your indignation upon them,
And let Your wrathful anger take hold of them.
25 [a]Let their dwelling place be desolate;
Let no one live in their tents.
26 For they persecute the *ones* [a]You have struck,
And talk of the grief of those You have wounded.
27 [a]Add iniquity to their iniquity,
[b]And let them not come into Your righteousness.
28 Let them [a]be blotted out of the book of the living,
[b]And not be written with the righteous.

29 But I *am* poor and sorrowful;
Let Your salvation, O God, set me up on high.
30 [a]I will praise the name of God with a song,
And will magnify Him with thanksgiving.
31 [a]*This* also shall please the LORD better than an ox *or* bull,
Which has horns and hooves.
32 [a]The humble shall see *this and* be glad;
And you who seek God, [b]your hearts shall live.
33 For the LORD hears the poor,
And does not despise [a]His prisoners.

34 [a]Let heaven and earth praise Him,
The seas [b]and everything that moves in them.
35 [a]For God will save Zion
And build the cities of Judah,
That they may dwell there and possess it.
36 Also, [a]the [1]descendants of His servants shall inherit it,
And those who love His name shall dwell in it.

19 [a]Ps. 22:6, 7; Heb. 12:2 **20** [a]Is. 63:5 [b]Job 16:2 [1]Lit. *sickness* **21** [a]Matt. 27:34, 48; Mark 15:23, 36; Luke 23:36; John 19:28–30 **22** [a]Rom. 11:9, 10 **23** [a]Is. 6:9, 10 **24** [a][Jer. 10:25; 1 Thess. 2:16] **25** [a]Matt. 23:38; Luke 13:35; Acts 1:20 **26** [a][Is. 53:4; 1 Pet. 2:24] **27** [a]Neh. 4:5; [Rom. 1:28] [b][Is. 26:10] **28** [a][Ex. 32:32]; Phil. 4:3; [Rev. 3:5; 13:8] [b]Ezek. 13:9; Luke 10:20; Heb. 12:23 **30** [a][Ps. 28:7] **31** [a]Ps. 50:13, 14, 23; 51:16 **32** [a]Ps. 34:2 [b]Ps. 22:26 **33** [a][Ps. 68:6]; Eph. 3:1 **34** [a]Ps. 96:11; Is. 44:23; 49:13 [b]Is. 55:12 **35** [a]Ps. 51:18; Is. 44:26 **36** [a]Ps. 102:28 [1]Lit. *seed*

PSALM 70

title [a]Ps. 38:title **1** [a]Ps. 40:13–17

PSALM 70†

Prayer for Relief from Adversaries

To the Chief Musician. *A Psalm* of David. [a]To bring to remembrance.

MAKE *haste,* [a]O God, to deliver me!
Make haste to help me, O LORD!

70 (69, LXX) All the enemies of God and of His people will be put to shame, but those who seek the Lord will rejoice. The early Desert Fathers used v. 1 as a text for "ceaseless prayer," thereby living out the exhortation of St. Paul in 1 Thess. 5:17 to "pray without

(continued on next page)

2 [a]Let them be ashamed and
confounded
Who seek my life;
Let them be [1]turned back and
confused
Who desire my hurt.
3 [a]Let them be turned back
because of their shame,
Who say, [1]"Aha, aha!"

4 Let all those who seek You
rejoice and be glad in You;
And let those who love Your
salvation say continually,
"Let God be magnified!"

5 [a]But I *am* poor and needy;
[b]Make haste to me, O God!
You *are* my help and my
deliverer;
O LORD, do not delay.

PSALM 71†

God the Rock of Salvation

IN [a]You, O LORD, I put my trust;
Let me never be put to shame.
2 [a]Deliver me in Your
righteousness, and cause me
to escape;
[b]Incline Your ear to me, and save
me.
3 [a]Be my [1]strong refuge,
To which I may resort
continually;
You have given the
[b]commandment to save me,
For You *are* my rock and my
fortress.

4 [a]Deliver me, O my God, out of
the hand of the wicked,
Out of the hand of the
unrighteous and cruel man.
5 For You are [a]my hope, O Lord
GOD;
You are my trust from my youth.
6 [a]By You I have been [1]upheld
from birth;
You are He who took me out
of my mother's womb.
My praise *shall be* continually of
You.

7 [a]I have become as a wonder to
many,
But You *are* my strong refuge.
8 Let [a]my mouth be filled *with*
Your praise
And with Your glory all the day.
9 Do not cast me off in the time
of old age;
Do not forsake me when my
strength fails.
10 For my enemies speak against
me;
And those who lie in wait for
my life [a]take counsel
together,
11 Saying, "God has forsaken him;
Pursue and take him, for *there
is* none to deliver *him*."

12 [a]O God, do not be far from me;
O my God, [b]make haste to help
me!
13 Let them be [1]confounded *and*
consumed
Who are adversaries of my life;
Let them be covered *with*
reproach and dishonor
Who seek my hurt.

14 But I will hope continually,
And will praise You yet more
and more.
15 My mouth shall tell of Your
righteousness
And Your salvation all the day,
For I do not know *their* limits.
16 I will go in the strength of the
Lord GOD;
I will make mention of Your
righteousness, of Yours only.

17 O God, You have taught me
from my [a]youth;

2 [a]Ps. 35:4, 26 [1]So with MT, LXX, Tg., Vg.; some Heb. mss., Syr. *appalled* (cf. 40:15)
3 [a]Ps. 40:15 [1]An expression of scorn
5 [a]Ps. 72:12, 13 [b]Ps. 141:1

PSALM 71

1 [a]Ps. 25:2, 3
2 [a]Ps. 31:1 [b]Ps. 17:6
3 [a]Ps. 31:2, 3 [b]Ps. 44:4 [1]Lit. *rock of refuge* or *rock of habitation*
4 [a]Ps. 140:1, 3
5 [a]Jer. 14:8; 17:7, 13, 17; 50:7
6 [a]Ps. 22:9, 10; Is. 46:3 [1]*sustained from the womb*
7 [a]Is. 8:18; Zech. 3:8; 1 Cor. 4:9
8 [a]Ps. 35:28
10 [a]2 Sam. 17:1
12 [a]Ps. 35:22 [b]Ps. 70:1
13 [1]*ashamed*
17 [a]Deut. 4:5; 6:7

(continued from previous page)
ceasing." This is often seen as the precursor to the now-famous Jesus Prayer, "O Lord Jesus Christ, Son of God, have mercy on me, a sinner," as the means of prayer without ceasing. This psalm is read during both Small and Great Compline (the late evening services).

71 (70, LXX) This psalm is a beautiful prayer for the aged Christian (see especially vv. 17, 18).

And to this *day* I declare Your
wondrous works.
18 Now also [a]when *I am* old and
grayheaded,
O God, do not forsake me,
Until I declare Your strength to
this generation,
Your power to everyone *who* is
to come.

19 Also [a]Your righteousness,
O God, *is* [1]very high,
You who have done great
things;
[b]O God, who *is* like You?
20 [a]*You,* who have shown me great
and severe troubles,
[b]Shall revive me again,
And bring me up again from the
depths of the earth.
21 You shall increase my
greatness,
And comfort me on every side.

22 Also [a]with the lute I will praise
You—
And Your faithfulness, O my
God!
To You I will sing with the harp,
O [b]Holy One of Israel.
23 My lips shall greatly rejoice
when I sing to You,
And [a]my soul, which You have
redeemed.
24 My tongue also shall talk of
Your righteousness all the day
long;
For they are confounded,
For they are brought to shame
Who seek my hurt.

PSALM 72†

Deliverance for the Poor

A Psalm [a]of Solomon.

GIVE the king Your judgments,
O God,
And Your righteousness to the
king's Son.
2 [a]He will judge Your people with
righteousness,
And Your poor with justice.
3 [a]The mountains will bring peace
to the people,
And the little hills, by
righteousness.
4 [a]He will bring justice to the poor
of the people;
He will save the children of the
needy,
And will [1]break in pieces the
oppressor.

5 [1]They shall fear You
[a]As long as the sun and moon
endure,
Throughout all generations.
6 [a]He shall come down like rain
upon the grass before
mowing,
Like showers *that* water the
earth.
7 In His days the righteous shall
flourish,
[a]And abundance of peace,
Until the moon is no more.

8 [a]He shall have dominion also
from sea to sea,
And from the River to the ends
of the earth.
9 [a]Those who dwell in the
wilderness will bow before
Him,
[b]And His enemies will lick the
dust.
10 [a]The kings of Tarshish and of the
isles
Will bring presents;
The kings of Sheba and Seba
Will offer gifts.
11 [a]Yes, all kings shall fall down
before Him;
All nations shall serve Him.

12 For He [a]will deliver the needy
when he cries,

18 [a][Is. 46:4] **19** [a]Deut. 3:24; Ps. 57:10 [b]Ps. 35:10 [1]*great,* lit. *to the height* of heaven **20** [a]Ps. 60:3 [b]Hos. 6:1, 2 **22** [a]Ps. 92:1–3 [b]2 Kin. 19:22; Is. 1:4 **23** [a]Ps. 103:4

PSALM 72

title [a]Ps. 127:title **2** [a][Is. 9:7; 11:2–5; 32:1] **3** [a]Ps. 85:10 **4** [a]Is. 11:4 [1]*crush* **5** [a]Ps. 72:7, 17; 89:36 [1]So with MT, Tg.; LXX, Vg. *They shall continue* **6** [a]Deut. 32:2; 2 Sam. 23:4; Hos. 6:3 **7** [a]Is. 2:4 **8** [a]Ex. 23:31; [Is. 9:6; Zech. 9:10] **9** [a]Ps. 74:14; Is. 23:13 [b]Is. 49:23; Mic. 7:17 **10** [a]1 Kin. 10:2; 2 Chr. 9:21 **11** [a]Is. 49:23 **12** [a]Job 29:12

72 (71, LXX) This is a messianic psalm, concerning how Messiah will deliver the poor (v. 2); save the children of the needy (v. 4); and rule the earth from sea to sea (v. 8). It is used all through the Christmas services. Christ Himself is the true Solomon, the peacemaker who will make the two (Jews and Gentiles) one, and will break down the dividing wall of hostility (see Eph. 2:14–16). Verses 10, 11 are a reference to the wise men, as seen in the liturgical prayers of the Church.

The poor also, and *him* who has
no helper.
13 He will spare the poor and
needy,
And will save the souls of the
needy.
14 He will redeem their life from
oppression and violence;
And [a]precious shall be their
blood in His sight.

15 And He shall live;
And the gold of [a]Sheba will be
given to Him;
Prayer also will be made for
Him continually,
And daily He shall be praised.

16 There will be an abundance of
grain in the earth,
On the top of the mountains;
Its fruit shall wave like
Lebanon;
[a]And *those* of the city shall
flourish like grass of the
earth.

17 [a]His name shall endure
forever;
His name shall continue as long
as the sun.
And [b]*men* shall be blessed in
Him;
[c]All nations shall call Him
blessed.

18 [a]Blessed *be* the LORD God, the
God of Israel,
[b]Who only does wondrous
things!
19 And [a]blessed *be* His glorious
name forever!
[b]And let the whole earth be filled
with His glory.
Amen and Amen.

20 The prayers of David the son of
Jesse are ended.

14 [a]1 Sam. 26:21; [Ps. 116:15]
15 [a]Is. 60:6
16 [a]1 Kin. 4:20
17 [a][Ps. 89:36] [b][Gen. 12:3] [c]Luke 1:48
18 [a]1 Chr. 29:10 [b]Ex. 15:11; Job 5:9
19 [a][Neh. 9:5] [b]Num. 14:21; Hab. 2:14

PSALM 73

title [a]Ps. 50:title
2 [a]Job 12:5
3 [a]Ps. 37:1, 7; [Prov. 23:17] [b]Job 21:5–16; Jer. 12:1
4 [1]*pains*
5 [a]Job 21:9
6 [a]Ps. 109:18
7 [a]Job 15:27; Jer. 5:28 [1]Tg. *face bulges;* LXX, Syr., Vg. *iniquity bulges*
8 [a]Ps. 53:1 [b]2 Pet. 2:18; Jude 16 [1]Proudly
9 [a]Rev. 13:6
10 [a][Ps. 75:8]
11 [a]Job 22:13

BOOK THREE: Psalms 73–89

PSALM 73†

The Goodness of God to His People

A Psalm of [a]Asaph.

TRULY God *is* good to Israel,
To such as are pure in heart.
2 But as for me, my feet had
almost stumbled;
My steps had nearly [a]slipped.
3 [a]For I *was* envious of the
boastful,
When I saw the prosperity of
the [b]wicked.

4 For *there are* no [1]pangs in their
death,
But their strength *is* firm.
5 [a]They *are* not in trouble *as other*
men,
Nor are they plagued like *other*
men.
6 Therefore pride serves as their
necklace;
Violence covers them [a]*like* a
garment.
7 [a]Their [1]eyes bulge with
abundance;
They have more than heart
could wish.
8 [a]They scoff and speak wickedly
concerning oppression;
They [b]speak [1]loftily.
9 They set their mouth [a]against
the heavens,
And their tongue walks through
the earth.

10 Therefore his people return
here,
[a]And waters of a full *cup* are
drained by them.
11 And they say, [a]"How does God
know?

73 (72, LXX) In this psalm, the end of the wicked is contrasted with that of the righteous. **Until I went into the sanctuary of God; then I understood their end** (v. 17): Whenever we enter into worship we ask the Lord to ". . . enlighten our hearts with the pure light of Your Divine Knowledge and open our minds to understand Your evangelical proclamations" (prayer before the Gospel in the Divine Liturgy of St. John Chrysostom). Often in worship, the Lord reveals knowledge to us, through our intuition, that we would not understand through a purely rational approach.

And is there knowledge in the
Most High?"
12 Behold, these *are* the ungodly,
Who are always at ease;
They increase *in* riches.
13 Surely I have [1]cleansed my heart
in [a]vain,
And washed my hands in
innocence.
14 For all day long I have been
plagued,
And chastened every morning.

15 If I had said, "I will speak thus,"
Behold, I would have been
untrue to the generation of
Your children.
16 When I thought *how* to
understand this,
It *was* [1]too painful for me—
17 Until I went into the sanctuary
of God;
Then I understood their
[a]end.

18 Surely [a]You set them in slippery
places;
You cast them down to
destruction.
19 Oh, how they are *brought* to
desolation, as in a moment!
They are utterly consumed with
terrors.
20 As a dream when *one* awakes,
So, Lord, when You awake,
You shall despise their image.

21 Thus my heart was grieved,
And I was [1]vexed in my mind.
22 [a]I *was* so foolish and ignorant;
I was *like* a beast before You.
23 Nevertheless I *am* continually
with You;
You hold *me* by my right hand.
24 [a]You will guide me with Your
counsel,
And afterward receive me *to*
glory.

13 [a]Job 21:15; 35:3; Mal. 3:14
[1]*kept my heart pure in vain*
16 [1]*trouble-some in my eyes*
17 [a][Ps. 37:38; 55:23]
18 [a]Ps. 35:6
21 [1]Lit. *pierced in my kidneys*
22 [a]Ps. 92:6
24 [a]Ps. 32:8; 48:14; Is. 58:11
25 [a][Phil. 3:8]
26 [a]Ps. 84:2
[b]Ps. 16:5
[1]Lit. *rock*
27 [a][Ps. 119:155]
[1]Are unfaithful to You
28 [a][Heb. 10:22; James 4:8]
[b]Ps. 116:10; 2 Cor. 4:13

PSALM 74
title [1]Heb. *Maschil*
4 [a]Lam. 2:7
[b]Num. 2:2

25 [a]Whom have I in heaven *but*
You?
And *there is* none upon earth
that I desire besides You.
26 [a]My flesh and my heart fail;
But God *is* the [1]strength of my
heart and my [b]portion
forever.

27 For indeed, [a]those who are far
from You shall perish;
You have destroyed all those
who [1]desert You for harlotry.
28 But *it is* good for me to
[a]draw near to God;
I have put my trust in the Lord
GOD,
That I may [b]declare all Your
works.

PSALM 74†

A Plea for Relief from Oppressors

A [1]Contemplation of Asaph.

O GOD, why have You cast *us* off
forever?
Why does Your anger smoke
against the sheep of Your
pasture?
2 Remember Your congregation,
which You have purchased of
old,
The tribe of Your inheritance,
which You have redeemed—
This Mount Zion where You
have dwelt.
3 Lift up Your feet to the
perpetual desolations.
The enemy has damaged
everything in the sanctuary.
4 [a]Your enemies roar in the midst
of Your meeting place;
[b]They set up their banners *for*
signs.
5 They seem like men who lift up
Axes among the thick trees.

---

74 (73, LXX) The psalmist describes the final captivity of Israel; God, however, still gives them a possibility of salvation. Verse 1 gives the context: Why have You done great things in the past and not today? Verse 12 is prophetic in that the God **of old** is the One who will come to work salvation on the Cross **in the midst of the earth;** this verse is used at the Exaltation of the Cross. Verses 13–15 are used on Epiphany Eve and seen as fulfilled in Christ's baptism. (See 1 Cor. 10:1–4, where St. Paul sees the passage through the Red Sea as a type of baptism.)

6 And now they break down its
carved work, all at once,
With axes and hammers.
7 They have set fire to Your
sanctuary;
They have defiled the dwelling
place of Your name to the
ground.
8 [a]They said in their hearts,
"Let us [1]destroy them
altogether."
They have burned up all the
meeting places of God in the
land.

9 We do not see our signs;
[a]*There is* no longer any prophet;
Nor *is there* any among us who
knows how long.
10 O God, how long will the
adversary [1]reproach?
Will the enemy blaspheme Your
name forever?
11 [a]Why do You withdraw Your
hand, even Your right hand?
Take it out of Your bosom and
destroy *them*.

12 For [a]God *is* my King from of
old,
Working salvation in the midst
of the earth.
13 [a]You divided the sea by Your
strength;
You broke the heads of the
[1]sea serpents in the waters.
14 You broke the heads of
[1]Leviathan in pieces,
And gave him *as* food to the
people inhabiting the
wilderness.
15 [a]You broke open the fountain
and the flood;
[b]You dried up mighty rivers.
16 The day *is* Yours, the night also
is [a]Yours;
[b]You have prepared the light and
the sun.
17 You have [a]set all the borders of
the earth;
[b]You have made summer and
winter.

18 Remember this, *that* the enemy
has reproached, O LORD,
And *that* a foolish people has
blasphemed Your name.
19 Oh, do not deliver the life of
Your turtledove to the wild
beast!
Do not forget the life of Your
poor forever.
20 [a]Have respect to the covenant;
For the [1]dark places of the earth
are full of the [2]haunts of
[3]cruelty.
21 Oh, do not let the oppressed
return ashamed!
Let the poor and needy praise
Your name.

22 Arise, O God, plead Your own
cause;
Remember how the foolish man
[1]reproaches You daily.
23 Do not forget the voice of Your
enemies;
The tumult of those who rise up
against You increases
continually.

PSALM 75†

Thanksgiving for God's Righteous Judgment

To the Chief Musician. Set to [a]"Do[1] Not Destroy." A Psalm of Asaph. A Song.

WE give thanks to You, O God,
we give thanks!
For Your wondrous works
declare *that* Your name is
near.

2 "When I choose the [1]proper time,
I will judge uprightly.
3 The earth and all its inhabitants
are dissolved;
I set up its pillars firmly. Selah

4 "I said to the boastful, 'Do not
deal boastfully,'
And to the wicked, [a]'Do not
[1]lift up the horn.
5 Do not lift up your horn on
high;

8 [a]Ps. 83:4 [1]*oppress*
9 [a]1 Sam. 3:1; Lam. 2:9; Ezek. 7:26; Amos 8:11
10 [1]*revile*
11 [a]Lam. 2:3
12 [a]Ps. 44:4
13 [a]Ex. 14:21 [1]*sea monsters*
14 [1]A large sea creature of unknown identity
15 [a]Ex. 17:5, 6; Num. 20:11; Ps. 105:41; Is. 48:21 [b]Ex. 14:21, 22; Josh. 2:10; 3:13
16 [a]Job 38:12 [b]Gen. 1:14–18
17 [a]Deut. 32:8; Acts 17:26 [b]Gen. 8:22
20 [a]Gen. 17:7, 8; Lev. 26:44, 45 [1]*hiding places* [2]*homes* [3]*violence*
22 [1]*reviles* or *taunts*

PSALM 75

title [a]Ps. 57:title [1]Heb. *Al Tashcheth*
2 [1]*appointed*
4 [a][1 Sam. 2:3]; Ps. 94:4 [1]Raise the head proudly like a horned animal

75 (74, LXX) The psalmist is troubled by the fact that God's people will be rejected if they do not seek refuge in God and find their consolation in Him.

Do *not* speak with [1]a stiff neck.' "

6 For exaltation *comes* neither from the east
Nor from the west nor from the south.
7 But [a]God *is* the Judge:
[b]He puts down one,
And exalts another.
8 For [a]in the hand of the LORD *there is* a cup,
And the wine is red;
It is fully mixed, and He pours it out;
Surely its dregs shall all the wicked of the earth
Drain *and* drink down.

9 But I will declare forever,
I will sing praises to the God of Jacob.

10 "All[a] the [1]horns of the wicked I will also cut off,
But [b]the horns of the righteous shall be [c]exalted."

5 [1]Insolent pride
7 [a]Ps. 50:6 [b]1 Sam. 2:7; Ps. 147:6; Dan. 2:21
8 [a]Job 21:20; Ps. 60:3; Jer. 25:15; Rev. 14:10; 16:19
10 [a]Ps. 101:8; Jer. 48:25 [b]Ps. 89:17; 148:14 [c]1 Sam. 2:1 [1]Strength

PSALM 76

The Majesty of God in Judgment

To the Chief Musician. On [1]stringed instruments. A Psalm of Asaph. A Song.

IN [a]Judah God *is* known;
His name *is* great in Israel.
2 In [1]Salem also is His tabernacle,
And His dwelling place in Zion.
3 There He broke the arrows of the bow,
The shield and sword of battle. Selah

4 You *are* more glorious and excellent
[a]*Than* the mountains of prey.
5 [a]The stouthearted were plundered;
[b]They [1]have sunk into their sleep;
And none of the mighty men have found the use of their hands.
6 [a]At Your rebuke, O God of Jacob,
Both the chariot and horse were cast into a dead sleep.

7 You, Yourself, *are* to be feared;
And [a]who may stand in Your presence
When once You are angry?
8 [a]You caused judgment to be heard from heaven;
[b]The earth feared and was still,
9 When God [a]arose to judgment,
To deliver all the oppressed of the earth. Selah

10 [a]Surely the wrath of man shall praise You;
With the remainder of wrath
You shall gird Yourself.

11 [a]Make vows to the LORD your God, and pay *them;*
[b]Let all who are around Him bring presents to Him who ought to be feared.
12 He shall cut off the spirit of princes;
[a]*He is* awesome to the kings of the earth.

PSALM 76
title [1]Heb. *neginoth*
1 [a]Ps. 48:1, 3
2 [1]Jerusalem
4 [a]Ezek. 38:12
5 [a]Is. 10:12; 46:12 [b]Ps. 13:3 [1]Lit. *have slumbered their sleep*
6 [a]Ex. 15:1–21; Ezek. 39:20; Nah. 2:13; Zech. 12:4
7 [a][Ezra 9:15; Nah. 1:6; Mal. 3:2; Rev. 6:17]
8 [a]Ex. 19:9 [b]1 Chr. 16:30; 2 Chr. 20:29
9 [a][Ps. 9:7–9]
10 [a]Ex. 9:16; Rom. 9:17
11 [a][Eccl. 5:4–6] [b]2 Chr. 32:22, 23
12 [a]Ps. 68:35

PSALM 77†

The Consoling Memory of God's Redemptive Works

To the Chief Musician. [a]To Jeduthun. A Psalm of Asaph.

I CRIED out to God with my voice—
To God with my voice;
And He gave ear to me.
2 In the day of my trouble I sought the Lord;
My hand was stretched out in the night without ceasing;
My soul refused to be comforted.

PSALM 77
title [a]Ps. 39:title

77 (76, LXX) This is a psalm of the remembrance of God's mighty caring works. Its center is vv. 13b and 14a, a beloved refrain in the Orthodox Church, used in Vespers at Easter, Pentecost and Christmas, the great days of God's caring works in Christian history. The God who did all these great works of old is with us today, and always.

3 I remembered God, and was troubled;
I complained, and my spirit was overwhelmed. Selah

4 You hold my eyelids *open;*
I am so troubled that I cannot speak.
5 I have considered the days of old,
The years of ancient times.
6 I call to remembrance my song in the night;
I meditate within my heart,
And my spirit [1]makes diligent search.

7 Will the Lord cast off forever?
And will He be favorable no more?
8 Has His mercy ceased forever?
Has *His* [a]promise failed [1]forevermore?
9 Has God forgotten to be gracious?
Has He in anger shut up His tender mercies? Selah

10 And I said, "This *is* my [1]anguish;
But I will remember the years of the right hand of the Most High."
11 I will remember the works of the LORD;
Surely I will remember Your wonders of old.
12 I will also meditate on all Your work,
And talk of Your deeds.
13 Your way, O God, *is* in [1]the [a]sanctuary;
Who *is* so great a God as *our* God?
14 You *are* the God who does wonders;
You have declared Your strength among the peoples.
15 You have with *Your* arm redeemed Your people,
The sons of Jacob and Joseph. Selah

16 The waters saw You, O God;
The waters saw You, they were [a]afraid;
The depths also trembled.
17 The clouds poured out water;
The skies sent out a sound;
Your arrows also flashed about.
18 The voice of Your thunder *was* in the whirlwind;
The lightnings lit up the world;
The earth trembled and shook.
19 Your way *was* in the sea,
Your path in the great waters,
And Your footsteps were not known.
20 You led Your people like a flock
By the hand of Moses and Aaron.

6 [1]*ponders diligently*
8 [a][2 Pet. 3:8, 9] [1]Lit. *unto generation and generation*
10 [1]Lit. *infirmity*
13 [a]Ps. 73:17 [1]Or *holiness*
16 [a]Ex. 14:21; Hab. 3:8, 10

PSALM 78†

God's Kindness to Rebellious Israel

A [a]Contemplation[1] of Asaph.

GIVE ear, O my people, *to* my law;
Incline your ears to the words of my mouth.
2 I will open my mouth in a [a]parable;
I will utter [1]dark sayings of old,
3 Which we have heard and known,
And our fathers have told us.
4 [a]We will not hide *them* from their children,
[b]Telling to the generation to come the praises of the LORD,
And His strength and His wonderful works that He has done.

5 For [a]He established a testimony in Jacob,
And appointed a law in Israel,

PSALM 78
title [a]Ps. 74:title [1]Heb. *Maschil*
2 [a]Matt. 13:34, 35 [1]*obscure sayings* or *riddles*
4 [a]Ex. 12:26, 27; Deut. 4:9; 6:7; Job 15:18; Is. 38:19; Joel 1:3 [b]Ex. 13:8, 14
5 [a]Ps. 147:19

78 (77, LXX) This psalm gives a lengthy history of Israel, starting with Jacob, who is Israel, and ending with God's choosing of David. When the Church prays a prayer of Israel's history, it sees Christ as its end or fulfillment in the Church, for from David comes forth the Savior of our souls. The events in vv. 14–16 are mentioned in 1 Cor. 10:1–5, where Paul attributes all these acts to Christ Himself, and goes on to relate this history to the sacraments.

Which He commanded our fathers,
That [b]they should make them known to their children;
6 [a]That the generation to come might know *them,*
The children *who* would be born,
That they may arise and declare *them* to their children,
7 That they may set their hope in God,
And not forget the works of God,
But keep His commandments;
8 And [a]may not be like their fathers,
[b]A stubborn and rebellious generation,
A generation [c]*that* did not [1]set its heart aright,
And whose spirit was not faithful to God.

9 The children of Ephraim, *being* armed *and* [1]carrying bows,
Turned back in the day of battle.
10 [a]They did not keep the covenant of God;
They refused to walk in His law,
11 And [a]forgot His works
And His wonders that He had shown them.

12 [a]Marvelous things He did in the sight of their fathers,
In the land of Egypt, [b]*in* the field of Zoan.
13 [a]He divided the sea and caused them to pass through;
And [b]He made the waters stand up like a heap.
14 [a]In the daytime also He led them with the cloud,
And all the night with a light of fire.
15 [a]He split the rocks in the wilderness,
And gave *them* drink in abundance like the depths.
16 He also brought [a]streams out of the rock,
And caused waters to run down like rivers.

17 But they sinned even more against Him
By [a]rebelling against the Most High in the wilderness.
18 And [a]they tested God in their heart
By asking for the food of their fancy.
19 [a]Yes, they spoke against God:
They said, "Can God prepare a table in the wilderness?
20 [a]Behold, He struck the rock,
So that the waters gushed out,
And the streams overflowed.
Can He give bread also?
Can He provide meat for His people?"

21 Therefore the LORD heard *this* and [a]was furious;
So a fire was kindled against Jacob,
And anger also came up against Israel,
22 Because they [a]did not believe in God,
And did not trust in His salvation.
23 Yet He had commanded the clouds above,
[a]And opened the doors of heaven,
24 [a]Had rained down manna on them to eat,
And given them of the [1]bread of [b]heaven.
25 Men ate angels' food;
He sent them food to [1]the full.

26 [a]He caused an east wind to blow in the heavens;
And by His power He brought in the south wind.
27 He also rained meat on them like the dust,
Feathered fowl like the sand of the seas;
28 And He let *them* fall in the midst of their camp,
All around their dwellings.
29 [a]So they ate and were well filled,
For He gave them their own desire.
30 They were not [1]deprived of their craving;
But [a]while their food *was* still in their mouths,
31 The wrath of God came against them,

5 [b]Deut. 4:9; 11:19
6 [a]Ps. 102:18
8 [a]2 Kin. 17:14; 2 Chr. 30:7; Ezek. 20:18 [b]Ex. 32:9; Deut. 9:7, 24; 31:27; Judg. 2:19; Is. 30:9 [c]Job 11:13; Ps. 78:37 [1]Lit. *prepare its heart*
9 [1]Lit. *bow shooters*
10 [a]2 Kin. 17:15
11 [a]Ps. 106:13
12 [a]Ex. 7—12 [b]Num. 13:22; Is. 19:11; 30:4; Ezek. 30:14
13 [a]Ex. 14:21 [b]Ex. 15:8
14 [a]Ex. 13:21
15 [a]Ex. 17:6; Num. 20:11; Is. 48:21; [1 Cor. 10:4]
16 [a]Num. 20:8, 10, 11
17 [a]Deut. 9:22; Is. 63:10; Heb. 3:16
18 [a]Ex. 16:2
19 [a]Ex. 16:3; Num. 11:4; 20:3; 21:5
20 [a]Num. 20:11
21 [a]Num. 11:1
22 [a]Deut. 1:32; 9:23; [Heb. 3:18]
23 [a]Gen. 7:11; [Mal. 3:10]
24 [a]Ex. 16:4 [b]John 6:31 [1]Lit. *grain*
25 [1]*satiation*
26 [a]Num. 11:31
29 [a]Num. 11:19, 20
30 [a]Num. 11:33 [1]Lit. *separated*

And slew the stoutest of them,
And struck down the choice *men* of Israel.

32 In spite of this [a]they still sinned,
And [b]did not believe in His wondrous works.
33 [a]Therefore their days He consumed in futility,
And their years in fear.

34 [a]When He slew them, then they sought Him;
And they returned and sought earnestly for God.
35 Then they remembered that [a]God *was* their rock,
And the Most High God [b]their Redeemer.
36 Nevertheless they [a]flattered Him with their mouth,
And they lied to Him with their tongue;
37 For their heart was not steadfast with Him,
Nor were they faithful in His covenant.
38 [a]But He, *being* full of [b]compassion, forgave *their* iniquity,
And did not destroy *them*.
Yes, many a time [c]He turned His anger away,
And [d]did not stir up all His wrath;
39 For [a]He remembered [b]that they *were but* flesh,
[c]A breath that passes away and does not come again.

40 How often they [a]provoked[1] Him in the wilderness,
And grieved Him in the desert!
41 Yes, [a]again and again they tempted God,
And limited the Holy One of Israel.
42 They did not remember His [1]power:
The day when He redeemed them from the enemy,
43 When He worked His signs in Egypt,
And His wonders in the field of Zoan;
44 [a]Turned their rivers into blood,
And their streams, that they could not drink.
45 [a]He sent swarms of flies among them, which devoured them,
And [b]frogs, which destroyed them.
46 He also gave their crops to the caterpillar,
And their labor to the [a]locust.
47 [a]He destroyed their vines with hail,
And their sycamore trees with frost.
48 He also gave up their [a]cattle to the hail,
And their flocks to fiery [1]lightning.
49 He cast on them the fierceness of His anger,
Wrath, indignation, and trouble,
By sending angels of destruction *among them*.
50 He made a path for His anger;
He did not spare their soul from death,
But gave [1]their life over to the plague,
51 And destroyed all the [a]firstborn in Egypt,
The first of *their* strength in the tents of Ham.
52 But He [a]made His own people go forth like sheep,
And guided them in the wilderness like a flock;
53 And He [a]led them on safely, so that they did not fear;
But the sea [b]overwhelmed their enemies.
54 And He brought them to His [a]holy border,
This mountain [b]*which* His right hand had acquired.
55 [a]He also drove out the nations before them,
[b]Allotted them an inheritance by [1]survey,
And made the tribes of Israel dwell in their tents.

56 [a]Yet they tested and provoked the Most High God,
And did not keep His testimonies,
57 But [a]turned back and acted unfaithfully like their fathers;

32 [a]Num. 14:16, 17 [b]Num. 14:11; Ps. 78:11, 22 **33** [a]Num. 14:29, 35 **34** [a]Num. 21:7; [Hos. 5:15] **35** [a][Deut. 32:4, 15] [b][Ex. 15:13]; Deut. 7:8; Is. 41:14; 44:6; 63:9 **36** [a]Ex. 24:7, 8; Ezek. 33:31 **38** [a][Num. 14:18–20] [b]Ex. 34:6 [c][Is. 48:9] [d]1 Kin. 21:29 **39** [a]Job 10:9; Ps. 103:14–16 [b]John 3:6 [c][Job 7:7, 16; James 4:14] **40** [a]Ps. 95:8–10; [Eph. 4:30]; Heb. 3:16 [1]*rebelled against Him* **41** [a]Num. 14:22; Deut. 6:16 **42** [1]Lit. *hand* **44** [a]Ex. 7:20
45 [a]Ex. 8:24 [b]Ex. 8:6 **46** [a]Ex. 10:14 **47** [a]Ex. 9:23–25 **48** [a]Ex. 9:19 [1]*lightning bolts* **50** [1]Or *their beasts* **51** [a]Ex. 12:29, 30 **52** [a]Ps. 77:20 **53** [a]Ex. 14:19, 20 [b]Ex. 14:27, 28 **54** [a]Ex. 15:17 [b]Ps. 44:3 **55** [a]Josh. 11:16–23; Ps. 44:2 [b]Josh. 13:7; 19:51; 23:4 [1]*surveyed measurement*, lit. *measuring cord* **56** [a]Judg. 2:11–13 **57** [a]Ezek. 20:27, 28

[a]They were turned aside
[b]like a deceitful bow.
58 [a]For they provoked Him to anger
with their [b]high places,
And moved Him to jealousy
with their carved images.
59 When God heard *this,* He was
furious,
And greatly abhorred Israel,
60 [a]So that He forsook the
tabernacle of Shiloh,
The tent He had placed among
men,
61 [a]And delivered His strength into
captivity,
And His glory into the enemy's
hand.
62 [a]He also gave His people over to
the sword,
And was furious with His
inheritance.
63 The fire consumed their young
men,
And [a]their maidens were not
given in marriage.
64 [a]Their priests fell by the sword,
And [b]their widows made no
lamentation.

65 Then the Lord awoke as *from*
sleep,
[a]Like a mighty man who shouts
because of wine.
66 And [a]He beat back His
enemies;
He put them to a perpetual
reproach.

67 Moreover He rejected the tent
of Joseph,
And did not choose the tribe of
Ephraim,
68 But chose the tribe of Judah,
Mount Zion [a]which He loved.
69 And He built His [a]sanctuary like
the heights,
Like the earth which He has
established forever.
70 [a]He also chose David His
servant,
And took him from the
sheepfolds;
71 From following [a]the ewes that
had young He brought him,
[b]To shepherd Jacob His people,
And Israel His inheritance.
72 So he shepherded them

57 [b]Hos. 7:16 **58** [a]Deut. 32:16, 21; Judg. 2:12; 1 Kin. 14:9; Is. 65:3 [b]Deut. 12:2 **60** [a]1 Sam. 4:11; Jer. 7:12–14; 26:6–9 **61** [a]Judg. 18:30 **62** [a]Judg. 20:21; 1 Sam. 4:10 **63** [a]Jer. 7:34; 16:9; 25:10 **64** [a]1 Sam. 4:17; 22:18 [b]Job 27:15; Ezek. 24:23 **65** [a]Is. 42:13 **66** [a]1 Sam. 5:6 **68** [a][Ps. 87:2] **69** [a]1 Kin. 6:1–38 **70** [a]1 Sam. 16:11, 12; 2 Sam. 7:8 **71** [a]2 Sam. 7:8; [Is. 40:11] [b]2 Sam. 5:2; 1 Chr. 11:2

72 [a]1 Kin. 9:4

PSALM 79

1 [a]Ps. 74:2 [b]2 Kin. 25:9, 10; 2 Chr. 36:17–19; Jer. 26:18; 52:12–14; Mic. 3:12 [1]*Gentiles* [2]*in ruins* **2** [a]Deut. 28:26; Jer. 7:33; 19:7; 34:20 **4** [a]Ps. 44:13; [Dan. 9:16] **5** [a]Ps. 74:1, 9 [b][Zeph. 3:8] **6** [a]Jer. 10:25; [Zeph. 3:8] [b]Is. 45:4, 5; 1 Thess. 4:5; [2 Thess. 1:8] [c]Ps. 53:4 [1]*Gentiles* **8** [a]Is. 64:9 [1]Or *against us the iniquities of those who were before us*

according to the [a]integrity of
his heart,
And guided them by the
skillfulness of his hands.

PSALM 79

The Nations Are Yours: Intercession for Israel

A Psalm of Asaph.

O GOD, the [1]nations have come
into [a]Your inheritance;
Your holy temple they have
defiled;
[b]They have laid Jerusalem
[2]in heaps.
2 [a]The dead bodies of Your
servants
They have given *as* food for the
birds of the heavens,
The flesh of Your saints to the
beasts of the earth.
3 Their blood they have shed like
water all around Jerusalem,
And *there was* no one to bury
them.
4 We have become a reproach to
our [a]neighbors,
A scorn and derision to those
who are around us.

5 [a]How long, LORD?
Will You be angry forever?
Will Your [b]jealousy burn like
fire?
6 [a]Pour out Your wrath on the
[1]nations that [b]do not know
You,
And on the kingdoms that
[c]do not call on Your name.
7 For they have devoured Jacob,
And laid waste his dwelling
place.

8 [a]Oh, do not remember [1]former
iniquities against us!
Let Your tender mercies come
speedily to meet us,
For we have been brought very
low.
9 Help us, O God of our
salvation,
For the glory of Your name;

And deliver us, and provide
atonement for our sins,
[a]For Your name's sake!
10 [a]Why should the [1]nations say,
"Where *is* their God?"
Let there be known among the
nations in our sight
The avenging of the blood of
Your servants *which has been*
shed.

11 Let [a]the groaning of the
prisoner come before You;
According to the greatness of
Your [1]power
Preserve those who are
appointed to die;
12 And return to our neighbors
[a]sevenfold into their bosom
[b]Their reproach with which they
have reproached You,
O Lord.

13 So [a]we, Your people and sheep
of Your pasture,
Will give You thanks forever;
[b]We will show forth Your praise
to all generations.

PSALM 80†

God's Vine

To the Chief Musician. [a]Set to [1]"The Lilies." A [2]Testimony of Asaph. A Psalm.

GIVE ear, O Shepherd of
Israel,
[a]You who lead Joseph [b]like a
flock;
You who dwell *between* the
cherubim, [c]shine forth!
2 Before [a]Ephraim, Benjamin,
and Manasseh,
Stir up Your strength,
And come *and* save us!

3 [a]Restore us, O God;
[b]Cause Your face to shine,
And we shall be saved!

4 O LORD God of hosts,
[a]How long will You be angry
Against the prayer of Your
people?
5 [a]You have fed them with the
bread of tears,
And given them tears to drink
in great measure.
6 You have made us a strife to our
neighbors,
And our enemies laugh among
themselves.

7 Restore us, O God of hosts;
Cause Your face to shine,
And we shall be saved!
8 You have brought [a]a vine out
of Egypt;
[b]You have cast out the [1]nations,
and planted it.
9 You prepared *room* for it,
And caused it to take deep root,
And it filled the land.
10 The hills were covered with its
shadow,
And the [1]mighty cedars with its
[a]boughs.
11 She sent out her boughs to
[1]the Sea,
And her branches to [2]the River.

12 Why have You [a]broken down
her [1]hedges,
So that all who pass by the way
pluck her *fruit?*
13 The boar out of the woods
uproots it,
And the wild beast of the field
devours it.

14 Return, we beseech You, O God
of hosts;
[a]Look down from heaven and
see,
And visit this vine
15 And the vineyard which Your
right hand has planted,
And the branch *that* You made
strong [a]for Yourself.

9 [a]Jer. 14:7, 21
10 [a]Ps. 42:10 [1]*Gentiles*
11 [a]Ps. 102:20 [1]Lit. *arm*
12 [a]Gen. 4:15; Lev. 26:21; Prov. 6:31; Is. 30:26 [b]Ps. 74:10, 18, 22
13 [a]Ps. 74:1; 95:7 [b]Is. 43:21

PSALM 80
title [a]Ps. 45:title [1]Heb. *Shoshannim* [2]Heb. *Eduth*
1 [a][Ex. 25:20–22]; 1 Sam. 4:4; 2 Sam. 6:2 [b]Ps. 77:20 [c]Deut. 33:2
2 [a]Ps. 78:9, 67
3 [a]Lam. 5:21 [b]Num. 6:25; Ps. 4:6
4 [a]Ps. 79:5
5 [a]Ps. 42:3; Is. 30:20
8 [a][Is. 5:1, 7]; Jer. 2:21; Ezek. 15:6; 17:6; 19:10 [b]Ps. 44:2; Acts 7:45 [1]*Gentiles*
10 [a]Lev. 23:40 [1]Lit. *cedars of God*
11 [1]The Mediterranean [2]The Euphrates
12 [a]Is. 5:5; Nah. 2:2 [1]*walls* or *fences*
14 [a]Is. 63:15
15 [a][Is. 49:5]

80 (79, LXX) The psalmist prays for all those who have been taken as captives by the Assyrians (2 Kin. 17:1–23). If the psalm is understood in a spiritual way, he is praying for those who have endured the spiritual captivity of Satan. He prays for God to come and deliver His people Israel, again fulfilled in the Church as shown by Jesus' teaching in John 15:1–5. It is interesting to note that when the bishop visits an Orthodox church, he blesses the people with the words of vv. 14, 15. The LXX makes a clarifying improvement on v. 17, rendering it ". . . upon the Son of Man whom You have raised up for Yourself."

16 *It is* burned with fire, *it is* cut down;
[a]They perish at the rebuke of Your countenance.
17 [a]Let Your hand be upon the man of Your right hand,
Upon the son of man *whom* You made strong for Yourself.
18 Then we will not turn back from You;
Revive us, and we will call upon Your name.

19 Restore us, O LORD God of hosts;
Cause Your face to shine,
And we shall be saved!

PSALM 81

An Appeal for Israel's Repentance

To the Chief Musician. [a]On[1] an instrument of Gath. A Psalm of Asaph.

SING aloud to God our strength;
Make a joyful shout to the God of Jacob.
2 Raise a song and strike the timbrel,
The pleasant harp with the lute.

3 Blow the trumpet at the time of the New Moon,
At the full moon, on our solemn feast day.
4 For [a]this *is* a statute for Israel,
A law of the God of Jacob.
5 This He established in Joseph *as* a testimony,
When He went throughout the land of Egypt,
[a]*Where* I heard a language I did not understand.

6 "I removed his shoulder from the burden;
His hands were freed from the baskets.
7 [a]You called in trouble, and I delivered you;
[b]I answered you in the secret place of thunder;
I [c]tested you at the waters of [1]Meribah. Selah

8 "Hear,[a] O My people, and I will admonish you!
O Israel, if you will listen to Me!
9 There shall be no [a]foreign god among you;
Nor shall you worship any foreign god.
10 [a]I *am* the LORD your God,
Who brought you out of the land of Egypt;
[b]Open your mouth wide, and I will fill it.

11 "But My people would not heed My voice,
And Israel would *have* [a]none of Me.
12 [a]So I gave them over to [1]their own stubborn heart,
To walk in their own counsels.

13 "Oh,[a] that My people would listen to Me,
That Israel would walk in My ways!
14 I would soon subdue their enemies,
And turn My hand against their adversaries.
15 [a]The haters of the LORD would pretend submission to Him,
But their [1]fate would endure forever.
16 He would [a]have fed them also with [1]the finest of wheat;
And with honey [b]from the rock I would have satisfied you."

PSALM 82†

A Plea for Justice

A Psalm of Asaph.

GOD [a]stands in the congregation of [1]the mighty;
He judges among [b]the [2]gods.

---

16 a[Ps. 39:11]
17 aPs. 89:21

PSALM 81

title aPs. 8:title
1Heb. *Al Gittith*
4 aLev. 23:24; Num. 10:10
5 aDeut. 28:49; Ps. 114:1; Jer. 5:15
7 aEx. 2:23; 14:10; Ps. 50:15
bEx. 19:19; 20:18
cEx. 17:6, 7; Num. 20:13
1Lit. *Strife* or *Contention*
8 a[Ps. 50:7]
9 a[Ex. 20:3; Deut. 5:7; 32:12]; Ps. 44:20; [Is. 43:12]
10 aEx. 20:2; Deut. 5:6
bPs. 103:5
11 aEx. 32:1; Deut. 32:15
12 a[Job 8:4; Acts 7:42; Rom. 1:24, 26]
1*the dictates of their heart*
13 a[Deut. 5:29; Is. 48:18]
15 aRom. 1:30
1Lit. *time*
16 aDeut. 32:14
bJob 29:6
1Lit. *fat of wheat*

PSALM 82

1 a[2 Chr. 19:6; Eccl. 5:8]
bPs. 82:6
1Heb. *El*, lit. *God*
2Judges; Heb. *elohim*, lit. *mighty ones* or *gods*

---

82 (81, LXX) This psalm is sung on Holy Saturday at the Liturgy of St. Basil, and again at Vespers with v. 8 repeated as a refrain after each verse. In the context of the Resurrection

(continued on next page)

2 How long will you judge
unjustly,
And [a]show partiality to the
wicked? Selah
3 [1]Defend the poor and fatherless;
Do justice to the afflicted and
[a]needy.
4 Deliver the poor and needy;
Free *them* from the hand of the
wicked.

5 They do not know, nor do they
understand;
They walk about in darkness;
All the [a]foundations of the earth
are [1]unstable.

6 I said, [a]"You *are* [1]gods,
And all of you *are* children of
the Most High.
7 But you shall die like men,
And fall like one of the princes."

8 Arise, O God, judge the earth;
[a]For You shall inherit all
nations.

PSALM 83†

The Craftiness of Enemies

A Song. A Psalm of Asaph.

Do[a] not keep silent, O God!
Do not hold Your peace,
And do not be still, O God!
2 For behold, [a]Your enemies
make a [1]tumult;
And those who hate You have
[2]lifted up their head.
3 They have taken crafty counsel
against Your people,
And consulted together
[a]against Your sheltered ones.
4 They have said, "Come, and
[a]let us cut them off from *being*
a nation,
That the name of Israel may be
remembered no more."
5 For they have consulted
together with one [1]consent;
They [2]form a confederacy
against You:
6 [a]The tents of Edom and the
Ishmaelites;
Moab and the Hagrites;
7 Gebal, Ammon, and Amalek;
Philistia with the inhabitants of
Tyre;
8 Assyria also has joined with
them;
They have helped the children
of Lot. Selah

9 Deal with them as *with*
[a]Midian,
As *with* [b]Sisera,
As *with* Jabin at the Brook
Kishon,
10 Who perished at En Dor,
[a]*Who* became *as* refuse on the
earth.
11 Make their nobles like [a]Oreb
and like Zeeb,
Yes, all their princes like
[b]Zebah and Zalmunna,
12 Who said, "Let us take for
ourselves
The pastures of God for a
possession."

13 [a]O my God, make them like the
whirling dust,
[b]Like the chaff before the wind!
14 As the fire burns the woods,
And as the flame [a]sets the
mountains on fire,
15 So pursue them with Your
tempest,
And frighten them with Your
storm.
16 Fill their faces with shame,
That they may seek Your name,
O LORD.

2 [a][Deut. 1:17]; Prov. 18:5
3 [a][Deut. 24:17; Is. 11:4; Jer. 22:16] [1]*Vindicate*
5 [a]Ps. 11:3 [1]*moved*
6 [a]John 10:34 [1]Judges; Heb. *elohim*, lit. *mighty ones* or *gods*
8 [a]Ps. 2:8; [Rev. 11:15]

PSALM 83
1 [a]Ps. 28:1
2 [a]Ps. 81:15; Is. 17:12; Acts 4:25 [1]*uproar* [2]Exalted themselves
3 [a][Ps. 27:5]
4 [a]Esth. 3:6, 9; Jer. 11:19; 31:36
5 [1]Lit. *heart* [2]Lit. *cut a covenant*
6 [a]2 Chr. 20:1, 10, 11
9 [a]Num. 31:7; Judg. 7:22 [b]Judg. 4:15–24; 5:20, 21
10 [a]Zeph. 1:17
11 [a]Judg. 7:25 [b]Judg. 8:12–21
13 [a]Is. 17:13 [b]Job 21:18; Ps. 35:5; Is. 40:24; Jer. 13:24
14 [a]Ex. 19:18; Deut. 32:22

(continued from previous page)
coming the following day, this psalm is the Church's confident invitation to God to judge her. Verse 6 is quoted by Christ in John 10:34 and is God's promise to supply us, by grace, with what He is by nature. In the Orthodox Church, this process of regaining the image and likeness of God is called *theosis* (Gr.), meaning deification (see article, "Deification," at 2 Pet. 1).

83 (82, LXX) The psalmist asks God to punish the Assyrians for their arrogance, and for their attack on Jerusalem.

17 Let them be [1]confounded and
dismayed forever;
Yes, let them be put to shame
and perish,
18 [a]That they may know that You,
whose [b]name alone *is* the
LORD,
Are [c]the Most High over all the
earth.

PSALM 84†

The Blessedness of Dwelling in the House of God

To the Chief Musician. [a]On[1] an instrument of Gath. A Psalm of the sons of Korah.

HOW [a]lovely [1]*is* Your tabernacle,
O LORD of hosts!
2 [a]My soul longs, yes, even faints
For the courts of the LORD;
My heart and my flesh cry out
for the living God.

3 Even the sparrow has found a
home,
And the swallow a nest for
herself,
Where she may lay her young—
Even Your altars, O LORD of
hosts,
My King and my God.
4 Blessed *are* those who dwell in
Your [a]house;
They will still be praising You.
Selah

5 Blessed *is* the man whose
strength *is* in You,
Whose heart *is* set on
pilgrimage.
6 *As they* pass through the Valley
[a]of [1]Baca,
They make it a spring;
The rain also covers it with
[2]pools.
7 They go [a]from strength to
strength;
[1]*Each one* [b]appears before God in
Zion.

8 O LORD God of hosts, hear my
prayer;
Give ear, O God of Jacob!
Selah
9 [a]O God, behold our shield,
And look upon the face of Your
[1]anointed.

10 For a day in Your courts *is* better
than a thousand.
I would rather [1]be a doorkeeper
in the house of my God
Than dwell in the tents of
wickedness.
11 For the LORD God *is* [a]a sun and
[b]shield;
The LORD will give grace and
glory;
[c]No good *thing* will He withhold
From those who walk uprightly.

12 O LORD of hosts,
[a]Blessed *is* the man who trusts
in You!

PSALM 85†

The Captives Have Come Back

To the Chief Musician. A Psalm [a]of the sons of Korah.

LORD, You have been favorable to
Your land;
You have [a]brought back the
captivity of Jacob.
2 You have forgiven the iniquity
of Your people;
You have covered all their sin.
Selah
3 You have taken away all Your
wrath;
You have turned from the
fierceness of Your anger.

4 [a]Restore us, O God of our
salvation,

17 [1]*ashamed*
18 [a]Ps. 59:13
[b]Ex. 6:3
[c][Ps. 92:8]

PSALM 84

title [a]Ps. 8:title
[1]Heb. *Al Gittith*
1 [a]Ps. 27:4; 46:4, 5
[1]*are Your dwellings*
2 [a]Ps. 42:1, 2
4 [a][Ps. 65:4]
6 [a]2 Sam. 5:22–25
[1]Lit. *Weeping*
[2]Or *blessings*
7 [a]Prov. 4:18; Is. 40:31; John 1:16; 2 Cor. 3:18
[b]Ex. 34:23; Deut. 16:16
[1]LXX, Syr., Vg. *The God of gods shall be seen*
9 [a]Gen. 15:1
[1]Commissioned one, Heb. *messiah*
10 [1]*stand at the threshold*
11 [a]Is. 60:19, 20; Mal. 4:2; Rev. 21:23
[b]Gen. 15:1
[c]Ps. 34:9, 10
12 [a][Ps. 2:12; 40:4]

PSALM 85

title [a]Ps. 42:title
1 [a]Ezra 1:11—2:1; Ps. 14:7; Jer. 30:18; 31:23; Ezek. 39:25; Hos. 6:11; Joel 3:1
4 [a]Ps. 80:3, 7

84 (83, LXX) This psalm of longing for the presence of the Lord is used daily at the Ninth Hour, and at the Feast of the Transfiguration of Christ.

85 (84, LXX) God will forgive the sins of His people if they return to Him. He asks the Jewish people to confess their sins, so that they may find mercy through the Messiah, Lord Jesus Christ. This psalm is sung at Ninth Hour prayers. Verses 10–13 are seen as being fulfilled in the Incarnation of the Son of God.

And cause Your anger toward
us to cease.
5 [a]Will You be angry with us
forever?
Will You prolong Your anger to
all generations?
6 Will You not [a]revive us again,
That Your people may rejoice in
You?
7 Show us Your mercy, LORD,
And grant us Your salvation.

8 I will hear what God the LORD
will speak,
For He will speak peace
To His people and to His saints;
But let them not turn back to
[1]folly.
9 Surely [a]His salvation *is* near to
those who fear Him,
[b]That glory may dwell in our
land.

10 Mercy and truth have met
together;
[a]Righteousness and peace have
kissed.
11 Truth shall spring out of the
earth,
And righteousness shall look
down from heaven.
12 [a]Yes, the LORD will give *what is*
good;
And our land will yield its
increase.
13 Righteousness will go before
Him,
And shall make His footsteps
our pathway.

PSALM 86†

A Prayer for Mercy

A Prayer of David.

BOW down Your ear, O LORD,
hear me;
For I *am* poor and needy.
2 Preserve my [1]life, for I *am* holy;
You are my God;

5 [a]Ps. 79:5
6 [a]Hab. 3:2
8 [1]*foolishness*
9 [a]Is. 46:13 [b]Hag. 2:7; Zech. 2:5; [John 1:14]
10 [a]Ps. 72:3; [Is. 32:17]; Luke 2:14
12 [a][Ps. 84:11; James 1:17]

PSALM 86
2 [1]Lit. *soul*
4 [a]Ps. 25:1; 143:8 [1]*Make glad*
5 [a]Ps. 130:7; 145:9; [Joel 2:13]
8 [a][Ex. 15:11]; 2 Sam. 7:22; 1 Kin. 8:23; Ps. 89:6; Jer. 10:6
10 [a][Ex. 15:11] [b]Deut. 6:4; Is. 37:16; Mark 12:29; 1 Cor. 8:4
11 [a]Ps. 27:11; 143:8 [1]Give me singleness of heart
13 [1]The abode of the dead

Save Your servant who trusts in
You!
3 Be merciful to me, O Lord,
For I cry to You all day long.
4 [1]Rejoice the soul of Your servant,
[a]For to You, O Lord, I lift up my
soul.
5 For [a]You, Lord, *are* good, and
ready to forgive,
And abundant in mercy to all
those who call upon You.

6 Give ear, O LORD, to my prayer;
And attend to the voice of my
supplications.
7 In the day of my trouble I will
call upon You,
For You will answer me.

8 [a]Among the gods *there is* none
like You, O Lord;
Nor *are there any works* like Your
works.
9 All nations whom You have
made
Shall come and worship before
You, O Lord,
And shall glorify Your name.
10 For You *are* great, and [a]do
wondrous things;
[b]You alone *are* God.

11 [a]Teach me Your way, O LORD;
I will walk in Your truth;
[1]Unite my heart to fear Your
name.
12 I will praise You, O Lord my
God, with all my heart,
And I will glorify Your name
forevermore.
13 For great *is* Your mercy toward
me,
And You have delivered my
soul from the depths of
[1]Sheol.

14 O God, the proud have risen
against me,
And a mob of violent *men* have
sought my life,
And have not set You before
them.

86 (85, LXX) Illumined by the Holy Spirit concerning the coming of the Only Begotten Son and the remission of our sins, the psalmist prays that he might be numbered among the saved through God's grace. This psalm is seen as an evening prayer and is used at the Ninth Hour.

15 But [a]You, O Lord, *are* a God full
of compassion, and gracious,
Longsuffering and abundant in
mercy and truth.

16 Oh, turn to me, and have mercy
on me!
Give Your strength to Your
servant,
And save the son of Your
maidservant.

17 Show me a sign for good,
That those who hate me may
see *it* and be ashamed,
Because You, LORD, have
helped me and comforted me.

PSALM 87†

The City of God

A Psalm of the sons of Korah. A Song.

HIS foundation *is* in the holy
mountains.

2 [a]The LORD loves the gates of Zion
More than all the dwellings of
Jacob.

3 [a]Glorious things are spoken of
you,
O city of God! Selah

4 "I will make mention of [1]Rahab
and Babylon to those who
know Me;
Behold, O Philistia and Tyre,
with Ethiopia:
'This *one* was born there.' "

5 And of Zion it will be said,
"This *one* and that *one* were born
in her;
And the Most High Himself
shall establish her."

6 The LORD will record,
When He [a]registers the peoples:
"This *one* was born there."
Selah

7 Both the singers and the players
on instruments *say,*
"All my springs *are* in you."

PSALM 88†

The Darkness of Death

A Song. A Psalm of the sons of Korah. To the Chief Musician. Set to "Mahalath Leannoth." A [1]Contemplation of [a]Heman the Ezrahite.

O LORD, [a]God of my salvation,
I have cried out day and night
before You.

2 Let my prayer come before You;
[1]Incline Your ear to my cry.

3 For my soul is full of troubles,
And my life [a]draws near to the
grave.

4 I am counted with those who
[a]go[1] down to the pit;
[b]I am like a man *who has* no
strength,

5 [1]Adrift among the dead,
Like the slain who lie in the
grave,
Whom You remember no more,
And who are cut off from Your
hand.

6 You have laid me in the lowest
pit,
In darkness, in the depths.

7 Your wrath lies heavy upon me,
And You have afflicted *me* with
all [a]Your waves. Selah

15 [a]Ex. 34:6; [Ps. 86:5]

PSALM 87

2 [a]Ps. 78:67, 68
3 [a]Is. 60:1
4 [1]Egypt
6 [a]Is. 4:3

PSALM 88

title [a]1 Kin. 4:31; 1 Chr. 2:6 [1]Heb. *Maschil*
1 [a]Ps. 27:9; [Luke 18:7]
2 [1]Listen to
3 [a]Ps. 107:18
4 [a][Ps. 28:1] [b]Ps. 31:12 [1]Die
5 [1]Lit. *Free*
7 [a]Ps. 42:7

87 (86, LXX) This psalm deals with the salvation of the Gentiles and has a unique liturgical usage. It is sung on Christmas Eve at the vesperal liturgy, with v. 6 being a reference both to the registry of the people by Caesar, and to the registry by God of His people in heaven.

88 (87, LXX) This is the psalm of the darkness of death, a picture of the grave with no glimpse of redemption. The psalmist speaks of the death of the Messiah, and questions how He is going to give resurrection to the spirits now in hell. In vv. 10–12 the ultimate questions of death are asked, but with no answer. Verse 15 shows the coming Christ as the Man of Sorrows, ready to die from His youth up. For v. 18, the LXX renders the concluding line, "My only companion is darkness." This psalm, prayed at Good Friday Vespers, is seen by the Church as being answered forever in the Resurrection of Jesus Christ. Psalm 88 is also the fourth of the six psalms of Matins (see note on Ps. 3).

8 [a]You have [1]put away my
acquaintances far from me;
You have made me an
abomination to them;
[b]*I am* shut up, and I cannot get
out;
9 My eye wastes away because of
affliction.

[a]LORD, I have called daily upon
You;
I have stretched out my hands
to You.
10 Will You work wonders for the
dead?
Shall [1]the dead arise *and* praise
You? Selah
11 Shall Your lovingkindness be
declared in the grave?
Or Your faithfulness in the place
of destruction?
12 Shall Your wonders be known
in the dark?
And Your righteousness in the
land of forgetfulness?

13 But to You I have cried out,
O LORD,
And in the morning my prayer
comes before You.
14 LORD, why do You cast off my
soul?
Why do You hide Your face from
me?
15 I *have been* afflicted and ready to
die from *my* youth;
I suffer Your terrors;
I am distraught.
16 Your fierce wrath has gone over
me;
Your terrors have [1]cut me off.
17 They came around me all day
long like water;
They engulfed me altogether.
18 [a]Loved one and friend You have
put far from me,
And my acquaintances into
darkness.

8 [a]Job 19:13, 19; Ps. 31:11; 142:4 [b]Lam. 3:7 [1]*taken away my friends* **9** [a]Ps. 86:3 **10** [1]*shades, ghosts* **16** [1]*destroyed me* **18** [a]Job 19:13; Ps. 31:11; 38:11

PSALM 89

title [a]1 Kin. 4:31 [1]Heb. *Maschil* **2** [a][Ps. 119:89, 90] **3** [a]1 Kin. 8:16 [b]2 Sam. 7:11; 1 Chr. 17:10–12 **4** [a][2 Sam. 7:13; Is. 9:7; Luke 1:33] **5** [a][Ps. 19:1] **6** [a]Ps. 86:8; 113:5 **7** [a]Ps. 76:7, 11 **9** [a]Ps. 65:7; 93:3, 4; 107:29 **10** [a]Ex. 14:26–28; Ps. 87:4; Is. 30:7; 51:9 [1]Egypt

PSALM 89†

God's Covenant with David

A [1]Contemplation of [a]Ethan the Ezrahite.

I WILL sing of the mercies of the
LORD forever;
With my mouth will I make
known Your faithfulness to all
generations.
2 For I have said, "Mercy shall be
built up forever;
[a]Your faithfulness You shall
establish in the very
heavens."

3 "I[a] have made a covenant with
My chosen,
I have [b]sworn to My servant
David:
4 'Your seed I will establish
forever,
And build up your throne
[a]to all generations.'" Selah

5 And [a]the heavens will praise
Your wonders, O LORD;
Your faithfulness also in the
assembly of the saints.
6 [a]For who in the heavens can be
compared to the LORD?
Who among the sons of the
mighty can be likened to the
LORD?
7 [a]God is greatly to be feared in
the assembly of the saints,
And to be held in reverence by
all *those* around Him.
8 O LORD God of hosts,
Who *is* mighty like You,
O LORD?
Your faithfulness also
surrounds You.
9 [a]You rule the raging of the sea;
When its waves rise, You still
them.
10 [a]You have broken [1]Rahab in
pieces, as one who is slain;

89 (88, LXX) This psalm concerns the covenant of the Son of God with David. In the historical context, it appears after David's glory years as king of Israel, asking whether God's **lovingkindnesses** are over (v. 49). He foretells the birth of Christ from the lineage of David and his kingdom (vv. 34–37)—and also foretells the passion of Christ (vv. 38–45). The Orthodox Church has seen vv. 5–18 as a prophecy of the Transfiguration, with the Son of David receiving greater glory on **Tabor** (v. 12), and she sings this song on the Feast of the Transfiguration.

You have scattered Your
enemies with Your mighty
arm.

11 [a]The heavens *are* Yours, the
earth also *is* Yours;
The world and all its fullness,
You have founded them.
12 The north and the south, You
have created them;
[a]Tabor and [b]Hermon rejoice in
Your name.
13 You have a mighty arm;
Strong is Your hand, *and* high
is Your right hand.
14 Righteousness and justice *are*
the foundation of Your
throne;
Mercy and truth go before Your
face.
15 Blessed *are* the people who
know the [a]joyful sound!
They walk, O LORD, in the light
of Your countenance.
16 In Your name they rejoice all
day long,
And in Your righteousness they
are exalted.
17 For You *are* the glory of their
strength,
And in Your favor our [1]horn is
[a]exalted.
18 For our shield *belongs* to the
LORD,
And our king to the Holy One
of Israel.

19 Then You spoke in a vision to
Your [1]holy one,
And said: "I have given help to
one who is mighty;
I have exalted one [a]chosen from
the people.
20 [a]I have found My servant
David;
With My holy oil I have
anointed him,
21 [a]With whom My hand shall be
established;
Also My arm shall strengthen
him.
22 The enemy shall not [1]outwit
him,
Nor the son of wickedness afflict
him.
23 I will beat down his foes before
his face,
And plague those who hate
him.
24 "But My faithfulness and My
mercy *shall be* with him,
And in My name his horn shall
be exalted.
25 Also I will [a]set his hand over
the sea,
And his right hand over the
rivers.
26 He shall cry to Me, 'You *are*
[a]my Father,
My God, and [b]the rock of my
salvation.'
27 Also I will make him [a]*My*
firstborn,
[b]The highest of the kings of the
earth.
28 [a]My mercy I will keep for him
forever,
And My covenant shall stand
firm with him.
29 His seed also I will make *to
endure* forever,
[a]And his throne [b]as the days of
heaven.

30 "If[a] his sons [b]forsake My law
And do not walk in My
judgments,
31 If they [1]break My statutes
And do not keep My
commandments,
32 Then I will punish their
transgression with the rod,
And their iniquity with stripes.
33 [a]Nevertheless My
lovingkindness I will not
[1]utterly take from him,
Nor [2]allow My faithfulness to
fail.
34 My covenant I will not break,
Nor [a]alter the word that has
gone out of My lips.
35 Once I have sworn [a]by My
holiness;
I will not lie to David:
36 [a]His seed shall endure forever,
And his throne [b]as the sun
before Me;
37 It shall be established forever
like the moon,
Even *like* the faithful witness in
the sky." Selah
38 But You have [a]cast off and
[b]abhorred,[1]

11 [a][Gen. 1:1; 1 Chr. 29:11] **12** [a]Josh. 19:22; Judg. 4:6; Jer. 46:18 [b]Deut. 3:8; Josh. 11:17; 12:1; Song 4:8 **15** [a]Lev. 23:24; Num. 10:10; Ps. 98:6 **17** [a]Ps. 75:10; 92:10; 132:17 [1]Strength **19** [a]1 Kin. 11:34 [1]So with many Heb. mss.; MT, LXX, Tg., Vg. *holy ones* **20** [a]1 Sam. 13:14; 16:1–12; Acts 13:22 **21** [a]Ps. 80:17 **22** [1]Or *exact usury from him*

25 [a]Ps. 72:8 **26** [a]2 Sam. 7:14; [1 Chr. 22:10]; Jer. 3:19 [b]2 Sam. 22:47 **27** [a]Ex. 4:22; Ps. 2:7; Jer. 31:9; [Col. 1:15, 18] [b]Num. 24:7; [Ps. 72:11]; Rev. 19:16 **28** [a]Is. 55:3 **29** [a][1 Kin. 2:4; Is. 9:7]; Jer. 33:17 [b]Deut. 11:21 **30** [a][2 Sam. 7:14] [b]Ps. 119:53 **31** [1]*profane* **33** [a]2 Sam. 7:14, 15 [1]Lit. *break off* [2]Lit. *deal falsely with My faithfulness* **34** [a][Num. 23:19]; Jer. 33:20–22 **35** [a][1 Sam. 15:29]; Amos 4:2; [Titus 1:2] **36** [a][Luke 1:33] [b]Ps. 72:17 **38** [a][1 Chr. 28:9] [b]Deut. 32:19 [1]*rejected*

You have been furious with
Your [2]anointed.
39 You have renounced the
covenant of Your servant;
[a]You have [1]profaned his crown
by casting it to the ground.
40 You have broken down all his
hedges;
You have brought his
[1]strongholds to ruin.
41 All who pass by the way
[a]plunder him;
He is a reproach to his
neighbors.
42 You have exalted the right hand
of his adversaries;
You have made all his enemies
rejoice.
43 You have also turned back the
edge of his sword,
And have not sustained him in
the battle.
44 You have made his [1]glory cease,
And cast his throne down to the
ground.
45 The days of his youth You have
shortened;
You have covered him with
shame. Selah

46 How long, LORD?
Will You hide Yourself forever?
Will Your wrath burn like fire?
47 Remember how short my time
[a]is;
For what [b]futility have You
created all the children of
men?
48 What man can live and not
[1]see [a]death?
Can he deliver his life from the
power of [2]the grave? Selah

49 Lord, where *are* Your former
lovingkindnesses,
Which You [a]swore to David
[b]in Your truth?
50 Remember, Lord, the reproach
of Your servants—
[a]*How* I bear in my bosom *the
reproach of* all the many
peoples,
51 [a]With which Your enemies have
reproached, O LORD,
With which they have
reproached the footsteps of
Your [1]anointed.

52 [a]Blessed *be* the LORD
forevermore!
Amen and Amen.

BOOK FOUR: Psalms 90–106

PSALM 90†

God Our Dwelling Place

A Prayer [a]of Moses the man of God.

LORD, [a]You have been our
[1]dwelling place in all
generations.
2 [a]Before the mountains were
brought forth,
Or ever You [1]had formed the
earth and the world,
Even from everlasting to
everlasting, You *are* God.

3 You turn man to destruction,
And say, [a]"Return, O children
of men."
4 [a]For a thousand years in Your
sight
Are like yesterday when it is
past,
And *like* a watch in the night.
5 You carry them away *like* a
flood;
[a]*They are* like a sleep.
In the morning [b]they are like
grass *which* grows up:
6 In the morning it flourishes and
grows up;
In the evening it is cut down
and withers.

38 [2]Commissioned one, Heb. *messiah*
39 [a]Ps. 74:7; Lam. 5:16 [1]*defiled*
40 [1]*fortresses*
41 [a]Ps. 80:12
44 [1]*splendor* or *brightness*
47 [a]Ps. 90:9 [b]Ps. 62:9
48 [a][Eccl. 3:19] [1]*experience death* [2]Or *Sheol*
49 [a][2 Sam. 7:15]; Jer. 30:9; Ezek. 34:23 [b]Ps. 54:5
50 [a]Ps. 69:9, 19
51 [a]Ps. 74:10, 18, 22 [1]Commissioned one, Heb. *messiah*
52 [a]Ps. 41:13

PSALM 90
title [a]Deut. 33:1
1 [a][Deut. 33:27; Ezek. 11:16] [1]LXX, Tg., Vg. *refuge*
2 [a]Job 15:7; [Prov. 8:25, 26] [1]Lit. *gave birth to*
3 [a]Gen. 3:19; Job 34:14, 15
4 [a]2 Pet. 3:8
5 [a]Ps. 73:20 [b]Is. 40:6

90 (89, LXX) This psalm is a morning prayer, used daily at the First Hour. There are several practical insights in this psalm. Verse 4 is paraphrased by Peter (2 Pet. 3:8) to show that the Second Coming of Christ is near, but its time is not predictable. Verse 10 describes the human life span as being between 70 and 80 years—yet a brief moment compared to the timelessness of eternity. In v. 17 it is God Himself who secures and gives meaning to the work we do on earth. Without Him, our work and our lives are without meaning and are void.

7 For we have been consumed by
Your anger,
And by Your wrath we are
terrified.
8 [a]You have set our iniquities
before You,
Our [b]secret *sins* in the light of
Your countenance.
9 For all our days have passed
away in Your wrath;
We finish our years like a sigh.
10 The days of our lives *are* seventy
years;
And if by reason of strength *they*
are eighty years,
Yet their boast *is* only labor and
sorrow;
For it is soon cut off, and we
fly away.
11 Who knows the power of Your
anger?
For as the fear of You, *so is* Your
wrath.
12 [a]So teach *us* to number our days,
That we may gain a heart of
wisdom.

13 Return, O LORD!
How long?
And [a]have compassion on Your
servants.
14 Oh, satisfy us early with Your
mercy,
[a]That we may rejoice and be glad
all our days!
15 Make us glad according to the
days *in which* You have
afflicted us,
The years *in which* we have seen
evil.
16 Let [a]Your work appear to Your
servants,
And Your glory to their
children.
17 [a]And let the beauty of the LORD
our God be upon us,
And [b]establish the work of our
hands for us;
Yes, establish the work of our
hands.

8 [a]Ps. 50:21; [Jer. 16:17] [b]Ps. 19:12; [Eccl. 12:14]
12 [a]Deut. 32:29; Ps. 39:4
13 [a]Ex. 32:12; Deut. 32:36
14 [a]Ps. 85:6
16 [a][Deut. 32:4]; Hab. 3:2
17 [a]Ps. 27:4 [b]Is. 26:12

PSALM 91†

The Psalm for the Departed

HE [a]who dwells in the secret
place of the Most High
Shall abide [b]under the shadow
of the Almighty.
2 [a]I will say of the LORD, *"He is* my
refuge and my fortress;
My God, in Him I will trust."

3 Surely [a]He shall deliver you
from the snare of the [1]fowler
And from the perilous
pestilence.
4 [a]He shall cover you with His
feathers,
And under His wings you shall
take refuge;
His truth *shall be your* shield and
[1]buckler.
5 [a]You shall not be afraid of the
terror by night,
Nor of the arrow *that* flies by
day,
6 *Nor* of the pestilence *that* walks
in darkness,
Nor of the destruction *that* lays
waste at noonday.

7 A thousand may fall at your
side,
And ten thousand at your right
hand;
But it shall not come near you.
8 Only [a]with your eyes shall you
look,
And see the reward of the
wicked.

9 Because you have made the
LORD, *who is* [a]my refuge,

PSALM 91
1 [a]Ps. 27:5; 31:20; 32:7 [b]Ps. 17:8; Is. 25:4; 32:2
2 [a]Ps. 142:5
3 [a]Ps. 124:7; Prov. 6:5 [1]One who catches birds in a trap or snare
4 [a]Ps. 17:8 [1]A small shield
5 [a][Job 5:19; Ps. 112:7; Is. 43:2]
8 [a]Ps. 37:34; Mal. 1:5
9 [a]Ps. 91:2

91 (90, LXX) This is the funeral psalm in the Orthodox Church, a song of confidence in God's protection. It is also a prayer before bedtime. Verse 6 explains why it is used additionally as a noontime or Sixth Hour prayer. In passing, this psalm describes Satan in various ways: **the terror by night, the arrow that flies by day, the pestilence that walks in darkness,** and **the destruction that lays waste at noonday** (vv. 5, 6). The LXX reads "the demon that lays waste at noonday." The psalmist proclaims, however, the triumph of the man of God over all of these manifestations (vv. 9–16).

Even the Most High, [b]your dwelling place,
10 [a]No evil shall befall you,
Nor shall any plague come near your dwelling;
11 [a]For He shall give His angels charge over you,
To keep you in all your ways.
12 In *their* hands they shall [1]bear you up,
[a]Lest you [2]dash your foot against a stone.
13 You shall tread upon the lion and the cobra,
The young lion and the serpent you shall trample underfoot.

14 "Because he has set his love upon Me, therefore I will deliver him;
I will [1]set him on high, because he has [a]known My name.
15 He shall [a]call upon Me, and I will answer him;
I *will be* [b]with him in trouble;
I will deliver him and honor him.
16 With [1]long life I will satisfy him,
And show him My salvation."

9 [b]Ps. 90:1
10 [a][Prov. 12:21]
11 [a]Ps. 34:7; Matt. 4:6; Luke 4:10; [Heb. 1:14]
12 [a]Matt. 4:6; Luke 4:11
[1]*lift*
[2]*strike*
14 [a][Ps. 9:10]
[1]*exalt him*
15 [a]Job 12:4; Ps. 50:15
[b]Is. 43:2
16 [1]Lit. *length of days*

PSALM 92
1 [a]Ps. 147:1
2 [a]Ps. 89:1
3 [a]1 Chr. 23:5

PSALM 92†

Praise to the Lord for His Love and Faithfulness

A Psalm. A Song for the Sabbath day.

IT *is* [a]good to give thanks to the LORD,
And to sing praises to Your name, O Most High;
2 To [a]declare Your lovingkindness in the morning,
And Your faithfulness every night,
3 [a]On an instrument of ten strings,
On the lute,
And on the harp,
With harmonious sound.
4 For You, LORD, have made me glad through Your work;
I will triumph in the works of Your hands.

5 [a]O LORD, how great are Your works!
[b]Your thoughts are very deep.
6 [a]A senseless man does not know,
Nor does a fool understand this.
7 When [a]the wicked [1]spring up like grass,
And when all the workers of iniquity flourish,
It is that they may be destroyed forever.

8 [a]But You, LORD, *are* on high forevermore.
9 For behold, Your enemies, O LORD,
For behold, Your enemies shall perish;
All the workers of iniquity shall [a]be scattered.

10 But [a]my [1]horn You have exalted like a wild ox;
I have been [b]anointed with fresh oil.
11 [a]My eye also has seen *my desire* on my enemies;
My ears hear *my desire* on the wicked
Who rise up against me.

12 [a]The righteous shall flourish like a palm tree,
He shall grow like a cedar in Lebanon.
13 Those who are planted in the house of the LORD
Shall flourish in the courts of our God.
14 They shall still bear fruit in old age;
They shall be [1]fresh and [2]flourishing,
15 To declare that the LORD is upright;

5 [a]Ps. 40:5; [Rev. 15:3]
[b]Ps. 139:17, 18; [Is. 28:29; Rom. 11:33, 34]
6 [a]Ps. 73:22
7 [a]Job 12:6; Ps. 37:1, 2; Jer. 12:1, 2; [Mal. 3:15]
[1]*sprout*
8 [a][Ps. 83:18]
9 [a]Ps. 68:1
10 [a]Ps. 89:17
[b]Ps. 23:5
[1]Strength
11 [a]Ps. 54:7
12 [a]Num. 24:6; Ps. 52:8; Jer. 17:8; Hos. 14:5, 6
14 [1]Full of oil or sap, lit. *fat*
[2]*green*

92 (91, LXX) This psalm is a great prayer of thanksgiving, with vv. 1, 2, and 4 being sung as the first antiphon (psalm sung responsively) on a regular Sunday. Verses 12 and 13 are a passage frequently used in reference to the saints. An allusion may be seen here to the Second Coming of the Lord, when God will reign with His saints forever.

[a]*He is* my rock, and [b]*there is* no
unrighteousness in Him.

PSALM 93†

The Eternal Reign of the Lord

THE [a]LORD reigns, He is clothed
with majesty;
The LORD is clothed,
[b]He has girded Himself with
strength.
Surely the world is established,
so that it cannot be [1]moved.
2 [a]Your throne *is* established from
of old;
You *are* from everlasting.

3 The floods have [1]lifted up,
O LORD,
The floods have lifted up their
voice;
The floods lift up their waves.
4 [a]The LORD on high *is* mightier
Than the noise of many waters,
Than the mighty waves of the
sea.

5 Your testimonies are very sure;
Holiness adorns Your house,
O LORD, [1]forever.

PSALM 94

God the Refuge of the Righteous

O LORD God, [a]to whom
vengeance belongs—
O God, to whom vengeance
belongs, shine forth!
2 Rise up, O [a]Judge of the earth;
[1]Render punishment to the
proud.
3 LORD, [a]how long will the
wicked,
How long will the wicked
triumph?

15 a[Deut. 32:4] b[Rom. 9:14]

PSALM 93

1 aPs. 96:10 bPs. 65:6 1*shaken*
2 aPs. 45:6; [Lam. 5:19]
3 1*raised up*
4 aPs. 65:7
5 1Lit. *for length of days*

PSALM 94

1 aDeut. 32:35; [Is. 35:4; Nah. 1:2; Rom. 12:19]
2 a[Gen. 18:25] 1*Repay with*
3 a[Job 20:5]
4 aPs. 31:18; Jude 15
7 aJob 22:13; Ps. 10:11 1*pay attention*
9 a[Ex. 4:11; Prov. 20:12]
10 1*disciplines* 2*Gentiles*
11 aJob 11:11; 1 Cor. 3:20
12 a[Deut. 8:5; Job 5:17; Ps. 119:71; Prov. 3:11, 12; Heb. 12:5, 6]
13 1*relief*
14 1*abandon*

4 They [a]utter speech, *and* speak
insolent things;
All the workers of iniquity boast
in themselves.
5 They break in pieces Your
people, O LORD,
And afflict Your heritage.
6 They slay the widow and the
stranger,
And murder the fatherless.
7 [a]Yet they say, "The LORD does
not see,
Nor does the God of Jacob
[1]understand."

8 Understand, you senseless
among the people;
And *you* fools, when will you
be wise?
9 [a]He who planted the ear, shall
He not hear?
He who formed the eye, shall
He not see?
10 He who [1]instructs the [2]nations,
shall He not correct,
He who teaches man
knowledge?
11 The LORD [a]knows the thoughts
of man,
That they *are* futile.

12 Blessed *is* the man whom You
[a]instruct, O LORD,
And teach out of Your law,
13 That You may give him
[1]rest from the days of
adversity,
Until the pit is dug for the
wicked.
14 For the LORD will not [1]cast off
His people,
Nor will He forsake His
inheritance.
15 But judgment will return to
righteousness,
And all the upright in heart will
follow it.

16 Who will rise up for me against
the evildoers?

93 (92, LXX) This is a psalm of enthronement of God as King. It is sung every Saturday evening at Great Vespers to inaugurate the Lord's Day, proclaiming Christ as King and Ruler over all. In Israel, as in the Orthodox Church, the day begins with sundown the night before (Gen. 1:5). Thus Sunday worship starts on Saturday at sundown with a service that Orthodox Christians consider of great importance. This psalm may be seen to refer to the first coming of the Lord, when he dwelt on earth, and established His Church.

Who will stand up for me
against the workers of
iniquity?
17 Unless the LORD *had been* my
help,
My soul would soon have
settled in silence.
18 If I say, "My foot slips,"
Your mercy, O LORD, will hold
me up.
19 In the multitude of my anxieties
within me,
Your comforts delight my soul.
20 Shall [a]the throne of iniquity,
which devises evil by law,
Have fellowship with You?
21 They gather together against the
life of the righteous,
And condemn [a]innocent blood.
22 But the LORD has been my
defense,
And my God the rock of my
refuge.
23 He has brought on them their
own iniquity,
And shall [1]cut them off in their
own wickedness;
The LORD our God shall cut
them off.

PSALM 95†

A Call to Worship and Obedience

OH come, let us sing to the LORD!
Let us shout joyfully to the Rock
of our salvation.
2 Let us come before His presence
with thanksgiving;
Let us shout joyfully to Him
with [a]psalms.
3 For [a]the LORD *is* the great God,
And the great King above all
gods.
4 [1]In His hand *are* the deep places
of the earth;
The heights of the hills *are* His
also.
5 [a]The sea *is* His, for He made it;
And His hands formed the dry
land.

6 Oh come, let us worship and
bow down;
Let [a]us kneel before the LORD
our Maker.
7 For He *is* our God,
And [a]we *are* the people of His
pasture,
And the sheep [1]of His hand.

[b]Today, if you will hear His
voice:
8 "Do not harden your hearts, as
in the [1]rebellion,
[a]As *in* the day of [2]trial in the
wilderness,
9 When [a]your fathers tested Me;
They tried Me, though they
[b]saw My work.
10 For [a]forty years I was [1]grieved
with *that* generation,
And said, 'It *is* a people who go
astray in their hearts,
And they do not know My
ways.'
11 So [a]I swore in My wrath,
'They shall not enter My rest.'"

PSALM 96†

A Song of Praise to God Coming in Judgment

OH, [a]sing to the LORD a new
song!
Sing to the LORD, all the earth.
2 Sing to the LORD, bless His
name;

20 [a]Amos 6:3
21 [a][Ex. 23:7]; Ps. 106:38; [Prov. 17:15]; Matt. 27:4
23 [1]*destroy them*

PSALM 95

2 [a]Eph. 5:19; James 5:13
3 [a][Ps. 96:4; 1 Cor. 8:5, 6]
4 [1]In His possession
5 [a]Gen. 1:9, 10; Jon. 1:9
6 [a]2 Chr. 6:13; Dan. 6:10; [Phil. 2:10]
7 [a]Ps. 79:13 [b]Heb. 3:7–11, 15; 4:7 [1]Under His care
8 [a]Ex. 17:2–7; Num. 20:13 [1]Or *Meribah*, lit. *Strife, Contention* [2]Or *Massah*, lit. *Trial, Testing*
9 [a]Ps. 78:18; [1 Cor. 10:9] [b]Num. 14:22
10 [a]Acts 7:36; 13:18; Heb. 3:10, 17 [1]*disgusted*
11 [a]Num. 14:23, 28–30; Deut. 1:35; Heb. 4:3, 5

PSALM 96

1 [a]1 Chr. 16:23–33

95 (94, LXX) This psalm is an invitation to worship, to fall down before God (v. 6). It is the third antiphon (psalm sung responsively) in the Divine Liturgy. Verses 7–11 are quoted in Heb. 3:7–11, showing the life of rest in God promised to His true worshipers, and secured for us through Jesus Christ. The psalm serves as a warning to those who fall short of God's rest through unbelief, here particularly directed to Israel.

96 (95, LXX) This, and the next four psalms (97—100), are psalms of praise and adoration. Verse 2b is sung as a refrain on the Day of the Annunciation. Throughout, the psalmist speaks about the call of the Gentiles, which will happen after their deliverance from their spiritual captivity when the Church has been established on earth.

Proclaim the good news of His
salvation from day to day.
3 Declare His glory among the
[1]nations,
His wonders among all peoples.

4 For [a]the LORD *is* great and
[b]greatly to be praised;
[c]He *is* to be feared above all
gods.
5 For [a]all the gods of the peoples
are idols,
[b]But the LORD made the
heavens.
6 Honor and majesty *are* before
Him;
Strength and [a]beauty *are* in His
sanctuary.

7 [a]Give[1] to the LORD, O families of
the peoples,
Give to the LORD glory and
strength.
8 [1]Give to the LORD the glory *due*
His name;
Bring an offering, and come into
His courts.
9 Oh, worship the LORD [a]in the
beauty of holiness!
Tremble before Him, all the
earth.

10 Say among the [1]nations,
[a]"The LORD reigns;
The world also is firmly
established,
It shall not be [2]moved;
[b]He shall judge the peoples
righteously."

11 [a]Let the heavens rejoice, and let
the earth be glad;
[b]Let the sea roar, and [1]all its
fullness;
12 Let the field be joyful, and all
that *is* in it.
Then all the trees of the woods
will rejoice before the LORD.
13 For He is coming, for He is
coming to judge the earth.
[a]He shall judge the world with
righteousness,
And the peoples with His truth.

3 [1]*Gentiles*
4 [a]Ps. 145:3
[b]Ps. 18:3
[c]Ps. 95:3
5 [a]1 Chr. 16:26; [Jer. 10:11]
[b]Ps. 115:15; Is. 42:5
6 [a]Ps. 29:2
7 [a]1 Chr. 16:28, 29; Ps. 29:1, 2
[1]*Ascribe*
8 [1]*Ascribe*
9 [a]1 Chr. 16:29; 2 Chr. 20:21; Ps. 29:2
10 [a]Ps. 93:1; 97:1; [Rev. 11:15; 19:6]
[b]Ps. 67:4
[1]*Gentiles*
[2]*shaken*
11 [a]Ps. 69:34; Is. 49:13
[b]Ps. 98:7
[1]*all that is in it*
13 [a][Rev. 19:11]

PSALM 97
1 [a][Ps. 96:10]
[1]Or *coastlands*
2 [a]Ex. 19:9; Deut. 4:11; 1 Kin. 8:12; Ps. 18:11
[b][Ps. 89:14]
3 [a]Ps. 18:8; Dan. 7:10; Hab. 3:5
4 [a]Ex. 19:18
5 [a]Ps. 46:6; Amos 9:5; Mic. 1:4; Nah. 1:5
6 [a]Ps. 19:1
7 [a][Ex. 20:4]
[b][Heb. 1:6]
9 [a]Ps. 83:18
[b]Ex. 18:11; Ps. 95:3; 96:4
10 [a][Ps. 34:14; Prov. 8:13; Amos 5:15; Rom. 12:9]
[b]Ps. 31:23; 145:20; Prov. 2:8
[c]Ps. 37:40; Jer. 15:21; Dan. 3:28
11 [a]Job 22:28; Ps. 112:4; Prov. 4:18

PSALM 97†

A Song of Praise to the Sovereign Lord

THE LORD [a]reigns;
Let the earth rejoice;
Let the multitude of [1]isles be
glad!

2 [a]Clouds and darkness surround
Him;
[b]Righteousness and justice *are*
the foundation of His throne.
3 [a]A fire goes before Him,
And burns up His enemies
round about.
4 [a]His lightnings light the world;
The earth sees and trembles.
5 [a]The mountains melt like wax at
the presence of the LORD,
At the presence of the Lord of
the whole earth.
6 [a]The heavens declare His
righteousness,
And all the peoples see His
glory.

7 [a]Let all be put to shame who
serve carved images,
Who boast of idols.
[b]Worship Him, all *you* gods.
8 Zion hears and is glad,
And the daughters of Judah
rejoice
Because of Your judgments,
O LORD.
9 For You, LORD, *are* [a]most high
above all the earth;
[b]You are exalted far above all
gods.

10 You who love the LORD,
[a]hate evil!
[b]He preserves the souls of His
saints;
[c]He delivers them out of the
hand of the wicked.
11 [a]Light is sown for the righteous,
And gladness for the upright in
heart.

97 (96, LXX) This psalm refers to the salvation of the world and the belief of all the nations in Christ.

12 [a]Rejoice in the LORD, you
righteous,
[b]And give thanks [1]at the
remembrance of [2]His holy
name.

PSALM 98†

Praise to the Lord for His Salvation and Judgment

A Psalm.

OH, [a]sing to the LORD a new
song!
For He has [b]done marvelous
things;
His right hand and His holy arm
have gained Him the victory.
2 [a]The LORD has made known His
salvation;
[b]His righteousness He has
revealed in the sight of the
[1]nations.
3 He has remembered His mercy
and His faithfulness to the
house of Israel;
[a]All the ends of the earth have
seen the salvation of our God.

4 Shout joyfully to the LORD, all
the earth;
Break forth in song, rejoice, and
sing praises.
5 Sing to the LORD with the harp,
With the harp and the sound of
a psalm,
6 With trumpets and the sound of
a horn;
Shout joyfully before the LORD,
the King.

7 Let the sea roar, and all its
fullness,
The world and those who dwell
in it;
8 Let the rivers clap *their* hands;
Let the hills be joyful together
before the LORD,
9 [a]For He is coming to judge the
earth.
With righteousness He shall
judge the world,
And the peoples with [1]equity.

PSALM 99†

The Footstool of the Lord

THE LORD reigns;
Let the peoples tremble!
[a]He dwells *between* the cherubim;
Let the earth be [1]moved!
2 The LORD *is* great in Zion,
And He *is* high above all the
peoples.
3 Let them praise Your great and
awesome name—
[1]He *is* holy.

4 The King's strength also loves
justice;
You have established equity;
You have executed justice and
righteousness in Jacob.
5 Exalt the LORD our God,
And worship at His footstool—
He *is* holy.

6 Moses and Aaron were among
His priests,
And Samuel was among those
who [a]called upon His name;
They called upon the LORD, and
He answered them.
7 He spoke to them in the cloudy
pillar;
They kept His testimonies and
the [1]ordinance He gave them.

8 You answered them, O LORD
our God;

12 [a]Ps. 33:1 [b]Ps. 30:4 [1]Or *for the memory* [2]Or *His holiness*

PSALM 98

1 [a]Ps. 33:3; Is. 42:10 [b]Ex. 15:11; Ps. 77:14
2 [a]Is. 52:10; [Luke 1:77; 2:30, 31] [b]Is. 62:2; Rom. 3:25 [1]*Gentiles*
3 [a][Is. 49:6]; Luke 3:6; [Acts 13:47; 28:28]
9 [a][Ps. 96:10, 13] [1]*uprightness*

PSALM 99

1 [a]Ex. 25:22; 1 Sam. 4:4; Ps. 80:1 [1]*shaken*
3 [1]Or *It*
6 [a]1 Sam. 7:9; 12:18
7 [1]*statute*

98 (97, LXX) This psalm is similar to Ps. 96. Verses 2, 3, which mention salvation for Jew and Gentile alike, are sung at the Feast of the Presentation of Christ in the Temple. Other portions of the psalm are sung on Palm Sunday. The psalmist sings of the first coming of Christ, as well as the faith of all the nations in Him—those who would realize all the promises given to the Fathers of the OT. For this reason he exhorts all believers to sing the triumphal hymn, **for He has done marvelous things** (v. 1).

99 (98, LXX) The footstool of the Lord is seen by most patristic and liturgical sources as His Cross. Thus, this psalm, highlighted by v. 5, is sung at the Feast of the Exaltation of the Cross. Verses 1–4 refer to the Kingdom of God. **Them** in v. 8 refers to the high priests.

You were to them God-Who-Forgives,
Though You took vengeance on their deeds.
9 Exalt the LORD our God,
And worship at His holy hill;
For the LORD our God *is* holy.

PSALM 100†

A Song of Procession

[a]A Psalm of Thanksgiving.

MAKE [a]a joyful shout to the LORD, [1]all you lands!
2 Serve the LORD with gladness;
Come before His presence with singing.
3 Know that the LORD, He *is* God;
[a]*It is* He *who* has made us, and [1]not we ourselves;
[b]*We are* His people and the sheep of His pasture.

4 [a]Enter into His gates with thanksgiving,
And into His courts with praise.
Be thankful to Him, *and* bless His name.
5 For the LORD *is* good;
[a]His mercy *is* everlasting,
And His truth *endures* to all generations.

PSALM 101†

Dedication to God

A Psalm of David.

I WILL sing of mercy and justice;
To You, O LORD, I will sing praises.
2 I will behave wisely in a [1]perfect way.
Oh, when will You come to me?
I will [a]walk within my house with a perfect heart.

3 I will set nothing [1]wicked before my eyes;
[a]I hate the work of those [b]who fall away;
It shall not cling to me.
4 A perverse heart shall depart from me;
I will not [a]know wickedness.

5 Whoever secretly slanders his neighbor,
Him I will destroy;
[a]The one who has a haughty look and a proud heart,
Him I will not endure.

6 My eyes *shall be* on the faithful of the land,
That they may dwell with me;
He who walks in a [1]perfect way,
He shall serve me.
7 He who works deceit shall not dwell within my house;
He who tells lies shall not [1]continue in my presence.
8 [a]Early I will destroy all the wicked of the land,
That I may cut off all the evildoers [b]from the city of the LORD.

PSALM 102†

A Prayer in Affliction

A Prayer of the afflicted, [a]when he is overwhelmed and pours out his complaint before the LORD.

HEAR my prayer, O LORD,
And let my cry come to You.

PSALM 100
title [a]Ps. 145:title
1 [a]Ps. 95:1 [1]Lit. *all the earth*
3 [a]Job 10:3, 8; Ps. 119:73; 139:13, 14; [Eph. 2:10] [b]Ps. 95:7; [Is. 40:11]; Ezek. 34:30, 31 [1]So with Kt., LXX, Vg.; Qr., many Heb. mss., Tg. *we are His*
4 [a]Ps. 66:13; 116:17–19
5 [a]Ps. 136:1

PSALM 101
2 [a]1 Kin. 11:4 [1]*blameless*
3 [a]Ps. 97:10 [b]Josh. 23:6 [1]*worthless*
4 [a][Ps. 119:115]
5 [a]Prov. 6:17
6 [1]*blameless*
7 [1]Lit. *be established*
8 [a][Ps. 75:10]; Jer. 21:12 [b]Ps. 48:2, 8

PSALM 102
title [a]Ps. 61:2

100 (99, LXX) The closing psalm of the series of five on the theme of praise is an OT processional hymn. A popular psalm for devotional reading, it has no special liturgical use apart from its place in the weekly psalm cycle. All those who embrace the faith are exhorted to give thanks and praises to God for everything accomplished on their behalf.
101 (100, LXX) This psalm is a morning prayer used daily at the First Hour—a day-by-day dedication of the worshiper to personal righteousness (see vv. 3, 4). Within the psalm the perfect man is described, the one who conducts His life according to God's will. We are taught godly behavior which characterizes all who desire to attain the Kingdom of God (vv. 1–5).
102 (101, LXX) This psalm is a prayer in affliction, with v. 13a sung on Easter morning *(continued on next page)*

2 [a]Do not hide Your face from me
in the day of my trouble;
Incline Your ear to me;
In the day that I call, answer me
speedily.

3 For my days [1]are [a]consumed
like smoke,
And my bones are burned like
a hearth.
4 My heart is stricken and
withered like grass,
So that I forget to eat my bread.
5 Because of the sound of my
groaning
My bones cling to my [1]skin.
6 I am like a pelican of the
wilderness;
I am like an owl of the desert.
7 I lie awake,
And am like a sparrow alone on
the housetop.

8 My enemies reproach me all day
long;
Those who deride me swear an
oath against me.
9 For I have eaten ashes like
bread,
And mingled my drink with
weeping,
10 Because of Your indignation
and Your wrath;
For You have lifted me up and
cast me away.
11 My days *are* like a shadow that
lengthens,
And I wither away like grass.

12 But You, O LORD, shall endure
forever,
And the remembrance of Your
name to all generations.
13 You will arise *and* have mercy
on Zion;
For the time to favor her,
Yes, the set time, has come.
14 For Your servants take pleasure
in her stones,
And show favor to her dust.

2 [a]Ps. 27:9; 69:17
3 [a]James 4:14 [1]Lit. *end in*
5 [1]*flesh*
15 [a]1 Kin. 8:43 [1]*Gentiles*
16 [a][Is. 60:1, 2]
17 [a]Neh. 1:6; Ps. 22:24
18 [a]Deut. 31:19; [Rom. 15:4; 1 Cor. 10:11] [b]Ps. 22:31
19 [a]Deut. 26:15; Ps. 14:2
20 [a]Ps. 79:11
21 [a]Ps. 22:22
22 [a][Is. 2:2, 3; 49:22, 23; 60:3]; Zech. 8:20–23
23 [a]Job 21:21
24 [a][Ps. 39:13]; Is. 38:10 [b]Job 36:26; [Ps. 90:2]; Hab. 1:12
25 [a][Gen. 1:1; Neh. 9:6; Heb. 1:10–12]
26 [a]Is. 34:4; 51:6; Matt. 24:35; [2 Pet. 3:7, 10–12]; Rev. 20:11 [1]*continue*

15 So the [1]nations shall [a]fear the
name of the LORD,
And all the kings of the earth
Your glory.
16 For the LORD shall build up
Zion;
[a]He shall appear in His glory.
17 [a]He shall regard the prayer of the
destitute,
And shall not despise their
prayer.

18 This will be [a]written for the
generation to come,
That [b]a people yet to be created
may praise the LORD.
19 For He [a]looked down from the
height of His sanctuary;
From heaven the LORD viewed
the earth,
20 [a]To hear the groaning of the
prisoner,
To release those appointed to
death,
21 To [a]declare the name of the
LORD in Zion,
And His praise in Jerusalem,
22 [a]When the peoples are gathered
together,
And the kingdoms, to serve the
LORD.

23 He weakened my strength in
the way;
He [a]shortened my days.
24 [a]I said, "O my God,
Do not take me away in the
midst of my days;
[b]Your years *are* throughout all
generations.
25 [a]Of old You laid the foundation
of the earth,
And the heavens *are* the work
of Your hands.
26 [a]They will perish, but You will
[1]endure;
Yes, they will all grow old like
a garment;
Like a cloak You will change
them,
And they will be changed.

(continued from previous page)
before the reading of the gospel. Verses 25–27 are quoted in Heb. 1:10–12 in the context of establishing the Son of God as eternal Creator. The psalmist implores God to have mercy on His people. He proclaims the call of all **the nations** (v. 15)—accomplished after the Incarnation of Jesus Christ.

27 But [a]You *are* the same,
And Your years will have no end.
28 [a]The children of Your servants will continue,
And their descendants will be established before You."

PSALM 103†

Praise for Mercy and Angelic Hosts

A Psalm of David.

BLESS [a]the LORD, O my soul;
And all that is within me, *bless* His holy name!
2 Bless the LORD, O my soul,
And forget not all His benefits:
3 [a]Who forgives all your iniquities,
Who [b]heals all your diseases,
4 Who redeems your life from destruction,
[a]Who crowns you with lovingkindness and tender mercies,
5 Who satisfies your mouth with good *things*,
So that [a]your youth is renewed like the eagle's.

6 The LORD executes righteousness
And justice for all who are oppressed.
7 [a]He made known His ways to Moses,
His acts to the children of Israel.
8 [a]The LORD *is* merciful and gracious,
Slow to anger, and abounding in mercy.
9 [a]He will not always strive *with us*,
Nor will He keep *His anger* forever.
10 [a]He has not dealt with us according to our sins,
Nor punished us according to our iniquities.
11 For as the heavens are high above the earth,
So great is His mercy toward those who fear Him;
12 As far as the east is from the west,
So far has He [a]removed our transgressions from us.
13 [a]As a father pities *his* children,
So the LORD pities those who fear Him.
14 For He [1]knows our frame;
He remembers that we *are* dust.

15 *As for* man, [a]his days *are* like grass;
As a flower of the field, so he flourishes.
16 [a]For the wind passes over it, and it is [1]gone,
And [b]its place remembers it no more.
17 But the mercy of the LORD *is* from everlasting to everlasting
On those who fear Him,
And His righteousness to children's children,
18 [a]To such as keep His covenant,
And to those who remember His commandments to do them.

19 The LORD has established His throne in heaven,
And [a]His kingdom rules over all.

20 [a]Bless the LORD, you His angels,
Who excel in strength, who [b]do His word,
Heeding the voice of His word.
21 Bless the LORD, all *you* His hosts,
[a]*You* [1]ministers of His, who do His pleasure.
22 Bless the LORD, all His works,
In all places of His dominion.

Bless the LORD, O my soul!

27 [a][Is. 41:4; 43:10; Mal. 3:6; Heb. 13:8]; James 1:17
28 [a]Ps. 69:36

PSALM 103
1 [a]Ps. 104:1, 35
3 [a]Ps. 130:8; Is. 33:24 [b][Ex. 15:26]; Ps. 147:3; [Is. 53:5]; Jer. 17:14
4 [a][Ps. 5:12]
5 [a][Is. 40:31]
7 [a]Ex. 33:12–17; Ps. 147:19
8 [a][Ex. 34:6, 7; Num. 14:18]; Deut. 5:10; Neh. 9:17; Ps. 86:15; Jer. 32:18; Jon. 4:2; James 5:11
9 [a][Ps. 30:5; Is. 57:16]; Jer. 3:5; [Mic. 7:18]
10 [a][Ezra 9:13; Lam. 3:22]
12 [a][2 Sam. 12:13; Is. 38:17; 43:25; Zech. 3:9; Heb. 9:26]
13 [a]Mal. 3:17
14 [1]Understands our constitution
15 [a]Is. 40:6–8; James 1:10, 11; 1 Pet. 1:24
16 [a][Is. 40:7] [b]Job 7:10 [1]*not*
18 [a][Deut. 7:9]; Ps. 25:10
19 [a][Ps. 47:2; Dan. 4:17, 25]
20 [a]Ps. 148:2 [b][Matt. 6:10]
21 [a][Heb. 1:14] [1]*servants*

103 (102, LXX) This is a beloved morning psalm, the fifth of the six Matins psalms (see note on Ps. 3). Psalm 103 is often used as the opening antiphon (psalm sung responsively) in the Orthodox Divine Liturgy. Verses 20, 21 speak of the angels, and this passage is sung on days on which the angels are honored in the Church. Within this psalm, the people of God are taught to praise Him for His great benevolence, which is proclaimed by Christ's banishing of sin and by the glory of His Resurrection.

PSALM 104†

A Poem of Creation

BLESS [a]the LORD, O my soul!

O LORD my God, You are very
great:
You are clothed with honor and
majesty,
2 Who cover *Yourself* with light as
with a garment,
Who stretch out the heavens
like a curtain.

3 [a]He lays the beams of His upper
chambers in the waters,
Who makes the clouds His
chariot,
Who walks on the wings of the
wind,
4 Who makes His angels spirits,
His [1]ministers a flame of fire.

5 *You who* [1]laid the foundations of
the earth,
So *that* it should not be moved
forever,
6 You [a]covered it with the deep
as *with* a garment;
The waters stood above the
mountains.
7 At Your rebuke they fled;
At the voice of Your thunder
they hastened away.
8 [1]They went up over the
mountains;
They went down into the
valleys,
To the place which You founded
for them.
9 You have [a]set a boundary that
they may not pass over,
[b]That they may not return to
cover the earth.

10 He sends the springs into the
valleys;
They flow among the hills.
11 They give drink to every beast
of the field;
The wild donkeys quench their
thirst.
12 By them the birds of the
heavens have their home;
They sing among the branches.
13 [a]He waters the hills from His
upper chambers;
The earth is satisfied with
[b]the fruit of Your works.

14 [a]He causes the grass to grow for
the cattle,
And vegetation for the service
of man,
That he may bring forth
[b]food from the earth,
15 And [a]wine *that* makes glad the
heart of man,
Oil to make *his* face shine,
And bread *which* strengthens
man's heart.
16 The trees of the LORD are full *of
sap*,
The cedars of Lebanon which
He planted,
17 Where the birds make their
nests;
The stork has her home in the
fir trees.
18 The high hills *are* for the wild
goats;
The cliffs are a refuge for the
[a]rock[1] badgers.

19 [a]He appointed the moon for
seasons;
The [b]sun knows its going
down.
20 [a]You make darkness, and it is
night,
In which all the beasts of the
forest creep about.
21 [a]The young lions roar after their
prey,
And seek their food from God.
22 *When* the sun rises, they gather
together
And lie down in their dens.

PSALM 104
1 [a]Ps. 103:1
3 [a][Amos 9:6]
4 [1]*servants*
5 [1]Lit. *founded the earth upon her bases*
6 [a]Gen. 1:6
8 [1]Or *The mountains rose up; The valleys sank down*
9 [a]Job 26:10; Ps. 33:7; [Jer. 5:22] [b]Gen. 9:11–15
13 [a]Ps. 147:8 [b]Jer. 10:13
14 [a]Gen. 1:29 [b]Job 28:5
15 [a]Judg. 9:13; Ps. 23:5; Prov. 31:6; Eccl. 10:19
18 [a]Lev. 11:5 [1]*rock hyraxes*
19 [a]Gen. 1:14 [b]Job 38:12; Ps. 19:6
20 [a][Ps. 74:16; Is. 45:7]
21 [a]Job 38:39

104 (103, LXX) The great psalm of Vespers, this psalm is a poetic rendition of Genesis 1. Since the new day begins at sundown (see note on Ps. 93), Ps. 104 is sung by the faithful to give praise and thanksgiving to the Creator. Because of v. 30, this psalm is also sung on Pentecost. The psalmist shows the providence of God: He provides for the heavens and the earth, and does not neglect even the smallest creatures.

23 Man goes out to [a]his work
And to his labor until the
evening.

24 [a]O LORD, how manifold are Your
works!
In wisdom You have made them
all.
The earth is full of Your
[b]possessions—
25 This great and wide sea,
In which *are* innumerable
teeming things,
Living things both small and
great.
26 There the ships sail about;
There is that [a]Leviathan[1]
Which You have [2]made to play
there.

27 [a]These all wait for You,
That You may give *them* their
food in due season.
28 *What* You give them they gather
in;
You open Your hand, they are
filled with good.
29 You hide Your face, they are
troubled;
[a]You take away their breath,
they die and return to their
dust.
30 [a]You send forth Your Spirit, they
are created;
And You renew the face of the
earth.

31 May the glory of the LORD
endure forever;
May the LORD [a]rejoice in His
works.
32 He looks on the earth, and it
[a]trembles;
[b]He touches the hills, and they
smoke.

33 [a]I will sing to the LORD as long
as I live;
I will sing praise to my God
while I have my being.
34 May my [a]meditation be sweet
to Him;
I will be glad in the LORD.
35 May [a]sinners be consumed from
the earth,
And the wicked be no more.

Bless the LORD, O my soul!
[1]Praise the LORD!

PSALM 105†

The Eternal Faithfulness of the Lord to Israel

OH, [a]give thanks to the LORD!
Call upon His name;
[b]Make known His deeds among
the peoples!
2 Sing to Him, sing psalms to
Him;
[a]Talk of all His wondrous works!
3 Glory in His holy name;
Let the hearts of those rejoice
who seek the LORD!
4 Seek the LORD and His strength;
[a]Seek His face evermore!
5 [a]Remember His marvelous
works which He has done,
His wonders, and the
judgments of His mouth,
6 O seed of Abraham His servant,
You children of Jacob, His
chosen ones!

7 He *is* the LORD our God;
[a]His judgments *are* in all the
earth.

23 [a]Gen. 3:19
24 [a]Ps. 40:5; Prov. 3:19; [Jer. 10:12]; 51:15 [b]Ps. 65:9
26 [a]Job 41:1; Is. 27:1 [1]A large sea creature of unknown identity [2]Lit. *formed*
27 [a]Job 36:31; Ps. 136:25
29 [a]Job 34:15; [Eccl. 12:7]
30 [a]Is. 32:15
31 [a]Gen. 1:31; Prov. 8:31
32 [a]Hab. 3:10 [b]Ex. 19:18; Ps. 144:5
33 [a]Ps. 63:4
34 [a]Ps. 19:14
35 [a]Ps. 37:38 [1]Heb. *Hallelujah*

PSALM 105
1 [a]1 Chr. 16:8–22, 34; Ps. 106:1; Is. 12:4 [b]Ps. 145:12
2 [a]Ps. 119:27
4 [a]Ps. 27:8
5 [a]Ps. 77:11
7 [a][Is. 26:9]

105—107 (104—106, LXX) These three are lengthy historical and poetic psalms, revealing the heritage of Israel.

Psalm 105 begins with praise to God for His deeds at the time of Abraham, continues telling of Isaac, Jacob, and Moses, and closes with the Exodus.

Psalm 106 continues with the days of Israel in Egypt and the Exodus, but also chastens the people for their faithlessness and disbelief—manifest in such actions as forgetting God's **works** (v. 13), making the golden **calf** (v. 19), despising the **pleasant** (Promised) **land** (v. 24), joining themselves to **Baal** (v. 28), and mingling with the pagans (vv. 35–38). But even with this, God is faithful and hears their cry (vv. 44–48) and does the same for us!.

Psalm 107 completes the trilogy of Israel's history. It reveals that no matter how great the desperation of God's people, God, who always does wonderful works for His people, will surely deliver them. And those who are wise to **observe** will **understand** His mercy (v. 43).

8 He [a]remembers His covenant forever,
The word *which* He commanded, for a thousand generations,
9 [a]*The covenant* which He made with Abraham,
And His oath to Isaac,
10 And confirmed it to Jacob for a statute,
To Israel *as* an everlasting covenant,
11 Saying, [a]"To you I will give the land of Canaan
As the allotment of your inheritance,"
12 [a]When they were few in number,
Indeed very few, [b]and strangers in it.

13 When they went from one nation to another,
From *one* kingdom to another people,
14 [a]He permitted no one to do them wrong;
Yes, [b]He rebuked kings for their sakes,
15 *Saying,* "Do not touch My anointed ones,
And do My prophets no harm."

16 Moreover [a]He called for a famine in the land;
He destroyed all the [b]provision of bread.
17 [a]He sent a man before them—
Joseph—*who* [b]was sold as a slave.
18 [a]They hurt his feet with fetters,
[1]He was laid in irons.
19 Until the time that his word came to pass,
[a]The word of the LORD tested him.
20 [a]The king sent and released him,
The ruler of the people let him go free.
21 [a]He made him lord of his house,
And ruler of all his possessions,
22 To [1]bind his princes at his pleasure,
And teach his elders wisdom.

23 [a]Israel also came into Egypt,
And Jacob dwelt [b]in the land of Ham.

24 [a]He increased His people greatly,
And made them stronger than their enemies.
25 [a]He turned their heart to hate His people,
To deal craftily with His servants.

26 [a]He sent Moses His servant,
And Aaron whom He had chosen.
27 They [a]performed His signs among them,
And wonders in the land of Ham.
28 He sent darkness, and made *it* dark;
And they did not rebel against His word.
29 [a]He turned their waters into blood,
And killed their fish.
30 [a]Their land abounded with frogs,
Even in the chambers of their kings.
31 [a]He spoke, and there came swarms of flies,
And lice in all their territory.
32 [a]He gave them hail for rain,
And flaming fire in their land.
33 [a]He struck their vines also, and their fig trees,
And splintered the trees of their territory.
34 [a]He spoke, and locusts came,
Young locusts without number,
35 And ate up all the vegetation in their land,
And devoured the fruit of their ground.
36 [a]He also [1]destroyed all the firstborn in their land,
[b]The first of all their strength.

37 [a]He also brought them out with silver and gold,
And *there was* none feeble among His tribes.
38 [a]Egypt was glad when they departed,
For the fear of them had fallen upon them.
39 [a]He spread a cloud for a covering,
And fire to give light in the night.

8 [a]Luke 1:72 **9** [a]Gen. 17:2; Luke 1:73; [Gal. 3:17]; Heb. 6:17 **11** [a]Gen. 13:15; 15:18 **12** [a]Gen. 34:30; [Deut. 7:7] [b]Gen. 23:4; Heb. 11:9 **14** [a]Gen. 35:5 [b]Gen. 12:17 **16** [a]Gen. 41:54 [b]Lev. 26:26; Is. 3:1; Ezek. 4:16 **17** [a][Gen. 45:5] [b]Gen. 37:28, 36; Acts 7:9 **18** [a]Gen. 40:15 [1]*His soul came into iron* **19** [a]Gen. 39:11–21; 41:25, 42, 43 **20** [a]Gen. 41:14 **21** [a]Gen. 41:40–44 **22** [1]Bind as prisoners **23** [a]Gen. 46:6; Acts 7:15 [b]Ps. 78:51

24 [a]Ex. 1:7, 9 **25** [a]Ex. 1:8–10; 4:21 **26** [a]Ex. 3:10; 4:12–15 **27** [a]Ex. 7—12; Ps. 78:43 **29** [a]Ex. 7:20, 21; Ps. 78:44 **30** [a]Ex. 8:6 **31** [a]Ex. 8:16, 17 **32** [a]Ex. 9:23–25 **33** [a]Ps. 78:47 **34** [a]Ex. 10:4 **36** [a]Ex. 12:29; 13:15; Ps. 135:8; 136:10 [b]Gen. 49:3 [1]Lit. *struck down* **37** [a]Ex. 12:35, 36 **38** [a]Ex. 12:33 **39** [a]Ex. 13:21; Neh. 9:12; Ps. 78:14; Is. 4:5

40 [a]*The people* asked, and He brought quail,
And [b]satisfied them with the bread of heaven.
41 [a]He opened the rock, and water gushed out;
It ran in the dry places *like* a river.

42 For He remembered [a]His holy promise,
And Abraham His servant.
43 He brought out His people with joy,
His chosen ones with [1]gladness.
44 [a]He gave them the lands of the [1]Gentiles,
And they inherited the labor of the nations,
45 [a]That they might observe His statutes
And keep His laws.

[1]Praise the LORD!

PSALM 106†

The Disbelief of Israel and God's Faithfulness

PRAISE[1] the LORD!

[a]Oh, give thanks to the LORD, for *He is* good!
For His mercy *endures* forever.
2 Who can [1]utter the mighty acts of the LORD?
Who can declare all His praise?
3 Blessed *are* those who keep justice,
And [1]he who [a]does righteousness at [b]all times!

4 [a]Remember me, O LORD, with the favor *You have toward* Your people.
Oh, visit me with Your salvation,
5 That I may see the benefit of Your chosen ones,
That I may rejoice in the gladness of Your nation,
That I may glory with [1]Your inheritance.

6 [a]We have sinned with our fathers,
We have committed iniquity,
We have done wickedly.
7 Our fathers in Egypt did not understand Your wonders;
They did not remember the multitude of Your mercies,
[a]But rebelled by the sea—the Red Sea.

8 Nevertheless He saved them for His name's sake,
[a]That He might make His mighty power known.
9 [a]He rebuked the Red Sea also, and it dried up;
So [b]He led them through the depths,
As through the wilderness.
10 He [a]saved them from the hand of him who hated *them*,
And redeemed them from the hand of the enemy.
11 [a]The waters covered their enemies;
There was not one of them left.
12 [a]Then they believed His words;
They sang His praise.

13 [a]They soon forgot His works;
They did not wait for His counsel,
14 [a]But lusted exceedingly in the wilderness,
And tested God in the desert.
15 [a]And He gave them their request,
But [b]sent leanness into their soul.

16 When [a]they envied Moses in the camp,
And Aaron the saint of the LORD,
17 [a]The earth opened up and swallowed Dathan,
And covered the faction of Abiram.
18 [a]A fire was kindled in their company;
The flame burned up the wicked.

19 [a]They made a calf in Horeb,
And worshiped the molded image.

---

40 [a]Ex. 16:12 [b]Ps. 78:24
41 [a]Ex. 17:6; Num. 20:11; Ps. 78:15; 114:8; Is. 48:21; [1 Cor. 10:4]
42 [a]Gen. 15:13, 14; Ps. 105:8
43 [1]*a joyful shout*
44 [a]Josh. 11:16–23; 13:7; Ps. 78:55 [1]*nations*
45 [a][Deut. 4:1, 40] [1]Heb. *Hallelujah*

PSALM 106
1 [a]1 Chr. 16:34, 41 [1]Heb. *Hallelujah*
2 [1]*express*
3 [a]Ps. 15:2 [b][Gal. 6:9] [1]LXX, Syr., Tg., Vg. *those who do*
4 [a]Ps. 119:132
5 [1]The people of Your inheritance
6 [a]1 Kin. 8:47; [Ezra 9:7; Neh. 1:7; Jer. 3:25; Dan. 9:5]
7 [a]Ex. 14:11, 12
8 [a]Ex. 9:16
9 [a]Ex. 14:21; Ps. 18:15; Is. 51:10; Nah. 1:4 [b]Is. 63:11–13
10 [a]Ex. 14:30
11 [a]Ex. 14:27, 28; 15:5
12 [a]Ex. 15:1–21
13 [a]Ex. 15:24; 16:2; 17:2
14 [a]Num. 11:4; 1 Cor. 10:6
15 [a]Num. 11:31 [b]Is. 10:16
16 [a]Num. 16:1–3
17 [a]Num. 16:31, 32; Deut. 11:6
18 [a]Num. 16:35, 46
19 [a]Ex. 32:1–4; Deut. 9:8; Acts 7:41

20 Thus [a]they changed their glory
Into the image of an ox that eats grass.
21 They forgot God their Savior,
Who had done great things in Egypt,
22 Wondrous works in the land of Ham,
Awesome things by the Red Sea.
23 [a]Therefore He said that He would destroy them,
Had not Moses His chosen one [b]stood before Him in the breach,
To turn away His wrath, lest He destroy *them.*

24 Then they despised [a]the pleasant land;
They [b]did not believe His word,
25 [a]But complained in their tents,
And did not heed the voice of the LORD.
26 [a]Therefore He raised up His hand *in an oath* against them,
[b]To [1]overthrow them in the wilderness,
27 [a]To [1]overthrow their descendants among the [2]nations,
And to scatter them in the lands.
28 [a]They joined themselves also to Baal of Peor,
And ate sacrifices [1]made to the dead.
29 Thus they provoked *Him* to anger with their deeds,
And the plague broke out among them.
30 [a]Then Phinehas stood up and intervened,
And the plague was stopped.
31 And that was accounted to him [a]for righteousness
To all generations forevermore.

32 [a]They angered *Him* also at the waters of [1]strife,
[b]So that it went ill with Moses on account of them;
33 [a]Because they rebelled against His Spirit,
So that he spoke rashly with his lips.

20 [a]Rom. 1:23
23 [a]Ex. 32:10 [b]Ezek. 22:30
24 [a]Deut. 8:7 [b][Heb. 3:18, 19]
25 [a]Num. 14:2, 27
26 [a]Ezek. 20:15, 16 [b]Num. 14:28–30 [1]*make them fall*
27 [a]Lev. 26:33 [1]*make their descendants fall also* [2]*Gentiles*
28 [a]Hos. 9:10 [1]*offered*
30 [a]Num. 25:7, 8
31 [a]Num. 25:11–13
32 [a]Num. 20:3–13 [b]Deut. 1:37; 3:26 [1]Or *Meribah*
33 [a]Num. 20:3, 10
34 [a]Judg. 1:21 [b][Deut. 7:2, 16]
35 [a]Judg. 3:5, 6
36 [a]Judg. 2:12 [b]Deut. 7:16
37 [a]2 Kin. 16:3; 17:17 [b][Lev. 17:7]
38 [a][Num. 35:33]
39 [a]Ezek. 20:18 [b][Lev. 17:7] [1]*became unclean* [2]Were unfaithful
40 [a]Judg. 2:14 [b][Deut. 9:29; 32:9]
41 [a]Judg. 2:14
43 [a]Judg. 2:16
44 [a]Judg. 3:9; 6:7; 10:10
45 [a][Lev. 26:41, 42] [b]Judg. 2:18 [c]Ps. 69:16
46 [a]Ezra 9:9
47 [a]1 Chr. 16:35, 36

34 [a]They did not destroy the peoples,
[b]Concerning whom the LORD had commanded them,
35 [a]But they mingled with the Gentiles
And learned their works;
36 [a]They served their idols,
[b]Which became a snare to them.
37 [a]They even sacrificed their sons
And their daughters to [b]demons,
38 And shed innocent blood,
The blood of their sons and daughters,
Whom they sacrificed to the idols of Canaan;
And [a]the land was polluted with blood.
39 Thus they [1]were [a]defiled by their own works,
And [b]played[2] the harlot by their own deeds.

40 Therefore [a]the wrath of the LORD was kindled against His people,
So that He abhorred [b]His own inheritance.
41 And [a]He gave them into the hand of the Gentiles,
And those who hated them ruled over them.
42 Their enemies also oppressed them,
And they were brought into subjection under their hand.
43 [a]Many times He delivered them;
But they rebelled in their counsel,
And were brought low for their iniquity.

44 Nevertheless He regarded their affliction,
When [a]He heard their cry;
45 [a]And for their sake He remembered His covenant,
And [b]relented [c]according to the multitude of His mercies.
46 [a]He also made them to be pitied
By all those who carried them away captive.

47 [a]Save us, O LORD our God,
And gather us from among the Gentiles,

To give thanks to Your holy
name,
To triumph in Your praise.

48 [a]Blessed *be* the LORD God of
Israel
From everlasting to everlasting!
And let all the people say,
"Amen!"

[1]Praise the LORD!

BOOK FIVE: Psalms 107–150

PSALM 107†

Thanksgiving to the Lord for His Great Works of Deliverance

OH, [a]give thanks to the LORD, for
He is good!
For His [1]mercy *endures* forever.
2 Let the redeemed of the LORD
say *so,*
Whom He has redeemed from
the hand of the enemy,
3 And [a]gathered out of the lands,
From the east and from the
west,
From the north and from the
south.

4 They wandered in [a]the
wilderness in a desolate way;
They found no city to dwell in.
5 Hungry and thirsty,
Their soul fainted in them.
6 [a]Then they cried out to the LORD
in their trouble,
And He delivered them out of
their distresses.
7 And He led them forth by the
[a]right way,
That they might go to a city for
a dwelling place.
8 [a]Oh, that *men* would give thanks
to the LORD *for* His goodness,
And *for* His wonderful works to
the children of men!
9 For [a]He satisfies the longing
soul,
And fills the hungry soul with
goodness.

10 Those who [a]sat in darkness and
in the shadow of death,
[b]Bound[1] in affliction and irons—

48 [a]Ps. 41:13 [1]Heb. *Halle-lujah*

PSALM 107

1 [a]1 Chr. 16:34; Ps. 106:1; Jer. 33:11 [1]Heb. same as *goodness,* vv. 8, 15, 21, 31, and *loving-kindness,* v. 43
3 [a]Is. 43:5, 6; Jer. 29:14; 31:8–10; [Ezek. 39:27, 28]
4 [a]Num. 14:33; 32:13; [Deut. 2:7; 32:10]; Josh. 5:6; 14:10
6 [a]Ps. 50:15; [Hos. 5:15]
7 [a]Ezra 8:21; Ps. 5:8; Jer. 31:9
8 [a]Ps. 107:15, 21
9 [a][Ps. 34:10; Luke 1:53]
10 [a][Is. 42:7; Mic. 7:8; Luke 1:79] [b]Job 36:8 [1]*Prisoners*
11 [a]Lam. 3:42 [b][Ps. 73:24] [1]*scorned*
12 [a]Ps. 22:11
14 [a]Ps. 68:6
16 [a]Is. 45:1, 2
17 [a][Is. 65:6, 7; Jer. 30:14, 15]; Lam. 3:39; Ezek. 24:23
18 [a]Job 33:20 [b]Job 33:22
20 [a]Matt. 8:8 [b]2 Kin. 20:5; Ps. 30:2 [c]Job 33:28, 30
22 [a]Lev. 7:12; Ps. 50:14; Heb. 13:15 [b]Ps. 9:11 [1]*joyful singing*

11 Because they [a]rebelled against
the words of God,
And [1]despised [b]the counsel of
the Most High,
12 Therefore He brought down
their heart with labor;
They fell down, and *there was*
[a]none to help.
13 Then they cried out to the LORD
in their trouble,
And He saved them out of their
distresses.
14 [a]He brought them out of
darkness and the shadow of
death,
And broke their chains in
pieces.
15 Oh, that *men* would give thanks
to the LORD *for* His goodness,
And *for* His wonderful works to
the children of men!
16 For He has [a]broken the gates of
bronze,
And cut the bars of iron in two.

17 Fools, [a]because of their
transgression,
And because of their iniquities,
were afflicted.
18 [a]Their soul abhorred all manner
of food,
And they [b]drew near to the
gates of death.
19 Then they cried out to the LORD
in their trouble,
And He saved them out of their
distresses.
20 [a]He sent His word and [b]healed
them,
And [c]delivered *them* from their
destructions.
21 Oh, that *men* would give thanks
to the LORD *for* His goodness,
And *for* His wonderful works to
the children of men!
22 [a]Let them sacrifice the sacrifices
of thanksgiving,
And [b]declare His works with
[1]rejoicing.

23 Those who go down to the sea
in ships,
Who do business on great
waters,
24 They see the works of the LORD,
And His wonders in the deep.

25 For He commands and [a]raises the stormy wind,
Which lifts up the waves of the sea.
26 They mount up to the heavens,
They go down again to the depths;
[a]Their soul melts because of trouble.
27 They reel to and fro, and stagger like a drunken man,
And [1]are at their wits' end.
28 Then they cry out to the LORD in their trouble,
And He brings them out of their distresses.
29 [a]He calms the storm,
So that its waves are still.
30 Then they are glad because they are quiet;
So He guides them to their desired haven.
31 [a]Oh, that *men* would give thanks to the LORD *for* His goodness,
And *for* His wonderful works to the children of men!
32 Let them exalt Him also
[a]in the assembly of the people,
And praise Him in the company of the elders.

33 He [a]turns rivers into a wilderness,
And the watersprings into dry ground;
34 A [a]fruitful land into [1]barrenness,
For the wickedness of those who dwell in it.
35 [a]He turns a wilderness into pools of water,
And dry land into watersprings.
36 There He makes the hungry dwell,
That they may establish a city for a dwelling place,
37 And sow fields and plant vineyards,
That they may yield a fruitful harvest.
38 [a]He also blesses them, and they multiply greatly;
And He does not let their cattle [b]decrease.

39 When they are [a]diminished and brought low
Through oppression, affliction and sorrow,
40 [a]He pours contempt on princes,
And causes them to wander in the wilderness *where there is* no way;
41 [a]Yet He sets the poor on high, far from affliction,
And [b]makes *their* families like a flock.
42 [a]The righteous see *it* and rejoice,
And all [b]iniquity stops its mouth.

43 [a]Whoever *is* wise will observe these *things*,
And they will understand the lovingkindness of the LORD.

PSALM 108†

Assurance of God's Victory over Enemies

A Song. A Psalm of David.

O [a]GOD, my heart is steadfast;
I will sing and give praise, even with my glory.
2 [a]Awake, lute and harp!
I will awaken the dawn.
3 I will praise You, O LORD, among the peoples,
And I will sing praises to You among the nations.
4 For Your mercy *is* great above the [1]heavens,
And Your truth *reaches* to the clouds.

5 [a]Be exalted, O God, above the heavens,
And Your glory above all the earth;
6 [a]That Your beloved may be delivered,
Save *with* Your right hand, and [1]hear me.

25 [a]Jon. 1:4
26 [a]Ps. 22:14
27 [1]Lit. *all their wisdom is swallowed up*
29 [a]Ps. 89:9; Matt. 8:26; Luke 8:24
31 [a]Ps. 107:8, 15, 21
32 [a]Ps. 22:22, 25
33 [a]1 Kin. 17:1, 7; Is. 50:2
34 [a]Gen. 13:10; Deut. 29:23 [1]Lit. *a salty waste*
35 [a]Ps. 114:8; [Is. 41:17, 18]
38 [a]Gen. 12:2; 17:16, 20 [b]Ex. 1:7; [Deut. 7:14]
39 [a]2 Kin. 10:32
40 [a]Job 12:21, 24
41 [a]1 Sam. 2:8; [Ps. 113:7, 8] [b]Ps. 78:52
42 [a]Job 5:15, 16 [b]Job 5:16; Ps. 63:11; [Rom. 3:19]
43 [a]Ps. 64:9; Jer. 9:12; [Hos. 14:9]

PSALM 108
1 [a]Ps. 57:7–11
2 [a]Ps. 57:8–11
4 [1]*skies*
5 [a]Ps. 57:5, 11
6 [a]Ps. 60:5–12 [1]Lit. *answer*

108 (107, LXX) This is a psalm of triumph. Verse 5 is used on Ascension Day and is also said by the priest after Holy Communion has been given to the faithful.

7 God has spoken in His holiness:
"I will rejoice;
I will divide Shechem
And measure out the Valley of
Succoth.
8 Gilead *is* Mine; Manasseh *is*
Mine;
Ephraim also *is* the [1]helmet for
My head;
[a]Judah *is* My lawgiver.
9 Moab *is* My washpot;
Over Edom I will cast My shoe;
Over Philistia I will triumph."

10 [a]Who will bring me *into* the
strong city?
Who will lead me to Edom?
11 *Is it* not *You*, O God, *who* cast
us off?
And *You*, O God, *who* did not
go out with our armies?
12 Give us help from trouble,
For the help of man is useless.
13 [a]Through God we will do
valiantly,
For *it is* He *who* shall tread down
our enemies.

PSALM 109†

The Judgment of the Betrayer

To the Chief Musician. A Psalm of David.

DO[a] not keep silent,
O God of my praise!
2 For the mouth of the wicked
and the mouth of the deceitful
Have opened against me;
They have spoken against me
with a [a]lying tongue.
3 They have also surrounded me
with words of hatred,
And fought against me
[a]without a cause.
4 In return for my love they are
my accusers,
But I *give myself to* prayer.

5 Thus [a]they have rewarded me
evil for good,
And hatred for my love.

6 Set a wicked man over him,
And let [a]an [1]accuser stand at his
right hand.
7 When he is judged, let him be
found guilty,
And [a]let his prayer become sin.
8 Let his days be [a]few,
And [b]let another take his office.
9 [a]Let his children be fatherless,
And his wife a widow.
10 Let his children [1]continually be
vagabonds, and beg;
Let them [2]seek *their bread* also
from their desolate places.
11 [a]Let the creditor seize all that he
has,
And let strangers plunder his
labor.
12 Let there be none to extend
mercy to him,
Nor let there be any to favor his
fatherless children.
13 [a]Let his [1]posterity be cut off,
And in the generation following
let their [b]name be blotted out.

14 [a]Let the iniquity of his fathers be
remembered before the LORD,
And let not the sin of his mother
[b]be blotted out.
15 Let them be continually before
the LORD,
That He may [a]cut off the
memory of them from the
earth;
16 Because he did not remember to
show mercy,
But persecuted the poor and
needy man,
That he might even slay the
[a]broken in heart.
17 [a]As he loved cursing, so let it
come to him;
As he did not delight in

8 [a][Gen. 49:10] [1]Lit. *protection*
10 [a]Ps. 60:9
13 [a]Ps. 60:12

PSALM 109

1 [a]Ps. 83:1
2 [a]Ps. 27:12
3 [a]Ps. 35:7; 69:4; John 15:25
5 [a]Ps. 35:7, 12; 38:20; Prov. 17:13
6 [a]Zech. 3:1 [1]Heb. *satan*
7 [a][Prov. 28:9]
8 [a][Ps. 55:23]; John 17:12 [b]Ps. 69:25; Acts 1:20
9 [a]Ex. 22:24
10 [1]*wander continuously* [2]So with MT, Tg.; LXX, Vg. *be cast out*
11 [a]Neh. 5:7; Job 5:5; 18:9
13 [a]Job 18:19; Ps. 37:28 [b]Prov. 10:7 [1]*descendants be destroyed*
14 [a][Ex. 20:5; Num. 14:18]; Is. 65:6; [Jer. 32:18] [b]Neh. 4:5; Jer. 18:23
15 [a]Job 18:17; [Ps. 34:16]
16 [a][Ps. 34:18]
17 [a]Prov. 14:14; [Matt. 7:2]

109 (108, LXX) This is the most violent of the so-called cursing psalms. Verse 8 is referred to in Acts 1:20 as a prophecy: the place of Judas among the Apostles will be given to another. The whole psalm, describing the cruelty of godless adversaries, is seen liturgically as a reference to Judas. Verses 21, 22 are seen as prophetic of the sufferings of Christ on the Cross: **my heart is wounded** (lit. "pierced"). Thus it is prayed at the Third Hour on Good Friday. The psalm ends with deliverance (vv. 30, 31), with special reference to the Lord's protection of the poor.

blessing, so let it be far from
him.
18 As he clothed himself with
cursing as with his garment,
So let it [a]enter his body like
water,
And like oil into his bones.
19 Let it be to him like the garment
which covers him,
And for a belt with which he
girds himself continually.
20 *Let* this *be* the LORD's reward to
my accusers,
And to those who speak evil
against my person.

21 But You, O GOD the Lord,
Deal with me for Your name's
sake;
Because Your mercy *is* good,
deliver me.
22 For I *am* poor and needy,
And my heart is wounded
within me.
23 I am gone [a]like a shadow when
it lengthens;
I am shaken off like a locust.
24 My [a]knees are weak through
fasting,
And my flesh is feeble from lack
of fatness.
25 I also have become [a]a reproach
to them;
When they look at me, [b]they
shake their heads.

26 Help me, O LORD my God!
Oh, save me according to Your
mercy,
27 [a]That they may know that this
is Your hand—
That You, LORD, have done it!
28 [a]Let them curse, but You
bless;
When they arise, let them be
ashamed,
But let [b]Your servant rejoice.
29 [a]Let my accusers be clothed with
shame,
And let them cover themselves
with their own disgrace as
with a mantle.

30 I will greatly praise the LORD
with my mouth;
Yes, [a]I will praise Him among
the multitude.
31 For [a]He shall stand at the right
hand of the poor,
To save *him* from those
[1]who condemn him.

18 [a]Num. 5:22
23 [a]Ps. 102:11
24 [a]Heb. 12:12
25 [a]Ps. 22:7; Jer. 18:16; Lam. 2:15 [b]Matt. 27:39; Mark 15:29
27 [a]Job 37:7
28 [a]2 Sam. 6:11, 12 [b]Is. 65:14
29 [a]Job 8:22; Ps. 35:26
30 [a]Ps. 35:18; 111:1
31 [a][Ps. 16:8] [1]Lit. *judging his soul*

PSALM 110†

Announcement of the Messiah's Reign

A Psalm of David.

THE [a]LORD said to my Lord,
"Sit at My right hand,
Till I make Your enemies Your
[b]footstool."
2 The LORD shall send the rod of
Your strength [a]out of Zion.
[b]Rule in the midst of Your
enemies!

3 [a]Your people *shall be* volunteers
In the day of Your power;
[b]In the beauties of holiness, from
the womb of the morning,
You have the dew of Your
youth.
4 The LORD has sworn
And [a]will not relent,
"You *are* a [b]priest forever

PSALM 110
1 [a]Matt. 22:44; Mark 12:36; 16:19; Luke 20:42, 43; Acts 2:34, 35; Col. 3:1; Heb. 1:13 [b][1 Cor. 15:25; Eph. 1:22]
2 [a][Rom. 11:26, 27] [b][Ps. 2:9; Dan. 7:13, 14]
3 [a]Judg. 5:2; Neh. 11:2 [b]1 Chr. 16:29; Ps. 96:9
4 [a][Num. 23:19] [b][Zech. 6:13]

110 (109, LXX) This is the psalm most often quoted in the NT. Verse 1 is referred to by Christ Himself in Matt. 22:44 when explaining who He is—the Son of God. Thus He establishes once for all that Ps. 110 is messianic, not just a reference to King David. It is crucial for us to understand the reading of the LXX for v. 3: "With You is dominion on the day of Your birth in the radiance of holiness; from the womb before the morning star have I begotten you." What a picture of the eternal birth and the earthly birth of the Son of God! This verse is therefore used all through the Christmas season services as a prophetic proclamation of the Incarnation of God's eternal Son.

Verse 4 is referred to repeatedly in the Book of Hebrews (Heb. 5:6, 10; 6:20). Here is the OT foundation for seeing Melchizedek as a type of the priesthood of Christ as Messiah, both fulfilling and infinitely surpassing the priesthood under the Law of Moses. Verses 5–7 speak of the triumph of the Messiah over His enemies.

According to the order of
[c]Melchizedek."

5 The Lord *is* [a]at Your right hand;
He shall [1]execute kings
[b]in the day of His wrath.
6 He shall judge among the
nations,
He shall fill *the places* with dead
bodies,
[a]He shall [1]execute the heads of
many countries.
7 He shall drink of the brook by
the wayside;
[a]Therefore He shall lift up the
head.

4 [c][Heb. 5:6, 10; 6:20]
5 [a][Ps. 16:8] [b]Ps. 2:5, 12; [Rom. 2:5; Rev. 6:17] [1]Lit. *break kings in pieces*
6 [a]Ps. 68:21 [1]Lit. *break in pieces*
7 [a][Is. 53:12]

PSALM 111†

Praise to God for His Faithfulness and Justice

PRAISE[1] the LORD!

[a]I will praise the LORD with *my*
whole heart,
In the assembly of the upright
and *in* the congregation.

2 [a]The works of the LORD *are* great,
[b]Studied by all who have
pleasure in them.
3 His work *is* [a]honorable and
glorious,
And His righteousness endures
forever.
4 He has made His wonderful
works to be remembered;
[a]The LORD *is* gracious and full of
compassion.
5 He has given food to those who
fear Him;
He will ever be mindful of His
covenant.
6 He has declared to His people
the power of His works,
In giving them the [1]heritage of
the nations.

7 The works of His hands *are*
[a]verity[1] and justice;
All His precepts *are* sure.
8 [a]They stand fast forever and
ever,
And are [b]done in truth and
uprightness.
9 [a]He has sent redemption to His
people;
He has commanded His
covenant forever:
[b]Holy and awesome *is* His name.

10 [a]The fear of the LORD *is* the
beginning of wisdom;
A good understanding have all
those who do *His*
commandments.
His praise endures forever.

PSALM 111

1 [a]Ps. 35:18 [1]Heb. *Hallelujah*
2 [a]Ps. 92:5 [b]Ps. 143:5
3 [a]Ps. 145:4, 5
4 [a][Ps. 86:5]
6 [1]*inheritance*
7 [a][Rev. 15:3] [1]*truth*
8 [a]Is. 40:8; Matt. 5:18 [b][Rev. 15:3]
9 [a]Luke 1:68 [b]Luke 1:49
10 [a]Job 28:28; [Prov. 1:7; 9:10]; Eccl. 12:13

PSALM 112†

The Blessed State of the Righteous

PRAISE[1] the LORD!

Blessed *is* the man *who* fears the
LORD,
Who [a]delights greatly in His
commandments.

2 [a]His descendants will be mighty
on earth;
The generation of the upright
will be blessed.
3 [a]Wealth and riches *will be* in his
house,
And his righteousness [1]endures
forever.
4 [a]Unto the upright there arises
light in the darkness;
He is gracious, and full of
compassion, and righteous.

PSALM 112

1 [a]Ps. 128:1 [1]Heb. *Hallelujah*
2 [a][Ps. 102:28]
3 [a]Prov. 3:16; 8:18; [Matt. 6:33] [1]*stands*
4 [a]Job 11:17; Ps. 97:11

---

111 (110, LXX) This psalm gives praise to the Lord for His mighty deeds of salvation. Liturgically this is used as a Christmas psalm. Verse 9a, the Lord **has sent redemption to His people,** is the communion hymn on Christmas Day.

112 (111, LXX) Of the psalms describing the righteous man, this is the most popular song in the Orthodox Church for use on days of commemoration of the saints. Verses 6b, 7a make up the communion hymn for most saints' days, for these righteous ones who have departed are present with us at the heavenly Eucharist (see Heb. 13:22–24), and are thus in everlasting remembrance in the sight of God and in our hearts and minds. Memory eternal!

5 [a]A good man deals graciously
and lends;
He will guide his affairs
[b]with discretion.
6 Surely he will never be shaken;
[a]The righteous will be in
everlasting remembrance.
7 [a]He will not be afraid of evil
tidings;
His heart is steadfast, trusting
in the LORD.
8 His [a]heart *is* established;
[b]He will not be afraid,
Until he [c]sees *his desire* upon his
enemies.

9 He has dispersed abroad,
He has given to the poor;
His righteousness endures
forever;
His [1]horn will be exalted with
honor.
10 The wicked will see *it* and be
grieved;
He will gnash his teeth and melt
away;
The desire of the wicked shall
perish.

5 [a]Ps. 37:26; [Luke 6:35] [b][Eph. 5:15; Col. 4:5]
6 [a]Prov. 10:7
7 [a][Prov. 1:33]
8 [a]Heb. 13:9 [b][Ps. 27:1; 56:11]; Prov. 1:33; 3:24; [Is. 12:2] [c]Ps. 59:10
9 [1]Strength

PSALM 113†

A Passover Hymn of Praise

PRAISE[1] the LORD!
[a]Praise, O servants of the LORD,
Praise the name of the LORD!
2 [a]Blessed be the name of the LORD

PSALM 113
1 [a]Ps. 135:1 [1]Heb. *Hallelujah*
2 [a][Dan. 2:20]

113—118 In the Hebrew Psalter these six psalms constitute what is called the *Hallel,* for each psalm begins or ends with "Hallelujah." They were specifically sung at the Passover as hymns of praise to the Lord for Israel's deliverance from Pharaoh.

Psalm 113 (112, LXX) teaches us to chant unceasingly to the deliverer. Verse 2 is sung at the close of every liturgy in the Orthodox Church, as the faithful go their way to be servants of Christ in the world.

Psalm 114 is the song of the Exodus as Israel went forth from Egypt. (Psalms 114 and 115 constitute Ps. 113 in the LXX.) This psalm, which includes descriptions of the people of God passing through the Red Sea (v. 3) and the Jordan River (v. 5), is sung to celebrate the Baptism of Christ at Epiphany, and at other feasts as well. The psalmist foretells the call of the Gentiles, teaching the OT is the work of God, and proclaiming that the salvation of Israel is the work of the Lord.

Psalm 115 describes the folly of idolatry. We read **the dead do not praise the LORD** (v. 17) . . . **but we will bless the LORD** (v. 18). The third kneeling prayer on Pentecost Sunday quotes this passage, but reveals that the "we" (v. 18) is a reference to those who are in Christ—both the living and the dead. *The dead* (v. 17) refers to those who have died outside of Christ.

Psalm 116:1–9 is Ps. 114 in the LXX; Ps. 116:10–19 is Ps. 115 in the LXX. Thus Ps. 116 in the NKJV is seen by the Orthodox Church as two separate psalms, and is used in two specific ways. The first section (vv. 1–9) is a psalm of deliverance from death, and is used on Palm Sunday in reference to the resurrection of Lazarus the day before. The second section (vv. 10–19) is a eucharistic song in the Church, one of several communion hymns. Note **the cup of salvation** (v. 13) and the **sacrifice of thanksgiving** (v. 17). Verse 15 is sung at the feasts of the Mother of God and of the saints, and is one of relatively few passages in the Psalms which describe death in the light of the resurrection.

Psalm 117 (116, LXX), the shortest psalm, is a Passover song in Israel and prophesies that one day the Gentiles will praise the Lord. It is seen in that light in Rom. 15:11, and is used liturgically each day at Vespers.

Psalm 118 (117, LXX) is rich in Orthodox liturgical usage. Historically, it concludes the songs sung at Passover, and is the hymn which was sung at the close of the Passover Christ ate with His disciples: "and when they had sung a hymn, they went out to the Mount of Olives" (Mark 14:26; see also Matt. 26:30).

Psalm 118:22 is quoted by Christ and by Peter (see center-column references) as speaking directly of Christ as the stone rejected by the builders, Israel, which becomes the chief cornerstone of the Church. In v. 25 **save now** is synonymous with "Hosannah." So when Christ is praised on the original Palm Sunday with "Hosannah!" the people are quoting vv. 25, 26 (see center-column references).

Liturgically, Ps. 118 is used heavily on Palm Sunday. But in addition, there are other

(continued on next page)

From this time forth and
forevermore!
3 [a]From the rising of the sun to its
going down
The LORD's name *is* to be
praised.
4 The LORD *is* [a]high above all
nations,
[b]His glory above the heavens.
5 [a]Who *is* like the LORD our God,
Who dwells on high,
6 [a]Who humbles Himself to behold
The things that are in the heavens
and in the earth?

7 [a]He raises the poor out of the
dust,
And lifts the [b]needy out of the
ash heap,
8 That He may [a]seat *him* with
princes—
With the princes of His people.
9 [a]He grants the [1]barren woman a
home,
Like a joyful mother of children.

Praise the LORD!

3 [a]Is. 59:19; Mal. 1:11
4 [a]Ps. 97:9; 99:2 [b][Ps. 8:1]
5 [a]Ps. 89:6; [Is. 57:15]
6 [a][Ps. 11:4; Is. 57:15]
7 [a]1 Sam. 2:8; Ps. 107:41 [b]Ps. 72:12
8 [a][Job 36:7]
9 [a]1 Sam. 2:5; Is. 54:1 [1]*childless*

PSALM 114†

The Power of God in His Deliverance of Israel

WHEN [a]Israel went out of Egypt,
The house of Jacob [b]from a
people [1]of strange language,
2 [a]Judah became His sanctuary,
And Israel His dominion.

3 [a]The sea saw *it* and fled;
[b]Jordan turned back.
4 [a]The mountains skipped like
rams,
The little hills like lambs.
5 [a]What ails you, O sea, that you
fled?
O Jordan, *that* you turned back?
6 O mountains, *that* you skipped
like rams?
O little hills, like lambs?

7 Tremble, O earth, at the
presence of the Lord,
At the presence of the God of
Jacob,
8 [a]Who turned the rock *into* a pool
of water,
The flint into a fountain of
waters.

PSALM 114
1 [a]Ex. 12:51; 13:3 [b]Ps. 81:5 [1]*who spoke unintelligibly*
2 [a]Ex. 6:7; 19:6; 25:8; 29:45, 46; Deut. 27:9
3 [a]Ex. 14:21; Ps. 77:16 [b]Josh. 3:13–16
4 [a]Ex. 19:18; Judg. 5:5; Ps. 29:6; Hab. 3:6
5 [a]Hab. 3:8
8 [a]Ex. 17:6; Num. 20:11; Ps. 107:35

PSALM 115†

The Futility of Idols and the Trustworthiness of God

NOT [a]unto us, O LORD, not unto
us,
But to Your name give glory,
Because of Your mercy,
Because of Your truth.
2 Why should the [1]Gentiles say,
[a]"So where *is* their God?"

3 [a]But our God *is* in heaven;
He does whatever He pleases.
4 [a]Their idols *are* silver and gold,
The work of men's hands.
5 They have mouths, but they do
not speak;
Eyes they have, but they do not
see;
6 They have ears, but they do not
hear;
Noses they have, but they do
not smell;
7 They have hands, but they do
not handle;
Feet they have, but they do not
walk;
Nor do they mutter through
their throat.
8 [a]Those who make them are like
them;

PSALM 115
1 [a][Is. 48:11]; Ezek. 36:32
2 [a]Ps. 42:3, 10 [1]*nations*
3 [a][1 Chr. 16:26]
4 [a]Deut. 4:28; 2 Kin. 19:18; Is. 37:19; 44:10, 20; Jer. 10:3
8 [a]Ps. 135:18; Is. 44:9–11

(continued from previous page)
usages. Verse 24 is used as the paschal hymn on Easter Sunday, the biblical "day of the Lord." Verses 26a, 27a are used daily at Matins, acclaiming Christ as God, the Light of the World, at Epiphany. The message is that the new people, made up of Jews and Gentiles, should learn to call upon the incarnate Word of God for help at the time of persecution, to give thanks to Him for their triumph, to follow the way of virtue, and to confess the Lord who is the cornerstone.

So is everyone who trusts in them.

9 [a]O Israel, trust in the LORD;
[b]He *is* their help and their shield.
10 O house of Aaron, trust in the LORD;
He *is* their help and their shield.
11 You who fear the LORD, trust in the LORD;
He *is* their help and their shield.

12 The LORD [1]has been mindful of *us;*
He will bless us;
He will bless the house of Israel;
He will bless the house of Aaron.
13 [a]He will bless those who fear the LORD,
Both small and great.

14 May the LORD give you increase more and more,
You and your children.
15 *May* you *be* [a]blessed by the LORD,
[b]Who made heaven and earth.

16 The heaven, *even* the heavens, *are* the LORD's;
But the earth He has given to the children of men.
17 [a]The dead do not praise the LORD,
Nor any who go down into silence.
18 [a]But we will bless the LORD
From this time forth and forevermore.

Praise the LORD!

PSALM 116†

Thanksgiving for Deliverance from Death

I [a]LOVE the LORD, because He has heard
My voice *and* my supplications.
2 Because He has inclined His ear to me,
Therefore I will call *upon Him* as long as I live.

3 [a]The [1]pains of death surrounded me,
And the [2]pangs of Sheol [3]laid hold of me;
I found trouble and sorrow.
4 Then I called upon the name of the LORD:
"O LORD, I implore You, deliver my soul!"

5 [a]Gracious *is* the LORD, and [b]righteous;
Yes, our God *is* merciful.
6 The LORD preserves the simple;
I was brought low, and He saved me.
7 Return to your [a]rest, O my soul,
For [b]the LORD has dealt bountifully with you.

8 [a]For You have delivered my soul from death,
My eyes from tears,
And my feet from falling.
9 I will walk before the LORD
[a]In the land of the living.
10 [a]I believed, therefore I spoke,
"I am greatly afflicted."
11 [a]I said in my haste,
[b]"All men *are* liars."

12 What shall I render to the LORD
For all His benefits toward me?
13 I will take up the cup of salvation,
And call upon the name of the LORD.
14 [a]I will pay my vows to the LORD
Now in the presence of all His people.

15 [a]Precious in the sight of the LORD
Is the death of His saints.

16 O LORD, truly [a]I *am* Your servant;
I *am* Your servant, [b]the son of Your maidservant;
You have loosed my bonds.
17 I will offer to You [a]the sacrifice of thanksgiving,
And will call upon the name of the LORD.
18 I will pay my vows to the LORD
Now in the presence of all His people,

9 [a]Ps. 118:2, 3 [b]Ps. 33:20
12 [1]*has remembered us*
13 [a]Ps. 128:1, 4
15 [a][Gen. 14:19] [b]Gen. 1:1; Acts 14:15; Rev. 14:7
17 [a]Ps. 6:5; 88:10–12; [Is. 38:18]
18 [a]Ps. 113:2; Dan. 2:20

PSALM 116

1 [a]Ps. 18:1
3 [a]Ps. 18:4–6 [1]Lit. *cords* [2]*distresses* [3]Lit. *found me*
5 [a][Ps. 103:8] [b][Ezra 9:15]; Neh. 9:8; [Ps. 119:137; 145:17; Jer. 12:1; Dan. 9:14]
7 [a][Jer. 6:16; Matt. 11:29] [b]Ps. 13:6
8 [a]Ps. 56:13
9 [a]Ps. 27:13
10 [a]2 Cor. 4:13
11 [a]Ps. 31:22 [b]Rom. 3:4
14 [a]Ps. 116:18
15 [a]Ps. 72:14; [Rev. 14:13]
16 [a]Ps. 119:125; 143:12 [b]Ps. 86:16
17 [a]Lev. 7:12; Ps. 50:14; 107:22

19 In the [a]courts of the LORD's
house,
In the midst of you,
O Jerusalem.

[1]Praise the LORD!

PSALM 117†

Let All Peoples Praise the Lord

PRAISE [a]the LORD, all you
Gentiles!
[1]Laud Him, all you peoples!
2 For His merciful kindness is
great toward us,
And [a]the truth of the LORD
endures forever.

Praise the LORD!

PSALM 118†

Praise to God for His Everlasting Mercy

OH, [a]give thanks to the LORD, for
He is good!
[b]For His mercy *endures* forever.

2 [a]Let Israel now say,
"His mercy *endures* forever."
3 Let the house of Aaron now say,
"His mercy *endures* forever."
4 Let those who fear the LORD
now say,
"His mercy *endures* forever."

5 [a]I called on the LORD in distress;
The LORD answered me *and*
[b]*set me* in a broad place.
6 [a]The LORD *is* on my side;
I will not fear.
What can man do to me?
7 [a]The LORD is for me among those
who help me;
Therefore [b]I shall see *my desire*
on those who hate me.
8 [a]*It is* better to trust in the LORD
Than to put confidence in man.
9 [a]*It is* better to trust in the LORD
Than to put confidence in
princes.

19 [a]Ps. 96:8
[1]Heb. *Halle-lujah*

PSALM 117
1 [a]Rom. 15:11
[1]*Praise*
2 [a][Ps. 100:5]

PSALM 118
1 [a]1 Chr. 16:8, 34; Jer. 33:11
[b]2 Chr. 5:13; 7:3; Ezra 3:11; [Ps. 136:1–26]
2 [a][Ps. 115:9]
5 [a]Ps. 120:1
[b]Ps. 18:19
6 [a]Ps. 27:1; 56:9; [Rom. 8:31; Heb. 13:6]
7 [a]Ps. 54:4
[b]Ps. 59:10
8 [a]2 Chr. 32:7, 8; Ps. 40:4; Is. 31:1, 3; 57:13; Jer. 17:5
9 [a]Ps. 146:3
11 [a]Ps. 88:17
12 [a]Deut. 1:44
[b]Eccl. 7:6; Nah. 1:10
[1]*cut them off*
14 [a]Ex. 15:2; Is. 12:2
16 [a]Ex. 15:6
17 [a][Ps. 6:5]; Hab. 1:12
[b]Ps. 73:28
18 [a]Ps. 73:14; Jer. 31:18; [1 Cor. 11:32]; 2 Cor. 6:9
[1]*disciplined*
19 [a]Is. 26:2
20 [a]Ps. 24:7
[b]Is. 35:8; [Rev. 21:27; 22:14, 15]
21 [a]Ps. 116:1
22 [a]Matt. 21:42; Mark 12:10, 11; Luke 20:17; Acts 4:11; [Eph. 2:20; 1 Pet. 2:7, 8]
23 [1]Lit. *This is from the LORD*

10 All nations surrounded me,
But in the name of the LORD I
will destroy them.
11 They [a]surrounded me,
Yes, they surrounded me;
But in the name of the LORD I
will destroy them.
12 They surrounded me [a]like bees;
They were quenched [b]like a fire
of thorns;
For in the name of the LORD I
will [1]destroy them.
13 You pushed me violently, that
I might fall,
But the LORD helped me.
14 [a]The LORD *is* my strength and
song,
And He has become my
salvation.

15 The voice of rejoicing and
salvation
Is in the tents of the righteous;
The right hand of the LORD does
valiantly.
16 [a]The right hand of the LORD is
exalted;
The right hand of the LORD does
valiantly.
17 [a]I shall not die, but live,
And [b]declare the works of the
LORD.
18 The LORD has [a]chastened[1] me
severely,
But He has not given me over
to death.

19 [a]Open to me the gates of
righteousness;
I will go through them,
And I will praise the LORD.
20 [a]This is the gate of the LORD,
[b]Through which the righteous
shall enter.

21 I will praise You,
For You have [a]answered me,
And have become my salvation.

22 [a]The stone *which* the builders
rejected
Has become the chief
cornerstone.
23 [1]This was the LORD's doing;
It *is* marvelous in our eyes.
24 This *is* the day the LORD has
made;

We will rejoice and be glad in
it.

25 Save now, I pray, O LORD;
O LORD, I pray, send now
prosperity.
26 [a]Blessed *is* he who comes in the
name of the LORD!
We have blessed you from the
house of the LORD.
27 God *is* the LORD,
And He has given us [a]light;
Bind the sacrifice with cords to
the horns of the altar.
28 You *are* my God, and I will
praise You;
[a]*You are* my God, I will exalt You.

29 Oh, give thanks to the LORD, for
He is good!
For His mercy *endures* forever.

PSALM 119†

The Law of the Lord

א ALEPH

BLESSED *are* the [1]undefiled in the
way,
[a]Who walk in the law of the
LORD!
2 Blessed *are* those who keep His
testimonies,
Who seek Him with the
[a]whole heart!
3 [a]They also do no iniquity;
They walk in His ways.
4 You have commanded *us*
To keep Your precepts
diligently.
5 Oh, that my ways were directed
To keep Your statutes!
6 [a]Then I would not be ashamed,
When I look into all Your
commandments.

26 [a]Matt. 21:9; 23:39; Mark 11:9; Luke 13:35; 19:38
27 [a]Esth. 8:16; [1 Pet. 2:9]
28 [a]Ex. 15:2; Is. 25:1

PSALM 119

1 [a]Ps. 128:1; [Ezek. 11:20; 18:17]; Mic. 4:2
[1]*blameless*
2 [a]Deut. 6:5; 10:12; 11:13; 13:3
3 [a][1 John 3:9; 5:18]
6 [a]Job 22:26

10 [a]2 Chr. 15:15
11 [a]Ps. 37:31; Luke 2:19
13 [a]Ps. 34:11
15 [1]*look into*
16 [a]Ps. 1:2
17 [a]Ps. 116:7
19 [a]Gen. 47:9; Lev. 25:23; 1 Chr. 29:15; Ps. 39:12; Heb. 11:13
20 [a]Ps. 42:1, 2; 63:1; 84:2
[1]*is crushed*

7 I will praise You with
uprightness of heart,
When I learn Your righteous
judgments.
8 I will keep Your statutes;
Oh, do not forsake me utterly!

ב BETH

9 How can a young man cleanse
his way?
By taking heed according to
Your word.
10 With my whole heart I have
[a]sought You;
Oh, let me not wander from
Your commandments!
11 [a]Your word I have hidden in my
heart,
That I might not sin against
You.
12 Blessed *are* You, O LORD!
Teach me Your statutes.
13 With my lips I have [a]declared
All the judgments of Your
mouth.
14 I have rejoiced in the way of
Your testimonies,
As *much as* in all riches.
15 I will meditate on Your
precepts,
And [1]contemplate Your ways.
16 I will [a]delight myself in Your
statutes;
I will not forget Your word.

ג GIMEL

17 [a]Deal bountifully with Your
servant,
That I may live and keep Your
word.
18 Open my eyes, that I may see
Wondrous things from Your
law.
19 [a]I *am* a stranger in the earth;
Do not hide Your
commandments from me.
20 [a]My soul [1]breaks with longing

---

119 (118, LXX) In this, the longest of the psalms, every verse speaks of the law, the commandments, the statutes, and the precepts of the Lord. Therein we learn of the fellowship of the saints, among whom the righteousness of the law and God's strength will prevail. Those who endure the troubles will receive their rewards. Christ is the only one who perfectly prays this psalm, for He alone obeys perfectly **the law of the LORD** (v. 1). But because He perfectly kept the Law, He was killed. Thus, this psalm is prayed in its entirety at Matins on Holy Saturday with the Church assembled around the tomb of Christ. Further, this is the Orthodox funeral psalm, the very core of the service, for all who die in Christ are justified by His righteousness.

For Your judgments at all times.
21 You rebuke the proud—the cursed,
Who stray from Your commandments.
22 [a]Remove from me reproach and contempt,
For I have kept Your testimonies.
23 Princes also sit *and* speak against me,
But Your servant meditates on Your statutes.
24 Your testimonies also *are* my delight
And my counselors.

ד DALETH

25 [a]My soul clings to the dust;
[b]Revive me according to Your word.
26 I have declared my ways, and You answered me;
[a]Teach me Your statutes.
27 Make me understand the way of Your precepts;
So [a]shall I meditate on Your wonderful works.
28 [a]My soul [1]melts from [2]heaviness;
Strengthen me according to Your word.
29 Remove from me the way of lying,
And grant me Your law graciously.
30 I have chosen the way of truth;
Your judgments I have laid *before me.*
31 I cling to Your testimonies;
O LORD, do not put me to shame!
32 I will run the course of Your commandments,
For You shall [a]enlarge my heart.

ה HE

33 [a]Teach me, O LORD, the way of Your statutes,
And I shall keep it *to* the end.
34 [a]Give me understanding, and I shall keep Your law;
Indeed, I shall observe it with *my* whole heart.
35 Make me walk in the path of Your commandments,
For I delight in it.
36 [1]Incline my heart to Your testimonies,
And not to [a]covetousness.
37 [a]Turn[1] away my eyes from [b]looking at worthless things,
And revive me in [2]Your way.
38 [a]Establish Your word to Your servant,
Who *is devoted* to fearing You.
39 Turn away my reproach which I dread,
For Your judgments *are* good.
40 Behold, I long for Your precepts;
Revive me in Your righteousness.

ו WAW

41 Let Your mercies come also to me, O LORD—
Your salvation according to Your word.
42 So shall I have an answer for him who [1]reproaches me,
For I trust in Your word.
43 And take not the word of truth utterly out of my mouth,
For I have hoped in Your ordinances.
44 So shall I keep Your law continually,
Forever and ever.
45 And I will walk [1]at [a]liberty,
For I seek Your precepts.
46 [a]I will speak of Your testimonies also before kings,
And will not be ashamed.
47 And I will delight myself in Your commandments,
Which I love.
48 My hands also I will lift up to Your commandments,
Which I love,
And I will meditate on Your statutes.

ז ZAYIN

49 Remember the word to Your servant,
Upon which You have caused me to hope.
50 This *is* my [a]comfort in my affliction,
For Your word has given me life.
51 The proud have me in great derision,

---

22 [a]Ps. 39:8
25 [a]Ps. 44:25 [b]Ps. 143:11
26 [a]Ps. 25:4; 27:11; 86:11
27 [a]Ps. 145:5, 6
28 [a]Ps. 107:26 [1]Lit. *drops* [2]*grief*
32 [a]1 Kin. 4:29; Is. 60:5; 2 Cor. 6:11, 13
33 [a][Matt. 10:22; Rev. 2:26]
34 [a][Prov. 2:6; James 1:5]
36 [a]Ezek. 33:31; [Mark 7:20–23]; Luke 12:15; [Heb. 13:5] [1]Cause me to long for
37 [a]Is. 33:15 [b]Prov. 23:5 [1]Lit. *Cause my eyes to pass away from* [2]So with MT, LXX, Vg.; Tg. *Your words*
38 [a]2 Sam. 7:25
42 [1]*taunts*
45 [a]Prov. 4:12 [1]Lit. *in a wide place*
46 [a]Ps. 138:1; Matt. 10:18; Acts 26
50 [a]Job 6:10; [Rom. 15:4]

Yet I do not turn aside from
Your law.
52 I remembered Your judgments
of old, O LORD,
And have comforted myself.
53 [a]Indignation has taken hold of
me
Because of the wicked, who
forsake Your law.
54 Your statutes have been my
songs
In the house of my pilgrimage.
55 [a]I remember Your name in the
night, O LORD,
And I keep Your law.
56 This has become mine,
Because I kept Your precepts.

ח HETH

57 [a]*You are* my portion, O LORD;
I have said that I would keep
Your words.
58 I entreated Your favor with *my*
whole heart;
Be merciful to me according to
Your word.
59 I [a]thought about my ways,
And turned my feet to Your
testimonies.
60 I made haste, and did not
delay
To keep Your commandments.
61 The cords of the wicked have
bound me,
But I have not forgotten Your
law.
62 [a]At midnight I will rise to give
thanks to You,
Because of Your righteous
judgments.
63 I *am* a companion of all who fear
You,
And of those who keep Your
precepts.
64 [a]The earth, O LORD, is full of
Your mercy;
Teach me Your statutes.

ט TETH

65 You have dealt well with Your
servant,
O LORD, according to Your
word.
66 Teach me good judgment and
[a]knowledge,
For I believe Your
commandments.
67 Before I was [a]afflicted I went
astray,
But now I keep Your word.
68 You *are* [a]good, and do good;
Teach me Your statutes.
69 The proud have [a]forged[1] a lie
against me,
But I will keep Your precepts
with *my* whole heart.
70 [a]Their heart is [1]as fat as grease,
But I delight in Your law.
71 *It is* good for me that I have been
afflicted,
That I may learn Your statutes.
72 [a]The law of Your mouth *is* better
to me
Than thousands of *coins of* gold
and silver.

י YOD

73 [a]Your hands have made me and
fashioned me;
Give me understanding, that I
may learn Your
commandments.
74 [a]Those who fear You will be glad
when they see me,
Because I have hoped in Your
word.
75 I know, O LORD, [a]that Your
judgments *are* [1]right,
And *that* in faithfulness You
have afflicted me.
76 Let, I pray, Your merciful
kindness be for my comfort,
According to Your word to Your
servant.
77 Let Your tender mercies come
to me, that I may live;
For Your law *is* my delight.
78 Let the proud [a]be ashamed,
For they treated me wrongfully
with falsehood;
But I will meditate on Your
precepts.
79 Let those who fear You turn to
me,
Those who know Your
testimonies.
80 Let my heart be blameless
regarding Your statutes,
That I may not be ashamed.

כ KAPH

81 [a]My soul faints for Your
salvation,
But I hope in Your word.

53 [a]Ex. 32:19; Ezra 9:3; Neh. 13:25
55 [a]Ps. 63:6
57 [a]Num. 18:20; Ps. 16:5; Jer. 10:16; Lam. 3:24
59 [a]Mark 14:72; Luke 15:17
62 [a]Acts 16:25
64 [a]Ps. 33:5
66 [a]Phil. 1:9
67 [a]Prov. 3:11; Jer. 31:18, 19; [Heb. 12:5–11]
68 [a]Ps. 106:1; 107:1; [Matt. 19:17]
69 [a]Job 13:4; Ps. 109:2 [1]Lit. *smeared me with a lie*
70 [a]Deut. 32:15; Job 15:27; Ps. 17:10; Is. 6:10; Jer. 5:28; Acts 28:27 [1]Insensible
72 [a]Ps. 19:10; Prov. 8:10, 11, 19
73 [a]Job 10:8; 31:15; [Ps. 139:15, 16]
74 [a]Ps. 34:2
75 [a][Heb. 12:10] [1]Lit. *righteous*
78 [a]Ps. 25:3
81 [a]Ps. 73:26; 84:2

82 My eyes fail *from searching* Your
word,
Saying, "When will You
comfort me?"
83 For [a]I have become like a
wineskin in smoke,
Yet I do not forget Your statutes.
84 [a]How many *are* the days of Your
servant?
[b]When will You execute
judgment on those who
persecute me?
85 [a]The proud have dug pits for me,
Which *is* not according to Your
law.
86 All Your commandments *are*
faithful;
They persecute me [a]wrongfully;
Help me!
87 They almost made an end of me
on earth,
But I did not forsake Your
precepts.
88 Revive me according to Your
lovingkindness,
So that I may keep the
testimony of Your mouth.

ל LAMED

89 [a]Forever, O LORD,
Your word [1]is settled in
heaven.
90 Your faithfulness *endures* to all
generations;
You established the earth, and
it [1]abides.
91 They continue this day
according to [a]Your
ordinances,
For all *are* Your servants.
92 Unless Your law *had been* my
delight,
I would then have perished in
my affliction.
93 I will never forget Your
precepts,
For by them You have given me
life.
94 I *am* Yours, save me;
For I have sought Your
precepts.
95 The wicked wait for me to
destroy me,
But I will [1]consider Your
testimonies.
96 [a]I have seen the consummation
of all perfection,
But Your commandment *is*
exceedingly broad.

מ MEM

97 Oh, how I love Your law!
[a]It *is* my meditation all the day.
98 You, through Your
commandments, make me
[a]wiser than my enemies;
For they *are* ever with me.
99 I have more understanding
than all my teachers,
[a]For Your testimonies *are* my
meditation.
100 [a]I understand more than the
[1]ancients,
Because I keep Your precepts.
101 I have restrained my feet from
every evil way,
That I may keep Your word.
102 I have not departed from Your
judgments,
For You Yourself have taught
me.
103 [a]How sweet are Your words to
my taste,
Sweeter than honey to my
mouth!
104 Through Your precepts I get
understanding;
Therefore I hate every false
way.

נ NUN

105 [a]Your word *is* a lamp to my feet
And a light to my path.
106 [a]I have sworn and confirmed
That I will keep Your righteous
judgments.
107 I am afflicted very much;
Revive me, O LORD, according
to Your word.
108 Accept, I pray, [a]the freewill
offerings of my mouth,
O LORD,
And teach me Your
judgments.
109 [a]My life *is* continually [1]in my
hand,
Yet I do not forget Your law.
110 [a]The wicked have laid a snare
for me,
Yet I have not strayed from
Your precepts.
111 [a]Your testimonies I have taken
as a [1]heritage forever,

83 [a]Job 30:30
84 [a]Ps. 39:4 [b]Rev. 6:10
85 [a]Ps. 35:7; Prov. 16:27; Jer. 18:22
86 [a]Ps. 35:19
89 [a]Ps. 89:2; Is. 40:8; Matt. 24:35; [1 Pet. 1:25] [1]Lit. *stands firm*
90 [1]Lit. *stands*
91 [a]Jer. 33:25
95 [1]*give attention to*
96 [a]Matt. 5:18
97 [a]Ps. 1:2
98 [a]Deut. 4:6
99 [a][2 Tim. 3:15]
100 [a][Job 32:7–9] [1]*aged*
103 [a]Ps. 19:10; Prov. 8:11
105 [a]Prov. 6:23
106 [a]Neh. 10:29
108 [a]Hos. 14:2; Heb. 13:15
109 [a]Judg. 12:3; Job 13:14 [1]In danger
110 [a]Ps. 140:5
111 [a]Deut. 33:4 [1]*inheritance*

For they *are* the rejoicing of my
heart.
112 I have inclined my heart to
perform Your statutes
Forever, to the very end.

ס SAMEK

113 I hate the [1]double-minded,
But I love Your law.
114 [a]You *are* my hiding place and
my shield;
I hope in Your word.
115 [a]Depart from me, you
evildoers,
For I will keep the
commandments of my
God!
116 Uphold me according to Your
word, that I may live;
And do not let me [a]be
ashamed of my hope.
117 [1]Hold me up, and I shall be
safe,
And I shall observe Your
statutes continually.
118 You reject all those who stray
from Your statutes,
For their deceit *is* falsehood.
119 You [1]put away all the wicked
of the earth [a]*like* [2]dross;
Therefore I love Your
testimonies.
120 [a]My flesh trembles for fear of
You,
And I am afraid of Your
judgments.

ע AYIN

121 I have done justice and
righteousness;
Do not leave me to my
oppressors.
122 Be [a]surety[1] for Your servant for
good;
Do not let the proud oppress
me.
123 My eyes fail *from seeking* Your
salvation
And Your righteous word.
124 Deal with Your servant
according to Your mercy,
And teach me Your statutes.
125 [a]I *am* Your servant;
Give me understanding,
That I may know Your
testimonies.
126 *It is* time for You to act, O LORD,
For they have [1]regarded Your
law as void.
127 [a]Therefore I love Your
commandments
More than gold, yes, than fine
gold!
128 Therefore all *Your* precepts
concerning all *things*
I consider *to be* right;
I hate every false way.

פ PE

129 Your testimonies are
wonderful;
Therefore my soul keeps them.
130 The entrance of Your words
gives light;
[a]It gives understanding to the
[b]simple.
131 I opened my mouth and
[a]panted,
For I longed for Your
commandments.
132 [a]Look upon me and be merciful
to me,
[b]As Your custom *is* toward
those who love Your name.
133 [a]Direct my steps by Your word,
And [b]let no iniquity have
dominion over me.
134 [a]Redeem me from the
oppression of man,
That I may keep Your precepts.
135 [a]Make Your face shine upon
Your servant,
And teach me Your statutes.
136 [a]Rivers of water run down from
my eyes,
Because *men* do not keep Your
law.

צ TSADDE

137 [a]Righteous *are* You, O LORD,
And upright *are* Your
judgments.
138 [a]Your testimonies, *which* You
have commanded,
Are righteous and very faithful.
139 [a]My zeal has [1]consumed me,
Because my enemies have
forgotten Your words.
140 [a]Your word *is* very [1]pure;
Therefore Your servant loves
it.
141 I *am* small and despised,
Yet I do not forget Your
precepts.

113 [1]Lit. *divided* in heart or mind
114 [a][Ps. 32:7]
115 [a]Ps. 6:8; Matt. 7:23
116 [a]Ps. 25:2; [Rom. 5:5; 9:33; 10:11; Phil. 1:20]
117 [1]*Uphold me*
119 [a]Is. 1:22, 25; Ezek. 22:18, 19 [1]*destroy,* lit. *cause to cease* [2]*slag* or *refuse*
120 [a]Job 4:14; Hab. 3:16
122 [a]Job 17:3; Heb. 7:22 [1]*guaranty*
125 [a]Ps. 116:16
126 [1]*broken Your law*
127 [a]Ps. 19:10
130 [a]Prov. 6:23 [b][Ps. 19:7]; Prov. 1:4
131 [a]Ps. 42:1
132 [a]Ps. 106:4 [b]Ps. 51:1; [2 Thess. 1:6]
133 [a]Ps. 17:5 [b][Ps. 19:13; Rom. 6:12]
134 [a]Luke 1:74
135 [a]Num. 6:25; Ps. 4:6
136 [a]Jer. 9:1, 18; 14:17; Lam. 3:48; Ezek. 9:4
137 [a]Ezra 9:15; Neh. 9:33; Jer. 12:1; Lam. 1:18; Dan. 9:7, 14
138 [a][Ps. 19:7–9]
139 [a]Ps. 69:9; John 2:17 [1]*put an end to*
140 [a]Ps. 12:6 [1]Lit. *refined* or *tried*

142 Your righteousness *is* an
everlasting righteousness,
And Your law *is* [a]truth.
143 Trouble and anguish have
[1]overtaken me,
Yet Your commandments *are*
my delights.
144 The righteousness of Your
testimonies *is* everlasting;
Give me understanding, and I
shall live.

ק QOPH

145 I cry out with *my* whole heart;
Hear me, O LORD!
I will keep Your statutes.
146 I cry out to You;
Save me, and I will keep Your
testimonies.
147 [a]I rise before the dawning of the
morning,
And cry for help;
I hope in Your word.
148 [a]My eyes are awake through the
night watches,
That I may meditate on Your
word.
149 Hear my voice according to
Your lovingkindness;
O LORD, revive me according
to Your justice.
150 They draw near who follow
after wickedness;
They are far from Your law.
151 You *are* [a]near, O LORD,
And all Your commandments
are truth.
152 Concerning Your testimonies,
I have known of old that You
have founded them [a]forever.

ר RESH

153 [a]Consider my affliction and
deliver me,
For I do not forget Your law.
154 [a]Plead my cause and redeem
me;
Revive me according to Your
word.
155 Salvation *is* far from the
wicked,
For they do not seek Your
statutes.
156 [1]Great *are* Your tender mercies,
O LORD;
Revive me according to Your
judgments.

142 [a][Ps. 19:9; John 17:17]
143 [1]Lit. *found*
147 [a]Ps. 5:3
148 [a]Ps. 63:1, 6
151 [a][Ps. 145:18]; Is. 50:8
152 [a]Luke 21:33
153 [a]Lam. 5:1
154 [a]1 Sam. 24:15; Mic. 7:9
156 [1]Or *Many*

157 [a]Ps. 44:18
158 [a]Ezek. 9:4
161 [a]1 Sam. 24:11; 26:18
165 [a]Prov. 3:2; [Is. 26:3; 32:17]
[1]Lit. *they have no stumbling block*
166 [a]Gen. 49:18
168 [a]Job 24:23; Prov. 5:21
169 [a]Ps. 119:27, 144
170 [1]Prayer of supplication
171 [a]Ps. 119:7

157 Many *are* my persecutors and
my enemies,
Yet I do not [a]turn from Your
testimonies.
158 I see the treacherous, and
[a]am disgusted,
Because they do not keep Your
word.
159 Consider how I love Your
precepts;
Revive me, O LORD, according
to Your lovingkindness.
160 The entirety of Your word *is*
truth,
And every one of Your
righteous judgments *endures*
forever.

ש SHIN

161 [a]Princes persecute me without
a cause,
But my heart stands in awe of
Your word.
162 I rejoice at Your word
As one who finds great
treasure.
163 I hate and abhor lying,
But I love Your law.
164 Seven times a day I praise You,
Because of Your righteous
judgments.
165 [a]Great peace have those who
love Your law,
And [1]nothing causes them to
stumble.
166 [a]LORD, I hope for Your
salvation,
And I do Your
commandments.
167 My soul keeps Your
testimonies,
And I love them exceedingly.
168 I keep Your precepts and Your
testimonies,
[a]For all my ways *are* before You.

ת TAU

169 Let my cry come before You,
O LORD;
[a]Give me understanding
according to Your word.
170 Let my [1]supplication come
before You;
Deliver me according to Your
word.
171 [a]My lips shall utter praise,

For You teach me Your statutes.
172 My tongue shall speak of Your word,
For all Your commandments *are* righteousness.
173 Let Your hand become my help,
For [a]I have chosen Your precepts.
174 [a]I long for Your salvation, O LORD,
And [b]Your law *is* my delight.
175 Let my soul live, and it shall praise You;
And let Your judgments help me.
176 [a]I have gone astray like a lost sheep;
Seek Your servant,
For I do not forget Your commandments.

173 [a]Josh. 24:22; Luke 10:42
174 [a]Ps. 119:166 [b]Ps. 119:16, 24
176 [a][Is. 53:6]; Jer. 50:6; Matt. 18:12; Luke 15:4; [1 Pet. 2:25]

PSALM 120†

Plea for Relief from Bitter Foes

A Song of Ascents.

IN [a]my distress I cried to the LORD,
And He heard me.
2 Deliver my soul, O LORD, from lying lips
And from a deceitful tongue.

3 What shall be given to you,
Or what shall be done to you,
You false tongue?
4 Sharp arrows of the [1]warrior,
With coals of the broom tree!

5 Woe is me, that I dwell in [a]Meshech,
[b]*That* I dwell among the tents of Kedar!
6 My soul has dwelt too long
With one who hates peace.
7 I *am for* peace;
But when I speak, they *are* for war.

PSALM 120

1 [a]Jon. 2:2
4 [1]*mighty one*
5 [a]Gen. 10:2; 1 Chr. 1:5; Ezek. 27:13; 38:2, 3; 39:1 [b]Gen. 25:13; Is. 21:16; 60:7; Jer. 2:10; 49:28; Ezek. 27:21

PSALM 121†

God the Help of Those Who Seek Him

A Song of Ascents.

I [a]WILL lift up my eyes to the hills—
From whence comes my help?
2 [a]My help *comes* from the LORD,
Who made heaven and earth.

3 [a]He will not allow your foot to [1]be moved;
[b]He who keeps you will not slumber.
4 Behold, He who keeps Israel
Shall neither slumber nor sleep.

5 The LORD *is* your [1]keeper;
The LORD *is* [a]your shade
[b]at your right hand.
6 [a]The sun shall not strike you by day,
Nor the moon by night.

7 The LORD shall [1]preserve you from all evil;
He shall [a]preserve your soul.
8 The LORD shall [a]preserve[1] your going out and your coming in
From this time forth, and even forevermore.

PSALM 121

1 [a][Jer. 3:23]
2 [a][Ps. 124:8]
3 [a]1 Sam. 2:9; Prov. 3:23, 26 [b][Ps. 127:1; Prov. 24:12]; Is. 27:3 [1]*slip*
5 [a]Is. 25:4 [b]Ps. 16:8 [1]*protector*
6 [a]Ps. 91:5; Is. 49:10; Jon. 4:8; Rev. 7:16
7 [a]Ps. 41:2 [1]*keep*
8 [a]Deut. 28:6; [Prov. 2:8; 3:6] [1]*keep*

PSALM 122†

The House of the Lord

A Song of Ascents. Of David.

I WAS glad when they said to me,
[a]"Let us go into the house of the LORD."

PSALM 122

1 [a][Is. 2:3; Mic. 4:2]; Zech. 8:21

120—134 (119—133, LXX) These are the Songs of Ascent or the "gradual" psalms. They were sung in Israel by the faithful as "pilgrimage songs" while the people processed from great distances up to Jerusalem for the Feasts of Passover, Pentecost and Tabernacles. From this usage, the principal liturgical use in the Orthodox Church comes as we progress through Lent toward Easter. These are the psalms sung each Wednesday and Friday at the Presanctified Liturgy as we make our pilgrimage to Easter with Christ our Passover.

In addition, Ps. 130, **out of the depths I have cried to You, O LORD** (v. 1), is a daily vesperal hymn. Psalm 132, a messianic psalm, is used at Christmas time and for feasts of Mary, for she, the Mother of God, gives to us **the fruit of** her **body** (v. 11), her Son our Savior.

2 Our feet have been standing
Within your gates, O Jerusalem!

3 Jerusalem is built
As a city that is [a]compact together,
4 [a]Where the tribes go up,
The tribes of the LORD,
[1]To [b]the Testimony of Israel,
To give thanks to the name of the LORD.
5 [a]For thrones are set there for judgment,
The thrones of the house of David.

6 [a]Pray for the peace of Jerusalem:
"May they prosper who love you.
7 Peace be within your walls,
Prosperity within your palaces."
8 For the sake of my brethren and companions,
I will now say, "Peace *be* within you."
9 Because of the house of the LORD our God
I will [a]seek your good.

PSALM 123†

Prayer for Relief from Contempt

A Song of Ascents.

UNTO You [a]I lift up my eyes,
O You [b]who dwell in the heavens.
2 Behold, as the eyes of servants *look* to the hand of their masters,
As the eyes of a maid to the hand of her mistress,
[a]So our eyes *look* to the LORD our God,
Until He has mercy on us.

3 Have mercy on us, O LORD, have mercy on us!
For we are exceedingly filled with contempt.
4 Our soul is exceedingly filled
With the scorn of those who are at ease,
With the contempt of the proud.

3 [a]2 Sam. 5:9
4 [a]Ex. 23:17; Deut. 16:16 [b]Ex. 16:34 [1]Or *As a testimony to*
5 [a]Deut. 17:8; 2 Chr. 19:8
6 [a]Ps. 51:18
9 [a]Neh. 2:10; Esth. 10:3

PSALM 123

1 [a]Ps. 121:1; 141:8 [b]Ps. 2:4; 11:4; 115:3
2 [a]Ps. 25:15

PSALM 124

1 [a]Ps. 118:6; [Rom. 8:31] [b]Ps. 129:1
3 [a]Num. 16:30; Ps. 56:1, 2; 57:3; Prov. 1:12
4 [1]*swept over*
5 [1]*swept over*
7 [a]Ps. 91:3 [b]Prov. 6:5; Hos. 9:8 [1]Persons who catch birds in a trap or snare
8 a[Ps. 121:2] [b]Gen. 1:1; Ps. 134:3

PSALM 125

3 [a]Prov. 22:8; Is. 14:5

PSALM 124†

The Lord the Defense of His People

A Song of Ascents. Of David.

"IF it had not been the LORD who was on our [a]side,"
[b]Let Israel now say—
2 "If it had not been the LORD who was on our side,
When men rose up against us,
3 Then they would have [a]swallowed us alive,
When their wrath was kindled against us;
4 Then the waters would have overwhelmed us,
The stream would have [1]gone over our soul;
5 Then the swollen waters
Would have [1]gone over our soul."

6 Blessed *be* the LORD,
Who has not given us *as* prey to their teeth.
7 [a]Our soul has escaped [b]as a bird from the snare of the [1]fowlers;
The snare is broken, and we have escaped.
8 [a]Our help *is* in the name of the LORD,
[b]Who made heaven and earth.

PSALM 125†

The Lord the Strength of His People

A Song of Ascents.

THOSE who trust in the LORD
Are like Mount Zion,
Which cannot be moved, *but* abides forever.
2 As the mountains surround Jerusalem,
So the LORD surrounds His people
From this time forth and forever.

3 For [a]the scepter of wickedness shall not rest
On the land allotted to the righteous,

Lest the righteous reach out
their hands to iniquity.

4 Do good, O LORD, to *those who are* good,
And to *those who are* upright in
their hearts.

5 As for such as turn aside to their
[a]crooked ways,
The LORD shall lead them away
With the workers of iniquity.

[b]Peace *be* upon Israel!

PSALM 126†

A Joyful Return to Zion

A Song of Ascents.

WHEN [a]the LORD brought back
[1]the captivity of Zion,
[b]We were like those who dream.
2 Then [a]our mouth was filled
with laughter,
And our tongue with singing.
Then they said among the
[1]nations,
"The LORD has done great things
for them."
3 The LORD has done great things
for us,
And we are glad.

4 Bring back our captivity,
O LORD,
As the streams in the South.
5 [a]Those who sow in tears
Shall reap in joy.
6 He who continually goes
[1]forth weeping,
Bearing [2]seed for sowing,
Shall doubtless come again
[3]with [a]rejoicing,
Bringing his sheaves *with him*.

PSALM 127†

The Home and Family

A Song of Ascents. Of Solomon.

UNLESS the LORD builds the
house,
They labor in vain who build it;
Unless [a]the LORD guards the
city,
The watchman stays awake in
vain.
2 *It is* vain for you to rise up early,
To sit up late,
To [a]eat the bread of sorrows;
For so He gives His beloved
sleep.

3 Behold, [a]children *are* a heritage
from the LORD,
[b]The fruit of the womb *is* a
[c]reward.
4 Like arrows in the hand of a
warrior,
So *are* the children of one's
youth.
5 [a]Happy *is* the man who has his
quiver full of them;
[b]They shall not be ashamed,
But shall speak with their
enemies in the gate.

PSALM 128†

Blessings of Those Who Fear the Lord

A Song of Ascents.

BLESSED [a]*is* every one who fears
the LORD,
Who walks in His ways.

2 [a]When you eat the [1]labor of your
hands,
You *shall be* happy, and *it shall*
be [b]well with you.
3 Your wife *shall be* [a]like a fruitful
vine
In the very heart of your house,
Your [b]children [c]like olive plants
All around your table.
4 Behold, thus shall the man be
blessed
Who fears the LORD.

5 [a]The LORD bless you out of Zion,
And may you see the good of
Jerusalem
All the days of your life.
6 Yes, may you [a]see your
children's children.

[b]Peace *be* upon Israel!

125:5 [a]Prov. 2:15; Is. 59:8 [b]Ps. 128:6; [Gal. 6:16]

PSALM 126

1 [a]Ps. 85:1; Jer. 29:14; Hos. 6:11; Joel 3:1 [b]Acts 12:9 [1]Those of the captivity
2 [a]Job 8:21 [1]*Gentiles*
5 [a]Is. 35:10; 51:11; 61:7; Jer. 31:9; [Gal. 6:9]
6 [a]Is. 61:3 [1]*to and fro* [2]Lit. *a bag of seed for sowing* [3]*with shouts of joy*

PSALM 127

1 [a][Ps. 121:3–5]
2 [a][Gen. 3:17, 19]
3 [a][Gen. 33:5; Josh. 24:3, 4; Ps. 113:9] [b]Deut. 7:13; 28:4; Is. 13:18 [c][Ps. 113:9]
5 [a]Ps. 128:2, 3 [b]Job 5:4; Prov. 27:11

PSALM 128

1 [a]Ps. 119:1
2 [a]Is. 3:10 [b]Deut. 4:40 [1]Fruit of the labor
3 [a]Ezek. 19:10 [b]Ps. 127:3–5 [c]Ps. 52:8; 144:12
5 [a]Ps. 134:3
6 [a]Gen. 48:11; 50:23; Job 42:16; Ps. 103:17; [Prov. 17:6] [b]Ps. 125:5

PSALM 129†

Victory over Adversaries

A Song of Ascents.

"MANY a time they have [a]afflicted[1] me from [b]my youth,"
[c]Let Israel now say—
2 "Many a time they have afflicted me from my youth;
Yet they have not prevailed against me.
3 The plowers plowed on my back;
They made their furrows long."
4 The LORD *is* righteous;
He has cut in pieces the cords of the wicked.

5 Let all those who hate Zion
Be put to shame and turned back.
6 Let them be as the [a]grass *on* the housetops,
Which withers before it grows up,
7 With which the reaper does not fill his hand,
Nor he who binds sheaves, his [1]arms.
8 Neither let those who pass by them say,
[a]"The blessing of the LORD *be* upon you;
We bless you in the name of the LORD!"

PSALM 130†

Waiting for the Redemption of the Lord

A Song of Ascents.

OUT [a]of the depths I have cried to You, O LORD;
2 Lord, hear my voice!
Let Your ears be attentive
To the voice of my supplications.

3 [a]If You, LORD, should [1]mark iniquities,
O Lord, who could [b]stand?
4 But *there is* [a]forgiveness with You,
That [b]You may be feared.

5 [a]I wait for the LORD, my soul waits,
And [b]in His word I do hope.
6 [a]My soul *waits* for the Lord
More than those who watch for the morning—
Yes, more than those who watch for the morning.

7 [a]O Israel, hope in the LORD;
For [b]with the LORD *there is* mercy,
And with Him *is* abundant redemption.
8 And [a]He shall redeem Israel
From all his iniquities.

PSALM 131†

Trust in the Lord

A Song of Ascents. Of David.

LORD, my heart is not [1]haughty,
Nor my eyes [2]lofty.
[a]Neither do I [3]concern myself with great matters,
Nor with things too [4]profound for me.

2 Surely I have calmed and quieted my soul,
[a]Like a weaned child with his mother;
Like a weaned child *is* my soul within me.

3 [a]O Israel, hope in the LORD
From this time forth and forever.

PSALM 132†

The Dwelling Place of God

A Song of Ascents.

LORD, remember David
And all his afflictions;
2 How he swore to the LORD,

PSALM 129
1 [a][Jer. 1:19; 15:20]; Matt. 16:18; 2 Cor. 4:8, 9 [b]Ezek. 23:3; Hos. 2:15 [c]Ps. 124:1 [1]*persecuted*
6 [a]Ps. 37:2
7 [1]*arms full,* lit. *bosom*
8 [a]Ruth 2:4

PSALM 130
1 [a]Lam. 3:55
3 [a][Ps. 143:2] [b][Nah. 1:6; Mal. 3:2]; Rev. 6:17 [1]*take note of*
4 [a][Ex. 34:7; Neh. 9:17; Ps. 86:5; Is. 55:7; Dan. 9:9] [b][1 Kin. 8:39, 40; Jer. 33:8, 9]
5 [a][Ps. 27:14] [b]Ps. 119:81
6 [a]Ps. 119:147
7 [a]Ps. 131:3 [b][Ps. 86:5, 15; Is. 55:7]
8 [a][Ps. 103:3, 4]; Luke 1:68; Titus 2:14

PSALM 131
1 [a]Jer. 45:5; [Rom. 12:16] [1]Proud [2]Arrogant [3]Lit. *walk in* [4]*difficult*
2 [a][Matt. 18:3; 1 Cor. 14:20]
3 [a][Ps. 130:7]

[a]*And* vowed to [b]the Mighty One
of Jacob:
3 "Surely I will not go into the
chamber of my house,
Or go up to the comfort of my
bed;
4 I will [a]not give sleep to my eyes
Or slumber to my eyelids,
5 Until I [a]find a place for the
LORD,
A dwelling place for the Mighty
One of Jacob."

6 Behold, we heard of it [a]in
Ephrathah;
[b]We found it [c]in the fields of
[1]the woods.
7 Let us go into His tabernacle;
[a]Let us worship at His
footstool.
8 [a]Arise, O LORD, to Your resting
place,
You and [b]the ark of Your
strength.
9 Let Your priests [a]be clothed
with righteousness,
And let Your saints shout for
joy.

10 For Your servant David's sake,
Do not turn away the face of
Your [1]Anointed.

11 [a]The LORD has sworn *in* truth to
David;
He will not turn from it:
"I will set upon your throne
[b]the [1]fruit of your body.
12 If your sons will keep My
covenant
And My testimony which I shall
teach them,
Their sons also shall sit upon
your throne forevermore."

13 [a]For the LORD has chosen
Zion;
He has desired *it* for His
[1]dwelling place:
14 "This[a] *is* My resting place
forever;
Here I will dwell, for I have
desired it.
15 [a]I will abundantly bless her
[1]provision;
I will satisfy her poor with
bread.
16 [a]I will also clothe her priests with
salvation,
[b]And her saints shall shout aloud
for joy.
17 [a]There I will make the [1]horn of
David grow;
[b]I will prepare a lamp for My
[2]Anointed.
18 His enemies I will [a]clothe with
shame,
But upon Himself His crown
shall flourish."

PSALM 133†

Blessed Unity of the People of God

A Song of Ascents. Of David.

BEHOLD, how good and how
pleasant *it is*
For [a]brethren to dwell together
in unity!

2 *It is* like the precious oil upon
the head,
Running down on the beard,
The beard of Aaron,
Running down on the edge of
his garments.
3 *It is* like the dew of [a]Hermon,
Descending upon the
mountains of Zion;
For [b]there the LORD
commanded the blessing—
Life forevermore.

PSALM 134†

A Prayer of Vigil

A Song of Ascents.

BEHOLD, bless the LORD,
All *you* servants of the LORD,
Who by night stand in the
house of the LORD!
2 [a]Lift up your hands *in* the
sanctuary,
And bless the LORD.

3 The LORD who made heaven
and earth
Bless you from Zion!

PSALM 132

2 [a]Ps. 65:1 [b]Gen. 49:24; Is. 49:26; 60:16
4 [a]Prov. 6:4
5 [a]1 Kin. 8:17; 1 Chr. 22:7; Ps. 26:8; Acts 7:46
6 [a]1 Sam. 17:12 [b]1 Sam. 7:1 [c]1 Chr. 13:5 [1]Heb. *Jaar*, lit. *Woods*
7 [a]Ps. 5:7; 99:5
8 [a]Num. 10:35 [b]Ps. 78:61
9 [a]Job 29:14
10 [1]Commissioned One, Heb. *Messiah*
11 [a][Ps. 89:3, 4, 33; 110:4] [b]2 Sam. 7:12; [1 Kin. 8:25; 2 Chr. 6:16; Luke 1:69; Acts 2:30] [1]*offspring*
13 [a][Ps. 48:1, 2] [1]*home*
14 [a]Ps. 68:16; Matt. 23:21
15 [a]Ps. 147:14 [1]*supply of food*
16 [a]2 Chr. 6:41; Ps. 132:9; 149:4 [b]1 Sam. 4:5; Hos. 11:12
17 [a]Ezek. 29:21; Luke 1:69 [b]1 Kin. 11:36; 15:4; 2 Kin. 8:19; 2 Chr. 21:7; Ps. 18:28 [1]Government [2]Heb. *Messiah*
18 [a]Job 8:22; Ps. 35:26

PSALM 133

1 [a]Gen. 13:8; Heb. 13:1
3 [a]Deut. 4:48 [b]Lev. 25:21; Deut. 28:8; Ps. 42:8

PSALM 134

2 [a][1 Tim. 2:8]

PSALM 135†

The Mercies of God in Creation and Redemption

PRAISE the LORD!

Praise the name of the LORD;
[a]Praise *Him,* O you servants of the LORD!
2 [a]You who stand in the house of the LORD,
In [b]the courts of the house of our God,
3 Praise the LORD, for [a]the LORD *is* good;
Sing praises to His name, [b]for *it is* pleasant.
4 For [a]the LORD has chosen Jacob for Himself,
Israel for His [1]special treasure.

5 For I know that [a]the LORD *is* great,
And our Lord *is* above all gods.
6 [a]Whatever the LORD pleases He does,
In heaven and in earth,
In the seas and in all deep places.
7 [a]He causes the [1]vapors to ascend from the ends of the earth;
[b]He makes lightning for the rain;
He brings the wind out of His [c]treasuries.

8 [a]He [1]destroyed the firstborn of Egypt,
[2]Both of man and beast.
9 [a]He sent signs and wonders into the midst of you, O Egypt,
[b]Upon Pharaoh and all his servants.
10 [a]He defeated many nations
And slew mighty kings—
11 Sihon king of the Amorites,
Og king of Bashan,
And [a]all the kingdoms of Canaan—
12 [a]And gave their land *as* a [1]heritage,
A heritage to Israel His people.

13 [a]Your name, O LORD, *endures* forever,
Your fame, O LORD, throughout all generations.
14 [a]For the LORD will judge His people,
And He will have compassion on His servants.

15 [a]The idols of the nations *are* silver and gold,
The work of men's hands.
16 They have mouths, but they do not speak;
Eyes they have, but they do not see;
17 They have ears, but they do not hear;
Nor is there *any* breath in their mouths.
18 Those who make them are like them;
So is everyone who trusts in them.

19 [a]Bless the LORD, O house of Israel!
Bless the LORD, O house of Aaron!
20 Bless the LORD, O house of Levi!
You who fear the LORD, bless the LORD!
21 Blessed be the LORD [a]out of Zion,
Who dwells in Jerusalem!

Praise the LORD!

PSALM 135
1 [a]Ps. 113:1
2 [a]Luke 2:37 [b]Ps. 116:19
3 [a][Ps. 119:68] [b]Ps. 147:1
4 [a][Ex. 19:5]; Mal. 3:17; [Titus 2:14; 1 Pet. 2:9] [1]*precious possession*
5 [a]Ps. 95:3; 97:9
6 [a]Ps. 115:3
7 [a]Jer. 10:13 [b]Job 28:25, 26; 38:24–28 [c]Jer. 51:16 [1]Water vapor
8 [a]Ex. 12:12; Ps. 78:51 [1]Lit. *struck down* [2]Lit. *From man to beast*
9 [a]Ex. 7:10; Deut. 6:22; Ps. 78:43 [b]Ps. 136:15
10 [a]Num. 21:24; Ps. 136:17
11 [a]Josh. 12:7–24
12 [a]Ps. 78:55; 136:21, 22 [1]*inheritance*
13 [a][Ex. 3:15; Ps. 102:12]
14 [a]Deut. 32:36
15 [a][Ps. 115:4–8]
19 [a][Ps. 115:9]
21 [a]Ps. 134:3

PSALM 136†

Thanksgiving to God for His Enduring Mercy

OH, [a]give thanks to the LORD, for *He is* good!
[b]For His mercy *endures* forever.

PSALM 136
1 [a]Ps. 106:1 [b]1 Chr. 16:34; Jer. 33:11

135; 136 (134; 135, LXX) These psalms go together both in content and in use. They are called in the Orthodox Church the *Polyeleos* or "Many Mercies." Psalm 136 is a responsive psalm, with the choir and the people singing alternately. These two psalms form the core of Matins for the great feast days of the Church.

2 Oh, give thanks to [a]the God of gods!
For His mercy *endures* forever.
3 Oh, give thanks to the Lord of lords!
For His mercy *endures* forever:

4 To Him [a]who alone does great wonders,
For His mercy *endures* forever;
5 [a]To Him who by wisdom made the heavens,
For His mercy *endures* forever;
6 [a]To Him who laid out the earth above the waters,
For His mercy *endures* forever;
7 [a]To Him who made great lights,
For His mercy *endures* forever—
8 [a]The sun to rule by day,
For His mercy *endures* forever;
9 The moon and stars to rule by night,
For His mercy *endures* forever.

10 [a]To Him who struck Egypt in their firstborn,
For His mercy *endures* forever;
11 [a]And brought out Israel from among them,
For His mercy *endures* forever;
12 [a]With a strong hand, and with [1]an outstretched arm,
For His mercy *endures* forever;
13 [a]To Him who divided the Red Sea in two,
For His mercy *endures* forever;
14 And made Israel pass through the midst of it,
For His mercy *endures* forever;
15 [a]But overthrew Pharaoh and his army in the Red Sea,
For His mercy *endures* forever;
16 [a]To Him who led His people through the wilderness,
For His mercy *endures* forever;
17 [a]To Him who struck down great kings,
For His mercy *endures* forever;
18 [a]And slew famous kings,
For His mercy *endures* forever—
19 [a]Sihon king of the Amorites,
For His mercy *endures* forever;
20 [a]And Og king of Bashan,
For His mercy *endures* forever—
21 [a]And gave their land as a [1]heritage,
For His mercy *endures* forever;
22 A heritage to Israel His servant,
For His mercy *endures* forever.

23 Who [a]remembered us in our lowly state,
For His mercy *endures* forever;
24 And [a]rescued us from our enemies,
For His mercy *endures* forever;
25 [a]Who gives food to all flesh,
For His mercy *endures* forever.

26 Oh, give thanks to the God of heaven!
For His mercy *endures* forever.

2 [a][Deut. 10:17]
4 [a]Deut. 6:22; Job 9:10; Ps. 72:18
5 [a]Gen. 1:1, 6–8; Prov. 3:19; Jer. 51:15
6 [a]Gen. 1:9; Ps. 24:2; [Is. 42:5]; Jer. 10:12
7 [a]Gen. 1:14–18
8 [a]Gen. 1:16
10 [a]Ex. 12:29; Ps. 135:8
11 [a]Ex. 12:51; 13:3, 16
12 [a]Ex. 6:6; Deut. 4:34; 5:15; 7:19; 9:29; 11:2; 2 Kin. 17:36; 2 Chr. 6:32; Jer. 32:17 [1]Mighty power
13 [a]Ex. 14:21
15 [a]Ex. 14:27
16 [a]Ex. 13:18; 15:22; Deut. 8:15
17 [a]Ps. 135:10–12
18 [a]Deut. 29:7
19 [a]Num. 21:21
20 [a]Num. 21:33
21 [a]Josh. 12:1 [1]*inheritance*
23 [a]Gen. 8:1; Deut. 32:36; Ps. 113:7
24 [a]Ps. 44:7
25 [a]Ps. 104:27; 145:15

PSALM 137†

A Prayer in Exile

BY the rivers of Babylon,
There we sat down, yea, we wept
When we remembered Zion.
2 We hung our harps
Upon the willows in the midst of it.
3 For there those who carried us away captive asked of us a song,
And those who [a]plundered us *requested* mirth,
Saying, "Sing us *one* of the songs of Zion!"

4 How shall we sing the LORD's song
In a foreign land?
5 If I forget you, O Jerusalem,

PSALM 137
3 [a]Ps. 79:1

137 (136, LXX) This psalm was sung in exile in the OT, while Israel was in captivity in Babylon. In Orthodox usage, it is prayed by the Christian community as being in exile in this world. In this context, it is used in the Matins service beginning just before Lent on the Sunday of the Prodigal Son (the exile returning home) and is used throughout Lent itself in the Matins services.

Let my right hand forget *its skill!*
6 If I do not remember you,
Let my [a]tongue cling to the roof
of my mouth—
If I do not exalt Jerusalem
Above my chief joy.

7 Remember, O LORD, against
[a]the sons of Edom
The day of Jerusalem,
Who said, [1]"Raze *it*, raze *it*,
To its very foundation!"

8 O daughter of Babylon,
[a]who are to be destroyed,
Happy the one [b]who repays you
as you have served us!
9 Happy the one who takes and
[a]dashes
Your little ones against the rock!

PSALM 138†

The Lord's Goodness to the Faithful

A Psalm of David.

I WILL praise You with my whole
heart;
[a]Before the gods I will sing
praises to You.
2 [a]I will worship [b]toward Your
holy temple,
And praise Your name
For Your lovingkindness and
Your truth;
For You have [c]magnified Your
word above all Your name.
3 In the day when I cried out, You
answered me,
And made me bold *with* strength
in my soul.

4 [a]All the kings of the earth shall
praise You, O LORD,

6 [a]Job 29:10; Ps. 22:15; Ezek. 3:26
7 [a]Jer. 49:7–22; Lam. 4:21; Ezek. 25:12–14; 35:2; Amos 1:11; Obad. 10–14 [1]Lit. *Make bare*
8 [a]Is. 13:1–6; 47:1 [b]Jer. 50:15; Rev. 18:6
9 [a]2 Kin. 8:12; Is. 13:16; Hos. 13:16; Nah. 3:10

PSALM 138

1 [a]Ps. 119:46
2 [a]Ps. 28:2 [b]1 Kin. 8:29 [c]Is. 42:21
4 [a]Ps. 102:15
6 [a][Ps. 113:4–7] [b]Prov. 3:34; [Is. 57:15]; Luke 1:48; [James 4:6; 1 Pet. 5:5]
7 [a][Ps. 23:3, 4]
8 [a]Ps. 57:2; [Phil. 1:6] [b]Job 10:3, 8 [1]*complete*

PSALM 139

1 [a]Ps. 17:3; Jer. 12:3
2 [a]2 Kin. 19:27 [b]Is. 66:18; Matt. 9:4
3 [a]Job 14:16; 31:4 [1]Lit. *winnow*

When they hear the words of
Your mouth.
5 Yes, they shall sing of the ways
of the LORD,
For great *is* the glory of the
LORD.
6 [a]Though the LORD *is* on high,
Yet [b]He regards the lowly;
But the proud He knows from
afar.

7 [a]Though I walk in the midst of
trouble, You will revive me;
You will stretch out Your hand
Against the wrath of my
enemies,
And Your right hand will save
me.
8 [a]The LORD will [1]perfect *that which*
concerns me;
Your mercy, O LORD, *endures*
forever;
[b]Do not forsake the works of
Your hands.

PSALM 139†

God's Perfect Knowledge of Man

For the Chief Musician. A Psalm of David.

O LORD, [a]You have searched me
and known *me*.
2 [a]You know my sitting down and
my rising up;
You [b]understand my thought
afar off.
3 [a]You [1]comprehend my path and
my lying down,
And are acquainted with all my
ways.
4 For *there is* not a word on my
tongue,

138 (137, LXX) The LXX clarifies v. 1: "I will praise You with my whole heart; in the presence of the angels I will sing Your praise." This psalm is thus used by the Orthodox Church on the feast days of the angels. The psalmist thanks God for the Gentiles who are going to see God and receive His grace, especially the kings of the Gentiles. This takes place after the Incarnation.

139 (138, LXX) Each of us is known by the Lord. The psalmist wonders at the depth of God's plan and foretells the calling of the Gentiles and the resistance of the Jews. Verse 8 is prophetic, and could only be true for us had God entered Sheol. Thus, Christ descended to Hades on our behalf, trampling down death by death, so that through God in the flesh dwelling in hell, we are not separated from Him even in death!

But behold, O LORD, [a]You know
it altogether.
5 You have [1]hedged me behind
and before,
And laid Your hand upon me.
6 [a]*Such* knowledge *is* too
wonderful for me;
It is high, I cannot *attain* it.

7 [a]Where can I go from Your
Spirit?
Or where can I flee from Your
presence?
8 [a]If I ascend into heaven, You *are*
there;
[b]If I make my bed in [1]hell,
behold, You *are there.*
9 *If* I take the wings of the
morning,
And dwell in the uttermost parts
of the sea,
10 Even there Your hand shall lead
me,
And Your right hand shall hold
me.
11 If I say, "Surely the darkness
shall [1]fall on me,"
Even the night shall be light
about me;
12 Indeed, [a]the darkness [1]shall not
hide from You,
But the night shines as the
day;
The darkness and the light *are*
both alike *to You.*

13 For You formed my inward
parts;
You [1]covered me in my
mother's womb.
14 I will praise You, for [1]I am
fearfully *and* wonderfully
made;
Marvelous are Your works,
And *that* my soul knows very
well.
15 [a]My [1]frame was not hidden from
You,
When I was made in secret,
And skillfully wrought in the
lowest parts of the earth.
16 Your eyes saw my substance,
being yet unformed.

4 [a][Heb. 4:13]
5 [1]*enclosed*
6 [a]Job 42:3; Ps. 40:5
7 [a][Jer. 23:24; Amos 9:2–4]
8 [a][Amos 9:2–4] [b][Job 26:6; Prov. 15:11] [1]Or *Sheol*
11 [1]Vg., Symmachus *cover*
12 [a]Job 26:6; 34:22; [Dan. 2:22; Heb. 4:13] [1]Lit. *is not dark*
13 [1]*wove*
14 [1]So with MT, Tg.; LXX, Syr., Vg. *You are fearfully wonderful*
15 [a]Job 10:8, 9; Eccl. 11:5 [1]Lit. *bones were*
17 [a][Ps. 40:5; Rom. 11:33]
19 [a][Is. 11:4] [b]Ps. 119:115 [1]Lit. *men of bloodshed*
20 [a]Jude 15 [1]LXX, Vg. *They take your cities in vain*
21 [a]2 Chr. 19:2
22 [1]*complete*
23 [a]Job 31:6; Ps. 26:2
24 [a]Ps. 5:8; 143:10

PSALM 140
2 [a]Ps. 56:6

And in Your book they all were
written,
The days fashioned for me,
When *as yet there were* none of
them.
17 [a]How precious also are Your
thoughts to me, O God!
How great is the sum of them!
18 *If* I should count them, they
would be more in number
than the sand;
When I awake, I am still with
You.
19 Oh, that You would [a]slay the
wicked, O God!
[b]Depart from me, therefore, you
[1]bloodthirsty men.
20 For they [a]speak against You
wickedly;
[1]Your enemies take *Your name* in
vain.
21 [a]Do I not hate them, O LORD,
who hate You?
And do I not loathe those who
rise up against You?
22 I hate them with [1]perfect hatred;
I count them my enemies.
23 [a]Search me, O God, and know
my heart;
Try me, and know my anxieties;
24 And see if *there is any* wicked
way in me,
And [a]lead me in the way
everlasting.

PSALM 140†

Prayer for Deliverance from Evil Men

To the Chief Musician. A Psalm of David.

DELIVER me, O LORD, from evil
men;
Preserve me from violent men,
2 Who plan evil things in *their*
hearts;
[a]They continually gather
together *for* war.

---

140 (139, LXX) This is the last of the Passion psalms as used by the Orthodox Church. It is sung at Sixth Hour on Good Friday.

3 They sharpen their tongues like a serpent;
The [a]poison of asps *is* under their lips. Selah

4 [a]Keep me, O LORD, from the hands of the wicked;
Preserve me from violent men,
Who have purposed to make my steps stumble.
5 The proud have hidden a [a]snare for me, and cords;
They have spread a net by the wayside;
They have set traps for me. Selah

6 I said to the LORD: "You *are* my God;
Hear the voice of my supplications, O LORD.
7 O GOD the Lord, the strength of my salvation,
You have [1]covered my head in the day of battle.
8 Do not grant, O LORD, the desires of the wicked;
Do not further his *wicked* scheme,
[a]*Lest* they be exalted. Selah

9 "*As for* the head of those who surround me,
Let the evil of their lips cover them;
10 [a]Let burning coals fall upon them;
Let them be cast into the fire,
Into deep pits, that they rise not up again.
11 Let not a slander be established in the earth;
Let evil hunt the violent man to overthrow *him*."

3 [a]Ps. 58:4; Rom. 3:13; James 3:8
4 [a]Ps. 71:4
5 [a]Ps. 35:7; Jer. 18:22
7 [1]*sheltered*
8 [a]Deut. 32:27
10 [a]Ps. 11:6
12 [a]1 Kin. 8:45; Ps. 9:4

PSALM 141
2 [a][Ex. 30:8]; Luke 1:10; [Rev. 5:8; 8:3, 4] [b]Ps. 134:2; [1 Tim. 2:8] [c]Ex. 29:39, 41; 1 Kin. 18:29, 36; Dan. 9:21
3 [a][Prov. 13:3; 21:23]
4 [a]Prov. 23:6
5 [a][Prov. 9:8; Eccl. 7:5; Gal. 6:1]

12 I know that the LORD will [a]maintain
The cause of the afflicted,
And justice for the poor.
13 Surely the righteous shall give thanks to Your name;
The upright shall dwell in Your presence.

PSALM 141†

Lord I Cry to You

A Psalm of David.

LORD, I cry out to You;
Make haste to me!
Give ear to my voice when I cry out to You.
2 Let my prayer be set before You [a]*as* incense,
[b]The lifting up of my hands *as* [c]the evening sacrifice.

3 Set a guard, O LORD, over my [a]mouth;
Keep watch over the door of my lips.
4 Do not incline my heart to any evil thing,
To practice wicked works
With men who work iniquity;
[a]And do not let me eat of their delicacies.

5 [a]Let the righteous strike me;
It shall be a kindness.
And let him rebuke me;
It shall be as excellent oil;
Let my head not refuse it.

For still my prayer *is* against the deeds of the wicked.

141; 142 (140; 141, LXX) These are the psalms of the evening incense. These two psalms are both sung at the evening prayers, or Vespers, with 141:2 sung both in Israel and in the Church during the offering of the incense to God. As Rev. 5:8 teaches, incense is the visible sign of the prayers of all God's people. The prophet Malachi foretold its continued use in "every place," including "among the Gentiles" (Mal. 1:11). Incense was brought to Christ as a gift at His birth, and it has been used in the worship of the Christian Church from her very start.

The Orthodox Church understands 141:3, 4 as a daily prayer for the purification of our words and thoughts. These verses appear early in the Vespers service.

The LXX clarifies 141:6, 7: "When they [the wicked] are given over to those who shall condemn them, they will learn that the Word of the Lord is true. As a rock which one breaks and shatters on the ground, so shall their [the wicked's] bones be strewn at the mouth of the grave."

6 Their judges are overthrown by the sides of the [1]cliff,
And they hear my words, for they are sweet.
7 Our bones are scattered at the mouth of the grave,
As when one plows and breaks up the earth.

8 But [a]my eyes *are* upon You, O GOD the Lord;
In You I take refuge;
[1]Do not leave my soul destitute.
9 Keep me from [a]the snares they have laid for me,
And from the traps of the workers of iniquity.
10 [a]Let the wicked fall into their own nets,
While I escape safely.

6 [1]*rock*
8 [a]2 Chr. 20:12; Ps. 25:15
[1]Lit. *Do not make my soul bare*
9 [a]Ps. 119:110
10 [a]Ps. 35:8

PSALM 142†

A Supplication for Protection from Evildoers

A [a]Contemplation[1] of David. A Prayer [b]when he was in the cave.

I CRY out to the LORD with my voice;
With my voice to the LORD I make my supplication.
2 I pour out my complaint before Him;
I declare before Him my trouble.

3 When my spirit [1]was [a]overwhelmed within me,
Then You knew my path.
In the way in which I walk
They have secretly [b]set a snare for me.
4 Look on *my* right hand and see,
For *there is* no one who acknowledges me;
Refuge has failed me;
No one cares for my soul.

5 I cried out to You, O LORD:
I said, "You *are* my refuge,
My portion in the land of the living.
6 [1]Attend to my cry,
For I am brought very low;
Deliver me from my persecutors,
For they are stronger than I.
7 Bring my soul out of prison,
That I may [a]praise Your name;
The righteous shall surround me,
For You shall deal bountifully with me."

PSALM 142
title [a]Ps. 32:title
[b]1 Sam. 22:1; Ps. 57:title
[1]Heb. *Maschil*
3 [a]Ps. 77:3
[b]Ps. 141:9
[1]Lit. *fainted*
6 [1]*Give heed*
7 [a]Ps. 34:1, 2

PSALM 143†

Waiting in Darkness for the Light

A Psalm of David.

HEAR my prayer, O LORD,
Give ear to my supplications!
In Your faithfulness answer me,
And in Your righteousness.
2 Do not enter into judgment with Your servant,
[a]For in Your sight no one living is righteous.

3 For the enemy has persecuted my soul;
He has crushed my life to the ground;
He has made me dwell in [1]darkness,
Like those who have long been dead.
4 [a]Therefore my spirit is overwhelmed within me;
My heart within me is distressed.

5 [a]I remember the days of old;
I meditate on all Your works;
I [1]muse on the work of Your hands.
6 I spread out my hands to You;
[a]My soul *longs* for You like a thirsty land. Selah

PSALM 143
2 [a][Ex. 34:7]; Job 4:17; 9:2; 25:4; Ps. 130:3; Eccl. 7:20; [Rom. 3:20–23; Gal. 2:16]
3 [1]*dark places*
4 [a]Ps. 77:3
5 [a]Ps. 77:5, 10, 11
[1]*ponder*
6 [a]Ps. 63:1

143 (142, LXX) This is the last of the six psalms of Matins (see note on Ps. 3). It is the song of one afflicted, waiting in the darkness for the light. It is a prayer which awaits the light of dawn (v. 8)—both physical and spiritual. Verse 10b is used at Pentecost with the LXX rendering: "Let your good Spirit lead me on a level path."

7 Answer me speedily, O LORD;
My spirit fails!
Do not hide Your face from me,
[a]Lest I [1]be like those who [2]go down into the pit.
8 Cause me to hear Your lovingkindness [a]in the morning,
For in You do I trust;
[b]Cause me to know the way in which I should walk,
For [c]I lift up my soul to You.

9 Deliver me, O LORD, from my enemies;
[1]In You I take shelter.
10 [a]Teach me to do Your will,
For You *are* my God;
[b]Your Spirit *is* good.
Lead me in [c]the land of uprightness.

11 [a]Revive me, O LORD, for Your name's sake!
For Your righteousness' sake bring my soul out of trouble.
12 In Your mercy [a]cut[1] off my enemies,
And destroy all those who afflict my soul;
For I *am* Your servant.

PSALM 144

A Blessing for the King

A Psalm of David.

BLESSED *be* the LORD my Rock,
[a]Who trains my hands for war,
And my fingers for battle—
2 My lovingkindness and my fortress,
My high tower and my deliverer,
My shield and *the One* in whom I take refuge,
Who subdues [1]my people under me.

3 [a]LORD, what *is* man, that You take knowledge of him?
Or the son of man, that You are mindful of him?
4 [a]Man is like a breath;
[b]His days *are* like a passing shadow.

5 [a]Bow down Your heavens, O LORD, and come down;
[b]Touch the mountains, and they shall smoke.
6 [a]Flash forth lightning and scatter them;
Shoot out Your arrows and destroy them.
7 Stretch out Your hand from above;
Rescue me and deliver me out of great waters,
From the hand of foreigners,
8 Whose mouth [a]speaks [1]lying words,
And whose right hand *is* a right hand of falsehood.

9 I will [a]sing a new song to You, O God;
On a harp of ten strings I will sing praises to You,
10 *The One* who gives [1]salvation to kings,
[a]Who delivers David His servant
From the deadly sword.

11 Rescue me and deliver me from the hand of foreigners,
Whose mouth speaks lying words,
And whose right hand *is* a right hand of falsehood—
12 That our sons *may be* [a]as plants grown up in their youth;
That our daughters *may be* as [1]pillars,
Sculptured in palace style;
13 *That* our barns *may be* full,
Supplying all kinds of produce;
That our sheep may bring forth thousands
And ten thousands in our fields;
14 *That* our oxen *may be* well laden;
That there be no [1]breaking in or going out;
That there be no outcry in our streets.
15 [a]Happy *are* the people who are in such a state;
Happy *are* the people whose God *is* the LORD!

143:7 [a]Ps. 28:1 [1]*become* [2]Die
8 [a]Ps. 46:5 [b]Ps. 5:8 [c]Ps. 25:1
9 [1]LXX, Vg. *To You I flee*
10 [a]Ps. 25:4, 5 [b]Neh. 9:20 [c]Is. 26:10
11 [a]Ps. 119:25
12 [a]Ps. 54:5 [1]*put an end to*

PSALM 144
1 [a]2 Sam. 22:35; Ps. 18:34
2 [1]So with MT, LXX, Vg.; Syr., Tg. *the peoples* (cf. 18:47)
3 [a]Job 7:17; Ps. 8:4; Heb. 2:6
4 [a]Ps. 39:11 [b]Job 8:9; 14:2; Ps. 102:11
5 [a]Ps. 18:9; Is. 64:1 [b]Ps. 104:32
6 [a]Ps. 18:13, 14
8 [a]Ps. 12:2 [1]*empty* or *worthless*
9 [a]Ps. 33:2, 3; 40:3
10 [a]Ps. 18:50 [1]*deliverance*
12 [a]Ps. 128:3 [1]*corner pillars*
14 [1]Lit. *breach*
15 [a]Deut. 33:29; [Ps. 33:12; Jer. 17:7]

PSALM 145†

A Song of God's Majesty and Love

[a]A Praise of David.

I WILL [1]extol You, my God,
O King;
And I will bless Your name
forever and ever.
2 Every day I will bless You,
And I will praise Your name
forever and ever.
3 [a]Great *is* the LORD, and greatly
to be praised;
And [b]His greatness *is*
[1]unsearchable.

4 [a]One generation shall praise
Your works to another,
And shall declare Your mighty
acts.
5 [1]I will meditate on the glorious
splendor of Your majesty,
And [2]on Your wondrous works.
6 *Men* shall speak of the might of
Your awesome acts,
And I will declare Your
greatness.
7 They shall [1]utter the memory of
Your great goodness,
And shall sing of Your
righteousness.

8 [a]The LORD *is* gracious and full of
compassion,
Slow to anger and great in
mercy.
9 [a]The LORD *is* good to all,
And His tender mercies *are* over
all His works.

10 [a]All Your works shall praise You,
O LORD,
And Your saints shall bless You.
11 They shall speak of the glory of
Your kingdom,
And talk of Your power,
12 To make known to the sons of
men His mighty acts,
And the glorious majesty of His
kingdom.
13 [a]Your kingdom *is* an everlasting
kingdom,
And Your dominion *endures*
throughout all [1]generations.

14 The LORD upholds all who fall,
And [a]raises up all *who are*
bowed down.
15 [a]The eyes of all look expectantly
to You,
And [b]You give them their food
in due season.
16 You open Your hand
[a]And satisfy the desire of every
living thing.

17 The LORD *is* righteous in all His
ways,
Gracious in all His works.
18 [a]The LORD *is* near to all who call
upon Him,
To all who call upon Him
[b]in truth.
19 He will fulfill the desire of those
who fear Him;
He also will hear their cry and
save them.
20 [a]The LORD preserves all who love
Him,
But all the wicked He will
destroy.
21 My mouth shall speak the praise
of the LORD,
And all flesh shall bless His holy
name
Forever and ever.

PSALM 146†

God Our Helper

PRAISE[1] the LORD!

[a]Praise the LORD, O my soul!

PSALM 145
title [a]Ps. 100:title
1 [1]*praise*
3 [a][Ps. 147:5] [b]Job 5:9; 9:10; 11:7; Is. 40:28; [Rom. 11:33] [1]Beyond our understanding
4 [a]Is. 38:19
5 [1]So with MT, Tg.; DSS, LXX, Syr., Vg. *They* [2]Lit. *on the words of Your wondrous works*
7 [1]*eagerly utter,* lit. *bubble forth*
8 [a][Ex. 34:6, 7; Num. 14:18]; Ps. 86:5, 15
9 [a][Ps. 100:5]; Jer. 33:11; Nah. 1:7; [Matt. 19:17; Mark 10:18]
10 [a]Ps. 19:1
13 [a]Dan. 2:44; 4:3; [1 Tim. 1:17; 2 Pet. 1:11] [1]So with MT, Tg.; DSS, LXX, Syr., Vg. add *The LORD is faithful in all His words, And holy in all His works*
14 [a]Ps. 146:8
15 [a]Ps. 104:27 [b]Ps. 136:25
16 [a]Ps. 104:21, 28
18 [a][Deut. 4:7] [b][John 4:24]
20 [a][Ps. 31:23]

PSALM 146
1 [a]Ps. 103:1 [1]Heb. *Hallelujah*

145 (144, LXX) Verse 2 is part of the Great Doxology at the close of Sunday Matins. Verses 15, 16 are frequently used in the monasteries as a giving of thanks before meals. In patristic literature we find the Fathers of the Church interpreting **Your works** (v. 10) as referring to the Incarnation, and the **generations** (v. 13) as referring to the Church.

146 (145, LXX) This psalm is a song of praise to God as our hope and as the Restorer and Healer of Israel. In many Orthodox Churches, this is the ordinary second antiphon (psalm sung responsively) of the Divine Liturgy.

2 [a]While I live I will praise the LORD;
I will sing praises to my God while I have my being.

3 [a]Do not put your trust in princes,
Nor in [1]a son of man, in whom *there is* no [2]help.
4 [a]His spirit departs, he returns to his earth;
In that very day [b]his plans perish.

5 [a]Happy *is he* who *has* the God of Jacob for his help,
Whose hope *is* in the LORD his God,
6 [a]Who made heaven and earth,
The sea, and all that *is* in them;
Who keeps truth forever,
7 [a]Who executes justice for the oppressed,
[b]Who gives food to the hungry.
[c]The LORD gives freedom to the prisoners.

8 [a]The LORD opens *the eyes of* the blind;
[b]The LORD raises those who are bowed down;
The LORD loves the righteous.
9 [a]The LORD watches over the strangers;
He relieves the fatherless and widow;
[b]But the way of the wicked He [1]turns upside down.
10 [a]The LORD shall reign forever—
Your God, O Zion, to all generations.

Praise the LORD!

PSALM 147†

Praise to God for His Word and Providence

PRAISE[1] the LORD!
For [a]*it is* good to sing praises to our God;
[b]For *it is* pleasant, *and* [c]praise is beautiful.

2 The LORD [a]builds up Jerusalem;
[b]He gathers together the outcasts of Israel.
3 [a]He heals the brokenhearted
And binds up their [1]wounds.
4 [a]He counts the number of the stars;
He calls them all by name.
5 [a]Great *is* our Lord, and [b]mighty in power;
[c]His understanding *is* infinite.
6 [a]The LORD lifts up the humble;
He casts the wicked down to the ground.

7 Sing to the LORD with thanksgiving;
Sing praises on the harp to our God,
8 [a]Who covers the heavens with clouds,
Who prepares rain for the earth,
Who makes grass to grow on the mountains.
9 [a]He gives to the beast its food,
And [b]to the young ravens that cry.

10 [a]He does not delight in the strength of the horse;
He takes no pleasure in the legs of a man.
11 The LORD takes pleasure in those who fear Him,
In those who hope in His mercy.

12 Praise the LORD, O Jerusalem!
Praise your God, O Zion!
13 For He has strengthened the bars of your gates;
He has blessed your children within you.
14 [a]He makes peace *in* your borders,
And [b]fills you with [1]the finest wheat.

15 [a]He sends out His command *to the* earth;

2 [a]Ps. 104:33
3 [a][Is. 2:22] [1]A human being [2]*salvation*
4 [a][Eccl. 12:7] [b][Ps. 33:10; 1 Cor. 2:6]
5 [a]Jer. 17:7
6 [a]Gen. 1:1; Ex. 20:11; Acts 4:24; Rev. 14:7
7 [a]Ps. 103:6 [b]Ps. 107:9 [c]Ps. 107:10; Is. 61:1
8 [a]Matt. 9:30; [John 9:7, 32, 33] [b]Luke 13:13
9 [a]Deut. 10:18; Ps. 68:5 [b]Ps. 147:6 [1]Lit. *makes crooked*
10 [a]Ex. 15:18; Ps. 10:16; [Rev. 11:15]

PSALM 147
1 [a]Ps. 92:1 [b]Ps. 135:3 [c]Ps. 33:1 [1]Heb. *Hallelujah*
2 [a]Ps. 102:16 [b]Deut. 30:3; Is. 11:12; 56:8; Ezek. 39:28
3 [a][Ps. 51:17]; Is. 61:1; Luke 4:18 [1]Lit. *sorrows*
4 [a]Is. 40:26
5 [a]Ps. 48:1 [b]Nah. 1:3 [c]Is. 40:28
6 [a]Ps. 146:8, 9
8 [a]Job 38:26; Ps. 104:13
9 [a]Job 38:41 [b][Matt. 6:26]
10 [a]Ps. 33:16, 17
14 [a]Is. 54:13; 60:17, 18 [b]Ps. 132:15 [1]Lit. *fat of wheat*
15 [a][Ps. 107:20]

147 Verses 1–11 here in the MT are Ps. 146 in the LXX. Verses 12–20 are Ps. 147 in the LXX, closing the section of numerical discrepancy between the two versions.

(continued on next page)

His word runs very swiftly.
16 [a]He gives snow like wool;
He scatters the frost like ashes;
17 He casts out His hail like [1]morsels;
Who can stand before His cold?
18 [a]He sends out His word and melts them;
He causes His wind to blow, *and* the waters flow.

19 [a]He declares His word to Jacob,
[b]His statutes and His judgments to Israel.
20 [a]He has not dealt thus with any nation;
And *as for His* judgments, they have not known them.

[1]Praise the LORD!

16 [a]Job 37:6
17 [1]*fragments of food*
18 [a]Job 37:10
19 [a]Deut. 33:4; Ps. 103:7 [b]Mal. 4:4
20 [a]Deut. 4:32–34; [Rom. 3:1, 2] [1]Heb. *Hallelujah*

PSALM 148†

Praise to the Lord from Creation

PRAISE[1] the LORD!

Praise the LORD from the heavens;
Praise Him in the heights!
2 Praise Him, all His angels;
Praise Him, all His hosts!
3 Praise Him, sun and moon;
Praise Him, all you stars of light!
4 Praise Him, [a]you heavens of heavens,
And [b]you waters above the heavens!

5 Let them praise the name of the LORD,
For [a]He commanded and they were created.
6 [a]He also established them forever and ever;
He made a decree which shall not pass away.

7 Praise the LORD from the earth,
[a]You great sea creatures and all the depths;
8 Fire and hail, snow and clouds;
Stormy wind, fulfilling His word;
9 [a]Mountains and all hills;
Fruitful trees and all cedars;
10 Beasts and all cattle;
Creeping things and flying fowl;
11 Kings of the earth and all peoples;
Princes and all judges of the earth;
12 Both young men and maidens;
Old men and children.

13 Let them praise the name of the LORD,
For His [a]name alone is exalted;
His glory *is* above the earth and heaven.
14 And He [a]has exalted the [1]horn of His people,
The praise of [b]all His saints—
Of the children of Israel,
[c]A people near to Him.

[2]Praise the LORD!

PSALM 148
1 [1]Heb. *Hallelujah*
4 [a]Deut. 10:14; 1 Kin. 8:27; [Neh. 9:6] [b]Gen. 1:7
5 [a]Gen. 1:1, 6
6 [a]Ps. 89:37; [Jer. 31:35, 36; 33:20, 25]
7 [a]Is. 43:20
9 [a]Is. 44:23; 49:13
13 [a]Ps. 8:1
14 [a]1 Sam. 2:1; Ps. 75:10 [b]Ps. 149:9 [c]Lev. 10:3; Eph. 2:17 [1]Strength or dominion [2]Heb. *Hallelujah*

PSALM 149†

Praise to God for His Salvation and Judgment

PRAISE[1] the LORD!

[a]Sing to the LORD a new song,
And His praise in the assembly of saints.

PSALM 149
1 [a]Ps. 33:3 [1]Heb. *Hallelujah*

(continued from previous page)
Verses 12, 13 (the beginning of the LXX Ps. 147) are used on the Sunday of St. Thomas, the Sunday after Easter. They are fulfilled in the meeting behind closed doors of the disciples in the Upper Room in Jerusalem where Thomas's faith is strengthened: **He has blessed your children within you** (v. 13).

148—150 These three psalms of praise, called "The Praises," form the conclusion to the Psalter. These psalms exhort all of creation to give praise to God. They are sung every morning in the Church as "The Praises" of Matins. Scholars have discovered this use as consistent in all historic Christian practice, East and West alike. The climax of the Psalter is reached in Ps. 150, where humanity and creation, everywhere and in all circumstances, are called upon to make this doxology to God.

2 Let Israel rejoice in their Maker;
Let the children of Zion be
joyful in their [a]King.
3 [a]Let them praise His name with
the dance;
Let them sing praises to Him
with the timbrel and harp.
4 For [a]the LORD takes pleasure in
His people;
[b]He will beautify the [1]humble
with salvation.

5 Let the saints be joyful in glory;
Let them [a]sing aloud on their
beds.
6 *Let* the high praises of God *be*
in their mouth,
And [a]a two-edged sword in
their hand,
7 To execute vengeance on the
nations,
And punishments on the
peoples;
8 To bind their kings with chains,
And their nobles with fetters of
iron;
9 [a]To execute on them the written
judgment—
[b]This honor have all His saints.

[1]Praise the LORD!

2 [a]Judg. 8:23; Zech. 9:9; Matt. 21:5
3 [a]Ex. 15:20; Ps. 81:2
4 [a]Ps. 35:27 [b]Ps. 132:16; Is. 61:3 [1]*meek*
5 [a]Job 35:10
6 [a]Heb. 4:12; Rev. 1:16
9 [a]Deut. 7:1, 2; Ezek. 28:26 [b]Ps. 148:14; 1 Cor. 6:2 [1]Heb. *Hallelujah*

PSALM 150
1 [a]Ps. 145:5, 6 [1]Heb. *Hallelujah* [2]*expanse* of heaven
2 [a]Deut. 3:24
3 [1]*cornet*
6 [1]Heb. *Hallelujah*

PSALM 150†

Let All Things Praise the Lord

PRAISE[a1] the LORD!

Praise God in His sanctuary;
Praise Him in His mighty
[2]firmament!

2 Praise Him for His mighty acts;
Praise Him according to His
excellent [a]greatness!

3 Praise Him with the sound of
the [1]trumpet;
Praise Him with the lute and
harp!
4 Praise Him with the timbrel and
dance;
Praise Him with stringed
instruments and flutes!
5 Praise Him with loud cymbals;
Praise Him with clashing
cymbals!

6 Let everything that has breath
praise the LORD.

[1]Praise the LORD!

Morning Prayers

The Trisagion Prayers

† In the Name of the Father, and of the Son, and of the Holy Spirit. Amen.

Glory to You, O Lord, glory to You.

O Heavenly King, O Comforter, the Spirit of Truth, who are in all places and fill all things, the treasury of good things and the giver of life: Come and abide in us, cleanse us from every stain, and save our souls, O Good One.

Holy God, Holy Mighty, Holy Immortal, have mercy on us (*three times*).

Glory to the Father, and to the Son, and to the Holy Spirit, now and ever, and unto ages of ages. Amen.

O Most Holy Trinity, have mercy on us. O Lord, cleanse us from our sins. O Master, pardon our transgressions. O Holy One, visit and heal our infirmities, for Your Name's sake.

Lord, have mercy (*three times*).

Glory to the Father, and to the Son, and to the Holy Spirit, now and ever, and unto ages of ages. Amen.

Our Father, who are in heaven, hallowed be Your Name. Your Kingdom come. Your will be done, on earth as it is in heaven. Give us this day our daily bread; and forgive us our trespasses, as we forgive those who trespass against us; and lead us not into temptation, but deliver us from evil.

For Yours is the Kingdom, and the power, and the glory, of the Father, and of the Son, and of the Holy Spirit, now and ever, and unto ages of ages. Amen.

Morning Prayer to the Holy Trinity

Arising from sleep, I thank You, O Most Holy Trinity, that, for the sake of Your great kindness and longsuffering, You have not had indignation against me, for I am slothful and sinful. Neither have You destroyed me in my transgressions, but You have shown Your customary love toward mankind, and have raised me up as I lay in heedlessness, that I might sing my morning hymn and glorify Your sovereignty. Now enlighten the eyes of my understanding, open my ears to receive Your words, and teach me Your commandments. Help me to do Your will, to sing to You, to confess You from my heart, and to praise Your All-Holy Name: of the Father, and of the Son, and of the Holy Spirit, now and ever, and unto ages of ages. Amen.

The Nicene Creed

I believe in one God, the Father Almighty, Maker of heaven and earth, and of all things visible and invisible; and in one Lord Jesus Christ, the Son of God, the Only-Begotten, begotten of the Father before all worlds, Light of Light, Very God of Very God, begotten, not made; of one essence with the

Father; by whom all things were made: who for us men and for our salvation came down from heaven and was incarnate of the Holy Spirit and the Virgin Mary, and was made man; and was crucified also for us under Pontius Pilate, and suffered and was buried. The third day He rose again, according to the Scriptures; and ascended into heaven, and sits at the right hand of the Father; and He shall come again with glory to judge the living and the dead; whose Kingdom shall have no end. And I believe in the Holy Spirit, the Lord and Giver of life, who proceeds from the Father, who with the Father and the Son together is worshiped and glorified, who spoke by the prophets. And I believe in One Holy Catholic and Apostolic Church. I acknowledge one baptism for the remission of sins. I look for the resurrection of the dead and the life of the world to come. Amen.

The Psalms

Sunday	Psalm 5
Monday	Psalm 90
Tuesday	Psalm 101
Wednesday	Psalm 3
Thursday	Psalm 63
Friday	Psalm 103
Saturday	Psalm 5

The Gospel and Epistle

Referring to the Lectionary in the back of *The Orthodox Study Bible*, you may, as time permits, read the Gospel and Epistle for this day.

Intercessory Prayers

Remember, O Lord Jesus Christ, our God, Your mercies and loving-kindnesses, which have been from everlasting, and for the sake of which You did become man and deign to endure crucifixion and death for the salvation of all who rightly believe in You. You rose from the dead and ascended into heaven, and sit at the right hand of God the Father, and regard the humble prayers of all who call upon You with their whole heart. Incline Your ear and hear the humble entreaty of me, Your unprofitable servant, who offers it for an odor of spiritual fragrance for all Your people.

And first of all remember Your Holy Catholic and Apostolic Church, which You have purchased with Your precious blood. Confirm and strengthen it, enlarge and multiply it, keep it in peace, and preserve it unconquerable by the gates of hell forever. Heal the schisms of the churches, quench the ragings of the heathen, speedily undo and root out the growths of heresies, and bring them to naught by the power of Your Holy Spirit.

Save, O Lord, and have mercy upon all world rulers, on our president (*name*), on (*names*), and on all our civil authorities. Speak peace and blessing in their hearts for Your Holy Church and for all Your people, in order that we may live a calm and peaceful life, in all godliness and dignity.

Save, O Lord, and have mercy upon patriarchs, metropolitans, archbishops, priests, ministers, and deacons, and the whole clergy of Your Church, which You have established to feed the flock of Your word, and by their prayers have mercy upon me, and save me, a sinner.

Save, O Lord, and have mercy upon my spiritual father (*name*) and by his holy prayers forgive me my transgressions.

Save, O Lord, and have mercy upon my parents (*names*), my spouse (*name*), my brothers and sisters (*names*), my children (*names*), my kinsmen after the flesh, and my friends, and grant them Your blessings both here and hereafter.

Save, O Lord, and have mercy upon the old, the young, the needy, the orphans and the widows, and on all that are in sickness and sorrow, in distress and affliction, in oppression and captivity, in prison and confinement. More especially have mercy upon Your servants who are under persecution for Your sake and for the sake of the Orthodox Faith at the hands of heathen nations, of apostates, and of heretics: remember them, visit, strengthen, keep, and comfort them, and make haste to grant them, by Your power, relief, freedom, and deliverance.

Save, O Lord, and have mercy upon all who are sent on duty, all who travel, our fathers, brothers, and sisters, and upon all true Christians.

Save, O Lord, and have mercy upon those who envy and affront me, and do me harm, and do not let them perish through me, a sinner.

Those who depart from the Orthodox Faith, dazzled by destroying heresies, enlighten by the light of Your holy wisdom, and unite them to Your Holy, Apostolic, Catholic Church.

[*Add here any additional petitions*]

Prayer for the Beginning of the Day

O Lord, grant me to greet the coming day in peace. Help me in all things to rely upon Your holy will. In every hour of the day reveal Your will to me. Bless my dealings with all who surround me. Teach me to treat all that comes to me throughout the day with peace of soul and with firm conviction that Your will governs all. In all my deeds and words, guide my thoughts and feelings. In unforeseen events, let me not forget that all are sent by You. Teach me to act firmly and wisely, without embittering and embarrassing others. Give me strength to bear the fatigue of the coming day with all that it shall bring. Direct my will, teach me to pray, and You, Yourself, pray in me. Amen.

It is truly right to bless you, O Theotokos, ever blessed and most pure, and the Mother of our God. More honorable than the cherubim, and more glorious beyond compare than the seraphim, without defilement you gave birth to God the Word: true Theotokos, we magnify you.

Glory to the Father, and to the Son, and to the Holy Spirit, now and ever, and unto ages of ages. Amen.

Lord, have mercy (*three times*).

Benediction

Through the prayers of our Holy Fathers, O Lord Jesus Christ our God, have mercy on us and save us. Amen.

Evening Prayers

The Trisagion Prayers

† In the Name of the Father, and of the Son, and of the Holy Spirit. Amen.

Glory to You, O Lord, glory to You.

O Heavenly King, O Comforter, the Spirit of Truth, who are in all places and fill all things, the treasury of good things and the giver of life: Come and abide in us, cleanse us from every stain, and save our souls, O Good One.

Holy God, Holy Mighty, Holy Immortal, have mercy on us (*three times*).

Glory to the Father, and to the Son, and to the Holy Spirit, now and ever, and unto ages of ages. Amen.

O Most Holy Trinity, have mercy on us. O Lord, cleanse us from our sins. O Master, pardon our transgressions. O Holy One, visit and heal our infirmities, for Your Name's sake.

Lord, have mercy (*three times*).

Glory to the Father, and to the Son, and to the Holy Spirit, now and ever, and unto ages of ages. Amen.

Our Father, who are in heaven, hallowed be Your Name. Your Kingdom come. Your will be done, on earth as it is in heaven. Give us this day our daily bread; and forgive us our trespasses, as we forgive those who trespass against us; and lead us not into temptation, but deliver us from evil.

For Yours is the Kingdom, and the power, and the glory, of the Father, and of the Son, and of the Holy Spirit, now and ever, and unto ages of ages. Amen.

Prayer for the Evening

O eternal God, King of all creation, who have kept me safe to attain to this hour, forgive me the sins which I have committed this day in thought, word, and deed. And cleanse, O Lord, my humble soul from every stain of flesh and spirit. Grant me, O Lord, to pass this night in peace, to rise from my bed, and to please Your Holy Name all the days of my life, and to vanquish the enemies, both corporeal and incorporeal, that contend against me. Deliver me, O Lord, from the vain thoughts that stain me, and from evil desires. For Yours is the Kingdom, and the power, and the glory, of the Father, and of the Son, and of the Holy Spirit, now and ever, and unto ages of ages. Amen.

The Nicene Creed

I believe in one God, the Father Almighty, Maker of heaven and earth, and of all things visible and invisible; and in one Lord Jesus Christ, the Son of God, the Only-Begotten, begotten of the Father before all worlds, Light of Light, Very God of Very God, begotten, not made; of one essence with the Father; by whom all things were made: who for us men and for our salvation came down from heaven and was incarnate of the Holy Spirit and the Virgin Mary, and was made man; and was crucified also for us under Pontius Pilate, and suffered and was buried. The third day He rose again, according to the Scriptures; and ascended into heaven, and sits at the right hand of the Father; and He shall come again with glory to judge the living and the dead; whose Kingdom shall have no end. And I believe in the Holy Spirit, the Lord and giver of life, who proceeds from the Father, who with the Father and the Son together is worshiped and glorified, who spoke by the prophets. And I believe in One Holy Catholic and Apostolic Church. I acknowledge one baptism for the remission of sins. I look for the resurrection of the dead and the life of the world to come. Amen.

The Psalms

Sunday	Psalm 70
Monday	Psalm 143
Tuesday	Psalm 141
Wednesday	Psalm 130
Thursday	Psalm 130
Friday	Psalm 17
Saturday	Psalm 51

The Gospel and Epistle

Referring to the Lectionary in the back of *The Orthodox Study Bible,* you may, as time permits, read the Gospel and Epistle for this day.

Intercessory Prayers

Remember, O Lord Jesus Christ, our God, Your mercies and loving-kindnesses, which have been from everlasting, and for the sake of which You did become man and deign to endure crucifixion and death for the salvation of all who rightly believe in You. You rose from the dead and ascended into heaven, and sit at the right hand of God the Father, and regard the humble prayers of all who call upon You with their whole heart. Incline Your ear and hear the humble entreaty of me, Your unprofitable servant, who offers it for an odor of spiritual fragrance for all Your people.

And first of all remember Your Holy Catholic and Apostolic Church, which You have purchased with Your precious blood. Confirm and strengthen it, enlarge and multiply it, keep it in peace, and preserve it unconquerable by the gates of hell forever. Heal the schisms of the churches, quench the ragings of the heathen, speedily undo and root out the growths of heresies, and bring them to naught by the power of Your Holy Spirit.

Save, O Lord, and have mercy upon all world rulers, on our president (*name*), on (*names*), and on all our civil authorities. Speak peace and blessing in their hearts for Your Holy Church and for all Your people, in order that we may live a calm and peaceful life, in all godliness and dignity.

Save, O Lord, and have mercy upon patriarchs, metropolitans, archbishops, priests, ministers, and deacons, and the whole clergy of Your Church, which You have established to feed the flock of Your word, and by their prayers have mercy upon me, and save me, a sinner.

Save, O Lord, and have mercy upon my spiritual father (*name*) and by his holy prayers forgive me my transgressions.

Save, O Lord, and have mercy upon my parents (*names*), my spouse (*name*), my brothers and sisters (*names*), my children (*names*), my kinsmen after the flesh, and my friends, and grant them Your blessings both here and hereafter.

Save, O Lord, and have mercy upon the old, the young, the needy, the orphans and the widows, and on all that are in sickness and sorrow, in distress and affliction, in oppression and captivity, in prison and confinement. More especially have mercy upon Your servants who are under persecution for Your sake and for the sake of the Orthodox Faith at the hands of heathen nations, of apostates, and of heretics: remember them, visit, strengthen, keep, and comfort them, and make haste to grant them, by Your power, relief, freedom, and deliverance.

Save, O Lord, and have mercy upon all who are sent on duty, all who travel, our fathers, brothers, and sisters, and upon all true Christians.

Save, O Lord, and have mercy upon those who envy and affront me, and do me harm, and do not let them perish through me, a sinner.

Those who depart from the Orthodox Faith, dazzled by destroying heresies, enlighten by the light of Your holy wisdom, and unite them to Your Holy, Apostolic, Catholic Church.

[*Add here any additional petitions*]

A Prayer

O Christ our God, who at all times and in every hour in heaven and on earth are worshiped and glorified; who are longsuffering, merciful, and compassionate; who love the just and show mercy upon sinners; who call all to salvation through the promise of the good things to come; O Lord, in this hour receive our supplications and direct our lives according to Your commandments. Sanctify our souls, purify our bodies, correct our thoughts, cleanse our minds; deliver us from all tribulation, evil, and distress. Surround us with Your holy angels, so that guided and guarded by them, we may attain to the unity of the Faith and to the full knowledge of Your unapproachable glory. For You are blessed unto ages of ages. Amen.

It is truly right to bless you, O Theotokos, ever blessed and most pure, and the Mother of our God. More honorable than the cherubim, and more glorious beyond compare than the seraphim, without defilement you gave birth to God the Word: true Theotokos, we magnify you.

Glory to the Father, and to the Son, and to the Holy Spirit, now and ever, and unto ages of ages. Amen.

Lord, have mercy (*three times*).

Just Before Going to Sleep

Into Your hands, O Lord Jesus Christ, I commend my spirit and body; bless me, save me, and grant me eternal life. Amen.

Benediction

Through the prayers of our Holy Fathers, O Lord Jesus Christ our God, have mercy on us and save us. Amen.

How to Read the Bible

Bishop KALLISTOS of Diokleia

All Scripture is given by inspiration of God
(2 Tim. 3:16)

"If an earthly king, our emperor," wrote Saint Tikhon of Zadonsk (1724–83), "wrote you a letter, would you not read it with joy? Certainly, with great rejoicing and careful attention." But what, he asks, is our attitude toward the letter that has been addressed to us by no one less than God Himself? "You have been sent a letter, not by any earthly emperor, but by the King of Heaven. And yet you almost despise such a gift, so priceless a treasure." To open and read this letter, Saint Tikhon adds, is to enter into a personal conversation face-to-face with the living God. "Whenever you read the Gospel, Christ Himself is speaking to you. And while you read, you are praying and talking to Him."

Such exactly is our Orthodox attitude to the reading of Scripture. I am to see the Bible as God's personal letter sent specifically to myself. The words are not intended merely for others, far away and long ago, but they are written particularly and directly to me, here and now. Whenever we open our Bible, we are engaging in a creative dialogue with the Savior. In listening, we also respond. "Speak, for Your servant hears," we reply to God as we read (1 Sam. 3:10); "Here am I" (Is. 6:8).

Two centuries after Saint Tikhon, at the Moscow Conference held in 1976 between the Orthodox and the Anglicans, the true attitude toward Scripture was expressed in different but equally valid terms. This joint statement, signed by the delegates of both traditions, forms an excellent summary of the Orthodox view: "The Scriptures constitute a coherent whole. They are at once divinely inspired and humanly expressed. They bear authoritative witness to God's revelation of Himself in creation, in the Incarnation of the Word, and in the whole history of salvation, and as such express the word of God in human language. We know, receive, and interpret Scripture through the Church and in the Church. Our approach to the Bible is one of obedience."

Combining Saint Tikhon's words and the Moscow statement, the four key characteristics which mark the Orthodox "Scriptural mind" may be distinguished. First, our reading of Scripture is *obedient*. Second, it is *ecclesial*, in union with the Church. Third, it is *Christ-centered*. Fourth, it is *personal*.

Reading the Bible with Obedience

First of all, we see Scripture as inspired by God, and we approach it in a spirit of *obedience*. The divine inspiration of the Bible is emphasized alike by Saint Tikhon and by the 1976 Moscow Conference: Scripture is "a letter" from "the King of Heaven," writes Saint Tikhon; "Christ Himself is speaking to you." The Bible, states the Conference, is God's "authoritative witness" of

Himself, expressing "the word of God in human language." Our response to this divine word is rightly one of obedient receptivity. As we read, we wait on the Spirit.

Since it is divinely inspired, the Bible possesses a fundamental unity, a total coherence, because the same Spirit speaks on every page. We do not refer to it as "the books" in the plural, *ta biblia*. We call it "the Bible," "the Book," in the singular. It is one book, one Holy Scripture, with the same message throughout—one composite and yet a single story from Genesis to Revelation.

At the same time, however, the Bible is also humanly expressed. It is an entire library of distinct writings, composed at varying times, by different persons in widely diverse situations. We find God speaking here "at various times and in various ways" (Heb. 1:1). Each work in the Bible reflects the outlook of the age in which it was written and the particular viewpoint of the author. For God does not abolish our created personhood but enhances it. Divine grace cooperates with human freedom: we are "fellow workers," cooperators with God (1 Cor. 3:9). In the words of the second-century *Letter to Diognetus*, "God persuades, He does not compel; for violence is foreign to the divine nature." So it is precisely in the writing of inspired Scripture. The author of each book was not just a passive instrument, a flute played by the Spirit, a dictation machine recording a message. Every writer of Scripture contributes his or her particular human gifts. Alongside the divine aspect, there is also a human element in Scripture, and we are to value both.

Each of the four Evangelists, for example, has his own particular standpoint. Matthew is the most "ecclesiastical" and the most Jewish of the four, with his special interest in the relationship of the gospel to the Jewish Law, and his understanding of Christianity as the "New Law." Mark writes in less polished Greek, closer to the language of daily life, and includes vivid narrative details not found in the other gospels. Luke emphasizes the universality of Christ's love and His all-embracing compassion that extends equally to Jew and Gentile. The Fourth Gospel expresses a more inward and mystical approach, and was aptly styled by Saint Clement of Alexandria "a spiritual Gospel." Let us explore and enjoy to the fullest this life-giving variety within the Bible.

Because Scripture is in this way the word of God expressed in human language, there is a place for honest and exacting critical inquiry when studying the Bible. Our reasoning brain is a gift from God, and we need not be afraid to use it to the utmost when reading Scripture. Orthodox Christians neglect at our peril the results of independent scholarly research into the origin, dates, and authorship of the books of the Bible, although we shall always want to test these results in the light of Holy Tradition.

Alongside this human element, however, we are always to see the divine aspect. These texts are not simply the work of the individual authors. What we hear in Scripture is not just human words, marked by a greater or lesser skill and perceptiveness, but the uncreated Word of God Himself—the Father's Word "coming forth from silence," to use the phrase of Saint Ignatius of Antioch—the eternal Word of salvation. Approaching the Bible, then, we come not merely out of curiosity or to gain historical information. We come with a specific question: "How can I be saved?"

Obedient receptivity to God's word means above all two things: *a sense of wonder* and *an attitude of listening*. (1) *Wonder* is easily quenched. Do we not feel all too often, as we read the Bible, that it has become overly familiar, even boring? Have we not lost our alertness, our sense of expectation? How far are we changed by what we read? Continually, we need to cleanse the doors of our perception and to look with new eyes, in awe and amazement, at the miracle that is set before us—the ever-present miracle of God's divine word of salvation expressed in human language. As Plato remarked, "The beginning of truth is to wonder at things."

Some years ago I had a dream that I still remember vividly. I was back in the house where, for three years as a child, I lived in boarding school. A friend took me first through the rooms already familiar to me from the waking life of my childhood. Then, in my dream we entered other rooms that I had never seen before—spacious, elegant, filled with light. Finally, we came to a small, dark chapel, with golden mosaics gleaming in the candlelight. "How strange," I said to my companion, "that I have lived here for so long, and yet I never knew about the existence of all these rooms." And he replied, "But it is always so." I awoke, and, behold, it was a dream.

Should we not react in the presence of the Bible with exactly the same surprise, the same feeling of joy and discovery, that I experienced in my dream? There are so many rooms in Scripture that we have never as yet entered. There is so much for us still to explore.

(2) If obedience means wonder, it also means *listening*. Such indeed is the literal meaning of the word for "obey" in both Greek and Latin—to hear. The trouble is that most of us are better at talking than at listening. An incident on the *Goon Show*, which I used to follow eagerly on the radio in my student days, sums up our predicament all too well. The telephone rings, and one of the characters picks it up. "Hello," he exclaims, "hello, hello." His volume rises. "Who is speaking? I can't hear you. Hello, who is speaking?" A voice at the other end says, "You are speaking." "Ah," he replies, "I thought the voice sounded familiar." And he puts the receiver down.

One of the primary requirements, if we are to acquire a "scriptural mind," is to stop talking and to start listening. When we enter an Orthodox Church decorated in the traditional way, and look up towards the sanctuary, we see there in the apse the figure of the Mother of God with her hands raised to heaven—the ancient scriptural manner of praying that many still use today. Such is also to be our attitude to Scripture—an attitude of openness and attentive receptivity, our hands invisibly outstretched to heaven.

As we read our Bible, then, we are to model ourselves in this way on the Blessed Virgin Mary, for she is supremely the one who listens. At the Annunciation, listening to the angel, she responds obediently, "Let it be to me according to your word" (Luke 1:38). Had she not first listened to God's word and received it spiritually in her heart, she would never have borne the Word of God bodily in her womb. Receptive listening continues to be her attitude throughout the Gospel story. At Christ's nativity, after the adoration of the shepherds, "Mary kept all these things and pondered them in her heart" (Luke 2:19). After the visit to Jerusalem when Jesus was twelve years old, "His Mother kept all these things in her heart" (Luke 2:51). The vital importance of listening is also indicated in the last words attributed to the Theotokos in Holy Scripture, at the wedding feast in Cana of Galilee. "Whatever He says to you, do it" (John 2:5), she says to the servants—and to each one of us.

In all this the Virgin serves as a mirror and living icon of the biblical Christian. Hearing God's word, we are to be like her: pondering, keeping all these things in our hearts, doing whatever He tells us. We are to listen in obedience while God speaks.

Understanding the Bible through the Church

As the Moscow Conference affirms, "We know, receive, and interpret Scripture through the Church and in the Church." Our approach to the Bible is not only obedient but ecclesial. The words of Scripture, while addressed to us personally, are at the same time addressed to us as members of a community. Book and Church are not to be separated.

The interdependence of Church and Bible is evident in at least two ways. First, we *receive* Scripture through and in the Church. The Church tells us what is Scripture. In the first three centuries of Christian history, a lengthy process of sifting and testing was needed in order to distinguish between that which is authentically "canonical" Scripture, bearing authoritative witness to Christ's person and message, and that which is "apocryphal," useful perhaps for teaching, but not a normative source of doctrine. Thus, the Church has decided which books form the Canon of the New Testament. A book is not part of Holy Scripture because of any particular theory about its date and authorship, but because the Church treats it as canonical. Suppose, for example, that it could be proved that the Fourth Gospel was not actually written by Saint John the beloved disciple of Christ—in my view, there are in fact strong reasons for continuing to accept John's authorship—yet, even so, this would not alter the fact that we regard the Fourth Gospel as Scripture. Why? Because the Fourth Gospel, whoever the author may be, is accepted by the Church and in the Church.

Secondly, we *interpret* Scripture through and in the Church. If it is the Church that tells us what is Scripture, equally it is the Church that tells us how Scripture is to be understood. Coming upon the Ethiopian as he read the Old Testament in his chariot, Philip the Deacon asked him, "Do you understand what you are reading?"

"How can I," answered the Ethiopian, "unless someone guides me?" (Acts 8:30, 31).

His difficulty is also ours. The words of Scripture are not always self-explanatory. The Bible has a marvelous underlying simplicity, but when studied in detail it can prove a difficult book. God does indeed speak directly to the heart of each one of us during our Scripture reading—as Saint Tikhon says, our reading is a personal dialogue between each one and Christ Himself—but we also need guidance. And our guide is the Church. We make full use of our private understanding, illuminated by the Spirit. We make full use of biblical commentaries and of the findings of modern research. But we submit individual opinions, whether our own or those of the scholars, to the judgment of the Church.

We read the Bible personally, but not as isolated individuals. We say not "I" but "we." We read as the members of a family, the family of the Orthodox Catholic Church. We read in communion with all the other members of the Body of Christ in all parts of the world and in all generations of time. This communal or *catholic* approach to the Bible is underlined in one of the questions asked of a convert at the reception service used in the Russian Church: "Do you acknowledge that the Holy Scripture must be accepted and interpreted in accordance with the belief which has been handed down by the Holy Fathers, and which the Holy Orthodox Church, our Mother, has always held and still does hold?" The decisive criterion of our understanding of what Scripture means is *the mind of the Church*.

To discover this "mind of the Church," where do we begin? A first step is to see how Scripture is used in worship. How in particular are biblical lessons chosen for reading at the different feasts? A second step is to consult the writings of the Church Fathers, especially St. John Chrysostom. How do they analyze and apply the text of Scripture? An ecclesial manner of reading the Bible is in this way both *liturgical* and *patristic*.

To illustrate what it means to interpret Scripture in a liturgical way, consider the Old Testament lessons at Vespers for the Feast of the Annunciation (March 25) and at Vespers on Holy Saturday, the first part of the ancient Paschal Vigil. At the Annunciation there are five readings:

(1) *Genesis 28:10-17*: Jacob's dream of a ladder set up from earth to heaven.

(2) *Ezekiel 43:27-44*: the prophet's vision of the Jerusalem temple, with the closed gate through which none but the Prince may pass.

(3) *Proverbs 9:1-11*: one of the great Sophianic passages in the Old Testament, beginning "Wisdom has built her house."

(4) *Exodus 3:1-8*: Moses at the Burning Bush.

(5) *Proverbs 8:22-30*: another Sophianic text, describing Wisdom's place in God's eternal providence: "I have been established from everlasting, from the beginning, before there was ever an earth."

In these passages from the Old Testament, we have a series of powerful images to indicate the role of the Theotokos in God's unfolding plan of salvation. She is Jacob's ladder, for by means of her, God comes down and enters our world, assuming the flesh that she supplies. She is both Mother and Ever-Virgin; Christ is born from her, yet she remains still inviolate, the gate of her virginity sealed. She provides the humanity or house which Christ the Wisdom of God (1 Cor. 1:24) takes as His dwelling; alternatively, she is herself to be regarded as God's Wisdom. She is the Burning Bush, who contains within her womb the uncreated fire of the Godhead and yet is not consumed. From all eternity, "before there was ever an earth," she was forechosen by God to be His Mother.

Reading these passages in their original context within the Old Testament, we might not at once appreciate that they foreshadow the Savior's Incarnation from the Virgin. But, by exploring the use made of the Old Testament in the Church lectionary, we can discover layer upon layer of meanings that are far from obvious at first sight.

The same thing happens when we consider how Scripture is used on Holy Saturday. Here there are no less than fifteen Old Testament lessons. Regrettably, in many of our parishes the majority of these are omitted, so God's people are starved of their proper biblical nourishment. This long sequence of readings sets before us the deeper significance of Christ's "passing over" through death to resurrection. First among the lessons is the account of the creation (Gen. 1:1-13): Christ's Resurrection is a new creation (2 Cor. 5:17; Rev. 21:5), the inauguration of a new age, the age to come. The third lesson describes the Jewish ritual of the Passover meal: Christ crucified and risen is the new Passover, the Paschal Lamb who alone can take away the sin of the world (1 Cor. 5:7; John 1:29). The fourth lesson is the book of Jonah in its entirety: the prophet's three days in the belly of the fish foreshadow Christ's resurrection after three days in the tomb (Matt. 12:40). The sixth lesson recounts the crossing of the Red Sea by the Israelites (Ex. 13:20—15:19): Christ leads us from the bondage of Egypt (sin), through the Red Sea (baptism), into the promised land (the Church). The final lesson is the story of the three Holy Children in the fiery furnace (Dan. 3), once more a "type" or foreshowing of Christ's rising from the tomb.

How can we develop this ecclesial and liturgical way of reading Scripture in the Bible study circles within our parishes? One person can be given the task of noting whenever a particular passage is used for a festival or saint's day, and the group can then discuss together the reasons why it has been so chosen. Others in the group may be assigned to do homework among the Fathers, relying above all upon the biblical homilies of St. John Chrysostom, which are available in English translation in the series *Nicene and Post-Nicene Fathers*, reissued by Eerdmans. Initially we may be disappointed: the Fathers' manner of thinking and speaking is often strikingly different from our own today. But there is gold in the patristic texts, if only we have the persistence and imagination to discover it.

Christ, the Heart of the Bible

The third requirement in our reading of Scripture is that it should be Christ-centered. If we agree with the 1976 Moscow Conference that the "Scriptures constitute a coherent whole," where are we to locate their wholeness and coherence? *In the person of Christ*. He is the unifying thread that runs through the entirety of the Bible from the first sentence to the last. Jesus meets us on every page. It all ties up because of Him. "In Him all things hold together" (Col. 1:17 NRSV).

Much study of Scripture by modern western scholars has adopted an analytical approach, breaking up each book into what are seen as its original sources. The connecting links are unravelled, and the Bible is reduced to a series of isolated units. Recently, there has been a reaction against this, with biblical critics in the west devoting much greater attention to the way in which these primary units have come to be joined together. This is something that we Orthodox may certainly welcome. We must see the unity of Scripture as well as the diversity, the all-embracing end as well as the scattered beginnings. Orthodoxy prefers for the most part a "synthetic" rather than an analytical style of hermeneutics, seeing the Bible as an integrated whole, with Christ everywhere as the bond of union.

Such, as we have just seen, is precisely the effect of reading Scripture within the context of the Church's worship. As the lessons for the Annunciation and Holy Saturday make clear, everywhere in the Old Testament we find signposts and waymarks pointing to the mystery of Christ and His Mother Mary. Interpreting the Old Testament in the light of the New, and the New in the light of the Old—as the Church lectionary encourages us to do—we discover how the whole of Scripture finds its point of convergence in the Savior.

Orthodoxy makes extensive use of this "typological" method of interpretation, whereby "types" of Christ, signs and symbols of His work, are to be detected throughout the Old Testament. Melchizedek, for example, the priest-king of Salem who offered bread and wine to Abraham (Gen. 14:18), is regarded as a "type" of Christ not only by the Fathers but equally in the New Testament itself (Heb. 5:6; 7:1-19). The rock that flowed with water in the wilderness of Sinai (Ex. 17:6; Num. 30:7-11) is likewise a symbol of Christ (1 Cor. 10:4). Typology explains the choice of lessons, not only on Holy Saturday, but throughout the second half of Lent. Why are the Genesis readings in the sixth week dominated by the figure of Joseph? Why read from the Book of Job in Holy Week? Because Joseph and Job, who both suffered innocently, foreshadow the redemptive suffering of Christ on the Cross.

We can discover many other correspondences between the Old and New

Testament by using a biblical concordance. Often the best commentary of all is simply a concordance, or an edition of the Bible with well-chosen marginal cross-references. Only connect. It all ties up. In the words of Father Alexander Schmemann, "A Christian is the one who, wherever he looks, finds everywhere Christ, and rejoices in Him." This is true in particular of the biblical Christian. Wherever he looks, on every page, he finds everywhere Christ.

The Bible as Personal

According to Saint Mark the Monk ("Mark the Ascetic," fifth/sixth century), "He who is humble in his thoughts and engaged in spiritual work, when he reads the Holy Scriptures, will apply everything to himself and not to his neighbor." We are to look throughout Scripture for a *personal* application. Our question is not simply "What does it mean?" but "What does it mean *for me?*" As Saint Tikhon insists, "Christ Himself is speaking to *you*." Scripture is a direct, intimate dialogue between the Savior and myself—Christ addressing me and my heart responding. That is the fourth criterion in our Bible reading.

I am to see all the narratives in Scripture as part of my own personal story. The description of Adam's fall is equally an account of something in my own experience. Who is Adam? His name means simply "man," "human": it is I who am Adam. It is to me that God says, "Where are *you*?" (Gen. 3:9). We often ask, "Where is *God*?" But the real question is the one that God puts to the Adam in each one of us: "Where are *you*?"

Who is Cain, the murderer of his brother? It is I. God's challenge, "Where is Abel your brother?" (Gen. 4:9), is addressed to the Cain in each of us. The way to God lies through love for other people, and there is no other way. Disowning my sister or brother, I replace the image of God with the mark of Cain, and deny my essential humanity.

The same personal application is evident in the Lenten services, and above all in the Great Canon of St. Andrew of Crete. "I am the man who fell among thieves," we say (see Luke 10:30); "I was Your younger son, and wasted the wealth that You gave me . . . and now I am starved and hungry" (see Luke 15:11-14). "Who are the sheep, and who are the goats?" the Desert Fathers of Egypt used to ask (see Matt. 25:31-46). "The sheep are known to God," they replied. "As for the goats—that means *me*."

There are three steps to be taken when reading Scripture. First, we reflect that what we have in Scripture is *sacred history*: the history of the world from the Creation, the history of God's chosen people, the history of God Himself incarnate in Palestine, the history of the "wonderful works" (Acts 2:11) after Pentecost. We are never to forget that what we find in the Bible is not an ideology, not a philosophical theory, but a historical faith.

Next, we observe the *particularity*, the specificity, of this sacred history. In the Bible we find God intervening at specific times and in particular places, entering into dialogue with individual humans. We see before us the distinctive calls issued by God to each different person, to Abraham, Moses, and David, to Rebekah and Ruth, to Isaiah and the prophets. We see God becoming incarnate once only, in a particular corner of the earth, at a particular moment and from a particular Mother. This particularity we are to regard not as a scandal but as a blessing. Divine love is universal in its scope, but always personal in its expression.

This sense of the specificity of the Bible is a vital element in the Orthodox "scriptural mind." If we really love the Bible, we will love genealogies and details of dating and geography. One of the best ways to enliven the study of Scripture is to go on a pilgrimage to the Holy Land. Walk where Christ walked. Go down near the Dead Sea, climb the mountain of the Temptation, scan the desolation, feel how Christ must have felt during His forty days alone in the wilderness. Drink from the well where Jesus spoke with the Samaritan woman. Take a boat out on the Sea of Galilee, have the sailors stop the engine, and gaze in silence across the water. Go at night to the Garden of Gethsemane, sit in the dark under the ancient olives, and look across the valley to the lights of the city. Taste to the utmost the characteristic "isness" of the historical setting, and take that experience back to the daily Scripture reading.

Then we are to take a third step. After reliving Bible history in all its particularity, we are to apply it *directly to ourselves*. We are to say to ourselves, "These are not just distant places, events in the remote past. They belong to my own encounter with the Lord. The stories include me."

Betrayal, for instance, is part of the personal story of everyone. Have we not all betrayed others at some time in our life, and have we not all known what it is to be betrayed? And does not the memory of these moments leave deep, continuing scars on our psyche? Reading, then, the account of Saint Peter's betrayal of Jesus and of his restoration after the resurrection, we can see ourselves as each an actor in the story. Imagining what both Peter and Christ experienced at the moment immediately after the betrayal, we make their feelings our own. I am Peter; in the situation of betrayal, can I also be Christ? Reflecting likewise on the moment of reconciliation—seeing how the risen Savior with a love utterly devoid of sentimentality restored the fallen Peter to fellowship, seeing how Peter on his side had the humility and courage to accept this restoration—we ask ourselves: How Christlike am I to those who have betrayed me? And—after my own acts of betrayal, am I able to accept the forgiveness of others—am I able to forgive myself?

Take, as another example, the "woman who was a sinner," who emptied the flask of ointment over Christ's feet (Luke 7:36-50), and whom some identify with Saint Mary Magdalene, although that is not the usual Orthodox interpretation. Can I see her mirrored in myself? Do I share in her generosity, in her spontaneity and loving impulsiveness? "Her sins, which are many, are forgiven, for she loved much." Or am I calculating, mean, timid, holding myself back, never willing to commit myself fully to anything, either good or bad? As the Desert Fathers say, "Better someone who has sinned, if he knows he has sinned and repents, than a person who has not sinned and thinks of himself as righteous."

A personal approach of this kind means that in reading the Bible we are not simply detached and objective observers, absorbing information, taking note of facts. The Bible is not merely a work of literature or a collection of historical documents, although certainly it can be approached on that level. It is, much more fundamentally, a *sacred* book, addressed to *believers*, to be read with faith and love. We shall not profit fully from reading the Gospels unless we are in love with Christ. "Heart speaks to heart:" I enter into the living truth of Scripture only when my heart responds with love to the heart of God.

Reading Scripture in this way—in obedience, as a member of the Church, finding Christ everywhere, and seeing everything as part of my own personal story—we shall sense something of the power and healing to be found in the Bible. Yet always in our biblical voyage of exploration we are only at the very beginning. We are like someone launching out in a tiny boat across a limitless ocean. But, however great the journey, we can embark on it today, at this very hour, in this very moment.

At the high point of his spiritual crisis, wrestling with himself alone in the garden, Saint Augustine heard a child's voice crying out, "Take up and read, take up and read." He took up his Bible and read, and what he read altered his entire life. Let us do the same: *Take up and read*.

"Your word is a lamp to my feet and a light to my path" (Psalm 118 [119]:105).

Lectionary

PASCHA

The Resurrection of Christ, the Passover (Pascha) of the Lord: Easter
Acts 1:1–8; John 1:1–17
Bright Monday
Acts 1:12–17; 21–26; John 1:18–28
Bright Tuesday
Acts 2:14–21; Luke 24:12–35
Bright Wednesday
Acts 2:22–36; John 1:35–51
Bright Thursday
Acts 2:38–43; John 3:1–15
Bright Friday
Acts 3:1–8; John 2:12–22
The Life-Giving Spring of the Most Holy Theotokos
Philippians 2:5–11; Luke 10:38–42; 11:27, 28
Bright Saturday
Acts 3:11–16; John 3:22–33
Second Sunday of Pascha: Thomas Sunday
Acts 5:12–20; John 20:19–31
Second Week of Pascha
Monday
Acts 3:19–26; John 2:1–11
Tuesday
Acts 4:1–10; John 3:16–21
Commemoration of the Departed
1 Corinthians 15:39–57; John 5:24–30
Wednesday
Acts 4:13–22; John 5:17–24
Thursday
Acts 4:23–31; John 5:24–30
Friday
Acts 5:1–11; John 5:30—6:2
Saturday
Acts 5:21–33; John 6:14–27
Third Sunday of Pascha: Sunday of the Myrrhbearing Women and Sunday of Joseph of Arimathea and Nicodemus
Acts 6:17; Mark 15:43—16:8
Third Week of Pascha
Monday
Acts 6:8—7:5, 47–60; John 4:46–54
Tuesday
Acts 8:5–17; John 6:27–33
Wednesday
Acts 8:18–25; John 6:35–39
Thursday
Acts 8:26–39; John 6:40–44
Friday
Acts 8:40—9:19; John 6:48–54
Saturday
Acts 9:19–31; John 15:17—16:2
Fourth Sunday of Pascha: Sunday of the Paralytic
Acts 9:32–42; John 5:1–15
Fourth Week of Pascha
Monday
Acts 10:1–16; John 6:56–69
Tuesday
Acts 10:21–33; John 7:1–13
Wednesday
Acts 14:6–18; John 7:14–30
Thursday
Acts 10:34–43; John 8:12–20
Friday
Acts 10:44—11:10; John 8:21–30
Saturday
Acts 12:1–11; John 8:31–42
Fifth Sunday of Pascha: Sunday of the Samaritan Woman
Acts 11:19–26, 29–30; John 4:5–42
Fifth Week of Pascha
Monday
Acts 12:12–17; John 8:42–51
Tuesday
Acts 12:25—13:12; John 8:51–59
Wednesday
Acts 13:13–24; John 6:5–14
Thursday
Acts 14:20–27; John 9:39—10:9
Friday
Acts 15:5–34; John 10:17–28
Saturday
Acts 15:35–41; John 10:27–38
Sixth Sunday of Pascha: Sunday of the Blind Man
Acts 16:16–34; John 9:1–38
Sixth Week of Pascha
Monday
Acts 17:1–15; John 11:47–57
Tuesday
Acts 17:19–28; John 12:19–36
Wednesday
Acts 18:22–28; John 12:36–47
Thursday: The Ascension of Our Lord
VESPERS: (1) Isaiah 2:1–3; (2) Isaiah 62:10—63:9; (3) Zechariah 14:1, 4, 8–11. MATINS: Mark 16:9–20. LITURGY: Acts 1:1–12; Luke 24:36–53
Friday
Acts 19:1–8; John 14:1–11
Saturday
Acts 20:7–12; John 14:10–21
Seventh Sunday of Pascha: Sunday of the Fathers of the First Ecumenical Council
Acts 20:16–18, 28–36; John 17:1–13
Seventh Week of Pascha
Monday
Acts 21:8–14; John 14:27—15:7
Tuesday
Acts 21:26–32; John 16:2–13
Wednesday
Acts 23:1–11; John 16:15–23

Thursday
Acts 25:13–19; John 16:23–33
Friday
Acts 27:1–44; John 17:18–26
Saturday
Acts 28:1–31; John 21:15–25

PENTECOST

Sunday of Pentecost: Trinity Sunday
Descent of the Holy Spirit on the Disciples
VESPERS: (1) Numbers 11:16, 17, 24–29; (2) Joel 2:23–32; (3) Ezekiel 36:24–28. MATINS: John 20:19–23. LITURGY: Acts 2:1–11; John 7:37–52; 8:12
First Week After Pentecost
Monday: Day of the Holy Spirit
Ephesians 5:9–19; Matthew 18:10–20
Tuesday
Romans 1:1–7, 13–17; Matthew 4:25—5:13
Wednesday
Romans 1:18–27; Matthew 5:20–26
Thursday
Romans 1:28—2:9; Matthew 5:27–32
Friday
Romans 2:14–29; Matthew 5:33–41
Saturday
Romans 1:7–12; Matthew 5:42–48
First Sunday After Pentecost: Sunday of All Saints
VESPERS: (1) Isaiah 43:9–14; (2) Wisdom 3:1–9; (3) Wisdom 5:15—6:3. LITURGY: Hebrews 11:33—12:2; Matthew 10:32, 33, 37, 38; 19:27–30
Second Week After Pentecost
Monday
Romans 2:28—3:18; Matthew 6:31–34; 7:9–11
Tuesday
Romans 4:4–12; Matthew 7:15–21
Wednesday
Romans 4:13–25; Matthew 7:21–23
Thursday
Romans 5:10–16; Matthew 8:23–27
Friday
Romans 5:17—6:2; Matthew 9:14–17
Saturday
Romans 3:19–26; Matthew 7:1–8
Second Sunday After Pentecost
LITURGY: Romans 2:10–16; Matthew 4:18–23
Third Week After Pentecost
Monday
Romans 7:1–13; Matthew 9:36—10:8
Tuesday
Romans 7:14—8:2; Matthew 10:9–15
Wednesday
Romans 8:1–13; Matthew 10:16–22
Thursday
Romans 8:22–27; Matthew 10:23–31
Friday
Romans 9:6–19; Matthew 10:32–36; 11:1
Saturday
Romans 3:28—4:3; Matthew 7:24—8:4

Third Sunday After Pentecost
LITURGY: Romans 5:1–10; Matthew 6:22–33
Fourth Week After Pentecost
Monday
Romans 9:18–33; Matthew 11:2–15
Tuesday
Romans 10:11—11:2; Matthew 11:16–20
Wednesday
Romans 11:2–12; Matthew 11:20–26
Thursday
Romans 11:13–24; Matthew 11:27–30
Friday
Romans 11:25–36; Matthew 12:1–8
Saturday
Romans 6:11–17; Matthew 8:14–23
Fourth Sunday After Pentecost: Sunday of the Holy Fathers of the First Six Ecumenical Councils (July 13–19)
LITURGY: Romans 6:18–23; Matthew 8:5–13
Fifth Week After Pentecost
Monday
Romans 12:4, 5, 15–21; Matthew 12:9–13
Tuesday
Romans 14:9–18; Matthew 12:14–16, 22–30
Wednesday
Romans 15:7–16; Matthew 12:38–45
Thursday
Romans 15:17–29; Matthew 12:46—13:3
Friday
Romans 16:1–16; Matthew 13:4–9
Saturday
Romans 8:14–21; Matthew 9:9–13
Fifth Sunday After Pentecost
LITURGY: Romans 10:1–10; Matthew 8:28—9:1
Sixth Week After Pentecost
Monday
Romans 16:17–24; Matthew 13:10–23
Tuesday
1 Corinthians 1:1–9; Matthew 13:24–30
Wednesday
1 Corinthians 2:9—3:8; Matthew 13:31–36
Thursday
1 Corinthians 3:18–23; Matthew 13:36–43
Friday
1 Corinthians 4:5–8; Matthew 13:44–54
Saturday
Romans 9:1–5; Matthew 9:18–26
Sixth Sunday After Pentecost
LITURGY: Romans 12:6–14; Matthew 9:1–8
Seventh Week After Pentecost
Monday
1 Corinthians 5:9—6:11; Matthew 13:54–58
Tuesday
1 Corinthians 6:20—7:12; Matthew 14:1–13
Wednesday
1 Corinthians 7:12–24; Matthew 14:35—15:11
Thursday
1 Corinthians 7:24–35; Matthew 15:12–21
Friday
1 Corinthians 7:35—8:7; Matthew 15:29–31
Saturday
Romans 12:1–3; Matthew 10:37—11:1

Seventh Sunday After Pentecost
LITURGY: Romans 15:1–7; Matthew 9:27–35

Eighth Week After Pentecost
Monday
1 Corinthians 9:13–18; Matthew 16:1–6
Tuesday
1 Corinthians 10:5–12; Matthew 16:6–12
Wednesday
1 Corinthians 10:12–22; Matthew 16:20–24
Thursday
1 Corinthians 10:28—11:7; Matthew 16:24–28
Friday
1 Corinthians 11:8–22; Matthew 17:10–18
Saturday
Romans 13:1–10; Matthew 12:30–37

Eighth Sunday After Pentecost
LITURGY: 1 Corinthians 1:10–18; Matthew 14:14–22

Ninth Week After Pentecost
Monday
1 Corinthians 11:31—12:6; Matthew 18:1–11
Tuesday
1 Corinthians 12:12–26; Matthew 18:18–22; 19:1, 2, 13–15
Wednesday
1 Corinthians 13:4—14:5; Matthew 20:1–16
Thursday
1 Corinthians 14:6–19; Matthew 20:17–28
Friday
1 Corinthians 14:26–40; Matthew 21:12–14, 17–20
Saturday
Romans 14:6–9; Matthew 15:32–39

Ninth Sunday After Pentecost
LITURGY: 1 Corinthians 3:9–17; Matthew 14:22–34

Tenth Week After Pentecost
Monday
1 Corinthians 15:12–19; Matthew 21:18–22
Tuesday
1 Corinthians 15:29–38; Matthew 21:23–27
Wednesday
1 Corinthians 16:4–12; Matthew 21:28–32
Thursday
2 Corinthians 1:1–7; Matthew 21:43–46
Friday
2 Corinthians 1:12–20; Matthew 22:23–33
Saturday
Romans 15:30–33; Matthew 17:24—18:4

Tenth Sunday After Pentecost
LITURGY: 1 Corinthians 4:9–16; Matthew 17:14–23

Eleventh Week After Pentecost
Monday
2 Corinthians 2:4–15; Matthew 23:13–22
Tuesday
2 Corinthians 2:14—3:3; Matthew 23:23–28
Wednesday
2 Corinthians 3:4–11; Matthew 23:29–39
Thursday
2 Corinthians 4:1–6; Matthew 24:13–28
Friday
2 Corinthians 4:13–18; Matthew 24:27–33, 42–51
Saturday
1 Corinthians 1:3–9; Matthew 19:3–12

Eleventh Sunday After Pentecost
LITURGY: 1 Corinthians 9:2–12; Matthew 18:23–35

Twelfth Week After Pentecost
Monday
2 Corinthians 5:10–15; Mark 1:9–15
Tuesday
2 Corinthians 5:15–21; Mark 1:16–22
Wednesday
2 Corinthians 6:11–16; Mark 1:23–28
Thursday
2 Corinthians 7:1–10; Mark 1:29–35
Friday
2 Corinthians 7:10–16; Mark 2:18–22
Saturday
1 Corinthians 1:26–29; Matthew 20:29–34

Twelfth Sunday After Pentecost: Sunday of the Holy Fathers of the Seventh Ecumenical Council (October 11–17)
LITURGY: 1 Corinthians 15:1–11; Matthew 19:16–26

Thirteenth Week After Pentecost
Monday
2 Corinthians 8:7–15; Mark 3:6–12
Tuesday
2 Corinthians 8:16—9:5; Mark 3:13–19
Wednesday
2 Corinthians 9:12—10:7; Mark 3:20–27
Thursday
2 Corinthians 10:7–18; Mark 3:28–35
Friday
2 Corinthians 11:5–12; Mark 4:1–9
Saturday
1 Corinthians 2:6–9; Matthew 22:15–22

Thirteenth Sunday After Pentecost
LITURGY: 1 Corinthians 16:13–24; Matthew 21:33–42

Fourteenth Week After Pentecost
Monday
2 Corinthians 12:10–19; Mark 4:10–23
Tuesday
2 Corinthians 12:20—13:2; Mark 4:24–34
Wednesday
2 Corinthians 13:3–13; Mark 4:35–41
Thursday
Galatians 1:1–10, 20–24—2:5; Mark 5:1–20
Friday
Galatians 2:6–10; Mark 5:22–24, 35—6:1
Saturday
1 Corinthians 4:1–5; Matthew 23:1–12

Fourteenth Sunday After Pentecost
LITURGY: 2 Corinthians 1:21—2:4; Matthew 22:1–14

Fifteenth Week After Pentecost
Monday
Galatians 2:11–16; Mark 5:24–34
Tuesday
Galatians 2:21—3:7; Mark 6:1–7

Wednesday
Galatians 3:15–22; Mark 6:7–13
Thursday
Galatians 3:23—4:5; Mark 6:30–45
Friday
Galatians 4:8–21; Mark 6:45–53
Saturday
1 Corinthians 4:17—5:5; Matthew 24:1–13
Fifteenth Sunday After Pentecost
LITURGY: 2 Corinthians 4:6–15; Matthew 22:35–46
Sixteenth Week After Pentecost
Monday
Galatians 4:28—5:10; Mark 6:54—7:8
Tuesday
Galatians 5:11–21; Mark 7:5–16
Wednesday
Galatians 6:2–10; Mark 7:14–24
Thursday
Ephesians 1:1–9; Mark 7:24–30
Friday
Ephesians 1:7–17; Mark 8:1–10
Saturday
1 Corinthians 10:23–28; Matthew 24:34–44
Sixteenth Sunday After Pentecost
LITURGY: 2 Corinthians 6:1–10; Matthew 25:14–30
Seventeenth Week After Pentecost
Monday
Ephesians 1:22—2:3; Mark 10:46–52
Tuesday
Ephesians 2:19—3:7; Mark 11:11–23
Wednesday
Ephesians 3:8–21; Mark 11:23–26
Thursday
Ephesians 4:14–19; Mark 11:27–33
Friday
Ephesians 4:17–25; Mark 12:1–12
Saturday
1 Corinthians 14:20–25; Matthew 25:1–13
Seventeenth Sunday After Pentecost
LITURGY: 2 Corinthians 6:16—7:1; Matthew 15:21–28
Eighteenth Week After Pentecost
Monday
Ephesians 4:25–32; Luke 3:19–22
Tuesday
Ephesians 5:20–26; Luke 3:23—4:1
Wednesday
Ephesians 5:25–33; Luke 4:1–15
Thursday
Ephesians 5:33—6:9; Luke 4:16–22
Friday
Ephesians 6:18–24; Luke 4:22–30
Saturday
1 Corinthians 15:39–45; Luke 4:31–36
Eighteenth Sunday After Pentecost
LITURGY: 2 Corinthians 9:6–11; Luke 5:1–11
Nineteenth Week After Pentecost
Monday
Philippians 1:1–7; Luke 4:37–44
Tuesday
Philippians 1:8–14; Luke 5:12–16
Wednesday
Philippians 1:12–20; Luke 5:33–39
Thursday
Philippians 1:20–27; Luke 6:12–19
Friday
Philippians 1:27—2:4; Luke 6:17–23
Saturday
1 Corinthians 15:58—16:3; Luke 5:17–26
Nineteenth Sunday After Pentecost
LITURGY: 2 Corinthians 11:31—12:9; Luke 6:31–36

NATIVITY

(Note: The Advent Cycle occurs from the twentieth Sunday after Pentecost to the twenty-sixth Sunday after Pentecost. Consult your local calendars for the exact date.)

Sunday of the Holy Ancestors of Christ
LITURGY: Colossians 3:4–11; Luke 14:16–24
Saturday Before the Nativity
Galatians 3:8–12; Luke 13:18–29
Sunday Before Nativity: Sunday of the Holy Fathers
LITURGY: Hebrews 11:9–10, 17–23, 32–40; Matthew 1:1–25
Eve of the Nativity of Christ (December 24–January 6)
ROYAL HOURS: FIRST HOUR: Micah 5:2–4; Hebrews 1:1–12; Matthew 1:18–25. THIRD HOUR: Baruch 3:36—4:4; Galatians 3:23–29; Luke 2:1–20. SIXTH HOUR: Isaiah 7:10–16; 8:1–4; 8:8–10; Hebrews 1:10—2:3; Matthew 2:1–12. NINTH HOUR: Isaiah 9:6, 7; Hebrews 2:11–18; Matthew 2:13–23. VESPERS: (1) Genesis 1:1–13; (2) Numbers 24:2, 3; 5–9, 17, 18; (3) Micah 4:6, 7; 5:2–4; (4) Isaiah 11:1–10; (5) Baruch 3:36—4:4; (6) Daniel 2:31–36; 44, 45; (7) Isaiah 9:6, 7; (8) Isaiah 7:10–16; 8:1–4, 8–10; LITURGY: Hebrews 1:1–12; Luke 2:1–20
The Nativity of Our Lord God and Savior Jesus Christ (December 25–January 7)
LITURGY: Galatians 4:4–7; Matthew 2:1–12
Saturday After Nativity
1 Timothy 6:11–16; Matthew 12:15–21
Sunday After the Nativity
Galatians 1:11–19; Matthew 2:13–23

THEOPHANY

Saturday Before Theophany
1 Timothy 3:14–4:5; Matthew 3:1–11
Sunday Before Theophany
2 Timothy 4:5–8; Mark 1:1–8
Eve of the Theophany (January 5–18)
THE ROYAL HOURS: FIRST HOUR: Isaiah 35:1–10; Acts 13:25–32; Matthew 3:1–11; THIRD HOUR: Isaiah 1:16–20; Acts 19:1–18; Mark 1:1–8; SIXTH HOUR: Isaiah 12:3–6; Romans 6:3–11; Mark 1:9–15; NINTH HOUR:

Isaiah 49:8–15; Titus 2:11–14; 3:4–7; Matthew 3:13–17. VESPERS: (1) Genesis 1:1–13; (2) Exodus 14:15–18, 21–23, 27–29; (3) Exodus 15:22–27; 16:1; (4) Joshua 3:7, 8, 15–17; (5) 2 Kings 2:6–14; (6) 2 Kings 5:9–14; (7) Isaiah 1:16–20; (8) Genesis 32:1–10; (9) Exodus 2:5–10; (10) Judges 6:36–40; (11) 1 Kings 18:30–39; (12) 2 Kings 2:19–22; (13) Isaiah 49:8–15. LITURGY: 1 Corinthians 9:19–27; Luke 3:1–18. BLESSING OF WATER: (1) Isaiah 35:1–10; (2) Isaiah 55:1–13; (3) Isaiah 12:3–6; 1 Corinthians 10:1–4; Mark 1:9–11

The Holy Theophany of Our Lord God and Savior Jesus Christ (January 6–19)
MATINS: Mark 1:9–11. LITURGY: Titus 2:11–14, 3:4–7; Matthew 3:13–17

Saturday After the Theophany
Ephesians 6:10–17; Matthew 4:1–11

Sunday After the Theophany
LITURGY: Ephesians 4:7–13; Matthew 4:12–17

Twentieth Week After Pentecost
Monday
Philippians 2:12–16; Luke 6:24–30
Tuesday
Philippians 2:17–23; Luke 6:37–45
Wednesday
Philippians 2:24–30; Luke 6:46—7:1
Thursday
Philippians 3:1–8; Luke 7:17–30
Friday
Philippians 3:8–19; Luke 7:31–35
Saturday
2 Corinthians 1:8–11; Luke 5:27–32

Twentieth Sunday After Pentecost
LITURGY: Galatians 1:11–19; Luke 7:11–16

Twenty-First Week After Pentecost
Monday
Philippians 4:10–23; Luke 7:36–50
Tuesday
Colossians 1:1, 2, 7–11; Luke 8:1–3
Wednesday
Colossians 1:18–23; Luke 8:22–25
Thursday
Colossians 1:24–29; Luke 9:7–11
Friday
Colossians 2:1–7; Luke 9:12–18
Saturday
2 Corinthians 3:12–18; Luke 6:1–10

Twenty-First Sunday After Pentecost
LITURGY: Galatians 2:16–20; Luke 8:5–15

Twenty-Second Week After Pentecost
Monday
Colossians 2:13–20; Luke 9:18–22
Tuesday
Colossians 2:20—3:3; Luke 9:23–27
Wednesday
Colossians 3:17—4:1; Luke 9:44–50
Thursday
Colossians 4:2–9; Luke 9:49–56
Friday
Colossians 4:10–18; Luke 10:1–15
Saturday
2 Corinthians 5:1–10; Luke 7:1–10

Twenty-Second Sunday After Pentecost
LITURGY: Galatians 6:11–18; Luke 16:19–31

Twenty-Third Week After Pentecost
Monday
1 Thessalonians 1:1–5; Luke 10:22–24
Tuesday
1 Thessalonians 1:6–10; Luke 11:1–10
Wednesday
1 Thessalonians 2:1–8; Luke 11:9–13
Thursday
1 Thessalonians 2:9–14; Luke 11:14–23
Friday
1 Thessalonians 2:14–19; Luke 11:23–26
Saturday
2 Corinthians 8:1–5; Luke 8:16–21

Twenty-Third Sunday After Pentecost
LITURGY: Ephesians 2:4–10: Luke 8:26–39

Twenty-Fourth Week After Pentecost
Monday
1 Thessalonians 2:20—3:8; Luke 11:29–33
Tuesday
1 Thessalonians 3:9–13; Luke 11:34–41
Wednesday
1 Thessalonians 4:1–12; Luke 11:42–46
Thursday
1 Thessalonians 5:1–8; Luke 11:47—12:1
Friday
1 Thessalonians 5:9–13, 24–28; Luke 12:2–12
Saturday
2 Corinthians 11:1–6; Luke 9:1–6

Twenty-Fourth Sunday After Pentecost
LITURGY: Ephesians 2:4–22; Luke 8:41–56

Twenty-Fifth Week After Pentecost
Monday
2 Thessalonians 1:1–10; Luke 12:13–15, 22–31
Tuesday
2 Thessalonians 1:10—2:2; Luke 12:42–48
Wednesday
2 Thessalonians 2:1–12; Luke 12:48–59
Thursday
2 Thessalonians 2:13—3:5; Luke 13:1–9
Friday
2 Thessalonians 3:6–18; Luke 13:31–35
Saturday
Galatians 1:3–10; Luke 9:37–43

Twenty-Fifth Sunday After Pentecost
LITURGY: Ephesians 4:1–6; Luke 10:25–37

Twenty-Sixth Week After Pentecost
Monday
1 Timothy 1:1–7; Luke 14:12–15
Tuesday
1 Timothy 1:8–14; Luke 14:25–35
Wednesday
1 Timothy 1:18–20; 2:8–15; Luke 15:1–10
Thursday
1 Timothy 3:1–13; Luke 16:1–9
Friday
1 Timothy 4:4–8, 16; Luke 16:15–18, 17:1–4
Saturday
Galatians 3:8–12; Luke 9:57–62

Twenty-Sixth Sunday After Pentecost
LITURGY: Ephesians 5:9–19; Luke 12:16–21

Twenty-Seventh Week After Pentecost
Monday
1 Timothy 5:1–10; Luke 17:20–25
Tuesday
1 Timothy 5:11–21; Luke 17:26–37
Wednesday
1 Timothy 5:22—6:11; Luke 18:15–17, 26–30
Thursday
1 Timothy 6:17–21; Luke 18:31–34
Friday
2 Timothy 1:1, 2, 8–18; Luke 19:12–28
Saturday
Galatians 5:22—6:2; Luke 10:19–21
Twenty-Seventh Sunday After Pentecost
LITURGY: Ephesians 6:10–17; Luke 13:10–17
Twenty-Eighth Week After Pentecost
Monday
2 Timothy 2:20–26; Luke 19:37–44
Tuesday
2 Timothy 3:16—4:4; Luke 19:45–48
Wednesday
2 Timothy 4:9–22; Luke 20:1–8
Thursday
Titus 1:5—2:1; Luke 20:9–18
Friday
Titus 1:15—2:10; Luke 20:19–26
Saturday
Ephesians 1:16–23; Luke 12:32–40
Twenty-Eighth Sunday After Pentecost
LITURGY: Colossians 1:12–18; Luke 18:35–43
Twenty-Ninth Week After Pentecost
Monday
Hebrews 3:5–11; Luke 20:27–44
Tuesday
Hebrews 4:1–13; Luke 21:12–19
Wednesday
Hebrews 5:11—6:8; Luke 21:5–7, 10, 11, 20–24
Thursday
Hebrews 7:1–6; Luke 21:28–33
Friday
Hebrews 7:18–25; Luke 21:37—22:8
Saturday
Ephesians 2:11–13; Luke 13:18–29
Twenty-Ninth Sunday After Pentecost
LITURGY: Colossians 3:12–16; Luke 17:12–19
Thirtieth Week After Pentecost
Monday
Hebrews 8:7–13; Mark 8:11–21
Tuesday
Hebrews 9:8–10, 15–23; Mark 8:22–26
Wednesday
Hebrews 10:1–18; Mark 8:30–34
Thursday
Hebrews 10:35—11:7; Mark 9:10–16
Friday
Hebrews 11:8, 11–16; Mark 9:33–41
Saturday
Ephesians 5:1–8; Luke 14:1–11
Thirtieth Sunday After Pentecost
LITURGY: Colossians 3:12–16; Luke 18:18–27
Thirty-First Week After Pentecost
Monday
Hebrews 11:17, 27–31; Mark 9:42—10:1
Tuesday
Hebrews 12:25, 26, 13:22–25; Mark 10:2–12
Wednesday
James 1:1–18; Mark 10:11–16
Thursday
James 1:19–27; Mark 10:17–27
Friday
James 2:1–13; Mark 10:23–32
Saturday
Colossians 1:3–6; Luke 16:10–15
Thirty-First Sunday After Pentecost
LITURGY: 1 Timothy 1:15–17; Luke 18:35–43
Thirty-Second Week After Pentecost
Monday
James 2:14–26; Mark 10:46–52
Tuesday
James 3:1–10; Mark 11:11–23
Wednesday
James 3:11—4:6; Mark 11:23–26
Thursday
James 4:7—5:9; Mark 11:27–33
Friday
1 Peter 1:1, 2, 10–12, 2:6–10; Mark 12:1–12
Saturday
1 Thessalonians 5:14–23; Luke 17:3–10
Thirty-Second Sunday After Pentecost
LITURGY: 1 Timothy 4:9–15; Luke 19:1–10

(*Note:* If Theophany readings still apply or Easter is late, Zacchaeus Sunday may be moved to a later date. Consult a current calendar. Zacchaeus Sunday is the Sunday before the Triodion.)

TRIODION AND GREAT LENT

Week Before the Triodion: Week of the Publican and Pharisee
(*Note:* Scripture readings for the Week of the Publican and Pharisee are the same as readings for the Thirty–Third Week After Pentecost.)
Monday
1 Peter 2:21—3:9; Mark 12:13–17
Tuesday
1 Peter 3:10–22; Mark 12:18–27
Wednesday
1 Peter 4:1–11; Mark 12:28–37
Thursday
1 Peter 4:12—5:5; Mark 12:38–44
Friday
2 Peter 1:1–10; Mark 13:1–8
Saturday
2 Timothy 2:11–19; Luke 18:2–8

TRIODION

Tenth Sunday Before Easter
Sunday of the Publican and Pharisee
LITURGY: 2 Timothy 3:10–15; Luke 18:10–14

Week of the Prodigal Son
Monday
2 Peter 1:20—2:9; Mark 13:9–13
Tuesday
2 Peter 2:9–22; Mark 13:14–23
Wednesday
2 Peter 3:1–18; Mark 13:24–31
Thursday
1 John 1:8—2:6; Mark 13:31—14:2
Friday
1 John 2:7–17; Mark 14:3–9
Saturday
2 Timothy 3:1–9; Luke 20:45—21:4
Sunday of the Prodigal Son
LITURGY: 1 Corinthians 6:12–20; Luke 15:11–32
Meat Fare Week
Monday
1 John 2:18—3:10; Mark 11:1–11
Tuesday
1 John 3:11–20; Mark 14:10–42
Wednesday
1 John 3:21—4:6; Mark 14:43—15:1
Thursday
1 John 4:20—5:21; Mark 15:1–15
Friday
2 John 1:1–13; Mark 15:22–25, 33–41
Saturday
1 Corinthians 10:23–28; Luke 21:8, 9, 25–27, 33–36
Commemoration of the Departed
1 Thessalonians 4:13–17; John 5:24–30
Meat Fare Sunday
LITURGY: 1 Corinthians 8:8—9:2; Matthew 25:31–46
Cheese Fare Week
Monday
3 John 1:1–14; Luke 19:29–40; 22:7–39
Tuesday
Jude 1–10; Luke 22:39–42, 45—23:1
Wednesday
Joel 2:12–26; Joel 3:12–21
Thursday
Jude 11–25; Luke 23:2–34, 44–56
Friday
Zechariah 8:7–14; Zechariah 8:19–23
Saturday
Romans 14:19–23; 16:25–27; Matthew 6:1–13
Commemoration of All the Holy and Godbearing Fathers Who Shone Forth in the Ascetic Life
Galatians 5:22—6:2; Matthew 11:27–30
Sunday: Seventh Sunday Before Easter (Also Forgiveness Sunday)
LITURGY: Romans 13:11—14:4; Matthew 6:14–21

GREAT LENT

First Week of Great Lent
Monday
Isaiah 1:1–20; Genesis 1:1–13; Proverbs 1:1–20
Tuesday
Isaiah 1:19—2:3; Genesis 1:14–23; Proverbs 1:20–33
Wednesday
Isaiah 2:3–11; Genesis 1:24—2:3; Proverbs 2:1–22
Thursday
Isaiah 2:11–22; Genesis 2:4–19; Proverbs 3:1–18
Friday
Isaiah 3:1–14; Genesis 2:20—3:20; Proverbs 3:19–34
Saturday
Hebrews 1:1–12; Mark 2:23—3:5
First Sunday of Great Lent: Sunday of Orthodoxy
LITURGY: Hebrews 11:24–26, 32—12:2; John 1:43–51
Second Week of Great Lent
Monday
Isaiah 4:2–6; 5:1–7; Genesis 3:21—4:7; Proverbs 3:34—4:22
Tuesday
Isaiah 5:7–16; Genesis 4:8–15; Proverbs 5:1–15
Wednesday
Isaiah 5:16–26; Genesis 4:16–26; Proverbs 5:15—6:3
Thursday
Isaiah 6:1–12; Genesis 5:1–24; Proverbs 6:3–20
Friday
Isaiah 7:1–14; Genesis 5:32—6:8; Proverbs 6:20—7:1
Saturday
Hebrews 3:12–16; Mark 1:35–44
Second Sunday of Great Lent: Commemoration of St. Gregory Palamas
LITURGY: Hebrews 1:10—2:3; Mark 2:1–12
Third Week of Great Lent
Monday
Isaiah 8:13—9:7; Genesis 6:9–22; Proverbs 8:1–21
Tuesday
Isaiah 9:9—10:4; Genesis 7:1–5; Proverbs 8:32—9:11
Wednesday
Isaiah 10:12–20; Genesis 7:6–9; Proverbs 9:12–18
Thursday
Isaiah 11:10—12:2; Genesis 7:11—8:3; Proverbs 10:1–22
Friday
Isaiah 13:2–13; Genesis 8:4–21; Proverbs 10:31—11:12
Saturday
Hebrews 10:32–38; Mark 2:14–17
Third Sunday of Great Lent: Adoration of the Holy Cross
LITURGY: Hebrews 4:14—5:6; Mark 8:34—9:1
Fourth Week of Great Lent
Monday
Isaiah 14:24–32; Genesis 8:21—9:7; Proverbs 11:19—12:6

Tuesday
Isaiah 25:1–9; Genesis 9:8–17; Proverbs 12:8–22
Wednesday
Isaiah 26:21—27:9; Genesis 9:18—10:1; Proverbs 12:23—13:9
Thursday
Isaiah 28:14–22; Genesis 10:32—11:9; Proverbs 13:20—14:6
Friday
Isaiah 29:13–23; Genesis 12:1–7; Proverbs 14:15–26
Saturday
Hebrews 6:9–12; Mark 7:31–37

Fourth Sunday of Great Lent: Commemoration of Saint John of the Ladder
LITURGY: Hebrews 6:13–20; Mark 9:17–31

Fifth Week of Great Lent
Monday
Isaiah 37:33—38:6; Genesis 13:12–18; Proverbs 14:27—15:4
Tuesday
Isaiah 40:18–31; Genesis 15:1–15; Proverbs 15:7–19
Wednesday
Isaiah 41:4–14; Genesis 17:1–9; Proverbs 15:20—16:9
Thursday
Isaiah 42:5–16: Genesis 18:20–33; Proverbs 16:17—17:17
Friday
Isaiah 45:11–17; Genesis 22:1–18; Proverbs 17:17—18:5
Saturday
Hebrews 9:24–28; Mark 8:27–31

Fifth Sunday of Great Lent: Commemoration of Saint Mary of Egypt
LITURGY: Hebrews 9:11–14; Mark 10:32–45

Sixth Week of Great Lent
Monday
Isaiah 48:17—49:4; Genesis 27:1–41; Proverbs 19:16–25
Tuesday
Isaiah 49:6–10; Genesis 31:3–16; Proverbs 21:3–21
Wednesday
Isaiah 58:1–11; Genesis 43:26–31; 45:1–16; Proverbs 21:23—22:4
Thursday
Isaiah 65:8–16; Genesis 46:1–7; Proverbs 23:15—24:5
Friday
Isaiah 66:10–24; Genesis 49:33—50:26; Proverbs 31:8–31

Saturday of Saint Lazarus the Righteous
Hebrews 12:28—13:8; John 11:1–45

The Entry of the Lord into Jerusalem: Palm Sunday
VESPERS: (1) Genesis 49:1, 2, 8–12; (2) Zephaniah 3:14–19; (3) Zechariah 9:9–15. MATINS: Matt. 21:1–11, 15–17. LITURGY: Philippians 4:4–9; John 12:1–18

HOLY WEEK

Holy Monday
MATINS: Matthew 21:18–43; SIXTH HOUR: Ezekiel 1:1–20. VESPERS: Exodus 1:1–20; Job 1:1–12. LITURGY OF THE PRESANCTIFIED GIFTS: Matthew 24:3–35

Holy Tuesday
MATINS: Matthew 22:15—23:39; SIXTH HOUR: Ezekiel 1:21—2:1. VESPERS: Exodus 2:5–10; Job 1:13–22. LITURGY OF THE PRESANCTIFIED GIFTS: Matthew 24:36—26:2

Holy Wednesday
MATINS: John 12:17–50; SIXTH HOUR: Ezekiel 2:3—3:3. VESPERS: Exodus 2:11–22; Job 2:1–10. LITURGY OF THE PRESANCTIFIED GIFTS: Matthew 26:6–16

Holy Thursday
MATINS: Luke 22:1–39; FIRST HOUR: Jeremiah 11:18—12:5, 9–11, 14, 15. VESPERS: (1) Exodus 19:10–19; (2) Job 38:1–23; 42:1–5; (3) Isaiah 50:4–11. LITURGY OF SAINT BASIL: 1 Corinthians 11:23–32; Matthew 26:1–20; John 13:3–17; Matthew 26:21–39; Luke 22:43–45; Matthew 26:40—27:2

Holy Friday (Thursday Evening) The Twelve Passion Gospels
(1) John 13:31—18:1; (2) John 18:1–28; (3) Matthew 26:57–75; (4) John 18:28—19:16; (5) Matthew 27:3–32; (6) Mark 15:16–32; (7) Matthew 27:33–54; (8) Luke 23:32–49; (9) John 19:25–37; (10) Mark 15:43–47; (11) John 19:38–42; (12) Matthew 27:62–66

Holy Friday
THE ROYAL HOURS: FIRST HOUR: Zechariah 11:10–13; Galatians 6:14–18; Matthew 27:1–56. THIRD HOUR: Isaiah 50:4–11; Romans 5:6–11; Mark 15:16–41. SIXTH HOUR: Isaiah 52:13—54:1; Hebrews 2:11–18; Luke 23:32–49. NINTH HOUR: Jeremiah 11:18–23; 12:1–5, 9–11, 14, 15; Hebrews 10:19–31; John 18:28—19:37. VESPERS: (1) Exodus 33:11–23; (2) Job 42:12–16; (3) Isaiah 52:13—54:1; 1 Corinthians 1:18—2:2; Matthew 27:1–38; Luke 23:39–43; Matthew 27:39–54; John 19:31–37; Matthew 27:55–61

Holy Saturday
MATINS: Ezekiel 37:1–14; 1 Corinthians 5:6–8; Galatians 3:13, 14; Matthew 27:62–66. VESPERS: (1) Genesis 1:1–13; (2) Isaiah 60:1–16; (3) Exodus 12:1–11; (4) The Book of Jonah; (5) Joshua 5:10–15; (6) Exodus 13:20—15:19; (7) Zephaniah 3:8–15; (8) 1 Kings 17:8–24; (9) Isaiah 61:10—62:5; (10) Genesis 22:1–18; (11) Isaiah 61:1–9; (12) 2 Kings 4:8–37; (13) Isaiah 63:11—64:5; (14) Jeremiah 31:31–34; (15) Daniel 3:1–23 and the Song of the Holy Children (Apocrypha)

Great and Holy Saturday
LITURGY: Romans 6:3–11; Matthew 28:1–20

MAJOR FIXED FEASTS

The Meeting of Our Lord and Savior Jesus Christ (February 2–15)
VESPERS: (1) Exodus 12:51—13:3, 10–12, 14–16, 22–29; Leviticus 12:1–4, 6–8; Numbers 8:16, 17; (2) Isaiah 6:1–12; (3) Isaiah 19:1–5, 12, 16, 19–21. MATINS: Luke 2:25–32.
LITURGY: Hebrews 7:7–17; Luke 2:22–40

The Annunciation of Our Most Holy Lady, the Theotokos and Ever-Virgin Mary (March 25–April 7)
VESPERS: Parables of the Feast (1) Genesis 28:10–17; (2) Ezekiel 43:27—44:4; (3) Proverbs 9:1–11. VESPERS: Exodus 3:1–8; Proverbs 8:22–30. MATINS: Luke 1:39–49, 56.
LITURGY: Hebrews 2:11–18; Luke 1:24–38

The Holy, Glorious and All-Praised Leaders of the Apostles, Peter and Paul (June 29–July 12)
VESPERS: (1) 1 Peter 1:3–9; (2) 1 Peter 1:13–19; (3) 1 Peter 2:11–24. MATINS: John 21:15–25. LITURGY: 2 Corinthians 11:21—12:9; Matthew 16:13–19

The Holy Transfiguration of Our Lord God and Savior Jesus Christ (August 6–19)
VESPERS: (1) Exodus 24:12–18; (2) Exodus 33:11–23; 34:4–6, 8; (3) 1 Kings 19:3–9, 11–13, 15, 16. MATINS: Luke 9:28–36. LITURGY: 2 Peter 1:10–19; Matthew 17:1–9

The Dormition of Our Most Holy Lady the Theotokos and Ever-Virgin Mary (August 15–28)
VESPERS: (1) Genesis 28:10–17; (2) Ezekiel 43:27—44:4; (3) Proverbs 9:1–11. MATINS: Luke 1:39–49, 56. LITURGY: Philippians 2:5–11; Luke 10:38–42; 11:27, 28

The Nativity of Our Most Holy Lady the Theotokos and Ever-Virgin Lady (September 8–21)
Readings are the same as for Dormition

Saturday Before the Exaltation of the Cross
1 Corinthians 2:6–9; Matthew 10:37—11:1

Sunday Before the Exaltation of the Cross
Galatians 6:11–18; John 3:13–17

The Exaltation of the Precious and Life-Giving Cross (September 14–27)
VESPERS: (1) Exodus 15:22–27; (2) Proverbs 3:11–18; (3) Isaiah 60:11–16. MATINS: John 12:28–36. LITURGY: 1 Corinthians 1:18–24; John 19:6–11, 13–20, 25–28, 30–35

Saturday After the Exaltation of the Cross
1 Corinthians 1:26–29; John 8:21–30

Sunday After the Exaltation of the Cross
Galatians 2:16–20; Mark 8:34—9:1

The Protection of Our Most Holy Lady the Theotokos and Ever-Virgin Mary (October 1–14)
VESPERS and MATINS same as Dormition, August 15.
LITURGY: Hebrews 9:1–7; Luke 10:38–42; 11:27, 28

The Entry of the Most Holy Theotokos into the Temple (November 21–December 4)
VESPERS: (1) Exodus 40:1–5, 9, 10, 16, 34, 35; (2) 1 Kings 7:51; 8:1, 3–7, 9–11; (3) Ezekiel 43:27—44:4. MATINS: Luke 1:39–49, 56.
LITURGY: Hebrews 9:1–7; Luke 10:38–42; 11:27, 28

OTHER SPECIAL AND GENERAL FEASTDAYS

Most Holy Theotokos
MATINS: Luke 1:39–49, 56.
LITURGY: Philippians 2:5–11 or *Hebrews 9:1–7; Luke 10:38–42; 11:27, 28.*

Apostles
1 Corinthians 4:9–16; Luke 10:1–15 or *Luke 10:16–21.*

Holy Monks:
Galatians 5:22—6:2; Matthew 11:27–30 or *Luke 6:17–23* (St. Basil January 1–14) or *Matthew 7:12–21* (St. Andrew of Crete July 4–17).

Holy Nuns:
Galatians 3:23–29; Matthew 25:1–13 or *Luke 7:36–50.*

Holy Confessors:
Ephesians 6:10–17; Luke 12:8–12.

Holy Martyr
2 Timothy 2:1–10; alternatively *Acts 12:1–11;* Luke 12:1–12 or *John 15:17—16:2.*

Holy Martyrs
Romans 8:28–39; Matthew 10:16–22 or *Luke 21:12–19.*

Hieromartyr
Hebrews 13:7–16; Luke 12:32–40.

Hieromartyrs
Hebrews 5:4–10 or *Philippians 3:20—4:3; Luke 6:17–23* or *Luke 10:22–24* or *Luke 14:25–35.*

Monk Martyr
1 Timothy 1:8–18; Mark 8:34—9:1.

Monk Martyrs
Romans 8:28–39; Matthew 10:32, 33, 37, 38; 19:27–30 or *Luke 12:8–12.*

Female Martyrs
2 Corinthians 6:1–10 or *Galatians 3:23–29; Matthew 15:21–28* or *Mark 5:24.*

Holy Unmercenary Healers
1 Corinthians 12:27—13:8; Matthew 10:1, 5–8.

Prophets
1 Corinthians 14:20–25; Hebrews 6:13–20; or *James 5:10–20; Matthew 23:29–39* or *Luke 11:47–54.*

St. John the Baptist
Conception (September 23–October 6)
Galatians 4:22–31; Luke 1:5–25.
Nativity (June 24–July 7)
VESPERS: (1) Genesis 17:15–17, 19, 18:11–14; 21:1–8; (2) Judges 13:2–8, 13, 14, 17, 18, 21; (3) Isaiah 40:1–3, 9; 41:17, 18; 45:8; 48:20, 21, 54:1. MATINS: Luke 1:24, 25, 57–68, 76, 80.

LITURGY: Romans 13:11—14:4; Luke 1:1–15, 57–68, 76, 80

Beheading (August 29–September 11)

MATINS: Matthew 14:1–13. LITURGY: Acts 13:25–32; Mark 6:14–30.

First and Second Finding (February 24–March 9

Third Finding of the Honorable Head (May 29–June 7

MATINS: Luke 7:17. LITURGY: 2 *Corinthians 4:6–12; Matthew 11:2–15. VESPERS for both above: (1) Isaiah 40:1–3, 9, 41:17, 18; 45:8; 48:20, 21; 54:1; (2) Malachi 3:1–3, 5–7, 12, 18; 4:4–6; (3) Wisdom 4:7, 16, 17, 19, 20, 5:1–7*

Archangels (November 8–21, etc.)

Hebrew 2:2–10; Luke 10:16–21 or *Matthew 13:24–30, 36, 43.*

Hierarch: St. John Chrysostom (November 13–26), St. Sava of Serbia (January 14–27, etc.)

Hebrews 7:26—8:2; John 10:9–16. Also see St. Aphrahat of Persia. *MATINS: John 21:15–25*

Hierarchs: St. Nicholas of Myra (December 6–19), Sts. Cyril and Methodius, St. Athanasius, etc.

MATINS: John 10:1–9. LITURGY: Hebrews 13:17–21; Matthew 5:14–19; John 10:9–16; or *Luke 6:17–23.*

Commemoration of the Departed

Monday

Romans 16:6–9; John 5:17–24.

Tuesday

1 Corinthians 15:39–57; John 5:24–30.

Wednesday

2 Corinthians 5:1–10; John 6:35–39.

Thursday

1 Corinthians 15:20–28; John 6:40–44.

Friday

1 Corinthians 15:47–57; John 6:48–54.

Saturday

1 Thessalonians 4:13–17; John 5:24–30.

How to Read the New Testament in a Year

MATTHEW

Jan. 1 1
Jan. 2 2
Jan. 3 3
Jan. 4 4
Jan. 5 5
Jan. 6 5
Jan. 7 6
Jan. 8 6
Jan. 9 7
Jan. 10 8:1–13
Jan. 11 8:14–34
Jan. 12 9:1–17
Jan. 13 9:18–38
Jan. 14 10:1–25
Jan. 15 10:26–42
Jan. 16 11
Jan. 17 12:1–21
Jan. 18 12:22–50
Jan. 19 13:1–30
Jan. 20 13:31–58
Jan. 21 14:1–21
Jan. 22 14:22–36
Jan. 23 15:1–20
Jan. 24 15:21–39
Jan. 25 16
Jan. 26 17
Jan. 27 18:1–20
Jan. 28 18:21–35
Jan. 29 19
Jan. 30 20:1–16
Jan. 31 20:17–34
Feb. 1 21:1–22
Feb. 2 21:23–46
Feb. 3 22:1–22
Feb. 4 22:23–46
Feb. 5 23:1–22
Feb. 6 23:23–39
Feb. 7 24:1–28
Feb. 8 24:29–51
Feb. 9 25:1–30
Feb. 10 25:31–46
Feb. 11 26:1–25
Feb. 12 26:26–46
Feb. 13 26:47–75
Feb. 14 27:1–26
Feb. 15 27:27–44
Feb. 16 27:28–66
Feb. 17 28

MARK

Feb. 18 1:1–20
Feb. 19 1:21–45
Feb. 20 2
Feb. 21 3:1–19
Feb. 22 3:20–35
Feb. 23 4:1–20
Feb. 24 4:21–41
Feb. 25 5:1–20
Feb. 26 5:21–43
Feb. 27 6:1–29
Feb. 28 6:30–56
Feb. 29 7:1–23
Mar. 1 7:24–37
Mar. 2 8:1–21
Mar. 3 8:22–38
Mar. 4 9:1–29
Mar. 5 9:30–50
Mar. 6 10:1–31
Mar. 7 10:32–52
Mar. 8 11:1–19
Mar. 9 11:20–33
Mar. 10 12:1–27
Mar. 11 12:28–44
Mar. 12 13:1–23
Mar. 13 13:24–37
Mar. 14 14:1–26
Mar. 15 14:27–52
Mar. 16 14:53–72
Mar. 17 15:1–20
Mar. 18 15:21–47
Mar. 19 16

LUKE

Mar. 20 1:1–25
Mar. 21 1:26–38
Mar. 22 1:39–56
Mar. 23 1:57–80
Mar. 24 2:1–20
Mar. 25 2:21–51
Mar. 26 3
Mar. 27 4:1–30
Mar. 28 4:31–44
Mar. 29 5:1–16
Mar. 30 5:17–39
Mar. 31 6:1–26
Apr. 1 6:27–49
Apr. 2 7:1–35
Apr. 3 7:36–50
Apr. 4 8:1–25
Apr. 5 8:26–56
Apr. 6 9:1–17
Apr. 7 9:18–36
Apr. 8 9:37–62
Apr. 9 10:1–24
Apr. 10 10:25–42
Apr. 11 11:1–28
Apr. 12 11:29–54
Apr. 13 12:1–34
Apr. 14 12:35–59
Apr. 15 13:1–21
Apr. 16 13:22–35
Apr. 17 14:1–24
Apr. 18 14:25–35
Apr. 19 15:1–10
Apr. 20 15:11–32
Apr. 21 16
Apr. 22 17:1–19
Apr. 23 17:20–37
Apr. 24 18:1–17
Apr. 25 18:18–43
Apr. 26 19:1–27
Apr. 27 19:28–47
Apr. 28 20:1–26
Apr. 29 20:27–47
Apr. 30 21:1–19
May 1 21:20–38
May 2 22:1–23
May 3 22:24–46
May 4 22:47–71
May 5 23:1–25
May 6 23:26–56
May 7 24:1–27
May 8 24:27–53

JOHN

May 9 1:1–28
May 10 1:29–51
May 11 2
May 12 3:1–21
May 13 3:22–36
May 14 4:1–30
May 15 4:31–54
May 16 5:1–15
May 17 5:16–47
May 18 6:1–21
May 19 6:22–45
May 20 6:46–71
May 21 7:1–24
May 22 7:25–52
May 23 8:1–30
May 24 8:31–59
May 25 9:1–23
May 26 9:24–41
May 27 10:1–30
May 28 10:31–42
May 29 11:1–31
May 30 11:32–57
May 31 12:1–26
June 1 12:27–50
June 2 13:1–17
June 3 13:18–38
June 4 14
June 5 15—16:1–4
June 6 16:5–33
June 7 17
June 8 18:1–18
June 9 18:20–38

June 10 18:39—19:16
June 11 19:17–42
June 12 20
June 13 21

ACTS

June 14 1
June 15 2:1–21
June 16 2:22–47
June 17 3
June 18 4:1–22
June 19 4:23–37
June 20 5:1–16
June 21 5:17–42
June 22 6
June 23 7:1–22
June 24 7:23–43
June 25 7:44—8:2
June 26 8:3–25
June 27 8:26–40
June 28 9:1–19
June 29 9:20–43
June 30 10:1–24
July 1 10:25–48
July 2 11
July 3 12
July 4 13:1–25
July 5 13:26–52
July 6 14:1—15:5
July 7 15:6–21
July 8 15:22–41
July 9 16:1–21
July 10 16:22–40
July 11 17:1–15
July 12 17:16–34
July 13 18
July 14 19:1–20
July 15 19:21–41
July 16 20:1–16
July 17 20:17–37
July 18 21:1–14
July 19 21:15–36
July 20 21:37—22:29
July 21 22:30—23:10
July 22 23:11–35
July 23 24
July 24 25
July 25 26
July 26 27:1–26
July 27 27:27–44
July 28 28

ROMANS

July 29 1
July 30 2:1—3:8
July 31 3:9–31
Aug. 1 4
Aug. 2 5
Aug. 3 6
Aug. 4 7
Aug. 5 8:1–17
Aug. 6 8:18–39
Aug. 7 9:1–29
Aug. 8 9:30—10:13
Aug. 9 10:14–21
Aug. 10 11:1–16
Aug. 11 11:17–36
Aug. 12 12
Aug. 13 13
Aug. 14 14
Aug. 15 15:1–13
Aug. 16 15:14–33
Aug. 17 16

1 CORINTHIANS

Aug. 18 1
Aug. 19 2
Aug. 20 3
Aug. 21 4
Aug. 22 5
Aug. 23 6
Aug. 24 7:1–24
Aug. 25 7:25–40
Aug. 26 8
Aug. 27 9
Aug. 28 10:1–13
Aug. 29 10:14—11:1
Aug. 30 11:2–16
Aug. 31 11:17–34
Sept. 1 12
Sept. 2 13
Sept. 3 14:1–25
Sept. 4 14:26–40
Sept. 5 15:1–34
Sept. 6 15:35–58
Sept. 7 16

2 CORINTHIANS

Sept. 8 1:1–22
Sept. 9 1:23—2:17
Sept. 10 3
Sept. 11 4:1–15
Sept. 12 4:16—5:18
Sept. 13 5:18—7:1
Sept. 14 7:2–16
Sept. 15 8
Sept. 16 9
Sept. 17 10
Sept. 18 11:1–21
Sept. 19 11:22–33
Sept. 20 12
Sept. 21 13

GALATIANS

Sept. 22 1
Sept. 23 2
Sept. 24 3:1—4:7
Sept. 25 4:7–31
Sept. 26 5
Sept. 27 6

EPHESIANS

Sept. 28 1
Sept. 29 2
Sept. 30 3
Oct. 1 4:1–16
Oct. 2 4:17—5:21
Oct. 3 5:22—6:9
Oct. 4 6:10–24

PHILIPPIANS

Oct. 5 1
Oct. 6 2
Oct. 7 3:1—4:1
Oct. 8 4:2–23

COLOSSIANS

Oct. 9 1
Oct. 10 2
Oct. 11 3
Oct. 12 4

1 THESSALONIANS

Oct. 13 1
Oct. 14 2
Oct. 15 3
Oct. 16 4
Oct. 17 5

2 THESSALONIANS

Oct. 18 1
Oct. 19 2
Oct. 20 3

1 TIMOTHY

Oct. 21 1
Oct. 22 2
Oct. 23 3
Oct. 24 4
Oct. 25 5
Oct. 26 6

2 TIMOTHY

Oct. 27 1
Oct. 28 2
Oct. 29 3
Oct. 30 4

TITUS

Oct. 31 1
Nov. 1 2
Nov. 2 3

PHILEMON

Nov. 3

HEBREWS

Nov. 4 1
Nov. 5 2
Nov. 6 3
Nov. 7 4
Nov. 8 5
Nov. 9 6
Nov. 10 7
Nov. 11 8
Nov. 12 9
Nov. 13 10:1–25
Nov. 14 10:26–39
Nov. 15 11:1–19

Nov. 16	11:20–40
Nov. 17	12
Nov. 18	13

JAMES

Nov. 19	1
Nov. 20	2
Nov. 21	3
Nov. 22	4
Nov. 23	5

1 PETER

Nov. 24	1
Nov. 25	2
Nov. 26	3
Nov. 27	4
Nov. 28	5

2 PETER

Nov. 29	1
Nov. 30	2
Dec. 1	3

1 JOHN

Dec. 2	1
Dec. 3	2
Dec. 4	3
Dec. 5	4
Dec. 6	5

2 JOHN

Dec. 7

3 JOHN

Dec. 8

JUDE

Dec. 9

REVELATION

Dec. 10	1
Dec. 11	2
Dec. 12	3
Dec. 13	4
Dec. 14	5
Dec. 15	6
Dec. 16	7
Dec. 17	8
Dec. 18	9
Dec. 19	10
Dec. 20	11
Dec. 21	12
Dec. 22	13
Dec. 23	14
Dec. 24	15
Dec. 25	16
Dec. 26	17
Dec. 27	18
Dec. 28	19
Dec. 29	20
Dec. 30	21
Dec. 31	22

Introducing the Orthodox Church

The publication of *The Orthodox Study Bible* begs a question: exactly what is the Orthodox Church? Many people have heard of the Russian Orthodox Church, which celebrated its one thousandth birthday in 1988, or the Greek Orthodox Church, which was born centuries earlier. But Orthodoxy itself—what is it, and what are its historic roots?

The Church in the New Testament

To answer the question, go back to the pages of the New Testament, specifically to the Book of Acts and the birth of the Church at Pentecost. On that day the Holy Spirit descended on the Twelve Apostles and those gathered in the Upper Room, and by afternoon some three thousand souls believed in Christ and were baptized. The Scriptures record that when the first Christian community began, "they continued steadfastly in the apostles' doctrine and fellowship, in the breaking of bread, and in prayers" (Acts 2:42).

From Jerusalem, faith in Christ spread throughout Judea, to Samaria (Acts 8:5–39), to Antioch and to the Gentiles (Acts 11:19–26). Soon there were new converts and new Churches throughout Asia Minor and the Roman Empire as recorded in Acts and the Epistles.

The Church, of course, was not simply another organization in Roman society. The Lord Jesus Christ had given the promise of the Holy Spirit to "guide you into all truth" (John 16:13). With the fulfillment of that promise beginning with Pentecost, the Church bore more than mere institutional status. She is not an organization with mystery, but a mystery with organization. St. Paul called the Church "a dwelling place of God in the Spirit" (Eph. 2:22). The Church is a dynamic organism, the living body of Jesus Christ. She makes an indelible impact in the world, and those who live in her life and faith are personally transformed.

But the New Testament also reveals that the Church had her share of problems. All was not perfection. Some individuals within the Church even sought to lead her off the path the apostles established, and they had to be dealt with along with the errors they invented. Even whole local communities lapsed on occasion and were called to repentance. The church in Laodicea is a vivid example (Rev. 3:14–22). Discipline was administered for the sake of purity in the Church. But there was growth and maturation, even as the Church was attacked from within and without. The same Spirit who gave her birth gave her power for purity and correction, and she stood strong and grew, eventually invading the whole of the Roman Empire.

The Early Centuries

As the Church moves from the pages of the New Testament and on into the succeeding centuries of her history, her growth and development can be traced in terms of specific categories. The first is a category important for all Christian people: *doctrine*. Did she maintain the truth of God as given by Christ and His Apostles? Second, what about *worship*? Is there a discernible way in which the people of God have offered a sacrifice of praise and thanksgiving to Him? Third, consider Church *government*. What sort of polity did the Church practice?

1. *Doctrine*: Not only did the Church begin under the teaching of the Apostles, but she was also instructed to "stand fast and hold the traditions which you were taught, whether by word or our epistle" (2 Thess. 2:15). The Apostle Paul insisted that those matters delivered by him and his fellow apostles, both in person and in the writings that would come to be called the New Testament, be adhered to carefully. Thus followed such appropriate warnings as "in the name of our Lord Jesus Christ . . . withdraw from every brother who walks disorderly and not according to the tradition which he received from us" (2 Thess. 3:6). The doctrines taught by Christ and His disciples are to be safeguarded by "the church of the living God, the pillar and ground of the truth" (1 Tim. 3:15) and are not open for renegotiation. And the Church was still young when a *way* had to be found for providing this safeguard.

Midway through the first century, a dispute arose in Antioch over adherence to Old Testament laws. The matter could not be settled there; outside help was needed. The leaders of the Antiochian Church, the community which had earlier dispatched Paul and Barnabas as missionaries, brought the matter to Jerusalem for consideration by the apostles and elders there. The matter was discussed, debated, and a written decision was forthcoming.

James, the brother of the Lord and the first bishop of Jerusalem, put forth the solution to the problem. This settlement, agreed to by all concerned at what is known as the Council of Jerusalem (Acts 15:1–35), set the pattern for the use of church councils in the centuries ahead to settle doctrinal and moral issues that arose. Thus, throughout the history of the Church, we find scores of such councils on various levels to settle matters of dispute and to deal with those who do not adhere to the apostolic faith.

The first three hundred years of Christian history were also marked by the appearance of certain heresies or false teachings such as secret philosophic schemes for the elite (Gnosticism), dazzling prophetic aberrations (Montanism), and grave errors regarding the three Persons of the Trinity (Sabellianism). Then, in the early fourth century, a heresy with potential for Church-wide disruption appeared, propagated by one Arius, a presbyter in Alexandria, Egypt. He denied the eternality of the Son of God, claiming contrary to the apostles' doctrine that the Son was a created being who came into existence at a point in time, and thus was not truly God. This deadly error struck the Church like a cancer. Turmoil spread almost everywhere. The first Church-wide, or Ecumenical, Council met in Nicea in A.D. 325 to address this issue. Some 318 bishops, along with many priests, deacons, and laymen rejected the new teaching of Arius and his associates, upholding the apostles' doctrine of Christ, affirming the eternality of the Son and His consubstantiality with the Father. Their proclamation of the apostolic teaching concerning Christ included a creed, which, with the additions concerning the Holy Spirit made in 381 at the Council of Constantinople, forms the document today called the Nicene Creed.

Between the years 325 and 787, seven such Church-wide conclaves were held, meeting in the cities of Nicea, Ephesus, Chalcedon, and Constantinople. Known as the Seven Ecumenical Councils, all dealt first and foremost with some specific challenge to the apostolic teaching about Jesus Christ. The Third Ecumenical Council (431 A.D.), for instance, condemned the Nestorians—those who would divide Christ into two persons, one human and the other divine. The Nestorians were concentrated in Persia and eastward, and when some of the Nestorian bishops would not accept the decision of the Council, the Church experienced the first territorial schism. Evangelistically active, the Nestorians formed communities in Arabia, India, and as far away as China. A remnant still carries on a precarious existence in Kurdistan, Iraq, Syria, and the United States.

Among the issues addressed by the Fourth Ecumenical Council (451 A.D.) was the heresy of the Monophysites, who claimed that there is but one nature in Christ. Some claimed that the two natures in Christ were mingled into one, making Him neither God nor man. Others believed that the divine nature had swallowed up the human nature, and still other Monophysites believed that the Son had left His divine nature behind when He became man. Again, a segment of the church departed with the heretics. The Monophysite church still exists in Syria, Armenian, and Egypt. There is encouraging news, however, for the churches which left after the Council have worked out an agreement with the Orthodox Church, satisfying Orthodox theologians of their doctrinal correctness. Consequently, a break of some 1500 years is on the verge of being healed.

For the first thousand years of Christian history, the entire Church, save for the heretics, embraced and defended the New Testament apostolic faith. There was no consequential division. This one faith, preserved through all trials, attacks and tests, this apostolic doctrine was called "the Orthodox faith."

2. *Worship*: Doctrinal purity was tenaciously maintained, but true Christianity is far more than adherence to a set of correct beliefs alone. The life of the Church is centrally expressed in her worship and adoration of God the Father, Son, and Holy Spirit. Jesus Himself told the woman at the well, "the hour is coming, and now is, when the true worshipers will worship the Father in spirit and truth; for the Father is seeking such to worship Him" (John 4:23).

At the Last Supper, Jesus instituted the Eucharist, the communion service, when He took bread and wine, gave a blessing, and said to His disciples, "This is My body which is given for you; do this in remembrance of Me" and "This cup is the new covenant in My blood, which is shed for you" (Luke 22:19, 21). The Church participated in communion at least each Lord's Day (Acts 20:7, 11). From such first and second century sources as the *Didache*, the letters of St. Ignatius of Antioch and the writings of St. Justin Martyr, we are assured the Eucharist is the very center of Christian worship from the apostolic era on.

Also, just as the Law, the Psalms, and the Prophets were read in the Temple worship and the synagogue in Israel, so the Church also immediately gave high priority to the public reading of Scripture and to preaching in her worship, along with the Eucharistic meal.

Even before the middle of the first century, Christian worship was known by the term liturgy which literally means "the common work" or "the work of the people." The early liturgy of the Church's worship was composed of two essential parts: (1) the liturgy of the word, including hymns, Scripture reading, and preaching and (2) the liturgy of the faithful, composed of intercessory prayers, the kiss of peace, and the Eucharist. From virtually the beginning, Christian worship has had a definable shape or form which continues to this day.

Modern Christians advocating freedom from liturgy in worship are sometimes surprised to learn that spontaneity was never the practice in the ancient Church! A basic pattern or shape of Christian worship was observed from the start, and, as the Church grew and matured, liturgy matured as well. Hymns, Scripture readings, and prayers were intertwined in the basic foundation. A clear, purposeful procession through the year was forthcoming, which marked and joined in word, song, and praise the birth, ministry, death, Resurrection, and Ascension of the Lord Jesus Christ, and sanctified crucial aspects of Christian life and experience. The Christian life was lived in reality in the worship of the Church. Far from being just a boring routine, the ritual worship of the historic Church participated in the unfolding drama of the richness and mystery of the Gospel itself!

Further, specific landmarks in our salvation and walk with Christ were celebrated and sanctified. Baptism and the anointing with oil, or chrismation, were there from the start. Marriage, healing, confession of sin, and ordination to the ministry of the gospel are other early rites in the Church. On each of these occasions Christians understood that in a great mystery, grace and power from God were being given according to the individual need of each person. The Church saw these events as holy moments in her life and called them mysteries or sacraments.

3. ***Government***: No one seriously questions whether the apostles of Christ led the Church at her beginning. They had been given the commission to preach the Gospel (Matt. 28:19, 20) and the authority to forgive or retain sins (John 20:23). Theirs was by no means a preaching-only mission! They built the Church under Christ's headship. To govern it, three definite and permanent offices, as taught in the New Testament, were in evidence.

a. *The office of bishop*. The apostles themselves were the first bishops in the Church. Even before Pentecost, after Judas had turned traitor, Peter declared in applying Psalm 109:8, "Let another take his office" (Acts 1:20). This refers, of course, to the office of bishop. Some have mistakenly argued the office of bishop was a later invention. Quite to the contrary, the apostles were themselves bishops, and they appointed bishops to succeed them to oversee the Church in each locality.

Occasionally, the objection is still heard that the office of bishop and presbyter were originally identical. The terms are used interchangeably in the New Testament while the apostles were present, with a bishop being the presiding elder in a local church. After the apostles' deaths, however, the offices of bishop and presbyter became distinct throughout the Church. Ignatius of Antioch, consecrated bishop by A.D. 70 in the Church from which Paul and Barnabas had been sent out, writes just after the turn of the century that bishops appointed by the apostles, surrounded by their presbyters, were everywhere in the Church.

b. *The office of presbyter*. Elders or presbyters are mentioned very early in the life of the Church in Acts and the Epistles. Evidently in each place a Christian community developed, elders were appointed by the apostles to pastor the people.

As time passed, presbyters were referred to in the short form of the word as "prests," then as "priests," in full view of the fact that the Old Covenant priesthood had been fulfilled in Christ and that the Church is corporately a priesthood of believers. The priest was not understood as an intermediary between God and the people nor as a dispenser of grace. The role of the priest was to be the presence of Christ in the Christian community, and in the very capacity of being the presence of the Chief Shepherd, Jesus Christ, the priest was to safeguard the flock of God.

c. *The office of deacon.* The third order or office in the government of the New Testament Church was the deacon. At first the apostles fulfilled this office themselves, but with the rapid growth of the Church, seven initial deacons were selected (Acts 6:1-7) to help carry the responsibility of service to those in need. One of these deacons, Stephen, became the first martyr of the Church.

Through the centuries, the deacons have not only served the material needs of the Church but have held a key role in the liturgical life of the Church as well. Often called "the eyes and ears of the bishop," many deacons have become priests and ultimately entered the episcopal office.

The authority of the bishop, presbyter, and deacon was not anciently understood as being apart from the people but always from among the people. In turn the people of God were called to submit to those who ruled over them (Heb. 13:17), and they were also called to give their agreement to the direction of the leaders for the Church. On a number of occasions in history, that "Amen" was not forthcoming, and the bishops of the Church took note and changed course. Later in history, many Church leaders departed from the ancient model and usurped authority for themselves. In the minds of some, this brought the ancient model into question, but the problem was not in the model. It was in the deviation.

Also it was the ministry of the apostles that brought the people of God together as the laity. Far from being just observers, the laity are vital in the effectiveness of the Church. They are the recipients and active users of the gifts and grace of the Spirit. Each member of the laity has a role in the life and function of the Church. Each is to supply something to the whole (1 Cor. 12:7). The responsibility of the bishops, the priests, and the deacons is to be sure that this is a reality for the laity.

The worship of the Church at the close of its first one thousand years had substantially the same shape from place to place. The doctrine was the same. The whole Church confessed one creed, the same in every place, and had weathered many attacks. The government of the Church was recognizably one everywhere, and this One Church was the Orthodox Church.

Disagreements Between West and East

Tensions began to mount as the first millennium was drawing to a close. While numerous doctrinal, political, economic, and cultural factors were working to separate the Church in an East-West division, two major issues ultimately emerged above others: (1) that one man, the Pope of Rome, considered himself the universal bishop of the Church and (2) the addition of a novel clause to the Church's creed.

1. *The Papacy:* Among the Twelve, Saint Peter was early acknowledged as the leader. He was spokesman for the Twelve before and after Pentecost. He was the first bishop of Antioch and later bishop of Rome. No one challenged his role.

After the death of the apostles, as leadership in the Church developed, the bishop of Rome came to be recognized as first in honor, even though all bishops were equals. But after nearly three hundred years, the bishop of Rome slowly began to assume a role of superiority over the others, ultimately claiming to be the only true successor to Peter. The vast majority of the other bishops of the Church never questioned Rome's primacy of honor, but they patently rejected the Roman bishop's claim as the universal head of the Church on earth. This assumption of papal power became one major factor in rending the Roman Church, and all those it could gather with it, from the historic Orthodox Church.

2. *The Addition to the Creed:* A disagreement concerning the Holy Spirit also began to develop in the Church. Does the Holy Spirit proceed from the Father? Or does He proceed from the Father and the Son?

Our Lord Jesus Christ teaches, "But when the Helper comes, whom I shall send to you from the Father, the Spirit of truth who *proceeds from the Father*, He will testify of Me" (John 15:26). This is the basic statement in the New Testament about the Holy Spirit "proceeding," and it is clear: He "proceeds from the Father." Thus, when the ancient council at Constantinople (A.D. 381) reaffirmed the Creed of Nicea (A.D. 325), it expanded that Creed to proclaim these familiar words: "And in the Holy Spirit, the Lord and Life-Giver, Who proceeds from the Father, Who is worshiped and glorified together with the Father and the Son . . ."

Two hundred years later, however, at a local council in Toledo, Spain (A.D. 589), King Reccared declared, "The Holy Spirit also should be confessed by us and taught to proceed from the Father and the Son." The king may have meant well, but he was contradicting Jesus' teaching, confessed by the entire Church, concerning the Holy Spirit. Unfortunately, the local Spanish council agreed with his error, and, centuries later, in what was at least partially a politically motivated move, the Pope of Rome unilaterally changed the universal creed of the Church *without* an ecumenical council. Though this change was initially rejected in both east and west even by some of Rome's closest neighboring bishops, the Pope managed to eventually get the West to capitulate. The consequence, of course, in the Western Church has been the tendency to relegate the Holy Spirit to a lesser place than God the Father and God the Son. The change may appear small, but the consequences have proven disastrously immense. This issue, with the Pope departing from the Orthodox doctrine of the Church, became another instrumental cause separating the Roman Church from the historic Orthodox Church, the New Testament Church.

The Great Schism

Conflict between the Roman Pope and the East mounted—especially in the Pope's dealings with the bishop, or patriarch, of Constantinople. The Pope even went so far as to claim the authority to decide who should be the bishop of Constantinople in marked violation of historical precedent. No longer operating within the government of the New Testament Church, the Pope appeared to be seeking by political means to bring the whole Church under his domination.

Bizarre intrigues followed, one upon the other, as a series of Roman popes pursued this unswerving goal of attempting to control all Christendom. Perhaps the most incredible incident of these political, religious, and even military schemes occurred in the year 1054. A cardinal, sent by the Pope, slapped a document on the altar of the Church of Holy Wisdom in Constantinople during the Sunday worship, excommunicating the Patriarch of Constantinople from the Church.

The Pope, of course, had no legitimate right to do this, but the repercussions were staggering. Some dismal chapters of Church history were written during the next decades. The ultimate consequence of the Pope's action was that the whole Roman Catholic Church ended up divided from the New Testament faith of Orthodox Christianity. The schism has never been healed.

As the centuries passed, conflict continued. Attempts at reunion failed, and the Roman Church drifted farther from its historical roots.

Further Divisions in the West

During the centuries after A.D. 1054, the growing distinction between east and west was becoming indelibly marked in history. The eastern Church maintained the full stream of New Testament faith, worship, and practice—all the while enduring great persecution. The western or Roman Church bogged down in many complex problems. Then, less than five centuries after Rome committed itself to its unilateral alteration of doctrine and practice, another upheaval occurred—this time *inside* the western gates.

Although many in the west had spoken out against Roman domination and practice in earlier years, now a little-known German monk named Martin Luther inadvertently launched an attack against certain Roman Catholic practices which ended up affecting world history. His list of Ninety-Five Theses was nailed to the Church door at Wittenberg in 1517, signaling the start of what came to be called the Protestant Reformation. Luther had intended no break with Rome, but he could not be reconciled to its papal system of government as well as other doctrinal issues. He was excommunicated in 1521, and the door to future unity in the west slammed shut with a resounding crash.

The reforms Luther sought in Germany were soon accompanied by demands of Ulrich Zwingli in Zurich, John Calvin in Geneva, and hundreds of others all over western Europe. Fueled by complex political, social, and economic factors in addition to the religious problems, the Reformation spread like a raging fire into virtually every nook and cranny of the Roman Church. The ecclesiastical monopoly to which it had grown accustomed was greatly diminished, and massive division replaced unity. The ripple effect of that division impacts even today as the Protestant movement continues to split.

If trouble on the European continent were not trouble enough, the Church of England was in the process of going its own way as well. Henry VIII, amidst his marital problems, replaced the Pope of Rome with himself as head of the Church of England. For only the few short years that Mary was on the throne did the Pope again have ascendency in England. Elizabeth I returned England to Protestantism, and the English Church would soon experience even more division.

As decade followed decade in the west, the branches of Protestantism continued to divide. There were even branches that insisted they were neither Protestant nor Roman Catholic. All seemed to share a mutual dislike for the Bishop of Rome and the practices of his Church, and most wanted far less centralized forms of leadership. While some, such as the Lutherans and Anglicans, held on to certain forms of liturgy and sacrament, others, such as the Reformed Churches and the even more radical Anabaptists and their descendants, questioned and rejected many biblical ideas of hierarchy, sacrament, historic tradition, thinking they were freeing themselves of only Roman Catholicism. To this day, many sincere, modern, professing Christians will reject even the biblical data that speaks of historic Christian practice, simply because they think such historic practices are "Roman Catholic." To use the old adage, they threw the baby out with the bathwater without even being aware of it.

Thus, while retaining in varying degrees portions of foundational Christianity, neither Protestantism nor Catholicism can lay historic claim to being the true New Testament Church. In dividing from the Orthodox Christianity, Rome forfeited its place in the Church of the New Testament. In the divisions of the Reformation, the Protestants—as well-meaning as they might have been— failed to return to the New Testament Church.

The Orthodox Church Today

That original Church, the Church of Peter, Paul, and the apostles—despite persecution, political oppression, and desertion on certain of its flanks—miraculously carries on today the same faith and life of the Church of the New Testament. Admittedly, the style of Orthodoxy looks complicated to the modern Protestant eye, but given a historical understanding of how the Church has progressed, it may be seen that the simple Christ-centered faith of the apostles is fully preserved in its doctrines, practices, services, and even in its architecture.

In Orthodoxy today, as in years gone by, the basics of Christian doctrine, worship, and government are never up for alteration. One cannot be an Orthodox priest, for example, and reject the divinity of Christ, His virgin birth, Resurrection, Ascension into heaven, and Second Coming. The Church simply has not left its course in nearly two thousand years. It is One, Holy, Catholic, and Apostolic. It is the New Testament Church.

Orthodoxy is also, in the words of one of her bishops, "the best kept secret in America." Although there are more than 225 million Orthodox Christians in the world today, many in the west are not familiar with the Church. In North America for example, the Orthodox Church has, until recently, been largely restricted to ethnic boundaries, not spreading much beyond the parishes of the committed immigrants that brought the Church to the shores of this continent.

Still, the Holy Spirit has continued His work, causing new people to discover this Church of the New Testament. People have begun to find Orthodox Christianity through the writings of the early Church Fathers and through the humble witness of contemporary Orthodox Christians. Significant numbers of evangelicals, Episcopalians, and mainline Protestants are becoming Orthodox, and Orthodox student groups are springing up on campuses worldwide. The word is getting out.

What, then, is the Orthodox Church? It is the first Christian Church in history, the Church founded by the Lord Jesus Christ, described in the pages of the New Testament. Her history can be traced in unbroken continuity all the way back to Christ and His Twelve Apostles.

What is it that's missing in the non-Orthodox Churches—even the best of them? Fullness. For the fullness of the New Testament faith is to be found only in the New Testament Church. Being in the Church does not guarantee all those in it will take advantage of the fullness of the faith, but that fullness is there for those who do.

For persons who seriously desire the fullness of Orthodox Christianity, action must be taken. Being aware of this ancient Church is not enough. There must be a return to this Church of the New Testament. In our day many people have taken ample time to investigate and decide about the Roman Catholic faith, the Baptist, the Lutheran, and so on, but relatively few have taken a serious look at the Orthodox Church. Three specific suggestions will provide those interested with a tangible means of becoming acquainted with Orthodox Christianity on a personal basis.

1. ***Visit:*** Look up "Orthodox" or "Eastern Orthodox" in the "Churches" section of the yellow pages or ask a neighbor the whereabouts of the nearest Orthodox parish. Pay a visit—several visits. Meet the priest, and ask him to help you study and learn. And be prepared to exercise patience—sometimes a portion of the liturgy is not in English! The Service Book in the pew will help.

2. ***Read:*** There are a number of books and periodicals immensely helpful to people seeking to learn about the Orthodox Church. *The Orthodox Church* by KALLISTOS (Timothy) Ware (Penguin); *For the Life of the World* by Alexander Schmemann (St. Vladimir Seminary Press); *The Apostolic Fathers* edited by Jack N. Sparks (Light and Life Publishers), *Becoming Orthodox* by Peter E. Gillquist, and *Divine Energy* by Jon E. Braun and *AGAIN Magazine* (both by Conciliar Press).

3. ***Write:*** The people at Conciliar Press (P.O. Box 76, Ben Lomond, CA 95005-0076) have volunteered to answer questions regarding the Orthodox Church from *The Orthodox Study Bible* readers and to suggest further reading. Send your name and address with a request for information.

In a day when Christians are realizing anew the centrality and importance of worship, of the Church as the body of Christ, and the need to preserve true Christian faith, the doors of Orthodoxy are open wide. The invitation is extended to "come and see." Examine her faith, her worship, her history, her commitment to Christ, her love for God the Father, and her communion with the Holy Spirit.

For two thousand years the Orthodox Church has, by God's mercy, kept the faith delivered to the saints. Within her walls is the fullness of the salvation which was realized when "God so loved the world that He gave His only begotten Son, that whoever believes in Him should not perish but have everlasting life" (John 3:16).

Glossary

Reverend John W. Morris, Ph.D.

ABBA The Aramaic term of intimacy used in addressing one's father, somewhat equivalent to the English "Daddy." Christ uses *Abba* in addressing God the Father. St. Paul tells believers that their relationship with God through the Holy Spirit is so personal that they too may speak to Him as intimately as to their own father (Mark 14:36; Rom. 8:15).

ABSOLUTION The prayer offered by a bishop or presbyter for the forgiveness of sins. Following His glorious Resurrection, Christ breathed on His Apostles and said, "Receive the Holy Spirit. If you forgive the sins of any, they are forgiven them; if you retain the sins of any, they are retained" (John 20:22, 23). This gift of proclaiming God's forgiveness of sins remains forever in the Church. It is exercised in the sacraments of baptism and confession—the reconciliation to the Church of Christian believers who have sinned and repented. The priest or bishop is the witness who bears testimony to the repentance; only God forgives sins (*see* article, "Confession," at 1 John 1).

ADVENT A forty-day period of prayer, repentance, and fasting in preparation for Christmas. The word stems from the Latin word for "coming"; during the fast the faithful prepare for the coming of Christ at Christmas. *See also* **FASTING.**

AGAPE Greek for the unconditional love which God extends to His people. *Agape* also designates a communal meal connected to the Eucharist which was a practice of the early Church (1 Cor. 11:20–34).

ALLEGORY A story filled with symbolism illustrating a spiritual reality beyond the actual historical event being described. In the ancient Church, scholars of the School of Alexandria tended to consider many incidents in the Bible as allegorical, whereas the School of Antioch practiced a more historical approach to Scripture. Although Scripture contains some pure allegory (some parables of Christ, portions of Revelation), overemphasis on allegory may tend to de-emphasize or even deny the historicity of Holy Scripture. On the other hand, a denial of allegory robs the Scriptures of their deeper meaning. It is possible for a story to be both historical and allegorical. The majority of Church Fathers combined both elements in interpreting the Bible. *See* Luke 15:4–7; Gal. 4:21–26. *See also* **TYPE.**

ALLELUIA The Greek form of the Hebrew word *Hallelujah,* which means "praise God." Orthodox Christians sing a chorus of *Alleluia* interspersed with psalm verses prior to the Gospel reading at the Divine Liturgy.

ALMS Works of mercy or monetary gifts given to help the poor. Throughout the Scriptures, God's people are called to help those less fortunate than themselves (*see* Matt. 25:31–46).

ALPHA AND OMEGA The letters which begin and end the Greek alphabet, and symbolize the beginning and the end. *The Alpha and the Omega* is also used as a title of Christ (Rev. 1:8).

AMEN "So be it" in Hebrew. *Amen* is said or sung at the close of a prayer or hymn, showing the agreement of the people to what has been said (Deut. 27:15–26; 1 Cor. 14:16).

ANGELS Bodiless powers created before the creation of the physical universe. The English word "angel" comes from the Greek word for "messenger." Throughout the Scripture, angels are messengers who carry the Word of God to earth (e.g. Gabriel's visit to Mary, Luke 1:26–38). The Orthodox Church teaches that there are nine "choirs" or groups of angels: Angels, Archangels, Powers, Authorities, Principalities, Dominions,

Thrones, Cherubim, and Seraphim (*see* Gen. 3:24; Is. 6:2; Eph. 1:21; Col. 1:16; 1 Thess. 4:16; 1 Pet. 3:22).

ANNUNCIATION The visit of the Archangel Gabriel to the Virgin Mary to inform her that she had been chosen to bear Christ, the Son of God. The Feast of the Annunciation is celebrated exactly nine months before Christmas. Mary's Son was no ordinary child, but God's divine Son and Word in human flesh (*see* article, "Mary," at Luke 1; Is. 7:14; Luke 1:26–38; John 1:1–14).

ANTICHRIST Literally, "against Christ" or "instead of Christ." *Antichrist* is used by John to refer to (a) the opponent of Christ who will arise at the end of this age, and (b) the "many antichrists" who stand against the Son of God (1 John 2:18, 22; 4:3).

APOSTASY Literally, "turning away." This sin is committed when a Christian or body of believers rejects the true faith of Christ (1 Tim. 1:5–7; 4:1–3).

APOSTLE Literally, "one who is sent." *Apostle* is used as a title for the Twelve Disciples who formed the foundation of the NT Church, replacing, symbolically, the twelve tribes of Israel. In order to maintain this symbolism, Matthias was elected to replace Judas (Acts 1:15–26). The word is also used of the Seventy (or 72) sent by Christ, as well as of Paul, the repentant persecutor whom the risen Jesus sent as "apostle to the Gentiles" (Rom. 11:13). Great missionaries in the Church, such as Mary Magdalene (the "apostle to the apostles"), Thekla, Nira, Vladimir, and Innocent of Alaska are called "equal to the apostles." The extension of the apostolic ministry in the Church today is in the episcopacy. *See also* **EPISCOPACY.**

ASCENSION The ascent of Christ to Heaven following His Resurrection as Son of God in the flesh (Luke 24:50, 51; Acts 1:9–11). Christ's Ascension completes the union of God and humanity, for a Man who is God now reigns in Heaven.

ASCETICISM (from Gr. *askesis*, "athlete") A life of struggle—the crucifixion of the desires of the flesh, through a life of prayer, fasting, and self-denial. Through asceticism the Christian fights temptation to sin and thereby grows in spiritual strength. Such spiritual classics as *The Philokalia* and *The Ladder of Divine Ascent* give directions for the ascetic life (*see* Luke 9:23; Gal. 5:24).

AUTHORITY The rule of God over the world and the legitimate authority given by God to those ordained to shepherd the faithful (Heb. 13:17). Also, one of the nine choirs of angels. *See also* **ANGELS.**

BAPTISM (from Gr. *baptizo*, "to be plunged") The sacrament whereby one is born again, buried with Christ, resurrected with Him and united to Him. In baptism, one becomes a Christian and is joined to the Church. In Christ's baptism, water was set apart unto God as the means by which the Holy Spirit would bring to us new life and entrance into the heavenly Kingdom (*see* article "Holy Baptism," at Rom. 6; Matt. 3:13–17; 28:19; Mark 16:16; Acts 2:38, 39; Rom. 6:3; Col. 2:12; 1 Pet. 3:21).

BEATITUDE Literally, "exalted happiness." The ninefold blessing of Christ in the Sermon on the Mount is called the Beatitudes (Matt. 5:3–12).

BELIEF The acceptance of the truths of the gospel. More than a mental assent, *belief* as used in the NT includes trusting in God from the heart. Such belief results from (1) hearing the Word of God (Rom. 10:17) and (2) a gift of the Holy Spirit (Eph. 2:8). Although a Christian is saved by belief in Christ, faith without action (that is, a distinct movement of the will to follow Christ) is hollow and void of the righteousness necessary to salvation (*see* article, "Justification by Faith," at Rom. 5; Matt. 7:21; John 3:16; James 2:14–26).

BENEDICTION Literally, "good word"; blessing. Benedictions were given by Christ (Luke 24:50, 51) and by the Apostles (2 Cor. 13:14), and are given by the bishop or priest at the close of every Divine Liturgy.

BISHOP (Gr. *episkopos*) Overseer. A bishop is the leader of a local community of Christians. In the New Testament there is no clear distinction between the offices of bishop and elder (presbyter), both of which function as leaders of the community. However, by the mid- to late first century, the Church began to reserve the title *bishop* for the men of spiritual qualification who were consecrated to follow the Apostles in their office of oversight (*see* article, "The Four 'Orders' in Church Government," at 1 Tim.; Acts 1:15–26; 14:23; 1 Tim. 3:1–7).

BORN AGAIN Literally, "born from above." A person must be born again to new life in Christ to enter God's eternal Kingdom. This new birth takes place through the sacrament of Holy Baptism (John 3:16; Rom. 6:3, 4; Gal. 3:27). Spiritual life begins by receiving the Holy Spirit in baptism, and it is a dynamic process which continues throughout life. *See* article, "The New Birth," at John 3.

BROTHERS OF THE LORD St. James, the first bishop of Jerusalem, Joses, Simon, and Judas are referred to as brothers of Christ (Matt. 13:55). In the ancient Middle East one's close relatives were frequently referred to as brothers and sisters. Also, there is an ancient tradition that the "brothers and sisters" of Christ were actually children of St. Joseph from an earlier marriage; they are called the children of Mary although they are actually her stepchildren. Thus, these references to siblings of Christ do not contradict the ancient belief of the Orthodox Church that the Virgin Mary was a virgin before, during, and after the birth of Christ. The absence of blood brothers is suggested by Christ's act of entrusting Mary to the care of the apostle John (John 19:26, 27), which would have been against the Mosaic Law had she had other natural children.

CANON Literally, "a rule." It describes (1) the inspired Books of the Bible—the Canon of Scripture; (2) the rules and decrees issued by the early Church (see Acts 15:23–29) and by Ecumenical Councils—Canon Law; and (3) certain parts of worship, such as the Liturgical Canon or the Canon of Matins.

CHRISMATION The sacrament completing baptism, whereby one receives the gift of the Holy Spirit through anointing with the Chrism, a specially prepared oil which must be consecrated by a bishop. On several occasions in Acts, a baptized Christian received the gift of the Holy Spirit through the laying on of the hands of an Apostle (*see* Acts 8:14–17; 19:6). Chrismation is a continuation of that ancient practice in the Church. *See* article, "Chrismation," at Acts 2.

CHURCH The faithful are called out of the world to be the Church: the body of Christ, the Bride of Christ, the New Israel, the ark of salvation, the assembly of the faithful. Through the Church, Christians are united to Christ and to each other. In this community, the believer receives the grace of God through the sacraments and hears the truth of the gospel. This mystical transformation of people into one body in Christ takes place in the Eucharist. Because Christ is the Head of the Church, the Church is a reflection of the Incarnation, with both human and divine qualities (*see* 1 Cor. 10:16, 17; Gal. 6:16; Eph. 4:12; 5:22–32).

COMMANDMENT The Law of God, given first in the Ten Commandments on Mt. Sinai, and completed or fulfilled by the teaching of Christ (Ex. 20:1–17; Matt. 5:1—7:27; John 15:12).

COMMUNION (Gr. *koinonia*) A common union of the most intimate kind, enjoyed by Christians with God and with each other in the Church. This communion is especially realized in the mystery of the Holy Eucharist (John 6:56; 1 Cor. 10:16, 17).

CONFESSION (1) The avowal or verbal witness of faith in Christ, leading to salvation (Rom. 10:9). (2) The sacrament of the forgiveness of sins, whereby the repentant sinner confesses his sins to Christ in the presence of the priest, who pronounces God's absolution of those sins (*see* article, "Confession," at 1 John; John 20:22, 23; 1 John 1:9).

CONVERSION The beginning of salvation, occurring when a person repents, believes the gospel, and enters into a personal relationship with Christ. Conversion is not merely a change of belief but the beginning of a new life in Christ (2 Cor. 5:17), which is a process of growth into the image and likeness of God. Our salvation is the working together of conversion, justification, and sanctification throughout life.

CORRUPTION The state of mortality and sinfulness, the universal condition of fallen humanity. All are born into a world suffering the consequences of the Fall, the sin of Adam and Eve. These consequences include physical suffering, death, lack of perfection and a tendency to sin. See Ps. 53:3; Is. 53:6; Rom. 3:23; 1 John 5:19.

COSMOS The universe, or "world," created by God from nothing. It is controlled by God; He is the life of the world. Sin has corrupted the entire cosmos, and the rule of evil will not be abolished until the Second Coming of Jesus Christ. The universe will finally be redeemed by Christ when He comes again to transform the cosmos into a new heaven and a new earth. See Gen. 1:1; Rom. 8:19–22; Rev. 21:1.

COUNCIL A group of Christians gathered to deliberate and ask for the guidance of the Holy Spirit to administer the Church and decide on various doctrinal, moral, and liturgical questions. The Orthodox Church is conciliar (operating by councils) on all levels, from a parish to a worldwide council. While councils are not seen as infallible, their decisions become part of Church life when they are received by the entire Church. Besides the Jerusalem Council recorded in Acts 15, the Church counts Seven Ecumenical Councils in her history.

COVENANT An agreement or testament between men or between God and His people. In the Old Testament, God chose the people of Israel, ending with John the Baptist, to prepare the way for the coming of His Only Begotten Son. Through Christ, the covenant was perfected, and the promises of God to Abraham and the Jews are fulfilled through the Church, the New Israel, the New Covenant people of God. *See* Gen. 13:14–16; Gal. 3:6–9; 1 Pet. 2:9, 10.

CREATION (Gr. *ktisis*) Everything made by God. The term *creation* is applied to the cosmos in general and to mankind in particular. Our regeneration in Christ and the resurrection of the dead are both often called the "new creation." Creation has no existence apart from God, but is nevertheless distinct from God. (That which is not created, such as divine grace, the divine energies, belongs to God the Father, Son, and Holy Spirit.)

CREED A statement of belief. Creeds in their earlier forms were used by the apostles, and many are recorded in the New Testament (Eph. 5:14; 1 Tim. 3:16; 2 Tim. 2:11–13). The creed used throughout the Church was adopted at the Council of Nicea in A.D. 325 and expanded at the Council of Constantinople in A.D. 381. The Nicene Creed is used at baptisms, the Divine Liturgy, and in personal daily prayers.

CRUCIFIXION A form of execution of criminals used by the ancient Romans in which the offender is nailed through his wrists and ankles to a cross. A crucified person usually died from suffocation after becoming too exhausted to pull himself up in order to breathe. Besides Christ Himself (Matt. 27:35–50), the Apostles Peter, Andrew, James the Less, and Simon were also crucified.

CURSE (Gr. *anathema*) To cut off, separate; the opposite of blessing. A divine curse is God's judgment. Christ delivers believers from the curse caused by their inability to live by the law of God (*see* Gen. 3:14–19; 9:25; Mark 11:21; Gal. 3:10–14).

DAMNATION Eternity spent in hell under sentence of personal condemnation for rejecting the love and truth of God as revealed perfectly in Jesus Christ and the Holy Spirit. *See* Matt. 25:31–46; John 3:18.

DARKNESS A symbol of sin and rejection of God, who is light and whose followers walk in the light of righteousness. *See* John 1:5; Rom. 13:12.

DEACON Literally, "servant." Originally seven deacons were ordained to assist the apostles with the temporal affairs of the Church (Acts 6:1–7). This established office has continued in the Church. A deacon assists the bishop and priest, but cannot preside over the Eucharist, give blessings or pronounce absolution. In the New Testament (Rom.

16:1) and the early Church, women also served as deacons or deaconesses (1 Tim. 3:8–13; see note on v. 11).

DEIFICATION The grace of God through which believers grow to become like Him and enjoy intimate communion with the Father through the Son in the Holy Spirit (*see* article, "Deification," at 2 Pet. 1; 2 Cor. 3:18; 5:17; 2 Pet. 1:2–4).

DEPARTED The dead. Following death and judgment, those who have accepted God's truth and love as fully revealed in Christ and the Holy Spirit inherit eternal life in heaven. Those who have rejected His gift inherit eternal darkness. *See* Luke 16:19–31; Heb. 9:27.

DEVIL Satan, the leader of the fallen angels. Called by Jesus the father of lies (John 8:44), Satan tempts the faithful to join his rebellion against God. The Greek word for devil means "separator"; he seeks to pull people away from God. Although not evil by nature, the devil turned by his free choice from what was according to nature to what was against it. At the end of time, Christ will judge the devil and his followers and cast them into hell. *See* Matt. 25:41; Luke 10:18; 1 Pet. 5:8.

DISCIPLESHIP The life of learning, growing, self-sacrifice, and commitment required of every Christian. A Christian not only believes in Christ but leaves everything to follow Him. *See* Matt. 4:18–22; 7:21–23; Luke 9:23; Gal. 5:24.

DOCTRINE The teaching of the Church, called variously the doctrine of Christ (2 John 9), the apostles' doctrine (Acts 2:42), or sound doctrine (Titus 1:9; *see* 2 Tim. 3:16; Rom. 16:17).

EASTER The Feast of the Resurrection of Christ, also known as Pascha (from the Hebrew word for Passover). Christ proclaimed Himself as the true Passover and offered Himself as a sacrifice. Orthodox Christians celebrate Easter according to the decree of the Council of Nicea in A.D. 325: the first Sunday following the first full moon following the spring equinox following the Jewish Passover. Thus, Orthodox Easter is often one, four, or five weeks after the western Easter.

ENERGY Used theologically, that which radiates from the hidden essence or nature of God. The energies of God, such as grace, are not created, and allow the believer to enter into a personal relationship with God while preserving the unique character of God, whose essence always remains hidden from humanity. Moses was permitted to see the glory of God, His energies, but was forbidden to gaze on the face of God, His hidden essence. *See* Ex. 33:18–23; 2 Pet. 1:2–4.

EPIPHANY Literally, "a breaking through from above"; the word means a manifestation of God. Examples of epiphanies are the burning bush (Ex. 3:1–6) and the Transfiguration of Christ (Matt. 17:1–13). Twelve days after Christmas, the Church celebrates the Feast of Epiphany to honor the manifestation of the Holy Trinity at the Baptism of Christ (Mark 1:9–11). *See also* **THEOPHANY.**

EPISCOPACY The order of bishops in the Church (from Gr. *episkopos*, "overseer"). *See also* **BISHOP.**

ESCHATOLOGY The study of the last days (Gr. *eschaton*). According to the Holy Scriptures, Christ will come again at the end of time to judge the living and the dead, destroy the power of evil, and fully reveal the everlasting Kingdom (Matt. 25:31–46; Rev. 20:10—21:1). *See also* **SECOND COMING.**

ESSENCE (Gr. *ousia*) Also translated as substance, nature or being. God the Father, the Son, and the Holy Spirit are "of one essence." Jesus Christ is "of one essence" with God the Father and the Holy Spirit in His divinity, and "of one essence" with all human beings in His humanity. God's essence is beyond the understanding and comprehension of His creatures. God can be known by humans through the divine energies and operations of the Father, Son, and Holy Spirit (Ex. 33:18–23). *See also* **ENERGY.**

EUCHARIST Taken from a Greek word meaning "thanksgiving," *Eucharist* designates Holy Communion, the central act of Christian worship. At the Last Supper Christ gave thanks (Matt. 26:27; 1 Cor. 11:24), and embodied in the communion service is our own thanksgiving. The word came into use very early, as exemplified by its use in the writings of the apostles ("Now concerning the Eucharist. . . ." *Didache* 9:1) and the letters of St. Ignatius of Antioch (Ign. Phil. 4:1, about A.D. 107).

EVANGELIST One who preaches the gospel; used especially of Matthew, Mark, Luke, and John, who wrote the four NT Gospels.

EXCOMMUNICATION Literally, "out of communion." This judgment is pronounced by the Church on willfully heretical, immoral, or divisive persons who refuse to repent of their sins; it excludes them from the sacramental life of the Church (1 Cor. 5:1–5). Excommunication is not viewed as eternal damnation but a discipline pertaining only to this life. It is administered for the salvation of the person cut off from communion, with the hope that this act will ultimately bring the sinner to repentance.

FAITH Belief and trust in Christ as one's Savior. The effects of this faith are freedom from the power of the devil, the attainment of virtue, and progress toward perfection and union with God. One is saved by faith through grace—a living faith manifested by a righteous life (*see* article, "Justification by Faith," at Rom. 5; Rom. 3:28; Gal. 2:16; Eph. 2:8; James 2:14–17).

FASTING An ascetic exercise whereby one gives up certain foods, usually meat and dairy products, as a means of disciplining the body. Fasting is a part of the ascetic life and a sign of repentance. Orthodox Christians fast on most Wednesdays and Fridays (in memory of the betrayal and crucifixion of Christ) and during four fasting seasons: (1) Advent, the forty days before Christmas; (2) Great Lent, forty days before Palm Sunday and the week before Easter; (3) two weeks before the Feast of Ss. Peter and Paul (June 29); and (4) two weeks before the Feast of the Falling Asleep of the Virgin Mary (Aug. 15). *See* Matt. 6:16; Rom. 13:14; Gal. 5:16, 17.

FATHER (1) God the Father is one of the three Persons of the Holy Trinity. God the Son is eternally begotten of God the Father. God the Holy Spirit eternally proceeds from God the Father (see Matt. 28:19; John 14:10; 15:26). (2) "Father" is a title given to one's spiritual father based on the custom of the Jews, who spoke of their father Abraham or their father David, and on the words of Paul, who called himself the father of his flock. *See* Luke 1:73; Acts 4:25 with center-column note; 1 Cor. 4:15.

FELLOWSHIP (Gr. *koinonia*) Literally, "communion"; the unity of believers through Christ based on the fellowship of the Father, Son, and Holy Spirit. Christians are united into a special fellowship through their love for one another and common union with Christ (Acts 2:42; 1 John 1:3, 7). *See also* **COMMUNION.**

FILIOQUE A Latin word meaning "and the Son." Western churches began adding this word to the Nicene Creed several centuries after it was written: "I believe in the Holy Spirit . . . who proceeds from the Father *and the Son.*" This "*filioque* clause" is judged by the Orthodox Church as error because it is contrary to what Jesus taught (John 15:26); thus, it confuses correct belief concerning the Holy Trinity. The addition of the *filioque* in the West was a major factor contributing to the Great Schism in A.D. 1054.

FLESH (1) In New Testament usage, *flesh* refers to fallen human nature, which, through its ties to the world and mortality, struggles against spiritual growth and leads one into sin. Christians are called to subdue the lusts of the flesh so that they may grow in union with Christ (*see* Rom. 8:4–9; Gal. 5:16–24). (2) In Christology, *flesh* refers to the sinless human nature of Christ, or the Body of Christ. In liturgical usage, there is reference to the flesh of Christ in the Eucharist.

FORGIVENESS: The remission of sin and guilt through the love of Christ. Forgiveness is given originally in baptism; forgiveness for continuing sin is reclaimed through repentance. As God has forgiven the sins of believers, so are Christians to forgive those who have sinned against them (Matt. 6:14, 15; 18:21–35; 1 John 1:9).

FORNICATION (Gr. *porneia*): The sin of sexual intercourse outside of marriage. The word is also applied to polygamy and to many successive marriages. The Greek term means sexual immorality in general. Fornication is strongly condemned in Scripture (*see* 1 Cor. 6:16–18; Gal. 5:19; Col. 3:5.)

FREE WILL The freedom to choose between good and evil, between God and sin, which is one aspect of humanity created in the image of God. According to Orthodox teaching, sin stains the image of God but does not destroy it. Human beings may choose to accept or reject the gospel, but must suffer the consequences of their decision (*see* Gen. 3:22, 23; Rev. 3:20).

GENTILE A non-Jew. Christ and His Apostles preached the gospel first to the Jews, who were chosen by God to prepare the way for the Messiah. Christ died for all, Jew and Gentile; thus, salvation is offered to the Gentiles as well as to the Jews. Those Gentiles who believe in Christ become the true sons of Abraham, who was chosen by God before the Law was given. *See* Acts 11; 15:1–29; Rom. 1:16; Gal. 3:6–9.

GIFTS Charismatic or spiritual gifts are blessings and abilities given by the Holy Spirit to believers for the building up of the body of Christ. The gifts of the Spirit serve the general good of the whole Church. It is possible to confuse spiritual gifts with natural talents and emotions, or to misuse the genuine gifts of the Holy Spirit, resulting in pride and self-righteousness. For this reason, the Orthodox Church has always stressed humility and obedience to spiritual authority in the use of the gifts. Note that the Holy Spirit Himself is a gift (Rom. 5:5), as are baptism and the other sacraments. *See* Rom. 12:6–8; 1 Cor. 12; 13; 1 John 3:24.

GLORY The divine splendor of God, or a specific manifestation of God's presence, frequently likened to a cloud, smoke, or brilliant light. To serve and worship God is to glorify Him. Through the Holy Spirit, Christians are being changed to be like God and to reflect His glory. (See Ex. 19:9, 16–18; Is. 60:1; Luke 2:9; Rom. 8:16–18; 2 Cor. 3:18; 4:6.) *See also* **SHEKINAH.**

GLOSSOLALIA Literally, "speaking in tongues." St. Paul uses the term to describe not an emotional experience but a spiritual gift (1 Cor. 12:10), though not one of the higher gifts (1 Cor. 14:1–5). At Pentecost the gift was given to allow those present to hear the gospel in their native language (Acts 2:6); in Corinth, the gift is an ecstatic utterance (1 Cor. 14:2). The Apostle warns against too much emphasis on this experience, urging instead that believers seek to manifest love (1 Cor. 13:1) and communicate the gospel intelligibly (1 Cor. 14:19). Glossolalia has never played a significant role in historic Orthodox spirituality. *See* 1 Cor. 12—14.

GNOSTICISM A very complex ancient heresy that was manifested in many different forms and beliefs. The Gnostics taught that Christ had imparted secret knowledge, "gnosis," to a select few, who in turn transmitted hidden truths to an elite. Central to Gnosticism is the denial of the goodness of matter, leading to a denial of the reality of the Incarnation of the Son of God and of His bodily Resurrection. Several schools of Gnosticism taught that salvation consisted of liberation from the physical body and of growth to a higher, non-physical, spiritual level of existence. Orthodoxy has always rejected Gnosticism, teaching that the world and man were created good and will be redeemed by Christ and transformed at the end of this age (Gen. 1:1–31; Rom. 8:19–22; 1 Cor. 15:35–55; Rev. 21:1).

GOSPEL Literally, "the good news." The term comes from the ancient title announcing the ascension of a new ruler to the throne. The Christian gospel is summarized in the statement, "Repent, for the kingdom of heaven is at hand!" (Matt. 3:2; 4:17).

GRACE The gift of God's own presence and action in His creation. Through grace, God forgives sins and transforms the believer into His image and likeness. Grace is not merely unmerited favor—an attitude of God toward the believer. Grace is God's uncreated energy bestowed in the sacraments and is therefore truly experienced. A Christian is saved through grace, which is a gift of God and not a reward for good works. However, because grace changes a person, he or she will manifest the effects of grace through righteous living. *See* John 1:17; Rom. 5:21; Eph. 1:7; 2:8; 2 Thess. 1:12; 1 Pet. 5:5.

HADES A Greek word equivalent to the Hebrew *Sheol*—the realm of the dead. Following His burial and before His glorious Resurrection, Christ liberated the righteous dead in Hades, enabling them to enter Paradise because He had destroyed sin and death by His life-giving death (1 Pet. 3:18–20).

HEART In scriptural terms, the spiritual center of one's being. The heart is the seat of divine presence and grace and the source of moral acts. The transformation of the heart is the major work of God's saving grace. *See* Matt. 5:8; 6:21; 22:37; Luke 6:45; John 7:38; Rom. 2:29; 10:9, 10; Heb. 13:9.

HERESY Following one's own choice or opinion instead of divine truth preserved by the Church, so as to cause division among Christians. Heresy is a system of thought which contradicts true doctrine. It is false teaching, which all true Christians must reject (Matt. 7:15; 2 Pet. 2:1).

HOLY Literally, "set apart" or separated unto God; also, blessed, righteous, sinless. The word, therefore, refers to God as the source of holiness, to the Church and its sacraments, to worshipers of the true God, and to those of outstanding virtue. Those who are transformed by the Holy Spirit become holy as God is holy (Rom. 12:1; 1 Pet. 1:14–16; 2:9).

HOPE An expectation of something desired. Christian hope is trust and confidence in the eternal goodness of God, a faith that Christ has overcome the suffering of this world. God is both the cause and goal of hope (John 16:20–24, 33; Rom. 5:2; 8:24, 25; 2 Thess. 2:16).

HYPOSTASIS A technical theological term for "person" or something which has an individual existence. The word is used to describe the three Persons of the Godhead: the Father, Son, and Holy Spirit. *Hypostasis* is also used to describe the one Person of Christ, who is both truly divine and truly human.

ICON Image. Christ is "the image of the invisible God" (Col. 1:15). Because Christ is God who became Man, He can Himself be pictured or imaged. Thus, icons of Christ—together with those of His saints—express the reality of the Incarnation. Orthodox Christians honor or venerate icons, but never worship them, for worship is due to God alone. The honor given to icons passes on to the one represented on the icon, as a means of thanksgiving for what God has done in that person's life.

IDOL A statue or other image of a false god; also, anything that is worshiped in place of the one true God. Money, possessions, fame, even family members can become idols if we put them ahead of God (*see* Lev. 26:1; Col. 3:5).

ILLUMINATION Enlightenment. In the Bible, darkness is often used as an image of sin and death. To be illuminated is to be shown the true path of righteousness in God, thereby being led out of the darkness of sin and death. Baptism is called *illumination*, because in it we are delivered from sin and death and regenerated by the Holy Spirit. *See* Ezra 9:8; Ps. 13:3; 18:28; Eph. 1:18.

IMAGE (Gr. *eikon*) Literally, "icon." The Bible teaches that man was created in the *image* and likeness of God. Men and women reflect the divine image in their ability to reason and to rule nature, and in freedom of action. Although sin has darkened or stained God's image, it has not annihilated it. Through Christ, the image of God is renewed in man as believers are transformed by the grace of the Holy Spirit. *See* Gen. 1:26; Rom. 8:29; 2 Cor. 3:18. *See also* **ICON.**

IMMANUEL "God is with us," a title of Christ the Messiah, God in the flesh (Is. 7:14; Matt. 1:22, 23).

IMMORTALITY Eternal life. Those who follow Christ will rise to eternal life with Him in heaven; those who reject Him will be resurrected to eternity in hell (John 3:16–18; 5:26–29).

INCARNATE From Latin, meaning "to become flesh." Christ is God Incarnate: He became flesh—that is, human—thereby sanctifying human flesh and reuniting all humanity to God. According to Orthodox doctrine, Jesus Christ is perfect God and perfect Man (Luke 1:26–38; John 1:1–14; Phil. 2:5–7).

INCENSE The sap of the frankincense tree, or other aromatic substances, dried and burned in honor of God. The offering of *incense* has been associated with the worship of God since God commanded Moses to burn incense to Him in the tabernacle. The prophet Malachi (1:11) predicts, "among the Gentiles [the Church] . . . incense shall be offered . . ." The Magi offered frankincense to the infant Christ. Incense manifests the prayers of the saints as they ascend to heaven. It is found in every revelation of the worship of God in heaven. *See* Ex. 30:1–8; Matt. 2:9–11; Rev. 5:8.

INFANT BAPTISM There are numerous biblical passages which support the ancient Christian practice of infant baptism, which was universal in the Church until the Anabaptist reaction after the Protestant Reformation. Among these are: "Let the little children come to Me, and do not forbid them; for of such is the kingdom of heaven" (Matt. 19:14); the baptism of whole households and families, presumably including children (Acts 16:14, 15, 25–33); and Paul's comparison between circumcision, which was given to infants, and baptism (Col. 2:11, 12). *See* John 3:3–6; Rom. 6:3, 4; Gal. 3:27; 1 Pet. 3:21.

INTERCESSION Supplication to God in behalf of another person. Christ intercedes before God the Father in behalf of the repentant sinner, and God's people intercede for one another (*see* Is. 53:12; Jer. 27:18; Rom. 8:34).

JEW Originally one of God's chosen people who followed the covenant given to Moses by God. In the Old Testament, the Jews are (1) citizens of Judah; (2) the postexilic people of Israel; or (3) the worshipers of Yahweh. God chose the Jews to prepare the way for the coming of the Messiah, Jesus Christ, the Only Begotten Son of God. Through Christ the distinction between Jew and Gentile has been overcome, and all those who follow Him have become the true chosen people of God. *See* Acts 22:3; Rom. 1:16; 2:28, 29; Gal. 3:28; 1 Pet. 2:9.

JUDGMENT In the biblical sense, God's decision on the worthiness of one to enter heaven or to be condemned to hell. Following death, all will be judged, and Christ will return again to confirm that judgment. Because of sin, no one can earn a place in heaven by his own righteousness. However, through Christ, sin is forgiven and overcome, and those who have followed Him are granted a place in heaven. *See* Matt. 25:31–46; John 5:24; 16:8–11; Heb. 9:27; Rev. 20:11–15.

JUSTIFICATION The act whereby God forgives the sins of a believer and begins to transform him or her into a righteous person. No person can earn *justification* by works of righteousness, for justification is the gift of God given to those who respond to the gospel with faith. God also helps those who cooperate with His grace to become righteous. Saving faith is not mere belief but a commitment to Christ that is manifested by works of righteousness (*see* article, "Justification by Faith," at Rom. 5; Rom. 5:1, 2; Gal. 2:16; Phil. 2:12, 13; James 2:24).

KENOSIS Literally, "emptying." The word is associated with humility or humiliation. God the Word humbled Himself by becoming man (with no change in His divinity), suffering death on the Cross for the world and its salvation (Phil. 2:5–8).

KINGDOM OF GOD God's rule over the world, showing (1) His absolute sovereignty as Creator and (2) His sovereignty over the faithful who voluntarily submit to Him. The *Kingdom of God* was made manifest by Christ and is present in the world through the Church. The fullness of the Kingdom will come when Christ returns to judge the living and the dead, creating a new heaven and earth. *See* Mark 1:15; John 3:3–5; Rom. 8:20, 21; 1 Cor. 6:9, 10; Rev. 21:1—22:5.

KISS OF PEACE A kiss on the cheek or the shoulder given by one believer to another as a sign of Christian unity and fellowship (see 1 Cor. 16:20). The clergy, and in some places the faithful, exchange the *kiss of peace* before saying the Nicene Creed during the Divine Liturgy of the Orthodox Church.

KNOWLEDGE Knowing and experiencing the truth of God and salvation through Jesus Christ. Spiritual knowledge (1) is frequently identified with Christian doctrine; (2) is applied to the spiritual meaning of the Scripture; and (3) refers to mystical and contemplative knowledge, not merely intellectual knowledge of God. Its aim and effects are to enhance man's responsibility, to aid in discernment of good and evil, and to lead people to God. *See* Luke 12:47, 48; 1 Cor. 13:2; 2 Cor. 4:6; Eph. 4:11–16.

KOINONIA A Greek word meaning communion or intimate fellowship. This relationship exists between the three Persons of the Holy Trinity and also between Christians who are united by love into one body in Christ. *See* Acts 2:41, 42; 2 Cor. 13:14; 1 John 1:1–7. *See also* **COMMUNION.**

LAMB OF GOD Jesus Christ, the *Lamb of God,* offered Himself as a perfect sacrifice for the sins of the world (John 1:29). In the preparation service, the bread and wine are made ready to be consecrated in the Eucharist service to follow. The priest cuts out the center section of the loaf, called "the Lamb," for use in Communion as the Body of Christ.

LEAVENED As in leavened bread, where a small amount of yeast will cause the whole loaf to rise, so a small amount of evil or good affects the whole body (*see* Luke 13:20, 21; 1 Cor. 5:7, 8). In contrast to the Old Testament bread, which was unleavened to show the Israelites' separation from the world (*see* Ex. 12:15–20), leavened bread—risen bread—is used in Orthodox Communion to show forth the Resurrection of Christ.

LIGHT The Bible frequently uses *light* as a symbol of God and of that which is good, that which overcomes the darkness of sin and death. Candles are used in churches to symbolize the light of Christ. Christians are lights shining in the world to show the way of righteousness and salvation (*see* Matt. 5:14; John 8:12).

LITURGY The work or public service of the people of God, which is the worship of the one true God. The Divine Liturgy is the Eucharistic service of the Orthodox Church.

LOVE Charity, union, affection, friendship; unselfish concern for another's good. The *love* of Christians for each other and for the world is a reflection of the love between the three Persons of the Holy Trinity. *See* John 11:3, 36; 1 Cor. 13; 1 John 4:8, 16.

MAGNIFICAT The prayer or hymn sung by the Virgin Mary when she visited St. Elizabeth, the mother of St. John the Baptist, shortly after the Annunciation (Luke 1:46–55). Sung frequently during Matins in the Orthodox Church, this hymn takes its title from the Latin for the beginning phrase, "My soul magnifies the Lord." *See* 1 Sam. 2:1–10.

MAN (Gr. *anthropos*) Frequently used in the Bible in the generic sense for both man and woman. Man is the pinnacle of God's creation, for only he among the creatures was made in the image and likeness of God. *See* Gen. 1:26, 27; Luke 4:4.

MARTYR (Gr. *martyria*) Literally, "a witness." Normally, the term is used to describe those who give their lives for Christ. *Martyria* has two meanings: (1) witness or testimony, especially that which God bears to Christians, and which Christians bear to the world; and (2) martyrdom, especially Christ's Passion, and the martyrdom of Christians for the faith (*see* John 1:6–15; Acts 6:8—7:60).

MATINS The early morning prayer service in the Orthodox Church.

MEDIATOR One who intervenes on behalf of another. Jesus Christ intervenes on behalf of the faithful before God the Father (1 Tim. 2:5).

MERCY The compassionate, steadfast love of God for sinners. Christians reflect the *mercy* of God by caring for others. The most frequent prayer in Orthodox worship is "Lord, have mercy." *See* Matt. 5:7; Eph. 2:4–7; Titus 3:4–7.

MESSIAH The Christ, the anointed one of God. Jesus Christ is the *Messiah,* fulfilling all the promises made by God to His chosen people (*see* Is. 7:14; 9:6; Matt. 16:13–17).

MILLENNIUM A thousand years. The Orthodox Church has traditionally taught that the thousand-year reign of Christ on earth before the final defeat of Satan, as recorded in Rev. 20:1–3, is symbolic of the rule of Christ through the Church, which is a manifestation of the Kingdom of God (*see* 2 Pet. 3:8).

MIND The intelligent faculty, the inner person; often used synonymously with "heart." There are two Greek words for mind: (1) *nous,* the mind which is separated from the sensible world and the passions (Rom. 8:7; 12:2); and (2) *dianoia,* the intellect (Matt. 22:37).

MIRACLE A sign whereby God supersedes the normal laws of nature in a mysterious way in order to manifest His power as Master of the universe. Jesus Christ performed many miracles—some showing His mastery over nature, others demonstrating His power over sin, disease, and death. The apostles continued to manifest the power of God through miracles. Healings, weeping icons, and other contemporary miracles also show His power in the world today. *See* Matt. 8:1–34; John 11:1–44; Acts 3:1–9.

MISSION A task given by God to His people. Christ sent the Seventy on a *mission* (Luke 10:1–24). St. Paul went on three missionary journeys to preach the gospel (Acts 13:1—14:28; 15:36—18:22; 18:23—21:16). The *mission* of the Church today is to proclaim Christ to the world.

MYSTERY The ways of God, especially God's plan for salvation, which cannot be known with the rational, finite human mind, but can be experienced only by the revelation of God. The Orthodox Church also uses the term *mystery* for the sacraments of the Church. *See* Mark 4:11; 1 Cor. 2:7, 8; Eph. 5:32. *See also* **SACRAMENT.**

NATURE The sum of the qualities shared by individuals of the same type. (The qualities which distinguish individuals of a type from one another make up the "person.") The Holy Trinity is one divine Nature in three Persons. Humanity is one human nature in many persons. Although stained by sin, human nature is good, having been created in the image of God. Through grace, the Holy Spirit restores the nature of believers to its true, uncorrupted state, so that they may grow into union with God. *See* Gen. 1:26–31; 2 Cor. 3:18; 5:17.

NEW MAN One who is being transformed or deified by the Holy Spirit into a new creature in communion with God (2 Cor. 5:17; Gal. 6:15).

NEW JERUSALEM The center of the Kingdom of God which will be established following the Second Coming of Christ and the Last Judgment. The heavenly Jerusalem will take the place of the old earthly Jerusalem, and is called by Paul, "the mother of us all" (Gal. 4:26). *See* Rev. 3:12; 21:2.

OLD MAN One not transformed by the Holy Spirit, still a slave to sin and death (Rom. 6:5–7; Eph. 4:20–24).

ORDINATION The sacramental act setting a man apart for the ministry of the Church by the laying on of hands of a bishop. The original meaning of ordination includes both election and imposing of hands (*see* article, "Ordination," at Acts 14; Acts 6:1–6; 14:23; 1 Tim. 4:14).

ORIGINAL SIN The fact that every person born comes into the world stained with the consequences of the sins of Adam and Eve and of their other ancestors. These consequences are chiefly: (1) mortality, (2) a tendency to sin, and (3) alienation from God and from other people. Original sin does not carry guilt, however, for a person is guilty only of his or her own sins, not of those of Adam. Therefore, the Orthodox Church does not believe that a baby who dies unbaptized is condemned to hell. *See* Gen. 3:1–24; Rom. 5:12–16.

PARABLE A story told to illustrate a greater truth through images related to the daily lives of the hearers. Christ's teaching is filled with parables (*see* article, "Parables," at Matt. 13; Matt. 13:1–54).

PARADISE The place of rest for the departed in Christ. The original Paradise, seen in Gen. 2:8–14, will be restored in its fullness following the Second Coming of Christ. *See* Luke 23:43; 2 Cor. 12:4; 2 Pet. 3:13; Rev. 2:7; 21:1.

PARADOX That which is true, but not conventionally logical: for example, that a virgin could bear a Son and yet remain a virgin, as did Mary; or that God can be One, yet three Persons. The Christian faith is full of paradoxes, because our intellect is not sufficient to comprehend the mind of God (*see* Is. 55:8, 9).

PASCHA Greek for "Passover." Originally *Pascha* designated the Jewish Passover; now, it is the Feast of the Resurrection of Christ. Christ is the Lamb of God whose sacrifice delivers the faithful from death, as the sacrifice of the Passover Lamb delivered the ancient Jews from slavery and death in Egypt (Ex. 12; 13; 1 Cor. 5:7, 8).

PASSION (1) A term used to describe the sacrifice of Christ on the Cross. (2) Holy Week is often called Passion Week, describing Christ's struggle and suffering in Jerusalem. (3) Passions are human appetites or urges—such as hunger, the desire for pleasure and sexual drives—which become a source of sin when not controlled or directed by submission to the will of God (Rom. 1:26; 7:5; Gal. 5:24; Col. 3:5).

PEACE (Heb. *shalom*) Tranquillity, harmony with God, self, and other people made possible through Christ, who unites human beings to God and to each other. *See* Rom. 14:17; Gal. 5:22; Eph. 2:13–16; Phil. 4:6, 7.

PENTECOST Originally an OT harvest festival celebrated fifty days following the Passover. In time, *Pentecost* became the commemoration of the giving of the Law to Moses on Mt. Sinai. Pentecost took on a new meaning with the descent of the Holy Spirit on the apostles at Pentecost. Through the Sacrament of Chrismation, Orthodox Christians experience their own personal Pentecost. Every Divine Liturgy becomes a Pentecost through the descent of the Holy Spirit on the faithful and the gifts (the bread and wine), transforming them into the Body and Blood of Christ. *See* Ex. 23:14–17; Lev. 23:15–21; Acts 2:1–41.

PERSON (Gr. *prosopon;* Lat. *persona*) Regarding the Holy Trinity, there are three Divine Persons: God the Father, Son, and Holy Spirit. The Person of God the Son became Man, Jesus Christ, "for us and for our salvation" (Matt. 28:19). *See also* **HYPOSTASIS.**

PHARISEES One of the parties of first–century Judaism. The Pharisees favored strict legalistic application of traditional interpretations of the Law stemming from oral Jewish traditions. Unlike the Sadducees, they believed in angels and in the resurrection of the dead. The Pharisees were generally hostile to the mission of Christ, who condemned their excessive legalism and their preoccupation with outward forms, ignoring true righteousness of the heart. *See* Matt. 3:7; 12:14; 22:34; 23:13–36. *See also* **SADDUCEES.**

PILGRIM One who makes a journey to a religious shrine or a spiritual journey from sin and suffering in this life to eternal life with Christ in heaven. *See* Ps. 42:4; Heb. 11:13; 1 Pet. 2:11.

POWER (1) A divine attribute or energy (Matt. 6:13; Luke 1:35; Rom. 1:16). (2) The authority and ability to act (Matt. 9:6). (3) A category of angelic beings (Eph. 1:21).

PRAISE To glorify and give thanks to God or to speak highly of someone or something (Judg. 5:3; Ps. 9:1–14; Rom. 15:11).

PRAYER Communion with God through words of praise, thanksgiving, repentance, supplication, and intercession. Prayer is "raising up the heart and mind to God" (St. John of Damascus). Usually prayer is verbal. However, prayer of the heart or in the Spirit, the highest form of prayer, is without words. *See* Matt. 6:5–13; 21:22; Rom. 8:26; Phil. 4:6; 1 Thess. 5:17.

PRESBYTER Literally, "elder"; now generally called "priest." *Presbyter* is one of the three orders of the ordained ministry of the Church: bishop, presbyter, and deacon (*see* article, "The Four 'Orders' in Church Government," at 1 Tim.; Acts 14:23; 15:4–23; 1 Tim. 5:17–19; Titus 1:5). *See also* **BISHOP.**

PROCEED To come forth from or come to. The Holy Spirit proceeds from the Father, the fountainhead of the Holy Trinity (John 15:26).

PROPHET One who proclaims the will of God and/or who foretells the future, especially the coming and mission of Christ, through the inspiration of the Holy Spirit. *See* Deut. 18:18; Acts 28:25.

PROPITIATION An offering that results in atonement, redemption, and reconciliation. Christ offered Himself on the Cross as a propitiation for our sins, to liberate humanity from sin and death. See Rom. 3:21–26; Heb. 2:17; 1 John 2:2; 4:10.

PROSELYTE Literally, "one who comes toward." A proselyte is a convert to the Faith, usually from another religion. In the New Testament, the word usually refers to a Gentile convert to Judaism (*see* Acts 2:10; 13:43).

PROVIDENCE God's sovereign care in governing His creation, especially His care for the faithful (Rom. 8:28).

PURIFICATION The Old Testament rite whereby one is cleansed of ritual impurity caused by such things as contact with leprosy or a dead body, or sexual functions. This cleansing consisted of making a sacrifice or being sprinkled with "water of purification" (Num. 19:9). Christ liberated the faithful from these rites. Christians are purified by the sacraments and by their spiritual struggle towards transforming their passions. *See* Lev. 12:6; Num. 19:9–21; Matt. 15:11; Luke 2:22–33; Acts 10:9–16; 15:1–29.

RAPTURE The gathering of the Church on earth in the presence of Christ when He comes again to judge the living and the dead (1 Thess. 4:15–17). Orthodox theologians reject the recent minority view that the Church will be taken out of the world before the time of trouble preceding the Second Coming. Christ specifically teaches the faithful will experience the trials of tribulation (Matt. 24:4–28). *See also* **SECOND COMING.**

RECONCILIATION The removal of hostility and barriers between humans and God, and between individuals, accomplished by Christ (Rom. 5:11; 2 Cor. 5:18, 19).

REDEMPTION The deliverance of humanity from sin and death by Christ, who assumed humanity by His Incarnation, conquered sin and death by His life-giving death and glorious Resurrection, releases those who are in captivity to the evil one, and unites humanity to God by His Ascension (Gal. 3:13; Heb. 9:15). *See also* **DEIFICATION** and **SALVATION.**

REMEMBRANCE (Gr. *anamnesis*) Making present by means of recollection. The Eucharist is not merely a calling to mind but a remembrance of and mystical participation in the very sacrifice of Christ, His Resurrection, His Ascension, and His coming again (1 Cor. 11:23–26).

REMISSION The forgiveness and putting aside of sins. As the faithful are released from their sins through the sacramental life of the Church, they in turn are called to remit the sins of any who have offended them. *See* John 20:23; Acts 2:37, 38.

REPENTANCE Literally, "a change of mind" or attitude, and thus of behavior. God is the author of *repentance,* which is an integral part of baptism, confession, and ongoing spiritual life. Repentance is not simply sorrow for sins but a firm determination to turn away from sin to a new life of righteousness in Jesus Christ. *See* Matt. 4:17; 2 Pet. 3:9; 1 John 1:9.

RESURRECTION The reunion of the soul and body after death which will revitalize and transform the physical body into a spiritual body. Jesus Himself is the firstfruits of perfect resurrection; He will never again be subject to death. Because He conquered death by His Resurrection, all will rise again: the righteous to life with Christ, the wicked to judgment. *See* John 5:28, 29; 1 Cor. 15:35–55.

RIGHTEOUSNESS Being good, just, and blameless. All are called to a life of humble obedience to God. However, acts of righteousness cannot earn salvation. Rather, righteousness is the fruit of the Holy Spirit, and the way in which Christians respond with living faith to God's gift of salvation. *See* Matt. 5:6, 20; Rom. 4:3; Gal. 5:22; James 2:14–26.

RITES Forms of worship, music, vestments, and architecture. Most Orthodox Christians follow the liturgical practice of the ancient Churches in the east (Antioch, Jerusalem, and Alexandria), the rite commonly known as the Liturgy of St. John Chrysostom. However, some Orthodox follow a Western Rite, forms that developed in the west before the separation of Rome from the Orthodox Church.

RITUAL Ceremonies and texts used in the worship of the Church. Having her roots in the temple and synagogue, the Church has employed ritual in her worship from the very beginning. *See also* **LITURGY** and **WORSHIP.**

SABBATH The seventh day of the week, originally a day of rest, for after creation "God rested on the seventh day" (Gen. 2:2). Since Christ rose from the dead on the first day of the week, Sunday, the Church gathers on this day instead of the seventh to worship God. Sunday is also called "the Lord's Day" and "the eighth day," because it transcends the Sabbath and is seen as being a part of heavenly time rather than earthly time. *See* Ex. 20:8–11; Acts 20:7.

SACRAMENT Literally, a "mystery." A sacrament is a way in which God imparts grace to His people. Orthodox Christians frequently speak of seven sacraments, but God's gift of grace is not limited only to these seven—the entire life of the Church is mystical and sacramental. The sacraments were instituted by Christ Himself (John 1:16, 17). The seven mysteries are baptism (Matt. 28:18–20; Rom. 6:4; Gal. 3:27), chrismation (Acts 8:15–17; 1 John 2:27), the Holy Eucharist (Matt. 26:26–28; John 6:30–58; 1 Cor. 10:16; 11:23–31), confession (John 20:22, 23; 1 John 1:8, 9), ordination (Mark 3:14; Acts 1:15–26; 6:1–6; 1 Tim. 3:1–13; 4:14), marriage (Gen. 2:18–25; Eph. 5:22–33), and healing or unction (Luke 9:1–6; James 5:14, 15).

SACRIFICE To offer something up to God. In the Old Covenant, God commanded His people to sacrifice animals, grain, or oil as an act of thanksgiving, praise, forgiveness, and cleansing. However, these sacrifices were only a foreshadowing of the one perfect sacrifice—Christ, the Word of God, who left the heavenly glory to humble Himself by becoming Man, giving His life as a sacrifice on the Cross to liberate humanity from the curse of sin and death. In the Eucharist, the faithful participate in the all–embracing, final and total sacrifice of Christ. *See* Lev. 1:1—7:38; 1 Cor. 11:23–26; Phil. 2:5–8; Heb. 9:1—10:18. *See also* **REMEMBRANCE.**

SADDUCEES A party in Judaism at the time of Christ. The Sadducees steadfastly held to a literal interpretation of the Law contained in the first five books of the Old Testament (the Pentateuch or Torah), and rejected traditional interpretations favored by other groups of Jews, especially the Pharisees. Sadducees came from the priestly class and rejected the resurrection of the dead and the existence of angels. Christ condemned these Jewish leaders for their preoccupation with outward forms, ignoring or neglecting true righteousness of the heart (Matt. 16:1–12).

SAINT Literally, "a holy person." With God as the source of true holiness, all Christians are called to be saints (*see* Rom. 16:2; 1 Cor. 1:1, 2). But from the earliest times, the Church has designated certain outstanding men and women who have departed this life and reached deification as worthy of veneration and canonization as saints or holy persons.

SALVATION The fulfillment of humanity in Christ, through deliverance from the curse of sin and death, to union with God through Christ the Savior. Salvation includes a process of growth of the whole person whereby the sinner is changed into the image and likeness of God. One is saved by faith through grace. However, saving faith is more than mere belief. It must be a living faith manifested by works of righteousness, whereby we cooperate with God to do His will. We receive the grace of God for salvation through participation in the sacramental life of the Church. *See* articles, "The New Birth," at John 3; "Justification by Faith," at Rom. 5; and "Deification," at 2 Pet. 1; 2 Cor. 3:18; 4:16; 5:17; Eph. 2:8, 9; Phil. 2:12, 13; James 2:14–26; 1 Pet. 2:2. *See also* **DEIFICATION, JUSTIFICATION, REDEMPTION** and **SACRAMENT.**

SANCTIFICATION Literally, "being set apart" to God. The process of growth in Christ whereby the believer is made holy as God is holy, through the Holy Spirit (*see* article, "Deification," at 2 Pet. 1; Rom. 6:22 with center-column note; Rom. 15:16). *See also* **DEIFICATION, JUSTIFICATION** and **SALVATION.**

SANCTUARY The Holy of Holies or Most Holy Place—the place in the Old Testament tabernacle or temple containing the ark of the covenant, the dwelling place of God. Only the High Priest could enter the Most Holy Place and only on the Day of Atonement. When the early Christians built churches, they followed the general pattern of the temple, and the altar area is often called the sanctuary. See Ex. 26:31–35; 40:34, 35; Lev. 16:1–5; 1 Kin. 6:1–38; 8:1–11.

SECOND COMING At the end of the ages, Christ will come again to judge the living and the dead. Following the judgment, a new heaven and new earth will take the place of the old earth, which has been scarred by sin. Because Christ is already present through the Church, Christians enter into the Kingdom through their participation in the sacramental life of the Church as they await the coming of the Lord (*see* article, "The Second Coming of Christ," at Titus 2; Matt. 25:31–46; Rom. 8:18–21; 1 Thess. 4:16, 17; Rev. 20:11—22:5). *See also* **RESURRECTION.**

SHEKINAH The glory of God, frequently revealed in the symbols of fire and cloud in the Old Testament. Although Christians experience the energies of God, including His glory, they never penetrate beyond the cloud to the inner essence of God, which remains hidden. *See* Ex. 13:21; 24:15–18; 33:18–23; 40:34, 35; 2 Chr. 7:1; Matt. 17:1–5. *See also* **ENERGY** and **ESSENCE.**

SIN (Gr. *hamartia*) Literally, "missing the mark." This word in ancient Greek could describe the action of an archer who failed to hit the target. All humans are sinners who miss the mark of perfection that God has set for His people, resulting in alienation from God, sinful actions that violate the law of God, and ultimately in death. *See* Matt. 5:48; Rom. 3:23; 6:23; 1 John 1:8.

SOJOURNER A stranger or foreigner. Because the Church exists in a sinful world that has rejected God, Christians—citizens of the Kingdom of God—are strangers in a foreign land. Therefore, faithful sojourners are on guard, lest they adopt the ways of the fallen society in which they live. See 1 Pet. 2:11; 1 John 2:15–17.

SON OF MAN An important messianic title of Christ, who is perfect God and perfect Man. The Gospels reveal that Jesus often applied this title to Himself. In Christ, the Second Adam, God assumed and perfected sinful humanity, freeing those who follow

Him from the consequences of the rebellion of the first man, Adam. *See* Mark 2:28; 9:31; Rom. 5:12–21; 1 Cor. 15:21, 22, 45–49. *See also* **INCARNATION.**

SORROW Sadness and grief caused by the realization of one's sins. The Scriptures distinguish between godly sorrow, which produces repentance, and ungodly sorrow, the sadness of being found out, which produces death (Matt. 5:4; 2 Cor. 7:9, 10). Christ has conquered suffering and death, the cause of sadness, and turns true sorrow to joy for His followers (John 16:20–22, 33).

SOUL A living substance, simple, bodiless, and invisible by nature, activating the body to which it brings life, growth, sensation and reproduction. The mind is not distinct from the soul but serves as a window to the soul. The soul is free, endowed with will, and the power to act. Along with the body, the soul is created by God in His image. The soul of man will never die (Gen. 1:26; 2:7; Matt. 10:28).

SPIRIT (Gr. *pneuma*) Literally, "breath"; that which is living but immaterial. *Spirit* is used in three ways in Scripture. (1) The Holy Spirit is one of the three Persons of the Trinity (John 4:24; 20:22). (2) The angels are called spirits (Ps. 104:4). (3) The human spirit possesses the intuitive ability to know and experience God (Rom. 8:16; 1 Cor. 2:10–12).

SPIRITUALITY The ascetic and pious struggle against sin through repentance, prayer, fasting, and participation in the sacramental life of the Church. *See* Gal. 5:16–26; Phil. 2:12, 13. *See also* **SYNERGISM.**

STEWARD(SHIP) A steward is one who manages property belonging to another. All a Christian has belongs to God. Thus, the Christian gives back to God out of the material blessings he has received from God for the work of the Church. In the Old Testament, God commanded the faithful to give ten percent of their goods to God; though not under law, Christians should give at least as much. Christians are also stewards of the spiritual knowledge which God has entrusted to us. We must preserve the heritage of apostolic doctrine intact for future generations. *See* Gen. 14:18–20; Lev. 27:30–33; 1 Cor. 4:1, 2; 2 Cor. 9:6–8; 1 Pet. 4:10.

SYMBOL In Orthodox usage, the manifestation in material form of a spiritual reality. A *symbol* does not merely stand for something else, as does a "sign'; it indicates the actual presence of its subject. For example, the dove is the symbol which brought to Jesus the descent of the Holy Spirit (Matt. 3:13–16).

SYNAXIS Literally, "gathering" or "assembly." *Synaxis* is the word used for the ancient Greek Senate. The first part of the Divine Liturgy is called the synaxis because the faithful gather to sing, to hear the Scriptures read, and to hear the homily. The saints' days are also called a synaxis, such as the Synaxis of St. Michael and all the angels.

SYNERGISM (from Gr. *syn:* same, together; *ergos*: energy, work) Working together, the act of cooperation. In referring to the New Testament, synergism is the idea of being "workers together with" God (2 Cor. 6:1), or of working "out your own salvation . . . for it is God who works in you" (Phil. 2:12, 13). This is not a cooperation between "equals," but finite man working together with Almighty God. Nor does synergism suggest working for, or earning, salvation. God offers salvation by His grace, and man's ability to cooperate also is a grace. Therefore, man responds to salvation through cooperation with God's grace in living faith, righteous works and rejection of evil (James 2:14–26). *See also* **FREE WILL** and **PASSIONS.**

SYNOPTIC (from Gr. *syn:* same, together; *optic*: eye, vision) The books of Matthew, Mark, and Luke, which hold essentially the same viewpoint and "look alike," are called the synoptic Gospels.

TEMPTATION The seductive attraction of sin. Christ was tempted by Satan and has overcome the power of temptation. Those united to Christ are given His power also to withstand the temptation of sin through patience, courage, and obedience. *See* Matt. 4:1–11; 1 Cor. 10:13; Heb. 2:17, 18; James 1:12.

THANKSGIVING To be grateful, to offer thanks, especially to God for His love and mercy. The Eucharistic prayer is called the thanksgiving (*see* 1 Thess. 5:18).

THEOPHANY A manifestation of God in His uncreated glory. It refers also to Christ's resurrection appearances. The revelation of the Holy Trinity at the Baptism of Christ (Luke 3:21, 22) is the greatest theophany; it is celebrated in the Orthodox Church on Epiphany (Jan. 6). Other theophanies are found throughout the Bible. For example, God appeared to Abraham in the form of three men (Gen. 18:1–15), and to Jacob in a dream (Gen. 28:10–17). *See also* **EPIPHANY.**

THEOTOKOS God-bearer, birth-giver, frequently translated "Mother of God." Because Jesus Christ is the divine Son of God, Mary is called the Mother of God to profess our faith that in the Incarnation, God was in her womb. Elizabeth called Mary "blessed" and "the mother of my Lord" (Luke 1:42, 43). At the Council of Ephesus in A.D. 431, the Church condemned Nestorius and other heretics who refused to call the Virgin Mary the Theotokos. For if it was not God in Mary's womb, there is no salvation for humanity. *See* article, "Mary," at Luke 1; Luke 1:26–43; John 1:1–14.) *See also* **INCARNATION.**

TRADITION That which is handed down, transmitted. Tradition is the life of the Church in the Holy Spirit, for the Holy Spirit leads the Church "into all truth" (John 16:13) and enables her to preserve the truth taught by Christ to His Apostles. The Holy Scriptures are the core of Holy Tradition, as interpreted through the writings of the Fathers, the Ecumenical Councils, and the worship of the Church. Together, these traditions manifest the faith of the ancient undivided Church, inspired by the Holy Spirit to preserve the fullness of the gospel. *See* John 21:25; Acts 15:1–29; 2 Thess. 2:15.

TRANSFIGURATION A change or transformation. Christ was transfigured on Mt. Tabor, showing He is God in the flesh (Matt. 17:1–8). Christians are called to be transformed by the Holy Spirit into the image and likeness of God (Rom. 12:1, 2). *See* article, "The Transfiguration," at Matt. 17. *See also* **DEIFICATION.**

TRIBULATION (THE) The Scriptures reveal that much trouble and violence—Great Tribulation—will engulf the world before the Second Coming of Christ (Matt. 24:4–29). *See also* **ESCHATOLOGY, RAPTURE,** and **SECOND COMING.**

TRISAGION Literally, "Thrice Holy." The biblical Trisagion, "Holy, Holy, Holy," is the hymn of the angels before the throne of God (Is. 6:1–3; Rev. 4:8), and is one of the most important hymns of the Divine Liturgy. In the Tradition of the Church, this hymn has been amplified into the Trisagion frequently sung during services and said during prayers: "Holy God, Holy Mighty, Holy Immortal One, have mercy on us." The biblical use of "Holy" three times is an indication of the three Persons in the Godhead.

TYPE A historical event that has a deeper meaning, pointing to our salvation in Christ. For example, the three days that Jonah spent in the belly of the fish is a type of the three days that Christ would spend in the tomb (Matt. 12:40). The serpent that Moses lifted up on the staff is a type of the lifting up of Christ on the Cross (John 3:14–16). The burning bush, aflame but not consumed, is a type of the Virgin Mary, who carried the incarnate God in her womb but was not consumed by His presence (Luke 1:26–38). Noah's ark, which saved Noah and his family from death in the flood, is a type of baptism, which brings the believer from death to life (1 Pet. 3:18–22). *See also* **ALLEGORY.**

TRINITY God the Father and His Son and His Holy Spirit: one in essence and undivided. God revealed the mystery of the Trinity at Christ's baptism (Matt. 3:13–17), but even before that event, numerous Old Testament references pointed to the Trinity. For example, the frequent use of plural pronouns referring to the one God (Gen. 1:26); the three angels who appeared to Abraham (Gen. 18:1–16); and the Triple Holy hymn sung by the angels in Isaiah's vision (Is. 6:1–4) all suggest one God in three Persons, the Father, Son, and Holy Spirit (Matt. 28:19).

UNCTION Anointing of the sick with blessed oil, for the healing of body and soul. The gift of healing is bestowed by the Holy Spirit through the anointing, together with the prayers of the Unction service. *See* article "Healing," at James 5; James 5:14, 15; 1 John 2:20.) *See also* **SACRAMENT.**

UNLEAVENED BREAD Bread baked without yeast. The Jews used unleavened bread for the Passover to symbolize the fact that they had no time to wait for the yeast to rise in the bread (Ex. 12:1–20). By contrast, the bread of the New Covenant is leavened. *See also* **LEAVEN.**

VESPERS The evening prayer service in the Orthodox Church.

VICE A particular immoral, depraved, or degrading habit, as contrasted with virtue. Christians are called to flee from the vices and preserve their purity (Rom. 13:13; Eph. 4:17–24). *See also* **VIRTUE.**

VIRTUE A righteous characteristic such as self-control, patience, or humility; the opposite of *vice* or *passion*. As a person grows spiritually, he or she grows in virtue while the passions are conquered by the grace of God. See Phil. 4:8; 2 Pet. 1:2–7. *See also* **PASSION.**

WISDOM (OF GOD) A name for God's Son and Word; Christ is the Wisdom of God. Also, wisdom is given to the Church as a gift of the Holy Spirit. *See* John 1:1; 1 Cor. 2:6–8; Col. 3:16.

WITNESS (Gr. *martyria*) One who testifies by word and deed. In the New Testament, the word is also rendered "martyr," a reference to those who give their lives for the gospel of Christ. Also, the Holy Spirit bears *witness* to the spirits of those who believe in Christ, that they belong to Him. *See* Rom. 8:16; Heb. 10:15; 12:1; 1 John 5:6–12; Rev. 11:3–12. *See also* **MARTYR.**

WORD OF GOD (Gr. *Logos*) The Son of God, who from the mystery of His eternal birth is called the Word of the Father. The "Word became flesh" (John 1:14) for the salvation of the world. The Holy Scriptures are also called the Word of God, for they reveal the truth of God (John 1:1–14; 2 Pet. 1:19–21). *See also* **INCARNATION.**

WORSHIP Literally, "to bow down." In the Christian sense worship is the adoration of God through participation in the services of the Church, the highest act of a Christian (John 4:19–24). *See also* **LITURGY.**

WORTHY (Gr. *axios*) Describes those who act in a manner befitting one who is a follower of Christ. No one is worthy of salvation in and of himself, but all are made worthy through Christ (*see* 1 Thess. 2:10–12).

ZEAL Devotion; enthusiastic obedience to God; a quality of divine diligence or fervor. Christians are (1) called to follow Christ with enthusiasm and zeal (Acts 18:25; Rom. 12:10, 11) and (2) warned against misguided enthusiasm, a zeal "not according to knowledge" (Rom. 10:2).

Index to Annotations

This is a thorough, but not exhaustive, index to topics and names discussed in the annotations of *The Orthodox Study Bible*. For further information on topics, see the Glossary. For further information on proper names, see the Concordance. Each *italic* entry refers to a single annotation. Entries in **boldface** refer to two or more annotations within a passage of Scripture.

The Seventy

NAME	COMMEMORATED	N.T. REFERENCE(S)
Achaicus	June 15	1 Cor. 16:17
Agabus	Apr. 1; May 26	Acts 11:28; 21:10
Amplias	Oct. 31	Rom. 16:8
Ananias	Oct. 1	Acts 9:10–17; 22:12
Andronicus	May 17; July 30	Rom. 16:7
Apelles	Sept. 10; Oct. 31	Rom. 16:10
Apollos	Mar. 30; Dec. 8	Acts 18:24; 19:1; 1 Cor. 1:12; 3:4–22; 4:6; 16:12; Titus 3:13
Aquila	July 14	Acts 18:2, 18, 26; Rom. 16:3; 1 Cor. 16:19; 2 Tim. 4:19
Archippus	Feb. 19; July 6	Col. 4:17; Philem. 2
Aristarchus	Apr. 15; Sept. 27	Acts 19:29; 20:4; 27:2; Col. 4:10; Philem. 24
Aristobulus	Mar. 16; Oct. 31	Rom. 16:10
Artemas	Oct. 30	Titus 3:12
Asyncritus	Apr. 8	Rom. 16:14
Barnabas	June 11	Acts 4:36; 9:27; 11—15; 1 Cor. 9:6; Gal. 2:1, 9, 13; Col. 4:10
Caesar	Mar. 30; Dec. 8	
Carpus	May 26	2 Tim. 4:13
Clement	Sept. 10	Phil. 4:3
Cephas	Mar. 30; Dec. 8	
Cleopas	Oct. 30	Luke 24:18; John 19:25
Crescens	July 30	2 Tim. 4:10
Crispus	Oct. 4	Acts 18:8; 1 Cor. 1:14
Epaphras	Jan. 4	Col. 1:7; 4:12; Philem. 23
Epaphroditus	Mar. 30; Dec. 8	Phil. 2:25; 4:18
Epaenetus	July 30	Rom. 16:5
Erastus	Nov. 10	Acts 19:22; Rom. 16:23; 2 Tim. 4:20
Euodia	Sept. 7	Phil. 4:2
Fortunatus	June 15	1 Cor. 16:17
Gaius	Nov. 5	Acts 19:29; 20:4; Rom. 16:23; 1 Cor. 1:14; 3 John 1
Hermas	Mar. 8; Nov. 5	Rom. 16:14
Hermes	Apr. 8; May 31	Rom. 16:14
Herodion	Mar. 28; Apr. 8; Nov. 10	Rom. 16:11
James, the brother of the Lord	Nov. 23	Matt. 13:55; Mark 6:3; Acts 12:17; 15:13; James
Jason	Apr. 22	Acts 17:5–9
Justus	Oct. 30	Acts 1:23; 18:7; Col. 4:11
Linus	Nov. 5	2 Tim. 4:21
Lucius	Sept. 10	Acts 13:1; Rom. 16:21
Luke, the Evangelist	Oct. 18	Col. 4:14; 2 Tim. 4:11; Philem. 24
Mark, the Evangelist (called John)	Apr. 25	Acts 12:12, 25; 15:37–39; Col. 4:10; 2 Tim. 4:11; Philem. 24; 1 Pet. 5:13
Mark	Sept. 27; Oct. 30	
Narcissus	Oct. 31	Rom. 16:11
Nicanor	July 28	Acts 6:5
Olympas	Nov. 10	Rom. 16:15
Onesimus	Feb. 15	Col. 4:9; Philem. 10
Onesiphorus	Sept. 7; Dec. 8	2 Tim. 1:16; 4:19
Parmenas	July 28	Acts 6:5
Patrobus	Nov. 5	Rom. 16:14

NAME	COMMEMORATED	N.T. REFERENCE(S)
Philemon	Feb. 19; July 6; Nov. 2	Philem. 1
Philip, the Deacon	Oct. 11	Acts 6; 8; 21:8
Philologus	Nov. 5	Rom. 16:15
Phlegon	Apr. 8	Rom. 16:14
Prochorus	July 28	Acts 6:5
Pudens	Apr. 15	2 Tim. 4:21
Quadratus	Sept. 21	
Quartus	Nov. 10	Rom. 16:23
Rufus	Apr. 8	Mark 15:21; Rom. 16:13
Silas (Silvanus)	July 30	Acts 15:22–40; 16:19–40; 17:4–15; 18:5; 2 Cor. 1:19; 1 Thess. 1:1; 2 Thess. 1:1; 1 Pet. 5:12
Simeon, son of Cleophas	Apr. 27	Matt. 13:55; Mark 6:3
Sosipater	Apr. 28; Nov. 10	Rom. 16:21
Sosthenes	Mar. 30; Dec. 8	1 Cor. 1:1
Stachys	Oct. 31	Rom. 16:9
Stephen, the Archdeacon	Dec. 27	Acts 6:5—7:60; 8:2; 11:19; 22:20
Tertius	Nov. 10; Dec. 30	Rom. 16:22
Thaddaeus	Aug. 21	Matt. 10:3; Mark 3:18
Timon	July 28; Dec. 30	Acts 6:5
Timothy	Jan. 22	Acts 16:1; 17:14, 15; 18:5; 19:22; 20:4; Rom. 16:21; 1 and 2 Timothy
Titus	Aug. 25	2 Cor. 2:13; 7:6–14; 8:6–23; 12:18; Gal. 2:1–3; Titus
Trophimus	Apr. 15	Acts 20:4; 21:29; 2 Tim. 4:20
Tychicus	Dec. 8	Acts 20:4; Eph. 6:21; Col. 4:7; 2 Tim. 4:12; Titus 3:12
Urbanus	Oct. 31	Rom. 16:9
Zenas	Sept. 27	Titus 3:13

Interpreting the Scriptures

Jack N. Sparks

What is the Bible?

What is the Bible and how shall it be interpreted? Recognizing that any book at all can be read simply as literature, we will deal here, rather, with the purpose of the Scriptures and how they can be understood in the context of that purpose. Therefore, we should consider:

- Is the Bible just another book any person can pick up and read, starting wherever it happens to fall open, and understand its true meaning without any background?
- Or is the Bible a book addressed to a specific group of people, the Church, which is more than *just* a group of people, but distinctly and expressly the body of Christ—and to people individually only in and through their membership in that body?
- Does the Bible as seen in its totality, with its diverse segments spanning so many centuries and so many cultures, have a single and definite message?

All these questions are absolutely essential to any analysis of the Bible as a revelation from God and to its interpretation in that context. Further, laying aside all questions of the origins of the various segments included in the Scriptures, we must admit that the collection, the Bible in its entirety, was a production of a particular community—that is, both in Israel and in the Church. Nor is it to be considered a comprehensive collection of all the writings of the nature of those included which might have been available. It is rather a selective collection of writings with roots in the liturgical practices of the community, passing on the apostolic tradition, and eventually (for that very reason) certified by the recognized authority structure of the Church. We may also be assured that there were specific purposes guiding this selection. For we recall the words of the Apostle John concerning his own collection: "And truly Jesus did many other signs in the presence of His disciples, which are not written in this book; but these are written that you may believe that Jesus is the Christ, the Son of God, and that believing you may have life in His name" (John 20:30, 31).

John's statement applies in some sense or other to all the books of the Bible. Each is there for a reason related to our salvation. Writings were chosen, edited and assembled, utilized and eventually passed on to the people as an authorized presentation of God's message to humanity. How is it that we have the ones we have? It is a matter of passing on the tradition.

The Bible and the Church

The Old Testament was read in the Church from the beginning, and the New Testament books which would become part of the Canon of Scripture began to be collected and read in the Church. Though there were some doubts about a few books, it all sorted out rather smoothly, for the fact is, the apostolic tradition, the rule of faith, was at stake.

The earliest list we have is found in a fragment found by L. A. Muratori in an eighth-century manuscript. This fragment is believed to date from the second century, because of the names mentioned in it. Some lines are missing at the beginning of the manuscript, but it lists all the New Testament books except Hebrews, James, 1 and 2 Peter. A number of other sources also show the formation of the New Testament Canon in the early centuries—ending in the eighth century with a list by St. John of Damascus. The individual Fathers were reflecting the tradition as they understood it in the churches with which they were acquainted or worked. The Councils, as always, set out to reflect what had been believed from the beginning. Thus, when they gave a list, they intended to reflect the apostolic tradition as they understood it.

That point is essential: *the message comes from God.* How do we know? It is actually the body of Christ which recognizes His Word and certifies its truth. How do we recognize the sacred nature of the Bible? By faith. As a book, a whole, the Bible was written and compiled in the community—*primarily for its enlightenment and guidance.* That is why the Bible and the Church cannot be separated, with either aside to be studied independently, as if under a microscope. The Book and the Covenant go together, and the Covenant is with people. In ancient times, Israel, the people of the Covenant, had been entrusted with the books of the Covenant—the Word of God—as St. Paul so carefully notes in his letter to the Church at Rome: "To them were committed the oracles of God" (Rom. 3:2).

With the giving of the New Covenant (Matt. 26:28; Heb. 12:24), the Church of the Incarnate Word, Jesus Christ the Son and Word of God is entrusted with and maintains the message of the Kingdom of God. Understand then: *the Bible is the Word of God*, but it is what it is by the witness of the Church. Those who would change the Canon of Scripture based upon their scholarly investigations have no authority to do so, for the Bible is compiled and certified by the Church for the purposes for which God has given it to her.

The Mission of the Church

From another direction, we must forever remember the background of the New Testament—the world in which it was written and put together. For the Church had a mission from the very beginning. The apostolic preaching recorded in the Bible had two inseparable purposes: 1) the enlightenment and instruction of the faithful, and 2) the conversion of the world.

Consequently, the New Testament has a background and mission somewhat different from that of the Old Testament. For the Old Testament was a book put together in and for a specific identifiable and essentially stable community: Israel. Not so the New Testament, for its missionary goal caused it to be more open-ended—though still protected by the community (the Church) from being taken over by outsiders. We do not find the early apologists setting out to argue the meaning of Scripture with outsiders. Justin Martyr, Irenaeus of

Lyons, even Tertullian, did not argue doctrines of Christian faith with pagans or heretics on this basis. The Bible belonged to the Church. The appeal of outsiders to the Book of the Church was unacceptable, for they had no right to tread on that private property. An unbeliever, by definition, has no access (nor do spurious churches) to the message of the Bible—for him there is no message because "the natural man does not receive the things of the Spirit of God, for they are foolishness to him; nor can he know them, because they are spiritually discerned" (1 Cor. 2:14).

How, indeed, could it have been that a conglomerate of writings, written at various times by a variety of writers, came to be considered a single Book? It was not by accident that the Scriptures make up one Holy Bible. There is one primary focus, one main message, throughout—forming a single story. And that word "story" is important, for the Bible *is* a story—the story of how God has worked with His chosen people.

Prominent throughout the Scriptures are God's acts and mighty deeds. Everything is, exists, and continues because God set it all in motion. There is a beginning, creation, and an end, the new heaven and new earth—the ultimate goal. Thus, from Genesis to Revelation, the story runs true, made up of many threads, yet a single story. Between the two points something definite has been going on and forming, heading in a definite direction. There is an ultimate goal—a true consummation is anticipated and will come to pass. Each and every moment in all of history, in all our lives, has a relationship to the beginning and the end and has, despite all our doubts, its fitting and particular place within the whole of the story. Not one moment of our lives, of the history of the Church—indeed of the world, can be properly understood except within the context and perspective of the whole.

The writer of Hebrews tells us God "at various times and in various ways spoke in time past to the fathers by the prophets" (Heb. 1:1). All through the ages He has revealed Himself over and again, leading His people from one truth to another, guiding all the way. We must take note of the fact that there were stages in His revelation, and that it was always appropriate to whom He spoke. But all along it was *the same God who spoke the same message*. The very fact that this message is identical unifies the writings in spite of the dissimilarity of their means of presentation. Different versions of the same story are often taken into the Scriptures, just as they are. Though some have promoted the concept of a single composite Gospel with no variations—as a substitute for the four Gospels with their diversity—the Church has rejected such proposals, sticking with the four, in spite of the difficulties which arise from trying to reconcile the contradictions between the evangelists. The fact is that the four Gospels maintain the unity of the message quite adequately, and perhaps in a more comprehensive manner than some composite could achieve.

History and the Bible

The Bible is a book about God present in His world, active and revealing Himself. In the Scriptures we see Him intervening in human life, and not just as a record of the interventions, as if in a history. Ultimately, the revelation is itself an intervention in our lives, for God's work with humanity through the ages forms a message in itself in which He challenges our lives. We do not need to escape time and the mundane events of history to find God, for He meets us, personally, just where we are.

History belongs to God and He is not outside our history looking on. He is here with us. Thus, the Bible is inescapably historical, setting for us especially the intervention of God in history. In it we are not given a description of His eternal mysteries but a record of how these have impacted the lives of people. John catches the essence of this when he writes, "No one has seen God at any time. The only begotten Son, who is in the bosom of the Father, He has declared Him" (John 1:18). How did He make God known? By coming into human history in His Incarnation, and in it we see how history forms the frame for God's revelation to us in both the Old and New Testaments. Neither revelation nor truth can be fully or accurately defined in abstract terms, for the Truth is a person, Christ the Incarnate Lord: "I am the way, the truth, and the life. No one comes to the Father except through Me" (John 14:6).

God has established the closest of relationships between Himself and mankind, and it is in the Scriptures that we see that relationship revealed. His Covenant with us, and His choosing and adopting us as His own dear children (Rom. 8:15, 23; 9:4; Gal. 4:5; Eph. 1:5), shown forth to the watching universe in the Incarnation of the Son (Gal. 4:4).

In the very same revelation that shows us God, then, we see also His dealings with us—how He loves us, desires the best for us, sets forth His plan for us. God actually speaks to human beings—Adam, Abraham, Moses, and on and on. As He does, He shows us the meaning of our very existence and the only true ultimate for our life. Consequently, not only does God reveal Himself to mankind, but human response as well, as men and women listen and answer. There in the Scriptures are: prayer, thanksgiving, adoration, sorrow, repentance and contrition, rejoicing, hope, and even despair.

The New Covenant

In the Covenant, God joins Himself with men and women, and from Abraham to the Church, the Scriptures reveal the mystery of the relationship between God and mankind in not only the voice of God but in human response as well—a true dialogue. So even the prayers and praises of the Psalms, reflecting our response, are God's message to us. For in them we learn more of what He expects of us—the very reason He reveals Himself to us and converses with us. His Covenant is there so we may come to Him.

Nevertheless, the intimate relationship God forms with us is one of a sovereign, transcendent Lord with His creation. God is indeed the One "who alone has immortality, dwelling in unapproachable light, whom no man has seen or can see" (1 Tim. 6:16). Yet we remember that this light is "the true Light which gives light to every man coming into the world" (John 1:9). Therein lies the mystery, the paradox, of God's revelation, of the opening of the age to come, the Kingdom of Heaven, to us.

In the Scriptures we also see the history of the Covenant of God with His people. This historical aspect is woven throughout the Bible: The Pentateuch (the five books of Moses), the historical books, the Prophets, and the Psalms all join to pass on to us the history of the Covenant. Thus, intermixed with wisdom, prayer, prophecy, and commandments, we find the pattern of God's works among us. And the ultimate, the summit, is to be found, of course, in the Incarnation of the Son and Word, God entering history as a man.

As the Nicene Creed so clearly puts it: ". . . one Lord Jesus Christ, the Son of God, the Only-begotten, begotten of the Father before all worlds. Light of Light, Very God of Very God, begotten, not made; of one essence with the Father, by Whom all things were made: Who for us men and for our salvation came down from heaven and was incarnate of the Holy Spirit and the Virgin Mary, and was made man."

Our Destiny

The Bible also shows us where we are going—our destiny. The creation of mankind by God, our fall, and our salvation by Him are, after all, the primary themes of the Book. For it is the true account of the long pathway of our salvation by God—and that makes the Bible *our* story. We are there in the story: in obedience, in stubborn defiance and rebellion, in fall from communion with God, and in restoration to Him.

The path and destiny of mankind is capsulized in the incredible account of God's dealings with Israel, His chosen people through Abraham—and with the New Israel, the Church, His chosen ones purchased by Christ, "who gave Himself for us, that He might redeem us from every lawless deed and purify for Himself His own special people, zealous for good works" (Titus 2:14)—truly "a chosen generation, a royal priesthood, a holy nation, His own special people" (1 Pet. 2:9). This choosing is an essential concept, for He *did* actually choose *just one people*, Israel, setting them apart from all others. Amidst the chaos of human tribes, nations, and kingdoms there stood this one chosen by God to be governed by Him. With them alone He established a priesthood, even though it was a temporary and imperfect one to be replaced by the one true High Priest (Heb. 7), and in Israel alone true prophets arose, giving the message passed on to them by the Spirit of God.

Though the world did not know it, this nation was truly a sacred center for the whole, a place where—in the midst of a fallen, sinful, lost, and unredeemed world—God's mercy was displayed. That truth is the very core of the message of the Bible, a truth which did not spring from any human merit (for Israel was sinful and fallen as surely as all the rest of the world) but from God alone. It was given, as is stated in the Creed, "for us men and for our salvation." For though Israel had certain advantages (Rom. 3:1, 2) not granted to others, those advantages were actually there to bring about the ultimate salvation of us all (Rom. 3:29, 30). As our Lord said, "salvation is of the Jews" (John 4:22). Yet we should not forget that Israel was inferior to the Church, as was the law to grace.

Though God's purpose is the salvation of all, He accomplished it by a plan which involved choosing a people and setting them apart. Now, in this age, the Church is the body of Christ, the set-apart people—also not taken out of the world (see John 17:15) but left in the midst as a witness of His goodness, love and grace.

The Incarnation

The Incarnation is, of course, a high point on the line of time, a point at which there is a new beginning. But that new beginning is not because God stops doing one thing and does another. From the very beginning the Incarnation was planned, and rather than forming a sharp dividing line between the Old and the New Testament, it is that which gives them their unity. Though we recognize the distinction between the two testaments, we recognize their unity in the person of Christ the Savior, God, and man. He belongs to both as the One who fulfills the Old ("Do not think that I came to destroy the Law or the Prophets. I did not come to destroy but to fulfill" Matt. 5:17) and initiates and installs the New ("For this is My blood of the new covenant, which is shed for many for the remission of sins" Matt. 26:28).

Ultimately, then, He fulfills both Testaments—the whole—for He is "the Alpha and the Omega, the Beginning and the End" (Rev. 1:8). And in a mystery, this place of Christ—the beginning, the center, and as the goal—does not demolish the notion of time as a reality, but actually brings true meaning to the concept of time. For now we see that which happens not as mere happenstances but as significant markings on the way. That which is to be comes to pass and there is achievement, and for the future there is a goal and there is hope, for Christ God says, "Behold, I make all things new" (Rev. 21:5).

Matthew opens his Gospel with the words, "The book of the genealogy of Jesus Christ, the Son of David, the Son of Abraham" (Matt. 1:1), and proceeds to delineate His ancestry on earth, starting with Abraham. In that presentation is an important truth: in actuality, the whole of the Old Testament must be seen as just that, the account of the events and activities which have culminated in the appearance of the Son on earth in human flesh. For the Old Testament tells us of the promises of God and the anticipations of His people, of His Covenant, and gives us prophecy.

Nor is that prophecy to be seen only in the words of the prophets, for events were prophecies as well. Indeed, the whole—all that was promised, all that was done, the triumphs and failures of humanity, the hope of all—is prophetic, pointing forward toward the coming fulfillment in the Incarnation. But when Matthew writes his Gospel, the time of anticipation has passed. Now the promise is fulfilled, the Lord has come. This was not passing appearance or a temporary visit, for He had come to live among His people forever!

Note, however, that His coming does not do away with the Old Testament, for it is fulfilled in the New. Those old books of Israel are sacred even to the new Israel, the Church, and we neither set them aside nor ignore them. They forever tell the story of salvation, and bear witness to Christ. The Church still reads these books as a history of what God has done, what He has accomplished, as sacred history. The prophecies have been fulfilled and law has been replaced by grace.

More prominent for us is the Gospel and the New Testament, for we are the people of the New Covenant which Christ established. When we read the Old Testament we recognize what is written there as inspired by the Holy Spirit, "who at various times and in various ways spoke in time past to the fathers by the prophets" (Heb. 1:1). We so recognize them because in the New Testament, God "has in these last days spoken to us by His Son, whom He has appointed heir of all things" (Heb. 1:2). To Him we look and to Him we listen, for "that which we have seen and heard we declare to you, that you also may have fellowship with us; and truly our fellowship is with the Father and with His Son Jesus Christ" (1 John 1:3). In very fact, we are called by God to be "in Christ," and all who are in Him are "a new creation; old things have passed away; behold, all things have become new" (2 Cor. 5:17. In the same connection, see also Rom. 6:11, 23; 8:1, 2, 39; 12:5; 1 Cor. 1:2, 30;

15:22; Gal. 3:28; Eph. 1:3; 2:6, 10, 13; Phil. 4:21; Col. 1:2, 28; 2 Tim. 3:12; Philem. vv. 6, 23; 1 Peter 5:14, and many other instances).

The New Testament

Jesus Christ, the Incarnate Son and Word of God, is the fullness of God's revelation, and the New Testament—with the Gospels which detail His life and works, the Acts of the Apostles which tell us how the Church got under way, the Letters, and the Revelation—is as historical as is the Old. *Actual events, which take place in time,* form the foundation upon which Christian faith rests.

What is the content of the New Testament? We have the facts of the birth, life, works, suffering, death, resurrection and ascension of our Lord. We have the works of Christ our Lord and those of His disciples. We have His teaching and the teachings of His disciples and their followers. Yes, and in truth we have much more, for there is the mystical side, which points us to God, points us beyond the experience of the senses to the full reality of the existence of God and the heavenly realm.

The witness of the Church, set forth in her preaching, stands on these historical facts. When Peter stood to preach on the Day of Pentecost, his sermon started with truth he knew by experience: "This Jesus God has raised up, of which we are all witnesses" (Acts 2:32). As he continued that sermon, he based it upon the salvation wrought by Christ and brought to fulfillment in His Resurrection. That was the nature of the preaching of all the apostles and of those who carried the word on from them. It is a historical witness upon which the Church stands. Her creeds are based upon it; they are truth, and they tell what happened to establish the truth:

> by Whom all things were made; Who for us men and our salvation came down from heaven and was incarnate of the Holy Spirit and the Virgin Mary, and was made man; And was crucified also for us under Pontius Pilate, and suffered and was buried; The third day He rose again, according to the Scriptures; And ascended into heaven, and sits at the right hand of the Father; And He shall come again with glory to judge the living and the dead.

We know who Christ is, and we witness to the mystery seen in that, "in Him dwells all the fullness of the Godhead bodily" (Col. 2:9). We also know that this is a mystery that cannot be understood if we deal only with the dimensions of this earthly realm in which we live. There is a dimension which goes beyond, within which all this is enclosed. That does not, however, deny the boundaries of history on the earth. When we envisage these sacred truths, we see quite clearly the historical aspects—that which happened on earth.

The Apostolic Preaching

As we said, apostolic preaching was narrative in form—it told what had happened (Acts 2; Acts 7, etc.)—but what had happened was new and startling, and it was definitive: "The Word became flesh and dwelt among us, and we beheld His glory, the glory as of the only begotten of the Father, full of grace and truth" (John 1:14). Yes, these are happenings, but they are events far beyond the mundane affairs of everyday life, for not only are they so unheard of as to be unbelievable to the skeptic, they are of such importance as to surpass the imagination and stagger hope and belief. When we tell of the Incarnation, the Resurrection, and the Ascension, we describe events whose truth and whose implications can only be grasped by faith.

The evangelists and the apostles did not write like reporters nor even like biographers. They did not set out to give us a complete record of the activities of Jesus throughout His life. Their accounts of His life and works are particular to His mission on earth. Thus, their accounts tell of those aspects of His life, including what He did and said, which show us Who He was and what He was about. As they write an image, an icon, emerges of God Incarnate. For that is He about whom they write, and their words are carefully chosen to show Him for who He is.

Our faith reaches out to see what the holy writers have seen, whom they have set forth, and we see—not with the eyes which read the words but with inner eyes of faith, which grasps what those eyes cannot, for "faith is the substance of things hoped for, the evidence of things not seen" (Heb. 11:1). Yes, He came, He worked, He spoke, He did, and people saw Him, but our faith has grasped more than eyes can see. As St. Paul so aptly writes, "no one can say that Jesus is Lord except by the Holy Spirit" (1 Cor. 12:3).

By Faith

Those words tell the story: the Gospel, the *full* Gospel, is not to be grasped from the observable facts (those we receive with our five outer senses) alone. No, it is known and received within our hearts only by faith, by spiritual experience. That does not make it less real than the cold, hard facts—it makes it more so. What we receive by faith is most truly grasped of all, for "God is Spirit, and those who worship Him must worship in spirit and truth" (John 4:24).

The Gospels where we encounter Him were written within the Church. They are Her testimony of Him, records of faith and spiritual experience, of her birth and infancy in the Lord.

Yet we must remember that this mystical aspect takes place in time and space. The Gospels are true narratives, history in its purest form, telling us what really took place in space and time. Though we learn much more by faith (Heb. 11:1) than by our five senses, that fact simply shows how inadequate those senses are when it comes to the spiritual realm. Though certain facts are clear enough to the senses, what really happened is of much greater importance, for God the Father, Son, and Holy Spirit, entering into the flow of human history, performed a truly world-shaking act of redemption. That fact and its meaning merge to give us reality—"what *really* happened."

Preservation and Transmission of the Revelation

In the Church that revelation is preserved, and therefore the Church is logically the proper and primary interpreter of that revelation. That interpretation is not the proper role of someone who comes along, reads a bit of the revelation, and decides what it means. The testimony of the Holy Spirit takes the written words and reveals their meaning. Here we are not referring to the enlightenment individuals may receive by the Holy Spirit from time to time. Rather, we mean that by the permanent presence of the Holy Spirit in the Church, He gives her aid and guidance, for she is "the church of the living God, the pillar and ground of the truth" (1 Tim. 3:15).

The Scriptures *must* be interpreted. There is no getting around that. The Church is the God-appointed and permanent witness to the truth and meaning of the message which is to be found in the Scriptures, for the Church herself belongs to the same revelation. She is truly the body of Christ, the Incarnate Lord (Eph. 1:22, 23; Col. 1:24). Who shall proclaim the Gospel? Who shall preach the Word of God? Certainly not just some isolated individual who happens to pick up a copy of the Bible. Proclamation and preaching are part of the being, the essence of the Church. They are part of what she is. The Church witnesses to her Lord, His Gospel and His call.

Yet the witness of the Church is not just a telling of history—a report of what her Lord once did. For the Church is forever in the process of experiencing the work of her Lord in her midst, and her experience involves a continuous outworking of the message of "the faith which was once for all delivered to the saints" (Jude v. 3), a message which must be continually experienced and renewed by faith. Consequently, with her members forever guided by the Holy Spirit, the Church is constantly living the message. Christ Himself is present within the Church, for "He is the head of the body, the church, who is the beginning, the firstborn from the dead, that in all things He may have the preeminence" (Col. 1:18).

Salvation is not simply proclaimed in and by the Church, it is constantly lived by her members, who are continually being saved and by new members who are also being saved. The great works of God are not just something of the past, recorded in the Scriptures, for His work goes on continually in the Church, and through the Church, in the world. So the Church is an inherent part of the New Testament message—of revelation, for Christ is in her and she in Him, she is in very truth His body (Eph. 1:22, 23). Only in the Church is the New Testament really alive, for she is the continuation of that message, carrying its truth through the centuries and bringing it into today. Thus, the very history of the Church is a continuing story of redemption (see Col. 1:1–14). Indeed, the truth of the Scriptures is both revealed and corroborated by the growth of the Church, the body of Christ.

Interpreting the Scriptures

One thing is inescapable: *the Bible is a difficult book*—sealed, so to speak, with seven seals (see Rev. 5:1). But the Bible is not difficult because it is written in some unknown language or in code. We may, in fact, be so bold as to suggest that the great difficulty with the Bible is its magnificent clarity and directness. For the mysteries of God are given to us in the context of the daily lives of ordinary people. It may be, in fact, that the whole story of our salvation seems just all too human—just as Jesus Christ, the Lord of all, God Incarnate, was to all appearances a very ordinary man, the son of a carpenter.

We know that the Bible is inspired by God, and is indeed the Word of God. The nature of that inspiration, however, is beyond definition, for it is a mystery. Those who would define it—or demand definition—quickly run into trouble. When they ask questions such as: "Well, were the men who wrote it just instruments, whose hands were guided by God?" or "Was the Holy Spirit just with them, so that they basically had access to the truth?" they miss the whole point. The Scriptures are a mystery of the encounter between God and man. We will never be able to comprehend fully what it means that holy men of God heard the Word of their God—nor how it could possibly be that they could put that communication into the words of their human language and write it down. For even when the words were formed and written, the message was still God's. That is where the mystery lies, where the miracle of the Bible comes to light: for, after all, the Scriptures are the Word of God in human language.

No matter how we believe the communication—the inspiration—comes about, one fact remains to be reckoned with: The Bible transmits to us and preserves for us the Word of God in a form which human beings can grasp. When God spoke to man, the communication had to be in a form we could hear and understand. Divine inspiration does not get rid of what is human: it transfigures what is human. We must not think that human language degrades or darkens the glory of revelation nor that it restricts the power of the Word of God. We must believe this: Human words can be used to quite adequately convey the Word of God to us. His Word does not become tarnished or cloudy when it is expressed in human language. We are created in the image and likeness of God (Gen. 1:27; 5:1; 9:6) and the very fact of this image and likeness makes communication possible. That God speaks to us in the forms which are our own thought and speech makes our language something greater, for now the Holy Spirit enables us to speak of God.

Theology (literally "words about God") is thus made possible through His revelation. And, yes, theology (truly defined) is our response to God who first spoke to us, whom we have heard, and of whose words we have a record—and now proclaim.

This process is never complete, for we are never perfect in our development of theology—we must keep working at it. We always go back to the very same point of beginning, God's Word, the Holy Scriptures, which is His revelation. Through the creeds, the doctrines of the Church, the Eucharistic liturgy and the various prayer liturgies, and other sacred signs and symbols, theology (and, indeed, true philosophy) witnesses to the meaning of that revelation.

We must also realize, however, that in one respect the Scriptures are themselves a response to God, for they are at one and the same time the Word of God and the response of humanity. The Bible is the Word of God brought to us through the faithful response of those people who wrote it and handed it down to us. Indeed, in every case in which someone wrote, by the inspiration of God, a work which became part of the Bible, the presentation carries some flavor of that person—partly response to God and partly interpretation of the message received from God. Thus, there is certainly a sense in which all parts of Scripture reflect the context in which the revelation was given. It would be impossible for it not to be.

Having received the revelation in the form of the Scriptures, the Church has, through her experience in the world through the centuries, found it necessary to produce explanations. These explanations, seen as a whole, form that which is the structure and pattern of beliefs which are to be found especially in the creeds and other decisions of the Ecumenical Councils, but also in the writings of the great theologians of the Church such as St. Gregory Nazianzus (called "the Theologian"), St. Basil the Great, St. John of Damascus, St. Symeon the New Theologian and others. They are also to be found in the liturgical services, especially in the hymns and prayers.

Bible and Doctrine

Within that which forms the belief structure of the Church, we can clearly discern the mutual interrelationships of the truths which make up the revelation. As we follow through, comparing the parts of this theological system with the Scriptures, we see a happy correspondence which should not surprise us, for the Church sees the doctrines and beliefs as derived from the Scriptures, not as something different from or in place of them.

Yet consider: how systematic can we get with the revelation we have from God? When we set out to interpret it, how do we put all these various works—historical, prophetic, dogmatic, liturgical, written over a space of many hundreds of years, into a theological outline? We must not doubt that the Bible is a unity—for it certainly is—but we still must reckon with the fact that it is a collection of varied writings. That is something we cannot avoid facing. We must find a solution, and that depends upon our view of the cosmos and how our notion of history and our perception of time fit into it.

Methods of Interpretation

To avoid facing the fact that the writings were produced at different times and that the whole Bible was produced over a very long period of time is tempting. This way of looking at the Scriptures has been an enticement from the very beginning, and has probably been at least a factor in the various allegorical systems of interpreting the Scriptures which have sprung up from time to time—Philo, for example, and some of the writings of Origen and others as well. And for mystics! Well, the temptation is almost unavoidable at times.

Yet when the Bible is studied as allegorical, the simplicity disappears. The Bible becomes a book in which everything has a hidden meaning—usually according to a sort of secret code—and discerning its meaning becomes a process of discovering that code and deciphering those hidden meanings. Consequently, the historical context and perspective, literal meanings, obvious truth, and simplicity have little place—and are usually considered irrelevant. When studied this way, the historical context simply provides a framework within which imagery is interpreted—for the search is for "hidden eternal meanings" within that context.

With an allegorical system of interpretation, then, the Bible as a whole is rearranged into a book of symbols and symbolic forms, of secret edification, which brings out a "mystic truth" only discernable to the initiated. The process may even begin with such an evident fact as the eternal and unchanging truth of God. Then, in the process of searching the Old Testament for confirmation and testimony to all of the crucial Christian doctrines and beliefs, the outlook becomes pointed. The Old and New Testaments must be one thing, time and history become blurred and the peculiar characteristics of each are lost to the interpreter. At this point, we can so clearly see the pitfalls of this hermeneutical method that we need go no further. Though we would not deny the value of an occasional allegorical application of Scripture, we simply must resist the temptation to build an allegorical system of interpretation.

We must, therefore, maintain historical perspective in interpretation of the Scriptures, for 1) the Bible truly is history; 2) the Bible is *not* a systematic theology; 3) although the Bible *is* history, it *is not* a history of human faith and belief in God; and 4) the Bible *is the* history of God's revelation to us.

We have a dilemma we must deal with: the Church needs both the history of God's revelation to us *and* system to the way in which the faith is spelled out (in the creeds, etc.). It is legitimate to ask why. And it is legitimate to ask why the Church has always insisted on maintaining both and relying upon them together.

One possible answer is that given in the Protestant Reformation: the Bible is *the* authoritative record of God's revelation and anything else can be considered, at best, as no more than commentary on the Scriptures. According to this view, no such auxiliary work can have the same authority as the Bible itself. Actually, this position has great appeal, for there is some truth in it, but it is not ultimately satisfactory, for it is actually oblique to the real problem we have to face, which may be summed up in the questions:

- Why don't the revelations which come later (specifically those set forth in the New Testament) overrule and replace the earlier ones (in the Old Testament)?
- Why do we still need the Law and the Prophets (the Old Testament) even under Christ's New Covenant—and having the same level of authority (to some degree, at least) as the Gospels and the other New Testament writings?

The answers to these questions are essential to our understanding of the Holy Scriptures. For the Church has, indeed, passed on the Old Testament as part of the Canon of Scripture—and not just as history for us to refer to incidentally and not just as something that happened and is over and done with. We must have an understanding of the appropriate use of the Old Testament in the Christian Church.

We can establish first of all that the Old Testament does indeed serve a historical use, but that use is not as a history of human beliefs and their development or growth. It is the history of God's dealing with mankind and not just as isolated incidents of God entering into the lives of individual people. Rather, the Old Testament records how God carried out His purpose with humanity so that there is a comprehensive unity to the account of His acts recorded there. His mighty deeds led and guided His chosen people to the pinnacle of His purpose in the Incarnation of His Son. There is, therefore, a sense in which His first and continuing acts are reflected in those which came later. In addition to the continuity in God's actions, His goal was the same all along.

This identity of purpose throughout is the foundation for that form of interpretation of the Scripture which is called "typological." The writings of the Fathers consistently reflect this form of interpretation. The distinction between "typology" and "allegory" is quite clear, for the differences stand out:

- Allegory as a method of interpretation concentrates on the text. St. Augustine writes extensively on allegories, but coming down to a simple definition: "There are several species of this kind of trope that is called allegory, and one of them is that which is called enigma. Now the definition of the generic term must necessarily embrace also all its species; and hence, as every horse is an animal, but not every animal is a horse, so every enigma is an allegory, but every allegory is not an enigma. *What then is an allegory, but a trope wherein one thing is understood from another.*" (*On the Trinity*, book XV, ch. 9, p. 15). An allegorist hunts for "the hidden meaning" of Scripture behind the actual words.

- Typology, however, is not an interpretation of the words but of the events. The concept of "types" reaches into the Testaments to detect events that correspond and points out the message of the type and its fulfillment.

Typology

Thus, types are historical in nature—particular words are not examined at all—and the types depend upon correlation or correspondence. Not all Old Testament occurrences can be said to be types, for not all have parallels in the New. However, in the New Testament writings themselves we are given certain Old Testament incidents which are "types" of the key events in the New. Their parallel was set by God, for they were sign posts along the way, steps in the one great program: the redemption of our race.

Consequently, we see typology in the writings of St. Paul:

> which things are symbolic (Gr. *allēgoreō*, literally "to speak allegorically"). For these are the two covenants: the one from Mount Sinai which gives birth to bondage, which is Hagar; for this Hagar is Mount Sinai in Arabia, and corresponds to Jerusalem which now is, and is in bondage with her children; but the Jerusalem above is free, which is the mother of us all. For it is written: 'Rejoice, O barren, you who do not bear! Break forth and shout, you who do not travail! for the desolate has many more children than she who has a husband.' Now we, brethren, as Isaac was, are children of promise. But, as he who was born according to the flesh then persecuted him who was born according to the Spirit, even so it is now. Nevertheless what does the Scripture say? 'Cast out the bondwoman and her son, for the son of the bondwoman shall not be heir with the son of the freewoman.' So then, brethren, we are not children of the bondwoman but of the free. Stand fast therefore in the liberty by which Christ has made us free, and do not be entangled again with a yoke of bondage" (Gal. 4:24—5:1).

As indicated, St. Paul did indeed call this an "allegory." Of this usage by St. Paul, St. John Chrysostom writes: "Contrary to usage he calls a type an allegory. His meaning, however, is as follows: this history not only declares that which appears on the face of it but tells of something to happen later. Therefore, it is called an allegory. And what is foretold? No less than all the things now present" (Commentary on Gal. ch. IV). Chrysostom took the incident as a "type," however, and after explaining it a bit, writes: "Thus the type of the Jerusalem below was Hagar, as is plain from the mountain being so called—but that which is above is the Church. Nevertheless he is not content with these types, but adds the testimony of Isaiah to what he has spoken.

Having said that Jerusalem which is above 'is our mother,' and having given that name to the Church, he cites the words of the Prophet in his favor."

Actually, this is not at all the only use of "types" by St. Paul. In his letter to the Romans he writes: "Nevertheless death reigned from Adam to Moses, even over those who had not sinned according to the likeness of the transgression of Adam, who is a *type* of Him who was to come" (Rom. 5:14). And we recognize, in a passage in which foreshadowings of the Eucharist are also connected with Israel in the wilderness (1 Cor. 10:1–6), the use of typology in his seeing baptism in the crossing of the Red Sea by Israel. Our Savior Himself pointed to Jonah as a symbol—a type—of His Resurrection (Matt. 12:39–41). Also, the writer of the Letter to the Hebrews points to Melchizedek as a foreshadowing of Christ (ch. 7).

The Church's position concerning the underlying unity of the two testaments led her, from the very beginning, to reject those teachers who would not accept it. Prominent in the early centuries were such heretics as Marcion, who saw the Old Testament as having been superseded and done away. He (along others who held similar positions) was anathematized by the Church. Orthodox writers and theologians, from the very beginning, continued to exegete the Old Testament in typological terms.

For the fact is that behind all of God's entering into human affairs there is just one aim, and it is fully revealed in Christ. It is He to whom the Old Testament points, not only in the sense that we can say that the prophets spoke of Him but in everything. All of sacred history both points and leads, in one way or another, to Him for it is truly focused upon Him. Consequently, the Old Testament cannot be interpreted properly except in the light of the revelation of Jesus Christ, the Incarnate Son of God. In His Incarnation its mysteries are brought to light, disclosed and opened for all who will to see.

In the illumination from His Incarnation, the writings of the prophets become clear, revealing the One who was to come. Thus, the prophecies, pointing forward, can only be fully interpreted after the fact with the Incarnation (their fulfillment) pointing back to them. That does not mean, however, that the Church is assigning a new meaning to the prophetic texts, for the meaning was always there, even though it could not be discerned. For when the Church saw Moses, as the giver of the Law foreshadowing Christ or recognized the Suffering Servant in Isaiah's prophecy (see Is. 42) as a prefiguring of Christ crucified, she was not simply making an application of an Old Testament vision to a New Testament event. What she saw was the meaning of the Old Testament passage, a meaning which could only have been discerned after the coming of Christ. Isaiah's vision of the Servant of the Lord is now seen as a historical fact, for Christ has come and He has fulfilled the vision.

There are, of course, other ways in which allegorical interpretation differs from typology. For one thing, in an allegory the images drawn from the words are supposed to be reflections of a preexisting prototype as per the idealism of Plato, who viewed the whole visible world as reflecting invisible realities. In typology, on the other hand, the view is toward the future. Types prefigure, anticipate, something which is to come, as the crossing of the Red Sea and the eating of manna in the wilderness prefigured baptism and the eucharist. Thus, once more we see that typology, rather than being primarily a philological method of interpretation (as is allegorical interpretation), is primarily an historical method.

This is far more important than might be seen on the surface. For typology recognizes from the outset that history is *real*—and that the history presented in the Scriptures in particular is real. Further, it recognizes *that history lies in the hands of God Who orders and directs it*. Typology fits especially well with the essential concept of God's covenant with His people. For the covenant joins past, present, and future in the unity of God's eternal purpose which is fulfilled in Christ. Consequently, the types seen in the Scriptures by the Church are Christological, and the Church herself is seen in this typology as well, for the Church is the body and the bride of Christ.

This is not to imply that the typology used by writers and teachers in the Church has always perfectly represented these truths. We know that even anciently there was some slippage from typology into allegory and that allegory especially found its way into homilies and devotional teachings. But in the catechetical teachings—which were, of course, closely tied to the sacraments of baptism and the eucharist—a clearer typology was maintained. A historically oriented typological methodology was ingrained in the tradition of the Church, and deviations from balance, particularly in the direction of allegory, were due primarily to the predilections of individual scholars. The Church, in her teaching and worship, was truly devoted to the historicity of the faith. To know so, we have only to read the dogmatic teachings of the Church—the creeds, the writings of the Fathers—and the hymns and prayers of the services. She taught her doctrine to her people and constantly read the Holy Scriptures in the prayer and worship services, always reminding her members of how their faith and hope was rooted in the history revealed in the Scriptures.

Old Testament Foundations

The foundation for all that the Church was to be and is may be found in the Old Testament. When Christ came, there already was, in a certain respect, a Church, Israel, for God did not treat Israel like a nation so much as like a church. The terms used to describe or designate other peoples or nations distinguished them from that nation which was God's people. Why did He give her the Law? Certainly not as just another nation. That Law covered all aspects of her life: the government of her day-to-day and broader activities; her relationships with other peoples; her moral behavior; and her whole system of worship and relationship with God.

Why was this so? Because these were not just *any* people, this was the Israel of God, His own people. In the first place, the departmentalization of our existence into those things which are "spiritual" activities and those which are not is rather ridiculous. For His people, all was under His government. They were a community of God, united by Him, following His Law and the true faith, carrying out all those activities He had designated for them. They even had a hierarchy of priests. All the essentials of the Church were there.

Nevertheless, old Israel was not destined to last forever: the old dispensation has been fulfilled in the new; the Old Covenant has been transformed to the New; and ancient Israel has been rejected because of her absolute unbelief.

Israel rejected her Messiah, and thus passed over the day God had appointed for her transformation. Ultimately, we must simply declare that the only true inheritor of the Old Covenant is the Church of Jesus Christ, Incarnate God. She is, in very fact, the new Israel—"the Israel of God" (Gal. 6:16), a truth implicit in the argument of St. Paul in chapters 8, 9, and 10 of his letter to the church in Rome, as well as elsewhere in the New Testament. In the middle of the second century, Justin Martyr clearly expressed in his *Dialogue with Trypho* the Church's recognition of her role in this respect. We should also note that prior works, of lesser note and extent, had also assumed that concept of the Church as "the new Israel." In the *Letter of Barnabas*, for example, was written of Christ that:

> He submitted so that he might fulfill the promise to the Fathers and, while he was preparing the new people for himself and while he was still on earth, to prove that after he has brought about the resurrection he will judge.

These are but a few of such references to the Church. Clearly, she knew she was the successor to Israel as the people of God. Consequently, the Church was (and is) also seen as the inheritor of the Old Testament, which is to be interpreted as a book of and on the Church. Beginning with the New Testament and Christ Himself, that is exactly how the Old Testament was and has been treated.

Not THE LAW

Since the law has been fulfilled in Christ, the Church learned early that she was not to lay its requirements on those who came to her to be in Christ (see Acts 15). This part, at least, of the Old Testament was no longer to be followed. In Christ, through the Holy Spirit, she learned a new way to use that which had been passed on. For the Old Testament could not be applied as the Jews had employed it; everything must be seen in the light of Christ, His work, and His purpose. The new commandment, that of love, superseded the Ten Commandments, which demanded less.

Most significantly, the Church was no longer limited to one tribe or nation of people. These boundaries were erased, "For there is no distinction between Jew and Greek, for the same Lord over all is rich to all who call upon Him" (Rom. 10:12). No longer does any of the Old Testament apply to a single nation, nor may it be interpreted in any way except as it applies to the whole Church. To put it as did St. Cyril of Jerusalem, who called Israel "the first Church":

> After the rejection of the first Church in Judea, the Churches of Christ are multiplied throughout the whole world, and of them it is said in the Psalms, "Sing to the Lord a new song of praise in the assembly of the faithful" (Ps. 149:1). In keeping with this the Prophet also said to the Jews: "I have no pleasure in you, says the Lord of hosts," and he immediately adds: "For from the rising of the sun, even to its setting, my name is great among the nations" (Mal. 1:10, 11). It is of this holy Catholic Church that Paul writes to Timothy: "[I write] so that you may know how you ought to conduct yourself in the house of God, which is the church of the living God, the pillar and ground of the truth" (1 Tim. 3:15) ("Catechesis XVIII," *The Works of Saint Cyril of Jerusalem*, Vol. 2, trans. by Leo P. McCauley and Anthony A. Stephenson, Fathers of the Church series, Vol. 64, Catholic University of America, 1970, pp. 133, 134).

We can learn so very much from the Old Testament about so many things: the vagaries of the human heart, the fickleness of God's own people, social justice, history, the patience of God, etc. All this can be useful for many purposes, but it is not really proper to use it to construct an economic, social or political ideal, or utopia. For the Scriptures were not written to give us a textbook on such issues or any other for that matter. Ultimately, the Scriptures lead us to just one thing: Christ and His body, the Church.

It is not that there are not sociological, historical and political lessons to be learned from the Bible, *but*, that is not its purpose, and we cannot say we have found "scriptural support" for our theories about such matters. The Bible is for and of Christ and His Church and that is where it leads. What we legitimately take from the Old Testament is that which applies to the Church—that which is permanent, as opposed to that which was specifically for the Old Covenant. Even in the New Testament we must distinguish between those elements which are historical and those which are prophetic.

A Chosen Generation . . . A Holy Nation

Let us repeat it a third time: the whole of the Scriptures are centered on and are for Christ and His Church. It is neither about nations, governments or societies, nor is about those incidental themes which appear—the earth and its history, the sky and the heavens, or any other thing. Old Israel was a "type" of the new Israel—the Church—and that which was written of it was not about America or present-day Israel or any other nation, past, present or future. There is, after Christ, one new nation, or as St. Peter put it, a holy nation:

> But you are a chosen generation, a royal priesthood, a holy nation, His own special people, that you may proclaim the praises of Him who called you out of darkness into His marvelous light; who once were not a people but are now the people of God, who had not obtained mercy but now have obtained mercy (1 Pet. 2:9, 10).

Thus, the Church, made up of all peoples, nations and tongues, is the *one and only Christian nation*, "the people of God," and we cannot give that designation to any other nation, tribe, or people. We cannot rightly speak of the United States as "the people of God," or of "Holy Russia," but only of the "royal priesthood, a holy nation, His own special people"—the Church.

Though the Canon of Scripture is closed, the history of the "holy nation" still goes on, and with it the history of nations and peoples, among whom are mingled the people of God. We look forward to the coming of Christ, the fulfillment of the prophecies concerning His Kingdom. Yet, since His first coming, the future has a different meaning in the eyes of all who will see. For in the Church there is a certain tension between a past, present, and future different from that which existed for Israel of old. Christ, our Lord and God and King, is all of that which is not only to come but is in the past and present as well. His Kingdom was, is, and yet shall be, without break in continuity.

These facts are essential to our understanding and interpretation of the Scriptures. No rules of interpretation or hermeneutical principles can be considered exempt from careful examination in the light of these truths of the Kingdom. Note, in particular:

- We must avoid attempting to find direct parallels between the Old and New Testaments. Such parallels do not exist, for the contexts are radically different. Their relationship is on the order of type and antitype, of figure and fulfillment. The holy Fathers, as they read the Old Testament, were constantly aware of the way in which the Word of God continuously and in different ways revealed Himself throughout the Old Testament record. Nevertheless, these revelations—these *theophanies*—were never on the same plane as the Incarnation of the Word. That critical event is of a different character entirely. A "type" is a prefiguring, but does not reveal the truth in fullness. In the Old Testament there is the type, in the New the truth itself. Consequently, in the New Testament there is more than a prefiguring of the Kingdom, for in Christ we see the actuality.

- Yet, the final event, the *eschaton*, has not yet occurred. Sacred history continues. Christ, who is the fulfillment, has already entered the stream of history, but it is not yet over. The Kingdom of God has been revealed, but its fulfillment has not yet come. The Word Incarnate is here, in His Church, and He is the center of our lives. The Canon of Scripture is complete because the Word of God has become Incarnate. Yet it retains its authority, both as a record of the work of God and as prophecy of that which is even yet to come.

Consequently, when we say that the history of redemption continues, there is a context for that statement: since His Incarnation, the history is of Him and His body, His Church to which He has sent another Helper (John 14:16), who is with us. We cannot offer a completed story of the Church and her people, for her journey continues. With us also we keep the Holy Scriptures, a record of God's continual, expected and unexpected, revelation to His people.

HARMONY OF THE GOSPELS

Date	Event	Location	Matthew	Mark	Luke	John	Related References
	Luke's Introduction				1:1–4		Acts 1:1
	Pre-fleshly state of Christ					1:1–18	Heb. 1:1–14
	Genealogy of Jesus Christ		1:1–17		3:23–38		Ruth 4:18–22 1 Chr. 1:1–4
	BIRTH, INFANCY, AND ADOLESCENCE OF JESUS AND JOHN THE BAPTIST IN 17 EVENTS						
7 B.C.	(1) Announcement of Birth of John	Jerusalem (Temple)			1:5–25		Num. 6:3
7 or 6 B.C.	(2) Announcement of Birth of Jesus to the Virgin	Nazareth			1:26–38		Is. 7:14
c. 5 B.C.	(3) Song of Elizabeth to Mary	Hill Country of Judea			1:39–45		
	(4) Mary's Song of Praise				1:46–56		Ps. 103:17
5 B.C.	(5) Birth, Infancy, and Purpose for Future of John the Baptist	Judea			1:57–80		Mal. 3:1
	(6) Announcement of Jesus' Birth to Joseph	Nazareth	1:18–25				Is. 9:6, 7
5–4 B.C.	(7) Birth of Jesus Christ	Bethlehem	1:24, 25		2:1–7		Is. 7:14
	(8) Proclamation by the Angels	Near Bethlehem			2:8–14		1 Tim. 3:16
	(9) The Visit of Homage by Shepherds	Bethlehem			2:15–20		
	(10) Jesus' Circumcision	Bethlehem			2:21		Lev. 12:3
4 B.C.	(11) First Temple Visit with Acknowledgments by Simeon and Anna	Jerusalem			2:22–38		Ex. 13:2 Lev. 12
	(12) Visit of the Wise Men	Jerusalem & Bethlehem	2:1–12				Num. 24:17
	(13) Flight into Egypt and Massacre of Innocents	Bethlehem, Jerusalem & Egypt	2:13–18				Jer. 31:15
	(14) From Egypt to Nazareth with Jesus		2:19–23		2:39		
Afterward	(15) Childhood of Jesus	Nazareth			2:40, 51		
A.D. 7–8	(16) Jesus, 12 Years Old, Visits the Temple	Jerusalem			2:41–50		Deut. 16:1–8
Afterward	(17) 18-Year Account of Jesus' Adolescence and Adulthood	Nazareth			2:51, 52		1 Sam. 2:26
	TRUTHS ABOUT JOHN THE BAPTIST						
c. A.D. 25–27	John's Ministry Begins	Judean Wilderness	3:1	1:1–4	3:1, 2	1:19–28	Mal. 3:1
	Man and Message		3:2–12	1:2–8	3:3–14		Is. 40:3
	His Picture of Jesus		3:11, 12	1:7, 8	3:15–18	1:26, 27	Acts 2:38
	His Courage		14:4–12		3:19, 20		
	BEGINNING OF JESUS' MINISTRY IN 12 EVENTS						
c. A.D. 27	(1) Jesus Baptized	Jordan River	3:13–17	1:9–11	3:21–23	1:29–34	Ps. 2:7
	(2) Jesus Tempted	Wilderness	4:1–11	1:12, 13	4:1–13		Ps. 91:11
	(3) Calls First Disciples	Beyond Jordan				1:35–51	
	(4) The First Miracle	Cana in Galilee				2:1–11	
	(5) First Stay in Capernaum	(Capernaum is "His" city)				2:12	
A.D. 27	(6) First Cleansing of the Temple	Jerusalem				2:13–22	Ps. 69:9
	(7) Received at Jerusalem	Judea				2:23–25	
	(8) Teaches Nicodemus about Second Birth	Judea				3:1–21	Num. 21:8, 9
	(9) Co-Ministry with John	Judea				3:22–30	

Date	Event	Location	Matthew	Mark	Luke	John	Related References
A.D. 27	(10) Leaves for Galilee	Judea	4:12	1:14	4:14	4:1–4	
	(11) Samaritan Woman at Jacob's Well	Samaria				4:5–42	Josh. 24:32
	(12) Returns to Galilee			1:15	4:15	4:43–45	
A.D. 27–29	**THE GALILEAN MINISTRY OF JESUS IN 55 EVENTS**						
A.D. 27	(1) Healing of the Nobleman's Son	Cana				4:46–54	
	(2) Rejected at Nazareth	Nazareth			4:16–30		Is. 61:1, 2
	(3) Moved to Capernaum	Capernaum	4:13–17				Is. 9:1, 2
	(4) Four Become Fishers of Men	Sea of Galilee	4:18–22	1:16–20	5:1–11		Ps. 33:9
	(5) Demoniac Healed on the Sabbath Day	Capernaum		1:21–28	4:31–37		
	(6) Peter's Mother-in-Law Cured, Plus Others	Capernaum	8:14–17	1:29–34	4:38–41		Is. 53:4
c. A.D. 27	(7) First Preaching Tour of Galilee	Galilee	4:23–25	1:35–39	4:42–44		
	(8) Leper Healed and Response Recorded	Galilee	8:1–4	1:40–45	5:12–16		Lev. 13:49
	(9) Paralytic Healed	Capernaum	9:1–8	2:1–12	5:17–26		Rom. 3:23
	(10) Matthew's Call and Reception Held	Capernaum	9:9–13	2:13–17	5:27–32		Hos. 6:6
	(11) Disciples Defended via a Parable	Capernaum	9:14–17	2:18–22	5:33–39		
A.D. 28	(12) Goes to Jerusalem for Second Passover; Heals Lame Man	Jerusalem				5:1–47	Ex. 20:10
	(13) Plucked Grain Precipitates Sabbath Controversy	En Route to Galilee	12:1–8	2:23–28	6:1–5		Deut. 5:14
	(14) Withered Hand Healed Causes Another Sabbath Controversy	Galilee	12:9–14	3:1–6	6:6–11		
	(15) Multitudes Healed	Sea of Galilee	12:15–21	3:7–12	6:17–19		
	(16) Twelve Apostles Selected After a Night of Prayer	Near Capernaum		3:13–19	6:12–16		
	(17) Sermon on the Mt.	Near Capernaum	5:1—7:29		6:20–49		
	(18) Centurion's Servant Healed	Capernaum	8:5–13		7:1–10		Is. 49:12, 13
	(19) Raises Widow's Son from Dead	Nain			7:11–17		Job 19:25
	(20) Jesus Allays John's Doubts	Galilee	11:2–19		7:18–35		Mal. 3:1
	(21) Woes Upon the Privileged		11:20–30				Gen. 19:24
	(22) A Sinful Woman Anoints Jesus	Simon's House, Capernaum			7:36–50		
	(23) Another Tour of Galilee	Galilee			8:1–3		
	(24) Jesus Accused of Blasphemy	Capernaum	12:22–37	3:20–30	11:14–23		
	(25) Jesus' Answer to a Demand for a Sign	Capernaum	12:38–45		11:24–26, 29–36		
	(26) Mother, Brothers Seek Audience	Capernaum	12:46–50	3:31–35	8:19–21		
	(27) Famous Parables of Sower, Seed, Tares, Mustard Seed, Leaven, Treasure, Pearl, Dragnet, Lamp Told	By Sea of Galilee	13:1–52	4:1–34	8:4–18		Joel 3:13
	(28) Sea Made Serene	Sea of Galilee	8:23–27	4:35–41	8:22–25		
	(29) Gadarene Demoniac Healed	E. Shore of Galilee	8:28–34	5:1–20	8:26–39		
	(30) Jairus' Daughter Raised and Woman with Hemorrhage Healed		9:18–26	5:21–43	8:40–56		
	(31) Two Blind Men's Sight Restored		9:27–31				

Date	Event	Location	Matthew	Mark	Luke	John	Related References
A.D. 28	(32) Mute Demoniac Healed		9:32–34				
	(33) Nazareth's Second Rejection of Christ	Nazareth	13:53–58	6:1–6			
	(34) Twelve Sent Out		9:35—11:1	6:6–13	9:1–6		1 Cor. 9:14
	(35) Fearful Herod Beheads John	Galilee	14:1–12	6:14–29	9:7–9		
Spring A.D. 29	(36) Return of 12, Jesus Withdraws, 5000 Fed	Near Bethsaida	14:13–21	6:30–44	9:10–17	6:1–14	
	(37) Walks on the Water	Sea of Galilee	14:22–33	6:45–52		6:15–21	
	(38) Sick of Gennesaret Healed	Gennesaret	14:34–36	6:53–56			
	(39) Peak of Popularity Passes in Galilee	Capernaum				6:22–71 7:1	Is. 54:13
A.D. 29	(40) Traditions Attacked		15:1–20	7:1–23			Ex. 21:17
	(41) Aborted Retirement in Phoenicia: Syro-Phoenician Healed	Phoenicia	15:21–28	7:24–30			
	(42) Afflicted Healed	Decapolis	15:29–31	7:31–37			
	(43) 4000 Fed	Decapolis	15:32–39	8:1–9			
	(44) Pharisees Increase Attack	Magdala	16:1–4	8:10–13			
	(45) Disciples' Carelessness Condemned; Blind Man Healed		16:5–12	8:14–26			Jer. 5:21
	(46) Peter Confesses Jesus Is the Christ	Near Caesarea Philippi	16:13–20	8:27–30	9:18–21		
	(47) Jesus Foretells His Death	Caesarea Philippi	16:21–26	8:31–37	9:22–25		
	(48) Kingdom Promised		16:27, 28	9:1	9:26, 27		Prov. 24:12
	(49) The Transfiguration	Mountain Unnamed	17:1–13	9:2–13	9:28–36		Is. 42:1
	(50) Epileptic Healed	Mt. of Transfiguration	17:14–21	9:14–29	9:37–42		
	(51) Again Tells of Death, Resurrection	Galilee	17:22, 23	9:30–32	9:43–45		
	(52) Taxes Paid	Capernaum	17:24–27				Ex. 30:11–15
	(53) Disciples Contend About Greatness; Jesus Defines; also Patience, Loyalty, Forgiveness	Capernaum	18:1–35	9:33–50	9:46–62		
	(54) Jesus Rejects Brothers' Advice	Galilee				7:2–9	
c. Sept. A.D. 29	(55) Galilee Departure and Samaritan Rejection		19:1		9:51–56	7:10	
A.D. 29–30	**LAST JUDEAN AND PEREAN MINISTRY OF JESUS IN 42 EVENTS**						
Oct. A.D. 29	(1) Feast of Tabernacles	Jerusalem				7:2, 11–52	
	(2) Forgiveness of Adulteress	Jerusalem				7:53—8:11	Lev. 20:10
A.D. 29	(3) Christ—the Light of the World	Jerusalem				8:12–20	
	(4) Pharisees Can't Meet the Prophecy Thus Try to Destroy the Prophet	Jerusalem—Temple				8:12–59	Is. 6:9
	(5) Man Born Blind Healed; Following Consequences	Jerusalem				9:1–41	
	(6) Parable of the Good Shepherd	Jerusalem				10:1–21	
	(7) The Service of the Seventy	Probably Judea			10:1–24		
	(8) Lawyer Hears the Story of the Good Samaritan	Judea (?)			10:25–37		
	(9) The Hospitality of Martha and Mary	Bethany			10:38–42		
	(10) Another Lesson on Prayer	Judea (?)			11:1–13		

Date	Event	Location	Matthew	Mark	Luke	John	Related References
A.D. 29	(11) Accused of Connection with Beelzebub				11:14–36		
	(12) Judgment Against Lawyers and Pharisees				11:37–54		Mic. 6:8
	(13) Jesus Deals with Hypocrisy, Covetousness, Worry, and Alertness				12:1–59		Mic. 7:6
	(14) Repent or Perish				13:1–5		
	(15) Barren Fig Tree				13:6–9		
	(16) Crippled Woman Healed on Sabbath				13:10–17		Deut. 5:12–15
	(17) Parables of Mustard Seed and Leaven	Probably Perea			13:18–21		
Winter A.D. 29	(18) Feast of Dedication	Jerusalem				10:22–39	Ps. 82:6
	(19) Withdrawal Beyond Jordan					10:40–42	
	(20) Begins Teaching Return to Jerusalem with Special Words About Herod	Perea			13:22–35		Ps. 6:8
	(21) Meal with a Pharisee Ruler Occasions Healing Man with Dropsy; Parables of Ox, Best Places, and Great Supper				14:1–24		
	(22) Demands of Discipleship	Perea			14:25–35		
	(23) Parables of Lost Sheep, Coin, Son				15:1–32		1 Pet. 2:25
	(24) Parables of Unjust Steward, Rich Man and Lazarus				16:1–31		
	(25) Lessons on Service, Faith, Influence				17:1–10		
	(26) Resurrection of Lazarus	Perea to Bethany				11:1–44	
	(27) Reaction to It: Withdrawal of Jesus					11:45–54	
A.D. 30	(28) Begins Last Journey to Jerusalem via Samaria & Galilee	Samaria, Galilee			17:11		
	(29) Heals Ten Lepers				17:12–19		Lev. 13:45, 46
	(30) Lessons on the Coming Kingdom				17:20–37		Gen. 6—7
	(31) Parables: Persistent Widow, Pharisee and Tax Collector				18:1–14		
	(32) Doctrine on Divorce		19:1–12	10:1–12			Deut. 24:1–4 Gen. 2:23–25
	(33) Jesus Blesses Children: Objections	Perea	19:13–15	10:13–16	18:15–17		Ps. 131:2
	(34) Rich Young Ruler	Perea	19:16–30	10:17–31	18:18–30		Ex. 20:1–17
	(35) Laborers of the 11th Hour		20:1–16				
	(36) Foretells Death and Resurrection	Near Jordan	20:17–19	10:32–34	18:31–34		Ps. 22
	(37) Ambition of James and John		20:20–28	10:35–45			
	(38) Blind Bartimaeus Healed	Jericho		10:46–52	18:35–43		
	(39) Interview with Zacchaeus	Jericho			19:1–10		
	(40) Parable: the Minas	Jericho			19:11–27		
	(41) Returns to Home of Mary and Martha	Bethany				11:55—12:1	
	(42) Plot to Kill Lazarus	Bethany				12:9–11	
Spring A.D. 30	JESUS' FINAL WEEK OF WORK AT JERUSALEM IN 41 EVENTS						
Sunday	(1) Triumphal Entry	Bethany, Jerusalem, Bethany	21:1–9	11:1–11	19:28–44	12:12–19	Zech. 9:9

Date	Event	Location	Matthew	Mark	Luke	John	Related References
Monday	(2) Fig Tree Cursed and Temple Cleansed	Bethany to Jerusalem	21:10–19	11:12–18	19:45–48		Jer. 7:11
	(3) The Attraction of Sacrifice	Jerusalem				12:20–50	Is. 6:10
Tuesday	(4) Withered Fig Tree Testifies	Bethany to Jerusalem	21:20–22	11:19–26			
	(5) Sanhedrin Challenges Jesus. Answered by Parables: Two Sons, Wicked Vinedressers and Marriage Feast	Jerusalem	21:23—22:14	11:27—12:12	20:1–19		Is. 5:1, 2
	(6) Tribute to Caesar	Jerusalem	22:15–22	12:13–17	20:20–26		
	(7) Sadducees Question the Resurrection	Jerusalem	22:23–33	12:18–27	20:27–40		Ex. 3:6
	(8) Pharisees Question Commandments	Jerusalem	22:34–40	12:28–34			
	(9) Jesus and David	Jerusalem	22:41–46	12:35–37	20:41–44		Ps. 110:1
	(10) Jesus' Last Sermon	Jerusalem	23:1–39	12:38–40	20:45–47		
	(11) Widow's Mite	Jerusalem		12:41–44	21:1–4		Lev. 27:30
	(12) Jesus Tells of the Future	Mt. Olives	24:1–51	13:1–37	21:5–36		Dan. 12:1
	(13) Parables: Ten Virgins, Talents. The Day of Judgment	Mt. Olives	25:1–46				Zech. 14:5
	(14) Jesus Tells Date of Crucifixion		26:1–5	14:1, 2	22:1, 2		
	(15) Anointing by Mary at Simon's Feast	Bethany	26:6–13	14:3–9		12:2–8	
	(16) Judas Contracts the Betrayal		26:14–16	14:10, 11	22:3–6		Zech. 11:12
Thursday	(17) Preparation for the Passover	Jerusalem	26:17–19	14:12–16	22:7–13		Ex. 12:14–28
Thursday P.M.	(18) Passover Eaten, Jealousy Rebuked	Jerusalem	26:20	14:17	22:14–16, 24–30		
	(19) Feet Washed	Upper Room				13:1–20	
	(20) Judas Revealed, Defects	Upper Room	26:21–25	14:18–21	22:21–23	13:21–30	Ps. 41:9
	(21) Jesus Warns About Further Desertion; Cries of Loyalty	Upper Room	26:31–35	14:27–31	22:31–38	13:31–38	Zech. 13:7
	(22) Institution of the Lord's Supper	Upper Room	26:26–29	14:22–25	22:17–20		1 Cor. 11:23–34
	(23) Last Speech to the Apostles and Intercessory Prayer	Jerusalem				14:1—17:26	Ps. 35:19
Thursday-Friday	(24) The Grief of Gethsemane	Mt. Olives	26:30, 36–46	14:26, 32–42	22:39–46	18:1	Ps. 42:6
Friday	(25) Betrayal, Arrest, Desertion	Gethsemane	26:47–56	14:43–52	22:47–53	18:2–12	
	(26) First Examined by Annas	Jerusalem				18:12–14, 19–23	
	(27) Trial by Caiaphas and Council; Following Indignities	Jerusalem	26:57, 59–68	14:53, 55–65	22:54, 63–65	18:24	Lev. 24:16
	(28) Peter's Triple Denial	Jerusalem	26:58, 69–75	14:54, 66–72	22:54–62	18:15–18, 25–27	
	(29) Condemnation by the Council	Jerusalem	27:1	15:1	22:66–71		Ps. 110:1
	(30) Suicide of Judas	Jerusalem	27:3–10				Acts 1:18, 19
	(31) First Appearance Before Pilate	Jerusalem	27:2, 11–14	15:1–5	23:1–7	18:28–38	
	(32) Jesus Before Herod	Jerusalem			23:6–12		
	(33) Second Appearance Before Pilate	Jerusalem	27:15–26	15:6–15	23:13–25	18:39—19:16	Deut. 21:6–9
	(34) Mockery by Roman Soldiers	Jerusalem	27:27–30	15:16–19			
	(35) Led to Golgotha	Jerusalem	27:31–34	15:20–23	23:26–33	19:16, 17	Ps. 69:21
	(36) 6 Events of First 3 Hours on Cross	Calvary	27:35–44	15:24–32	23:33–43	19:18–27	Ps. 22:18
	(37) Last 3 Hours on Cross	Calvary	27:45–50	15:33–37	23:44–46	19:28–30	Ps. 22:1
	(38) Events Attending Jesus' Death		27:51–56	15:38–41	23:45, 47–49		
	(39) Burial of Jesus	Jerusalem	27:57–60	15:42–46	23:50–54	19:31–37	Ex. 12:46
Friday-Saturday	(40) Tomb Sealed	Jerusalem	27:61–66		23:55, 56		Ex. 20:8–11
	(41) Women Watch	Jerusalem		15:47			

Date	Event	Location	Matthew	Mark	Luke	John	Related References
A.D. 30	**THE RESURRECTION THROUGH THE ASCENSION IN 12 EVENTS**						
Dawn of First Day (Sunday, "Lord's Day")	(1) Women Visit the Tomb	Near Jerusalem	28:1–10	16:1–8	24:1–11		
	(2) Peter and John See the Empty Tomb				24:12	20:1–10	
	(3) Jesus' Appearance to Mary Magdalene	Jerusalem		16:9–11		20:11–18	
	(4) Jesus' Appearance to the Other Women	Jerusalem	28:9, 10				
	(5) Guards' Report of the Resurrection		28:11–15				
Sunday Afternoon	(6) Jesus' Appearance to Two Disciples on Way to Emmaus			16:12, 13	24:13–35		1 Cor. 15:5
Late Sunday	(7) Jesus' Appearance to Ten Disciples Without Thomas	Jerusalem		16:14	24:36–43	20:19–25	
One Week Later	(8) Appearance to Disciples with Thomas	Jerusalem				20:26–31	
During 40 Days until Ascension	(9) Jesus' Appearance to Seven Disciples by Sea of Galilee	Galilee				21:1–25	
	(10) Appearance to 500	Mt. in Galilee					1 Cor. 15:6
	(11) Great Commission		28:16–20	16:15–18	24:44–49		
	(12) The Ascension	Mt. Olivet		16:19, 20	24:50–53		Acts 1:4–11

MONIES, WEIGHTS, AND MEASURES

The Hebrews probably first used coins in the Persian period (500–350 B.C.). However, minting began around 700 B.C. in other nations. Prior to this, precious metals were weighed, not counted as money.

Some units appear as both measures of money and measures of weights. This comes from naming the coins after their weight. For example, the shekel was a weight long before it became the name of a coin.

It is helpful to relate biblical monies to current values. But we cannot make exact equivalents. The fluctuating value of money's purchasing power is difficult to determine in our own day. It is even harder to evaluate currencies used two- to three-thousand years ago.

Therefore, it is best to choose a value meaningful over time, such as a common laborer's daily wage. One day's wage corresponds to the ancient Jewish system (a silver shekel is four days' wages) as well as to the Greek and Roman systems (the drachma and the denarius were each coins representing a day's wage).

The monies chart below takes a current day's wage as thirty-two dollars. Though there are differences of economies and standards of living, this measure will help us apply meaningful values to the monetary units in the chart and in the biblical text.

Monies

Unit	*Monetary Value*	*Equivalents*	*Translations*
Jewish Weights			
Talent	gold—$5,760,000[1] silver—$384,000	3,000 shekels; 6,000 bekas	talent
Shekel	gold—$1,920 silver—$128	4 days' wages; 2 bekas; 20 gerahs	shekel
Beka	gold—$960 silver—$64	½ shekel; 10 gerahs	bekah
Gerah	gold—$96 silver—$6.40	1/20 shekel	gerah
Persian Coins			
Daric	gold—$1,280[2] silver—$64	2 days' wages; ½ Jewish silver shekel	drachma
Greek Coins			
Tetradrachma (Stater)	$128	4 drachmas	piece of money
Didrachma	$64	2 drachmas	tribute
Drachma	$32	1 day's wage	piece of silver
Lepton	$.25	½ of a Roman kodrantes	mite
Roman Coins			
Aureus	$800	25 denarii	
Denarius	$32	1 day's wage	denarius
Assarius	$2	1/16 of a denarius	copper coin
Kodrantes	$.50	¼ of an assarius	penny, quadrans

[1]Value of gold is fifteen times the value of silver.
[2]Value of gold is twenty times the value of silver.

Weights

Unit	*Weight*	*Equivalents*	*Translations*
Jewish Weights			
Talent	c. 75 pounds for common talent, c. 150 pounds for royal talent	60 minas; 3,000 shekels	talent
Mina	1.25 pounds	50 shekels	mina
Shekel	c. .4 ounce (11.4 grams) for common shekel c. .8 ounce for royal shekel	2 bekas; 20 gerahs	shekel
Beka	c. .2 ounce (5.7 grams)	½ shekel; 10 gerahs	half a shekel
Gerah	c. .02 ounce (.57 grams)	1/20 shekel	gerah
Roman Weight			
Litra	12 ounces		pound

Measures of Length

Unit	*Length*	*Equivalents*	*Translations*
Day's journey	c. 20 miles		day's journey
Roman mile	4,854 feet	8 stadia	mile
Sabbath day's journey	3,637 feet	6 stadia	Sabbath day's journey
Stadion	606 feet	⅛ Roman mile	furlong
Rod	9 feet (10.5 feet in Ezekiel)	3 paces; 6 cubits	measuring reed, reed
Fathom	6 feet	4 cubits	fathom
Pace	3 feet	⅓ rod; 2 cubits	pace
Cubit	18 inches	½ pace; 2 spans	cubit
Span	9 inches	½ cubit; 3 handbreadths	span
Handbreadth	3 inches	⅓ span; 4 fingers	handbreadth
Finger	.75 inches	¼ handbreadth	finger

Dry Measures

Unit	*Measure*	*Equivalents*	*Translations*
Homer	6.52 bushels	10 ephahs	homer
Kor	6.52 bushels	1 homer; 10 ephahs	kor, measure
Lethech	3.26 bushels	½ kor	half homer
Ephah	.65 bushel, 20.8 quarts	1/10 homer	ephah

Dry Measures—Continued

Unit	*Measure*	*Equivalents*	*Translations*
Modius	7.68 quarts		basket
Seah	7 quarts	⅓ ephah	measure
Omer	2.08 quarts	⅒ ephah; 1⅘ kab	omer
Kab	1.16 quarts	4 logs	kab
Choenix	1 quart		measure
Xestes	1⅙ pints		pot
Log	.58 pint	¼ kab	log

Liquid Measures

Unit	*Measure*	*Equivalents*	*Translations*
Kor	60 gallons	10 baths	kor
Metretes	10.2 gallons		gallons
Bath	6 gallons	6 hins	measure, bath
Hin	1 gallon	2 kabs	hin
Kab	2 quarts	4 logs	kab
Log	1 pint	¼ kab	log

CONCORDANCE

This Concordance is designed to help you locate important occurrences of significant words, phrases, and proper names found in the Bible. Words and phrases are referenced with Scripture quotations, in which the first letter of the word or phrase, italicized, stands for the entire word or phrase. Phrases are cross-referenced under every major word of the phrase except the first. When looking up a word, be sure to check for related forms of the word and for phrases beginning with that word.

Proper names are defined by descriptive phrases and Scripture references. If a name applies to more than one person, place, or group (see ABIJAH, below), the different identities are distinguished by the dash ("———").

AARON
Ancestry and family of, Ex 6:16–20, 23
Helper and prophet to Moses, Ex 4:13–31; 7:1, 2
Appears before Pharaoh, Ex 5:1–4
Performs miracles, Ex 7:9, 10, 19, 20
Supports Moses' hands, Ex 17:10–12
Ascends Mt. Sinai; sees God's glory, Ex 19:24; 24:1, 9, 10
Judges Israel in Moses' absence, Ex 24:14
Chosen by God as priest, Ex 28:1
Consecrated, Ex 29; Lev 8
Duties prescribed, Ex 30:7–10
Tolerates Israel's idolatry, Ex 32
Priestly ministry begins, Lev 9
Sons offer profane fire; Aaron's humble response, Lev 10
Conspires against Moses, Num 12:1–16
Rebelled against by Korah, Num 16
Intercedes to stop plague, Num 16:45–48
Rod buds to confirm his authority, Num 17:1–10
With Moses, fails at Meribah, Num 20:1–13
Dies; son succeeds him as priest, Num 20:23–29
His priesthood compared:
with Melchizedek's, Heb 7:11–19
with Christ's, Heb 9:6–15, 23–28

ABADDON
Angel of the bottomless pit, Rev 9:11

ABASED
I know how to be *a* . . . . Phil 4:12

ABBA
And He said, "*A* . . . . Mark 14:36
by whom we cry out, "*A* . . . Rom 8:15
crying out, "*A* . . . . Gal 4:6

ABED-NEGO
Babylonian name given to Azariah, a Hebrew captive, Dan 1:7
Appointed by Nebuchadnezzar, Dan 2:49
Refuses to serve idols; cast into furnace but delivered, Dan 3:12–30

ABEL
Adam's second son, Gen 4:2
His offering accepted, Gen 4:4
Murdered by Cain, Gen 4:8
His sacrifice offered by faith, Heb 11:4

ABEL BETH MAACHAH
Captured by Tiglath-Pileser, 2 Kin 15:29
Refuge of Sheba; saved from destruction, 2 Sam 20:14–22
Seized by Ben-Hadad, 1 Kin 15:20

ABEL MEHOLAH
A city a few miles east of Jabesh Gilead, Judg 7:22; 1 Kin 4:12
Elisha's native city, 1 Kin 19:16

ABHOR
My soul shall not *a* . . . . Lev 26:11
Therefore I *a* myself . . . . Job 42:6
nations will *a* him . . . . Prov 24:24
a the pride of Jacob . . . . Amos 6:8
A what is evil . . . . Rom 12:9

ABHORRED
a His own inheritance . . . . . . Ps 106:40
he who is *a* by the . . . . Prov 22:14
and their soul also *a* . . . . Zech 11:8

ABHORRENCE
They shall be an *a* . . . . Is 66:24

ABHORRENT
you have made us *a* . . . . Ex 5:21

ABHORS
So that his life *a* . . . . Job 33:20

ABIATHAR
A priest who escapes Saul at Nob, 1 Sam 22:20–23
Becomes high priest under David, 1 Sam 23:6, 9–12
Remains faithful to David, 2 Sam 15:24–29
Informs David about Ahithophel, 2 Sam 15:34–36
Supports Adonijah's usurpation, 1 Kin 1:7, 9, 25
Deposed by Solomon, 1 Kin 2:26, 27, 35

ABIDE
nor *a* in its paths . . . . Job 24:13
LORD, who may *a* . . . . Ps 15:1
He shall *a* before God . . . . Ps 61:7
the Most High shall *a* . . . . Ps 91:1
"If you *a* in My word . . . . John 8:31
And a slave does not *a* . . . . . John 8:35
Helper, that He may *a* . . . . John 14:16
A in Me and I in you . . . . . . John 15:4
If you *a* in Me . . . . John 15:7
a in My love . . . . John 15:9
And now *a* faith . . . . 1 Cor 13:13
does the love of God *a* . . . 1 John 3:17
this we know that we *a* . . . 1 John 4:13

ABIDES
even He who *a* from of old . . Ps 55:19
He who *a* in Me . . . . John 15:5
lives and *a* forever . . . . 1 Pet 1:23
will of God *a* forever . . . . . . 1 John 2:17

ABIDING
not have His word *a* . . . . John 5:38
has eternal life *a* . . . . 1 John 3:15

ABIEZRITES
Relatives of Gideon; rally to his call, Judg 6:11, 24, 34

ABIGAIL
Wise wife of foolish Nabal, 1 Sam 25:3
Appeases David and becomes his wife, 1 Sam 25:14–42
Mother of Chileab, 2 Sam 3:3

ABIHU
Second son of Aaron, Ex 6:23
Offers profane fire and dies, Lev 10:1–7

ABIJAH
Samuel's second son; follows corrupt ways, 1 Sam 8:2, 3
——— Descendant of Aaron; head of an office of priests, 1 Chr 24:3, 10
Zechariah belongs to division of, Luke 1:5
——— Son of Jeroboam I, 1 Kin 14:1–18
——— Another name for King Abijam, 2 Chr 11:20

ABIJAM (or Abijah)
King of Judah, 1 Kin 14:31
Follows the sins of his father, 1 Kin 15:1–7
Defeats Jeroboam and takes cities, 2 Chr 13:13–20

ABILENE
A province or tetrarchy of Syria, Luke 3:1

ABILITY
who had *a* to serve . . . . Dan 1:4
according to his own *a* . . . . Matt 25:15
and beyond their *a* . . . . 2 Cor 8:3
a which God supplies . . . . . . 1 Pet 4:11

ABIMELECH
King of Gerar; takes Sarah in ignorance, Gen 20:1–18
Makes treaty with Abraham, Gen 21:22–34
——— A second king of Gerar; sends Isaac away, Gen 26:1–16
Makes treaty with Isaac, Gen 26:17–33
——— Gideon's son by a concubine, Judg 8:31
Conspires to become king, Judg 9

ABINADAB
A man of Kirjath Jearim in whose house the ark was kept, 1 Sam 7:1, 2
——— The second of Jesse's eight sons, 1 Sam 16:8
Serves in Saul's army, 1 Sam 17:13
——— A son of Saul slain at Mt. Gilboa, 1 Sam 31:1–8
Bones of, buried by men of Jabesh, 1 Chr 10:1–12

ABIRAM
Reubenite who conspired against Moses, Num 16:1–50

ABISHAG
A Shunammite employed as David's nurse, 1 Kin 1:1–4, 15
Witnessed David's choice of Solomon as successor, 1 Kin 1:15–31
Adonijah slain for desiring to marry her, 1 Kin 2:13–25

ABISHAI
David's nephew; joins Joab in blood revenge against Abner, 2 Sam 2:18–24
Loyal to David during Absalom's and Sheba's rebellion, 2 Sam 16:9–12; 20:1–6, 10

Rebuked by David, 2 Sam 16:9–12; 19:21–23
His exploits, 2 Sam 21:16, 17; 23:18; 1 Chr 18:12, 13

ABLE
you are *a* to number ... Gen 15:5
the LORD was not *a* ... Num 14:16
shall give as he is *a* ... Deut 16:17
For who is *a* to judge ... 1 Kin 3:9
should be *a* to offer ... 1 Chr 29:14
who is *a* to build Him ... 2 Chr 2:6
"The LORD is *a* ... 2 Chr 25:9
Who then is *a* to stand ... Job 41:10
gold will not be *a* to ... Ezek 7:19
God whom we serve is *a* ... Dan 3:17
in pride He is *a* to abase ... Dan 4:37
God is *a* to raise up ... Matt 3:9
believe that I am *a* ... Matt 9:28
fear Him who is *a* ... Matt 10:28
Are you *a* to drink the ... Matt 20:22
enter and will not be *a* ... Luke 13:24
was not *a* to finish ... Luke 14:30
be *a* to contradict or ... Luke 21:15
shall be *a* to separate ... Rom 8:39
God is *a* to make him ... Rom 14:4
Now to Him who is *a* ... Rom 16:25
beyond what you are *a* ... 1 Cor 10:13
And God is *a* to make ... 2 Cor 9:8
may be *a* to comprehend ... Eph 3:18
that you may be *a* to ... Eph 6:13
hospitable, *a* to teach ... 1 Tim 3:2
persuaded that He is *a* ... 2 Tim 1:12
learning and never *a* ... 2 Tim 3:7
being tempted, He is *a* ... Heb 2:18
Therefore He is also *a* to ... Heb 7:25
that God was *a* to ... Heb 11:19
a also to bridle the ... James 3:2
to Him who is *a* ... Jude 24
was *a* to open the scroll, ... Rev 5:3
has come, and who is *a* ... Rev 6:17

ABNER
Saul's cousin; commander of his army, 1 Sam 14:50, 51
Rebuked by David, 1 Sam 26:5, 14–16
Supports Ishbosheth; defeated by David's men; kills Asahel, 2 Sam 2:8–32
Makes covenant with David, 2 Sam 3:6–21
Killed by Joab; mourned by David, 2 Sam 3:22–39

ABODE
but left their own *a* ... Jude 6

ABOLISHED
your works may be *a* ... Ezek 6:6
having *a* in His flesh ... Eph 2:15
Christ, who has *a* ... 2 Tim 1:10

ABOMINABLE
not make yourselves *a* ... Lev 11:43
They have done *a* ... Ps 14:1
your grave like an *a* ... Is 14:19
Oh, do not do this *a* ... Jer 44:4
they deny Him, being *a* ... Titus 1:16
and *a* idolatries ... 1 Pet 4:3
unbelieving, *a*, murderers ... Rev 21:8

ABOMINATION
every shepherd is an *a* ... Gen 46:34
If we sacrifice the *a* ... Ex 8:26
You have made me an *a* ... Ps 88:8
yes, seven are an *a* ... Prov 6:16
wickedness is an *a* ... Prov 8:7
Dishonest scales are an *a* ... Prov 11:1
the scoffer is an *a* ... Prov 24:9
even his prayer is an *a* ... Prov 28:9
An unjust man is an *a* ... Prov 29:27
incense is an *a* to Me ... Is 1:13
and place there the *a* ... Dan 11:31
the *a* of desolation ... Dan 12:11
the '*a* of desolation,' ... Matt 24:15
among men is an *a* ... Luke 16:15

ABOMINATIONS
to follow the *a* ... Deut 18:9
delights in their *a* ... Is 66:3
will put away your *a* ... Jer 4:1
your harlotry, your *a* ... Jer 13:27
will see greater *a* ... Ezek 8:6
a which they commit ... Ezek 8:17
you, throw away the *a* ... Ezek 20:7
show her all her *a* ... Ezek 22:2
a golden cup full of *a* ... Rev 17:4
of the *a* of the earth ... Rev 17:5

ABOUND
lawlessness will *a* ... Matt 24:12
the offense might *a* ... Rom 5:20
sin that grace may *a* ... Rom 6:1
thanksgiving to *a* ... 2 Cor 4:15
to make all grace *a* ... 2 Cor 9:8
and I know how to *a* ... Phil 4:12
that you should *a* ... 1 Thess 4:1
things are yours and *a* ... 2 Pet 1:8

ABOUNDED
But where sin *a* ... Rom 5:20

ABOUNDING
and *a* in goodness and ... Ex 34:6
and *a* in mercy ... Ps 103:8
immovable, always *a* ... 1 Cor 15:58
a in it with thanksgiving ... Col 2:7

ABOVE
that is in heaven *a* ... Ex 20:4
"He sent from *a* ... 2 Sam 22:17
A it stood seraphim ... Is 6:2
nor a servant *a* his ... Matt 10:24
He who comes from *a* ... John 3:31
beneath; I am from *a* ... John 8:23
been given you from *a* ... John 19:11
of all, who is *a* all ... Eph 4:6
the name which is *a* ... Phil 2:9
things which are *a* ... Col 3:1
perfect gift is from *a* ... James 1:17

ABRAHAM
Ancestry and family, Gen 11:26–31
Receives God's call; enters Canaan, Gen 12:1–6
Promised Canaan by God; pitches tent near Bethel, Gen 12:7, 8
Deceives Egyptians concerning Sarai, Gen 12:11–20
Separates from Lot; inherits Canaan, Gen 13
Rescues Lot from captivity, Gen 14:11–16
Gives a tithe to Melchizedek; refuses spoil, Gen 14:18–24
Covenant renewed; promised a son, Gen 15
Takes Hagar as concubine; Ishmael born, Gen 16
Name changed from Abram; circumcision commanded, Gen 17
Entertains Lord and angels, Gen 18:1–15
Intercedes for Sodom, Gen 18:16–33
Deceives Abimelech concerning Sarah, Gen 20
Birth of Isaac, Gen 21:1–7
Sends Hagar and Ishmael away, Gen 21:9–14
Offers Isaac in obedience to God, Gen 22:1–19
Finds wife for Isaac, Gen 24
Marries Keturah; fathers other children; dies, Gen 25:1–10
Friend of God, 2 Chr 20:7
Justified by faith, Rom 4:1–12
Father of true believers, Rom 4:11–25
In the line of faith, Heb 11:8–10
Eternal home of, in heaven, Luke 16:19–25
A was circumcised ... Gen 17:26
bore *A* a son in his ... Gen 21:2
A circumcised his son ... Gen 21:4
A was one hundred ... Gen 21:5
God tested *A*, and ... Gen 22:1
A said, "My son, God ... Gen 22:8
A begot Isaac ... Gen 25:19
His covenant with *A* ... Ex 2:24
I swore to give to *A* ... Ex 6:8
which I swore to *A* ... Num 32:11
which He made with *A* ... 1 Chr 16:16
O seed of *A* His servant ... Ps 105:6
LORD, who redeemed *A* ... Is 29:22
descendants of *A* My ... Is 41:8
David, the Son of *A* ... Matt 1:1
to you, before *A* was ... John 8:58
For if *A* was justified ... Rom 4:2
A believed God, and ... Rom 4:3
are of the faith of *A* ... Rom 4:16
of *A* might come upon ... Gal 3:14
Now to *A* and his Seed ... Gal 3:16
that *A* had two sons ... Gal 4:22
also *A* gave a tenth ... Heb 7:2
By faith *A* obeyed when ... Heb 11:8
By faith *A*, when he ... Heb 11:17
A believed God, and ... James 2:23
as Sarah obeyed *A*, ... 1 Pet 3:6

ABRAM
See ABRAHAM

ABRONAH
Israelite encampment, Num 33:34

ABSALOM
Son of David, 2 Sam 3:3
Kills Amnon for raping Tamar; flees from David, 2 Sam 13:20–39
Returns through Joab's intrigue; reconciled to David, 2 Sam 14
Attempts to usurp throne, 2 Sam 15:1—18:8
Caught and killed by Joab, 2 Sam 18:9–18
Mourned by David, 2 Sam 18:19—19:8

ABSENT
For I indeed, as *a* ... 1 Cor 5:3
in the body we are *a* ... 2 Cor 5:6

ABSTAIN
we write to them to *a* ... Acts 15:20
A from every form ... 1 Thess 5:22
and commanding to *a* ... 1 Tim 4:3
a from fleshly lusts ... 1 Pet 2:11

ABUNDANCE
is the sound of *a* ... 1 Kin 18:41
workmen with you in *a* ... 1 Chr 22:15
flourish, and *a* of peace ... Ps 72:7
eyes bulge with *a* ... Ps 73:7
nor he who loves *a* ... Eccl 5:10
delight itself in *a* ... Is 55:2
out of the *a* of the heart ... Matt 12:34
put in out of their *a* ... Mark 12:44
not consist in the *a* ... Luke 12:15
of affliction the *a* ... 2 Cor 8:2
above measure by the *a* ... 2 Cor 12:7
rich through the *a* ... Rev 18:3

ABUNDANT
in judgment and *a* ... Job 37:23
a in mercy to all those ... Ps 86:5
Longsuffering and *a* ... Ps 86:15
Him is *a* redemption ... Ps 130:7
placed it by *a* waters ... Ezek 17:5
lovely and its fruit *a* ... Dan 4:21
slow to anger and *a* ... Jon 4:2
in labors more *a* ... 2 Cor 11:23
may be more *a* in Jesus ... Phil 1:26
Lord was exceedingly *a* ... 1 Tim 1:14
a mercy has begotten ... 1 Pet 1:3

ABUNDANTLY
a satisfied with the ... Ps 36:8
may have it more *a* ... John 10:10
to do exceedingly *a* ... Eph 3:20
to show more *a* to the ... Heb 6:17

It was *a* because of ....Gal 3:19

ADDS
and He *a* no sorrow ......Prov 10:22
no one annuls or *a* to it .....Gal 3:15
If anyone *a* to these ....Rev 22:18

ADMINISTERS
a justice for the ....Deut 10:18

ADMONISH
also to *a* one another .....Rom 15:14
a him as a brother ......2 Thess 3:15

ADMONISHED
further, my son, be *a* ......Eccl 12:12
Angel of the LORD *a* ....Zech 3:6

ADMONISHING
a one another in ....Col 3:16

ADMONITION
were written for our *a* ....1 Cor 10:11
in the training and *a* ....Eph 6:4

ADONI-ZEDEK
An Amorite king of Jerusalem, Josh 10:1–5
Defeated and slain by Joshua, Josh 10:6–27

ADONIJAH
David's fourth son, 2 Sam 3:2, 4
Attempts to usurp throne, 1 Kin 1:5–53
Desires Abishag as wife, 1 Kin 2:13–18
Executed by Solomon, 1 Kin 2:19–25

ADONIRAM (or Adoram)
Official under David, Solomon, and Rehoboam, 2 Sam 20:24; 1 Kin 5:14; 12:18
Stoned by angry Israelites, 1 Kin 12:18
Called Hadoram, 2 Chr 10:18

ADOPTION
received the Spirit of *a* .....Rom 8:15
waiting for the *a*............Rom 8:23
to whom pertain the *a* ......Rom 9:4
we might receive the *a* ....Gal 4:5
a as sons by Jesus ....Eph 1:5

ADORN
a the monuments ....Matt 23:29
also, that the women *a* .....1 Tim 2:9

ADORNED
By His Spirit He *a* ....Job 26:13
You shall again be *a* ....Jer 31:4
temple, how it was *a* ......Luke 21:5
also *a* themselves ....1 Pet 3:5
prepared as a bride *a* ....Rev 21:2

ADRIFT
A among the dead ....Ps 88:5

ADULLAM
A town of Canaan, Gen 38:1, 12, 20; Josh 12:7, 15; 15:20, 35
David seeks refuge in caves of, 1 Sam 23:13–17

ADULTERER
the *a* and the adulteress....Lev 20:10
The eye of the *a* ....Job 24:15

ADULTERERS
the land is full of *a* ....Jer 23:10
nor idolaters, nor *a* ....1 Cor 6:9
a God will judge ....Heb 13:4
A and adulteresses ....James 4:4

ADULTERIES
I have seen your *a* ....Jer 13:27
her sight, and her *a* ....Hos 2:2
evil thoughts, *a* ....Mark 7:21

ADULTEROUS
evil and *a* generation ....Matt 12:39

ADULTERY
You shall not commit *a* .....Ex 20:14
You shall not commit *a* ....Deut 5:18
Whoever commits *a* ....Prov 6:32
Israel had committed *a* ....Jer 3:8
have committed *a* with .....Jer 29:23
a with their idols ....Ezek 23:37
and is committing *a* ....Hos 3:1
already committed *a* ....Matt 5:28
is divorced commits *a* ......Matt 5:32
You shall not commit *a* ...Matt 19:18
another commits *a* ....Mark 10:11
husband commits *a*.........Luke 16:18
a woman caught in *a* ....John 8:3
which are: *a*, fornication,.......Gal 5:19
having eyes full of *a* ....2 Pet 2:14
those who commit *a* ....Rev 2:22

ADVANCED
Joshua was old, *a* in ....Josh 13:1
I am old, *a* in age ....Josh 23:2
David was old, *a* in years ...1 Kin 1:1
were both well *a* in years ...Luke 1:7
wife is well *a* in years .....Luke 1:18
I *a* in Judaism beyond ....Gal 1:14

ADVANTAGE
a will it be to You ....Job 35:3
man has no *a* over ....Eccl 3:19
a that I go away ....John 16:7
What *a* then has the ....Rom 3:1
Satan should take *a* ....2 Cor 2:11
no one should take *a* .....1 Thess 4:6
people to gain *a* ....Jude 16

ADVERSARIES
The *a* of the LORD ....1 Sam 2:10
rid Myself of My *a* ....Is 1:24
a will not be able ....Luke 21:15
and there are many *a* .....1 Cor 16:9
terrified by your *a* ....Phil 1:28
will devour the *a* ....Heb 10:27

ADVERSARY
in the way as an *a* ....Num 22:22
battle he become our *a* ...1 Sam 29:4
how long will the *a* ....Ps 74:10
a has spread his hand ....Lam 1:10
Agree with your *a* ....Matt 5:25
for me from my *a* ....Luke 18:3
opportunity to the *a*.........1 Tim 5:14
your *a* the devil walks ....1 Pet 5:8

ADVERSITIES
you from all your *a* ......1 Sam 10:19
known my soul in *a* ....Ps 31:7

ADVERSITY
them with every *a* ....2 Chr 15:6
I shall never be in *a* ....Ps 10:6
from the days of *a* ....Ps 94:13
brother is born for *a* ....Prov 17:17
faint in the day of *a*.......Prov 24:10
the day of *a* consider ....Eccl 7:14
you the bread of *a* ....Is 30:20

ADVICE
And blessed is your *a* ....1 Sam 25:33
in this I give my *a* ....2 Cor 8:10

ADVOCATE
we have an *A* with the ....1 John 2:1

AENON
A place near Salim where John the Baptist baptized, John 3:22, 23

AFAR
and worship from *a* ....Ex 24:1
sons shall come from *a* ....Is 60:4
and not a God *a* ....Jer 23:23
and saw Abraham *a* ......Luke 16:23
to all who are *a* ....Acts 2:39
to you who were *a* ....Eph 2:17
but having seen them *a* ....Heb 11:13

AFFAIRS
he will guide his *a* ....Ps 112:5
I may hear of your *a* ....Phil 1:27
himself with the *a* ....2 Tim 2:4

AFFECTION
to his wife the *a*............1 Cor 7:3
for you all with the *a* ....Phil 1:8
if any *a* and mercy ....Phil 2:1

AFFECTIONATE
Be kindly *a* to one ....Rom 12:10

AFFIRM
you to *a* constantly ....Titus 3:8

AFFLICT
a them with their ....Ex 1:11
oath to *a* her soul ....Num 30:13
may be bound to *a* you .....Judg 16:6
a the descendants ....1 Kin 11:39
will hear, and *a* them ....Ps 55:19
a Your heritage ....Ps 94:5
a man to *a* his soul ....Is 58:5
to destroy, and to *a* ....Jer 31:28
For He does not *a* ....Lam 3:33
deal with all who *a* ....Zeph 3:19

AFFLICT YOUR SOULS
shall *a*, and do no work ....Lev 16:29
you shall *a*, and offer ......Lev 23:27
You shall *a*; you shall not ..Num 29:7

AFFLICTED
"Why have You *a* ....Num 11:11
and the Almighty has *a* ....Ruth 1:21
To him who is *a* ....Job 6:14
hears the cry of the *a* ......Job 34:28
You *a* the peoples ....Ps 44:2
Before I was *a* ....Ps 119:67
I am *a* very much ....Ps 119:107
Many a time they have *a* .....Ps 129:1
the cause of the *a* ....Ps 140:12
days of the *a* are evil .....Prov 15:15
Smitten by God, and *a* ....Is 53:4
oppressed and He was *a* ......Is 53:7
"O you *a* one, tossed ....Is 54:11
Why have we *a* our............Is 58:3
and satisfy the *a* ....Is 58:10
her virgins are *a* ....Lam 1:4
she has relieved the *a* .....1 Tim 5:10
being destitute, *a* ....Heb 11:37

AFFLICTING
A the just and taking .....Amos 5:12

AFFLICTION
in the land of my *a* ....Gen 41:52
the bread of *a* ....Deut 16:3
indeed look on the *a* ......1 Sam 1:11
LORD saw that the *a*.......2 Kin 14:26
a take hold of me ....Job 30:16
days of *a* confront me .....Job 30:27
held in the cords of *a* ....Job 36:8
of death, bound in *a* ....Ps 107:10
is my comfort in my *a* .....Ps 119:50
and it is an evil *a* ....Eccl 6:2
a He was afflicted ....Is 63:9
refuge in the day of *a* ......Jer 16:19
"O LORD, behold my *a*.......Lam 1:9
not grieved for the *a* ....Amos 6:6
For our light *a* ....2 Cor 4:17
supposing to add *a* ....Phil 1:16
the word in much *a* ......1 Thess 1:6

AFFLICTIONS
Many are the *a* of the ......Ps 34:19
in the *a* of Christ ....Col 1:24
shaken by these *a* ....1 Thess 3:3
persecutions, *a*, which ....2 Tim 3:11
in all things, endure *a*, ...2 Tim 4:5

AFFORD
poor and cannot *a* it ....Lev 14:21
such as he can *a* ....Lev 14:30

AFRAID
See DO NOT BE AFRAID
garden, and I was *a* ....Gen 3:10
saying, "Do not be *a* ....Gen 15:1
his face, for he was *a* ....Ex 3:6
none will make you *a* ....Lev 26:6
you shall not be *a* in ....Deut 1:17
of whom you are *a* ....Deut 7:19
do not be *a* of them ....Deut 20:1
Do not be *a* of the ....2 Kin 25:24

David was *a* of God . . . . . . 1 Chr 13:12
I will not be *a* of ten . . . . Ps 3:6
ungodliness made me *a* . . . . Ps 18:4
Of whom shall I be *a* . . . . Ps 27:1
Do not be *a* when one . . . . Ps 49:16
Whenever I am *a* . . . . Ps 56:3
farthest parts are *a* . . . . Ps 65:8
you will not be *a* . . . . Prov 3:24
nor be *a* of their threats . . . . Is 8:12
be *a* of the Assyrian . . . . Is 10:24
I will trust and not be *a* . . . . Is 12:2
no one will make them *a* . . . . . . Is 17:2
Do not fear, nor be *a* . . . . Is 44:8
that you should be *a* . . . . Is 51:12
Do not be *a* of their faces, ... Jer 1:8
dream which made me *a* . . . . . Dan 4:5
Then the mariners were *a* . . . . Jon 1:5
It is I; do not be *a* . . . . Matt 14:27
Do not be *a*; only believe . . Mark 5:36
Do not be *a*, Zacharias, ... Luke 1:13
Do not be *a*, Mary, for . . . . . Luke 1:30
not be *a* of those who . . . . . Luke 12:4
neither let it be *a* . . . . John 14:27
"Do not be *a*, Paul . . . . Acts 27:24
if you do evil, be *a* . . . . Rom 13:4
do good and are not *a* . . . . 1 Pet 3:6

AFTERWARD
A he will let you go . . . . Ex 11:1
a we will speak . . . . Job 18:2
a receive me to glory . . . . Ps 73:24
you shall follow Me *a* . . . . . John 13:36
the firstfruits, *a* . . . . 1 Cor 15:23

AGAG
A king of Amalek in Balaam's prophecy, Num 24:7
—— Amalekite king spared by Saul, but slain by Samuel, 1 Sam 15:8, 9, 20–24, 32, 33

AGAIN
See BORN AGAIN
day He will rise *a* . . . . Matt 20:19
'You must be born *a* . . . . John 3:7
to renew them *a* . . . . Heb 6:6
having been born *a* . . . . 1 Pet 1:23

AGAINST
See SINNED AGAINST THE LORD; SINNED AGAINST YOU
his hand shall be *a* . . . . Gen 16:12
I will set My face *a* . . . . Lev 20:3
come to 'set a man *a* . . . . . . Matt 10:35
or house divided *a* . . . . Matt 12:25
not with Me is *a* Me . . . . . . Matt 12:30
blasphemy *a* the Spirit . . . . Matt 12:31
For nation will rise *a* . . . . Matt 24:7
out, as *a* a robber . . . . Matt 26:55
I have sinned *a* . . . . Luke 15:18
lifted up his heel *a* . . . . John 13:18
LORD and *a* His Christ . . . . . . Acts 4:26
to kick *a* the goads . . . . Acts 9:5
all men everywhere *a* . . . . . Acts 21:28
let us not fight *a* . . . . Acts 23:9
a the promises of God . . . . Gal 3:21
we do not wrestle *a* . . . . Eph 6:12
I have a few things *a* . . . . Rev 2:20

AGE
well advanced in *a* . . . . Gen 18:11
Israel were dim with *a* . . . . Gen 48:10
the flower of their *a* . . . . . . 1 Sam 2:33
the grave at a full *a* . . . . Job 5:26
a is as nothing . . . . Ps 39:5
and in the *a* to come . . . . . Mark 10:30
"The sons of this *a* . . . . Luke 20:34
He is of *a*; ask him . . . . John 9:21
who are of full *a* . . . . Heb 5:14
the powers of the *a* . . . . Heb 6:5

AGE TO COME
in this age or in the *a* . . . . . Matt 12:32
in the *a*, eternal life . . . . . . Mark 10:30
in the *a* eternal life . . . . Luke 18:30
the powers of the *a* . . . . Heb 6:5

AGED
Wisdom is with *a* . . . . Job 12:12
a one as Paul, the *a* . . . . Philem 9

AGES
ordained before the *a* . . . . 1 Cor 2:7
in other *a* was not . . . . Eph 3:5
at the end of the *a* . . . . Heb 9:26

AGONY
And being in *a* . . . . Luke 22:44

AGREE
A with your adversary . . . . . Matt 5:25
that if two of you *a* . . . . Matt 18:19
testimonies did not *a* . . . . . Mark 14:56
and these three *a* . . . . 1 John 5:8

AGREED
unless they are *a* . . . . Amos 3:3
they were glad, and *a* . . . . . Luke 22:5

AGREEMENT
with Sheol we are in *a* . . . . Is 28:15
the North to make an *a* . . . . . Dan 11:6
what *a* has the temple . . . . . 2 Cor 6:16

AHAB
A wicked king of Israel, 1 Kin 16:29
Marries Jezebel; promotes Baal worship, 1 Kin 16:31–33; 18:17–46
Denounced by Elijah, 1 Kin 17:1
Wars against Ben-Hadad, 1 Kin 20:1–43
Covets Naboth's vineyard, 1 Kin 21:1–16
Death predicted; repentance delays judgment, 1 Kin 21:17–29
Goes to war in spite of Micaiah's warning; killed in battle, 1 Kin. 22:1–37
Prophecy concerning, fulfilled, 1 Kin 22:38
—— Lying prophet, Jer 29:21–23

AHASUERUS
The father of Darius the Mede, Dan 9:1
—— Persian king, probably Xerxes I, 486–465 B.C., Ezra 4:6; Esth 1:1
Makes Esther queen, Esth 2:16, 17
Orders Jews annihilated, by Haman's advice, Esth 3:8–15
Reverses decree at Esther's request, Esth 7; 8
Exalts Mordecai, Esth 10:1–3

AHAZ
King of Judah; pursues idolatry; submits to Assyrian rule; desecrates the temple, 2 Kin 16
Defeated by Syria and Israel, 2 Chr 28:5–15
Comforted by Isaiah; refuses to ask a sign, Is 7:1–17

AHAZIAH
King of Israel; son of Ahab and Jezebel; worships Baal, 1 Kin 22:51–53
Falls through lattice; calls on Baal-Zebub; dies according to Elijah's word, 2 Kin 1:2–18
—— King of Judah; Ahab's son-in-law; reigns wickedly, 2 Kin 8:25–29; 2 Chr 22:1–6
Killed by Jehu, 2 Kin 9:27–29; 2 Chr 22:7–9

AHIJAH
A prophet of Shiloh who foretells division of Solomon's kingdom, 1 Kin 11:29–39
Foretells elimination of Jeroboam's line, 1 Kin 14:1–18
A writer of prophecy, 2 Chr 9:29

AHIKAM
Sent in Josiah's mission to Huldah, 2 Kin 22:12–14
Protects Jeremiah, Jer 26:24
The father of Gedaliah, governor under Nebuchadnezzar, 2 Kin 25:22; Jer 39:14

AHIMAAZ
A son of Zadok the high priest, 1 Chr 6:8, 9
Warns David of Absalom's plans, 2 Sam 15:27, 36
First to tell David of Absalom's defeat, 2 Sam 18:19–30

AHIMELECH
High priest in Saul's reign; helps David, 1 Sam 21:1–9
Betrayed and killed by Doeg; son Abiathar escapes, 1 Sam 22:9–20
David writes concerning, Ps 52:title

AHINOAM
Wife of David, 1 Sam 25:43; 27:3; 30:5, 18
Mother of Amnon, 2 Sam 3:2

AHITHOPHEL
David's counselor, 2 Sam 15:12
Joins Absalom's insurrection; counsels him, 2 Sam 15:31; 16:20–23
His counsel rejected; commits suicide, 2 Sam 17:1–23

AI
Israel defeated at, Josh 7:2–5
Israel destroys completely, Josh 8:1–28

AIDE
the king's personal *a* . . . . . . Acts 12:20

AIJALON
Amorites not driven from, Judg 1:35
Miracle there, Josh 10:12, 13
City of refuge, 1 Chr 6:66–69
Fortified by Rehoboam, 2 Chr 11:5, 10
Captured by Philistines, 2 Chr 28:18

AIR
the birds of the *a* . . . . Gen 1:26
of the *a* have nests . . . . Luke 9:58
as one who beats the *a* . . . . 1 Cor 9:26
be speaking into the *a* . . . . . 1 Cor 14:9
of the power of the *a* . . . . Eph 2:2
the Lord in the *a* . . . . 1 Thess 4:17
his bowl into the *a* . . . . Rev 16:17

AKEL DAMA
Field called "Field of Blood," Acts 1:19

AKRABBIM
An "ascent" on the south of the Dead Sea, Num 34:4
One border of Judah, Josh 15:3

ALABASTER
mosaic pavement of *a* . . . . Esth 1:6
an *a* flask of very costly . . . . Matt 26:7
woman came having an *a* . Mark 14:3
brought an *a* flask of . . . . Luke 7:37

ALARM
to sound the *a* against . . . . 2 Chr 13:12
A day of trumpet and *a* . . . . . . Zeph 1:16

ALEXANDER
A member of the high-priestly family, Acts 4:6
—— A Jew in Ephesus, Acts 19:33, 34
—— An apostate condemned by Paul, 1 Tim 1:19, 20

ALEXANDRIA
Men of, persecute Stephen, Acts 6:9
Paul sails in ship of, Acts 27:6

ALGUM
a logs from Lebanon, ... 2 Chr 2:8
Ophir, brought *a* wood . . . . 2 Chr 9:10
a wood for the house . . . . . 2 Chr 9:11

ALIEN
because you were an *a* . . . . . Deut 23:7
I am an *a* in their . . . . Job 19:15
who turn away an *a* . . . . Mal 3:5

ALIENATED
a herself from them ...... Ezek 23:17
darkened, being *a* .... Eph 4:18
you, who once were *a* .... Col 1:21

ALIENS
For we are *a* and .... 1 Chr 29:15
For I have loved *a* .... Jer 2:25
A have devoured his .... Hos 7:9
without Christ, being *a* ..... Eph 2:12
the armies of the *a* .... Heb 11:34

ALIGHTING
dove and *a* upon Him .... Matt 3:16

ALIKE
All things come *a* .... Eccl 9:2
esteems every day *a* .... Rom 14:5

ALIVE
in the ark remained *a* .... Gen 7:23
with them went down *a* ... Num 16:33
LORD your God are *a* .... Deut 4:4
I kill and I make *a* .... Deut 32:39
Let them go down *a* .... Ps 55:15
he preserves himself *a* .... Ezek 18:27
heard that He was *a* ..... Mark 16:11
son was dead and is *a* ..... Luke 15:24
presented Himself *a* .... Acts 1:3
dead indeed to sin, but *a* ... Rom 6:11
I was *a* once without .... Rom 7:9
all shall be made *a* ..... 1 Cor 15:22
trespasses, made us *a* .... Eph 2:5
flesh, He has made *a* .... Col 2:13
that we who are *a* .... 1 Thess 4:15
the flesh but made *a* .... 1 Pet 3:18
and behold, I am *a* .... Rev 1:18
a name that you are *a* .... Rev 3:1
These two were cast *a* ...... Rev 19:20

ALL
See WITH ALL YOUR HEART
for this is man's *a* .... Eccl 12:13

ALL THE DAYS OF HIS LIFE
he shall read it *a* .... Deut 17:19
give him to the LORD *a* .... 1 Sam 1:11
I have made him ruler *a* ... 1 Kin 11:34
He commanded him *a* ..... 1 Kin 15:5
toils under the sun *a* .... Eccl 5:18
before the king *a* .... Jer 52:33

ALL THE EARTH
over the cattle, over *a* ...... Gen 1:26
alive on the face of *a* .... Gen 7:3
confused the language of *a* . Gen 11:9
Shall not the Judge of *a* ... Gen 18:25
there is none like Me in *a* .... Ex 9:14
going the way of *a* .... Josh 23:14
I go the way of *a*; .... 1 Kin 2:2
a sought the presence .... 1 Kin 10:24
Sing to the LORD, *a*; ...... 1 Chr 16:23
Let *a* fear the LORD; .... Ps 33:8
A shall worship You .... Ps 66:4
I have gathered *a* .... Is 10:14
that made *a* drunk .... Jer 51:7
which shall rule over *a* ..... Dan 2:39
Let *a* keep silence .... Hab 2:20
was darkness over *a* ..... Luke 23:44
sound has gone out to *a* ... Rom 10:18
of God sent out into *a* .... Rev 5:6

ALL THE SAINTS
God will come, and *a* ...... Zech 14:5
your love for *a* .... Eph 1:15
less than the least of *a* ...... Eph 3:8
able to comprehend with *a* .. Eph 3:18
and supplication for *a* .... Eph 6:18
your love for *a* .... Col 1:4
with the prayers of *a* .... Rev 8:3

ALLELUIA
Again they said, "*A* .... Rev 19:3

ALLOW
a Your Holy One .... Ps 16:10
a My faithfulness .... Ps 89:33
nor do you *a* those .... Matt 23:13
a Your Holy One .... Acts 2:27
who will not *a* you to be . 1 Cor 10:13

ALLOWED
bygone generations *a* ..... Acts 14:16

ALLURE
behold, I will *a* .... Hos 2:14
they *a* through the lusts ..... 2 Pet 2:18

ALMIGHTY
I am *A* God; walk before .... Gen 17:1
May God *A* bless you, and .. Gen 28:3
and to Jacob, as God *A* .... Ex 6:3
for the *A* has dealt very ..... Ruth 1:20
does the *A* pervert justice ..... Job 8:3
find out the limits of the *A* .. Job 11:7
of the wrath of the *A* ...... Job 21:20
your delight in the *A* .... Job 22:26
breath of the *A* gives me .... Job 33:4
under the shadow of the *A* ... Ps 91:1
as destruction from the *A* ..... Is 13:6
as destruction from the *A* .... Joel 1:15
and who is to come, the *A* ... Rev 1:8
holy, holy, Lord God *A* .... Rev 4:8
Even so, Lord God *A* .... Rev 16:7
fierceness and wrath of *A* .. Rev 19:15

ALMOND
a blossoms on one .... Ex 25:33
a tree blossoms .... Eccl 12:5
branch of an *a* tree .... Jer 1:11

ALMOST
for me, my feet had *a* .... Ps 73:2
a persuade me to .... Acts 26:28
a all things are .... Heb 9:22

ALMS
But rather give *a* .... Luke 11:41
you have and give *a* ...... Luke 12:33
I came to bring *a* .... Acts 24:17

ALOES
with myrrh and *a* .... Ps 45:8
my bed with myrrh, *a* ...... Prov 7:17
mixture of myrrh and *a* ... John 19:39

ALOUD
And he wept *a*, and the .... Gen 45:2
many shouted *a* for joy .... Ezra 3:12
them sing *a* on their beds .... Ps 149:5
Wisdom calls *a* outside ...... Prov 1:20
Cry *a* at Beth Aven .... Hos 5:8

ALPHA
I am the *A* and the .... Rev 1:8
I am the *A* and the .... Rev 22:13

ALTAR
Then Noah built an *a* .... Gen 8:20
he built an *a* to the LORD ..... Gen 12:7
built an *a* there .... Gen 13:18
Abraham built an *a* .... Gen 22:9
son and laid him on the *a* ... Gen 22:9
So he built an *a* there ..... Gen 26:25
make an *a* there to God ..... Gen 35:1
And Moses built an *a* .... Ex 17:15
An *a* of earth you .... Ex 20:24
two sides of the *a* .... Ex 27:7
incense *a* of acacia wood .... Ex 37:25
a shall be kept .... Lev 6:9
it to you upon the *a* .... Lev 17:11
offering for the *a* .... Num 7:84
a to the LORD your God .... Deut 27:5
Joshua built an *a* .... Josh 8:30
a great, impressive *a* ...... Josh 22:10
called the *a* Witness ...... Josh 22:34
and tear down the *a* .... Judg 6:25
early and built an *a* .... Judg 21:4
built an *a* to the LORD ..... 1 Sam 7:17
Saul built an *a* .... 1 Sam 14:35
"Go up, erect an *a* .... 2 Sam 24:18
built there an *a* .... 2 Sam 24:25
a which he had made .... 1 Kin 12:33
cried out against the *a* ..... 1 Kin 13:2
set up an *a* for Baal ...... 1 Kin 16:32
he repaired the *a* .... 1 Kin 18:30
a according to all that .... 2 Kin 16:11
built there an *a* .... 1 Chr 21:26
made a bronze *a* .... 2 Chr 4:1
a of gold and the tables .... 2 Chr 4:19
he restored the *a* .... 2 Chr 15:8
worship before one *a* .... 2 Chr 32:12
repaired the *a* of the ..... 2 Chr 33:16
the *a* of the God of .... Ezra 3:2
I will go to the *a* .... Ps 43:4
tongs from the *a* .... Is 6:6
there will be an *a* .... Is 19:19
Lord has spurned His *a* ..... Lam 2:7
The *a* was in front .... Ezek 40:47
you cover the *a* .... Mal 2:13
your gift to the *a* .... Matt 5:23
swears by the *a* .... Matt 23:18
I even found an *a* .... Acts 17:23
the offerings of the *a* ..... 1 Cor 9:13
partakers of the *a* .... 1 Cor 10:18
We have an *a* from .... Heb 13:10
Isaac his son on the *a* .... James 2:21
under the *a* the souls .... Rev 6:9
and stood at the *a* .... Rev 8:3
horns of the golden *a* .... Rev 9:13
angel came out from the *a* . Rev 14:18

ALTARS
a Hezekiah has taken .... 2 Kin 18:22
Even Your *a*, O LORD .... Ps 84:3
on the horns of your *a* .... Jer 17:1
a shall be broken .... Ezek 6:4
has made many *a* .... Hos 8:11
a shall be heaps .... Hos 12:11
destruction on the *a* .... Amos 3:14
and torn down Your *a* ..... Rom 11:3

ALTER
put their hand to *a* it .... Ezra 6:12
Nor *a* the word .... Ps 89:34
Persians, which does not *a* ... Dan 6:8
Persians, which does not *a* .. Dan 6:12

ALTERED
of His face was *a* .... Luke 9:29

ALWAYS
delight, rejoicing *a* .... Prov 8:30
the poor with you *a* .... Matt 26:11
Me you do not have *a* ..... Matt 26:11
lo, I am with you *a* .... Matt 28:20
'Son, you are *a* .... Luke 15:31
men *a* ought to pray .... Luke 18:1
immovable, *a* abounding 1 Cor 15:58
Rejoice in the Lord *a* .... Phil 4:4
thus we shall *a* .... 1 Thess 4:17
a be ready to give a .... 1 Pet 3:15

AM
See HERE I AM; I AM WITH YOU
to Moses, "I *A* WHO I *A* ...... Ex 3:14
First and I *a* the Last .... Is 44:6
in My name, I *a* there ..... Matt 18:20
I *a* the bread of life .... John 6:35
I *a* the light of the .... John 8:12
I *a* from above .... John 8:23
Abraham was, I *A* .... John 8:58
I *a* the door .... John 10:9
I *a* the good shepherd ..... John 10:11
I *a* the resurrection .... John 11:25
to him, "I *a* the way .... John 14:6
of God I *a* what I *a* .... 1 Cor 15:10

AMALEK
Grandson of Esau, Gen 36:11, 12
A chief of Edom, Gen 36:16
First among nations, Num 24:20

AMALEKITES
Destruction predicted, Ex 17:14; Deut 25:17–19
Defeated by Israel, Ex 17:8–13; Judg 7:12–25; 1 Sam 14:47, 48; 27:8, 9; 1 Chr 4:42, 43
Overcome Israel, Num 14:39–45; Judg 3:13

AMASA
Commands Absalom's rebels, 2 Sam 17:25

Made David's commander, 2 Sam 19:13
Treacherously killed by Joab, 2 Sam 20:9–12
Death avenged, 1 Kin 2:28–34

AMAZED
the multitudes were *a* ..... Matt 12:23
trembled and were *a* .... Mark 16:8
saw Him, they were *a* ..... Luke 2:48
Then they were all *a* and .... Acts 2:7
with Philip, and was *a* ...... Acts 8:13

AMAZIAH
King of Judah; kills his father's assassinators, 2 Kin 14:1–6; 2 Chr 25:1–4
Hires troops from Israel; is rebuked by a man of God; sends troops home, 2 Chr 25:5–10
Defeats Edomites; worships their gods, 2 Chr 25:11–16
Wars with Israel, 2 Kin 14:8–14; 2 Chr 25:17–24
Killed by conspirators, 2 Chr 25:25–28

AMBASSADOR
but a faithful *a* .... Prov 13:17
for which I am an *a* .... Eph 6:20

AMBASSADORS
which sends *a* by sea .... Is 18:2
cry outside, the *a* .... Is 33:7
we are *a* for Christ .... 2 Cor 5:20

AMBITION
Christ from selfish *a* .... Phil 1:16
through selfish *a* .... Phil 2:3

AMBUSH
Lay an *a* for the city .... Josh 8:2
a all around Gibeah ...... Judg 20:29
son heard of their *a* .... Acts 23:16
they lay in *a* along .... Acts 25:3

AMEN
shall say, "*A*, so be it ...... Num 5:22
answer and say, '*A* .... Deut 27:15
the people said, "*A!*" ..... 1 Chr 16:36
all the people say, "*A!*" .... Ps 106:48
and the glory forever. *A*. .... Matt 6:13
to the end of the age." *A*. .. Matt 28:20
accompanying signs. *A*. .. Mark 16:20
and blessing God. *A*. ..... Luke 24:53
that would be written. *A*. . John 21:25
uninformed say "*A* .... 1 Cor 14:16
are Yes, and in Him *A* ..... 2 Cor 1:20
These things says the *A* ..... Rev 3:14
creatures said, "*A* .... Rev 5:14
I am coming quickly." *A*. .. Rev 22:20

AMEND
A your ways and your .... Jer 7:3
from his evil way, *a* .... Jer 35:15

AMETHYST
an agate, and an *a* .... Ex 28:19
the twelfth *a* .... Rev 21:20

AMMON
A nation fathered by Lot, Gen 19:36, 38

AMMONITES
Excluded from assembly for hostility to Israel, Deut 23:3–6
Propose cruel treaty; conquered by Saul, 1 Sam 11:1–3, 11
Abuse David's ambassadors; conquered by his army, 2 Sam 10:1–14
Harass postexilic Jews, Neh 4:3, 7, 8
Defeated by Israel and Judah, Judg 11:4–33; 2 Chr 20:1–25; 27:5, 6
Prophecies concerning, Ps 83:1–18; Jer 25:9–21; Ezek 25:1–7; Amos 1:13–15; Zeph 2:9–11

AMNON
A son of David, 2 Sam 3:2
Rapes his half sister, 2 Sam 13:1–18
Killed by Absalom, 2 Sam 13:19–29

AMON
King of Judah, 2 Kin 21:18, 19
Follows evil, 2 Chr 33:22, 23
Killed by conspiracy, 2 Kin 21:23, 24
——— A governor of Samaria, 1 Kin 22:10, 26

AMORITES
Defeated by Joshua, Josh 10:1–43
Not driven out of Canaan, Judg 1:34–36
Put to forced labor under Solomon, 1 Kin 9:20, 21

AMOS
A prophet of Israel, Amos 1:1
Pronounces judgment against nations, Amos 1:1–3, 15
Denounces Israel's sins, Amos 4:1—7:9
Condemns Amaziah, the priest of Bethel, Amos 7:10–17
Predicts Israel's downfall, Amos 9:1–10
Foretells great blessings, Amos 9:11–15

AMPHIPOLIS
A city in Macedonia visited by Paul, Acts 17:1

AMRAM
Son of Kohath, Num 3:17–19
The father of Aaron, Moses and Miriam, Ex 6:18–20; 1 Chr 6:3

ANAKIM
A race of giants; very strong, Num 13:28–33; Deut 2:10, 11, 21
Defeated:
by Joshua, Josh 10:36–39; 11:21
by Caleb, Josh 14:6–15

ANANIAS
Disciple at Jerusalem; slain for lying to God, Acts 5:1–11
——— A Christian disciple at Damascus, Acts 9:10–19; 22:12–16
——— A Jewish high priest, Acts 23:1–5

ANATHOTH
A Levitical city in Benjamin, Josh 21:18
Jeremiah's birthplace; he buys property there, Jer 1:1; 32:6–15
To be invaded by Assyria, Is 10:30

ANCHOR
hope we have as an *a* .... Heb 6:19

ANCIENT
Do not remove the *a* ...... Prov 23:10
a times that I .... Is 37:26
until the *A* of Days .... Dan 7:22

ANDREW
A disciple of John the Baptist, then of Christ, Matt 4:18, 19; John 1:40–42
Enrolled among the Twelve, Matt 10:2
Mentioned, Mark 13:3, 4; John 6:8, 9; 12:20–22; Acts 1:13

ANGEL
Now the *A* of the LORD ...... Gen 16:7
A who has redeemed me ... Gen 48:16
"Behold, I send an *A* .... Ex 23:20
the donkey saw the *A* .... Num 22:23
For I have seen the *A* ...... Judg 6:22
Manoah said to the *A* ...... Judg 13:17
in my sight as an *a* .... 1 Sam 29:9
a who was destroying ... 2 Sam 24:16
night that the *a* .... 2 Kin 19:35
the *A* of His Presence .... Is 63:9
struggled with the *A* .... Hos 12:4
standing before the *A* .... Zech 3:3
like God, like the *A* .... Zech 12:8
things, behold, an *a* .... Matt 1:20
for an *a* of the Lord .... Matt 28:2
Then an *a* of the Lord ..... Luke 1:11
And behold, an *a* .... Luke 2:9
a appeared to Him from .. Luke 22:43
For an *a* went down at .... John 5:4
a has spoken to Him ...... John 12:29
But at night an *a* .... Acts 5:19
A who appeared to him .... Acts 7:35
Then immediately an *a* ... Acts 12:23
and no *a* or spirit .... Acts 23:8
a has spoken to him .... Acts 23:9
by me this night an *a* ...... Acts 27:23
himself into an *a* .... 2 Cor 11:14
even if we, or an *a* .... Gal 1:8
Then I saw a strong *a* .... Rev 5:2
over them the *a* .... Rev 9:11
Then I saw an *a* .... Rev 19:17
Jesus, have sent My *a* ..... Rev 22:16

ANGEL OF GOD
the *a* called to Hagar .... Gen 21:17
Then the *A* spoke to me .... Gen 31:11
A, who went before the ..... Ex 14:19
the *A* came to the woman .. Judg 13:9
the king is like the *a* ..... 2 Sam 19:27
in a vision an *a* coming ...... Acts 10:3
you received me as an *a*, ... Gal 4:14

ANGEL OF THE LORD
A found her by a spring ...... Gen 16:7
the *A* called to Abraham .... Gen 22:15
A appeared to him in a flame .. Ex 3:2
the donkey saw the *A* .... Num 22:23
the *A* came up from Gilgal .. Judg 2:1
the *A* appeared to him ..... Judg 6:12
A appeared to the woman .. Judg 13:3
A was by the threshing .. 2 Sam 24:16
a said to Elijah .... 2 Kin 1:3
a went out, and killed .... 2 Kin 19:35
in the land, with the *a* .... 1 Chr 21:12
The *a* encamps all around ..... Ps 34:7
let the *a* pursue them .... Ps 35:6
A, who stood among the ... Zech 1:11
priest standing before the *A*. Zech 3:1
like the *A* before them ..... Zech 12:8
a appeared to him in a ..... Matt 1:20
an *a* appeared to Joseph ... Matt 2:13
a descended from heaven, .. Matt 28:2
an *a* appeared to him, ... Luke 1:11
an *a* opened the prison ...... Acts 5:19
a spoke to Philip, saying ... Acts 8:26
an *a* stood by him, ... Acts 12:7
an *a* struck him, ... Acts 12:23

ANGELS
If He charges His *a* .... Job 4:18
lower than the *a* .... Ps 8:5
He shall give His *a* .... Ps 91:11
Praise Him, all His *a* .... Ps 148:2
He shall give His *a* .... Matt 4:6
a will come forth .... Matt 13:49
a always see the face ..... Matt 18:10
but are like *a* of God ...... Matt 22:30
not even the *a* of heaven .. Matt 24:36
and all the holy *a* .... Matt 25:31
twelve legions of *a* .... Matt 26:53
the presence of the *a* ...... Luke 15:10
was carried by the *a* ...... Luke 16:22
are equal to the *a* .... Luke 20:36
And she saw two *a* .... John 20:12
that we shall judge *a* .... 1 Cor 6:3
head, because of the *a* .... 1 Cor 11:10
and worship of *a* .... Col 2:18
with His mighty *a* .... 2 Thess 1:7
the Spirit, seen by *a* .... 1 Tim 3:16
much better than the *a* .... Heb 1:4
does not give aid to *a* .... Heb 2:16
company of *a*, to the .... Heb 12:22
unwittingly entertained *a* ... Heb 13:2
things which *a* desire .... 1 Pet 1:12
did not spare the *a* .... 2 Pet 2:4
a who did not keep .... Jude 6
Michael and his *a* .... Rev 12:7

ANGER
See SLOW TO ANGER
Cursed be their *a* .... Gen 49:7

sun, that the fierce *a* ...... Num 25:4
fierceness of His *a* .... Deut 13:17
heat of this great *a* .... Deut 29:24
So the *a* of the LORD .... Judg 10:7
to provoke Me to *a* .... 1 Kin 16:2
For His *a* is but for a .... Ps 30:5
let Your wrathful *a* .... Ps 69:24
a time He turned His *a* ...... Ps 78:38
made a path for His *a* .... Ps 78:50
You prolong Your *a* .... Ps 85:5
the power of Your *a* .... Ps 90:11
gracious, slow to *a* .... Ps 103:8
Nor will He keep His *a* ...... Ps 103:9
harsh word stirs up *a* ...... Prov 15:1
a sins against his own ..... Prov 20:2
a rests in the bosom .... Eccl 7:9
a the Holy One of .... Is 1:4
a is not turned away .... Is 5:25
a is turned away .... Is 12:1
'I will not cause My *a* .... Jer 3:12
For great is the *a* .... Jer 36:7
and I will send My *a* .... Ezek 7:3
does not retain His *a* .... Mic 7:18
fierceness of His *a* .... Nah 1:6
a is kindled against .... Zech 10:3
around at them with *a* ...... Mark 3:5
bitterness, wrath, *a* .... Eph 4:31

ANGER OF THE LORD

a was kindled against Moses, . Ex 4:14
a was aroused against .... Num 25:3
a burned against the .... Josh 7:1
a was hot against Israel .... Judg 2:14
a was aroused against .... 2 Sam 6:7
a was aroused against ..... 2 Kin 13:3
a is aroused against His .... Is 5:25
a will not turn back .... Jer 23:20
because of the *a* this .... Jer 52:3

ANGRY

Cain, "Why are you *a* .... Gen 4:6
"Let not the Lord be *a* ..... Gen 18:30
the Son, lest He be *a* .... Ps 2:12
judge, and God is *a* .... Ps 7:11
When once You are *a* .... Ps 76:7
Will you be *a* forever .... Ps 79:5
friendship with an *a* ...... Prov 22:24
backbiting tongue an *a* .... Prov 25:23
a man stirs up strife ...... Prov 29:22
in your spirit to be *a* .... Eccl 7:9
I was *a* with My people .... Is 47:6
nor will I always be *a* .... Is 57:16
covetousness I was *a* .... Is 57:17
right for you to be *a* .... Jon 4:4
LORD has been very *a* .... Zech 1:2
I am exceedingly *a* .... Zech 1:15
you that whoever is *a* ...... Matt 5:22
"Be *a*, and do not sin" .... Eph 4:26
Therefore I was *a* .... Heb 3:10
with whom was He *a* .... Heb 3:17
The nations were *a* .... Rev 11:18

ANGUISH

a has come upon me .... 2 Sam 1:9
a make him afraid .... Job 15:24
I will be in *a* over my .... Ps 38:18
and *a* have overtaken ..... Ps 119:143
longer remembers the *a* ... John 16:21
tribulation and *a* .... Rom 2:9
much affliction and *a* .... 2 Cor 2:4

ANIMAL

of every clean *a* .... Gen 7:2
Whoever kills an *a* .... Lev 24:18
the life of his *a* .... Prov 12:10
set him on his own *a* ..... Luke 10:34

ANIMALS

of *a* after their kind .... Gen 6:20
sacrifices of fat *a* .... Ps 66:15
of four-footed *a* .... Acts 10:12
and four-footed *a* .... Rom 1:23

ANISE

tithe of mint and *a* .... Matt 23:23

ANNA

Aged prophetess, Luke 2:36–38

ANNAS

A Jewish high priest, Luke 3:2
Christ appeared before, John 18:12–24
Peter and John appeared before, Acts 4:6

ANNUL

and who will *a* .... Is 14:27
years later, cannot *a* .... Gal 3:17

ANNULLING

one hand there is an *a* ...... Heb 7:18

ANNULS

is confirmed, no one *a* ...... Gal 3:15

ANOINT

You shall *a* them .... Ex 28:41
but you shall not *a* .... Deut 28:40
you shall *a* for Me the .... 1 Sam 16:3
a yourself with oil .... 2 Sam 14:2
a my head with oil .... Ps 23:5
Arise, you princes, *a* .... Is 21:5
a the Most Holy .... Dan 9:24
when you fast, *a* .... Matt 6:17
a My body for burial ...... Mark 14:8
they might come and *a* .... Mark 16:1
a your eyes with eye .... Rev 3:18

ANOINTED

See LORD'S ANOINTED
the priest, who is *a* .... Lev 16:32
"Surely the LORD's *a* ..... 1 Sam 16:6
destroy the LORD's *a* ..... 2 Sam 1:14
he cursed the LORD's *a* .. 2 Sam 19:21
shows mercy to His *a* .... 2 Sam 22:51
"Do not touch My *a* ...... 1 Chr 16:22
the LORD saves His *a* .... Ps 20:6
because the LORD has *a* .... Is 61:1
"These are the two *a* ...... Zech 4:14
Because He has *a* .... Luke 4:18
but this woman has *a* ..... Luke 7:46
a the eyes of the .... John 9:6
It was that Mary who *a* ... John 11:2
Jesus, whom You *a* .... Acts 4:27
and has *a* us is God .... 2 Cor 1:21

ANOINTING

also made the holy *a* .... Ex 37:29
pray over him, *a* him ..... James 5:14
But you have an *a* .... 1 John 2:20
but as the same *a* .... 1 John 2:27

ANOTHER

See LOVE ONE ANOTHER
that you love one *a* .... John 13:34
and He will give you *a* .... John 14:16
'Let *a* take his office .... Acts 1:20

ANSWER

will give Pharaoh an *a* .... Gen 41:16
a I should take back ..... 2 Sam 24:13
Him, he could not *a* .... Job 9:3
Call, and I will *a* .... Job 13:22
how shall I *a* Him .... Job 31:14
and you shall *a* .... Job 40:7
the day that I call, *a* .... Ps 102:2
In Your faithfulness *a* .... Ps 143:1
a turns away wrath .... Prov 15:1
A man has joy by the *a* ... Prov 15:23
He who gives a right *a* .... Prov 24:26
a a fool according .... Prov 26:4
was there none to *a* .... Is 50:2
for there is no *a* .... Mic 3:7
or what you should *a* ..... Luke 12:11
you may have an *a* .... 2 Cor 5:12
ought to *a* each one .... Col 4:6

ANSWERS

a a matter before he ...... Prov 18:13
but the rich *a* roughly ..... Prov 18:23
money *a* everything .... Eccl 10:19

ANT

Go to the *a*, you sluggard ... Prov 6:6

ANTICHRIST

heard that the *A* .... 1 John 2:18
a who denies the .... 1 John 2:22
is the spirit of the *A* .... 1 John 4:3
is a deceiver and an *a* .... 2 John 7

ANTIOCH

—— In Syria:
First Gentile church established, Acts 11:19–21
Disciples first called "Christians" in, Acts 11:26
Church commissions Paul, Acts 13:1–4; 15:35–41
Church troubled by Judaizers, Acts 15:1–4; Gal 2:11–21
—— In Pisidia:
Paul visits; Jews reject the gospel, Acts 13:14, 42–51

ANTIPATRIS

A city between Jerusalem and Caesarea, Acts 23:31

ANTITYPE

a which now saves us ..... 1 Pet 3:21

ANXIETIES

the multitude of my *a* .... Ps 94:19
Try me, and know my *a* .... Ps 139:23

ANXIETY

A in the heart of man ..... Prov 12:25
eat their bread with *a* .... Ezek 12:19

ANXIOUS

drink, nor have an *a* ..... Luke 12:29
Be *a* for nothing .... Phil 4:6

APART

See SET APART
that you shall set *a* .... Ex 13:12
she shall be set *a* .... Lev 15:19
the LORD has set *a* .... Ps 4:3
justified by faith *a* .... Rom 3:28

APHEK

A town in the Plain of Sharon, Josh 12:18
Site of Philistine camp, 1 Sam 4:1; 29:1
—— A city in Jezreel, 1 Kin 20:26–30
Syria's defeat prophesied here, 2 Kin 13:14–19

APOLLOS

An Alexandrian Jew; instructed by Aquila and Priscilla and sent to Achaia, Acts 18:24–28
Referred to as having ministered in Corinth, 1 Cor 1:12; 3:4, 22; 4:6; 16:12

APOLLONIA

A town between Amphipolis and Thessalonica, Acts 17:1

APOLLYON

Angel of the bottomless pit, Rev 9:11

APOSTLE

called to be an *a* .... Rom 1:1
inasmuch as I am an *a* .... Rom 11:13
Am I not an *a* .... 1 Cor 9:1
the signs of an *a* were .... 2 Cor 12:12
a preacher and an *a* .... 1 Tim 2:7
consider the *A* and High ..... Heb 3:1

APOSTLES

See TWELVE APOSTLES
names of the twelve *a* ..... Matt 10:2
whom He also named *a* .... Luke 6:13
displayed us, the *a* .... 1 Cor 4:9
am the least of the *a* ...... 1 Cor 15:9
to the most eminent *a* ..... 2 Cor 11:5
themselves into *a* .... 2 Cor 11:13
none of the other *a* .... Gal 1:19
gave some to be *a* .... Eph 4:11
who say they are *a* .... Rev 2:2
heaven, and you holy *a* .... Rev 18:20

APOSTLESHIP

in this ministry and *a* ...... Acts 1:25

received grace and *a* .... Rom 1:5
are the seal of my *a* .... 1 Cor 9:2
in Peter for the *a* .... Gal 2:8

APPAREL

is glorious in His *a* .... Is 63:1
clothed with foreign *a* ...... Zeph 1:8
by them in white *a* .... Acts 1:10
themselves in modest *a* ..... 1 Tim 2:9
gold rings, in fine *a* .... James 2:2
or putting on fine *a* .... 1 Pet 3:3

APPEAL

I *a* to Caesar .... Acts 25:11
love's sake I rather *a* .... Philem 9

APPEAR

and let the dry land *a* .... Gen 1:9
all your males shall *a* .... Ex 23:17
all Israel comes to *a* ...... Deut 31:11
shall I come and *a* .... Ps 42:2
Let Your work *a* .... Ps 90:16
He shall *a* in His .... Ps 102:16
doings your sins *a* .... Ezek 21:24
faces that they may *a* .... Matt 6:16
also outwardly *a* .... Matt 23:28
kingdom of God would *a* . Luke 19:11
For we must all *a* .... 2 Cor 5:10
for Him He will *a* .... Heb 9:28
and the sinner *a* .... 1 Pet 4:18

APPEARANCE

Do not look at his *a* ...... 1 Sam 16:7
a is blacker than soot .... Lam 4:8
As He prayed, the *a* .... Luke 9:29
judge according to *a* .... John 7:24
those who boast in *a* .... 2 Cor 5:12
to the outward *a* .... 2 Cor 10:7
found in *a* as a man .... Phil 2:8
indeed have an *a* .... Col 2:23

APPEARED

See LORD APPEARED TO
an angel of the Lord *a* ...... Luke 1:11
who *a* in glory and .... Luke 9:31
brings salvation has *a* ..... Titus 2:11
of the ages, He has *a* .... Heb 9:26

APPEARING

Lord Jesus Christ's *a* ...... 1 Tim 6:14
been revealed by the *a* .... 2 Tim 1:10
and the dead at His *a* ...... 2 Tim 4:1
who have loved His *a* ...... 2 Tim 4:8
hope and glorious *a* .... Titus 2:13

APPEARS

can stand when He *a* .... Mal 3:2
who is our life *a* .... Col 3:4
the Chief Shepherd *a* .... 1 Pet 5:4
in Him, that when He *a* ... 1 John 2:28

APPETITE

or satisfy the *a* .... Job 38:39
are a man given to *a* .... Prov 23:2

APPII FORUM

A town about 40 miles south of Rome where Christians came to meet Paul, Acts 28:15

APPLE

He kept him as the *a* ...... Deut 32:10
And my law as the *a* .... Prov 7:2
Like an *a* tree among .... Song 2:3
touches the *a* of His eye .... Zech 2:8

APPLES

fitly spoken is like *a* ...... Prov 25:11
refresh me with *a* .... Song 2:5

APPLIED

a my heart to know .... Eccl 7:25

APPOINT

I will even *a* terror .... Lev 26:16
a each of them to his .... Num 4:19
a me ruler over the .... 2 Sam 6:21
a salvation for walls .... Is 26:1
For God did not *a* .... 1 Thess 5:9
a elders in every city .... Titus 1:5

APPOINTED

You have *a* his limits .... Job 14:5
To release those *a* .... Ps 102:20
And as it is *a* for men .... Heb 9:27

APPOINTED FEASTS

to the LORD at your *a* ...... Num 29:39
your *a* my soul hates .... Is 1:14
her Sabbaths, all her *a* ...... Hos 2:11
O Judah, keep your *a* .... Nah 1:15

APPOINTED TIME

At the *a* I will return to .... Gen 18:14
keep the Passover at its *a* ... Num 9:2
the morning till the *a* .... 2 Sam 24:15
at the *a* the end shall be .... Dan 8:19
end will still be at the *a* .... Dan 11:27
vision is yet for an *a* .... Hab 2:3

APPROACH

a anyone who is near .... Lev 18:6
And cause to *a* You .... Ps 65:4
year, make those who *a* .... Heb 10:1

APPROACHING

take delight in *a* God .... Is 58:2
as you see the Day *a* .... Heb 10:25

APPROVE

their posterity who *a* .... Ps 49:13
do the same but also *a* .... Rom 1:32
a the things that .... Rom 2:18
a the things that are .... Phil 1:10

APPROVED

to God and *a* by men ...... Rom 14:18
to present yourself *a* ...... 2 Tim 2:15
when he has been *a* .... James 1:12

APRONS

a were brought from his .. Acts 19:12

AQUEDUCT

stood by the *a* .... 2 Kin 18:17
at the end of the *a* .... Is 7:3
he stood by the *a* .... Is 36:2

AQUILA

Paul's host in Corinth, Acts 18:2, 3
Travels to Syria and Ephesus with Paul, Acts 18:18, 19
Instructs Apollos, Acts 18:24–26
Esteemed by Paul, Rom 16:3, 4

AR

A chief Moabite city, Num 21:15
On Israel's route, Deut 2:18
Destroyed by Sihon, Num 21:28
Destroyed by God, Is 15:1

ARABIA

Pays tribute to Solomon, 1 Kin 10:14, 15
Plunders Jerusalem, 2 Chr 21:16, 17
Defeated by Uzziah, 2 Chr 26:1, 7
Denounced by prophets, Is 21:13–17

ARARAT

Site of ark's landing, Gen 8:4
Assassins flee to, 2 Kin 19:37; Is 37:38

ARAUNAH (or Ornan)

A Jebusite, 2 Sam 24:15–25
His threshing floor bought by David, 2 Sam 24:18–25
becomes site of temple, 2 Chr 3:1
Also called Ornan, 1 Chr 21:18–28

ARBITRATOR

a judge or an *a* over .... Luke 12:14

ARCHANGEL

with the voice of an *a* ... 1 Thess 4:16
Yet Michael the *a* .... Jude 9

ARCHELAUS

Son of Herod the Great, Matt 2:22

AREOPAGUS

Paul preaches at, Acts 17:18–34

ARGUMENTS

fill my mouth with *a* .... Job 23:4
casting down *a* and .... 2 Cor 10:5

ARIEL

Ezra's friend, Ezra 8:15–17
—— Name applied to Jerusalem, Is 29:1, 2, 7

ARISE

needy, now I will *a* .... Ps 12:5
A for our help .... Ps 44:26
Let God *a* .... Ps 68:1
A, shine; for your light .... Is 60:1
But the LORD will *a* .... Is 60:2
Righteousness shall *a* .... Mal 4:2
I will *a* and go to .... Luke 15:18
you who sleep, *a* .... Eph 5:14

ARISTARCHUS

A Macedonian Christian, Acts 19:29
Accompanies Paul, Acts 20:1, 4
Imprisoned with Paul, Col 4:10

ARK

Make yourself an *a* .... Gen 6:14
two of every sort into the *a* . Gen 6:19
Then the *a* rested .... Gen 8:4
she took an *a* of bulrushes .... Ex 2:3
in the *a* you shall put .... Ex 25:21
Bezalel made the *a* .... Ex 37:1
seat which is on the *a* .... Lev 16:2
the *a* which I had made .... Deut 10:5
"Cross over before the *a* .... Josh 4:5
"Take up the *a* .... Josh 6:6
Let us bring the *a* .... 1 Sam 4:3
Also the *a* of God .... 1 Sam 4:11
a of God was captured .... 1 Sam 4:19
Philistines took the *a* ...... 1 Sam 5:1
the *a* remained in Kirjath .. 1 Sam 7:2
out his hand to the *a* .... 2 Sam 6:6
brought the *a* of the ...... 2 Sam 6:17
Nothing was in the *a* .... 1 Kin 8:9
his hand to hold the *a* ...... 1 Chr 13:9
the holy *a* in the house .... 2 Chr 35:3
golden censer and the *a* ..... Heb 9:4
prepared an *a* for the .... Heb 11:7
of Noah, while the *a* .... 1 Pet 3:20
in heaven, and the *a* .... Rev 11:19

ARM

with an outstretched *a* .... Ex 6:6
"Has the LORD's *a* .... Num 11:23
With him is an *a* .... 2 Chr 32:8
a that has no strength .... Job 26:2
Have you an *a* like God .... Job 40:9
Break the *a* of the .... Ps 10:15
You have a mighty *a* .... Ps 89:13
a have gained Him the .... Ps 98:1
a shall rule for Him .... Is 40:10
therefore His own *a* .... Is 59:16
strength with His *a* .... Luke 1:51
with an uplifted *a* .... Acts 13:17
a yourselves also with .... 1 Pet 4:1

ARMAGEDDON

See MEGIDDO
Possible site of final battle, Rev 16:16

ARMED

You have *a* me with ..... 2 Sam 22:40
a strong man, fully *a* ..... Luke 11:21

ARMIES

make captains of the *a* .... Deut 20:9
"I defy the *a* of Israel .... 1 Sam 17:10
any number to His *a* .... Job 25:3
not go out with our *a* .... Ps 60:10
And he sent out his *a* .... Matt 22:7
surrounded by *a* .... Luke 21:20
And the *a* in heaven .... Rev 19:14
the earth, and their *a* .... Rev 19:19

ARMOR

but he put his *a* .... 1 Sam 17:54
spears, put on the *a* .... Jer 46:4
let us put on the *a* .... Rom 13:12
Put on the whole *a* .... Eph 6:11

ARMORBEARER

to the young man, his *a* .... Judg 9:54

Jonathan said to his *a* ... 1 Sam 14:12
he became his *a* ... 1 Sam 16:21
Saul said to his *a* ... 1 Sam 31:4
his *a* would not, for he ... 1 Chr 10:4
when his *a* saw that Saul .. 1 Chr 10:5

ARMS
are the everlasting *a* ... Deut 33:27
into the clash of *a* ... Job 39:21
It is God who *a* ... Ps 18:32
My *a* will judge the ... Is 51:5
wounds between your *a* ... Zech 13:6
took them up in His *a* ... Mark 10:16
took Him up in his *a* ... Luke 2:28

ARMY
the multitude of an *a* ... Ps 33:16
an exceedingly great *a* ... Ezek 37:10
the number of the *a* ... Rev 9:16

ARNON
Boundary between Moab and Ammon, Num 21:13, 26
Border of Reuben, Deut 3:12, 16
Ammonites reminded of, Judg 11:18–26

AROER
A town in east Jordan; rebuilt by Gadites, Num 32:34; Deut 2:36
Assigned to Reuben, Deut 3:12
Ruled by Amorites, Josh 12:2; 13:9, 10, 16

AROMA
smelled a soothing *a* ... Gen 8:21
To the one we are the *a* ... 2 Cor 2:16
for a sweet-smelling *a* ... Eph 5:2
a sweet-smelling *a* ... Phil 4:18

AROSE
younger *a* and lay with ... Gen 19:35
a and crossed the river ... Gen 31:21
behold, my sheaf *a* ... Gen 37:7
there *a* a new king ... Ex 1:8
Deborah *a* and went ... Judg 4:9
until I, Deborah, *a* ... Judg 5:7
a a mother in Israel ... Judg 5:7
Samuel *a* and went to Eli, .. 1 Sam 3:6
David *a* and fled ... 1 Sam 21:10
LORD *a* against His ... 2 Chr 36:16
Then I *a* in the night ... Neh 2:12
Esther *a* and stood before ... Esth 8:4
I *a* to open for my beloved .. Song 5:5
the king *a* very early ... Dan 6:19
afterward I *a* and went ... Dan 8:27
Jonah *a* to flee to ... Jon 1:3
And she *a* and served ... Matt 8:15
tempest *a* on the sea ... Matt 8:24
He *a* and rebuked ... Matt 8:26
all those virgins *a* and ... Matt 25:7
a great windstorm *a* ... Mark 4:37
a and rebuked the wind .. Mark 4:39
a against the church ... Acts 8:1
he *a* and was baptized ... Acts 9:18
with Him after He *a* ... Acts 10:41
a dissension *a* between ... Acts 23:7
smoke *a* out of the pit ... Rev 9:2

AROUSED
the LORD was greatly *a* ... Num 11:10
his wrath was *a* because ... Job 32:2
Then Joseph, being *a* ... Matt 1:24

ARPHAXAD
A son of Shem, Gen 10:22, 24
Born two years after the flood, Gen 11:10–13
An ancestor of Christ, Luke 3:36

ARRAY
a against Gibeah ... Judg 20:30
battle *a* against Israel ... 1 Sam 4:2
drew up in battle *a* ... 1 Sam 17:2
a yourself with glory ... Job 40:10

ARRAYED
his glory was not *a* ... Matt 6:29
"Who are these *a* ... Rev 7:13
The woman was *a* ... Rev 17:4

ARREST
come up to *a* Samson ... Judg 15:10
the altar, saying, "*A* him ... 1 Kin 13:4
when they *a* you ... Mark 13:11

ARROGANCE
Pride and *a* and the ... Prov 8:13
I will halt the *a* ... Is 13:11

ARROGANT
the fruit of the *a* ... Is 10:12
sanctuary, your *a* boast ... Ezek 24:21

ARROW
deliverance and the *a* ... 2 Kin 13:17
a cannot make him flee ... Job 41:28
make ready their *a* ... Ps 11:2
a that flies by day ... Ps 91:5
a sword, and a sharp *a* ... Prov 25:18
Their tongue is an *a* ... Jer 9:8
as a target for the *a* ... Lam 3:12

ARROWS
He sent out *a* and ... 2 Sam 22:15
a pierce me deeply ... Ps 38:2
There He broke the *a* ... Ps 76:3
Like *a* in the hand of ... Ps 127:4
He has caused the *a* ... Lam 3:13
were sworn over Your *a* ... Hab 3:9

ARTAXERXES
Artaxerxes I, king of Persia (465–425 B.C.), authorizes Ezra's mission to Jerusalem, Ezra 7:1–28
Temporarily halts rebuilding program at Jerusalem, Ezra 4:7–23
Authorizes Nehemiah's mission, Neh 2:1–10
Permits Nehemiah to return, Neh 13:6

ARTISAN
gifted *a* in whom ... Ex 36:1
the skillful *a*, and the expert ... Is 3:3

ARTISTIC
a designs of cherubim ... Ex 26:1
to design *a* works ... Ex 31:4
a designs of cherubim ... Ex 36:8
linen, into *a* designs ... Ex 39:3

AS IT IS WRITTEN
A in the Law of Moses, ... Dan 9:13
of Man indeed goes just *a* . Matt 26:24
A in the Prophets: "Behold, . Mark 1:2
of you hypocrites, *a* ... Mark 7:6
whatever they wished, *a* ... Mark 9:13
a, 'He gave them bread ... John 6:31
donkey, sat on it; *a* ... John 12:14
a, "The just shall live ... Rom 1:17
Israel will be saved, *a* ... Rom 11:26
but *a*, "The reproaches of .. Rom 15:3

ASA
Third king of Judah; restores true worship, 1 Kin 15:8–15; 2 Chr 14; 15
Hires Ben-Hadad against Baasha; rebuked by a prophet, 1 Kin 15:16–22; 2 Chr 16:1–10
Diseased, seeks physicians rather than the Lord, 2 Chr 16:12
Death and burial, 2 Chr 16:13, 14

ASAHEL
David's nephew; captain in his army; noted for valor, 2 Sam 2:18; 23:24; 1 Chr 2:16; 27:7
Killed by Abner, 2 Sam 2:19–23
Avenged by Joab, 2 Sam 3:27, 30

ASAPH
A Levite choir leader under David and Solomon, 1 Chr 15:16–19; 16:1–7; 2 Chr 5:6, 12
Twelve psalms assigned to, 2 Chr 29:30; Ps 50; 73—83

ASCEND
Who may *a* into the ... Ps 24:3
If I *a* into heaven ... Ps 139:8
'I will *a* into heaven ... Is 14:13
a as high as the eagle ... Obad 4
see the Son of Man *a* ... John 6:62

ASCENDED
You have *a* on high ... Ps 68:18
Who has *a* into heaven ... Prov 30:4
No one has *a* to heaven ... John 3:13
"When He *a* on high ... Eph 4:8
also the One who *a* ... Eph 4:10
And they *a* to heaven ... Rev 11:12

ASCENDING
angels of God were *a* ... Gen 28:12
the angels of God *a* ... John 1:51

ASCRIBE
a greatness to our God ... Deut 32:3
I will *a* righteousness to ... Job 36:3
A strength to God ... Ps 68:34

ASENATH
Daughter of Poti-Pherah and wife of Joseph, Gen 41:45
Mother of Manasseh and Ephraim, Gen 41:50–52; 46:20

ASHAMED
O my God, I am too *a* and ... Ezra 9:6
all my enemies be *a* ... Ps 6:10
Let me not be *a* ... Ps 25:2
who waits on You be *a* ... Ps 25:3
The wise men are *a* ... Jer 8:9
forsake You shall be *a* ... Jer 17:13
And Israel shall be *a* ... Hos 10:6
For whoever is *a* ... Mark 8:38
am not *a* of the gospel ... Rom 1:16
nothing I shall be *a* ... Phil 1:20
Therefore God is not *a* ... Heb 11:16
in Christ may be *a* ... 1 Pet 3:16
let him not be *a* ... 1 Pet 4:16
and not be *a* before ... 1 John 2:28

ASHDOD
One of five Philistine cities, Josh 13:3
Seat of Dagon worship, 1 Sam 5:1–8
Opposes Nehemiah, Neh 4:7
Women of, marry Jews, Neh 13:23, 24
Called Azotus, Acts 8:40

ASHER
Jacob's second son by Zilpah, Gen 30:12, 13
Goes to Egypt with Jacob, Gen 46:8, 17
Blessed by Jacob, Gen 49:20
—— Tribe of:
Census of, Num 1:41; 26:47
Slow to fight against Canaanites, Judg 1:31, 32; 5:17
Among Gideon's army, Judg 6:35; 7:23
A godly remnant among, 2 Chr 30:11

ASHERAH
The female counterpart of Baal, Judg 3:7; 1 Kin 18:19
Image of, erected by Manasseh in the temple, 2 Kin 21:7
Vessels of, destroyed by Josiah, 2 Kin 23:4
—— Translated "wooden images," idols used in the worship of Asherah, Ex 34:13; Deut 12:3; 16:21; 1 Kin 16:32, 33; 2 Kin 23:6, 7

ASHES
are proverbs of *a* ... Job 13:12
become like dust and *a* ... Job 30:19
For I have eaten *a* ... Ps 102:9
He feeds on *a*; a deceived ... Is 44:20
sackcloth and sat in *a* ... Jon 3:6
in sackcloth and *a* ... Luke 10:13
and the *a* of a heifer ... Heb 9:13

ASHKELON
One of five Philistine cities, Josh 13:3; Jer 47:5, 7

Captured by Judah, Judg 1:18
Men of, killed by Samson, Judg 14:19, 20
Repossessed by Philistines, 1 Sam 6:17; 2 Sam 1:20
Doom of, pronounced by the prophets, Jer 47:5, 7; Amos 1:8; Zeph 2:4, 7; Zech 9:5

ASHTAROTH

A city in Bashan; residence of King Og, Deut 1:4; Josh 12:4
Captured by Israel, Josh 9:10
—— A general designation of the Canaanite female deities, 1 Sam 7:3, 4; 31:10

ASHTORETH

A mother-goddess worshiped by the Philistines, 1 Sam 31:10
Israel ensnared by, Judg 2:13; 10:6
Worshiped by Solomon, 1 Kin 11:5, 33
Destroyed by Josiah, 2 Kin 23:13

ASIA

Paul forbidden to preach in, Acts 16:6
Paul's later ministry in, Acts 19:1–26
Seven churches of, Rev 1:4, 11

ASIDE

See TURN ASIDE
lay something *a*, storing ... 1 Cor 16:2
lay *a* all filthiness ... James 1:21
Therefore, laying *a* ... 1 Pet 2:1

ASK

"Why is it that you *a* ... Gen 32:29
when your children *a* ... Josh 4:6
"*A* a sign for yourself ... Is 7:11
They shall *a* the way ... Jer 50:5
the young children *a* ... Lam 4:4
A the LORD for rain in ... Zech 10:1
whatever things you *a* ... Matt 21:22
a, and it will be ... Luke 11:9
that whatever You *a* ... John 11:22
a anything in My ... John 14:14
in that day you will *a* ... John 16:23
something, let them *a* ... 1 Cor 14:35
above all that we *a* ... Eph 3:20
wisdom, let him *a* ... James 1:5
But let him *a* in faith ... James 1:6
because you do not *a* ... James 4:2
hears us, whatever we *a* .. 1 John 5:15

ASKS

For everyone who *a* ... Matt 7:8
if his son *a* for bread ... Matt 7:9
Or if he *a* for a fish ... Luke 11:11

ASLEEP

down, and was fast *a* ... Jon 1:5
But He was *a* ... Matt 8:24
but some have fallen *a* ... 1 Cor 15:6
those who are *a* ... 1 Thess 4:15
the fathers fell *a* ... 2 Pet 3:4

ASSEMBLE

A the men of Judah ... 2 Sam 20:4
a the outcasts of Israel ... Is 11:12
A yourselves, and let ... Jer 4:5
I will *a* them in the midst ... Jer 21:4
A yourselves and come ... Ezek 39:17
a a multitude of great ... Dan 11:10
A and come, all you ... Joel 3:11
I will surely *a* all of you ... Mic 2:12

ASSEMBLED

a all the congregation ... Num 1:18
Israel *a* together at Shiloh .. Josh 18:1
Solomon *a* the elders ... 1 Kin 8:1
David *a* the children of ... 1 Chr 15:4
of the God of Israel *a* ... Ezra 9:4
Israel were *a* with fasting ... Neh 9:1
who were at Shushan *a* ... Esth 9:18
behold, the kings *a* ... Ps 48:4
elders of the people *a* at ... Matt 26:3
with him were *a* all the .. Mark 14:53
the disciples were *a* ... John 20:19
a together was shaken ... Acts 4:31
being *a* with one accord, .. Acts 15:25

ASSEMBLING

not forsaking the *a* ... Heb 10:25

ASSEMBLY

to kill this whole *a* ... Ex 16:3
It is a sacred *a* ... Lev 23:36
a I will praise You ... Ps 22:22
I have hated the *a* ... Ps 26:5
also in the *a* of the ... Ps 89:5
to be feared in the *a* ... Ps 89:7
will rest in the *a* of the ... Prov 21:16
fast, call a sacred *a* ... Joel 1:14
people, sanctify the *a* ... Joel 2:15
a I will sing praise ... Heb 2:12
to the general *a* ... Heb 12:23
come into your *a* ... James 2:2

ASSHUR

One of the sons of Shem; progenitor of the Assyrians, Gen 10:22; 1 Chr 1:17
—— The chief god of the Assyrians; seen in names like Ashurbanipal (Osnapper), Ezra 4:10
—— A city in Assyria or the nation of Assyria, Num 24:22, 24

ASSOS

A seaport of Mysia in Asia to which Paul walked, Acts 20:13

ASSURANCE

night, and have no *a* ... Deut 28:66
riches of the full *a* ... Col 2:2
Spirit and in much *a* ... 1 Thess 1:5
to the full *a* of hope ... Heb 6:11
a true heart in full *a* ... Heb 10:22

ASSURE

a our hearts before ... 1 John 3:19

ASSURED

I will give you *a* peace ... Jer 14:13
learned and been *a* ... 2 Tim 3:14

ASSUREDLY, I SAY TO YOU

"For *a*, till heaven and ... Matt 5:18
"*A*, you will by no means .. Matt 5:26
A, they have their reward. ... Matt 6:2
"*A*, I have not found such .. Matt 8:10
"*A*, it will be more ... Matt 10:15
For *a*, you will not have ... Matt 10:23
a, he shall by no means .. Matt 10:42
"*A*, among those born of .. Matt 11:11
"*a* that many prophets ... Matt 13:17
"*A*, there are some ... Matt 16:28
for *a*, if you have faith ... Matt 17:20
"*A*, unless you are ... Matt 18:3
a, he rejoices more over .. Matt 18:13
"*A*, whatever you bind ... Matt 18:18
"*A* that it is hard for a ... Matt 19:23
"*A*, that in the ... Matt 19:28
"*A*, if you have faith and .. Matt 21:21
"*A* that tax collectors ... Matt 21:31
"*A*, all these things will . Matt 23:36
A, not one stone shall be ... Matt 24:2
"*A*, this generation will ... Matt 24:34
"*A* that he will make ... Matt 24:47
'*A*, I do not know you.' ... Matt 25:12
'*A*, inasmuch as you did .. Matt 25:40
'*A*, inasmuch as you did .. Matt 25:45
A, wherever this gospel ... Matt 26:13
"*A*, one of you will betray . Matt 26:21
"*A* that this night, before . Matt 26:34
"*A*, all sins will be ... Mark 3:28
A, no sign shall be given .. Mark 8:12
A, whoever does not ... Mark 10:15
"*A*, there is no one who .. Mark 10:29
a, whoever says to this ... Mark 11:23
"*A* that this poor widow . Mark 12:43
"*A*, I will no longer ... Mark 14:25
"*A*, no prophet is accepted . Luke 4:24
A that he will gird ... Luke 12:37
a, you shall not see Me ... Luke 13:35
"*A*, today you will be ... Luke 23:43
"Most *a*, hereafter you ... John 1:51
"Most *a*, unless one is born . John 3:3
"Most *a*, We speak what ... John 3:11
"Most *a*, the Son can do ... John 5:19
"Most *a*, he who hears ... John 5:24
"Most *a*, the hour is ... John 5:25
"Most *a*, you seek Me, not . John 6:26
"Most *a*, Moses did not ... John 6:32
"Most *a*, he who believes . John 6:47
"Most *a*, unless you eat ... John 6:53
"Most *a*, whoever commits . John 8:34
"Most *a*, if anyone keeps ... John 8:51
"Most *a*, before Abraham .. John 8:58
"Most *a*, he who does not .. John 10:1
"Most *a*, I am the door of .. John 10:7
"Most *a*, unless a grain ... John 12:24
Most *a*, he who receives .. John 13:20
"Most *a*, he who believes . John 14:12
"Most *a* that you will ... John 16:20
Most *a*, whatever you ask . John 16:23
"Most *a*, when you were .. John 21:18

ASSYRIA (or Asshur)

Founded by Nimrod, Gen 10:8–12; Mic 5:6
Agent of God's purposes, Is 7:17–20; 10:5, 6
Attacks and finally conquers Israel, 2 Kin 15:19, 20, 29; 17:3–41
Invades and threatens Judah, 2 Kin 18:13–37
Hezekiah prays for help against; army miraculously slain, 2 Kin 19:1–35
Prophecies concerning, Num 24:22–24; Is 10:12–19; 14:24, 25; 19:23–25; Hos 10:6; 11:5; Nah 3:1–19

ASTONISHED

dwell in it shall be *a* ... Lev 26:32
who passes by it will be *a* .. 1 Kin 9:8
I sat *a* until the evening ... Ezra 9:4
are *a* at His rebuke ... Job 26:11
Just as many were *a* ... Is 52:14
Be *a*, O heavens, at ... Jer 2:12
remained there *a* ... Ezek 3:15
was *a* for a time, and his ... Dan 4:19
that the people were *a* ... Matt 7:28
so that they were *a* ... Matt 13:54
disciples were *a* at His ... Mark 10:24
who heard Him were *a* ... Luke 2:47
a at the catch of fish ... Luke 5:9
her parents were *a*, ... Luke 8:56
at the tomb early, *a* us ... Luke 24:22
So he, trembling and *a*, ... Acts 9:6
who believed were *a*, ... Acts 10:45
saw him, they were *a* ... Acts 12:16
being *a* at the teaching ... Acts 13:12

ASTONISHMENT

you shall become an *a* ... Deut 28:37
a has taken hold ... Jer 8:21

ASTRAY

is a people who go *a* ... Ps 95:10
a fool, shall not go *a* ... Is 35:8
Their lies lead them *a* ... Amos 2:4
and one of them goes *a* .. Matt 18:12
'They always go *a* ... Heb 3:10
like sheep going *a* ... 1 Pet 2:25

ASTROLOGERS

the *a*, the stargazers ... Is 47:13
the magicians, the *a* ... Dan 2:2
bring in the *a* ... Dan 5:7

AT THE RIGHT HAND

Son of Man sitting *a* ... Matt 26:64
heaven, and sat down *a* .. Mark 16:19
Jesus standing *a* of God ... Acts 7:55
who is even *a* of God, ... Rom 8:34
sat down *a* of the Majesty ... Heb 1:3
Priest, who is seated *a* ... Heb 8:1
heaven and is *a* of God, ... 1 Pet 3:22

ATE
she took of its fruit and *a* ... Gen 3:6
near to him, and he *a* ... Gen 27:25
I *a* all of it before ... Gen 27:33
gaunt cows *a* up the seven ... Gen 41:4
a manna forty years ... Ex 16:35
died, you arose and *a* ... 2 Sam 12:21
Men *a* angels' food ... Ps 78:25
I *a* them, and Your word ... Jer 15:16
I *a* it, and it was in my ... Ezek 3:3
all *a* and were filled ... Matt 14:20
all *a* and were filled ... Matt 15:37
he *a* locusts and wild ... Mark 1:6
a the showbread ... Mark 2:26
all *a* and were filled ... Mark 6:42
they *a* and were filled ... Mark 8:8
all *a* and were filled ... Luke 9:17
Our fathers *a* the manna ... John 6:31
men and *a* with them ... Acts 11:3
a the same spiritual ... 1 Cor 10:3
a it, and it was as sweet ... Rev 10:10

ATHALIAH
Daughter of Ahab and Jezebel, 2 Kin 8:18, 26; 2 Chr 22:2, 3
Kills royal children; usurps throne, 2 Kin 11:1–3; 2 Chr 22:10, 11
Killed in priestly uprising, 2 Kin 11:4–16; 2 Chr 23:1–21

ATHENS
Paul preaches in, Acts 17:15–34
Paul resides in, 1 Thess 3:1

ATONEMENT
a year he shall make *a* ... Ex 30:10
priest shall make *a* ... Lev 16:30
the blood that makes *a* ... Lev 17:11
for it is the Day of *A* ... Lev 23:28
what shall I make *a* ... 2 Sam 21:3
offerings to make *a* ... Neh 10:33
a is provided for ... Prov 16:6
there will be no *a* ... Is 22:14
I provide you an *a* ... Ezek 16:63

ATTACK
the Midianites, and *a* ... Num 25:17
men go up and *a* Ai ... Josh 7:3
a Amalek, and utterly ... 1 Sam 15:3
got ready to *a* the city ... 1 Kin 20:12
a Jerusalem and create ... Neh 4:8
king of the South shall *a* ... Dan 11:40
no one will *a* you to hurt ... Acts 18:10

ATTACKED
a the Rephaim in ... Gen 14:5
who *a* Midian in the ... Gen 36:35
they *a* them until they left ... Josh 11:8
he *a* the army while the ... Judg 8:11
Jonathan *a* the garrison ... 1 Sam 13:3
a Ziklag and burned it ... 1 Sam 30:1
David *a* the Philistines ... 2 Sam 8:1
a Judah, and carried ... 2 Chr 28:17
a the ram, and broke ... Dan 8:7
a the house of Jason ... Acts 17:5

ATTAIN
It is high, I cannot *a* ... Ps 139:6
understanding will *a* ... Prov 1:5
How long until they *a* ... Hos 8:5
worthy to *a* that age ... Luke 20:35
by any means, I may *a* ... Phil 3:11

ATTALIA
A seaport of Pamphylia from which Paul sailed to Antioch, Acts 14:25

ATTEND
just cause, O LORD, *a* ... Ps 17:1
And *a* to the voice of ... Ps 86:6
behold, I will *a* ... Jer 23:2

ATTENTION
My son, give *a* to my ... Prov 4:20
Till I come, give *a* ... 1 Tim 4:13
and you pay *a* to the ... James 2:3

ATTENTIVE
Let Your ears be *a* ... Ps 130:2
the people were very *a* ... Luke 19:48

ATTESTED
a Man *a* by God to you ... Acts 2:22

AUSTERE
because you are an *a* ... Luke 19:21

AUTHOR
For God is not the *a* ... 1 Cor 14:33
He became the *a* ... Heb 5:9
unto Jesus, the *a* ... Heb 12:2

AUTHORITIES
magistrates and *a* ... Luke 12:11
a that exist are ... Rom 13:1
subject to rulers and *a* ... Titus 3:1
of God, angels and *a* ... 1 Pet 3:22

AUTHORITY
Jew, wrote with full *a* ... Esth 9:29
the righteous are in *a* ... Prov 29:2
them as one having *a* ... Matt 7:29
a man under *a* ... Matt 8:9
who are great exercise *a* ... Matt 20:25
"All *a* has been given ... Matt 28:18
ones exercise *a* over ... Mark 10:42
By what *a* are You ... Mark 11:28
a I will give You ... Luke 4:6
His word was with *a* ... Luke 4:32
a over all demons ... Luke 9:1
and has given Him *a* ... John 5:27
You have given Him *a* ... John 17:2
has put in His own *a* ... Acts 1:7
For there is no *a* ... Rom 13:1
a over her own body ... 1 Cor 7:4
to have a symbol of *a* ... 1 Cor 11:10
end to all rule and all *a* ... 1 Cor 15:24
and all who are in *a* ... 1 Tim 2:2
have *a* over a man ... 1 Tim 2:12
and rebuke with all *a* ... Titus 2:15
defile the flesh, reject *a* ... Jude 8
his throne, and great *a* ... Rev 13:2
they receive *a* for one ... Rev 17:12

AUTUMN
a trees without fruit ... Jude 12

AVAILS
nor uncircumcision *a* ... Gal 5:6
of a righteous man *a* ... James 5:16

AVEN
The city of On in Egypt near Cairo; known as Heliopolis, Gen 41:45; Ezek 30:17
—— A name contemptuously applied to Bethel, Hos 10:5, 8
—— Valley in Syria, Amos 1:5

AVENGE
for He will *a* the ... Deut 32:43
you that He will *a* ... Luke 18:8
Beloved, do not *a* ... Rom 12:19
a our blood on those ... Rev 6:10

AVENGER
The *a* of blood ... Num 35:19
the enemy and the *a* ... Ps 8:2
God's minister, an *a* ... Rom 13:4
the Lord is the *a* ... 1 Thess 4:6

AVENGES
It is God who *a* ... 2 Sam 22:48
When He *a* blood ... Ps 9:12

AVOID
a foolish and ignorant ... 2 Tim 2:23
a foolish disputes ... Titus 3:9

AWAKE
be satisfied when I *a* ... Ps 17:15
I lie *a* and am like ... Ps 102:7
A, lute and harp ... Ps 108:2
My eyes are *a* through ... Ps 119:148
A, O north wind ... Song 4:16
but my heart is *a* ... Song 5:2
of the earth shall *a* ... Dan 12:2
it is high time to *a* ... Rom 13:11
A to righteousness ... 1 Cor 15:34
"*A*, you who sleep ... Eph 5:14

AWARE
Before I was even *a* ... Song 6:12
hour that he is not *a* of ... Matt 24:50
But Jesus, being *a* of it ... Mark 8:17
hour when he is not *a* ... Luke 12:46
his wife also being *a* ... Acts 5:2

AWAY
the wind drives *a* ... Ps 1:4
Do not cast me *a* ... Ps 51:11
A time to cast *a* ... Eccl 3:5
fair one, and come *a* ... Song 2:10
and the shadows flee *a* ... Song 2:17
minded to put her *a* ... Matt 1:19
and earth will pass *a* ... Matt 24:35
and steal Him *a* ... Matt 27:64
the rich He has sent *a* ... Luke 1:53
of God who takes *a* ... John 1:29
"I am going *a*, and you ... John 8:21
they cried out, "*A* ... John 19:15
"They have taken *a* ... John 20:2
crying out, "*A* with him ... Acts 21:36
the veil is taken *a* ... 2 Cor 3:14
Barnabas was carried *a* ... Gal 2:13
unless the falling *a* ... 2 Thess 2:3
in Asia have turned *a* ... 2 Tim 1:15
heard, lest we drift *a* ... Heb 2:1
if they fall *a*, to renew ... Heb 6:6
which can never take *a* ... Heb 10:11
that does not fade *a* ... 1 Pet 5:4
the world is passing *a* ... 1 John 2:17
and the heaven fled *a* ... Rev 20:11
if anyone takes *a* ... Rev 22:19

AWE
the world stand in *a* ... Ps 33:8
my heart stands in *a* ... Ps 119:161

AWESOME
How *a* is this place ... Gen 28:17
a thing that I will do ... Ex 34:10
God, the great and *a* ... Deut 7:21
God, mighty and *a* ... Deut 10:17
a things which your eyes ... Deut 10:21
a name, THE LORD ... Deut 28:58
Angel of God, very *a* ... Judg 13:6
a deeds for Your land ... 2 Sam 7:23
a deeds, by driving out ... 1 Chr 17:21
heaven, O great and *a* ... Neh 1:5
the Lord, great and *a* ... Neh 4:14
a God, Who keeps ... Neh 9:32
show Yourself *a* ... Job 10:16
with God is *a* majesty ... Job 37:22
hand shall teach You *a* ... Ps 45:4
LORD Most High is *a* ... Ps 47:2
By *a* deeds in ... Ps 65:5
a are Your works ... Ps 66:3
He is *a* in His doing ... Ps 66:5
O God, You are more *a* ... Ps 68:35
He is *a* to the kings ... Ps 76:12
Your great and *a* name ... Ps 99:3
a things by the Red Sea ... Ps 106:22
Holy and *a* is His name ... Ps 111:9
of the might of Your *a* ... Ps 145:6
When You did *a* things ... Is 64:3
with me as a mighty, *a* ... Jer 20:11
her collapse was *a* ... Lam 1:9
so high they were *a* ... Ezek 1:18
color of an *a* crystal ... Ezek 1:22
its form was *a* ... Dan 2:31
"O Lord, great and *a* ... Dan 9:4
The LORD will be *a* ... Zeph 2:11

AWL
his ear with an *a* ... Ex 21:6
you shall take an *a* ... Deut 15:17

AWOKE
Noah *a* from his wine ... Gen 9:24
Jacob *a* from his sleep ... Gen 28:16
I *a*, for the LORD sustained ... Ps 3:5
Then the Lord *a* as ... Ps 78:65
came to Him and *a* Him ... Matt 8:25
they *a* Him and said to ... Mark 4:38

came to Him and *a* Him, . . . Luke 8:24

AX
a stroke with the *a* . . . . Deut 19:5
Abimelech took an *a* . . . . Judg 9:48
a tree, the iron *a* . . . . 2 Kin 6:5
If the *a* is dull, and one . . . . Eccl 10:10
a boast itself against . . . . Is 10:15
And even now the *a* . . . . Matt 3:10

AZARIAH
A prophet who encourages King Asa, 2 Chr 15:1–8
—— Son of King Jehoshaphat, 2 Chr 21:2
—— King of Judah, 2 Kin 15:1
—— A high priest who rebukes King Uzziah, 2 Chr 26:16–20
—— Chief priest in the time of Hezekiah, 2 Chr 31:9, 10
—— The Hebrew name of Abed-Nego, Dan 1:7

AZEKAH
Camp of Goliath, 1 Sam 17:1, 4, 17
Besieged by Nebuchadnezzar, Jer 34:7

AZMAVETH
A village near Jerusalem, Neh 12:29
Also called Beth Azmaveth, Neh 7:28

AZOTUS
A city which Philip the evangelist visited, Acts 8:40

BAAL (or Baals)
Deities of Canaanite polytheism, Judg 10:10–14
The male god of the Phoenicians and Canaanites; the counterpart of the female Ashtaroth, 2 Kin 23:5
Nature of the worship of, 1 Kin 18:26, 28; 19:18; Ps 106:28; Jer 7:9; 19:5; Hos 9:10; 13:1, 2
Worshiped by Israelites, Num 25:1–5; Judg 2:11–14; 3:7; 6:28–32; 1 Kin 16:31, 32; 2 Kin 21:3; Jer 11:13; Hos 2:8
Ahaz makes images to, 2 Chr 28:1–4
Overthrown by Elijah, 1 Kin 18:17–40 by Josiah, 2 Kin 23:4, 5
Denounced by prophets, Jer 19:4–6; Ezek 16:1, 2, 20, 21
Historic retrospect, Rom 11:4

BAAL PEOR (or Baal of Peor)
A Moabite god; worshiped by Israelites, Num 25:1–9

BAAL PERAZIM
Site of David's victory over the Philistines, 2 Sam 5:18–20
Same as Perazim, Is 28:21

BAAL-ZEBUB
A Philistine god at Ekron, 2 Kin 1:2
Ahaziah inquires of, 2 Kin 1:2, 6, 16
Also called Beelzebub, Matt 10:25; 12:24

BAALAH
A town also known as Kirjath Jearim, Josh 15:9, 10

BAALS
Deities of Canaanite polytheism, Judg 10:10–14
Ensnare Israelites, Judg 2:11–14; 3:7
Ahaz makes images to, 2 Chr 28:1–4

BAANAH
A murderer of Ishbosheth, 2 Sam 4:1–12

BAASHA
Usurps throne of Israel; his evil reign; wars with Judah, 1 Kin 15:16—16:7

BABBLER
b is no different . . . . Eccl 10:11
"What does this *b* . . . . Acts 17:18

BABBLINGS
the profane and idle *b* . . . . 1 Tim 6:20

BABE
the *b* leaped in my . . . . Luke 1:44
You will find a *B* . . . . Luke 2:12
righteousness, for he is a *b* . Heb 5:13

BABEL, TOWER OF
A huge brick structure intended to magnify man and preserve the unity of the race, Gen 11:1–4
Objectives of, thwarted by God, Gen 11:5–9

BABES
Out of the mouth of *b* . . . . Ps 8:2
b shall rule over them . . . . Is 3:4
revealed them to *b* . . . . Matt 11:25
'Out of the mouth of *b* . . . . . Matt 21:16
foolish, a teacher of *b* . . . . Rom 2:20
as to carnal, as to *b* . . . . 1 Cor 3:1
as newborn *b*, desire . . . . 1 Pet 2:2

BABYLON
Built by Nimrod; Tower of Babel, Gen 10:8–10; 11:1–9
Descriptions of, Is 13:19; 14:4; Jer 51:44; Dan 4:30
Jews carried captive to, 2 Kin 25:1–21; 2 Chr 36:5–21
Inhabitants of, described, Is 47:1, 9–13; Jer 50:35–38; Dan 5:1–3
Prophecies concerning, Is 13:1–22; Jer 21:1–7; 25:9–12; 27:5–8; 29:10; Jer 50:1–46; Dan 2:31–38; 7:2–4
The prophetic city, Rev 14:8; 16:19; 17:1—18:24

BACK
Jordan turned *b* . . . . Ps 114:3
but a rod is for the *b* . . . . . . Prov 10:13
a rod for the fool's *b* . . . . Prov 26:3
I gave My *b* to those . . . . Is 50:6
cast Me behind your *b* . . . . Ezek 23:35
found Him, bring *b* word . . . . Matt 2:8
plow, and looking *b* . . . . Luke 9:62
they drew *b* and fell . . . . John 18:6
I am sending him *b* . . . . Philem 12
of those who draw *b* . . . . . . Heb 10:39
someone turns him *b* . . . . . James 5:19
inside and on the *b* . . . . Rev 5:1

BACKBITERS
b, haters of God . . . . Rom 1:30

BACKBITING
b tongue an angry . . . . Prov 25:23

BACKSLIDER
The *b* in heart will be . . . . . Prov 14:14

BACKSLIDINGS
b will rebuke you . . . . Jer 2:19
And I will heal your *b* . . . . Jer 3:22
b have increased . . . . Jer 5:6
for our *b* are many . . . . Jer 14:7

BACKWARD
fell off the seat *b* . . . . 1 Sam 4:18
shadow ten degrees *b* . . . . 2 Kin 20:11

BAD
speak to you either *b* . . . . . . Gen 24:50
good for *b* or *b* for good . . . Lev 27:10
trouble is like a *b* tooth . . . Prov 25:19
as the *b* figs which cannot . . . Jer 24:8
if your eye is *b*, your . . . . Matt 6:23
b tree bears *b* fruit . . . . Matt 7:17
a *b* tree bear good . . . . Luke 6:43
whether good or *b* . . . . 2 Cor 5:10

BADGER
covering of *b* skins . . . . Ex 26:14
sandals of *b* skin . . . . Ezek 16:10

BAG
is sealed up in a *b* . . . . Job 14:17
wages to put into a *b* . . . . Hag 1:6
nor *b* for your journey . . . . Matt 10:10

BAKE
b twelve cakes with it . . . . Lev 24:5

BAKED
b unleavened cakes . . . . Ex 12:39
b unleavened bread . . . . . . 1 Sam 28:24

BAKER
the butler and the *b* . . . . Gen 40:1
an oven heated by a *b* . . . . Hos 7:4

BAKERS
of bread from the *b* . . . . Jer 37:21

BAKES
kindles it and *b* bread . . . . Is 44:15

BALAAM
Sent by Balak to curse Israel, Num 22:5–7; Josh 24:9
Hindered by talking donkey, Num 22:22–35; 2 Pet 2:16
Curse becomes a blessing, Deut 23:4, 5; Josh 24:10
Prophecies of, Num 23:7–10, 18–24; 24:3–9, 15–24
N.T. references to, 2 Pet 2:15, 16; Jude 11; Rev 2:14

BALAK
A Moabite king, Num 22:4
Hires Balaam to curse Israel, Num 22—24

BALANCE
and the hills in a *b* . . . . Is 40:12

BALANCES
weighed in the *b* . . . . Dan 5:27

BALD
shall not make any *b* . . . . Lev 21:5
every head shall be *b* . . . . Jer 48:37
completely *b* because . . . . . Ezek 27:31

BALDHEAD
Go up, you *b* . . . . 2 Kin 2:23

BALM
a little *b* and a little . . . . Gen 43:11
Is there no *b* in Gilead . . . . Jer 8:22

BAN
No person under the *b* . . . . . Lev 27:29

BAND
A *b* of robbers takes . . . . Hos 7:1
with a golden *b* . . . . Rev 1:13

BANDS
their *b* shall be silver . . . . Ex 27:10
broken the *b* of your yoke . Lev 26:13
broken the *b* of their . . . . . . Ezek 34:27
with *b* of love, and I was . . . . Hos 11:4
girded with golden *b* . . . . Rev 15:6

BANDAGED
him, and *b* his wounds . . . Luke 10:34

BANISHED
bring his *b* one home . . . . 2 Sam 14:13
he *b* the perverted . . . . 1 Kin 15:12

BANK
cows on the *b* of the river . . . Gen 41:3
the reeds by the river's *b* . . . . . . Ex 2:3
along the *b* of the river, ... Ezek 47:7
put my money in the *b* . . . Luke 19:23

BANKERS
my money with the *b* . . . . . Matt 25:27

BANKS
the *b* of the Jordan . . . . Num 13:29
overflows all its *b* . . . . Josh 3:15
overflowed all its *b* . . . . 1 Chr 12:15
b of scented herbs . . . . Song 5:13
the *b* of the Ulai . . . . Dan 8:16

BANNER
his *b* over me was love . . . . . . Song 2:4
a *b* to the people . . . . Is 11:10

a *b* for the nations . . . . Is 11:12
lift up a *b* for the peoples . . . . . Is 62:10
Set up a *b* in the land . . . . . . Jer 51:27
a *b* over His land . . . . Zech 9:16

BANNERS
we will set up our *b* . . . . Ps 20:5
They set up their *b* . . . . Ps 74:4
as an army with *b* . . . . Song 6:4

BANQUET
b that I have prepared . . . . Esth 5:4
companions make a *b* . . . . Job 41:6
lords, came to the *b* . . . . Dan 5:10

BANQUETING
He brought me to the *b* . . . . . Song 2:4

BANQUETS
b shall be removed . . . . Amos 6:7

BAPTISM
coming to his *b* . . . . Matt 3:7
b that I am baptized . . . . . . Matt 20:22
The *b* of John—where . . . . Matt 21:25
a *b* of repentance . . . . Mark 1:4
baptized with the *b* that . . Mark 10:38
The *b* of John—was it . . . . Mark 11:30
a *b* of repentance . . . . Luke 3:3
But I have a *b* to be . . . . . . Luke 12:50
The *b* of John—was it . . . . . Luke 20:4
from the *b* of John . . . . Acts 1:22
b which John preached . . . Acts 10:37
b of repentance to all . . . . . Acts 13:24
only the *b* of John . . . . Acts 18:25
said, "Into John's *b* . . . . Acts 19:3
a *b* of repentance, ... Acts 19:4
with Him through *b* . . . . Rom 6:4
Lord, one faith, one *b* . . . . Eph 4:5
buried with Him in *b* . . . . Col 2:12
now saves us—*b* . . . . 1 Pet 3:21

BAPTISMS
of the doctrine of *b* . . . . Heb 6:2

BAPTIZE
I indeed *b* you with . . . . Matt 3:11
He will *b* you with . . . . Mark 1:8
b you with the Holy . . . . Luke 3:16
"Why then do you *b* . . . . John 1:25
me to *b* with water . . . . John 1:33
Himself did not *b* . . . . John 4:2
did not send me to *b* . . . . . . 1 Cor 1:17

BAPTIZED
b by him in the Jordan, ... Matt 3:6
at the Jordan to be *b* by . . . . Matt 3:13
"I need to be *b* by You . . . . . Matt 3:14
When He had been *b* . . . . Matt 3:16
were all *b* by him . . . . Mark 1:5
was *b* by John . . . . Mark 1:9
b with the baptism that . . Mark 10:38
b with you will be *b* . . . . . . Mark 10:39
and is *b* will be saved . . . . Mark 16:16
came out to be *b* . . . . Luke 3:7
also came to be *b* . . . . Luke 3:12
Jesus also was *b* . . . . Luke 3:21
not having been *b* . . . . Luke 7:30
with them and *b* . . . . John 3:22
b more disciples . . . . John 4:1
for John truly *b* with water . . Acts 1:5
every one of you be *b* . . . . . . Acts 2:38
received his word were *b* . . . Acts 2:41
men and women were *b* . . . . Acts 8:12
he was *b* he continued . . . . . Acts 8:13
only been *b* in the name . . . Acts 8:16
hinders me from being *b* . . . Acts 8:36
water, and he *b* him . . . . Acts 8:38
he arose and was *b* . . . . Acts 9:18
these should not be *b* . . . . . Acts 10:47
be *b* in the name . . . . Acts 10:48
you shall be *b* with . . . . Acts 11:16
her household were *b* . . . . . Acts 16:15
all his family were *b* . . . . . . Acts 16:33
believed and were *b* . . . . Acts 18:8
Into what then were you *b* . . Acts 19:3
Arise and be *b*, and wash . Acts 22:16
were *b* into Christ . . . . Rom 6:3
I thank God that I *b* . . . . 1 Cor 1:14
b the household . . . . 1 Cor 1:16
all were *b* into Moses . . . . . . 1 Cor 10:2
Spirit we were all *b* . . . . 1 Cor 12:13
who are *b* for the dead . . . 1 Cor 15:29
as many of you as were *b* . . . Gal 3:27

BAPTIZING
b them in the name of . . . . Matt 28:19
b in the wilderness . . . . Mark 1:4
where John was *b* . . . . John 1:28
therefore I came *b* . . . . John 1:31
John also was *b* in Aenon . . John 3:23
behold, He is *b* . . . . John 3:26
where John was *b* . . . . John 10:40

BAR-JESUS (or Elymas)
A Jewish false prophet, Acts 13:6–12

BAR-JONAH
Surname of Simon (Peter), Matt 16:17

BARABBAS
A murderer released in place of Jesus, Matt 27:16–26; Acts 3:14, 15

BARAK
Defeats Jabin, Judg 4:1–24
A man of faith, Heb 11:32

BARBARIAN
nor uncircumcised, *b* . . . . Col 3:11

BARBARIANS
to Greeks and to *b* . . . . Rom 1:14

BARE
make yourselves *b* . . . . Is 32:11
The LORD has made *b* . . . . Is 52:10

BAREFOOT
covered and went *b* . . . . . 2 Sam 15:30
walking naked and *b* . . . . Is 20:2

BARLEY
a land of wheat and *b* . . . . Deut 8:8
loaf of *b* bread tumbled . . . . Judg 7:13
beginning of *b* harvest . . . . . . Ruth 1:22
who has five *b* loaves . . . . John 6:9
and three quarts of *b* . . . . Rev 6:6

BARN
seed still in the *b* . . . . Hag 2:19
the wheat into my *b* . . . . Matt 13:30
storehouse nor *b* . . . . Luke 12:24

BARNABAS
A disciple from Cyprus; gives property, Acts 4:36, 37
Supports Paul, Acts 9:27
Ministers in Antioch, Acts 11:22–30
Travels with Paul, Acts 12:25; 13—15
Breaks with Paul over John Mark, Acts 15:36–39

BARNS
so your *b* will be filled . . . . . Prov 3:10
b are broken down . . . . Joel 1:17
reap nor gather into *b* . . . . . . Matt 6:26
I will pull down my *b* . . . . . . Luke 12:18

BARREN
But Sarai was *b* . . . . Gen 11:30
b has borne seven . . . . 1 Sam 2:5
He grants the *b* . . . . Ps 113:9
"Sing, O *b*, you who have . . . . . Is 54:1
'Blessed are the *b* . . . . Luke 23:29
"Rejoice, O *b*, you who do . . . Gal 4:27
you will be neither *b* . . . . 2 Pet 1:8

BARRENNESS
A fruitful land into *b* . . . . Ps 107:34

BARS
has strengthened the *b* . . . . . Ps 147:13
bronze and cut the *b* . . . . Is 45:2
the earth with its *b* . . . . Jon 2:6

BARSABAS
Nominated to replace Judas, Acts 1:23
Sent to Antioch, Acts 15:22

BARTHOLOMEW
Called Nathanael, John 1:45, 46
One of the twelve apostles, Matt 10:3; Acts 1:13

BARTIMAEUS
Blind beggar healed by Jesus, Mark 10:46–52

BARUCH
Son of Neriah, Jer 32:12, 13
Jeremiah's faithful friend and scribe, Jer 36:4–32

BARZILLAI
Supplies David with food, 2 Sam 17:27–29
Age restrains him from following David, 2 Sam 19:31–39

BASE
the elder, and the *b* . . . . Is 3:5
and the *b* things of . . . . 1 Cor 1:28

BASHAN
Conquered by Israel, Num 21:33–35
Assigned to Manasseh, Deut 3:13
Conquered by Hazael, king of Syria, 2 Kin 10:32, 33

BASIC
to the *b* principles . . . . Col 2:8
b principles of the world . . . . Col 2:20

BASIN
poured water into a *b* . . . . . . John 13:5

BASINS
its shovels and its *b* . . . . Ex 27:3
b of silver, trimmers . . . . . 2 Kin 12:13
gold for the forks, the *b* . . 1 Chr 28:17
filled with blood like *b* . . . . . Zech 9:15

BASKET
the *b* on my head . . . . Gen 40:17
the *b* out of your hand . . . . . Deut 26:4
Blessed shall be your *b* . . . . Deut 28:5
Cursed shall be your *b* . . . . Deut 28:17
b had very good figs . . . . Jer 24:2
"A *b* of summer fruit . . . . Amos 8:2
lifted up the *b* between . . . . . Zech 5:9
and put it under a *b* . . . . Matt 5:15
under a *b*, but on a . . . . Luke 11:33
I was let down in a *b* . . . . . . 2 Cor 11:33

BASKETS
there were three white *b* . . Gen 40:16
and there were two *b* . . . . Jer 24:1
they took up twelve *b* . . . . . . Matt 14:20
took up seven large *b* . . . . . Matt 15:37

BATHED
My sword shall be *b* . . . . Is 34:5
to him, "He who is *b* . . . . John 13:10

BATHSHEBA
Wife of Uriah, taken by David, 2 Sam 11
Her first child dies, 2 Sam 12:14–19
Bears Solomon, 2 Sam 12:24
Secures throne for Solomon, 1 Kin 1:15–31
Deceived by Adonijah, 1 Kin 2:13–25

BATS
To the moles and *b* . . . . Is 2:20

BATTLE
b is the LORD's . . . . 1 Sam 17:47
out to God in the *b* . . . . 1 Chr 5:20
strength for the *b* . . . . Ps 18:39
shield and sword of *b* . . . . Ps 76:3
for the day of *b* . . . . Prov 21:31
the *b* to the strong . . . . Eccl 9:11
who turn back the *b* . . . . Is 28:6
A sound of *b* is in the . . . . . Jer 50:22
who will prepare for *b*? . . . . 1 Cor 14:8
became valiant in *b* . . . . Heb 11:34
gather them to the *b* . . . . Rev 16:14

BATTLE-AX
You are My *b* . . . . Jer 51:20

each with his *b* in his hand .. Ezek 9:2

BATTLEMENT

upon her a *b* of silver .... Song 8:9

BATTLES

before us and fight our *b* .. 1 Sam 8:20
to fight our *b* .... 2 Chr 32:8

BDELLIUM

B and the onyx stone .... Gen 2:12
like the color of *b* .... Num 11:7

BE FRUITFUL AND MULTIPLY

blessed them, saying, "*B* .... Gen 1:22
on the earth, and *b* .... Gen 8:17
"*B*, and fill the earth .... Gen 9:1
B; a nation and a .... Gen 35:11

BE GLAD AND REJOICE

I will *b* in You; I will .... Ps 9:2
I will *b* in Your mercy, ... Ps 31:7
We will *b* in you .... Song 1:4
we will *b* in His salvation .... Is 25:9
you also *b* with me .... Phil 2:18
us *b* and give Him glory, ... Rev 19:7

BE OF GOOD CHEER

to the paralytic, "Son, *b* ...... Matt 9:2
her He said, "*B*, daughter .. Matt 9:22
to them, saying, "*B* .... Matt 14:27
man, saying to him, "*B* ... Mark 10:49
b, I have overcome .... John 16:33
by him and said, "*B* .... Acts 23:11

BEAM

on a carrying *b* .... Num 4:10
like a weaver's *b* .... 1 Sam 17:7
the *b* from the timbers ...... Hab 2:11

BEAMS

paneled the temple with *b* .. 1 Kin 6:9
cedar *b* on the pillars .... 1 Kin 7:2
the *b* and doorposts .... 2 Chr 3:7
make *b* for the gates .... Neh 2:8
bones are like *b* .... Job 40:18
He lays the *b* of His .... Ps 104:3
b of our houses are cedar .. Song 1:17

BEAR

greater than I can *b* .... Gen 4:13
whom Sarah shall *b* .... Gen 17:21
not *b* false witness .... Ex 20:16
from the paw of the *b* ... 1 Sam 17:37
they shall *b* you up in .... Ps 91:12
b a broken spirit .... Prov 18:14
be clean, you who *b* .... Is 52:11
b their iniquities .... Is 53:11
LORD could no longer *b* ...... Jer 44:22
b deprived of her cubs ...... Hos 13:8
lion, and a *b* met him ...... Amos 5:19
He shall *b* the glory .... Zech 6:13
child, and *b* a Son .... Matt 1:23
A good tree cannot *b* .... Matt 7:18
how long shall I *b* .... Matt 17:17
by, to *b* His cross .... Mark 15:21
wife Elizabeth will *b* .... Luke 1:13
And whoever does not *b* .. Luke 14:27
in Me that does not *b* ...... John 15:2
for he does not *b* .... Rom 13:4
are strong ought to *b* .... Rom 15:1
you may be able to *b* .... 1 Cor 10:13
B one another's .... Gal 6:2
I *b* in my body the .... Gal 6:17
b the sins of many .... Heb 9:28
like the feet of a *b* .... Rev 13:2

BEAR FRUIT

take root downward, and *b* .. Is 37:31
bring forth branches, *b*, ... Ezek 17:8
shall the vine fail to *b* .... Mal 3:11
the word, accept it, and *b* .. Mark 4:20
it and *b* with patience ...... Luke 8:15
does not *b* He takes away .. John 15:2
branch cannot *b* of itself, .. John 15:4
that we should *b* to God ..... Rom 7:4
our members to *b* to death .. Rom 7:5

BEAR WITNESS

you *b* that you approve ... Luke 11:48
to *b* of the Light, ... John 1:7
If I *b* of Myself, ... John 5:31
"You *b* of Yourself .... John 8:13
Father's name, they *b* ..... John 10:25
And you also will *b* .... John 15:27
I should *b* to the truth .... John 18:37
must also *b* at Rome .... Acts 23:11
we have seen, and *b*, and .. 1 John 1:2
three who *b* in heaven .... 1 John 5:7
three that *b* on earth: ..... 1 John 5:8

BEARD

the edges of your *b* .... Lev 19:27
I caught it by its *b* .... 1 Sam 17:35
took Amasa by the *b* ..... 2 Sam 20:9
Running down on the *b* ..... Ps 133:2

BEARING

goes forth weeping, *b* .... Ps 126:6
And He, *b* His cross ...... John 19:17
b with one another .... Col 3:13
the camp, *b* His reproach .. Heb 13:13

BEARS

Every branch that *b* .... John 15:2
b all things, believes ...... 1 Cor 13:7
it is the Spirit who *b* ...... 1 John 5:6

BEAST

b has devoured him .... Gen 37:20
You preserve man and *b* ..... Ps 36:6
I was like a *b* before .... Ps 73:22
to the *b* its food .... Ps 147:9
b touches the mountain .... Heb 12:20
And I saw a *b* rising .... Rev 13:1
Then I saw another *b* ...... Rev 13:11
the mark of the *b* .... Rev 19:20

BEASTS

are we counted as *b* .... Job 18:3
The *b* go into dens .... Job 37:8
like the *b* that perish .... Ps 49:12
I have fought with *b* ...... 1 Cor 15:32
naturally, like brute *b* ...... Jude 10

BEAT

I will *b* down his foes .... Ps 89:23
You shall *b* him with a ..... Prov 23:14
b their swords into .... Is 2:4
you shall *b* in pieces .... Mic 4:13
spat in His face and *b* ..... Matt 26:67
but *b* his breast .... Luke 18:13

BEATEN

and you will be *b* .... Mark 13:9
his will, shall be *b* .... Luke 12:47
Three times I was *b* ...... 2 Cor 11:25
when you are *b* for your ... 1 Pet 2:20

BEATS

one who *b* the air .... 1 Cor 9:26

BEAUTIFUL

of men, that they were *b* ...... Gen 6:2
woman of *b* countenance .. Gen 12:11
that she was very *b* .... Gen 12:14
woman was very *b* .... Gen 24:16
she is *b* to behold .... Gen 26:7
but Rachel was *b* .... Gen 29:17
he was a *b* child .... Ex 2:2
the captives a *b* woman ... Deut 21:11
a *b* Babylonian garment ..... Josh 7:21
and *b* appearance .... 1 Sam 25:3
woman was very *b* .... 2 Sam 11:2
a woman of *b* .... 2 Sam 14:27
she was *b* to behold .... Esth 1:11
woman was lovely and *b* ...... Esth 2:7
b as the daughters of Job .. Job 42:15
B in elevation, the joy .... Ps 48:2
has made everything *b* ...... Eccl 3:11
my love, you are as *b* .... Song 6:4
How *b* are your feet .... Song 7:1
of the LORD shall be *b* .... Is 4:2
How *b* upon the .... Is 52:7
a *b* heritage of the hosts ..... Jer 3:19
became very *b* .... Ezek 16:7
a *b* crown on your head .. Ezek 16:12
You were exceedingly *b* .. Ezek 16:13
b crowns on their heads .. Ezek 23:42
b with a multitude .... Ezek 31:9
indeed appear *b* .... Matt 23:27
adorned with *b* stones ...... Luke 21:5
temple which is called *B* ..... Acts 3:2
begging alms at the *B* ...... Acts 3:10
How *b* are the feet .... Rom 10:15
they saw he was a *b* .... Heb 11:23
b appearance perishes ... James 1:11

BEAUTIFY

b the humble with .... Ps 149:4
b the place of My .... Is 60:13

BEAUTY

for glory and for *b* .... Ex 28:2
"The *b* of Israel is .... 2 Sam 1:19
in the *b* of holiness .... 1 Chr 16:29
show her *b* to the people ... Esth 1:11
let *b* preparations be given .. Esth 2:3
yourself with glory and *b* .. Job 40:10
To behold the *b* .... Ps 27:4
greatly desire your *b* .... Ps 45:11
Zion, the perfection of *b* ...... Ps 50:2
b of the LORD our God .... Ps 90:17
do not lust after her *b* ...... Prov 6:25
and *b* is passing .... Prov 31:30
branding instead of *b* .... Is 3:24
glorious *b* is a fading .... Is 28:1
see the King in His *b* .... Is 33:17
no *b* that we should .... Is 53:2
to give them *b* for ashes ...... Is 61:3
'the perfection of *b* .... Lam 2:15
b to be abhorred .... Ezek 16:25
said, 'I am perfect in *b* ..... Ezek 27:3
wisdom and perfect in *b* .. Ezek 28:12
of God was like it in *b* ..... Ezek 31:8
the one I called *B* .... Zech 11:7
the incorruptible *b* .... 1 Pet 3:4

BECAME

man *b* a living being .... Gen 2:7
to the Jews I *b* as a Jew ... 1 Cor 9:20
like me, for I *b* like you ...... Gal 4:12

BED

house, if I make my *b* ...... Job 17:13
I remember You on my *b* ...... Ps 63:6
if I make my *b* in hell .... Ps 139:8
Also our *b* is green .... Song 1:16
b is too short to stretch ...... Is 28:20
you have set your *b* .... Is 57:7
"Arise, take up your *b* ...... Matt 9:6
be two men in one *b* ...... Luke 17:34
and the *b* undefiled .... Heb 13:4

BEDRIDDEN

had been *b* eight years ..... Acts 9:33

BEDROOM

lying on his bed in his *b* ... 2 Sam 4:7
her brother in the *b* ...... 2 Sam 13:10
and his nurse in the *b* ...... 2 Kin 11:2

BEDS

sing aloud on their *b* .... Ps 149:5
shall rest in their *b* .... Is 57:2
who lie on *b* of ivory .... Amos 6:4

BEDSTEAD

his *b* was an iron *b* .... Deut 3:11

BEE

Egypt, and for the *b* .... Is 7:18

BEELZEBUB

Jesus accused of serving, Matt 10:25; 12:24–27

BEER LAHAI ROI

Angel meets Hagar there, Gen 16:7–14
Isaac dwells in, Gen 24:62

BEERSHEBA

God appears there to Hagar, Gen 21:14–19

to Isaac, Gen 26:23–25
to Jacob, Gen 46:1–5
to Elijah, 1 Kin 19:3–7
Oaths sworn there by Abraham, Gen 21:31–33
by Isaac, Gen 26:26–33

BEFALL
calamity *b* him .... Gen 42:4
b you in the last days .... Gen 49:1
No evil shall *b* you .... Ps 91:10

BEFOREHAND
do not worry *b* .... Mark 13:11
told you all things *b* .... Mark 13:23
not to meditate *b* .... Luke 21:14
when He testified *b* .... 1 Pet 1:11

BEG
I would *b* mercy of my .... Job 9:15
I am ashamed to *b* .... Luke 16:3
b you as sojourners .... 1 Pet 2:11

BEGAN
Then men *b* to call on .... Gen 4:26
since the world *b* .... Luke 1:70

BEGETS
b a scoffer does .... Prov 17:21
b a wise child will .... Prov 23:24
b a hundred children .... Eccl 6:3

BEGGAR
lifts the *b* from the ash .... 1 Sam 2:8
there was a certain *b* .... Luke 16:20

BEGGARLY
weak and *b* elements .... Gal 4:9

BEGGED
So the demons *b* Him, ... Matt 8:31
they *b* Him to depart .... Matt 8:34
b him, saying, 'Have .... Matt 18:29
b Him to put His hand .... Mark 7:32
b Him earnestly, saying .... Luke 7:4
b Him to come to his .... Luke 8:41
not this he who sat and *b* .... John 9:8
the Gentiles *b* that these .... Acts 13:42
those who heard it *b* .... Heb 12:19

BEGINNING
b God created the .... Gen 1:1
Though your *b* was .... Job 8:7
of the LORD is the *b* .... Ps 111:10
that God does from *b* .... Eccl 3:11
who made them at the *b* .... Matt 19:4
In the *b* was the Word .... John 1:1
This *b* of signs Jesus .... John 2:11
a murderer from the *b* .... John 8:44
with Me from the *b* .... John 15:27
the *b*, the firstborn .... Col 1:18
having neither *b* .... Heb 7:3
True Witness, the *B* .... Rev 3:14
and the Omega, the *B* .... Rev 21:6

BEGOTTEN
See ONLY BEGOTTEN SON
today I have *b* You .... Ps 2:7
heart, 'Who has *b* .... Is 49:21
glory as of the only *b* .... John 1:14
Christ Jesus I have *b* .... 1 Cor 4:15
abundant mercy has *b* .... 1 Pet 1:3
loves him who is *b* .... 1 John 5:1

BEGUN
Having *b* in the Spirit .... Gal 3:3
that He who has *b* .... Phil 1:6

BEHALF
to speak on God's *b* .... Job 36:2
you on Christ's *b* .... 2 Cor 5:20
has been granted on *b* .... Phil 1:29

BEHAVE
I will *b* wisely in a .... Ps 101:2
does not *b* rudely .... 1 Cor 13:5

BEHAVED
sent him, and *b* wisely .... 1 Sam 18:5
and blamelessly we *b* .... 1 Thess 2:10

BEHAVIOR
of good *b*, hospitable .... 1 Tim 3:2
they be reverent in *b* .... Titus 2:3

BEHEADED
he sent and had John *b* .... Matt 14:10
those who had been *b* .... Rev 20:4

BEHEMOTH
Described, Job 40:15–24

BEHOLD
the eyes to *b* the sun .... Eccl 11:7
B, you are fair .... Song 1:15
B, the virgin shall .... Is 7:14
Judah, "*B* your God .... Is 40:9
B the Lamb of God .... John 1:36
I am, that they may *b* .... John 17:24
to them, "*B* the Man .... John 19:5
B what manner of love .... 1 John 3:1

BEHOLDING
with unveiled face, *b* .... 2 Cor 3:18

BEING
man became a living *b* .... Gen 2:7
God while I have my *b* .... Ps 104:33
move and have our *b* .... Acts 17:28
who, *b* in the form of .... Phil 2:6

BEL
Patron god of Babylon, Is 46:1; Jer 50:2; 51:44

BELIEF
by the Spirit and *b* .... 2 Thess 2:13

BELIEVE
b me or listen to my voice .... Ex 4:1
will they not *b* Me .... Num 14:11
did not *b* the LORD .... Deut 1:32
I did not *b* the words .... 1 Kin 10:7
B in the LORD your God .... 2 Chr 20:20
did not *b* in His wondrous .... Ps 78:32
which you would not *b* .... Hab 1:5
ones who *b* in Me to sin .... Matt 18:6
'Why then did you not *b* .... Matt 21:25
cross, and we will *b* Him .... Matt 27:42
Repent, and *b* .... Mark 1:15
Do not be afraid; only *b* .... Mark 5:36
tears, "Lord, I *b* .... Mark 9:24
b in Me to stumble .... Mark 9:42
b that you receive .... Mark 11:24
that we may see and *b* .... Mark 15:32
because they did not *b* .... Mark 16:14
have no root, who *b* .... Luke 8:13
only *b*, and she will .... Luke 8:50
will by no means *b* .... Luke 22:67
and slow of heart to *b* .... Luke 24:25
all through him might *b* .... John 1:7
to those who *b* .... John 1:12
how will you *b* .... John 3:12
Now we *b*, not because .... John 4:42
sent, Him you do not *b* .... John 5:38
we may see it and *b* .... John 6:30
we have come to *b* .... John 6:69
brothers did not *b* in Him .... John 7:5
not *b* that I am He .... John 8:24
to him, "Do you *b* .... John 9:35
not *b*, because you .... John 10:26
b that the Father is in Me .... John 10:38
b that You are the Christ .... John 11:27
this, that they may *b* .... John 11:42
they did not *b* in Him .... John 12:37
may *b* that I am He .... John 13:19
you *b* in God, *b* also in .... John 14:1
B Me that I am in .... John 14:11
we *b* that You came .... John 16:30
b that You sent Me .... John 17:21
truth, so that you may *b* .... John 19:35
into His side, I will not *b* .... John 20:25
written that you may *b* .... John 20:31
word of the gospel and *b* .... Acts 15:7
"*B* on the Lord Jesus .... Acts 16:31
b on Him who would .... Acts 19:4
King Agrippa, do you *b* .... Acts 26:27
to all and on all who *b* .... Rom 3:22
father of all those who *b* .... Rom 4:11
the Lord Jesus and *b* .... Rom 10:9
And how shall they *b* .... Rom 10:14
to save those who *b* .... 1 Cor 1:21
a wife who does not *b* .... 1 Cor 7:12
I spoke," we also *b* .... 2 Cor 4:13
given to those who *b* .... Gal 3:22
Christ, not only to *b* .... Phil 1:29
if we *b* that Jesus died .... 1 Thess 4:14
should *b* the lie .... 2 Thess 2:11
of those who *b* .... 1 Tim 4:10
comes to God must *b* .... Heb 11:6
Even the demons *b* .... James 2:19
to you who *b*, He .... 1 Pet 2:7
should *b* on the name .... 1 John 3:23
Beloved, do not *b* .... 1 John 4:1
written to you who *b* .... 1 John 5:13

BELIEVED
And he *b* in the LORD .... Gen 15:6
So the people *b* .... Ex 4:31
b that I would see the .... Ps 27:13
Who has *b* our report .... Is 53:1
people of Nineveh *b* .... Jon 3:5
Blessed is she who *b* .... Luke 1:45
they *b* the Scripture .... John 2:22
because he has not *b* .... John 3:18
of that city *b* in Him .... John 4:39
you *b* Moses, you would .... John 5:46
Jesus did, *b* in Him .... John 11:45
who has *b* our report .... John 12:38
and he saw and *b* .... John 20:8
seen Me, you have *b* .... John 20:29
who heard the word *b* .... Acts 4:4
of those who *b* were of .... Acts 4:32
appointed to eternal life *b* .... Acts 13:48
Holy Spirit when you *b* .... Acts 19:2
"Abraham *b* God .... Rom 4:3
in whom they have not *b* .... Rom 10:14
than when we first *b* .... Rom 13:11
unless you *b* in vain .... 1 Cor 15:2
'I *b* and therefore I spoke .... 2 Cor 4:13
b God, and it was accounted .... Gal 3:6
b on in the world .... 1 Tim 3:16
I know whom I have *b* .... 2 Tim 1:12
b the love that God has .... 1 John 4:16

BELIEVERS
be an example to the *b* .... 1 Tim 4:12
are benefited are *b* .... 1 Tim 6:2

BELIEVES
See HE WHO BELIEVES
The simple *b* every .... Prov 14:15
possible to him who *b* .... Mark 9:23
b that those things he .... Mark 11:23
He who *b* and is .... Mark 16:16
that whoever *b* in Him .... John 3:16
He who *b* in the Son .... John 3:36
b in Him who sent Me .... John 5:24
who *b* in Me shall never .... John 6:35
b in Him may have .... John 6:40
he who *b* in Me has .... John 6:47
He who *b* in Me, as the .... John 7:38
He who *b* in Me, though .... John 11:25
He who *b* in Me .... John 12:44
whoever *b* in Him .... Acts 10:43
Him everyone who *b* is .... Acts 13:39
for everyone who *b* .... Rom 1:16
to everyone who *b* .... Rom 10:4
with the heart one *b* .... Rom 10:10
b all things, hopes all .... 1 Cor 13:7
Whoever *b* that Jesus is .... 1 John 5:1
he who *b* that Jesus is .... 1 John 5:5
b in the Son of God .... 1 John 5:10

BELIEVING
you ask in prayer, *b* .... Matt 21:22
b you may have life .... John 20:31
take along a *b* wife .... 1 Cor 9:5
blessed with *b* Abraham .... Gal 3:9
those who have *b* masters .... 1 Tim 6:2

BELLY
On your *b* you shall go .... Gen 3:14

And Jonah was in the *b* ..... Jon 1:17
three nights in the *b* ...... Matt 12:40
whose god is their *b* .... Phil 3:19

BELONG

interpretations *b* to God .... Gen 40:8
highest heavens *b* to ...... Deut 10:14
secret things *b* to .... Deut 29:29
"Dominion and fear *b* .... Job 25:2
shields of the earth *b* .... Ps 47:9
things also *b* to the wise .. Prov 24:23
To the Lord our God *b* .... Dan 9:9
My name, because you *b* .. Mark 9:41
to whom *b* the glory .... 1 Pet 4:11

BELONGS

offering that *b* to the LORD .. Lev 7:20
Salvation *b* to the LORD .... Ps 3:8
that power *b* to God .... Ps 62:11
to You, O Lord, *b* mercy .... Ps 62:12
shield *b* to the LORD.......... Ps 89:18
to whom vengeance *b* .... Ps 94:1
righteousness *b* to You ...... Dan 9:7
solid food *b* to those .... Heb 5:14
b to another tribe .... Heb 7:13
"Salvation *b* to our God ..... Rev 7:10

BELOVED

"The *b* of the Lord .... Deut 33:12
so He gives His *b* .... Ps 127:2
of myrrh is my *b* .... Song 1:13
My *b* is mine, and I am .... Song 2:16
b more than another .... Song 5:9
Where has your *b* .... Song 6:1
leaning upon her *b* .... Song 8:5
a song of my *B* .... Is 5:1
for you are greatly *b* .... Dan 9:23
"This is My *b* Son .... Matt 3:17
election they are *b* .... Rom 11:28
us accepted in the *B* .... Eph 1:6
Luke the *b* physician .... Col 4:14
than a slave as a *b* .... Philem 16
"This is My *b* Son .... 2 Pet 1:17
our *b* brother Paul .... 2 Pet 3:15
the saints and the *b* .... Rev 20:9

BELOVED SON

saying, "This is My *b*, ... Matt 3:17
"This is My *b*, in whom .... Matt 17:5
I will send my *b*. .... Luke 20:13
To Timothy, a *b*: .... 2 Tim 1:2

BELSHAZZAR

King of Babylon; Daniel interprets his dream, Dan 5

BELT

with a leather *b* .... Matt 3:4
us, he took Paul's *b* .... Acts 21:11

BELTESHAZZAR

Daniel's Babylonian name, Dan 1:7

BEMOAN

Or who will *b* you .... Jer 15:5
for the dead, nor *b* .... Jer 22:10

BEN-AMMI

Son of Lot; father of the Ammonites, Gen 19:38

BEN-HADAD

Ben-Hadad I, king of Damascus; hired by Asa, king of Judah, to attack Baasha, king of Israel, 1 Kin 15:18–21
——— Ben-Hadad II, king of Damascus; makes war on Ahab, king of Israel, 1 Kin 20
Falls in siege against Samaria, 2 Kin 6:24–33; 7:6–20
Killed by Hazael, 2 Kin 8:7–15
——— Ben-Hadad III, king of Damascus; loses all Israelite conquests made by Hazael, his father, 2 Kin 13:3–25

BEN-ONI

Rachel's name for Benjamin, Gen 35:16–18

BENAIAH

The son of Jehoiada; a mighty man, 2 Sam 23:20–23
Faithful to David, 2 Sam 15:18; 20:23
Escorts Solomon to the throne, 1 Kin 1:38–40
Executes Adonijah, Joab and Shimei, 1 Kin 2:25, 29–34, 46
——— A Pirathonite; another of David's mighty men, 2 Sam 23:30
Divisional commander, 1 Chr 27:14

BEND

The wicked *b* their bow ...... Ps 11:2

BENEATH

and on the earth *b* .... Deut 4:39
"You are from *b* .... John 8:23

BENEFACTORS

them are called '*b* .... Luke 22:25

BENEFIT

That I may see the *b* .... Ps 106:5
people who could not *b* .... Is 30:5
might have a second *b* .... 2 Cor 1:15

BENEFITS

daily loads us with *b* .... Ps 68:19
forget not all His *b* .... Ps 103:2
for all His *b* toward me .... Ps 116:12

BENJAMIN

Jacob's youngest son, Gen 35:16–20
Taken to Egypt against Jacob's wishes, Gen 42—45
Jacob's prophecy concerning, Gen 49:27
——— Tribe of:
Families of, Num 26:38–41
Territory allotted to, Josh 18:11–28
Attacked by remaining tribes for condoning sin of Gibeah, Judg 20:12–48
Wives provided for remnant of, Judg 21:1–23
Tribe of Saul, 1 Sam 9:1, 2
of Paul, Phil 3:5

BENT

have *b* their bow, ... Ps 37:14
and all their bows *b* .... Is 5:28
behold, this vine *b* .... Ezek 17:7
hearts shall be *b* on evil ... Dan 11:27
I have *b* Judah, My bow, ... Zech 9:13
was *b* over and could ...... Luke 13:11

BEREA

A city of Macedonia; visited by Paul, Acts 17:10–15

BEREAVE

I will *b* them of .... Jer 15:7
no more shall you *b* .... Ezek 36:12
children, yet I will *b* .... Hos 9:12

BERNICE

Sister of Herod Agrippa II, Acts 25:13, 23
Hears Paul's defense, Acts 26:1–30

BERODACH-BALADAN

See MERODACH-BALADAN
A king of Babylon, 2 Kin 20:12–19

BERYL

fourth row, a *b* .... Ex 28:20
a *b*, an onyx .... Ex 39:13
rods of gold set with *b* ..... Song 5:14
was like the color of *b* ..... Ezek 1:16
the color of a *b* .... Ezek 10:9
topaz, and diamond, *b* .... Ezek 28:13
His body was like *b* .... Dan 10:6
chrysolite, the eighth *b* .... Rev 21:20

BESEECH

Return, we *b* You .... Ps 80:14
b you therefore .... Rom 12:1
of the LORD, *b* you to .... Eph 4:1

BESIDE

He leads me *b* the .... Ps 23:2

"Paul, you are *b* .... Acts 26:24
For if we are *b* .... 2 Cor 5:13

BESIEGED

Joab *b* the city .... 2 Sam 11:16
went up and *b* Samaria .... 2 Kin 6:24
and the city was *b* .... 2 Kin 24:10
of cucumbers, as a *b* city .... Is 1:8
army *b* Jerusalem .... Jer 32:2
to Jerusalem and *b* it .... Dan 1:1

BEST

with the *b* ointments .... Amos 6:6
b seats in the synagogues .. Matt 23:6
b places at feasts .... Mark 12:39
sit down in the *b* place .... Luke 14:8
'Bring out the *b* .... Luke 15:22
earnestly desire the *b* .... 1 Cor 12:31

BESTOW

LORD, that He may *b* .... Ex 32:29
b greater honor .... 1 Cor 12:23

BESTOWED

love the Father has *b* ...... 1 John 3:1

BETH HORON

Twin towns of Ephraim, Josh 16:3, 5
Fortified by Solomon, 2 Chr 8:3–5
Prominent in battles, Josh 10:10–14; 1 Sam 13:18

BETH PEOR

Town near Pisgah, Deut 3:29
Moses buried near, Deut 34:6
Assigned to Reubenites, Josh 13:15, 20

BETH SHAN (or Beth Shean)

A town in Issachar, Josh 17:11–16
Saul's corpse hung up at, 1 Sam 31:10–13; 2 Sam 21:12–14

BETH SHEMESH

Ark brought to, 1 Sam 6:12–19
Joash defeats Amaziah at, 2 Kin 14:11
Taken by Philistines, 2 Chr 28:18

BETHABARA

A place beyond the Jordan where John baptized, John 1:28

BETHANY

A town on the Mt. of Olives, Luke 19:29
Home of Lazarus, John 11:1
Home of Simon, the leper, Matt 26:6
Jesus visits there, Mark 11:1, 11, 12
Scene of the ascension, Luke 24:50, 51

BETHEL

Abram settles near, Gen 12:7, 8
Site of Abram's altar, Gen 13:3, 4
Site of Jacob's vision of the ladder, Gen 28:10–19
Jacob returns to, Gen 35:1–15
Samuel judges there, 1 Sam 7:15, 16
Site of worship and sacrifice, 1 Sam 10:3
Center of idolatry, 1 Kin 12:28–33
Josiah destroys altars of, 2 Kin 23:4, 15–20
Denounced by prophets, 1 Kin 13:1–10; Amos 7:10–13; Jer 48:13; Hos 10:15

BETHESDA

Jerusalem pool, John 5:2–4

BETHLEHEM

Originally called Ephrath, Gen 35:16
Rachel buried there, Gen 35:19
Home of Naomi and Boaz, Ruth 1:1, 19; 4:9–11
Home of David, 1 Sam 16:1–18
Predicted place of Messiah's birth, Mic 5:2
Christ born there, Matt 2:1; Luke 2:4–7; John 7:42
Infants of, killed by Herod, Matt 2:16–18

BETHPHAGE

Village near Bethany, Mark 11:1

Near Mt. of Olives, Matt 21:1

BETHSAIDA
A city of Galilee, Mark 6:45
Home of Andrew, Peter and Philip, John 1:44; 12:21
Blind man healed there, Mark 8:22, 23
5,000 fed nearby, Luke 9:10–17
Unbelief of, denounced, Matt 11:21; Luke 10:13

BETRAY
the outcasts, do not *b* . . . . Is 16:3
you, one of you will *b* . . . . . Matt 26:21
Now brother will *b* . . . . Mark 13:12

BETRAYED
Man is about to be *b* . . . . . . Matt 17:22
in which He was *b* . . . . 1 Cor 11:23

BETRAYER
See, My *b* is at hand . . . . . Matt 26:46

BETRAYING
"Judas, are you *b* . . . . Luke 22:48

BETRAYS
who is the one who *b* . . . . . . John 21:20

BETROTH
"You shall *b* a wife . . . . Deut 28:30
"I will *b* you to Me . . . . Hos 2:19

BETROTHED
a virgin who is not *b* . . . . Ex 22:16
finds a *b* young woman . . . . Deut 22:25
I *b* to myself for a . . . . 2 Sam 3:14
mother Mary was *b* to . . . . . Matt 1:18
to a virgin *b* to a man . . . . . . Luke 1:27
For I have *b* you to . . . . 2 Cor 11:2

BETTER
obey is *b* than sacrifice . . 1 Sam 15:22
It is *b* to trust in . . . . Ps 118:8
B is a little with the . . . . . . Prov 15:16
B is a dry morsel . . . . Prov 17:1
B is the poor who . . . . Prov 19:1
B to dwell in . . . . Prov 21:19
b is a neighbor . . . . Prov 27:10
B a handful with . . . . Eccl 4:6
Two are *b* than one . . . . Eccl 4:9
B a poor and wise . . . . Eccl 4:13
were the former days *b* . . . . . Eccl 7:10
features appeared *b* . . . . Dan 1:15
For it is *b* to marry . . . . 1 Cor 7:9
Christ, which is far *b* . . . . Phil 1:23
b than the angels . . . . Heb 1:4
b things concerning . . . . Heb 6:9
b things than that . . . . Heb 12:24

BEULAH
A symbol of true Israel, Is 62:4, 5

BEVERAGE
lacks no blended *b* . . . . Song 7:2

BEWAIL
Israel, *b* the burning . . . . Lev 10:6
b my virginity . . . . Judg 11:37
I will *b* the vine . . . . Is 16:9

BEWARE
"*B* of false prophets . . . . Matt 7:15
b of evil workers . . . . Phil 3:2
B lest anyone cheat . . . . Col 2:8

BEWILDERED
"They are *b* by the land . . . . . . Ex 14:3

BEWITCHED
b you that you should . . . . Gal 3:1

BEYOND
b what is written . . . . 1 Cor 4:6
yes, and *b* their ability . . . . . . 2 Cor 8:3
advanced in Judaism *b* . . . . . . Gal 1:14

BEZALEL
Hur's grandson, 1 Chr 2:20
Tabernacle builder, Ex 31:1–11; 35:30–35

BEZER
A city of refuge in the territory of Reuben, Deut 4:43; John 20:8

BILDAD
One of Job's friends, Job 2:11
Makes three speeches, Job 8:1–22; 18:1–21; 25:1–6

BILHAH
Rachel's maid, Gen 29:29
The mother of Dan and Naphtali, Gen 30:1–8
Commits incest with Reuben, Gen 35:22

BILLOWS
b have gone over me . . . . Ps 42:7
all Your *b* and Your . . . . Jon 2:3

BIND
b them as a sign . . . . Deut 6:8
b this line of scarlet . . . . Josh 2:18
b the cluster of the . . . . Job 38:31
b the wild ox in the . . . . Job 39:10
b the sacrifice with cords . . . Ps 118:27
b them around your . . . . Prov 3:3
B them continually upon . . . . . Prov 6:21
B them on your fingers . . . . Prov 7:3
B up the testimony . . . . Is 8:16
but He will *b* us up . . . . Hos 6:1
and whatever you *b* . . . . Matt 16:19
'*B* him hand and foot . . . . Matt 22:13
b heavy burdens . . . . Matt 23:4
b the man who owns this . . . Acts 21:11

BINDS
first *b* the strong man . . . . . . Matt 12:29

BIRD
the blood of the *b* . . . . Lev 14:52
with him as with a *b* . . . . Job 41:5
soul, "Flee as a *b* . . . . Ps 11:1
has escaped as a *b* . . . . Ps 124:7
b hastens to the snare . . . . Prov 7:23
for a *b* of the air may . . . . . . Eccl 10:20
fly away like a *b* . . . . Hos 9:11
unclean and hated *b* . . . . Rev 18:2

BIRDS
b will eat your flesh . . . . Gen 40:19
b make their nests . . . . Ps 104:17
b caught in a snare . . . . Eccl 9:12
Look at the *b* of the air . . . . . Matt 6:26
"Foxes have holes and *b* . . . . Matt 8:20

BIRTH
cursed the day of his *b* . . . . Job 3:1
heaven, who gives it *b* . . . . . . Job 38:29
makes the deer give *b* . . . . Ps 29:9
the day of one's *b* . . . . Eccl 7:1
bring to the time of *b* . . . . Is 66:9
the deer also gave *b* . . . . Jer 14:5
no *b*, no pregnancy . . . . Hos 9:11
Now the *b* of Jesus . . . . Matt 1:18
will rejoice at his *b* . . . . Luke 1:14
who was blind from *b* . . . . John 9:1
labors with *b* pangs . . . . Rom 8:22
conceived, it gives *b* . . . . James 1:15

BIRTHDAY
which was Pharaoh's *b* . . . . Gen 40:20
b gave a feast for his . . . . Mark 6:21

BIRTHRIGHT
"Sell me your *b* . . . . Gen 25:31
Esau despised his *b* . . . . Gen 25:34
according to his *b* . . . . Gen 43:33
of food sold his *b* . . . . Heb 12:16

BIRTHSTOOLS
see them on the *b* . . . . Ex 1:16

BISHOP
the position of a *b* . . . . 1 Tim 3:1
b must be blameless . . . . Titus 1:7

BIT
and they *b* the people . . . . Num 21:6
be harnessed with *b* . . . . Ps 32:9

BITE
A serpent may *b* . . . . Eccl 10:11
But if you *b* and . . . . Gal 5:15

BITHYNIA
The Spirit keeps Paul from, Acts 16:7
Peter writes to Christians of, 1 Pet 1:1

BITS
the great house into *b* . . . . . Amos 6:11
Indeed, we put *b* . . . . James 3:3

BITTER
made their lives *b* . . . . Ex 1:14
b herbs they shall eat it . . . . . . Ex 12:8
to those who are *b* . . . . Prov 31:6
who put *b* for sweet . . . . Is 5:20
and do not be *b* . . . . Col 3:19
But if you have *b* . . . . James 3:14
make your stomach *b* . . . . Rev 10:9

BITTERLY
has dealt very *b* . . . . Ruth 1:20
And Hezekiah wept *b* . . . . 2 Kin 20:3
he went out and wept *b* . . . . Matt 26:75

BITTERNESS
man dies in the *b* . . . . Job 21:25
heart knows its own *b* . . . . . Prov 14:10
all my years in the *b* . . . . Is 38:15
you are poisoned by *b* . . . . Acts 8:23
b springing up cause . . . . Heb 12:15

BLACK
My skin grows *b* . . . . Job 30:30
wavy, and *b* as a raven . . . . . . Song 5:11
one hair white or *b* . . . . Matt 5:36
a *b* horse and he who sat . . . . . . Rev 6:5
and the sun became *b* . . . . Rev 6:12

BLACKNESS
the heavens with *b* . . . . Is 50:3
whom is reserved the *b* . . . . Jude 13

BLACKSMITH
no *b* to be found . . . . 1 Sam 13:19
The *b* with the tongs . . . . Is 44:12
I have created the *b* . . . . Is 54:16

BLADE
went in after the *b* . . . . Judg 3:22
first the *b*, then the head . . . . . Mark 4:28

BLAME
that anyone should *b* . . . . 2 Cor 8:20
be holy and without *b* . . . . Eph 1:4

BLAMELESS
walk before Me and be *b* . . . Gen 17:1
You shall be *b* . . . . Deut 18:13
b before Him, and I . . . . . . 2 Sam 22:24
and that man was *b* . . . . Job 1:1
a *b* and upright man . . . . Job 1:8
a *b* and upright man . . . . Job 2:3
will not cast away the *b* . . . . Job 8:20
though I were *b* . . . . Job 9:20
b who is ridiculed . . . . Job 12:4
make your ways *b* . . . . Job 22:3
I was also *b* before Him . . . . Ps 18:23
Then I shall be *b* . . . . Ps 19:13
Mark the *b* man . . . . Ps 37:37
when You speak, and *b* . . . . Ps 51:4
Let my heart be *b* . . . . Ps 119:80
the *b* will remain . . . . Prov 2:21
righteousness of the *b* . . . . Prov 11:5
the *b* in their ways . . . . Prov 11:20
the *b* will inherit good . . . . . . Prov 28:10
Sabbath, and are *b* . . . . Matt 12:5
end, that you may be *b* . . . . 1 Cor 1:8
that you may become *b* . . . . Phil 2:15
which is in the law, *b* . . . . Phil 3:6
you holy, and *b* . . . . Col 1:22
your hearts *b* in . . . . 1 Thess 3:13
body be preserved *b* . . . . 1 Thess 5:23
bishop then must be *b* . . . . 1 Tim 3:2
deacons, being found *b* . . . . . . 1 Tim 3:10
man is *b*, the husband . . . . Titus 1:6
a bishop must be *b* . . . . Titus 1:7
without spot and *b* . . . . 2 Pet 3:14

BLAMELESSLY
b we behaved . . . . 1 Thess 2:10

BLANKET
covered him with a *b* . . . . . Judg 4:18

BLASPHEME
b Your name forever . . . . Ps 74:10
compelled them to *b* . . . . Acts 26:11
may learn not to *b* . . . . 1 Tim 1:20
b that noble name . . . . James 2:7
God, to *b* His name . . . . Rev 13:6

BLASPHEMED
a foolish people has *b* . . . . Ps 74:18
b continually every . . . . Is 52:5
who passed by *b* Him . . . . . Matt 27:39
who were hanged *b* . . . . Luke 23:39
The name of God is *b* . . . . . . Rom 2:24
doctrine may not be *b* . . . . . . 1 Tim 6:1
On their part He is *b* . . . . 1 Pet 4:14
great heat, and they *b* . . . . . . Rev 16:9

BLASPHEMER
I was formerly a *b* . . . . 1 Tim 1:13

BLASPHEMERS
boasters, proud, *b* . . . . 2 Tim 3:2

BLASPHEMES
b the name of the LORD . . . . Lev 24:16
"This Man *b*!" . . . . Matt 9:3
who *b* against the Holy . . . . Mark 3:29
to him who *b* against . . . . . . Luke 12:10

BLASPHEMIES
false witness, *b* . . . . Matt 15:19
is this who speaks *b* . . . . Luke 5:21
great things and *b* . . . . Rev 13:5

BLASPHEMY
trouble and rebuke and *b* . . . . . Is 37:3
but the *b* against . . . . Matt 12:31
"He has spoken *b* . . . . Matt 26:65
You have heard the *b* . . . . Mark 14:64
not stone You, but for *b* . . John 10:33
mouth in *b* against God . . . . . Rev 13:6
was full of names of *b* . . . . . . Rev 17:3

BLAST
By the *b* of God they . . . . Job 4:9
for the *b* of the terrible . . . . Is 25:4

BLASTED
"I *b* you with blight . . . . Amos 4:9

BLEATING
"What then is this *b* . . . . . 1 Sam 15:14

BLEMISH
shall be without *b* . . . . Ex 12:5
LORD, a ram without *b* . . . . Lev 6:6
be holy and without *b* . . . . . . Eph 5:27
as of a lamb without *b* . . . . . . 1 Pet 1:19

BLEMISHED
to the Lord what is *b* . . . . Mal 1:14

BLESS
I will *b* you and make . . . . . . Gen 12:2
b those who *b* you . . . . Gen 12:3
blessing I will *b* you . . . . Gen 22:17
I will *b* you and multiply . . Gen 26:24
b you before I die . . . . Gen 27:4
"*B* me—me also . . . . Gen 27:34
You go unless You *b* . . . . . . Gen 32:26
He will *b* your bread . . . . Ex 23:25
"The LORD *b* you and . . . . . . Num 6:24
whom you *b* is blessed . . . . . . Num 22:6
Gerizim to *b* the people . . . . Deut 27:12
returned to *b* his house . . . 1 Chr 16:43
b the LORD at all . . . . Ps 34:1
b with their mouth . . . . Ps 62:4
b You while I live . . . . Ps 63:4
b His holy name . . . . Ps 103:1
b the house of Israel . . . . Ps 115:12
b those who fear the . . . . Ps 115:13
b you in the name of . . . . Ps 129:8
I will abundantly *b* . . . . Ps 132:15
this day forward I will *b* . . . . . Hag 2:19
b those who curse . . . . Luke 6:28
B those who persecute . . . . Rom 12:14
Being reviled, we *b* . . . . 1 Cor 4:12
of blessing which we *b* . . . 1 Cor 10:16
"blessing I will *b* you . . . . . . Heb 6:14
With it we *b* our God . . . . . . James 3:9

BLESS THE LORD
then you shall *b* your God . . Deut 8:10
the assembly, "Now *b* . . . . 1 Chr 29:20
Stand up and *b* . . . . Neh 9:5
I will *b* who has given . . . . Ps 16:7
the congregations I will *b* . . . . Ps 26:12
I will *b* at all times; . . . . Ps 34:1
B, O my soul; and all . . . . Ps 103:1
B, O my soul! O LORD . . . . Ps 104:1
we will *b* from this time . . . . Ps 115:18
b, all you servants . . . . Ps 134:1
B, O house of Israel! . . . . Ps 135:19

BLESSED
And God *b* them . . . . Gen 1:22
God *b* the seventh day . . . . Gen 2:3
God *b* Noah and his sons . . . . . . Gen 9:1
the earth shall be *b* . . . . Gen 12:3
b be those who . . . . Gen 27:29
indeed he shall be *b* . . . . Gen 27:33
b the Sabbath day . . . . Ex 20:11
he whom you bless is *b* . . . . . Num 22:6
b, and I cannot reverse . . . Num 23:20
B is he who blesses . . . . Num 24:9
B shall you be in the city . . . Deut 28:3
b among women is Jael . . . . . Judg 5:24
grew, and the LORD *b* . . . . . . Judg 13:24
the LORD *b* Obed-Edom . . . 2 Sam 6:11
You have *b* the work of . . . . . . Job 1:10
B is the man who walks . . . . Ps 1:1
B is the man to whom . . . . Ps 32:2
B is the nation whose . . . . Ps 33:12
B is he who considers . . . . Ps 41:1
B are those who keep . . . . Ps 106:3
B is he who comes . . . . Ps 118:26
b who fears the LORD . . . . Ps 128:4
rise up and call her *b* . . . . . Prov 31:28
nations will call you *b* . . . . . . Mal 3:12
B are the poor in . . . . Matt 5:3
B are those who mourn . . . . . . Matt 5:4
B are the meek . . . . Matt 5:5
B are those who hunger . . . . . . Matt 5:6
B are the merciful . . . . Matt 5:7
B are the pure in . . . . Matt 5:8
B are the peacemakers . . . . Matt 5:9
B are those who are . . . . Matt 5:10
B are you when they . . . . Matt 5:11
b is he who is not . . . . Matt 11:6
b are your eyes . . . . Matt 13:16
B is He who comes . . . . Matt 21:9
hand, 'Come, you *b* . . . . Matt 25:34
Jesus took bread, *b* . . . . Matt 26:26
b are you among women . . Luke 1:28
'*B* is He who comes . . . . . . Luke 13:35
know these things, *b* . . . . . John 13:17
B are those who have . . . . . John 20:29
'It is more *b* to give . . . . Acts 20:35
the Creator, who is *b* . . . . Rom 1:25
all, the eternally *b* . . . . Rom 9:5
B be the God and Father . . . 2 Cor 1:3
b with believing Abraham . . . . Gal 3:9
B be the God and . . . . Eph 1:3
b God which was . . . . 1 Tim 1:11
the lesser is *b* by the better . . Heb 7:7
this one will be *b* . . . . James 1:25
B is he who reads . . . . Rev 1:3
'*B* are the dead who . . . . Rev 14:13
B is he who watches . . . . Rev 16:15
B are those who are . . . . Rev 19:9
B and holy is he who . . . . Rev 20:6
B is he who keeps the . . . . . . Rev 22:7
B are those who do His . . . . . Rev 22:14

BLESSED BE THE LORD
B God of my master . . . . Gen 24:27
"*B*, who has delivered you . . Ex 18:10
"*B*, who has not left you . . . Ruth 4:14
"*B*, who has pleaded . . . . . 1 Sam 25:39
'*B* God of Israel, who . . . . . . 1 Kin 1:48
B God of Israel from . . . . . 1 Chr 16:36
B God of our fathers, ... Ezra 7:27
B, because He has heard . . . . . Ps 28:6
B, for he has shown me . . . . . . Ps 31:21
B, who daily loads us . . . . Ps 68:19
B, who has not given us . . . . . Ps 124:6
B my Rock, who trains . . . . . . Ps 144:1

BLESSING
and you shall be a *b* . . . . Gen 12:2
the *b* of Abraham . . . . Gen 28:4
I will command My *b* . . . . Lev 25:21
before you today a *b* . . . . . . Deut 11:26
LORD will command the *b* . . Deut 28:8
life and death, *b* . . . . Deut 30:19
exalted above all *b* . . . . Neh 9:5
The *b* of a perishing . . . . Job 29:13
Your *b* is upon Your . . . . Ps 3:8
did not delight in *b* . . . . Ps 109:17
The *b* of the LORD . . . . Prov 10:22
My *b* on your offspring . . . . Is 44:3
shall be showers of *b* . . . . . . Ezek 34:26
relent, and leave a *b* . . . . Joel 2:14
and you shall be a *b* . . . . Zech 8:13
pour out for you such *b* . . . . . Mal 3:10
the fullness of the *b* . . . . Rom 15:29
b which we bless . . . . 1 Cor 10:16
that the *b* of Abraham . . . . Gal 3:14
with every spiritual *b* . . . . Eph 1:3
cultivated, receives *b* . . . . Heb 6:7
"Surely *b* I will bless you . . . . . Heb 6:14
to inherit the *b* . . . . Heb 12:17
same mouth proceed *b* . . . . . James 3:10
honor and glory and *b* . . . . Rev 5:12

BLESSINGS
of the law, the *b* . . . . Josh 8:34
B are on the head of . . . . Prov 10:6

BLEW
b them into the Red Sea . . . . . Ex 10:19
b the trumpets, and the . . . . . Josh 6:8
Then Saul *b* the trumpet . . 1 Sam 13:3
the priests regularly *b* . . . . . 1 Chr 16:6
came, and the winds *b* . . . . . Matt 7:25

BLIGHT
"I blasted you with *b* . . . . . Amos 4:9
I struck you with *b* . . . . Hag 2:17

BLIND
I was eyes to the *b* . . . . Job 29:15
B yourselves and be . . . . Is 29:9
To open *b* eyes . . . . Is 42:7
I will bring the *b* . . . . Is 42:16
b people who have eyes . . . . Is 43:8
His watchmen are *b* . . . . Is 56:10
They wandered *b* . . . . Lam 4:14
when you offer the *b* . . . . Mal 1:8
The *b* see and the lame . . . . . . Matt 11:5
if the *b* leads the *b* . . . . Matt 15:14
of sight to the *b* . . . . Luke 4:18
to Him, "Are we *b* . . . . John 9:40
miserable, poor, *b* . . . . Rev 3:17

BLINDED
b their eyes and . . . . John 12:40
and the rest were *b* . . . . Rom 11:7
of this age has *b* . . . . 2 Cor 4:4
the darkness has *b* . . . . 1 John 2:11

BLINDFOLD
to *b* Him, and to beat . . . . Mark 14:65

BLINDS
a bribe, for a bribe *b* . . . . . . Deut 16:19

BLOCK
See STUMBLING BLOCK
not to put a stumbling *b* . . . Rom 14:13
the Jews a stumbling *b* . . . . 1 Cor 1:23

BLOOD
See FLESH AND BLOOD; INNOCENT BLOOD
of your brother's *b* . . . . Gen 4:10
life, that is, its *b* . . . . Gen 9:4
b shall be shed . . . . Gen 9:6
the tunic in the *b* . . . . Gen 37:31

you are a husband of *b* ... Ex 4:25
river were turned to *b* ... Ex 7:20
when I see the *b*, I will ... Ex 12:13
the *b* of the covenant ... Ex 24:8
b that makes atonement ... Lev 17:11
b sustains its life ... Lev 17:14
do not cover my *b* ... Job 16:18
is there in my *b* ... Ps 30:9
And condemn innocent *b* ... Ps 94:21
hands are full of *b* ... Is 1:15
also disclose her *b* ... Is 26:21
to you in your *b* ... Ezek 16:6
And the moon into *b* ... Joel 2:31
to the *b* of Zechariah ... Matt 23:35
For this is My *b* ... Matt 26:28
betraying innocent *b* ... Matt 27:4
called the Field of *B* ... Matt 27:8
b of this just Person ... Matt 27:24
"His *b* be on us and ... Matt 27:25
new covenant in My *b* ... Luke 22:20
b falling down ... Luke 22:44
were born, not of *b* ... John 1:13
b has eternal life ... John 6:54
that is, Field of *B* ... Acts 1:19
the moon into *b* ... Acts 2:20
b every nation of men ... Acts 17:26
with His own *b* ... Acts 20:28
propitiation by His *b* ... Rom 3:25
justified by His *b* ... Rom 5:9
communion of the *b* ... 1 Cor 10:16
b cannot inherit ... 1 Cor 15:50
confer with flesh and *b* ... Gal 1:16
redemption through His *b* ... Eph 1:7
brought near by the *b* ... Eph 2:13
against flesh and *b* ... Eph 6:12
peace through the *b* ... Col 1:20
His own *b* He entered ... Heb 9:12
"This is the *b* of the ... Heb 9:20
are purified with *b* ... Heb 9:22
the Holiest by the *b* ... Heb 10:19
sprinkling of the *b* ... 1 Pet 1:2
with the precious *b* ... 1 Pet 1:19
b of Jesus Christ His ... 1 John 1:7
the water, and the *b* ... 1 John 5:8
our sins in His own *b* ... Rev 1:5
us to God by Your *b* ... Rev 5:9
moon became like *b* ... Rev 6:12
them white in the *b* ... Rev 7:14
the sea became *b* ... Rev 8:8
overcame him by the *b* ... Rev 12:11
with the *b* of the martyrs ... Rev 17:6
a robe dipped in *b* ... Rev 19:13

BLOODSHED
me from the guilt of *b* ... Ps 51:14
the land is full of *b* ... Ezek 9:9
build up Zion with *b* ... Mic 3:10

BLOODTHIRSTY
The LORD abhors the *b* ... Ps 5:6
B and deceitful men ... Ps 55:23

BLOSSOM
Israel shall *b* and bud ... Is 27:6
and *b* as the rose ... Is 35:1
the fig tree may not *b* ... Hab 3:17

BLOT
b me out of Your book ... Ex 32:32
say that He would *b* ... 2 Kin 14:27
from my sins, and *b* ... Ps 51:9
and I will not *b* ... Rev 3:5

BLOTTED
Let them be *b* out of ... Ps 69:28
I have *b* out, like a thick ... Is 44:22
your sins may be *b* ... Acts 3:19

BLOW
b the trumpets over ... Num 10:10
priests shall *b* the ... Josh 6:4
When I *b* the trumpet ... Judg 7:18
an east wind to *b* ... Ps 78:26
B upon my garden ... Song 4:16
with a very severe *b* ... Jer 14:17
B the trumpet in Zion ... Joel 2:1
Lord GOD will *b* the ... Zech 9:14

BLOWS
B that hurt cleanse ... Prov 20:30
breath of the LORD *b* ... Is 40:7
The wind *b* where it ... John 3:8

BLUE
b, purple, and scarlet ... Ex 25:4
pomegranates of *b* ... Ex 28:33
tabernacle door, of *b* ... Ex 36:37
spread a *b* cloth ... Num 4:7
put a *b* thread in the ... Num 15:38
made the veil of *b* ... 2 Chr 3:14
royal apparel of *b* ... Esth 8:15
of fiery red, hyacinth *b* ... Rev 9:17

BLUSH
did they know how to *b* ... Jer 6:15

BOANERGES
Surname of James and John, Mark 3:17

BOAST
puts on his armor *b* ... 1 Kin 20:11
soul shall make its *b* ... Ps 34:2
God we *b* all day long ... Ps 44:8
and make your *b* ... Rom 2:17
that we are your *b* ... 2 Cor 1:14
you, and not to *b* ... 2 Cor 10:16
that I also may *b* ... 2 Cor 11:16
lest anyone should *b* ... Eph 2:9
your hearts, do not *b* ... James 3:14

BOASTERS
God, violent, proud, *b* ... Rom 1:30
lovers of money, *b* ... 2 Tim 3:2

BOASTFUL
b shall not stand ... Ps 5:5
I was envious of the *b* ... Ps 73:3

BOASTING
Where is *b* then ... Rom 3:27
should make my *b* ... 1 Cor 9:15
you, great is my *b* ... 2 Cor 7:4
All such *b* is evil ... James 4:16

BOASTS
Whoever falsely *b* ... Prov 25:14

BOAT
in the *b* with Zebedee ... Matt 4:21
So He got into a *b* ... Matt 9:1
disciples get into the *b* ... Matt 14:22
by *b* to the other side ... Mark 5:21
in the *b* by themselves ... Mark 6:32
b was in the middle ... Mark 6:47
b with His disciples ... Luke 8:22
immediately the *b* was ... John 6:21

BOAZ
A wealthy Bethlehemite, Ruth 2:1, 4–18
Husband of Ruth, Ruth 4:10–13
Ancestor of Christ, Matt 1:5
——— Pillar of the temple, 1 Kin 7:21

BODIES
valley of the dead *b* ... Jer 31:40
b a living sacrifice ... Rom 12:1
not know that your *b* ... 1 Cor 6:15
also celestial *b* ... 1 Cor 15:40
wives as their own *b* ... Eph 5:28
and chariots, and *b* ... Rev 18:13

BODILY
b form like a dove ... Luke 3:22
b presence is weak ... 2 Cor 10:10
of the Godhead *b* ... Col 2:9
b exercise profits ... 1 Tim 4:8

BODY
b clings to the ground ... Ps 44:25
b is carved ivory ... Song 5:14
b was wet with the dew ... Dan 4:33
of the *b* is the eye ... Matt 6:22
those who kill the *b* ... Matt 10:28
Take, eat; this is My *b* ... Matt 26:26
and asked for the *b* ... Matt 27:58
around his naked *b* ... Mark 14:51
of the temple of His *b* ... John 2:21
deliver me from this *b* ... Rom 7:24
redemption of our *b* ... Rom 8:23
members in one *b* ... Rom 12:4
and the Lord for the *b* ... 1 Cor 6:13
against his own *b* ... 1 Cor 6:18
not know that your *b* ... 1 Cor 6:19
glorify God in your *b* ... 1 Cor 6:20
But I discipline my *b* ... 1 Cor 9:27
one bread and one *b* ... 1 Cor 10:17
b which is broken ... 1 Cor 11:24
be guilty of the *b* ... 1 Cor 11:27
For as the *b* is one ... 1 Cor 12:12
baptized into one *b* ... 1 Cor 12:13
b is not one member ... 1 Cor 12:14
are the *b* of Christ ... 1 Cor 12:27
though I give my *b* ... 1 Cor 13:3
It is sown a natural *b* ... 1 Cor 15:44
both to God in one *b* ... Eph 2:16
be magnified in my *b* ... Phil 1:20
in the *b* of His flesh ... Col 1:22
by putting off the *b* ... Col 2:11
and neglect of the *b* ... Col 2:23
were called in one *b* ... Col 3:15
b You have prepared ... Heb 10:5
the offering of the *b* ... Heb 10:10
For as the *b* without ... James 2:26
our sins in His own *b* ... 1 Pet 2:24

BOILS
Job with painful *b* ... Job 2:7

BOISTEROUS
that the wind was *b* ... Matt 14:30

BOLD
the righteous are *b* ... Prov 28:1
whatever anyone is *b* ... 2 Cor 11:21
are much more *b* ... Phil 1:14

BOLDLY
I may open my mouth *b* ... Eph 6:19
therefore come *b* ... Heb 4:16
So we may *b* say ... Heb 13:6

BOLDNESS
Great is my *b* of ... 2 Cor 7:4
in whom we have *b* ... Eph 3:12
but with all *b* ... Phil 1:20
standing and great *b* ... 1 Tim 3:13
brethren, having *b* ... Heb 10:19
that we may have *b* ... 1 John 4:17

BOND
bring you into the *b* ... Ezek 20:37
of the Spirit in the *b* ... Eph 4:3
love, which is the *b* ... Col 3:14

BONDAGE
because of the *b* ... Ex 2:23
out of the house of *b* ... Ex 13:14
receive the spirit of *b* ... Rom 8:15
might bring us into *b* ... Gal 2:4
which gives birth to *b* ... Gal 4:24
again with a yoke of *b* ... Gal 5:1
lifetime subject to *b* ... Heb 2:15
he is brought into *b* ... 2 Pet 2:19

BONDS
"Let us break Their *b* ... Ps 2:3
the other I called *B* ... Zech 11:7

BONDSERVANT
Paul, a *b* of Jesus Christ, ... Rom 1:1
would not be a *b* of Christ ... Gal 1:10
who is one of you, a *b* ... Col 4:12
Paul, a *b* of God and an ... Titus 1:1
James, a *b* of God and of ... James 1:1
Simon Peter, a *b* and ... 2 Pet 1:1
Jude, a *b* of Jesus Christ, ... Jude 1

BONDSERVANTS
your *b* for Jesus' sake ... 2 Cor 4:5
B, be obedient to ... Eph 6:5
as men-pleasers, but as *b* ... Eph 6:6
Paul and Timothy, *b* of ... Phil 1:1
B, obey in all things ... Col 3:22

Masters, give your *b* . . . . Col 4:1
Exhort *b* to be obedient . . . . . Titus 2:9
for vice, but as *b* . . . . 1 Pet 2:16

BONDWOMAN
"Cast out this *b* . . . . Gen 21:10
the one by a *b* . . . . Gal 4:22

BONE
"This is now *b* of my . . . . Gen 2:23
b clings to my skin . . . . Job 19:20
bonds came together, *b* . . . . Ezek 37:7

BONES
shall carry up my *b* . . . . Gen 50:25
which made all my *b* . . . . Job 4:14
His *b* are like beams . . . . Job 40:18
I can count all My *b* . . . . Ps 22:17
and my *b* waste away . . . . Ps 31:10
I kept silent, my *b* . . . . Ps 32:3
the wind, or how the *b* . . . . . Eccl 11:5
say to them, 'O dry *b* . . . . . . Ezek 37:4
b are the whole house . . . . Ezek 37:11
of dead men's *b* . . . . Matt 23:27
b shall be broken . . . . John 19:36
concerning his *b* . . . . Heb 11:22

BOOK
you will find in the *b* . . . . Ezra 4:15
distinctly from the *b* . . . . Neh 8:8
were inscribed in a *b* . . . . Job 19:23
"Search from the *b* . . . . Is 34:16
'Write in a *b* for . . . . Jer 30:2
found written in the *b* . . . . . . Dan 12:1
so a *b* of remembrance . . . . . Mal 3:16
are written in the *b* . . . . Gal 3:10
sprinkled both the *b* . . . . Heb 9:19
in the Lamb's *B* . . . . Rev 21:27
the prophecy of this *b* . . . . . Rev 22:18
the words of the *b* . . . . Rev 22:19

BOOK OF LIFE
whose names are in the *B* . . . . Phil 4:3
out his name from the *B* . . . . . Rev 3:5
written in the *B* of the . . . . . . Rev 13:8
not written in the *B* . . . . Rev 17:8
opened, which is the *B* . . . . . Rev 20:12
found written in the *B* . . . . . Rev 20:15
written in the Lamb's *B* . . . . Rev 21:27
away his part from the *B* . . Rev 22:19

BOOK OF THE LAW
are written in this *B*, ... Deut 30:10
Take this *B*, and put it . . . . Deut 31:26
This *B* shall not depart . . . . . . Josh 1:8
that is written in the *B* . . . . . Josh 8:34
that is written in the *B* . . . . . Josh 23:6
"I have found the *B* . . . . 2 Kin 22:8
the words of the *B* . . . . 2 Kin 22:11
in Judah, and had the *B* . . . 2 Chr 17:9
the scribe to bring the *B* . . . . . Neh 8:1
written in the *b* . . . . Gal 3:10

BOOKS
b there is no end . . . . Eccl 12:12
not contain the *b* . . . . John 21:25
magic brought their *b* . . . . . Acts 19:19
God, and *b* were opened . . . Rev 20:12

BOOTH
b which a watchman . . . . Job 27:18
of Zion is left as a *b* . . . . Is 1:8

BOOTHS
dwell in *b* for seven . . . . Lev 23:42
in *b* during the feast . . . . Neh 8:14

BORDER
pillar to the LORD at its *b* . . . . Is 19:19

BORDERS
and enlarge your *b* . . . . Ex 34:24
makes peace in your *b* . . . . . Ps 147:14
and enlarge the *b* . . . . Matt 23:5

BORE
conceived and *b* Cain . . . . Gen 4:1
And to Sarah who *b* . . . . Is 51:2
b the sin of many . . . . Is 53:12

and He *b* them and . . . . Is 63:9
b our sicknesses . . . . Matt 8:17
who Himself *b* our sins . . . . . 1 Pet 2:24
b a male Child who was . . . . . Rev 12:5

BORN
"Every son who is *b* . . . . Ex 1:22
yet man is *b* to trouble . . . . Job 5:7
"Man who is *b* . . . . Job 14:1
'This one was *b* . . . . Ps 87:4
A time to be *b* . . . . Eccl 3:2
unto us a Child is *b* . . . . Is 9:6
Or shall a nation be *b* . . . . Is 66:8
b Jesus who is called . . . . Matt 1:16
For there is *b* to you . . . . Luke 2:11
unless one is *b* again . . . . John 3:3
That which is *b* . . . . John 3:6
For this cause I was *b* . . . . John 18:37
me also, as by one *b* . . . . . . 1 Cor 15:8
of the bondwoman was *b* . . . . Gal 4:23
having been *b* again . . . . 1 Pet 1:23
who loves is *b* of God . . . . . . 1 John 4:7
is the Christ is *b* . . . . 1 John 5:1
know that whoever is *b* . . 1 John 5:18

BORN AGAIN
unless one is *b*, ... John 3:3
'You must be *b* . . . . John 3:7
having been *b*, not of . . . . . . 1 Pet 1:23

BORNE
had *b* him no children . . . . . . Gen 16:1
the barren has *b* seven . . . . 1 Sam 2:5
not my son whom I had *b* . 1 Kin 3:21
'I have *b* chastening . . . . Job 34:31
Surely He has *b* our griefs . . . . Is 53:4
you who have not *b* . . . . Is 54:1
you have *b* the shame . . . . . Ezek 36:6
who have *b* the burden . . . Matt 20:12
And as we have *b* . . . . 1 Cor 15:49

BORROWER
b is servant to the . . . . Prov 22:7
lender, so with the *b* . . . . Is 24:2

BORROWS
The wicked *b* and does . . . . . . Ps 37:21

BOSOM
man take fire to his *b* . . . . . . Prov 6:27
consolation of her *b* . . . . Is 66:11
angels to Abraham's *b* . . . . Luke 16:22
Son, who is in the *b* . . . . John 1:18
leaning on Jesus' *b* . . . . John 13:23

BOTTLE
tears into Your *b* . . . . Ps 56:8
b shall be filled . . . . Jer 13:12

BOTTOM
they sank to the *b* . . . . Ex 15:5
in two from top to *b* . . . . . . Matt 27:51
in two from top to *b* . . . . . Mark 15:38

BOTTOMLESS
given the key to the *b* . . . . Rev 9:1
ascend out of the *b* . . . . Rev 17:8
the key to the *b* . . . . Rev 20:1

BOTTOMLESS PIT
given the key to the *b* . . . . Rev 9:1
the angel of the *b*, ... Rev 9:11
ascends out of the *b* . . . . Rev 11:7
ascend out of the *b* . . . . Rev 17:8
having the key to the *b* . . . . . . Rev 20:1
cast him into the *b* . . . . Rev 20:3

BOUGH
Joseph is a fruitful *b* . . . . . . Gen 49:22
cut down a *b* from the . . . . . Judg 9:48
lop off the *b* with terror . . . . . . Is 10:33
will be as a forsaken *b* . . . . Is 17:9

BOUGHS
cedars with its *b* . . . . Ps 80:10
She sent out her *b* . . . . Ps 80:11

BOUGHT
the hand of him who *b* . . . . Lev 25:28
not your Father, who *b* . . . . . Deut 32:6

b the threshing floor . . . . . 2 Sam 24:24
b the field from . . . . Jer 32:9
all that he had and *b* . . . . . Matt 13:46
For you were *b* at a . . . . 1 Cor 6:20
denying the Lord who *b* . . . . . 2 Pet 2:1

BOUND
he *b* Isaac his son . . . . Gen 22:9
she *b* the scarlet cord . . . . . . Josh 2:21
b him with two new . . . . Judg 15:13
b him with bronze . . . . Judg 16:21
of the wicked have *b* . . . . Ps 119:61
cast three men *b* . . . . Dan 3:24
b the waters in a . . . . Prov 30:4
not been closed or *b* . . . . Is 1:6
on earth will be *b* . . . . Matt 16:19
b hand and foot with . . . . . John 11:44
b at the four corners . . . . . . Acts 10:11
And see, now I go *b* . . . . . . Acts 20:22
of Israel I am *b* . . . . Acts 28:20
who has a husband is *b* . . . . . Rom 7:2
Are you *b* to a wife . . . . 1 Cor 7:27
Devil and Satan, and *b* . . . . . Rev 20:2

BOUNDARY
b that they may not . . . . Ps 104:9

BOUNDS
You shall set *b* . . . . Ex 19:12
I will set your *b* . . . . Ex 23:31

BOUNTIFUL
the miser said to be *b* . . . . Is 32:5
you into a *b* country . . . . Jer 2:7

BOUNTIFULLY
Because He has dealt *b* . . . . Ps 13:6
and he who sows *b* . . . . 2 Cor 9:6

BOW
sons *b* down to you . . . . Gen 27:29
brothers indeed come to *b* . Gen 37:10
b remained in strength . . . . . Gen 49:24
You shall not *b* . . . . Ex 23:24
to serve them and *b* . . . . Judg 2:19
b is renewed in my . . . . Job 29:20
Judah the Song of the *B* . . 2 Sam 1:18
will not trust in my *b* . . . . Ps 44:6
He breaks the *b* . . . . Ps 46:9
like a deceitful *b* . . . . Ps 78:57
let us worship and *b* . . . . Ps 95:6
B down Your heavens . . . . Ps 144:5
Me every knee shall *b* . . . . Is 45:23
not save them by *b* . . . . Hos 1:7
knee shall *b* to Me . . . . Rom 14:11
For this reason I *b* . . . . Eph 3:14
Jesus every knee should *b* . . Phil 2:10
who sat on it had a *b* . . . . Rev 6:2

BOWED
stood all around and *b* . . . . . . Gen 37:7
b the heavens also . . . . 2 Sam 22:10
whose knees have not *b* . . 1 Kin 19:18
They have *b* down and . . . . Ps 20:8
And they *b* the knee . . . . Matt 27:29
men who have not *b* . . . . Rom 11:4

BOWED THEIR HEADS
then they *b* and worshiped . . . Ex 4:31
So the people *b* . . . . Ex 12:27
b and prostrated . . . . 1 Chr 29:20
b and worshiped the Lord . . . Neh 8:6

BOWL
his hand in the *b* . . . . Prov 19:24
or the golden *b* . . . . Eccl 12:6
and poured out his *b* . . . . Rev 16:2

BOWLS
who drink wine from *b* . . . . . Amos 6:6
a harp, and golden *b* . . . . Rev 5:8
Go and pour out the *b* . . . . . . Rev 16:1
who had the seven *b* . . . . Rev 21:9

BOWS
"The *b* of the mighty . . . . 1 Sam 2:4

BOWSTRING
He has loosed my *b* . . . . Job 30:11

BOX
Judas had the money *b* . . . John 13:29

BOY
b to Hagar, and sent her . . . Gen 21:14
Do not sin against the *b*' . . Gen 42:22
the *b* Samuel ministered . . . 1 Sam 3:1
B Jesus lingered behind . . . Luke 2:43

BOYS
Shall be full of *b* . . . . Zech 8:5

BOZRAH
City of Edom, Gen 36:33
Destruction of, foretold, Amos 1:12
Figurative of Messiah's victory, Is 63:1

BRACELET
b that was on his arm, ... 2 Sam 1:10

BRACELETS
two *b* for her wrists . . . . Gen 24:22
of gold: armlets and *b* . . . . Num 31:50
b on their wrists . . . . Ezek 23:42

BRAIDED
not with *b* hair or . . . . 1 Tim 2:9

BRAMBLE
gather grapes from a *b* . . . . Luke 6:44

BRANCH
blossoms on one *b* . . . . Ex 25:33
b will not be green . . . . Job 15:32
from Israel, palm *b* . . . . Is 9:14
B shall grow out of . . . . Is 11:1
raise to David a *B* . . . . Jer 23:5
grow up to David a *B* . . . . Jer 33:15
forth My Servant the *B* . . . . . . Zech 3:8
whose name is the *B* . . . . Zech 6:12
b has already become . . . . . Matt 24:32
b that bears fruit He . . . . John 15:2
b cannot bear fruit . . . . John 15:4
he is cast out as a *b* . . . . John 15:6

BRANCHES
in the sun, and his *b* . . . . Job 8:16
and bring forth *b* . . . . Job 14:9
and cut down the *b* . . . . Is 18:5
and its *b* are broken . . . . Jer 11:16
His *b* shall spread . . . . Hos 14:6
of the air nested in its *b* . . Luke 13:19
vine, you are the *b* . . . . John 15:5
root is holy, so are the *b* . . . Rom 11:16
b were broken off . . . . Rom 11:17

BRAND
Is this not a *b* plucked . . . . . . Zech 3:2

BRASS
become sounding *b* . . . . 1 Cor 13:1
feet were like fine *b* . . . . Rev 1:15

BRAVE
in the faith, be *b* . . . . 1 Cor 16:13

BREACH
before Him in the *b* . . . . Ps 106:23
the Repairer of the *B* . . . . Is 58:12

BREACHES
Heal its *b*, for it is . . . . Ps 60:2

BREAD
See FEAST OF UNLEAVENED BREAD; UNLEAVENED BREAD
face you shall eat *b* . . . . Gen 3:19
of Salem brought out *b* . . . . Gen 14:18
"Behold, I will rain *b* . . . . Ex 16:4
shall eat unleavened *b* . . . . Ex 23:15
not live by *b* alone . . . . Deut 8:3
lives, I do not have *b* . . . . . 1 Kin 17:12
new wine, a land of *b* . . . . 2 Kin 18:32
that his life abhors *b* . . . . Job 33:20
people as they eat *b* . . . . Ps 14:4
Can He give *b* also . . . . Ps 78:20
up late, to eat the *b* . . . . Ps 127:2
her poor with *b* . . . . Ps 132:15
For they eat the *b* . . . . Prov 4:17
b eaten in secret is . . . . Prov 9:17
B gained by deceit is . . . . Prov 20:17
Go, eat your *b* with . . . . Eccl 9:7
Cast your *b* upon the . . . . Eccl 11:1
b will be given him . . . . Is 33:16
for what is not *b* . . . . Is 55:2
to share your *b* . . . . Is 58:7
We get our *b* at the . . . . Lam 5:9
who give me my *b* . . . . Hos 2:5
For their *b* shall be . . . . Hos 9:4
And lack of *b* in all . . . . Amos 4:6
these stones become *b* . . . . Matt 4:3
not live by *b* alone . . . . Matt 4:4
this day our daily *b* . . . . Matt 6:11
eating, Jesus took *b* . . . . Matt 26:26
no bag, no *b*, no copper . . . . Mark 6:8
is he who shall eat *b* . . . . Luke 14:15
gives you the true *b* . . . . John 6:32
I am the *b* of life . . . . John 6:48
having dipped the *b* . . . . John 13:26
b which we break . . . . 1 Cor 10:16
He was betrayed took *b* . . 1 Cor 11:23
as you eat this *b* . . . . 1 Cor 11:26
did we eat anyone's *b* . . . . . 2 Thess 3:8
and eat their own *b* . . . . 2 Thess 3:12

BREADTH
is as great as its *b* . . . . Rev 21:16

BREAK
that you shall *b* his yoke . . Gen 27:40
nor shall you *b* one of its . . . . Ex 12:46
lest the LORD *b* out against . . Ex 19:22
B off the golden earrings . . . . . Ex 32:2
b their bones and . . . . Num 24:8
never *b* My covenant . . . . Judg 2:1
torment my soul, and *b* . . . . . . Job 19:2
They *b* up my path . . . . Job 30:13
B their teeth in their . . . . Ps 58:6
And now they *b* down . . . . Ps 74:6
b My statutes and do . . . . Ps 89:31
covenant I will not *b* . . . . Ps 89:34
reed He will not *b* . . . . Is 42:3
and that you *b* every yoke . . . . . Is 58:6
your light shall *b* forth . . . . Is 58:8
Remember, do not *b* . . . . Jer 14:21
b your fallow ground, ... Hos 10:12
and where thieves *b* in . . . . . Matt 6:19
reed He will not *b* . . . . Matt 12:20
they did not *b* His legs . . . . . John 19:33
together to *b* bread . . . . Acts 20:7
bread which we *b*, ... 1 Cor 10:16
B forth and shout, ... Gal 4:27

BREAKING
in the *b* of bread . . . . Acts 2:42
b bread from house to . . . . Acts 2:46
weeping and *b* my heart . . Acts 21:13
dishonor God through *b* . . . . . Rom 2:23

BREAKS
He *b* in pieces mighty . . . . . . Job 34:24
My soul *b* with longing . . . . . Ps 119:20
Until the day *b* . . . . Song 2:17
Whoever therefore *b* . . . . Matt 5:19

BREAST
back on Jesus' *b* . . . . John 13:25

BREASTPLATE
a *b*, an ephod . . . . Ex 28:4
righteousness as a *b* . . . . Is 59:17
having put on the *b* . . . . Eph 6:14

BREASTS
blessings of the *b* . . . . Gen 49:25
on My mother's *b* . . . . Ps 22:9
doe, let her *b* satisfy . . . . Prov 5:19
Your two *b* are like . . . . Song 4:5
b which nursed You . . . . Luke 11:27
done, beat their *b* . . . . Luke 23:48

BREATH
nostrils the *b* of life . . . . Gen 2:7
at the blast of the *b* . . . . . . 2 Sam 22:16
that there was no *b* . . . . 1 Kin 17:17
perish, and by the *b* . . . . Job 4:9
as long as my *b* . . . . Job 27:3
has made me, and the *b* . . . . . Job 33:4
You take away their *b* . . . . . . Ps 104:29
Man is like a *b* . . . . Ps 144:4
everything that has *b* . . . . Ps 150:6
they all have one *b* . . . . Eccl 3:19
from it, who gives *b* . . . . Is 42:5
"Surely I will cause *b* . . . . Ezek 37:5
God who holds your *b* . . . . . . Dan 5:23
gives to all life, *b* . . . . Acts 17:25
consume with the *b* . . . . . . 2 Thess 2:8
power to give *b* . . . . Rev 13:15

BREATH OF LIFE
into his nostrils the *b* . . . . Gen 2:7
flesh in which is the *b* . . . . Gen 6:17
flesh in which is the *b* . . . . Gen 7:15
b from God entered them . . Rev 11:11

BREATHE
me, and such as *b* . . . . Ps 27:12
winds, O breath, and *b* . . . . . Ezek 37:9

BREATHED
and *b* into his nostrils the . . . . Gen 2:7
a loud voice, and *b* His . . . . Mark 15:37
He *b* on them, and said . . . John 20:22
fell down and *b* his last . . . . . . Acts 5:5
at his feet and *b* her last . . . . Acts 5:10

BREATHES
indeed he *b* his last . . . . Job 14:10

BRETHREN
presence of all his *b* . . . . Gen 16:12
be lifted above his *b* . . . . . . Deut 17:20
how good it is for *b* to . . . . . . Ps 133:1
and you are all *b* . . . . Matt 23:8
least of these My *b* . . . . . . Matt 25:40
Go and tell My *b* . . . . Matt 28:10
Men and *b*, this Scripture . . . Acts 1:16
six *b* accompanied me . . . . . Acts 11:12
firstborn among many *b* . . . . Rom 8:29
to judge between his *b* . . . . . 1 Cor 6:5
thus sin against the *b* . . . . . . 1 Cor 8:12
over five hundred *b* . . . . 1 Cor 15:6
perils among false *b* . . . . . 2 Cor 11:26
b secretly brought . . . . Gal 2:4
Finally, my *b*, be strong . . . . . Eph 6:10
Greet all the *b* with . . . . . . 1 Thess 5:26
to be made like His *b* . . . . Heb 2:17
sincere love of the *b* . . . . 1 Pet 1:22
because we love the *b* . . . . 1 John 3:14
our lives for the *b* . . . . 1 John 3:16
does not receive the *b* . . . . . 3 John 10
for the accuser of our *b* . . . . Rev 12:10
of your *b* the prophets . . . . . . Rev 22:9

BRIBE
you shall take no *b* . . . . Ex 23:8
b blinds the eyes . . . . Deut 16:19
b debases the heart . . . . Eccl 7:7

BRIBERY
consume the tents of *b* . . . . . Job 15:34

BRIBES
hand is full of *b* . . . . Ps 26:10
but he who hates *b* . . . . Prov 15:27
but he who receives *b* . . . . Prov 29:4
everyone loves *b* . . . . Is 1:23
the just and taking *b* . . . . Amos 5:12

BRICK
people straw to make *b* . . . . Ex 5:7
incense on altars of *b* . . . . Is 65:3
Make strong the *b* . . . . Nah 3:14

BRICKS
"Come, let us make *b* . . . . Gen 11:3
b which they made . . . . Ex 5:8
deliver the quota of *b* . . . . Ex 5:18
b have fallen down . . . . Is 9:10

BRIDE
them on you as a *b* . . . . Is 49:18
He who has the *b* . . . . John 3:29
I will show you the *b* . . . . Rev 21:9
the Spirit and the *b* . . . . Rev 22:17

BRIDEGROOM
righteousness, as a *b* . . . . Is 61:10

and as the *b* rejoices ... Is 62:5
mourn as long as the *b* ... Matt 9:15
b will be taken away ... Matt 9:15
went out to meet the *b* ... Matt 25:1
b fast while the ... Mark 2:19
the friend of the *b* ... John 3:29

BRIDLE
harnessed with bit and *b* ... Ps 32:9
b the whole body ... James 3:2

BRIER
b shall come up the ... Is 55:13
longer be a pricking *b* ... Ezek 28:24
of them is like a *b* ... Mic 7:4

BRIERS
there shall come up *b* ... Is 5:6
their words, though *b* ... Ezek 2:6

BRIGHTER
Her Nazirites were *b* ... Lam 4:7
a light from heaven, *b* ... Acts 26:13

BRIGHTNESS
From the *b* before Him ... 2 Sam 22:13
and kings to the *b* ... Is 60:3
goes forth as *b* ... Is 62:1
very dark, with no *b* ... Amos 5:20
who being the *b* ... Heb 1:3

BRIMSTONE
Then the LORD rained *b* ... Gen 19:24
b is scattered on his ... Job 18:15
fire, smoke, and *b* ... Rev 9:17
the lake of fire and *b* ... Rev 20:10

BRING
LORD your God will *b* ... Deut 30:3
b back his soul ... Job 33:30
for they *b* down ... Ps 55:3
Lord said, "I will *b* ... Ps 68:22
B forth your strong ... Is 41:21
He will *b* forth justice ... Is 42:3
b My righteousness ... Is 46:13
Though they *b* up their ... Hos 9:12
she will *b* forth a Son ... Matt 1:21
b no fruit to maturity ... Luke 8:14
b this Man's blood ... Acts 5:28
Who shall *b* a charge ... Rom 8:33
b Christ down from ... Rom 10:6
b Christ up from the ... Rom 10:7
even so God will *b* ... 1 Thess 4:14

BROAD
set me in a *b* place ... Ps 118:5
b is the way that ... Matt 7:13
their phylacteries *b* ... Matt 23:5

BROKE
b them at the foot of ... Ex 32:19
b open the fountain ... Ps 74:15
covenant which they *b* ... Jer 31:32
He blessed and *b* ... Matt 14:19
b the flask and poured ... Mark 14:3
b the legs of the ... John 19:32

BROKEN
he has *b* My covenant ... Gen 17:14
I am like a *b* vessel ... Ps 31:12
their bows shall be *b* ... Ps 37:15
He has *b* his covenant ... Ps 55:20
heart the spirit is *b* ... Prov 15:13
b spirit dries the ... Prov 17:22
but who can bear a *b* ... Prov 18:14
in the staff of this *b* ... Is 36:6
heart within me is *b* ... Jer 23:9
is oppressed and *b* ... Hos 5:11
this stone will be *b* ... Matt 21:44
Scripture cannot be *b* ... John 10:35
is My body which is *b* ... 1 Cor 11:24

BROKENHEARTED
He heals the *b* and ... Ps 147:3
sent Me to heal the *b* ... Is 61:1
sent Me to heal the *b* ... Luke 4:18

BRONZE
So Moses made a *b* ... Num 21:9
your head shall be *b* ... Deut 28:23
b serpent that Moses ... 2 Kin 18:4
Or is my flesh *b* ... Job 6:12
b as rotten wood ... Job 41:27
broken the gates of *b* ... Ps 107:16
b I will bring ... Is 60:17
b walls against the ... Jer 1:18
people a fortified *b* ... Jer 15:20
a third kingdom of *b* ... Dan 2:39
make your hooves *b* ... Mic 4:13
were mountains of *b* ... Zech 6:1

BROOD
The *b* of evildoers ... Is 14:20
B of vipers ... Matt 12:34
hen gathers her *b* ... Luke 13:34

BROOD OF VIPERS
he said to them, "*B* ... Matt 3:7
B! How can you, being ... Matt 12:34
Serpents, *b!* How can ... Matt 23:33
baptized by him, "*B* ... Luke 3:7

BROOK
stones from the *b* ... 1 Sam 17:40
shall drink of the *b* ... Ps 110:7
disciples over the *B* ... John 18:1

BROOK CHERITH
God hides Elijah here and the ravens feed him, 1 Kin 17:3–6

BROOKS
good land, a land of *b* ... Deut 8:7
b that pass away ... Job 6:15
for the water *b* ... Ps 42:1

BROTHER
"Where is Abel your *b* ... Gen 4:9
he were my friend or *b* ... Ps 35:14
speak against your *b* ... Ps 50:20
and a *b* is born for ... Prov 17:17
b offended is harder ... Prov 18:19
has neither son nor *b* ... Eccl 4:8
and do not trust any *b* ... Jer 9:4
he pursued his *b* ... Amos 1:11
Was not Esau Jacob's *b* ... Mal 1:2
b will deliver up ... Matt 10:21
how often shall my *b* ... Matt 18:21
"Teacher, tell my *b* ... Luke 12:13
b will rise again ... John 11:23
do you judge your *b* ... Rom 14:10
b goes to law against ... 1 Cor 6:6
shall the weak *b* ... 1 Cor 8:11
slave—a beloved *b* ... Philem 16
He who loves his *b* ... 1 John 2:10
and murdered his *b* ... 1 John 3:12
Whoever hates his *b* ... 1 John 3:15
b sinning a sin which ... 1 John 5:16
I, John, both your *b* ... Rev 1:9

BROTHERHOOD
the covenant of *b* ... Amos 1:9
I might break the *b* ... Zech 11:14
Love the *b* ... 1 Pet 2:17
experienced by your *b* ... 1 Pet 5:9

BROTHERLY
to one another with *b* ... Rom 12:10
b love continue ... Heb 13:1

BROTHER'S
Am I my *b* keeper ... Gen 4:9
at the speck in your *b* ... Matt 7:3

BROTHERS
My *b* have dealt ... Job 6:15
a stranger to my *b* ... Ps 69:8
is My mother, or My *b* ... Mark 3:33
b are these who hear ... Luke 8:21
b did not believe ... John 7:5
love as *b*, be tenderhearted ... 1 Pet 3:8

BROUGHT
He *b* out His people ... Ps 105:43
The king has *b* me into ... Song 1:4
to heaven, will be *b* ... Luke 10:15

BRUISE
He shall *b* your head ... Gen 3:15
LORD binds up the *b* ... Is 30:26
the LORD to *b* Him ... Is 53:10

BRUISED
b reed He will not ... Is 42:3
He was *b* for our ... Is 53:5
b reed He will not ... Matt 12:20

BRUTAL
b men who are ... Ezek 21:31

BUCKET
are as a drop in a *b* ... Is 40:15

BUCKLER
be your shield and *b* ... Ps 91:4

BUD
it bring forth and *b* ... Is 55:10

BUFFET
of Satan to *b* me ... 2 Cor 12:7

BUILD
b ourselves a city ... Gen 11:4
cities which you did not *b* ... Deut 6:10
shall *b* with whole stones ... Deut 27:6
b an altar to the LORD ... Judg 6:26
will *b* him a sure house ... 1 Sam 2:35
"Would you *b* a house ... 2 Sam 7:5
b a temple for the name ... 1 Kin 8:17
that the LORD will *b* ... 1 Chr 17:10
Solomon who shall *b* ... 1 Chr 28:6
able to *b* Him a temple ... 2 Chr 2:6
b the house of the LORD ... Ezra 1:5
and let us *b* the wall of ... Neh 2:17
B the walls of Jerusalem ... Ps 51:18
labor in vain who *b* ... Ps 127:1
afterward *b* your house ... Prov 24:27
down, and a time to *b* ... Eccl 3:3
house that you will *b* ... Is 66:1
I will *b* them and not ... Jer 24:6
Who *b* up Zion with ... Mic 3:10
b the desolate places ... Mal 1:4
'This man began to *b* ... Luke 14:30
What house will you *b* ... Acts 7:49
b you up and give you ... Acts 20:32
named, lest I should *b* ... Rom 15:20
For if I *b* again ... Gal 2:18

BUILDER
me, as a wise master *b* ... 1 Cor 3:10
foundations, whose *b* ... Heb 11:10

BUILDERS
The stone which the *b* ... Ps 118:22
The stone which the *b* ... Matt 21:42
The stone which the *b* ... Mark 12:10
The stone which the *b* ... Luke 20:17
was rejected by you *b* ... Acts 4:11
The stone which the *b* ... 1 Pet 2:7

BUILDING
field, you are God's *b* ... 1 Cor 3:9
destroyed, we have a *b* ... 2 Cor 5:1
in whom the whole *b* ... Eph 2:21
But you, beloved, *b* ... Jude 20

BUILDS
The LORD *b* up ... Ps 147:2
The wise woman *b* ... Prov 14:1
one take heed how he *b* ... 1 Cor 3:10

BUILT
Wisdom has *b* her house ... Prov 9:1
my works great, I *b* ... Eccl 2:4
Babylon, that I have *b* ... Dan 4:30
to a wise man who *b* ... Matt 7:24
a foolish man who *b* ... Matt 7:26
work which he has *b* ... 1 Cor 3:14
having been *b* on the ... Eph 2:20
rooted and *b* up in Him ... Col 2:7
For every house is *b* ... Heb 3:4
stones, are being *b* ... 1 Pet 2:5

BULL
I will not take a *b* ... Ps 50:9
like an untrained *b* ... Jer 31:18

BULLS
in the blood of *b* ... Is 1:11

For if the blood of *b* .... Heb 9:13

BULRUSHES
she took an ark of *b* .... Ex 2:3

BULWARKS
Mark well her *b* .... Ps 48:13
for walls and *b* .... Is 26:1

BUNDLE
each man's *b* of money .... Gen 42:35
A *b* of myrrh is my .... Song 1:13

BURDEN
You have laid the *b* .... Num 11:11
one knows his own *b* ..... 2 Chr 6:29
so that I am a *b* .... Job 7:20
Cast your *b* on the .... Ps 55:22
the grasshopper is a *b* ...... Eccl 12:5
in that day that his *b* .... Is 10:27
its reproach is a *b* .... Zeph 3:18
easy and My *b* is light .... Matt 11:30
upon you no greater *b* .... Acts 15:28
as it may, I did not *b* ..... 2 Cor 12:16
we might not be a *b* .... 1 Thess 2:9
on you no other *b* .... Rev 2:24

BURDENED
but you have *b* Me with ...... Is 43:24
were *b* beyond measure .... 2 Cor 1:8
this tent groan, being *b* ..... 2 Cor 5:4
be eased and you *b* .... 2 Cor 8:13
not let the church be *b* .... 1 Tim 5:16

BURDENS
and looked at their *b* .... Ex 2:11
For they bind heavy *b* ..... Matt 23:4
Bear one another's *b* .... Gal 6:2

BURDENSOME
b task God has given .... Eccl 1:13
his life will be *b* .... Is 15:4
I myself was not *b* .... 2 Cor 12:13
commandments are not *b* .. 1 John 5:3

BURIAL
as property for a *b* place .. Gen 23:20
indeed he has no *b* .... Eccl 6:3
she did it for My *b* .... Matt 26:12
to anoint My body for *b* ... Mark 14:8
for the day of My *b* .... John 12:7
Stephen to his *b* .... Acts 8:2

BURIED
and there will I be *b* .... Ruth 1:17
I saw the wicked *b* .... Eccl 8:10
away the body and *b* ..... Matt 14:12
also died and was *b* ...... Luke 16:22
Therefore we were *b* .... Rom 6:4
and that He was *b* .... 1 Cor 15:4
b with Him in baptism ...... Col 2:12

BURN
the bush does not *b* .... Ex 3:3
that My wrath may *b* .... Ex 32:10
b their chariots .... Josh 11:6
both will *b* together .... Is 1:31
"Did not our heart *b* ..... Luke 24:32
eat her flesh and *b* .... Rev 17:16

BURNED
If anyone's work is *b* ...... 1 Cor 3:15
my body to be *b* .... 1 Cor 13:3
whose end is to be *b* .... Heb 6:8
be touched and that *b* ..... Heb 12:18
are *b* outside the camp .... Heb 13:11
in it will be *b* .... 2 Pet 3:10
all green grass was *b* .... Rev 8:7

BURNING
b torch that passed .... Gen 15:17
with severe *b* fever .... Deut 28:22
on his lips like a *b* .... Prov 16:27
b fire shut up in my .... Jer 20:9
b jealousy against the ..... Ezek 36:5
plucked from the *b* .... Amos 4:11
a great mountain *b* .... Rev 8:8
fell from heaven, *b* .... Rev 8:10

BURNT
offered *b* offerings .... Gen 8:20
lamb for a *b* offering .... Gen 22:7
and *b* offerings, that .... Ex 10:25
took a *b* offering and .... Ex 18:12
shall set the altar of the *b* .... Ex 40:6
is a *b* sacrifice of the herd .... Lev 1:3
And they offered on it *b* ..... Josh 8:31
offer a *b* sacrifice with ...... Judg 6:26
if you offer a *b* offering ... Judg 13:16
accepted a *b* offering ...... Judg 13:23
b offerings on that altar .... 1 Kin 3:4
offered *b* offerings .... 1 Kin 9:25
offer *b* offerings on it, ... Ezra 3:2
delight in *b* offering .... Ps 51:16
b offerings are not .... Jer 6:20
sacrificing *b* offerings ..... Ezek 43:18
Though you offer Me *b* ... Amos 5:22

BURST
it is ready to *b* .... Job 32:19
with doors, when it *b* .... Job 38:8
the new wine will *b* .... Luke 5:37
falling headlong, he *b* ...... Acts 1:18

BURY
b your dead in the .... Gen 23:6
was no one to *b* them .... Ps 79:3
go and *b* my father .... Matt 8:21
and let the dead *b* .... Matt 8:22

BUSH
from the midst of a *b* .... Ex 3:2
Him who dwelt in the *b* ... Deut 33:16
to him in the *b* .... Acts 7:35

BUSINESS
in ships, who do *b* .... Ps 107:23
farm, another to his *b* ...... Matt 22:5
about My Father's *b* .... Luke 2:49

BUSYBODIES
at all, but are *b* .... 2 Thess 3:11
but also gossips and *b* .... 1 Tim 5:13

BUT I SAY TO YOU
B that whoever is angry ... Matt 5:22
B that whoever looks ...... Matt 5:28
B that whoever divorces .... Matt 5:32
B, do not swear at all ...... Matt 5:34
B, love your enemies, ... Matt 5:44
B, it will be more .... Matt 11:22
B that for every idle ...... Matt 12:36
B that Elijah has come .... Matt 17:12
B, I will not drink of ...... Matt 26:29
B that Elijah has also ...... Mark 9:13
B who hear: Love .... Luke 6:27
B that it will be more .... Luke 10:12

BUTLER
b did not remember .... Gen 40:23

BUTTER
So he took *b* and milk ...... Gen 18:8
were smoother than *b* .... Ps 55:21
of milk produces *b* .... Prov 30:33

BUY
in Egypt to *b* grain .... Gen 41:57
B it back in the presence .... Ruth 4:4
b the threshing floor .... 2 Sam 24:21
B the truth, and do not .... Prov 23:23
Yes, come, *b* wine and .... Is 55:1
B the field for money, and .. Jer 32:25
will *b* fields for money ...... Jer 32:44
that we may *b* the poor ...... Amos 8:6
b food for all these .... Luke 9:13
"*B* those things we .... John 13:29
rejoice, those who *b* .... 1 Cor 7:30
spend a year there, *b* ..... James 4:13
I counsel you to *b* .... Rev 3:18
and that no one may *b* ..... Rev 13:17

BUYER
nothing," cries the *b* ...... Prov 20:14
as with the *b*, so with .... Is 24:2
'Let not the *b* rejoice .... Ezek 7:12

BUYS
a field and *b* it .... Prov 31:16
has and *b* that field .... Matt 13:44
b their merchandise .... Rev 18:11

BYGONE
b generations .... Acts 14:16

BYWORD
But He has made me a *b* .... Job 17:6
You made us a *b* .... Ps 44:14

CAESAR
—— Augustus Caesar (31 B.C.–A.D. 14):
Decree of brings Joseph and Mary to Bethlehem, Luke 2:1
—— Tiberius Caesar (A.D. 14–37):
Christ's ministry dated by, Luke 3:1–23
Tribute paid to, Matt 22:17–21
Jews side with, John 19:12
—— Claudius Caesar (A.D. 41–54):
Famine in time of, Acts 11:28
Banished Jews from Rome, Acts 18:2
—— Nero Caesar (A.D. 54–68):
Paul appealed to, Acts 25:8–12
Christian converts in household of, Phil 4:22
Paul tried before, 2 Tim 4:16–18
Called Augustus, Acts 25:21

CAESAREA
Roman capital of Palestine, Acts 12:19; 23:33
Paul escorted to, Acts 23:23–33
Paul imprisoned at; appeals to Caesar, Acts 25:4, 8–13
Peter preaches at, Acts 10:34–43
Paul preaches at, Acts 9:26–30; 18:22; 21:8

CAESAREA PHILIPPI
A city in northern Palestine; scene of Peter's great confession, Matt 16:13–20
Probable site of the transfiguration, Matt 17:1–3

CAGE
c is full of birds .... Jer 5:27
foul spirit, and a *c* .... Rev 18:2

CAIAPHAS
Son-in-law of Annas; high priest, John 18:13
Makes prophecy, John 11:49–52
Jesus appears before, John 18:23, 24
Apostles appear before, Acts 4:1–22

CAIN
Adam's first son, Gen 4:1
His offering rejected, Gen 4:2–7; Heb 11:4
Murders Abel; is exiled; settles in Nod, Gen 4:8–17
A type of evil, Jude 11

CAKE
Ephraim is a *c* .... Hos 7:8

CAKES
Sustain me with *c* .... Song 2:5
and love the raisin *c* .... Hos 3:1

CALAMITIES
refuge, until these *c* .... Ps 57:1

CALAMITY
for the day of their *c* ...... Deut 32:35
will laugh at your *c* .... Prov 1:26
c shall come suddenly ...... Prov 6:15
If there is *c* in a .... Amos 3:6

CALCULATED
c the dust of the .... Is 40:12

CALDRON
this city is the *c* .... Ezek 11:3

CALEB
Sent as spy; gives good report; rewarded, Num 13:2, 6, 27, 30; 14:5–9, 24–38

Inherits Hebron, Josh 14:6–15
Conquers his territory with Othniel's help, Josh 15:13–19

CALF
and made a molded *c* . . . . Ex 32:4
They made a *c* in Horeb . . . . Ps 106:19
is, than a fatted *c* . . . . Prov 15:17
like a stubborn *c* . . . . Hos 4:16
Your *c* is rejected . . . . Hos 8:5
And bring the fatted *c* . . . . Luke 15:23
creature like a *c* . . . . Rev 4:7

CALL
Then men began to *c* . . . . Gen 4:26
I *c* heaven and earth . . . . Deut 4:26
I did not *c*, my son . . . . 1 Sam 3:6
I will *c* to the LORD . . . . . . 1 Sam 12:17
c their lands after . . . . Ps 49:11
To you, O men, I *c* . . . . Prov 8:4
c upon Him while He . . . . Is 55:6
c the Sabbath a delight, ... Is 58:13
'C to Me, and I will . . . . Jer 33:3
Arise, *c* on your God . . . . Jon 1:6
They will *c* on My name . . . Zech 13:9
c His name JESUS . . . . Matt 1:21
c the righteous . . . . Matt 9:13
Why do you *c* Me good . . Mark 10:18
shall *c* his name John . . . . . Luke 1:13
shall *c* His name JESUS . . . . Luke 1:31
Lord our God will *c* . . . . Acts 2:39
you must not *c* common . . . Acts 10:15
c them My people . . . . Rom 9:25
then shall they *c* . . . . Rom 10:14
For God did not *c* . . . . 1 Thess 4:7
Let him *c* for the elders . . . James 5:14
c and election sure . . . . 2 Pet 1:10

CALLED
c the light Day . . . . Gen 1:5
c his wife's name Eve . . . . Gen 3:20
"I, the LORD, have *c* . . . . Is 42:6
I have *c* you by your . . . . Is 43:1
The LORD has *c* Me from . . . . . . Is 49:1
and out of Egypt I *c* . . . . Hos 11:1
"Out of Egypt I *c* . . . . Matt 2:15
a city *c* Nazareth . . . . Matt 2:23
For many are *c* . . . . Matt 20:16
to those who are the *c* . . . . . Rom 8:28
these He also *c* . . . . Rom 8:30
But God has *c* us to . . . . 1 Cor 7:15
praises of Him who *c* . . . . 1 Pet 2:9
knowledge of Him who *c* . . . . 2 Pet 1:3
c children of God . . . . 1 John 3:1

CALLED BY MY NAME
if My people who are *c* . . . 2 Chr 7:14
everyone who is *c*, ... Is 43:7
a nation that was not *c* . . . . Is 65:1
this house which is *c* . . . . Jer 7:10
the city which is *c* . . . . Jer 25:29
house which is *c* . . . . Jer 32:34
the Gentiles who are *c* . . . . Amos 9:12
the Gentiles who are *c* . . . . Acts 15:17

CALLING
the gifts and the *c* . . . . Rom 11:29
For you see your *c* . . . . 1 Cor 1:26
remain in the same *c* . . . . . . 1 Cor 7:20
to walk worthy of the *c* . . . . . . Eph 4:1
in one hope of your *c* . . . . Eph 4:4
us with a holy *c* . . . . 2 Tim 1:9
of the heavenly *c* . . . . Heb 3:1

CALLS
c them all by name . . . . Ps 147:4
there is no one who *c* . . . . Is 64:7
David himself *c* . . . . Mark 12:37
c his own sheep . . . . John 10:3
For "whoever *c* . . . . Rom 10:13

CALM
the sea will become *c* . . . . Jon 1:12
there was a great *c* . . . . Matt 8:26

CALMED
Surely I have *c* . . . . Ps 131:2

CALVARY
Christ crucified there, Luke 23:33
Same as "Golgotha" in Hebrew, John 19:17

CALVES
made two *c* of gold . . . . 1 Kin 12:28
their cow *c* without . . . . Job 21:10
like stall-fed *c* . . . . Mal 4:2
blood of goats and *c* . . . . Heb 9:12
he took the blood of *c* . . . . . . Heb 9:19

CAMEL
it is easier for a *c* . . . . Matt 19:24
and swallow a *c* . . . . Matt 23:24

CAMEL'S
John was clothed with *c* . . . . Mark 1:6

CAMP
"This is God's *c* . . . . Gen 32:2
who went before the *c* . . . . . . Ex 14:19
to Him, outside the *c* . . . . . . Heb 13:13

CAN
I *c* do all things . . . . Phil 4:13

CANA
A village of upper Galilee; home of Nathanael, John 21:2
Site of Christ's first miracle, John 2:1–11
Healing at, John 4:46–54

CANAAN
A son of Ham, Gen 10:6
Cursed by Noah, Gen 9:20–25
—— Promised Land, Gen 12:5
Boundaries of, Gen 10:19
God's promises concerning, given to Abraham, Gen 12:1–3
to Isaac, Gen 26:2, 3
to Jacob, Gen 28:10–13
to Israel, Ex 3:8
Conquest of, announced, Gen 15:7–21
preceded by spying expedition, Num 13:1–33
delayed by unbelief, Num 14:1–35
accomplished by the Lord, Josh 23:1–16
achieved only in part, Judg 1:21, 27–36

CANAANITES
Israelites commanded to:
drive them out; not serve their gods, Ex 23:23–33
shun their abominations, Lev 18:24–30
not make covenants or intermarry with them, Deut 7:1–3

CANCER
will spread like *c* . . . . 2 Tim 2:17

CANE
bought Me no sweet *c* . . . . Is 43:24
Sheba, and sweet *c* . . . . Jer 6:20

CANOPIES
He made darkness *c* . . . . . 2 Sam 22:12

CANOPY
His *c* around Him was . . . . . . Ps 18:11

CAPERNAUM
Simon Peter's home, Mark 1:21, 29
Christ performs healings there, Matt 8:5–17; 9:1–8; Mark 1:21–28; John 4:46–54
preaches there, Mark 9:33–50; John 6:24–71
uses as headquarters, Matt 4:13–17
pronounces judgment upon, Matt 11:23, 24

CAPPADOCIA
Jews from, at Pentecost, Acts 2:1, 9
Christians of, addressed by Peter, 1 Pet 1:1

CAPSTONE
bring forth the *c* . . . . Zech 4:7

CAPTAIN
c of the guard, an . . . . Gen 39:1
made Amasa *c* of the . . . . 2 Sam 17:25
Nebuzaradan the *c* . . . . 2 Kin 25:11
which, having no *c* . . . . Prov 6:7
of troops and the *c* . . . . John 18:12
to the *c* of the guard . . . . . . Acts 28:16

CAPTIVE
have led captivity *c* . . . . Ps 68:18
of your neck, O *c* . . . . Is 52:2
they shall now go *c* . . . . Amos 6:7
and be led away *c* . . . . Luke 21:24
He led captivity *c* . . . . Eph 4:8

CAPTIVES
will bring back the *c* . . . . . . Amos 9:14
and return their *c* . . . . Zeph 2:7
make *c* of gullible women . . 2 Tim 3:6

CAPTIVITY
bring you back from *c* . . . . . Deut 30:3
high, You have led *c* . . . . Ps 68:18
Judah has gone into *c* . . . . Lam 1:3
from David until the *c* . . . . . . Matt 1:17
and bringing me into *c* . . . . . Rom 7:23
every thought into *c* . . . . 2 Cor 10:5
on high, He led *c* . . . . Eph 4:8
shall go into *c* . . . . Rev 13:10

CARCASS
honey were in the *c* . . . . Judg 14:8
For wherever the *c* . . . . Matt 24:28

CARE
and let her *c* for him . . . . 1 Kin 1:2
into the *c* of Hegai the . . . . Esth 2:8
Your *c* has preserved my . . Job 10:12
the LORD will take *c* of me . . . Ps 27:10
do You *c* about anyone, . . . Matt 22:16
to an inn, and took *c* of . . . Luke 10:34
"Lord, do You not *c* . . . . . . Luke 10:40
not *c* about the sheep . . . . . John 10:13
you to be without *c* . . . . 1 Cor 7:32
same *c* for one another . . . 1 Cor 12:25
but that our *c* for you . . . . . 2 Cor 7:12
who will sincerely *c* . . . . Phil 2:20
that now at last your *c* for . . Phil 4:10
how will he take *c* . . . . 1 Tim 3:5
that You take *c* of him . . . . Heb 2:6
casting all your *c* . . . . 1 Pet 5:7

CARED
he said, not that he *c* . . . . . . John 12:6

CAREFUL
c to observe all the . . . . Deut 17:19
shall be *c* to observe . . . . . 2 Kin 17:37
c to maintain good works . . . Titus 3:8

CAREFULLY
c keep all these . . . . Deut 11:22
choose his friends *c* . . . . Prov 12:26
than love *c* concealed . . . . . . Prov 27:5
I shall walk *c* all my . . . . Is 38:15
you have *c* followed . . . . 1 Tim 4:6

CARELESS
but he who is *c* . . . . Prov 19:16

CARES
no one *c* for my soul . . . . Ps 142:4
and are choked with *c* . . . . . Luke 8:14
He who is unmarried *c* . . . . 1 Cor 7:32
for He *c* for you . . . . 1 Pet 5:7

CARMEL
City of Judah, Josh 15:55
Site of Saul's victory, 1 Sam 15:12
—— A mountain of Palestine, Josh 19:26
Scene of Elijah's triumph, 1 Kin 18:19–45
Elisha visits, 2 Kin 2:25

CARNAL
spiritual, but I am *c* . . . . Rom 7:14

c mind is enmity . . . . Rom 8:7
for you are still c . . . . 1 Cor 3:3
our warfare are not c . . . . . 2 Cor 10:4

CARNALLY
we may know them c . . . . Gen 19:5
that we may know him c . . Judg 19:22
c minded is death . . . . Rom 8:6

CAROUSE
count it pleasure to c . . . . . 2 Pet 2:13

CAROUSING
be weighed down with c . . Luke 21:34

CARPENTER
Is this not the c . . . . Mark 6:3

CARRIED
the LORD your God c . . . . Deut 1:31
and c our sorrows . . . . Is 53:4
parted from them and c . . Luke 24:51
c me away in the . . . . Rev 17:3

CARRY
shall c me out of Egypt . . . . Gen 47:30
you shall c up my bones . . . . Ex 13:19
longer c the tabernacle . . . 1 Chr 23:26
their hands cannot c . . . . Job 5:12
c them away like a . . . . Ps 90:5
to gray hairs I will c you . . . . . . Is 46:4
and c out great exploits . . . Dan 11:32
I am not worthy to c . . . . Matt 3:11
C neither money bag . . . . . . Luke 10:4
for you to c your bed . . . . . . John 5:10
c you where you do not . . . John 21:18
it is certain we can c . . . . 1 Tim 6:7

CARRYING
a man will meet you c . . . Mark 14:13
always c about in the . . . . . 2 Cor 4:10

CART
ark of the LORD on the c . . 1 Sam 6:11
ark of God on a new c . . . . . 2 Sam 6:3
Every c had four bronze . . 1 Kin 7:30
and sin as if with a c rope . . . . Is 5:18
as a c is weighed down . . . Amos 2:13

CARTS
and Joseph gave them c. . . Gen 45:21
made ten c of bronze . . . . . . 1 Kin 7:27
the ten c, and ten lavers . . . 1 Kin 7:43
one Sea, and the c . . . . . . 2 Kin 25:16

CARVE
that its maker should c it . . . Hab 2:18

CARVED
for yourself a c image . . . . Ex 20:4
shall burn the c images . . . . Deut 7:25
the c images of their gods . . Deut 12:3
son, to make a c image . . . . Judg 17:3
Micah's c image which . . . . Judg 18:31
Then he c cherubim . . . . 1 Kin 6:35
He even set a c image, ... 2 Chr 33:7
to shame who serve c . . . . Ps 97:7
workman to prepare a c . . . . . Is 40:20
the c images of Babylon . . . . Jer 51:47
I will cut off the c image . . . . Nah 1:14

CASE
God has judged my c . . . . Gen 30:6
c that is too hard . . . . Deut 1:17
I have prepared my c . . . . . . Job 13:18
I would present my c . . . . Job 23:4
"Present your c . . . . Is 41:21
plead His c with all flesh . . . Jer 25:31
My c with you face to . . . . Ezek 20:35
plead your c before the . . . . . . Mic 6:1
Him, until He pleads my c . . . Mic 7:9
Festus laid Paul's c . . . . Acts 25:14

CASSIA
myrrh and aloes and c . . . . Ps 45:8

CAST
C out this bondwoman . . . . Gen 21:10
c him into this pit which . . . Gen 37:22
c longing eyes on Joseph . . . Gen 39:7
c it before Pharaoh, ... Ex 7:9
army He has c into the sea . . . Ex 15:4
that I may c lots for you . . . . Josh 18:6
c two pillars of bronze . . . . 1 Kin 7:15
they c lots for their duty, . . 1 Chr 25:8
they c Pur (that is, the lot) . . . Esth 3:7
had c Pur (that is, the lot), . . Esth 9:24
When they c you down . . . . . Job 22:29
c away Their cords from . . . . . . Ps 2:3
c upon You from birth . . . . Ps 22:10
for My clothing they c lots . . Ps 22:18
Why are you c down . . . . Ps 42:5
But You have c us off . . . . Ps 44:9
c me away from Your . . . . Ps 51:11
C your burden on the . . . . Ps 55:22
He c on them the . . . . Ps 78:49
the LORD will not c . . . . Ps 94:14
me up and c me away . . . . Ps 102:10
The lot is c into the lap, ... Prov 16:33
the people c off restraint . . Prov 29:18
and the earth shall c . . . . Is 26:19
My sight, as I have c . . . . Jer 7:15
C away from you all . . . . . . Ezek 18:31
Did we not c three men . . . . . Dan 3:24
brought Daniel and c . . . . Dan 6:16
c all our sins into . . . . Mic 7:19
whole body to be c . . . . Matt 5:29
c out demons in Your . . . . . . Matt 7:22
the kingdom will be c . . . . . . Matt 8:12
spirits, to c them out . . . . Matt 10:1
And if I c out demons by . . Matt 12:27
My clothing they c lots . . . . Matt 27:35
can Satan c out Satan . . . . . Mark 3:23
In My name they will c . . . Mark 16:17
do your sons c them out . . Luke 11:19
has power to c into hell . . . . Luke 12:5
His garments and c lots . . Luke 23:34
by no means c out . . . . John 6:37
C the net on the right . . . . . . John 21:6
c away His people . . . . Rom 11:1
C out the bondwoman . . . . Gal 4:30
c away your confidence . . . Heb 10:35
c their crowns before . . . . Rev 4:10
the great dragon was c . . . . . Rev 12:9
c him into the bottomless . . . Rev 20:3
was c into the lake of fire . . Rev 20:15

CAST OUT DEMONS
c in Your name, ... Matt 7:22
raise the dead, c . . . . Matt 10:8
"This fellow does not c . . . Matt 12:24
heal sicknesses and to c . . . Mark 3:15
In My name they will c . . . Mark 16:17
And if I c by Beelzebub, . . Luke 11:19
that fox, 'Behold, I c . . . . . . Luke 13:32

CASTING
nation which I am c . . . . Lev 20:23
Andrew his brother, c . . . . . . Matt 4:18
c down arguments . . . . 2 Cor 10:5
c all your care . . . . 1 Pet 5:7

CASTING OUT DEMONS
all Galilee, and c . . . . Mark 1:39
who does not follow us c . . . Mark 9:38
someone c in Your name, . . Luke 9:49

CASTLE
are like the bars of a c . . . . Prov 18:19

CASTS
If Satan c out Satan . . . . . . Matt 12:26
perfect love c out . . . . 1 John 4:18

CATASTROPHE
bring such a c on this place . . Jer 19:3
not rise from the c that I . . . . Jer 51:64

CATCH
in wait to c the poor . . . . Ps 10:9
c Him in His words . . . . Mark 12:13
down your nets for a c . . . . . Luke 5:4
From now on you will c . . . Luke 5:10
seeking to c Him in . . . . . . Luke 11:54
they could not c Him in . . Luke 20:26

CATCHES
and the wolf c the . . . . John 10:12
c the wise in their . . . . 1 Cor 3:19

CATERPILLAR
their crops to the c . . . . Ps 78:46

CATTLE
c you shall take as . . . . Josh 8:2
does not let their c . . . . Ps 107:38

CAUGHT
behind him was a ram c . . . Gen 22:13
and that night they c . . . . John 21:3
Spirit of the Lord c . . . . Acts 8:39
her Child was c up . . . . Rev 12:5

CAUSE
I would commit my c . . . . Job 5:8
my enemy without c . . . . Ps 7:4
hate me without a c . . . . Ps 35:19
c His face to shine . . . . Ps 67:1
C me to know the way . . . . . . Ps 143:8
one to plead his c . . . . Prov 18:17
God, Who pleads the c . . . . Is 51:22
He judged the c . . . . Jer 22:16
brother without a c . . . . Matt 5:22
hated Me without a c . . . . . John 15:25
For this c I was born . . . . . John 18:37

CAUSED
not c it to rain on the earth . . Gen 2:5
LORD God c a deep sleep . . . . Gen 2:21
LORD c the sea to go back . . . Ex 14:21
Jonathan again c . . . . 1 Sam 20:17
pagan women c even him . . Neh 13:26
c the dawn to know its . . . . . Job 38:12
which You have c me . . . . . . Ps 119:49
I have c to be carried . . . . Jer 29:4
the LORD has c the . . . . Lam 2:6
He c me to eat that scroll . . . Ezek 3:2

CAVALRY
and cities for his c . . . . 1 Kin 9:19
on a horse with the c . . . . . 1 Kin 20:20
their c comes from afar . . . . . . Hab 1:8

CAVE
daughters dwelt in a c . . . . . Gen 19:30
field and the c that is in . . . Gen 23:11
him in the c of Machpelah . . Gen 25:9
in a c at Makkedah . . . . Josh 10:16
escaped to the c of . . . . 1 Sam 22:1
hidden them, fifty to a c . . . 1 Kin 18:4
It was a c, and a stone . . . . John 11:38

CAVES
the people hid in c . . . . 1 Sam 13:6
rocks, and into the c . . . . Is 2:19
in dens and c of the . . . . Heb 11:38

CEASE
and night shall not c . . . . Gen 8:22
Why should the work c . . . . Neh 6:3
There the wicked c . . . . Job 3:17
He makes wars c . . . . Ps 46:9
C listening to . . . . Prov 19:27
when the grinders c . . . . Eccl 12:3
C to do evil . . . . Is 1:16
eyes flow and do not c, ... Lam 3:49
cause all her mirth to c . . . . . Hos 2:11
they did not c teaching . . . . . Acts 5:42
tongues, they will c . . . . 1 Cor 13:8
do not c to give . . . . Eph 1:16
do not c to pray for . . . . Col 1:9

CEASED
c building the city . . . . Gen 11:8
the sea, and the sea c . . . . Jon 1:15
this woman has not c to . . . Luke 7:45
offense of the cross has c . . . . Gal 5:11

CEASES
for the godly man c . . . . Ps 12:1

CEASING
c your work of faith . . . . . . 1 Thess 1:3
thank God without c . . . . . 1 Thess 2:13
pray without c . . . . 1 Thess 5:17

CEDAR
dwell in a house of c . . . . 2 Sam 7:2

He shall grow like a *c* .... Ps 92:12
of our houses are *c* .... Song 1:17
it, paneling it with *c* .... Jer 22:14
Indeed Assyria was a *c* .... Ezek 31:3

CEDARS
the LORD breaks the *c* .... Ps 29:5
c of Lebanon which He .... Ps 104:16

CELEBRATE
you shall *c* your sabbath ... Lev 23:32
You shall *c* it in the .... Lev 23:41
to *c* the dedication with .... Neh 12:27
c yearly the fourteenth ..... Esth 9:21

CELEBRATED
Herod's birthday was *c* .... Matt 14:6

CELESTIAL
but the glory of the *c* ..... 1 Cor 15:40

CENCHREA
A harbor of Corinth, Acts 18:18
Home of Phoebe, Rom 16:1

CENSER
Aaron, each took his *c* ...... Lev 10:1
Each man had a *c* .... Ezek 8:11
which had the golden *c* ...... Heb 9:4
the angel took the *c* .... Rev 8:5

CENSUS
When you take the *c* of ...... Ex 30:12
"Take a *c* of all the .... Num 1:2
Take a *c* of the people ..... Num 26:4
Israel because of this *c* ... 1 Chr 27:24
the *c* in which David .... 2 Chr 2:17
c first took place while ..... Luke 2:2
in the days of the *c* .... Acts 5:37

CENTER
the sanctuary in the *c* ...... Ezek 48:8
side, and Jesus in the *c* ... John 19:18

CENTURION
c came to Him, pleading .... Matt 8:5
when the *c*, who stood ... Mark 15:39
when the *c* saw what ..... Luke 23:47
Cornelius the *c*, a just ..... Acts 10:22
said to the *c* who stood .... Acts 22:25
a *c* of the Augustan .... Acts 27:1

CENTURION'S
a certain *c* servant, who .... Luke 7:2

CEPHAS
Aramaic for Peter, John 1:42

CERAMIC
the iron mixed with *c* clay .. Dan 2:41

CEREMONIALLY
Israel and cleanse them *c* ... Num 8:6

CEREMONIES
rites and *c* you shall keep ... Num 9:3
as in the *c* of your fathers, ... Jer 34:5

CERTAIN
a *c* man of Bethlehem, ... Ruth 1:1
Know for *c* that on the .... 1 Kin 2:42
a *c* man clothed in linen, ... Dan 10:5
was a *c* landowner .... Matt 21:33
into the city to a *c* man ... Matt 26:18
But a *c* Samaritan, as he .. Luke 10:33
A *c* man had a fig tree ..... Luke 13:6
A *c* man gave a great ..... Luke 14:16
A *c* man had two sons .... Luke 15:11
There was a *c* rich man .... Luke 16:1
there was a *c* beggar ..... Luke 16:20
there was a *c* nobleman .... John 4:46
c we can carry nothing ..... 1 Tim 6:7
He designates a *c* day .... Heb 4:7
a *c* fearful expectation ..... Heb 10:27

CERTAINLY NOT
C! Indeed, let God be true ... Rom 3:4
C! For then how will God .... Rom 3:6
the law through faith? *C!* ... Rom 3:31
C! How shall we who died .. Rom 6:2
law but under grace? *C* .... Rom 6:15
Is the law sin? *C* .... Rom 7:7
C! But sin, that it might .... Rom 7:13
with God? *C* .... Rom 9:14
cast away His people? *C* .... Rom 11:1
C! But through their fall, .. Rom 11:11
members of a harlot? *C* .... 1 Cor 6:15
a minister of sin? *C* .... Gal 2:17
C! For if there had been ..... Gal 3:21

CERTAINTY
make you know the *c* ..... Prov 22:21
you may know the *c* .... Luke 1:4

CERTIFICATE
writes her a *c* of divorce ... Deut 24:1
Where is the *c* of your .... Is 50:1
given her a *c* of divorce .... Jer 3:8
a man to write a *c* .... Mark 10:4

CERTIFIED
His testimony has *c* .... John 3:33

CHAFF
c that a storm .... Job 21:18
c which the wind .... Ps 1:4
Let them be like *c* .... Ps 35:5
be chased like the *c* .... Is 17:13
You shall conceive *c* .... Is 33:11
the day passes like *c* .... Zeph 2:2
He will burn up the *c* .... Matt 3:12

CHAIN
He has made my *c* .... Lam 3:7
pit and a great *c* .... Rev 20:1

CHAINED
of God is not *c* .... 2 Tim 2:9
the prisoners as if *c* .... Heb 13:3

CHAINS
their kings with *c* .... Ps 149:8
your neck with *c* .... Song 1:10
And his *c* fell off .... Acts 12:7
am, except for these *c* ..... Acts 26:29
Remember my *c* .... Col 4:18
minister to me in my *c* ..... Philem 13
delivered them into *c* .... 2 Pet 2:4

CHAINWORK
with wreaths of *c* .... 1 Kin 7:17
carved palm trees and *c* .... 2 Chr 3:5

CHAIR
and a table and a *c* .... 2 Kin 4:10

CHALCEDONY
sapphire, the third *c* .... Rev 21:19

CHALDEA
Originally, the southern portion of Babylonia, Gen 11:31
Applied later to all Babylonia, Dan 3:8
Abram came from, Gen 11:28–31

CHALDEANS
Attack Job, Job 1:17
Nebuchadnezzar, king of, 2 Kin 24:1
Jerusalem defeated by, 2 Kin 25:1–21
Babylon, "the glory of," Is 13:19
Predicted captivity of Jews among, Jer 25:1–26
God's agent, Hab 1:6

CHALK
he marks one out with *c* ..... Is 44:13

CHALKSTONES
c that are beaten to dust ...... Is 27:9

CHAMBER
went into his *c* and wept .. Gen 43:30
in his cool private *c*) .... Judg 3:20
into an inner *c* to hide .... 2 Chr 18:24
go out from his *c* .... Joel 2:16

CHAMBERS
and the *c* of the south .... Job 9:9
brought me into his *c* .... Song 1:4
and his *c* by injustice .... Jer 22:13

CHAMPION
And a *c* went out from .... 1 Sam 17:4

CHANCE
time and *c* happen to .... Eccl 9:11

CHANGE
c his countenance .... Job 14:20
c the night into day .... Job 17:12
and who can make Him *c* .. Job 23:13
Because they do not *c* .... Ps 55:19
a cloak You will *c* .... Ps 102:26
with those given to *c* ..... Prov 24:21
Can the Ethiopian *c* .... Jer 13:23
c times and law .... Dan 7:25
c their glory into .... Hos 4:7
the LORD, I do not *c* .... Mal 3:6
now and to *c* my tone .... Gal 4:20
there is also a *c* .... Heb 7:12

CHANGED
c my wages ten times, ... Gen 31:7
c his clothing, and came ... Gen 41:14
them, and they will be *c* ... Ps 102:26
But My people have *c* .... Jer 2:11
his countenance was *c*, ... Dan 5:9
c the glory of the .... Rom 1:23
but we shall all be *c* ...... 1 Cor 15:51
up, and they will be *c* .... Heb 1:12
the priesthood being *c* ...... Heb 7:12

CHANGERS'
and poured out the *c* .... John 2:15

CHANGES
c the times and the .... Dan 2:21

CHANNELS
c of the sea were seen .... Ps 18:15

CHANT
who *c* "Peace" while .... Mic 3:5

CHARACTER
and *c*, hope .... Rom 5:4
you know his proven *c* ..... Phil 2:22

CHARCOAL
As *c* is to burning coals, .. Prov 26:21

CHARGE
My voice and kept My *c* .... Gen 26:5
shall not *c* him interest ..... Ex 22:25
You shall not *c* interest ... Deut 23:19
in *c* of the music .... 1 Chr 15:22
kept the *c* of their God .... Neh 12:45
not sin nor *c* God with ...... Job 1:22
His angels *c* over you .... Ps 91:11
His angels *c* over you .... Matt 4:6
His angels *c* over You ..... Luke 4:10
not *c* them with this sin .... Acts 7:60
shall bring a *c* against ..... Rom 8:33
of Christ without *c* .... 1 Cor 9:18
of God to you free of *c* .... 2 Cor 11:7
anyone's bread free of *c* .. 2 Thess 3:8
This *c* I commit to you, ... 1 Tim 1:18

CHARGED
May it not be *c* .... 2 Tim 4:16

CHARIOT
He took off their *c* .... Ex 14:25
that suddenly a *c* .... 2 Kin 2:11
makes the clouds His *c* ...... Ps 104:3
and overtake this *c* .... Acts 8:29

CHARIOTEERS
killed seven hundred *c* .. 2 Sam 10:18

CHARIOTS
the clatter of his *c* .... Judg 5:28
Some trust in *c* .... Ps 20:7
The *c* of God are .... Ps 68:17

CHARITABLE
you do not do your *c* .... Matt 6:1
that your *c* deed .... Matt 6:4
c deeds which she .... Acts 9:36

CHARM
C is deceitful and .... Prov 31:30

CHARMED
may bite when it is not *c* .. Eccl 10:11
vipers which cannot be *c* .... Jer 8:17

CHARMERS
heed the voice of *c* .... Ps 58:5

CHARMS
the perfume boxes, the *c*, ... Is 3:20
have scattered your *c* to . . . . . Jer 3:13
who sew magic *c* . . . . Ezek 13:18

CHASE
Five of you shall *c* . . . . Lev 26:8
How could one *c* . . . . Deut 32:30
angel of the LORD *c* . . . . Ps 35:5

CHASTE
may present you as a *c* . . . . 2 Cor 11:2
to be discreet, *c* . . . . Titus 2:5
c conduct accompanied . . . . . 1 Pet 3:2

CHASTEN
C your son while there . . . . Prov 19:18
is My desire, I will *c* . . . . Hos 10:10
a father does not *c* . . . . Heb 12:7
I love, I rebuke and *c* . . . . Rev 3:19

CHASTENED
c my soul with fasting . . . . Ps 69:10
c every morning . . . . Ps 73:14
The LORD has *c* me . . . . Ps 118:18
In vain I have *c* . . . . Jer 2:30
c us as seemed best . . . . . . Heb 12:10

CHASTENING
have not seen the *c* . . . . Deut 11:2
do not despise the *c* . . . . Job 5:17
'I have borne *c* . . . . Job 34:31
a prayer when Your *c* . . . . Is 26:16
if you are without *c* . . . . Heb 12:8
Now no *c* seems to be . . . . . Heb 12:11

CHASTENS
the LORD your God *c* you . . . . Deut 8:5
the LORD loves He *c* . . . . Heb 12:6

CHASTISE
and I, even I, will *c* . . . . Lev 26:28
c them according . . . . Hos 7:12
I will therefore *c* . . . . Luke 23:22

CHASTISED
father *c* you with whips, . . 1 Kin 12:11
have *c* me, and I was *c* . . . . Jer 31:18

CHASTISEMENT
the *c* for our peace . . . . Is 53:5

CHATTER
c leads only to poverty . . . . Prov 14:23

CHEAT
'You shall not *c* . . . . Lev 19:13
Beware lest anyone *c* . . . . Col 2:8

CHEATED
let yourselves be *c* . . . . 1 Cor 6:7
we have *c* no one . . . . 2 Cor 7:2

CHEBAR
River in Babylonia, Ezek 1:3
Site of Ezekiel's visions, Ezek 10:15, 20

CHEDORLAOMER
A king of Elam; invaded Canaan, Gen 14:1–16

CHEEK
Let him give his *c* . . . . Lam 3:30
with a rod on the *c* . . . . Mic 5:1
on your right *c* . . . . Matt 5:39

CHEEKBONE
my enemies on the *c* . . . . Ps 3:7

CHEEKS
c are lovely with . . . . Song 1:10
His *c* are like a bed . . . . Song 5:13
struck Me, and My *c* . . . . Is 50:6

CHEER
See BE OF GOOD CHEER
and let your heart *c* . . . . Eccl 11:9
"Son, be of good *c* . . . . Matt 9:2

CHEERFUL
makes a *c* countenance . . . Prov 15:13
for God loves a *c* . . . . 2 Cor 9:7
Is anyone *c*? Let him . . . . . James 5:13

CHEERFULNESS
shows mercy, with *c* . . . . Rom 12:8

CHEESE
and curdle me like *c* . . . . Job 10:10

CHEMOSH
The god of the Moabites, Num 21:29
Children sacrificed to, 2 Kin 3:26, 27
Solomon builds altars to, 1 Kin 11:7
Josiah destroys altars of, 2 Kin 23:13

CHERISHES
but nourishes and *c* . . . . Eph 5:29
as a nursing mother *c* . . . . 1 Thess 2:7

CHERUB
Make one *c* at one end, ... Ex 25:19
c at one end on this side . . . . . . Ex 37:8
He rode upon a *c* . . . . 2 Sam 22:11
other *c* was ten cubits . . . . . 1 Kin 6:25
And He rode upon a *c*, ... Ps 18:10
the wheels, under the *c* . . . . . Ezek 10:2
anointed *c* who covers . . . . . Ezek 28:14
tree between *c* and *c* . . . . . . Ezek 41:18

CHERUBIM
and He placed *c* . . . . Gen 3:24
shall make two *c* of gold . . . . Ex 25:18
an artistic design of *c* . . . . Ex 26:31
dwells between the *c* . . . . 2 Sam 6:2
two *c* of olive wood . . . . 1 Kin 6:23
out the wings of the *c* so . . 1 Kin 6:27
were lions, oxen, and *c* . . . . 1 Kin 7:29
its panels he engraved *c* . . . 1 Kin 7:36
under the wings of the *c* . . . . 1 Kin 8:6
c overshadowed the ark . . . . . 2 Chr 5:8
dwell between the *c* . . . . Ps 80:1
who dwells between the *c* . . . . Is 37:16
fire from among the *c* . . . . . . Ezek 10:2
above it were the *c* . . . . Heb 9:5

CHEST
offering in a *c* by its side . . 1 Sam 6:8
the *c* with the gold rats . . . 1 Sam 6:11
the priest took a *c* . . . . 2 Kin 12:9
came and emptied the *c* . . 2 Chr 24:11

CHESTNUT
c trees, peeled white . . . . . . Gen 30:37

CHEW
or does not *c* the cud, is . . . . Lev 11:26

CHEWING
What the *c* locust left, the . . . . Joel 1:4
the *c* locust, my great . . . . Joel 2:25

CHICKS
gathers her *c* under her . . . Matt 23:37

CHIEF
is white and ruddy, *c* . . . . . . Song 5:10
of whom I am *c* . . . . 1 Tim 1:15
Zion a *c* cornerstone . . . . 1 Pet 2:6
has become the *c* . . . . 1 Pet 2:7
C Shepherd appears . . . . 1 Pet 5:4

CHILD
See WITH CHILD
she is with *c* by harlotry . . . Gen 38:24
that he was a beautiful *c* . . . . . . Ex 2:2
c grew, and she brought . . . . . Ex 2:10
the *c* shall be a Nazirite . . . . Judg 13:5
the *c* ministered to the . . . . 1 Sam 2:11
c Samuel grew in stature . . 1 Sam 2:26
named the *c* Ichabod . . . . . 1 Sam 4:21
her dead *c* in my bosom . . . 1 Kin 3:20
Divide the living *c* in two . . 1 Kin 3:25
soul of the *c* came back . . . 1 Kin 17:22
flesh of the *c* became . . . . . 2 Kin 4:34
Like a weaned *c* . . . . Ps 131:2
c is known by his . . . . Prov 20:11
Train up a *c* in the . . . . Prov 22:6
before the *C* shall know . . . . Is 7:16
For unto us a *C* . . . . Is 9:6
c shall lead them . . . . Is 11:6
When Israel was a *c* . . . . Hos 11:1
with *c* of the Holy Spirit . . . . . Matt 1:18
virgin shall be with *c* . . . . Matt 1:23
He took a little *c* . . . . Mark 9:36
of God as a little *c* . . . . Mark 10:15
kind of *c* will this be . . . . Luke 1:66
So the *c* grew and . . . . Luke 1:80
the circumcision of the *C* . . Luke 2:21
When I was a *c* . . . . 1 Cor 13:11
She bore a male *C* . . . . Rev 12:5

CHILDBEARING
she will be saved in *c* . . . . . 1 Tim 2:15

CHILDBIRTH
pain as a woman in *c* . . . . Is 13:8

CHILDHOOD
from your flesh, for *c* . . . . . . Eccl 11:10
And he said, "From *c* . . . . . Mark 9:21
c you have known . . . . 2 Tim 3:15

CHILDISH
I put away *c* things . . . . . . 1 Cor 13:11

CHILDLESS
give me, seeing I go *c* . . . . . . Gen 15:2
this man down as *c* . . . . Jer 22:30

CHILDREN
See LITTLE CHILDREN
she bore Jacob no *c* . . . . Gen 30:1
and all of you are *c* . . . . Ps 82:6
c are a heritage . . . . Ps 127:3
He has blessed your *c* . . . . . . Ps 147:13
let the *c* of Zion be . . . . Ps 149:2
c are blessed after . . . . Prov 20:7
c rise up and call her . . . . . Prov 31:28
c are their oppressors . . . . Is 3:12
c whom the LORD has . . . . Is 8:18
be the peace of your *c* . . . . Is 54:13
they are My people, *c* . . . . Is 63:8
the hearts of the *c* . . . . Mal 4:6
c will rise up against . . . . . . Matt 10:21
and become as little *c* . . . . . . Matt 18:3
c were brought to Him . . . . Matt 19:13
"Let the little *c* . . . . Matt 19:14
the right to become *c* . . . . John 1:12
you were Abraham's *c* . . . . . . John 8:39
spirit that we are *c* . . . . Rom 8:16
but as my beloved *c* . . . . 1 Cor 4:14
Brethren, do not be *c* . . . . . 1 Cor 14:20
c ought not to lay up . . . . . 2 Cor 12:14
and were by nature *c* . . . . Eph 2:3
should no longer be *c* . . . . Eph 4:14
Walk as *c* of light . . . . Eph 5:8
and harmless, *c* of God . . . . . Phil 2:15
now we are *c* of God . . . . 1 John 3:2
that we love the *c* . . . . 1 John 5:2
to hear that my *c* . . . . 3 John 4

CHILDREN'S
are really ours and our *c* . . Gen 31:16
the *c* children to the third . . . . Ex 34:7
His righteousness to *c* . . . . . . Ps 103:17
you see your *c* children . . . . . Ps 128:6
inheritance to his *c* . . . . Prov 13:22
C children are the crown . . . . Prov 17:6
the *c* teeth are set on edge . . Jer 31:29
good to take the *c* bread . . Matt 15:26
eat from the *c* crumbs . . . . . Mark 7:28

CHILION
Elimelech's son, Ruth 1:2
Orpah's deceased husband, Ruth 1:4, 5
Boaz redeems his estate, Ruth 4:9

CHINNERETH (or Chinneroth)
Fortified city in Naphtali, Deut 3:17
A region bordering the Sea of Galilee, 1 Kin 15:20
Same as the plain of Gennesaret, Matt 14:34
—— The O.T. name for the Sea of Galilee, Num 34:11
Also called Lake of Gennesaret, Luke 5:1

CHOICE
rather than *c* gold . . . . Prov 8:10

CHOIR
c went the opposite way, . . Neh 12:38

CHOKE
things entering in *c* the . . . . Mark 4:19

CHOKED
thorns sprang up and *c* . . . . Matt 13:7
are *c* with cares, riches, ... Luke 8:14

CHOOSE
therefore *c* life . . . . Deut 30:19
c none of his ways . . . . Prov 3:31
evil and *c* the good . . . . Is 7:15
will still *c* Israel . . . . Is 14:1
will again *c* Jerusalem . . . . . Zech 1:17
You did not *c* Me, but I . . . John 15:16
yet what I shall *c* . . . . Phil 1:22

CHOOSES
in the way He *c* . . . . Ps 25:12

CHOSE
a good while ago God *c* . . . . Acts 15:7
just as He *c* us in Him . . . . Eph 1:4
from the beginning *c* . . . . 2 Thess 2:13

CHOSEN
the LORD has *c* you to be . . . Deut 14:2
has *c* them to minister to . . . Deut 21:5
c the son of Jesse to . . . . . 1 Sam 20:30
of Jacob, His *c* . . . . 1 Chr 16:13
I have *c* Jerusalem, that . . . . 2 Chr 6:6
I have *c* David to be over . . . 2 Chr 6:6
people He has *c* . . . . Ps 33:12
a covenant with My *c* . . . . Ps 89:3
c the way of truth . . . . Ps 119:30
A good name is to be *c* . . . . Prov 22:1
servant whom I have *c* . . . . Is 43:10
Is it a fast that I have *c* . . . . Is 58:5
c that good part . . . . Luke 10:42
I know whom I have *c* . . . . John 13:18
c you that you should . . . . . Acts 22:14
c the foolish things . . . . 1 Cor 1:27
Has God not *c* the poor . . . . James 2:5
But you are a *c* . . . . 1 Pet 2:9

CHRIST
See JESUS; LORD JESUS CHRIST; LOVE OF CHRIST; YOU ARE THE CHRIST
Preexistence of, Ps 2:7; John 8:58; Col 1:15–18
Birth of, from a virgin, Is 7:14; Matt 1:18–25
Deity of, Is 9:6; John 1:1, 14, 18; 20:28, 29; Rom 9:5; Heb 1:8
Humanity of, Gen 3:15; Matt 22:45; Luke 3:38; John 1:14; 1 Cor 15:45–47; Gal 4:4; Phil 2:5–11; 1 Tim 2:5
Character of:
omnipotent, Matt 28:18
omniscient, Col 2:3
omnipresent, Matt 18:20
eternal, John 1:1, 2, 15
holy, Luke 1:35
righteous, Is 53:11
just, Zech 9:9
guileless, 1 Pet 2:22
sinless, 2 Cor 5:21
spotless, 1 Pet 1:19
innocent, Matt 27:4
gentle, Matt 11:29
merciful, Heb 2:17
humble, Phil 2:8
forgiving, Luke 23:34
Mission of:
do God's will, John 6:38
save sinners, Luke 19:10
destroy Satan's works, Heb 2:14; 1 John 3:8
fulfill the O.T., Matt 5:17
give life, John 10:10, 28
complete revelation, Heb 1:1
Worshiped by:
O.T. saints, Josh 5:13–15
demons, Mark 5:2, 6
men, John 9:38
angels, Heb 1:6
disciples, Luke 24:52
saints in glory, Rev 7:9, 10
all, Phil 2:10, 11
O.T. types of:
Adam, Rom 5:14
Abel, Heb 12:24
Moses, Deut 18:15
Passover, 1 Cor 5:7
manna, John 6:32
bronze serpent, John 3:14
genealogy of Jesus *C* . . . . Matt 1:1
Jesus who is called *C* . . . . . Matt 1:16
"You are the *C* . . . . Matt 16:16
do you think about the *C* . . Matt 22:42
if You are the *C* . . . . Matt 26:63
of the gospel of Jesus *C*, ... Mark 1:1
You are the *C* . . . . Mark 8:29
Are You the *C*, the Son . . Mark 14:61
a Savior, who is *C* . . . . Luke 2:11
and said, "The *C* of God . . . Luke 9:20
that He Himself is *C* . . . . Luke 23:2
is translated, the *C*) . . . . John 1:41
the law that the *C* . . . . John 12:34
believe that Jesus is the *C* . John 20:31
crucified, both Lord and *C* . . Acts 2:36
preaching Jesus as the *C* . . . Acts 5:42
he preached the *C* . . . . Acts 9:20
that this Jesus is the *C* . . . . . . Acts 9:22
Jesus the *C* heals . . . . Acts 9:34
the *C* had to suffer and . . . . . Acts 17:3
that Jesus is the *C* . . . . Acts 18:28
that the *C* would suffer, . . . Acts 26:23
His Son Jesus *C* our Lord . . . Rom 1:3
faith in Jesus *C* to all and . . . Rom 3:22
through our Lord Jesus *C* . . . Rom 5:1
in due time *C* died for the . . . Rom 5:6
through our Lord Jesus *C* . . Rom 5:11
through the One, Jesus *C* . . Rom 5:17
that just as *C* was raised . . . . Rom 6:4
life in *C* Jesus our Lord . . . . Rom 6:23
law through the body of *C* . . Rom 7:4
those who are in *C* Jesus . . . . Rom 8:1
have the Spirit of *C* . . . . Rom 8:9
and joint heirs with *C* . . . . . Rom 8:17
It is *C* who died . . . . Rom 8:34
C came, who is over all . . . . . Rom 9:5
C is the end of the law . . . . . Rom 10:4
many, are one body in *C* . . . Rom 12:5
put on the Lord Jesus *C* . . . Rom 13:14
For to this end *C* died . . . . . . Rom 14:9
C did not please . . . . Rom 15:3
just as *C* also received us, . . Rom 15:7
serve our Lord Jesus *C* . . . Rom 16:18
are sanctified in *C* Jesus . . . . 1 Cor 1:2
Is *C* divided . . . . 1 Cor 1:13
For *C* did not send me to . . 1 Cor 1:17
we preach *C* crucified . . . . 1 Cor 1:23
Him you are in *C* Jesus . . . . 1 Cor 1:30
among you except Jesus *C* . 1 Cor 2:2
is laid, which is Jesus *C* . . . 1 Cor 3:11
indeed *C*, our Passover, ... 1 Cor 5:7
bodies are members of *C* . . 1 Cor 6:15
Lord Jesus *C*, through . . . . . . 1 Cor 8:6
you sin against *C* . . . . 1 Cor 8:12
and that Rock was *C* . . . . . . 1 Cor 10:4
just as I also imitate *C* . . . . 1 Cor 11:1
head of every man is *C* . . . . 1 Cor 11:3
you are the body of *C* . . . . 1 Cor 12:27
that *C* died for our sins . . . . 1 Cor 15:3
if *C* is not risen, then . . . . 1 Cor 15:14
even so in *C* all shall be . . 1 Cor 15:22
our Lord Jesus *C* . . . . 1 Cor 15:57
sufferings of *C* abound . . . . . 2 Cor 1:5
leads us in triumph in *C*, . . 2 Cor 2:14
you are an epistle of *C* . . . . 2 Cor 3:3
veil is taken away in *C* . . . . 2 Cor 3:14
gospel of the glory of *C* . . . . 2 Cor 4:4
the judgment seat of *C* . . . . 2 Cor 5:10
if anyone is in *C* . . . . 2 Cor 5:17
accord has *C* with Belial . . 2 Cor 6:15
and gentleness of *C* . . . . 2 Cor 10:1
as a chaste virgin to *C* . . . . 2 Cor 11:2
to pervert the gospel of *C* . . . . Gal 1:7
which we have in *C* Jesus, ... Gal 2:4
to be justified by *C* . . . . Gal 2:17
been crucified with *C* . . . . Gal 2:20
your Seed," who is *C* . . . . Gal 3:16
before by God in *C* . . . . Gal 3:17
through faith in *C* Jesus . . . . Gal 3:26
until *C* is formed in you, ... Gal 4:19
which *C* has made us free . . . . Gal 5:1
become estranged from *C* . . . . Gal 5:4
cross of our Lord Jesus *C* . . . Gal 6:14
the heavenly places in *C* . . . . Eph 1:3
in one all things in *C*, ... Eph 1:10
which He worked in *C* . . . . . . Eph 1:20
C (by grace you have been . . . Eph 2:5
time you were without *C* . . . . Eph 2:12
Jesus *C* Himself being . . . . . . Eph 2:20
unsearchable riches of *C* . . . . . Eph 3:8
C may dwell in your . . . . Eph 3:17
stature of the fullness of *C* . . Eph 4:13
Him who is the head—*C* . . . Eph 4:15
even as God in *C* forgave . . . Eph 4:32
C will give you light . . . . Eph 5:14
C is head of the church . . . . . Eph 5:23
just as *C* also loved the . . . . . Eph 5:25
or in truth, *C* is preached . . . Phil 1:18
to me, to live is *C* . . . . Phil 1:21
to depart and be with *C* . . . . . Phil 1:23
worthy of the gospel of *C* . . . Phil 1:27
which was also in *C* Jesus . . . Phil 2:5
confess that Jesus *C* . . . . Phil 2:11
I have counted loss for *C* . . . . Phil 3:7
enemies of the cross of *C* . . . Phil 3:18
C who strengthens . . . . Phil 4:13
riches in glory by *C* Jesus . . Phil 4:19
of your faith in *C* Jesus . . . . Col 1:4
which is *C* in you . . . . Col 1:27
every man perfect in *C* . . . . . . Col 1:28
of the Father and of *C* . . . . Col 2:2
received *C* Jesus the Lord . . . Col 2:6
but the substance is of *C* . . . . Col 2:17
you were raised with *C* . . . . Col 3:1
hidden with *C* in God . . . . Col 3:3
C who is our life . . . . Col 3:4
C is all and in all . . . . Col 3:11
Let the word of *C* dwell . . . . . Col 3:16
dead in *C* will rise first . . 1 Thess 4:16
our Lord Jesus *C*, ... 1 Thess 5:9
and the Lord Jesus *C* . . . . . 2 Thess 1:2
of our Lord Jesus *C* . . . . . . 2 Thess 2:1
of our Lord Jesus *C* . . . . . 2 Thess 2:14
I thank *C* Jesus our Lord . . 1 Tim 1:12
that *C* Jesus came into . . . 1 Tim 1:15
first Jesus *C* might show . . 1 Tim 1:16
and men, the Man *C* . . . . 1 Tim 2:5
in *C* Jesus before time . . . . . 2 Tim 1:9
good soldier of Jesus *C* . . . . 2 Tim 2:3
in *C* Jesus with eternal . . . . 2 Tim 2:10
in *C* Jesus will suffer . . . . . . 2 Tim 3:12
faith which is in *C* Jesus . . 2 Tim 3:15
and the Lord Jesus *C*, ... 2 Tim 4:1
God and Savior Jesus *C* . . . Titus 2:13
of our confession, *C* Jesus, . . . Heb 3:1
C as a Son over His own . . . . Heb 3:6
C if we hold the beginning . . Heb 3:14
So also *C* did not glorify . . . . . Heb 5:5
elementary principles of *C* . . . Heb 6:1
But *C* came as High Priest . . Heb 9:11
more shall the blood of *C* . . . Heb 9:14
For *C* has not entered the . . . Heb 9:24
C was offered once to bear . . Heb 9:28
body of Jesus *C* once for . . Heb 10:10
Jesus *C* is the same . . . . Heb 13:8
of the blood of Jesus *C* . . . . . . 1 Pet 1:2
Spirit of *C* who was in . . . . . . 1 Pet 1:11
the precious blood of *C* . . . . . 1 Pet 1:19
because *C* also suffered . . . . 1 Pet 2:21
For *C* also suffered once . . . 1 Pet 3:18
resurrection of Jesus *C* . . . . . 1 Pet 3:21

for the name of C ....1 Pet 4:14
God and Savior Jesus C .....2 Pet 1:1
of our Lord Jesus C ....2 Pet 1:16
C His Son cleanses us .....1 John 1:7
Jesus C the righteous .....1 John 2:1
denies that Jesus is the C .1 John 2:22
name of His Son Jesus C .1 John 3:23
confesses that Jesus C .....1 John 4:2
that Jesus is the C ....1 John 5:1
true, in His Son Jesus C ..1 John 5:20
of C does not have God .....2 John 9
and our Lord Jesus C ....Jude 4
The Revelation of Jesus C ....Rev 1:1
from Jesus C, the faithful ....Rev 1:5
the testimony of Jesus C .....Rev 1:9
of our Lord and of His C, ..Rev 11:15
of His C have come ....Rev 12:10
and reigned with C ....Rev 20:4
be priests of God and of C ..Rev 20:6

CHRISTIAN
me to become a C ....Acts 26:28
anyone suffers as a C ......1 Pet 4:16

CHRISTIANS
were first called C ....Acts 11:26

CHRIST'S
you are C, and Christ is ....1 Cor 3:23
We are fools for C sake, ...1 Cor 4:10
are C at His coming ....1 Cor 15:23
in himself that he is C, ...2 Cor 10:7
if you are C, then you are ...Gal 3:29
partake of C sufferings .....1 Pet 4:13

CHRISTS
For false c and ....Matt 24:24

CHRYSOLITE
sardius, the seventh c ......Rev 21:20

CHRYSOPRASE
ninth topaz, the tenth c ....Rev 21:20

CHURCH
rock I will build My c .....Matt 16:18
them, tell it to the c ....Matt 18:17
c daily those who were .....Acts 2:47
elders in every c ....Acts 14:23
do you despise the c .....1 Cor 11:22
persecuted the c of God ...1 Cor 15:9
over all things to the c ......Eph 1:22
be made known by the c ......Eph 3:10
also loved the c ....Eph 5:25
Himself a glorious c ....Eph 5:27
as the Lord does the c ......Eph 5:29
no c shared with me ....Phil 4:15
body, which is the c ....Col 1:24
is the c of the living .....1 Tim 3:15
and do not let the c ....1 Tim 5:16
general assembly and c ....Heb 12:23
To the angel of the c ....Rev 2:1

CHURCHES
strengthening the c ....Acts 15:41
The c of Christ greet ....Rom 16:16
imitators of the c ....1 Thess 2:14
John, to the seven c ....Rev 1:4
angels of the seven c ....Rev 1:20
these things in the c ....Rev 22:16

CHURNING
For as the c of milk ....Prov 30:33

CHURNS
My heart c within Me ....Hos 11:8

CILICIA
Paul's homeland, Acts 21:39
Students from, argued with Stephen, Acts 6:9
Paul labors in, Gal 1:21

CINNAMON
sweet-smelling c ....Ex 30:23
saffron, calamus and c, ...Song 4:14
c and incense, fragrant ....Rev 18:13

CIRCLE
He walks above the c ......Job 22:14
when He drew a c ....Prov 8:27
who sits above the c ....Is 40:22

CIRCUIT
of heaven, and its c ....Ps 19:6
comes again on its c ....Eccl 1:6

CIRCUMCISE
c the foreskin of your .....Deut 10:16
LORD your God will c ....Deut 30:6
C yourselves to the ....Jer 4:4
is necessary to c them ......Acts 15:5

CIRCUMCISED
among you shall be c ....Gen 17:10
day Abraham was c ....Gen 17:26
Abraham c his son Isaac ....Gen 21:4
every male was c, all ......Gen 34:24
let all his males be c ....Ex 12:48
of Egypt, had not been c ....Josh 5:5
c him on the eighth day ......Acts 7:8
who will justify the c ......Rom 3:30
While he was c ....Rom 4:10
the gospel for the c ....Gal 2:7
if you become c ....Gal 5:2
c the eighth day ....Phil 3:5
In Him you were also c .....Col 2:11

CIRCUMCISION
him the covenant of c ....Acts 7:8
c that which is outward ....Rom 2:28
c is that of the heart ....Rom 2:29
a servant to the c ....Rom 15:8
C is nothing and ....1 Cor 7:19
Christ Jesus neither c ....Gal 5:6
For we are the c ....Phil 3:3
circumcised with the c ......Col 2:11
those of the c ....Titus 1:10

CIRCUMSPECTLY
then that you walk c ....Eph 5:15

CISTERN
waters of his own c ......2 Kin 18:31
from your own c ....Prov 5:15

CISTERNS
and hewn themselves c ......Jer 2:13
went to the c and found .....Jer 14:3

CITIES
He overthrew those c .....Gen 19:25
repair the ruined c ....Is 61:4
c are a wilderness ....Is 64:10
c will be laid waste ....Jer 4:7
three parts, and the c ......Rev 16:19

CITIZEN
But I was born a c ....Acts 22:28

CITIZENS
But his c hated him ......Luke 19:14
but fellow c with the ....Eph 2:19

CITIZENSHIP
sum I obtained this c ......Acts 22:28
For our c is in heaven ......Phil 3:20

CITY
See HOLY CITY
And he built a c ....Gen 4:17
shall make glad the c ....Ps 46:4
c shall flourish ....Ps 72:16
They found no c ....Ps 107:4
c that is compact ....Ps 122:3
the LORD guards the c ....Ps 127:1
at the entry of the c ....Prov 8:3
c has become a harlot ....Is 1:21
upon Zion, the c ....Is 33:20
after the holy c ....Is 48:2
How lonely sits the c ....Lam 1:1
Nineveh, that great c ....Jon 4:11
c that dwelt securely ......Zeph 2:15
to the oppressing c ....Zeph 3:1
c called Nazareth ....Matt 2:23
c that is set on a ....Matt 5:14
He has prepared a c ....Heb 11:16
Zion and to the c ....Heb 12:22
have no continuing c ......Heb 13:14
will tread the holy c ....Rev 11:2
fallen, that great c ....Rev 14:8
and the beloved c ....Rev 20:9
John, saw the holy c ....Rev 21:2
c was pure gold ....Rev 21:18
c had no need of the ....Rev 21:23
the gates into the c ....Rev 22:14

CITY OF DAVID
of Zion (that is, the C ......2 Sam 5:7
with him into the C ....2 Sam 6:10
was buried in the C ....1 Kin 2:10
of the Lord from the C .....1 Kin 8:1
was buried in the C ....1 Kin 11:43
for himself in the C ....1 Chr 15:1
the Millo in the C ....2 Chr 32:5
the west side of the C ....2 Chr 32:30
that go down from the C ....Neh 3:15
up the stairs of the C, ...Neh 12:37
the damage to the c, ...Is 22:9
into Judea, to the c, ...Luke 2:4
this day in the c a Savior, ..Luke 2:11

CLAD
was c with zeal as a cloak ...Is 59:17

CLAMOROUS
A foolish woman is c ....Prov 9:13

CLANGING
brass or a c cymbal ....1 Cor 13:1

CLAP
c their hands at him ....Job 27:23
Oh, c your hands ....Ps 47:1
let the rivers c ....Ps 98:8
of the field shall c ....Is 55:12

CLAUDIUS LYSIAS
Roman commander who protected Paul, Acts 24:22–24, 26

CLAY
dwell in houses of c ....Job 4:19
have made me like c ....Job 10:9
are defenses of c ....Job 13:12
been formed out of c ....Job 33:6
takes on form like c ....Job 38:14
pit, out of the miry c ....Ps 40:2
be esteemed as the c ....Is 29:16
Shall the c say to him ....Is 45:9
We are the c, and You ....Is 64:8
"Look, as the c ....Jer 18:6
iron and partly of c ....Dan 2:33
blind man with the c ....John 9:6
have power over the c ....Rom 9:21
but also of wood and c ......2 Tim 2:20

CLEAN
seven each of every c ....Gen 7:2
outside the camp to a c ....Lev 4:12
all who are c may eat of it ..Lev 7:19
between unclean and c .....Lev 10:10
shall be c from the flow .....Lev 12:7
shall pronounce him c .....Lev 13:23
wash his clothes and be c ...Lev 13:34
wash in them and be c ....2 Kin 5:12
all of them were ritually c ..Ezra 6:20
pure, and I am c in your ....Job 11:4
Who can bring a c ....Job 14:4
He who has c hands and .....Ps 24:4
hyssop, and I shall be c ....Ps 51:7
Create in me a c heart, ...Ps 51:10
I have made my heart c, ...Prov 20:9
make yourselves c ....Is 1:16
the midst of her, be c ....Is 52:11
Then I will sprinkle c .....Ezek 36:25
c out His threshing ....Matt 3:12
You can make me c ....Matt 8:2
outside of them may be c . Matt 23:26
wrapped it in a c linen ....Matt 27:59
all things are c ....Luke 11:41
but is completely c ....John 13:10
"You are not all c ....John 13:11
You are already c ....John 15:3
your own heads; I am c ....Acts 18:6

in fine linen, *c* .... Rev 19:8

CLEANNESS
according to the *c* of ..... 2 Sam 22:21
According to the *c* of my .... Ps 18:20
Also I gave you *c* of teeth .. Amos 4:6

CLEANSE
You shall *c* the altar .... Ex 29:36
and *c* them ceremonially .... Num 8:6
and *c* my hands with soap, .. Job 9:30
C me from secret .... Ps 19:12
and *c* me from my sin .... Ps 51:2
How can a young man *c* .... Ps 119:9
I will *c* you from all .... Ezek 36:25
they shall *c* the altar ...... Ezek 43:22
c the lepers, raise .... Matt 10:8
For you *c* the outside .... Matt 23:25
let us *c* ourselves from all .. 2 Cor 7:1
might sanctify and *c* .... Eph 5:26
c your conscience .... Heb 9:14
C your hands .... James 4:8
us our sins and to *c* .... 1 John 1:9

CLEANSED
He who is to be *c* shall ...... Lev 14:8
Surely I have *c* .... Ps 73:13
and you were not *c* .... Ezek 24:13
the sanctuary shall be *c* .... Dan 8:14
I am willing; be *c*." .... Matt 8:3
the lepers are *c* .... Matt 11:5
they went, they were *c* ... Luke 17:14
"Were there not ten *c* .... Luke 17:17
God has *c* you must .... Acts 10:15

CLEANSES
Therefore if anyone *c* ..... 2 Tim 2:21
Jesus Christ His Son *c* .... 1 John 1:7

CLEAR
c shining after rain .... 2 Sam 23:4
fair as the moon, *c* .... Song 6:10
yourselves to be *c* .... 2 Cor 7:11
like a jasper stone, *c* .... Rev 21:11
of life, *c* as crystal .... Rev 22:1

CLEARLY
I not *c* reveal Myself ..... 1 Sam 2:27
you will see *c* to remove .... Matt 7:5
hour of the day he saw *c* ... Acts 10:3
c portrayed among you .... Gal 3:1
men's sins are *c* evident .. 1 Tim 5:24

CLEARS
by no means *c* the guilty .. Num 14:18

CLEFTS
to go into the *c* .... Is 2:21
valleys and in the *c* .... Is 7:19
you who dwell in the *c* ..... Jer 49:16

CLERK
c had quieted the .... Acts 19:35

CLIFF
secret places of the *c* ...... Song 2:14

CLIMB
go into thickets and *c* .... Jer 4:29
mighty men, they *c* .... Joel 2:7
though they *c* up to .... Amos 9:2

CLIMBED
c up into a sycamore tree .. Luke 19:4

CLIMBS
c up some other way ...... John 10:1

CLING
and that you may *c* .... Deut 30:20
to her, "Do not *c* .... John 20:17
C to what is good .... Rom 12:9

CLINGS
and My tongue *c* .... Ps 22:15
My soul *c* to the dust .... Ps 119:25

CLOAK
c You will change them .... Ps 102:26
let him have your *c* .... Matt 5:40
c You will fold them .... Heb 1:12
using liberty as a *c* .... 1 Pet 2:16

CLODS
The *c* of the valley .... Job 21:33

CLOSE
c friends abhor me .... Job 19:19
of Christ he came *c* .... Phil 2:30

CLOSED
c up the flesh in its place ... Gen 2:21
LORD had *c* her womb ...... 1 Sam 1:5
and has *c* your eyes .... Is 29:10
for the words are *c* .... Dan 12:9
the deep *c* around me .... Jon 2:5
Then He *c* the book, and .. Luke 4:20
their eyes they have *c* ..... Acts 28:27

CLOSER
sticks *c* than a brother .... Prov 18:24

CLOTH
a piece of unshrunk *c* ...... Matt 9:16
in a clean linen *c* .... Matt 27:59

CLOTHE
c them with tunics .... Ex 40:14
c me with skin and .... Job 10:11
c her priests with .... Ps 132:16
His enemies I will *c* .... Ps 132:18
Though you *c* yourself .... Jer 4:30
He not much more *c* .... Matt 6:30

CLOTHED
of skin, and *c* them .... Gen 3:21
Have you *c* his neck .... Job 39:19
off my sackcloth and *c* ..... Ps 30:11
The pastures are *c* .... Ps 65:13
the LORD is *c* .... Ps 93:1
You are *c* with honor .... Ps 104:1
c himself with cursing ..... Ps 109:18
Let Your priests be *c* .... Ps 132:9
all her household is *c* .... Prov 31:21
c you with fine linen ...... Ezek 16:10
A man *c* in soft .... Matt 11:8
I was naked and you *c* .... Matt 25:36
legion, sitting and *c* .... Mark 5:15
And they *c* Him with ..... Mark 15:17
rich man who was *c* ...... Luke 16:19
desiring to be *c* .... 2 Cor 5:2
that you may be *c* .... Rev 3:18
a woman *c* with the sun ..... Rev 12:1
He was *c* with a robe ...... Rev 19:13

CLOTHES
See TORE HIS CLOTHES
c will abhor me .... Job 9:31
c became shining .... Mark 9:3
many spread their *c* ...... Luke 19:36
laid down their *c* .... Acts 7:58
and tore off their *c* .... Acts 22:23
a poor man in filthy *c* .... James 2:2

CLOTHING
c they cast lots .... Ps 22:18
c is woven with gold .... Ps 45:13
will provide your *c* .... Prov 27:26
and honor are her *c* ...... Prov 31:25
of vengeance for *c* .... Is 59:17
the body more than *c* ...... Matt 6:25
do you worry about *c* ...... Matt 6:28
to you in sheep's *c* .... Matt 7:15
those who wear soft *c* ...... Matt 11:8
c as white as snow .... Matt 28:3
c they cast lots .... John 19:24
before me in bright *c* ..... Acts 10:30

CLOTHS
wrapped in swaddling *c* ... Luke 2:12
in, saw the linen *c* .... John 20:5

CLOUD
My rainbow in the *c* .... Gen 9:13
rainbow shall be in the *c* .... Gen 9:16
day in a pillar of *c* .... Ex 13:21
c covered the mountain ..... Ex 24:15
c descended and stood .... Ex 33:9
the *c* above the mercy seat .. Lev 16:2
that the *c* of incense may ... Lev 16:13
that the *c* filled the house .. 1 Kin 8:10
LORD, was filled with a *c* .. 2 Chr 5:13
would dwell in the dark *c* .. 2 Chr 6:1
c did not depart .... Neh 9:19
He led them with the *c* ...... Ps 78:14
his favor is like a *c* ...... Prov 16:15
like a *c* of dew in the heat ..... Is 18:4
these who fly like a *c* .... Is 60:8
rainbow in a *c* on a .... Ezek 1:28
like a morning *c* .... Hos 6:4
behold, a bright *c* .... Matt 17:5
c came and overshadowed . Luke 9:34
of Man coming in a *c* ..... Luke 21:27
c received Him out of .... Acts 1:9
were under the *c* .... 1 Cor 10:1
by so great a *c* .... Heb 12:1
ascended to heaven in a *c* .. Rev 11:12

CLOUDS
a morning without *c* ...... 2 Sam 23:4
c poured out water .... Ps 77:17
and hail, snow and *c* .... Ps 148:8
c drop down the dew ...... Prov 3:20
he who regards the *c* .... Eccl 11:4
of Man coming on the *c* ... Matt 24:30
with them in the *c* ...... 1 Thess 4:17
are *c* without water .... Jude 12
He is coming with *c* .... Rev 1:7

CLOUDY
them by day with a *c* .... Neh 9:12
spoke to them in the *c* .... Ps 99:7

CLOVEN
the hoof, having *c* .... Lev 11:3
chew the cud or have *c* .... Deut 14:7

CLUNG
but Ruth *c* to her .... Ruth 1:14
Solomon *c* to these in ..... 1 Kin 11:2

CLUSTER
beloved is to me a *c* .... Song 1:14
wine is found in the *c* .... Is 65:8

CNIDUS
City of Asia Minor on Paul's voyage, Acts 27:7

COAL
in his hand a live *c* .... Is 6:6
it shall not be a *c* .... Is 47:14

COALS
wicked He will rain *c* .... Ps 11:6
c were kindled by it .... Ps 18:8
let burning *c* fall .... Ps 140:10
Can one walk on hot *c* ...... Prov 6:28
so you will heap *c* .... Prov 25:22
doing you will heap *c* .... Rom 12:20

COARSE
robe of *c* hair to deceive .... Zech 13:4
nor *c* jesting, which are ...... Eph 5:4

COBRA
it becomes *c* venom .... Job 20:14
c that stops its ear .... Ps 58:4
the lion and the *c* .... Ps 91:13

COBRA'S
shall play by the *c* .... Is 11:8

CODE
even with your written *c* .... Rom 2:27

COFFIN
and he was put in a *c* ..... Gen 50:26
David followed the *c* ..... 2 Sam 3:31
touched the open *c* .... Luke 7:14

COIN
sold for a copper *c* .... Matt 10:29
if she loses one *c* .... Luke 15:8

COLD
and harvest, *c* and .... Gen 8:22
can stand before His *c* ..... Ps 147:17
Like the *c* of snow in ..... Prov 25:13
c water to a weary .... Prov 25:25
c water in the name of .... Matt 10:42
of many will grow *c* ...... Matt 24:12

that you are neither *c* . . . . Rev 3:15

COLLECTED
coming I might have *c* . . . . Luke 19:23

COLLECTION
from Jerusalem the *c* . . . . . . 2 Chr 24:6
concerning the *c* . . . . 1 Cor 16:1

COLLECTOR
See TAX COLLECTOR; TAX COLLECTORS AND SINNERS

COLOR
c like the *c* of bdellium . . . . Num 11:7
the *c* of burnished bronze . . . Ezek 1:7
c of an awesome crystal . . . Ezek 1:22
the *c* of a beryl stone . . . . . Ezek 10:9
all faces are drained of *c* . . . . . Joel 2:6

COLORS
him a tunic of many *c* . . . . . . Gen 37:3
on a robe of many *c* . . . . 2 Sam 13:18
stones of various *c*, all . . . . 1 Chr 29:2

COLOSSE
A city in Asia Minor, Col 1:2
Evangelized by Epaphras, Col 1:7
Not visited by Paul, Col 2:1
Paul writes against errors of, Col 2:16–23

COLT
and his donkey's *c* . . . . Gen 49:11
on a donkey, a *c* . . . . Zech 9:9
on a donkey, a *c* . . . . Matt 21:5
own clothes on the *c* . . . . . Luke 19:35

COME
then does wisdom *c* . . . . Job 28:20
of glory shall *c* . . . . Ps 24:7
Our God shall *c* . . . . Ps 50:3
You all flesh will *c* . . . . Ps 65:2
C with me from Lebanon . . . Song 4:8
He will *c* and save you . . . . Is 35:4
who have no money, *C* . . . . Is 55:1
Your kingdom *c* . . . . Matt 6:10
C to Me . . . . Matt 11:28
For many will *c* . . . . Matt 24:5
Israel, let Him now *c* . . . . . Matt 27:42
If anyone desires to *c* . . . . . . Luke 9:23
kingdom of God has *c* . . . . . . Luke 10:9
I have *c* in My . . . . John 5:43
and I have not *c* . . . . John 7:28
thirsts, let him *c* . . . . John 7:37
c that they may have . . . . . John 10:10
c as a light into the . . . . John 12:46
I will *c* to you . . . . John 14:18
If I had not *c* . . . . John 15:22
savage wolves will *c* . . . . . . Acts 20:29
O Lord, *c* . . . . 1 Cor 16:22
the door, I will *c* . . . . Rev 3:20
the bride say, "*C* . . . . Rev 22:17

COMELINESS
He has no form or *c* . . . . Is 53:2

COMES
Who is this who *c* . . . . Is 63:1
'Come,' and he *c* . . . . Matt 8:9
Lord's death till He *c* . . . . . 1 Cor 11:26
Then *c* the end . . . . 1 Cor 15:24

COMFORT
one will *c* us concerning . . . . Gen 5:29
daughters arose to *c* him . . Gen 37:35
speak *c* to your servants . . 2 Sam 19:7
with him, and to *c* him . . . . . . Job 2:11
and Your staff, they *c* . . . . Ps 23:4
And *c* me on every side . . . . . Ps 71:21
is my *c* in my affliction . . . . Ps 119:50
kindness be for my *c* . . . . Ps 119:76
When will you *c* . . . . Ps 119:82
go up to the *c* of my bed . . . . Ps 132:3
yes, *c* My people . . . . Is 40:1
For the LORD will *c* . . . . Is 51:3
c all who mourn . . . . Is 61:2
comforts, so I will *c* you . . . . . Is 66:13
she has none to *c* her . . . . Lam 1:2
wilderness, and speak *c* to . . Hos 2:14
the LORD will again *c* . . . . . . Zech 1:17
c them concerning their . . John 11:19
in the *c* of the Holy Spirit, . . . Acts 9:31
c of the Scriptures might . . . Rom 15:4
and exhortation and *c* to . . 1 Cor 14:3
and God of all *c* . . . . 2 Cor 1:3
trouble, with the *c* . . . . 2 Cor 1:4
that he may *c* your hearts . . . Eph 6:22
in Christ, if any *c* . . . . Phil 2:1
and *c* your hearts, ... Col 4:8
c one another . . . . 1 Thess 4:18
c each other and edify . . . 1 Thess 5:11
c your hearts and . . . . 2 Thess 2:17

COMFORTED
So Isaac was *c* after . . . . . . Gen 24:67
c them and spoke kindly . . Gen 50:21
David *c* Bathsheba . . . . 2 Sam 12:24
soul refused to be *c* . . . . Ps 77:2
For the LORD has *c* . . . . Is 49:13
refusing to be *c* . . . . Jer 31:15
children, refusing to be *c* . . . Matt 2:18
mourn, for they shall be *c* . . . Matt 5:4
but now he is *c* . . . . Luke 16:25
they were not a little *c* . . . . Acts 20:12
ourselves are *c* by God . . . . . 2 Cor 1:4

COMFORTER
but they have no *c* . . . . Eccl 4:1
She had no *c* . . . . Lam 1:9

COMFORTERS
because he has sent *c* to . . 2 Sam 10:3
miserable *c* are you all . . . . . . Job 16:2
for *c*, but I found none . . . . . . Ps 69:20

COMFORTS
the army, as one who *c* . . . . Job 29:25
I, even I, am He who *c* . . . . Is 51:12
him, and restore *c* . . . . Is 57:18
one whom his mother *c* . . . . . . Is 66:13
who *c* us in all our . . . . 2 Cor 1:4
who *c* the downcast . . . . 2 Cor 7:6

COMING
your salvation is *c* . . . . Is 62:11
behold, the day is *c* . . . . Mal 4:1
but He who is *c* . . . . Matt 3:11
"Are You the *C* . . . . Matt 11:3
be the sign of Your *c* . . . . Matt 24:3
is delaying his *c* . . . . Matt 24:48
see the Son of Man *c* . . . . . Mark 13:26
mightier than I is *c* . . . . Luke 3:16
are Christ's at His *c* . . . . . . 1 Cor 15:23
to you the power and *c* . . . . 2 Pet 1:16
the promise of His *c* . . . . 2 Pet 3:4
Behold, I am *c* . . . . Rev 3:11
"Behold, I am *c* . . . . Rev 22:7
"Surely I am *c* . . . . Rev 22:20

COMMAND
in order that he may *c* . . . . . Gen 18:19
shall speak all that I *c* you . . . . Ex 7:2
transgress the *c* of the . . . . Num 14:41
add to the word which I *c* . . . Deut 4:2
I *c* you today you must be . . . Deut 8:1
Whatever I *c* you, be . . . . . . Deut 12:32
therefore I *c* you, saying . . Deut 15:11
"The LORD will *c* . . . . Deut 28:8
in that I *c* you . . . . Deut 30:16
today, which you shall *c* . . Deut 32:46
c His lovingkindness . . . . Ps 42:8
c victories for Jacob . . . . Ps 44:4
you, and whatever I *c* you . . . . Jer 1:7
to them all that I *c* you . . . . . . Jer 1:17
to all that I *c* . . . . Jer 11:4
that I *c* you to speak to . . . . . Jer 26:2
c that these stones . . . . Matt 4:3
if it is You, *c* . . . . Matt 14:28
c fire to come down . . . . Luke 9:54
c I have received . . . . John 10:18
And I know that His *c* . . . . John 12:50
if you do whatever I *c* . . . . John 15:14
These things I *c* you, ... John 15:17
do the things we *c* . . . . 2 Thess 3:4
C those who are rich in . . . 1 Tim 6:17
kept My *c* to persevere . . . . Rev 3:10

COMMANDED
See LORD COMMANDED
the LORD God *c* the man . . . . Gen 2:16
to all that the LORD *c* him . . . . Gen 7:5
Joseph *c* his servants the . . . Gen 50:2
just as the LORD *c* them, ... Ex 7:6
which the LORD *c* him . . . . Ex 19:7
just as the LORD my God *c* . . Deut 4:5
LORD *c* us to observe all . . . . Deut 6:24
Have I not *c* you . . . . Josh 1:9
did so, as the LORD *c* . . . . . 2 Sam 5:25
which I *c* your fathers . . . . 2 Kin 17:13
to all that I have *c* them . . . 2 Kin 21:8
do all that I have *c* them . . 2 Chr 33:8
"Have you *c* the . . . . Job 38:12
He *c*, and it stood fast . . . . Ps 33:9
Which He *c* our fathers, ... Ps 78:5
c His covenant forever . . . . Ps 111:9
For there the LORD *c* . . . . Ps 133:3
of the LORD, for He *c* . . . . Ps 148:5
things that I have *c* you . . . Matt 28:20
Even so the Lord has *c* . . . . 1 Cor 9:14
it is the God who *c* . . . . 2 Cor 4:6
not endure what was *c* . . . . . . Heb 12:20

COMMANDER
the *c* of his army, spoke . . . Gen 21:22
but as *C* of the army of . . . . . Josh 5:14
c of his army was Sisera, ... Judg 4:2
c over His inheritance . . . . 1 Sam 10:1
Abner, the *c* of the . . . . 1 Sam 17:55
Joab the *c* of the army . . . . 1 Kin 1:19
have a message for you, *C* . . 2 Kin 9:5
Rehum the *c* and Shimshai . . Ezra 4:8
news came to the *c* of . . . . . Acts 21:31
But the *c* Lysias came by . . . Acts 24:7

COMMANDMENT
to the *c* of the LORD, ... Ex 17:1
numbered at the *c* of the . . . Num 3:39
shall keep every *c* which . . . Deut 11:8
heed to do the *c* . . . . Josh 22:5
observe the law and the *c* . 2 Chr 14:4
according to the *c* of . . . . 2 Chr 29:25
c of the LORD is pure . . . . Ps 19:8
c is exceedingly broad . . . . . Ps 119:96
For the *c* is a lamp . . . . Prov 6:23
Me is taught by the *c* . . . . Is 29:13
which is the great *c* . . . . Matt 22:36
is the first and great *c* . . . . Matt 22:38
no other *c* greater than . . . Mark 12:31
according to the *c* . . . . Luke 23:56
A new *c* I give to . . . . John 13:34
the Father gave Me *c* . . . . . John 14:31
is My *c*, that you love . . . . . John 15:12
whom we gave no such *c* . . Acts 15:24
law, but when the *c* . . . . Rom 7:9
the *c* might become . . . . Rom 7:13
and if there is any other *c* . . Rom 13:9
as a concession, not as a *c* . . 1 Cor 7:6
I speak not by *c*, but . . . . 2 Cor 8:8
which is the first *c* . . . . Eph 6:2
have a *c* to receive tithes . . . . . . Heb 7:5
the holy *c* delivered to . . . . 2 Pet 2:21
of the *c* of us, the apostles . . 2 Pet 3:2
c is the word which . . . . 1 John 2:7
And this is His *c* . . . . 1 John 3:23
as we received *c* . . . . 2 John 4
I wrote a new *c* to you . . . . . . 2 John 5
This is the *c* that as you . . . . . 2 John 6

COMMANDMENTS
love Me and keep My *c* . . . . . . Ex 20:6
c which I have written, ... Ex 24:12
covenant, the Ten *C* . . . . Ex 34:28
he gave them as *c* all that . . . Ex 34:32
you shall keep My *c* . . . . Lev 22:31
all the *c* of the LORD and . . Num 15:39
perform the Ten *C* . . . . Deut 4:13
love Me and keep My *c* . . . . . Deut 5:10
to observe all these *c* . . . . . . Deut 6:25

COMMANDS

COMMEND

COMMENDABLE

COMMENDED

COMMENDING

COMMENDS

COMMIT

COMMITS

COMMITTED

COMMON

COMMOTION

COMMUNED

COMMUNION

COMPANION

COMPANIONS

COMPANY

COMPARABLE

COMPARE

COMPARED

COMPASSION

COMPASSIONATE

COMPASSIONS

COMPEL

COMPELLED

COMPELS

COMPETES

COMPLACENCY

COMPLAIN

COMPLAINED

COMPLAINERS

COMPLAINING

COMPLAINT

COMPLAINTS

COMPLETE

COMPLETED

COMPLETELY

CONVULSED
unclean spirit had *c* him ... Mark 1:26
immediately the spirit *c* ... Mark 9:20

COOKED
c their own children .... Lam 4:10

COOL
in the garden in the *c* .... Gen 3:8
and *c* my tongue .... Luke 16:24

COPIES
necessary that the *c* .... Heb 9:23
hands, which are *c* .... Heb 9:24

COPPER
hills you can dig *c* .... Deut 8:9
c in your money belts ...... Matt 10:9
of cups, pitchers, *c* .... Mark 7:4
sold for two *c* coins .... Luke 12:6

COPPERSMITH
c did me much harm ...... 2 Tim 4:14

COPY
who serve the *c* .... Heb 8:5

CORBAN
from me is C (that is, ... Mark 7:11

CORD
this line of scarlet *c* .... Josh 2:18
And a threefold *c* .... Eccl 4:12
before the silver *c* .... Eccl 12:6

CORDS
cut in pieces the *c* .... Ps 129:4
he is caught in the *c* .... Prov 5:22
draw iniquity with *c* .... Is 5:18
them with gentle *c* .... Hos 11:4
had made a whip of *c* ...... John 2:15

CORIANDER
it was like white *c* seed ..... Ex 16:31
manna was like *c* seed ..... Num 11:7

CORINTH
Paul labors at, Acts 18:1–18
Site of church, 1 Cor 1:2
Visited by Apollos, Acts 19:1

CORNELIUS
A religious Gentile, Acts 10:1–48

CORNER
cut off a *c* of Saul's robe .. 1 Sam 24:4
Jerusalem at the C Gate ... 2 Chr 26:9
dwell in a *c* of a housetop .. Prov 21:9
in the *c* of a bed and on ... Amos 3:12
was not done in a *c* .... Acts 26:26

CORNERS
its horns on its four *c* .... Ex 27:2
in the tassels of the *c* ...... Num 15:38
sheet bound at the four *c* .. Acts 10:11
at the four *c* of the earth ..... Rev 7:1

CORNERSTONE
Or who laid its *c* .... Job 38:6
has become the chief *c* ..... Ps 118:22
stone, a precious *c* .... Is 28:16
become the chief *c* .... Matt 21:42
has become the chief *c* ..... Acts 4:11
Himself being the chief *c* ... Eph 2:20
in Zion a chief *c* .... 1 Pet 2:6

CORPSE
c was thrown on the ..... 1 Kin 13:24
c trodden underfoot .... Is 14:19

CORRECT
with rebukes You *c* .... Ps 39:11
C your son, and he will ... Prov 29:17
But I will *c* you in .... Jer 30:11

CORRECTED
human fathers who *c* .... Heb 12:9

CORRECTION
nor detest His *c* .... Prov 3:11
but he who refuses *c* ...... Prov 10:17
but he who hates *c* .... Prov 12:1
rod of *c* will drive it ...... Prov 22:15
Do not withhold *c* .... Prov 23:13
they received no *c* .... Jer 2:30
for reproof, for *c* .... 2 Tim 3:16

CORRECTS
is the man whom God *c* ..... Job 5:17
the LORD loves He *c* .... Prov 3:12

CORRODED
and silver are *c* .... James 5:3

CORRUPT
earth also was *c* before ..... Gen 6:11
the sons of Eli were *c* ..... 1 Sam 2:12
have together become *c* .... Ps 14:3
have together become *c* .... Ps 53:3
old man which grows *c* ..... Eph 4:22
Let no *c* word .... Eph 4:29
men of *c* minds .... 2 Tim 3:8
in these things they *c* .... Jude 10

CORRUPTED
for all flesh had *c* .... Gen 6:12
we have *c* no one .... 2 Cor 7:2
so your minds may be *c* ... 2 Cor 11:3
Your riches are *c* .... James 5:2
the great harlot who *c* ...... Rev 19:2

CORRUPTIBLE
For this *c* must put on .... 1 Cor 15:53
redeemed with *c* things ..... 1 Pet 1:18

CORRUPTION
Your Holy One to see *c* ...... Ps 16:10
God raised up saw no *c* ... Acts 13:37
from the bondage of *c* ...... Rom 8:21
The body is sown in *c* .... 1 Cor 15:42
c inherit incorruption .... 1 Cor 15:50
of the flesh reap *c* .... Gal 6:8
having escaped the *c* .... 2 Pet 1:4
perish in their own *c* ...... 2 Pet 2:12

COST
and count the *c* .... Luke 14:28

COSTLY
foundation was of *c* .... 1 Kin 7:10
of very *c* oil of spikenard .. Mark 14:3
or pearls or *c* clothing ...... 1 Tim 2:9

COSTS
which *c* me nothing ..... 2 Sam 24:24

COUCH
He went up to my *c* .... Gen 49:4
I drench my *c* with my .... Ps 6:6
Behold, it is Solomon's *c* .... Song 3:7

COULD
has done what she *c* ...... Mark 14:8
c remove mountains .... 1 Cor 13:2
which no one *c* number ...... Rev 7:9

COUNCIL
shall be in danger of the *c* .. Matt 5:22
all the *c* sought false ...... Matt 26:59
a prominent *c* member, .. Mark 15:43
Pharisees gathered a *c* .... John 11:47
and called the *c* together ... Acts 5:21
all the *c* of the elders, ... Acts 22:5

COUNCILS
deliver you up to *c* .... Mark 13:9

COUNSEL
and strength, He has *c* ..... Job 12:13
the *c* of the wicked is ...... Job 21:16
when the friendly *c* .... Job 29:4
is this who darkens *c* .... Job 38:2
who walks not in the *c* .... Ps 1:1
We took sweet *c* .... Ps 55:14
guide me with Your *c* .... Ps 73:24
you disdained all my *c* ..... Prov 1:25
have none of my *c* .... Prov 1:30
Where there is no *c* .... Prov 11:14
C in the heart of man .... Prov 20:5
by wise *c* wage war .... Prov 20:18
whom did He take *c* .... Is 40:14
You are great in *c* .... Jer 32:19
according to the *c* .... Eph 1:11
immutability of His *c* .... Heb 6:17
I *c* you to buy from .... Rev 3:18

COUNSELOR
be called Wonderful, C .... Is 9:6
but there was no *c* .... Is 41:28
Has your *c* perished .... Mic 4:9
who has become His *c* .... Rom 11:34

COUNSELORS
c there is safety .... Prov 11:14

COUNT
c the people of Israel ..... 2 Sam 24:4
I can *c* all My bones .... Ps 22:17
all *c* John as a prophet .... Matt 21:26
c my life dear to .... Acts 20:24
c me as a partner .... Philem 17
c it all joy when you fall ... James 1:2
His promise, as some *c* ...... 2 Pet 3:9

COUNTED
Even a fool is *c* .... Prov 17:28
c as the small dust .... Is 40:15
the wages are not *c* .... Rom 4:4
me, these I have *c* loss for .... Phil 3:7
He *c* me faithful .... 1 Tim 1:12
who rule well be *c* .... 1 Tim 5:17
c the blood of the .... Heb 10:29

COUNTENANCE
The LORD lift up His *c* ..... Num 6:26
c they did not cast .... Job 29:24
up the light of Your *c* .... Ps 4:6
His *c* is like Lebanon ...... Song 5:15
hypocrites, with a sad *c* .... Matt 6:16
His *c* was like .... Matt 28:3
of the glory of his *c* .... 2 Cor 3:7
sword, and His *c* .... Rev 1:16

COUNTRY
See FAR COUNTRY
"Get out of your *c* .... Gen 12:1
but you shall go to my *c* .... Gen 24:4
us pass through your *c* .. Num 20:17
Israel to search out the *c* .... Josh 2:2
an end of dividing the *c* ... Josh 19:51
the *c* was quiet for forty ... Judg 8:28
dwell in the *c* of Moab ...... Ruth 1:1
the *c* of the Philistines ... 1 Sam 27:11
good news from a far *c* ... Prov 25:25
you into a bountiful *c*, ... Jer 2:7
their own *c* another way ... Matt 2:12
honor except in his own *c* . Matt 13:57
and went into a far *c* ..... Matt 21:33
the *c* of the Gadarenes .... Mark 5:1
go into the surrounding *c* .. Mark 6:36
and went into a far *c* .... Mark 12:1
there were in the same *c* .... Luke 2:8
journeyed to a far *c*, ... Luke 15:13
as in a foreign *c* .... Heb 11:9
that is, a heavenly *c* .... Heb 11:16

COUNTRYMEN
for my brethren, my *c* .... Rom 9:3

COUNTS
c the number of the stars .... Ps 147:4

COURAGE
strong and of good *c* .... Deut 31:6
c in anyone because of ...... Josh 2:11
the prophet, he took *c* ..... 2 Chr 15:8
Be of good *c*, and do it ..... Ezra 10:4
his *c* against the king of ... Dan 11:25
thanked God and took *c* .. Acts 28:15

COURAGEOUS
Only be strong and very *c*. .. Josh 1:7
Be strong and *c* .... 2 Chr 32:7

COURSE
and sets on fire the *c* ...... James 3:6

COURT
the *c* of the tabernacle .... Ex 27:9
men, and they come to *c*, ... Deut 25:1
made the *c* of the priests .... 2 Chr 4:9
the inner *c* to the king ..... Esth 4:11
appoint my day in *c* .... Job 9:19
many would *c* your favor .. Job 11:19
Do not go hastily to *c* .... Prov 25:8

up in the c of the prison ..... Jer 32:2
cloud filled the inner c ..... Ezek 10:3
me into the outer c .... Ezek 40:17
by you or by a human c .... 1 Cor 4:3
They zealously c you .... Gal 4:17

COURTEOUS
be tenderhearted, be c ...... 1 Pet 3:8

COURTS
he may dwell in Your c ...... Ps 65:4
even faints for the c .... Ps 84:2
flourish in the c .... Ps 92:13
and into His c .... Ps 100:4
drink it in My holy c .... Is 62:9

COVENANT
See NEW COVENANT
I will establish My c .... Gen 6:18
I establish My c with you .... Gen 9:9
the LORD made a c .... Gen 15:18
I will make My c between .. Gen 17:2
for Me, behold, My c .... Gen 17:4
My voice and keep My c ..... Ex 19:5
he took the Book of the C .... Ex 24:7
as a perpetual c .... Ex 31:16
it is a c of salt .... Num 18:19
c which He commanded .... Deut 4:13
the c which He made ...... Deut 29:1
never break My c with ...... Judg 2:1
a c before the LORD ..... 1 Sam 23:18
is the c of the LORD .... 1 Kin 8:21
You, who keep Your c ..... 1 Kin 8:23
of the Book of the C .... 2 Kin 23:2
Remember His c forever . 1 Chr 16:15
You, who keep Your c .... 2 Chr 6:14
of the Book of the C ..... 2 Chr 34:30
You who keep Your c .... Neh 1:5
"I have made a c .... Job 31:1
will show them His c .... Ps 25:14
c shall stand firm .... Ps 89:28
has remembered His c ...... Ps 105:8
sons will keep My c .... Ps 132:12
forgets the c of her God .... Prov 2:17
and give You as a c .... Is 42:6
with them an everlasting c .... Is 61:8
the words of this c .... Jer 11:2
I will make a new c .... Jer 31:31
'I made a c with your .... Jer 34:13
a c of peace with them .... Ezek 37:26
c with many for one week .. Dan 9:27
they transgressed the c ...... Hos 6:7
I might break the c ...... Zech 11:10
and your wife by c .... Mal 2:14
the Messenger of the c .... Mal 3:1
is My blood of the new c .. Matt 26:28
My blood of the new c ... Mark 14:24
cup is the new c .... Luke 22:20
the new c in My blood .... 1 Cor 11:25
as ministers of the new c ... 2 Cor 3:6
c that was confirmed .... Gal 3:17
Mediator of a better c .... Heb 8:6
c had been faultless .... Heb 8:7
He says, "A new c .... Heb 8:13
the Mediator of the new c ... Heb 9:15
Mediator of the new c .... Heb 12:24
of the everlasting c .... Heb 13:20

COVENANTED
your kingdom, as I c .... 2 Chr 7:18
to the word that I c .... Hag 2:5

COVENANTS
the glory, the c .... Rom 9:4
these are the two c .... Gal 4:24

COVER
the rock, and will c .... Ex 33:22
He shall c you with .... Ps 91:4
c Yourself with light .... Ps 104:2
LORD as the waters c .... Is 11:9
and will no more c .... Is 26:21
from the wind and a c .... Is 32:2
and to the hills, 'C us ..... Luke 23:30
not to c his head .... 1 Cor 11:7
c a multitude of sins ...... James 5:20
love will c a multitude of .... 1 Pet 4:8

COVERED
The depths have c .... Ex 15:5
c my transgressions as ..... Job 31:33
Whose sin is c .... Ps 32:1
the wings of a dove c .... Ps 68:13
You have c all their sin ...... Ps 85:2
You c me in my .... Ps 139:13
with two he c his face .... Is 6:2
of Jacob will be c .... Is 27:9
You have c Yourself .... Lam 3:44
For there is nothing c ..... Matt 10:26

COVERING
spread a cloud for a c ...... Ps 105:39
make sackcloth their c .... Is 50:3
given to her for a c .... 1 Cor 11:15

COVERINGS
and made themselves c ...... Gen 3:7

COVET
"You shall not c .... Ex 20:17
c fields and take them .... Mic 2:2
You murder and c .... James 4:2

COVETED
c no one's silver .... Acts 20:33

COVETOUS
nor thieves, nor c .... 1 Cor 6:10
trained in c practices ...... 2 Pet 2:14

COVETOUSNESS
but he who hates c .... Prov 28:16
for nothing but your c ...... Jer 22:17
heed and beware of c ..... Luke 12:15
would not have known c .... Rom 7:7
all uncleanness or c .... Eph 5:3
conduct be without c .... Heb 13:5

COWARDLY
the c, unbelieving .... Rev 21:8

COWS
out of the river seven c ..... Gen 41:2
c ate up the first seven .... Gen 41:20
take two milk c which ..... 1 Sam 6:7
you c of Bashan, who are ... Amos 4:1

CRAFTILY
His people, to deal c .... Ps 105:25

CRAFTINESS
wise in their own c .... Job 5:13
not walking in c .... 2 Cor 4:2
deceived Eve by his c ..... 2 Cor 11:3
in the cunning c .... Eph 4:14

CRAFTSMAN
instructor of every c .... Gen 4:22
c encouraged the .... Is 41:7
c stretches out his .... Is 44:13

CRAFTSMEN
all the c who were doing ..... Ex 36:4
and the Valley of C .... Neh 11:35
no small profit to the c .... Acts 19:24

CRAFTY
Jonadab was a very c .... 2 Sam 13:3
the devices of the c .... Job 5:12
They have taken c .... Ps 83:3
of a harlot, and a c .... Prov 7:10
Nevertheless, being c ..... 2 Cor 12:16

CRANE
Like a c or a swallow .... Is 38:14

CRAVES
and his soul still c .... Is 29:8

CRAVING
yielded to intense c .... Num 11:4
who had yielded to c ...... Num 11:34

CREAM
she brought out c .... Judg 5:25
were bathed with c .... Job 29:6

CREATE
C in me a clean heart, ... Ps 51:10
then the LORD will c above ..... Is 4:5
peace and c calamity .... Is 45:7
Who did not c it in vain ..... Is 45:18
For behold, I c .... Is 65:17
to c in Himself one new .... Eph 2:15

CREATED
God c the heavens .... Gen 1:1
God c great sea creatures ... Gen 1:21
So God c man in His .... Gen 1:27
earth when they were c ...... Gen 2:4
the day that God c man .... Gen 5:1
man whom I have c .... Gen 6:7
God c man on the earth .... Deut 4:32
south, You have c them ..... Ps 89:12
You c all the children of ..... Ps 89:47
c may praise the LORD ..... Ps 102:18
Spirit, they are c .... Ps 104:30
and they were c .... Ps 148:5
and see who has c .... Is 40:26
of Israel has c .... Is 41:20
LORD, Who c the heavens ..... Is 42:5
says the LORD, who c you .... Is 43:1
I, the LORD, have c it .... Is 45:8
They are c now and not .... Is 48:7
I have c the blacksmith ...... Is 54:16
For the LORD has c .... Jer 31:22
place where you were c ... Ezek 21:30
on the day you were c .... Ezek 28:13
Has not one God c .... Mal 2:10
which God c until this .... Mark 13:19
nor any other c thing ...... Rom 8:39
Nor was man c for the .... 1 Cor 11:9
c in Christ Jesus .... Eph 2:10
hidden in God who c .... Eph 3:9
new man which was c ...... Eph 4:24
Him all things were c .... Col 1:16
from foods which God c .... 1 Tim 4:3
for You c all things .... Rev 4:11
who c heaven and the ...... Rev 10:6

CREATION
the beginning of the c ..... Mark 10:6
beginning of the c which . Mark 13:19
since the c of the world .... Rom 1:20
c was subjected .... Rom 8:20
know that the whole c ...... Rom 8:22
Christ, he is a new c ...... 2 Cor 5:17
anything, but a new c .... Gal 6:15
firstborn over all c .... Col 1:15
that is, not of this c .... Heb 9:11
from the beginning of c ..... 2 Pet 3:4
Beginning of the c of God ... Rev 3:14

CREATOR
Remember now your C ..... Eccl 12:1
God, the LORD, the C .... Is 40:28
rather than the C .... Rom 1:25
good, as to a faithful C .... 1 Pet 4:19

CREATURE
See LIVING CREATURE
every living c that is with ... Gen 9:12
living c with its four .... Ezek 1:15
the gospel to every c ...... Mark 16:15
For every c of God is .... 1 Tim 4:4
And there is no c .... Heb 4:13
And every c which is .... Rev 5:13
and every living c .... Rev 16:3

CREATURES
See LIVING CREATURES
created great sea c .... Gen 1:21
firstfruits of His c .... James 1:18
were four living c .... Rev 4:6

CREDIT
who love you, what c ...... Luke 6:32
For what c is it if .... 1 Pet 2:20

CREDITOR
Every c who has lent ...... Deut 15:2
c is coming to take my ..... 2 Kin 4:1
c seize all that he .... Ps 109:11
There was a certain c ..... Luke 7:41

CREEP
beasts of the forest c .... Ps 104:20

sort are those who c . . . . 2 Tim 3:6

CREEPING
c thing and beast of . . . . Gen 1:24
every sort of c thing . . . . Ezek 8:10
animals and c things . . . . Rom 1:23

CREPT
For certain men have c . . . . Jude 4

CRETE
Paul visits, Acts 27:7–21
Titus dispatched to, Titus 1:5
Inhabitants of, evil and lazy, Titus 1:12

CRIB
donkey its master's c . . . . Is 1:3

CRIED
he c with an exceedingly . . Gen 27:34
the poor who c out . . . . Job 29:12
They c to You . . . . Ps 22:5
of the depths I have c . . . . Ps 130:1
of the belly of Sheol I c . . . . . . Jon 2:2
beginning to sink he c . . . . Matt 14:30
Jesus c out and said . . . . John 12:44
they c out, "Away with . . . John 19:15

CRIES
your brother's blood c . . . . . . Gen 4:10
with vehement c . . . . Heb 5:7

CRIMES
land is filled with c . . . . Ezek 7:23

CRIMINALS
also two others, c . . . . Luke 23:32

CRIMSON
blue, and purple, and c . . . . 2 Chr 3:14
though they are red like c . . . . . Is 1:18

CRIPPLE
c from his mother's womb . . Acts 14:8

CRISPUS
Chief ruler of synagogue of Corinth, Acts 18:8
Baptized by Paul, 1 Cor 1:14

CROOKED
perverse and c generation . . Deut 32:5
turn aside to their c . . . . Ps 125:5
whose ways are c . . . . Prov 2:15
What is c cannot be made . . Eccl 1:15
what He has made c . . . . Eccl 7:13
c places shall be made . . . . Is 40:4
c places straight . . . . Is 45:2
c places shall be made . . . . . . Luke 3:5
in the midst of a c . . . . Phil 2:15

CROSS
I would not c over the . . . . . Deut 4:21
But when you c over the . . Deut 12:10
does not take his c . . . . Matt 10:38
and take up his c . . . . Matt 16:24
compelled to bear His c . . . Matt 27:32
down from the c . . . . Matt 27:40
and take up his c . . . . Mark 8:34
and take up his c daily, ... Luke 9:23
does not bear his c . . . . Luke 14:27
And He, bearing His c, ... John 19:17
lest the c of Christ . . . . 1 Cor 1:17
offense of the c has ceased . . Gal 5:11
persecution for the c . . . . Gal 6:12
boast except in the c . . . . Gal 6:14
one body through the c . . . . . . Eph 2:16
even the death of the c . . . . . . Phil 2:8
the enemies of the c . . . . Phil 3:18
through the blood of His c . . . Col 1:20
having nailed it to the c . . . . . Col 2:14
Him endured the c . . . . Heb 12:2

CROW
rooster will not c this . . . . . Luke 22:34

CROWD
shall not follow a c . . . . Ex 23:2

CROWN
the holy c on the turban . . . . . Ex 29:6
You set a c of pure . . . . Ps 21:3
c the year with Your . . . . Ps 65:11
have profaned his c . . . . Ps 89:39
upon Himself His c . . . . Ps 132:18
The c of the wise is . . . . Prov 14:24
head is a c of glory . . . . Prov 16:31
Woe to the c of pride . . . . Is 28:1
hosts will be for a c . . . . Is 28:5
c has fallen from our . . . . Lam 5:16
they had twisted a c . . . . . . Matt 27:29
wearing the c of thorns . . . . John 19:5
obtain a perishable c . . . . . . 1 Cor 9:25
brethren, my joy and c . . . . Phil 4:1
or joy, or c of rejoicing . . 1 Thess 2:19
laid up for me the c . . . . . . 2 Tim 4:8
he will receive the c . . . . . . James 1:12
you will receive the c of . . . . 1 Pet 5:4
I will give you the c of life . . . Rev 2:10
no one may take your c . . . . . Rev 3:11
on His head a golden c . . . . . Rev 14:14

CROWNED
angels, and You have c . . . . Ps 8:5
but the prudent are c . . . . . . Prov 14:18
athletics, he is not c . . . . 2 Tim 2:5
You have c him with glory . . . Heb 2:7

CROWNS
and they had c of gold . . . . Rev 4:4
on his horns ten c . . . . Rev 13:1
His head were many c . . . . . . Rev 19:12

CRUCIFIED
be delivered up to be c . . . . . Matt 26:2
"Let Him be c . . . . Matt 27:22
robbers were c with Him . . Matt 27:38
you seek Jesus who was c . . Matt 28:5
scourged Him, to be c . . . . . Mark 15:15
third hour, and they c . . . . . Mark 15:25
of Nazareth, who was c . . . . . Mark 16:6
Calvary, there they c . . . . . . Luke 23:33
of sinful men, and be c . . . . . Luke 24:7
to death, and c Him . . . . . . Luke 24:20
Him to them to be c . . . . John 19:16
c there was a garden . . . . . . John 19:41
lawless hands, have c . . . . Acts 2:23
of Nazareth, whom you c, . . . Acts 4:10
that our old man was c . . . . . . Rom 6:6
Was Paul c for you . . . . 1 Cor 1:13
but we preach Christ c, ... 1 Cor 1:23
Jesus Christ and Him c . . . . . . 1 Cor 2:2
they would not have c . . . . 1 Cor 2:8
though He was c . . . . 2 Cor 13:4
I have been c with Christ . . . . Gal 2:20
portrayed among you as c . . . . Gal 3:1
c the flesh with its passions . . Gal 5:24
the world has been c to me . . Gal 6:14
where also our Lord was c . . Rev 11:8

CRUCIFY
and to scourge and to c . . . Matt 20:19
them you will kill and c . . . Matt 23:34
out again, "C Him . . . . Mark 15:13
saying, "C Him, c Him . . . . Luke 23:21
I have power to c You . . . . John 19:10
"Shall I c your King . . . . . . John 19:15
since they c again . . . . Heb 6:6

CRUEL
wrath, for it is c . . . . Gen 49:7
spirit and c bondage . . . . Ex 6:9
hate me with c hatred . . . . Ps 25:19
of the wicked are c . . . . Prov 12:10

CRUELTY
of c are in their . . . . Gen 49:5
the haunts of c . . . . Ps 74:20
c you have ruled . . . . Ezek 34:4

CRUMBS
eat from the children's c . . Mark 7:28
c which fell from the . . . . . Luke 16:21

CRUSH
that a foot may c . . . . Job 39:15
that your foot may c . . . . Ps 68:23
the poor, who c . . . . Amos 4:1
of peace will c . . . . Rom 16:20

CRUSHED
in the dust, who are c . . . . Job 4:19
c my life to the . . . . Ps 143:3
every side, yet not c . . . . 2 Cor 4:8

CRUST
man is reduced to a c . . . . . . Prov 6:26

CRY
and their c came up to . . . . Ex 2:23
of oppressions they c . . . . Job 35:9
heart and my flesh c . . . . Ps 84:2
I c out with my whole . . . . . Ps 119:145
Does not wisdom c . . . . Prov 8:1
"What shall I c . . . . Is 40:6
nor lift up a c . . . . Jer 7:16
c mightily to God . . . . Jon 3:8
at midnight a c . . . . Matt 25:6
His own elect who c . . . . Luke 18:7

CRYING
"The voice of one c . . . . Matt 3:3
nor sorrow, nor c . . . . Rev 21:4

CRYSTAL
nor c can equal it . . . . Job 28:17
your gates of c . . . . Is 54:12
of an awesome c . . . . Ezek 1:22
a sea of glass, like c . . . . Rev 4:6

CUBIT
shall finish it to a c . . . . Gen 6:16
can add one c . . . . Matt 6:27

CUCUMBERS
in Egypt, the c . . . . Num 11:5
a hut in a garden of c . . . . Is 1:8

CUD
c or those that have cloven . . Lev 11:4
the c or have cloven . . . . Deut 14:7

CUMI
Talitha, c," which is . . . . Mark 5:41

CUNNING
the serpent was more c . . . . Gen 3:1
c comes quickly . . . . Job 5:13
c craftiness of deceitful . . . . . . Eph 4:14

CUP
My c runs over . . . . Ps 23:5
waters of a full c are . . . . Ps 73:10
the LORD there is a c . . . . Ps 75:8
I will take up the c . . . . Ps 116:13
the dregs of the c . . . . Is 51:17
men give them the c . . . . Jer 16:7
"Take this wine c . . . . Jer 25:15
The c of the LORD's . . . . Hab 2:16
make Jerusalem a c . . . . Zech 12:2
little ones only a c . . . . Matt 10:42
will indeed drink My c . . . . . Matt 20:23
cleanse the inside of the c . Matt 23:26
Then He took the c . . . . Matt 26:27
possible, let this c . . . . Matt 26:39
c of water to drink in My . . Mark 9:41
the outside of the c . . . . Luke 11:39
c is the new covenant . . . . . Luke 22:20
this c away from Me . . . . Luke 22:42
cannot drink the c . . . . 1 Cor 10:21
c is the new covenant . . . . . 1 Cor 11:25
the c of His indignation . . . . Rev 14:10
to give her the c . . . . Rev 16:19
c full of abominations . . . . Rev 17:4

CURE
but they could not c . . . . . . Matt 17:16
and to c diseases . . . . Luke 9:1

CURES
and perform c . . . . Luke 13:32

CURSE
c the ground for man's . . . . Gen 8:21
will c him who curses you . . . Gen 12:3
your c be on me, my son . . . Gen 27:13
c a ruler of your . . . . Ex 22:28
You shall not c the deaf . . . . Lev 19:14
c this people for me . . . . Num 22:6
Balaam, "Neither c . . . . Num 23:25

your God turned the *c* ..... Deut 23:5
on Mount Ebal to *c* .... Deut 27:13
c which I have set before .. Deut 30:1
said to him, '*C* David .... 2 Sam 16:10
the *c* into a blessing .... Neh 13:2
C God and die .... Job 2:9
mouth, but they *c* .... Ps 62:4
Let them *c*, but You bless .. Ps 109:28
The *c* of the LORD is .... Prov 3:33
So a *c* without cause shall .. Prov 26:2
Do not *c* the king .... Eccl 10:20
the *c* has devoured .... Is 24:6
a byword, a taunt and a *c* .... Jer 24:9
This is the *c* that goes out ... Zech 5:3
a *c* among the nations ..... Zech 8:13
"I will send a *c* .... Mal 2:2
are cursed with a *c* .... Mal 3:9
bless those who *c* you, ... Luke 6:28
bless and do not *c* .... Rom 12:14
law are under the *c* .... Gal 3:10
us from the *c* of the law, ... Gal 3:13
Father, and with it we *c* ... James 3:9
there shall be no more *c* ... Rev 22:3

CURSED
c more than all cattle .... Gen 3:14
C is the man who .... Jer 17:5
c is he who keeps .... Jer 48:10
'Depart from Me, you *c* ... Matt 25:41
C is everyone who hangs .... Gal 3:13
and near to being *c* .... Heb 6:8

CURSES
I will curse him who *c* ...... Gen 12:3
'For everyone who *c* .... Lev 20:9
write these *c* in a book ..... Num 5:23
c his father or his .... Prov 20:20
'He who *c* father or .... Mark 7:10

CURSINGS
by the sword for the *c* ...... Hos 7:16

CURTAIN
of each *c* shall be .... Ex 26:2
the heavens like a *c* .... Ps 104:2

CUSH
Ham's oldest son, 1 Chr 1:8–10
——— Another name for Ethiopia, Is 18:1

CUSHAN-RISHATHAIM
Mesopotamian king; oppresses Israel, Judg 3:8
Othniel delivers Israel from, Judg 3:9, 10

CUSTOM
to me, as Your *c* .... Ps 119:132
according to the *c* .... Acts 15:1
we have no such *c* .... 1 Cor 11:16

CUT
confidence shall be *c* .... Job 8:14
evildoers shall be *c* .... Ps 37:9
the wicked will be *c* .... Prov 2:22
c off your supply of bread .. Ezek 5:16
your navel cord was not *c* .. Ezek 16:4
stone was *c* out without .... Dan 2:34
that I will *c* off the names .. Zech 13:2
not bear good fruit is *c* ..... Matt 3:10
causes you to sin, *c* .... Matt 5:30
and will *c* him in .... Matt 24:51
him whose ear Peter *c* .... John 18:26
He had his hair *c* .... Acts 18:18

CYMBAL
or a clanging *c* .... 1 Cor 13:1

CYPRUS
Mentioned in prophecies, Num 24:24; Is 23:1–12; Jer 2:10
Christians preach to Jews of, Acts 11:19, 20
Paul and Barnabas visit, Acts 13:4–13; 15:39

CYRENE
A Greek colonial city in North Africa; home of Simon the cross-bearer, Matt 27:32
Synagogue of, Acts 6:9
Christians from, become missionaries, Acts 11:20

CYRUS
King of Persia, referred to as God's anointed, Is 44:28—45:1

DAGON
The national god of the Philistines, Judg 16:23
Falls before ark, 1 Sam 5:1–5

DAILY
much as they gather *d* .... Ex 16:5
d He shall be praised .... Ps 72:15
to me, watching *d* .... Prov 8:34
Yet they seek Me *d* .... Is 58:2
Give us this day our *d* ...... Matt 6:11
I sat *d* with you .... Matt 26:55
take up his cross *d* .... Luke 9:23
the Scriptures *d* .... Acts 17:11
our Lord, I die *d* .... 1 Cor 15:31
stands ministering *d* .... Heb 10:11

DALMATIA
A region east of the Adriatic Sea; Titus departs for, 2 Tim 4:10

DAMASCUS
Capital of Syria; captured by David; ruled by enemy kings, 2 Sam 8:5, 6; 1 Kin 11:23, 24; 15:18
Elisha's prophecy in, 2 Kin 8:7–15
Taken by Assyrians, 2 Kin 16:9
Prophecy concerning, Is 8:3, 4
Paul converted on road to; first preaches there, Acts 9:1–22
escapes from, 2 Cor 11:32, 33
revisits, Gal 1:17

DAN
Jacob's son by Bilhah, Gen 30:5, 6
Prophecy concerning, Gen 49:16, 17
——— Tribe of:
Numbered, Num 1:38, 39
Blessed, Deut 33:22
Receive their inheritance, Josh 19:40–47
Fall into idolatry, Judg 18:1–31
——— Town, northern boundary of Israel, Judg 20:1
Called Leshem; captured by Danites, Josh 19:47
Center of idolatry, 1 Kin 12:28–30
Destroyed by Ben-Hadad, 1 Kin 15:20

DANCE
and their children *d* .... Job 21:11
His name with the *d* .... Ps 149:3
mourn, and a time to *d* ...... Eccl 3:4
d has turned into .... Lam 5:15
and you did not *d* .... Matt 11:17

DANCED
Then David *d* before ...... 2 Sam 6:14
daughter of Herodias *d* ..... Matt 14:6

DANCING
saw the calf and the *d* ...... Ex 32:19
me my mourning into *d* ..... Ps 30:11
he heard music and *d* .... Luke 15:25

DANIEL
Taken to Babylon; refuses Nebuchadnezzar's foods, Dan 1
Interprets dreams; honored by king, Dan 2
Interprets handwriting on wall; honored by Belshazzar, Dan 5:10–29
Appointed to high office; conspired against and thrown to lions, Dan 6:1–23
Visions of four beasts, ram and goat, Dan 7; 8
Intercedes for Israel, Dan 9:1–19
Further visions, Dan 9:20—12:13

DARE
someone would even *d* ...... Rom 5:7
D any of you .... 1 Cor 6:1

DARIUS
Darius the Mede, son of Ahasuerus; made king of the Chaldeans, Dan 9:1
Succeeds Belshazzar, Dan 5:30, 31
Co-ruler with Cyrus, Dan 6:28
——— Darius Hystaspis (522–486 B.C.), king of all Persia; temple work dated by his reign, Ezra 4:5, 24
Confirms Cyrus's royal edict, Ezra 6:1–14
——— Darius the Persian (423–404 B.C.); priestly records kept during his reign, Neh 12:22

DARK
dwell in the *d* cloud .... 1 Kin 8:12
I am *d*, but lovely .... Song 1:5
d place of the earth .... Is 45:19
d places like the dead .... Lam 3:6
and makes the day *d* .... Amos 5:8
and the day shall be *d* .... Mic 3:6
I tell you in the *d* .... Matt 10:27
while it was still *d* .... John 20:1
shines in a *d* place .... 2 Pet 1:19

DARKENED
so that the land was *d* ...... Ex 10:15
Let their eyes be *d* .... Ps 69:23
their understanding *d* .... Eph 4:18

DARKNESS
d He called Night .... Gen 1:5
shall enlighten my *d* ..... 2 Sam 22:29
through the deep *d* .... Job 22:13
Those who sat in *d* .... Ps 107:10
d shall not hide .... Ps 139:12
d have seen a great light .... Is 9:2
I will make *d* light .... Is 42:16
and deep *d* the people .... Is 60:2
Israel, or a land of *d* .... Jer 2:31
body will be full of *d* .... Matt 6:23
cast out into outer *d* .... Matt 8:12
and the power of *d* .... Luke 22:53
d rather than light .... John 3:19
d does not know .... John 12:35
For you were once *d* .... Eph 5:8
the rulers of the *d* .... Eph 6:12
us from the power of *d* ...... Col 1:13
of the night nor of *d* ...... 1 Thess 5:5
and to blackness and *d* .... Heb 12:18
called you out of *d* .... 1 Pet 2:9
blackness of *d* forever ..... 2 Pet 2:17
and in Him is no *d* .... 1 John 1:5
Him, and walk in *d* .... 1 John 1:6
d is passing away .... 1 John 2:8
blackness of *d* forever .... Jude 13

DARTS
quench all the fiery *d* ...... Eph 6:16

DASH
You shall *d* them to .... Ps 2:9
lest you *d* your foot .... Matt 4:6

DASHED
hand, O LORD, has *d* .... Ex 15:6
also will be *d* to .... Is 13:16
infants shall be *d* .... Hos 13:16

DATHAN
Joins Korah's rebellion, Num 16:1–35
Swallowed up by the earth, Ps 106:17

DAUGHTER
I am the *d* of Bethuel, ... Gen 24:24
Dinah the *d* of Leah .... Gen 34:1
Jochebed the *d* of Levi .... Num 26:59
had neither son nor *d* ..... Judg 11:34
cry of the *d* of my people .... Jer 8:19
the virgin *d* of my people ... Jer 14:17

O virgin, the *d* of Egypt . . . . Jer 46:11
"Rejoice greatly, O *d* . . . . Zech 9:9
My *d* has just died, ... Matt 9:18
Be of good cheer, *d* . . . . Matt 9:22
being a *d* of Abraham, ... Luke 13:16
"Fear not, *d* of Zion . . . . . . John 12:15
the son of Pharaoh's *d* . . . . . Heb 11:24

DAUGHTER-IN-LAW

Judah said to Tamar his *d* . Gen 38:11
the Moabitess her *d* with . . . Ruth 1:22
lewdly defiles his *d* . . . . Ezek 22:11
d against her . . . . Mic 7:6
a *d* against her . . . . Matt 10:35

DAUGHTERS

he had sons and *d* . . . . Gen 5:4
of God saw the *d* . . . . Gen 6:2
Thus both the *d* of Lot . . . . . Gen 19:36
years for your two *d* . . . . . . Gen 31:41
the *d* of Zelophehad . . . . Num 27:1
not give them our *d* as . . . . . Judg 21:7
Turn back, my *d* . . . . Ruth 1:11
O *d* of Israel, weep over . . 2 Sam 1:24
d wore such apparel . . . . . 2 Sam 13:18
beautiful as the *d* of Job . . . Job 42:15
Kings' *d* are among Your . . . . . Ps 45:9
Let the *d* of Judah be glad, . . Ps 48:11
The leech has two *d* . . . . . . Prov 30:15
"Many *d* have done well . . Prov 31:29
a bird, and all the *d* . . . . Eccl 12:4
O *d* of Jerusalem, like the . . . Song 1:5
"Because the *d* of Zion are . . . . Is 3:16
d shall go into captivity . . . Ezek 30:18
your *d* shall prophesy . . . . Joel 2:28
D of Jerusalem, do not . . . . Luke 23:28
d shall prophesy . . . . Acts 2:17
man had four virgin *d* . . . . . . Acts 21:9
shall be My sons and *d* . . . . 2 Cor 6:18
whose *d* you are if you . . . . . . 1 Pet 3:6

DAVID

See CITY OF DAVID; HOUSE OF DAVID; SEED OF DAVID; SON OF DAVID; THRONE OF DAVID
Anointed by Samuel, 1 Sam 16:1–13
Becomes royal harpist, 1 Sam 16:14–23
Defeats Goliath, 1 Sam 17
Makes covenant with Jonathan, 1 Sam 18:1–4
Honored by Saul; loved by the people; Saul becomes jealous, 1 Sam 18:5–16
Wins Michal as wife, 1 Sam 18:17–30
Flees from Saul, 1 Sam 19; 20; 21:10—22:5; 23:14–29
Eats the holy bread, 1 Sam 21:1–6; Matt 12:3, 4
Saves Keilah from Philistines, 1 Sam 23:1–13
Twice spares Saul's life, 1 Sam 24:1–22; 26:1–25
Anger at Nabal appeased by Abigail; marries her, 1 Sam 25:2–42
Allies with the Philistines, 1 Sam 27:1—28:2
Rejected by them, 1 Sam 29
Avenges destruction of Ziklag, 1 Sam 30
Mourns death of Saul and Jonathan, 2 Sam 1
Anointed king of Judah, 2 Sam 2:1–7
War with Saul's house; Abner defects to David, 2 Sam 3:1, 6–21
Mourns Abner's death, 2 Sam 3:28–39
Punishes Ishbosheth's murderers, 2 Sam 4
Anointed king of all Israel, 2 Sam 5:1–5
Conquers Jerusalem; makes it his capital, 2 Sam 5:6–16
Defeats Philistines, 2 Sam 5:17–25
Brings ark to Jerusalem, 2 Sam 6
Receives eternal covenant, 2 Sam 7
Further conquests, 2 Sam 8; 10
Shows mercy to Mephibosheth, 2 Sam 9
Commits adultery and murder, 2 Sam 11
Rebuked by Nathan; repents, 2 Sam 12:1–23; Ps 32; 51
Absalom's rebellion, 2 Sam 15—18
Mourns Absalom's death, 2 Sam 18:33—19:8
Shows himself merciful, 2 Sam 19:18–39
Sheba's rebellion, 2 Sam 19:40—20:22
Avenges the Gibeonites, 2 Sam 21:1–14
Song of deliverance, 2 Sam 22
Sins by numbering the people, 2 Sam 24:1–17
Buys threshing floor to build altar, 2 Sam 24:18–25
Secures Solomon's succession, 1 Kin 1:5–53
Instructions to Solomon, 1 Kin 2:1–11
Last words, 2 Sam 23:1–7
Inspired by Spirit, Matt 22:43
As prophet, Acts 2:29–34
Faith of, Heb 11:32–34

DAY

See LAST DAY; THIRD DAY
God called the light *D* . . . . Gen 1:5
blessed the seventh *d* . . . . Gen 2:3
garden in the cool of the *d* . . . Gen 3:8
on that *d* all the fountains . . Gen 7:11
and *d* and night . . . . Gen 8:22
"Swear to me as of this *d* . . Gen 25:33
shall observe this *d* . . . . Ex 12:17
a certain quota every *d* . . . . . . Ex 16:4
sixth *d* bread for two days . . Ex 16:29
rested on the seventh *d* . . . . . Ex 16:30
Remember the Sabbath *d* . . . . . Ex 20:8
eaten the same *d* . . . . Lev 19:6
seventh *d* shall be a holy . . . . Lev 23:8
be the *D* of Atonement . . . . . Lev 23:27
clothes on the seventh *d* . . Num 31:24
and in the cloud by *d* . . . . . . Deut 1:33
This *d* you are to cross . . . . . Deut 2:18
witness against you this *d* . . Deut 4:26
the *d* of their calamity . . . . Deut 32:35
you shall meditate in it *d* . . . . Josh 1:8
"This *d* I have rolled away . . . Josh 5:9
grain, on the very same *d* . . Josh 5:11
has been no *d* like that . . . . . Josh 10:14
rebel this *d* against the . . . . Josh 22:16
You are witnesses this *d* . . . Ruth 4:10
on the *d* of battle, that . . . 1 Sam 13:22
the victory that *d* was . . . . 2 Sam 19:2
This *d* is a *d* of good news, . . 2 Kin 7:9
This *d* is a *d* of trouble, . . . 2 Kin 19:3
of a pit on a snowy *d* . . . . 1 Chr 11:22
d of the foundation of . . . . . 2 Chr 8:16
Be still, for the *d* is holy . . . . Neh 8:11
made it a *d* of feasting . . . . . Esth 9:18
and cursed the *d* . . . . Job 3:1
for the *d* of battle and . . . . . . Job 38:23
d utters speech . . . . Ps 19:2
For a *d* in Your courts . . . . Ps 84:10
In the *d* of my trouble . . . . Ps 86:7
d the LORD has made . . . . Ps 118:24
not strike you by *d* . . . . Ps 121:6
night shines as the *d* . . . . Ps 139:12
unto the perfect *d* . . . . Prov 4:18
do not know what a *d* . . . . . . Prov 27:1
the *d* when the keepers . . . . . Eccl 12:3
Until the *d* breaks and . . . . . . Song 4:6
In that *d* the Branch of the . . . . . Is 4:2
in the *d* of your fast you . . . . . . Is 58:3
tears, that I might weep *d* . . . . Jer 9:1
My covenant with the *d* . . . . Jer 33:20
a cloud on a rainy *d*, so . . . . Ezek 1:28
Behold, the *d* . . . . Ezek 7:10
on the *d* of the LORD . . . . Ezek 13:5
the *d* you were created . . . Ezek 28:15
life, in the *d* of your fall . . Ezek 32:10
knees three times that *d* . . . . Dan 6:10
you shall stumble in the *d* . . . . Hos 4:5
a *d* of clouds and thick . . . . . . Joel 2:2
For the *d* of the LORD . . . . Joel 2:11
who put far off the *d* . . . . Amos 6:3
next *d* God prepared a . . . . Jon 4:7
the *d* of your watchman . . . . . . Mic 7:4
for the *d* of the LORD . . . . Zeph 1:7
who has despised the *d* . . . . . Zech 4:10
neither *d* nor night . . . . Zech 14:7
who can endure the *d* . . . . Mal 3:2
d our daily bread . . . . Matt 6:11
and Gomorrah in the *d* . . . . Matt 10:15
d when I drink it new . . . . . Matt 26:29
this *d* in the city of David . . Luke 2:11
you seven times in a *d* . . . . . Luke 17:4
and the third *d* rise again . . Luke 24:7
sent Me while it is *d* . . . . John 9:4
great and awesome *d* . . . . Acts 2:20
person esteems one *d* . . . . Rom 14:5
D will declare it . . . . 1 Cor 3:13
again the third *d* . . . . 1 Cor 15:4
d I have been in the . . . . . . 2 Cor 11:25
perfectly that the *d* . . . . 1 Thess 5:2
and sons of the *d* . . . . 1 Thess 5:5
He designates a certain *d* . . . . . Heb 4:7
God in the *d* of visitation . . . 1 Pet 2:12
with the Lord one *d* . . . . 2 Pet 3:8
great *d* of God Almighty . . . Rev 16:14

DAY OF THE LORD

For the *d* of hosts shall . . . . Is 2:12
Wail, for the *d* is at hand . . . . . . Is 13:6
the holy *d* honorable, ... Is 58:13
is the *d* God of hosts, ... Jer 46:10
stand in battle on the *d* . . . Ezek 13:5
is near, even the *d* . . . . Ezek 30:3
For the *d* is at hand; . . . . Joel 1:15
the great and awesome *d* . . . Joel 2:31
For what good is the *d* . . . . Amos 5:18
d upon all the nations . . . . Obad 15
for the *d* is at hand, ... Zeph 1:7
the great and dreadful *d* . . . . . Mal 4:5
the great and awesome *d* . . . Acts 2:20
may be saved in the *d* . . . . . . 1 Cor 5:5
also are ours, in the *d* . . . . . 2 Cor 1:14
d will come as a thief . . . . 2 Pet 3:10

DAYS

See ALL THE DAYS OF HIS LIFE; LAST DAYS
seasons, and for *d* . . . . Gen 1:14
rain on the earth forty *d* . . . . . . Gen 7:4
He who is eight *d* old . . . . Gen 17:12
Seven *d* you shall eat . . . . Ex 12:15
Six *d* you shall gather it, ... Ex 16:26
Six *d* you shall labor . . . . Ex 20:9
that your *d* may be long . . . . Deut 5:16
d are swifter than a . . . . Job 7:6
Let me alone, for my *d* . . . . Job 7:16
of woman is of few *d* . . . . Job 14:1
blessed the latter *d* . . . . Job 42:12
me all the *d* of my life . . . . Ps 23:6
The *d* of our lives are . . . . Ps 90:10
teach us to number our *d* . . . . Ps 90:12
For my *d* are consumed . . . . . . Ps 102:3
I remember the *d* of old . . . . . . Ps 143:5
for length of *d* and long . . . . . Prov 3:2
of the LORD prolongs *d* . . . . Prov 10:27
evil all the *d* of her life . . . . Prov 31:12
"Why were the former *d* . . . . Eccl 7:10
Before the difficult *d* . . . . Eccl 12:1
and tested them ten *d* . . . . Dan 1:14
He had fasted forty *d* . . . . Matt 4:2
But the *d* will come when . . Matt 9:15
those *d* were shortened . . . Matt 24:22
had shortened those *d* . . . . Mark 13:20
the *d* were completed . . . . Luke 2:6
But the *d* will come when . . Luke 5:35
raise it up in three *d* . . . . John 2:20
he has been dead four *d* . . John 11:39
by them during forty *d* . . . . Acts 1:3

You observe *d* and .... Gal 4:10
life and see good *d* .... 1 Pet 3:10
will come in the last *d*, ... 2 Pet 3:3
two hundred and sixty *d*, ... Rev 11:3

DAYSPRING

with which the *D* .... Luke 1:78

DEACONS

with the bishops and *d* .... Phil 1:1
d must be reverent .... 1 Tim 3:8
d be the husbands .... 1 Tim 3:12

DEAD

See RAISED FROM THE DEAD; RAISED HIM FROM THE DEAD
"We shall all be *d* .... Ex 12:33
he stood between the *d* ... Num 16:48
work wonders for the *d* .... Ps 88:10
who have long been *d* .... Ps 143:3
But the *d* know nothing .... Eccl 9:5
shall cast out the *d* .... Is 26:19
d bury their own *d* .... Matt 8:22
d are raised up and .... Matt 11:5
not the God of the *d* ...... Matt 22:32
for this my son was *d* .... Luke 15:24
d will hear the voice .... John 5:25
was raised from the *d* .... Rom 6:4
yourselves to be *d* .... Rom 6:11
from the law sin was *d* .... Rom 7:8
be Lord of both the *d* .... Rom 14:9
resurrection of the *d* ..... 1 Cor 15:12
baptized for the *d* .... 1 Cor 15:29
made alive, who were *d* .... Eph 2:1
And the *d* in Christ ...... 1 Thess 4:16
d while she lives .... 1 Tim 5:6
without works is *d* .... James 2:26
d did not live again .... Rev 20:5
And the *d* were judged ...... Rev 20:12

DEAD SEA

Called the:
Salt Sea, Gen 14:3
Sea of the Arabah, Deut 3:17

DEADLY

they drink anything *d* .... Mark 16:18
evil, full of *d* poison ...... James 3:8
d wound was healed .... Rev 13:3

DEADNESS

the *d* of Sarah's womb .... Rom 4:19

DEAF

makes the mute, the *d* .... Ex 4:11
d shall hear the words .... Is 29:18
d shall be unstopped .... Is 35:5
d as My messenger .... Is 42:19
d who have ears .... Is 43:8
their ears shall be *d* .... Mic 7:16
are cleansed and the *d* ..... Matt 11:5

DEAL

Do you thus *d* with the ..... Deut 32:6
My Servant shall *d* .... Is 52:13

DEAR

servant, who was *d* to him .. Luke 7:2
count my life *d* to myself .. Acts 20:24
of God as *d* children .... Eph 5:1
you had become *d* to us .. 1 Thess 2:8

DEARLY

I have given the *d* beloved ... Jer 12:7
rulers *d* love dishonor .... Hos 4:18

DEATH

See SECOND DEATH; SHADOW OF DEATH
Let me die the *d* .... Num 23:10
d parts you and me .... Ruth 1:17
and the shadow of *d* .... Job 10:21
You will bring me to *d* ..... Job 30:23
For in *d* there is no .... Ps 6:5
I sleep the sleep of *d* .... Ps 13:3
of the shadow of *d* .... Ps 23:4
my soul from *d* .... Ps 56:13
can live and not see *d* .... Ps 89:48
house leads down to *d* .... Prov 2:18
who hate me love *d* .... Prov 8:36
D and life are in the ...... Prov 18:21
swallow up *d* forever .... Is 25:8
no pleasure in the *d* ...... Ezek 18:32
redeem them from *d* .... Hos 13:14
turns the shadow of *d* .... Amos 5:8
who shall not taste *d* ..... Matt 16:28
but has passed from *d* ..... John 5:24
he shall never see *d* .... John 8:51
Nevertheless *d* reigned ..... Rom 5:14
as sin reigned in *d* .... Rom 5:21
D no longer has .... Rom 6:9
the wages of sin is *d* .... Rom 6:23
to bear fruit to *d* .... Rom 7:5
proclaim the Lord's *d* .... 1 Cor 11:26
since by man came *d* ..... 1 Cor 15:21
D is swallowed up in ..... 1 Cor 15:54
The sting of *d* is sin .... 1 Cor 15:56
we are the aroma of *d* ..... 2 Cor 2:16
d is working in us .... 2 Cor 4:12
the world produces *d* ...... 2 Cor 7:10
to the point of *d* .... Phil 2:8
d crowned with glory .... Heb 2:9
who had the power of *d* .... Heb 2:14
that he did not see *d* .... Heb 11:5
brings forth *d* .... James 1:15
to God, being put to *d* ..... 1 Pet 3:18
is sin leading to *d* .... 1 John 5:16
Be faithful until *d* .... Rev 2:10
Over such the second *d* ..... Rev 20:6
shall be no more *d* .... Rev 21:4
which is the second *d* .... Rev 21:8

DEBATE

D your case with your ...... Prov 25:9
you fast for strife and *d* .... Is 58:4

DEBIR

City of Judah; captured by Joshua, Josh 10:38, 39
Recaptured by Othniel; formerly called Kirjath Sepher, Josh 15:15–17; Judg 1:11–13

DEBORAH

A prophetess and judge, Judg 4:4–14
Composed song of triumph, Judg 5:1–31

DEBT

everyone who was in *d* ... 1 Sam 22:2
sell the oil and pay your *d* .. 2 Kin 4:7
the exacting of every *d* .... Neh 10:31
and forgave him the *d* .... Matt 18:27
counted as grace but as *d* ... Rom 4:4

DEBTOR

I am a *d* both to .... Rom 1:14
that he is a *d* to keep .... Gal 5:3

DEBTORS

as we forgive our *d* .... Matt 6:12
of his master's *d* .... Luke 16:5
brethren, we are *d* .... Rom 8:12
and they are their *d* .... Rom 15:27

DEBTS

forgive us our *d*, as we ..... Matt 6:12

DECAPOLIS

Multitudes from follow Jesus, Matt 4:25
Jesus heals demon-possessed, preaches in, Mark 5:20

DECEIT

spirit there is no *d* .... Ps 32:2
from speaking *d* .... Ps 34:13
d shall not dwell .... Ps 101:7
D is in the heart of .... Prov 12:20
Nor was any *d* in His .... Is 53:9
They hold fast to *d* .... Jer 8:5
in whom is no *d* .... John 1:47
"O full of all *d* .... Acts 13:10
philosophy and empty *d* ...... Col 2:8
no sin, nor was *d* .... 1 Pet 2:22
mouth was found no *d* ...... Rev 14:5

DECEITFUL

deliver me from the *d* .... Ps 43:1
d men shall not .... Ps 55:23
of the wicked are *d* .... Prov 12:5
of an enemy are *d* .... Prov 27:6
"The heart is *d* .... Jer 17:9
are false apostles, *d* ...... 2 Cor 11:13

DECEITFULLY

an idol, nor sworn *d* .... Ps 24:4
the word of God *d* .... 2 Cor 4:2

DECEITFULNESS

this world and the *d* ...... Matt 13:22
hardened through the *d* ..... Heb 3:13

DECEIVE

'Do not *d* yourselves .... Jer 37:9
rise up and *d* many .... Matt 24:11
signs and wonders to *d* ... Matt 24:24
Let no one *d* himself ...... 1 Cor 3:18
Let no one *d* you with .... Eph 5:6
we have no sin, we *d* ..... 1 John 1:8
children, let no one *d* you ... 1 John 3:7
go out to *d* the nations ...... Rev 20:8

DECEIVED

"The serpent *d* .... Gen 3:13
Why then have you *d* me .. Gen 29:25
Why have you *d* us .... Josh 9:22
d heart has turned him ...... Is 44:20
heed that you not be *d* ..... Luke 21:8
Are you also *d* .... John 7:47
by the commandment, *d* ... Rom 7:11
Do not be *d* .... 1 Cor 6:9
as the serpent *d* .... 2 Cor 11:3
Do not be *d*, God is not .... Gal 6:7
but the woman being *d* .... 1 Tim 2:14
deceiving and being *d* ..... 2 Tim 3:13
Do not be *d*, my beloved .. James 1:16
all the nations were *d* ...... Rev 18:23
who *d* them .... Rev 20:10

DECEIVER

"But cursed be the *d* .... Mal 1:14
how that *d* said .... Matt 27:63
This is a *d* and an .... 2 John 7

DECEIVES

heed that no one *d* .... Matt 24:4
d his own heart .... James 1:26
Satan, who *d* the whole ..... Rev 12:9

DECEIVING

giving heed to *d* spirits ...... 1 Tim 4:1
and worse, *d* and being .... 2 Tim 3:13
hearers only, *d* .... James 1:22

DECENTLY

all things be done *d* .... 1 Cor 14:40

DECEPTION

d all the day long .... Ps 38:12

DECEPTIVE

you with *d* words .... 2 Pet 2:3

DECISION

but its every *d* .... Prov 16:33
in the valley of *d* .... Joel 3:14

DECLARE

D His glory among the .... 1 Chr 16:24
I will *d* the decree .... Ps 2:7
The heavens *d* the .... Ps 19:1
d Your name to My .... Ps 22:22
d what He had done .... Ps 66:16
d that the LORD is .... Ps 92:15
d His generation .... Is 53:8
what is Mine and *d* it to .. John 16:14
who will *d* His generation .. Acts 8:33
we *d* to you glad tidings ... Acts 13:32
"I will *d* Your name .... Heb 2:12
seen and heard we *d* ...... 1 John 1:3

DECLARED

the Father, He has *d* .... John 1:18
and *d* to be the Son of ...... Rom 1:4

DECREE

King Cyrus issued a *d* to ... Ezra 5:13
Moreover I issue a *d* as to ... Ezra 6:8
let a royal *d* go out from .... Esth 1:19

let a *d* be written that they . . Esth 3:9
"I will declare the *d* . . . . Ps 2:7
d which shall not pass . . . . . . Ps 148:6
Woe to those who *d* . . . . Is 10:1
by a perpetual *d* . . . . Jer 5:22
is by the *d* of the watchers . . Dan 4:17
Nineveh by the *d* of the . . . . . . Jon 3:7
in those days that a *d* . . . . Luke 2:1

DEDICATED
house and has not *d* . . . . Deut 20:5
every *d* thing in . . . . Ezek 44:29
first covenant was *d* . . . . Heb 9:18

DEDICATION
sacrifices at the *d* . . . . Ezra 6:17
it was the Feast of *D* . . . . . John 10:22

DEED
What *d* is this you have . . . Gen 44:15
d has been done . . . . Judg 19:30
So I took the purchase *d*, . . . Jer 32:11
you do a charitable *d* . . . . Matt 6:2
a Prophet mighty in *d* . . . . Luke 24:19
you do in word or *d* . . . . Col 3:17
us from every lawless *d* . . . . Titus 2:14
your good *d* might not . . . . . Philem 14
or in tongue, but in *d* . . . . . 1 John 3:18

DEEDS
works and Your mighty *d* . . Deut 3:24
make known His *d* . . . . 1 Chr 16:8
Declare His *d* among . . . . Ps 9:11
them according to their *d* . . . . Ps 28:4
d You did in their days, ... Ps 44:1
awesome *d* in righteousness . . Ps 65:5
vengeance on their *d* . . . . Ps 99:8
Make known His *d* . . . . Ps 105:1
harlot by their own *d* . . . . . . Ps 106:39
against the *d* of the wicked . . Ps 141:5
man according to his *d* . . . . Prov 24:12
declare His *d* among . . . . Is 12:4
they surpass the *d* . . . . Jer 5:28
their *d* on their own head . . Ezek 9:10
charitable *d* before men . . . . . Matt 6:1
the *d* of your fathers . . . . . Luke 11:48
because their *d* . . . . John 3:19
You do the *d* of your . . . . John 8:41
mighty in words and *d* . . . . Acts 7:22
one according to his *d* . . . . Rom 2:6
apart from the *d* of the law . Rom 3:28
you put to death the *d* . . . . . . Rom 8:13
off the old man with his *d* . . . . . Col 3:9
shares in his evil *d* . . . . 2 John 11
that you hate the *d* of the . . . . Rev 2:6
did not repent of their *d* . . . . Rev 16:11

DEEP
LORD God caused a *d* . . . . Gen 2:21
He lays up the *d* . . . . Ps 33:7
D calls unto *d* . . . . Ps 42:7
In His hand are the *d* . . . . Ps 95:4
His wonders in the *d* . . . . Ps 107:24
put out in *d* darkness . . . . . Prov 20:20
led them through the *d* . . . . . . Is 63:13
d closed around me . . . . Jon 2:5
d uttered its voice . . . . Hab 3:10
"Launch out into the *d* . . . . Luke 5:4
I have been in the *d* . . . . . . 2 Cor 11:25

DEEPER
D than Sheol . . . . Job 11:8

DEEPLY
Drink, yes, drink *d* . . . . Song 5:1
But He sighed *d* . . . . Mark 8:12

DEER
"Naphtali is a *d* . . . . Gen 49:21
my feet like the feet of *d* . . . . Ps 18:33
As the *d* pants for the . . . . Ps 42:1
shall leap like a *d* . . . . Is 35:6

DEER'S
will make my feet like *d* . . . . Hab 3:19

DEFEATED
and Israel was *d* . . . . 1 Sam 4:10

DEFECT
who has any *d* . . . . Lev 21:17

DEFEND
'For I will *d* this . . . . 2 Kin 19:34
d my own ways before . . . . . . Job 13:15
for joy, because You *d* . . . . Ps 5:11
of the God of Jacob *d* you . . . . Ps 20:1
D the poor and . . . . Ps 82:3
d the fatherless . . . . Is 1:17
of hosts *d* Jerusalem . . . . Is 31:5
The LORD of hosts will *d* . . . Zech 9:15

DEFENDER
a *d* of widows . . . . Ps 68:5

DEFENSE
For wisdom is a *d* . . . . Eccl 7:12
d will be the fortress . . . . Is 33:16
am appointed for the *d* . . . . . Phil 1:17
d no one stood with me . . . 2 Tim 4:16
be ready to give a *d* . . . . 1 Pet 3:15

DEFERRED
Hope *d* makes the heart . . . Prov 13:12

DEFILE
the heart, and they *d* . . . . . Matt 15:18
also these dreamers *d* . . . . Jude 8

DEFILED
had *d* Dinah his daughter . . . Gen 34:5
d the dwelling place . . . . Ps 74:7
For your hands are *d* . . . . Is 59:3
lest they should be *d* . . . . . John 18:28
and has *d* this holy place . . Acts 21:28
being weak, is *d* . . . . 1 Cor 8:7
and conscience are *d* . . . . . . Titus 1:15
even the garment *d* . . . . Jude 23
have not *d* their garments . . . . Rev 3:4

DEFILES
mouth, this *d* a man . . . . . . Matt 15:11
d the temple of God . . . . 1 Cor 3:17
it anything that *d* . . . . Rev 21:27

DEFRAUD
d his brother in this . . . . . . 1 Thess 4:6

DEGENERATE
before Me into the *d* . . . . Jer 2:21
d is your heart . . . . Ezek 16:30

DEGREES
go forward ten *d* . . . . 2 Kin 20:9

DELAIAH
Son of Shemaiah; urges Jehoiakim not to burn Jeremiah's scroll, Jer 36:12, 25

DELICACIES
let me eat of their *d* . . . . Ps 141:4
Do not desire his *d* . . . . Prov 23:3
of the king's *d* . . . . Dan 1:5

DELICATE
Leah's eyes were *d*, but . . . . Gen 29:17
be called tender and *d* . . . . Is 47:1
a lovely and *d* woman . . . . Jer 6:2

DELIGHT
the LORD as great *d* . . . . . . 1 Sam 15:22
And his heart took *d* . . . . 2 Chr 17:6
your *d* in the Almighty . . . . . Job 22:26
Will he *d* himself in . . . . Job 27:10
But his *d* is in the . . . . Ps 1:2
ones, in whom is all my *d* . . . . Ps 16:3
D yourself also in the . . . . Ps 37:4
I *d* to do Your will . . . . Ps 40:8
You do not *d* in burnt . . . . Ps 51:16
They *d* in lies . . . . Ps 62:4
the peoples who *d* in war . . . . Ps 68:30
I will *d* myself in Your . . . . . Ps 119:16
commandments, For I *d* . . . . Ps 119:35
For Your law is my *d* . . . . . . Ps 119:77
Your law had been my *d* . . . Ps 119:92
And Your law is my *d* . . . . Ps 119:174
does not *d* in the strength . . Ps 147:10
For scorners *d* in their . . . . Prov 1:22
d in the perversity of the . . . Prov 2:14
d ourselves with love . . . . . . Prov 7:18
And I was daily His *d* . . . . . . Prov 8:30
but a just weight is His *d* . . . Prov 11:1
truthfully are His *d* . . . . Prov 12:22
will give *d* to your soul . . . . Prov 29:17
in his shade with great *d* . . . . Song 2:3
His *d* is in the fear of the . . . . . Is 11:3
gold, they will not *d* in it . . . . . Is 13:17
And let your soul *d* . . . . Is 55:2
call the Sabbath a *d* . . . . Is 58:13
that in which I do not *d* . . . . Is 65:12
For in these I *d*," says the . . . . Jer 9:24
eyes, the *d* of your soul . . . Ezek 24:21
For I *d* in the law of . . . . Rom 7:22
taking *d* in false humility . . . . Col 2:18

DELIGHTED
The LORD *d* only in . . . . Deut 10:15
d greatly in David . . . . 1 Sam 19:1
because He *d* in me . . . . . . 2 Sam 22:20
who *d* in you, setting you . . . 2 Chr 9:8
me because He *d* in me . . . . . Ps 18:19

DELIGHTS
whom the king *d* to honor . . . Esth 6:6
Him, since He *d* in Him . . . . . . Ps 22:8
the LORD, and He *d* in his . . . . Ps 37:23
the son in whom he *d* . . . . . . Prov 3:12
O love, with your *d* . . . . Song 7:6
For the LORD *d* in you . . . . Is 62:4
forever, because He *d* . . . . Mic 7:18

DELILAH
Deceives Samson, Judg 16:4–22

DELIVER
d them out of the hand . . . . Ex 3:8
will *d* him into your hand' . . . Judg 4:7
The LORD will *d* us . . . . 2 Kin 18:32
He shall *d* you in six . . . . Job 5:19
is no one who can *d* . . . . Job 10:7
'*D* him from going down . . . Job 33:24
Let Him *d* Him . . . . Ps 22:8
d their soul from . . . . Ps 33:19
I will *d* him and honor . . . . . . Ps 91:15
d you from the immoral . . . . . Prov 2:16
wickedness will not *d* . . . . Eccl 8:8
have I no power to *d* . . . . Is 50:2
we serve is able to *d* . . . . Dan 3:17
into temptation, but *d* . . . . . . Matt 6:13
let Him *d* Him now if . . . . . Matt 27:43
d such a one to Satan . . . . . . 1 Cor 5:5
And the Lord will *d* . . . . 2 Tim 4:18
d the godly out of . . . . 2 Pet 2:9

DELIVERANCE
d He gives to His king . . . . Ps 18:50
but *d* is of the LORD . . . . Prov 21:31
not accepting *d* . . . . Heb 11:35

DELIVERED
d the poor who cried . . . . Job 29:12
for You have *d* my soul . . . . . . Ps 56:13
For He has *d* the life . . . . Jer 20:13
All things have been *d* . . . . . Matt 11:27
who was *d* up because . . . . Rom 4:25
But now we have been *d* . . . . . Rom 7:6
who *d* us from so great . . . . 2 Cor 1:10
was once for all *d* . . . . Jude 3

DELIVERER
the LORD raised up a *d* . . . . . . Judg 3:9
LORD raised up a *d* for . . . . . Judg 3:15
my fortress and my *d* . . . . . 2 Sam 22:2
LORD gave Israel a *d*. . . . . 2 Kin 13:5
You are my help and my *d* . . . Ps 40:17
My high tower and my *d* . . . . Ps 144:2
d by the hand of the Angel . Acts 7:35
D will come out of . . . . Rom 11:26

DELIVERERS
d who saved them . . . . Neh 9:27

DELIVERS
d the kingdom to God . . . . 1 Cor 15:24
even Jesus who *d* . . . . 1 Thess 1:10

DELUSION
send them strong *d* . . . . . . 2 Thess 2:11

DEMAS
Follows Paul, Col 4:14
Forsakes Paul, 2 Tim 4:10

DEMETRIUS
A silversmith at Ephesus, Acts 19:24–31
—— A good Christian, 3 John 12

DEMON
when the *d* was cast out ... Matt 9:33
they say, 'He has a *d* ... Matt 11:18
Jesus rebuked the *d* ... Matt 17:18
the *d* out of her daughter ... Mark 7:26
a spirit of an unclean *d* ... Luke 4:33
you say, 'He has a *d* ... Luke 7:33
was driven by the *d* into ... Luke 8:29
d threw him down and ... Luke 9:42
He was casting out a *d* ... Luke 11:14
You have a *d* ... John 7:20
and have a *d* ... John 8:48
He has a *d* and is mad ... John 10:20

DEMON-POSSESSED
and those who were *d* ... Matt 4:24
to Him many who were *d* ... Matt 8:16
there met Him two *d* men, ... Matt 8:28
Him a man, mute and *d* ... Matt 9:32
to Him who was *d* ... Matt 12:22
daughter is severely *d* ... Matt 15:22
and those who were *d* ... Mark 1:32
one who had been *d* ... Mark 5:15
had been *d* was healed ... Luke 8:36

DEMONIC
is earthly, sensual, *d* ... James 3:15

DEMONS
See CAST OUT DEMONS; CASTING OUT DEMONS
They sacrificed to *d* ... Deut 32:17
their daughters to *d* ... Ps 106:37
cast out *d* in Your name ... Matt 7:22
d begged Him, saying, ... Matt 8:31
He casts out *d* ... Matt 9:34
raise the dead, cast out *d* ... Matt 10:8
except by Beelzebub ... Matt 12:24
and cast out many *d* ... Mark 1:34
and to cast out *d* ... Mark 3:15
d begged Him, saying, ... Mark 5:12
they cast out many *d* ... Mark 6:13
out *d* in Your name ... Mark 9:38
He had cast seven *d* ... Mark 16:9
name they will cast out *d* ... Mark 16:17
And *d* also came out of ... Luke 4:41
whom had come seven *d* ... Luke 8:2
many *d* had entered ... Luke 8:30
authority over all *d* ... Luke 9:1
casting out *d* in Your ... Luke 9:49
the *d* are subject ... Luke 10:17
casts out *d* by Beelzebub ... Luke 11:15
fox, 'Behold, I cast out *d* ... Luke 13:32
Lord and the cup of *d* ... 1 Cor 10:21
spirits and doctrines of *d* ... 1 Tim 4:1
Even the *d* believe ... James 2:19
they should not worship *d* ... Rev 9:20
For they are spirits of *d* ... Rev 16:14
a dwelling place of *d* ... Rev 18:2

DEMONSTRATE
faith, to *d* His ... Rom 3:25

DEMONSTRATES
d His own love toward ... Rom 5:8

DEMONSTRATION
but in *d* of the Spirit and ... 1 Cor 2:4

DEN
in the viper's *d* ... Is 11:8
by My name, become a *d* ... Jer 7:11
cast him into the *d* ... Dan 6:16
it a '*d* of thieves ... Matt 21:13

DENARIUS
the laborers for a *d* ... Matt 20:2
they brought Him a *d* ... Matt 22:19
quart of wheat for a *d* ... Rev 6:6

DENIED
before men will be *d* ... Luke 12:9
Peter then *d* again ... John 18:27
d the Holy One and the ... Acts 3:14
things cannot be *d* ... Acts 19:36
household, he has *d* ... 1 Tim 5:8
word, and have not *d* ... Rev 3:8

DENIES
But whoever *d* Me ... Matt 10:33
d that Jesus is the ... 1 John 2:22

DENS
lie down in their *d* ... Ps 104:22
and mountains, in *d* ... Heb 11:38

DENY
lest you *d* your God ... Josh 24:27
place, then it will *d* him ... Job 8:18
lest I be full and *d* ... Prov 30:9
him I will also *d* before ... Matt 10:33
let him *d* himself ... Matt 16:24
will *d* Me three times ... Matt 26:34
who *d* that there is a ... Luke 20:27
confessed, and did not *d* ... John 1:20
He cannot *d* Himself ... 2 Tim 2:13
in works they *d* ... Titus 1:16
d the only Lord ... Jude 4
d My faith even ... Rev 2:13

DENYING
but *d* its power ... 2 Tim 3:5
d ungodliness and ... Titus 2:12
d the Lord who bought ... 2 Pet 2:1

DEPART
scepter shall not *d* ... Gen 49:10
they say to God, '*D* ... Job 21:14
D from evil and do good ... Ps 34:14
fear the LORD and *d* ... Prov 3:7
the mountains, shall *d* ... Is 54:10
on the left hand, '*D* ... Matt 25:41
will *d* from the faith ... 1 Tim 4:1

DEPARTED
the day that you *d* ... Deut 9:7

DEPARTING
heart of unbelief in *d* ... Heb 3:12

DEPARTS
His spirit *d*, he returns to ... Ps 146:4
But if the unbeliever *d* ... 1 Cor 7:15

DEPARTURE
d savage wolves will ... Acts 20:29
and the time of my *d* ... 2 Tim 4:6

DEPRESSION
of man causes *d* ... Prov 12:25

DEPRIVE
d myself of good ... Eccl 4:8
d one another except ... 1 Cor 7:5

DEPRIVED
like a bear *d* of her cubs ... Hos 13:8

DEPTH
because they had no *d* ... Matt 13:5
nor height nor *d* ... Rom 8:39
Oh, the *d* of the ... Rom 11:33
width and length and *d* ... Eph 3:18

DEPTHS
d have covered them ... Ex 15:5
The *d* also trembled ... Ps 77:16
my soul from the *d* ... Ps 86:13
led them through the *d* ... Ps 106:9
go down again to the *d* ... Ps 107:26
d I was brought forth ... Prov 8:24
our sins into the *d* ... Mic 7:19
have not known the *d* ... Rev 2:24

DERANGED
the nations are *d* ... Jer 51:7

DERBE
Paul visits, Acts 14:6, 20
Paul meets Timothy at, Acts 16:1

DERISION
shall hold them in *d* ... Ps 2:4
I am in *d* daily ... Jer 20:7

DESCEND
His glory shall not *d* ... Ps 49:17
d now from the cross ... Mark 15:32
Lord Himself will *d* ... 1 Thess 4:16
This wisdom does not *d* ... James 3:15

DESCENDANTS
All you *d* of Jacob ... Ps 22:23
d shall inherit the ... Ps 25:13
pour My Spirit on your *d* ... Is 44:3
In the LORD all the *d* ... Is 45:25
none of his *d* shall prosper ... Jer 22:30
"We are Abraham's *d* ... John 8:33
So shall your *d* be ... Rom 4:18

DESCENDED
because the LORD *d* ... Ex 19:18
that He also first *d* ... Eph 4:9
He who *d* is also the ... Eph 4:10

DESCENDING
were ascending and *d* ... Gen 28:12
"I saw the Spirit *d* ... John 1:32
God ascending and *d* ... John 1:51
the holy Jerusalem, *d* ... Rev 21:10

DESERT
And tested God in the *d* ... Ps 106:14
d shall rejoice and blossom ... Is 35:1
and rivers in the *d* ... Is 43:19
her *d* like the garden of ... Is 51:3
'Look, He is in the *d* ... Matt 24:26
ate the manna in the *d* ... John 6:31

DESERTED
d place by Himself ... Matt 14:13

DESERTS
led them through the *d* ... Is 48:21
They wandered in *d* ... Heb 11:38

DESERVE
to them what they *d* ... Ps 28:4
d I will judge them ... Ezek 7:27

DESIGN
with an artistic *d* ... Ex 26:31
may keep its whole *d* ... Ezek 43:11

DESIRABLE
the eyes, and a tree *d* ... Gen 3:6
d that we should leave ... Acts 6:2

DESIRE
d shall be for your ... Gen 3:16
and you shall not *d* your ... Deut 5:21
is all the *d* of Israel ... 1 Sam 9:20
salvation and all my *d* ... 2 Sam 23:5
I *d* to reason with God ... Job 13:3
for we do not *d* ... Job 21:14
boasts of his heart's *d* ... Ps 10:3
heard the *d* of the humble ... Ps 10:17
him his heart's *d* ... Ps 21:2
and offering You did not *d* ... Ps 40:6
Behold, You *d* truth in ... Ps 51:6
confused Who *d* my hurt ... Ps 70:2
upon earth that I *d* ... Ps 73:25
the *d* of the wicked ... Ps 112:10
and satisfy the *d* ... Ps 145:16
all the things you may *d* ... Prov 3:15
all the things one may *d* ... Prov 8:11
d of the righteous will ... Prov 10:24
The *d* of the righteous is ... Prov 11:23
The *d* of the lazy ... Prov 21:25
nor *d* to be with them ... Prov 24:1
a burden, and *d* fails ... Eccl 12:5
and his *d* is toward me ... Song 7:10
the *d* of our soul is ... Is 26:8
beauty that we should *d* ... Is 53:2
the *d* of their eyes, and ... Ezek 24:25
For I *d* mercy and not ... Hos 6:6
great man utters his evil *d* ... Mic 7:3
d mercy and not sacrifice ... Matt 9:13
d I have desired ... Luke 22:15
"Father, I *d* that ... John 17:24
all manner of evil *d* ... Rom 7:8
Brethren, my heart's *d* ... Rom 10:1

give place to the *d* .... Eph 4:27
the wiles of the *d* .... Eph 6:11
condemnation as the *d* ..... 1 Tim 3:6
the snare of the *d* .... 2 Tim 2:26
of death, that is, the *d* ...... Heb 2:14
Resist the *d* and he .... James 4:7
d walks about like a .... 1 Pet 5:8
the works of the *d* .... 1 John 3:8
contending with the *d* .... Jude 9
Indeed, the *d* is about .... Rev 2:10
serpent of old, called the *D* .. Rev 12:9
the *d* has come down to .... Rev 12:12
serpent of old, who is the *D* . Rev 20:2
d, who deceived them ...... Rev 20:10

DEVIOUS
crooked, and who are *d* .... Prov 2:15

DEVISE
Do not *d* evil against .... Prov 3:29
Woe to those who *d* .... Mic 2:1

DEVISES
d wickedness on his .... Ps 36:4
he *d* evil continually .... Prov 6:14
d wicked plans to .... Is 32:7
But a generous man *d* .... Is 32:8

DEVOID
He who is *d* of wisdom .... Prov 11:12

DEVOTE
d rashly something as .... Prov 20:25

DEVOTED
d offering is most .... Lev 27:28
"Every *d* thing in .... Num 18:14
Your servant, who is *d* ..... Ps 119:38

DEVOUR
A fire shall *d* before .... Ps 50:3
For you *d* widows' .... Matt 23:14
bite and *d* one another ...... Gal 5:15
seeking whom he may *d* .... 1 Pet 5:8
d her Child as .... Rev 12:4

DEVOURED
Some wild beast has *d* ..... Gen 37:20
rebel, you shall be *d* .... Is 1:20
the curse has *d* .... Is 24:6
Your sword has *d* .... Jer 2:30
For shame has *d* .... Jer 3:24
have *d* their judges .... Hos 7:7
trees, the locust *d* .... Amos 4:9
birds came and *d* them ..... Matt 13:4
of heaven and *d* them .... Rev 20:9

DEVOURER
I will rebuke the *d* .... Mal 3:11

DEVOURING
You love all *d* words .... Ps 52:4
the flame of *d* fire .... Is 29:6

DEVOUT
man was just and *d* .... Luke 2:25
d men carried Stephen ...... Acts 8:2
d soldier from among ...... Acts 10:7
d proselytes followed Paul . Acts 13:43

DEW
God give you of the *d* ..... Gen 27:28
shall also drop *d* .... Deut 33:28
have the *d* of Your youth .... Ps 110:3
his favor is like *d* .... Prov 19:12
a cloud of *d* in the heat .... Is 18:4
your *d* is like the *d* .... Is 26:19
like the early *d* .... Hos 6:4
many peoples, like *d* .... Mic 5:7

DIADEM
LORD, and a royal *d*........... Is 62:3

DIADEMS
ten horns, and seven *d* ...... Rev 12:3

DIAL
d by which it had gone .... Is 38:8

DIAMOND
a sapphire, and a *d* .... Ex 28:18
d it is engraved .... Jer 17:1

the sardius, topaz, and *d* .. Ezek 28:13

DIANA
Worship of at Ephesus creates uproar, Acts 19:23–41

DIBON
Amorite town, Num 21:30
Taken by Israel, Num 32:2–5
Destruction of, foretold, Jer 48:18, 22

DICTATES
according to the *d* .... Jer 23:17

DIE
it you shall surely *d* .... Gen 2:17
you touch it, lest you *d* ...... Gen 3:3
the land of Egypt shall *d* ...... Ex 11:5
Where you *d*, I will *d*, ... Ruth 1:17
but a person shall *d* .... 2 Chr 25:4
Curse God and *d* .... Job 2:9
sees wise men *d* .... Ps 49:10
I shall not *d*, but live .... Ps 118:17
He shall *d* for lack of ...... Prov 5:23
but fools *d* for lack of ..... Prov 10:21
hates correction will *d* .... Prov 15:10
with a rod, he will not *d* .. Prov 23:13
who are appointed to *d* .... Prov 31:8
how does a wise man *d* ..... Eccl 2:16
born, and a time to *d* .... Eccl 3:2
why should you *d* .... Eccl 7:17
drink, for tomorrow we *d* .... Is 22:13
their worm does not *d* .... Is 66:24
every one shall *d* for his .... Jer 31:30
wicked way, he shall *d* .... Ezek 3:19
the soul who sins shall *d* ... Ezek 18:4
man, you shall surely *d* ... Ezek 33:8
"Even if I have to *d* .... Matt 26:35
'their worm does not *d* .... Mark 9:44
nor can they *d* .... Luke 20:36
eat of it and not *d* .... John 6:50
to you that you will *d* ...... John 8:24
though he may *d* .... John 11:25
that one man should *d* .... John 11:50
that Jesus would *d* .... John 11:51
our law He ought to *d* ...... John 19:7
righteous man will one *d* .... Rom 5:7
the flesh you will *d* .... Rom 8:13
if we *d*, we *d* to the Lord .... Rom 14:8
For as in Adam all *d* ..... 1 Cor 15:22
Jesus our Lord, I *d* daily .. 1 Cor 15:31
and to *d* is gain .... Phil 1:21
for men to *d* once .... Heb 9:27
are the dead who *d* .... Rev 14:13

DIED
And all flesh *d* .... Gen 7:21
"Oh, that we had *d* .... Ex 16:3
himself with fire, and *d* .. 1 Kin 16:18
Hadad *d* also .... 1 Chr 1:51
So Saul *d* for his .... 1 Chr 10:13
was that the beggar *d* .... Luke 16:22
in due time Christ *d* .... Rom 5:6
Christ *d* for us .... Rom 5:8
For he who has *d* .... Rom 6:7
Now if we *d* with .... Rom 6:8
sin revived and I *d* .... Rom 7:9
For to this end Christ *d* .... Rom 14:9
perish, for whom Christ *d* . 1 Cor 8:11
that Christ *d* for our sins .. 1 Cor 15:3
that if One *d* for all .... 2 Cor 5:14
and He *d* for all .... 2 Cor 5:15
through the law *d* .... Gal 2:19
if you *d* with Christ from .... Col 2:20
For you *d*, and your life is .... Col 3:3
believe that Jesus *d* ..... 1 Thess 4:14
who *d* for us .... 1 Thess 5:10
for if we *d* with Him ...... 2 Tim 2:11
These all *d* in faith .... Heb 11:13
having *d* to sins .... 1 Pet 2:24

DIES
If a man *d*, shall he live .... Job 14:14
When a wicked man *d* ..... Prov 11:7
into the ground and *d* .... John 12:24
if the husband *d*, she is ...... Rom 7:2

and no one *d* to himself ..... Rom 14:7
made alive unless it *d* .... 1 Cor 15:36

DIFFERENCE
the LORD will make a *d* .... Ex 9:4
d between the unclean .... Ezek 22:26
the *d* between the holy .... Ezek 44:23
For there is no *d* .... Rom 3:22
were, it makes no *d* to me .... Gal 2:6

DIFFERENCES
There are *d* of ministries, .. 1 Cor 12:5

DIFFERENT
he has a *d* spirit in him ... Num 14:24
with *d* kinds of seed .... Deut 22:9
each *d* from the other .... Dan 7:3
d kinds of tongues .... 1 Cor 12:10
if you receive a *d* spirit .... 2 Cor 11:4
of Christ, to a *d* gospel, ... Gal 1:6

DIFFERING
Having then gifts *d* .... Rom 12:6

DIFFERS
for one star *d* from .... 1 Cor 15:41

DIFFICULT
d is the way which leads ... Matt 7:14

DIFFUSED
By what way is light *d* ..... Job 38:24

DIFFUSES
us *d* the fragrance .... 2 Cor 2:14

DIG
wells which you did not *d* .. Deut 6:11
Son of man, *d* into the ...... Ezek 8:8
Though they *d* into hell .... Amos 9:2
I cannot *d*; I am ashamed .. Luke 16:3

DIGNITARIES
afraid to speak evil of *d* .... 2 Pet 2:10
and speak evil of *d* .... Jude 8

DILIGENCE
your heart with all *d* .... Prov 4:23
d is man's precious .... Prov 12:27
he who leads, with *d* .... Rom 12:8
not lagging in *d*, fervent .. Rom 12:11
d it produced in you .... 2 Cor 7:11
of your love by the *d* .... 2 Cor 8:8
giving all *d*, add to your ..... 2 Pet 1:5

DILIGENT
d in sanctifying .... 2 Chr 29:34
and my spirit makes *d* .... Ps 77:6
hand of the *d* makes rich ... Prov 10:4
of the *d* will rule .... Prov 12:24
d shall be made rich .... Prov 13:4
proved *d* in many things ... 2 Cor 8:22
d to come to me quickly .... 2 Tim 4:9
Let us therefore be *d* .... Heb 4:11
be *d* to be found by Him ... 2 Pet 3:14

DILIGENTLY
if you *d* obey the voice of .. Deut 28:1
seek me *d* will find me ..... Prov 8:17
d followed every good ..... 1 Tim 5:10
he sought it *d* with tears .. Heb 12:17

DIM
His eyes were not *d* .... Deut 34:7
the windows grow *d* .... Eccl 12:3
the gold has become *d* ...... Lam 4:1

DIMINISH
stars *d* their brightness ..... Joel 2:10
the lights will *d* .... Zech 14:6

DIMLY
we see in a mirror, *d* ..... 1 Cor 13:12

DINAH
Daughter of Leah, Gen 30:20, 21
Defiled by Shechem, Gen 34:1–24
Avenged by brothers, Gen 34:25–31

DINE
asked Him to *d* with ...... Luke 11:37
come in to him and *d* .... Rev 3:20

DINNER
Better is a *d* of herbs ..... Prov 15:17

I have prepared my *d* ...... Matt 22:4
invites you to *d* .... 1 Cor 10:27

DIOTREPHES
Unruly church member, 3 John 9, 10

DIP
d them in the blood .... Lev 14:51
d it in the water, ... Num 19:18
let him *d* his foot in oil .... Deut 33:24
d your piece of bread ...... Ruth 2:14
d the tip of his finger in .. Luke 16:24

DIPPED
d the tunic in the blood .... Gen 37:31
d his finger in the .... Lev 9:9
d seven times in the .... 2 Kin 5:14
of bread when I have *d* .... John 13:26
clothed with a robe *d* .... Rev 19:13

DIRECT
the morning I will *d* .... Ps 5:3
and He shall *d* your paths ..... Prov 3:6
d their work in truth .... Is 61:8
Now may the Lord *d* ..... 2 Thess 3:5

DIRT
I cast them out like *d* .... Ps 18:42
cast up mire and *d* .... Is 57:20

DISAPPEARS
As water *d* from the .... Job 14:11

DISARMED
d principalities .... Col 2:15

DISARMS
and *d* the mighty .... Job 12:21

DISASTER
bring *d* on the house ..... 1 Kin 14:10
I am fashioning a *d* .... Jer 18:11
war and *d* and pestilence .... Jer 28:8
D will come upon .... Ezek 7:26
you shall see *d* .... Zeph 3:15
voyage will end with *d* .... Acts 27:10

DISCERN
Can I *d* between the .... 2 Sam 19:35
Then you shall again *d* .... Mal 3:18
d the face of the sky .... Matt 16:3
senses exercised to *d* .... Heb 5:14

DISCERNED
they are spiritually *d* .... 1 Cor 2:14

DISCERNER
d of the thoughts .... Heb 4:12

DISCERNING
not *d* the Lord's body ..... 1 Cor 11:29
another *d* of spirits, to ..... 1 Cor 12:10

DISCERNMENT
and takes away the *d* .... Job 12:20

DISCERNS
a wise man's heart *d* .... Eccl 8:5

DISCIPLE
d is not above his .... Matt 10:24
in the name of a *d* .... Matt 10:42
he cannot be My *d* .... Luke 14:26
the *d* whom He loved ..... John 19:26
d whom Jesus loved .... John 21:7
the *d* whom Jesus loved .. John 21:20

DISCIPLES
See TWELVE DISCIPLES
but Your *d* do not fast ..... Matt 9:14
called His twelve *d* to ...... Matt 10:1
d transgress the .... Matt 15:2
took the twelve *d* .... Matt 20:17
all the *d* forsook Him ..... Matt 26:56
make *d* of all the nations, . Matt 28:19
with His *d* to the sea .... Mark 3:7
called His *d* to Himself ..... Luke 6:13
His *d* believed in Him ...... John 2:11
many of His *d* went back .... John 6:66
My word, you are My *d* ...... John 8:31
to become His *d* .... John 9:27
but we are Moses' *d* .... John 9:28
His *d* did not understand .. John 12:16
know that you are My *d* .. John 13:35
so you will be My *d* .... John 15:8
Then the *d* were glad .... John 20:20
of the *d* was multiplying, ... Acts 6:1
the *d* were first called ..... Acts 11:26
souls of the *d*, exhorting ... Acts 14:22
strengthening all the *d* .... Acts 18:23

DISCIPLES'
began to wash the *d* feet .... John 13:5

DISCIPLINE
Harsh *d* is for him who ... Prov 15:10
I *d* my body and bring ...... 1 Cor 9:27

DISCIPLINES
but he who loves him *d* ... Prov 13:24

DISCLOSE
d my dark saying .... Ps 49:4

DISCORD
and one who sows *d* .... Prov 6:19

DISCOURAGE
why will you *d* the heart .... Num 32:7

DISCOURAGED
do not fear or be *d* .... Deut 1:21
will not fail nor be *d* .... Is 42:4
lest they become *d* .... Col 3:21
you become weary and *d* .... Heb 12:3
d when you are rebuked .... Heb 12:5

DISCREET
d, chaste, homemakers, ... Titus 2:5

DISCRETION
D will preserve you .... Prov 2:11
out knowledge and *d* .... Prov 8:12
woman who lacks *d* .... Prov 11:22
The *d* of a man makes ..... Prov 19:11
the heavens at His *d* .... Jer 10:12

DISEASE
Shall I recover from this *d* .. 2 Kin 8:8
in his *d* he did not seek .. 2 Chr 16:12
all kinds of *d* among the .... Matt 4:23
every *d* among the people .. Matt 9:35
well of whatever *d* he had ... John 5:4

DISEASES
Who heals all your *d*, ... Ps 103:3
afflicted with various *d* ...... Matt 4:24
various *d* brought them ...... Luke 4:40
all demons, and to cure *d* ... Luke 9:1
d left them and the evil .... Acts 19:12

DISFIGURE
nor shall you *d* the edges ... Lev 19:27
d their faces that .... Matt 6:16

DISGRACE
plead my *d* against me, ... Job 19:5
do not *d* the throne of .... Jer 14:21

DISGRACEFUL
he had done a *d* thing ...... Gen 34:7
done a *d* thing in Israel ...... Josh 7:15
Do not do this *d* thing ... 2 Sam 13:12

DISGUISES
and he *d* his face .... Job 24:15
He who hates, *d* .... Prov 26:24

DISHONEST GAIN
turned aside after *d* .... 1 Sam 8:3
for the sake of *d* .... Titus 1:11
not for *d* but eagerly .... 1 Pet 5:2

DISHONESTY
Wealth gained by *d* will ... Prov 13:11

DISHONOR
d who wish me evil .... Ps 40:14
with *d* comes reproach ...... Prov 18:3
d the pride of all .... Is 23:9
Her rulers dearly love *d* .... Hos 4:18
My Father, and you *d* Me .. John 8:49
d their bodies among .... Rom 1:24
and another for *d* .... Rom 9:21
long hair, it is a *d* to ...... 1 Cor 11:14
It is sown in *d* .... 1 Cor 15:43
by honor and *d* .... 2 Cor 6:8
honor and some for *d* ...... 2 Tim 2:20

DISHONORED
but we are *d* .... 1 Cor 4:10
But you have *d* the .... James 2:6

DISHONORS
For son *d* father .... Mic 7:6
covered, *d* his head .... 1 Cor 11:4

DISOBEDIENCE
d many were made .... Rom 5:19
works in the sons of *d* .... Eph 2:2
d received a just .... Heb 2:2

DISOBEDIENT
Nevertheless they were *d* ..... Neh 9:26
the *d* to the wisdom of ...... Luke 1:17
out My hands to a *d* .... Rom 10:21
you were once *d* to God .... Rom 11:30
d to parents, unthankful, ... 2 Tim 3:2
d, deceived, serving .... Titus 3:3
They stumble, being *d* .... 1 Pet 2:8
who formerly were *d* .... 1 Pet 3:20

DISORDERLY
for this *d* gathering .... Acts 19:40
brother who walks *d* ..... 2 Thess 3:6

DISPENSATION
d of the fullness of .... Eph 1:10
d of the grace of God .... Eph 3:2

DISPERSE
d them throughout the .... Ezek 20:23

DISPERSION
intend to go to the *D* .... John 7:35
the pilgrims of the *D* .... 1 Pet 1:1

DISPLEASE
LORD see it, and it *d* .... Prov 24:18

DISPLEASED
that David had done *d* ... 2 Sam 11:27
You have been *d* .... Ps 60:1
they were greatly *d* .... Matt 20:24
it, He was greatly *d* .... Mark 10:14

DISPUTE
Now there was also a *d* ... Luke 22:24

DISPUTED
when he *d* about the body ..... Jude 9

DISPUTER
Where is the *d* of this ...... 1 Cor 1:20

DISPUTES
d rather than godly .... 1 Tim 1:4
but is obsessed with *d* .... 1 Tim 6:4
foolish and ignorant *d* ...... 2 Tim 2:23
But avoid foolish *d* .... Titus 3:9

DISQUALIFIED
myself should become *d* ... 1 Cor 9:27
indeed you are *d* .... 2 Cor 13:5
though we may seem *d* ..... 2 Cor 13:7

DISQUIETED
And why are you *d* .... Ps 42:5

DISSENSION
had no small *d* and .... Acts 15:2
this, a *d* arose between ...... Acts 23:7
a creator of *d* among all .... Acts 24:5

DISSENSIONS
selfish ambitions, *d* .... Gal 5:20

DISSIPATION
not accused of *d* .... Titus 1:6
in the same flood of *d* .... 1 Pet 4:4

DISSOLVED
of heaven shall be *d* .... Is 34:4
the heavens will be *d* ...... 2 Pet 3:12

DISTINCTION
and made no *d* .... Acts 15:9
For there is no *d* .... Rom 10:12
compassion, making a *d* .... Jude 22

DISTRACTED
But Martha was *d* with ... Luke 10:40

DISTRESS
me in the day of my *d* ...... Gen 35:3
When you are in *d* .... Deut 4:30
my life from every *d* ...... 1 Kin 1:29
you out of dire *d* .... Job 36:16
keep you from *d* .... Job 36:19
d them in His deep .... Ps 2:5
on the LORD in *d* .... Ps 118:5
a whirlwind, when *d* .... Prov 1:27
and on the earth *d* .... Luke 21:25
tribulation, or *d* .... Rom 8:35
of the present *d* .... 1 Cor 7:26

DISTRESSED
was greatly afraid and *d* .... Gen 32:7
Israel was severely *d* .... Judg 10:9
David was greatly *d* ...... 1 Sam 30:6
the queen was deeply *d* ..... Esth 4:4
heart within me is *d* .... Ps 143:4
not be upon her who is *d* .... Is 9:1
troubled and deeply *d* .... Mark 14:33
and how *d* I am till it is ... Luke 12:50

DISTRESSES
bring me out of my *d* .... Ps 25:17

DISTRESSING
d spirit from the LORD ... 1 Sam 16:14
Now the *d* spirit from ..... 1 Sam 19:9

DISTRIBUTE
that you have and *d* ...... Luke 18:22

DISTRIBUTED
and they *d* to each as .... Acts 4:35
But as God has *d* .... 1 Cor 7:17

DISTRIBUTING
d to the needs of the .... Rom 12:13

DITCH
will fall into a *d* .... Matt 15:14

DIVERSE
D weights are an .... Prov 20:23

DIVERSITIES
There are *d* of gifts .... 1 Cor 12:4
there are *d* of activities, ... 1 Cor 12:6

DIVIDE
D the living child .... 1 Kin 3:25
d My garments among .... Ps 22:18
d their tongues .... Ps 55:9
d the spoil with the .... Prov 16:19
d the inheritance .... Luke 12:13
"Take this and *d* .... Luke 22:17

DIVIDED
and the waters were *d* .... Ex 14:21
death they were not *d* ..... 2 Sam 1:23
And You *d* the sea .... Neh 9:11
"Who has *d* a channel ...... Job 38:25
shall they ever be *d* .... Ezek 37:22
kingdom has been *d* .... Dan 5:28
your land shall be *d* .... Amos 7:17
"Every kingdom *d* .... Matt 12:25
and a house *d* against ..... Luke 11:17
in one house will be *d* ..... Luke 12:52
So he *d* to them his .... Luke 15:12
they *d* His garments and .. Luke 23:34
d My garments among ..... John 19:24
appeared to them *d* .... Acts 2:3
d them among all .... Acts 2:45
Is Christ *d*? Was Paul ..... 1 Cor 1:13
the great city was *d* .... Rev 16:19

DIVIDES
at home *d* the spoil .... Ps 68:12

DIVIDING
rightly *d* the word of ...... 2 Tim 2:15

DIVINATION
shall you practice *d* .... Lev 19:26
D is on the lips of .... Prov 16:10
darkness without *d* .... Mic 3:6
a spirit of *d* met us .... Acts 16:16

DIVINE
futility and who *d* .... Ezek 13:9
and her prophets *d* .... Mic 3:11
d service and the .... Heb 9:1
d power has given .... 2 Pet 1:3

DIVINERS
your prophets, your *d* .... Jer 27:9

DIVISION
So there was a *d* .... John 7:43
piercing even to the *d* .... Heb 4:12

DIVISIONS
note those who cause *d* .... Rom 16:17
and that there be no *d* ...... 1 Cor 1:10
envy, strife, and *d* .... 1 Cor 3:3
hear that there are *d* ...... 1 Cor 11:18
persons, who cause *d* .... Jude 19

DIVISIVE
Reject a *d* man after .... Titus 3:10

DIVORCE
cannot *d* her all his days ... Deut 22:19
her a certificate of *d* .... Deut 24:1
of your mother's *d* .... Is 50:1
given her a certificate of *d* ...... Jer 3:8
Israel says that He hates *d* ... Mal 2:16
give her a certificate of *d* ... Matt 5:31
to *d* his wife for just any ... Matt 19:3
a certificate of *d* .... Mark 10:4
husband is not to *d* his ..... 1 Cor 7:11

DIVORCED
d from her husband .... Lev 21:7
A widow or a *d* woman ...... Lev 21:14
daughter is a widow or *d* .. Lev 22:13
vow of a widow or a *d* .... Num 30:9
d her must not take her ..... Deut 24:4
a widow or a *d* woman ... Ezek 44:22
is *d* commits adultery .... Matt 5:32
is *d* from her husband ...... Luke 16:18

DIVORCES
say, 'If a man *d* his wife .... Jer 3:1
said, 'Whoever *d* his wife .. Matt 5:31
whoever *d* his wife .... Matt 19:9
Whoever *d* his wife .... Mark 10:11
Whoever *d* his wife .... Luke 16:18

DO
set in them to *d* evil .... Eccl 8:11
I will also *d* it .... Is 46:11
men to *d* to you, *d* .... Matt 7:12
d this and you will .... Luke 10:28
He sees the Father *d* .... John 5:19
without Me you can *d* ...... John 15:5
"Sirs, what must I *d* ...... Acts 16:30
d evil that good may .... Rom 3:8
For what I will to *d* .... Rom 7:15
good that I will to *d* .... Rom 7:19
or whatever you *d*, *d* .... 1 Cor 10:31
d all things through .... Phil 4:13
d in word or deed, *d* .... Col 3:17
d good and to share .... Heb 13:16
and *d* this or that .... James 4:15

DO NOT BE AFRAID
vision, saying, "*D*, Abram .... Gen 15:1
said to the people, "*D* ..... Ex 14:13
d, and do not tremble .... Deut 20:3
Lord said to Joshua, "*D* .... Josh 11:6
d of him." So he arose ...... 2 Kin 1:15
D of the words .... 2 Kin 19:6
D of sudden terror, ... Prov 3:25
D of their faces, for .... Jer 1:8
"*D* to serve the Chaldeans ... Jer 40:9
And you, son of man, *d* ..... Ezek 2:6
D, you beasts of the .... Joel 2:22
"Joseph, son of David, *d* ... Matt 1:20
It is I; *d* .... Matt 14:27
"Arise, and *d* .... Matt 17:7
said to the women, "*D* ..... Matt 28:5
of the synagogue, "*D* ...... Mark 5:36
angel said to him, "*D* ...... Luke 1:13
"*D*, Mary, for you have ..... Luke 1:30
angel said to them, "*D*, ... Luke 2:10
Jesus said to Simon, "*D* ... Luke 5:10
d of those who kill the ..... Luke 12:4
"*D*, but speak .... Acts 18:9
"*D*, Paul; you must .... Acts 27:24
saying to me, "*D* .... Rev 1:17

DO NOT FEAR
d, for I am with you. ...... Gen 26:24
d to go down to Egypt, ... Gen 46:3
D; for God has come .... Ex 20:20
d or be discouraged .... Deut 1:21
d the gods of the .... Judg 6:10
d, you shall not die .... Judg 6:23
D. You have done all .... 1 Sam 12:20
D, for I will surely .... 2 Sam 9:7
Elijah said to her, "*D*; .... 1 Kin 17:13
D, for those who are with .. 2 Kin 6:16
d or be fainthearted .... Is 7:4
fearful-hearted, "Be strong, *d* . Is 35:4
d the reproach of men, ... Is 51:7
d, O My servant Jacob,' ..... Jer 30:10
said to me, "*D*, Daniel ...... Dan 10:12
remains among you; *d* .... Hag 2:5
D, let your hands be .... Zech 8:13
d them. For there is .... Matt 10:26
D therefore; you are of .... Luke 12:7
D any of those things .... Rev 2:10

DOCTRINE
said, 'My *d* is pure .... Job 11:4
for I give you good *d* .... Prov 4:2
idol is a worthless *d* .... Jer 10:8
of bread, but of the *d* ..... Matt 16:12
What new *d* is this .... Mark 1:27
"My *d* is not Mine .... John 7:16
Jerusalem with your *d* .... Acts 5:28
heart that form of *d* .... Rom 6:17
with every wind of *d* .... Eph 4:14
is contrary to sound *d* ..... 1 Tim 1:10
followed my *d* .... 2 Tim 3:10
is profitable for *d* .... 2 Tim 3:16
not endure sound *d* .... 2 Tim 4:3
in *d* showing integrity .... Titus 2:7
they may adorn the *d* .... Titus 2:10
not abide in the *d* .... 2 John 9

DOCTRINES
the commandments and *d* ..... Col 2:22
spirits and *d* of demons .... 1 Tim 4:1
various and strange *d* ..... Heb 13:9

DOEG
An Edomite; chief of Saul's herdsmen, 1 Sam 21:7
Betrays David, 1 Sam 22:9, 10
Kills 85 priests, 1 Sam 22:18, 19

DOERS
of God, but the *d* .... Rom 2:13
But be *d* of the word ..... James 1:22

DOG
to David, "Am I a *d* ...... 1 Sam 17:43
they growl like a *d* .... Ps 59:6
d returns to his own .... Prov 26:11
d is better than a .... Eccl 9:4
d returns to his own .... 2 Pet 2:22

DOGS
you shall throw it to the *d* ... Ex 22:31
The *d* shall eat whoever .. 1 Kin 14:11
The *d* shall eat Jezebel .... 2 Kin 9:10
Yes, they are greedy *d* .... Is 56:11
what is holy to the *d* .... Matt 7:6
d eat the crumbs which .... Matt 15:27
Moreover the *d* came ...... Luke 16:21
But outside are *d* .... Rev 22:15

DOMINION
let them have *d* .... Gen 1:26
"*D* and fear belong .... Job 25:2
made him to have *d* .... Ps 8:6
let them not have *d* .... Ps 19:13
besides You have had *d* ...... Is 26:13
d is an everlasting .... Dan 4:34
sin shall not have *d* .... Rom 6:14
Not that we have *d* .... 2 Cor 1:24
glory and majesty, *d* .... Jude 25

DONKEY
d saw the Angel ... Num 22:23
Does the wild *d* ... Job 6:5
d its master's crib ... Is 1:3
and riding on a *d* ... Zech 9:9
colt, the foal of a *d* ... Matt 21:5
He had found a young *d* .. John 12:14
d speaking with a ... 2 Pet 2:16

DONKEY'S
d colt is born a man ... Job 11:12

DONKEYS
d quench their thirst ... Ps 104:11
a chariot of *d* ... Is 21:7
And the wild *d* stood ... Jer 14:6

DOOM
for the day of *d* ... Prov 16:4

DOOR
sin lies at the *d* ... Gen 4:7
keep watch over the *d* ... Ps 141:3
d turns on its hinges ... Prov 26:14
stone against the *d* ... Matt 27:60
to you, I am the *d* ... John 10:7
and effective *d* ... 1 Cor 16:9
d was opened to me by ... 2 Cor 2:12
would open to us a *d* ... Col 4:3
is standing at the *d* ... James 5:9
before you an open *d* ... Rev 3:8
I stand at the *d* ... Rev 3:20
and behold, a *d* ... Rev 4:1

DOORKEEPER
I would rather be a *d* ... Ps 84:10
To him the *d* ... John 10:3

DOORPOSTS
write them on the *d* ... Deut 6:9
"Strike the *d* ... Amos 9:1

DOORS
up, you everlasting *d* ... Ps 24:7
the entrance of the *d* ... Prov 8:3
when the *d* are shut in ... Eccl 12:4
who would shut the *d* ... Mal 1:10

DOR
City captured by Joshua and assigned to Manasseh, Josh 12:23; 17:11; Judg 1:27

DORCAS
Disciple at Joppa, also called Tabitha; raised to life, Acts 9:36–42

DOTHAN
Ancient town where Joseph was sold, Gen 37:14–25
Elisha strikes Syrians at, 2 Kin 6:8–23

DOUBLE
Please let a *d* portion of ... 2 Kin 2:9
from the LORD's hand *d* ... Is 40:2
first I will repay *d* ... Jer 16:18
worthy of *d* honor ... 1 Tim 5:17
and repay her *d* ... Rev 18:6

DOUBLE-MINDED
I hate the *d* ... Ps 119:113
he is a *d* man ... James 1:8
your hearts, you *d* ... James 4:8

DOUBT
life shall hang in *d* ... Deut 28:66
faith, why did you *d* ... Matt 14:31
does not *d* in his heart ... Mark 11:23
No *d* this man is a ... Acts 28:4

DOUBTING
without wrath and *d* ... 1 Tim 2:8
in faith, with no *d* ... James 1:6

DOUBTS
And why do *d* arise in ... Luke 24:38
for I have *d* about you ... Gal 4:20
doubting, for he who *d* ... James 1:6

DOUGH
d before it was leavened, ... Ex 12:34

DOVE
d found no resting ... Gen 8:9
I had wings like a *d* ... Ps 55:6
I mourned like a *d* ... Is 38:14
also is like a silly *d* ... Hos 7:11
descending like a *d* ... Matt 3:16

DOVES
and moan sadly like *d* ... Is 59:11
and harmless as *d* ... Matt 10:16
of those who sold *d* ... Matt 21:12

DOWNCAST
who comforts the *d* ... 2 Cor 7:6

DRAGNET
gather them in their *d* ... Hab 1:15
d that was cast ... Matt 13:47

DRAGON
a great, fiery red *d* ... Rev 12:3
fought with the *d* ... Rev 12:7
they worshiped the *d* ... Rev 13:4
He laid hold of the *d* ... Rev 20:2

DRAIN
wicked of the earth *d* ... Ps 75:8

DRAINED
all faces are *d* ... Joel 2:6

DRANK
them, and they all *d* ... Mark 14:23
d with Him after He ... Acts 10:41
d the same spiritual ... 1 Cor 10:4

DRAW
d honey from the rock ... Deut 32:13
me to *d* near to God ... Ps 73:28
and the years *d* ... Eccl 12:1
D me away ... Song 1:4
Woe to those who *d* ... Is 5:18
with joy you will *d* ... Is 12:3
"*D* some out now ... John 2:8
You have nothing to *d* ... John 4:11
will *d* all peoples ... John 12:32
let us *d* near with a ... Heb 10:22
who *d* back to perdition ... Heb 10:39
D near to God and He ... James 4:8

DRAWN
The wicked have *d* ... Ps 37:14
tempted when he is *d* ... James 1:14

DRAWS
and my life *d* near to ... Ps 88:3
your redemption *d* ... Luke 21:28
the Father who sent Me *d* .. John 6:44
but if anyone *d* back ... Heb 10:38

DREAD
fear of you and the *d* ... Gen 9:2
begin to put the *d* ... Deut 2:25

DREADFUL
of the great and *d* ... Mal 4:5

DREAM
Now Joseph had a *d* ... Gen 37:5
We each have had a *d* ... Gen 40:8
I speak to him in a *d* ... Num 12:6
will fly away like a *d* ... Job 20:8
As a *d* when one awakes ... Ps 73:20
like those who *d* ... Ps 126:1
For a *d* comes through ... Eccl 5:3
her, shall be as a *d* ... Is 29:7
prophet who has a *d* ... Jer 23:28
do not let the *d* ... Dan 4:19
your old men shall *d* ... Joel 2:28
to Joseph in a *d* ... Matt 2:13
things today in a *d* ... Matt 27:19
your old men shall *d* ... Acts 2:17

DREAMERS
d defile the flesh ... Jude 8

DREAMS
in the multitude of *d* ... Eccl 5:7
when a hungry man *d* ... Is 29:8
Nebuchadnezzar had *d* ... Dan 2:1

DREGS
d shall all the wicked ... Ps 75:8
has settled on his *d* ... Jer 48:11

DREW
and *d* for all his camels ... Gen 24:20
Because I *d* him out of ... Ex 2:10
d me out of many waters ... Ps 18:16
and *d* his sword, struck ... Matt 26:51

DRIED
My strength is *d* ... Ps 22:15
of her blood was *d* ... Mark 5:29
saw the fig tree *d* ... Mark 11:20
and its water was *d* ... Rev 16:12

DRIFT
have heard, lest we *d* ... Heb 2:1

DRINK
"What shall we *d* ... Ex 15:24
"Do not *d* wine or ... Lev 10:9
and let him *d* of the ... Job 21:20
gave me vinegar to *d* ... Ps 69:21
D water from your own ... Prov 5:15
mocker, strong *d* ... Prov 20:1
lest they *d* and forget ... Prov 31:5
Give strong *d* to him ... Prov 31:6
Let him *d* and forget ... Prov 31:7
d your wine with a ... Eccl 9:7
follow intoxicating *d* ... Is 5:11
mixing intoxicating *d* ... Is 5:22
d the milk of the ... Is 60:16
My servants shall *d* ... Is 65:13
bosom, that you may *d* ... Is 66:11
d water by measure ... Ezek 4:11
"Bring wine, let us *d* ... Amos 4:1
to you of wine and *d* ... Mic 2:11
and you gave Me no *d* ... Matt 25:42
that day when I *d* ... Matt 26:29
mingled with gall to *d* ... Matt 27:34
with myrrh to *d* ... Mark 15:23
to her, "Give Me a *d* ... John 4:7
him come to Me and *d* ... John 7:37
d wine nor do anything ... Rom 14:21
do, as often as you *d* ... 1 Cor 11:25
all been made to *d* ... 1 Cor 12:13
No longer *d* only water ... 1 Tim 5:23
has made all nations *d* ... Rev 14:8

DRINKS
to her, "Whoever *d* ... John 4:13
d My blood has eternal ... John 6:54
For he who eats and *d* ... 1 Cor 11:29
For the earth which *d* ... Heb 6:7

DRIP
immoral woman *d* honey ... Prov 5:3
d as the honeycomb ... Song 4:11
shall *d* with new wine, the .. Joel 3:18

DRIPPED
my hands *d* with myrrh, ... Song 5:5

DRIPPING
wife are a continual *d* ... Prov 19:13
His lips are lilies, *d* ... Song 5:13

DRIVE
Little by little I will *d* ... Ex 23:30
then you shall *d* out all ... Num 33:52
not utterly *d* them out ... Josh 17:13
but they could not *d* out ... Judg 1:19
of the wicked *d* ... Ps 36:11
so *d* them away ... Ps 68:2
will *d* it far from him ... Prov 22:15
They shall *d* you from ... Dan 4:25
I will *d* them from My ... Hos 9:15
temple and began to *d* ... Mark 11:15

DRIVEN
They were *d* out from ... Job 30:5
Let them be *d* backward ... Ps 40:14
sail and so were *d* ... Acts 27:17
a wave of the sea *d* ... James 1:6

DROP
They *d* on the pastures ... Ps 65:12
the nations are as a *d* ... Is 40:15

DROSS
of the earth like *d* ... Ps 119:119
Take away the *d* ... Prov 25:4
purge away your *d* ... Is 1:25
of Israel has become *d* ... Ezek 22:18

DROUGHT
through a land of *d* .... Jer 2:6
in the year of *d* .... Jer 17:8
For I called for a *d* .... Hag 1:11

DROVE
So He *d* out the man .... Gen 3:24
temple of God and *d* ...... Matt 21:12
a whip of cords, He *d* ...... John 2:15

DROWN
nor can the floods *d* .... Song 8:7
harmful lusts which *d* ...... 1 Tim 6:9

DROWSINESS
d will clothe a .... Prov 23:21

DRUNK
of the wine and was *d* ...... Gen 9:21
d my wine with my milk .... Song 5:1
you afflicted, and *d* .... Is 51:21
My anger, made them *d* .... Is 63:6
be satiated and made *d* ..... Jer 46:10
the guests have well *d* ...... John 2:10
For these are not *d* .... Acts 2:15
and another is *d* .... 1 Cor 11:21
And do not be *d* .... Eph 5:18
and those who get *d* ...... 1 Thess 5:7
the earth were made *d* .... Rev 17:2
I saw the woman, *d* .... Rev 17:6

DRUNKARD
d could be included .... Deut 29:19
d is a proverb in the .... Prov 26:9
to and fro like a *d* .... Is 24:20
or a reviler, or a *d* .... 1 Cor 5:11

DRUNKEN
I am like a *d* man .... Jer 23:9

DRUNKENNESS
will be filled with *d* .... Ezek 23:33
Jerusalem a cup of *d* .... Zech 12:2
with carousing, *d* .... Luke 21:34
not in revelry and *d* .... Rom 13:13
envy, murders, *d* .... Gal 5:21
lusts, *d*, revelries .... 1 Pet 4:3

DRUSILLA
Wife of Felix; hears Paul, Acts 24:24, 25

DRY
place, and let the *d* .... Gen 1:9
made the sea into *d* .... Ex 14:21
It was *d* on the fleece ...... Judg 6:40
I will *d* up her sea .... Jer 51:36
d tree flourish .... Ezek 17:24
will make the rivers *d* .... Ezek 30:12
will be done in the *d* ..... Luke 23:31

DUE
because it is your *d* .... Lev 10:13
their food in *d* season ...... Ps 104:27
pay all that was *d* .... Matt 18:34
d time Christ died .... Rom 5:6
to whom taxes are *d* .... Rom 13:7
d season we shall .... Gal 6:9
exalt you in *d* time .... 1 Pet 5:6

DUG
that I have *d* this well ..... Gen 21:30
father's servants had *d* .... Gen 26:15
in my grave which I *d* for ... Gen 50:5
They have *d* a pit before ..... Ps 57:6
the pit is *d* for the wicked ... Ps 94:13
proud have *d* pits for me ... Ps 119:85
He *d* it up and cleared out ..... Is 5:2
to the Euphrates and *d* ...... Jer 13:7
d a winepress in it and .... Matt 21:33
d in the ground, and hid .. Matt 25:18
who *d* deep and laid .... Luke 6:48

DULL
heart of this people *d* .... Is 6:10
people have grown *d* ..... Matt 13:15
you have become *d* .... Heb 5:11

DUMB
the tongue of the *d* .... Is 35:6
"Deaf and *d* spirit .... Mark 9:25

DUNGHILL
the land nor for the *d* ..... Luke 14:35

DUST
formed man of the *d* .... Gen 2:7
d you shall return .... Gen 3:19
descendants as the *d* ...... Gen 13:16
now, I who am but *d* .... Gen 18:27
"Who can count the *d* .... Num 23:10
lay your gold in the *d* ...... Job 22:24
and repent in *d* .... Job 42:6
Will the *d* praise You .... Ps 30:9
like the whirling *d* .... Ps 83:13
show favor to her *d* .... Ps 102:14
remembers that we are *d* ... Ps 103:14
or the primal *d* .... Prov 8:26
all are from the *d* .... Eccl 3:20
counted as the small *d* .... Is 40:15
They shall lick the *d* .... Mic 7:17
city, shake off the *d* .... Matt 10:14
image of the man of *d* .... 1 Cor 15:49

DUTY
the *d* of a husband's .... Deut 25:5
d of a close relative .... Ruth 3:13
done what was our *d* ..... Luke 17:10

DWELL
O LORD, make me *d* .... Ps 4:8
Who may *d* in Your holy ...... Ps 15:1
He himself shall *d* .... Ps 25:13
d in the land, and feed on .... Ps 37:3
the LORD God might *d* .... Ps 68:18
of my God than *d* .... Ps 84:10
Him, that glory may *d* .... Ps 85:9
Woe is me, that I *d* .... Ps 120:5
better to *d* in a corner ..... Prov 25:24
he will *d* on high .... Is 33:16
into Egypt to *d* there .... Is 52:4
"I *d* in the high and .... Is 57:15
Restorer of Streets to *D* In ... Is 58:12
"They shall no longer *d* .... Lam 4:15
they enter and *d* there .... Matt 12:45
of Judea and all who *d* ..... Acts 2:14
"I will *d* in them .... 2 Cor 6:16
that Christ may *d* .... Eph 3:17
the fullness should *d* .... Col 1:19
the word of Christ *d* .... Col 3:16
men, and He will *d* .... Rev 21:3

DWELLER
fled and became a *d* .... Acts 7:29

DWELLING
A people *d* alone .... Num 23:9
is the way to the *d* .... Job 38:19
built together for a *d* .... Eph 2:22
a foreign country, *d* .... Heb 11:9

DWELLS
He who *d* in the secret .... Ps 91:1
but the Father who *d* ..... John 14:10
do it, but sin that *d* .... Rom 7:17
the Spirit of God *d* .... Rom 8:9
from the dead *d* .... Rom 8:11
the Spirit of God *d* .... 1 Cor 3:16
d all the fullness .... Col 2:9
which righteousness *d* ..... 2 Pet 3:13
you, where Satan *d* .... Rev 2:13

DWELT
Egypt, and Jacob *d* .... Ps 105:23
became flesh and *d* .... John 1:14
By faith he *d* in the .... Heb 11:9

DYING
I do not object to *d* .... Acts 25:11
in the body the *d* .... 2 Cor 4:10
Jacob, when he was *d* ..... Heb 11:21

EAGLE
As an *e* stirs up its .... Deut 32:11
e swooping on its prey ...... Job 9:26
fly away like an *e* .... Prov 23:5
The way of an *e* .... Prov 30:19
nest as high as the *e* .... Jer 49:16
had the face of an *e* .... Ezek 1:10
like a flying *e* .... Rev 4:7
two wings of a great *e* ..... Rev 12:14

EAGLES
up with wings like *e* .... Is 40:31
are swifter than *e* .... Jer 4:13
e will be gathered .... Matt 24:28

EAGLES'
how I bore you on *e* .... Ex 19:4

EAR
shall pierce his *e* .... Ex 21:6
Does not the *e* test .... Job 12:11
Bow down Your *e* .... Ps 31:2
And the *e* of the wise ...... Prov 18:15
He awakens My *e* .... Is 50:4
e is uncircumcised .... Jer 6:10
what you hear in the *e* .... Matt 10:27
cut off his right *e* .... John 18:10
not seen, nor *e* heard .... 1 Cor 2:9
if the *e* should say .... 1 Cor 12:16
He who has an *e* .... Rev 2:7

EARLY
Very *e* in the morning ..... Mark 16:2
arrived at the tomb *e* ..... Luke 24:22

EARNEST
must give the more *e* .... Heb 2:1

EARNESTLY
if you *e* obey My .... Deut 11:13
He prayed more *e* .... Luke 22:44
in this we groan, *e* .... 2 Cor 5:2
e that it would not .... James 5:17
you to contend *e* .... Jude 3

EARS
both his *e* will tingle ..... 2 Kin 21:12
Whoever shuts his *e* ...... Prov 21:13
And hear with their *e* .... Is 6:10
He who has *e* .... Matt 11:15
e are hard of hearing ..... Matt 13:15
they have itching *e* .... 2 Tim 4:3
e are open to their .... 1 Pet 3:12

EARS TO HEAR
eyes to see and *e*, ... Deut 29:4
e but does not hear .... Ezek 12:2
He who has *e*, ... Matt 11:15
He who has *e* .... Matt 13:9
He who has *e*, ... Matt 13:43
"He who has *e*, ... Mark 4:9
If anyone has *e*, ... Mark 4:23
If anyone has *e*, ... Mark 7:16
"He who has *e*, ... Luke 8:8
He who has *e*, ... Luke 14:35

EARTH
See ALL THE EARTH; HEAVEN AND EARTH

The *e* was without form ..... Gen 1:2
God called the dry land *E* ... Gen 1:10
caused it to rain on the *e* ...... Gen 2:5
The *e* also was corrupt ...... Gen 6:11
a wind to pass over the *e* .... Gen 8:1
and multiply, and fill the *e* ... Gen 9:1
the whole *e* was populated .. Gen 9:19
and struck the dust of the *e* .. Ex 8:17
the *e* is the LORD'S .... Ex 9:29
the *e* swallowed them .... Ex 15:12
"Lest the *e* swallow us .... Num 16:34
or that is in the *e* beneath ... Deut 5:8
e which is under you ..... Deut 28:23
e to witness against .... Deut 31:28
fell to the *e* on his face ...... Josh 7:6
the *e* trembled .... Judg 5:4
e ares .... the LORD' 1 Sam 2:8
the *e* .... 1 quaked .. Sam 14:15
"I gof all the *e* .. the way o . 1 Kin 2:2
the eed .... was divid 1 Chr 1:19
to th the *e* ..... le LORD, all Chr 16:23
comi the *e* .... lng to judg Chr 16:33

service for man on *e* . . . . Job 7:1
He hangs the *e* on . . . . Job 26:7
foundations of the *e* . . . . Job 38:4
tried in a furnace of *e* . . . . Ps 12:6
e is the LORD's . . . . Ps 24:1
the shields of the *e* . . . . Ps 47:9
You visit the *e* . . . . Ps 65:9
You had formed the *e* . . . . Ps 90:2
let the *e* be moved . . . . Ps 99:1
glory is above the *e* . . . . Ps 148:13
wisdom founded the *e* . . . . . Prov 3:19
there was ever an *e* . . . . Prov 8:23
For three things the *e* . . . . . Prov 30:21
e abides forever . . . . Eccl 1:4
heaven, and you on *e* . . . . Eccl 5:2
the fruit of the *e* . . . . Is 4:2
for the meek of the *e* . . . . Is 11:4
the *e* shall be full of . . . . Is 11:9
curse has devoured the *e* . . . . . Is 24:6
a dark place of the *e* . . . . Is 45:19
the foundations of the *e* . . . . . . Is 51:16
are higher than the *e* . . . . Is 55:9
e is My footstool . . . . Is 66:1
new *e* which I will make . . . . . Is 66:22
O *e*, *e*, *e*, hear the word . . . . . Jer 22:29
lifted me up between *e* . . . . . . Ezek 8:3
and the *e* shone with . . . . Ezek 43:2
a tree in the midst of the *e* . . Dan 4:10
in heaven and on *e* . . . . Dan 6:27
The *e* shall answer . . . . Hos 2:22
I will darken the *e* . . . . Amos 8:9
e will be filled . . . . Hab 2:14
Let all the *e* keep silence . . . . Hab 2:20
shall inherit the *e* . . . . Matt 5:5
heaven and *e* pass away . . . . Matt 5:18
e as it is in heaven . . . . Matt 6:10
treasures on *e*, where . . . . Matt 6:19
whatever you bind on *e* . . . Matt 18:18
of the *e* will mourn . . . . Matt 24:30
Me in heaven and on *e* . . . . Matt 28:18
all the seeds on *e* . . . . Mark 4:31
and *e* will pass away . . . . . Mark 13:31
on *e* peace, goodwill . . . . Luke 2:14
power on *e* to forgive . . . . Luke 5:24
find faith on the *e* . . . . Luke 18:8
e is My footstool . . . . Acts 7:49
then shook the *e* . . . . Heb 12:26
e which are now . . . . 2 Pet 3:7
heavens and a new *e* . . . . 2 Pet 3:13
all the tribes of the *e* . . . . Rev 1:7
"Do not harm the *e* . . . . Rev 7:3
he was cast to the *e* . . . . Rev 12:9
the *e* helped the woman . . . . . . Rev 12:16
on the *e* will worship him . . . . Rev 13:8
and the *e* was reaped . . . . . . Rev 14:16
the *e* was illuminated . . . . Rev 18:1
from whose face the *e* . . . . . Rev 20:11
new heaven and a new *e* . . . . . Rev 21:1

EARTHEN
holy water in an *e* vessel . . . Num 5:17
a potter's *e* flask . . . . Jer 19:1
treasure in *e* vessels . . . . 2 Cor 4:7

EARTHLY
If I have told you *e* . . . . John 3:12
that if our *e* house . . . . 2 Cor 5:1
their mind on *e* things . . . . Phil 3:19
from above, but is *e* . . . . James 3:15

EARTHQUAKE
LORD was not in the *e* . . . . 1 Kin 19:11
as you fled from the *e* . . . . . Zech 14:5
there was a great *e* . . . . Matt 28:2
there was a great *e* . . . . Acts 16:26
there was a great *e* . . . . Rev 6:12
e as had not occurred . . . . . . Rev 16:18

EARTHQUAKES
And there will be *e* . . . . Mark 13:8

EASE
I was at *e*, but He has . . . . . . Job 16:12
you women who are at *e* . . . . . . Is 32:9
to you who are at *e* . . . . Amos 6:1

take your *e*; eat, drink . . . . Luke 12:19

EASIER
Which is *e*, to say . . . . Mark 2:9
It is *e* for a camel . . . . Mark 10:25
e for heaven and earth . . . . . Luke 16:17

EAST
goes toward the *e* . . . . Gen 2:14
e of the garden of Eden . . . . . Gen 3:24
the LORD brought an *e* . . . . . . Ex 10:13
e wind scattered . . . . Job 38:24
As far as the *e* . . . . Ps 103:12
descendants from the *e* . . . . Is 43:5
wise men from the *E* . . . . Matt 2:1
many will come from *e* . . . . . Matt 8:11
will come from the *e* . . . . . Luke 13:29
e might be prepared . . . . Rev 16:12

EASTWARD
planted a garden *e* in Eden . . . Gen 2:8

EASY
My yoke is *e* and My . . . . . Matt 11:30

EAT
you may freely *e* . . . . Gen 2:16
e dust all the days . . . . Gen 3:14
'You shall not *e* . . . . Gen 3:17
you shall *e* the herb . . . . Gen 3:18
e of my game . . . . Gen 27:19
brethren to *e* bread . . . . Gen 31:54
you shall *e* it in haste . . . . Ex 12:11
No foreigner shall *e* it . . . . . . Ex 12:43
may not *e* the life . . . . Deut 12:23
dogs shall *e* Jezebel . . . . 2 Kin 9:10
my people as they *e* . . . . Ps 53:4
love it will *e* its fruit . . . . . . Prov 18:21
E only as much as you . . . . Prov 25:16
good to *e* much honey . . . . . Prov 25:27
e your bread with joy . . . . Eccl 9:7
Curds and honey He shall *e* . . . . Is 7:15
You shall *e* this year such . . . Is 37:30
lion shall *e* straw . . . . Is 65:25
e this scroll . . . . Ezek 3:1
on your couches, *e* . . . . Amos 6:4
e the flesh of My . . . . Mic 3:3
life, what you will *e* . . . . Matt 6:25
even the little dogs *e* . . . . . . Matt 15:27
You to *e* the Passover . . . . . Matt 26:17
I may *e* the Passover . . . . . Mark 14:14
e; this is My body . . . . Mark 14:22
what you will *e* . . . . Luke 12:22
food to *e* of which you . . . . . . John 4:32
give us His flesh to *e* . . . . John 6:52
"Rise, Peter; kill and *e*." . . . Acts 10:13
e nor drink till they have . . . Acts 23:21
one believes he may *e* . . . . . . Rom 14:2
e meat nor drink wine . . . . . Rom 14:21
I will never again *e* . . . . 1 Cor 8:13
e whatever is set . . . . 1 Cor 10:27
e; this is My body . . . . 1 Cor 11:24
neither shall he *e* . . . . 2 Thess 3:10
have no right to *e* . . . . Heb 13:10
e your flesh like fire . . . . James 5:3
"Take and *e* it . . . . Rev 10:9

EATEN
Have you *e* from the . . . . Gen 3:11
It shall be *e* the same day . . . Lev 19:6
Your house has *e* me up . . . . . . Ps 69:9
e my honeycomb with my . . . Song 5:1
bad figs which cannot be *e* . . Jer 24:8
e the fruit of lies . . . . Hos 10:13
And he was *e* by worms . . Acts 12:23

EATING
by *e* with the blood . . . . 1 Sam 14:33
sons and daughters were *e* . . Job 1:13
e swine's flesh . . . . Is 66:17
neither *e* nor drinking . . . . Matt 11:18
the flood, they were *e* . . . . . Matt 24:38
as they were *e*, He said . . . Matt 26:21
Pharisees saw Him *e* . . . . . . Mark 2:16
in the same house, *e* . . . . Luke 10:7
e in an idol's temple . . . . 1 Cor 8:10

in *e*, each one takes . . . . . . 1 Cor 11:21

EATS
The righteous *e* . . . . Prov 13:25
receives sinners and *e* . . . . . Luke 15:2
Whoever *e* My flesh . . . . John 6:54
e this bread will live . . . . John 6:58
e despise him who does . . . . Rom 14:3
He who *e*, *e* to the . . . . Rom 14:6
an unworthy manner *e* . . . 1 Cor 11:29

EBAL
Mountain in Samaria, Deut 27:12, 13
Stones of the Law erected upon, Deut 27:1–8; Josh 8:30–35

EBED-MELECH
Ethiopian eunuch; rescues Jeremiah, Jer 38:7–13
Promised divine protection, Jer 39:15–18

EBENEZER
Site of Israel's defeat, 1 Sam 4:1–10
Ark transferred from, 1 Sam 5:1
Site of memorial stone, 1 Sam 7:10, 12

EBER
Great-grandson of Shem, Gen 10:21–24; 1 Chr 1:25
Progenitor of the:
Hebrews, Gen 11:16–26
Arabians and Arameans, Gen 10:25–30
Ancestor of Christ, Luke 3:35

EDEN
First home of mankind, Gen 2:8–15
Zion becomes like, Is 51:3
Called the "garden of God," Ezek 28:13

EDIFICATION
his good, leading to *e* . . . . . . Rom 15:2
prophesies speaks *e* . . . . . . 1 Cor 14:3
things be done for *e* . . . . . . 1 Cor 14:26
the Lord gave us for *e* . . . . . 2 Cor 10:8
has given me for *e* . . . . 2 Cor 13:10
rather than godly *e* . . . . 1 Tim 1:4

EDIFIES
puffs up, but love *e* . . . . 1 Cor 8:1
he who prophesies *e* . . . . . . 1 Cor 14:4

EDIFY
but not all things *e* . . . . 1 Cor 10:23
and *e* one another . . . . 1 Thess 5:11

EDIFYING
of the body for the *e* . . . . Eph 4:16

EDOM
Name given to Esau, Gen 25:30
—— Land of Esau; called Seir, Gen 32:3
Called Edom and Idumea, Mark 3:8
People of, cursed, Is 34:5, 6

EDOMITES
Descendants of Esau, Gen 36:9
Refuse passage to Israel, Num 20:18–20
Hostile to Israel, Gen 27:40; 1 Sam 14:47; 2 Chr 20:10; Ps 137:7
Prophecies concerning, Gen 27:37; Is 34:5–17; Ezek 25:12–14; 35:5–7; Amos 9:11, 12

EDREI
Capital of Bashan, Deut 3:10
Site of Og's defeat, Num 21:33–35

EFFECT
of the peoples of no *e* . . . . Ps 33:10
of no *e* by your tradition . . . Matt 15:6
promise made of no *e* . . . . Rom 4:14
make the promise of no *e* . . . . Gal 3:17

EFFECTIVELY
for He who worked *e* . . . . Gal 2:8
e works in you who . . . . . 1 Thess 2:13

EGG
in the white of an *e* . . . . Job 6:6

Or if he asks for an *e* ..... Luke 11:12

EGLON
City of Judah, Josh 15:39

EGYPT
Abram visits, Gen 12:10
Joseph sold into, Gen 37:28, 36
Joseph becomes leader in, Gen 39:1–4
Hebrews move to, Gen 46:5–7
Hebrews persecuted in, Ex 1:15–22
Plagues on, Ex 7—11
Israel leaves, Ex 12:31–33
Army of, perishes, Ex 14:26–28
Prophecies concerning, Gen 15:13; Is 19:18–25; Ezek 29:14, 15; 30:24, 25; Matt 2:15

EHUD
Son of Gera, Judg 3:15
Slays Eglon, Judg 3:16–26

EIGHT
Isaac when he was *e* days .. Gen 21:4
Jesse, and who had *e* .... 1 Sam 17:12
Josiah was *e* years old .... 2 Kin 22:1
e days were completed .... Luke 2:21
about *e* days after these .... Luke 9:28
bedridden *e* years .... Acts 9:33
a few, that is, *e* .... 1 Pet 3:20
saved Noah, one of *e* .... 2 Pet 2:5

EIGHTH
shall sow in the *e* year ..... Lev 25:22
So it was, on the *e* day .... Luke 1:59
circumcised the *e* day, of ..... Phil 3:5

EIGHTY
Moses was *e* years old .... Ex 7:7
land had rest for *e* years .... Judg 3:30
I am today *e* years old ... 2 Sam 19:35
with him were *e* priests .. 2 Chr 26:17
strength they are *e* years .... Ps 90:10
your bill, and write *e* ...... Luke 16:7

EKRON
Philistine city, Josh 13:3
Captured by Judah, Judg 1:18
Assigned to Dan, Josh 19:40, 43
Ark sent to, 1 Sam 5:10
Denounced by the prophets, Jer 25:9, 20

EL BETHEL
Site of Jacob's altar, Gen 35:6, 7

ELAH
King of Israel, 1 Kin 16:6, 8–10

ELAMITES
Descendants of Shem, Gen 10:22
Destruction of, Jer 49:34–39
In Persian Empire, Ezra 4:9
Jews from, at Pentecost, Acts 2:9

ELATH
Seaport on Red Sea, 1 Kin 9:26
Built by Azariah, 2 Kin 14:21, 22
Captured by Syrians, 2 Kin 16:6
Same as Ezion Geber, 2 Chr 8:17

ELDER
clothes of her *e* son Esau .. Gen 27:15
The *e* and honorable .... Is 9:15
against an *e* except .... 1 Tim 5:19
I who am a fellow *e* .... 1 Pet 5:1
The *E*, To the elect lady ..... 2 John 1
The *E*, To the beloved .... 3 John 1

ELDERS
See TWENTY-FOUR ELDERS
and seventy of the *e* .... Ex 24:1
called for the *e* of Israel ..... Josh 24:1
the advice of the *e* .... 2 Chr 10:13
And teach his *e* .... Ps 105:22
in the company of the *e* .... Ps 107:32
and counsel from the *e* .... Ezek 7:26
the tradition of the *e* .... Matt 15:2
many things from the *e* ... Matt 16:21
e of the people plotted ..... Matt 27:1
be rejected by the *e* .... Luke 9:22
e who had come to Him .. Luke 22:52
the people, the *e* .... Acts 6:12
they had appointed *e* ..... Acts 14:23
e came together to .... Acts 15:6
and called for the *e* .... Acts 20:17
e who rule well be .... 1 Tim 5:17
lacking, and appoint *e* .... Titus 1:5
e obtained a good .... Heb 11:2
Let him call for the *e* ..... James 5:14
e who are among you I ..... 1 Pet 5:1
I saw twenty-four *e* .... Rev 4:4
twenty-four *e* fall down ..... Rev 4:10
the twenty-four *e* fell down .. Rev 5:8

ELDERSHIP
of the hands of the *e* ...... 1 Tim 4:14

ELEAZAR
Son of Aaron; succeeds him as high priest, Ex 6:23, 25; 28:1; Lev 10:6, 7; Num 3:32; 20:25–28; Josh 14:1; 24:33

ELECT
whom I uphold, My *E* .... Is 42:1
and Israel My *e* .... Is 45:4
e shall long enjoy the .... Is 65:22
gather together His *e* ..... Matt 24:31
e have obtained it .... Rom 11:7
e according to the .... 1 Pet 1:2
a chief cornerstone, *e* .... 1 Pet 2:6
e sister greet you .... 2 John 13

ELECTION
e they are beloved .... Rom 11:28
call and *e* sure .... 2 Pet 1:10

ELEMENTS
weak and beggarly *e* .... Gal 4:9
e will melt with .... 2 Pet 3:10

ELEVEN
and his *e* sons .... Gen 32:22
the *e* stars bowed down ..... Gen 37:9
e disciples went away ..... Matt 28:16
and found the *e* .... Luke 24:33
numbered with the *e* .... Acts 1:26

ELI
Officiates in Shiloh, 1 Sam 1:3
Blesses Hannah, 1 Sam 1:12–19
Becomes Samuel's guardian, 1 Sam 1:20–28
Samuel ministers before, 1 Sam 2:11
Sons of, 1 Sam 2:12–17
Rebukes sons, 1 Sam 2:22–25
Rebuked by a man of God, 1 Sam 2:27–36
Instructs Samuel, 1 Sam 3:1–18
Death of, 1 Sam 4:15–18

ELIAB
Brother of David, 1 Sam 16:5–13
Fights in Saul's army, 1 Sam 17:13
Discounts David's worth, 1 Sam 17:28, 29

ELIAKIM
Son of Hilkiah, 2 Kin 18:18
Confers with Rabshakeh, Is 36:4, 11–22
Sent to Isaiah, Is 37:2–5
Becomes type of the Messiah, Is 22:20–25
——— Son of King Josiah, 2 Kin 23:34
Name changed to Jehoiakim, 2 Chr 36:4

ELIASHIB
High priest, Neh 12:10
Rebuilds Sheep Gate, Neh 3:1, 20, 21
Allies with foreigners, Neh 13:4, 5, 28

ELIHU
David's brother, 1 Chr 27:18
Called Eliab, 1 Sam 16:6
——— One who reproved Job and his friends, Job 32:2, 4–6

ELIJAH
Denounces Ahab; goes into hiding; fed by ravens, 1 Kin 17:1–7
Dwells with widow; performs miracles for her, 1 Kin 17:8–24
Sends message to Ahab; overthrows prophets of Baal, 1 Kin 18:1–40
Brings rain, 1 Kin 18:41–45
Flees from Jezebel; fed by angels, 1 Kin 19:1–8
Receives revelation from God, 1 Kin 19:9–18
Condemns Ahab, 1 Kin 21:15–29
Condemns Ahaziah; fire consumes troops sent against him, 2 Kin 1:1–16
Taken up to heaven, 2 Kin 2:1–15
Appears with Christ in transfiguration, Matt 17:1–4
Type of John the Baptist, Mal 4:5, 6; Luke 1:17

ELIMELECH
Naomi's husband, Ruth 1:1–3; 2:1, 3; 4:3–9

ELIPHAZ
One of Job's friends, Job 2:11
Rebukes Job, Job 4:1, 5
Is forgiven, Job 42:7–9

ELISHA
Chosen as Elijah's successor; follows him, 1 Kin 19:16–21
Witnesses Elijah's translation; receives his spirit and mantle, 2 Kin 2:1–18
Performs miracles, 2 Kin 2:19–25; 4:1—6:23
Prophesies victory over Moab; fulfilled, 2 Kin 3:11–27
Prophesies end of siege; fulfilled, 2 Kin 7
Prophesies death of Ben-Hadad, 2 Kin 8:7–15
Sends servant to anoint Jehu, 2 Kin 9:1–3
Last words and death; miracle performed by his bones, 2 Kin 13:14–21

ELIZABETH
Barren wife of Zacharias, Luke 1:5–7
Conceives a son, Luke 1:13, 24, 25
Salutation to Mary, Luke 1:36–45
Mother of John the Baptist, Luke 1:57–60

ELIZAPHAN
Chief of Kohathites, Num 3:30
Heads family, 1 Chr 15:5, 8
Family consecrated, 2 Chr 29:12–16

ELKANAH
Father of Samuel, 1 Sam 1:1–23
——— Son of Korah, Ex 6:24
Escapes judgment, Num 26:11

ELNATHAN
Father of Nehushta, 2 Kin 24:8
Goes to Egypt, Jer 26:22
Entreats with king, Jer 36:25

ELOQUENT
"O my Lord, I am not *e* ...... Ex 4:10
an *e* man and mighty ..... Acts 18:24

ELYMAS
Arabic name of Bar-Jesus, a false prophet, Acts 13:6–12

EMBALM
to *e* his father .... Gen 50:2

EMBANKMENT
will build an *e* .... Luke 19:43

EMBRACE
you shall *e* a son .... 2 Kin 4:16
a time to *e*, and a time .... Eccl 3:5

EMBRACED
and have *e* other gods ...... 1 Kin 9:9

be *e* in the arms of .... Prov 5:20
e them, and departed to .... Acts 20:1
e them, and confessed ..... Heb 11:13

EMBRACES
his right hand *e* me .... Song 2:6

EMERALD
sardius, a topaz, and an *e* ... Ex 28:17
turquoise, and *e* with ..... Ezek 28:13
chalcedony, the fourth *e* ... Rev 21:19

EMERALDS
for your wares *e* .... Ezek 27:16

EMMAUS
Town near Jerusalem, Luke 24:13–18

EMPTY
And the pit was *e* .... Gen 37:24
appear before Me *e* .... Ex 23:15
e pitchers, and torches ..... Judg 7:16
after *e* things which ...... 1 Sam 12:21
comfort me with *e* words ... Job 21:34
not listen to *e* talk .... Job 35:13
LORD makes the earth *e* .... Is 24:1
trust in *e* words .... Is 59:4
comes, he finds it *e* .... Matt 12:44
He has sent away *e* .... Luke 1:53
you with *e* words .... Eph 5:6

EMPTY-HANDED
sent me away *e* .... Gen 31:42
appear before Me *e* .... Ex 34:20
'Do not go *e* to your .... Ruth 3:17
and sent him away *e* ...... Mark 12:3

EMPTY-HEADED
e man will be wise .... Job 11:12

EN DOR
Town of Manasseh which was the home of the witch whom Saul consulted, Josh 17:11; 1 Sam 28:1–10; Ps 83:9, 10

EN GEDI
Occupied by the Amorites, Gen 14:7
Assigned to Judah, Josh 15:62, 63
David's hiding place, 1 Sam 23:29
Noted for vineyards, Song 1:14

EN HAKKORE
Miraculous spring, Judg 15:14–19

EN ROGEL
Fountain outside Jerusalem, 2 Sam 17:17
Seat of Adonijah's plot, 1 Kin 1:5–9

ENABLED
our Lord who has *e* .... 1 Tim 1:12

ENCHANTER
and the expert *e* .... Is 3:3

ENCOURAGE
e him and strengthen him .. Deut 3:28
e you concerning your .... 1 Thess 3:2

ENCOURAGED
is, that I may be *e* .... Rom 1:12
and all may be *e* .... 1 Cor 14:31
their hearts may be *e* .... Col 2:2

ENCOURAGEMENT
Hezekiah gave *e* to .... 2 Chr 30:22
translated Son of *E*) .... Acts 4:36
they rejoiced over its *e* .... Acts 15:31

END
at the *e* of forty days .... Gen 8:6
one cherub at one *e* .... Ex 25:19
at the *e* of forty days ...... Deut 9:11
the *e* of every seven years .. Deut 15:1
made an *e* of dividing ..... Josh 19:51
yet your latter *e* .... Job 8:7
Man puts an *e* to darkness .. Job 28:3
from one *e* of heaven .... Ps 19:6
make me to know my *e* .... Ps 39:4
Your years will have no *e* .. Ps 102:27
shall keep it to the *e* ...... Ps 119:33
e is the way of death .... Prov 14:12
not be blessed at the *e* .... Prov 20:21
There was no *e* of all .... Eccl 4:16
The *e* of a thing is better ..... Eccl 7:8
and peace there will be no *e* ..... Is 9:7
Declaring the *e* .... Is 46:10
Our *e* was near .... Lam 4:18
whose iniquity shall *e* ..... Ezek 21:25
shall endure to the *e* .... Dan 6:26
the time of the *e* .... Dan 8:17
until the time of the *e* ...... Dan 11:35
what shall be the *e* .... Dan 12:8
e has come upon my .... Amos 8:2
to the *e* will be saved ..... Matt 10:22
the harvest is the *e* .... Matt 13:39
to pass, but the *e* .... Matt 24:6
always, even to the *e* ...... Matt 28:20
there will be no *e* .... Luke 1:33
He loved them to the *e* ...... John 13:1
to the *e* of the earth .... Acts 1:8
the *e* of those things is ...... Rom 6:21
For Christ is the *e* .... Rom 10:4
the hope firm to the *e* .... Heb 3:6
steadfast to the *e* .... Heb 3:14
but now, once at the *e* .... Heb 9:26
of Job and seen the *e* ...... James 5:11
the *e* of your faith .... 1 Pet 1:9
But the *e* of all .... 1 Pet 4:7
what will be the *e* .... 1 Pet 4:17
the latter *e* is worse .... 2 Pet 2:20
My works until the *e* .... Rev 2:26
Beginning and the *E* .... Rev 22:13

ENDEAVORING
e to keep the unity .... Eph 4:3

ENDED
the seventh day God *e* His ... Gen 2:2
that her warfare is *e* .... Is 40:2
is past, the summer is *e* .... Jer 8:20
Jesus had *e* these sayings .. Matt 7:28
had *e* every temptation ..... Luke 4:13
supper being *e*, the devil ... John 13:2

ENDLESS
and *e* genealogies .... 1 Tim 1:4
to the power of an *e* .... Heb 7:16

ENDS
cherubim at the two *e* of ... Ex 25:19
judge the *e* of the earth ... 1 Sam 2:10
looks to the *e* of the earth .. Job 28:24
All the *e* of the world .... Ps 22:27
all the *e* of the earth have ..... Ps 98:3
established all the *e* .... Prov 30:4
Creator of the *e* of the .... Is 40:28
from the *e* of the earth .... Is 42:10
she came from the *e* ...... Matt 12:42
salvation to the *e* .... Acts 13:47
their words to the *e* .... Rom 10:18

ENDURANCE
For you have need of *e* .... Heb 10:36
run with *e* the race that ..... Heb 12:1

ENDURE
But the LORD shall *e* .... Ps 9:7
weeping may *e* for a night .... Ps 30:5
as the sun and moon *e* .... Ps 72:5
His name shall *e* .... Ps 72:17
heart, Him I will not *e* .... Ps 101:5
glory of the LORD *e* .... Ps 104:31
nor does a crown *e* .... Prov 27:24
Can your heart *e* .... Ezek 22:14
e only for a time .... Mark 4:17
persecuted, we *e* .... 1 Cor 4:12
must *e* hardship .... 2 Tim 2:3
Therefore I *e* all .... 2 Tim 2:10
If you *e* chastening .... Heb 12:7
them blessed who *e* .... James 5:11

ENDURED
what persecutions I *e* .... 2 Tim 3:11
he had patiently *e* .... Heb 6:15
e as seeing Him who .... Heb 11:27
For consider Him who *e* ..... Heb 12:3

ENDURES
See HIS MERCY ENDURES FOREVER

goodness of God *e* .... Ps 52:1
And His truth *e* .... Ps 100:5
his righteousness *e* forever ... Ps 112:3
truth of the LORD *e* forever .. Ps 117:2
For His mercy *e* .... Ps 136:1
But he who *e* to the .... Matt 10:22
e only for a while .... Matt 13:21
for the food which *e* .... John 6:27
he has built on it *e* .... 1 Cor 3:14
hopes all things, *e* .... 1 Cor 13:7
is the man who *e* .... James 1:12
word of the LORD *e* .... 1 Pet 1:25

ENDURING
the LORD is clean, *e* .... Ps 19:9
e possession for .... Heb 10:34

ENEMIES
See LOVE YOUR ENEMIES
an enemy to your *e* .... Ex 23:22
Your *e* be scattered .... Num 10:35
I took you to curse my *e* .. Num 23:11
LORD will cause your *e* ..... Deut 28:7
from the hand of our *e* .. 1 Sam 12:10
your *e* from before you ..... 2 Sam 7:9
be saved from my *e* .... 2 Sam 22:4
Let all my *e* be ashamed ...... Ps 6:10
be saved from my *e* .... Ps 18:3
delivers me from my *e* ...... Ps 18:48
the presence of my *e* .... Ps 23:5
Let not my *e* triumph .... Ps 25:2
But my *e* are vigorous .... Ps 38:19
arise, let His *e* be scattered ... Ps 68:1
e will lick the dust .... Ps 72:9
Your *e* with Your mighty .... Ps 89:10
Your *e* Your footstool .... Ps 110:1
me wiser than my *e* .... Ps 119:98
rescued us from our *e* ...... Ps 136:24
I count them my *e* .... Ps 139:22
makes even his *e* to be ..... Prov 16:7
e are the men of his .... Mic 7:6
darkness will pursue His *e* ... Nah 1:8
to you, love your *e* .... Matt 5:44
a man's *e* will be those .... Matt 10:36
be saved from our *e* .... Luke 1:71
Your *e* Your footstool ...... Luke 20:43
e we were reconciled .... Rom 5:10
the gospel they are *e* ..... Rom 11:28
till He has put all *e* .... 1 Cor 15:25
were alienated and *e* .... Col 1:21
His *e* are made His .... Heb 10:13
and devours their *e* .... Rev 11:5

ENEMY
then I will be an *e* .... Ex 23:22
out the *e* from before ..... Deut 33:27
David's *e* continually ...... 1 Sam 18:29
delivered your *e* into ..... 1 Sam 26:8
Haman, the *e* of the Jews ..... Esth 8:1
regard me as Your *e* .... Job 13:24
He counts me as His *e* ..... Job 33:10
or have plundered my *e* .... Ps 7:4
You may silence the *e* .... Ps 8:2
e does not triumph .... Ps 41:11
e who reproaches me .... Ps 55:12
a strong tower from the *e* ...... Ps 61:3
e has persecuted my .... Ps 143:3
If your *e* is hungry .... Prov 25:21
kisses of an *e* are .... Prov 27:6
the *e* comes in like .... Is 59:19
with the wound of an *e* ..... Jer 30:14
rejoice over me, my *e* .... Mic 7:8
and hate your *e* .... Matt 5:43
The *e* who sowed them ... Matt 13:39
all the power of the *e* ..... Luke 10:19
"If your *e* hungers .... Rom 12:20
last *e* that will be .... 1 Cor 15:26
become your *e* because .... Gal 4:16
not count him as an *e* ... 2 Thess 3:15
makes himself an *e* .... James 4:4

ENGRAVE
two onyx stones and *e* .... Ex 28:9
e its inscription .... Zech 3:9

ENJOY
e its sabbaths as long ...... Lev 26:34
therefore *e* pleasure .... Eccl 2:1
e the good of all his labor .... Eccl 3:13
richly all things to *e* .... 1 Tim 6:17
than to *e* the passing ...... Heb 11:25

ENJOYMENT
So I commended *e* .... Eccl 8:15

ENLARGES
He *e* nations .... Job 12:23
e his desire as hell .... Hab 2:5

ENLIGHTEN
E my eyes, lest I sleep .... Ps 13:3
the LORD my God will *e* ..... Ps 18:28

ENLIGHTENED
those who were once *e* ...... Heb 6:4

ENMITY
And I will put *e* .... Gen 3:15
the carnal mind is *e* .... Rom 8:7
in His flesh the *e* .... Eph 2:15
putting to death the *e* .... Eph 2:16
with the world is *e* .... James 4:4

ENOCH
Father of Methuselah, Gen 5:21
Walks with God, Gen 5:22
Taken up to heaven, Gen 5:24
Prophecy of, cited, Jude 14, 15

ENOUGH
four never say, "*E* .... Prov 30:15
It is *e*! The hour has ..... Mark 14:41
servants have bread *e* .... Luke 15:17

ENRAGED
being exceedingly *e* .... Acts 26:11
And the dragon was *e* ..... Rev 12:17

ENRAPTURED
And always be *e* .... Prov 5:19

ENRICHED
that you were *e* .... 1 Cor 1:5
while you are *e* .... 2 Cor 9:11

ENSNARED
The wicked is *e* .... Prov 12:13

ENSNARES
sin which so easily *e* .... Heb 12:1

ENTANGLE
how they might *e* .... Matt 22:15

ENTANGLES
engaged in warfare *e* .... 2 Tim 2:4

ENTER
'They shall not *e* My rest .... Ps 95:11
E into His gates .... Ps 100:4
Do not *e* into judgment ...... Ps 143:2
E into the rock .... Is 2:10
He shall *e* into peace .... Is 57:2
Jonah began to *e* the city on .. Jon 3:4
you will by no means *e* ..... Matt 5:20
"*E* by the narrow .... Matt 7:13
Lord,' shall *e* the kingdom .. Matt 7:21
city or town you *e* .... Matt 10:11
e into life with one eye ..... Matt 18:9
e the kingdom of God ..... Matt 19:24
E into the joy of your ..... Matt 25:21
and pray, lest you *e* .... Matt 26:41
e a strong man's .... Mark 3:27
child will by no means *e* . Mark 10:15
e the kingdom of God .... Mark 10:24
Whatever house you *e* .... Luke 9:4
"Strive to *e* through .... Luke 13:24
Can he *e* a second time .... John 3:4
cannot *e* the kingdom .... John 3:5
you, he who does not *e* ..... John 10:1
who have believed do *e* ...... Heb 4:3
e the Holiest by the .... Heb 10:19
e the temple till the .... Rev 15:8
e through the gates .... Rev 22:14

ENTERED
day that Noah *e* the ark ... Matt 24:38
went out and *e* the swine .. Mark 5:13
as they *e* the cloud .... Luke 9:34
day that Noah *e* the ark .. Luke 17:27
Then Satan *e* Judas .... Luke 22:3
through one man sin *e* ..... Rom 5:12
ear heard, nor have *e* .... 1 Cor 2:9
he who has *e* His rest .... Heb 4:10
the forerunner has *e* .... Heb 6:20
e the Most Holy Place ...... Heb 9:12

ENTERS
If anyone *e* by Me .... John 10:9
e the Presence behind ...... Heb 6:19

ENTHRONED
You are holy, *e* in .... Ps 22:3
LORD sat *e* at the Flood ...... Ps 29:10

ENTICED
his own desires and *e* .... James 1:14

ENTICING
e speech she caused .... Prov 7:21
e unstable souls .... 2 Pet 2:14

ENTIRELY
give yourself *e* to them .... 1 Tim 4:15

ENTRANCE
The *e* of Your words ...... Ps 119:130
e will be supplied .... 2 Pet 1:11

ENTREAT
"*E* me not to leave you .... Ruth 1:16
"But now *e* God's favor ...... Mal 1:9
being defamed, we *e* .... 1 Cor 4:13

ENTREATED
man of God *e* the LORD .... 1 Kin 13:6
e our God for this .... Ezra 8:23

ENTRUSTED
e with a stewardship ...... 1 Cor 9:17
e with the gospel .... 1 Thess 2:4

ENVIOUS
For I was *e* of the .... Ps 73:3
Do not be *e* of evil .... Prov 24:1
patriarchs, becoming *e* ...... Acts 7:9

ENVY
e slays a simple .... Job 5:2
e the oppressor .... Prov 3:31
e is rottenness .... Prov 14:30
not let your heart *e* .... Prov 23:17
e have now perished .... Eccl 9:6
Him over because of *e* .... Matt 27:18
full of *e*, murder .... Rom 1:29
not in strife and *e* .... Rom 13:13
where there are *e*, strife ..... 1 Cor 3:3
love does not *e* .... 1 Cor 13:4
e, murders, drunkenness .... Gal 5:21
preach Christ even from *e* .. Phil 1:15
living in malice and *e* .... Titus 3:3
For where *e* and .... James 3:16
deceit, hypocrisy, *e* .... 1 Pet 2:1

EPAPHRAS
Leader of the Colossian church, Col 1:7, 8
Suffers as a prisoner in Rome, Philem 23

EPAPHRODITUS
Messenger from Philippi, Phil 2:25–27
Brings a gift to Paul, Phil 4:18

EPHES DAMMIM
Philistine encampment, 1 Sam 17:1
Called Pasdammim, 1 Chr 11:13

EPHESUS
Paul visits, Acts 18:18–21
Miracles done here, Acts 19:11–21
Demetrius stirs up riot in, Acts 19:24–29
Elders of, addressed by Paul at Miletus, Acts 20:17–38
Letter sent to, Eph 1:1
Site of one of seven churches, Rev 1:11

EPHOD
stones to be set in the *e* ...... Ex 25:7
a breastplate, an *e* .... Ex 28:4
made the *e* of gold, blue ..... Ex 39:2
and put the *e* on him .... Lev 8:7
Gideon made it into an *e* ... Judg 8:27
a shrine, and made an *e* .... Judg 17:5
a child, wearing a linen *e* . 1 Sam 2:18
was wearing an *e* .... 1 Sam 14:3
"Bring the *e* here .... 1 Sam 23:9
brought the *e* to David .... 1 Sam 30:7
was wearing a linen *e* .... 2 Sam 6:14

EPHRAIM
Joseph's younger son, Gen 41:52
Obtains Jacob's blessing, Gen 48:8–20
—— Tribe of:
Predictions concerning, Gen 48:20
Territory assigned to, Josh 16:1–10
Assist Deborah, Judg 5:14, 15
Assist Gideon, Judg 7:24, 25
Quarrel with Gideon, Judg 8:1–3
Quarrel with Jephthah, Judg 12:1–4
Leading tribe of kingdom of Israel, Is 7:2–17
Provoke God by sin, Hos 12:7–14
Many of, join Judah, 2 Chr 15:8, 9
Captivity of, predicted, Hos 9:3–17
Messiah promised to, Zech 9:9–13

EPHRATHAH
Ancient name of Bethlehem, Ruth 4:11
Prophecy concerning, Mic 5:2

EPHRON
Hittite who sold Machpelah to Abraham, Gen 23:8–20

EPICUREANS
Sect of pleasure-loving philosophers, Acts 17:18

EPISTLE
You are our *e* written ...... 2 Cor 3:2
you are an *e* .... 2 Cor 3:3
by word or our *e* .... 2 Thess 2:15
our word in this *e* .... 2 Thess 3:14
is a sign in every *e* ...... 2 Thess 3:17

EPISTLES
e of commendation to ...... 2 Cor 3:1
as also in all his *e* .... 2 Pet 3:16

EQUAL
it was you, a man my *e* ...... Ps 55:13
and you made them *e* ..... Matt 20:12
they are *e* to the angels ... Luke 20:36
making Himself *e* .... John 5:18
it robbery to be *e* .... Phil 2:6

EQUALITY
that there may be *e* .... 2 Cor 8:14

EQUITY
You have established *e* .... Ps 99:4
judgment, and *e* .... Prov 1:3
and *e* cannot enter .... Is 59:14
and pervert all *e* .... Mic 3:9
with Me in peace and *e* .... Mal 2:6

ER
Son of Judah, Gen 38:1–7; 46:12

ERASTUS
Paul's friend at Ephesus, Acts 19:21, 22; 2 Tim 4:20
Treasurer of Corinth, Rom 16:23

ERR
you cause you to *e* .... Is 3:12
My people Israel to *e* .... Jer 23:13

ERROR
God that it was an *e* .... Eccl 5:6
utter *e* against the LORD, ... Is 32:6
nor was there any *e* .... Dan 6:4
e which was due .... Rom 1:27
a sinner from the *e* .... James 5:20
led away with the *e* .... 2 Pet 3:17
and the spirit of *e* .... 1 John 4:6
run greedily in the *e* .... Jude 11

ERRORS
can understand his *e* .... Ps 19:12

ESARHADDON
Son of Sennacherib; king of Assyria (681–669 B.C.), 2 Kin 19:36, 37

ESAU
Isaac's favorite son, Gen 25:25–28
Sells his birthright, Gen 25:29–34
Deprived of blessing; seeks to kill Jacob, Gen 27
Reconciled to Jacob, Gen 33:1–17
Descendants of, Gen 36

ESCAPE
E to the mountains ....Gen 19:17
Do not let one of them *e* .. 1 Kin 18:40
and they shall not *e* ....Job 11:20
Shall they *e* by ....Ps 56:7
speaks lies will not *e* ....Prov 19:5
who fears God will *e* ....Eccl 7:18
and how shall we *e* ....Is 20:6
who does such things *e* ....Ezek 17:15
nothing shall *e* them ....Joel 2:3
How can you *e* the ....Matt 23:33
e all these things ....Luke 21:36
same, that you will *e* ....Rom 2:3
also make the way of *e* ... 1 Cor 10:13
And they shall not *e* ...... 1 Thess 5:3
e the snare of the devil .... 2 Tim 2:26
how shall we *e* if we ....Heb 2:3
e who refused Him who ... Heb 12:25

ESCAPED
I alone have *e* to tell ....Job 1:15
my flesh, and I have *e* .....Job 19:20
Our soul has *e* as a ....Ps 124:7
all *e* safely to land ....Acts 27:44
having *e* the corruption .....2 Pet 1:4
after they have *e* ....2 Pet 2:20

ESH-BAAL
Son of Saul, 1 Chr 8:33

ESHCOL
Valley near Hebron, Num 13:22–27; Deut 1:24

ESTABLISH
But I will *e* My covenant ....Gen 6:18
I will *e* the throne of his ..2 Sam 7:13
to *e* them forever............2 Chr 9:8
'Your seed I will *e* ....Ps 89:4
e the work of our ....Ps 90:17
E Your word to Your ......Ps 119:38
e an everlasting ....Ezek 16:60
e justice in the gate ....Amos 5:15
seeking to *e* their own ......Rom 10:3
to Him who is able to *e* ...Rom 16:25
He may *e* your hearts ... 1 Thess 3:13
e you in every good .....2 Thess 2:17
faithful, who will *e* ....2 Thess 3:3
that He may *e* the second ...Heb 10:9
E your hearts ....James 5:8
a while, perfect, *e* ....1 Pet 5:10

ESTABLISHED
He not made you and *e* ....Deut 32:6
also is firmly *e* ....1 Chr 16:30
David my father be *e* ....2 Chr 1:9
e it upon the waters ....Ps 24:2
a rock, and *e* my steps ....Ps 40:2
e a testimony in Jacob ....Ps 78:5
It shall be *e* forever ....Ps 89:37
Your throne is *e* ....Ps 93:2
LORD has *e* His throne .....Ps 103:19
let all your ways be *e* ......Prov 4:26
e the clouds above ....Prov 8:28
lip shall be *e* forever ......Prov 12:19
your thoughts will be *e* ....Prov 16:3
by understanding it is *e* ....Prov 24:3
house shall be *e* ....Is 2:2
In mercy the throne will be *e* ..Is 16:5
by His power, He has *e* .....Jer 10:12
every word may be *e* .....Matt 18:16
built up in Him and *e* ....Col 2:7
covenant, which was *e* ....Heb 8:6
that the heart be *e* ....Heb 13:9

ESTABLISHES
The king *e* the land by .....Prov 29:4
Now He who *e* us with ....2 Cor 1:21

ESTEEM
high wall in his own *e* ....Prov 18:11
and we did not *e* ....Is 53:3
e others better than ....Phil 2:3
and hold such men in *e* ......Phil 2:29
e them very highly ....1 Thess 5:13

ESTEEMED
For what is highly *e* ....Luke 16:15
those who are least *e* ....1 Cor 6:4

ESTEEMS
One person *e* one day ....Rom 14:5

ESTHER
Selected for harem, Esth 2:7–16
Chosen to be queen, Esth 2:17, 18
Agrees to intercede for her people, Esth 4
Invites king to banquet, Esth 5:1–8
Denounces Haman; obtains reversal of decree, Esth 7:1—8:8
Establishes Purim, Esth 9:29–32

ESTRANGED
The wicked are *e* ....Ps 58:3
because they are all *e* ......Ezek 14:5
You have become *e* ....Gal 5:4

ETAM
Rock where Samson took refuge, Judg 15:8–19

ETERNAL
e God is your refuge ......Deut 33:27
For man goes to his *e* ....Eccl 12:5
I do that I may have *e* ....Matt 19:16
and inherit *e* life ....Matt 19:29
the righteous into *e* life ...Matt 25:46
that I may inherit *e* life ...Mark 10:17
in the age to come, *e* .....Mark 10:30
not perish but have *e* ....John 3:15
gathers fruit for *e* life ......John 4:36
you think you have *e* ....John 5:39
drinks My blood has *e* life ..John 6:54
the words of *e* life ....John 6:68
And I give them *e* life .....John 10:28
that He should give *e* ....John 17:2
And this is *e* life ....John 17:3
e life to those who by ......Rom 2:7
righteousness to *e* ....Rom 5:21
the gift of God is *e* ....Rom 6:23
e weight of glory ....2 Cor 4:17
are not seen are *e* ....2 Cor 4:18
not made with hands, *e* ....2 Cor 5:1
to the King *e*, immortal .....1 Tim 1:17
lay hold on *e* life ....1 Tim 6:12
e life which God ....Titus 1:2
to the hope of *e* life ....Titus 3:7
and of *e* judgment ....Heb 6:2
obtained *e* redemption ......Heb 9:12
e life which was ....1 John 1:2
has promised us—*e* life ...1 John 2:25
that no murderer has *e* ...1 John 3:15
God has given us *e* ....1 John 5:11
that you have *e* life ....1 John 5:13
the true God and *e* life ....1 John 5:20
Jesus Christ unto *e* ....Jude 21

ETERNAL LIFE
that I may have *e* ....Matt 19:16
the righteous into *e* ....Matt 25:46
in the age to come, *e* .....Mark 10:30
I do to inherit *e* ....Luke 10:25
not perish but have *e* ....John 3:15
and gathers fruit for *e* ......John 4:36
you think you have *e* ....John 5:39
You have the words of *e* ...John 6:68
will keep it for *e* ....John 12:25
is *e*, that they may know ...John 17:3
had been appointed to *e* ...Acts 13:48
e to those who by patient ...Rom 2:7
righteousness to *e* ....Rom 5:21
the gift of God is *e* ....Rom 6:23
lay hold on *e* ....1 Tim 6:12
in hope of *e* which God.......Titus 1:2
declare to you that *e* ....1 John 1:2
He has promised us *e* .....1 John 2:25
no murderer has *e* ....1 John 3:15
that God has given us *e* ...1 John 5:11
Lord Jesus Christ unto *e* .....Jude 21

ETERNITY
Also He has put *e* ....Eccl 3:11
One who inhabits *e* ....Is 57:15

ETHAM
Israel's encampment, Ex 13:20

ETHIOPIA
See CUSH
Hostile to Israel and Judah, 2 Chr 12:2, 3; 14:9–15; Is 43:3; Dan 11:43
Prophecies against, Is 20:1–6; Ezek 30:4–9

ETHIOPIANS
Skin of, unchangeable, Jer 13:23

EUNICE
Mother of Timothy, 2 Tim 1:5

EUNUCH
eczema or scab, or is a *e* ...Lev 21:20
Hegai the king's *e* ....Esth 2:3
of Ethiopia, a *e* ....Acts 8:27

EUNUCHS
seven *e* who served ....Esth 1:10
be *e* in the palace ....Is 39:7
Ethiopian, one of the *e* ....Jer 38:7
the master of his *e* ....Dan 1:3
have made themselves *e* ..Matt 19:12

EUPHRATES
River of Eden, Gen 2:14
Boundary of Promised Land, Gen 15:18; 1 Kin 4:21, 24
Scene of battle, Jer 46:2, 6, 10
Angels bound there, Rev 9:14

EUTYCHUS
Sleeps during Paul's sermon, Acts 20:9
Restored to life, Acts 20:12

EVANGELIST
house of Philip the *e* ....Acts 21:8
do the work of an *e* ....2 Tim 4:5

EVANGELISTS
some prophets, some *e* ......Eph 4:11

EVEN
E in laughter the heart ....Prov 14:13
E a child is known ....Prov 20:11
e nature itself teach ......1 Cor 11:14
e denying the Lord who .....2 Pet 2:1

EVENING
the *e* and the morning were ..Gen 1:5
quails came up at *e* ....Ex 16:13
At *e* they return ....Ps 59:6
e it is cut down and ....Ps 90:6
of my hands as the *e* ....Ps 141:2
e do not withhold your .....Eccl 11:6
and more fierce than *e* ....Hab 1:8
When it is *e* you say, 'It .....Matt 16:2
when *e* came, the boat .....Mark 6:47
in the *e*, at midnight .....Mark 13:35
it is toward *e* ....Luke 24:29

EVER
shall reign forever and *e* ....Ex 15:18
No razor has *e* come ....Judg 16:17
were the upright *e* cut off .....Job 4:7
Let them *e* shout for joy, ...Ps 5:11
eyes are *e* toward the LORD ..Ps 25:15
He is *e* merciful ....Ps 37:26
Or *e* You had formed ....Ps 90:2
Your name forever and *e* ....Ps 145:1
shines *e* brighter unto ......Prov 4:18
there was *e* an earth ....Prov 8:23
even forever and *e* ....Dan 7:18
time, no, nor *e* shall be ....Matt 24:21
eat fruit from you *e* ....Mark 11:14

all things that I *e* did ...... John 4:29
"No man *e* spoke like ...... John 7:46
be glory forever and *e* .... Gal 1:5
no one *e* hated his own ..... Eph 5:29
the angels has He *e* said .... Heb 1:13
to the Lamb, forever and *e* .. Rev 5:13
shall reign forever and *e* ... Rev 11:15

EVERLASTING

for an *e* covenant .... Gen 17:7
are the *e* arms .... Deut 33:27
God of Israel from *e* ..... 1 Chr 16:36
His mercy is *e* .... Ps 100:5
of the LORD is from *e* .... Ps 103:17
to Israel as an *e* covenant .. Ps 105:10
righteousness is an *e* ..... Ps 119:142
lead me in the way *e* .... Ps 139:24
Your kingdom is an *e* ...... Ps 145:13
E Father, Prince of Peace ...... Is 9:6
in YAH, the LORD, is *e* .... Is 26:4
e joy on their heads .... Is 35:10
I will make an *e* covenant ..... Is 55:3
will be to you an *e* .... Is 60:19
from *E* is Your name .... Is 63:16
loved you with an *e* love ..... Jer 31:3
awake, some to *e* life .... Dan 12:2
cast into the *e* fire .... Matt 18:8
away into *e* punishment .. Matt 25:46
not perish but have *e* ...... John 3:16
springing up into *e* life ..... John 4:14
Him who sent Me has *e* .... John 5:24
endures to *e* life .... John 6:27
in Him may have *e* .... John 6:40
believes in Me has *e* .... John 6:47
unworthy of *e* life .... Acts 13:46
and the end, *e* life .... Rom 6:22
of the Spirit reap *e* .... Gal 6:8
e destruction from the .... 2 Thess 1:9
reserved in *e* chains .... Jude 6

EVERLASTING LIFE

Some to *e*, some to shame .. Dan 12:2
not perish but have *e* ...... John 3:16
springing up into *e* .... John 4:14
e and shall not come .... John 5:24
food which endures to *e* ... John 6:27
His command is *e* .... John 12:50
yourselves unworthy of *e* . Acts 13:46
holiness, and the end, *e* .... Rom 6:22
will of the Spirit reap *e* .... Gal 6:8
to believe on Him for *e* .... 1 Tim 1:16

EVERYONE

said, 'Repent now *e* .... Jer 25:5
e who is born of the .... John 3:8
E who is of the truth ..... John 18:37

EVIDENCE

my *e* is on high .... Job 16:19
e of things not seen .... Heb 11:1

EVIDENT

the sight of God is *e* .... Gal 3:11
of some are clearly *e* ...... 1 Tim 5:25
e that our Lord arose .... Heb 7:14

EVIL

knowledge of good and *e* .... Gen 2:9
knowing good and *e* .... Gen 3:5
his heart was only *e* .... Gen 6:5
repaid *e* for good .... Gen 44:4
e have been the .... Gen 47:9
you meant *e* against me ... Gen 50:20
follow a crowd to do *e* .... Ex 23:2
e in the sight of the .... Num 32:13
the *e* from your midst ...... Deut 13:5
and good, death and *e* .... Deut 30:15
Saul plotted *e* against ..... 1 Sam 23:9
rebellious and *e* city .... Ezra 4:12
feared God and shunned *e* .... Job 1:1
e shall touch you .... Job 5:19
I looked for good, *e* .... Job 30:26
nor shall *e* dwell .... Ps 5:4
Nor does *e* to his neighbor .... Ps 15:3
I will fear no *e* .... Ps 23:4
Keep your tongue from *e* .... Ps 34:13
E shall slay the .... Ps 34:21
he does not abhor *e* .... Ps 36:4
Depart from *e*, and do .... Ps 37:27
done this *e* in Your sight ..... Ps 51:4
e more than good .... Ps 52:3
e shall befall you .... Ps 91:10
love the LORD, hate *e* .... Ps 97:10
not be afraid of *e* tidings .... Ps 112:7
feet from every *e* way .... Ps 119:101
preserve you from all *e* ..... Ps 121:7
secure, without fear of *e* ... Prov 1:33
LORD and depart from *e* ..... Prov 3:7
of the LORD is to hate *e* .... Prov 8:13
To do *e* is like sport .... Prov 10:23
shall be filled with *e* ...... Prov 12:21
e will bow before the ..... Prov 14:19
Keeping watch on the *e* .... Prov 15:3
is to depart from *e* .... Prov 16:17
Whoever rewards *e* .... Prov 17:13
A prudent man forsees *e* ... Prov 22:3
e all the days of her ...... Prov 31:12
vanity and a great *e* .... Eccl 2:21
There is a severe *e* .... Eccl 5:13
of men are full of *e* .... Eccl 9:3
put away *e* from your ..... Eccl 11:10
to those who call *e* .... Is 5:20
his eyes from seeing *e* .... Is 33:15
is taken away from *e* .... Is 57:1
of peace and not of *e* .... Jer 29:11
commit this great *e* .... Jer 44:7
Seek good and not *e* ...... Amos 5:14
turn from his *e* way .... Jon 3:8
"Turn now from your *e* ..... Zech 1:4
not to resist an *e* person ... Matt 5:39
His sun rise on the *e* .... Matt 5:45
deliver us from the *e* .... Matt 6:13
If you then, being *e* .... Matt 7:11
"Why do you think *e* .... Matt 9:4
e treasure brings .... Matt 12:35
"An *e* and adulterous ..... Matt 12:39
to do good or to do *e* .... Mark 3:4
proceed *e* thoughts .... Mark 7:21
what *e* has He done ...... Mark 15:14
to the unthankful and *e* .... Luke 6:35
e treasure of his heart ..... Luke 6:45
If you then, being *e* .... Luke 11:13
everyone practicing *e* ...... John 3:20
them from the *e* one ...... John 17:15
bear witness of the *e* ..... John 18:23
the *e* spirits went out ..... Acts 19:12
'You shall not speak *e* of ... Acts 23:5
e I will not to do .... Rom 7:19
then a law, that *e* .... Rom 7:21
done any good or *e* .... Rom 9:11
Abhor what is *e* .... Rom 12:9
Repay no one *e* for .... Rom 12:17
not be overcome by *e* ..... Rom 12:21
to good works, but to *e* .... Rom 13:3
good be spoken of as *e* .... Rom 14:16
simple concerning *e* ...... Rom 16:19
provoked, thinks no *e* ..... 1 Cor 13:5
"*E* company corrupts ..... 1 Cor 15:33
from this present *e* age .... Gal 1:4
e speaking be put away ..... Eph 4:31
withstand in the *e* day ...... Eph 6:13
from every form of *e* .... 1 Thess 5:22
a root of all kinds of *e* .... 1 Tim 6:10
an *e* heart of unbelief .... Heb 3:12
cannot be tempted by *e* ... James 1:13
speaks *e* of a brother ... James 4:11
envy, and all *e* speaking ..... 1 Pet 2:1
refrain his tongue from *e* .. 1 Pet 3:10
against those who do *e* .... 1 Pet 3:12
he who does *e* has not ..... 3 John 11

EVIL-MERODACH

Babylonian king (562–560 B.C.), 2 Kin 25:27–30

EVIL-MINDEDNESS

strife, deceit, *e* .... Rom 1:29

EVIL ONE

than these is from the *e* .... Matt 5:37
But deliver us from the *e* ... Matt 6:13
But deliver us from the *e* .. Luke 11:4
keep them from the *e* ..... John 17:15
guard you from the *e* ..... 2 Thess 3:3

EVILDOER

LORD shall repay the *e* .... 2 Sam 3:39
An *e* gives heed to false .... Prov 17:4
"If He were not an *e* ...... John 18:30
suffer trouble as an *e* .... 2 Tim 2:9
a thief, an *e* .... 1 Pet 4:15

EVILDOERS

Do not fret because of *e* ...... Ps 37:1
e shall be cut off .... Ps 37:9
Depart from me, you *e* .... Ps 119:115
iniquity, a brood of *e* .... Is 1:4
e shall never be .... Is 14:20
against you as *e* .... 1 Pet 2:12

EVILS

e have surrounded me .... Ps 40:12
have committed two *e* .... Jer 2:13

EXALT

God, and I will *e* .... Ex 15:2
do you *e* yourselves .... Num 16:3
e the horn of His .... 1 Sam 2:10
e His name together .... Ps 34:3
E the LORD our God .... Ps 99:5
Let them *e* Him .... Ps 107:32
are my God, I will *e* .... Ps 118:28
if I do not *e* Jerusalem ...... Ps 137:6
E her, and she will .... Prov 4:8
into heaven, I will *e* .... Is 14:13
I will *e* You, I will praise ...... Is 25:1
E the humble .... Ezek 21:26
and he shall *e* himself ...... Dan 8:25
He may *e* you in due time ... 1 Pet 5:6

EXALTATION

e comes neither from .... Ps 75:6
who rejoice in My *e* .... Is 13:3
brother glory in his *e* ...... James 1:9

EXALTED

Let God be *e* .... 2 Sam 22:47
So the LORD *e* Solomon .. 1 Chr 29:25
built You an *e* house .... 2 Chr 6:2
name, which is *e* .... Neh 9:5
e for a little while .... Job 24:24
God is *e* by His power .... Job 36:22
when vileness is *e* .... Ps 12:8
God of my salvation be *e* .... Ps 18:46
Be *e*, O LORD, in Your .... Ps 21:13
I will be *e* among the .... Ps 46:10
Be *e*, O God, above .... Ps 57:5
righteous shall be *e* .... Ps 75:10
favor our horn is *e* .... Ps 89:17
You are *e* far above .... Ps 97:9
hand of the LORD is *e* .... Ps 118:16
His name alone is *e* .... Ps 148:13
upright the city is *e* ...... Prov 11:11
LORD alone shall be *e* .... Is 2:11
His name is *e* .... Is 12:4
The LORD is *e*, for He dwells .. Is 33:5
valley shall be *e* .... Is 40:4
and humble the *e* .... Ezek 21:26
e above the hills .... Mic 4:1
humbles himself will be *e* . Matt 23:12
Him God has *e* .... Acts 5:31
And lest I should be *e* ..... 2 Cor 12:7
also has highly *e* .... Phil 2:9

EXALTS

down one, and *e* another ..... Ps 75:7
Righteousness *e* .... Prov 14:34
whoever *e* himself will ... Luke 14:11
high thing that *e* .... 2 Cor 10:5
e himself above all .... 2 Thess 2:4

EXAMINE

E me, O LORD .... Ps 26:2
e our ways, and turn .... Lam 3:40
But let a man *e* .... 1 Cor 11:28
But let each one *e* .... Gal 6:4

EXAMPLE
to make her a public *e* ..... Matt 1:19
I have given you an *e* ..... John 13:15
in following my *e* ..... Phil 3:17
to make ourselves an *e* ..... 2 Thess 3:9
youth, but be an *e* ..... 1 Tim 4:12
us, leaving us an *e* ..... 1 Pet 2:21
making them an *e* ..... 2 Pet 2:6
are set forth as an *e* ..... Jude 7

EXAMPLES
happened to them as *e* ..... 1 Cor 10:11
so that you became *e* ..... 1 Thess 1:7
to you, but being *e* ..... 1 Pet 5:3

EXCEEDING
for us a far more *e* ..... 2 Cor 4:17
the *e* greatness of ..... Eph 1:19
He might show the *e* ..... Eph 2:7
also be glad with *e* joy ..... 1 Pet 4:13

EXCEEDINGLY
prevailed *e* on the earth ..... Gen 7:19
your *e* great reward ..... Gen 15:1
your descendants *e* ..... Gen 16:10
and grew *e* mighty ..... Ex 1:7
for the LORD must be *e* ..... 1 Chr 22:5
You have made him *e* ..... Ps 21:6
let them rejoice *e* ..... Ps 68:3
and I love them *e* ..... Ps 119:167
is far off and *e* deep ..... Eccl 7:24
it displeased Jonah *e* ..... Jon 4:1
rejoiced with *e* great joy ..... Matt 2:10
e high mountain ..... Matt 4:8
Rejoice and be *e* ..... Matt 5:12
they were *e* sorrowful ..... Matt 26:22
e white, like snow ..... Mark 9:3
"My soul is *e* sorrowful ..... Mark 14:34
Him who is able to do *e* ..... Eph 3:20
our Lord was *e* abundant ..... 1 Tim 1:14
given to us *e* great ..... 2 Pet 1:4

EXCEEDS
your righteousness *e* ..... Matt 5:20

EXCEL
you His angels, who *e* ..... Ps 103:20
but you *e* them all ..... Prov 31:29
that you seek to *e* ..... 1 Cor 14:12

EXCELLENCE
e You have overthrown ..... Ex 15:7
did not come with *e* ..... 1 Cor 2:1
the *e* of the power ..... 2 Cor 4:7
things loss for the *e* ..... Phil 3:8

EXCELLENT
He is *e* in power ..... Job 37:23
How *e* is Your name in all ..... Ps 8:1
It shall be as *e* oil ..... Ps 141:5
to His *e* greatness ..... Ps 150:2
will speak of *e* things ..... Prov 8:6
An *e* wife is the crown of ..... Prov 12:4
like Lebanon, *e* ..... Song 5:15
for He has done *e* ..... Is 12:5
in counsel and *e* ..... Is 28:29
Inasmuch as an *e* ..... Dan 5:12
the things that are *e* ..... Rom 2:18
show you a more *e* way ..... 1 Cor 12:31
the things that are *e* ..... Phil 1:10
a more *e* name ..... Heb 1:4
e sacrifice than Cain ..... Heb 11:4
came to Him from the *E* ..... 2 Pet 1:17

EXCELS
Do you see a man who *e* ..... Prov 22:29
I saw that wisdom *e* ..... Eccl 2:13
of the glory that *e* ..... 2 Cor 3:10

EXCHANGE
give in *e* for his soul ..... Matt 16:26

EXCHANGED
Nor can it be *e* ..... Job 28:17
e the truth of God for ..... Rom 1:25
For even their women *e* ..... Rom 1:26

EXCLUDE
you, and when they *e* ..... Luke 6:22
they want to *e* you ..... Gal 4:17

EXCUSE
God be angry at your *e* ..... Eccl 5:6
but now they have no *e* ..... John 15:22
they are without *e* ..... Rom 1:20
do you think that we *e* ..... 2 Cor 12:19

EXCUSES
began to make *e* ..... Luke 14:18

EXECUTE
nor *e* His fierce wrath ..... 1 Sam 28:18
e vengeance on the ..... Ps 149:7
if you thoroughly *e* ..... Jer 7:5
E judgment and ..... Jer 22:3
e the fierceness ..... Hos 11:9
'*E* true justice ..... Zech 7:9
e judgment also ..... John 5:27
e wrath on him who ..... Rom 13:4

EXECUTES
by the judgment He *e* ..... Ps 9:16
e righteousness ..... Ps 103:6
e justice for the ..... Ps 146:7
One whose *e* His word ..... Joel 2:11
e justice for me ..... Mic 7:9

EXERCISE
those who are great *e* ..... Matt 20:25
e yourself toward ..... 1 Tim 4:7
e profits a little ..... 1 Tim 4:8

EXERCISED
have their senses *e* ..... Heb 5:14

EXHORT
we command and *e* ..... 2 Thess 3:12
I *e* first of all ..... 1 Tim 2:1
e him as a father ..... 1 Tim 5:1
and *e* these things ..... 1 Tim 6:2
Convince, rebuke, *e* ..... 2 Tim 4:2
doctrine, both to *e* ..... Titus 1:9
e the young men ..... Titus 2:6
Speak these things, *e* ..... Titus 2:15
e one another ..... Heb 3:13

EXHORTATION
you have any word of *e* ..... Acts 13:15
he who exhorts, in *e* ..... Rom 12:8
to reading, to *e* ..... 1 Tim 4:13
with the word of *e* ..... Heb 13:22

EXHORTED
For I earnestly *e* ..... Jer 11:7
e and strengthened ..... Acts 15:32
as you know how we *e* ..... 1 Thess 2:11

EXILE
and also an *e* from ..... 2 Sam 15:19
The captive *e* hastens ..... Is 51:14

EXIST
things which do not *e* ..... Rom 4:17
by Your will they *e* ..... Rev 4:11

EXPECT
an hour you do not *e* ..... Luke 12:40

EXPECTATION
The *e* of the poor ..... Ps 9:18
God alone, for my *e* ..... Ps 62:5
the people were in *e* ..... Luke 3:15
For the earnest *e* ..... Rom 8:19
a certain fearful *e* ..... Heb 10:27

EXPECTING
e to receive something ..... Acts 3:5

EXPEDIENT
e for us that one man ..... John 11:50

EXPERT
and the *e* enchanter ..... Is 3:3
those of an *e* warrior ..... Jer 50:9
because you are *e* ..... Acts 26:3

EXPLAIN
was no one who could *e* ..... Gen 41:24
days they could not *e* ..... Judg 14:14
"*E* this parable to us ..... Matt 15:15
to say, and hard to *e* ..... Heb 5:11

EXPLAINED
He *e* all things to His ..... Mark 4:34
e to him the way of God ..... Acts 18:26

EXPLOIT
e all your laborers ..... Is 58:3
against those who *e* ..... Mal 3:5
they will *e* you with ..... 2 Pet 2:3

EXPOSED
his deeds should be *e* ..... John 3:20
all things that are *e* ..... Eph 5:13

EXPOUNDED
He *e* to them in all ..... Luke 24:27

EXPRESS
man cannot *e* it ..... Eccl 1:8
of His glory and the *e* ..... Heb 1:3

EXPRESSLY
of the LORD came *e* ..... Ezek 1:3
Now the Spirit *e* ..... 1 Tim 4:1

EXTEND
none to *e* mercy to him ..... Ps 109:12
"Behold, I will *e* ..... Is 66:12
did not *e* to you ..... 2 Cor 10:14

EXTINGUISHED
broken, my days are *e* ..... Job 17:1
They are *e*, they are ..... Is 43:17

EXTOL
I will *e* You ..... Ps 30:1
e Him who rides ..... Ps 68:4

EXTOLLED
e with my tongue ..... Ps 66:17
shall be exalted and *e* ..... Is 52:13

EXTORTION
e gathers it for him ..... Prov 28:8
your neighbors by *e* ..... Ezek 22:12
they are full of *e* ..... Matt 23:25

EXTORTIONERS
nor *e* will inherit ..... 1 Cor 6:10

EXULT
in anguish I would *e* ..... Job 6:10

EYE
e for *e*, tooth for tooth ..... Ex 21:24
your *e* be evil against ..... Deut 15:9
the ear, but now my *e* ..... Job 42:5
me as the apple of Your *e* ..... Ps 17:8
guide you with My *e* ..... Ps 32:8
Behold, the *e* of the ..... Ps 33:18
He who formed the *e* ..... Ps 94:9
with the *e* causes trouble ..... Prov 10:10
and the seeing *e* ..... Prov 20:12
who has a generous *e* ..... Prov 22:9
A man with an evil *e* ..... Prov 28:22
e that mocks his ..... Prov 30:17
e is not satisfied ..... Eccl 1:8
labors, nor is his *e* ..... Eccl 4:8
for they shall see *e* ..... Is 52:8
e seen any God besides ..... Is 64:4
the apple of His *e* ..... Zech 2:8
If your right *e* causes ..... Matt 5:29
it was said, 'An *e* ..... Matt 5:38
lamp of the body is the *e* ..... Matt 6:22
plank in your own *e* ..... Matt 7:3
e causes you to sin ..... Matt 18:9
Or is your *e* evil ..... Matt 20:15
e causes you to sin ..... Mark 9:47
when your *e* is good ..... Luke 11:34
the *e* of a needle ..... Luke 18:25
"*E* has not seen ..... 1 Cor 2:9
"Because I am not an *e* ..... 1 Cor 12:16
whole body were an *e* ..... 1 Cor 12:17
the twinkling of an *e* ..... 1 Cor 15:52
every *e* will see Him ..... Rev 1:7
your eyes with *e* salve ..... Rev 3:18

EYELIDS
His eyes behold, His *e* ..... Ps 11:4
e look right before ..... Prov 4:25
slumber to your *e* ..... Prov 6:4

EYES
e will be opened ....Gen 3:5
"Lift your *e* now and ......Gen 13:14
Abraham lifted his *e* ......Gen 22:13
the *e* of Israel were dim ...Gen 48:10
and you can be our *e* .....Num 10:31
hallow Me in the *e* of .....Num 20:12
Your *e* have seen what the ..Deut 4:3
frontlets between your *e* ....Deut 6:8
right in his own *e* ....Deut 12:8
in the *e* of the LORD.......Deut 13:18
e to see and ears to hear ...Deut 29:4
thorns in your *e* ....Josh 23:13
found favor in your *e* ......Ruth 2:10
open his *e* that he may .....2 Kin 6:17
she put paint on her *e* .....2 Kin 9:30
My *e* will be open ....2 Chr 7:15
For the *e* of the LORD.......2 Chr 16:9
God may enlighten our *e* ....Ezra 9:8
Do You have *e* of flesh ......Job 10:4
And my *e* shall behold ......Job 19:27
His *e* are on their ways .....Job 24:23
I was *e* to the blind ....Job 29:15
e observe from afar ....Job 39:29
e are secretly fixed ....Ps 10:8
His *e* behold, His eyelids .....Ps 11:4
enlightening the *e* ....Ps 19:8
e are ever toward the ....Ps 25:15
is before my *e* ....Ps 26:3
The *e* of the LORD are ....Ps 34:15
His *e* observe the nations .....Ps 66:7
e fail while I wait ....Ps 69:3
e shall you look ....Ps 91:8
E they have, but they ....Ps 115:5
marvelous in our *e* ....Ps 118:23
Open my *e*, that I may see ..Ps 119:18
I will lift up my *e* ....Ps 121:1
our *e* look to the LORD ......Ps 123:2
not give sleep to my *e* ....Ps 132:4
e saw my substance.........Ps 139:16
wise in your own *e* ....Prov 3:7
not depart from your *e* .....Prov 3:21
e look straight ahead ......Prov 4:25
is right in his own *e* ......Prov 12:15
The *e* of the LORD are......Prov 15:3
but the *e* of a fool ....Prov 17:24
Will you set your *e* ....Prov 23:5
Who has redness of *e* .....Prov 23:29
be wise in his own *e* ....Prov 26:5
so the *e* of man are ....Prov 27:20
pure in its own *e* ....Prov 30:12
The wise man's *e* ....Eccl 2:14
e than the wandering ....Eccl 6:9
You have dove's *e* ....Song 1:15
the *e* of the lofty ....Is 5:15
e have seen the King ....Is 6:5
lest they see with their *e* ......Is 6:10
of the book, and the *e* ....Is 29:18
open Your *e*, O LORD ....Is 37:17
e fail from looking ....Is 38:14
O LORD, are not Your *e* ....Jer 5:3
Who have *e* and see ....Jer 5:21
e will weep bitterly ....Jer 13:17
For I will set My *e* ....Jer 24:6
your *e* from tears ....Jer 31:16
rims were full of *e* ....Ezek 1:18
full of *e* all around ....Ezek 10:12
e to see but does ....Ezek 12:2
that horn which had *e* ......Dan 7:20
horn between his *e* ....Dan 8:5
e like torches of fire, ...Dan 10:6
the *e* of the Lord GOD ......Amos 9:8
You are of purer *e* ....Hab 1:13
their *e* were opened ....Matt 9:30
But blessed are your *e* ....Matt 13:16
their *e* were heavy ....Matt 26:43
it is marvelous in our *e* ...Mark 12:11
Hades, he lifted up his *e* ..Luke 16:23
raise his *e* to heaven ......Luke 18:13
lift up your *e* and look .....John 4:35
"He put clay on my *e* ......John 9:15
e of one who was born ....John 9:32
fixing his *e* on him ....Acts 3:4
e they have closed ....Acts 28:27
e that they should not ......Rom 11:8
plucked out your own *e* .....Gal 4:15
e of your understanding ....Eph 1:18
have seen with our *e* ......1 John 1:1
the lust of the *e* ....1 John 2:16
as snow, and His *e* ....Rev 1:14
and anoint your *e* ....Rev 3:18
creatures full of *e* ....Rev 4:6
horns and seven *e* ....Rev 5:6
tear from their *e* ....Rev 21:4

EYESERVICE
not with *e*, as ....Eph 6:6
the flesh, not with *e* ....Col 3:22

EYEWITNESSES
the beginning were *e* ....Luke 1:2
e of His majesty ....2 Pet 1:16

EZEKIEL
Sent to rebellious Israel, Ezek 2; 3
Prophesies by symbolic action:
siege of Jerusalem, Ezek 4
destruction of Jerusalem, Ezek 5
captivity of Judah, Ezek 12:1–20
destruction of the temple, Ezek 24:15–27
Visions of:
God's glory, Ezek 1:4–28
abominations, Ezek 8:5–18
valley of dry bones, Ezek 37:1–14
messianic times, Ezek 40—48
river of life, Ezek 47:1–5
Parables, allegories, dirges of, Ezek 15; 16; 17; 19; 23; 24

EZION GEBER
See ELATH
Town on the Red Sea, 1 Kin 9:26
Israelite encampment, Num 33:35
Seaport of Israel's navy, 1 Kin 22:48

EZRA
Scribe, priest and reformer of post-exilic times; commissioned by Artaxerxes, Ezra 7
Returns with exiles to Jerusalem, Ezra 8
Institutes reforms, Ezra 9
Reads the Law, Neh 8
Assists in dedication of wall, Neh 12:27–43

FABLES
nor give heed to *f* ....1 Tim 1:4
be turned aside to *f* ....2 Tim 4:4
cunningly devised *f* ....2 Pet 1:16

FACE
was on the *f* of the deep .....Gen 1:2
In the sweat of your *f* you ..Gen 3:19
"For I have seen God *f* ....Gen 32:30
shall see my *f* no more ....Gen 44:23
Joseph fell on his father's *f* .Gen 50:1
LORD spoke to Moses *f* to *f* ..Ex 33:11
f shone while he ....Ex 34:29
he put a veil on his *f* ....Ex 34:33
the LORD make His *f* ....Num 6:25
I will hide My *f* from ......Deut 31:17
his *f* in his mantle ....1 Kin 19:13
Then he turned his *f* ....2 Kin 20:2
seek His *f* evermore .....1 Chr 16:11
and pray and seek My *f* ....2 Chr 7:14
not turn His *f* from you ...2 Chr 30:9
Why is your *f* sad, since .....Neh 2:2
curse You to Your *f* ....Job 1:11
I will put off my sad *f* and ...Job 9:27
and lift up your *f* to God ..Job 22:26
He shall see His *f* with joy .Job 33:26
me, I will see Your *f* ....Ps 17:15
"Your *f*, LORD, I will seek.....Ps 27:8
Do not hide Your *f* from ......Ps 27:9
Why do You hide Your *f* .....Ps 44:24
and cause His *f* to shine ......Ps 67:1
Do not hide Your *f* from .....Ps 102:2
Make Your *f* shine upon ..Ps 119:135
As in water *f* reflects ....Prov 27:19
of his *f* is changed ....Eccl 8:1
I have set My *f* like a flint .....Is 50:7
sins have hidden His *f* ....Is 59:2
I have made your *f* ....Ezek 3:8
set your *f* against Gog, of ..Ezek 38:2
but to us shame of *f* ....Dan 9:7
before Your *f* who ....Matt 11:10
to discern the *f* of the sky ..Matt 16:3
f shone like the sun ....Matt 17:2
of His *f* was altered........Luke 9:29
His *f* to go to Jerusalem ...Luke 9:51
they struck Him on the *f* ..Luke 22:64
always before my *f* ....Acts 2:25
his *f* as the *f* of an angel ....Acts 6:15
dimly, but then *f* ....1 Cor 13:12
look steadily at the *f* ....2 Cor 3:7
with unveiled *f* ....2 Cor 3:18
one strikes you on the *f* ..2 Cor 11:20
withstood him to his *f* ....Gal 2:11
that we may see your *f* ..1 Thess 3:10
his natural *f* in a ....James 1:23
but the *f* of the LORD.......1 Pet 3:12
creature had a *f* like a man ...Rev 4:7
They shall see His *f* ....Rev 22:4

FACE TO FACE
For I have seen God *f*, ...Gen 32:30
the Lord spoke to Moses *f* ...Ex 33:11
I speak with him *f* ....Num 12:8
the LORD talked with you *f* .Deut 5:4
whom the LORD knew *f* ...Deut 34:10
Angel of the LORD *f* ....Judg 6:22
My case with you *f* ....Ezek 20:35
mirror, dimly, but then *f* ..1 Cor 13:12

FACES
f were not ashamed ....Ps 34:5
wipe away tears from all *f* ....Is 25:8
hid, as it were, our *f* ....Is 53:3
be afraid of their *f* ....Jer 1:8
and all *f* turned pale ....Jer 30:6
Each one had four *f* ....Ezek 1:6
the gate that *f* toward the ..Ezek 43:1
your *f* looking worse than ..Dan 1:10
all *f* are drained of color .....Joel 2:6
they disfigure their *f* ....Matt 6:16
fell on their *f* before the .....Rev 7:11

FACTIONS
there must also be *f* ......1 Cor 11:19

FADE
we all *f* as a leaf ....Is 64:6
and the leaf shall *f* ....Jer 8:13
rich man also will *f* ....James 1:11
and that does not *f* ....1 Pet 1:4
of glory that does not *f* .....1 Pet 5:4

FADES
withers, the flower *f* ....Is 40:7

FAIL
eyes shall look and *f* ......Deut 28:32
man's heart *f* because ....1 Sam 17:32
You shall not *f* to have a ..1 Kin 8:25
eyes of the wicked will *f* ...Job 11:20
flesh and my heart *f* ....Ps 73:26
of the thirsty to *f* ....Is 32:6
not one of these shall *f* ....Is 34:16
their tongues *f* ....Is 41:17
whose waters do not *f* ....Is 58:11
have caused wine to *f* ......Jer 48:33
His compassions *f* not ....Lam 3:22
of the olive may *f* ....Hab 3:17
nor shall the vine *f* ....Mal 3:11
heavens that does not *f* ...Luke 12:33
that when you *f* ....Luke 16:9
tittle of the law to *f* ....Luke 16:17
faith should not *f* ....Luke 22:32
prophecies, they will *f* .....1 Cor 13:8

Your years will not *f* . . . . . Heb 1:12
For the time would *f* . . . . . . Heb 11:32

FAILED
Not a word *f* of any . . . . . . Josh 21:45
My relatives have *f* . . . . . . Job 19:14
Has His promise *f* . . . . Ps 77:8
refuge has *f* me . . . . Ps 142:4

FAILING
men's hearts *f* . . . . Luke 21:26

FAILS
my strength *f* because . . . . . . Ps 31:10
Therefore my heart *f* me . . . . . Ps 40:12
my spirit *f* . . . . Ps 143:7
and every vision *f* . . . . Ezek 12:22
wine is dried up, the oil *f* . . . Joel 1:10
He never *f*, but the unjust . . . Zeph 3:5
Love never *f* . . . . 1 Cor 13:8

FAINT
If you *f* in the day of . . . . . Prov 24:10
the youths shall *f* . . . . Is 40:30
shall walk and not *f* . . . . Is 40:31
my heart is *f* in me . . . . Jer 8:18
and the infants *f* . . . . Lam 2:11

FAINTED
thirsty, their soul *f* . . . . Ps 107:5

FAINTHEARTED
unruly, comfort the *f* . . . . 1 Thess 5:14

FAINTS
longs, yes, even *f* . . . . Ps 84:2
My soul *f* for Your . . . . Ps 119:81
And the whole heart *f* . . . . Is 1:5
the earth, neither *f* . . . . Is 40:28

FAIR
Behold, you are *f* . . . . Song 1:15
How *f* and how pleasant . . . . Song 7:6
of the Lord is not *f* . . . . . . Ezek 18:25
My ways which are *f* . . . . . Ezek 18:29
say, 'It will be *f* weather . . . . Matt 16:2
to a place called *F* . . . . Acts 27:8
what is just and *f* . . . . Col 4:1

FAIR HAVENS
Harbor of Crete at which Paul landed, Acts 27:8

FAIR-MINDED
These were more *f* . . . . Acts 17:11

FAIRER
f than the sons . . . . Ps 45:2

FAIREST
another beloved, O *f* . . . . Song 5:9
your beloved gone, O *f* . . . . . . Song 6:1

FAITH
in whom is no *f* . . . . Deut 32:20
shall live by his *f* . . . . Hab 2:4
you, O you of little *f* . . . . Matt 6:30
not found such great *f* . . . . Matt 8:10
your *f* has made you well . . Matt 9:22
"O you of little *f* . . . . Matt 14:31
woman, great is your *f* . . . . Matt 15:28
f as a mustard seed . . . . Matt 17:20
that you have no *f* . . . . Mark 4:40
to them, "Have *f* . . . . Mark 11:22
not found such great *f* . . . . . . Luke 7:9
you, O you of little *f* . . . . . . Luke 12:28
"Increase our *f* . . . . Luke 17:5
will He really find *f* . . . . Luke 18:8
through *f* in His name . . . . Acts 3:16
a man full of *f* . . . . Acts 6:5
the Holy Spirit and of *f* . . . . Acts 11:24
that he had *f* to be healed . . Acts 14:9
were strengthened in the *f* . . Acts 16:5
are sanctified by *f* . . . . Acts 26:18
for obedience to the *f* . . . . Rom 1:5
that your *f* is spoken of . . . . . Rom 1:8
God is revealed from *f* . . . . . Rom 1:17
God, through *f* . . . . Rom 3:22
f apart from the deeds . . . . . . Rom 3:28
his *f* is accounted for . . . . Rom 4:5
f which he had while still . . . Rom 4:11
f is made void and the . . . . . . Rom 4:14
those who are of the *f* . . . . Rom 4:16
And not being weak in *f* . . . . Rom 4:19
having been justified by *f* . . . Rom 5:1
of *f* speaks in this way . . . . . Rom 10:6
f which we preach . . . . Rom 10:8
f comes by hearing . . . . Rom 10:17
and you stand by *f* . . . . Rom 11:20
each one a measure of *f* . . . . Rom 12:3
in proportion to our *f* . . . . . . Rom 12:6
Do you have *f* . . . . Rom 14:22
whatever is not from *f* . . . . Rom 14:23
that your *f* should not be . . . 1 Cor 2:5
though I have all *f* . . . . 1 Cor 13:2
And now abide *f* . . . . 1 Cor 13:13
your *f* is also empty . . . . . . 1 Cor 15:14
stand fast in the *f* . . . . 1 Cor 16:13
For we walk by *f* . . . . 2 Cor 5:7
as your *f* is increased . . . . . 2 Cor 10:15
now preaches the *f* which . . . Gal 1:23
law but by *f* in Jesus Christ . . Gal 2:16
the flesh I live by *f* . . . . Gal 2:20
or by the hearing of *f* . . . . Gal 3:2
f are sons of Abraham . . . . Gal 3:7
the just shall live by *f* . . . . . . Gal 3:11
the law is not of *f* . . . . Gal 3:12
of the Spirit through *f* . . . . . . Gal 3:14
But before *f* came . . . . Gal 3:23
But after *f* has come . . . . Gal 3:25
f working through love . . . . Gal 5:6
of the household of *f* . . . . Gal 6:10
been saved through *f* . . . . Eph 2:8
one Lord, one *f* . . . . Eph 4:5
to the unity of the *f* . . . . Eph 4:13
taking the shield of *f* . . . . Eph 6:16
for the *f* of the gospel . . . . . . Phil 1:27
established in the *f* . . . . Col 2:7
your work of *f* . . . . 1 Thess 1:3
on the breastplate of *f* . . . . 1 Thess 5:8
work of *f* with power . . . . . 2 Thess 1:11
for not all have *f* . . . . 2 Thess 3:2
a true son in the *f* . . . . 1 Tim 1:2
edification which is in *f* . . . . . 1 Tim 1:4
having *f* and a good . . . . 1 Tim 1:19
if they continue in *f*, love . . 1 Tim 2:15
the mystery of the *f* . . . . 1 Tim 3:9
great boldness in the *f* . . . . . 1 Tim 3:13
in love, in spirit, in *f* . . . . . . 1 Tim 4:12
he has denied the *f* . . . . 1 Tim 5:8
righteousness, godliness, *f*. 1 Tim 6:11
Fight the good fight of *f* . . . 1 Tim 6:12
I have kept the *f* . . . . 2 Tim 4:7
in our common *f* . . . . Titus 1:4
temperate, sound in *f* . . . . . . Titus 2:2
not being mixed with *f* . . . . Heb 4:2
of *f* toward God, ... Heb 6:1
those who through *f* . . . . Heb 6:12
in full assurance of *f* . . . . . . Heb 10:22
the just shall live by *f* . . . . . Heb 10:38
f is the substance . . . . Heb 11:1
without *f* it is . . . . Heb 11:6
These all died in *f* . . . . Heb 11:13
good testimony through *f* . . Heb 11:39
author and finisher of our *f* . Heb 12:2
whose *f* follow . . . . Heb 13:7
your *f* produces patience . . . James 1:3
But let him ask in *f* . . . . James 1:6
someone says he has *f* . . . . . James 2:14
Show me your *f* . . . . James 2:18
f without works is dead . . . James 2:20
and not by *f* only . . . . James 2:24
f will save the sick . . . . James 5:15
the genuineness of your *f* . . . 1 Pet 1:7
receiving the end of your *f* . . . 1 Pet 1:9
him, steadfast in the *f* . . . . . . 1 Pet 5:9
add to your *f* virtue . . . . 2 Pet 1:5
on your most holy *f* . . . . Jude 20
works, love, service, *f* . . . . . . Rev 2:19
the patience and the *f* . . . . . . Rev 13:10
of God and the *f* . . . . Rev 14:12

FAITHFUL
he is *f* in all My house . . . . . Num 12:7
God, He is God, the *f* . . . . Deut 7:9
found his heart *f* . . . . Neh 9:8
f disappear from among . . . . . . Ps 12:1
LORD preserves the *f* . . . . Ps 31:23
whose spirit was not *f* . . . . Ps 78:8
eyes shall be on the *f* . . . . Ps 101:6
commandments are *f* . . . . Ps 119:86
are righteous and very *f* . . Ps 119:138
f spirit conceals a . . . . Prov 11:13
A *f* witness does not lie . . . . Prov 14:5
But who can find a *f* . . . . Prov 20:6
A *f* man will abound . . . . . . Prov 28:20
the LORD who is *f* . . . . Is 49:7
f witness between us . . . . Jer 42:5
or fault, because he was *f* . . . . Dan 6:4
the Holy One who is *f* . . . . . . Hos 11:12
"Who then is a *f* . . . . Matt 24:45
good and *f* servant . . . . Matt 25:23
"Who then is that *f* . . . . Luke 12:42
He who is *f* in what . . . . Luke 16:10
if you have not been *f* . . . . Luke 16:12
have judged me to be *f* . . . . Acts 16:15
God is *f*, by whom . . . . 1 Cor 1:9
that one be found *f* . . . . 1 Cor 4:2
is my beloved and *f* . . . . 1 Cor 4:17
God is *f*, who will not . . . . . 1 Cor 10:13
But as God is *f* . . . . 2 Cor 1:18
f minister in the LORD . . . . Eph 6:21
f brethren in Christ . . . . Col 1:2
He who calls you is *f* . . . . 1 Thess 5:24
because He counted me *f* . . . 1 Tim 1:12
This is a *f* saying and . . . . . 1 Tim 1:15
temperate, *f* in all things . . 1 Tim 3:11
commit these to *f* men . . . . . . 2 Tim 2:2
f High Priest in . . . . Heb 2:17
as Moses also was *f* . . . . Heb 3:2
Moses indeed was *f* . . . . Heb 3:5
He who promised is *f* . . . . . . Heb 10:23
judged Him *f* who had . . . . . Heb 11:11
He is *f* and just to . . . . 1 John 1:9
Be *f* until death . . . . Rev 2:10
words are true and *f* . . . . Rev 21:5

FAITHFULNESS
righteousness and his *f* . . 1 Sam 26:23
for in their *f* they . . . . 2 Chr 31:18
f reaches to the clouds . . . . Ps 36:5
I have declared Your *f* . . . . . . Ps 40:10
Your *f* to all generations . . . . . Ps 89:1
f You shall establish . . . . Ps 89:2
Your *f* also surrounds . . . . Ps 89:8
allow My *f* to fail . . . . Ps 89:33
and Your *f* every night . . . . Ps 92:2
f endures to all . . . . Ps 119:90
In Your *f* answer me . . . . Ps 143:1
counsels of old are *f* . . . . Is 25:1
great is Your *f* . . . . Lam 3:23
your *f* is like a morning . . . . . . Hos 6:4
unbelief make the *f* . . . . Rom 3:3
kindness, goodness, *f* . . . . Gal 5:22

FAITHLESS
the words of the *f* . . . . Prov 22:12
"O *f* and perverse . . . . Matt 17:17
"O *f* generation . . . . Mark 9:19
If we are *f*, He remains . . . . 2 Tim 2:13

FALL
a deep sleep to *f* . . . . Gen 2:21
but do not let me *f* . . . . 2 Sam 24:14
Let them *f* by their . . . . Ps 5:10
Though he *f*, he shall not . . . . Ps 37:24
For I am ready to *f* . . . . Ps 38:17
Yes, all kings shall *f* . . . . Ps 72:11
A thousand may *f* at your . . . . . Ps 91:7
Let the wicked *f* into their . . Ps 141:10
LORD upholds all who *f* . . . . . Ps 145:14
but a prating fool will *f* . . . . Prov 10:8
the wicked will *f* by his . . . . Prov 11:5
no counsel, the people *f* . . . Prov 11:14
trusts in his riches will *f* . . Prov 11:28
haughty spirit before a *f* . . Prov 16:18

but the wicked shall *f* . . . . . Prov 24:16
digs a pit will *f* . . . . Prov 26:27
For if they *f*, one will lift . . . . Eccl 4:10
both he who helps will *f* . . . . . . Is 31:3
all their host shall *f* . . . . Is 34:4
men shall utterly *f* . . . . Is 40:30
"Will they *f* and not rise . . . . . . Jer 8:4
F and rise no more . . . . Jer 25:27
proud shall stumble and *f* . . . Jer 50:32
of music, you shall *f* . . . . Dan 3:5
if You will *f* down . . . . Matt 4:9
And great was its *f* . . . . Matt 7:27
the blind, both will *f* . . . . . . Matt 15:14
f from their masters' . . . . Matt 15:27
the stars will *f* . . . . Matt 24:29
Child is destined for the *f* . . Luke 2:34
"I saw Satan *f* . . . . Luke 10:18
they will *f* by the edge . . . . Luke 21:24
might *f* on some . . . . Acts 5:15
f short of the glory of . . . . . . Rom 3:23
that they should *f* . . . . Rom 11:11
block or a cause to *f* in . . . . Rom 14:13
take heed lest he *f* . . . . 1 Cor 10:12
with pride he *f* . . . . 1 Tim 3:6
be rich *f* into temptation . . . . 1 Tim 6:9
if they *f* away . . . . Heb 6:6
to *f* into the hands of the . . Heb 10:31
lest anyone *f* short of . . . . . . Heb 12:15
it all joy when you *f* . . . . . . James 1:2
and rocks, "*F* on us . . . . Rev 6:16

FALLEN
has your countenance *f* . . . . . . Gen 4:6
terror of you has *f* on us . . . . Josh 2:9
f on its face to the earth . . . 1 Sam 5:3
who reproach You have *f* . . . . . Ps 69:9
you are *f* from heaven . . . . Is 14:12
"Babylon is *f* . . . . Is 21:9
Babylon has suddenly *f* . . . . . . Jer 51:8
you have *f* from grace . . . . Gal 5:4
who have *f* asleep . . . . 1 Thess 4:13
And I saw a star *f* . . . . Rev 9:1
"Babylon is *f* . . . . Rev 14:8

FALLING
and my feet from *f* . . . . Ps 116:8
and *f* down before Him . . . . Luke 8:47
great drops of blood *f* . . . . Luke 22:44
f away comes first . . . . 2 Thess 2:3

FALLS
when your enemy *f* . . . . Prov 24:17
who is alone when he *f* . . . . . Eccl 4:10
not one of them *f* to the . . . . Matt 10:29
And whoever *f* . . . . Matt 21:44
divided against a house *f* . Luke 11:17
wheat *f* into the ground . . . John 12:24
master he stands or *f* . . . . Rom 14:4
grass; its flower *f* . . . . James 1:11
withers, and its flower *f* . . . . 1 Pet 1:24
so that no rain *f* . . . . Rev 11:6

FALSE
"You shall not bear *f* . . . . Ex 20:16
shall not bear *f* witness . . . . Deut 5:20
I hate every *f* way . . . . Ps 119:104
f witness who speaks lies . . Prov 6:19
gives heed to *f* lips . . . . Prov 17:4
f witness shall perish . . . . . Prov 21:28
the *f* pen of the scribe . . . . Jer 8:8
walk in a *f* spirit . . . . Mic 2:11
and do not love a *f* . . . . Zech 8:17
"Beware of *f* prophets . . . . . . Matt 7:15
shall not bear *f* witness . . . Matt 19:18
f christs and *f* . . . . Matt 24:24
at last two *f* witnesses . . . . Matt 26:60
f prophets will rise . . . . Mark 13:22
and we are found *f* . . . . 1 Cor 15:15
among *f* brethren . . . . 2 Cor 11:26
of *f* brethren secretly . . . . Gal 2:4
taking delight in *f* humility . . . Col 2:18
f prophets have gone . . . . 1 John 4:1
f teachers among you . . . . 2 Pet 2:1
mouth of the *f* prophet . . . . . Rev 16:13

FALSE PROPHETS
Beware of *f*, who come to . . Matt 7:15
many *f* will rise up . . . . Matt 24:11
false christs and *f* . . . . Matt 24:24
f will rise and show . . . . . . Mark 13:22
their fathers to the *f* . . . . Luke 6:26
But there were also *f* . . . . 2 Pet 2:1
many *f* have gone out . . . . . . 1 John 4:1

FALSE WITNESS
You shall not bear *f* . . . . Ex 20:16
a *f* who speaks lies, ... Prov 6:19
But a *f*, deceit . . . . Prov 12:17
f will not go unpunished . . . Prov 19:5
A man who bears *f* . . . . Prov 25:18
thefts, *f*, blasphemies . . . . . . Matt 15:19
bore *f* against Him . . . . Mark 14:56

FALSEHOOD
since *f* remains in your . . . . Job 21:34
If I have walked with *f* . . . . . Job 31:5
those who speak *f* . . . . Ps 5:6
and brings forth *f* . . . . Ps 7:14
For their deceit is *f* . . . . Ps 119:118
remove *f* and lies far . . . . Prov 30:8
under *f* we have hidden . . . . . . Is 28:15
offspring of *f* . . . . Is 57:4
and trusted in *f* . . . . Jer 13:25

FALSELY
it, and swears *f* . . . . Lev 6:3
shall not steal, nor deal *f* . . . Lev 19:11
nor have we dealt *f* . . . . Ps 44:17
Whoever *f* boasts of . . . . Prov 25:14
surely they swear *f* . . . . Jer 5:2
prophesy *f* to you . . . . Jer 29:9
words, swearing *f* . . . . Hos 10:4
of evil against you *f* . . . . Matt 5:11
anyone or accuse *f* . . . . Luke 3:14
f called knowledge . . . . 1 Tim 6:20

FAME
his *f* spread throughout . . . . Josh 6:27
Sheba heard of the *f* . . . . 1 Kin 10:1
exceed the *f* of which . . . . . . 1 Kin 10:7
his *f* spread throughout all . . Esth 9:4
endures forever, Your *f* . . . . . Ps 135:13
heard My *f* nor seen . . . . Is 66:19
Your *f* went out . . . . Ezek 16:14
them for praise and *f* . . . . Zeph 3:19
Then His *f* went . . . . Matt 4:24

FAMILIAR
to mediums and *f* spirits . . . . Lev 19:31
and *f* spirits, to prostitute . . . Lev 20:6
Even my own *f* friend . . . . Ps 41:9

FAMILIES
in you all the *f* . . . . Gen 12:3
in your seed all the *f* of . . . . Gen 28:14
and all the *f* of the nations . . Ps 22:27
God sets the solitary in *f* . . . . . Ps 68:6
and makes their *f* . . . . Ps 107:41
the God of all the *f* . . . . Jer 31:1
f which the LORD has . . . . Jer 33:24
of all the *f* of the earth . . . . . . Amos 3:2
in your seed all the *f* . . . . Acts 3:25

FAMILY
that man and against his *f* . . . Lev 20:5
against the whole *f* . . . . Amos 3:1
shall mourn, every *f* . . . . Zech 12:12
Joseph's *f* became known . . Acts 7:13
sons of the *f* of Abraham . . Acts 13:26
f were baptized . . . . Acts 16:33
from whom the whole *f* . . . . . Eph 3:15

FAMINE
Now there was a *f* . . . . Gen 12:10
besides the first *f* that was . . . Gen 26:1
seven years of *f* will arise . . Gen 41:30
the *f* was severe in the . . . . . . Gen 43:1
the LORD has called for a *f* . . 2 Kin 8:1
In *f* He shall redeem you . . . . Job 5:20
keep them alive in *f* . . . . Ps 33:19
He called for a *f* . . . . Ps 105:16
and destruction, *f* . . . . Is 51:19
shall die by the sword, by *f* . . Jer 21:9
send the sword, the *f* . . . . Jer 24:10
of the fever of *f* . . . . Lam 5:10
I will increase the *f* . . . . Ezek 5:16
there arose a severe *f* . . . . . Luke 15:14
a *f* and great trouble came . . Acts 7:11
or persecution, or *f*, or . . . . . Rom 8:35

FAMINES
And there will be *f* . . . . Matt 24:7

FAMISH
righteous soul to *f* . . . . Prov 10:3

FAMISHED
honorable men are *f* . . . . Is 5:13

FAMOUS
and may his name be *f* . . . . . Ruth 4:14

FAN
not to *f* or to cleanse . . . . Jer 4:11
His winnowing *f* . . . . Matt 3:12

FANCIES
with their own *f* . . . . Prov 1:31

FAR
removed my brothers *f* . . . . Job 19:13
Your judgments are *f* . . . . Ps 10:5
Be not *f* from Me . . . . Ps 22:11
those who are *f* . . . . Ps 73:27
The LORD is *f* from the . . . . Prov 15:29
but it was *f* from me . . . . Eccl 7:23
removed their hearts *f* . . . . Is 29:13
Those near and those *f* . . . . Ezek 22:5
their heart is *f* from . . . . Matt 15:8
going to a *f* country . . . . Mark 13:34
though He is not *f* . . . . Acts 17:27
you who once were *f* . . . . Eph 2:13

FAR BE IT FROM ME
"*F* that I should do so . . . . . . Gen 44:17
'*F*; for those who honor . . . 1 Sam 2:30
f that I should sin . . . . 1 Sam 12:23
F! Let not the king . . . . . . 1 Sam 22:15
f, that I should swallow . . 2 Sam 20:20
"*F*, O LORD, that . . . . 2 Sam 23:17
"*F*, O my God, that . . . . 1 Chr 11:19
F that I should say . . . . Job 27:5

FAR COUNTRY
"We have come from a *f* . . . . Josh 9:6
good news from a *f* . . . . Prov 25:25
f, from the end of heaven . . . . . Is 13:5
from a *f*, from Babylon . . . . Is 39:3
and went into a *f* . . . . Matt 21:33
man traveling to a *f* . . . . Matt 25:14
a *f*, and there wasted . . . . . Luke 15:13
nobleman went into a *f* . . . Luke 19:12
and went into a *f* . . . . Luke 20:9

FARMER
The hard-working *f* . . . . 2 Tim 2:6
See how the *f* waits . . . . James 5:7

FASHIONED
have made me and *f* . . . . Job 10:8

FASHIONS
He *f* their hearts . . . . Ps 33:15

FAST
"But you who held *f* to the . . Deut 4:4
serve Him and hold *f* to . . . . Deut 13:4
For he held *f* to the LORD . . 2 Kin 18:6
My maids and I will *f* . . . . . . Esth 4:16
commanded, and it stood *f* . . . . Ps 33:9
of your *f* you find pleasure . . . . Is 58:3
f that I have chosen . . . . Is 58:5
they *f*, I will not hear . . . . Jer 14:12
Consecrate a *f*, call a . . . . Joel 1:14
believed God, proclaimed a *f* . Jon 3:5
"Moreover, when you *f* . . . . . Matt 6:16
disciples do not *f* . . . . Matt 9:14
f while the bridegroom is . . Mark 2:19
I *f* twice a week . . . . Luke 18:12
if you hold *f* that word . . . . . 1 Cor 15:2
stand *f* in the faith, be . . . . 1 Cor 16:13
holding *f* the word of life . . . . Phil 2:16
you stand *f* in the Lord . . . . 1 Thess 3:8

holding *f* the faithful word . . Titus 1:9
hold *f* our confession . . . . Heb 4:14
hold *f* the confession . . . . . . Heb 10:23
Hold *f* what you have . . . . Rev 3:11

FASTED

and *f* seven days . . . . 1 Sam 31:13
the child, and David *f* . . . 2 Sam 12:16
f and entreated our God . . . . Ezra 8:23
'Why have we *f* . . . . Is 58:3
'When you *f* and . . . . Zech 7:5
And when He had *f* . . . . Matt 4:2
Then, having *f* and prayed . . Acts 13:3

FASTENED

were its foundations *f* . . . . Job 38:6
'the peg that is *f* . . . . Is 22:25

FASTING

I was *f* and praying before . . . Neh 1:4
humbled myself with *f* . . . . . . Ps 35:13
are weak through *f* . . . . Ps 109:24
house on the day of *f* . . . . Jer 36:6
and spent the night *f* . . . . Dan 6:18
with all your heart, with *f* . . . Joel 2:12
not appear to men to be *f* . . Matt 6:18
except by prayer and *f* . . . . Matt 17:21
I was *f* until this hour . . . . . Acts 10:30
give yourselves to *f* . . . . 1 Cor 7:5

FASTINGS

but served God with *f* . . . . . Luke 2:37
in sleeplessness, in *f* . . . . 2 Cor 6:5

FAT

the first seven, the *f* cows . . Gen 41:20
and you will eat the *f* . . . . . . Gen 45:18
f is the LORD's . . . . Lev 3:16
Now Eglon was a very *f* . . . Judg 3:17
have closed up their *f* . . . . Ps 17:10

FATHER

See GOD THE FATHER; HEAVENLY FATHER

man shall leave his *f* . . . . Gen 2:24
saw the nakedness of his *f* . . Gen 9:22
and you shall be a *f* . . . . Gen 17:4
the lineage of our *f* . . . . Gen 19:32
his *f* blessed him . . . . Gen 27:41
God of my *f* has been with . . Gen 31:5
Esau was the *f* of the . . . . . . Gen 36:43
f loved him more than all . . . Gen 37:4
Thus his *f* wept for him . . . . Gen 37:35
'Is your *f* still alive . . . . Gen 43:7
bring my *f* down here . . . . . . Gen 45:13
God, the God of your *f* . . . . . . Gen 46:3
to meet his *f* Israel . . . . Gen 46:29
went up to bury his *f* . . . . Gen 50:7
Honor your *f* and your . . . . . . Ex 20:12
Honor your *f* and your . . . . . Deut 5:16
obey the voice of his *f* . . . . Deut 21:18
of Jesse, the *f* of David . . . . Ruth 4:17
son, and I will be his *F* . . . 1 Chr 22:10
son, and I will be his *F* . . . . 1 Chr 28:6
'You are my *f* . . . . Job 17:14
I was a *f* to the poor . . . . Job 29:16
When my *f* and my mother . . Ps 27:10
A *f* of the fatherless . . . . Ps 68:5
f pities his children . . . . Ps 103:13
the instruction of a *f* . . . . Prov 4:1
wise son makes a glad *f* . . . . Prov 10:1
wise son makes a *f* glad . . . Prov 15:20
glory of children is their *f* . . Prov 17:6
the *f* of a fool has no joy . . Prov 17:21
son is a grief to his *f* . . . . . . Prov 17:25
curses his *f* or his . . . . Prov 20:20
f of the righteous will . . . . . Prov 23:24
makes his *f* rejoice . . . . Prov 29:3
that curses its *f* . . . . Prov 30:11
God, Everlasting *F* . . . . Is 9:6
Your first *f* sinned . . . . Is 43:27
You, O LORD, are our *F* . . . . . . Is 63:16
time cry to Me, My *F* . . . . Jer 3:4
for I am a *F* to Israel . . . . Jer 31:9
for the iniquity of his *f* . . . Ezek 18:17
not bear the guilt of the *f* . Ezek 18:20
"A son honors his *f* . . . . Mal 1:6
Have we not all one *F* . . . . . . Mal 2:10
your *F* who sees in secret . . . Matt 6:4
your heavenly *F* will also . . Matt 6:14
neither will your *F* forgive . . Matt 6:15
your heavenly *F* knows . . . . Matt 6:32
much more will your *F* . . . . . Matt 7:11
He who loves *f* . . . . Matt 10:37
does anyone know the *F* . . Matt 11:27
'He who curses *f* . . . . Matt 15:4
My *F* who is in heaven . . . . Matt 18:10
a man shall leave his *f* . . . . . Matt 19:5
for One is your *F* . . . . Matt 23:9
you blessed of My *F* . . . . . . Matt 25:34
"O My *F*, if this cup . . . . . . Matt 26:42
in the name of the *F* . . . . . . Matt 28:19
F with the holy angels . . . . Mark 8:38
a man shall leave his *f* . . . . Mark 10:7
the Son, but only the *F* . . . Mark 13:32
"Abba, *F*, all things are . . Mark 14:36
Your *f* and I have sought . . . Luke 2:48
just as your *F* also is . . . . . . Luke 6:36
first go and bury my *f* . . . . . Luke 9:59
who the Son is but the *F* . . Luke 10:22
bread from any *f* among . . Luke 11:11
F give the Holy Spirit to . . Luke 11:13
F will be divided . . . . Luke 12:53
does not hate his *f* . . . . Luke 14:26
arise and go to my *f* . . . . . . Luke 15:18
'I beg you therefore, *f* . . . . Luke 16:27
"*F*, if it is Your will . . . . Luke 22:42
"*F*, forgive them, for . . . . . . Luke 23:34
only begotten of the *F* . . . . . John 1:14
F loves the Son . . . . John 3:35
worship the *F* in spirit . . . . . John 4:23
F has been working . . . . John 5:17
what He sees the *F* do . . . . . John 5:19
F raises the dead . . . . John 5:21
F judges no one . . . . John 5:22
not honor the *F* who sent . . John 5:23
All that the *F* gives Me . . . . John 6:37
He has seen the *F* . . . . John 6:46
F who sent Me bears . . . . . . John 8:18
but as My *F* taught Me, I . . . John 8:28
we have one *F* . . . . John 8:41
he is a liar and the *f* of it . . . John 8:44
I and My *F* are one . . . . John 10:30
and believe that the *F* . . . . John 10:38
"*F*, I thank You that . . . . . . John 11:41
F, glorify Your name . . . . . . John 12:28
"Lord, show us the *F* . . . . . . John 14:8
seen Me has seen the *F* . . . . John 14:9
believe that I am in the *F* . John 14:10
because I go to My *F* . . . . . John 14:12
And I will pray the *F* . . . . . John 14:16
will be loved by My *F* . . . . John 14:21
'I am going to the *F* . . . . . . John 14:28
F is the vinedresser . . . . John 15:1
whatever you ask the *F* . . . John 15:16
you ask the *F* in My . . . . . . John 16:23
came forth from the *F* . . . . . John 16:28
And now, O *F*, glorify Me . . John 17:5
yet ascended to My *F* . . . . John 20:17
F the promise of the Holy . . Acts 2:33
that he might be the *f* . . . . . . Rom 4:11
"I have made you a *f* . . . . Rom 4:17
we cry out, "Abba, *F*." . . . . . Rom 8:15
F of our Lord Jesus . . . . Rom 15:6
F of mercies and God of . . . . 2 Cor 1:3
"I will be a *F* to you . . . . 2 Cor 6:18
by one Spirit to the *F* . . . . Eph 2:18
I bow my knees to the *F* of . . Eph 3:14
one God and *F* of all . . . . Eph 4:6
a man shall leave his *f* and . . . Eph 5:31
F be glory forever and . . . . . . Phil 4:20
For it pleased the *F* that in . . Col 1:19
f does his own children . . 1 Thess 2:11
but exhort him as a *f* . . . . 1 Tim 5:1
"I will be to Him a *F* . . . . Heb 1:5
without *f*, without mother . . . . Heb 7:3
whom a *f* does not chasten . . Heb 12:7
comes down from the *F* . . James 1:17
we bless our God and *F* . . . . James 3:9
if you call on the *F* . . . . 1 Pet 1:17
an Advocate with the *F* . . . . 1 John 2:1
love of the *F* is not in . . . . 1 John 2:15
love the *F* has bestowed . . . 1 John 3:1
and testify that the *F* . . . . . 1 John 4:14
F, the Word, and the . . . . . . 1 John 5:7
his name before My *F* . . . . Rev 3:5

FATHER IN HEAVEN

and glorify your *F* . . . . Matt 5:16
may be sons of your *F* . . . . . Matt 5:45
just as your *F* is perfect . . . . Matt 5:48
no reward from your *F* . . . . . . Matt 6:1
Our *F*, hallowed be Your . . . . Matt 6:9
who does the will of My *F* . . Matt 7:21
does the will of My *F* . . . . . . Matt 12:50
done for them by My *F* . . . Matt 18:19
F may also forgive you . . . Mark 11:25
Our *F*, hallowed be . . . . Luke 11:2

FATHER'S

Joseph fell on his *f* face . . . . . Gen 50:1
he and his *f* household . . . . Gen 50:22
my *f* God, and I will exalt . . . . Ex 15:2
When I was my *f* son . . . . Prov 4:3
keep your *f* command . . . . . . Prov 6:20
heeds his *f* instruction . . . . . . Prov 13:1
you in My *F* kingdom . . . . . Matt 26:29
I must be about My *F* . . . . . . Luke 2:49
many of my *f* hired . . . . Luke 15:17
Do not make My *F* house . . John 2:16
works that I do in My *F* . . John 10:25
F house are many . . . . John 14:2
the *F* who sent Me . . . . John 14:24
that a man has his *f* . . . . 1 Cor 5:1

FATHERLESS

afflict any widow or *f* child . . Ex 22:22
and your children *f* . . . . Ex 22:24
justice for the *f* . . . . Deut 10:18
my hand against the *f* . . . . . . Job 31:21
the helper of the *f* . . . . Ps 10:14
to do justice to the *f* . . . . Ps 10:18
father of the *f*, a defender . . . . Ps 68:5
Let his children be *f* . . . . Ps 109:9
He relieves the *f* . . . . Ps 146:9
the fields of the *f* . . . . Prov 23:10
do not defend the *f* . . . . Is 1:23
they may rob the *f* . . . . Is 10:2
You the *f* finds mercy . . . . Hos 14:3
the widow or the *f* . . . . Zech 7:10

FATHERS

bury me with my *f* . . . . Gen 49:29
swore to your *f* to give you . . . Ex 13:5
the iniquity of the *f* . . . . Ex 20:5
the LORD swore to your *f* . . . . Deut 1:8
f make you a thousand . . . . . Deut 1:11
the iniquity of the *f* upon . . . . Deut 5:9
the LORD God of our *f* . . . . . . Ezra 7:27
f trusted in You . . . . Ps 22:4
sojourner, as all my *f* were . . Ps 39:12
our ears, O God, our *f* . . . . Ps 44:1
He commanded our *f* . . . . Ps 78:5
did in the sight of their *f* . . . . Ps 78:12
have sinned with our *f* . . . . . . Ps 106:6
that I gave to your *f* forever . . . Jer 7:7
f have eaten sour grapes . . . . Jer 31:29
f have eaten sour grapes . . . Ezek 18:2
for the iniquities of our *f* . . . . Dan 9:16
f provoked Me to wrath . . . . Zech 8:14
For so did their *f* to the . . . . Luke 6:26
Our *f* worshiped on this . . . . John 4:20
f ate the manna . . . . John 6:31
f nor we were able to . . . . . Acts 15:10
of whom are the *f* . . . . Rom 9:5
you do not have many *f* . . . 1 Cor 4:15
unaware that all our *f* . . . . . 1 Cor 10:1
f, do not provoke . . . . Eph 6:4
F, do not provoke your . . . . . . Col 3:21
where your *f* tested Me . . . . . . Heb 3:9

FATLING

and the *f* together . . . . Is 11:6

FATNESS
as with marrow and *f* . . . . Ps 63:5
of the root and *f* . . . . Rom 11:17

FATTED
f cattle are killed . . . . Matt 22:4
has killed the *f* . . . . Luke 15:27

FATTENED
f your hearts as . . . . James 5:5

FATTER
f in flesh than all the . . . . Dan 1:15

FAULT
find no charge or *f* . . . . Dan 6:4
tell him his *f* between . . . . . Matt 18:15
I have found no *f* . . . . Luke 23:14
does He still find *f* . . . . Rom 9:19
of God without *f* . . . . Phil 2:15
for they are without *f* . . . . Rev 14:5

FAULTLESS
covenant had been *f* . . . . Heb 8:7
to present you *f* . . . . Jude 24

FAULTS
"I remember my *f* . . . . Gen 41:9
me from secret *f* . . . . Ps 19:12
are beaten for your *f* . . . . 1 Pet 2:20

FAVOR
Joseph found *f* in his sight . . Gen 39:4
nor show *f* to the young . . . Deut 28:50
"Let me find *f* in your . . . . . Ruth 2:13
f in his sight more than all . . Esth 2:17
granted me life and *f* . . . . Job 10:12
with *f* You will surround . . . . . Ps 5:12
His *f* is for life . . . . Ps 30:5
who *f* my righteous cause . . . Ps 35:27
the *f* You have toward . . . . . . Ps 106:4
find *f* and high esteem . . . . . . Prov 3:4
obtains *f* from the LORD . . . . Prov 8:35
A good man obtains *f* . . . . . . Prov 12:2
understanding gains *f* . . . . . Prov 13:15
his *f* is like a cloud . . . . Prov 16:15
but his *f* is like dew . . . . Prov 19:12
loving *f* rather than silver . . Prov 22:1
in My *f* I have had mercy . . . . Is 60:10
and seek the LORD's *f* . . . . Jer 26:19
brought Daniel into the *f* . . . . Dan 1:9
have found *f* with God . . . . . Luke 1:30
and stature, and in *f* . . . . Luke 2:52
God and having *f* . . . . Acts 2:47
troubles, and gave him *f* . . . . Acts 7:10
to do the Jews a *f* . . . . Acts 24:27

FAVORABLE
And will He be *f* . . . . Ps 77:7
LORD, You have been *f* . . . . Ps 85:1

FAVORED
because You *f* them . . . . Ps 44:3
"Rejoice, highly *f* . . . . Luke 1:28

FAVORITISM
do not show personal *f* . . . Luke 20:21
God shows personal *f* . . . . Gal 2:6

FEAR
See DO NOT FEAR
do not *f*, for I am with . . . . . Gen 26:24
this and live, for I *f* God . . . Gen 42:18
not *f* to go down to Egypt . . . Gen 46:3
f the people of the . . . . Num 14:9
not *f* or be discouraged . . . . Deut 1:21
to put the dread and *f* . . . . . . Deut 2:25
f Me all the days . . . . Deut 4:10
You shall *f* the LORD . . . . Deut 6:13
f Him, and keep His . . . . Deut 13:4
book, that you may *f* . . . . . . Deut 28:58
do not *f* nor be dismayed . . . Deut 31:8
said, "Does Job *f* . . . . Job 1:9
Yes, you cast off *f* . . . . Job 15:4
houses are safe from *f* . . . . . . Job 21:9
"Dominion and *f* belong . . . . . Job 25:2
Surely no *f* of me will . . . . Job 33:7
He mocks at *f* . . . . Job 39:22
they are in great *f* . . . . Ps 14:5
You who *f* the LORD . . . . Ps 22:23
of death, I will *f* . . . . Ps 23:4
with those who *f* Him . . . . Ps 25:14
whom shall I *f* . . . . Ps 27:1
me, my heart shall not *f* . . . . . . Ps 27:3
Let all the earth *f* . . . . Ps 33:8
on those who *f* Him . . . . Ps 33:18
around those who *f* Him . . . . . . Ps 34:7
Oh, *f* the LORD . . . . Ps 34:9
there is no *f* of God . . . . Ps 36:1
they are in great *f* . . . . Ps 53:5
hear, all you who *f* . . . . Ps 66:16
ends of the earth shall *f* . . . . . . Ps 67:7
f You as long as the . . . . Ps 72:5
heart to *f* Your name . . . . Ps 86:11
LORD pities those who *f* . . . . Ps 103:13
those who *f* the LORD. . . . . . . Ps 115:13
Let those who *f* the LORD . . . . Ps 118:4
f You will be glad . . . . Ps 119:74
pleasure in those who *f* . . . . Ps 147:11
by the *f* of the LORD one . . . . Prov 16:6
The *f* of man brings a . . . . . Prov 29:25
it, that men should *f* . . . . Eccl 3:14
F God and keep His . . . . Eccl 12:13
let Him be your *f* . . . . Is 8:13
their *f* toward Me is taught . . . Is 29:13
"Be strong, do not *f* . . . . Is 35:4
F not, for I am with you . . . . . Is 41:10
F not, for I have redeemed . . . . Is 43:1
not *f* the reproach of men . . . . . Is 51:7
Do not *f*, for you will not . . . . . Is 54:4
the *f* of Me is not in you . . . . . Jer 2:19
Do you not *f* Me . . . . Jer 5:22
who would not *f* . . . . Jer 10:7
but I will put My *f* . . . . Jer 32:40
greatly beloved, *f* not . . . . . . Dan 10:19
who *f* My name the Sun . . . . . Mal 4:2
f Him who is able . . . . Matt 10:28
serve Him without *f* . . . . Luke 1:74
Then *f* came upon all . . . . . . Luke 7:16
"Do not *f*, little flock . . . . . . Luke 12:32
a judge who did not *f* . . . . . . Luke 18:2
failing them from *f* . . . . Luke 21:26
"Do you not even *f* . . . . Luke 23:40
of bondage again to *f* . . . . . . Rom 8:15
f to whom *f*, honor to . . . . . . Rom 13:7
holiness in the *f* of God . . . . . 2 Cor 7:1
another in the *f* of God . . . . . . Eph 5:21
your own salvation with *f* . . . Phil 2:12
the rest also may *f* . . . . 1 Tim 5:20
given us a spirit of *f* . . . . 2 Tim 1:7
those who through *f* . . . . Heb 2:15
His rest, let us *f* . . . . Heb 4:1
because of His godly *f* . . . . Heb 5:7
F God. Honor the king . . . . . 1 Pet 2:17
love casts out *f* . . . . 1 John 4:18
Do not *f* any of . . . . Rev 2:10
"*F* God and give glory . . . . . . Rev 14:7
servants and those who *f* . . . . Rev 19:5

FEAR OF THE LORD
f fell on the people . . . . 1 Sam 11:7
f fell on all the . . . . 2 Chr 17:10
f, that is wisdom, ... Job 28:28
The *f* is clean, enduring . . . . . . Ps 19:9
I will teach you the *f* . . . . Ps 34:11
The *f* is the beginning of . . . . Ps 111:10
The *f* is the beginning of . . . . Prov 1:7
The *f* is to hate evil; . . . . Prov 8:13
The *f* is the beginning of . . . Prov 9:10
The *f* prolongs days . . . . Prov 10:27
The *f* is a fountain of . . . . . . Prov 14:27
a little with the *f* . . . . Prov 15:16
The *f* is the instruction . . . . Prov 15:33
The *f* leads to life, ... Prov 19:23
By humility and the *f* . . . . Prov 22:4
of knowledge and of the *f* . . . . . Is 11:2
His delight is in the *f*, ... Is 11:3
And walking in the *f* . . . . Acts 9:31

FEAR THE LORD
That you may *f* your God, . . . Deut 6:2
require of you, but to *f* . . . . Deut 10:12
that they may learn to *f* . . . . Deut 31:12
f, serve Him in sincerity . . . Josh 24:14
them how they should *f* . . 2 Kin 17:28
he honors those who *f* . . . . Ps 15:4
who *f*, trust in the LORD; . . . . Ps 115:11
F and depart from evil . . . . . . Prov 3:7
"Let us now *f* . . . . Jer 5:24
I *f*, the God of heaven, ... Jon 1:9

FEARED
But the midwives *f* . . . . Ex 1:17
so the people *f* the LORD . . . Ex 14:31
He is also to be *f* . . . . 1 Chr 16:25
f God more than . . . . Neh 7:2
thing I greatly *f* has come . . . Job 3:25
Yourself, are to be *f* . . . . Ps 76:7
God is greatly to be *f* . . . . Ps 89:7
He is to be *f* above all gods . . . Ps 96:4
Then those who *f* . . . . Mal 3:16
they *f* greatly, saying . . . . . Matt 27:54
Him, for they *f* the people . . Luke 22:2
one who *f* God with all his . . Acts 10:2

FEARFUL
f in praises, doing . . . . Ex 15:11
them, "Why are you *f* . . . . . . Matt 8:26
there will be *f* sights . . . . . . Luke 21:11
It is a *f* thing to . . . . Heb 10:31

FEARFUL-HEARTED
to those who are *f* . . . . Is 35:4

FEARFULLY
f and wonderfully made . . . . . Ps 139:14

FEARFULNESS
F and trembling have . . . . Ps 55:5
f has seized the . . . . Is 33:14

FEARING
is devoted to *f* You . . . . Ps 119:38
woman, *f* and trembling . . . Mark 5:33
sincerity of heart, *f* . . . . Col 3:22
forsook Egypt, not *f* . . . . Heb 11:27

FEARS
upright man, one who *f* . . . . . . Job 1:8
Who is the man that *f* . . . . Ps 25:12
me from all my *f* . . . . Ps 34:4
every one who *f* the LORD . . . Ps 128:1
in his uprightness *f* . . . . Prov 14:2
a woman who *f* the LORD . . Prov 31:30
an oath as he who *f* . . . . Eccl 9:2
every nation whoever *f* . . . . Acts 10:35
f has not been made . . . . 1 John 4:18

FEAST
Then he made them a *f* . . . . . Gen 19:3
F of Unleavened Bread . . . . . Ex 12:17
keep a *f* to Me in the year . . . Ex 23:14
and the *F* of Harvest . . . . Ex 23:16
F of Ingathering . . . . Ex 23:16
observe the *F* of Weeks . . . . . Ex 34:22
F of the Passover be left . . . . Ex 34:25
F of Tabernacles for . . . . Lev 23:34
and you shall keep a *f* . . . . Num 29:12
the *F* of Esther, for all his . . Esth 2:18
moon, on our solemn *f* day . . . Ps 81:3
f is made for laughter . . . . . Eccl 10:19
f day the terrors that . . . . Lam 2:22
hate, I despise your *f* . . . . . Amos 5:21
"Not during the *f*, lest . . . . . Mark 14:2
every year at the *F* . . . . Luke 2:41
by anyone to a wedding *f* . . Luke 14:8
when you give a *f* . . . . Luke 14:13
Now the Passover, a *f* . . . . John 6:4
the *f* Jesus went up into . . . . John 7:14
great day of the *f* . . . . John 7:37
Now before the *f* of the . . . . John 13:1
let us keep the *f* . . . . 1 Cor 5:8

FEAST OF DEDICATION
Now it was the *F* . . . . John 10:22

FEAST OF HARVEST
and the *F*, the firstfruits . . . . . Ex 23:16

FEAST OF INGATHERING
F at the end of the year. ... Ex 23:16
and the *F* at the year's end .. Ex 34:22

FEAST OF TABERNACLES
the *F* for seven days ... Lev 23:34
observe the *F* seven ... Deut 16:13
year of release, at the *F* ... Deut 31:10
They also kept the *F*, ... Ezra 3:4
and to keep the *F* ... Zech 14:16
Now the Jews' *F* ... John 7:2

FEAST OF UNLEAVENED BREAD
you shall observe the *F* ... Ex 12:17
You shall keep the *F* ... Ex 23:15
F you shall keep. Seven ... Ex 34:18
Jerusalem to keep the *F* .. 2 Chr 30:13
And they kept the *F* ... Ezra 6:22
on the first day of the *F* ... Matt 26:17
the Passover and the *F* ... Mark 14:1
Now the *F* drew near, ... Luke 22:1

FEAST OF WEEKS
you shall observe the *F* ... Ex 34:22
at your *f*, you shall have .. Num 28:26
you shall keep the *F* ... Deut 16:10

FEASTING
house full of *f* with strife ... Prov 17:1
go to the house of *f* ... Eccl 7:2

FEASTS
See APPOINTED FEASTS
These are the *f* of the LORD .. Lev 23:4
in your appointed *f* ... Num 10:10
Moons and on the set *f* ... 1 Chr 23:31
I will turn your *f* ... Amos 8:10
the best places at *f* ... Luke 20:46
spots in your love *f* ... Jude 12

FEATHERS
shall cover you with His *f* ... Ps 91:4

FED
f me all my life long ... Gen 48:15
and *f* you with manna ... Deut 8:3
but the shepherds *f* ... Ezek 34:8
They *f* him with grass like .. Dan 5:21
So those who *f* the swine .. Mark 5:14
desiring to be *f* with the .. Luke 16:21
f you with milk and ... 1 Cor 3:2

FEEBLE
strengthened the *f* ... Job 4:4
And there was none *f* ... Ps 105:37
And my flesh is *f* ... Ps 109:24
and make firm the *f* knees ... Is 35:3
Every hand will be *f* ... Ezek 7:17
hang down, and the *f* ... Heb 12:12

FEED
ravens to *f* you there ... 1 Kin 17:4
and *f* on His faithfulness ... Ps 37:3
death shall *f* on them ... Ps 49:14
of the righteous *f* ... Prov 10:21
He will *f* His flock like a ... Is 40:11
and *f* your flocks ... Is 61:5
f you with knowledge ... Jer 3:15
over them who will *f* them ... Jer 23:4
I will *f* My flock, and I ... Ezek 34:15
to him, "*F* My lambs ... John 21:15
to him, "*F* My sheep ... John 21:17
your enemy hungers, *f* ... Rom 12:20
my goods to *f* the poor ... 1 Cor 13:3

FEEDS
"Ephraim *f* on the wind ... Hos 12:1
your heavenly Father *f* ... Matt 6:26
he who *f* on Me will live ... John 6:57

FEET
See UNDER HIS FEET
your sandals off your *f* ... Ex 3:5
not worn out on your *f* ... Deut 29:5
f touched the dry land ... Josh 4:18
So she lay at his *f* ... Ruth 3:14
was lame in both his *f* ... 2 Sam 9:13
so my *f* did not slip ... 2 Sam 22:37
in places forgotten by *f* ... Job 28:4
I was *f* to the lame ... Job 29:15
all things under his *f* ... Ps 8:6
He makes my *f* like the ... Ps 18:33
pierced My hands and My *f* . Ps 22:16
You have set my *f* ... Ps 31:8
and set my *f* upon a rock ... Ps 40:2
does not allow our *f* ... Ps 66:9
f had almost stumbled ... Ps 73:2
and my *f* from falling ... Ps 116:8
f from every evil way ... Ps 119:101
word is a lamp to my *f* ... Ps 119:105
f have been standing ... Ps 122:2
For their *f* run to ... Prov 1:16
Her *f* go down to death ... Prov 5:5
f that are swift in running .. Prov 6:18
spreads a net for his *f* ... Prov 29:5
with two he covered his *f* ... Is 6:2
sandals off your *f* ... Is 20:2
called him to His *f* ... Is 41:2
up the dust of your *f* ... Is 49:23
mountains are the *f* ... Is 52:7
place of My *f* glorious ... Is 60:13
have not restrained their *f* ... Jer 14:10
its *f* partly of iron and ... Dan 2:33
f like burnished bronze in ... Dan 10:6
are the dust of His *f* ... Nah 1:3
on the mountains the *f* of ... Nah 1:15
make my *f* like deer's *f* ... Hab 3:19
in that day His *f* ... Zech 14:4
off the dust from your *f* ... Matt 10:14
two hands or two *f* ... Matt 18:8
saw Him, he fell at His *f* ... Mark 5:22
she came and fell at His *f* .. Mark 7:25
rather than having two *f* ... Mark 9:45
began to wash His *f* ... Luke 7:38
sitting at the *f* of Jesus ... Luke 8:35
also sat at Jesus' *f* ... Luke 10:39
and sandals on his *f* ... Luke 15:22
My hands and My *f* ... Luke 24:39
wash the disciples' *f* ... John 13:5
wash one another's *f* ... John 13:14
and the other at the *f* ... John 20:12
up, and immediately his *f* ... Acts 3:7
at the apostles' *f* ... Acts 4:35
your sandals off your *f* ... Acts 7:33
his own hands and *f* ... Acts 21:11
f are swift to shed ... Rom 3:15
beautiful are the *f* ... Rom 10:15
all things under His *f* ... 1 Cor 15:27
put all things under His *f* ... Eph 1:22
and having shod your *f* ... Eph 6:15
straight paths for your *f* ... Heb 12:13
fell at His *f* as dead ... Rev 1:17
And I fell at his *f* ... Rev 19:10

FELIX
Governor of Judea; letter addressed to, Acts 23:24–30
Paul's defense before, Acts 24:1–27

FELL
f on his neck and kissed ... Gen 33:4
Joseph *f* on his father's ... Gen 50:1
Saul took a sword and *f* .. 1 Sam 31:4
ax head *f* into the water ... 2 Kin 6:5
Saul took a sword and *f* ... 1 Chr 10:4
fear of the Jews *f* upon ... Esth 8:17
fire of God *f* from heaven ... Job 1:16
foes, they stumbled and *f* ... Ps 27:2
f on my face, and I heard .. Ezek 1:28
Spirit of the LORD *f* upon ... Ezek 11:5
f down bound into the ... Dan 3:23
lots, and the lot *f* on Jonah ... Jon 1:7
on that house; and it *f* ... Matt 7:27
seed *f* by the wayside ... Matt 13:4
others *f* on good ground ... Matt 13:8
saw Him, he *f* at His feet .. Mark 5:22
as they sailed He *f* asleep .. Luke 8:23
f among thieves ... Luke 10:30
the tower in Siloam *f* ... Luke 13:4
f from the rich man's ... Luke 16:21
she *f* down at His feet ... John 11:32
and the lot *f* on Matthias ... Acts 1:26
f down and breathed his ... Acts 5:5
had said this, he *f* asleep ... Acts 7:60
ready, he *f* into a trance ... Acts 10:10
the Holy Spirit *f* upon all .. Acts 10:44
his chains *f* off his hands ... Acts 12:7
he *f* down from the third ... Acts 20:9
who reproached You *f* on ... Rom 15:3
f down after they were ... Heb 11:30
elders *f* down before ... Rev 5:8
of heaven *f* to the earth ... Rev 6:13
a great star *f* from heaven .. Rev 8:10
four living creatures *f* ... Rev 19:4

FELLOW
f servants who owed ... Matt 18:28
begins to beat his *f* ... Matt 24:49
f worker concerning ... 2 Cor 8:23
f citizens with the ... Eph 2:19
Gentiles should be *f* ... Eph 3:6
rest of my *f* workers ... Phil 4:3
These are my only *f* ... Col 4:11
that we may become *f* ... 3 John 8
I am your *f* servant ... Rev 19:10

FELLOWSHIP
doctrine and *f* ... Acts 2:42
were called into the *f* ... 1 Cor 1:9
not want you to have *f* ... 1 Cor 10:20
f has righteousness ... 2 Cor 6:14
the right hand of *f* ... Gal 2:9
And have no *f* with the ... Eph 5:11
for your *f* in the ... Phil 1:5
of love, if any *f* ... Phil 2:1
and the *f* of His ... Phil 3:10
also may have *f* ... 1 John 1:3
we say that we have *f* ... 1 John 1:6
the light, we have *f* ... 1 John 1:7

FEMALE
male and *f* He created ... Gen 1:27
they shall be male and *f* ... Gen 6:19
ark to Noah, male and *f* ... Gen 7:9
has borne a male or a *f* ... Lev 12:7
made them male and *f* ... Matt 19:4
there is neither male nor *f* ... Gal 3:28

FENCE
and a tottering *f* ... Ps 62:3

FENCED
He has *f* up my way ... Job 19:8

FERTILIZE
I dig around it and *f* ... Luke 13:8

FERVENT
f desire I have desired ... Luke 22:15
and being *f* in spirit ... Acts 18:25
f in spirit, serving the ... Rom 12:11
f prayer of a ... James 5:16
all things have *f* ... 1 Pet 4:8
will melt with *f* ... 2 Pet 3:10

FERVENTLY
you, always laboring *f* ... Col 4:12
love one another *f* ... 1 Pet 1:22

FESTIVAL
night when a holy *f* ... Is 30:29
or regarding a *f* ... Col 2:16

FESTUS
Governor of Judea, Acts 24:27
Paul's defense made to, Acts 25:1–22

FETCH
f my knowledge from ... Job 36:3

FETTERS
hurt his feet with *f* ... Ps 105:18
their nobles with *f* ... Ps 149:8

FEVER
f which shall consume ... Lev 26:16
my bones burn with *f* ... Job 30:30
mother lying sick with a *f* .. Matt 8:14
immediately the *f* left her .. Mark 1:31
and rebuked the *f* ... Luke 4:39
of Publius lay sick of a *f* ... Acts 28:8

FEW
f and evil have been . . . . Gen 47:9
f days and full of . . . . Job 14:1
Let his days be *f* . . . . Ps 109:8
let your words be *f* . . . . Eccl 5:2
there are *f* who find it . . . . . . Matt 7:14
but the laborers are *f* . . . . Matt 9:37
called, but *f* chosen . . . . Matt 20:16
"Lord, are there *f* . . . . Luke 13:23
prepared, in which a *f* . . . . . 1 Pet 3:20
I have a *f* things . . . . Rev 2:20

FIDELITY
but showing all good *f* . . . . . Titus 2:10

FIELD
and to every beast of the *f* . . Gen 2:20
f which the LORD has . . . . Gen 27:27
gleaned in the *f* after the . . . . Ruth 2:3
even the beasts of the *f* . . . . Ps 8:7
Let the *f* be joyful . . . . Ps 96:12
as a flower of the *f*, so he . . Ps 103:15
went by the *f* of the lazy . . Prov 24:30
She considers a *f* and . . . . . Prov 31:16
to house; they add *f* . . . . Is 5:8
becomes a fruitful *f* . . . . Is 32:15
is like the flower of the *f* . . . . . . Is 40:6
beast of the *f* will honor . . . . . Is 43:20
all the trees of the *f* shall . . . . Is 55:12
"Buy the *f* for money . . . . Jer 32:25
thrive like a plant in the *f* . . Ezek 16:5
shall be plowed like a *f* . . . . . Mic 3:12
Consider the lilies of the *f* . . Matt 6:28
clothes the grass of the *f* . . . Matt 6:30
The *f* is the world . . . . Matt 13:38
and buys that *f* . . . . Matt 13:44
let him who is in the *f* . . . Matt 24:18
f has been called the . . . . Matt 27:8
which today is in the *f* . . . . Luke 12:28
Two men will be in the *f* . . Luke 17:36
you are God's *f* . . . . 1 Cor 3:9
the *f* he will pass away . . . James 1:10

FIELD OF BLOOD
A field bought as a cemetery for Judas's burial, Matt 27:1–10
Predicted in the O.T., Zech 11:12, 13

FIELDS
and sends waters on the *f* . . . Job 5:10
nor enter the *f* of the . . . . . . Prov 23:10
f yield no food . . . . Hab 3:17
living out in the *f* . . . . Luke 2:8
eyes and look at the *f* . . . . . John 4:35

FIERCE
the *f* wrath of our God . . . . Ezra 10:14
f wrath has gone over me . . . Ps 88:16
A *f* lion is in the streets . . . Prov 26:13
the *f* anger of the LORD . . . . Jer 4:8
in the day of His *f* anger . . . Lam 1:12
turn away from His *f* anger . . Jon 3:9
the tombs, exceedingly *f* . . . . Matt 8:28
are driven by *f* winds . . . . . . James 3:4

FIERCENESS
f has deceived you . . . . Jer 49:16
the winepress of the *f* . . . . . . Rev 19:15

FIERY
the LORD sent *f* serpents. . . . Num 21:6
right hand came a *f* . . . . Deut 33:2
shall make them as a *f* . . . . Ps 21:9
their flocks to *f* lightning . . . . Ps 78:48
offspring will be a *f* . . . . Is 14:29
burning *f* furnace . . . . Dan 3:6
from the burning *f* furnace . . Dan 3:17
f darts of the wicked one . . . . Eph 6:16
concerning the *f* trial . . . . . . 1 Pet 4:12
horse, *f* red, went out . . . . Rev 6:4
f red dragon having . . . . Rev 12:3

FIFTEEN
about *f* thousand all who . . . Judg 8:10
add to your days *f* years . . . 2 Kin 20:6
remained with him *f* days . . . Gal 1:18

FIFTH
morning were the *f* day . . . . . Gen 1:23
He opened the *f* seal . . . . Rev 6:9
the *f* angel poured out . . . . . Rev 16:10

FIFTY
nine hundred and *f* years . . . Gen 9:29
Suppose there were *f* . . . . . . Gen 18:24
f prophets of Baal, and . . . 1 Kin 18:19
denarii, and the other *f* . . . . Luke 7:41
sit down in groups of *f* . . . . Luke 9:14
down quickly and write *f* . . Luke 16:6
"You are not yet *f* years . . . John 8:57

FIG
f leaves together . . . . Gen 3:7
f trees and pomegranates . . . . Deut 8:8
his vine and his *f* . . . . 1 Kin 4:25
from his own *f* tree . . . . . . 2 Kin 18:31
fruit falling from a *f* . . . . Is 34:4
and the *f* tree has withered . . . Joel 1:12
f tree and the vine yield . . . . Joel 2:22
f tree may not blossom . . . . . Hab 3:17
immediately the *f* tree . . . . . Matt 21:19
parable from the *f* tree . . . . Matt 24:32
saw the *f* tree dried up . . . Mark 11:20
fruit on this *f* . . . . Luke 13:7
"Look at the *f* . . . . Luke 21:29
'I saw you under the *f* . . . . . John 1:50
Can a *f* tree . . . . James 3:12
f tree drops its late . . . . Rev 6:13

FIGHT
The LORD will *f* for you . . . . . . Ex 14:14
like men, and *f* . . . . 1 Sam 4:9
you go with me to *f* . . . . 1 Kin 22:4
Our God will *f* for us . . . . Neh 4:20
My servants would *f* . . . . . John 18:36
to him, let us not *f* . . . . Acts 23:9
Thus I *f*: not as one who . . . 1 Cor 9:26
F the good *f* . . . . 1 Tim 6:12
have fought the good *f* . . . . . 2 Tim 4:7
You *f* and war . . . . James 4:2

FIGHTS
your God is He who *f* . . . . . Josh 23:10
because my lord *f* . . . . 1 Sam 25:28
f come from among . . . . James 4:1

FIGS
puts forth her green *f* . . . . . . Song 2:13
f set before the . . . . Jer 24:1
from thornbushes or *f* . . . . . . Matt 7:16
men do not gather *f* . . . . Luke 6:44
or a grapevine bear *f* . . . . . . James 3:12

FIGURATIVELY
brethren, I have *f* . . . . 1 Cor 4:6

FIGURE
using no *f* of speech . . . . . . John 16:29

FILL
f the earth and subdue . . . . . . Gen 1:28
multiply, and *f* the earth . . . . . . Gen 9:1
f their sacks with grain . . . . Gen 42:25
"*F* four waterpots . . . . 1 Kin 18:33
He will yet *f* your mouth . . . . . . Job 8:21
f my mouth with . . . . Job 23:4
wealth, that I may *f* . . . . Prov 8:21
out of his wings will *f* the . . . . . . Is 8:8
"Do I not *f* heaven . . . . Jer 23:24
f this temple with . . . . Hag 2:7
f such a great multitude . . . Matt 15:33
"*F* the waterpots . . . . John 2:7
hope *f* you with all joy . . . . Rom 15:13
that He might *f* . . . . Eph 4:10
so as always to *f* . . . . 1 Thess 2:16

FILLED
f her pitcher, and came . . . . Gen 24:16
you shall be *f* with bread . . . . Ex 16:12
the LORD *f* the tabernacle. . . . Ex 40:34
all the earth shall be *f* . . . . Num 14:21
f the house of the LORD . . . . 1 Kin 8:11
So they ate and were *f* . . . . . . Neh 9:25
the whole earth be *f* . . . . Ps 72:19
they are *f* with good . . . . Ps 104:28
Then our mouth was *f* . . . . Ps 126:2
barns will be *f* with . . . . Prov 3:10
of his lips he shall be *f* . . . . Prov 18:20
for they shall be *f* . . . . Matt 5:6
they all ate and were *f* . . . . Matt 14:20
"Let the children be *f* . . . . . Mark 7:27
in spirit, *f* with wisdom . . . . Luke 2:40
f with the Holy Spirit . . . . Luke 4:1
were *f* with fear, saying . . . . Luke 5:26
he would gladly have *f* . . . Luke 15:16
they *f* them up to the brim . . . John 2:7
f twelve baskets with the . . . John 6:13
sorrow has *f* your heart . . . . John 16:6
were all *f* with the Holy . . . . . Acts 2:4
why has Satan *f* your heart . . Acts 5:3
being *f* with all . . . . Rom 1:29
full of goodness, *f* . . . . Rom 15:14
that you may be *f* . . . . Eph 3:19
but be *f* with the Spirit . . . . . Eph 5:18
being *f* with the fruits . . . . Phil 1:11
peace, be warmed and *f* . . James 2:16

FILLED WITH THE HOLY SPIRIT
He will also be *f* . . . . Luke 1:15
and Elizabeth was *f* . . . . Luke 1:41
father Zacharias was *f* . . . . . . Luke 1:67
Then Jesus, being *f* . . . . Luke 4:1
And they were all *f* . . . . Acts 2:4
Peter, *f*, said to them . . . . Acts 4:8
and they were all *f*, ... Acts 4:31
your sight and be *f* . . . . Acts 9:17
who also is called Paul, *f*, . . . Acts 13:9

FILTH
has washed away the *f* . . . . Is 4:4
been made as the *f* . . . . 1 Cor 4:13
the removal of the *f* . . . . 1 Pet 3:21

FILTHINESS
from all your *f* . . . . Ezek 36:25
ourselves from all *f* . . . . 2 Cor 7:1
lay aside all *f* . . . . James 1:21
abominations and the *f* . . . . . Rev 17:4

FILTHY
is abominable and *f* . . . . Job 15:16
with *f* garments . . . . Zech 3:3
malice, blasphemy, *f* . . . . Col 3:8
poor man in *f* clothes . . . . . . James 2:2
oppressed by the *f* . . . . 2 Pet 2:7
let him be *f* . . . . Rev 22:11

FIND
"If I *f* in Sodom fifty . . . . . Gen 18:26
not *f* the household idols . . . Gen 31:35
Can we *f* such a one as . . . . Gen 41:38
straw where you can *f* it . . . . . Ex 5:11
that I may *f* grace in Your . . Ex 33:13
sure your sin will *f* . . . . Num 32:23
you will *f* Him if you seek . . Deut 4:29
"Let me *f* favor in your . . . . Ruth 2:13
f the arrows which I . . . . . 1 Sam 20:36
f in the book of the . . . . Ezra 4:15
Can you *f* out the limits of . . Job 11:7
knew where I might *f* Him . . Job 23:3
Almighty, we cannot *f* . . . . . Job 37:23
but they will not *f* me . . . . . . Prov 1:28
life to those who *f* . . . . Prov 4:22
seek me diligently will *f* . . . . Prov 8:17
word wisely will *f* good . . . Prov 16:20
can *f* a virtuous wife . . . . . . Prov 31:10
that no one can *f* . . . . Eccl 3:11
waters, for you will *f* . . . . Eccl 11:1
if you *f* my beloved . . . . Song 5:8
f Me, when you search for . . . Jer 29:13
seek, and you will *f* . . . . Matt 7:7
and there are few who *f* it . . . Matt 7:14
for My sake will *f* . . . . Matt 10:39
will *f* a piece of money . . . . Matt 17:27
when he comes, will *f* . . . . . Matt 24:46
you will *f* a colt tied . . . . Mark 11:2
he *f* you sleeping . . . . Mark 13:36
f a Babe wrapped . . . . Luke 2:12
seek, and you will *f* . . . . Luke 11:9
you will *f* a colt tied . . . . . . Luke 19:30

f no fault in this Man ...... Luke 23:4
seek Me and not *f* Me ...... John 7:34
not *f* them in the prison ...... Acts 5:22
I *f* then a law ...... Rom 7:21
f grace to help in ...... Heb 4:16
seek death and will not *f* it ... Rev 9:6

FINDING
great things past *f* ...... Job 9:10
rest; and *f* none ...... Luke 11:24
and His ways past *f* ...... Rom 11:33

FINDS
one who *f* great treasure .. Ps 119:162
the man who *f* wisdom ...... Prov 3:13
whoever *f* me *f* life ...... Prov 8:35
f a wife *f* a good ...... Prov 18:22
Whatever your hand *f* ...... Eccl 9:10
You the fatherless *f* mercy ... Hos 14:3
and he who seeks *f* ...... Matt 7:8
f his life will lose ...... Matt 10:39
he *f* it empty, swept, and .. Matt 12:44
and he who seeks *f* ...... Luke 11:10
carefully until she *f* it ...... Luke 15:8

FINE
ate up the seven *f* looking ... Gen 41:4
Then I beat them as *f* .... 2 Sam 22:43
gold, yea, than much *f* ...... Ps 19:10
than gold, yes, than *f* gold .. Prov 8:19
f gold is a wise ...... Prov 25:12
her clothing is *f* linen ...... Prov 31:22
set on bases of *f* gold ...... Song 5:15
more rare than *f* ...... Is 13:12
and for *f* clothing ...... Is 23:18
how changed the *f* ...... Lam 4:1
Then he bought *f* linen ... Mark 15:46
rings, in *f* apparel ...... James 2:2
His feet were like *f* brass .... Rev 1:15
for the *f* linen is the ...... Rev 19:8

FINGER
written with the *f* ...... Ex 31:18
written with the *f* of God ... Deut 9:10
f shall be thicker ...... 1 Kin 12:10
the pointing of the *f* ...... Is 58:9
demons with the *f* of ...... Luke 11:20
dip the tip of his *f* ...... Luke 16:24
the ground with His *f* ...... John 8:6
"Reach your *f* ...... John 20:27

FINGERS
the work of Your *f* ...... Ps 8:3
he points with his *f* ...... Prov 6:13
Bind them on your *f* ...... Prov 7:3
that which their own *f* ...... Is 2:8
In the same hour the *f* of a ... Dan 5:5
with one of their *f* ...... Matt 23:4
put His *f* in his ears ...... Mark 7:33

FINISH
We *f* our years like a sigh .... Ps 90:9
to *f* the transgression ...... Dan 9:24
he has enough to *f* ...... Luke 14:28
has given Me to *f* ...... John 5:36
so that I may *f* ...... Acts 20:24

FINISHED
house of the LORD was *f* ... 1 Kin 7:51
f the work which You ...... John 17:4
He said, "It is *f* ...... John 19:30
I have *f* the race ...... 2 Tim 4:7
thousand years were *f* ...... Rev 20:3

FIRE
rained brimstone and *f* .... Gen 19:24
to him in a flame of *f* ...... Ex 3:2
the pillar of *f* by night ...... Ex 13:22
descended upon it in *f* ...... Ex 19:18
made, burned it in the *f* ...... Ex 32:20
by day, and *f* was over ...... Ex 40:38
profane *f* before the LORD ... Lev 10:1
through the *f* to Molech .... Lev 18:21
like the appearance of *f* ...... Num 9:15
the *f* was quenched ...... Num 11:2
from the midst of the *f* ...... Deut 5:24
God, who answers by *f* ... 1 Kin 18:24
the *f* of the LORD fell ...... 1 Kin 18:38
LORD was not in the *f* ...... 1 Kin 19:12
of *f* appeared with horses .. 2 Kin 2:11
I was musing, the *f* ...... Ps 39:3
we went through *f* ...... Ps 66:12
they have set *f* ...... Ps 74:7
f goes before Him ...... Ps 97:3
His ministers a flame of *f* .... Ps 104:4
f and hail, snow and ...... Ps 148:8
burns as the *f* ...... Is 9:18
says the LORD, whose *f* ...... Is 31:9
you walk through the *f* ...... Is 43:2
f that burns all the ...... Is 65:5
My fury come forth like *f* ...... Jer 4:4
their daughters in the *f* ...... Jer 7:31
His waist and downward, *f* .. Ezek 8:2
in the midst of the *f* ...... Dan 3:25
the smell of *f* was not on ...... Dan 3:27
He break out like *f* ...... Amos 5:6
for conflict by *f* ...... Amos 7:4
a brand plucked from the *f* .. Zech 3:2
like a refiner's *f* ...... Mal 3:2
the Holy Spirit and *f* ...... Matt 3:11
chaff with unquenchable *f* .. Matt 3:12
shall be in danger of hell *f* .. Matt 5:22
he often falls into the *f* .... Matt 17:15
into the everlasting *f* ...... Matt 25:41
f is not quenched ...... Mark 9:44
"I came to send *f* ...... Luke 12:49
tongues, as of *f* ...... Acts 2:3
off the creature into the *f* .. Acts 28:5
coals of *f* on his head ...... Rom 12:20
f taking vengeance ...... 2 Thess 1:8
His ministers a flame of *f* .... Heb 1:7
and that burned with *f* ...... Heb 12:18
our God is a consuming *f* .. Heb 12:29
And the tongue is a *f* ...... James 3:6
vengeance of eternal *f* ...... Jude 7
His eyes like a flame of *f* .. Rev 1:14
f came down from God ...... Rev 20:9
into the lake of *f* ...... Rev 20:14

FIREBRAND
f plucked from the ...... Amos 4:11

FIREBRANDS
a madman who throws *f* .. Prov 26:18
two stubs of smoking *f* ...... Is 7:4

FIRM
their strength is *f* ...... Ps 73:4
shall stand *f* with him ...... Ps 89:28
Take *f* hold of instruction .. Prov 4:13
f the feeble knees ...... Is 35:3
of the hope *f* to the ...... Heb 3:6

FIRMAMENT
Thus God made the *f* ...... Gen 1:7
f shows His handiwork ...... Ps 19:1
in His mighty *f* ...... Ps 150:1
brightness of the *f* ...... Dan 12:3

FIRST
the morning were the *f* day .. Gen 1:5
cows ate up the *f* seven .... Gen 41:20
The *f* of the firstfruits of ...... Ex 23:19
"Give the *f* woman the .... 1 Kin 3:27
The *f* one to plead his ..... Prov 18:17
f father sinned ...... Is 43:27
the *F* and I am the Last ...... Is 44:6
f was like a lion, and had ...... Dan 7:4
F be reconciled to your .... Matt 5:24
seek *f* the kingdom of ...... Matt 6:33
F remove the plank from .... Matt 7:5
unless he *f* binds the ...... Matt 12:29
man is worse than the *f* ... Matt 12:45
who are *f* will be last ...... Matt 19:30
desires to be *f* ...... Matt 20:27
This is the *f* and great ...... Matt 22:38
f the blade, then the ...... Mark 4:28
that Elijah must come *f* .... Mark 9:11
f shall be slave ...... Mark 10:44
the *f* commandment ...... Mark 12:30
And the gospel must *f* .... Mark 13:10
He appeared *f* to Mary .... Mark 16:9
let me *f* go and bury my ... Luke 9:59
f He must suffer many .... Luke 17:25
f took a wife, and died .... Luke 20:29
f found his own brother .... John 1:41
him throw a stone at her *f* .. John 8:7
disciples were *f* called ...... Acts 11:26
evil, of the Jew *f* ...... Rom 2:9
"Or who has *f* given ...... Rom 11:35
f apostles, second ...... 1 Cor 12:28
f man Adam became a ... 1 Cor 15:45
f a willing mind ...... 2 Cor 8:12
that we who *f* trusted ...... Eph 1:12
the *f* commandment with ...... Eph 6:2
in Christ will rise *f* ...... 1 Thess 4:16
the falling away comes *f* .. 2 Thess 2:3
Therefore I exhort *f* of all .. 1 Tim 2:1
For Adam was formed *f* ... 1 Tim 2:13
let them *f* learn to show ..... 1 Tim 5:4
to teach you again the *f* .... Heb 5:12
f covenant had been ...... Heb 8:7
from above is *f* pure ...... James 3:17
knowing this *f*, that no ...... 2 Pet 1:20
this *f*: that scoffers will ...... 2 Pet 3:3
love Him because He *f* ... 1 John 4:19
I am the *F* and the ...... Rev 1:17
you have left your *f* ...... Rev 2:4
The *f* angel sounded ...... Rev 8:7
is the *f* resurrection ...... Rev 20:5
f earth had passed away ...... Rev 21:1

FIRST AND THE LAST
and the Omega, the *F* ...... Rev 1:11
not be afraid; I am the *F* ...... Rev 1:17
'These things says the *F*, ... Rev 2:8
and the End, the *F* ...... Rev 22:13

FIRST-RIPE
f fruit which my soul ...... Mic 7:1

FIRSTBORN
"I am Esau your *f* ...... Gen 27:19
"Israel is My son, My *f* ...... Ex 4:22
LORD struck all the *f* ...... Ex 12:29
"Consecrate to Me all the *f* ... Ex 13:2
was the *f* of Israel ...... Num 26:5
destroyed all the *f* in Egypt .. Ps 78:51
I will make him My *f* ...... Ps 89:27
Shall I give my *f* ...... Mic 6:7
as one grieves for a *f* ...... Zech 12:10
brought forth her *f* ...... Matt 1:25
brought forth her *f* Son .... Luke 2:7
that He might be the *f* ...... Rom 8:29
invisible God, the *f* ...... Col 1:15
the beginning, the *f* ...... Col 1:18
witness, the *f* from ...... Rev 1:5

FIRSTFRUIT
For if the *f* is holy ...... Rom 11:16

FIRSTFRUITS
the *f* of your harvest to ...... Lev 23:10
bring the *f* of our ground .. Neh 10:35
with the *f* of all your ...... Prov 3:9
also who have the *f* ...... Rom 8:23
and has become the *f* ...... 1 Cor 15:20
order: Christ the *f* ...... 1 Cor 15:23
might be a kind of *f* ...... James 1:18
among men, being *f* ...... Rev 14:4

FISH
over the *f* of the sea ...... Gen 1:28
f taken in a cruel net ...... Eccl 9:12
had prepared a great *f* ...... Jon 1:17
do You make men like *f* ...... Hab 1:14
Or if he asks for a *f* ...... Matt 7:10
belly of the great *f* ...... Matt 12:40
five loaves and two *f* ...... Matt 14:17
and likewise the *f* ...... John 21:13

FISHERMEN
The *f* also will mourn ...... Is 19:8
I will send for many *f* ...... Jer 16:16

FISHERS
and I will make you *f* ...... Matt 4:19

FIT
and looking back, is *f* ...... Luke 9:62

FITTING
Therefore it is not *f* for the .. Esth 3:8
Is it *f* to say to a .... Job 34:18
Luxury is not *f* .... Prov 19:10
so honor is not *f* .... Prov 26:1
things which are not *f* .... Rom 1:28
husbands, as is *f* in the ...... Col 3:18
a High Priest was *f* .... Heb 7:26

FIVE
bring out those *f* kings .... Josh 10:22
f smooth stones .... 1 Sam 17:40
about *f* thousand men ..... Matt 14:21
and *f* were foolish .... Matt 25:2
to one he gave *f* talents ... Matt 25:15
Are not *f* sparrows sold .... Luke 12:6
bought *f* yoke of oxen .... Luke 14:19
you have had *f* husbands .. John 4:18
speak *f* words with my ... 1 Cor 14:19

FIXED
f My limit for it .... Job 38:10
is a great gulf *f* .... Luke 16:26

FLAME
appeared to him in a *f* .... Ex 3:2
f will dry out his .... Job 15:30
His ministers a *f* of fire ...... Ps 104:4
f consumes the chaff .... Is 5:24
and his Holy One for a *f* ...... Is 10:17
and tempest and the *f* .... Is 29:6
nor shall the *f* scorch you ..... Is 43:2
hot, the *f* of the fire killed .. Dan 3:22
behind them a *f* .... Joel 2:3
am tormented in this *f* .... Luke 16:24
and His ministers a *f* .... Heb 1:7
and His eyes like a *f* .... Rev 1:14

FLAMES
the LORD divides the *f* .... Ps 29:7

FLAMING
f sword which turned .... Gen 3:24
f fire in their land .... Ps 105:32
in *f* fire taking .... 2 Thess 1:8

FLANKS
Strengthen your *f* .... Nah 2:1

FLASK
alabaster *f* of fragrant oil .. Luke 7:37

FLATTER
I do not know how to *f* ..... Job 32:22
They *f* with their .... Ps 5:9

FLATTERED
Nevertheless they *f* .... Ps 78:36

FLATTERING
f mouth works ruin .... Prov 26:28
f speech deceive .... Rom 16:18
any time did we use *f* ..... 1 Thess 2:5
swelling words, *f* .... Jude 16

FLATTERS
with one who *f* with .... Prov 20:19
f his neighbor spreads ...... Prov 29:5

FLATTERY
shall corrupt with *f* .... Dan 11:32

FLAVOR
the salt loses its *f* .... Matt 5:13

FLAVORLESS
f food be eaten .... Job 6:6

FLAX
f He will not quench .... Is 42:3
f He will not quench ...... Matt 12:20

FLED
Moses *f* from the face of ...... Ex 2:15
f before the men of Ai .... Josh 7:4
The sea saw it and *f* .... Ps 114:3
who have *f* for refuge .... Heb 6:18

FLEE
f away secretly .... Gen 31:27
those who hate You *f* ..... Num 10:35
such a man as I *f* .... Neh 6:11
who see me outside *f* .... Ps 31:11
Or where can I *f* .... Ps 139:7
wicked *f* when no one ..... Prov 28:1
And the shadows *f* .... Song 2:17
f to Egypt, and stay there .. Matt 2:13
who are in Judea *f* .... Matt 24:16
F sexual immorality .... 1 Cor 6:18
f these things and .... 1 Tim 6:11
F also youthful lusts ...... 2 Tim 2:22
devil and he will *f* .... James 4:7

FLEECE
there is dew on the *f* only .. Judg 6:37

FLESH
See ACCORDING TO THE FLESH
bone of my bones and *f* ..... Gen 2:23
shall become one *f* .... Gen 2:24
f had corrupted their .... Gen 6:12
f I shall see God .... Job 19:26
My *f* also will rest in .... Ps 16:9
What can *f* do to me .... Ps 56:4
f longs for You in a dry ...... Ps 63:1
that they were but *f* .... Ps 78:39
my heart and my *f* .... Ps 84:2
Who gives food to all *f* ..... Ps 136:25
f shall bless His holy .... Ps 145:21
It will be health to your *f* .... Prov 3:8
and health to all their *f* .... Prov 4:22
mouth cause your *f* to sin .... Eccl 5:6
is wearisome to the *f* .... Eccl 12:12
And all *f* shall see it .... Is 40:5
"All *f* is grass .... Is 40:6
give them a heart of *f* ..... Ezek 11:19
of stone out of your *f* .. Ezek 36:26
out My Spirit on all *f* .... Joel 2:28
Be silent, all *f*, before the .. Zech 2:13
two shall become one *f* ..... Matt 19:5
were shortened, no *f* .... Matt 24:22
is willing, but the *f* is ..... Matt 26:41
shall become one *f* .... Mark 10:8
but the *f* is weak .... Mark 14:38
f shall see the salvation ..... Luke 3:6
And the Word became *f* ...... John 1:14
is born of the *f* is *f* .... John 3:6
I shall give is My *f* .... John 6:51
unless you eat the *f* .... John 6:53
Whoever eats My *f* and .... John 6:54
For My *f* is food indeed .... John 6:55
f profits nothing .... John 6:63
according to the *f* .... John 8:15
Him authority over all *f* .... John 17:2
out of My Spirit on all *f* .... Acts 2:17
did His *f* see corruption ..... Acts 2:31
no *f* will be justified in ...... Rom 3:20
when we were in the *f* .... Rom 7:5
in my *f*) nothing good .... Rom 7:18
of God, but with the *f* ...... Rom 7:25
not walk according to the *f* .. Rom 8:1
on the things of the *f* .... Rom 8:5
in the *f* cannot please God .... Rom 8:8
you are not in the *f* .... Rom 8:9
to the *f* you will die .... Rom 8:13
no provision for the *f* ..... Rom 13:14
f should glory in His .... 1 Cor 1:29
for the destruction of the *f* .. 1 Cor 5:5
"shall become one *f* .... 1 Cor 6:16
there is one kind of *f* ..... 1 Cor 15:39
no one according to the *f* .. 2 Cor 5:16
from all filthiness of the *f* ... 2 Cor 7:1
war according to the *f* ..... 2 Cor 10:3
immediately confer with *f* ... Gal 1:16
law no *f* shall be justified .... Gal 2:16
which I now live in the *f* .... Gal 2:20
not fulfill the lust of the *f* ..... Gal 5:16
For the *f* lusts .... Gal 5:17
have crucified the *f* .... Gal 5:24
his *f* will of the *f* reap .... Gal 6:8
good showing in the *f* .... Gal 6:12
may boast in your *f* .... Gal 6:13
one ever hated his own *f* .... Eph 5:29
two shall become one *f* ...... Eph 5:31
have no confidence in the *f* .. Phil 3:3
of His *f* through death .... Col 1:22
was manifested in the *f* ... 1 Tim 3:16
the veil, that is, His *f* ...... Heb 10:20
f has ceased from sin .... 1 Pet 4:1
of his time in the *f* .... 1 Pet 4:2
the lust of the *f* .... 1 John 2:16
has come in the *f* .... 1 John 4:2
dreamers defile the *f* .... Jude 8

FLESH AND BLOOD
f has not revealed this .... Matt 16:17
f cannot inherit the ...... 1 Cor 15:50
do not wrestle against *f* .... Eph 6:12
have partaken of *f* .... Heb 2:14

FLESHLY
f wisdom but by the ...... 2 Cor 1:12
law of a *f* commandment ...... Heb 7:16
f lusts which war against .. 1 Pet 2:11

FLIES
will send swarms of *f* .... Ex 8:21
He sent swarms of *f* .... Ps 78:45
of the arrow that *f* by day .... Ps 91:5
Dead *f* putrefy the .... Eccl 10:1

FLIGHT
put ten thousand to *f* ..... Deut 32:30
f shall perish from .... Amos 2:14
And pray that your *f* ...... Matt 24:20
turned to *f* the armies of ... Heb 11:34

FLINT
will seem like *f* .... Is 5:28
set My face like a *f* .... Is 50:7

FLINTY
out of the *f* rock .... Deut 8:15
oil from the *f* rock .... Deut 32:13

FLOAT
and he made the iron *f* ..... 2 Kin 6:6

FLOCK
of the firstborn of his *f* .... Gen 4:4
Go now to the *f* and bring .. Gen 27:9
pass through all your *f* .... Gen 30:32
put them with Laban's *f* ... Gen 30:40
Moses was tending the *f* ...... Ex 3:1
Your people like a *f* .... Ps 77:20
wilderness like a *f* .... Ps 78:52
lead Joseph like a *f* .... Ps 80:1
their families like a *f* .... Ps 107:41
the footsteps of the *f* .... Song 1:8
He will feed His *f* .... Is 40:11
with the shepherd of His *f* ... Is 63:11
"You have scattered My *f* .... Jer 23:2
gather the remnant of My *f* .. Jer 23:3
oil, for the young of the *f* ... Jer 31:12
you do not feed the *f* .... Ezek 34:3
are My *f*, the *f* .... Ezek 34:31
though the *f* be cut .... Hab 3:17
my God, "Feed the *f* .... Zech 11:4
sheep of the *f* will be ...... Matt 26:31
watch over their *f* by night .. Luke 2:8
"Do not fear, little *f* ...... Luke 12:32
there will be one *f* .... John 10:16
and to all the *f* .... Acts 20:28
not sparing the *f* .... Acts 20:29
of the milk of the *f* .... 1 Cor 9:7
Shepherd the *f* of God ...... 1 Pet 5:2
examples to the *f* .... 1 Pet 5:3

FLOCKS
fed the rest of Laban's *f* ... Gen 30:36
their little ones, their *f* ...... Gen 50:8
Also take your *f* and your ... Ex 12:32
are clothed with *f* .... Ps 65:13
the *f* of your companions ... Song 1:7
lion among *f* of sheep .... Mic 5:8
for they shall feed their *f* .. Zeph 3:13

FLOOD
the waters of the *f* .... Gen 7:10
a *f* to destroy all flesh ...... Gen 9:15
on the earth after the *f* .... Gen 10:32
sat enthroned at the *F* .... Ps 29:10
them away like a *f* .... Ps 90:5
enemy comes in like a *f* ...... Is 59:19

the days before the *f* ..... Matt 24:38
when the *f* arose, the ..... Luke 6:48
bringing in the *f* ..... 2 Pet 2:5
of his mouth like a *f* ..... Rev 12:15

FLOODS
me, and the *f* of ..... Ps 18:4
f on the dry ground ..... Is 44:3
and the *f* surrounded me ..... Jon 2:3
rain descended, the *f* ..... Matt 7:25

FLOOR
down to the threshing *f* ..... Ruth 3:6
came to the threshing *f* ..... Ruth 3:14
bought the threshing *f* ... 2 Sam 24:24
clean out His threshing *f* ... Matt 3:12
clean out His threshing *f* ... Luke 3:17

FLOUR
a handful of *f* in a bin ..... 1 Kin 17:12
bin of *f* was not used up .. 1 Kin 17:16
"Then bring some *f* ..... 2 Kin 4:41

FLOURISH
the righteous shall *f* ..... Ps 72:7
f in the courts of our God ..... Ps 92:13
tent of the upright will *f* ... Prov 14:11

FLOURISHED
your care for me has *f* ..... Phil 4:10

FLOURISHES
In the morning it *f* ..... Ps 90:6

FLOW
f away as waters which ..... Ps 58:7
and the waters *f* ..... Ps 147:18
that its spices may *f* ..... Song 4:16
all nations shall *f* ..... Is 2:2
and peoples shall *f* to it ..... Mic 4:1
who had a *f* of blood ..... Matt 9:20
f of blood for twelve ..... Mark 5:25
immediately her *f* of ..... Luke 8:44
of his heart will *f* ..... John 7:38

FLOWER
comes forth like a *f* ..... Job 14:2
as a *f* of the field ..... Ps 103:15
beauty is a fading *f* ..... Is 28:4
is like the *f* of the ..... Is 40:6
grass withers, the *f* ..... Is 40:7
if she is past the *f* ..... 1 Cor 7:36
of man as the *f* ..... 1 Pet 1:24

FLOWERS
f appear on the earth ..... Song 2:12

FLOWING
'a land *f* with milk ..... Deut 6:3
of wisdom is a *f* ..... Prov 18:4
the Gentiles like a *f* ..... Is 66:12

FLUTE
play the harp and *f* ..... Gen 4:21
sound of the horn, *f* ..... Dan 3:5
saw the *f* players ..... Matt 9:23
"We played the *f* for you .. Luke 7:32

FLUTES
instruments and *f* ..... Ps 150:4

FLUTISTS
harpists, musicians, *f* ..... Rev 18:22

FLY
let birds *f* above the earth ... Gen 1:20
I would *f* away and be ..... Ps 55:6
soon cut off, and we *f* ..... Ps 90:10
they *f* away like an ..... Prov 23:5
being caused to *f* swiftly ..... Dan 9:21

FLYING
a *f* swallow, so a curse ..... Prov 26:2

FOAL
a colt, the *f* of a donkey ..... Zech 9:9
a colt, the *f* of a donkey ..... Matt 21:5

FOAMS
so that he *f* at the mouth ... Luke 9:39

FOE
and scattered the *f* ..... Ps 18:14

FOES
my enemies and *f* ..... Ps 27:2
I will beat down his *f* ..... Ps 89:23

FOLD
are not of this *f* ..... John 10:16
a cloak You will *f* ..... Heb 1:12

FOLDING
slumber, a little *f* ..... Prov 6:10
f of the hands to sleep ..... Prov 24:33

FOLLOW
willing to *f* me to this land .. Gen 24:5
f what is altogether ..... Deut 16:20
If the LORD is God, *f* ..... 1 Kin 18:21
shall *f* me all the days ..... Ps 23:6
to Me, you who *f* ..... Is 51:1
"*F* Me, and I will make ..... Matt 4:19
f You wherever You go ..... Matt 8:19
"*F* Me, and let the dead ..... Matt 8:22
He said to him, "*F* ..... Matt 9:9
f after Me is not worthy ... Matt 10:38
his cross, and *f* Me ..... Matt 16:24
up his cross, and *f* ..... Mark 8:34
someone who does not *f* ... Mark 9:38
the cross, and *f* Me ..... Mark 10:21
signs will *f* those who ..... Mark 16:17
he does not *f* with us ..... Luke 9:49
I will *f* You wherever ..... Luke 9:57
said to another, "*F* Me ..... Luke 9:59
not go after them or *f* ..... Luke 17:23
and come, *f* Me ..... Luke 18:22
f him into the house ..... Luke 22:10
the sheep *f* him, for they ... John 10:4
will by no means *f* ..... John 10:5
serves Me, let him *f* ..... John 12:26
on your garment and *f* ..... Acts 12:8
those of some men *f* ..... 1 Tim 5:24
God to you, whose faith *f* ... Heb 13:7
that you should *f* ..... 1 Pet 2:21
f the Lamb wherever He ..... Rev 14:4
and their works *f* ..... Rev 14:13

FOLLOWED
f the LORD my God ..... Josh 14:8
LORD took me as I *f* ..... Amos 7:15
left their nets and *f* Him ..... Matt 4:20
great multitudes *f* Him ..... Matt 8:1
Peter *f* Him at a distance .. Matt 26:58
women who *f* Jesus ..... Matt 27:55
we have left all and *f* ..... Mark 10:28
sight and *f* Jesus ..... Mark 10:52
This girl *f* Paul and us ..... Acts 16:17
spiritual Rock that *f* ..... 1 Cor 10:4
diligently *f* every good ..... 1 Tim 5:10
carefully *f* my doctrine ..... 2 Tim 3:10

FOLLOWING
if you turn away from *f* ... Num 32:15
away this day from *f* the ... Josh 22:16
back from *f* after you ..... Ruth 1:16
continue *f* the LORD ..... 1 Sam 12:14
f the sheep, to be ruler ..... 2 Sam 7:8
away from *f* the LORD ..... 2 Chr 25:27
turned, and seeing them *f* .. John 1:38
whom Jesus loved *f* ..... John 21:20
join in *f* my example ..... Phil 3:17
f the way of Balaam ..... 2 Pet 2:15

FOLLOWS
My soul *f* close behind ..... Ps 63:8
but he who *f* frivolity is ... Prov 12:11
loves him who *f* ..... Prov 15:9
f Me shall not walk ..... John 8:12

FOLLY
taken much notice of *f* ..... Job 35:15
not turn back to *f* ..... Ps 85:8
F is joy to him who is ..... Prov 15:21
correction of fools is *f* ..... Prov 16:22
F is set in great ..... Eccl 10:6

FOOD
you it shall be for *f* ..... Gen 1:29
that lives shall be *f* ..... Gen 9:3
stranger, giving him *f* ..... Deut 10:18
He gives *f* in abundance ..... Job 36:31
he may bring forth *f* ..... Ps 104:14
Who gives *f* to all ..... Ps 136:25
Much *f* is in the ..... Prov 13:23
feed me with the *f* ..... Prov 30:8
their *f* in the summer ..... Prov 30:25
night, and provides *f* ..... Prov 31:15
f which you eat shall ..... Ezek 4:10
I ate no pleasant *f* ..... Dan 10:3
the fields yield no *f* ..... Hab 3:17
that there may be *f* ..... Mal 3:10
is worthy of his *f* ..... Matt 10:10
to give them *f* in due ..... Matt 24:45
and you gave Me *f* ..... Matt 25:35
and he who has *f* ..... Luke 3:11
Life is more than *f* ..... Luke 12:23
I have *f* to eat of which ..... John 4:32
f is to do the will of Him ... John 4:34
for the *f* which perishes ..... John 6:27
have you any *f* ..... John 21:5
they ate their *f* ..... Acts 2:46
our hearts with *f* ..... Acts 14:17
destroy with your *f* ..... Rom 14:15
f makes my brother ..... 1 Cor 8:13
the same spiritual *f* ..... 1 Cor 10:3
sower, and bread for *f* ..... 2 Cor 9:10
And having *f* and ..... 1 Tim 6:8
and not solid *f* ..... Heb 5:12
But solid *f* belongs to ..... Heb 5:14
of *f* sold his birthright ..... Heb 12:16
destitute of daily *f* ..... James 2:15

FOODS
F for the stomach ..... 1 Cor 6:13
f which God created ..... 1 Tim 4:3

FOOL
I have played the *f* ..... 1 Sam 26:21
Should Abner die as a *f* .. 2 Sam 3:33
f has said in his ..... Ps 14:1
or as a *f* to the correction .. Prov 7:22
is like sport to a *f* ..... Prov 10:23
f will be servant ..... Prov 11:29
f is right in his own ..... Prov 12:15
f lays open his folly ..... Prov 13:16
A *f* despises his father's ..... Prov 15:5
a hundred blows on a *f* ... Prov 17:10
is too lofty for a *f* ..... Prov 24:7
Do not answer a *f* ..... Prov 26:4
"As it happens to the *f*, it ... Eccl 2:15
A *f* also multiplies words .. Eccl 10:14
whoever says, 'You *f* ..... Matt 5:22
But God said to him, '*F* ... Luke 12:20
let him become a *f* that ..... 1 Cor 3:18
I speak as a *f* ..... 2 Cor 11:23
I have become a *f* ..... 2 Cor 12:11

FOOLISH
of the *f* women speaks ..... Job 2:10
I was so *f* and ..... Ps 73:22
f pulls it down with ..... Prov 14:1
f man squanders it ..... Prov 21:20
"For My people are *f* ..... Jer 4:22
f hearts were darkened ..... Rom 1:21
Has not God made *f* ..... 1 Cor 1:20
But God has chosen the *f* .. 1 Cor 1:27
O *f* Galatians ..... Gal 3:1
nor *f* talking, nor coarse ..... Eph 5:4
But avoid *f* and ignorant .. 2 Tim 2:23
were also once *f* ..... Titus 3:3
But avoid *f* disputes ..... Titus 3:9

FOOLISHLY
man acts *f*, and a man ..... Prov 14:17
I speak *f*—I am bold ..... 2 Cor 11:21

FOOLISHNESS
O God, You know my *f* ..... Ps 69:5
Forsake *f* and live ..... Prov 9:6
of fools proclaims *f* ..... Prov 12:23
The *f* of a man twists ..... Prov 19:3
F is bound up in the ..... Prov 22:15
devising of *f* is sin ..... Prov 24:9
person will speak *f* ..... Is 32:6
of the cross is *f* ..... 1 Cor 1:18

Because the *f* of God ...... 1 Cor 1:25
this world is *f* with God ... 1 Cor 3:19

FOOLS
f despise wisdom .... Prov 1:7
folly of *f* is deceit .... Prov 14:8
F mock at sin .... Prov 14:9
has no pleasure in *f* .... Eccl 5:4
F and blind! .... Matt 23:17
to be wise, they became *f* .. Rom 1:22
We are *f* for Christ's ...... 1 Cor 4:10
not as *f* but as wise .... Eph 5:15

FOOT
your *f* will tread upon .... Josh 1:3
your sandal off your *f* ...... Josh 5:15
f has trodden shall be ...... Josh 14:9
dash your *f* against a stone .. Ps 91:12
will not allow your *f* .... Ps 121:3
f will not stumble .... Prov 3:23
From the sole of the *f* .... Is 1:6
you turn away your *f* .... Is 58:13
dash your *f* against a stone .. Matt 4:6
f causes you to sin .... Matt 18:8
you dash your *f* .... Luke 4:11
If the *f* should say .... 1 Cor 12:15

FOOTMEN
have run with the *f* .... Jer 12:5

FOOTSTEPS
f were not known .... Ps 77:19
and shall make His *f* .... Ps 85:13

FOOTSTOOL
God, and worship at His *f* .... Ps 99:5
Your enemies Your *f* .... Ps 110:1
throne, and earth is My *f* ..... Is 66:1
by the earth, for it is His *f* .. Matt 5:35
Your enemies Your *f* ..... Matt 22:44
throne, and earth is My *f* ... Acts 7:49
"Sit here at my *f* .... James 2:3

FORBID
come to Me, and do not *f* .. Matt 19:14
said, "Do not *f* him .... Mark 9:39
"Can anyone *f* water ...... Acts 10:47
prophesy, and do not *f* ... 1 Cor 14:39
f that I should boast .... Gal 6:14

FORBIDDEN
LORD your God has *f* you ... Deut 4:23
they were *f* by the Holy .... Acts 16:6

FORBIDDING
confidence, no one *f* ...... Acts 28:31
f us to speak to the ...... 1 Thess 2:16
f to marry .... 1 Tim 4:3

FORCE
violent take it by *f* .... Matt 11:12
come and take Him by *f* ... John 6:15
a testament is in *f* .... Heb 9:17

FORCEFUL
f are right words .... Job 6:25

FORCES
Though they join *f* .... Prov 11:21

FOREFATHERS
f who refused to hear .... Jer 11:10
and oppressed our *f* .... Acts 7:19
conscience, as my *f* .... 2 Tim 1:3

FOREHEADS
strong against their *f* .... Ezek 3:8
put a mark on the *f* .... Ezek 9:4
seal of God on their *f* .... Rev 9:4
his mark on their *f* .... Rev 20:4

FOREIGN
been a stranger in a *f* land ... Ex 2:22
put away the *f* gods .... Josh 24:23
loved many *f* women ...... 1 Kin 11:1
the LORD's song in a *f* land .. Ps 137:4
set out *f* seedlings .... Is 17:10
promise as in a *f* country ... Heb 11:9

FOREIGN GODS
"put away the *f* .... Gen 35:2
to jealousy with *f*; .... Deut 32:16
the LORD and serve *f* ...... Josh 24:20
So they put away the *f* .... Judg 10:16
then put away the *f* .... 1 Sam 7:3
the altars of the *f* .... 2 Chr 14:3
He took away the *f* ...... 2 Chr 33:15
forsaken Me and served *f* .... Jer 5:19
to be a proclaimer of *f* .... Acts 17:18

FOREIGNER
"I am a *f* and a .... Gen 23:4
of me, since I am a *f* .... Ruth 2:10
to God except this *f* ...... Luke 17:18
who speaks will be a *f* .... 1 Cor 14:11

FOREIGNERS
from the hand of *f* .... Ps 144:11
with the children of *f* .... Is 2:6
f shall build up your .... Is 60:10
f who were there .... Acts 17:21
longer strangers and *f* ...... Eph 2:19

FOREKNEW
For whom He *f* .... Rom 8:29
His people whom He *f* ..... Rom 11:2

FOREKNOWLEDGE
purpose and *f* of God .... Acts 2:23
according to the *f* .... 1 Pet 1:2

FOREORDAINED
He indeed was *f* .... 1 Pet 1:20

FORERUNNER
f has entered for us .... Heb 6:20

FORESAW
'I *f* the LORD .... Acts 2:25

FORESEEING
f that God would .... Gal 3:8

FORESEES
A prudent man *f* .... Prov 22:3

FORESKINS
in the flesh of your *f* .... Gen 17:11
f of the Philistines .... 1 Sam 18:25

FOREST
beast of the *f* is Mine .... Ps 50:10
See how great a *f* .... James 3:5

FORESTS
and strips the *f* .... Ps 29:9

FORETOLD
have also *f* these days ..... Acts 3:24
killed those who *f* .... Acts 7:52

FOREVER
See HIS MERCY ENDURES FOREVER
and eat, and live *f* .... Gen 3:22
shall not strive with man *f* .. Gen 6:3
This is My name *f* .... Ex 3:15
and they shall inherit it *f* .... Ex 32:13
to our children *f* .... Deut 29:29
has loved Israel *f* .... 1 Kin 10:9
for His mercy endures *f* ... 2 Chr 5:13
for His mercy endures *f* .... 2 Chr 7:3
I would not live *f* .... Job 7:16
from this generation *f* .... Ps 12:7
LORD sits as King *f* .... Ps 29:10
Do not cast us off *f* .... Ps 44:23
throne, O God, is *f* .... Ps 45:6
"You are a priest *f* .... Ps 110:4
His mercy endures *f* .... Ps 118:1
F, O LORD, Your word is .... Ps 119:89
be moved, but abides *f* ...... Ps 125:1
From this time forth and *f* ... Ps 125:2
This is My resting place *f* ... Ps 132:14
name, O LORD, endures *f* ... Ps 135:13
His mercy endures *f* .... Ps 136:1
will bless Your name *f* .... Ps 145:1
bless His holy name *f* .... Ps 145:21
who keeps truth *f* .... Ps 146:6
The LORD shall reign *f* .... Ps 146:10
also established them *f* .... Ps 148:6
lip shall be established *f* .. Prov 12:19
for riches are not *f* .... Prov 27:24
Trust in the LORD *f* .... Is 26:4
of our God stands *f* .... Is 40:8
My salvation will be *f* .... Is 51:6
will not cast off *f* .... Lam 3:31
be the name of God *f* .... Dan 2:20
Like the stars *f* .... Dan 12:3
of the LORD our God *f* .... Mic 4:5
and the glory *f* .... Matt 6:13
eats this bread will live *f* ... John 6:58
the Christ remains *f* .... John 12:34
He may abide with you *f* .. John 14:16
righteousness endures *f* .... 2 Cor 9:9
who is blessed *f* .... 2 Cor 11:31
to whom be glory *f* .... Gal 1:5
generation, *f* and ever ...... Eph 3:21
and Father be glory *f* .... Phil 4:20
throne, O God, is *f* .... Heb 1:8
"You are a priest *f* .... Heb 5:6
f according to the order of .. Heb 6:20
has been perfected *f* .... Heb 7:28
one sacrifice for sins *f* ...... Heb 10:12
yesterday, today, and *f* ...... Heb 13:8
lives and abides *f* .... 1 Pet 1:23
of the LORD endures *f* ..... 1 Pet 1:25
blackness of darkness *f* .... Jude 13
power, both now and *f* .... Jude 25
throne, and to the Lamb, *f* .. Rev 5:13
And they shall reign *f* ...... Rev 22:5

FOREVERMORE
Blessed be the LORD *f* .... Ps 89:52
this time forth and *f* .... Ps 113:2
behold, I am alive *f* .... Rev 1:18

FOREWARNED
all such, as we also *f* ..... 1 Thess 4:6

FORGAVE
f the iniquity of my .... Ps 32:5
and *f* him the debt .... Matt 18:27
I *f* you all that debt .... Matt 18:32
to repay, he freely *f* .... Luke 7:42
the one whom he *f* more ... Luke 7:43
God in Christ *f* .... Eph 4:32
even as Christ *f* .... Col 3:13

FORGED
The proud have *f* .... Ps 119:69

FORGERS
But you *f* of lies .... Job 13:4

FORGET
"For God has made me *f* .. Gen 41:51
yourselves, lest you *f* .... Deut 4:23
f the covenant of your .... Deut 4:31
f the LORD who brought .... Deut 6:12
the paths of all who *f* .... Job 8:13
all the nations that *f* .... Ps 9:17
this, you who *f* God .... Ps 50:22
f the works of God .... Ps 78:7
I will not *f* Your word ...... Ps 119:16
If I *f* you, O Jerusalem ...... Ps 137:5
My son, do not *f* .... Prov 3:1
f her nursing child .... Is 49:15
f the LORD your Maker .... Is 51:13
virgin *f* her ornaments .... Jer 2:32
f your work and labor .... Heb 6:10
Do not *f* to entertain .... Heb 13:2
But do not *f* to do good .... Heb 13:16
do not *f* this one thing ...... 2 Pet 3:8

FORGETFUL
not a *f* hearer but a doer .. James 1:25

FORGETFULNESS
in the land of *f* .... Ps 88:12

FORGETS
f the covenant of her .... Prov 2:17
and immediately *f* .... James 1:24

FORGETTING
f those things which .... Phil 3:13

FORGIVE
please *f* my sin only this .... Ex 10:17
if You will *f* their sin ...... Ex 32:32
dwelling place, and *f* ...... 1 Kin 8:39
f their sin and heal .... 2 Chr 7:14

good, and ready to *f* .... Ps 86:5
For I will *f* their iniquity .... Jer 31:34
O Lord, hear! O Lord, *f* .... Dan 9:19
And *f* us our debts .... Matt 6:12
Father will also *f* .... Matt 6:14
f men their trespasses .... Matt 6:15
sin against me, and I *f* ...... Matt 18:21
his heart, does not *f* .... Matt 18:35
Who can *f* sins but God .... Mark 2:7
f him, that your Father ...... Mark 11:25
if you do not *f*, neither ..... Mark 11:26
power on earth to *f* sins ...... Luke 5:24
F, and you will be .... Luke 6:37
f us our sins, for we also .... Luke 11:4
and if he repents, *f* him ...... Luke 17:3
'I repent,' you shall *f* him ... Luke 17:4
f them, for they do not ...... Luke 23:34
f the sins of any .... John 20:23
you ought rather to *f* .... 2 Cor 2:7
anything, I also *f* .... 2 Cor 2:10
F me this wrong .... 2 Cor 12:13
f us our sins and to .... 1 John 1:9

FORGIVEN

transgression is *f* .... Ps 32:1
sins be *f* them .... Mark 4:12
to whom little is *f* .... Luke 7:47
of your heart may be *f* .... Acts 8:22
indeed I have *f* .... 2 Cor 2:10
f you all trespasses .... Col 2:13
sins, he will be *f* .... James 5:15
your sins are *f* .... 1 John 2:12

FORGIVENESS

But there is *f* with .... Ps 130:4
God belong mercy and *f* .... Dan 9:9
never has *f*, but is subject .. Mark 3:29
preached to you the *f* .... Acts 13:38
they may receive *f* .... Acts 26:18
His blood, the *f* .... Eph 1:7
His blood, the *f* of sins ...... Col 1:14

FORGIVES

f all your iniquities .... Ps 103:3
"Who is this who even *f* ..... Luke 7:49

FORGIVING

tenderhearted, *f* .... Eph 4:32
and *f* one another .... Col 3:13

FORGOT

remember Joseph, but *f* ...... Gen 40:23
f the LORD their God .... Judg 3:7
f His works and His .... Ps 78:11
They soon *f* His works .... Ps 106:13

FORGOTTEN

f the God who fathered .... Deut 32:18
needy shall not always be *f* ... Ps 9:18
"Why have You *f* .... Ps 42:9
If we had *f* the name .... Ps 44:20
memory of them is *f* .... Eccl 9:5
you will not be *f* .... Is 44:21
And my Lord has *f* .... Is 49:14
I have *f* prosperity .... Lam 3:17
not one of them is *f* .... Luke 12:6
f the exhortation .... Heb 12:5
f that he was cleansed .... 2 Pet 1:9

FORM

earth was without *f* .... Gen 1:2
he sees the *f* of the LORD ... Num 12:8
of the words, but saw no *f* .. Deut 4:12
Who would *f* a god or .... Is 44:10
f the light and create .... Is 45:7
He has no *f* or comeliness ..... Is 53:2
descended in bodily *f* .... Luke 3:22
time, nor seen His *f* .... John 5:37
having the *f* of knowledge .. Rom 2:20
For the *f* of this .... 1 Cor 7:31
who, being in the *f* .... Phil 2:6
the *f* of a bondservant .... Phil 2:7
Abstain from every *f* ...... 1 Thess 5:22
having a *f* of godliness .... 2 Tim 3:5

FORMED

And the LORD God *f* .... Gen 2:7
And His hands *f* .... Ps 95:5
f my inward parts .... Ps 139:13
f everything gives the ..... Prov 26:10
say of him who *f* .... Is 29:16
Me there was no God *f* .... Is 43:10
This people I have *f* .... Is 43:21
No weapon *f* against you ..... Is 54:17
"Before I *f* you in .... Jer 1:5
Will the thing *f* say to .... Rom 9:20
until Christ is *f* .... Gal 4:19
For Adam was *f* first .... 1 Tim 2:13

FORMER

according to the *f* .... Gen 40:13
not remember *f* inquiries ...... Ps 79:8
f lovingkindness .... Ps 89:49
f days better than .... Eccl 7:10
Who gives rain, both the *f* ..... Jer 5:24
f rain to the earth .... Hos 6:3
the *f* rain, and the latter .... Joel 2:23
f prophets preached .... Zech 1:4
through the *f* prophets .... Zech 7:12
The *f* account I made, O .... Acts 1:1
f conduct in Judaism .... Gal 1:13
your *f* conduct, the old .... Eph 4:22
yourselves to the *f* lusts ...... 1 Pet 1:14
in *f* times, the holy women .... 1 Pet 3:5
f things have passed .... Rev 21:4

FORMS

clay say to him who *f* .... Is 45:9
f the spirit of man .... Zech 12:1

FORNICATION

"We were not born of *f* .... John 8:41
adultery, *f*, uncleanness .... Gal 5:19
of the wrath of her *f* .... Rev 14:8

FORNICATOR

you know, that no *f* .... Eph 5:5
lest there be any *f* .... Heb 12:16

FORNICATORS

but *f* and adulterers .... Heb 13:4

FORSAKE

but if you *f* Him .... 2 Chr 15:2
and did not *f* them .... Neh 9:17
mercies You did not *f* .... Neh 9:19
Do not leave me nor *f* me .... Ps 27:9
father and my mother *f* me .. Ps 27:10
Cease from anger, and *f* .... Ps 37:8
And does not *f* His saints ..... Ps 37:28
"If his sons *f* My law .... Ps 89:30
f His inheritance .... Ps 94:14
But I did not *f* Your .... Ps 119:87
father, and do not *f* .... Prov 1:8
Let not mercy and truth *f* .... Prov 3:3
worthless idols *f* .... Jon 2:8
of you does not *f* .... Luke 14:33
never leave you nor *f* .... Heb 13:5

FORSAKEN

My God, why have You *f* .... Ps 22:1
seen the righteous *f* .... Ps 37:25
you dread will be *f* .... Is 7:16
cities will be as a *f* .... Is 17:9
a mere moment I have *f* .... Is 54:7
no longer be termed *F* .... Is 62:4
they have *f* Me .... Jer 2:13
My God, why have You *f* ... Matt 27:46
persecuted, but not *f* .... 2 Cor 4:9
for Demas has *f* .... 2 Tim 4:10
f the right way .... 2 Pet 2:15

FORSAKES

f the companion of her ...... Prov 2:17
and *f* them will have .... Prov 28:13

FORSAKING

f the assembling .... Heb 10:25

FORSOOK

f God who made him .... Deut 32:15
all the disciples *f* .... Matt 26:56
with me, but all *f* .... 2 Tim 4:16
By faith he *f* Egypt .... Heb 11:27

FORT

Man the *f*! .... Nah 2:1

FORTRESS

LORD is my rock, my *f* ...... 2 Sam 22:2
my rock of refuge, a *f* .... Ps 31:2
He is my refuge and my *f* ...... Ps 91:2

FORTUNE-TELLING

masters much profit by *f* .. Acts 16:16

FORTY

to rain on the earth *f* days ... Gen 7:4
to pass, at the end of *f* days .. Gen 8:6
not do it for the sake of *f* .. Gen 18:29
Isaac was *f* years old .... Gen 25:20
Esau was *f* years old .... Gen 26:34
F days were required .... Gen 50:3
Israel ate manna *f* years .... Ex 16:35
mountain *f* days and *f* .... Ex 24:18
LORD *f* days and *f* nights .... Ex 34:28
out the land after *f* days ... Num 13:25
in the wilderness *f* years ... Num 14:33
f days, for each day you .... Num 14:34
in the wilderness *f* years .. Num 32:13
These *f* years the LORD .... Deut 2:7
f years in the wilderness ..... Deut 8:2
foot swell these *f* years .... Deut 8:4
first, *f* days and *f* nights ..... Deut 9:18
f nights I kept prostrating .. Deut 9:25
mountain *f* days and *f* ..... Deut 10:10
F blows he may give him .. Deut 25:3
f years old when Moses .... Josh 14:7
land had rest for *f* years .... Judg 5:31
the Philistines for *f* years ... Judg 13:1
judged Israel *f* years .... 1 Sam 4:18
presented himself *f* .... 1 Sam 17:16
f nights as far as Horeb ...... 1 Kin 19:8
For *f* years I was grieved ..... Ps 95:10
f days, and Nineveh shall ...... Jon 3:4
when He had fasted *f* days .. Matt 4:2
for *f* days by the devil .... Luke 4:2
seen by them during *f* days .. Acts 1:3
when he was *f* years old ..... Acts 7:23
when *f* years had passed .... Acts 7:30
f who had formed this ..... Acts 23:13
more than *f* of them lie .... Acts 23:21
f stripes minus one .... 2 Cor 11:24
and saw My works *f* years ..... Heb 3:9
was He angry *f* years .... Heb 3:17

FORWARD

David from that day *f* ... 1 Sam 16:13
David from that day *f* ..... 1 Sam 18:9

FOUGHT

f against me without .... Ps 109:3
I have *f* the good fight, I .... 2 Tim 4:7

FOUL

My wounds are *f* .... Ps 38:5
f weather today .... Matt 16:3
a prison for every *f* .... Rev 18:2

FOUND

f a helper comparable .... Gen 2:20
Why have I *f* favor in .... Ruth 2:10
where can wisdom be *f* ..... Job 28:12
when You may be *f* .... Ps 32:6
f My servant David .... Ps 89:20
a thousand I have *f* .... Eccl 7:28
this only I have *f* .... Eccl 7:29
f the one I love .... Song 3:4
LORD while He may be *f* .... Is 55:6
none was *f* like Daniel .... Dan 1:19
he *f* them ten times better .. Dan 1:20
balances, and *f* wanting ...... Dan 5:27
any error or fault *f* in him .... Dan 6:4
f Daniel praying and .... Dan 6:11
your fruit is *f* .... Hos 14:8
and when you have *f* Him .... Matt 2:8
not *f* such great faith .... Matt 8:10
when he had *f* one pearl .. Matt 13:46
f nothing on it but leaves .. Matt 21:19
f them sleeping, and said .. Matt 26:40
have *f* favor with God .... Luke 1:30
they *f* Him in the temple ... Luke 2:46
fruit on it and *f* none .... Luke 13:6

he was lost and is *f* .... Luke 15:24
they *f* the stone rolled .... Luke 24:2
f the Messiah" (which ..... John 1:41
we *f* the prison shut .... Acts 5:23
I even *f* an altar with .... Acts 17:23
I *f* to bring death .... Rom 7:10
that one be *f* faithful .... 1 Cor 4:2
and be *f* in Him .... Phil 3:9
being *f* blameless .... 1 Tim 3:10
be diligent to be *f* .... 2 Pet 3:14
anyone not *f* written in ..... Rev 20:15

FOUNDATION
he shall lay its *f* .... Josh 6:26
His *f* is in the holy .... Ps 87:1
and justice are the *f* .... Ps 89:14
Of old You laid the *f* .... Ps 102:25
has an everlasting *f* .... Prov 10:25
deep and laid the *f* .... Luke 6:48
the earth without a *f* .... Luke 6:49
loved Me before the *f* ...... John 17:24
I have laid the *f* .... 1 Cor 3:10
f can anyone lay than ...... 1 Cor 3:11
us in Him before the *f* .... Eph 1:4
the solid *f* of God .... 2 Tim 2:19
not laying again the *f* .... Heb 6:1
Lamb slain from the *f* .... Rev 13:8
the first *f* was jasper .... Rev 21:19

FOUNDATIONS
when I laid the *f* .... Job 38:4
f are destroyed .... Ps 11:3
You who laid the *f* .... Ps 104:5
shall raise up the *f* .... Is 58:12
that the *f* of the prison .... Acts 16:26
The *f* of the wall .... Rev 21:19

FOUNDED
For He has *f* it upon .... Ps 24:2
by wisdom *f* the earth .... Prov 3:19
shake it, for it was *f* .... Luke 6:48

FOUNTAIN
Let your *f* be blessed .... Prov 5:18
Immediately the *f* of her ... Mark 5:29
will become in him a *f* ...... John 4:14
I will give of the *f* of the .... Rev 21:6

FOUNTAINS
on that day all the *f* .... Gen 7:11
f be dispersed abroad .... Prov 5:16
when there were no *f* .... Prov 8:24
lead them to living *f* .... Rev 7:17

FOUR
became *f* riverheads .... Gen 2:10
prophets are *f* hundred ... 1 Kin 18:22
Each one had *f* faces ...... Ezek 10:14
and each one *f* wings ...... Ezek 10:21
I see *f* men loose, walking .. Dan 3:25
f great beasts came up .... Dan 7:3
f kingdoms shall arise .... Dan 8:22
are *f* spirits of heaven .... Zech 6:5
ate were *f* thousand .... Matt 15:38
been in the tomb *f* days ... John 11:17
sheet bound at the *f* .... Acts 10:11
Now this man had *f* virgin .. Acts 21:9
were *f* living creatures full ... Rev 4:6
the *f* angels to whom it was ... Rev 7:2

FOWLER
you from the snare of the *f* ... Ps 91:3
bird from the hand of the *f* .. Prov 6:5

FOX
build, if even a *f* .... Neh 4:3
"Go, tell that *f* .... Luke 13:32

FOXES
caught three hundred *f* ...... Judg 15:4
f that spoil the vines .... Song 2:15
F have holes and birds ...... Luke 9:58

FRAGMENTS
f that remained .... Matt 14:20
of the leftover *f* .... Luke 9:17
baskets with the *f* .... John 6:13

FRAGRANCE
garments is like the *f* ...... Song 4:11
was filled with the *f* .... John 12:3
we are to God the *f* .... 2 Cor 2:15

FRAGRANT
the merchant's *f* powders ... Song 3:6
flask of very costly *f* oil .... Matt 26:7
an alabaster flask of *f* oil .. Luke 7:37
prepared spices and *f* .... Luke 23:56
was this *f* oil not sold .... John 12:5
f oil and frankincense .... Rev 18:13

FRAIL
that I may know how *f* .... Ps 39:4

FRAME
For He knows our *f* .... Ps 103:14
f was not hidden .... Ps 139:15

FRAMED
that the worlds were *f* .... Heb 11:3

FRANKINCENSE
oil on it, and put *f* on it .... Lev 2:1
with myrrh and *f* .... Song 3:6
gold, *f*, and myrrh .... Matt 2:11
incense, fragrant oil and *f* .. Rev 18:13

FREE
and the servant is *f* .... Job 3:19
let the oppressed go *f* .... Is 58:6
'You will be made *f* .... John 8:33
if the Son makes you *f* .... John 8:36
And having been set *f* .... Rom 6:18
now having been set *f* .... Rom 6:22
Jesus has made me *f* .... Rom 8:2
Am I not *f* .... 1 Cor 9:1
is neither slave nor *f* .... Gal 3:28
Jerusalem above is *f* .... Gal 4:26
Christ has made us *f* .... Gal 5:1
he is a slave or *f* .... Eph 6:8
poor, *f* and slave .... Rev 13:16

FREED
has died has been *f* .... Rom 6:7

FREEDMAN
slave is the Lord's *f* .... 1 Cor 7:22

FREEDOM
The LORD gives *f* to the ...... Ps 146:7

FREELY
the garden you may *f* .... Gen 2:16
I will love them *f* .... Hos 14:4
F you have received .... Matt 10:8
f give us all things .... Rom 8:32
that have been *f* .... 1 Cor 2:12
the water of life *f* .... Rev 22:17

FREEWOMAN
the other by a *f* .... Gal 4:22
with the son of the *f* .... Gal 4:30

FRESH
My glory is *f* within .... Job 29:20
they shall be *f* .... Ps 92:14
both salt water and *f* ...... James 3:12

FRETS
and his heart *f* .... Prov 19:3

FRIEND
a man speaks to his *f* .... Ex 33:11
of Abraham Your *f* .... 2 Chr 20:7
though he were my *f* .... Ps 35:14
f You have put far from me . Ps 88:18
f loves at all times .... Prov 17:17
f who sticks closer .... Prov 18:24
not forsake your own *f* .... Prov 27:10
a *f* of tax collectors .... Matt 11:19
of you shall have a *f* .... Luke 11:5
f Lazarus sleeps .... John 11:11
you are not Caesar's *f* .... John 19:12
Philemon our beloved *f* ..... Philem 1
he was called the *f* .... James 2:23
wants to be a *f* .... James 4:4

FRIENDLY
friends must himself be *f* .. Prov 18:24

FRIENDS
and hate your *f* .... 2 Sam 19:6
My *f* scorn me .... Job 16:20
f have forgotten me .... Job 19:14
the rich has many *f* .... Prov 14:20
one's life for his *f* .... John 15:13
You are My *f* .... John 15:14
I have called you *f* .... John 15:15
to forbid any of his *f* .... Acts 24:23

FRIENDSHIP
no *f* with an angry man ... Prov 22:24
that *f* with the world .... James 4:4

FROGS
your territory with *f* .... Ex 8:2
f coming out of the .... Rev 16:13

FRONTLETS
on your hand and as *f* ...... Ex 13:16
and they shall be as *f* .... Deut 6:8

FROZEN
the broad waters are *f* ...... Job 37:10

FRUIT
See BEAR FRUIT
and showed them the *f* .... Num 13:26
Blessed shall be the *f* .... Deut 28:4
brings forth its *f* .... Ps 1:3
f is better than gold .... Prov 8:19
The *f* of the righteous ..... Prov 11:30
with good by the *f* .... Prov 12:14
f was sweet to my .... Song 2:3
they shall eat the *f* .... Is 3:10
like the first *f* .... Is 28:4
"I create the *f* .... Is 57:19
f is found in Me .... Hos 14:8
does not bear good *f* .... Matt 3:10
good tree bears good *f* ...... Matt 7:17
not drink of this *f* .... Matt 26:29
and blessed is the *f* .... Luke 1:42
life, and bring no *f* .... Luke 8:14
and he came seeking *f* .... Luke 13:6
And if it bears *f* .... Luke 13:9
branch that bears *f* .... John 15:2
that you bear much *f* .... John 15:8
should go and bear *f* .... John 15:16
f did you have then in .... Rom 6:21
God, you have your *f* .... Rom 6:22
that we should bear *f* .... Rom 7:4
But the *f* of the Spirit is ...... Gal 5:22
(for the *f* of the Spirit is .... Eph 5:9
but I seek the *f* .... Phil 4:17
yields the peaceable *f* .... Heb 12:11
the *f* of our lips, giving ...... Heb 13:15
Now the *f* of .... James 3:18
precious *f* of the earth ...... James 5:7
autumn trees without *f* .... Jude 12
tree yielding its *f* .... Rev 22:2

FRUITFUL
See BE FRUITFUL AND MULTIPLY
them, saying, "Be *f* .... Gen 1:22
a *f* bough, a *f* .... Gen 49:22
wife shall be like a *f* .... Ps 128:3
heaven and *f* seasons ...... Acts 14:17
pleasing Him, being *f* .... Col 1:10

FRUITS
Therefore bear *f* .... Matt 3:8
know them by their *f* .... Matt 7:16
and increase the *f* .... 2 Cor 9:10
being filled with the *f* of .... Phil 1:11
of mercy and good *f* .... James 3:17
which bore twelve *f* .... Rev 22:2

FUEL
people shall be as *f* .... Is 9:19
into the fire for *f* .... Ezek 15:4

FUGITIVE
A *f* and a vagabond .... Gen 4:12

FULFILL
the LORD, to *f* his vow ...... Lev 22:21
And you shall *f* .... 1 Kin 5:9
f all your petitions .... Ps 20:5

f the desire of those .... Ps 145:19
for us to *f* all .... Matt 3:15
come to destroy but to *f* .... Matt 5:17
for the flesh, to *f* its lusts .. Rom 13:14
f the law of Christ .... Gal 6:2
f my joy by being .... Phil 2:2
and *f* all the good .... 2 Thess 1:11
evangelist, *f* your ministry .. 2 Tim 4:5
If you really *f* .... James 2:8

FULFILLED
be *f* which was spoken by .. Matt 1:22
the law till all is *f* .... Matt 5:18
could the Scriptures be *f* .. Matt 26:54
is *f*, and the kingdom ..... Mark 1:15
is *f* in your hearing .... Luke 4:21
of the Gentiles are *f* ...... Luke 21:24
all things must be *f* .... Luke 24:44
this joy of mine is *f* .... John 3:29
the Scripture may be *f* .... John 13:18
My joy *f* in themselves .... John 17:13
this Scripture had to be *f* ... Acts 1:16
they had *f* their ministry .. Acts 12:25
of the law might be *f* .... Rom 8:4
loves another has *f* .... Rom 13:8
For all the law is *f* .... Gal 5:14
the words of God are *f* ..... Rev 17:17

FULFILLMENT
for there will be a *f* .... Luke 1:45
love is the *f* of the .... Rom 13:10

FULL
I went out *f* .... Ruth 1:21
For I am *f* of words .... Job 32:18
of the LORD is *f* .... Ps 29:4
who has his quiver *f* .... Ps 127:5
Lest I be *f* and deny ...... Prov 30:9
yet the sea is not *f* .... Eccl 1:7
the whole earth is *f* .... Is 6:3
and it was *f* of bones ...... Ezek 37:1
But truly I am *f* .... Mic 3:8
whole body will be *f* .... Matt 6:22
of the Father, *f* of grace .... John 1:14
your joy may be *f* .... John 15:11
chose Stephen, a man *f* ...... Acts 6:5
You are already *f* .... 1 Cor 4:8
learned both to be *f* .... Phil 4:12
I am *f*, having received ...... Phil 4:18
in *f* assurance of faith ..... Heb 10:22
that your joy may be *f* ..... 1 John 1:4
we may receive a *f* reward .. 2 John 8

FULL-GROWN
and sin, when it is *f* ...... James 1:15

FULLNESS
satisfied with the *f* .... Ps 36:8
f we have all received ..... John 1:16
to Israel until the *f* .... Rom 11:25
But when the *f* of the .... Gal 4:4
dispensation of the *f* .... Eph 1:10
filled with all the *f* .... Eph 3:19
Him dwells all the *f* .... Col 2:9

FULLY
did not *f* follow the LORD .. 1 Kin 11:6
time has not yet *f* come ..... John 7:8
Pentecost had *f* come .... Acts 2:1
being *f* convinced that .... Rom 4:21
f preached the gospel ..... Rom 15:19
f pleasing Him, being .... Col 1:10
preached *f* through me .... 2 Tim 4:17
rest your hope *f* upon the .. 1 Pet 1:13

FUME
Why do you *f* with envy ..... Ps 68:16

FUNCTION
do not have the same *f* ..... Rom 12:4

FURIOUS
You have been *f* .... Ps 89:38
f man do not go .... Prov 22:24
fury and in *f* rebukes ...... Ezek 5:15
LORD avenges and is *f* .... Nah 1:2
this, they were *f* .... Acts 5:33

FURIOUSLY
for he drives *f* .... 2 Kin 9:20

FURNACE
you out of the iron *f* .... Deut 4:20
tested you in the *f* .... Is 48:10
of a burning fiery *f* .... Dan 3:6
cast them into the *f* .... Matt 13:42
the smoke of a great *f* .... Rev 9:2

FURNISHED
also *f* her table .... Prov 9:2
a large upper room, *f* ..... Mark 14:15

FURNISHINGS
and the pattern of all its *f* .... Ex 25:9
tabernacle and all its *f* ..... Num 1:50
Solomon had all the *f* .... 1 Kin 7:48
all the holy *f* that were in .... 2 Chr 5:5

FURY
F is not in Me .... Is 27:4
they are full of the *f* .... Is 51:20
f to His adversaries .... Is 59:18
My own *f*, it sustained .... Is 63:5
even in anger and *f* .... Jer 21:5
and I will cause My *f* .... Ezek 5:13
Thus will I spend My *f* ..... Ezek 6:12
in anger and *f* on the .... Mic 5:15

FUTILE
For it is not a *f* thing ...... Deut 32:47
of the peoples are *f* .... Jer 10:3
wise, that they are *f* .... 1 Cor 3:20
risen, your faith is *f* ...... 1 Cor 15:17

FUTILITY
allotted months of *f* .... Job 7:3
f have You created all ...... Ps 89:47
was subjected to *f* .... Rom 8:20

FUTURE
for the *f* of that man .... Ps 37:37
the *f* of the wicked .... Ps 37:38
to give you a *f* and a hope .. Jer 29:11
to many days in the *f* .... Dan 8:26

GAAL
Son of Ebed; vilifies Abimelech, Judg 9:26–41

GAASH
Hill of Ephraim, Judg 2:9
Joshua buried near, Josh 24:30

GABBATHA
Place of Pilate's court, John 19:13

GABRIEL
Messenger archangel; interprets Daniel's vision, Dan 8:16–27
Reveals the prophecy of 70 weeks, Dan 9:21–27
Announces John's birth, Luke 1:11–22
Announces Christ's birth, Luke 1:26–38
Stands in God's presence, Luke 1:19

GAD
Son of Jacob by Zilpah, Gen 30:10, 11
Blessed by Jacob, Gen 49:19
——— Tribe of:
Census of, Num 1:24, 25
Territory of, Num 32:20–36
Captivity of, 1 Chr 5:26
Later references to, Rev 7:5
——— Prophet in David's reign, 1 Sam 22:5
Message of, to David, 2 Sam 24:10–16

GADARENES (or Gergesenes)
People east of the Sea of Galilee, Mark 5:1
Healing of demon-possessed in territory of, Matt 8:28–34

GAIN
See DISHONEST GAIN
aside after dishonest *g* ..... 1 Sam 8:3
they did not *g* possession ...... Ps 44:3
That we may *g* a heart of .... Ps 90:12
g than fine gold .... Prov 3:14
He who is greedy for *g* .... Prov 15:27
will have no lack of *g* ..... Prov 31:11
a time to *g* .... Eccl 3:6
to get dishonest *g* .... Ezek 22:27
him who covets evil *g* .... Hab 2:9
and to die is *g* .... Phil 1:21
what things were *g* to me .... Phil 3:7
rubbish, that I may *g* .... Phil 3:8
is a means of *g* .... 1 Tim 6:5
contentment is great *g* ..... 1 Tim 6:6
the sake of dishonest *g* .... Titus 1:11
for dishonest *g* .... 1 Pet 5:2
people to *g* advantage .... Jude 16

GAINED
which he had *g* .... Gen 31:18
g in the land of Canaan ..... Gen 36:6
have *g* Him the victory .... Ps 98:1
Wealth *g* by dishonesty .... Prov 13:11
Bread *g* by deceit is .... Prov 20:17
An inheritance *g* hastily .. Prov 20:21
g more wisdom than all .... Eccl 1:16
you have *g* your brother .. Matt 18:15
received two *g* two more .. Matt 25:17
g five more talents .... Matt 25:20

GAINS
understanding *g* favor .... Prov 13:15
g the whole world .... Matt 16:26

GAIUS
Companion of Paul, Acts 19:29
——— Convert at Derbe, Acts 20:4
——— Paul's host at Corinth, Rom 16:23; 1 Cor 1:14

GALATIA
Paul visits, Acts 16:6; 18:23
Paul writes to Christians in, Gal 1:1
Peter writes to Christians in, 1 Pet 1:1

GALILEANS
Speech of, Mark 14:70
Faith of, John 4:45
Pilate's cruelty toward, Luke 13:1, 2

GALILEE
Prophecies concerning, Deut 33:18–23; Is 9:1, 2
Dialect of, distinctive, Matt 26:73
Herod's jurisdiction over, Luke 3:1
Christ's contacts with, Matt 2:22; 4:12–25; 26:32; 27:55; John 4:1, 3

GALILEE, SEA OF
Scene of many events in Christ's life, Mark 7:31
Called Chinnereth, Num 34:11
Later called Gennesaret, Luke 5:1

GALL
grapes are grapes of *g* .... Deut 32:32
They also gave me *g* .... Ps 69:21
the wormwood and the *g* ... Lam 3:19
turned justice into *g* ...... Amos 6:12
wine mingled with *g* ...... Matt 27:34

GALLIO
Roman proconsul of Achaia, dismisses charges against Paul, Acts 18:12–17

GALLONS
twenty or thirty *g* apiece .... John 2:6

GALLOWS
both were hanged on a *g* ... Esth 2:23
should be hanged on the *g* .. Esth 9:25

GAMALIEL
Famous Jewish teacher, Acts 22:3
Respected by people, Acts 5:34–39

GAME
because he ate of his *g* .... Gen 25:28
Bring me *g* and make .... Gen 27:7

GAP
and stand in the *g* .... Ezek 22:30

GARDEN
LORD God planted a *g* . . . . Gen 2:8
g enclosed is my . . . . Song 4:12
like a watered *g* . . . . Is 58:11
Eden, the *g* of God . . . . Ezek 28:13
raise up for them a *g* . . . . . Ezek 34:29
where there was a *g* . . . . John 18:1
in the *g* a new tomb . . . . . . John 19:41

GARDENER
Him to be the *g* . . . . John 20:15

GARDENS
I made myself *g* . . . . Eccl 2:5
plant *g* and eat their . . . . Jer 29:5

GARLANDS
brought oxen and *g* . . . . Acts 14:13

GARLIC
the onions, and the *g* . . . . . . Num 11:5

GARMENT
and Japheth took a *g* . . . . Gen 9:23
like a hairy *g* all over . . . . . . Gen 25:25
she caught him by his *g* . . . Gen 39:12
she kept his *g* with her . . . . Gen 39:16
beautiful Babylonian *g* . . . . . Josh 7:21
put on your best *g* . . . . Ruth 3:3
g that is moth-eaten . . . . Job 13:28
made sackcloth my *g* . . . . Ps 69:11
with light as with a *g* . . . . Ps 104:2
one who takes away a *g* . . Prov 25:20
the *g* of praise for the . . . . Is 61:3
the hem of His *g* . . . . Matt 9:20
have on a wedding *g* . . . . . Matt 22:11
cloth on an old *g* . . . . Mark 2:21
throwing aside his *g* . . . . . Mark 10:50
all grow old like a *g* . . . . Heb 1:11
hating even the *g* . . . . Jude 23

GARMENTS
took off her widow's *g* . . . . . Gen 38:14
the *g* of her widowhood . . . Gen 38:19
g did not wear out on . . . . Deut 8:4
and old *g* on themselves . . . . . Josh 9:5
our *g* and our sandals . . . . . . Josh 9:13
cut off their *g* in the . . . . . . 2 Sam 10:4
Why are your *g* hot . . . . Job 37:17
They divide My *g* . . . . Ps 22:18
She makes linen *g* and . . . . Prov 31:24
g always be white . . . . Eccl 9:8
g rolled in blood . . . . Is 9:5
from Edom, with dyed *g* . . . . . . Is 63:1
nor were their *g* affected . . . . Dan 3:27
your heart, and not your *g* . . Joel 2:13
Take away the filthy *g* . . . . . . Zech 3:4
man clothed in soft *g* . . . . . . Matt 11:8
and divided His *g* . . . . Matt 27:35
by them in shining *g* . . . . . . Luke 24:4
and laid aside His *g* . . . . John 13:4
divided My *g* among . . . . . . John 19:24
g which Dorcas had made . . Acts 9:39
g are moth-eaten . . . . James 5:2
be clothed in white *g* . . . . Rev 3:5

GARRISON
gathered the whole *g* . . . . . Matt 27:27
Damascenes with a *g* . . . . . 2 Cor 11:32

GATE
sitting in the *g* of Sodom . . . . Gen 19:1
Boaz went up to the *g* . . . . Ruth 4:1
people who were at the *g* . . Ruth 4:11
This is the *g* of the . . . . Ps 118:20
by the narrow *g* . . . . Matt 7:13
Because narrow is the *g* . . . . Matt 7:14
by the Sheep *G* a pool . . . . . . John 5:2
laid daily at the *g* . . . . Acts 3:2
she did not open the *g* . . . . Acts 12:14
suffered outside the *g* . . . . . Heb 13:12
each individual *g* . . . . Rev 21:21

GATES
possess the *g* of those . . . . . Gen 24:60
g are burned with fire . . . . Neh 1:3
I commanded the *g* to be . . Neh 13:19
they go down to the *g* . . . . . . Job 17:16
up your heads, O you *g* . . . . Ps 24:7
The LORD loves the *g* . . . . Ps 87:2
Enter into His *g* with . . . . Ps 100:4
Open to me the *g* . . . . Ps 118:19
watching daily at my *g* . . . . . Prov 8:34
is known in the *g* . . . . Prov 31:23
praise her in the *g* . . . . Prov 31:31
go through the *g* . . . . Is 62:10
and the *g* of Hades . . . . Matt 16:18
wall with twelve *g* . . . . Rev 21:12
g were twelve pearls . . . . Rev 21:21
g shall not be shut . . . . Rev 21:25

GATH
Philistine city, 1 Sam 6:17
Ark carried to, 1 Sam 5:8
David takes refuge in, 1 Sam 21:10–15
David's second flight to, 1 Sam 27:3–12
Captured by David, 1 Chr 18:1
Destruction of, prophetic, Amos 6:1–3
Name becomes proverbial, Mic 1:10

GATH HEPHER
Birthplace of Jonah, 2 Kin 14:25

GATHER
g my soul with sinners . . . . Ps 26:9
G My saints together . . . . Ps 50:5
and a time to *g* stones . . . . Eccl 3:5
g the lambs with His . . . . Is 40:11
g His wheat into the . . . . Matt 3:12
sow nor reap nor *g* . . . . Matt 6:26
Do men *g* grapes from . . . . . Matt 7:16
g where I have not . . . . Matt 25:26
g together His elect . . . . . . Mark 13:27
who does not *g* with Me . . Luke 11:23
often I wanted to *g* your . . Luke 13:34
G up the fragments that . . . . John 6:12
of the times He might *g* . . . . Eph 1:10

GATHERED
g little had no lack . . . . Ex 16:18
And *g* out of the lands . . . . . . Ps 107:3
g some of every kind . . . . . . Matt 13:47
g together in My name . . . . Matt 18:20
the nations will be *g* . . . . . . Matt 25:32
many were *g* together . . . . . Acts 12:12
g the church together . . . . . Acts 14:27
when Paul had *g* a bundle . . Acts 28:3
when you are *g* together . . . . 1 Cor 5:4
who *g* much had nothing . . 2 Cor 8:15
they *g* them together . . . . . . Rev 16:16

GATHERING
g together of the waters . . . . Gen 1:10
widow was there *g* . . . . 1 Kin 17:10
I am *g* a couple of sticks . . 1 Kin 17:12
they were three days *g* . . . 2 Chr 20:25
He gives the work of *g* . . . . . Eccl 2:26
g where you have not . . . . . Matt 25:24
g a mob, set all the city in . . Acts 17:5
for this disorderly *g* . . . . Acts 19:40
g together to Him . . . . 2 Thess 2:1

GATHERS
g the waters of the . . . . Ps 33:7
His heart *g* iniquity . . . . Ps 41:6
He *g* together the outcasts . . . Ps 147:2
g her food in the . . . . Prov 6:8
He who *g* in summer is a . . Prov 10:5
he who *g* by labor will . . . . Prov 13:11
extortion *g* it for him who . . Prov 28:8
The Lord GOD, who *g* . . . . Is 56:8
together, as a hen *g* . . . . Matt 23:37

GAUNT
out of the river, ugly and *g* . . Gen 41:3
g and ugly cows ate up . . . . Gen 41:20

GAVE
So Adam *g* names to all . . . . Gen 2:20
She also *g* to her husband . . . Gen 3:6
to be with me, she *g* . . . . Gen 3:12
he *g* him a tithe of all . . . . . Gen 14:20
g her to her husband . . . . Gen 16:3
and *g* the lad a drink . . . . . . Gen 21:19
hand, and *g* him a drink . . . Gen 24:18
Abraham *g* all that he had . . Gen 25:5
Jacob *g* Esau bread and . . . Gen 25:34
which God *g* to Abraham . . . Gen 28:4
g him favor in the sight . . . . Gen 39:21
Joseph *g* a command . . . . . . Gen 42:25
it *g* light by night to the . . . . . Ex 14:20
He *g* Moses two tablets of . . . Ex 31:18
So they *g* it to me, and I . . . . Ex 32:24
g the children of Israel . . . . Num 13:32
stone and *g* them to me . . . . Deut 5:22
the LORD *g* me the two . . . . . Deut 9:11
g you on this side of the . . . . Josh 1:14
g it as an inheritance . . . . . Josh 11:23
So he *g* her the upper . . . . . Josh 15:19
The LORD *g* them rest all . . Josh 21:44
Samson *g* a feast there . . . . Judg 14:10
g the changes of clothing . Judg 14:19
therefore I *g* her to your . . . Judg 15:2
LORD *g* her conception . . . . . Ruth 4:13
g birth, for her labor . . . . . 1 Sam 4:19
God *g* him another heart . . 1 Sam 10:9
g it to David, with his . . . . . 1 Sam 18:4
Saul *g* him Michal . . . . 1 Sam 18:27
So the priest *g* him holy . . 1 Sam 21:6
g him the sword of . . . . 1 Sam 22:10
this woman also *g* birth . . . 1 Kin 3:18
God *g* Solomon wisdom . . . 1 Kin 4:29
Hiram *g* Solomon cedar . . . 1 Kin 5:10
g to King Solomon . . . . 1 Kin 10:10
g a commandment . . . . 1 Chr 14:12
David *g* his son . . . . 1 Chr 28:11
g it to the workmen . . . . . . 2 Chr 34:10
Hilkiah *g* the book to . . . . 2 Chr 34:15
Josiah *g* the lay people . . . . 2 Chr 35:7
so he readily *g* beauty . . . . . . Esth 2:9
g gifts according to the . . . . Esth 2:18
He also *g* him a copy of . . . . . Esth 4:8
and *g* it to Mordecai . . . . Esth 8:2
return to God who *g* it . . . . . . Eccl 12:7
of the eunuchs *g* names . . . . . Dan 1:7
and *g* them vegetables . . . . . . Dan 1:16
God *g* them knowledge . . . . . Dan 1:17
g him many great gifts . . . . . Dan 2:48
Belshazzar *g* the command . . Dan 5:2
g thanks before his God . . . . Dan 6:10
He *g* them power over . . . . . Matt 10:1
g You this authority . . . . . Matt 21:23
hungry and you *g* Me . . . . . Matt 25:35
g thanks, and *g* it to . . . . . Matt 26:27
g Him sour wine . . . . Matt 27:34
platter, and *g* it to . . . . Mark 6:28
To many blind He *g* sight . . Luke 7:21
g Me no water for My . . . . . Luke 7:44
g them to the innkeeper . . Luke 10:35
no one *g* him anything . . . Luke 15:16
saw it, *g* praise to God . . . . Luke 18:43
to them He *g* the right to . . . John 1:12
that He *g* His only . . . . John 3:16
Those whom You *g* . . . . John 17:12
glory which You *g* Me . . . . John 17:22
head, He *g* up His spirit . . . John 19:30
tongues, as the Spirit *g* . . . . . . Acts 2:4
great power the apostles *g* . . Acts 4:33
who *g* alms generously to . . Acts 10:2
g us rain from heaven . . . . . Acts 14:17
God also *g* them up . . . . Rom 1:24
but God *g* the increase . . . . . 1 Cor 3:6
but first *g* themselves to . . . . 2 Cor 8:5
but God *g* it to Abraham . . . . Gal 3:18
g Him to be head over all . . . Eph 1:22
captive, and *g* gifts to men . . . Eph 4:8
He Himself *g* some to be . . . . Eph 4:11
Abraham *g* a tenth part of . . . Heb 7:2
and the heaven *g* rain . . . . . James 5:18
g Him glory, so that your . . 1 Pet 1:21
He *g* us commandment . . . 1 John 3:23
which God *g* Him to show . . . . Rev 1:1
g to the seven angels . . . . Rev 15:7
The sea *g* up the dead . . . . . Rev 20:13

"If you knew the *g* .... John 4:10
the *g* of the Holy Spirit ..... Acts 2:38
thought that the *g* of God ... Acts 8:20
the *g* of the Holy .... Acts 10:45
same *g* as He gave us ..... Acts 11:17
to you some spiritual *g* ..... Rom 1:11
But the free *g* is not .... Rom 5:15
of the *g* of righteousness ... Rom 5:17
but the *g* of God is .... Rom 6:23
each one has his own *g* ..... 1 Cor 7:7
though I have the *g* .... 1 Cor 13:2
it is the *g* of God .... Eph 2:8
Not that I seek the *g* .... Phil 4:17
Do not neglect the *g* ...... 1 Tim 4:14
you to stir up the *g* .... 2 Tim 1:6
tasted the heavenly *g* .... Heb 6:4
Every good *g* and every .. James 1:17
one has received a *g* .... 1 Pet 4:10

GIFTED
the women who were *g* ..... Ex 35:25
but good-looking, *g* .... Dan 1:4

GIFTS
g you shall offer .... Num 18:29
You have received *g* .... Ps 68:18
and Seba will offer *g* .... Ps 72:10
though you give many *g* ... Prov 6:35
to one who gives *g* .... Prov 19:6
how to give good *g* .... Matt 7:11
rich putting their *g* .... Luke 21:1
Having then *g* differing .... Rom 12:6
are diversities of *g* .... 1 Cor 12:4
and desire spiritual *g* ...... 1 Cor 14:1
captive, and gave *g* .... Eph 4:8

GIHON
River of Eden, Gen 2:13
—— Spring outside Jerusalem, 1 Kin 1:33–45
Source of water supply, 2 Chr 32:30

GILBOA
Range of limestone hills in Issachar, 1 Sam 28:4
Scene of Saul's death, 1 Sam 31:1–9
Under David's curse, 2 Sam 1:17, 21

GILEAD
Plain east of the Jordan; taken from the Amorites and assigned to Gad, Reuben, and Manasseh, Num 21:21–31; 32:33–40; Deut 3:12, 13; Josh 13:24–31
Ishbosheth rules over, 2 Sam 2:8, 9
David takes refuge in, 2 Sam 17:21–26
Conquered by Hazael, 2 Kin 10:32, 33
Balm of, figurative of national healing, Jer 8:22

GILGAL
Site of memorial stones, circumcision, first Passover in the Promised Land, Josh 4:19—5:12
Site of Gibeonite covenant, Josh 9:3–15
One location on Samuel's circuit, 1 Sam 7:15, 16
Saul made king and later rejected, 1 Sam 11:15; 13:4–15
Denounced for idolatry, Hos 9:15

GIRD
G Your sword upon Your .... Ps 45:3
of wrath You shall *g* .... Ps 76:10
I will *g* you, though you .... Is 45:5
and another will *g* .... John 21:18
Therefore *g* up the .... 1 Pet 1:13

GIRDED
a towel and *g* Himself ..... John 13:4
down to the feet and *g* ...... Rev 1:13

GIRGASHITES
Descendants of Canaan, Gen 10:15, 16
Land of, given to Abraham's descendants, Gen 15:18, 21
Delivered to Israel, Josh 24:11

GITTITES
600 follow David, 2 Sam 15:18–23

GIVE
g thanks to the LORD ...... 1 Chr 16:8
g me wisdom and .... 2 Chr 1:10
G ear to my prayer .... Ps 17:1
G to them according .... Ps 28:4
g you the desires .... Ps 37:4
Yes, the LORD will *g* .... Ps 85:12
G me understanding .... Ps 119:34
g me your heart .... Prov 23:26
You will *g* truth to .... Mic 7:20
G to him who asks .... Matt 5:42
G us this day our .... Matt 6:11
what you have and *g* ..... Matt 19:21
authority I will *g* .... Luke 4:6
g them eternal life .... John 10:28
new commandment I *g* .. John 13:34
but what I do have I *g* .... Acts 3:6
g us all things .... Rom 8:32
G no offense .... 1 Cor 10:32
So let each one *g* .... 2 Cor 9:7
nor *g* place to the devil ..... Eph 4:27
g him who has need .... Eph 4:28
g thanks to God .... 2 Thess 2:13
g yourself entirely .... 1 Tim 4:15
good works, ready to *g* .... 1 Tim 6:18
and always be ready to *g* .. 1 Pet 3:15
They will *g* an account to ... 1 Pet 4:5
I will *g* you the crown of .... Rev 2:10
I will *g* him a white stone, .. Rev 2:17
I will *g* him the morning .... Rev 2:28
"*G* me the little book .... Rev 10:9
I will *g* of the fountain of .... Rev 21:6
g to every one according ... Rev 22:12

GIVEN
I have *g* every green herb .. Gen 1:30
land which He has *g* you ... Deut 8:10
will tread upon I have *g* ...... Josh 1:3
I had *g* rest to Israel from .. Josh 23:1
see, I have *g* you a wise ... 1 Kin 3:12
He has *g* us rest on .... 2 Chr 14:7
she was *g* whatever she .... Esth 2:13
You have *g* me wisdom ..... Dan 2:23
Ask and it will be *g* to you . Matt 7:7
to him more will be *g* ..... Matt 13:12
nor are *g* in marriage ..... Matt 22:30
has, more will be *g* ...... Matt 25:29
to whom much is *g* .... Luke 12:48
and are *g* in marriage ..... Luke 20:34
My body which is *g* for .... Luke 22:19
law was *g* through Moses .. John 1:17
has *g* Him authority to ..... John 5:27
g Me I should lose .... John 6:39
Spirit was not yet *g* .... John 7:39
have been freely *g* .... 1 Cor 2:12
g us the Spirit in our ...... 2 Cor 1:22
g according to the .... Eph 4:7
utterance may be *g* to me ... Eph 6:19
not *g* to wine .... 1 Tim 3:3
God has not *g* us a spirit ... 2 Tim 1:7
All Scripture is *g* by ...... 2 Tim 3:16
robe was *g* to each of .... Rev 6:11

GIVES
He who *g* to the poor ...... Prov 28:27
For God *g* wisdom and ..... Eccl 2:26
g life to the world .... John 6:33
All that the Father *g* .... John 6:37
The good shepherd *g* ..... John 10:11
not as the world *g* .... John 14:27
g us richly all things ...... 1 Tim 6:17
who *g* to all liberally ...... James 1:5
g grace to the humble ...... James 4:6

GLAD
See BE GLAD AND REJOICE
g of heart for the good .... 2 Chr 7:10
I will be *g* and .... Ps 9:2
my heart is *g* .... Ps 16:9
Be *g* in the LORD and .... Ps 32:11
streams shall make *g* .... Ps 46:4
And wine that makes *g* .... Ps 104:15
I will be *g* in the LORD ...... Ps 104:34
I was *g* when they said ...... Ps 122:1
son makes a *g* father .... Prov 10:1
We will be *g* and rejoice ..... Song 1:4
Be *g* and rejoice with all ... Zeph 3:14
shall see it and be *g* .... Zech 10:7
and be exceedingly *g* .... Matt 5:12
bring you these *g* tidings .. Luke 1:19
bringing the *g* tidings of .... Luke 8:1
make merry and be *g* ..... Luke 15:32
he saw it and was *g* .... John 8:56
Let us be *g* and rejoice ...... Rev 19:7

GLADNESS
in the day of your *g* ...... Num 10:10
day of feasting and *g* .... Esth 9:17
You have put *g* in my .... Ps 4:7
me hear joy and *g* .... Ps 51:8
Serve the LORD with *g* .... Ps 100:2
shall obtain joy and *g* .... Is 35:10
They shall obtain joy and *g* .. Is 51:11
over you with *g* .... Zeph 3:17
receive it with *g* .... Mark 4:16
they ate their food with *g* ... Acts 2:46
You with the oil of *g* more ... Heb 1:9

GLASS
there was a sea of *g* .... Rev 4:6
like transparent *g* .... Rev 21:21

GLORIFIED
the people I must be *g* .... Lev 10:3
and they *g* the God of ..... Matt 15:31
Jesus was not yet *g* .... John 7:39
when Jesus was *g* .... John 12:16
By this My Father is *g* ..... John 15:8
I have *g* You on the .... John 17:4
g His Servant Jesus .... Acts 3:13
these He also *g* .... Rom 8:30
things God may be *g* ...... 1 Pet 4:11

GLORIFY
My altar, and I will *g* .... Is 60:7
g your Father in .... Matt 5:16
"Father, *g* Your name ..... John 12:28
He will *g* Me .... John 16:14
And now, O Father, *g* .... John 17:5
what death he would *g* ... John 21:19
God, they did not *g* .... Rom 1:21
therefore *g* God in .... 1 Cor 6:20
also Christ did not *g* .... Heb 5:5
ashamed, but let him *g* .... 1 Pet 4:16

GLORIOUS
g in holiness, fearful in ...... Ex 15:11
daughter is all *g* .... Ps 45:13
And blessed be His *g* .... Ps 72:19
G things are spoken .... Ps 87:3
is honorable and *g* .... Ps 111:3
g splendor of Your .... Ps 145:5
habitation, holy and *g* .... Is 63:15
also enter the *G* Land ...... Dan 11:41
engraved on stones, was *g* .. 2 Cor 3:7
it to Himself a *g* .... Eph 5:27
be conformed to His *g* ...... Phil 3:21
g appearing of our .... Titus 2:13

GLORY
"Please, show me Your *g* ... Ex 33:18
filled with the *g* of the ..... Num 14:21
g has departed from .... 1 Sam 4:21
G in His holy name ...... 1 Chr 16:10
a shield for me, my *g* .... Ps 3:3
who have set Your *g* .... Ps 8:1
Who is this King of *g* .... Ps 24:8
the place where Your *g* .... Ps 26:8
Your power and Your *g* ...... Ps 63:2
shall speak of the *g* .... Ps 145:11
wise shall inherit *g* .... Prov 3:35
head is a crown of *g*, if ... Prov 16:31
The *g* of young men is .... Prov 20:29
It is the *g* of God to .... Prov 25:2
"*G* to the righteous .... Is 24:16
g I will not give .... Is 42:8
g will be seen upon .... Is 60:2

brightness of the LORD's *g* . . Ezek 10:4
then be likened in *g* . . . . . . Ezek 31:18
I will set My *g* among . . . . Ezek 39:21
I will change their *g* . . . . Hos 4:7
and I will be the *g* . . . . Zech 2:5
He shall bear the *g* . . . . Zech 6:13
that they may have *g* . . . . Matt 6:2
the power and the *g* . . . . Matt 6:13
g was not arrayed . . . . Matt 6:29
Man will come in the *g* . . . Matt 16:27
with power and great *g* . . . Matt 24:30
"*G* to God in the . . . . Luke 2:14
and we beheld His *g* . . . . John 1:14
and manifested His *g* . . . . . . John 2:11
I do not seek My own *g* . . . . John 8:50
"Give God the *g* . . . . John 9:24
g which I had with You . . . . John 17:5
g which You gave Me I . . . John 17:22
he did not give *g* . . . . Acts 12:23
doing good seek for *g* . . . . Rom 2:7
in faith, giving *g* . . . . Rom 4:20
the adoption, the *g* . . . . Rom 9:4
the riches of His *g* . . . . Rom 9:23
God, alone wise, be *g* . . . . . Rom 16:27
who glories, let him *g* . . . . . 1 Cor 1:31
but woman is the *g* . . . . 1 Cor 11:7
of the *g* that excels . . . . 2 Cor 3:10
of the gospel of the *g* . . . . 2 Cor 4:4
eternal weight of *g* . . . . 2 Cor 4:17
who glories, let him *g* . . . . 2 Cor 10:17
to His riches in *g* . . . . Phil 4:19
appear with Him in *g* . . . . Col 3:4
For you are our *g* . . . . 1 Thess 2:20
You crowned him with *g* . . . . . Heb 2:7
many sons to *g* . . . . Heb 2:10
grass, and all the *g* . . . . 1 Pet 1:24
to whom belong the *g* . . . . . . 1 Pet 4:11
for the Spirit of *g* . . . . 1 Pet 4:14
To Him be the *g* and the . . . 1 Pet 5:11
the presence of His *g* . . . . Jude 24
O Lord, to receive *g* . . . . Rev 4:11

GLORY OF GOD
The heavens declare the *g* . . . . Ps 19:1
unto death, but for the *g* . . . John 11:4
into heaven and saw the *g* . . Acts 7:55
fall short of the *g* . . . . Rom 3:23
do all to the *g* . . . . 1 Cor 10:31
he is the image and *g* . . . . 1 Cor 11:7
g in the face of Jesus . . . . 2 Cor 4:6
with smoke from the *g* . . . . . . Rev 15:8
having the *g*. . . . . Rev 21:11
for the *g* illuminated it . . . . . Rev 21:23

GLORY OF THE LORD
g appeared in the cloud . . . . . Ex 16:10
g rested on Mount Sinai, ... Ex 24:16
g filled the tabernacle . . . . Ex 40:34
the *g* will appear to you . . . . . . Lev 9:6
g appeared in the . . . . Num 14:10
the *g* appeared to all . . . . . Num 16:19
and the *g* appeared . . . . Num 16:42
the *g* appeared to them . . . . Num 20:6
the *g* filled the house . . . . . . 1 Kin 8:11
the *g* filled the temple . . . . 2 Chr 7:1
May the *g* endure forever . . Ps 104:31
They shall see the *g* . . . . Is 35:2
the *g* shall be revealed, ... Is 40:5
the *g* is risen upon you . . . . Is 60:1
of the likeness of the *g* . . . . . Ezek 1:28
behold, the *g* stood there . . . Ezek 3:23
the *g* went up . . . . Ezek 10:4
the *g* came into the . . . . Ezek 43:4
g filled the house of the . . . . Ezek 44:4
the knowledge of the *g* . . . . . . Hab 2:14
the *g* shone around them, . . . Luke 2:9
as in a mirror the *g*, ... 2 Cor 3:18
by us to the *g* . . . . 2 Cor 8:19

GLORYING
Your *g* is not good . . . . 1 Cor 5:6

GLUTTON
g will come to poverty . . . . Prov 23:21
you say, 'Look, a *g* . . . . Luke 7:34

GLUTTONS
companion of *g* shames . . . . Prov 28:7
evil beasts, lazy *g* . . . . Titus 1:12

GNASHING
will be weeping and *g* . . . . . . Matt 8:12

GO
He said, "Let Me *g* . . . . Gen 32:26
'Let My people *g* . . . . Ex 5:1
Presence does not *g* . . . . Ex 33:15
for wherever you *g* . . . . Ruth 1:16
"Look, I *g* forward . . . . Job 23:8
For I used to *g* with the . . . . . . Ps 42:4
g astray as soon as . . . . Ps 58:3
I will *g* in the strength of . . . . Ps 71:16
Those who *g* down to . . . . Ps 107:23
Where can I *g* from . . . . Ps 139:7
G to the ant . . . . Prov 6:6
All *g* to one place . . . . Eccl 3:20
of mourning than to *g* . . . . Eccl 7:2
out of Zion shall *g* forth . . . . Is 2:3
You wherever You *g* . . . . Matt 8:19
do not *g* out . . . . Matt 24:26
He said to them, "*G* . . . . . . Mark 16:15
And I say to one, '*G* . . . . Luke 7:8
also want to *g* away . . . . John 6:67
to whom shall we *g* . . . . John 6:68
g you cannot come . . . . John 8:21
I *g* to prepare a place . . . . . . John 14:2
will do, because I *g* . . . . John 14:12
seek Me, let these *g* . . . . John 18:8
and he shall *g* out no more . . Rev 3:12

GOADS
of the wise are like *g* . . . . . . Eccl 12:11
to kick against the *g* . . . . Acts 9:5

GOAL
I press toward the *g* . . . . Phil 3:14

GOATS
drink the blood of *g* . . . . Ps 50:13
his sheep from the *g* . . . . . . Matt 25:32
with the blood of *g* . . . . Heb 9:12
g could take away . . . . Heb 10:4

GOD
See ANGEL OF GOD; GLORY OF GOD; HAND OF GOD; HOUSE OF GOD; KINGDOM OF GOD; LORD GOD OF HOSTS; LORD GOD OF ISRAEL; LOVE OF GOD; LOVE THE LORD YOUR GOD; MAN OF GOD; PEOPLE OF GOD; POWER OF GOD; RIGHTEOUSNESS OF GOD; SON OF GOD; SONS OF GOD; SPIRIT OF GOD; THINGS OF GOD; THRONE OF GOD; WILL OF GOD; WORD OF GOD; WRATH OF GOD

Names of:
God, Gen 1:1
LORD God, Gen 2:4
God Most High, Gen 14:18–22
Lord GOD, Gen 15:2, 8
Almighty God, Gen 17:1, 2
I AM, Ex 3:14
Jealous, Ex 34:14
Eternal God, Deut 33:27
Living God, Josh 3:10
God of hosts, Ps 80:7
LORD of hosts, Is 1:24
Holy One of Israel, Is 43:3, 14, 15
Mighty God, Jer 32:18
God of heaven, Jon 1:9
Heavenly Father, Matt 6:26
King eternal, 1 Tim 1:17
only Potentate, 1 Tim 6:15
Father of lights, James 1:17

Manifestations of:
face of, Gen 32:30
voice of, Deut 5:22–26
glory of, Ex 40:34, 35
Angel of, Gen 16:7–13
name of, Ex 34:5–7
form of, Num 12:6–8

Nature of:
spirit, John 4:24
one, Deut 6:4
personal, John 17:1–3
trinitarian, 2 Cor 13:14

Attributes of:
incomparable, 2 Sam 7:22
invisible, John 1:18
inscrutable, Is 40:28
unchangeable, Num 23:19
unequaled, Is 40:13–25
unsearchable, Rom 11:33, 34
infinite, 1 King 8:27
eternal, Is 57:15
omnipotent, Jer 32:17, 27
omnipresent, Ps 139:7–12
omniscient, 1 John 3:20
foreknowing, Is 48:3, 5
wise, Acts 15:18
holy, Rev 4:8
impartial, 1 Pet 1:17
just, Ps 89:14
longsuffering, Ex 34:6, 7
love, 1 John 4:8, 16
mercy, Lam 3:22, 23
truth, Ps 117:2
vengeance, Deut 32:34–41
wrath, Deut 32:22

G created the heavens . . . . Gen 1:1
Abram of *G* Most High . . . . Gen 14:19
and I will be their *G* . . . . Gen 17:8
hands of the Mighty *G* . . . . Gen 49:24
the *G* of Abraham . . . . Ex 3:6
He is my *G* . . . . Ex 15:2
Stand before *G* for the . . . . . . Ex 18:19
"I am the LORD your *G* . . . . Ex 20:2
"This is your *g* . . . . Ex 32:4
G is not a man . . . . Num 23:19
G is a consuming fire . . . . . . Deut 4:24
great and awesome *G* . . . . . . Deut 7:21
my people, and your *G* . . . . Ruth 1:16
know that there is a *G* . . . 1 Sam 17:46
a rock, except our *G* . . . . . 2 Sam 22:32
If the LORD is *G* . . . . 1 Kin 18:21
G is greater than all . . . . 2 Chr 2:5
G is greater than . . . . Job 33:12
"Behold, *G* is mighty . . . . Job 36:5
"Behold, *G* is great . . . . Job 36:26
You have been My *G* . . . . Ps 22:10
"Where is your *G* . . . . Ps 42:3
G is our refuge . . . . Ps 46:1
G is in the midst of . . . . Ps 46:5
G is the King of all . . . . Ps 47:7
The Mighty One, *G* . . . . Ps 50:1
I am *G*, your *G* . . . . Ps 50:7
me a clean heart, O *G* . . . . Ps 51:10
Our *G* is the *G* . . . . Ps 68:20
Who is so great a *G* . . . . Ps 77:13
Restore us, O *G* . . . . Ps 80:7
You alone are *G* . . . . Ps 86:10
Exalt the LORD our *G* . . . . Ps 99:9
Yes, our *G* is merciful . . . . Ps 116:5
give thanks to the *G* . . . . Ps 136:26
For *G* is in heaven . . . . Eccl 5:2
Counselor, Mighty *G* . . . . Is 9:6
G is my salvation . . . . Is 12:2
Behold, this is our *G* . . . . Is 25:9
"Behold your *G* . . . . Is 40:9
Is there a *G* besides . . . . Is 44:8
to Zion, "Your *G* . . . . Is 52:7
stricken, smitten by *G* . . . . Is 53:4
and I will be their *G* . . . . Jer 31:33
and I saw visions of *G* . . . . . . Ezek 1:1
Who is a *G* like You . . . . Mic 7:18
translated, "*G* with us." . . . . Matt 1:23
in *G* my Savior . . . . Luke 1:47
the Word was with *G* . . . . John 1:1
enter the kingdom of *G* . . . . . John 3:5
For *G* so loved the . . . . John 3:16
has certified that *G* . . . . John 3:33
G is Spirit, and those . . . . . . John 4:24

"My Lord and my *G* ...... John 20:28
Christ is the Son of *G* ...... Acts 8:37
To the Unknown *G* .... Acts 17:23
Indeed, let *G* be true .... Rom 3:4
If *G* is for us .... Rom 8:31
G is faithful .... 1 Cor 1:9
us there is one *G* .... 1 Cor 8:6
G shall supply all .... Phil 4:19
and I will be their *G* .... Heb 8:10
G is a consuming fire ..... Heb 12:29
G is greater than our ..... 1 John 3:20
for *G* is love .... 1 John 4:8
No one has seen *G* .... 1 John 4:12
in the temple of My *G* .... Rev 3:12
gave glory to the *G* .... Rev 11:13
G Himself will be .... Rev 21:3
and I will be his *G* .... Rev 21:7

GOD THE FATHER
G has set His seal on Him .. John 6:27
the kingdom to *G* .... 1 Cor 15:24
through Jesus Christ and *G* ... Gal 1:1
G and our Lord Jesus Christ .. Gal 1:3
for all things to *G* .... Eph 5:20
love with faith, from *G* ...... Eph 6:23
to the glory of *G* .... Phil 2:11
giving thanks to *G* .... Col 3:17
in *G* and the Lord Jesus .. 1 Thess 1:1
mercy, and peace from *G* ... 2 Tim 1:2
mercy, and peace from *G* .... Titus 1:4
the foreknowledge of *G* ...... 1 Pet 1:2
For He received from *G* .... 2 Pet 1:17
G and from the Lord Jesus .. 2 John 3
sanctified by *G*, and .... Jude 1

GODDESS
after Ashtoreth the *g* .... 1 Kin 11:5
of the great *g* Diana ...... Acts 19:35

GODHEAD
eternal power and *G* .... Rom 1:20
the fullness of the *G* .... Col 2:9

GODLINESS
is the mystery of *g* .... 1 Tim 3:16
g is profitable .... 1 Tim 4:8
Now *g* with contentment ... 1 Tim 6:6
having a form of *g* .... 2 Tim 3:5
pertain to life and *g* .... 2 Pet 1:3
to perseverance *g* .... 2 Pet 1:6

GODLY
Himself him who is *g* .... Ps 4:3
everyone who is *g* .... Ps 32:6
who desire to live *g* .... 2 Tim 3:12
righteously, and *g* .... Titus 2:12
reverence and *g* fear ...... Heb 12:28
to deliver the *g* .... 2 Pet 2:9

GODS
See FOREIGN GODS
your God is God of *g* ..... Deut 10:17
the household *g* .... 2 Kin 23:24
He judges among the *g* .... Ps 82:1
I said, "You are *g* .... Ps 82:6
yourselves with *g* .... Is 57:5
If He called them *g* .... John 10:35
g have come down to ..... Acts 14:11

GOG
Prince of Rosh, Meshech, and Tubal, Ezek 38:2, 3
——— Leader of the final battle, Rev 20:8–15

GOLAN
City of refuge, Josh 20:8, 21:27

GOLD
And the *g* of that land ...... Gen 2:12
a mercy seat of pure *g* ...... Ex 25:17
multiply silver and *g* ..... Deut 17:17
"If I have made *g* .... Job 31:24
yea, than much fine *g* .... Ps 19:10
is like apples of *g* .... Prov 25:11
is Mine, and the *g* .... Hag 2:8
g I do not have .... Acts 3:6
with braided hair or *g* ...... 1 Tim 2:9
a man with *g* rings .... James 2:2
Your *g* and silver are ...... James 5:3
more precious than *g* .... 1 Pet 1:7
like silver or *g* .... 1 Pet 1:18
of the city was pure *g* ...... Rev 21:21

GOLDEN
g bell and a pomegranate ... Ex 28:34
g tumors and five *g* rats .... 1 Sam 6:4
from the *g* calves that .... 2 Kin 10:29
or the *g* bowl is broken, or .. Eccl 12:6
the seven *g* lampstands ...... Rev 1:20
and *g* bowls full of incense, .. Rev 5:8
g altar which is before .... Rev 9:13
having in her hand a *g* cup .. Rev 17:4

GOLGOTHA
Where Jesus died, Matt 27:33–35

GOLIATH
Giant of Gath, 1 Sam 17:4
Killed by David, 1 Sam 17:50
——— Brother of above; killed by Elhanan, 2 Sam 21:19

GOMER
Son of Japheth, Gen 10:2, 3; 1 Chr 1:5, 6
Northern nation, Ezek 38:6
——— Wife of Hosea, Hos 1:2, 3

GOMORRAH
See SODOM AND GOMORRAH
With Sodom, defeated by Chedorlaomer; Lot captured, Gen 14:8–12
Destroyed by God, Gen 19:23–29
Later references to, Is 1:10; Amos 4:11; Matt 10:15

GONE
I am *g* like a shadow .... Ps 109:23
I have *g* astray like a ..... Ps 119:176
the word has *g* out of .... Is 45:23
like sheep have *g* .... Is 53:6

GOOD
See BE OF GOOD CHEER; LORD IS GOOD
God saw that it was *g* ...... Gen 1:10
but God meant it for *g* ..... Gen 50:20
LORD has promised *g* ..... Num 10:29
you have spoken is *g* ..... 2 Kin 20:19
seeking the *g* of his .... Esth 10:3
Shall we indeed accept *g* .... Job 2:10
"Who will show us any *g* .... Ps 4:6
is none who does *g* .... Ps 14:1
G and upright is the .... Ps 25:8
that he may see *g* .... Ps 34:12
Truly God is *g* to .... Ps 73:1
g man deals graciously ...... Ps 112:5
Your Spirit is *g* .... Ps 143:10
g man obtains favor .... Prov 12:2
g word makes it glad ..... Prov 12:25
on the evil and the *g* .... Prov 15:3
A merry heart does *g* ..... Prov 17:22
who knows what is *g* .... Eccl 6:12
learn to do *g* .... Is 1:17
Zion, you who bring *g* .... Is 40:9
tidings of *g* things .... Is 52:7
talked to me, with *g* .... Zech 1:13
said, "Be of *g* cheer .... Matt 9:22
A *g* man out of the .... Matt 12:35
"*G* Teacher, what *g* .... Matt 19:16
No one is *g* but One ...... Matt 19:17
For she has done a *g* ..... Matt 26:10
behold, I bring you *g* ...... Luke 2:10
love your enemies, do *g* .... Luke 6:35
"Can anything *g* come ..... John 1:46
Some said, "He is *g* .... John 7:12
who went about doing *g* .. Acts 10:38
For he was a *g* man .... Acts 11:24
in that He did *g* .... Acts 14:17
g man someone would .... Rom 5:7
in my flesh) nothing *g* ...... Rom 7:18
overcome evil with *g* ...... Rom 12:21
according to the *g* pleasure .. Eph 1:5
fruitful in every *g* .... Col 1:10
know that the law is *g* ...... 1 Tim 1:8
may wage the *g* warfare .. 1 Tim 1:18
For this is *g* and .... 1 Tim 2:3
bishop, he desires a *g* ...... 1 Tim 3:1
for this is *g* and .... 1 Tim 5:4
a *g* soldier of Jesus Christ .. 2 Tim 2:3
prepared for every *g* ...... 2 Tim 2:21
I have fought the *g* fight .... 2 Tim 4:7
and have tasted the *g* .... Heb 6:5
obtained a *g* testimony ..... Heb 11:2
Every *g* gift and every .... James 1:17
g days, let him refrain ..... 1 Pet 3:10
to suffer for doing *g* .... 1 Pet 3:17
g stewards of the .... 1 Pet 4:10

GOOD WORKS
that they may see your *g* ... Matt 5:16
"Many *g* I have shown .... John 10:32
woman was full of *g* .... Acts 9:36
in Christ Jesus for *g*, ... Eph 2:10
godliness, with *g* .... 1 Tim 2:10
well reported for *g*; .... 1 Tim 5:10
g of some are clearly, ... 1 Tim 5:25
that they be rich in *g* ..... 1 Tim 6:18
to be a pattern of *g* .... Titus 2:7
stir up love and *g* .... Heb 10:24
by your *g* which they ...... 1 Pet 2:12

GOODNESS
"I will make all My *g* .... Ex 33:19
and abounding in *g* .... Ex 34:6
"You are my Lord, my *g* ...... Ps 16:2
Surely *g* and mercy .... Ps 23:6
that I would see the *g* .... Ps 27:13
how great is Your *g* .... Ps 31:19
The *g* of God endures .... Ps 52:1
how great is its *g* .... Zech 9:17
the riches of His *g* .... Rom 2:4
consider the *g* and .... Rom 11:22
kindness, *g* .... Gal 5:22

GOODS
When *g* increase .... Eccl 5:11
and plunder his *g* .... Matt 12:29
ruler over all his *g* .... Matt 24:47
"Soul, you have many *g* .. Luke 12:19
man was wasting his *g* .... Luke 16:1
I give half of my *g* .... Luke 19:8
has this world's *g* .... 1 John 3:17

GOSHEN
District of Egypt where Israel lived; the best of the land, Gen 45:10; 46:28, 29; 47:1–11

GOSPEL
See PREACH THE GOSPEL
The beginning of the *g* ..... Mark 1:1
and believe in the *g* .... Mark 1:15
g must first be preached .. Mark 13:10
to testify to the *g* .... Acts 20:24
separated to the *g* .... Rom 1:1
not ashamed of the *g* .... Rom 1:16
should live from the *g* ..... 1 Cor 9:14
if our *g* is veiled .... 2 Cor 4:3
to a different *g* .... Gal 1:6
of truth, the *g* .... Eph 1:13
the mystery of the *g* .... Eph 6:19
g which you heard .... Col 1:23
the everlasting *g* .... Rev 14:6

GOSSIPS
only idle but also *g* .... 1 Tim 5:13

GOVERNMENT
and the *g* will be upon .... Is 9:6

GRACE
But Noah found *g* .... Gen 6:8
G is poured upon Your .... Ps 45:2
The LORD will give *g* .... Ps 84:11
the Spirit of *g* .... Zech 12:10
and the *g* of God was .... Luke 2:40
g and truth came .... John 1:17
And great *g* was upon ...... Acts 4:33
G to you and peace .... Rom 1:7

receive abundance of *g* .... Rom 5:17
g is no longer *g* .... Rom 11:6
The *g* of our Lord .... Rom 16:20
For you know the *g* .... 2 Cor 8:9
"My *g* is sufficient .... 2 Cor 12:9
The *g* of the Lord .... 2 Cor 13:14
you have fallen from *g* .... Gal 5:4
to the riches of His *g* .... Eph 1:7
g you have been saved .... Eph 2:8
dispensation of the *g* .... Eph 3:2
g was given according .... Eph 4:7
G be with all those .... Eph 6:24
G to you and peace .... 1 Thess 1:1
according to the *g* of .... 2 Thess 1:12
and good hope by *g* ..... 2 Thess 2:16
be strong in the *g* that is ... 2 Tim 2:1
the *g* of God that brings ... Titus 2:11
been justified by His *g* we ... Titus 3:7
G be with you all .... Titus 3:15
insulted the Spirit of *g* ..... Heb 10:29
shaken, let us have *g* ...... Heb 12:28
But He gives more *g* .... James 4:6
who prophesied of the *g* ... 1 Pet 1:10
together of the *g* of life ..... 1 Pet 3:7
this is the true *g* .... 1 Pet 5:12
but grow in the *g* .... 2 Pet 3:18

GRACIOUS
he said, "God be *g* .... Gen 43:29
I will be *g* to whom I .... Ex 33:19
then He is *g* to him .... Job 33:24
wise man's mouth are *g* ... Eccl 10:12
of hosts will be *g* .... Amos 5:15
know that You are a *g* .... Jon 4:2
that He may be *g* .... Mal 1:9
at the *g* words which ...... Luke 4:22
that the Lord is *g* .... 1 Pet 2:3

GRACIOUSLY
God has dealt *g* with me ... Gen 33:11
A good man deals *g* and .... Ps 112:5
receive us *g*, for we will .... Hos 14:2

GRAFT
able to *g* them in again ... Rom 11:23

GRAFTED
in unbelief, will be *g* ...... Rom 11:23

GRAIN
Israel went to buy *g* .... Gen 42:5
it treads out the *g* .... Deut 25:4
You provide their *g* .... Ps 65:9
be an abundance of *g* .... Ps 72:16
him who withholds *g* ..... Prov 11:26
be revived like *g* .... Hos 14:7
G shall make the young .... Zech 9:17
to pluck heads of *g* .... Matt 12:1
unless a *g* of wheat .... John 12:24
it treads out the *g* .... 1 Cor 9:9

GRAINFIELDS
the *g* on the Sabbath .... Matt 12:1
He went through the *g* ...... Luke 6:1

GRANT
and *g* us Your salvation ...... Ps 85:7
G that these two .... Matt 20:21
who overcomes I will *g* ..... Rev 3:21

GRANTED
has *g* me my petition ..... 1 Sam 1:27
It shall be *g* you .... Esth 5:6
he *g* the body to Joseph .. Mark 15:45
g to him by My Father ..... John 6:65
it was *g* to harm the earth .... Rev 7:2
He was *g* power to give .... Rev 13:15

GRAPEVINE
olives, or a *g* bear figs ... James 3:12

GRAPES
in the blood of *g* .... Gen 49:11
their *g* are *g* of gall .... Deut 32:32
g give a good smell .... Song 2:13
vines have tender *g* .... Song 2:15
brought forth wild *g* .... Is 5:2
Yet gleaning *g* will be .... Is 17:6
No *g* shall be on the vine ..... Jer 8:13
have eaten sour *g* .... Ezek 18:2
Do men gather *g* .... Matt 7:16
g are fully ripe .... Rev 14:18

GRASPING
all is vanity and *g* .... Eccl 1:14

GRASS
they were as the *g* .... 2 Kin 19:26
offspring like the *g* .... Job 5:25
g which grows up .... Ps 90:5
his days are like *g* .... Ps 103:15
The *g* withers .... Is 40:7
so clothes the *g* .... Matt 6:30
to sit down on the *g* ...... Matt 14:19
"All flesh is as *g* .... 1 Pet 1:24

GRASSHOPPERS
inhabitants are like *g* .... Is 40:22
generals like great *g* .... Nah 3:17

GRAVE
g does not come .... Job 7:9
for the *g* as my house ...... Job 17:13
my soul up from the *g* .... Ps 30:3
the power of the *g* .... Ps 49:15
or wisdom in the *g* .... Eccl 9:10
And they made His *g* .... Is 53:9
the power of the *g* .... Hos 13:14

GRAVES
there were no *g* .... Ex 14:11
and the *g* were opened .... Matt 27:52
g which are not .... Luke 11:44
g will hear His voice .... John 5:28

GRAY
would bring down my *g* ... Gen 42:38
the man of *g* hairs .... Deut 32:25
of old men is their *g* ...... Prov 20:29

GRAZE
cow and bear shall *g* .... Is 11:7
let him *g* with the beasts .... Dan 4:15

GREAT
God made two *g* lights ...... Gen 1:16
and make your name *g* .... Gen 12:2
With *g* wrestlings I have .... Gen 30:8
there was a *g* cry in Egypt .. Ex 12:30
have committed a *g* sin ..... Ex 32:30
shall shout with a *g* shout .... Josh 6:5
were *g* resolves of heart .... Judg 5:15
He has done us this *g* ...... 1 Sam 6:9
For the LORD is *g* .... 1 Chr 16:25
I build will be *g* .... 2 Chr 2:5
"The work is *g* .... Neh 4:19
Who does *g* things .... Job 5:9
G men are not always .... Job 32:9
in the *g* assembly .... Ps 22:25
g are Your works .... Ps 92:5
my God, You are very *g* ...... Ps 104:1
"The LORD has done *g* ...... Ps 126:2
g is the sum of them ...... Ps 139:17
in the place of the *g* .... Prov 25:6
g is the Holy One .... Is 12:6
And do you seek *g* .... Jer 45:5
g is Your faithfulness ...... Lam 3:23
The *g* day of the LORD ..... Zeph 1:14
he shall be called *g* .... Matt 5:19
one pearl of *g* price .... Matt 13:46
desires to become *g* .... Matt 20:26
and *g* commandment ...... Matt 22:38
a *g* windstorm arose, and .. Mark 4:37
g multitude followed .... Mark 5:24
he had *g* possessions ...... Mark 10:22
She was of a *g* age, and ... Luke 2:36
g drops of blood .... Luke 22:44
before the coming of the *g* .. Acts 2:20
did *g* wonders and signs ..... Acts 6:8
that he was someone *g* ...... Acts 8:9
"*G* is Diana of the .... Acts 19:28
that I have *g* sorrow .... Rom 9:2
a *g* and effective door ..... 1 Cor 16:9
because of His *g* love with ... Eph 2:4
This is a *g* mystery, but I ... Eph 5:32
without controversy *g* ..... 1 Tim 3:16
with contentment is *g* ...... 1 Tim 6:6
But in a *g* house .... 2 Tim 2:20
appearing of our *g* .... Titus 2:13
See how *g* a forest .... James 3:5
g men, the rich men .... Rev 6:15
Babylon the *G* .... Rev 17:5
Then I saw a *g* white ...... Rev 20:11
the dead, small and *g* ..... Rev 20:12

GREATER
the throne will I be *g* ...... Gen 41:40
g than all the gods .... Ex 18:11
whose appearance was *g* ... Dan 7:20
kingdom of heaven is *g* ... Matt 11:11
place there is One *g* .... Matt 12:6
g than Jonah is here ...... Matt 12:41
g than Solomon is here ... Matt 12:42
g things than these .... John 1:50
g than our father .... John 4:12
a servant is not *g* .... John 13:16
G love has no one .... John 15:13
'A servant is not *g* .... John 15:20
parts have *g* modesty .... 1 Cor 12:23
he who prophesies is *g* .... 1 Cor 14:5
swear by no one *g* .... Heb 6:13
condemns us, God is *g* ... 1 John 3:20
witness of God is *g* .... 1 John 5:9

GREATEST
little child is the *g* .... Matt 18:4
be considered the *g* .... Luke 22:24
but the *g* of these is ...... 1 Cor 13:13

GREATNESS
And in the *g* of Your .... Ex 15:7
According to the *g* .... Ps 79:11
g is unsearchable .... Ps 145:3
I will declare Your *g* .... Ps 145:6
I have attained *g* .... Eccl 1:16
traveling in the *g* .... Is 63:1
is the exceeding *g* .... Eph 1:19

GREECE
Paul preaches in, Acts 17:16–31
Daniel's vision of, Dan 8:21

GREED
part is full of *g* .... Luke 11:39

GREEDINESS
all uncleanness with *g* ...... Eph 4:19
the faith in their *g* .... 1 Tim 6:10

GREEDY
of everyone who is *g* .... Prov 1:19
not violent, not *g* .... 1 Tim 3:3
not violent, not *g* .... Titus 1:7

GREEK
written in Hebrew, *G* ..... John 19:20
and also for the *G* .... Rom 1:16
with me, being a *G* .... Gal 2:3
is neither Jew nor *G* .... Gal 3:28

GREEKS
Natives of Greece, Joel 3:6; Acts 16:1
Spiritual state of, Rom 10:12
Some believe, Acts 14:1

GREEN
and under every *g* tree ... 2 Kin 17:10
lie down in *g* pastures .... Ps 23:2

GREET
g your brethren only .... Matt 5:47
G one another with a ..... 1 Cor 16:20
into your house nor *g* ...... 2 John 10
G the friends by name ..... 3 John 14

GREETED
and *g* Elizabeth .... Luke 1:40

GREW
Pharaoh's heart *g* hard .... Ex 7:13
Samuel *g* before the ...... 1 Sam 2:21
and you *g*, matured, and ... Ezek 16:7
g exceedingly great toward .. Dan 8:9
and the thorns *g* up and .... Mark 4:7
And the Child *g* .... Luke 2:40

But the word of God *g* .... Acts 12:24
the word of the Lord *g* .... Acts 19:20

GRIEF
burden and his own *g* ..... 2 Chr 6:29
g were fully weighed .... Job 6:2
Though I speak, my *g* .... Job 16:6
observe trouble and *g* .... Ps 10:14
of mirth may be *g* .... Prov 14:13
much wisdom is much *g* .... Eccl 1:18
and acquainted with *g* .... Is 53:3
joy and not with *g* .... Heb 13:17

GRIEVE
g the children of men ...... Lam 3:33
g the Holy Spirit .... Eph 4:30

GRIEVED
earth, and He was *g* .... Gen 6:6
Has not my soul *g* .... Job 30:25
forty years I was *g* .... Ps 95:10
a woman forsaken and *g* ...... Is 54:6
g His Holy Spirit .... Is 63:10
with anger, being *g* .... Mark 3:5
Peter was *g* because ...... John 21:17

GRINDERS
when the *g* cease .... Eccl 12:3

GRINDING
the sound of *g* is low .... Eccl 12:4
g the faces of the poor .... Is 3:15
Two women will be *g* ..... Matt 24:41

GROAN
The dying *g* in the .... Job 24:12
even we ourselves *g* .... Rom 8:23
who are in this tent *g* .... 2 Cor 5:4

GROANED
He *g* in the spirit and ..... John 11:33

GROANING
So God heard their *g* .... Ex 2:24
I am weary with my *g* .... Ps 6:6
Then Jesus, again *g* ...... John 11:38

GROANINGS
g which cannot .... Rom 8:26

GROPE
And you shall *g* .... Deut 28:29
They *g* in the dark .... Job 12:25
We *g* for the wall like .... Is 59:10
hope that they might *g* ..... Acts 17:27

GROUND
"Cursed is the *g* .... Gen 3:17
you stand is holy *g* .... Ex 3:5
up your fallow *g* .... Jer 4:3
give its fruit, the *g* .... Zech 8:12
others fell on good *g* .... Matt 13:8
bought a piece of *g* .... Luke 14:18
God, the pillar and *g* ...... 1 Tim 3:15

GROUNDED
being rooted and *g* .... Eph 3:17

GROUPS
sit down in *g* of fifty .... Luke 9:14

GROW
they will all *g* old like ...... Ps 102:26
the horn of David *g* .... Ps 132:17
the earth will *g* old like .... Is 51:6
you shall go out and *g* .... Mal 4:2
truth in love, may *g* .... Eph 4:15
and they will all *g* .... Heb 1:11
but *g* in the grace and ..... 2 Pet 3:18

GROWN
plants *g* up in their youth .. Ps 144:12
They have *g* fat, they are .... Jer 5:28
this people have *g* dull .... Matt 13:15
this people have *g* dull .... Acts 28:27

GROWS
shall eat every tree which *g* .. Ex 10:5
what *g* of its own accord ... Lev 25:11
It *g* old because of all my ...... Ps 6:7
when it is sown, it *g* up .... Mark 4:32
g into a holy temple in the .. Eph 2:21

your faith *g* exceedingly .. 2 Thess 1:3

GROWTH
causes *g* of the body for .... Eph 4:16

GRUDGINGLY
in his heart, not *g* .... 2 Cor 9:7

GRUMBLERS
These are *g* .... Jude 16

GUARANTEE
in our hearts as a *g* .... 2 Cor 1:22
us the Spirit as a *g* .... 2 Cor 5:5
who is the *g* of our .... Eph 1:14

GUARD
g the way to the tree .... Gen 3:24
I will *g* my ways, lest I sin .... Ps 39:1
will be your rear *g* .... Is 52:12
g the doors of your .... Mic 7:5
we were kept under *g* .... Gal 3:23
to the whole palace *g* .... Phil 1:13
g your hearts and minds ..... Phil 4:7
g you from the evil one ... 2 Thess 3:3
G what was committed .... 1 Tim 6:20

GUARDIANS
but is under *g* and .... Gal 4:2

GUARDS
Unless the LORD *g* .... Ps 127:1
And the *g* shook for .... Matt 28:4

GUIDANCE
and excellent in *g* .... Is 28:29

GUIDE
I will *g* you with My eye ..... Ps 32:8
He will be our *g* .... Ps 48:14
Father, You are the *g* .... Jer 3:4
g our feet into the .... Luke 1:79
has come, He will *g* .... John 16:13
Judas, who became a *g* ..... Acts 1:16
you yourself are a *g* .... Rom 2:19

GUIDES
Woe to you, blind *g* .... Matt 23:16
unless someone *g* .... Acts 8:31

GUILT
they accept their *g* .... Lev 26:41
g has grown up to the .... Ezra 9:6
of your fathers' *g* .... Matt 23:32

GUILTLESS
g who takes His name .... Ex 20:7
have condemned the *g* ..... Matt 12:7

GUILTY
"We are truly *g* .... Gen 42:21
we have been very *g* .... Ezra 9:7
the world may become *g* ... Rom 3:19
in one point, he is *g* ...... James 2:10

GULF
you there is a great *g* ..... Luke 16:26

HABAKKUK
Prophet in Judah just prior to Babylonian invasion, Hab 1:1
Prayer of, in praise of God, Hab 3:1–19

HABITATION
to Your holy *h* .... Ex 15:13
Is God in His holy *h* .... Ps 68:5
in a peaceful *h* .... Is 32:18
from His holy *h* .... Zech 2:13
be clothed with our *h* .... 2 Cor 5:2

HACHILAH
Hill in the Wilderness of Ziph where David hid, 1 Sam 23:19–26

HADADEZER
King of Zobah, 2 Sam 8:3–13
Defeated by David, 2 Sam 10:6–19

HADASSAH
Esther's Jewish name, Esth 2:7

HADES
be brought down to *H* .... Matt 11:23
H shall not prevail .... Matt 16:18
being in torments in *H* .... Luke 16:23
not leave my soul in *H* ..... Acts 2:27
I have the keys of *H* .... Rev 1:18
H were cast into the ...... Rev 20:14

HAGAR
Sarah's servant; bears Ishmael to Abraham, Gen 16
Abraham sends her away; God comforts her, Gen 21:9–21
Paul explains symbolic meaning of, Gal 4:22–31

HAGGAI
Postexilic prophet; contemporary of Zechariah, Ezra 5:1, 2; 6:14; Hag 1:1

HAGGITH
One of David's wives, 2 Sam 3:4
Mother of Adonijah, 1 Kin 1:5

HAIL
cause very heavy *h* .... Ex 9:18
seen the treasury of *h* ...... Job 38:22
He casts out His *h* .... Ps 147:17
h will sweep away the .... Is 28:17
of the plague of the *h* ...... Rev 16:21

HAILSTONES
clouds passed with *h* .... Ps 18:12

HAIR
bring down my gray *h* ..... Gen 42:38
shaved his consecrated *h* .. Num 6:19
h of his head began to .... Judg 16:22
he cut the *h* of his .... 2 Sam 14:26
the *h* on my body stood ..... Job 4:15
Your *h* is like a flock .... Song 4:1
h had grown like eagles' .... Dan 4:33
you cannot make one *h* .... Matt 5:36
clothed with camel's *h* ...... Mark 1:6
But not a *h* of your .... Luke 21:18
wiped His feet with her *h* .. John 11:2
He had his *h* cut off at .... Acts 18:18
since not a *h* will fall ..... Acts 27:34
if a woman has long *h* .... 1 Cor 11:15
not with braided *h* .... 1 Tim 2:9
arranging the *h* .... 1 Pet 3:3
h were white like wool, ... Rev 1:14
black as sackcloth of *h*, ... Rev 6:12
h like women's *h* .... Rev 9:8

HAIRS
are more than the *h* .... Ps 40:12
h I will carry you .... Is 46:4
yes, gray *h* are here .... Hos 7:9
But the very *h* .... Matt 10:30

HAIRY
h garment all over .... Gen 25:25
A *h* man wearing a leather .. 2 Kin 1:8

HAKKOZ
Descendant of Aaron, 1 Chr 24:1, 10
Called Koz, Ezra 2:61, 62
Descendants of, kept from priesthood, Neh 7:63, 64

HALF
h of it in the morning and ... Lev 6:20
h the tribe of Manasseh .... Josh 22:9
h of the people followed .. 1 Kin 16:21
up to *h* the kingdom .... Esth 5:6
you, up to *h* my kingdom .. Mark 6:23
I give *h* of my goods to .... Luke 19:8
h a time, from the .... Rev 12:14

HALLOW
hosts, Him you shall *h* .... Is 8:13
h the Holy One of .... Is 29:23
h the Sabbath day .... Jer 17:24

HALLOWED
the Sabbath day and *h* ...... Ex 20:11
but I will be *h* .... Lev 22:32
who is holy shall be *h* .... Is 5:16

heaven, *h* be Your name . . . . Matt 6:9

HAM
Noah's youngest son, Gen 5:32
Enters ark, Gen 7:7
His immoral behavior merits Noah's curse, Gen 9:22–25
Father of descendants of repopulated earth, Gen 10:6–20

HAMAN
Plots to destroy Jews, Esth 3:3–15
Invited to Esther's banquet, Esth 5:1–14
Forced to honor Mordecai, Esth 6:5–14
Hanged on his own gallows, Esth 7:1–10

HAMATH
Israel's northern boundary, Num 34:8; 1 Kin 8:65; Ezek 47:16–20
Conquered, 2 Kin 18:34; Jer 49:23
Israelites exiled there, Is 11:11

HAMMER
h that breaks the rock . . . . . . Jer 23:29
How the *h* of the whole . . . . . . Jer 50:23

HAMOR
Sells land to Jacob, Gen 33:18–20; Acts 7:16
Killed by Jacob's sons, Gen 34:1–31

HAMSTRUNG
their self-will they *h* an ox . . Gen 49:6
David *h* all the chariot . . . . . . 2 Sam 8:4

HANANI
Father of Jehu the prophet, 1 Kin 16:1, 7
Rebukes Asa; confined to prison, 2 Chr 16:7–10
——— Nehemiah's brother; brings news concerning the Jews, Neh 1:2
Becomes a governor of Jerusalem, Neh 7:2

HANANIAH
False prophet who contradicts Jeremiah, Jer 28:1–17
——— Hebrew name of Shadrach, Dan 1:6, 7, 11

HAND
See AT THE RIGHT HAND; HIS RIGHT HAND; MY RIGHT HAND; STRETCH OUT MY HAND; STRETCHED OUT HIS HAND
lest he put out his *h* . . . . Gen 3:22
h shall be against . . . . Gen 16:12
your *h* under my thigh . . . . Gen 24:2
h toward Israel's right *h* . . . . Gen 48:13
What is that in your *h* . . . . Ex 4:2
took the rod of God in his *h* . . Ex 4:20
tooth for tooth, *h* . . . . Ex 21:24
lay his *h* on the bull's head . . . Lev 4:4
Egypt with a mighty *h* . . . . . Deut 9:26
and strengthened his *h* . . . 1 Sam 23:16
Uzzah put out his *h* . . . . 2 Sam 6:6
let us fall into the *h* . . . . . 2 Sam 24:14
Then, by the good *h* . . . . Ezra 8:18
He would loose His *h* . . . . Job 6:9
he stretches out his *h* . . . . . . Job 15:25
that your own right *h* . . . . Job 40:14
h has held me up . . . . Ps 18:35
My times are in Your *h* . . . . . Ps 31:15
and night Your *h* . . . . Ps 32:4
Your right *h* is full . . . . Ps 48:10
Let Your *h* be upon the . . . . . . Ps 80:17
h shall be established . . . . Ps 89:21
"Sit at My right *h* . . . . Ps 110:1
days is in her right *h* . . . . . . Prov 3:16
heart is in the *h* . . . . Prov 21:1
Whatever your *h* finds . . . . . . Eccl 9:10
is at his right *h* . . . . Eccl 10:2
do not withhold your *h* . . . . . . Eccl 11:6
His left *h* is under my . . . . Song 8:3
My *h* has laid the . . . . Is 48:13
Behold, the LORD's *h* . . . . Is 59:1
are the work of Your *h* . . . . Is 64:8
the clay is in the potter's *h* . . . Jer 18:6
Am I a God near at *h* . . . . Jer 23:23
and incense in their *h*, to . . . . Jer 41:5
h under their wings . . . . Ezek 10:8
a measuring rod in his *h* . . . Ezek 40:3
of a man's *h* appeared . . . . Dan 5:5
a *h* touched me, which . . . . . Dan 10:10
of heaven is at *h* . . . . Matt 3:2
if your right *h* causes . . . . . . Matt 5:30
do not let your left *h* . . . . Matt 6:3
h causes you to sin . . . . Mark 9:43
sitting at the right *h* . . . . . . Mark 14:62
delivered from the *h* . . . . Luke 1:74
Sit at My right *h*, ... Acts 2:34
at the right *h* of God . . . . Acts 7:55
is even at the right *h* . . . . Rom 8:34
Because I am not a *h* . . . . . . 1 Cor 12:15
with my own *h* . . . . 1 Cor 16:21
the right *h* of fellowship . . . . . . Gal 2:9
by the *h* of a mediator . . . . Gal 3:19
to you with my own *h* . . . . Gal 6:11
The Lord is at *h* . . . . Phil 4:5
sitting at the right *h* of God . . . Col 3:1
"Sit at My right *h* . . . . Heb 1:13
right *h* of the throne of the . . . Heb 8:1
down at the right *h* . . . . Heb 10:12
of the Lord is at *h* . . . . James 5:8
in His right *h* seven stars . . . . Rev 1:16
stars in His right *h* . . . . Rev 2:1

HAND OF GOD
the *h* was very heavy . . . . . 1 Sam 5:11
the *h* was on Judah . . . . . . 2 Chr 30:12
the *h* has struck me . . . . Job 19:21
was from the *h* . . . . Eccl 2:24
their works are in the *h* . . . . . . Eccl 9:1
under the mighty *h*, ... 1 Pet 5:6

HAND OF THE LORD
the *h* was against them, ... Deut 2:15
earth may know the *h*, ... Josh 4:24
of Israel out of the *h* . . . . . . Josh 22:31
h has gone out against . . . . . . Ruth 1:13
h was heavy on the . . . . 1 Sam 5:6
h was against the . . . . 1 Sam 7:13
let us fall into the *h* . . . . . 2 Sam 24:14
h came upon Elijah; . . . . . . 1 Kin 18:46
the *h* came upon him . . . . . . 2 Kin 3:15
according to the *h* . . . . Ezra 7:6
h my God was upon me . . . . . Ezra 7:28
the *h* has done this . . . . Job 12:9
the right *h* does valiantly . . . Ps 118:15
king's heart is in the *h* . . . . . . Prov 21:1
crown of glory in the *h* . . . . Is 62:3
the *h* shall be known . . . . Is 66:14
the *h* was strong upon me . . Ezek 3:14
the *h* came upon me . . . . Ezek 37:1
And the *h* was with him . . . Luke 1:66
And the *h* was with them . . Acts 11:21
the *h* is upon you, ... Acts 13:11

HANDIWORK
firmament shows His *h* . . . . Ps 19:1

HANDKERCHIEFS
so that even *h* or aprons . . Acts 19:12

HANDLE
h the law did not know . . . . . . Jer 2:8
H Me and see . . . . Luke 24:39
do not taste, do not *h* . . . . Col 2:21

HANDLED
and our hands have *h* . . . . . . 1 John 1:1

HANDS
the *h* are the *h* . . . . Gen 27:22
and Hur supported his *h* . . . . Ex 17:12
Moses had laid his *h* on . . . Deut 34:9
here we are, in your *h* . . . . . . Josh 9:25
took his life in his *h* . . . . 1 Sam 19:5
put my life in my *h* . . . . 1 Sam 28:21
but His *h* make whole . . . . Job 5:18
and cleanse my *h* . . . . Job 9:30
h have made me and . . . . Job 10:8
They pierced My *h* . . . . Ps 22:16
washed my *h* in innocence . . Ps 73:13
establish the work of our *h* . . Ps 90:17
In their *h* they shall bear . . . . Ps 91:12
h formed the dry land . . . . Ps 95:5
stretches out her *h* . . . . Prov 31:19
say, 'He has no *h* . . . . Is 45:9
strike your *h* together . . . . Ezek 21:14
was cut out without *h* . . . . Dan 2:34
on the palms of my *h* . . . . Dan 10:10
The *h* of Zerubbabel have . . . Zech 4:9
than having two *h* . . . . Matt 18:8
will lay *h* on the sick . . . . . . Mark 16:18
into Your *h* I commit . . . . . . Luke 23:46
Behold My *h* and My . . . . . Luke 24:39
only, but also my *h* . . . . John 13:9
h the print of the . . . . John 20:25
his chains fell off his *h* . . . . . Acts 12:7
know that these *h* . . . . Acts 20:34
and he laid his *h* on him . . . . Acts 28:8
a house not made with *h* . . . . 2 Cor 5:1
his *h* what is good . . . . Eph 4:28
made without *h* . . . . Col 2:11
lifting up holy *h* . . . . 1 Tim 2:8
the laying on of the *h* . . . . . . 1 Tim 4:14
Do not lay *h* on anyone . . . . . 1 Tim 5:22
the laying on of my *h* . . . . 2 Tim 1:6
baptisms, of laying on of *h* . . . Heb 6:2
not made with *h* . . . . Heb 9:11
to fall into the *h* . . . . Heb 10:31
Cleanse your *h*, you . . . . James 4:8
and our *h* have handled, . . . 1 John 1:1
foreheads or on their *h* . . . . . . Rev 20:4

HANDWRITING
having wiped out the *h* . . . . . . Col 2:14

HANG
They will *h* on him all the . . . . Is 22:24
commandments *h* all the . . . Matt 22:40
the hands which *h* down . . . Heb 12:12

HANGED
for he who is *h* . . . . Deut 21:23
went and *h* himself . . . . Matt 27:5

HANGS
h the earth on nothing . . . . . . Job 26:7
is everyone who *h* . . . . Gal 3:13

HANNAH
Barren wife of Elkanah; prays for a son, 1 Sam 1:1–18
Bears Samuel and dedicates him to the Lord, 1 Sam 1:19–28
Magnifies God, 1 Sam 2:1–10

HANUN
King of Ammon; disgraces David's ambassadors and is defeated by him, 2 Sam 10:1–14

HAPPEN
show us what will *h* . . . . Is 41:22
understand what will *h* . . . . Dan 10:14
not know what will *h* . . . . . James 4:14

HAPPINESS
one year, and bring *h* . . . . . . Deut 24:5

HAPPY
h are these your servants . . . 2 Chr 9:7
H is the man who has . . . . Ps 127:5
H are the people who . . . . . . Ps 144:15
H is the man who finds . . . . Prov 3:13
mercy on the poor, *h* . . . . . . Prov 14:21
trusts in the LORD, *h* . . . . . . Prov 16:20
h is he who keeps . . . . Prov 29:18
H is he who does not . . . . . . Rom 14:22

HARAN
Abraham's younger brother, Gen 11:26–31
——— City of Mesopotamia, Gen 11:31
Abraham leaves, Gen 12:4, 5
Jacob dwells at, Gen 29:4–35

HARASS
and Judah shall not *h* .... Is 11:13
h some from the church .... Acts 12:1

HARD
Is anything too *h* .... Gen 18:14
Pharaoh's heart is *h* .... Ex 7:14
test him with *h* questions .. 1 Kin 10:1
His heart is as *h* .... Job 41:24
shown Your people *h* .... Ps 60:3
of the unfaithful is *h* ...... Prov 13:15
h to bear, and lay them .... Matt 23:4
I knew you to be a *h* ...... Matt 25:24
"This is a *h* saying .... John 6:60
It is *h* for you to kick .... Acts 9:5
are some things *h* .... 2 Pet 3:16

HARDEN
But I will *h* his heart .... Ex 4:21
Do not *h* your hearts .... Ps 95:8
h your hearts as .... Heb 3:8

HARDENED
But Pharaoh *h* his .... Ex 8:32
Who has *h* himself .... Job 9:4
their heart was *h* .... Mark 6:52
eyes and *h* their hearts .... John 12:40
lest any of you be *h* .... Heb 3:13

HARDENS
A wicked man *h* his ...... Prov 21:29
h his heart will fall ...... Prov 28:14
whom He wills He *h* .... Rom 9:18

HARDER
brother offended is *h* to ... Prov 18:19
their faces *h* than rock .... Jer 5:3
h than flint, I have made ..... Ezek 3:9

HARDSHIP
h that has befallen us ..... Num 20:14
h as a good soldier .... 2 Tim 2:3

HARLOT
play the *h* with their gods ... Ex 34:16
shall be no ritual *h* .... Deut 23:17
of a *h* named Rahab .... Josh 2:1
h is a deep pit .... Prov 23:27
the deeds of a brazen *h* ... Ezek 16:30
Oholah played the *h* .... Ezek 23:5
you, Israel, play the *h*, let .... Hos 4:15
h is one body with .... 1 Cor 6:16
h Rahab did not perish .... Heb 11:31
of the great *h* who .... Rev 17:1

HARLOTRIES
the land with your *h* .... Jer 3:2
Let her put away her *h* .... Hos 2:2

HARLOTRY
through her casual *h* .... Jer 3:9
the lewdness of your *h* ..... Jer 13:27
let them put their *h* .... Ezek 43:9
are the children of *h* .... Hos 2:4
Ephraim, you commit *h* .... Hos 5:3
for the spirit of *h* .... Hos 5:4

HARLOTS
his blood while the *h* .... 1 Kin 22:38
h enter the kingdom ...... Matt 21:31
Great, The Mother of *H* ..... Rev 17:5

HARM
do My prophets no *h* ..... 1 Chr 16:22
they thought to do me *h* ..... Neh 6:2
those who sought their *h* .... Esth 9:2
it only causes *h* .... Ps 37:8
and do My prophets no *h* .. Ps 105:15
and I will not *h* you .... Jer 25:6
Do yourself no *h*, for we .... Acts 16:28
Love does no *h* to a .... Rom 13:10
and do not *h* the oil .... Rev 6:6
Do not *h* the earth, the .... Rev 7:3

HARMLESS
become blameless and *h* ..... Phil 2:15
for us, who is holy, *h* .... Heb 7:26

HARMONIOUS
the harp, with *h* sound .... Ps 92:3

HAROD
Well near Gideon's camp, Judg 7:1

HARP
those who play the *h* .... Gen 4:21
skillful player on the *h* .. 1 Sam 16:16
Praise the LORD with the *h* .. Ps 33:2
Sing to the LORD with the *h* .. Ps 98:5
On a *h* of ten strings I will .. Ps 144:9
with the lute and *h* .... Ps 150:3
Lamb, each having a *h* .... Rev 5:8

HARPS
to direct with *h* on the .... 1 Chr 15:21
We hung our *h* upon the .... Ps 137:2
playing their *h* .... Rev 14:2
of glass, having *h* of God .... Rev 15:2

HARSH
a *h* word stirs up anger .... Prov 15:1
"Your words have been *h* ... Mal 3:13
but also to the *h* .... 1 Pet 2:18

HARVEST
See FEAST OF HARVEST
seedtime and *h* .... Gen 8:22
to death in the days of *h* .. 2 Sam 21:9
He who sleeps in *h* is a .... Prov 10:5
to the joy of *h* .... Is 9:3
cloud of dew in the heat of *h* .. Is 18:4
shall eat up your *h* .... Jer 5:17
"The *h* is past .... Jer 8:20
of her *h* will come .... Jer 51:33
the sickle, for the *h* is ripe ... Joel 3:13
h truly is plentiful .... Matt 9:37
pray the Lord of the *h* ..... Matt 9:38
sickle, because the *h* ...... Mark 4:29
pray the Lord of the *h* to ... Luke 10:2
already white for *h* .... John 4:35
the *h* of the earth is .... Rev 14:15

HASTE
you shall eat it in *h* .... Ex 12:11
For I said in my *h* .... Ps 31:22
And they came with *h* ...... Luke 2:16
"Zacchaeus, make *h* .... Luke 19:5

HASTEN
be multiplied who *h* .... Ps 16:4
Do not *h* in your .... Eccl 7:9
I, the LORD, will *h* .... Is 60:22

HASTENING
h the coming of the .... 2 Pet 3:12

HASTENS
and he sins who *h* .... Prov 19:2
with an evil eye *h* .... Prov 28:22
is near and *h* quickly ...... Zeph 1:14

HASTILY
utter anything *h* .... Eccl 5:2
lay hands on anyone *h* .... 1 Tim 5:22

HASTY
Do you see a man *h* ...... Prov 29:20

HATE
'You shall not *h* .... Lev 19:17
h all workers of .... Ps 5:5
h the righteous shall .... Ps 34:21
love the LORD, *h* evil .... Ps 97:10
h every false way .... Ps 119:104
h the double-minded ...... Ps 119:113
I *h* and abhor lying .... Ps 119:163
love, and a time to *h* .... Eccl 3:8
h robbery for burnt .... Is 61:8
H evil, love good .... Amos 5:15
I *h*, I despise your feast ... Amos 5:21
You who *h* good and .... Mic 3:2
either he will *h* the one ..... Matt 6:24
but what I *h*, that I do .... Rom 7:15
Nicolaitans, which I also *h* ... Rev 2:6
these will *h* the harlot, ... Rev 17:16

HATED
So Esau *h* Jacob because .. Gen 27:41
they *h* knowledge .... Prov 1:29
Therefore I *h* life .... Eccl 2:17
h all my labor in .... Eccl 2:18
but Esau I have *h* .... Mal 1:3
And you will be *h* .... Matt 10:22
have seen and also *h* ..... John 15:24
h Me without a cause ..... John 15:25
world has *h* them .... John 17:14
but Esau I have *h* .... Rom 9:13
For no one ever *h* .... Eph 5:29
and *h* lawlessness .... Heb 1:9

HATEFUL
h woman when she is ..... Prov 30:23
in malice and envy, *h* .... Titus 3:3

HATERS
The *h* of the LORD .... Ps 81:15
backbiters, *h* of God .... Rom 1:30

HATES
six things the LORD *h* ...... Prov 6:16
lose it, and he who *h* ..... John 12:25
"If the world *h* .... John 15:18
h his brother is .... 1 John 2:11

HATING
h even the garment defiled ... Jude 23

HATRED
I hate them with perfect *h* .. Ps 139:22

HAUGHTY
Your eyes are on the *h* .. 2 Sam 22:28
bring down *h* looks .... Ps 18:27
my heart is not *h* .... Ps 131:1
h spirit before a fall .... Prov 16:18
A proud and *h* man .... Prov 21:24
Do not be *h*, but fear ...... Rom 11:20
age not to be *h* .... 1 Tim 6:17

HAUNTS
are full of the *h* .... Ps 74:20

HAURAN
District southeast of Mt. Hermon, Ezek 47:16

HAVE MERCY
h on me, and hear my prayer .. Ps 4:1
h on me, for I am .... Ps 25:16
H upon me, O God, ... Ps 51:1
arise and *h* on Zion; .... Ps 102:13
and forsakes them will *h* .. Prov 28:13
nor *h* on their fatherless ...... Is 9:17
the Lord will *h* .... Is 14:1
will *h* on His afflicted .... Is 49:13
not pity nor spare nor *h* .... Jer 13:14
I will surely *h* on him," ..... Jer 31:20
captives of Jacob, and *h* .. Ezek 39:25
I will no longer *h* .... Hos 1:6
how long will You not *h* .. Zech 1:12
"Son of David, *h* on us ..... Matt 9:27
"*H* on me, O Lord .... Matt 15:22
Lord, *h* on my son, ... Matt 17:15
"*H* on us, O Lord, ... Matt 20:30
"Jesus, Son of David, *h* .. Mark 10:47
'Father Abraham, *h* .... Luke 16:24
"Jesus, Master, *h* on us .. Luke 17:13
"Jesus, Son of David, *h* ... Luke 18:38
"I will *h* on whomever ..... Rom 9:15
that He might *h* on all .... Rom 11:32

HAVEN
shall dwell by the *h* .... Gen 49:13
to their desired *h* .... Ps 107:30

HAVOC
for Saul, he made *h* .... Acts 8:3

HAY
precious stones, wood, *h* .. 1 Cor 3:12

HAZAEL
Anointed king of Syria by Elijah, 1 Kin 19:15–17
Elisha predicts his taking the throne, 2 Kin 8:7–15
Oppresses Israel, 2 Kin 8:28, 29; 10:32, 33; 12:17, 18; 13:3–7, 22

HAZAR ENAN
Village of north Palestine, Num 34:9, 10

HAZEROTH
Scene of sedition of Miriam and Aaron, Num 11:35—12:16

HAZOR
Royal Canaanite city destroyed by Joshua, Josh 11:1–13
Rebuilt and assigned to Naphtali, Josh 19:32, 36
Army of, defeated by Deborah and Barak, Judg 4:1–24

HE WHO BELIEVES
H and is baptized .... Mark 16:16
H in Him is not .... John 3:18
H in the Son has .... John 3:36
h in Me shall never thirst .. John 6:35
h in Me has everlasting .... John 6:47
H in Me, as the Scripture ... John 7:38
H, though he may die, ... John 11:25
and said, "*H* in Me, ... John 12:44
h in Me, the works that ... John 14:12
precious, and *h* on Him ..... 1 Pet 2:6
the world, but *h* .... 1 John 5:5
H in the Son of God ...... 1 John 5:10

HEAD
He shall bruise your *h* ...... Gen 3:15
white baskets on my *h* .... Gen 40:16
on the *h* of the bed .... Gen 47:31
your right hand on his *h* ... Gen 48:18
shall come upon his *h* .... 1 Sam 1:11
a bronze helmet on his *h* .. 1 Sam 17:5
and cut off his *h* with .... 1 Sam 17:51
crown from his *h* .... 2 Sam 12:30
put ashes on her *h* .... 2 Sam 13:19
and dust on his *h* .... 2 Sam 15:32
My *h*, my *h!*" .... 2 Kin 4:19
is with us as our *h* .... 2 Chr 13:12
my skin, and laid my *h* .... Job 16:15
return upon his own *h* .... Ps 7:16
of pure gold upon his *h* .... Ps 21:3
the lip, they shake the *h* ...... Ps 22:7
You anoint my *h* with oil ..... Ps 23:5
than the hairs of my *h* .... Ps 40:12
the precious oil upon the *h* .. Ps 133:2
The silver-haired *h* is a ... Prov 16:31
old men is their gray *h* .... Prov 20:29
coals of fire on his *h* ...... Prov 25:22
h is covered with dew ...... Song 5:2
The whole *h* is sick .... Is 1:5
it to bow down his *h* .... Is 58:5
For every *h* shall be bald ... Jer 48:37
visions of my *h* troubled ..... Dan 4:5
could lift up his *h* .... Zech 1:21
you swear by your *h* .... Matt 5:36
you fast, anoint your *h* ..... Matt 6:17
Baptist's *h* here on a .... Matt 14:8
first the blade, then the *h* .. Mark 4:28
and poured it on His *h* .... Mark 14:3
thorns, put it on His *h* .... Mark 15:17
did not anoint My *h* with .. Luke 7:46
has nowhere to lay His *h* .. Luke 9:58
bowing His *h*, He gave .... John 19:30
coals of fire on his *h* ...... Rom 12:20
having his *h* covered .... 1 Cor 11:4
or prophesies with her *h* ... 1 Cor 11:5
and gave Him to be *h* .... Eph 1:22
For the husband is *h* .... Eph 5:23
His *h* and his hair .... Rev 1:14
having on His *h* a golden .. Rev 14:14
His *h* were many crowns .. Rev 19:12

HEADS
See BOWED THEIR HEADS
men to ride over our *h* ...... Ps 66:12
Him, wagging their *h* ..... Matt 27:39
dragon having seven *h* ...... Rev 12:3

HEAL
I wound and I *h* .... Deut 32:39
surely I will *h* you .... 2 Kin 20:5
O LORD, *h* me .... Ps 6:2
H my soul, for I have .... Ps 41:4
time to kill, and a time to *h* .. Eccl 3:3
sent Me to *h* the .... Is 61:1
h your backslidings .... Jer 3:22
who can *h* you .... Lam 2:13
torn, but He will *h* .... Hos 6:1
h all kinds of sickness ..... Matt 10:1
H the sick, cleanse .... Matt 10:8
to *h* on the Sabbath .... Matt 12:10
so that I should *h* .... Matt 13:15
power to *h* sicknesses ...... Mark 3:15
sent Me to *h* the .... Luke 4:18
Physician, *h* yourself ...... Luke 4:23

HEALED
I have *h* this water .... 2 Kin 2:21
His word and *h* them .... Ps 107:20
And return and be *h* .... Is 6:10
His stripes we are *h* .... Is 53:5
h the hurt of My .... Jer 6:14
When I would have *h* .... Hos 7:1
and He *h* them .... Matt 4:24
and my servant will be *h* .... Matt 8:8
and *h* all who were sick, ... Matt 8:16
Jesus' feet, and He *h* ...... Matt 15:30
be *h* of their diseases, ... Luke 6:17
demon-possessed was *h* ... Luke 8:36
h the child, and gave him .. Luke 9:42
touched his ear and *h* .... Luke 22:51
and they were all *h* .... Acts 5:16
he had faith to be *h* .... Acts 14:9
but rather be *h* .... Heb 12:13
that you may be *h* .... James 5:16
whose stripes you were *h* .. 1 Pet 2:24
his deadly wound was *h* .... Rev 13:3

HEALING
h shall spring forth .... Is 58:8
so that there is no *h* .... Jer 14:19
Your injury has no *h* .... Nah 3:19
shall arise with *h* .... Mal 4:2
and *h* all kinds of .... Matt 4:23
h all who were oppressed . Acts 10:38
tree were for the *h* .... Rev 22:2

HEALINGS
to another gifts of *h* ...... 1 Cor 12:9
Do all have gifts of *h* ..... 1 Cor 12:30

HEALS
h all your diseases .... Ps 103:3
He *h* the broken-hearted .... Ps 147:3
h the stroke of their .... Is 30:26
Jesus the Christ *h* .... Acts 9:34

HEALTH
It will be *h* to your flesh, ... Prov 3:8
and *h* to all their flesh ..... Prov 4:22
of the wise promotes *h* .... Prov 12:18
to the soul and *h* .... Prov 16:24
and for a time of *h* .... Jer 8:15
no recovery for the *h* .... Jer 8:22
For I will restore *h* to you .. Jer 30:17
all things and be in *h* .... 3 John 2

HEAP
This *h* is a witness .... Gen 31:48
I could *h* up words .... Job 16:4
sea together as a *h* .... Ps 33:7
so you will *h* coals of ..... Prov 25:22
ears, they will *h* .... 2 Tim 4:3

HEAPS
Though he *h* up silver ..... Job 27:16

HEAR
See EARS TO HEAR
with us, and we will *h* ...... Ex 20:19
Me, I will surely *h* their ..... Ex 22:23
"*H*, O Israel: The LORD ...... Deut 6:4
Him you shall *h* .... Deut 18:15
of the oxen which I *h* .... 1 Sam 15:14
You *h* the supplication of .. 1 Kin 8:30
h in heaven Your .... 1 Kin 8:43
H me when I call .... Ps 4:1
O You who *h* prayer .... Ps 65:2
h what God the LORD .... Ps 85:8
ear, shall He not *h* .... Ps 94:9
h the words of the .... Prov 22:17
h rather than to give .... Eccl 5:1
H, O heavens, and give ear ..... Is 1:2
H, you who are afar .... Is 33:13
Let the earth *h* .... Is 34:1
I have made you *h* new .... Is 48:6
I spoke, you did not *h* .... Is 65:12
cleansed and the deaf *h* .... Matt 11:5
'Hearing you will *h* ...... Matt 13:14
if he will not *h* .... Matt 18:16
"Take heed what you *h* .... Mark 4:24
ears, do you not *h* .... Mark 8:18
h the sound of it .... John 3:8
that God does not *h* .... John 9:31
My sheep *h* My voice ...... John 10:27
And how shall they *h* ..... Rom 10:14
man be swift to *h* .... James 1:19
those who *h* the words of .... Rev 1:3
h what the Spirit says .... Rev 2:7
has an ear, let him *h* ...... Rev 13:9

HEARD
h the sound of the .... Gen 3:8
h their cry because of .... Ex 3:7
you only *h* a voice .... Deut 4:12
certainly God has *h* .... Ps 66:19
quietly, should be *h* .... Eccl 9:17
Have you not *h* .... Is 40:21
world men have not *h* .... Is 64:4
Who has *h* such a thing .... Is 66:8
h Ephraim bemoaning ...... Jer 31:18
that they will be *h* .... Matt 6:7
h the word believed .... Acts 4:4
I say, have they not *h* ..... Rom 10:18
not seen, nor ear *h* .... 1 Cor 2:9
h inexpressible words ..... 2 Cor 12:4
things that you have *h* ..... 2 Tim 2:2
the things we have *h* .... Heb 2:1
the word which they *h* .... Heb 4:2
from death, and was *h* .... Heb 5:7
which we have *h* .... 1 John 1:1
Lord's Day, and I *h* .... Rev 1:10

HEARER
if anyone is a *h* .... James 1:23
is not a forgetful *h* .... James 1:25

HEARERS
for not the *h* of the .... Rom 2:13
impart grace to the *h* .... Eph 4:29
of the word, and not *h* ..... James 1:22

HEARING
and read in the *h* .... Ex 24:7
Book of Moses in the *h* ..... Neh 13:1
Do not speak in the *h* ...... Prov 23:9
'Keep on *h*, but do not .... Is 6:9
h they do not .... Matt 13:13
h they may hear .... Mark 4:12
If the whole were *h* ...... 1 Cor 12:17
or by the *h* of faith .... Gal 3:2
have become dull of *h* ...... Heb 5:11

HEARS
for Your servant *h* .... 1 Sam 3:9
out, and the LORD *h* .... Ps 34:17
He who *h* you *h* Me ...... Luke 10:16
of God *h* God's words ..... John 8:47
And if anyone *h* .... John 12:47
who is of the truth *h* ...... John 18:37
He who knows God *h* ..... 1 John 4:6
And let him who *h* .... Rev 22:17

HEART
See UPRIGHT IN HEART; WITH ALL YOUR HEART
h was only evil .... Gen 6:5
for you know the *h* .... Ex 23:9
as many as had a willing *h* .. Ex 35:22
h the LORD had put .... Ex 36:2
seek Him with all your *h* ... Deut 4:29
the foreskin of your *h* ..... Deut 10:16
whatever your *h* desires .. Deut 14:26
and confusion of *h* .... Deut 28:28
will circumcise your *h* ..... Deut 30:6
incline your *h* to the ...... Josh 24:23
great searchings of *h* ...... Judg 5:16

Hannah spoke in her *h* ... 1 Sam 1:13
h rejoices in the LORD ... 1 Sam 2:1
God gave him another *h* ... 1 Sam 10:9
a man after His own *h* ... 1 Sam 13:14
LORD looks at the *h* ... 1 Sam 16:7
his *h* died within him, ... 1 Sam 25:37
despised him in her *h* ... 2 Sam 6:16
David's *h* condemned ... 2 Sam 24:10
and understanding *h* ... 1 Kin 3:12
largeness of *h* like the ... 1 Kin 4:29
h to build a temple for ... 1 Kin 8:18
My eyes and My *h* will be ... 1 Kin 9:3
his wives turned his *h* ... 1 Kin 11:4
Ezra had prepared his *h* ... Ezra 7:10
He pierces my *h* ... Job 16:13
How my *h* yearns within ... Job 19:27
For God made my *h* ... Job 23:16
My *h* is in turmoil and ... Job 30:27
within your *h* on your bed ... Ps 4:4
My *h* also instructs me ... Ps 16:7
your *h* live forever ... Ps 22:26
h is overflowing ... Ps 45:1
My *h* is steadfast ... Ps 57:7
Thus my *h* was grieved ... Ps 73:21
my *h* and my flesh cry ... Ps 84:2
h is set on pilgrimage ... Ps 84:5
may gain a *h* of wisdom ... Ps 90:12
h shall depart from me ... Ps 101:4
look and a proud *h* ... Ps 101:5
with my whole *h* ... Ps 111:1
With my whole *h* I have ... Ps 119:10
I have hidden in my *h* ... Ps 119:11
h is not haughty ... Ps 131:1
O God, and know my *h* ... Ps 139:23
h makes a cheerful ... Prov 15:13
The king's *h* is in the ... Prov 21:1
as he thinks in his *h* ... Prov 23:7
with a wicked *h* ... Prov 26:23
h reveals the man ... Prov 27:19
trusts in his own *h* ... Prov 28:26
The *h* of the wise is ... Eccl 7:4
and a wise man's *h* ... Eccl 8:5
h yearned for him ... Song 5:4
and the whole *h* ... Is 1:5
h shall resound ... Is 16:11
the yearning of Your *h* ... Is 63:15
the mind and the *h* ... Jer 11:20
h is deceitful above ... Jer 17:9
I will give them a *h* ... Jer 24:7
therefore My *h* yearns ... Jer 31:20
and take the stony *h* ... Ezek 11:19
get yourselves a new *h* ... Ezek 18:31
uncircumcised in *h* ... Ezek 44:7
are the pure in *h* ... Matt 5:8
is, there your *h* ... Matt 6:21
of the *h* proceed evil ... Matt 15:19
does not doubt in his *h* ... Mark 11:23
Did not our *h* burn ... Luke 24:32
h will flow rivers ... John 7:38
"Let not your *h* ... John 14:1
believed were of one *h* ... Acts 4:32
Satan filled your *h* ... Acts 5:3
h is not right in the ... Acts 8:21
is that of the *h* ... Rom 2:29
h that God has raised ... Rom 10:9
with the *h* one believes ... Rom 10:10
in sincerity of *h* ... Eph 6:5
refresh my *h* in the ... Philem 20
always go astray in their *h* ... Heb 3:10
and shuts up his *h* ... 1 John 3:17
if our *h* condemns us ... 1 John 3:20

HEARTILY
you do, do it *h* ... Col 3:23

HEARTS
God tests the *h* ... Ps 7:9
who seek God, your *h* ... Ps 69:32
let the *h* of those ... Ps 105:3
And he will turn the *h* ... Mal 4:6
h failing them from ... Luke 21:26
purifying their *h* ... Acts 15:9
will guard your *h* ... Phil 4:7
of God rule in your *h* ... Col 3:15

HEAT
and harvest, cold and *h*, ... Gen 8:22
storm, a shade from the *h* ... Is 25:4
in the *h* of my spirit ... Ezek 3:14
will melt with fervent *h* ... 2 Pet 3:12

HEATHEN
repetitions as the *h* ... Matt 6:7
him be to you like a *h* ... Matt 18:17

HEAVEN
See FATHER IN HEAVEN; HOST OF HEAVEN; KINGDOM OF HEAVEN
called the firmament *H* ... Gen 1:8
High, Possessor of *h* ... Gen 14:19
called to him from *h* ... Gen 22:11
multiply as the stars of *h* ... Gen 26:4
give you of the dew of *h* ... Gen 27:28
and this is the gate of *h* ... Gen 28:17
with blessings of *h* above ... Gen 49:25
out his rod toward *h* ... Ex 9:23
rain bread from *h* for you ... Ex 16:4
Out of *h* He let you hear ... Deut 4:36
precious things of *h* ... Deut 33:13
foundations of *h* quaked ... 2 Sam 22:8
the host of *h* standing ... 1 Kin 22:19
came down from *h* ... 2 Kin 1:12
Elijah into *h* by a ... 2 Kin 2:1
would make windows in *h* ... 2 Kin 7:2
Behold, *h* and the *h* of ... 2 Chr 6:18
The LORD's throne is in *h* ... Ps 11:4
LORD looks down from *h* ... Ps 14:2
Whom have I in *h* but You ... Ps 73:25
word is settled in *h* ... Ps 119:89
For God is in *h* ... Eccl 5:2
"*H* is My throne ... Is 66:1
"If *h* above can be ... Jer 31:37
and the birds of the *h* ... Dan 2:38
come to know that *H* ... Dan 4:26
though they climb up to *h* ... Amos 9:2
These are four spirits of *h* ... Zech 6:5
for the kingdom of *h* ... Matt 3:2
your Father in *h* ... Matt 5:16
Our Father in *h*, hallowed ... Matt 6:9
on earth as it is in *h* ... Matt 6:10
H and earth will ... Matt 24:35
from Him a sign from *h* ... Mark 8:11
but are like angels in *h* ... Mark 12:25
with the clouds of *h* ... Mark 14:62
prayed, the *h* was opened ... Luke 3:21
fall like lightning from *h* ... Luke 10:18
names are written in *h* ... Luke 10:20
done on earth as it is in *h* ... Luke 11:2
will be more joy in *h* ... Luke 15:7
have sinned against *h* ... Luke 15:18
descending from *h* like a ... John 1:32
you shall see *h* open ... John 1:51
one has ascended to *h* ... John 3:13
the true bread from *h* ... John 6:32
a voice came from *h* ... John 12:28
sheet, let down from *h* ... Acts 11:5
the whole family in *h* ... Eph 3:15
laid up for you in *h* ... Col 1:5
and the *h* gave rain ... James 5:18
there was silence in *h* ... Rev 8:1
sign appeared in *h* ... Rev 12:1
Now I saw a new *h* ... Rev 21:1

HEAVEN AND EARTH
High, Possessor of *h* ... Gen 14:19
"I call *h* to witness ... Deut 4:26
You have made *h* ... 2 Kin 19:15
of Israel, who made *h* ... 2 Chr 2:12
servants of the God of *h* ... Ezra 5:11
Let *h* praise Him, the seas ... Ps 69:34
the LORD, who made *h* ... Ps 121:2
LORD who made *h* bless ... Ps 134:3
who made *h*, the sea, and ... Ps 146:6
You have made *h* ... Is 37:16
"do I not fill *h*?" says ... Jer 23:24
the ordinances of *h* ... Jer 33:25
I will shake *h*, the sea and ... Hag 2:6
till *h* pass away, one jot ... Matt 5:18
Father, Lord of *h* ... Matt 11:25
"*H* will pass away, but ... Matt 24:35
You are God, who made *h* ... Acts 4:24
the whole family in *h* ... Eph 3:15
worship Him who made *h* ... Rev 14:7

HEAVENLY
h host praising God ... Luke 2:13
if I tell you *h* things ... John 3:12
are those who are *h* ... 1 Cor 15:48
the image of the *h* Man ... 1 Cor 15:49
blessing in the *h* ... Eph 1:3
the *h* places in Christ Jesus ... Eph 2:6
and powers in the *h* places ... Eph 3:10
wickedness in the *h* places ... Eph 6:12
and have tasted the *h* ... Heb 6:4
h things themselves ... Heb 9:23
a better, that is, a *h* ... Heb 11:16
the living God, the *h* ... Heb 12:22

HEAVENLY FATHER
your *h* will also forgive ... Matt 6:14
yet your *h* feeds them ... Matt 6:26
h knows that you need ... Matt 6:32
My *h* has not planted ... Matt 15:13
"So My *h* also will do ... Matt 18:35
your *h* give the Holy ... Luke 11:13

HEAVENS
I will make your *h* ... Lev 26:19
and the highest *h* ... Deut 10:14
h cannot contain ... 1 Kin 8:27
the LORD made the *h* ... 1 Chr 16:26
Till the *h* are no more ... Job 14:12
in the *h* shall laugh ... Ps 2:4
h declare the glory ... Ps 19:1
Let the *h* declare His ... Ps 50:6
h can be compared ... Ps 89:6
The *h* are Yours ... Ps 89:11
For as the *h* are high ... Ps 103:11
When He prepared the *h* ... Prov 8:27
h are higher than the ... Is 55:9
behold, I create new *h* ... Is 65:17
and behold, the *h* ... Matt 3:16
h will be shaken ... Matt 24:29
h are the work of Your ... Heb 1:10
h will pass away ... 2 Pet 3:10

HEAVINESS
and I am full of *h* ... Ps 69:20
My soul melts from *h* ... Ps 119:28

HEAVY
the bondage was *h* ... Neh 5:18

HEBREW
Term applied to:
- Abram, Gen 14:13
- Israelites, 1 Sam 4:6, 9
- Jews, Acts 6:1
- Paul, Phil 3:5

HEBRON
Abram, Isaac, and Jacob dwell there, Gen 13:18; 23:2–20; 35:27
Visited by spies, Num 13:21, 22
Defeated by Joshua, Josh 10:1–37
Caleb's inheritance, Josh 14:12–15
David's original capital; sons born there, 2 Sam 2:1–3, 11; 3:2–5
Site of Absalom's rebellion, 2 Sam 15:7–10

HEDGE
behold, I will *h* up your ... Hos 2:6
sharper than a thorn *h* ... Mic 7:4
a vineyard and set a *h* ... Mark 12:1

HEDGED
and whom God has *h* ... Job 3:23
You have *h* me behind ... Ps 139:5
He has *h* me in so that ... Lam 3:7

HEED
See TAKE HEED
By taking *h* according ... Ps 119:9
if you *h* Me carefully ... Jer 17:24

and let us not give *h* .... Jer 18:18
Take *h*, watch and pray .. Mark 13:33
stands take *h* lest he ..... 1 Cor 10:12
nor give *h* to fables .... 1 Tim 1:4
giving *h* to deceiving ...... 1 Tim 4:1
the more earnest *h* .... Heb 2:1

HEEDS
h counsel is wise .... Prov 12:15

HEEL
you shall bruise His *h* ...... Gen 3:15
took hold of Esau's *h* ...... Gen 25:26
has lifted up his *h* .... Ps 41:9
Me has lifted up his *h* ..... John 13:18

HEIFER
a red *h* without blemish .... Num 19:2
not plowed with my *h* ..... Judg 14:18
goats and the ashes of a *h* .. Heb 9:13

HEIGHT
"Is not God in the *h* .... Job 22:12
looked down from the *h* .... Ps 102:19
nor *h* nor depth .... Rom 8:39
length and depth and *h* ..... Eph 3:18

HEIR
own body shall be your *h* ... Gen 15:4
Has he no *h* .... Jer 49:1
Now I say that the *h* .... Gal 4:1
if a son, then an *h* .... Gal 4:7
He has appointed *h* .... Heb 1:2
the world and became *h* .... Heb 11:7

HEIRS
of God and joint *h* .... Rom 8:17
should be fellow *h* .... Eph 3:6
be rich in faith and *h* ...... James 2:5
vessel, and as being *h* .... 1 Pet 3:7

HELAM
Place between Damascus and Hamath where David defeated Syrians, 2 Sam 10:16–19

HELL
shall be turned into *h* .... Ps 9:17
go down alive into *h* .... Ps 55:15
house is the way to *h* ...... Prov 7:27
his soul from *h* .... Prov 23:14
H and Destruction are .... Prov 27:20
"*H* from beneath is .... Is 14:9
be in danger of *h* fire .... Matt 5:22
to be cast into *h* .... Matt 18:9
the condemnation of *h* .... Matt 23:33
power to cast into *h* .... Luke 12:5
it is set on fire by *h* .... James 3:6

HELLENISTS
Greek-speaking Jews, Acts 6:1
Hostile to Paul, Acts 9:29
Gospel preached to, Acts 11:20

HELMET
a breastplate, and a *h* .... Is 59:17
And take the *h* of .... Eph 6:17
and love, and as a *h* ...... 1 Thess 5:8

HELP
the shield of your *h* .... Deut 33:29
Is my *h* not within me .... Job 6:13
"There is no *h* for him .... Ps 3:2
May He send you *h* .... Ps 20:2
He is our *h* and our .... Ps 33:20
yet praise Him, the *h* .... Ps 42:11
A very present *h* .... Ps 46:1
Give us *h* from trouble ...... Ps 60:11
God, make haste to *h* .... Ps 71:12
"I have given *h* .... Ps 89:19
the LORD had been my *h* .... Ps 94:17
there was none to *h* .... Ps 107:12
He is their *h* and .... Ps 115:9
Our *h* is in the name .... Ps 124:8
let no one *h* him .... Prov 28:17
h my unbelief .... Mark 9:24
tell her to *h* me .... Luke 10:40
and find grace to *h* .... Heb 4:16

HELPED
far the LORD has *h* .... 1 Sam 7:12

h the people to .... Neh 8:7
fall, but the LORD *h* .... Ps 118:13
of salvation I have *h* .... Is 49:8
h His servant Israel .... Luke 1:54

HELPER
I will make him a *h* .... Gen 2:18
Behold, God is my *h* .... Ps 54:4
give you another *H* ...... John 14:16
"But when the *H* .... John 15:26
she has been a *h* .... Rom 16:2
"The LORD is my *h* .... Heb 13:6

HELPFUL
all things are not *h* .... 1 Cor 6:12

HELPS
the Spirit also *h* .... Rom 8:26
gifts of healings, *h* .... 1 Cor 12:28

HEM
and touched the *h* .... Matt 9:20
might only touch the *h* ..... Matt 14:36

HEMAN
Composer of a psalm, Ps 88:title

HEMLOCK
judgment springs up like *h* .. Hos 10:4

HEN
as a *h* gathers her chicks .. Matt 23:37
as a *h* gathers her brood .. Luke 13:34

HENNA
is to me a cluster of *h* ..... Song 1:14
fragrant *h* with spikenard .. Song 4:13

HERB
the *h* that yields seed, and .. Gen 1:11
every green *h* for food ...... Gen 1:30
struck every *h* of the field .... Ex 9:25
ate every *h* of the land .... Ex 10:15
raindrops on the tender *h* .. Deut 32:2
field and the green *h* ..... 2 Kin 19:26
And wither as the green *h* .... Ps 37:2
the field and the green *h* ...... Is 37:27

HERBS
with bitter *h* they shall eat ... Ex 12:8
bread and bitter *h* .... Num 9:11
a dinner of *h* where love .. Prov 15:17

HERD
And Abraham ran to the *h* .. Gen 18:7
a burnt sacrifice of the *h* ...... Lev 1:3
tithe of the *h* or the flock .. Lev 27:32
there be no *h* in the stalls ... Hab 3:17
into the *h* of swine .... Matt 8:31

HERE
Then I said, "*H* am I .... Is 6:8

HERE I AM
And he said, "*H* .... Gen 22:1
And he answered him, "*H* .. Gen 27:1
'Jacob.' And I said, '*H* ..... Gen 31:11
So he said to him, "*H* ..... Gen 37:13
Jacob!" And he said, "*H* .... Gen 46:2
Moses!" And he said, "*H* ...... Ex 3:4
And he answered, "*H* ...... 1 Sam 3:4
"*H*. Witness against me ... 1 Sam 12:3
h, let Him do to me as ... 2 Sam 15:26
h, the first to come ...... 2 Sam 19:20
nor let the eunuch say, "*H* .... Is 56:3
cry, and He will say, '*H* .... Is 58:9
I said, '*H*, *h*,' to a nation ..... Is 65:1
h, in your hand; do with .... Jer 26:14
And he said, "*H* .... Acts 9:10

HERESIES
dissensions, *h* .... Gal 5:20
in destructive *h* .... 2 Pet 2:1

HERITAGE
give it to you as a *h* .... Ex 6:8
have given me the *h* .... Ps 61:5
for that is his *h* .... Eccl 3:22
for it is his *h* .... Eccl 5:18
This is the *h* of the .... Is 54:17
of My people, My *h* .... Joel 3:2

The flock of Your *h* .... Mic 7:14

HERMES
Paul acclaimed as, Acts 14:12

HERMON
Highest mountain (9,166 ft.) in Syria; also called Sirion, Shenir, Deut 3:8, 9

HEROD
—— Herod the Great, procurator of Judea (37–4 B.C.), Luke 1:5
Inquires about Jesus' birth, Matt 2:3–8
Slays infants of Bethlehem, Matt 2:12–18
—— Herod Antipas, the tetrarch, ruler of Galilee and Perea (4 B.C.–A.D. 39), Luke 3:1
Imprisons John the Baptist, Luke 3:18–21
Has John the Baptist beheaded, Matt 14:1–12
Disturbed about Jesus, Luke 9:7–9
Jesus sent to him, Luke 23:7–11
—— Herod Agrippa I (A.D. 37–44), Acts 12:1, 19
Kills James, Acts 12:1, 2
Imprisons Peter, Acts 12:3–11, 19
Slain by an angel, Acts 12:20–23
—— Herod Agrippa II (A.D. 53–70); called Agrippa and King Agrippa, Acts 25:22–24, 26
Festus tells him about Paul, Acts 25:13–27
Paul makes a defense before, Acts 26:1–32

HERODIANS
Join Pharisees against Jesus, Mark 3:6
Seek to trap Jesus, Matt 22:15–22
Jesus warns against, Mark 8:15

HERODIAS
Granddaughter of Herod the Great; plots John's death, Matt 14:3–12
Married her uncle, Mark 6:17, 18

HESHBON
Ancient Moabite city; taken by Moses, Num 21:23–34
Assigned to Reubenites, Num 32:1–37
Prophecies concerning, Is 15:1–4; 16:8–14; Jer 48:2, 34, 35

HETH
Son of Canaan, Gen 10:15
Abraham buys field from sons of, Gen 23:3–20
Esau marries daughters of, Gen 27:46

HEW
H for yourself two tablets .. Deut 10:1

HEWN
she has *h* out her seven ..... Prov 9:1
in a tomb that was *h* ..... Luke 23:53

HEZEKIAH
Righteous king of Judah; reforms temple and worship, 2 Chr 29—31
Wars with Assyria; prayer for deliverance is answered, 2 Kin 18:7—19:37
His sickness and recovery; thanksgiving, 2 Kin 20:1–11; Is 38:9–22
Boasts to Babylonian ambassadors, 2 Kin 20:12–19
Death, 2 Kin 20:20, 21

HID
naked; and I *h* myself ...... Gen 3:10
child, she *h* him three .... Ex 2:2
Egyptian and *h* him in the .... Ex 2:12
she *h* the messengers .... Josh 6:25
David *h* in the field ...... 1 Sam 20:24
they *h* him and his nurse .. 2 Kin 11:2
And we *h*, as it were, our ...... Is 53:3
and *h* his lord's money .... Matt 25:18

says the *H*, "So shall the . . Acts 21:11
out in our hearts by the *H* . . . Rom 5:5
me witness in the *H* . . . . Rom 9:1
peace and joy in the *H* . . . . Rom 14:17
sanctified by the *H* . . . . . . Rom 15:16
but which the *H* teaches . . . 1 Cor 2:13
is the temple of the *H* . . . . 1 Cor 6:19
is Lord except by the *H* . . . . 1 Cor 12:3
by kindness, by the *H* . . . . . . 2 Cor 6:6
were sealed with the *H* of . . . Eph 1:13
And do not grieve the *H* . . . . Eph 4:30
by the *H* who dwells . . . . 2 Tim 1:14
and renewing of the *H* . . . . . . Titus 3:5
miracles, and gifts of the *H* . . Heb 2:4
become partakers of the *H* . . . Heb 6:4
were moved by the *H* . . . . . . 2 Pet 1:21
the Word, and the *H* . . . . . . 1 John 5:7

HOME

LORD has brought me *h* . . . . Ruth 1:21
sparrow has found a *h* . . . . . Ps 84:3
the stork has her *h* . . . . Ps 104:17
to his eternal *h* . . . . Eccl 12:5
said to him, "Go *h* . . . . Mark 5:19
into an everlasting *h* . . . . Luke 16:9
to him and make Our *h* . . . John 14:23
took her to his own *h* . . . . . John 19:27
let him eat at *h* . . . . 1 Cor 11:34
own husbands at *h* . . . . 1 Cor 14:35
that while we are at *h* . . . . . . 2 Cor 5:6
to show piety at *h* . . . . 1 Tim 5:4

HOMELESS

and beaten, and *h* . . . . 1 Cor 4:11

HOMEMAKERS

be discreet, chaste, *h* . . . . Titus 2:5

HOMOSEXUALS

nor adulterers, nor *h*, nor . . . 1 Cor 6:9

HONEST

we are *h* men . . . . Gen 42:11

HONEY

See MILK AND HONEY
flowing with milk and *h* . . Num 16:13
"What is sweeter than *h* . . Judg 14:18
I tasted a little of this *h* . . 1 Sam 14:29
Sweeter also than *h* and . . . . Ps 19:10
and with *h* from the . . . . Ps 81:16
sweeter than *h* to my . . . . . Ps 119:103
My son, eat *h* because . . . . Prov 24:13
not good to eat much *h* . . . . Prov 25:27
h and milk are under . . . . . . Song 4:11
was locusts and wild *h* . . . . Matt 3:4
sweet as *h* in my mouth . . . . Rev 10:10

HONEYCOMB

than honey and the *h* . . . . Ps 19:10
words are like a *h* . . . . Prov 16:24
fish and some *h* . . . . Luke 24:42

HONOR

H your father and your . . . . . Ex 20:12
both riches and *h* . . . . 1 Kin 3:13
the king delights to *h* . . . . Esth 6:6
earth, and lay my *h* . . . . Ps 7:5
A man who is in *h* . . . . Ps 49:20
Sing out the *h* of His . . . . Ps 66:2
will deliver him and *h* . . . . Ps 91:15
H and majesty are . . . . Ps 96:6
h have all His saints . . . . Ps 149:9
H the LORD with your . . . . Prov 3:9
before *h* is humility . . . . Prov 15:33
h is not fitting . . . . Prov 26:1
spirit will retain *h* . . . . Prov 29:23
Father, where is My *h* . . . . Mal 1:6
is not without *h* . . . . Matt 13:57
'*H* your father and your . . . Matt 15:4
h the Son just as they . . . . John 5:23
"I do not receive *h* . . . . John 5:41
but I *h* My Father . . . . John 8:49
"If I *h* Myself . . . . John 8:54
him My Father will *h* . . . . . John 12:26
make one vessel for *h* . . . . Rom 9:21
to whom fear, *h* . . . . Rom 13:7
we bestow greater *h* . . . . . 1 Cor 12:23
sanctification and *h* . . . . . . 1 Thess 4:4
alone is wise, be *h* . . . . 1 Tim 1:17
worthy of double *h* . . . . 1 Tim 5:17
and clay, some for *h* . . . . 2 Tim 2:20
no man takes this *h* . . . . Heb 5:4
H the king . . . . 1 Pet 2:17
from God the Father *h* . . . . . 2 Pet 1:17
give glory and *h* . . . . Rev 4:9

HONORABLE

of God, and he is an *h* . . . . 1 Sam 9:6
His work is *h* and . . . . Ps 111:3
It is *h* for a man to . . . . Prov 20:3
traders are the *h* . . . . Is 23:8
holy day of the LORD *h* . . . . . . Is 58:13
providing *h* things . . . . 2 Cor 8:21
Marriage is *h* among . . . . Heb 13:4
having your conduct *h* . . . . . . 1 Pet 2:12

HONORABLY

desiring to live *h* . . . . Heb 13:18

HONORS

h those who fear the . . . . Ps 15:4
'This people *h* Me . . . . Mark 7:6
It is My Father who *h* . . . . . . John 8:54

HOOKS

will lament who cast *h* . . . . Is 19:8
spears into pruning *h* . . . . Mic 4:3

HOOVES

those that have cloven *h* . . . . Lev 11:4
I will make your *h* bronze . . . . Mic 4:13

HOPE

I should say I have *h* . . . . . . Ruth 1:12
are spent without *h* . . . . Job 7:6
so You destroy the *h* . . . . Job 14:19
where then is my *h* . . . . Job 17:15
h He has uprooted . . . . Job 19:10
also will rest in *h* . . . . Ps 16:9
heart, all you who *h* . . . . Ps 31:24
My *h* is in You . . . . Ps 39:7
For You are my *h* . . . . Ps 71:5
I *h* in Your word . . . . Ps 119:147
O Israel, *h* in the . . . . Ps 130:7
h will not be cut . . . . Prov 23:18
There is more *h* . . . . Prov 26:12
the living there is *h* . . . . Eccl 9:4
O the *H* of Israel . . . . Jer 14:8
good that one should *h* . . . . . Lam 3:26
Achor as a door of *h* . . . . Hos 2:15
you prisoners of *h* . . . . Zech 9:12
I have *h* in God . . . . Acts 24:15
to *h*, in *h* believed . . . . Rom 4:18
and rejoice in *h* . . . . Rom 5:2
h does not disappoint . . . . Rom 5:5
h that is seen is . . . . Rom 8:24
But if we *h* for what . . . . Rom 8:25
And now abide faith, *h* . . . 1 Cor 13:13
life only we have *h* . . . . 1 Cor 15:19
may know what is the *h* . . . . Eph 1:18
were called in one *h* . . . . Eph 4:4
h which is laid . . . . Col 1:5
Christ in you, the *h* . . . . Col 1:27
For what is our *h* . . . . 1 Thess 2:19
others who have no *h* . . . 1 Thess 4:13
and as a helmet the *h* . . . . . 1 Thess 5:8
Jesus Christ, our *h* . . . . 1 Tim 1:1
in *h* of eternal life . . . . Titus 1:2
for the blessed *h* . . . . Titus 2:13
to lay hold of the *h* . . . . Heb 6:18
of a better *h* . . . . Heb 7:19
us again to a living *h* . . . . 1 Pet 1:3
you a reason for the *h* . . . . . 1 Pet 3:15
who has this *h* in Him . . . . . 1 John 3:3

HOPED

substance of things *h* . . . . Heb 11:1

HOPHNI

Wicked son of Eli, 1 Sam 1:3; 2:12–17, 22–25
Prophecy against, 1 Sam 2:27–36; 3:11–14
Carries ark into battle; killed, 1 Sam 4:1–11

HOR

Mountain of Edom; scene of Aaron's death, Num 20:22–29; 33:37–39

HOREB

See SINAI
God appears to Moses at, Ex 3:1–22
Water flows from, Ex 17:6
Elijah lodged here 40 days, 1 Kin 19:8, 9

HORITES

Inhabitants of Mt. Seir, Gen 36:20
Defeated by Chedorlaomer, Gen 14:5, 6
Driven out by Esau's descendants, Gen 36:20–29; Deut 2:12, 22

HORMAH

Destroyed by Israel, Num 21:1–3

HORN

my shield and the *h* . . . . Ps 18:2
h will be exalted . . . . Ps 112:9
goat had a notable *h* . . . . Dan 8:5
and has raised up a *h* . . . . Luke 1:69

HORRIBLE

h thing has been . . . . Jer 5:30
I have seen a *h* . . . . Hos 6:10

HORROR

and behold, *h* and . . . . Gen 15:12
sorrow, the cup of *h* . . . . . . Ezek 23:33
you will become a *h* . . . . . . Ezek 27:36

HORSE

The *h* and its rider He . . . . Ex 15:1
Have you given the *h* . . . . . . Job 39:19
h is a vain hope . . . . Ps 33:17
the strength of the *h* . . . . Ps 147:10
h is prepared for the . . . . . . Prov 21:31
and behold, a white *h* . . . . Rev 6:2
and behold, a black *h* . . . . Rev 6:5
and behold, a pale *h* . . . . Rev 6:8
and behold, a white *h* . . . . Rev 19:11

HORSES

seen servants on *h* . . . . Eccl 10:7
h are swifter than . . . . Jer 4:13
Do *h* run on rocks . . . . Amos 6:12
we put bits in *h* . . . . James 3:3

HOSANNA

H in the highest . . . . Matt 21:9

HOSEA

Son of Beeri, prophet of the northern kingdom, Hos 1:1

HOSHEA

Original name of Joshua, the son of Nun, Deut 32:44; Num 13:8, 16
—— Israel's last king; usurps throne, 2 Kin 15:30
Reigns wickedly; Israel taken to Assyria during his reign, 2 Kin 17:1–23

HOSPITABLE

of good behavior, *h* . . . . 1 Tim 3:2
Be *h* to one another . . . . 1 Pet 4:9

HOST

who brings out their *h* . . . . Is 40:26
of the heavenly *h* . . . . Luke 2:13

HOST OF HEAVEN

all the *h*, you feel driven . . . . Deut 4:19
throne, and all the *h* . . . . 1 Kin 22:19
worshiped all the *h* . . . . 2 Kin 17:16
and for all the *h* . . . . 2 Kin 23:4
The *h* worships You . . . . Neh 9:6
All the *h* shall be dissolved . . . . Is 34:4
the moon and all the *h* . . . . Jer 8:2
burned incense to all the *h* . . . Jer 19:13
the *h* cannot be numbered . . . Jer 33:22
And it grew up to the *h* . . . . . . Dan 8:10
them up to worship the *h* . . . Acts 7:42

HOSTILITY

Him who endured such *h* . . . Heb 12:3

HOSTS
See LORD GOD OF HOSTS; LORD OF HOSTS
name of the LORD of *h* . . . 1 Sam 17:45
As the LORD of *h* lives . . . . 1 Kin 18:15
The LORD of *h* is with . . . . Ps 46:7
LORD, all you His *h* . . . . Ps 103:21
praise Him, all His *h* . . . . Ps 148:2
word of the LORD of *h* . . . . Is 39:5
LORD of *h* is His name . . . . Is 47:4
against spiritual *h* . . . . Eph 6:12

HOT
of the LORD was *h* . . . . Judg 2:14
My heart was *h* within . . . . Ps 39:3
are neither cold nor *h* . . . . Rev 3:15

HOUND
My enemies would *h* . . . . Ps 56:2

HOUR
h what you should . . . . Matt 10:19
day and *h* no one knows . . Matt 24:36
Man is coming at an *h* . . . . Matt 24:44
Behold, the *h* is at . . . . Matt 26:45
But this is your *h* . . . . Luke 22:53
h has not yet come . . . . John 2:4
But the *h* is coming . . . . John 4:23
h has come that the . . . . John 12:23
save Me from this *h* . . . . . . John 12:27
"Father, the *h* has come . . . . John 17:1
will not know what *h* . . . . Rev 3:3
keep you from the *h* . . . . Rev 3:10

HOURS
Are there not twelve *h* . . . . . John 11:9

HOUSE
from your father's *h* . . . . Gen 12:1
But as for me and my *h* . . . Josh 24:15
h appointed for all . . . . Job 30:23
with them to the *h* . . . . Ps 42:4
the goodness of Your *h* . . . . Ps 65:4
For her *h* leads down . . . . . . Prov 2:18
Through wisdom a *h* . . . . Prov 24:3
better to go to the *h* . . . . Eccl 7:2
of the *h* tremble . . . . Eccl 12:3
to the *h* of the God of . . . . Is 2:3
to those who join *h* . . . . Is 5:8
h was filled with . . . . Is 6:4
'Set your *h* in order . . . . Is 38:1
h shall be called a . . . . Is 56:7
built his *h* on the rock . . . . . Matt 7:24
and beat on that *h* . . . . Matt 7:25
blew and beat on that *h* . . . . Matt 7:27
had come into Peter's *h* . . . . Matt 8:14
came into the ruler's *h* . . . . . Matt 9:23
sheep of the *h* of Israel . . . . . Matt 10:6
h divided against . . . . Matt 12:25
enter a strong man's *h* . . . . Matt 12:29
h shall be called a . . . . Matt 21:13
Your *h* is left to you . . . . . . Matt 23:38
the *h* of Simon the leper . . . . Matt 26:6
no one who has left *h* . . . . Mark 10:29
My *h* shall be called a *h* . . Mark 11:17
the *h* of Zacharias . . . . Luke 1:40
bed, and go to your *h* . . . . . . Luke 5:24
ruin of that *h* was great . . . . Luke 6:49
Whatever *h* you enter . . . . . . Luke 9:4
h may be filled . . . . Luke 14:23
light a lamp, sweep the *h* . . Luke 15:8
has come to this *h* . . . . Luke 19:9
make My Father's *h* . . . . John 2:16
for Your *h* has eaten Me . . . John 2:17
the *h* was filled with the . . . John 12:3
h are many mansions . . . . . . John 14:2
bread from *h* to *h*, they . . . . . Acts 2:46
hour I prayed in my *h* . . . . . Acts 10:30
in the *h* of Simon . . . . Acts 10:32
publicly and from *h* . . . . Acts 20:20
in his own rented *h* . . . . Acts 28:30
church that is in their *h* . . . . Rom 16:5
a *h* not made with hands, . . . 2 Cor 5:1
who rules his own *h* . . . . 1 Tim 3:4
children, manage the *h* . . . . 1 Tim 5:14
in a great *h* there are . . . . . 2 Tim 2:20
the church in your *h* . . . . Philem 2
has more honor than the *h* . . . Heb 3:3
For every *h* is built . . . . Heb 3:4
His own *h*, whose *h* . . . . Heb 3:6
Priest over the *h* of God . . . Heb 10:21
being built up a spiritual *h* . . 1 Pet 2:5
to begin at the *h* of God . . . . 1 Pet 4:17
him into your *h* . . . . 2 John 1:10

HOUSE OF DAVID
a covenant with the *h* . . . . 1 Sam 20:16
house of Saul and the *h* . . . . 2 Sam 3:1
rebellion against the *h* . . . . . 1 Kin 12:19
may return to the *h* . . . . 1 Kin 12:26
shall be born to the *h* . . . . . . 1 Kin 13:2
away from the *h* . . . . 1 Kin 14:8
shall not dwell in the *h* . . . . 2 Chr 8:11
would not destroy the *h* . . . 2 Chr 21:7
the wall, beyond the *h* . . . . . Neh 12:37
the thrones of the *h* . . . . Ps 122:5
And it was told to the *h* . . . . Is 7:2
The key of the *h* I will lay . . . . Is 22:22
'O *h*! Thus says the LORD: . . . Jer 21:12
h shall be like God . . . . Zech 12:8
was Joseph, of the *h* . . . . Luke 1:27

HOUSE OF GOD
none other than the *h* . . . . . Gen 28:17
the *h* was in Shiloh . . . . Judg 18:31
of the tabernacle of the *h* . . 1 Chr 6:48
stones to build the *h* . . . . . . 1 Chr 22:2
all the service of the *h* . . . . 1 Chr 28:21
King Solomon for the *h* . . . 2 Chr 4:11
of the LORD filled the *h* . . . . 2 Chr 5:14
people dedicated the *h* . . . . . 2 Chr 7:5
also brought into the *h* . . . 2 Chr 15:18
with them in the *h* . . . . 2 Chr 22:12
articles from the *h* . . . . 2 Chr 36:18
freewill offerings for the *h* . . Ezra 1:4
oversee the work of the *h* . . . Ezra 3:8
or the courts of the *h* . . . . Neh 8:16
"Why is the *h* forsaken?" . . Neh 13:11
I went with them to the *h* . . . . . Ps 42:4
a green olive tree in the *h* . . . . Ps 52:8
walked to the *h* in the . . . . Ps 55:14
when you go to the *h* . . . . Eccl 5:1
the articles of the *h* . . . . Dan 1:2
from the temple of the *h* . . . . . Dan 5:3
how he entered the *h* and . . Matt 12:4
conduct yourself in the *h* . . 1 Tim 3:15
High Priest over the *h* . . . . Heb 10:21
to begin at the *h* . . . . 1 Pet 4:17

HOUSE OF THE LORD
you shall bring into the *h* . . . Ex 23:19
price of a dog to the *h* . . . . . Deut 23:18
into the treasury of the *h* . . . Josh 6:24
she went up to the *h* . . . . 1 Sam 1:7
brought him to the *h* . . . . . 1 Sam 1:24
he went into the *h* and . . . 2 Sam 12:20
his own house, and the *h* . . . 1 Kin 3:1
he began to build the *h* . . . . . 1 Kin 6:1
the cloud filled the *h* . . . . . . 1 Kin 8:10
hidden with her in the *h* . . . 2 Kin 11:3
the damage of the *h* . . . . . . 2 Kin 12:12
service of song in the *h* . . . . 1 Chr 6:31
David said, "This is the *h* . . 1 Chr 22:1
began to build the *h* . . . . 2 Chr 3:1
for the *h* was finished . . . . . . 2 Chr 5:1
So the *h* was completed. . . 2 Chr 8:16
heart on repairing the *h* . . . 2 Chr 24:4
cut off from the *h* . . . . 2 Chr 26:21
of the *h* to cleanse it . . . . . 2 Chr 29:16
built altars in the *h* . . . . 2 Chr 33:4
of the Law in the *h* . . . . 2 Chr 34:15
from the *h* to Babylon . . . . . 2 Chr 36:7
build the *h* God of Israel . . . . Ezra 1:3
heart, to beautify the *h* . . . . . Ezra 7:27
I will dwell in the *h* forever . . . Ps 23:6
that I may dwell in the *h* . . . . . Ps 27:4
who are planted in the *h* . . . . Ps 92:13
"Let us go into the *h* . . . . Ps 122:1
Hezekiah went up to the *h* . . . Is 37:14
these words in the *h* . . . . Jer 26:7
of praise into the *h*. For I . . . Jer 33:11
He burned the *h* and the . . . . Jer 52:13
noise in the *h* as on the . . . . . Lam 2:7
LORD filled the *h*; and I . . . . Ezek 44:4
it shall not come into the *h* . . . Hos 9:4
shall flow from the *h* . . . . Joel 3:18
came and worked on the *h* . . Hag 1:14
priests who were in the *h* . . . Zech 7:3

HOUSEHOLD
over the ways of her *h* . . . . Prov 31:27
If the *h* is worthy . . . . Matt 10:13
be those of his own *h* . . . . . Matt 10:36
make ruler over his *h* . . . . . Luke 12:42
h were baptized . . . . Acts 16:15
saved, you and your *h* . . . . Acts 16:31
also baptized the *h* . . . . 1 Cor 1:16
the *h* of Stephanas . . . . 1 Cor 16:15
those who are of the *h* . . . . . . Gal 6:10
who are of Caesar's *h* . . . . . . Phil 4:22
mercy to the *h* of . . . . 2 Tim 1:16
ark for the saving of his *h* . . . Heb 11:7

HOUSEHOLDER
h who brings out of . . . . Matt 13:52

HOUSEHOLDS
that He provided *h* for . . . . Ex 1:21
heads of the fathers' *h* . . . . Ezra 10:16
those who creep into *h* . . . . . 2 Tim 3:6
who subvert whole *h* . . . . . . Titus 1:11

HOUSES
h are safe from fear . . . . Job 21:9
Yet He filled their *h* . . . . Job 22:18
is that their *h* will last . . . . Ps 49:11
H and riches are an . . . . Prov 19:14
who has left *h* or . . . . Matt 19:29
you devour widows' *h* . . . . Matt 23:14
Do you not have *h* . . . . 1 Cor 11:22

HOUSETOP
dwell in a corner of a *h* . . . Prov 25:24
they went up on the *h* . . . . . Luke 5:19
went up on the *h* to pray, . . . Acts 10:9

HOUSETOPS
herb, as the grass on the *h* . . . Is 37:27
ear, preach on the *h* . . . . . . Matt 10:27
be proclaimed on the *h* . . . . Luke 12:3

HOVERING
Spirit of God was *h* . . . . Gen 1:2

HOW
"*H* can this be . . . . Luke 1:34
H long do You keep . . . . John 10:24
h you turned to God . . . . . . 1 Thess 1:9

HULDAH
Wife of Shallum, 2 Kin 22:14
Foretells Jerusalem's ruin, 2 Kin 22:15–17; 2 Chr 34:22–25
Exempts Josiah from trouble, 2 Kin 22:18–20

HUMAN
broken without *h* means . . . . Dan 8:25
for joy that a *h* being . . . . . John 16:21
I speak in *h* terms . . . . Rom 6:19
words of *h* wisdom . . . . 1 Cor 2:4
we have had *h* fathers . . . . . . Heb 12:9

HUMBLE
man Moses was very *h* . . . . Num 12:3
h you and test you . . . . Deut 8:2
who is proud, and *h* . . . . Job 40:11
the cry of the *h* . . . . Ps 9:12
Do not forget the *h* . . . . Ps 10:12
the desire of the *h* . . . . Ps 10:17
h He guides in justice . . . . Ps 25:9
h shall hear of it and . . . . Ps 34:2
LORD lifts up the *h* . . . . Ps 147:6
h spirit with the . . . . Prov 16:19
contrite and *h* spirit . . . . Is 57:15
a meek and *h* people . . . . . . Zeph 3:12
associate with the *h* . . . . Rom 12:16
gives grace to the *h* . . . . James 4:6

H yourselves in the .... James 4:10
gives grace to the *h* .... 1 Pet 5:5
h yourselves under the ...... 1 Pet 5:6

HUMBLED
h himself greatly .... 2 Chr 33:12
as a man, He *h* Himself ...... Phil 2:8

HUMBLES
h Himself to behold .... Ps 113:6

HUMILIATION
to plunder, and to *h* .... Ezra 9:7
h His justice was .... Acts 8:33
but the rich in his *h* .... James 1:10

HUMILITY
By *h* and the fear of .... Prov 22:4
righteousness, seek *h* .... Zeph 2:3
the Lord with all *h* .... Acts 20:19
delight in false *h* .... Col 2:18
mercies, kindness, *h* .... Col 3:12
h correcting those .... 2 Tim 2:25
gentle, showing all *h* .... Titus 3:2
and be clothed with *h* .... 1 Pet 5:5

HUNDRED
Adam lived were nine *h* ..... Gen 5:5
of Lamech were seven *h* ..... Gen 5:31
of Jacob's life was one *h* ... Gen 47:28
Joseph lived one *h* and ..... Gen 50:22
one *h* cubits long for one ..... Ex 27:9
of which was one *h* .... Num 7:13
for a *h* foreskins of the ... 2 Sam 3:14
one *h* summer fruits ...... 2 Sam 16:1
had taken one *h* prophets .. 1 Kin 18:4

HUNDREDFOLD
in the same year a *h* .... Gen 26:12
some a *h*, some sixty .... Matt 13:8
receive a *h* now in this ... Mark 10:30
up, and yielded a crop a *h* .. Luke 8:8

HUNGER
you, allowed you to *h* .... Deut 8:3
lack and suffer *h* .... Ps 34:10
They shall neither *h* .... Is 49:10
likely to die from *h* .... Jer 38:9
are those who *h* .... Matt 5:6
for you shall *h* .... Luke 6:25
to Me shall never *h* .... John 6:35
present hour we both *h* .... 1 Cor 4:11
They shall neither *h* .... Rev 7:16

HUNGRY
bread from the *h* .... Job 22:7
and fills the *h* .... Ps 107:9
gives food to the *h* .... Ps 146:7
h soul every bitter .... Prov 27:7
your soul to the *h* .... Is 58:10
for I was *h* and you .... Matt 25:35
when did we see You *h* ... Matt 25:37
and one is *h* and .... 1 Cor 11:21
But if anyone is *h* .... 1 Cor 11:34
to be full and to be *h* .... Phil 4:12

HUNT
Yet you *h* my life to ..... 1 Sam 24:11
h the violent man .... Ps 140:11
h the souls of My .... Ezek 13:18

HUNTER
Nimrod the mighty *h* .... Gen 10:9
Esau was a skillful *h* ...... Gen 25:27

HUR
Man of Judah; of Caleb's house, 1 Chr 2:18–20

Supports Moses' hands, Ex 17:10–12

Aids Aaron, Ex 24:14

HURAM
Master craftsman of Solomon's temple, 1 Kin 7:13–40, 45; 2 Chr 2:13, 14

HURT
h a woman with child .... Ex 21:22
who plot my *h* .... Ps 35:4
but I was not *h* .... Prov 23:35
another to his own *h* .... Eccl 8:9
They shall not *h* .... Is 11:9
of my people I am *h* .... Jer 8:21
Woe is me for my *h* .... Jer 10:19
it will by no means *h* ..... Mark 16:18
shall not be *h* by the .... Rev 2:11

HUSBAND
She also gave to her *h* .... Gen 3:6
desire shall be for your *h* ... Gen 3:16
"Surely you are a *h* .... Ex 4:25
Uriah her *h* was dead .... 2 Sam 11:26
h safely trusts her .... Prov 31:11
Her *h* is known in the ..... Prov 31:23
your Maker is your *h* .... Is 54:5
though I was a *h* .... Jer 31:32
you will call Me "My *H* ...... Hos 2:16
I have no *h* .... John 4:17
now have is not your *h* .... John 4:18
But if the *h* dies, she is ...... Rom 7:2
woman have her own *h* ..... 1 Cor 7:2
For the unbelieving *h* ...... 1 Cor 7:14
you will save your *h* .... 1 Cor 7:16
betrothed you to one *h* .... 2 Cor 11:2
For the *h* is head of .... Eph 5:23
the *h* of one wife .... 1 Tim 3:2
a bride adorned for her *h* ... Rev 21:2

HUSBANDS
them ask their own *h* ..... 1 Cor 14:35
H, love your wives .... Eph 5:25
H, love your wives and do ... Col 3:19
Let deacons be the *h* ...... 1 Tim 3:12
women to love their *h* ...... Titus 2:4
submissive to your own *h* .... 1 Pet 3:1

HUSHAI
Archite; David's friend, 2 Sam 15:32–37

Feigns sympathy with Absalom, 2 Sam 16:16–19

Defeats Ahithophel's advice, 2 Sam 17:5–23

HYACINTH
h blue, and sulfur yellow ..... Rev 9:17

HYMENAEUS
False teacher excommunicated by Paul, 1 Tim 1:19, 20

HYMN
they had sung a *h* .... Matt 26:30

HYMNS
praying and singing *h* .... Acts 16:25
in psalms and *h* .... Eph 5:19

HYPOCRISY
you are full of *h* .... Matt 23:28
Pharisees, which is *h* .... Luke 12:1
Let love be without *h* .... Rom 12:9
away with their *h* .... Gal 2:13
and without *h* .... James 3:17
malice, all deceit, *h* .... 1 Pet 2:1

HYPOCRITE
of the *h* shall perish .... Job 8:13
and the joy of the *h* .... Job 20:5
is the hope of the *h* .... Job 27:8
for everyone is a *h* .... Is 9:17
also played the *h* .... Gal 2:13

HYPOCRITES
"But the *h* in heart .... Job 36:13
will I go in with *h* .... Ps 26:4
For you were *h* .... Jer 42:20
not be like the *h* .... Matt 6:5
do you test Me, you *h* ..... Matt 22:18
and Pharisees, *h* .... Matt 23:13

HYSSOP
Purge me with *h* .... Ps 51:7
sour wine, put it on *h* ..... John 19:29

I AM WITH YOU
do not fear, for *I*. I will .... Gen 26:24
"Behold, *I* and will keep ... Gen 28:15
Fear not, for *I*; be not .... Is 41:10
I to deliver you," says the ..... Jer 1:8
prevail against you; for *I* ... Jer 15:20
For *I*,' says the LORD, 'to .... Jer 30:11
I, to save you and deliver ... Jer 42:11
saying, "*I*, says the LORD." .. Hag 1:13
and lo, *I* always, even to .. Matt 28:20
I, and no one will attack .. Acts 18:10
absent in the flesh, yet *I* in .... Col 2:5

I WILL BE WITH YOU
"Dwell in this land, and *I* ... Gen 26:3
to your family, and *I* .... Gen 31:3
I swore to them, and *I* ..... Deut 31:23
as I was with Moses, so *I* .... Josh 1:5
"Surely *I*, and you shall .... Judg 6:16
David did, then *I* .... 1 Kin 11:38
pass through the waters, *I* .... Is 43:2

IBZAN
Judge of Israel; father of 60 children, Judg 12:8, 9

ICE
dark because of the *i* .... Job 6:16

ICHABOD
Son of Phinehas, 1 Sam 4:19–22

ICONIUM
City of Asia Minor; visited by Paul, Acts 13:51

Many converts in, Acts 14:1–6

IDDO
Leader of Jews at Casiphia, Ezra 8:17–20

——— Seer whose writings are cited, 2 Chr 9:29

IDLE
For they are *i* .... Ex 5:8
i person will suffer .... Prov 19:15
i word men may speak .... Matt 12:36
saw others standing *i* .... Matt 20:3
they learn to be *i* .... 1 Tim 5:13
both *i* talkers and .... Titus 1:10

IDLENESS
not eat the bread of *i* ..... Prov 31:27
through *i* of hands the ..... Eccl 10:18
food, and abundance of *i* .. Ezek 16:49

IDLY
They speak *i* everyone with .. Ps 12:2

IDOL
lifted up his soul to an *i* ...... Ps 24:4
if he blesses an *i* .... Is 66:3
a wooden *i* is a worthless ..... Jer 10:8
that an *i* is nothing .... 1 Cor 8:4
thing offered to an *i* .... 1 Cor 8:7
That an *i* is anything ..... 1 Cor 10:19

IDOLATER
or covetous, or an *i* .... 1 Cor 5:11
man, who is an *i* .... Eph 5:5

IDOLATERS
fornicators, nor *i* .... 1 Cor 6:9
immoral, sorcerers, *i* .... Rev 21:8
and murderers and *i* .... Rev 22:15

IDOLATRIES
and abominable *i* .... 1 Pet 4:3

IDOLATROUS
he removed the *i* priests ... 2 Kin 23:5
I have not sat with *i* mortals .. Ps 26:4
pay for your *i* sins .... Ezek 23:49
the names of the *i* priests ..... Zeph 1:4

IDOLATRY
beloved, flee from *i* .... 1 Cor 10:14
i, sorcery, hatred .... Gal 5:20
covetousness, which is *i* .... Col 3:5

IDOLS
stolen the household *i* ..... Gen 31:19
of the peoples are *i* .... Ps 96:5
i are silver and gold .... Ps 115:4
land is also full of *i* .... Is 2:8

insane with their *i* .... Jer 50:38
in the room of his *i* .... Ezek 8:12
from their wooden *i* .... Hos 4:12
who regard worthless *i* .... Jon 2:8
i speak delusion .... Zech 10:2
things polluted by *i* .... Acts 15:20
You who abhor *i* .... Rom 2:22
This was offered to *i* ..... 1 Cor 10:28
keep yourselves from *i* ... 1 John 5:21
worship demons, and *i* ...... Rev 9:20

IDUMEA
Name used by Greeks and Romans to designate Edom, Mark 3:8

IGNORANCE
unintentionally or in *i* .... Ezek 45:20
that you did it in *i* .... Acts 3:17
i God overlooked .... Acts 17:30
sins committed in *i* .... Heb 9:7
to silence the *i* .... 1 Pet 2:15

IGNORANT
I was so foolish and *i* .... Ps 73:22
though Abraham was *i* ...... Is 63:16
For they being *i* of God's ... Rom 10:3
be *i* of this mystery .... Rom 11:25
not want you to be *i* .... 1 Cor 12:1
But if anyone is *i* .... 1 Cor 14:38
i disputes, knowing that ... 2 Tim 2:23
on those who are *i* .... Heb 5:2

IGNORANTLY
because I did it *i* .... 1 Tim 1:13

IJON
Town of Naphtali; captured by Ben-Hadad, 1 Kin 15:20
Captured by Tiglath-Pileser, 2 Kin 15:29

ILL
God sent a spirit of *i* will ... Judg 9:23
David, and it became *i* ... 2 Sam 12:15
bed and pretend to be *i* ... 2 Sam 13:5
go *i* with him who is .... Job 20:26

ILLEGITIMATE
then you are *i* .... Heb 12:8

ILLUMINATED
after you were *i* .... Heb 10:32
and the earth was *i* .... Rev 18:1
for the glory of God *i* ...... Rev 21:23

ILLYRICUM
Paul preaches in, Rom 15:19

IMAGE
See WOODEN IMAGE; WOODEN IMAGES
Us make man in Our *i* ...... Gen 1:26
yourselves a carved *i* .... Deut 4:16
shall despise their *i* .... Ps 73:20
the king made an *i* .... Dan 3:1
to them, "Whose *i* .... Matt 22:20
since he is the *i* .... 1 Cor 11:7
He is the *i* of the .... Col 1:15
and not the very *i* .... Heb 10:1
the beast and his *i* .... Rev 14:9
who worshiped his *i* .... Rev 19:20

IMAGINATION
although the *i* of man's ..... Gen 8:21
the proud in the *i* .... Luke 1:51

IMITATE
I urge you, *i* me .... 1 Cor 4:16
as I also *i* Christ .... 1 Cor 11:1
i those who through .... Heb 6:12

IMMANUEL
shall call His name *I* .... Is 7:14
shall call His name *I* .... Matt 1:23

IMMEDIATELY
I the fig tree withered ..... Matt 21:19
i the Spirit drove Him ...... Mark 1:12
i they left their nets and ... Mark 1:18
hear, Satan comes *i* .... Mark 4:15
i he puts in the sickle, ... Mark 4:29
I his mouth was opened ... Luke 1:64
i her flow of blood .... Luke 8:44
stones would *i* cry out .... Luke 19:40
I sent to you *i*, and you .... Acts 10:33
i an angel of the Lord ..... Acts 12:23
I did not *i* confer with flesh .. Gal 1:16
i forgets what kind of .... James 1:24
I I was in the Spirit .... Rev 4:2

IMMORAL
lips of an *i* woman drip ..... Prov 5:3
i woman is a deep pit ..... Prov 22:14
with sexually *i* people ...... 1 Cor 5:9
murderers, sexually *i* .... Rev 21:8

IMMORALITY
except sexual *i* .... Matt 5:32
wife, except for sexual *i* .... Matt 19:9
and from sexual *i* .... Acts 15:29
unrighteousness, sexual *i* .. Rom 1:29
i as is not even named ...... 1 Cor 5:1
Flee sexual *i* .... 1 Cor 6:18
abstain from sexual *i* ..... 1 Thess 4:3
themselves over to sexual *i* .... Jude 7
to repent of her sexual *i* .... Rev 2:21

IMMORTAL
to the King eternal, *i* ...... 1 Tim 1:17

IMMORTALITY
glory, honor, and *i* .... Rom 2:7
mortal must put on *i* ..... 1 Cor 15:53
who alone has *i* .... 1 Tim 6:16
and brought life and *i* ..... 2 Tim 1:10

IMMOVABLE
be steadfast, *i* .... 1 Cor 15:58

IMMUTABLE
that by two *i* things .... Heb 6:18

IMPART
see you, that I may *i* .... Rom 1:11
that it may *i* grace .... Eph 4:29

IMPENITENT
i heart you are .... Rom 2:5

IMPERISHABLE
but we for an *i* crown ..... 1 Cor 9:25

IMPLANTED
with meekness the *i* ...... James 1:21

IMPORTED
had horses *i* from Egypt .. 1 Kin 10:28
i from Egypt a chariot ..... 2 Chr 1:17

IMPOSSIBLE
and nothing will be *i* ..... Matt 17:20
"With men this is *i* .... Matt 19:26
God nothing will be *i* ...... Luke 1:37
It is *i* that no offenses ..... Luke 17:1
For it is *i* for those who ...... Heb 6:4
which it is *i* for God to lie ... Heb 6:18
without faith it is *i* .... Heb 11:6

IMPOSTORS
i will grow worse .... 2 Tim 3:13

IMPRISONMENT
and of chains and *i* .... Heb 11:36

IMPRISONMENTS
in stripes, in *i* .... 2 Cor 6:5

IMPULSIVE
but he who is *i* .... Prov 14:29

IMPURITY
during her *i* shall be .... Lev 15:20
cleansed from her *i* .... 2 Sam 11:4
end to another with their *i* .. Ezra 9:11
a woman during her *i* ...... Ezek 18:6

IMPUTE
"Do not let my lord *i* .... 2 Sam 19:19
the LORD does not *i* .... Ps 32:2
the LORD shall not *i* .... Rom 4:8

IMPUTED
bloodshed shall be *i* .... Lev 17:4
might be *i* to them .... Rom 4:11
alone that it was *i* .... Rom 4:23
but sin is not *i* .... Rom 5:13

IMPUTES
i righteousness apart .... Rom 4:6

IN MY NAME
which He speaks *i* .... Deut 18:19
to speak a word *i* .... Deut 18:20
i his horn shall be exalted. .. Ps 89:24
prophets prophesy lies *i* .... Jer 14:14
prophesy falsely to you *i* ..... Jer 29:9
little child like this *i* .... Matt 18:5
are gathered together *i* .... Matt 18:20
many will come *i*, saying ... Matt 24:5
who works a miracle *i* .... Mark 9:39
cup of water to drink *i* .... Mark 9:41
I they will cast out .... Mark 16:17
whatever you ask *i* .... John 14:13
the Father will send *i* ..... John 14:26
you ask the Father *i* ...... John 15:16
day you will ask *i* .... John 16:26

IN THE WORLD
He was *i*, and the world .... John 1:10
"As long as I am *i*, I am ..... John 9:5
His own who were *i* .... John 13:1
I you will have .... John 16:33
"Now I am no longer *i* .... John 17:11
I was with them *i* .... John 17:12
until the law sin was *i* ..... Rom 5:13
an idol is nothing *i* .... 1 Cor 8:4
we conducted ourselves *i* .. 2 Cor 1:12
no hope and without God *i* .. Eph 2:12
you shine as lights *i* .... Phil 2:15
why, as though living *i* ...... Col 2:20
believed on *i*, received .... 1 Tim 3:16
the corruption that is *i* ...... 2 Pet 1:4
the world or the things *i* .. 1 John 2:15
greater than he who is *i* ... 1 John 4:4

INCENSE
oil and for the sweet *i* .... Ex 25:6
lamps, he shall burn *i* on it ... Ex 30:7
perpetual *i* before the LORD .. Ex 30:8
the pure *i* of sweet spices, ... Ex 37:29
the cloud of *i* may cover ... Lev 16:13
put *i* in it, and each of .... Num 16:17
burned *i* at the high places .. 1 Kin 3:3
be set before You as *i* .... Ps 141:2
i is an abomination to Me ..... Is 1:13
i to the queen of heaven .... Jer 44:18
oil and My *i* before them .. Ezek 16:18
In every place *i* shall be ..... Mal 1:11
his lot fell to burn *i* when ... Luke 1:9
right side of the altar of *i* .. Luke 1:11
golden bowls full of *i* .... Rev 5:8
the smoke of the *i*, with ...... Rev 8:4
cinnamon and *i*, fragrant .. Rev 18:13

INCLINE
i your heart to the .... Josh 24:23
I Your ear to me, and hear ... Ps 17:6
I Your ear to my cry .... Ps 88:2
I my heart to Your .... Ps 119:36
i my heart to any evil .... Ps 141:4
i your ear to my sayings ... Prov 4:20
not obey Me or *i* their ear .... Jer 7:26
O my God, *i* Your ear and .. Dan 9:18

INCORRUPTIBLE
the glory of the *i* .... Rom 1:23
dead will be raised *i* ..... 1 Cor 15:52
to an inheritance *i* .... 1 Pet 1:4
corruptible seed but *i* ...... 1 Pet 1:23
i beauty of a gentle .... 1 Pet 3:4

INCORRUPTION
it is raised in *i* .... 1 Cor 15:42
corruption inherit *i* .... 1 Cor 15:50
must put on *i* .... 1 Cor 15:53

INCREASE
if riches *i*, do not set .... Ps 62:10
the LORD give you *i* .... Ps 115:14
hear and *i* learning .... Prov 1:5
When goods *i*, they .... Eccl 5:11
Of the *i* of His .... Is 9:7
and knowledge shall *i* ...... Dan 12:4

Lord, "*I* our faith . . . Luke 17:5
He must *i*, but I must . . . John 3:30
but God gave the *i* . . . 1 Cor 3:6
grows with the *i* . . . Col 2:19
for they will *i* . . . 2 Tim 2:16

INCREASED
The waters *i* and . . . Gen 7:17
i your mercy which you . . Gen 19:19
nation and *i* its joy . . . Is 9:3
And Jesus *i* in wisdom . . . Luke 2:52

INCREASES
i knowledge *i* sorrow . . . Eccl 1:18
who have no might He *i* . . . Is 40:29

INCREDIBLE
should it be thought *i* . . . Acts 26:8

INCURABLE
My wound is *i* . . . Job 34:6
'Your affliction is *i* . . . Jer 30:12
Your sorrow is *i* . . . Jer 30:15

INDEBTED
everyone who is *i* . . . Luke 11:4

INDEED
i it was very good . . . Gen 1:31
"But will God *i* . . . 1 Kin 8:27
"Behold, an Israelite *i* . . . John 1:47

INDIA
Eastern limit of Persian Empire, Esth 1:1

INDICATING
the Holy Spirit *i* . . . Heb 9:8
who was in them was *i* . . . 1 Pet 1:11

INDIGNANT
saw it, they were *i* . . . Matt 26:8

INDIGNATION
of His anger, wrath, *i* . . . Ps 78:49
I has taken hold . . . Ps 119:53
in whose hand is My *i* . . . Is 10:5
For the *i* of the LORD . . . Is 34:2
have filled me with *i* . . . Jer 15:17
can stand before His *i* . . . Nah 1:6
i which will devour . . . Heb 10:27
into the cup of His *i* . . . Rev 14:10

INDIVIDUALLY
He fashions their hearts *i* . . . Ps 33:15
i members of one another . . Rom 12:5
Christ, and members *i* . . . 1 Cor 12:27

INDUCED
O LORD, You *i* me . . . Jer 20:7
if the prophet is *i* . . . Ezek 14:9

INDULGENCE
no value against the *i* . . . Col 2:23

INEXCUSABLE
Therefore you are *i* . . . Rom 2:1

INEXPRESSIBLE
Paradise and heard *i* . . . 2 Cor 12:4
you rejoice with joy *i* . . . 1 Pet 1:8

INFALLIBLE
suffering by many *i* . . . Acts 1:3

INFANTS
i who never saw . . . Job 3:16
i You have ordained . . . Ps 8:2
i You have perfected . . . Matt 21:16
they also brought *i* . . . Luke 18:15

INFERIOR
another kingdom *i* . . . Dan 2:39
that I am not at all *i* . . . 2 Cor 11:5

INFIRMITIES
"He Himself took our *i* . . . Matt 8:17
boast, except in my *i* . . . 2 Cor 12:5
and your frequent *i* . . . 1 Tim 5:23

INFIRMITY
a spirit of *i* eighteen . . . Luke 13:11
had an *i* thirty-eight years . . John 5:5
i I preached the gospel to . . . Gal 4:13

INFLAMING
i yourselves with gods . . . Is 57:5

INGATHERING
the Feast of *I* at the year's . . Ex 34:22

INHABIT
the wicked will not *i* . . . Prov 10:30
cities and *i* them . . . Amos 9:14

INHABITANT
Cry out and shout, O *i* . . . Is 12:6
And the *i* will not say . . . Is 33:24

INHABITANTS
He looks on all the *i* . . . Ps 33:14
give ear, all *i* . . . Ps 49:1
Let the *i* of Sela sing . . . Is 42:11
Woe to the *i* of the . . . Rev 12:12

INHABITED
rejoicing in His *i* . . . Prov 8:31
'You shall be *i* . . . Is 44:26
who formed it to be *i* . . . Is 45:18

INHERIT
i the iniquities . . . Job 13:26
descendants shall *i* . . . Ps 25:13
The righteous shall *i* . . . Ps 37:29
The wise shall *i* . . . Prov 3:35
love me to *i* wealth . . . Prov 8:21
The simple *i* folly . . . Prov 14:18
the blameless will *i* . . . Prov 28:10
i the kingdom prepared . . . Matt 25:34
I do that I may *i* . . . Mark 10:17
unrighteous will not *i* . . . 1 Cor 6:9
you may *i* a blessing . . . 1 Pet 3:9
who overcomes shall *i* . . . Rev 21:7

INHERITANCE
"You shall have no *i* . . . Num 18:20
is the place of His *i* . . . Deut 32:9
the portion of my *i* . . . Ps 16:5
yes, I have a good *i* . . . Ps 16:6
i shall be forever . . . Ps 37:18
He will choose our *i* . . . Ps 47:4
You confirmed Your *i* . . . Ps 68:9
the tribe of Your *i* . . . Ps 74:2
i gained hastily . . . Prov 20:21
right of *i* is yours . . . Jer 32:8
i has been turned . . . Lam 5:2
will arise to your *i* . . . Dan 12:13
And God gave him no *i* . . . Acts 7:5
and give you an *i* . . . Acts 20:32
For if the *i* is of the . . . Gal 3:18
we have obtained an *i* . . . Eph 1:11
be partakers of the *i* . . . Col 1:12
receive as an *i* . . . Heb 11:8
to an *i* incorruptible . . . 1 Pet 1:4

INIQUITIES
How many are my *i* . . . Job 13:23
i have overtaken me . . . Ps 40:12
I prevail against me . . . Ps 65:3
forgives all your *i* . . . Ps 103:3
LORD, should mark *i* . . . Ps 130:3
was bruised for our *i* . . . Is 53:5
He shall bear their *i* . . . Is 53:11
i have separated you . . . Is 59:2

INIQUITY
See WORKERS OF INIQUITY
God, visiting the *i* of the . . . Ex 20:5
He has not observed *i* . . . Num 23:21
wicked brings forth *i* . . . Ps 7:14
O LORD, pardon my *i* . . . Ps 25:11
i I have not hidden . . . Ps 32:5
was brought forth in *i* . . . Ps 51:5
If I regard *i* in my . . . Ps 66:18
Add *i* to their *i* . . . Ps 69:27
workers of *i* flourish . . . Ps 92:7
i boast in themselves . . . Ps 94:4
Shall the throne of *i* . . . Ps 94:20
let no *i* have dominion . . . Ps 119:133
i will reap sorrow . . . Prov 22:8
a people laden with *i* . . . Is 1:4
i is taken away . . . Is 6:7
has laid on Him the *i* . . . Is 53:6
will remember their *i* . . . Hos 9:9
to those who devise *i* . . . Mic 2:1
like You, pardoning *i* . . . Mic 7:18
all you workers of *i* . . . Luke 13:27
a fire, a world of *i* . . . James 3:6

INJUSTICE
of truth and without *i* . . . Deut 32:4
i shuts her mouth . . . Job 5:16
i have your fathers . . . Jer 2:5

INK
us, written not with *i* . . . 2 Cor 3:3
do so with paper and *i* . . . 2 John 12

INN
room for them in the *i* . . . Luke 2:7
brought him to an *i* . . . Luke 10:34

INNOCENCE
of my heart and *i* . . . Gen 20:5
washed my hands in *i* . . . Ps 73:13

INNOCENT
do not kill the *i* . . . Ex 23:7
a bribe to slay an *i* . . . Deut 27:25
i will divide the . . . Job 27:17
a bribe against the *i* . . . Ps 15:5
because I was found *i* . . . Dan 6:22
by betraying *i* blood . . . Matt 27:4
saying, "I am *i* . . . Matt 27:24
this day that I am *i* . . . Acts 20:26

INNOCENT BLOOD
"lest *i* be shed in the . . . Deut 19:10
against *i*, to kill David . . . 1 Sam 19:5
the *i* which Joab shed . . . 1 Kin 2:31
shed very much *i* . . . 2 Kin 21:16
righteous, and condemn *i* . . . Ps 94:21
And shed *i*, the blood . . . Ps 106:38
tongue, hands that shed *i* . . Prov 6:17
they make haste to shed *i* . . . Is 59:7
do not shed *i* in this place . . . Jer 7:6
you will surely bring *i* . . . Jer 26:15
for they have shed *i* . . . Joel 3:19
do not charge us with *i* . . . Jon 1:14
sinned by betraying *i* . . . Matt 27:4

INNUMERABLE
i as the sand which is . . . Heb 11:12
i company of angels . . . Heb 12:22

INQUIRE
went to *i* of the LORD . . . Gen 25:22
a man went to *i* of God . . . 1 Sam 9:9
I may go to her and *i* . . . 1 Sam 28:7
sent you to Me to *i* of Me . . . Jer 37:7
i who in it is worthy . . . Matt 10:11
to *i* more fully about him . . Acts 23:20

INQUIRED
children of Israel *i* . . . Judg 20:27
Therefore David *i* . . . 1 Sam 23:2
the LORD, nor *i* of Him . . . Zeph 1:6
the prophets have *i* . . . 1 Pet 1:10

INQUIRY
shall make careful *i* . . . Deut 19:18

INSANE
images, and they are *i* . . . Jer 50:38
the spiritual man is *i* . . . Hos 9:7

INSCRIBED
Oh, that they were *i* . . . Job 19:23
See, I have *i* you on . . . Is 49:16

INSCRIPTION
wrote on it an *i* like the . . . Ex 39:30
image and *i* is this . . . Matt 22:20
the *i* of His accusation . . . Mark 15:26
found an altar with this *i* . . Acts 17:23

INSPIRATION
is given by *i* of God . . . 2 Tim 3:16

INSTRUCT
good Spirit to *i* them . . . Neh 9:20
I will *i* you and teach . . . Ps 32:8
is the man whom You *i* . . . Ps 94:12

Jacob rejoice and *I* be glad . . . Ps 14:7
Redeem *I,* O God, out of . . . . . Ps 25:22
Truly God is good to *I* . . . . Ps 73:1
O *I,* if you will listen to Me . . . Ps 81:8
When *I* went out of Egypt, . . . Ps 114:1
Let *I* now say, "His mercy . . . Ps 118:2
O *I,* hope in the LORD . . . . Ps 130:7
Let *I* rejoice in their Maker . . Ps 149:2
will shepherd My people *I* . . . Matt 2:6
great faith, not even in *I* . . . . Matt 8:10
sheep of the house of *I* . . . . . Matt 10:6
the twelve tribes of *I* . . . . . . Matt 19:28
If He is the King of *I,* let . . Matt 27:42
helped His servant *I* . . . . Luke 1:54
of his manifestation to *I* . . . Luke 1:80
Are you the teacher of *I,* . . . John 3:10
restore the kingdom to *I* . . . . . Acts 1:6
God raised up for *I* a . . . . . . Acts 13:23
because for the hope of *I* . . Acts 28:20
For they are not all *I* . . . . Rom 9:6
so all *I* will be saved . . . . . . Rom 11:26
Observe *I* after the flesh . . 1 Cor 10:18
and upon the *I* of God . . . . Gal 6:16
eighth day, of the stock of *I* . . Phil 3:5
with the house of *I* . . . . Heb 8:8
children of *I* were sealed . . . . . Rev 7:4
tribes of the children of *I* . . Rev 21:12

ISRAELITES
Afflicted in Egypt, Ex 1:12–22
Escape from Egypt, Ex 12:29–42, 50; 13:17–22
Receive law at Sinai, Ex 19
Idolatry and rebellion of, Ex 32; Num 13; 14
Wander in the wilderness, Num 14:26–39
Cross Jordan; conquer Canaan, Josh 4; 12
Ruled by judges, Judg 2
Saul chosen as king, 1 Sam 10
Kingdom divided, 1 Kin 12
Northern kingdom carried captive, 2 Kin 17
Southern kingdom carried captive, 2 Kin 24
70 years in exile, 2 Chr 36:20, 21
Return after exile, Ezra 1:1–5
Nation rejects Christ, Matt 27:20–27
Nation destroyed, Luke 21:20–24

ISSACHAR
Jacob's fifth son, Gen 30:17, 18
—— Tribe of:
Genealogy of, 1 Chr 7:1–5
Prophecy concerning, Gen 49:14, 15
Census at Sinai, Num 1:28, 29
Inheritance of, Josh 19:17–23

ISSUED
King Darius *i* a decree . . . . . . Ezra 6:1
be *i* as law in every . . . . Esth 3:14
i as a decree in every . . . . Esth 8:13
A fiery stream *i* and came . . . Dan 7:10
before the decree is *i,* . . . . Zeph 2:2

IT IS WRITTEN
as *i* in the Law of Moses . . . . 1 Kin 2:3
as *i* in this Book of . . . . 2 Kin 23:21
Feast of Tabernacles, as *i* . . . . Ezra 3:4
trees, to make booths, as *i* . . Neh 8:15
in the scroll of the Book *i* . . . . . Ps 40:7
"Behold, *i* before Me: I will . . . . Is 65:6
"As *i* in the Law of Moses . . . Dan 9:13
for thus *i* by the prophet: . . . . Matt 2:5
"*I,* 'Man shall not live by . . . . Matt 4:4
throw Yourself down. For *i* . . Matt 4:6
"*I* again, 'You shall not . . . . . . Matt 4:7
i, 'You shall worship . . . . Matt 4:10
"For this is he of whom *i* . . Matt 11:10
"*I,* 'My house shall be . . . . . Matt 21:13
i: 'I will strike the . . . . Matt 26:31
"Thus *i,* and thus it was . . . Luke 24:46
"*I* in the prophets, 'And . . . . John 6:45
i in the book of Psalms . . . . . . Acts 1:20
i, 'You shall not speak . . . . . Acts 23:5
volume of the book *i* . . . . Heb 10:7
because *i,* "Be holy, for . . . . . 1 Pet 1:16

ITALIAN
was called the *I* Regiment . . Acts 10:1

ITALY
Jews expelled from, Acts 18:2
Paul sails for, Acts 27:1, 6
Christians in, Acts 28:14

ITCHING
they have *i* ears . . . . 2 Tim 4:3

ITHAMAR
Youngest son of Aaron, Ex 6:23
Consecrated as priest, Ex 28:1
Duty entrusted to, Ex 38:21
Jurisdiction over Gershonites and Merarites, Num 4:21–33

ITINERANT
i Jewish exorcists . . . . Acts 19:13

ITUREA
Region ruled by Herod Philip, Luke 3:1

IVORY
made a great throne of *i* . . 1 Kin 10:18
Out of the *i* palaces . . . . Ps 45:8
neck is like an *i* tower . . . . . . Song 7:4
lie on beds of *i,* stretch . . . . . Amos 6:4

JABBOK
River entering the Jordan about 20 miles north of the Dead Sea, Num 21:24
Scene of Jacob's conflict, Gen 32:22–32
Boundary marker, Deut 3:16

JABESH GILEAD
Consigned to destruction, Judg 21:8–15
Saul defeats the Ammonites at, 1 Sam 11:1–11
Citizens of, rescue Saul's body, 1 Sam 31:11–13
David thanks citizens of, 2 Sam 2:4–7

JABIN
Canaanite king of Hazor; leads confederacy against Joshua, Josh 11:1–14
—— Another king of Hazor; oppresses Israelites, Judg 4:2
Defeated by Deborah and Barak, Judg 4:3–24
Immortalized in poetry, Judg 5:1–31

JACHIN
One of two pillars in front of Solomon's temple, 1 Kin 7:21, 22

JACINTH
third row, a *j,* an agate, ... Ex 28:19
the eleventh *j* . . . . Rev 21:20

JACKALS
it shall be a habitation of *j* . . . Is 34:13
make a wailing like the *j* . . . . . Mic 1:8

JACOB
Son of Isaac and Rebekah; Rebekah's favorite, Gen 25:21–28
Obtains birthright, Gen 25:29–34
Obtains blessing meant for Esau; flees, Gen 27:1—28:5
Sees vision of ladder, Gen 28:10–22
Serves Laban for Rachel and Leah, Gen 29:1–30
Fathers children, Gen 29:31—30:24
Flees from, makes covenant with Laban, Gen 30:25—31:55
Makes peace with Esau, Gen 32:1–21; 33:1–17
Wrestles with God, Gen 32:22–32
Returns to Bethel; renamed Israel, Gen 35:1–15
Shows preference for Joseph, Gen 37:3
Mourns Joseph's disappearance, Gen 37:32–35
Sends sons to Egypt for food, Gen 42:1–5
Reluctantly allows Benjamin to go, Gen 43:1–15
Moves his household to Egypt, Gen 45:25—47:12
Blesses his sons and grandsons; dies, Gen 48; 49
Buried in Canaan, Gen 50:1–14

JACOB'S WELL
Christ teaches a Samaritan woman at, John 4:5–26

JAEL
Wife of Heber the Kenite; kills Sisera, Judg 4:17–22
Praised by Deborah, Judg 5:24–27

JAIR
Manassite warrior; conquers towns in Gilead, Num 32:41; Deut 3:14
—— Eighth judge of Israel, Judg 10:3–5

JAIRUS
Ruler of the synagogue; Jesus raises his daughter, Mark 5:22–24, 35–43

JAMES
Son of Zebedee, called as disciple, Matt 4:21, 22; Luke 5:10, 11
One of the Twelve, Matt 10:2; Mark 3:17
Zealous for the Lord, Luke 9:52–54
Ambitious for honor, Mark 10:35–45
Witnesses transfiguration, Matt 17:1–9
Martyred by Herod Agrippa, Acts 12:2
—— Son of Alphaeus; one of the Twelve, Matt 10:3, 4
Called "the Less," Mark 15:40
—— Jesus' half brother, Matt 13:55, 56; Gal 1:19
Becomes leader of Jerusalem Council and Jerusalem church, Acts 15:13–22; Gal 2:9
Author of an epistle, James 1:1

JANNES AND JAMBRES
Two Egyptian magicians; oppose Moses, Ex 7:11–22; 2 Tim 3:8

JANOAH
Town of Naphtali, 2 Kin 15:29

JAPHETH
One of Noah's three sons, Gen 5:32
Receives blessing, Gen 9:20–27
His descendants occupy Asia Minor and Europe, Gen 10:2–5

JARED
Father of Enoch, Gen 5:15–20
Ancestor of Noah, 1 Chr 1:2
Ancestor of Christ, Luke 3:37

JASHER
Book of, quoted, Josh 10:13

JASON
Welcomes Paul at Thessalonica, Acts 17:5–9
Described as Paul's kinsman, Rom 16:21

JASPER
a beryl, an onyx, and a *j* . . . . Ex 28:20
beryl, onyx, and *j* . . . . Ezek 28:13
stone, like a *j* stone, clear . . Rev 21:11

JAVAN
Son of Japheth, Gen 10:2, 4
Descendants of, to receive good news, Is 66:19, 20

JAVELINS
bows and arrows, the *j* . . . . . Ezek 39:9

JAW
or pierce his *j* with a hook . . Job 41:2

JAWBONE
a fresh *j* of a donkey . . . . . . Judg 15:15

JAWS
My tongue clings to My *j* . . . . Ps 22:15
bridle in the *j* of the people . . Is 30:28
I will put hooks in your *j* . . . Ezek 29:4
put hooks into your *j* . . . . . . Ezek 38:4

JEALOUS
your God, am a *j* God . . . . Ex 20:5
LORD, whose name is *J* . . . . . . Ex 34:14
he becomes *j* of his wife, . . . Num 5:14
a consuming fire, a *j* . . . . Deut 4:24
I will be *j* for My holy . . . . Ezek 39:25
For I am *j* for you . . . . 2 Cor 11:2

JEALOUSY
They provoked Him to *j* . . . Deut 32:16
Will Your *j* burn like . . . . Ps 79:5
j is a husband's . . . . Prov 6:34
as strong as death, *j* . . . . Song 8:6
will provoke you to *j* . . . . . . Rom 10:19
fall, to provoke them to *j* . . Rom 11:11
provoke the Lord to *j* . . . . 1 Cor 10:22
for you with godly *j* . . . . 2 Cor 11:2

JEBUS
Canaanite name of Jerusalem before captured by David, 1 Chr 11:4–8

JEBUSITES
Descendants of Canaan, Gen 15:18–21; Num 13:29
Defeated by Joshua, Josh 11:1–12
Not driven from Jerusalem; later conquered by David, Judg 1:21; 2 Sam 5:6–8
Put to forced labor under Solomon, 1 Kin 9:20, 21

JECONIAH
See JEHOIACHIN
Variant form of Jehoiachin, 1 Chr 3:16, 17
Abbreviated to Coniah, Jer 22:24, 28

JEDIDIAH
Name given to Solomon by Nathan, 2 Sam 12:24, 25

JEDUTHUN
Levite musician appointed by David, 1 Chr 16:41, 42
Heads a family of musicians, 2 Chr 5:12
Name appears in psalm titles, Ps 39; 62; 77

JEGAR SAHADUTHA
Name given by Laban to memorial stones, Gen 31:46, 47

JEHOAHAZ
Son and successor of Jehu, king of Israel, 2 Kin 10:35
Seeks the Lord in defeat, 2 Kin 13:2–9
——— Son and successor of Josiah, king of Judah, 2 Kin 23:30–34
Called Shallum, 1 Chr 3:15
——— Another form of Ahaziah, youngest son of King Joram, 2 Chr 21:17

JEHOASH
See JOASH

JEHOIACHIN
Son of Jehoiakim; next to the last king of Judah, 2 Kin 24:8
Deported to Babylon, 2 Kin 24:8–16
Liberated by Evil-Merodach, Jer 52:31–34

JEHOIADA
High priest during reign of Joash, 2 Kin 11:4—12:16
Instructs Joash, 2 Kin 12:2

JEHOIAKIM
Wicked king of Judah; son of Josiah; serves Pharaoh and Nebuchadnezzar, 2 Kin 23:34—24:7
Taken captive to Babylon, 2 Chr 36:6–8
Kills prophet Urijah, Jer 26:20–23
Destroys Jeremiah's scroll; cursed by God, Jer 36

JEHORAM (or Joram)
Wicked king of Judah; son of Jehoshaphat, 2 Kin 8:16–24
Marries Athaliah, 2 Kin 8:18, 19
Kills his brothers, 2 Chr 21:2, 4
Elijah prophesies against him; prophecy fulfilled, 2 Chr 21:12–20
——— Wicked king of Israel; son of Ahab, 2 Kin 3:1–3
Counseled by Elisha, 2 Kin 3; 5:8; 6:8–12
Wounded in battle, 2 Kin 8:28, 29
Killed by Jehu, 2 Kin 9:14–26

JEHOSHAPHAT
Righteous king of Judah; son of Asa, 1 Kin 22:41–50
Goes to war with Ahab against Syria, 1 Kin 22:1–36
Institutes reforms; sends out teachers of the Law, 2 Chr 17:6–9; 19
His enemies defeated through his faith, 2 Chr 20:1–30

JEHOZABAD
Son of a Moabitess; assassinates Joash, 2 Kin 12:20, 21
Put to death, 2 Chr 25:3

JEHU
Prophet; denounces Baasha, 1 Kin 16:1–7
Rebukes Jehoshaphat, 2 Chr 19:2, 3
——— Commander under Ahab; anointed king, 1 Kin 19:16; 2 Kin 9:1–13
Destroys the house of Ahab, 2 Kin 9:14—10:30
Turns away from the Lord; dies, 2 Kin 10:31–36

JEHUDI
Reads Jeremiah's scroll, Jer 36:14, 21, 23

JEOPARDY
stand in *j* every hour . . . . . 1 Cor 15:30

JEPHTHAH
Gilead's son by a harlot, Judg 11:1
Driven out, then brought back to command army against Ammonites, Judg 11:2–28
Sacrifices his daughter to fulfill a vow, Judg 11:29–40
Chastises Ephraim, Judg 12:1–7

JEREMIAH
Prophet under Josiah, Jehoiakim, and Zedekiah, Jer 1:1–3
Called by God, Jer 1:4–9
Forbidden to marry, Jer 16:2
Imprisoned by Pashhur, Jer 20:1–6
Prophecy written, destroyed, rewritten, Jer 36
Accused of defection and imprisoned; released by Zedekiah, Jer 37
Cast into dungeon; rescued; prophesies to Zedekiah, Jer 38
Set free by Nebuchadnezzar, Jer 39:11—40:6
Forcibly taken to Egypt, Jer 43:5–7

JERICHO
City near the Jordan, Num 22:1
Called the city of palm trees, Deut 34:3; 2 Chr 28:15
Miraculously defeated by Joshua, Josh 6
Rebuilt by Hiel, 1 Kin 16:34
Visited by Jesus, Matt 20:29–34; Luke 19:1–10

JEROBOAM
Son of Nebat; receives prophecy that he will be king, 1 Kin 11:26–40
Made king; leads revolt against Rehoboam, 1 Kin 12:1–24
Sets up idols, 1 Kin 12:25–33
Rebuked by a man of God, 1 Kin 13:1–10
Judgment on house of, 1 Kin 13:33—14:20
——— Wicked king of Israel; son of Joash; successful in war, 2 Kin 14:23–29
Prophecy concerning, Amos 7:7–13

JERUBBAAL
Name given to Gideon for destroying Baal's altar, Judg 6:32

JERUSALEM
Originally called Salem, Gen 14:18
Jebusite city, Josh 15:8; Judg 1:8, 21
King of, defeated by Joshua, Josh 10:5–23
Conquered by David; made capital, 2 Sam 5:6–9
Ark brought to, 2 Sam 6:12–17; 1 Kin 8:1–13
Saved from plague, 2 Sam 24:16
Temple built and dedicated here, 1 Kin 6; 8:14–66
Suffers in war, 1 Kin 14:25–27; 2 Kin 14:13, 14; Is 7:1
Miraculously saved, 2 Kin 19:31–36
Captured by Babylon, 2 Kin 24:10—25:21; Jer 39:1–8
Exiles return and rebuild temple, Ezra 1:1–4; 2:1
Walls of, dedicated, Neh 12:27–47
Christ enters as King, Matt 21:4–11
Christ laments for, Matt 23:37; Luke 19:41–44
Church born in, Acts 2
Christians of, persecuted, Acts 4

Jebusite city (which is *J*) . . . Josh 15:8
in *J* he reigned . . . . 2 Sam 5:5
were born to him in *J* . . . . . 2 Sam 5:14
ark of God back to *J* . . . . 2 Sam 15:29
yourself a house in *J* . . . . . . 1 Kin 2:36
a lamp before Me in *J* . . . . . 1 Kin 11:36
Solomon reigned in *J* . . . . . 1 Kin 11:42
Rehoboam came to *J* . . . . . 1 Kin 12:21
gave him a lamp in *J* . . . . . . 1 Kin 15:4
down the wall of *J* from . . 2 Kin 14:13
up to *J* to make war . . . . 2 Kin 16:5
before this altar in *J*' . . . . 2 Kin 18:22
should deliver *J* from . . . . 2 Kin 18:35
J shall not be given into . . 2 Kin 19:10
daughter of *J* has . . . . 2 Kin 19:21
I will stretch over *J* the . . . 2 Kin 21:13
(She dwelt in *J* in the . . . 2 Kin 22:14
elders of Judah and *J* to . . . 2 Kin 23:1
burned them outside *J* . . . . . 2 Kin 23:4
from *J* to Babylon . . . . 2 Kin 24:15
his army came against *J* . . . 2 Kin 25:1
the walls of *J* all around . . 2 Kin 25:10
J into captivity by the . . . . 1 Chr 6:15
house of the LORD in *J* . . . . 1 Chr 6:32
Now in *J* the children of . . . . 1 Chr 9:3
and all Israel went to *J* . . . . 1 Chr 11:4
took more wives in *J* . . . . . . 1 Chr 14:3

all Israel together at *J*, to . . 1 Chr 15:3
angel to *J* to destroy it . . . 1 Chr 21:15
they may dwell in *J* . . . . . . 1 Chr 23:25
David assembled at *J* all . . 1 Chr 28:1
gold as common in *J* as . . . 2 Chr 1:15
the LORD at *J* on Mount . . . . 2 Chr 3:1
Solomon reigned in *J* . . . . . 2 Chr 9:30
So Rehoboam dwelt in *J*, . . 2 Chr 11:5
of Judah and came to *J* . . . . 2 Chr 12:4
him in the city, in *J* . . . . 2 Chr 28:27
the altars that were in *J* . . 2 Chr 30:14
against the God of *J* . . . . . 2 Chr 32:19
the inhabitants of *J* . . . . . . 2 Chr 32:26
to *J* into his kingdom . . . . 2 Chr 33:13
and the inhabitants of *J* . . 2 Chr 35:18
of the LORD which is in *J* . . . Ezra 2:68
together as one man to *J* . . . Ezra 3:1
out of the captivity to *J* . . . . . . Ezra 3:8
the temple which is in *J* . . . . Ezra 6:5
to bring them to *J* to the . . . . Ezra 8:30
a wall in Judah and *J* . . . . . . Ezra 9:9
that they must gather at *J* . . Ezra 10:7
I came to *J* and was there . . Neh 2:11
let us build the wall of *J* . . . . Neh 2:17
to come and attack *J* . . . . Neh 4:8
it was, at the gates of *J* . . . . Neh 13:19
build the walls of *J* . . . . Ps 51:18
In the midst of you, O *J* . . . . Ps 116:19
J is built as a city that is . . . . Ps 122:3
If I forget you, O *J*, let my . . . Ps 137:5
The LORD builds up *J* . . . . Ps 147:2
was king over Israel in *J* . . . . . Eccl 1:12
you, O daughters of *J* . . . . . . Song 5:8
as Tirzah, lovely as *J*, ... Song 6:4
snare to the inhabitants of *J* . . . Is 8:14
of Zion, the hill of *J* . . . . Is 10:32
numbered the houses of *J* . . . . Is 22:10
watchmen on your walls, O *J* . . Is 62:6
a wilderness, *J* a desolation . . Is 64:10
yes, proclaim against *J*, ... Jer 4:16
Be instructed, O *J*, lest My . . . . Jer 6:8
will make *J* a heap of ruins . . Jer 9:11
the cry of *J* has gone up . . . . . Jer 14:2
reigned eleven years in *J* . . . . Jer 52:1
J has become an unclean . . . Lam 1:17
and portray on it a city, *J* . . . Ezek 4:1
me in visions of God to *J* . . . . Ezek 8:3
Oholah, and *J* is Oholibah . . Ezek 23:4
build *J* until Messiah the . . . . Dan 9:25
then *J* shall be holy, and . . . . Joel 3:17
utters His voice from *J* . . . . Amos 1:2
The captives of *J* who are . . . Obad 20
You not have mercy on *J* . . Zech 1:12
To measure *J*, to see what . . . Zech 2:2
again in her own place—*J*. . Zech 12:6
to *J* to worship the King . . Zech 14:17
from the East came to *J* . . . . . Matt 2:1
that He must go to *J* . . . . . Matt 16:21
O *J*, *J*, the one who . . . . Matt 23:37
we are going up to *J* . . . . . Mark 10:33
Jesus lingered behind in *J* . Luke 2:43
you see *J* surrounded . . . . . Luke 21:20
Daughters of *J*, do not . . . . Luke 23:28
but tarry in the city of *J* . . Luke 24:49
J before the Passover . . . . . John 11:55
be witnesses to Me in *J* . . . . . . Acts 1:8
were gathered together at *J* . . Acts 4:6
you have filled *J* with . . . . . . Acts 5:28
Lord, they returned to *J* . . . . Acts 8:25
bring them bound to *J* . . . . . . Acts 9:2
when Saul had come to *J* . . . Acts 9:26
when Peter came up to *J* . . . Acts 11:2
came from *J* to Antioch . . . Acts 11:27
bound in the spirit to *J* . . . . Acts 20:22
shall the Jews at *J* bind . . . Acts 21:11
I went up to *J* to worship . . Acts 24:11
he was willing to go to *J* . . Acts 25:20
the saints who are in *J* . . . . Rom 15:26
to bear your gift to *J* . . . . . . 1 Cor 16:3
corresponds to *J* which . . . . . Gal 4:25
city of My God, the New *J* . . Rev 3:12
saw the holy city, New *J* . . . . Rev 21:2

JESHIMON
Wilderness west of the Dead Sea, 1 Sam 23:19, 24

JESHUA (or Joshua)
Postexilic high priest; returns with Zerubbabel, Ezra 2:2
Aids in rebuilding temple, Ezra 3:2–8
Also called Joshua; seen in vision, Zech 3:1–10

JESHURUN
Poetic name of endearment for Israel, Deut 32:15

JESSE
Grandson of Ruth and Boaz, Ruth 4:17–22
Father of David, 1 Sam 16:1–13
Mentioned in prophecy, Is 11:1, 10

JESTING
talking, nor coarse *j* . . . . Eph 5:4

JESUS
See CHRIST; LORD JESUS CHRIST
birth of *J* Christ was as . . . . Matt 1:18
shall call His name *J* . . . . Matt 1:21
J was led up by the . . . . Matt 4:1
These twelve *J* sent . . . . Matt 10:5
and laid hands on *J* . . . . . . Matt 26:50
Barabbas and destroy *J* . . . Matt 27:20
we to do with You, *J* . . . . . . Mark 1:24
J withdrew with His . . . . Mark 3:7
J said, "Do not forbid . . . . . Mark 9:39
J went into Jerusalem . . . . Mark 11:11
as they were eating, *J* . . . . Mark 14:22
and he delivered *J* . . . . . . Mark 15:15
J increased in wisdom . . . . . Luke 2:52
J said, "Who touched . . . . . . Luke 8:45
J rebuked the unclean . . . . . Luke 9:42
J said to him, "Foxes . . . . . . Luke 9:58
sought to see who *J* was . . Luke 19:3
near to *J* to kiss Him . . . . . Luke 22:47
J Himself stood in the . . . . Luke 24:36
truth came through *J* . . . . . . John 1:17
J said to him, "Rise, take . . . . John 5:8
J lifted up His eyes . . . . John 6:5
they saw *J* walking on . . . . . John 6:19
But *J* stooped down and . . . . . John 8:6
J wept . . . . John 11:35
anointed the feet of *J* . . . . . . John 12:3
J was crucified . . . . John 19:20
other things that *J* did . . . John 21:25
This *J* God has raised . . . . . . Acts 2:32
of Your holy Servant *J* . . . . . . Acts 4:30
believed on the Lord *J* . . . . Acts 11:17
baptized into Christ *J* . . . . Rom 6:3
Spirit of life in Christ *J* . . . . . . Rom 8:2
your mouth the Lord *J* . . . . . Rom 10:9
among you except *J* . . . . 1 Cor 2:2
the day of the Lord *J* . . . . 1 Cor 5:5
heavenly places in Christ *J* . . . Eph 2:6
that at the name of *J* every . . Phil 2:10
perfect in Christ *J* . . . . Col 1:28
exhort in the Lord *J* . . . . . 1 Thess 4:1
But we see *J*, who was . . . . . . Heb 2:9
J the Son of God, let us . . . . . Heb 4:14
looking unto *J*, the author . . . Heb 12:2
J Christ the righteous . . . . . 1 John 2:1
that *J* is the Son of God . . . 1 John 5:5
Revelation of *J* Christ . . . . Rev 1:1
Even so, come, Lord *J* . . . . . Rev 22:20

JETHER
Gideon's oldest son, Judg 8:20, 21

JETHRO
Priest of Midian; becomes Moses' father-in-law, Ex 2:16–22
Blesses Moses' departure, Ex 4:18
Visits and counsels Moses, Ex 18
Also called Reuel, Num 10:29

JEW
J whose name was . . . . Esth 2:5
is it that You, being a *J* . . . . . John 4:9
Am I a *J*? . . . . John 18:35
found out that he was a *J* . Acts 19:34
I am indeed a *J*, born in . . . . Acts 22:3
believes, for the *J* first . . . . . Rom 1:16
who does evil, of the *J* first . . Rom 2:9
he is not a *J* who is one . . . . Rom 2:28
advantage then has the *J* . . . . Rom 3:1
no distinction between *J* . . Rom 10:12
Jews I became as a *J* . . . . . . 1 Cor 9:20
If you, being a *J*, live in . . . . . Gal 2:14
is neither *J* nor Greek . . . . . . Gal 3:28
is neither Greek nor *J* . . . . Col 3:11

JEWELS
your thighs are like *j* . . . . . . Songs 7:1
that I make them My *j* . . . . Mal 3:17

JEWISH
against their *J* brethren . . . . . . Neh 5:1
J descent, you will not . . . . . Esth 6:13
a *J* brother in bondage . . . . Jer 34:9
expectation of the *J* . . . . Acts 12:11
J exorcists took it upon . . . Acts 19:13
light to the *J* people and . . Acts 26:23
giving heed to *J* fables . . . . . Titus 1:14

JEWS
See KING OF THE JEWS
Jesus born King of the, Matt 2:2
Salvation comes through the, John 4:22; Acts 11:19; Rom 1:16; 2:9, 10
Reject Christ, Matt 27:21–25
Reject the gospel, Acts 13:42–46

the elders of the *J* build . . . . . Ezra 6:7
are these feeble *J* doing . . . . . . Neh 4:2
J who were at Shushan . . . . . Esth 9:18
sent letters to all the *J* . . . . . . Esth 9:30
I am afraid of the *J* who . . . . . Jer 38:19
of the *J* seven hundred . . . . . Jer 52:30
There are certain *J* whom . . . Dan 3:12
You the King of the *J* . . . . . Matt 27:11
of purification of the *J*, ... John 2:6
for salvation is of the *J* . . . . John 4:22
those *J* who believed Him . . John 8:31
the *J* took up stones . . . . . . John 10:31
The King of the *J* . . . . John 19:19
dwelling in Jerusalem *J* . . . . . Acts 2:5
confounded the *J* who . . . . . . Acts 9:22
in the land of the *J* . . . . Acts 10:39
in the synagogues of the *J* . . Acts 13:5
But the *J* stirred up the . . . . Acts 13:50
refuted the *J* publicly, ... Acts 18:28
the God of the *J* only . . . . . . Rom 3:29
J a stumbling block . . . . 1 Cor 1:23
whether *J* or Greeks, ... 1 Cor 12:13
From the *J* five times I . . . 2 Cor 11:24
compel Gentiles to live as *J* . . Gal 2:14
of those who say they are *J* . . Rev 2:9
Satan, who say they are *J* . . . . Rev 3:9

JEZEBEL
Ahab's idolatrous wife, 1 Kin 16:31
Her abominable acts, 1 Kin 18:4, 13; 19:1, 2; 21:1–16
Death prophesied; prophecy fulfilled, 1 Kin 21:23; 2 Kin 9:7, 30–37
—— Type of paganism in the church, Rev 2:20

JEZREEL
Ahab's capital, 1 Kin 18:45; 21:1
Ahab's family destroyed at, 1 Kin 21:23; 2 Kin 9:30–37; 10:1–11

JOAB
David's nephew; commands his army, 2 Sam 2:10–32; 8:16; 10:1–14; 11:1, 14–25; 20:1–23
Kills Abner, 2 Sam 3:26, 27
Intercedes for Absalom, 2 Sam 14:1–33
Remains loyal to David; kills Absalom, 2 Sam 18:1–5, 9–17
Demoted; kills Amasa, 2 Sam 19:13; 20:8–10

Opposes census, 2 Sam 24:1–9; 1 Chr 21:1–6
Supports Adonijah, 1 Kin 1:7
Solomon orders his death in obedience to David's command, 1 Kin 2:1–6, 28–34

JOANNA
Wife of Chuza, Herod's steward, Luke 8:1–3
With others, heralds Christ's resurrection, Luke 23:55, 56

JOASH (or Jehoash)
Son of Ahaziah; saved from Athaliah's massacre and crowned by Jehoiada, 2 Kin 11:1–12
Repairs the temple, 2 Kin 12:1–16
Turns away from the Lord and is killed, 2 Chr 24:17–25
—— Wicked king of Israel; son of Jehoahaz, 2 Kin 13:10–25
Defeats Amaziah in battle, 2 Kin 14:8–15; 2 Chr 25:17–24

JOB
Model of righteousness, Job 1:1–5
His faith tested, Job 1:6—2:10
Debates with his three friends; complains to God, Job 3—33
Elihu intervenes, Job 34—37
God's answer, Job 38—41
Humbles himself and repents, Job 42:1–6
Restored to prosperity, Job 42:10–17

JOCHEBED
Daughter of Levi; mother of Miriam, Aaron, and Moses, Ex 6:20

JOEL
Preexilic prophet, Joel 1:1
Quoted in N.T., Acts 2:16

JOGBEHAH
Town in Gilead, Judg 8:11

JOHANAN
Military leader of Judah; warns Gedaliah of Ishmael's plot, Jer 40:13–16
Avenges Gedaliah; takes the people to Egypt, Jer 41:11–18

JOHN
The apostle, son of Zebedee; called as disciple, Matt 4:21, 22; Luke 5:1–11
Chosen as one of the Twelve, Matt 10:2
Especially close to Christ, Matt 17:1–9; Mark 13:3; John 13:23–25; 19:26, 27; 20:2–8; 21:7, 20
Ambitious and overzealous, Mark 10:35–41; Luke 9:54–56
Sent to prepare the Passover, Luke 22:8–13
With Peter, heals a man and is arrested, Acts 3:1—4:22
Goes on missionary trip with Peter, Acts 8:14–25
Exiled on Patmos, Rev 1:9
Author of Gospel, three epistles, and the Revelation, John 21:23–25; 1 John; 2 John; 3 John; Rev 1:1
—— The Baptist; O.T. prophecy concerning, Is 40:3–5; Mal 4:5
His birth announced and accomplished, Luke 1:11–20, 57–80
Preaches repentance, Luke 3:1–20
Bears witness to Christ, John 1:19–36; 3:25–36
Baptizes Jesus, Matt 3:13–17
Jesus speaks about, Matt 11:7–19
Identified with Elijah, Matt 11:13, 14
Herod imprisons and kills, Matt 14:3–12
—— Surnamed Mark: *see* MARK

JOIN
Woe to those who *j* . . . . Is 5:8
'Come and let us *j* . . . . Jer 50:5
of the rest dared *j* . . . . Acts 5:13

JOINED
and mother and be *j* . . . . Gen 2:24
for him who is *j* . . . . Eccl 9:4
"Ephraim is *j* . . . . Hos 4:17
what God has *j* . . . . Matt 19:6
you be perfectly *j* . . . . 1 Cor 1:10
But he who is *j* . . . . 1 Cor 6:17
the whole body, *j* . . . . Eph 4:16

JOINT
j as He wrestled . . . . Gen 32:25
My bones are out of *j* . . . . Ps 22:14
j heirs with Christ . . . . Rom 8:17
by what every *j* . . . . Eph 4:16

JOINTS
and knit together by *j* . . . . . . Col 2:19
and spirit, and of *j* . . . . Heb 4:12

JOKTAN
See ARABIA
Descendants of Shem, Gen. 10:21, 25

JONADAB (or Jehonadab)
David's nephew; encourages Amnon in sin, 2 Sam 13:3–5, 32–36
—— Son of Rechab; father of the Rechabites, Jer 35:5–19
Helps Jehu overthrow Baal, 2 Kin 10:15–28

JONAH
Prophet sent to Nineveh; rebels and is punished, Jon 1
Repents and is saved, Jon 2
Preaches in Nineveh, Jon 3
Becomes angry at God's mercy, Jon 4
Type of Christ's resurrection, Matt 12:39, 40

JONATHAN
King Saul's eldest son; his exploits in battle, 1 Sam 13:2, 3; 14:1–14, 49
Saved from his father's wrath, 1 Sam 14:24–45
Makes covenant with David; protects him from Saul, 1 Sam 18:1–4; 19:1–7; 20:1–42; 23:15–18
Killed by Philistines, 1 Sam 31:2, 8
Mourned by David; his son provided for, 2 Sam 1:17–27; 9:1–8
—— Son of high priest Abiathar; faithful to David, 2 Sam 15:26–36; 17:15–22
Informs Adonijah of Solomon's coronation, 1 Kin 1:41–49

JOPPA
Scene of Peter's vision, Acts 10:5–23, 32

JORAM
See JEHORAM

JORDAN RIVER
Lot dwells near, Gen 13:8–13
Canaan's eastern boundary, Num 34:12
Moses forbidden to cross, Deut 3:27
Miraculous dividing of, for Israel, Josh 3:1–17
by Elijah, 2 Kin 2:5–8
by Elisha, 2 Kin 2:13,14
Naaman healed in, 2 Kin 5:10–14
John baptizes in, Matt 3:6, 13–17

JOSEPH
Son of Jacob by Rachel, Gen 30:22–24
Loved by Jacob; hated by his brothers, Gen 37:3–11
Sold into slavery, Gen 37:12–36
Unjustly imprisoned in Egypt, Gen 39:1–23
Interprets dreams in prison, Gen 40:1–23
Wins Pharaoh's favor, Gen 41:1–44
Prepares Egypt for famine, Gen 41:45–57
Sells grain to his brothers, Gen 42—44
Reveals identity and reconciles with brothers; sends for Jacob, Gen 45:1–28
Settles family in Egypt, Gen 47:1–12
His sons blessed by Jacob, Gen 48:1–22
Blessed by Jacob, Gen 49:22–26
Buries his father; reassures his brothers, Gen 50:1–21
His death, Gen 50:22–26
—— Husband of Mary, Jesus' mother, Matt 1:16
Visited by angel, Matt 1:19–25
Takes Mary to Bethlehem, Luke 2:3–7
Protects Jesus from Herod, Matt 2:13–23
Jesus subject to, Luke 2:51
—— Secret disciple from Arimathea; donates tomb and assists in Christ's burial, Mark 15:42–46; Luke 23:50–53; John 19:38–42

JOSES
One of Jesus' half brothers, Matt 13:55
—— The name of Barnabas, Acts 4:36

JOSHUA
See JESHUA
—— Leader of Israel succeeding Moses, Num 27:18–23
Leads battle against Amalek, Ex 17:8–16
Sent as spy into Canaan; reports favorably, Num 13:16–25; 14:6–9
Assumes command, Josh 1:1–18
Sends spies to Jericho, Josh 2:1
Leads Israel across Jordan, Josh 3:1–17
Sets up commemorative stones, Josh 4:1–24
Circumcises the people, Josh 5:2–9
Conquers Jericho, Josh 5:13—6:27
Punishes Achan, Josh 7:10–26
Conquers Canaan, Josh 8—12
Divides the land, Josh 13—19
Addresses rulers, Josh 23:1–16
Addresses the people, Josh 24:1–28
His death, Josh 24:29, 30

JOSIAH
Righteous king of Judah; son of Amon, 2 Kin 22:1, 2
Repairs the temple, 2 Kin 22:3–9
Hears the Law; spared for his humility, 2 Kin 22:10–20
Institutes reforms, 2 Kin 23:1–25
Killed in battle, 2 Chr 35:20–25

JOT
one *j* or one tittle . . . . Matt 5:18

JOTHAM
Gideon's youngest son; escapes Abimelech's massacre, Judg 9:5
Utters prophetic parable, Judg 9:7–21
—— Righteous king of Judah; son of Azariah, 2 Kin 15:32–38; 2 Chr 27:1–9

JOURNEY
us go three days' *j* . . . . Ex 3:18
busy, or he is on a *j* . . . . . . 1 Kin 18:27
he has gone on a long *j* . . . . Prov 7:19
city, a three-day *j* in extent . . . Jon 3:3
nor bag for your *j*, nor . . . . Matt 10:10
he went on a *j* . . . . Matt 25:15
Nevertheless I must *j* . . . . . Luke 13:33
wearied from His *j* . . . . John 4:6
may send me on my *j* . . . . . 1 Cor 16:6
j in a manner worthy of . . . . . 3 John 6

JOY
LORD your God with *j* ..... Deut 28:47
of Obed-Edom with *j* ..... 1 Chr 15:25
the *j* of the LORD is your .... Neh 8:10
heart to sing for *j* .... Job 29:13
presence is fullness of *j* ..... Ps 16:11
j comes in the morning .... Ps 30:5
To God my exceeding *j* .... Ps 43:4
me the *j* of Your salvation ... Ps 51:12
sow in tears shall reap in *j* .. Ps 126:5
You according to the *j* .... Is 9:3
j you will draw water .... Is 12:3
everlasting *j* on their heads .. Is 51:11
ashes, the oil of *j* .... Is 61:3
j shall be theirs .... Is 61:7
shall sing for *j* .... Is 65:14
word was to me the *j* ...... Jer 15:16
I will *j* in the God of my .... Hab 3:18
receives it with *j* .... Matt 13:20
Enter into the *j* .... Matt 25:21
in my womb for *j* .... Luke 1:44
good tidings of great *j* ..... Luke 2:10
there will be more *j* .... Luke 15:7
did not believe for *j* ...... Luke 24:41
My *j* may remain in ...... John 15:11
will be turned into *j* ...... John 16:20
that your *j* may be full .... John 16:24
they may have My *j* ...... John 17:13
finish my race with *j* ...... Acts 20:24
peace and *j* in the Holy ... Rom 14:17
fill you with all *j* .... Rom 15:13
that my *j* is the *j* .... 2 Cor 2:3
the Spirit is love, *j* .... Gal 5:22
brethren, my *j* and .... Phil 4:1
longsuffering with *j* .... Col 1:11
with *j* of the Holy Spirit, .. 1 Thess 1:6
are our glory and *j* ...... 1 Thess 2:20
that I may be filled with *j* .. 2 Tim 1:4
j that was set before .... Heb 12:2
count it all *j* .... James 1:2
j inexpressible and full ...... 1 Pet 1:8
with exceeding *j* .... 1 Pet 4:13
that your *j* may be full .... 1 John 1:4
that our *j* may be full ..... 2 John 12
I have no greater *j* .... 3 John 4
His glory with exceeding *j* ... Jude 24

JOYFUL
And my soul shall be *j* .... Ps 35:9
Make a *j* shout to the .... Ps 100:1
of prosperity be *j* .... Eccl 7:14
and make them *j* .... Is 56:7
soul shall be *j* in my God .... Is 61:10
I am exceedingly *j* .... 2 Cor 7:4
to be *j* for the present ..... Heb 12:11

JOYFULLY
Let us shout *j* to the Rock .... Ps 95:1
shout *j* before the LORD, ... Ps 98:6
j accepted the plundering .. Heb 10:34

JOZACHAR
Assassin of Joash, 2 Kin 12:19–21
Called Zabad, 2 Chr 24:26

JUBAL
Son of Lamech, Gen 4:21

JUBILEE
cause the trumpet of the *J* ... Lev 25:9
For it is the *J* .... Lev 25:12
his field after the *J*, then ... Lev 27:18
In the Year of *J* the field ... Lev 27:24
the *J* of the children .... Num 36:4

JUDAH
Son of Jacob and Leah, Gen 29:30–35
Intercedes for Joseph, Gen 37:26, 27
Fails in duty to Tamar, Gen 38:1–30
Offers himself as Benjamin's ransom, Gen 44:18–34
Jacob bestows birthright on, Gen 49:3–10
Ancestor of Christ, Matt 1:3, 16
——— Tribe of:
Prophecy concerning, Gen 49:8–12
Numbered at Sinai, Num 1:26, 27
Territory assigned to, Josh 15:1–63
Leads in conquest of Canaan, Judg 1:1–19
Makes David king, 2 Sam 2:1–11
Loyal to David and his house, 2 Sam 20:1, 2; 1 Kin 12:20
Becomes leader of southern kingdom, 1 Kin 14:21, 22
Taken to Babylon, 2 Kin 24:1–16
Returns after exile, 2 Chr 36:20–23

JUDAISM
And I advanced in *J* .... Gal 1:14

JUDAS
Judas Lebbaeus, surnamed Thaddaeus, Matt 10:3
One of the Twelve, Luke 6:13, 16
Offers a question, John 14:22
——— Judas Barsabas, a chief deputy, Acts 15:22–32
——— Betrayer of Christ: *see* ISCARIOT

JUDE (or Judas)
Half brother of Christ, Matt 13:55
Does not believe in Christ, John 7:5
Becomes Christ's disciple, Acts 1:14
Writes an epistle, Jude 1

JUDEA
Christ born in, Matt 2:1, 5, 6
Hostile toward Christ, John 7:1
Gospel preached in, Acts 8:1, 4
Churches established in, Acts 9:31

JUDGE
The LORD *j* between .... Gen 16:5
Dan shall *j* his people as .. Gen 49:16
you a price and a *j* over us ... Ex 2:14
Moses sat to *j* the people .... Ex 18:13
For the LORD will *j* .... Deut 32:36
the LORD was with the *j* .... Judg 2:18
coming to *j* the earth ..... 1 Chr 16:33
and judges who may *j* all ... Ezra 7:25
He shall *j* the world in .... Ps 9:8
How long will you *j* unjustly .. Ps 82:2
Arise, O God, *j* the earth ..... Ps 82:8
Rise up, O *J* of the .... Ps 94:2
He is coming to *j* the earth .. Ps 96:13
He shall *j* the world, and ..... Ps 98:9
the LORD will *j* His people .. Ps 135:14
j righteously, and plead .... Prov 31:9
sword the LORD will *j* .... Is 66:16
deliver you to the *j* .... Matt 5:25
"*J* not, that you be not ...... Matt 7:1
"Man, who made Me a *j* .. Luke 12:14
j who did not fear God .... Luke 18:2
As I hear, I *j* .... John 5:30
Do not *j* according .... John 7:24
I *j* no one .... John 8:15
j the world but to .... John 12:47
this, O man, you who *j* ...... Rom 2:3
then how will God *j* .... Rom 3:6
Therefore let us not *j* ..... Rom 14:13
the saints will *j* the world ... 1 Cor 6:2
that we shall *j* angels .... 1 Cor 6:3
J among yourselves ...... 1 Cor 11:13
let no one *j* you in .... Col 2:16
Christ, who will *j* .... 2 Tim 4:1
Lord, the righteous *J* .... 2 Tim 4:8
heaven, to God the *J* .... Heb 12:23
and adulterers God will *j* ... Heb 13:4
are you to *j* another .... James 4:12
the *J* is standing at the ..... James 5:9
who is ready to *j* the living .. 1 Pet 4:5
holy and true, until You *j* ... Rev 6:10

JUDGED
God has *j* my case .... Gen 30:6
So they *j* the people at all ... Ex 18:26
upon him, and he *j* Israel ... Judg 3:10
Samuel *j* Israel all the .... 1 Sam 7:15
condemn him when he is *j* ... Ps 37:33
He *j* the cause of the poor .. Jer 22:16
You who *j* your sisters, ... Ezek 16:52
Judge not, that you be not *j* .. Matt 7:1
You have rightly *j* .... Luke 7:43
ruler of this world is *j* .... John 16:11
being *j* by you this day .... Acts 24:21
law will be *j* by the law .... Rom 2:12
overcome when You are *j* ... Rom 3:4
world will be *j* by you ...... 1 Cor 6:2
But when we are *j* .... 1 Cor 11:32
be *j* by the law of liberty .. James 2:12
the dead were *j* according .. Rev 20:12

JUDGES
j who delivered .... Judg 2:16
in the days when the *j* .... Ruth 1:1
said to the *j*, "Take heed .... 2 Chr 19:6
Surely He is God who *j* ..... Ps 58:11
He *j* among the gods .... Ps 82:1
He makes the *j* of the .... Is 40:23
j are evening wolves .... Zeph 3:3
For the Father *j* .... John 5:22
he who is spiritual *j* .... 1 Cor 2:15
j me is the Lord .... 1 Cor 4:4
who without partiality *j* .... 1 Pet 1:17
Him who *j* righteously ..... 1 Pet 2:23

JUDGMENT
Aaron shall bear the *j* of ..... Ex 28:30
show partiality in *j* .... Deut 1:17
David administered *j* ..... 2 Sam 8:15
Does God subvert *j* .... Job 8:3
Teach me good *j* .... Ps 119:66
instructs him in right *j* .... Is 28:26
from prison and from *j* .... Is 53:8
I will also speak *j* .... Jer 4:12
j was made in favor of ...... Dan 7:22
be in danger of the *j* .... Matt 5:21
For with what *j* you judge ... Matt 7:2
in the day of *j* than for .... Matt 11:22
will rise up in the *j* ...... Matt 12:42
shall not come into *j* .... John 5:24
and My *j* is righteous ...... John 5:30
but judge with righteous *j* .. John 7:24
if I do judge, My *j* .... John 8:16
For *j* I have come into ..... John 9:39
Now is the *j* of this .... John 12:31
the righteous *j* of God .... Rom 1:32
j which came from one .... Rom 5:16
all stand before the *j* ..... Rom 14:10
yet I give *j* as one whom .. 1 Cor 7:25
eats and drinks *j* .... 1 Cor 11:29
appear before the *j* .... 2 Cor 5:10
preceding them to *j* ...... 1 Tim 5:24
after this the *j* .... Heb 9:27
For *j* is without mercy .... James 2:13
receive a stricter *j* .... James 3:1
time has come for *j* .... 1 Pet 4:17
a long time their *j* .... 2 Pet 2:3
boldness in the day of *j* .. 1 John 4:17
darkness for the *j* .... Jude 6
the hour of His *j* has come .. Rev 14:7
hour your *j* has come .... Rev 18:10
j was committed to them .... Rev 20:4

JUDGMENTS
The *j* of the LORD are .... Ps 19:9
j are a great deep .... Ps 36:6
I dread, for Your *j* .... Ps 119:39
statutes nor kept My *j* ...... Ezek 5:7
had not executed My *j* .... Ezek 20:24
unsearchable are His *j* .... Rom 11:33
righteous are His *j* .... Rev 19:2

JUG
So she opened a *j* of milk .. Judg 4:19
j of water by Saul's ..... 1 Sam 26:12

JULIUS
Roman centurion assigned to guard Paul, Acts 27:1–44

JUST
Noah was a *j* man .... Gen 6:9
I have done *j* as you told .. Gen 27:19
j as the LORD commanded ... Num 26:4
J as the gazelle and the ... Deut 12:22
a perfect and *j* weight ..... Deut 25:15

j as my strength was . . . . . . Josh 14:11
Hear a *j* cause . . . . Ps 17:1
the path of the *j* is like . . . . . Prov 4:18
j weight is His delight . . . . . Prov 11:1
It is a joy for the *j* . . . . Prov 21:15
j man who perishes . . . . Eccl 7:15
For there is not a *j* . . . . Eccl 7:20
way of the *j* is uprightness . . . . Is 26:7
the blood of the *j* . . . . Lam 4:13
j shall live by his . . . . Hab 2:4
He is *j* and having . . . . Zech 9:9
her husband, being a *j* . . . . . . Matt 1:19
resurrection of the *j* . . . . Luke 14:14
j persons who need no . . . . . . Luke 15:7
the Holy One and the *J* . . . . . Acts 3:14
dead, both of the *j* . . . . Acts 24:15
j shall live by faith . . . . Rom 1:17
that He might be *j* . . . . Rom 3:26
the *j* shall live by faith . . . . . . Gal 3:11
j as you were called in one . . . Eph 4:4
j as Christ also loved the . . . . Eph 5:25
whatever things are *j* . . . . Phil 4:8
received a *j* reward, ... Heb 2:2
j men made perfect . . . . Heb 12:23
have murdered the *j* . . . . James 5:6
He is faithful and *j* . . . . 1 John 1:9
J and true are Your . . . . Rev 15:3

JUSTICE

to do righteousness and *j* . . Gen 18:19
after many to pervert *j* . . . . Ex 23:2
for all His ways are *j* . . . . Deut 32:4
bribes, and perverted *j* . . . . . 1 Sam 8:3
to discern *j* . . . . 1 Kin 3:11
the Almighty pervert *j* . . . . Job 8:3
gives *j* to the oppressed . . . . . . Job 36:6
j as the noonday . . . . Ps 37:6
and Your poor with *j* . . . . Ps 72:2
Do *j* to the afflicted . . . . Ps 82:3
and *j* are the . . . . Ps 89:14
j for all who are oppressed . . Ps 103:6
He guards the paths of *j*, ... Prov 2:8
revenues without *j* . . . . Prov 16:8
do not understand *j* . . . . Prov 28:5
j the measuring line . . . . Is 28:17
the LORD is a God of *j* . . . . Is 30:18
He will bring forth *j* . . . . Is 42:1
No one calls for *j* . . . . Is 59:4
J is turned back . . . . Is 59:14
I, the LORD, love *j* . . . . Is 61:8
you, O home of *j* . . . . Jer 31:23
plundering, execute *j* . . . . . . Ezek 45:9
truth, and His ways *j* . . . . Dan 4:37
observe mercy and *j* . . . . Hos 12:6
who turn *j* to wormwood . . . . Amos 5:7
'Execute true *j* . . . . Zech 7:9
"Where is the God of *j* . . . . Mal 2:17
And He will declare *j* . . . . . . Matt 12:18
of herbs, and pass by *j* . . . . Luke 11:42
His humiliation His *j* . . . . Acts 8:33

JUSTIFICATION

because of our *j* . . . . Rom 4:25
offenses resulted in *j* . . . . Rom 5:16
men, resulting in *j* . . . . Rom 5:18

JUSTIFIED

Me that you may be *j* . . . . Job 40:8
of Israel shall be *j* . . . . Is 45:25
words you will be *j* . . . . Matt 12:37
But wisdom is *j* . . . . Luke 7:35
j rather than the . . . . Luke 18:14
who believes is *j* . . . . Acts 13:39
"That You may be *j* . . . . Rom 3:4
law no flesh will be *j* . . . . Rom 3:20
j freely by His grace . . . . Rom 3:24
having been *j* by . . . . Rom 5:1
these He also *j* . . . . Rom 8:30
but you were *j* . . . . 1 Cor 6:11
that we might be *j* . . . . Gal 2:16
who attempt to be *j* . . . . Gal 5:4
j in the Spirit . . . . 1 Tim 3:16
then that a man is *j* . . . . James 2:24
the harlot also *j* . . . . James 2:25

JUSTIFIER

be just and the *j* . . . . Rom 3:26

JUSTIFIES

He who *j* the wicked . . . . Prov 17:15
It is God who *j* . . . . Rom 8:33

JUSTIFY

j the wicked for a . . . . Is 5:23
wanting to *j* himself . . . . Luke 10:29
"You are those who *j* . . . . . . Luke 16:15
is one God who will *j* . . . . Rom 3:30
that God would *j* . . . . Gal 3:8

JUSTLY

of you but to do *j* . . . . Mic 6:8
And we indeed *j* . . . . Luke 23:41
how devoutly and *j* . . . . 1 Thess 2:10

JUSTUS

Surname of Joseph, a disciple, Acts 1:23
—— Man of Corinth; befriends Paul, Acts 18:7
—— Fellow worker of Paul, also called Jesus, Col 4:11

KADESH

Spies sent from, Num 13:3, 26
Moses strikes rock at, Num 20:1–13
Boundary in the new Israel, Ezek 47:19

KADESH BARNEA

Boundary of Promised Land, Num 34:1–4
Limit of Joshua's military campaign, Josh 10:41

KARNAIM

Conquered region, Amos 6:13

KEDESH

Town in south Judah, Josh 15:23
—— Levite city in Issachar, 1 Chr 6:72

KEDESH NAPHTALI

City of refuge, Josh 21:27, 32
Home of Barak, Judg 4:6

KEEP

k you wherever you . . . . Gen 28:15
day, to *k* it holy . . . . Ex 20:8
and *k* My judgments . . . . Lev 25:18
k all My commandments . . . . . 1 Kin 6:12
and that You would *k* . . . . 1 Chr 4:10
Even he who cannot *k* . . . . Ps 22:29
K my soul, and deliver me . . . . Ps 25:20
do not *k* silence . . . . Ps 35:22
k Your righteous . . . . Ps 119:106
k them in the midst of . . . . . . Prov 4:21
K your heart with all . . . . Prov 4:23
a time to *k* silence . . . . Eccl 3:7
k your appointed feasts, ... Nah 1:15
Let all the earth *k* . . . . Hab 2:20
k the commandments . . . . . . Matt 19:17
charge over you, to *k* . . . . Luke 4:10
If you love Me, *k* . . . . John 14:15
k through Your name . . . . John 17:11
orderly and *k* the law . . . . Acts 21:24
and *k* the traditions . . . . 1 Cor 11:2
Let your women *k* . . . . 1 Cor 14:34
a debtor to *k* the whole law . . . . Gal 5:3
k the unity of the . . . . Eph 4:3
k yourself pure . . . . 1 Tim 5:22
He is able to *k* what I . . . . . . 2 Tim 1:12
to *k* oneself unspotted . . . . . . James 1:27
k His commandments . . . . 1 John 2:3
k His commandments . . . . . . 1 John 3:22
k yourselves from idols . . . 1 John 5:21
k yourselves in the . . . . Jude 21
k you from stumbling . . . . Jude 24
k those things . . . . Rev 1:3
I also will *k* you from the . . . . Rev 3:10
of those who *k* the words . . . . Rev 22:9

KEEPER

Am I my brother's *k* . . . . Gen 4:9
of the *k* of the prison . . . . Gen 39:21
The LORD is your *k* . . . . Ps 121:5
me the *k* of the vineyards . . . . Song 1:6
to the *k* of his vineyard . . . . . Luke 13:7
of the prison, awaking . . . . . . Acts 16:27

KEEPERS

in the day when the *k* . . . . Eccl 12:3

KEEPS

the faithful God who *k* . . . . Deut 7:9
God, Who *k* covenant and . . . Neh 9:32
who *k* you will not slumber . . Ps 121:3
k truth forever . . . . Ps 146:6
k his way preserves . . . . Prov 16:17
k the commandment . . . . Prov 19:16
Whoever *k* the law is a . . . . . . Prov 28:7
none of you *k* the law . . . . John 7:19
born of God *k* himself . . . . . 1 John 5:18
and *k* his garments . . . . Rev 16:15

KEILAH

Town of Judah; rescued from Philistines by David, 1 Sam 23:1–5
Prepares to betray David; he escapes, 1 Sam 23:6–13

KENITES

Canaanite tribe whose land is promised to Abraham's seed, Gen 15:19
Subjects of Balaam's prophecy, Num 24:20–22
Settle with Judahites, Judg 1:16
Spared by Saul in war with Amalekites, 1 Sam 15:6

KEPT

shall be *k* burning on it . . . . . . Lev 6:9
be *k* as a sign against . . . . . . Num 17:10
He *k* him as the apple of . . . Deut 32:10
For I have *k* the ways . . . . 2 Sam 22:22
k what You promised . . . . 2 Chr 6:15
Now Josiah *k* a Passover . . 2 Chr 35:1
desolate she *k* Sabbath . . . 2 Chr 36:21
brethren who *k* the gates, . . . Neh 11:19
gatekeepers *k* the charge . . . Neh 12:45
that *k* a pilgrim feast . . . . Ps 42:4
vineyard I have not *k* . . . . Song 1:6
when a holy festival is *k* . . . . . Is 30:29
k charge of My . . . . Ezek 44:15
we have *k* His ordinance . . . . . . Mal 3:14
these things I have *k* . . . . . . Matt 19:20
But Jesus *k* silent . . . . Matt 26:63
she *k* asking Him to cast . . . Mark 7:26
all these things I have *k* . . Mark 10:20
k all these things . . . . Luke 2:19
love, just as I have *k* . . . . John 15:10
If they *k* My word, they . . . . John 15:20
You gave Me I have *k* . . . . . John 17:12
k back part of the . . . . Acts 5:2
k secret since the world . . . Rom 16:25
I have *k* the faith . . . . 2 Tim 4:7
who are *k* by the power . . . . . . 1 Pet 1:5
Because you have *k* My . . . . . . Rev 3:10

KETURAH

Abraham's second wife, Gen 25:1
Sons of:
listed, Gen 25:1, 2
given gifts and sent away, Gen 25:6

KEY

The *k* of the house of . . . . Is 22:22
have taken away the *k* . . . Luke 11:52
"He who has the *k* . . . . Rev 3:7
heaven, having the *k* . . . . Rev 20:1

KEYS

I will give you the *k* . . . . . . Matt 16:19
And I have the *k* . . . . Rev 1:18

KIBROTH HATTAAVAH

Burial site of Israelites slain by God, Num 11:33–35

KICK

is hard for you to *k* . . . . Acts 9:5

KIDNAPPERS

for sodomites, for *k* . . . . 1 Tim 1:10

KIDNAPS

“He who *k* a man and ... Ex 21:16

KIDRON

Valley near Jerusalem; crossed by David and Christ, 2 Sam 15:23; John 18:1
Idols dumped there, 2 Chr 29:16

KILL

who finds me will *k* ... Gen 4:14
k the Passover lamb ... Ex 12:21
I *k* and I make alive ... Deut 32:39
“Am I God, to *k* ... 2 Kin 5:7
a time to *k* ... Eccl 3:3
to save life or to *k* ... Mark 3:4
of them they will *k* ... Luke 11:49
afraid of those who *k* ... Luke 12:4
Why do you seek to *k* ... John 7:19
except to steal, and to *k* ... John 10:10
“Rise, Peter; *k* and eat ... Acts 10:13
was about to *k* himself ... Acts 16:27
to *k* with sword, with ... Rev 6:8

KILLED

Abel his brother and *k* ... Gen 4:8
For I have *k* a man for ... Gen 4:23
LORD *k* all the firstborn ... Ex 13:15
Your servant has *k* ... 1 Sam 17:36
for Your sake we are *k* ... Ps 44:22
and scribes, and be *k* ... Matt 16:21
Siloam fell and *k* them ... Luke 13:4
k the Prince of life ... Acts 3:15
me, and by it *k* me ... Rom 7:11
“For Your sake we are *k* ... Rom 8:36
who *k* both the Lord ... 1 Thess 2:15
martyr, who was *k* ... Rev 2:13

KILLS

“The LORD *k* and ... 1 Sam 2:6
the one who *k* the ... Matt 23:37
for the letter *k* ... 2 Cor 3:6

KIND

animals after their *k* ... Gen 6:20
breed with another *k* ... Lev 19:19
k can come out by ... Mark 9:29
For He is *k* to the ... Luke 6:35
suffers long and is *k* ... 1 Cor 13:4
is one *k* of flesh of men, ... 1 Cor 15:39
And be *k* to one ... Eph 4:32
forgets what *k* of man ... James 1:24

KINDLED

When His wrath is *k* ... Ps 2:12
I, the LORD, have *k* ... Ezek 20:48
wish it were already *k* ... Luke 12:49
they *k* a fire and made us ... Acts 28:2

KINDLY

The LORD deal *k* ... Ruth 1:8
Julius treated Paul *k* ... Acts 27:3
k affectionate to one ... Rom 12:10

KINDNESS

may the LORD show *k* ... 2 Sam 2:6
anger, abundant in *k* ... Neh 9:17
me His marvelous *k* ... Ps 31:21
For His merciful *k* ... Ps 117:2
tongue is the law of *k* ... Prov 31:26
k shall not depart ... Is 54:10
I remember you, the *k* ... Jer 2:2
by longsuffering, by *k* ... 2 Cor 6:6
longsuffering, *k* ... Gal 5:22
But when the *k* and the ... Titus 3:4
and to brotherly *k* ... 2 Pet 1:7

KING

Then Melchizedek *k* ... Gen 14:18
days there was no *k* ... Judg 17:6
said, “Give us a *k* ... 1 Sam 8:6
“Long live the *k* ... 1 Sam 10:24
they anointed David *k* ... 2 Sam 2:4
Yet I have set My *K* ... Ps 2:6
The LORD is *K* forever ... Ps 10:16
K answer us when we ... Ps 20:9
And the *K* of glory ... Ps 24:7
k is saved by the ... Ps 33:16
k Your judgments ... Ps 72:1
For God is my *K* ... Ps 74:12
do who succeeds the *k* ... Eccl 2:12
out of prison to be *k* ... Eccl 4:14
when your *k* is a child ... Eccl 10:16
In the year that *K* ... Is 6:1
k will reign in ... Is 32:1
the LORD is our *K* ... Is 33:22
Is not her *K* in her ... Jer 8:19
and the everlasting *K* ... Jer 10:10
k of Babylon, *k* ... Ezek 26:7
I gave you a *k* in My ... Hos 13:11
the LORD shall be *K* ... Zech 14:9
He who has been born *K* ... Matt 2:2
This Is Jesus the *K* ... Matt 27:37
by force to make Him *k* ... John 6:15
“Behold your *K* ... John 19:14
there is another *k* ... Acts 17:7
Now to the *K* eternal ... 1 Tim 1:17
only Potentate, the *K* ... 1 Tim 6:15
this Melchizedek, *k* ... Heb 7:1
Honor the *k* ... 1 Pet 2:17
K of kings and Lord of ... Rev 19:16

KING OF THE JEWS

He who has been born *K* ... Matt 2:2
saying, “Are You the *K* ... Matt 27:11
This Is Jesus the *K* ... Matt 27:37
to release to you the *K* ... Mark 15:9
salute Him, “Hail, *K* ... Mark 15:18
“If You are the *K* ... Luke 23:37
‘He said, “I am the *K* ... John 19:21

KINGDOM

you shall be to Me a *k* ... Ex 19:6
LORD has torn the *k* ... 1 Sam 15:28
Yours is the *k* ... 1 Chr 29:11
k is the LORD's ... Ps 22:28
the scepter of Your *k* ... Ps 45:6
in heaven, and His *k* ... Ps 103:19
is an everlasting *k* ... Ps 145:13
k which shall never be ... Dan 2:44
High rules in the *k* ... Dan 4:17
Your *k* has been divided, ... Dan 5:28
and glory and a *k*, ... Dan 7:14
k shall be the LORD's ... Obad 21
for Yours is the *k* ... Matt 6:13
Baptist until now the *k* ... Matt 11:12
are the sons of the *k* ... Matt 13:38
k all things that offend ... Matt 13:41
up to half of my *k* ... Mark 6:23
Blessed is the *k* of our ... Mark 11:10
nation, and *k* against *k* ... Mark 13:8
of His *k* there will be no ... Luke 1:33
k of God has come near ... Luke 10:9
k come. Your will be done ... Luke 11:2
k divided against ... Luke 11:17
to give you the *k* ... Luke 12:32
of such is the *k* of God ... Luke 18:16
against nation, and *k* ... Luke 21:10
at My table in My *k* ... Luke 22:30
You come into Your *k* ... Luke 23:42
he cannot enter the *k* ... John 3:5
If My *k* were of this ... John 18:36
preaching the *k* of God ... Acts 20:25
when He delivers the *k* ... 1 Cor 15:24
in the *k* of Christ and God ... Eph 5:5
you into His own *k* ... 1 Thess 2:12
the scepter of Your *k* ... Heb 1:8
we are receiving a *k* ... Heb 12:28
into the everlasting *k* ... 2 Pet 1:11

KINGDOM OF GOD

But seek first the *k* ... Matt 6:33
k has come upon you ... Matt 12:28
rich man to enter the *k* ... Matt 19:24
harlots enter the *k* ... Matt 21:31
the *k* will be taken ... Matt 21:43
the gospel of the *k* ... Mark 1:14
the *k* is at hand ... Mark 1:15
the mystery of the *k* ... Mark 4:11
what shall we liken the *k* ... Mark 4:30
death till they see the *k* ... Mark 9:1
enter the *k* with one eye ... Mark 9:47
for of such is the *k* ... Mark 10:14
riches to enter the *k* ... Mark 10:23
are not far from the *k* ... Mark 12:34
I drink it new in the *k* ... Mark 14:25
waiting for the *k* ... Mark 15:43
“I must preach the *k* ... Luke 4:43
poor, for yours is the *k* ... Luke 6:20
he who is least in the *k* ... Luke 7:28
preach the *k* and to heal ... Luke 9:2
you go and preach the *k* ... Luke 9:60
back, is fit for the *k* ... Luke 9:62
all the prophets in the *k* ... Luke 13:28
shall eat bread in the *k* ... Luke 14:15
k has been preached ... Luke 16:16
k does not come with ... Luke 17:20
the *k* is within you ... Luke 17:21
for the sake of the *k* ... Luke 18:29
thought the *k* would ... Luke 19:11
know that the *k* is near ... Luke 21:31
he cannot see the *k* ... John 3:3
things pertaining to the *k* ... Acts 1:3
tribulations enter the *k* ... Acts 14:22
testified of the *k* ... Acts 28:23
the *k* is not eating and ... Rom 14:17
the *k* is not in word ... 1 Cor 4:20
will not inherit the *k* ... 1 Cor 6:9
cannot inherit the *k* ... 1 Cor 15:50
will not inherit the *k* ... Gal 5:21
fellow workers for the *k* ... Col 4:11
counted worthy of the *k* ... 2 Thess 1:5

KINGDOM OF HEAVEN

“Repent, for the *k* ... Matt 3:2
for theirs is the *k* ... Matt 5:10
by no means enter the *k* ... Matt 5:20
Lord, shall enter the *k* ... Matt 7:21
Isaac, and Jacob in the *k* ... Matt 8:11
‘The *k* is at hand ... Matt 10:7
who is least in the *k* ... Matt 11:11
the mysteries of the *k* ... Matt 13:11
The *k* is like a man ... Matt 13:24
k is like a mustard seed, ... Matt 13:31
The *k* is like leaven, ... Matt 13:33
the *k* is like treasure ... Matt 13:44
k is like a dragnet ... Matt 13:47
you the keys of the *k* ... Matt 16:19
then is greatest in the *k* ... Matt 18:1
by no means enter the *k* ... Matt 18:3
is the greatest in the *k* ... Matt 18:4
k is like a certain king ... Matt 18:23
for of such is the *k* ... Matt 19:14
a rich man to enter the *k* ... Matt 19:23
k is like a landowner ... Matt 20:1
k is like a certain king ... Matt 22:2
you shut up the *k* ... Matt 23:13
k shall be likened ... Matt 25:1
the *k* is like a man ... Matt 25:14

KINGDOMS

the *k* were moved ... Ps 46:6
tremble, who shook *k* ... Is 14:16
showed Him all the *k* ... Matt 4:8
have become the *k* ... Rev 11:15

KINGS

The *k* of the earth set ... Ps 2:2
k shall fall down ... Ps 72:11
He is awesome to the *k* ... Ps 76:12
By me *k* reign ... Prov 8:15
He will stand before *k* ... Prov 22:29
k is unsearchable ... Prov 25:3
that which destroys *k* ... Prov 31:3
it is not for *k* to drink ... Prov 31:4
K shall be your foster ... Is 49:23
“They set up *k* ... Hos 8:4
before governors and *k* ... Matt 10:18
k have desired to see ... Luke 10:24
You have reigned as *k* ... 1 Cor 4:8
and has made us *k* ... Rev 1:6
that the way of the *k* ... Rev 16:12
may eat the flesh of *k* ... Rev 19:18

KIR HARESETH

Fortified city of Moab, 2 Kin 3:25; Is 15:1; 16:7

KIRJATH ARBA
Ancient name of Hebron, Gen 23:2
Possessed by Judah, Judg 1:10

KIRJATH JEARIM
Gibeonite town, Josh 9:17
Ark taken from, 1 Chr 13:5

KISH
Benjamite of Gibeah; father of King Saul, 1 Sam 9:1–3

KISHON
River of north Palestine; Sisera's army swept away by, Judg 4:7, 13
Elijah executes prophets of Baal at, 1 Kin 18:40

KISS
K the Son, lest He be . . . . Ps 2:12
Let him *k* me with the . . . . . . Song 1:2
who sacrifice *k* the calves . . . Hos 13:2
Whomever I *k*, He is . . . . . Mark 14:44
You gave Me no *k* . . . . Luke 7:45
drew near to Jesus to *k* . . . Luke 22:47
another with a holy *k* . . . . . Rom 16:16
another with a holy *k* . . . . 2 Cor 13:12
with a holy *k* . . . . 1 Thess 5:26
one another with a *k* . . . . . . 1 Pet 5:14

KISSED
they *k* one another . . . . . . 1 Sam 20:41
and peace have *k* each. . . . . . . Ps 85:10
Rabbi!" and *k* Him . . . . Matt 26:49
and she *k* His feet and . . . . . Luke 7:38

KITTIM
See CYPRUS
Descendants of Javan, Gen 10:4

KNEE
that to Me every *k* . . . . Is 45:23
And they bowed the *k* . . . . Matt 27:29
have not bowed the *k* . . . . . . Rom 11:4
every *k* shall bow to . . . . . . Rom 14:11
of Jesus every *k* . . . . Phil 2:10

KNEES
make firm the feeble *k* . . . . Is 35:3
be dandled on her *k* . . . . Is 66:12
this reason I bow my *k* . . . . . Eph 3:14
and the feeble *k* . . . . Heb 12:12

KNEW
k that they were naked . . . . . . Gen 3:7
Adam *k* Eve his wife . . . . Gen 4:1
in the womb I *k* . . . . Jer 1:5
to them, 'I never *k* . . . . Matt 7:23
k what was in man . . . . John 2:25
For He made Him who *k* . . 2 Cor 5:21

KNIFE
fire in his hand, and a *k* . . . . Gen 22:6
his house he took a *k* . . . . . Judg 19:29
put a *k* to your throat if . . . . Prov 23:2
cut it with the scribe's *k* . . . . Jer 36:23

KNIT
of Jonathan was *k* . . . . 1 Sam 18:1
k me together with . . . . Job 10:11
be encouraged, being *k* . . . . Col 2:2

KNOCK
k, and it will be . . . . Matt 7:7
at the door and *k* . . . . Rev 3:20

KNOW
k good and evil . . . . Gen 3:22
and I did not *k* . . . . Gen 28:16
Egypt, who did not *k* Joseph . . Ex 1:8
k that I am the LORD . . . . Ex 6:7
'I *k* you by name, and you . . Ex 33:12
way, that I may *k* You . . . . . . Ex 33:13
to *k* how to do all manner . . . . Ex 36:1
Therefore *k* that the LORD . . . Deut 7:9
k what was in your heart . . . . Deut 8:2
You should *k* in your heart . . Deut 8:5
that you may *k* the way by . . Josh 3:4
might be taught to *k* war, . . . Judg 3:2
Samuel did not yet *k* the . . . 1 Sam 3:7
k that there is a God . . . . . 1 Sam 17:46
I *k* that this is a holy man . . 2 Kin 4:9
k that there is no God . . . . . 2 Kin 5:15
you, my son Solomon, *k* . . . 1 Chr 28:9
Hear it, and *k* for . . . . Job 5:27
and *k* nothing, because . . . . Job 8:9
k that my Redeemer . . . . Job 19:25
'What does God *k* . . . . Job 22:13
k Your name will put . . . . Ps 9:10
Now I *k* that the LORD saves . . Ps 20:6
k that I am God . . . . Ps 46:10
make me to *k* wisdom . . . . Ps 51:6
O God, and *k* my heart . . . . . Ps 139:23
k wisdom and instruction, . . . Prov 1:2
to *k* understanding . . . . Prov 4:1
set my heart to *k* wisdom . . . Eccl 1:17
that He may *k* to refuse the . . . Is 7:15
Egyptians will *k* the LORD . . . . Is 19:21
But I *k* your dwelling place, . . Is 37:28
do not *k* nor understand . . . . . Is 44:18
All flesh shall *k* that I, the . . . Is 49:26
My people shall *k* My name . . . Is 52:6
call a nation you do not *k* . . . . Is 55:5
language you do not *k* . . . . Jer 5:15
nor did they *k* how to blush . . Jer 6:15
Who can *k* it . . . . Jer 17:9
saying, 'K the LORD . . . . Jer 31:34
you shall *k* that I am . . . . Ezek 6:13
of the field shall *k* that I . . Ezek 17:24
Gentiles shall *k* that . . . . . . Ezek 39:23
is anxious to *k* the dream . . . . Dan 2:3
you may *k* the thoughts . . . . Dan 2:30
I wished to *k* the truth . . . . . . Dan 7:19
you shall *k* no God but Me . . Hos 13:4
For I *k* your manifold . . . . Amos 5:12
for you to *k* justice . . . . Mic 3:1
did not *k* her till she had . . . Matt 1:25
You *k* how to discern the . . . Matt 16:3
k that summer is near . . . . Matt 24:32
k what hour your Lord . . . . Matt 24:42
an oath, "I do not *k* . . . . Matt 26:72
I do not *k* the Man . . . . Matt 26:74
k the mystery of the . . . . Mark 4:11
k the commandments . . . . Mark 10:19
do not *k* what you ask . . . . Mark 10:38
do not *k* what manner of . . Luke 9:55
k how to give good gifts . . Luke 11:13
k that its desolation is . . . . Luke 21:20
the world did not *k* . . . . John 1:10
We speak what We *k* . . . . . . John 3:11
k what we worship . . . . John 4:22
k that You are the Christ . . John 6:69
k that you are Abraham's . . John 8:37
we *k* that God does not . . . . John 9:31
hear My voice, and I *k* . . . . John 10:27
If you *k* these things . . . . . . John 13:17
k whom I have chosen . . . . John 13:18
we are sure that You *k* . . . John 16:30
k that I love You . . . . John 21:15
k times or seasons . . . . Acts 1:7
and said, "Jesus I *k* . . . . Acts 19:15
we *k* that all things work . . Rom 8:28
wisdom did not *k* . . . . 1 Cor 1:21
nor can he *k* them . . . . 1 Cor 2:14
For we *k* in part and . . . . . . 1 Cor 13:9
k a man in Christ who . . . . . 2 Cor 12:2
when you did not *k* God, ... Gal 4:8
k the love of Christ . . . . Eph 3:19
k Him and the power . . . . Phil 3:10
abased, and I *k* how to . . . . . Phil 4:12
k how to possess his . . . . . 1 Thess 4:4
k what is restraining . . . . . 2 Thess 2:6
k whom I have believed . . . 2 Tim 1:12
so that they may *k* . . . . 2 Tim 2:25
this we *k* that we *k* Him . . . 1 John 2:3
He who says, "I *k* . . . . 1 John 2:4
and you *k* all things . . . . . . 1 John 2:20
By this we *k* love . . . . 1 John 3:16
k that we are of the . . . . . . 1 John 3:19
k that He abides . . . . 1 John 3:24
k that we are of God . . . . . 1 John 5:19
"I *k* your works . . . . Rev 2:2

KNOWING
like God, *k* good and evil . . . . Gen 3:5
k their thoughts, said, ... Matt 9:4
not *k* the Scriptures nor . . . Matt 22:29
k all things that would . . . . . . John 18:4
k that tribulation produces . . Rom 5:3
k that your labor is not . . . 1 Cor 15:58
k that He who raised up . . . 2 Cor 4:14
k that while we are at . . . . . . 2 Cor 5:6
k that I am appointed for . . . Phil 1:17
k that you also have a . . . . Col 4:1
k that you have a better . . . Heb 10:34
not *k* where he was going . . Heb 11:8
k that the testing of your . . James 1:3
k that the same sufferings . . . 1 Pet 5:9

KNOWLEDGE
and the tree of the *k* . . . . Gen 2:9
and understanding, in *k* . . . . . Ex 35:31
LORD is the God of *k*. . . . . . . 1 Sam 2:3
give me wisdom and *k*, ... 2 Chr 1:10
Can anyone teach God *k* . . . Job 21:22
who is perfect in *k* . . . . Job 36:4
unto night reveals *k* . . . . Ps 19:2
me good judgment and *k* . . . Ps 119:66
k is too wonderful . . . . Ps 139:6
LORD is the beginning of *k* . . Prov 1:7
k the depths were . . . . Prov 3:20
k rather than choice . . . . Prov 8:10
Wise people store up *k* . . . . Prov 10:14
prudent man conceals *k* . . . Prov 12:23
k is easy to him who . . . . Prov 14:6
k spares his words . . . . Prov 17:27
a soul to be without *k* . . . . . . Prov 19:2
by *k* the rooms are filled . . . Prov 24:4
of *k* increases strength . . . . . Prov 24:5
and he who increases *k* . . . . . Eccl 1:18
k is that wisdom . . . . Eccl 7:12
no work or device or *k* . . . . . Eccl 9:10
Whom will he teach *k* . . . . Is 28:9
His *k* My righteous Servant . . Is 53:11
k shall increase . . . . Dan 12:4
you have rejected *k* . . . . Hos 4:6
taken away the key of *k* . . Luke 11:52
having more accurate *k* . . . Acts 24:22
to retain God in their *k* . . . . Rom 1:28
having the form of *k* . . . . Rom 2:20
by the law is the *k* of sin . . . Rom 3:20
K puffs up, but love . . . . 1 Cor 8:1
to another the word of *k* . . 1 Cor 12:8
all mysteries and all *k* . . . . . 1 Cor 13:2
whether there is *k* . . . . 1 Cor 13:8
of His *k* in every place . . . . 2 Cor 2:14
to give the light of the *k* . . . . 2 Cor 4:6
by purity, by *k*, by . . . . 2 Cor 6:6
against the *k* of God . . . . . . 2 Cor 10:5
Christ which passes *k* . . . . Eph 3:19
k of His will in all wisdom . . . . Col 1:9
treasures of wisdom and *k* . . . . Col 2:3
is falsely called *k* . . . . 1 Tim 6:20
faith virtue, to virtue *k* . . . . . . 2 Pet 1:5
in the grace and *k* . . . . 2 Pet 3:18

KNOWN
In Judah God is *k* . . . . Ps 76:1
my mouth will I make *k* . . . . . . Ps 89:1
If you had *k* Me . . . . John 8:19
My sheep, and am *k* . . . . . . John 10:14
The world has not *k* . . . . . . John 17:25
peace they have not *k* . . . . . . Rom 3:17
I would not have *k* . . . . Rom 7:7
"For who has *k* . . . . Rom 11:34
after you have *k* . . . . Gal 4:9
requests be made *k* . . . . Phil 4:6
k the Holy Scriptures . . . . . . 2 Tim 3:15
have not *k* the depths of . . . . Rev 2:24

KNOWS
For God *k* that in . . . . Gen 3:5
k the secrets of the . . . . Ps 44:21
he understands and *k* . . . . Jer 9:24
k what is in the . . . . Dan 2:22
k those who trust . . . . Nah 1:7
k the things you have . . . . Matt 6:8

and hour no one *k* . . . . Matt 24:36
k who the Son is . . . . Luke 10:22
but God *k* your hearts . . . . Luke 16:15
searches the hearts *k* . . . . . . Rom 8:27
k the things of God . . . . 1 Cor 2:11
The LORD *k* the thoughts . . 1 Cor 3:20
k those who are His . . . . 2 Tim 2:19
to him who *k* to do . . . . James 4:17
and *k* all things . . . . 1 John 3:20
written which no one *k* . . . . . Rev 2:17

KOHATH

Second son of Levi, Gen 46:8, 11
Brother of Jochebed, mother of Aaron and Moses, Ex 6:16–20

KOHATHITES

Numbered, Num 3:27, 28
Duties assigned to, Num 4:15–20
Leaders of temple music, 1 Chr 6:31–38; 2 Chr 20:19

KORAH

Leads rebellion against Moses and Aaron; supernaturally destroyed, Num 16:1–35
Sons of, not destroyed, Num 26:9–11

LABAN

Son of Bethuel; brother of Rebekah; father of Leah and Rachel, Gen 24:15, 24, 29; 29:16
Agrees to Rebekah's marriage to Isaac, Gen 24:50, 51
Entertains Jacob, Gen 29:1–14
Substitutes Leah for Rachel, Gen 29:15–30
Agrees to division of cattle; grows resentful of Jacob, Gen 30:25—31:2
Pursues Jacob and makes covenant with him, Gen 31:21–55

LABOR

Six days you shall *l* . . . . Ex 20:9
why then do I *l* . . . . Job 9:29
their boast is only *l* . . . . Ps 90:10
The *l* of the righteous . . . . . Prov 10:16
l will increase . . . . Prov 13:11
l there is profit . . . . Prov 14:23
things are full of *l* . . . . Eccl 1:8
has man for all his *l* . . . . Eccl 2:22
He shall see the *l* . . . . Is 53:11
"Before she was in *l* . . . . Is 66:7
from the womb to see *l* . . . . . Jer 20:18
to Me, all you who *l* . . . . Matt 11:28
Do not *l* for the . . . . John 6:27
knowing that your *l* . . . . . . 1 Cor 15:58
but rather let him *l* . . . . Eph 4:28
mean fruit from my *l* . . . . Phil 1:22
your work of faith, *l* . . . . . . 1 Thess 1:3
forget your work and *l* . . . . Heb 6:10
your works, your *l* . . . . Rev 2:2

LABORED

l more abundantly than . . 1 Cor 15:10
for you, lest I have *l* . . . . Gal 4:11

LABORERS

but the *l* are few . . . . Matt 9:37

LABORING

of a *l* man is sweet . . . . Eccl 5:12
l night and day . . . . 1 Thess 2:9

LABORS

The person who *l* . . . . Prov 16:26
is no end to all his *l* . . . . Eccl 4:8
entered into their *l* . . . . John 4:38
creation groans and *l* . . . . . . Rom 8:22
l more abundant . . . . 2 Cor 11:23
may rest from their *l* . . . . Rev 14:13

LACHISH

Defeated by Joshua, Josh 10:3–33
Taken by Sennacherib, 2 Kin 18:13–17; Is 36:1, 2; 37:8

LACK

the city for *l* of five . . . . Gen 18:28
gathered little had no *l* . . . . . . Ex 16:18
'you shall not *l* a man on . . . 1 Kin 2:4
anyone perish for *l* . . . . Job 31:19
the LORD shall not *l* . . . . Ps 34:10
fools die for *l* of wisdom . . Prov 10:21
for *l* of justice there is . . . . Prov 13:23
to the poor will not *l* . . . . . . Prov 28:27
l a man to stand before . . . . . Jer 35:19
for *l* of knowledge . . . . Hos 4:6
What do I still *l* . . . . Matt 19:20
"One thing you *l* . . . . Mark 10:21
did you *l* anything . . . . Luke 22:35
of your *l* of self-control . . . . 1 Cor 7:5
may supply their *l* . . . . 2 Cor 8:14
gathered little had no *l* . . . . . 2 Cor 8:15

LACKED

among them who *l* . . . . Acts 4:34

LACKING

is *l* cannot be numbered . . . . Eccl 1:15
to supply what was *l* in . . . . . Phil 2:30
the things that are *l* . . . . Titus 1:5
and complete, *l* nothing . . . . . James 1:4

LACKS

woman who *l* discretion . . Prov 11:22
who *l* understanding . . . . Prov 28:16
to that part which *l* . . . . 1 Cor 12:24
If any of you *l* wisdom . . . . . James 1:5
he who *l* these things is . . . . . 2 Pet 1:9

LAD

and gave the *l* a drink . . . . . Gen 21:19
lay your hand on the *l* . . . . . Gen 22:12
said, "The *l* is no more . . . . Gen 37:30
'The *l* cannot leave his . . . . . Gen 44:30
As the *l* ran, he shot an . . 1 Sam 20:36
"There is a *l* here who has . . John 6:9

LADDER

and behold, a *l* . . . . Gen 28:12

LADEN

nation, a people *l* . . . . Is 1:4
and are heavy *l* . . . . Matt 11:28

LADIES

wisest *l* answered her . . . . . . Judg 5:29
very day the noble *l* . . . . Esth 1:18

LADY

'I shall be a *l* . . . . Is 47:7
To the elect *l* . . . . 2 John 1

LAGGING

not *l* in diligence . . . . Rom 12:11

LAHAI ROI

Name of a well, Gen 16:7, 14
Same as Beer Lahai Roi, Gen 24:62

LAID

l him on the altar . . . . Gen 22:9
l up the food in the cities . . Gen 41:48
and *l* it in the reeds by the . . . . Ex 2:3
l the staff on the face of . . . 2 Kin 4:31
l the foundation of the . . . . . Ezra 5:16
But man dies and is *l* . . . . Job 14:10
You *l* the foundation . . . . Ps 102:25
He has *l* waste My vine . . . . Joel 1:7
have *l* the foundation of . . . . . Zech 4:9
even now the ax is *l* to . . . . . . Matt 3:10
the place where they *l* . . . . . Mark 16:6
l Him in a manger . . . . Luke 2:7
l the foundation on the . . . . . Luke 6:48
"Where have you *l* . . . . John 11:34
l aside His garments . . . . John 13:4
where You have *l* Him . . . . John 20:15
l it at the apostles' feet . . . . . Acts 4:37
and he *l* his hands on him . . Acts 28:8
I have *l* the foundation . . . . . 1 Cor 3:10
He *l* down His life . . . . 1 John 3:16
He *l* His right hand on me . . Rev 1:17

LAISH

Called Leshem, Josh 19:47; Judg 18:29
Taken by Danites, Judg 18:7, 14, 27

LAKE

by the *L* of Gennesaret . . . . . . Luke 5:1
to the other side of the *l* . . . Luke 8:22
cast alive into the *l* . . . . Rev 19:20

LAMB

but where is the *l* . . . . Gen 22:7
a *l* for a household . . . . Ex 12:3
and kill the Passover *l* . . . . Ex 12:21
took the poor man's *l* . . . . . 2 Sam 12:4
shall dwell with the *l* . . . . Is 11:6
He was led as a *l* . . . . Is 53:7
l shall feed together . . . . Is 65:25
The *L* of God who takes . . . . . John 1:29
as a *l* before its shearer . . . . Acts 8:32
of Christ, as of a *l* . . . . 1 Pet 1:19
the elders, stood a *L* . . . . Rev 5:6
"Worthy is the *L* . . . . Rev 5:12
by the blood of the *L* . . . . Rev 12:11
Book of Life of the *L* . . . . Rev 13:8
supper of the *L* . . . . Rev 19:9

LAMB'S

the bride, the *L* wife . . . . Rev 21:9
in the *L* Book of Life . . . . Rev 21:27

LAMBS

slaughtered the Passover *l* . . Ezra 6:20
O little hills, like *l* . . . . Ps 114:6
with the blood of *l* and . . . . Is 34:6
gather the *l* with His arm . . . . Is 40:11
out as *l* among wolves . . . . . . Luke 10:3
"Feed My *l* . . . . John 21:15

LAME

l take the prey . . . . Is 33:23
l shall leap like a . . . . Is 35:6
when you offer the *l* . . . . Mal 1:8
blind see and the *l* . . . . Matt 11:5
And a certain man *l* . . . . Acts 3:2
so that what is *l* . . . . Heb 12:13

LAMECH

Son of Methushael, of Cain's race, Gen 4:17, 18
——Son of Methuselah; father of Noah, Gen 5:25–31

LAMENT

l the daughter of . . . . Judg 11:40
king sang a *l* over Abner . . 2 Sam 3:33
Her gates shall *l* and mourn . . . Is 3:26
"They shall not *l* for him, . . . Jer 22:18
they shall *l* for her . . . . Ezek 32:16
to you, and you did not *l* . . Matt 11:17
that you will weep and *l* . . John 16:20
L and mourn and weep . . . . James 4:9
l for her, when they see . . . . . . Rev 18:9

LAMENTATION

a great and very solemn *l* . . Gen 50:10
with this *l* over Saul and . . 2 Sam 1:17
was heard in Ramah, *l* . . . . . . Jer 31:15
l in the daughter of Judah . . . Lam 2:5
was heard in Ramah, *l* . . . . . . Matt 2:18
and made great *l* . . . . Acts 8:2

LAMP

For You are my *l* . . . . 2 Sam 22:29
"How often is the *l* . . . . Job 21:17
You will light my *l* . . . . Ps 18:28
Your word is a *l* . . . . Ps 119:105
the *l* of the wicked . . . . Prov 13:9
his *l* will be put out . . . . Prov 20:20
Nor do they light a *l* . . . . Matt 5:15
"The *l* of the body . . . . Matt 6:22
when he has lit a *l* . . . . Luke 8:16
l gives you light . . . . Luke 11:36
does not light a *l* . . . . Luke 15:8
burning and shining *l* . . . . . . John 5:35
l shall not shine . . . . Rev 18:23
They need no *l* nor . . . . Rev 22:5

LAMPS

he made its seven *l* . . . . Ex 37:23
Jerusalem with *l* . . . . Zeph 1:12

and trimmed their *l* .... Matt 25:7
Seven *l* of fire .... Rev 4:5

LAMPSTAND
branches of the *l* .... Ex 25:32
and there is a *l* .... Zech 4:2
a basket, but on a *l* .... Matt 5:15
in which was the *l* .... Heb 9:2
and remove your *l* .... Rev 2:5

LAND
and let the dry *l* appear ...... Gen 1:9
God called the dry *l* Earth .. Gen 1:10
dwelt in the *l* of Nod .... Gen 4:16
l that I will show you .... Gen 12:1
I will give this *l* .... Gen 12:7
was a famine in the *l* .... Gen 12:10
Is not the whole *l* before .... Gen 13:9
walk in the *l* through its ... Gen 13:17
I have given this *l* .... Gen 15:18
arise, get out of this *l* ...... Gen 31:13
the best of the *l* of Egypt .. Gen 45:18
dwell in the *l* of Goshen .... Gen 46:34
a stranger in a foreign *l* ...... Ex 2:22
l flowing with milk .... Ex 3:8
to a *l* flowing with milk and .. Ex 3:17
the *l* of their pilgrimage .... Ex 6:4
firstborn in the *l* of Egypt ... Ex 12:12
and the *l* vomits out its .... Lev 18:25
for the *l* is Mine .... Lev 25:23
I will give peace in the *l* ..... Lev 26:6
And all the tithe of the *l* ... Lev 27:30
spy out the *l* of Canaan ... Num 13:17
evil report about the *l* ..... Num 14:37
l is subdued before the .... Num 32:22
possess the good *l* .... Deut 6:18
a *l* of wheat and barley ..... Deut 8:8
He will bless you in the *l* ... Deut 28:8
the produce of your *l* ...... Deut 28:51
l which I am giving .... Josh 1:2
to go in to possess the *l* .... Josh 1:11
Joshua took the whole *l* ... Josh 11:23
Joshua divided the *l* .... Josh 18:10
to return to the *l* of Judah ... Ruth 1:7
sold the piece of *l* which .... Ruth 4:3
spiritists from the *l* .... 1 Sam 28:9
In the *l* of the living .... Ps 27:13
dwell in the *l*, and feed on .... Ps 37:3
turned the sea into dry *l* ...... Ps 66:6
in the *l* of forgetfulness ...... Ps 88:12
l was polluted with blood ... Ps 106:38
dry *l* into watersprings ..... Ps 107:35
for You like a thirsty *l* ...... Ps 143:6
is heard in our *l* .... Song 2:12
they will see the *l* .... Is 33:17
a *l* of grain and new wine .... Is 36:17
and your *l* shall be married ... Is 62:4
Bethlehem, in the *l* .... Matt 2:6
put out a little from the *l* .... Luke 5:3
price of the *l* for yourself .... Acts 5:3
and his left foot on the *l* .... Rev 10:2

LAND OF THE LIVING
nor is it found in the *l* ...... Job 28:13
of the LORD in the *l* .... Ps 27:13
uproot you from the *l* .... Ps 52:5
before the LORD in the *l* ..... Ps 116:9
my portion in the *l* .... Ps 142:5
the LORD in the *l* .... Is 38:11
cut off from the *l* .... Is 53:8
establish glory in the *l* .... Ezek 26:20

LANDMARK
your neighbor's *l* .... Deut 19:14
remove the ancient *l* ...... Prov 22:28
those who remove a *l* .... Hos 5:10

LANDS
We have mortgaged our *l* .... Neh 5:3
to scatter them in the *l* ..... Ps 106:27
or wife or children or *l* .... Matt 19:29
of *l* or houses sold them .... Acts 4:34

LANGUAGE
whole earth had one *l* ...... Gen 11:1
there confuse their *l* .... Gen 11:7
is no speech nor *l* .... Ps 19:3
a people of strange *l* .... Ps 114:1
the peoples a pure *l* .... Zeph 3:9
speak in his own *l* .... Acts 2:6
blasphemy, filthy *l* .... Col 3:8

LANGUAGES
according to their *l* .... Gen 10:20
be, so many kinds of *l* .... 1 Cor 14:10

LAODICEA
Paul's concern for, Col 2:1; 4:12–16
Letter to church of, Rev 3:14–22

LAST
See FIRST AND THE LAST
He shall stand at *l* .... Job 19:25
First and I am the *L* .... Is 44:6
l man the same as .... Matt 20:14
l will be first .... Matt 20:16
are first who will be *l* ..... Luke 13:30
raise him up at the *l* day ... John 6:40
On the *l* day, that great .... John 7:37
come to pass in the *l* days .. Acts 2:17
The *l* enemy that will be .. 1 Cor 15:26
eye, at the *l* trumpet ...... 1 Cor 15:52
has in these *l* days spoken ... Heb 1:2
children, it is the *l* .... 1 John 2:18
the First and the *L* .... Rev 1:11
l are more than the first ..... Rev 2:19

LAST DAY
raise it up at the *l* .... John 6:39
the resurrection at the *l* ... John 11:24
will judge him in the *l* .... John 12:48

LAST DAYS
shall befall you in the *l* ..... Gen 49:1
come to pass in the *l* .... Acts 2:17
in the *l* perilous times ...... 2 Tim 3:1
these *l* spoken to us .... Heb 1:2
up treasure in the *l* .... James 5:3
will come in the *l* .... 2 Pet 3:3

LATE
to rise up early, to sit up *l* ... Ps 127:2
and already the hour is *l* .. Mark 6:35
l autumn trees without ...... Jude 12
as a fig tree drops its *l* ...... Rev 6:13

LATIN
in Hebrew, Greek, and *L* .. John 19:20

LATTER
people in the *l* days .... Dan 10:14
former rain, and the *l* .... Joel 2:23
The glory of this *l* temple .... Hag 2:9
l times some will .... 1 Tim 4:1
the early and *l* rain .... James 5:7
l end is worse for them .... 2 Pet 2:20

LATTICE
I looked through my *l* .... Prov 7:6
gazing through the *l* .... Song 2:9

LAUGH
Why did Sarah *l* .... Gen 18:13
"God has made me *l* .... Gen 21:6
sits in the heavens shall *l* ...... Ps 2:4
You, O LORD, shall *l* .... Ps 59:8
to weep, and a time to *l* ...... Eccl 3:4
Woe to you who *l* .... Luke 6:25

LAUGHS
he *l* at the threat of .... Job 41:29
The Lord *l* at him .... Ps 37:13

LAUGHTER
was filled with *l* .... Ps 126:2
your *l* be turned to .... James 4:9

LAUNDERER
such as no *l* on earth can ... Mark 9:3

LAVER
also make a *l* of bronze ..... Ex 30:18
l contained forty baths .... 1 Kin 7:38

LAW
See ACCORDING TO THE LAW; BOOK OF THE LAW; UNDER THE LAW; WORKS OF THE LAW
stones a copy of the *l* ...... Josh 8:32
When He made a *l* .... Job 28:26
The *l* of the LORD is .... Ps 19:7
The *l* of his God is in .... Ps 37:31
I delight in Your *l* .... Ps 119:70
The *l* of Your mouth is ..... Ps 119:72
l is my delight .... Ps 119:77
Oh, how I love Your *l* ...... Ps 119:97
And Your *l* is truth .... Ps 119:142
and the *l* a light .... Prov 6:23
is he who keeps the *l* ..... Prov 29:18
shall go forth the *l* .... Is 2:3
l will proceed from Me .... Is 51:4
in whose heart is My *l* .... Is 51:7
the *L* is no more .... Lam 2:9
The *l* of truth was in .... Mal 2:6
to destroy the *L* .... Matt 5:17
for this is the *L* .... Matt 7:12
l prophesied until John .... Matt 11:13
hang all the *L* and the .... Matt 22:40
one tittle of the *l* to fail ... Luke 16:17
l was given through .... John 1:17
"Does our *l* judge a .... John 7:51
a teacher of the *l* held in .... Acts 5:34
and keep the *l* .... Acts 15:24
are all zealous for the *l* .... Acts 21:20
man according to the *l* .... Acts 22:12
l is the knowledge .... Rom 3:20
By what *l*? Of works? .... Rom 3:27
because the *l* brings .... Rom 4:15
when there is no *l* .... Rom 5:13
you are not under *l* .... Rom 6:14
have become dead to the *l* ... Rom 7:4
Is the *l* sin .... Rom 7:7
For we know that the *l* .... Rom 7:14
warring against the *l* .... Rom 7:23
For the *l* of the Spirit of ..... Rom 8:2
For what the *l* could .... Rom 8:3
A wife is bound by *l* as .... 1 Cor 7:39
who are without *l* .... 1 Cor 9:21
strength of sin is the *l* .... 1 Cor 15:56
l that I might live .... Gal 2:19
Spirit by the works of the *l* ... Gal 3:2
under guard by the *l* .... Gal 3:23
the *l* was our tutor .... Gal 3:24
born under the *l* .... Gal 4:4
l is fulfilled in one .... Gal 5:14
and so fulfill the *l* of Christ ... Gal 6:2
concerning the *l*, a Pharisee .. Phil 3:5
to be teachers of the *l* ...... 1 Tim 1:7
l is not made for a .... 1 Tim 1:9
and strivings about the *l* .... Titus 3:9
into the perfect *l* .... James 1:25
fulfill the royal *l* .... James 2:8

LAW AND THE PROPHETS
them, for this is the *L* .... Matt 7:12
hang all the *L* .... Matt 22:40
The *l* were until John. .... Luke 16:16
being witnessed by the *L* ... Rom 3:21

LAW OF MOSES
the stones a copy of the *l* ... Josh 8:32
a skilled scribe in the *L* ..... Ezra 7:6
bring the Book of the *L* ...... Neh 8:1
oath written in the *L* .... Dan 9:11
the *L*, My servant .... Mal 4:4
according to the *l* .... Luke 2:22
were written in the *L* ..... Luke 24:44
Sabbath, so that the *l* ...... John 7:23
not be justified by the *l* .... Acts 13:39
them to keep the *l* .... Acts 15:5

LAW OF THE LORD
that you may keep the *l* .. 1 Chr 22:12
that he forsook the *l* ...... 2 Chr 12:1
themselves to the *L* .... 2 Chr 31:4
his heart to seek the *L* ..... Ezra 7:10
his delight is in the *l* .... Ps 1:2
l is perfect, converting .... Ps 19:7
way, who walk in the *l* ...... Ps 119:1
they have rejected the *l* .... Is 5:24
who will not hear the *l* .... Is 30:9
'We are wise, and the *l* .... Jer 8:8

they have despised the *l*, . . . Amos 2:4
things according to the *l* . . . Luke 2:39

LAWFUL
doing what is not *l* . . . . Matt 12:2
Is it *l* to pay taxes . . . . Matt 22:17
All things are *l* . . . . 1 Cor 6:12

LAWGIVER
Judah is My *l* . . . . Ps 60:7
the LORD is our *L* . . . . Is 33:22
There is one *L* . . . . James 4:12

LAWLESS
l one will be revealed . . . . . 2 Thess 2:8
and hearing their *l* . . . . 2 Pet 2:8

LAWLESSNESS
Me, you who practice *l* . . . . . Matt 7:23
l is already at work . . . . 2 Thess 2:7
and hated *l* . . . . Heb 1:9
and sin is *l* . . . . 1 John 3:4

LAWYERS
l rejected the will of . . . . Luke 7:30
Woe to you also, *l* . . . . Luke 11:46

LAY
l it on the wood, but put . . 1 Kin 18:23
I *l* down and slept . . . . Ps 3:5
I will *l* your stones with . . . . . . Is 54:11
Do not *l* up for yourselves . . Matt 6:19
nowhere to *l* His head . . . . . . Matt 8:20
I have power to *l* it down . John 10:18
Will you *l* down your life . John 13:38
l hands may receive . . . . Acts 8:19
Do not *l* hands on . . . . 1 Tim 5:22
let us *l* aside every weight, . . Heb 12:1
l aside all filthiness . . . . James 1:21
"Behold, I *l* in Zion a chief . . 1 Pet 2:6

LAYING
l on of the apostles' hands . . Acts 8:18
the *l* on of my hands . . . . 2 Tim 1:6
not *l* again the foundation . . . . Heb 6:1
of *l* on of hands, of . . . . Heb 6:2
l aside all malice, all deceit . . 1 Pet 2:1

LAYS
'God *l* up one's iniquity . . . . Job 21:19
He *l* up the deep in . . . . Ps 33:7
He *l* the beams of His . . . . Ps 104:3
which the LORD *l* on him . . . . . Is 30:32
l the foundation of the . . . . . Zech 12:1
he who *l* up treasure . . . . . Luke 12:21
he *l* it on his shoulders, ... Luke 15:5

LAZARUS
Beggar described in a parable, Luke 16:20–25
——— Brother of Mary and Martha; raised from the dead, John 11:1–44
Attends a supper, John 12:1, 2
Jews seek to kill, John 12:9–11

LAZINESS
L casts one into a . . . . Prov 19:15
l the building decays . . . . . . Eccl 10:18

LAZY
l man will be put to . . . . Prov 12:24
l man does not roast . . . . . . Prov 12:27
soul of a *l* man desires . . . . . Prov 13:4
l man buries his hand . . . . . Prov 19:24
by the field of the *l* . . . . Prov 24:30
l man is wiser in his . . . . . . Prov 26:16
wicked and *l* servant . . . . . . Matt 25:26
liars, evil beasts, *l* . . . . Titus 1:12

LEAD
pillar of cloud to *l* the way . . Ex 13:21
they sank like *l* . . . . Ex 15:10
L me in Your truth and . . . . Ps 25:5
And *l* me in a smooth path . . Ps 27:11
L me and guide me . . . . Ps 31:3
L me to the rock that is . . . . . . Ps 61:2
Your hand shall *l* . . . . Ps 139:10
a little child shall *l* them . . . . . . Is 11:6
I will *l* them in paths they . . . . Is 42:16
l is consumed by the fire . . . . . Jer 6:29
bronze, tin, iron, and *l* . . . . Ezek 22:18
tin, and *l* for your goods . . Ezek 27:12
threw the *l* cover over its . . . . Zech 5:8
And do not *l* us into . . . . Matt 6:13
"Can the blind *l* . . . . Luke 6:39
not *l* us into temptation . . . . Luke 11:4
someone to *l* him by the . . . . Acts 13:11
aspire to *l* a quiet life . . . . 1 Thess 4:11
that we may *l* a quiet and . . 1 Tim 2:2
to *l* them out of the land of . . . Heb 8:9
sin which does not *l* to . . . 1 John 5:16
l them to living fountains . . . Rev 7:17

LEADING
l men among the . . . . Acts 15:22
not a few of the *l* women . . . Acts 17:4
of lawlessness *l* to more . . . . Rom 6:19
his good, *l* to edification . . . . Rom 15:2
sin not *l* to death . . . . 1 John 5:16

LEADS
He *l* me beside the . . . . Ps 23:2
He *l* me in the paths . . . . Ps 23:3
And if the blind *l* . . . . Matt 15:14
by name and *l* them out . . . . John 10:3
the goodness of God *l* . . . . Rom 2:4

LEAF
plucked olive *l* . . . . Gen 8:11
Will You frighten a *l* . . . . Job 13:25
l will be green . . . . Jer 17:8

LEAH
Laban's eldest daughter; given to Jacob deceitfully, Gen 29:16–27
Unloved by Jacob, but bears children, Gen 29:30–35; 30:16–21

LEAN
all your heart, and *l* . . . . Prov 3:5
Yet they *l* on the LORD . . . . . . Mic 3:11

LEANING
Then, *l* back on Jesus' . . . . John 13:25
l on the top of his . . . . Heb 11:21

LEANNESS
request, but sent *l* . . . . Ps 106:15
of hosts, will send *l* . . . . Is 10:16

LEAP
by my God I can *l* . . . . Ps 18:29
Then the lame shall *l* . . . . Is 35:6

LEAPED
the rams which *l* upon . . . . . Gen 31:10
they *l* about the altar . . . . . 1 Kin 18:26
the babe *l* in her womb . . . . Luke 1:41
and he *l* and walked . . . . . . Acts 14:10

LEAPING
saw King David *l* . . . . 2 Sam 6:16
walking, *l*, and praising . . . . . Acts 3:8

LEARN
it, may hear and *l* . . . . Deut 31:13
l Your statutes . . . . Ps 119:71
lest you *l* his ways . . . . Prov 22:25
l to do good . . . . Is 1:17
neither shall they *l* . . . . Is 2:4
My yoke upon you and *l* . . Matt 11:29
Let a woman *l* in . . . . 1 Tim 2:11
let our people also *l* . . . . Titus 3:14
no one could *l* that song . . . . Rev 14:3

LEARNED
Me the tongue of the *l* . . . . Is 50:4
who has heard and *l* . . . . John 6:45
have not so *l* Christ . . . . Eph 4:20
in all things I have *l* . . . . Phil 4:12
l obedience by the . . . . Heb 5:8

LEARNING
hear and increase *l* . . . . Prov 1:5
l is driving you mad . . . . . . Acts 26:24
were written for our *l* . . . . . . Rom 15:4

LEAST
Judah, are not the *l* . . . . Matt 2:6
so, shall be called *l* . . . . Matt 5:19
For I am the *l* of the . . . . 1 Cor 15:9

LEATHER
everything made of *l* . . . . . Num 31:20
wearing a *l* belt around . . . . . 2 Kin 1:8
with a *l* belt around his . . . . . Mark 1:6

LEAVE
a man shall *l* his . . . . Gen 2:24
He will not *l* you nor . . . . Deut 31:6
For You will not *l* . . . . Ps 16:10
do not *l* me nor . . . . Ps 27:9
"I will never *l* . . . . Heb 13:5

LEAVEN
day you shall remove *l* . . . . . . Ex 12:15
of heaven is like *l* . . . . Matt 13:33
and beware of the *l* . . . . Matt 16:6
know that a little *l* . . . . 1 Cor 5:6
l leavens the whole . . . . Gal 5:9

LEAVENED
For whoever eats *l* bread . . . . Ex 12:15
shall eat no *l* bread with . . . Deut 16:3
of meal till it was all *l* . . . . Matt 13:33

LEAVES
and they sewed fig *l* . . . . Gen 3:7
nothing on it but *l* . . . . Matt 21:19
l the sheep and flees . . . . . . John 10:12
The *l* of the tree . . . . Rev 22:2

LEBANON
Part of Israel's inheritance, Josh 13:5–7
Not completely conquered, Judg 3:1–3
Source of materials for temple, 1 Kin 5:2–18; Ezra 3:7
Mentioned in prophecy, Is 10:34; 29:17; 35:2; Ezek 17:3; Hos 14:5–7

LEBBAEUS
See JUDAS
Surname of Judas (Jude), Matt 10:3

LEBONAH
Town north of Shiloh, Judg 21:19

LED
l the people around by . . . . . . Ex 13:18
I have *l* you forty years in . . Deut 29:5
so the LORD alone *l* . . . . Deut 32:12
have *l* captivity captive . . . . . . Ps 68:18
l them forth by the . . . . Ps 107:7
He was *l* as a lamb to the . . . . . Is 53:7
and be *l* out with peace . . . . . . Is 55:12
l them by the right . . . . Is 63:12
have *l* them astray . . . . Jer 50:6
Then Jesus was *l* up by the . . Matt 4:1
l Him out to crucify . . . . . . Mark 15:20
"He was *l* as a sheep to . . . . . Acts 8:32
For as many as are *l* . . . . Rom 8:14
sorrow *l* to repentance . . . . . 2 Cor 7:9
if you are *l* by the Spirit . . . . . Gal 5:18
l captivity captive . . . . Eph 4:8
l away by various . . . . 2 Tim 3:6

LEFT
Lie also on your *l* side . . . . . . Ezek 4:4
l hand know what your . . . . . Matt 6:3
"See, we have *l* . . . . Matt 19:27
And everyone who has *l* . . Matt 19:29
on My *l* is not Mine to . . . . Mark 10:40
right hand and on the *l* . . . . . 2 Cor 6:7

LEGACY
shame shall be the *l* . . . . Prov 3:35

LEGION
"My name is *L* . . . . Mark 5:9
"*L*," because many . . . . Luke 8:30

LEGIONS
twelve *l* of angels . . . . Matt 26:53

LEGS
Like the *l* of the lame . . . . Prov 26:7
l are pillars of . . . . Song 5:15
did not break His *l* . . . . John 19:33

LEHI
Samson kills Philistines at, Judg 15:9–19

LEMUEL
King taught by his mother, Prov 31:1–31

LEND
"If you *l* money to ....Ex 22:25
l him sufficient ....Deut 15:8
And if you *l* to those ....Luke 6:34
l me three loaves ....Luke 11:5

LENDER
is servant to the *l* ....Prov 22:7
as with the *l* ....Is 24:2

LENDING
and my servants, am *l* ......Neh 5:10

LENDS
ever merciful, and *l* ....Ps 37:26
deals graciously and *l* ....Ps 112:5
has pity on the poor *l* ......Prov 19:17

LENGTH
The *l* of the ark shall ....Gen 6:15
is your life and the *l* ......Deut 30:20
L of days is in her ....Prov 3:16
l is as great as its ....Rev 21:16

LENGTHENS
a shadow when it *l* ....Ps 109:23

LEOPARD
the *l* shall lie down ....Is 11:6
or the *l* its spots ....Jer 13:23

LEPER
put out of the camp every *l* .. Num 5:2
and there she was, a *l* ......Num 12:10
King Uzziah was a *l* ......2 Chr 26:21
l came and worshiped ....Matt 8:2
house of Simon the *l* ......Mark 14:3

LEPERS
And when these *l* ....2 Kin 7:8
the sick, cleanse the *l* ......Matt 10:8
And many *l* were in ....Luke 4:27
ten men who were *l* ......Luke 17:12

LEPROSY
This is the law of *l* ....Lev 14:57
he would heal him of his *l* ...2 Kin 5:3
l broke out on his ....2 Chr 26:19
immediately the *l* left him ....Luke 5:13

LEPROUS
out, behold, his hand was *l* ....Ex 4:6
Miriam became *l* ....Num 12:10
out from his presence *l* ......2 Kin 5:27
his forehead, he was *l* ......2 Chr 26:20

LET
"*L* there be light" ....Gen 1:3
L the little children ....Matt 19:14

LETTER
they delivered the *l* ....Acts 15:30
the Spirit, and not in the *l* ..Rom 2:29
the oldness of the *l* ....Rom 7:6
for the *l* kills ....2 Cor 3:6
you sorry with my *l* ....2 Cor 7:8
or by word or by *l* ....2 Thess 2:2

LETTERS
does this Man know *l* ......John 7:15
or *l* of commendation ....2 Cor 3:1
"For his *l*," they say ......2 Cor 10:10
with what large *l* ....Gal 6:11

LEVI
Third son of Jacob and Leah, Gen 29:34
Avenges rape of Dinah, Gen 34:25–31
Jacob's prophecy concerning, Gen 49:5–7
Ancestor of Moses and Aaron, Ex 6:16–27

LEVIATHAN
"Can you draw out *L* ....Job 41:1
L which You have made ......Ps 104:26

LEVITE
"Is not Aaron the *L* ....Ex 4:14
Likewise a *L*, when he ......Luke 10:32
a *L* of the country of ....Acts 4:36

LEVITES
Rewarded for dedication, Ex 32:26–29
Appointed over tabernacle, Num 1:47–54
Substituted for Israel's firstborn, Num 3:12–45
Consecrated to the Lord's service, Num 8:5–26
Cities assigned to, Num 35:2–8; Josh 14:3, 4; 1 Chr 6:54–81
Organized for temple service, 1 Chr 9:14–34; 23:1—26:28

LEVITICAL
were through the *L* ....Heb 7:11

LEWDNESS
wickedness, deceit, *l* ....Mark 7:22
drunkenness, not in *l* ......Rom 13:13
themselves over to *l* ....Eph 4:19
when we walked in *l* ....1 Pet 4:3

LIAR
a *l* listens eagerly to a ......Prov 17:4
for he is a *l* and the ....John 8:44
but every man a *l* ....Rom 3:4
we make Him a *l* ....1 John 1:10
Who is a *l* but he who ......1 John 2:22
his brother, he is a *l* ......1 John 4:20
God has made Him a *l* ......1 John 5:10

LIARS
"All men are *l* ....Ps 116:11
Cretans are always *l* ....Titus 1:12
and have found them *l* ....Rev 2:2
l shall have their ....Rev 21:8

LIBERALITY
he who gives, with *l* ....Rom 12:8
the riches of their *l* ....2 Cor 8:2

LIBERALLY
who gives to all *l* ....James 1:5

LIBERTY
year, and proclaim *l* ....Lev 25:10
And I will walk at *l* ....Ps 119:45
to proclaim *l* to the ....Is 61:1
to proclaim *l* to the ....Luke 4:18
into the glorious *l* ....Rom 8:21
For why is my *l* ....1 Cor 10:29
Lord is, there is *l* ....2 Cor 3:17
therefore in the *l* ....Gal 5:1
l as an opportunity ....Gal 5:13
the perfect law of *l* ....James 1:25
yet not using *l* ....1 Pet 2:16

LIBNAH
Canaanite city, captured by Joshua, Josh 10:29, 30
Given to Aaron's descendants, Josh 21:13

LIBYA
Mentioned in prophecy, Ezek 30:5; Dan 11:43
Jews from, present at Pentecost, Acts 2:1–10

LICE
so that it may become *l* ....Ex 8:16
and *l* in all their territory ......Ps 105:31

LIE
man, that He should *l* ......Num 23:19
to Samuel, "Go, *l* down ......1 Sam 3:9
For now I will *l* ....Job 7:21
I will not *l* to David ....Ps 89:35
forged a *l* against me ......Ps 119:69
leopard shall *l* down with ......Is 11:6
prophesy a *l* to you in My ..Jer 29:21
heart to *l* to the Holy Spirit ..Acts 5:3
Do not *l* to one ....Col 3:9
God, who cannot *l* ....Titus 1:2

do not boast and *l* ....James 3:14
know it, and that no *l* ......1 John 2:21
an abomination or a *l* ......Rev 21:27

LIED
They have *l* about the ....Jer 5:12
You have not *l* to men ....Acts 5:4

LIES
sin *l* at the door ....Gen 4:7
not say, "Here *l* Jezebel ....2 Kin 9:37
He *l* in wait secretly ....Ps 10:9
speak *l* shall be stopped ......Ps 63:11
and he who speaks *l* ....Prov 19:5
She also *l* in wait as for ....Prov 23:28
prophesy *l* in My name ......Jer 14:14
they shall speak *l* at the ....Dan 11:27
l in the name of the LORD ..Zech 13:3
speaking *l* in hypocrisy ......1 Tim 4:2
and the whole world *l* ......1 John 5:19

LIFE
See ALL THE DAYS OF HIS LIFE; BOOK OF LIFE; BREATH OF LIFE; ETERNAL LIFE; EVERLASTING LIFE; TREE OF LIFE; WATER OF LIFE
the breath of *l* ....Gen 2:7
l was also in the ....Gen 2:9
I will require the *l* of man ....Gen 9:5
then you shall give *l* ....Ex 21:23
For the *l* of the ....Lev 17:11
before you today *l* ....Deut 30:15
You have granted me *l* ......Job 10:12
in whose hand is the *l* ......Job 12:10
God takes away his *l* ....Job 27:8
with the light of *l* ....Job 33:30
He will redeem their *l* ......Ps 72:14
word has given me *l* ....Ps 119:50
blessing—*L* forevermore ....Ps 133:3
regain the paths of *l* ....Prov 2:19
She is a tree of *l* ....Prov 3:18
so they will be *l* ....Prov 3:22
finds me finds *l* ....Prov 8:35
the *l* of his animal ....Prov 12:10
LORD is a fountain of *l* ....Prov 14:27
l winds upward for the ......Prov 15:24
thief hates his own *l* ....Prov 29:24
is that wisdom gives *l* ......Eccl 7:12
I have cut off my *l* ....Is 38:12
you the way of *l* ....Jer 21:8
l shall be as a prize ....Jer 39:18
not worry about your *l* ......Matt 6:25
l does not consist ....Luke 12:15
L is more than food ....Luke 12:23
l was the light ....John 1:4
so the Son gives *l* ....John 5:21
as the Father has *l* ....John 5:26
spirit, and they are *l* ....John 6:63
have the light of *l* ....John 8:12
and I lay down My *l* ......John 10:15
resurrection and the *l* ......John 11:25
you lay down your *l* ......John 13:38
God, who gives *l* ....Rom 4:17
that pertain to this *l* ....1 Cor 6:3
Lord Jesus, that the *l* ......2 Cor 4:10
l which I now live ....Gal 2:20
l is hidden with ....Col 3:3
of God who gives *l* ....1 Tim 6:13
For what is your *l* ....James 4:14
that pertain to *l* ....2 Pet 1:3
l was manifested ....1 John 1:2
and the pride of *l* ....1 John 2:16
has given us eternal *l* ......1 John 5:11
who has the Son has *l* ....1 John 5:12
the Lamb's Book of *L* ......Rev 21:27
right to the tree of *l* ....Rev 22:14
the water of *l* freely ....Rev 22:17
from the Book of *L* ....Rev 22:19

LIFT
"*L* your eyes now and ......Gen 13:14
l up His countenance ......Num 6:26
L up your heads ....Ps 24:7
I will *l* up my hands ....Ps 63:4

I will *l* up my eyes to ....Ps 121:1
l up your voice like a ....Is 58:1
l up a banner for the ....Is 62:10
l our hearts and hands .....Lam 3:41
Nation shall not *l* up sword ...Mic 4:3
Lord, and He will *l* ....James 4:10

LIFTED
l up the ark, and it rose .....Gen 7:17
Then Abraham *l* his eyes ...Gen 22:13
Esau *l* up his voice and ....Gen 27:38
he *l* up the rod and struck ....Ex 7:20
when your heart is *l* up ....Deut 8:14
O LORD, for You have *l*.......Ps 30:1
l up his heel against me ......Ps 41:9
your heart is *l* up ....Ezek 28:2
l like a banner over His ....Zech 9:16
He *l* up His eyes toward ...Luke 6:20
in Hades, he *l* up his .....Luke 16:23
l up His hands and ....Luke 24:50
the Son of Man be *l* ....John 3:14
And I, if I am *l* ....John 12:32
of Man must be *l* ....John 12:34
l up his heel against Me ..John 13:18
l up His eyes to heaven ....John 17:1

LIFTING
while *l* up their hands ....Neh 8:6
The *l* up of my hands as .....Ps 141:2
l up holy hands, without ....1 Tim 2:8

LIFTS
He brings low and *l* up ....1 Sam 2:7
the One who *l* up my head .....Ps 3:3
The LORD *l* up the humble ...Ps 147:6

LIGAMENTS
together by joints and *l* .....Col 2:19

LIGHT
"Let there be *l* ....Gen 1:3
God called the *l* Day ....Gen 1:5
had *l* in their dwellings ......Ex 10:23
pillar of fire to give them *l* ..Ex 13:21
of pressed olives for the *l* ....Ex 27:20
he shall be like the *l* of ...2 Sam 23:4
by night, to show them *l* ......Neh 9:19
"The *l* of the wicked ....Job 18:5
l will shine on your ....Job 22:28
the wicked their *l* ....Job 38:15
to the dwelling of *l* ....Job 38:19
LORD, lift up the *l* ....Ps 4:6
For You will *l* my lamp ....Ps 18:28
The LORD is my *l*...............Ps 27:1
Oh, send out Your *l* ....Ps 43:3
L is sown for the ....Ps 97:11
and He has given us *l* ......Ps 118:27
and a *l* to my path ....Ps 119:105
Him, all you stars of *l* ....Ps 148:3
The *l* of the righteous ....Prov 13:9
The *l* of the eyes ....Prov 15:30
The LORD gives *l* ....Prov 29:13
Truly the *l* is sweet ....Eccl 11:7
let us walk in the *l* ....Is 2:5
l is darkened by the ....Is 5:30
because there is no *l* ....Is 8:20
moon will be as the *l* ....Is 30:26
darkness *l* before them ....Is 42:16
l shall break forth ....Is 58:8
for your *l* has come ....Is 60:1
shall come to your *l* ....Is 60:3
be your everlasting *l* ....Is 60:20
gives the sun for a *l* ....Jer 31:35
moon shall not give her *l* ...Ezek 32:7
like *l* that goes forth ....Hos 6:5
have seen a great *l* ....Matt 4:16
"You are the *l* ....Matt 5:14
Let your *l* so shine ....Matt 5:16
body will be full of *l* ....Matt 6:22
moon will not give its *l* ....Matt 24:29
take heed that the *l* ....Luke 11:35
than the sons of *l* ....Luke 16:8
and the life was the *l* ....John 1:4
That was the true *L* ....John 1:9
darkness rather than *l* ......John 3:19
evil hates the *l* ....John 3:20
truth comes to the *l* ....John 3:21
saying, "I am the *l* ....John 8:12
believe in the *l* ....John 12:36
I have come as a *l* ....John 12:46
to *l* the hidden things ....1 Cor 4:5
God who commanded *l* ......2 Cor 4:6
Walk as children of *l* ....Eph 5:8
You are all sons of *l* ......1 Thess 5:5
and immortality to *l*........2 Tim 1:10
into His marvelous *l* ....1 Pet 2:9
do well to heed as a *l* ....2 Pet 1:19
to you, that God is *l* ....1 John 1:5
l as He is in the ....1 John 1:7
says he is in the *l* ....1 John 2:9
l of a lamp shall not ....Rev 18:23
The Lamb is its *l* ....Rev 21:23
Lord God gives them *l* ......Rev 22:5

LIGHTEN
L the yoke which ....1 Kin 12:9
the sea, to *l* the load ....Jon 1:5

LIGHTLY
this, did I do it *l* ....2 Cor 1:17

LIGHTNING
For as the *l* comes ....Matt 24:27
countenance was like *l* ....Matt 28:3
saw Satan fall like *l* ....Luke 10:18

LIGHTNINGS
were thunderings and *l* .....Ex 19:16
the *l* lit up the world ....Ps 77:18
l light the world ....Ps 97:4
the throne proceeded *l* ....Rev 4:5

LIGHTS
"Let there be *l* ....Gen 1:14
when Aaron *l* the lamps at ....Ex 30:8
Him who made great *l* ....Ps 136:7
whom you shine as *l*..........Phil 2:15
from the Father of *l* ....James 1:17

LIKE
"Who is *l* You ....Ex 15:11
L a lily among thorns ....Song 2:2
be made *l* His brethren ....Heb 2:17

LIKE-MINDED
grant you to be *l*..............Rom 15:5
For I have no one *l* ....Phil 2:20

LIKEN
To whom will you *l* Me ....Is 46:5
shall I *l* this generation ....Matt 11:16
shall I *l* the kingdom ....Luke 13:20

LIKENESS
according to Our *l*.............Gen 1:26
carved image—any *l* ....Ex 20:4
when I awake in Your *l* ....Ps 17:15
in the *l* of His death ....Rom 6:5
His own Son in the *l* ....Rom 8:3
and coming in the *l* ....Phil 2:7

LILIES
were in the shape of *l* .....1 Kin 7:22
his lips are *l*, dripping .....Song 5:13
feeds his flock among the *l*..Song 6:3
the *l*, how they grow ....Luke 12:27

LILY
the *l* of the valleys ....Song 2:1
Like a *l* among thorns ....Song 2:2
shall grow like the *l* ....Hos 14:5

LIMIT
Do you *l* wisdom to ....Job 15:8
to the sea its *l* ....Prov 8:29

LIMITED
l the Holy One of ....Ps 78:41

LINE
l has gone out through ....Ps 19:4
upon precept, *l* upon *l* ....Is 28:10
I am setting a plumb *l* ....Amos 7:8

LINEAGE
was of the house and *l* ....Luke 2:4

LINEN
him in garments of fine *l* ..Gen 41:42
artistically woven of fine *l* ..Ex 39:27
shall put on his *l* garment ....Lev 6:10
with the *l* turban he shall.....Lev 16:4
take off the *l* garments ......Lev 16:23
child, wearing a *l* ephod ..1 Sam 2:18
David also wore a *l* ....1 Chr 15:27
her clothing is fine *l* ....Prov 31:22
get yourself a *l* sash ....Jer 13:1
to the man clothed with *l*....Ezek 9:3
heard the man clothed in *l* ..Dan 12:7
wrapped it in a clean *l* ....Matt 27:59
wrapped Him in the *l* .....Mark 15:46
in purple and fine *l* ....Luke 16:19
strips of *l* with the spices ..John 19:40
saw the *l* cloths lying ....John 20:5
that was clothed in fine *l* ...Rev 18:16
l is the righteous ....Rev 19:8

LINGER
Those who *l* long at ....Prov 23:30
salvation shall not *l* ....Is 46:13

LINGERED
the Boy Jesus *l* behind ....Luke 2:43

LINTEL
on the *l* of the houses ....Ex 12:7
the *l* and doorposts were ...1 Kin 6:31

LION
he lies down as a *l* ....Gen 49:9
he tore the *l* apart as one ...Judg 14:6
when a *l* or a bear ....1 Sam 17:34
is like the heart of a *l* ...2 Sam 17:10
l standing by the corpse ...1 Kin 13:28
Killed a *l* in the midst ....1 Chr 11:22
like a fierce *l* ....Job 10:16
l shall eat straw ....Is 11:7
face of a *l* on the right .....Ezek 1:10
the third the face of a *l* ....Ezek 10:14
the face of a young *l* ....Ezek 41:19
For I will be like a *l* ....Hos 5:14
about like a roaring *l* ....1 Pet 5:8
living creature was like a *l* ...Rev 4:7
the *L* of the tribe of Judah ...Rev 5:5

LION'S
Judah is a *l* whelp ....Gen 49:9

LIONS
Twelve *l* stood there ....1 Kin 10:20
My soul is among *l*..............Ps 57:4
be cast into the den of *l* ....Dan 6:7
the mouths of *l* ....Heb 11:33
were like the heads of *l* .....Rev 9:17

LIPS
of uncircumcised *l* ....Ex 6:12
off all flattering *l*.................Ps 12:3
Let the lying *l* ....Ps 31:18
The *l* of the righteous .....Prov 10:21
but the *l* of knowledge .....Prov 20:15
am a man of unclean *l* ....Is 6:5
with stammering *l* and ....Is 28:11
I create the fruit of the *l* ....Is 57:19
offer the sacrifices of our *l* ..Hos 14:2
honors Me with their *l* ....Mark 7:6
asps is under their *l* ....Rom 3:13
other *l* I will speak ....1 Cor 14:21
that is, the fruit of our *l* ....Heb 13:15
from evil, and his *l* ....1 Pet 3:10

LISTEN
L now to my voice ....Ex 18:19
would not *l* to Balaam .....Deut 23:5
not *l* to their judges ....Judg 2:17
But do not *l* to Hezekiah ..2 Kin 18:32
L carefully to Me ....Is 55:2
O Lord, *l* and act ....Dan 9:19
"*L*! Behold, a sower went ...Mark 4:3
you are not able to *l* ....John 8:43
Why do you *l* to Him ......John 10:20
you who fear God, *l* ....Acts 13:16

LISTENED
God *l* to Leah, and she ....Gen 30:17

the LORD *l* to the voice of .. Num 21:3
But the LORD *l* to me .... Deut 9:19
l to the voice of Manoah ... Judg 13:9
and the LORD *l* to him ...... 2 Kin 13:4
the LORD *l* to Hezekiah ... 2 Chr 30:20
Yet you have not *l* to Me .... Jer 25:7
"Men, you should have *l* .. Acts 27:21

LISTENS

but whoever *l* to me .... Prov 1:33

LITTLE

l foxes that spoil the .... Song 2:15
We have a *l* sister .... Song 8:8
upon line, here a *l* .... Is 28:10
though you are *l* .... Mic 5:2
indeed it came to *l* .... Hag 1:9
for I was a *l* angry .... Zech 1:15
l ones only a cup .... Matt 10:42
"O you of *l* faith .... Matt 14:31
Whoever receives one *l* .... Matt 18:5
to whom *l* is forgiven ...... Luke 7:47
"Let the *l* children come .. Luke 18:16
faithful in a very *l* .... Luke 19:17
gathered *l* had no lack ..... 2 Cor 8:15
l leaven leavens the whole .... Gal 5:9
exercise profits a *l* .... 1 Tim 4:8
made him a *l* lower than ..... Heb 2:7
"For yet a *l* while .... Heb 10:37
the tongue is a *l* member .. James 3:5
L children, keep .... 1 John 5:21
"Give me the *l* book .... Rev 10:9

LITTLE CHILDREN

converted and become as *l* . Matt 18:3
l were brought to Him .... Matt 19:13
receives one of these *l* ..... Mark 9:37
"Let the *l* come to Me, ... Mark 10:14
L, I shall be with you ..... John 13:33
My *l*, for whom I labor ...... Gal 4:19
l, these things I write ...... 1 John 2:1
I write to you, *l*, ... 1 John 2:12
now, *l*, abide in Him, ... 1 John 2:28
L, let no one deceive ...... 1 John 3:7
You are of God, *l*, ... 1 John 4:4
L, keep yourselves from .. 1 John 5:21

LIVE

eat, and *l* forever .... Gen 3:22
a man does, he shall *l* .... Lev 18:5
I would not *l* forever .... Job 7:16
L joyfully with the .... Eccl 9:9
by these things men *l* .... Is 38:16
sin, he shall surely *l* .... Ezek 3:21
"Seek Me and *l* .... Amos 5:4
but the just shall *l* .... Hab 2:4
l by bread alone .... Matt 4:4
who feeds on Me will *l* ..... John 6:57
Because I *l*, you will *l* ..... John 14:19
for in Him we *l* .... Acts 17:28
those who *l* according to .... Rom 8:5
l peaceably with all .... Rom 12:18
should *l* from the gospel ... 1 Cor 9:14
as dying, and behold we *l* ... 2 Cor 6:9
l in the manner of Gentiles .. Gal 2:14
the life which I now *l* .... Gal 2:20
"the just shall *l* by faith ..... Gal 3:11
If we *l* in the Spirit .... Gal 5:25
to me, to *l* is Christ .... Phil 1:21
l godly in Christ .... 2 Tim 3:12
the just shall *l* by faith .... Heb 10:38
Father of spirits and *l* .... Heb 12:9
to *l* honorably .... Heb 13:18
l according to God in .... 1 Pet 4:6
l again until the thousand .... Rev 20:5

LIVED

our religion I *l* a Pharisee .. Acts 26:5
died and rose and *l* .... Rom 14:9
walked when you *l* in them ... Col 3:7
And they *l* and reigned ..... Rev 20:4

LIVES

but man *l* by every .... Deut 8:3
know that my Redeemer *l* .. Job 19:25
days of our *l* are seventy .... Ps 90:10
have risked their *l* .... Acts 15:26
He *l* to God .... Rom 6:10
For none of us *l* .... Rom 14:7
He *l* by the power of God .. 2 Cor 13:4
but Christ *l* in me .... Gal 2:20
at all while the testator *l* .... Heb 9:17
to lay down our *l* .... 1 John 3:16
I am He who *l* .... Rev 1:18

LIVING

See LAND OF THE LIVING
and man became a *l* .... Gen 2:7
in the light of the *l* .... Ps 56:13
l will take it to heart .... Eccl 7:2
l know that they will .... Eccl 9:5
Why should a *l* man .... Lam 3:39
the dead, but of the *l* ...... Matt 22:32
Why do you seek the *l* ..... Luke 24:5
I am the *l* bread .... John 6:51
will flow rivers of *l* water .. John 7:38
to be Judge of the *l* .... Acts 10:42
your bodies a *l* sacrifice .... Rom 12:1
the church of the *l* God .... 1 Tim 3:15
who will judge the *l* .... 2 Tim 4:1
the word of God is *l* .... Heb 4:12
the hands of the *l* God ..... Heb 10:31
to Him as to a *l* stone .... 1 Pet 2:4
ready to judge the *l* .... 1 Pet 4:5
l creature was like a .... Rev 4:7
the four *l* creatures .... Rev 7:11

LIVING CREATURE

earth bring forth the *l* ...... Gen 1:24
Adam called each *l*, ... Gen 2:19
every *l* that is with you: .... Gen 9:10
and every *l* of all flesh ...... Gen 9:15
every *l* that moves .... Lev 11:46
each *l* with its four .... Ezek 1:15
This was the *l* I saw ...... Ezek 10:15
the spirit of the *l* .... Ezek 10:17
first *l* was like a lion, ... Rev 4:7
I heard the second *l* .... Rev 6:3
l in the sea died .... Rev 16:3

LIVING CREATURES

with an abundance of *l*, ... Gen 1:20
likeness of four *l* .... Ezek 1:5
the wings of the *l* .... Ezek 3:13
four *l* full of eyes .... Rev 4:6
four *l* said, "Amen!" .... Rev 5:14
the *l* in the sea died, ... Rev 8:9
before the four *l* .... Rev 14:3
one of the four *l* .... Rev 15:7
l fell down and worshiped .. Rev 19:4

LO-AMMI

Symbolic name of Hosea's son, Hos 1:8, 9

LO-RUHAMAH

Symbolic name of Hosea's daughter, Hos 1:6

LOAD

into the sea, to lighten the *l* .. Jon 1:5
you *l* men with burdens .. Luke 11:46
shall bear his own *l* .... Gal 6:5

LOADED

they *l* their donkeys with .. Gen 42:26
l them on donkeys .... 1 Sam 25:18
women *l* down with sins .... 2 Tim 3:6

LOAF

l of barley bread tumbled .. Judg 7:13
l with them in the boat .... Mark 8:14

LOATHE

I *l* my life .... Job 7:16
l themselves for the .... Ezek 6:9

LOATHSOME

but a wicked man is *l* ...... Prov 13:5

LOAVES

have here only five *l* ...... Matt 14:17
He took the seven *l* .... Matt 15:36
lend me three *l* .... Luke 11:5
you ate of the *l* .... John 6:26

LOCKS

If you weave the seven *l* .. Judg 16:13
his *l* are wavy, and black .. Song 5:11

LOCUST

What the chewing *l* .... Joel 1:4
left, the swarming *l* .... Joel 1:4

LOCUSTS

as numerous as *l* .... Judg 7:12
He spoke, and *l* came .... Ps 105:34
the *l* have no king .... Prov 30:27
and his food was *l* .... Matt 3:4
waist, and he ate *l* .... Mark 1:6
out of the smoke *l* .... Rev 9:3

LODGED

them in and *l* them .... Acts 10:23
children, if she has *l* ...... 1 Tim 5:10

LOFTILY

they speak *l* .... Ps 73:8

LOFTY

haughty, nor my eyes *l* ...... Ps 131:1
Wisdom is too *l* .... Prov 24:7
l are their eyes .... Prov 30:13
and *L* One who .... Is 57:15

LOINS

gird up the *l* of your .... 1 Pet 1:13

LONELY

How *l* sits the city that was .. Lam 1:1

LONG

your days may be *l* .... Deut 5:16
said, "*L* live the king .... 1 Sam 10:24
who *l* for death .... Job 3:21
me the thing that I *l* .... Job 6:8
I *l* for Your salvation ..... Ps 119:174
the appointed time was *l* .... Dan 10:1
l as the bridegroom is ...... Matt 9:15
How *l* shall I bear with .... Mark 9:19
go around in *l* robes ..... Mark 12:38
make *l* prayers .... Luke 20:47
we are killed all day *l* ...... Rom 8:36
Love suffers *l* and is kind .. 1 Cor 13:4
how greatly I *l* .... Phil 1:8
"How *l*, O LORD, holy and ... Rev 6:10

LONGING

wife cast *l* eyes on Joseph .. Gen 39:7
David said with *l*, "Oh ... 2 Sam 23:15
For He satisfies the *l* soul .... Ps 107:9
since he was *l* for you all ... Phil 2:26

LONGSUFFERING

and gracious, *l* .... Ps 86:15
is love, joy, peace, *l* .... Gal 5:22
and gentleness, with *l* .... Eph 4:2
for all patience and *l* .... Col 1:11
might show all *l* .... 1 Tim 1:16
when once the Divine *l* .... 1 Pet 3:20
and consider that the *l* ..... 2 Pet 3:15

LOOK

Do not *l* behind you .... Gen 19:17
l down from heaven .... Ps 80:14
who has a haughty *l* .... Ps 101:5
A proud *l*, a lying .... Prov 6:17
that day a man will *l* .... Is 17:7
L upon Zion .... Is 33:20
"*L* to Me, and be saved ...... Is 45:22
l to the rock from which ...... Is 51:1
we *l* for light .... Is 59:9
we *l* for justice .... Is 59:11
"*L* among the nations .... Hab 1:5
l on Me whom they .... Zech 12:10
L at the birds of the air .... Matt 6:26
why do you *l* at the speck ... Matt 7:3
say to you, '*L* here .... Luke 17:23
L at the fig tree .... Luke 21:29
and *l* at My hands .... John 20:27
l on their threats .... Acts 4:29
L! see the heavens .... Acts 7:56
of Israel could not *l* .... 2 Cor 3:7
while we do not *l* .... 2 Cor 4:18
Let each of you *l* .... Phil 2:4

angels desire to *l* into . . . . . . 1 Pet 1:12
l for new heavens and a . . . 2 Pet 3:13
L to yourselves . . . . 2 John 8
open the scroll, or to *l* at it . . . Rev 5:3

LOOKED
But when I *l* for good . . . . . . Job 30:26
They *l* to Him and were . . . . . . Ps 34:5
For He *l* down from the . . . . Ps 102:19
He *l* for justice . . . . Is 5:7
"We *l* for peace . . . . Jer 8:15
"You *l* for much . . . . Hag 1:9
the Lord turned and *l* . . . . . Luke 22:61
for he *l* to the reward . . . . . Heb 11:26

LOOKING
the plow, and *l* back . . . . Luke 9:62
l for the blessed hope . . . . . . Titus 2:13
l unto Jesus, the author . . . . . Heb 12:2
l carefully lest . . . . Heb 12:15
l for the mercy of . . . . Jude 21

LOOKS
Absalom for his good *l* . . 2 Sam 14:25
Then he *l* at men and . . . . . . Job 33:27
God *l* down from heaven . . . . . Ps 53:2
The lofty *l* of man . . . . Is 2:11
to you that whoever *l* . . . . Matt 5:28

LOOM
and the web from the *l* . . . . Judg 16:14
cuts me off from the *l* . . . . Is 38:12

LOOSE
l the armor of kings . . . . Is 45:1
and whatever you *l* . . . . . . Matt 16:19
said to them, "*L* him . . . . . . John 11:44

LOOSED
You have *l* my bonds . . . . . . Ps 116:16
the silver cord is *l* . . . . Eccl 12:6
on earth will be *l* in . . . . Matt 16:19
his tongue was *l*, and he . . . Mark 7:35
l from your infirmity . . . . . Luke 13:12
be *l* from this bond . . . . Luke 13:16
l the pains of death . . . . Acts 2:24
everyone's chains were *l* . . Acts 16:26
Do not seek to be *l* . . . . 1 Cor 7:27

LORD
See ANGEL OF THE LORD; ANGER OF THE LORD; BLESS THE LORD; BLESSED BE THE LORD; DAY OF THE LORD; FEAR OF THE LORD; FEAR THE LORD; GLORY OF THE LORD; HAND OF THE LORD; HOUSE OF THE LORD; LAW OF THE LORD; LOVE THE LORD YOUR GOD; PRAISE THE LORD; REJOICE IN THE LORD; SEEK THE LORD; SERVE THE LORD; SINNED AGAINST THE LORD; SPIRIT OF THE LORD; VOICE OF THE LORD; VOW TO THE LORD; WAIT ON THE LORD; WAY OF THE LORD; WRATH OF THE LORD
L is my strength . . . . Ex 15:2
L is a man of war . . . . Ex 15:3
L our God, the *L* . . . . Deut 6:4
sacrifice to the *L* your . . . . . Deut 17:1
may know that the *L* . . . . 1 Kin 8:60
If the *L* is God . . . . 1 Kin 18:21
You alone are the *L* . . . . Neh 9:6
The *L* of hosts . . . . Ps 24:10
belongs to the *L* . . . . Ps 89:18
let us sing to the *L* . . . . Ps 95:1
L is the great God . . . . Ps 95:3
Gracious is the *L* . . . . Ps 116:5
L surrounds His people . . . . . Ps 125:2
The *L* is righteous . . . . Ps 129:4
L is near to all who . . . . Ps 145:18
L is a God of justice . . . . Is 30:18
L Our Righteousness . . . . Jer 23:6
L has done marvelous . . . . . . Joel 2:21
L God is my strength . . . . Hab 3:19
"The *L* is one . . . . Zech 14:9
shall not tempt the *L* . . . . Matt 4:7
shall worship the *L* . . . . Matt 4:10
Son of Man is also *L* . . . . . . Mark 2:28
who is Christ the *L* . . . . Luke 2:11
why do you call Me '*L* . . . . . Luke 6:46
L is risen indeed . . . . Luke 24:34
call Me Teacher and *L* . . . . John 13:13
He is *L* of all . . . . Acts 10:36
'Who are You, *L* . . . . Acts 26:15
with your mouth the *L* . . . . . Rom 10:9
Greek, for the same *L* . . . . . . Rom 10:12
say that Jesus is *L* . . . . 1 Cor 12:3
second Man is the *L* . . . . . . 1 Cor 15:47
the Spirit of the *L* . . . . 2 Cor 3:17
that Jesus Christ is *L* . . . . Phil 2:11
and deny the only *L* . . . . Jude 4
L God Omnipotent . . . . Rev 19:6

LORD APPEARED TO
Then the *L* Abram and . . . . . . Gen 12:7
the *L* Abram and said to . . . . Gen 17:1
L him by the terebinth . . . . . . Gen 18:1
Then the *L* him and said . . . . Gen 26:2
Then the glory of the *L* . . . . . Lev 9:23
glory of the *L* them . . . . Num 20:6
L Solomon in a dream . . . . 1 Kin 3:5
L Solomon the second . . . . . . 1 Kin 9:2

LORD COMMANDED
all that the *L* him . . . . Gen 7:5
L Moses and Aaron, ... Ex 12:50
words which the *L* him . . . . Ex 19:7
the thing which the *L*, ... Ex 35:4
The *L* this to be given . . . . Lev 7:36
which the *L* Moses . . . . Lev 27:34
As the *L* Moses, so he . . . . . . Num 1:19
as the *L* Moses, all . . . . Num 15:36
Moses did as the *L* . . . . Num 27:22
statutes which the *L* . . . . Num 30:16
the *L* us to observe . . . . Deut 6:24
not kept what the *L* . . . . . . 1 Sam 13:14
David did so, as the *L* . . . . . 2 Sam 5:25
So the *L* the angel, ... 1 Chr 21:27
there the *L* the blessing . . . . . Ps 133:3
the Euphrates, as the *L* . . . . . . Jer 13:5
did as the angel of the *L* . . . . Matt 1:24

LORD GOD OF HOSTS
the *L* was with him . . . . 2 Sam 5:10
very zealous for the *L* . . . . . 1 Kin 19:10
who wait for You, O *L*, ... Ps 69:6
Restore us, O *L*; . . . . Ps 80:19
O *L*, hear my prayer; . . . . Ps 84:8
Therefore thus says the *L*: . . . . Is 10:24
L in the Valley of Vision . . . . . . Is 22:5
I have heard from the *L*, ... Is 28:22
called by Your name, O *L* . . Jer 15:16
this is the day of the *L* . . . . . Jer 46:10
the work of the *L* . . . . Jer 50:25
the *L* is his name . . . . Amos 4:13
The *L*, he who touches . . . . . . Amos 9:5

LORD GOD OF ISRAEL
Pharaoh, "Thus says the *L* . . . . Ex 5:1
before the Lord, the *L* . . . . Ex 34:23
give glory to the *L*, ... Josh 7:19
built an altar to the *L* . . . . Josh 8:30
sworn to them by the *L* . . . . . . Josh 9:19
the *L* fought for Israel . . . . . Josh 10:42
L was their inheritance . . . . . Josh 13:33
your heart to the *L* . . . . Josh 24:23
will sing praise to the *L* . . . . . . Judg 5:3
"O *L*, why has this come . . . Judg 21:3
be given you by the *L*, ... Ruth 2:12
Saul said to the *L* . . . . 1 Sam 14:41
"O *L*, Your servant . . . . 1 Sam 23:10
Blessed is the *L* . . . . 1 Sam 25:32
L: 'I anointed you . . . . 2 Sam 12:7
'Blessed be the *L* . . . . 1 Kin 1:48
for the name of the *L* . . . . 1 Kin 8:17
turned away from the *L* . . . . . 1 Kin 11:9
provoked the *L* to anger . . . 1 Kin 15:30
O *L*, the One who . . . . 2 Kin 19:15
the ark of the *L* . . . . 1 Chr 15:12
build a house for the *L* . . . . . . 1 Chr 22:6
"The *L* has given rest . . . . . . 1 Chr 23:25
their heart to seek the *L* . . 2 Chr 11:16
they turned to the *L* . . . . 2 Chr 15:4
the Passover to the *L* . . . . . . 2 Chr 30:1
build the house of the *L* . . . . . Ezra 1:3
in order to seek the *L* . . . . . . Exra 6:21
Blessed be the *L*, from . . . . . . Ps 41:13
Blessed is the *L*, for he . . . . Luke 1:68

LORD HAS SPOKEN
son's wife, as the *L* . . . . Gen 24:51
that the *L* we will do . . . . Ex 19:8
the statutes which the *L* . . . . Lev 10:11
which the *L* to Moses . . . . . . Num 15:22
For the *L* of David . . . . 2 Sam 3:18
the sign which the *L* . . . . 1 Kin 13:3
the mouth of the *L* . . . . Is 1:20
for the mouth of the *L* . . . . Is 40:5
not be proud, for the *L* . . . . . . Jer 13:15
Hear this word that the *L* . . . Amos 3:1

LORD IS GOOD
taste and see that the *L* . . . . Ps 34:8
For the *L*; His mercy . . . . Ps 100:5
Praise the Lord, for the *L* . . . . . Ps 135:3
L to all, and His . . . . Ps 145:9
Lord of hosts, for the *L* . . . . . Jer 33:11
The *L* to those who wait . . . . Lam 3:25
The *L*, a stronghold . . . . Nah 1:7

LORD JESUS CHRIST
we believed on the *L* . . . . . . Acts 11:17
the grace of the *L* . . . . Acts 15:11
for the name of our *L* . . . . . Acts 15:26
"Believe on the *L* . . . . Acts 16:31
with God through our *L* . . . . . . Rom 5:1
in God through our *L* . . . . Rom 5:11
But put on the *L* . . . . Rom 13:14
do not serve our *L* . . . . Rom 16:18
the revelation of our *L* . . . . . . 1 Cor 1:7
in the day of our *L* . . . . 1 Cor 1:8
victory through our *L* . . . . . . 1 Cor 15:57
does not love the *L* . . . . 1 Cor 16:22
know the grace of our *L* . . . . 2 Cor 8:9
in the cross of our *L* . . . . Gal 6:14
in the name of our *L* . . . . Eph 5:20
for the Savior, the *L* . . . . Phil 3:20
presence of our *L* . . . . 1 Thess 2:19
salvation through our *L* . . . 1 Thess 5:9
at the coming of our *L* . . . 1 Thess 5:23
obey the gospel of our *L* . . 2 Thess 1:8
the coming of our *L* . . . . 2 Thess 2:1
hold the faith of our *L* . . . . . . James 2:1
in the knowledge of *L* . . . . 2 Pet 1:8
just as our *L* showed me . . . 2 Pet 1:14
Lord God and our *L* . . . . Jude 4
by the apostles of our *L* . . . . . . Jude 17
The grace of our *L* . . . . Rev 22:21

LORD OF HOSTS
to the *L* in Shiloh . . . . 1 Sam 1:3
"O *L*, if You will indeed . . 1 Sam 1:11
L, who dwells between . . . . 1 Sam 4:4
in the name of the *L* . . . . . 1 Sam 17:45
'*L* is the God over Israel . . 2 Sam 7:26
The zeal of the *L* . . . . 2 Kin 19:31
the *L* was with him . . . . 1 Chr 11:9
The *L*, He is the King . . . . Ps 24:10
The *L* is with us; . . . . Ps 46:7
Your tabernacle, O *L* . . . . Ps 84:1
Unless the *L* had left to . . . . Is 1:9
For the day of the *L* . . . . Is 2:12
vineyard of the *L* . . . . Is 5:7
Holy, holy, holy is the *L* . . . . Is 6:3
The *L*, Him you shall . . . . Is 8:13
The zeal of the *L* . . . . Is 9:7
Through the wrath of the *L* . . . Is 9:19
in the wrath of the *L* . . . . Is 13:13
L will reign on Mount Zion . . Is 24:23
In that day the *L* . . . . Is 28:5
O *L*, God of Israel . . . . Is 37:16
his Redeemer, the *L* . . . . Is 44:6
is your husband, the *L* . . . . Is 54:5
But, O *L*, You who test . . . . . Jer 20:12
of the living God, the *L* . . . . . Jer 23:36

intercession to the *L* .... Jer 27:18
the *L* is His name .... Jer 31:35
Praise the *L*, for the Lord ... Jer 33:11
by his God, the *L* .... Jer 51:5
The *L* has sworn .... Jer 51:14
the people of the *L* .... Zeph 2:10
on the house of the *L* .... Hag 1:14
with glory,' says the *L* ...... Hag 2:7
"Return to me," says the *L* .. Zech 1:3
"O *L*, how long will You ... Zech 1:12
L has sent me .... Zech 2:9
My Spirit,' says the *L* .... Zech 4:6
wrath came from the *L* .... Zech 7:12
the Mountain of the *L* .... Zech 8:3
shall come to seek the *L* ... Zech 8:22
The *L* will defend them .... Zech 9:15
worship the King, the *L* ... Zech 14:16
a great King," says the *L* .... Mal 1:14
is the messenger of the *L* .... Mal 2:7
return to you, says the *L* ...... Mal 3:7

LORD OF LORDS
God of gods and *L* .... Deut 10:17
give thanks to the *L* .... Ps 136:3
King of kings and *L* .... 1 Tim 6:15
He is *L* and King of kings .. Rev 17:14
King of kings and *L* .... Rev 19:16

LORD WAS WITH HIM
master saw that the *L* ...... Gen 39:3
Samuel grew, and the *L* .. 1 Sam 3:19
David, because the *L* .... 1 Sam 18:12
ways, and the *L* .... 1 Sam 18:14
The *L*; he prospered .... 2 Kin 18:7
And the hand of the *L* ...... Luke 1:66

LORD'S ANOINTED
"Surely the *L* is before .... 1 Sam 16:6
to my master, the *L* .... 1 Sam 24:6
his hand against the *L* .... 1 Sam 26:9
hand to destroy the *L* ..... 2 Sam 1:14
he cursed the *L* .... 2 Sam 19:21

LORDS
many gods and many *l* ..... 1 Cor 8:5
nor as being *l* over .... 1 Pet 5:3
for He is Lord of *l* .... Rev 17:14

LORDSHIP
Gentiles exercise *l* .... Luke 22:25

LOSE
gain, and a time to *l* .... Eccl 3:6
save his life will *l* .... Matt 16:25
reap if we do not *l* .... Gal 6:9
that we do not *l* .... 2 John 8

LOSES
but if the salt *l* .... Matt 5:13
and *l* his own soul .... Matt 16:26
if she *l* one coin .... Luke 15:8
l his life will preserve .... Luke 17:33

LOSS
he will suffer *l* .... 1 Cor 3:15
count all things *l* .... Phil 3:8

LOST
are dry, our hope is *l* ..... Ezek 37:11
save that which was *l* ..... Matt 18:11
the one which is *l* .... Luke 15:4
my sheep which was *l* ..... Luke 15:6
the piece which I *l* .... Luke 15:9
and none of them is *l* ..... John 17:12
You gave Me I have *l* ...... John 18:9

LOT
Abram's nephew; accompanies him, Gen 11:27—12:5; 13:1
Separates from Abram, Gen 13:5–12
Rescued by Abram, Gen 14:12–16
Saved from Sodom for his hospitality, Gen 19:1–29
Tricked into committing incest, Gen 19:30–38

LOT
shall be divided by *l* ...... Num 26:55
You maintain my *l* .... Ps 16:5
cast in your *l* among .... Prov 1:14
l is cast into the lap .... Prov 16:33

LOT'S WIFE
Disobedient, becomes pillar of salt, Gen 19:26
Event to be remembered, Luke 17:32

LOTS
l causes contentions ...... Prov 18:18
garments, casting *l* .... Mark 15:24
And they cast their *l* .... Acts 1:26

LOUD
I cried out with a *l* .... Gen 39:14
Him with *l* cymbals .... Ps 150:5
cried out with a *l* .... Matt 27:46
I heard behind me a *l* .... Rev 1:10

LOVE
l your neighbor as .... Lev 19:18
l the LORD your God .... Deut 6:5
your *l* to me was .... 2 Sam 1:26
How long will you *l* .... Ps 4:2
Oh, *l* the LORD .... Ps 31:23
l righteousness .... Ps 45:7
he has set his *l* .... Ps 91:14
Oh, how I *l* Your law .... Ps 119:97
peace have those who *l* ... Ps 119:165
preserves all who *l* .... Ps 145:20
us take our fill of *l* .... Prov 7:18
l covers all sins .... Prov 10:12
a time to *l* .... Eccl 3:8
People know neither *l* .... Eccl 9:1
l is better than wine .... Song 1:2
banner over me was *l* .... Song 2:4
stir up nor awaken *l* .... Song 3:5
I will give you my *l* .... Song 7:12
l is as strong as death .... Song 8:6
waters cannot quench *l* ...... Song 8:7
time was the time of *l* ...... Ezek 16:8
backsliding, I will *l* .... Hos 14:4
do justly, to *l* mercy .... Mic 6:8
to you, *l* your enemies ..... Matt 5:44
l those who *l* you .... Matt 5:46
which of them will *l* .... Luke 7:42
you do not have the *l* ...... John 5:42
if you have *l* for one ...... John 13:35
"If you *l* Me, keep My .... John 14:15
and My Father will *l* .... John 14:23
l one another as I .... John 15:12
l has no one than this ..... John 15:13
l Me more than these ..... John 21:15
of Jonah, do you *l* .... John 21:16
because the *l* of God .... Rom 5:5
Let *l* be without .... Rom 12:9
to *l* one another .... Rom 13:8
L does no harm to a ..... Rom 13:10
up, but *l* edifies .... 1 Cor 8:1
L suffers long and is ...... 1 Cor 13:4
L never fails .... 1 Cor 13:8
greatest of these is *l* ..... 1 Cor 13:13
For the *l* of Christ .... 2 Cor 5:14
and the God of *l* .... 2 Cor 13:11
of the Spirit is *l* .... Gal 5:22
rooted and grounded in *l* .... Eph 3:17
the edifying of itself in *l* .... Eph 4:16
Husbands, *l* your wives ..... Eph 5:25
if any comfort of *l* .... Phil 2:1
of the Son of His *l* .... Col 1:13
being knit together in *l* .... Col 2:2
l your wives and do .... Col 3:19
breastplate of faith and *l* .. 1 Thess 5:8
the commandment is *l* ...... 1 Tim 1:5
continue in faith, *l* .... 1 Tim 2:15
word, in conduct, in *l* ..... 1 Tim 4:12
For the *l* of money is ...... 1 Tim 6:10
l their husbands .... Titus 2:4
Let brotherly *l* .... Heb 13:1
having not seen you *l* .... 1 Pet 1:8
L the brotherhood .... 1 Pet 2:17
for "*l* will cover a .... 1 Pet 4:8
with a kiss of *l* .... 1 Pet 5:14
brotherly kindness *l* .... 2 Pet 1:7
loves the world, the *l* ..... 1 John 2:15
we *l* the brethren .... 1 John 3:14
By this we know *l* .... 1 John 3:16
him, how does the *l* ...... 1 John 3:17
Beloved, let us *l* .... 1 John 4:7
know God, for God is *l* .... 1 John 4:8
In this is *l* .... 1 John 4:10
If we *l* one another .... 1 John 4:12
L has been perfected ...... 1 John 4:17
There is no fear in *l* ...... 1 John 4:18
l Him because He first .... 1 John 4:19
who loves God must *l* .... 1 John 4:21
For this is the *l* .... 1 John 5:3
and *l* be multiplied to you ..... Jude 2
are spots in your *l* feasts ..... Jude 12
have left your first *l* .... Rev 2:4
your works, *l*, service .... Rev 2:19
and they did not *l* .... Rev 12:11

LOVE OF CHRIST
separate us from the *l* ...... Rom 8:35
For the *l* compels us .... 2 Cor 5:14
l which passes knowledge .. Eph 3:19

LOVE OF GOD
pass by justice and the *l* .. Luke 11:42
you do not have the *l* ...... John 5:42
the *l* has been poured .... Rom 5:5
separate us from the *l* ...... Rom 8:39
l is perfected in him .... 1 John 2:5
the *l* abide in him .... 1 John 3:17
In this the *l* .... 1 John 4:9
For this is the *l* .... 1 John 5:3
keep yourselves in the *l* ...... Jude 21

LOVE ONE ANOTHER
l; as I have loved you ..... John 13:34
that you *l* as I have .... John 15:12
anything except to *l* .... Rom 13:8
are taught by God to *l* .... 1 Thess 4:9
l fervently with a pure ..... 1 Pet 1:22
that we should *l* .... 1 John 3:11
Beloved, let us *l* .... 1 John 4:7
the beginning: that we *l* ..... 2 John 5

LOVE THE LORD YOUR GOD
You shall *l* with all your .... Deut 6:5
to *l* with all your heart ..... Deut 30:6
l, to walk in all His ways ... Josh 22:5
"You shall *l* with .... Matt 22:37
l with all your heart ...... Mark 12:30
l with all your heart .... Luke 10:27

LOVE YOUR ENEMIES
in that you *l* .... 2 Sam 19:6
But I say to you, *l* .... Matt 5:44
L, do good to those .... Luke 6:27

LOVE YOUR NEIGHBOR
you shall *l* as yourself ..... Lev 19:18
l and hate your enemy ..... Matt 5:43
'You shall *l* as yourself .... Matt 19:19
l as yourself .... Gal 5:14
"You shall *l* as yourself ..... James 2:8

LOVED
Because the LORD has *l* ..... 1 Kin 10:9
L one and friend You .... Ps 88:18
Yet Jacob I have *l* .... Mal 1:2
forgiven, for she *l* .... Luke 7:47
so *l* the world that .... John 3:16
"See how He *l* .... John 11:36
whom Jesus *l* .... John 13:23
"As the Father *l* .... John 15:9
l them as You have .... John 17:23
"Jacob I have *l* .... Rom 9:13
the Son of God, who *l* .... Gal 2:20
l the church and gave .... Eph 5:25
l righteousness .... Heb 1:9
God, but that He *l* .... 1 John 4:10
Beloved, if God so *l* ...... 1 John 4:11
To Him who *l* us and .... Rev 1:5

LOVELY
l are your tents, O Jacob ... Num 24:5
of David had a *l* sister .... 2 Sam 13:1
The young woman was *l* ..... Esth 2:7
l is Your tabernacle .... Ps 84:1

l woman who lacks .... Prov 11:22
I am dark, but *l* .... Song 1:5
he is altogether *l* .... Song 5:16
whatever things are *l* .... Phil 4:8

LOVER
a *l* of what is good .... Titus 1:8

LOVERS
the harlot with many *l* .... Jer 3:1
your *l* have forgotten you ... Jer 30:14
"I will go after my *l* .... Hos 2:5
Ephraim has hired *l* .... Hos 8:9
who were *l* of money ..... Luke 16:14
For men will be *l* .... 2 Tim 3:2

LOVES
l righteousness .... Ps 33:5
life, and *l* many days .... Ps 34:12
A friend *l* at all .... Prov 17:17
He who *l* father or .... Matt 10:37
l his life will lose .... John 12:25
l Me will be loved .... John 14:21
l a cheerful giver .... 2 Cor 9:7
who *l* his wife *l* .... Eph 5:28
If anyone *l* the world ...... 1 John 2:15
l God must love his .... 1 John 4:21
l him who is .... 1 John 5:1

LOVESICK
apples, for I am *l* .... Song 2:5
you tell him I am *l* .... Song 5:8

LOVINGKINDNESS
not concealed Your *l* .... Ps 40:10
l is better than life .... Ps 63:3
to declare Your *l* .... Ps 92:2
Who crowns you with *l* ..... Ps 103:4
l I have drawn .... Jer 31:3
You show *l* to thousands ... Jer 32:18
justice, in *l* and mercy ...... Hos 2:19
abundant in *l* .... Jon 4:2

LOVINGKINDNESSES
mercies and Your *l* .... Ps 25:6
where are Your former *l* .... Ps 89:49
the multitude of His *l* .... Is 63:7

LOW
He brings *l* and lifts .... 1 Sam 2:7
both *l* and high .... Ps 49:2
it *l*, He lays it *l* .... Is 26:5
and hill brought *l* .... Luke 3:5

LOWER
made him a little *l* .... Ps 8:5
shall go into the *l* .... Ps 63:9
made him a little *l* .... Heb 2:7

LOWEST
and sets over it the *l* .... Dan 4:17

LOWLINESS
with all *l* and .... Eph 4:2
or conceit, but in *l* .... Phil 2:3

LOWLY
yet He regards the *l* .... Ps 138:6
for I am gentle and *l* ...... Matt 11:29
He has regarded the *l* ...... Luke 1:48
and exalted the *l* .... Luke 1:52
in presence am *l* .... 2 Cor 10:1
l body that it may be .... Phil 3:21
l brother glory .... James 1:9

LOYAL
be *l* to the LORD our God .. 1 Kin 8:61
truth and with a *l* heart .... 2 Kin 20:3
with a *l* heart they .... 1 Chr 29:9
faithfully and with a *l* ..... 2 Chr 19:9
or else he will be *l* .... Matt 6:24

LUCIFER
Name applied to Satan, Is 14:12

LUD
See LYDIA
A people descended from Shem, 1 Chr 1:17

LUKE
"The beloved physician," Col 4:14
Paul's last companion, 2 Tim 4:11
Author of third Gospel, Luke (title)

LUKEWARM
because you are *l* .... Rev 3:16

LUMP
from the same *l* .... Rom 9:21
you may be a new *l* .... 1 Cor 5:7

LUST
Do not *l* after her .... Prov 6:25
caught by their *l* .... Prov 11:6
looks at a woman to *l* ...... Matt 5:28
not fulfill the *l* .... Gal 5:16
not in passion of *l* .... 1 Thess 4:5
You *l* and do not have ..... James 4:2
the *l* of the flesh .... 1 John 2:16

LUSTS
to fulfill its *l* .... Rom 13:14
l which drown men .... 1 Tim 6:9
also youthful *l* .... 2 Tim 2:22
and worldly *l* .... Titus 2:12
to the former *l* .... 1 Pet 1:14
abstain from fleshly *l* .... 1 Pet 2:11
to their own ungodly *l* .... Jude 18

LUTE
Awake, *l* and harp .... Ps 57:8
l I will praise You .... Ps 71:22
harp with the *l* .... Ps 81:2
ten strings, on the *l* .... Ps 92:3
Awake, *l* and harp .... Ps 108:2
Praise Him with the *l* .... Ps 150:3

LUXURY
L is not fitting .... Prov 19:10
l are in kings' courts .... Luke 7:25
in pleasure and *l* .... James 5:5
the abundance of her *l* ...... Rev 18:3

LYCAONIA
District of Asia Minor where Paul preached, Acts 14:6, 11

LYCIA
Province of Asia Minor visited by Paul, Acts 21:1, 2; 27:5, 6

LYDDA
Aeneas healed at, Acts 9:32–35

LYDIA
Woman of Thyatira; Paul's first European convert, Acts 16:14, 15, 40
——— District of Asia Minor containing Ephesus, Smyrna, Thyatira, and Sardis, Rev 1:11

LYING
has put a *l* spirit .... 1 Kin 22:23
I hate and abhor *l* .... Ps 119:163
proud look, a *l* tongue ..... Prov 6:17
L lips are an .... Prov 12:22
righteous man hates *l* ...... Prov 13:5
not trust in these *l* .... Jer 7:4
a paralytic *l* on a bed .... Matt 9:2
in swaddling cloths, *l* ...... Luke 2:12
the Babe *l* in a manger .... Luke 2:16
cloths *l* by themselves .... Luke 24:12
saw the linen cloths *l* .... John 20:5
putting away *l* .... Eph 4:25
signs, and *l* wonders ..... 2 Thess 2:9

LYRE
the horn, flute, harp, *l* .... Dan 3:15

LYSIAS, CLAUDIUS
See CLAUDIUS LYSIAS

LYSTRA
Paul visits; is worshiped by people of and stoned by Jews, Acts 14:6–20
Home of Timothy, Acts 16:1, 2

MAACAH (or Maachah)
Small Syrian kingdom near Mt. Hermon, Deut 3:14
Not possessed by Israel, Josh 13:13
——— David's wife; mother of Absalom, 2 Sam 3:3
——— Wife of Rehoboam; mother of King Abijah, 2 Chr 11:18–21
Makes idol; is deposed as queen mother, 1 Kin 15:13

MACEDONIA
Paul preaches in, Acts 16:9—17:14
Paul's troubles in, 2 Cor 7:5
Churches of, generous, Rom 15:26; 2 Cor 8:1–5

MACHIR
Manasseh's only son, Gen 50:23
Founder of the family of Machirites, Num 26:29
Conqueror of Gilead, Num 32:39, 40

MACHPELAH
Field containing a cave; bought by Abraham, Gen 23:9–18
Sarah and Abraham buried here, Gen 23:19; 25:9, 10
Isaac, Rebekah, Leah, and Jacob buried here, Gen 49:29–31

MAD
has a demon and is *m* .... John 10:20
he said, "I am not *m* ...... Acts 26:25

MADE
m the stars also .... Gen 1:16
everything that He had *m* ... Gen 1:31
wife the LORD God *m* .... Gen 3:21
God *m* a wind to pass over ... Gen 8:1
'I have *m* Abram rich' ..... Gen 14:23
LORD *m* a covenant with ... Gen 15:18
I have *m* you a father of .... Gen 17:5
he *m* him a tunic of many .. Gen 37:3
Joseph *m* himself known ... Gen 45:1
they *m* their lives bitter ...... Ex 1:14
m the sea into dry land ..... Ex 14:21
tool, and *m* a molded calf ..... Ex 32:4
He also *m* the mercy seat .... Ex 37:6
LORD *m* between Himself .. Lev 26:46
Moses *m* a bronze serpent .. Num 21:9
m a covenant .... 1 Sam 20:16
has *m* Solomon king ...... 1 Kin 1:43
he *m* the Most Holy Place .. 2 Chr 3:8
had *m* to praise the LORD, .. 2 Chr 7:6
Have You not *m* a hedge .... Job 1:10
You have *m* me like clay .... Job 10:9
He has *m* me a byword of ... Job 17:6
For You have *m* him a little ... Ps 8:5
You have *m* him to have ...... Ps 8:6
You *m* Me trust while on ..... Ps 22:9
by which they have *m* You ... Ps 45:8
have *m* summer and winter .. Ps 74:17
you have *m* the LORD .... Ps 91:9
It is He who has *m* us, and ... Ps 100:3
m known His ways to .... Ps 103:7
LORD, who *m* heaven and .. Ps 115:15
the day the LORD has *m* ... Ps 118:24
by wisdom *m* the heavens ... Ps 136:5
and wonderfully *m* .... Ps 139:14
generous soul will be *m* ... Prov 11:25
m everything beautiful ..... Eccl 3:11
A feast is *m* for laughter ... Eccl 10:19
hear long ago how I *m* .... Is 37:26
I have *m* the earth, and ...... Is 45:12
things My hand has *m* .... Is 66:2
He has *m* the earth by His .. Jer 10:12
I have *m* you a watchman .. Ezek 3:17
king *m* a great feast for a .... Dan 5:1
your faith has *m* you well .. Matt 9:22
you have *m* it a den of .... Matt 21:13
m another five talents ...... Matt 25:16
God '*m* them male and .... Mark 10:6
temple *m* with hands ...... Mark 14:58
places shall be *m* straight ... Luke 3:5
she was *m* straight, and ... Luke 13:13
All things were *m* .... John 1:3
the water that was *m* wine .. John 2:9

in temples *m* with hands . . . Acts 7:48
he *m* havoc of the church, . . . Acts 8:3
are heirs, faith is *m* void . . Rom 4:14
m me free from the law of . . Rom 8:2
confession is *m* unto . . . . . . Rom 10:10
Has not God *m* foolish . . . . 1 Cor 1:20
all shall be *m* alive . . . . 1 Cor 15:22
m Him who knew no . . . . . 2 Cor 5:21
strength is *m* perfect . . . . . . 2 Cor 12:9
Seed were the promises *m* . . . Gal 3:16
And you He *m* alive, who . . . . Eph 2:1
and *m* us sit together in . . . . . . Eph 2:6
of God might be *m* . . . . Eph 3:10
but *m* Himself of no . . . . Phil 2:7
requests be *m* known to . . . . . Phil 4:6
He has *m* alive together . . . . . Col 2:13
m him a little lower than . . . . . Heb 2:7
are *m* His footstool . . . . Heb 10:13
but *m* alive by the Spirit . . . 1 Pet 3:18
not been *m* perfect in . . . . . 1 John 4:18
has *m* us kings and priests . . . Rev 1:6
m them white in the blood . . Rev 7:14
worship Him who *m* . . . . Rev 14:7
of the earth were *m* drunk . . Rev 17:2

MADNESS
pretended *m* in . . . . 1 Sam 21:13
wisdom and to know *m* . . . . . Eccl 1:17
m is in their hearts . . . . Eccl 9:3

MAGDALA
City of Galilee, Matt 15:39

MAGDALENE
See MARY

MAGIC
women who sew *m* . . . . Ezek 13:18
m brought their books . . . . Acts 19:19

MAGNIFICENCE
m I cannot endure . . . . Job 31:23

MAGNIFIED
So let Your name be *m* . . . 2 Sam 7:26
"Let the LORD be *m* . . . . Ps 35:27
The LORD be *m* . . . . Ps 40:16
for You have *m* Your . . . . Ps 138:2
The LORD is *m* beyond the. . . . Mal 1:5
the Lord Jesus was *m* . . . . . Acts 19:17
also Christ will be *m* . . . . Phil 1:20

MAGNIFIES
"My soul *m* the Lord . . . . . . Luke 1:46

MAGNIFY
m the LORD with me . . . . Ps 34:3
m himself above every . . . . Dan 11:36

MAGOG
People among Japheth's descendants, Gen 10:2
Associated with Gog, Ezek 38:2
Representatives of final enemies, Rev 20:8

MAHANAIM
Name given by Jacob to a sacred site, Gen 32:2
Becomes Ishbosheth's capital, 2 Sam 2:8–29
David flees to, during Absalom's rebellion, 2 Sam 17:24, 27

MAHER-SHALAL-HASH-BAZ
Symbolic name of Isaiah's second son; prophetic of the fall of Damascus and Samaria, Is 8:1–4

MAHLON
Husband of Ruth; without child, Ruth 1:2–5

MAIDENS
Both young men and *m* . . . . Ps 148:12
She has sent out her *m* . . . . . Prov 9:3

MAIDSERVANT
"I am Ruth, your *m* . . . . Ruth 3:9
save the son of Your *m* . . . . . Ps 86:16
"Behold the *m* . . . . Luke 1:38
lowly state of His *m* . . . . Luke 1:48

MAIDSERVANTS
m shall lead her as . . . . Nah 2:7
m I will pour out My . . . . Acts 2:18

MAIMED
to enter into life *m* . . . . Mark 9:43
the poor and the *m* . . . . Luke 14:21

MAINTAIN
and *m* their cause . . . . 1 Kin 8:45
careful to *m* good works . . . . Titus 3:8

MAINTAINED
For You have *m* my . . . . Ps 9:4

MAJESTIC
thunders with His *m* voice . . Job 37:4
which are *m* in pace . . . . . . Prov 30:29
But there the *m* LORD will . . . . Is 33:21

MAJESTY
Honor and *m* are before . . 1 Chr 16:27
the victory and the *m* . . . . 1 Chr 29:11
with God is awesome *m* . . . . Job 37:22
of the LORD is full of *m* . . . . . . Ps 29:4
He is clothed with *m* . . . . Ps 93:1
Honor and *m* are before . . . . . . Ps 96:6
splendor of Your *m* . . . . Ps 145:5
LORD and the glory of His *m* . . Is 2:10
in the *m* of the name of the . . . Mic 5:4
right hand of the *M* . . . . Heb 1:3
eyewitnesses of His *m* . . . . . 2 Pet 1:16
wise, be glory and *m* . . . . Jude 25

MAKE
"Let Us *m* man in Our . . . . . . Gen 1:26
desirable to *m* one wise . . . . . . Gen 3:6
let us *m* a name for . . . . Gen 11:4
m you a great nation . . . . Gen 12:2
m My covenant between . . . . Gen 17:2
"You shall not *m* . . . . Ex 20:4
I will *m* of you a great . . . . . . Ex 32:10
m your belly swell and . . . . Num 5:22
LORD *m* His face shine . . . . . Num 6:25
M a fiery serpent, and . . . . . Num 21:8
husband may *m* it void . . . Num 30:13
m yourself an ark of . . . . Deut 10:1
Now *m* us a king to judge . . 1 Sam 8:5
m me a small cake from . . 1 Kin 17:13
m confession to the . . . . Ezra 10:11
I *m* my bed in the . . . . Job 17:13
LORD, *m* me dwell in safety . . . . Ps 4:8
M Your face shine upon . . . . . Ps 31:16
My soul shall *m* its boast in . . Ps 34:2
shall *m* glad the city of God . . Ps 46:4
wings I will *m* my refuge . . . . . Ps 57:1
m His praise glorious . . . . Ps 66:2
my mouth will I *m* known . . . . Ps 89:1
M a joyful shout to the . . . . . . Ps 100:1
I *m* my bed in hell, behold . . . Ps 139:8
M haste, my beloved, and . . Song 8:14
m mention that His name . . . . . Is 12:4
m the crooked places . . . . Is 45:2
I will *m* an everlasting . . . . . . Jer 32:40
writing and *m* known to . . . . Dan 5:15
m it plain on tablets, that . . . . Hab 2:2
m me walk on my high . . . . . . Hab 3:19
no one shall *m* them . . . . Zeph 3:13
m you fishers of men . . . . Matt 4:19
till I *m* Your enemies . . . . . Matt 22:44
let us *m* three tabernacles . . Mark 9:5
there *m* ready for us . . . . . . Mark 14:15
M them sit down in . . . . Luke 9:14
M me like one of your . . . . . Luke 15:19
m haste and come down, . . Luke 19:5
not *m* My Father's house . . . John 2:16
the truth shall *m* you free . . John 8:32
m Our home with him . . . . John 14:23
we then *m* void the law . . . . Rom 3:31
m no provision for the . . . . Rom 13:14
m my brother stumble . . . . . 1 Cor 8:13
m the way of escape . . . . . 1 Cor 10:13
God is able to *m* all grace . . . 2 Cor 9:8
to *m* known the mystery . . . . Eph 6:19
Lord *m* you increase . . . . . 1 Thess 3:12
till I *m* Your enemies Your . . Heb 1:13
m you complete in every . . . Heb 13:21
diligent to *m* your call . . . . . 2 Pet 1:10
we *m* Him a liar, and . . . . . 1 John 1:10
will *m* your stomach bitter . . Rev 10:9
Behold, I *m* all things new . . Rev 21:5

MAKER
where is God my *M* . . . . Job 35:10
before the LORD our *M* . . . . Ps 95:6
the LORD is the *m* of them . . Prov 22:2
man will look to his *M* . . . . Is 17:7
who strives with his *M* . . . . Is 45:9
M is your husband . . . . Is 54:5
has forgotten his *M* . . . . Hos 8:14
builder and *m* is God . . . . . . Heb 11:10

MAKES
He *m* nations great, and . . . . Job 12:23
He *m* my feet like the feet . . . Ps 18:33
He *m* me to lie down in . . . . . . Ps 23:2
He *m* wars cease to the end . . . Ps 46:9
Who *m* His angels spirits, . . . Ps 104:4
son *m* a glad father, ... Prov 10:1
Hope deferred *m* the . . . . . . Prov 13:12
he *m* even his enemies to . . Prov 16:7
He *m* lightnings for the . . . . . Jer 51:16
for He *m* His sun rise on . . . . Matt 5:45
m both the deaf to hear . . . Mark 7:37
He *m* intercession . . . . Rom 8:27
m himself an enemy of . . . . . James 4:4

MAKING
is sure, *m* wise the simple . . . Ps 19:7
m the word of God of no . . Mark 7:13
m mention of you in my . . . . Eph 1:16
m melody in your heart to . . . Eph 5:19

MAKKEDAH
Canaanite town assigned to Judah, Josh 15:20, 41

MALACHI
Prophet and writer, Mal 1:1

MALCHISHUA
Son of King Saul, 1 Sam 14:49
Killed at Gilboa, 1 Sam 31:2

MALCHUS
Servant of the high priest, John 18:10

MALE
He created them *m* and . . . . . . Gen 5:2
into the ark to Noah, *m* . . . . Gen 7:9
every *m* child in your . . . . . . Gen 17:12
who has borne a *m* or a . . . . . Lev 12:7
lie with a *m* as with a . . . . . . Lev 18:22
utterly destroy every *m* . . . Judg 21:11
came, she delivered a *m* . . . . . . Is 66:7
beginning 'made them *m* . . . Matt 19:4
is neither *m* nor female . . . . . Gal 3:28
gave birth to the *m* Child . . Rev 12:13

MALICE
in *m* be babes . . . . 1 Cor 14:20
away from you, with all *m* . . Eph 4:31
wrath, *m*, blasphemy, ... Col 3:8
pleasures, living in *m* . . . . Titus 3:3
laying aside all *m* . . . . 1 Pet 2:1

MALICIOUSNESS
covetousness, *m* . . . . Rom 1:29

MALIGN
m a servant to his . . . . Prov 30:10

MALTA
Site of Paul's shipwreck, Acts 28:1–8

MAMMON
cannot serve God and *m* . . . Matt 6:24
by unrighteous *m* . . . . Luke 16:9

MAMRE
Town or district near Hebron, Gen 23:19
Abram dwells by the oaks of, Gen 13:18

MAN
See NEW MAN; OLD MAN; RIGHTEOUS MAN; SON OF MAN; WISE MAN

"Let Us make *m* ....Gen 1:26
she was taken out of *M* .....Gen 2:23
Therefore a *m* shall leave ...Gen 2:24
were both naked, the *m*.....Gen 2:25
I will destroy *m* whom I .....Gen 6:7
M wrestled with him ....Gen 32:24
God is not a *m*, that He ...Num 23:19
but *m* lives by every word ...Deut 8:3
No *m* shall be able to .....Deut 11:25
m looks at the outward ...1 Sam 16:7
"You are the *m* ....2 Sam 12:7
and prove yourself a *m* .....1 Kin 2:2
"What is *m*................Job 7:17
For an empty-headed *m* ....Job 11:12
"Are you the first *m* ....Job 15:7
Blessed is the *m* who ....Ps 1:1
m that You are mindful ....Ps 8:4
The steps of a good *m* are ...Ps 37:23
Blessed is that *m* who ....Ps 40:4
What can *m* do to me ....Ps 118:6
Happy is the *m* who finds ..Prov 3:13
rebuke a wise *m*, and he ....Prov 9:8
A good *m* obtains favor ....Prov 12:2
that seems right to a *m* ...Prov 16:25
The spirit of a *m* is the ....Prov 20:27
Let another *m* praise you, ..Prov 27:2
shall take hold of one *m*, ...Is 4:1
Because I am a *m* of unclean ...Is 6:5
marred more than any *m* ....Is 52:14
M of sorrows and ....Is 53:3
mighty *m* glory in his ....Jer 9:23
Blessed is the *m* who trusts ..Jer 17:7
Son of *m*, can these ....Ezek 37:3
He has shown you, O *m*, ...Mic 6:8
Will a *m* rob God ....Mal 3:8
M shall not live by bread ....Matt 4:4
A good *m* out of the ......Matt 12:35
the mouth defiles a *m* .....Matt 15:11
For this reason a *m* shall ...Matt 19:5
coming of the Son of *M* ...Matt 24:27
first binds the strong *m* ...Mark 3:27
within and defile a *m* .....Mark 7:23
what will it profit a *m* .....Mark 8:36
m had two sons ....Luke 15:11
a certain rich *m* ....Luke 16:19
a *m* named Zacchaeus .....Luke 19:2
can a *m* be born when he ...John 3:4
blind *m* with the clay ....John 9:6
m should die for the ....John 11:50
"Behold the *M* ....John 19:5
name, has made this *m* .....Acts 3:16
a *m* full of faith and the .....Acts 6:5
you are inexcusable, O *m*, ...Rom 2:1
blessed is the *m* to whom ...Rom 4:8
m is not from woman .....1 Cor 11:8
I became a *m*, I put ......1 Cor 13:11
since by *m* came death ...1 Cor 15:21
though our outward *m* ....2 Cor 4:16
for whatever a *m* sows, that ..Gal 6:7
in Himself one new *m* ......Eph 2:15
that the *m* of God may ....2 Tim 3:17
m can tame the tongue ....James 3:8
a righteous *m* avails ......James 5:16
is the number of a *m* .....Rev 13:18

MAN OF GOD

Moses the *m* blessed ....Deut 33:1
"A *m* came to me, and ....Judg 13:6
a *m* came to Eli and said ..1 Sam 2:27
there is in this city a *m* ....1 Sam 9:6
to Shemaiah the *m* ....1 Kin 12:22
a *m* went from Judah to ...1 Kin 13:1
m who was disobedient ..1 Kin 13:26
I to do with you, O *m* ....1 Kin 17:18
a *m* came and spoke to ...1 Kin 20:28
"*M*, the king has said ....2 Kin 1:9
this a holy *m*..................2 Kin 4:9
M, there is death ....2 Kin 4:40
m sent to the king ....2 Kin 6:9
he died, just as the *m* ......2 Kin 7:17
the *m* was angry with ....2 Kin 13:19
"It is the tomb of the *m* ..2 Kin 23:17
for so David the *m* ....2 Chr 8:14
But a *m* came to him ....2 Chr 25:7
Law of Moses the *m* ....Ezra 3:2
command of David the *m* ..Neh 12:24
son of Igdaliah, a *m* ....Jer 35:4
But you, O *m*, flee these ...1 Tim 6:11
m may be complete ....2 Tim 3:17

MAN'S

curse the ground for *m* .....Gen 8:21
every *m* hand against .....Gen 16:12
We are all one *m* sons .....Gen 42:11
each *m* money was in the ..Gen 43:21
The rich *m* wealth is his ..Prov 10:15
When a *m* ways please ....Prov 16:7
A *m* heart plans his way ...Prov 16:9
The rich *m* wealth is his ..Prov 18:11
A *m* gift makes room for ..Prov 18:16
m steps are of the LORD ...Prov 20:24
A *m* pride will bring him ..Prov 29:23
a righteous *m* reward .....Matt 10:41
enter a strong *m* house ....Mark 3:27
from the rich *m* table .....Luke 16:21
one *m* offense many died ..Rom 5:15
on another *m* foundation ..Rom 15:20

MANASSEH

Joseph's firstborn son, Gen 41:50, 51
Adopted by Jacob, Gen 48:5, 6
Loses his birthright to Ephraim, Gen 48:13–20
—— Tribe of:
Numbered, Num 1:34, 35
Half-tribe of, settle east of Jordan, Num 32:33–42; Deut 3:12–15
Help Joshua against Canaanites, Josh 1:12–18
Land assigned to western half-tribe, Josh 17:1–13
Eastern half-tribe builds altar, Josh 22:9–34
Some of, help David, 1 Chr 12:19–31
—— Wicked king of Judah; son of Hezekiah, 2 Kin 21:1–18; 2 Chr 33:1–9
Captured and taken to Babylon; repents and is restored, 2 Chr 33:10–13
Removes idols and altars, 2 Chr 33:14–20

MANGER

Will he bed by your *m* ......Job 39:9
and laid Him in a *m* ....Luke 2:7
the Babe lying in a *m* ......Luke 2:16

MANIFEST

m Myself to him ....John 14:21
is it that You will *m* ....John 14:22
be known of God is *m* in ...Rom 1:19
but now made *m*, and ....Rom 16:26
that I may make it *m*, as I ....Col 4:4
was *m* in these last times ...1 Pet 1:20

MANIFESTATION

But the *m* of the ....1 Cor 12:7
deceitfully, but by *m* ....2 Cor 4:2

MANIFESTED

Galilee, and *m* His glory ....John 2:11
"I have *m* Your name ....John 17:6
God was *m* in the flesh ....1 Tim 3:16
the life was *m* ....1 John 1:2
the Son of God was *m* .....1 John 3:8
the love of God was *m* ....1 John 4:9

MANIFOLD

m are Your works ....Ps 104:24
the *m* wisdom of God ....Eph 3:10
good stewards of the *m* ....1 Pet 4:10

MANKIND

called them *M* in the day ....Gen 5:2
of *m* may seek the LORD ..Acts 15:17
to kill a third of *m*..............Rev 9:15
But the rest of *m*, who ....Rev 9:20

MANNA

of Israel ate *m*..............Ex 16:35
the *m* was like coriander ...Num 11:7
the *m* ceased on the day.....Josh 5:12
Your *m* from their mouth ...Neh 9:20
had rained down *m* ....Ps 78:24
Our fathers ate the *m* ....John 6:31
golden pot that had the *m*....Heb 9:4
of the hidden *m* ....Rev 2:17

MANNER

in all *m* of workmanship, ...Ex 31:3
Is this the *m* of man ....2 Sam 7:19
In this *m*, therefore, pray ....Matt 6:9
m of life from my youth, ...Acts 26:4
same *m* He also took .....1 Cor 11:25
in an unworthy *m* ....1 Cor 11:27
sorrowed in a godly *m* ...2 Cor 7:11
m of life, purpose, faith, ...2 Tim 3:10
as is the *m* of some ....Heb 10:25
what *m* of persons ....2 Pet 3:11
Behold what *m* of love ....1 John 3:1
m worthy of God ....3 John 6

MANOAH

Danite; father of Samson, Judg 13:1–25

MANSIONS

house are many *m*........John 14:2

MANTLE

Then he took the *m* ....2 Kin 2:14

MAON

Village in Judah, Josh 15:55
David stays at, 1 Sam 23:24, 25
Nabal's house here, 1 Sam 25:2

MARA

Name chosen by Naomi, Ruth 1:20

MARAH

First Israelite camp after passing through the Red Sea, Num 33:8, 9

MARCHED

people, when You *m* ....Ps 68:7

MARK (John)

Son of Mary of Jerusalem; travels with Barnabas and Saul, Acts 12:12, 25
Leaves Paul at Perga, Acts 13:13
Barnabas and Paul separate because of him, Acts 15:37–40
Later approved by Paul, Col 4:10; 2 Tim 4:11
Companion of Peter, 1 Pet 5:13
Author of the second Gospel, Mark 1:1

MARK

And the LORD set a *m*.........Gen 4:15
M the blameless man ....Ps 37:37
slave, to receive a *m* ....Rev 13:16
whoever receives the *m* ...Rev 14:11

MARKET

is sold in the meat *m* ....1 Cor 10:25

MARRED

so His visage was *m* ....Is 52:14
he made of clay was *m* ....Jer 18:4

MARRIAGE

join in *m* with the people ...Ezra 9:14
were not given in *m* ....Ps 78:63
nor are given in *m* ....Matt 22:30
they were given in *m* .....Luke 17:27
her in *m* does well ....1 Cor 7:38
M is honorable among ......Heb 13:4
the *m* of the Lamb has ......Rev 19:7

MARRIED

and *m* Pharaoh's daughter ..1 Kin 3:1
woman when she is *m* ....Prov 30:23
"for I am *m* to you ....Jer 3:14
first died after he had *m* ..Matt 22:25
said, 'I have *m* a wife .....Luke 14:20
m wives, they were ....Luke 17:27
But he who is *m* ....1 Cor 7:33
But she who is *m* ....1 Cor 7:34

MARRIES

If a man *m* a woman and ..Lev 20:14

as a young man *m* a virgin ..... Is 62:5
m another, commits .... Matt 19:9
she *m* another man, she ..... Rom 7:3
if a virgin *m*, she has not .. 1 Cor 7:28

MARROW
and of joints and *m* .... Heb 4:12

MARRY
m her, and raise up an ...... Gen 38:8
battle and another man *m* .. Deut 20:7
it is better not to *m* .... Matt 19:10
they neither *m* nor are ...... Matt 22:30
The sons of this age *m* .... Luke 20:34
let them *m* .... 1 Cor 7:9
forbidding to *m* .... 1 Tim 4:3
the younger widows *m* .... 1 Tim 5:14

MARRYING
and drinking, *m* .... Matt 24:38

MARTHA
Sister of Mary and Lazarus; loved by Jesus, John 11:1–5
Affirms her faith, John 11:19–28
Offers hospitality to Jesus, Luke 10:38; John 12:1, 2
Gently rebuked by Christ, Luke 10:39–42

MARTYR
m Stephen was shed ...... Acts 22:20
was My faithful *m* .... Rev 2:13

MARTYRS
the blood of the *m* .... Rev 17:6

MARVEL
do not *m* at the matter .... Eccl 5:8
Do not *m* that I said to you .. John 3:7
Do not *m* at this .... John 5:28
Israel, why do you *m* at .... Acts 3:12
I *m* that you are turning ...... Gal 1:6
Do not *m*, my brethren ... 1 John 3:13

MARVELED
Jesus heard it, He *m* .... Matt 8:10
And the multitudes *m* ...... Matt 9:33
these words, they *m* ...... Matt 22:22
the governor *m* greatly .... Matt 27:14
He *m* because of their .... Mark 6:6
so that Pilate *m* .... Mark 15:5
His mother *m* at those ..... Luke 2:33
believe for joy, and *m* .... Luke 24:41
were all amazed and *m* ...... Acts 2:7
And all the world *m* .... Rev 13:3
when I saw her, I *m* .... Rev 17:6

MARVELOUS
Remember His *m* works .. 1 Chr 16:12
m things without number ..... Job 5:9
will tell of all Your *m* works ... Ps 9:1
m things He did .... Ps 78:12
For He has done *m* things .... Ps 98:1
It is *m* in our eyes .... Ps 118:23
M are Your works .... Ps 139:14
I will again do a *m* work ..... Is 29:14
LORD has done *m* things .... Joel 2:21
If it is *m* in the eyes of ...... Zech 8:6
Why, this is a *m* thing ...... John 9:30
of darkness into His *m* .... 1 Pet 2:9
m are Your works, Lord ...... Rev 15:3

MARVELS
people I will do *m* .... Ex 34:10

MARY
Mother of Christ, Matt 1:16
Visited by angel, Luke 1:26–38
Visits Elizabeth and offers praise, Luke 1:39–56
Gives birth to Jesus, Luke 2:6–20
Flees to Egypt, Matt 2:13–18
Visits Jerusalem with Jesus, Luke 2:41–52
Entrusted to John's care, John 19:25–27
—— Mother of James and Joses; present at crucifixion and burial, Matt 27:55–61
Sees the risen Lord; informs disciples, Matt 28:1–10
—— Magdalene; delivered from seven demons; supports Christ's ministry, Luke 8:2, 3
Present at crucifixion and burial, Matt 27:55–61
First to see the risen Lord, Mark 16:1–10; John 20:1–18
—— Sister of Martha and Lazarus; loved by Jesus, John 11:1–5
Grieves for Lazarus, John 11:19, 20, 28–33
Anoints Jesus, Matt 26:6–13; John 12:1–8
Commended by Jesus, Luke 10:38–42
—— Mark's mother, Acts 12:12–17

MASSAH AND MERIBAH
First, at Rephidim, Israel just out of Egypt, Ex 17:1–7
Second, at Kadesh Barnea, 40 years later, Num 20:1–13

MASTER
of Abraham his *m* .... Gen 24:9
If she does not please her *m* .. Ex 21:8
for your *m* Saul is dead .... 2 Sam 2:7
If only my *m* were with ..... 2 Kin 5:3
m! For it was borrowed ..... 2 Kin 6:5
no longer call Me 'My *M* .... Hos 2:16
a servant like his *m* .... Matt 10:25
before him, saying, '*M* .... Matt 18:26
servant whom his *m* ...... Matt 24:46
M, *M*, we are perishing .... Luke 8:24
M, it is good for us to be .... Luke 9:33
m of that servant will ..... Luke 12:46
So the *m* commended the .. Luke 16:8
Jesus, *M*, have mercy ..... Luke 17:13
the *m* of the feast called .... John 2:9
is not greater than his *m* .. John 13:16
greater than his *m* .... John 15:20
m builder I have laid ...... 1 Cor 3:10
own *M* also is in heaven ..... Eph 6:9
and useful for the *M* ...... 2 Tim 2:21

MASTERS
look to the hand of their *m* .. Ps 123:2
the soul of his *m* .... Prov 25:13
m besides You have .... Is 26:13
can serve two *m* .... Luke 16:13
her *m* much profit .... Acts 16:16
And you, *m*, do the same .... Eph 6:9
M, give your bondservants ... Col 4:1
who have believing *m* ...... 1 Tim 6:2
be obedient to their own *m* .. Titus 2:9

MATTANIAH
King Zedekiah's original name, 2 Kin 24:17

MATTER
m is found in me .... Job 19:28
He who answers a *m* ..... Prov 18:13

MATTERS
the weightier *m* .... Matt 23:23
judge the smallest *m* .... 1 Cor 6:2

MATTHEW
Becomes Christ's follower, Matt 9:9
Chosen as one of the Twelve, Matt 10:2, 3
Called Levi, the son of Alphaeus, Mark 2:14
Author of the first Gospel, Matt (title)

MATTHIAS
Chosen by lot to replace Judas, Acts 1:15–26

MATURE
among those who are *m* .... 1 Cor 2:6
understanding be *m* ...... 1 Cor 14:20
us, as many as are *m* .... Phil 3:15

MEAN
What do you *m* .... Ex 12:26
What does this parable *m* ... Luke 8:9
what these things *m* ...... Acts 17:20
I do not *m* that others ..... 2 Cor 8:13

MEANING
'What is the *m* .... Deut 6:20
if I do not know the *m* .... 1 Cor 14:11

MEANS
or one tittle will by no *m* ... Matt 5:18
you will by no *m* enter ..... Matt 5:20
he shall by no *m* lose his .. Matt 10:42
you will by no *m* enter ..... Matt 18:3
words will by no *m* pass .. Matt 24:35
will by no *m* hurt them ... Mark 16:18
shall by any *m* hurt you .. Luke 10:19
to Me I will by no *m* cast ... John 6:37
I must by all *m* keep this .. Acts 18:21
I might by all *m* save ...... 1 Cor 9:22
if, by any *m*, I may attain ... Phil 3:11
godliness is a *m* of gain .... 1 Tim 6:5
by no *m* be put to shame .... 1 Pet 2:6

MEANT
but God *m* it for good ..... Gen 50:20

MEASURE
a perfect and just *m* ...... Deut 25:15
give us a *m* of revival in ...... Ezra 9:8
apportion the waters by *m* . Job 28:25
what is the *m* of my days ..... Ps 39:4
and the short *m* .... Mic 6:10
and with the *m* you use, it ... Matt 7:2
good *m*, pressed down, ... Luke 6:38
give the Spirit by *m* .... John 3:34
to each one a *m* .... Rom 12:3
lest I be exalted above *m* .. 2 Cor 12:7
to the *m* of the stature of ... Eph 4:13
m the temple of God .... Rev 11:1

MEASURED
m heaven with a span .... Is 40:12
If heaven above can be *m* ... Jer 31:37
nor the sand of the sea *m* ... Jer 33:22
cannot be *m* or numbered .. Hos 1:10
you use, it will be *m* .... Matt 7:2
it will be *m* back to you .... Luke 6:38
Then he *m* its wall .... Rev 21:17

MEASURES
your house differing *m* .... Deut 25:14
weights and diverse *m* .... Prov 20:10

MEASURING
will make justice the *m* line .. Is 28:17
the man's hand was a *m* ... Ezek 40:5
behold, a man with a *m* ..... Zech 2:1
m themselves by .... 2 Cor 10:12
given a reed like a *m* .... Rev 11:1

MEAT
you *m* to eat in the evening .. Ex 16:8
But while the *m* was still .. Num 11:33
Can He provide *m* .... Ps 78:20
He also rained *m* .... Ps 78:27
good neither to eat *m* ..... Rom 14:21
will never again eat *m* ..... 1 Cor 8:13
is sold in the *m* .... 1 Cor 10:25

MEDDLE
why should you *m* .... 2 Kin 14:10

MEDEBA
Moabite town assigned to Judah, Num 21:29, 30; Josh 13:9, 16

MEDES, MEDIA
Part of Medo-Persian Empire, Esth 1:19
Israel deported to, 2 Kin 17:6
Babylon falls to, Dan 5:30, 31
Daniel rises high in kingdom of, Dan 6:1–28
Cyrus, king of, allows Jews to return, 2 Chr 36:22, 23
Agents in Babylon's fall, Is 13:17–19

MEDIATE
a mediator does not *m* ...... Gal 3:20

MEDIATOR
Nor is there any *m* .... Job 9:33

by the hand of a *m* .... Gal 3:19
is one God and one *M* ...... 1 Tim 2:5
as He is also *M* .... Heb 8:6
to Jesus the *M* of the ...... Heb 12:24

MEDICINE
does good, like *m* .... Prov 17:22

MEDICINES
you will use many *m* .... Jer 46:11

MEDITATE
Isaac went out to *m* .... Gen 24:63
but you shall *m* .... Josh 1:8
M within your heart on .... Ps 4:4
I *m* within my heart .... Ps 77:6
I will *m* on Your .... Ps 119:15
Your heart will *m* .... Is 33:18
m beforehand on what ... Luke 21:14
m on these things .... Phil 4:8

MEDITATES
in His law he *m* .... Ps 1:2

MEDITATION
O LORD, consider my *m* .... Ps 5:1
of my mouth and the *m* ..... Ps 19:14
the *m* of my heart shall ...... Ps 49:3
m be sweet to Him .... Ps 104:34
It is my *m* all the day ...... Ps 119:97

MEDITERRANEAN SEA
Described as:
Sea, Gen 49:13
Great Sea, Josh 1:4; 9:1
Sea of the Philistines, Ex 23:31
Western Sea, Deut 11:24; Joel 2:20; Zech 14:8

MEDIUM
a woman who is a *m* ...... Lev 20:27
a woman who is a *m* ..... 1 Sam 28:7

MEDIUM'S
shall be like a *m* .... Is 29:4

MEDIUMS
"Seek those who are *m* .... Is 8:19

MEEK
But the *m* shall inherit the ... Ps 37:11
with equity for the *m* .... Is 11:4
all you *m* of the earth .... Zeph 2:3
Blessed are the *m* .... Matt 5:5

MEEKNESS
with you by the *m* .... 2 Cor 10:1
are done in the *m* .... James 3:13
that is in you, with *m* ...... 1 Pet 3:15

MEET
from the tent door to *m* ..... Gen 18:2
For You *m* him with the ...... Ps 21:3
mercies come speedily to *m* .. Ps 79:8
prepare to *m* your God .... Amos 4:12
out to *m* the bridegroom ... Matt 25:1
go out to *m* him .... Matt 25:6
a man will *m* you .... Luke 22:10
m the Lord in the air .... 1 Thess 4:17

MEETING
In the tabernacle of *m* ...... Ex 27:21
burned up all the *m* .... Ps 74:8

MEGIDDO
City of Canaan; scene of battles, Judg 5:19–21; 2 Kin 23:29, 30
Fortified by Solomon, 1 Kin 9:15
Possible site of Armageddon, Rev 16:16

MELCHIZEDEK
Priest and king of Salem, Gen 14:18–20
Type of Christ's eternal priesthood, Heb 7:1–22

MELODY
make sweet *m* .... Is 23:16
singing and making *m* ...... Eph 5:19

MELT
You make his beauty *m* ..... Ps 39:11
The mountains *m* like wax ... Ps 97:5

man's heart will *m* .... Is 13:7
mountains will *m* under ...... Mic 1:4
the elements will *m* .... 2 Pet 3:10

MEMBER
body is not one *m* .... 1 Cor 12:14
if they were all one *m* .... 1 Cor 12:19
if one *m* suffers, all the ... 1 Cor 12:26
tongue is a little *m* .... James 3:5

MEMBERS
you that one of your *m* ..... Matt 5:29
do not present your *m* ...... Rom 6:13
have many *m* in one body .. Rom 12:4
that your bodies are *m* .... 1 Cor 6:15
there are many *m* .... 1 Cor 12:20
neighbor, for we are *m* ..... Eph 4:25
m that it defiles the .... James 3:6

MEMORIAL
and this is My *m* .... Ex 3:15
day shall be to you a *m* ..... Ex 12:14
as a *m* between your eyes, ... Ex 13:9
also be told as a *m* .... Matt 26:13
be told of as a *m* .... Mark 14:9
come up for a *m* before .... Acts 10:4

MEMORY
The *m* of him perishes ..... Job 18:17
He may cut off the *m* .... Ps 109:15
The *m* of the righteous ..... Prov 10:7

MEMPHIS (or Noph)
Ancient capital of Egypt, Hos 9:6
Prophesied against by Isaiah, Is 19:13
Jews flee to, Jer 44:1
Denounced by the prophets, Jer 46:19

MEN
See WISE MEN
m began to call on the .... Gen 4:26
saw the daughters of *m* ...... Gen 6:2
But the *m* of Sodom were .. Gen 13:13
Hebrew *m* were fighting ..... Ex 2:13
Send *m* to spy out the ..... Num 13:2
So Gideon took ten *m* ..... Judg 6:27
with the LORD and *m* ..... 1 Sam 2:26
reproach of *m*, and despised .. Ps 22:6
All *m* shall fear, and shall .... Ps 64:9
received gifts among *m* ..... Ps 68:18
you shall die like *m* .... Ps 82:7
with wise *m* will be wise .. Prov 13:20
are the crown of old *m* ..... Prov 17:6
not be envious of evil *m* .... Prov 24:1
m should fear before Him .. Eccl 3:14
the Egyptians are *m* .... Is 31:3
despised and rejected by *m* ... Is 53:3
I see four *m* loose .... Dan 3:25
make you fishers of *m* ..... Matt 4:19
light so shine before *m* ..... Matt 5:16
forgive *m* their trespasses .. Matt 6:14
confesses Me before *m* .... Matt 10:32
will not be forgiven *m* .... Matt 12:31
every idle word *m* may .... Matt 12:36
was carried by four *m* .... Mark 2:3
Who do *m* say that I am ... Mark 8:27
With *m* it is impossible ... Mark 10:27
goodwill toward *m* .... Luke 2:14
when all *m* speak well of .. Luke 6:26
m always ought to pray .... Luke 18:1
from heaven or from *m* .... Luke 20:4
the life was the light of *m* ... John 1:4
loved the praise of *m* .... John 12:43
old *m* shall dream dreams .. Acts 2:17
have not lied to *m* but to .... Acts 5:4
m everywhere to repent ... Acts 17:30
Likewise also the *m* .... Rom 1:27
in the sight of all *m* .... Rom 12:17
let no one boast in *m* ...... 1 Cor 3:21
all things to all *m* .... 1 Cor 9:22
with the tongues of *m* ..... 1 Cor 13:1
speak to *m* but to God ..... 1 Cor 14:2
the Lord, and not to *m* .... Eph 6:7
to the tradition of *m*, ... Col 2:8
between God and *m* .... 1 Tim 2:5
rejected indeed by *m* .... 1 Pet 2:4

In those days *m* will seek .... Rev 9:6
to scorch *m* with fire .... Rev 16:8

MENAHEM
Cruel king of Israel, 2 Kin 15:14–18

MENSERVANTS
And also on My *m* .... Joel 2:29
And on My *m* and on My ... Acts 2:18

MENTION
I will make *m* of Your .... Ps 71:16
make *m* that His name is ...... Is 12:4
by You only we make *m* ..... Is 26:13
He has made *m* of My name .. Is 49:1
You who make *m* of the ...... Is 62:6
will *m* the lovingkindnesses ... Is 63:7
Make *m* to the nations, ... Jer 4:16
m of you always in my .... Rom 1:9
he was dying, made *m* .... Heb 11:22

MEPHIBOSHETH
Son of King Saul, 2 Sam 21:8
——— Grandson of King Saul; crippled son of Jonathan, 2 Sam 4:4–6
Sought out and honored by David, 2 Sam 9:1–13
Accused by Ziba, 2 Sam 16:1–4
Later explains himself to David, 2 Sam 19:24–30
Spared by David, 2 Sam 21:7

MERAB
King Saul's eldest daughter, 1 Sam 14:49
Saul promises her to David, but gives her to Adriel, 1 Sam 18:17–19

MERARI
Third son of Levi, Gen 46:11
——— Descendants of, called Merarites:
Duties in the tabernacle, Num 3:35–37
Cities assigned to, Josh 21:7, 34–40
Duties in the temple, 1 Chr 26:10–19
Assist Ezra after Exile, Ezra 8:18, 19

MERCHANDISE
perceives that her *m* ...... Prov 31:18
house a house of *m* .... John 2:16

MERCHANTS
set it in a city of *m* .... Ezek 17:4
have multiplied your *m* ..... Nah 3:16
m were the great men ..... Rev 18:23

MERCIES
for His *m* are great .... 2 Sam 24:14
in Your manifold *m* You .... Neh 9:19
multitude of Your tender *m* ... Ps 51:1
I will sing of the *m* of the ..... Ps 89:1
and His tender *m* .... Ps 145:9
give you the sure *m* ...... Acts 13:34
brethren, by the *m* of God .. Rom 12:1
the Father of *m* .... 2 Cor 1:3
beloved, put on tender *m* .... Col 3:12

MERCIFUL
LORD, the LORD God, *m* ...... Ex 34:6
your God is a *m* God .... Deut 4:31
With the *m* You will show ... Ps 18:25
He is ever *m* .... Ps 37:26
God be *m* to us and .... Ps 67:1
for He is gracious and *m* ... Joel 2:13
Blessed are the *m* .... Matt 5:7
Therefore be *m*, just as .... Luke 6:36
saying, 'God be *m* .... Luke 18:13
For I will be *m* .... Heb 8:12
compassionate and *m* ... James 5:11

MERCY
See HAVE MERCY; HIS MERCY ENDURES FOREVER
but showing *m* to .... Ex 20:6
You shall put the *m* seat .... Ex 26:34
and abundant in *m* .... Num 14:18
m endures forever .... 1 Chr 16:34
I have trusted in Your *m* ..... Ps 13:5
to Your *m* remember me ..... Ps 25:7
I trust in the *m* .... Ps 52:8

come, buy wine and *m* .... Is 55:1
and whiter than *m* .... Lam 4:7
shall flow with *m* .... Joel 3:18
have come to need *m* .... Heb 5:12
m is unskilled in the .... Heb 5:13
desire the pure *m* .... 1 Pet 2:2

MILK AND HONEY
to a land flowing with *m* ...... Ex 3:8
It truly flows with *m* ...... Num 13:27
land flowing with *m* .... Deut 6:3
land flowing with *m* .... Josh 5:6
land flowing with *m* .... Jer 11:5
m, the glory of all .... Ezek 20:6

MILL
be grinding at the *m* ...... Matt 24:41

MILLO
Fort at Jerusalem, 2 Sam 5:9
Prepared by Solomon, 1 Kin 9:15
Strengthened by Hezekiah, 2 Chr 32:5
Scene of Joash's death, 2 Kin 12:20, 21

MILLSTONE
m were hung around his ... Matt 18:6
a stone like a great *m* ...... Rev 18:21

MIND
the people had a *m* to work .. Neh 4:6
put wisdom in the *m* .... Job 38:36
perfect peace, whose *m* .... Is 26:3
and with all your *m* .... Matt 22:37
and in his right *m* .... Mark 5:15
nor have an anxious *m* ... Luke 12:29
m I myself serve the .... Rom 7:25
Because the carnal *m* is ..... Rom 8:7
the *m* of the Spirit is .... Rom 8:27
who has known the *m* ... Rom 11:34
renewing of your *m* .... Rom 12:2
Be of the same *m* .... Rom 12:16
convinced in his own *m* .... Rom 14:5
have the *m* of Christ .... 1 Cor 2:16
you are out of your *m* .... 1 Cor 14:23
Let this *m* be in you .... Phil 2:5
Set your *m* on things above, .. Col 3:2
to *m* your own .... 1 Thess 4:11
love and of a sound *m* ...... 2 Tim 1:7
put My laws in their *m* ..... Heb 8:10
the loins of your *m* .... 1 Pet 1:13

MINDFUL
is man that You are *m* .... Ps 8:4
The LORD has been *m* ...... Ps 115:12
for you are not *m* .... Matt 16:23
is man that You are *m* .... Heb 2:6

MINDS
people change their *m* ...... Ex 13:17
put My law in their *m* ...... Jer 31:33
I stir up your pure *m* .... 2 Pet 3:1
He who searches the *m* ..... Rev 2:23

MINISTER
to make you a *m* .... Acts 26:16
for he is God's *m* .... Rom 13:4
you will be a good *m* .... 1 Tim 4:6
spirits sent forth to *m* for ... Heb 1:14
a *M* of the sanctuary .... Heb 8:2

MINISTERED
But the child *m* .... 1 Sam 2:11
a thousand thousands *m* .... Dan 7:10
angels came and *m* to ...... Matt 4:11
As they *m* to the Lord ...... Acts 13:2

MINISTERS
angels spirits, His *m* .... Ps 104:4
for they are God's *m* .... Rom 13:6
commend ourselves as *m* ... 2 Cor 6:4
Are they *m* of Christ ..... 2 Cor 11:23
If anyone *m* .... 1 Pet 4:11

MINISTRIES
are differences of *m* .... 1 Cor 12:5

MINISTRY
I magnify my *m* .... Rom 11:13
But if the *m* of death .... 2 Cor 3:7
since we have this *m* .... 2 Cor 4:1
and has given us the *m* .... 2 Cor 5:18
for the work of *m* .... Eph 4:12
m which you have .... Col 4:17
fulfill your *m* .... 2 Tim 4:5
a more excellent *m* .... Heb 8:6

MINT
For you pay tithe of *m* .... Matt 23:23

MIRACLE
saying, 'Show a *m* .... Ex 7:9
no one who works a *m* .... Mark 9:39
see some *m* done by Him .. Luke 23:8
that a notable *m* .... Acts 4:16

MIRACLES
God worked unusual *m* ... Acts 19:11
the working of *m* .... 1 Cor 12:10
Are all workers of *m* ..... 1 Cor 12:29
with various *m* .... Heb 2:4

MIRIAM
Sister of Aaron and Moses, Num 26:59
Chosen by God; called a prophetess, Ex 15:20
Punished for rebellion, Num 12:1–16
Buried at Kadesh, Num 20:1

MIRTH
I will test you with *m* .... Eccl 2:1
is in the house of *m* .... Eccl 7:4
joy is darkened, the *m* .... Is 24:11

MISER
eat the bread of a *m* .... Prov 23:6

MISERIES
m that are coming .... James 5:1

MISERY
would forget your *m* .... Job 11:16
and remember his *m* .... Prov 31:7

MISTREATED
But the Egyptians *m* .... Deut 26:6
those who are *m* .... Heb 13:3

MISTREATS
m his father and .... Prov 19:26

MITES
widow putting in two *m* ... Luke 21:2

MITYLENE
Visited by Paul, Acts 20:13–15

MIZPAH
Site of covenant between Jacob and Laban, Gen 31:44–53
——— Town of Benjamin; outraged Israelites gather here, Josh 18:21, 26; Judg 20:1, 3
Samuel gathers Israel, 1 Sam 7:5–16; 10:17–25
Residence of Gedaliah, 2 Kin 25:23, 25

MOAB
Son of Lot, Gen 19:33–37
——— Country of the Moabites, Deut 1:5

MOABITES
Descendants of Lot, Gen 19:36, 37
Join Midian in cursing Israel, Num 22:4
Excluded from Israel, Deut 23:3–6
Kindred of Ruth, Ruth 1:4
Subdued by Israel, 1 Sam 14:47; 2 Sam 8:2; 2 Kin 3:4–27
Women of, lead Solomon astray, 1 Kin 11:1–8
Prophecies concerning, Is 11:14; 15:1–9; Jer 48:1–47; Amos 2:1–3

MOAN
m sadly like doves .... Is 59:11

MOCK
I will *m* when your .... Prov 1:26
Fools *m* at sin .... Prov 14:9
to the Gentiles to *m* .... Matt 20:19

MOCKED
at noon, that Elijah *m* .... 1 Kin 18:27
"I am one *m* by his .... Job 12:4
knee before Him and *m* ... Matt 27:29
deceived, God is not *m* .... Gal 6:7

MOCKER
Wine is a *m* .... Prov 20:1

MOCKERS
that there would be *m* .... Jude 18

MOCKINGS
others had trial of *m* ...... Heb 11:36

MOCKS
He who *m* the poor .... Prov 17:5

MODERATION
with propriety and *m* .... 1 Tim 2:9

MOLECH
God of the Ammonites; worshiped by Solomon, 1 Kin 11:7
Human sacrifice made to, Lev 18:21; 2 Kin 23:10

MOMENT
consume them in a *m* ..... Num 16:21
In a *m* they die .... Job 34:20
For His anger is but for a *m* .. Ps 30:5
face from you for a *m* .... Is 54:8
of the world in a *m* of time .. Luke 4:5
m, in the twinkling .... 1 Cor 15:52
which is but for a *m* .... 2 Cor 4:17

MONEY
man's *m* to his sack .... Gen 42:25
does not put out his *m* .... Ps 15:5
m answers every .... Eccl 10:19
be redeemed without *m* ...... Is 52:3
and you who have no *m* ...... Is 55:1
of the *m* changers .... Matt 21:12
and hid his lord's *m* ...... Matt 25:18
put *m* into the treasury ... Mark 12:41
promised to give him *m* .. Mark 14:11
Carry neither *m* .... Luke 10:4
I sent you without *m* ..... Luke 22:35
the *m* changers doing ...... John 2:14
a thief, and had the *m* ..... John 12:6
be purchased with *m* .... Acts 8:20
not greedy for *m* .... 1 Tim 3:3
m is a root of all .... 1 Tim 6:10
not greedy for *m* .... Titus 1:7

MONSTER
me up like a *m* .... Jer 51:34
of Egypt, O great *m* .... Ezek 29:3

MONTH
ark rested in the seventh *m* .. Gen 8:4
first *m* of the year to you ..... Ex 12:2
will bear fruit every *m* .. Ezek 47:12
latter rain in the first *m* ..... Joel 2:23
in the sixth *m* the angel .... Luke 1:26
this is now the sixth *m* .... Luke 1:36
yielding its fruit every *m* .... Rev 22:2

MONTHS
child, she hid him three *m* ..... Ex 2:2
with her about three *m*, ... Luke 1:56
up three years and six *m* .. Luke 4:25
You observe days and *m* .... Gal 4:10
to torment them for five *m* ... Rev 9:5
continue for forty-two *m* .... Rev 13:5

MOON
this time, the sun, the *m* .... Gen 37:9
and the *m* stopped, till .... Josh 10:13
of Your fingers, the *m* .... Ps 8:3
until the *m* is no more .... Ps 72:7
the *m* for seasons .... Ps 104:19
by day, nor the *m* by night .. Ps 121:6
morning, fair as the *m* ..... Song 6:10
sun and *m* grow dark .... Joel 2:10
the *m* into blood, before .... Joel 2:31
and *m* will grow dark, and .. Joel 3:15
sun and *m* stood still in ...... Hab 3:11
m will not give its .... Mark 13:24
in the sun, in the *m* .... Luke 21:25
or a new *m* or sabbaths, ... Col 2:16

and a thick cloud on the *m* . . Ex 19:16
Moses was on the *m* forty . . . Ex 24:18
"But as a *m* falls . . . . Job 14:18
You have made my *m* . . . . Ps 30:7
of many peaks is the *m* . . . . . . Ps 68:15
let us go up to the *m* . . . . Is 2:3
be exalted, and every *m* . . . . Is 40:4
image became a great *m* . . . . Dan 2:35
an alarm in My holy *m* . . . . . . Joel 2:1
Who are you, O great *m* . . . . Zech 4:7
on an exceedingly high *m* . . . Matt 4:8
He went up on a *m* . . . . Matt 5:1
you will say to this *m* . . . . . Matt 17:20
came down from the *m* . . . . . Mark 9:9
whoever says to this *m* . . . Mark 11:23
shall be filled and every *m* . . Luke 3:5
feeding there on the *m* . . . . . Luke 8:32
worshiped on this *m* . . . . John 4:20
with Him on the holy *m* . . . . 2 Pet 1:18
it is rolled up, and every *m* . . Rev 6:14
to a great and high *m* . . . . . . Rev 21:10

MOUNTAINS

tops of the *m* were seen . . . . . Gen 8:5
He removes the *m* . . . . Job 9:5
Surely the *m* yield . . . . Job 40:20
though the *m* be carried . . . . . . Ps 46:2
m will bring peace . . . . Ps 72:3
excellent than the *m* . . . . Ps 76:4
m were brought forth . . . . Ps 90:2
m melt like wax at the . . . . Ps 97:5
m skipped like rams . . . . Ps 114:4
m surround Jerusalem . . . . . . Ps 125:2
forth into singing, you *m* . . . . . Is 44:23
How beautiful upon the *m* . . . . Is 52:7
m shall depart and the . . . . Is 54:10
m shook at Your presence . . . . . Is 64:3
m shall be thrown down . . Ezek 38:20
in Judea flee to the *m* . . . . Matt 24:16
and day, he was in the *m* . . . . Mark 5:5
begin 'to say to the *m* . . . . Luke 23:30
that I could remove *m* . . . . . 1 Cor 13:2
in deserts and *m* . . . . Heb 11:38
m were not found . . . . Rev 16:20

MOURN

and you *m* at last . . . . Prov 5:11
a time to *m* . . . . Eccl 3:4
to comfort all who *m*, ... Is 61:2
will *m* for Him as one . . . . Zech 12:10
are those who *m* . . . . Matt 5:4
m as long as the . . . . Matt 9:15
Lament and *m* and weep . . . James 4:9
of the earth will *m* . . . . Rev 1:7

MOURNED

we *m* to you . . . . Matt 11:17
and have not rather *m* . . . . 1 Cor 5:2

MOURNING

This is a deep *m* . . . . Gen 50:11
for me my *m* into dancing . . . . Ps 30:11
m all the day long . . . . Ps 38:6
m shall be ended . . . . Is 60:20
ashes, the oil of joy for *m* . . . . Is 61:3
men break bread in *m* . . . . Jer 16:7
I will turn their *m* . . . . Jer 31:13
shall be a great *m* . . . . Zech 12:11
be turned to *m* and . . . . James 4:9

MOURNS

heavily, as one who *m* . . . . . . Ps 35:14
The earth *m* and fades . . . . Is 24:4
for Him as one *m* . . . . Zech 12:10

MOUTH

"Who has made man's *m* . . . . . Ex 4:11
and put the words in his *m* . . . Ex 4:15
the earth opened its *m* . . . . Num 16:32
the *m* of the donkey . . . . Num 22:28
from the *m* of the LORD . . . . . Deut 8:3
near you, in your *m* . . . . Deut 30:14
not depart from your *m* . . . . . . Josh 1:8
Out of the *m* of babes . . . . Ps 8:2
Let the words of my *m* and . . . Ps 19:14
shall continually be in my *m* . . Ps 34:1
The *m* of the righteous . . . . . . Ps 37:30
m shall speak wisdom . . . . Ps 49:3
my *m* shall show forth . . . . . . Ps 51:15
with my *m* will I make . . . . Ps 89:1
iniquity stops its *m* . . . . Ps 107:42
Then our *m* was filled with . . Ps 126:2
by the words of your *m* . . . . . Prov 6:2
knowledge, but the *m* . . . . . Prov 10:14
by the fruit of his *m* . . . . . . Prov 12:14
m preserves his life . . . . Prov 13:3
The *m* of an immoral . . . . . Prov 22:14
and a flattering *m* . . . . Prov 26:28
her *m* with wisdom . . . . Prov 31:26
And he touched my *m* with . . . . Is 6:7
yet He opened not His *m* . . . . . . Is 53:7
not depart from your *m* . . . . . . Is 59:21
put My words in your *m* . . . . Jer 1:9
it was in my *m* like honey . . . Ezek 3:3
m speaking pompous . . . . Dan 7:8
the doors of your *m* . . . . Mic 7:5
from the *m* of God . . . . Matt 4:4
near to Me with their *m* . . . . Matt 15:8
m defiles a man . . . . Matt 15:11
that 'by the *m* of two or . . . Matt 18:16
'Out of the *m* of babes . . . . Matt 21:16
m I will judge you . . . . Luke 19:22
I will give you a *m* . . . . Luke 21:15
so He opened not His *m* . . . . Acts 8:32
is near you, in your *m* . . . . . . Rom 10:8
with your *m* the Lord . . . . Rom 10:9
m confession is made . . . . . Rom 10:10
proceed out of your *m*, but . . Eph 4:29
the same *m* proceed . . . . . . James 3:10
m great swelling words . . . . . . Jude 16
vomit you out of My *m* . . . . . Rev 3:16
sweet as honey in your *m* . . . Rev 10:9
m was found no deceit . . . . . . Rev 14:5

MOUTHS

gape at Me with their *m* . . . . . Ps 22:13
food was still in their *m* . . . . . Ps 78:30
have *m*, but they do not . . . . . Ps 115:5
near to Me with their *m* . . . . . Is 29:13
and shut the lions' *m* . . . . Dan 6:22

MOVE

and the earth will *m* . . . . Is 13:13
the mountain shall *m* . . . . . . Zech 14:4
M from here to there,' . . . . Matt 17:20
m them with one of their . . . Matt 23:4
in Him we live and *m* . . . . . Acts 17:28

MOVED

shall never be *m* . . . . Ps 15:5
right hand I shall not be *m* . . . Ps 16:8
she shall not be *m* . . . . Ps 46:5
I shall not be greatly *m* . . . . Ps 62:2
m Him to jealousy with . . . . . . Ps 78:58
m with compassion . . . . Matt 14:14
all the city was *m* . . . . Matt 21:10
spoke as they were *m* . . . . . . 2 Pet 1:21

MUCH

m study is wearisome . . . . . . Eccl 12:12
m better than wine is . . . . . . Song 4:10
to whom *m* is given . . . . . . Luke 12:48
M more then . . . . Rom 5:9

MULTIPLIED

the more they *m* and grew . . . . Ex 1:12
sorrows shall be *m* . . . . Ps 16:4
your days will be *m* . . . . Prov 9:11
When the wicked are *m*, . . Prov 29:16
m before You, and our sins . . Is 59:12
of the disciples *m* . . . . Acts 6:7
Holy Spirit, they were *m* . . . Acts 9:31
word of God grew and *m* . . Acts 12:24
peace, and love be *m* to you . . . Jude 2

MULTIPLY

See BE FRUITFUL AND MULTIPLY
"Be fruitful and *m* . . . . Gen 1:22
will greatly *m* your sorrow . . Gen 3:16
m your descendants . . . . Gen 16:10
multiplying I will *m* your . . Gen 22:17
m my days as the . . . . Job 29:18
m the descendants . . . . Jer 33:22
m the seed you have . . . . . . 2 Cor 9:10

MULTITUDE

stars of heaven in *m* . . . . Deut 1:10
m of years should teach . . . Job 32:7
Your house in the *m* . . . . Ps 5:7
m that kept a pilgrim . . . . Ps 42:4
in the *m* of Your mercy, ... Ps 69:13
In the *m* of words sin . . . . . . Prov 10:19
In a *m* of people is a . . . . . . Prov 14:28
bury Gog and all his *m* . . . Ezek 39:11
to the *m* in parables . . . . . . Matt 13:34
compassion on the *m* . . . . . Matt 15:32
commanded the *m* to sit . . Matt 15:35
a great *m* followed Him . . . Matt 20:29
with the angel a *m* . . . . Luke 2:13
whole *m* sought to touch . . . Luke 6:19
because of the *m* of fish . . . John 21:6
stars of the sky in *m* . . . . . . Heb 11:12
"love will cover a *m* . . . . 1 Pet 4:8
and behold, a great *m* . . . . Rev 7:9
voice of a great *m* in . . . . Rev 19:1

MULTITUDES

M, *m* in the valley of . . . . Joel 3:14
when the *m* saw it, they . . . . . Matt 9:8
all the *m* were amazed . . . . Matt 12:23
He commanded the *m* to . . Matt 14:19
taught the *m* from the . . . . . . Luke 5:3
m throng and press You . . . Luke 8:45
m from sacrificing to . . . . . . Acts 14:18

MURDER

"You shall not *m* . . . . Ex 20:13
Will you steal, *m*, commit . . . . . Jer 7:9
'You shall not *m* . . . . Matt 5:21
they had committed *m* in . . . Mark 15:7
threats and *m* against . . . . Acts 9:1
full of envy, *m*, strife . . . . Rom 1:29
You *m* and covet and . . . . . . James 4:2

MURDERED

sons of those who *m* . . . . . . Matt 23:31
Jesus whom you *m* . . . . Acts 5:30
one and *m* his brother . . . . 1 John 3:12

MURDERER

He was a *m* from the . . . . John 8:44
and asked for a *m* . . . . Acts 3:14
of you suffer as a *m* . . . . 1 Pet 4:15
his brother is a *m* . . . . 1 John 3:15

MURDERERS

in it, but now *m* . . . . Is 1:21
and profane, for *m* . . . . 1 Tim 1:9
abominable, *m* . . . . Rev 21:8

MURDERS

whoever *m* will be in . . . . Matt 5:21
evil thoughts, *m* . . . . Matt 15:19
envy, *m*, drunkenness . . . . Gal 5:21
did not repent of their *m* . . . . Rev 9:21

MUSIC

So David played *m* . . . . . . 1 Sam 18:10
I will play *m* before the . . . 2 Sam 6:21
Israel played *m* before . . . . . 1 Chr 13:8
whirling and playing *m* . . 1 Chr 15:29
but Asaph made *m* with . . . 1 Chr 16:5
the *m* of the LORD, which . . . 2 Chr 7:6
m are brought low . . . . Eccl 12:4
the house, he heard *m* . . . . Luke 15:25

MUSING

while I was *m*, the fire . . . . Ps 39:3

MUST

touches the altar *m* be . . . . . . Ex 29:37
I *m* be regarded as holy . . . . . Lev 10:3
m be careful to observe . . . . . Deut 8:1
is sleeping and *m* be . . . . . . 1 Kin 18:27
Him, and you *m* wait for . . . Job 35:14
he *m* restore sevenfold . . . . . . Prov 6:31
precept *m* be upon precept . . . Is 28:10
that Elijah *m* come first . . . Matt 17:10
offenses *m* come, but woe . . Matt 18:7
Man *m* suffer many . . . . Mark 8:31

such things *m* happen ..... Mark 13:7
And the gospel *m* first ... Mark 13:10
m be about My Father's .... Luke 2:49
you, 'You *m* be born again .. John 3:7
He *m* increase, but I .... John 3:30
Him *m* worship in spirit .... John 4:24
I *m* work the works of ...... John 9:4
that He *m* rise again from .. John 20:9
by which we *m* be saved .... Acts 4:12
m suffer for My name's ..... Acts 9:16
you *m* not call common ... Acts 10:15
m put on incorruption, ... 1 Cor 15:53
If I *m* boast, I will .... 2 Cor 11:30
bishop then *m* be .... 1 Tim 3:2
deacons *m* be reverent ..... 1 Tim 3:8
servant of the Lord *m* ..... 2 Tim 2:24
to God *m* believe that He ... Heb 11:6
m love his brother also ... 1 John 4:21
things which *m* shortly ...... Rev 1:1
m be released for a little .... Rev 20:3
m shortly take place .... Rev 22:6

MUSTARD
heaven is like a *m* seed ... Matt 13:31
have faith as a *m* seed .... Matt 17:20

MUTE
Or who makes the *m* .... Ex 4:11
m who does not open .... Ps 38:13
I was *m* with silence .... Ps 39:2
was cast out, the *m* spoke .. Matt 9:33
who has a *m* spirit .... Mark 9:17
But behold, you will be *m* .. Luke 1:20
demon, and it was *m* ...... Luke 11:14

MUTILATION
beware of the *m* .... Phil 3:2

MUTUAL
by the *m* faith both .... Rom 1:12

MUZZLE
"You shall not *m* .... Deut 25:4
"You shall not *m* .... 1 Tim 5:18

MY RIGHT HAND
Because He is at *m* .... Ps 16:8
You hold me by *m* .... Ps 73:23
my Lord, "Sit at *M* .... Ps 110:1
let *m* forget its skill .... Ps 137:5
Look on *m* and see .... Ps 142:4
and *M* has stretched out ..... Is 48:13
but to sit on *M* .... Matt 20:23
to my Lord, "Sit at *M* ..... Matt 22:44
for He is at *m* .... Acts 2:25
Sit at *M*, till I make .... Heb 1:13
stars which you saw in *M* ... Rev 1:20

MYRA
Paul changes ships here, Acts 27:5, 6

MYRRH
perfumed my bed with *m* .. Prov 7:17
my hands dripped with *m* ... Song 5:5
gold, frankincense, and *m* .. Matt 2:11
wine mingled with *m* to .. Mark 15:23

MYSIA
Paul and Silas pass through here, Acts 16:7, 8

MYSTERIES
to you to know the *m* ..... Matt 13:11
and understand all *m* ...... 1 Cor 13:2
the spirit he speaks *m* ..... 1 Cor 14:2

MYSTERIOUS
today is not too *m* .... Deut 30:11

MYSTERY
given to know the *m* .... Mark 4:11
wisdom of God in a *m* ...... 1 Cor 2:7
Behold, I tell you a *m* .... 1 Cor 15:51
made known to us the *m* ..... Eph 1:9
This is a great *m* .... Eph 5:32
m which has been .... Col 1:26
the *m* of godliness .... 1 Tim 3:16

NAAMAN
Captain in the Syrian army, 2 Kin 5:1–11
Healed of his leprosy, 2 Kin 5:14–17
Referred to by Christ, Luke 4:27

NABAL
Refuses David's request, 1 Sam 25:2–12
Escapes David's wrath but dies of a stroke, 1 Sam 25:13–39

NABOTH
Murdered for his vineyard by King Ahab, 1 Kin 21:1–16
His murder avenged, 1 Kin 21:17–25

NADAB
Eldest of Aaron's four sons, Ex 6:23
Takes part in affirming covenant, Ex 24:1, 9–12
Becomes priest, Ex 28:1
Consumed by fire, Lev 10:1–7
——— King of Israel, 1 Kin 14:20
Killed by Baasha, 1 Kin 15:25–31

NAHASH
King of Ammon; makes impossible demands, 1 Sam 11:1–15

NAHOR
Grandfather of Abraham, Gen 11:24–26
——— Son of Terah, brother of Abraham, Gen 11:17

NAHUM
Prophet to Judah concerning Nineveh, Nah 1:1

NAILED
n it to the cross .... Col 2:14

NAIN
Village south of Nazareth; Jesus raises widow's son here, Luke 7:11–17

NAIOTH
Prophets' school in Ramah, 1 Sam 19:18, 19, 22, 23

NAKED
And they were both *n* ...... Gen 2:25
knew that they were *n* .... Gen 3:7
told you that you were *n* ..... Gen 3:11
"*N* I came from my .... Job 1:21
Sheol is *n* before Him, and .. Job 26:6
Isaiah has walked *n* .... Is 20:3
I was *n* and you .... Matt 25:36
and fled from them *n* ..... Mark 14:52
shall not be found *n* .... 2 Cor 5:3
but all things are *n* .... Heb 4:13
brother or sister is *n* ..... James 2:15
poor, blind, and *n* .... Rev 3:17

NAKEDNESS
of Canaan, saw the *n* .... Gen 9:22
The *n* of your father's wife .. Lev 18:8
in hunger, in thirst, in *n* ... Deut 28:48
or famine, or *n* .... Rom 8:35
often, in cold and *n* ...... 2 Cor 11:27
n may not be revealed .... Rev 3:18

NAME
See CALLED BY MY NAME; HOLY NAME; IN MY NAME
creature, that was its *n* ..... Gen 2:19
called his wife's *n* Eve ...... Gen 3:20
and make your *n* great ..... Gen 12:2
Abram called on the *n* ...... Gen 13:4
your *n* shall be Abraham .... Gen 17:5
but Sarah shall be her *n* ... Gen 17:15
Israel shall be your *n* ...... Gen 35:10
So she called his *n* Moses .... Ex 2:10
This is My *n* forever .... Ex 3:15
My *n* may be declared in ..... Ex 9:16
the LORD is His *n* .... Ex 15:3
Israel called its *n* Manna .... Ex 16:31
shall not take the *n* .... Ex 20:7
whose *n* is Jealous, is a ...... Ex 34:14
are called by the *n* .... Deut 28:10
glorious and awesome *n* .. Deut 28:58
by My *n* will humble ...... 2 Chr 7:14
and he has no *n* .... Job 18:17
excellent is Your *n* .... Ps 8:1
n will put their trust .... Ps 9:10
LORD the glory due to His *n* .. Ps 29:2
let us exalt His *n* together .... Ps 34:3
lift up my hands in Your *n* ... Ps 63:4
the clouds, by His *n* YAH ..... Ps 68:4
be His glorious *n* .... Ps 72:19
n is great in Israel .... Ps 76:1
do not call on Your *n* .... Ps 79:6
whose *n* alone is the LORD ... Ps 83:18
to Him, and bless His *n* ..... Ps 100:4
to Your *n* give glory .... Ps 115:1
above all Your *n* .... Ps 138:2
He calls them all by *n* .... Ps 147:4
The *n* of the LORD is a .... Prov 18:10
A good *n* is to be .... Prov 22:1
what is His Son's *n* .... Prov 30:4
And His *n* will be called .... Is 9:6
mention that His *n* is exalted .. Is 12:4
make mention of Your *n* ..... Is 26:13
the LORD, that is My *n* .... Is 42:8
be to the LORD for a *n* .... Is 55:13
be called by a new *n* .... Is 62:2
Everlasting is Your *n* .... Is 63:16
who calls on Your *n* .... Is 64:7
it shall be to Me a *n* .... Jer 33:9
and made Yourself a *n* ..... Dan 9:15
we will walk in the *n* .... Mic 4:5
They will call on My *n* ...... Zech 13:9
n shall be great .... Mal 1:11
to you who fear My *n* .... Mal 4:2
you shall call His *n* .... Matt 1:21
hallowed be Your *n* .... Matt 6:9
prophesied in Your *n* .... Matt 7:22
righteous man in the *n* .... Matt 10:41
n Gentiles will trust .... Matt 12:21
together in My *n* .... Matt 18:20
will come in My *n* .... Matt 24:5
"My *n* is Legion .... Mark 5:9
children in My *n* receives .. Mark 9:37
In My *n* they will cast .... Mark 16:17
The virgin's *n* was .... Luke 1:27
for me, and holy is His *n* .. Luke 1:49
"His *n* is John .... Luke 1:63
and cast out your *n* .... Luke 6:22
who believe in His *n* .... John 1:12
comes in his own *n* .... John 5:43
his own sheep by *n* .... John 10:3
you ask in My *n* .... John 14:13
Father will send in My *n* .. John 14:26
keep through Your *n* ...... John 17:11
whoever calls on the *n* ...... Acts 2:21
through faith in His *n* .... Acts 3:16
there is no other *n* .... Acts 4:12
suffer shame for His *n* ..... Acts 5:41
baptized in the *n* of .... Acts 10:48
whoever calls on the *n* .... Rom 10:13
every *n* that is named, not ... Eph 1:21
which is above every *n* .... Phil 2:9
at the *n* of Jesus every ...... Phil 2:10
deed, do all in the *n* .... Col 3:17
a more excellent *n* .... Heb 1:4
giving thanks to His *n* ..... Heb 13:15
blaspheme that noble *n* ..... James 2:7
with oil in the *n* of the .... James 5:14
reproached for the *n* .... 1 Pet 4:14
n of the Son of God ...... 1 John 5:13
you hold fast to My *n* .... Rev 2:13
n that you are alive .... Rev 3:1
and have not denied My *n* .... Rev 3:8
or the *n* of the beast .... Rev 13:17
having His Father's *n* .... Rev 14:1
and glorify Your *n* .... Rev 15:4
n written that no one ...... Rev 19:12

NAME'S
by all for My *n* sake ...... Matt 10:22

or lands, for My *n* sake, . . . Matt 19:29
saved them for His *n* . . . . Ps 106:8
forgiven you for His *n* . . . . 1 John 2:12

NAMED

let my name be *n* . . . . Gen 48:16
I have *n* you . . . . Is 45:4
of a young man *n* Saul . . . . . Acts 7:58
not even *n* among the . . . . . . 1 Cor 5:1
and every name that is *n* . . . . Eph 1:21

NAMES

So Adam gave *n* to all . . . . . . Gen 2:20
lands after their own *n* . . . . . . Ps 49:11
Now the *n* of the twelve . . . . Matt 10:2
n are written in heaven . . . . Luke 10:20
whose *n* are in the Book of . . Phil 4:3
Let everyone who *n* the . . . 2 Tim 2:19
whose *n* are not written in . . Rev 17:8
the *n* of the twelve . . . . Rev 21:12
on them were the *n* of the . . Rev 21:14

NAOMI

Widow of Elimelech, Ruth 1:1–3
Returns to Bethlehem with Ruth, Ruth 1:14–19
Arranges Ruth's marriage to Boaz, Ruth 3; 4

NAPHTALI

Son of Jacob by Bilhah, Gen 30:1–8
Receives Jacob's blessing, Gen 49:21, 28
—— Tribe of:
Numbered, Num 1:42, 43
Territory assigned to, Josh 19:32–39
Joins Gideon's army, Judg 7:23
Attacked by Ben-Hadad and Tiglath-Pileser, 1 Kin 15:20; 2 Kin 15:29
Prophecy of great light in; fulfilled in Christ's ministry, Is 9:1–7; Matt 4:12–16

NARROW

"Enter by the *n* gate . . . . Matt 7:13
n is the gate and . . . . Matt 7:14

NATHAN

Son of David, 2 Sam 5:14
Mary's lineage traced through, Zech 12:12
—— Prophet under David and Solomon, 1 Chr 29:29
Reveals God's plan to David, 2 Sam 7:2–29
Rebukes David's sin, 2 Sam 12:1–15
Reveals Adonijah's plot, 1 Kin 1:10–46

NATHANAEL

One of Christ's disciples, John 1:45–51

NATION

make you a great *n* . . . . Gen 12:2
You slay a righteous *n* . . . . . . Gen 20:4
priests and a holy *n* . . . . Ex 19:6
Blessed is the *n* whose . . . . . . Ps 33:12
dealt thus with any *n* . . . . Ps 147:20
Righteousness exalts a *n* . . Prov 14:34
lift up sword against *n* . . . . Is 2:4
that the righteous *n* . . . . Is 26:2
call a *n* you do not know . . . . . Is 55:5
a small one a strong *n* . . . . Is 60:22
n that was not called . . . . Is 65:1
Or shall a *n* be born at once . . . Is 66:8
n changed its gods . . . . Jer 2:11
I will make them one *n* . . . Ezek 37:22
since there was a *n* . . . . Dan 12:1
N shall not lift up sword . . . . . Mic 4:3
Me, even this whole *n* . . . . Mal 3:9
n will rise against . . . . Matt 24:7
for he loves our *n* . . . . Luke 7:5
N will rise against *n*, ... Luke 21:10
whole *n* should perish . . . . John 11:50
those who are not a *n* . . . . . Rom 10:19
royal priesthood, a holy *n* . . . 1 Pet 2:9
tribe, tongue, and *n* . . . . Rev 13:7

NATIONS

Two *n* are in your womb . . Gen 25:23
itself among the *n* . . . . Num 23:9
shall lend to many *n* . . . . . . Deut 28:12
Why do the *n* rage . . . . Ps 2:1
I will give You the *n* . . . . Ps 2:8
be exalted among the *n* . . . . . Ps 46:10
n shall serve Him . . . . Ps 72:11
n shall call Him . . . . Ps 72:17
n shall fear the name . . . . . . Ps 102:15
is high above all *n* . . . . Ps 113:4
All *n* before Him are . . . . Is 40:17
n who do not know . . . . Is 55:5
a house of prayer for all *n* . . . . Is 56:7
the wise men of the *n* . . . . Jer 10:7
a reproach to the *n* . . . . Ezek 22:4
come to the Desire of All *N* . . Hag 2:7
n shall be joined . . . . Zech 2:11
speak peace to the *n* . . . . Zech 9:10
For I will gather all the *n* . . Zech 14:2
disciples of all the *n* . . . . . . Matt 28:19
in His name to all *n* . . . . . . Luke 24:47
the father of many *n* . . . . Rom 4:18
In you all the *n* shall be . . . . . . Gal 3:8
who was to rule all *n* . . . . Rev 12:5
For all the *n* have drunk of . . Rev 18:3
the healing of the *n* . . . . Rev 22:2

NATURAL

nor his *n* vigor abated . . . . . Deut 34:7
women exchanged the *n* . . . Rom 1:26
the men, leaving the *n* . . . . . Rom 1:27
did not spare the *n* . . . . Rom 11:21
n man does not receive . . . . 1 Cor 2:14
It is sown a *n* body . . . . 1 Cor 15:44
not first, but the *n* . . . . 1 Cor 15:46
his *n* face in a mirror . . . . . James 1:23

NATURE

men with the same *n* . . . . . . Acts 14:15
that the Divine *N* is . . . . Acts 17:29
for what is against *n* . . . . Rom 1:26
by *n* do the things in . . . . Rom 2:14
n itself teach you . . . . 1 Cor 11:14
We who are Jews by *n* . . . . . . Gal 2:15
by *n* children of wrath . . . . Eph 2:3
on fire the course of *n* . . . . . James 3:6
man with a *n* like ours . . . . James 5:17
of the divine *n* . . . . 2 Pet 1:4

NAZARENE

Jesus to be called, Matt 2:23
Descriptive of Jesus' followers, Acts 24:5

NAZARETH

Town in Galilee; considered obscure, John 1:46
City of Jesus' parents, Matt 2:23
Early home of Jesus, Luke 2:39–51
Jesus rejected by, Luke 4:16–30

NEAPOLIS

Seaport of Philippi, Acts 16:11

NEAR

that has God so *n* to it . . . . . . Deut 4:7
But the word is very *n* . . . . Deut 30:14
The LORD is *n* to all . . . . Ps 145:18
upon Him while He is *n* . . . . Is 55:6
know that it is *n* . . . . Matt 24:33
kingdom of God is *n* . . . . . . Luke 21:31
"The word is *n* . . . . Rom 10:8
to those who were *n* . . . . Eph 2:17
for the time is *n* . . . . Rev 1:3

NEARER

now our salvation is *n* . . . . Rom 13:11

NEBO

Babylonian god, Is 46:1
—— Summit of Pisgah; Moses dies here, Deut 32:49; 34:1, 5

NEBUCHADNEZZAR

Monarch of the Neo-Babylonian Empire (605–562 B.C.); carries Jews captive to Babylon, Dan 1:1–3
Crushes Jehoiachin's revolt, 2 Kin 24:10–17
Destroys Jerusalem; captures Zedekiah, Jer 39:5–8
Prophecies concerning, Is 14:4–27; Jer 21:7–10; 25:8, 9; 27:4–11; 32:28–36; 43:10–13; Ezek 26:7–12

NEBUZARADAN

Nebuchadnezzar's captain at siege of Jerusalem, 2 Kin 25:8–20
Protects Jeremiah, Jer 39:11–14

NECESSARY

mouth more than my *n* . . . . . Job 23:12
and thus it was *n* . . . . Luke 24:46
n that the word of God . . . . Acts 13:46
It is *n* to circumcise them, . . Acts 15:5
burden than these *n* . . . . Acts 15:28
to be weaker are *n* . . . . 1 Cor 12:22
Therefore it is *n* that this . . . . Heb 8:3
Therefore it was *n* that the . . Heb 9:23
I found it *n* to write . . . . Jude 3

NECESSITIES

have provided for my *n* . . . Acts 20:34
and again for my *n* . . . . Phil 4:16

NECESSITY

n is laid upon me . . . . 1 Cor 9:16
not grudgingly or of *n* . . . . . . 2 Cor 9:7
there must also of *n* be the . . Heb 9:16

NECK

smooth part of his *n* . . . . Gen 27:16
wept on his *n* a good . . . . . . Gen 46:29
bind them around your *n*, . . . Prov 3:3
and grace to your *n* . . . . Prov 3:22
and hardens his *n* . . . . Prov 29:1
Your *n* is like an ivory . . . . . . Song 7:4
and his yoke from your *n* . . . . Is 10:27
n was an iron sinew . . . . Is 48:4
were hung around his *n* . . . . Matt 18:6
ran and fell on his *n* . . . . . . Luke 15:20

NECKS

stiffened their *n* . . . . Neh 9:29
with outstretched *n* . . . . Is 3:16
who risked their own *n* . . . . Rom 16:4

NEED

in nakedness, and in *n* . . Deut 28:48
a prowler, and your *n* . . . . . Prov 24:34
the things you have *n* . . . . Matt 6:8
no *n* of a physician . . . . Matt 9:12
'The Lord has *n* . . . . Matt 21:3
did when he was in *n* . . . . . Mark 2:25
say, 'The Lord has *n* of it . . Mark 11:3
testimony do we *n* . . . . Luke 22:71
all, as anyone had *n* . . . . Acts 2:45
each as anyone had *n* . . . . . . Acts 4:35
hand, "I have no *n* . . . . 1 Cor 12:21
who ministered to my *n* . . . . . Phil 2:25
to abound and to suffer *n* . . . Phil 4:12
supply all your *n* . . . . Phil 4:19
not *n* to be ashamed . . . . . . 2 Tim 2:15
to help in time of *n* . . . . Heb 4:16
you *n* someone to teach . . . . . Heb 5:12
do not *n* that anyone . . . . . 1 John 2:27
sees his brother in *n* . . . . . 1 John 3:17
The city had no *n* . . . . Rev 21:23

NEEDY

your poor and your *n* . . . . . Deut 15:11
They push the *n* . . . . Job 24:4
n shall not always be . . . . Ps 9:18
He will deliver the *n* . . . . Ps 72:12
and lifts the *n* . . . . Ps 113:7
Him has mercy on the *n* . . Prov 14:31
out her hands to the *n* . . . . Prov 31:20
to rob the *n* of . . . . Is 10:2
n will lie down in . . . . Is 14:30
a strength to the *n* . . . . Is 25:4

NEGLECT

n the gift that is . . . . 1 Tim 4:14
if we *n* so great a . . . . Heb 2:3

NEGLECTED

n the weightier . . . . Matt 23:23
their widows were *n* . . . . Acts 6:1

NEHEMIAH
Jewish cupbearer to King Artaxerxes; prays for restoration of Jerusalem, Neh 1:4–11
King commissions him to rebuild walls, Neh 2:1–8
Overcomes opposition and accomplishes rebuilding, Neh 4—6
Appointed governor, Neh 5:14
Participates with Ezra in restored worship, Neh 8—10
Registers the people and the priests and Levites, Neh 11:1—12:26
Dedicates the wall, Neh 12:27–43
Returns to Jerusalem after absence and institutes reforms, Neh 13:4–31

NEIGHBOR
See LOVE YOUR NEIGHBOR
every man ask from his *n* .... Ex 11:2
witness against your *n* ....Ex 20:16
you shall love your *n* .... Lev 19:18
witness against your *n* ..... Deut 5:20
secretly slanders his *n*.......... Ps 101:5
Do not say to your *n*, "Go .. Prov 3:28
He who despises his *n* .... Prov 14:21
against your *n* without .... Prov 24:28
for better is a *n* .... Prov 27:10
every man teach his *n* ...... Jer 31:34
gives drink to his *n* .... Hab 2:15
man the truth to his *n* ..... Zech 8:16
'You shall love your *n* ...... Matt 5:43
love your *n* as yourself .... Matt 22:39
"And who is my *n* .... Luke 10:29
do you think was *n* .... Luke 10:36
"You shall love your *n* ..... Rom 13:9
love your *n* as yourself .... Gal 5:14
of them shall teach his *n* .... Heb 8:11

NEIGHBOR'S
shall not covet your *n* wife .. Ex 20:17
n garment as a pledge ...... Ex 22:26
or anything that is your *n* .. Deut 5:21
remove your *n* landmark .. Deut 19:14
goes in to his *n* wife .... Prov 6:29

NEIGHBORS
from all your *n* .... 2 Kin 4:3
Who speak peace to their *n* ... Ps 28:3
a reproach to our *n* .... Ps 44:13
return to our *n* sevenfold .... Ps 79:12
nor your rich *n*............. Luke 14:12
Therefore the *n* and those ... John 9:8

NEST
As an eagle stirs up its *n* .. Deut 32:11
and make its *n* .... Job 39:27
n is a man who wanders ...... Prov 27:8
though you set your *n* .... Obad 4
that he may set his *n* .... Hab 2:9
and *n* in its branches ..... Matt 13:32

NET
me with His *n* .... Job 19:6
pluck my feet out of the *n* ... Ps 25:15
have hidden their *n* .... Ps 35:7
They have prepared a *n* ...... Ps 57:6
an antelope in a *n* .... Is 51:20
catch in their *n* .... Hab 1:15
casting a *n* into the sea ..... Matt 4:18
I will let down the *n* .... Luke 5:5
to them, "Cast the *n* .... John 21:6
so many, the *n* was not ... John 21:11

NETHINIM
Servants of the Levites, Ezra 8:20
Possible origins of:
Gibeonites, Josh 9:23–27
Solomon's forced laborers, 1 Kin 9:20, 21
Mentioned, 1 Chr 9:2; Ezra 2:43–54; 7:24; 8:17; Neh 3:31; 7:46–60, 73; 10:28, 29; 11:21

NETS
fall into their own *n* .... Ps 141:10
immediately left their *n* .... Matt 4:20
down your *n* for a catch .... Luke 5:4

NEVER
in Me shall *n* thirst .... John 6:35
in Me shall *n* die .... John 11:26
Love *n* fails .... 1 Cor 13:8
n take away sins .... Heb 10:11
"I will *n* leave you .... Heb 13:5
prophecy *n* came by .... 2 Pet 1:21

NEW
Now there arose a *n* .... Ex 1:8
the LORD creates a *n*...... Num 16:30
man has taken a *n* wife ..... Deut 24:5
They chose *n* gods .... Judg 5:8
him with two *n* ropes ..... Judg 15:13
ark of God on a *n* cart ..... 2 Sam 6:3
He has put a *n* song in my .... Ps 40:3
sing to the LORD a *n* song..... Ps 96:1
will overflow with *n* wine . Prov 3:10
and there is nothing *n* .... Eccl 1:9
Behold, I will do a *n* .... Is 43:19
shall be called by a *n* name ... Is 62:2
For behold, I create *n* .... Is 65:17
when I will make a *n* .... Jer 31:31
n every morning .... Lam 3:23
I will give you a *n* heart ... Ezek 36:26
shall overflow with *n* wine .. Joel 2:24
wine into *n* wineskins ...... Matt 9:17
of the *n* covenant .... Matt 26:28
laid it in his *n* tomb .... Matt 27:60
speak with *n* tongues ...... Mark 16:17
n commandment I give .... John 13:34
tell or to hear some *n* ...... Acts 17:21
he is a *n* creation .... 2 Cor 5:17
n man who is renewed ...... Col 3:10
when I will make a *n* .... Heb 8:8
Mediator of the *n* covenant . Heb 9:15
n heavens and a *n* .... 2 Pet 3:13
n commandment I write ... 1 John 2:8
n name written which .... Rev 2:17
the *N* Jerusalem, which ..... Rev 3:12
And they sang a *n* .... Rev 5:9
And I saw a *n* heaven .... Rev 21:1
I make all things *n* .... Rev 21:5

NEW COVENANT
I will make a *n* with .... Jer 31:31
this is My blood of the *n* .. Matt 26:28
"This cup is the *n* in .... Luke 22:20
"This cup is the *n* .... 1 Cor 11:25
as ministers of the *n* .... 2 Cor 3:6
"when I will make a *n* .... Heb 8:8
Mediator of the *n*........... Heb 9:15
the Mediator of the *n* ...... Heb 12:24

NEW MAN
create in Himself one *n* ..... Eph 2:15
that you put on the *n* .... Eph 4:24
and have put on the *n* .... Col 3:10

NEWNESS
also should walk in *n* .... Rom 6:4
should serve in the *n* .... Rom 7:6

NEWS
heard this bad *n* .... Ex 33:4
Proclaim the good *n* of His ... Ps 96:2
soul, so is good *n* .... Prov 25:25
him who brings good *n* ...... Is 52:7
n of Him went out .... Luke 4:14
good *n* of your faith .... 1 Thess 3:6

NICANOR
One of the first seven deacons, Acts 6:1–5

NICODEMUS
Pharisee; converses with Jesus, John 3:1–12
Protests unfairness of Christ's trial, John 7:50–52
Brings gifts to anoint Christ's body, John 19:39, 40

NICOLAITANS
Group teaching moral laxity, Rev 2:6–15

NICOLAS
One of the first seven deacons, Acts 6:5

NIGHT
darkness He called *N* .... Gen 1:5
day and *n* shall not cease ... Gen 8:22
father drink wine that *n* ... Gen 19:33
It is a *n* of solemn .... Ex 12:42
pillar of fire by *n* .... Ex 13:22
strong east wind all that *n* .. Ex 14:21
came to Balaam at *n* ...... Num 22:20
meditate in it day and *n* ..... Josh 1:8
and the *n* be ended .... Job 7:4
gives songs in the *n* .... Job 35:10
law he meditates day and *n* .... Ps 1:2
instructs me in the *n* seasons .. Ps 16:7
n reveals knowledge .... Ps 19:2
Weeping may endure for a *n* . Ps 30:5
be afraid of the terror by *n* ... Ps 91:5
Your faithfulness every *n* ...... Ps 92:2
awake through the *n* ...... Ps 119:148
and stars to rule by *n* .... Ps 136:9
the *n* shines as the day ..... Ps 139:12
rises while it is yet *n* .... Prov 31:15
Watchman, what of the *n* ..... Is 21:11
desired You in the *n* .... Is 26:9
and perished in a *n* .... Jon 4:10
Child and His mother by *n* . Matt 2:14
His disciples come by *n* ... Matt 27:64
over their flock by *n* .... Luke 2:8
and continued all *n* .... Luke 6:12
man came to Jesus by *n* .... John 3:2
n is coming when no .... John 9:4
came to Jesus by *n* .... John 19:39
that *n* Peter was sleeping, .. Acts 12:6
stood by me this *n* .... Acts 27:23
The *n* is far spent .... Rom 13:12
as a thief in the *n* .... 1 Thess 5:2
We are not of the *n* .... 1 Thess 5:5
they do not rest day or *n* ..... Rev 4:8
before our God day and *n* .. Rev 12:10
there shall be no *n* .... Rev 21:25
there shall be no *n* .... Rev 22:5

NIGHTS
earth forty days and forty *n* .. Gen 7:4
forty days and forty *n* .... Ex 24:18
forty days and forty *n* .... Matt 4:2
three *n* in the belly of ..... Matt 12:40

NILE
Hebrew children drowned in, Ex 1:22
Moses hidden in, Ex 2:3–10
Water of, turned to blood, Ex 7:14–21
Mentioned in prophecies, Is 19:5–8; 23:3; 27:12; Jer 46:7–9; Amos 9:5

NIMROD
Ham's grandson, Gen 10:6–12

NINE
Adam lived were *n* hundred .. Gen 5:5
of Methuselah were *n* .... Gen 5:27
where are the *n* .... Luke 17:17

NINETY-NINE
he not leave the *n* .... Matt 18:12
n just persons .... Luke 15:7

NINEVEH
Capital of Assyria, 2 Kin 19:36
Jonah preaches to; people repent, Jon 3:1–10; Matt 12:41
Prophecy against, Nah 2:13—3:19; Zeph 2:13–15

NOAH
Son of Lamech, Gen 5:28–32
Finds favor with God; commissioned to build the ark, Gen 6:8–22
Fills ark and survives flood, Gen 7
Leaves ark; builds altar; receives God's promise, Gen 8
God's covenant with, Gen 9:1–17
Blesses and curses his sons; dies, Gen 9:18–29

NO AMON (or Thebes)
Nineveh compared to, Nah 3:8

NOB
City of priests; David flees to, 1 Sam 21:1–9
Priests of, killed by Saul, 1 Sam 22:9–23

NOBLE
of the king's most *n* princes . Esth 6:9
I had planted you a *n* vine . . . Jer 2:21
heard the word with a *n* . . . Luke 8:15
most *n* Festus, but speak . . Acts 26:25
mighty, not many *n* . . . . 1 Cor 1:26
whatever things are *n* . . . . Phil 4:8
not blaspheme that *n* . . . . . . James 2:7

NOBLES
voice of *n* was hushed . . . . . Job 29:10
king is the son of *n* . . . . Eccl 10:17
n have sent their lads . . . . Jer 14:3
your *n* rest in the . . . . Nah 3:18

NOD
Place (east of Eden) of Cain's exile, Gen 4:16, 17

NOISE
There is a *n* of war in the . . . Ex 32:17
any *n* with your voice . . . . . . Josh 6:10
the *n* of a great army . . . . 2 Kin 7:6
Than the *n* of many waters . . . Ps 93:4
The *n* of a multitude . . . . Is 13:4
people who make a *n* . . . . Is 17:12
of Egypt, is but a *n* . . . . Jer 46:17
They have made a *n* . . . . Lam 2:7
the *n* of many waters . . . . . . Ezek 1:24
the *n* of the wheels beside . . Ezek 3:13
the *n* of your songs . . . . Amos 5:23
n of the day of the . . . . Zeph 1:14
away with a great *n* . . . . 2 Pet 3:10

NORTH
Zion on the sides of the *n* . . . . Ps 48:2
O *n* wind, and come . . . . Song 4:16
I will say to the *n*, 'Give . . . . Is 43:6
Israel from the land of . . . . Jer 16:15
Togarmah from the far *n* . . Ezek 38:6
place out of the far *n* . . . . . Ezek 38:15
the west, from the *n* . . . . . . Luke 13:29

NOSTRILS
n the breath of life . . . . Gen 2:7
breath of God in my *n* . . . . . . Job 27:3
breath is in his *n* . . . . Is 2:22

NOTE
urge you, brethren, *n* . . . . . Rom 16:17
n those who so walk . . . . Phil 3:17

NOTHING
For now you are *n* . . . . Job 6:21
rich, yet has *n* . . . . Prov 13:7
"It is good for *n* . . . . Prov 20:14
before Him are as *n* . . . . Is 40:17
their works are *n* . . . . Is 41:29
I can of Myself do *n* . . . . John 5:30
Me you can do *n* . . . . John 15:5
men, it will come to *n* . . . . . . Acts 5:38
bring to *n* the things . . . . 1 Cor 1:28
For I know of *n* against . . . . . . 1 Cor 4:4
have not love, I am *n* . . . . . . 1 Cor 13:2
love, it profits me *n* . . . . 1 Cor 13:3
Be anxious for *n* . . . . Phil 4:6
For we brought *n* . . . . 1 Tim 6:7
complete, lacking *n* . . . . James 1:4
name's sake, taking *n* . . . . 3 John 7

NOTORIOUS
n prisoner called . . . . Matt 27:16

NOURISHED
"I have *n* and . . . . Is 1:2
n and knit together . . . . Col 2:19
n in the words of . . . . 1 Tim 4:6

NOURISHES
n and cherishes it . . . . Eph 5:29

NOVICE
not a *n*, lest being . . . . 1 Tim 3:6

NUMBER
if a man could *n* . . . . Gen 13:16
fulfill the *n* of your days . . . . . Ex 23:26
that I may know the *n* . . . . 2 Sam 24:2
and moved David to *n* . . . . 1 Chr 21:1
things without *n* . . . . Job 5:9
For now You *n* my steps . . . . Job 14:16
n the clouds by wisdom . . . . Job 38:37
teach us to *n* our days . . . . Ps 90:12
He counts the *n* . . . . Ps 147:4
Me days without *n* . . . . Jer 2:32
in *n* about five thousand . . . John 6:10
a great *n* believed and . . . . Acts 11:21
and increased in *n* daily . . . . Acts 16:5
which no one could *n* . . . . Rev 7:9
His *n* is 666 . . . . Rev 13:18

NUMBERED
David *n* the people . . . . 2 Sam 18:1
he had *n* the people . . . . . 2 Sam 24:10
are more than can be *n* . . . . Ps 40:5
death, and He was *n* with . . . . Is 53:12
God has *n* your kingdom . . . Dan 5:26
of your head are all *n* . . . . . . Matt 10:30
n among the twelve . . . . Luke 22:3
'And He was *n* with . . . . . . Luke 22:37
was *n* with the eleven . . . . . . Acts 1:26

OAKS
Wail, O *o* of Bashan . . . . Zech 11:2

OARSMEN
o brought you into . . . . Ezek 27:26

OATH
two of them swore an *o* . . . Gen 21:31
the *o* which He swore to . . . . Deut 7:8
people feared the *o* . . . . . . 1 Sam 14:26
Judah rejoiced at the *o* . . 2 Chr 15:15
o to walk in God's Law . . . . Neh 10:29
for the sake of your *o* . . . . Eccl 8:2
I may establish the *o* . . . . Jer 11:5
And you shall be an *o* . . . . . . Jer 42:18
raised My hand in an *o* . . . . Ezek 20:5
the *o* written in the Law . . . . Dan 9:11
he denied with an *o* . . . . Matt 26:72
o which He swore . . . . Luke 1:73
themselves under an *o* . . . . Acts 23:12
made priest without an *o* . . . Heb 7:20
or with any other *o* . . . . James 5:12

OATHS
shall perform your *o* . . . . Matt 5:33
because of the *o* . . . . Matt 14:9

OBADIAH
King Ahab's steward, 1 Kin 18:3–16
—— Prophet of Judah, Obad 1

OBED
Son of Boaz and Ruth, Ruth 4:17–22

OBED-EDOM
Philistine from Gath; ark of the Lord left in his house, 2 Sam 6:10–12; 1 Chr 13:13, 14

OBEDIENCE
scorns *o* to his mother . . . . Prov 30:17
and apostleship for *o* . . . . Rom 1:5
o many will be made . . . . Rom 5:19
For your *o* has become . . . . Rom 16:19
glorify God for the *o* of . . . . 2 Cor 9:13
captivity to the *o* . . . . 2 Cor 10:5
confidence in your *o* . . . . Philem 21
yet He learned *o* . . . . Heb 5:8
for *o* and sprinkling . . . . 1 Pet 1:2

OBEDIENT
said we will do, and be *o* . . . . Ex 24:7
you are willing and *o* . . . . Is 1:19
of the priests were *o* . . . . Acts 6:7
make the Gentiles *o* . . . . Rom 15:18

bondservants, be *o* to . . . . Eph 6:5
Himself and became *o* . . . . . . Phil 2:8
homemakers, good, *o* . . . . Titus 2:5
as *o* children . . . . 1 Pet 1:14

OBEY
LORD, that I should *o* . . . . Ex 5:2
God and *o* His voice . . . . Deut 4:30
o the commandments . . . . . Deut 11:27
if you diligently *o* the . . . . . . Deut 28:1
if you do not *o* the voice . . Deut 28:15
His voice we will *o* . . . . Josh 24:24
o is better than . . . . 1 Sam 15:22
they hear of me they *o* . . . . . . Ps 18:44
O My voice, and I will be . . . . . Jer 7:23
O My voice, and do . . . . Jer 11:4
we will *o* the voice of the . . . . Jer 42:6
shall serve and *o* Him . . . . . . Dan 7:27
if you diligently *o* . . . . Zech 6:15
winds and the sea *o* Him . . . Matt 8:27
spirits, and they *o* Him . . . . . Mark 1:27
o God rather than men . . . . . Acts 5:29
and do not *o* the truth . . . . Rom 2:8
yourselves slaves to *o* . . . . Rom 6:16
o your parents in all . . . . Col 3:20
Bondservants, *o* in all . . . . Col 3:22
on those who do not *o* . . . . 2 Thess 1:8
salvation to all who *o* Him . . . Heb 5:9
O those who rule . . . . Heb 13:17
mouths that they may *o* . . . . James 3:3
if some do not *o* . . . . 1 Pet 3:1

OBEYED
Abraham *o* My voice . . . . Gen 26:5
you have not *o* My voice . . . . . Judg 2:2
bondage anymore, they *o* . . . . Jer 34:10
of sin, yet you *o* . . . . Rom 6:17
they have not all *o* . . . . Rom 10:16
By faith Abraham *o* . . . . Heb 11:8
as Sarah *o* Abraham . . . . 1 Pet 3:6

OBEYING
o the truth through . . . . 1 Pet 1:22

OBSCURITY
shall see out of *o* . . . . Is 29:18

OBSERVANCE
the LORD, a solemn *o* . . . . Ex 12:42

OBSERVATION
does not come with *o* . . . . . Luke 17:20

OBSERVE
So you shall *o* the Feast of . . Ex 12:17
to *o* the Sabbath . . . . Ex 31:16
which I teach you to *o* . . . . . . Deut 4:1
night, that you may *o* to do . . Josh 1:8
man, and *o* the upright . . . . . . Ps 37:37
is wise will *o* these things . . Ps 107:43
and let your eyes *o* . . . . Prov 23:26
o mercy and justice . . . . Hos 12:6
teaching them to *o* all . . . . . . Matt 28:20
who does not *o* the day . . . . . Rom 14:6
o days and months and . . . . . . Gal 4:10
o your chaste conduct . . . . 1 Pet 3:2

OBSERVES
o the wind will not . . . . Eccl 11:4
He who *o* the day . . . . Rom 14:6

OBSERVING
o his natural face . . . . James 1:23

OBSESSED
nothing, but is *o* . . . . 1 Tim 6:4

OBSOLETE
Now what is becoming *o* . . . . . Heb 8:13

OBSTINATE
and made his heart *o* . . . . Deut 2:30
I knew that you were *o* . . . . Is 48:4

OBTAIN
They shall *o* joy and . . . . Is 35:10
for they shall *o* mercy . . . . Matt 5:7
they also may *o* mercy . . . . Rom 11:31
way that you may *o* it . . . . . . 1 Cor 9:24
o salvation through . . . . 1 Thess 5:9

o for themselves a good . . . 1 Tim 3:13
that they might *o* a better . . Heb 11:35
and covet and cannot *o* . . . . James 4:2

OBTAINED

Esther *o* favor in the sight . . Esth 2:15
o a part in this . . . . Acts 1:17
yet have now *o* mercy . . . . Rom 11:30
have *o* an inheritance . . . . Eph 1:11
He has by inheritance *o* . . . . . Heb 1:4
endured, he *o* the . . . . Heb 6:15
o eternal redemption . . . . Heb 9:12
o promises, stopped the . . . Heb 11:33
To those who have *o* . . . . 2 Pet 1:1

OBTAINS

o favor from the LORD . . . . . Prov 8:35

ODED

Prophet of Samaria, 2 Chr 28:9–15

OF THE WORLD

men *o* who have . . . . Ps 17:14
their words to the end *o* . . . . . . Ps 19:4
the ends *o* shall remember . . Ps 22:27
all inhabitants *o* . . . . Ps 49:1
All inhabitants *o* . . . . Is 18:3
proclaimed to the end *o* . . . . . Is 62:11
all the kingdoms *o* . . . . Matt 4:8
You are the light *o* . . . . Matt 5:14
from the foundation *o* . . . . . Matt 13:35
since the beginning *o* . . . . . . Matt 24:21
nations *o* seek after . . . . Luke 12:30
takes away the sin *o* . . . . John 1:29
The Christ, the Savior *o* . . . . John 4:42
give for the life *o* . . . . John 6:51
"I am the light *o* . . . . John 8:12
If you were *o* . . . . John 15:19
have given Me out *o* . . . . John 17:6
he would be the heir *o* . . . . . Rom 4:13
is the reconciling *o* . . . . Rom 11:15
foolish things *o* to put . . . . . 1 Cor 1:27
not the spirit *o* . . . . 1 Cor 2:12
made as the filth *o* . . . . 1 Cor 4:13
cares about the things *o* . . . 1 Cor 7:33
sorrow *o* produces death . . 2 Cor 7:10
under the elements *o* . . . . Gal 4:3
before the foundation *o* . . . . . . Eph 1:4
basic principles *o* . . . . Col 2:8
wants to be a friend *o* . . . . . James 4:4
escaped the pollutions *o* . . . 2 Pet 2:20
of the Father but is *o* . . . . . 1 John 2:16
sent the Son as Savior *o* . . 1 John 4:14
from the foundation *o* . . . . Rev 17:8

OF THIS WORLD

word, and the cares *o* . . . . . Matt 13:22
o, the deceitfulness . . . . Mark 4:19
sons *o* are more shrewd . Luke 16:8
You are *o*; I am not *o* . . . . . . John 8:23
he sees the light *o* . . . . John 11:9
Now is the judgment *o* . . . . John 12:31
for the ruler *o* is coming . . John 14:30
the ruler *o* is judged . . . . . . John 16:11
"My kingdom is not *o* . . . John 18:36
foolish the wisdom *o* . . . . . . 1 Cor 1:20
wisdom *o* is foolishness . . . 1 Cor 3:19
immoral people *o* . . . . 1 Cor 5:10
form *o* is passing away . . . . 1 Cor 7:31
according to the course *o* . . . . Eph 2:2
not chosen the poor *o* . . . . . James 2:5
kingdoms *o* have become . . Rev 11:15

OFFEND

I will *o* no more . . . . Job 34:31
that devour him will *o* . . . . Jer 2:3
lest we *o* them . . . . Matt 17:27
than that he should *o* . . . . . . Luke 17:2
them, "Does this *o* . . . . John 6:61

OFFENDED

How have I *o* you, that . . . . . Gen 20:9
A brother *o* is harder . . . . . Prov 18:19
is not *o* because of Me . . . . . Matt 11:6
So they were *o* at Him . . . . Matt 13:57
And then many will be *o* . . Matt 24:10
have I *o* in anything at all . . Acts 25:8
stumbles or is *o* . . . . Rom 14:21

OFFENDER

who make a man an *o* . . . . Is 29:21
For if I am an *o* . . . . Acts 25:11

OFFENSE

and a rock of *o* . . . . Is 8:14
You are an *o* to Me . . . . Matt 16:23
by whom the *o* comes . . . . . . Matt 18:7
one man's *o* many died . . . . Rom 5:15
by the one man's *o* . . . . Rom 5:17
stone and rock of *o* . . . . Rom 9:33
Give no *o*, either to . . . . 1 Cor 10:32
the *o* of the cross . . . . Gal 5:11
sincere and without *o* . . . . Phil 1:10
and a rock of *o* . . . . 1 Pet 2:8

OFFENSES

For *o* must come . . . . Matt 18:7
impossible that no *o* . . . . . . Luke 17:1
up because of our *o* . . . . Rom 4:25

OFFER

and *o* him there as a burnt . . Gen 22:2
You shall not *o* strange . . . . . . Ex 30:9
o for a sweet aroma to the . . Lev 6:21
to *o* willingly to You . . . . . 1 Chr 29:17
o up for yourselves a burnt . . Job 42:8
Therefore I will *o* sacrifices . . . Ps 27:6
o to You the sacrifice . . . . . . Ps 116:17
o the blind as a . . . . Mal 1:8
come and *o* your gift . . . . Matt 5:24
one cheek, *o* the other . . . . . Luke 6:29
egg, will he *o* him a . . . . Luke 11:12
to *o* up sacrifices, first for . . . Heb 7:27
which they *o* continually . . . . Heb 10:1
let us continually *o* . . . . Heb 13:15
to *o* up spiritual sacrifices . . . 1 Pet 2:5

OFFERED

Jacob *o* a sacrifice on . . . . . Gen 31:54
eaten the same day it is *o* . . . Lev 7:15
o profane fire before the . . . . Lev 10:1
Solomon *o* a thousand . . . . . . 1 Kin 3:4
who willingly *o* a . . . . Ezra 3:5
he *o* them money, ... Acts 8:18
from things *o* to idols . . . . . Acts 15:29
to eat those things *o* . . . . 1 Cor 8:10
"This was *o* to idols," . . . . . 1 Cor 10:28
when He *o* up Himself . . . . Heb 7:27
the eternal Spirit *o* . . . . Heb 9:14
so Christ was *o* . . . . Heb 9:28
in them" (which are *o* . . . . . . Heb 10:8
o one sacrifice . . . . Heb 10:12
By faith Abel *o* . . . . Heb 11:4

OFFERING

not respect Cain and his *o* . . . Gen 4:5
poured a drink *o* on it . . . . . Gen 35:14
a freewill *o* to the LORD, all . . Ex 35:29
you shall bring your *o* . . . . Lev 1:2
This is the law of the sin *o* . . Lev 6:25
Do not respect their *o* . . . . Num 16:15
fifty men who were *o* . . . . . . Num 16:35
he offered the burnt *o* . . . . . 1 Sam 13:9
at the time of the *o* of . . . . 1 Kin 18:36
the *o* for the house of our . . Ezra 8:25
of God, with the grain *o* . . . . Neh 13:9
o You did not require . . . . Ps 40:6
You make His soul an *o* . . . . . Is 53:10
they should present an *o* . . . . Dan 2:46
drink *o* have been cut off . . . . Joel 1:9
I accept an *o* from your . . . . . Mal 1:10
to the LORD an *o* . . . . Mal 3:3
an *o* for your cleansing, . . . Luke 5:14
Himself for us, an *o* . . . . Eph 5:2
out as a drink *o* . . . . Phil 2:17
o You did not . . . . Heb 10:5
o of the body of Jesus . . . . . Heb 10:10
o He has perfected . . . . Heb 10:14
is no longer an *o* . . . . Heb 10:18

OFFERINGS

and offered burnt *o* . . . . Gen 8:20
It is most holy of the *o* . . . . Lev 2:3
My food for My *o* made . . . . Num 28:2
on it burnt *o* to the LORD . . . Josh 8:31
delight in burnt *o* . . . . 1 Sam 15:22
burnt *o* and peace *o* . . . . . 2 Sam 24:25
heart brought burnt *o* . . . . 2 Chr 29:31
He remember all your *o* . . . . Ps 20:3
freewill *o* of my mouth . . . Ps 119:108
enough of burnt *o* of rams . . . . Is 1:11
In burnt *o* and . . . . Heb 10:6

OFFERS

Whoever *o* praise glorifies . . Ps 50:23
o sacrifices in the high . . . . . Jer 48:35
that he *o* God service . . . . John 16:2

OFFICE

He restored me to my *o* . . . . Gen 41:13
let another take his *o* . . . . Ps 109:8
sitting at the tax *o* . . . . Matt 9:9
Levi, sitting at the tax *o* . . . Luke 5:27
'Let another take his *o* . . . . . Acts 1:20

OFFICERS

appoint *o* over the land . . . . Gen 41:34
also make your *o* . . . . Is 60:17
the *o* struck Him with . . . . Mark 14:65
o answered, "No man . . . . . John 7:46
o saw Him, they cried . . . . . John 19:6

OFFSCOURING

You have made us an *o* . . . . Lam 3:45
the *o* of all things . . . . 1 Cor 4:13

OFFSPRING

You have given me no *o* . . . . Gen 15:3
also shown me your *o* . . . . Gen 48:11
because of the *o* which . . . . Ruth 4:12
your *o* like the grass of the . . Job 5:25
My blessing on your *o* . . . . Is 44:3
He seeks godly *o* . . . . Mal 2:15
wife and raise up *o* . . . . . . Matt 22:24
had her and left no *o* . . . . Mark 12:22
For we are also His *o* . . . . . Acts 17:28
we are the *o* of God . . . . Acts 17:29
am the Root and the O . . . . . Rev 22:16

OFTEN

o I wanted to gather . . . . . . Luke 13:34
as *o* as you eat this . . . . 1 Cor 11:26
in sleeplessness *o* . . . . 2 Cor 11:27
should offer Himself *o* . . . . . . Heb 9:25

OG

Amorite king of Bashan, Deut 3:1–13
Defeated and killed by Israel, Num 21:32–35

OHOLAH

Symbolic name of Samaria, Ezek 23:4, 5, 36

OIL

for the anointing *o* . . . . Ex 25:6
o to Me throughout your . . . . Ex 30:31
shall take the anointing *o* . . . Ex 40:9
anointing *o* on Aaron's . . . . Lev 8:12
land of olive *o* and honey . . . Deut 8:8
I cease giving my *o* . . . . Judg 9:9
a bin, and a little *o* . . . . 1 Kin 17:12
the jar of *o* run dry . . . . 1 Kin 17:16
So the *o* ceased . . . . 2 Kin 4:6
o to the storehouse . . . . Neh 13:12
poured out rivers of *o* . . . . Job 29:6
You anoint my head with *o* . . . Ps 23:5
anointed with fresh *o* . . . . Ps 92:10
the heart of man, *o* . . . . Ps 104:15
like the precious *o* . . . . Ps 133:2
be as excellent *o* . . . . Ps 141:5
the *o* of joy for mourning, ... Is 61:3
and I anointed you with *o* . . Ezek 16:9
with new wine and *o* . . . . Joel 2:24
thousand rivers of *o* . . . . Mic 6:7
and took no *o* with them, . . . Matt 25:3
the wise took *o* in their . . . . . Matt 25:4
'Give us some of your *o* . . . . Matt 25:8
very costly fragrant *o* . . . . . . Matt 26:7
o might have been sold . . . . Matt 26:9

costly *o* of spikenard ...... Mark 14:3
anoint My head with *o* .... Luke 7:46
wounds, pouring on *o* .... Luke 10:34
Why was this fragrant *o* ... John 12:5
anointing him with *o* ..... James 5:14
and do not harm the *o* .... Rev 6:6

OINTMENT

O and perfume delight ..... Prov 27:9
your name is *o* .... Song 1:3

OLD

was five hundred years *o* ... Gen 5:32
was ninety-nine years *o* ... Gen 17:1
who is ninety years *o* ..... Gen 17:17
Remember the days of *o*, ... Deut 32:7
o lion perishes for lack ...... Job 4:11
So Job died, *o* and full of .. Job 42:17
young, and now am *o* .... Ps 37:25
me off in the time of *o* age .... Ps 71:9
will utter dark sayings of *o* ... Ps 78:2
still bear fruit in *o* age ...... Ps 92:14
are the crown of *o* men .... Prov 17:6
and when he is *o* he will ... Prov 22:6
all manner, new and *o* ..... Song 7:13
die one hundred years *o* ..... Is 65:20
o men shall dream dreams .. Joel 2:28
was said to those of *o* ...... Matt 5:21
wine into *o* wineskins ...... Matt 9:17
He was twelve years *o* ..... Luke 2:42
man be born when he is *o* .. John 3:4
yet fifty years *o* .... John 8:57
but when you are *o* .... John 21:18
Your *o* men shall dream .... Acts 2:17
o man was crucified .... Rom 6:6
of the *O* Testament .... 2 Cor 3:14
o things have passed ...... 2 Cor 5:17
have put off the *o* man .... Col 3:9
o wives' fables, and .... 1 Tim 4:7
obsolete and growing *o* ..... Heb 8:13
that serpent of *o* .... Rev 20:2

OLD MAN

the presence of an *o* .... Lev 19:32
there will not be an *o* ..... 1 Sam 2:31
nor an *o* who has not .... Is 65:20
I am an *o*, and my wife .... Luke 1:18
our *o* was crucified .... Rom 6:6
the *o* which grows corrupt .. Eph 4:22
put off the *o* with his .... Col 3:9

OLDER

o shall serve the .... Gen 25:23
o than your father .... Job 15:10
"Now his *o* son was ...... Luke 15:25
not rebuke an *o* man .... 1 Tim 5:1
o women as mothers .... 1 Tim 5:2
that the *o* men be sober, ... Titus 2:2
the *o* women likewise, that .. Titus 2:3

OLDEST

beginning with the *o* .... John 8:9

OLIVE

a freshly plucked *o* .... Gen 8:11
o trees which you did not .. Deut 6:11
a land of *o* groves .... 2 Kin 18:32
I am like a green *o* .... Ps 52:8
Your children like *o* plants .. Ps 128:3
of the *o* may fail .... Hab 3:17
the *o* tree have not yielded .. Hag 2:19
and you, being a wild *o* ... Rom 11:17
o tree which is wild .... Rom 11:24
These are the two *o* trees ... Rev 11:4

OLIVES, MOUNT OF

David flees to, 2 Sam 15:30
Prophecy concerning, Zech 14:4
Christ's triumphal entry from, Matt 21:1
Prophetic discourse delivered from, Matt 24:3
Christ's ascension from, Acts 1:9–12

OMNIPOTENT

For the Lord God *O* .... Rev 19:6

OMRI

Made king of Israel by army, 1 Kin 16:16, 21, 22
Builds Samaria; reigns wickedly, 1 Kin 16:23–27

ON

City of Lower Egypt; center of sun worship, Gen 41:45, 50
Called Beth Shemesh, Jer 43:13

ONAN

Second son of Judah; slain for failure to give his brother an heir, Gen 38:8–10

ONCE

please come at *o* .... Num 22:6
marched around the city *o* . Josh 6:14
o more with the fleece ..... Judg 6:39
God has spoken *o*, twice I ... Ps 62:11
shall a nation be born at *o* .... Is 66:8
died, He died to sin *o* ...... Rom 6:10
alive *o* without the law ...... Rom 7:9
o I was stoned .... 2 Cor 11:25
o were far off have been ... Eph 2:13
who *o* was unprofitable .... Philem 11
for this He did *o* for all ..... Heb 7:27
Most Holy Place *o* for all ... Heb 9:12
for men to die *o* .... Heb 9:27
so Christ was offered *o* to ... Heb 9:28
who *o* were not a people ... 1 Pet 2:10
also suffered *o* .... 1 Pet 3:18

ONE

See EVIL ONE; HOLY ONE OF ISRAEL; LOVE ONE ANOTHER; WITH ONE ACCORD

He took *o* of his ribs, and ... Gen 2:21
they shall become *o* flesh ... Gen 2:24
desirable to make *o* wise ..... Gen 3:6
o language and *o* speech .... Gen 11:1
our God, the LORD is *o* ...... Deut 6:4
Blessed be the *o* who ...... Ruth 2:19
on a mountain on *o* side .. 1 Sam 17:3
kissed *o* another .... 1 Sam 20:41
in two, and give half to *o* .. 1 Kin 3:25
failed *o* word of all His .... 1 Kin 8:56
I told no *o* what my God .... Neh 2:12
no *o* could withstand them, .. Esth 9:2
o who feared God and .... Job 1:1
o mocked by his friends, ... Job 12:4
find *o* wise man among .... Job 17:10
God may speak in *o* way ... Job 33:14
who does good, no, not *o* ..... Ps 53:3
limited the Holy *O* of Israel .. Ps 78:41
Blessed is every *o* who ..... Ps 128:1
there is *o* who withholds .. Prov 11:24
flee when no *o* pursues .... Prov 28:1
Two are better than *o* .... Eccl 4:9
up, my love, my fair *o* ..... Song 2:10
I will seek the *o* I love ...... Song 3:2
shall take hold of *o* man, ... Is 4:1
open, and no *o* shall shut ..... Is 22:22
you will be gathered *o* .... Is 27:12
Return now every *o* from ... Jer 18:11
wings touched *o* another .... Ezek 1:9
Each *o* had four faces ..... Ezek 10:21
o who is found written ..... Dan 12:1
Holy *O* who is faithful ..... Hos 11:12
Has not *o* God created us ... Mal 2:10
deliver us from the evil *o* ... Matt 6:13
whoever causes *o* of .... Matt 18:6
two shall become *o* flesh' ... Matt 19:5
and hour no *o* knows ...... Matt 24:36
watch with Me *o* hour .... Matt 26:40
receives *o* of these .... Mark 9:37
"*O* thing you lack .... Mark 10:21
o on Your right hand .... Mark 10:37
Surely you are *o* of ...... Mark 14:70
The voice of *o* crying in .... Luke 3:4
No *o*, when he has lit a .... Luke 8:16
o thing is needed .... Luke 10:42
o sinner who repents ..... Luke 15:10
You still lack *o* thing ..... Luke 18:22
O sows and another .... John 4:37
Has no *o* condemned you .. John 8:10
I and My Father are *o* .... John 10:30
you love *o* another .... John 13:34
Me, that they may be *o* ... John 17:11
Not *o* of His bones .... John 19:36
Holy *O* to see corruption ... Acts 2:27
o accord in the temple ..... Acts 2:46
none righteous, no, not *o* ... Rom 3:10
each *o* a measure of faith .. Rom 12:3
Repay no *o* evil for evil ... Rom 12:17
Owe no *o* anything except . Rom 13:8
that *o* be found faithful ..... 1 Cor 4:2
to *o* is given the word ..... 1 Cor 12:8
body is not *o* member .... 1 Cor 12:14
if *o* strikes you on the .... 2 Cor 11:20
for you are all *o* .... Gal 3:28
love serve *o* another .... Gal 5:13
Bear *o* another's burdens, ... Gal 6:2
to create in Himself *o* .... Eph 2:15
o body and *o* Spirit .... Eph 4:4
o Lord, *o* faith, *o* .... Eph 4:5
o God and Father of .... Eph 4:6
but *o* thing I do, forgetting .. Phil 3:13
o Mediator between God ... 1 Tim 2:5
the husband of *o* wife ...... 1 Tim 3:2
Let no *o* despise your ..... 1 Tim 4:12
But each *o* is tempted ..... James 1:14
love *o* another fervently ... 1 Pet 1:22
Be hospitable to *o* another .. 1 Pet 4:9
a thousand years as *o* .... 2 Pet 3:8
and these three are *o* ...... 1 John 5:7
I will give to each *o* of you .. Rev 2:23
Lamb opened *o* of the seals .. Rev 6:1
on the cloud sat *O* like ..... Rev 14:14

ONESIMUS

Slave of Philemon converted by Paul in Rome, Philem 10–17
With Tychicus, carries Paul's letters to Colosse and to Philemon, Col 4:7–9

ONESIPHORUS

Ephesian Christian commended for his service, 2 Tim 1:16–18

ONLY BEGOTTEN SON

The *o*, who is in .... John 1:18
world that He gave His *o* .. John 3:16
offered up his *o* .... Heb 11:17
God has sent His *o* .... 1 John 4:9

OPEN

o his eyes that he may .... 2 Kin 6:17
o the eyes of these men ... 2 Kin 6:20
o His lips against you .... Job 11:5
His ears are *o* to their cry ..... Ps 34:15
You *o* Your hand .... Ps 104:28
O my eyes, that I may see .. Ps 119:18
O rebuke is better than .... Prov 27:5
O your mouth for the ...... Prov 31:8
and no one shall *o* .... Is 22:22
I will *o* your mouth to .... Ezek 29:21
o toward Jerusalem .... Dan 6:10
a lamb in *o* country .... Hos 4:16
o My mouth in parables ... Matt 13:35
Can a demon *o* the eyes .. John 10:21
she did not *o* the gate ..... Acts 12:14
our heart is wide *o* .... 2 Cor 6:11
things are naked and *o* ..... Heb 4:13
set before you an *o* door ..... Rev 3:8
o the scroll and to .... Rev 5:2

OPENED

eat of it your eyes will be *o* .. Gen 3:5
the earth *o* its mouth ..... Num 16:32
the LORD *o* the mouth ..... Num 22:28
the LORD *o* the eyes .... 2 Kin 6:17
Ezra *o* the book in the sight .. Neh 8:5
o not His mouth .... Is 53:7
that the heavens were *o* ..... Ezek 1:1
knock, and it will be *o* to .... Matt 7:7
our eyes may be *o* .... Matt 20:33
his ears were *o* .... Mark 7:35

when He had *o* the book . . . Luke 4:17
Then their eyes were *o* . . . Luke 24:31
o the Scriptures . . . Luke 24:32
o their understanding . . . Luke 24:45
clay and *o* his eyes . . . John 9:14
Lord *o* the prison doors . . . Acts 5:19
I see the heavens *o* and . . . Acts 7:56
effective door has *o* . . . 1 Cor 16:9
when the Lamb *o* . . . Rev 6:1
he *o* the bottomless pit, and . . Rev 9:2
Now I saw heaven *o* . . . Rev 19:11
God, and books were *o* . . . Rev 20:12

OPENLY

will Himself reward you *o* . . . Matt 6:4
to the feast, not *o* . . . John 7:10
o among the Jews, . . . John 11:54
and showed Him *o* . . . Acts 10:40
They have beaten us *o*, . . . Acts 16:37

OPENS

o the ears of men . . . Job 33:16
The LORD *o* the eyes of . . . Ps 146:8
him the doorkeeper *o* . . . John 10:3
and shuts and no one *o* . . . Rev 3:7
o the door, I will come in . . . Rev 3:20

OPHEL

Hill, southeast of Jerusalem, Neh 3:15–27
Fortified by Manasseh, 2 Chr 27:3
Residence of Nethinim, Neh 3:26

OPHIR

Famous for gold, 1 Chr 29:4

OPHRAH

Town in Manasseh; home of Gideon, Judg 6:11, 15
Site of Gideon's burial, Judg 8:32

OPINION

dared not declare my *o* . . . Job 32:6
be wise in your own *o* . . . Rom 11:25

OPINIONS

falter between two *o* . . . 1 Kin 18:21

OPPORTUNITY

sought *o* to betray Him . . . Matt 26:16
o to answer for himself . . . Acts 25:16
But sin, taking *o* . . . Rom 7:8
but give you *o* to boast . . . 2 Cor 5:12
that I may cut off the *o* . . . 2 Cor 11:12
liberty as an *o* for the flesh . . Gal 5:13
as we have *o* . . . Gal 6:10
but you lacked *o* . . . Phil 4:10
no *o* to the adversary . . . 1 Tim 5:14
they would have had *o* . . . Heb 11:15

OPPOSES

who *o* and exalts . . . 2 Thess 2:4

OPPOSITE

wrote *o* the lampstand on . . . Dan 5:5
Go into the village *o* you . . . Matt 21:2
Mary, sitting *o* the tomb . . Matt 27:61
Jesus sat *o* the treasury . . Mark 12:41
Gadarenes, which is *o* . . . Luke 8:26

OPPRESS

mistreat a stranger nor *o* . . . Ex 22:21
you shall not *o* . . . Lev 25:17
You that You should *o* . . . Job 10:3
He does not *o* . . . Job 37:23
no more *o* My people . . . Ezek 45:8
he loves to *o* . . . Hos 12:7
they *o* a man and his house, . . Mic 2:2
o the widow or the . . . Zech 7:10
o them four hundred years . . Acts 7:6
Do not the rich *o* . . . James 2:6

OPPRESSED

Whom have I *o* . . . 1 Sam 12:3
For he has *o* and . . . Job 20:19
fatherless and the *o* . . . Ps 10:18
for all who are *o* . . . Ps 103:6
The tears of the *o* . . . Eccl 4:1
He was *o* and He was . . . Is 53:7
her midst, and the *o* . . . Amos 3:9
at liberty those who are *o* . . Luke 4:18
healing all who were *o* . . . Acts 10:38
Lot, who was *o* by . . . 2 Pet 2:7

OPPRESSES

o the poor reproaches . . . Prov 14:31
o the poor to increase . . . Prov 22:16
A poor man who *o* . . . Prov 28:3

OPPRESSION

have surely seen the *o* . . . Ex 3:7
"For the *o* of the . . . Ps 12:5
Do not trust in *o* . . . Ps 62:10
their life from *o* . . . Ps 72:14
brought low through *o* . . . Ps 107:39
Redeem me from the *o* . . . Ps 119:134
considered all the *o* . . . Eccl 4:1
o destroys a wise . . . Eccl 7:7
justice, but behold, *o* . . . Is 5:7
surely seen the *o* . . . Acts 7:34

OPPRESSIONS

of *o* they cry out . . . Job 35:9

OPPRESSOR

the voice of the *o* . . . Job 3:18
Do not envy the *o* . . . Prov 3:31
is a great *o* . . . Prov 28:16
of the fury of the *o* . . . Is 51:13
No more shall an *o* . . . Zech 9:8

OPPRESSORS

me from the hand of *o* . . . Job 6:23
not leave me to my *o* . . . Ps 119:121
o there is power . . . Eccl 4:1
LORD because of the *o* . . . Is 19:20

ORACLES

received the living *o* . . . Acts 7:38
were committed the *o* . . . Rom 3:2
principles of the *o* . . . Heb 5:12
let him speak as the *o* . . . 1 Pet 4:11

ORDAINED

infants You have *o* . . . Ps 8:2
the stars, which You have *o* . . . Ps 8:3
o you a prophet . . . Jer 1:5
the Man whom He has *o* . . Acts 17:31
God *o* before the ages . . . 1 Cor 2:7

ORDER

in *o* that you may know . . . Ex 8:22
'Set your house in *o* . . . 2 Kin 20:1
of the LORD was set in *o* . . 2 Chr 29:35
in *o* to seek the LORD . . . Ezra 6:21
set your words in *o* . . . Job 33:5
you, and set them in *o* . . . Ps 50:21
to the *o* of Melchizedek . . . Ps 110:4
in *o* to cleanse the land . . . Ezek 39:12
swept, and put in *o* . . . Matt 12:44
it swept and put in *o* . . . Luke 11:25
done decently and in *o* . . . 1 Cor 14:40
each one in his own *o* . . . 1 Cor 15:23
to see your good *o* . . . Col 2:5
according to the *o* . . . Heb 5:6
in *o* to stir up love . . . Heb 10:24

ORDERED

man did as Joseph *o* . . . Gen 43:17
for so the LORD has *o* . . . 2 Sam 16:11
for so the king had *o* all . . . Esth 1:8
a good man are *o* by the . . . Ps 37:23

ORDERS

o his conduct aright I . . . Ps 50:23
as I have given *o* to the . . . 1 Cor 16:1

ORDINANCE

the *o* of the Passover . . . Ex 12:43
you shall keep My *o* . . . Lev 18:30
an *o* forever throughout . . . Num 10:8
o for Israel to this day . . . 1 Sam 30:25
required by *o* for each day . . Ezra 3:4
forsake the *o* of their God . . . Is 58:2
that we have kept His *o* . . . Mal 3:14
resists the *o* of God . . . Rom 13:2
yourselves to every *o* . . . 1 Pet 2:13

ORDINANCES

shall you walk in their *o* . . . Lev 18:3
o by the hand of Moses . . . 2 Chr 33:8
and gave them just *o* . . . Neh 9:13
Do you know the *o* . . . Job 38:33
according to Your *o* . . . Ps 119:91
"If those *o* depart . . . Jer 31:36
not appointed the *o* . . . Jer 33:25
gone away from My *o* . . . Mal 3:7
contained in *o* . . . Eph 2:15
and fleshly *o* imposed . . . Heb 9:10

ORION

Brilliant constellation, Job 9:9

ORNAMENT

will be a graceful *o* . . . Prov 1:9
of gold and an *o* . . . Prov 25:12
with them all as an *o* . . . Is 49:18

ORNAMENTS

cheeks are lovely with *o* . . . Song 1:10
a virgin forget her *o* . . . Jer 2:32
I adorned you with *o*, put . Ezek 16:11

ORPAH

Ruth's sister-in-law, Ruth 1:4, 14

ORPHANS

We have become *o* . . . Lam 5:3
I will not leave you *o* . . . John 14:18
to visit *o* and widows . . . James 1:27

OSNAPPER

Called "the great and noble," Ezra 4:10

OSTRICHES

o will dwell there . . . Is 13:21
is cruel, like *o* . . . Lam 4:3
a mourning like the *o* . . . Mic 1:8

OTHNIEL

Son of Kenaz, Caleb's youngest brother, Judg 1:13
Captures Kirjath Sepher; receives Caleb's daughter as wife, Josh 15:15–17
First judge of Israel, Judg 3:9–11

OUGHT

what Israel *o* to do . . . 1 Chr 12:32
These you *o* to have . . . Matt 23:23
pray for as we *o* . . . Rom 8:26
how you *o* to conduct . . . 1 Tim 3:15
which they *o* not . . . 1 Tim 5:13
persons *o* you to be . . . 2 Pet 3:11

OUTCAST

they called you an *o* . . . Jer 30:17
the lame, I will gather the *o* . . . Mic 4:6
and the *o* a strong nation . . . Mic 4:7

OUTCASTS

gathers together the *o* . . . Ps 147:2
will assemble the *o* . . . Is 11:12
hide the *o*, do not betray . . . Is 16:3
Let My *o* dwell with . . . Is 16:4

OUTCRY

because the *o* against . . . Gen 19:13
that there be no *o* . . . Ps 144:14
Then there arose a loud *o* . . Acts 23:9

OUTGOINGS

You make the *o* of the . . . Ps 65:8

OUTRAGE

lewdness and *o* in . . . Judg 20:6

OUTRAN

the other disciple *o* . . . John 20:4

OUTSIDE

and dish, that the *o* . . . Matt 23:26
Pharisees make the *o* . . . Luke 11:39
toward those who are *o* . . . Col 4:5
to Him, *o* the camp . . . Heb 13:13
But *o* are dogs and . . . Rev 22:15

OUTSTRETCHED

power and by Your *o* arm . . Deut 9:29
and with an *o* arm . . . Deut 26:8
an *o* arm, Him you shall . . 2 Kin 17:36
against you with an *o* . . . Jer 21:5

OUTWARD
at the *o* appearance ...... 1 Sam 16:7
Even though our *o* man ... 2 Cor 4:16
to the *o* appearance .... 2 Cor 10:7
adornment be merely *o* ..... 1 Pet 3:3

OUTWARDLY
appear beautiful *o* .... Matt 23:27
not a Jew who is one *o* .... Rom 2:28

OUTWIT
The enemy shall not *o* .... Ps 89:22

OVEN
make them as a fiery *o* .... Ps 21:9
burning like an *o* .... Mal 4:1
is thrown into the *o* .... Matt 6:30

OVERCAME
My throne, as I also *o* .... Rev 3:21
And they *o* him by .... Rev 12:11

OVERCOME
we are well able to *o* it ... Num 13:30
for they have *o* me .... Song 6:5
to those who are *o* with wine .. Is 28:1
good cheer, I have *o* ...... John 16:33
o when You are judged ...... Rom 3:4
o evil with good .... Rom 12:21
entangled in them and *o* ... 2 Pet 2:20
because you have *o* ...... 1 John 2:13
and have *o* them, ... 1 John 4:4
that has *o* the world ...... 1 John 5:4
and the Lamb will *o* .... Rev 17:14

OVERCOMES
of God *o* the world .... 1 John 5:4
he who *o* the world .... 1 John 5:5
o I will give to eat .... Rev 2:7
o shall not be hurt .... Rev 2:11
To him who *o* I will give .... Rev 2:17
He who *o* shall be clothed .... Rev 3:5
To him who *o* I will grant .... Rev 3:21
o shall inherit all .... Rev 21:7

OVERFLOW
Let not the floodwater *o* ..... Ps 69:15
vats will *o* with new wine .. Prov 3:10
shall *o* with righteousness ... Is 10:22
rivers, they shall not *o* you .... Is 43:2
vats shall *o* with new wine .. Joel 2:24

OVERFLOWING
My heart is *o* with a .... Ps 45:1
a flood of mighty waters *o* ..... Is 28:2
and shall be an *o* flood .... Jer 47:2
But with an *o* flood He will ... Nah 1:8

OVERSEER
Then he made him *o* .... Gen 39:4
having no captain, *o* .... Prov 6:7
to the Shepherd and *O* ..... 1 Pet 2:25

OVERSEERS
Spirit has made you *o* ..... Acts 20:28
you, serving as *o* .... 1 Pet 5:2

OVERSHADOW
of the Highest will *o* .... Luke 1:35

OVERTAKE
some evil *o* me and I die ... Gen 19:19
o you, because you obey ... Deut 28:2
upon you and *o* you .... Deut 28:15
and *o* you, until you are ... Deut 28:45
lest he *o* us suddenly .... 2 Sam 15:14
does righteousness *o* .... Is 59:9
you feared shall *o* .... Jer 42:16
lest darkness *o* you .... John 12:35
and *o* this chariot .... Acts 8:29
that this Day should *o* ... 1 Thess 5:4

OVERTAKEN
and anguish have *o* me ... Ps 119:143
No temptation has *o* ...... 1 Cor 10:13
if a man is *o* in any .... Gal 6:1

OVERTHREW
So He *o* those cities .... Gen 19:25
will be as when God *o* .... Is 13:19
As God *o* Sodom and .... Jer 50:40
"I *o* some of you .... Amos 4:11

OVERTHROW
you shall utterly *o* .... Ex 23:24
o them in the wilderness ... Ps 106:26
o their descendants .... Ps 106:27
o the righteous in .... Prov 18:5
As in the *o* of Sodom and ... Jer 49:18
o the throne of .... Hag 2:22
of God, you cannot *o* it ..... Acts 5:39
o the faith of some .... 2 Tim 2:18

OVERTHROWN
Their judges are *o* .... Ps 141:6
but it is *o* by the mouth ... Prov 11:11
The wicked are *o* and are .. Prov 12:7
desolate, as *o* by strangers ..... Is 1:7
of Sodom, which was *o* ..... Lam 4:6
I will make it *o* .... Ezek 21:27
and Nineveh shall be *o* .... Jon 3:4

OVERTHROWS
and *o* the mighty .... Job 12:19
o them in the night .... Job 34:25
o the words of the .... Prov 22:12

OVERTURNED
my heart is *o* within .... Lam 1:20
o the tables of the .... Matt 21:12
money and *o* the tables .... John 2:15

OVERWHELM
o the fatherless .... Job 6:27
sends them out, they *o* ..... Job 12:15

OVERWHELMED
when my heart is *o* .... Ps 61:2
and my spirit was *o* .... Ps 77:3
o their enemies .... Ps 78:53
waters would have *o* .... Ps 124:4
my spirit is *o* within .... Ps 143:4

OVERWORK
Do not *o* to be rich .... Prov 23:4

OWE
Pay me what you *o* .... Matt 18:28
'How much do you *o* .... Luke 16:5
O no one anything .... Rom 13:8
o me even your own .... Philem 19

OWED
o him ten thousand .... Matt 18:24
fellow servants who *o* ..... Matt 18:28
o five hundred denarii ..... Luke 7:41

OWN
created man in His *o* .... Gen 1:27
interpretation of his *o* ..... Gen 41:11
of his *o* people as wife ..... Lev 21:14
grasshoppers in our *o* .... Num 13:33
is right in his *o* eyes .... Deut 12:8
each to his *o* inheritance .. Josh 24:28
a man after His *o* heart .. 1 Sam 13:14
loved him as his *o* soul ... 1 Sam 18:1
Your very *o* people .... 2 Sam 7:24
Your *o* we have given .... 1 Chr 29:14
everyone to his *o* city ...... Ezra 2:1
reproach on their *o* heads .... Neh 4:4
wise in their *o* craftiness .... Job 5:13
He who swears to his *o* hurt .. Ps 15:4
Even my *o* familiar friend in .. Ps 41:9
on your *o* understanding .... Prov 3:5
not be wise in your *o* eyes .. Prov 3:7
troubles his *o* house ...... Prov 11:29
a fool is right in his *o* .... Prov 12:15
a man are pure in his *o* .... Prov 16:2
wisdom loves his *o* soul .... Prov 19:8
no rule over his *o* spirit ... Prov 25:28
forsake your *o* friend ..... Prov 27:10
her *o* works praise her .... Prov 31:31
over another to his *o* hurt ... Eccl 8:9
the work of their *o* hands ...... Is 2:8
every one from his *o* fig ..... Is 36:16
dictates of their *o* heart ...... Jer 9:14
return upon your *o* head .... Obad 15
idols forsake their *o* Mercy ... Jon 2:8
men of his *o* household ...... Mic 7:6
the plank in your *o* eye ..... Matt 7:3
dead bury their *o* dead ..... Matt 8:22
and loses his *o* soul .... Matt 16:26
honor except in his *o* .... Mark 6:4
is known by its *o* fruit ..... Luke 6:44
He came to His *o* .... John 1:11
not to do My *o* will .... John 6:38
I do not seek My *o* glory ... John 8:50
and am known by My *o* .. John 10:14
having loved His *o* .... John 13:1
world would love its *o* .... John 15:19
took her to his *o* home .... John 19:27
speak in his *o* language ..... Acts 2:6
by our *o* power or .... Acts 3:12
His *o* love toward us ...... Rom 5:8
did not spare His *o* Son ... Rom 8:32
and you are not your *o* .... 1 Cor 6:19
But each one has his *o* ..... 1 Cor 7:7
ask their *o* husbands at .. 1 Cor 14:35
plucked out your *o* eyes ..... Gal 4:15
submit to your *o* husbands .. Eph 5:22
ought to love their *o* wives .. Eph 5:28
work out your *o* salvation .. Phil 2:12
For all seek their *o* .... Phil 2:21
who rules his *o* house ...... 1 Tim 3:4
but with His *o* blood He .... Heb 9:12
in His *o* body on the tree ... 1 Pet 2:24
but left their *o* abode .... Jude 6
from our sins in His *o* .... Rev 1:5

OX
shall not muzzle an *o* ..... Deut 25:4
"Will the wild *o* .... Job 39:9
you bind the wild *o* .... Job 39:10
like a young wild *o* .... Ps 29:6
exalted like a wild *o* .... Ps 92:10
o knows its owner .... Is 1:3
had the face of an *o* .... Ezek 1:10
Sabbath loose his *o* ...... Luke 13:15
shall not muzzle an *o* .... 1 Cor 9:9

PACE
are majestic in *p* .... Prov 30:29

PACIFIES
A gift in secret *p* .... Prov 21:14
for conciliation *p* .... Eccl 10:4

PADAN ARAM
Same as Mesopotamia, Gen 24:10; *see* MESOPOTAMIA
Home of Isaac's wife, Gen 25:20
Jacob flees to, Gen 28:2–7
Jacob returns from, Gen 31:17, 18
People of, called Syrians, Gen 31:24
Language of, called Aramaic, 2 Kin 18:26

PAGAN
have taken *p* wives from ... Ezra 10:2
by marrying *p* women ..... Neh 13:27
have begotten *p* children ..... Hos 5:7
priests with the *p* priests ..... Zeph 1:4

PAID
today I have *p* my vows .... Prov 7:14
p the very last mite .... Luke 12:59
p tithes through Abraham .... Heb 7:9

PAILS
p are full of milk .... Job 21:24

PAIN
p you shall bring .... Gen 3:16
Because I bore him in *p* .... 1 Chr 4:9
on my affliction and my *p* ... Ps 25:18
p as a woman in .... Is 13:8
are filled with *p* .... Is 21:3
before her *p* came .... Is 66:7
Why is my *p* perpetual ..... Jer 15:18
labor and in *p* to give birth .. Rev 12:2
shall be no more *p* .... Rev 21:4

PAINED
My heart is severely *p* .... Ps 55:4
I am *p* in my very .... Jer 4:19

PAINFUL
this, it was too *p* ....Ps 73:16
for the present, but *p* ......Heb 12:11

PAINS
The *p* of death ....Ps 116:3
having loosed the *p* ....Acts 2:24
upon them, as labor *p* ....1 Thess 5:3

PAINT
and she put *p* on her ......2 Kin 9:30
your eyes with *p* ....Jer 4:30

PAINTING
it with cedar and *p* ....Jer 22:14

PALACE
support from the *p* ....Ezra 4:14
was taken to the king's *p* ....Esth 2:8
was great in the king's *p* ....Esth 9:4
enter the King's *p* ....Ps 45:15
a *p* of foreigners ....Is 25:2
to serve in the king's *p* ......Dan 1:4
the king went to his *p* ......Dan 6:18
at the *p* of the high priest ..Matt 26:3
guards his own *p* ....Luke 11:21
evident to the whole *p* ......Phil 1:13

PALACES
out of the ivory *p* ....Ps 45:8
God is in her *p* ....Ps 48:3
has entered our *p* ....Jer 9:21
has swallowed up all her *p* ..Lam 2:5
in the *p* at Ashdod ....Amos 3:9

PALANQUIN
the King made himself a *p* ..Song 3:9

PALE
his face now grow *p* ....Is 29:22
and all faces turned *p* ....Jer 30:6
behold, a *p* horse ....Rev 6:8

PALM
of water and seventy *p* .....Ex 15:27
p trees, and open flowers ..1 Kin 6:29
of yours is like a *p* tree .....Song 7:7
p branch and bulrush in ....Is 9:14
p branch or bulrush, may ......Is 19:15
and *p* trees were carved ..Ezek 41:20
p trees and went out ......John 12:13
p branches in their ....Rev 7:9

PALMS
you on the *p* of My hands ....Is 49:16
struck Him with the *p* .....Matt 26:67

PALTI (or Paltiel)
Man to whom Saul gives Michal, David's wife, in marriage, 1 Sam 25:44; 2 Sam 3:15

PAMPERS
p his servant from ....Prov 29:21

PAMPHYLIA
People from, at Pentecost, Acts 2:10
Paul visits; John Mark returns home from, Acts 13:13; 15:38
Paul preaches in cities of, Acts 14:24, 25

PANGS
The *p* of death ....Ps 18:4
P and sorrows will ....Is 13:8
labors with birth *p* ....Rom 8:22

PANICKED
the men of Benjamin *p* ....Judg 20:41

PANT
They *p* after the dust ....Amos 2:7

PANTS
As the deer *p* for the ....Ps 42:1

PAPHOS
Paul blinds Elymas at, Acts 13:6–13

PAPYRUS
"Can the *p* grow up ....Job 8:11

PARABLE
open my mouth in a *p* ....Ps 78:2
speak a *p* to the house of ..Ezek 17:2
utter a *p* to the rebellious ..Ezek 24:3
p He did not speak ....Matt 13:34
learn this *p* from the fig ...Matt 24:32
spoken the *p* against .....Mark 12:12
do You speak this *p* ....Luke 12:41

PARABLES
'Does he not speak *p* ....Ezek 20:49
understand all the *p* ....Mark 4:13
rest it is given in *p* ....Luke 8:10

PARADE
love does not *p* ....1 Cor 13:4

PARADISE
will be with Me in *P* ......Luke 23:43
was caught up into *P* ......2 Cor 12:4
in the midst of the *P* ....Rev 2:7

PARALYTIC
then He said to the *p* ....Matt 9:6
on which the *p* was lying ....Mark 2:4

PARALYZED
servant is lying at home *p* ...Matt 8:6
sick people, blind, lame, *p* ...John 5:3
who were *p* and lame ....Acts 8:7

PARAN
Residence of exiled Ishmael, Gen 21:21
Israelites camp in, Num 10:12
Headquarters of spies, Num 13:3, 26
Site of David's refuge, 1 Sam 25:1

PARCHMENTS
especially the *p* ....2 Tim 4:13

PARDON
p your transgressions ....Ex 23:21
You are God, ready to *p* .....Neh 9:17
not *p* my transgression ....Job 7:21
O LORD, *p* my iniquity..........Ps 25:11
He will abundantly *p* ....Is 55:7
p all their iniquities ....Jer 33:8

PARDONED
ended, that her iniquity is *p* ...Is 40:2

PARDONING
is a God like You, *p* ....Mic 7:18

PARENTS
will rise up against *p* ....Matt 10:21
His *p* went to Jerusalem ...Luke 2:41
has left house or *p* ....Luke 18:29
sinned, this man or his *p* ....John 9:2
disobedient to *p* ....Rom 1:30
to lay up for the *p* ....2 Cor 12:14
obey your *p* in all things, ...Col 3:20
disobedient to *p* ....2 Tim 3:2

PARMENAS
One of the first seven deacons, Acts 6:5

PART
You have no *p* in the ....Josh 22:25
has chosen that good *p* ...Luke 10:42
you, you have no *p* ....John 13:8
And he kept back *p* of the ...Acts 5:2
that blindness in *p* has ....Rom 11:25
to that *p* which lacks it, ...1 Cor 12:24
For we know in *p* ....1 Cor 13:9
p has a believer ....2 Cor 6:15
Abraham gave a tenth *p* ......Heb 7:2
shall take away his *p* ....Rev 22:19

PARTAKE
for we all *p* of that ....1 Cor 10:17
you cannot *p* of the ....1 Cor 10:21

PARTAKER
and have been a *p* ....Ps 50:18
in hope should be *p* ....1 Cor 9:10
Christ, and also a *p* ....1 Pet 5:1

PARTAKERS
Gentiles have been *p* ....Rom 15:27
of the sacrifices *p* ....1 Cor 10:18
know that as you are *p* ......2 Cor 1:7
gospel, you all are *p* ....Phil 1:7
qualified us to be *p* ....Col 1:12
For we have become *p* ......Heb 3:14

PARTED
them, that He was *p* ......Luke 24:51
so sharp that they *p* ....Acts 15:39

PARTIAL
You shall not be *p* ....Lev 19:15

PARTIALITY
You shall not show *p* ....Deut 1:17
unjustly, and show *p* ....Ps 82:2
is not good to show *p* ....Prov 18:5
but have shown *p* ....Mal 2:9
that God shows no *p* ....Acts 10:34
For there is no *p* ....Rom 2:11
doing nothing with *p* ....1 Tim 5:21
but if you show *p* ....James 2:9
good fruits, without *p* ....James 3:17

PARTIES
revelries, drinking *p* ....1 Pet 4:3

PARTING
at the *p* of the road ....Ezek 21:21

PARTITION
the Testimony, and *p* ....Ex 40:3

PARTNER
Whoever is a *p* with a ....Prov 29:24
you count me as a *p* ....Philem 17

PARTRIDGE
when one hunts a *p* ....1 Sam 26:20

PARTS
anything but death *p* ....Ruth 1:17
in the inward *p* ....Ps 51:6
uttermost *p* of the sea ....Ps 139:9
Shout, you lower *p* ....Is 44:23
and made four *p* ....John 19:23
but our presentable *p* ....1 Cor 12:24
into the lower *p* ....Eph 4:9

PASHHUR
Official opposing Jeremiah, Jer 21:1; 38:1–13
—— Priest who puts Jeremiah in jail, Jer 20:1–6

PASS
I will *p* over you ....Ex 12:13
of the sea that *p* ....Ps 8:8
When you *p* through the ....Is 43:2
"I will make you *p* ....Ezek 20:37
seven times shall *p* over ....Dan 4:32
I will not *p* by them ....Amos 7:8
and earth will *p* ....Matt 24:35
let this cup *p* from Me ....Matt 26:39
will by no means *p* ....Mark 13:31
p away with a great noise ..2 Pet 3:10

PASSED
And behold, the LORD *p* ..1 Kin 19:11
and Your waves *p* over me ....Jon 2:3
p by on the other side ....Luke 10:31
forbearance God had *p* ....Rom 3:25
all *p* through the sea ....1 Cor 10:1
old things have *p* away ....2 Cor 5:17
High Priest who has *p* ....Heb 4:14
By faith they *p* through .....Heb 11:29
know that we have *p* ....1 John 3:14
former things have *p* away ..Rev 21:4

PASSES
For the wind *p* over it ....Ps 103:16
of Christ which *p* ....Eph 3:19

PASSING
days are like a *p* shadow ....Ps 144:4
and *p* by, to bear His .....Mark 15:21
Jesus of Nazareth was *p* ..Luke 18:37
which glory was *p* away, ...2 Cor 3:7
the *p* pleasures of sin ......Heb 11:25
the darkness is *p* away ....1 John 2:8

PASSION
than to burn with *p* ....1 Cor 7:9
uncleanness, *p*, evil ....Col 3:5

PASSIONS
gave them up to vile *p* ..... Rom 1:26

PASSOVER
It is the LORD's *P* .... Ex 12:11
of the Feast of the *P* be left ... Ex 34:25
at twilight is the LORD's *P* ... Lev 23:5
the *P* at its appointed time .. Num 9:2
to the rite of the *P* and ..... Num 9:14
sacrifice the *P* at twilight ... Deut 16:6
the *P* on the fourteenth ...... Josh 5:10
of King Josiah this *P* ..... 2 Kin 23:23
P in the second month .... 2 Chr 30:2
of the slaughter of the *P* .. 2 Chr 30:17
Now Josiah kept a *P* to .... 2 Chr 35:1
the *P* lambs for all the ..... Ezra 6:20
you shall observe the *P* ... Ezek 45:21
I will keep the *P* .... Matt 26:18
P with My disciples ...... Mark 14:14
the *P* must be killed .... Luke 22:7
Now the *P* of the Jews ..... John 2:13
Now the *P*, a feast of the ..... John 6:4
P of the Jews was near .... John 11:55
six days before the *P* ...... John 12:1
that they might eat the *P* .. John 18:28
Preparation Day of the *P* . John 19:14
indeed Christ, our *P* .... 1 Cor 5:7
By faith he kept the *P* ..... Heb 11:28

PAST
My days are *p* .... Job 17:11
lo, the winter is *p* .... Song 2:11
harvest is *p*, the summer ...... Jer 8:20
and His ways *p* finding .... Rom 11:33
resurrection is already *p* .. 2 Tim 2:18
ways spoke in time *p* .... Heb 1:1
p lifetime in doing .... 1 Pet 4:3

PASTORS
and some *p* and .... Eph 4:11

PASTURE
the sheep of Your *p* .... Ps 74:1
the people of His *p* .... Ps 95:7
feed them in good *p* ...... Ezek 34:14
in and out and find *p* ...... John 10:9

PASTURES
to lie down in green *p* .... Ps 23:2

PATARA
Port of Lycia where Paul changes ships, Acts 21:1, 2

PATH
You enlarged my *p* ...... 2 Sam 22:37
p no bird knows .... Job 28:7
You will show me the *p* ...... Ps 16:11
lead me in a smooth *p* .... Ps 27:11
comprehend my *p* and my ... Ps 139:3
But the *p* of the just .... Prov 4:18
You weigh the *p* of the just .... Is 26:7
Him in the *p* of justice .... Is 40:14
way in the sea and a *p* .... Is 43:16

PATHROS
Described as a lowly kingdom, Ezek 29:14–16
Refuge for dispersed Jews, Jer 44:1–15
Jews to be regathered from, Is 11:11

PATHS
He leads me in the *p* .... Ps 23:3
Teach me Your *p* .... Ps 25:4
and all her *p* are .... Prov 3:17
p they have not .... Is 42:16
themselves crooked *p* .... Is 59:8
Make His *p* straight .... Matt 3:3
and make straight *p* .... Heb 12:13

PATIENCE
'Master, have *p* .... Matt 18:26
and bear fruit with *p* ...... Luke 8:15
p possess your souls ..... Luke 21:19
Now may the God of *p* ..... Rom 15:5
labor of love, and *p* ...... 1 Thess 1:3
faith, love, *p* .... 1 Tim 6:11
and *p* inherit the promises .. Heb 6:12
your faith produces *p* .... James 1:3
p have its perfect .... James 1:4
of suffering and *p* .... James 5:10
in the kingdom and *p* .... Rev 1:9
Here is the *p* and the .... Rev 13:10

PATIENT
rejoicing in hope, *p* .... Rom 12:12
uphold the weak, be *p* ... 1 Thess 5:14

PATIENTLY
the LORD, and wait *p* .... Ps 37:7
if you take it *p* .... 1 Pet 2:20

PATMOS
John, banished here, receives the Revelation, Rev 1:9

PATRIARCHS
begot the twelve *p* .... Acts 7:8

PATTERN
p which you were .... Ex 26:30
as you have us for a *p* ...... Phil 3:17
Hold fast the *p* .... 2 Tim 1:13
p shown you on the .... Heb 8:5

PAUL
Roman citizen from Tarsus; studied under Gamaliel, Acts 22:3, 25–28
Originally called Saul; persecutes the church, Acts 7:58; 8:1, 3; 9:1, 2
Converted on road to Damascus, Acts 9:3–19
Preaches in Damascus; escapes to Jerusalem and then to Tarsus, Acts 9:20–30
Ministers in Antioch; sent to Jerusalem, Acts 11:25–30
First missionary journey, Acts 13; 14
Speaks for Gentiles at Jerusalem Council, Acts 15:1–5, 12
Second missionary journey, Acts 15:36—18:22
Third missionary journey, Acts 18:23—21:14
Arrested in Jerusalem; defense before Roman authorities, Acts 21:15—26:32
Sent to Rome, Acts 27:1—28:31
His epistles, Rom; 1 and 2 Cor; Gal; Eph; Phil; Col; 1 and 2 Thess; 1 and 2 Tim; Titus; Philem

PAULUS, SERGIUS
Roman proconsul of Cyprus, Acts 13:4, 7

PAVED
a *p* work of sapphire stone .. Ex 24:10

PAVEMENT
that is called The *P* .... John 19:13

PAVILION
shall hide me in His *p* .... Ps 27:5
them secretly in a *p* .... Ps 31:20

PAW
from the *p* of the lion .... 1 Sam 17:37

PAWS
He *p* in the valley .... Job 39:21

PAY
sell the oil and *p* your debt .. 2 Kin 4:7
p attention to my wisdom ... Prov 5:1
with which to *p* .... Prov 22:27
priests teach for *p* .... Mic 3:11
with me, and I will *p* ..... Matt 18:26
p taxes to Caesar .... Matt 22:17
For you *p* tithe of .... Matt 23:23
to *p* taxes to Caesar ..... Mark 12:14

PEACE
"These men are at *p* .... Gen 34:21
sacrifice of the *p* offering ..... Lev 3:9
I will give *p* in the .... Lev 26:6
you, and give you *p* ...... Num 6:26
Joshua made *p* with them .. Josh 9:15
had made *p* with Israel ..... Josh 10:1
'Make *p* with me by a .... 2 Kin 18:31
If you ever return in *p* ... 2 Chr 18:27
field shall be at *p* .... Job 5:23
both lie down in *p* .... Ps 4:8
seek *p* and pursue it .... Ps 34:14
for He will speak *p* .... Ps 85:8
p have those who .... Ps 119:165
I am for *p* .... Ps 120:7
for the *p* of Jerusalem .... Ps 122:6
P be within your walls ...... Ps 122:7
P be upon Israel .... Ps 125:5
war, and a time of *p* .... Eccl 3:8
Father, Prince of *P* .... Is 9:6
keep him in perfect *p* .... Is 26:3
p they have not .... Is 59:8
slightly, saying, '*P* .... Jer 6:14
"We looked for *p* .... Jer 8:15
give you assured *p* .... Jer 14:13
they will seek *p* .... Ezek 7:25
My people, saying, '*P* ..... Ezek 13:10
P be multiplied .... Dan 4:1
this One shall be *p* .... Mic 5:5
place I will give *p* .... Hag 2:9
speak *p* to the nations ...... Zech 9:10
is worthy, let your *p* ...... Matt 10:13
that I came to bring *p* ...... Matt 10:34
and on earth *p* .... Luke 2:14
if a son of *p* is there .... Luke 10:6
that make for your *p* ..... Luke 19:42
I leave with you, My *p* .... John 14:27
in Me you may have *p* .... John 16:33
Grace to you and *p* .... Rom 1:7
by faith, we have *p* .... Rom 5:1
minded is life and *p* .... Rom 8:6
of *p* will crush Satan ..... Rom 16:20
God has called us to *p* .... 1 Cor 7:15
p will be with you ...... 2 Cor 13:11
Spirit is love, joy, *p* .... Gal 5:22
He Himself is our *p* .... Eph 2:14
the Spirit in the bond of *p* .... Eph 4:3
of the gospel of *p* .... Eph 6:15
and the *p* of God .... Phil 4:7
heaven, having made *p* ...... Col 1:20
And let the *p* of God .... Col 3:15
Be at *p* among .... 1 Thess 5:13
faith, love, *p* .... 2 Tim 2:22
meaning "king of *p*," .... Heb 7:2
Pursue *p* with all people ... Heb 12:14
is sown in *p* by those ...... James 3:18
p be multiplied .... 2 Pet 1:2
it to take *p* from the earth .... Rev 6:4

PEACEABLE
and *p* life in all .... 1 Tim 2:2
is first pure, then *p* .... James 3:17

PEACEABLY
Do you come *p* .... 1 Sam 16:4
p?" And he said, "*P*." ..... 1 Kin 2:13
speaks *p* to his neighbor ...... Jer 9:8
He shall enter *p*, even ..... Dan 11:24
on you, live *p* .... Rom 12:18

PEACEFUL
in a *p* habitation .... Is 32:18

PEACEMAKERS
Blessed are the *p* .... Matt 5:9

PEARL
had found one *p* .... Matt 13:46
gate was of one *p* .... Rev 21:21

PEARLS
nor cast your *p* .... Matt 7:6
hair or gold or *p* .... 1 Tim 2:9
gates were twelve *p* .... Rev 21:21

PEG
wife, took a tent *p* .... Judg 4:21
will fasten him as a *p* .... Is 22:23

PEKAH
Son of Remaliah; usurps Israel's throne, 2 Kin 15:25–28
Forms alliance with Rezin of Syria against Ahaz, Is 7:1–9

Alliance defeated; captives returned, 2 Kin 16:5–9
Territory of, overrun by Tiglath-Pileser, 2 Kin 15:29
Assassinated by Hoshea, 2 Kin 15:30

PEKAHIAH
Son of Menahem; king of Israel, 2 Kin 15:22–26
Assassinated by Pekah, 2 Kin 15:23–25

PEN
My tongue is the *p* .... Ps 45:1
on it with a man's *p* .... Is 8:1
to write to you with *p* ...... 3 John 13

PENNY
have paid the last *p* .... Matt 5:26

PENTECOST
P had fully come .... Acts 2:1
on the Day of *P* .... Acts 20:16
tarry in Ephesus until *P* ... 1 Cor 16:8

PENUEL
Place east of Jordan; site of Jacob's wrestling with angel, Gen 32:24–31
Inhabitants of, slain by Gideon, Judg 8:8, 9, 17

PEOPLE
will take you as My *p* .... Ex 6:7
Who is like you, a *p* ...... Deut 33:29
p shall be my *p* .... Ruth 1:16
p who know the joyful ...... Ps 89:15
We are His *p* and the .... Ps 100:3
Happy are the *p* .... Ps 144:15
"Blessed is Egypt My *p* ...... Is 19:25
this is a rebellious *p* .... Is 30:9
p who provoke Me .... Is 65:3
and they shall be My *p* ...... Jer 24:7
Then they shall be My *p* .. Ezek 37:23
for you are not My *p* .... Hos 1:9
like *p*, like priest .... Hos 4:9
to make ready a *p* .... Luke 1:17
taught the *p* in the .... Luke 20:1
Unless you *p* see signs ..... John 4:48
a great multitude of sick *p* .. John 5:3
all the *p* came to Him .... John 8:2
man should die for the *p* .. John 11:50
favor with all the *p* .... Acts 2:47
were done among the *p* .... Acts 5:12
for they feared the *p*, lest ... Acts 5:26
and signs among the *p* ...... Acts 6:8
the *p* grew and multiplied .. Acts 7:17
of My *p* who are in Egypt .. Acts 7:34
astonished the *p* of .... Acts 8:9
a great many *p* were ...... Acts 11:24
take out of them a *p* ...... Acts 15:14
his defense to the *p* .... Acts 19:33
of this *p* has grown dull ... Acts 28:27
who were not My *p* .... Rom 9:25
and contrary *p* .... Rom 10:21
His *p* whom He foreknew ... Rom 11:2
and they shall be My *p* .... 2 Cor 6:16
His own special *p* .... Titus 2:14
and they shall be My *p* ...... Heb 8:10
LORD will judge His *p* ..... Heb 10:30
His own special *p* .... 1 Pet 2:9
but are now the *p* .... 1 Pet 2:10
tribe and tongue and *p* .... Rev 5:9
tribe, tongue, and *p* .... Rev 14:6
they shall be His *p* .... Rev 21:3

PEOPLE OF GOD
in the assembly of the *p* .... Judg 20:2
a thing against the *p* ..... 2 Sam 14:13
a rest for the *p* .... Heb 4:9
affliction with the *p* .... Heb 11:25
people but are now the *p* .. 1 Pet 2:10

PEOPLES
Let *p* serve you .... Gen 27:29
separated you from the *p* ... Lev 20:26
scatter you among all *p* ... Deut 28:64
His deeds among the *p* .... 1 Chr 16:8
The LORD shall judge the *p* .... Ps 7:8
clap your hands, all you *p* .... Ps 47:1
Let all the *p* praise You ...... Ps 67:5
of the earth and all *p* .... Ps 148:11
lift up a banner for the *p* ..... Is 62:10
customs of the *p* are futile ..... Jer 10:3
to the *p* a pure language, ... Zeph 3:9
sow them among the *p* ..... Zech 10:9
heavy stone for all *p* .... Zech 12:3
will draw all *p* to Myself .. John 12:32

PEOR
Mountain of Moab opposite Jericho, Num 23:28
Israel's camp seen from, Num 24:2
——— Moabite god called Baal of Peor, Num 25:3, 5, 18
Israelites punished for worship of, Num 31:16

PERCEIVE
given you a heart to *p* ...... Deut 29:4
but I cannot *p* .... Job 23:8
seeing, but do not *p* .... Is 6:9
may see and not *p* .... Mark 4:12
not yet *p* nor understand .. Mark 8:17
In truth I *p* that God ...... Acts 10:34

PERCEIVED
not heard nor *p* by the ear .... Is 64:4
Jesus *p* their wickedness .. Matt 22:18
when Jesus *p* in His spirit .. Mark 2:8
Jesus *p* their thoughts ..... Luke 5:22
for I *p* power going out .... Luke 8:46
p the grace that had been .... Gal 2:9

PERDITION
except the son of *p* .... John 17:12
to them a proof of *p* .... Phil 1:28
revealed, the son of *p* .... 2 Thess 2:3
who draw back to *p* .... Heb 10:39
day of judgment and *p* ...... 2 Pet 3:7

PEREZ
One of Judah's twin sons by Tamar, Gen 38:24–30

PERFECT
Noah was a just man, *p* ...... Gen 6:9
His work is *p* .... Deut 32:4
Give a *p* lot .... 1 Sam 14:41
one who is *p* in .... Job 36:4
for God, His way is *p* .... Ps 18:30
The law of the LORD is *p*, ... Ps 19:7
I hate them with *p* hatred .. Ps 139:22
will keep him in *p* peace ...... Is 26:3
You were *p* in your .... Ezek 28:15
Father in heaven is *p* .... Matt 5:48
"If you want to be *p* ...... Matt 19:21
they may be made *p* ...... John 17:23
and *p* will of God .... Rom 12:2
when that which is *p* ..... 1 Cor 13:10
is made *p* in weakness .... 2 Cor 12:9
present every man *p* .... Col 1:28
the law made nothing *p* ..... Heb 7:19
more *p* tabernacle .... Heb 9:11
of just men made *p* .... Heb 12:23
patience have its *p* work ... James 1:4
good gift and every *p* ..... James 1:17
in word, he is a *p* .... James 3:2
p love casts out fear ...... 1 John 4:18

PERFECTED
third day I shall be *p* ..... Luke 13:32
or am already *p* .... Phil 3:12
the Son who has been *p* .... Heb 7:28
the love of God is *p* .... 1 John 2:5

PERFECTION
the *p* of beauty .... Ps 50:2
consummation of all *p* .... Ps 119:96
You were the seal of *p* .... Ezek 28:12
let us go on to *p* .... Heb 6:1

PERFORM
p the duty .... Ruth 3:13
p Your statutes .... Ps 119:112
am ready to *p* My word ..... Jer 1:12
he is obliged to *p* it .... Matt 23:16
What sign will You *p* ...... John 6:30
how to *p* what is good ..... Rom 7:18

PERFORMED
They *p* His signs .... Ps 105:27
works are *p* by His hands ... Mark 6:2
John *p* no sign .... John 10:41
who *p* the service perfect in .. Heb 9:9

PERFUMER'S
putrefy the *p* ointment .... Eccl 10:1

PERGA
Visited by Paul, Acts 13:13, 14; 14:25

PERGAMOS
Site of one of the seven churches, Rev 1:11
Special message to, Rev 2:12–17

PERIL
or nakedness, or *p* .... Rom 8:35

PERILOUS
from the *p* pestilence .... Ps 91:3
in the last days *p* .... 2 Tim 3:1

PERILS
journeys often, in *p* ...... 2 Cor 11:26

PERISH
"Surely we die, we *p* ..... Num 17:12
until you *p* from this ...... Josh 23:13
and if I *p*, I *p* .... Esth 4:16
Why did I not *p* .... Job 3:11
All flesh would *p* .... Job 34:15
way of the ungodly shall *p* .... Ps 1:6
He is like the beasts that *p* .. Ps 49:12
they *p* at the rebuke .... Ps 80:16
very day his plans *p* .... Ps 146:4
he who speaks lies shall *p* .. Prov 19:9
But those riches *p* through .. Eccl 5:14
they all will *p* together .... Is 31:3
the remnant in Judah *p* ..... Jer 40:15
so that we may not *p* .... Jon 1:6
one of your members *p* ..... Matt 5:29
little ones should *p* .... Matt 18:14
will *p* by the sword .... Matt 26:52
will all likewise *p* .... Luke 13:3
in Him should not *p* .... John 3:16
they shall never *p* .... John 10:28
whole nation should *p* .... John 11:50
Your money *p* with you, ... Acts 8:20
will also *p* without law ..... Rom 2:12
shall the weak brother *p* ... 1 Cor 8:11
concern things which *p* ..... Col 2:22
among those who *p* ..... 2 Thess 2:10
They will *p*, ... Heb 1:11
that any should *p* .... 2 Pet 3:9

PERISHABLE
do it to obtain a *p* .... 1 Cor 9:25

PERISHED
p being innocent .... Job 4:7
Truth has *p* and has .... Jer 7:28
The faithful man has *p* .... Mic 7:2

PERISHES
The old lion *p* for lack of .... Job 4:11
The righteous *p*, ... Is 57:1
for the food which *p* .... John 6:27
precious than gold that *p* ... 1 Pet 1:7

PERISHING
We are *p* .... Matt 8:25
to those who are *p* .... 2 Cor 4:3

PERIZZITES
One of seven Canaanite nations, Deut 7:1
Possessed Palestine in Abraham's time, Gen 13:7
Jacob's fear of, Gen 34:30
Many of, slain by Judah, Judg 1:4, 5

PERJURER
p shall be expelled .... Zech 5:3

PERMIT
the Spirit did not *p* .... Acts 16:7
I do not *p* a woman .... 1 Tim 2:12

PERMITS
you, if the Lord *p* ....1 Cor 16:7
we will do if God *p* ....Heb 6:3

PERMITTED
p no one to do them ....Ps 105:14

PERPETUAL
p incense before the LORD....Ex 30:8
It shall be a *p* statute for ..Num 19:21
Why is my pain *p* ....Jer 15:18
make it a *p* desolation ......Jer 25:12
saltpits, and a *p* desolation ..Zeph 2:9

PERPETUATED
Your name shall be *p*.......Nah 1:14

PERPLEXED
at one another, *p* ....John 13:22
we are *p*...................2 Cor 4:8

PERSECUTE
p me as God does ....Job 19:22
p me wrongfully ....Ps 119:86
when they revile and *p* .....Matt 5:11
Bless those who *p* ....Rom 12:14

PERSECUTED
p the poor and needy ......Ps 109:16
p the prophets who ....Matt 5:12
If they *p* Me..............John 15:20
p the church of God ....1 Cor 15:9
p, but not forsaken ....2 Cor 4:9
p us now preaches the ......Gal 1:23

PERSECUTES
wicked in his pride *p* ....Ps 10:2

PERSECUTION
p arises because of ....Matt 13:21
At that time a great *p* ....Acts 8:1
do I still suffer *p* ....Gal 5:11

PERSECUTIONS
and lands, with *p* ....Mark 10:30
in needs, in *p* ....2 Cor 12:10
p, afflictions, which ....2 Tim 3:11

PERSECUTOR
a blasphemer, a *p*.........1 Tim 1:13

PERSECUTORS
Deliver me from my *p*, for ...Ps 142:6
vengeance for me on my *p* ..Jer 15:15
all her *p* overtake her in .....Lam 1:3

PERSEVERANCE
tribulation produces *p*.......Rom 5:3
to this end will all *p* ....Eph 6:18
longsuffering, love, *p* .....2 Tim 3:10
heard of the *p* of Job .....James 5:11
to self-control *p* ....2 Pet 1:6

PERSEVERE
kept My command to *p* .....Rev 3:10

PERSISTENCE
p he will rise and ....Luke 11:8

PERSON
In whose eyes a vile *p*........Ps 15:4
p will suffer hunger ....Prov 19:15
do not regard the *p* ....Matt 22:16
One *p* esteems one day ....Rom 14:5
to eat with such a *p* ....1 Cor 5:11
no fornicator, unclean *p* .....Eph 5:5
that such a *p* is warped ....Titus 3:11
express image of His *p* ......Heb 1:3
let it be the hidden *p* ....1 Pet 3:4
by whom a *p* is overcome ..2 Pet 2:19

PERSUADE
Who will *p* Ahab to ......1 Kin 22:20
"You almost *p* me ....Acts 26:28
the Lord, we *p* men ....2 Cor 5:11
For do I now *p* men ....Gal 1:10

PERSUADED
a ruler is *p* ....Prov 25:15
neither will they be *p* .....Luke 16:31
p that He is able ....2 Tim 1:12

PERSUASIVE
p words of human ....1 Cor 2:4
you with *p* words ....Col 2:4

PERTAINING
Priest in things *p* ....Heb 2:17
for men in things *p* ....Heb 5:1

PERTURBED
things the earth is *p* ......Prov 30:21

PERVERSE
your way is *p* ....Num 22:32
for the *p* person is an ......Prov 3:32
p lips far from you ....Prov 4:24
p heart will be ....Prov 12:8
p man sows strife ....Prov 16:28
but he who is *p* ....Prov 28:18
from this *p* generation .....Acts 2:40

PERVERSITY
in oppression and *p* ....Is 30:12

PERVERT
You shall not *p* ....Deut 16:19
and *p* all equity ....Mic 3:9
p the gospel of Christ ....Gal 1:7

PERVERTING
We found this fellow *p* ....Luke 23:2
will you not cease *p*......Acts 13:10

PERVERTS
p the words of the ....Ex 23:8
p his ways will become ....Prov 10:9

PESTILENCE
from the perilous *p* ....Ps 91:3
p that walks in ....Ps 91:6
Before Him went *p* ....Hab 3:5

PESTILENCES
will be famines, *p* ....Matt 24:7

PETER
Fisherman; called to discipleship, Matt 4:18–20; John 1:40–42
Called as apostle, Matt 10:2–4
Walks on water, Matt 14:28–33
Confesses Christ's deity, Matt 16:13–19
Rebuked by Christ, Matt 16:21–23
Witnesses transfiguration, Matt 17:1–8; 2 Pet 1:16–18
Denies Christ three times, Matt 26:69–75
Commissioned to feed Christ's sheep, John 21:15–17
Leads disciples, Acts 1:15–26
Preaches at Pentecost, Acts 2:1–41
Performs miracles, Acts 3:1–11; 5:14–16; 9:32–43
Called to minister to Gentiles, Acts 10
Defends his visit to Gentiles, Acts 11:1–18
Imprisoned and delivered, Acts 12:3–19
Speaks at Jerusalem Council, Acts 15:7–14
Writes epistles, 1 Pet 1:1; 2 Pet 1:1

PETITION
of Israel grant your *p* .....1 Sam 1:17
What is your *p* ....Esth 5:6
present your *p* before Him ...Jer 42:9
makes his *p* three times .....Dan 6:13

PETITIONS
fulfill all your *p* ....Ps 20:5
p that we have asked .....1 John 5:15

PHARAOH
Kings of Egypt, contemporaries of:
Abraham, Gen 12:15–20
Joseph, Gen 40; 41
Moses in youth, Ex 1:8–11
the Exodus, Ex 5—14
Solomon, 1 Kin 3:1; 11:17–20
Other Pharaohs, 1 Kin 14:25, 26; 2 Kin 17:4; 18:21; 19:9; 23:29; Jer 44:30

PHARISEE
"Blind *P*, first cleanse .....Matt 23:26
P who had invited Him .....Luke 7:39
P asked Him to dine ......Luke 11:37
temple to pray, one a *P* ...Luke 18:10
P named Gamaliel ....Acts 5:34
I am a *P*, the son of a *P* ....Acts 23:6
our religion I lived a *P* .....Acts 26:5
concerning the law, a *P* ......Phil 3:5

PHARISEES
See SCRIBES AND PHARISEES
when he saw many of the *P* .Matt 3:7
when the *P* saw it, they ....Matt 9:11
we and the *P* fast often .....Matt 9:14
P said, "He casts out ....Matt 9:34
P saw it, they said to ....Matt 12:2
P were offended when ....Matt 15:12
of the leaven of the *P* ......Matt 16:6
P also came to Him ....Matt 19:3
P heard His parables ......Matt 21:45
P went and plotted how ...Matt 22:15
P heard that He had ....Matt 22:34
P gathered together to .....Matt 27:62
P came out and began to ..Mark 8:11
P and teachers of the law ..Luke 5:17
P and lawyers rejected .....Luke 7:30
you *P* make the outside ...Luke 11:39
"But woe to you *P*! For ....Luke 11:42
of the leaven of the *P* ......Luke 12:1
P came, saying to Him .....Luke 13:31
to the lawyers and *P* ....Luke 14:3
P and scribes murmured ....Luke 15:2
P, who were lovers of .....Luke 16:14
P when the kingdom of ....Luke 17:20
of the *P* named Nicodemus ..John 3:1
P heard the crowd ....John 7:32
P therefore said to Him ....John 8:13
P also asked him again .....John 9:15
went away to the *P* ....John 11:46
P had given a command ...John 11:57
because of the *P* they .....John 12:42
of the *P* who believed ....Acts 15:5
Sadducees and the other *P* .Acts 23:6

PHILADELPHIA
City of Lydia in Asia Minor; church established here, Rev 1:11

PHILEMON
Christian at Colosse to whom Paul writes, Philem 1
Paul appeals to him to receive Onesimus, Philem 9–21

PHILETUS
False teacher, 2 Tim 2:17, 18

PHILIP
Son of Herod the Great, Matt 14:3
——— One of the twelve apostles, Matt 10:3
Brings Nathanael to Christ, John 1:43–48
Tested by Christ, John 6:5–7
Introduces Greeks to Christ, John 12:20–22
Gently rebuked by Christ, John 14:8–12
——— One of the first seven deacons, Acts 6:5
Called an evangelist, Acts 21:8
Preaches in Samaria, Acts 8:5–13
Leads the Ethiopian eunuch to Christ, Acts 8:26–40

PHILIPPI
City of Macedonia (named after Philip of Macedon); visited by Paul, Acts 16:12; 20:6
Paul writes letter to church of, Phil 1:1

PHILISTIA
The land of the Philistines, Gen 21:32, 34; Josh 13:2; Ps 60:8

PHILISTINES
Not attacked by Joshua, Josh 13:1–3

Left to test Israel, Judg 3:1–4
God delivers Israel to, as punishment, Judg 10:6, 7
Israel delivered from, by Samson, Judg 13—16
Capture, then return the ark of the Lord, 1 Sam 4—6
Wars and dealings with Saul and David, 1 Sam 13:15—14:23; 17:1–52; 18:25–27; 21:10–15; 27:1—28:6; 29:1–11; 31:1–13; 2 Sam 5:17–25
Originally on the island of Caphtor, Jer 47:4
Prophecies concerning, Is 9:11, 12; Jer 25:15–20; 47:1–7; Ezek 25:15–17; Zeph 2:4–6

PHILOSOPHERS
p encountered him .... Acts 17:18

PHILOSOPHY
cheat you through *p* .... Col 2:8

PHINEHAS
Aaron's grandson; executes God's judgment, Num 25:1–18; Ps 106:30, 31
Settles dispute over memorial altar, Josh 22:11–32
—— Younger son of Eli; abuses his office, 1 Sam 1:3; 2:12–17, 22–36
Killed by Philistines, 1 Sam 4:11, 17

PHOENICIA
Mediterranean coastal region including the cities of Ptolemais, Tyre, Zarephath and Sidon; evangelized by early Christians, Acts 11:19
Jesus preaches here, Matt 15:21

PHRYGIA
Jews from, at Pentecost, Acts 2:1, 10
Visited twice by Paul, Acts 16:6

PHYLACTERIES
They make their *p* .... Matt 23:5

PHYSICIAN
Gilead, is there no *p* .... Jer 8:22
have no need of a *p* .... Matt 9:12
Luke the beloved *p* .... Col 4:14

PHYSICIANS
are all worthless *p* .... Job 13:4
her livelihood on *p* .... Luke 8:43

PI HAHIROTH
Israel camps there before crossing the Red Sea, Ex 14:2, 9; Num 33:7, 8

PICTURE
what parable shall we *p* .... Mark 4:30

PIECE
placed each *p* opposite .... Gen 15:10
hammered *p* of pure gold ... Ex 25:36
one *p* with the mercy seat .... Ex 37:8
two legs or a *p* of an ear .. Amos 3:12
No one puts a *p* .... Matt 9:16
bought a *p* of ground ..... Luke 14:18
Him a *p* of a broiled fish .. Luke 24:42
from the top in one *p* .... John 19:23

PIECES
for my wages thirty *p* ..... Zech 11:12
they took the thirty *p* ...... Matt 27:9
shall be dashed to *p* .... Rev 2:27

PIERCE
and his master shall *p* .... Ex 21:6
a sword will *p* .... Luke 2:35

PIERCED
p My hands and My feet .... Ps 22:16
Me whom they have *p* .... Zech 12:10
of the soldiers *p* .... John 19:34
p themselves through ...... 1 Tim 6:10
and they also who *p* .... Rev 1:7

PIERCING
p even to the division .... Heb 4:12

PIETY
first learn to show *p* .... 1 Tim 5:4

PILATE, PONTIUS
Governor of Judea (A.D. 26–36), Luke 3:1
Questions Jesus and delivers Him to Jews, Matt 27:2, 11–26; John 18:28—19:16

PILGRIMAGE
heart is set on *p* .... Ps 84:5
In the house of my *p* .... Ps 119:54

PILGRIMS
we are aliens and *p* ...... 1 Chr 29:15
were strangers and *p* .... Heb 11:13

PILLAR
and she became a *p* .... Gen 19:26
where you anointed the *p* .. Gen 31:13
and by night in a *p* .... Ex 13:21
standing by a *p* .... 2 Kin 11:14
a *p* to the LORD .... Is 19:19
the living God, the *p* .... 1 Tim 3:15
I will make him a *p* in the ... Rev 3:12

PILLARS
break their sacred *p* .... Ex 34:13
between the *p* .... Judg 16:25
And he cast two *p* .... 1 Kin 7:15
bronze *p* that were in ..... 2 Kin 25:13
I set up its *p* firmly .... Ps 75:3
out her seven *p* .... Prov 9:1
blood and fire and *p* .... Joel 2:30
who seemed to be *p* .... Gal 2:9
and his feet like *p* .... Rev 10:1

PILOT
rudder wherever the *p* ...... James 3:4

PIM
p for the plowshares ..... 1 Sam 13:21

PINE
cypress tree and the *p* .... Is 41:19
for these *p* away .... Lam 4:9

PINNACLE
set Him on the *p* .... Luke 4:9

PISGAH
Mountain in Moab where Balaam offers sacrifice, Num 23:14
Moses views Promised Land from, Deut 3:27
Site of Moses' death, Deut 34:1–7

PISHON
One of Eden's four rivers, Gen 2:10, 11

PISIDIA
Twice visited by Paul, Acts 13:13, 14; 14:24

PIT
See BOTTOMLESS PIT
cast him into some *p* .... Gen 37:20
soul draws near the *P* ...... Job 33:22
who go down to the *p* .... Ps 28:1
woman is a deep *p* .... Prov 22:14
a harlot is a deep *p* .... Prov 23:27
fall into his own *p* .... Prov 28:10
my life in the *p* .... Lam 3:53
who descend into the *P* ... Ezek 31:16
up my life from the *p* .... Jon 2:6
from the waterless *p* .... Zech 9:11
if it falls into a *p* .... Matt 12:11
ox that has fallen into a *p* .. Luke 14:5
the key to the bottomless *p* ... Rev 9:1
into the bottomless *p* .... Rev 20:3

PITCH
inside and outside with *p* .... Gen 6:14
Israel would *p* their tents ... Num 9:17

PITCHER
her *p* on her shoulder ..... Gen 24:15
or the *p* shattered at the .... Eccl 12:6
carrying a *p* of water ...... Luke 22:10

PITCHERS
and torches inside the *p* .... Judg 7:16
the *p* of pure gold .... 1 Chr 28:17
the washing of cups, *p* .... Mark 7:4

PITHOM
Egyptian city built by Hebrew slaves, Ex 1:11

PITIABLE
of all men the most *p* ..... 1 Cor 15:19

PITS
The proud have dug *p* ...... Ps 119:85

PITY
eye shall have no *p* .... Deut 7:16
"Have *p* on me .... Job 19:21
for someone to take *p* .... Ps 69:20
He who has *p* on the ...... Prov 19:17
p He redeemed them .... Is 63:9
land, and *p* His people .... Joel 2:18
And should I not *p* .... Jon 4:11
just as I had *p* .... Matt 18:33

PLACE
See HIGH PLACE; HOLY PLACE; MOST HOLY PLACE
p know him anymore .... Job 7:10
All go to one *p* .... Eccl 3:20
return again to My *p* .... Hos 5:15
Come, see the *p* .... Matt 28:6
My word has no *p* .... John 8:37
I go to prepare a *p* .... John 14:2
might go to his own *p* ...... Acts 1:25

PLACES
See HIGH PLACES
set them in slippery *p* .... Ps 73:18
dark *p* of the earth .... Ps 74:20
and the rough *p* .... Is 40:4
They love the best *p* .... Matt 23:6
in the heavenly *p* .... Eph 1:3

PLAGUE
bring yet one more *p* .... Ex 11:1
with a very great *p* .... Num 11:33
those who died in the *p* .... Num 25:9
three days' *p* in your .... 2 Sam 24:13
p come near your .... Ps 91:10
and the *p* was stopped ..... Ps 106:30
And this shall be the *p* .... Zech 14:12
because of the *p* of the ..... Rev 16:21

PLAGUES
I will send all My *p* .... Ex 9:14
I will be your *p* .... Hos 13:14
p that are written .... Rev 22:18

PLAINLY
the Christ, tell us *p* .... John 10:24
now You are speaking *p* .. John 16:29
such things declare *p* .... Heb 11:14

PLAN
p evil things in their .... Ps 140:2
Let none of you *p* .... Zech 7:10
p according to the flesh .... 2 Cor 1:17

PLANK
First remove the *p* .... Matt 7:5

PLANS
He makes the *p* of the .... Ps 33:10
in that very day his *p* .... Ps 146:4
that devises wicked *p* .... Prov 6:18
A man's heart *p* .... Prov 16:9
P are established .... Prov 20:18

PLANT
A time to *p* .... Eccl 3:2
Him as a tender *p* .... Is 53:2
they shall *p* vineyards .... Is 65:21
p of an alien vine .... Jer 2:21
the LORD God prepared a *p* ... Jon 4:6
p which My heavenly ...... Matt 15:13

PLANTED
The LORD God *p* a garden .... Gen 2:8
and he *p* a vineyard .... Gen 9:20
Abraham *p* a tamarisk .... Gen 21:33

shall be like a tree *p* ... Ps 1:3
Your right hand has *p* ... Ps 80:15
p it with the choicest vine ... Is 5:2
shall they be *p* ... Is 40:24
like a tree *p* by the waters ... Jer 17:8
by the roots and be *p* ... Luke 17:6
I *p*, Apollos watered ... 1 Cor 3:6

PLANTS
our sons may be as *p* ... Ps 144:12
down its choice *p* ... Is 16:8
neither he who *p* ... 1 Cor 3:7

PLASTERED
p with untempered ... Ezek 13:14
Her prophets *p* them ... Ezek 22:28

PLATFORM
scribe stood on a *p* ... Neh 8:4

PLATTER
head here on a *p* ... Matt 14:8

PLAY
and rose up to *p* ... Ex 32:6
p skillfully with a ... Ps 33:3
nursing child shall *p* ... Is 11:8
and rose up to *p* ... 1 Cor 10:7

PLAYED
So David *p* music with ... 1 Sam 18:10
We *p* the flute for you ... Matt 11:17

PLEAD
the one who would *p* ... Judg 6:31
Oh, that one might *p* ... Job 16:21
p my cause against an ... Ps 43:1
p with your friend ... Prov 6:3
Behold, I will *p* ... Jer 2:35
p His case with all ... Jer 25:31

PLEADED
Then Moses *p* with the ... Ex 32:11
this thing I *p* with ... 2 Cor 12:8

PLEADING
though God were *p* ... 2 Cor 5:20

PLEASANT
food, that it was *p* ... Gen 3:6
fallen to me in *p* places ... Ps 16:6
they despised the *p* ... Ps 106:24
how good and how *p* ... Ps 133:1
and knowledge is *p* ... Prov 2:10
words of the pure are *p* ... Prov 15:26
P words are like a ... Prov 16:24
p places of the ... Jer 23:10
Is he a *p* child ... Jer 31:20
I ate no *p* food ... Dan 10:3

PLEASANTNESS
Her ways are ways of *p* ... Prov 3:17

PLEASE
P say you are my sister, ... Gen 12:13
P, go in to my maid ... Gen 16:2
p let me escape there ... Gen 19:20
P come near, ... Gen 27:21
P hear this dream which I ... Gen 37:6
Now, *p*, forgive the ... Gen 50:17
P, let us go three days' ... Ex 5:3
P inquire of God, ... Judg 18:5
p pardon my sin, ... 1 Sam 15:25
yet honor me now, *p*, ... 1 Sam 15:30
P bring the ephod here ... 1 Sam 30:7
P let my sister Tamar ... 2 Sam 13:5
p let my brother ... 2 Sam 13:26
When a man's ways *p* ... Prov 16:7
do those things that *p* ... John 8:29
in the flesh cannot *p* ... Rom 8:8
p his neighbor for his ... Rom 15:2
how he may *p* the Lord ... 1 Cor 7:32
how he may *p* his wife ... 1 Cor 7:33
may *p* her husband ... 1 Cor 7:34
Or do I seek to *p* men ... Gal 1:10
is impossible to *p* Him ... Heb 11:6

PLEASED
and she *p* Samson well ... Judg 14:7
Then You shall be *p* ... Ps 51:19
The LORD is well *p* ... Is 42:21
Yet it *p* the LORD to bruise ... Is 53:10
Would he be *p* with you ... Mal 1:8
in whom I am well *p* ... Matt 3:17
danced before them and *p* ... Matt 14:6
God was not well *p* ... 1 Cor 10:5
But when it *p* God, who ... Gal 1:15
testimony, that he *p* ... Heb 11:5
in whom I am well *p* ... 2 Pet 1:17

PLEASES
dwell where it *p* you ... Gen 20:15
He does whatever He *p* ... Ps 115:3
Whatever the LORD *p* ... Ps 135:6
who *p* God shall escape ... Eccl 7:26
nor awaken love until it *p* ... Song 2:7

PLEASING
sacrifice, well *p* ... Phil 4:18
for this is well *p* ... Col 3:20
in you what is well *p* ... Heb 13:21

PLEASURE
grown old, shall I have *p* ... Gen 18:12
not a God who takes *p* ... Ps 5:4
has *p* in the prosperity ... Ps 35:27
Do good in Your good *p* ... Ps 51:18
Your servants take *p* ... Ps 102:14
The LORD takes *p* in those ... Ps 147:11
p will be a poor man ... Prov 21:17
for He has no *p* ... Eccl 5:4
shall perform all My *p* ... Is 44:28
your fast you find *p* ... Is 58:3
nor finding your own *p* ... Is 58:13
Do I have any *p* ... Ezek 18:23
I have no *p* in you ... Mal 1:10
your Father's good *p* ... Luke 12:32
to the good *p* of His ... Eph 1:5
to do for His good *p* ... Phil 2:13
fulfill all the good *p* ... 2 Thess 1:11
p is dead while ... 1 Tim 5:6
for sin You had no *p* ... Heb 10:6
back, My soul has no *p* ... Heb 10:38
p that war in your ... James 4:1
on the earth in *p* ... James 5:5

PLEASURES
Your right hand are *p* ... Ps 16:11
cares, riches, and *p* ... Luke 8:14
to enjoy the passing *p* ... Heb 11:25
may spend it on your *p* ... James 4:3

PLEDGE
give me a *p* till you send ... Gen 38:17
hands in *p* for a stranger ... Prov 6:1
shakes hands in a *p*, and ... Prov 17:18
who shakes hands in a *p* ... Prov 22:26

PLEIADES
Part of God's creation, Job 9:9; Amos 5:8

PLENTIFUL
You, O God, sent a *p* ... Ps 68:9
The harvest truly is *p* ... Matt 9:37

PLENTIFULLY
rich man yielded *p* ... Luke 12:16

PLENTY
p which were in the ... Gen 41:53
LORD will grant you *p* ... Deut 28:11
barns will be filled with *p* ... Prov 3:10
diligent lead surely to *p* ... Prov 21:5
his land will have *p* ... Prov 28:19

PLIGHT
He laughs at the *p* ... Job 9:23

PLOT
in the *p* at Jezreel, so that ... 2 Kin 9:37
and the people *p* ... Ps 2:1
near the *p* of ground that ... John 4:5
p became known to Saul ... Acts 9:24

PLOTS
The wicked *p* against ... Ps 37:12

PLOTTED
and *p* to take Jesus by ... Matt 26:4
chief priests *p* ... John 12:10

PLOW
lazy man will not *p* ... Prov 20:4
Does one *p* there with ... Amos 6:12
put his hand to the *p* ... Luke 9:62
he who plows should *p* ... 1 Cor 9:10

PLOWED
"Zion shall be *p* ... Jer 26:18
You have *p* wickedness ... Hos 10:13
of you Zion shall be *p* ... Mic 3:12

PLOWMAN
p shall overtake the ... Amos 9:13

PLOWSHARES
beat their swords into *p* ... Is 2:4
Beat your *p* into swords ... Joel 3:10
beat their swords into *p* ... Mic 4:3

PLUCK
grain, you may *p* ... Deut 23:25
who pass by the way *p* ... Ps 80:12
obey, I will utterly *p* ... Jer 12:17
p the heads of grain ... Mark 2:23

PLUCKED
p the victim from his ... Job 29:17
cheeks to those who *p* ... Is 50:6
And His disciples *p* ... Luke 6:1
you would have *p* ... Gal 4:15

PLUMB
a *p* line, with a *p* ... Amos 7:7
rejoice to see the *p* ... Zech 4:10

PLUNDER
p the Egyptians ... Ex 3:22
who pass by the way *p* ... Ps 89:41
The *p* of the poor is ... Is 3:14
p you shall become ... Jer 30:16
house and *p* his goods ... Matt 12:29

PLUNDERED
stouthearted were *p* ... Ps 76:5
a people robbed and *p* ... Is 42:22
"And when you are *p* ... Jer 4:30
Because you have *p* ... Hab 2:8

PLUNDERING
me because of the *p* ... Is 22:4
accepted the *p* of your ... Heb 10:34

POETS
some of your own *p* ... Acts 17:28

POINT
obedient to the *p* of death ... Phil 2:8
even to the *p* of chains ... 2 Tim 2:9
Now this is the main *p* ... Heb 8:1
yet stumble in one *p* ... James 2:10

POINTS
but was in all *p* tempted ... Heb 4:15

POISON
the *p* of asps is under ... Ps 140:3
"The *p* of asps is ... Rom 3:13
evil, full of deadly *p* ... James 3:8

POISONED
p by bitterness ... Acts 8:23
p their minds against ... Acts 14:2

POLLUTIONS
have escaped the *p* ... 2 Pet 2:20

POMEGRANATE
a golden bell and a *p*, a ... Ex 28:34
the *p* tree, the palm tree ... Joel 1:12

POMEGRANATES
you shall make *p* of blue ... Ex 28:33
brought some of the *p* ... Num 13:23
grain or figs or vines or *p* ... Num 20:5
of vines and fig trees and *p* ... Deut 8:8

POMP
multitude and their *p* ... Is 5:14
p is brought down to ... Is 14:11
had come with great *p* ... Acts 25:23

POMPOUS
and a mouth speaking *p* ... Dan 7:8

PONDER
P the path of your . . . . Prov 4:26

PONDERED
p them in her heart . . . . Luke 2:19

PONDERS
p all his paths . . . . Prov 5:21

PONTUS
Jews from, at Pentecost, Acts 2:5, 9
Home of Aquila, Acts 18:2
Christians of, addressed by Peter, 1 Pet 1:1

POOL
the rock into a *p* of water . . . Ps 114:8
the wilderness a *p* . . . . Is 41:18
by the Sheep Gate a *p* . . . . . . John 5:2
at a certain time into the *p* . . John 5:4
wash in the *p* of Siloam . . . . . John 9:7
'Go to the *p* of Siloam . . . . . John 9:11

POOLS
also covers it with *p* . . . . Ps 84:6
a wilderness into *p* . . . . Ps 107:35
your eyes like the *p* . . . . Song 7:4

POOR
p shall not give less . . . . Ex 30:15
be partial to the *p* . . . . Lev 19:15
p will never cease . . . . Deut 15:11
whether *p* or rich . . . . Ruth 3:10
raises the *p* from the dust . . 1 Sam 2:8
seeing I am a *p* . . . . 1 Sam 18:23
one rich and the other *p* . . 2 Sam 12:1
left some of the *p* . . . . 2 Kin 25:12
and gifts to the *p* . . . . Esth 9:22
So the *p* have hope . . . . Job 5:16
and forsaken the *p* . . . . Job 20:19
I delivered the *p* . . . . Job 29:12
soul grieved for the *p* . . . . . . Job 30:25
The expectation of the *p* . . . . . Ps 9:18
p shall eat and be . . . . Ps 22:26
p man cried out . . . . Ps 34:6
delivering the *p* from him . . . Ps 35:10
to cast down the *p* . . . . Ps 37:14
But I am *p* and needy . . . . Ps 40:17
is he who considers the *p* . . . . . Ps 41:1
goodness for the *p* . . . . Ps 68:10
For the LORD hears the *p*, ... Ps 69:33
and Your *p* with justice . . . . . . Ps 72:2
Let the *p* and needy . . . . Ps 74:21
Defend the *p* and fatherless . . Ps 82:3
yet He sets the *p* . . . . Ps 107:41
at the right hand of the *p* . . . Ps 109:31
He has given to the *p* . . . . Ps 112:9
He raises the *p* . . . . Ps 113:7
satisfy her *p* with bread . . . . Ps 132:15
and justice for the *p* . . . . Ps 140:12
a slack hand becomes *p* . . . . Prov 10:4
one who makes himself *p* . . Prov 13:7
p man is hated even . . . . Prov 14:20
p reproaches his Maker . . . . . Prov 17:5
p man uses entreaties . . . . . Prov 18:23
Better is the *p* who . . . . Prov 19:1
p will also cry himself . . . . Prov 21:13
p have this in common . . . . . Prov 22:2
p man who oppresses . . . . Prov 28:3
Better is the *p* who . . . . Prov 28:6
the cause of the *p* . . . . Prov 29:7
Or lest I be *p* and steal . . . . . Prov 30:9
to devour the *p* from . . . . . . Prov 30:14
plead the cause of the *p* . . . Prov 31:9
her hand to the *p* . . . . Prov 31:20
remembered that same *p* . . . . Eccl 9:15
He shall judge the *p*, and . . . . . Is 11:4
the *p* of His people shall . . . . . Is 14:32
a strength to the *p* . . . . Is 25:4
The *p* and needy seek . . . . Is 41:17
preach good tidings to the *p* . . Is 61:1
on him who is *p* and of a . . . . . Is 66:2
delivered the life of the *p* . . . Jer 20:13
land of Judah the *p* people . . Jer 39:10
the hand of the *p* . . . . Ezek 16:49
and mistreated the *p* . . . . . Ezek 22:29
by showing mercy to the *p* . . Dan 4:27
for silver, and the *p* . . . . Amos 2:6
you tread down the *p* . . . . . . Amos 5:11
the alien or the *p* . . . . Zech 7:10
in particular the *p* . . . . Zech 11:7
"Blessed are the *p* . . . . Matt 5:3
p have the gospel . . . . Matt 11:5
have and give to the *p* . . . . Matt 19:21
For you have the *p* . . . . Matt 26:11
one *p* widow came . . . . Mark 12:42
the gospel to the *p* . . . . Luke 4:18
Blessed are you *p*, ... Luke 6:20
the *p* have the gospel . . . . Luke 7:22
give a feast, invite the *p* . . Luke 14:13
half of my goods to the *p* . . Luke 19:8
contribution for the *p* . . . . . Rom 15:26
my goods to feed the *p* . . . . 1 Cor 13:3
as *p*, yet making many . . . . 2 Cor 6:10
your sakes He became *p* . . . . 2 Cor 8:9
He has given to the *p* . . . . 2 Cor 9:9
should remember the *p* . . . . Gal 2:10
and say to the *p* man . . . . James 2:3
God not chosen the *p* . . . . . . James 2:5
wretched, miserable, *p* . . . . Rev 3:17
and great, rich and *p* . . . . . . Rev 13:16

POORLY
we are *p* clothed, ... 1 Cor 4:11

POPLAR
himself rods of green *p* . . . . Gen 30:37

POPULATED
the whole earth was *p* . . . . Gen 9:19

POPULOUS
great, mighty, and *p* . . . . Deut 26:5

PORCH
p which is called . . . . Acts 3:11

PORCHES
Bethesda, having five *p* . . . . . John 5:2

PORCIUS FESTUS
Paul stands trial before, Acts 25:1–22

PORCUPINE
the *p* shall possess it, also . . . . Is 34:11

PORTION
For the LORD's *p* . . . . Deut 32:9
This is the *p* from God . . . . . Job 20:29
O LORD, You are the *p* . . . . Ps 16:5
heart and my *p* forever . . . . . . Ps 73:26
You are my *p* . . . . Ps 119:57
p for her maidservants . . . . Prov 31:15
I will divide Him a *p* . . . . Is 53:12
rejoice in their *p* . . . . Is 61:7
The *P* of Jacob is not . . . . Jer 10:16
they have trodden My *p* . . . . Jer 12:10
"The LORD is my *p* . . . . Lam 3:24
p of the king's delicacies . . . . . Dan 1:8
and appoint him his *p* . . . . Matt 24:51
to give them their *p* . . . . Luke 12:42
give me the *p* . . . . Luke 15:12
part nor *p* in this matter . . . . Acts 8:21

PORTRAYED
Christ was clearly *p* . . . . Gal 3:1

POSITION
If a man desires the *p* . . . . . . 1 Tim 3:1

POSSESS
descendants shall *p* . . . . Gen 22:17
which you are going to *p* . . Deut 28:21
land which you go to *p* . . . Deut 28:63
p the land which . . . . Josh 1:11
told them to go in to *p* the . . Neh 9:15
fathers to go in and *p* . . . . Neh 9:23
may dwell there and *p* it . . . . Ps 69:35
tithes of all that I *p* . . . . Luke 18:12
By your patience *p* . . . . Luke 21:19
as though they did not *p* . . 1 Cor 7:30
p his own vessel . . . . 1 Thess 4:4

POSSESSED
much land yet to be *p* . . . . . . Josh 13:1
"The LORD *p* me at . . . . Prov 8:22
of the things he *p* . . . . Acts 4:32
that a certain slave girl *p* . . Acts 16:16

POSSESSING
p knowledge and quick to . . . Dan 1:4
and yet *p* all things . . . . 2 Cor 6:10

POSSESSION
as an everlasting *p* . . . . Gen 17:8
ends of the earth for Your *p* . . . Ps 2:8
the rest of their *p* . . . . Ps 17:14
they did not gain *p* . . . . Ps 44:3
is man's precious *p* . . . . Prov 12:27
Sapphira his wife, sold a *p* . . Acts 5:1
to give it to him for a *p* . . . . . . Acts 7:5
of the purchased *p* . . . . Eph 1:14
and an enduring *p* . . . . Heb 10:34

POSSESSIONS
is full of Your *p* . . . . Ps 104:24
kinds of precious *p* . . . . Prov 1:13
the LORD with your *p* . . . . Prov 3:9
Yes, I had greater *p* . . . . Eccl 2:7
for he had great *p* . . . . Mark 10:22
and there wasted his *p* . . . Luke 15:13
and sold their *p* . . . . Acts 2:45

POSSESSOR
P of heaven and earth . . . . . . Gen 14:19

POSSESSORS
all who were *p* of lands . . . . Acts 4:34

POSSIBLE
God all things are *p* . . . . Matt 19:26
O My Father, if it is *p* . . . . . Matt 26:39
all things are *p* to him . . . . . Mark 9:23
God all things are *p* . . . . . . Mark 10:27
men are *p* with God . . . . . . Luke 18:27
If it is *p*, as much as . . . . . . Rom 12:18
bear you witness that, if *p* . . . Gal 4:15
p that the blood . . . . Heb 10:4

POSTERITY
to preserve a *p* . . . . Gen 45:7
p shall serve Him . . . . Ps 22:30
p who approve their . . . . Ps 49:13
the *p* of the righteous . . . . . . Prov 11:21

POSTPONED
it will no more be *p* . . . . Ezek 12:25

POT
to Aaron, "Take a *p* . . . . Ex 16:33
from a boiling *p* . . . . Job 41:20
The refining *p* is for . . . . Prov 17:3
p that had the manna . . . . Heb 9:4

POTENTATE
the blessed and only *P* . . . . 1 Tim 6:15

POTI-PHERAH
Egyptian priest of On (Heliopolis), Gen 41:45–50
Father of Asenath, Joseph's wife, Gen 46:20

POTIPHAR
High Egyptian officer, Gen 39:1
Puts Joseph in jail, Gen 39:20

POTS
when we sat by the *p* . . . . Ex 16:3
also took away the *p* . . . . Jer 52:18
are regarded as clay *p* . . . . Lam 4:2

POTSHERD
for himself a *p* . . . . Job 2:8
is dried up like a *p* . . . . Ps 22:15
Let the *p* strive with . . . . Is 45:9

POTTER
Shall the *p* be esteemed as . . . Is 29:16
the clay, and You our *p* . . . . Is 64:8
seemed good to the *p* . . . . Jer 18:4
Does not the *p* have . . . . Rom 9:21

POTTER'S FIELD
Judas's money used for purchase of, Matt 27:7, 8

POUND
Mary took a *p* of very . . . . . John 12:3

POUNDS
about a hundred *p* ... John 19:39

POUR
p out your heart ... Ps 62:8
P out Your wrath ... Ps 79:6
p My Spirit on your ... Is 44:3
and let the skies *p* ... Is 45:8
P out Your fury ... Jer 10:25
that I will *p* out My ... Joel 2:28
"And I will *p* ... Zech 12:10
p out for you such blessing .. Mal 3:10
that I will *p* out of My ... Acts 2:17
My maidservants I will *p* ... Acts 2:18
angels, "Go and *p* ... Rev 16:1

POURED
And now my soul is *p* ... Job 30:16
I am *p* out like water ... Ps 22:14
grace is *p* upon Your ... Ps 45:2
name is ointment *p* ... Song 1:3
visited You, they *p* ... Is 26:16
strong, because He *p* ... Is 53:12
and My fury will be *p* ... Jer 7:20
His fury is *p* out like ... Nah 1:6
broke the flask and *p* ... Mark 14:3
of God has been *p* ... Rom 5:5
if I am being *p* ... Phil 2:17
I am already being *p* ... 2 Tim 4:6
whom He *p* out on us ... Titus 3:6

POVERTY
of the poor is their *p* ... Prov 10:15
but it leads to *p* ... Prov 11:24
P and shame will come ... Prov 13:18
leads only to *p* ... Prov 14:23
lest you come to *p* ... Prov 20:13
give me neither *p* ... Prov 30:8
p put in all the ... Luke 21:4
and their deep *p* ... 2 Cor 8:2
p might become rich ... 2 Cor 8:9
tribulation, and *p* ... Rev 2:9

POWER
that I may show My *p* ... Ex 9:16
become glorious in *p* ... Ex 15:6
for God has *p* to help ... 2 Chr 25:8
him who is without *p* ... Job 26:2
p who can understand ... Job 26:14
p belongs to God ... Ps 62:11
p Your enemies shall ... Ps 66:3
gives strength and *p* ... Ps 68:35
when it is in the *p* of your .. Prov 3:27
in the *p* of the tongue ... Prov 18:21
a king is, there is *p* ... Eccl 8:4
No one has *p* over the ... Eccl 8:8
the strength of His *p* ... Is 40:26
bodies the fire had no *p* ... Dan 3:27
truly I am full of *p* ... Mic 3:8
anger and great in *p* ... Nah 1:3
'Not by might nor by *p* ... Zech 4:6
the kingdom and the *p* ... Matt 6:13
the Son of Man has *p* ... Matt 9:6
who had given such *p* ... Matt 9:8
gave them *p* over unclean .. Matt 10:1
Scriptures nor the *p* ... Matt 22:29
the Son of Man has *p* ... Mark 2:10
p to heal sicknesses ... Mark 3:15
that *p* had gone out ... Mark 5:30
Scriptures nor the *p* of ... Mark 12:24
p of the Spirit to Galilee ... Luke 4:14
And the *p* of the Lord ... Luke 5:17
the Son of Man has *p* ... Luke 5:24
p went out from Him ... Luke 6:19
I perceived *p* going out ... Luke 8:46
and gave them *p* ... Luke 9:1
all the *p* of the enemy ... Luke 10:19
and the *p* of darkness ... Luke 22:53
you are endued with *p* ... Luke 24:49
I have *p* to lay it ... John 10:18
not know that I have *p* ... John 19:10
"You could have no *p* ... John 19:11
you shall receive *p* ... Acts 1:8
as though by our own *p* ... Acts 3:12
Stephen, full of faith and *p* .. Acts 6:8
man is the great *p* ... Acts 8:10
"Give me this *p* ... Acts 8:19
Holy Spirit and with *p* ... Acts 10:38
the *p* of Satan to God, ... Acts 26:18
the Son of God with *p* ... Rom 1:4
for it is the *p* ... Rom 1:16
even His eternal *p* ... Rom 1:20
My *p* in you ... Rom 9:17
potter have *p* over the ... Rom 9:21
the *p* of the Holy Spirit ... Rom 15:13
by the *p* of the Spirit of ... Rom 15:19
saved it is the *p* ... 1 Cor 1:18
Greeks, Christ the *p* ... 1 Cor 1:24
of the Spirit and of *p*, ... 1 Cor 2:4
men but in the *p* of God ... 1 Cor 2:5
is not in word but in *p* ... 1 Cor 4:20
be brought under the *p* ... 1 Cor 6:12
and all authority and *p* ... 1 Cor 15:24
it is raised in *p* ... 1 Cor 15:43
of the *p* may be of God ... 2 Cor 4:7
of truth, by the *p* of God ... 2 Cor 6:7
that the *p* of Christ ... 2 Cor 12:9
He lives by the *p* of God .. 2 Cor 13:4
greatness of His *p* ... Eph 1:19
all principality and *p* ... Eph 1:21
prince of the *p* of the air ... Eph 2:2
working of His *p* ... Eph 3:7
to the *p* that works in us ... Eph 3:20
the Lord and in the *p* ... Eph 6:10
the *p* of His resurrection ... Phil 3:10
to His glorious *p* ... Col 1:11
us from the *p* of darkness ... Col 1:13
of all principality and *p* ... Col 2:10
only, but also in *p* ... 1 Thess 1:5
the glory of His *p* ... 2 Thess 1:9
work of faith with *p* ... 2 Thess 1:11
of Satan, with all *p* ... 2 Thess 2:9
of fear, but of *p* ... 2 Tim 1:7
according to the *p* of God ... 2 Tim 1:8
godliness but denying its *p* .2 Tim 3:5
by the word of His *p* ... Heb 1:3
p of death, that ... Heb 2:14
but according to the *p* ... Heb 7:16
since it has no *p* at all ... Heb 9:17
are kept by the *p* of God ... 1 Pet 1:5
as His divine *p* ... 2 Pet 1:3
made known to you the *p* .. 2 Pet 1:16
who are greater in *p* ... 2 Pet 2:11
dominion and *p* ... Jude 25
to him I will give *p* ... Rev 2:26
glory and honor and *p* ... Rev 4:11
honor and glory and *p* ... Rev 5:13
and honor and *p* ... Rev 7:12
and *p* belong to the Lord ... Rev 19:1
the second death has no *p* .. Rev 20:6

POWER OF GOD
the Scriptures nor the *p* ... Matt 22:29
the right hand of the *p* ... Luke 22:69
"This man is the great *p* ... Acts 8:10
it is the *p* to salvation ... Rom 1:16
being saved it is the *p* ... 1 Cor 1:18
Christ the *p* and the ... 1 Cor 1:24
word of truth, by the *p* ... 2 Cor 6:7
yet He lives by the *p* ... 2 Cor 13:4
gospel according to the *p* ... 2 Tim 1:8
who are kept by the *p* ... 1 Pet 1:5

POWERFUL
of the LORD is *p* ... Ps 29:4
of God is living and *p* ... Heb 4:12

POWERS
the *p* of the heavens ... Matt 24:29
nor principalities nor *p*, ... Rom 8:38
p in the heavenly places, ... Eph 3:10
principalities, against *p* ... Eph 6:12
or principalities or *p* ... Col 1:16
principalities and *p* ... Col 2:15
word of God and the *p* ... Heb 6:5
p having been made ... 1 Pet 3:22

PRACTICE
to do, that I do not *p* ... Rom 7:15
I will not to do, that I *p* ... Rom 7:19
those who *p* such things ... Gal 5:21
and do not *p* the truth ... 1 John 1:6
Whoever does not *p* ... 1 John 3:10

PRACTICED
p witchcraft and ... 2 Kin 17:17
previously *p* sorcery in ... Acts 8:9
those who had *p* magic ... Acts 19:19
they have *p* deceit ... Rom 3:13
which they have *p* ... 2 Cor 12:21

PRACTICES
wrath on him who *p* evil ... Rom 13:4
trained in covetous *p* ... 2 Pet 2:14
p righteousness is born .. 1 John 2:29
whoever loves and *p* a lie .. Rev 22:15

PRACTICING
For everyone *p* evil hates .. John 3:20
judge those *p* such things ... Rom 2:3

PRAETORIUM
Pilate's palace in Jerusalem, Mark 15:16; John 18:28; Matt 27:27
——— Herod's palace at Caesarea, Acts 23:35

PRAISE
Now I will *p* the LORD ... Gen 29:35
your brothers shall *p* ... Gen 49:8
He is my God, and I will *p* ... Ex 15:2
He is your *p* ... Deut 10:21
which He has made, in *p* .. Deut 26:19
I will sing *p* to the ... Judg 5:3
to *p* the LORD God of ... 1 Chr 16:4
to triumph in Your *p* ... 1 Chr 16:35
David, "for giving *p*." ... 1 Chr 23:5
p the LORD, and ... 1 Chr 23:30
and to *p* the LORD ... 1 Chr 25:3
p Your glorious name ... 1 Chr 29:13
offered *p* by their ministry .. 2 Chr 7:6
for their duties (to *p* and .. 2 Chr 8:14
"*P* the LORD, for His ... 2 Chr 20:21
began to sing and to *p* .. 2 Chr 20:22
the Levites to sing *p* ... 2 Chr 29:30
to *p* in the gates of the ... 2 Chr 31:2
to *p* the LORD, according ... Ezra 3:10
above all blessing and *p* ... Neh 9:5
singers, and songs of *p* ... Neh 12:46
I will *p* You, O LORD ... Ps 9:1
p shall be of You in ... Ps 22:25
For *p* from the upright ... Ps 33:1
p shall continually be ... Ps 34:1
of Your *p* all the day long ... Ps 35:28
the people shall *p* ... Ps 45:17
Whoever offers *p* ... Ps 50:23
P is awaiting You ... Ps 65:1
make His *p* glorious ... Ps 66:2
let all the peoples *p* ... Ps 67:3
Let heaven and earth *p* ... Ps 69:34
p shall be continually ... Ps 71:6
And the heavens will *p* ... Ps 89:5
and into His courts with *p* ... Ps 100:4
silent, O God of my *p* ... Ps 109:1
Seven times a day I *p* ... Ps 119:164
All Your works shall *p* ... Ps 145:10
shall speak the *p* ... Ps 145:21
P the LORD ... Ps 148:1
P Him with high sounding ... Ps 150:5
that has breath *p* ... Ps 150:6
Let another man *p* ... Prov 27:2
let her own works *p* ... Prov 31:31
And your gates *P* ... Is 60:18
the garment of *p* for the ... Is 61:3
He makes Jerusalem a *p* ... Is 62:7
For You are my *p* ... Jer 17:14
Me a name of joy, a *p* ... Jer 33:9
p You, O God of my ... Dan 2:23
Nebuchadnezzar, *p* and ... Dan 4:37
p the name of the LORD ... Joel 2:26
give you fame and *p* ... Zeph 3:20
You have perfected *p* ... Matt 21:16
saw it, gave *p* to God ... Luke 18:43
p God with a loud voice .. Luke 19:37

of men more than the *p* ... John 12:43
p is not from men but ... Rom 2:29
will have *p* from the same .. Rom 13:3
"*P* the LORD, ... Rom 15:11
Then each one's *p* ... 1 Cor 4:5
Now I *p* you, brethren ... 1 Cor 11:2
I do not *p* you ... 1 Cor 11:22
the brother whose *p* ... 2 Cor 8:18
to the *p* of the glory of His ... Eph 1:6
should be to the *p* ... Eph 1:12
to the *p* of His glory ... Eph 1:14
to the glory and *p* ... Phil 1:11
I will sing *p* to You ... Heb 2:12
the sacrifice of *p* ... Heb 13:15
and for the *p* of those ... 1 Pet 2:14
saying, "*P* our God ... Rev 19:5

PRAISE THE LORD

and said, "Now I will *p* ... Gen 29:35
to thank, and to *p* ... 1 Chr 16:4
King David had made to *p* .. 2 Chr 7:6
"*P*, for His mercy ... 2 Chr 20:21
with cymbals, to *p* ... Ezra 3:10
Those who seek Him will *p* .. Ps 22:26
P with the harp ... Ps 33:2
yet to be created may *p* ... Ps 102:18
the Lord, O my soul! *P* ... Ps 104:35
P! Oh, give thanks ... Ps 106:1
The dead do not *p* ... Ps 115:17
p, all you Gentiles ... Ps 117:1
while I live I will *p* ... Ps 146:2
P! *P* from the heavens ... Ps 148:1
that has breath *p* ... Ps 150:6
P, call upon His name ... Is 12:4
shall eat it, and *p* ... Is 62:9
P! For He has delivered ... Jer 20:13
P, all you Gentiles ... Rom 15:11

PRAISED

who is worthy to be *p* ... 2 Sam 22:4
and greatly to be *p* ... 1 Chr 16:25
and *p* the LORD ... 1 Chr 16:36
thousand *p* the LORD ... 1 Chr 23:5
music, and *p* the LORD, ... 2 Chr 5:13
and *p* the LORD, saying ... 2 Chr 7:3
the priests *p* the LORD ... 2 Chr 30:21
when they *p* the LORD ... Ezra 3:11
and *p* the LORD ... Neh 5:13
daily He shall be *p* ... Ps 72:15
LORD's name is to be *p* ... Ps 113:3
and greatly to be *p* ... Ps 145:3
the LORD, she shall be *p* ... Prov 31:30
where our fathers *p* ... Is 64:11
the Most High and *p* ... Dan 4:34

PRAISES

in holiness, fearful in *p* ... Ex 15:11
sang *p* with gladness, ... 2 Chr 29:30
enthroned in the *p* ... Ps 22:3
O LORD, I will sing *p* ... Ps 101:1
it is good to sing *p* ... Ps 147:1
and he *p* her ... Prov 31:28
shall proclaim the *p* ... Is 60:6
you may proclaim the *p* ... 1 Pet 2:9

PRAISEWORTHY

if there is anything *p* ... Phil 4:8

PRAISING

they sang responsively, *p* .. Ezra 3:11
they will still be *p* ... Ps 84:4
of the heavenly host *p* ... Luke 2:13
p God for all the things ... Luke 2:20
in the temple *p* ... Luke 24:53
p God and having favor ... Acts 2:47
leaping, and *p* God ... Acts 3:8

PRATING

p fool will fall ... Prov 10:8
p against us with ... 3 John 10

PRAY

heal her, O God, I *p* ... Num 12:13
of this people, I *p* ... Num 14:19
p to the LORD that He ... Num 21:7
Strengthen me, I *p*. ... Judg 16:28
LORD in ceasing to *p* ... 1 Sam 12:23
my God, for to You I will *p* ... Ps 5:2
p to You in a time when ... Ps 32:6
at noon I will *p* ... Ps 55:17
I *p*, send now prosperity. ... Ps 118:25
who hate you, and *p* ... Matt 5:44
"And when you *p* ... Matt 6:5
But you, when you *p* ... Matt 6:6
when you *p*, do not use ... Matt 6:7
manner, therefore, *p* ... Matt 6:9
Therefore *p* the LORD of ... Matt 9:38
by Himself to *p* ... Matt 14:23
hands on them and *p* ... Matt 19:13
while I go and *p* over ... Matt 26:36
Watch and *p* ... Matt 26:41
I cannot now *p* ... Matt 26:53
to the mountain to *p* ... Mark 6:46
you ask when you *p* ... Mark 11:24
Take heed, watch and *p* .. Mark 13:33
Sit here while I *p* ... Mark 14:32
"Watch and *p*, lest you ... Mark 14:38
out to the mountain to *p* ... Luke 6:12
p for those who spitefully .. Luke 6:28
up on the mountain to *p* ... Luke 9:28
"Lord, teach us to *p* ... Luke 11:1
men always ought to *p* ... Luke 18:1
up to the temple to *p* ... Luke 18:10
P that you may not ... Luke 22:40
Rise and *p*, lest you ... Luke 22:46
And I will *p* ... John 14:16
I shall *p* the Father for ... John 16:26
I do not *p* for the ... John 17:9
I do not *p* that You ... John 17:15
"I do not *p* for ... John 17:20
p God if perhaps the ... Acts 8:22
P to the Lord for me, that .. Acts 8:24
up on the housetop to *p* ... Acts 10:9
know what we should *p* ... Rom 8:26
to *p* to God with her ... 1 Cor 11:13
p that he may interpret ... 1 Cor 14:13
For if I *p* in a tongue ... 1 Cor 14:14
I will *p* with the ... 1 Cor 14:15
Now I *p* to God ... 2 Cor 13:7
And this also we *p* ... 2 Cor 13:9
And this I *p*, that your love .. Phil 1:9
do not cease to *p* for you ... Col 1:9
p without ceasing ... 1 Thess 5:17
Brethren, *p* for us ... 1 Thess 5:25
we also *p* always ... 2 Thess 1:11
p for us, that the word ... 2 Thess 3:1
therefore that the men *p* ... 1 Tim 2:8
P for us, for we are ... Heb 13:18
Let him *p* ... James 5:13
to one another, and *p* ... James 5:16
say that he should *p* ... 1 John 5:16
p that you may prosper ... 3 John 2

PRAYED

So Abraham *p* to God ... Gen 20:17
So Moses *p* for the people . Num 21:7
Manoah *p* to the LORD ... Judg 13:8
For this child I *p*, and ... 1 Sam 1:27
Then Hezekiah *p* before .. 2 Kin 19:15
times that day, and *p* ... Dan 6:10
Then Jonah *p* to the LORD ... Jon 2:1
So he *p* to the LORD, ... Jon 4:2
into the wilderness and *p* .. Luke 5:16
Pharisee stood and *p* ... Luke 18:11
p more earnestly ... Luke 22:44
p earnestly that it ... James 5:17

PRAYER

God heeded the *p* ... 2 Sam 21:14
in heaven their *p* ... 1 Kin 8:45
p made in this place ... 2 Chr 7:15
the thanksgiving with *p* ... Neh 11:17
fear, and restrain *p* ... Job 15:4
And my *p* is pure ... Job 16:17
p would return to my ... Ps 35:13
A *p* to the God of my ... Ps 42:8
P also will be made ... Ps 72:15
Let my *p* come before ... Ps 88:2
He shall regard the *p* ... Ps 102:17
but I give myself to *p* ... Ps 109:4
to the LORD, but the *p* ... Prov 15:8
hears the *p* of the ... Prov 15:29
hear the *p* of Your servant .. Dan 9:17
while I was speaking in *p* ... Dan 9:21
not go out except by *p* ... Matt 17:21
things you ask in *p* ... Matt 21:22
out by nothing but *p* ... Mark 9:29
a house of *p* for all ... Mark 11:17
all night in *p* to God ... Luke 6:12
My house is a house of *p* . Luke 19:46
with one accord in *p* and ... Acts 1:14
the temple at the hour of *p* .. Acts 3:1
continually to *p* ... Acts 6:4
your *p* has been heard ... Acts 10:31
where *p* was ... Acts 16:13
as we went up to *p* ... Acts 16:16
p to God for Israel is that .. Rom 10:1
steadfastly in *p* ... Rom 12:12
to fasting and *p* ... 1 Cor 7:5
always with all *p* ... Eph 6:18
always in every *p* of mine ... Phil 1:4
deliverance through your *p* . Phil 1:19
but in everything by *p* ... Phil 4:6
Continue earnestly in *p*, ... Col 4:2
the word of God and *p* ... 1 Tim 4:5
And the *p* of faith ... James 5:15

PRAYERS

though you make many *p* ... Is 1:15
pretense make long *p* ... Matt 23:14
fastings and *p* night and ... Luke 2:37
pretense make long *p* ... Luke 20:47
of bread, and in *p* ... Acts 2:42
Your *p* and your alms ... Acts 10:4
always in my *p* ... Rom 1:9
me in *p* to God for me ... Rom 15:30
fervently for you in *p* ... Col 4:12
that supplications, *p* ... 1 Tim 2:1
and *p* night and day ... 1 Tim 5:5
always in my *p* ... Philem 4
when He had offered up *p* ... Heb 5:7
p may not be hindered ... 1 Pet 3:7
are open to their *p* ... 1 Pet 3:12
and watchful in your *p* ... 1 Pet 4:7
which are the *p* ... Rev 5:8

PRAYING

and found Daniel *p* ... Dan 6:11
whenever you stand *p* ... Mark 11:25
Paul and Silas were *p* ... Acts 16:25
p always with all prayer ... Eph 6:18
faith, *p* in the Holy Spirit, ... Jude 20

PRAYS

every woman who *p* or ... 1 Cor 11:5
tongue, my spirit *p* ... 1 Cor 14:14

PREACH

to *p* good tidings ... Is 61:1
that great city, and *p* ... Jon 3:2
time Jesus began to *p* ... Matt 4:17
you hear in the ear, *p* ... Matt 10:27
p the gospel to every ... Mark 16:15
P the gospel to the ... Luke 4:18
p the kingdom of God ... Luke 9:60
to *p* the word in Asia ... Acts 16:6
ready to *p* the gospel ... Rom 1:15
word of faith which we *p*) .. Rom 10:8
And how shall they *p* ... Rom 10:15
it my aim to *p* the gospel .. Rom 15:20
p Christ crucified ... 1 Cor 1:23
is me if I do not *p* ... 1 Cor 9:16
I or they, so we *p* ... 1 Cor 15:11
For we do not *p* ... 2 Cor 4:5
p any other gospel to you ... Gal 1:8
that I might *p* Him among ... Gal 1:16
gospel which I *p* ... Gal 2:2
p Christ even from ... Phil 1:15
The former *p* Christ from ... Phil 1:16
P the word ... 2 Tim 4:2

PREACH THE GOSPEL

into all the world and *p* .. Mark 16:15
He has anointed Me to *p* ... Luke 4:18

Lord had called us to *p* .... Acts 16:10
I am ready to *p* .... Rom 1:15
the feet of those who *p* .... Rom 10:15
made it my aim to *p* .... Rom 15:20
to baptize, but to *p* .... 1 Cor 1:17
who *p* should live from .... 1 Cor 9:14
to *p* in the regions .... 2 Cor 10:16

PREACHED

have the gospel *p* to them .. Matt 11:5
p that people .... Mark 6:12
p to all the nations .... Mark 13:10
wherever this gospel is *p* .. Mark 14:9
out and *p* everywhere .... Mark 16:20
have the gospel *p* to them .. Luke 7:22
of sins should be *p* .... Luke 24:47
p in Jesus the resurrection ... Acts 4:2
p Christ to them .... Acts 8:5
p the word of the Lord, ... Acts 8:25
baptism which John *p* .... Acts 10:37
through this Man is *p* .... Acts 13:38
of God was *p* by Paul .... Acts 17:13
he *p* to them Jesus .... Acts 17:18
lest, when I have *p* .... 1 Cor 9:27
whom we have not *p* .... 2 Cor 11:4
than what we have *p* .... Gal 1:8
in truth, Christ is *p* .... Phil 1:18
was *p* to every creature .... Col 1:23
might be *p* fully through .. 2 Tim 4:17
the gospel was *p* .... Heb 4:2
also He went and *p* .... 1 Pet 3:19

PREACHER

The words of the *P* .... Eccl 1:1
they hear without a *p* .... Rom 10:14
I was appointed a *p* .... 1 Tim 2:7
I was appointed a *p* .... 2 Tim 1:11
of eight people, a *p* .... 2 Pet 2:5

PREACHES

the Jesus whom Paul *p* .... Acts 19:13
p another Jesus whom .... 2 Cor 11:4
p any other gospel .... Gal 1:9
p the faith which he .... Gal 1:23

PREACHING

at the *p* of Jonah .... Matt 12:41
p a baptism of repentance .. Mark 1:4
every city and village, *p* .... Luke 8:1
p the gospel and healing .... Luke 9:6
p Jesus as the .... Acts 5:42
went everywhere *p* .... Acts 8:4
to my gospel and the *p* .... Rom 16:25
p were not with .... 1 Cor 2:4
not risen, then our *p* .... 1 Cor 15:14
His word through *p* .... Titus 1:3

PRECEDE

p those who are asleep .. 1 Thess 4:15

PRECEDING

p them to judgment, ... 1 Tim 5:24

PRECEPT

p must be upon *p* .... Is 28:10
P upon *p*, *p* upon *p* .... Is 28:13
walked by human *p* .... Hos 5:11
heart he wrote you this *p* .. Mark 10:5
p to all the people .... Heb 9:19

PRECEPTS

and commanded them *p* .... Neh 9:14
all His *p* are sure .... Ps 111:7
us to keep Your *p* .... Ps 119:4
Behold, I long for Your *p* ... Ps 119:40
will meditate on Your *p* .... Ps 119:78
because I keep Your *p* .... Ps 119:100
how I love Your *p* .... Ps 119:159
and kept all his *p* .... Jer 35:18
by departing from Your *p* .... Dan 9:5

PRECIOUS

gave *p* things to her .... Gen 24:53
because my life was *p* ... 1 Sam 26:21
with *p* stones .... 2 Sam 12:30
P in the sight of the .... Ps 116:15
How *p* also are Your .... Ps 139:17
She is more *p* than .... Prov 3:15
rooms are filled with all *p* .. Prov 24:4
a *p* cornerstone, a sure .... Is 28:16
Since you were *p* .... Is 43:4
p things shall not .... Is 44:9
if you take out the *p* .... Jer 15:19
The *p* sons of Zion .... Lam 4:2
p stones, wood, hay .... 1 Cor 3:12
farmer waits for the *p* .... James 5:7
more *p* than gold .... 1 Pet 1:7
but with the *p* blood of .... 1 Pet 1:19
but chosen by God and *p* ... 1 Pet 2:4
chief cornerstone, elect, *p* ... 1 Pet 2:6
who believe, He is *p* .... 1 Pet 2:7
p in the sight of .... 1 Pet 3:4
like *p* faith with us by the ... 2 Pet 1:1
and *p* promises, ... 2 Pet 1:4

PREDESTINED

He foreknew, He also *p* .... Rom 8:29
having *p* us to .... Eph 1:5
inheritance, being *p* .... Eph 1:11

PREEMINENCE

He may have the *p* .... Col 1:18
loves to have the *p* .... 3 John 9

PREFERENCE

in honor giving *p* .... Rom 12:10

PREFERRED

comes after me is *p* .... John 1:15

PREGNANCY

no birth, no *p*, and no .... Hos 9:11

PREGNANT

woe to those who are *p* ... Matt 24:19
pains upon a *p* woman ... 1 Thess 5:3

PREJUDICE

these things without *p* .... 1 Tim 5:21

PREMEDITATE

p what you will .... Mark 13:11

PREPARATION

Now it was the *P* .... John 19:14
your feet with the *p* .... Eph 6:15

PREPARATIONS

p of the heart belong .... Prov 16:1

PREPARE

P provisions for .... Josh 1:11
'Let us now *p* to build .... Josh 22:26
p your hearts for the .... 1 Sam 7:3
p it for myself and my ... 1 Kin 17:12
which I will *p* for them .... Esth 5:8
p a table before me in .... Ps 23:5
p mercy and truth .... Ps 61:7
P your outside work, ... Prov 24:27
yet they *p* their food in .... Prov 30:25
P the way of the LORD .... Is 40:3
P the way for the .... Is 62:10
p the ambushes .... Jer 51:12
P the way of the LORD, ... Matt 3:3
do You want us to *p* .... Matt 26:17
P the way of the LORD .... Mark 1:3
to *p* for Him .... Luke 9:52
will, and did not *p* .... Luke 12:47
p the Passover for us .... Luke 22:8
p a place for you .... John 14:2

PREPARED

place which I have *p* .... Ex 23:20
You *p* room for it .... Ps 80:9
When He *p* the heavens .... Prov 8:27
for the LORD has *p* .... Zeph 1:7
for whom it is *p* .... Matt 20:23
fire *p* for the devil and .... Matt 25:41
which You have *p* .... Luke 2:31
mercy, which He had *p* .... Rom 9:23
things which God has *p* .... 1 Cor 2:9
Now He who has *p* .... 2 Cor 5:5
p beforehand that we .... Eph 2:10
p for every good work .... 2 Tim 2:21
God, for He has *p* .... Heb 11:16
p as a bride adorned for .... Rev 21:2

PRESENCE

themselves from the *p* .... Gen 3:8
went out from the *p* .... Gen 4:16
the *p* of my mistress Sarai .. Gen 16:8
we die in your *p* .... Gen 47:15
P will go with you .... Ex 33:14
and honor the *p* .... Lev 19:32
afraid in any man's *p* .... Deut 1:17
am terrified at His *p* .... Job 23:15
p is fullness of joy .... Ps 16:11
shall dwell in Your *p* .... Ps 140:13
not tremble at My *p* .... Jer 5:22
shall shake at My *p* .... Ezek 38:20
fled from the *p* of the LORD .. Jon 1:10
Be silent in the *p* .... Zeph 1:7
stands in the *p* of God .... Luke 1:19
and drank in Your *p* .... Luke 13:26
in the *p* of the people .... Luke 20:26
full of joy in Your *p* .... Acts 2:28
to God in the *p* of them ... Acts 27:35
the *p* of Him whom he .... Rom 4:17
should glory in His *p* .... 1 Cor 1:29
in the *p* of Christ .... 2 Cor 2:10
who in *p* am lowly .... 2 Cor 10:1
but his bodily *p* .... 2 Cor 10:10
obeyed, not as in my *p* .... Phil 2:12
p of many witnesses .... 1 Tim 6:12
the *P* behind the veil .... Heb 6:19
appear in the *p* of God .... Heb 9:24

PRESENT

a very *p* help in trouble .... Ps 46:1
we are all *p* before .... Acts 10:33
not *p* your members .... Rom 6:13
for to will is *p* with me .... Rom 7:18
evil is *p* with me .... Rom 7:21
p time are not worthy to ... Rom 8:18
nor things *p* nor things to .. Rom 8:38
p your bodies a living .... Rom 12:1
or death, or things *p* .... 1 Cor 3:22
absent in body but *p* .... 1 Cor 5:3
because of the *p* distress .. 1 Cor 7:26
p the gospel of Christ .. 1 Cor 9:18
to be *p* with the Lord .... 2 Cor 5:8
may *p* you as a chaste .... 2 Cor 11:2
not only when I am *p* .... Gal 4:18
that He might *p* .... Eph 5:27
to *p* you holy, ... Col 1:22
to *p* yourself .... 2 Tim 2:15
and godly in the *p* age, ... Titus 2:12
established in the *p* truth .. 2 Pet 1:12
p you faultless .... Jude 24

PRESENTED

p them to Pharaoh .... Gen 47:2
p themselves before God ... Josh 24:1
treasures, they *p* .... Matt 2:11
And He *p* him to his .... Luke 7:15
to whom He also *p* Himself .. Acts 1:3
they also *p* Paul to him .... Acts 23:33
For just as you *p* .... Rom 6:19

PRESENTING

p my supplication before ... Dan 9:20

PRESENTS

kings will bring *p* .... Ps 68:29

PRESERVE

before you to *p* life .... Gen 45:5
You shall *p* me from .... Ps 32:7
O LORD, You *p* man and .... Ps 36:6
He shall *p* your soul .... Ps 121:7
The LORD shall *p* .... Ps 121:8
discretion will *p* you .... Prov 2:11
lips of the wise will *p* .... Prov 14:3
the LORD *p* knowledge .... Prov 22:12
children, I will *p* .... Jer 49:11
pardon those whom I *p* .... Jer 50:20
loses his life will *p* .... Luke 17:33
every evil work and *p* .... 2 Tim 4:18

PRESERVED

and my life is *p* .... Gen 32:30
p us in all the way that .... Josh 24:17

the LORD *p* David .... 2 Sam 8:6
Your care has *p* my spirit .. Job 10:12
soul, and body be *p* ..... 1 Thess 5:23

PRESERVES
For the LORD *p* the .... Ps 31:23
p the souls of His .... Ps 97:10
The LORD *p* the simple ...... Ps 116:6
p the way of His saints ...... Prov 2:8
who guards his mouth *p* ... Prov 13:3
he who keeps his way *p* .. Prov 16:17

PRESS
but I *p* on, that I may lay ... Phil 3:12
I *p* toward the goal .... Phil 3:14

PRESSED
p her virgin bosom .... Ezek 23:8
p about Him to touch ...... Mark 3:10
the multitude *p* about Him .. Luke 5:1
p down, shaken together, .. Luke 6:38
We are hard *p* on every .... 2 Cor 4:8
For I am hard *p* .... Phil 1:23

PRESUMPTUOUS
servant also from *p* .... Ps 19:13
They are *p*, self-willed ..... 2 Pet 2:10

PRETENDED
them, *p* madness .... 1 Sam 21:13

PRETENSE
whole heart, but in *p* .... Jer 3:10
p make long prayers ...... Matt 23:14

PREVAIL
He did not *p* against him .. Gen 32:25
no man shall *p* .... 1 Sam 2:9
do not let man *p* .... 2 Chr 14:11
our tongue we will *p* .... Ps 12:4
He shall *p* against His .... Is 42:13
but they shall not *p* .... Jer 1:19
but he will not *p* .... Dan 11:12
of Hades shall not *p* .... Matt 16:18
but they did not *p*, ... Rev 12:8

PREVAILED
The waters *p* and greatly ... Gen 7:18
hand, that Israel *p* .... Ex 17:11
Judah *p* over his brothers .. 1 Chr 5:2
with the Angel and *p* .... Hos 12:4
grew mightily and *p* ...... Acts 19:20
has *p* to open the scroll and .. Rev 5:5

PREVIOUSLY
who *p* practiced sorcery in .. Acts 8:9

PREY
the mountains of *p* .... Ps 76:4
has not given us as *p* .... Ps 124:6
Shall the *p* be taken .... Is 49:24
evil makes himself a *p* .... Is 59:15
shall no longer be a *p* ..... Ezek 34:22
when he has no *p* .... Amos 3:4

PRICE
be weighed for its *p* .... Job 28:15
a fool the purchase *p* ...... Prov 17:16
one pearl of great *p* .... Matt 13:46
back part of the *p* .... Acts 5:3
you were bought at a *p* .... 1 Cor 6:20
You were bought at a *p* ... 1 Cor 7:23

PRIDE
p come against me .... Ps 36:11
p serves as their necklace .... Ps 73:6
p and arrogance and .... Prov 8:13
By *p* comes nothing .... Prov 13:10
P goes before .... Prov 16:18
p will bring him low .... Prov 29:23
and her daughter had *p* ... Ezek 16:49
p He is able to put down .... Dan 4:37
was hardened in *p* .... Dan 5:20
has sworn by the *p* .... Amos 8:7
For the *p* of the .... Zech 11:3
evil eye, blasphemy, *p* ..... Mark 7:22
p he fall into the .... 1 Tim 3:6
eyes, and the *p* of life .... 1 John 2:16

PRIEST
See HIGH PRIEST

he was the *p* of God .... Gen 14:18
That son who becomes *p* .... Ex 29:30
The sons of Aaron the *p* ...... Lev 1:7
the *p* shall burn all on the ..... Lev 1:9
p shall lay them in order ..... Lev 1:12
p shall make atonement .... Lev 19:22
for the *p* is holy to his God .. Lev 21:7
Eleazar the *p* spoke .... Num 26:3
and Eleazar the *p* .... Num 26:63
Eleazar the *p*, Joshua ..... Josh 19:51
when Phinehas the *p* ...... Josh 22:30
The *p* stood at the .... Judg 18:17
Eli the *p* was sitting .... 1 Sam 1:9
Myself a faithful *p* .... 1 Sam 2:35
Eli, the LORD's *p* in .... 1 Sam 14:3
Saul talked to the *p* ...... 1 Sam 14:19
to Ahimelech the *p* .... 1 Sam 21:2
p gave him holy bread .... 1 Sam 21:6
Urijah the *p* built an ..... 2 Kin 16:11
Jehoiada the *p* brought .. 2 Chr 23:14
the *p* found the Book .... 2 Chr 34:14
gave Ezra the *p* .... Ezra 7:11
p could consult .... Neh 7:65
p forever according .... Ps 110:4
the *p* and the prophet .... Is 28:7
So He shall be a *p* .... Zech 6:13
of a *p* should keep .... Mal 2:7
show yourself to the *p* .... Matt 8:4
to Caiaphas the high *p* .. Matt 26:57
And the high *p* arose ..... Matt 26:62
away to the high *p* .... Mark 14:53
well as Annas the high *p* .... Acts 4:6
and faithful High *P* .... Heb 2:17
High *P* of our confession, ... Heb 3:1
we have a great High *P* ...... Heb 4:14
we do not have a High *P* ..... Heb 4:15
p forever according .... Heb 5:6
We have such a High *P*, ... Heb 8:1
high *p* went alone .... Heb 9:7
Christ came as High *P* ...... Heb 9:11

PRIEST'S
the high *p* servant .... John 18:10

PRIESTHOOD
be an everlasting *p* .... Ex 40:15
have defiled the *p* .... Neh 13:29
p being changed .... Heb 7:12
has an unchangeable *p* ...... Heb 7:24
house, a holy *p* .... 1 Pet 2:5
generation, a royal *p* .... 1 Pet 2:9

PRIESTS
to Me a kingdom of *p* .... Ex 19:6
may minister to Me as *p* .... Ex 28:41
and the *p*, Aaron's sons, ... Lev 1:5
"Command the *p* .... Josh 4:16
and let seven *p* bear seven .. Josh 6:6
the *p* blew the trumpets .... Josh 6:20
had killed the LORD's *p* .. 1 Sam 22:21
removed the idolatrous *p* .. 2 Kin 23:5
Jahaziel the *p* .... 1 Chr 16:6
and Benjamin, and the *p* ...... Ezra 1:5
yet told the Jews, the *p* ..... Neh 2:16
Their *p* fell by the sword, ... Ps 78:64
Aaron were among His *p* ..... Ps 99:6
Let Your *p* be clothed with .. Ps 132:9
her *p* with salvation .... Ps 132:16
named the *p* of the LORD ...... Is 61:6
which the *p* ministered ..... Jer 52:18
and the iniquities of her *p* .. Lam 4:13
p have violated My law ... Ezek 22:26
the *p* shall throw salt on .. Ezek 43:24
"Hear this, O *p*! .... Hos 5:1
the *p* mourn, who minister ... Joel 1:9
her *p* teach for pay .... Mic 3:11
p in the temple profane ..... Matt 12:5
But when the chief *p* ...... Matt 21:15
went to the chief *p* .... Matt 26:14
of silver to the chief *p* and .. Matt 27:3
the chief *p* stirred up ...... Mark 15:11
Caiaphas being high *p* ...... Luke 3:2
show yourselves to the *p* .. Luke 17:14
Jesus said to the chief *p* .. Luke 22:52
Pilate said to the chief *p* .... Luke 23:4
But the chief *p* plotted .... John 12:10
become *p* without an oath ..... Heb 7:21
need daily, as those high *p* .. Heb 7:27
high *p* men who have .... Heb 7:28
since there are *p* who offer ... Heb 8:4
made us kings and *p* .... Rev 1:6
but they shall be *p* .... Rev 20:6

PRIESTS'
where the *p* feet stood firm .. Josh 4:3
and the soles of the *p* feet .. Josh 4:18

PRINCE
"Who made you a *p* .... Ex 2:14
is the house of the *p* .... Job 21:28
is the downfall of a *p* ..... Prov 14:28
Everlasting Father, *P* .... Is 9:6
against the *P* of princes ..... Dan 8:25
until Messiah the *P* .... Dan 9:25
with the *p* of Persia .... Dan 10:20
except Michael your *p* ..... Dan 10:21
days without king or *p* .... Hos 3:4
p asks for gifts .... Mic 7:3
and killed the *P* .... Acts 3:15
His right hand to be *P* ...... Acts 5:31
the *p* of the power .... Eph 2:2

PRINCES
He is not partial to *p* .... Job 34:19
to bind his *p* at his .... Ps 105:22
He may seat him with *p* ..... Ps 113:8
to put confidence in *p* .... Ps 118:9
P also sit and speak .... Ps 119:23
p and all judges of .... Ps 148:11
good, nor to strike *p* ...... Prov 17:26
is a child, and your *p* .... Eccl 10:16
of nobles, and your *p* .... Eccl 10:17
children to be their *p* .... Is 3:4
p will rule with .... Is 32:1
He brings the *p* .... Is 40:23

PRINCIPAL
Wisdom is the *p* .... Prov 4:7

PRINCIPALITIES
nor *p* nor powers .... Rom 8:38
and blood, but against *p* ..... Eph 6:12
dominions or *p* or powers ... Col 1:16
disarmed *p* and powers, ... Col 2:15

PRINCIPALITY
far above all *p* .... Eph 1:21
is the head of all *p* .... Col 2:10

PRINCIPLES
from the basic *p* .... Col 2:20
again the first *p* .... Heb 5:12

PRINT
hands the *p* of the nails ... John 20:25

PRISCILLA (or Prisca)
Wife of Aquila, Acts 18:1–3
With Aquila, instructs Apollos, Acts 18:26
Mentioned by Paul, Rom 16:3; 1 Cor 16:19; 2 Tim 4:19

PRISON
and put him into the *p* .... Gen 39:20
Bring my soul out of *p* .... Ps 142:7
in darkness from the *p* .... Is 42:7
the opening of the *p* .... Is 61:1
should put him in *p* .... Jer 29:26
John had been put in *p* ..... Matt 4:12
John had heard in *p* .... Matt 11:2
had John beheaded in *p* ... Matt 14:10
I was in *p* and you .... Matt 25:36
we see You sick, or in *p* .. Matt 25:39
or naked or sick or in *p* ... Matt 25:44
after John was put in *p* ..... Mark 1:14
put them in the common *p* .. Acts 5:18
Lord opened the *p* doors .... Acts 5:19
did not find them in the *p* .. Acts 5:22
was therefore kept in *p* ...... Acts 12:5
of the *p* were shaken .... Acts 16:26
seeing the *p* doors open ... Acts 16:27

So the keeper of the *p* .... Acts 16:36
to the spirits in *p* .... 1 Pet 3:19
a *p* for every foul spirit, ... Rev 18:2
will be released from his *p* .. Rev 20:7

PRISONER
the groaning of the *p* .... Ps 79:11
p called Barabbas .... Matt 27:16
releasing one *p* to them ... Mark 15:6
reason I, Paul, the *p* .... Eph 3:1
the *p* of the Lord, beseech ... Eph 4:1
Lord, nor of me His *p* ...... 2 Tim 1:8
Paul, a *p* of Christ Jesus, ... Philem 1

PRISONERS
p rest together .... Job 3:18
does not despise His *p* ...... Ps 69:33
gives freedom to the *p* ...... Ps 146:7
the stronghold, you *p* ...... Zech 9:12
the *p* were listening to .... Acts 16:25
and my fellow *p* .... Rom 16:7
Remember the *p* as if .... Heb 13:3

PRISONS
the synagogues and *p* .... Luke 21:12
p more frequently .... 2 Cor 11:23

PRIVATE
is of any *p* interpretation .. 2 Pet 1:20

PRIVATELY
disciples came to Jesus *p* .. Matt 17:19
Andrew asked Him *p* ..... Mark 13:3
aside *p* into a deserted ..... Luke 9:10

PRIZE
life shall be as a *p* .... Jer 21:9
but one receives the *p* ..... 1 Cor 9:24
the goal for the *p* .... Phil 3:14

PROCEED
For they *p* from evil .... Jer 9:3
heart *p* evil thoughts ...... Matt 15:19
p evil thoughts, adulteries . Mark 7:21
not permitting us to *p* ...... Acts 27:7
p out of your mouth, ... Eph 4:29
of the same mouth *p* ..... James 3:10

PROCEEDED
for I *p* forth .... John 8:42
p from the mouth of Him .. Rev 19:21

PROCEEDINGS
he adjourned the *p* .... Acts 24:22

PROCEEDS
by every word that *p* .... Deut 8:3
by every word that *p* .... Matt 4:4
Spirit of truth who *p* ...... John 15:26
back part of the *p* .... Acts 5:2

PROCESS
in the *p* of time .... 1 Sam 1:20

PROCESSION
They have seen Your *p* .... Ps 68:24

PROCHORUS
One of the first seven deacons, Acts 6:5

PROCLAIM
you, and I will *p* .... Ex 33:19
p the name of the LORD .... Deut 32:3
p it not in the .... 2 Sam 1:20
and they shall *p* .... Is 60:6
to *p* liberty to the captives, ... Is 61:1
to *p* the acceptable year of .... Is 61:2
began to *p* it freely .... Mark 1:45
knowing, Him I *p* .... Acts 17:23
drink this cup, you *p* ...... 1 Cor 11:26
that you may *p* the praises .. 1 Pet 2:9

PROCLAIMED
p the good news .... Ps 40:9
company of those who *p* .... Ps 68:11
p a fast, and put on .... Jon 3:5
he went his way and *p* ..... Luke 8:39
inner rooms will be *p* ...... Luke 12:3

PROCLAIMER
"He seems to be a *p* ...... Acts 17:18

PROCLAIMS
good news, who *p* .... Is 52:7

PROCONSUL
seeking to turn the *p* .... Acts 13:8
When Gallio was *p* .... Acts 18:12

PRODIGAL
with *p* living .... Luke 15:13

PRODUCE
land shall yield its *p* .... Lev 26:4
all kinds of *p* .... Ps 144:13
p the righteousness of ..... James 1:20

PRODUCED
p in me all manner of evil ... Rom 7:8
What diligence it *p* in ...... 2 Cor 7:11

PRODUCES
forcing of wrath *p* strife ... Prov 30:33
indeed bears fruit and *p* .. Matt 13:23
if it dies, it *p* much grain .. John 12:24
tribulation *p* perseverance .. Rom 5:3
sorrow *p* repentance .... 2 Cor 7:10
of your faith *p* patience .... James 1:3

PRODUCING
p death in me through ...... Rom 7:13

PROFANE
and offered *p* fire .... Lev 10:1
and priest are *p* .... Jer 23:11
"But you *p* it .... Mal 1:12
tried to *p* the temple .... Acts 24:6
But reject *p* and old .... 1 Tim 4:7
p person like Esau .... Heb 12:16

PROFANED
p his crown by casting ...... Ps 89:39
and *p* My Sabbaths .... Ezek 22:8
p the LORD's holy .... Mal 2:11

PROFANENESS
of Jerusalem *p* has .... Jer 23:15

PROFANING
p the covenant of the .... Mal 2:10

PROFESS
They *p* to know God .... Titus 1:16

PROFESSING
P to be wise .... Rom 1:22
is proper for women *p* .... 1 Tim 2:10

PROFIT
p is there in my blood .... Ps 30:9
p has a man from all .... Eccl 1:3
There was no *p* under .... Eccl 2:11
for they will not *p* .... Is 57:12
words that cannot *p* .... Jer 7:8
p which you have made .. Ezek 22:13
p is it that we have .... Mal 3:14
For what *p* is it to .... Matt 16:26
For what will it *p* .... Mark 8:36
For what *p* is it to .... Luke 9:25
her masters much *p* .... Acts 16:16
hope of *p* was gone .... Acts 16:19
brought no small *p* .... Acts 19:24
what is the *p* of .... Rom 3:1
not seeking my own *p* .... 1 Cor 10:33
Christ will *p* you .... Gal 5:2
about words to no *p* .... 2 Tim 2:14
them, but He for our *p* .... Heb 12:10
What does it *p* .... James 2:14
and sell, and make a *p* .... James 4:13

PROFITABLE
"Can a man be *p* .... Job 22:2
It is doubtless not *p* .... 2 Cor 12:1
godliness is *p* for all .... 1 Tim 4:8
of God, and is *p* .... 2 Tim 3:16
things are good and *p* .... Titus 3:8
to you, but now is *p* .... Philem 11

PROFITS
p a man nothing that .... Job 34:9
from her *p* she plants a ... Prov 31:16
the flesh *p* nothing .... John 6:63
have not love, it *p* .... 1 Cor 13:3
exercise *p* a little .... 1 Tim 4:8

PROFOUND
with things too *p* .... Ps 131:1

PROGRESS
your *p* may be evident .... 1 Tim 4:15

PROLONG
you will not *p* your .... Deut 4:26
p Your anger to all .... Ps 85:5
nor will he *p* his days ...... Eccl 8:13

PROLONGED
and his days are *p* .... Eccl 8:12

PROLONGS
The fear of the LORD *p* .... Prov 10:27

PROMISE
of all His good *p* .... 1 Kin 8:56
Has His *p* failed .... Ps 77:8
remembered His holy *p* .... Ps 105:42
Behold, I send the *P* ...... Luke 24:49
but to wait for the *P* .... Acts 1:4
p of the Holy Spirit, He ..... Acts 2:33
For the *p* is to you .... Acts 2:39
p drew near which God .... Acts 7:17
for the hope of the *p* .... Acts 26:6
is made void and the *p* ...... Rom 4:14
p might be sure .... Rom 4:16
p of God through unbelief .. Rom 4:20
For this is the word of *p* .... Rom 9:9
make the *p* of no effect ...... Gal 3:17
it is no longer of *p* .... Gal 3:18
heirs according to the *p* ..... Gal 3:29
Isaac was, are children of *p* . Gal 4:28
first commandment with *p* ... Eph 6:2
having *p* of the life that .... 1 Tim 4:8
Therefore, since a *p* .... Heb 4:1
endured, he obtained the *p* .. Heb 6:15
to the heirs of *p* .... Heb 6:17
did not receive the *p* ..... Heb 11:39
they *p* them liberty .... 2 Pet 2:19
not slack concerning His *p* .. 2 Pet 3:9
p that He has promised ... 1 John 2:25

PROMISED
bless you as He has *p* ..... Deut 1:11
that what He had *p* .... Rom 4:21
Him faithful who had *p* ... Heb 11:11

PROMISES
For all the *p* of God .... 2 Cor 1:20
his Seed were the *p* .... Gal 3:16
patience inherit the *p* .... Heb 6:12
having received the *p* ...... Heb 11:13
great and precious *p* .... 2 Pet 1:4

PROMOTE
Exalt her, and she will *p* .... Prov 4:8

PROMOTED
Then the king *p* Daniel ..... Dan 2:48
Then the king *p* Shadrach, .. Dan 3:30

PROMOTES
tongue of the wise *p* ...... Prov 12:18

PROMPTLY
him disciplines him *p* ..... Prov 13:24

PRONOUNCE
for he could not *p* it right .. Judg 12:6
P them guilty, O God .... Ps 5:10

PROOF
which is to them a *p* .... Phil 1:28

PROOFS
by many infallible *p* .... Acts 1:3

PROPER
you, but for what is *p* ..... 1 Cor 7:35
Is it *p* for a woman to .... 1 Cor 11:13
but, which is *p* .... 1 Tim 2:10
are *p* for sound doctrine .... Titus 2:1

PROPERLY
Let us walk *p* .... Rom 13:13
that you may walk *p* .... 1 Thess 4:12

PROPHECIES
Do not despise *p* .... 1 Thess 5:20

PROPHECY
if *p*, let us prophesy in ... Rom 12:6
miracles, to another *p* ... 1 Cor 12:10
I have the gift of *p* ... 1 Cor 13:2
p with the laying on of ... 1 Tim 4:14
for *p* never came by ... 2 Pet 1:21
is the spirit of *p* ... Rev 19:10
of the book of this *p* ... Rev 22:19

PROPHESIED
upon them, that they *p* ... Num 11:25
to them, yet they *p* ... Jer 23:21
Lord, have we not *p* ... Matt 7:22
prophets and the law *p* ... Matt 11:13
virgin daughters who *p* ... Acts 21:9
even more that you *p* ... 1 Cor 14:5

PROPHESIES
for the prophet who *p* ... Jer 28:9
woman who prays or *p* ... 1 Cor 11:5
p edifies the church ... 1 Cor 14:4

PROPHESY
prophets, "Do not *p* ... Is 30:10
The prophets *p* falsely ... Jer 5:31
your daughters shall *p* ... Joel 2:28
Who can but *p* ... Amos 3:8
saying, "*P* to us ... Matt 26:68
and to say to Him, "*P!*" ... Mark 14:65
your daughters shall *p* ... Acts 2:17
if prophecy, let us *p* ... Rom 12:6
know in part and we *p* ... 1 Cor 13:9
that you may *p* ... 1 Cor 14:1
For you can all *p* one ... 1 Cor 14:31
desire earnestly to *p* ... 1 Cor 14:39

PROPHESYING
he had finished *p* ... 1 Sam 10:13
Every man praying or *p*, ... 1 Cor 11:4
p is not for unbelievers ... 1 Cor 14:22

PROPHET
shall be your *p* ... Ex 7:1
raise up for you a *P* ... Deut 18:15
arisen in Israel a *p* ... Deut 34:10
"I alone am left a *p* ... 1 Kin 18:22
is no longer any *p* ... Ps 74:9
I ordained you a *p* ... Jer 1:5
p is induced to speak ... Ezek 14:9
The *p* is a fool ... Hos 9:7
nor was I a son of a *p* ... Amos 7:14
send you Elijah the *p* ... Mal 4:5
p shall receive a ... Matt 10:41
the sign of the *p* Jonah ... Matt 12:39
p is not without honor ... Matt 13:57
by Daniel the *p* ... Mark 13:14
no *p* is accepted in his ... Luke 4:24
is not a greater *p* ... Luke 7:28
it cannot be that a *p* ... Luke 13:33
Nazareth, who was a *P* ... Luke 24:19
"Are you the *P* ... John 1:21
"This is truly the *P* ... John 6:14
for no *p* has arisen out of ... John 7:52
p named Agabus ... Acts 21:10
with him the false *p* ... Rev 19:20

PROPHET'S
shall receive a *p* reward ... Matt 10:41

PROPHETESS
Then Miriam the *p*, ... Ex 15:20
Now Deborah, a *p*, ... Judg 4:4
there was one, Anna, a *p* ... Luke 2:36

PROPHETIC
by the *p* Scriptures ... Rom 16:26
p word confirmed ... 2 Pet 1:19

PROPHETS
See FALSE PROPHETS; LAW AND THE PROPHETS
LORD's people were *p* ... Num 11:29
Saul also among the *p* ... 1 Sam 10:12
the mouth of all his *p* ... 1 Kin 22:22
Where now are your *p* ... Jer 37:19
prophesy against the *p* ... Ezek 13:2
Her *p* are insolent ... Zeph 3:4
the Law or the *P* ... Matt 5:17
is the Law and the *P* ... Matt 7:12
or one of the *p* ... Matt 16:14
the tombs of the *p* ... Matt 23:29
indeed, I send you *p* ... Matt 23:34
one who kills the *p* ... Matt 23:37
Then many false *p* ... Matt 24:11
have Moses and the *p* ... Luke 16:29
You are sons of the *p* ... Acts 3:25
p did your fathers not ... Acts 7:52
To Him all the *p* ... Acts 10:43
do you believe the *p* ... Acts 26:27
before through His *p* ... Rom 1:2
by the Law and the *P* ... Rom 3:21
have killed Your *p* ... Rom 11:3
p are subject to the ... 1 Cor 14:32
to be apostles, some *p* ... Eph 4:11
brethren, take the *p* ... James 5:10
this salvation the *p* ... 1 Pet 1:10
were also false *p* ... 2 Pet 2:1
because many false *p* ... 1 John 4:1
blood of saints and *p* ... Rev 16:6
found the blood of *p* ... Rev 18:24
of your brethren the *p* ... Rev 22:9

PROPITIATION
set forth as a *p* ... Rom 3:25
to God, to make *p* ... Heb 2:17
He Himself is the *p* ... 1 John 2:2
His Son to be the *p* ... 1 John 4:10

PROPORTION
let us prophesy in *p* ... Rom 12:6

PROPOSED
And they *p* two ... Acts 1:23

PROPRIETY
modest apparel, with *p* ... 1 Tim 2:9

PROSECUTOR
answer me, that my *P* ... Job 31:35

PROSELYTE
and sea to win one *p* ... Matt 23:15
Nicolas, a *p* from Antioch, ... Acts 6:5

PROSELYTES
Rome, both Jews and *p* ... Acts 2:10

PROSPER
made all he did to *p* ... Gen 39:3
you shall not *p* ... Deut 28:29
LORD, God made him *p* ... 2 Chr 26:5
they *p* who love you ... Ps 122:6
his sins will not *p* ... Prov 28:13
of the LORD shall *p* ... Is 53:10
against you shall *p* ... Is 54:17
please, and it shall *p* ... Is 55:11
of the wicked *p* ... Jer 12:1
King shall reign and *p* ... Jer 23:5
storing up as he may *p* ... 1 Cor 16:2
I pray that you may *p* ... 3 John 2

PROSPERED
since the LORD has *p* ... Gen 24:56
he *p* wherever he went ... 2 Kin 18:7
David his father, and *p* ... 1 Chr 29:23
all his heart. So he *p* ... 2 Chr 31:21
Hezekiah *p* in all his ... 2 Chr 32:30
and they *p* through the ... Ezra 6:14
in the LORD will be *p* ... Prov 28:25
Daniel *p* in the reign ... Dan 6:28
He did all this and *p* ... Dan 8:12

PROSPERING
His ways are always *p* ... Ps 10:5

PROSPERITY
p all your days ... Deut 23:6
p exceed the fame ... 1 Kin 10:7
p the destroyer ... Job 15:21
spend their days in *p* ... Job 36:11
Now in my *p* I said ... Ps 30:6
has pleasure in the *p* ... Ps 35:27
When I saw the *p* ... Ps 73:3
I pray, send now *p* ... Ps 118:25
the day of *p* be joyful ... Eccl 7:14
that we have our *p* ... Acts 19:25

PROSPEROUS
had made his journey *p* ... Gen 24:21
will make your way *p* ... Josh 1:8

PROSPERS
he turns, he *p* ... Prov 17:8
just as your soul *p* ... 3 John 2

PROSTRATE
of the proud lie *p* ... Job 9:13

PROTECTED
holy man, and he *p* him ... Mark 6:20

PROUD
p waves must stop ... Job 38:11
tongue that speaks *p* ... Ps 12:3
and fully repays the *p* ... Ps 31:23
does not respect the *p* ... Ps 40:4
a haughty look and a *p* ... Ps 101:5
p He knows from afar ... Ps 138:6
the house of the *p* ... Prov 15:25
Everyone *p* in heart ... Prov 16:5
p heart stirs up ... Prov 28:25
is better than the *p* ... Eccl 7:8
by wine, he is a *p* ... Hab 2:5
He has scattered the *p* ... Luke 1:51
boasters, *p* ... 2 Tim 3:2
"God resists the *p*, but ... James 4:6
"God resists the *p* ... 1 Pet 5:5

PROVE
p yourself a man ... 1 Kin 2:2
does your arguing *p* ... Job 6:25
mind, that you may *p* ... Rom 12:2

PROVERB
an astonishment, a *p* ... Deut 28:37
incline my ear to a *p* ... Ps 49:4
that hang limp is a *p* ... Prov 26:7
of a drunkard is a *p* ... Prov 26:9
one shall take up a *p* ... Mic 2:4
to the true *p* ... 2 Pet 2:22

PROVERBS
spoke three thousand *p* ... 1 Kin 4:32
The *p* of Solomon the ... Prov 1:1
are *p* of Solomon ... Prov 25:1
in order many *p* ... Eccl 12:9

PROVIDE
"My son, God will *p* ... Gen 22:8
Can He *p* meat for His ... Ps 78:20
lambs will *p* your ... Prov 27:26
prosperity that I *p* ... Jer 33:9
P neither gold nor ... Matt 10:9
if anyone does not *p* ... 1 Tim 5:8

PROVIDED
I have *p* Myself a king ... 1 Sam 16:1
p for her from the king's ... Esth 2:9
p from Your godness ... Ps 68:10
atonement is *p* for iniquity . Prov 16:6
these hands have *p* ... Acts 20:34
p something better ... Heb 11:40

PROVIDES
p food for the raven ... Job 38:41
p her supplies in the ... Prov 6:8
p food for her household . Prov 31:15

PROVIDING
p honorable things, ... 2 Cor 8:21

PROVISION
bread of their *p* was dry ... Josh 9:5
Now Solomon's *p* ... 1 Kin 4:22
abundantly bless her *p* ... Ps 132:15
p of the king's delicacies ... Dan 1:5
no *p* for the flesh ... Rom 13:14

PROVOKE
do not *p* Him ... Ex 23:21
p God are secure ... Job 12:6
Do they *p* Me to ... Jer 7:19
p them to jealousy ... Rom 11:11
you, fathers, do not *p* ... Eph 6:4
do not *p* your children, lest . Col 3:21

PROVOKED
How often they *p* ... Ps 78:40

p the Most High . . . . Ps 78:56
Thus they *p* Him to . . . . Ps 106:29
his spirit was *p* . . . . Acts 17:16
seek its own, is not *p* . . . . . . 1 Cor 13:5

PROVOKING
p one another, envying one . . Gal 5:26

PROWLER
poverty come like a *p* . . . . . Prov 24:34

PRUDENCE
son, endowed with *p* . . . . . . 2 Chr 2:12
To give *p* to the . . . . Prov 1:4
wisdom, dwell with *p* . . . . . . Prov 8:12
us in all wisdom and *p* . . . . Eph 1:8

PRUDENT
p man covers shame . . . . . . Prov 12:16
A *p* man conceals . . . . Prov 12:23
The wisdom of the *p* . . . . Prov 14:8
p considers well . . . . Prov 14:15
receives correction is *p* . . . . Prov 15:5
heart will be called *p* . . . . . Prov 16:21
p acquires knowledge . . . . . . Prov 18:15
p wife is from the . . . . Prov 19:14
p man foresees evil . . . . Prov 22:3
perished from the *p* . . . . Jer 49:7
Therefore the *p* . . . . Amos 5:13
from the wise and *p* . . . . . . Matt 11:25

PRUDENTLY
Servant shall deal *p* . . . . Is 52:13

PRUNES
that bears fruit He *p* . . . . John 15:2

PSALM
and the sound of a *p* . . . . Ps 98:5
in the second *P* . . . . Acts 13:33
each of you has a *p* . . . . . . 1 Cor 14:26

PSALMIST
And the sweet *p* . . . . 2 Sam 23:1

PSALMS
Sing to Him, sing *p* . . . . 1 Chr 16:9
to one another in *p* . . . . Eph 5:19
one another in *p* . . . . Col 3:16
Let him sing *p* . . . . James 5:13

PSALTERY
harp, lyre, and *p* . . . . Dan 3:10

PTOLEMAIS
Seaport city south of Tyre; Paul lands at, Acts 21:7

PUBLIC
to make her a *p* example . . . Matt 1:19

PUBLISHED
to be proclaimed and *p* . . . . Jon 3:7

PUBLIUS
Roman official; entertains Paul, Acts 28:7, 8

PUFFED
Now some are *p* up . . . . 1 Cor 4:18
itself, is not *p* . . . . 1 Cor 13:4
a novice, lest being *p* . . . . 1 Tim 3:6

PUFFS
Knowledge *p* up . . . . 1 Cor 8:1

PUL
King of Assyria; same as Tiglath-Pileser, 2 Kin 15:19
—— Country and people in Africa, Is 66:19

PULL
P me out of the net . . . . Ps 31:4
I will *p* down my barns . . . Luke 12:18

PULLING
for *p* down strongholds . . . . 2 Cor 10:4

PUNISH
take that man and *p* . . . . Deut 22:18
p the righteous is . . . . Prov 17:26
"I will *p* the world . . . . Is 13:11
Shall I not *p* them for . . . . Jer 5:9
p all who oppress them . . . . . Jer 30:20
p your iniquity . . . . Lam 4:22
So I will *p* them for . . . . Hos 4:9

PUNISHED
You our God have *p* . . . . Ezra 9:13
because He has not *p* . . . . . . Job 35:15
p them often in every . . . . . Acts 26:11
These shall be *p* . . . . 2 Thess 1:9

PUNISHES
will you say when He *p* . . . . . Jer 13:21

PUNISHMENT
p is greater than I . . . . Gen 4:13
you do in the day of *p* . . . . Is 10:3
p they shall be cast . . . . Jer 8:12
p they shall perish . . . . Jer 10:15
a man for the *p* . . . . Lam 3:39
The *p* of the iniquity . . . . Lam 4:6
days of *p* have come . . . . Hos 9:7
not turn away its *p* . . . . Amos 1:3
into everlasting *p* . . . . Matt 25:46
p which was inflicted . . . . 2 Cor 2:6
Of how much worse *p* . . . . . . Heb 10:29
sent by him for the *p* . . . . 1 Pet 2:14
the unjust under *p* . . . . 2 Pet 2:9

PUNON
Israelite camp, Num 33:42, 43

PURCHASED
(Now this man *p* a field . . . . Acts 1:18
of God could be *p* . . . . Acts 8:20
of the *p* possession . . . . Eph 1:14

PURE
a mercy seat of *p* gold . . . . . . Ex 25:17
Can a man be more *p* . . . . Job 4:17
if you were *p* and . . . . Job 8:6
'My doctrine is *p* . . . . Job 11:4
that he could be *p* . . . . Job 15:14
the heavens are not *p* . . . . . . Job 15:15
the stars are not *p* . . . . Job 25:5
of the LORD are *p* . . . . Ps 12:6
will show Yourself *p* . . . . Ps 18:26
To such as are *p* . . . . Ps 73:1
of the *p* are pleasant . . . . . . Prov 15:26
ways of a man are *p* . . . . Prov 16:2
my heart clean, I am *p* . . . . . Prov 20:9
but as for the *p* . . . . Prov 21:8
a generation that is *p* . . . . . . Prov 30:12
Shall I count *p* . . . . Mic 6:11
Blessed are the *p* in heart . . . Matt 5:8
things indeed are *p* . . . . Rom 14:20
whatever things are *p* . . . . Phil 4:8
with a *p* conscience . . . . 1 Tim 3:9
keep yourself *p* . . . . 1 Tim 5:22
serve with a *p* conscience . . 2 Tim 1:3
p all things are *p* . . . . Titus 1:15
bodies washed with *p* . . . . . Heb 10:22
P and undefiled religion . . James 1:27
above is first *p* . . . . James 3:17
babes, desire the *p* . . . . 1 Pet 2:2
just as He is *p* . . . . 1 John 3:3

PURER
p eyes than to behold . . . . Hab 1:13

PURGE
P me with hyssop . . . . Ps 51:7
p them as gold and . . . . Mal 3:3

PURGED
away, and your sin *p* . . . . Is 6:7
He had by Himself *p* . . . . Heb 1:3

PURIFICATION
for the water of *p* . . . . Num 19:9
with the water of *p* . . . . Num 31:23

PURIFIED
earth, *p* seven times . . . . Ps 12:6
all things are *p* . . . . Heb 9:22
Since you have *p* . . . . 1 Pet 1:22

PURIFIES
hope in Him *p* himself . . . . . 1 John 3:3

PURIFY
p the sons of Levi . . . . Mal 3:3
and *p* your hearts . . . . James 4:8

PURIFYING
thus *p* all foods . . . . Mark 7:19
p their hearts by . . . . Acts 15:9
sanctifies for the *p* . . . . Heb 9:13

PURIM
called these days *P* . . . . Esth 9:26

PURITY
be delivered by the *p* . . . . Job 22:30
He who loves *p* of . . . . Prov 22:11
by *p*, by knowledge . . . . 2 Cor 6:6
spirit, in faith, in *p* . . . . 1 Tim 4:12

PURPLE
who was clothed in *p* . . . . Luke 16:19
they put on Him a *p* . . . . John 19:2
She was a seller of *p* . . . . Acts 16:14

PURPOSE
and fulfill all your *p* . . . . Ps 20:4
A time for every *p* . . . . Eccl 3:1
p that is purposed . . . . Is 14:26
But for this *p* I came . . . . . . John 12:27
by the determined *p* . . . . Acts 2:23
them all that with *p* . . . . Acts 11:23
called according to His *p* . . . Rom 8:28
to the eternal *p* . . . . Eph 3:11
sent to you for this very *p* . . . Eph 6:22
Now the *p* of the . . . . 1 Tim 1:5
manner of life, *p* . . . . 2 Tim 3:10
For this *p* the Son of God . . 1 John 3:8
to fulfill His *p* . . . . Rev 17:17

PURPOSED
For the LORD had *p* . . . . . . 2 Sam 17:14
LORD of hosts has *p* . . . . Is 23:9
But Daniel *p* in his . . . . Dan 1:8
Paul *p* in the Spirit . . . . Acts 19:21
pleasure which He *p* . . . . Eph 1:9

PURPOSELY
the bundles fall *p* for her . . . Ruth 2:16

PURPOSES
each one give as he *p* . . . . 2 Cor 9:7

PURSE
let us all have one *p* . . . . Prov 1:14

PURSES
p his lips and brings . . . . . . Prov 16:30

PURSUE
And will You *p* dry . . . . Job 13:25
p my honor as the wind . . . . Job 30:15
The sword shall *p* . . . . Jer 48:2
but their hearts *p* . . . . Ezek 33:31
Let us know, let us *p* . . . . Hos 6:3
p righteousness . . . . Rom 9:30
P love, and desire . . . . 1 Cor 14:1
p what is good . . . . 1 Thess 5:15
p righteousness . . . . 1 Tim 6:11
p righteousness, faith . . . . . 2 Tim 2:22
P peace with all people . . . . Heb 12:14
him seek peace and *p* . . . . 1 Pet 3:11

PURSUES
Evil *p* sinners . . . . Prov 13:21
flee when no one *p* . . . . Prov 28:1

PURSUING
but Israel, *p* the law . . . . Rom 9:31

PUT
Also He has *p* eternity . . . . . . Eccl 3:11
pride He is able to *p* down . . Dan 4:37
what you will *p* on . . . . Matt 6:25
p my hand into His . . . . John 20:25
But *p* on the Lord . . . . Rom 13:14

PUT OFF
I will *p* my sad face . . . . Job 9:27
You have *p* my sackcloth . . . . Ps 30:11
you *p*, concerning your . . . . Eph 4:22
you yourselves are to *p* all . . . . Col 3:8
shortly I must *p* my tent . . . . . 2 Pet 1:14

PUT ON
I *p* righteousness . . . . Job 29:14

awake, *p* strength, O arm . . . . Is 51:9
For He *p* righteousness . . . . . . Is 59:17
body, what you will *p* . . . . . . Matt 6:25
they *p* Him a purple robe . . John 19:2
p the armor of light . . . . Rom 13:12
p the Lord Jesus Christ . . . . . Rom 13:14
must *p* incorruption . . . . . . 1 Cor 15:53
into Christ have *p* Christ . . . . Gal 3:27
you *p* the new man . . . . Eph 4:24
P the whole armor of God . . Eph 6:11
having *p* the breastplate . . . . Eph 6:14
have *p* the new man . . . . Col 3:10
p tender mercies . . . . Col 3:12
all these things *p* love . . . . . Col 3:14
I will *p* you no other . . . . Rev 2:24

PUTEOLI
Seaport of Italy, Acts 28:13

PUTREFYING
bruises and *p* sores . . . . Is 1:6

QUAIL
and it brought *q* . . . . Num 11:31
and He brought *q* . . . . Ps 105:40

QUAKED
the whole mountain *q* . . . . Ex 19:18
and the earth *q* . . . . Matt 27:51

QUAKES
The earth *q* before . . . . Joel 2:10

QUALIFIED
the Father who has *q* . . . . Col 1:12

QUARREL
see how he seeks a *q* . . . . 2 Kin 5:7
any fool can start a *q* . . . . . . Prov 20:3
He will not *q* nor cry . . . . . Matt 12:19
of the Lord must not *q* . . . . . 2 Tim 2:24

QUARRELSOME
but gentle, not *q* . . . . 1 Tim 3:3

QUARTER
in the Second *Q* . . . . 2 Kin 22:14
from the Second *Q* . . . . Zeph 1:10

QUARTZ
be made of coral or *q* . . . . . . Job 28:18

QUEEN
Q Vashti also made a . . . . Esth 1:9
stands the *q* in gold . . . . Ps 45:9
burn incense to the *q* . . . . Jer 44:17
The *q* of the South . . . . Matt 12:42
under Candace the *q* . . . . Acts 8:27
heart, 'I sit as *q* . . . . Rev 18:7

QUEENS
There are sixty *q* . . . . Song 6:8
q your nursing mothers . . . . . . Is 49:23

QUENCH
Many waters cannot *q* . . . . Song 8:7
so that no one can *q* . . . . Jer 4:4
flax He will not *q* . . . . Matt 12:20
q all the fiery . . . . Eph 6:16
Do not *q* the Spirit . . . . 1 Thess 5:19

QUENCHED
LORD, the fire was *q* . . . . Num 11:2
they were *q* like a . . . . Ps 118:12
their fire is not *q* . . . . Is 66:24
that shall never be *q* . . . . Mark 9:43
and the fire is not *q* . . . . Mark 9:44
q the violence of fire . . . . . . Heb 11:34

QUESTIONS
test him with hard *q* . . . . 1 Kin 10:1
and asking them *q* . . . . Luke 2:46
market, asking no *q* . . . . . . 1 Cor 10:25

QUICK-TEMPERED
q man acts foolishly . . . . . . Prov 14:17
not self-willed, not *q* . . . . Titus 1:7

QUICKLY
have turned aside *q* . . . . Ex 32:8
with your adversary *q* . . . . . . Matt 5:25
"What you do, do *q* . . . . John 13:27
Behold, I am coming *q* . . . . . . Rev 3:11
"Surely I am coming *q* . . . . . Rev 22:20

QUIET
lain still and been *q* . . . . Job 3:13
'Take heed, and be *q* . . . . Is 7:4
earth is at rest and *q* . . . . Is 14:7
gladness, He will *q* . . . . Zeph 3:17
warned him to be *q* . . . . . . Mark 10:48
aspire to lead a *q* . . . . 1 Thess 4:11
we may lead a *q* and . . . . 1 Tim 2:2
a gentle and *q* spirit . . . . 1 Pet 3:4

QUIETED
calmed and *q* my soul . . . . Ps 131:2
the city clerk had *q* . . . . Acts 19:35

QUIETNESS
will give peace and *q* . . . . . . 1 Chr 22:9
When He gives *q* . . . . Job 34:29
a handful with *q* . . . . Eccl 4:6
in *q* and confidence . . . . Is 30:15
of righteousness, *q* . . . . Is 32:17
that they work in *q* . . . . 2 Thess 3:12

QUIETS
q the earth by the . . . . Job 37:17

QUIVER
q rattles against him . . . . Job 39:23
the man who has his *q* . . . . Ps 127:5
q He has hidden Me . . . . Is 49:2
Their *q* is like an . . . . Jer 5:16

RAAMSES
Treasure city built by Hebrew slaves, Ex 1:11

RABBAH
Capital of Ammon, Amos 1:14
Besieged by Joab; defeated and enslaved by David, 2 Sam 12:26–31
Destruction of, foretold, Jer 49:2, 3

RABBI
be called by men, '*R* . . . . Matt 23:7
do not be called '*R* . . . . Matt 23:8

RABBONI
Mary addresses Christ as, John 20:16

RABMAG
Title applied to Babylonian prince, Jer 39:3, 13

RABSARIS
Title applied to:
Assyrian officials sent by Sennacherib, 2 Kin 18:17
Babylonian prince, Jer 39:3, 13

RABSHAKEH
Sent by king of Assyria to threaten Hezekiah, 2 Kin 18:17–37; Is 36:2–22
The Lord sends rumor to take him away, 2 Kin 19:6–8; Is 37:6–8

RACA
to his brother, '*R* . . . . Matt 5:22

RACE
man to run its *r* . . . . Ps 19:5
r is not to the swift . . . . Eccl 9:11
who run in a *r* all run . . . . . 1 Cor 9:24
I have finished the *r* . . . . 2 Tim 4:7
with endurance the *r* . . . . Heb 12:1

RACHEL
Laban's younger daughter; Jacob's favorite wife, Gen 29:28–30
Supports her husband's position, Gen 31:14–16
Mother of Joseph and Benjamin, Gen 30:22–25
Prophecy concerning; quoted, Jer 31:15; Matt 2:18

RADIANT
to Him and were *r* . . . . Ps 34:5

RAGE
Disperse the *r* of your . . . . . . Job 40:11
Why do the nations *r* . . . . Ps 2:1
'Why did the nations *r* . . . . . . Acts 4:25

RAGES
he *r* against all wise . . . . Prov 18:1

RAGS
clothe a man with *r* . . . . Prov 23:21
are like filthy *r* . . . . Is 64:6

RAHAB
Prostitute in Jericho; helps Joshua's spies, Josh 2:1–21
Spared in battle, Josh 6:17–25
Mentioned in the N.T., Matt 1:5; Heb 11:31; James 2:25
——— Used figuratively of Egypt, Ps 87:4

RAIN
had not caused it to *r* . . . . Gen 2:5
And the *r* was on the . . . . Gen 7:12
I will *r* bread from heaven . . . Ex 16:4
early *r* and the latter *r* . . . . Deut 11:14
my teaching drop as the *r* . . Deut 32:2
be dew nor *r* these years . . 1 Kin 17:1
sound of abundance of *r* . . 1 Kin 18:41
He gives *r* on the . . . . Job 5:10
to the gentle *r* . . . . Job 37:6
sent a plentiful *r* . . . . Ps 68:9
clouds, who prepares *r* . . . . . . Ps 147:8
snow in summer and *r* . . . . . . Prov 26:1
r which leaves no food . . . . . Prov 28:3
not return after the *r* . . . . Eccl 12:2
the *r* is over and gone . . . . . . Song 2:11
our God, who gives *r* . . . . Jer 5:24
I will *r* down on him . . . . . . Ezek 38:22
given you the former *r* . . . . Joel 2:23
there will be no *r* . . . . Zech 14:17
the good, and sends *r* . . . . Matt 5:45
and the *r* descended . . . . Matt 7:25
He did good, gave us *r* . . . . . Acts 14:17
r that often comes . . . . Heb 6:7
the early and latter *r* . . . . James 5:7
that it would not *r* . . . . James 5:17
and the heaven gave *r* . . . . . James 5:18

RAINBOW
I set My *r* in the . . . . Gen 9:13
the appearance of a *r* . . . . Ezek 1:28
and there was a *r* . . . . Rev 4:3

RAINED
had *r* down manna on . . . . Ps 78:24
r fire and brimstone . . . . . . Luke 17:29

RAINS
r righteousness . . . . Hos 10:12

RAISE
shall *r* up the tabernacle . . . . Ex 26:30
that I will *r* to David a . . . . Jer 23:5
third day He will *r* . . . . Hos 6:2
that God is able to *r* . . . . Matt 3:9
in three days I will *r* . . . . John 2:19
and I will *r* him up at . . . . . . John 6:40
Lord and will also *r* . . . . 1 Cor 6:14
will also *r* us up with . . . . . . 2 Cor 4:14
and the Lord will *r* . . . . James 5:15

RAISED
this purpose I have *r* . . . . Ex 9:16
the LORD *r* up judges . . . . Judg 2:16
LORD has *r* up prophets . . . . . . Jer 29:15
be killed, and be *r* . . . . Matt 16:21
whom God *r* up . . . . Acts 2:24
just as Christ was *r* . . . . Rom 6:4
Spirit of Him who *r* . . . . Rom 8:11
And God both *r* up the . . . . . . 1 Cor 6:14
"How are the dead *r* . . . . . 1 Cor 15:35
and the dead will be *r* . . . . 1 Cor 15:52
and *r* us up together . . . . Eph 2:6
then you were *r* . . . . Col 3:1

RAISED FROM THE DEAD
beheaded; he has been *r* . . . Mark 6:16

whom He had *r* .... John 12:1
disciples after He was *r* ... John 21:14
Prince of life, whom God *r* . Acts 3:15
Christ was *r* by the glory .... Rom 6:4
been *r*, dies no more .... Rom 6:9
that He has been *r* .... 1 Cor 15:12
heaven, whom He *r* ..... 1 Thess 1:10
r according to my gospel ... 2 Tim 2:8

RAISED HIM FROM THE DEAD
out of his tomb and *r* ..... John 12:17
But God *r* .... Acts 13:30
your heart that God has *r* .. Rom 10:9
God the Father who *r* .... Gal 1:1
in Christ when He *r* .... Eph 1:20
the working of God, who *r* .. Col 2:12
believe in God, who *r* ...... 1 Pet 1:21

RAISES
r the poor out of the .... Ps 113:7
r those who are bowed ...... Ps 146:8
For as the Father *r* .... John 5:21
but in God who *r* .... 2 Cor 1:9

RAM
r which had two horns ...... Dan 8:3

RAMAH
Fortress built, 1 Kin 15:17–22
Samuel's headquarters, 1 Sam 7:15, 17
David flees to, 1 Sam 19:18–23

RAMOTH GILEAD
City of refuge east of Jordan, Deut 4:43; Josh 20:8; 1 Chr 6:80
Site of Ahab's fatal conflict with Syrians, 1 Kin 22:1–39

RAMPART
and it stood by the *r* ..... 2 Sam 20:15
whose *r* was like the sea, ... Nah 3:8
and set myself on the *r* ...... Hab 2:1

RAMS
the sweet aroma of *r* .... Ps 66:15
r of Nebaioth shall .... Is 60:7

RAN
they both *r* together .... John 20:4
You *r* well .... Gal 5:7

RANKS
r out of the land of Egypt ... Ex 13:18
war, who could keep *r* . 1 Chr 12:38
and they do not break *r* ...... Joel 2:7

RANSOM
r would not help you .... Job 36:18
nor give to God a *r* .... Ps 49:7
The *r* of a man's life .... Prov 13:8
"I will *r* them from .... Hos 13:14
to give His life a *r* .... Mark 10:45
who gave Himself a *r* ...... 1 Tim 2:6

RANSOMED
and the *r* of the LORD .... Is 35:10
redeemed Jacob, and *r* ...... Jer 31:11

RARE
of the LORD was *r* .... 1 Sam 3:1
make a mortal more *r* .... Is 13:12

RASH
Do not be *r* with your .... Eccl 5:2

RASHLY
so that he spoke *r* .... Ps 106:33
and do nothing *r* .... Acts 19:36

RATS
tumors and five golden *r* ... 1 Sam 6:4

RAVEN
Then he sent out a *r*, ... Gen 8:7
food for the *r* .... Job 38:41
and black as a *r* .... Song 5:11
and the *r* shall dwell in it .... Is 34:11

RAVENOUS
inwardly they are *r* .... Matt 7:15

RAVENS
and to the young *r* .... Ps 147:9
Consider the *r* .... Luke 12:24

RAVISHED
You have *r* my heart .... Song 4:9
r the women in Zion .... Lam 5:11

RAYS
He had *r* flashing from His .. Hab 3:4

RAZOR
no *r* shall come upon his .... Num 6:5
no *r* shall come upon his .. Judg 13:5
r has ever come upon .... Judg 16:17
like a sharp *r* .... Ps 52:2
will shave with a hired *r* ...... Is 7:20

REACHED
earth, and its top *r* .... Gen 28:12
For her sins have *r* .... Rev 18:5

REACHING
r forward to those .... Phil 3:13

READ
saying, "*R* this, please" ...... Is 29:11
if you can *r* the writing ..... Dan 5:16
"Have you never *r* .... Matt 21:42
day, and stood up to *r* ..... Luke 4:16
hearts, known and *r* .... 2 Cor 3:2
when Moses is *r* .... 2 Cor 3:15
when this epistle is *r* .... Col 4:16
r the scroll, or to look at ..... Rev 5:4

READER
let the *r* understand ...... Mark 13:14

READINESS
the word with all *r* .... Acts 17:11
that as there was a *r* ...... 2 Cor 8:11

READING
r the prophet Isaiah .... Acts 8:30
give attention to *r* .... 1 Tim 4:13

READS
that he may run who *r* .... Hab 2:2
Blessed is he who *r* .... Rev 1:3

READY
"The LORD was *r* .... Is 38:20
and those who were *r* ..... Matt 25:10
"Lord, I am *r* .... Luke 22:33
and being *r* to punish ..... 2 Cor 10:6
Be *r* in season and out ..... 2 Tim 4:2
and always be *r* .... 1 Pet 3:15

REAFFIRM
r your love to him .... 2 Cor 2:8

REAP
in tears shall *r* .... Ps 126:5
the clouds will not *r* .... Eccl 11:4
r the whirlwind .... Hos 8:7
r in mercy .... Hos 10:12
You shall sow, but not *r* ..... Mic 6:15
they neither sow nor *r* ..... Matt 6:26
you knew that I *r* .... Matt 25:26
if we *r* your material ...... 1 Cor 9:11
that he will also *r* .... Gal 6:7
due season we shall *r* .... Gal 6:9
in Your sickle and *r* ...... Rev 14:15

REAPED
wheat but *r* thorns .... Jer 12:13
you have *r* iniquity .... Hos 10:13
earth, and the earth was *r* .. Rev 14:16

REAPER
r does not fill his .... Ps 129:7
shall overtake the *r* .... Amos 9:13

REAPERS
I will say to the *r* .... Matt 13:30
r are the angels .... Matt 13:39

REAPING
r what I did not .... Luke 19:22

REAPS
One sows and another *r* ... John 4:37

REASON
out wisdom and the *r* .... Eccl 7:25
Come now, and let us *r* .... Is 1:18

faith, why do you *r* .... Matt 16:8
words of truth and *r* .... Acts 26:25
who asks you a *r* .... 1 Pet 3:15

REASONED
for three Sabbaths *r* .... Acts 17:2
r about righteousness ..... Acts 24:25

REBEKAH
Great-niece of Abraham, Gen 22:20–23
Becomes Isaac's wife, Gen 24:15–67
Mother of Esau and Jacob, Gen 25:21–28
Encourages Jacob to deceive Isaac, then to flee, Gen 27:1–29, 42–46

REBEL
Only do not *r* .... Num 14:9
Will you *r* against the .... Neh 2:19
There are those who *r* ..... Job 24:13
and they did not *r* .... Ps 105:28
if you refuse and *r* .... Is 1:20

REBELLED
r against You, cast Your .... Neh 9:26
for they have *r* against You ... Ps 5:10
and they have *r* against Me ..... Is 1:2
nation that has *r* against .... Ezek 2:3
have done wickedly and *r* .... Dan 9:5
For who, having heard, *r* .... Heb 3:16

REBELLING
more against Him by *r* ...... Ps 78:17

REBELLION
r is as the sin .... 1 Sam 15:23
For he adds *r* to his .... Job 34:37
evil man seeks only *r* ..... Prov 17:11
you have taught *r* .... Jer 28:16
hearts as in the *r* .... Heb 3:8
and perished in the *r* .... Jude 11

REBELLIOUS
r exalt themselves .... Ps 66:7
but the *r* dwell in a .... Ps 68:6
day long to a *r* people .... Is 65:2
a defiant and *r* heart .... Jer 5:23
their princes are *r* .... Hos 9:15

REBELS
are all stubborn *r* .... Jer 6:28

REBUILD
God, to *r* its ruins .... Ezra 9:9
tombs, that I may *r* .... Neh 2:5
they shall *r* the old ruins .... Is 61:4
r it as in the days of .... Amos 9:11
will *r* the tabernacle of .... Acts 15:16

REBUILDING
we are *r* the temple that .... Ezra 5:11
heard that we were *r* the ..... Neh 4:1

REBUILT
be *r* on its former site ...... Ezra 5:15
heard that I had *r* the wall ... Neh 6:1
and the ruins shall be *r* ... Ezek 36:33

REBUKE
He will surely *r* .... Job 13:10
astonished at His *r* .... Job 26:11
they perish at the *r* .... Ps 80:16
At Your *r* they fled .... Ps 104:7
And let him *r* me .... Ps 141:5
Turn at my *r* .... Prov 1:23
r a wise man .... Prov 9:8
R is more effective .... Prov 17:10
r is better than love .... Prov 27:5
better to hear the *r* .... Eccl 7:5
r the oppressor .... Is 1:17
sake I have suffered *r* .... Jer 15:15
r strong nations .... Mic 4:3
sins against you, *r* .... Luke 17:3
r Your disciples .... Luke 19:39
Do not *r* an older man ...... 1 Tim 5:1
who are sinning *r* .... 1 Tim 5:20
r them sharply .... Titus 1:13
"The Lord *r* you .... Jude 9
As many as I love, I *r* .... Rev 3:19

REBUKED
r the winds and the . . . . Matt 8:26
r their unbelief . . . . Mark 16:14
when you are *r* by Him . . . . Heb 12:5
but he was *r* for his . . . . 2 Pet 2:16

REBUKES
with *r* You correct . . . . Ps 39:11
r a wicked man . . . . Prov 9:7
ear that hears the *r* . . . . Prov 15:31
r a man will find more . . . . Prov 28:23

RECALL
r the former days . . . . Heb 10:32

RECEDED
waters *r* continually from . . . . Gen 8:3
Then the sky *r* as a scroll . . . Rev 6:14

RECEIVE
He shall *r* blessing . . . . Ps 24:5
r us graciously . . . . Hos 14:2
you are willing to *r* . . . . Matt 11:14
believing, you will *r* . . . . Matt 21:22
and His own did not *r* . . . . John 1:11
"I do not *r* honor . . . . John 5:41
will come again and *r* . . . . . . John 14:3
the world cannot *r* . . . . John 14:17
Ask, and you will *r* . . . . John 16:24
"*R* the Holy Spirit . . . . John 20:22
"Lord Jesus, *r* . . . . Acts 7:59
r the Holy Spirit . . . . Acts 19:2
R one who is weak . . . . Rom 14:1
that each one may *r* . . . . 2 Cor 5:10
r the grace of God in . . . . 2 Cor 6:1
r the Spirit by the . . . . Gal 3:2
R him therefore in the . . . . . . Phil 2:29
suppose that he will *r* . . . . James 1:7
whatever we ask we *r* . . . . . 1 John 3:22

RECEIVED
Freely you have *r*, freely . . . Matt 10:8
r your consolation . . . . Luke 6:24
in your lifetime you *r* . . . . . Luke 16:25
But as many as *r* . . . . John 1:12
and ankle bones *r* strength . . Acts 3:7
for God has *r* him . . . . Rom 14:3
For I *r* from the Lord . . . . . 1 Cor 11:23
I *r* forty stripes minus . . . . 2 Cor 11:24
but you *r* me as an angel . . . . Gal 4:14
have *r* Christ Jesus . . . . Col 2:6
tradition which he *r* . . . . . . 2 Thess 3:6
r up in glory . . . . 1 Tim 3:16
r the knowledge of the . . . . Heb 10:26
r strength to conceive . . . . . Heb 11:11
who had *r* the promises . . . . Heb 11:17
Women *r* their dead . . . . Heb 11:35
As each one has *r* a gift, . . . 1 Pet 4:10
For He *r* from God the . . . . . 2 Pet 1:17
r the mark of the beast . . . . Rev 19:20

RECEIVES
r correction is prudent . . . . . Prov 15:5
r you *r* Me . . . . Matt 10:40
immediately *r* it with joy . . Matt 13:20
r one little child . . . . Matt 18:5
and whoever *r* Me . . . . Mark 9:37
For everyone who asks *r* . Luke 11:10
This man *r* sinners and . . . . Luke 15:2
run, but one *r* the prize . . . . 1 Cor 9:24
who *r* tithes, paid tithes . . . . . . Heb 7:9
every son whom He *r* . . . . Heb 12:6

RECEIVING
r a kingdom which . . . . Heb 12:28

RECHAB
Assassin of Ishbosheth, 2 Sam 4:2, 6
—— Father of Jehonadab, founder of the Rechabites, 2 Kin 10:15–23
Related to the Kenites, 1 Chr 2:55

RECHABITES
Kenite clan fathered by Rechab, committed to nomadic life, Jer 35:1–19

RECOMPENSE
Vengeance is Mine, and *r* . Deut 32:35
He will accept no *r* . . . . Prov 6:35
not say, "I will *r* . . . . Prov 20:22
the LORD is the God of *r* . . . . . Jer 51:56
days of *r* have come . . . . Hos 9:7

RECOMPENSED
of my hands He has *r* . . . . 2 Sam 22:21
the LORD has *r* me . . . . 2 Sam 22:25

RECONCILE
and that He might *r* . . . . Eph 2:16
r all things to . . . . Col 1:20

RECONCILED
First be *r* to your . . . . Matt 5:24
were enemies we were *r* . . . Rom 5:10
Christ's behalf, be *r* . . . . 2 Cor 5:20

RECONCILIATION
now received the *r* . . . . Rom 5:11
to us the word of *r* . . . . 2 Cor 5:19

RECONCILING
cast away is the *r* . . . . Rom 11:15
God was in Christ *r* . . . . 2 Cor 5:19

RECORD
r My name I will come . . . . . . Ex 20:24

RECOVER
Shall I *r* from this disease . . 2 Kin 8:8
So Jeroboam did not *r* . . . 2 Chr 13:20
sick, and they will *r* . . . . Mark 16:18

RED
the first came out *r* . . . . Gen 25:25
though they are *r* . . . . Is 1:18
Why is Your apparel *r* . . . . Is 63:2
for the sky is *r* . . . . Matt 16:2
fiery *r* dragon having . . . . Rev 12:3

RED SEA
Divided for Israelites, Ex 14:15–31
Boundary of Promised Land, Ex 23:31

REDEEM
man you shall surely *r* . . . . Num 18:15
in our power to *r* them . . . . . Neh 5:5
In famine He shall *r* . . . . Job 5:20
R me from the hand of . . . . Job 6:23
can by any means *r* . . . . Ps 49:7
But God will *r* my soul . . . . Ps 49:15
r their life from . . . . Ps 72:14
And He shall *r* Israel . . . . Ps 130:8
all that it cannot *r* . . . . Is 50:2
I will *r* them from . . . . Hos 13:14
was going to *r* Israel . . . . . Luke 24:21
r those who were . . . . Gal 4:5
us, that He might *r* . . . . Titus 2:14

REDEEMED
people whom You have *r* . . . Ex 15:13
r them from the hand . . . . . . Ps 106:10
Let the *r* of the LORD . . . . Ps 107:2
r shall walk there . . . . Is 35:9
sea a road for the *r* . . . . Is 51:10
and you shall be *r* . . . . Is 52:3
and *r* His people . . . . Luke 1:68
Christ has *r* us from . . . . Gal 3:13
that you were not *r* . . . . 1 Pet 1:18
were slain, and have *r* . . . . Rev 5:9
These were *r* from . . . . Rev 14:4

REDEEMER
For I know that my *R* . . . . . . Job 19:25
Most High God their *R* . . . . . . Ps 78:35
for their *R* is mighty . . . . . . Prov 23:11
the LORD and your *R* . . . . Is 41:14
R will come to Zion . . . . Is 59:20
our *R* from Everlasting . . . . Is 63:16
Their *R* is strong . . . . Jer 50:34

REDEEMING
r the time . . . . Eph 5:16

REDEMPTION
For the *r* of their . . . . Ps 49:8
with Him is abundant *r* . . . . . Ps 130:7
r is yours to buy it . . . . Jer 32:7
those who looked for *r* . . . . . Luke 2:38
your *r* draws near . . . . Luke 21:28
grace through the *r* . . . . Rom 3:24
the adoption, the *r* . . . . Rom 8:23
sanctification and *r* . . . . 1 Cor 1:30
In Him we have *r* . . . . Eph 1:7
for the day of *r* . . . . Eph 4:30
obtained eternal *r* . . . . Heb 9:12

REED
r He will not break . . . . Is 42:3
r shaken by the wind . . . . Matt 11:7
A bruised *r* He will not . . . . Matt 12:20
on the head with a *r* . . . . Mark 15:19
sour wine, put it on a *r* . . . Mark 15:36
Then I was given a *r* like a . . Rev 11:1
the city with the *r* . . . . Rev 21:16

REEDS
r flourish without . . . . Job 8:11
the beasts of the *r* . . . . Ps 68:30

REFINED
where gold is *r* . . . . Job 28:1
us as silver is *r* . . . . Ps 66:10
Behold, I have *r* you, but . . . . . Is 48:10
refine them as silver is *r* . . . Zech 13:9
from Me gold *r* in the fire . . . . Rev 3:18

REFINER
He will sit as a *r* . . . . Mal 3:3

REFINER'S
For He is like a *r* fire . . . . Mal 3:2

REFORMATION
until the time of *r* . . . . Heb 9:10

REFRAIN
R from meddling with . . . . 2 Chr 35:21
who have no right to *r* . . . . . . 1 Cor 9:6
good days, let him *r* . . . . 1 Pet 3:10

REFRESH
bread, that you may *r* . . . . Gen 18:5
r my heart in the Lord . . . . . Philem 20

REFRESHED
of God, and may be *r* . . . . . Rom 15:32
r my spirit and yours . . . . . 1 Cor 16:18
his spirit has been *r* . . . . 2 Cor 7:13
for he often *r* . . . . 2 Tim 1:16

REFRESHES
r the soul of his . . . . Prov 25:13

REFRESHING
r may come from the . . . . Acts 3:19

REFUGE
six cities of *r* . . . . Num 35:6
eternal God is your *r* . . . . . Deut 33:27
you have come for *r* . . . . Ruth 2:12
but the LORD is his *r* . . . . Ps 14:6
God is our *r* and . . . . Ps 46:1
wings I will make my *r* . . . . Ps 57:1
God is a *r* for us . . . . Ps 62:8
You are my strong *r* . . . . Ps 71:7
His wings you shall take *r* . . . . Ps 91:4
You are my *r*, my . . . . Ps 142:5
the heat, for a place of *r* . . . . Is 4:6
a *r* from the storm, a shade . . . . Is 25:4
who have fled for *r* . . . . Heb 6:18

REFUSE
you *r* to let My people go . . . . Ex 10:4
let my head not *r* it . . . . Ps 141:5
but if you *r* and rebel, you . . . . Is 1:20
r the evil and choose . . . . Is 7:15
through deceit they *r* . . . . Jer 9:6
who *r* to hear My words, . . . Jer 13:10
hear or whether they *r* . . . . . . Ezek 2:5
r the younger widows . . . . . 1 Tim 5:11
See that you do not *r* . . . . . . Heb 12:25

REFUSED
They *r* to obey . . . . Neh 9:17
Queen Vashti *r* to come at . . Esth 1:12
my soul *r* to be comforted . . . . Ps 77:2
Inasmuch as these people *r* . . . . Is 8:6
because they *r* to repent . . . . . Hos 11:5
nothing is to be *r* if it is . . . . 1 Tim 4:4

REFUSES
My soul *r* to touch . . . . Job 6:7
he who *r* correction goes . . Prov 10:17
he who *r*, let him refuse . . . . Ezek 3:27
And if he *r* to hear . . . . Matt 18:17

REGARD
Yet *r* the prayer of Your . . . 1 Kin 8:28
r the rich more than . . . . Job 34:19
r iniquity in my heart . . . . Ps 66:18
r the prayer of the . . . . Ps 102:17
You do not *r* the person . . . Matt 22:16
did not fear God nor *r* . . . . . Luke 18:2
we *r* no one according to . . 2 Cor 5:16

REGARDED
I must be *r* as holy . . . . Lev 10:3
my hand and no one *r* . . . . . Prov 1:24
r the lowly state . . . . Luke 1:48

REGARDS
on high, yet He *r* the lowly . . Ps 138:6
r a rebuke will be . . . . Prov 13:18
He no longer *r* them . . . . Lam 4:16

REGENERATION
to you, that in the *r* . . . . . . Matt 19:28
the washing of *r* . . . . Titus 3:5

REGISTERED
So all went to be *r* . . . . Luke 2:3
firstborn who are *r* . . . . Heb 12:23

REGRETTED
but afterward he *r* . . . . Matt 21:29

REGULATIONS
yourselves to *r* . . . . Col 2:20

REHOBOAM
Son and successor of Solomon; refuses reform, 1 Kin 11:43—12:15
Ten tribes revolt against, 1 Kin 12:16–24
Reigns over Judah 17 years, 1 Kin 14:21–31; 2 Chr 11:5–23
Apostasizes, then repents, 2 Chr 12:1–16

REHOBOTH
Name of a well dug by Isaac, Gen 26:22

REIGN
The LORD shall *r* forever . . . . Ex 15:18
but a king shall *r* . . . . 1 Sam 12:12
hypocrite should not *r* . . . . . Job 34:30
so the LORD will *r* . . . . Mic 4:7
And He will *r* . . . . Luke 1:33
not have this man to *r* . . . . Luke 19:14
righteousness will *r* . . . . Rom 5:17
so grace might *r* . . . . Rom 5:21
do not let sin *r* . . . . Rom 6:12
to *r* over the Gentiles . . . . . . Rom 15:12
For He must *r* till He . . . . . 1 Cor 15:25
and we shall *r* on the . . . . Rev 5:10
and He shall *r* forever . . . . . Rev 11:15
of Christ, and shall *r* . . . . Rev 20:6

REIGNED
death *r* from Adam to . . . . . . Rom 5:14
so that as sin *r* . . . . Rom 5:21
You have *r* as kings . . . . 1 Cor 4:8
And they lived and *r* . . . . Rev 20:4

REIGNS
God *r* over the nations . . . . Ps 47:8
The LORD *r* . . . . Ps 93:1
to Zion, "Your God *r* . . . . Is 52:7
Lord God Omnipotent *r* . . . . . Rev 19:6

REJECT
will these people *r* . . . . Num 14:11
r all those who stray . . . . . Ps 119:118
"All too well you *r* . . . . Mark 7:9
R a divisive man . . . . Titus 3:10

REJECTED
r has become the chief . . . . . Ps 118:22
He is despised and *r* . . . . Is 53:3
Israel has *r* the . . . . Hos 8:3
r has become the chief . . . . Matt 21:42
many things and be *r* . . . . . . Luke 17:25
This Moses whom they *r* . . . Acts 7:35
to a living stone, *r* . . . . 1 Pet 2:4
r has become the chief . . . . 1 Pet 2:7

REJECTION
you shall know My *r* . . . . . Num 14:34

REJECTS
he who *r* Me *r* . . . . Luke 10:16
r this does not reject . . . . . 1 Thess 4:8

REJOICE
See BE GLAD AND REJOICE
so the LORD will *r* . . . . Deut 28:63
let the field *r* . . . . 1 Chr 16:32
and let Your saints *r* . . . . . . 2 Chr 6:41
r who put their trust . . . . Ps 5:11
people, let Jacob *r* . . . . Ps 14:7
R in the LORD . . . . Ps 33:1
mutual confusion who *r* . . . . . Ps 35:26
The righteous shall *r* . . . . Ps 58:10
of Your wings I will *r* . . . . Ps 63:7
But the king shall *r* . . . . Ps 63:11
Let them *r* before God . . . . Ps 68:3
In Your name they *r* . . . . Ps 89:16
Let the heavens *r* . . . . Ps 96:11
Let the earth *r* . . . . Ps 97:1
righteous see it and *r* . . . . Ps 107:42
we will *r* and be glad . . . . Ps 118:24
who *r* in doing evil . . . . Prov 2:14
be blessed, and *r* . . . . Prov 5:18
she shall *r* in time to . . . . . . Prov 31:25
R, O young man . . . . Eccl 11:9
We will be glad and *r* . . . . Song 1:4
among men shall *r* . . . . Is 29:19
I will greatly *r* . . . . Is 61:10
My servants shall *r* . . . . Is 65:13
your heart shall *r* . . . . Is 66:14
Yes, I will *r* . . . . Jer 32:41
Do not *r* over me . . . . Mic 7:8
He will *r* over you . . . . Zeph 3:17
do not *r* in this . . . . Luke 10:20
loved Me, you would *r* . . . . John 14:28
but the world will *r* . . . . John 16:20
and your heart will *r* . . . . . John 16:22
R with those who . . . . Rom 12:15
and in this I *r* . . . . Phil 1:18
faith, I am glad and *r* . . . . Phil 2:17
R in the Lord always . . . . Phil 4:4
R always . . . . 1 Thess 5:16
yet believing, you *r* . . . . 1 Pet 1:8

REJOICE IN THE LORD
R, O you righteous . . . . Ps 33:1
R, you righteous . . . . Ps 97:12
you shall *r*, and glory in . . . . . Is 41:16
I will greatly *r* . . . . Is 61:10
you children of Zion and *r* . . . Joel 2:23
Yet I will *r*, I will joy . . . . Hab 3:18
their heart shall *r* . . . . Zech 10:7
Finally, my brethren, *r* . . . . Phil 3:1
R always. Again I will say . . . Phil 4:4

REJOICED
for good as He *r* . . . . Deut 30:9
for my heart *r* . . . . Eccl 2:10
and my spirit has *r* . . . . Luke 1:47
In that hour Jesus *r* . . . . . . Luke 10:21
Your father Abraham *r* . . . . John 8:56
But I *r* in the Lord . . . . Phil 4:10

REJOICES
My heart *r* in the LORD . . . . 1 Sam 2:1
glad, and my glory *r* . . . . Ps 16:9
bridegroom *r* over the bride . . . Is 62:5
r more over that sheep . . . . Matt 18:13
but *r* in the truth . . . . 1 Cor 13:6

REJOICING
His works with *r* . . . . Ps 107:22
The voice of *r* and . . . . Ps 118:15
for they are the *r* . . . . Ps 119:111
come again with *r* . . . . Ps 126:6
r in His inhabited . . . . Prov 8:31
he went on his way *r* . . . . Acts 8:39
yet always *r* . . . . 2 Cor 6:10
or joy, or crown of *r* . . . . . 1 Thess 2:19
confidence and the *r* . . . . Heb 3:6

RELATIVES
r stand afar off . . . . Ps 38:11

RELEASE
shall grant a *r* of debts . . . . . Deut 15:1
time in the year of *r*, at . . . Deut 31:10
do you want me to *r* . . . . Matt 27:17
and power to *r* You . . . . John 19:10
"*R* the four angels . . . . Rev 9:14

RELEASED
r him, and forgave him . . . Matt 18:27
he *r* Barabbas to them . . . . Matt 27:26
she is *r* from the law of . . . . . Rom 7:2
Satan will be *r* from his . . . . . Rev 20:7

RELEASING
of strife is like *r* water . . . . Prov 17:14
to *r* one prisoner to them . . Mark 15:6

RELENT
sworn and will not *r* . . . . Ps 110:4
and will not *r* . . . . Jer 4:28
then the LORD will *r* . . . . Jer 26:13
if He will turn and *r* . . . . Joel 2:14
sworn and will not *r* . . . . Heb 7:21

RELENTED
So the LORD *r* from the . . . . . . Ex 32:14
the LORD looked and *r* . . . . 1 Chr 21:15
and God *r* from the . . . . Jon 3:10

RELENTING
I am weary of *r* . . . . Jer 15:6

RELIEF
saw that there was *r* . . . . Ex 8:15
that I may find *r* . . . . Job 32:20

RELIEVE
of my lips would *r* . . . . Job 16:5
r those who are really . . . . . 1 Tim 5:16

RELIEVED
You have *r* me when I . . . . Ps 4:1

RELIEVES
r the fatherless . . . . Ps 146:9

RELIGION
about their own *r* . . . . Acts 25:19
in self-imposed *r* . . . . Col 2:23
heart, this one's *r* . . . . James 1:26
and undefiled *r* . . . . James 1:27

RELIGIOUS
things you are very *r* . . . . . . Acts 17:22
you thinks he is *r* . . . . James 1:26

RELY
name of the LORD and *r* . . . . . . Is 50:10
You *r* on your sword . . . . . Ezek 33:26

REMAIN
shall let none of it *r* . . . . Ex 12:10
r angry forever . . . . Jer 3:5
and this city shall *r* . . . . Jer 17:25
that if ten men *r* . . . . Amos 6:9
you, that My joy may *r* . . . John 15:11
your fruit should *r* . . . . John 15:16
"If I will that he *r* . . . . John 21:22
the greater part *r* . . . . 1 Cor 15:6
Nevertheless to *r* . . . . Phil 1:24
we who are alive and *r* . . 1 Thess 4:15
the things which *r* . . . . Rev 3:2

REMAINDER
with the *r* of wrath . . . . Ps 76:10
I am deprived of the *r* . . . . Is 38:10

REMAINED
Also my wisdom *r* . . . . Eccl 2:9
And Mary *r* with her . . . . . . Luke 1:56
like a dove, and He *r* . . . . . . John 1:32

REMAINS
"While the earth *r* . . . . Gen 8:22
Therefore your sin *r* . . . . John 9:41

There *r* therefore a ... Heb 4:9
sin, for His seed *r* ... 1 John 3:9

REMEMBER

But *r* me when it is ... Gen 40:14
R the Sabbath day ... Ex 20:8
r that you were a ... Deut 15:15
R His marvelous works .. 1 Chr 16:12
but we will *r* the name ... Ps 20:7
r the sins of my youth ... Ps 25:7
r Your name in the ... Ps 119:55
R now your Creator ... Eccl 12:1
r your love more than ... Song 1:4
r the former things ... Is 43:18
"I *r* you, the kindness ... Jer 2:2
and their sin I will *r* ... Jer 31:34
r the covenant of ... Amos 1:9
in wrath *r* mercy ... Hab 3:2
or *r* the five loaves of the ... Matt 16:9
and to *r* His holy ... Luke 1:72
R Lot's wife ... Luke 17:32
r me when You come ... Luke 23:42
r the words of the ... Acts 20:35
that we should *r* the poor ... Gal 2:10
R my chains ... Col 4:18
R that Jesus Christ ... 2 Tim 2:8
deeds I will *r* no more ... Heb 8:12
R those who rule ... Heb 13:7
R therefore from where you .. Rev 2:5

REMEMBERED

Then God *r* Noah ... Gen 8:1
r His covenant with ... Ex 2:24
I *r* God, and was ... Ps 77:3
r Your judgments ... Ps 119:52
Who *r* us in our lowly ... Ps 136:23
yea, we wept when we *r* ... Ps 137:1
r that same poor man ... Eccl 9:15
r the days of old ... Is 63:11
And Peter *r* the word ... Matt 26:75
r the word of the Lord ... Acts 11:16

REMEMBERS

r His covenant forever ... Ps 105:8
My soul still *r* ... Lam 3:20

REMEMBRANCE

in death there is no *r* ... Ps 6:5
I call to *r* my song ... Ps 77:6
There is no *r* of ... Eccl 1:11
Put Me in *r* ... Is 43:26
do this in *r* of Me ... Luke 22:19
do this in *r* of Me ... 1 Cor 11:24

REMIND

r you always of these ... 2 Pet 1:12
But I want to *r* you ... Jude 5

REMINDER

there is a *r* of sins ... Heb 10:3
you always have a *r* ... 2 Pet 1:15
pure minds by way of *r* ... 2 Pet 3:1

REMISSION

repentance for the *r* ... Mark 1:4
Jesus Christ for the *r* ... Acts 2:38
where there is *r* ... Heb 10:18

REMNANT

Jerusalem shall go a *r* ... 2 Kin 19:31
r of you who have ... 2 Chr 30:6
would be no *r* or survivor .. Ezra 9:14
to us a very small *r* ... Is 1:9
The *r* will return ... Is 10:21
be well with your *r* ... Jer 15:11
I will gather the *r* ... Jer 23:3
and all the *r* of Judah ... Jer 44:28
Yet I will leave a *r* ... Ezek 6:8
r whom the LORD calls ... Joel 2:32
I will not treat the *r* ... Zech 8:11
time there is a *r* ... Rom 11:5

REMORSEFUL

been condemned, was *r* ... Matt 27:3

REMOVE

I will also *r* Judah from .. 2 Kin 23:27
R Your plague from me ... Ps 39:10
R Your gaze from me ... Ps 39:13
r your foot from evil ... Prov 4:27
r falsehood and lies ... Prov 30:8
Therefore *r* sorrow ... Eccl 11:10
R violence and ... Ezek 45:9
I will *r* the iniquity of that ... Zech 3:9
let me *r* the speck that ... Luke 6:42
r your lampstand ... Rev 2:5

REMOVED

Though the earth be *r* ... Ps 46:2
r our transgressions ... Ps 103:12
will never be *r* ... Prov 10:30
and the hills be *r* ... Is 54:10
this mountain, 'Be *r* ... Matt 21:21

REMOVES

r the mountains ... Job 9:5

REND

So *r* your heart ... Joel 2:13

RENDER

What shall I *r* to the ... Ps 116:12
who will *r* to him the ... Matt 21:41
"*R* therefore to Caesar ... Matt 22:21
r to each one according ... Rom 2:6
R to her just as she ... Rev 18:6

RENDERS

See that no one *r* evil ... 1 Thess 5:15

RENEW

r a steadfast spirit ... Ps 51:10
r the face of the ... Ps 104:30
on the LORD shall *r* ... Is 40:31

RENEWED

that your youth is *r* ... Ps 103:5
inward man is being *r* ... 2 Cor 4:16
and be *r* in the spirit ... Eph 4:23
the new man who is *r* ... Col 3:10

RENEWING

transformed by the *r* ... Rom 12:2
of regeneration and *r* ... Titus 3:5

RENOUNCE

Why do the wicked *r* ... Ps 10:13

RENOUNCED

r the covenant of Your ... Ps 89:39
r the hidden things ... 2 Cor 4:2

RENOUNCES

greedy and *r* the LORD ... Ps 10:3

RENOWN

were of old, men of *r* ... Gen 6:4

RENTED

years in his own *r* house .. Acts 28:30

REPAID

done, so God has *r* ... Judg 1:7
And he has *r* me evil ... 1 Sam 25:21
good shall be *r* ... Prov 13:21
Shall evil be *r* ... Jer 18:20

REPAIR

r the house of your ... 2 Chr 24:5
r the ruined cities ... Is 61:4

REPAY

He will *r* him to his ... Deut 7:10
silence, but will *r* ... Is 65:6
He will surely *r* ... Jer 51:56
again, I will *r* ... Luke 10:35
because they cannot *r* ... Luke 14:14
R no one evil for evil ... Rom 12:17
is Mine, I will *r* ... Rom 12:19
r their parents ... 1 Tim 5:4
I will *r* ... Philem 19

REPAYS

and who *r* him for what ... Job 21:31
r the proud person ... Ps 31:23
shall he be who *r* ... Ps 137:8
the LORD, who fully *r* ... Is 66:6

REPEATS

r a matter separates ... Prov 17:9

REPENT

of man, that He should *r* .. Num 23:19
I abhor myself, and *r* ... Job 42:6
R now everyone of his evil ... Jer 25:5
R, turn away from your ... Ezek 14:6
because they refused to *r* ... Hos 11:5
"*R*, for the kingdom ... Matt 3:2
R, and believe in the ... Mark 1:15
you *r* you will all ... Luke 13:3
said to them, "*R* ... Acts 2:38
R therefore and be ... Acts 3:19
men everywhere to *r* ... Acts 17:30
and do the first works, or ... Rev 2:5
be zealous and *r* ... Rev 3:19

REPENTANCE

bear fruits worthy of *r*, ... Matt 3:8
you with water unto *r* ... Matt 3:11
a baptism of *r* for the ... Mark 1:4
but sinners, to *r* ... Mark 2:17
persons who need no *r* ... Luke 15:7
to the Gentiles *r* to life ... Acts 11:18
of God leads you to *r* ... Rom 2:4
sorrow produces *r* ... 2 Cor 7:10
will grant them *r* ... 2 Tim 2:25
of *r* from dead works and ... Heb 6:1
renew them again to *r* ... Heb 6:6
found no place for *r* ... Heb 12:17
all should come to *r* ... 2 Pet 3:9

REPENTED

No man *r* of his ... Jer 8:6
after my turning, I *r* ... Jer 31:19
it, because they *r* ... Matt 12:41

REPETITIONS

r as the heathen do ... Matt 6:7

REPHAIM

Valley near Jerusalem, 2 Sam 23:13, 14
Scene of Philistine defeats, 2 Sam 5:18–22

REPHIDIM

Israelite camp, Num 33:12–15
Moses strikes rock at, Ex 17:1–7
Amalek defeated at, Ex 17:8–16

REPORT

circulate a false *r* ... Ex 23:1
For it is not a good *r* ... 1 Sam 2:24
r makes the bones ... Prov 15:30
Who has believed our *r* ... Is 53:1
who has believed our *r* ... Rom 10:16
things are of good *r* ... Phil 4:8

REPRIMANDED

And they *r* him sharply ... Judg 8:1

REPROACH

has taken away my *r* ... Gen 30:23
away the *r* of Egypt from ... Josh 5:9
and bring *r* on all Israel .. 1 Sam 11:2
we may no longer be a *r* ... Neh 2:17
r me as long as I live ... Job 27:6
does he take up a *r* ... Ps 15:3
You make us a *r* ... Ps 44:13
sake I have borne *r* ... Ps 69:7
R has broken my heart ... Ps 69:20
Remove from me *r* and ... Ps 119:22
nation, but sin is a *r* ... Prov 14:34
with dishonor comes *r* ... Prov 18:3
do not fear the *r* ... Is 51:7
not remember the *r* ... Is 54:4
bring an everlasting *r* ... Jer 23:40
because I bore the *r* ... Jer 31:19
become a desolation, a *r* ... Jer 49:13
you shall bear the *r* ... Mic 6:16
to take away my *r* among .. Luke 1:25
these things You *r* ... Luke 11:45
lest he fall into *r* ... 1 Tim 3:7
esteeming the *r* ... Heb 11:26
the camp, bearing His *r* ... Heb 13:13
and without *r* ... James 1:5

REPROACHED

of those who *r* You fell ... Rom 15:3
If you are *r* for the ... 1 Pet 4:14

REPROACHES

is not an enemy who *r* ... Ps 55:12

oppresses the poor *r* . . . . Prov 14:31
curse, and Israel to *r* . . . . Is 43:28
in infirmities, in *r* . . . . 2 Cor 12:10

REPROACHFULLY
they strike me *r* . . . . Job 16:10

REPROOF
for doctrine, for *r* . . . . 2 Tim 3:16

REPROOFS
R of instruction are . . . . Prov 6:23

REPUTATION
seven men of good *r* . . . . Acts 6:3
to those who were of *r* . . . . Gal 2:2
made Himself of no *r* . . . . Phil 2:7

REQUEST
not withheld the *r* . . . . Ps 21:2
He gave them their *r* . . . . Ps 106:15
the Lord God to make *r* . . . . Dan 9:3
For Jews *r* a sign . . . . 1 Cor 1:22
of mine making *r* . . . . Phil 1:4

REQUESTS
r be made known . . . . Phil 4:6

REQUIRE
the LORD your God *r* . . . . Deut 10:12
a foreigner you may *r* . . . . Deut 15:3
"You will not *r* . . . . Ps 10:13
offering You did not *r* . . . . Ps 40:6
what does the LORD *r* . . . . Mic 6:8

REQUIRED
of the world may be *r* . . . . Luke 11:50
your soul will be *r* . . . . Luke 12:20
him much will be *r* . . . . Luke 12:48
Moreover it is *r* . . . . 1 Cor 4:2

REQUIREMENTS
keeps the righteous *r* . . . . Rom 2:26
r that was against us . . . . Col 2:14

RESCUE
R me from their . . . . Ps 35:17
and no one shall *r* . . . . Hos 5:14

RESERVE
r the unjust under . . . . 2 Pet 2:9

RESERVED
Have you not *r* a blessing . . Gen 27:36
I have *r* seven thousand . . 1 Kin 19:18
which I have *r* for the . . . . Job 38:23
"I have *r* for Myself . . . . Rom 11:4
r in heaven for you . . . . 1 Pet 1:4
of darkness, to be *r* . . . . 2 Pet 2:4
habitation, He has *r* . . . . Jude 6

RESERVES
He *r* wrath for His enemies . . Nah 1:2

RESIDUE
The *r* of My people . . . . Zeph 2:9

RESIST
r an evil person . . . . Matt 5:39
not able to *r* the wisdom . . . . Acts 6:10
r the Holy Spirit . . . . Acts 7:51
these also *r* the truth . . . . 2 Tim 3:8
R the devil and he . . . . James 4:7
R him, steadfast in the . . . . 1 Pet 5:9

RESISTED
For who has *r* His will . . . . Rom 9:19
Jannes and Jambres *r* . . . . 2 Tim 3:8
for he has greatly *r* . . . . 2 Tim 4:15
You have not yet *r* . . . . Heb 12:4

RESISTS
"God *r* the proud . . . . James 4:6
for "God *r* the proud . . . . 1 Pet 5:5

RESOLVED
I have *r* what to do . . . . Luke 16:4

RESORT
to which I may *r* . . . . Ps 71:3

RESOUND
my heart shall *r* . . . . Is 16:11

RESPECT
Have *r* to the covenant . . . . Ps 74:20
his eyes will have *r* . . . . Is 17:7
saying, 'They will *r* . . . . Matt 21:37
of the law held in *r* . . . . Acts 5:34
and we paid them *r* . . . . Heb 12:9

RESPECTED
And the LORD *r* Abel . . . . Gen 4:4
little folly to one *r* . . . . Eccl 10:1

RESPONSE
in whose mouth is no *r* . . . . Ps 38:14

REST
is the Sabbath of *r* . . . . Ex 31:15
you shall find no *r* . . . . Deut 28:65
to build a house of *r* . . . . 1 Chr 28:2
I would have been at *r* . . . . Job 3:13
the weary are at *r* . . . . Job 3:17
My flesh also will *r* in hope . . . . Ps 16:9
R in the LORD . . . . Ps 37:7
fly away and be at *r* . . . . Ps 55:6
of the LORD shall *r* . . . . Is 11:2
whole earth is at *r* . . . . Is 14:7
"This is the *r* . . . . Is 28:12
sake I will not *r* . . . . Is 62:1
is the place of My *r* . . . . Is 66:1
then you will find *r* . . . . Jer 6:16
and I will give you *r* . . . . Matt 11:28
and you will find *r* . . . . Matt 11:29
you who are troubled *r* . . . . 2 Thess 1:7
shall not enter My *r* . . . . Heb 3:11
remains therefore a *r* . . . . Heb 4:9
to enter that *r* . . . . Heb 4:11
And they do not *r* . . . . Rev 4:8
that they should *r* . . . . Rev 6:11
"that they may *r* . . . . Rev 14:13
But the *r* of the dead . . . . Rev 20:5

RESTED
He had done, and He *r* . . . . Gen 2:2
glory of the LORD *r* . . . . Ex 24:16
when the Spirit *r* . . . . Num 11:25
"And God *r* on the . . . . Heb 4:4

RESTING
the dove found no *r* place . . . . Gen 8:9
foot have a *r* place . . . . Deut 28:65
do not plunder his *r* . . . . Prov 24:15
r place shall be . . . . Is 11:10
all the earth is *r* . . . . Zech 1:11
still sleeping and *r* . . . . Matt 26:45

RESTLESS
I am *r* in my complaint . . . . Ps 55:2

RESTORATION
until the times of *r* . . . . Acts 3:21

RESTORE
R to me the joy . . . . Ps 51:12
I still must *r* . . . . Ps 69:4
r your judges as . . . . Is 1:26
r them to this place . . . . Jer 27:22
For I will *r* health to . . . . Jer 30:17
"So I will *r* to you . . . . Joel 2:25
declare that I will *r* . . . . Zech 9:12
and will *r* all things . . . . Matt 17:11
I *r* fourfold . . . . Luke 19:8
You at this time *r* . . . . Acts 1:6
who are spiritual *r* . . . . Gal 6:1

RESTORED
it was *r* like his other flesh . . . . Ex 4:7
whose son he had *r* to life . . 2 Kin 8:1
LORD *r* Job's losses when . . . Job 42:10
hand was *r* as whole as . . . . Mark 3:5
that I may be *r* to you the . . Heb 13:19

RESTORER
may he be to you a *r* . . . . Ruth 4:15

RESTORES
with joy, for He *r* . . . . Job 33:26
He *r* my soul . . . . Ps 23:3

RESTRAIN
now *r* Your hand . . . . 2 Sam 24:16
Therefore I will not *r* . . . . Job 7:11
Will You *r* Yourself . . . . Is 64:12
no one can *r* His hand . . . . Dan 4:35

RESTRAINED
r my feet from every . . . . Ps 119:101
Are they *r* . . . . Is 63:15

RESTRAINS
For nothing *r* the LORD . . . . 1 Sam 14:6
r his lips is wise . . . . Prov 10:19
only He who now *r* . . . . 2 Thess 2:7

RESTRAINT
they have cast off *r* . . . . Job 30:11
they break all *r* . . . . Hos 4:2

RESTS
r quietly in the heart . . . . Prov 14:33

RESURRECTION
who say there is no *r* . . . . Matt 22:23
Therefore, in the *r* . . . . Matt 22:28
of the graves after His *r* . . . . Matt 27:53
Therefore, in the *r* . . . . Mark 12:23
repaid at the *r* of the . . . . Luke 14:14
being sons of the *r* . . . . Luke 20:36
done good, to the *r* . . . . John 5:29
to her, "I am the *r* . . . . John 11:25
a witness with us of His *r* . . Acts 1:22
them Jesus and the *r* . . . . Acts 17:18
heard of the *r* of the . . . . Acts 17:32
that there will be a *r* . . . . Acts 24:15
the likeness of His *r* . . . . Rom 6:5
say that there is no *r* . . . . 1 Cor 15:12
and the power of His *r* . . . . Phil 3:10
that the *r* is already . . . . 2 Tim 2:18
obtain a better *r* . . . . Heb 11:35
the *r* of Jesus Christ . . . . 1 Pet 3:21
This is the first *r* . . . . Rev 20:5

RETAIN
happy are all who *r* . . . . Prov 3:18
spirit to *r* the spirit . . . . Eccl 8:8
r the sins of any . . . . John 20:23
like to *r* God in their . . . . Rom 1:28

RETURN
So the LORD will *r* . . . . 1 Kin 2:32
and *r* to our neighbors . . . . Ps 79:12
R, O LORD . . . . Ps 90:13
none who go to her *r* . . . . Prov 2:19
womb, naked shall he *r* . . . . Eccl 5:15
the clouds do not *r* . . . . Eccl 12:2
let him *r* to the LORD . . . . Is 55:7
it shall not *r* to Me . . . . Is 55:11
"If you will *r* . . . . Jer 4:1
for they shall *r* . . . . Jer 24:7
me, and I will *r* . . . . Jer 31:18
say, 'I will go and *r* . . . . Hos 2:7
help of your God, *r* . . . . Hos 12:6
"*R* to Me," says the LORD . . . . Zech 1:3
R to Me, and I will *r* to . . . . Mal 3:7
he says, 'I will *r* . . . . Matt 12:44
if not, it will *r* to you . . . . Luke 10:6
reviled, did not revile in *r* . . 1 Pet 2:23

RETURNED
and they *r* and sought . . . . Ps 78:34
yet you have not *r* . . . . Amos 4:6
astray, but have now *r* . . . . 1 Pet 2:25

RETURNING
"I am *r* to Jerusalem . . . . Zech 1:16
r evil for evil or . . . . 1 Pet 3:9

RETURNS
spirit departs, he *r* . . . . Ps 146:4
As a dog *r* to his own . . . . Prov 26:11
"A dog *r* to his own . . . . 2 Pet 2:22

REUBEN
Jacob's eldest son, Gen 29:31, 32
Lies with Bilhah; loses preeminence, Gen 35:22; 49:3, 4
Plots to save Joseph, Gen 37:21–30
Offers sons as pledge for Benjamin, Gen 42:37
—— Tribe of:
Numbered, Num 1:20, 21; 26:5–11
Settle east of Jordan, Num 32:1–42

Join in war against Canaanites, Josh 1:12–18
Erect memorial altar, Josh 22:10–34

REVEAL
The heavens will *r* .... Job 20:27
I will heal them and *r* .... Jer 33:6
the Son wills to *r* Him .... Matt 11:27
r His Son in me .... Gal 1:16
otherwise, God will *r* ...... Phil 3:15

REVEALED
things which are *r* .... Deut 29:29
of the LORD shall be *r* .... Is 40:5
righteousness to be *r* .... Is 56:1
Then the secret was *r* .... Dan 2:19
blood has not *r* this to .... Matt 16:17
which will not be *r* .... Mark 4:22
covered that will not be *r* .. Luke 12:2
the Son of Man is *r* .... Luke 17:30
the wrath of God is *r* .... Rom 1:18
glory which shall be *r* ...... Rom 8:18
But God has *r* them to ..... 1 Cor 2:10
secrets of his heart are *r* . 1 Cor 14:25
as it has now been *r* .... Eph 3:5
but now has been *r* .... Col 1:26
the Lord Jesus is *r* .... 2 Thess 1:7
lawless one will be *r* ..... 2 Thess 2:8
ready to be *r* in the .... 1 Pet 1:5
when His glory is *r* .... 1 Pet 4:13
r what we shall be .... 1 John 3:2

REVEALER
Lord of kings, and a *r* ...... Dan 2:47

REVEALING
waits for the *r* .... Rom 8:19

REVEALS
as a talebearer *r* .... Prov 20:19
r deep and secret .... Dan 2:22
r secrets has made .... Dan 2:29
r His secret to His .... Amos 3:7

REVELATION
was no widespread *r* ...... 1 Sam 3:1
Where there is no *r* .... Prov 29:18
to bring *r* to the Gentiles ... Luke 2:32
the day of wrath and *r* .... Rom 2:5
eagerly waiting for the *r* .... 1 Cor 1:7
has a tongue, has a *r* ..... 1 Cor 14:26
it came through the *r* .... Gal 1:12
And I went up by *r*, and ...... Gal 2:2
spirit of wisdom and *r* ...... Eph 1:17
r He made known to .... Eph 3:3
and glory at the *r* .... 1 Pet 1:7
The *R* of Jesus Christ .... Rev 1:1

REVELATIONS
come to visions and *r* ..... 2 Cor 12:1

REVELRIES
drunkenness, *r* .... Gal 5:21
lusts, drunkenness, *r* .... 1 Pet 4:3

REVENGE
and we will take our *r* ...... Jer 20:10

REVENUES
than vast *r* without .... Prov 16:8

REVERENCE
and *r* My sanctuary .... Lev 19:30
and to be held in *r* .... Ps 89:7
Master, where is My *r* .... Mal 1:6
submission with all *r* .... 1 Tim 3:4
God acceptably with *r* ..... Heb 12:28

REVERENT
man who is always *r* ...... Prov 28:14
their wives must be *r* ..... 1 Tim 3:11
older men be sober, *r* .... Titus 2:2

REVILE
are you when they *r* .... Matt 5:11
r God's high priest .... Acts 23:4
evildoers, those who *r* ..... 1 Pet 3:16

REVILED
crucified with Him *r* ..... Mark 15:32
who, when He was *r* .... 1 Pet 2:23

REVILER
or an idolater, or a *r* .... 1 Cor 5:11

REVILERS
nor drunkards, nor *r* ...... 1 Cor 6:10

REVILING
come envy, strife, *r* .... 1 Tim 6:4

REVIVAL
give us a measure of *r* .... Ezra 9:8

REVIVE
troubles, shall *r* .... Ps 71:20
Will You not *r* us .... Ps 85:6
r me according to Your .... Ps 119:25
r the spirit of the .... Is 57:15
two days He will *r* .... Hos 6:2
r Your work in the .... Hab 3:2

REVIVED
they shall be *r* .... Hos 14:7
came, sin *r* and I died .... Rom 7:9

REVOLT
You will *r* more and .... Is 1:5

REVOLTED
Israel have deeply *r* .... Is 31:6
they have *r* and .... Jer 5:23

REVOLTERS
r are deeply involved .... Hos 5:2

REWARD
exceedingly great *r* .... Gen 15:1
them there is great *r* .... Ps 19:11
r me evil for good .... Ps 35:12
"Surely there is a *r* .... Ps 58:11
look, and see the *r* .... Ps 91:8
will a sure *r* .... Prov 11:18
and the LORD will *r* .... Prov 25:22
and this was my *r* .... Eccl 2:10
behold, His *r* is with .... Is 40:10
r them for their deeds .... Hos 4:9
for great is your *r* .... Matt 5:12
you have no *r* from .... Matt 6:1
you, they have their *r* .... Matt 6:2
receive a prophet's *r* ...... Matt 10:41
by no means lose his *r* .... Matt 10:42
r will be great .... Luke 6:35
we receive the due *r* ...... Luke 23:41
will receive his own *r* .... 1 Cor 3:8
cheat you of your *r* .... Col 2:18
for he looked to the *r* .... Heb 11:26
may receive a full *r* .... 2 John 8
quickly, and My *r* .... Rev 22:12

REWARDED
Thus they have *r* .... Ps 109:5

REWARDER
and that He is a *r* .... Heb 11:6

REWARDS
Whoever *r* evil for .... Prov 17:13
and follows after *r* .... Is 1:23
and give your *r* .... Dan 5:17

REZIN
King of Damascus; joins Pekah against Ahaz, 2 Kin 15:37
Confederacy of, inspires Isaiah's great messianic prophecy, Is 7:1—9:12

REZON
Son of Eliadah; establishes Syrian kingdom, 1 Kin 11:23–25

RHEGIUM
City in Italy where Paul visits, Acts 28:13

RHODA
Servant girl, Acts 12:13–16

RHODES
Island off coast of Asia Minor which Paul passes, Acts 21:1

RIBLAH
Headquarters of:
Pharaoh Necho, 2 Kin 23:31–35
Nebuchadnezzar, 2 Kin 25:6, 20, 21
Zedekiah blinded here, Jer 39:5–7

RICH
Abram was very *r* .... Gen 13:2
makes poor and makes *r* ... 1 Sam 2:7
r man will lie down .... Job 27:19
the *r* among the people ...... Ps 45:12
when one becomes *r* .... Ps 49:16
soul will be made *r* .... Prov 11:25
who makes himself *r* .... Prov 13:7
r has many friends .... Prov 14:20
The *r* and the poor .... Prov 22:2
r rules over the poor .... Prov 22:7
r man is wise in his .... Prov 28:11
do not curse the *r* .... Eccl 10:20
it is hard for a *r* .... Matt 19:23
to you who are *r* .... Luke 6:24
from the *r* man's table .... Luke 16:21
for he was very *r* .... Luke 18:23
Lord over all is *r* .... Rom 10:12
You are already *r* .... 1 Cor 4:8
though He was *r* .... 2 Cor 8:9
who desire to be *r* .... 1 Tim 6:9
but the *r* in his .... James 1:10
So the *r* man also will ..... James 1:11
of this world to be *r* .... James 2:5
you say, 'I am *r* .... Rev 3:17

RICHES
Both *r* and honor come ... 1 Chr 29:12
He swallows down *r* .... Job 20:15
he heaps up *r* .... Ps 39:6
the abundance of his *r* ..... Ps 52:7
if *r* increase .... Ps 62:10
r will be in his house .... Ps 112:3
in her left hand *r* .... Prov 3:16
R and honor are .... Prov 8:18
R do not profit .... Prov 11:4
in his *r* will fall .... Prov 11:28
yet has great *r* .... Prov 13:7
of the wise is their *r* ...... Prov 14:24
Houses and *r* are an ...... Prov 19:14
of the LORD are *r* .... Prov 22:4
r are not forever .... Prov 27:24
r kept for their owner ...... Eccl 5:13
darkness and hidden *r* .... Is 45:3
you shall eat the *r* .... Is 61:6
so is he who gets *r* .... Jer 17:11
have increased your *r* ...... Ezek 28:5
for those who have *r* ... Mark 10:23
do you despise the *r* .... Rom 2:4
might make known the *r* ... Rom 9:23
what are the *r* .... Eph 1:18
show the exceeding *r* .... Eph 2:7
the unsearchable *r* .... Eph 3:8
trust in uncertain *r* .... 1 Tim 6:17
r than the treasures .... Heb 11:26
r are corrupted .... James 5:2
to receive power and *r* ...... Rev 5:12

RICHLY
Christ dwell in you *r* .... Col 3:16
God, who gives us *r* .... 1 Tim 6:17

RIDDLE
"Let me pose a *r* .... Judg 14:12

RIDDLES
the wise and their *r* .... Prov 1:6

RIDE
wind and cause me to *r* .... Job 30:22
in Your majesty *r* .... Ps 45:4
have caused men to *r* .... Ps 66:12

RIDER
r He has thrown .... Ex 15:1
the horse and its *r* .... Job 39:18

RIDES
Behold, the LORD *r* .... Is 19:1

RIDGES
You water its *r* .... Ps 65:10

RIDICULE
those who see Me *r* Me .... Ps 22:7
Whom do you *r* .... Is 57:4

RINGS
a man with gold *r* . . . . James 2:2

RIPE
figs that are first *r* . . . . Jer 24:2

RISE
is vain for you to *r* . . . . Ps 127:2
"Now I will *r* . . . . Is 33:10
for He makes His sun *r* . . . . Matt 5:45
of Nineveh will *r* . . . . Matt 12:41
third day He will *r* . . . . Matt 20:19
false prophets will *r* . . . . . . Matt 24:24
persuaded though one *r* . . Luke 16:31
third day He will *r* . . . . Luke 18:33
had to suffer and *r* . . . . Acts 17:3
be the first to *r* . . . . Acts 26:23
fact the dead do not *r* . . . . 1 Cor 15:15
in Christ will *r* . . . . 1 Thess 4:16

RISEN
of the LORD is *r* . . . . Is 60:1
women there has not *r* . . . . Matt 11:11
disciples that He is *r* . . . . . . Matt 28:7
"The Lord is *r* . . . . Luke 24:34
furthermore is also *r* . . . . Rom 8:34
then Christ is not *r* . . . . 1 Cor 15:13
if Christ is not *r* . . . . 1 Cor 15:17
But now Christ is *r* . . . . 1 Cor 15:20

RISES
shall I do when God *r* . . . . . . Job 31:14
every tongue which *r* . . . . Is 54:17

RISING
may know from the *r* . . . . Is 45:6
questioning what the *r* . . . . Mark 9:10
for the fall and *r* . . . . Luke 2:34

RIVER
Indeed the *r* may rage . . . . . . Job 40:23
them drink from the *r* . . . . Ps 36:8
r whose streams shall . . . . Ps 46:4
the *r* of God is full . . . . Ps 65:9
went through the *r* . . . . Ps 66:6
peace to her like a *r* . . . . Is 66:12
in the Jordan *R* . . . . Mark 1:5
he showed me a pure *r* . . . . . Rev 22:1

RIVERS
He turns *r* into a . . . . Ps 107:33
R of water run down . . . . . . Ps 119:136
By the *r* of Babylon . . . . Ps 137:1
All the *r* run into the . . . . Eccl 1:7
us a place of broad *r* . . . . Is 33:21
the wilderness and *r* . . . . Is 43:19
the sea, I make the *r* . . . . Is 50:2
his heart will flow *r* . . . . John 7:38

RIZPAH
Saul's concubine taken by Abner, 2 Sam 3:6–8
Sons of, killed, 2 Sam 21:8, 9
Grief-stricken, cares for corpses, 2 Sam 21:10–14

ROAD
I will even make a *r* . . . . Is 43:19
depths of the sea a *r* . . . . Is 51:10
seen the Lord on the *r* . . . . Acts 9:27

ROAR
Let the sea *r* . . . . 1 Chr 16:32
though its waters *r* . . . . Ps 46:3
The young lions *r* . . . . Ps 104:21
'The LORD will *r* . . . . Jer 25:30
He will *r* like a lion . . . . Hos 11:10
The LORD also will *r* . . . . Joel 3:16
Will a lion *r* in the . . . . Amos 3:4

ROARING
wrath is like the *r* . . . . Prov 19:12
Like a *r* lion and a . . . . Prov 28:15
and the waves *r* . . . . Luke 21:25
walks about like a *r* . . . . 1 Pet 5:8

ROARS
their voice *r* like the . . . . Jer 6:23
"The LORD *r* from . . . . Amos 1:2
as when a lion *r* . . . . Rev 10:3

ROB
r the poor because he . . . . . . Prov 22:22
r the needy of justice . . . . Is 10:2
"Will a man *r* God . . . . Mal 3:8
do you *r* temples . . . . Rom 2:22

ROBBED
r their treasuries . . . . Is 10:13
But this is a people *r* . . . . Is 42:22
Yet you have *r* Me . . . . Mal 3:8
r other churches . . . . 2 Cor 11:8

ROBBER
a son who is a *r* . . . . Ezek 18:10
is a thief and a *r* . . . . John 10:1
Barabbas was a *r* . . . . John 18:40

ROBBERS
and Israel to the *r* . . . . Is 42:24
also crucified two *r* . . . . Mark 15:27
Me are thieves and *r* . . . . John 10:8
here who are neither *r* . . . . Acts 19:37
waters, in perils of *r* . . . . . . 2 Cor 11:26

ROBBERY
nor vainly hope in *r* . . . . Ps 62:10
I hate *r* for burnt . . . . Is 61:8
did not consider it *r* . . . . Phil 2:6

ROBE
r of the ephod, the ephod . . . . . Ex 29:5
off a corner of Saul's *r* . . . . 1 Sam 24:4
her *r* of many colors . . . . . 2 Sam 13:19
with a *r* of fine linen, ... 1 Chr 15:27
let a royal *r* be brought . . . . . . Esth 6:8
justice was like a *r* . . . . Job 29:14
instead of a rich *r* . . . . Is 3:24
covered me with the *r* . . . . Is 61:10
His *r* became white and . . . . Luke 9:29
'Bring out the best *r* . . . . Luke 15:22
on Him a purple *r* . . . . John 19:2
Then a white *r* was . . . . Rev 6:11
with a *r* dipped in blood, ... Rev 19:13

ROBES
to the King in *r* . . . . Ps 45:14
have stained all My *r* . . . . Is 63:3
clothe you with rich *r* . . . . Zech 3:4
go around in long *r* . . . . Luke 20:46
clothed with white *r* . . . . Rev 7:9

ROCK
you shall strike the *r* . . . . Ex 17:6
put you in the cleft of the *r* . . Ex 33:22
and struck the *r* . . . . Num 20:11
R who begot you . . . . Deut 32:18
For their *r* is not . . . . Deut 32:31
and fire rose out of the *r* . . . Judg 6:21
nor is there any *r* . . . . 1 Sam 2:2
"The LORD is my *r* . . . . 2 Sam 22:2
And who is a *r* . . . . 2 Sam 22:32
Blessed be my *R* . . . . 2 Sam 22:47
away, and as a *r* . . . . Job 14:18
set me high upon a *r* . . . . Ps 27:5
For You are my *r* . . . . Ps 31:3
r that is higher than . . . . Ps 61:2
and my God the *r* . . . . Ps 94:22
who turned the *r* . . . . Ps 114:8
been mindful of the *R* . . . . Is 17:10
shadow of a great *r* . . . . Is 32:2
look to the *r* from which . . . . Is 51:1
that breaks the *r* in pieces . . Jer 23:29
dwell in the clefts of the *r* . . . . Obad 3
his house on the *r* . . . . Matt 7:24
r I will build My . . . . Matt 16:18
Some fell on *r* . . . . Luke 8:6
stumbling stone and *r* . . . . Rom 9:33
R that followed them . . . . . . 1 Cor 10:4
and a *r* of offense . . . . 1 Pet 2:8

ROCKS
and the *r* were split . . . . Matt 27:51
to the mountains and *r* . . . . Rev 6:16

ROD
And Moses took the *r* . . . . Ex 4:20
man threw down his *r* . . . . Ex 7:12
passes under the *r* . . . . Lev 27:32
the rock twice with his *r* . . Num 20:11
chasten him with the *r* . . . . 2 Sam 7:14
break them with a *r* of iron . . . . Ps 2:9
Your *r* and Your staff . . . . Ps 23:4
The *r* and rebuke give . . . . Prov 29:15
shall come forth a *R* . . . . Is 11:1
you pass under the *r* . . . . . . Ezek 20:37
measuring *r* six cubits . . . . . . Ezek 40:5
I come to you with a *r* . . . . . 1 Cor 4:21
Aaron's *r* that budded, ... Heb 9:4
rule them with a *r* . . . . Rev 2:27
rule them with a *r* of iron . . Rev 19:15

ROLL
ruinous storm they *r* . . . . Job 30:14
r away the stone . . . . Mark 16:3

ROLLED
the heavens shall be *r* . . . . Is 34:4
the stone had been *r* . . . . Mark 16:4

ROMAN
Tell me, are you a *R* . . . . . . Acts 22:27
learned that he was a *R* . . . Acts 23:27

ROME
Jews expelled from, Acts 18:2
Paul:
writes to Christians of, Rom 1:7
desires to go to, Acts 19:21
comes to, Acts 28:14
imprisoned in, Acts 28:16

ROOF
the *r* he saw a woman . . . . . 2 Sam 11:2
stuck the the *r* of their . . . . . Job 29:10
cling to the *r* of my mouth . . . Ps 137:6
uncovered the *r* where He . . Mark 2:4

ROOM
See UPPER ROOM
You prepared *r* for it . . . . Ps 80:9
until no more *r* . . . . Zech 10:10
you a large upper *r* . . . . Mark 14:15
no *r* for them in the . . . . Luke 2:7
still there is *r* . . . . Luke 14:22
into the upper *r* . . . . Acts 1:13

ROOMS
make *r* in the ark . . . . Gen 6:14
He is in the inner *r* . . . . Matt 24:26

ROOSTER
him, "Before the *r* . . . . Matt 26:75

ROOT
r bearing bitterness . . . . Deut 29:18
the foolish taking *r* . . . . Job 5:3
r may grow old in the . . . . Job 14:8
day there shall be a *R* . . . . Is 11:10
shall again take *r* . . . . Is 37:31
because they had no *r* . . . . . . Matt 13:6
and if the *r* is holy . . . . Rom 11:16
of money is a *r* . . . . 1 Tim 6:10
lest any *r* of . . . . Heb 12:15
I am the *R* and the . . . . Rev 22:16

ROOTED
that you, being *r* . . . . Eph 3:17
r and built up in Him . . . . Col 2:7

ROOTS
because its *r* reached . . . . . . Ezek 31:7
and lengthen his *r* . . . . Hos 14:5
dried up from the *r* . . . . Mark 11:20
pulled up by the *r* . . . . Jude 12

ROSE
I am the *r* of Sharon . . . . Song 2:1
and blossom as the *r* . . . . Is 35:1
end Christ died and *r* . . . . Rom 14:9
buried, and that He *r* . . . . 1 Cor 15:4
that Jesus died and *r* . . . . . 1 Thess 4:14

ROTTENNESS
is like *r* in his bones . . . . Prov 12:4

ROUGH
and the *r* places smooth . . . . Is 40:4
and the *r* ways smooth . . . . . Luke 3:5

ROUGHLY
answered the people *r* .... 1 Kin 12:13

ROYAL
dwell in the *r* city with .... 1 Sam 27:5
son was over the *r* house .. 2 Kin 15:5
and a *r* house for himself .... 2 Chr 2:1
destroyed all the *r* heirs .. 2 Chr 22:10
so he set the *r* crown .... Esth 2:17
a *r* diadem in the hand of .... Is 62:3
to establish a *r* statute and ... Dan 6:7
the *r* law according to the .. James 2:8
r priesthood, a holy nation .. 1 Pet 2:9

RUBBISH
things, and count them as *r* .. Phil 3:8

RUBIES
of wisdom is above *r* .... Job 28:18
more precious than *r* .... Prov 3:15
is better than *r* .... Prov 8:11
worth is far above *r* .... Prov 31:10
your pinnacles of *r* .... Is 54:12
ruddy in body than *r* .... Lam 4:7

RUDDY
Now he was *r* .... 1 Sam 16:12
beloved is white and *r* ..... Song 5:10

RUIN
r those two can bring ..... Prov 24:22
flattering mouth works *r* .. Prov 26:28
have made a city a *r* .... Is 25:2
I will *r* the pride of Judah .... Jer 13:9
will not be your *r* .... Ezek 18:30
And the *r* of that .... Luke 6:49
to no profit, to the *r* .... 2 Tim 2:14

RUINED
shall be utterly *r* .... Is 60:12
the mighty trees are *r* ...... Zech 11:2
wineskins will be *r* .... Luke 5:37

RUINS
rebuild the old *r* .... Is 61:4
of My house that is in *r*, ... Hag 1:9
I will rebuild its *r*, and I ... Acts 15:16

RULE
greater light to *r* the day .... Gen 1:16
and he shall *r* .... Gen 3:16
r the raging of the .... Ps 89:9
R in the midst of Your ...... Ps 110:2
A wise servant will *r* .... Prov 17:2
Whoever has no *r* over .... Prov 25:28
Yet he will *r* over all .... Eccl 2:19
sit and *r* on His throne ...... Zech 6:13
puts an end to all *r* .... 1 Cor 15:24
us walk by the same *r* ...... Phil 3:16
let the peace of God *r* .... Col 3:15
Let the elders who *r* ...... 1 Tim 5:17
Remember those who *r* ..... Heb 13:7
He shall *r* them with a rod .. Rev 2:27
He Himself will *r* them ..... Rev 19:15

RULER
the sheep, to be *r* .... 2 Sam 7:8
down to eat with a *r* .... Prov 23:1
bear is a wicked *r* .... Prov 28:15
r pays attention .... Prov 29:12
to Me the One to be *r* .... Mic 5:2
by Beelzebub, the *r* .... Matt 12:24
I will make you *r* .... Matt 25:21
the *r* of this world .... John 12:31
because the *r* of this ...... John 16:11
'Who made you a *r* .... Acts 7:27
speak evil of a *r* .... Acts 23:5

RULER OF THE SYNAGOGUE
He said to the *r* .... Mark 5:36
Jairus, and he was a *r* ..... Luke 8:41
r answered with .... Luke 13:14
r, believed on the Lord ...... Acts 18:8
took Sosthenes, the *r* ..... Acts 18:17

RULERS
and the *r* take counsel .... Ps 2:2
r decree justice .... Prov 8:15
"You know that the *r* ..... Matt 20:25
Have any of the *r* .... John 7:48
r are not a terror .... Rom 13:3
which none of the *r* .... 1 Cor 2:8
powers, against the *r* .... Eph 6:12
to be subject to *r* .... Titus 3:1

RULES
'He who *r* over men ...... 2 Sam 23:3
them know that God *r* .... Ps 59:13
He *r* by His power .... Ps 66:7
r his spirit than he .... Prov 16:32
that the Most High *r* .... Dan 4:17
that the Most High *r* .... Dan 4:32
r his own house well .... 1 Tim 3:4
according to the *r* .... 2 Tim 2:5

RULING
r their children .... 1 Tim 3:12

RUMOR
r will be upon *r* .... Ezek 7:26

RUMORS
hear of wars and *r* .... Matt 24:6
you hear of wars and *r* .... Mark 13:7

RUN
I will *r* the course of .... Ps 119:32
r and not be weary .... Is 40:31
many shall *r* to and .... Dan 12:4
Therefore I *r* thus .... 1 Cor 9:26
I might *r*, or had *r* .... Gal 2:2
that I have not *r* .... Phil 2:16
us, and let us *r* .... Heb 12:1
that you do not *r* .... 1 Pet 4:4

RUNNER
are swifter than a *r* .... Job 9:25
r will run to meet .... Jer 51:31

RUNS
word *r* very swiftly .... Ps 147:15
nor of him who *r* .... Rom 9:16

RUSH
The nations will *r* .... Is 17:13

RUSHING
like the *r* of the seas .... Is 17:12
as of a *r* mighty wind, and ... Acts 2:2

RUST
r destroy and where .... Matt 6:19

RUTH
Moabitess, Ruth 1:4
Follows Naomi, Ruth 1:6–18
Marries Boaz, Ruth 4:9–13
Ancestress of Christ, Ruth 4:13, 21, 22

SABAOTH
S had left us a .... Rom 9:29
ears of the Lord of *S* ...... James 5:4

SABBATH
'Tomorrow is a *S* .... Ex 16:23
"Remember the *S* .... Ex 20:8
You shall keep the *S* .... Ex 31:14
a *S* of rest to the LORD .... Ex 35:2
day is a *S* of solemn rest .... Lev 23:3
shall keep a *s* to the LORD ... Lev 25:2
'Observe the *S* day, to ...... Deut 5:12
bear no burden on the *S* .... Jer 17:21
the grainfields on the *S* .... Matt 12:1
S was made for man ...... Mark 2:27
is also Lord of the *S* .... Mark 2:28
"Is it lawful on the *S* to do . Mark 3:4
Is it lawful on the *S* to do ... Luke 6:9
It is the *S*; it is not lawful .. John 5:10
not only broke the *S* .... John 5:18
circumcise a man on the *S* . John 7:22
the synagogues every *S* ... Acts 15:21

SABBATHS
S you shall keep .... Ex 31:13
You shall keep My *S* .... Lev 26:2
The New Moons, the *S* .... Is 1:13
also gave them My *S* ..... Ezek 20:12
for three *S* reasoned with ... Acts 17:2
festival or a new moon or *s* .. Col 2:16

SACKCLOTH
I have sewn *s* over my ..... Job 16:15
You have put off my *s* .... Ps 30:11
and remove the *s* .... Is 20:2
with fasting, *s*, and ashes .... Dan 9:3
a fast, and put on *s* .... Jon 3:5
repented long ago in *s* .... Matt 11:21

SACRED
have a *s* assembly .... Num 29:35
iniquity and the *s* .... Is 1:13
call a *s* assembly .... Joel 1:14

SACRIFICE
I *s* to the LORD all males .... Ex 13:15
is a burnt *s* of the herd .... Lev 1:3
is a *s* of peace offering .... Lev 3:1
the law of the *s* of peace .... Lev 7:11
a *s* of a peace offering to ... Num 6:17
you shall *s* the Passover ... Deut 16:2
s to the LORD of hosts ..... 1 Sam 1:3
do you kick at My *s* ...... 1 Sam 2:29
to *s* to the LORD your .... 1 Sam 15:15
S and offering You did .... Ps 40:6
offer to You the *s* .... Ps 116:17
to the LORD than *s* .... Prov 21:3
The *s* of the wicked is .... Prov 21:27
than to give the *s* of fools .... Eccl 5:1
in that day, and will make *s* .. Is 19:21
For the LORD has a *s* .... Is 34:6
who will bring the *s* .... Jer 33:11
I desire mercy and not *s* ..... Hos 6:6
of My offerings they *s* ...... Hos 8:13
But I will *s* to You .... Jon 2:9
LORD has prepared a *s* ...... Zeph 1:7
offer the blind as a *s* .... Mal 1:8
desire mercy and not *s* ..... Matt 9:13
'I desire mercy and not *s* ... Matt 12:7
s will be seasoned .... Mark 9:49
your bodies a living *s* .... Rom 12:1
an offering and a *s* .... Eph 5:2
aroma, an acceptable *s* ...... Phil 4:18
put away sin by the *s* .... Heb 9:26
He had offered one *s* ...... Heb 10:12
no longer remains a *s* ..... Heb 10:26
God a more excellent *s* ..... Heb 11:4
offer the *s* of praise .... Heb 13:15

SACRIFICED
s their sons and their ...... Ps 106:37
They *s* to the Baals .... Hos 11:2
our Passover, was *s* for us .. 1 Cor 5:7
to eat things *s* .... Rev 2:14

SACRIFICES
He who *s* to any god .... Ex 22:20
burnt offerings, your *s* ..... Deut 12:6
The *s* of God are a .... Ps 51:17
the *s* of thanksgiving .... Ps 107:22
multitude of your *s* .... Is 1:11
Bring no more futile *s* .... Is 1:13
he who *s* a lamb .... Is 66:3
acceptable, nor your *s* .... Jer 6:20
bringing *s* of praise to the .. Jer 17:26
by him the daily *s* .... Dan 8:11
burnt offerings and *s* ..... Mark 12:33
priests, to offer up *s* .... Heb 7:27
with better *s* than these ..... Heb 9:23
s for sin you had no .... Heb 10:6
s God is well pleased ...... Heb 13:16
offer up spiritual *s* .... 1 Pet 2:5

SAD
"Why is your face *s* .... Neh 2:2
s countenance the .... Eccl 7:3
whom I have not made *s* .. Ezek 13:22
as you walk and are *s* .... Luke 24:17

SADDUCEES
Rejected by John, Matt 3:7
Test Jesus, Matt 16:1–12

Silenced by Jesus, Matt 22:23–34
Disturbed by teaching of resurrection, Acts 4:1, 2
Oppose apostles, Acts 5:17–40

SAFE
and I shall be *s* .... Ps 119:117
in the LORD shall be *s* ..... Prov 29:25
he has received him *s* ...... Luke 15:27

SAFELY
And He led them on *s* .... Ps 78:53
make them lie down *s* .... Hos 2:18

SAFETY
sons are far from *s* .... Job 5:4
take your rest in *s* .... Job 11:18
will set him in the *s* .... Ps 12:5
the needy will lie down in *s* .. Is 14:30
say, "Peace and *s* .... 1 Thess 5:3

SAFETY'S
by you for *s* sake .... Prov 3:29

SAINTS
See ALL THE SAINTS
ten thousands of *s* .... Deut 33:2
the feet of His *s* .... 1 Sam 2:9
puts no trust in His *s* .... Job 15:15
s who are on the earth .... Ps 16:3
does not forsake His *s* .... Ps 37:28
"Gather My *s* .... Ps 50:5
the souls of His *s* .... Ps 97:10
is the death of His *s* .... Ps 116:15
the way of His *s* .... Prov 2:8
war against the *s* .... Dan 7:21
shall persecute the *s* .... Dan 7:25
Jesus, called to be *s* .... 1 Cor 1:2
the least of all the *s* .... Eph 3:8
Christ with all His *s* ...... 1 Thess 3:13
be glorified in His *s* ...... 2 Thess 1:10
all delivered to the *s* .... Jude 3
ways, O King of the *s* .... Rev 15:3
shed the blood of *s* .... Rev 16:6
the camp of the *s* .... Rev 20:9

SAKE
My servant Abraham's *s* ... Gen 26:24
has blessed me for your *s* .. Gen 30:27
the Egyptians for Israel's *s* .... Ex 18:8
for His great name's *s* .... 1 Sam 12:22
kindness for Jonathan's *s* .. 2 Sam 9:1
for the *s* of your father .... 1 Kin 11:12
the *s* of Your great name .. 2 Chr 6:32
save me for Your mercies' *s* .... Ps 6:4
For His name's *s* .... Ps 23:3
Your name's *s*, O LORD .... Ps 25:11
for Your name's *s* .... Ps 31:3
sins, for Your name's *s* .... Ps 79:9
for His name's *s* .... Ps 106:8
me for Your name's *s* ...... Ps 109:21
LORD, for Your name's *s* .... Ps 143:11
for Your *s* I have .... Jer 15:15
for righteousness' *s* .... Matt 5:10
you falsely for My *s* .... Matt 5:11
and kings for My *s* .... Matt 10:18
by all for My name's *s* ...... Matt 10:22
life for My *s* will find it ..... Matt 10:39
life for My *s* will find it ..... Matt 16:25
kingdom of heaven's *s* ...... Matt 19:12
lands, for My name's *s* ...... Matt 19:29
nations for My name's *s* ...... Matt 24:9
elect's *s* those days will .... Matt 24:22
loses his life for My *s* ...... Mark 8:35
rulers and kings for My *s* .. Mark 13:9
men for My name's *s* .... Mark 13:13
but for the elect's *s* .... Mark 13:20
life for My *s* will save it .... Luke 9:24
s of the kingdom of .... Luke 18:29
rulers for My name's *s* ..... Luke 21:12
by all for My name's *s* ..... Luke 21:17
my life for Your *s* .... John 13:37
down your life for My *s* ... John 13:38
to you for My name's *s* .... John 15:21
suffer for My name's *s* .... Acts 9:16
are fools for Christ's *s* ...... 1 Cor 4:10
I do for the gospel's *s* .... 1 Cor 9:23
s of him who had done ...... 2 Cor 7:12
for your stomach's *s* .... 1 Tim 5:23
suffer for righteousness' *s* .. 1 Pet 3:14
for His name's *s* .... 1 John 2:12
labored for My name's *s* .... Rev 2:3

SAKES
for their *s* I sanctify .... John 17:19
your *s* He became poor .... 2 Cor 8:9

SALAMIS
Paul preaches here, Acts 13:4, 5

SALEM
Jerusalem's original name, Gen 14:18
Used poetically, Ps 76:2

SALIM
Place near Aenon, John 3:23

SALOME
One of the ministering women, Mark 15:40, 41
Visits empty tomb, Mark 16:1
—— Herodias' daughter (not named in the Bible), Matt 14:6–11

SALT
she became a pillar of *s* .... Gen 19:26
shall season with *s* .... Lev 2:13
covenant of *s* forever .... Num 18:19
city and sowed it with *s* ...... Judg 9:45
s nor wrapped in .... Ezek 16:4
"You are the *s* .... Matt 5:13
s loses its flavor .... Mark 9:50
with grace, seasoned with *s* ..... Col 4:6

SALT SEA
O.T. name for the Dead Sea, Gen 14:3; Num 34:3, 12

SALVATION
still, and see the *s* .... Ex 14:13
the Rock of my *s* .... 2 Sam 22:47
For this is all my *s* .... 2 Sam 23:5
the good news of His *s* .... 1 Chr 16:23
S belongs to the LORD .... Ps 3:8
I will rejoice in Your *s* .... Ps 9:14
shield and the horn of my *s* .... Ps 18:2
We will rejoice in your *s* .... Ps 20:5
You are the God of my *s* .... Ps 25:5
is my light and my *s* .... Ps 27:1
to me the joy of Your *s* .... Ps 51:12
From Him comes my *s* .... Ps 62:1
on earth, Your *s* .... Ps 67:2
God is the God of *s* .... Ps 68:20
and Your *s* all the day .... Ps 71:15
Restore us, O God of our *s* ...... Ps 85:4
Surely His *s* is near .... Ps 85:9
and He has become my *s* ...... Ps 118:14
S is far from the .... Ps 119:155
LORD, I hope for Your *s* ...... Ps 119:166
forgotten the God of your *s* ...... Is 17:10
God will appoint *s* .... Is 26:1
with an everlasting *s* .... Is 45:17
for My *s* is about to .... Is 56:1
call your walls *S* .... Is 60:18
s as a lamp that burns .... Is 62:1
LORD our God is the *s* .... Jer 3:23
joy in the God of my *s* .... Hab 3:18
is just and having *s* .... Zech 9:9
raised up a horn of *s* .... Luke 1:69
eyes have seen Your *s* .... Luke 2:30
to him, "Today *s* .... Luke 19:9
what we worship, for *s* .... John 4:22
Nor is there *s* in any .... Acts 4:12
you should be for *s* .... Acts 13:47
the power of God to *s* .... Rom 1:16
is made unto *s* .... Rom 10:10
s has come to the .... Rom 11:11
s is nearer than .... Rom 13:11
now is the day of *s* .... 2 Cor 6:2
And take the helmet of *s* .... Eph 6:17
work out your own *s* .... Phil 2:12
wrath, but to obtain *s* .... 1 Thess 5:9
chose you for *s* .... 2 Thess 2:13
also may obtain the *s* .... 2 Tim 2:10
of God that brings *s* .... Titus 2:11
neglect so great a *s* .... Heb 2:3
s perfect through .... Heb 2:10
s the prophets have .... 1 Pet 1:10
"*S* belongs to our God .... Rev 7:10
S and glory and honor .... Rev 19:1

SAMARIA
Capital of Israel, 1 Kin 16:24–29
Besieged by Ben-Hadad, 1 Kin 20:1–21
Besieged again; miraculously delivered, 2 Kin 6:24—7:20
Inhabitants deported by Assyria; repopulated with foreigners, 2 Kin 17:5, 6, 24–41
—— District of Palestine in Christ's time, Luke 17:11–19
Disciples forbidden to preach in, Matt 10:5
Gospel preached there after the ascension, Acts 1:8; 9:31; 15:3

SAMARITAN
But a certain *S* .... Luke 10:33
a drink from me, a *S* .... John 4:9

SAMARITANS
People of mixed heredity, 2 Kin 17:24–41
Christ preaches to, John 4:5–42
Story of "the good Samaritan," Luke 10:30–37
Converts among, Acts 8:5–25

SAMOS
Paul visits, Acts 20:15

SAMSON
Birth predicted and accomplished, Judg 13:2–25
Marries Philistine; avenges betrayal, Judg 14
Defeats Philistines singlehandedly, Judg 15
Betrayed by Delilah; loses strength, Judg 16:4–22
Destroys many in his death, Judg 16:23–31

SAMUEL
Born in answer to prayer; dedicated to God, 1 Sam 1:1–28
Receives revelation; recognized as prophet, 1 Sam 3:1–21
Judges Israel, 1 Sam 7:15–17
Warns Israel against a king, 1 Sam 8:10–18
Anoints Saul, 1 Sam 9:15—10:1
Rebukes Saul, 1 Sam 15:10–35
Anoints David, 1 Sam 16:1–13
Death of, 1 Sam 25:1

SANBALLAT
Influential Samaritan; attempts to thwart Nehemiah's plans, Neh 2:10; 4:7, 8; 6:1–14

SANCTIFICATION
righteousness and *s* .... 1 Cor 1:30
will of God, your *s* .... 1 Thess 4:3
salvation through *s* .... 2 Thess 2:13

SANCTIFIED
s it, because in it He rested .. Gen 2:3
s the people, and they .... Ex 19:14
I *s* to Myself all the .... Num 3:13
s this house, that My .... 2 Chr 7:16
I have commanded My *s* .... Is 13:3
you were born I *s* .... Jer 1:5
Him whom the Father *s* .... John 10:36
they also may be *s* .... John 17:19
might be acceptable, *s* ...... Rom 15:16
to those who are *s* .... 1 Cor 1:2
washed, but you were *s* ...... 1 Cor 6:11
husband is *s* by the .... 1 Cor 7:14
for it is *s* by the .... 1 Tim 4:5
those who are being *s* .... Heb 2:11

will we have been *s* ... Heb 10:10
who are called, *s* ... Jude 1

SANCTIFIES
or the temple that *s* ... Matt 23:17
For both He who *s* ... Heb 2:11

SANCTIFY
"*S* yourselves ... Josh 3:5
would send and *s* them ... Job 1:5
s My great name ... Ezek 36:23
that I, the LORD, *s* ... Ezek 37:28
Myself and *s* Myself ... Ezek 38:23
S them by Your ... John 17:17
for their sakes I *s* ... John 17:19
that He might *s* ... Eph 5:26
s you completely ... 1 Thess 5:23

SANCTUARY
let them make Me a *s* ... Ex 25:8
I went into the *s* ... Ps 73:17
set fire to Your *s* ... Ps 74:7
O God, is in the *s* ... Ps 77:13
He will be as a *s* ... Is 8:14
He has abandoned His *s* ... Lam 2:7
I shall be a little *s* ... Ezek 11:16
to shine on Your *s* ... Dan 9:17
and the earthly *s* ... Heb 9:1
is brought into the *s* ... Heb 13:11

SAND
descendants as the *s* ... Gen 32:12
be heavier than the *s* ... Job 6:3
in number than the *s* ... Ps 139:18
O Israel, be as the *s* ... Is 10:22
innumerable as the *s* ... Heb 11:12

SANDAL
remove his *s* from his ... Deut 25:9
So he took off his *s* ... Ruth 4:8
s strap I am not worthy ... Mark 1:7

SANDALS
Take your *s* off your feet ... Ex 3:5
beautiful are your feet in *s* .. Song 7:1
whose *s* I am not worthy ... Matt 3:11
bag, knapsack, nor *s* ... Luke 10:4
tie on your *s* ... Acts 12:8

SANG
s this song to the LORD ... Ex 15:1
worshiped, the singers *s* ... 2 Chr 29:28
The singers *s* loudly ... Neh 12:42
morning stars *s* together ... Job 38:7
They *s* His praise ... Ps 106:12
they *s* a new song, saying ... Rev 5:9
s as it were a new song ... Rev 14:3

SAPPHIRA
Wife of Ananias; struck dead for lying, Acts 5:1–11

SAPPHIRE
shall be a turquoise, a *s* ... Ex 28:18
was jasper, the second *s* ... Rev 21:19

SAPPHIRES
are the source of *s* ... Job 28:6

SARAH (or Sarai)
Barren wife of Abram, Gen 11:29–31
Represented as Abram's sister, Gen 12:10–20
Gives Abram her maid, Gen 16:1–3
Receives promise of a son, Gen 17:15–21
Gives birth to Isaac, Gen 21:1–8

SARDIS
Site of one of the seven churches, Rev 1:11

SARDONYX
the fifth *s*, the sixth ... Rev 21:20

SASH
tunic, a turban, and a *s* ... Ex 28:4
get yourself a linen *s* ... Jer 13:1

SASHES
girded them with *s* ... Lev 8:13
s for the merchants ... Prov 31:24

SAT
of Babylon, there we *s* ... Ps 137:1
I *s* down in his shade ... Song 2:3
s alone because of ... Jer 15:17
people who *s* in darkness ... Matt 4:16
Now Peter *s* outside in ... Matt 26:69
into heaven, and *s* ... Mark 16:19
s down again, He said ... John 13:12
s down at the right hand ... Heb 1:3
And He who *s* there was ... Rev 4:3
Him who *s* on the horse ... Rev 19:19

SATAN
See DEVIL
S stood up against ... 1 Chr 21:1
before the LORD, and *S* ... Job 1:6
And the LORD said to *S* ... Zech 3:2
"Away with you, *S* ... Matt 4:10
"Get behind Me, *S* ... Matt 16:23
forty days, tempted by *S* .. Mark 1:13
"How can *S* cast out ... Mark 3:23
to them, "I saw *S* ... Luke 10:18
Then *S* entered Judas ... Luke 22:3
S has asked for you ... Luke 22:31
S filled your heart ... Acts 5:3
S under your feet shortly .. Rom 16:20
such a one to *S* ... 1 Cor 5:5
For *S* himself ... 2 Cor 11:14
messenger of *S* to buffet ... 2 Cor 12:7
to the working of *S* ... 2 Thess 2:9
whom I delivered to *S* ... 1 Tim 1:20
are a synagogue of *S* ... Rev 2:9
you, where *S* dwells ... Rev 2:13
known the depths of *S* ... Rev 2:24
called the Devil and *S* ... Rev 12:9
years have expired, *S* ... Rev 20:7

SATIATED
s the weary soul ... Jer 31:25
It shall be *s* and made ... Jer 46:10

SATISFIED
I shall be *s* when I ... Ps 17:15
his land will be *s* ... Prov 12:11
a good man will be *s* ... Prov 14:14
s soul loathes the ... Prov 27:7
that are never *s* ... Prov 30:15
silver will not be *s* ... Eccl 5:10
left hand and not be *s* ... Is 9:20
of His soul, and be *s* ... Is 53:11
My people shall be *s* ... Jer 31:14
still were not *s* ... Ezek 16:28
but they were not *s* ... Amos 4:8
and cannot be *s* ... Hab 2:5

SATISFIES
s your mouth with good ... Ps 103:5
s the longing soul ... Ps 107:9

SATISFY
s us early with Your ... Ps 90:14
long life I will *s* ... Ps 91:16
s her poor with bread ... Ps 132:15
for what does not *s* ... Is 55:2

SATISFYING
eats to the *s* of his ... Prov 13:25

SAUL
Becomes first king of Israel, 1 Sam 9—11
Sacrifices unlawfully, 1 Sam 13:1–14
Wars with Philistines, 1 Sam 13:15—14:52
Disregards the Lord's command; rejected by God, 1 Sam 15
Suffers from distressing spirits, 1 Sam 16:14–23
Becomes jealous of David; attempts to kill him, 1 Sam 18:5—19:22
Pursues David; twice spared by him, 1 Sam 22—24; 26
Consults medium, 1 Sam 28:7–25
Defeated, commits suicide; buried, 1 Sam 31

——— of Tarsus, apostle to the Gentiles: *see* PAUL

SAVE
will *s* Israel by my hand ... Judg 6:37
the LORD does not *s* ... 1 Sam 17:47
there was none to *s* ... 2 Sam 22:42
s the humble person ... Job 22:29
Oh, *s* me for Your ... Ps 6:4
s me from all those who ... Ps 7:1
S Your people, and bless ... Ps 28:9
send from heaven and *s* ... Ps 57:3
Your ear to me, and *s* me ... Ps 71:2
s the children of the ... Ps 72:4
s the souls of the ... Ps 72:13
s me, and I will keep ... Ps 119:146
LORD, and He will *s* ... Prov 20:22
He will come and *s* ... Is 35:4
LORD was ready to *s* ... Is 38:20
s your children ... Is 49:25
that it cannot *s* ... Is 59:1
mighty to *s* ... Is 63:1
one who cannot *s* ... Jer 14:9
s you and deliver you ... Jer 15:20
s me, and I shall be ... Jer 17:14
O LORD, *s* Your people ... Jer 31:7
other, That he may *s* ... Hos 13:10
Assyria shall not *s* ... Hos 14:3
the Mighty One, will *s* ... Zeph 3:17
JESUS, for He will *s* ... Matt 1:21
Him, saying, "Lord, *s* us ... Matt 8:25
s his life will lose it ... Matt 16:25
s that which was ... Matt 18:11
three days, *s* Yourself ... Matt 27:40
s life or to kill ... Mark 3:4
to *s* his life will lose it ... Mark 8:35
s Yourself, and come ... Mark 15:30
to *s* life or to destroy ... Luke 6:9
life for My sake will *s* it ... Luke 9:24
seeks to *s* his life ... Luke 17:33
let Him *s* Himself if ... Luke 23:35
You are the Christ, *s* ... Luke 23:39
'Father, *s* Me from ... John 12:27
but to *s* the world ... John 12:47
and *s* some of them ... Rom 11:14
to *s* those who believe ... 1 Cor 1:21
by all means *s* some ... 1 Cor 9:22
the world to *s* sinners ... 1 Tim 1:15
doing this you will *s* ... 1 Tim 4:16
able to *s* Him from death ... Heb 5:7
able to *s* your souls ... James 1:21
Can faith *s* him ... James 2:14
who is able to *s* ... James 4:12
will *s* a soul from death ... James 5:20

SAVED
See WILL BE SAVED
the LORD *s* Israel that day ... Ex 14:30
you will be *s* from your ... Num 10:9
like you, a people *s* ... Deut 33:29
But You have *s* us from ... Ps 44:7
blamelessly will be *s* ... Prov 28:18
Look to Me, and be *s* ... Is 45:22
and we are not *s* ... Jer 8:20
"Who then can be *s* ... Matt 19:25
to the end shall be *s* ... Matt 24:13
"He *s* others ... Matt 27:42
"Who then can be *s* ... Mark 10:26
to the end shall be *s* ... Mark 13:13
no flesh would be *s* ... Mark 13:20
"He *s* others ... Mark 15:31
and is baptized will be *s* .. Mark 16:16
That we should be *s* ... Luke 1:71
"Your faith has *s* ... Luke 7:50
through Him might be *s* ... John 3:17
enters by Me, he will be *s* .. John 10:9
of the LORD shall be *s* ... Acts 2:21
them, saying, "Be *s* ... Acts 2:40
of Moses, you cannot be *s* .. Acts 15:1
what must I do to be *s* ... Acts 16:30
For we were *s* in this ... Rom 8:24
is that they may be *s* ... Rom 10:1
all Israel will be *s* ... Rom 11:26

his spirit may be *s* .... 1 Cor 5:5
that they may be *s* .... 1 Cor 10:33
which also you are *s* ...... 1 Cor 15:2
those who are being *s* ..... 2 Cor 2:15
grace you have been *s* .... Eph 2:8
that they might be *s* ..... 2 Thess 2:10
all men to be *s* .... 1 Tim 2:4
she will be *s* in .... 1 Tim 2:15
to His mercy He *s* .... Titus 3:5
eight souls, were *s* .... 1 Pet 3:20
of those who are *s* .... Rev 21:24

SAVES
s the needy from the .... Job 5:15
s such as have a .... Ps 34:18
antitype which now *s* ...... 1 Pet 3:21

SAVIOR
forgot God their *S* .... Ps 106:21
He will send them a *S* .... Is 19:20
of Israel, your *S* .... Is 43:3
Me, a just God and a *S* ...... Is 45:21
I, the LORD, am your *S* .... Is 60:16
So He became their *S* .... Is 63:8
his *S* in time of trouble .... Jer 14:8
for there is no *s* .... Hos 13:4
rejoiced in God my *S* ...... Luke 1:47
the city of David a *S* .... Luke 2:11
the Christ, the *S* .... John 4:42
to be Prince and *S* .... Acts 5:31
up for Israel a *S* .... Acts 13:23
and He is the *S* .... Eph 5:23
of God our *S* and the .... 1 Tim 1:1
God, who is the *S* .... 1 Tim 4:10
of our *S* Jesus Christ ..... 2 Tim 1:10
God and *S* Jesus Christ ..... Titus 2:13
God our *S* toward man ...... Titus 3:4
Son as *S* of the world .... 1 John 4:14
to God our *S*, who alone is ... Jude 25

SAVIORS
s shall come to Mount .... Obad 21

SAVOR
days, and I do not *s* .... Amos 5:21

SAWN
stoned, they were *s* .... Heb 11:37

SAY
But I *s* to you that .... Matt 5:22
"But who do you *s* .... Matt 16:15
s that we have no sin .... 1 John 1:8

SAYING
disclose my dark *s* .... Ps 49:4
cannot accept this *s* ...... Matt 19:11
"This is a hard *s* .... John 6:60
This is a faithful *s* .... 1 Tim 1:15

SAYINGS
I will utter dark *s* .... Ps 78:2
whoever hears these *s* ..... Matt 7:24

SCALES
You shall have honest *s* .... Lev 19:36
be weighed on honest *s* ..... Job 31:6
deceitful *s* are in his .... Hos 12:7
his eyes something like *s* ... Acts 9:18
on it had a pair of *s* .... Rev 6:5

SCARLET
midwife took a *s* thread ... Gen 38:28
s thread, fine linen .... Ex 25:4
s cord in the window .... Josh 2:18
is clothed with *s* .... Prov 31:21
are like a strand of *s* .... Song 4:3
your sins are like *s* .... Is 1:18
and put a *s* robe on Him .. Matt 27:28
s beast which was full ...... Rev 17:3

SCATTER
I will *s* you among the ..... Lev 26:33
S the peoples who .... Ps 68:30
s the sheep of My .... Jer 23:1
I will *s* to all winds .... Jer 49:32
s seed on the ground ...... Mark 4:26

SCATTERED
lest we be *s* abroad .... Gen 11:4
let His enemies be *s* .... Ps 68:1
of iniquity shall be *s* .... Ps 92:9
"You have *s* My flock .... Jer 23:2
s Israel will gather .... Jer 31:10
"Israel is like *s* sheep .... Jer 50:17
they were weary and *s* ..... Matt 9:36
where I have not *s* seed ... Matt 25:26
of the flock will be *s* ...... Matt 26:31
the sheep will be *s* .... Mark 14:27
that you will be *s* .... John 16:32
tribes which are *s* abroad .. James 1:1

SCATTERS
s the frost like ashes .... Ps 147:16
There is one who *s* .... Prov 11:24
throne of judgment *s* .... Prov 20:8
not gather with Me *s* ..... Matt 12:30

SCEPTER
s shall not depart .... Gen 49:10
S shall rise out of .... Num 24:17
holds out the golden *s* ...... Esth 4:11
a *s* of righteousness .... Ps 45:6
a *s* of righteousness .... Heb 1:8

SCHEME
perfected a shrewd *s* .... Ps 64:6

SCHEMER
will be called a *s* .... Prov 24:8

SCHEMES
who brings wicked *s* .... Ps 37:7
sought out many *s* .... Eccl 7:29

SCHISM
there should be no *s* ...... 1 Cor 12:25

SCHOOL
daily in the *s* of .... Acts 19:9

SCOFF
They *s* and speak .... Ps 73:8
They *s* at kings .... Hab 1:10

SCOFFER
"He who corrects a *s* .... Prov 9:7
s does not listen .... Prov 13:1
s seeks wisdom and .... Prov 14:6
s is an abomination .... Prov 24:9

SCOFFERS
S ensnare a city .... Prov 29:8
s will come in the .... 2 Pet 3:3

SCORCHED
sun was up they were *s* ..... Matt 13:6
And men were *s* with .... Rev 16:9

SCORN
My friends *s* me .... Job 16:20
to our neighbors, a *s* ...... Ps 44:13
laughed you to *s* .... Is 37:22

SCORNED
consider, for I am *s* .... Lam 1:11
and princes are *s* .... Hab 1:10

SCORNFUL
nor sits in the seat of the *s* .... Ps 1:1
the *s* one is consumed .... Is 29:20

SCORNS
He *s* the scornful .... Prov 3:34
s obedience to his .... Prov 30:17

SCORPION
will he offer him a *s* ...... Luke 11:12

SCORPIONS
and you dwell among *s* .... Ezek 2:6
on serpents and *s* .... Luke 10:19
They had tails like *s* .... Rev 9:10

SCOURGE
from the *s* of the tongue ..... Job 5:21
hosts will stir up a *s* .... Is 10:26
up to councils and *s* ...... Matt 10:17
will mock Him, and *s* .... Mark 10:34
s a man who is a Roman .. Acts 22:25

SCOURGES
will chastise you with *s* .. 1 Kin 12:11
s every son whom .... Heb 12:6

SCRIBE
a skilled *s* in the Law .... Ezra 7:6
"Where is the *s* .... Is 33:18
the false pen of the *s* .... Jer 8:8
gave it to Baruch the *s* ..... Jer 36:32
a certain *s* came and said .. Matt 8:19
s said to Him, "Well ..... Mark 12:32
Where is the *s*? .... 1 Cor 1:20

SCRIBES
and not as the *s* .... Matt 7:29
"Beware of the *s* .... Mark 12:38
s sought how they might .. Mark 14:1

SCRIBES AND PHARISEES
righteousness of the *s* ...... Matt 5:20
s answered, saying .... Matt 12:38
s who were from .... Matt 15:1
But woe to you, *s* .... Matt 23:13
the *s* saw him eating .... Mark 2:16
s watched Him closely ...... Luke 6:7
Woe to you, *s* .... Luke 11:44
s brought to him a woman .. John 8:3

SCRIPTURE
what is noted in the *S* ..... Dan 10:21
S was fulfilled which ..... Mark 15:28
"Today this *S* .... Luke 4:21
S cannot be broken .... John 10:35
that the *S* might be .... John 19:24
place in the *S* which he ..... Acts 8:32
For what does the *S* .... Rom 4:3
S has confined all .... Gal 3:22
All *S* is given by .... 2 Tim 3:16
that the *S* says in vain ..... James 4:5
that no prophecy of *S* ...... 2 Pet 1:20

SCRIPTURES
not knowing the *S* .... Matt 22:29
S must be fulfilled .... Mark 14:49
and mighty in the *S* .... Acts 18:24
have known the Holy *S* ... 2 Tim 3:15
also the rest of the *S* .... 2 Pet 3:16

SCROLL
in the *s* of the book .... Ps 40:7
and note it on a *s* .... Is 30:8
Baruch wrote on a *s* .... Jer 36:4
the king had burned the *s* .. Jer 36:27
eat this *s*, and go .... Ezek 3:1
saw there a flying *s* .... Zech 5:1
on the throne a *s* .... Rev 5:1
was able to open the *s* .... Rev 5:3
the sky receded as a *s* .... Rev 6:14

SEA
drowned in the Red *S* .... Ex 15:4
this great and wide *s* .... Ps 104:25
who go down to the *s* ...... Ps 107:23
to the *s* its limit .... Prov 8:29
rebuke I dry up the *s* .... Is 50:2
the waters cover the *s* .... Hab 2:14
and the *s* obey Him .... Matt 8:27
Him walking on the *s* .... Matt 14:26
throne there was a *s* .... Rev 4:6
standing on the *s* .... Rev 15:2
there was no more *s* .... Rev 21:1

SEAL
Set me as a *s* upon .... Song 8:6
the *s* of perfection .... Ezek 28:12
therefore *s* up the vision ..... Dan 8:26
has set His *s* on Him .... John 6:27
of circumcision, a *s* .... Rom 4:11
the *s* of my apostleship ..... 1 Cor 9:2
stands, having this *s* ...... 2 Tim 2:19
He opened the second *s* .... Rev 6:3
He opened the seventh *s* ...... Rev 8:1
Do not *s* the words of the .. Rev 22:10

SEALED
My transgression is *s* ...... Job 14:17
s till the time of the end .... Dan 12:9
who also has *s* us and ..... 2 Cor 1:22
by whom you were *s* .... Eph 4:30
of those who were *s* .... Rev 7:4

SEALS
sealed with seven *s* .... Rev 5:1

SEAM
tunic was without *s* ... John 19:23

SÉANCE
"Please conduct a *s* ... 1 Sam 28:8

SEARCH
"Can you *s* out the ... Job 11:7
would not God *s* ... Ps 44:21
glory of kings is to *s* ... Prov 25:2
found it by secret *s* ... Jer 2:34
I, the LORD, *s* the ... Jer 17:10
s the Scriptures ... John 5:39
S and look, for no ... John 7:52

SEARCHED
O LORD, You have *s* ... Ps 139:1
s the Scriptures ... Acts 17:11
and *s* carefully ... 1 Pet 1:10

SEARCHES
for the LORD *s* all ... 1 Chr 28:9
s the hearts knows ... Rom 8:27
For the Spirit *s* ... 1 Cor 2:10
that I am He who *s* ... Rev 2:23

SEASON
I will give you rain in its *s* ... Lev 26:4
bring forth its fruit in its *s* ... Ps 1:3
their food in due *s* ... Ps 104:27
a word spoken in due *s* ... Prov 15:23
To everything there is a *s* ... Eccl 3:1
word in *s* to him who is ... Is 50:4
give them food in due *s* ... Matt 24:45
flavor, how will you *s* it ... Mark 9:50
for in due *s* we shall reap ... Gal 6:9
Be ready in *s* and out ... 2 Tim 4:2

SEASONED
how shall it be *s* ... Matt 5:13
"For everyone will be *s* ... Mark 9:49

SEASONS
let them be for signs and *s* ... Gen 1:14
appointed the moon for *s* ... Ps 104:19
the times and the *s* ... Dan 2:21
for you to know times or *s* ... Acts 1:7
days and months and *s* ... Gal 4:10
the times and the *s* ... 1 Thess 5:1

SEAT
See MERCY SEAT
shall make a mercy *s* ... Ex 25:17
I might come to His *s* ... Job 23:3
that He may *s* him with ... Ps 113:8
sit in Moses' *s* ... Matt 23:2
before the judgment *s* ... 2 Cor 5:10
the mercy *s* ... Heb 9:5

SEATED
the Ancient of Days was *s* ... Dan 7:9
s Him at His right hand ... Eph 1:20
who is *s* at the right hand ... Heb 8:1

SEATS
at feasts, the best *s* ... Matt 23:6
you love the best *s* ... Luke 11:43

SECOND
morning were the *s* day ... Gen 1:8
And the *s* is like it ... Matt 22:39
Can he enter a *s* time into ... John 3:4
the *s* Man is the Lord ... 1 Cor 15:47
and behind the *s* veil, the ... Heb 9:3
He will appear a *s* time ... Heb 9:28
the *s* living creature like a ... Rev 4:7
Then the *s* angel sounded ... Rev 8:8

SECOND DEATH
not be hurt by the *s* ... Rev 2:11
Over such the *s* has no ... Rev 20:6
of fire. This is the *s* ... Rev 20:14
brimstone, which is the *s* ... Rev 21:8

SECRET
s things belong ... Deut 29:29
The *s* of the LORD is ... Ps 25:14
in the *s* place of His ... Ps 27:5
when I was made in *s* ... Ps 139:15
do not disclose the *s* ... Prov 25:9
I have not spoken in *s* ... Is 45:19
Father who is in the *s* ... Matt 6:6
s from the foundation of ... Matt 13:35
For nothing is *s* that will ... Luke 8:17
in *s* I have said nothing ... John 18:20
s since the world began ... Rom 16:25
are done by them in *s* ... Eph 5:12

SECRETLY
"Now a word was *s* ... Job 4:12
He lies in wait *s* ... Ps 10:9
minded to put her away *s* ... Matt 1:19
a disciple of Jesus, but *s* ... John 19:38

SECRETS
would show you the *s* ... Job 11:6
For He knows the *s* ... Ps 44:21
A talebearer reveals *s* ... Prov 11:13
heaven who reveals *s* ... Dan 2:28
God will judge the *s* ... Rom 2:16
And thus the *s* of his ... 1 Cor 14:25

SECT
him (which is the *s* ... Acts 5:17
to the strictest *s* ... Acts 26:5

SECURE
while the camp felt *s* ... Judg 8:11
dwell safely, and will be *s* ... Prov 1:33
him as a peg in a *s* place ... Is 22:23
made *s* until the third ... Matt 27:64

SECURELY
pleasures, who dwell *s* ... Is 47:8
nation that dwells *s* ... Jer 49:31

SECURES
he *s* it for himself among ... Is 44:14

SECURITY
gives them *s*, and they ... Job 24:23

SEDUCED
flattering lips she *s* ... Prov 7:21
because they have *s* ... Ezek 13:10

SEE
for no man shall *s* ... Ex 33:20
the LORD does not *s* ... 1 Sam 16:7
in my flesh I shall *s* ... Job 19:26
s the works of God ... Ps 66:5
lest they *s* with their ... Is 6:10
for sin, He shall *s* ... Is 53:10
for they shall *s* God ... Matt 5:8
seeing they do not *s* ... Matt 13:13
s greater things than ... John 1:50
rejoiced to *s* My day ... John 8:56
we wish to *s* Jesus ... John 12:21
and the world will *s* ... John 14:19
Him, for we shall *s* ... 1 John 3:2
They shall *s* His face ... Rev 22:4

SEED
s shall be called ... Gen 21:12
s shall be its stump ... Is 6:13
He shall see His *s* ... Is 53:10
you a noble vine, a *s* ... Jer 2:21
s is the word of God ... Luke 8:11
had left us a *s* ... Rom 9:29
to each *s* its own body ... 1 Cor 15:38
S were the promises ... Gal 3:16
you are Abraham's *s* ... Gal 3:29
of corruptible *s* ... 1 Pet 1:23
not sin, for His *s* ... 1 John 3:9

SEED OF DAVID
Christ comes from the *s* ... John 7:42
who was born of the *s* ... Rom 1:3
Jesus Christ, of the *s* ... 2 Tim 2:8

SEEDS
the good *s* are the ... Matt 13:38
not say, "And to *s* ... Gal 3:16

SEEK
will find Him if you *s* ... Deut 4:29
pray and *s* My face ... 2 Chr 7:14
your heart to *s* God ... 2 Chr 19:3
s your God as you do ... Ezra 4:2
may God above not *s* ... Job 3:4
countenance does not *s* ... Ps 10:4
LORD, that will I *s* ... Ps 27:4
You said, "*S* My face ... Ps 27:8
early will I *s* You ... Ps 63:1
s me diligently will ... Prov 8:17
s one's own glory ... Prov 25:27
s justice, rebuke ... Is 1:17
Should they *s* the dead ... Is 8:19
the Gentiles shall *s* ... Is 11:10
Jacob, '*S* Me in vain ... Is 45:19
Yet they *s* Me daily ... Is 58:2
s great things for ... Jer 45:5
s what was lost ... Ezek 34:16
"*S* Me and live ... Amos 5:4
and people should *s* ... Mal 2:7
things the Gentiles *s* ... Matt 6:32
s, and you will find ... Matt 7:7
of Man has come to *s* ... Luke 19:10
because I do not *s* ... John 5:30
You will *s* Me and ... John 7:34
in doing good *s* ... Rom 2:7
Because they did not *s* ... Rom 9:32
Let no one *s* his own ... 1 Cor 10:24
for I do not *s* yours ... 2 Cor 12:14
For all *s* their own ... Phil 2:21
s those things which ... Col 3:1
s the one to come ... Heb 13:14

SEEK THE LORD
from there you will *s* ... Deut 4:29
of those rejoice who *s* ... 1 Chr 16:10
heart and your soul to *s* ... 1 Chr 22:19
set their heart to *s* ... 2 Chr 11:16
disease he did not *s* ... 2 Chr 16:12
set himself to *s* ... 2 Chr 20:3
of the land in order to *s* ... Ezra 6:21
who *s* shall not lack ... Ps 34:10
S and His strength ... Ps 105:4
those who *s* understand ... Prov 28:5
righteousness, you who *s* ... Is 51:1
S while He may be found ... Is 55:6
Israel shall return and *s* ... Hos 3:5
S and live, lest He ... Amos 5:6
S, all you meek ... Zeph 2:3
nations shall come to *s* ... Zech 8:22
rest of mankind may *s* ... Acts 15:17
so that they should *s* ... Acts 17:27

SEEKING
run to and fro, *s* ... Amos 8:12
and he came *s* fruit ... Luke 13:6
for the Father is *s* ... John 4:23
like a roaring lion, *s* ... 1 Pet 5:8

SEEKS
Zion; no one *s* her ... Jer 30:17
receives, and he who *s* ... Matt 7:8
There is none who *s* ... Rom 3:11

SEEMS
There is a way which *s* ... Prov 14:12
have, even what he *s* ... Luke 8:18
If anyone among you *s* ... 1 Cor 3:18

SEEN
s God face to face ... Gen 32:30
All this I have *s* ... Eccl 8:9
s the one I love ... Song 3:3
Who has *s* such things ... Is 66:8
s strange things today ... Luke 5:26
No one has *s* God at ... John 1:18
time, nor *s* His form ... John 5:37
I speak what I have *s* ... John 8:38
s Me has *s* the ... John 14:9
things which we have *s* ... Acts 4:20
s Jesus Christ our ... 1 Cor 9:1
things which are not *s* ... 2 Cor 4:18
whom no man has *s* ... 1 Tim 6:16
heard, which we have *s* ... 1 John 1:1

SEES
here seen Him who *s* ... Gen 16:13
s all the sons of men ... Ps 33:13
s his brother in need ... 1 John 3:17
s his brother sinning ... 1 John 5:16

SEIR
Home of Esau, Gen 32:3
Horites of, dispossessed by Esau's descendants, Deut 2:12
Desolation of, Ezek 35:15

SEIZE
s the city, for the LORD ...... Josh 8:7
Will not pangs *s* you, like ... Jer 13:21
also houses, and *s* them ...... Mic 2:2
s his inheritance .... Matt 21:38
you did not *s* Me .... Matt 26:55
further to *s* Peter also .... Acts 12:3

SEIZED
pangs have *s* you like a ...... Mic 4:9
For it had often *s* him ..... Luke 8:29
profit was gone, they *s* ... Acts 16:19
Jews *s* me in the temple ... Acts 26:21

SELF-CONFIDENT
a fool rages and is *s* ...... Prov 14:16

SELF-CONTROL
about righteousness, *s* .... Acts 24:25
because of your lack of *s* ... 1 Cor 7:5
they cannot exercise *s* ...... 1 Cor 7:9
gentleness, *s* .... Gal 5:23
love, and holiness, with *s* . 1 Tim 2:15
slanderers, without *s* .... 2 Tim 3:3
to knowledge *s* .... 2 Pet 1:6

SELF-CONTROLLED
just, holy, *s* .... Titus 1:8

SELF-SEEKING
envy and *s* exist .... James 3:16

SELFISH
s ambitions, backbitings .. 2 Cor 12:20
s ambitions, dissensions ...... Gal 5:20
preach Christ from *s* .... Phil 1:16
s ambition or conceit .... Phil 2:3

SELL
said, "*S* me your .... Gen 25:31
s Your people for .... Ps 44:12
s the righteous .... Amos 2:6
s whatever you have .... Mark 10:21
no sword, let him *s* ...... Luke 22:36
no one may buy or *s* ...... Rev 13:17

SEND
He shall *s* from heaven .... Ps 57:3
"Whom shall I *s* .... Is 6:8
s them a Savior .... Is 19:20
"Behold, I *s* you out ...... Matt 10:16
The Son of Man will *s* .... Matt 13:41
S the multitudes away .... Matt 14:15
He will *s* His angels ...... Matt 24:31
"*S* us to the swine, that .. Mark 5:12
s them out two by two ...... Mark 6:7
S them away, that they .... Mark 6:36
I *s* you out as lambs .... Luke 10:3
I will *s* them prophets .... Luke 11:49
s Lazarus that he .... Luke 16:24
s the Promise of My ...... Luke 24:49
God did not *s* His Son ..... John 3:17
whom the Father will *s* ... John 14:26
has sent Me, I also *s* ...... John 20:21

SENDING
I am *s* you to Jesse .... 1 Sam 16:1
God did by *s* His own Son .. Rom 8:3

SENDS
s rain on the just and ...... Matt 5:45
till He *s* forth justice to ... Matt 12:20

SENNACHERIB
Assyrian king (705–681 B.C.); son and successor of Sargon II, 2 Kin 18:13
Death of, by assassination, 2 Kin 19:36, 37

SENSELESS
Understand, you *s* .... Ps 94:8

SENSES
of use have their *s* .... Heb 5:14

SENSIBLY
who can answer *s* .... Prov 26:16

SENSUAL
but is earthly, *s* .... James 3:15
These are *s* persons .... Jude 19

SENT
s out the dove .... Gen 8:12
'I AM has *s* me to you .... Ex 3:14
s to spy out the land ...... Num 13:16
LORD *s* me to anoint you . 1 Sam 15:1
and His Spirit have *s* .... Is 48:16
s these prophets .... Jer 23:21
s this commandment .... Mal 2:4
receives Him who *s* Me ... Matt 10:40
not Me but Him who *s* .... Mark 9:37
he *s* a servant to the ...... Mark 12:2
He has *s* Me to heal the .... Luke 4:18
Baptist has *s* us to You ..... Luke 7:20
receives Him who *s* Me ..... Luke 9:48
rejects Him who *s* Me .... Luke 10:16
a man *s* from God .... John 1:6
the will of Him who *s* Me ... John 6:38
Father who *s* Me bears ..... John 8:18
is he who is *s* greater ..... John 13:16
You *s* Me into the world .. John 17:18
As the Father has *s* .... John 20:21
unless they are *s* .... Rom 10:15
Spirit *s* from heaven .... 1 Pet 1:12
s His Son to be the ..... 1 John 4:10
s His angel to show His ..... Rev 22:6

SEPARATE
he shall *s* himself .... Num 6:3
s yourselves from the ..... Ezra 10:11
let not man *s* .... Matt 19:6
Who shall *s* us from .... Rom 8:35
harmless, undefiled, *s* .... Heb 7:26

SEPARATED
but the poor is *s* .... Prov 19:4
"The LORD has utterly *s* .... Is 56:3
to be an apostle, *s* .... Rom 1:1
it pleased God, who *s* .... Gal 1:15

SEPARATES
who repeats a matter *s* ...... Prov 17:9

SEPARATION
the middle wall of *s* .... Eph 2:14

SERAPHIM
Above it stood *s* .... Is 6:2

SERGIUS PAULUS
Roman proconsul of Cyprus, converted by Paul, Acts 13:7–12

SERIOUS
therefore be *s* and .... 1 Pet 4:7

SERPENT
s was more cunning .... Gen 3:1
"The *s* deceived me .... Gen 3:13
"Make a fiery *s* .... Num 21:8
like the poison of a *s* .... Ps 58:4
s you shall trample .... Ps 91:13
their tongues like a *s* .... Ps 140:3
air, the way of a *s* .... Prov 30:19
s may bite when it is ...... Eccl 10:11
be a fiery flying *s* .... Is 14:29
and wounded the *s* .... Is 51:9
will he give him a *s* .... Matt 7:10
Moses lifted up the *s* .... John 3:14
was cast out, that *s* .... Rev 12:9

SERPENTS
is the poison of *s* .... Deut 32:33
be wise as *s* .... Matt 10:16
to trample on *s* .... Luke 10:19

SERVANT
a *s* of servants he .... Gen 9:25
take a gift from your *s* .... 2 Kin 5:15
the *s* of the man of God .... 2 Kin 8:4
s who earnestly .... Job 7:2
bountifully with Your *s* ... Ps 119:17
and the fool will be *s* ..... Prov 11:29
s will rule over a son ...... Prov 17:2
A *s* will not be .... Prov 29:19
Who is blind but My *s* .... Is 42:19
"Is Israel a *s* .... Jer 2:14
and a *s* his master .... Mal 1:6
nor a *s* above his master .. Matt 10:24
My *S* whom I have .... Matt 12:18
you, let him be your *s* ..... Matt 20:26
good and faithful *s* .... Matt 25:21
'You wicked and lazy *s* .... Matt 25:26
the unprofitable *s* .... Matt 25:30
be last of all and *s* of all .... Mark 9:35
you shall be your *s* .... Mark 10:43
a *s* to the vinedressers ..... Mark 12:2
to my *s*, 'Do this,' .... Luke 7:8
that *s* who knew his .... Luke 12:47
I am, there My *s* will be .. John 12:26
s does not know what .... John 15:15
'A *s* is not greater than .. John 15:20
struck the high priest's *s* .. John 18:10
against Your holy *S* .... Acts 4:27
Christ has become a *s* .... Rom 15:8

SERVANTS
puts no trust in His *s* .... Job 4:18
for all your *s* .... Ps 119:91
on the ground like *s* .... Eccl 10:7
shall call you the *s* .... Is 61:6
S rule over us .... Lam 5:8
Again he sent other *s* ...... Matt 21:36
the king said to the *s* ..... Matt 22:13
s whom the master .... Luke 12:37
are unprofitable *s* .... Luke 17:10
longer do I call you *s* ..... John 15:15
My *s* would fight, so ...... John 18:36
so consider us, as *s* .... 1 Cor 4:1

SERVE
people go, that they may *s* .... Ex 8:1
s you until the Year of .... Lev 25:40
LORD your God and *s* ...... Deut 6:13
S the LORD .... Josh 24:14
land, so you shall *s* aliens ..... Jer 5:19
s Him with one accord .... Zeph 3:9
You cannot *s* God and ...... Matt 6:24
to be served, but to *s* ..... Matt 20:28
to be served, but to *s* ..... Mark 10:45
the mind I myself *s* .... Rom 7:25
but through love *s* .... Gal 5:13
s the living God .... Heb 9:14
s Him day and night in ...... Rev 7:15

SERVE THE LORD
men go, that they may *s* ...... Ex 10:7
go, *s* as you have said .... Ex 12:31
So you shall *s* .... Ex 23:25
to *s* your God with all ..... Deut 10:12
Because you did not *s* ..... Deut 28:47
and my house, we will *s* .. Josh 24:15
s with all your heart ..... 1 Sam 12:20
commanded Judah to *s* ... 2 Chr 33:16
S with fear, and rejoice .... Ps 2:11
S with gladness .... Ps 100:2
the kingdoms, to *s* .... Ps 102:22
But they shall *s* their God .... Jer 30:9
s without distraction .... 1 Cor 7:35
inheritance, for you *s* .... Col 3:24

SERVED
did not come to be *s* ...... Matt 20:28
did not come to be *s* ...... Mark 10:45
s the creature rather than .. Rom 1:25

SERVES
If anyone *s* Me .... John 12:26

SERVICE
do you mean by this *s* ...... Ex 12:26
that he offers God *s* .... John 16:2
is your reasonable *s* .... Rom 12:1
with goodwill doing *s* .... Eph 6:7
your works, love, *s* .... Rev 2:19

SERVING
years I have been *s* .... Luke 15:29
s the Lord with all .... Acts 20:19

fervent in spirit, *s* .... Rom 12:11
you, *s* as overseers .... 1 Pet 5:2

SET
"See, I have *s* .... Deut 30:15
s the LORD always .... Ps 16:8
I will *s* him on high .... Ps 91:14
s aside the grace .... Gal 2:21

SET APART
will *s* the land of Goshen ..... Ex 8:22
s to the Lord all that .... Ex 13:12
she shall be *s* seven days .. Lev 15:19
Then Moses *s* three cities .. Deut 4:41
as a dog laps, you shall *s* .... Judg 7:5
It was *s* for you .... 1 Sam 9:24
Aaron was *s*, he and his .. 1 Chr 23:13
the Lord has *s* for Himself ..... Ps 4:3
s a district for the Lord .... Ezek 45:1

SETH
Third son of Adam, Gen 4:25
In Christ's ancestry, Luke 3:38

SETTLE
Therefore *s* it in .... Luke 21:14

SETTLED
and my speech *s* .... Job 29:22
O LORD, Your word is *s* .... Ps 119:89
the mountains were *s* .... Prov 8:25
s accounts with them ..... Matt 25:19

SEVEN
Then *s* priests bearing ..... Josh 6:13
he had *s* hundred wives ... 1 Kin 11:3
the child sneezed *s* times ... 2 Kin 4:35
Joash was *s* years old .... 2 Chr 24:1
S times a day I praise ..... Ps 119:164
may fall *s* times and rise .. Prov 24:16
there are *s* abominations .. Prov 26:25
in that day *s* women shall ...... Is 4:1
Passover, a feast of *s* ..... Ezek 45:21
s times more than it was .... Dan 3:19
let *s* times pass over him ... Dan 4:16
there shall be *s* weeks and .. Dan 9:25
He took the *s* loaves ...... Matt 15:36
forgive him? Up to *s* ...... Matt 18:21
wife of the *s* will she be ... Matt 22:28
had come *s* demons .... Luke 8:2
s other spirits more .... Luke 11:26
s times in a day .... Luke 17:4
out from among you *s* .... Acts 6:3
s churches which are .... Rev 1:4
I saw *s* golden lampstands .. Rev 1:12
The mystery of the *s* stars .. Rev 1:20
He who holds the *s* stars ..... Rev 2:1
has the *s* Spirits of God ...... Rev 3:1
S lamps of fire were .... Rev 4:5
sealed with *s* seals .... Rev 5:1
saw the *s* angels who stand .. Rev 8:2
s thunders uttered their ..... Rev 10:3
earthquake *s* thousand ..... Rev 11:13
red dragon having *s* heads .. Rev 12:3
of the sea, having *s* heads ... Rev 13:1
s angels having the *s* last ... Rev 15:1
who had the *s* bowls .... Rev 17:1
s last plagues came to me ... Rev 21:9

SEVENFOLD
light of the sun will be *s* ..... Is 30:26

SEVENTH
the *s* day God ended His ..... Gen 2:2
ark rested in the *s* month ..... Gen 8:4
on the *s* day there shall ..... Ex 12:16
gather it, but on the *s* day ... Ex 16:26
When He opened the *s* seal .. Rev 8:1
the sounding of the *s* angel .. Rev 10:7
Then the *s* angel sounded .. Rev 11:15
the *s* angel poured out ..... Rev 16:17
s chrysolite, the eighth ..... Rev 21:20

SEVENTY
S weeks are .... Dan 9:24
up to *s* times seven .... Matt 18:22
Then the *s* returned ...... Luke 10:17

SEVERE
My wound is *s* .... Jer 10:19
not to be too *s* .... 2 Cor 2:5

SEVERITY
the goodness and *s* .... Rom 11:22

SEWS
s a piece of unshrunk ..... Mark 2:21

SEXUAL
s immorality causes her .... Matt 5:32
except for *s* immorality .... Matt 19:9
from *s* immorality, from .. Acts 15:20
s immorality, wickedness .. Rom 1:29
s immorality among you .... 1 Cor 5:1
the body is not for *s* .... 1 Cor 6:13
Flee *s* immorality .... 1 Cor 6:18
commit *s* immorality .... 1 Cor 10:8
abstain from *s* .... 1 Thess 4:3
to commit *s* immorality ..... Rev 2:14
repent of her *s* immorality .. Rev 2:21

SEXUALLY
company with *s* immoral .... 1 Cor 5:9
s immoral, sorcerers .... Rev 21:8

SHADE
I sat down in his *s* .... Song 2:3
be a tabernacle for *s* .... Is 4:6
may nest under its *s* .... Mark 4:32

SHADOW
May darkness and the *s* ..... Job 3:5
He flees like a *s* .... Job 14:2
hide me under the *s* .... Ps 17:8
walks about like a *s* .... Ps 39:6
like a passing *s* .... Ps 144:4
he passes like a *s* .... Eccl 6:12
and to trust in the *s* .... Is 30:2
In the *s* of His hand .... Is 49:2
which are a *s* of .... Col 2:17
the law, having a *s* .... Heb 10:1
is no variation or *s* ...... James 1:17

SHADOW OF DEATH
of darkness and the *s* ...... Job 10:21
my eyelids is the *s* .... Job 16:16
seen the doors of the *s* ..... Job 38:17
the valley of the *s* .... Ps 23:4
out of darkness and the *s* .. Ps 107:14
s, upon them a light .... Is 9:2
turns the *s* into morning .... Amos 5:8
s light has dawned .... Matt 4:16
in darkness and the *s* ...... Luke 1:79

SHADOWS
my members are like *s* ...... Job 17:7
and the *s* flee away .... Song 2:17

SHADRACH
Hananiah's Babylonian name, Dan 1:3, 7
Cast into the fiery furnace, Dan 3:1–28

SHAKE
Who is he who will *s* .... Job 17:3
their loins *s* continually ..... Ps 69:23
s the earth .... Is 2:19
S yourself from the .... Is 52:2
you *s* your head in scorn .... Jer 48:27
s their heads at the .... Lam 2:15
that the thresholds may *s* .. Amos 9:1
and the knees *s* .... Nah 2:10
hiss and *s* his fist .... Zeph 2:15
little while) I will *s* heaven ... Hag 2:6
I will *s* all nations .... Hag 2:7
s off the dust from your ... Matt 10:14
s off the dust under your .. Mark 6:11
house, and could not *s* it ... Luke 6:48
s not only the earth .... Heb 12:26

SHAKEN
reed is *s* in the water ..... 1 Kin 14:15
quaked and were *s* .... Ps 18:7
he will never be *s* .... Ps 112:6
A reed *s* by the wind .... Matt 11:7
of the heavens will be *s* ... Matt 24:29
the heavens will be *s* ..... Mark 13:25
s together, and running .... Luke 6:38
together was *s* .... Acts 4:31
of the prison were *s* .... Acts 16:26
not to be soon *s* .... 2 Thess 2:2
which cannot be *s* .... Heb 12:28

SHAKES
s the earth out of its .... Job 9:6
s the Wilderness .... Ps 29:8
The earth *s* at the noise ..... Jer 49:21

SHALLUM
King of Israel, 2 Kin 15:10–15

SHALMANESER
Assyrian king, 2 Kin 17:3

SHAME
you turn my glory to *s* .... Ps 4:2
let them be put to *s* .... Ps 83:17
s who serve carved .... Ps 97:7
hate Zion be put to *s* .... Ps 129:5
s shall be the .... Prov 3:35
is a son who causes *s* ...... Prov 10:5
hide My face from *s* .... Is 50:6
S has covered our .... Jer 51:51
their glory into *s* .... Hos 4:7
never be put to *s* .... Joel 2:26
Pass by in naked *s*, you ..... Mic 1:11
the unjust knows no *s* ...... Zeph 3:5
worthy to suffer *s* .... Acts 5:41
will not be put to *s* .... Rom 9:33
to put to *s* the wise .... 1 Cor 1:27
I say this to your *s* .... 1 Cor 6:5
glory is in their *s* .... Phil 3:19
put Him to an open *s* .... Heb 6:6
the cross, despising the *s* ... Heb 12:2

SHAMEFUL
committing what is *s* .... Rom 1:27
for it is *s* for women ..... 1 Cor 14:35
For it is *s* even to .... Eph 5:12

SHAMGAR
Judge of Israel; strikes down 600 Philistines, Judg 3:31

SHAMMAH
Son of Jesse, 1 Sam 16:9
Called Shimea, 1 Chr 2:13
——— One of David's mighty men, 2 Sam 23:11
Also called Shammoth the Harorite, 1 Chr 11:27

SHAPHAN
Scribe under Josiah, 2 Kin 22:3–14

SHARE
a stranger does not *s* ..... Prov 14:10
s in anything done under .... Eccl 9:6
s your bread with the .... Is 58:7
is taught the word *s* .... Gal 6:6
to give, willing to *s* .... 1 Tim 6:18
to do good and to *s* .... Heb 13:16
lest you *s* in her sins, and ... Rev 18:4

SHARING
for your liberal *s* .... 2 Cor 9:13

SHARON
Coastal plain between Joppa and Mt. Carmel, 1 Chr 27:29
Famed for roses, Song 2:1
Inhabitants of, turn to the Lord, Acts 9:35

SHARP
destruction, like a *s* razor .... Ps 52:2
S as a two-edged sword ..... Prov 5:4
sledge with *s* teeth .... Is 41:15
My mouth like a *s* sword ..... Is 49:2
son of man, take a *s* sword .. Ezek 5:1
went a *s* two-edged sword .... Rev 1:16
who has the *s* two-edged .... Rev 2:12
and in His hand a *s* sickle .. Rev 14:14

SHARPEN
s their tongue like a .... Ps 64:3
and one does not *s* .... Eccl 10:10

SHARPENS
My adversary *s* His . . . . Job 16:9

SHARPNESS
I should use *s* . . . . 2 Cor 13:10

SHATTERED
at ease, but He has *s* . . . . Job 16:12

SHAVE
Then the Nazirite shall *s* . . . Num 6:18
s off the seven locks . . . . . . Judg 16:19
will *s* with a hired razor . . . . . . Is 7:20
they may *s* their heads . . . . . Acts 21:24

SHAVED
s off half of their beards . . 2 Sam 10:4
as if her head were *s* . . . . . . 1 Cor 11:5

SHEALTIEL
Son of King Jeconiah and father of Zerubbabel, 1 Chr 3:17

SHEAR-JASHUB
Symbolic name given to Isaiah's son, Is 7:3

SHEATH
'Return it to its *s* . . . . Ezek 21:30
your sword into the *s* . . . . . John 18:11

SHEAVES
bringing his *s* . . . . Ps 126:6
nor he who binds *s* . . . . Ps 129:7
gather them like *s* . . . . Mic 4:12

SHEBA
Land of, occupied by Sabeans, famous traders, Job 1:15; Ps 72:10
Queen of, visits Solomon; marvels at his wisdom, 1 Kin 10:1–13
Mentioned by Christ, Matt 12:42

SHEBAH
Name given to a well and town (Beersheba), Gen 26:31–33

SHEBNA
Treasurer under Hezekiah, Is 22:15
Demoted to position of scribe, 2 Kin 19:2
Man of pride and luxury, replaced by Eliakim, Is 22:19–21

SHECHEM
Son of Hamor; rapes Dinah, Jacob's daughter, Gen 34:1–31
——— Ancient city of Ephraim, Gen 33:18
Joshua's farewell address delivered at, Josh 24:1–25
Supports Abimelech; destroyed, Judg 9
Rebuilt by Jeroboam I, 1 Kin 12:25

SHED
s blood without cause . . . 1 Sam 25:31
s innocent blood . . . . Ps 106:38
which is *s* for many . . . . . . Matt 26:28
which is *s* for many . . . . . . Mark 14:24
s from the foundation of . . Luke 11:50
blood, which is *s* for . . . . . . Luke 22:20
martyr Stephen was *s* . . . . . Acts 22:20
feet are swift to *s* blood . . . . Rom 3:15
they have *s* the blood of . . . . . Rev 16:6
of His servants *s* by her . . . . . Rev 19:2

SHEDDING
blood, and without *s* . . . . Heb 9:22

SHEEP
spared the best of the *s* . . 1 Sam 15:15
as *s* that have no . . . . 2 Chr 18:16
like *s* intended for food . . . . Ps 44:11
as *s* for the slaughter . . . . Ps 44:22
s of Your pasture . . . . Ps 79:13
and the *s* of His hand . . . . Ps 95:7
and the *s* of His pasture . . . . . . Ps 100:3
astray like a lost *s* . . . . Ps 119:176
All we like *s* have gone . . . . Is 53:6
slaughter, and as a *s* . . . . Is 53:7
Pull them out like *s* . . . . Jer 12:3
scatter the *s* of My pasture . . . Jer 23:1
have been lost *s* . . . . Jer 50:6
My *s* wandered through . . . . Ezek 34:6
will search for My *s* . . . . . . Ezek 34:11
shall judge between *s* . . . . . Ezek 34:17
lion among flocks of *s* . . . . Mic 5:8
s will be scattered . . . . Zech 13:7
like *s* having no shepherd . . Matt 9:36
rather to the lost *s* . . . . Matt 10:6
I send you out as *s* . . . . Matt 10:16
lost *s* of the house of . . . . . . Matt 15:24
If a man has a hundred *s* . . Matt 18:12
his *s* from the goats . . . . Matt 25:32
And He will set the *s* . . . . . . Matt 25:33
s not having a shepherd . . . Mark 6:34
s will be scattered . . . . Mark 14:27
having a hundred *s* . . . . Luke 15:4
plowing or tending *s* . . . . Luke 17:7
the shepherd of the *s* . . . . John 10:2
and he calls his own *s* . . . . . John 10:3
and I know My *s* . . . . John 10:14
s I have which are not . . . . John 10:16
you are not of My *s* . . . . John 10:26
said to him, "Tend My *s* . . John 21:16
said to him, "Feed My *s*. . John 21:17
"He was led as a *s* . . . . Acts 8:32
as *s* for the slaughter . . . . Rom 8:36
great Shepherd of the *s* . . . . Heb 13:20
like *s* going astray . . . . 1 Pet 2:25

SHEEPFOLDS
lie down among the *s* . . . . . . Ps 68:13

SHEET
object like a great *s* . . . . Acts 10:11

SHELTER
I will trust in the *s* . . . . Ps 61:4
in You I take *s* . . . . Ps 143:9
the LORD will be a *s* . . . . Joel 3:16

SHELTERS
s him all the day long . . . . . Deut 33:12
be pastures, with *s* . . . . Zeph 2:6

SHEM
Oldest son of Noah, Gen 5:32
Escapes the flood, Gen 7:13
Receives a blessing, Gen 9:23, 26
Ancestor of Semitic people, Gen 10:22–32

SHEMAIAH
Prophet of Judah, 1 Kin 12:22–24
Explains Shishak's invasion as divine punishment, 2 Chr 12:5–8
Records Rehoboam's reign, 2 Chr 12:15

SHEMER
Sells Omri the hill on which Samaria is built, 1 Kin 16:23, 24

SHEOL
down to the gates of *S* . . . . . Job 17:16
not leave my soul in *S*. . . . . . . Ps 16:10
S laid hold of me . . . . Ps 116:3
S cannot thank . . . . Is 38:18
the belly of *S* I cried . . . . Jon 2:2

SHEPHERD
s is an abomination . . . . Gen 46:34
s My people Israel . . . . 2 Sam 5:2
The LORD is my *s* . . . . Ps 23:1
s Jacob His people . . . . Ps 78:71
His flock like a *s* . . . . Is 40:11
of Cyrus, 'He is My *s* . . . . Is 44:28
s who follows You . . . . Jer 17:16
because there was no *s* . . . . Ezek 34:5
I will establish one *s* . . . . . . Ezek 34:23
"As a *s* takes from . . . . Amos 3:12
to the worthless *s* . . . . Zech 11:17
'I will strike the *S* . . . . Matt 26:31
"I am the good *s* . . . . John 10:11
s the church of God . . . . Acts 20:28
the dead, that great *S* . . . . . . Heb 13:20
S the flock of God . . . . 1 Pet 5:2
when the Chief *S* . . . . 1 Pet 5:4
of the throne will *s* . . . . Rev 7:17

SHEPHERDS
your sons shall be *s* . . . . . . Num 14:33
And they are *s* who . . . . Is 56:11
And I will give you *s* . . . . Jer 3:15
s who destroy and . . . . Jer 23:1
s who feed My people . . . . Jer 23:2
s have led them astray . . . . Jer 50:6
s fed themselves . . . . Ezek 34:8
in the same country *s* . . . . Luke 2:8

SHESHACH
Symbolic of Babylon, Jer 25:26

SHESHBAZZAR
Prince of Judah, Ezra 1:8, 11

SHETHAR-BOZNAI
Official of Persia, Ezra 5:3, 6

SHIELD
I am your *s* . . . . Gen 15:1
the *s* of your help and . . . . Deut 33:29
s of Saul, not anointed . . . . 2 Sam 1:21
whom I will trust: my *s* . . . 2 Sam 22:3
He is a *s* to all who . . . . . . 2 Sam 22:31
gold went into each *s* . . . . . 2 Chr 9:15
are a *s* for me, my glory . . . . . . Ps 3:3
surround him as with a *s* . . . . . Ps 5:12
my *s* and the horn of . . . . Ps 18:2
He is a *s* to all who trust in . . Ps 18:30
me the *s* of Your salvation . . Ps 18:35
my strength and my *s* . . . . Ps 28:7
He is our help and our *s* . . . . . Ps 33:20
God is a sun and *s* . . . . Ps 84:11
truth shall be your *s* . . . . Ps 91:4
He is their help and their *s* . . Ps 115:9
hiding place and my *s* . . . . . Ps 119:114
all, taking the *s* . . . . Eph 6:16

SHIHOR
Name given to the Nile, Is 23:3
Israel's southwestern border, Josh 13:3

SHILOH
Center of worship, Judg 18:31
Headquarters for division of Promised Land, Josh 18:1, 10
Benjamites seize women of, Judg 21:19–23
Ark of the covenant taken from, 1 Sam 4:3–11
Punishment given to, Jer 7:12–15
——— Messianic title, Gen 49:10

SHIMEI
Benjamite; insults David, 2 Sam 16:5–13
Pardoned, but confined, 2 Sam 19:16–23
Breaks agreement; executed by Solomon, 1 Kin 2:39–46

SHIMSHAI
Scribe opposing the Jews, Ezra 4:8–24

SHINAR
Tower built at, Gen 11:2–9

SHINE
LORD make His face *s* . . . . . . Num 6:25
even the moon does not *s* . . . Job 25:5
Make Your face *s* upon . . . . . . Ps 31:16
cause His face to *s* . . . . Ps 67:1
the cherubim, *s* . . . . Ps 80:1
Make Your face *s* . . . . Ps 119:135
will not cause its light to *s* . . Is 13:10
Arise, *s*; for your light . . . . Is 60:1
who are wise shall *s* . . . . Dan 12:3
your light so *s* before men . . Matt 5:16
the righteous will *s* . . . . Matt 13:43
among whom you *s* . . . . Phil 2:15
a third of the day did not *s* . . Rev 8:12
sun or of the moon to *s* . . . . . Rev 21:23

SHINED
them a light has *s* . . . . Is 9:2

SHINES
But the night *s* as the day . . . Ps 139:12
that *s* ever brighter unto . . . Prov 4:18
And the light *s* . . . John 1:5
light that *s* in a dark . . . 2 Pet 1:19

SHINING
the earth, by clear *s* . . . 2 Sam 23:4
the just is like the *s* sun . . . Prov 4:18
His clothes became *s* . . . Mark 9:3
by them in *s* garments . . . Luke 24:4
light is already *s* . . . 1 John 2:8
was like the sun *s* . . . Rev 1:16

SHIP
the way of a *s* in the . . . Prov 30:19
found a *s* going to Tarshish . . Jon 1:3
finding a *s* sailing over to . . Acts 21:2
some on parts of the *s* . . . Acts 27:44

SHIPHRAH
Hebrew midwife, Ex 1:15

SHIPS
pass by like swift *s* . . . Job 9:26
down to the sea in *s* . . . Ps 107:23
like the merchant *s* . . . Prov 31:14
Look also at *s* . . . James 3:4

SHIPWRECK
faith have suffered *s* . . . 1 Tim 1:19

SHONE
the skin of Moses' face *s* . . Ex 34:35
His face *s* like the sun . . . Matt 17:2
of the Lord *s* around them . . Luke 2:9
a light *s* around him . . . Acts 9:3
and a light *s* in the prison . . Acts 12:7

SHOOK
so loudly that the earth *s* . . 1 Sam 4:5
the earth *s* and trembled . . 2 Sam 22:8
earth *s*; the heavens also . . . Ps 68:8
The earth trembled and *s* . . Ps 77:18
guards *s* for fear of him . . . Matt 28:4
they *s* off the dust from . . . Acts 13:51

SHOOT
they *s* out the lip . . . Ps 22:7
But God shall *s* . . . Ps 64:7

SHORT
of the wicked is *s* . . . Job 20:5
Remember how *s* my time . . . Ps 89:47
for he was of *s* stature . . . Luke 19:3
have sinned and fall *s* . . . Rom 3:23
the work and cut it *s* . . . Rom 9:28
fall *s* of the grace of God . . Heb 12:15
knows that he has a *s* . . . Rev 12:12

SHORTENED
his youth You have *s* . . . Ps 89:45
the wicked will be *s* . . . Prov 10:27
those days were *s* . . . Matt 24:22
Lord had *s* those days . . . Mark 13:20

SHORTLY
which must *s* take place . . . Rev 1:1
which must *s* take place . . . Rev 22:6

SHOT
shall be stoned or *s* . . . Heb 12:20

SHOULDER
will be upon His *s* . . . Is 9:6

SHOUT
shall *s* with a great *s* . . . Josh 6:5
s for joy, all you upright in . . Ps 32:11
skillfully with a *s* of joy . . . Ps 33:3
s for joy and be glad . . . Ps 35:27
S to God with the voice of . . . Ps 47:1
Make a joyful *s* to God, all . . Ps 66:1
Make a joyful *s* to the God . . . Ps 81:1
s joyfully to the Rock . . . Ps 95:1
S joyfully to the LORD . . . Ps 98:4
Make a joyful *s* . . . Ps 100:1
from heaven with a *s* . . . 1 Thess 4:16

SHOUTED
So the people *s* when the . . . Josh 6:20
they *s*, saying, "Crucify . . . Luke 23:21

SHOW
a land that I will *s* . . . Gen 12:1
will *s* Yourself merciful . . 2 Sam 22:26
will *s* Yourself merciful . . . Ps 18:25
S me Your ways . . . Ps 25:4
I will *s* the salvation of . . . Ps 50:23
mouth shall *s* forth Your . . . Ps 51:15
S us Your mercy, LORD . . . Ps 85:7
and *s* us what will happen . . . Is 41:22
s yourselves men . . . Is 46:8
s mercy and compassion . . . Zech 7:9
s them a sign from . . . Matt 16:1
S Me the tax money . . . Matt 22:19
s great signs and . . . Matt 24:24
s signs and wonders to . . . Mark 13:22
s Him greater works . . . John 5:20
s Yourself to the world . . . John 7:4
s us the Father . . . John 14:8
you say, '*S* us the Father . . . John 14:9
I *s* you a more excellent . . 1 Cor 12:31
S me your faith without . . James 2:18
I will *s* you things which . . . Rev 4:1

SHOWBREAD
you shall set the *s* . . . Ex 25:30
s which had been taken . . . 1 Sam 21:6
s which was not lawful . . . Matt 12:4

SHOWED
s him mercy, and He . . . Gen 39:21
and the LORD *s* him a tree . . . Ex 15:25
s Him all the kingdoms . . . Matt 4:8
s Him all the kingdoms . . . Luke 4:5
But even Moses *s* in the . . Luke 20:37
s them His hands and . . . Luke 24:40
s them His hands and . . . John 20:20
Jesus *s* Himself again to . . . John 21:1
third day, and *s* Him . . . Acts 10:40
s me the great city, the . . . Rev 21:10

SHOWERS
make it soft with *s* . . . Ps 65:10
s have been withheld . . . Jer 3:3
can the heavens give *s* . . . Jer 14:22
from the LORD, like *s* . . . Mic 5:7

SHOWN
You have *s* Your servant . . Gen 32:10
have *s* more kindness . . . Ruth 3:10
grace be *s* to the wicked . . . Is 26:10
s you from My Father . . . John 10:32

SHOWS
firmament *s* His handiwork . . . Ps 19:1
that God *s* no partiality . . . Acts 10:34
God *s* personal favoritism . . . Gal 2:6

SHREWDLY
because he had dealt *s* . . . Luke 16:8

SHRINES
who made silver *s* . . . Acts 19:24

SHRIVELED
You have *s* me up . . . Job 16:8

SHUFFLES
with his eyes, he *s* . . . Prov 6:13

SHULAMITE
Beloved of the bridegroom king, Song 6:13

SHUNAMMITE
Abishag, David's nurse, 1 Kin 1:3, 15
—— Woman who cared for Elisha, 2 Kin 4:8–12

SHUNEM
Town of Issachar, Josh 19:18

SHUNNED
feared God and *s* evil . . . Job 1:1

SHUR
Wilderness in south Palestine, Gen 16:7
Israel went from Red Sea to, Ex 15:22
Hagar fled here, Gen 16:7

SHUSHAN
Residence of Persian monarchs, Esth 1:2

SHUT
s the door behind him . . . Gen 19:6
Let her be *s* out of the . . . Num 12:14
"Or who *s* in the sea . . . Job 38:8
Has He in anger *s* . . . Ps 77:9
For you *s* up the . . . Matt 23:13
came, the doors being *s* . . . John 20:26
door, and no one can *s* it . . . Rev 3:8
have power to *s* heaven . . . Rev 11:6

SHUTS
s his ears to the cry . . . Prov 21:13
s his eyes from seeing . . . Is 33:15
brother in need, and *s* . . . 1 John 3:17
who opens and no one *s* . . . Rev 3:7

SICK
have made him *s* . . . Hos 7:5
I was *s* and you . . . Matt 25:36
he whom You love is *s* . . . John 11:3
many are weak and *s* . . . 1 Cor 11:30
have left in Miletus *s* . . . 2 Tim 4:20
faith will save the *s* . . . James 5:15

SICKLE
Put in the *s* . . . Joel 3:13
"Thrust in Your *s* . . . Rev 14:15

SICKNESS
will sustain him in *s* . . . Prov 18:14
"This *s* is not unto . . . John 11:4

SICKNESSES
And bore our *s* . . . Matt 8:17

SIDE
two rings shall be on one *s* . . Ex 25:12
And a cubit on one *s* . . . Ex 26:13
For the south *s* there shall . . . Ex 27:9
this *s* of the Jordan in the . . . Deut 1:1
on this *s* of the Jordan . . . Josh 1:14
me down on every *s* . . . Job 19:10
wicked prowl on every *s* . . . Ps 12:8
Fear is on every *s* . . . Ps 31:13
hills rejoice on every *s* . . . Ps 65:12
comfort me on every *s* . . . Ps 71:21
The LORD is on my *s* . . . Ps 118:6
Lie also on your left *s* . . . Ezek 4:4
gate chambers on one *s* . . . Ezek 40:10
robe sitting on the right *s* . . Mark 16:5
pierced His *s* with a . . . John 19:34
His hands and His *s* . . . John 20:20
put my hand into His *s* . . . John 20:25
the net on the right *s* . . . John 21:6

SIDON
See TYRE AND SIDON
Canaanite city; inhabitants not expelled, Judg 1:31
Hostile relations with Israel, Judg 10:12; Is 23:12; Joel 3:4–6
Jesus preaches to, Matt 15:21; Luke 6:17

SIFT
s the nations with the . . . Is 30:28
s the house of Israel . . . Amos 9:9
for you, that he may *s* . . . Luke 22:31

SIFTS
A wise king *s* out the . . . Prov 20:26

SIGH
our years like a *s* . . . Ps 90:9
the merry-hearted *s* . . . Is 24:7
of the men who *s* . . . Ezek 9:4

SIGHING
For my *s* comes before . . . Job 3:24
s is not hidden . . . Ps 38:9

SIGHT
and see this great *s* . . . Ex 3:3
evil in the *s* of the LORD . . . Judg 2:11
as stupid in your *s* . . . Job 18:3
of human waste in their *s* . . Ezek 4:12
seemed good in Your *s* . . . Matt 11:26
he received his *s* . . . Mark 10:52
abomination in the *s* of . . . Luke 16:15

washed, and I received *s* ... John 9:11
he marveled at the *s* .... Acts 7:31
three days without *s* .... Acts 9:9
are just in the *s* of God ..... Rom 2:13
will be justified in His *s* .... Rom 3:20
by faith, not by *s* .... 2 Cor 5:7
precious in the *s* of God ..... 1 Pet 3:4

SIGN
Show me a *s* for good .... Ps 86:17
will give you a *s* .... Is 7:14
for an everlasting *s* .... Is 55:13
we want to see a *s* .... Matt 12:38
seeks after a *s* .... Matt 12:39
And what will be the *s* ..... Matt 24:3
s which will be spoken .... Luke 2:34
again is the second *s* ...... John 4:54
For Jews request a *s* ...... 1 Cor 1:22
Now a great *s* appeared ..... Rev 12:1

SIGNS
and let them be for *s* .... Gen 1:14
you not know their *s* .... Job 21:29
They performed His *s* ...... Ps 105:27
We are for *s* and .... Is 8:18
How great are His *s* .... Dan 4:3
cannot discern the *s* .... Matt 16:3
the accompanying *s* ...... Mark 16:20
s Jesus did in Cana of ..... John 2:11
no one can do these *s* .... John 3:2
because you saw the *s* ..... John 6:26
is a sinner do such *s* .... John 9:16
this Man works many *s* ... John 11:47
Jesus did many other *s* ... John 20:30
demons, performing *s* ..... Rev 16:14

SIGNS AND WONDERS
Lord showed *s* .... Deut 6:22
great terror and with *s* ..... Deut 26:8
s against Pharaoh .... Neh 9:10
He sent *s* .... Ps 135:9
We are for *s* in Israel .... Is 8:18
good to declare the *s* .... Dan 4:2
He works *s* in heaven ...... Dan 6:27
rise and show great *s* ..... Matt 24:24
"Unless you people see *s* .. John 4:48
s may be done through ..... Acts 4:30
of the apostles many *s* ..... Acts 5:12
His grace, granting *s* .... Acts 14:3
mighty *s*, by the power .... Rom 15:19
in *s* and mighty deeds .... 2 Cor 12:12
bearing witness both with *s* .. Heb 2:4

SIHON
Amorite king; defeated by Israel, Num 21:21–32
Territory of, assigned to Reuben and Gad, Num 32:1–38

SILAS (or Silvanus)
Leader in Jerusalem church; sent to Antioch, Acts 15:22–35
Travels with Paul, Acts 15:40, 41
Jailed and released, Acts 16:25–40
Mentioned in epistles, 2 Cor 1:19; 1 Thess 1:1; 2 Thess 1:1; 1 Pet 5:12

SILENCE
that You may *s* .... Ps 8:2
I was mute with *s* .... Ps 39:2
soon have settled in *s* .... Ps 94:17
"Sit in *s* .... Is 47:5
I will not keep *s*, but will ..... Is 65:6
in *s* with all submission ... 1 Tim 2:11
s the ignorance of foolish .. 1 Pet 2:15
seal, there was *s* .... Rev 8:1

SILENT
the wicked shall be *s* ...... 1 Sam 2:9
Oh, that you would be *s* ..... Job 13:5
season, and am not *s* .... Ps 22:2
Do not be *s* to me .... Ps 28:1
praise to You and not be *s* .. Ps 30:12
Let them be *s* in the .... Ps 31:17
come, and shall not keep *s* ... Ps 50:3
before its shearers is *s* .... Is 53:7

Be *s* in the presence .... Zeph 1:7
But Jesus kept *s* .... Matt 26:63
His answer and kept *s* .... Luke 20:26
before its shearer is *s* ...... Acts 8:32
Let your women keep *s* .. 1 Cor 14:34

SILK
and covered you with *s* ... Ezek 16:10

SILLY
They are *s* children .... Jer 4:22

SILOAM
Tower of, falls and kills 18 people, Luke 13:4
Blind man washes in pool of, John 9:1–11

SILVER
and your precious *s* .... Job 22:25
Though he heaps up *s* ..... Job 27:16
s tried in a furnace .... Ps 12:6
have refined us as *s* .... Ps 66:10
than the profits of *s* .... Prov 3:14
chosen rather than *s* ...... Prov 16:16
refining pot is for *s* .... Prov 17:3
He who loves *s* will .... Eccl 5:10
s has become dross .... Is 1:22
call them rejected *s* .... Jer 6:30
may buy the poor for *s* ..... Amos 8:6
him thirty pieces of *s* ..... Matt 26:15

SIMEON
Son of Jacob by Leah, Gen 29:32, 33
Avenges his sister's dishonor, Gen 34:25–31
Held hostage by Joseph, Gen 42:18–20, 24
Rebuked by Jacob, Gen 49:5–7
—— Tribe of:
Numbered, Num 1:23; 26:12–14
Receive inheritance, Josh 19:1–9
Fight Canaanites with Judah, Judg 1:1–3, 17–20
—— Just man; blesses infant Jesus, Luke 2:25–35

SIMILITUDE
been made in the *s* .... James 3:9

SIMON
Simon Peter: *see* PETER
—— One of the Twelve; called "the Cananite," Matt 10:4
—— One of Jesus' half brothers, Matt 13:55
—— Pharisee, Luke 7:36–40
—— Man of Cyrene, bears Jesus' cross, Matt 27:32
—— Sorcerer, Acts 8:9–24
—— Tanner in Joppa, Acts 9:43

SIMPLE
making wise the *s* .... Ps 19:7
LORD preserves the *s* .... Ps 116:6
understanding to the *s* .... Ps 119:130
s believes every word ..... Prov 14:15
the hearts of the *s* .... Rom 16:18

SIMPLICITY
ones, will you love *s* .... Prov 1:22
in the world in *s* .... 2 Cor 1:12
corrupted from the *s* ...... 2 Cor 11:3

SIN
not well, *s* lies at the door .... Gen 4:7
because their *s* is very ..... Gen 18:20
brothers and their *s* .... Gen 50:17
It is a *s* offering .... Ex 29:14
committed a great *s* .... Ex 32:30
offer to the LORD for his *s* .... Lev 4:3
the *s* which they have .... Lev 4:14
a lamb as his *s* offering ..... Lev 4:32
of the goats as a *s* offering ... Lev 5:6
is the law of the *s* offering ... Lev 6:25
They shall bear their *s* ..... Lev 20:20
his God shall bear his *s* .... Lev 24:15
any *s* that men commit in ... Num 5:6

If you *s* unintentionally ... Num 15:22
flesh, shall one man *s* ..... Num 16:22
he died in his own *s* .... Num 27:3
goats as a *s* offering .... Num 29:5
and be sure your *s* .... Num 32:23
because of all your *s* .... Deut 9:18
it become *s* among you .... Deut 15:9
or any *s* that he commits .. Deut 19:15
you *s* against the LORD ...... Deut 20:18
a *s* deserving of death .... Deut 21:22
no *s* deserving of death ... Deut 22:26
to death for his own *s* ..... Deut 24:16
forgive the *s* of Your ...... 1 Kin 8:34
When they *s* against You .. 1 Kin 8:46
this thing became a *s* ..... 1 Kin 12:30
in his *s* by which .... 1 Kin 15:26
and made Israel *s* .... 1 Kin 21:22
to death for his own *s* ..... 2 Kin 14:6
made Judah *s* with his .... 2 Kin 21:11
forgive the *s* of Your .... 2 Chr 6:25
and will forgive their *s* .... 2 Chr 7:14
shall die for his own *s* .... 2 Chr 25:4
do not let their *s* be blotted .. Neh 4:5
In all this Job did not *s* nor .. Job 1:22
all this Job did not *s* .... Job 2:10
and search out my *s* .... Job 10:6
he adds rebellion to his *s* ... Job 34:37
Be angry, and do not *s* .... Ps 4:4
whose *s* is covered .... Ps 32:1
I acknowledged my *s* .... Ps 32:5
my bones because of my *s* .... Ps 38:3
my ways, lest I *s* .... Ps 39:1
And cleanse me from my *s* ... Ps 51:2
s is always before me .... Ps 51:3
in *s* my mother .... Ps 51:5
the *s* of their mouth .... Ps 59:12
I might not *s* against You .. Ps 119:11
of the wicked to *s* .... Prov 10:16
Fools mock at *s* .... Prov 14:9
s is a reproach .... Prov 14:34
I am pure from my *s* .... Prov 20:9
mouth cause your flesh to *s* .. Eccl 5:6
good and does not *s* .... Eccl 7:20
away, and your *s* purged .... Is 6:7
soul an offering for *s* .... Is 53:10
And He bore the *s* .... Is 53:12
what is our *s* that we have .. Jer 16:10
your high places of *s* .... Jer 17:3
s I will remember no .... Jer 31:34
he shall die in his *s* .... Ezek 3:20
and confessing my *s* .... Dan 9:20
They eat up the *s* .... Hos 4:8
Now they *s* more and .... Hos 13:2
right eye causes you to *s* ... Matt 5:29
I say to you, every *s* and .. Matt 12:31
who believe in Me to *s* ..... Matt 18:6
hand causes you to *s* ...... Mark 9:43
who takes away the *s* ...... John 1:29
S no more .... John 5:14
"He who is without *s* .... John 8:7
go and *s* no more .... John 8:11
Me, and will die in your *s* .. John 8:21
commits *s* is a slave of *s* ... John 8:34
of you convicts Me of *s* .... John 8:46
you would have no *s* .... John 9:41
convict the world of *s* ...... John 16:8
they are all under *s* .... Rom 3:9
law is the knowledge of *s* .. Rom 3:20
LORD shall not impute *s* ..... Rom 4:8
s entered the world .... Rom 5:12
s is not imputed .... Rom 5:13
where *s* abounded, grace ... Rom 5:20
s that grace may .... Rom 6:1
that the body of *s* might be .. Rom 6:6
died to *s* once for all ...... Rom 6:10
s shall not have .... Rom 6:14
Shall we *s* because we ..... Rom 6:15
you were slaves of *s* .... Rom 6:17
been set free from *s* .... Rom 6:22
the wages of *s* is death ..... Rom 6:23
Is the law *s*? .... Rom 7:7
s revived and I died .... Rom 7:9

s that dwells in me .... Rom 7:17
me free from the law of s ... Rom 8:2
body is dead because of s .. Rom 8:10
Every s that a man does ... 1 Cor 6:18
you s against Christ .... 1 Cor 8:12
The sting of death is s .... 1 Cor 15:56
Him who knew no s .... 2 Cor 5:21
man of s is revealed ...... 2 Thess 2:3
we are, yet without s .... Heb 4:15
appeared to put away s ..... Heb 9:26
longer an offering for s .... Heb 10:18
s willfully after we .... Heb 10:26
it gives birth to s .... James 1:15
partiality, you commit s .... James 2:9
do it, to him it is s .... James 4:17
"Who committed no s .... 1 Pet 2:22
the flesh has ceased from s .. 1 Pet 4:1
that cannot cease from s ... 2 Pet 2:14
cleanses us from all s ..... 1 John 1:7
say that we have no s ..... 1 John 1:8
that you may not s .... 1 John 2:1
s is lawlessness .... 1 John 3:4
in Him there is no s .... 1 John 3:5
and he cannot s .... 1 John 3:9
s which does not lead .... 1 John 5:16
there is s not leading to .. 1 John 5:17

SINAI

Mountain (same as Horeb) where the law was given, Ex 19:1–25
Used allegorically by Paul, Gal 4:24, 25

SINCERE

Holy Spirit, by s love .... 2 Cor 6:6
that you may be s .... Phil 1:10
and from s faith .... 1 Tim 1:5
s love of the brethren ...... 1 Pet 1:22

SINCERITY

LORD, serve Him in s...... Josh 24:14
unleavened bread of s ...... 1 Cor 5:8
simplicity and godly s ..... 2 Cor 1:12
as of s, but as from God, .. 2 Cor 2:17
testing the s of your love ... 2 Cor 8:8
in s of heart, as to Christ .... Eph 6:5
our Lord Jesus Christ in s .. Eph 6:24
men-pleasers, but in s .... Col 3:22

SINFUL

place, a brood of s men ... Num 32:14
Alas, s nation .... Is 1:4
and s generation .... Mark 8:38
from me, for I am a s ...... Luke 5:8
the hands of s men .... Luke 24:7
become exceedingly s ...... Rom 7:13
likeness of s flesh .... Rom 8:3

SING

"S to the LORD .... Ex 15:21
Awake, awake, s a song ... Judg 5:12
s praises to Your name .. 2 Sam 22:50
S to the LORD, all the..... 1 Chr 16:23
when they began to s .... 2 Chr 20:22
the widow's heart to s .... Job 29:13
S praises to the LORD, who ... Ps 9:11
I will s to the LORD........... Ps 13:6
S to Him a new song .... Ps 33:3
my tongue shall s aloud of .. Ps 51:14
shout for joy, they also s .... Ps 65:13
S out the honor .... Ps 66:2
nations be glad and s for ..... Ps 67:4
You I will s with the harp ... Ps 71:22
I will s of the mercies of ..... Ps 89:1
s to the LORD a new song..... Ps 98:1
I will s of mercy and .... Ps 101:1
I will s to the LORD as ...... Ps 104:33
S praises to His name .... Ps 135:3
"S us one of the songs ...... Ps 137:3
they shall s of the ways of ... Ps 138:5
S to the LORD a new song ... Ps 149:1
S to the LORD, for He has ..... Is 12:5
up their voice, they shall s ... Is 24:14
S to the LORD a new song.... Is 42:10
My servants shall s .... Is 65:14
she shall s there, as in the .. Hos 2:15
S and rejoice, O daughter .. Zech 2:10
I will s with the .... 1 Cor 14:15
assembly I will s .... Heb 2:12
Let him s psalms .... James 5:13
They s the song of Moses ... Rev 15:3

SINGERS

instruments for s .... 1 Kin 10:12
who bore the ark, the s .. 1 Chr 15:27
instruments for s .... 2 Chr 9:11
s with musical .... 2 Chr 23:13
s sang, and the .... 2 Chr 29:28
The s sang loudly with .... Neh 12:42
The s went before........... Ps 68:25
male and female s .... Eccl 2:8

SINGING

rejoicing and with s .... 2 Chr 23:18
s to the LORD .... 2 Chr 30:21
with thanksgivings and s .. Neh 12:27
His presence with s .... Ps 100:2
and our tongue with s .... Ps 126:2
the time of s has come ..... Song 2:12
break forth into s .... Is 14:7
even with joy and s .... Is 35:2
come to Zion with s .... Is 35:10
With a voice of s, declare .... Is 48:20
and come to Zion with s ..... Is 51:11
and s hymns to God ...... Acts 16:25
and spiritual songs, s .... Eph 5:19
s with grace in your hearts .. Col 3:16

SINGLENESS

them s of heart to obey .. 2 Chr 30:12

SINISTER

who understands s .... Dan 8:23

SINK

I s in deep mire .... Ps 69:2
to s he cried out .... Matt 14:30

SINNED

had ceased, he s yet more .... Ex 9:34
has s a young bull without ... Lev 4:3
promised, for we have s .. Num 14:40
s against their own souls .. Num 16:38
to the LORD, "We have s .. Judg 10:15
Saul said, "I have s ..... 1 Sam 26:21
may be that my sons have s .. Job 1:5
Have I s? What have I ...... Job 7:20
those who have s .... Job 24:19
for I have s against You .... Ps 41:4
You only, have I s .... Ps 51:4
you say, 'I have not s .... Jer 2:35
Jerusalem has s .... Lam 1:8
Our fathers s and are .... Lam 5:7
we have s and committed .... Dan 9:5
the more they s against Me .. Hos 4:7
you have s from the days ... Hos 10:9
"I have s by betraying ..... Matt 27:4
"Father, I have s .... Luke 15:18
"Rabbi, who s .... John 9:2
For as many as have s ...... Rom 2:12
for all have s and .... Rom 3:23
marries, she has not s ..... 1 Cor 7:28
not spare the angels who s .. 2 Pet 2:4
say that we have not s ..... 1 John 1:10
for the devil has s .... 1 John 3:8

SINNED AGAINST THE LORD

"I have s your God .... Ex 10:16
s your God—had made ..... Deut 9:16
"Indeed I have s .... Josh 7:20
said there, "We have s..... 1 Sam 7:6
to Nathan, "I have s ..... 2 Sam 12:13
For we have s .... Jer 3:25
because we have s .... Jer 8:14
because you have s .... Jer 44:23
because they have s .... Zeph 1:17

SINNED AGAINST YOU

saying, "We have s .... Judg 10:10
I have not s, but you ...... Judg 11:27
I have not s .... 1 Sam 24:11
because they have s .... 1 Kin 8:33
Your people who have s .. 2 Chr 6:39
Israel which we have s ...... Neh 1:6
heal my soul, for I have s ..... Ps 41:4
many, we have s .... Jer 14:7
fathers, because we have s ... Dan 9:8

SINNER

the ungodly and the s ...... Prov 11:31
overthrows the s............ Prov 13:6
of the s is stored up for ... Prov 13:22
s He gives the work .... Eccl 2:26
s shall be trapped by her ... Eccl 7:26
s does evil a hundred .... Eccl 8:12
As is the good, so is the s .... Eccl 9:2
s destroys much good ...... Eccl 9:18
the city who was a s....... Luke 7:37
s who repents than .... Luke 15:7
be merciful to me a s ..... Luke 18:13
can a man who is a s ...... John 9:16
know that this Man is a s .. John 9:24
the ungodly and the s...... 1 Pet 4:18

SINNERS

See TAX COLLECTORS AND SINNERS
utterly destroy the s ..... 1 Sam 15:18
in the path of s .... Ps 1:1
nor s in the congregation ...... Ps 1:5
therefore He teaches s .... Ps 25:8
soul with s .... Ps 26:9
s be consumed from the .... Ps 104:35
son, if s entice you .... Prov 1:10
Evil pursues s, but to the .. Prov 13:21
not let your heart envy s .. Prov 23:17
The s in Zion are .... Is 33:14
All the s of My people ..... Amos 9:10
s came and sat down with .. Matt 9:10
the righteous, but s .... Matt 9:13
tax collectors and s .... Matt 11:19
into the hands of s .... Matt 26:45
and s also sat together .... Mark 2:15
into the hands of s .... Mark 14:41
call the righteous, but s .... Luke 5:32
s love those who love ...... Luke 6:32
of tax collectors and s ..... Luke 7:34
Galileans were worse s .... Luke 13:2
man receives s and eats ... Luke 15:2
God does not hear s .... John 9:31
while we were still s .... Rom 5:8
many were made s .... Rom 5:19
the ungodly and for s ...... 1 Tim 1:9
the world to save s........ 1 Tim 1:15
separate from s .... Heb 7:26
such hostility from s .... Heb 12:3
things which ungodly s ...... Jude 15

SINS

'If a person s .... Lev 4:2
s unintentionally in regard .. Lev 5:15
of the s of Jeroboam ..... 1 Kin 14:16
my iniquities and s .... Job 13:23
from presumptuous s........ Ps 19:13
the s of my youth .... Ps 25:7
pain, and forgive all my s ... Ps 25:18
Hide Your face from my s .... Ps 51:9
s are not hidden from You .... Ps 69:5
atonement for our s .... Ps 79:9
You, our secret s .... Ps 90:8
but he who s against .... Prov 8:36
but love covers all s ...... Prov 10:12
despises his neighbor s ... Prov 14:21
s against his own life ...... Prov 20:2
s have hidden His face .... Is 59:2
your s have withheld good ... Jer 5:25
He will uncover your s ...... Lam 4:22
the soul who s shall .... Ezek 18:4
to make an end of s .... Dan 9:24
His people from their s .... Matt 1:21
Jordan, confessing their s ... Matt 3:6
power on earth to forgive s .. Matt 9:6
if your brother s .... Matt 18:15
for the remission of s ..... Matt 26:28
for the remission of s .... Mark 1:4
forgive s but God alone ...... Mark 2:7
for the remission of s .... Luke 3:3

on earth to forgive *s* .... Luke 5:24
brother *s* against you ...... Luke 17:3
that you will die in your *s* .. John 8:24
I take away their *s* .... Rom 11:27
s according to the .... 1 Cor 15:3
are still in your *s* .... 1 Cor 15:17
who gave Himself for our *s* ... Gal 1:4
the forgiveness of *s* .... Eph 1:7
blood, the forgiveness of *s* ... Col 1:14
s are clearly evident .... 1 Tim 5:24
by Himself purged our *s* ...... Heb 1:3
once to bear the *s* .... Heb 9:28
one sacrifice for *s* forever .. Heb 10:12
cover a multitude of *s* .... James 5:20
that we, having died to *s* ... 1 Pet 2:24
If we confess our *s* .... 1 John 1:9
propitiation for our *s* .... 1 John 2:2
s are forgiven you .... 1 John 2:12
Whoever *s* has neither .... 1 John 3:6
He who *s* is of the devil ... 1 John 3:8
propitiation for our *s* ..... 1 John 4:10
you share in her *s* .... Rev 18:4

SION
See ZION
Name given to all or part of Mt. Hermon, Deut 4:48

SISERA
Canaanite commander of Jabin's army; slain by Jael, Judg 4:2–22

SISTER
Please say you are my *s* ... Gen 12:13
And he said, "She is my *s* .. Gen 26:7
of David had a lovely *s* ... 2 Sam 13:1
are my mother and my *s* ... Job 17:14
fair is your love, my *s* ..... Song 4:10
We have a little *s* .... Song 8:8
treacherous *s* Judah saw it ..... Jer 3:7
Your elder *s* is Samaria ... Ezek 16:46
is My brother and *s* .... Matt 12:50
You not care that my *s* ... Luke 10:40
loved Martha and her *s* .... John 11:5
to you Phoebe our *s* .... Rom 16:1
s is not under bondage .... 1 Cor 7:15

SIT
he shall *s* on my throne ... 1 Kin 1:13
Those who *s* in the .... Ps 69:12
"Come down and *s* .... Is 47:1
"Why do we *s* still .... Jer 8:14
but to *s* on My right ...... Matt 20:23
and the Pharisees *s* .... Matt 23:2
Grant us that we may *s* .. Mark 10:37
"*S* at My right hand ..... Mark 12:36
those who *s* in darkness ... Luke 1:79
s down in the lowest ..... Luke 14:10
"*S* at My right hand .... Heb 1:13
say to him, "You *s* .... James 2:3
I will grant to *s* .... Rev 3:21
heart, 'I *s* as queen .... Rev 18:7

SITS
God *s* on His holy .... Ps 47:8
It is He who *s* above .... Is 40:22
so that he *s* as God .... 2 Thess 2:4
Him who *s* on the throne ..... Rev 4:9
harlot who *s* on many .... Rev 17:1
where the harlot *s* .... Rev 17:15

SITTING
Eli the priest was *s* on ..... 1 Sam 1:9
LORD *s* on His throne..... 1 Kin 22:19
LORD *s* on His throne .... 2 Chr 18:18
You know my *s* down and ... Ps 139:2
s on a donkey, a colt, the ... Matt 21:5
see the Son of Man *s* ..... Mark 14:62
s on a donkey's colt ...... John 12:15
two angels in white *s* ..... John 20:12
where Christ is, *s* .... Col 3:1
I saw twenty-four elders *s* ... Rev 4:4
a woman *s* on a scarlet ..... Rev 17:3

SIX
S days you shall gather it, .. Ex 16:26
S days you shall labor .... Ex 20:9

SKIES
thick clouds of the *s* ..... 2 Sam 22:12
have you spread out the *s* .. Job 37:18
the *s* sent out a sound .... Ps 77:17
and is lifted up to the *s* .... Jer 51:9

SKILL
hand forget its *s* .... Ps 137:5
nor favor to men of *s* .... Eccl 9:11
them knowledge and *s* .... Dan 1:17
forth to give you *s* .... Dan 9:22

SKILLFUL
Esau was a *s* hunter, a .... Gen 25:27
a *s* player on the harp ... 1 Sam 16:16
all types of *s* men for .... 1 Chr 22:15
s work a man is envied ...... Eccl 4:4
the hands of a *s* workman .. Song 7:1
send for *s* wailing women .... Jer 9:17
who are *s* to destroy ...... Ezek 21:31

SKILLFULNESS
guided them by the *s* .... Ps 78:72

SKIN
God made tunics of *s* .... Gen 3:21
s of his face shone while .... Ex 34:29
LORD and said, "*S* .... Job 2:4
sewn sackcloth over my *s* .. Job 16:15
have escaped by the *s* ...... Job 19:20
My bones cling to my *s* ..... Ps 102:5
nation tall and smooth of *s* .... Is 18:2
Ethiopian change his *s* ..... Jer 13:23
s is hot as an oven .... Lam 5:10
who strip the *s* from My ..... Mic 3:2

SKINS
she put the *s* of the kids ... Gen 27:16

SKIP
He makes them also *s* .... Ps 29:6

SKIPPING
upon the mountains, *s* ...... Song 2:8

SKULL
to say, Place of a *S* .... Matt 27:33

SKY
the faithful witness in the *s* .. Ps 89:37
weather, for the *s* is red .... Matt 16:2
stars of the *s* in multitude .. Heb 11:12
s receded as a scroll .... Rev 6:14

SLACK
He will not be *s* .... Deut 7:10
s hand becomes poor ...... Prov 10:4
The Lord is not *s* .... 2 Pet 3:9

SLAIN
s his thousands .... 1 Sam 18:7
beauty of Israel is *s* ...... 2 Sam 1:19
the dead, like the *s* .... Ps 88:5
and all who were *s* .... Prov 7:26
I shall be *s* in the .... Prov 22:13
s men are not *s* .... Is 22:2
no more cover her *s* .... Is 26:21
and the *s* of the LORD .... Is 66:16
and night for the *s* .... Jer 9:1
Those *s* by the sword .... Lam 4:9
the prophets, I have *s* .... Hos 6:5
is the Lamb who was *s* ..... Rev 5:12

SLANDER
s your own mother's .... Ps 50:20
and whoever spreads *s* .... Prov 10:18

SLANDERERS
be reverent, not *s* .... 1 Tim 3:11
unforgiving, *s* .... 2 Tim 3:3
in behavior, not *s* .... Titus 2:3

SLANDEROUSLY
as we are *s* reported .... Rom 3:8

SLAUGHTER
as sheep for the *s* .... Ps 44:22
led as a lamb to the *s* .... Is 53:7
but the Valley of *S* .... Jer 7:32
lamb brought to the *s* .... Jer 11:19

"Feed the flock for *s* ...... Zech 11:4
led as a sheep to the *s* ...... Acts 8:32
as sheep for the *s* .... Rom 8:36

SLAVE
that you were a *s* .... Deut 15:15
first shall be *s* of all ...... Mark 10:44
commits sin is a *s* .... John 8:34
you called while a *s* .... 1 Cor 7:21
there is neither *s* nor free .... Gal 3:28
you are no longer a *s* .... Gal 4:7
s nor free, but Christ is all ... Col 3:11

SLAVES
here we are, my lord's *s* ... Gen 44:16
they shall not be sold as *s* .. Lev 25:42
free his male and female *s* .. Jer 34:10
should no longer be *s* .... Rom 6:6
though you were *s* .... Rom 6:17
your members as *s* .... Rom 6:19
having become *s* of God ... Rom 6:22
do not become *s* .... 1 Cor 7:23
whether *s* or free .... 1 Cor 12:13
are *s* of corruption .... 2 Pet 2:19

SLAY
s the righteous .... Gen 18:25
s a righteous nation .... Gen 20:4
Evil shall *s* the .... Ps 34:21
Oh, that You would *s* .... Ps 139:19
s them before me .... Luke 19:27

SLEEP
God caused a deep *s* .... Gen 2:21
Jacob awoke from his *s* ... Gen 28:16
him to *s* on her knees ..... Judg 16:19
the night, when deep *s* ...... Job 4:13
my eyes, lest I *s* .... Ps 13:3
Why do You *s* .... Ps 44:23
have sunk into their *s* .... Ps 76:5
they are like a *s* .... Ps 90:5
neither slumber nor *s* .... Ps 121:4
He gives His beloved *s* ...... Ps 127:2
I will not give *s* .... Ps 132:4
s will be sweet .... Prov 3:24
For they do not *s* .... Prov 4:16
A little *s* .... Prov 6:10
Do not love *s* .... Prov 20:13
a little *s*, a little slumber .. Prov 24:33
The *s* of a laboring .... Eccl 5:12
I *s*, but my heart is awake .. Song 5:2
the spirit of deep *s* .... Is 29:10
Also his *s* went from .... Dan 6:18
I was in a deep *s* .... Dan 8:18
him were heavy with *s* .... Luke 9:32
them, "Why do you *s* ..... Luke 22:46
He was overcome by *s* ...... Acts 20:9
time to awake out of *s* .... Rom 13:11
among you, and many *s* .. 1 Cor 11:30
We shall not all *s* .... 1 Cor 15:51
"Awake, you who *s* .... Eph 5:14
with Him those who *s* ... 1 Thess 4:14
Therefore let us not *s* ..... 1 Thess 5:6

SLEEPERS
gently the lips of *s* .... Song 7:9

SLEEPING
or perhaps he is *s* .... 1 Kin 18:27
is not dead, but *s* .... Matt 9:24
"Are you still *s* .... Matt 26:45
suddenly, he find you *s* ... Mark 13:36
that night Peter was *s* ...... Acts 12:6

SLEEPLESSNESS
in labors, in *s* .... 2 Cor 6:5
and toil, in *s* often .... 2 Cor 11:27

SLEEPS
wise son; he who *s* .... Prov 10:5
"Our friend Lazarus *s* .... John 11:11

SLEPT
I lay down and *s* .... Ps 3:5
but while men *s* .... Matt 13:25

SLIGHTED
is the one who is *s* .... Prov 12:9

SLING
he had, and his *s* ....1 Sam 17:40
a stone in a *s* is he ....Prov 26:8

SLIP
their foot shall *s* ....Deut 32:35
my footsteps may not *s* ....Ps 17:5

SLIPPERY
way be dark and *s* ....Ps 35:6
set them in *s* places ....Ps 73:18
be to them like *s* ....Jer 23:12

SLOOPS
all the beautiful *s* ....Is 2:16

SLOW
but I am *s* of speech ....Ex 4:10
S to anger, and abounding .....Ps 103:8
He who is *s* to wrath .....Prov 14:29
the LORD is *s* to anger ....Nah 1:3
s of heart to believe in ....Luke 24:25
hear, *s* to speak, *s* ....James 1:19

SLOW TO ANGER
s, abundant in kindness ....Neh 9:17
merciful and gracious, *s* ......Ps 103:8
full of compassion, *s* ....Ps 145:8
but he who is *s* allays .....Prov 15:18
gracious and merciful, *s* ....Joel 2:13
merciful God, *s* ....Jon 4:2
the Lord is *s* and great ......Nah 1:3

SLUGGARD
will you slumber, O *s* ....Prov 6:9

SLUMBER
who keeps you will not *s* ....Ps 121:3
lying down, loving to *s* ....Is 56:10
destruction does not *s* ....2 Pet 2:3

SLUMBERED
delayed, they all *s* ....Matt 25:5

SLUMBERING
upon men, while *s* ....Job 33:15

SMALL
'The place is too *s* ....Is 49:20
I will make you *s* ....Jer 49:15
may stand, for he is *s* ......Amos 7:2
I will make you *s* ....Obad 2
the day of *s* things ....Zech 4:10
And I saw the dead, *s* ....Rev 20:12

SMELL
and he smelled the *s* ......Gen 27:27
s there will be a ....Is 3:24

SMELLS
s the battle from afar ......Job 39:25

SMITTEN
Him stricken, *s* ....Is 53:4

SMOKE
went up like the *s* ....Gen 19:28
s is driven away ....Ps 68:2
are consumed like *s* ....Ps 102:3
like a wineskin in *s* ....Ps 119:83
like pillars of *s* ....Song 3:6
s shall ascend forever ....Is 34:10
vanish away like *s* ....Is 51:6
fire and vapor of *s* ....Acts 2:19
s arose out of the pit ....Rev 9:2
was filled with *s* ....Rev 15:8
Her *s* rises up ....Rev 19:3

SMOKING
two stubs of *s* firebrands ....Is 7:4
s flax He will not quench ......Is 42:3
s flax He will not quench . Matt 12:20

SMOOTH
speak to us *s* things ....Is 30:10
And the rough places *s* ....Is 40:4
though they speak *s* ....Jer 12:6
the rough ways *s* ....Luke 3:5

SMOOTH-SKINNED
man, and I am a *s* ....Gen 27:11

SMYRNA
Site of one of the seven churches, Rev 1:11

SNAIL
s which melts away as ....Ps 58:8

SNARE
it will surely be a *s* ....Ex 23:33
It became a *s* to ....Judg 8:27
that she may be a *s* ......1 Sam 18:21
s snatches their ....Job 5:5
and he walks into a *s* ....Job 18:8
their table become a *s* ....Ps 69:22
as a bird from the *s* ....Ps 124:7
birds caught in a *s* ....Eccl 9:12
and the pit and the *s* ....Is 24:17
I have laid a *s* ....Jer 50:23
s have come upon us ....Lam 3:47
is a fowler's *s* ....Hos 9:8
a bird fall into a *s* ....Amos 3:5
it will come as a *s* ....Luke 21:35
temptation and a *s* ....1 Tim 6:9
and escape the *s* ....2 Tim 2:26

SNARED
The wicked is *s* ....Ps 9:16
and be broken, be *s* ....Is 8:15
all of them are *s* ....Is 42:22

SNARES
the *s* of death ....Ps 18:5
who seek my life lay *s* ....Ps 38:12
and built great *s* ....Eccl 9:14
wait as one who sets *s* ....Jer 5:26

SNATCH
s the fatherless ....Job 24:9
neither shall anyone *s* ....John 10:28

SNATCHES
s away what was ....Matt 13:19

SNEER
and you *s* at it ....Mal 1:13

SNIFFED
they *s* at the wind ....Jer 14:6

SNORTING
s strikes terror ....Job 39:20

SNOW
See WHITE AS SNOW
and heat consume the *s* ....Job 24:19
For He says to the *s* ....Job 37:6
the treasury of *s* ....Job 38:22
shall be whiter than *s* ....Ps 51:7
He gives *s* like wool ....Ps 147:16
As *s* in summer and ....Prov 26:1
She is not afraid of *s* .....Prov 31:21
shall be as white as *s* ....Is 1:18
garment was white as *s* ....Dan 7:9
clothing as white as *s* ....Matt 28:3
wool, as white as *s* ....Rev 1:14

SOAKED
their land shall be *s* ....Is 34:7

SOAP
lye, and use much *s* ....Jer 2:22

SOBER
of the day be *s* ....1 Thess 5:8
the older men be *s* ....Titus 2:2

SOBERLY
think, but to think *s* ....Rom 12:3
we should live *s* ....Titus 2:12

SOCHOH
Town in Judah where David kills Goliath, Josh 15:1, 35; 1 Sam 17:1, 49

SOCKET
touched the *s* of his hip ....Gen 32:25
arm be torn from the *s* .....Job 31:22

SODA
and like vinegar on *s* .....Prov 25:20

SODOM
Lot chooses to live there, Gen 13:10–13
Plundered by Chedorlaomer, Gen 14:8–24
Abraham intercedes for, Gen 18:16–33
Destroyed by God, Gen 19:1–29
Cited as example of sin and destruction, Deut 29:23; 32:32; Is 1:9, 10; 3:9; Jer 23:14; 49:18; Lam 4:6; Ezek 16:46–63; Matt 11:23, 24; 2 Pet 2:6; Jude 7

SODOM AND GOMORRAH
and the kings of *S* ....Gen 14:10
the outcry against *S* ....Gen 18:20
brimstone and fire on *S* ...Gen 19:24
like the overthrow of *S* ....Deut 29:23
As God overthrew *S* ....Jer 50:40
as God overthrew *S* ....Amos 4:11
for the land of *S* ....Matt 10:15
more tolerable for *S* ....Mark 6:11
turning the cities of *S* ....2 Pet 2:6
as *S*, and the cities ....Jude 7

SODOMITES
nor homosexuals, nor *s* .....1 Cor 6:9
for fornicators, for *s* ......1 Tim 1:10

SOFT
s answer turns away ....Prov 15:1
clothed in *s* garments ......Matt 11:8

SOFTER
his words were *s* ....Ps 55:21

SOJOURNER
But no *s* had to lodge ....Job 31:32

SOJOURNERS
are strangers and *s* ....Lev 25:23
I beg you as *s* ....1 Pet 2:11

SOLD
s his birthright ....Gen 25:33
the house that was *s* ....Lev 25:33
their Rock had *s* ....Deut 32:30
and He *s* them into the ......Judg 2:14
s themselves to do ....2 Kin 17:17
Had we been *s* as male ......Esth 7:4
who was *s* as a slave ....Ps 105:17
s all that he had ....Matt 13:46
they bought, they *s* ....Luke 17:28
s their possessions ....Acts 2:45
but I am carnal, *s* ....Rom 7:14
Eat whatever is *s* ....1 Cor 10:25

SOLDIER
hardship as a good *s* ....2 Tim 2:3
enlisted him as a *s* ....2 Tim 2:4

SOLDIERS
sum of money to the *s* ....Matt 28:12
The *s* also mocked ....Luke 23:36
s twisted a crown ....John 19:2

SOLEMN
and very *s* lamentation ....Gen 50:10
a *s* observance for all the ....Ex 12:42
a sabbath of *s* rest for ....Lev 16:31
"Proclaim a *s* assembly ...2 Kin 10:20
the refuse of your *s* feasts ....Mal 2:3

SOLEMNLY
saying, "The man *s* ....Gen 43:3
s testified of the ....Acts 28:23

SOLID
milk and not with *s* food ...1 Cor 3:2
the *s* foundation ....2 Tim 2:19
need milk and not *s* food ...Heb 5:12

SOLITARILY
heritage, who dwell *s* ....Mic 7:14

SOLITARY
God sets the *s* in ....Ps 68:6

SOLOMON
David's son by Bathsheba, 2 Sam 12:24
Becomes king, 1 Kin 1:5–53
Receives and carries out David's instructions, 1 Kin 2
Prays for and demonstrates wisdom, 1 Kin 3:3–28; 4:29–34
Builds and dedicates temple; builds palace, 1 Kin 5—8

Lord appears to, 1 Kin 9:1–9
His fame and glory, 1 Kin 9:10—10:29
Falls into idolatry; warned by God, 1 Kin 11:1–13
Adversaries arise, 1 Kin 11:14–40
Death of, 1 Kin 11:41–43
Writings credited to him, Ps 72; 127; Prov 1:1; 10:1; 25:1; Eccl 1:1; Song 1:1

SOMEBODY

up, claiming to be *s* .... Acts 5:36

SOMETHING

"Simon, I have *s* .... Luke 7:40
thinks himself to be *s* .... Gal 6:3

SON

See BELOVED SON; ONLY BEGOTTEN SON

wife shall bear you a *s* .... Gen 17:19
Abraham a *s* in his old ..... Gen 21:2
your *s*, your only *s* Isaac .... Gen 22:2
the knife to slay his *s* ..... Gen 22:10
he called Esau his older *s* ... Gen 27:1
"I am your *s*, your .... Gen 27:32
conceived and bore a *s* .... Gen 29:32
Joseph my *s* is still alive ... Gen 45:28
And she bore him a *s* .... Ex 2:22
a *s* born to Naomi .... Ruth 4:17
"Send me your *s* David .. 1 Sam 16:19
she bore a *s*, and he ..... 2 Sam 12:24
king is grieved for his *s* .. 2 Sam 19:2
he charged Solomon his *s* .. 1 Kin 2:1
"My *s*, as for me, it was ... 1 Chr 22:7
gave his *s* Solomon ...... 1 Chr 28:11
Me, 'You are My *S* .... Ps 2:7
Upon the *s* of man whom .... Ps 80:17
I was my father's *s* .... Prov 4:3
s makes a glad father .... Prov 10:1
s is a grief to his .... Prov 17:25
Correct your *s*, and he .... Prov 29:17
And what, *s* of my womb .. Prov 31:2
shall conceive and bear a *S* ... Is 7:14
is born, unto us a *S* .... Is 9:6
heaven, O Lucifer, *s* .... Is 14:12
out of Egypt I called My *s* .. Hos 11:1
He is an unwise *s* .... Hos 13:13
prophet, nor was I a *s* ..... Amos 7:14
s honors his father .... Mal 1:6
will bring forth a *S* .... Matt 1:21
"This is My beloved *S* ...... Matt 3:17
no one knows the *S* .... Matt 11:27
not the carpenter's *s* ...... Matt 13:55
are the Christ, the *S* .... Matt 16:16
For the *S* of Man will ..... Matt 16:27
of all he sent his *s* .... Matt 21:37
Whose *S* is He .... Matt 22:42
'Lord,' how is He his *S* .... Matt 22:45
as much a *s* of hell .... Matt 23:15
of the *S* of Man .... Matt 24:37
'I am the *S* of God .... Matt 27:43
of Jesus Christ, the *S* .... Mark 1:1
S of Man has power .... Mark 2:10
"This is My beloved *S* .... Mark 9:7
'They will respect my *s* .... Mark 12:6
this Man was the *S* .... Mark 15:39
called the *S* of the .... Luke 1:32
"You are My beloved *S* ..... Luke 3:22
the Christ, the *S* of God .... Luke 4:41
S of Man has power .... Luke 5:24
S of Man is also Lord .... Luke 6:5
out, the only *s* .... Luke 7:12
S of Man has come .... Luke 7:34
And if a *s* of peace .... Luke 10:6
will be divided against *s* .. Luke 12:53
to be called your *s* .... Luke 15:19
because he also is a *s* ...... Luke 19:9
I will send my beloved *s* .. Luke 20:13
You then the *S* of God .... Luke 22:70
The only begotten *S* .... John 1:18
gave His only begotten *S* .. John 3:16
God did not send His *S* ...... John 3:17
the Father loves the *S* ...... John 3:35
S can do nothing .... John 5:19
For the Father loves the *S* .. John 5:20
everyone who sees the *S* ... John 6:40
s abides forever .... John 8:35
if the *S* makes you free ..... John 8:36
S of Man must be lifted .... John 12:34
"Woman, behold your *s* ... John 19:26
S of Encouragement .... Acts 4:36
Jesus Christ is the *S* .... Acts 8:37
in the gospel of His *S* .... Rom 1:9
by sending His own *S* .... Rom 8:3
not spare His own *S* .... Rom 8:32
S Himself will also be .... 1 Cor 15:28
God sent forth His *S* .... Gal 4:4
longer a slave but a *s* .... Gal 4:7
you for my *s* Onesimus .... Philem 10
"You are My *S* .... Heb 1:5
but Christ as a *S* over His ..... Heb 3:6
though He was a *S* .... Heb 5:8
to be called the *s* .... Heb 11:24
"This is My beloved *S* ...... 2 Pet 1:17
S cleanses us from all sin .. 1 John 1:7
Whoever denies the *S* .... 1 John 2:23
sent His *S* to be the ...... 1 John 4:10
Jesus is the *S* of God ..... 1 John 4:15
God has given of His *S* ... 1 John 5:10
who has the *S* has life .... 1 John 5:12

SON OF DAVID

the *s* had a lovely .... 2 Sam 13:1
Solomon the *s* king ...... 1 Chr 29:22
proverbs of Solomon the *s* .. Prov 1:1
of the Preacher, the *s* .... Eccl 1:1
Jesus Christ, the *S* .... Matt 1:1
"Joseph, *s*, do not be .... Matt 1:20
S, have mercy on us .... Matt 9:27
"Could this be the *S* .... Matt 12:23
on me, O Lord, *S* .... Matt 15:22
Hosanna to the *S* .... Matt 21:9
said to Him, "The *S* ...... Matt 22:42
"Jesus, *S*, have mercy .... Mark 10:47
that the Christ is the *S* .. Mark 12:35
son of Nathan, the *s* .... Luke 3:31
"Jesus, *S*, have mercy ..... Luke 18:38

SON OF GOD

the fourth is like the *S* ...... Dan 3:25
"If you are the *S* .... Matt 4:3
with You, Jesus, You *S* ..... Matt 8:29
"Truly You are the *S* ..... Matt 14:33
You are the Christ, the *S* .. Matt 26:63
If You are the *S* .... Matt 27:40
"Truly this was the *S* ..... Matt 27:54
born will be called the *S* ... Luke 1:35
of Adam, the *s* .... Luke 3:38
testified that this is the *S* ... John 1:34
"Rabbi, You are the *S* ...... John 1:49
the only begotten *S* .... John 3:18
hear the voice of the *S* ..... John 5:25
"Do you believe in the *S* ... John 9:35
I said, 'I am the *S* .... John 10:36
the *S* may be glorified ..... John 11:4
You are the Christ, the *S* .. John 11:27
He made Himself the *S* ...... John 19:7
is the Christ, the *S* .... John 20:31
declared to be the *S* .... Rom 1:4
I live by faith in the *S* .... Gal 2:20
of the knowledge of the *S* ... Eph 4:13
heavens, Jesus the *S* .... Heb 4:14
again for themselves the *S* ... Heb 6:6
but made like the *S* .... Heb 7:3
trampled the *S* underfoot .. Heb 10:29
For this purpose the *S* ..... 1 John 3:8
that Jesus is the *S* .... 1 John 5:5
'These things says the *S* .... Rev 2:18

SON OF MAN

s that You visit him .... Ps 8:4
s, that You are mindful ...... Ps 144:3
in princes, nor in a *s* .... Ps 146:3
"*S*, stand on your feet .... Ezek 2:1
"*S*, eat what you find .... Ezek 3:1
behold One like the *S* ...... Dan 7:13
the *S* has nowhere to .... Matt 8:20
S has power on earth .... Matt 9:6
Israel before the *S* .... Matt 10:23
The *S* came eating and .... Matt 11:19
the *S* is Lord even .... Matt 12:8
a word against the *S* ...... Matt 12:32
will the *S* be three days ... Matt 12:40
the good seed is the *S* ..... Matt 13:37
men say that I, the *S* ..... Matt 16:13
S coming in His .... Matt 16:28
until the *S* is risen .... Matt 17:9
S is about to be betrayed .. Matt 17:22
S has come to save .... Matt 18:11
S sits on the throne .... Matt 19:28
S will be betrayed .... Matt 20:18
S did not come to be ...... Matt 20:28
will the coming of the *S* ... Matt 24:27
S will be delivered up ...... Matt 26:2
S indeed goes as it is ..... Matt 26:24
S must suffer many .... Mark 8:31
S also will be ashamed ..... Mark 8:38
the *S* also will confess .... Luke 12:8
one of the days of the *S* .. Luke 17:22
S has come to seek .... Luke 19:10
to stand before the *S* ...... Luke 21:36
betraying the *S* with a ..... Luke 22:48
descending upon the *S* ...... John 1:51
heaven, that is the *S* .... John 3:13
because He is the *S* .... John 5:27
which the *S* will give you ... John 6:27
eat the flesh of the *S* .... John 6:53
"When you lift up the *S* .... John 8:28
S should be glorified ...... John 12:23
"Now the *S* is glorified ..... John 13:31
heavens opened and the *S* .. Acts 7:56
S that You take care .... Heb 2:6
One like the *S* .... Rev 1:13
cloud sat One like the *S* .... Rev 14:14

SONG

is my strength and *s* .... Ex 15:2
Then Israel sang this *s* .... Num 21:17
Sing to Him a new *s* .... Ps 33:3
He has put a new *s* .... Ps 40:3
in the night His *s* .... Ps 42:8
me, and I am the *s* .... Ps 69:12
sing to the LORD a new *s* ...... Ps 96:1
LORD is my strength and *s* .. Ps 118:14
asked of us a *s* .... Ps 137:3
I will sing a new *s* .... Ps 144:9
Sing to the LORD a new *s* ... Ps 149:1
The *s* of songs, which is .... Song 1:1
to my Well-beloved a *s* .... Is 5:1
my strength and my *s* .... Is 12:2
Sing to the LORD a new *s* ..... Is 42:10
their taunting *s* .... Lam 3:14
I am their taunting *s* .... Lam 3:63
as a very lovely *s* .... Ezek 33:32
They sang a new *s* .... Rev 5:9
a new *s* before the throne .... Rev 14:3
And they sing the *s* .... Rev 15:3

SONGS

my Maker, who gives *s* .... Job 35:10
surround me with *s* .... Ps 32:7
have been my *s* in the ...... Ps 119:54
Sing us one of the *s* .... Ps 137:3
is one who sings *s* .... Prov 25:20
the noise of your *s* .... Amos 5:23
and spiritual *s* .... Eph 5:19

SONS

s of Jacob were twelve .... Gen 35:22
circumcise the *s* of Israel ..... Josh 5:2
the *s* of Eli were corrupt .. 1 Sam 2:12
the *s* of the prophets who .... 2 Kin 2:3
s of the prophets cried out .. 2 Kin 4:1
the *s* of the prophets .... 2 Kin 4:38
these were the *s* of David ... 1 Chr 3:1
s come to honor .... Job 14:21
exalted among the *s* of .... Ps 12:8
shall be Your *s* .... Ps 45:16
s of men to do under .... Eccl 2:3
my beloved among the *s* .... Song 2:3
Your *s* shall make haste ..... Is 49:17

s shall come from afar .... Is 60:4
"Has Israel no s .... Jer 49:1
The precious s of Zion ...... Lam 4:2
eat their s in your midst .... Ezek 5:10
'You are the s .... Hos 1:10
He will purify the s .... Mal 3:3
to him, "Then the s ...... Matt 17:26
A man had two s, and ..... Matt 21:28
be forgiven the s of men .. Mark 3:28
and you will be s .... Luke 6:35
that you may become s ... John 12:36
You are s of the .... Acts 3:25
called s of the living God ... Rom 9:26
and you shall be My s ..... 2 Cor 6:18
who are of faith are s .... Gal 3:7
the adoption as s .... Gal 4:5
because you are s .... Gal 4:6
us to adoption as s by Jesus .. Eph 1:5
You are all s of light ..... 1 Thess 5:5
in bringing many s .... Heb 2:10
speaks to you as to s .... Heb 12:5
illegitimate and not s .... Heb 12:8

SONS OF GOD

s saw the daughters of men .. Gen 6:2
s came to present .... Job 1:6
all the s shouted for .... Job 38:7
for they shall be called s .... Matt 5:9
to the angels and are s ... Luke 20:36
Spirit of God, these are s ... Rom 8:14
for the revealing of the s ... Rom 8:19
For you are all s .... Gal 3:26

SOON

for it is s cut off .... Ps 90:10
s forgot His works .... Ps 106:13

SOOTHED

or bound up, or s .... Is 1:6

SOOTHSAYERS

your dreamers, your s, or .... Jer 27:9
A sword is against the s .... Jer 50:36
the s cannot declare to the .. Dan 2:27

SORCERER

omens, or a s .... Deut 18:10
But Elymas the s .... Acts 13:8

SORCERERS

soothsayers, or your s .... Jer 27:9
outside are dogs and s ..... Rev 22:15

SORCERESS

shall not permit a s .... Ex 22:18

SORCERY

For there is no s .... Num 23:23
idolatry, s .... Gal 5:20

SORES

and putrefying s .... Is 1:6
Lazarus, full of s .... Luke 16:20

SORROW

multiply your s .... Gen 3:16
s dances before him .... Job 41:22
in my soul, having s .... Ps 13:2
s is continually .... Ps 38:17
I found trouble and s .... Ps 116:3
And He adds no s .... Prov 10:22
the heart may s .... Prov 14:13
S is better than .... Eccl 7:3
Therefore remove s .... Eccl 11:10
and desperate s .... Is 17:11
you shall cry for s .... Is 65:14
to see labor and s .... Jer 20:18
Your s is incurable .... Jer 30:15
added grief to my s .... Jer 45:3
gather those who s .... Zeph 3:18
them sleeping from s ..... Luke 22:45
s has filled your .... John 16:6
s will be turned .... John 16:20
that I have great s .... Rom 9:2
s produces repentance ..... 2 Cor 7:10
lest I should have s .... Phil 2:27
s as others who have .... 1 Thess 4:13
no more death, nor s .... Rev 21:4

SORROWFUL

am a woman of s spirit ... 1 Sam 1:15
But I am poor and s .... Ps 69:29
For all his days are s .... Eccl 2:23
replenished every s .... Jer 31:25
were exceedingly s .... Matt 17:23
saying, he went away s ... Matt 19:22
soul is exceedingly s ...... Matt 26:38
and went away s .... Mark 10:22
and you will be s .... John 16:20
if I make you s .... 2 Cor 2:2
and I may be less s .... Phil 2:28

SORROWS

the s of Sheol .... 2 Sam 22:6
s God distributes .... Job 21:17
s shall be multiplied .... Ps 16:4
by men, a Man of s .... Is 53:3
are the beginning of s ...... Matt 24:8
through with many s ...... 1 Tim 6:10

SORRY

s that He had made man ..... Gen 6:6
who will be s for you .... Is 51:19
And the king was s .... Matt 14:9
For you were made s .... 2 Cor 7:9

SOSTHENES

Ruler of the synagogue at Corinth, Acts 18:17
—— Paul's Christian brother, 1 Cor 1:1

SOUGHT

I s the LORD .... Ps 34:4
whole heart I have s ...... Ps 119:10
s the one I love .... Song 3:1
shall be called S Out .... Is 62:12
So I s for a man .... Ezek 22:30
s what was lost .... Ezek 34:4
s favor from Him .... Hos 12:4
LORD, and have not s .... Zeph 1:6
s it diligently .... Heb 12:17

SOUL

s enter their council .... Gen 49:6
with all your s .... Deut 6:5
was knit to the s .... 1 Sam 18:1
your heart and your s .... 1 Chr 22:19
"My s loathes my life .... Job 10:1
as you do, if your s .... Job 16:4
s draws near the Pit .... Job 33:22
will not leave my s .... Ps 16:10
converting the s .... Ps 19:7
He restores my s .... Ps 23:3
s shall make its boast .... Ps 34:2
s shall be joyful .... Ps 35:9
you cast down, O my s .... Ps 42:5
s silently waits .... Ps 62:1
He has done for my s .... Ps 66:16
Let my s live .... Ps 119:175
s knows very well .... Ps 139:14
No one cares for my s .... Ps 142:4
so destroys his own s .... Prov 6:32
me wrongs his own s .... Prov 8:36
it is not good for a s .... Prov 19:2
A satisfied s loathes .... Prov 27:7
When You make His s .... Is 53:10
s delight itself .... Is 55:2
and your s shall live .... Is 55:3
you have heard, O my s ...... Jer 4:19
the s of the father as .... Ezek 18:4
the proud, his s .... Hab 2:4
able to destroy both s ..... Matt 10:28
and loses his own s .... Matt 16:26
with all your s .... Matt 22:37
"My s magnifies the Lord . Luke 1:46
through your own s also ... Luke 2:35
And I will say to my s .... Luke 12:19
Now My s is troubled .... John 12:27
not leave my s in Hades .... Acts 2:27
of one heart and one s .... Acts 4:32
your whole spirit, s ...... 1 Thess 5:23
to the saving of the s ...... Heb 10:39
his way will save a s ..... James 5:20
which war against the s ... 1 Pet 2:11
his righteous s .... 2 Pet 2:8
health, just as your s .... 3 John 2

SOULS

See AFFLICT YOUR SOULS
and will save the s .... Ps 72:13
and he who wins s .... Prov 11:30
s shall be like a .... Jer 31:12
who made our very s .... Jer 38:16
will find rest for your s ... Matt 11:29
patience possess your s ... Luke 21:19
unsettling your s .... Acts 15:24
is able to save your s ..... James 1:21
the salvation of your s .... 1 Pet 1:9
and bodies and s of men .... Rev 18:13
I saw the s of those who ..... Rev 20:4

SOUND

He stores up s wisdom ...... Prov 2:7
s heart is life .... Prov 14:30
one rises up at the s .... Eccl 12:4
to you at the s of your cry .... Is 30:19
voice was like the s .... Ezek 43:2
s an alarm in My holy .... Joel 2:1
do not s a trumpet .... Matt 6:2
For the trumpet will s .... 1 Cor 15:52
is contrary to s doctrine ... 1 Tim 1:10
s words which you .... 2 Tim 1:13
that they may be s .... Titus 1:13
as the s of many waters ...... Rev 1:15
s of their wings was like ...... Rev 9:9

SOUNDED

The first angel s .... Rev 8:7

SOUNDNESS

There is no s in my .... Ps 38:3
him this perfect s .... Acts 3:16

SOUNDS

Dreadful s are in his .... Job 15:21
a distinction in the s ...... 1 Cor 14:7

SOUTH

s comes the whirlwind ...... Job 37:9
as the streams in the S ...... Ps 126:4
And to the s, 'Do not keep .... Is 43:6
the S shall become strong .. Dan 11:5
The queen of the S will .. Matt 12:42

SOW

s trouble reap .... Job 4:8
then let me s .... Job 31:8
s fields and plant .... Ps 107:37
Those who s in tears .... Ps 126:5
the wind will not s .... Eccl 11:4
Blessed are you who s .... Is 32:20
ground, and do not s .... Jer 4:3
"They s the wind .... Hos 8:7
S for yourselves .... Hos 10:12
You shall s, but not reap .... Mic 6:15
s is not made alive .... 1 Cor 15:36
they neither s nor reap ... Luke 12:24

SOWED

s tares among the wheat . Matt 13:25

SOWER

may give seed to the s .... Is 55:10
"Behold, a s went .... Matt 13:3
a s went out to sow .... Mark 4:3
The s sows the word ...... Mark 4:14
A s went out to sow .... Luke 8:5

SOWN

shall they be s .... Is 40:24
a land not s .... Jer 2:2
"You have s much .... Hag 1:6
where you have not s ..... Matt 25:24
that was s in their hearts .. Mark 4:15
s spiritual things .... 1 Cor 9:11
It is s in weakness .... 1 Cor 15:43
of righteousness is s ...... James 3:18

SOWS

s righteousness will .... Prov 11:18
s the good seed is the .... Matt 13:37
'One s and another .... John 4:37

s sparingly will ....2 Cor 9:6
for whatever a man *s* ....Gal 6:7

SPAN
My life *s* is gone, taken ......Is 38:12
measured heaven with a *s* ...Is 40:12

SPARE
The LORD would not *s*.....Deut 29:20
hand, but *s* his life ....Job 2:6
S the poor and needy ....Ps 72:13
I will not pity nor *s* ....Jer 13:14
say, "*S* Your people ....Joel 2:17
s them as a man spares ....Mal 3:17
He who did not *s* ....Rom 8:32
s the natural branches ....Rom 11:21
flesh, but I would *s* ....1 Cor 7:28
if God did not *s* ....2 Pet 2:4

SPARES
s his rod hates his ....Prov 13:24

SPARK
the work of it as a *s* ....Is 1:31

SPARKLES
it is red, when it *s* ....Prov 23:31

SPARKS
to trouble, as the *s* ....Job 5:7
s you have kindled ....Is 50:11

SPARROW
s has found a home ....Ps 84:3
awake, and am like a *s* ......Ps 102:7

SPARROWS
more value than many *s* ..Matt 10:31

SPAT
Then they *s* on Him.......Matt 27:30
in his ears, and He *s* ......Mark 7:33

SPEAK
only the word that I *s* .....Num 22:35
s just once more ....Judg 6:39
s good words to them .....1 Kin 12:7
oh, that God would *s*........Job 11:5
Will you *s* wickedly..........Job 13:7
For God may *s* in one ......Job 33:14
Will he *s* softly to...........Job 41:3
Do not *s* in the ....Prov 23:9
and a time to *s* ....Eccl 3:7
If they do not *s* ....Is 8:20
tongue He will *s*..............Is 28:11
s anymore in His name ......Jer 20:9
and *s* comfort to her ....Hos 2:14
at the end it will *s*...........Hab 2:3
s each man the truth ....Zech 8:16
But only *s* a word, and my ..Matt 8:8
or what you should *s* ....Matt 10:19
it is not you who *s* ....Matt 10:20
to you when all men *s* .....Luke 6:26
s what We know and ....John 3:11
"I who *s* to you am He .....John 4:26
s what I have seen ....John 8:38
The words that I *s* to .....John 14:10
He hears He will *s*.........John 16:13
Spirit and began to *s* ....Acts 2:4
Do all *s* with tongues .....1 Cor 12:30
I *s* with the tongues ....1 Cor 13:1
I would rather *s* ....1 Cor 14:19
So *s* and so do as ....James 2:12

SPEAKING
s your own words ....Is 58:13
while they are still *s* ....Is 65:24
a proof of Christ *s* ....2 Cor 13:3
envy, and all evil *s* ....1 Pet 2:1

SPEAKS
to face, as a man *s* ....Ex 33:11
this day that God *s* ....Deut 5:24
day that I am He who *s* ....Is 52:6
the one who *s* uprightly ...Amos 5:10
He whom God has sent *s* ..John 3:34
When he *s* a lie ....John 8:44
he who *s* with tongues ....1 Cor 14:5
If anyone *s* in a tongue ...1 Cor 14:27
he being dead still *s* ....Heb 11:4

of sprinkling that *s* ....Heb 12:24
s evil of a brother ....James 4:11

SPEAR
lay hold on bow and *s* ....Jer 6:23
His side with a *s* ....John 19:34

SPEARS
whose teeth are *s* ....Ps 57:4
and their *s* into ....Is 2:4
pruning hooks into *s* ....Joel 3:10

SPECIAL
you shall be a *s* treasure .....Ex 19:5
you to be His *s* people ....Deut 26:18
Israel for His *s* treasure .....Ps 135:4
His own *s* people ....Titus 2:14
nation, His own *s* people ....1 Pet 2:9

SPECK
do you look at the *s* ....Matt 7:3

SPECTACLE
and make you a *s* ....Nah 3:6
we have been made a *s* ......1 Cor 4:9
He made a public *s* ....Col 2:15
you were made a *s* ....Heb 10:33

SPEECH
one language and one *s* ....Gen 11:1
drop as the rain, my *s* .....Deut 32:2
s settled on them as ....Job 29:22
There is no *s* nor ....Ps 19:3
s is not becoming ....Prov 17:7
your *s* shall be low ....Is 29:4
a people of obscure *s* ....Is 33:19
not understand My *s* ....John 8:43
s deceive the hearts ....Rom 16:18
and his *s* contemptible ....2 Cor 10:10
I am untrained in *s* ....2 Cor 11:6
s always be with grace ....Col 4:6

SPEECHLESS
your mouth for the *s* ....Prov 31:8
And he was *s* ....Matt 22:12

SPEED
they shall come with *s* ....Is 5:26

SPEEDILY
judgment be executed *s* .....Ezra 7:26
to me, deliver me *s*...........Ps 31:2
I call, answer me *s* ....Ps 102:2

SPEND
Why do you *s* money for ....Is 55:2
whatever more you *s* ....Luke 10:35
I will very gladly *s* ....2 Cor 12:15
amiss, that you may *s* .....James 4:3

SPENT
strength shall be *s* ....Lev 26:20
For my life is *s* ....Ps 31:10
in vain, I have *s* ....Is 49:4
"But when he had *s* ....Luke 15:14

SPICES
s for the anointing oil ....Ex 25:6
s in great quantity ....1 Kin 10:10
that its *s* may flow out .....Song 4:16
and Salome bought *s* ....Mark 16:1
s which they had ....Luke 24:1
strips of linen with the *s* ..John 19:40

SPIDER
s skillfully grasps ....Prov 30:28

SPIES
to them, "You are *s* ....Gen 42:9
men who had been *s* ....Josh 6:23
s who pretended ....Luke 20:20

SPIKENARD
fragrant henna with *s* .....Song 4:13
of very costly oil of *s* ......Mark 14:3

SPIN
neither toil nor *s* ....Matt 6:28

SPINDLE
her hand holds the *s* ....Prov 31:19

SPIRIT
See HOLY SPIRIT; FILLED WITH THE HOLY SPIRIT; UNCLEAN SPIRIT

S shall not strive ....Gen 6:3
the breath of the *s* of life ....Gen 7:22
filled with the *s* of wisdom ...Ex 28:3
and everyone whose *s* ......Ex 35:21
S that is upon you ....Num 11:17
And the *S* rested upon ....Num 11:26
LORD would put His *S*.....Num 11:29
he has a different *s*.......Num 14:24
in whom is the *S* ....Num 27:18
God sent a *s* of ill will ......Judg 9:23
portion of your *s* ....2 Kin 2:9
I will send a *s* upon him ...2 Kin 19:7
there was no more *s*.........2 Chr 9:4
s came forward and ......2 Chr 18:20
also gave Your good *S* .....Neh 9:20
against them by Your *S* .....Neh 9:30
Then a *s* passed before ....Job 4:15
care has preserved my *s* ...Job 10:12
And whose *s* came from .....Job 26:4
hand I commit my *s* ....Ps 31:5
Your Holy *S* from me ....Ps 51:11
s was not faithful ....Ps 78:8
You send forth Your *S* .....Ps 104:30
Your *S* is good ....Ps 143:10
I will pour out my *s* on ....Prov 1:23
The *s* of a man is the ....Prov 20:27
Who knows the *s* ....Eccl 3:21
s will return to God ....Eccl 12:7
night, yes, by my *s* ....Is 26:9
out on you the *s* ....Is 29:10
are flesh, and not *s* ....Is 31:3
S has gathered them ....Is 34:16
is the life of my *s*...............Is 38:16
I have put My *S* ....Is 42:1
and His *S* have sent Me ......Is 48:16
s would fail before Me ....Is 57:16
S entered me when He ....Ezek 2:2
the *S* lifted me up ....Ezek 3:12
who follow their own *s* .....Ezek 13:3
new heart and a new *s* ....Ezek 18:31
be feeble, every *s* ....Ezek 21:7
I will put My *S* ....Ezek 36:27
in him is the *S* ....Dan 4:8
as an excellent *s* ....Dan 5:12
walk in a false *s* ....Mic 2:11
and forms the *s* ....Zech 12:1
with child of the Holy *S* .....Matt 1:18
"Blessed are the poor in *s* ...Matt 5:3
I will put My *S* ....Matt 12:18
S descending upon Him .....Mark 1:10
Immediately the *S* ....Mark 1:12
s indeed is willing ....Mark 14:38
go before Him in the *s* ......Luke 1:17
in the power of the *S* ......Luke 4:14
manner of *s* you are of .....Luke 9:55
When an unclean *s* goes ..Luke 11:24
against the Holy *S* ....Luke 12:10
hands I commit My *s* ......Luke 23:46
they had seen a *s* ....Luke 24:37
s does not have flesh ....Luke 24:39
I saw the *S* descending .....John 1:32
born of water and the *S* .....John 3:5
God is *S* ....John 4:24
I speak to you are *s* ....John 6:63
He groaned in the *s*........John 11:33
He was troubled in *s* ....John 13:21
all filled with the Holy *S* ......Acts 2:4
but if a *s* or an angel ....Acts 23:9
to the *S* of holiness, by the ..Rom 1:4
whom I serve with my *s* ....Rom 1:9
but according to the *S* ....Rom 8:1
according to the *S* ....Rom 8:5
the flesh but in the *S* ....Rom 8:9
s that we are children ....Rom 8:16
what the mind of the *S* .....Rom 8:27
to us through His *S* ....1 Cor 2:10
gifts, but the same *S* ....1 Cor 12:4
in a tongue, my *s* ....1 Cor 14:14
but the *S* gives life ....2 Cor 3:6
Now the Lord is the *S* ......2 Cor 3:17
we have the same *s* ....2 Cor 4:13
Having begun in the *S* ....Gal 3:3

has sent forth the *S* .... Gal 4:6
Walk in the *S*, and you ....Gal 5:16
But if you are led by the *S* ... Gal 5:18
the fruit of the *S* is love ..... Gal 5:22
If we live in the *S*, let us ..... Gal 5:25
he who sows to the *S* .... Gal 6:8
with the Holy *S* .... Eph 1:13
may give to you the *s* .... Eph 1:17
the unity of the *S* .... Eph 4:3
is one body and one *S* .... Eph 4:4
stand fast in one *s* .... Phil 1:27
yet I am with you in *s* .... Col 2:5
Do not quench the *S* .... 1 Thess 5:19
and may your whole *s* ... 1 Thess 5:23
sanctification by the *S* ... 2 Thess 2:13
flesh, justified in the *S* .... 1 Tim 3:16
S expressly says that .... 1 Tim 4:1
not given us a *s* of fear ..... 2 Tim 1:7
division of soul and *s* .... Heb 4:12
through the eternal *S* .... Heb 9:14
body without the *s* is ..... James 2:26
S who dwells in us .... James 4:5
S of Christ who was in .... 1 Pet 1:11
made alive by the *S* .... 1 Pet 3:18
S whom He has given .... 1 John 3:24
do not believe every *s* ..... 1 John 4:1
has given us of His *S* ..... 1 John 4:13
S who bears witness ...... 1 John 5:6
not having the *S* .... Jude 19
I was in the *S* on the .... Rev 1:10
him hear what the *S* .... Rev 2:7
Immediately I was in the *S* ... Rev 4:2
And the *S* and the .... Rev 22:17

SPIRIT OF GOD
S was hovering over the ..... Gen 1:2
a man in whom is the *S* ... Gen 41:38
filled him with the *S* .... Ex 31:3
the *S* came upon him .... Num 24:2
S came upon him .... 1 Sam 10:10
the *S* came upon Saul .... 1 Sam 11:6
S came upon the .... 1 Sam 19:20
The *S* has made me .... Job 33:4
in a vision by the *S* .... Ezek 11:24
that the *S* is in you .... Dan 5:14
S descending like a dove ... Matt 3:16
out demons by the *S* ...... Matt 12:28
indeed the *S* dwells in you .. Rom 8:9
by the power of the *S* ..... Rom 15:19
the things of the *S* .... 1 Cor 2:14
the *S* dwells in you .... 1 Cor 3:16
I think I also have the *S* ... 1 Cor 7:40
no one speaking by the *S* .. 1 Cor 12:3
By this you know the *S* .... 1 John 4:2

SPIRIT OF THE LORD
The *S* came upon him ...... Judg 3:10
the *S* came upon Gideon ... Judg 6:34
S came mightily upon ...... Judg 14:6
S will come upon you .... 1 Sam 10:6
S came upon David ..... 1 Sam 16:13
S departed from Saul .... 1 Sam 16:14
S will carry you .... 1 Kin 18:12
S has taken him up ...... 2 Kin 2:16
The *S* shall rest upon Him .... Is 11:2
The *S* GOD is upon Me .... Is 61:1
Then the *S* fell upon me ... Ezek 11:5
Is the *S* restricted .... Mic 2:7
am full of power by the *S* .... Mic 3:8
The *S* is upon Me .... Luke 4:18
together to test the *S* .... Acts 5:9
S caught Philip away .... Acts 8:39

SPIRIT OF TRUTH
S, whom the world .... John 14:17
S who proceeds from ..... John 15:26
He, the *S* has come .... John 16:13
By this we know the *s* .... 1 John 4:6

SPIRITS
See UNCLEAN SPIRITS
God, the God of the *s* ..... Num 16:22
who makes His angels *s* ..... Ps 104:4
the LORD weighs the *s* ..... Prov 16:2
power over unclean *s* ...... Matt 10:1
discerning of *s* .... 1 Cor 12:10
heed to deceiving *s* .... 1 Tim 4:1
not all ministering *s* .... Heb 1:14
to the Father of *s* .... Heb 12:9
and preached to the *s* ...... 1 Pet 3:19
spirit, but test the *s* .... 1 John 4:1

SPIRITUAL
the *s* man is insane .... Hos 9:7
we know that the law is *s* .. Rom 7:14
s judges all things .... 1 Cor 2:15
s people but as to .... 1 Cor 3:1
Now concerning *s* gifts .... 1 Cor 12:1
to be a prophet or *s* ...... 1 Cor 14:37
However, the *s* is not ..... 1 Cor 15:46
s restore such a one .... Gal 6:1
being built up a *s* house ..... 1 Pet 2:5

SPIRITUALLY
s minded is life .... Rom 8:6
because they are *s* .... 1 Cor 2:14

SPIT
He had *s* on his eyes ...... Mark 8:23
s on Him, and kill Him ... Mark 10:34
some began to *s* on Him .. Mark 14:65
insulted and *s* upon ...... Luke 18:32

SPITEFULLY
for those who *s* .... Matt 5:44

SPITTING
face from shame and *s* .... Is 50:6

SPLENDOR
with majesty and *s* .... Job 40:10
Like the *s* of the meadows ... Ps 37:20
on the glorious *s* .... Ps 145:5
the *s* of old men is their .... Prov 20:29
of Zion all her *s* .... Lam 1:6
wisdom, and defile your *s* .. Ezek 28:7

SPLIT
ground *s* apart under ..... Num 16:31
pierced his head, she *s* ..... Judg 5:26
the altar shall *s* apart ..... 1 Kin 13:3
of Olives shall be *s* in two .. Zech 14:4
and the rocks were *s* ..... Matt 27:51

SPOIL
hate us have taken *s* .... Ps 44:10
when they divide the *s* .... Is 9:3
He shall divide the *s* .... Is 53:12
Take *s* of silver .... Nah 2:9
s will be divided .... Zech 14:1

SPOILER
I have created the *s* .... Is 54:16

SPOKE
God *s* to Moses and said ...... Ex 6:2
s they did not hear .... Is 66:4
who feared the LORD *s* ...... Mal 3:16
"No man ever *s* .... John 7:46
We know that God *s* .... John 9:29
I was a child, I *s* .... 1 Cor 13:11
in various ways *s* .... Heb 1:1
s as they were moved ...... 2 Pet 1:21

SPOKEN
See LORD HAS SPOKEN
'just as you have *s* .... Num 14:28
God has *s* once .... Ps 62:11
I have not *s* in secret .... Is 45:19
LORD has *s* against you ..... Amos 3:1
'What have we *s* .... Mal 3:13
s this parable against ..... Luke 20:19
the prophets have *s* ...... Luke 24:25
why am I evil *s* .... 1 Cor 10:30

SPOKESMAN
So he shall be your *s* .... Ex 4:16

SPONGE
them ran and took a *s* .... Matt 27:48

SPOT
and there is no *s* .... Song 4:7
church, not having *s* .... Eph 5:27
commandment without *s* .. 1 Tim 6:14
Himself without *s* .... Heb 9:14
blemish and without *s* ..... 1 Pet 1:19

SPOTS
They are *s* and .... 2 Pet 2:13
These are *s* in your .... Jude 12

SPOUSE
your love, my sister, my *s* .. Song 4:10
Israel served for a *s* .... Hos 12:12

SPREAD
fell on my knees and *s* ...... Ezra 9:5
they have *s* a net by .... Ps 140:5
Then He *s* it before me .... Ezek 2:10
Then the word of God *s* ..... Acts 6:7
the Lord was being *s* ...... Acts 13:49
their message will *s* .... 2 Tim 2:17

SPREADS
He alone *s* out the .... Job 9:8
s them out like a tent .... Is 40:22
Zion *s* out her hands .... Lam 1:17

SPRING
Truth shall *s* out of .... Ps 85:11
is like a murky *s* .... Prov 25:26
sister, my spouse, a *s* ...... Song 4:12
s forth I tell you .... Is 42:9
of Israel to *s* forth .... Ezek 29:21
s shall become dry .... Hos 13:15
s send forth fresh .... James 3:11

SPRINGING
a fountain of water *s* ...... John 4:14
of bitterness *s* .... Heb 12:15

SPRINGS
"Have you entered the *s* ... Job 38:16
He sends the *s* into .... Ps 104:10
and the thirsty land *s* .... Is 35:7
and the dry land *s* .... Is 41:18

SPRINKLE
He *s* many nations .... Is 52:15
Then I will *s* .... Ezek 36:25

SPRINKLED
s dust on his head .... Job 2:12
and hyssop, and *s* .... Heb 9:19
having our hearts *s* .... Heb 10:22

SPRINKLING
s that speaks .... Heb 12:24
for obedience and *s* .... 1 Pet 1:2

SPROUT
down, that it will *s* .... Job 14:7
and the seed should *s* ...... Mark 4:27

SPY
men to *s* out the land .... Num 13:2
sent to *s* out Jericho .... Josh 6:25
to *s* out the land and .... Judg 18:2
to *s* out our liberty .... Gal 2:4

SQUARE
the night in the open *s* ..... Gen 19:2
in the open *s* of the city ... Judg 19:15
took my seat in the open *s* .. Job 29:7
the city is laid out as a *s* ... Rev 21:16

SQUARES
voice in the open *s* .... Prov 1:20
s I will seek the one .... Song 3:2

STABILITY
will be the *s* of your .... Is 33:6

STAFF
this Jordan with my *s* ..... Gen 32:10
your feet, and your *s* .... Ex 12:11
the donkey with his *s* .... Num 22:27
Your rod and Your *s* .... Ps 23:4
LORD has broken the *s* .... Is 14:5
'How the strong *s* .... Jer 48:17
they have been a *s* .... Ezek 29:6
And I took my *s*, Beauty .. Zech 11:10
for the journey except a *s* ... Mark 6:8
on the top of his *s* .... Heb 11:21

STAG
like a gazelle or a young *s* .. Song 2:9

STAGGER
and He makes them *s* . . . . . . Job 12:25
they will drink and *s* . . . . Jer 25:16

STAGGERS
as a drunken man *s* . . . . Is 19:14

STAKES
s will ever be removed . . . . Is 33:20

STALLS
be no herd in the *s* . . . . Hab 3:17

STAMMERERS
s will be ready . . . . Is 32:4

STAMMERING
For with *s* lips and . . . . Is 28:11
s tongue that you . . . . Is 33:19

STAMPING
At the noise of the *s* . . . . Jer 47:3

STAND
where you *s* is holy ground . . . . Ex 3:5
S still, and see the . . . . Ex 14:13
one shall be able to *s* . . . . . . Deut 7:24
"Who is able to *s* . . . . 1 Sam 6:20
took a *s* for the covenant . . 2 Kin 23:3
we are not able to *s* . . . . Ezra 10:13
but it does not *s* . . . . Job 8:15
lives, and He shall *s* . . . . Job 19:25
ungodly shall not *s* . . . . Ps 1:5
Why do You *s* afar off . . . . Ps 10:1
Or who may *s* in His . . . . Ps 24:3
the world *s* in awe of Him . . . . . Ps 33:8
Who will *s* up for me . . . . Ps 94:16
and let an accuser *s* . . . . Ps 109:6
They *s* fast forever . . . . Ps 111:8
he will not *s* before . . . . Prov 22:29
Do not take your *s* . . . . Eccl 8:3
"It shall not *s* . . . . Is 7:7
"*S* in the ways and . . . . Jer 6:16
not lack a man to *s* . . . . Jer 35:19
whose words will *s* . . . . Jer 44:28
s in the gap before Me . . . . Ezek 22:30
and it shall *s* . . . . Dan 2:44
but she shall not *s* . . . . Dan 11:17
Who can *s* before His . . . . Nah 1:6
s on the Mount of Olives . . . Zech 14:4
And who can *s* when He . . . . . Mal 3:2
against itself will not *s* . . . . Matt 12:25
that kingdom cannot *s* . . . . . Mark 3:24
how will his kingdom *s* . . . Luke 11:18
why do you *s* gazing up . . . . Acts 1:11
you *s* is holy ground . . . . Acts 7:33
this grace in which we *s* . . . . Rom 5:2
he will be made to *s* . . . . Rom 14:4
Watch, *s* fast in the . . . . . . 1 Cor 16:13
for by faith you *s* . . . . 2 Cor 1:24
S fast therefore in the . . . . Gal 5:1
having done all, to *s* . . . . Eph 6:13
S therefore . . . . Eph 6:14
s fast in the Lord . . . . Phil 4:1
now we live, if you *s* . . . . . 1 Thess 3:8
of God in which you *s* . . . . . . 1 Pet 5:12
Behold, I *s* at the . . . . Rev 3:20

STANDARD
LORD will lift up a *s* . . . . Is 59:19
Set up the *s* toward . . . . Jer 4:6

STANDING
the Lord *s* by the altar . . . . . Amos 9:1
the LORD, and Satan *s* . . . . Zech 3:1
they love to pray *s* . . . . Matt 6:5
and saw others *s* idle . . . . Matt 20:3
s here who will not taste . . . Mark 9:1
the woman *s* in the midst . . . John 8:9
and the Son of Man *s* . . . . . Acts 7:56
the Judge is *s* at the door . . James 5:9
Then I saw an angel *s* . . . . . Rev 19:17

STANDS
Nor *s* in the path of sinners . . . . Ps 1:1
counsel of the LORD *s* . . . . Ps 33:11
my heart *s* in awe of . . . . . . Ps 119:161
The LORD *s* up to plead . . . . Is 3:13

there *s* One among you . . . . . John 1:26
him who thinks he *s* . . . . . . 1 Cor 10:12
foundation of God *s* . . . . 2 Tim 2:19

STAR
S shall come out of . . . . Num 24:17
For we have seen His *s* . . . . . Matt 2:2
for one *s* differs from . . . . . 1 Cor 15:41
give him the morning *s* . . . . . Rev 2:28
And a great *s* fell . . . . Rev 8:10
Bright and Morning *S* . . . . . . Rev 22:16

STARS
He made the *s* also . . . . Gen 1:16
as the *s* of the heaven . . . . . . Gen 22:17
s bowed down to me . . . . Gen 37:9
s are not pure in His . . . . Job 25:5
when the morning *s* . . . . Job 38:7
the moon and the *s* . . . . Ps 8:3
s to rule by night, for His . . . . Ps 136:9
praise Him, all you *s* . . . . Ps 148:3
the *s* will diminish their . . . . . . Joel 3:15
the *s* of heaven will fall . . Mark 13:25
born as many as the *s* . . . . . . Heb 11:12
wandering *s* for whom . . . . Jude 13
in His right hand seven *s* . . . . . Rev 1:16
a garland of twelve *s* . . . . Rev 12:1

STARVED
His strength is *s* . . . . Job 18:12

STATE
man at his best *s* . . . . Ps 39:5
us in our lowly *s* . . . . Ps 136:23
and the last *s* of that . . . . . . Matt 12:45
learned in whatever *s* . . . . Phil 4:11

STATURE
add one cubit to his *s* . . . . . . Matt 6:27
in wisdom and *s* . . . . Luke 2:52
add one cubit to his *s* . . . . . . Luke 12:25
for he was of short *s* . . . . Luke 19:3
the measure of the *s* . . . . Eph 4:13

STATUTE
It shall be a *s* forever to . . . . Ex 27:21
be theirs for a perpetual *s* . . Ex 29:9
shall be a perpetual *s* . . . . Lev 3:17
it shall be a *s* forever . . . . . . Lev 23:14
For this is a *s* for Israel . . . . Ps 81:4
to establish a royal *s* . . . . Dan 6:7

STATUTES
shall therefore keep My *s* . . . Lev 18:5
My ways, to keep My *s* . . . . 1 Kin 3:14
not put away His *s* from . . . . . Ps 18:22
the *s* of the LORD are . . . . Ps 19:8
Teach me Your *s* . . . . Ps 119:12
s have been my songs . . . . . . Ps 119:54
observe Your *s* . . . . Ps 119:117
not walked in My *s* . . . . Ezek 5:6
did not walk in My *s* . . . . Ezek 20:21

STAY
her feet would not *s* . . . . Prov 7:11
S here and watch with . . . . . . Matt 26:38
for today I must *s* . . . . Luke 19:5
the time of your *s* . . . . 1 Pet 1:17

STEADFAST
yes, you could be *s* . . . . Job 11:15
O God, my heart is *s* . . . . Ps 57:7
their heart was not *s* . . . . Ps 78:37
his heart is *s* . . . . Ps 112:7
God, and *s* forever . . . . Dan 6:26
brethren, be *s* . . . . 1 Cor 15:58
faith, grounded and *s* . . . . Col 1:23
angels proved *s* . . . . Heb 2:2
of our confidence *s* . . . . Heb 3:14
soul, both sure and *s* . . . . Heb 6:19
Resist him, *s* in the . . . . 1 Pet 5:9

STEADFASTLY
s set His face to go . . . . Luke 9:51
And they continued *s* . . . . Acts 2:42
continuing *s* in . . . . Rom 12:12

STEADFASTNESS
good order and the *s* . . . . Col 2:5
from your own *s* . . . . 2 Pet 3:17

STEADILY
could not look *s* . . . . 2 Cor 3:13

STEADY
and his hands were *s* . . . . Ex 17:12

STEAL
"You shall not *s* . . . . Ex 20:15
Will you *s* . . . . Jer 7:9
s My words every one . . . . . . Jer 23:30
thieves break in and *s* . . . . Matt 6:19
night and *s* Him away . . . . Matt 27:64
murder, 'Do not *s* . . . . Mark 10:19
not come except to *s* . . . . John 10:10
a man should not *s* . . . . Rom 2:21
Let him who stole *s* . . . . Eph 4:28

STEEP
s places shall fall . . . . Ezek 38:20
waters poured down a *s* . . . . . . Mic 1:4
violently down the *s* . . . . Matt 8:32

STEM
forth a Rod from the *s* . . . . Is 11:1

STENCH
there will be a *s* . . . . Is 3:24
this time there is a *s* . . . . John 11:39

STEP
there is but a *s* . . . . 1 Sam 20:3
s has turned from the . . . . Job 31:7

STEPHEN
One of the first seven deacons, Acts 6:1–8
Falsely accused by Jews; gives defense, Acts 6:9—7:53
Becomes first Christian martyr, Acts 7:54–60

STEPS
has held fast to His *s* . . . . Job 23:11
and count all my *s* . . . . Job 31:4
and He sees all his *s* . . . . Job 34:21
Uphold my *s* in Your . . . . Ps 17:5
The *s* of a good man . . . . Ps 37:23
of his *s* shall slide . . . . Ps 37:31
and established my *s* . . . . Ps 40:2
hide, they mark my *s* . . . . Ps 56:6
s had nearly slipped . . . . Ps 73:2
Direct my *s* by Your . . . . Ps 119:133
s will not be hindered . . . . Prov 4:12
the LORD directs his *s* . . . . Prov 16:9
A man's *s* are of the . . . . Prov 20:24
to direct his own *s* . . . . Jer 10:23
should follow His *s* . . . . 1 Pet 2:21

STEWARD
faithful and wise *s* . . . . Luke 12:42
you can no longer be *s* . . . . . . Luke 16:2
commended the unjust *s* . . . Luke 16:8
be blameless, as a *s* . . . . Titus 1:7

STEWARDS
of Christ and *s* . . . . 1 Cor 4:1
one another, as good *s* . . . . . . 1 Pet 4:10

STEWARDSHIP
entrusted with a *s* . . . . 1 Cor 9:17

STICK
and his bones *s* . . . . Job 33:21
and *s* out the tongue . . . . Is 57:4
'For Joseph, the *s* . . . . Ezek 37:16

STICKS
a man gathering *s* . . . . Num 15:32
was there gathering *s* . . . . 1 Kin 17:10
And the *s* on which . . . . Ezek 37:20

STIFF
rebellion and your *s* . . . . Deut 31:27
do not speak with a *s* . . . . Ps 75:5

STIFF-NECKED
Now do not be *s* . . . . 2 Chr 30:8
"You *s* and uncircumcised . . Acts 7:51

STILL
on your bed, and be *s* . . . . Ps 4:4

of the LORD is *s* ... Prov 10:29
knowledge increases *s* ... Prov 24:5
S and honor are her ... Prov 31:25
is better than *s* ... Eccl 9:16
for *s* and not for ... Eccl 10:17
For You have been a *s* ... Is 25:4
him take hold of My *s* ... Is 27:5
of His might and the *s* ... Is 40:26
might He increases *s* ... Is 40:29
works it with the *s* ... Is 44:12
righteousness and *s* ... Is 45:24
Put on your *s* ... Is 52:1
O LORD, my *s* and my ... Jer 16:19
I will destroy the *s* ... Hag 2:22
He has shown *s* with ... Luke 1:51
were still without *s* ... Rom 5:6
s is made perfect ... 2 Cor 12:9
you have a little *s* ... Rev 3:8

STRENGTHEN
and He shall *s* ... Ps 27:14
S the weak hands ... Is 35:3
"So I will *s* them in ... Zech 10:12
s your brethren ... Luke 22:32
s the hands ... Heb 12:12
s the things ... Rev 3:2

STRENGTHENED
weak you have not *s* ... Ezek 34:4
unbelief, but was *s* ... Rom 4:20
of His glory, to be *s* ... Eph 3:16
stood with me and *s* ... 2 Tim 4:17

STRENGTHENING
s the souls of the ... Acts 14:22

STRENGTHENS
s the wise more than ... Eccl 7:19
through Christ who *s* ... Phil 4:13

STRETCH
will quickly *s* out her ... Ps 68:31
said to the man, "*S* ... Matt 12:13
are old, you will *s* ... John 21:18

STRETCH OUT MY HAND
I will *s* and strike Egypt ... Ex 3:20
when I *s* on Egypt ... Ex 7:5
Lord's anointed, to *s* ... 1 Sam 24:6
forbid that I should *s* ... 1 Sam 26:11
s against the inhabitants ... Jer 6:12
And I will *s* against you ... Jer 51:25
I will *s* against them ... Ezek 6:14
I will *s* against you ... Ezek 25:7
I will *s* against Judah ... Zeph 1:4

STRETCHED
s himself out on the ... 1 Kin 17:21
s himself out on him ... 2 Kin 4:35
I have *s* out my hands ... Ps 88:9
but His hand is *s* out still ... Is 5:25
Who *s* out the heavens ... Is 51:13
His wisdom, and has *s* ... Jer 10:12
"All day long I have *s* ... Rom 10:21

STRETCHED OUT HIS HAND
Abraham *s* and took the ... Gen 22:10
Aaron *s* over the waters ... Ex 8:6
Aaron *s* with his rod ... Ex 8:17
Moses *s* toward heaven ... Ex 10:22
Moses *s* over the sea ... Ex 14:21
as soon as he had *s* ... Josh 8:19
And when the angel *s* ... 2 Sam 24:16
he has *s* against them ... Is 5:25
He *s* over the sea ... Is 23:11
And the cherub *s* ... Ezek 10:7
Jesus *s* and caught him ... Matt 14:31
Herod the king *s* to ... Acts 12:1

STRETCHES
For he *s* out his hand ... Job 15:25

STRICKEN
My heart is *s* and ... Ps 102:4
yet we esteemed Him *s* ... Is 53:4
of My people He was *s* ... Is 53:8
You have *s* them ... Jer 5:3
He has *s*, but He will ... Hos 6:1

STRIFE
let there be no *s* ... Gen 13:8
You have made us a *s* ... Ps 80:6
at the waters of *s* ... Ps 106:32
Hatred stirs up *s* ... Prov 10:12
comes nothing but *s* ... Prov 13:10
man stirs up *s* ... Prov 15:18
transgression loves *s* ... Prov 17:19
borne me, a man of *s* ... Jer 15:10
and lust, not in *s* ... Rom 13:13
even from envy and *s* ... Phil 1:15
which come envy, *s* ... 1 Tim 6:4

STRIKE
said, "*S* this people ... 2 Kin 6:18
The sun shall not *s* ... Ps 121:6
Let the righteous *s* ... Ps 141:5
S a scoffer ... Prov 19:25
s your hands ... Ezek 21:14
s the waves of the sea ... Zech 10:11
"*S* the Shepherd ... Zech 13:7
s the earth with a ... Mal 4:6
'I will *s* the Shepherd ... Matt 26:31
'I will *s* the Shepherd ... Mark 14:27
if well, why do you *s* ... John 18:23
the sun shall not *s* ... Rev 7:16
s the earth with all ... Rev 11:6

STRIKES
To him who *s* you on the ... Luke 6:29
if one *s* you on the face ... 2 Cor 11:20
a scorpion when it *s* ... Rev 9:5

STRINGED
of your *s* instruments ... Is 14:11
of your *s* instruments ... Amos 5:23

STRIP
S yourselves ... Is 32:11
s her naked and expose ... Hos 2:3

STRIPES
their iniquity with *s* ... Ps 89:32
s we are healed ... Is 53:5
be beaten with many *s* ... Luke 12:47
I received forty *s* ... 2 Cor 11:24
s you were healed ... 1 Pet 2:24

STRIVE
"My Spirit shall not *s* ... Gen 6:3
He will not always *s* ... Ps 103:9
Do not *s* with a man ... Prov 3:30
Let the potsherd *s* ... Is 45:9
"*S* to enter through ... Luke 13:24
the Lord not to *s* ... 2 Tim 2:14

STRIVING
for a man to stop *s* ... Prov 20:3

STROKE
with a mighty *s* ... Jer 14:17

STRONG
with a *s* hand he will let ... Ex 6:1
Be *s* and of good courage ... Deut 31:6
be *s* and very courageous ... Josh 1:7
Be *s* and conduct ... 1 Sam 4:9
indeed He is *s* ... Job 9:19
The LORD *s* and mighty ... Ps 24:8
bring me to the *s* ... Ps 60:9
a *s* tower from the enemy ... Ps 61:3
s is Your hand ... Ps 89:13
there is *s* confidence ... Prov 14:26
the LORD is a *s* tower ... Prov 18:10
A wise man is *s* ... Prov 24:5
s shall be as tinder ... Is 1:31
"We have a *s* city ... Is 26:1
She had *s* branches for ... Ezek 19:11
shall be as *s* as iron ... Dan 2:40
the weak say, 'I am *s* ... Joel 3:10
enter a *s* man's house ... Matt 12:29
one can enter a *s* man's ... Mark 3:27
When a *s* man ... Luke 11:21
We then who are *s* ... Rom 15:1
weak, but you are *s* ... 1 Cor 4:10
I am weak, then I am *s* ... 2 Cor 12:10
are weak and you are *s* ... 2 Cor 13:9
my brethren, be *s* ... Eph 6:10
weakness were made *s* ... Heb 11:34
men, because you are *s* ... 1 John 2:14
s is the Lord God ... Rev 18:8

STRONGER
weakness of God is *s* ... 1 Cor 1:25

STRONGHOLD
crag of the rock and the *s* ... Job 39:28
of my salvation, my *s* ... Ps 18:2
down the trusted *s* ... Prov 21:22

STRUCK
s the rock twice ... Num 20:11
the hand of God has *s* ... Job 19:21
s all my enemies ... Ps 3:7
Behold, He *s* the rock ... Ps 78:20
I was angry and *s* ... Is 57:17
in My wrath I *s* ... Is 60:10
s the head from the ... Hab 3:13
I *s* you with blight ... Hag 2:17
took the reed and *s* ... Matt 27:30
the officers *s* Him with ... Mark 14:65
they *s* Him on the head ... Mark 15:19
Him, they *s* Him on the ... Luke 22:64
s Him with their hands ... John 19:3
and *s* down the Egyptian ... Acts 7:24

STUBBLE
shall bring forth *s* ... Is 33:11
his sword, as driven *s* ... Is 41:2
they shall be as *s* ... Is 47:14
s that passes ... Jer 13:24
do wickedly will be *s* ... Mal 4:1

STUBBORN
when Pharaoh was *s* about ... Ex 13:15
If a man has a *s* ... Deut 21:18
and *s* children ... Ezek 2:4

STUBBORN-HEARTED
"Listen to Me, you *s* ... Is 46:12

STUBBORNNESS
do not look on the *s* ... Deut 9:27

STUDENT
the teacher with the *s* ... 1 Chr 25:8

STUDIED
having never *s* ... John 7:15

STUMBLE
causes them to *s* ... Ps 119:165
to make my steps *s* ... Ps 140:4
your foot will not *s* ... Prov 3:23
know what makes them *s* ... Prov 4:19
one will be weary or *s* ... Is 5:27
among them shall *s* ... Is 8:15
we *s* at noonday as at ... Is 59:10
that they might not *s* ... Is 63:13
before your feet *s* ... Jer 13:16
they will *s* and fall ... Jer 46:6
have caused many to *s* ... Mal 2:8
you will be made to *s* ... Matt 26:31
if all are made to *s* ... Matt 26:33
immediately they *s* ... Mark 4:17
who believe in Me to *s* ... Mark 9:42
s because of Me this ... Mark 14:27
the day, he does not *s* ... John 11:9
Who is made to *s* ... 2 Cor 11:29
whole law, and yet *s* ... James 2:10
For we all *s* in many ... James 3:2

STUMBLED
and those who *s* ... 1 Sam 2:4
God, for you have *s* ... Hos 14:1
s that they should ... Rom 11:11

STUMBLES
word, immediately he *s* ... Matt 13:21

STUMBLING
the deaf, nor put a *s* ... Lev 19:14
but a stone of *s* ... Is 8:14
Behold, I will lay *s* ... Jer 6:21
watched for my *s* ... Jer 20:10
it became their *s* ... Ezek 7:19
stumbled at that *s* ... Rom 9:32

I lay in Zion a *s* .... Rom 9:33
this, not to put a *s* .... Rom 14:13
to the Jews a *s* .... 1 Cor 1:23
of yours become a *s* .... 1 Cor 8:9
and "A stone of *s* .... 1 Pet 2:8
is no cause for *s* .... 1 John 2:10
to keep you from *s* .... Jude 24

STUMBLING BLOCK
s out of the way .... Is 57:14
I lay a *s* before him .... Ezek 3:20
it became their *s* .... Ezek 7:19
s and a recompense .... Rom 11:9
not to put a *s* .... Rom 14:13
to the Jews a *s* .... 1 Cor 1:23
of yours become a *s* .... 1 Cor 8:9
taught Balak to put a *s* ..... Rev 2:14

STUMP
whose *s* remains when it is .... Is 6:13
leave the *s* and roots .... Dan 4:15

STUPID
and regarded as *s* .... Job 18:3
who hates correction is *s* ... Prov 12:1
Surely I am more *s* .... Prov 30:2

SUBDUE
s the peoples under us .... Ps 47:3
shall *s* three kings .... Dan 7:24
s our iniquities .... Mic 7:19
s all things to .... Phil 3:21

SUBDUED
land was *s* before them ...... Josh 18:1
So the Philistines were *s* .. 1 Sam 7:13
You have *s* under me those ... Ps 18:39
through faith *s* kingdoms .. Heb 11:33

SUBJECT
for it is not *s* .... Rom 8:7
Let every soul be *s* .... Rom 13:1
all things are made *s* ..... 1 Cor 15:28
Remind them to be *s* .... Titus 3:1
all their lifetime *s* .... Heb 2:15
having been made *s* .... 1 Pet 3:22

SUBJECTED
because of Him who *s* ..... Rom 8:20

SUBJECTION
put all things in *s* .... Heb 2:8
more readily be in *s* .... Heb 12:9

SUBMISSION
in silence with all *s* .... 1 Tim 2:11
his children in *s* .... 1 Tim 3:4

SUBMISSIVE
Wives, likewise, be *s* .... 1 Pet 3:1
Yes, all of you be *s* .... 1 Pet 5:5

SUBMIT
s yourself under her hand .. Gen 16:9
Your enemies shall *s* .... Ps 66:3
Wives, *s* to your own .... Eph 5:22
s to your own husbands ..... Col 3:18
Therefore *s* to God .... James 4:7
s yourselves to every ...... 1 Pet 2:13
you younger people, *s* .... 1 Pet 5:5

SUBSIDED
and the waters *s* .... Gen 8:1
the king's wrath *s* .... Esth 7:10

SUBSTANCE
Bless his *s* .... Deut 33:11
Your eyes saw my *s* .... Ps 139:16
up all the *s* of his house ..... Prov 6:31
the LORD, and their *s* .... Mic 4:13
Now faith is the *s* of .... Heb 11:1

SUCCEED
For this will not *s* .... Num 14:41
you shall not *s* .... Jer 32:5

SUCCESS
please give me *s* .... Gen 24:12
You spoil my *s* .... Job 30:22
but wisdom brings *s* .... Eccl 10:10

SUCCESSFUL
Joseph, and he was a *s* ..... Gen 39:2

SUCCOTH
Place east of the Jordan, Judg 8:4, 5
Jacob's residence here, Gen 33:17
—— Israel's first camp, Ex 12:37

SUDDENLY
whom you seek, will *s* .... Mal 3:1
s there was with the .... Luke 2:13

SUE
s you and take away .... Matt 5:40

SUFFER
for a stranger will *s* .... Prov 11:15
Son of Man must *s* many .. Mark 8:31
He must *s* many things .... Mark 9:12
Son of Man must *s* many .. Luke 9:22
He must *s* many things ... Luke 17:25
for the Christ to *s* .... Luke 24:46
that the Christ would *s* ..... Acts 3:18
to *s* shame for His name .... Acts 5:41
s for My name's sake .... Acts 9:16
that the Christ had to *s* ..... Acts 17:3
that the Christ would *s* .... Acts 26:23
Christ, if indeed we *s* ...... Rom 8:17
all the members *s* .... 1 Cor 12:26
sufferings which we also *s* .. 2 Cor 1:6
that they may not *s* .... Gal 6:12
in Him, but also to *s* .... Phil 1:29
we would *s* tribulation .... 1 Thess 3:4
s trouble as an .... 2 Tim 2:9
Jesus will *s* persecution ... 2 Tim 3:12
choosing rather to *s* .... Heb 11:25
when you do good and *s* ... 1 Pet 2:20
even if you should *s* for .... 1 Pet 3:14
the will of God, to *s* .... 1 Pet 3:17
s as a murderer .... 1 Pet 4:15
Therefore let those who *s* .. 1 Pet 4:19
you are about to *s* .... Rev 2:10

SUFFERED
I have *s* many things ..... Matt 27:19
s many things from .... Mark 5:26
s these things and to ..... Luke 24:26
Have you *s* so many .... Gal 3:4
for whom I have *s* .... Phil 3:8
in that He Himself has *s* .... Heb 2:18
by the things which He *s* ..... Heb 5:8
with His own blood, *s* ..... Heb 13:12
because Christ also *s* ...... 1 Pet 2:21
when He *s*, He did not ..... 1 Pet 2:23
For Christ also *s* .... 1 Pet 3:18
since Christ *s* .... 1 Pet 4:1
after you have *s* .... 1 Pet 5:10

SUFFERING
My eyes bring *s* .... Lam 3:51
Himself alive after His *s* by .. Acts 1:3
for the *s* of death crowned ..... Heb 2:9
as an example of *s* .... James 5:10
Is anyone among you *s* ... James 5:13
forth as an example, *s* .... Jude 7

SUFFERINGS
I consider that the *s* .... Rom 8:18
share with me in the *s* ...... 2 Tim 1:8
perfect through *s* .... Heb 2:10
great struggle with *s* ...... Heb 10:32
beforehand the *s* .... 1 Pet 1:11

SUFFERS
Love *s* long and is .... 1 Cor 13:4

SUFFICIENCY
but our *s* is from God .... 2 Cor 3:5
always having all *s* .... 2 Cor 9:8

SUFFICIENT
S for the day is its .... Matt 6:34
by the majority is *s* .... 2 Cor 2:6
Not that we are *s* .... 2 Cor 3:5

SUITABLE
by the hand of a *s* .... Lev 16:21

SUM
How great is the *s* .... Ps 139:17
s I obtained this .... Acts 22:28

SUMMED
commandment, are all *s* .... Rom 13:9

SUMMER
and heat, winter and *s* ..... Gen 8:22
into the drought of *s* .... Ps 32:4
You have made *s* .... Ps 74:17
you know that *s* .... Matt 24:32

SUMPTUOUSLY
fine linen and fared *s* ..... Luke 16:19

SUN
So the *s* stood still .... Josh 10:13
love Him be like the *s* ...... Judg 5:31
grows green in the *s* .... Job 8:16
a tabernacle for the *s* .... Ps 19:4
the LORD God is a *s* .... Ps 84:11
s shall not strike you .... Ps 121:6
the *s* to rule by day .... Ps 136:8
to behold the *s* .... Eccl 11:7
while the *s* and the .... Eccl 12:2
moon, clear as the *s* .... Song 6:10
s will be sevenfold .... Is 30:26
s returned ten degrees .... Is 38:8
s shall no longer be .... Is 60:19
s has gone down while .... Jer 15:9
LORD, who gives the *s* .... Jer 31:35
the *s* and moon grow .... Joel 2:10
s shall be turned .... Joel 2:31
s shall go down on the .... Mic 3:6
The *s* and moon stood .... Hab 3:11
for He makes His *s* .... Matt 5:45
the *s* was darkened .... Luke 23:45
is one glory of the *s* ...... 1 Cor 15:41
do not let the *s* .... Eph 4:26
s became black as .... Rev 6:12
s shall not strike .... Rev 7:16
had no need of the *s* .... Rev 21:23

SUPPER
man gave a great *s* .... Luke 14:16
to eat the Lord's *S* ...... 1 Cor 11:20
took the cup after *s* ...... 1 Cor 11:25
together for the *s* .... Rev 19:17

SUPPLICATION
s that you have made .... 1 Kin 9:3
and make your *s* .... Job 8:5
LORD has heard my *s* .... Ps 6:9
to the LORD I made *s* .... Ps 30:8
Yourself from my *s* .... Ps 55:1
Let my *s* come before ..... Ps 119:170
They will make *s* .... Is 45:14
with all prayer and *s* .... Eph 6:18
by prayer and *s* .... Phil 4:6

SUPPLICATIONS
Will he make many *s* to ..... Job 41:3
of my *s* when I cry to You ..... Ps 28:2
To the voice of my *s* .... Ps 130:2
request by prayer and *s* ..... Dan 9:3
and continues in *s* and ..... 1 Tim 5:5
offered up prayers and *s* ..... Heb 5:7

SUPPLIES
Now may He who *s* .... 2 Cor 9:10
Therefore He who *s* .... Gal 3:5
by what every joint *s* .... Eph 4:16

SUPPLY
s what was lacking .... Phil 2:30
And my God shall *s* .... Phil 4:19

SUPPORT
but the LORD was my *s* .. 2 Sam 22:19
this, that you must *s* ...... Acts 20:35

SUPPOSE
S there were fifty .... Gen 18:24
"But *s* they will not believe .... Ex 4:1
s that I came to give ...... Luke 12:51
not drunk, as you *s* .... Acts 2:15
who *s* that godliness is a .... 1 Tim 6:5
man *s* that he will receive .. James 1:7

SUPREME
to the king as *s* .... 1 Pet 2:13

SURE
s your sin will find .... Num 32:23
build him a s house ...... 1 Sam 2:35
but no man is s .... Job 24:22
testimony of the LORD is s ...... Ps 19:7
all His precepts are s .... Ps 111:7
call and election s .... 2 Pet 1:10

SURETY
Be s for Your servant ..... Ps 119:122
one who hates being s ..... Prov 11:15
Jesus has become a s .... Heb 7:22

SURROUND
But you shall s .... 2 Kin 11:8
LORD, mercy shall s .... Ps 32:10

SURROUNDED
the waves of death s ...... 2 Sam 22:5
The pangs of death s .... Ps 18:4
The pains of death s .... Ps 116:3
All nations s me .... Ps 118:10
their own deeds have s ...... Hos 7:2
and the floods s .... Jon 2:3
also, since we are s .... Heb 12:1

SURVIVOR
was no refugee or s .... Lam 2:22

SUSANNA
Believing woman ministering to Christ, Luke 8:2, 3

SUSPICIONS
reviling, evil s .... 1 Tim 6:4

SUSTAIN
You will s him on his .... Ps 41:3
of a man will s .... Prov 18:14
S me with cakes of .... Song 2:5

SUSTAINED
Forty years You s them ..... Neh 9:21
I awoke, for the LORD s me ..... Ps 3:5
and My own fury, it s Me .... Is 63:5

SWADDLING
thick darkness its s .... Job 38:9
Him in s cloths .... Luke 2:7

SWALLOW
like a flying s .... Prov 26:2
Like a crane or a s .... Is 38:14
s observe the time .... Jer 8:7
great fish to s Jonah .... Jon 1:17
a gnat and s a camel ...... Matt 23:24

SWALLOWED
Aaron's rod s up their rods ... Ex 7:12
the earth s them .... Ex 15:12
s me up like a monster ...... Jer 51:34
He has s up Israel .... Lam 2:5
"Death is s up in victory .. 1 Cor 15:54
s up with too much sorrow .. 2 Cor 2:7

SWEAR
shall I make you s .... 1 Kin 22:16
in the earth shall s .... Is 65:16
s oaths by the LORD .... Zeph 1:5
'You shall not s .... Matt 5:33
began to curse and s .... Matt 26:74
because He could s .... Heb 6:13
my brethren, do not s .... James 5:12

SWEARING
By s and lying .... Hos 4:2

SWEARS
he who s to his own .... Ps 15:4
everyone who s by Him ..... Ps 63:11
but whoever s by the ..... Matt 23:18

SWEAT
In the s of your face .... Gen 3:19
Then His s became like ... Luke 22:44

SWEET
it is a s aroma, an offering .. Ex 29:18
a s aroma to the LORD .... Lev 1:9
by fire as a s aroma to ..... Num 28:2
Though evil is s .... Job 20:12
valley shall be s to him .... Job 21:33
s are Your words .... Ps 119:103
my words, for they are s .... Ps 141:6
his fruit was s to my taste .. Song 2:3
for your voice is s .... Song 2:14
His mouth is most s .... Song 5:16
shall drip with s wine ...... Amos 9:13
but it will be as s .... Rev 10:9

SWEETER
"What is s than honey ..... Judg 14:18
S also than honey and the ... Ps 19:10
s than honey to my .... Ps 119:103

SWEETNESS
'Should I cease my s .... Judg 9:11
called prudent, and s .... Prov 16:21
s of a man's friend gives ... Prov 27:9
mouth like honey in s .... Ezek 3:3

SWELL
thigh rot and your belly s .... Num 5:21
their feet did not s .... Neh 9:21
your heart shall s with joy ..... Is 60:5

SWELLING
they speak great s .... 2 Pet 2:18

SWEPT
his army shall be s away .. Dan 11:26
he finds it empty, s .... Matt 12:44

SWIFT
s as the eagle flies .... Deut 28:49
pass by like s ships .... Job 9:26
handles the bow, the s ..... Amos 2:15
let every man be s .... James 1:19

SWIFTLY
His word runs very s .... Ps 147:15

SWIM
night I make my bed s .... Ps 6:6

SWINE
the s, though it divides .... Lev 11:7
cast your pearls before s ...... Matt 7:6
went into the herd of s ...... Matt 8:32
the pods that the s ate ...... Luke 15:16

SWINE'S
ring of gold in a s snout ... Prov 11:22
in the midst, eating s flesh ..... Is 66:17

SWOON
as they s like the .... Lam 2:12

SWORD
See TWO-EDGED SWORD
s which turned every .... Gen 3:24
but not with your s .... Josh 24:12
the wicked with Your s .... Ps 17:13
land by their own s .... Ps 44:3
my bow, nor shall my s .... Ps 44:6
their tongue a sharp s .... Ps 57:4
shall not lift up s .... Is 2:4
But he shall flee from the s .... Is 31:8
s shall be bathed .... Is 34:5
The s of the LORD is .... Is 34:6
And I will send a s .... Jer 9:16
will die by the s .... Ezek 7:15
'A s, a s is sharpened ...... Ezek 21:9
'A s, a s is drawn .... Ezek 21:28
Bow and s of battle I .... Hos 2:18
people shall die by the s .. Amos 9:10
not lift up s against nation ..... Mic 4:3
"Awake, O s .... Zech 13:7
to bring peace but a s ...... Matt 10:34
for all who take the s ..... Matt 26:52
s will pierce through .... Luke 2:35
he does not bear the s ...... Rom 13:4
the s of the Spirit .... Eph 6:17
than any two-edged s .... Heb 4:12
a sharp two-edged s .... Rev 1:16
mouth goes a sharp s ...... Rev 19:15

SWORDS
yet they were drawn s .... Ps 55:21
shall beat their s .... Is 2:4
beat their s into plowshares .. Mic 4:3
look, here are two s .... Luke 22:38

SWORE
So I s in My wrath .... Ps 95:11
So I s in My wrath .... Heb 3:11
and s by Him who lives ...... Rev 10:6

SWORN
"By Myself I have s .... Gen 22:16
The LORD has s in .... Ps 132:11
I have s by Myself .... Is 45:23
"The LORD has s .... Heb 7:21

SYCAMORE
into a s tree to see Him .... Luke 19:4

SYCHAR
Town of Samaria; Jesus talks to woman at well here, John 4:5–39

SYMBOLIC
which things are s .... Gal 4:24
It was s for the .... Heb 9:9

SYMBOLS
I have given s through ..... Hos 12:10

SYMPATHIZE
Priest who cannot s .... Heb 4:15

SYMPATHY
My s is stirred .... Hos 11:8

SYNAGOGUE
See RULER OF THE SYNAGOGUE
He went into the s .... Luke 4:16
he was a ruler of the s ...... Luke 8:41
in the s every Sabbath ...... Acts 18:4
but are a s of Satan .... Rev 2:9

SYRACUSE
City visited by Paul, Acts 28:12

SYRIANS
Abraham's kindred, Gen 22:20–23; 25:20
Hostile to Israel, 2 Sam 8:11–13; 10:6–19; 1 Kin 20:1–34; 22:1–38; 2 Kin 6:8—7:7
Defeated by Assyria, 2 Kin 16:9
Destruction of, foretold, Is 17:1–3
Gospel preached to, Acts 15:23, 41

SYRO-PHOENICIAN
Daughter of, freed of demon, Mark 7:25–31

TABERAH
Israelite camp; fire destroys many there, Num 11:1–3

TABERNACLE
that is, the pattern of the t .. Ex 25:9
you shall make the t .... Ex 26:1
called it the t of meeting ...... Ex 33:7
did not depart from the t .... Ex 33:11
covered the t of meeting, ... Ex 40:34
t He shall hide me .... Ps 27:5
I will abide in Your t .... Ps 61:4
In Salem also is His t .... Ps 76.2
How lovely is Your t .... Ps 84:1
Let us go into His t .... Ps 132:7
quiet home, a t .... Is 33:20
has done violence to His t ... Lam 2:6
My t also shall be with .... Ezek 37:27
You also took up the t ...... Acts 7:43
and will rebuild the t ..... Acts 15:16
the true t which the Lord .... Heb 8:2
and more perfect t .... Heb 9:11
the temple of the t of the .... Rev 15:5
Behold, the t .... Rev 21:3

TABERNACLES
See FEAST OF TABERNACLES
T for seven days to the .... Lev 23:34
Feast of T seven days ...... Deut 16:13
us make here three t .... Matt 17:4
Feast of T was at hand ...... John 7:2

TABITHA
See DORCAS

TABLE
shall also make a *t* . . . . Ex 25:23
prepare a *t* before me . . . . Ps 23:5
t become a snare . . . . Ps 69:22
a *t* in the wilderness . . . . Ps 78:19
head as He sat at the *t* . . . . . Matt 26:7
dogs under the *t* . . . . Mark 7:28
t in the Pharisee's house . . . Luke 7:37
t become a snare . . . . Rom 11:9
of the Lord's *t* . . . . 1 Cor 10:21

TABLES
t are full of vomit . . . . Is 28:8
and overturned the *t* . . . . . . Matt 21:12
of God and serve *t* . . . . Acts 6:2

TABLET
write them on the *t* . . . . Prov 3:3
is engraved on the *t* . . . . Jer 17:1

TABLETS
I will give you *t* of stone . . . . Ex 24:12
Cut two *t* of stone like the . . . Ex 34:1
wrote on the *t* the words . . . . Ex 34:28
the two *t* of the Testimony . . Ex 34:29
wrote them on two *t* of . . . . Deut 4:13
God, not on *t* of stone . . . . . . 2 Cor 3:3
and the *t* of the covenant . . . . Heb 9:4

TABOR
Scene of rally against Sisera, Judg 4:6, 12, 14

TADMOR
Trading center near Damascus, 2 Chr 8:4

TAHPANHES (or Tehaphnehes)
City of Egypt; refuge of fleeing Jews, Jer 2:16; 44:1; Ezek 30:18

TAIL
hand and take it by the *t*" . . . . Ex 4:4
the head and not the *t* . . . . Deut 28:13
turned the foxes *t* to *t* . . . . . Judg 15:4
He moves his *t* like a . . . . . Job 40:17
t drew a third of the . . . . Rev 12:4

TAILS
They had *t* like scorpions, . . . Rev 9:10
for their *t* are like serpents . . Rev 9:19

TAKE
You shall *t* with you seven . . . Gen 7:2
T now your son, your only . . Gen 22:2
I will *t* you as My people, ... Ex 6:7
You shall not *t* the name of . . Ex 20:7
I will *t* sickness away . . . . . . Ex 23:25
t off your ornaments, that . . . . Ex 33:5
I will *t* away My hand . . . . . . Ex 33:23
t us as Your inheritance . . . . . Ex 34:9
T heed to yourself, lest . . . . . Ex 34:12
shall not *t* vengeance . . . . . . Lev 19:18
to *t* the vow of a Nazirite . . . . Num 6:2
T heed to yourselves, lest . . . Deut 4:23
You shall not *t* the name . . . Deut 5:11
shall *t* oaths in His name . . . . Deut 6:13
add to it nor *t* away . . . . . . Deut 12:32
T your sandal off your . . . . . . Josh 5:15
God does not *t* away . . . . . 2 Sam 14:14
How long shall I *t* counsel . . . . Ps 13:2
t Your Holy Spirit . . . . Ps 51:11
I will not utterly *t* from . . . . . Ps 89:33
His wings you shall *t* refuge . . Ps 91:4
I will *t* up the cup of . . . . Ps 116:13
t not the word of . . . . Ps 119:43
In You I *t* refuge . . . . Ps 141:8
in You I *t* shelter . . . . Ps 143:9
T firm hold of instruction, . . . Prov 4:13
and *t* away all your alloy . . . . . Is 1:25
will *t* the heart of stone . . . Ezek 36:26
t words with you . . . . Hos 14:2
t away your tunic, let him . . Matt 5:40
does not *t* his cross . . . . Matt 10:38
T My yoke upon . . . . Matt 11:29
t up his cross, and . . . . Matt 16:24
T what is yours and . . . . . . Matt 20:14
t You in, or naked and . . . . Matt 25:38
and you did not *t* Me in . . . Matt 25:43
T, eat; this is My body . . . . . Matt 26:26
and *t* up his cross . . . . Mark 8:34
t up the cross, and . . . . Mark 10:21
T, eat; this is My body . . . Mark 14:22
T this cup away . . . . Mark 14:36
t up his cross daily, and . . . Luke 9:23
My life that I may *t* . . . . John 10:17
I urge you to *t* heart . . . . . . Acts 27:22
T, eat; this is My body . . . . 1 Cor 11:24
Therefore *t* up the whole . . . Eph 6:13

TAKE HEED
T to yourself and see . . . . Ex 10:28
'*T* to yourselves that . . . . Ex 19:12
T to yourself, lest you . . . . . . Ex 34:12
t to speak what the Lord . . Num 23:12
t, lest you lift your eyes . . . . . Deut 4:19
your sons *t* to their way . . . . 1 Kin 2:4
T, do not turn to iniquity . . . Job 36:21
T, and be quiet . . . . Is 7:4
t, you peoples from afar . . . . . . Is 49:1
Everyone *t* to his neighbor . . . . Jer 9:4
t to your spirit . . . . Mal 2:15
T that you do not do . . . . Matt 6:1
"*T* and beware of the . . . . . . Matt 16:6
T that you do not . . . . Matt 18:10
"*T* that no one deceives . . . . Matt 24:4
"*T* what you hear . . . . Mark 4:24
t; see, I have told you . . . . Mark 13:23
T, watch and pray . . . . Mark 13:33
t that the light . . . . Luke 11:35
"*T* and beware . . . . Luke 12:15
t to yourselves, lest . . . . Luke 21:34
t how he builds on it . . . . . . 1 Cor 3:10
stands *t* lest he fall . . . . 1 Cor 10:12
"*T* to the ministry . . . . Col 4:17
T to yourself and to . . . . 1 Tim 4:16

TAKEN
t from man He made into . . . Gen 2:22
because she was *t* out of . . . . Gen 2:23
for out of it you were *t* . . . . . Gen 3:19
have you *t* us away to die . . . Ex 14:11
But the LORD has *t* you . . . . Deut 4:20
t the wife of Uriah . . . . . . 2 Sam 12:10
and the LORD has *t* away . . . . Job 1:21
God has *t* away my justice . . Job 34:5
you are *t* by the words . . . . . . Prov 6:2
He was *t* from prison . . . . Is 53:8
righteous is *t* away from . . . . . . Is 57:1
of God will be *t* from . . . . Matt 21:43
one will be *t* and the . . . . Matt 24:40
what he has will be *t* . . . . . . Mark 4:25
He was *t* up . . . . Acts 1:9
veil is *t* away in Christ . . . . 2 Cor 3:14
until He is *t* out of . . . . 2 Thess 2:7
By faith Enoch was *t* . . . . Heb 11:5

TAKES
who *t* His name in vain . . . . . . Ex 20:7
LORD *t* pleasure in those . . . . . Ps 147:11
For the LORD *t* pleasure in . . Ps 149:4
than he who *t* a city . . . . . . Prov 16:32
does not bear fruit He *t* . . . . John 15:2

TAKING
the fruit of *t* away his sin . . . . . Is 27:9
t Him up on a high . . . . Luke 4:5
t the shield of faith with . . . . Eph 6:16
t the form of a bondservant . . Phil 2:7

TALEBEARER
not go about as a *t* . . . . Lev 19:16
t reveals secrets . . . . Prov 11:13

TALENT
went and hid your *t* . . . . Matt 25:25

TALENTS
owed him ten thousand *t* . . Matt 18:24
to one he gave five *t* . . . . . . Matt 25:15

TALITHA
T, cumi," which is . . . . Mark 5:41

TALK
shall *t* of them when . . . . Deut 6:7
t be vindicated . . . . Job 11:2
with unprofitable *t* . . . . Job 15:3
My tongue also shall *t* . . . . . . Ps 71:24
entangle Him in His *t* . . . . Matt 22:15
I will no longer *t* . . . . John 14:30
turned aside to idle *t* . . . . 1 Tim 1:6

TALKED
within us while He *t* . . . . . . Luke 24:32

TALKERS
both idle *t* and . . . . Titus 1:10

TALL
and *t* as the Anakim . . . . Deut 2:10
to a nation *t* and . . . . Is 18:2

TAMAR
Wife of Er and mother of Perez and Zerah, Gen 38:6–30
——— Absalom's sister, 2 Sam 13:1–32

TAMBOURINE
They sing to the *t* . . . . Job 21:12
The mirth of the *t* . . . . Is 24:8

TAME
no man can *t* the tongue . . . James 3:8

TANNER
in Joppa with Simon, a *t* . . . Acts 9:43

TAPESTRY
She makes *t* for herself . . . Prov 31:22

TARES
the *t* also appeared . . . . Matt 13:26

TARGET
You set me as Your *t* . . . . Job 7:20
and set me up as a *t* . . . . Lam 3:12

TARRY
who turns aside to *t* . . . . Jer 14:8
come and will not *t* . . . . Heb 10:37

TARSHISH
City at a great distance from Palestine, Jon 1:3
Ships of, noted in commerce, Ps 48:7

TARSUS
Paul's birthplace, Acts 21:39
Saul sent to, Acts 9:30
Visited by Barnabas, Acts 11:25

TARTAN
Sent to fight against Jerusalem, 2 Kin 18:17

TASK
your *t* in making brick both . . Ex 5:14
this burdensome *t* . . . . Eccl 1:13

TASKMASTERS
Therefore they set *t* over . . . . . Ex 1:11

TASSELS
Tell them to make *t* on . . . . Num 15:38
shall make *t* on the four . . Deut 22:12

TASTE
the *t* of it was like wafers . . . Ex 16:31
and its *t* was like the . . . . Num 11:8
Oh, *t* and see that the . . . . Ps 34:8
are Your words to my *t* . . . Ps 119:103
was sweet to my *t* . . . . Song 2:3
not *t* death till they see . . . . . Mark 9:1
shall *t* my supper . . . . Luke 14:24
Do not touch, do not *t* . . . . Col 2:21
might *t* death for . . . . Heb 2:9

TASTED
But when He had *t* . . . . Matt 27:34
t the heavenly gift . . . . Heb 6:4
t the good word . . . . Heb 6:5
t that the Lord is . . . . 1 Pet 2:3

TATTENAI
Persian governor opposing the Jews, Ezra 5:3, 6

TAUGHT
O God, You have *t* . . . . Ps 71:17
as His counselor has *t* . . . . Is 40:13

the synagogue and *t* ...... Mark 1:21
He *t* them many things by .. Mark 4:2
presence, and You *t* ...... Luke 13:26
they shall all be *t* .... John 6:45
but as My Father *t* .... John 8:28
that they *t* the people and ... Acts 4:2
t accurately the things of .. Acts 18:25
from man, nor was I *t* .... Gal 1:12
and have been *t* by Him .... Eph 4:21
the faith, as you have been *t* .. Col 2:7
which you were *t* .... 2 Thess 2:15

TAUNT
and a byword, a *t* .... Jer 24:9

TAX
t collectors do the .... Matt 5:46
received the temple *t* ..... Matt 17:24
I say to you that *t* ...... Matt 21:31
Show Me the *t* .... Matt 22:19

TAX COLLECTOR
Matthew the *t* .... Matt 10:3
like heathen and a *t* ..... Matt 18:17
a *t* named Levi .... Luke 5:27
and the other a *t* .... Luke 18:10
who was a chief *t* .... Luke 19:2

TAX COLLECTORS AND SINNERS
your Teacher eat with *t* ... Matt 9:11
He eats and drinks with *t* . Mark 2:16
winebibber, a friend of *t* ... Luke 7:34

TAXES
take customs or *t* .... Matt 17:25
Is it lawful to pay *t* ...... Matt 22:17
forbidding to pay *t* .... Luke 23:2
t to whom *t* .... Rom 13:7

TEACH
t them to your children ..... Deut 4:9
t them diligently .... Deut 6:7
t Jacob Your judgments .. Deut 33:10
t you the good and the .. 1 Sam 12:23
"Can anyone *t* .... Job 21:22
"I will *t* you about .... Job 27:11
t me what I do not see ..... Job 34:32
t me Your paths .... Ps 25:4
T me Your way .... Ps 27:11
t you the fear of the .... Ps 34:11
t You awesome things .... Ps 45:4
t transgressors Your .... Ps 51:13
So *t* us to number our .... Ps 90:12
T me Your statutes .... Ps 119:12
He will *t* us His ways .... Is 2:3
"Whom will he *t* .... Is 28:9
every man *t* his neighbor ... Jer 31:34
a bribe, her priests *t* .... Mic 3:11
t the way of God in ...... Matt 22:16
He began to *t* them .... Mark 6:34
t us to pray, as John also .. Luke 11:1
the Holy Spirit will *t* ..... Luke 12:12
in My name, He will *t* .... John 14:26
you not to *t* in this name ... Acts 5:28
therefore, who *t* another ... Rom 2:21
even nature itself *t* .... 1 Cor 11:14
permit a woman to *t* ...... 1 Tim 2:12
things command and *t* ..... 1 Tim 4:11
T and exhort these .... 1 Tim 6:2
t you again the first .... Heb 5:12
not need that anyone *t* ... 1 John 2:27

TEACHER
for One is your *T* .... Matt 23:8
T, do You not care that .... Mark 4:38
asked Him, "Good *T* ..... Mark 10:17
know that You are a *t* ...... John 3:2
T, this woman was caught .. John 8:4
T has come and is .... John 11:28
You call Me *T* .... John 13:13
named Gamaliel, a *t* .... Acts 5:34
a *t* of babes, having .... Rom 2:20
a *t* of the Gentiles in .... 1 Tim 2:7

TEACHERS
than all my *t* .... Ps 119:99
t will not be moved .... Is 30:20
prophets, third *t* .... 1 Cor 12:28
and some pastors and *t* ..... Eph 4:11
desiring to be *t* .... 1 Tim 1:7
time you ought to be *t* ...... Heb 5:12
of you become *t* .... James 3:1
there will be false *t* .... 2 Pet 2:1

TEACHES
therefore He *t* sinners .... Ps 25:8
He who *t* man knowledge ... Ps 94:10
t men so, shall be called .... Matt 5:19
the Holy Spirit *t* .... 1 Cor 2:13
If anyone *t* otherwise ...... 1 Tim 6:3
the same anointing *t* ..... 1 John 2:27

TEACHING
t them to observe all ...... Matt 28:20
were astonished at His *t* ... Mark 1:22
Me, *t* as doctrines the ...... Mark 7:7
they did not cease *t* .... Acts 5:42
he who teaches, in *t* .... Rom 12:7
by prophesying, or by *t* .... 1 Cor 14:6
t every man in all .... Col 1:28
t things which they .... Titus 1:11
t us that .... Titus 2:12

TEAR
t yourself in anger .... Job 18:4
lest they *t* me like a .... Ps 7:2
I, even I, will *t* .... Hos 5:14
feet, and turn and *t* .... Matt 7:6
will wipe away every *t* ...... Rev 21:4

TEARS
I have seen your *t* .... 2 Kin 20:5
my couch with my *t* .... Ps 6:6
t have been my food .... Ps 42:3
with the bread of *t* .... Ps 80:5
drench you with my *t* .... Is 16:9
GOD will wipe away *t* .... Is 25:8
eyes may run with *t* .... Jer 9:18
My eyes fail with *t* .... Lam 2:11
His feet with her *t* .... Luke 7:38
night and day with *t* ...... Acts 20:31
mindful of your *t* .... 2 Tim 1:4
vehement cries and *t* .... Heb 5:7
it diligently with *t* .... Heb 12:17

TEETH
t whiter than milk .... Gen 49:12
by the skin of my *t* .... Job 19:20
You have broken the *t* .... Ps 3:7
As vinegar to the *t* .... Prov 10:26
you cleanness of *t* .... Amos 4:6
and gnashing of *t* .... Matt 8:12

TEKOA
Home of a wise woman, 2 Sam 14:2, 4, 9
Home of Amos, Amos 1:1

TELL
that you may *t* it to .... Ps 48:13
the message that I *t* .... Jon 3:2
Who can *t* if God .... Jon 3:9
t him his fault .... Matt 18:15
whatever they *t* .... Matt 23:3
He comes, He will *t* .... John 4:25

TEMAN
Tribe in northeast Edom, Gen 36:34
Judgment pronounced against, Amos 1:12
God appears from, Hab 3:3

TEMPERATE
for the prize is *t* in all ..... 1 Cor 9:25
husband of one wife, *t* ..... 1 Tim 3:2

TEMPEST
the windy storm and *t* .... Ps 55:8
one, tossed with *t* .... Is 54:11
And suddenly a great *t* ..... Matt 8:24

TEMPLE
So Solomon built the *t* .... 1 Kin 6:14
build a *t* for the LORD ..... 2 Chr 2:12
t for the name of the LORD .. 2 Chr 6:7
of the LORD filled the *t* ..... 2 Chr 7:1
LORD is in His holy *t* .... Ps 11:4
to inquire in His *t* .... Ps 27:4
The *t* of the LORD .... Jer 7:4
suddenly come to His *t* ...... Mal 3:1
One greater than the *t* ..... Matt 12:6
murdered between the *t* .. Matt 23:35
veil of the *t* was torn ...... Matt 27:51
found Him in the *t* .... Luke 2:46
"Destroy this *t* .... John 2:19
was speaking of the *t* ...... John 2:21
one accord in the *t* .... Acts 2:46
the Beautiful Gate of the *t* .. Acts 3:10
that you are the *t* .... 1 Cor 3:16
your body is the *t* .... 1 Cor 6:19
grows into a holy *t* .... Eph 2:21
sits as God in the *t* .... 2 Thess 2:4
Then the *t* of God was ..... Rev 11:19
But I saw no *t* in it .... Rev 21:22
and the Lamb are its *t* ..... Rev 21:22

TEMPLES
t made with hands .... Acts 7:48

TEMPORARY
which are seen are *t* ...... 2 Cor 4:18

TEMPT
Why do you *t* the LORD ...... Ex 17:2
You shall not *t* the LORD ... Deut 6:16
they even *t* God .... Mal 3:15
t the LORD your God .... Matt 4:7
that Satan does not *t* .... 1 Cor 7:5
nor let us *t* Christ .... 1 Cor 10:9
nor does He Himself *t* .... James 1:13

TEMPTATION
do not lead us into *t* .... Matt 6:13
lest you enter into *t* .... Matt 26:41
in time of *t* fall away .... Luke 8:13
And do not lead us into *t* .. Luke 11:4
t has overtaken you ...... 1 Cor 10:13
to be rich fall into *t* .... 1 Tim 6:9
the man who endures *t* ... James 1:12

TEMPTED
because they *t* the LORD ..... Ex 17:7
again and again they *t* God .. Ps 78:41
forty days, *t* by Satan ..... Mark 1:13
being *t* for forty days by .... Luke 4:2
not allow you to be *t* ..... 1 Cor 10:13
lest you also be *t* .... Gal 6:1
has suffered, being *t* .... Heb 2:18
in all points *t* .... Heb 4:15
he is *t*, "I am *t* by God" ... James 1:13
But each one is *t* .... James 1:14

TEMPTER
Now when the *t* came .... Matt 4:3

TEN
t should be found .... Gen 18:32
the *T* Commandments ...... Ex 34:28
David his *t* thousands .... 1 Sam 18:7
or go backward *t* .... 2 Kin 20:9
an instrument of *t* strings .... Ps 92:3
test your servants for *t* .... Dan 1:12
before it, and it had *t* horns .. Dan 7:7
The *t* horns are *t* kings ..... Dan 7:24
owed him *t* thousand ...... Matt 18:24
him who has *t* talents ..... Matt 25:28
there met Him *t* men ..... Luke 17:12
t horns, and seven .... Rev 12:3
seven heads and *t* horns .... Rev 13:1
The *t* horns which you ..... Rev 17:12

TEND
to him, "*T* My sheep ...... John 21:16

TENDER
your heart was *t* .... 2 Kin 22:19
t shoots will not .... Job 14:7
Let Your *t* mercies come ..... Ps 79:8
Your *t* mercies come to .... Ps 119:77
no more be called *t* .... Is 47:1
through the *t* mercy of .... Luke 1:78
put on *t* mercies .... Col 3:12

TENDERHEARTED
to one another, *t* ....Eph 4:32
love as brothers, be *t* ....1 Pet 3:8

TENDS
t a flock and does not ....1 Cor 9:7

TENT
pitched his *t* in the ....Gen 26:17
it was, hidden in his *t* ....Josh 7:22
Israel, every man to his *t* ....Judg 7:8
shall know that your *t* ....Job 5:24
like a shepherd's *t* ....Is 38:12
the place of your *t* ....Is 54:2
My *t* is plundered ....Jer 10:20
earthly house, this *t* ....2 Cor 5:1
long as I am in this *t* ......2 Pet 1:13
I must put off my *t* ....2 Pet 1:14

TENTH
I will surely give a *t* to ....Gen 28:22
the *t* one shall be holy to ..Lev 27:32
to the LORD, a *t* of the ....Num 18:26
shall bring up a *t* of ....Neh 10:38
Abraham gave a *t* part of ....Heb 7:2

TENTMAKERS
occupation they were *t* .....Acts 18:3

TENTS
those who dwell in *t* ....Gen 4:20
"How lovely are your *t* ....Num 24:5
The *t* of robbers ....Job 12:6
than dwell in the *t* ....Ps 84:10
is in the *t* of the righteous ..Ps 118:15
I dwell among the *t* ....Ps 120:5
LORD will save the *t* ....Zech 12:7

TERAH
Father of Abram, Gen 11:26
Idolater, Josh 24:2
Dies in Haran, Gen 11:25–32

TEREBINTH
far as the *t* tree of Moreh ....Gen 12:6
dwelt by the *t* trees of .....Gen 13:18
sat under the *t* tree which ..Judg 6:11
as a *t* tree or as an oak, ...Is 6:13

TERRESTRIAL
bodies and *t* bodies ....1 Cor 15:40

TERRIBLE
t wilderness ....Deut 1:19
haughtiness of the *t* ....Is 13:11
is great and very *t* ....Joel 2:11

TERRIFIED
to you, 'Do not be *t* ....Deut 1:29
Therefore I am *t* at His .....Job 23:15
by Your wrath we are *t* ......Ps 90:7
But they were *t* ....Luke 24:37
and not in any way *t* ....Phil 1:28

TERRIFIES
and the Almighty *t* ....Job 23:16

TERRIFY
me with dreams and *t* ....Job 7:14
not let dread of Him *t* ....Job 9:34
are coming to *t* them ....Zech 1:21

TERRIFYING
t was the sight ....Heb 12:21

TERRITORY
smite all your *t* with frogs .....Ex 8:2
bring locusts into your *t* .....Ex 10:4
the *t* of their inheritance ...Josh 19:41
all the *t* of Israel ....Judg 19:29
He restored the *t* of ....2 Kin 14:25

TERROR
the *t* of God was upon the ..Gen 35:5
there shall be *t* ....Deut 32:25
are nothing, you see *t* ....Job 6:21
from God is a *t* ....Job 31:23
not be afraid of the *t* ....Ps 91:5
from the *t* of the LORD and ....Is 2:10
t to fall on them suddenly ....Jer 15:8
I will make you a *t* ....Jer 20:4
but a great *t* fell ....Dan 10:7
the *t* of the Lord, we ......2 Cor 5:11

TERRORS
the *t* of God are ....Job 6:4
T frighten him on ....Job 18:11
before the king of *t* ....Job 18:14
T overtake him like a ....Job 27:20
consumed with *t* ....Ps 73:19

TERTULLUS
Orator who accuses Paul, Acts 24:1–8

TEST
God has come to *t* you ......Ex 20:20
that He might *t* Israel by ....Judg 3:1
t him with hard ....1 Kin 10:1
behold, His eyelids *t* ....Ps 11:4
ask, nor will I *t* the LORD ....Is 7:12
You who *t* the righteous, ...Jer 20:12
t them as gold is ....Zech 13:9
said, "Why do you *t* ......Matt 22:18
But this He said to *t* him ....John 6:6
t the Spirit of the ....Acts 5:9
why do you *t* God by .....Acts 15:10
and the fire will *t* ....1 Cor 3:13
T yourselves ....2 Cor 13:5
T all things ....1 Thess 5:21
but *t* the spirits ....1 John 4:1
to *t* those who dwell on ......Rev 3:10

TESTAMENT
where there is a *t* ....Heb 9:16
For a *t* is in force ....Heb 9:17

TESTATOR
be the death of the *t* ....Heb 9:16

TESTED
that God *t* Abraham ....Gen 22:1
You have *t* my heart ....Ps 17:3
And they *t* God in ....Ps 78:18
t you at the waters of ....Ps 81:7
When your fathers *t* ....Ps 95:9
t them ten days ....Dan 1:14
also first be *t* ....1 Tim 3:10
Where your fathers *t* ....Heb 3:9
though it is *t* by fire ....1 Pet 1:7
t those who say they ....Rev 2:2

TESTIFIED
Yet the LORD *t* against....2 Kin 17:13
who sent Me, has *t* of Me ..John 5:37
he who has seen has *t* ....John 19:35
for as you have *t* ....Acts 23:11
t beforehand the ....1 Pet 1:11
of God which He has *t* ......1 John 5:9
t of the truth that is in you ...3 John 3

TESTIFIES
and heard, that He *t* ....John 3:32
that the Holy Spirit *t* ......Acts 20:23

TESTIFY
yes, your own lips *t* ....Job 15:6
You, and our sins *t* ....Is 59:12
T against Me ....Mic 6:3
t what We have ....John 3:11
these are they which *t* .....John 5:39
to *t* to the gospel of the ...Acts 20:24
t that the Father ....1 John 4:14
sent My angel to *t* ....Rev 22:16

TESTIFYING
was righteous, God *t* ....Heb 11:4
t that this is ....1 Pet 5:12

TESTIMONIES
those who keep His *t* ....Ps 119:2
for I have kept Your *t* ......Ps 119:22
t are my meditation ....Ps 119:99
I love Your *t* ....Ps 119:119
t are wonderful ....Ps 119:129

TESTIMONY
two tablets of the *T* ....Ex 31:18
be put to death on the *t* ....Deut 17:6
For He established a *t* ....Ps 78:5
that I may keep the *t* ....Ps 119:88
Bind up the *t* ....Is 8:16
under your feet as a *t* .....Mark 6:11
Now this is the *t* ....John 1:19
no one receives His *t* ......John 3:32
who has received His *t* .....John 3:33
in your law that the *t* ......John 8:17
and we know that his *t* ....John 21:24
declaring to you the *t* ......1 Cor 2:1
obtained a good *t* ....Heb 11:2
he had this *t* ....Heb 11:5
not believed the *t* ....1 John 5:10
And this is the *t* ....1 John 5:11
for the *t* which they held .....Rev 6:9
and by the word of their *t* ..Rev 12:11
For the *t* of Jesus is .....Rev 19:10

TESTING
is *t* you to know whether ..Deut 13:3
t the mind and the heart, ...Jer 11:20
came to Him, *t* Him ....Matt 19:3
knowing that the *t* ....James 1:3

TESTS
the righteous God *t* ....Ps 7:9
The LORD *t* the righteous .....Ps 11:5
gold, but the LORD *t*........Prov 17:3
men, but God who *t* ......1 Thess 2:4

TETRARCH
Herod being *t* of Galilee ....Luke 3:1
Now Herod the *t* heard of ..Luke 9:7
with Herod the *t* ....Acts 13:1

THADDAEUS
One of the Twelve, Mark 3:18

THANK
t offerings into the ....2 Chr 29:31
"I *t* You and praise ....Dan 2:23
"I *t* You, Father ....Matt 11:25
t that servant because .....Luke 17:9
t You that I am not ....Luke 18:11
First, I *t* my God ....Rom 1:8
t God without ceasing ...1 Thess 2:13
t Christ Jesus our ....1 Tim 1:12

THANKFUL
Be *t* to Him........Ps 100:4
Him as God, nor were *t* ....Rom 1:21

THANKFULNESS
Felix, with all *t* ....Acts 24:3

THANKS
give *t* to the LORD, for....1 Chr 16:34
and giving *t* to the LORD....Ezra 3:11
grave who will give You *t* ......Ps 6:5
give *t*! For Your wondrous ....Ps 75:1
is good to give *t* to the LORD ..Ps 92:1
give *t* to the LORD, for He.....Ps 107:1
give *t* to the LORD, for He.....Ps 136:1
the cup, and gave *t* ....Matt 26:27
she gave *t* to the Lord ....Luke 2:38
at His feet, giving Him *t* ..Luke 17:16
t He distributed them ....John 6:11
for he gives God *t* ....Rom 14:6
when He had given *t* ......1 Cor 11:24
But *t* be to God, who ......1 Cor 15:57
T be to God for His ....2 Cor 9:15
giving *t* always for ....Eph 5:20
t can we render ....1 Thess 3:9
in everything give *t* .....1 Thess 5:18
We give You *t*, O Lord .....Rev 11:17

THANKSGIVING
with the voice of *t* ....Ps 26:7
Offer to God *t* ....Ps 50:14
His presence with *t* ....Ps 95:2
into His gates with *t* ....Ps 100:4
the sacrifices of *t* ....Ps 107:22
supplication, with *t* ....Phil 4:6
vigilant in it with *t* ....Col 4:2
to be received with *t* ....1 Tim 4:3
glory and wisdom, *t* and ....Rev 7:12

THE-LORD-IS-MY-BANNER
and called its name, *T* ......Ex 17:15

THE-LORD-IS-PEACE
the LORD, and called it *T* ...Judg 6:24

THE-LORD-WILL-PROVIDE
the name of the place, *T* ... Gen 22:14

THEATER
and rushed into the *t* ..... Acts 19:29

THEOPHILUS
Luke addresses his writings to, Luke 1:3; Acts 1:1

THESSALONICA
Paul preaches in, Acts 17:1–13
Paul writes letters to churches of, 1 Thess 1:1

THICK
T swarms of flies came into .. Ex 8:24
there was *t* darkness in all .. Ex 10:22
I come to you in the *t* cloud .. Ex 19:9
cloud, and *t* darkness ...... Deut 4:11
T clouds cover Him, so ..... Job 22:14
t darkness its swaddling .... Job 38:9
and *t* clouds of the skies .... Ps 18:11
t darkness, like the .... Joel 2:2
of clouds and *t* darkness, .. Zeph 1:15

THIEF
When you saw a *t* .... Ps 50:18
do not despise a *t* .... Prov 6:30
t hates his own life .... Prov 29:24
t is ashamed when he .... Jer 2:26
the windows like a *t* .... Joel 2:9
t shall be expelled .... Zech 5:3
known what hour the *t* ... Matt 24:43
t approaches nor moth ... Luke 12:33
way, the same is a *t* .... John 10:1
because he was a *t* .... John 12:6
Lord will come as a *t* ...... 2 Pet 3:10
upon you as a *t* .... Rev 3:3
I am coming as a *t* .... Rev 16:15

THIEVES
And companions of *t* .... Is 1:23
a den of *t* in your eyes ...... Jer 7:11
destroy and where *t* .... Matt 6:19
have made it a den of *t* ... Matt 21:13
and fell among *t* .... Luke 10:30
before Me and *t* .... John 10:8

THIGH
put your hand under my *t* .. Gen 24:2
Also the right *t* you shall .... Lev 7:32
LORD makes your *t* rot ..... Num 5:21
them hip and *t* with a ...... Judg 15:8
Your sword upon Your *t* ..... Ps 45:3
good piece, the *t* .... Ezek 24:4

THINGS
in heaven give good *t* ...... Matt 7:11
evil, speak good *t* .... Matt 12:34
kept all these *t* .... Luke 2:51
Lazarus evil *t* .... Luke 16:25
the Scriptures the *t* .... Luke 24:27
share in all good *t* .... Gal 6:6

THINGS OF GOD
search out the deep *t* .... Job 11:7
not mindful of the *t* .... Matt 16:23
not mindful of the *t* .... Mark 8:33
things, yes, the deep *t* ..... 1 Cor 2:10

THINK
nor does his heart *t* .... Is 10:7
let none of you *t* evil in .... Zech 8:17
Do not *t* that I came to ..... Matt 5:17
t that they will be .... Matt 6:7
t you have eternal .... John 5:39
not to *t* of himself .... Rom 12:3
I *t* I also have the Spirit ... 1 Cor 7:40
of ourselves to *t* .... 2 Cor 3:5
let no one *t* me a fool .... 2 Cor 11:16
all that we ask or *t* .... Eph 3:20

THINKS
yet the LORD *t* upon me ..... Ps 40:17
for as he *t* in his .... Prov 23:7
t that he knows .... 1 Cor 8:2
t he stands take heed .... 1 Cor 10:12
For if anyone *t* .... Gal 6:3
t he is religious .... James 1:26

THIRD
morning were the *t* day ..... Gen 1:13
the end of every *t* year .... Deut 14:28
the *t* the face of a lion .... Ezek 10:14
a *t* kingdom of bronze, ... Dan 2:39
on the *t* day He will raise .... Hos 6:2
and be raised the *t* day ... Matt 16:21
went out about the *t* hour .. Matt 20:3
again, and prayed the *t* .. Matt 26:44
He will rise the *t* day ...... Mark 9:31
the *t* day He will rise ..... Mark 10:34
He came the *t* time .... Mark 14:41
Now it was the *t* hour .... Mark 15:25
and be raised the *t* day .... Luke 9:22
the *t* day He will rise ..... Luke 18:33
and the *t* day rise again ... Luke 24:7
rise from the dead the *t* .. Luke 24:46
He said to him the *t* ...... John 21:17
caught up to the *t* heaven . 2 Cor 12:2
the *t* living creature had a .... Rev 4:7
When He opened the *t* seal .. Rev 6:5
t of the trees were burned .... Rev 8:7
the *t* woe is coming .... Rev 11:14
Then the *t* angel poured .... Rev 16:4

THIRD DAY
the morning were the *t* ..... Gen 1:13
t the Lord will come down .. Ex 19:11
t must be burned .... Lev 7:17
any remains until the *t* ...... Lev 19:6
the unclean on the *t* ...... Num 19:19
t you shall go up .... 2 Kin 20:5
t He will raise us up .... Hos 6:2
be raised again the *t* ..... Matt 16:21
t He will be raised up ..... Matt 17:23
t He will rise again .... Matt 20:19
made secure until the *t* ... Matt 27:64
He will rise the *t* .... Mark 9:31
t He will rise again ...... Mark 10:34
and be raised the *t* .... Luke 9:22
t I shall be perfected ..... Luke 13:32
t He will rise again ...... Luke 18:33
and the *t* rise again .... Luke 24:7
today is the *t* since ...... Luke 24:21
rise from the dead the *t* .. Luke 24:46
God raised up on the *t* .... Acts 10:40
He rose again the *t* .... 1 Cor 15:4

THIRST
out of the rock for their *t* ... Neh 9:15
tongues fail for *t* .... Is 41:17
those who hunger and *t* ..... Matt 5:6
give him will never *t* ...... John 4:14
in Me shall never *t* .... John 6:35
said, "I *t*!" .... John 19:28
we both hunger and *t* ..... 1 Cor 4:11
anymore nor *t* anymore ..... Rev 7:16

THIRSTS
My soul *t* for God .... Ps 42:2
saying, "If anyone *t* .... John 7:37
freely to him who *t* .... Rev 21:6
And let him who *t* .... Rev 22:17

THIRSTY
and *t* land where there is ..... Ps 63:1
longs for You like a *t* land .. Ps 143:6
and if he is *t* .... Prov 25:21
as when a *t* man dreams ...... Is 29:8
the drink of the *t* .... Is 32:6
t land springs of .... Is 35:7
on him who is *t* .... Is 44:3
but you shall be *t* .... Is 65:13
in a dry and *t* land .... Ezek 19:13
I was *t* and you gave ..... Matt 25:35
we see You hungry or *t* ... Matt 25:44
if he is *t* .... Rom 12:20

THIRTY
Joseph was *t* years old .... Gen 41:46
t years old and above .... Num 4:3
t pieces of silver .... Matt 26:15
at about *t* years of age, ... Luke 3:23

THIS GENERATION
righteous before me in *t* ..... Gen 7:1
preserve them from *t* .... Ps 12:7
what shall I liken *t* .... Matt 11:16
in the judgment with *t* .... Matt 12:41
things will come upon *t* ... Matt 23:36
t will by no means pass ... Matt 24:34
"Why does *t* seek a sign .. Mark 8:12
Son of Man will be to *t* .. Luke 11:30
it shall be required of *t* ... Luke 11:51
and be rejected by *t* ...... Luke 17:25
t will by no means .... Luke 21:32

THISTLES
t grow instead of .... Job 31:40
or figs from *t* .... Matt 7:16

THOMAS
Apostle of Christ, Matt 10:3
Ready to die with Christ, John 11:16
Doubts Christ's resurrection, John 20:24–29

THORN
t that goes into the .... Prov 26:9
t shall come up the .... Is 55:13
a *t* in the flesh was .... 2 Cor 12:7

THORNBUSHES
gather grapes from *t* .... Matt 7:16

THORNS
Both *t* and thistles it .... Gen 3:18
T and snares are .... Prov 22:5
all overgrown with *t* ...... Prov 24:31
the crackling of *t* .... Eccl 7:6
Like a lily among *t* .... Song 2:2
and do not sow among *t* ...... Jer 4:3
wheat but reaped *t* .... Jer 12:13
And some fell among *t* ...... Matt 13:7
twisted a crown of *t* ...... Matt 27:29
the ones sown among *t* .... Mark 4:18
wearing the crown of *t* .... John 19:5

THOUGHT
t is that their houses .... Ps 49:11
You *t* that I was .... Ps 50:21
Both the inward *t* .... Ps 64:6
I *t* about my ways .... Ps 119:59
You understand my *t* .... Ps 139:2
"Surely, as I have *t* .... Is 14:24
to man what his *t* .... Amos 4:13
perceiving the *t* .... Luke 9:47
And he *t* within .... Luke 12:17
because you *t* that the gift .. Acts 8:20
t he was seeing a vision .... Acts 12:9
I *t* as a child .... 1 Cor 13:11
God, bringing every *t* ..... 2 Cor 10:5
will he be *t* worthy who ... Heb 10:29

THOUGHTS
the intent of the *t* .... 1 Chr 28:9
is in none of his *t* .... Ps 10:4
t toward us .... Ps 40:5
t are very deep .... Ps 92:5
The LORD knows the *t* .... Ps 94:11
t will be established .... Prov 16:3
unrighteous man his *t* .... Is 55:7
For My *t* are not your .... Is 55:8
long shall your evil *t* .... Jer 4:14
they do not know the *t* ..... Mic 4:12
Jesus, knowing their *t* ...... Matt 9:4
heart proceed evil *t* ...... Matt 15:19
futile in their *t* .... Rom 1:21
The LORD knows the *t* ..... 1 Cor 3:20
and is a discerner of the *t* ... Heb 4:12

THOUSAND
one *t* from each tribe ...... Num 31:5
two *t* three hundred days ... Dan 8:14
one *t* two hundred .... Dan 12:11
eaten were about five *t* ... Matt 14:21
who ate were four *t* men .. Matt 15:38
loaves were about five *t* ... Mark 6:44
eaten were about four *t* ..... Mark 8:9
were about five *t* men ..... Luke 9:14
one day is as a *t* years ...... 2 Pet 3:8

hundred and forty-four *t* .... Rev 14:1
bound him for a *t* years ..... Rev 20:2

THREAT
shall flee at the *t* .... Is 30:17

THREATEN
suffered, He did not *t* ...... 1 Pet 2:23

THREATENING
to them, giving up *t* .... Eph 6:9

THREATS
Lord, look on their *t* .... Acts 4:29
still breathing *t* .... Acts 9:1

THREE
the vine were *t* branches .. Gen 40:10
were *t* white baskets .... Gen 40:16
child, she hid him *t* months .. Ex 2:2
T times you shall keep a .... Ex 23:14
T times in the year all ...... Ex 34:23
T times a year all your .... Deut 16:16
t hundred concubines ..... 1 Kin 11:3
on the child *t* times, and .. 1 Kin 17:21
so he struck *t* times ...... 2 Kin 13:18
either *t* years of famine .. 1 Chr 21:12
Now when Job's *t* friends .... Job 2:11
There are *t* things that .... Prov 30:15
Did we not cast *t* men ...... Dan 3:24
his petition *t* times a day ... Dan 6:13
came up, before which *t* .... Dan 7:20
t more kings will arise in ... Dan 11:2
For *t* transgressions of ..... Amos 1:3
Son of Man be *t* days ..... Matt 12:40
make here *t* tabernacles .... Matt 17:4
For where two or *t* are .... Matt 18:20
you will deny Me *t* .... Matt 26:34
temple and build it in *t* ... Matt 27:40
After *t* days I will rise .... Matt 27:63
after *t* days rise again ...... Mark 8:31
will deny Me *t* times ..... Mark 14:30
and build it in *t* days ..... Mark 15:29
will deny Me *t* times ..... Luke 22:61
that day about *t* thousand .. Acts 2:41
was *t* days without sight .... Acts 9:9
This was done *t* times ..... Acts 10:16
spoke boldly for *t* months .. Acts 19:8
hope, love, these *t* .... 1 Cor 13:13
and these *t* are one .... 1 John 5:7
By these *t* plagues a third ... Rev 9:18
I saw *t* unclean spirits ..... Rev 16:13

THRESH
he does not *t* it .... Is 28:28
t the mountains .... Is 41:15
it is time to *t* her .... Jer 51:33
"Arise and *t* .... Mic 4:13

THRESHING
t shall last till the .... Lev 26:5
fleece of wool on the *t* ..... Judg 6:37
went down to the *t* floor .... Ruth 3:6
David bought the *t* floor . 2 Sam 24:24
like the dust at *t* .... 2 Kin 13:7
t floor of Ornan the ...... 1 Chr 21:18
Oh, my *t* and the grain ...... Is 21:10
clean out His *t* floor .... Matt 3:12

THRESHOLD
with her hands on the *t* ... Judg 19:27
were broken off on the *t* ... 1 Sam 5:4
been, to the *t* of the temple .. Ezek 9:3

THREW
every man *t* down his rod .... Ex 7:12
he *t* stones at David ...... 2 Sam 16:6
t him into the sea, and the .. Jon 1:15
t him into prison till he ... Matt 18:30
he *t* down the pieces .... Matt 27:5
t their own clothes on .... Luke 19:35
they *t* them into prison, ... Acts 16:23
t it into the great .... Rev 14:19
t it into the sea, saying, ... Rev 18:21

THROAT
t is an open tomb .... Ps 5:9
put a knife to your *t* .... Prov 23:2
unshod, and your *t* .... Jer 2:25
t is an open tomb .... Rom 3:13

THRONE
LORD sitting on His *t* ..... 1 Kin 22:19
He has prepared His *t* .... Ps 9:7
temple, the LORD's *t* .... Ps 11:4
Your *t*, O God, is .... Ps 45:6
has established His *t* .... Ps 103:19
he upholds his *t* .... Prov 20:28
Lord sitting on a *t* .... Is 6:1
"Heaven is My *t* .... Is 66:1
shall be called The *T* .... Jer 3:17
do not disgrace the *t* .... Jer 14:21
A glorious high *t* .... Jer 17:12
t was a fiery flame .... Dan 7:9
sit and rule on His *t* .... Zech 6:13
for it is God's *t* .... Matt 5:34
will give Him the *t* .... Luke 1:32
"Your *t*, O God, is .... Heb 1:8
come boldly to the *t* .... Heb 4:16
where Satan's *t* .... Rev 2:13
My Father on His *t* .... Rev 3:21
I saw a great white *t* .... Rev 20:11

THRONE OF DAVID
set up the *t* over Israel .... 2 Sam 3:10
and set me on the *t* .... 1 Kin 2:24
t shall be established .... 1 Kin 2:45
t and over His kingdom .... Is 9:7
princes sitting on the *t* ..... Jer 17:25
you who sit on the *t* .... Jer 22:2
king who sits on the *t* ...... Jer 29:16
no one to sit on the *t* .... Jer 36:30

THRONE OF GOD
swears by the *t* .... Matt 23:22
right hand of the *t* .... Heb 12:2
they are before the *t* .... Rev 7:15
without fault before the *t* ... Rev 14:5
proceeding from the *t* .... Rev 22:1

THRONES
t are set there .... Ps 122:5
also sit on twelve *t* .... Matt 19:28
mighty from their *t* .... Luke 1:52
invisible, whether *t* .... Col 1:16
t I saw twenty-four .... Rev 4:4

THRONG
house of God in the *t* .... Ps 55:14

THROW
he said, "*T* her down ...... 2 Kin 9:33
keep, and a time to *t* away .. Eccl 3:6
the LORD will *t* you away .... Is 22:17
of your land and *t* .... Mic 5:11
me, "*T* it to the potter" ... Zech 11:13
may build, but I will *t* down .. Mal 1:4
t Yourself down .... Matt 4:6
children's bread and *t* .... Matt 15:26
let him *t* a stone at her ..... John 8:7
t them into the fire, and .... John 15:6

THROWN
rider He has *t* into the sea ... Ex 15:1
their slain shall be *t* .... Is 34:3
mountains shall be *t* .... Ezek 38:20
down and *t* into the fire .... Matt 3:10
neck, and he were *t* .... Mark 9:42
down and *t* into the fire .... Luke 3:9

THRUST
and rose up and *t* .... Luke 4:29
T in Your sickle and reap .. Rev 14:15

THUMMIM
the Urim and the *T* .... Ex 28:30
Your *T* and Your Urim ..... Deut 33:8
with the Urim and *T* .... Ezra 2:63
with the Urim and *T* .... Neh 7:65

THUNDER
But the *t* of His power ..... Job 26:14
The voice of Your *t* .... Ps 77:18
the secret place of *t* .... Ps 81:7
t they hastened away .... Ps 104:7
that is, "Sons of *T*" .... Mark 3:17
the voice of loud *t* .... Rev 14:2

THUNDERED
"The LORD *t* from .... 2 Sam 22:14
The LORD *t* .... Ps 18:13

THUNDERINGS
people witnessed the *t* ...... Ex 20:18
the sound of mighty *t* .... Rev 19:6

THUNDERS
t marvelously with His ...... Job 37:5
The God of glory *t* .... Ps 29:3

THYATIRA
Residence of Lydia, Acts 16:14
Site of one of the seven churches, Rev 2:18–24

TIBERIAS
Sea of Galilee called, John 6:1, 23

TIDINGS
be afraid of evil *t* .... Ps 112:7
you who bring good *t*, lift ..... Is 40:9
brings glad *t* of good things ... Is 52:7
preach good *t* to the poor ..... Is 61:1
of him who brings good *t* ... Nah 1:15
I bring you good *t* .... Luke 2:10
who bring glad *t* .... Rom 10:15

TIGLATH-PILESER
Powerful Assyrian king who invades Samaria, 2 Kin 15:29

TILL
no man to *t* the ground ...... Gen 2:5

TILLER
but Cain was a *t* .... Gen 4:2

TILLS
t his land will be .... Prov 12:11
t his land will have .... Prov 28:19

TIMBREL
took the *t* in her hand ...... Ex 15:20
Praise Him with the *t* and ... Ps 150:4

TIMBRELS
out to meet him with *t* .... Judg 11:34

TIME
See APPOINTED TIME
in the appointed *t* of the .... Ex 34:18
LORD at its appointed *t* ..... Num 9:13
children ask in *t* to come .... Josh 4:6
t I shall be blameless ...... Judg 15:3
For in the *t* of trouble He ..... Ps 27:5
pray to You in a *t* .... Ps 32:6
ashamed in the evil *t* .... Ps 37:19
strength in the *t* of trouble .. Ps 37:39
how short my *t* is .... Ps 89:47
t for every purpose under .... Eccl 3:1
A *t* to be born .... Eccl 3:2
but *t* and chance .... Eccl 9:11
LORD, will hasten it in its *t* .. Is 60:22
But in the *t* of their trouble .. Jer 2:27
the *t* of their punishment .... Jer 8:12
you in the *t* of adversity .... Jer 15:11
in the *t* of Your anger ...... Jer 18:23
your *t* was the *t* .... Ezek 16:8
a *t* and times and half a *t* ... Dan 7:25
at that *t* your people shall .. Dan 12:1
The *t* has not come .... Hag 1:2
says, "My *t* is at hand .... Matt 26:18
A second *t* the rooster .... Mark 14:72
t of temptation fall away .. Luke 8:13
you did not know the *t* ... Luke 19:44
has seen God at any *t* ..... John 1:18
Can he enter a second *t* ..... John 3:4
t has not yet come .... John 7:6
the *t* is coming when I .... John 16:25
to him again a second *t* ... John 21:16
I have a convenient *t* ..... Acts 24:25
be revealed in his own *t* .. 2 Thess 2:6
Jesus before *t* began .... 2 Tim 1:9
for the *t* is near .... Rev 1:3
that he has a short *t* .... Rev 12:12
a *t* and times and half a *t* .. Rev 12:14

TIME OF TROUBLE
I have reserved for the *t* . . . Job 38:23
in the *t* He shall hide me . . . . . Ps 27:5
their strength in the *t* . . . . Ps 37:39
Lord will deliver him in *t* . . . . . Ps 41:1
unfaithful man in *t* . . . . Prov 25:19
salvation also in the *t* . . . . Is 33:2
his Savior in *t* . . . . Jer 14:8
And there shall be a *t* . . . . . . Dan 12:1

TIMES
Three *t* you shall keep a . . . . Ex 23:14
seven *t* in the same . . . . Josh 6:15
in the Jordan seven *t* . . . . . . 2 Kin 5:10
understanding of the *t* . . . 1 Chr 12:32
t are not hidden . . . . Job 24:1
t are in Your hand . . . . Ps 31:15
will bless the LORD at all *t* . . . . Ps 34:1
Trust in Him at all *t*, you . . . . . Ps 62:8
Seven *t* a day I praise . . . . Ps 119:164
A friend loves at all *t* . . . . . Prov 17:17
may fall seven *t* and rise . . Prov 24:16
does evil a hundred *t* . . . . Eccl 8:12
he found them ten *t* better . . Dan 1:20
let seven *t* pass over him . . . Dan 4:16
in those *t* many shall rise . . Dan 11:14
the signs of the *t* . . . . Matt 16:3
up to seventy *t* seven . . . . Matt 18:22
Gentiles until the *t* . . . . . . Luke 21:24
not for you to know *t* . . . . Acts 1:7
their preappointed *t* . . . . . . Acts 17:26
last days perilous *t* . . . . 2 Tim 3:1
God, who at various *t* . . . . Heb 1:1

TIMON
One of the first seven deacons, Acts 6:1–5

TIMOTHY
Paul's companion, Acts 16:1–3; 18:5; 20:4, 5; 2 Cor 1:19; Phil 1:1; 2 Tim 4:9, 21
Ministers independently, Acts 17:14, 15; 19:22; 1 Cor 4:17; Phil 2:19, 23; 1 Thess 3:1–6; 1 Tim 1:1–3; 4:14

TINGLE
who hears it will *t* . . . . 1 Sam 3:11
hears of it, his ears will *t* . . . . Jer 19:3

TIP
on the *t* of the right ear of . . . Ex 29:20
the *t* of his finger in . . . . Luke 16:24

TIRZAH
Seat of Jeroboam's rule, 1 Kin 14:17
Capital of Israel until Omri's reign, 1 Kin 16:6–23

TITHE
And he gave him a *t* . . . . Gen 14:20
LORD, a tenth of the *t* . . . . . Num 18:26
t of your grain or your . . . . Deut 12:17
"You shall truly *t* . . . . Deut 14:22
shall bring out the *t* . . . . Deut 14:28
laying aside all the *t* . . . . . . Deut 26:12
in abundantly the *t* . . . . 2 Chr 31:5
Judah brought the *t* . . . . Neh 13:12
For you pay *t* of mint . . . . . . Matt 23:23

TITHES
to redeem any of his *t* . . . . . Lev 27:31
t which you receive . . . . Num 18:28
and to bring the *t* . . . . Neh 10:37
firstfruits, and the *t* . . . . Neh 12:44
the articles, the *t* . . . . Neh 13:5
Bring all the *t* . . . . Mal 3:10
I give *t* of all that I . . . . . . Luke 18:12
to receive *t* from the . . . . Heb 7:5
mortal men receive *t* . . . . Heb 7:8
Levi, who receives *t* . . . . Heb 7:9

TITHING
the year of *t* . . . . Deut 26:12

TITLE
Now Pilate wrote a *t* . . . . . . John 19:19

TITTLE
away, one jot or one *t* . . . . . . Matt 5:18

TITUS
Ministers in Crete, Titus 1:4, 5
Paul's representative in Corinth, 2 Cor 7:6, 7, 13, 14; 8:6–23

TOBIAH
Ammonite servant; ridicules the Jews, Neh 2:10

TODAY
Bake what you will bake *t* . . Ex 16:23
yourselves *t* to the LORD, ... Ex 32:29
for *t* the LORD will appear . . . . Lev 9:4
t shall be in your heart . . . . . . Deut 6:6
God makes with you *t* . . . . . . Deut 29:12
have departed from me *t* . . 1 Sam 10:2
you have *t* rejected . . . . . . 1 Sam 10:19
this day, for *t* the LORD . . 1 Sam 11:13
t I have begotten You . . . . Ps 2:7
of the field, which *t* . . . . Matt 6:30
work *t* in my vineyard . . . . Matt 21:28
T this Scripture is . . . . Luke 4:21
the grass, which *t* . . . . Luke 12:28
T salvation has come to . . . Luke 19:9
t you will be with Me . . . . . . Luke 23:43
t I have begotten You . . . . Heb 1:5
"*T*, if you will hear . . . . Heb 3:7
the same yesterday, *t* . . . . Heb 13:8

TOGARMAH
Northern country inhabited by descendants of Gomer, Gen 10:3
Supplied horses to Tyrians and soldiers to the army of Gog, Ezek 27:14; 38:6

TOIL
t you shall eat of . . . . Gen 3:17
whom do I *t* and deprive . . . . . Eccl 4:8
they neither *t* nor . . . . Matt 6:28
our labor and *t* . . . . 1 Thess 2:9

TOILED
I had *t* under the sun . . . . Eccl 2:18
"Master, we have *t* . . . . Luke 5:5

TOLD
Behold, I have *t* . . . . Matt 28:7
things which were *t* . . . . Luke 2:18
t me all things that I . . . . John 4:29
t you the truth which . . . . John 8:40
so, I would have *t* . . . . John 14:2
"And now I have *t* . . . . John 14:29

TOLERABLE
you, it will be more *t* . . . . . Matt 10:15

TOMB
throat is an open *t* . . . . Ps 5:9
sitting opposite the *t* . . . . Matt 27:61
corpse and laid it in a *t* . . . . Mark 6:29
laid Him in a *t* which . . . . . Mark 15:46
rolled away from the *t* . . . . . . Luke 24:2
been in the *t* four days . . . . . John 11:17
Lazarus out of his *t* . . . . John 12:17
in the garden a new *t* . . . . . John 19:41
Magadalene went to the *t* . . John 20:1
throat is an open *t* . . . . Rom 3:13

TOMBS
like whitewashed *t* . . . . Matt 23:27
you build the *t* . . . . Matt 23:29
For you build the *t* . . . . Luke 11:47

TOMORROW
yourselves for *t* . . . . Num 11:18
Sanctify yourselves for *t* . . . Josh 7:13
Do not boast about *t*, for . . . Prov 27:1
drink, for *t* we die . . . . Is 22:13
t will be as today . . . . Is 56:12
t is thrown into the . . . . Matt 6:30
do not worry about *t* . . . . Matt 6:34
I must journey today, *t*, . . . Luke 13:33
drink, for *t* we die . . . . 1 Cor 15:32
what will happen *t* . . . . James 4:14

TONGUE
of speech and slow of *t* . . . . . . Ex 4:10
the scourge of the *t* . . . . Job 5:21
me, and I will hold my *t* . . . . . Job 6:24
hides it under his *t* . . . . Job 20:12
the *t* that speaks proud . . . . Ps 12:3
Keep your *t* from evil . . . . Ps 34:13
t shall speak of Your . . . . Ps 35:28
lest I sin with my *t* . . . . Ps 39:1
t shall sing aloud of Your . . . Ps 51:14
and their *t* a sharp sword . . . . Ps 57:4
to you, you false *t* . . . . Ps 120:3
laughter, and our *t* . . . . Ps 126:2
remember you, let my *t* . . . . . . Ps 137:6
is not a word on my *t* . . . . Ps 139:4
The *t* of the righteous is . . . Prov 10:20
but the perverse *t* . . . . Prov 10:31
forever, but a lying *t* . . . . . . Prov 12:19
The *t* of the wise uses . . . . . . Prov 15:2
A wholesome *t* is a . . . . Prov 15:4
perverse *t* falls into evil . . Prov 17:20
t keeps his soul . . . . Prov 21:23
t breaks a bone . . . . Prov 25:15
who flatters with the *t* . . . . . Prov 28:23
and on her *t* is the law . . . . Prov 31:26
another *t* He will speak to . . . Is 28:11
t shall take an oath . . . . Is 45:23
GOD has given Me the *t* . . . . Is 50:4
of his *t* was loosed . . . . Mark 7:35
his *t* loosed, and he . . . . Luke 1:64
in water and cool my *t* . . . . Luke 16:24
t shall confess to God . . . . . Rom 14:11
he who speaks in a *t* . . . . . . 1 Cor 14:2
t should confess that . . . . Phil 2:11
does not bridle his *t* . . . . . . James 1:26
t is a little member . . . . James 3:5
And the *t* is a fire . . . . James 3:6
no man can tame the *t* . . . . . . James 3:8
love in word or in *t* . . . . 1 John 3:18
every nation, tribe, *t* . . . . Rev 14:6

TONGUES
From the strife of *t* . . . . Ps 31:20
speak with new *t* . . . . Mark 16:17
to them divided *t*, as of fire . . Acts 2:3
speaking in our own *t* . . . . Acts 2:11
and they spoke with *t* . . . . Acts 19:6
I speak with the *t* . . . . 1 Cor 13:1
Therefore *t* are for a . . . . 1 Cor 14:22
many peoples, nations, *t*, . . Rev 10:11

TOOK
He *t* one of his ribs, and . . . . Gen 2:21
t of every clean animal . . . . . Gen 8:20
Abram *t* Sarai his wife . . . . . . Gen 12:5
they *t* stones and made a . . Gen 31:46
Then Joseph *t* an oath . . . . . Gen 50:25
Then Moses *t* his wife and . . . Ex 4:20
Moses *t* the rod of God in . . . . Ex 4:20
Then they *t* ashes from the . . . Ex 9:10
t the bones of Joseph . . . . Ex 13:19
t outside the camp him . . . . Lev 24:23
Moses *t* the redemption . . . . Num 3:49
t of the Spirit that was . . . . Num 11:25
Israel *t* all these cities . . . . . Num 21:25
they *t* all the spoil and . . . . . Num 31:11
Then I *t* the two tablets . . . . Deut 9:17
Then I *t* your sin, the calf . . Deut 9:21
t up twelve stones from the . . Josh 4:8
Samson *t* hold of the . . . . Judg 16:29
Tamar *t* the cakes . . . . 2 Sam 13:10
he *t* hold of her and . . . . . . 2 Sam 13:11
Jehu *t* no heed to walk . . . 2 Kin 10:31
Then David *t* more wives . . . 1 Chr 14:3
He *t* away the foreign . . . . . 2 Chr 33:15
You are He who *t* me out of . . Ps 71:6
t all the remnant of Judah . . . Jer 43:5
Then the Spirit *t* me up . . . Ezek 11:24
he *t* the young Child and . . . Matt 2:14
Then the devil *t* Him up . . . . . Matt 4:5
Himself *t* our infirmities . . . . Matt 8:17
He *t* the five loaves and . . . . Matt 14:19
they *t* up twelve baskets . . . Matt 14:20
He *t* the seven loaves . . . . . . Matt 15:36
t up seven large baskets . . . Matt 15:37
Then Peter *t* Him aside . . . . Matt 16:22
virgins who *t* their lamps . . . Matt 25:1
a stranger and you *t* Me . . Matt 25:35

Then He *t* the cup, and ... Matt 26:27
Peter *t* Him aside and ..... Mark 8:32
Then He *t* a little child .... Mark 9:36
He *t* the cup, and gave ... Luke 22:17

TOOTH
eye for eye, *t* .... Ex 21:24
eye for eye, *t* for *t* .... Lev 24:20
t for *t*, hand for hand, ... Deut 19:21
is like a bad *t* .... Prov 25:19
eye for an eye and a *t* ...... Matt 5:38

TOP
a tower whose *t* is in the .... Gen 11:4
consuming fire on the *t* of ... Ex 24:17
mercy seat on *t* of the ark .. Ex 25:21
in two from *t* to bottom ... Matt 27:51
torn in two from *t* to ..... Mark 15:38

TOPHET
See HINNOM, VALLEY OF THE SON OF
T was established .... Is 30:33
the high places of *T* .... Jer 7:31
make this city like *T* .... Jer 19:12
like the place of *T* .... Jer 19:13

TORCH
and a burning *t* that ...... Gen 15:17
and like a fiery *t* .... Zech 12:6

TORCHES
When he had set the *t* ..... Judg 15:5
his eyes like *t* .... Dan 10:6
come with flaming *t* .... Nah 2:3

TORE
that he *t* his clothes, and .. Judg 11:35
t his garments and lay ... 2 Sam 13:31
t it into twelve pieces .... 1 Kin 11:30
t down the temple of ..... 2 Kin 10:27
temple of Baal, and *t* it ... 2 Chr 23:17
t his robe, and shaved his .... Job 1:20
and each one *t* his robe ...... Job 2:12

TORE HIS CLOTHES
in the pit, and he *t* .... Gen 37:29
Then Jacob *t*, put .... Gen 37:34
Then Joshua *t*, and fell ...... Josh 7:6
he *t* and put sackcloth .... 1 Kin 21:27
the letter, that he *t* .... 2 Kin 5:7
of the Law, that he *t* ..... 2 Kin 22:11
of the Law, that he *t* ..... 2 Chr 34:19
he *t* and put on sackcloth .... Esth 4:1
heard it, that he *t* .... Is 37:1
Then the high priest *t* ..... Matt 26:65
Then the high priest *t* .... Mark 14:63

TORMENT
"How long will you *t* .... Job 19:2
shall lie down in *t* .... Is 50:11
You come here to *t* .... Matt 8:29
to this place of *t* .... Luke 16:28
fear involves *t* .... 1 John 4:18
to *t* them for five months .... Rev 9:5
t ascends forever .... Rev 14:11

TORMENTED
t with unclean spirits ...... Luke 6:18
for I am *t* in this .... Luke 16:24
He shall be *t* with fire ..... Rev 14:10
And they will be *t* .... Rev 20:10

TORMENTS
And being in *t* .... Luke 16:23

TORN
Joseph is *t* to pieces .... Gen 37:33
the altar of Baal, *t* down ... Judg 6:28
has *t* the kingdom .... 1 Sam 15:28
lion, which has *t* him ..... 1 Kin 13:26
aside my ways and *t* .... Lam 3:11
for He has *t* .... Hos 6:1
of the temple was *t* .... Matt 27:51
t in two from top to ...... Mark 15:38

TORTURED
Others were *t* .... Heb 11:35

TOSSED
t with tempest .... Is 54:11
t to and fro and .... Eph 4:14

TOTTER
drunkard, and shall *t* .... Is 24:20

TOUCH
eat it, nor shall you *t* it ...... Gen 3:3
the mountain or *t* its base ... Ex 19:12
carcasses you shall not *t* ..... Lev 11:8
seven no evil shall *t* .... Job 5:19
t no unclean thing .... Is 52:11
"If only I may *t* .... Matt 9:21
that they might only *t* ..... Matt 14:36
If only I may *t* His .... Mark 5:28
and begged Him to *t* him .. Mark 8:22
that He might *t* them ...... Luke 18:15
a man not to *t* a woman .... 1 Cor 7:1
Do not *t* what is unclean, .. 2 Cor 6:17
wicked one does not *t* .... 1 John 5:18

TOUCHED
whoever has *t* any slain ... Num 31:19
whose hearts God had *t* . 1 Sam 10:26
t my mouth with it .... Is 6:7
hand and *t* my mouth .... Jer 1:9
but he *t* me, and stood me .. Dan 8:18
said, "Who *t* My clothes .. Mark 5:30
t the open coffin, and .... Luke 7:14
Jesus said, "Who *t* Me? ..... Luke 8:45
mountain that may be *t* .... Heb 12:18

TOUCHES
if a person *t* any unclean ..... Lev 5:2
whoever *t* the carcass of ... Lev 11:24
Whoever *t* those things .... Lev 15:27
whoever *t* anything made ... Lev 22:4
He *t* the hills .... Ps 104:32
t you *t* the .... Zech 2:8

TOWEL
His garments, took a *t* ..... John 13:4

TOWER
t whose top is in the .... Gen 11:4
t which the sons of men .... Gen 11:5
the *t* of salvation to ..... 2 Sam 22:51
for me, a strong *t* .... Ps 61:3
my fortress, my high *t* ...... Ps 144:2
like an ivory *t* .... Song 7:4
a watchman in the *t* .... Is 21:5
in it and built a *t* .... Matt 21:33
whom the *t* in Siloam fell .. Luke 13:4
intending to build a *t* ..... Luke 14:28

TOWN
Neither go into the *t* .... Mark 8:26
from the *t* of Bethlehem, ... John 7:42

TOWNS
of Megiddo and its *t* ...... Josh 17:11
as *t* without walls .... Zech 2:4

TRACE
no *t* of them was found ...... Dan 2:35

TRACKED
t our steps so that we ...... Lam 4:18

TRADERS
Then Midianite *t* passed ... Gen 37:28
are princes, whose *t* .... Is 23:8

TRADITION
transgress the *t* .... Matt 15:2
of no effect by your *t* ...... Matt 15:6
holding the *t* of the elders .. Mark 7:3
according to the *t* .... Col 2:8
t which he received ...... 2 Thess 3:6
conduct received by *t* ..... 1 Pet 1:18

TRADITIONS
zealous for the *t* .... Gal 1:14
t which you were .... 2 Thess 2:15

TRAIN
T up a child in the .... Prov 22:6
t of His robe filled .... Is 6:1

TRAINED
who is perfectly *t* .... Luke 6:40
those who have been *t* .... Heb 12:11

TRAINING
bring them up in the *t* .... Eph 6:4

TRAITOR
also became a *t* .... Luke 6:16

TRAITORS
t, headstrong .... 2 Tim 3:4

TRAMPLE
Your name we will *t* .... Ps 44:5
serpent you shall *t* .... Ps 91:13
hand, to *t* My courts .... Is 1:12
You shall *t* the wicked .... Mal 4:3
swine, lest they *t* .... Matt 7:6
you the authority to *t* .... Lk 10:19

TRAMPLED
wall, and it shall be *t* down ..... Is 5:5
as straw is *t* down for the ... Is 25:10
t them in My fury .... Is 63:3
The Lord has *t* underfoot .. Lam 1:15
now she will be *t* .... Mic 7:10
t the nations in anger .... Hab 3:12
Jerusalem will be *t* .... Luke 21:24
t the Son of God .... Heb 10:29
the winepress was *t* .... Rev 14:20

TRANCE
he fell into a *t* .... Acts 10:10
t I saw a vision .... Acts 11:5

TRANSFIGURED
and was *t* before them ..... Matt 17:2

TRANSFORMED
this world, but be *t* .... Rom 12:2
the Lord, are being *t* ...... 2 Cor 3:18

TRANSFORMING
t themselves into .... 2 Cor 11:13

TRANSFORMS
Satan himself *t* himself ... 2 Cor 11:14

TRANSGRESS
t the command of the ..... Num 14:41
the LORD's people *t* ..... 1 Sam 2:24
my mouth shall not *t* .... Ps 17:3
his mouth must not *t* ..... Prov 16:10
of bread a man will *t* ..... Prov 28:21
those who *t* against Me ... Ezek 20:38
in which you *t* against ..... Zeph 3:11
do Your disciples *t* .... Matt 15:2

TRANSGRESSED
t My covenant .... Josh 7:11
they had *t* against the ..... 2 Chr 12:2
your mediators have *t* .... Is 43:27
the rulers also *t* .... Jer 2:8
who have *t* My covenant .... Jer 34:18
their fathers have *t* .... Ezek 2:3
Yes, all Israel has *t* .... Dan 9:11
t your commandment ..... Luke 15:29

TRANSGRESSES
"Indeed, because he *t* .... Hab 2:5
Whoever *t* and does not ...... 2 John 9

TRANSGRESSING
God, in *t* His covenant, ... Deut 17:2
t against our God by ...... Neh 13:27

TRANSGRESSION
iniquity and *t* and sin .... Ex 34:7
Make me know my *t* .... Job 13:23
t is sealed up in a .... Job 14:17
I am pure, without *t* .... Job 33:9
though I am without *t* .... Job 34:6
be innocent of great *t* .... Ps 19:13
is he whose *t* is forgiven .... Ps 32:1
their *t* with the rod .... Ps 89:32
because of their *t* .... Ps 107:17
He who covers a *t* .... Prov 17:9
He who loves *t* loves ...... Prov 17:19
By *t* an evil man is .... Prov 29:6
man abounds in *t* .... Prov 29:22
tell My people their *t* .... Is 58:1
and the *t* of desolation ...... Dan 8:13
at Gilgal multiply *t* .... Amos 4:4
my firstborn for my *t* .... Mic 6:7

and passing over the *t* ... Mic 7:18
no law there is no *t* ... Rom 4:15
deceived, fell into *t* ... 1 Tim 2:14
steadfast, and every *t* ... Heb 2:2

TRANSGRESSIONS
He will not pardon your *t* ... Ex 23:21
forgive your *t* nor your ... Josh 24:19
if I have covered my *t* ... Job 31:33
"I will confess my *t* ... Ps 32:5
me from all my *t* ... Ps 39:8
mercies, blot out my *t* ... Ps 51:1
For I acknowledge my *t* ... Ps 51:3
has He removed our *t* ... Ps 103:12
who blots out your *t* ... Is 43:25
was wounded for our *t* ... Is 53:5
for the *t* of My people ... Is 53:8
for our *t* are with us, and ... Is 59:12
yoke of my *t* was bound ... Lam 1:14
from you all the *t* ... Ezek 18:31
I punish Israel for their *t* .. Amos 3:14
was added because of *t* ... Gal 3:19
redemption of the *t* ... Heb 9:15

TRANSGRESSOR
and were called a *t* ... Is 48:8
are a *t* of the law ... Rom 2:27
I make myself a *t* ... Gal 2:18
become a *t* of the law ... James 2:11

TRANSGRESSORS
the *t* shall be destroyed ... Ps 37:38
Then I will teach *t* ... Ps 51:13
to any wicked *t* ... Ps 59:5
The destruction of *t* and of ... Is 1:28
numbered with the *t* ... Is 53:12
when the *t* have reached ... Dan 8:23
numbered with the *t* ... Mark 15:28
numbered with the *t* ... Luke 22:37
convicted by the law as *t* .. James 2:9

TRANSLATED
Immanuel," which is *t* ... Matt 1:23
cumi," which is *t* ... Mark 5:41
Golgotha, which is *t* ... Mark 15:22
which is *t*, "My God ... Mark 15:34
the Messiah" (which is *t* ... John 1:41
Cephas" (which is *t* ... John 1:42

TRAP
of Israel, as a *t* ... Is 8:14
where there is no *t* ... Amos 3:5
become a snare and a *t* ... Rom 11:9

TRAPS
they have set *t* ... Ps 140:5
for me, and from the *t* ... Ps 141:9

TRAVEL
For you *t* land and sea ... Matt 23:15
Paul's *t* companions ... Acts 19:29

TRAVELER
t who turns aside ... Jer 14:8

TRAVELING
lodge, O you *t* companies ... Is 21:13
lie waste, the *t* ... Is 33:8
t in the greatness of His ... Is 63:1
a man *t* to a far country .. Matt 25:14
two of them were *t* that .. Luke 24:13

TRAVERSE
t the way of ... Prov 8:20

TREACHEROUS
the *t* dealer deals ... Is 21:2
The *t* dealers have dealt ... Is 24:16
yet her *t* sister Judah did ... Jer 3:8
an assembly of *t* men ... Jer 9:2
are insolent, *t* ... Zeph 3:4

TREACHEROUSLY
and you who deal *t* ... Is 33:1
have you dealt *t* with Me ... Jer 3:20
happy who deal so *t* ... Jer 12:1
even they have dealt *t* ... Jer 12:6
They have dealt *t* ... Hos 5:7
Why do we deal *t* ... Mal 2:10
that you do not deal *t* ... Mal 2:16
This man dealt *t* ... Acts 7:19

TREAD
t down the wicked in ... Job 40:12
it is He who shall *t* ... Ps 60:12
You shall *t* upon the ... Ps 91:13
shout, as those who *t* ... Jer 25:30
because you *t* down the ... Amos 5:11
will come down and *t* ... Mic 1:3
And they will *t* ... Rev 11:2

TREADS
like one who *t* in the ... Is 63:2
t the high places ... Amos 4:13
an ox while it *t* ... 1 Tim 5:18
t the winepress ... Rev 19:15

TREASURE
a special *t* above all the ... Deut 7:6
to you His good *t* ... Deut 28:12
one who finds great *t* ... Ps 119:162
for His special *t* ... Ps 135:4
t my commands within ... Prov 2:1
there is much *t* ... Prov 15:6
There is desirable *t* ... Prov 21:20
of the LORD is His *t* ... Is 33:6
For where your *t* ... Matt 6:21
t brings forth evil ... Matt 12:35
is like *t* hidden in a field .. Matt 13:44
t things new and old ... Matt 13:52
and you will have *t* ... Matt 19:21
will have *t* in heaven ... Mark 10:21
So is he who lays up *t* ... Luke 12:21
t in the heavens that ... Luke 12:33
For where your *t* is ... Luke 12:34
will have *t* in heaven ... Luke 18:22
But we have this *t* ... 2 Cor 4:7
You have heaped up *t* ... James 5:3

TREASURED
t the words of His ... Job 23:12

TREASURER
Erastus, the *t* of the ... Rom 16:23

TREASURES
sealed up among My *t* ... Deut 32:34
t hidden in the sand ... Deut 33:19
it more than hidden *t* ... Job 3:21
her as for hidden *t* ... Prov 2:4
t of wickedness profit ... Prov 10:2
Getting *t* by a lying ... Prov 21:6
is no end to their *t* ... Is 2:7
I will give you the *t* ... Is 45:3
in your works and your *t*, ... Jer 48:7
Are there yet the *t* ... Mic 6:10
for yourselves *t* ... Matt 6:19
are hidden all the *t* ... Col 2:3
riches than the *t* ... Heb 11:26

TREASURIES
that I may fill their *t* ... Prov 8:21

TREASURING
t up for yourself wrath in ... Rom 2:5

TREASURY
you entered the *t* of snow .. Job 38:22
who have given to the *t* .. Mark 12:43
their gifts into the *t* ... Luke 21:1

TREAT
Should he *t* our sister ... Gen 34:31
not *t* her brutally ... Deut 21:14

TREATED
He *t* Abram well for her ... Gen 12:16
t them spitefully, and ... Matt 22:6
and be *t* with contempt ... Mark 9:12
were spitefully *t* at ... 1 Thess 2:2

TREATS
Cursed is the one who *t* ... Deut 27:16

TREATY
Now Solomon made a *t* ... 1 Kin 3:1
Let there be a *t* between ... 1 Kin 15:19
So he made a *t* with ... 1 Kin 20:34
Let there be a *t* between .. 2 Chr 16:3

TREE
LORD God made every *t* ... Gen 2:9
but of the *t* ... Gen 2:17
you eaten from the *t* ... Gen 3:11
tamarisk *t* in Beersheba ... Gen 21:33
for the *t* of the field is ... Deut 20:19
they said to the olive *t* ... Judg 9:8
the Diviners' Terebinth *T* .. Judg 9:37
the cedar *t* of Lebanon ... 1 Kin 4:33
down under a broom *t* ... 1 Kin 19:4
there is hope for a *t* ... Job 14:7
t planted by the ... Ps 1:3
like a native green *t* ... Ps 37:35
shall flourish like a palm *t* .. Ps 92:12
t falls to the south ... Eccl 11:3
Like an apple *t* ... Song 2:3
the cedar and the acacia *t* ... Is 41:19
for as the days of a *t* ... Is 65:22
are upright, like a palm *t* ... Jer 10:5
your name, Green Olive *T*, .. Jer 11:16
t planted by the ... Jer 17:8
and set it like a willow *t* ... Ezek 17:5
brought down the high *t* .. Ezek 17:24
The *t* that you saw, which .. Dan 4:20
and the fig *t* has withered ... Joel 1:12
t bears good fruit ... Matt 7:17
t is known by its fruit ... Matt 12:33
And seeing a fig *t* by the .. Matt 21:19
fig *t* which You cursed ... Mark 11:21
For every *t* is known by ... Luke 6:44
a sycamore *t* to see Him ... Luke 19:4
everyone who hangs on a *t* .. Gal 3:13
His own body on the *t* ... 1 Pet 2:24
as a fig *t* drops its late ... Rev 6:13

TREE OF LIFE
The *t* was also in the midst .. Gen 2:9
and take also of the *t* ... Gen 3:22
guard the way to the *t* ... Gen 3:24
She is a *t* to those ... Prov 3:18
of the righteous is a *t* ... Prov 11:30
desire comes, it is a *t* ... Prov 13:12
wholesome tongue is a *t* ... Prov 15:4
to eat from the *t* ... Rev 2:7
t, which bore twelve fruits .. Rev 22:2
have the right to the *t* ... Rev 22:14

TREES
and the *t* of the field shall ... Lev 26:4
t once went forth ... Judg 9:8
Then all the *t* said to the ... Judg 9:14
Also he spoke of *t* ... 1 Kin 4:33
Then all the *t* of the ... Ps 96:12
The *t* of the LORD are ... Ps 104:16
all kinds of fruit *t* ... Eccl 2:5
all the *t* of the field shall ... Is 55:12
they may be called *t* ... Is 61:3
and on beast, on the *t* ... Jer 7:20
all the *t* of the field shall .. Ezek 17:24
so that all the *t* ... Ezek 31:9
"I see men like *t* ... Mark 8:24
took branches of palm *t* .. John 12:13
late autumn *t* without ... Jude 12
the sea, or the *t* ... Rev 7:3
third of the *t* were burned ... Rev 8:7

TREMBLE
T before Him ... 1 Chr 16:30
The dead *t*, those under ... Job 26:5
have made the earth *t* ... Ps 60:2
T before Him, all the earth ... Ps 96:9
let the peoples *t* ... Ps 99:1
T, O earth, at the presence .. Ps 114:7
who made the earth *t* ... Is 14:16
That the nations may *t* ... Is 64:2
LORD, you who *t* at His ... Is 66:5
'Will you not *t* ... Jer 5:22
wrath the earth will *t* ... Jer 10:10
they shall fear and *t* ... Jer 33:9
my kingdom men must *t* ... Dan 6:26
the inhabitants of the land *t* .. Joel 2:1
before them, the heavens *t* .. Joel 2:10
demons believe—and *t*! ... James 2:19

T You are the Son of . . . . . Matt 14:33
T this was the Son of . . . . . Matt 27:54
T this Man was the Son . . Mark 15:39
T, I say to you that he . . . . Luke 12:44
t the Son of Man goes . . . . Luke 22:22
that this is *t* the Christ . . . . . John 7:26
"*T* this is the Prophet . . . . . . John 7:40
that God is *t* among you . . . . 1 Cor 14:25
T the signs of an . . . . 2 Cor 12:12
t righteousness would have . . Gal 3:21
t the love of God is . . . . 1 John 2:5

TRUMPET
When the *t* sounds long, ... Ex 19:13
you hear the sound of the *t* . . Josh 6:5
LORD with the sound of a *t* . . . Ps 47:5
Blow the *t* at the time . . . . Ps 81:3
and when he blows a *t*, you . . . Is 18:3
"Blow the *t* in the . . . . Jer 4:5
Lord GOD will blow the *t* . . . Zech 9:14
deed, do not sound a *t* . . . . . . Matt 6:2
t makes an uncertain . . . . . . 1 Cor 14:8
For the *t* will sound . . . . 1 Cor 15:52
and with the *t* of God . . . . 1 Thess 4:16
loud voice, as of a *t* . . . . Rev 1:10
t of the three angels who . . . Rev 8:13
sixth angel who had the *t* . . . Rev 9:14

TRUMPETS
the priests shall blow the *t* . . Josh 6:4
and their *t* in their hands . . . . Judg 7:8
With *t* and the sound of a . . . . Ps 98:6
to them were given seven *t* . . Rev 8:2

TRUST
in whom I will *t* . . . . 2 Sam 22:3
a shield to all who *t* in . . . 2 Sam 22:31
We *t* in the LORD our . . . . . 2 Kin 18:22
they put their *t* in Him . . . . 1 Chr 5:20
t is a spider's web . . . . Job 8:14
He slay me, yet will I *t* . . . . . Job 13:15
If God puts no *t* . . . . Job 15:15
and put your *t* in the LORD . . . . Ps 4:5
who put their *t* in You . . . . Ps 5:11
strength, in whom I will *t* . . . . Ps 18:2
shield to all who *t* in Him . . . Ps 18:30
you made Me *t* . . . . Ps 22:9
as for me, I *t* in You, O . . . . . . Ps 31:14
T in the LORD . . . . Ps 37:3
t also in Him, and He shall . . . Ps 37:5
I *t* in the mercy of God . . . . Ps 52:8
In You, O LORD, I put my *t* . . . Ps 71:1
You are my *t* from my . . . . Ps 71:5
my God, in Him I will *t* . . . . Ps 91:2
It is better to *t* in the LORD . . Ps 118:8
T in the LORD with all . . . . Prov 3:5
that your *t* may be in . . . . . Prov 22:19
who put their *t* in Him . . . . . Prov 30:5
my salvation, I will *t* . . . . Is 12:2
T in the LORD forever, for in . . Is 26:4
We *t* in the LORD our God,' . . . . Is 36:7
Let him *t* in the name . . . . Is 50:10
But he who puts his *t* in Me . . Is 57:13
Do not *t* in these . . . . Jer 7:4
My name, in which you *t* . . . . . Jer 7:14
you have put your *t* in Me . . Jer 39:18
Do not *t* in a friend . . . . Mic 7:5
He knows those who *t* in . . . . . Nah 1:7
name Gentiles will *t* . . . . . . Matt 12:21
those who *t* in riches . . . . . Mark 10:24
such *t* through Christ . . . . 2 Cor 3:4
committed to your *t* . . . . 1 Tim 6:20
I will put My *t* in Him . . . . . . Heb 2:13

TRUSTED
He *t* in the LORD God of . . . 2 Kin 18:5
"He *t* in the LORD . . . . Ps 22:8
Because we have *t* in His . . . . Ps 33:21
t in the abundance of his . . . . . Ps 52:7
He *t* in God . . . . Matt 27:43
that we who first *t* . . . . Eph 1:12
the holy women who *t* . . . . . . 1 Pet 3:5

TRUSTS
But he who *t* in the . . . . Ps 32:10
is the man who *t* in Him . . . . . Ps 34:8
whoever *t* in the LORD, ... Prov 16:20
he who *t* in the LORD . . . . . . Prov 28:25
He who *t* in his own . . . . Prov 28:26
whoever *t* in the LORD . . . . . . Prov 29:25
the man who *t* in the LORD . . . Jer 17:7

TRUTH
See SPIRIT OF TRUTH; WORD OF TRUTH
led me in the way of *t* . . . . . Gen 24:48
justice, a God of *t* . . . . Deut 32:4
Him in sincerity and in *t*, . . Josh 24:14
serve Him in *t* with all . . . . 1 Sam 12:24
the *t* in the name of the . . 2 Chr 18:15
and speaks the *t* . . . . Ps 15:2
me in Your *t* and teach me . . . Ps 25:5
all His work is done in *t* . . . . . Ps 33:4
t continually preserve . . . . Ps 40:11
Behold, You desire *t* . . . . Ps 51:6
T shall spring out of . . . . Ps 85:11
t shall be your shield . . . . Ps 91:4
And His *t* endures to all . . . . . Ps 100:5
the *t* of the LORD endures . . . . Ps 117:2
t utterly out of my . . . . Ps 119:43
and Your law is *t* . . . . Ps 119:142
commandments are *t* . . . . . Ps 119:151
of Your word is *t* . . . . Ps 119:160
who speaks *t* declares . . . . . . Prov 12:17
t belong to those who . . . . . . Prov 14:22
t atonement is provided . . . . . Prov 16:6
walked before You in *t* . . . . Is 38:3
t is fallen in the . . . . Is 59:14
not valiant for the *t* . . . . Jer 9:3
cast *t* down to the ground . . . Dan 8:12
in the Scripture of *T* . . . . Dan 10:21
"There is no *t* . . . . Hos 4:1
called the City of *T* . . . . Zech 8:3
speak each man the *t* . . . . . . Zech 8:16
love *t* and peace . . . . Zech 8:19
t was in his mouth . . . . Mal 2:6
t came through Jesus . . . . John 1:17
worship in spirit and *t* . . . . . . John 4:24
you shall know the *t* . . . . John 8:32
"I am the way, the *t* . . . . John 14:6
He, the Spirit of *t* . . . . John 16:13
Your word is *t* . . . . John 17:17
be sanctified by the *t* . . . . . John 17:19
to Him, "What is *t* . . . . John 18:38
speak the words of *t* . . . . . . Acts 26:25
who suppress the *t* . . . . Rom 1:18
of sincerity and *t* . . . . 1 Cor 5:8
but rejoices in the *t* . . . . 1 Cor 13:6
but, speaking the *t* . . . . Eph 4:15
each one speak *t* with his . . . Eph 4:25
your waist with *t* . . . . Eph 6:14
in the word of the *t* . . . . Col 1:5
the love of the *t* . . . . 2 Thess 2:10
I am speaking the *t* . . . . 1 Tim 2:7
they may know the *t* . . . . . . 2 Tim 2:25
the knowledge of the *t* . . . . . . 2 Tim 3:7
in the present *t* . . . . 2 Pet 1:12
way of *t* will be . . . . 2 Pet 2:2
but in deed and in *t* . . . . 1 John 3:18
that we are of the *t* . . . . 1 John 3:19
we know the spirit of *t* . . . . . 1 John 4:6
the Spirit is *t* . . . . 1 John 5:6
t that is in you . . . . 3 John 3

TRUTHFUL
The *t* lip shall be . . . . Prov 12:19

TRUTHFULLY
deal *t* are His delight . . . . . Prov 12:22

TRY
t my mind and my heart . . . . . Ps 26:2
t me, and know my . . . . Ps 139:23
refine them and *t* them . . . . Jer 9:7
t Me now in this . . . . Mal 3:10
which is to *t* you . . . . 1 Pet 4:12

TUBAL
Son of Japheth, Gen 10:2
—— Tribe associated with Javan and Meshech, Is 66:19
In Gog's army, Ezek 38:2, 3
Punishment of, Ezek 32:26, 27

TUBAL-CAIN
Son of Lamech, Gen 4:19–22

TUMORS
the boils of Egypt, with *t* . . Deut 28:27
and struck them with *t* . . . . 1 Sam 5:6
Five golden *t* and five . . . . . 1 Sam 6:4

TUMULT
their waves, and the *t* . . . . Ps 65:7
Your enemies make a *t* . . . . Ps 83:2

TUNIC
Also he made him a *t* . . . . Gen 37:3
and take away your *t* . . . . . . Matt 5:40
not withhold your *t* . . . . Luke 6:29
the *t* was without seam, . . . John 19:23

TUNICS
the LORD God made *t* . . . . Gen 3:21
not to put on two *t* . . . . Mark 6:9
He who has two *t*, let him . Luke 3:11
weeping, showing the *t* . . . . . Acts 9:39

TURBAN
like a robe and a *t* . . . . Job 29:14
"Remove the *t* . . . . Ezek 21:26

TURN
T from Your fierce wrath, . . . Ex 32:12
Do not *t* to idols, nor make . . . Lev 19:4
you shall not *t* . . . . Deut 17:11
LORD may *t* away from . . . . Num 25:4
do not *t* from it to the right . . Josh 1:7
t from their sin because . . . . 1 Kin 8:35
T from your evil ways, . . . 2 Kin 17:13
do not *t* to iniquity, for . . . . . Job 36:21
t to the LORD, and all the . . . . Ps 22:27
T Yourself to me, and have . . Ps 25:16
do not *t* Your servant away . . Ps 27:9
Then we will not *t* . . . . Ps 80:18
but let them not *t* . . . . Ps 85:8
t to me, and have mercy . . . . Ps 86:16
yet I do not *t* . . . . Ps 119:51
T at my rebuke . . . . Prov 1:23
Do not *t* to the right or . . . . Prov 4:27
not let your heart *t* . . . . Prov 7:25
I will *t* My hand against you, . . Is 1:25
every man will *t* to his own . . Is 13:14
'*T* now everyone from . . . . . . Jer 35:15
T us back to You, O . . . . Lam 5:21
"Repent, *t* away from . . . . . . Ezek 14:6
Repent, and *t* from all . . . . Ezek 18:30
T, *t* from your evil ways . . Ezek 33:11
T to me with all your . . . . Joel 2:12
yes, let every one *t* . . . . Jon 3:8
"*T* now from your evil . . . . Zech 1:4
those who *t* away an alien . . . Mal 3:5
he will *t* the hearts of the . . . . Mal 4:6
on your right cheek, *t* . . . . . . Matt 5:39
t the hearts of the . . . . Luke 1:17
you that you should *t* . . . . . Acts 14:15
t them from darkness . . . . . . Acts 26:18
repent, *t* to God, and do . . . Acts 26:20
Let him *t* away from . . . . 1 Pet 3:11
waters to *t* them to blood . . . Rev 11:6

TURN ASIDE
t and see this great . . . . Ex 3:3
t after many to pervert . . . . . . Ex 23:2
t and serve other gods . . . . Deut 11:16
So you shall not *t* . . . . Deut 28:14
Law of Moses, lest you *t* . . . Josh 23:6
they went, and did not *t* . . . 1 Sam 6:12
t from following the . . . . . 1 Sam 12:20
He did not *t* from them . . . 1 Kin 22:43
did not *t* from it . . . . 2 Chr 20:32
The paths of their way *t* . . . . Job 6:18
nor such as *t* to lies . . . . Ps 40:4
I do not *t* from Your law . . . Ps 119:51
such as *t* to their crooked . . . Ps 125:5
Do not let your heart *t* . . . . . Prov 7:25
to *t* the justice due . . . . Lam 3:35

did not *t* when they went .. Ezek 1:17
did not *t* when they ...... Ezek 10:11

TURNED
in the river were *t* to blood ... Ex 7:20
who *t* to the LORD with ... 2 Kin 23:25
t to the LORD God of ...... 2 Chr 15:4
and *t* their backs on ...... 2 Chr 29:6
t me over to the hands of .. Job 16:11
I love have *t* against .... Job 19:19
kept His way and not *t* .... Job 23:11
The wicked shall be *t* .... Ps 9:17
let them be *t* back and .... Ps 70:2
t my feet to Your .... Ps 119:59
of Israel, they have *t* .... Is 1:4
LORD has not *t* back from ..... Jer 4:8
shall be *t* into darkness ..... Joel 2:31
that they *t* from their evil ... Jon 3:10
Then He *t* to the woman ... Luke 7:44
sorrow will be *t* into joy .. John 16:20
sun shall be *t* into .... Acts 2:20
saw him and *t* to the Lord .. Acts 9:35
number believed and *t* .... Acts 11:21
and how you *t* to God ..... 1 Thess 1:9

TURNING
Gentiles who are *t* to ..... Acts 15:19
marvel that you are *t* .... Gal 1:6
or shadow of *t* .... James 1:17
and *t* the cities of Sodom .... 2 Pet 2:6

TURNS
of the wicked He *t* .... Ps 146:9
A soft answer *t* .... Prov 15:1
he *t*, he prospers .... Prov 17:8
One who *t* away his ear .... Prov 28:9
when a righteous man *t* .... Ezek 3:20
But if a wicked man *t* .... Ezek 18:21
a wicked man *t* away ..... Ezek 18:27
he *t* from his sin and ..... Ezek 33:14
t from his wickedness .... Ezek 33:19
but no one *t* back .... Nah 2:8
that he who *t* .... James 5:20

TURTLEDOVE
the life of Your *t* .... Ps 74:19
t is heard in our land ...... Song 2:12

TURTLEDOVES
of *t* or young pigeons .... Lev 1:14
A pair of *t* or two young .. Luke 2:24

TUTOR
the law was our *t* .... Gal 3:24
no longer under a *t* .... Gal 3:25

TWELVE
the sons of Jacob were *t* ... Gen 35:22
are the *t* tribes of Israel ... Gen 49:28
were *t* stones according ..... Ex 39:14
t men, each one .... Num 1:44
Joshua set up *t* stones .... Josh 4:9
Solomon had *t* governors ... 1 Kin 4:7
Elijah took *t* stones, ... 1 Kin 18:31
Manasseh was *t* years ..... 2 Kin 21:1
called His *t* disciples to .... Matt 10:1
These *t* Jesus sent out ..... Matt 10:5
they took up *t* baskets .... Matt 14:20
more than *t* legions of .... Matt 26:53
Then He appointed *t* ...... Mark 3:14
of blood for *t* years .... Mark 5:25
took up *t* baskets full ..... Mark 6:43
when He was *t* years old .. Luke 2:42
He chose *t* whom He .... Luke 6:13
a flow of blood for *t* .... Luke 8:43
t baskets of the leftover ... Luke 9:17
filled *t* baskets with the .... John 6:13
I not choose you, the *t* ..... John 6:70
head a garland of *t* stars .... Rev 12:1
t gates were *t* pearls .... Rev 21:21

TWELVE APOSTLES
Now the names of the *t* .... Matt 10:2
and the *t* with Him .... Luke 22:14
the names of the *t* .... Rev 21:14

TWELVE DISCIPLES
when He had called His *t* .. Matt 10:1
commanding His *t* .... Matt 11:1
took the *t* aside on the .... Matt 20:17
Then He called His *t* .... Luke 9:1

TWELVE TRIBES
these are the *t* of Israel .... Gen 49:28
pillars according to the *t* ...... Ex 24:4
name according to the *t* ..... Ex 39:14
inheritance among the *t* .. Ezek 47:13
judging the *t* .... Matt 19:28
To this promise our *t* .... Acts 26:7
the *t* which are scattered .. James 1:1
the names of the *t* .... Rev 21:12

TWENTY-FOUR ELDERS
on the thrones I saw *t* .... Rev 4:4
t fall down before Him ..... Rev 4:10
t fell down before the .... Rev 5:8
t fell down and worshiped .. Rev 5:14
t who sat before God ...... Rev 11:16
t and the four living .... Rev 19:4

TWICE
the rock *t* with his rod .... Num 20:11
t as much as he had .... Job 42:10
the rooster crows *t* .... Mark 14:30
the rooster crows *t* .... Mark 14:72

TWILIGHT
at *t* is the LORD's Passover .. Lev 23:5
sacrifice the Passover at *t* .. Deut 16:6

TWIN
figurehead was the *T* ..... Acts 28:11

TWINS
there were *t* in her womb .. Gen 25:24
behold, *t* were in her ...... Gen 38:27
two fawns, *t* of a gazelle .... Song 7:3

TWIST
All day they *t* my .... Ps 56:5
unstable people *t* to .... 2 Pet 3:16

TWO
God made *t* great lights ..... Gen 1:16
t each of animals that are ..... Gen 7:2
the ark to Noah, *t* .... Gen 7:15
T nations are in your ...... Gen 25:23
t rams without blemish, ... Ex 29:1
He gave Moses *t* tablets of .. Ex 31:18
shall be unclean *t* weeks .... Lev 12:5
t young pigeons .... Lev 12:8
t tablets of the covenant ... Deut 9:15
hewed *t* tablets of stone .... Deut 10:3
by the mouth of *t* or .... Deut 19:15
the *t* middle pillars .... Judg 16:29
divided the Red Sea in *t* .... Ps 136:13
T are better than one .... Eccl 4:9
t he covered his .... Is 6:2
a ram which had *t* horns .... Dan 8:3
saw, having the *t* horns .... Dan 8:20
there stood *t* others, one .... Dan 12:5
one mile, go with him *t* .... Matt 5:41
five loaves and *t* fish ...... Matt 14:17
'by the mouth of *t* or ...... Matt 18:16
For where *t* or three are .. Matt 18:20
t shall become one .... Matt 19:5
A man had *t* sons, and .... Matt 21:28
five talents, to another *t* .. Matt 25:15
t robbers were crucified .. Matt 27:38
in *t* from top to bottom .. Matt 27:51
said, "Five, and *t* fish ..... Mark 6:38
t shall become one flesh' .. Mark 10:8
and threw in *t* mites, ... Mark 12:42
also crucified *t* robbers ... Mark 15:27
in *t* from top to bottom ... Mark 15:38
t young pigeons .... Luke 2:24
t fish, unless we go and .... Luke 9:13
certain man had *t* sons ... Luke 15:11
servant can serve *t* .... Luke 16:13
widow putting in *t* mites ... Luke 21:2
were also *t* others, ... Luke 23:32
temple was torn in *t* ...... Luke 23:45
t of them were traveling .. Luke 24:13
T hundred denarii worth .... John 6:7
t small fish, but what are ... John 6:9
these are the *t* covenants .... Gal 4:24
new man from the *t* .... Eph 2:15
t shall become one flesh .... Eph 5:31
from *t* or three witnesses .. 1 Tim 5:19
was *t* hundred million; I .... Rev 9:16
power to my *t* witnesses .... Rev 11:3
had *t* horns like a lamb .... Rev 13:11

TWO-EDGED SWORD
and a *t* in their hand .... Ps 149:6
as wormwood, sharp as a *t* .. Prov 5:4
sharper than any *t* .... Heb 4:12
His mouth went a sharp *t* .... Rev 1:16
He who has the sharp *t* ..... Rev 2:12

TYCHICUS
Paul's companion, Acts 20:1, 4
Paul's messenger, Eph 6:21, 22; Col 4:7–9; 2 Tim 4:12

TYPE
of Adam, who is a *t* .... Rom 5:14

TYRE
City of Phoenicia noted for its commerce, Josh 19:29; 2 Sam 5:11; Jer 25:22

TYRE AND SIDON
cut off from *T* every helper .. Jer 47:4
you to do with Me, O *T* ...... Joel 3:4
had been done in *T* .... Matt 11:21
to the region of *T* .... Matt 15:21
more tolerable for *T* at ... Luke 10:14
with the people of *T* ..... Acts 12:20

UGLY
And the *u* and gaunt cows .. Gen 41:4

ULAI
Scene of Daniel's visions, Dan 8:2–16

UNAFRAID
Do you want to be *u* .... Rom 13:3

UNAWARE
I do not want you to be *u* .. Rom 1:13
not want you to be *u* ..... 1 Cor 10:11

UNBELIEF
because of their *u* .... Matt 13:58
Because of your *u* .... Matt 17:20
help my *u* .... Mark 9:24
and He rebuked their *u* .. Mark 16:14
promise of God through *u* .. Rom 4:20
did it ignorantly in *u* ..... 1 Tim 1:13
you an evil heart of *u* .... Heb 3:12
enter in because of *u* .... Heb 3:19

UNBELIEVER
But if the *u* departs, let ..... 1 Cor 7:15
has a believer with an *u* ... 2 Cor 6:15
and is worse than an *u* ..... 1 Tim 5:8

UNBELIEVERS
his portion with the *u* .... Luke 12:46
who believe but to *u* ..... 1 Cor 14:22
are uninformed or *u* ...... 1 Cor 14:23
yoked together with *u* ..... 2 Cor 6:14

UNBELIEVING
Do not be *u* .... John 20:27
u Jews stirred up the .... Acts 14:2
For the *u* husband is ...... 1 Cor 7:14
u nothing is pure .... Titus 1:15
But the cowardly, *u* .... Rev 21:8

UNCIRCUMCISED
heed me, for I am of *u* lips ... Ex 6:12
Behold, I am of *u* lips, and ... Ex 6:30
For no *u* person shall eat it .. Ex 12:48
u hearts are humbled ...... Lev 26:41
is this *u* Philistine .... 1 Sam 17:26
of Israel are *u* in the heart ... Jer 9:26
u in heart and *u* in flesh ... Ezek 44:7
You stiff-necked and *u* ...... Acts 7:51
not the physically *u* .... Rom 2:27
by faith and the *u* .... Rom 3:30
only, or upon the *u* also ..... Rom 4:9

u had been committed . . . . Gal 2:7
nor Jew, circumcised nor *u* . . Col 3:11

UNCIRCUMCISION
has become *u* . . . . Rom 2:25
u is nothing, but keeping . . 1 Cor 7:19
who are called *U* by . . . . Eph 2:11

UNCLEAN
of animals that are *u* . . . . Gen 7:2
person touches any *u* thing . . . Lev 5:2
u thing shall not be eaten . . . Lev 7:19
to the LORD, while he is *u* . . . Lev 7:20
who touches any *u* . . . . Lev 7:21
They are *u* to you . . . . Lev 11:8
these you shall become *u* . . Lev 11:24
I am a man of *u* lips . . . . Is 6:5
u shall no longer come . . . . Is 52:1
we are all like an *u* thing . . . . . . Is 64:6
I pronounced them *u* . . . . . Ezek 20:26
He commands even the *u* . . Mark 1:27
commands the *u* spirits . . . . Luke 4:36
any man common or *u* . . . . Acts 10:28
there is nothing *u* . . . . Rom 14:14
your children would be *u* . . 1 Cor 7:14
Do not touch what is *u* . . . 2 Cor 6:17
that no fornicator, *u* . . . . Eph 5:5

UNCLEAN SPIRIT
u to depart from the land . . Zech 13:2
u goes out of a man . . . . Matt 12:43
synagogue with an *u* . . . . Mark 1:23
u had convulsed him . . . . Mark 1:26
"He has an *u* . . . . Mark 3:30
a man with an *u* . . . . Mark 5:2
daughter had an *u* . . . . Mark 7:25
He rebuked the *u* . . . . Mark 9:25
He had commanded the *u* . . Luke 8:29
Jesus rebuked the *u* . . . . Luke 9:42
u goes out of a man . . . . . . Luke 11:24

UNCLEAN SPIRITS
them power over *u* . . . . Matt 10:1
He commands even the *u* . . Mark 1:27
u, whenever they saw . . . . . Mark 3:11
u went out and entered . . . . Mark 5:13
tormented with *u* . . . . Luke 6:18
who were tormented by *u* . . Acts 5:16
u, crying with a loud . . . . Acts 8:7
three *u* like frogs . . . . Rev 16:13

UNCLEANNESS
of Israel from their *u*, lest . . Lev 15:31
for sin and for *u* . . . . Zech 13:1
men's bones and all *u* . . . . . Matt 23:27
also gave them up to *u* . . . . . Rom 1:24
members as slaves of *u* . . . . . Rom 6:19
adultery, fornication, *u*, ... Gal 5:19
fornication, *u*, passion, evil . . . Col 3:5
did not call us to *u* . . . . 1 Thess 4:7
flesh in the lust of *u* . . . . 2 Pet 2:10

UNCLEANNESSES
from all your *u* . . . . Ezek 36:29

UNCLOTHED
we want to be *u* . . . . 2 Cor 5:4

UNCOVER
Do not *u* your heads nor . . . . Lev 10:6
shall not *u* her nakedness . . . Lev 18:7
u the woman's head, and . . Num 5:18
the LORD will *u* their secret . . . . Is 3:17
skirt, *u* the thigh . . . . Is 47:2
he will *u* your sins . . . . Lam 4:22

UNCOVERED
and became *u* in his tent . . . . Gen 9:21
of the world were *u* . . . . . 2 Sam 22:16
I have *u* his secret places, . . Jer 49:10
its foundation will be *u* . . . Ezek 13:14
transgressions are *u* . . . . . . Ezek 21:24
they *u* the roof where He . . . Mark 2:4
head *u* dishonors her . . . . . . 1 Cor 11:5
to God with her head *u* . . . . 1 Cor 11:13

UNCOVERS
u her nakedness, he has . . . Lev 20:18
u deep things out of . . . . Job 12:22

UNDEFILED
Blessed are the *u* . . . . Ps 119:1
all, and the bed *u* . . . . Heb 13:4
u religion before God . . . . . James 1:27
incorruptible and *u* . . . . 1 Pet 1:4

UNDER HIS FEET
And there was *u* . . . . Ex 24:10
down with darkness *u* . . . 2 Sam 22:10
You have put all things *u* . . . . . Ps 8:6
has put all enemies *u* . . . . 1 Cor 15:25
And He put all things *u* . . . . . Eph 1:22
things in subjection *u* . . . . Heb 2:8

UNDER THE LAW
to those who are *u* . . . . Rom 3:19
to those who are *u* . . . . 1 Cor 9:20
of a woman, born *u* . . . . Gal 4:4
you who desire to be *u* . . . . . Gal 4:21
Spirit, you are not *u* . . . . Gal 5:18

UNDERFOOT
Lord has trampled *u* all . . . . Lam 1:15
the Son of God *u* . . . . Heb 10:29

UNDERMINE
And you *u* your friend . . . . . . Job 6:27

UNDERSTAND
u one another's speech . . . . . Gen 11:7
cause me to *u* wherein I . . . . . Job 6:24
of His power who can *u* . . . . Job 26:14
can anyone *u* the . . . . Job 36:29
uttered what I did not *u* . . . . . Job 42:3
if there are any who *u* . . . . Ps 14:2
Who can *u* his errors . . . . Ps 19:12
in Egypt did not *u* . . . . Ps 106:7
Make me *u* the way of . . . . . Ps 119:27
then you will *u* the fear of . . . Prov 2:5
you will *u* righteousness . . . . . Prov 2:9
is to *u* his way . . . . Prov 14:8
Evil men do not *u* . . . . Prov 28:5
hearing, but do not *u* . . . . Is 6:9
so that they cannot *u* . . . . Is 44:18
and quick to *u* . . . . Dan 1:4
set your heart to *u* . . . . Dan 10:12
u shall instruct many . . . . . . Dan 11:33
of the wicked shall *u* . . . . . . Dan 12:10
people who do not *u* . . . . Hos 4:14
Let him *u* these things . . . . . . Hos 14:9
nor do they *u* His counsel . . . . Mic 4:12
will hear and shall not *u* . . Matt 13:14
should *u* with their heart . . Matt 13:15
they may hear and not *u* . . Mark 4:12
hearing they may not *u* . . . . Luke 8:10
Why do you not *u* . . . . John 8:43
u with their hearts and . . . . John 12:40
I am doing you do not *u* . . . John 13:7
u what you are reading . . . . . Acts 8:30
lest they should *u* . . . . Acts 28:27
I am doing, I do not *u* . . . . . . Rom 7:15
have not heard shall *u* . . . . . Rom 15:21
u all mysteries . . . . 1 Cor 13:2
some things hard to *u* . . . . . 2 Pet 3:16

UNDERSTANDING
of God, in wisdom, in *u*, in . . . Ex 31:3
a woman of good *u* . . . . 1 Sam 25:3
asked for yourself *u* . . . . 1 Kin 3:11
and exceedingly great *u* . . . . 1 Kin 4:29
filled with wisdom and *u* . . . 1 Kin 7:14
He has counsel and *u* . . . . . . Job 12:13
He takes away the *u* of . . . . Job 12:24
by His *u* He breaks up . . . . . Job 26:12
is the place of *u* . . . . Job 28:12
depart from evil is *u* . . . . Job 28:28
Almighty gives him *u* . . . . Job 32:8
If you have *u*, hear this . . . . . Job 34:16
has given *u* to the heart . . . . . Job 38:36
not endow her with *u* . . . . Job 39:17
my heart shall give *u* . . . . Ps 49:3
a good *u* have all those . . . . . Ps 111:10
Give me *u* . . . . Ps 119:34
give me *u*, that I may . . . . . . Ps 119:73
Your precepts I get *u* . . . . . Ps 119:104
give me *u*, that I may . . . . . Ps 119:125
give me *u*, and I shall . . . . . Ps 119:144
give me *u* according to . . . . Ps 119:169
His *u* is infinite . . . . Ps 147:5
a man of *u* will attain wise . . Prov 1:5
apply your heart to *u* . . . . Prov 2:2
u will keep you . . . . Prov 2:11
lean not on your own *u* . . . . . Prov 3:5
u He established . . . . Prov 3:19
with a woman lacks *u* . . . . . Prov 6:32
As for him who lacks *u*, ... Prov 9:4
and go in the way of *u* . . . . . Prov 9:6
of the Holy One is *u* . . . . Prov 9:10
a man of *u* has wisdom . . . . Prov 10:23
but a man of *u* holds his . . Prov 11:12
frivolity is devoid of *u* . . . . . Prov 12:11
Good *u* gains favor, but . . . . Prov 13:15
to wrath has great *u* . . . . . . Prov 14:29
him who has *u* seeks . . . . . . Prov 15:14
but a man of *u* walks . . . . . . Prov 15:21
who heeds rebuke gets *u* . . Prov 15:32
And to get *u* is to be . . . . . . Prov 16:16
U is a wellspring . . . . Prov 16:22
A man devoid of *u* . . . . Prov 17:18
A fool has no delight in *u* . . Prov 18:2
u will find good . . . . Prov 19:8
the way of *u* will rest in . . . Prov 21:16
and instruction and *u* . . . . . . Prov 23:23
but the poor who has *u* . . . . Prov 28:11
A ruler who lacks *u* is a . . Prov 28:16
Spirit of wisdom and *u* . . . . Is 11:2
For it is a people of no *u* . . . . . Is 27:11
His *u* is unsearchable . . . . Is 40:28
the heaven by His *u* . . . . Jer 51:15
also still without *u* . . . . Matt 15:16
heart, with all the *u* . . . . Mark 12:33
And He opened their *u* . . . . Luke 24:45
also pray with the *u* . . . . . . 1 Cor 14:15
five words with my *u* . . . . . . 1 Cor 14:19
but in *u* be mature . . . . 1 Cor 14:20
having their *u* darkened, ... Eph 4:18
God, which surpasses all *u* . . . Phil 4:7
and spiritual *u* . . . . Col 1:9
the Lord give you *u* . . . . 2 Tim 2:7
Who is wise and *u* . . . . James 3:13
and has given us an *u* . . . . 1 John 5:20
him who has *u* calculate . . . Rev 13:18

UNDERSTANDS
God *u* its way, and He . . . . . Job 28:23
all plain to him who *u* . . . . . . Prov 8:9
is easy to him who *u* . . . . Prov 14:6
there is none who *u* . . . . Rom 3:11

UNDERSTOOD
all Israel *u* that day . . . . 2 Sam 3:37
my ear has heard and *u* it . . . . Job 13:1
Then I *u* their end . . . . Ps 73:17
My heart has *u* great . . . . Eccl 1:16
Have you not *u* from . . . . Is 40:21
u all these things . . . . Matt 13:51
clearly seen, being *u* . . . . Rom 1:20
I *u* as a child, I thought . . . 1 Cor 13:11

UNDESIRABLE
gather together, O *u* . . . . Zeph 2:1

UNDIGNIFIED
I will be even more *u* . . . . . 2 Sam 6:22

UNDISCERNING
u, untrustworthy . . . . Rom 1:31

UNDONE
He left nothing *u* of all . . . . Josh 11:15
"Woe is me, for I am *u* . . . . Is 6:5
leaving the others *u* . . . . Matt 23:23

UNEDUCATED
that they were *u* . . . . Acts 4:13

UNEQUALLY
Do not be *u* yoked . . . . 2 Cor 6:14

UNEXPECTEDLY
that Day come on you *u* . . Luke 21:34

UNFAITHFUL
they were *u* to the God . . . . 1 Chr 5:25
u will be uprooted . . . . Prov 2:22
but the *u* will be taken by . . Prov 11:6
way of the *u* is hard . . . . . . Prov 13:15
they were *u* to Me . . . . Ezek 39:23

UNFAITHFULLY
back and acted *u* . . . . Ps 78:57

UNFAITHFULNESS
because of their *u* . . . . 1 Chr 9:1
So Saul died for his *u* . . . . 1 Chr 10:13
they have persisted in *u*,' . . Ezek 15:8

UNFAMILIAR
to a people of *u* speech . . . . . Ezek 3:5

UNFORGIVING
unloving, *u* . . . . Rom 1:31
unloving, *u*, slanderers, ... 2 Tim 3:3

UNFORMED
substance, being yet *u* . . . . . Ps 139:16

UNFRUITFUL
and it becomes *u* . . . . Mark 4:19
my understanding is *u* . . . . 1 Cor 14:14
the *u* works of darkness . . . . . Eph 5:11
that they may not be *u* . . . . Titus 3:14

UNGODLINESS
u made me afraid . . . . Ps 18:4
heaven against all *u* . . . . Rom 1:18
He will turn away *u* . . . . Rom 11:26

UNGODLY
delivered me to the *u* . . . . Job 16:11
u shall not stand . . . . Ps 1:5
of the *u* shall perish . . . . Ps 1:6
my cause against an *u* . . . . Ps 43:1
u man digs up evil . . . . Prov 16:27
who justifies the *u* . . . . Rom 4:5
Christ died for the *u* . . . . Rom 5:6
and perdition of *u* men . . . . . . 2 Pet 3:7
convict all who are *u* . . . . Jude 15

UNHOLY
the holy and *u* . . . . Ezek 22:26
for sinners, for the *u* . . . . 1 Tim 1:9

UNINFORMED
the place of the *u* . . . . 1 Cor 14:16

UNINHABITED
shall be *u* forty years . . . . . Ezek 29:11
and your cities shall be *u* . . Ezek 35:9

UNINTENDED
the LORD, for their *u* sin . . Num 15:25

UNINTENTIONAL
them, for it was *u* . . . . Num 15:25

UNINTENTIONALLY
If a person sins *u* against . . . . . Lev 4:2
If you sin *u*, and do not . . . . Num 15:22
kills his neighbor *u* . . . . Deut 4:42
sinned *u* or in ignorance . . Ezek 45:20

UNITE
U my heart to fear . . . . Ps 86:11

UNITY
to dwell together in *u* . . . . . . Ps 133:1
to keep the *u* of the . . . . Eph 4:3
we all come to the *u* . . . . Eph 4:13

UNJUST
hope of the *u* perishes . . . . . Prov 11:7
u knows no shame . . . . Zeph 3:5
on the just and on the *u* . . . . Matt 5:45
commended the *u* . . . . Luke 16:8
he who is *u* in what is . . . . Luke 16:10
extortioners, *u* . . . . Luke 18:11
of the just and the *u* . . . . Acts 24:15
u who inflicts wrath . . . . Rom 3:5
For God is not *u* . . . . Heb 6:10
the just for the *u* . . . . 1 Pet 3:18
let him be *u* still . . . . Rev 22:11

UNJUSTLY
long will you judge *u* . . . . Ps 82:2
he will deal *u* . . . . Is 26:10

UNKNOWN
not stand before *u* . . . . Prov 22:29
To The *U* God . . . . Acts 17:23
And I was *u* by face to . . . . . Gal 1:22

UNLAWFUL
You know how *u* it is . . . . . . Acts 10:28

UNLEAVENED
See FEAST OF UNLEAVENED BREAD
the Feast of *U* Bread . . . . . . Mark 14:1
since you truly are *u* . . . . 1 Cor 5:7

UNLEAVENED BREAD
feast, and baked *u* . . . . Gen 19:3
roasted in fire, with *u* . . . . Ex 12:8
observe the Feast of *U* . . . . . . Ex 12:17
u and parched grain . . . . Josh 5:11
the meat and the *u* . . . . Judg 6:20
u among their brethren . . . . . 2 Kin 23:9
to keep the Feast of *U* . . . . 2 Chr 30:13
they kept the Feast of *U* . . . . Ezra 6:22
day of the Feast of the *U* . . Matt 26:17
Feast of *U* . . . . Luke 22:1
during the Days of *U* . . . . Acts 12:3
u of sincerity and truth . . . . . 1 Cor 5:8

UNLOVED
saw that Leah was *u* . . . . Gen 29:31
both the loved and the *u*, . . . Deut 21:15

UNLOVING
untrustworthy, *u* . . . . Rom 1:31

UNMARRIED
But I say to the *u* and . . . . . . 1 Cor 7:8

UNMERCIFUL
unforgiving, *u* . . . . Rom 1:31

UNPREPARED
with me and find you *u* . . . . . 2 Cor 9:4

UNPRESENTABLE
u parts have greater . . . . . . 1 Cor 12:23

UNPROFITABLE
And cast the *u* . . . . Matt 25:30
'We are *u* servants . . . . Luke 17:10
have together become *u* . . . . . Rom 3:12
who once was *u* to you . . . . . . Philem 11
for that would be *u* . . . . Heb 13:17

UNPROFITABLENESS
of its weakness and *u* . . . . Heb 7:18

UNPUNISHED
wicked will not go *u* . . . . Prov 11:21
witness will not go *u* . . . . Prov 19:9
be rich will not go *u* . . . . . . Prov 28:20
You shall not go *u*, but . . . . . Jer 49:12

UNQUENCHABLE
up the chaff with *u* . . . . Matt 3:12
He will burn with *u* . . . . Luke 3:17

UNRESTRAINED
that the people were *u* . . . . . . Ex 32:25

UNRIGHTEOUS
u man his thoughts . . . . Is 55:7
been faithful in the *u* . . . . . Luke 16:11
u will not inherit the . . . . 1 Cor 6:9

UNRIGHTEOUSNESS
and there is no *u* . . . . Ps 92:15
builds his house by *u* . . . . Jer 22:13
Him is true, and no *u* . . . . . . John 7:18
all ungodliness and *u* . . . . Rom 1:18
the truth, but obey *u* . . . . Rom 2:8
as instruments of *u* to sin . . . . Rom 6:13
Is there *u* with God . . . . Rom 9:14
but had pleasure in *u* . . . . 2 Thess 2:12
will be merciful to their *u* . . . Heb 8:12
receive the wages of *u* . . . . . . 2 Pet 2:13
cleanse us from all *u* . . . . . . 1 John 1:9
All *u* is sin . . . . 1 John 5:17

UNRULY
those who are *u* . . . . 1 Thess 5:14
It is an *u* evil . . . . James 3:8

UNSEARCHABLE
does great things, and *u* . . . . . . Job 5:9
heart of kings is *u* . . . . Prov 25:3
u are His judgments . . . . Rom 11:33

UNSHRUNK
No one puts a piece of *u* . . . Matt 9:16

UNSKILLED
only of milk is *u* . . . . Heb 5:13

UNSPOTTED
to keep oneself *u* . . . . James 1:27

UNSTABLE
U as water . . . . Gen 49:4
man, *u* in all his ways . . . . . James 1:8
from sin, enticing *u* souls . . . 2 Pet 2:14

UNSTOPPED
of the deaf shall be *u* . . . . Is 35:5

UNTAUGHT
which *u* and unstable . . . . 2 Pet 3:16

UNTHANKFUL
disobedient to parents, *u* . . . 2 Tim 3:2

UNTRAINED
and *u* men, they marveled . . Acts 4:13
Even though I am *u* in . . . . . 2 Cor 11:6

UNTRUSTWORTHY
undiscerning, *u* . . . . Rom 1:31

UNUSUAL
to pass His act, His *u* act . . . . . Is 28:21
God worked *u* miracles . . . . . . Acts 19:11

UNVEILED
But we all, with *u* face, ... 2 Cor 3:18

UNWASHED
but to eat with *u* hands . . . Matt 15:20
eat bread with *u* hands . . . . . Mark 7:5

UNWISE
He is an *u* son . . . . Hos 13:13
both to wise and to *u* . . . . Rom 1:14
Therefore do not be *u* . . . . Eph 5:17

UNWITTINGLY
have *u* entertained angels . . . Heb 13:2

UNWORTHY
and judge yourselves *u* . . . . Acts 13:46
u manner will be . . . . 1 Cor 11:27

UPHOLD
u the evildoers . . . . Job 8:20
u me with Your generous . . . . Ps 51:12
U me according to . . . . Ps 119:116
you, I will *u* you with My . . . . . Is 41:10
My Servant whom I *u* . . . . Is 42:1
there was no one to *u* . . . . Is 63:5
u the weak, be patient . . . 1 Thess 5:14

UPHOLDING
u all things by the . . . . Heb 1:3

UPHOLDS
the LORD *u* the righteous . . . . Ps 37:17
Your right hand *u* . . . . Ps 63:8
LORD *u* all who fall . . . . Ps 145:14

UPPER ROOM
shut the doors of the *u* . . . . . Judg 3:23
carried him to the *u* . . . . . . 1 Kin 17:19
the lattice of his *u* . . . . 2 Kin 1:2
let us make a small *u* . . . . . . 2 Kin 4:10
And in his *u* . . . . Dan 6:10
show you a large *u* . . . . Mark 14:15
they went up into the *u* . . . . . . Acts 1:13
they laid her in an *u* . . . . Acts 9:37
many lamps in the *u* . . . . Acts 20:8

UPRIGHT
righteous and *u* is He . . . . . . Deut 32:4
man was blameless and *u* . . . . . . Job 1:1
u man, one who fears God . . . . Job 1:8
where were the *u* . . . . Job 4:7
Good and *u* is the LORD . . . . Ps 25:8
u shall have dominion . . . . Ps 49:14
declare that the LORD is *u* . . . Ps 92:15

u will be blessed ....Ps 112:2
u there arises light ....Ps 112:4
For the *u* will dwell in the .. Prov 2:21
is strength for the *u* ....Prov 10:29
u will guide them ....Prov 11:3
u will deliver them ....Prov 11:6
u will flourish ....Prov 14:11
u is His delight ....Prov 15:8
of the *u* is a highway ....Prov 15:19
Whoever causes the *u* to .. Prov 28:10
that God made man *u* ....Eccl 7:29
and there is no one *u* ....Mic 7:2
his soul is not *u* ....Hab 2:4

UPRIGHT IN HEART
God, Who saves the *u* ....Ps 7:10
shoot secretly at the *u* ....Ps 11:2
shout for joy, all you *u* ....Ps 32:11
righteousness to the *u* ....Ps 36:10
all the *u* shall glory ....Ps 64:10
all the *u* will follow it ....Ps 94:15
gladness for the *u* ....Ps 97:11

UPRIGHTLY
He who walks *u*, and works .. Ps 15:2
from those who walk *u* ....Ps 84:11
shield to those who walk *u* .. Prov 2:7
understanding walks *u* ... Prov 15:21
good to him who walks *u* ....Mic 2:7

UPRIGHTNESS
to show man His *u* ....Job 33:23
praise You with *u* of heart ... Ps 119:7
me in the land of *u* ....Ps 143:10
of *u* to walk in the ways ... Prov 2:13
walks in his *u* fears the .... Prov 14:2
princes for their *u* ....Prov 17:26
of the just is *u* ....Is 26:7
land of *u* he will deal ....Is 26:10

UPROAR
so that the city is in an *u* .. 1 Kin 1:45
be an *u* of the people ....Mark 14:2
After the *u* had ceased, ...Acts 20:1

UPROOT
He will *u* Israel from ....1 Kin 14:15
then I will *u* ....2 Chr 7:20
u you from the land ....Ps 52:5
u the wheat with ....Matt 13:29

UPROOTED
LORD *u* them from their ... Deut 29:28
my hope He has *u* like a ... Job 19:10
unfaithful will be *u* from ... Prov 2:22

UPWARD
prevailed fifteen cubits *u* ... Gen 7:20
trouble, as the sparks fly *u* ... Job 5:7
winds *u* for the wise ....Prov 15:24
downward, and bear fruit *u* .. Is 37:31
my eyes fail from looking *u* .. Is 38:14

UR OF THE CHALDEANS
City of Abram's early life, Gen 11:28–31; 15:7
Located in Mesopotamia by Stephen, Acts 7:2, 4

URGE
I *u* you to take heart, ...Acts 27:22
I *u* you, imitate ....1 Cor 4:16
Therefore I *u* you to ....2 Cor 2:8
I *u* you to become like me ... Gal 4:12
I *u* you in the sight of ....1 Tim 6:13

URGED
the angels *u* Lot to hurry, .. Gen 19:15
His disciples *u* Him ....John 4:31
I strongly *u* him to ....1 Cor 16:12

URIAH
Hittite; one of David's warriors, 2 Sam 23:39
Husband of Bathsheba; condemned to death by David, 2 Sam 11:1–27

URIJAH
High priest in Ahaz's time, 2 Kin 16:10–16
——— Prophet in Jeremiah's time, Jer 26:20–23

URIM
of judgment of *U* ....Ex 28:30
the judgment of the *U* ....Num 27:21
Thummim and Your *U* ....Deut 33:8
could consult with the *U* ... Ezra 2:63
could consult with the *U* ....Neh 7:65

US
"God with *u* ....Matt 1:23
who is not against *u* ....Mark 9:40
If God is for *u* ....Rom 8:31
They went out from *u* ....1 John 2:19

USE
who spitefully *u* you ....Matt 5:44
leaving the natural *u* ....Rom 1:27
u this world as not ....1 Cor 7:31
u liberty as an ....Gal 5:13
u a little wine ....1 Tim 5:23
reason of *u* have their ....Heb 5:14

USEFUL
Is it *u* for any work ....Ezek 15:4
u for the Master ....2 Tim 2:21
you, for he is *u* to me for .. 2 Tim 4:11

USELESS
all of them are *u* ....Is 44:9
are unprofitable and *u* ....Titus 3:9
one's religion is *u* ....James 1:26

USES
if one *u* it lawfully ....1 Tim 1:8

USING
u no figure of speech ....John 16:29
perish with the *u* ....Col 2:22
u liberty as a ....1 Pet 2:16

USURY
Take no *u* or ....Lev 25:36
exacting *u* from his brother .. Neh 5:7
put out his money at *u* ....Ps 15:5

UTTER
u words from their heart ....Job 8:10
nor my tongue *u* deceit ....Job 27:4
u pure knowledge ....Job 33:3
u dark sayings of old ....Ps 78:2
My lips shall *u* praise ....Ps 119:171
a false witness will *u* lies ... Prov 14:5
heart will *u* perverse ....Prov 23:33
let not your heart *u* ....Eccl 5:2
I will *u* My judgments ....Jer 1:16
lawful for a man to *u* ....2 Cor 12:4

UTTERANCE
the Spirit gave them *u* ....Acts 2:4
u may be given to me ....Eph 6:19

UTTERED
The deep *u* its voice ....Hab 3:10
which cannot be *u* ....Rom 8:26
the seven thunders *u* ....Rev 10:4

UTTERLY
that I will *u* blot out the ....Ex 17:14
they *u* destroyed all that ....Josh 6:21
lands by *u* destroying ....2 Kin 19:11
he shall not be *u* cast down .. Ps 37:24
Oh, do not forsake me *u* ....Ps 119:8
it would be *u* despised ....Song 8:7
You have *u* rejected ....Lam 5:22
u destroyed from among ... Acts 3:23
she will be *u* burned with ... Rev 18:8

UTTERMOST
upon them to the *u* ....1 Thess 2:16
u those who come ....Heb 7:25

UTTERS
Day unto day *u* speech ....Ps 19:2
u His voice from ....Amos 1:2
and the great man *u* ....Mic 7:3

UZZAH
Son of Abinadab, struck down for touching the ark of the covenant, 2 Sam 6:3–11

UZZIAH
King of Judah, called Azariah, 2 Kin 14:21; 15:1–7
Reigns righteously, 2 Chr 26:1–15
Usurps priestly function; stricken with leprosy, 2 Chr 26:16–21
Life of, written by Isaiah, 2 Chr 26:22, 23

VAGABOND
v you shall be on the ....Gen 4:12

VAIN
of the LORD your God in *v* ... Ex 20:7
of the LORD your God in *v* .. Deut 5:11
the people plot a *v* ....Ps 2:1
they labor in *v* who build it .. Ps 127:1
v life which he passes ....Eccl 6:12
'I have labored in *v* ....Is 49:4
And in *v* they worship Me .. Matt 15:9
And in *v* they worship Me, .. Mark 7:7
you believed in *v* ....1 Cor 15:2
labor is not in *v* in the ....1 Cor 15:58
law, then Christ died in *v* ....Gal 2:21
run in *v* or labored in *v* ....Phil 2:16

VALIANT
Only be *v* for me ....1 Sam 18:17
They are not *v* for the ....Jer 9:3
v men swept away ....Jer 46:15

VALIANTLY
while Israel does *v* ....Num 24:18
God we will do *v* ....Ps 60:12
of the LORD does *v* ....Ps 118:15

VALLEY
in the *V* of Megiddo ....2 Chr 35:22
I walk through the *v* ....Ps 23:4
pass through the *V* ....Ps 84:6
the verdure of the *v* ....Song 6:11
v shall be exalted ....Is 40:4
in the midst of the *v* ....Ezek 37:1
in the *v* of decision ....Joel 3:14
v shall be filled ....Luke 3:5

VALLEYS
He is not God of the *v* ... 1 Kin 20:28
and the lily of the *v* ....Song 2:1
the *v* will split like wax ....Mic 1:4

VALOR
a mighty man of *v* ....1 Sam 16:18

VALUE
does not know its *v* ....Job 28:13
of more *v* than they ....Matt 6:26
you are of more *v* than ... Matt 10:31
Of how much more *v* ....Matt 12:12
you are of more *v* than ....Luke 12:7
Of how much more *v* ....Luke 12:24
they counted up the *v* ....Acts 19:19
but are of no *v* against the .. Col 2:23

VALUED
It cannot be *v* in the ....Job 28:16
is *v* by what others say ... Prov 27:21

VANISH
when it is hot, they *v* ....Job 6:17
For the heavens will *v* ....Is 51:6
knowledge, it will *v* ....1 Cor 13:8
old is ready to *v* away ....Heb 8:13

VANISHED
Has their wisdom *v* ....Jer 49:7
and He *v* from their ....Luke 24:31

VANITY
of vanities, all is *v* ....Eccl 1:2
This also is *v* and grasping .. Eccl 6:9
iniquity with cords of *v* ....Is 5:18

VANQUISH
God will *v* him, not man ... Job 32:13

VAPOR
best state is but *v* ....Ps 39:5

have night without *v* .... Mic 3:6
they had also seen a *v* .... Luke 24:23
in a *v* he has seen a man .... Acts 9:12
in a trance I saw a *v* .... Acts 11:5
v appeared to Paul in .... Acts 16:9
to the heavenly *v* .... Acts 26:19

VISIONS
thoughts from the *v* .... Job 4:13
opened and I saw *v* of God .. Ezek 1:1
These were the *v* of my ..... Dan 4:10
young men shall see *v* .... Joel 2:28
young men shall see *v* ...... Acts 2:17
I will come to *v* .... 2 Cor 12:1

VISIT
but God will surely *v* ...... Gen 50:24
in the day when I *v* .... Ex 32:34
v the earth and water .... Ps 65:9
Oh, *v* me with Your .... Ps 106:4
and you did not *v* Me ..... Matt 25:43
v orphans and widows .... James 1:27

VISITATION
the time of your *v* .... Luke 19:44
God in the day of *v* .... 1 Pet 2:12

VISITED
he will not be *v* .... Prov 19:23
many days you will be *v* ... Ezek 38:8
I was sick and you *v* Me .. Matt 25:36
Israel, for He has *v* .... Luke 1:68
"God has *v* His people ..... Luke 7:16
how God at the first *v* ..... Acts 15:14

VISITING
v the iniquity of the fathers .. Ex 20:5

VISITOR
am a foreigner and a *v* ..... Gen 23:4

VITALITY
v was turned into the .... Ps 32:4

VOICE
"I heard Your *v* .... Gen 3:10
God heard the *v* of the .... Gen 21:17
you have obeyed My *v* .... Gen 22:18
only obey my *v*, and go, ... Gen 27:13
v is Jacob's *v* .... Gen 27:22
I should obey His *v* .... Ex 5:2
God answered him by *v* ..... Ex 19:19
your God and obey His *v* ... Deut 4:30
obey the *v* of the LORD .... Deut 30:10
wept with a loud *v* ...... 2 Sam 15:23
heard the *v* of Elijah ..... 1 Kin 17:22
fire a still small *v* .... 1 Kin 19:12
and my flute to the *v* .... Job 30:31
you thunder with a *v* .... Job 40:9
cried to the LORD with my *v* ... Ps 3:4
with the *v* of thanksgiving .... Ps 26:7
the *v* of my supplications ..... Ps 28:6
He uttered His *v* .... Ps 46:6
Hear my *v*, O God, in my ..... Ps 64:1
He sends out His *v* .... Ps 68:33
cried out to God with my *v* ... Ps 77:1
have lifted up their *v* .... Ps 93:3
if you will hear His *v* .... Ps 95:7
word, heeding the *v* .... Ps 103:20
for your *v* is sweet .... Song 2:14
their *v* shall be heard as far ... Is 15:4
The *v* of one crying in .... Is 40:3
the *v* of weeping shall .... Is 65:19
A *v* from the temple .... Is 66:6
the *v* of the LORD our God ... Jer 3:25
that does not obey the *v* of ... Jer 7:28
v was heard in Ramah ..... Jer 31:15
the *v* of joy and .... Jer 33:11
I heard a *v* of One .... Ezek 1:28
who has a pleasant *v* ..... Ezek 33:32
like the *v* of a multitude .... Dan 10:6
with the *v* of thanksgiving .... Jon 2:9
v was heard in Ramah ..... Matt 2:18
"The *v* of one crying .... Matt 3:3
And suddenly a *v* .... Matt 3:17
will anyone hear His *v* .... Matt 12:19
and suddenly a *v* .... Matt 17:5
cried out with a loud *v* .... Matt 27:46
a loud *v* glorified God, ... Luke 17:15
hear the *v* of the Son of .... John 5:25
for they know his *v* .... John 10:4
v did not come because ... John 12:30
the truth hears My *v* .... John 18:37
the *v* of an archangel .... 1 Thess 4:16
whose *v* then shook the .... Heb 12:26
glory when such a *v* .... 2 Pet 1:17
If anyone hears My *v* .... Rev 3:20
I heard a *v* from heaven, ... Rev 14:2

VOICE OF THE LORD
diligently heed the *v* .... Ex 15:26
if we hear the *v* .... Deut 5:25
they did not obey the *v* .... Josh 5:6
as in obeying the *v* ...... 1 Sam 15:22
you did not obey the *v* ... 1 Sam 28:18
v is over the waters .... Ps 29:3
did not heed the *v* .... Ps 106:25
Also I heard the *v* .... Is 6:8
v, who fully repays .... Is 66:6
they did not obey the *v* .... Jer 43:7
We have not obeyed the *v* .. Dan 9:10
people, obeyed the *v* .... Hag 1:12
diligently obey the *v* .... Zech 6:15
the *v* came to him .... Acts 7:31

VOICES
God of Israel with *v* ..... 2 Chr 20:19
shall lift up their *v* .... Is 52:8
demanding with loud *v* ... Luke 23:23
And there were loud *v* ..... Rev 11:15

VOID
was without form, and *v* ..... Gen 1:2
they are a nation *v* .... Deut 32:28
the LORD had made a *v* .... Judg 21:15
regarded Your law as *v* ... Ps 119:126
it shall not return to Me *v* .... Is 55:11
Do we then make *v* .... Rom 3:31
heirs, faith is made *v* .... Rom 4:14
make my boasting *v* .... 1 Cor 9:15

VOLUME
in the *v* of the book .... Heb 10:7

VOLUNTEERS
Your people shall be *v* ...... Ps 110:3

VOMIT
lest the land *v* .... Lev 18:28
dog returns to his own *v* .. Prov 26:11
man staggers in his *v* .... Is 19:14
returns to his own *v* .... 2 Pet 2:22
cold nor hot, I will *v* .... Rev 3:16

VOW
Then Jacob made a *v* ...... Gen 28:20
to take the *v* of a Nazirite ... Num 6:2
he carried out his *v* .... Judg 11:39
v shall be performed .... Ps 65:1
When you make a *v* .... Eccl 5:4
not to *v* than to *v* .... Eccl 5:5
for he had taken a *v* ...... Acts 18:18
men who have taken a *v* .. Acts 21:23

VOW TO THE LORD
So Israel made a *v* .... Num 21:2
Or if a woman makes a *v* .. Num 30:3
When you make a *v* ...... Deut 23:21
And Jephthah made a *v* ... Judg 11:30
yes, they will make a *v* ...... Is 19:21

VOWED
If she *v* in her husband's .. Num 30:10
v to the Mighty One of ...... Ps 132:2
Pay what you have *v* .... Eccl 5:4
I will pay what I have *v* ...... Jon 2:9

VOWS
v to the LORD the offering .. Num 6:21
you will pay your *v* .... Job 22:27
I will pay My *v* .... Ps 22:25
V made to You are .... Ps 56:12
Make *v* to the LORD .... Ps 76:11
today I have paid my *v* ..... Prov 7:14
to reconsider his *v* .... Prov 20:25
And what, son of my *v* ..... Prov 31:2
to the LORD and took *v* ...... Jon 1:16

WAFERS
like *w* made with honey .... Ex 16:31

WAGE
those who exploit *w* .... Mal 3:5
w the good warfare .... 1 Tim 1:18

WAGES
I will give you your *w* .... Ex 2:9
the *w* of the wicked .... Prov 10:16
the transgressor his *w* .... Prov 26:10
w will be troubled .... Is 19:10
and he who earns *w* .... Hag 1:6
to you, give me my *w* ..... Zech 11:12
and give them their *w* ...... Matt 20:8
be content with your *w* ..... Luke 3:14
is worthy of his *w* .... Luke 10:7
him who works, the *w* ...... Rom 4:4
For the *w* of sin is .... Rom 6:23
is worthy of his *w* .... 1 Tim 5:18
Indeed the *w* of the .... James 5:4
and will receive the *w* of ... 2 Pet 2:13

WAIL
streets everyone will *w* .... Is 15:3
everyone shall *w* .... Is 16:7
My heart shall *w* .... Jer 48:36
"Son of man, *w* .... Ezek 32:18

WAILING
w is heard from Zion .... Jer 9:19
shall be *w* in all streets ... Amos 5:16
of heart and bitter *w* ..... Ezek 27:31
There will be *w* .... Matt 13:42
cried out, weeping and *w* .. Rev 18:19

WAIST
than my father's *w* .... 1 Kin 12:10
Your *w* is a heap of wheat .. Song 7:2
put it around your *w* .... Jer 13:1
the appearance of His *w* ... Ezek 1:27
w was girded with gold ..... Dan 10:5
Let your *w* be girded ..... Luke 12:35
girded your *w* with truth .... Eph 6:14

WAIT
if he did not lie in *w* .... Ex 21:13
would you *w* for them till .. Ruth 1:13
w until you have .... 1 Sam 1:23
hard service I will *w* .... Job 14:14
If I *w* for the grave .... Job 17:13
w patiently for Him .... Ps 37:7
my eyes fail while I *w* .... Ps 69:3
These all *w* for You .... Ps 104:27
let us lie in *w* to shed ...... Prov 1:11
And I will *w* on the .... Is 8:17
the LORD will *w* .... Is 30:18
not be ashamed who *w* ...... Is 49:23
w quietly for the .... Lam 3:26
I will *w* for the God .... Mic 7:7
Though it tarries, *w* for it .... Hab 2:3
be like men who *w* .... Luke 12:36
but to *w* for the Promise ...... Acts 1:4
see, we eagerly *w* .... Rom 8:25
w for one another .... 1 Cor 11:33
the Spirit eagerly *w* .... Gal 5:5
we also eagerly *w* .... Phil 3:20
and to *w* for His Son .... 1 Thess 1:10
To those who eagerly *w* .... Heb 9:28

WAIT ON THE LORD
W, be of good courage ...... Ps 27:14
But those who *w* .... Ps 37:9
W, and keep His way .... Ps 37:34
And I will *w* .... Is 8:17
w shall renew their .... Is 40:31

WAITED
w for your salvation .... Gen 49:18
and when I *w* for light ..... Job 30:26
w patiently for the .... Ps 40:1
we have *w* for Him .... Is 25:9

WASTE
who are left shall *w* . . . . . . Lev 26:39
the cities are laid *w* . . . . Is 6:11
empty and makes it *w* . . . . Is 24:1
w the mountains . . . . Is 42:15
"Why this *w* . . . . Matt 26:8

WASTED
The field is *w* . . . . Joel 1:10
this fragrant oil *w* . . . . Mark 14:4
w his possessions . . . . Luke 15:13

WASTELAND
w shall be glad . . . . Is 35:1

WASTES
His flesh *w* away from . . . . . Job 33:21
My eye *w* away because of . . . . Ps 6:7
cities shall be perpetual *w* . . Jer 49:13

WASTING
w and destruction are . . . . Is 59:7
that this man was *w* . . . . Luke 16:1

WATCH
Therefore *w* yourselves . . . . . Deut 2:4
of them we set a *w* . . . . Neh 4:9
my steps, but do not *w* . . . . . Job 14:16
is past, and like a *w* . . . . Ps 90:4
keep *w* over the door . . . . Ps 141:3
and all who *w* for . . . . Is 29:20
W the road . . . . Nah 2:1
W therefore, for you . . . . . . Matt 24:42
"What! Could you not *w* . . Matt 26:40
W and pray, lest you . . . . . Matt 26:41
W therefore, for you do . . Mark 13:35
Could you not *w* one . . . . . Mark 14:37
W and pray, lest you . . . . . Mark 14:38
keeping *w* over their flock . . Luke 2:8
W therefore, and pray . . . . Luke 21:36
W, stand fast in the . . . . . . 1 Cor 16:13
submissive, for they *w* . . . . . Heb 13:17

WATCHED
in the days when God *w* . . . . . Job 29:2
w while a stone was cut . . . . Dan 2:34
come, he would have *w* . . . Matt 24:43
Pharisees *w* Him closely . . . . Luke 6:7

WATCHER
I done to You, O *w* of men . . Job 7:20

WATCHES
w the righteous . . . . Ps 37:32
LORD *w* over the strangers . . Ps 146:9
She *w* over the ways of . . . Prov 31:27
Blessed is he who *w* . . . . Rev 16:15

WATCHFUL
But you be *w* in all . . . . 2 Tim 4:5
be serious and *w* . . . . 1 Pet 4:7
Be *w*, and strengthen the . . . . . Rev 3:2

WATCHING
who listens to me, *w* . . . . . . Prov 8:34
the flock, who were *w* . . . . Zech 11:11
he comes, will find *w* . . . . . Luke 12:37

WATCHMAN
guards the city, the *w* . . . . . . Ps 127:1
W, what of the night . . . . Is 21:11
I have made you a *w* . . . . . . Ezek 3:17
the day of your *w* . . . . Mic 7:4

WATCHMEN
w who go about the . . . . Song 3:3
w shall lift up their . . . . Is 52:8
His *w* are blind . . . . Is 56:10
I have set *w* on your . . . . Is 62:6
Also, I set *w* over you . . . . Jer 6:17
strong, set up the *w* . . . . Jer 51:12

WATER
Eden to *w* the garden . . . . Gen 2:10
Unstable as *w* . . . . Gen 49:4
your bread and your *w* . . . . . Ex 23:25
of affliction and *w* . . . . 1 Kin 22:27
w disappears from the . . . . Job 14:11
w wears away stones . . . . Job 14:19
drinks iniquity like *w* . . . . Job 15:16
not given the weary *w* . . . . Job 22:7
He binds up the *w* . . . . Job 26:8
I am poured out like *w* . . . . Ps 22:14
where there is no *w* . . . . Ps 63:1
they have shed like *w* . . . . Ps 79:3
Drink *w* from your own . . . . Prov 5:15
"Stolen *w* is sweet . . . . Prov 9:17
the whole supply of *w* . . . . Is 3:1
and needy seek *w* . . . . Is 41:17
For I will pour *w* . . . . Is 44:3
silence and given us *w* . . . . Jer 8:14
eye overflows with *w* . . . . . . Lam 1:16
will be as weak as *w* . . . . Ezek 7:17
w the land with the . . . . Ezek 32:6
you gave Me no *w* . . . . Luke 7:44
there was much *w* . . . . John 3:23
given you living *w* . . . . John 4:10
rivers of living *w* . . . . John 7:38
blood and *w* came out . . . . John 19:34
"Can anyone forbid *w* . . . . . Acts 10:47
with the washing of *w* . . . . Eph 5:26
can yield both salt *w* . . . . . . James 3:12
were saved through *w* . . . . . 1 Pet 3:20
is He who came by *w* . . . . . . 1 John 5:6
the Spirit, the *w* . . . . 1 John 5:8
are clouds without *w* . . . . Jude 12

WATER OF LIFE
w freely to him who . . . . Rev 21:6
a pure river of *w* . . . . Rev 22:1
let him take the *w* . . . . Rev 22:17

WATERED
w the whole face . . . . Gen 2:6
that it was well *w* . . . . Gen 13:10
I planted, Apollos *w* . . . . 1 Cor 3:6

WATERPOTS
"Fill four *w* with water . . . 1 Kin 18:33
"Fill the *w* with water . . . . John 2:7

WATERS
and struck the *w* . . . . Ex 7:20
If He withholds the *w* . . . . Job 12:15
me beside the still *w* . . . . Ps 23:2
though its *w* roar and . . . . Ps 46:3
w have come up to my . . . . Ps 69:1
then the *w* would have . . . . Ps 124:4
rich, and he who *w* . . . . Prov 11:25
Who has bound the *w* . . . . Prov 30:4
your bread upon the *w* . . . . Eccl 11:1
a well of living *w* . . . . Song 4:15
w cannot quench love . . . . . . Song 8:7
of the LORD as the *w* . . . . Is 11:9
w will fail from the . . . . Is 19:5
because I give *w* . . . . Is 43:20
have sworn that the *w* . . . . Is 54:9
thirsts, come to the *w* . . . . Is 55:1
fountain of living *w* . . . . Jer 2:13
w flowed over my head . . . . . . Lam 3:54
the sound of many *w* . . . . Ezek 43:2
w surrounded me . . . . Jon 2:5
shall be that living *w* . . . . Zech 14:8
often, in perils of *w* . . . . 2 Cor 11:26
living fountains of *w* . . . . Rev 7:17
w became wormwood . . . . Rev 8:11

WAVE
you shall *w* them as a *w* . . . . Ex 29:24
w offering before the LORD . . Lev 7:30
the priest shall *w* them . . . . . . Num 6:20
Its fruit shall *w* . . . . Ps 72:16
is like a *w* of the sea . . . . James 1:6

WAVER
He did not *w* at the . . . . Rom 4:20

WAVERING
of our hope without *w* . . . . . Heb 10:23

WAVES
and here your proud *w* . . . . . Job 38:11
all Your *w* and billows . . . . Ps 42:7
the noise of their *w* . . . . Ps 65:7
the multitude of its *w* . . . . Jer 51:42
was covered with the *w* . . . . Matt 8:24
sea, tossed by the *w* . . . . Matt 14:24
raging *w* of the sea . . . . Jude 13

WAX
My heart is like *w* . . . . Ps 22:14
w melts before the . . . . Ps 68:2
mountains melt like *w* . . . . Ps 97:5

WAY
and show them the *w* . . . . Ex 18:20
day I am going the *w* . . . . . . Josh 23:14
and the right *w* . . . . 1 Sam 12:23
As for God, His *w* . . . . 2 Sam 22:31
to a man whose *w* . . . . Job 3:23
But He knows the *w* . . . . Job 23:10
"Where is the *w* . . . . Job 38:19
the LORD knows the *w* . . . . Ps 1:6
you perish in the *w* . . . . Ps 2:12
Teach me Your *w* . . . . Ps 27:11
This is the *w* of those . . . . Ps 49:13
w may be known on . . . . Ps 67:2
Your *w* was in the sea . . . . Ps 77:19
where there is no *w* . . . . Ps 107:40
I have chosen the *w* . . . . Ps 119:30
I hate every false *w* . . . . Ps 119:104
in the *w* everlasting . . . . Ps 139:24
and preserves the *w* . . . . Prov 2:8
The *w* of the wicked is . . . . . . Prov 4:19
instruction are the *w* . . . . Prov 6:23
w that seems right . . . . Prov 14:12
not know what is the *w* . . . . . Eccl 11:5
of terrors in the *w* . . . . Eccl 12:5
The *w* of the just is . . . . Is 26:7
"This is the *w* . . . . Is 30:21
LORD, who makes a *w* . . . . Is 43:16
wicked forsake his *w* . . . . Is 55:7
O LORD, I know the *w* . . . . Jer 10:23
one heart and one *w* . . . . Jer 32:39
Israel, is it not My *w* . . . . . Ezek 18:25
w which is not fair . . . . Ezek 33:17
and pervert the *w* . . . . Amos 2:7
the LORD has His *w* . . . . Nah 1:3
he will prepare the *w* . . . . Mal 3:1
and broad is the *w* . . . . Matt 7:13
and difficult is the *w* . . . . Matt 7:14
will prepare Your *w* . . . . Matt 11:10
and teach the *w* . . . . Matt 22:16
and the *w* you know . . . . John 14:4
to him, "I am the *w* . . . . John 14:6
proclaim to us the *w* . . . . Acts 16:17
explained to him the *w* . . . . . Acts 18:26
you a more excellent *w* . . . . . 1 Cor 12:31
w which He consecrated . . . . Heb 10:20
forsaken the right *w* . . . . 2 Pet 2:15
to have known the *w* . . . . 2 Pet 2:21
have gone in the *w* . . . . Jude 11

WAY OF THE LORD
that they keep the *w* . . . . . . Gen 18:19
did not walk in the *w* . . . . . 2 Kin 21:22
w is strength for the . . . . . . Prov 10:29
Prepare the *w*, make . . . . Is 40:3
for they do not know the *w* . . . . Jer 5:4
"The *w* is not fair . . . . Ezek 18:25
Prepare the *w*, make His . . . . . Matt 3:3
Prepare the *w*, make His . . . . . Mark 1:3
Prepare the *w*, make His . . . . . Luke 3:4
Make straight the *w* . . . . John 1:23
instructed in the *w* . . . . Acts 18:25

WAYS
for all His *w* are . . . . Deut 32:4
they do not know its *w* . . . . . . Job 24:13
is the first of the *w* . . . . Job 40:19
Show me Your *w* . . . . Ps 25:4
transgressors Your *w* . . . . Ps 51:13
would walk in My *w* . . . . Ps 81:13
w were directed . . . . Ps 119:5
I thought about my *w* . . . . Ps 119:59
righteous in all His *w* . . . . Ps 145:17
For the *w* of man are . . . . Prov 5:21
w please the LORD . . . . Prov 16:7
He will teach us His *w* . . . . Is 2:3
nor are your *w* . . . . Is 55:8
"Stand in the *w* . . . . Jer 6:16

that I sat down and *w* .... Neh 1:4
Have I not *w* for him .... Job 30:25
I *w* and chastened my soul .. Ps 69:10
down, yea, we *w* .... Ps 137:1
out and *w* bitterly .... Matt 26:75
He saw the city and *w* .... Luke 19:41
Jesus *w* .... John 11:35
as she *w* she stooped ..... John 20:11
So I *w* much .... Rev 5:4

WEST
in the *w* are astonished .... Job 18:20
as the east is from the *w* ... Ps 103:12
of the LORD from the *w* ...... Is 59:19
male goat came from the *w* .. Dan 8:5
in two, from east to *w* ..... Zech 14:4
east and flashes to the *w* .. Matt 24:27
rising out of the *w* .... Luke 12:54

WET
They are *w* with the .... Job 24:8
his body was *w* with .... Dan 4:33

WHEAT
with the finest of *w* .... Ps 81:16
we may trade *w* .... Amos 8:5
even sell the bad *w* .... Amos 8:6
but gather the *w* .... Matt 13:30
w falls into the .... John 12:24
perhaps *w* or some .... 1 Cor 15:37
oil, fine flour and *w* ...... Rev 18:13

WHEEL
brings the threshing *w* .... Prov 20:26
the fountain, or the *w* .... Eccl 12:6
in the middle of a *w* .... Ezek 1:16

WHEELS
off their chariot *w* .... Ex 14:25
the rumbling of his *w* .... Jer 47:3
appearance of the *w* .... Ezek 1:16
noise of rattling *w* .... Nah 3:2

WHERE
not knowing *w* he was ...... Heb 11:8

WHIP
A *w* for the horse .... Prov 26:3
The noise of a *w* .... Nah 3:2

WHIPS
chastised you with *w* ..... 1 Kin 12:11

WHIRLING
saw King David *w* .... 1 Chr 15:29

WHIRLWIND
Elijah went up by a *w* ..... 2 Kin 2:11
Job out of the *w* .... Job 38:1
them away as with a *w* .... Ps 58:9
w will take them away .... Is 40:24
w shall scatter them .... Is 41:16
w shall be raised .... Jer 25:32
has His way in the *w* .... Nah 1:3

WHISPER
my ear received a *w* .... Job 4:12
and wizards, who *w* .... Is 8:19

WHISPERER
w separates the best ...... Prov 16:28

WHISPERERS
they are *w* .... Rom 1:29

WHISPERINGS
backbitings, *w* .... 2 Cor 12:20

WHISTLE
w for the fly that is in the ..... Is 7:18

WHITE
like *w* coriander seed .... Ex 16:31
leprous, as *w* as snow .... Num 12:10
My beloved is *w* .... Song 5:10
they shall be as *w* as snow .... Is 1:18
and make them *w* .... Dan 11:35
be purified, made *w* .... Dan 12:10
red, sorrel, and *w* .... Zech 1:8
make one hair *w* or black .. Matt 5:36
his clothing as *w* as snow .. Matt 28:3
shining, exceedingly *w* ..... Mark 9:3
for they are already *w* ..... John 4:35
saw two angels in *w* ...... John 20:12
by them in *w* apparel .... Acts 1:10
and hair were *w* like wool .. Rev 1:14
walk with Me in *w* .... Rev 3:4
clothed in *w* garments .... Rev 3:5
behold, a *w* horse .... Rev 6:2
and made them *w* .... Rev 7:14
Then I saw a great *w* ...... Rev 20:11

WHITE AS SNOW
became leprous, as *w* ..... Num 12:10
presence leprous, as *w* .... 2 Kin 5:27
they shall be as *w* .... Is 1:18
His garment was *w* .... Dan 7:9
his clothing as *w* .... Matt 28:3
white like wool, as *w* .... Rev 1:14

WHITEN
launderer on earth can *w* ... Mark 9:3

WHITER
and I shall be *w* than snow ... Ps 51:7

WHITEWASHED
you are like *w* tombs ..... Matt 23:27
strike you, you *w* wall ...... Acts 23:3

WHOLE
the face of the *w* earth ...... Gen 11:4
Is not the *w* land before .... Gen 13:9
w house of Israel, bewail .... Lev 10:6
shall build with *w* stones ... Deut 27:6
down for about a *w* day ... Josh 10:13
let the *w* earth be filled ..... Ps 72:19
Who seek Him with the *w* ... Ps 119:2
my *w* heart I have sought .. Ps 119:10
observe it with my *w* .... Ps 119:34
You with my *w* heart .... Ps 138:1
the *w* earth is full of His .... Is 6:3
to Me with her *w* heart ...... Jer 3:10
The *w* earth will rejoice ... Ezek 35:14
on the *w* house of Israel .. Ezek 39:25
than for your *w* body to .... Matt 5:29
your *w* body will be full .... Matt 6:22
if he gains the *w* world ... Matt 16:26
if he gains the *w* world .... Mark 8:36
if he gains the *w* world .... Luke 9:25
the *w* body will be full .... Luke 11:36
the *w* creation groans ...... Rom 8:22
w body were an eye ...... 1 Cor 12:17
a debtor to keep the *w* law ... Gal 5:3
on the *w* armor of God ..... Eph 6:11
may your *w* spirit, soul .. 1 Thess 5:23
also to bridle the *w* body .. James 3:2
that it defiles the *w* body .. James 3:6
who deceives the *w* world ... Rev 12:9

WHOLESOME
w tongue is a tree .... Prov 15:4
not consent to *w* words ...... 1 Tim 6:3

WHOLLY
w followed the LORD .... Deut 1:36
I will not leave you *w* ...... Jer 46:28

WICKED
were exceedingly *w* .... Gen 13:13
the righteous with the *w* ... Gen 18:25
For I will not justify the *w* .... Ex 23:7
a *w* thought in your heart .. Deut 15:9
from every *w* thing .... Deut 23:9
and condemn the *w* .... Deut 25:1
w shall be silent .... 1 Sam 2:9
proceeds from the *w* .... 1 Sam 24:13
was *w* in the sight of the ... 1 Chr 2:3
turn from their *w* ways .... 2 Chr 7:14
Should you help the *w* .... 2 Chr 19:2
turn from their *w* works .... Neh 9:35
on the counsel of the *w* ..... Job 10:3
You know that I am not *w* ... Job 10:7
w man writhes with pain ... Job 15:20
triumphing of the *w* is ...... Job 20:5
Why do the *w* live and .... Job 21:7
w are reserved for the ...... Job 21:30
to nobles, 'You are *w* ...... Job 34:18
of the *w* come to an end .... Ps 7:9
with the *w* every day .... Ps 7:11
You have destroyed the *w* ...... Ps 9:5
w is snared in the .... Ps 9:16
w shall be turned .... Ps 9:17
do the *w* renounce God ..... Ps 10:13
w bend their bow .... Ps 11:2
w He will rain coals .... Ps 11:6
the *w* who oppress me .... Ps 17:9
Evil shall slay the *w* .... Ps 34:21
w shall be no more .... Ps 37:10
The *w* watches the .... Ps 37:32
But to the *w* God says .... Ps 50:16
So let the *w* perish at the ..... Ps 68:2
of the *w* I will also cut off ... Ps 75:10
how long will the *w* .... Ps 94:3
nothing *w* before my eyes ... Ps 101:3
and the *w* be no more ...... Ps 104:35
of the *w* shall perish .... Ps 112:10
is far from the *w* .... Ps 119:155
if there is any *w* .... Ps 139:24
the way of the *w* He turns ... Ps 146:9
w will be cut off from ...... Prov 2:22
The way of the *w* is like .... Prov 4:19
heart that devises *w* plans .. Prov 6:18
he who rebukes a *w* man ..... Prov 9:7
the wages of the *w* to sin .. Prov 10:16
of the *w* will perish .... Prov 10:28
w will fall by his own ...... Prov 11:5
w man does deceptive .... Prov 11:18
w will not go .... Prov 11:21
expectation of the *w* is .... Prov 11:23
words of the *w* are, "Lie ... Prov 12:6
mercies of the *w* are ...... Prov 12:10
w covet the catch of evil .. Prov 12:12
The way of the *w* is an ..... Prov 15:9
thoughts of the *w* are an ... Prov 15:26
LORD is far from the *w* ... Prov 15:29
He who says to the *w* ..... Prov 24:24
w flee when no one .... Prov 28:1
the righteous and the *w* .... Eccl 3:17
Do not be overly *w* .... Eccl 7:17
not be well with the *w* ...... Eccl 8:13
Woe to the *w*! It shall be ill ... Is 3:11
w forsake his way .... Is 55:7
But the *w* are like the .... Is 57:20
the way of the *w* prosper .... Jer 12:1
from the hand of the *w* ..... Jer 15:21
and desperately *w* .... Jer 17:9
if a *w* man turns from .... Ezek 18:21
a *w* man turns away ...... Ezek 18:27
if you warn the *w* to turn .. Ezek 33:9
when the *w* turns from ... Ezek 33:19
w shall do wickedly .... Dan 12:10
at all acquit the *w* .... Nah 1:3
the righteous and the *w* ..... Mal 3:18
You shall trample the *w* ...... Mal 4:3
with this *w* generation .... Matt 12:45
separate the *w* from .... Matt 13:49
A *w* and adulterous .... Matt 16:4
fiery darts of the *w* one ..... Eph 6:16
have overcome the *w* .... 1 John 2:14
w one does not touch ..... 1 John 5:18
the sway of the *w* .... 1 John 5:19

WICKEDLY
brethren, do not do so *w* .... Gen 19:7
beg you, do not act so *w* .. Judg 19:23
and I have done *w* ...... 2 Sam 24:17
Will you speak *w* .... Job 13:7
God will never do *w* .... Job 34:12
iniquity, we have done *w* .... Ps 106:6
Those who do *w* .... Dan 11:32
yes, all who do *w* .... Mal 4:1

WICKEDNESS
LORD saw that the *w* .... Gen 6:5
can I do this great *w* .... Gen 39:9
the land become full of *w* .. Lev 19:29
may be no *w* among .... Lev 20:14
'*W* proceeds from the .... 1 Sam 24:13
w oppress them .... 2 Sam 7:10
if *w* is found in him, he .... 1 Kin 1:52
do *w* in the sight of the .. 1 Kin 21:25

be, that even the *w* ... Matt 8:27
holding the four *w* ... Rev 7:1

WINDSTORM
And a great *w* arose ... Mark 4:37

WINE
Noah awoke from his *w* ... Gen 9:24
Do not drink *w* or ... Lev 10:9
Nazirite may drink *w* ... Num 6:20
drink *w* or similar drink ... Judg 13:4
I have drunk neither *w* ... 1 Sam 1:15
w for those who are ... 2 Sam 16:2
king was merry with *w* ... Esth 1:10
drinking *w* in their oldest ... Job 1:13
drink the *w* of confusion ... Ps 60:3
w that makes glad ... Ps 104:15
W is a mocker ... Prov 20:1
Do not look on the *w* ... Prov 23:31
w makes merry ... Eccl 10:19
love is better than *w* ... Song 1:2
w goes down smoothly ... Song 7:9
w inflames them ... Is 5:11
are drunk, but not with *w* ... Is 29:9
Yes, come, buy *w* ... Is 55:1
Take this *w* cup of fury ... Jer 25:15
We will drink no *w*, for ... Jer 35:6
new *w* into old wineskins ... Matt 9:17
they gave Him sour *w* ... Matt 27:34
w nor strong drink ... Luke 1:15
pouring on oil and *w* ... Luke 10:34
when they ran out of *w* ... John 2:3
"They are full of new *w* ... Acts 2:13
do not be drunk with *w* ... Eph 5:18
given to *w*, nor violent ... 1 Tim 3:3
but use a little *w* ... 1 Tim 5:23
not given to much *w* ... Titus 2:3
not harm the oil and the *w* ... Rev 6:6
the *w* of the wrath of her ... Rev 14:8
her the cup of the *w* ... Rev 16:19

WINEBIBBER
'Look, a glutton and a *w* ... Luke 7:34

WINEBIBBERS
Do not mix with *w* ... Prov 23:20

WINEPRESS
"I have trodden the *w* ... Is 63:3
for the *w* is full ... Joel 3:13
into the great *w* ... Rev 14:19
Himself treads the *w* ... Rev 19:15

WINESKIN
I have become like a *w* ... Ps 119:83

WINESKINS
new wine into old *w* ... Matt 9:17

WING
maidservant under your *w* ... Ruth 3:9
One *w* of the cherub ... 1 Kin 6:24
so I spread My *w* ... Ezek 16:8

WINGS
I bore you on eagles' *w* ... Ex 19:4
w you have come ... Ruth 2:12
the shadow of Your *w* ... Ps 17:8
He flew upon the *w* ... Ps 18:10
the shadow of Your *w* ... Ps 36:7
w I will make my refuge ... Ps 57:1
If I take the *w* ... Ps 139:9
each one had six *w* ... Is 6:2
up with *w* like eagles ... Is 40:31
a lion, and had eagle's *w* ... Dan 7:4
with healing in His *w* ... Mal 4:2
her chicks under her *w* ... Matt 23:37
each having six *w* ... Rev 4:8
woman was given two *w* ... Rev 12:14

WINNOW
You shall *w* them ... Is 41:16

WINNOWING
His *w* fan is in His hand ... Luke 3:17

WINS
w souls is wise ... Prov 11:30

WINTER
have made summer and *w* ... Ps 74:17
For lo, the *w* is past ... Song 2:11
w it shall occur ... Zech 14:8
flight may not be in *w* ... Matt 24:20

WIPE
the Lord GOD will *w* ... Is 25:8
w them with the towel ... John 13:5
w away every tear ... Rev 21:4

WIPED
reproach will not be *w* ... Prov 6:33
w them with the hair of ... Luke 7:38
w out the handwriting ... Col 2:14

WIPES
eats and *w* her mouth ... Prov 30:20

WISDOM
for this is your *w* ... Deut 4:6
God gave Solomon *w* ... 1 Kin 4:29
w will die with you ... Job 12:2
where can *w* be found ... Job 28:12
fear of the Lord, that is *w* ... Job 28:28
Who has put *w* in the ... Job 38:36
of the righteous speaks *w* ... Ps 37:30
will make me to know *w* ... Ps 51:6
is the beginning of *w* ... Ps 111:10
but fools despise *w* and ... Prov 1:7
For the LORD gives *w* ... Prov 2:6
is the man who finds *w* ... Prov 3:13
Get *w*! Get understanding! ... Prov 4:5
W is the principal ... Prov 4:7
is the beginning of *w* ... Prov 9:10
W rests in the heart ... Prov 14:33
to get *w* than gold ... Prov 16:16
W is in the sight of him ... Prov 17:24
w loves his own soul ... Prov 19:8
W is too lofty for a ... Prov 24:7
w is much grief ... Eccl 1:18
gives *w* and knowledge ... Eccl 2:26
W is better than ... Eccl 9:16
W is better than weapons ... Eccl 9:18
He gives *w* to the wise ... Dan 2:21
w is justified by her ... Matt 11:19
Jesus increased in *w* ... Luke 2:52
the *w* of God also ... Luke 11:49
riches both of the *w* ... Rom 11:33
the gospel, not with *w* ... 1 Cor 1:17
Greeks seek after *w* ... 1 Cor 1:22
For the *w* of this world ... 1 Cor 3:19
not with fleshly *w* ... 2 Cor 1:12
now the manifold *w* ... Eph 3:10
all the treasures of *w* ... Col 2:3
Walk in *w* toward those ... Col 4:5
If any of you lacks *w* ... James 1:5
power and riches and *w* ... Rev 5:12
and glory and *w* ... Rev 7:12

WISE
great nation is a *w* ... Deut 4:6
He catches the *w* ... Job 5:13
God is *w* in heart and ... Job 9:4
not find one *w* man ... Job 17:10
men are not always *w* ... Job 32:9
when will you be *w* ... Ps 94:8
w will observe these ... Ps 107:43
Do not be *w* in your ... Prov 3:7
The *w* in heart will ... Prov 10:8
W people store up ... Prov 10:14
he who wins souls is *w* ... Prov 11:30
w son heeds his father's ... Prov 13:1
The *w* woman builds her ... Prov 14:1
w man fears and departs ... Prov 14:16
The *w* in heart will be ... Prov 16:21
folly, lest he be *w* ... Prov 26:5
w men turn away wrath ... Prov 29:8
they are exceedingly *w* ... Prov 30:24
The words of the *w* ... Eccl 12:11
They are *w* to do evil ... Jer 4:22
is *w*? Let him understand ... Hos 14:9
Therefore be *w* as ... Matt 10:16
five of them were *w* ... Matt 25:2
barbarians, both to *w* ... Rom 1:14
to God, alone *w* ... Rom 16:27
Where is the *w* ... 1 Cor 1:20
sake, but you are *w* ... 1 Cor 4:10
not as fools but as *w* ... Eph 5:15
to God who alone is *w* ... 1 Tim 1:17
are able to make you *w* ... 2 Tim 3:15

WISE MAN
select a discerning and *w* ... Gen 41:33
w answer with empty ... Job 15:2
I shall not find one *w* ... Job 17:10
A *w* will hear and ... Prov 1:5
rebuke a *w*, and he will ... Prov 9:8
w fears and departs ... Prov 14:16
w will appease it ... Prov 16:14
w holds them back ... Prov 29:11
what more has the *w* ... Eccl 6:8
found in it a poor *w* ... Eccl 9:15
Let not the *w* glory ... Jer 9:23
w who built his house ... Matt 7:24
that there is not a *w* ... 1 Cor 6:5

WISE MEN
Egypt and all its *w* ... Gen 41:8
Pharaoh also called the *w* ... Ex 7:11
the king said to the *w* ... Esth 1:13
For he sees *w* die ... Ps 49:10
Where are your *w* ... Is 19:12
the wisdom of their *w* ... Is 29:14
all the *w* of the nations ... Jer 10:7
to destroy all the *w* ... Dan 2:12
all the *w* of Babylon ... Dan 2:48
Now all the king's *w* ... Dan 5:8
w from the East came ... Matt 2:1
secretly called the *w* ... Matt 2:7
he was deceived by the *w* ... Matt 2:16
prophets, *w*, and scribes ... Matt 23:34
I speak as to *w* ... 1 Cor 10:15

WISELY
I will behave *w* ... Ps 101:2
who heeds the word *w* ... Prov 16:20
you do not inquire *w* ... Eccl 7:10
saw that he answered *w* ... Mark 12:34

WISER
he was *w* than all men ... 1 Kin 4:31
w than the birds ... Job 35:11
w than my enemies ... Ps 119:98
of God is *w* than men ... 1 Cor 1:25

WISH
for me to do what I *w* ... Matt 20:15
w it were already ... Luke 12:49
where you do not *w* ... John 21:18
For I *w* that all men were ... 1 Cor 7:7
I could *w* you were cold or ... Rev 3:15

WISHED
Then he *w* death for ... Jon 4:8
him whatever they *w* ... Mark 9:13

WISHES
turns it wherever He *w* ... Prov 21:1
wind blows where it *w* ... John 3:8

WITCHCRAFT
is as the sin of *w* ... 1 Sam 15:23

WITH ALL YOUR HEART
if you seek Him *w* ... Deut 4:29
love the Lord your God *w* ... Deut 6:5
the Lord your God *w* ... Deut 10:12
and to serve Him *w* ... Josh 22:5
but serve the Lord *w* ... 1 Sam 12:20
Trust in the Lord *w* ... Prov 3:5
you search for Me *w* ... Jer 29:13
Lord, "Turn to me *w* ... Joel 2:12
Be glad and rejoice *w* ... Zeph 3:14
the Lord your God *w* ... Matt 22:37
the Lord your God *w* ... Mark 12:30
the Lord your God *w* ... Luke 10:27
"If you believe *w* ... Acts 8:37

WITH CHILD
you are *w*, and you shall ... Gen 16:11
daughters of Lot were *w* ... Gen 19:36
she is *w* by harlotry." So ... Gen 38:24
fight, and hurt a woman *w* ... Ex 21:22
David, and said, "I am *w* ... 2 Sam 11:5

womb of her who is *w* . . . . . . Eccl 11:5
As a woman *w* is in pain . . . . . Is 26:17
who have not travailed *w!* . . . . Is 54:1
a man is ever in labor *w* . . . . . Jer 30:6
women *w* ripped open . . . . . Hos 13:16
found *w* of the Holy Spirit . . Matt 1:18
a virgin shall be *w* . . . . Matt 1:23
betrothed wife, who was *w* . . Luke 2:5
being *w*, she cried out . . . . . Rev 12:2

WITH ONE ACCORD

words of the prophets *w* . . 1 Kin 22:13
the Lord, to serve Him *w* . . . Zeph 3:9
w began to make . . . . Luke 14:18
continued *w* in prayer . . . . Acts 1:14
with *w* in one place . . . . Acts 2:1
So continuing daily *w* . . . . . . Acts 2:46
their voice to God *w* . . . . Acts 4:24
w in Solomon's Porch . . . . . . Acts 5:12
multitudes *w* heeded . . . . Acts 8:6
being assembled *w* . . . . Acts 15:25

WITHDRAW

God will not *w* His . . . . Job 9:13
He does not *w* His eyes . . . . . Job 36:7
From such *w* yourself . . . . . . 1 Tim 6:5

WITHER

also shall not *w* . . . . Ps 1:3
w as the green . . . . Ps 37:2
leaves will not *w* . . . . Ezek 47:12
How did the fig tree *w* . . . . Matt 21:20

WITHERED

behold, seven heads, *w* . . . . Gen 41:23
stricken and *w* like grass . . . . Ps 102:4
surely joy has *w* away . . . . . . Joel 1:12
the plant that it *w* . . . . Jon 4:7
man who had a *w* hand . . . Matt 12:10
had no root they *w* away . . . Matt 13:6
the fig tree *w* away . . . . Matt 21:19
out as a branch and is *w* . . . John 15:6

WITHERS

The grass *w* . . . . Is 40:7
burning heat than it *w* . . . . James 1:11
The grass *w* . . . . 1 Pet 1:24

WITHHELD

and your sins have *w* . . . . Jer 5:25

WITHHOLD

w Your tender mercies . . . . Ps 40:11
good thing will He *w* . . . . Ps 84:11
Do not *w* good from . . . . Prov 3:27
your cloak, do not *w* . . . . . . Luke 6:29

WITHOUT

having no hope and *w* . . . . . . Eph 2:12
pray *w* ceasing . . . . 1 Thess 5:17
w controversy . . . . 1 Tim 3:16
w works is dead . . . . James 2:26

WITHSTAND

no one is able to *w* You . . . 2 Chr 20:6
no animal could *w* him . . . . . . Dan 8:4
was I that I could *w* . . . . Acts 11:17
you may be able to *w* . . . . Eph 6:13

WITHSTOOD

Persia *w* me twenty-one . . . Dan 10:13
I *w* him to his face . . . . Gal 2:11

WITNESS

See BEAR WITNESS; FALSE WITNESS
see, God is *w* between . . . . . Gen 31:50
Surely even now my *w* . . . . . Job 16:19
like the faithful *w* . . . . Ps 89:37
w does not lie . . . . Prov 14:5
have given him as a *w* . . . . Is 55:4
a true and faithful *w* . . . . Jer 42:5
I will be a swift *w* . . . . Mal 3:5
all the world as a *w* . . . . Matt 24:14
This man came for a *w* . . . . . John 1:7
do not receive Our *w* . . . . . . John 3:11
"If I bear *w* of . . . . John 5:31
is another who bears *w* . . . . John 5:32
But I have a greater *w* . . . . . John 5:36
who was bearing *w* . . . . Acts 14:3
For you will be His *w* . . . . . Acts 22:15
For God is my *w* . . . . Phil 1:8
are three who bear *w* . . . . . 1 John 5:7
If we receive the *w* . . . . 1 John 5:9
who bore *w* to the word . . . . . Rev 1:2
Christ, the faithful *w* . . . . Rev 1:5
beheaded for their *w* . . . . Rev 20:4

WITNESSED

is revealed, being *w* . . . . Rom 3:21
w the good confession . . . . . 1 Tim 6:13

WITNESSES

of two or three *w* . . . . Deut 17:6
for Myself faithful *w* . . . . Is 8:2
"You are My *w* . . . . Is 43:10
the presence of many *w* . . . 1 Tim 6:12
the Holy Spirit also *w* . . . . . Heb 10:15
so great a cloud of *w* . . . . Heb 12:1
give power to my two *w* . . . . . Rev 11:3

WIVES

two *w*, one loved . . . . Deut 21:15
he had seven hundred *w* . . . . 1 Kin 11:3
daughters as *w* for . . . . Ezra 9:2
you to divorce your *w* . . . . . . Matt 19:8
W, submit to your own . . . . . Eph 5:22
Husbands, love your *w* . . . . . Eph 5:25
Husbands, love your *w* . . . . . . Col 3:19
w must be reverent . . . . 1 Tim 3:11
by the conduct of their *w* . . . 1 Pet 3:1

WIZARDS

who are mediums and *w* . . . . . . Is 8:19

WOE

W is me, that I dwell in . . . . . Ps 120:5
Who has *w*? . . . . Prov 23:29
W to the wicked . . . . Is 3:11
W to those who call evil . . . . . . Is 5:20
W to you, O Jerusalem . . . . . Jer 13:27
"*W* to the bloody city . . . . . . Ezek 24:9
'*W* to him who increases . . . . . . Hab 2:6
"*W* to you, Chorazin . . . . . . Matt 11:21
w to that man by whom . . . . Matt 18:7
But *w* to you, scribes . . . . . . Matt 23:13
But *w* to those who are . . Mark 13:17
W to you who are full . . . . . . Luke 6:25
w is me if I do not . . . . 1 Cor 9:16
W, *w*, *w* to the inhabitants . . Rev 8:13
One *w* is past . . . . Rev 9:12

WOLF

The *w* and the lamb . . . . Is 65:25
the sheep, sees the *w* . . . . . John 10:12

WOLVES

they are ravenous *w* . . . . Matt 7:15
out as lambs among *w* . . . . . Luke 10:3
savage *w* will come in . . . . Acts 20:29

WOMAN

she shall be called *W* . . . . Gen 2:23
every *w* shall ask of her . . . . . Ex 3:22
A widow or a divorced *w* . . Lev 21:14
stand the *w* before the . . . . . Num 5:18
w shall not wear anything . . Deut 22:5
the *w* took the two men . . . . . Josh 2:4
that you are a virtuous *w* . . Ruth 3:11
keep you from the evil *w* . . . Prov 6:24
adultery with a *w* lacks . . . . Prov 6:32
A foolish *w* is clamorous . . . Prov 9:13
A gracious *w* retains . . . . . . Prov 11:16
w builds her house . . . . Prov 14:1
w who fears the LORD . . . . . Prov 31:30
Can a *w* forget her nursing . . Is 49:15
w shall encompass a . . . . Jer 31:22
whoever looks at a *w* . . . . . . Matt 5:28
a *w* of Canaan came . . . . . . Matt 15:22
"O *w*, great is your faith . . Matt 15:28
if a *w* divorces . . . . Mark 10:12
w came having an . . . . Mark 14:3
"Do you see this *w* . . . . Luke 7:44
Then the *w* of Samaria . . . . . . John 4:9
brought to Him a *w* . . . . John 8:3
"*W*, behold your . . . . John 19:26
w was full of good . . . . Acts 9:36
Jewish *w* who believed . . . . . Acts 16:1
natural use of the *w* . . . . Rom 1:27
a man not to touch a *w* . . . . . 1 Cor 7:1
the head of *w* is man . . . . . . 1 Cor 11:3
For if a *w* is not covered . . . 1 Cor 11:6
w is the glory of man . . . . . 1 Cor 11:7
but *w* from man . . . . 1 Cor 11:8
but *w* for the man . . . . 1 Cor 11:9
this reason the *w* ought . . 1 Cor 11:10
His Son, born of a *w* . . . . Gal 4:4
Let a *w* learn in . . . . 1 Tim 2:11
I do not permit a *w* . . . . 1 Tim 2:12
w being deceived . . . . 1 Tim 2:14
you allow that *w* Jezebel . . . . Rev 2:20
w clothed with the sun . . . . . . Rev 12:1
the earth helped the *w* . . . . . Rev 12:16
And I saw a *w* sitting on a . . Rev 17:3
the *w* whom you saw is . . . . Rev 17:18

WOMB

nations are in your *w* . . . . . Gen 25:23
LORD had closed her *w* . . . 1 Sam 1:5
took Me out of the *w* . . . . Ps 22:9
formed you from the *w* . . . . Is 44:2
called Me from the *w* . . . . Is 49:1
in the *w* I knew you . . . . Jer 1:5
is the fruit of your *w* . . . . . . Luke 1:42
"Blessed is the *w* . . . . Luke 11:27

WOMEN

the Hebrew *w* are not . . . . Ex 1:19
All the *w* who were gifted . . . Ex 35:25
ten *w* shall bake your . . . . . . Lev 26:26
blessed is she among *w* . . . . Judg 5:24
loved many foreign *w* . . . . . 1 Kin 11:1
pagan *w* caused . . . . Neh 13:26
among Your honorable *w* . . . . Ps 45:9
O fairest among *w* . . . . Song 1:8
w rule over them . . . . Is 3:12
new wine the young *w* . . . . . Zech 9:17
thousand men, besides *w* . . Matt 14:21
thousand men, besides *w* . . Matt 15:38
w will be grinding . . . . Matt 24:41
w who followed Jesus . . . . Matt 27:55
are you among *w* . . . . Luke 1:28
it just as the *w* had said . . Luke 24:24
devout and prominent *w* . . . Acts 13:50
not a few of the leading *w* . . Acts 17:4
w keep silent in the . . . . . . 1 Cor 14:34
the *w* adorn themselves . . . . 1 Tim 2:9
which is proper for *w* . . . . . 1 Tim 2:10
admonish the young *w* . . . . . . Titus 2:4
times, the holy *w* . . . . 1 Pet 3:5
not defiled with *w* . . . . Rev 14:4

WONDER

gives you a sign or a *w* . . . . Deut 13:1
I have become as a *w* . . . . Ps 71:7
marvelous work and a *w* . . . . Is 29:14
they were filled with *w* . . . . . Acts 3:10

WONDERFUL

name, seeing it is *w* . . . . Judg 13:18
Your love to me was *w* . . . 2 Sam 1:26
things too *w* for me . . . . Job 42:3
Your *w* works Which You . . . . Ps 40:5
He has made His *w* works . . . Ps 111:4
Your testimonies are *w* . . . Ps 119:129
things which are too *w* . . . Prov 30:18
name will be called *W* . . . . Is 9:6
of hosts, who is *w* . . . . Is 28:29
all His *w* works . . . . Jer 21:2
and scribes saw the *w* . . . . Matt 21:15
our own tongues the *w* . . . . . Acts 2:11

WONDERFULLY

fearfully and *w* made . . . . . . Ps 139:14

WONDERS

See SIGNS AND WONDERS
w which I will do . . . . Ex 3:20
LORD will do *w* among you . . Josh 3:5
are the God who does *w* . . . . Ps 77:14
Shall Your *w* be known . . . . . Ps 88:12
heavens will praise Your *w* . . . Ps 89:5
who alone does great *w* . . . . . Ps 136:4

Egypt with signs and *w* ... Jer 32:21
and how mighty His *w* ... Dan 4:3
He works signs and *w* ... Dan 6:27
"And I will show *w* ... Joel 2:30
and done many *w* ... Matt 7:22
w were done among ... Acts 5:12
w God had worked ... Acts 15:12
signs, and lying *w* ... 2 Thess 2:9
both with signs and *w* ... Heb 2:4

WONDROUS
the *w* works of God ... Job 37:14
and tell of all Your *w* ... Ps 26:7
I declare Your *w* works ... Ps 71:17
w works declare that ... Ps 75:1
w works in the land of ... Ps 106:22
for they are a *w* ... Zech 3:8

WONDROUSLY
God, who has dealt *w* ... Joel 2:26

WOOD
precious stones, *w* ... 1 Cor 3:12

WOODCUTTERS
but let them be *w* ... Josh 9:21

WOODEN IMAGE
any tree, as a *w* ... Deut 16:21
cut down the *w* ... Judg 6:25
And Ahab made a *w* ... 1 Kin 16:33
a *w* and worshiped ... 2 Kin 17:16
cut down the *w* ... 2 Kin 18:4
and burned the *w* ... 2 Kin 23:15

WOODEN IMAGES
cut down their *w* ... Ex 34:13
burn their *w* with fire ... Deut 12:3
they have made their *w* ... 1 Kin 14:15
w on every high hill ... 2 Kin 17:10
you have removed the *w* ... 2 Chr 19:3
served *w* and idols ... 2 Chr 24:18
the altars and the *w* ... 2 Chr 34:7
w nor the incense altars ... Is 17:8
w and incense altars ... Is 27:9
w by the green trees ... Jer 17:2
I will pluck your *w* ... Mic 5:14

WOOL
She seeks *w* and flax ... Prov 31:13
they shall be as *w* ... Is 1:18
head was like pure *w* ... Dan 7:9
hair were white like *w* ... Rev 1:14

WORD
See ACCORDING TO THE WORD OF THE LORD
w that proceeds ... Deut 8:3
w is very near you ... Deut 30:14
w of the LORD is proven ... Ps 18:30
For the *w* of the LORD is ... Ps 33:4
w I have hidden ... Ps 119:11
w has given me life ... Ps 119:50
w is a lamp to my feet ... Ps 119:105
w makes it glad ... Prov 12:25
a harsh *w* stirs up anger ... Prov 15:1
w spoken in due season ... Prov 15:23
He who heeds the *w* ... Prov 16:20
w fitly spoken is ... Prov 25:11
The LORD sent a *w* ... Is 9:8
the *w* of our God ... Is 40:8
w has gone out of My ... Is 45:23
w be that goes forth ... Is 55:11
But His *w* was in my ... Jer 20:9
w will be his oracle ... Jer 23:36
w which I speak will ... Ezek 12:28
But only speak a *w* ... Matt 8:8
for every idle *w* ... Matt 12:36
mighty in deed and *w* ... Luke 24:19
beginning was the *W* ... John 1:1
W became flesh and ... John 1:14
if anyone keeps My *w* ... John 8:51
w which you hear is ... John 14:24
Your *w* is truth ... John 17:17
and glorified the *w* ... Acts 13:48
to one is given the *w* ... 1 Cor 12:8
of water by the *w* ... Eph 5:26
holding fast the *w* ... Phil 2:16
Let the *w* of Christ ... Col 3:16
come to you in *w* only ... 1 Thess 1:5
in every good *w* ... 2 Thess 2:17
by the *w* of His power ... Heb 1:3
w which they heard did ... Heb 4:2
the implanted *w* ... James 1:21
does not stumble in *w* ... James 3:2
that by the *w* of God ... 2 Pet 3:5
whoever keeps His *w* ... 1 John 2:5
let us not love in *w* ... 1 John 3:18
the Father, the *W* ... 1 John 5:7

WORD OF GOD
announce to you the *w* ... 1 Sam 9:27
w came to Nathan ... 1 Chr 17:3
Every *w* is pure ... Prov 30:5
the *w* of no effect ... Mark 7:13
the *w* came to John ... Luke 3:2
alone, but by every *w* ... Luke 4:4
about Him to hear the *w* ... Luke 5:1
The seed is the *w* ... Luke 8:11
who hear the *w* and do it ... Luke 8:21
spoke the *w* with boldness ... Acts 4:31
leave the *w* and serve ... Acts 6:2
then the *w* spread ... Acts 6:7
had also received the *w* ... Acts 11:1
necessary that the *w* ... Acts 13:46
that the *w* has taken no ... Rom 9:6
and hearing by the *w* ... Rom 10:17
w come originally ... 1 Cor 14:36
peddling the *w* ... 2 Cor 2:17
the *w* deceitfully ... 2 Cor 4:2
Spirit, which is the *w* ... Eph 6:17
sanctified by the *w* ... 1 Tim 4:5
w is not chained ... 2 Tim 2:9
w is living and powerful ... Heb 4:12
were framed by the *w* ... Heb 11:3
through the *w* ... 1 Pet 1:23
w abides in you ... 1 John 2:14
who bore witness to the *w* ... Rev 1:2
had been slain for the *w* ... Rev 6:9
His name is called The *W* ... Rev 19:13
to Jesus and for the *w* ... Rev 20:4

WORD OF TRUTH
And take not the *w* ... Ps 119:43
by the *w*, by the power ... 2 Cor 6:7
after you heard the *w* ... Eph 1:13
rightly dividing the *w* ... 2 Tim 2:15
us forth by the *w* ... James 1:18

WORDS
I waited for your *w* ... Job 32:11
his *w* are without wisdom ... Job 34:35
Give ear to my *w* ... Ps 5:1
Let the *w* of my mouth ... Ps 19:14
How sweet are Your *w* ... Ps 119:103
I will make my *w* known ... Prov 1:23
pay attention to the *w* ... Prov 7:24
hear the *w* of the wise ... Prov 22:17
The *w* of the wise are ... Eccl 12:11
And I have put My *w* ... Is 51:16
Take *w* with you ... Hos 14:2
Do not My *w* do good to ... Mic 2:7
pass away, but My *w* ... Matt 24:35
at the gracious *w* ... Luke 4:22
w that I speak to you ... John 6:63
You have the *w* of ... John 6:68
My *w* abide in you, you ... John 15:7
And remember the *w* ... Acts 20:35
not with wisdom of *w* ... 1 Cor 1:17
those who hear the *w* ... Rev 1:3
is he who keeps the *w* ... Rev 22:7
keep the *w* of this book ... Rev 22:9

WORK
day God ended His *w* ... Gen 2:2
Moses finished the *w* ... Ex 40:33
people had a mind to *w* ... Neh 4:6
You shall desire the *w* ... Job 14:15
for they are all the *w* ... Job 34:19
the *w* of Your fingers ... Ps 8:3
I hate the *w* of those ... Ps 101:3
the heavens are the *w* ... Ps 102:25
Man goes out to his *w* ... Ps 104:23
w is honorable and ... Ps 111:3
man does deceptive *w* ... Prov 11:18
then I saw all the *w* ... Eccl 8:17
for there is no *w* ... Eccl 9:10
God will bring every *w* ... Eccl 12:14
that He may do His *w* ... Is 28:21
and all we are the *w* ... Is 64:8
him nothing for his *w* ... Jer 22:13
and mighty in *w* ... Jer 32:19
For I will *w* a *w* ... Hab 1:5
and said, 'Son, go, *w* ... Matt 21:28
could do no mighty *w* ... Mark 6:5
we do, that we may *w* ... John 6:28
"This is the *w* of God ... John 6:29
I must *w* the works ... John 9:4
w which You have given ... John 17:4
know that all things *w* ... Rom 8:28
He will finish the *w* ... Rom 9:28
w is no longer *w* ... Rom 11:6
Do not destroy the *w* ... Rom 14:20
w will become manifest ... 1 Cor 3:13
Are you not my *w* ... 1 Cor 9:1
abounding in the *w* ... 1 Cor 15:58
without ceasing your *w* ... 1 Thess 1:3
good word and *w* ... 2 Thess 2:17
If anyone will not *w* ... 2 Thess 3:10
but a doer of the *w* ... James 1:25

WORKED
with one hand they *w* ... Neh 4:17
and wonders God had *w* ... Acts 15:12
which He *w* in Christ ... Eph 1:20

WORKER
w is worthy of his ... Matt 10:10
Timothy, my fellow *w* ... Rom 16:21
w who does not need ... 2 Tim 2:15

WORKERS
You hate all *w* of ... Ps 5:5
we are God's fellow *w* ... 1 Cor 3:9
dogs, beware of evil *w* ... Phil 3:2

WORKERS OF INIQUITY
in company with the *w* ... Job 34:8
You hate all *w* ... Ps 5:5
Depart from me, all you *w* ... Ps 6:8
nor be envious of the *w* ... Ps 37:1
Deliver me from the *w* ... Ps 59:2
when all the *w* flourish ... Ps 92:7
from the traps of the *w* ... Ps 141:9
will come to the *w* ... Prov 10:29
from Me, all you *w* ... Luke 13:27

WORKING
everywhere, the Lord *w* ... Mark 16:20
My Father has been *w* ... John 5:17
according to the *w* ... Eph 1:19
through faith in the *w* ... Col 2:12
manner, not *w* at all ... 2 Thess 3:11

WORKMANSHIP
For we are His *w* ... Eph 2:10

WORKS
See GOOD WORKS
the wondrous *w* of God ... Job 37:14
are Your wonderful *w* ... Ps 40:5
Come and see the *w* ... Ps 66:5
how great are Your *w* ... Ps 92:5
manifold are Your *w* ... Ps 104:24
The *w* of the LORD are ... Ps 111:2
w shall praise You ... Ps 145:10
and let her own *w* ... Prov 31:31
"For I know their *w* ... Is 66:18
of whose *w* are truth ... Dan 4:37
show Him greater *w* ... John 5:20
w that I do in My ... John 10:25
w that I do he will do ... John 14:12
w righteousness ... Acts 10:35
might stand, not of *w* ... Rom 9:11
let us cast off the *w* ... Rom 13:12
is the same God who *w* ... 1 Cor 12:6
Now the *w* of the flesh ... Gal 5:19

the spirit who now *w* . . . . Eph 2:2
not of *w*, lest anyone . . . . Eph 2:9
with the unfruitful *w* . . . . Eph 5:11
for it is God who *w* . . . . Phil 2:13
w they deny Him . . . . Titus 1:16
zealous for good *w* . . . . Titus 2:14
repentance from dead *w* . . . . . Heb 6:1
but does not have *w* . . . . James 2:14
also justified by *w* . . . . James 2:25
He might destroy the *w* . . . . 1 John 3:8
"I know your *w* . . . . Rev 2:2
their *w* follow them . . . . Rev 14:13
according to their *w* . . . . Rev 20:12

WORKS OF THE LAW
as it were, by the *w* . . . . Rom 9:32
not justified by the *w* . . . . Gal 2:16
the Spirit by the *w* . . . . Gal 3:2
does He do it by the *w* . . . . Gal 3:5
w are under the curse . . . . Gal 3:10

WORLD
See IN THE WORLD; OF THE WORLD; OF THIS WORLD
He shall judge the *w* . . . . Ps 9:8
For the *w* is Mine . . . . Ps 50:12
w is established . . . . Ps 93:1
The field is the *w* . . . . Matt 13:38
w are more shrewd . . . . Luke 16:8
He was in the *w* . . . . John 1:10
For God so loved the *w* . . . . . . John 3:16
His Son into the *w* . . . . John 3:17
the Savior of the *w* . . . . John 4:42
w cannot hate you . . . . John 7:7
You are of this *w* . . . . John 8:23
Look, the *w* has gone . . . . John 12:19
w will see Me no more . . . . . . John 14:19
"If the *w* hates you . . . . John 15:18
If you were of the *w* . . . . John 15:19
I have overcome the *w* . . . . . John 16:33
do not pray for the *w* . . . . John 17:9
w has not known You . . . . John 17:25
w may become guilty . . . . Rom 3:19
be conformed to this *w* . . . . Rom 12:2
things of the *w* . . . . 1 Cor 1:27
w is foolishness . . . . 1 Cor 3:19
w has been crucified . . . . Gal 6:14
without God in the *w* . . . . Eph 2:12
loved this present *w* . . . . 2 Tim 4:10
He has not put the *w* . . . . Heb 2:5
unspotted from the *w* . . . . . . James 1:27
w is enmity with God . . . . James 4:4
Do not love the *w* . . . . 1 John 2:15
all that is in the *w* . . . . 1 John 2:16
w is passing away . . . . 1 John 2:17
w does not know us . . . . 1 John 3:1
They are of the *w* . . . . 1 John 4:5
so are we in this *w* . . . . 1 John 4:17
And all the *w* marveled . . . . Rev 13:3

WORLDS
also He made the *w* . . . . Heb 1:2

WORM
w should feed sweetly . . . . Job 24:20
But I am a *w* . . . . Ps 22:6
"Fear not, you *w* . . . . Is 41:14
their *w* does not die . . . . Is 66:24
w does not die and the . . . . . Mark 9:44

WORMS
flesh is caked with *w* . . . . Job 7:5
you, and *w* cover you . . . . Is 14:11
And he was eaten by *w* . . . . Acts 12:23

WORMWOOD
end she is bitter as *w* . . . . Prov 5:4
who turn justice to *w* . . . . Amos 5:7
of the star is *W* . . . . Rev 8:11

WORRIED
Martha, you are *w* . . . . Luke 10:41

WORRY
to you, do not *w* . . . . Matt 6:25
Therefore do not *w* . . . . Matt 6:31

WORRYING
by *w* can add one cubit . . . . . . Matt 6:27

WORSE
w than their fathers . . . . Jer 7:26

WORSHIP
I will go yonder and *w* . . . . . Gen 22:5
shall not *w* the LORD . . . . . . Deut 12:31
w the LORD in the . . . . 1 Chr 16:29
He is your Lord, *w* . . . . Ps 45:11
Oh come, let us *w* . . . . Ps 95:6
and have come to *w* Him . . . . . Matt 2:2
will fall down and *w* . . . . Matt 4:9
"You shall *w* the LORD . . . . . . Matt 4:10
And in vain they *w* . . . . Matt 15:9
w what you do not know . . . . . John 4:22
true worshipers will *w* . . . . . . John 4:23
the One whom you *w* . . . . Acts 17:23
w the God of my . . . . Acts 24:14
false humility and *w* . . . . Col 2:18
the angels of God *w* . . . . Heb 1:6
make them come and *w* . . . . Rev 3:9
w Him who lives . . . . Rev 4:10
w Him who made . . . . Rev 14:7

WORSHIPED
w the LORD, and blessed . . . Gen 24:48
w it and sacrificed to it . . . . Ex 32:8
w the LORD their God . . . . Neh 9:3
fell to the ground and *w* . . . . . . Job 1:20
w the works of their own . . . . Jer 1:16
leper came and *w* Him . . . . Matt 8:2
she came and *w* Him . . . . Matt 15:25
they saw Him, they *w* . . . . Matt 28:17
w Him, and returned . . . . Luke 24:52
Our fathers *w* . . . . John 4:20
down at his feet and *w* . . . . Acts 10:25
of God for the lie, and *w* . . . . Rom 1:25
w Him who lives . . . . Rev 5:14
on their faces and *w* . . . . Rev 11:16
w God who sat on the . . . . Rev 19:4

WORSHIPER
if anyone is a *w* . . . . John 9:31

WORSHIPERS
destroying the *w* of Baal . . 2 Kin 10:19
the true *w* will worship . . . . . . John 4:23
with the Gentile *w* . . . . Acts 17:17

WORTH
and make my speech *w* . . . . . . Job 24:25
of the wicked is *w* . . . . Prov 10:20
her *w* is far above rubies . . Prov 31:10

WORTHLESS
looking at *w* things . . . . Ps 119:37
A *w* person, a wicked . . . . Prov 6:12
Indeed they are all *w* . . . . Is 41:29
wooden idol is a *w* doctrine . . Jer 10:8

WORTHLESSNESS
long will you love *w* . . . . Ps 4:2

WORTHY
I am not *w* of the . . . . Gen 32:10
LORD, who is *w* to be . . . . . 2 Sam 22:4
who is *w* to be praised . . . . Ps 18:3
sandals I am not *w* . . . . Matt 3:11
inquire who in it is *w* . . . . . . Matt 10:11
more than Me is not *w* . . . . . Matt 10:37
invited were not *w* . . . . Matt 22:8
I am not *w* to stoop down . . Mark 1:7
and I am no longer *w* . . . . . . Luke 15:19
strap I am not *w* to loose . . John 1:27
feet I am not *w* to loose . . . Acts 13:25
present time are not *w* . . . . Rom 8:18
apostles, who am not *w* . . . . 1 Cor 15:9
to walk *w* of the calling . . . . . . Eph 4:1
w of the gospel of Christ . . . . Phil 1:27
may walk *w* of the Lord . . . . . . Col 1:10
w of God who calls . . . . 1 Thess 2:12
w of the kingdom of . . . . . . 2 Thess 1:5
count you *w* of this . . . . 2 Thess 1:11
"The laborer is *w* . . . . 1 Tim 5:18
the world was not *w* . . . . Heb 11:38
in a manner *w* of God . . . . 3 John 6
white, for they are *w* . . . . Rev 3:4
"You are *w*, O Lord . . . . Rev 4:11
Who is *w* to open the scroll . . Rev 5:2
"*W* is the Lamb who . . . . Rev 5:12

WOUND
I *w* and I heal . . . . Deut 32:39
My *w* is incurable . . . . Job 34:6
But God will *w* the . . . . Ps 68:21
and my *w* incurable . . . . Jer 15:18
and *w* their weak . . . . 1 Cor 8:12
and his deadly *w* . . . . Rev 13:3

WOUNDED
and my heart is *w* . . . . Ps 109:22
They struck me, they *w* . . . . . . Song 5:7
and *w* the serpent . . . . Is 51:9
But He was *w* for our . . . . Is 53:5
there remained only *w* . . . . Jer 37:10
with which I was *w* . . . . Zech 13:6
w him, and departed . . . . Luke 10:30
house naked and *w* . . . . Acts 19:16
to the beast who was *w* . . . . . . Rev 13:14

WOUNDING
killed a man for *w* . . . . Gen 4:23

WOUNDS
He *w*, but His hands make . . . . Job 5:18
and binds up their *w* . . . . Ps 147:3
Faithful are the *w* . . . . Prov 27:6
For her *w* are incurable . . . . Mic 1:9
and bandaged his *w* . . . . Luke 10:34

WOVEN
Her clothing is *w* with gold . . Ps 45:13
w from the top in one . . . . . . John 19:23

WRANGLINGS
useless *w* of men of . . . . 1 Tim 6:5

WRAPPED
weeds were *w* around my . . . . . . Jon 2:5
he *w* it in a clean linen . . . . . Matt 27:59
w Him in swaddling cloths . . Luke 2:7
his face was *w* with a . . . . John 11:44

WRATH
w has gone out from . . . . . . Num 16:46
provoked the LORD to *w* . . . . Deut 9:22
Had I not feared the *w* . . . . Deut 32:27
w kills a foolish . . . . Job 5:2
speak to them in His *w* . . . . Ps 2:5
living and burning *w* . . . . Ps 58:9
Surely the *w* of man . . . . Ps 76:10
Your fierce *w* has gone . . . . Ps 88:16
Will Your *w* burn like . . . . Ps 89:46
w we are terrified . . . . Ps 90:7
So I swore in My *w* . . . . Ps 95:11
in the day of His *w* . . . . Ps 110:5
death is the king's *w* . . . . Prov 16:14
The king's *w* is like . . . . Prov 19:12
of great *w* will suffer . . . . Prov 19:19
w is heavier than . . . . Prov 27:3
W is cruel and anger a . . . . . . Prov 27:4
w I will give him . . . . Is 10:6
With a little *w* . . . . Is 54:8
in My *w* I struck you . . . . Is 60:10
I will pour out my *w* . . . . Hos 5:10
w remember mercy . . . . Hab 3:2
you to flee from the *w* . . . . Matt 3:7
see life, but the *w* . . . . John 3:36
For the *w* of God is . . . . Rom 1:18
up for yourself *w* . . . . Rom 2:5
the law brings about *w* . . . . Rom 4:15
wanting to show His *w* . . . . Rom 9:22
rather give place to *w* . . . . Rom 12:19
not only because of *w* . . . . Rom 13:5
outbursts of *w* . . . . 2 Cor 12:20
nature children of *w* . . . . Eph 2:3
sun go down on your *w* . . . . Eph 4:26
Let all bitterness, *w* . . . . Eph 4:31
delivers us from the *w* . . . . . 1 Thess 1:10
w has come upon them . . . 1 Thess 2:16
holy hands, without *w* . . . . 1 Tim 2:8
So I swore in My *w* . . . . Heb 3:11
not fearing the *w* . . . . Heb 11:27

for the *w* of man does .... James 1:20
throne and from the *w* ...... Rev 6:16
to you, having great *w* ..... Rev 12:12
of the wine of the *w* .... Rev 14:8
winepress of the *w* .... Rev 14:19
for in them the *w* .... Rev 15:1
fierceness of His *w* .... Rev 16:19

WRATH OF GOD
w abides on him .... John 3:36
w is revealed from .... Rom 1:18
w comes upon the sons of .... Eph 5:6
of the wine of the *w* .... Rev 14:10
great winepress of the *w* ... Rev 14:19
the *w* is complete .... Rev 15:1
the bowls of the *w* .... Rev 16:1

WRATH OF THE LORD
w was aroused against .... Num 11:33
for great is the *w* .... 2 Kin 22:13
w turned from him .... 2 Chr 12:12
fierce *w* is upon you ..... 2 Chr 28:11
w fell upon Judah .... 2 Chr 29:8
w did not come upon ..... 2 Chr 32:26
w arose against His ...... 2 Chr 36:16
w was kindled against ..... Ps 106:40
w of hosts the land .... Is 9:19
w of hosts and in the day .... Is 13:13
in the day of the *w* .... Ezek 7:19

WRATHFUL
w man stirs up strife ...... Prov 15:18

WRESTLE
For we do not *w* .... Eph 6:12

WRESTLED
I have *w* with my sister ..... Gen 30:8
a Man *w* with him until .... Gen 32:24

WRETCHED
w man that I am .... Rom 7:24
know that you are *w* .... Rev 3:17

WRETCHEDNESS
do not let me see my *w* ... Num 11:15

WRINGING
w the nose produces ...... Prov 30:33

WRINKLE
not having spot or *w* .... Eph 5:27

WRITE
I will *w* on these tablets ...... Ex 34:1
"*W* these words .... Ex 34:27
w bitter things .... Job 13:26
w them on the tablet of ..... Prov 3:3
w them on the tablet .... Prov 7:3
'*W* this man down as .... Jer 22:30
and *w* it on their hearts ..... Jer 31:33
w them on their hearts ..... Heb 8:10
their minds I will *w* .... Heb 10:16
w no new commandment .. 1 John 2:7
a new commandment I *w* .. 1 John 2:8
I had many things to *w* .... 3 John 13
W the things which you ..... Rev 1:19
w on him My new name .... Rev 3:12

WRITER
is the pen of a ready *w* .... Ps 45:1

WRITING
the *w* was the *w* .... Ex 32:16
read the *w* to the king ...... Dan 5:17
And the *w* was: Jesus ...... John 19:19

WRITINGS
do not believe his *w* .... John 5:47

WRITTEN
See AS IT IS WRITTEN; IT IS WRITTEN
which I have *w* .... Ex 24:12
tablets of stone, *w* .... Ex 31:18
tablets were *w* on both ...... Ex 32:15
book which You have *w* ... Ex 32:32
w with the finger of God ... Deut 9:10
law that are *w* in this .... Deut 28:58
w in this Book of the ..... Deut 29:21
as it is *w* in the Book of .... Josh 8:31
w in the Law of the ...... 1 Chr 16:40
scroll of the Book it is *w* ..... Ps 40:7
be *w* with the righteous ..... Ps 69:28
book they all were *w* .... Ps 139:16
Have I not *w* to you .... Prov 22:20
is found *w* in the book ..... Dan 12:1
thus it is *w* by the prophet ... Matt 2:5
your names are *w* .... Luke 10:20
are *w* may be fulfilled ..... Luke 21:22
"What I have *w* .... John 19:22
as it is *w*, "The just shall ... Rom 1:17
law *w* in their hearts .... Rom 2:15
it is *w*, "Vengeance is ..... Rom 12:19
our epistle *w* in our hearts .. 2 Cor 3:2
ministered by us, *w* .... 2 Cor 3:3
for it is *w*, "Cursed is .... Gal 3:10
because it is *w*, "Be holy ... 1 Pet 1:16
the stone a new name *w* ..... Rev 2:17
names have not been *w* ..... Rev 13:8
name *w* on their foreheads .. Rev 14:1
forehead a name was *w* ...... Rev 17:5
the plagues that are *w* ..... Rev 22:18

WRONG
sinned, we have done *w* ... 2 Chr 6:37
sin nor charge God with *w* .. Job 1:22
I cry out concerning *w* .... Job 19:7
not charge them with *w* .... Job 24:12
no one to do them *w* .... Ps 105:14
Do no *w* and do no .... Jer 22:3
I am doing you no *w* ...... Matt 20:13
has done nothing *w* .... Luke 23:41
of them suffer *w* .... Acts 7:24
Jews I have done no *w* .... Acts 25:10
Forgive me this *w* .... 2 Cor 12:13
But he who does *w* .... Col 3:25

WRONGDOING
say if they found any *w* ... Acts 24:20

WRONGED
give it to the one he has *w* .. Num 5:7
have seen how I am *w* .... Lam 3:59
then that God has *w* .... Job 19:6
We have *w* no one .... 2 Cor 7:2
But if he has *w* .... Philem 18

WRONGFULLY
hate me *w* have multiplied .. Ps 38:19
endures grief, suffering *w* .. 1 Pet 2:19

WRONGS
me *w* his own soul .... Prov 8:36

WROTE
w on the tablets the words .. Ex 34:28
of the hand that *w* .... Dan 5:5
stooped down and *w* .... John 8:6

WROUGHT
And skillfully *w* .... Ps 139:15

YEAR
first month of the *y* .... Ex 12:2
That fiftieth *y* shall be a .... Lev 25:11
In this *Y* of Jubilee, each .. Lev 25:13
we eat in the seventh *y* .... Lev 25:20
In the *Y* of Jubilee .... Lev 27:24
crown the *y* with Your ...... Ps 65:11
the acceptable *y* .... Is 61:2
be his until the *y* .... Ezek 46:17
to Jerusalem every *y* ...... Luke 2:41
went alone once a *y* .... Heb 9:7
of sins every *y* .... Heb 10:3

YEARS
and for days and *y* .... Gen 1:14
Are Your *y* like the .... Job 10:5
y should teach .... Job 32:7
I will remember the *y* .... Ps 77:10
For a thousand *y* .... Ps 90:4
lives are seventy *y* .... Ps 90:10
Your *y* are throughout ..... Ps 102:24
y will have no end .... Ps 102:27
when He was twelve *y* ..... Luke 2:42
are not yet fifty *y* .... John 8:57
y will not fail .... Heb 1:12
for a thousand *y* .... Rev 20:2
with Him a thousand *y* ...... Rev 20:6

YES
let your '*Y*' be '*Y*,' .... Matt 5:37
No, but in Him was *Y* ..... 2 Cor 1:19

YESTERDAY
For we were born *y* .... Job 8:9
Are like *y* when it is past ..... Ps 90:4
Jesus Christ is the same *y* .. Heb 13:8

YIELD
the land will *y* its fruit ...... Lev 25:19
y yourselves to the LORD ... 2 Chr 30:8
That they may *y* a fruitful .. Ps 107:37
shall *y* her increase .... Ezek 34:27
But do not *y* to them ...... Acts 23:21
gentle, willing to *y*, full ... James 3:17

YIELDED
y to intense craving .... Num 11:4
y their bodies, that they ..... Dan 3:28
good ground and *y* a crop .. Matt 13:8
voice, *y* up His spirit ...... Matt 27:50
rich man *y* plentifully .... Luke 12:16

YIELDS
the herb that *y* seed .... Gen 1:11
of the righteous *y* fruit .... Prov 12:12
it *y* the peaceable .... Heb 12:11

YOKE
you shall break his *y* ...... Gen 27:40
and He will put a *y* .... Deut 28:48
Your father made our *y* .... 1 Kin 12:4
You have broken the *y* .... Is 9:4
a man to bear the *y* .... Lam 3:27
Take My *y* upon you ...... Matt 11:29
as are under the *y* .... 1 Tim 6:1

YOKED
Do not be unequally *y* ..... 2 Cor 6:14

YOU ARE THE CHRIST
answered and said, "*Y* .... Matt 16:16
God: Tell us if *Y* .... Matt 26:63
and said to Him, "*Y* .... Mark 8:29
crying out and saying, "*Y* .. Luke 4:41
If *Y*, tell us .... Luke 22:67
"If *Y*, save Yourself ...... Luke 23:39
believe and know that *Y* ... John 6:69
If *Y*, tell us plainly .... John 10:24
Lord I believe that *Y* ..... John 11:27

YOUNG
His flesh shall be *y* .... Job 33:25
I have been *y* .... Ps 37:25
she may lay her *y* .... Ps 84:3
How can a *y* man cleanse .... Ps 119:9
The glory of *y* men is ...... Prov 20:29
y ones shall lie .... Is 11:7
dream dreams, your *y* ...... Joel 2:28
y man followed Him ..... Mark 14:51
they admonish the *y* .... Titus 2:4
I write to you, *y* .... 1 John 2:13

YOUNGER
they mock at me, men *y* ..... Job 30:1
y son gathered all .... Luke 15:13
let him be as the *y* .... Luke 22:26
y women as sisters .... 1 Tim 5:2
Likewise you *y* people ...... 1 Pet 5:5

YOURS
all that I have are *y* .... 1 Kin 20:4
the battle is not *y* .... 2 Chr 20:15
I am *Y*, save me .... Ps 119:94
Y is the kingdom .... Matt 6:13
Take what is *y* .... Matt 20:14
y is the kingdom .... Luke 6:20
And all Mine are *Y* .... John 17:10
For all things are *y* .... 1 Cor 3:21
for I do not seek *y* .... 2 Cor 12:14

YOUTH
for he was only a *y* ...... 1 Sam 17:42
the LORD from my *y* ...... 1 Kin 18:12
the sins of my *y* .... Ps 25:7
the companion of her *y* .... Prov 2:17
with the wife of your *y* ..... Prov 5:18
in the days of your *y* .... Eccl 11:9
and *y* are vanity .... Eccl 11:10
in the days of your *y* .... Eccl 12:1
the shame of your *y* .... Is 54:4
speak, for I am a *y* .... Jer 1:6
Do not say, 'I am a *y*,' for ..... Jer 1:7
the kindness of your *y* .... Jer 2:2
the days of your *y* .... Ezek 16:22
with the wife of his *y* .... Mal 2:15
I have kept from my *y* .... Matt 19:20
I have kept from my *y* .... Mark 10:20
I have kept from my *y* .... Luke 18:21
the flower of her *y* .... 1 Cor 7:36
no one despise your *y* ..... 1 Tim 4:12

YOUTHFUL
Flee also *y* lusts .... 2 Tim 2:22

YOUTHS
perceived among the *y* ...... Prov 7:7
y shall faint and be .... Is 40:30

ZACCHAEUS
Wealthy tax collector converted to Christ, Luke 19:1–10

ZACHARIAS
Father of John the Baptist, Luke 1:5–17

ZADOK
Co-priest with Abiathar; remains loyal to David, 2 Sam 15:24–29; 20:25
Rebuked by David, 2 Sam 19:11, 12
Does not follow Adonijah; anoints Solomon, 1 Kin 1:8–45
Takes Abiathar's place, 1 Kin 2:35

ZALMUNNA
Midianite king, Judg 8:4–21

ZAREPHATH
Town of Sidon where Elijah revives widow's son, 1 Kin 17:8–24; Luke 4:26

ZEAL
The *z* of the LORD of ..... 2 Kin 19:31
z has consumed me .... Ps 119:139
He shall stir up His *z* .... Is 42:13
have spoken it in My *z* .... Ezek 5:13
for Zion with great *z* .... Zech 8:2
"*Z* for Your house has ..... John 2:17
that they have a *z* .... Rom 10:2
z has stirred up the .... 2 Cor 9:2

ZEALOUS
he was *z* for his God ..... Num 25:13
"I have been very *z* ...... 1 Kin 19:10
'I am *z* for Zion with .... Zech 8:2
they are all *z* for the law .. Acts 21:20
since you are *z* .... 1 Cor 14:12
But it is good to be *z* .... Gal 4:18
z for good works .... Titus 2:14
Therefore be *z* and repent .. Rev 3:19

ZEBAH
King of Midian killed by Gideon, Judg 8:4–28

ZEBEDEE
Galilean fisherman; father of James and John, Matt 4:21, 22

ZEBULUN
Sixth son of Jacob and Leah, Gen 30:19, 20
Prophecy concerning, Gen 49:13
—— Tribe of:
Numbered, Num 1:30, 31; 26:27
Territory assigned to, Josh 19:10–16
Joins Gideon in battle, Judg 6:34, 35
Some respond to Hezekiah's reforms, 2 Chr 30:10–18
Christ visits territory of, Matt 4:13–16

ZECHARIAH
King of Israel; last ruler of Jehu's dynasty, 2 Kin 15:8–12
—— Postexilic prophet and priest, Ezra 5:1; Zech 1:1, 7

ZEDEKIAH
Last king of Judah; uncle and successor of Jehoiachin; reigns wickedly, 2 Kin 24:17–19; 2 Chr 36:10
Rebels against Nebuchadnezzar, 2 Chr 36:11–13
Denounced by Jeremiah, Jer 34:1–22
Consults Jeremiah, Jer 37; 38
Captured and taken to Babylon, 2 Kin 25:1–7; Jer 39:1–7

ZELOPHEHAD
Manassite whose five daughters secure female rights, Num 27:1–7

ZEPHANIAH
Author of Zephaniah, Zeph 1:1
—— Priest and friend of Jeremiah during Zedekiah's reign, Jer 21:1

ZERUBBABEL
Descendant of David, 1 Chr 3:1–19
Leader of Jewish exiles, Neh 7:6, 7; Hag 2:21–23
Rebuilds the temple, Ezra 3:1–10; Zech 4:1–14

ZIBA
Saul's servant, 2 Sam 9:9
Befriends David, 2 Sam 16:1–4
Accused of deception by Mephibosheth, 2 Sam 19:17–30

ZIKLAG
City on the border of Judah, Josh 15:1, 31
Held by David, 1 Sam 27:6
Overthrown by Amalekites, 1 Sam 30:1–31

ZILPAH
Leah's maid, Gen 29:24
Mother of Gad and Asher, Gen 30:9–13

ZIMRI
Simeonite prince slain by Phinehas, Num 25:6–14
—— King of Israel for seven days, 1 Kin 16:8–20

ZIN
Wilderness through which the Israelites passed, Num 20:1
Border between Judah and Edom, Josh 15:1–3

ZION
Literally, an area in Jerusalem; called the City of David, 2 Sam 5:6–9; 2 Chr 5:2
Used figuratively of God's kingdom, Ps 125:1; Heb 12:22; Rev 14:1
City of David, which is *Z* ... 1 Kin 8:1
City of David, which is *Z* ... 2 Chr 5:2
the LORD, who dwells in *Z* .... Ps 9:11
Is Mount *Z* on the sides of .... Ps 48:2
in Your good pleasure to *Z* .. Ps 51:18
God will save *Z* and build ... Ps 69:35
And of *Z* it will be said .... Ps 87:5
the LORD shall build up *Z* .. Ps 102:16
the name of the LORD in *Z* .. Ps 102:21
back the captivity of *Z* ...... Ps 126:1
the LORD has chosen *Z* ..... Ps 132:13
when we remembered *Z* ..... Ps 137:1
Z shall be redeemed with ..... Is 1:27
For out of *Z* shall go forth ..... Is 2:3
My people, who dwell in *Z* ... Is 10:24
shout, O Inhabitant of *Z* ...... Is 12:6
hosts will reign on Mount *Z* .. Is 24:23
I lay in *Z* a stone for a .... Is 28:16
down to fight for Mount *Z* .... Is 31:4
come to *Z* with singing ...... Is 35:10
virgin, the daughter of *Z* ..... Is 37:22
I will place salvation in *Z* .... Is 46:13
the LORD will comfort *Z* .... Is 51:3
come to *Z* with singing ...... Is 51:11
Redeemer will come to *Z* .... Is 59:20
Z of the Holy One of Israel .. Is 60:14
Arise, and let us go up to *Z* .. Jer 31:6
to be forgotten in *Z* .... Lam 2:6
Blow the trumpet in *Z* .... Joel 2:1
for the LORD dwells in *Z* .... Joel 3:21
on Mount *Z* there shall be ... Obad 17
For out of *Z* the law shall .... Mic 4:2
Sing, O daughter of *Z* ..... Zeph 3:14
LORD will gain comfort *Z* .. Zech 1:17
rejoice, O daughter of *Z* .... Zech 2:10
Fear not, daughter of *Z* ... John 12:15
in *Z* a stumbling stone ..... Rom 9:33
will come out of *Z* .... Rom 11:26
Behold, I lay in *Z* a chief .... 1 Pet 2:6

ZIPPORAH
Daughter of Jethro; wife of Moses, Ex 18:1, 2

ZOAR
Ancient city of Canaan originally named Bela, Gen 14:2, 8
Spared destruction at Lot's request, Gen 19:20–23

ZOPHAR
Naamathite; friend of Job, Job 2:11

Index to Maps

The following index is divided into two parts, one for Map 5, Jerusalem, and the other for all the other maps. Place names are given as shown on the maps. Where a place name refers to a large area, the index gives the location of the name. Where a name refers to a river, the index gives the source and mouth of the river.

In the index to Maps 1 through 4 and 6 through 9, major political divisions, such as countries and regions, are shown in capital letters (examples: EGYPT, PALESTINE). Cities are shown in upper and lower case as usual (example: Hebron). Geographical features are shown in italics (example: *Jordan River*).

INDEX TO MAPS

Map 1. The Nations of Genesis 10
Map 2. The Exodus of Israel
Map 3. The Conquest of Canaan
Map 4. The Kingdom Years
Map 6. Palestine in Christ's Time
Map 7. Paul's First and Second Journeys
Map 8. Paul's Third and Fourth Journeys
Map 9. The Holy Land in Modern Times

Map 5. Jerusalem—From David to Christ

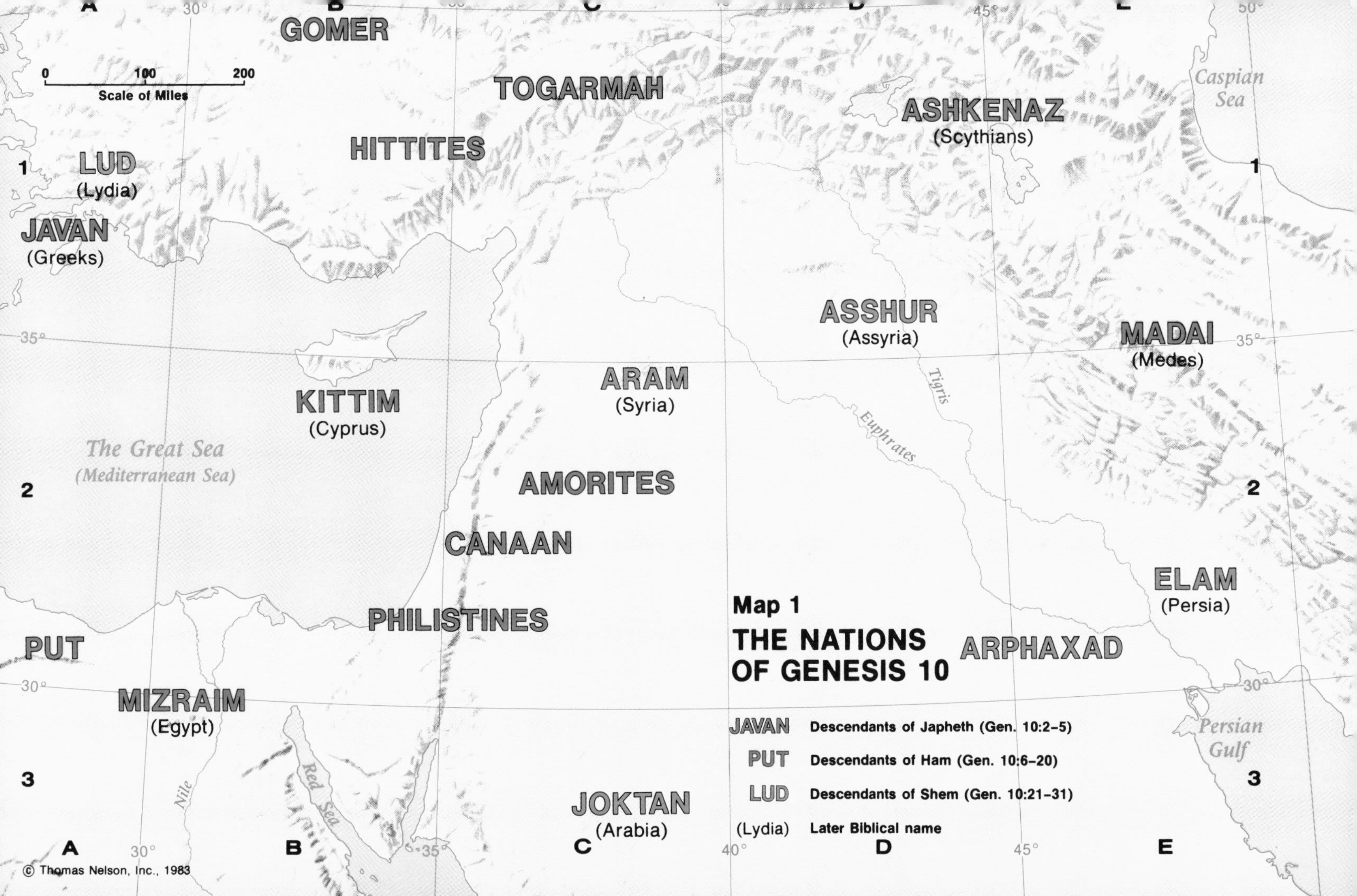
Map 1
THE NATIONS OF GENESIS 10
JAVAN Descendants of Japheth (Gen. 10:2–5)
PUT Descendants of Ham (Gen. 10:6–20)
LUD Descendants of Shem (Gen. 10:21–31)
(Lydia) Later Biblical name
0 100 200
Scale of Miles
GOMER
TOGARMAH
ASHKENAZ
(Scythians)
HITTITES
LUD
(Lydia)
JAVAN
(Greeks)
Caspian Sea
ASSHUR
(Assyria)
MADAI
(Medes)
ARAM
(Syria)
KITTIM
(Cyprus)
The Great Sea
(Mediterranean Sea)
Tigris
Euphrates
AMORITES
CANAAN
ELAM
(Persia)
PHILISTINES
ARPHAXAD
PUT
MIZRAIM
(Egypt)
Persian Gulf
Nile
Red Sea
JOKTAN
(Arabia)
30°
35°
40°
45°
50°
A B C D E
1 2 3

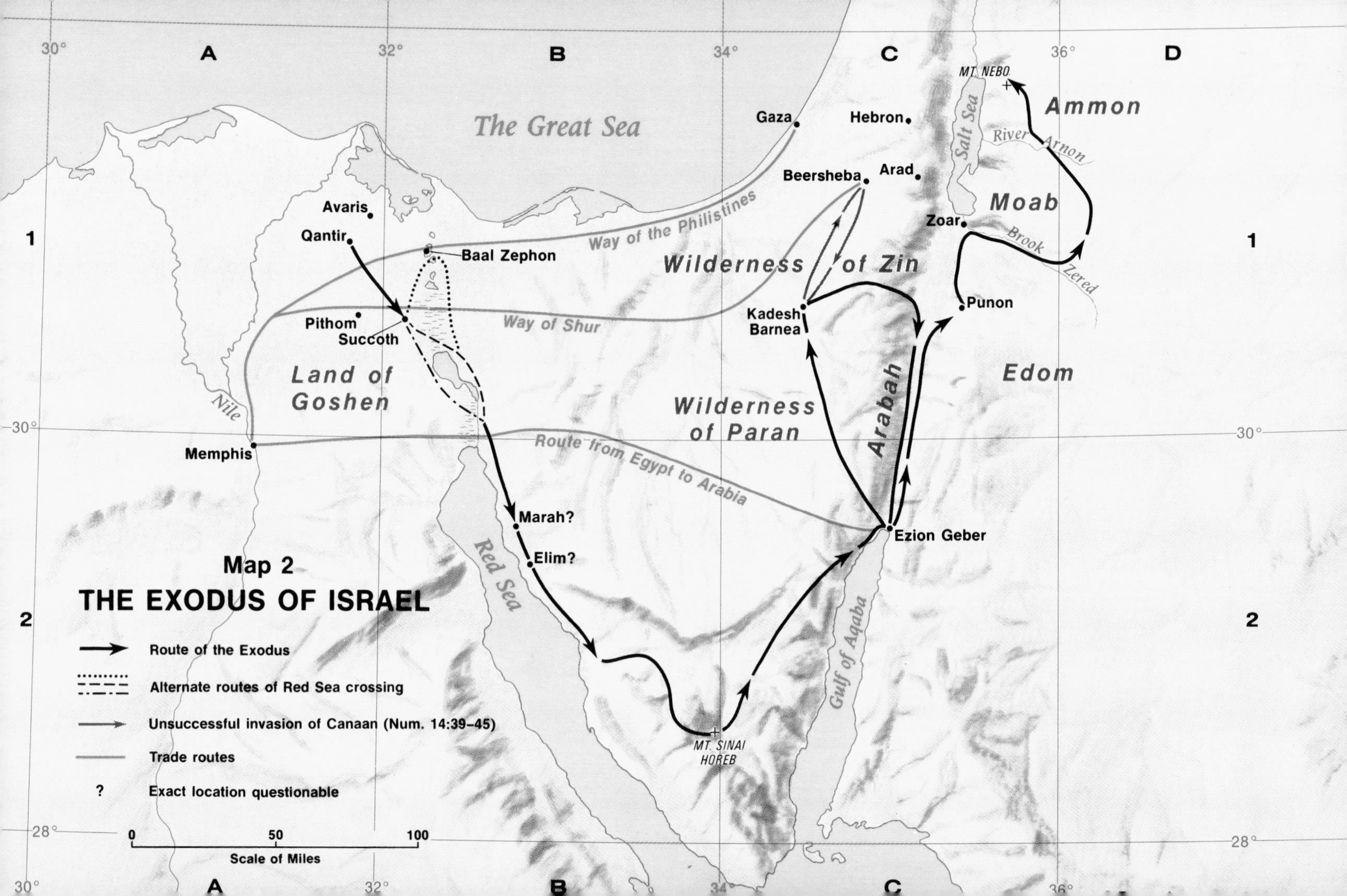

Map 2
THE EXODUS OF ISRAEL
Route of the Exodus
Alternate routes of Red Sea crossing
Unsuccessful invasion of Canaan (Num. 14:39–45)
Trade routes
? Exact location questionable
0 50 100
Scale of Miles
The Great Sea
Gaza
Hebron
Beersheba
Arad
Avaris
Qantir
Baal Zephon
Pithom
Succoth
Land of Goshen
Nile
Memphis
Way of the Philistines
Way of Shur
Route from Egypt to Arabia
Wilderness of Zin
Wilderness of Paran
Kadesh Barnea
Arabah
Marah?
Elim?
Red Sea
MT. SINAI HOREB
Gulf of Aqaba
Ezion Geber
Punon
Edom
Zoar
Moab
Salt Sea
MT. NEBO
Ammon
River Arnon
Brook Zered

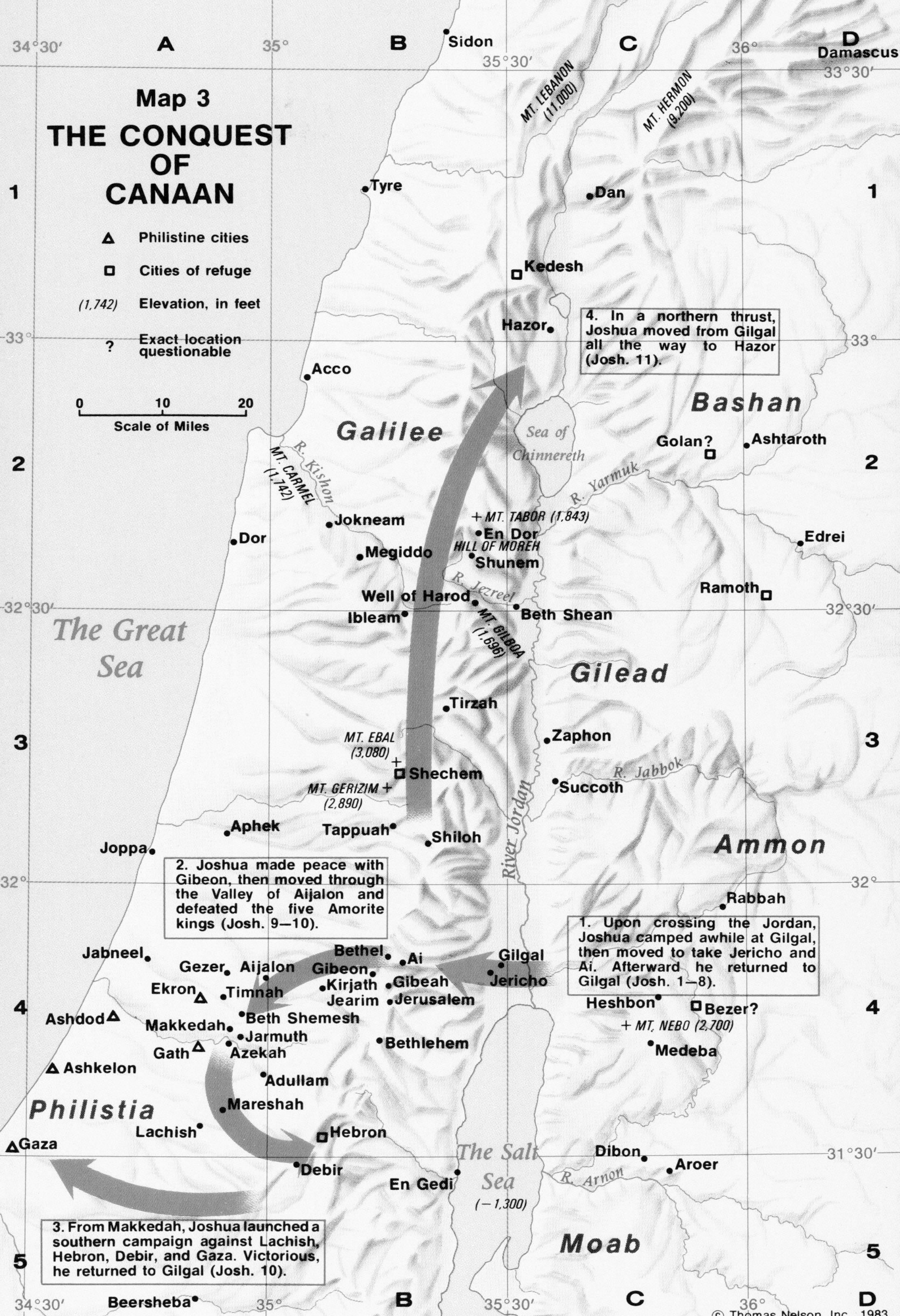

Map 3
THE CONQUEST OF CANAAN
Philistine cities
Cities of refuge
(1,742) Elevation, in feet
? Exact location questionable
0 10 20
Scale of Miles
34°30′
A
35°
B
35°30′
C
36°
D
33°30′
33°
32°30′
32°
31°30′
1
2
3
4
5
Sidon
Damascus
MT. LEBANON (11,000)
MT. HERMON (9,200)
Tyre
Dan
Kedesh
Hazor
4. In a northern thrust, Joshua moved from Gilgal all the way to Hazor (Josh. 11).
Acco
Bashan
Galilee
Sea of Chinnereth
Golan?
Ashtaroth
R. Kishon
MT. CARMEL (1,742)
R. Yarmuk
MT. TABOR (1,843)
Jokneam
En Dor
HILL OF MOREH
Dor
Megiddo
Shunem
Edrei
R. Jezreel
Ramoth
Well of Harod
Beth Shean
Ibleam
MT. GILBOA (1,696)
The Great Sea
Gilead
Tirzah
MT. EBAL (3,080)
Zaphon
Shechem
R. Jabbok
MT. GERIZIM (2,890)
Succoth
River Jordan
Aphek
Tappuah
Shiloh
Joppa
Ammon
2. Joshua made peace with Gibeon, then moved through the Valley of Aijalon and defeated the five Amorite kings (Josh. 9—10).
Rabbah
1. Upon crossing the Jordan, Joshua camped awhile at Gilgal, then moved to take Jericho and Ai. Afterward he returned to Gilgal (Josh. 1—8).
Jabneel
Bethel
Ai
Gilgal
Gezer
Aijalon
Gibeon
Jericho
Ekron
Timnah
Kirjath Jearim
Gibeah
Jerusalem
Heshbon
Bezer?
Ashdod
Makkedah
Beth Shemesh
MT. NEBO (2,700)
Jarmuth
Bethlehem
Gath
Azekah
Medeba
Ashkelon
Adullam
Philistia
Mareshah
Lachish
Hebron
Gaza
The Salt Sea
(–1,300)
Dibon
Aroer
Debir
En Gedi
R. Arnon
3. From Makkedah, Joshua launched a southern campaign against Lachish, Hebron, Debir, and Gaza. Victorious, he returned to Gilgal (Josh. 10).
Moab
Beersheba

Map 4
THE KINGDOM YEARS
Probable extent of Israelite control during the Kingdom of Solomon, c. 950 B.C.
The Kingdoms of Israel and Judah, c. 860 B.C.
Boundary between Israel and Judah
? Exact location questionable
0 25 50
Scale of Miles
34° A 35° B 36° C 37°
1 2 3 4 5 6
34° 33° 32° 31° 30°
Riblah
Zobah
Byblos
Phoenicia
MT. LEBANON
MT. HERMON
Sidon
Zarephath
Damascus
Tyre
Dan
Kedesh
Syria
Hazor
Acco
Sea of Chinnereth
Ashtaroth
R. Yarmuk
Golan?
The Great Sea
MT. CARMEL
Jokneam
Dor
Megiddo
Jezreel
Ramoth Gilead
Taanach
MT. GILBOA
Dothan
Jabesh Gilead
Tirzah
Zaphon
Samaria
Succoth
Shechem
Jordan R.
R. Jabbok
Aphek
Shiloh
Ammon
Joppa
ISRAEL
Rabbah
Mizpah
Bethel
Jabneh
Gezer
Ramah
Heshbon
Philistia
Jerusalem
Beth Shemesh
Bethlehem
Medeba
Ashkelon
Tekoa
Adullam
Eglon?
Dibon
Gaza
The Salt Sea
Hebron
Aroer
Debir
R. Arnon
Ziklag?
Arad
Moab
Beersheba
Kir Hareseth
Zoar
R. Zered
JUDAH
Bozrah
Kadesh Barnea
River of Egypt
Edom
Teman
Note: Other place names significant during the time of the Kingdoms are found on Map 3.
Ezion Geber
Elath

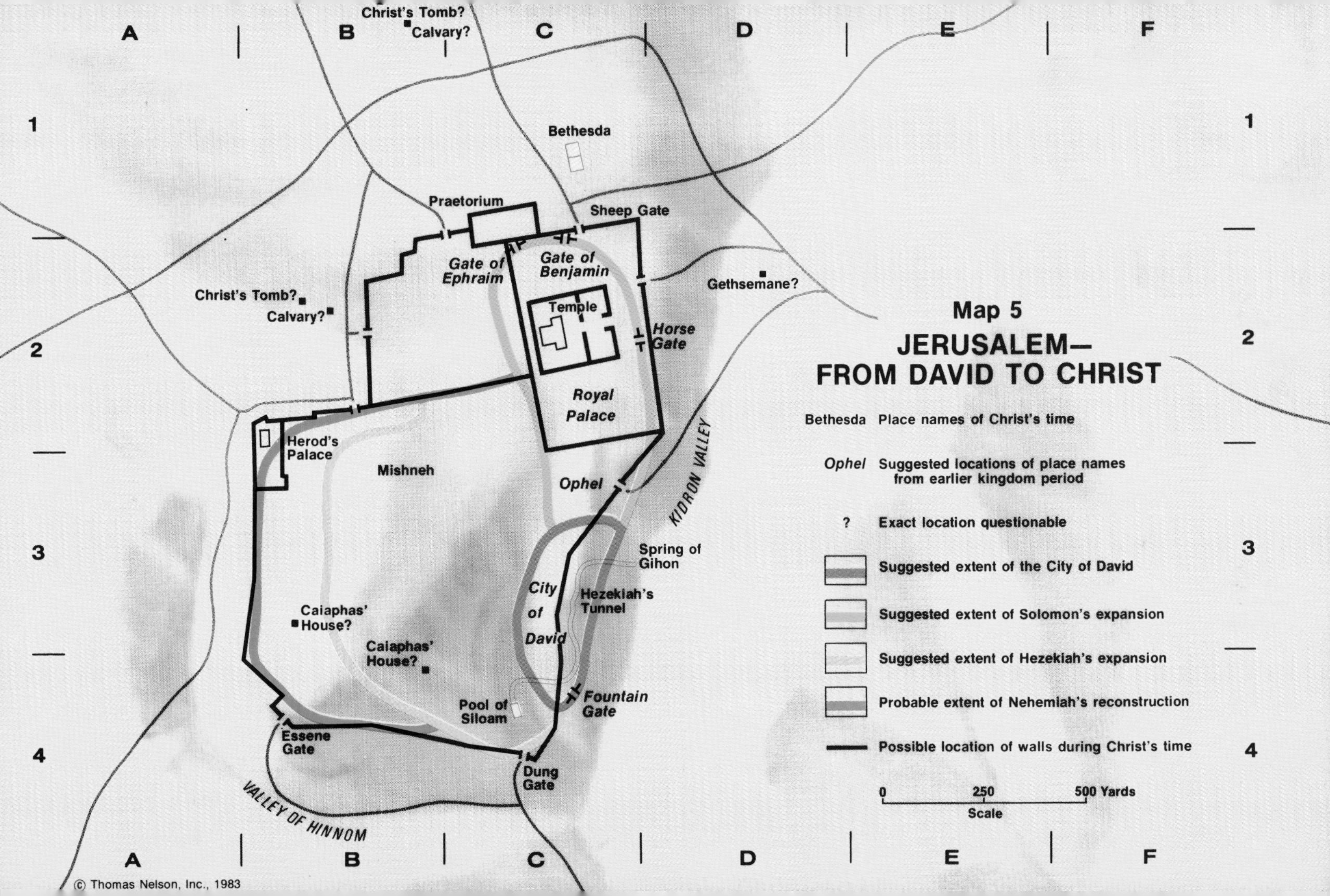

Map 5
JERUSALEM—
FROM DAVID TO CHRIST
Bethesda Place names of Christ's time
Ophel Suggested locations of place names from earlier kingdom period
? Exact location questionable
Suggested extent of the City of David
Suggested extent of Solomon's expansion
Suggested extent of Hezekiah's expansion
Probable extent of Nehemiah's reconstruction
Possible location of walls during Christ's time
0
250
500 Yards
Scale
Christ's Tomb?
Calvary?
Bethesda
Praetorium
Sheep Gate
Gate of Ephraim
Gate of Benjamin
Gethsemane?
Christ's Tomb?
Calvary?
Temple
Horse Gate
Royal Palace
Herod's Palace
Mishneh
Ophel
KIDRON VALLEY
Spring of Gihon
City of David
Hezekiah's Tunnel
Caiaphas' House?
Caiaphas' House?
Pool of Siloam
Fountain Gate
Essene Gate
Dung Gate
VALLEY OF HINNOM
A
B
C
D
E
F
1
2
3
4

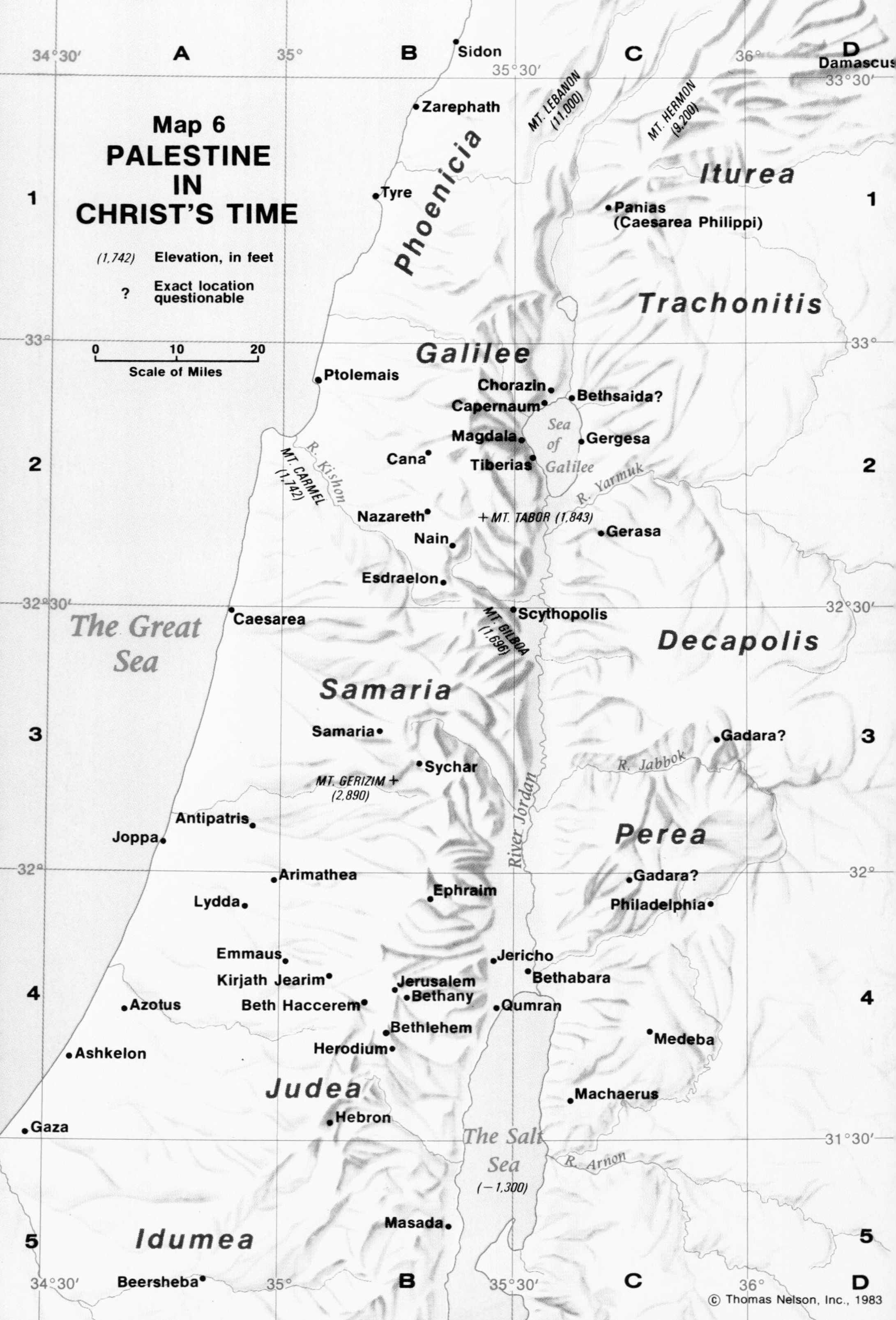

Map 6
PALESTINE IN CHRIST'S TIME
(1,742) Elevation, in feet
? Exact location questionable
0 10 20
Scale of Miles
A
B
C
D
1
2
3
4
5
34°30′
35°
35°30′
36°
33°30′
33°
32°30′
32°
31°30′
Sidon
Damascus
Zarephath
MT. LEBANON (11,000)
MT. HERMON (9,200)
Phoenicia
Iturea
Tyre
Panias (Caesarea Philippi)
Trachonitis
Galilee
Ptolemais
Chorazin
Capernaum
Bethsaida?
Sea of Galilee
Magdala
Gergesa
Cana
Tiberias
MT. CARMEL (1,742)
R. Kishon
R. Yarmuk
Nazareth
MT. TABOR (1,843)
Gerasa
Nain
Esdraelon
Caesarea
Scythopolis
MT. GILBOA (1,696)
The Great Sea
Decapolis
Samaria
Samaria
Gadara?
Sychar
R. Jabbok
MT. GERIZIM (2,890)
River Jordan
Antipatris
Joppa
Perea
Arimathea
Gadara?
Ephraim
Lydda
Philadelphia
Emmaus
Jericho
Kirjath Jearim
Bethabara
Jerusalem
Bethany
Azotus
Beth Haccerem
Qumran
Bethlehem
Medeba
Ashkelon
Herodium
Judea
Machaerus
Hebron
Gaza
The Salt Sea
R. Arnon
(−1,300)
Masada
Idumea
Beersheba

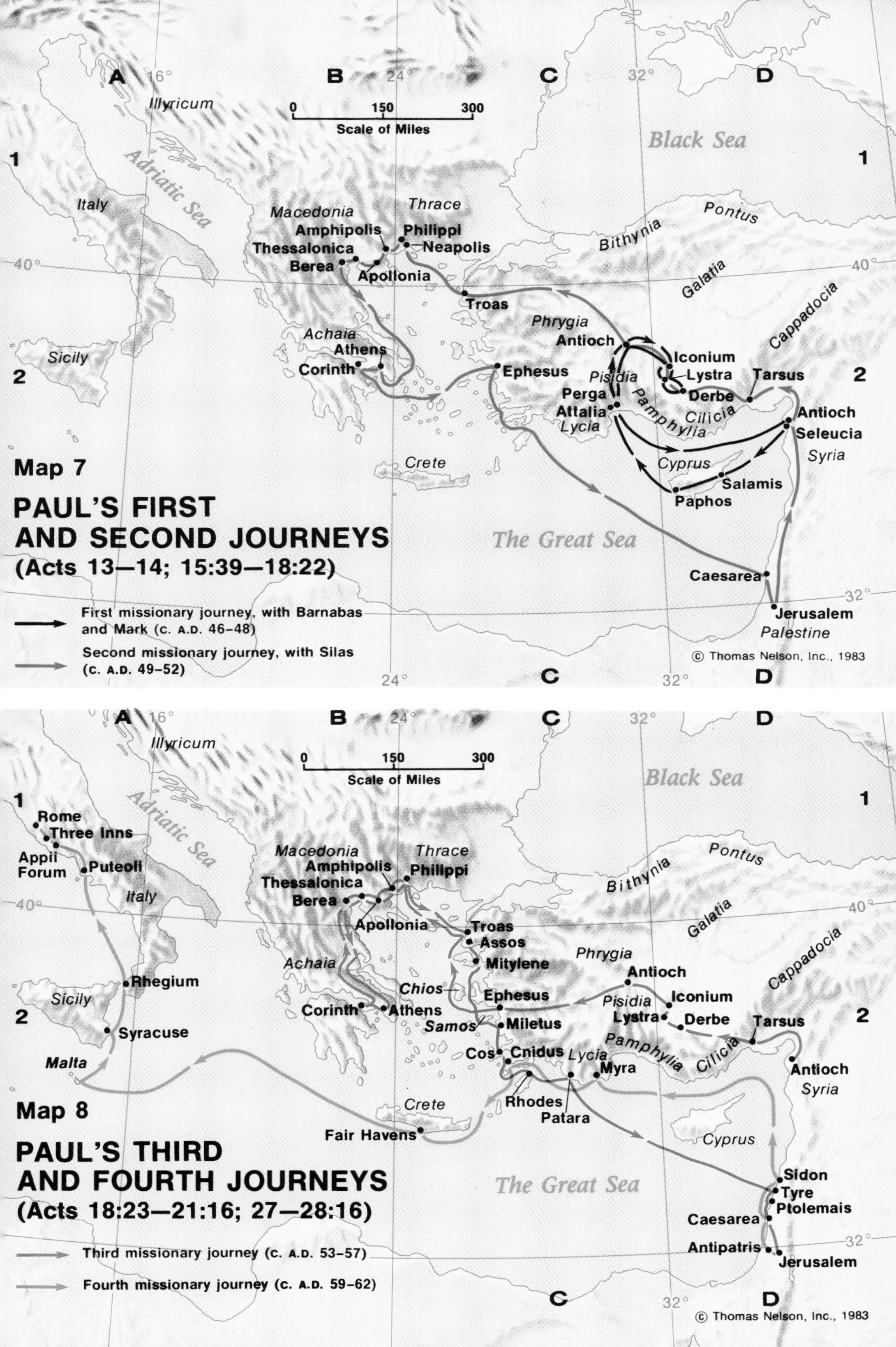
Map 7
PAUL'S FIRST AND SECOND JOURNEYS
(Acts 13—14; 15:39—18:22)
First missionary journey, with Barnabas and Mark (c. A.D. 46–48)
Second missionary journey, with Silas (c. A.D. 49–52)
Scale of Miles
0
150
300
A
B
C
D
1
2
16°
24°
32°
40°
Illyricum
Adriatic Sea
Italy
Sicily
Black Sea
Macedonia
Thrace
Amphipolis
Philippi
Thessalonica
Neapolis
Berea
Apollonia
Troas
Achaia
Athens
Corinth
Ephesus
Bithynia
Pontus
Galatia
Cappadocia
Phrygia
Antioch
Iconium
Lystra
Derbe
Pisidia
Perga
Attalia
Lycia
Pamphylia
Cilicia
Tarsus
Antioch
Seleucia
Syria
Cyprus
Salamis
Paphos
Crete
The Great Sea
Caesarea
Jerusalem
Palestine
© Thomas Nelson, Inc., 1983
Map 8
PAUL'S THIRD AND FOURTH JOURNEYS
(Acts 18:23—21:16; 27—28:16)
Third missionary journey (c. A.D. 53–57)
Fourth missionary journey (c. A.D. 59–62)
Scale of Miles
0
150
300
Rome
Three Inns
Appii Forum
Puteoli
Italy
Rhegium
Sicily
Syracuse
Malta
Illyricum
Adriatic Sea
Macedonia
Thrace
Amphipolis
Philippi
Thessalonica
Berea
Apollonia
Troas
Assos
Mitylene
Achaia
Chios
Corinth
Athens
Samos
Ephesus
Miletus
Cos
Cnidus
Rhodes
Patara
Lycia
Myra
Crete
Fair Havens
Black Sea
Bithynia
Pontus
Galatia
Cappadocia
Phrygia
Antioch
Pisidia
Iconium
Lystra
Derbe
Pamphylia
Cilicia
Tarsus
Antioch
Syria
Cyprus
The Great Sea
Sidon
Tyre
Ptolemais
Caesarea
Antipatris
Jerusalem
© Thomas Nelson, Inc., 1983

Map 9
THE HOLY LAND IN MODERN TIMES
Area occupied by Israel since June, 1967
0 25 50
Scale of Miles
A B C D E
34° 35° 36° 37°
1 2 3 4 5 6
34° 33° 32° 31° 30°
Tripoli
LEBANON
BEKAA VALLEY
Beirut
LEBANON MTS.
ANTI-LEBANON MTS.
Sidon
Damascus
U.N. Buffer Zone
1973 Line
Tyre
Dan
SYRIA
Qiryat Shemona
Quneitra
Nahariyya
1967 Cease-Fire Line
Safad
Golan Heights
Akko
Sea of Galilee
Haifa
Tiberias
Dera
Nazareth
Mediterranean Sea
Afula
Ramtha
Beth Shean
Hadera
Netanya
Tulkarm
Jarash
Nablus
Herzliyya
Jordan River
Tel Aviv
West Bank
Yafo
Petah Tiqwa
Rishon le Zion
Lod
Amman
Ramla
Ramalah
Ashdod
Jericho
Jerusalem
Bethlehem
Ashqelon
Madaba
Qiryat Gat
Gaza
Hebron
Dead Sea
Dhiban
En Gedi
Beersheba
Al-Arish
Karak
JORDAN
ISRAEL
EGYPT
Negev
Arabah
Sinai
Elat
Aqaba